27347

THE

HOLY BIBLE

CONTAINING THE

OLD AND NEW TESTAMENTS

THE TEXT CAREFULLY PRINTED FROM THE
MOST CORRECT COPIES OF THE PRESENT
AUTHORIZED TRANSLATION, INCLUDING THE
MARGINAL READINGS AND PARALLEL TEXTS

WITH

A COMMENTARY AND CRITICAL NOTES

DESIGNED AS A HELP TO A BETTER UNDERSTANDING
OF THE SACRED WRITINGS

BY ADAM CLARKE, LL.D., F.S.A., &c.

A NEW EDITION, WITH THE
AUTHOR'S FINAL CORRECTIONS

For whatsoever things were written aforetime were written for our learning, that we through
patience and comfort of the Scriptures might have hope.—Rom. xv. 4.

THE OLD TESTAMENT

VOLUME III.—JOB TO SOLOMON'S SONG

ABINGDON PRESS
NASHVILLE   ●   NEW YORK

ISBN 0-687-09125-X

Printed in the United States of America

PREFACE

TO THE

BOOK OF JOB

THIS is the most singular book in the whole of the Sacred Code: though written by the same inspiration, and in reference to the same end, the salvation of men, it is so different from every other book of the Bible, that it seems to possess nothing in common with them, for even the *language*, in its construction, is dissimilar from that in the *Law*, the *Prophets*, and the *historical books*. But on all hands it is accounted a work that contains "the purest *morality*, the sublimest *philosophy*, the simplest *ritual*, and the most majestic *creed*." Except the *two first chapters* and the *ten last verses*, which are merely *prose*, all the rest of the book is *poetic;* and is every where reducible to the *hemistich* form, in which all the other poetic books of the Bible are written: it is therefore properly called a POEM; but whether it belongs to the *dramatic* or *epic* species has not been decided by learned men. To try it by those *rules* which have been derived from *Aristotle*, and are still applied to ascertain compositions in these departments of poetry, is, in my opinion, as absurd as it is ridiculous. Who ever made a poem on these rules? And is there a poem in the universe worth reading that is strictly conformable to these rules? *Not one*. The rules, it is true, were deduced from compositions of this description:—and although they may be very useful, in assisting poets to methodize their compositions, and to keep the different parts distinct; yet they have often acted as a species of critical trammels, and have cramped genius. Genuine poetry is like a mountain flood: it pours down, resistless, bursts all bounds, scoops out its own channel, carries woods and rocks before it, and spreads itself abroad, both deep and wide, over all the plain. Such, indeed, is the poetry which the reader will meet with in this singular and astonishing book. As to Aristotle himself, although he was a keen-eyed plodder of nature, and a prodigy for his time; yet if we may judge from his *poetics*, he had a soul as incapable of feeling the true *genie createur*, as *Racine* terms the *spirit of poetry*, as he was, by his physics, metaphysics, and analogies, of discovering the true system of the universe.

As to the book of Job, it is most evidently a *poem*, and a *poem* of the highest order; dealing in *subjects* the most grand and sublime; using *imagery* the most chaste and appropriate; described by language the most happy and energetic; conveying *instruction*, both in Divine and human things, the most ennobling and useful; abounding in *precepts* the most pure and exalted, which are enforced by *arguments* the most strong and conclusive, and illustrated by *examples* the most natural and striking.

All these points will appear in the strongest light to every attentive reader of the book; and to such its great *end* will be answered: they will learn from it, that God has way every where: that the *wicked*, though bearing rule for a time, can never be ultimately prosperous and happy; and that the *righteous*, though oppressed with sufferings and calamities, can never be forgotten by Him in whose hands are his saints, and with whom their lives are precious; that in this world neither are the wicked ultimately punished, nor the righteous ultimately rewarded; that God's judgments are a great deep, and his ways past finding out; but the issues of all are to the glory of his wisdom and grace, and to the eternal happiness of those who trust in him. This is the grand design of the book, and this design will be strikingly evident to the simplest and most unlettered reader, whose heart is right with God, and who is seeking instruction, in order that he may glorify his Maker, by receiving and by doing good.

Notwithstanding all this, there is not a book in Scripture on the subject of which more *difficulties* have been started. None, says *Calmet*, has furnished more subjects of doubt and embarrassment; and none has afforded less information for the solution of those doubts. On this subject the great questions which have been agitated refer, principally, 1. To the *person* of Job. 2. To his *existence*. 3. To the *time* in which he lived. 4. To his *country*. 5. To his *stock* or *kindred*. 6. To his *religion*. 7. To the *author* of the book. 8. To its *truth*. 9. To its *authenticity*; and, 10. To the *time* and *occasion* on which it was written.

With respect to the *first* and *second*, several writers of eminent note have denied the *personality* of Job; according to them, no such person ever existed; he is merely *fabulous*, and is like the *Il penseroso*, or *sorrowful man* of Milton; sorrow, distress, affliction, and persecution personified, as the name imports. According to them, he is a mere *ideal being*, created by the genius of the poet; clothed with such attributes, and placed in such circumstances, as gave the poet scope and materials for his work.

Thirdly, as to the *time* in which those place him who receive this as a *true history*, there is great variety. According to some, he flourished in the *patriarchal age;* some make him *contemporary* with *Moses;* that he was in the captivity in Egypt, and that he lived at the time of the *exodus*. Some place him in the time of the Israelitish *judges;* others in the days of *David;* others, in those of *Solomon;* and others, in the time of the *Babylonish captivity*, having been teacher of a school at Tiberias in Palestine, and, with the rest of his countrymen, carried away into Babylon; and that he lived under *Ahasuerus* and *Esther*. *Fourthly*, as to his *country:* some make him an *Arab;* others, an *Egyptian;* others, a *Syrian;* some an *Israelite;* and some, an *Idumean*. *Fifthly*, as to his *origin:* some derive him from *Nachor*, and others from *Esau*, and make him the *fifth* in descent *from Abraham*. *Sixthly*, as to his *religion:* some suppose it to have been *Sabæism;* others, that it was *patriarchal;* and others, that he was bred up in the *Jewish* faith. *Seventhly*, as to the *author* of the work, learned men are greatly divided: some suppose the author to have been *Elihu;* others, *Job;* others, *Job* and *his friends;* others, *Moses;* some, *Solomon;* others, *Isaiah;* and others, *Ezra*, or some *unknown Jew*, posterior to the captivity. *Eighthly*, as to the book: some maintain that it is a history of *fact*, given by one best qualified to record it; and others, that it is an instructive *fiction*—facts, persons, dialogues and all, being supposititious; given, however, by the inspiration of God, in a sort of *parabolic* form, like those employed in the Gospel; and similar to that of the *rich man and Lazarus*. *Ninthly*, as to its *authenticity:* while some, and those not well qualified to judge, have asserted it to be a mere *human production*, of no Divine authority; others have clearly shown that the book itself, whatever questions may arise concerning the *person, author, time, place,* &c., was ever received by the Jewish *Church* and *people* as authentic, genuine, and divinely inspired; and incorporated, with the highest propriety, among the most instructive, sublime, and excellent portions of Divine revelation. *Tenthly*, as to the *occasion* on which it was written, there are considerable differences of opinion: some will have it to be written for the *consolation* of the *Hebrews* in their peregrinations through the *wilderness;* and others, for the comfort and encouragement of the Israelites in the *Babylonish captivity:* these state that *Job* represents *Nehemiah*, and that his three professed friends, but real enemies, *Eliphaz* the *Temanite*, *Bildad* the *Shuhite*, and *Zophar* the *Naamathite*, represent *Sanballat* the *Horonite*, *Tobiah* the *Ammonite*, and *Geshem* the *Arabian!* and that the whole book should be understood and interpreted on this ground; and that, with a little allowance for poetic colouring, all its parts perfectly harmonize, thus understood; showing, in a word, that into whatsoever troubles or persecutions God may permit his people to be brought, yet he will sustain them in the fire, bring them safely through it, and discomfit all their enemies: and that whatsoever is true on this *great scale*, is true also on that which is more *contracted;* as he will equally support, defend, and finally render conqueror, every individual that trusts in him.

I shall not trouble my readers with the arguments which have been used by learned men, *pro* and *con*, relative to the particulars already mentioned: were I to do this, I must transcribe a vast mass of matter, which, though it might display great learning in the authors, would most certainly afford little edification to the great bulk of my readers. My own opinion on those points they may naturally wish to know; and to that opinion they have a right: it is such as I dare avow, and such as I feel no disposition to conceal. I believe Job to have been a *real person*, and his history to be a *statement* of *facts*.

As the preface to this book (I mean the first chapter) states him to have lived in the land of *Uz*, or *Uts*, I believe, with Mr. *Good* and several other learned men, this place to have been "situated in *Arabia Petræa*, on the south-western coast of the lake *Asphaltites*, in a line between Egypt and Philistia, surrounded with Kedar, Teman, and Midian; all of which were districts of Arabia Petræa; situated in Idumea, the land of Edom or Esau; and comprising so large a part of it, that *Idumea* and *Ausitis*, or the land of *Uz*, and the land of *Edom*, were convertible terms, and equally employed to import the same region: thus, Lam. iv. 21: 'Rejoice and be glad, O daughter of Edom, that dwellest in the land of Uz.' " See Mr. *Good's Introductory Dissertation;* who proceeds to observe: "Nothing is clearer than that all the persons introduced into this poem were *Idumeans*, dwelling in Idumea; or, in other words, Edomite Arabs. These characters are, *Job* himself, dwelling in the land of *Uz; Eliphaz* of *Teman*, a district of as much repute as *Uz*, and (upon the joint testimony of *Jer.* xlix. 7, 20; *Ezek.* xxv. 13; *Amos* i. 11, 12, and *Obadiah* ver. 8, 9) a part, and a principal part, of *Idumea; Bildad* of *Shuah*, always mentioned in conjunction with *Sheba* and *Dedan*, all of them being uniformly placed in the vicinity of Idumea; *Zophar* of *Naamah*, a city whose name imports *pleasantness*, which is also stated, in Josh. xv. 21, 41, to have been situated in Idumea, and to have lain in a southern direction towards its coast, or the shores of the Red Sea; and *Elihu* of *Buz*, which as the name of a place occurs but once in sacred writ, but is there (Jer. xxv. 22) mentioned in conjunction with *Teman* and *Dedan;* and hence necessarily, like themselves, a border city upon *Ausitis*, *Uz*, or *Idumea*. It had a number of names: it was at first called *Horitis*, from the *Horim* or *Horites*, who appear to have first settled there. Among the descendants of these, the most distinguished was *Seir;* and from him the land was known by the name of the *Land of Seir*. This *chief* had a numerous family, and among the most signalized of his grandsons was *Uz*, or *Uts;* and from him, and not from *Uz* the son of Nahor, it seems to have been called *Ausitis*, or the *Land of Uz*. The family of *Hor*, *Seir*, or *Uz*, were at length dispossessed of the entire region by *Esau*, or *Edom;* who strengthened himself by his marriage with one of the daughters of *Ishmael;* and the conquered territory was denominated *Idumea*, or the land of Edom." I think this is conclusive as to the *country* of Job and his friends. See Mr. *Good* as above.

The *man* and his *country* being thus ascertained, the *time* in which he lived is the point next to be considered.

I feel all the difficulties of the various chronologies of learned men: all that has been offered on the subject is only *opinion* or *probable conjecture;* and, while I differ from many respectable authors, I dare not say that I have more to strengthen my opinion than they have to support theirs.

I do not believe that he lived under the *patriarchal* dispensation; nor in any time *previous* to the *giving of the Law*, or to the *death of Moses*. I have examined the opposite arguments, and they have brought no conviction to my mind. That he lived *after* the giving of the Law appears to me very probable, from what I consider frequent references to the Mosaic institutions occurring in the book, and which I shall notice in their respective places. I know it has been asserted *there are no such references;* and I am astonished at the assertion: the reader will judge whether a plain case is made out where the supposed references occur. An obstinate adherence to a preconceived system is like *prejudice;* it has neither *eyes* nor *ears.*

With this question, that relative to the *author* of the book is nearly connected. Were we to suppose that *Job* himself, or *Elihu,* or *Job* and *his friends,* wrote the work, the question would at once be answered that regards the *time;* but all positive evidence on this point is wanting: and while other suppositions have certain *arguments* to support them, the above claimants who are supported only by critical *conjecture,* must stand where they are for want of evidence. The opinions that appear the most probable, and have plausible arguments to support them, are the following: 1. *Moses* was the author of this book, as many portions of it harmonize with his acknowledged writings. 2. *Solomon* is the most likely author, as many of the sentiments contained in it are precisely the same with those in the Proverbs; and they are delivered often in nearly the same words. 3. The book was written by some *Jew,* in or soon after the time of the Babylonish captivity.

1. That *Moses* was the author has been the opinion of most learned men; and none has set the arguments in support of this opinion in so strong a light as Mr. *Mason Good,* in his *Introductory Dissertation* to his *translation* and *notes* on this book. Mr. G. is a gentleman of great knowledge, great learning, and correct thinking; and whatever he says or writes is entitled to respect. If he have *data,* his deductions are most generally consecutive and solid. He contends, "that the writer of this poem must in his style have been equally master of the *simple* and of the *sublime;* that he must have been minutely and elaborately acquainted with *Astronomy, Natural History,* and the *general science* of his age; that he must have been a *Hebrew* by birth and *native language,* and an *Arabian* by long residence and local study; and, finally, that he must have flourished and composed the work before the exodus." And he thinks that "every one of these features is consummated in *Moses,* and in *Moses* alone; and that the whole of them give us his complete lineaments and portraiture. Instructed in all the learning of Egypt, it appears little doubtful that he composed it during some part of his forty years' residence with the hospitable Jethro, in that district of Idumea which was named Midian." In addition to these external proofs of identity, Mr. *Good* thinks, "a little attention will disclose to us an internal proof, of peculiar force, in the close and striking similarity of diction and idiom which exists between the book of Job and those pieces of poetry which *Moses* is usually admitted to have composed." This point he proceeds to examine; and thinks that the following examples may make some progress toward settling the question, by exhibiting a very singular proof of general *parallelism.*

"The order of creation, as detailed in the first chapter of Genesis, is precisely similar to that described in Job xxxviii. 1–20, the general arrangement that occupied the *first* day;—the formation of the *clouds,* which employed the *second;*—the separation of the *sea,* which took up a part of the *third;*—and the establishment of the *luminaries* in the skies, which characterized the *fourth.*

"In this general description, as given in Genesis, the vapour in the clouds, and the fluid in the sea, are equally denominated *waters:* thus, ver. 5, 6, 7, 'And God said, Let there be a firmament *in the midst of the waters,* and let it divide the *waters from the waters.* And God made the firmament, and divided the *waters which were under* the firmament from the *waters which were above* the firmament.'

"Let us compare this passage with Job xxvi. 8–10:—

> He driveth together the *waters* into His thick clouds;
> And the cloud is not rent under them.—
> He setteth a bow on the face of the *waters,*
> Till the consummation of light and of darkness.

"These are, perhaps, the only instances in the Bible in which the cloudy vapours are denominated *waters,* before they become concentrated into rain; and they offer an identity of thought, which strongly suggests an identity of person. The following is another very striking peculiarity of the same kind, occurring in the same description, and is perhaps still more in point. The combined simplicity and sublimity of Gen. i. 3, 'And God said, Be light! and light was,' has been felt and praised by critics of every age, Pagan and Mohammedan, as well as Jewish and Christian; and has by all of them been regarded as a characteristic feature in the Mosaic style. In the poem before us we have the following proof of identity of manner, chap. xxxvii. 6:—

> Behold! He saith to the snow, Be!
> On earth then falleth it.
> To the rain—and it falleth;—
> The rains of his might.

"This can hardly be regarded as an allusion, but as an instance of identity of manner. In the psalmist we have an allusion: and it occurs thus, xxxiii. 9, הוא אמר ויהי *hu amar vaiyehi,* 'He spake, and it existed;' and I copy it that the reader may see the difference. The eulogy of Longinus upon the passage in Genesis is a eulogy also upon that in Job; and the Koran, in verbally copying the psalmist, has bestowed an equal panegyric upon all of them:—

قال لَهُ كُن فَيَكُونُ

Dixit, 'Esto;' et fuit.—*He said,* Be thou; *and it* was.

"With reference to the description of the creation, in the book of Genesis, I shall only farther observe, that the same simplicity of style, adapted to so lofty a subject, characteristically distinguishes the writer of the book of Job, who commonly employs a diction peculiarly magnificent, as though trusting to the subject to support itself, without the feeble aid of rhetorical ornaments. Of this the description of the tribunal of the Almighty, given in the first and second chapters of the ensuing poem, is a striking example, as indeed I have already remarked; and that of the midnight apparition in the fourth chapter is no less so.

"The following instances are of a more general nature, and lead, upon a broader principle, to the same conclusion:—

Ch. ver.	JOB	Ch. ver.	EXODUS
xiii. 24.	Wherefore accountest thou me thine enemy? Wouldst thou hunt down the parched stubble?	xv. 7.	Thou sentest forth thy wrath, Consuming them as stubble.
iv. 9.	By the blast of God they perish; And by the breath of His nostrils they are consumed.	8.	And with the blast of thy nostrils The waters were gathered together.
xv. 24.	*Distress* and *anguish* dismay him; They overwhelm him as a king ready for battle.	10.	Thou didst blow with thy wind: The sea covered them.
xx. 26.	Terrors shall be upon him— [him.	16.	Terror and dread shall fall upon them: By the might of thine arm they shall be still as a stone.
26.	Every *horror* treasured up in reserve for A fire unblown shall consume him.		

Ch. ver.	JOB	Ch. ver.	DEUTERONOMY
27.	The heavens shall disclose his iniquity, And the earth shall rise up against him.	xxviii. 22.	And Jehovah shall smite thee with a consumption; And with a fever, and with an inflammation, And with an extreme burning.
xviii. 15.	Brimstone shall be rained down upon his dwelling.	23.	And the heaven over thy head shall be brass; And the earth under thee, iron.
16.	Below shall his root be burnt up, And above shall his branch be cut off.	24.	And Jehovah shall make the rain of thy land powder and dust; From heaven shall it come down upon thee, Until thou be destroyed. [tion,
xii. 17.	Counsellors he leadeth captive, And judges he maketh distracted.	28.	Jehovah shall smite thee with destruction, And blindness, and astonishment of heart.
24.	He bewildereth the judgment of the leaders of the people of a land, And causeth them to wander in a pathless desert:		

Ch. ver.	JOB	Ch. ver.	DEUTERONOMY
vii. 25.	They grope about in darkness, even without a glimpse; Yea, he maketh them to reel like the drunkard.	xxviii. 29.	And thou shalt grope at noonday, As the blind gropeth in darkness: And thou shalt not prosper in thy ways: And thou shalt only be oppressed. And consumed continually.
viii. 17.	His roots shall be entangled in a rock; With a bed of stones shall he grapple;		
18.	Utterly shall it drink him up from his place; Yea, it shall renounce him, and say, "I never knew thee."	63.	And it shall come to pass, As Jehovah exulted over you, To do you good, and to multiply you, So will Jehovah exult over you, To destroy you, and reduce you to naught.
19.	Behold the Eternal exulting in his course; Even over his dust shall rise up another.		

"In this specimen of comparison it is peculiarly worthy of remark, that not only the same train of ideas is found to recur, but in many instances the same words, where others might have been employed, and perhaps have answered as well; the whole obviously resulting from the habit of thinking upon subjects in the same manner, and by means of the same terms which is common to every one, and which distinguishes original identity from intentional imitation. I will only advert to one instance: the use of the very powerful, but not very common verb שׂשׂ *sis*, 'to exult,' *exulto, glorior,* γαυριαω, which occurs in the last verse of both the above passages, and is in each instance equally appropriate: ישׂישׂ יהוה *yasis Yehovah*—הוא משׂישׂ *hu mesos,* يستمو مش

"The same term is again employed, Job xxxix. 21, to express the spirited prancing of the high mettled war-horse.

"The above passage from chap. viii. 19 has not been generally understood, and has been given erroneously in the translations." Mr. *Good*, in his notes, p. 101–103, enters at large into a defence of his version of this passage.

Ch. ver.	JOB	Ch. ver.	DEUTERONOMY
viii. 8.	For examine, I beseech thee, the past age; Yea, gird thyself to the study of its forefathers;	xxxii. 7.	Reflect on the days of old; Contemplate the times of ages beyond ages; Inquire of thy father, and he will show thee; Thine elders, *and they will* instruct thee.
10.	Shall not they instruct thee, counsel thee, And swell forth the sayings of their wisdom?		
xx. 17.	He shall not behold the branches of the river, Brooks of honey and butter.—	13.	He gave him to suck honey out of the rock, And oil out of the flinty rock,
xxix. 6.	When my path flowed with butter, And the rock *poured out* for me rivers of oil.	14.	Butter of kine, and milk of sheep.
xv. 27.	Though his face be enveloped with fatness, And heaped up with fatness on his loins.	15.	But Jeshurun waxed fat, and kicked: Thou art waxen fat, thou art grown thick; Thou art *enveloped with* fatness.
vi. 4.	The arrows of the Almighty are within me; Their poison drinketh up my spirit: The *terrors* of God set themselves in array against me;	23.	I will heap mischiefs upon them, I will spend my arrows upon them.
xvi. 13.	His arrows fly around me; He pierceth my reins without mercy.	42.	I will make mine arrows drunk with blood.

"The fine pathetic elegy of the *ninetieth* psalm has been usually ascribed to Moses; and Dathé imagines it was written by him a little before his death.

"Kennicott and Geddes have some doubt upon this point, chiefly because the ultimate period assigned in it to the life of man is fourscore years; while Moses was at his death a hundred and twenty years old, yet 'his eye was not dim, nor his natural force abated;' Deut. xxxiv. 7.

"The following comparison will, perhaps, have a tendency to confirm the general opinion, by rendering it probable that its author and the author of the Book of Job were the same person.

Ch. ver.	JOB	Psa. ver.	PSALM
xiv. 2.	He springeth up as a flower, and is cut down; Yea, he fleeth as a shadow, and endureth not.	xc. 5.	They are like the passing grass of the morning; [groweth:
3.	And dost thou cast thine eyes upon such a one? And wouldst thou bring me into judgment with thyself?	6.	In the morning it springeth up and In the evening it is cut down and withereth.
16.	Yet now art thou numbering my steps; Thou overlookest nothing of my sins:—	7.	For we are consumed by thine anger, And by thy wrath are we troubled.
18.	And for ever, as the crumbling mountain dissolveth, And the rock mouldereth away from his place,	8.	Thou hast set our iniquities before thee: Our secret sins in the light of thy countenance.
19.	So consumest thou the hope of man, Thou harassest him continually till he perish.	9.	Behold, all our days are passed away in thy wrath, We spend our years as a tale that is told.
vii. 21.	Why wilt thou not turn away from my transgression, And let my calamity pass by?	10.	Their strength is labour and sorrow; It is soon cut off, and we flee away.
xi. 14.	If the iniquity of thy hand thou put away, And let not wickedness dwell in thy tabernacles,	12.	So teach us to number our days That we may apply our hearts unto wisdom.
16.	Lo! then shalt thou forget affliction; As waters passed by shalt thou remember it:	14.	O satisfy us early with thy mercy, [days, That we may rejoice and be glad all our
17.	And brighter shall the time be than noontide; Thou shalt shine forth, thou shalt grow vigorous, like the day-spring.	15.	Make us glad according to the days of our affliction, To the years we have seen evil:
		16.	Let thy wonders be shown unto thy servants And thy glory unto their children;
		17.	And let the beauty of Jehovah, our God, be upon us, And establish thou the work of our hands.

"The strictly and decidedly acknowledged productions of Moses are but few; and in the above examples I have taken a specimen from by far the greater number. It is, indeed, not a little astonishing that, being so few, they should offer a resemblance in so many points.

"There may at times be some difficulty in determining between the similarity of style and diction resulting from established habit, and that produced by intentional imitation; yet, in the former case, it will commonly, if I mistake not, be found looser, but more general; in the latter, stricter, but more confined to particular words or idioms; the whole of the features not having been equally caught, while those which have been laid hold of are given more minutely than in the case of habit. The *manner* runs carelessly through every part, and is perpetually striking us unawares; the *copy* walks after it with measured but unequal pace, and is restless in courting our attention. The specimens of resemblance now produced are obviously of the former kind: both sides have an equal claim to originality, and seem very powerfully to establish a unity of authorship."

Thus far Mr. Good; who has, on his own side of the question, most certainly exhausted the subject. The case he has made out is a strong one: we shall next examine whether a stronger cannot be made out in behalf of *Solomon*, as the second candidate for the authorship of this most excellent book.

2. That this book was the work of Solomon was the opinion of some early Christian writers, among whom was Gregory Nazianzen; and of several moderns, among whom were Spanheim and Hardouin. The latter has gone so far as to place the death of Job in the *thirty-fifth* year of the reign of David; and he supposes that Solomon wrote the work in question, about the *second* or *third* year of his reign. On this last opinion no stress whatever should be placed.

As the argument for Moses has been supported by supposed *parallelisms* between his acknowledged works and the Book of Job, so has that which attributes the latter to Solomon. That Solomon, from his *vast learning* and *wisdom*, was capable of such a work, none can deny. His knowledge in *astronomy, natural history, politics, theology, languages,* and the *general science* of *his* age, must have given him at least equal qualifications to those possessed by Moses. And if *he* was the author of the Book of Canticles, which most men believe, he had certainly a *poetic mind*, equal, if not superior, to all the writers who had existed previously to his time. The Book of Proverbs and that of Ecclesiastes are almost universally attributed to him: now, in the Book of Job, there are a multitude of *sentiments*, *sentences, terms*, and *modes of speech*, which are almost peculiar to Solomon, as will appear from the whole books.

In both we find the most exalted eulogium of *wisdom*. See Job xxviii. 12; Prov. viii. 11, &c. Job says, "The *fear of the Lord*, that is *wisdom;* and to depart from evil, that is *understanding;*" chap. xxviii. 28. Solomon says, "The *fear of the Lord* is the beginning of *knowledge*, but *fools* despise *wisdom* and *instruction;*" Prov. i. 7.

Job speaks of the *state of the dead* nearly in the same terms as Solomon: compare chap. xxi. 33, xii. 22, xxxvi. 5, with Prov. ix. 18.

Job says, chap. xxvi. 6, "*Hell* is naked before him, and *destruction* hath no covering." Solomon says, Prov. xv. 11, "*Hell* and *destruction* are before the Lord; how much more the hearts of the children of men?" Job says, "Man drinketh iniquity like water;" chap. xv. 16. And *Elihu* charges him with "drinking *up* scorning like water;" chap. xxxiv. 7. The same image occurs in *Solomon*, Prov. xxvi. 6: "He that sendeth a message by the hand of a fool *drinketh* damage."

In Job xv. 34 it is said, "Fire shall consume the tabernacle of *bribery*." The same turn of thought occurs Prov. xv. 27: "He that is greedy of gain troubleth his own house; but he that hateth *gifts* shall live."

Both speak of *weighing the spirits* or *winds*. See Job xxviii. 25; Prov. xvi. But to me the parallelism in these cases is not evident, as both the reason of the saying, and some of the terms in the original, are different. Job tells his friends, "If they would *hold their peace*, it would be their *wisdom;*" chap. xiii. 5. Solomon has the same sentiment in nearly the same words, Prov. xvii. 28: "Even a fool, when he *holdeth his peace*, is counted *wise;* and he that shutteth his lips is esteemed a man of understanding."

Solomon represents the *rephaim* or *giants* as in *hell*, or the *great deep;* Prov. ii. 18; ix. 18, vii. 27. The like sentiment is in Job xxvi. 5. See the Hebrew.

In Job xxvii. 16, 17, it is said that "If the wicked heap up silver as the dust, and prepare raiment as the clay; the just shall put it on, and the innocent shall divide the silver." The like sentiment is found, Prov. xxviii. 8: "He that by usury and unjust gain increaseth his substance, he shall gather for him that will pity the poor." Solomon says, Prov. xvi. 18: "Pride goeth before destruction, and a haughty spirit before a fall:" and, "Before destruction the heart of man is haughty; and before honour is humility;" xviii. 12: and, "A man's pride shall bring him low; but honour shall uphold the humble in spirit." The same sentiment is expressed in Job xxii. 29: "When men are *cast down*, then thou shalt say, There is a *lifting up;* and he shall save the *humble* person."

Both speak nearly in the same way concerning the *creation* of the *earth* and the *sea*. "Where wast thou when I *laid the foundations of the earth?—*Who *shut up the sea* with doors, when it brake forth as if it had issued from the womb?" Job xxxviii. 4–8. This seems a reference to the *flood*. In Prov. vii. 22–29 *Wisdom* says: "The Lord possessed me in the beginning of his way—when as yet he had not *made the earth*—when he gave to the *sea* his decree that the *waters* should not *pass his commandment:* when he *appointed* the *foundations of the earth*." These are precisely the same kind of conceptions, and nearly the same phraseology.

In Job xx. 7 it is said, "The wicked shall *perish* for ever, like his own DUNG." And in Prov. x. 7 it is said, "The name of the wicked shall ROT."

It would not be difficult to enlarge this list of correspondences by a collation of passages in *Job* and in *Proverbs;* but most of them will occur to the attentive reader. There is, however, another *class of evidence* that appears still more forcible, viz.: There are several *terms* used frequently in the Book of Job and in the books of Solomon which are almost *peculiar* to those books, and which argue an *identity* of *authorship*. The noun תושיה *tushi-yah*, which may signify *essence, substance, reality, completeness*, occurs in Job and Proverbs. See Job v. 12, vi. 13, xi. 6, xii. 16, xxvi. 3, and xxx. 22; Proverbs ii. 7, iii. 21, viii. 14, and xviii. 1. And it occurs only *twice*, as far as I can recollect, in all the Bible besides; viz., Isa. xxviii. 29, and Mic. vi. 9. The word הוה *havvah*, used in the sense of *misfortune, ruinous downfall, calamity*, occurs Job vi. 2, 30, xxx. 13, and in Prov. x. 3, xi. 6, xvii. 4, and xix. 13. It occurs nowhere else, except once in Ezek. vii. 26, once in Micah vii. 3, and a few times in the Psalms, v. 9, lii. 2, 7, lv. 12, xci. 3, xciv. 20, xxxvii. 12, and lxii. 3.

The word תחבלות *tachbuloth, wise counsels*, occurs only in Job xxxvii. 12, and in Prov. i. 5, xi. 14, xii. 5, xx. 18, and xxiv. 6; and nowhere else in the Bible in this form. And פתה *potheh, the silly one, simpleton, fool*, is used precisely in the same sense in Job v. 2, Prov. xix. 7, and in various other parts of the same book. The word אבדון, *abaddon, destruction*, Job xxvi. 6, xxviii. 22, xxxi. 12, connected sometimes with שאול *sheol, hell*, or the *grave*; and מות *maveth, death*, occurs as above, and in Prov. xv. 11, and xxvii. 20.

Calmet, who refers to several of the above places, adds: It would be easy to collect a great number of similar parallel passages; but it must make a forcible impression in favour of this opinion when we observe in Job and Proverbs the same *principles*, the same sentiments, the same *terms*, and some that are found only in Job and Solomon. We may add farther, the beauty of the *style*, the sublimity of the *thoughts*, the dignity of the *matter*, the *form* and *order* in which the *materials* of this writer are laid down, the vast *erudition* and astonishing *fecundity* of *genius*, all of which perfectly characterize Solomon.

Besides the above, we find many *forms of expression* in this book which prove that its author had a *knowledge of the law of God*, and *many* which show that he was acquainted with the *Psalms* of David, and a few very like what we find in the *writings of the prophets*. I shall insert a few more:—

Job xv. 27: Because he covereth his face with *fatness*.
Job xxxiv. 14: If he set his heart upon man, he shall gather unto himself his *spirit* and his *breath*.

Job xxi. 9: Their houses are safe from fear; neither is the rod of God upon them.
Job xxi. 10: Their bull gendereth, and faileth not; their cow calveth, and casteth not her calf.
Job xxi. 18: They (the wicked) are as *stubble* before the *wind;* and as *chaff* that the storm carrieth away.
Job xxii. 19: The *righteous see it*, and are *glad;* and the innocent laugh them to scorn.

Job xxxviii. 41: Who provideth for the *raven his* food? when his *young ones cry unto God*.
Job xii. 21: *He poureth contempt upon princes*, and weakeneth the strength of the mighty.
Job iii. 3: *Let the day perish in which I was born;* and the night in which it was said, There is a man-child conceived. See also chap. x. 18.

Job xxi. 7: *Wherefore do the wicked live*, become old, and are *mighty in power?*
Job xxviii. 12: But where shall *wisdom be found*, and where is the place of *understanding?* 13: Man knoweth not the price thereof; neither is it found in the land of the living.

Psa. xvii. 10: They are *inclosed* in their own *fat.* lxxiii. 7: Their eyes stand out with *fatness*.
Psa. civ. 29: Thou hidest thy face, and they are troubled: thou *takest away* their *breath;* they die, and return to their dust.

Psa. lxxiii. 5: They are not in trouble as other men; neither are they plagued like other men.
Psa. cxliv. 13, 14: Let our sheep bring forth thousands;—and our oxen be strong to labour.
Psa. i. 4: The ungodly are like the *chaff* which the *wind* driveth away.

Psa. lviii. 10: The *righteous shall rejoice* when he seeth the *vengeance;* he shall wash his feet in the blood of the wicked.
Psa. cxlvii. 9: He giveth to the *beast his* food; and to the *young ravens which cry*.
Psa. cvii. 40: *He poureth contempt upon princes*, and causeth them to wander in the wilderness.
Jer. xv. 10: *Wo is me, my mother, that thou hast borne me, a man of strife*. xx. 14, 15: *Cursed be the day wherein I was born*—let not the day wherein my mother bare me be blessed.

Jer. xii. 1, 2: *Wherefore doth the way of the wicked prosper? they grow;* yea, they *bring forth fruit*.
Collate these verses with *Baruch* iii. 14, 15, 29, and see Prov. i. 20–23, ii. 2–7, iii. 13–18, iv. 5–9, viii. 10–35.

The remarkable sentiment that "God, as Sovereign of the world, does treat the righteous and the wicked, independently of their respective merits, with a similar lot in this life, and that like events often happen to both," is maintained in the Book of Job and the Ecclesiastes of Solomon. Job ix. 22–24: "He *destroyeth* the *perfect* and the *wicked*. If the scourge slay suddenly, he will laugh at the trial of the *innocent*. The *earth* is *given* into the *hand* of the *wicked;* he covereth the faces of the judges thereof; if not, where and who is he?" x. 15: "If I be *wicked,* wo unto me; and if I be *righteous,* yet will I not lift up my head." ix. 15: "*Whom,* though I were *righteous,* yet would I not *answer;* I would make supplication to my Judge." xii. 6: "The tabernacles of *robbers prosper,* and they that *provoke God* are *secure;* into whose hand God bringeth abundantly." xxi. 7–9: "Wherefore do the *wicked live, become old,* yea are *mighty* in *power?* Their *seed* is *established* in their *sight,* and their *offspring before their eyes.* Their *houses* are *safe* from *fear,* neither is the *rod of God upon them.*"

Similar sentiments, with a great similarity of expression, are found in the following passages from *Solomon.* Eccles. vi. 8: "For what hath the *wise* more than the *fool?*" viii. 14: "There be *just men* to whom it happeneth *according* to the *work* of the *wicked.* Again, there be *wicked men* to whom it happeneth *according* to the *work* of the *righteous.*" ix. 2: "*All things come alike to all:* there is *one event to the righteous* and to the *wicked;* to the *good* and to the *clean,* and to the *unclean;* to him that *sacrificeth,* and to him that *sacrificeth not.* As is the *good,* so is the *sinner;* and he that *sweareth,* as he that *feareth* an *oath.*" vii. 15: "There is a *just man* that *perisheth* in his *righteousness;* and there is a *wicked man* that *prolongeth* his life in *his wickedness.*"

I may conclude this with the words of a learned translator of the book of Job, and apply in reference to *Solomon* what he applies to *Moses:* "The specimens of resemblance now produced have an equal claim to originality, and seem very powerfully to establish a unity of authorship." I think the argument much stronger in favour of Solomon as its author than of Moses: and while even here I hesitate, I must enter my protest against the conclusions drawn by others; and especially those who profess to show where *David, Solomon, Isaiah, Jeremiah, Ezekiel,* &c., have *copied* and *borrowed* from Job! Some of them, in all probability, never saw the book; and those who did had an *inspiration, dignity, manner,* and *power* of their own, that rendered it quite unnecessary to borrow from him. Such plagiarism would appear, in common cases, neither requisite nor graceful. I have a high opinion of the book of Job, but God forbid that I should ever bring it on a level with the *compositions* of the *sweet singer of Israel,* the inimitable *threnodies* of *Jeremiah,* or the *ultra-sublime* effusions of the *evangelical prophet.* Let each keep his place, and let God be acknowledged as the inspirer of all.

Thus, by exactly the same process, we come to different conclusions; for the evidence is now as strong *that Job lived posterior to the days of Moses;* that he was acquainted with the *Law* and the *Prophets;* that either he took much from the *Psalms* and *Proverbs,* or that *David* and *Solomon* borrowed much from him; or that *Solomon,* the son of *David,* wrote the history; as it is that he lived in the days of *Moses.*

For my own part, I think the *later date* by far the most probable; and although I think the arguments that go to prove *Solomon* to be the *author* are *weightier* than those so skilfully brought forth by learned men in behalf of *Moses,* yet I think if possible that it was the work of *neither,* but rather of *some learned Idumean,* well acquainted with the Jewish religion and writers; and I still hold the opinion which I formed more than *thirty* years ago, when I read over this book in the *Septuagint,* and afterwards in the *Hebrew,* that it is most probable the work was originally composed in *Arabic,* and afterwards translated into *Hebrew* by a person who either had not the same command of the *Hebrew* as he had of the *Arabic,* or else purposely affected the *Arabic idiom,* retaining many *Arabic words* and *Arabisms;* either because he could not find appropriate expressions in the *Hebrew,* or because he wished to *adorn* and *enrich* the *one language* by borrowing copiously from the other. The *Hebrew* of the book of Job differs as much from the pure Hebrew of *Moses* and the *early prophets,* as the Persian of *Ferdoosy* differs from that of *Saady.* Both these were *Persian poets;* the *former* wrote in the simplicity and purity of his elegant native language, adopting very few *Arabic* words; while *the latter* labours to introduce them at every turn, and has thus produced a language neither *Persian* nor *Arabic*. And so prevalent is this custom become with all Persian writers, both in *prose* and *verse*, that the pure Persian becomes daily more and more corrupted, insomuch that there is reason to fear that in process of time it will be swallowed up in the language of the conquerors of that country, in which it was formerly esteemed the most polished language of Asia. Such influence has the language of a conqueror on the country he has subdued; witness our own, where a paltry *French phraseology*, the remnant of one of the evils brought upon us by our *Norman conqueror* and *tyrant*, has greatly weakened the strong current of our mother tongue; so that, however amalgamated, filed, and polished by eminent authors, we only speak a very tolerable jargon, *enriched*, as we foolishly term it, by the spoils of other tongues. The best specimen of our ancient language exists in the *Lord's prayer*, which is pure *English*, or what is called *Anglo-Saxon*, with the exception of three frenchified words, *trespasses, temptation*, and *deliver*.

But to return to the book of Job. The collections of Mr. Good, Dr. Magee, and others, if they do not prove that *Moses was the author of the book*, prove that the author was well acquainted with the Mosaic writings; and prove that he was also acquainted with the ninetieth Psalm; and this last circumstance will go far to prove that he lived *after* the days of *David*, for we have no evidence whatever that the ninetieth Psalm was *published* previously to the collection and publication of the Psalms now generally termed the *Psalms of David*, though many of them were written by other hands, and not a few even *after the Babylonish captivity*. And, as to the *inscription* to this Psalm, תפלה משה איש האלהים *tephillah Mosheh ish haelohim*, "A prayer of Moses, the man of God;" 1. We know not that *Moses* the *Jewish lawgiver* is meant: it might be another person of the same name. 2. And even in that case it does not positively state that this Moses was the *author* of it. 3. The *inscriptions* to the Psalms are of *dubious*, and many of them of *no authority*: some of them evidently *misplaced;* and others either bearing *no relation* to the *matter* of the *Psalms* to which they are prefixed, or evidently contradictory to that matter. Hence our translators have considered these inscriptions as of *no authority;* and have not admitted them, in any case, into the *body* of their respective Psalms. The *parallelism*, therefore, drawn from this Psalm, will not help much to prove that *Moses was the author of the book of Job;* but it will go far to prove, as will be seen in other cases, that the author of this book was acquainted with the *book of Psalms*, as several of the preceding collections testify; and that there is a probability that he had read the *prophets* that lived and wrote in the *time*, and *after* the time, of the *Babylonish captivity*, which appears to me the only thing that shakes the argument in favour of *Solomon;* unless we take the *converse* of the question, and say that *Moses, David, Solomon, Isaiah, Jeremiah,* and *Micah,* all knew and borrowed from the *book of Job*. But this supposition will, in its turn, be shaken by the consideration that there are several things in the book of Job which evidently refer to the *law as already given*, and to some of the *principal occurrences* in the Israelitish history, if such references can be made out. These considerations have led me to think it probable that the book was written *after the captivity* by some unknown but highly eminent and inspired man. We may wonder, indeed, that the author of such an eminent work has not been handed down to posterity; and that the question should be left at the discretion of the whole *limbus* of conjecture; but we find, not only several books in the Bible, but also other works of minor importance and a later date, similarly circumstanced. We have no certain evidence of the *author* of the books of *Judges, Samuel, Kings, Chronicles, Ruth, Ezra, Nehemiah,* or *Esther;* we can, in reference to them, make *probable conjectures,* but this is all. Even in the *New Testament* the author of the *Epistle to the Hebrews* is still unknown; though a pretty general tradition, and strong internal evidence, give it to St. Paul; yet this point is not *so proved* as to exclude all doubt.

The finest poems of heathen antiquity, the *Iliad* and *Odyssey*, cannot be certainly traced to their author. Of the person called *Homer*, to whom they have been attributed, no one knows any thing. He is still, for aught we know, a *fabulous* person; and the relations concerning him are entitled to little more credit than is due to the *Life of Æsop* by *Planudes*. *Seven* different *cities* have claimed the honour of being his birth-place. They are expressed in the following distich:—

'Επτα πολεις διεριζουσι περι ριζαν 'Ομηρου,
Σμυρνα, 'Ροδος, Κολοφον, Σαλαμις, Χιος, Αργος, Αθηναι.

Smyrna, Rhodos, Colophon, Salamis, Chios, Argos, Athenæ,
Orbis de Patria certat, HOMERE, *tua.*

Nor have these claims ever been adjusted. Some have gone so far as to attribute the work to *Solomon*, king of Israel, composed *after* his defection from the true religion to idolatry! that the word *Homer*, 'Ομηρος *Homeros*, is merely *Hebrew*, אמרים *omerim*, with a *Greek* termination, signifying the *sayings* or *discourses*, from אמר *amar, he spoke;* the whole work being little more than the *dialogues* or *conversations* of the eminent characters of which it is composed. Even the *battles* of Homer are full of *parleys;* and the principal information conveyed by the poem is through the *conversation* of the respective chiefs.

The *Makamaton*, or *assemblies*, of the celebrated Arabic author *Hariri*, show us how *conversations* were anciently carried on among the *Arabs*, and even in the same country in which the plan of the poem of Job is laid; and were we closely to compare the *sex concessus* of that author, published by *Schultens*, we might find many analogies between them and the turn of conversation in the book of Job. But the *uncertainty* relative to the *author* detracts nothing from the *merit* and *excellency* of the *poem*. As it is the most singular, so it is the best, as a whole, in the *Hebrew* canon. It exhibits a full view of the opinions of the eastern sages on the most important points; not only their *religion* and *system* of *morals* are frequently introduced, but also their philosophy, astronomy, natural history, mineralogy, and *arts* and *sciences* in general; as well those that were *ornamental*, as those which ministered to the comforts and necessities of life. And on a careful examination, we shall probably find that several arts, which are supposed to be the discoveries of the *moderns*, were not unknown to those who lived in a very remote antiquity, and whom it is fashionable to consider as *unlettered* and *uncultivated barbarians*.

As the person, family, time, and descendants of Job are so very uncertain, I shall not trouble my readers with the many *genealogical tables* which have been constructed by chronologists and commentators; yet it might be considered a *defect* were I not to notice what is inserted at the end of the *Greek* and *Arabic* Versions relative to this point; to which I shall add Dr. *Kennicott's* Tables, and the substance of a letter which contains some curious particulars.

"And he (Job) dwelt in the land of *Ausitis*, in the confines of Idumea and Arabia; and his former name was *Jobab*. And he took to wife Arabissa, and begat a son whose name was Ennon. And his (Jobab's) father's name was Zarith, one of the sons of the children of Esau; and his mother's name was Bosora; and thus he was the *fifth* from Abraham."

"And these are the kings who reigned in Edom; which region he also governed; the first was *Balak*, the son of Beor, the name of whose city was Dennaba. And after Balak reigned *Jobab*, who is also called Job. And after him *Assom*, the governor of the country of the Temanites. After him *Adad*, the son of Basad, who cut off Madian in the plain of Moab; and the name of his city was Gethaim."

"The *friends* who came to visit him were *Eliphaz*, son of Sophan, of the children of Esau, king of the Temanites. *Baldad*, the son of Amnon, of Chobar, tyrant of the Sauchites. *Sophar*, king of the Minaites. *Thaiman*, son of Eliphaz, governor of the Idumeans."

"This is translated from the Syriac copy. He dwelt in the land of *Ausitis*, on the borders of the Euphrates; and his former name was *Jobab;* and his father was Zareth, who came from the east." This is verbatim from the *Codex Alexandrinus*.

The *Arabic* is not so circumstantial, but is the same in substance. "And Job dwelt in the land of *Auz*, between the boundaries of Edom and Arabia; and he was at first called *Jobab*. And he married a strange woman, and to her was born a son called *Anun*. But Job was the son of *Zara*, a descendant of the children of *Esau;* his mother's name was *Basra*, and he was the *sixth* from Abraham. Of the kings who reigned in Edom, the first who reigned over that land was *Balak*, the son of Beor, and the name of his city was Danaba. And after him *Jobab*, the same who is called Job. And after Job, he (Assom) who was prince of the land of Teman. And after him (Adad) the son of Barak, he who slew and put to flight Madian, in the plains of Moab; and the name of his city was Jatham. And of the *friends* of Job who visited him was *Eliphaz*, the son of Esau, king of the Temanites."

Dr. Kennicott says, When Job lived seems deducible from his being contemporary with Eliphaz, the Temanite, thus:—

ABRAHAM

	ISAAC		
1			1
2 Esau.		Jacob.	2
3 Eliphaz.		Levi.	3
4 Teman.		Kohath.	4
5 Eliphaz the Temanite.		Amram—Job.	5
		Moses.	

The late Miss Mary Freeman Shepherd, well known for her strong masculine genius, and knowledge of various languages, sent me the following genealogy and remarks, which she thought would clearly ascertain the time of Job. I faithfully transcribe them from her letter to me, a short time before her death.

"Shem, two years after the flood, begat Arphaxad and Uz, and also Aram	2
Arphaxad begat Salah at	35
Salah begat Eber at	30
Eber begat Peleg at	34
Peleg, in whose time the earth was divided, begat Reu at	30
Reu begat Serug at	32
Serug begat Nahor at	30
Nahor begat Terah at	29
Terah begat Abraham at	70
Abraham begat Ishmael at eighty-six, Israel at	100
Isaac married at forty, soon after, probably at forty-three, Esau and Jacob born	43
Jacob married at forty, had Reuben his first-born, and Levi born of Leah, by the time he was forty-four	44
Levi begat Kohath, suppose at	40
Kohath begat Amram, suppose at	40
Amram begat Moses, suppose at	40
After the deluge	599

"Shem was the father of Aram, who gave his name to the Aramites, *i. e.*, the Syrians; and he was the father of Uz, who gave his name to the *land of Uz*, in which JOB *dwelt*, not was *born*, for the text says, *There was a man in the land of Uz, called Job.*

"In Gen. xlvi. 13, one of the sons of Issachar is named *Job*. In the genealogies of Num. xxvi. 24, and in 1 Chron. vii. 1, he is called *Jashub*. It is remarkable that there is no mention in Chronicles of the sons of Jashub, or of any of the sons of Issachar, among the thousands of Israel, sons of Tola, where, might not *Job* be called *Jashub?* Mitzraim, *i. e.*, Egypt, was a son of Ham; Uz and Aram, sons of Shem; Ishmael by Hagar, and Midian by Keturah, both sons to Abram. How well does this account for the nearness of the languages of these people, being scions from the same mother tongue!

"Ishmael, the father of the tribes of Arabia; Arabic was, therefore, not their mother tongue. The roots of these languages germinated from the Hebrew roots, and so a new language sprang up, afterwards formed according to grammatic rules, and enriched as arts and sciences, and cultivated genius, added new inventions. Things new and unknown before gave rise to new words or names. Nouns, and the action, operation, and effects of arts and sciences, produced verbs or roots. Thus the Arabic become so copious and rich, and has roots not in the pure original Hebrew. All this considered, might not Moses have written the book of Job, as parts of Ezra, Nehemiah, and Daniel were written, after the captivity, in a mixed language, in order that it might be the better understood by those for whom it was written; those of the people who, being left in Jerusalem, had retained their native Hebrew; and those who had, by long residence in Babylon, corrupted and mingled it with the Chaldaic, which is a dialect of the Hebrew, like the modern language of Italy when compared with that of ancient Rome, or our modern Latin when compared with that of the Augustan age.

"By the influence of climate upon the organs of speech, the different avocations, usages, diet, turn of mind, and genius of men, the dialects which all streamed from one language, and *pronounced* in one and the same *speech*, confounded, (not annihilated, troubled, but not dried up,) no new language then created, yet so confounded in utterance that they understood not one another's speech. The operation was upon the ear of the heart, as in the day of pentecost: one man spoke, and all, though of different tongues, understood; the ear suggested the various sounds to the tongue, and from thence the varied pronunciations of one and the same language often makes it misunderstood.

"*Shem*, who lived five hundred and two years after the deluge, being still alive, and in the three hundred and ninety-third year of his life, when Abram was born, therefore the Jewish tradition that Shem was the Melchisedek, (my righteous king of Salem,) an epithet, or title of honour and respect, not a proper name, and, as the head and father of his race, Abraham paid tithes to him; this seems to me well founded, and the idea confirmed by these remarkable words, Psalm cx., *Jehovah hath sworn, and will not repent,* אתה כהן לעולם על דברתי מלכי־צדק *attah cohen leolam al dibrathi malki-tsedek.* As if he had said, *Thou,* my only-begotten Son, first-born of many brethren; not according to the *substituted* priesthood of the sons of Levi, who, after the sin of the golden calf, stood up in lieu of all the first-born of Israel, invested with their forfeited rights of primogeniture of king and priest; the Lord hath sworn, and will not repent, (change,) Thou art a priest for ever after the (my order of Melchisedek, my own original primitive) order of primogeniture; even as *Shem* the *man of name*, the *Shem* that stands the *first* and foremost of the sons of Noah. The *righteous prince and priest of the most high God* meets his descendant Abraham after the slaughter of the kings, with refreshments; blessed him as the head and father of his race, and as such, he receives from Abraham the tithe of all the spoil.

"How beautifully does Paul of Tarsus, writing to the Hebrews, point through Melchisedek,—Shem, the head and father of their race, invested in all the original rights of primogeniture, priest of the most high God, blessing Abraham as such, as Levi even had existence, and as such receiving tithe from Abraham, and in him from Levi yet in the loins of his forefathers, when Moses on this great and solemn occasion records simply this: Melchisedek, king of Salem, priest of the most high God, *sine genealogia;* his pedigree not mentioned, but standing, as *Adam* in St. Luke's genealogy, without father and without mother, *Adam of God,* Luke iii., last verse;—how beautifully, I say, doth St. Paul point through Melchisedek to Jehoshua our great High Priest and King, whose eternal generation who shall declare! *Hammashiach,* the Lord's Anointed, Priest, and King, after the order of Melchisedek, only begotten first-born Son! The Levitical priesthood that arose from the sin of the golden calf and the forfeited rights of the first-born, in whose stead stood the sons of Levi, (the reward of their zeal for God, on that sad occasion.) This right of primogeniture, as the streams of Jordan at the presence of God, *conversus est retrorsum,* to its fountain head; and *Judah was his sanctuary,* Psalm cxiv. Reuben forfeited by incest his *excellence;* Simeon and Levi, the right in priority of birth, theirs; and Judah, he to whom his brethren should bow down as their head. From the time of Abraham, who married a sister of Haran, prince of the tribe of Judah, to the time of *Jesus,* the tribes of Levi and Judah intermarried: thus was incorporated the source and streams in one. And the very names of all the sons of the tribes of Israel lost in *one,* that of Jehudah, from which they call themselves Jehudim.

"The *shebit*, tribe, not sceptre, the rod or ensign of the chief of a tribe. 'The *tribe*, *genealogy*, shall not recede from Jehudah until Shiloh come;' for whose genealogy they subsist. Ten, by the schism of Jeroboam, may be carried away beyond the river, and heard of no more; but Jehudah, Levi, and Benjamin, shall be tribes; and their registers shall be clear and unbroken until the temple and city and all the registers of genealogy are destroyed. The people are one; one people worshipping one God. 'I have prayed,' said Jehoshua Mashiach, 'that ye might be one in me, as I and my Father are one.'

"Ham, the son of Noah, begat Cush, and Cush begat Nimrod, and Saba, and others. Nimrod began a monarchy, and founded Babel. Out of that land went forth Asshur, and builded Nineveh. Nimrod was therefore contemporary with Peleg. Compare Gen. ii. 8, 9, with Gen. ix. 10–25.

"Thus, in about two hundred and ten or twenty years after the deluge, by the confusion of tongues, was the earth divided; as its inhabitants, dispersing no doubt in families together formed themselves into nations, people, and tribes and kindreds, and from thence into *tongues*.

"From the knowledge I have of the Hebrew, I have caught a glance of the genius, spirit, and tone of the general march of the oriental tongues, and even of the expression of their character. To me the book of Job seems to have much of the Chaldee, both in words and idiom, and much of the sublimity and spirit of the writings of Moses. His grand descriptions of the Most High, his wondrous works, his power, wisdom, justice, and truth, all speak the historian of Genesis, the legislator of Israel, the unconsumed fire of the burning bush, the loud thunders of Sinai, and the shinings of the light of God. That pointed exactness and conciseness of narration that distinguish Moses, are also conspicuous in the book of Job. If Moses did indeed write this book, he wrote it for the *nations*, as well as for Israel; and took, as the best vehicle of a general conveyance, a language most generally understood. At this day, for the facilitating of intercourse in the Levant, Mediterranean, Archipelago, &c., there is a language called *Lingua Franca*, the language of the Franks. To Israel Moses conveyed the pure language of their fathers; but rather than the nations should be famished for bread, or die for thirst, he put *manna* in their coarse earthen vessels, and wine in their wooden cups.

"You see, my dear sir, how strong is female obstinacy; I struggle and contend for the body of Moses. I admire Moses; I admire Job. God, by the prophet Ezekiel and the apostle St. James, ascertains the history of Job to be a fact, not a fiction. And thus inspiration sustains its inspiration.

"Will you, dear sir, think it worth while to collect and put together these scattered scraps, as little pegs to better shelves, which you must furbish, smooth, and point;—too hard a work for *Mary* the aged? Blessed are the pure of heart, for they shall see God: and in him see all truth."—*M. F. S.*

Miss Shepherd is a strong auxiliary to Mr. Good; still I remain unconvinced. My readers must choose for themselves.

The history of Job, but strangely disguised, is well known among the Asiatics. He is called by the Arabic and Persian historians ایّوب *Ayoub*, which is exactly the same as the Hebrew איוב *Ayoub*, which Europeans have strangely metamorphosed into *Job*. In the *Tareekh Muntekheb* his genealogy is given thus: Ayoub the son of Anosh, the son of Razakh, the son of Ais, (Esau,) the son of Isaac. He was a prophet, and was afflicted by a grievous malady *three years*, or according to others, *seven years;* at the end of which, when eighty years of age, he was restored to perfect health, and had a son named *Bash ben Ayoub.* Other writers say he had *five* sons, with whom he made war on a brutal people called *Dsul Kefel*, whom he exterminated because they refused to receive the knowledge of the true God, whom he preached to them. *Khondemir*, who entitles him *Job the patient*, gives us his history in the following manner:—

"*Job*, by his father's side, was descended from *Esau*, and by his mother from *Lot*. *Abou Giaffer al Tabary* relates that God sent him to preach to the inhabitants of *Thaniah*, a people who dwelt between Remla and Damascus; but *three* persons only received the truth. Nevertheless, as he was very zealous in the service of God, he rewarded his faith and obedience by heaping riches upon him, and giving him a numerous family. This excited the envy of the devil, who, presenting himself before God, accused Job as one who was *selfish* in his devotion; and, were it not for the temporal blessings which he received from his Maker, he would not worship even once in the day. God having given Satan permission to spoil Job of his goods, and deprive him of his children, he gave the same proofs of his piety, worshipping God as before, and patiently bearing his great losses. Satan, enraged to be thus baffled, presented himself once more before God, and asserted that Job continued thus faithful because he knew that God would reward his constancy with an equal or even greater portion of earthly blessings: but if he would afflict his *body* by some grievous disease, he would soon abandon his service, and be at the end of his patience. In order fully to show the piety of this exemplary man, God permitted Satan to afflict his body as he pleased, with the exception of his *eyes*, his *ears*, and his *tongue*. The devil, having received this permission, blew up the nostrils of Job such a pestilential heat as immediately turned his whole mass of blood into corruption, so that his whole body became one ulcer, the smell of which was so offensive that his greatest intimates could not approach him; and he was obliged to be carried out of the city, and laid in a distant place entirely by himself. Notwithstanding, Job continued both his patience and piety. His wife, *Rosina*, never forsook him, but continued daily to bring him the necessaries of life. Satan observing this, stole from her the provision she had made for her husband; and when reduced to the lowest ebb, he appeared to her under the form of an old *bald woman*, and told her, that if she would give her the two tresses of hair that hung down on her neck, she would provide her daily with what was necessary for her husband's support. This offer appearing so very advantageous in behalf of her afflicted husband, she accepted the offer, and gave the two tresses to the old woman.

"Satan, overjoyed at the success of his plots, went to Job, told him that his wife had been caught in the act of adultery, and that her tresses had been cut off, and here was the proof of the fact. Job, seeing this, and finding his wife without her tresses, not supposing that he was deceived by the devil, lost his patience, and bound himself by an oath, that if he should ever recover his health he would inflict on her the most exemplary punishment. Satan, supposing he had now gained his end, transformed himself into an *angel of light*, and went throughout the country as a messenger of God, informing the people that Job, who was counted a prophet, had fallen from his piety and brought the wrath of God upon him; that they should no more listen to his preaching, but banish him from among them, lest the curse of God should fall on the whole country.

"Job, coming to understand how the matter stood, had recourse to God by faith and prayer, and said these remarkable words, which are found in the KORAN: 'Distress closes me in on every side: but thou, O Lord, art more merciful than all those who can feel compassion.' On this all his pains and sufferings immediately ceased; for Gabriel, the faithful servant of the Most High, descended from heaven, took Job by the hand, and lifting him up from the place where he lay, stamped on the ground with his foot, and immediately a spring of water rose up from the earth, out of which Job having drunk, and washed his body, he was instantly cleansed of all his ulcers, and restored to perfect health.

"God, having thus restored him, greatly multiplied his goods, so that the rain and the snow which fell around his dwelling were precious; and his riches became so abundant, as if showers of gold had descended upon him."

This is the sum of the account given by the oriental historians, who, forsaking the truth of the sacred history, have blended the story with their own fables. The great facts are however the same in the main; and we find that with them the personality, temptation, and deliverance of Job, are matters of serious credibility. Abul Faragius says that the trial of Job happened in the twenty-fifth year of Nahor, son of Serug; thus making him prior to Abraham. He calls him ايوب الطديق *Ayoub assadeek, Job the righteous.* See *Abul Faragius, Ebn Batric, D'Herbelot,* &c.

Commentators have considered this book as being divided into distinct parts. Mr. Good, who considers it a regular Hebrew epic, divides it into *six parts* or books, which he considers to be its natural division, and unquestionably intended by the author. These six parts are, an *opening* or *exordium*, containing the introductory history or decree concerning Job; *three* distinct series of arguments, in each of which the speakers are regularly allowed their respective turns; the *summing* up of the controversy; and the *close* of the *catastrophe*, consisting of the suffering hero's grand and glorious acquittal, and restoration to prosperity and happiness.

PART I.—*The* TEMPTATION *of Job decreed*

Which contains.—1. A brief narrative of Job. 2. The tribunal of the *Almighty.* 3. His remarks to *Satan* concerning Job's fidelity. 4. Satan's reply. 5. The *Almighty* consents to his temptation. 6. Return of the celestial tribunal. 7. The fidelity of Job proved and declared. 8. *Satan* insinuates that he would not have proved true had the attack been made on his person. 9. The *Almighty* consents to a second trial. 10. The trial made. 11. Job's utter misery. 12. The visit of his three friends to condole with him. Chap. i. and ii.

PART II.—*First Series of Controversy*

1. Exclamation of *Job* on his miserable condition. 2. Speech of *Eliphaz*, accusing him of want of firmness, and suspecting his integrity, on account of the affliction with which he is visited. 3. *Job's* reply, reproaching his friends with cruelty; bewailing the disappointment he had felt in them; calling for death as the termination of his miseries; then longing for life, expostulating with the Almighty, and supplicating his forgiveness. 4. *Bildad* resumes the argument of Eliphaz with great severity; openly accuses Job of hypocrisy; and exhorts him to repentance, in order that he may avoid utter ruin. 5. *Job* in reply longs to plead his cause before God, but is overwhelmed at his majesty. 6. He again desponds, and calls for death as the only refuge from his sorrows. 7. *Zophar* continues the argument on the side of his companions; condemns Job acrimoniously for still daring to assert his innocence; and once more exhorts him to repentance, as the only means of obtaining a restoration to the favour of the *Almighty.* 8. *Job* is stimulated to a still severer reply. 9. Accuses his companions of declaiming on the part of God, with the base hope of propitiating him. 10. Boldly demands his trial at the tribunal of the Almighty; and, realizing the tribunal before him, commences his pleading, in an address variegated on every side by opposite feelings: fear, triumph, humiliation, expostulation, despondency. Chap. iii.–xiv.

PART III.—*Second Series of Controversy*

1. *Eliphaz* commences the discussion in his regular turn; accuses Job of vehemence and vanity; asserts that no man is innocent; and that his own conduct sufficiently proves himself not to be so. 2. *Job* replies; and complains bitterly of the unjust reproaches heaped upon him; and accuses his companions of holding him up to public derision. 3. He pathetically bemoans his lot; and looks forward to the grave with glimmering, through despair, of a resurrection from its ruins. 4. *Bildad* perseveres in his former argument of Job's certain wickedness, from his signal sufferings; and, in a string of lofty traditions, points out the constant attendance of misery upon wickedness. 5. *Job* rises superior to this attack; appeals to the piety and generosity of his friends; asserts the Almighty to have afflicted him for purposes altogether unknown; and then soars to a full and triumphant hope of a

future resurrection, and vindication of his innocence. 6. *Zophar* repeats the former charge; and *Job* replies, by directly controverting his argument, and proving, from a variety of examples, that in the present world the wicked are chiefly prosperous, and the just for the most part subject to affliction. Chap. xv.–xxi.

PART IV.—*Third Series of Controversy*

1. *Eliphaz*, in direct opposition to Job's last remarks, contends that certain and utter ruin is the uniform lot of the wicked; and adduces the instances of the *deluge*, and of Sodom and the other cities of the plain. 2. *Job* supports his position by fresh and still more forcible examples. Though he admits that, in the mystery of Providence, prosperity and adversity are often equally the lot of both the righteous and the wicked; yet he denies that this ought to be held as an argument in favour of the last, whose prosperity is in the utmost degree precarious, and who in calamity are wholly destitute of hope and consolation. 3. *Bildad* replies in a string of lofty but general apophthegms, tending to prove that Job cannot be without sin, since no man is so in the sight of God. 4. *Job* rejoins with indignation; takes a general survey of his life, in the different capacities of a magistrate, a husband, and a master; and challenges his companions to point out a single act of injustice he had committed. Chap. xxii.–xxxi.

PART V.—*The Summing up of the Controversy*

1. *Zophar*, who ought to have concluded the last series, having declined to prosecute the debate any farther, the general argument is summed up by *Elihu*, who has not hitherto spoken, though present from the first. 2. He condemns the subject matter of the opponents of Job, as altogether irrelevant; accuses Job himself, not of suffering for any past impiety, but of speaking irreverently during the controversy. 3. He contests several of Job's positions; asserts that afflictions are often sent by the Almighty for the wisest and most merciful purposes; and that, in every instance, our duty is submission. 4. He closes with describing the Creator as supreme and uncontrollable; and as creating, upholding, and regulating all nature according to his own will and pleasure; incomprehensibly and mysteriously yet ever wisely and benevolently. Chap. xxxii.–xxxvii.

PART VI.—*The Acquittal and Restoration of Job*

1. The *Almighty* appears to pronounce judgment; speaks to Job in a sublime and magnificent address out of a whirlwind. 2. *Job* humbles himself before God, and is accepted. 3. His *friends* are severely reproved for their conduct during the controversy, a sacrifice is demanded of them, and Job is appointed their intercessor. 4. He prays for his friends, and his prayer is accepted. 5. He is restored to his former state of prosperity, and his substance in every instance doubled. Chap. xxxviii.–xlii.

On this plan Mr. Good has constructed his learned translation and excellent observations on this book.

The following *Synopsis* or general view of this book is very intelligible, and may serve as an index to the work:—

I. The Historical Exordium, written in *prose.*—Chap. i., ii.

II. The threefold Series of Controversy, written in *poetry.*—Chap. iii.–xlii. ver. 1–6.

III. The *issue* of Job's trial; restoration to health and prosperity, in *prose.*—Chap. xlii. ver. 7–17.

> 1. Job's Disputation with his three friends, who came to visit him, in a *threefold* series, chap. iii.–xxxi.; including Job's speech, in which he curses the day of his birth, chap. iii.: this gives rise to the

First Series of Controversy, comprehended in chap. iv.–xiv.

    1. With Eliphaz, chap. iv.–vii.
        a. The Speech of *Eliphaz*, chap. iv., v.
        b. The Answer of *Job*, chap. vi., vii.
    2. With Bildad, chap. viii.–x.
        a. The Speech of *Bildad*, chap. viii.
        b. The Answer of *Job*, chap. ix., x.
    3. With Zophar, chap. xi.–xiv.
        a. The Speech of *Zophar*, chap. xi.
        b. The Answer of *Job*, chap. xii.–xiv.

Second Series of Controversy, included in chap. xv.–xxi.

    1. With Eliphaz, chap. xv., xvii.
        a. The Speech of *Eliphaz*, chap. xv.
        b. The Answer of *Job*, chap. xvi., xvii.
    2. With Bildad, chap. xviii., xix.
        a. The Speech of *Bildad*, chap. xviii.
        b. The Answer of *Job*, chap. xix.
    3. With Zophar, chap. xx., xxi.
        a. *Zophar's* Speech, chap. xx.
        b. The Answer of *Job*, chap. xxi.

Third Series of Controversy, included in chap. xxii.–xxxi.

    1. With Eliphaz, chap. xxii.–xxiv.
        a. The Speech of *Eliphaz*, chap. xxii.
        b. The Answer of *Job*, chap. xxiii., xxiv.
    2. With Bildad, chap. xxv.–xxxi.
        a. The Speech of *Bildad*, chap. xxv.
        b. The Answer of *Job*, chap. xxvi.–xxxi.

Elihu's judgment concerning the Controversy, delivered at *four* different intervals, pausing for Job's answer, chap. xxxii.–xxxvii.

        a. Elihu's *first* Speech, chap. xxxii., xxxiii.
        b. Elihu's *second* Speech, chap. xxxiv.
        c. Elihu's *third* Speech, chap. xxxv.
        d. Elihu's *fourth* Speech, chap. xxxvi., xxxvii.

The Almighty appears, speaks out of a whirlwind, and determines the Controversy, chap. xxxviii.–xli.

        a. The first Speech of the *Almighty*, chap. xxxviii., xxxix.
        b. The second Speech of the *Almighty*, chap. xl., xli.
        c. The Answer and *humiliation* of *Job*, chap. xlii., ver. 1–6.

Historical Narration concerning the restoration of Job to health and great worldly prosperity; with the account of his age and death, chap. xlii., ver. 7–17.

Some have contended that the *whole* of this book is written in *verse;* but I can see no rule or method by which the *two first chapters,* and the *ten last verses* of chap. xlii. can be reduced to poetry or poetic arrangement. They are merely *narrative;* and are utterly destitute of that dignity and pathos everywhere evident in this poem, and in every part of the Hebrew hemistich poetry wherever it occurs. I could almost suppose these places the work of *another hand;* a *Preface* and a *Conclusion* written by some person who was well acquainted with the fact of Job's temptation, and who found such additions necessary to cast light upon the poem. But they are most probably the work of the same hand. There are, in different parts of the body of the poem, *sentences in prose,* which are the *headings* to the different speeches. This is frequent among the Arabic and Persian poets. Such headings are generally in *rubric,* and should here stand by themselves.

THE
BOOK OF JOB

As the time in which Job lived is so very uncertain, (see the *preface*, and the *observations* at the end of the notes on the first chapter,) the date found in our common English Bibles, which is upon the supposition that Moses wrote the book while among the Midianites, about *one thousand five hundred and twenty years* before the commencement of the Christian era, is inserted in the margin, not because it is the most probable, but because it is the most generally received.

CHAPTER I

Character of Job, 1. His family, 2. His substance, 3. Care of his family, 4, 5. Satan accuses him to God as a selfish person, who served God only for the hope of secular rewards, 6–11. Satan is permitted to strip him of all his children and property, 12–19. Job's remarkable resignation and patience, 20–22.

A. M. cir. 2484
B. C. cir. 1520
Ante I. Olymp.
cir. 744
Ante U. C. cir.
767

THERE was a man ªin the land of Uz, whose name *was* ᵇJob, and that man was ᶜperfect and upright, and one that feared God, and eschewed evil.

2 And there were born unto him seven sons and three daughters.

3 His ᵈsubstance also was seven thousand sheep, and three thousand camels, and five hundred yoke of oxen, and five hundred she-asses, and a very great ᵉhousehold; so that this man was the greatest of all the ᶠmen of the East.

4 And his sons went and feasted in *their* houses, every one his day, and sent and called for their three sisters to eat and to drink with them.

5 And it was so, when the days of *their* feasting were gone about, that Job sent and sanctified them, and rose up early in the morning, ᵍand offered burnt-offerings *according* to the number of them all: for Job said, It may

A. M. cir. 2484
B. C. cir. 1520
Ante I. Olymp.
cir. 744
Ante U. C. cir.
767

ªGen. xxii. 20, 21——ᵇEzek. xiv. 14; James v. 11
ᶜChap. ii. 3——ᵈOr, *cattle*

ᵉOr, *husbandry*——ᶠHeb. *sons of the East*——ᵍGen. viii. 20; chap. xlii. 8

NOTES ON CHAP. I

Verse 1. In the land of Uz] This country was situated in Idumea, or the land of *Edom*, in *Arabia Petræa*, of which it comprised a very large district. See the *preface*.

Whose name was Job] The original is איוב *Aiyob;* and this orthography is followed by the *Chaldee, Syriac,* and *Arabic.* From the *Vulgate* we borrow *Job*, not very dissimilar from the Ιωβ *Iob* of the *Septuagint.* The name signifies *sorrowful,* or *he that weeps.* He is supposed to have been called *Jobab.* See more in the *preface.*

Perfect and upright] תם וישר *tam veyashar;* COMPLETE as to his *mind* and *heart,* and STRAIGHT or CORRECT as to his *moral deportment.*

Feared God.] Had him in continual reverence as the fountain of justice, truth, and goodness.

Eschewed evil.] סר מרע *sar mera,* departing from, or avoiding evil. We have the word *eschew* from the old French *eschever,* which signifies to *avoid.* All *within* was holy, all *without* was righteous; and his whole life was employed in *departing* from *evil,* and *drawing nigh to God.* Coverdale translates **an innocent anb bertuous man, soch one as feareð Goð, an eschueð**

ebell. From this translation we retain the word *eschew.*

Verse 3. His substance also was seven thousand sheep] A thousand, says the Chaldee, *for each of his sons. Three thousand camels: a thousand for each of his daughters. Five hundred yoke of oxen* for *himself.* And *five hundred she-asses* for his *wife.* Thus the *Targum* divides the substance of this eminent man.

A very great household] עבדה רבה מאד *abuddah rabbah meod,* "a very great estate." The word עבדה *abuddah* refers chiefly to husbandry, including *all manner of labour* in the *field,* with *cattle,* and every description of *servants.*

The greatest of all the men of the East.] He was more eminent than any other person in that region in wisdom, wealth, and piety. He was the chief *emir* of that district.

Verse 4. Feasted in their houses, every one his day] It is likely that a *birthday festival* is here intended. When the birthday of one arrived, he invited his brothers and sisters to feast with *him;* and each observed the same custom.

Verse 5. When the days of their feasting were gone about] At the conclusion of the year, when the birthday of each had been celebrated,

A. M. cir. 2484
B. C. cir. 1520
Ante I. Olymp.
cir. 744
Ante U. C. cir.
767

be that my sons have sinned,
and [h]cursed God in their
hearts. Thus did Job [i]con-
tinually.

6 Now [k]there was a day [l]when
the sons of God came to present
themselves before the LORD, and
[m]Satan came also [n]among them.

A. M. cir. 2484
B. C. cir. 1520
Ante I. Olymp.
cir. 744
Ante U. C. cir.
767

---

[h]1 Kings xxi. 10, 13——[i]Heb. *all the days*——[k]Chap.
ii. 1——[l]1 Kings xxii. 19; chap. xxxviii. 7

[m]Hebrew, *the adversary*, 1 Chron. xxi. 1; Rev. xii. 9, 10
[n]Heb. *in the midst of them*

---

the pious father appears to have gathered them all together, that the whole family might hold a *feast to the Lord*, offering burnt-offerings in order to make an atonement for sins of all kinds, whether presumptuous or committed through ignorance. This we may consider as a general custom among the godly in those ancient times.

And cursed God in their hearts.] וברכו אלהים *uberechu Elohim.* In this book, according to most interpreters, the verb ברך *barach* signifies both to *bless* and to *curse;* and the noun אלהים *Elohim* signifies the *true God, false gods,* and *great* or *mighty.* The reason why Job offered the burnt-offerings appears to have been this: in a country where idolatry flourished, he thought it possible that his children might, in their festivity, have given way to idolatrous thoughts, or done something prescribed by idolatrous rites; and therefore the words may be rendered thus: *It may be that my children have blessed the gods in their hearts.* Others think that the word ברך *barach* should be understood as implying *farewell, bidding adieu*—lest my children have *bidden adieu* to God, that is, *renounced* him, and *cast off his fear.* To me this is very unlikely. Mr. *Mason Good* contends that the word should be understood in its regular and general sense, *to bless;* and that the conjunction ו *vau* should be translated *nor.* "Peradventure my sons may have sinned, *nor* blessed God in their hearts." This version he supports with great learning. I think the sense given above is more plain, and less embarrassed. They might have been guilty of some species of *idolatry.* This is possible even among those called *Christians,* in their *banquets;* witness their songs to Bacchus, Venus, &c., which are countless in number, and often sung by persons who would think themselves injured, not to be reputed Christians. Coverdale, in his translation, (1535,) renders the passage thus: 𝔓𝔢𝔯𝔞𝔡𝔳𝔢𝔫𝔱𝔲𝔯𝔢 𝔪𝔶 𝔰𝔬𝔫𝔫𝔢𝔰 𝔥𝔞𝔟𝔢 𝔡𝔬𝔫𝔢 𝔰𝔬𝔪𝔢 𝔬𝔣𝔣𝔢𝔫𝔠𝔢, 𝔞𝔫𝔡 𝔥𝔞𝔳𝔢 𝔟𝔢𝔢𝔫 𝔲𝔫𝔱𝔥𝔞𝔫𝔨𝔣𝔲𝔩 𝔱𝔬 𝔊𝔬𝔡 𝔦𝔫 𝔱𝔥𝔢𝔦𝔯 𝔥𝔢𝔯𝔱𝔢𝔰.

Thus did Job continually.] At the end of every year, when all the birthday festivals had gone round.

Verse 6. *There was a day when the sons of God*] All the *versions,* and indeed all the critics, are puzzled with the phrase *sons of God;* בני האלהים *beney haelohim,* literally, *sons of the God,* or *sons of the gods.* The *Vulgate* has simply *filii dei, sons of God.* The *Septuagint,* οἱ ἀγγελοι του θεου, *the angels of God.* The *Chaldee,* כתי מלאכיא *kittey malachaiya, troops of angels.* The *Syriac* retains the Hebrew words and letters, only leaving out the demonstrative ה *he* in the word האלהים *haelohim,* thus, ܒܢܝ ܐܠܗܝܡ *baney Elohim.* The *Arabic* nearly copies the Hebrew also, بنوا الوهيم *banoa Iloheem;* to which, if we give not the literal translation of the *Hebrew,* we may give

what translation we please. *Coverdale* (1535) translates it, 𝔰𝔢𝔯𝔟𝔞𝔲𝔫𝔱𝔢𝔰 𝔬𝔣 𝔊𝔬𝔡. The *Targum* supposes that this assembly took place on the day of the *great atonement,* which occurred once each year. *And there was a day of judgment in the beginning of the year; and the troops of angels came, that they might stand in judgment before the Lord.* But what are we to make of this whole account? Expositions are endless. That of Mr. *Peters* appears to me to be at once the most simple and the most judicious: "The Scripture speaks of God after the manner of men, for there is a necessity of condescending to our capacities, and of suiting the revelation to our apprehension. As kings, therefore, transact their most important affairs in a *solemn council* or *assembly,* so God is pleased to represent himself as having *his council* likewise; and as passing the decrees of his providence in an *assembly* of his *holy angels.* We have here, in the case of *Job,* the same grand assembly held, as was before in that of *Ahab,* 1 Kings xxii.; the same host of heaven, called here the *sons of God,* presenting themselves *before* Jehovah, as in the vision of *Micaiah* they are said to stand *on his right hand and on his left.* A *wicked spirit* appearing among them, here called *Satan* or the *adversary,* and there a *lying spirit;* both bent on mischief, and ready to do all the hurt they were permitted to do; for both were under the *control* of his power. The *imagery* is just the same; and the only *difference* is in the *manner* of the relation. That mentioned above, Micaiah, as a *prophet,* and in the actual exercise of his prophetic office, delivers it, as he received it, in a *vision. I saw the Lord sitting on his throne, and all the* HOST *of* HEAVEN *standing by him, on his right hand and on his left; and there came forth a* LYING SPIRIT, *and stood* BEFORE *the Lord, and said,* 1 Kings xxii. 19-22. The other, as a *historian,* interweaves it with his history; and tells us, in his plain narrative style, *There was a day when the* SONS *of God came to* PRESENT *themselves* BEFORE *the Lord; and* SATAN *came also among them.* And this he delivers in the same manner as he does, *There was a man in the land of Uz, whose name was Job.*

"The things delivered to us by these two inspired writers are the same in substance, equally high, and above the reach of human sight and knowledge; but the *manner* of delivering them is different, each as suited best to his particular purpose. This, then is the prophetical way of representing things, as to the manner of doing them, which, whether done exactly in the same manner, concerns us not to know; but which are really done: and God would have them described as done in this manner, to make the more lively and lasting impression on us. At the same time, it must not be forgotten that representations of this kind are founded in a well-known and established truth, viz., the doctrine of *good and bad angels,* a point revealed from the beginning, and with-

A. M. cir. 2484
B. C. cir. 1520
Ante I. Olymp. cir. 744
Ante U. C. cir. 767

7 And the LORD said unto
Satan, Whence comest thou?
Then Satan answered the LORD,
and said, From [o]going to and
fro in the earth, and from walking up and
down in it.
8 And the LORD said unto Satan, [p]Hast
thou considered my servant Job, that *there is*
none like him in the earth, a perfect and an
upright man, one that feareth God and escheweth evil?
9 Then Satan answ
LORD, and said, Doth
God for naught?
10 Hast not thou m
about him, and abou
that he hath on eve
ed the work of his hands, an
is increased in the land.
11 [r]But put forth thine hand now, and
touch all that he hath, [s]and he will curse
thee to thy face.

[o]Chap. ii. 2; Matt. xii. 43; 1 Pet. v. 8——[p]Heb. *Hast thou set thine heart on*

[q]Or, *cattle*——[r]Chap. ii. 5; xix. 21——[s]Heb. *if he curse thee not to thy face*

out a previous knowledge of which, the visions of the prophets could scarcely be intelligible." See Gen. xxviii.

And Satan came also] This word *also* is emphatic in the original, השטן *hassatan, the Satan,* or *the adversary;* translated by the *Septuagint* ὁ Διαβολος. The original word is preserved by the *Chaldee, Syriac,* and *Arabic;* indeed, in each of them the word signifies an *adversary.* St. *Peter,* 1st Epist., ch. v., ver. 8, plainly refers to this place; and fully proves that השטן *hassatan,* which he literally translates ὁ αντιδικος, the ADVERSARY, is no other than ὁ Διαβολος, the DEVIL, or chief of bad demons, which he adds to others by way of explanation. There are many δαιμονες, *demons,* mentioned in Scripture; but the word *Satan* or *devil* is never found in the originals of the Old and New Testaments in the *plural* number. Hence we reasonably infer, that all evil spirits are under the government of ONE *chief,* the DEVIL, who is more powerful and more wicked than the rest. From the GREEK Διαβολος comes the LATIN *Diabolus,* the SPANISH *Diablo,* the FRENCH *Diable,* the ITALIAN *Diavolo,* the German **Teuffel**, the DUTCH *Duivel,* the ANGLO-SAXON **deofle**, and the ENGLISH *Devil,* which some would derive from the compound THE-EVIL; ὁ πονηρος, the *evil one,* or *wicked one.*

It is now fashionable to deny the existence of this evil spirit; and this is one of what St. John (Rev. ii. 24) calls τα βαθη του σατανα, *the depths of Satan;* as he well knows that they who deny his being will not be afraid of his power and influence; will not watch against his wiles and devices; will not pray to God for deliverance from the evil one; will not expect him to be trampled down under their feet, who has no existence; and, consequently, they will become an easy and unopposing prey to the enemy of their souls. By leading men to disbelieve and deny his existence, he throws them off their guard; and is then their complete master, and they are led captive by him at his will. It is well known that, among all those who make any profession of religion, those who deny the existence of the devil are they who pray little or none at all; and are, apparently, as careless about the existence of God as they are about the being of a devil. Piety to God is with them out of the question; for those who do not pray, especially in *private,* (and I never met with a devil-denier who did,) have no *religion* of any kind, whatsoever pretensions they may choose to make.

Verse 7. *From going to and fro in the earth*] The translation of the *Septuagint* is curious: Περιελθων την γην και εμπεριπατησας την ὑπ' ουρανον, παρειμι; "Having gone round the earth, and walked over all that is under heaven, I am come hither." The *Chaldee* says, "I am come from going round the earth to examine the works of the children of men; and from walking through it." *Coverdale,* who generally hits the sense, translates thus: **I have gone aboute the londe and walked thorow it.** Mr. *Good* has it, *from roaming round the earth, and walking about it.*

St. Peter, as has been already stated, ver. 6, refers to this: *Be sober, be vigilant; for your* ADVERSARY *the* DEVIL GOETH ABOUT, *as a roaring lion, seeking whom he may devour.* I rather think, with *Coverdale,* that ארץ *arets* here signifies rather that *land,* than the *habitable globe.* The words are exceedingly emphatic; and the latter verb התהלך *hithhallech* being in the *hithpael* conjugation shows how *earnest* and *determined* the devil is in his work: he *sets himself to walk;* he is *busily employed in it;* he is seeking the destruction of men; and while they sleep, he wakes—while they are careless, he is alert. The spirit of this saying is often expressed by the simple inhabitants of the country: when they perceive a man plotting mischief, and frequent in transgression, they say, *The devil is* BUSY *with him.*

Verse 8. *Hast thou considered my servant Job*] Literally, *Hast thou placed thy heart on my servant Job?* Hast thou viewed his conduct with attention, whilst thou wert roaming about, seeking whom thou mightest devour? viz., the careless, prayerless, and profligate in general.

Verse 9. *Doth Job fear God for naught?*] Thou hast made it his interest to be exemplary in his conduct: for this assertion Satan gives his reasons in what immediately follows.

Verse 10. *Hast not thou made a hedge about him*] Thou hast *fortified* him with *spikes* and *spears.* Thou hast defended him as by an unapprochable hedge. He is an object of thy peculiar care; and is not exposed to the common trials of life.

Verse 11. *But put forth thine hand*] Shoot the dart of poverty and affliction against him.

And he will curse thee to thy face.] אם לא על פניך יברכך *im lo al paneycha yebarechecca,* "If he will not bless thee to thy appearances." He will bless thee only in proportion to the temporal good thou bestowest upon him; to the provi-

A. M. cir. 2484
B. C. cir. 1520
Ante I. Olymp.
cir. 744
Ante U. C. cir.
767

12 And the LORD said unto Satan, Behold, all that he hath *is* in thy 'power, only upon himself put not forth thine hand. So Satan went forth from the presence of the LORD.

13 And there was a day when his sons and his daughters *were* eating and drinking wine in their eldest brother's house:

14 And there came a messenger unto Job, and said, The oxen were ploughing, and the asses feeding beside them:

15 And the Sabeans fell *upon them,* and took them away; yea, they have slain the servants with the edge of the sword; and I only am escaped alone to tell thee.

16 While he *was* yet speaking, there came also another, and said, ᵘThe fire of God is fallen from heaven, and hath burned up the sheep, and the servants, and consumed them; and I only am escaped alone to tell thee.

A. M. cir. 2484
B. C. cir. 1520
Ante I. Olymp.
cir. 744
Ante U. C. cir.
767

17 While he *was* yet speaking, there came also another, and said, The Chaldeans made out three bands, and ᵛfell upon the camels, and have carried them away, yea, and slain the servants with the edge of the sword; and I only am escaped alone to tell thee.

18 While he *was* yet speaking, there came also another, and said, Thy sons and thy daughters *were* eating and drinking wine in their eldest brother's house;

19 And behold, there came a great wind ʷfrom the wilderness, and smote the four corners of the house, and it fell upon the young men, and they are dead; and I only am escaped alone to tell thee.

ᵗHeb. *hand*——ᵘOr, *A great fire*

ᵛHeb. *rushed*——ʷHeb. *from aside, &c.*

---

dential and gracious *appearances* or *displays* of thy power in his behalf. If *thou* wilt be gracious, *he* will be pious. The exact maxim of a great statesman, Sir Robert Walpole: *Every man has his price.* "But you have not bought such a one?" "No, because I would not go up to his price. He valued himself at more than I thought him worth; and I could get others cheaper, who, in the general muster, would do as well." No doubt Sir R. met with many such; and the devil many more. But still God has multitudes that will neither sell their souls, their consciences, nor their country, for any price; who, though God should slay them, will nevertheless trust in him; and be honest men, howsoever tempted by the devil and his vicegerents. So did Job; so have done thousands; so will all do, in whose hearts Christ dwells by faith.

Verse 12. *All that he hath is in thy power*] Satan cannot deprive a man even of an *ass*, a *sheep*, or a *pig*, but by especial permission of God. His power and malice are ever bounded, and under control.

So Satan went forth] The Targum adds, *with authority from the presence of the Lord.*

Verse 13. *There was a day*] *The first day of the week,* says the *Targum.* It no doubt refers to one of those *birthday festivals* mentioned before.

Verse 14. *The asses feeding beside them*] אתנות *athonoth,* the *she-asses,* which appear to have been more domesticated, as of more worth and use than the others, both for their milk and their work.

Verse 15. *And the Sabeans fell*] The *Vulgate* alone understands this of a *people.* The *Septuagint, Syriac,* and *Arabic,* understand it as implying a *marauding party.* The *Chaldee* says, "Lilith, queen of Zamargad, rushed suddenly upon them, and carried them away." The *Sabeans* mentioned here are supposed to have been the same with those who were the descendants of Abraham by Keturah, whose son Jok-

shan begat Sheba. The sons of Keturah were sent by Abraham into the east, Gen. xxv. 6, and inhabited Arabia Deserta, on the east of the land of Uz. Hordes of predatory banditti were frequent in those countries and continue so to the present day. They made sudden incursions, and carried off *men, women, children, cattle,* and *goods* of every description; and immediately retired to the desert, whither it was in vain to pursue them.

Verse 16. *The fire of God is fallen*] Though *the fire of God* may mean a *great,* a *tremendous* fire, yet it is most natural to suppose *lightning* is meant; for as *thunder* was considered to be the *voice of God,* so *lightning* was the *fire of God.* And as the *prince of the power of the air* was permitted now to arm himself with this dreadful artillery of heaven, he might easily direct the zigzag lightning to every part of the fields where the sheep were feeding, and so destroy the whole in a moment.

Verse 17. *The Chaldeans made out three bands*] The *Chaldeans* inhabited each side of the Euphrates near to Babylon, which was their capital. They were also mixed with the wandering *Arabs,* and lived like them on *rapine.* They were the descendants of *Chesed,* son of Nahor and brother of Huz, from whom they had their name *Casdim,* which we translate *Chaldeans.* They divided themselves into *three bands,* in order the more speedily and effectually to encompass, collect, and drive off the three thousand camels: probably they mounted the camels and rode off.

Verse 19. *A great wind from the wilderness*] Here was another proof of the influence of *the prince of the power of the air.* What mischief might he not do with this tremendous agent, were he not constantly under the control of the Almighty! He seems to have directed four different currents, which, blowing against the four corners or sides of the house, crushed it together, and involved all within in one common ruin.

A. M. cir. 2484
B. C. cir. 1520
Ante I. Olymp.
cir. 744
Ante U. C. cir.
767
20 Then Job arose, ˣand rent his ʸmantle, and shaved his head, and fell down upon the ground, and worshipped,

21 And said, ᶻNaked came I out of my mother's womb, and naked shall I return thither: the LORD gave, and the LORD hath taken away; blessed be the name of the LORD.

A. M. cir. 2484
B. C. cir. 1520
Ante I. Olymp.
cir. 744
Ante U. C. cir.
767

22 ᵃIn all this Job sinned not, nor ᵇcharged God foolishly.

ˣGen. xxxvii. 29; Ezra ix. 3——ʸOr, *robe*
ᵃChap. ii. 10——ᵇOr,

ᶻPsa. xlix. 17; Eccles. v. 15; 1 Tim. vi. 7
attributed folly to God

Verse 20. *Rent his mantle*] Tearing the garments, shaving or pulling off the hair of the head, throwing dust or ashes on the head, and sitting on the ground, were acts by which immoderate grief was expressed. Job must have felt the bitterness of anguish when he was told that, in addition to the loss of all his *property*, he was deprived of his *ten children* by a violent death. Had he not felt this most poignantly, he would have been unworthy of the name of *man*.

Worshipped] *Prostrated himself;* lay all along upon the ground, with his face in the dust.

Verse 21. *Naked came I out of my mother's womb*] I had no earthly possessions when I came into the world; I cannot have less going out of it. What I have the *Lord gave:* as it was his *free gift*, he has a right to resume it when he pleases; and I owe him *gratitude* for the time he has permitted me to enjoy this gift.

Naked shall I return thither] Whither? Not to his *mother's womb* surely; nor does he call the *earth* his *mother* in this place. In the first clause of the verse he speaks without a *metaphor*, and in the latter he speaks in reference to the *ground* on which he was about to fall. As I came out of my mother's womb destitute of the earthly possessions, so shall I return שׁמה *shammah*, THERE; i. e., to the earth on which he was now falling. That *mother earth* was a common expression in different nations, I allow; but I believe no such metaphor was now in the mind of Job.

The Lord gave] The *Chaldee* has, "The WORD of the Lord, מימרא דיי *meymera dayai*, gave; and the WORD of the Lord and the house of his judgment, have taken away!" WORD is used here *personally*, as in many other places of all the *Targums*.

Blessed be the name of the Lord.] The following is a fine paraphrase on the sentiment in this verse:—

"*Good* when he *gives, supremely good;*
  Nor less when he *denies;*
Afflictions from his sovereign hand,
  Are *blessings* in disguise."

Seeing I have lost my temporal goods, and all my domestic comforts, may God alone be all my portion! The *Vulgate, Septuagint,* and *Covedale*, add, *The Lord hath done as he pleased.*

Verse 22. *In all this Job sinned not*] He did not give way to any action, passion, or expression, offensive to his Maker. He did not charge God with acting unkindly towards him, but felt as perfectly satisfied with the *privation* which the hand of God had occasioned, as he was with the *affluence* and *health* which that hand had bestowed. This is the transaction that gave the strong and vivid colouring to the character of Job; in this, and in *this alone*, he was a *pattern* of *patience* and *resignation*. In

this Satan was utterly disappointed; he found a man who loved his God more than his earthly portion. This was a rare case, even in the experience of the devil. He had seen multitudes who bartered their God for money, and their hopes of blessedness in the world to come for secular possessions in the present. He had been so often successful in this kind of temptation, that he made no doubt he should succeed again. He saw many who, when riches increased, set their hearts on them, and forgot God. He saw many also who, when deprived of earthly comforts, blasphemed their Maker. He therefore inferred that Job, in similar circumstances, would act like the others; he was disappointed. Reader, has he, by *riches* or *poverty*, succeeded with thee? Art thou pious when affluent, and patient and contented when in poverty?

THAT Job lived *after* the giving of the law, seems to me clear from many references to the rites and ceremonies instituted by Moses. In chap. i. 5, we are informed that he *sanctified* his children, and *offered burnt-offerings daily in the morning for each of them*. This was a general ordinance of the law, as we may see, Lev. ix. 7: "Moses said unto Aaron, Go unto the altar, and offer thy sin-offering and thy *burnt-offering*, and make an atonement for thyself and for the people." Ver. 22: "And Aaron lifted up his hands towards the people, and blessed them, and came down from offering the *burnt-offering*."

This sort of offering, we are told above, *Job offered continually;* and this also was according to the law, Exod. xxix. 42: "This shall be a *continual* burnt-offering throughout your generations." See also Num. xxviii. 3, 6, 10, 15, 24, 31.

This custom was observed *after the captivity*, Ezra iii. 5: "They offered the *continual burnt-offering:* and of every one that offered a freewill-offering." See also Neh. x. 33. Ezekiel, who prophesied during the captivity, enjoins this positively, chap. xlvi. 13-15: "Thou shalt daily prepare a *burnt-offering* unto the Lord; thou shalt prepare it *every morning*."

Job appears to have thought that his children might have *sinned* through *ignorance*, or sinned *privately;* and it was consequently necessary to make the due sacrifices to God in order to prevent his wrath and their punishment; he therefore offered the burnt-offering, which was prescribed by the law in cases of sins committed *through ignorance*. See the ordinances Lev. iv. 1-35; v. 15-19, and particularly Num. xv. 24-29. I think it may be fairly presumed that the offerings which Job made for his children were in reference to these laws.

The *worship* of the *sun, moon,* and *stars*, as being the most prevalent and most seductive idolatry, was very expressly forbidden by the law, Deut. iv. 19: "Take heed, lest thou lift up thine eyes to heaven; and when thou seest the *sun*, and the *moon*, and the *stars*, even all the *host* of *heaven*, shouldest be driven to worship them, and serve them." Job purges himself from this species of idolatry, chap. xxxi. ver. 26-28: "If I beheld the *sun* when it shined, or the *moon* walking in brightness, and my heart hath been secretly enticed, or my mouth hath kissed my hand: this also were an iniquity *to be punished by* the judge; for I should have *denied the God* that is *above*."

He clears himself also from *adultery* in reference to the law enacted against that sin, Job xxxi. 9-12: "If mine heart have been deceived by a woman, or if I have laid wait at my neighbour's door; then let my wife grind to another: for this is a heinous crime; yea, it is an iniquity *to be punished by* the judges." See the law against this sin, Exod. xx. 14, 17: "Thou shalt not commit *adultery:* thou shalt not *covet* thy *neighbour's wife*." Lev. xx. 10: "The man that committeth *adultery* with another man's wife shall surely be put to death;" see Deut. xxii. 22. And for the *judge's* office in such cases, see Deut. xvii. 9-12: "Thou shalt come unto the priests and Levites, and unto the *judge* that shall be in those days; and they shall show thee the sentence of *judgment*." 1 Sam. ii. 25: "If one man sin against another, the *judge* shall *judge* him."

The following will, I think, be considered an evident allusion to the *passage of the Red Sea*, and the destruction of the *proud Egyptian king:* Job xxvi. 11, 12: "The pillars of heaven tremble, and are astonished at his reproof. He *divideth* the *sea* with his power; and by his understanding he *smiteth* through the *proud*." These, with several others that might be adduced, are presumptive proofs that the *writer* of this book lived after the giving and establishment of the law, if not much later, let Job himself live when he might. See other proofs in the notes.

CHAPTER II

The sons of God once more present themselves before him; and Satan comes also, accusing Job as a person whose steadfastness would be soon shaken, provided his body were to be subjected to sore afflictions, 1–5. He receives permission to afflict Job, and smites him with sore boils, 6–8. His wife reviles him, 9. His pious reproof, 10. His three friends come to visit and mourn with him.

A. M. cir. 2484
B. C. cir. 1520
Ante I. Olymp.
cir. 744
Ante U. C. cir. 767

A GAIN [a]there was a day when the sons of God came to present themselves before the LORD, and Satan came also among them to present himself before the LORD.

2 And the LORD said unto Satan, From whence comest thou? And [b]Satan answered the LORD, and said, From going to and fro in the earth, and from walking up and down in it.

3 And the LORD said unto Satan, Hast thou considered my servant Job, that *there is* none like him in the earth, [c]a perfect and an upright man, one that feareth God, and escheweth evil? and still he [d]holdeth fast his integrity, although thou movedst me against him, [e]to [f]destroy him without cause.

4 And Satan answered the LORD, and said,

A. M. cir. 2484
B. C. cir. 1520
Ante I. Olymp.
cir. 744
Ante U. C. cir. 767

---

[a]Chap. i. 6——[b]Chap. i. 7——[c]Chap. i. 1, 8——[d]Chap. xxvii. 5, 6——[e]Heb. *to swallow him up*——[f]Chap. ix. 17

NOTES ON CHAP. II

Verse 1. *Again there was a day*] How long this was after the former trial, we know not: probably *one whole year*, when, as the *Targum* intimates, it was the time of the annual atonement; which, if so, must have been at least one whole year after the former; and during which period the patience and resignation of Job had sufficient scope to show themselves. This appearance of the *sons of God* and *Satan* is to be understood metaphorically—there could be nothing *real* in it—but it is intended to instruct us in the doctrine of the existence of good and evil spirits; that Satan pursues man with implacable enmity, and that he can do no man hurt, either in his person or property, but by the especial permission of God; and that God gives him permission only when he purposes to overrule it for the greater manifestation of his own glory, and the greater good of his tempted followers.

Verse 3. *To destroy him without cause.*] Thou wishedst me to permit thee to destroy a man whose sins have not called for so heavy a judgment. This seems to be the meaning of this saying. The original word, לבלע *leballeo*, signifies to *swallow down* or *devour;* and this word St. Peter had no doubt in view in the place quoted on verse 7 of the preceding chapter: "Your adversary the devil goeth about as a *roaring lion, seeking whom he may* DEVOUR; ζητων, τινα καταπιη, *seeking whom he may* SWALLOW or GULP DOWN. See the note on 1 Pet. v. 8.

Verse 4. *Skin for skin*] That is, A man will part with all he has in the world to save his life; and he will part with all by piecemeal, till he has nothing left on earth, and even be thankful, provided his life be spared. Thou hast only destroyed his *property;* thou hast left him his *life* and his health. Thou hast not touched his *flesh* nor his *bone;* therefore he is patient and resigned. Man, through the love of life, will go much farther: he will give up one *member* to save the *rest;* yea, *limb* after *limb*, as long as there is hope that, by such sacrifices, life may be spared or *prolonged*. This is the meaning given to the passage by the *Targum;* and, I believe, the true one; hence, ver. 6, the Lord says, *Save his life.*

A. M. cir. 2484
B. C. cir. 1520
Ante I. Olymp.
cir. 744
Ante U. C. cir.
767

Skin for skin, yea, all that a man hath will he give for his life.

5 ᵍBut put forth thine hand now, and touch his ʰbone and his flesh, and he will curse thee to thy face.

6 ¹And the LORD said unto Satan, Behold, he *is* in thine hand; ᵏbut save his life.

7 So went Satan forth from the presence of the LORD, and smote Job with sore boils

¹from the sole of his foot unto his crown.

A. M. cir. 2484
B. C. cir. 1520
Ante I. Olymp.
cir. 744
Ante U. C. cir.
767

8 And he took him a potsherd to scrape himself withal; ᵐand he sat down among the ashes.

9 Then said his wife unto him, ⁿDost thou still °retain thine integrity? curse God, and die.

10 But he said unto her, Thou speakest as one of the foolish women speaketh. What?

ᵍChap. i. 11——ʰChap. xix. 20——ⁱChap. i. 12——ᵏOr, *only*——ˡIsa. i. 6

ᵐ2 Sam. xiii. 19; chap. xlii. 6; Ezek. xxvii. 30; Matt. xi. 21——ⁿChap. xxi. 15——°Ver. 3

Verse 5. *He will curse thee to thy face.*] Literally, *If he will not bless thee to thy face or appearances.* His *piety to thee* will be always regulated by thy *bounty* to him. See the note on chap. i. 11.

Verse 6. *But save his life.*] His *body* thou shalt have permission to afflict, but against his *life* thou shalt have no power; therefore take care of his life. The original, נפשו שמר naphsho shemor, may be translated, *keep his soul;* but the word also signifies *life;* yet in the hands of the destroyer the life of this holy man is placed! How astonishing is the economy of salvation! It is so manged, by the unlimited power and skill of God, that the grand adversary of souls becomes himself, by the order of God, the *preserver* of that which the evil of his nature incessantly prompts him to destroy!

Verse 7. *Sore boils*] בשחין רע bischin ra, "with an evil inflammation." What this diabolical disorder was, interpreters are not agreed. Some think it was the *leprosy;* and this is the reason why he dwelt by himself, and had his habitation in an unclean place, *without the city,* (Septuagint, ἔξω τῆς πωλεως,) or in the open air: and the reason why his friends beheld him *afar off,* ver. 12, was because they knew that the disorder was infectious.

His *scraping* himself with a *potsherd* indicates a disease accompanied with intolerable *itching,* one of the characteristics of the *smallpox.* Query, Was it not this disorder? And in order to save his life (for that he had in especial command) did not Satan himself direct him to the *cool regimen,* without which, humanly speaking, the disease must have proved fatal? In the *elephantiasis* and *leprosy* there is, properly speaking, no boil or *detached inflammation,* or *swelling,* but *one uniform disordered state* of the *whole surface,* so that the whole body is covered with loathsome scales, and the skin appears like that of the *elephant,* thick and wrinkled, from which appearance the disorder has its name. In the *smallpox* it is different; each *pock* or *pustule* is a separate inflammation, tending to suppuration; and during this process, the fever is in general very high, and the anguish and distress of the patient intolerable. When the suppuration is pretty far advanced, the *itching* is extreme; and the hands are often obliged to be confined to prevent the patient from literally *tearing* his own flesh.

Verse 9. *Then said his wife*] To this verse the *Septuagint* adds the following words: "Much time having elapsed, his wife said unto him, How long dost thou stand steadfast, saying, 'Behold, I wait yet a little longer looking for the hope of my salvation?' Behold thy memorial is already blotted out from the earth, together with thy sons and thy daughters, the fruits of my pains and labours, for whom with anxiety I have laboured in vain. Thyself also sittest in the rottenness of worms night and day, while I am a wanderer from place to place, and from house to house, waiting for the setting of the sun, that I may rest from my labours, and from the griefs which oppress me. Speak therefore some word against God, and die." We translate ברך אלהים ומת *barech Elohim vamuth, Curse God, and die.* The verb ברך *barach* is supposed to include in it the ideas of *cursing* and *blessing;* but it is not clear that it has the former meaning in any part of the sacred writings, though we sometimes translate it so.

Here it seems to be a strong *irony. Job* was exceedingly afflicted, and apparently dying through sore disease; yet his soul was filled with gratitude to God. His *wife,* destitute of the salvation which her husband possessed, gave him this *ironical* reproof. *Bless God, and die*— What! bless him for his *goodness,* while he is destroying all that thou hast! bless him for his support, while he is casting thee down and destroying thee! Bless on, and die.

The *Targum* says that Job's wife's name was *Dinah,* and that the words which she spake to him on this occasion were ברך מימרא דיי ומית *berich meymera dayai umith. Bless the word of the Lord, and die.*

Ovid has such an *irony* as I suppose this to have been:—

Quid vos sacra juvant? quid nunc Ægyptia prosunt
    Sistra?——
Cum rapiant mala fata bonos, ignoscite fasso,
    Sollicitor nullos esse putare deos.
Vive pius, moriere pius; cole sacra, colentem
    Mors gravis a templis in cava busta trahet.
                    AMOR. lib. iii., *Eleg.* ix. ver. 33.

"In vain to gods (if gods there are) we pray,
And needless victims prodigally pay;
Worship their sleeping deities: yet death
Scorns votaries, and stops the praying breath.
To hallow'd shrines intruding fate will come,
And drag you from the altar to the tomb."
                    STEPNEY.

Verse 10. *Thou speakest as one of the foolish*] Thou speakest like an infidel; like one who has

A. M. cir. 2484
B. C. cir. 1520
Ante I. Olymp.
cir. 744
Ante U. C. cir.
767

Pshall we receive good at the hand of God, and shall we not receive evil? qIn all this did not Job rsin with his lips.

11 Now when Job's three sfriends heard of all this evil that was come upon him, they came every one from his own place; Eliphaz the tTemanite, and Bildad the uShuhite, and Zophar the Naamathite: for they had made an appointment together to come vto mourn with him and to comfort him.

12 And when they lifted up their eyes afar·off, and knew him not, they lifted up their voice, and wept; and they rent every one his mantle, and wsprinkled dust upon their heads toward heaven.

A. M. cir. 2484
B. C. cir. 1520
Ante I. Olymp.
cir. 744
Ante U. C. cir.
767

13 So they sat down with him upon the ground xseven days and seven nights, and none spake a word unto him: for they saw that *his* grief was very great.

PCh. i. 21; Rom. xii. 12; James v. 10, 11——qCh. i. 22
rPsa. xxxix. 1——sProv. xvii. 17——tGen. xxxvi. 11;

Jer. xlix. 7——uGen. xxv. 2——vCh. xlii. 11; Rom. xii.15
wNeh. ix. 1; Lam. ii. 10; Ezek. xxvii. 30——xGen. l. 10

---

no knowledge of God, of religion, or of a future state.

The Targum, who calls this woman *Dinah*, translates thus: "Thou speakest like one of those women who have wrought folly in the house of their father." This is in reference to an ancient rabbinical opinion, that Job lived in the days of the patriarch Jacob, whose daughter Dinah he had married.

Shall we receive good] This we have received in great abundance for many years:—

And shall we not receive evil?] Shall we murmur when He *afflicts* us for a *day*, who has given us *health* for so *many years?* Shall we blaspheme his name for *momentary privations*, who has given us such a *long succession of enjoyments?* His blessings are his own: he never *gave* them to us; they were only *lent.* We have had the long, the free, the unmerited use of them; and shall we be offended at the *Owner*, when he comes to reclaim his own property? This would be foolish, ungrateful, and wicked. So may every one reason who is suffering from adversity. But who, besides Job, reasons thus? Man is naturally discontented and ungrateful.

In all this did not Job sin with his lips.] The Chaldee adds, *But in his heart he thought words.* He had surmisings of heart, though he let nothing escape from his lips.

Verse 11. *Job's three friends*] The first was *Eliphaz the Temanite;* or, as the *Septuagint* has it, Ελιφαζ ὁ Θαιμανων βασιλευς, *Eliphaz the king of the Thaimanites.* Eliphaz was one of the sons of Esau; and Teman, of Eliphaz, Gen. xxxvi. 10, 11. Teman was a city of Edom, Jer. xlix. 7-20; Ezek. xxv. 13; Amos i. 11, 12.

Bildad the Shuhite] Or, as the *Septuagint*, Βαλδαδ ὁ Συχεων τυραννος, *Baldad, tyrant of the Suchites.* *Shuah* was the son of Abraham by Keturah; and his posterity is reckoned among the Easterns. It is supposed he should be placed with his brother *Midian*, and his brother's sons *Sheba* and *Dedan.* See Gen. xxv. 2, 3. Dedan was a city of Edom, see Jer. xlix. 8, and seems to have been situated in its southern boundary, as Teman was in its western. Ezek. xxv. 13.

Zophar the Naamathite] Or, according to the *Septuagint*, Σωφαρ Μιναιων Βασιλευς, *Sophar king of the Minaites.* He most probably came from that *Naamah*, which was bordering upon the Edomites to the south and fell by lot to the tribe of Judah, Josh. xv. 21-41. These circum-

stances, which have already been mentioned in the *introduction*, prove that Job must have dwelt in the land of *Edom*, and that all his friends dwelt in *Arabia Petræa*, or in the countries immediately adjacent. That some of those Eastern people were highly *cultivated*, we have at least indirect proof in the case of *the Temanites*, Jer. xlix. 7: *Concerning Edom thus saith the Lord of hosts, Is wisdom no more in Teman? Is counsel perished from the prudent? Is their wisdom vanished?* They are celebrated also in *Baruch*, iii. 22, 23. Speaking of *wisdom* he says: *It hath not been heard of in Chanaan; neither hath it been seen in Theman. The Agarenes that seek wisdom upon earth, the merchants of Meran and of Theman, the expounders of fables, and searchers out of understanding, none of these have known the way of wisdom.* It is evident enough from these quotations that the inhabitants of those districts were celebrated for their knowledge; and the sayings of Job's three friends are proofs that their reputation for wisdom stood on a very solid foundation.

Verse 12. *They rent every one his mantle*] I have already had frequent occasions to point out and illustrate, by quotations from the ancients, the actions that were used in order to express profound grief; such as wrapping themselves in sackcloth, covering the face, strewing dust or ashes upon the head, sitting upon the bare ground, &c., &c.; significant actions which were in use among all nations.

Verse 13. *They sat down with him upon the ground seven days*] They were astonished at the unprecedented change which had taken place in the circumstances of this most eminent man; they could not reconcile his present situation with any thing they had met with in the history of Divine providence. The *seven days* mentioned here were the period appointed for mourning. The Israelites mourned for Jacob *seven days*, Gen. l. 10. And the men of Jabesh mourned so long for the death of Saul, 1 Sam. xxxi. 13; 1 Chron. x. 12. And Ezekiel sat on the ground with the captives at Chebar, and mourned with and for them *seven days.* Ezek. iii. 15. The wise son of Sirach says, "*Seven days* do men mourn for him that is dead;" Ecclus. xxii. 12. So calamitous was the state of Job, that they considered him as a dead man: and went through the prescribed period of mourning for him.

They saw that his *grief was very great.*]

This is the reason why they did *not speak* to him: they believed him to be suffering for heavy crimes, and, seeing him suffer so much, they were not willing to add to his distresses by invectives or reproach. Job himself first broke silence.

CHAPTER III

Job curses the day of his birth, and regrets that he ever saw the light, 1–12. Describes the empire of death and its inhabitants, 13–19. Regrets that he is appointed to live in the midst of sorrows, for the calamities which he feared had overtaken him, 20–26.

A. M. cir. 2484
B. C. cir. 1520
Ante I. Olymp.
cir. 744
A. U. C. cir.
767

AFTER this opened Job his mouth and cursed his day.

2 And Job ªspake, and said,

3 ᵇLet the day perish wherein I was born, and the night *in which* it was said, There is a man-child conceived.

A. M. cir. 2484
B. C. cir. 1520
Ante I. Olymp.
cir. 744
A. U. C. cir.
767

4 Let that day be darkness; let not God regard it from above, neither let the light shine upon it.

5 Let darkness and ᶜthe shadow of death

ªHebrew, *answered*——ᵇChapter x. 18, 19; Jeremiah xv. 10; xx. 14

ᶜChap. x. 21, 22; xvi. 16; xxviii. 3; Psa. xxiii. 4; xliv. 19; cvii. 10, 14; Jer. xiii. 16; Amos v. 8

NOTES ON CHAP. III

Verse 1. *After this opened Job his mouth*] After the *seven days' mourning* was over, there being no prospect of relief, Job is represented as thus *cursing the day of his birth.* Here the *poetic* part of the book *begins;* for most certainly there is nothing in the preceding chapters either in the *form* or *spirit* of *Hebrew poetry.* It is easy indeed to break the sentences into *hemistichs;* but this does not constitute them *poetry:* for, although *Hebrew poetry* is in general in hemistichs, yet it does not follow that the division of *narrative* into hemistichs must necessarily constitute it *poetry.*

In many cases the Asiatic poets introduce their compositions with *prose narrative;* and having in this way prepared the reader for what he is to expect, begin their *deevans, cassidehs, gazels,* &c. This appears to be the plan followed by the author of this book. Those who still think, after examining the structure of those chapters, and comparing them with the undoubted poetic parts of the book, that *they* also, and the *ten* concluding verses, are *poetry,* have my consent, while I take the liberty to believe most decidedly the opposite.

Cursed his day.] That is, the day of his birth; and thus he gave vent to the agonies of his soul, and the distractions of his mind. His execrations have something in them awfully solemn, tremendously deep, and strikingly sublime. But let us not excuse all the things which he said in his haste, and in the bitterness of his soul, because of his former well established character of patience. He bore all his *privations* with becoming resignation to the Divine will and providence: but now, feeling himself the subject of continual sufferings, being in heaviness through manifold temptation, and probably having the light of God withdrawn from his mind, as his consolations most undoubtedly were, he regrets that ever he was born; and in a very high strain of impassioned poetry curses his day. We find a similar execration to this in Jeremiah, chap. xx. 14-18, and in other places; which, by the way, are **no** proofs that the one borrowed from the other;

but that this was the common mode of Asiatic thinking, speaking, and feeling, on such occasions.

Verse 3. *There is a man-child conceived.*] The word הרה *harah* signifies to *conceive;* yet here, it seems, it should be taken in the sense of *being born,* as it is perfectly unlikely that the night of conception should be either distinctly known or published.

Verse 4. *Let that day be darkness*] The meaning is exactly the same with our expression, "Let it be blotted out of the calendar." However distinguished it may have been, as the birthday of a man once celebrated for his possessions, liberality, and piety, let it no longer be thus noted; as he who was thus celebrated is now the sport of adversity, the most impoverished, most afflicted, and most wretched of human beings.

Let not God regard it from above] אל ידרשהו *al yidreshehu,* "Let Him not *require* it"—let Him not consider it essential to the completion of the days of the year; and therefore he adds, *neither let the light shine upon it.* If it must be a part of *duration,* let it not be distinguished by the light of the sun.

Verse 5. *Let darkness and the shadow of death stain it*] יגאלהו *yigaluhu,* "pollute or avenge it," from גאל *gaal,* to *vindicate, avenge, &c.;* hence גאל *goel,* the nearest of kin, whose right it was to *redeem* an inheritance, and *avenge* the death of his relative by slaying the murderer. Let this day be pursued, overtaken, and destroyed. Let natural darkness, the total privation of the solar light, rendered still more intense by death's shadow projected over it, *seize on* and destroy this day, εκλαβοι αυτην, *Septuagint;* alluding, perhaps, says Mr. *Parkhurst,* to the avenger of blood seizing the offender.

Let a cloud dwell upon it] 𝔏𝔢𝔱 𝔱𝔥𝔢 𝔡𝔶𝔪𝔪𝔢 𝔠𝔩𝔬𝔲𝔡𝔢 𝔣𝔞𝔩𝔩 𝔲𝔭𝔬𝔫 𝔦𝔱.—*Coverdale.* Let the thickest clouds have there their dwelling-place—let that be the period of time on which they shall constantly rest, and never be *dispersed.* This seems to be the import of the original, חשכן עליו אננה *tishcan alaiv ananah.* Let it be the

A. M. cir. 2484
B. C. cir. 1520
Ante I. Olymp.
cir. 744
Ante U. C. cir.
767

^dstain it; let a cloud dwell upon it; ^elet the blackness of the day terrify it.

6 *As for* that night, let darkness seize upon it; ^flet it not be joined unto the days of the year, let it not come into the number of the months.

7 Lo, let that night be solitary, let no joyful voice come therein.

8 Let them curse it that curse the day, ^gwho are ready to raise up ^htheir mourning.

9 Let the stars of the twilight thereof be dark; let it look for light, but *have* none;

A. M. cir. 2484
B. C. cir. 1520
Ante I. Olymp.
cir. 744
Ante U. C. cir.
767

---

^dOr, *challenge it*——^eOr, *let them terrify it, as those who have a bitter day;* Amos viii. 10

^fOr, *let it not rejoice among the days*——^gJer. ix. 17, 18
^hOr, *a leviathan*

---

place in which *clouds* shall be continually *gathered together,* so as to be the storehouse of the densest vapours, still in the act of being increasingly condensed.

Let the blackness of the day terrify it.] **And let it be lapped in with sorrow.**—*Coverdale.* This is very expressive: *lap* signifies to fold up, or envelope any particular thing with fold upon fold, so as to *cover it everywhere* and *secure it in all points.* Leaving out the semicolon, we had better translate the whole clause thus: "Let the thickest cloud have its dwelling-place upon it, and let the bitterness of a day fill it with terror." *A day* similar to that, says the *Targum,* in which *Jeremiah was distressed for the destruction of the house of the sanctuary;* or like that in which *Jonah was cast into the sea of Tarsis;* such a day as that on which some great or national misfortune has happened: probably in allusion to that in which *the darkness that might be felt* enveloped the whole land of Egypt, and the night in which the destroying angel slew all the first-born in the land.

Verse 6. As for *that night, let darkness seize upon it*] I think the *Targum* has hit the sense of this whole verse: "Let darkness seize upon that night; let it not be reckoned among the annual festivals; in the number of the months of the calendar let it not be computed."

Some understand the word אֹפֶל *ophel* as signifying a *dark storm;* hence the Vulgate, *tenebrosus turbo,* "a dark whirlwind." And hence *Coverdale,* **Let the darck storme obercome that night, let it not be reckoned amonge the dayes off the yeare, nor counted in the monethes.** Every thing is here personified; *day, night, darkness, shadow of death, cloud, &c.;* and the same idea of the total extinction of that portion of time, or its being rendered ominous and portentous, is pursued through all these verses, from the *third* to the *ninth,* inclusive. The *imagery* is diversified, the *expressions* varied, but the *idea* is the same.

Verse 7. Lo, *let that night be solitary*] The word הִנֵּה *hinneh, behold,* or *lo,* is wanting in one of *De Rossi's* MSS., nor is it expressed in the *Septuagint, Vulgate, Syriac,* or *Arabic.*

The word גַּלְמוּד *galmud,* which we translate *solitary,* is properly *Arabic.* From جلم *ghalama* or *jalama,* signifying to *cut off, make bare, amputate,* comes جلمود *jalmud,* a *rock,* a *great stone;* and جلاميد *jalameedet, weight,* a *burden, trouble,* from which we may gather Job's meaning: "Let that night be grievous, oppressive, as destitute of good as a bare rock is of verdure." The *Targum* gives the sense, *In that night let there be tribulation.*

Let no joyful voice come therein.] Let there be no choirs of singers; no pleasant music heard; no dancing or merriment. The word רְנָנָה *renanah* signifies any brisk *movement,* such as the vibration of the rays of light, or the brisk modulation of the voice in a cheerful ditty. The *Targum* has, *Let not the crowing of the rural or wild cock resound in it.* Let all work be intermitted; let there be no sportive exercises; and let all animals be totally silent.

Verse 8. *Let them curse it that curse the day*] This translation is scarcely intelligible. I have waded through a multitude of interpretations, without being able to collect from them such a notion of the verse as could appear to me probable. *Schultens, Rosenmüller,* and after them Mr. *Good,* have laboured much to make it plain. They think the custom of *sorcerers* who had *execrations* for peoples, places, things, days, &c., is here referred to; such as Balaam, Elymas, and many others were: but I cannot think that a man who knew the Divine Being and his sole government of the world so well as Job did, would make such an allusion, who must have known that such *persons* and their *pretensions* were impostors and execrable vanities. I shall give as near a translation as I can of the words, and subjoin a short paraphrase:

יִקְּבֻהוּ אֹרְרֵי יוֹם הָעֲתִידִים עֹרֵר לִוְיָתָן *yikkebuhu orerey yom haathidim orer livyathan;* "Let them curse it who detest the day; them who are ready to raise up the leviathan." That is, Let them curse my birthday who hate daylight, such as adulterers, murderers, thieves, and banditti, for whose practices the *night* is more convenient; and let them curse it who, being like me *weary of life,* are desperate enough to provoke the leviathan, the crocodile, to tear them to pieces. This version is nearly the same as that given by *Coverdale.* **Let them that curse the daye gibe it their curse also, then those that be ready to rayse up lebiathan.** By *leviathan* some understand the greatest and most *imminent dangers;* and others, the *devil,* whom the *enchanters* are desperate enough to attempt to raise by their incantations.

Calmet understands the whole to be spoken of the *Atlantes,* a people of *Ethiopia,* who *curse the sun* because it parches their fields and their bodies; and who *fearlessly attack, kill,* and *eat the crocodile.* This seems a good sense.

Verse 9. *Let the stars of the twilight thereof*] The stars of the twilight may here refer to the planets *Venus, Jupiter, Mars,* and *Mercury,* as well as to the brighter fixed stars.

Let it look for light] Here the prosopopoeia or personification is still carried on. The *darkness* is represented as *waiting* for the lustre of the *evening star,* but is disappointed; and then for the *aurora* or *dawn,* but equally in vain.

A. M. cir. 2484
B. C. cir. 1520
Ante I. Olymp.
cir. 744
Ante U. C. cir.
767

neither let it see [l]the dawning of the day:

10 Because it shut not up the doors of my *mother's* womb, nor his sorrow from mine eyes.

11 [k]Why died I not from the womb? *why* did I *not* give up the ghost when I came out of the belly?

12 [l]Why did the knees prevent me? or why the breast that I should suck?

13 For now should I have lain still and

been quiet, I should have slept: then had I been at rest,

14 With kings and counsellors of the earth, which [m]built desolate places for themselves;

15 Or with princes that had gold, who filled their houses with silver.

16 Or [n]as a hidden untimely birth I had not been; as infants *which* never saw light.

17 There the wicked cease *from* troubling; and there the [o]weary be at rest.

A. M. cir. 2484
B. C. cir. 1520
Ante I. Olymp.
cir. 744
Ante U. C. cir.
767

---

[l]Heb. *the eyelids of the morning*, chap. xli. 18——[k]Chap. x. 18——[l]Gen. xxx. 3; Isa. lxvi. 12

[m]Chapter xv. 28——[n]Psa. lviii. 8——[o]Heb. *wearied in strength*

He had prayed that its *light*, the sun, should not shine upon it, ver. 4; and here he prays that its *evening star* may be totally obscured, and that it might never see the *dawning of the day.* Thus his execration comprehends every thing that might *irradiate* or *enliven* it.

Verse 10. *Because it shut not up the doors*] Here is the reason why he curses the day and the night in which he was conceived and born; because, had he never been brought into existence, he would never have seen trouble. It seems, however, very harsh that he should have wished the destruction of his *mother*, in order that his birth might have been prevented; and I rather think Job's execration did not extend thus far. The *Targum* understands the passage as speaking of the *umbilical cord*, by which the fœtus is nourished in its mother's womb: had this been shut up, there must have been a miscarriage, or he must have been *dead born;* and thus *sorrow would have been hidden from his eyes.* This seeming gloss is much nearer the letter and spirit of the Hebrew than is generally imagined. I shall quote the words: כי

לא סגר דלתי בטני *ki lo sagar dalthey bitni, because it did not shut up the doors of my belly.* This is much more consistent with the feelings of humanity, than to wish his mother's womb to have been his grave.

Verse 11. *Why died I not from the womb*] As the other circumstance did not take place, why was I not *still-born*, without the possibility of *reviviscence?* or, as this did not occur, why did I not *die as soon as born?* These *three* things appear to me to be clearly intended here:—1. Dying in the womb, or never coming to maturity, as in the case of an *abortion.* 2. Being still-born, without ever being able to breathe. 3. Or, if born alive, dying within a short time after. And to these states he seems to refer in the following verses.

Verse 12. *Why did the knees prevent me?*] Why was I dandled on the knees? Why was I nourished by the breasts? In either of the above cases I had neither been received into a mother's lap, nor hung upon a mother's breasts.

Verse 13. *For now should I have lain still*] In that case I had been insensible; *quiet*—without these overwhelming agitations; *slept*—unconscious of evil; *been at rest*—been out of the reach of calamity and sorrow.

Verse 14. *With kings and counsellors of the earth*] I believe this translation to be perfectly correct. The *counsellors*, יעצי *yoatsey*, I

suppose to mean the privy council, or advisers of kings; those without whose advice kings seldom undertake wars, expeditions, &c. These mighty agitators of the world are at rest in their graves, after the lives of commotion which they have led among men: most of whom indeed have been the troublers of the peace of the globe.

Which built desolate places] Who erect mausoleums, funeral monuments, sepulchral pyramids, &c., to keep their *names* from *perishing*, while their *bodies* are turned to *corruption.* I cannot think, with some learned men, that Job is here referring to those patriotic princes who employed themselves in repairing the ruins and desolations which others had occasioned. His simple idea is, that, had he died from the womb, he would have been equally at rest, neither troubling nor troubled, as those defunct kings and planners of wars and great designs are, who have nothing to keep even their *names* from perishing, but the monuments which they have raised to contain their corrupting flesh, mouldering bones, and dust.

Verse 15. *Or with princes that had gold*] Chief or mighty men, lords of the soil, or fortunate adventurers in merchandise, who got gold in abundance, filled their houses with silver, left all behind, and had nothing reserved for themselves but the *empty places* which they had made for their last dwelling, and where their dust now sleeps, devoid of care, painful journeys, and anxious expectations. He alludes here to the case of the *covetous, whom nothing can satisfy,* as an Asiatic writer has observed, *but the dust that fills his mouth when laid in the grave.*—SAADY.

Verse 16. *Or as a hidden untimely birth*] An early miscarriage, which was scarcely perceptible by the parent herself; and in this case he *had not been*—he had never had the distinguishable form of a human being, whether *male* or *female.*

As infants] Little ones; those farther advanced in maturity, but miscarried long before the time of birth.

Verse 17. *There the wicked cease*] In the grave the oppressors of men cease from irritating, harassing, and distressing their fellow creatures and dependents.

And there the weary be at rest.] Those who were worn out with the cruelties and tyrannies of the above. The troubles and the troubled, the restless and the submissive, the toils of the

A. M. cir. 2484
B. C. cir. 1520
Ante I. Olymp. cir. 744
Ante U. C. cir. 767

18 *There* the prisoners rest to-gether; Pthey hear not the voice of the oppressor.

19 The small and great are there; and the servant *is* free from his master.

20 qWherefore is light given to him that is in misery, and life unto the rbitter *in* soul;

21 Which slong tfor death, but it *cometh* not; and dig for it more than ufor hid treasures;

22 Which rejoice exceedingly, *and* are glad, when they can find the grave?

A. M. cir. 2484
B. C. cir. 1520
Ante I. Olymp. cir. 744
Ante U. C. cir. 767

23 *Why is light given* to a man whose way is hid, vand whom God hath whedged in?

24 For my sighing cometh xbe-fore I eat, and my roarings are poured out like the waters.

25 For ythe thing which I greatly feared is come upon me, and that which I was afraid of is come unto me.

26 I was not in safety, neither had I rest, neither was I quiet; yet trouble came.

PChapter xxxix. 7——qJeremiah xx. 18——r1 Samuel i. 10; 2 Kings iv. 27; Proverbs xxxi. 6——sHebrew, *wait*——tRevelation ix. 6——uProverbs ii. 4——vCh.

xxix. 8; Lamentations iii. 7——wChapter i. 10——xHe-brew, *before my meat*——yHebrew, *I feared a fear, and it came upon me*

---

great and the labours of the slave, are here put in opposition.

Verse 18. *The prisoners rest together*] Those who were slaves, feeling all the troubles, and scarcely tasting any of the pleasures of life, are quiet in the grave together; and the voice of the oppressor, the hard, unrelenting task-master, which was more terrible than death, is heard no more. *They* are free from his exactions, and *his* mouth is silent in the dust. This may be a reference to the Egyptian bondage. The chil-dren of Israel cried by reason of their oppres-sors or task-masters.

Verse 19. *The small and great are there.*] All sorts and conditions of men are equally blended in the grave, and ultimately reduced to one common dust; and between the bond and free there is no difference. The *grave* is

"The appointed place of rendezvous, where all These travellers meet."

Equality is absolute among the sons of men in their *entrance* into and *exit* from the world: all the intermediate state is *disparity.* All men *begin* and *end life alike;* and there is no differ-ence between the king and the cottager. A con-templation of this should equally humble the *great* and the *small.* The saying is *trite,* but it is *true:—*

Pallida mors æquo pulsat pede pauperum ta-bernas,
Regumque turres.
            HOR. Odar. lib. i., Od. iv., ver. 13.

"With equal pace impartial Fate Knocks at the palace as the cottage gate."

Death is that state,
"Where they an equal honour share Who buried or unburied are.
Where *Agamemnon* knows no more Than *Irus* he contemn'd before.
Where fair *Achilles* and *Thersites* lie, Equally *naked, poor,* and *dry.*"

And why do not the *living* lay these things to heart?

There is a fine saying in *Seneca ad Marciam,* cap. 20, on this subject, which may serve as a comment on this place: MORS—servitutem invito domino remittit; hæc captivorum catenas levat; hæc e carcere eduxit, quos exire imperium im-potens vetuerat. Hæc est in quo nemo humili-tatem suam sensit; hæc quæ nulli paruit; hæc, quæ nihil quicquam alieno fecit arbitrio. Hæc,

ubi res communes fortuna male divisit, et æquo jure genitos alium alii donavit, exæquat omnia. —"Death, in spite of the master, manumits the slave. It loosens the chains of the prisoners. It brings out of the dungeon those whom im-potent authority had forbidden to go at large. This is the state in which none is sensible of his humiliation. Death obeys no man. It does nothing according to the will of another. It reduces, by a just law, to a state of equality, all who in their families and circumstances had unequal lots in life."

Verse 20. *Wherefore is light given*] Why is life granted to him who is incapable of enjoy-ing it, or of performing its functions?

Verse 21. *Which long for death*] They look to it as the *end* of all their miseries; and long more for a separation from life, than those who love gold do for a rich mine.

Verse 22. *Which rejoice exceedingly.* Liter-ally, *They rejoice with joy,* and *exult when they find the grave.*

There is a various reading here in one of *Kennicott's* MSS., which gives a different sense. Instead of *who rejoice,* אלי גיל *eley gil,* with JOY, it has אלי גל *eley gal, who rejoice at the* TOMB, *and exult when they find the grave.*

Verse 23. *To a man whose way is hid*] Who knows not what is before him in either world, but is full of fears and trembling concerning both.

God hath hedged in?] Leaving him no way to escape; and not permitting him to see one step before him.

There is an exact parallel to this passage in Lam. iii. 7, 9: *He hath hedged me about that I cannot get out. He hath inclosed my ways with hewn stone.* Mr. *Good* translates the verse thus: *To the man whose path is broken up, and whose futurity God hath overwhelmed.* But I cannot see any necessity for departing from the com-mon text, which gives both an *easy* and a *natural* sense.

Verse 24. *For my sighing cometh*] Some think that this refers to the *ulcerated state* of Job's *body, mouth, hands,* &c. He longed for food, but was not able to lift it to his mouth with his hands, nor masticate it when brought thither. This is the sense in which *Origen* has taken the words. But perhaps it is most natural to suppose that he means his sighing took away all appetite, and served him in place of meat. There is the same thought in Psa. xlii. 3: *My tears have been my meat day and night;* which place is not an imitation of Job, but more likely *Job* an imitation of it, or, rather, both an imitation of *nature.*

My roarings are poured out] My lamentations are like the noise of the murmuring stream, or the dashings of the overswollen torrent.

Verse 25. *For the thing which I greatly feared*] Literally, *the fear that I feared;* or, *I feared a fear,* as in the *margin.* While I was in prosperity I thought adversity might come, and I had a dread of it. I feared the loss of my family and my property; and both have occurred. I was not lifted up: I knew that what I possessed I had from Divine Providence, and that he who gave might take away. I am not stripped of my all as a punishment for my self-confidence.

Verse 26. *I was not in safety*] If this verse be read *interrogatively,* it will give a good and easy sense: *Was I not in safety? Had I not rest? Was I not in comfort? Yet trouble came.* It is well known that, previously to this attack of Satan, Job was in great prosperity and peace. Mr. *Good* translates, *I had no peace; yea, I had no rest. Yea, I had no respite, as the trouble came on;* and refers the whole to the quick succession of the series of heavy evils by which he was tried. There is a similar thought in the Psalmist: *Deep crieth unto deep at the noise of thy water-spouts; all thy waves and thy billows have gone over me;* Psa. xlii. 7. One evil treads on the heels of another.

In this chapter Job's conflict begins. *Now,* and not *before,* Satan appears to have access to his *mind.* When he deprived him of his *property,* and, what was still dearer, of his *sons* and his *daughters,* the hope of his family, he bore all with the most exemplary patience, and the deepest resignation to the Divine will. When his adversary was permitted to touch his *body,* and afflict it in the most grievous and distressing manner, rendered still more intolerable by his being previously deprived of all the *comforts* and *necessaries* of life; still he held fast his integrity; no complaint, no murmur was heard. From the Lord's hand he received his *temporal good;* and from that hand he received his *temporal evil,* the privation of that good. Satan was, therefore, baffled in all his attempts; Job continued to be *a perfect and upright man, fearing God, and avoiding evil.* This was Job's triumph, or rather the triumph of Divine grace; and Satan's defeat and confusion.

It is indeed very seldom that God permits Satan to waste the *substance* or afflict the *body* of any man; but at all times this malevolent spirit may have access to the *mind* of any man, and inject doubts, fears, diffidence, perplexities, and even *unbelief.* And here is the spiritual conflict. Now, *their wrestling is not with flesh and blood*—with *men* like themselves, nor about *secular* affairs; but they have to contend with *angels, principalities and powers, and the rulers of the darkness of this world, and spiritual wickednesses in heavenly places.* In such cases Satan is often permitted to diffuse *darkness* into the understanding, and envelope the heavens with clouds. Hence are engendered *false views* of God and his providence, of men, of the spiritual world, and particularly of the person's own state and circumstances. Every thing is distorted, and all seen through a false medium. Indescribable distractions and uneasiness are hereby induced; the mind is like a troubled sea, tossed by a tempest that seems to confound both heaven and earth. Strong *temptations* to things which the soul contemplates with abhorrence are injected; and which are followed by immediate *accusations,* as if the injections were the *offspring of the heart itself;* and the trouble and dismay produced are represented as the sense of guilt, from a consciousness of having, in heart, committed these evils. Thus Satan tempts, accuses, and upbraids, in order to perplex the soul, induce skepticism, and destroy the empire of faith. Behold here the *permission* of God, and behold also his *sovereign control:* all this time the grand tempter is not permitted to touch the *heart,* the seat of the affections, nor offer even the slightest violence to the *will.* The soul is cast down, but not destroyed; perplexed, but not in despair. It is on all sides harassed; without are fightings, within are fears: but the *will* is inflexible on the side of God and truth, and the heart, with all its train of affections and passions, follows it. The man does not wickedly depart from his God; the outworks are violently *assailed,* but not *taken;* the city is still safe, and the citadel impregnable. Heaviness may endure for the night, but joy cometh in the morning. Jesus is soon seen walking upon the waters. He speaks peace to the winds and the sea: immediately there is a calm. Satan is bruised down under the feet of the sufferer, the clouds are dispersed, the heavens re-appear, and the soul, to its surprise, finds that the storm, instead of hindering, has driven it nearer to the haven whither it would be.

The reader who closely examines the subject will find that this was the case of Job. The following chapters show the conflict of the soul; the end of the book, God's victory and his exaltation. Satan sifted Job as wheat, but his faith failed not.

CHAPTER IV

Eliphaz answers; and accuses Job of impatience, and of despondence in the time of adversity, 1–6; asserts that no innocent man ever perished, and that the wicked are afflicted for their sins, 7–11; relates a vision that he had, 12–16, and what was said to him on the occasion, 17–21.

A. M. cir. 2484
B. C. cir. 1520
Ante I. Olymp.
cir. 744
Ante U. C. cir.
767

THEN Eliphaz the Temanite answered and said,

2 *If* we assay [a]to commune with thee, wilt thou be grieved? but [b]who can withhold himself from speaking?

3 Behold, thou hast instructed many, and thou [c]hast strengthened the weak hands.

4 Thy words have upholden him that was falling, and thou [d]hast strengthened [e]the feeble knees.

5 But now it is come upon thee, and thou

faintest: it toucheth thee, and thou art troubled.

A. M. cir. 2484
B. C. cir. 1520
Ante I. Olymp.
cir. 744
Ante U. C. cir.
767

6 *Is* not *this* [f]thy fear, [g]thy confidence, thy hope, and the uprightness of thy ways?

7 Remember, I pray thee, [h]who *ever* perished, being innocent? or where were the righteous cut off?

8 Even as I have seen, [i]they that plough iniquity, and sow wickedness, reap the same.

---

[a]Heb. *a word*——[b]Heb. *who can refrain from words?* [c]Isa. xxxv. 3——[d]Isa. xxxv. 3——[e]Heb. *the bowing knees;* Heb. xii. 12

[f]Ch. i. 1——[g]Prov. iii. 26——[h]Psalm xxxvii. 25 [i]Psalm vii. 14; Proverbs xxii. 8; Hosea x. 13; Galatians vi. 7, 8

NOTES ON CHAP. IV

Verse 1. *Then Eliphaz the Temanite answered*] For *seven days* this person and his two friends had observed a profound silence, being awed and confounded at the sight of Job's unprecedented affliction. Having now sufficiently contemplated his afflicted state, and heard his bitter complaint, forgetting that he came as a *comforter,* and not as a *reprover,* he loses the feeling of the *friend* in the haughtiness of the *censor,* endeavouring to strip him of his only consolation,—the testimony of his conscience, that in simplicity and godly sincerity, not in fleshly wisdom, but by the grace of God, he had his conversation among men,—by insinuating that if his ways had been upright, he would not have been abandoned to such distress and affliction; and if his heart possessed that righteousness of which he boasted, he would not have been so suddenly cast down by adversity.

Verse 2. *If we assay to commune with thee*] As if he had said, Should I and my friends endeavour to reason with thee ever so mildly, because we shall have many things to say by way of reprehension, thou wilt be grieved and faint; and this we may reasonably infer from the manner in which thou bearest thy present afflictions. Yet as thou hast uttered words which are injurious to thy Maker, who can forbear speaking? It is our duty to rise up on the part of God, though thereby we shall grieve him who is our friend. This was a plausible beginning, and certainly was far from being insincere.

Verse 3. *Thou hast instructed many*] Thou hast seen many in affliction and distress, and thou hast given them such advice as was suitable to their state, and effectual to their relief; and by this means thou hast *strengthened the weak hands,* and the *feeble knees*—the desponding have been encouraged, and the irresolute confirmed and excited to prompt and proper actions, by thy counsel and example.

Verse 5. *But now it is come upon thee*] Now it is thy turn to suffer, and give an example of the efficacy of thy own principles; but instead of this, behold, thou faintest. Either, therefore, thou didst *pretend* to what thou hadst not; or thou art not making a proper use of the principles which thou didst recommend to others.

Verse 6. *Is not this thy fear*] I think *Coverdale* hits the true meaning: 𝔚𝔥𝔢𝔯𝔢 𝔦𝔰 𝔫𝔬𝔴 𝔱𝔥𝔶 𝔣𝔢𝔞𝔯𝔢 𝔬𝔣 𝔊𝔬𝔡, 𝔱𝔥𝔶 𝔰𝔱𝔢𝔡𝔣𝔞𝔰𝔱𝔫𝔢𝔰𝔰𝔢, 𝔱𝔥𝔶 𝔭𝔞𝔠𝔦𝔢𝔫𝔠𝔢, 𝔞𝔫𝔡 𝔱𝔥𝔢 𝔭𝔢𝔯𝔣𝔢𝔠𝔱𝔫𝔢𝔰𝔰𝔢 𝔬𝔣 𝔱𝔥𝔶 𝔩𝔦𝔣𝔢? If these be genuine, surely there is no cause for all this complaint, vexation, and

despair. That this is the meaning, the next words show.

Verse 7. *Remember, I pray thee*] Recollect, if thou canst, a single instance where God abandoned an innocent man, or suffered him to perish. Didst thou ever hear of a case in which God abandoned a righteous man to destruction? Wert thou a righteous man, and innocent of all hidden crimes, would God abandon thee thus to the malice of Satan? or let loose the plagues of affliction and adversity against thee?

Verse 8. *They that plough iniquity*] A proverbial form of speech drawn from nature. Whatever seed a man sows in the ground, he reaps the same kind; for every seed produces its like. Thus *Solomon,* Prov. xxii. 8: "He that soweth iniquity shall reap vanity." And St. Paul, Gal. vi. 7, 8: "Be not deceived, God is not mocked; for whatsoever a man soweth, that shall he also reap. For he that soweth to his flesh, shall of the flesh reap corruption; but he who soweth to the Spirit, shall of the Spirit reap life everlasting." And of the same nature is that other saying of the apostle, *He that soweth sparingly, shall reap sparingly,* 2 Cor. ix. 6.

The same figure is employed by the Prophet Hosea viii. 7: *They have sown the wind, and they shall reap the whirlwind;* and chap. x. 12, 13: *Sow to yourselves in righteousness; reap in mercy. Ye have ploughed wickedness; ye have reaped iniquity.* The last sentence contains, not only the same *image,* but almost the *same words* as those used by Eliphaz.

Our Lord expresses the same thing, in the following words: Matt. vii. 16-18: *Do men gather grapes of thorns, or figs of thistles? Every good tree bringeth forth good fruit, but a corrupt tree bringeth forth evil fruit.* So the Greeks:—

Ατης αρουρα θανατον εκκαρπιζεται.
ÆSCH. Ἑπτα επι Θηβαις, ver. 607.

"The field of iniquity produces the fruit of death."

Ὑβρις γαρ εξανθους ̇ εκαρπωσε σταχυν
Ατης, ὁθεν παγκλαυτον εξαμα θερος.
ΙΒ. Περσαι, ver. 823.

"For oppression, when it springs,
Puts forth the blade of vengeance; and its fruit
Yields a ripe harvest of repentant wo."—POTTER.

The image is common every where, because it is a universal law of nature.

A. M. cir. 2484
B. C. cir. 1520
Ante I. Olymp.
cir. 744
Ante U. C. cir.
767

9 By the blast of God they perish, and [k]by the breath of his nostrils are they consumed.

10 The roaring of the lion, and the voice of the fierce lion, and [l]the teeth of the young lions, are broken.

11 [m]The old lion perisheth for lack of prey, and the stout lion's whelps are scattered abroad.

12 Now a thing was [n]secretly brought to me, and mine ear received a little thereof.

A. M. cir. 2484
B. C. cir. 1520
Ante I. Olymp.
cir. 744
Ante U. C. cir.
767

13 [o]In thoughts from the visions of the night, when deep sleep falleth on men,

14 Fear [p]came upon me, and [q]trembling, which made [r]all my bones to shake.

15 Then a spirit passed before my face; the hair of my flesh stood up:

16 It stood still, but I could not discern the form thereof: an image *was* before mine eyes, [s]*there was* silence, and I heard a voice, *saying,*

17 [t]Shall mortal man be more just than

---

[k]That is, *by his anger;* as Isa. xxx. 33; see Exod. xv. 8; chap. i. 19; xv. 30; Isa. xi. 4; 2 Thess. ii. 8——[l]Psa. lviii. 6——[m]Psa. xxxiv. 10

[n]Heb. *by stealth*——[o]Chap. xxxiii. 15——[p]Heb. *met me*——[q]Hab. iii. 16——[r]Heb. *the multitude of my bones*——[s]Or, *I heard a still voice*——[t]Chap. ix. 2

Verse 9. *By the blast of God they perish*] As the noxious and parching east wind blasts and destroys vegetation, so the wicked perish under the indignation of the Almighty.

Verse 10. *The roaring of the lion*] By the roaring lion, fierce lion, old lion, stout lion, and lion's whelps, tyrannous rulers of all kinds are intended. The design of Eliphaz in using these figures is to show that even those who are possessed of the greatest *authority* and *power*—the *kings, rulers,* and *princes* of the earth—when they become wicked and oppressive to their subjects are cast down, broken to pieces, and destroyed, by the incensed justice of the Lord; and their *whelps*—their children and intended *successors,* scattered without possessions over the face of the earth.

Verse 11. *The old lion perisheth*] In this and the preceding verse the word *lion* occurs *five times;* and in the original the words are all different:—

1. אריה *aryeh,* from ארה *arah,* to tear off.
2. שחל *shachal,* which as it appears to signify *black* or *dark,* may mean the *black lion,* which is said to be found in Ethiopia and India. 3. כפיר *kephir,* a *young lion,* from כפר *caphar, to cover,* because he is said to *hide* himself in order to surprise his prey, which the *old one* does not. 4. ליש *layish,* from לש *lash, to knead, trample upon;* because of his method of seizing his prey. 5. לביא *labi,* from לבא *laba, to suckle with the first milk;* a lioness giving suck; at which time they are peculiarly fierce. All these words may point out some *quality* of the lion; and this was probably the cause why they were originally given: but it is likely that, in process of time, they served only to designate the beast, without any particular reference to any of his properties. We have one and the same idea when we say the *lion,* the *king of beasts,* the *monarch of the forest,* the *most noble of quadrupeds,* &c.

Verse 12. *Now a thing was secretly brought to me*] To give himself the more authority, he professes to have received a vision from God, by which he was taught the secret of the Divine dispensations in providence; and a confirmation of the doctrine which he was now stating to Job; and which he applied in a different way to what was designed in the Divine communication.

Mine ear received a little thereof.] Mr. *Good* translates, "And mine ear received a whisper along with it." The *apparition* was the general subject; and the *words* related ver. 17, &c., were the *whispers* which he heard when the apparition stood still.

Verse 13. *From the visions of the night*] "It is in vain," says Mr. *Good,* "to search through ancient or modern poetry for a description that has any pretensions to rival that upon which we are now entering. Midnight—solitude—the deep sleep of all around—the dreadful chill and horripilation or erection of the hair over the whole body—the shivering, not of the *muscles* only, but of the *bones* themselves—the gliding approach of the spectre—the abruptness of his pause—his undefined and indescribable form—are all powerful and original characters, which have never been given with equal effect by any other writer."

Mr. *Hervey's* illustration is also striking and natural. "'Twas in the *dead of night;* all nature lay shrouded in darkness; every creature was buried in *sleep.* The most *profound silence* reigned through the universe. In these solemn moments Eliphaz, alone, all wakeful and solitary, was musing on sublime subjects. When, lo! an awful being burst into his apartment. *A spirit passed before his face.* Astonishment seized the beholder. His bones shivered within him; his flesh trembled all over him; and the hair of his head stood erect with horror. *Sudden* and *unexpected* was its appearance; not such its departure. *It stood still,* to present itself more fully to his view. It made a solemn pause, to prepare his mind for some momentous message. After which *a voice was heard.* A *voice,* for the importance of its meaning, worthy to be had in everlasting remembrance. It spoke, and these were its words:"

Verse 17. *Shall mortal man*] אנוש *enosh;* Greek βροτος· poor, weak, dying man.

Be more just than God?] Or, האנוש מאלוה יצדק *haenosh meeloah yitsdak;* shall poor, weak, sinful man be justified before God?

Shall a man] גבר *gaber,* shall even the *strong* and *mighty man,* be pure before his Maker? Is any man, considered merely in and of himself, either holy in his conduct, or pure in his heart? No. He must be justified by the mercy of God, through an *atoning sacrifice;* he must be *sanctified* by the Holy Spirit of God, and thus made a partaker of the Divine nature. Then he is justified before God, and pure in the sight of his Maker: and this is a work which God himself alone can do; so the work is not *man's*

A. M. cir. 2484
B. C. cir. 1520
Ante I. Olymp.
cir. 744
Ante U. C. cir.
767

God? shall a man be more pure than his Maker?

18 Behold, he ᵘput no trust in his servants; ᵛand his angels he charged with folly:

19 ʷHow much less *in* them that dwell in ˣhouses of clay, whose foundation *is* in the

---

A. M. cir. 2484
B. C. cir. 1520
Ante I. Olymp.
cir. 744
Ante U. C. cir.
767

dust, *which* are crushed before the moth?

20 ʸThey are ᶻdestroyed from morning to evening: they perish for ever without any regarding *it.*

21 ᵃDoth not their excellency *which is* in them go away? ᵇthey die, even without wisdom.

ᵘChap. xv. 15; xxv. 5; 2 Pet. ii. 4——ᵛOr, *nor in his angels* in whom *he put light*——ʷChap. xv. 16

ˣ2 Cor. iv. 7; v. 1——ʸPsa. xc. 5, 6——ᶻHeb. *beaten in pieces*——ᵃPsa. xxxix. 11; xlix. 14——ᵇCh. xxxvi. 12

---

work, but God's. It is false to infer, from the words of this spectre, (whether it came from heaven or hell, we know not, for its communication shows and rankles a wound, without providing a cure,) that no man can be justified, and that no man can be purified, when God both justifies the ungodly, and sanctifies the unholy. The meaning can be no more than this: no man can make an atonement for his own sins, nor purify his own heart. Hence all *boasting* is for ever excluded. Of this Eliphaz believed Job to be guilty, as he appeared to talk of his righteousness and purity, as if they had been his own acquisition.

Verse 18. *Behold, he put no trust in his servants*] This verse is generally understood to refer to the fall of angels; for there were some of those heavenly beings *who kept not their first estate:* they did not persevere to the end of their probation, and therefore fell into condemnation, and are *reserved in chains of darkness unto the judgment of the great day;* Jude 6. It is said *he put no trust in them*—he knew that nothing could be *absolutely immutable* but himself; and that no intelligent beings could *subsist* in a state of *purity,* unless continually dependent on himself, and deriving constant supplies of grace, power, and light, from him who gave them their being.

And his angels he charged with folly] Not *chargeth,* as many quote the passage. He *charged* those with folly who kept not their first estate. It does not appear that he is *charging* the others in the same way, who continue steadfast.

The several translations of this verse, both ancient and modern, are different from each other. Here are the chief:—

In angelis suis reperit pravitatem, "In his angels he found perverseness," VULGATE. The SEPTUAGINT is nearly the same. *Il met la lumiere dans ses anges,* "He puts light into his angels," FRENCH BIBLE. Even those pure intelligences have continual need of being irradiated by the Almighty. ܩܫܝܫ̈ܐ ܡܢ ܩܕ̈ܡܘܗܝ

wa-bemalakui neshim temcho, "And he hath put amazement in his angels," SYRIAC. The ARABIC is the same. *In angelis suis ponet gloriationem,* "In his angels he will put exultation," MONTANUS. The Hebrew is תהלה *toholah, irradiation,* from הלה *halah, to irradiate, glister,* or *shine.* In this place we may consider angels (מלאכים *malachim*) as heavenly or earthly messengers or angels of the Lord; and the *glory, influence,* and *honour* of their office as being *put in them* by the Most High. They are as planets which shine with a *borrowed light.* They have nothing but what they have received. Coverdale translates the whole verse thus:

𝕭𝖊𝖍𝖔𝖑𝖉𝖊 𝖍𝖊 𝖍𝖆𝖙𝖍 𝖋𝖔𝖚𝖓𝖉𝖊 𝖚𝖓𝖋𝖆𝖞𝖙𝖍𝖋𝖚𝖑𝖓𝖊𝖘𝖘𝖊 𝖆𝖒𝖔𝖓𝖌𝖊 𝖍𝖎𝖘 𝖔𝖜𝖓𝖊 𝖘𝖊𝖗𝖇𝖆𝖚𝖓𝖙𝖘 𝖆𝖓𝖉 𝖕𝖗𝖔𝖚𝖉𝖊 𝖉𝖎𝖘𝖔𝖇𝖊𝖉𝖎𝖊𝖓𝖈𝖊 𝖆𝖒𝖔𝖓𝖌𝖊 𝖍𝖎𝖘 𝖆𝖓𝖌𝖊𝖑𝖘. The sense is among all these interpreters; and if the *fallen angels* are meant, the passage is plain enough.

Verse 19. *How much less*] Rather, with the VULGATE, *How much more?* If angels may be unstable, how can man arrogate stability to himself who dwells in an earthly tabernacle, and who must shortly return to dust?

Crushed before the moth? The slightest accident oftentimes destroys. "A *fly,* a *grapestone,* or a *hair* can kill." Great men have fallen by all these. This is the general idea in the text; and it is useless to *sift* for meanings.

Verse 20. *They are destroyed from morning to evening*] In almost every moment of time some human being comes into the world, and some one departs from it. Thus are they "destroyed from morning to evening."

They perish for ever] יאבדו *yobedu; peribunt,* they *pass by;* they *go out of sight;* they moulder with the dust, and are soon forgotten. Who regards the past generation now among the dead?

Isaiah has a similar thought, chap. lvii. 1: "The righteous perisheth, and NO MAN LAYETH IT TO HEART: and merciful men are taken away, none considering that the righteous is taken away from the evil to come." Some think that Isaiah borrowed from Job; this will appear possible when it has been *proved,* which has never yet been done, that the writer of this book flourished *before* Isaiah. If, however, he borrowed the above thought, it must be allowed that it has been wondrously improved by coming through his hands.

Verse 21. *Doth not their excellency—go away?*] Personal beauty, corporeal strength, powerful eloquence, and various mental endowments, pass away, or are *plucked up by the roots;* they are no more seen or heard among men, and their memory soon perisheth.

They die, even without wisdom.] If wisdom means *the pursuit of the best end, by the most legitimate and appropriate means,* the great mass of mankind appear to perish without it. But, if we consider the subject more closely, we shall find that all men die in a state of comparative ignorance. With all our boasted science and arts, how little do we know! Do we know any thing to *perfection* that belongs either to the *material* or *spiritual* world? Do we understand even what *matter* is? What is its *essence?* Do we understand what *spirit* is? Then, what is its *essence?* Almost all the phenomena of nature, its grandest operations, and the laws of the heavenly bodies, have been explained on the principle of *gravitation* or *attraction;* but in *what does this consist?* Who can answer? We can traverse every part of the huge and trackless ocean by means of the *compass;* but who understands the nature of *magnetism* on which all this depends? We eat and drink in order to maintain life; but what is *nutrition,* and how is it effected? This has never been explained. Life depends on *respiration* for its continuance; but by what kind of action is it, that *in a moment* the *lungs* separate the *oxygen,* which is friendly to life, from the *nitrogen,* which would destroy it; suddenly absorbing the *one,* and expelling the *other?* Who, among the generation of *hypothesis-framers,* has *guessed* this out? Life is continued by the

circulation of the blood; but by what power and law does it circulate? Have the *systole* and *diastole* of the heart, on which this circulation depends, ever been satisfactorily explained? Most certainly not. Alas, *we die without wisdom;* and must *die,* to know these, and ten thousand other matters equally unknown, and equally important. To be safe, in reference to eternity, we must know the only true God, and Jesus Christ whom he has sent; whom to know is life eternal. This knowledge, obtained and retained, will entitle us to all the rest in the eternal world.

CHAPTER V

Eliphaz proceeds to show that the wicked are always punished by the justice of God, though they may appear to flourish for a time, 1–8; extols the providence of God, by which the counsels of the wicked are brought to naught, and the poor fed and supported, 9–16; shows the blessedness of being corrected by God, in the excellent fruits that result from it; and exhorts Job to patience and submission, with the promise of all secular prosperity, and a happy death in a mature and comfortable old age, 17–27.

A. M. cir. 2484
B. C. cir. 1520
Ante I. Olymp. cir. 744
Ante U. C. cir. 767

CALL now, if there be any that will answer thee; and to which of the saints wilt thou [a]turn?

2 For wrath killeth the foolish man, and [b]envy slayeth the silly one.

3 [c]I have seen the foolish taking root:

but suddenly I cursed his habitation.

4 [d]His children are far from safety, and they are crushed in the gate, [e]neither *is there* any to deliver *them.*

5 Whose harvest the hungry eateth up, and taketh it even out of the thorns, and [f]the

A. M. cir. 2484
B. C. cir. 1520
Ante I. Olymp. cir. 744
Ante U. C. cir. 767

[a]Or, *look*——[b]Or, *indignation*——[e]Psa. xxxvii. 35, 36; Jer. xii. 2, 3

[d]Psa. cxix. 155; cxxvii. 5——[e]Psa. cix. 12——[f]Chap. xviii. 9

NOTES ON CHAP. V

Verse 1. *Call now, if there be any*] This appears to be a strong *irony.* From whom among those *whose foundations are in the dust, and who are crushed before the moth,* canst thou expect succour?

To which of the saints wilt thou turn?] To whom among the *holy ones,* (קדשים *kedoshim,*) or among those who are equally dependent on Divine support with thyself, and can do no good but as influenced and directed by God, *canst thou turn* for help? Neither angel nor saint can help any man unless sent especially from God; and all prayers to *them* must be foolish and absurd, not to say impious. Can the *channel* afford me water, if the *fountain* cease to emit it?

Verse 2. *For wrath killeth the foolish man*] *Foolish, silly,* and *simple,* are epithets given by *Solomon* to sinners and transgressors of all kinds. Such parallelisms have afforded a presumptive argument that Solomon was the author of this book. See the *preface.* The words of Eliphaz may be considered as a sort of *maxim,* which the wisdom and experience of ages had served to establish; viz., The wrath of God is manifested only against the wicked and impious; and if thou wert not such, God would not thus contend with thee.

Verse 3. *I have seen the foolish taking root*] I have seen wicked men for a time in prosperity, and becoming established in the earth; but I well knew, from God's manner of dealing with men, that they must soon be blasted. I even ventured to *pronounce their doom;* for I

knew that, in the order of God's providence, that was inevitable. *I cursed his habitation.*

Verse 4. *His children are far from safety*] His posterity shall not continue in prosperity. *Ill gotten, ill spent;* whatever is got by wrong must have God's curse on it.

They are crushed in the gate] The Targum says, *They shall be bruised in the gate of hell, in the day of the great judgment.* There is reference here to a custom which I have often had occasion to notice: viz., that in the Eastern countries the *court-house,* or *tribunal of justice,* was at the GATE *of the city;* here the magistrates attended, and hither the plaintiff and defendant came for justice.

Verse 5. *Whose harvest*] Their possessions, because acquired by unjust means, shall not be under the protection of God's providence; he shall abandon them to be pillaged and destroyed by the wandering *half-starved* hordes of the *desert banditti.* They shall carry it suddenly off; *even the thorns*—grain, weeds, thistles, and all, shall they carry off in their rapacious hurry.

The robber swalloweth us] Or, more properly, the *thirsty,* צמים *tsammim,* as is plain from their *swallowing up* or *gulping down;* opposed to the *hungry* or *half-starved,* mentioned in the preceding clause. The *hungry* shall *eat up* their grain, and the *thirsty* shall *drink down* their wine and oil, here termed חילם *cheylam,* their *strength* or *power,* for the most obvious reasons.

There seem to be *two* allusions in this verse: 1. To the hordes of wandering predatory banditti, or half-starved Arabs of the desert, who have their scanty maintenance by the plunder

A. M. cir. 2484
B. C. cir. 1520
Ante I. Olymp.
cir. 744
Ante U. C. cir.
767

robber swalloweth up their sub-stance.

6 Although [g]affliction cometh not forth of the dust, neither doth trouble spring out of the ground;

7 Yet man is [h]born unto [i]trouble, as [k]the sparks fly upward.

8 I would seek unto God, and unto

A. M. cir. 2484
B. C. cir. 1520
Ante I. Olymp.
cir. 744
Ante U. C. cir.
767

God would I commit my cause:

9 [l]Which doeth great things [m]and unsearchable; marvellous things [n]without number:

10 [o]Who giveth rain upon the earth, and sendeth waters upon the [p]fields:

11 [q]To set up on high those that be low;

---

[g]Or, *iniquity*——[h]Gen. iii. 17, 18, 19; 1 Cor. x. 13
[i]Or, *labour*——[k]Heb. *the sons of the burning coal lift up to fly*——[l]Chap. ix. 10; xxxvii. 5; Psa. xl. 5; lxxii. 18; cxlv. 3; Rom. xi. 33

[m]Heb. *and there is no search*——[n]Heb. *till there be no number*——[o]Chap. xxviii. 26; Psa. lxv. 9, 10; cxlvii. 8; Jer. v. 24; x. 13; li. 16; Acts xiv. 47——[p]Heb. *out-places*——[q]1 Sam. ii. 7; Psa. cxiii. 7

---

of others. These descendants of Ishmael have ever had their hands against all men, and live to this day in the same predatory manner in which they have lived for several thousands of years. M. *Volney's* account of them is striking: "These men are smaller, leaner, and blacker, than any of the Bedouins yet discovered. Their wasted legs had only tendons without calves. Their belly was shrunk to their back. They are in general small, lean, and swarthy, and more so in the bosom of the desert than on the borders of the more cultivated country. They are ordinarily about five feet or *five feet two inches* high; they seldom have more than about six ounces of food for the whole day. Six or seven dates, soaked in melted butter, a little milk, or curd, serve a man for twenty-four hours; and he seems happy when he can add a small portion of coarse flour, or a little ball of rice. Their *camels* also, which are their only support, are remarkably meagre, living on the meanest and most scanty provision. *Nature* has given it a small head without ears, at the end of a long neck without flesh. She has taken from its legs and thighs every muscle not immediately requisite for motion; and in short has bestowed on its withered body only the vessels and tendons necessary to connect its frame together. She has furnished it with a strong jaw, that it may grind the hardest aliments; and, lest it should consume too much, she has straitened its stomach, and obliged it to chew the cud." Such is the description given of the Bedouin and his camel, by M. Volney. who, while he denies the true God, finds out a deity which he calls *Nature*, whose works evince the highest providence, wisdom, and design! And where does this most wonderful and intelligent *goddess* dwell? Nowhere but in the creed of the infidel; while the genuine believer knows that *nature* is only the *agent* created and employed by the great and wise God to accomplish, under his direction, the greatest and most stupendous beneficial effects.

The *second allusion* in the verse I suppose to be to the loss Job had sustained of his cattle by the predatory *Sabeans;* and all this Eliphaz introduces for the support of his grand argument, to convict Job of hidden crimes, on which account his enemies were permitted to destroy his property; that property, because of this wickedness, being placed out of the protection of God's providence.

Verse 6. *Affliction cometh not forth of the dust*] If there were not an adequate cause, thou couldst not be so grievously afflicted.

Spring out of the ground] It is not from mere

natural causes that affliction and trouble come; God's justice inflicts them upon offending man.

Verse 7. *Yet man is born unto trouble*] לעמל *leamal*, to *labour*. He must *toil* and be *careful;* and if in the course of his labour he meet with trials and difficulties, he should rise superior to them, and not *sink* as thou dost.

As the sparks fly upward.] ובני רשף יגביהו עוף *ubeney resheph yagbihu uph; And the sons of the coal lift up their flight*, or *dart upwards.* And who are *the sons of the coal?* Are they not bold, intrepid, ardent, fearless men, who rise superior to all their trials; combat what are termed chance and occurrence; succumb under no difficulties; and rise superior to time, tide, fate, and fortune? I prefer this to all the various meanings of the place with which I have met. *Coverdale* translates, ᵗIt iȿ man tḫat iȿ borne unto mẏȿerẏ, like aȿ tḫe bẏrde for to flẏ Most of the ancient *versions* give a similar sense.

Verse 8. *I would seek unto God*] Were I in your place, instead of wasting my time, and irritating my soul with useless complaints, I would apply to my Maker, and, if conscious of my innocence, would confidently commit my cause to him.

Verse 9. *Which doeth great things*] No work, however complicated, is too deep for his counsel to plan; none, however stupendous, is too great for his power to execute. He who is upright is always safe in referring his cause to God, and trusting in him.

Verse 10. *Who giveth rain upon the earth*] The *Chaldee* gives this verse a fine turn: "Who gives rain on the face of the land of *Israel*, and sends waters on the face of the *provinces* of the *people.*" Similar to our Lord's saying, which is expressed in the half of the compass: *Your Father which is in heaven*—SENDETH RAIN ON THE JUST AND ON THE UNJUST; Matt. v. 45.

Sendeth waters upon the fields] The term הוצות *chutsoth*, which we translate *fields*, and generally signifies *streets*, may here mean those *plantations* which are *laid out* in *ridges* or *plats*, in an *orderly*, *regular* manner. God does not only send rain upon the *earth* in a *general* manner, but, by an *especial providence*, waters the *cultivated ground*, so that not one ridge is destitute of its due proportion of fructifying moisture.

Verse 11. *To set up on high those that be low*] He so distributes his providential blessings without partiality, that the land of the *poor man* is as well *sunned* and *watered* as that of the *rich;* so that he is thus set upon a level with the lords of the soil.

A. M. cir. 2484
B. C. cir. 1520
Ante I. Olymp.
cir. 744
Ante U. C. cir.
767

that those which mourn may be exalted to safety.

12 [r]He disappointeth the devices of the crafty, so that the hands [s]cannot perform *their* enterprise.

13 [t]He taketh the wise in their own craftiness: and the counsel of the froward is carried headlong.

14 [u]They [v]meet with darkness in the daytime, and grope in the noonday as in the night.

15 But [w]he saveth the poor from the sword,

from their mouth, and from the hand of the mighty.

A. M. cir. 2484
B. C. cir. 1520
Ante I. Olymp.
cir. 744
Ante U. C. cir.
767

16 [x]So the poor hath hope, and iniquity stoppeth her mouth.

17 [y]Behold, happy *is* the man whom God correcteth: therefore despise not thou the chastening of the Almighty:

18 [z]For he maketh sore, and bindeth up: he woundeth, and his hands make whole.

19 [a]He shall deliver thee in six troubles: yea, in seven [b]there shall no evil touch thee.

---

[r]Neh. iv. 15; Psa. xxxiii. 10; Isa. viii. 10——[s]Or, *cannot perform any thing*——[t]Psa. ix. 15; 1 Cor. iii. 19 [u]Deut. xxviii. 29; Isa. lix. 10; Amos viii. 9——[v]Or, *run into*——[w]Psa. xxxv. 10

[x]1 Sam. ii. 9; Psa. cvii. 42——[y]Psa. xciv. 12; Prov. iii. 11, 12; Heb. xii. 5; James i. 12; Rev. iii. 19——[z]Deut. xxxii. 39; 1 Sam. ii. 6; Isa. xxx. 26; Hos. vi. 1——[a]Psa. xxxiv. 19; xci. 3; Prov. xxiv. 16; 1 Cor. x. 13——[b]Psa. xci. 10

Verse 12. *He disappointeth the devices of the crafty*] All these sayings refer to God's *particular providence*, by which he is ever working for the *good*, and counterworking the plots of the *wicked*. And as various as are the contingent, capricious, and malevolent acts of men, so varied are his providential interferences; disappointing the devices, snares, and plots of the crafty, so that their plans being confounded, and their machinery broken in pieces, *their hands cannot perform their enterprises.*

Verse 13. *He taketh the wise in their own craftiness*] So counterworks them as to cause their feet to be taken in their own snares, and their evil dealings to fall on their own pate. Such frequent proofs has God given of his especial interference in behalf of the innocent, who have been the objects of the plots and evil designs of the wicked, by turning those evil devices against their framers, that *he who digs a pit for his neighbour shall fall into it himself* has become a universal *adage*, and has passed, either in so many words or in sense, into all the languages of all the people of the earth. *Lucretius* expresses it strongly:

Circumrretit enim vis atque injuria quemque,
Atque, unde exorta est, ad eum plerumque re-
   vortit.   LUCRET. lib. v., ver. 1151.

"For force and wrong entangle the man that uses them;
And, for the most part, recoil on the head of the contriver."

Verse 14. *They meet with darkness in the daytime*] God confounds them and their measures; and, with all their cunning and dexterity, they are outwitted, and often act on their own projects, planned with care and skill, as if they had been the crudest conceptions of the most disordered minds. They act in *noonday* as if the *sun were extinct*, and their *eyes put out.* Thus does God "abate their pride, assuage their malice, and confound their devices."

Verse 15. *He saveth the poor from the sword, from their mouth*] This is rather a harsh construction. To avoid this, some have proposed to render מחרב *mechereb*, which we translate *from the sword, the persecuted*, but, I am afraid, on very slender authority. Instead of מחרב מפיהם *mechereb mippihem*, "from the sword,

from their mouth," *eleven of Kennicott and De Rossi's* MSS. read מחרב פיהם *mechereb pihem, from the sword of their mouth;* and with these MSS. the *Chaldee, Vulgate, Syriac,* and *Arabic* agree. The verse, therefore, may be translated thus:—

He saveth from the sword of their mouth;
The poor from the hand of the mighty.

Or thus:—

He saveth from the sword of their mouth;
And with a strong hand the impoverished.

Verse 16. *So the poor*] דל *dal*, he who is made *thin*, who is *wasted, extenuated; hath hope*—he sees what God is accustomed to do, and he expects a repetition of gracious dealings in his own behalf; and because God deals thus with those who trust in him, therefore the *mouth of impiety is stopped.*

Religion is kept alive in the earth, because of God's signal interventions in behalf of the bodies and souls of his followers.

Verse 17. *Behold, happy is the man*] הנה *hinneh behold*, is wanting in *five* of *Kennicott's* and *De Rossi's* MSS., and also in the *Syriac, Vulgate,* and *Arabic.*

We have had *fathers of our flesh*, who corrected us for their pleasure, or according to their caprices, and we were subject to them: how much more should we be subject to the *Father of spirits*, and live? for he corrects that we may be partakers of his holiness, in order that we may be rendered fit for his glory. See Heb. xii. 5; James i. 12; and Prov. iii. 12.

Verse 18. *For he maketh sore, and bindeth up* Thus nervously rendered by *Coverdale*, ꝺFor t'ough he make a wounde, he gibeth a medicyne agapne; though he smpte, his honde maketh whole agapne.

Verse 19. *He shall deliver thee in six troubles*] The numbers *six* and *seven* are put here for *many.* Though a number of troubles should come upon thee *all at once*, and there should be no hope, humanly speaking, yet God would rid thee out of them all; for he saves as well from *many* as from *few.* We may also understand the words, He who hath been thy deliverer in past troubles, will not deny his help in those which are to come.

A. M. cir. 2484
B. C. cir. 1520
Ante I. Olymp.
cir. 744
Ante U. C. cir.
767

20 [c]In famine he shall redeem thee from death: and in war [d]from the power of the sword.

21 [e]Thou shalt be hid [f]from the scourge of the tongue: neither shalt thou be afraid of destruction when it cometh.

22 At destruction and famine thou shalt laugh: [g]neither shalt thou be afraid of the beasts of the earth.

23 [h]For thou shalt be in league with the stones of the field: and the beasts of the field shall be at peace with thee.

24 And thou shalt know [i]that thy tabernacle *shall be* in peace; and thou shalt visit thy habitation, and shalt not [k]sin.

A. M. cir. 2484
B. C. cir. 1520
Ante I. Olymp.
cir. 744
Ante U. C. cir.
767

25 Thou shalt know also that [l]thy seed *shall be* [m]great, and thine offspring [n]as the grass of the earth.

26 [o]Thou shalt come to *thy* grave in a full age, like as a shock of corn [p]cometh in his season.

27 Lo this, we have [q]searched it, so it *is;* hear it, and know thou *it* [r]for thy good.

[c]Psa. xxxiii. 19; xxxvii. 19——[d]Heb. *from the hands*
[e]Psalm xxxi. 20——[f]Or, *when the tongue scourgeth*
[g]Isa. xi. 9; xxxv. 9; lxv. 25; Ezek. xxxiv. 25——[h]Psa. xci. 12; Hos. ii. 18

[i]Or, *that peace is thy tabernacle*——[k]Or, *err*——[l]Psa. cxii. 2——[m]Or, *much*——[n]Psa. lxxii. 16——[o]Prov. ix. 11; x. 27——[p]Heb. *ascendeth*——[q]Psa. cxi. 2——[r]Heb. *for thyself;* Prov. ix. 12

Verse 20. *In famine he shall redeem thee*] The *Chaldee,* which understands this chapter as speaking of the *troubles and deliverances of the Israelites in Egypt and the wilderness,* renders this verse as follows: "In the famine of Egypt he redeemed thee from death; and in the war of Amalek, from the slaying of the sword."

Verse 21. *Thou shalt be hid from the scourge of the tongue*] The *Targum* refers this to the *incantations of Balaam:* "From injury by the tongue of Balaam thou shalt be hidden in the clouds; and thou shalt not fear from the blasting of the Midianites, when it shall come."

Perhaps no evil is more dreadful than the *scourge of the tongue:* evil-speaking, detraction, backbiting, calumny, slander, tale-bearing, whispering, and scandalizing, are some of the terms which we use when endeavouring to express the baleful influence and effects of that member, which is a *world of fire,* kindled from the nethermost hell. The Scripture abounds with invectives and execrations against it. See Psa. xxxi. 20, lii. 2-4; Prov. xii. 18, xiv. 3; James iii. 5-8.

Neither shalt thou be afraid] "Thou shouldst have such strong confidence in God, that even in the presence of destruction thou shouldst not fear death," the God of life and power being with thee.

Verse 22. *At destruction and famine thou shalt laugh*] This most forcibly expresses the strongest security, and confidence in that security. "In the desolation of Sihon, and in the famine of the desert, thou shalt laugh; and of the camps of Og, who is compared to a wild beast of the earth, thou shalt not be afraid."—*Targum.*

Verse 23. *Thou shalt be in league with the stones of the field*] Instead of אבני *abney, stones,* Mr. *Good* reads בני *beney, sons,* or *produce;* but this reading is not supported by any ancient version, nor, as far as I know, by any MS. yet collated. We must, therefore, take up the text as we find it, and make the best we can of the present reading.

The *Chaldee* gives a plausible sense: Thou needest not to fear, "because thy covenant is on tables of stone, which are publicly erected in the field; and the Canaanites, which are compared to the beasts of the field, have made peace with thee."

Perhaps the reference is to those *rocks* or

strong holds, where banditti secured themselves and their prey, or where the *emirs* or neighbouring *chiefs* had their ordinary residence. Eliphaz may be understood as saying: Instead, then, of taking advantage of thee, as the *Sabeans* have done, the circumjacent chieftains will be confederate with thee; and the very beasts of the field will not be permitted to harm thy flocks.

Coverdale seems to have had an idea of this kind, as we find he translates the verse thus:—

But the castels in the londe shall be confederate with the,

And the beastes of the felde shall gŭe the peace.

I believe the above to be the meaning of the place. See the next verse.

Verse 24. *Thou shalt know*] Thou shalt be so fully satisfied of the friendly disposition of all thy neighbours, that thou shalt rest secure in thy bed, and not be afraid of any danger, though sleeping in thy *tent* in the *field;* and when thou returnest from thy country excursions, thou shalt find that thy *habitation* has been preserved in peace and prosperity, and that thou hast *made no mistake* in thy trust, in thy confidence, or in thy confederates.

The word אהלך *oholecha,* "thy tabernacle," means simply a *tent,* or *moveable dwelling,* composed of *poles, pins,* and *cloth,* or *skin,* to be pitched any where in a few moments, and struck again with the same ease.

The word נוך *navecha,* which we properly translate thy *habitation,* signifies a *solid, permanent dwelling-place.* See Josh. xxii. 4, 6, 7, 8; 2 Sam. xviii. 17; xix. 8; 1 Kings xii. 16; Psa. lii. 7; xci. 10; cxxxii. 3; Lam. ii. 4; Mal. ii. 12; and with these passages compare the place in the text.

As to תחטא *techeta,* which we translate thou shalt not SIN, it comes from חטא *chata,* to *err,* to *mistake,* to *miss the mark:* hence to *sin, transgress God's laws,* seeking for happiness in forbidden and unlawful things, and therefore *missing the mark,* because in *them* happiness is not to be found: and it is very likely, from the connection above, that to *mistake* or *err* is its meaning in this place. I need not add, that the Arab chiefs, who had their castles and strong holds, frequently in their country excursions lodged in *tents* in the open fields; and

that on such occasions a hostile neighbour sometimes took advantage of their absence, attacked
and pillaged their houses, and carried off their
families and household. See at the end of this
chapter.

Verse 25. *Thine offspring as the grass*] Thou
shalt have a numerous and permanent issue.

Verse 26. *Thou shalt come to thy grave*]
Thou shalt not die before thy time; thou shalt
depart from life like a full-fed guest; happy in
what thou hast known, and in what thou hast
enjoyed.

Like as a shock of corn] Thou shalt completely run through the round of the *spring,
summer, autumn,* and *winter* of life; and thou
shalt be buried like a wholesome seed in the
earth; from which thou shalt again rise up
into an eternal *spring!*

Verse 27. *Lo this, we have searched it*] What
I have told thee is the sum of our wisdom and
experience on these important points. These are
established maxims, which universal experience
supports. *Know*—understand, and reduce them
to practice *for thy good.* Thus ends *Eliphaz,*
the *Temanite,* "full of wise saws and ancient
instances;" but he miserably perverted them
in his application of them to Job's case and
character. They contain, however, many wholesome truths, of which the wise in heart may
make a very advantageous practical use.

THE predatory excursions referred to in verse
23 were not unfrequent among our own barbarous ancestors. An affecting picture of this
kind is drawn by *Shakspeare,* from *Holinshed's
Chronicles,* of the case of *Macduff,* whose castle
was attacked in his absence by *Macbeth* and his
wife and all his children murdered. A similar
incident was the ground of the old heroic ballad
of *Hardicanute.* When the veteran heard that
a host of Norwegians had landed to pillage the
country, he armed, and posted to the field to
meet the invading foe. He slew the chief in
battle, and routed his pillaging banditti. While
this was taking place, another party took the
advantage of his absence, attacked his castle,
and carried off or murdered his lovely wife and
family; which, being perceived on his return
by the war and age-worn chief, is thus affectingly described by the unknown poet:—

Loud and chill blew the westlin wind,
    Sair beat the heavy showir,
Mirk grew the nicht eir *Hardyknute*
    Wan neir his stately tower:

His tower that us'd with torches bleise
    To shine sae far at nicht,
Seim'd now as black as mourning weid,
    Nae marvel, sair he sich'd.

"Thair's nae light in my lady's bowir,
    Thair's nae light in my hall;
Nae blink shynes round my *Fairly* fair,
    Nor *ward* stands on my wall.

"What bodes it, *Thomas! Robert!* say?"
    Nae answer—speaks their dreid;
"Stand back, my sons, I'll be your gyde;"
    But bye they pass'd with speid.

"As fast I haif sped owr Scotland's foes"—
    There ceis'd his brag of weir.
Sair schamt to mind ocht but his dame,
    And maiden *Fairly* fair.

Black feir he felt; but what to feir
    He wist not yet with dreid;
Sair schook his body, sair his limbs,
    And all the warrior fled.

The ending of this poem is lost; but we here
see that the castle of *Hardicanute* was surprised, and his family destroyed, or carried off,
while he and his sons had been employed in
defeating the invading Norwegians. Thank
God! *civilization,* the offspring of the spread
of *Christianity,* has put an end to these barbarous practices among us; but in the *East,* where
Christianity is not, they flourish still. Britons!
send out your Bible and your missionaries to
tame these barbarians; for whom *heathenism*
has done nothing, and the *Koran* next to nothing. *Civilization* itself, without the *Bible,* will
do as little; for the civilized Greeks and Romans
were barbarians, fell and murderous; living in
envy and malice, hateful, hating one another,
and offering *hundreds* at a time of *human victims* to their ruthless deities. Nothing but
Christianity ever did, or even can, cure these
evils.

CHAPTER VI

*Job answers, and vindicates himself; and shows that the great affliction which he suffered was the cause of his
complaining, by which life was rendered burdensome to him, 1–13. He complains that, whereas he expected
consolation from his friends, he had received nothing but the bitterest reproaches, on the assumed ground that
he must be a wicked man, else God would not so grievously afflict him, 14–20. He shows them that they knew
nothing of his case, and that they had no compassion, 21–23. And then entreats them, if they can, to show him
in what he has offended, as he is ready to acknowledge and correct every trespass, 24–30.*

A. M. cir. 2484
B. C. cir. 1520
Ante I. Olymp.
cir. 744
Ante U. C. cir.
767

BUT Job answered and said,
2 O, that my grief were
thoroughly weighed, and my
calamity ªlaid in the balances
together!

3 For now it would be heavier ᵇthan the
sand of the sea: therefore ᶜmy words are
swallowed up.

4 ᵈFor the arrows of the Almighty *are*
within me, the poison whereof drinketh up my
spirit: ᵉthe terrors of God do set themselves
in array against me.

5 Doth the wild ass bray ᶠwhen he hath
grass? or loweth the ox over his fodder?

6 Can that which is unsavoury
be eaten without salt? or is there
any taste in the white of an
egg?

A. M. cir. 2484
B. C. cir. 1520
Ante I. Olymp.
cir. 744
Ante U. C. cir.
767

7 The things *that* my soul refuseth to touch
are as my sorrowful meat.

8 O that I might have my request; and
that God would grant *me* ᵍthe thing that I
long for!

9 Even ʰthat it would please God to destroy me; that he would let loose his hand,
and cut me off!

10 Then should I yet have comfort; yea, I
would harden myself in sorrow: let him not

ªHeb. *lifted up*——ᵇProv. xxvii. 3——ᶜThat is, *I want words to express my grief;* Psa. lxxvii. 4

ᵈPsa. xxxviii. 2——ᵉPsa. lxxxviii. 15, 16——ᶠHeb. *at grass*——ᵍHeb. *my expectation*——ʰ1 Kings xix. 4

NOTES ON CHAP. VI

Verse 2. O that my grief were thoroughly weighed] Job wished to be dealt with according to justice; as he was willing that his sins,
if they could be proved, should be weighed
against his sufferings; and if this could not be
done, he wished that his sufferings and his
complainings might be weighed together; and
it would then be seen that, bitter as his complaint had been, it was little when compared
with the distress which occasioned it.

Verse 3. Heavier than the sand of the sea]
This includes *two ideas:* their *number* was too
great to be counted; their *weight* was too great
to be estimated.

Verse 4. The arrows of the Almighty] There
is an evident reference here to *wounds inflicted
by poisoned arrows;* and to the burning fever
occasioned by such *wounds*, producing such an
intense parching thirst as to dry up all the
moisture in the system, stop all the salivary
ducts, thicken and inflame the blood, induce
putrescency, and terminate in raging mania,
producing the most terrifying images, from
which the patient is relieved only by death.
This is strongly expressed in the fine figure:
The POISON DRINKETH *up my* SPIRIT; *the* TERRORS
of GOD SET THEMSELVES *in* ARRAY *against me.*
That *calamities* are represented among the
Eastern writers as the *arrows of the Almighty*,
we have abundant proofs. In reference to this,
I shall adduce that fine saying attributed to
Aaly, the son-in-law of *Mohammed*, in the *Too-
zuki Teemour;* which I have spoken of elsewhere. "It was once demanded of the fourth
califf, (*Aaly*,) 'If the canopy of *heaven* were a
bow; and if the *earth* were the *cord thereof;*
and if *calamities* were the *arrows;* if *mankind*
were the *mark* for those arrows; and if *Almighty
God*, the tremendous and glorious, were the unerring *Archer;* to whom could the sons of Adam
flee for protection?' The califf answered, 'The
sons of Adam must flee unto the Lord.'" This
fine image Job keeps in view in the eighth and
ninth verses, wishing that the *unerring marks-
man* may *let fly* these arrows, *let loose his hand,*
to destroy and cut him off.

Verse 5. Doth the wild ass] פרא *pere*, translated *onager*, by the *Vulgate*, from the ονος αγριος
of the *Septuagint*, which we properly enough,

translate *wild ass.* It is the same with the
tame ass; only in a wild state it grows to a
larger size, is stronger, and more fleet. The
meaning of Job appears to be this: You condemn me for complaining; do I complain without a cause? The *wild ass* will not *bray*, and
the *ox* will not low, unless in *want.* If they
have plenty of provender, they are silent. Were
I at rest, at ease, and happy, I would not complain.

Verse 6. Can that which is unsavoury] Mr.
Good renders this verse as follows: *Doth insipid food without a mixture of salt, yea, doth
the white of the egg give forth pungency?*
Which he thus illustrates: "Doth that which
hath nothing of seasoning, nothing of a pun-
gent or irritable power within it, produce pungency or irritation? I too should be quiet and
complain not, if I had nothing provocative or
acrimonious, but, alas! the food I am doomed
to partake of is the very calamity which is
most acute to my soul—that which I most
loathe, and which is most grievous or trying
to my palate." Some render the original, *Is
there any dependence on the drivel of dreams?*
There have been a great variety of interpretations given of this verse. I could add another;
but that of Mr. *Good* is as likely to be correct
as that of any other critic.

Verse 8. O that I might have] As Job had
no hope that he should ever be redeemed from
his present helpless state, he earnestly begs God
to shorten it by taking away his life.

Verse 9. Let loose his hand] A metaphor
taken from *an archer drawing his arrow to the
head,* and then *loosing his hold, that the arrow
may fly to the mark.* See on ver. 4.

Verse 10. Then should I yet have comfort]
Instead of עוד *od*, YET, three of *Kennicott's* and
De Rossi's MSS. have זאת *zoth*, THIS. *And* THIS
should be my comfort. The expectation that
he will speedily make an end of me would cause
me to rejoice with great joy. This reading is
supported by the *Vulgate* and the *Chaldee.*

I would harden myself in sorrow] To know
that I should shortly have an end put to my
miseries would cause me to endure the present
with determinate resolution. *Let him not spare*
—let him use whatever *means* he chooses, for
I will not resist his decree; he is *holy*, and his
decrees must be just.

A. M. cir. 2484
B. C. cir. 1520
Ante I. Olymp. cir. 744
Ante U. C. cir. 767

spare; for [1]I have not concealed the words of [k]the Holy One.

11 What *is* my strength, that I should hope? and what *is* mine end, that I should prolong my life?

12 *Is* my strength the strength of stones? or *is* my flesh [1]of brass?

---

[1]Acts xx. 20——[k]Lev. xix. 2; Isa. lvii. 15; Hos. xi. 9
[1]Heb. *brazen*

Verse 11. *What is my strength*] I can never suppose that my strength will be restored; and, were that possible, have I any comfortable prospect of a happy termination of my life? Had I any prospect of *future* happiness, I might well bear my *present* ills; but the state of my *body* and the state of my *circumstances* preclude all hope.

Verse 12. Is *my strength the strength of stones?*] I am neither a *rock*, nor is my flesh *brass*, that I can endure all these calamities. This is a proverbial saying, and exists in all countries. Cicero says, *Non enim est e saxo sculptus, aut e* ROBORE *dolatus* HOMO; *habet corpus, habet animum; movetur mente, movetur sensibus.* "For man is not chiselled out of the *rock*, nor hewn out of the *oak*; he has a body, and he has a soul; the one is actuated by intellect, the other by the senses." Quæst. Acad. iv. 31. So *Homer*, where he represents Apollo urging the Trojans to attack the Greeks:—

Νεμεσησε δ' Απολλων,

Περγαμου εκκατιδων· Τρωεσσι δε κεκλετ' αυσας·
Ορνυσθ', Ιπποδαμοι Τρωες, μηδ' εικετε χαρμης
Αργειοις· επει ου σφιλιθος χρως, ουδε σιδηρος,
Χαλκον ανασχεσθαι ταμεσιχροα βαλλομενοισιν.

ILIAD, lib. iv., ver. 507.

But Phœbus now from Ilion's towering height
Shines forth reveal'd, and animates the fight.
Trojans, be bold, and force to force oppose;
Your foaming steeds urge headlong on the foes!
Nor are their bodies ROCKS, nor ribb'd with STEEL;
Your weapons enter, and your strokes they feel.
POPE.

These are almost the same expressions as those in Job.

Verse 13. Is *not my help in me?*] My help is all in myself; and, alas! that is perfect weakness: *and my subsistence,* תושיה *tushiyah,* all that is *real, stable,* and *permanent, is driven quite from me.* My *friends* have forsaken me, and I am abandoned to *myself;* my *property* is all taken away, and I have no *resources* left. I believe Job neither said, nor intended to say, as some interpreters have it, *Reason is utterly driven from me.* Surely there is no mark in this chapter of his being deranged, or at all impaired in his intellect.

Verse 14. *To him that is afflicted pity should be showed from his friend; but he forsaketh the fear of the Almighty.*] The *Vulgate* gives a better sense, *Qui tollit ab amico suo misericordiam, timorem Domini dereliquit,* "He who takes away mercy from his friend, hath cast off the fear of the Lord." The word ממס *lammas,* which we render *to him who is* AFFLICTED, from מסח *masuh, to dissolve,* or *waste away,* is in

---

13 *Is* not my help in me? and is wisdom driven quite from me?

A. M. cir. 2484
B. C. cir. 1520
Ante I. Olymp. cir. 744
Ante U. C. cir. 767

14 [m]To [n]him that is afflicted pity *should be showed* from his friend; but he forsaketh the fear of the Almighty.

15 [o]My brethren have dealt deceitfully as

---

[m]Heb. *To him that melteth*——[n]Prov. xvii. 17——[o]Psa. xxxviii. 11; xli. 9

---

thirty-two of Dr. *Kennicott's* and *De Rossi's* MSS. למאס *lemoes,* "to him that *despiseth* his friend;" and hence the passage may be read: *To him who despiseth his friend, it is a reproach; and he will forsake the fear of the Almighty:* or, as Mr. *Good* translates,

"Shame to the man who despiseth his friend! He indeed hath departed from the fear of the Almighty."

Eliphaz had, in effect, *despised* Job; and on this ground had acted any thing but the part of a *friend* towards him; and he well deserved the severe stroke which he here receives. A heathen said, *Amicus certus in re incerta cernitur;* the full sense of which we have in our common adage:—

A FRIEND IN NEED *is a* FRIEND INDEED

Job's *friends,* so called, supported *each other* in their attempts to blacken the character of this worthy man; and their hand became the heavier, because they supposed the hand of God was upon him. To each of them, individually, might be applied the words of another heathen:—

————Absentem qui rodit amicum,
Qui non defendit alio culpante; solutos
Qui captat risus hominum, famamque dicacis,
Fingere qui non visa potest; commissa tacere
Qui nequit; hic niger est; hunc tu, Romane, caveto.

HOR. Satyr. lib. i., s. iv., ver. 81.

He who, malignant, tears an absent friend;
Or, when attack'd by others, don't defend;
Who trivial bursts of laughter strives to raise,
And courts, of prating petulance, the praise;
Of things he never saw who tells his tale,
And friendship's secrets knows not to conceal;—
This man is *vile;* here, Roman, fix your mark;
His *soul's* as *black* as his complexion's dark.
FRANCIS.

Verse 15. *Have dealt deceitfully as a brook*] There is probably an allusion here to those *land torrents* which make a sudden appearance, and as suddenly vanish; being produced by the rains that fall upon the mountains during the rainy season, and are soon absorbed by the thirsty sands over which they run. At first they seem to promise a *permanent stream,* and are noticed with delight by the people, who fill their tanks or reservoirs from their waters; but sometimes they are so large and rapid as to carry every thing before them: and then suddenly fail, so that there is no time to fill the tanks. The approach of Job's friends promised much of sympathy and compassion; his expectations were raised: but their conduct soon con-

A. M. cir. 2484
B. C. cir. 1520
Ante I. Olymp.
cir. 744
Ante U. C. cir.
767 a brook, *and* ᴾas the stream of brooks they pass away;

16 Which are blackish by reason of the ice, *and* wherein the snow is hid:

17 What time they wax warm, �q they vanish: ʳwhen it is hot, they are ˢconsumed out of their place.

18 The paths of their way are turned aside; they go to nothing, and perish.

19 The troops of ᵗTema looked, the companies of ᵘSheba waited for them.

20 They were ᵛconfounded because they had hoped; they came thither, and were ashamed.

21 ʷFor now ˣye are ʸnothing; ye see

A. M. cir. 2484
B. C. cir. 1520
Ante I. Olymp.
cir. 744
Ante U. C. cir.
767 *my* casting down, and ᶻare afraid.

22 Did I say, Bring unto me? or, Give a reward for me of your substance?

23 Or, Deliver me from the enemy's hand? or, Redeem me from the hand of the mighty?

24 Teach me, and I will hold my tongue: and cause me to understand wherein I have erred.

25 How forcible are right words! but what doth your arguing reprove?

26 Do ye imagine to reprove words, and the speeches of one that is desperate, *which are* as wind?

ᵖJer. xv. 18——�q Heb. *they are cut off*——ʳHeb. *in the heat thereof*——ˢHeb. *extinguished*——ᵗGen. xxv. 15——ᵘ1 Kings x. 1; Psa. lxxii. 10; Ezek. xxvii. 22, 23——ᵛJer. xiv. 3

ʷOr, *For now ye are* like *to them;* Hebrew, *to it* ˣChapter xiii. 4——ʸHebrew, *not*——ᶻPsalm xxxviii. 11

---

vinced him that they were physicians of no value; therefore he compares them to the *deceitful torrents* that soon *pass away.*

Verse 16. *Blackish by reason of the ice*] He represents the waters as being sometimes suddenly frozen, their foam being turned into the semblance of snow or hoar-frost: when the heat comes, they are speedily liquefied; and the evaporation is so strong from the heat, and the absorption so powerful from the sand, that they soon disappear.

Verse 18. *The paths of their way*] They sometimes forsake their *ancient channels,* which is a frequent case with the river *Ganges;* and, growing smaller and smaller from being divided into numerous streams, *they go to nothing and perish*—are at last utterly lost in the sands.

Verse 19. *The troops of Tema looked*] The *caravans* coming from *Tema* are represented as arriving at those places where it was well known torrents did descend from the mountains, and they were full of expectation that here they could not only slake their thirst, but fill their *girbas* or *water-skins;* but when they arrive, they find the waters totally dissipated and lost. In vain did the caravans of Sheba *wait for them;* they did not reappear: and they *were confounded, because they had hoped* to find here refreshment and rest.

Verse 21. *For now ye are nothing*] Ye are just to me as those deceitful torrents to the caravans of Tema and Sheba; they were *nothing* to them; ye are *nothing* to me.

Ye see my *casting down*] Ye see that I have been hurried from my eminence into want and misery, as the flood from the top of the mountains, which is divided, evaporated, and lost in the desert.

And are afraid.] Ye are terrified at the calamity that has come upon me; and instead of drawing near to comfort me, ye start back at my appearance.

Verse 22. *Did I say, Bring unto me?*] Why do you stand aloof? Have I asked you to bring me any presents? or to supply my wants out of your stores?

Verse 23. *Or, Deliver me*] Did I send to you

to come and avenge me of the destroyers of my property, or to rescue my substance out of the hands of my enemies?

Verse 24. *Teach me*] Show me where I am mistaken. Bring proper arguments to convince me of my errors; and you will soon find that I shall gladly receive your counsels, and abandon the errors of which I may be convicted.

Verse 25. *How forcible are right words*] A well-constructed argument, that has truth for its basis, is *irresistible.*

But what doth your arguing reprove?] Your *reasoning* is defective, because your *premises* are false; and your *conclusions* prove nothing, because of the falsity of the premises whence they are drawn. The last clause, literally rendered, is, *What reproof, in a reproof from you?* As you have *proved no fault* you have consequently *reproved* no vice. Instead of מה נמרצו *mah nimretsu,* "how forcible," מה נמלצו *mah nimletsu,* "how savoury or pleasant," is the reading of two MSS., the *Chaldee,* and some of the *rabbins.* Both senses are good, but the common reading is to be preferred.

Verse 26. *Do ye imagine to reprove words*] Is it some expressions which in my hurry, and under the pressure of unprecedented affliction, I have uttered, that ye catch at? You can find no flaw in my conduct; would ye *make me an* OFFENDER *for a* WORD? Why endeavour to take such advantage of a man who complains in the bitterness of his heart, through despair of life and happiness?

Verse 27. *Ye overwhelm the fatherless*] Ye see that I am as destitute as the most *miserable orphan;* would ye overwhelm such a one? and would you *dig a pit for your friend*—do ye lay wait for me, and endeavour to entangle me in my talk? I believe this to be the spirit of Job's words.

Verse 28. *Look upon me*] View me; consider my circumstances; compare my words; and you must be convinced that I have spoken nothing but truth.

Verse 29. *Return, I pray you*] Reconsider *the whole subject. Do not be offended. Yea,*

A. M. cir. 2484
B. C. cir. 1520
Ante I. Olymp. cir. 744
Ante U. C. cir. 767

27 Yea, [a]ye overwhelm the fatherless, and ye [b]dig *a pit* for your friend.

28 Now therefore be content, look upon me; for *it is* [c]evident unto you if I lie.

29 [d]Return, I pray you, let it not be iniquity; yea, return again, my righteousness *is* [e]in it.

30 Is there iniquity in my tongue? cannot [f]my taste discern perverse things?

A. M. cir. 2484
B. C. cir. 1520
Ante I. Olymp. cir. 744
Ante U. C. cir. 767

---

[a]Hebrew, *ye cause to fall upon*——[b]Psa. lvii. 6
[c]Heb. *before your face*——[d]Chap. xvii. 10

[e]That is, *in this matter*——[f]Heb. *my palate*, chap. xii. 11; xxxiv. 3

---

reconsider the subject; *my righteousness is in it*—my argumentation is a sufficient proof of my innocence.

Verse 30. *Is there iniquity in my tongue?*] Am I not an *honest* man? and if in my haste my tongue had uttered *falsity*, would not my conscience discern it? and do you think that such a man as your friend is would defend what he knew to be wrong?

I HAVE done what I could to make this chapter plain, to preserve the connection, and show the dependence of the several parts on each other; without which many of the sayings would have been very obscure. The whole chapter is an inimitable apology for what he had uttered, and a defence of his conduct. This might have ended the controversy, had not his friends been determined to bring him in guilty. They had prejudged his cause, and assumed a certain position, from which they were determined not to be driven.

CHAPTER VII

Job continues to deplore his helpless and afflicted state, 1–6. He expostulates with God concerning his afflictions, 7–12; describes the disturbed state of his mind by visions in the night season; abhors life, 13–16; and, showing that he is unworthy of the notice of God, begs pardon and respite, 17–21.

A. M. cir. 2484
B. C. cir. 1520
Ante I. Olymp. cir. 744
Ante U. C. cir. 767

*I*S there not [a]an [b]appointed time to man upon earth? are not his days also like the days of a hireling?

2 As a servant [c]earnestly desireth the shadow, and as a hireling looketh for *the reward of* his work:

3 So am I made to possess [d]months of vanity, and wearisome nights are appointed to me.

A. M. cir. 2484
B. C. cir. 1520
Ante I. Olymp. cir. 744
Ante U. C. cir. 767

---

[a]Or, *a warfare*——[b]Chap. xiv. 5, 13, 14; Psa. xxxix. 4

[c]Heb. *gapeth after*——[d]See chap. xxix. 2

NOTES ON CHAP. VII

Verse 1. *Is there not an appointed time to man*] The *Hebrew*, with its literal rendering, is as follows: חלא צבא לאנוש עלי ארץ *halo tsaba leenosh aley arets*, "Is there not a warfare to miserable man upon the earth?" And thus most of the *versions* have understood the words. The SEPTUAGINT: Ποτερον ουχι πειρατηριον εστι ὁ βιος ανθρωπου επι της γης; "Is not the life of man a place of trial upon earth?" The VULGATE: *Militia est* vita hominis super terram, "The life of man is a warfare upon earth." The CHALDEE is the same. *N'y a-t-il pas comme un train de guerre ordonné aux mortels sur la terre?* "Is there not a continual campaign ordained for mortals upon the earth?" FRENCH BIBLE. The GERMAN and DUTCH the same. COVERDALE: Is not the life off man upon earth a very bataple? CARMARDEN, Rouen, 1566: Hath man any certayne tyme upon earth? SYRIAC and ARABIC: "Now, man has time upon the earth." *Non è egli il tempo determinato à l'huomo sopra la terra?* "Is there not a determined time to man upon the earth?" BIB. ITAL., 1562. All these are nearer to the true sense than ours; and of a bad translation, worse use has been made by many theologians. I believe the simple sentiment which the writer wished to convey is this: *Human life is a state of probation;* and every day and place is a time and place of *exercise*, to *train us up* for eternal life. *Here* is the exercise, and here the *warfare:* we are *enlisted* in the *bands of the Church militant*, and must accomplish our *time of service*, and be honourably *dismissed* from the *warfare*, having *conquered* through the blood of the Lamb; and then receive the *reward* of the heavenly inheritance.

Verse 2. *Earnestly desireth the shadow*] As a man who labours hard in the *heat* of the day earnestly desires to get under a *shade*, or wishes for the *long evening shadows*, that he may rest from his labour, get his day's wages, retire to his food, and then go to rest. *Night* is probably what is meant by the *shadow;* as in VIRGIL, Æn. iv., ver. 7: Humentemque Aurora *polo dimoverat* UMBRAM. "The morning had removed the humid shadow, i. e., *night*, from the world." Where SERVIUS justly observes: *Nihil interest, utrum* UMBRAM *an* NOCTEM *dicat:* NOX enim UMBRA *terræ est*, "It makes no difference whether he says *shadow* or *night;* for night is the *shadow* of the earth."

Verse 3. *So am I made to possess*] But night is no relief to me; it is only a continuance of my anxiety and labour. I am like the *hireling*, I have my *appointed* labour for the *day*. I am like the *soldier* harassed by the enemy: I am obliged to be continually on the watch, always on the look out, with scarcely any rest.

A. M. cir. 2484
B. C. cir. 1520
Ante I. Olymp.
cir. 744
Ante U. C. cir.
767

4 ᵉWhen I lie down, I say, When shall I arise, and ᶠthe night be gone? and I am full of tossings to and fro unto the dawning of the day.

5 My flesh is ᵍclothed with worms and clods of dust; my skin is broken, and become loathsome.

6 ʰMy days are swifter than a weaver's shuttle, and are spent without hope.

7 O remember that ⁱmy life *is* wind: mine eye ᵏshall no more ˡsee good.

8 ᵐThe eye of him that hath seen me shall see me no *more:* thine eyes *are* upon me, ⁿand I *am* not.

A. M. cir. 2484
B. C. cir. 1520
Ante I. Olymp.
cir. 744
Ante U. C. cir.
767

ᵉDeut. xxviii. 67; chap. xvii. 12——ᶠHeb. *the evening be measured*——ᵍIsa. xiv. 11——ʰChap. ix. 25; xvi. 22; xvii. 14; Psa. xc. 6; cii. 11; ciii. 15; cxliv. 4; Isa. xxxviii. 12; xl. 6; James iv. 14——ⁱPsa. lxxviii. 39; lxxxix. 47 ᵏHeb. *shall not return*——ˡ*To see*, that is, *to enjoy* ᵐChap. xx. 9——ⁿ*That is, I can live no longer*

Verse 4. *When I lie down*] I have so little rest, that when I do lie down I long for the return of the light, that I may rise. Nothing can better depict the state of a man under continual afflictions, which afford him no respite, his days and his nights being spent in constant anguish, utterly unable to be in any one posture, so that he is continually changing his position in his bed, finding ease nowhere: thus, as himself expresses it, he is *full of tossings.*

Verse 5. *My flesh is clothed with worms*] This is perhaps no figure, but is literally true: the miserably ulcerated state of his body, exposed to the open air, and in a state of great destitution, was favourable to those insects that sought such places in which to deposit their *ova*, which might have produced the animals in question. But the figure is too horrid to be farther illustrated.

Clods of dust] I believe all the commentators have here missed the sense. I suppose Job to allude to those *incrustations* of indurated or dried *pus*, which are formed on the tops of pustules in a state of decay: such as the *scales* which fall from the pustules of the smallpox, when the patient becomes convalescent. Or, if Job's disease was the *elephantiasis*, it may refer to the *furfuraceous scales* which are continually falling off the body in that disorder. It is well known, that in this disease the *skin* becomes very *rigid*, so as to *crack* across, especially at the different *joints*, out of which fissures a loathsome *ichor* is continually exuding. To something like this the words may refer, *My* SKIN is BROKEN, and become LOATHSOME.

Verse 6. *Swifter than a weaver's shuttle*] The word ארג *areg* signifies rather the *weaver* than his *shuttle.* And it has been doubted whether any such instrument were in use in the days of Job. Dr. Russell, in his account of Aleppo, shows that though they wove many kinds of curious cloth, yet no *shuttle* was used, as they conducted every thread of the *woof* by their *fingers.* That some such instrument as the *shuttle* was in use from time immemorial, there can be no doubt: and it is certain that such an instrument must have been in the view of Job, without which the figure would lose its expression and force. In almost every nation the whole of human existence has been compared to a *web;* and the principle of life, through the continual succession of moments, hours, days, weeks, months, and years, *to a thread woven through that web.* Hence arose the fable of the *Parcæ* or *Fates*, called also the *Destinies* or *Fatal Sisters.* They were the daughters of *Erebus* and *Nox*, darkness and night; and were *three* in number, and named *Clotho, Lachesis*,

and *Atropos.* Clotho held the distaff; Lachesis spun off the thread; and Atropos cut it off with her scissors, when it was determined that life should end. Job represents the *thread of his life* as being *spun out* with great rapidity and tenuity, and about to be *cut off.*

And are spent without hope.] Expectation of future good was at an end; *hope* of the alleviation of his miseries no longer existed. The *hope* of future good is the *balm of life*: where that is not, there is *despair;* where despair is, there is *hell.* The fable above mentioned is referred to by *Virgil*, Ecl. iv., ver. 46, but is there applied to *time:*——

Talia Secla, suis dixerunt, currite, fusis
Concordes stabili fatorum numine Parcæ.

"The FATES, when they this happy *thread* have spun
Shall bless the sacred *clue*, and bit it *smoothly run.*"   DRYDEN.

Isaiah uses the same figure, chap. xxxviii. 12:——

My *life* is cut off, as by the *weaver:*
He will sever me from the *loom.*
In the course of the day thou wilt finish my web.   LOWTH.

Coverdale translates thus: 𝔐𝔶 𝔡𝔞𝔶𝔢𝔰 𝔭𝔞𝔰𝔰𝔢 𝔬𝔳𝔢𝔯 𝔪𝔬𝔯𝔢 𝔰𝔭𝔢𝔡𝔢𝔩𝔶 𝔱𝔥𝔢𝔫 𝔞 𝔴𝔢𝔞𝔳𝔢𝔯 𝔠𝔞𝔫 𝔴𝔢𝔞𝔳𝔢 𝔬𝔲𝔱 𝔥𝔦𝔰 𝔴𝔢𝔟𝔟𝔢 𝔞𝔫𝔡 𝔞𝔯𝔢 𝔤𝔬𝔫𝔢 𝔬𝔯 𝔍 𝔞𝔪 𝔞𝔴𝔞𝔯𝔯𝔢.

A fine example of this figure is found in the *Teemour Nameh*, which I shall give in Mr. *Good's* translation:——
"Praise be to God, who hath *woven* the *web* of human affairs in the *loom* of his will and of his wisdom, and hath made *waves of times* and of *seasons* to *flow* from the *fountain* of his *providence* into the *ocean* of his *power*." The simile is fine, and elegantly expressed.

Verse 7. *My life* is *wind*] Mr. *Good* translates, "O remember that, if my life pass away, mine eye turn no more to scenes of goodness;" which he paraphrases thus: "O remember that, if my life pass away, never more shall I witness those scenes of Divine favour, never more adore thee for those proofs of unmerited mercy, which till now have been so perpetually bestowed on me." I think the *common translation* gives a very good sense.

Verse 8. *Shall see me no more*] If I die in my present state, with all this load of undeserved odium which is cast upon me by my friends, I shall never have an opportunity of vindicating my character, and regaining the good opinion of mankind.

Thine eyes are *upon me, and I am not.*] Thou canst look me into nothing. Or, Let thine eye

A. M. cir. 2484
B. C. cir. 1520
Ante I. Olymp. cir. 744
Ante U. C. cir. 767

9 *As* the cloud is consumed and vanisheth away; so °he that goeth down to the grave shall come up no *more.*

10 He shall return no more to his house, Pneither shall his place know him any more.

11 Therefore I will ᑫnot refrain my mouth; I will speak in the anguish of my spirit; I will ʳcomplain in the bitterness of my soul.

12 *Am* I a sea, or a whale, that thou settest a watch over me?

13 ˢWhen I say, My bed shall comfort me, my couch shall ease my complaint;

A. M. cir. 2484
B. C. cir. 1520
Ante I. Olymp. cir. 744
Ante U. C. cir. 767

14 Then thou scarest me with dreams, and terrifiest me through visions:

15 So that my soul chooseth strangling, *and* death rather ᵗthan my life.

16 ᵘI loathe *it;* I would not live alway: ᵛlet me alone; ʷfor my days *are* vanity.

17 ˣWhat *is* man, that thou shouldest mag-

°2 Sam. xii. 23——PChap. viii. 18; xx. 9; Psa. ciii. 16
ᑫPsa. xxxix. 1, 9; xl. 9——ʳ1 Sam. i. 10; chap. x. 1
ˢChap. ix. 27

ᵗHeb. *than my bones*——ᵘChap. x. 1——ᵛChap. x. 20; xiv. 6; Psa. xxxix. 13——ʷPsa. lxii. 9——ˣPsa. viii. 4; cxliv. 3; Heb. ii. 6

be upon me as judged to death, and I shall immediately cease to live among men.

Verse 9. *As the cloud is consumed*] As the cloud is dissipated, so is the breath of those that go down to the grave. As that cloud shall never return, so shall it be with the dead; they return no more to sojourn with the living. See on the following verses.

Verse 10. *He shall return no more to his house, neither shall his place know him any more.*] He does not mean that he shall be *annihilated*, but that he shall never more become an inhabitant of the earth.

The word שאול, which we properly enough translate *grave*, here signifies also the *state of the dead, hades*, and sometimes any *deep pit*, or even *hell* itself.

Verse 11. *Therefore I will not refrain*] All is hopeless; I will therefore indulge myself in complaining.

Verse 12. *Am I a sea, or a whale*] "Am I condemned as the Egyptians were who were drowned in the Red Sea? or am I as Pharaoh, who was drowned in it in his sins, that thou settest a keeper over me?" *Targum.* Am I as dangerous as the sea, that I should be encompassed about with barriers, lest I should hurt mankind? Am I like an ungovernable *wild beast* or *dragon*, that I must be put under locks and bars? I think our own version less exceptionable than any other hitherto given of this verse. The meaning is sufficiently plain. Job was hedged about and shut in with insuperable difficulties of various kinds; he was entangled as a wild beast in a net; the more he struggled, the more he lost his strength, and the less probability there was of his being extricated from his present situation. The *sea* is shut in with barriers, over which it cannot pass; for God has "placed the sand for the *bound* of the sea by a perpetual decree, that it cannot pass it: and though the waves thereof toss themselves, yet can they not prevail; though they roar, yet can they not pass over it;" Jer. v. 22. "*For* thou hast set a *bound* that they may not pass over; that they turn not again to cover the earth;" Psa. civ. 9. "Or *who* shut up the sea with *doors*, when it brake forth, *as if* it had issued out of the womb? When I made the cloud the *garment* thereof, and thick darkness a *swaddling band* for it, and brake up for it my *decreed place*, and set *bars* and *doors;* and said, Hitherto shalt thou come, but no farther: and here shall thy proud waves be stayed;" chap. xxxviii. 8.

Here then is Job's allusion: the *bounds, doors, garment, swaddling bands, decreed place,* and *bars*, are the *watchers* or *keepers* which God has set to prevent the *sea* from *overflowing the earth;* so Job's *afflictions* and *distresses* were the *bounds* and *bars* which God had apparently set to prevent him from injuring his fellow creatures. At least Job, in his complaint, so takes it. Am I like the *sea*, which thou hast imprisoned within bounds, ready to overwhelm and destroy the country? or am I like a *dragon*, which must be cooped up in the same way, that it may not have the power to kill and destroy? Surely in my prosperity I gave no evidence of such a disposition; therefore should not be treated as a man dangerous to society. In this Job shows that *he will not refrain his mouth.*

Verse 14. *Thou scarest me with dreams*] There is no doubt that Satan was permitted to haunt his *imagination* with dreadful dreams and terrific appearances; so that, as soon as he fell asleep, he was suddenly roused and alarmed by those appalling images. He needed rest by sleep, but was afraid to close his eyes because of the horrid images which were presented to his imagination. Could there be a state more deplorable than this?

Verse 15. *Chooseth strangling*] It is very likely that he felt, in those interrupted and dismal slumbers, an oppression and difficulty of breathing something like the *incubus* or *nightmare;* and, distressing as this was, he would prefer death by this means to any longer life in such miseries.

Verse 16. *I loathe* it; *I would not live alway*] Life, in such circumstances, is hateful to me; and though I wish for long life, yet if length of days were offered to me with the sufferings which I now undergo, I would despise the offer and spurn the boon.

Mr. *Good* is not satisfied with our common version, and has adopted the following, which in his *notes* he endeavours to illustrate and defend:

Verse 15. So that my soul coveteth suffocation, And death in comparison with my suffering.

16. No longer would I live! O, release me! How are my days vanity!

Verse 17. *What is man that thou shouldest magnify him? and that thou shouldest set thine heart upon him?*] Two different ideas have been drawn from these words:—

1. Man is not worth thy notice; why therefore dost thou contend with him?

A. M. cir. 2484
B. C. cir. 1520
Ante I. Olymp.
cir. 744
Ante U. C. cir.
767

nify him? and that thou shouldest set thine heart upon him?

18 And *that* thou shouldest
visit him every morning, *and* try
him every moment?

19 How long wilt thou not depart from me,
nor let me alone till I swallow down my spittle?

20 I have sinned; what shall I do unto

thee, [y]O thou Preserver of men?
why [z]hast thou set me as a mark
against thee, so that I am a burden to myself?

21 And why dost thou not pardon my transgression, and take away mine iniquity? for
now shall I sleep in the dust; and thou shalt
seek me in the morning, but I *shall* not *be*.

A. M. cir. 2484
B. C. cir. 1520
Ante I. Olymp.
cir. 744
Ante U. C. cir.
767

---

[y]Psa. xxxvi. 6

[z]Chap. xvi. 12; Psa. xxi. 12; Lam. iii. 12

---

2. How astonishing is thy kindness that thou shouldest *fix thy heart*—thy strongest affections, on such a poor, base, vile, impotent creature as man, (אנוש *enosh*,) that thou shouldest so highly exalt him beyond all other creatures, and mark him with the most particular notice of thy providence and grace!

The paraphrase of *Calmet* is as follows: "Does man, such as he at present is, merit thy attention! What is man that God should make it his business to examine, try, prove, and afflict him? Is it not doing him too much honour to think thus seriously about him? O Lord! I am not worthy that thou shouldest concern thyself about *me!*"

Verse 19. *Till I swallow down my spittle?*] This is a proverbial expression, and exists among the Arabs to the present day; the very language being nearly the same. It signifies the same as, *Let me draw my breath; give me a moment's space; let me have even the twinkling of an eye.* I am urged by my sufferings to continue my complaint; but my strength is exhausted, my *mouth dry* with speaking. Suspend my sufferings even for so short a space as is necessary to swallow my spittle, that my parched tongue may be moistened, so that I may renew my complaint.

Verse 20. *I have sinned; what shall I do*] Dr. *Kennicott* contends that these words are spoken to *Eliphaz*, and not to God, and would paraphrase them thus: "You say I must have been a sinner. What then? I have not sinned against thee, O thou spy upon mankind! Why hast thou set up *me* as a butt or mark to shoot at? Why am *I* become a burden unto thee? Why not rather overlook my transgression, and pass by mine iniquity? I am now sinking to the dust! To-morrow, perhaps, I shall be sought in vain!" See his vindication of Job at the end of *these notes* on this book. Others

consider the address as made to God. Taken in this light, the sense is plain enough.

Those who suppose that the address is made to God, translate the 20th verse thus: "Be it that I have sinned, what injury can I do unto thee, O thou Observer of man? Why hast thou set me up as a mark for thee, and why am I made a burden to thee?" The *Septuagint* is thus: Ει εγω ἡμαρτον, τι δυνησομαι πραξαι, ὁ επισταμενος τον νουν των ανθρωπων; *If I have sinned, what can I do, O thou who knowest the mind of men?* Thou knowest that it is impossible for *me* to make any restitution. I cannot blot out my offences; but whether I have sinned so as to bring all these calamities upon me, thou knowest, who searchest the hearts of men.

Verse 21. *And why dost thou not pardon*] These words are spoken *after the manner of men.* If thou have any design to save me, if I have sinned, why dost thou not pardon my transgression, as thou seest that I am a dying man; and to-morrow morning thou mayest seek me to do me good, but in all probability I shall then be no more, and all thy kind thoughts towards me shall be unavailing? If I have sinned, then why should not I have a part in that mercy that flows so freely to all mankind?

That Job does not criminate himself here, as our text intimates, is evident enough from his own repeated assertions of his innocence. And it is most certain that *Bildad*, who immediately answers, did not consider him as criminating but as *justifying* himself; and this is the very ground on which *he* takes up the subject. Were we to admit the contrary, we should find strange inconsistencies, if not contradictions, in Job's speeches: on such a ground the controversy must have immediately terminated, as he would then have acknowledged that of which his friends accused him; and here the book of Job would have ended.

CHAPTER VIII

Bildad answers, and reproves Job for his justifying himself, 1, 2. Shows that God is just, and never punishes
but for iniquity; and intimates that it was on account of their sins that his children were cut off, 3, 4. States
that, if Job would humble himself to the Almighty, provided he were innocent, his captivity would soon be
turned, and his latter end be abundantly prosperous, 5-7. Appeals to the ancients for the truth of what he
says; and draws examples from the vegetable world, to show how soon the wicked may be cut off, and the hope
of the hypocrite perish, 8-19. Asserts that God never did cast off a perfect man nor help the wicked; and that,
if Job be innocent, his end shall be crowned with prosperity, 20-22.

A. M. cir. 2484
B. C. cir. 1520
Ante I. Olymp.
cir. 744
Ante U. C. cir.
767

THEN answered Bildad the Shuhite, and said,

2 How long wilt thou speak these *things?* and *how long shall* the words of thy mouth *be like* a strong wind?

3 ᵃDoth God pervert judgment? or doth the Almighty pervert justice?

4 If ᵇthy children have sinned against him, and if he have cast them away ᶜfor their transgression;

5 ᵈIf thou wouldest seek unto God betimes, and make thy supplication to the Almighty;

6 If thou *wert* pure and upright, surely now he would awake for thee, and make the habitation of thy righteousness prosperous.

A. M. cir. 2484
B. C. cir. 1520
Ante I. Olymp.
cir. 744
Ante U. C. cir.
767

7 Though thy beginning was small, yet thy latter end should greatly increase.

8 ᵉFor inquire, I pray thee, of the former age, and prepare thyself to the search of their fathers:

9 (For ᶠwe *are but of* yesterday, and know ᵍnothing, because our days upon earth *are* a shadow:)

ᵃGen. xviii. 25; Deut. xxxii. 4; 2 Chron. xix. 7; chap. xxxiv. 12, 17; Dan. ix. 14; Rom. iii. 5——ᵇChap. i. 5, 18 ᶜHeb. *in the hand of their transgression*

ᵈCh. v. 8; xi. 13; xxii. 23, &c.——ᵉDeut. iv. 32; xxxii. 7; ch. xv. 18——ᶠGen. xlvii. 9; 1 Chron. xxix. 15; ch. vii. 6; Psa. xxxix. 5; cii. 11; cxliv. 14——ᵍHeb. *not*

NOTES ON CHAP. VIII

Verse 1. *Bildad the Shuhite*] Supposed to be a descendant of *Shuah*, one of the sons of Abraham, by Keturah, who dwelt in Arabia Deserta, called in Scripture the *east country.* See Gen. xxv. 1, 2, 6.

Verse 2. *How long wilt thou speak these things?*] Wilt thou still go on to charge God foolishly? Thy heavy affliction proves that thou art under his wrath; and his wrath, thus manifested, proves that it is for thy sins that he punisheth thee.

Be like *a strong wind?*] The *Arabic*, with which the *Syriac* agrees, is روح العظمة *ruch-olazomati, the spirit of pride.* Wilt thou continue to *breathe forth a tempest of words?* This is more literal.

Verse 3. *Doth God pervert judgment?*] God afflicts thee; can he afflict thee for naught? As he is just, his judgment is just; and he could not inflict punishment unless there be a cause.

Verse 4. *If thy children have sinned*] I know thy children have been cut off by a terrible judgment; but was it not because by transgression they had filled up the measure of their iniquity?

And he have cast them away] Has sent them off, says the Targum, *to the place of their transgression*—to that punishment due to their sins.

Verse 5. *If thou wouldest seek unto God*] Though God has so severely afflicted thee, and removed thy children by a terrible judgment; yet if thou wilt now humble thyself before him, and implore his mercy, thou shalt be saved. He cut *them* off in their sins, but he spares *thee;* and this is a proof that he waits to be gracious to thee.

Verse 6. *If thou* wert *pure and upright*] Concerning thy guilt there can be no doubt; for if thou hadst been a holy man, and these calamities had occurred through accident, or merely by the malice of thy enemies, would not God, long ere this, have manifested his power and justice in thy behalf, punished thy enemies, and restored thee to affluence?

The habitation of thy righteousness] Strongly ironical. If thy house had been as a temple of God, in which his worship had been performed, and his commandments obeyed, would it now be in a state of ruin and desolation?

Verse 7. *Though thy beginning was small*] Thy *former state*, compared to that into which God would have brought thee, would be small; for to show his respect for thy piety, because thou hadst, through thy faithful attachment to him, suffered the loss of all things, he would have greatly multiplied thy former prosperity, so that thou shouldest now have vastly more than thou didst ever before possess.

Verse 8. *Inquire—of the former age*] לדור רישון *ledor rishon,* of the *first age;* of the *patriarchs;* the first generation of men that dwelt upon the earth: not of the *age that was just past,* as Mr. *Peters* and several others have imagined, in order to keep up the presumption of Job's high antiquity. *Bildad* most evidently refers to an antiquity exceedingly remote.

Verse 9. *For we are but of yesterday, and know nothing*] It is evident that Bildad refers to those times in which human life was protracted to a much *longer date* than that in which Job lived; when men, from the long period of *eight* or *nine hundred years,* had the opportunity of making many observations, and treasuring up a vast fund of knowledge and experience. In comparison with *them,* he considers *that age* as *nothing,* and that generation as being only of *yesterday,* not having had opportunity of laying up knowledge: nor could they expect it, as their days upon earth would be but a *shadow,* compared with that *substantial* time in which the fathers had lived. Perhaps there may be an allusion here to the *shadow* projected by the *gnomon of a dial,* during the time the sun is above the horizon. As is a single *solar day,* so is our *life.* The following beautiful motto I have seen on a sundial: UMBRÆ SUMUS! "We are shadows!" referring to the different shadows by which the gnomon marked the hours, during the course of the day; and all intended to convey this moral lesson to the passengers: Your life is composed of time, marked out by such shadows as these. Such as time *is,* such are *you;* as fleeting, as transitory, as unsubstantial. These *shadows* lost, *time* is lost; *time* lost, *soul* lost! Reader, take heed!

The writer of this book probably had before his eyes these words of David, in his last prayer, 1 Chron. xxix. 15: "For we are strangers before thee, and sojourners, as all our fathers *were;*

A. M. cir. 2484
B. C. cir. 1520
Ante I. Olymp.
cir. 744
Ante U. C. cir.
767

10 Shall not they teach thee, *and* tell thee, and utter words out of their heart?

11 Can the rush grow without mire? can the flag grow without water?

12 [h]Whilst it *is* yet in his greenness, *and*

not cut down, it withereth before any *other* herb.

13 So *are* the paths of all that forget God; and the [i]hypocrite's hope shall perish:

14 Whose hope shall be cut off, and

A. M. cir. 2484
B. C. cir. 1520
Ante I. Olymp.
cir. 744
Ante U. C. cir.
767

---

[h]Psa. cxxix. 6; Jer. xvii. 6——[i]Ch. xi. 20;   xviii. 14; xxvii. 8; Psa. cxii. 10; Prov. x. 28

---

our days upon earth are as a SHADOW, and there is no *expectation.* There is no reason to *hope* that they shall be *prolonged;* for our lives are limited down to *threescore years* and *ten,* as the average of the life even of *old men.*

Verse 10. *Shall not they teach thee*] Wilt thou not treat their maxims with the utmost deference and respect? They *utter words from their heart*—what they say is the fruit of long and careful experience.

Verse 11. *Can the rush grow*] The word נמא *gome,* which we translate *rush,* is, without doubt, the Egyptian flag *papyrus,* on which the ancients *wrote,* and from which our *paper* derives its name. The *Septuagint,* who made their Greek translation in Egypt, (if this book made a part of it,) and knew well the import of each word in both languages, render נמא *gome* by παπυρος *papyrus,* thus: Μη θαλλει παπυρος ανευ ὑδατος; *Can the* PAPYRUS *flourish without water?* Their translation leaves no doubt concerning the meaning of the original. They were probably *writing on* the *very substance* in question, while making their translation. The technical language of no science is so thoroughly barbarous as that of *botany:* the description of this plant by *Linnæus,* shall be a proof. The plant he calls "*Cyperus Papyrus;* CLASS *Triandria;* ORDER *Monogynia;* Culm three-sided, naked; umbel longer than the involucres; involucels three-leaved, setaceous, longer; spikelets in threes.— Egypt, &c. *Involucre* eight-leaved; general *umbel* copious, the rays sheathing at the base; *partial* on very short peduncles; *spikelets* alternate, sessile; *culm* leafy at the base; *leaves* hollow, ensiform."

Hear our plain countryman *John Gerarde,* who describes the same plant: "*Papyrus Nilotica,* Paper Reed, hath many large flaggie leaves, somewhat triangular and smooth, not much unlike those of cats-taile, rising immediately from a tuft of roots, compact of many strings; amongst the which it shooteth up two or three naked stalkes, square, and rising some six or seven cubits high above the water; at the top whereof there stands a tuft or bundle off chaffie threds, set in comely order, resembling a tuft of floures, but barren and void of seed;" GERARDE's *Herbal,* p. 40. Which of the two descriptions is easiest to b⌣ understood by common sense, either with or without a knowledge of the Latin language? This plant grows in the *muddy* banks of the Nile, as it requires an abundance of water for its nourishment.

Can the flag grow without water?] Parkhurst supposes that the word אחו *achu,* which we render *flag,* is the same with that species of *reed* which Mr. *Hasselquist* found growing near the river Nile. He describes it (p. 97) as "having scarcely any branches, but numerous leaves, which are narrow, smooth, channelled on the upper surface; and the plant about eleven feet

high. The Egyptians make *ropes* of the leaves. They lay the plant in water, like hemp, and then make good and strong *cables* of them." As אח *ach* signifies to *join, connect, associate,* hence אחי *achi,* a *brother.* אחו *achu* may come from the same root, and have its name from its usefulness in making *ropes, cables,* &c., which are composed of *associated* threads, and serve to *tie, bind together,* &c.

Verse 12. *Whilst it* is *yet in his greenness*] We do not know enough of the natural history of this plant to be able to discern the strength of this allusion; but we learn from it that, although this plant be very succulent, and grow to a great size, yet it is short-lived, and speedily withers; and this we may suppose to be in the *dry season,* or on the retreat of the waters of the Nile. However, *Soon* RIPE, *soon* ROTTEN, is a maxim in horticulture.

Verse 13. *So* are *the paths*] The *papyrus* and the *rush* flourish while they have a plentiful supply of *ooze* and *water;* but take these away, and their prosperity is speedily at an end; so it is with the *wicked* and profane; their prosperity is of short duration, however great it may appear to be in the beginning. Thou also, O thou enemy of God, hast flourished for a time; but the blast of God is come upon thee, and now thou art dried up from the very roots.

The hypocrite's hope shall perish] A *hypocrite,* or rather *profligate,* has no inward religion, for his heart is not right with God; he has only *hope,* and that *perishes* when he gives up the ghost.

This is the first place in which the word *hypocrite* occurs, or the noun חנף *chaneph,* which *rather* conveys the idea of *pollution* and *defilement* than of *hypocrisy.* A hypocrite is one who only *carries the mask of godliness,* to serve secular purposes; who wishes to be taken for a religionist, though he is conscious he has *no religion.* Such a person cannot have *hope* of any good, because he knows he is *insincere:* but the person in the text has hope; therefore *hypocrite* cannot be the meaning of the original word. But all the *vile,* the *polluted,* and the *profligate* have *hope;* they hope to end their iniquities before they end life; and they hope to get at last to the kingdom of heaven. *Hypocrite* is a very improper translation of the Hebrew.

Verse 14. *Whose hope shall be cut off*] Such persons, subdued by the strong habits of sin, hope on fruitlessly, till the last thread of the web of life is cut off from the beam; and then they find no more strength in their hope than is in the threads of the spider's web.

Mr. *Good* renders, *Thus shall their support rot away.* The foundation on which they trust 'is rotten, and by and by the whole superstructure of their confidence shall tumble into ruin.

A. M. cir. 2484
B. C. cir. 1520
Ante I. Olymp.
cir. 744
Ante U. C. cir.
767

whose trust *shall be* [k]a spider's web.

15 [l]He shall lean upon his house, but it shall not stand: he shall hold it fast, but it shall not endure.

16 He *is* green before the sun, and his branch shooteth forth in his garden.

17 His roots are wrapped about the heap, *and* seeth the place of stones.

18 [m]If he destroy him from his place, then *it* shall deny him, *saying,* I have not seen thee.

19 Behold, this *is* the joy of his way, and [n]out of the earth shall others grow.

20 Behold, God will not cast away a perfect *man,* neither will he [o]help the evil doers:

21 Till he fill thy mouth with laughing, and thy lips with [p]rejoicing.

22 They that hate thee shall be [q]clothed with shame; and the dwelling-place of the wicked [r]shall come to naught.

A. M. cir. 2484
B. C. cir. 1520
Ante I. Olymp.
cir. 744
Ante U. C. cir.
767

---

[k]Heb. *a spider's house;* Isa. lix. 5, 6——[l]Ch. xxvii. 18
[m]Ch. vii. 10; xx. 9; Psa. xxxvii. 36——[n]Psa. cxiii. 7

[o]Heb. *take the ungodly by the hand*——[p]Heb. *shouting for joy*——[q]Psa. xxxv. 26; cix. 29——[r]Heb. *shall not be*

Verse 15. *He shall lean upon his house*] This is an allusion to the spider. When he suspects his *web,* here called his *house,* to be frail or unsure, he leans upon it in different parts, propping himself on his hinder legs, and pulling with his fore claws, to see if all be safe. If he find any part of it injured, he immediately adds new cordage to that part, and attaches it strongly to the wall. When he finds all safe and strong, he retires into his hole at one corner, supposing himself to be in a state of complete security, when in a moment the *brush* or the *besom* sweeps away both himself, his house, and his confidence. This I have several times observed; and it is in this that the strength and *point* of the comparison consist. The *wicked,* whose hope is in his temporal possessions, strengthens and keeps his house in repair; and thus *leans* on his earthly supports; in a moment, as in the case of the *spider,* his house is overwhelmed by the blast of God's judgments, and himself probably buried in its ruins. This is a very fine and expressive metaphor, which not one of the commentators that I have seen has ever discovered.

Verse 16. *He is green before the sun*] This is another metaphor. The wicked is represented as a luxuriant plant, in a good soil, with all the advantages of a good situation; well exposed to the sun; the roots intervolving themselves with stones, so as to render the tree more stable; but suddenly a blast comes, and the tree begins to die. The sudden fading of its leaves, &c., shows that its root is become as rottenness, and its vegetable life destroyed. I have often observed sound and healthy trees, which were flourishing in all the pride of vegetative health, suddenly struck by some unknown and incomprehensible blast, begin to die away, and perish from the roots. I have seen also the prosperous wicked, in the inscrutable dispensations of the Divine providence, blasted, stripped, made bare, and despoiled, in the same way.

Verse 18. *If he destroy him from his place*] Is not this a plain reference to the *alienation of his inheritance?* God destroys him from it; it becomes the property of another; and on his revisiting it, the place, by a striking *prosopopœia,* says, "I know thee not; I have never seen thee." This also have I witnessed; I looked on it, felt regret, received instruction, and hasted away.

Verse 19. *Behold this is the joy of his way*] A strong irony. Here is the issue of all his

mirth, of his sports, games, and pastimes! See the unfeeling, domineering, polluting and polluted scape-grace, levelled with those whom he had despised, a servant of servants, or unable to work through his debaucheries, cringing for a morsel of bread, or ingloriously ending his days in that bane of any well-ordered and civilized state, a *parish workhouse.* This also I have most literally witnessed.

Out of the earth shall others grow.] As in the preceding case, when *one* plant or tree is blasted or cut down, *another* may be planted in the same place; so, when a spendthrift has run through his property, another possesses his inheritance, and grows up from that soil in which he himself might have continued to flourish, had it not been for his extravagance and folly.

This verse Mr. *Good* applies to GOD *himself,* with no advantage to the argument, nor elucidation of the sense, that I can see. I shall give his translation, and refer to his learned notes for his vindication of the version he has given:—

"Behold the Eternal (הוא) exulting in his course;
Even over his dust shall raise up another."

In this way none of the ancient *versions* have understood the passage. I believe it to be a strong *irony,* similar to that which some think flowed from the pen of the *same writer: Rejoice, O young man, in thy youth; and let thy heart cheer thee in the days of thy youth; and walk in the ways of thine heart, and in the sight of thine eyes. But know thou, that for all these God will bring thee into judgment;* Eccles. xi. 9. These two places illustrate each other.

Verse 20. *Behold, God will not cast away a perfect* man] This is another of the *maxims* of the *ancients,* which Bildad produces: "As sure as he will punish and root out the wicked, so surely will he defend and save the righteous."

Verse 21. *Till he fill thy mouth with laughing*] Perhaps it may be well to translate after Mr. *Good* "Even yet may he fill thy mouth with laughter!" The two verses may be read as a *prayer;* and probably they were thus expressed by Bildad, who speaks with less virulence than his predecessor, though with equal positiveness in respect to the grand charge, viz., *If thou wert not a sinner of no mean magnitude, God would not have inflicted such unprecedented calamities upon thee.*

This most exceptionable position, which is so contrary to matter of fact, was founded upon maxims which they derived from the *ancients*. Surely *observation* must have, in numberless instances, corrected this mistake. They must have seen many *worthless men* in high *prosperity*, and many of the *excellent of the earth* in deep *adversity* and *affliction;* but the opposite was an article of their *creed*, and all appearances and facts must take its colouring.

Job's friends must have been acquainted, at least, with the history of the ancient *patriarchs;* and most certainly they contained facts of an opposite nature. Righteous *Abel* was persecuted and murdered by his wicked brother *Cain*. *Abram* was obliged to leave his own country on account of worshipping the true God; *so* all tradition has said. *Jacob* was persecuted by his brother *Esau; Joseph* was sold into slavery by his brothers; *Moses* was obliged to flee from Egypt, and was variously tried and afflicted, even by his own brethren. Not to mention *David*, and almost all the *prophets*. All these were proofs that the best of men were frequently exposed to sore afflictions and heavy calamities; and it is not by the prosperity or adversity of men in this world, that we are to judge of the approbation or disapprobation of God towards them. In every case our Lord's rule is infallible: *By their fruits ye shall know them.*

CHAPTER IX

Job acknowledges God's justice and man's sinfulness, 1–3. Celebrates his almighty power as manifested in the earth and in the heavens, 4–10. Maintains that God afflicts the innocent as well as the wicked, without any respect to their works: and hath delivered the earth into the hands of the wicked, 11–24. Complains of his lot, and maintains his innocence, 25–35.

A. M. cir. 2484
B. C. cir. 1520
Ante I. Olymp.
cir. 744
Ante U. C. cir.
767

THEN Job answered and said,

2 I know *it is* so of a truth: but how should [a]man be just [b]with God?

3 If he will contend with him, he cannot answer him one of a thousand.

4 [c]*He is* wise in heart, and mighty in strength; who hath hardened *himself* against him, and hath prospered?

5 Which removeth the mountains, and they know not: which overturneth them in his anger.

6 Which [d]shaketh the earth out of her place, and [e]the pillars thereof tremble.

7 Which commandeth the sun, and it

A. M. cir. 2484
B. C. cir. 1520
Ante I. Olymp.
cir. 744
Ante U. C. cir.
767

---

[a]Psa. cxliii. 2; Rom. iii. 20——[b]Or, *before God*——[c]Ch. xxxvi. 5

[d]Isa. ii. 19, 21; Hag. ii. 6, 21; Heb. xii. 26——[e]Chap. xxvi. 11

NOTES ON CHAP. IX

Verse 2. *I know* it is *so of a truth*] I acknowledge the general truth of the maxims you have advanced. God will not ultimately punish a righteous person, nor shall the wicked finally triumph; and though righteous before man, and truly sincere in my piety, yet I know, when compared with the immaculate holiness of God, all my righteousness is nothing.

Verse 3. *If he will contend with him*] God is so holy, and his law so strict, that if he will enter into judgment with his creatures, the most upright of them cannot be justified in his sight.

One of a thousand.] Of a thousand offences of which he may be accused he cannot vindicate himself even in *one*. How little that any man does, even in the way of righteousness, truth, and mercy, can stand the penetrating eye of a just and holy God, when all *motives*, *feelings*, and *objects*, come to be scrutinized! In his sight, on this ground, no man living can be justified. O, how necessary to fallen, weak, miserable, imperfect and sinful man, is the doctrine of justification by faith, and sanctification through the Divine Spirit, by the sacrificial death and mediation of the Lord Jesus Christ!

Verse 4. He is *wise in heart, and mighty in strength*] By his infinite knowledge he searches out and sees all things, and by his almighty power he can punish all delinquencies. He that rebels against him must be destroyed.

Verse 5. *Removeth the mountains, and they know not*] This seems to refer to earthquakes. By those strong convulsions, mountains, valleys, hills, even whole islands, are removed in an instant; and to this latter circumstance the words, *they know not*, most probably refer. The work is done in the twinkling of an eye; no warning is given; the mountain, that seemed to be as firm as the earth on which it rested, was in the same moment both *visible* and *invisible;* so suddenly was it swallowed up.

Verse 6. *The pillars thereof tremble.*] This also refers to an earthquake, and to that *tremulous motion* which sometimes gives warning of the approaching catastrophe, and from which this violent convulsion of nature has received its name. *Earthquakes*, in Scripture language, signify also violent commotions and disturbances in *states; mountains* often signify *rulers; sun, empires; stars, petty states*. But it is most likely that the expressions here are to be understood literally.

Verse 7. *Which commandeth the sun*] Obscures it either with clouds, with thick darkness, or with an eclipse.

A. M. cir. 2484
B. C. cir. 1520
Ante I. Olymp.
cir. 744
Ante U. C. cir.
767

riseth not; and sealeth up the stars.

8 [f]Which alone spreadeth out the heavens, and treadeth upon the [g]waves of the sea.

9 [h]Which maketh [i]Arcturus, Orion, and Pleiades, and the chambers of the south.

10 [k]Which doeth great things past finding

out; yea, and wonders without number.

11 [l]Lo, he goeth by me, and I see *him* not: he passeth on also, but I perceive him not.

12 [m]Behold, he taketh away, [n]who can hinder him? who will say unto him, What doest thou?

A. M. cir. 2484
B. C. cir. 1520
Ante I. Olymp.
cir. 744
Ante U. C. cir.
767

---

[f]Gen. i. 6; Psa. civ. 2, 3——[g]Heb. *heights*——[h]Gen. i. 16; chap. xxxviii. 31, &c.; Amos v. 8——[i]Heb. *Ash, Cesil, and Cimah*

[k]Chap. v. 9; Psa. lxxi. 15——[l]Chap. xiii. 8, 9; xxxv. 14——[m]Isa. xlv. 9; Jer. xviii. 6; Rom. ix. 20——[n]Heb. *who can turn him away?* chap. xi. 10

Sealeth up the stars.] Like the contents of a letter, wrapped up and sealed, so that it cannot be read. Sometimes the heavens become as black as ebony, and no star, figure, or character, in this great book of God can be read.

Verse 8. *And treadeth upon the waves*] This is a very majestic image. God not only walks upon the waters, but, when the sea runs mountains high, he steps from billow to billow in his almighty and essential majesty. There is a similar sentiment in David, Psa. xxix. 10: "The Lord sitteth upon the flood; yea, the Lord sitteth King for ever." But both are far outdone by the Psalmist, Psa. xviii. 9-15, and especially in these words, ver. 10, *He did fly on the wings of the wind*. Job is great, but in every respect David is greater.

Verse 9. *Which maketh Arcturus, Orion, and Pleiades, and the chambers of the south*.] For this translation the original words are עשה עש

כסיל וכימה והדרי תמן *oseh ash, kesil, vechimah vehadrey theman*, which are thus rendered by the Septuagint: Ὁ ποιων Πλειαδα, και Ἑσπερον, και Αρκτουρον, και ταμεια νοτου; "Who makes the Pleiades, and Hesperus, and Arcturus, and Orion, and the chambers of the south."

The Vulgate, *Qui facit Arcturum, et Oriona, et Hyadas, et interiora Austri;* "Who maketh Arcturus, and Orion, and the Hyades, and the innermost chambers of the south."

The Targum follows the Hebrew, but paraphrases the latter clause thus: "and the chambers or houses of the planetary domination in the southern hemisphere."

The Syriac and Arabic, "Who maketh the Pleiades, and Arcturus, and the giant, (*Orion* or *Hercules*,) and the boundaries of the south."

Coverdale has, 𝔥𝔢 maketh the waynes of heaven, the Orions, the vii starres and the secrete places of the south. And on the *vii starres* he has this marginal note: some call these seven starres, the clock henne with hir chickens. See below.

Edmund Becke, in his edition, 1549, follows *Coverdale;* but puts vaynes *of heaven* for *waynes*, which *Carmarden*, in his Bible, Rouen, 1566, mistaking, changes into waves *of heaven.*

Barker's Bible, 1615, reads, "He maketh the *starres* Arcturus, Orion, and Pleiades, and the climates of the south." On which he has this note, "These are the names of certain starres, whereby he meaneth that all starres, both knowen and unknowen, are at His appointment."

Our early translators seem to agree much with the German and Dutch: 𝔈r machet ben

wagen am himmel, unb Orion, unb bie Glucken, unb bie Sterne gegen mittag; "He maketh the wagon of heaven, (*Charles's wain,*) and Orion, and the clucking hen, (*the Pleiades,*) and the stars of the mid-day region." See above, under *Coverdale.*

The *Dutch* version is not much unlike the *German*, from which it is taken: Die ben wagen maecht, ben Orion, enbe het sebengesternte, enb be binnenkameren ban't Zupben.

The *European* versions, in general, copy one or other of the above, or make a compound translation from the whole; but all are derived ultimately from the *Septuagint* and *Vulgate*.

As to the *Hebrew* words, they might as well have been applied to any of the other constellations of heaven: indeed, it does not appear that *constellations* are at all meant. *Parkhurst* and *Bate* have given, perhaps, the best interpretation of the words, which is as follows:—

"כימה *kimah*, from כמה *camah, to be hot* or *warm*, denotes genial heat or warmth, as opposed to עש *ash*, a parching, biting air, on the one side; and כסיל *kesil*, the rigid, contracting *cold*, on the other; and the chambers (thick clouds) of the south." See more in *Parkhurst*, under כמה.

I need scarcely add that these words have been variously translated by critics and commentators. Dr. *Hales* translates *kimah* and *kesil* by *Taurus* and *Scorpio;* and, if this translation were indubitably correct, we might follow him to his conclusions, viz., that Job lived 2337 years before Christ! See at the end of this chapter.

Verse 10. *Great things past finding out*] Great things without end; wonders without number.—*Targum*.

Verse 11. *Lo, he goeth by me, and I see* him *not*] He is incomprehensible in all his ways, and in all his works; and he must be so if he be God, and *work* as God; for his own nature and his operations are past finding out.

Verse 12. *He taketh away*] He never *gives*, but he is ever *lending:* and while the gift is useful or is improved, he permits it to remain; but when it becomes useless or is misused, he recalls it.

Who can hinder him?] Literally, *Who can cause him to restore it?*

What doest thou?] He is supreme, and will give account of none of his matters. He is infinitely wise, and cannot mistake. He is infinitely kind, and can do nothing cruel. He is infinitely good, and can do nothing wrong. No one, therefore, should question either his motives or his operations.

A. M. cir. 2484 B. C. cir. 1520 Ante I. Olymp. cir. 744 Ante U. C. cir. 767

13 *If* God will not withdraw
his anger, °the ᵖproud helpers
do stoop under him.
14 How much less shall I answer him, *and* choose out my words *to reason* with him?
15 ᵠWhom, though I were righteous, *yet* would I not answer, *but* I would make supplication to my Judge.
16 If I had called, and he had answered me; *yet* would I not believe that he had hearkened unto my voice.
17 For he breaketh me with a tempest, and multiplieth my wounds ʳwithout cause.
18 He will not suffer me to take my breath, but filleth me with bitterness.

A. M. cir. 2484 B. C. cir. 1520 Ante I. Olymp. cir. 744 Ante U. C. cir. 767

19 If *I speak* of strength, lo
he is strong: and if of judgment,
who shall set me a time *to*
plead?
20 If I justify myself, mine own mouth shall condemn me: *if I say* I *am* perfect, it shall also prove me perverse.
21 *Though* I *were* perfect, *yet* would I not know my soul: I would despise my life.
22 This *is* one *thing,* therefore I said *it,* ˢHe destroyeth the perfect and the wicked.
23 If the scourge slay suddenly, he will laugh at the trial of the innocent.
24 The earth is given into the hand of the wicked: ᵗhe covereth the faces of the judges thereof; if not, where, *and* who *is* he?

°Chap. xxvi. 12; Isa. xxx. 7——ᵖHeb. *helpers of pride* or *strength*——ᵠChap. x. 15

ʳChap. ii. 3; xxxiv. 6——ˢEccles. ix. 2, 3; Ezek. xxi. 3——ᵗ2 Sam. xv. 30; xix. 4; Jer. xiv. 4

Verse 13. If *God will not withdraw his anger*] It is of no use to contend with God; he cannot be successfully resisted; all his opposers must perish.

Verse 14. *How much less shall I answer*] I cannot contend with my Maker. He is the *Lawgiver* and the *Judge.* How shall I stand in judgment before *him?*

Verse 15. *Though I were righteous*] Though clear of all the crimes, public and secret, of which you accuse me, yet I would not dare to stand before his immaculate holiness. Man's holiness may profit man, but in the sight of the infinite purity of God it is nothing. Thus sung an eminent poet:—

"I loathe myself when God I see,
And into nothing fall;
Content that thou exalted be,
And Christ be all in all."

I would make supplication to my Judge.] Though not conscious of any sin, I should not think myself thereby justified; but would, from a conviction of the exceeding breadth of the commandment, and the limited nature of my own perfection, cry out, "Cleanse thou me from secret faults!"

Verse 16. *If I had called, and he had answered*] I could scarcely suppose, such is his majesty and such his holiness, that he could condescend to notice a being so *mean,* and in every respect so infinitely *beneath* his notice. These sentiments sufficiently confuted that slander of his friends, who said he was presumptuous, had not becoming notions of the majesty of God, and used blasphemous expressions against his sovereign authority.

Verse 17. *He breaketh me with a tempest*] The *Targum, Syriac,* and *Arabic* have this sense: *He powerfully smites even every hair of my head, and multiplies my wounds without cause.* That is, There is no reason known to myself, or to any man, why I should be thus most oppressively afflicted. It is, therefore, cruel, and inconsequent to assert that *I suffer for my crimes.*

Verse 18. *He will not suffer me to take my breath*] I have no respite in my afflictions; I suffer continually in my body, and my mind is incessantly harassed.

Verse 19. *If* I speak *of strength, lo,* he is *strong*] Human wisdom, power, and influence avail nothing before him.

Who shall set me a time] מי יועידני *mi yoideni,* "Who would be a witness for me?" or, Who would dare to appear in my behalf? Almost all the *terms* in this part of the speech of Job, from ver. 11 to ver. 24, are *forensic* or *juridical,* and are taken from *legal processes* and *pleadings* in their *gates* or *courts of justice.*

Verse 20. *If I justify myself*] God must have some reason for his conduct towards me; I therefore do not pretend to justify myself; the attempt to do it would be an insult to his majesty and justice. Though I am conscious of none of the crimes of which you accuse me; and know not *why* he contends with me; yet he must have some reason, and that reason he does not choose to explain.

Verse 21. Though *I* were *perfect*] Had I the fullest conviction that, in every thought, word, and deed, I were blameless before him, yet I would not plead this; nor would I think it any security for a life of ease and prosperity, or any proof that my days should be prolonged.

Verse 22. *This* is *one* thing] My own observation shows, that in the course of providence the righteous and the wicked have an equal lot; for when any sudden calamity comes, the *innocent* and the *guilty* fall alike. There may be a few exceptions, but they are very extraordinary, and very rare.

Verse 24. *The earth is given into the hand of the wicked*] Is it not most evident that the worst men possess most of this world's goods, and that the righteous are scarcely ever in power or affluence? This was the case in Job's time; it is the case still. Therefore *prosperity* and *adversity* in this life are no marks either of God's approbation or disapprobation.

He covereth the faces of the judges thereof] Or, *The faces of its decisions he shall cover.* God is often stated in Scripture as *doing* a thing

A. M. cir. 2484
B. C. cir. 1520
Ante I. Olymp. cir. 744
Ante U. C. cir. 767

25 Now [u]my days are swifter than a post: they flee away, they see no good.

26 They are passed away as the [v]swift [w]ships: [x]as the eagle *that* hasteth to the prey.

27 [y]If I say, I will forget my complaint, I will leave off my heaviness, and comfort *myself:*

28 [z]I am afraid of all my sorrows, I know that thou [a]wilt not hold me innocent.

29 *If* I be wicked, why then labour I in vain?

30 [b]If I wash myself with snow water, and make my hands never so clean;

31 Yet shalt thou plunge me in the ditch, and mine own clothes shall [c]abhor me.

A. M. cir. 2484
B. C. cir. 1520
Ante I. Olymp. cir. 744
Ante U. C. cir. 767

---

[u]Chap. vii. 6, 7——[v]Heb. *ships of desire*——[w]Or, *ships of Ebeh*——[x]Hab. i. 8——[y]Chap. vii. 13

[z]Psa. cxix. 120——[a]Exod. xx. 7——[b]Jer. ii. 22——[c]Or, *make me to be abhorred*

---

which he only *permits* to be done. So he permits the eyes of judgment to be blinded; and hence false decisions. Mr. *Good* translates the verse thus:—

"The earth is given over to the hand of IN-JUSTICE;
She hoodwinketh the faces of its judges.
Where every one liveth is it not so?"

And vindicates the translation in his learned notes: but I think the Hebrew will not bear this rendering; especially that in the *third* line.

Where, and *who* is *he?*] If this be not the case, *who* is he that acts in this way, and *where* is he to be found? If God does not *permit* these things, who is it that *orders* them?

Coverdale translates, As for the worlde, he geueth it ouer into the power of the wicked, such as the rulers be wherof all londes are full. Is it not so? Where is there eny, but he is soch one? This sense is clear enough, if the original will bear it. The last clause is thus rendered by the *Syriac* and *Arabic, Who can bear his indignation?*

Verse 25. *Swifter than a post*] מני רץ *minni rats, than a runner.* The light-footed messenger or *courier* who carries messages from place to place.

They flee away] The *Chaldee* says, *My days are swifter than the shadow of a flying bird.* So swiftly do they flee away that I cannot discern them; and when past they cannot be recalled. There is a sentiment like this in VIRGIL, *Geor.* lib. iii., ver. 284:—

Sed FUGIT *interea,* FUGIT IRREPARABILE *tempus!*—

"But in the meanwhile time flies! irreparable time flies away!"

Verse 26. *As the swift ships*] אניות אבה *oniyoth ebeh.* Ships of desire, or *ships of Ebeh,* says our *margin;* perhaps more correctly, *inflated ships,* the sails bellying out with a fair brisk wind, the tide favourable, and the vessels themselves lightly freighted.

The *Vulgate* has, *Like ships freighted with apples. Ships laden with the best fruits.*—TARGUM. *Ships well adapted for sailing.*—ARABIC. Shipes that be good under sale.—COVERDALE. Probably this relates to the light fast-sailing ships on the Nile, which were made of *reeds* or *papyrus.*

Perhaps the idea to be seized is not so much the *swiftness* of the passage, as their leaving *no trace* or *track* behind them. But instead of אבר *ebeh,* איבה *eybah, hostile ships* or the *ships*

VOL. III

of enemies, is the reading of *forty-seven* of *Kennicott's* and *De Rossi's* MSS., and of the *Syriac* version. If this be the true reading, what is its sense? My days are gone off like the light vessels of the pirates, having stripped me of my property, and carried all irrecoverably away, under the strongest press of sail, that they may effect their escape, and secure their booty.

The next words, *As the eagle* that *hasteth to the prey,* seem at least to countenance, if not confirm, the above reading: the idea of *robbery* and *spoil, prompt attack* and *sudden retreat,* is preserved in both images.

Verse 27. *I will forget my complaint*] I will *forsake* or *forego* my complaining. *I will leave off my heaviness.* VULGATE, *I will change my countenance*—force myself to smile, and endeavour to assume the *appearance of comfort.*

Verse 28. *I am afraid of all my sorrows*] *Coverdale* translates, after the *Vulgate,* Then am I afrayed of all my workes. Even were I to cease from complaining, I fear lest not one of my works, however well intentioned, would stand thy scrutiny, or meet with thy approbation.

Thou wilt not hold me innocent.] *Coverdale,* after the *Vulgate,* For I knowe thou fauourest not an euil doer; but this is not the sense of the original: Thou wilt not acquit me so as to take away my afflictions from me.

Verse 29. *If I be wicked*] If I am the sinner you suppose me to be, in vain should I labour to counterfeit joy, and cease to complain of my sufferings.

Verse 30. *If I wash myself with snow water*] Supposed to have a more detergent quality than common water; and it was certainly preferred to common water by the ancients. Of this we find an example in an elegant but licentious author: *Tandem ergo discubuimus, pueris Alexandrinis* AQUAM *in manus* NIVATAM *infundentibus, aliisque insequentibus ad pedes.*—PETR. *Satyr.,* cap. xxxi. "At length we sat down, and had *snow water* poured on our hands by lads of Alexandria," &c.

Mr. *Good* supposes that there is an allusion here to the ancient rite of *washing the hands* in token of *innocence.* See Psa. xxvi. 6: *I will* WASH *my hands in* INNOCENCY; and lxxiii. 13: *Verily I have cleansed my heart in vain, and* WASHED *my* HANDS IN INNOCENCY. And by this ceremony *Pilate* declared himself *innocent* of the blood of Christ, Matt. xxvii. 24.

Verse 31. *And mine own clothes shall abhor me.*] Such is thine infinite purity, when put in opposition to the purity of man, that it will bear no comparison. Searched and tried by the

A. M. cir. 2484
B. C. cir. 1520
Ante I. Olymp.
cir. 744
Ante U. C. cir.
767

32 For *[d]he is* not a man as I *am, that* I should answer him, and we should come together in judgment.

33 *[e]*Neither is there *[f]any* *[g]*day's-man betwixt us, *that* might lay his hand upon us both.

A. M. cir. 2484
B. C. cir. 1520
Ante I. Olymp.
cir. 744
Ante U. C. cir.
767

34 *[h]*Let him take his rod away from me, and let not his fear terrify me:

35 *Then* would I speak, and not fear him; *[i]*but *it is* not so with me.

---

[d]Eccles. vi. 10; Isa. xlv. 9; Jer. xlix. 19; Rom. ix. 20 ——— [e]Ver. 19; 1 Sam. ii. 25——[f]Heb. *one that should argue*

[g]Or, *umpire*——[h]Chap. xiii. 20, 21, 22; xxxiii. 7; Psa. xxxix. 10——[i]Heb. *but I am not so with myself*

---

eye of God, I should be found as a *leper*, so that my *own clothes* would dread to touch me, for fear of being infected by my corruption. This is a strong and bold figure; and is derived from the corrupted state of his *body*, which his clothes dreaded to touch, because of the contagious nature of his disorder.

Verse 32. *For* he is *not a man as I* am] I cannot contend with him as with one of my fellows in a court of justice.

Verse 33. *Neither is there any day's-man*] בינינו מוכיח *beyneynu mochiach*, a *reprover, arguer,* or *umpire between us.* DAY'S-MAN, in our law, means an arbitrator, or umpire between party and party; as it were bestowing a *day,* or certain time on a *certain day,* to decree, judge, or decide a matter.—*Minshieu.* DAY is used in law for the *day of appearance in court,* either originally or upon assignation, for hearing a matter for trial.—*Idem.* But *arbitrator* is the proper meaning of the term here: one who is, by the consent of both parties, to judge between them, and settle their differences.

Instead of לא יש *lo yesh, there is not,* fifteen of *Kennicott's* and *De Rossi's* MSS., with the *Septuagint, Syriac,* and *Arabic,* read לו יש *lu yesh, I wish there were:* or, O that there were! Ειθε ην ο μεσιτης ημων, και ελεγχων και διακουων αναμεσον αμφοτερων; *O that we had a mediator, an advocate, and judge between us both!*—SEPT. Poor Job! He did not yet know the *Mediator* between God and man: the only means by which God and man can be brought together and reconciled. Had St. Paul this in his eye when he wrote 1 Tim. ii. 5, 6? *For there is one God, and one Mediator between God and men, the man Christ Jesus; who gave himself a ransom for all.* Without this *Mediator,* and the *ransom price* which he has laid down, God and man can never be united: and that this union might be made possible, Jesus took the human into conjunction with his Divine nature; and thus *God was manifest in the flesh.*

Verse 34. *Let him take his rod away*] In the Masoretic Bibles, the word שבטו *shibto, his rod,* is written with a large ט *teth,* as above; and as the letter in numerals stands for 9, the *Masora* says the word was thus written to show the *nine calamities* under which Job had suffered, and which he wished God to remove.

As שבט *shebet* signifies, not only *rod,* but also *sceptre* or the *ensign of royalty,* Job might here refer to God sitting in his majesty upon the judgment-seat; and this sight so appalled him, that, filled with terror, he was unable to speak. When a sinful soul sees God in his majesty, terror seizes upon it, and prayer is impossible. We have a beautiful illustration of this, Isa. vi. 1-5: "I saw the Lord sitting upon a throne, high and lifted up, and his train filled the temple. Then said I, Wo is me, for I am undone, because

I am a man of unclean lips; for mine eyes have seen the King, the Lord of hosts."

Verse 35. *But* it is *not so with me.*] I am not in such circumstances as to plead with my Judge. I believe the sense of these words is nearly as *Coverdale* has expressed it:—𝔉or as longe as 𝔍 am in soch fearfulnesse, 𝔍 can make no answere. A natural picture of the state of a penitent soul, which needs no additional colouring.

ON the names of the constellations mentioned ver. 9, and again chap. xxxviii. 31, &c., much has been written, and to little effect. I have already, in the notes, expressed my doubts whether any constellation be intended. Dr. *Hales,* however, finds in these names, as he thinks, astronomical data, by which he ascertains the time of Job. I shall give his words:—

"The cardinal constellations of spring and autumn, in *Job's* time, were *Chimah,* and *Chesil* or *Taurus,* and *Scorpio;* noticed ix. 9, and again, xxxviii. 31, 32; of which the principal stars are, *Aldebaran,* the bull's eye, and *Antares,* the scorpion's heart. Knowing, therefore, the longitudes of these stars, at present, the interval of time from thence to the assumed date of *Job's* trial will give the difference of the longitudes; and ascertain their positions then, with respect to the vernal and autumnal points of intersection of the equinoctial and ecliptic; according to the usual rate of the *precession of the equinoxes,* one degree in 71 years. See that article, vol. i., p. 185.

"The following calculations I owe to the kindness and skill of the respectable *Dr. Brinkley, Andrew's* Professor of Astronomy in the University of Dublin.

"In A. D. 1800 *Aldebaran* was in 2 signs, 7 degrees, east longitude. But since the date of *Job's* trial, B. C. 2338, i. e., 4138 years, the precession of the equinoxes amounted to 1 sign, 27 degrees, 53 minutes; which, being subtracted from the former quantity, left *Aldebaran* in only 9 degrees, 7 minutes longitude, or distance from the *vernal* intersection; which, falling within the constellation *Taurus,* consequently rendered it the cardinal constellation of *spring,* as *Pisces* is at present.

"In A. D. 1800 *Antares* was in 8 signs, 6 degrees, 58 minutes, east longitude; or 2 signs, 6 degrees, 58 minutes, east of the *autumnal* intersection: from which subtracting as before the amount of the precession, *Antares* was left only 9 degrees, 5 minutes east. Since then, the autumnal equinox was found within *Scorpio,* this was the cardinal constellation of *autumn,* as *Virgo* is at present.

"Such a combination and coincidence of various rays of evidence, derived from widely different sources, *history,* sacred and profane, *chronology,* and *astronomy,* and all converging to the same focus, tend strongly to establish the time of *Job's* trial, as rightly assigned to the year B. C. 2337, or 818 years after the deluge, 184 years before the birth of Abram; 474 years before the settlement of *Jacob's* family in *Egypt;* and 689 years before their *exode* or departure from thence." *New Analysis of Chronology*, vol. ii., p. 57.

Now all this is specious; and, were the *foundation* sound, we might rely on the permanence of the building, though the rains should descend, the floods come, and the winds blow and beat on that house. But all these deductions and conclusions are founded on the *assumption* that *Chimah* and *Chesil* mean *Taurus* and *Scorpio:* but this is the very point that is to be proved; for proof of this is not offered, nor, indeed, can be offered; and such assumptions are palpably nugatory. That עשׁ *ash* has been generally understood to signify the *Great Bear;* כסיל *Kesil, Orion;* and בימה *Kimah,* the *Pleiades;* may be seen everywhere: but that they do signify these constellations is perfectly uncertain. We have only conjectures concerning their meaning; and on such conjectures no *system* can be built. Genuine *data,* in Dr. *Hales's* hands, are sure to be conducted to legitimate conclusions: but neither he nor any one else can construct an astronomical fabric in the limbus of conjecture. *When* JOB lived is perfectly uncertain: but that this book was written 818 years after the deluge; 184 years before the birth of Abram, and 689 years before the exodus; and that all this is demonstrable from *Chimah* and *Chesil* signifying *Taurus* and *Scorpio,*

whence the positions of the equinoxes at the time of Job's trial can be ascertained; can never be proved, and should never be credited.

In what many learned men have written on this subject, I find as much solidity and satisfaction as from what is piously and gravely stated in the *Glossa Ordinaria:*—

Qui facit Arcturum. Diversæ sunt constellationes, varios status ecclesiæ signantes. Per Arcturum, qui semper super orizontem nostrum apparet, significatur status apostolorum qui in episcopis remanet. Per Oriona, qui est tempestatis signum, significatur status martyrum. Per Hyadas, quæ significant pluvios, status doctorum doctrinæ pluvium effundentium. Per interiora austri, quæ sunt nobis occulta, status Anachoretarum, hominum aspectus declinantium. "These different constellations signify *various states* of the Church. By *Arcturus,* which always appears above our horizon, is signified the *apostolic state,* which still remains in *episcopacy.* By *Orion,* which is a tempestuous sign, is signified the *state* of the *martyrs.* By the *Hyades,* (kids,) which indicate rain, the *state* of the *doctors,* pouring out the rain of doctrine, is signified. And by the *inner chambers of the south,* which are hidden from us, the *state* of the *Anchorets* (hermits) is signified, who always shun the sight of men."

Much more of the same allegorical matter may be found in the same place, the *Glossa Ordinaria* of *Strabus* of *Fulda,* on the ninth chapter of Job. But how unreal and empty are all these things! What an *uncertain* sound do such trumpets give!

CHAPTER X

Job is weary of life, and expostulates with God, 1–6. He appeals to God for his innocence; and pleads on the weakness of his frame, and the manner of his formation, 7–13. Complains of his sufferings, and prays for respite, 14–20. Describes the state of the dead, 21, 22.

A. M. cir. 2484
B. C. cir. 1520
Ante I. Olymp. cir. 744
Ante U. C. cir. 767

MY [a]soul is [b]weary of my life; I will leave my complaint upon myself; [c]I will speak in the bitterness of my soul.

2 I will say unto God, Do not condemn me;

show me wherefore thou contendest with me.

3 *Is it* good unto thee that thou shouldest oppress, that thou shouldest despise [d]the work of thine hands, and shine upon the counsel of the wicked?

A. M. cir. 2484
B. C. cir. 1520
Ante I. Olymp. cir. 744
Ante U. C. cir. 767

---

[a]1 Kings xix. 4; chap. vii. 16; Jonah iv. 3, 8——[b]Or, *cut off while I live*

[c]Chap. vii. 11——[d]Heb. *the labour of thine hands?* Psa. cxxxviii. 8; Isa. lxiv. 8

NOTES ON CHAP. X

Verse 1. *My soul is weary of my life*] Here is a proof that נפש *nephesh* does not signify the animal life, but the soul or immortal mind, as distinguished from חי *chai,* that animal life; and is a strong proof that Job believed in the distinction between these two principles; was no materialist; but, on the contrary, credited the proper immortality of the soul. This is worthy of observation. See chap. xii. 10.

I will leave my complaint] I will charge myself with the cause of my own calamities; and shall not charge my Maker foolishly: but I must deplore my wretched and forlorn state.

Verse 2. *Do not condemn me*] Let me not be afflicted in thy wrath.

Show me wherefore thou contendest] If I am afflicted because of my sins, show me what that sin is. God never afflicts but for past sin, or to try his followers; or for the greater manifestation of his grace in their support and deliverance.

Verse 3. *Is it good unto thee*] Surely it can be no gratification to thee to distress the children of men, as if thou didst despise the work of thy own hands.

And shine upon the counsel] For by my afflictions the harsh judgments of the wicked will appear to be confirmed: viz., that God regards

A. M. cir. 2484
B. C. cir. 1520
Ante I. Olymp.
cir. 744
Ante U. C. cir.
767

4 Hast thou eyes of flesh? or [e]seest thou as man seeth?

5 *Are* thy days as the days of man? *are* thy years as man's days,

6 That thou inquirest after mine iniquity, and searchest after my sin?

7 [f]Thou [g]knowest that I am not wicked; and *there is* none that can deliver out of thine hand.

8 [h]Thine hands [i]have made me and fashioned me together round about; yet thou dost destroy me.

9 Remember, I beseech thee, that [k]thou hast made me as the clay; and wilt thou bring me into dust again?

A. M. cir. 2484
B. C. cir. 1520
Ante I. Olymp.
cir. 744
Ante U. C. cir.
767

10 [l]Hast thou not poured me out as milk, and curdled me like cheese?

11 Thou hast clothed me with skin and flesh, and hast [m]fenced me with bones and sinews.

12 Thou hast granted me life and favour, and thy visitation hath preserved my spirit.

13 And these *things* hast thou hid in thine

---

[e]1 Sam. xvi. 7——[f]Heb. It is *upon thy knowledge*
[g]Psa. cxxxix. 1, 2——[h]Psa. cxix. 73

[i]Heb. *took pains about me*——[k]Gen. ii. 7; iii. 19; Isa. lxiv. 8——[l]Psa. cxxxix. 14, 15, 16——[m]Heb. *hedged*

---

not his most fervent worshippers; and it is no benefit to lead a religious life.

Verse 4. *Hast thou eyes of flesh?*] Dost thou judge as *man* judges? Illustrated by the next clause, *Seest thou as man seeth?*

Verse 5. Are *thy days as the days of man*] אנוש *enosh*, wretched, miserable man. Thy *years as man's days;* גבר *gaber*, the strong man. Thou art not short-lived, like man in his present imperfect state; nor can the years of the long-lived patriachs be compared with thine. The difference of the phraseology in the original justifies this view of the subject. Man in his *low estate* cannot be likened unto thee; nor can he in his *greatest excellence*, though made in thy own image and likeness, be compared to thee.

Verse 6. *That thou inquirest*] Is it becoming thy infinite dignity to concern thyself so much with the affairs or transgressions of a despicable mortal? A word spoken in the heart of most sinners.

Verse 7. *Thou knowest that I am not wicked*] While thou hast this knowledge of me and my conduct, why appear to be sifting me as if in order to find out sin; and though none can be found, treating me as though I were a transgressor?

Verse 8. *Thine hands have made me*] Thou art well acquainted with human nature, for thou art its author.

And fashioned me together round about] All my powers and faculties have been planned and executed by thyself. It is thou who hast refined the materials out of which I have been formed, and modified them into that excellent symmetry and order in which they are now found; so that the union and harmony of the different parts, (יחד *yachad*,) and their arrangement and completion, (סביב *sabib*,) proclaim equally thy wisdom, skill, power, and goodness.

Yet thou dost destroy me.] ותבלעני *vattebal-leeni*, "and thou wilt swallow me up." Men generally care for and prize those works on which they have spent most time, skill, and pains: but, although thou hast formed me with such incredible skill and labour, yet thou art about to destroy me! How dreadful an evil must sin be, when, on its account, God has pronounced the sentence of death on all mankind; and that body, so curiously and skilfully formed, must be decomposed, and reduced to dust!

Verse 9. *Thou hast made me as the clay*]

Thou hast fashioned me, according to thy own mind, out of a mass of clay: after so much skill and pains expended, men might naturally suppose they were to have a permanent being; but thou hast decreed to turn them into dust!

Verse 10. *Hast thou not poured me out as milk*] After all that some learned men have said on this subject, in order to confine the images here to simple *nutrition*, I am satisfied that *generation* is the true notion. *Respicit ad* fetus *in* matris utero *primam formationem, quum in embryonem ex* utriusque *parentis* semine *coalescit.—Ex* semine líquido, lac *quodammodo* referente, *me formasti.—In interpretando, inquit Hieronymus, omnino his accedo qui de* genitali semine *accipiunt, quod ipsa tanquam natura* emulget, *ac dein concrescere in* utero ac coalescere jubet. I make no apology for leaving this untranslated.

The different expressions in this and the following verse are very appropriate: *the pouring out like milk*—coagulating, *clothing with skin and flesh, fencing with bones* and *sinews*, are well imagined, and delicately, and at the same time forcibly, expressed.

If I believed that Job referred to *nutrition*, which I do not, I might speak of the *chyle*, the *chylopoietic* organs, the *lacteal* vessels, and the generation of all the solids and fluids from this substance, which itself is derived from the food taken into the *stomach*. But this process, properly speaking, does not take place till the human being is brought into the world, it being previously nourished by the *mother* by means of the *funis umbilicus*, without that action of the *stomach* by which the *chyle* is prepared.

Verse 12. *Thou hast granted me life and favour*] Thou hast brought me from my mother's womb; given me an actual existence among men; by thy favour or mercy thou hast provided me with the means of life; and *thy visitation*—thy continual providential care, has *preserved* me *in life*—has given me the air I breathe, and furnished me with those powers which enable me to respire it as an agent and preserver of life. It is by God's continued visitation or influence that the life of any man is preserved; *in him we live, move, and have our being.*

Verse 13. *And these* things *hast thou hid in thine heart*] Thou hast had many gracious purposes concerning me which thou hast not made known; but thy visitations and mercy are

A. M. cir. 2484
B. C. cir. 1520
Ante I. Olymp.
cir. 744
Ante U. C. cir.
767

heart: I know that this *is* with thee.

14 If I sin, then [n]thou markest me, and thou wilt not acquit me from mine iniquity.

15 If I be wicked, [o]wo unto me; [p]and *if* I be righteous, *yet* will I not lift up my head. *I am* full of confusion; therefore [q]see thou mine affliction;

16 For it increaseth. [r]Thou huntest me as a fierce lion: and again thou showest thyself marvellous upon me.

17 Thou renewest [s]thy witnesses against me, and increasest thine indignation upon me; changes and war *are* against me.

18 [t]Wherefore then hast thou brought me forth out of the womb? O that I had given up the ghost, and no eye had seen me!

A. M. cir. 2484
B. C. cir. 1520
Ante I. Olymp.
cir. 744
Ante U. C. cir.
767

19 I should have been as though I had not been; I should have been carried from the womb to the grave.

20 [u]*Are* not my days few? [v]cease *then, and* [w]let me alone, that I may take comfort a little,

21 Before I go *whence* I shall not return, [x]*even* to the land of darkness [y]and the shadow of death;

22 A land of darkness, as darkness *itself; and* of the shadow of death, without any order, and *where* the light *is* as darkness.

---

[n]Psa. cxxxix. 1——[o]Isa. iii. 11——[p]Chap. ix. 12, 15, 20, 21——[q]Psa. xxv. 18——[r]Isa. xxxviii. 13; Lam. iii. 10 [s]That is, *thy plagues,* Ruth i. 21

[t]Chap. iii. 11——[u]See chap. vii. 6, 16; viii. 9; Psa. xxxix. 5——[v]Psa. xxxix. 13—— [w]Chap. vii. 16, 19 [x]Psa. lxxxviii. 12——[y]Psa. xxiii. 4

---

sufficient proofs of kindness towards me; though for purposes unknown to me thou hast sorely afflicted me, and continuest to treat me as an enemy.

Verse 14. *If I sin*] From thee nothing can be hidden; if I sin, thou takest account of the transgression, and canst not hold me for innocent when thou knowest I am guilty.

Verse 15. *If I be wicked*] I must meet with that punishment that is due to the workers of iniquity.

If *I be righteous*] I am only in the state which my duty to my Creator requires me to be in; and I cannot therefore suppose that on this account I can deserve any thing by way of *favour* from the justice of my Maker.

I am *full of confusion*] I am confounded at my state and circumstances. I know that thou art merciful, and dost not afflict willingly the children of men; I know I have not wickedly departed from thee; and yet I am treated by thee as if I were an apostate from every good. I am therefore full of confusion. See thou to my affliction; and bring me out of it in such a way as shall at once prove my innocence, the righteousness of thy ways, and the mercy of thy nature.

Verse 16. *For it increaseth.*] Probably this refers to the *affliction* mentioned above, which is increased in proportion to its duration. Every day made his escape from such a load of evils less and less probable.

Thou huntest me as a fierce lion] As the hunters attack the king of beasts in the forest, so my friends attack me. They assail me on every side.

Thou showest thyself marvellous] Thy designs, thy ways, thy works, are all incomprehensible to me; thou dost both confound and overpower me. Mr. *Good* translates thus:—

"For uprousing as a ravenous lion dost thou
    spring upon me.
And again thou showest over me thy vast
    power."

Verse 17. *Thou renewest thy witnesses*] In **this** speech of Job he is ever referring to *trials*

in courts of judicature, and almost all his terms are *forensic.* Thou bringest witnesses in continual succession to confound and convict me.

Changes and war] I am as if attacked by successive troops; one company being wearied, another succeeds to the attack, so that I am harassed by continual warfare.

Verse 18. *Wherefore then*] Why didst thou give me a being, when thou didst foresee I should be exposed to such incredible hardships? See on chap. iii. 10, &c.

Verse 19. *I should have been as though*] Had I given up the ghost as soon as born, as I could not then have been conscious of existence, it would have been, as it respects myself, as though I had never been; being immediately transported from my mother's womb to the grave.

Verse 20. *Are not my days few?*] My life cannot be long; let me have a little respite before I die.

Verse 21. *I shall not return*] I shall not return again from the *dust* to have a dwelling among *men.*

To the land of darkness] See the notes on chap. iii. 5. There are here a crowd of obscure and dislocated terms, admirably expressive of the obscurity and uncertainty of the subject. What do we know of the state of separate spirits? What do we know of the spiritual world? How do souls exist separate from their respective bodies? Of what are they capable, and what is their employment? Who can answer these questions? Perhaps nothing can be said much better of the state than is here said, *a land of obscurity, like darkness.*

The shadow of death] A place where death rules, over which he projects his shadow, intercepting every light of every kind of life.

Without any order, ולא סדרים *velo sedarim,* having no arrangements, no distinctions of inhabitants; the poor and the rich are there, the master and his slave, the king and the beggar, their bodies in equal corruption and disgrace, their souls distinguished only by their moral character. Stripped of their flesh, they stand in their naked simplicity before God in that place.

Verse 22. *Where the light is as darkness.*]

A palpable obscure: it is space and place, and has only such light or capability of distinction as renders "darkness visible." The following words of *Sophocles* convey the same idea: Ιω σκοτος εμοι φαος; "Thou darkness be my light." It is, as the *Vulgate* expresses it, *Terra tenebrosa, et operta mortis caligine: Terra miseriæ et tenebrarum, ubi umbra mortis, et nullus ordo, sed sempiternus horror inhabitat:* "A murky land, covered with the thick darkness of death: a land of wretchedness and obscurities, where is the shadow of death, and no order, but sempiternal horror dwells everywhere." Or, as *Coverdale* expresses this last clause, 𝔚𝔥𝔢𝔯𝔢𝔞𝔰 𝔦𝔰 𝔫𝔬 𝔬𝔯𝔡𝔯𝔢 𝔟𝔲𝔱 𝔱𝔢𝔯𝔯𝔦𝔟𝔩𝔢 𝔣𝔢𝔞𝔯𝔢 𝔞𝔰 𝔦𝔫 𝔱𝔥𝔢 𝔡𝔞𝔯𝔨𝔫𝔢𝔰𝔰𝔢. A *duration* not characterized or measured by any of the attributes of time; where

there is *no order* of darkness and light, night and day, heat and cold, summer and winter. It is the *state of the dead!* The *place of separate spirits!* It is *out of time, out of probation, beyond change* or *mutability*. It is on the *confines* of *eternity!* But *what* is THIS? and *where! Eternity!* how can I form any conception of thee? In thee there is no order, no bounds, no substance, no progression, no change, no past, no present, no future! Thou art an indescribable something, to which there is no analogy in the compass of creation. Thou art infinity and incomprehensibility to all finite beings. Thou art what, living, I know not, and what I must die to know; and even then I shall apprehend no more of thee than merely that thou art E-T-E-R-N-I-T-Y !

CHAPTER XI

Zophar answers Job, and reproves him severely for his attempts to justify himself; charges him with secret iniquity, and contends that God inflicts less punishment on him than his iniquities deserve, 1–6. Shows the knowledge and perfections of God to be unsearchable, and that none can resist his power, 7–11. Warns him against vanity of mind, and exhorts him to repentance on the ground that his acceptance with God is still a possible case, and that his latter days may yet become happy and prosperous, 12–20.

A. M. cir. 2484
B. C. cir. 1520
Ante I. Olymp.
cir. 744
Ante U. C. cir.
767

THEN answered Zophar the Naamathite, and said,

2 Should not the multitude of words be answered? and should ᵃa man full of talk be justified?

3 Should thy ᵇlies make men hold their peace? and when thou mockest, shall no man make thee ashamed?

4 For ᶜthou hast said, My doctrine is pure, and I am clean in thine eyes.

5 But O that God would speak, and open his lips against thee;

6 And that he would show thee the secrets of wisdom, that *they are* double to that which is! Know therefore that ᵈGod exacteth of

A. M. cir. 2484
B. C. cir. 1520
Ante I. Olymp.
cir. 744
Ante U. C. cir
767

ᵃHeb. *a man of lips*——ᵇOr, *devices*

ᶜChap. vi. 10; x. 7——ᵈEzra ix. 13

NOTES ON CHAP. XI

Verse 1. *Zophar the Naamathite*] Of this man and his friends, see chap. ii. 11. He is the most inveterate of Job's accusers, and generally speaks without feeling or pity. In *sour godliness* he excelled all the rest. This chapter and the twentieth comprehends all that he said. He was too crooked to speak much in measured verse.

Verse 2. *Should not the multitude of words be answered?*] Some translate, "To multiply words profiteth nothing."

And should a man full of talk be justified] שפתים איש *ish sephathayim*, "a man of lips," a proper appellation for a great talker: he is "a man of lips," i. e., his *lips* are the only active parts of his system.

Verse 3. *Should thy lies make men hold their peace?*] This is a very severe reproof, and not justified by the occasion.

And when thou mockest] As thou despisest others, shall no man put thee to scorn? Zophar could never think that the solemn and awful manner in which Job spoke could be called *babbling*, as some would translate the term לעג *laag*. He might consider Job's speech as *sarcastic* and *severe*, but he could not consider it as *nonsense*.

Verse 4. *My doctrine is pure*] לקחי *likchi*, "my assumptions." What I assume or take as right, and just. and true, are so; the precepts

which I have formed, and the practice which I have founded on them, are all correct and perfect. Job had not exactly said, *My doctrine and way of life are pure,* and *I am clean in thine eyes;* but he had vindicated himself from their charges of *secret sins* and *hypocrisy,* and appealed to God for his general uprightness and sincerity: but Zophar here begs the question, in order that he may have something to say, and room to give vent to his invective.

Verse 5. *But O that God would speak*] How little feeling, humanity, and charity is there in this prayer!

Verse 6. *The secrets of wisdom*] All the depths of his own counsels; the heights, lengths, and breadths, of holiness. *That they are double to that which is.* תושיה *tushiyah*, which we translate *that which is.* is a word frequent in *Job* and in the *Book of Proverbs,* and is one of the evidences brought in favour of *Solomon* as the author of this book. It signifies *substance* or *essence*, and is translated by a great variety of terms; enterprise, completeness, substance, the whole constitution, wisdom, law, sound wisdom, solid complete happiness, solidity of reason and truth, the complete total sum, &c., &c. See Taylor's Hebrew and English Concord., under ישה. In this place the versions are various. *Coverdale,* following the *Vulgate,* translates: 𝔗𝔥𝔞𝔱 𝔥𝔢 𝔪𝔦𝔤𝔥𝔱 𝔰𝔥𝔢𝔴𝔢 𝔱𝔥𝔢 (𝔬𝔲𝔱 𝔬𝔣 𝔥𝔦𝔰 𝔰𝔢𝔠𝔯𝔦𝔱𝔢 𝔴𝔦𝔰𝔰𝔡𝔬𝔪𝔢) 𝔥𝔬𝔴 𝔪𝔞𝔫𝔶𝔣𝔬𝔩𝔡𝔢 𝔥𝔦𝔰 𝔩𝔞𝔴𝔢 𝔦𝔰. The *Septuagint,* οτι διπλους εσται των κατα σε, that

A. M. cir. 2484
B. C. cir. 1520
Ante I. Olymp.
cir. 744
Ante U. C. cir.
767

thee *less* than thine iniquity *de-serveth.*

7 [e]Canst thou by searching find out God? canst thou find out the Almighty unto perfection?

8 *It is* [f]as high as heaven; what canst thou do? deeper than hell; what canst thou know?

9 The measure thereof *is* longer than the earth, and broader than the sea.

10 [g]If he [h]cut off, and shut up, or gather together, then [i]who can hinder him?

A. M. cir. 2484
B. C. cir. 1520
Ante I. Olymp.
cir. 744
Ante U. C. cir.
767

11 For [k]he knoweth vain men: he seeth wickedness also; will he not then consider *it?*

12 For [l]vain [m]man would be wise, though man be born *like* a wild ass's colt.

13 [n]If thou [o]prepare thine heart, and

---

[e]Eccles. iii. 11; Rom. xi. 33——[f]Heb. *the heights of heaven*——[g]Ch. ix. 12; xii. 14; Rev. iii. 7——[h]Or, *make a change*——[i]Heb. *who can turn him away?* chap. ix. 12

[k]Psa. x. 11, 14; xxxv. 22; xciv. 11——[l]Heb. *empty* [m]Psa. lxxiii. 22; xcii. 6; Eccles. iii. 18; Rom. i. 22 [n]Chap. v. 8; xxii. 21——[o]1 Sam. vii. 3; Psa. lxxviii. 8

---

it is double to what it is with thee. Mr. *Good* translates, "For they are intricacies to INIQUITY." This is a meaning never before given to תושיה *tushiyah*, and a meaning which even his own learned note will not make generally prevalent. Perhaps Zophar is here, in mind, comparing the wisdom which has been *revealed* with the wisdom *not revealed.* The perfection and excellence of the Divine nature and the purity of his law, are, in substance and essence, double or manifold to the revelation already made.

Less than thine iniquity deserveth.] Mr. *Good* translates, *And the knowledge hath withdrawn from thee because of thy sins;* and represents Zophar as praying that God would reveal to him the secrets of wisdom, and the knowledge which he had withdrawn from him because of his transgressions. That Zophar intends to insinuate that God afflicted Job because of his iniquities, is evident; and that he thought that God had inflicted less chastisement upon him than his sins deserved, is not less so; and that, therefore, Job's complaining of harsh treatment was not at all well founded.

Verse 7. Canst thou by searching find out God?] What is God? A Being self-existent, eternal, infinite, immense, without bounds, incomprehensible either by mind, or time, or space. Who then can find this Being out? Who can fathom his depths, ascend to his heights, extend to his breadths, and comprehend the infinitude of his perfections?

Verse 8. It is as high as heaven] High as the heavens, what canst thou work? Deep below *sheol*, (the invisible world,) what canst thou know? Long beyond the earth, and broad beyond the sea, is its measure. These are instances in the immensity of created things, and all out of the reach of human power and knowledge; and if these things are so, how incomprehensible must he be, who designed, created, preserves, and governs the whole!

We find the same thought in Milton:—

"These are thy glorious works, Parent of good!
Almighty! Thine this universal frame:
How wondrous fair! Thyself how wondrous
   then!"

Verse 10. If he cut off] As he is unlimited and almighty, he cannot be *controlled.* He will do whatsoever he pleases; and he is pleased with nothing but what is *right.* Who then will dare to find fault? Perhaps Zophar may refer to Job's former state, his losses and afflictions. *If he cut off,* as he has done, thy children; *if he*

shut up, as he has done, thyself by this sore disease; or *gather together* hostile bands to invade thy territories and carry away thy property; who can hinder him? He is sovereign, and has a right to dispose of his own property as he pleases.

Verse 11. He knoweth vain men] מתי שוא *methey shav,* "men of falsehood."

He seeth wickedness] He sees as well what is in man, as what man *does;* and of his actions and propensities he cannot be an indifferent spectator.

Verse 12. For vain man would be wise] The original is difficult and uncertain, ואיש נבוב ילבב *veish nabub yillabeb,* "And shall the hollow man assume courage," or "pride himself?" Or, as Mr. *Good* rather paraphrases it, *Will he then accept the hollow-hearted person?* The *Chaldee* gives *two* renderings: *An eloquent man shall become wiser in his heart, and the colt of the wild ass is born as the son of man.* Or, *The wise man shall ponder it; and the refractory youth, who at last becomes prudent, shall make a great man.* Coverdale:—𝔄 𝔟𝔞𝔶𝔫𝔢 𝔟𝔬𝔡𝔶 𝔢𝔵𝔞𝔩𝔱𝔢𝔱𝔥 𝔥𝔦𝔪 𝔰𝔢𝔩𝔣; 𝔞𝔫𝔡 𝔱𝔥𝔢 𝔰𝔬𝔫 𝔬𝔣 𝔪𝔞𝔫 𝔦𝔰 𝔩𝔦𝔨𝔢 𝔞 𝔴𝔶𝔩𝔡𝔢 𝔞𝔰𝔰𝔢'𝔰 𝔣𝔬𝔞𝔩𝔢. *Houbigant* translates thus:—*A man who hath understanding will become prudent; but he who is as the wild ass hath no heart,* i. e., *sense.* According to this critic, the meaning is this:—A man of sense, should he at any time transgress, will learn wisdom from it; but a man of a brutish mind, uncultivated and unreflecting, will plunge yet deeper into iniquity.

Though man be born like *a wild ass's colt*] Is translated by Mr. *Good, Or shall the wild ass colt assume the man?* This is making a sense, but such as I fear the original will never allow. There is no end to the translations of this verse, and conjectures relative to its meaning. I shall conclude with the *Vulgate:*—*Vir vanus in superbiam erigitur, et tanquam pullum onagri se liberum natum putat,* "Vain man is puffed up with pride; and he supposes himself to be born free like the wild ass's colt." Man is full of self-conceit; and imagines himself born to act as he pleases, to roam at large, to be under no control, and to be accountable to none for his actions.

Verse 13. If thou prepare thine heart] Make use of the powers which God has given thee, and be determined to seek him with all thy soul.

And stretch out thine hands toward him] Making fervent prayer and supplication, putting away *iniquity* out of thy *hand,* and not permitting *wickedness to dwell in thy tabernacle;* then

A. M. cir. 2484
B. C. cir. 1520
Ante I. Olymp.
cir. 744
Ante U. C. cir.
767

[P]stretch out thine hands toward him;

14 If iniquity *be* in thine hand, put it far away, and [q]let not wickedness dwell in thy tabernacles.

15 [r]For then shalt thou lift up thy face without spot; yea, thou shalt be steadfast, and shalt not fear:

16 Because thou shalt [s]forget *thy* misery, *and* remember *it* as waters *that* pass away:

17 And *thine* age [t]shall [u]be clearer than

the noonday; thou shalt shine forth, thou shalt be as the morning.

A. M. cir. 2484
B. C. cir. 1520
Ante I. Olymp.
cir. 744
Ante U. C. cir.
767

18 And thou shalt be secure, because there is hope; yea, thou shalt dig *about thee, and* [v]thou shalt take thy rest in safety.

19 Also thou shalt lie down, and none shall make *thee* afraid; yea, many shall [w]make suit unto thee.

20 But [x]the eyes of the wicked shall fail, and [y]they shall not escape, and [z]their hope *shall be as* [a]the giving up of the ghost.

---

[p]Psa. lxxxviii. 9; cxliii. 6——[q]Psa. ci. 3——[r]See Gen. iv. 5, 6; chap. xxii. 26; Psa. cxix. 6; 1 John iii. 21 [s]Isa. lxv. 16——[t]Heb. *shall arise above the noonday* [u]Psa. xxxvii. 6; cxii. 4; Isa. lviii. 8, 10

[v]Lev. xxvi. 5, 6; Psalm iii. 5; iv. 8; Proverbs iii. 24 [w]Heb. *entreat thy face;* Psa. xlv. 12——[x]Lev. xxvi. 16; Deut. xxviii. 65——[y]Heb. *flight shall perish from them* [z]Ch. viii. 14; xviii. 14; Prov. xi. 7——[a]Or, *a puff of breath*

---

thou shalt *lift up thy face without a blush,* thou wilt become *established,* and *have nothing to fear,* ver. 14, 15.

There is a sentiment in Prov. xvi. 1, very similar to that in the 13th verse, which we translate very improperly:—

לאדם מערכי לב *leadam maarchey leb.*
To man are the preparations of the heart:
ומהוה מענה לשן *umeyehovah maaneh lashon.*
But from Jehovah is the answer to the tongue.

It is man's duty to pray; it is God's prerogative to answer. Zophar, like all the rest, is true to his principle. Job must be a wicked man, else he had not been afflicted. There must be some iniquity in his hand, and some wickedness tolerated in his family. So they all supposed.

Verse 16. *Because thou shalt forget* thy *misery*] Thou shalt have such long and complete rest, that thou shalt scarcely remember thy *labour.*

As waters that *pass away*] Like as the mountain floods, which sweep every thing before them, houses, tents, cattle, and the produce of the field, and are speedily absorbed by the sandy plains over which they run; so shalt thou remember thy sufferings: they were wasting and ruinous for the time, but were soon over and gone.

Verse 17. Thine *age shall be clearer than the noonday*] The *rest of thy life* shall be unclouded prosperity.

Thou shalt shine forth] Thou shalt be in this unclouded state, as the sun in the firmament of heaven, giving light and heat to all around thee.

Thou shalt be as the morning.] Thus the sun of thy prosperity shall arise, and shine more and more unto the perfect day. This is the image which the sacred writer employs, and it is correct and elegant.

Verse 18. *And thou shalt be secure*] Thou shalt not fear any farther evils to disturb thy prosperity, for thou shalt have a well-grounded *hope* and confidence that thou shalt no more be visited by adversity.

Yea, thou shalt dig] I believe this neither refers to *digging his* grave, nor to *curiously investigating* surrounding circumstances; but to the custom of *digging for water* in the places where they pitched their tents. It was a matter

of high importance in Asiatic countries to find good wells of wholesome water; and they were frequently causes of contention among neighbouring chiefs, who sometimes stopped them up, and at other times seized them as their own. Through envy of Isaac's prosperity the Philistines stopped up all the wells which Abraham had digged, Gen. xxvi. 12-16. And we find the herdsmen of Gerar contending with Isaac's servants about the wells which the latter had digged; so that they were obliged to abandon two of the chief of them, and remove to a distance in order to dig and find quiet possession. See Gen. xxxi. 17-22. Zophar, in reference to all these sorts of contentions and petty wars about *wells* and *springs,* tells Job that in the state of prosperity to which he shall be brought by the good providence of God, he shall *dig*—find wells of living water; none shall contend with him; and he shall rest in safety, all the neighbouring chieftains cultivating friendship with him; see on chap. v. 23, 24; and that this is the meaning of the passage the following verse shows: *Thou shalt lie down, and none shall make thee afraid; yea, many shall make suit unto thee.* Thou shalt be in perfect security; no enemy shall molest thee, and many shall seek thy friendship.

Verse 20. *The eyes of the wicked shall fail*] They shall be continually looking out for help and deliverance; but their expectation shall be cut off.

And they shall not escape] They shall receive the punishment due to their deserts; for God has his eye continually upon them. ומנוס אבר מנהם *umanos abad minnehem,* literally, "And escape perishes from them." *Flight* from impending destruction is impossible.

And their hope shall be as the giving up of the ghost.] ותקותם מפח נפש *vethikvatham mappach naphesh,* "And their hope an exhalation of breath," or *a mere wish of the mind.* They retain their hope to the last; and the *last breath* they breathe is the final and eternal termination of their hope. They give up their *hope* and their *ghost* together; for a *vain* hope cannot enter into that place where *shadow* and *representation* exist not; all being *substance* and *reality.* And thus endeth Zophar the Naamathite; whose premises were in general good, his conclusions legitimate, but his *application* of them to Job's case totally erroneous; because he still proceeded on the ground that Job was a wicked man, if not *ostensibly,* yet *secretly;* and that the sufferings he was undergoing were the means by which God was unmasking him to the view of men.

But, allowing that Job had been a bad man, the exhortations of Zophar were well calculated to enforce repentance and excite confidence in the Divine mercy. Zophar seems to have had a full conviction of the all-governing providence of God; and that those who served him with an

honest and upright heart would be ever distinguished in the distribution of temporal good. He seems however to think that rewards and punishments were distributed in this *life,* and does not refer, at least very evidently, to a *future state.* Probably his information on subjects of divinity did not extend much beyond the grave; and we have much cause to thank God for a clearer dispensation. *Deus nobis hæc otia fecit.* God grant that we may make a good use of it!

CHAPTER XII

Job reproves the boasting of his friends, and shows their uncharitableness towards himself, 1–5; asserts that even the tabernacles of robbers prosper; and that, notwithstanding, God is the Governor of the world; a truth which is proclaimed by all parts of the creation whether animate of inanimate, and by the revolutions which take place in states, 6–25.

A. M. cir. 2484
B. C. cir. 1520
Ante I. Olymp. cir. 744
Ante U. C. cir. 767

AND Job answered and said, 2 No doubt but ye *are* the people, and wisdom shall die with you.

3 But [a]I have [b]understanding as well as you; [c]I *am* not inferior to you: yea, [d]who knoweth not such things as these?

4 [e]I am *as* one mocked of his neighbour, who [f]calleth upon God, and he answereth him: the just upright *man is* laughed to scorn.

5 [g]He that is ready to slip with *his* feet *is as* a lamp despised in the thought of him that is at ease.

6 [h]The tabernacles of robbers prosper, and they that provoke God are secure; into whose hand God bringeth *abundantly.*

7 But ask now the beasts, and they shall teach thee; and the fowls of the air, and they shall tell thee:

A. M. cir. 2484
B. C. cir. 1520
Ante I. Olymp. cir. 744
Ante U. C. cir. 767

[a]Chap. xiii. 2——[b]Heb. *a heart*——[c]Heb. *I fall not lower than you*——[d]Heb. *with whom* are *not such as these?*

[e]Ch. xvi. 10; xvii. 2, 6; xxi. 3; xxx. 1——[f]Psa. xci. 15 [g]Prov. xiv. 2——[h]Ch. xxi. 7; Psa. xxxvii. 1, 35; lxxiii. 11, 12; xcii. 7; Jer. xii. 1; Mal. iii. 15

NOTES ON CHAP. XII

Verse 2. *No doubt but ye* are *the people*] Doubtless ye are the wisest men in the world; all wisdom is concentrated in you; and when ye die, there will no more be found on the face of the earth! This is a strong irony.

Verse 3. *I am not inferior to you*] I do not fall short of any of you in understanding, wisdom, learning, and experience.

Who knoweth not such things as these?] All your boasted wisdom consists only in *strings of proverbs* which are in every person's mouth, and are no proof of wisdom and experience in them that use them.

Verse 4. *I am as one mocked of his neighbour*] Though I am invoking God for help and salvation, yet my friends mock me in this most solemn and sacred work. But God answereth me.

The just upright man is *laughed to scorn*] This is a very difficult verse, on which no two critics seem to be agreed. Mr. *Good* translates the fourth and fifth verses thus:—

"Thus brother is become a laughing-stock to his companions,
While calling upon God that he would succour him.
The just, the perfect man, is a laughing-stock to the proud,
A derision amidst the sunshine of the prosperous,
While ready to slip with his foot."

For a vindication of this version, I must refer to his notes. *Coverdale* gives at least a good sense. Thus he that calleth upon God, and whom God heareth, is mocked of his neighboure: the godly and innocent man is laughed to scorne. Godlynesse is a light despysed in the hertes of the rich; and is set for them to stomble upon. The *fifth* verse is thus rendered by Mr. *Parkhurst:* "A torch of contempt, or contemptible link, (see Isa. vii. 4, xl. 2, 3,) לעשתות *leashtoth,* to the splendours of the prosperous (is he who is) ready (נכון *nachon,* Job xv. 23, xviii. 12; Psa. xxxviii. 17) to slip with his foot." The general sense is tolerably plain; but to *emendations* and *conjectures* there is no end.

Verse 6. *The tabernacles of robbers prosper.*] Those who live by the plunder of their neighbours are often found in great secular prosperity; and they that provoke God by impiety and blasphemy live in a state of security and affluence. These are administrations of Providence which cannot be accounted for; yet the Judge of all the earth does right. Therefore prosperity and adversity are no evidences of a man's spiritual state, nor of the place he holds in the approbation or disapprobation of God.

Verse 7. *But ask now the beasts, and they shall teach thee*] Mr. *Good's* paraphrase here is very just: "Why tell ye me that the Almighty hath brought this calamity upon me? Every thing in nature, the beasts of the field, the fowls of the heaven, every inhabitant of earth and sea, and every thing that befalls them, are the

A. M. cir. 2484
B. C. cir. 1520
Ante I. Olymp.
cir. 744
Ante U. C. cir.
767

8 Or speak to the earth, and it shall teach thee: and the fishes of the sea shall declare unto thee.

9 Who knoweth not in all these that the hand of the LORD hath wrought this?

10 [i]In whose hand *is* the [k]soul of every living thing, and the breath of [l]all mankind.

11 [m]Doth not the ear try words? and the [n]mouth taste his meat?

12 [o]With the ancient *is* wisdom; and in length of days understanding.

13 [p]With [q]him *is* wisdom and strength, he hath counsel and understanding.

A. M. cir. 2484
B. C. cir. 1520
Ante I. Olymp.
cir. 744
Ante U. C. cir.
767

14 Behold, [r]he breaketh down, and it cannot be built again: he [s]shutteth [t]up a man, and there can be no opening.

15 Behold, he [u]withholdeth the waters, and they dry up: also he [v]sendeth them out, and they overturn the earth.

16 [w]With him *is* strength and wisdom: the deceived and the deceiver *are* his.

---

[i]Num. xvi. 22; Dan. v. 23; Acts xvii. 28——[k]Or, *life* [l]Heb. *all flesh of man*——[m]Chap. xxxiv. 3——[n]Heb. *palate*, chap. vi. 30——[o]Chap. xxxii. 7

[p]That is, *with God*——[q]Ch. ix. 4; xxxvi. 5——[r]Ch. xi. 10——[s]Isa. xxii. 22; Rev. iii. 7——[t]Heb. *upon*——[u]1 Kings viii. 35; xvii. 1——[v]Gen. vii. 11——[w]Ver. 13

---

work of his hands; and every thing feels and acknowledges him to be the universal Creator and Controller. It is the common doctrine of all nature; but to apply it as *ye* would apply it to me, and to assert that I am suffering from being guilty of hypocrisy, is equally impertinent. He ordains every thing in wisdom as well as in power; but why events happen as they happen, why good and evil are promiscuously scattered throughout nature or human life, ye are as ignorant of as myself."

Verse 10. *In whose hand is the soul of every living thing*] נפש כל חי *nephesh col chai*, "the soul of all life."

And the breath of all mankind.] ורוח כל בשר *veruach col besar*, "and the spirit or breath of all flesh." Does not the *first* refer to the *immortal soul*, the principle of all *intellectual life;* and the *latter* to the *breath, respiration*, the grand means by which *animal existence* is continued? See chap. x. 1.

Verse 11. *Doth not the ear try words?*] All these are common-place sayings. Ye have advanced nothing new; ye have cast no light upon the dispensations of Providence.

Verse 12. *With the ancient is wisdom*] Men who have lived in those primitive times, when the great facts of nature were recent, such as the creation, fall, flood, confusion of tongues, migration of families, and consequent settlement of nations, had much knowledge from those facts; and their *length of days*—the many hundreds of years to which they lived, gave them such an opportunity of accumulating wisdom by *experience*, that they are deservedly considered as oracles.

Verse 13. *With him is wisdom and strength*] But all these things come from GOD; he is the Fountain of wisdom and the Source of power. He alone can give us unerring counsel, and understanding to comprehend and act profitably by it. See on ver. 16.

Verse 14. *He breaketh down*] He alone can *create*, and he alone can *destroy*. Nothing can be annihilated but by the same Power that created it. This is a most remarkable fact. No power, skill, or cunning of man can annihilate the smallest particle of matter. Man, by chemical agency, may change its *form;* but to reduce it to *nothing* belongs to God alone. In the course of his providence God breaks down, so that it cannot be built up again. See proofs of

this in the total political destruction of *Nineveh, Babylon, Persepolis, Tyre*, and other cities, which have broken down never to be rebuilt; as well as the Assyrian, Babylonian, Grecian, and Roman empires, which have been dismembered and almost annihilated, never more to be regenerated.

He shutteth up a man] He often frustrates the best laid purposes, so that they can never be brought to good effect.

Verse 15. *He withholdeth the waters*] This is, I think, an allusion to the *third* day's work of the creation, Gen. i. 9: *And God said, Let the waters be gathered together unto one place, and let the dry land appear.* Thus the earth was drained, and the waters collected into seas, and bound to their particular places.

Also he sendeth them out] Here is also an allusion to the *flood*, for when he broke up the fountains of the great deep, then the *earth was overturned*.

Verse 16. *With him is strength and wisdom*] עז ותושיה *oz vethushiyah*, strength and sufficiency. Strength or power, springing from an exhaustless and infinite source of potency. In the *thirteenth* verse it is said, With him is wisdom and strength; but the expressions are not the same, חכמה וגבורה *chochmah ugeburah*, intelligence and fortitude, or strength in action, the wisdom ever guiding the exertions of *power;* but here is strength or power in essence, and an eternal *potentiality*. With him is every excellence, *in potentia* and *in esse*. He *borrows* nothing, he *derives* nothing. As he is self-existent, so is he self-sufficient. We have had the word *tushiyah* before. See the note on chap. xi. 6.

The deceived and the deceiver are his.] Some think this refers to the *fall;* even *Satan* the deceiver or beguiler, and *Adam* and *Eve*, the *deceived* or beguiled, are his. Satan, as this book shows, cannot act without especial *permission;* and *man*, whom the seducer thought to make his own property for ever, is claimed as the *peculium* or especial property of God, for the *seed of the woman* was then appointed to *bruise the head of the serpent;* and Jesus Christ has assumed the nature of man, and thus brought human nature into a *state of fellowship with himself*. Thus *he who sanctifieth and they who are sanctified are all of one, for which cause he is not ashamed to call them brethren;* Heb. ii, 11.

A. M. cir. 2484
B. C. cir. 1520
Ante I. Olymp.
cir. 744
Ante U. C. cir.
767

17 He leadeth counsellors away spoiled, and [x]maketh the judges fools.

18 He looseth the bond of kings, and girdeth their loins with a girdle.

19 He leadeth princes away spoiled, and overthroweth the mighty.

20 [y]He removeth away [z]the speech of the trusty, and taketh away the understanding of the aged.

21 [a]He poureth contempt upon princes, and [b]weakeneth the strength of the mighty.

22 [c]He discovereth deep things out of darkness, and bringeth out to light the shadow of death.

23 [d]He increaseth the nations, and destroyeth them: he enlargeth the nations, and [e]straiteneth them *again*.

24 He taketh away the heart of the chief of

A. M. cir. 2484
B. C. cir. 1520
Ante I. Olymp.
cir. 744
Ante U. C. cir.
767

---

[x]2 Sam. xv. 31; xvii. 14, 23; Isa. xix. 12; xxix. 14; 1 Cor. i. 19——[y]Chap. xxxii. 9; Isa. iii. 1, 2, 3——[z]Heb. *the lip of the faithful*——[a]Psa. cvii. 40; Dan. ii. 21

[b]Or, *looseth the girdle of the strong*——[c]Dan. ii. 22; Matt. x. 26; 1 Cor. iv. 5——[d]Psa. cvii. 38; Isa. ix. 3; xxvi. 15——[e]Heb. *leadeth in*

Verse 17. *He leadeth counsellors away spoiled*] The events of *war* are also in his hand. It is he who gives *victory;* through him even the *counsellors*—the great men and chief men, are often led into captivity, and found among the *spoils*.

And maketh the judges fools.] He infatuates the judges. Does this refer to the foolish conduct of some of the *Israelitish judges*, such as *Samson?*

Verse 18. *He looseth the bond of kings*] He takes away their splendid robes, and clothes them with sackcloth; or, he dissolves their authority, permits their subjects to rebel and overthrow the state, to bind them as captives, and despoil them of all power, authority, and liberty. Many proofs of this occur in the Israelitish history and in the history of the principal nations of the earth, and not a few in the history of Britain.

Verse 19. *He leadeth princes away spoiled, and overthroweth the mighty.*] What multitudes of proofs of this does the history of the world present! Even the late disastrous war with the French republic and empire, which began in 1793, and continued without intermission till 1814, was afterwards renewed, and had a catastrophe that went nearly to ruin Europe. How many princes, or rather *priests*, כהנים *cohanim*, have been spoiled of their power, influence, and authority; and how many *mighty men*—captains, generals, admirals, &c., have been overthrown! But supposing that the writer of the Book of Job lived, as some think, *after* the *captivity*, how many *priests* were led away spoiled, both from Israel and Judah; and how many *kings* and *mighty men* were overthrown in the disastrous wars between the Assyrians, Babylonians, and Jews!

Verse 20. *He removeth away the speech of the trusty*] The faithful counsellor and the eloquent orator avail nothing: *Quos Deus vult perdere, prius dementat;* "God infatuates those whom he is determined to destroy." The writer might have had his eyes on Isa. iii. 1-3, which the reader will do well to consult.

The understanding of the aged.] זקנים *zekenim* signifies the same here as our word *elders* or *elder-men;* which includes in itself the two ideas of *seniority*, or considerably advanced age, and *official authority*. These can do no more to save a state which God designs to destroy, notwithstanding their great political wisdom and knowledge, than the child who can neither reason nor speak.

Verse 21. *He poureth contempt upon princes*]

נדיבים *nedibim*, "those of royal extraction;" widely different from the כהנים *cohanim* mentioned ver. 19.

Weakeneth the strength of the mighty.] אפיקים *aphikim*, the *compact;* the *well-strung together;* the *nervous* and *sinewy*. Perhaps there is a reference here to the *crocodile*, as the same term is applied, chap. xl. 13, to the *compactness* of his bones: and as רפה מזיח *rippah meziach*, which we translate *weakeneth the strength*, signifies more properly *looseth the girdle*, as the *margin* has properly rendered it, the reference seems still more pointed; for it is known that "the crocodile, from the shoulders to the extremity of the tail, is covered with large *square scales*, disposed like *parallel girdles, fifty-two* in number. In the middle of each *girdle* are *four protuberances*, which become higher as they approach the end of the tail, and compose *four rows*." See the quotation in *Parkhurst*, under the word אפק *aphak*. What is human strength against this? We may say as the Lord said, Job xl. 19: *He that made him can make his sword to approach* unto him. He alone can loose the girdles of this mighty one.

Verse 22. *He discovereth deep things out of darkness*] This may refer either to God's works in the great deep, or to the plots and stratagems of wicked men, conspiracies that were deeply laid, well digested, and about to be produced into existence, when *death*, whose *shadow* had hitherto concealed them, is to glut himself with *carnage*.

Verse 23. *He increaseth the nations*] Mr. *Good* translates, *He letteth the nations grow licentious*. Pride, fulness of bread, with extensive trade and commerce, produce luxury; and this is ever accompanied with profligacy of manners. When, then, the cup of this iniquity is full, God destroys the nation, by bringing or permitting to come against it a nation less pampered, more necessitous, and inured to toil.

He enlargeth the nations] Often permits a nation to acquire an accession of territory, and afterwards shuts them up within their ancient boundaries, and often contracts even those. All these things seem to occur as natural events, and the consequences of state intrigues, and such like causes; but when Divine inspiration comes to pronounce upon them, they are shown to be the consequence of God's acting in his judgment and mercy; for it is by *him* that kings reign; it is *he* who putteth down one and raiseth up another.

Verse 24. *He taketh away the heart of the*

A. M. cir. 2484
B. C. cir. 1520
Ante I. Olymp.
cir. 744
Ante U. C. cir.
767
the people of the earth, and ʰcauseth them to wander in a wilderness *where there is* no way.

25 ᵍThey grope in the dark without light, and he maketh them to ʰstagger ⁱlike *a* drunken man.

A. M. cir. 2484
B. C. cir. 1520
Ante I. Olymp.
cir. 744
Ante U. C. cir.
767

ᶠPsa. cvii. 4, 40——ᵍDeut. xxviii. 29; chap. v. 14

ʰHeb. *wonder*——ⁱPsa. cvii. 27

---

chief] Suddenly deprives the leaders of great counsels, or mighty armies of courage; so that, panic-struck, they flee when none pursueth, or are confounded when about to enter on the accomplishment of important designs.

And causeth them to wander in a wilderness] A plain allusion to the journeyings of the Israelites in the deserts of Arabia, on their way to the promised land. Their *chief*, Aaron, had his *courage all taken away* by the clamours of the people; and so made them a molten calf to be the object of their worship, which defection from God was the cause of their wandering nearly *forty* years in the trackless wilderness. The reference is so marked, that it scarcely admits of a doubt; yet *Houbigant* and some others have called it in question, and suppose that those *chiefs* or *heads of families* which led out colonies into distant parts are principally intended. It answers too well to the case of the Israelites in the wilderness to admit of any other interpretation.

Verse 25. *They grope in the dark*] The writer seems to have had his eye on those words of Moses, Deut. xxviii. 28, 29: *The Lord shall smite thee with madness, and blindness, and astonishment of heart; and thou shalt* GROPE AT NOONDAY, *as the* BLIND GROPETH IN DARKNESS. And this also may refer to the unaccountable errors, transgressions, and judicial blindness of the Israelites in their journeying to the promised land; but it will apply also to the state of wicked nations under judicial blindness. The writer is principally indebted for his *imagery*, and indeed for the *chief expressions* used here, to Psa. cvii. 27: *They reel to and fro, and stagger like a drunken man.* 39, 40: *Again, they are minished and brought low through oppression, affliction, and sorrow. He* POURETH CONTEMPT UPON PRINCES, *and* CAUSETH THEM TO WANDER IN THE WILDERNESS, *where there is* NO WAY.

Mr. *Good* has some judicious reflections on this chapter, particularly on ver. 13-22: "It should be observed," says he, "that the entire passage has a reference to the machinery of a regular and political government; and that its general drift is to imprint on the mind of the hearer the important doctrine that the whole of the constituent principles of such a government, its officers and institutions; its monarchs and princes; its privy-counsellors, judges, and ministers of state; its chieftains, public orators, and assembly of elders; its nobles, or men of hereditary rank; and its stout robust peasantry, as we should express it in the present day; nay, the deep designing villains that plot in secret its destruction;—that the nations themselves. and the heads or sovereigns of the nations, are all and equally in the hands of the Almighty; that with him human pomp is poverty; human excellence, turpitude; human judgment, error; human wisdom, folly; human dignity, contempt; human strength, weakness."

CHAPTER XIII

Job defends himself against the accusations of his friends, and accuses them of endeavouring to pervert truth, 1-8. Threatens them with God's judgments, 9-12. Begs some respite, and expresses strong confidence in God, 13-19. He pleads with God, and deplores his severe trials and sufferings, 20-28.

A. M. cir. 2484
B. C. cir. 1520
Ante I. Olymp.
cir. 744
Ante U. C. cir.
767

LO, mine eye hath seen all *this,* mine ear hath heard and understood it.

2 ᵃWhat ye know, *the same* do I know also: I *am* not inferior unto you.

3 ᵇSurely I would speak to the Almighty, and I desire to reason with God.

4 But ye *are* forgers of lies, ᶜye *are* all physicians of no value.

A. M. cir. 2484
B. C. cir. 1520
Ante I. Olymp.
cir. 744
Ante U. C. cir.
767

ᵃChap. xii. 3——ᵇChap. xxiii. 3; xxxi. 35

ᶜChap. vi. 21; xvi. 2

NOTES ON CHAP. XIII

Verse 1. *Lo, mine eye hath seen all* this] Ye have brought nothing *new* to me; I know those maxims as well as you: nor have you any knowledge of which I am not possessed.

Verse 3. *Surely I would speak to the Almighty*] אולם *ulam,* O that:—I *wish I could speak to the Almighty!*

I desire to reason with God.] He speaks here in reference to the proceedings in a court of justice. Ye pretend to be advocates for God, but ye are forgers of lies: O that God himself would appear! Before him I could soon prove

my innocence of the evils with which ye charge me.

Verse 4. *Ye are forgers of lies*] Ye frame deceitful arguments: ye reason sophistically, and pervert truth and justice, in order to support your cause.

Physicians of no value.] Ye are as feeble in your reasonings as ye are inefficient in your skill. Ye can neither heal the wound of my mind, nor the disease of my body. In ancient times every wise man professed skill in the healing art, and probably Job's friends had tried their skill on his *body* as well as on his *mind.* He therefore had, in his argument

A. M. cir. 2484
B. C. cir. 1520
Ante I. Olymp.
cir. 744
Ante U. C. cir.
767

5 O that ye would altogether hold your peace! and ^dit should be your wisdom.

6 Hear now my reasoning, and hearken to the pleadings of my lips.

7 ^eWill ye speak wickedly for God? and talk deceitfully for him?

8 Will ye accept his person? will ye contend for God?

9 Is it good that he should search you out? or as one man mocketh another, do ye *so* mock him?

10 He will surely reprove you, if ye do secretly accept persons.

A. M. cir. 2484
B. C. cir. 1520
Ante I. Olymp.
cir. 744
Ante U. C. cir.
767

11 Shall not his excellency make you afraid? and his dread fall upon you?

12 Your remembrances *are* like unto ashes, your bodies to bodies of clay.

13 ^fHold your peace, let me alone, that I may speak, and let come on me what *will*.

14 Wherefore ^gdo I take my flesh in my teeth, and ^hput my life in mine hand?

15 ⁱThough he slay me, yet will I trust in

---

^dProv. xvii. 28——^eChap. xvii. 5; xxxii. 21; xxxvi. 4
^fHeb. *be silent from me*

^gChap. xviii. 4——^h1 Sam. xxviii. 21; Psa. cxix. 109
ⁱPsa. xxiii. 4; Prov. xiv. 32

---

against their teaching, a double advantage: Your skill in *divinity* and *physic* is equal: in the former ye are *forgers of lies;* in the latter, ye are *good-for-nothing* physicians. I can see no reason to depart from the general meaning of the original to which the ancient versions adhere. The Chaldee says: "Ye are idle physicians; and, like the mortified flesh which is cut off with the knife, so are the whole of you." The imagery in the former clause is *chirurgical,* and refers to the *sewing together,* or *connecting the divided sides* of wounds; for טפלי *topheley,* which we translate *forgers,* comes from טפל *taphal,* to fasten, tie, connect, sew together. And I question whether טפלי *topheley* here may not as well express SURGEONS, as רפאי *ropheey,* in the latter clause, PHYSICIANS. Ye are CHIRURGEONS of *falsity,* and *worthless* PHYSICIANS.

Verse 5. *Hold your peace! and it should be your wisdom.*] In Prov. xvii. 28 we have the following *apophthegm:* "Even a fool, when he holdeth his peace, is counted wise; and he that shutteth his lips, a man of understanding." There is no reason to say that Solomon quotes from Job: I have already expressed my opinion that the high antiquity attributed to this *book* is perfectly unfounded, and that there is much more evidence that *Solomon* was its *author,* than there is that it was the composition of *Moses.* But, whenever Job lived, whether *before* Abraham or *after* Moses, the book was not written till the time of Solomon, if not later. But as to the saying in question, it is a general apophthegm, and may be found among the wise sayings of all nations.

I may observe here, that a *silent man* is not likely to be a *fool;* for *a fool will be always prating,* or, according to another adage, *a fool's bolt is soon shot.* The Latins have the same proverb: *Vir sapit, qui pauca loquitur,* "A wise man speaks little."

Verse 6. *Hear now my reasoning*] The speeches in this book are conceived as if delivered in a *court of justice,* different counsellors pleading against each other. Hence most of the terms are *forensic.*

Verse 7. *Will ye speak wickedly for God?*] In order to support your own cause, in contradiction to the evidence which the whole of my life bears to the uprightness of my heart, will ye continue to assert that God could not thus afflict me, unless flagrant iniquity were

found in my ways; for it is on this ground alone that ye pretend to vindicate the providence of God. Thus ye tell lies for God's sake, and thus ye wickedly contend for your Maker.

Verse 8. *Will ye accept his person?*] Do you think to act by him as you would by a *mortal;* and, by telling lies in his favour, attempt to conciliate his esteem?

Verse 9. *Is it good that he should search you out?*] Would it be to your credit if God should try your hearts, and uncover the motives of your conduct? Were you tried as I am, how would you appear?

Do ye so mock him?] Do ye think that you can deceive him; and by flattering speeches bring him to your terms, as you would bring an undiscerning, empty mortal, like yourselves?

Verse 10. *He will surely reprove you*] You may expect, not only his disapprobation, but his hot displeasure.

Verse 11. *His dread fall upon you?*] The very apprehension of his wrath is sufficient to crush you to nothing.

Verse 12. *Your remembrances* are *like unto ashes*] Your *memorable sayings* are *proverbs of dust.* This is properly the meaning of the original: זכרניכם משלי אפר *zichroneycem mishley epher.* This he speaks in reference to the ancient and reputedly wise sayings which they had so copiously quoted against him.

Your bodies to bodies of clay.] This clause is variously translated: *Your swelling heaps are swelling heaps of mire.* That is, *Your high-flown speeches* are dark, involved, and incoherent; they are all sound, no sense; great swelling words, either of difficult or no meaning, or of no point as applicable to my case.

Verse 13. *Hold your peace*] You have perverted righteousness and truth, and your pleadings are totally irrelevant to the case; you have travelled out of the road; you have left law and justice behind you; it is high time that you should have done.

Let come on me what will.] I will now defend myself against you, and leave the cause to its issue.

Verse 14. *Wherefore do I take my flesh in my teeth*] A proverbial expression. I risk every thing on the justice of my cause. *I put my life in my hand,* 1 Sam. xxviii. 21. I run all hazards; I am fearless of the consequences.

Verse 15. *Though he slay me*] I have no dependence but God; I trust in him alone. Should

A. M. cir. 2484
B. C. cir. 1520
Ante I. Olymp.
cir. 744
Ante U. C. cir.
767

him: ᵏbut I will ˡmaintain mine own ways before him.

16 He also *shall be* my salvation: for a hypocrite shall not come before him.

17 Hear diligently my speech, and my declaration with your ears.

18 Behold now, I have ordered *my* cause; I know that I shall be justified.

19 ᵐWho *is* he *that* will plead with me? for now, if I hold my tongue, I shall give up the ghost.

20 ⁿOnly do not two *things* unto me: then will I not hide myself from thee.

21 ᵒWithdraw thine hand far from me: and let not thy dread make me afraid.

22 Then call thou and I will answer: or let

me speak, and answer thou me.

23 How many *are* mine iniquities and sins? make me to know my transgression and my sin.

24 ᵖWherefore hidest thou thy face, and ᑫholdest me for thine enemy?

25 ʳWilt thou break a leaf driven to and fro? and wilt thou pursue the dry stubble?

26 For thou writest bitter things against me, and ˢmakest me to possess the iniquities of my youth.

27 ᵗThou puttest my feet also in the stocks, and ᵘlookest narrowly unto all my paths; thou settest a print upon the ᵛheels of my feet.

28 And he, as a rotten thing, consumeth, as a garment that is moth-eaten.

A. M. cir. 2484
B. C. cir. 1520
Ante I. Olymp.
cir. 744
Ante U. C. cir.
767

ᵏChap. xxvii. 5——ˡHeb. *prove* or *argue*——ᵐChap. xxxiii. 6; Isa. l. 8——ⁿChap. ix. 34; xxxiii. 7——ᵒPsa. xxxix. 10——ᵖDeut. xxxii. 20; Psa. xiii. 1; xliv. 24; lxxxviii. 14; Isa. viii. 17

ᑫDeut. xxxii. 42; Ruth i. 21; chap. xvi. 9; xix. 11; xxxiii. 10; Lam. ii. 5——ʳIsa. xlii. 3——ˢChap. xx. 11; Psa. xxv. 7——ᵗChap. xxxiii. 11——ᵘHeb. *observest* ᵛHeb. *roots*

---

he even destroy my life by this affliction, yet will I hope that when he has tried me, I shall come forth as gold. In the common printed Hebrew text we have לֹא אֲיַחֵל *lo ayachel, I will* NOT *hope;* but the Vulgate, Syriac, Arabic, and Chaldee have read לוֹ *lo*, HIM, instead of לֹא *lo*, NOT; with *twenty-nine* of Kennicott's and De Rossi's MSS., and the Complutensian and Antwerp Polyglots. Our translators have followed the best reading. Coverdale renders the verse thus: 𝕷𝖔, 𝖙𝖍𝖊𝖗𝖊 𝖎𝖘 𝖓𝖊𝖙𝖍𝖊𝖗 𝖈𝖔𝖒𝖋𝖔𝖗𝖙𝖊 𝖓𝖊𝖗 𝖍𝖔𝖕𝖊 𝖋𝖔𝖗 𝖒𝖊, 𝖞𝖋 𝖍𝖊 𝖙𝖜𝖎𝖑 𝖘𝖑𝖆𝖞𝖊 𝖒𝖊.

But I will maintain mine own ways] I am so conscious of my innocence, that I fear not to defend myself from your aspersions, even in the presence of my Maker.

Verse 16. *He also shall be my salvation*] He will save me, *because* I trust in him.

A hypocrite] A *wicked man* shall never be able to stand before him. I am conscious of this; and were I, as you suppose, *a secret sinner*, I should not dare to make this appeal.

Verse 18. *Behold now, I have ordered*] I am now ready to come into court, and care not how many I have to contend with, provided they speak truth.

Verse 19. *Who is he that will plead with me?*] Let my accuser, the *plaintiff*, come forward; I will defend my cause against him.

I shall give up the ghost.] I shall cease to breathe. Defending myself will be as respiration unto me; or, While he is stating his case, I will be *so silent* as scarcely to *appear to breathe.*

Verse 20. *Only do not two things unto me*] These *two* things are the following: 1. *Withdraw thine hand far from me*—remove the heavy affliction which thy hand has inflicted. 2. *Let not thy dread make me afraid*—terrify me not with dreadful displays of thy majesty. The *reasons* of this request are sufficiently evident: 1. How can a man stand in a court of justice and plead for his life, when under grievous

bodily affliction? *Withdraw thy hand far from me.* 2. Is it to be expected that a man can be sufficiently recollected, and in self-possession, to plead for his life, when he is overwhelmed with the awful appearance of the judge, the splendour of the court, and the various ensigns of justice? *Let not thy dread make me afraid.*

Verse 22. *Then call thou*] Begin thou first to plead, and I will answer for myself; or, I will first state and defend my own case, and then answer *thou* me.

Verse 23. *How many are mine iniquities*] Job being permitted to begin first, enters immediately upon the subject; and as it was a fact that he was grievously afflicted, and this his friends asserted was in consequence of grievous iniquities, he first desires to have them specified. What are the *specific* charges in this indictment? To say I must be a *sinner* to be thus afflicted, is saying nothing; tell me *what* are the *sins*, and show me the *proofs*.

Verse 24. *Wherefore hidest thou thy face*] Why is it that I no longer enjoy thy *approbation?*

Holdest me for thine enemy?] Treatest me as if I were the vilest of sinners?

Verse 25. *Wilt thou break a leaf*] Is it becoming thy dignity to concern thyself with a creature so contemptible?

Verse 26. *Thou writest bitter things against me*] The indictment is filled with bitter or grievous charges, which, if proved, would bring me to bitter punishment.

The iniquities of my youth] The levities and indiscretions of my *youth* I acknowledge; but is this a *ground* on which to form charges against a man, the integrity of whose *life* is unimpeachable?

Verse 27. *Thou puttest my feet also in the stocks*] בַּסַּד *bassad*, "in a clog," such as was tied to the feet of slaves, to prevent them from running away. This is still used in the West Indies, among *slave-dealers;* and is there called the *pudding*, being a large collar of iron, locked round the ankle of the unfortunate man. Some have had them *twenty* pounds' weight; and, having been condemned to carry them for several years, when released could not walk without them! A case of this kind I knew: The slave had learned to walk well with his *pudding*, but when taken off, if he attempted to walk, he fell down, and was obliged to resume it occasionally, till practice had taught him the proper centre of gravity, which had been so materially altered by wearing so large a weight; the badge at once of *his oppression*, and of the *cruelty* of his *task-masters!*

And lookest narrowly] Thou hast seen all my goings out and comings in; and there is no step I have taken in life with which thou art unacquainted.

Thou settest a print upon the heels of my feet.] Some understand this as the *mark* left on the foot by the clog; or the *owner's mark* indented on this clog; or, Thou hast pursued me as a hound does his game, by the *scent*.

Verse 28. *And he, as a rotten thing*] I am like a *vessel* made of *skin;* rotten, because of old age; or like a *garment* corroded by the *moth.* So the *Septuagint, Syriac,* and *Arabic* understood it. The word *he* may refer to himself.

CHAPTER XIV

The shortness, misery, and sinfulness of man's life, 1–4. The unavoidable necessity of death; and the hope of a general resurrection, 5–15. Job deplores his own state, and the general wretchedness of man, 16–22.

A. M. cir. 2484
B. C. cir. 1520
Ante I. Olymp.
cir. 744
Ante U. C. cir.
767

MAN *that is* born of a woman is ªof few days, and ᵇfull of trouble.

2 ᶜHe cometh forth like a flower, and is cut down: he fleeth also as a shadow, and continueth not.

3 And ᵈdost thou open thine eyes upon such a one, and ᵉbringest me into judgment with thee?

A. M. cir. 2484
B. C. cir. 1520
Ante I. Olymp.
cir. 744
Ante U. C. cir.
767

4 ᶠWho ᵍcan bring a clean *thing* out of an unclean? not one.

5 ʰSeeing his days *are* determined, the number of his months *are* with thee, thou hast appointed his bounds that he cannot pass:

ªHeb. *short of days*——ᵇChapter v. 7; Eccles. ii. 23 ᶜChap. viii. 9; Psa. xc. 5, 6, 9; cii. 11; ciii. 15; cxliv. 4; Isa. xl. 6; James i. 10, 11; iv. 14; 1 Pet. i. 24

ᵈPsa. cxliv. 3——ᵉPsa. cxliii. 2——ᶠHeb. *who will give?*——ᵍGen. v. 3; Psa. li. 5; John iii. 6; Rom. v. 12; Eph. ii. 3——ʰChap. vii. 1; xxx. 23; Heb. ix. 27

NOTES ON CHAP. XIV

Verse 1. *Man—born of a woman*] There is a delicacy in the original, not often observed: אדם ילוד אשה *Adam yelud ishah,* "Adam born of a woman, few of days, and full of tremor." *Adam,* who did *not* spring from *woman,* but was immediately formed by God, had *many days,* for he lived *nine hundred* and *thirty* years; during which time neither sin nor death had multiplied in the earth, as they were found in the days of Job. But the *Adam* who springs *now from woman,* in the way of ordinary generation, has *very few years.* Seventy, on an average, being the highest term, may be well said to be *few in days;* and all matter of fact shows that they are full of fears and apprehensions, רגז *rogez,* cares, anxieties, and tremors. He seems born, not indeed to *live,* but to *die;* and, by living, he forfeits the title to life.

Verse 2. *He cometh forth like a flower*] This is a frequent image both in the Old and New Testament writers; I need not quote the places here, as the readers will find them all in the *margin.*

He fleeth also as a shadow] Himself, as he appears among men, is only the *shadow* of his *real, substantial,* and *eternal* being. He is here compared to a *vegetable;* he springs up, bears his flower, is often nipped by disease, blasted by afflictions, and at last cut down by death. The bloom of youth, even in the most prosperous state, is only the forerunner of hoary hairs, enfeebled muscles, impaired senses, general debility, anility, and dissolution All these images are finely embodied, and happily expressed, in the beautiful lines of a very nervous and correct poet, too little known, but whose compositions deserve the *first place* among what may be called the *minor poets* of Britain. See at the end of the chapter.

Verse 3. *Dost thou open thine eyes upon such a one*] The whole of this chapter is directed to God alone; in no part of it does he take any notice of his friends.

Verse 4. *Who can bring a clean* thing] This verse is thus rendered by the *Chaldee:* "Who will produce a clean thing from man, who is polluted with sins, except God, who is one?" By *Coverdale* thus: 𝔚𝔥𝔬 𝔠𝔞𝔫 𝔪𝔞𝔨𝔢 𝔦𝔱 𝔠𝔩𝔢𝔞𝔫𝔢, 𝔱𝔥𝔞𝔱 𝔠𝔬𝔪𝔪𝔢𝔱𝔥 𝔬𝔣 𝔞𝔫 𝔲𝔫𝔠𝔩𝔢𝔞𝔫𝔢 𝔱𝔥𝔦𝔫𝔤𝔢? 𝔑𝔬 𝔟𝔬𝔡𝔶.

The text refers to man's *original* and corrupt nature. Every man that is born into the world comes into it in a corrupt or sinful state. This is called *original sin;* and is derived from *fallen Adam,* who is the stock, to the utmost ramifications of the human family. Not one human spirit is born into the world without this corruption of nature. All are impure and unholy; and from this principle of depravity all transgression is produced; and from this corruption of nature God alone can save.

The *Septuagint,* in the *Codex Alexandrinus,* reads the verse thus: Τις γαρ εσται καθαρο· απο ρυπου; ουδε εις, εαν και μιας ημερας γενηται ὁ βιος αυτου επι της γης; "Who is pure from corruption? Not one, although he had lived but one day upon the earth."

Verse 5. *Seeing his days* are *determined*] The general *term* of human life is fixed by God himself; in vain are all attempts to prolong it beyond this term. Several attempts have been made in all nations to find an *elixir* that would expel all the seeds of disease, and keep men in

A. M. cir. 2484
B. C. cir. 1520
Ante I. Olymp.
cir. 744
Ante U. C. cir.
767

6 'Turn from him, that he may
krest, till he shall accomplish,
las a hireling, his day.

7 For there is hope of a tree, if it be cut down, mthat it will sprout again, and that the tender branch thereof will not cease.

8 Though the root thereof wax old in the earth, and the stock thereof die in the ground;

9 *Yet* through the scent of water it will bud, and bring forth boughs like a plant.

10 But man dieth, and nwasteth away: yea, man giveth up the ghost, and where *is* he?

11 *As* the waters fail from the sea, and

A. M. cir. 2484
B. C. cir. 1520
Ante I. Olymp.
cir. 744
Ante U. C. cir.
767

---

lChap. vii. 16, 19; x. 20; Psa. xxxix. 13——kHeb. *cease*

lCh. vii. 1——mVer. 14——nHeb. *is weakened* or *cut off*

---

continual health; but all these attempts have failed. *Basil, Valentine, Norton, Dastin, Ripley, Sandivogius, Artephius, Geber, Van Helmont, Paracelsus, Philalethes,* and several others. both in Europe and Asia, have written copiously on the subject, and have endeavoured to prove that a *tincture* might be produced, by which all *imperfect metals* may be transmuted into *perfect;* and an *elixir* by which the *human body* may be kept in a state of endless repair and health. And these profess to teach the method by which this *tincture* and this *elixir* may be made! Yet all these are dead; and dead, for aught we know, comparatively young! *Artephius* is, indeed, said to have lived *ninety* years, which is probable; but some of his foolish disciples, to give credit to their thriftless craft, added another *cipher,* and made his age *nine hundred!* Man may endeavour to pass the *bound;* and God may, here and there, produce a *Thomas Parr,* who died in 1635, aged *one hundred* and *fifty-two;* and a *Henry Jenkins,* who died in 1670, aged *one hundred* and *sixty-nine;* but these are rare instances, and do not affect the general *term.* Nor can death be avoided. *Dust thou art, and unto dust thou shalt return,* is the *law;* and that will ever render nugatory all such pretended *tinctures* and *elixirs.*

But, although man *cannot pass his appointed bounds,* yet he may so live as *never to reach them;* for folly and wickedness abridge the term of human life; and therefore the psalmist says, *Bloody and deceitful men shall not live out* HALF *their days,* Psa. lv. 23, for by indolence, intemperance, and disorderly passions, the life of man is shortened in cases innumerable. We are not to understand the *bounds* as applying to *individuals,* but to the *race* in general. Perhaps there is no case in which God has determined absolutely that man's age shall be so long, and shall neither be more nor less. The contrary supposition involves innumerable absurdities.

Verse 6. *Turn from him, that he may rest*] Cease to try him by afflictions and distresses, that he may enjoy some of the comforts of life, before he be removed from it: and thus, like a *hireling,* who is permitted by his master to take a little repose in the heat of the day, from severe labour, I shall also have a breathing time from affliction, before I come to that bound over which I cannot pass. See chap. x. 20, where there is a similar request.

Verse 7. *For there is hope of a tree*] We must not, says *Calmet,* understand this of an *old tree,* the stem and roots of which are *dried up* and *rotted:* but there are some trees which grow from *cuttings;* and some which, though pulled out of the earth, and having had their roots dried and withered by long exposure to the sun and wind, will, on being replanted, take root and resume their verdure. There are also certain trees, the fibres of which are so solid, that if after several years they be steeped in water, they resume their vigour, the tubes dilate, and the blossoms or flowers which were attached to them expand; as I have often witnessed in what is called the *rose of Jericho.* There are few trees which will not send forth new shoots, when the stock is cut down level with the earth.

Verse 9. *Through the scent of water it will bud*] A fine metaphor: the water acts upon the decaying and perishing tree, as strong and powerful odours from musk, otto of roses, ammonia, &c., act on a fainting or swooning person.

Verse 10. *But man dieth*] No human being ever can spring from the dead body of man; *that* wasteth away, corrupts, and is dissolved; for the man dies; and when he breathes out his last breath, and his body is reduced to dust, then, *where is he?* There is a beautiful verse in the Persian poet *Khosroo,* that is not unlike this saying of Job:—

رفتم سویِ خطیره و بگریستم بزار
از هٔخّرهٔ دوستانِ کر اسپیر فنا شدند
گفتم ایشان کجا شدند و خطر
داداز مرا جواب ایشان کجا

"I went towards the burying ground, and wept
To think of the departure of friends which were captives to death;
I said, *Where are they?* and *Fate*
Gave back this answer by *Echo, Where are they?*"

Thus paraphrased by a learned friend:—

Beneath the cypress' solemn shade,
As on surrounding tombs I gazed,
I wept, and thought of friends there laid,
Whose hearts with warmest love had blazed,
Where are those friends my heart doth lack,
Whose words, in grief, gave peace? *Ah, where?*
And *Fate,* by *Echo,* gave me back
This short but just reply, *Ah, where?*

Verse 11. *The waters fail from the sea*] I believe this refers to *evaporation,* and nothing else. As the waters are evaporated from the sea, and the river in passing over the sandy desert is partly exsiccated, and partly absorbed; and yet the waters of the sea are not exhausted, as these vapours, being condensed, fall down in rain, and by means of rivers return again into the sea: so man is imperceptibly removed from

A. M. cir. 2484
B. C. cir. 1520
Ante I. Olymp. cir. 744
Ante U. C. cir. 767

the flood decayeth and drieth
up:
12 So man lieth down, and
riseth not: [o]till the heavens *be*
no more, they shall not awake, nor be raised
out of their sleep.
13 O that thou wouldest hide me in the
grave, that thou wouldest keep me secret, until
thy wrath be past, that thou
wouldest appoint me a set time,
and remember me!
14 If a man die, shall he live
again? all the days of my appointed time
[p]will I wait, [q]till my change come.
15 [r]Thou shalt call, and I will answer thee:
thou wilt have a desire to the work of thine hands.

A. M. cir. 2484
B. C. cir. 1520
Ante I. Olymp. cir. 744
Ante U. C. cir. 767

[o]Psa. cii. 26; Isa. li. 6; lxv. 17; lxvi. 22; Acts iii. 21; Rom. viii. 20; 2 Pet. iii. 7, 10, 11; Rev. xx. 11; xxi. 1

[p]Chap. xiii. 15——[q]Ver. 7; 1 Cor. xv. 51; 2 Cor. iii. 18; Phil. iii. 21——[r]Chap. xiii. 22

his fellows by death and dissolution; yet the human race is still continued, the population of the earth being kept up by perpetual generations.

Verse 12. *So man lieth down*] He falls asleep in his bed of earth.

And riseth not] Men shall not, like cut down trees and plants, reproduce their like; nor shall they arise till the heavens are no more, till the earth and all its works are burnt up, and the general resurrection of human beings shall take place. Surely it would be difficult to twist this passage to the denial of the resurrection of the body. Neither can these expressions be fairly understood as implying Job's belief in the *materiality* of the soul, and that the whole man *sleeps* from the day of his death to the morning of the resurrection. We have already seen that Job makes a distinction between the animal life and rational soul in man; and it is most certain that the doctrine of the *materiality of the soul*, and its *sleep* till the resurrection, has no place in the sacred records. There is a most beautiful passage to the same purpose, and with the same imagery, in Moschus's epitaph on the death of Bion:—

Αι, αι, ται μαλαχαι μεν επαν κατα καπον ολωνται,
Η τα χλωρα σελινα, το τ' ευθαλες ουλον ανηθον,
'Υστερον αυ ζωοντι, και εις ετος αλλο φυοντι·
Αμμες δ', οἱ μεγαλοι, και καρτεροι, η σοφοι ανδρες,
'Οπποτε πρωτα θανωμες, ανακοοι εν χθονι κοιλᾳ
Εὑδομες ευ μαλα μακρον, ατερμονα, νηγρετον ὑπνον.

Idyll. iii., ver. 100.

Alas! alas! the mallows, when they die,
Or garden herbs, and sweet Anethum's pride,
Blooming in vigour, wake again to life,
And flourish beauteous through another year:
But we, the great, the mighty, and the wise,
When once we die, unknown in earth's dark womb
Sleep, long and drear, the endless sleep of death.

J. B. B. C.

A more cold and comfortless philosophy was never invented. The next verse shows that Job did not entertain this view of the subject.

Verse 13. *O that thou wouldest hide me in the grave*] Dreadful as death is to others, I shall esteem it a high privilege; it will be to me a covert from the wind and from the tempest of this affliction and distress.

Keep me secret] Hide my soul with thyself, where my enemies cannot invade my repose; or, as the poet expresses it:—

"My spirit hide with saints above,
My body in the tomb."

Job does not appear to have the *same thing* in view when he entreats God to *hide him in the grave;* and to *keep him secret, until his wrath be past.* The former relates to the *body;* the latter to the *spirit.*

That thou wouldest appoint me a set time] As he had spoken of the death of his body before, and the secreting of his spirit in the invisible world, he must refer here to the *resurrection;* for what else can be said to be an object of desire to one whose body is mingled with the dust?

And remember me!] When my body has paid that debt of death which it owes to thy Divine justice, and the morning of the resurrection is come, when it may be said thy *wrath*, אפך *appecha*, "thy displeasure," against the body is past, it having suffered the sentence denounced by thyself: *Dust thou art, and unto dust thou shalt return,* for *in the day thou eatest thereof thou shalt surely die;* then *remember me*—raise my body, unite my spirit to it, and receive both into thy glory for ever.

Verse 14. *If a man die, shall he live* again?] The *Chaldee* translates, If a wicked man die, can he ever live again? or, *he can never live again.* The *Syriac* and *Arabic* thus: "If a man die, shall he revive? Yea, all the days of his youth he awaits till his old age come." The *Septuagint:* "If a man die, shall he live, having accomplished the days of his life? I will endure till I live again." Here is no doubt, but a strong persuasion, of the certainty of the general resurrection.

All the days of my appointed time] צבאי *tsebai,* "of my warfare;" see on chap. vii. 1.

Will I await till חליפתי *chaliphathi, my renovation, come.* This word is used to denote the springing again of grass, Psa. xc. 5, 6, after it had once withered, which is in itself a very expressive emblem of the resurrection.

Verse 15. *Thou shalt call*] Thou shalt say, *There shall be time no longer: Awake, ye dead! and come to judgment!*

And I will answer thee] My dissolved frame shall be united at thy call; and body and soul shall be rejoined.

Thou wilt have a desire] תכסף *tichsoph,* "Thou wilt *pant* with desire;" or, "Thou wilt *yearn* over the work of thy hands." God has subjected the creature to vanity, in *hope;* having determined the resurrection. Man is one of the noblest works of God. He has exhibited him as a master-piece of his creative skill, power, and goodness. Nothing less than the strongest call upon justice could have induced him thus to destroy the work of his hands. No wonder that he has an earnest desire towards it; and that although *man dies, and is as water*

A. M. cir. 2484
B. C. cir. 1520
Ante I. Olymp.
cir. 744
Ante U. C. cir.
767

16 ˢFor now thou numberest my steps: dost thou not watch over my sin?

17 ᵗMy transgression *is* sealed up in a bag, and thou sewest up mine iniquity.

18 And surely the mountain falling ᵘcometh to naught, and the rock is removed out of his place.

19 The waters wear the stones: thou ᵛwashest away the things which grow *out* of the

dust of the earth; and thou destroyest the ᵂhope of man.

A. M. cir. 2484
B. C. cir. 1520
Ante I. Olymp.
cir. 744
Ante U. C. cir.
767

20 Thou prevailest for ever against him, and he passeth: thou changest his countenance, and sendest him away.

21 His sons come to honour, and ˣhe knoweth *it* not; and they are brought low, but he perceiveth *it* not of them.

22 But his flesh upon him shall have pain, and his soul within him shall mourn.

ˢChapter x. 6, 14; xiii. 27; xxxi. 4; xxxiv. 21; Psalm lvi. 8; cxxxix. 1, 2, 3; Proverbs v. 21; Jeremiah xxxii. 19——ᵗDeuteronomy xxxii. 34; Hosea xiii. 12

ᵘHebrew, *fadeth*——ᵛHebrew, *overflowest*——ᵂChapter xi. 20; xxvii. 8——ˣEcclesiastes ix. 5; Isaiah lxiii. 16

---

spilt upon the ground that cannot be gathered up again; yet doth he devise means that his banished be not expelled from him. Even God is represented as *earnestly longing* for the ultimate reviviscence of the sleeping dust. He cannot, he will not, forget the work of his hands.

Verse 16. *For now thou numberest my steps*] כי עתה *ki attah*, ALTHOUGH *thou*, &c. Though thou, by thy conduct towards me, seemest bent on my utter destruction, yet thou delightest in mercy, and I shall be saved.

Verse 17. *My transgression* is *sealed up in a bag*] An allusion to the custom of collecting evidence of state transgressions, *sealing them up in a bag*, and presenting them to the judges and officers of state to be examined, in order to trial and judgment. Just at this time (July, 1820) charges of state transgressions, *sealed up in a* GREEN BAG, and presented to the two houses of parliament, for the examination of a secret committee, are making a considerable noise in the land. Some suppose the allusion is to *money sealed up in bags;* which is common in the East. This includes two ideas: 1. Job's transgressions were all *numbered;* not one was passed by. 2. They were sealed up; so that none of them could be lost. These bags were indifferently *sewed* or *sealed*, the two words in the text.

Verse 18. *The mountain falling cometh to naught*] Every thing in nature is exposed to mutability and decay:—even mountains themselves may fall from their bases, and be dashed to pieces; or be suddenly swallowed up by an earthquake; and, by the same means, the strongest and most massive rocks may be removed.

Verse 19. *The waters wear the stones*] Even the common stones are affected in the same way. Were even *earthquakes* and violent concussions of nature wanting, the action of *water*, either *running* over them as a *stream*, or *even falling* upon them in *drops*, will wear these stones. Hence the proverb:—

Gutta cavat lapidem non vi sed sæpe cadendo.

"Constant droppings will make a hole in a flint."

Εκ θαμινης ραθαμιγγος, ὁκως λογος, αιες ιοισας,
Χ' ὁ λιθος ες ρωχμον κοιλαινεται.

"From frequent dropping, as the proverb says, perpetually falling, even a stone is hollowed into a hole."

Thou washest away the things] Alluding to sudden falls of rain occasioning floods, by which the fruits of the earth are swept away; and thus *the hope of man*—the *grain* for his household, and *provender* for his cattle, *is destroyed*.

Verse 20. *Thou prevailest for ever against him*] It is impossible for him to withstand thee: every stroke of thine brings him down.

Thou changest his countenance] Probably an allusion to the custom of *covering the face*, when the person was condemned, and *sending him away* to execution. See the case of Haman, in the note on *Esther*, chap. vii. 8.

Verse 21. *His sons come to honour*] When dead, he is equally indifferent and unconscious whether his children have met with a splendid or oppressive lot in life; for as to this world, when man dies, *in that day all his thoughts perish.*

Verse 22. *But his flesh upon him shall have pain*] The sum of the life of man is this, *pain of body* and *distress of soul;* and he is seldom without the one or the other, and often oppressed by both. Thus ends Job's discourse on the miserable state and condition of man.

THE last verse of the preceding chapter has been differently translated and explained.

Mr. *Good's* version is the following, which he vindicates in a learned note:—

For his flesh shall drop away from him;
And his soul shall become a waste from him.

The *Chaldee* thus: "Nevertheless his flesh, on account of the worms, shall grieve over him; and his soul, in the house of judgment, shall wail over him." In another copy of this version it is thus: "Nevertheless his flesh, before the window is closed over him, shall grieve; and his soul, for seven days of mourning, shall bewail him in the house of his burial." I shall give the *Hebrew:*—

אך בשרו עליו יכאב

Ach besaro alaiv yichab,

ונפשו עליו תאבל:

Venaphsho alaiv teebal.

Which Mr. *Stock* translates thus, both to the spirit and letter:—

But over him his flesh shall grieve;
And over him his breath shall mourn.

"In the daring spirit of oriental poetry," says he, "the *flesh*, or body, and the *breath*, are made conscious beings; the former lamenting its putrefaction in the grave, the latter mourning over the mouldering clay which it once enlivened."

This version is, in my opinion, the most natural yet offered. The *Syriac* and *Arabic* present nearly the same sense: "But his body shall grieve over him; and his soul be astonished over him."

Coverdale follows the Vulgate: 𝔚𝔥𝔶𝔩𝔢 𝔥𝔢 𝔩𝔶𝔟𝔢𝔱𝔥 𝔥𝔦𝔰 𝔣𝔩𝔢𝔰𝔥 𝔪𝔲𝔰𝔱 𝔥𝔞𝔟𝔢 𝔱𝔯𝔞𝔟𝔞𝔶𝔩𝔢; 𝔞𝔫𝔡 𝔴𝔥𝔶𝔩𝔢 𝔱𝔥𝔢 𝔰𝔬𝔲𝔩 𝔦𝔰 𝔦𝔫 𝔥𝔦𝔪, 𝔥𝔢 𝔪𝔲𝔰𝔱 𝔟𝔢 𝔦𝔫 𝔰𝔬𝔯𝔬𝔴𝔢.

On ver. 2. I have referred to the following beautiful lines, which illustrate these finely figurative texts:—

He cometh forth as a FLOWER, *and is* CUT DOWN; *he fleeth also as a shadow, and continueth not.*

All flesh is GRASS, *and all the goodliness thereof is as the* FLOWER *of the field.*

The GRASS *withereth, the* FLOWER *fadeth; but the word of our God shall stand for ever.*

The morning flowers display their sweets,
　　And gay their silken leaves unfold;
As careless of the noonday heats,
　　As fearless of the evening cold.

Nipp'd by the wind's untimely blast,
　　Parch'd by the sun's directer ray,
The momentary glories waste,
　　The short-lived beauties die away.

So blooms the human face divine,
　　When youth its pride of beauty shows;
Fairer than spring the colours shine,
　　And sweeter than the virgin rose.

Or worn by slowly-rolling years,
　　Or broke by sickness in a day,
The fading glory disappears,
　　The short-lived beauties die away.

Yet these, new rising from the tomb,
　　With lustre brighter far shall shine;
Revive with ever-during bloom,
　　Safe from diseases and decline.

Let sickness blast, let death devour,
　　If heaven must recompense our pains:
Perish the grass and fade the flower,
　　If firm the word of God remains.

See a Collection of Poems on Sundry Occasions, by the Rev. *Samuel Wesley*, Master of *Blundell's* School, *Tiverton*.

CHAPTER XV

Eliphaz charges Job with impiety in attempting to justify himself, 1–13; asserts the utter corruption and abominable state of man, 14–16; and, from his own knowledge and the observations of the ancients, shows the desolation to which the wicked are exposed, and insinuates that Job has such calamities to dread, 17–35.

A. M. cir. 2484
B. C. cir. 1520
Ante I. Olymp. cir. 744
Ante U. C. cir. 767

THEN answered Eliphaz the Temanite, and said,

2 Should a wise man utter [a]vain knowledge, and fill his belly with the east wind?

3 Should he reason with unprofitable talk?

or with speeches wherewith he can do no good?

4 Yea, [b]thou castest off fear, and restrainest [c]prayer before God.

5 For thy mouth [d]uttereth thine iniquity, and thou choosest the tongue of the crafty.

A. M. cir. 2484
B. C. cir. 1520
Ante I. Olymp. cir. 744
Ante U. C. cir. 767

---

[a]Heb. *knowledge of wind*——[b]Heb. *thou makest void*——[c]Or, *speech*——[d]Heb. *teacheth*

NOTES ON CHAP. XV

Verse 2. *Should a wise man utter vain knowledge*] Or rather, *Should a wise man utter the science of wind?* A science without solidity or certainty.

And fill his belly with the east wind?] בטן *beten*, which we translate *belly*, is used to signify any part of the cavity of the body, whether the region of the *thorax* or *abdomen;* here it evidently refers to the *lungs*, and may include the *cheeks* and *fauces.* The *east wind*, קדים *kadim*, is a very *stormy wind* in the Levant, or the eastern part of the Mediterranean Sea, supposed to be the same with that called by the Greeks ευροκλυδων, *euroclydon*, the *east storm*, mentioned Acts xxvii. 14. Eliphaz, by these words, seems to intimate that Job's speech was a perfect *storm* or *tempest of words*.

Verse 3. *Should he reason with unprofitable talk?*] Should a man talk disrespectfully of his Maker, or speak to him without reverence? and should he suppose that he has *proved* any thing, when he has uttered words of little meaning, and used *sound* instead of *sense?*

Verse 4. *Thou castest off fear*] Thou hast no reverence for God.

And restrainest prayer] Instead of *humbling* thyself, and making *supplication* to thy Judge, thou spendest thy time in arraigning his providence and justifying thyself.

When a man has any doubts whether he has grieved God's Spirit, and his mind feels troubled, it is much better for him to go immediately to God, and ask *forgiveness*, than spend any time in finding excuses for his conduct, or labouring to divest it of its seeming obliquity. *Restraining* or suppressing *prayer*, in order to find excuses or palliations for infirmities, indiscretions, or improprieties of any kind, which appear to trench on the sacred limits of *morality* and *godliness*, may be to a man the worst of evils: humiliation and prayer for *mercy* and *pardon* can never be out of their place to any soul of man who, surrounded with evils, is ever liable to offend.

Verse 5. *For thy mouth uttereth*] In attempting to justify thyself, thou hast added iniquity to sin, and hast endeavoured to impute blame to thy Maker.

The tongue of the crafty.] Thou hast var-

A. M. cir. 2484
B. C. cir. 1520
Ante I. Olymp. cir. 744
Ante U. C. cir. 767

6 ^eThine own mouth con-demneth thee, and not I: yea, thine own lips testify against thee.

7 *Art* thou the first man *that* was born? ^for wast thou made before the hills?

8 ^gHast thou heard the secret of God? and dost thou restrain wisdom to thyself?

9 ^hWhat knowest thou, that we know not?

what understandest thou, which *is* not in us?

A. M. cir. 2484
B. C. cir. 1520
Ante I. Olymp. cir. 744
Ante U. C. cir. 767

10 ⁱWith us *are* both the gray-headed and very aged men, much elder than thy father.

11 *Are* the consolations of God small with thee? is there any secret thing with thee?

12 Why doth thine heart carry thee away? and what do thy eyes wink at,

---

^eLuke xix. 22; Psa. xc. 2——^fProv. viii. 25——^gRom.

xi. 34; 1 Cor. ii. 11——^hCh. xiii. 2——ⁱCh. xxxii. 6, 7

---

nished thy own conduct, and used *sophistical* arguments to defend thyself. Thou resemblest those *cunning persons,* עֲרוּמִים *arumim,* who derive their *skill* and *dexterity* from the *old serpent,* "the *nachash,* who was עָרוּם *arum,* subtle, or *crafty,* beyond all the beasts of the field;" Gen. iii. 1. Thy wisdom is not from *above,* but from *beneath.*

Verse 7. Art *thou the first man* that *was born?*] Literally, "Wert thou born before Adam?" Art thou in the pristine state of purity and innocence? Or art thou like Adam in his *first state?* It does not become the fallen descendant of a fallen parent to talk as thou dost.

Made before the hills?] Did God create thee the beginning of his ways? or wert thou the first intelligent creature which his hands have formed?

Verse 8. *Hast thou heard the secret of God?*] "Hast thou hearkened in God's council?" Wert thou one of the *celestial cabinet,* when God said, *Let* us *make man in* our *image, and in* our *likeness?*

Dost thou restrain wisdom to thyself?] Dost thou wish us to understand that God's counsels were revealed to none but thyself? And dost thou desire that we should give implicit credence to whatsoever thou art pleased to speak? These are all strong sarcastic questions, and apparently uttered with great contempt.

Verse 9. *What knowest thou*] Is it likely that thy intellect is greater than ours; and that thou hast cultivated it better than we have done ours?

What *understandest thou*] Or, *Dost thou understand* any thing, *and it is not with us?* Show us any point of knowledge possessed by thyself, of which we are ignorant.

Verse 10. *With us* are *both the gray-headed*] One copy of the *Chaldee Targum* paraphrases the verse thus: "Truly Eliphaz the hoary-headed, and Bildad the long-lived, are among us; and Zophar, who in age surpasseth thy father." It is very likely that Eliphaz refers to himself and his friends in this verse, and not either to the old men of their tribes, or to the masters by whom they themselves were instructed. Eliphaz seems to have been the *eldest* of these sages; and, therefore, he takes the lead in each part of this dramatic poem.

Verse 11. Are *the consolations of God small with thee?*] Various are the renderings of this verse. Mr. *Good* translates the verse thus: "Are then the mercies of God of no account with thee?" or, "the addresses of kindness before thee?"

The VULGATE thus:—"Can it be a difficult thing for God to comfort thee? But thou hinderest this by thy intemperate speeches."

The SYRIAC and ARABIC thus:—"Remove from thee the threatenings (*Arabic,* reproaches) of God, and speak tranquilly with thy own spirit."

The SEPTUAGINT thus:—"Thou hast been scourged lightly for the sins which thou hast committed; and thou hast spoken greatly beyond measure; or, with excessive insolence."

Houbigant thus:—"Dost thou not regard the threatenings of God; or, has there been any thing darkly revealed to thee."

Coverdale:—Dost thou no more regarde the comforte of God? But thy wicked wordes wil not suffre the.

Scarcely any two translators or interpreters agree in the *translation,* or even *meaning* of this verse. The *sense,* as expressed in the *Vulgate,* or in our own *version,* or that of *Coverdale,* is plain enough:—"Hast thou been so unfaithful to God, that he has withdrawn his consolations from thy heart? And is there any secret thing, any bosom sin, which thou wilt not give up, that has thus provoked thy Maker?" This is the sense of our version: and I believe it to be as near the original as any yet offered. I may just add the *Chaldee:*—"Are the consolations of God few to thee? And has a word in secret been spoken unto thee?" And I shall close all these with the *Hebrew text,* and the literal version of *Arius Montanus:*—

המעט ממך תנחומות אל

hameat mimmecha tanchumoth el.

ודבר לאט עמך:

vedabar laat immak.

Nonne parum a te consolationes Dei? Et verbum latet tecum?

"Are not the consolations of God small to thee? And does a word (or thing) lie hidden with thee?"

Now, let the reader choose for himself.

Verse 12. *Why doth thine heart carry thee away?*] Why is it that thou dost conceive and entertain such high sentiments of thyself?

And what do thy eyes wink at] With what splendid opinion of thyself is thine eye dazzled? Perhaps there is an allusion here to that *sparkling in the eye* which is excited by sensations of joy and pleasing objects of sight, or to that furious *rolling of the eyes* observed in deranged persons. *Rosenmüller* translates thus:—

> Quo te tuus animus rapit?
> Quid occuli tui vibrantes?

> "Whither does thy soul hurry thee?
> What mean thy rolling eyes?"

A. M. cir. 2484
B. C. cir. 1520
Ante I. Olymp.
cir. 744
Ante U. C. cir.
767

13 That thou turnest thy spirit against God, and lettest *such* words go out of thy mouth?

14 [k]What *is* man, that he should be clean? and *he which is* born of a woman, that he should be righteous?

15 [l]Behold, he putteth no trust in his saints; yea, the heavens are not clean in his sight.

16 [m]How much more abominable and filthy *is* man, [n]which drinketh iniquity like water?

17 I will show thee, hear me; and that *which* I have seen I will declare;

18 Which wise men have told [o]from their fathers, and have not hid *it:*

A. M. cir. 2484
B. C. cir. 1520
Ante I. Olymp.
cir. 744
Ante U. C. cir.
767

19 Unto whom alone the earth was given, and [p]no stranger passed among them.

20 The wicked man travaileth with pain all *his* days, [q]and the number of years is hidden to the oppressor.

21 [r]A dreadful sound *is* in his ears: [s]in prosperity the destroyer shall come upon him.

22 He believeth not that he shall return out of darkness, and he is waited for of the sword.

---

[k]1 Kings viii. 46; 2 Chron. vi. 36; chap. xiv. 4; Psa. xiv. 3; Prov. xx. 9; Eccles. vii. 20; 1 John i. 8, 10 [l]Chap. iv. 18; xxv. 5

[m]Ch. iv. 19; Psa. xiv. 3; liii. 3——[n]Ch. xxxiv. 7; Prov. xix. 28——[o]Chap. viii. 8——[p]Joel iii. 17——[q]Psa. xc. 12——[r]Heb. *a sound of fears*——[s]1 Thess. v. 3

Thou seemest transported beyond thyself; thou art actuated by a furious spirit. Thou art *beside thyself;* thy *words* and thy *eyes* show it.

None but a *madman* could speak and act as thou dost; for *thou turnest thy spirit against God, and lettest such words go out of thy mouth,* ver. 13. This latter sense seems to agree best with the words of the text, and with the context.

Verse 13. *That thou turnest thy spirit against God*] The ideas here seem to be taken from an *archer,* who *turns his eye* and his *spirit*—his *desire*—against the object which he wishes to hit; and then *lets loose* his arrow that it may attain the mark.

Verse 14. *What is man, that he should be clean?*] מה אנוש *mah enosh;* what is *weak, sickly, dying, miserable* man, that he should be clean? This is the import of the original word *enosh.*

And—born of a woman, that he should be righteous?] It appears, from many passages in the sacred writings, that *natural birth* was supposed to be a defilement; and that every man born into the world was in a state of moral pollution. Perhaps the word יצדק *yitsdak* should be translated, *that he should justify himself,* and not *that he should be righteous.*

Verse 15. *Behold, he putteth no trust in his saints; yea, the heavens are not clean in his sight.*] The *Vulgate* has, "Behold, among his saints, none is immutable; and the heavens are not clean in his sight."

Coverdale:—Beholde, he hath found unfaithfulnesse amonge his owne sanctes, yea, the very heavens are unclene in his sight.

Eliphaz uses the same mode of speech, chap. iv. 17, 18; where see the notes. Nothing is immutable but GOD: *saints* may fall; *angels* may fall; all their goodness is *derived* and *dependent.* The *heavens* themselves have no purity compared with his.

Verse 16. *How much more abominable and filthy is man*] As in the preceding verse it is said, *he putteth no trust in his saints,* it has appeared both to translators and commentators that the original words, אף כי *aph ki,* should be rendered *how much* LESS, not *how much* MORE: How much less would he put confidence in man, who is filthy and abominable in his nature, and profligate in his practice, as he

drinks *down iniquity like water?* A man who is under the power of sinful propensities commits sin as greedily as the *thirsty man* or *camel* drinks down water. He thinks he can never have enough. This is a finished character of a BAD *man; he hungers and thirsts after* SIN: on the contrary, the GOOD *man hungers and thirsts after* RIGHTEOUSNESS.

Verse 17. *I will show thee, hear me; and that which I have seen I will declare*] Eliphaz is now about to quote a whole collection of *wise sayings* from the ancients; all good enough in themselves, but sinfully misapplied to the case of Job.

Verse 19. *Unto whom alone the earth was given*] He very likely refers to the *Israelites,* who got possession of the promised land from God himself; no *stranger* being permitted to dwell in it, as the old inhabitants were to be exterminated. Some think that *Noah* and *his* sons may be intended; as it is certain that the *whole earth* was *given to them,* when there were no *strangers*—no other family of mankind—in being. But, *system* apart, the words seem to apply more clearly to the *Israelites.*

Verse 20. *The wicked man travaileth with pain*] This is a most forcible truth: a life of sin is a life of misery; and he that WILL *sin* MUST *suffer.* One of the *Targums* gives it a strange turn:—"All the days of the ungodly Esau he was expected to repent, but he did not repent; and the number of years was hidden from the sturdy Ishmael." The sense of the original, מתחולל *mithcholel,* is *he torments himself:* he is a true *heautontimoreumenos,* or self-tormentor; and he alone is author of his own sufferings, and of his own ruin.

Verse 21. *A dreadful sound is in his ears*] If he be an oppressor or tyrant, he can have no rest; he is full of suspicions that the cruelties he has exercised on others shall be one day exercised on himself; for even in his prosperity he may expect the destroyer to rush upon him.

Verse 22. *That he shall return out of darkness*] If he take but a few steps in the dark, he expects the *dagger* of the assassin. This appears to be the only meaning of the place. Some think the passage should be understood to signify that he has no hope of a *resurrection;* he can never escape from the tomb. This I

A. M. cir. 2484
B. C. cir. 1520
Ante I. Olymp.
cir. 744
Ante U. C. cir.
767

23 He 'wandereth abroad for bread, *saying,* Where *is it?* he knoweth that "the day of darkness is ready at his hand.

24 Trouble and anguish shall make him afraid; they shall prevail against him, as a king ready to the battle.

25 For he stretcheth out his hand against God, and strengtheneth himself against the Almighty.

26 He runneth upon him, *even on his* neck, upon the thick bosses of his bucklers;

27 ᵛBecause he covereth his face with his fatness, and maketh collops of fat on *his* flanks.

A. M. cir. 2484
B. C. cir. 1520
Ante I. Olymp.
cir. 744
Ante U. C. cir.
767

28 And he dwelleth in desolate cities, *and* in houses which no man inhabiteth, which are ready to become heaps.

29 He shall not be rich, neither shall his substance continue, neither shall he prolong the perfection thereof upon the earth.

30 He shall not depart out of darkness; the flame shall dry up his branches, and ʷby the breath of his mouth shall he go away.

'Psa. lix. 15; cix. 10——ᵘChap. xviii. 12

ᵛChap. xvii. 10——ʷChap. iv. 9

---

doubt: in the days of the writer of this book, the doctrine of a future judgment was understood in every part of the East where the knowledge of the true God was diffused.

Verse 23. *He wandereth abroad for bread*] He is reduced to a state of the utmost indigence; he who was once in affluence requires a morsel of bread, and can scarcely by begging procure enough to sustain life.

Is ready at his hand.] *Is* בידו *beyado, in his hand*—in his possession. As he cannot get *bread,* he must soon meet *death.*

Verse 24. *Trouble and anguish shall make him afraid*] He shall be in continual fear of death; being now brought down by adversity, and stripped of all the goods which he had got by oppression, his life is a mark for the meanest assassin.

As a king ready to the battle.] The acts of his wickedness and oppression are as numerous as the troops he commands; and when he comes to meet his enemy in the field, he is not only deserted but slain by his troops. How true are the words of the poet:—

Ad generum Cereris sine cæde et vulnere pauci
Descendunt reges, et sicca morte tyranni.
                              JUV. Sat., ver. 112.

"For few usurpers to the shades descend
By a dry death, or with a quiet end."

Verse 25. *He stretcheth out his hand against God*] While in *power* he thought himself *supreme.* He not only did not acknowledge God, by whom kings reign, but *stretched out his hand*—used his *power,* not to *protect,* but to *oppress* those over whom he had supreme rule; and thus *strengthened himself against the Almighty.*

Verse 26. *He runneth upon him*] Calmet has properly observed that this refers to GOD, who, like a mighty conquering hero, marches against the ungodly, rushes upon him, seizes him by the throat, which the *mail* by which it is encompassed cannot protect; neither his shield nor spear can save him when the *Lord of hosts* comes against him.

Verse 27. *Because he covereth his face*] He has lived in luxury and excess; and like a man overloaded with flesh, he cannot defend himself against the strong gripe of his adversary.

The *Arabic,* for *maketh collops of fat on his flanks,* has وجِدِّ التَّرِيا فوقَ العَيوقَ *He lays the Pleiades upon the Hyades,* or, *He places Surreea upon aiyuk,* a proverbial expression for, *His ambition is boundless; He aspires as high as heaven; His head touches the stars;* or, is like the *giants* of old, who were fabled to have attempted to scale heaven by placing one high mountain upon another:—

Ter sunt conati imponere Pelio Ossam
Scilicet, atque Ossæ frondosum involvere
 Olympum
Ter Pater extructos disjecit fulmine montes.
                              VIRG. Geor. i., ver. 281.

"With mountains piled on mountains, thrice
 they strove
To scale the steepy battlements of Jove;
And thrice his lightning and red thunder
 play'd,
And their demolish'd works in ruins laid."
                              DRYDEN.

To the lust of power and the schemes of ambition there are no bounds; but see the end of such persons: the haughty spirit precedes a fall; their palaces become desolate; and their heaven is reduced to a chaos.

Verse 28. *He dwelleth in desolate cities*] It is sometimes the fate of a tyrant to be obliged to take up his habitation in some of those cities which have been ruined by his wars, and in a house so ruinous as to be ready to fall into heaps. Ancient and modern history afford abundance of examples to illustrate this.

Verse 29. *He shall not be rich*] The whole of what follows, to the end of the chapter, seems to be directed against Job himself, whom Eliphaz indirectly accuses of having been a *tyrant* and *oppressor.* The threatened evils are, 1. *He shall not be rich,* though he labours greatly to acquire riches. 2. *His substance shall not continue*—God will blast it, and deprive him of *power* to preserve it. 3. *Neither shall he prolong the perfection thereof*—all his works shall perish, for God will blot out his remembrance from under heaven.

Verse 30. *He shall not depart out of darkness*] 4. He shall be in continual afflictions and distress. 5. *The flame shall dry up his branches* —his *children* shall be cut off by sudden judg-

A. M. cir. 2484
B. C. cir. 1520
Ante I. Olymp.
cir. 744
Ante U. C. cir.
767

31 Let not him that is deceived ˣtrust in vanity: for vanity shall be his recompense.

32 It shall be ʸaccomplished ᶻbefore his time, and his branch shall not be green.

33 He shall shake off his unripe grape as

the vine, and shall cast off his flower as the olive.

34 For the congregation of hypocrites *shall be* desolate, and fire shall consume the tabernacles of bribery.

35 ᵃThey conceive mischief, and bring forth ᵇvanity, and their belly prepareth deceit.

A. M. cir. 2484
B. C. cir. 1520
Ante I. Olymp.
cir. 744
Ante U. C. cir.
767

ˣIsa. lix. 4——ʸOr, *cut off*——ᶻCh. xxii. 16; Psa. lv. 23

ᵃPsa. vii. 14; Isa. lix. 4; Hos. x. 13——ᵇOr, *iniquity*

---

ments. 6. *He shall pass away by the breath of his mouth;* for by the breath of his mouth doth God slay the wicked.

Verse 31. *Let not him that is deceived*] 7. He has many *vain imaginations* of obtaining wealth, power, pleasure, and happiness; but he is *deceived;* and he finds that he has trusted בשׁוא *bashshav, in a lie;* and this lie is his recompense.

Verse 32. *It shall be accomplished before his time*] I believe the *Vulgate* gives the true sense: *Antequam dies ejus impleantur, peribit;* "He shall perish before his time; before his days are completed." 8. He shall be removed by a violent death, and not live out half his days. 9. *And his branch shall not be green*— there shall be no *scion* from his roots; all his *posterity* shall fail.

Verse 33. *He shall shake off his unripe grape*] 10. Whatever *children* he may have, they shall never survive him, nor come to mature age. They shall be like *wind-fall grapes* and *blasted olive blossoms.* As the *vine* and *olive,* which are among the most *useful* trees, affording *wine* and *oil,* so necessary for the worship of God and the comfort of man, are mentioned here they may be intended to refer to the hopeful progeny of the oppressor; but who fell, like the untimely grape or the blasted olive flower, without having the opportunity of realizing the public expectation.

Verse 34. *The congregation of hypocrites*] 11. Job is here classed with *hypocrites,* or

rather the *impious* of all kinds. The *congregation,* or ערת *adath, society,* of such, shall be *desolate,* or a *barren rock,* גלמוד *galmud.* See this Arabic word explained in the note on chap. iii. 7.

Fire shall consume the tabernacles of bribery.] 12. Another insinuation against Job, that he had perverted justice and judgment, and had taken *bribes.*

Verse 35. *They conceive mischief*] The figure here is both elegant and impressive. The wicked *conceive* mischief, from the seed which Satan sows in their hearts; in producing which they *travail* with many pangs, (for sin is a sore labour,) and at last their *womb* produces *fraud* or *deception.* This is an *accursed* birth, from an *iniquitous* conception. St. *James* gives the figure at full length, most beautifully touched in all its parts: *When lust hath conceived it bringeth forth sin; and sin, when it is finished, bringeth forth death;* James i. 15, where see the note.

Poor Job! what a fight of affliction had he to contend with! His *body* wasted and tortured with sore *disease;* his *mind* harassed by *Satan;* and his *heart* wrung with the unkindness, and false accusations of his *friends.* No wonder he was greatly agitated, often distracted, and sometimes even thrown off his guard. However, all his enemies were chained; and beyond that chain they could not go. God was his unseen Protector, and did not suffer his faithful servant to be greatly moved.

CHAPTER XVI

Job replies to Eliphaz, and through him to all his friends, who, instead of comforting him, had added to his misfortunes; and shows that, had they been in his circumstances, he would have treated them in a different manner, 1–5. Enters into an affecting detail of his suffering, 6–16. Consoles himself with the consciousness of his own innocence, of which he takes God to witness, and patiently expects a termination of all his sufferings by death, 17–22.

A. M. cir. 2484
B. C. cir. 1520
Ante I. Olymp.
cir. 744
Ante U. C. cir.
767

THEN Job answered and said, 2 I have heard many such things: ᵃmiserable ᵇcomforters *are* ye all.

3 Shall ᶜvain words have an end? or what emboldeneth thee that thou answerest?

4 I also could speak as ye *do:*

A. M. cir. 2484
B. C. cir. 1520
Ante I. Olymp.
cir. 744
Ante U. C. cir.
767

ᵃOr, *troublesome*——ᵇChap. xiii. 4

ᶜHeb. *words of wind*

NOTES ON CHAP. XVI

Verse 2. *I have heard many such things*] These sayings of the ancients are not strange to me; but they do not apply to my case: ye see me in affliction; ye should endeavour to console me. This ye do not; and yet ye pretend to do it! *Miserable comforters* are ye all.

Verse 3. *Vain words*] Literally, *words of air.*
What emboldeneth thee] Thou art totally ignorant of the business; what then can induce thee to take part in this discussion?

Verse 4. *I also could speak*] It is probably better to render some of these *permissives* or *potential verbs* literally in the *future tense,* as in the Hebrew: *I also* WILL *speak.* Mr. *Good* has adopted this mode.

A. M. cir. 2484
B. C. cir. 1520
Ante I. Olymp. cir. 744
Ante U. C. cir. 767

if your soul were in my soul's stead, I could heap up words against you, and ^dshake mine head at you.

5 *But* I would strengthen you with my mouth, and the moving of my lips should assuage *your grief.*

6 Though I speak, my grief is not assuaged: and *though* I forbear, ^ewhat am I eased?

7 But now he hath made me weary: thou hast made desolate all my company.

8 And thou hast filled me with wrinkles, *which* is a witness *against me:* and my leanness rising up in me beareth witness to my face.

9 ^fHe teareth *me* in his wrath, who hateth me: he gnasheth upon me with his teeth; ^gmine enemy sharpeneth his eyes upon me.

A. M. cir. 2484
B. C. cir. 1520
Ante I. Olymp. cir. 744
Ante U. C. cir. 767

10 They have ^hgaped upon me with their mouth; they ⁱhave smitten me upon the cheek reproachfully; they have ^kgathered themselves together against me.

11 God ^lhath ^mdelivered me to the ungodly, and turned me over into the hands of the wicked.

12 I was at ease, but he hath broken me asunder: he hath also taken *me* by my neck, and shaken me to pieces, and ⁿset me up for his mark.

13 His archers compass me round about, he cleaveth my reins asunder, and doth not spare; he poureth out my gall upon the ground.

14 He breaketh me with breach upon breach, he runneth upon me like a giant.

15 I have sewed sackcloth upon my skin,

---

^dPsa. xxii. 7; cix. 25; Lam. ii. 15——^eHeb. *what goeth from me?*——^fCh. x. 16, 17——^gCh. xiii. 24——^hPsa. xxii. 13——ⁱLam. iii. 30; Mic. v. 1——^kPsa. xxxv. 15 ^lCh. i. 15, 17——^mHeb. *hath shut me up*——ⁿCh. vii. 20

If your soul were in my soul's stead] If you were in my place, I also could quote many wise sayings that might tend to show that you were hypocrites and wicked men; but would this be fair? Even when I might not choose to go farther in *assertion,* I might *shake my head* by way of *insinuation* that there was much more behind, of which I did not choose to speak; but would this be right? That such sayings are in memory, is no proof that they were either made for me, or apply to my case.

Verse 5. *I would strengthen you with my mouth*] Mr. *Good* translates thus:—

"With my own mouth will I overpower you,
Till the quivering of my lips shall fail;"

for which rendering he contends in his learned notes. This translation is countenanced by the *Septuagint, Syriac,* and *Arabic* versions.

Verse 6. *Though I speak*] But it will be of no avail thus to speak; for reprehensions of *your* conduct will not serve to mitigate *my* sufferings.

Verse 7. *But now he hath made me weary*] The *Vulgate* translates thus:—*Nunc autem oppressit me dolor meus; et in nihilum redacti sunt omnes artus mei;* "But now my grief oppresses me, and all my joints are reduced to nothing." Perhaps Job alluded here to his *own afflictions,* and the *desolation of his family.* Thou hast made me weary with continual affliction; my strength is quite exhausted; and thou hast made desolate all my company, not leaving me a single child to continue my name, or to comfort me in sickness or old age. Mr. *Good* translates:—

"Here, indeed, hath he distracted me;
Thou hast struck apart all my witnesses."

Verse 8. *Thou hast filled me with wrinkles*] If Job's disease were the *elephantiasis,* in which the whole skin is *wrinkled* as the skin of the *elephant,* from which this species of leprosy has taken its name, these words would apply most forcibly to it; but the whole passage, through its obscurity, has been variously rendered. *Calmet* unites it with the preceding, and *Houbigant* is not very different. He translates thus:—"For my trouble hath now weakened all my frame, and brought wrinkles over me: he is present as a witness, and ariseth against me, who telleth lies concerning me; he openly contradicts me to my face." Mr. *Good* translates nearly in the same way; others still differently.

Verse 9. *He teareth me in his wrath*] Who the person is that is spoken of in this verse, and onward to the end of the *fourteenth,* has been a question on which commentators have greatly differed. Some think God, others Eliphaz, is intended: I think *neither.* Probably God permitted *Satan* to *show* himself to Job, and the *horrible* form which he and his *demons* assumed increased the misery under which Job had already suffered so much. All the expressions, from this to the end of the *fourteenth* verse, may be easily understood on this principle; *e. g.,* ver. 9: "He (*Satan*) gnasheth upon me with his teeth; mine enemy sharpeneth his eyes upon me." Ver. 10: "They (*demons*) have gaped on me with their mouth;—they have gathered themselves together against me." Ver. 11: "God hath delivered me to the ungodly, (עויל *avil,* to the EVIL ONE,) and turned me over into the hands of the wicked." He hath abandoned me to be tortured by the *tempter* and his *host.*

If we consider all these expressions as referring to Job's *three friends,* we must, in that case, acknowledge that the *figures* are all strained to an insufferable height, so as not to be justified by any *figure* of speech.

Verse 13. *His archers compass me*] רביו *rabbaiv* "his great ones." The *Vulgate* and *Septuagint* translate this *his spears;* the *Syriac, Arabic,* and *Chaldee, his arrows.* On this and the following verse Mr. *Heath* observes: "The metaphor is here taken from huntsmen: first, they surround the beast; then he is shot dead; his entrails are next taken out; and then his body is broken up limb by limb."

Verse 15. *I have sewed sackcloth*] שק *sak,*

A. M. cir. 2484
B. C. cir. 1520
Ante I. Olymp.
cir. 744
Ante U. C. cir.
767
and °defiled my horn in the dust.

16 My face is foul with weeping, and on my eyelids *is* the shadow of death.

17 Not for *any* injustice in mine hands: also my prayer *is* pure.

18 O earth, cover not thou my blood, and Plet my cry have no place.

19 Also now, behold, qmy witness *is* in heaven, and my record *is* on rhigh.

20 My friends sscorn me: *but* mine eye poureth out *tears* unto God.

21 'O that one might plead for a man with God, as a man *pleadeth* for his uneighbour!

22 When va few years are come, then I shall wgo the way *whence* I shall not return.

A. M. cir. 2484
B. C. cir. 1520
Ante I. Olymp.
cir. 744
Ante U. C. cir.
767

°Chap. xxx. 19; Psa. vii. 5—— PChap. xxvii. 9; Psa. lxvi. 18, 19——qRom. i. 9——rHeb. *in the high places* sHeb. are *my scorners*

tChap. xxxi. 35; Eccles. vi. 10; Isa. xlv. 9; Rom. ix. 20——uOr, *friend*——vHebrew, *years of number* wEccles. xii. 5

a word that has passed into almost all languages, as I have already had occasion to notice in other parts of this work.

Defiled my horn in the dust.] The *horn* was an emblem of *power;* and the metaphor was originally taken from beasts, such as the urus, wild ox, *buffalo,* or perhaps the *rhinoceros,* who were perceived to have so much power in their horns. Hence a horn was frequently worn on crowns and helmets, as is evident on ancient coins; and to this day it is an appendage to the diadem of the kings and chiefs of Abyssinia. In the second edition of Mr. Bruce's Travels in Abyssinia, vol. viii., plates 2 and 3, we have engravings of two chiefs, *Kefla Yasous,* and *Woodage Ashahel,* who are represented with this emblem of *power* on their forehead. Mr. Bruce thus describes it: "One thing remarkable in this cavalcade, which I observed, was the head dress of the *governors of provinces.* A large broad fillet was bound upon their forehead, and tied behind their head. In the middle of this was a *horn,* or a conical piece of silver, gilt, about *four* inches in length, much in the shape of our common candle extinguishers. This is called *kirn,* or horn; and is only worn in reviews, or *parades after victory.* This, I apprehend, like all others of their usages, is taken from the Hebrews; and the several allusions made in Scripture to it arise from this practice. 'I said unto the fools, Deal not foolishly; and to the wicked, Lift not up the *horn.*' 'Lift not up your *horn* on high, speak not with a stiff neck; for promotion cometh not,' &c. 'But my *horn* shalt thou *exalt* like the horn of a unicorn.' 'And the *horn* of the righteous shall be *exalted* with honour.' And so in many other places throughout the Psalms." In a note on the same page we have the following observation: "The crooked manner in which they hold their neck when this ornament is on their forehead, for fear it should fall forward, perfectly shows the meaning of 'Speak not with a stiff neck when you hold the horn on high (or erect) like the horn of the unicorn.' "—Bruce's Travels, vol. iv., p. 407.

Defiling or *rolling the horn in the dust,* signifies the disgrace or destruction of power, authority, and eminence.

Mr. *Good* translates, *I have rolled my* turban *in the dust,* which he endeavours to justify in a long note. But in this, I think, this very learned man is mistaken. The Hebrew קרן *keren* is the same as the Æthiopic *kirn,* and both mean exactly, in such connection, what Mr. Bruce has noticed above. The *horn* on the

diadem is the emblem of power, authority, and eminence.

Verse 16. *On my eyelids* is *the shadow of death*] Death is now *fast approaching* me; already his *shadow* is projected over me.

Verse 17. *Not for* any *injustice*] I must assert, even with my last breath, that the charges of my friends against me are groundless. I am afflicted unto death, but not on account of my iniquities.

Also my prayer is pure.] I am no hypocrite, God knoweth.

Verse 18. *O earth, cover not thou my blood*] This is evidently an allusion to the murder of Abel, and the verse has been understood in *two* different ways: 1. Job here calls for justice against his destroyers. His *blood* is his *life,* which he considers as taken away by *violence,* and therefore calls for vengeance. Let my blood cry against my murderers, as the blood of Abel cried against Cain. My innocent life is taken away by violence, as his innocent life was; as therefore the *earth* was not permitted *to cover his blood,* so that his murderer should be concealed, let my death be avenged in the same way. 2. It has been supposed that the passage means that Job considered himself accused of shedding innocent blood; and, conscious of his own perfect innocence, he prays that the earth may not cover any blood shed by him. Thus Mr. Scott:—

"O earth, the blood accusing me reveal;
  Its piercing voice in no recess conceal."

And this notion is followed by Mr. *Good.* But, with all deference to these learned men, I do not see that this meaning can be supported by the Hebrew text; nor was the passage so understood by any of the ancient versions. I therefore prefer the first sense, which is sufficiently natural, and quite in the manner of Job in his impassioned querulousness.

Verse 19. *My witness* is *in heaven*] I appeal to God for my innocence.

Verse 20. *My friends scorn me*] They deride and insult me, but my eye is towards God; I look to him to vindicate my cause.

Verse 21. *O that one might plead*] Let me only have liberty to plead with God, as a man hath with his fellow.

Verse 22. *When a few years are come*] I prefer Mr. *Good's* version:—

"But the years numbered to me are come,
  And I must go the way whence I shall not return."

Job could not, in his present circumstances, expect *a few years of longer life;* from his own conviction he was expecting death every hour. The next verse, the *first* of the following chapter, should come in here: *My breath is corrupt, &c.*] He felt himself as in the arms of death: he saw the grave as already digged which was to receive his dead body. This verse shows that our translation of the *twenty-second* verse is improper, and vindicates Mr. *Good's* version.

I HAVE said on ver. 9 that a part of Job's sufferings probably arose from appalling representations made to his eye or to his imagination by Satan and his agents. I think this neither irrational nor improbable. That he and his demons have power to make themselves manifest on especial occasions, has been credited in all ages of the world; not by the weak, credulous, and superstitious only, but also by the wisest, the most learned, and the best of men. I am persuaded that many passages in the Book of Job refer to this, and admit of an easy interpretation on this ground.

CHAPTER XVII

Job complains of the injustice of his friends, and compares his present state of want and wo with his former honour and affluence, 1–6. God's dealings with him will even astonish upright men; yet the righteous shall not be discouraged, but hold on his way, 7–9. Asserts that there is not a wise man among his friends, and that he has no expectation but of a speedy death, 10–16.

A. M. cir. 2484
B. C. cir. 1520
Ante I. Olymp.
cir. 744
Ante U. C. cir.
767

MY ᵃbreath is corrupt, my days are extinct, ᵇthe graves *are ready* for me.

2 *Are there* not mockers with me? and doth not mine eye ᶜcontinue in their ᵈprovocation?

3 Lay down now, put me in a surety with thee; who *is* he *that* ᵉwill strike hands with me?

4 For thou hast hid their heart from understanding: therefore shalt thou not exalt *them.*

A. M. cir. 2484
B. C. cir. 1520
Ante I. Olymp.
cir. 744
Ante U. C. cir.
767

5 He that speaketh flattery to *his* friends, even the eyes of his children shall fail.

6 He hath made me also a ᶠby-word of the people; and ᵍaforetime I was as a tabret.

ᵃOr, *spirit is spent*——ᵇPsa. lxxxviii. 3, 4——ᶜHeb. *lodge*——ᵈ1 Sam. i. 6, 7

ᵉProv. vi. 1; xvii. 18; xxii. 26——ᶠChap. xxx. 9——ᵍOr, *before them*

NOTES ON CHAP. XVII

Verse 1. *My breath is corrupt*] Rather, *My spirit is oppressed,* רוחי חבלה *ruchi chubbalah: My days are extinct, and the sepulchral cells are ready for me.*—PARKHURST. There is probably a reference here to cemeteries, where were several niches, in each of which a corpse was deposited. See on ver. 16.

For חבלה *chubbalah, corrupted* or *oppressed,* some MSS. have חלה *chalah, is made weak;* and one has נבלה *is worn down, consumed:* this is agreeable to the *Vulgate, Spiritus meus attenuebatur;* "My spirit is exhausted."

Verse 2. Are there *not mockers with me?*] This has been variously translated. The VULGATE: "I have not sinned, and yet my eye dwells upon afflictions." SEPTUAGINT: "I conjure you, labouring under afflictions, what evil have I done? Yet strangers have robbed me of my substance." Mr. GOOD: "But are not revilers before me? Alas, mine eye penetrateth their rebukes." CALMET thinks the Hebrew might be translated thus: "If I have not been united in friendship with the wicked, why are my eyes in bitterness?" COVERDALE translates both verses thus: 𝔐𝔶 𝔟𝔯𝔢𝔱𝔥 𝔣𝔞𝔶𝔩𝔢𝔱𝔥, 𝔪𝔶 𝔡𝔞𝔶𝔢𝔰 𝔞𝔯𝔢 𝔰𝔥𝔬𝔯𝔱𝔢𝔫𝔢𝔡, 𝔍 𝔞𝔪 𝔥𝔞𝔯𝔡𝔢 𝔞𝔱 𝔡𝔢𝔞𝔱𝔥𝔢𝔰 𝔡𝔬𝔯𝔢. 𝔍 𝔥𝔞𝔳𝔢 𝔡𝔦𝔰𝔠𝔢𝔞𝔳𝔢𝔡 𝔫𝔬 𝔪𝔞𝔫, 𝔶𝔢𝔱 𝔪𝔲𝔰𝔱 𝔪𝔶𝔫𝔢 𝔢𝔶𝔢 𝔠𝔬𝔫𝔱𝔦𝔫𝔲𝔢 𝔦𝔫 𝔥𝔢𝔟𝔶𝔫𝔢𝔰𝔰𝔢. Mr. HEATH: "Were it not so, I have sarcasms enow in store; and I could spend the whole night unmoved at their aggravations." The general meaning is sufficiently plain, and the reader has got translations enough.

Verse 3. *Lay down now*] Deposit a pledge; stake your conduct against mine, and your life and soul on the issue; let the cause come before God; let him try it; and see whether any of you shall be justified by him, while I am condemned.

Verse 4. *For thou hast hid their heart*] This address is to *God;* and here he is represented as *doing* that which in the course of his providence he only *permits* to be done.

Shalt thou not exalt them.] This was exactly fulfilled: not one of Job's friends was exalted; on the contrary, God condemned the whole; and they were not received into the Divine favour till Job sacrificed, and made intercession for them.

Verse 5. *He that speaketh flattery*] There is a great variety of meaning given to the terms in this verse. The general sense is, The man who expects much from his friends will be disappointed: while depending on them his children's eyes may fail in looking for bread.

Verse 6. *He hath made me also a by-word*] My afflictions and calamities have become a subject of general conversation, so that my poverty and affliction are proverbial. *As poor as Job, As afflicted as Job,* are proverbs that have even reached our times and are still in use.

Aforetime I was as a tabret.] This is not the translation of the Hebrew ותפת לפנים אהיה *vethopheth lephanim eheyeh.* Instead of לפנים *lephanim,* I would read לפניהם *liphneyhem,* and then the clause might be translated thus: *I shall be as a furnace,* or *consuming fire* (Topheth) *before them.* They shall have little reason to mock when they see the end of the Lord's dealings with me; my example will be a consuming fire to them, and my false friends

A. M. cir. 2484
B. C. cir. 1520
Ante I. Olymp.
cir. 744
Ante U. C. cir.
767
7 hMine eye also is dim by reason of sorrow, and all lmy members *are* as a shadow.

8 Upright *men* shall be astonied at this, and the innocent shall stir up himself against the hypocrite.

9 The righteous also shall hold on his way, and he that hath kclean hands lshall be stronger and stronger.

10 But as for you all, mdo ye return, and come now: for I cannot find *one* wise *man* among you.

11 nMy days are past, my purposes are broken off, *even* othe thoughts of my heart.

12 They change the night into day: the light *is* pshort because of darkness.

A. M. cir. 2484
B. C. cir. 1520
Ante I. Olymp.
cir. 744
Ante U. C. cir.
767
13 If I wait, the grave *is* mine house: I have made my bed in the darkness.

14 I have qsaid to corruption, Thou *art* my father: to the worm, *Thou art* my mother, and my sister.

15 And where *is* now my hope? as for my hope, who shall see it?

16 They shall go down rto the bars of the pit, when *our* srest together *is* in the dust.

---

hPsalm vi. 7; xxxi. 9——iOr, *my thoughts*——kPsalm xxiv. 4——lHebrew, *shall add strength*——mChapter vi. 29——nChapter vii. 6; ix. 25——oHebrew, *the possessions*——pHebrew, *near*——qHebrew, *cried* or *called*——rChapter xviii. 13——sChapter iii. 17, 18, 19

---

will be confounded. COVERDALE translates thus: He hath made me as it were a bywordе of the comon people. I am his gestinge stocke amonge them.

Verse 7. *Mine eye also is dim*] Continual weeping impairs the sight; and indeed any affliction that debilitates the frame generally, weakens the *sight* in the same proportion.

All my members are *as a shadow.*] Nothing is left but *skin* and *bone.* I am but the *shadow* of my *former self.*

Verse 8. *Upright* men *shall be astonied*] In several of these verses Job is supposed to speak prophetically of his future restoration, and of the good which religious society should derive from the history of his original affluence, consequent poverty and affliction, and final restoration to health, peace, and prosperity. The *upright* will receive the account with astonishment, and wonder at the dispensations of the Almighty; while *hypocrites,* false professors and the *sour-headed,* godly, shall be unmasked, and *innocent* men, whether in affliction or affluence, shall be known to be favourites of the Almighty.

Verse 9. *The righteous also shall hold on his way*] There shall be no doubt concerning the dispensations of the Divine providence. My case shall illustrate all seemingly intricate displays of God's government. None shall be stumbled at seeing a godly man under oppression, knowing that God never permits any thing of the kind but for the good of the subject, and the manifestation of his own mercy, wisdom, and love. Therefore, whatever occurs to the righteous man, he will take it for granted that all is well and justly managed, and that the end will be glorious.

Shall be stronger and stronger.] He shall take encouragement from my case, stay himself on the Lord, and thus gain strength by every blast of adversity. This is one grand use of the book of Job. It casts much light on seemingly partial displays of Divine providence: and has ever been the great *text-book* of godly men in a state of persecution and affliction. This is what Job seems prophetically to declare.

Verse 10. *But as for you all*] Ye are too proud, and too full of self-importance, to profit by what ye see. *Return*—enter into yourselves, consider your ways, go again to school, get back to your own houses, and endeavour to acquire humility and knowledge; for there is not one wise man among you.

Verse 11. *My days are past*] Job seems to relapse here into his former state of gloom. These *transitions* are very frequent in this poem; and they strongly mark the struggle of piety and resignation with continued affliction, violent temptation, and gloomy providences.

The thoughts of my heart.] All my purposes are interrupted; and all my schemes and plans, in relation to myself and family, are torn asunder, destroyed, and dissipated.

Verse 12. *They change the night into day*] These purposes and thoughts are so very gloomy, that they change day into night.

The light is *short because of darkness.*] אור קרוב מפני חשך *or karob mippeney choshek,* "The light is near from the face of darkness." I have scarcely any light: what is called *light* is so near akin to darkness, that it is scarcely severed from it. There is either *no light,* or merely such as is sufficient to render *darkness visible.* A fine picture of the state of his mind—he was generally in darkness; but had occasional *gleams* of hope.

Verse 13. *The grave* is *mine house*] Let my life be long or short, the grave at last will be my *home.* I expect soon to lie down in darkness—there is my end: I cannot reasonably hope for any thing else.

Verse 14. *I have said to corruption*] I came from a corrupted stock, and I must go to corruption again. The Hebrew might be thus rendered: *To the ditch I have called, Thou* art *my father. To the worm,* Thou art *my mother and my sister.* I am in the nearest state of affinity to *dissolution* and *corruption:* I may well call them my *nearest relations,* as I shall soon be blended with them.

Verse 15. *And where* is *now my hope?*] In the circumstances in which I am found, of what use can *hope* be? Were I to form the expectation of future good, who could ever see it realized? Is it then any wonder that I should complain and bemoan my wretched lot?

Verse 16. *They shall go down to the bars of the pit*] All that I have must descend into the depths of the grave. Thither are we all going; and there alone can I *rest.*

בַּדֵּי *baddey*, which we translate *bars*, signifies also *branches, distended limbs,* or *claws,* and may here refer either to a personification of the grave, a monster who seizes on human bodies, and keeps them fast in his *deadly gripe;* or to the different *branching-off-alleys* in subterranean cemeteries, or catacombs, in which *niches* are made for the reception of different bodies.

When our *rest together* is *in the dust.*] That is, according to some critics, My *hope* and *myself* shall descend together into the grave. It shall never be realized, for the time of my departure is at hand.

IN those times what deep shades hung on the state of man after death, and on every thing pertaining to the eternal world! Perplexity and uncertainty were the consequences; and a corresponding gloom often dwelt on the minds of even the best of the Old Testament believers. Job's friends, though learned in all the wisdom of the Arabians, connected with the advantages derivable from the Mosaic writings, and perhaps those of the earlier prophets, had little clear or distinct in their minds relative to all subjects *post mortem,* or of the invisible world. Job himself, though sometimes strongly confident, is often harassed with doubts and fears upon the subject, insomuch that his sayings and experience often appear contradictory. Perhaps it could not be otherwise; the true light was not then come: Jesus alone brought life and immortality to light by his Gospel.

CHAPTER XVIII

Bildad, in a speech of passionate invective, accuses Job of impatience and impiety, 1–4; shows the fearful end of the wicked and their posterity; and apparently applies the whole to Job, whom he threatens with the most ruinous end, 5–21.

A. M. cir. 2484
B. C. cir. 1520
Ante I. Olymp.
cir. 744
Ante U. C. cir.
767

THEN answered Bildad the Shuhite, and said,

2 How long *will it be ere* ye make an end of words? mark, and afterwards we will speak.

3 Wherefore are we counted ^aas beasts, *and* reputed vile in your sight?

4 ^bHe teareth ^chimself in his anger: shall the earth be forsaken for thee?

A. M. cir. 2484
B. C. cir. 1520
Ante I. Olymp.
cir. 744
Ante U. C. cir.
767

---

^aPsa. lxxiii. 22——^bChap. xiii. 14

^cHeb. *his soul*

NOTES ON CHAP. XVIII

Verse 1. *Then answered Bildad*] The following analysis of this speech, by Mr. *Heath,* is judicious: "Bildad, irritated to the last degree that Job should treat their advice with so much contempt, is no longer able to keep his passions within the bounds of decency. He proceeds to downright abuse; and finding little attention given by Job to his arguments, he tries to terrify him into a compliance. To that end he draws a yet more terrible picture of the final end of wicked men than any yet preceding, throwing in all the circumstances of Job's calamities, that he might plainly perceive the resemblance; and at the same time insinuating that he had much worse still to expect, unless he prevented it by a speedy change of behaviour. That it was the highest arrogance in him to suppose that he was of consequence enough to be the cause of altering the general rules of Providence, ver. 4. And that it was much more expedient for the good of the whole, that he, by his example, should deter others from treading in the same path of wickedness and folly;" ver. 5–7.

Verse 2. *How long* will it be ere *ye make an end*] It is difficult to say to whom this address is made: being in the *plural* number, it can hardly be supposed to mean Job only. It probably means all present; as if he had said, It is vain to talk with this man, and follow him through all his quibbles: take notice of this, and then let us all deliver our sentiments fully to him, without paying any regard to his self-vindications. It must be owned that this is the plan which Bildad followed; and he amply unburdens a mind that was labouring under the spirit of rancour and abuse. Instead of *How long* will it be ere *ye make an end of words?*

Mr. *Good* translates: "*How long will ye plant thorns* (irritating, lacerating, wounding invectives) *among words?*" translating the unusual term קִנְצֵי *kintsey, thorns,* instead of *bounds* or *limits.* The word קִנְצֵי *kintsey* may be the Chaldee form for קֵצִי *kitsey,* the נ *nun* being inserted by the Chaldeans for the sake of *euphony,* as is frequently done; and it may be considered as the contracted plural from קִין *kats,* a *thorn,* from קַץ *kats,* to lacerate, rather than קֵץ *kets,* an *end,* from קָצָה *katsah,* to cut off.

Schultens and others have contended that קִין *kanats,* is an Arabic word, used also in Hebrew; that كَنَصَ *kanasa,* signifies to *hunt,* to *lay snares;* and hence مَقْنَص *maknas,* a snare: and that the words should be translated, "How long will you put captious snares in words?" But I prefer קִנְצֵי *kintsey,* as being the *Chaldee* form for קֵצִי *kitsey,* whether it be considered as expressing *limits* or *thorns;* as the whole instance is formed after the Chaldee model, as is evident, not only in the word in question, but also in לְמִלִּין *lemillin, to words,* the Chaldee plural instead of לְמִלִּים *lemillim,* the Hebrew plural.

Verse 3. *Counted as beasts*] Thou treatest us as if we had neither reason nor understanding.

Verse 4. *He teareth himself in his anger*] Literally, *Rending his own soul in his anger;* as if he had said, Thou art a madman: thy fury has such a sway over thee that thou eatest thy own flesh. While thou treatest us as beasts, we see thee to be a furious maniac, destroying thy own life.

Shall the earth be forsaken for thee?] To say

A. M. cir. 2484
B. C. cir. 1520
Ante I. Olymp.
cir. 744
Ante U. C. cir.
767

and shall the rock be removed out of his place?

5 Yea, [d]the light of the wicked shall be put out, and the spark of his fire shall not shine.

6 The light shall be dark in his tabernacle, [e]and his [f]candle shall be put out with him.

7 The steps of his strength shall be straitened, and [g]his own counsel shall cast him down.

8 For [h]he is cast into a net by his own feet, and he walketh upon a snare.

9 The gin shall take *him* by the heel, *and* [i]the robber shall prevail against him.

A. M. cir. 2484
B. C. cir. 1520
Ante I. Olymp.
cir. 744
Ante U. C. cir.
767

10 The snare *is* [k]laid for him in the ground, and a trap for him in the way.

11 [l]Terrors shall make him afraid on every side, and shall [m]drive him to his feet.

12 His strength shall be hunger-bitten, and [n]destruction *shall be* ready at his side.

13 It shall devour the [o]strength of his skin: *even* the first-born of death shall devour his strength.

14 [p]His confidence shall be rooted out of

---

[d]Prov. xiii. 9; xx. 20; xxiv. 20——[e]Ch. xxi. 17; Psa. xviii. 28——[f]Or, *lamp*——[g]Ch. v. 13——[h]Ch. xxii. 10; Psa. ix. 15; xxxv. 8——[i]Ch. v. 5——[k]Heb. *hidden*

[l]Ch. xv. 21; xx. 25; Jer. vi. 25; xx. 3; xlvi. 5; xlix. 29 [m]Heb. *scatter him*——[n]Ch. xv. 23——[o]Heb. *bars* [p]Ch. viii. 14; xi. 20; Psa. cxii. 10; Prov. x. 28

---

the least, afflictions are the common lot of men. Must God work a miracle in providence, in order to exempt thee from the operation of natural causes? Dost thou wish to engross all the attention and care of providence to thyself alone? What pride and insolence!

Verse 5. *The light of the wicked shall be put out*] Some think it would be better to translate the original, "Let the light of the wicked be extinguished!" Thou art a bad man, and thou hast perverted the understanding which God hath given thee. Let that understanding, that abused gift, be taken away. From this verse to the end of the chapter is a continual invective against Job.

Verse 6. *The light shall be dark in his tabernacle*] His *property* shall be destroyed, his house pillaged, and himself and his family come to an untimely end.

His candle shall be put out] He shall have no *posterity*.

Verse 7. *The steps of his strength*] Even in his greatest prosperity he shall be in straits and difficulties.

His own counsel] He shall be the dupe and the victim of his own airy, ambitious, and impious schemes.

Verse 8. *For he is cast into a net*] His own conduct will infallibly bring him to ruin. He shall be like a wild beast taken in a net; the more he flounces in order to extricate himself, the more he shall be entangled.

He walketh upon a snare.] He is continually walking on the meshes of a net, by which he must soon be entangled and overthrown.

Verse 9. *The gin shall take* him] Houbigant reads the *tenth* before the *ninth* verse, thus: "The snare is laid for him in the ground, and a trap for him in the way. The gin shall take him by the heel, and the robber shall prevail against him."

From the beginning of the *seventh* verse to the end of the *thirteenth* there is an allusion to the various arts and methods practised in hunting. 1. A number of persons extend themselves in a forest, and drive the game before them, still straitening the space from a broad base to a narrow point in form of a triangle, so that the farther they go the less room have they on the right and left, the hunters lining each side, while the drovers with their dogs are

coming up behind. "The steps of his strength shall be straitened," ver. 7. 2. *Nets, gins,* and *pitfalls,* are laid or formed in different places, so that many are taken before they come to the point where the two lines close. "He is cast into a net, he walketh upon a snare—the trap is laid for him in the way—the snare in the ground," ver. 8, 9, 10. 3. The *howling of the dogs,* with the *shouts* of the *huntsmen,* fill him with dismay, and cause him to run himself beyond his strength and out of breath. "Terrors shall make him afraid on every side, and shall drive him to his feet," ver. 11. 4. While spent with hunger and fatigue, he is entangled in the spread nets; and the huntsman either pierces him with an arrow or spear, or cuts the sinews of his legs, so that he is easily captured and destroyed. "The robbers shall prevail against him," ver. 9. "His strength is hunger-bitten, and destruction is ready at his side," ver. 12. This latter verse is thus paraphrased by the Chaldee: "Let his first-born son be famished; and affliction be prepared for his wife."

Verse 13. *It shall devour the strength of his skin*] This may refer to the *elephant,* or to the *rhinoceros,* whose skin scarcely any dart can pierce: but in the case referred to above, the animal is taken in a pitfall, and then the *first-born of death*—a sudden and *overwhelming stroke*—deprives him of life. See the account of hunting the *elephant* in the East at the end of the chapter. The Chaldee has: "The strength of his skin shall devour his flesh; and the angel of death shall consume his children."

Verse 14. *His confidence shall be rooted out*] His dwelling-place, how well soever fortified, shall now be deemed utterly insecure.

And it shall bring him to the king of terrors.] Or, as Mr. *Good* translates, "And dissolution shall invade him as a monarch." He shall be completely and finally overpowered.

The phrase *king of terrors* has been generally thought to mean *death;* but it is not used in any such way in the text. For לְמֶלֶךְ בַּלָּהוֹת *lemelech ballahoth, to the king of destructions,* one of *De Rossi's* MSS. has כְּמֶלֶךְ *kemelech,* "as a king;" and one, instead of בַּלָּהוֹת *ballahoth,* with ו *vau holem,* to indicate the *plural, terrors* or *destructions,* has בַּלָּהוּת *ballahuth,* with ו *vau shurek,* which is *singular,* and singnifies *terror,*

A. M. cir. 2484
B. C. cir. 1520
Ante I. Olymp.
cir. 744
Ante U. C. cir.
767

his tabernacle, and it shall bring him to the king of terrors.

15 It shall dwell in his tabernacle, because *it is* none of his:

brimstone shall be scattered upon his habitation.

16 ᑫHis roots shall be dried up beneath, and above

A. M. cir. 2484
B. C. cir. 1520
Ante I. Olymp.
cir. 744
Ante U. C. cir.
767

ᑫChap. xxix. 19; Isa. v. 24;   Amos ii. 9; Mal. iv. 1

---

destruction. So the Vulgate seems to have read, as it translates, *Et calcet super eum, quasi rex, interitus;* "And shall tread upon him as a king or destroyer. Or as a king who is determined utterly to destroy him." On this verse the bishop of Killala, Dr. Stock, says, "I am sorry to part with a beautiful phrase in our common version, *the king of terrors,* as descriptive of *death;* but there is no authority for it in the Hebrew text."

It may however be stated that death has been denominated by similar epithets both among the Greeks and Romans.

So *Virgil,* Æn. vi., ver. 100.
————Quando hic *inferni* janua *regis*
Dicitur.

"The gates of the *king of hell* are reported to be here."

And OVID, Metam. lib. v., ver. 356, 359.

Inde tremit tellus: et rex pavit ipse silentum.
Hanc metuens cladem, tenebrosa sede tyrannus
Exierat.

"Earth's inmost bowels quake, and nature groans;
His terrors reach the direful KING of HELL.
Fearing this destruction, the *tyrant* left his *gloomy court.*"

And in SOPHOCLES, (Œdip. Colon., ver. 1628, edit. Johnson.)

Εννυχιων αναξ,
Αιδωνευ.

"O Pluto, *king of shades.*" That is, the invisible demon, who dwells in darkness impenetrable.

Old COVERDALE translates: 𝔙𝔢𝔯𝔶 𝔣𝔢𝔞𝔯𝔣𝔲𝔩𝔫𝔢𝔰𝔰𝔢 𝔰𝔥𝔞𝔩𝔩 𝔟𝔯𝔦𝔫𝔤𝔢 𝔥𝔦𝔪 𝔱𝔬 𝔱𝔥𝔢 𝔨𝔶𝔫𝔤𝔢.

Verse 15. *It shall dwell in his tabernacle*] *Desolation* is here *personified,* and it is said that it shall be the inhabitant, its former owner being destroyed. *Brimstone shall be scattered upon his habitation,* so that, like Sodom and Gomorrah, it may be an everlasting monument of the Divine displeasure.

In the Persian poet *Saady,* we find a couplet which contains a similar sentiment:—

پرده داری میكند در قصر قیصر عنكبوت
بومی نوبت میزند بر كنبد افراسیاب

Purdeh daree meekund dar keesri Keesar anke-boot
Boomee Noobat meezund ber kumbed Afraseeab.

"The spider holds the veil in the palace of Cæsar;
The owl stands sentinel on the watchtower of Afrasiab."

The palaces of those mighty kings are so desolate that the *spider* is the only *chamberlain,* and the *owl* the only *sentinel.* The *web* of the former is all that remains as a substitute for the *costly veil* furnished by the *chamberlain* in the palace of the *Roman monarch;* and the *hooting* of the latter is the only remaining substitute for the sound of *drums* and *trumpets* by which the *guards* were accustomed *to be relieved* at the watchtower of the *Persian king.*

The word قیصر *Keesur,* the same as Καισαρ or *Cæsar,* is the term which the Asiatics always use when they designate the *Roman emperor.*

Afrasiab was an ancient king who invaded and conquered Persia about *seven hundred* years before the Christian era. After having reigned *twelve* years, he was defeated and slain by *Zalzer* and his son, the famous *Rustem.* The present reigning family of Constantinople claim descent from this ancient monarch.

Brimstone shall be scattered upon his habitation.] This may either refer to the destruction of Sodom and Gomorrah, as has already been intimated, or to an ancient custom of *fumigating houses* with brimstone, in order to *purify* them from defilement. PLINY says, Hist. Nat., lib. xxxv., c. 15, speaking of the uses of sulphur, *Habet et in religionibus locum ad expiandas suffitu domos;* which Dr. *Holland* paraphrases thus: "Moreover brimstone is employed ceremoniously in hallowing of houses; for many are of opinion that the perfume and burning thereof will keep out all enchantments; yea, and drive away foul fiends and evil sprites that do haunt a place."

OVID refers to the same, *De Arte. Am.,* lib. ii., ver. 329.

Et veniat, quæ *lustret* anus *lectumque locumque:*
Præferat et tremula *sulphur* et ova manu.

This alludes to the ceremony of purifying the *bed* or place in which a sick person was confined; an *old woman* or *nurse* was the operator, and *eggs* and *sulphur* were the instruments of *purification.*

On this and other methods of purgation see an excellent note in Servius on these words of Virgil, Æn. vi., ver. 740.

————— Aliæ panduntur inanes
Suspensæ ad ventos: aliis sub gurgite vasto
Infectum eluitur scelus, aut exuritur igni.

"For this are various penances subjoin'd;
And some are hung to bleach upon the wind;
Some plunged in waters, others, plunged in fires."

Unde etiam, says *Servius,* in sacris Liberi omnibus tres sunt istæ purgationes: nam aut *tæda* purgantur et *sulphure,* aut *aqua* abluuntur, aut *aëre* ventilantur.

"These three kinds of purgation are used in the rites of Bacchus: they are purged by flame and sulphur, or washed in water, or ventilated by the winds."

A. M. cir. 2484
B. C. cir. 1520
Ante I. Olymp.
cir. 744
Ante U. C. cir.
767

shall his branch be cut off. 17 ʳHis remembrance shall perish from the earth, and he shall have no name in the street.

18 ˢHe shall be driven from light into darkness, and chased out of the world.

19 ᵗHe shall neither have son nor nephew among his people, nor any remaining in his dwellings.

A. M. cir. 2484
B. C. cir. 1520
Ante I. Olymp.
cir. 744
Ante U. C. cir.
767

20 They that come after *him* shall be astonied at ᵘhis day, as they that ᵛwent before ʷwere affrighted.

21 Surely such *are* the dwellings of the wicked, and this *is* the place *of him that* ˣknoweth not God.

ʳPsa. xxxiv. 16; cix. 13; Prov. ii. 22; x. 7——ˢHeb. *they shall drive him*——ᵗIsa. xiv. 32; Jer. xxii. 30 ᵘPsa. xxxvii. 16

ᵛOr, *lived with him*——ʷHebrew, *laid hold on horror* ˣJeremiah ix. 3; x. 25; 1 Thess. iv. 5; 2 Thess. i. 8; Tit. i. 16

But it is most likely that Bildad, in his usual uncharitable manner, alludes to the destruction of Job's property and family by *winds* and *fire: for the* FIRE OF GOD *fell from heaven and burnt up the sheep and the servants, and* CONSUMED *them; and a great wind,* probably the *sulphureous suffocating simoom, smote the four corners of the house,* where Job's children were feasting, and killed them; see chap. i. 16, 19.

Verse 16. *His roots shall be dried up—his branch be cut off.*] He shall be as utterly destroyed, both in *himself,* his *posterity,* and his *property,* as a tree is whose branches are all lopped off, and whose every root is cut away.

Verse 17. *His remembrance shall perish*] He shall have none to survive him, to continue his name among men.

No name in the street.] He shall never be a man of reputation; after his demise, none shall talk of his *fame.*

Verse 18. *He shall be driven from light*] He shall be taken off by a violent death.

And chased out of the world.] The wicked is DRIVEN AWAY in *his iniquity.* This shows his reluctance to depart from life.

Verse 19. *He shall neither have son nor nephew*] *Coverdale,* following the *Vulgate,* translates thus: 𝔥𝔢 𝔰𝔥𝔞𝔩 𝔫𝔢𝔦𝔱𝔥𝔢𝔯 𝔥𝔞𝔟𝔢 𝔠𝔥𝔦𝔩𝔡𝔯𝔢𝔫 𝔫𝔢𝔯 𝔨𝔭𝔫𝔰𝔰 𝔣𝔬𝔩𝔨 𝔞𝔪𝔬𝔫𝔤 𝔥𝔦𝔰 𝔭𝔢𝔬𝔭𝔩𝔢, 𝔫𝔬 𝔫𝔢𝔯 𝔢𝔫𝔭 𝔭𝔬𝔰𝔱𝔢𝔯𝔦𝔱𝔢 𝔦𝔫 𝔥𝔦𝔰 𝔠𝔬𝔲𝔫𝔱𝔯𝔦𝔢 : 𝔭𝔬𝔫𝔤𝔢 𝔞𝔫𝔡 𝔬𝔩𝔡𝔢 𝔰𝔥𝔞𝔩 𝔟𝔢 𝔞𝔰𝔱𝔬𝔫𝔭𝔰𝔥𝔢𝔡 𝔞𝔱 𝔥𝔦𝔰 𝔡𝔢𝔞𝔱𝔥.

Verse 20. *They that come after* him] The *young* shall be struck with astonishment when they hear the relation of the judgments of God upon this wicked man. *As they that went before.* The *aged* who were his contemporaries, and who saw the judgments that fell on him, were affrighted, אחזו שער *achazu saar, seized with horror*—were horrified; or, as Mr. *Good* has well expressed it, *were panic-struck.*

Verse 21. *Such are the dwellings*] This is the common lot of the wicked; and it shall be particularly the case with him *who knoweth not God,* that is *Job,* for it is evident he alludes to him. Poor Job! hard was thy lot, severe were thy sufferings.

ON the elephant hunt to which I have referred, ver. 13, I shall borrow the following account extracted from Mr. Cordiner's History of Ceylon, by Mr. *Good:*—

"We have a curious description of the elephant hunt, which is pursued in a manner not essentially different from the preceding, except that the snares are pallisadoed with the strongest possible stakes, instead of being netted, and still farther fortified by interlacings. They are numerous, but connected together; every snare or inclosure growing gradually narrower, and opening into each other by a gate or two that will only admit the entrance of a single animal at a time.

"The wood in which elephants are known to abound is first surrounded, excepting at the end where the foremost and widest inclosure is situated, with fires placed on moveable pedestals, which in every direction are drawn closer and closer, and, aided by loud and perpetual shouts, drive the animals forward till they enter into the outer snare. After which the same process is continued, and they are driven by fear into a second, into a third, and into a fourth; till at length the elephants become so much subdivided, that by the aid of cordage fastened carefully round their limbs, and the management of decoy elephants, they are easily capable of being led away one by one, and tamed. A single hunt thus conducted will sometimes occupy not less than two months of unremitting labour; and the entrance of the elephants into the snares is regarded as an amusement or sport of the highest character, and as such is attended by all the principal families of the country." *Account of Ceylon,* p. 218-226.

CHAPTER XIX

Job complains of the cruelty of his friends, 1–5. Pathetically laments his sufferings, 6–12. Complains of his being forsaken by all his domestics, friends, relatives, and even his wife, 13–19. Details his sufferings in an affecting manner, calls upon his friends to pity him, and earnestly wishes that his speeches may be recorded, 20–24. Expresses his hope in a future resurrection, 25–27. And warns his persecutors to desist, lest they fall under God's judgments, 28, 29.

A. M. cir. 2484
B. C. cir. 1520
Ante I. Olymp.
cir. 744
Ante U. C. cir.
767

THEN Job answered and said, 2 How long will ye vex my soul, and break me in pieces with words?

3 These [a]ten times have ye reproached me: ye are not ashamed *that* ye [b]make yourselves strange to me.

4 And be it indeed *that* I have erred, mine error remaineth with myself.

5 If indeed ye will [c]magnify *yourselves* against me, and plead against me my reproach:

6 Know now that God hath overthrown me, and hath compassed me with his net.

A. M. cir. 2484
B. C. cir. 1520
Ante I. Olymp.
cir. 744
Ante U. C. cir.
767

7 Behold, I cry out of [d]wrong, but I am not heard: I cry aloud, but *there is* no judgment.

8 [e]He hath fenced up my way that I cannot pass, and he hath set darkness in my paths.

9 [f]He hath stripped me of my glory, and taken the crown *from* my head.

10 He hath destroyed me on every side,

---

[a]Gen. xxxi. 7; Lev. xxvi. 26——[b]Or, *harden yourselves against me*——[c]Psa. xxxviii. 16

[d]Or, *violence*——[e]Chap. iii. 23; Psa. lxxxviii. 8——[f]Psa. lxxxix. 44

NOTES ON CHAP. XIX

Verse 2. *How long will ye vex my soul*] Every thing that was irritating, vexatious, and opprobrious, his friends had recourse to, in order to support their own system, and overwhelm him. Not one of them seems to have been touched with a feeling of tenderness towards him, nor does a kind expression drop at any time from their lips! They were called *friends;* but this term, in reference to them, must be taken in the sense of *cold-blooded acquaintances.* However, there are many in the world that go under the sacred name of *friends*, who, in times of difficulty, act a similar part. Job's friends have been, by the general consent of posterity, consigned to endless infamy. May all those who follow their steps be equally enrolled in the annals of bad fame!

Verse 3. *These ten times*] The exact arithmetical number is not to be regarded; *ten times* being put for many times, as we have already seen. See particularly the note on Gen. xxxi. 7.

Ye make yourselves strange to me.] When I was in affluence and prosperity, ye were my intimates, and appeared to rejoice in my happiness; but now ye scarcely know me, or ye profess to consider me a wicked man because I am in adversity. Of this you had no suspicion when I was in prosperity! Circumstances change men's minds.

Verse 4. *And be it indeed* that *I have erred*] Suppose indeed that I have been mistaken in any thing, that in the simplicity of my heart I have gone astray, and that this matter remains with myself, (for most certainly there is no public stain on my life,) you must grant that this error, whatsoever it is, has hurt no person except myself. Why then do ye treat me as a person whose life has been a general blot, and whose example must be a public curse?

Verse 6. *Know now that God hath overthrown me*] The matter is between him and me, and he has not commissioned *you* to add reproaches to *his* chastisements.

And hath compassed me with his net.] There may be an allusion here to the different modes of *hunting* which have been already referred to in the preceding chapter. But if we take the whole verse together, and read the latter clause before the former, thus, "Know, therefore, that God hath encompassed me with his net, and overthrown me;" the allusion may be to an ancient mode of combat practised among the ancient Persians, ancient Goths, and among the

Romans. The custom among the Romans was this: "One of the combatants was armed with a *sword* and *shield*, the other with a *trident* and *net*. The *net* he endeavoured to cast over the head of his adversary, in which, when he succeeded, the entangled person was soon pulled down by a noose that fastened round the neck, and then despatched. The person who carried the *net* and *trident* was called *Retiarius*, and the other who carried the sword and shield was termed *Secutor*, or the *pursuer*, because, when the *Retiarius* missed his throw, he was obliged to run about the ground till he got his net in order for a second throw, while the *Secutor* followed hard to prevent and despatch him." The *Persians* in old times used what was called كُمُنْد *kumund*, *the noose*. It was not a *net*, but a sort of *running loop*, which horsemen endeavoured to cast over the heads of their enemies that they might pull them off their horses.

That the *Goths* used a *hoop net* fastened to a pole, which they endeavoured to throw over the heads of their foes, is attested by *Olaus Magnus, Hist. de Gentibus Septentrionalibus*, Rom. 1555, lib. xi., cap. 13, *De diversis Modis præliandi Finnorum*. His words are, Quidam restibus instar *retium* ferinorum ductilibus sublimi jactatione utuntur: ubi enim cum hoste congressi sunt, injiciunt eos restes quasi laqueos in caput resistentis, ut equum aut hominem ad se trahant. "Some use elastic ropes, formed like hunting nets, which they throw aloft; and when they come in contact with the enemy, they throw these ropes over the head of their opponent, and by this means they can then drag either man or horse to themselves." At the head of the page he gives a wood-cut representing the *net*, and the manner of throwing it over the head of the enemy. To such a device Job might allude, *God hath encompassed me with his* NET, *and overthrown me.*

Verse 7. *I cry out of wrong*] I complain of violence and of injustice; but no one comes to my help.

Verse 8. *He hath fenced up my way*] This may allude to the mode of hunting the elephant, described at the conclusion of the preceding chapter; or to the operations of an invading army. See under ver. 11.

Verse 9. *He hath stripped me of my glory*] I am reduced to such circumstances, that I have lost all my honour and respect.

Verse 10. *Mine hope hath he removed like a tree.*] There is no more hope of my restoration to affluence, authority, and respect, than there

A. M. cir. 2484
B. C. cir. 1520
Ante I. Olymp.
cir. 744
Ante U. C. cir.
767

and I am gone: and mine hope hath he removed like a tree.

11 He hath also kindled his wrath against me, and ᵍhe counteth me unto him as *one of* his enemies.

12 His troops come together, and ʰraise up their way against me, and encamp round about my tabernacle.

13 ⁱHe hath put my brethren far from me, and mine acquaintance are verily estranged from me.

14 My kinsfolk have failed, and my familiar friends have forgotten me.

15 They that dwell in mine house, and my maids, count me for a stranger: I am an alien in their sight.

A. M. cir. 2484
B. C. cir. 1520
Ante I. Olymp.
cir. 744
Ante U. C. cir.
767

16 I called my servant, and he gave *me* no answer; I entreated him with my mouth.

17 My breath is strange to my wife, though I entreated for the children's *sake* of ᵏmine own body.

18 Yea, ˡyoung ᵐchildren despised me; I arose, and they spake against me.

19 ⁿAll ᵒmy inward friends abhorred me: and they whom I loved are turned against me.

20 ᵖMy bone cleaveth to my skin, ᑫand to

ᵍChapter xiii. 24; Lam. ii. 5——ʰChapter xxx. 12
ⁱPsalm xxxi. 11; xxxviii. 11; lxix. 8; lxxxviii. 8, 18
ᵏHeb. *my belly*——ˡOr, *the wicked*

ᵐ2 Kings ii. 23——ⁿPsalm xli. 9; lv. 13, 14, 20
ᵒHebrew, *the men of my secret*——ᵖChap. xxx. 30;
Psa. cii. 5; Lam. iv. 8——ᑫOr, *as*

---

is that a tree shall grow and flourish, whose roots are extracted from the earth. I am pulled up by the roots, withered, and *gone*.

Verse 11. *And he counteth me unto him as one of his enemies*.] From the *seventh* to the *thirteenth* verse there seems to be an allusion to a hostile invasion, battles, sieges, &c. 1. A neighbouring chief, *without provocation*, invades his neighbour's territories, and none of his friends will come to his help. "I cry out of wrong, but I am not heard," ver. 7. 2. The foe has seized on all the passes, and he is hemmed up. "He hath fenced up my way that I cannot pass," ver. 8. 3. He has surprised and carried by assault the regal city, seized and possessed the treasures. "He hath stripped me of my glory, and taken the crown from my head," ver. 9. 4. All his armies are routed in the field, and his strong places carried. "He hath destroyed me on every side," ver. 10. 5. The enemy proceeds to the greatest length of outrage, wasting every thing with fire and sword. "He hath kindled his wrath against me, and treateth me like one of his adversaries, ver. 11. 6. He is cooped up in a small camp with the wrecks of his army; and in this he is closely besieged by all the power of his foes, who encompass the place, and *raise forts* against it. "His troops come together, and raise up their way against me, and encamp round about my tabernacle." 7. Not receiving any assistance from friends or neighbours, he abandons all hope of being able to keep the field, escapes with the utmost difficulty, and is despised and neglected by his friends and domestics because he has been unfortunate. "I am escaped with the skin of my teeth," ver. 20. "My kinsfolk have failed—all my intimate friends abhorred me," ver. 14-19.

Verse 14. *My kinsfolk have failed*] Literally, *departed*: they have all left my house now there is no more hope of *gain*.

Verse 15. *They that dwell in mine house*] In this and the following verses the disregard and contempt usually shown to men who have fallen from affluence and authority into poverty and dependence, are very forcibly described: formerly reverenced by *all*, now esteemed by none. Pity to those who have fallen into adversity is rarely shown; the *rich have many friends*, and

to him who appears to be gaining worldly substance much court is paid; for *many worship the rising sun, who think little of that which is gone down*. Some are even reproached with that eminence which they have lost, though not culpable for the loss. A *bishop*, perhaps *Bale*, of *Ossory*, being obliged to leave his country and fly for his life, in the days of bloody Queen Mary, and who never regained his bishopric, was met one morning by one like those whom Job describes, who, intending to be witty at the expense of the venerable prelate, accosted him thus: "Good morrow, ʙɪsʜᴏᴘ *quondam*." To which the bishop smartly replied, "Adieu, ᴋɴᴀᴠᴇ *semper*."

Verse 17. *Though I entreated for the children's sake of mine own body*.] This may imply no more than adjuring her by the tenderest ties, by their affectionate intercourse, and consequently by the *children* which had been the seals of their mutual affection, though these children were no more.

But the mention of his *children* in this place may intimate that he had still some remaining; that there might have been *young ones*, who, not being of a proper age to attend the festival of their elder brothers and sisters, escaped that sad catastrophe. The *Septuagint* have, Προσεκαλουμην δε κολακευων υιους παλλακιδων μου, "I affectionately entreated the *children of my concubines*." But there is no ground in the Hebrew text for such a strange exceptionable rendering. *Coverdale* has, 𝔍 am fayne to speake fayre to the chíldren of myne own body.

Verse 19. *My inward friends*] Those who were my greatest *intimates*.

Verse 20. *My bone cleaveth to my skin*.] My flesh is entirely wasted away, and nothing but skin and bone left.

I am escaped with the skin of my teeth.] I have had the most narrow escape. If I still live, it is a thing to be wondered at, my sufferings and privations have been so great. To *escape with the skin of the teeth* seems to have been a proverbial expression, signifying great difficulty. I had as narrow an escape from death, as the thickness of the enamel on the teeth. I was within a hair's breadth of destruction; see on verse 11.

A. M. cir. 2484
B. C. cir. 1520
Ante I. Olymp.
cir. 744
Ante U. C. cir.
767

my flesh, and I am escaped with the skin of my teeth.

21 Have pity upon me, have pity upon me, O ye my friends; ʳfor the hand of God hath touched me.

22 Why do ye ˢpersecute me as God, and are not satisfied with my flesh?

ʳChap. i. 11; Psa. xxxviii. 2

---

23 ᵗO that my words were now written! O that they were printed in a book!

A. M. cir. 2484
B. C. cir. 1520
Ante I. Olymp.
cir. 744
Ante U. C. cir.
767

24 That they were graven with an iron pen and lead in the rock for ever!

25 For I know *that* my Redeemer liveth, and

ˢPsa. lxix. 26——ᵗHeb. *Who will give*, &c.

Verse 21. *Have pity upon me*] The iteration here strongly indicates the depth of his distress, and that his spirit was worn down with the length and severity of his suffering.

Verse 22. *Why do ye persecute me as God*] Are not the afflictions which God sends enough? Do ye not see that I have as much as I can bear? When the papists were burning Dr. Taylor at Oxford, while wrapped in the flames, one of the true sons of the Church took a stick out of the faggots, and threw it at his head, and split open his face. To whom he calmly said, *Man, why this wrong? Do not I suffer enough?*

And are not satisfied with my flesh?] Will ye persecute my *soul*, while God is persecuting my *body?* Is it not enough that my *body* is destroyed? Why then labour to torment my *mind?*

Verse 23. *O that my words were now written!*] Job introduces the important subject which follows in a manner unusually solemn; and he certainly considers the words which he was about to utter of great moment, and therefore wishes them to be *recorded* in every possible way. All the modes of writing then in use he appears to refer to. As to *printing*, that should be out of the question, as no such art was *then* discovered, nor for nearly *two thousand* years after. Our translators have made a strange mistake by rendering the verb יחקו *yuchaku, printed,* when they should have used *described, traced out.* O that my words were fairly traced out in a book! It is necessary to make this remark, because superficial readers have imagined that the *art of printing* existed in Job's time, and that it was not a discovery of the *fifteenth* century of the Christian era: whereas there is no proof that it ever existed in the world before A. D. 1440, or thereabouts, for the first printed book with a date is a *psalter* printed by *John Fust,* in 1457, and the first *Bible* with a date is that by the same artist in 1460.

Three kinds of writing Job alludes to, as being practised in his time: 1. *Writing in a book,* formed either of the leaves of the *papyrus,* already described, (see on chap. viii. 11,) or on a sort of *linen cloth.* A roll of this kind, with unknown characters, I have seen taken out of the envelopments of an Egyptian mummy. *Denon,* in his travels in Egypt, gives an account of a book of this kind, with an engraved *facsimile,* taken also out of an Egyptian mummy. 2. *Cutting with an iron stile on plates of lead.* 3. *Engraving on large stones* or *rocks,* many of which are still found in different parts of Arabia.

To the present day the *leaves* of the *palm tree* are used in the East instead of *paper,* and a *stile* of brass, silver, iron, &c., with a *steel point,* serves for a pen. By this instrument the letters are cut or engraved on the substance of the leaf, and afterwards some black colouring matter is rubbed in, in order to make the letters apparent. This was probably the oldest mode of writing, and it continues among the Cingalese to the present day. It is worthy of remark that Pliny (*Hist. Nat.*, lib. xiii., c. 11) mentions most of these methods of writing, and states that the *leaves* of the *palm tree* were used before other substances were invented. After showing that *paper* was not used before the conquest of Egypt by Alexander the Great, he proceeds: In palmarum foliis primo scriptitatum; deinde quarundam arborum libris: postea publica monumenta plumbeis voluminibus, mox et privata linteis confici cœpta, aut ceris. "At first men wrote on palm tree leaves, and afterwards on the bark or rind of other trees. In process of time, public monuments were written on *rolls of lead,* and those of a private nature on *linen books,* or tables covered with *wax.*"

Pausanias, lib. xii., c. 31, giving an account of the Bœotians, who dwelt near fount Helicon, states the following fact:—Και μοι μολιβδον εδεικνυσαν, ενθα ἡ πηγη, τα πολλα ὑπο του χρονου λελυμασμενον, εγγεγραπται γαρ αυτῳ τα εργα; "They showed me a *leaden table* near to the fountain, on which his works (*Hesiod's*) were written; but a great part had perished by the injuries of time."

Verse 24. *Iron pen and lead*] Some suppose that the meaning of this place is this: the *iron pen* is the *chisel* by which the letters were to be *deeply cut* in the *stone* or *rock;* and the *lead* was melted into those cavities in order to preserve the engraving distinct. But this is not so natural a supposition as what is stated above; that Job refers to the different kinds of writing or perpetuating public events, used in his time: and the quotations from *Pliny* and *Pausanias* confirm the opinion already expressed.

Verse 25. *For I know that my Redeemer liveth*] Any attempt to establish the *true meaning* of this passage is almost hopeless. By learned men and eminent critics the words have been understood very differently; some vehemently contending that they refer to the *resurrection of the body, and the redemption of the human race by Jesus Christ;* while others, with equal vehemence and show of argument, have contended that they refer only *to Job's restoration to health, family comforts, and general prosperity, after the present trial should be ended.* In defence of these two opinions larger treatises have been written than the whole book of Job would amount to, if written even in *capitals.* To discuss the arguments on either side the nature of this work forbids; but my own view of the subject will be reasonably expected by the reader. I shall therefore lay down *one principle,* without which no mode of interpreta-

A. M. cir. 2484
B. C. cir. 1520
Ante I. Olymp.
cir. 744
Ante U. C. cir.
767

that he shall stand at the latter *day* upon the earth:

26 ᵘAnd *though* after my skin *worms* destroy this *body,* yet ᵛin my flesh shall I see God:

27 Whom I shall see for myself, and mine eyes shall behold, and not ᵂanother; ˣ*though* my reins be consumed ʸwithin me.

A. M. cir. 2484
B. C. cir. 1520
Ante I. Olymp.
cir. 744
Ante U. C. cir.
767

ᵘOr, *After I shall awake, though this* body *be destroyed, yet out of my flesh shall I see God*——ᵛPsa. xvii. 15; 1 Cor. xiii. 12; 1 John iii. 2

ᵂHeb. *a stranger*——ˣOr, *my veins within me are consumed with earnest desire* [for that day]——ʸHeb. *in my bosom*

---

tion hitherto offered can have any weight. The principle is this: *Job was now under the especial inspiration of the Holy Spirit, and spoke prophetically.*

Now, whether we allow that the passage refers to the *general resurrection* and *the redemption by Christ,* or to Job's *restoration to health, happiness, and prosperity,* this principle is equally necessary. 1. In those times no man could speak so clearly concerning the general resurrection and the redemption by Jesus Christ as Job, by one class of interpreters, is supposed here to do, unless especially inspired for this very purpose. 2. Job's restoration to health and happiness, which, though it did take place, was so totally improbable to himself all the way through, so wholly unexpected, and, in every sense, impossible, except to the almighty power of God, that it could not be *inferred* from any thing that had already taken place, and must be foreshown by direct inspiration. Now, that it was *equally easy* to predict either of these events, will be at once evident, because both were in *futurity,* and both were *previously determined.* Nothing *contingent* could exist in either; with them *man* had nothing to do; and they were equally within the knowledge of Him to whose *ubiquity* there can be neither *past* nor *future time;* in whose *presence absolute and contingent events* subsist in their own *distinctive characters,* and are never resolved into each other.

But another question may arise, *Which was most likely to be the subject of this oracular declaration, the general resurrection and redemption by Christ; or the restoration of Job to health and affluence?*

If we look only to the *general importance* of these things, this question may be soon decided; for the doctrine of human redemption, and the general resurrection to an eternal life, are of infinitely greater importance than any thing that could affect the personal welfare of Job. We may therefore say, of two things which only the power of God can effect, and one of which only shall be done, it is natural to conclude he will do that which is of most importance; and that is of most importance by which a greater measure of glory is secured to himself, and a greater sum of good produced to mankind.

As, therefore, a revelation by which the *whole human race,* in all its successive generations, to the end of time, may be most essentially benefited, is superior in its worth and importance to that by which *one man* only can be benefited, it is natural to conclude here, that the revelation relative to the general resurrection, &c., is that which most likely the text includes.

But to this it may be answered, God does not do always in the first instance that which is most necessary and important *in itself,* as every

thing is done in that *order* and in that *time* which seems best to his godly wisdom; therefore, a thing of *less importance* may be done *now,* and a thing of *greater importance* left to a *future time.* So, God made the *earth* before he made *man,* produced *light* before he formed the *celestial luminaries,* and instituted the *Mosaic economy* before the *Christian dispensation.* This is all true, for every thing is done in that *season* in which it may best fulfil the designs of providence and grace. But the question still recurs, Which of the predictions was most congruous to the circumstances of Job, and those of his companions; and which of them was most likely to do most good on that occasion, and to be most useful through the subsequent ages of the world? The subject is now considerably narrowed; and, if this question could be satisfactorily answered, the true meaning of the passage would be at once found out. 1. For the sake of righteousness, justice, and truth, and to vindicate the ways of God with man, it was necessary that Job's *innocence* should be cleared; that the false judgments of his friends should be corrected; and that, as Job was now reduced to a state of the lowest distress, it was worthy the kindness of God to give him some direct intimation that his sufferings should have a happy termination. That such an event *ought* to take place, there can be no question: and that it did take place, is asserted in the book; and that Job's friends *saw* it, were reproved, corrected, and admitted into his favour of whom they *did not speak that which was right,* and who had, in consequence, *God's wrath kindled against them,* are also attested facts. But surely there was no need of *so solemn a revelation* to inform them of what was shortly to take place, when they lived to see it; nor can it be judged essentially necessary to the support of Job, when the ordinary consolations of God's Spirit, and the excitement of a good hope through grace, might have as completely answered the end.

2. On the other hand, to give men, who were the chiefs of their respective tribes, proper notice of a doctrine of which they appear to have had no adequate conception, and which was so necessary to the peace of society, the good government of men, and the control of unruly and wayward passions, which the doctrine of the general resurrection and consequent judgment is well calculated to produce; and to stay and support the suffering godly under the afflictions and calamities of life; were objects worthy the highest regards of infinite philanthropy and justice, and of the most pointed and solemn revelation which could be given on such an occasion. In short, they are the *grounds* on which *all revelation* is given to the sons of men: and the prophecy in question, viewed in this light, was, in that dark age and country, *a light shining in a dark place;* for the doctrine of the gen-

A. M. cir. 2484
B. C. cir. 1520
Ante I. Olymp.
cir. 744
Ante U. C. cir.
767

28 But ye should say, ᶻWhy persecute we him, ᵃseeing the root of the matter is found in me?

29 Be ye afraid of the sword: for wrath *bringeth* the punishments of the sword, ᵇthat ye may know *there is* a judgment.

A. M. cir. 2484
B. C. cir. 1520
Ante I. Olymp
cir. 744
Ante U. C. cir.
767

ᶻVer. 22——ᵃOr, *and* what *root of matter is found in me?*——ᵇPsa. lviii. 10, 11

---

eral resurrection, and of future rewards and punishments, existed among the *Arabs* from time immemorial, and was a part of the public creed of the different tribes when Mohammed endeavoured to establish his own views of that resurrection and of future rewards and punishments, by the edge of the sword. I have thus endeavoured dispassionately to view this subject; and having instituted the preceding mode of reasoning, without foreseeing where it would tend, being only desirous to find out truth, I arrive at the conclusion, that the prophecy in question was not designed to point out the *future prosperity of Job;* but rather the *future redemption of mankind by Jesus Christ, and the general resurrection of the human race.*

After what has been stated above, a short paraphrase on the words of the text will be all that is necessary to be added.

I know, ידעתי *yadati,* I have a firm and full persuasion, *that my Redeemer,* גאלי *goali,* my *Kinsman,* he whose right it was among the ancient Hebrews to redeem the forfeited heritages belonging to the family, to vindicate its honour, and to avenge the death of any of his relatives by slaying the murderer; (Lev. xxv. 25; Num. xxxv. 12; Ruth iii. 13;) but here it must refer to *Christ,* who has truly the *right* of redemption, being of the *same kindred,* who was *born of woman, flesh of flesh and bone of our bone.*

Liveth, חי *chai,* is the living One, who has the keys of hell and death: the Creator and Lord of the spirits of all flesh, and the principle and support of all *life.*

And that *he shall stand at the latter* day *upon the earth.* The latter day, אחרון *acharon,* the latter day, or *time,* when God comes to judgment; or *finally,* or *at last,* or *in the last time,* or *latter days,* as the Gospel is termed, he shall be manifested in the flesh.

He shall stand, יקום *yakum,* he shall arise, or stand up, i. e., to give sentence in judgment: or he himself shall arise from the dust, as the passage has been understood by some to refer to the resurrection of Christ from the dead.

Upon the earth, על עפר *al aphar,* over the dead, or those who are reduced to *dust.* This is the meaning of עפר *aphar* in Psa. xxx. 9: *What profit is there in my blood when I go down to the pit? Shall the* DUST *(i. e., the dead) praise thee? He shall arise over the dust* —over them who sleep in the dust, whom he shall also raise up.

Verse 26. *And though after my skin* worms *destroy this* body] *My skin,* which is now almost all that remains *of* my former self, except the bones; see ver. 20. *They destroy this*—not body. נקפו זאת *nikkephu zoth, they*—diseases and affliction, destroy THIS wretched composition of misery and corruption.

Yet in my flesh shall I see God] Either, I shall arise from the dead, have a renewed body, and see him with eyes of flesh and blood, though what I have now shall shortly moulder into

dust; or, I shall see him *in the flesh;* my *Kinsman,* who shall partake of my flesh and blood, in order that he may ransom the lost inheritance.

Verse 27. *Whom I shall see for myself*] Have a personal interest in the *resurrection,* as I shall have in the *Redeemer.*

And mine eyes shall behold] That very person who shall be the *resurrection,* as he is the *life.*

And not another] ולא זר *velo zar,* and not a *stranger,* one who has *no relation* to human nature; but גאלי *goali,* my redeeming Kinsman.

Though my reins be consumed within me.] Though I am now apparently on the brink of death, the thread of life being spun out to extreme tenuity.

This, on the mode of interpretation which I have assumed, appears to be the meaning of this passage. The words may have a somewhat different colouring put on them; but the basis of the interpretation will be the same.

I shall conclude with the version of *Coverdale:*—

𝔉or 𝔍 am sure that my 𝔯edeemer liveth;
𝔄nd that 𝔍 shal ryse out of the earth in the latter daye;
𝔗hat 𝔍 shal be clothed againe with this skynne
𝔄nd se 𝔊od in my flesh.
𝔜ee, 𝔍 myself shal beholde him,
𝔑ot with other, but with these same eyes.
𝔐y reins are consumed within me, when ye saye,
𝔚hy do not we persecute him?
𝔚e have founde an occasion against him.

Verse 28. *But ye should say*] Or, *Then ye shall say.*

Why persecute we him] Or, as Mr. *Good,* How did we persecute him! Alas! we are now convinced that we did wrong.

Seeing the root of the matter] A *pure practice,* and a *sound hope,* resting on the solid ground of *sound faith,* received from God himself. Instead of בי *bi, in* ME, בו *bo, in* HIM, is the reading of more than *one hundred* of Kennicott's and De Rossi's MSS., and in several of the *versions. Seeing the root of the matter is found in* HIM.

Verse 29. *Be ye afraid of the sword*] Of God's judgments.

For wrath bringeth] Such anger as ye have displayed against me God will certainly resent and punish.

That ye may know there is a judgment.] That ye may know that God will judge the world; and that the unequal distribution of riches and poverty, afflictions and health, in the present life, is a proof that there must be a future judgment, where evil shall be punished and virtue rewarded.

IT would not be fair, after all the discussion of the preceding verses in reference to the two grand opinions and modes of interpretation instituted by learned men, not to inform the reader that a *third* method of solving all difficulties has been proposed, viz., that Job refers to a Divine conviction which he had just then received, that God would appear in the most evident manner to vindicate his innocence, and give the fullest proofs to his friends and to the world that his afflictions had not been sent as a scourge for his iniquities. Dr. Kennicott was the proposer of this third mode of solving these difficulties, and I shall give his method in his own words.

"These five verses, though they contain but *twelve* lines, have occasioned controversies without number, as to the general meaning of Job in this place, whether he here expressed his firm belief of a *resurrection to happiness after death*, or of *a restoration to prosperity during the remainder of his life.*

"Each of these positions has found powerful as well as numerous advocates; and the short issue of the whole seems to be, that each party has confuted the opposite opinion, yet without establishing its own. For how could Job here express his conviction of a reverse of things in *this* world, and of a restoration to *temporal prosperity*, at the very time when he strongly asserts that his miseries would soon be terminated by death? See chap. vi. 11; vii. 21; xvii. 11-15; xix. 10, and particularly in chap. vii. 7: *O remember that my life is wind; mine eye shall no more see good.*

"Still less could Job here express *a hope full of immortality*, which sense cannot be extorted from the words without every violence. And as the *possession* of such belief is not to be reconciled with Job's so bitterly cursing the day of his birth in chap. iii., so the declaration of such belief would have solved at once the whole difficulty in dispute.

"But if neither of the preceding and opposite opinions can be admitted, if the words are not meant to express Job's belief either of a *restoration* or of a *resurrection*, what then are we to do? It does not appear to me that any other interpretation has *yet* been proposed by the learned; yet I will now venture to offer a *third* interpretation, different from both the former, and which, whilst it is free from the preceding difficulties, does not seem liable to equal objections.

"The conviction, then, which I suppose Job to express here, is this: That though his dissolution was hastening on amidst the unjust accusations of his pretended friends, and the cruel insults of his hostile relations; and though, whilst he was thus singularly oppressed with anguish of mind, he was also tortured with pains of body, torn by sores and ulcers from head to foot, and sitting upon dust and ashes; yet still, out of that miserable body, in his flesh thus stripped of skin, and nearly dropping into the grave, HE SHOULD SEE GOD, who would *appear in his favour*, and vindicate THE INTEGRITY *of his character.* This opinion may perhaps be fairly and fully supported by the sense of the words themselves, by the context, and by the following remarks.

"We read in chap. ii. 7, that *Job* was smitten with *sore boils from the sole of his foot unto his crown;* and ver. 8, 'He sat down among the *ashes.*' In chap. vii. 5, Job says, 'My flesh is clothed with worms, and clods of *dust;* my skin is broken, and become loathsome.' In chap. xvi. 19: 'Also now, behold, my witness is in heaven, and my record is on high.' Then come the words of Job, chap. xix. 25-29. And then,

in opposition to what Job had just said, that God would soon appear to vindicate him, and that even his accusing *friends* would acquit him, Zophar says, chap. xx. 27, that '*the heaven* would reveal his iniquity, and the *earth* would rise up against him.' Lastly, this opinion concerning Job's words, as to God's *vindication* of him, is confirmed strongly at the end of the book, which records the conclusion of Job's history. His firm hope is here supposed to be that, *before his death*, he should, *with his bodily eyes*, see GOD *appearing and vindicating his character.* And from the conclusion we learn that God did thus appear: *Now*, says Job, *mine eye seeth thee.* And then did God most effectually and for ever brighten the glory of Job's fame, by *four* times calling him HIS SERVANT; and, as his anger was kindled against Job's *friends*, by speaking to them in the following words: 'Ye have not spoken of me the thing that is right, as *my servant* Job hath. Go to *my servant* Job,— and *my servant* Job shall pray for you,—in that ye have not spoken of me the thing which is right, like *my servant* Job,' chap. xl. 7, 8."

Dr. K. then gives the common version, and proposes the following as a new version:—

Ver. 25. For I know that my Vindicator liveth,
And he at last shall arise over *this* dust.
26. And after that mine adversaries have mangled *me* thus,
Even in my flesh shall I see God.
27. Whom I shall see on my side;
And mine eyes shall behold, but not estranged *from me:*
All this have I made up in mine own bosom.
28. Verily ye shall say, Why have we persecuted him;
Seeing the truth of the matter is found with him?
29. Tremble for yourselves at the face of the sword;
For the sword waxeth hot against iniquities:
Therefore be assured that judgment will take place.

KENNICOTT'S *Remarks on Select Passages of Scripture*, p. 165.

There is something very plausible in this plan of Dr. Kennicott; and in the conflicting opinions relative to the meaning of this celebrated and much controverted passage, no doubt some will be found who will adopt it as a middle course. The theory, however, is better than some of the arguments by which it is supported. Yet had I not been led, by the evidence mentioned before, to the conclusion there drawn, I should probably have adopted Dr. K.'s opinion with some modification: but as to his *new version*, it is what I am persuaded the Hebrew text can never bear. It is even too loose a paraphrase of the original, as indeed are most of the new versions of this passage. Dr. Kennicott says, that such a confidence as those cause Job to express, who make him speak concerning the *future resurrection*, ill comports with his cursing so bitterly the day of his birth, &c. But this objection has little if any strength, when we consider that it is not at all probable that Job had this confidence any time before the moment in which he uttered it: it was then a *direct revelation*, nothing of which he ever had before, else he had never dropped those words of impatience and irritation which we find in several of his speeches. And this may be safely inferred from the consideration, that *after this time* no such words escaped his lips: he bears the rest of his sufferings with great patience and fortitude; and seems to look forward with steady hope to that day in which all tears shall be wiped away from off all faces, and it be fully proved that the Judge of all the earth has done right.

CHAPTER XX

Zophar answers Job, and largely details the wretchedness of the wicked and the hypocrite; shows that the rejoicing of such is short and transitory, 1–9. That he is punished in his family and in his person, 10–14. That he shall be stripped of his ill-gotten wealth, and shall be in misery, though in the midst of affluence, 15–23. He shall at last die a violent death, and his family and property be finally destroyed, 24–29.

A. M. cir. 2484
B. C. cir. 1520
Ante I. Olymp.
cir. 744
Ante U. C. cir.
767

THEN answered Zophar the Naamathite, and said,

2 Therefore do my thoughts cause me to answer, and for *this* [a]I make haste.

3 I have heard the check of my reproach, and the spirit of my understanding causeth me to answer.

4 Knowest thou *not* this of old, since man was placed upon earth,

5 [b]That the triumphing of the wicked *is* [c]short, and the joy of the hypocrite *but* for a moment?

A. M. cir. 2484
B. C. cir. 1520
Ante I. Olymp.
cir. 744
Ante U. C. cir.
767

6 [d]Though his excellency mount up to the heavens, and his head reach unto [e]the clouds;

7 *Yet* he shall perish for ever [f]like his own dung: they which have seen him shall say, Where *is* he?

---

[a]Hebrew, *my haste* is *in me*——[b]Psalm xxxvii. 35, 36 [c]Heb. *from near*

[d]Isa. xiv. 13, 14; Obad. 3, 4——[e]Heb. *cloud*——[f]Psa. lxxxiii. 10

NOTES ON CHAP. XX

Verse 2. *Therefore do my thoughts*] It has already been observed that Zophar was the most inveterate of all Job's *enemies*, for we really must cease to call them *friends*. He sets no bounds to his invective, and outrages every rule of charity. A man of such a bitter spirit must have been, in general, very unhappy. With him Job is, by insinuation, every thing that is base, vile, and hypocritical. Mr. *Good* translates this verse thus: "Whither would my tumult transport me? And how far my agitation within me?" This is all the modesty that appears in Zophar's discourse. He acknowledges that he is pressed by the impetuosity of his spirit to reply to Job's self-vindication. The original is variously translated, but the sense is as above.

For this *I make haste.*] ובעבור חושי בי *ubaabur chushi bi, there is sensibility in me,* and my *feelings* provoke me to reply.

Verse 3. *I have heard the check of my reproach*] Some suppose that Zophar quotes the words of Job, and that some words should be supplied to indicate this meaning; *e. g.*, "I have heard (sayest thou) the check or charge of my reproach?" Or it may refer to what Job says of Zophar and his companions, chap. xix. 2, 3: *How long will ye vex my soul—these ten times have ye reproached me.* Zophar therefore assumes his old ground, and retracts nothing of what he had said. Like many of his own complexion in the present day, he was determined to believe that *his* judgment was infallible, and that *he* could not err.

Verse 4. *Knowest thou* not *this of old*] This is a maxim as ancient as the world; it began with the first man: A wicked man shall triumph but a short time; God will destroy the proud doer.

Since man was placed upon earth] Literally, *since* ADAM *was placed on the earth;* that is, since the fall, wickedness and hypocrisy have *existed;* but they have never *triumphed* long. Thou hast lately been expressing confidence in reference to a general judgment; but such is thy character, that thou hast little reason to anticipate with any joy the decisions of that day.

Verse 6. *Though his excellency mount up to the heavens*] Probably referring to the original state of Adam, of whose fall he appears to have spoken, ver. 4. He was created in the *image of God;* but by his sin against his Maker he fell into wretchedness, misery, death, and destruction.

Verse 7. *He shall perish for ever*] He is *dust*, and shall return to the dust from which he was taken. Zophar here hints his disbelief in that doctrine, the resurrection of the body, which Job had so solemnly asserted in the preceding chapter. Or he might have been like some in the present day, who believe that the wicked shall be annihilated, and the bodies of the righteous only be raised from the dead; but I know of no scripture by which such a doctrine is confirmed.

Like his own dung] His reputation shall be abominable, and his putrid carcass shall resemble his own excrement. A speech that partakes as much of the malevolence as of the asperity of Zophar's spirit.

A. M. cir. 2484
B. C. cir. 1520
Ante I. Olymp.
cir. 744
Ante U. C. cir.
767

8 He shall fly away ᵍas a dream, and shall not be found: yea, he shall be chased away as a vision of the night.

9 ʰThe eye also *which* saw him shall *see him* no more; neither shall his place any more behold him.

10 ¹His children shall seek to please the poor, and his hands ᵏshall restore their goods.

11 His bones are full *of* ¹*the sin* of his youth, ᵐwhich shall lie down with him in the dust.

12 Though wickedness be sweet in his mouth,

though he hide it under his tongue;

13 *Though* he spare it, and forsake it not; but keep it still ⁿwithin his mouth:

14 *Yet* his meat in his bowels is turned, *it is* the gall of asps within him.

15 He hath swallowed down riches, and he shall vomit them up again: God shall cast them out of his belly.

16 He shall suck the poison of asps: the viper's tongue shall slay him.

17 He shall not see ᵒthe rivers, ᵖthe

A. M. cir. 2484
B. C. cir. 1520
Ante I. Olymp.
cir. 744
Ante U. C. cir.
767

ᵍPsa. lxxiii. 20; xc. 5——ʰChap. vii. 8, 10; viii. 18; Psa. xxxvii. 36; ciii. 16——ⁱOr, *The poor shall oppress his children*——ᵏVer. 18

¹Chap. xiii. 26; Psa. xxv. 7——ᵐChap. xxi. 26 ⁿHeb. *in the midst of his palate*——ᵒPsa. xxxvi. 9; Jer. xvii. 6——ᵖOr, *streaming brooks*

Verse 8. *He shall fly away as a dream*] Instead of rising again from corruption, as thou hast asserted, (chap. xix. 26,) with a new body, his flesh shall rot in the earth, and his spirit be dissipated like a vapour; and, like a vision of the night, nothing shall remain but the bare impression that such a creature had once existed, but shall appear no more for ever.

Verse 10. *His children shall seek to please the poor*] They shall be reduced to the lowest degree of poverty and want, so as to be obliged to become servants to the poor. *Cursed be Ham, a servant of servants shall he be.* There are cases where the poor actually serve the poor; and this is the lowest or most abject state of poverty.

His hands shall restore their goods.] He shall be obliged to restore the goods that he has taken by violence.

Mr. *Good* translates: *His branches shall be involved in his iniquity;* i. e., his children shall suffer on his account. "His own hands shall render to himself the evil that he has done to others."—*Calmet.* The clause is variously translated.

Verse 11. *His bones are full* of the sin *of his youth*] Our translators have followed the Vulgate, *Ossa ejus implebuntur vitiis adolescentiæ ejus;* "his bones shall be filled with the sins of his youth." The Syriac and Arabic have, *his bones are full of marrow;* and the Targum is to the same sense. At first view it might appear that Zophar refers to those infirmities in old age, which are the consequences of youthful vices and irregularities. עלומו *alumav*, which we translate *his youth*, may be rendered *his hidden things;* as if he had said, *his secret vices* bring down his strength to the dust. For this rendering *Rosenmüller* contends, and several other German critics. Mr. *Good* contends for the same.

Verse 12. *Though wickedness be sweet in his mouth*] This seems to refer to the *secret sins* mentioned above.

Hide it under his tongue] This and the *four* following verses contain an allegory; and the reference is to a man who, instead of taking wholesome food, takes what is *poisonous*, and is so delighted with it because it is sweet, that he rolls it under his tongue, and will scarcely let

it down into his stomach, he is so delighted with the taste; "he spares it, and forsakes it not, but keeps it still within his mouth," ver. 13. "But when he swallows it, it is turned to the gall of asps within him," ver. 14, which shall corrode and torture his bowels.

Verse 15. *He shall vomit them up again*] This is also an allusion to an effect of most ordinary *poisons;* they occasion a nausea, and often excruciating *vomiting;* nature striving to eject what it knows, if retained, will be its bane.

Verse 16. *He shall suck the poison of asps*] That delicious morsel, that *secret, easily-besetting sin,* so palatable, and so pleasurable, shall act on the life of his soul, as the poison of asps would do on the life of his body.

The poison is called *the gall of asps*, it being anciently supposed that the *poison of serpents* consists in their *gall*, which is thought to be copiously exuded when those animals are *enraged;* as it has been often seen that their bite is *not poisonous* when they are *not angry.* Pliny, in speaking of the various parts of animals, *Hist. Nat.* lib. xi., c. 37, states, from this circumstance, that in the gall the poison of serpents consists; *ne quis miretur id* (fel) *venenum esse serpentum.* And in lib. xxviii., c. 9, he ranks the *gall* of horses among the poisons: *Damnatur* (fel) *equinum tantum inter venena.* We see, therefore, that the *gall* was considered to be the source whence the poison of serpents was generated, not only in Arabia, but also in Italy.

Verse 17. *He shall not see the rivers*] Mr. *Good* has the following judicious note on this passage: "Honey and butter are the common results of a rich, well-watered pasturage, offering a perpetual banquet of grass to kine, and of nectar to bees; and thus loading the possessor with the most luscious luxuries of pastoral life, peculiarly so before the discovery of the means of obtaining *sugar.* The expression appears to have been proverbial; and is certainly used here to denote a very high degree of temporal prosperity." See also chap. xxix. 6. To the Hebrews such expressions were quite familiar. See Exod. iii. 8; xiii. 5; xxxiii. 3; 2 Kings xviii. 32; Deut. xxxi. 20, and elsewhere.

The Greek and Roman writers abound in such images.

A. M. cir. 2484
B. C. cir. 1520
Ante I. Olymp.
cir. 744
Ante U. C. cir.
767

floods, the brooks of honey and butter.

18 That which he laboured for �qshall he restore, and shall not

swallow *it* down : ʳaccording to his substance *shall* the restitution *be,* and he shall not rejoice *therein.*

19 Because he hath ˢoppressed

A. M. cir. 2484
B. C. cir. 1520
Ante I. Olymp.
cir. 744
Ante U. C. cir.
767

�q Ver. 10, 15——ʳ Heb. *according to the sub-*   *stance of his exchange*——ˢ Heb. *crushed*

Milk and honey were such delicacies with the ancients, that *Pindar* compares his song to them for its *smoothness* and *sweetness:*—

Χαιρε

Φιλος. Εγω τοδε τοι
Πεμπω μεμιγμενον μελι λευκῳ
Συν γαλακτι· κιρναμενα δ' εερσ' αμ-
φεπει πομ' αοιδιμον, Αιο-
λισιν εν πνοαισιν αυλων.

PIND. Nem. iii., ver. 133.

"Hail, friend! to thee I tune my song;
For thee its *mingled sweets* prepare;
Mellifluous accents pour along;
Verse, *pure as milk*, to thee I bear;
On all thy actions falls the dew of praise;
Pierian draughts thy thirst of fame assuage,
And breathing flutes thy songs of triumph
raise."   J. B. C.

Qui te, Pollio, amat, veniat, quo te quoque
gaudet;
*Mel*la fluant illi, ferat et *rubus* asper *amomum.*
VIRG. Ecl. iii., ver. 88.

"Who Pollio loves, and who his muse admires;
Let Pollio's fortune crown his full desires
Let *myrrh*, instead of *thorn*, his fences fill;
And *showers* of *honey* from his *oaks* distil!"
DRYDEN.

OVID, describing the *golden age*, employs the same image:—

Flumina *jam* lactis, *jam* flumina nectaris *ibant;*
Flavaque *de viridi stillabant* ilice mella.
Metam. lib. i., ver. 3.

"*Floods* were with *milk*, and *floods* with *nectar*,
fill'd;
And *honey* from the sweating *oak* distill'd."
DRYDEN.

HORACE employs a similar image in nearly the same words:—

Mella *cava manant ex* ilice, *montibus altis;*
Levis crepante lympha desilit pede.
Epod. xvi., ver. 46.

"From hollow *oaks*, where *honey'd streams*
distil,
And bounds with noisy foot the pebbled rill."
FRANCIS.

Job employs the same metaphor, chap. xxix. 6:—

When I washed my steps with *butter*,
And the rock poured out to me rivers of *oil.*

Isaiah, also, chap. vii. 22, uses the same when describing the produce of a *heifer* and two *ewes:*—

From the plenty of *milk* that they shall produce,
He shall eat *butter: butter* and *honey* shall he
eat,
Whosoever is left in the midst of the land.

And *Joel*, iii. 18:—

And it shall come to pass in that day,
The *mountains* shall drop down *new wine*,
And the hills shall flow with *milk;*
And all the *rivers* of Judah shall flow with
waters.

These expressions denote *fertility* and *abundance;* and are often employed to point out the *excellence* of the promised land, which is frequently denominated *a land flowing with milk and honey:* and even the superior blessings of the *Gospel* are thus characterized, Isa. li. 1.

Verse 18. *That which he laboureth for shall he restore*] I prefer here the reading of the *Arabic*, which is also supported by the *Syriac*, and is much nearer to the *Hebrew* text than the common version. *He shall return to labour, but he shall not eat; he shall toil, and not be permitted to enjoy the fruit of his labour.* The whole of this verse Mr. *Good* thus translates:—

"To labour shall he return, but he shall not
eat.
A *dearth* his *recompense:* yea, nothing shall he
taste."

It may be inquired how Mr. *Good* arrives at this meaning. It is by considering the word יעלם *yaalos*, which we translate *he shall rejoice*, as the Arabic علس *alasa*, "he ate, drank, tasted;" and the word כהיל *kehil*, which we make a compound word, *keeheyl*, "according to substance," to be the pure Arabic word كحل *kahala*, "it was fruitless," applied to a year of *dearth:* hence *kahlan*, "a barren year." Conceiving these two to be pure *Arabic* words, for which he seems to have sufficient authority, he renders תמורתו *temuratho*, *his recompense*, as in chap. xv. 31, and not *restitution*, as here. The general meaning is, He shall labour and toil, but shall not reap, for God shall send on his land blasting and mildew. *Houbigant* translates the verse thus: *Reddet labore partum; neque id absumet; copiosæ fuerunt mercaturæ ejus, sed illis non fruetur.* "He shall restore what he gained by labour, nor shall he consume it; his merchandises were abundant, but he shall not enjoy them." O, how doctors disagree! Old *Coverdale* gives a good sense, which is no unfrequent thing with this venerable translator:—

𝕭ut laboure 𝔰hal he, and yet habe nothinge to eate; great trabayle 𝔰hal he make for riche𝔰, but he 𝔰hal not enjoye them.

Verse 19. *He hath oppressed* and *hath forsaken the poor*] Literally, *He hath broken in pieces the forsaken of the poor;* כי רצץ עזב דלים *ki ritstsats azab dallim.* The poor have fled from famine, and left their children behind them; and this hard-hearted wretch, meaning Job all the while, has suffered them to perish, when he might have saved them alive.

A. M. cir. 2484
B. C. cir. 1520
Ante I. Olymp. cir. 744
Ante U. C. cir. 767

and hath forsaken the poor; *be-cause* he hath violently taken away a house which he builded not;

20 [t]Surely he shall not [u]feel quietness in his belly, he shall not save of that which he desired.

21 [v]There shall none of his meat be left; therefore shall no man look for his goods.

22 In the fulness of his sufficiency he shall be in straits: every hand of the [w]wicked shall come upon him.

23 *When* he is about to fill his belly, *God* shall cast the fury of his wrath upon him, and shall rain *it* upon him [x]while he is eating.

A. M. cir. 2484
B. C. cir. 1520
Ante I. Olymp. cir. 744
Ante U. C. cir. 767

24 [y]He shall flee from the iron weapon, *and* the bow of steel shall strike him through.

25 It is drawn, and cometh out of the body; yea, [z]the glittering sword cometh out of his gall: [a]terrors *are* upon him.

26 All darkness *shall be* hid in his secret places: [b]a fire not blown shall consume him;

---

[t]Eccles. v. 13, 14——[u]Heb. *know*——[v]Or, *There shall be none left for his meat*——[w]Or, *troublesome*——[x]Num. xi. 33;

Psa. lxxviii. 30, 31——[y]Isa. xxiv. 18; Jer. xlviii. 43; Amos v. 19——[z]Chap. xvi. 13——[a]Chap. xviii. 11——[b]Psa. xxi. 9

He hath violently taken away a house which he builded not] Or rather, He hath thrown down a house, and hath not rebuilt it. By neglecting or destroying the forsaken orphans of the poor, mentioned above, he has destroyed a house, (*a family*,) while he might, by helping the wretched, have preserved the family from becoming extinct.

Verse 20. *Surely he shall not feel quietness in his belly*] I have already remarked that the word בטן *beten*, which we translate *belly*, often means in the sacred Scriptures the whole of the human trunk; the regions of the *thorax* and *abdomen*, with their contents; the heart, lungs, liver, &c., and consequently all the *thoughts*, *purposes*, and *inclinations* of the mind, of which those viscera were supposed to be the functionaries. The meaning seems to be, "He shall never be satisfied; he shall have an endless desire after secular good, and shall never be able to obtain what he covets."

Verse 21. *There shall none of his meat be left*] *Coverdale* translates thus: He devoured so gredily, that he left nothinge behynde, therefore his goodes shal not prospere. He shall be stripped of every thing.

Verse 22. *In the fulness of his sufficiency he shall be in straits*] This is a fine saying, and few of the menders of Job's text have been able to improve the version. It is literally true of every great, rich, wicked man; he has no God, and anxieties and perplexities torment him, notwithstanding he has his portion in this life.

Every hand of the wicked shall come upon him.] All *kinds* of misery shall be his portion. *Coverdale* translates: Though he had plenteousnesse of every thinge, yet was he poore; and, therefore, he is but a wretch on every syde.

Verse 23. *When he is about to fill his belly*] Here seems a plain allusion to the *lustings of the children of Israel in the desert*. God showered down *quails* upon them, and showered down his wrath while the flesh was in their mouth. The allusion is too plain to be mistaken; and this gives some countenance to the bishop of Killala's version of the 20th verse:—

"Because he acknowledged not the *quail* in his stomach,
In the midst of his delight he shall not escape."

That שלו, which we translate *quietness*, means a *quail*, also the history of the Hebrews' lustings, Exod. xvi. 2-11, and Num. xi. 31-35, suffi-

ciently proves. Let the reader mark all the expressions here, from ver. 20 to 23, and compare them with Num. xi. 31-35, and he will probably be of opinion that Zophar has that history immediately in view, which speaks of the Hebrews' murmurings for bread and flesh, and the miraculous *showers* of *manna* and *quails*, and the judgments that fell on them for their murmurings. Let us compare a few passages:—

Verse 20. *He shall not feel quietness*] שלו *selav*, the quail. "He shall not save of that which he desired." Verse 21: "There shall none of his meat be left." Exod. xvi. 19: "Let no man leave of it till the morning."

Verse 22. *In the fulness of his sufficiency, he shall be in straits.*] Exod. xvi. 20: "But some of them left of it until the morning, and it bred worms and stank."

Verse 23. *When he is about to* fill his belly, *God shall cast the* fury of his wrath *upon him, and shall* rain it *upon him while he is eating.*] Num. xi. 33: "And while the flesh was yet between their teeth, ere it was chewed, the wrath of the Lord was kindled against the people, and the Lord smote the people with a very great plague." Psa. lxxviii. 26-30: "He rained flesh upon them as dust, and feathered fowls like as the sand of the sea: so they did eat and were filled—but, while the meat was in their mouth, the wrath of God came upon them," &c. These show to what Zophar refers.

Verse 24. *He shall flee from the iron weapon*] Or, "Though he should flee from the iron armour, the brazen bow should strike him through." So that yf he fle the yron weapens, he shal be shott with the stele bow.—*Coverdale*. That is, he shall most certainly perish: all kinds of deaths await him.

Verse 25. *It is drawn, and cometh out*] This refers to *archery*: The arrow is *drawn out* of the sheaf or quiver, and discharged from the bow against its mark, and pierces the vitals, and passes through the body. So *Coverdale*:— The arowe shal be taken forth, and go out at his backe.

Verse 26. *A fire not blown shall consume him*] As Zophar is here showing that the wicked cannot escape from the Divine judgments; so he points out the different instruments which God employs for their destruction. The *wrath of God*—any secret or supernatural curse. The *iron weapon*—the spear or such like. The *bow*, and its swift-flying *arrow*. *Darkness*—deep horror and perplexity. *A fire not blown*—a supernatural fire; *lightning*: such as fell on

A. M. cir. 2484
B. C. cir. 1520
Ante I. Olymp.
cir. 744
Ante U. C. cir.
767

it shall go ill with him that is left in his tabernacle.

27 The heaven shall reveal his iniquity; and the earth shall rise up against him.

28 The increase of his house shall depart,

ᵉChap. xxvii. 13; xxxi. 2, 3

Korah, and his company, to whose destruction there is probably here an allusion: hence the words, *It shall go ill with him who is left in his tabernacle.* "And the Lord spake unto Moses and Aaron, Separate yourselves from among this congregation, that I may consume them in a moment. *Get ye up from about the tabernacle* of Korah, Dathan, and Abiram. *Depart* from the *tents* of these wicked men. There came out a fire from the Lord and consumed the two hundred and fifty men that offered incense;" Num. xvi. 20, &c.

Verse 27. *The heaven shall reveal his iniquity; and the earth shall rise up against him.*] Another allusion, if I mistake not, to the destruction of Korah and his company. The heaven revealed their iniquity; God declared out of heaven his judgment of their rebellion. "And the glory of the Lord appeared unto all the congregation;" Num. xvi. 20, &c. And then *the earth rose up against them.* "The ground clave asunder that was under them, and the earth opened her mouth and swallowed them up; and they went down alive into the pit, and the earth closed upon them;" Num. xvi. 31-33.

Verse 28. *The increase of his house shall depart,* and his goods *shall flow away in the day of his wrath.*] A farther allusion to the punishment of the rebellious company of Korah, who not only perished *themselves,* but their *houses* also, and their *goods.* Num. xvi. 32.

These examples were all in point, on the ground assumed by Zophar; and such well-attested facts would not be passed over by him, had he known the record of them; and that he did know it, alludes to it, and quotes the very circumstances, is more than probable.

Verse 29. *This is the portion*] As God has dealt with the *murmuring Israelites,* and with the *rebellious sons* of *Korah,* so will he deal with those who *murmur* against the *dispensations* of his *providence,* and rebel against his *authority.* Instead of an *earthly portion,* and an *ecclesiastical heritage,* such as Korah, Dathan, and Abiram sought; they shall have *fire* from God to *scorch them,* and the *earth* to *swallow them up.*

Dr. *Stock,* bishop of Killala, who has noticed the allusion to the *quails,* and for which he has been most unmeritedly ridiculed, gives us the following note on the passage:—

"Here I apprehend is a fresh example of the known usage of Hebrew poets, in adorning their compositions by allusions to facts in the history of their own people. It has escaped all the interpreters; and it is the more important, because it fixes the date of this poem, so far as to prove its having been composed *subsequently* to the transgression of Israel, at Kibroth Hattaavah, recorded in Num. xi. 33, 34. Because the wicked acknowledges not the *quail,* that is,

and his goods shall flow away in the day of his wrath.

29 ᶜThis *is* the portion of a wicked man from God, and the heritage ᵈappointed unto him by God.

A. M. cir. 2484
B. C. cir. 1520
Ante I. Olymp.
cir. 744
Ante U. C. cir.
767

ᵈHeb. *of his decree from God*

---

the meat with which God has filled his stomach; but, like the ungrateful Israelites, *crammed,* and *blasphemed his feeder,* as *Milton* finely expresses it, he shall experience the same punishment with them, and be cut off in the midst of his enjoyment, as Moses tells us the people were who lusted."

If I mistake not, I have added considerable strength to the prelate's reasoning, by showing that there is a reference also to the history of the *manna,* and to that which details the *rebellion of Korah* and his company; and if so, (and they may dispute who please,) it is a proof that the Book of Job is not *so* old as, much less *older* than, the *Pentateuch,* as some have endeavoured to prove, but with no evidence of success, at least to my mind: a point which never has been, and I am certain never can be, proved; which has multitudes of presumptions against it, and not one clear incontestable fact for it. Mr. *Good* has done more in this case than any of his predecessors, and yet Mr. *Good* has failed; no wonder then that *others,* unmerciful criticisers of the bishop of Killala, have failed also, who had not a tenth part of Mr. *Good's* learning, nor one-hundredth part of his critical acumen.

It is, however, strange that men cannot suffer others to differ from them on a subject of confessed difficulty and comparatively little importance, without raising up the cry of *heresy* against them, and treating them with superciliousness and contempt! These should know, if they are *clergymen,* whether *dignified* or *not,* that such conduct ill becomes the *sacerdotal* character; and that *ante barbam docet senes* cannot be always spoken to the *teacher's* advantage.

As *a good story is not the worse for being twice told,* the following lines from a clergyman, who, for his *humility* and piety, was as much an honour to his *vocation* as he was to human nature, may not be amiss, in point of advice to all *Warburtonian* spirits:—

"Be *calm* in arguing, for *fierceness* makes
    Error a *fault,* and *truth discourtesy.*
    Why should I feel another man's mistakes
More than his *sickness* or his *poverty?*
In love I should: but anger is not love
Nor *wisdom* neither; therefore, gently move.
    Calmness is great advantage: he that lets
    Another chafe, may warm him at *his* fire,
Mark all his wanderings, and enjoy his frets;
    As cunning fencers suffer heat to tire.
Truth dwells not in the clouds: the bow that's
    there
Doth often aim at, never hit, the sphere."

                 HERBERT.

Dr. *Stock's* work on the Book of Job will stand honourably on the same shelf with the best on this difficult subject.

CHAPTER XXI

Job expresses himself as puzzled by the dispensations of Divine Providence, because of the unequal distribution of temporal goods; he shows that wicked men often live long, prosper in their families, in their flocks, and in all their substance, and yet live in defiance of God and sacred things, 1–16. At other times their prosperity is suddenly blasted, and they and their families come to ruin, 17–21. God, however, is too wise to err; and he deals out various lots to all according to his wisdom: some come sooner, others later, to the grave: the strong and the weak, the prince and the peasant, come to a similar end in this life; but the wicked are reserved for a day of wrath, 22–33. He charges his friends with falsehood in their pretended attempts to comfort him, 34.

A. M. cir. 2484
B. C. cir. 1520
Ante I. Olymp.
cir. 744
Ante U. C. cir.
767

BUT Job answered and said,

2 Hear diligently my speech, and let this be your consolations.

3 Suffer me that I may speak; and after that I have spoken, [a]mock on.

4 As for me, *is* my complaint to man? and if *it were so,* why should not my spirit be [b]troubled?

5 [c]Mark me, and be astonished, [d]and lay *your* hand upon *your* mouth.

6 Even when I remember I am afraid, and trembling taketh hold on my flesh.

7 [e]Wherefore do the wicked live, be-come old, yea, are mighty in power?

A. M. cir. 2484
B. C. cir. 1520
Ante I. Olymp.
cir. 744
Ante U. C. cir.
767

8 Their seed is established in their sight with them, and their offspring before their eyes.

9 Their houses [f]*are* safe from fear, [g]neither *is* the rod of God upon them.

10 Their bull gendereth, and faileth not; their cow calveth, and [h]casteth not her calf.

11 They send forth their little ones like a flock, and their children dance.

12 They take the timbrel and harp, and re-joice at the sound of the organ.

---

[a]Chap. xvi. 10; xxvii. 2——[b]Heb. *shortened*——[c]Heb. *look unto me*——[d]Judg. xviii. 19; chap. xxix. 9; xl. 4; Psa. xxxix. 9

[e]Chap. xii. 6; Psa. xvii. 10, 14; lxxiii. 3, 12; Jer. xii. 1; Hab. i. 16——[f]Heb. *are peace from fear*——[g]Psa. lxxiii. 5——[h]Exod. xxiii. 26

NOTES ON CHAP. XXI

Verse 2. *Let this be your consolations.*] ותהי זאת תנחומתיכם *uthehi zoth tanchumotheychem* may be translated, "And let this be your retractations." Let what I am about to say induce you to *retract* what you have said, and to *recall* your false judgments.

נחם *nacham* signifies, not only to *comfort,* but to *change one's mind,* to *repent;* hence the *Vulgate* translates *et agite pœnitentiam,* "and re-pent," which *Coverdale* follows in his version, *and amende yourselves.* Some suppose the verse to be understood ironically: I am now about to give you consolations for those you have given me. When I have done, then turn them into *mockery* if you please.

Verse 4. *As for me*] האנכי *heanochi,* "Alas for me!" Is it not with a man that I speak? And, if this be the case, why should not my spirit be troubled? I do not reply against my *Maker:* I suffer much from God and man; why then may I not have the privilege of complain-ing to creatures like myself?

Verse 5. *Mark me, and be astonished*] Con-sider and compare the state in which I was once, with that in which I am now; and be astonished at the judgments and dispensations of God. You will then be confounded; you will put your hands upon your mouths, and keep silent.

Putting the hand on the mouth, or the *finger on the lips,* was the token of silence. The Egyptian god *Harpocrates,* who was the *god of silence,* is represented with his finger compress-ing his upper lip.

Verse 6. *I am afraid* I am about to speak of the mysterious workings of Providence; and I tremble at the thought of entering into a detail on such a subject; my very flesh trembles.

Verse 7. *Wherefore do the wicked live*] You have frequently asserted that the wicked are invariably punished in this life; and that the righteous are ever distinguished by the strong-est marks of God's providential kindness; how then does it come that many wicked men live long and prosperously, and at last die in peace, without any evidence whatever of God's dis-pleasure? This is a fact that is occurring daily; none can deny it; how then will you reconcile it with your maxims?

Verse 8. *Their seed is established*] They see their own *children* grow up, and become settled in the land; and behold their *children's chil-dren* also; so that their generations are not cut off. Even the posterity of the wicked continue.

Verse 9. *Neither* is *the rod of God upon them.*] They are not afflicted as other men.

Verse 10. *Their bull gendereth*] עבר *ibbar, passes over, i. e.,* on the cow, referring to the actions of the bull when coupling with the female. Their flocks multiply greatly, they bring forth in time, and none of them is barren.

Verse 11. *They send forth their little ones*] It is not very clear whether this refers to the *young of the flocks* or to their *children.* The first clause may mean the former, the next clause the latter; while the *young* of their *cattle* are in flocks, their numerous *children* are healthy and vigorous, *and dance for joy.*

Verse 12. *They take the timbrel and harp*] ישאו *yisu,* they *rise up* or *lift themselves up,*

A. M. cir. 2484
B. C. cir. 1520
Ante I. Olymp.
cir. 744
Ante U. C. cir.
767

13 They ¹spend their days ᵏin wealth, and in a moment go down to the grave.

14 ¹Therefore they say unto God, Depart from us; for we desire not the knowledge of thy ways.

15 ᵐWhat *is* the Almighty, that we should serve him? and ⁿwhat profit should we have, if we pray unto him?

A. M. cir. 2484
B. C. cir. 1520
Ante I. Olymp.
cir. 744
Ante U. C. cir.
767

16 Lo, their good *is* not in their hand: ᵒthe counsel of the wicked is far from me.

17 ᵖHow oft is the qcandle of the wicked

ⁱCh. xxxvi. 11——ᵏOr, *in mirth*——ˡCh. xxii. 17
ᵐExod. v. 2; ch. xxxiv. 9——ⁿCh. xxxv. 3; Mal. iii. 14

ᵒCh. xxii. 18; Psa. i. 1; Prov. i. 10; Ezek. xi. 2; Luke xxiii. 51; Acts v. 33——ᵖCh. xviii. 6——qOr, *lamp*

---

probably alluding to the rural exercise of dancing.

תֹּף *toph*, which we translate *timbrel*, means a sort of *drum*, such as the *tom-tom* of the Asiatics.

כִּנּוֹר *kinnor* may mean something of the *harp* kind.

עוּגָב *ugab*, organ, means nothing like the instrument now called the *organ*, though thus translated both by the *Septuagint* and *Vulgate;* it probably means the *syrinx*, composed of several unequal pipes, close at the bottom, which, when blown into at the top, gives a very *shrill* and *lively* sound. To these instruments the youth are represented as *dancing joyfully*. Mr. *Good* translates: "They trip merrily to the sound of the pipe." And illustrates his translation with the following verse:—

> "Now pursuing, now retreating,
> Now in circling troops they meet;
> To brisk notes in cadence beating,
> Glance their many twinkling feet."

The original is intended to convey the true notion of the gambols of the rustic nymphs and swains on festival occasions; and let it be observed that this is spoken of the children of those who say unto God, "Depart from us; for we desire not the knowledge of thy ways. What is the Almighty, that we should serve him? and what profit should we have if we pray unto him?" ver. 14, 15. Is it any wonder that the children of such parents should be living to the flesh, and serving the lusts of the flesh? for neither they nor their parents know God, nor pray unto him.

Verse 13. *They spend their days in wealth*] There is a various reading here of some importance. In the text we have יבלו *yeballu, they grow old*, or wear out as with old age, *terent vetustate;* and in the *margin*, יכלו *yechallu, they consume;* and the *Masora* states that this is one of the *eleven* words which are written with ב *beth* and must be read with כ *caph*. Several *editions* have the former word in the *text*, and the latter in the *margin;* the former being what is called the *kethib*, the latter *keri*.

יבלו *yeballu, they grow old*, or *wear out*, is the reading of the *Antwerp, Paris*, and *London* Polyglots; יכלו *yechallu, they accomplish* or *spend*, is the reading of the *Complutensian Polyglot*, thirteen of *Kennicott's* and *De Rossi's* MSS., the *Septuagint, Chaldee, Syriac*, and *Arabic*. The *Vulgate* has *ducunt*, "they lead or spend," from which our translation is borrowed. I incline to the former, as Job's argument derives considerable strength from this circum-

stance; they not only *spend* their days in faring sumptuously every day; but they even *wear out* so as to *grow old* in it; they are not cut off by any sudden judgment of God. This is fact; therefore your doctrine, that the wicked are cut off suddenly and have but a short time, is far from the truth.

In a moment go down to the grave.] They wear out their years in pleasure; grow old in their gay and giddy life; and die, as in a moment, without previous sickness; or, as Mr. *Good* has it, *They quietly descend into the grave*.

Verse 14. *They say unto God*] This is the language of their *conduct*, though not directly of their *lips*.

Depart from us] Let us alone; we do not trouble thee. Thy ways are painful; we do not like cross-bearing. Thy ways are spiritual; we wish to live after the flesh. We have learned to do our own will; we do not wish to study thine.

Verse 15. *What is the Almighty*] What allegiance do we owe to him? We feel no *obligation* to *obey* him; and what profit can we derive from *prayer?* We are as happy as flesh and blood can make us: our kingdom is of this world; we wish for no other portion than that which we have.

Those who have never prayed as they ought know nothing of the benefits of prayer.

Verse 16. *Their good is not in their hand*] With all their boasting and self-dependence, God only *lends* them his bounty; and though it appears to be their own, yet it is at his disposal. Some of the wicked he permits to live and die in *affluence*, provided it be acquired in the ordinary way of his providence, by trade, commerce, &c. Others he permits to possess it for a *while* only, and then strips them of their illegally procured property.

The counsel of the wicked is far from me.] Some understand the words thus: "Far be it from me to advocate the cause of the wicked." I have nothing in common with them, and am not their apologist. I state a fact: they are often found in continual prosperity. I state another fact: they are often found in wretchedness and misery.

Verse 17. *How oft is the candle of the wicked put out?*] The *candle* or *lamp* is often used, both as the emblem of *prosperity* and of *posterity*. Oftentimes the rejoicing of the wicked is short; and, not unfrequently, his *seed* is cut off from the earth. The *root* is dried up, and the *branch* is withered.

God *distributeth sorrows in his anger*.] He must be incensed against those who refuse to *know, serve*, and *pray* unto him. In his anger, therefore, he portions out to each his due share of misery, vexation, and wo.

A. M. cir. 2484
B. C. cir. 1520
Ante I. Olymp.
cir. 744
Ante U. C. cir.
767

put out? and *how oft* cometh their destruction upon them? God [r]distributeth sorrows in his anger.

18 [s]They are as stubble before the wind, and as chaff that the storm [t]carrieth away.

19 God layeth up [u]his iniquity [v]for his children: he rewardeth him, and he shall know *it*.

20 His eyes shall see his destruction, and [w]he shall drink of the wrath of the Almighty.

21 For what pleasure *hath* he in his house

after him, when the number of his months is cut off in the midst?

22 [x]Shall *any* teach God knowledge? seeing he judgeth those that are high.

23 One dieth [y]in his full strength, being wholly at ease and quiet.

24 His [z]breasts are full of milk, and his bones are moistened with marrow.

25 And another dieth in the bitterness of his soul, and never eateth with pleasure.

A. M. cir. 2484
B. C. cir. 1520
Ante I. Olymp.
cir. 744
Ante U. C. cir.
767

---

[r]Luke xii. 46——[s]Psalm i. 4; xxxv. 5; Isaiah xvii. 13; xxix. 5; Hosea xiii. 3——[t]Hebrew, *stealeth away* [u]That is, *the punishment of his iniquity*——[v]Exodus xx. 5——[w]Psalm lxxv. 8; Isaiah li. 17; Jeremiah xxv. 15; Revelation xiv. 10; xix. 15——[x]Isaiah xl. 13; xlv. 9; Romans xi. 34; 1 Cor. ii. 16——[y]Hebrew, *in his very perfection*, or *in the strength of his perfection* [z]Or, *milk pails*

Verse 18. *They are as stubble before the wind*] "His fan is in his hand; he will thoroughly cleanse his floor, and the chaff he will burn with unquenchable fire. Therefore the wicked shall not stand in the judgment, but shall be like the *chaff* which the wind driveth away." Were not this a common thought, I should have supposed that the author of this book borrowed it from Psa. i. 4. The original signifies that they shall be *carried away by a furious storm;* and borne off as *booty* is by the swift-riding robbers of the desert, who make a sudden irruption, and then set off at full speed with their prey.

Verse 19. *God layeth up his iniquity for his children*] This is according to the declaration of God, Exod. xx. 5: "Visiting the iniquity of the fathers upon the children, unto the third and fourth generation of them that hate me." This always supposes that the *children*, who are thus visited, have *copied their parents' example;* or that *ill-gotten property* is found in their hands, which has descended to them from their wicked fathers; and of this God, in his judgments, strips them. It is, however, very natural to suppose that children brought up without the fear of God will walk in the sight of their own eyes, and according to the imaginations of their own hearts.

He rewardeth him, and he shall know it.] He shall so visit his transgressions upon him, that he shall at last discern that it is God who hath done it. And thus they will find that there would have been *profit* in *serving* him, and *safety* in *praying* unto him. But this they have neglected, and now it is too late.

Verse 20. *His eyes shall see his destruction*] He shall perceive its approach, and have the double punishment of *fearing* and *feeling; feeling* a THOUSAND deaths in *fearing* ONE.

He shall drink of the wrath] The cup of God's wrath, the cup of trembling, &c., is frequently expressed or referred to in the sacred writings, Deut. xxxii. 33; Isa. li. 17-22; Jer. xxv. 15; Rev. xiv. 8. It appears to be a metaphor taken from those cups of poison which certain criminals were obliged to drink. A *cup of the juice of hemlock* was the *wrath* or *punishment* assigned by the Athenian magistrates to the philosopher *Socrates*.

Verse 21. *For what pleasure* hath *he in his house after him*] What may happen to his

posterity he neither knows nor cares for, as he is now numbered with the dead, and numbered with them before he had lived out half his years. Some have translated the verse thus: "Behold how speedily God destroys the house of the wicked after him! How he shortens the number of his months!"

Verse 22. *Shall* any *teach God knowledge?*] Who among the sons of men can pretend to teach GOD how to govern the world, who himself teaches *those that are high*—the heavenly inhabitants, that excel us infinitely both in knowledge and wisdom? Neither angels nor men can comprehend the reasons of the Divine providence. It is a depth known only to God.

Verse 23. *One dieth in his full strength*] In this and the three following verses Job shows that the inequality of fortune, goods, health, strength, &c., decides nothing either for or against persons in reference to the approbation or disapprobation of God, as these various lots are no indications of their *wickedness* or *innocence*. One has a *sudden*, another a *lingering* death; but by none of these can their eternal states be determined.

Verse 24. *His breasts are full of milk*] The word עטיני *atinaiv*, which occurs nowhere else in the Hebrew Bible, is most likely an *Arabic* term, but probably so *provincial* as to be now lost.　عطن *atana* signifies to macerate hides so as to take off the hair: hence Mr. *Good* thinks it means here, that *sleekness of skin* which is the effect of *fatness* both in man and beast. But as the radical idea signifies to *stink*, as leather does which is thus macerated, I cannot see how this meaning can apply here. Under the root עטן *atan*, Mr. *Parkhurst* gives the following definitions: "עטן occurs, not as a verb, but as a noun masculine plural, in construction, עטיני *atiney, the bowels, intestines;* once Job xxi. 24, עטיניו *atinaiv*, his bowels or intestines, *are full of*, or *abound with*, חלב *chalab, fat*. So the LXX.: Τα δε εγκατα αυτου πληρη στεατος. The VULGATE: Viscera, ejus *plena sunt adipe*, 'his intestines are full of fat.' May not עטינים *atinim* be a noun masculine plural from עטה *atah*, to involve, formed as גליונים *gailyonim, mirrors*, from גלה *galah*, to reveal? And may not the *intestines*, including those fatty parts, the mesentery and omentum, be so called on account of their wonderful *involutions?*" I think

A. M. cir. 2484
B. C. cir. 1520
Ante I. Olymp.
cir. 744
Ante U. C. cir.
767

26 They shall [a]lie down alike in the dust, and the worms shall cover them.

27 Behold, I know your thoughts, and the devices *which* ye wrongfully imagine against me.

28 For ye say, [b]Where *is* the house of the prince? and where *are* [c]the dwelling-places of the wicked?

29 Have ye not asked them that go by the way? and do ye not know their tokens,

30 [d]That the wicked is reserved to the day of destruction? they shall be brought forth to [e]the day of wrath.

A. M. cir. 2484
B. C. cir. 1520
Ante I. Olymp.
cir. 744
Ante U. C. cir.
767

31 Who shall declare his way [f]to his face? and who shall repay him *what* he hath done?

32 Yet shall he be brought to the [g]grave and shall [h]remain in the tomb.

33 The clods of the valley shall be sweet unto him, and [i]every man shall draw after him, as *there are* innumerable before him.

34 How then comfort ye me in vain, seeing in your answers there remaineth [k]falsehood?

---

[a]Chapter xx. 11; Eccles. ix. 2——[b]Chapter xx. 7
[c]Heb. *the tent of the tabernacles of the wicked*——[d]Prov. xvi. 4; 2 Pet. ii. 9

[e]Heb. *the day of wraths*——[f]Gal. ii. 11——[g]Heb. *graves*——[h]Heb. *watch in the heap*——[i]Heb. ix. 27
[k]Heb. *transgression*

---

this conjecture to be as likely as any that has yet been formed.

Verse 26. *They shall lie down alike in the dust*] Death levels all distinctions, and the grave makes all equal. There may be a difference in the grave itself; but the human corpse is the same in all. Splendid monuments enshrine *corruption;* but the *sod* must lie close and heavy upon the putrefying carcass, to prevent it from becoming the bane of the living.

Verse 27. *I know your thoughts*] Ye still think that, because I am grievously afflicted, I must therefore be a felonious transgressor.

Verse 28. *For ye say, Where* is *the house of the prince?*] In order to prove your point, ye *ask, Where is the house of the tyrant and oppressor?* Are they not overthrown and destroyed? And is not this a proof that God does not permit the wicked to enjoy prosperity?

Verse 29. *Have ye not asked them that go by the way?*] This appears to be Job's answer. Consult travellers who have gone through different countries; and they will tell you that they have seen both examples—the wicked in great prosperity in some instances, while suddenly destroyed in others. See at the end of the chapter.

Do ye not know their tokens] Mr. *Good* translates the whole verse thus: "Surely thou canst never have inquired of men of travel; or thou couldst not have been ignorant of their tokens. Hadst thou made proper inquiries, thou wouldst have heard of their awful end in a thousand instances. And also of their *prosperity.*" See at the end of this chapter.

Verse 30. *That the wicked is reserved to the day of destruction?*] Though every one can tell that he has seen the wicked in prosperity, and even spend a long life in it; yet this is no proof that God loves him, or that he shall enjoy a prosperous lot in the next world. There, he shall meet with the *day of wrath.* There, the wicked shall be punished, and the just rewarded.

Verse 31. *Who shall declare his way to his face?*] But while the wicked is in power, who shall dare to tell him to his face what his true character is? or, who shall dare to repay him the evil he has done? As such a person cannot have his punishment in this life, he must have it in another; and for this the *day of wrath*—the day of judgment, is prepared.

Verse 32. *Yet shall he be brought to the grave*] He shall die like other men; and the

corruption of the grave shall prey upon him. Mr. Carlyle, in his specimens of Arabic poetry, Translations, p. 16, quotes this verse, which he translates and paraphrases, והוא לקברות יובל "He shall be brought to the grave," ועל נדיש ישקוד "And shall *watch upon the high-raised heap.*"

It was the opinion of the pagan Arabs, that upon the death of any person, a bird, by them called *Manah,* issued from the brain, and haunted the sepulchre of the deceased, uttering a lamentable scream. This notion, he adds, is evidently alluded to in Job xxi. 32. Thus *Abusahel,* on the death of his mistress:—

"If her *ghost's* funereal *screech*
Through the earth my grave should reach,
On *that voice* I loved so well
My transported ghost would dwell."

Verse 33. *The clods of the valley shall be sweet unto him*] Perhaps there is an allusion here to the Asiatic mode of interment for princes, saints, and nobles: a well-watered valley was chosen for the tomb, where a perpetual spring might be secured. This was intended to be the emblem of a *resurrection,* or of a *future life;* and to *conceal* as much as possible the disgrace of the rotting carcass.

Every man shall draw after him] There seem to be two allusions intended here: 1. To *death,* the common lot of all. *Millions have gone before him* to the tomb; and כל אדם *col adam, all men, shall follow him:* all past generations have died; all succeeding generations shall die also. 2. To pompous *funeral processions;* multitudes *preceding,* and multitudes *following,* the corpse.

Verse 34. *How then comfort ye me in vain*] Mr. *Good* translates: "How vainly then would ye make me retract!" See the note on ver. 2. I cannot *retract* any thing I have said, as I have proved by fact and testimony that your positions are false and unfounded. Your pretensions to comfort me are as hollow as the arguments you bring in support of your exceptionable doctrines.

THIS chapter may be called Job's triumph over the insinuated calumnies, and specious but false doctrines, of his opponents. The irritability of his temper no longer appears: from the time he got that glorious discovery of his *Redeemer,* and the joyous hope of an *eternal in-*

heritance, chap. xix. 25, &c., we find no more murmurings, nor unsanctified complainings. He is now full master of himself; and reasons conclusively, because he reasons coolly. Impassioned transports no longer carry him away: his mind is serene; his heart, fixed; his hope, steady; and his faith, strong. Zophar the Naamathite is now, in his presence, as an infant in the gripe of a mighty giant. Another of these pretended friends but real enemies comes forward to renew the attack with virulent invective, malevolent insinuation, and unsupported assertion. Him, Job meets, and vanquishes by pious resignation and fervent prayer. Though, at different times after this, Job had his buffetings from his grand adversary, and some seasons of comparative darkness, yet his faith is unshaken, and he stands as a beaten anvil to the stroke. He effectually exculpates himself, and vindicates the dispensations of his Maker.

There appears to be something in the 29th verse which requires to be farther examined: *Have ye not asked them that go by the way? And do ye not know their tokens?* It is probable that this verse may allude to the custom of *burying the dead by the way-side*, and raising up *specious* and *descriptive* monuments over them. Job argues that the lot of outward prosperity fell alike to the just and to the unjust, and that the sepulchral monuments by the way-side were proofs of his assertion; for his friends, as well as himself and others, had noted them, and asked the history of such and such persons, from the nearest inhabitants of the place; and the answers, in a great variety of cases, had been: "*That* monument points out the place where a wicked man lies, who was all his lifetime in prosperity and affluence, yet oppressed the poor, and shut up the bowels of his compas-sion against the destitute; and *this* belongs to a man who lived only to serve his God, and to do good to man according to his power, yet had not a day of health, nor an hour of prosperity; God having given to the former *his portion in this life*, and reserved the recompense of the latter to a *future state*."

The *Septuagint* render the verse thus:— Ερωτησατε παραπορευμενους ὁδον, και τα σημεια αυτων ουκ απαλλοτριωσατε, "Inquire of those who pass by the way; and their signs [monuments] ye will not alienate." That is, When ye hear the history of these persons, ye will not then assert that the man who lived in prosperity was a genuine worshipper of the true God, and therefore was blessed with temporal good; and that he who lived in adversity was an enemy to God, and was consequently cursed with the want of secular blessings. Of the *former* ye will hear a different account from those who dare now speak the truth, because the prosperous oppressor is no more; and of the *latter* ye shall learn that, though afflicted, destitute, and distressed, he was one of those who acknowledged God in all his ways, and never performed an act of religious service to him in hope of *secular gain;* sought his approbation only, and met death cheerfully, in the hope of being eternally with the Lord.

Neither good nor evil can be known by the occurrences of this life. Every thing argues the certainty of a future state, and the necessity of a day of judgment. They who are in the habit of marking casualties, especially if those whom they love not are the subjects of them, as tokens of Divine displeasure, only show an ignorance of God's dispensations, and a malevolence of mind that would fain arm itself with the celestial thunders, in order to transfix those whom they deem their enemies.

CHAPTER XXII

Eliphaz reproves Job for his attempts to clear his character and establish his innocence, 1–4. Charges him with innumerable transgressions; with oppressions towards his brethren, cruelty to the poor, hard-heartedness to the needy, and uncharitableness towards the widow and the orphan; and says it is on these accounts that snares and desolations are come upon him, 5–11. Speaks of the majesty and justice of God: how he cut off the antediluvians, the inhabitants of Sodom and the cities of the plain, 12–20. Exhorts him to repent and acknowledge his sins, and promises him great riches and prosperity, 21–30.

A. M. cir. 2484
B. C. cir. 1520
Ante I. Olymp. cir. 744
Ante U. C. cir. 767

THEN Eliphaz the Temanite answered and said,

2 ªCan a man be profitable unto God, ᵇas he that is wise may be profitable unto himself?

3 *Is it* any pleasure to the Almighty, that thou art righteous? or *is it* gain *to him,* that thou makest thy ways perfect?

4 Will he reprove thee for fear of thee? will he enter with thee into judgment?

5 *Is* not thy wickedness great? and thine iniquities infinite?

A. M. cir. 2484
B. C. cir. 1520
Ante I. Olymp. cir. 744
Ante U. C. cir. 767

ªChap. xxxv. 7; Psa. xvi. 2; Luke xvii. 10——ᵇOr, *if he* *may be profitable* doth his *good success* depend *thereon?*

NOTES ON CHAP. XXII

Verse 2. *Can a man be profitable unto God*] God does not afflict thee because thou hast *deprived* him of any excellency. A man may be profitable to a man, but no man can profit his Maker. He has no interest in thy conduct; he does not punish thee because thou hast offended and deprived him of some good. Thy iniquities are against justice, and justice requires thy punishment.

Verse 3. Is it *any pleasure to the Almighty*] Infinite in his perfections, he can neither *gain* nor *lose* by the wickedness or righteousness of men.

A. M. cir. 2484
B. C. cir. 1520
Ante I. Olymp. cir. 744
Ante U. C. cir. 767

6 For thou hast ^ctaken a pledge from thy brother for naught, and ^dstripped the naked of their clothing.

7 Thou hast not given water to the weary to drink, and thou ^ehast withholden bread from the hungry.

8 But *as for* ^fthe mighty man, he had the earth; and the ^ghonourable man dwelt in it.

9 Thou hast sent widows away empty, and the arms of ^hthe fatherless have been broken.

10 Therefore ⁱsnares *are* round about thee, and sudden fear troubleth thee;

11 Or darkness, *that* thou canst not see; and abundance of ^kwaters cover thee.

12 *Is* not God in the height of heaven? and behold ^lthe height of the stars, how high they are!

13 And thou sayest, ^mHow ⁿdoth God know? can he judge through the dark cloud?

14 ^oThick clouds *are* a covering to him, that

A. M. cir. 2484
B. C. cir. 1520
Ante I. Olymp. cir. 474
Ante U. C. cir. 767

---

^cExodus xxii. 26, 27; Deuteronomy xxiv. 10, &c.; chap. xxiv. 3, 9; Ezekiel xviii. 12——^dHebrew, *stripped the clothes of the naked*——^eSee chap. xxxi. 17; Deuteronomy xv. 7, &c.; Isaiah lviii. 7; Ezekiel xviii. 7, 16; Matt. xxv. 42——^fHeb. *the man of arm*——^gHeb.

eminent or *accepted for countenance*——^hChapter xxxi. 21; Isa. x. 2; Ezek. xxii. 7——ⁱChap. xviii. 8, 9, 10; xix. 6——^kPsalm lxix. 1, 2; cxxiv. 4; Lam. iii. 54
^lHeb. *the head of the stars*——^mOr, *What*——ⁿPsa. x. 11; lix. 7; lxxiii. 11; xciv. 7——^oPsa. cxxxix. 11, 12

Verse 4. *For fear of thee?*] Is it because he is afraid that thou wilt do him some *injury*, that he has stripped thee of thy power and wealth?

Verse 5. Is *not thy wickedness great?*] Thy sins are not only *many*, but they are *great;* and of thy continuance in them *there is no end*, אֵין קֵץ *ein kets*.

Verse 6. *Thou hast taken a pledge*] Thou hast been vexatious in all thy doings, and hast exacted where nothing was due, so that through thee the poor have been unable to procure their necessary clothing.

Verse 7. *Thou hast not given water*] It was esteemed a great virtue in the East to furnish thirsty travellers with water; especially in the deserts, where scarcely a *stream* was to be found, and where *wells* were very rare. Some of the Indian devotees are accustomed to stand with a *girbah* or skin full of water, on the public roads, to give drink to weary travellers who are parched with thirst.

Verse 8. *But* as for *the mighty man, he had the earth*] אִישׁ זְרֹעַ *ish zeroa, the man of arm*. Finger, hand, and arm, are all emblems of strength and power. The *man of arm* is not only the *strong man*, but the *man of power* and *influence*, the man of *rapine* and *plunder*.

The honourable man] Literally, the man whose *face is accepted*, the respectable man, the man of *wealth*. Thou wert an enemy to the *poor* and *needy*, but thou didst favour and flatter the *rich* and *great*.

Verse 9. *The arms of the fatherless*] Whatever *strength* or *power* or property they had, of that thou hast deprived them. Thou hast been hard-hearted and cruel, and hast enriched thyself with the spoils of the poor and the defenceless.

Verse 10. *Therefore snares*] As thou hast dealt with others, so has God, in his retributive providence, dealt with thee. As thou hast spoiled, so art thou spoiled. Thou art taken in a net from which thou canst not escape. There is an allusion here to the hunting of the elephant: he is driven into an inclosure in the woods, passing from strait to strait, till brought into a narrow point, from which he cannot escape; and then his consternation is great, and his roaring terrible. God hath hunted thee down, as men hunt down those wild and dangerous beasts. See on chap. xviii.

Verse 11. *Or darkness, that thou canst not*

see] The sense of this passage, in the connection that the particle *or* gives it with the preceding verse, is not easy to be ascertained. To me it seems very probable that a letter has been lost from the first word; and that אֹו *o*, which we translate OR, was originally אֹור *or*, LIGHT. The copy used by the *Septuagint* had certainly this reading; and therefore they translate the verse thus: Τὸ φῶς σοι εἰς σκότος ἀπέβη; *Thy* LIGHT *is changed into darkness;* that is, Thy *prosperity* is turned into *adversity*.

Houbigant corrects the text thus: instead of אֹו חֹשֶׁךְ לֹא תִרְאֶה *o chosech lo tireh, or darkness thou canst not see*, he reads חֹשֶׁךְ לֹא אֹור תִרְאֶה *chosech lo or tireh, darkness, not light, shalt thou behold;* that is, Thou shalt dwell in thick darkness. Mr. *Good* translates: "Or darkness which thou canst not penetrate, and a flood of waters shall cover thee." Thou shalt either be enveloped in deep darkness, or overwhelmed with a flood.

The versions all translate differently; and neither they nor the MSS. give any light, except what is afforded by the Septuagint. *Coverdale* is singular: **Shuldest thou then send darcknesse? Shulde not the water floude runne ober the?** Perhaps the meaning is: "Thou art so encompassed with darkness, that thou canst not see thy way; and therefore fallest into the snares and traps that are laid for thee."

Verse 12. Is *not God in the height of heaven?*] It appears, from this and the following verses, that Eliphaz was attributing infidel and blasphemous speeches or sentiments to Job. As if he had said: "Thou allowest that there is a God, but thou sayest that he is infinitely exalted above the heavens and the stars, and that there is so much dense ether and thick cloud between his throne and the earth, that he can neither see it nor its inhabitants." These were sentiments which Job never held, and never uttered; but if a man be dressed in a bear's skin, he may be hunted and worried by his own dogs. Job's friends attribute falsities to him, and then dilate upon them, and draw inferences from them injurious to his character. *Polemic writers*, both in *theology* and *politics*, often act in this way.

Verse 14. *He walketh in the circuit of heaven*] He confines himself to those infinitely exalted regions and cares nothing for the inhabitants of the earth.

A. M. cir. 2484
B. C. cir. 1520
Ante I. Olymp.
cir. 744
Ante U. C. cir.
767

he seeth not; and he walketh in the circuit of heaven.

15 Hast thou marked the old way which wicked men have trodden?

16 Which ᵖwere cut down out of time, �q whose foundation was overflown with a flood:

17 ʳWhich said unto God, Depart from us: and ˢwhat can the Almighty do ᵗfor them?

18 Yet he filled their houses with good *things:* but ᵘthe counsel of the wicked is far from me.

19 ᵛThe righteous see *it,* and are glad: and

the innocent laugh them to scorn.

A. M. cir. 2484
B. C. cir. 1520
Ante I. Olymp.
cir. 744
Ante U. C. cir.
767

20 Whereas our ʷsubstance is not cut down, but ˣthe remnant of them the fire consumeth.

21 Acquaint now thyself ʸwith him, and ᶻbe at peace: thereby good shall come unto thee.

22 Receive, I pray thee, the law from his mouth, and ᵃlay up his words in thine heart.

23 ᵇIf thou return to the Almighty, thou shalt be built up, thou shalt put away iniquity far from thy tabernacles.

ᵖCh. xv. 32; Psa. lv. 23; cii. 24; Eccles. vii. 17
�q Heb. *a flood was poured upon their foundation;* Gen. vii. 11; 2 Pet. ii. 5——ʳCh. xxi. 14——ˢPsa. iv. 6——ᵗOr, *to them*

ᵘChap. xxi. 16——ᵛPsa. lviii. 10; cvii. 42——ʷOr, *estate*——ˣOr, *their excellency*——ʸThat is, *with God*
ᶻIsa. xxvii. 5——ᵃPsa. cxix. 11——ᵇChap. viii. 5, 6; xi. 13, 14

Verse 15. *Hast thou marked the old way*] This is supposed to be another accusation; as if he had said, "Thou followest the same way that the wicked of old have walked in." Here is an evident allusion to the FLOOD, as is particularly noted in the next verse.

Verse 16. *Whose foundation was overflown with a flood*] The unrighteous in the days of Noah, who appear to have had an abundance of all temporal good, (ver. 18,) and who surpassed the deeds of all the former wicked, said in effect to God, *Depart from us.* And when Noah preached unto them the terrors of the Lord, and the necessity of repentance, they rejected his preaching with, *What can the Almighty do for us?* Let him do his worst; we care not for him, ver. 17.

For למו *lamo, to* THEM, the *Septuagint, Syriac,* and *Arabic* have evidently read לנו *lanu, to* US. This reading quotes their *own saying;* the former reading narrates it in *the third person.* The meaning, however, is the same.

Verse 18. *But the counsel of the wicked is far from me.*] Sarcastically quoting Job's words, chap. xxi. 14, 16. Job, having in the preceding chapter described the wicked, who said unto the Almighty, "Depart from us," &c., adds, *But the counsel of the wicked is far from me.* Eliphaz here, having described the impious, among whom he evidently ranks Job, makes use of the same expression, as if he had said, "Thank God, I have no connection with you nor your companions; nor is my mind contaminated by your creed."

Verse 19. *The righteous see it, and are glad*] They see God's judgments on the incorrigibly wicked, and know that the Judge of all the earth does right; hence they rejoice in all the dispensations of his providence.

Verse 20. *Whereas our substance is not cut down*] We, who fear the Lord, still continue in health and peace; whereas they who have departed from him are destroyed even to their very remnant.

Mr. *Good* thinks that קימנו *kimanu,* which we translate *our substance,* is the same as the Arabic قومنا *our people* or *tribe;* and hence he translates the clause thus: "For our tribe is not

cut off; while even the remnant of these a conflagration consumed." The reference here is supposed to be to the destruction of the men of Sodom and Gomorrah. A judgment by a *flood* took off the world of the ungodly in the days of *Noah.* Their remnant, those who lived in the same ungodly way, were taken off by a judgment of fire, in the days of *Lot.* Eliphaz introduces these two examples in order to terrify Job into a compliance with the exhortation which immediately follows.

Verse 21. *Acquaint now thyself with him*] Perhaps the verb הסכן *hasken* should be translated here, *treasure up,* or *lay up. Lay up* or procure an *interest now with him, and be at peace.* Get the Divine favour, and then thou wilt be at peace with God, and have happiness in thy own soul.

Thereby good shall come unto thee.] בהם *bahem,* "in them," shall good come unto thee. That is, in getting an interest in the Divine favour, and in having thy soul brought into a state of peace with him; thereby, in them, that is, these two things, good will come unto thee. First, thou wilt have an interest in his favour, from which thou mayest expect all blessings; and, secondly, from his peace in thy conscience thou wilt feel unutterable happiness. Get these blessings *now,* for thou knowest not what a day may bring forth. Reader, hast *thou* these blessings?

Verse 22. *Receive, I pray thee, the law from his mouth*] Some, who wish to place Job *before* the law given by Moses, say that this means the *Noahic precepts;* others, that the *law of nature* is intended! Stuff and vanity! The allusion is plainly to the *law* given by God to the children of Israel, called here by way of emphasis, תורה *torah, the* LAW, which contained אמריו *amaraiv, his* WORDS, the *words* or *sayings of God* himself; consequently, it is not the *Noahic precepts,* nor the *law of nature,* neither of which were ever *written* or *registered* as the *words of God's mouth.*

Verse 23. *Thou shalt be built up*] God will restore thee to thy wonted state of prosperity; and thou shalt again have a *household,* not only of *servants,* but of *children* also. So much may be implied in the words, *Thou shalt be* BUILT UP. See my sermon on ver. 21-23.

A. M. cir. 2484
B. C. cir. 1520
Ante I. Olymp. cir. 744
Ante U. C. cir. 767

24 Then shalt thou ^clay up gold ^das dust, and the *gold* of Ophir as the stones of the brooks.

25 Yea, the Almighty shall be thy ^edefence, and thou shalt have ^fplenty of silver.

26 For then shalt thou have thy ^gdelight in the Almighty, and ^hshalt lift up thy face unto God.

27 ⁱThou shalt make thy prayer unto him, and he shall hear thee, and thou shalt pay thy vows.

28 Thou shalt also decree a thing, and it shall be established unto thee: and the light shall shine upon thy ways.

A. M. cir. 2484
B. C. cir. 1520
Ante I. Olymp. cir. 744
Ante U. C. cir. 767

29 When *men* are cast down, then thou shalt say, *There is* lifting up; and ^khe shall save ^lthe humble person.

30 ^mHe shall deliver the island of the innocent: and it is delivered by the pureness of thine hands.

---

^c2 Chron. i. 15——^dOr, *on the dust*——^eOr, *gold* ^fHeb. *silver of strength*——^gChap. xxvii. 10; Isa. lviii. 14 ^hChap. xi. 15——ⁱPsa. l. 14, 15; Isa. lviii. 9

^kProv. xxix. 23; James iv. 6; 1 Pet. v. 5——^lHeb. *him that hath low eyes*——^mOr, *The innocent shall deliver the island*, Gen. xviii. 26, &c.

Verse 24. *Then shalt thou lay up gold as dust*] The original is not fairly rendered in this translation, וְשִׁית עַל עָפָר בֶּצֶר *veshith al aphar batser,* which *Montanus* renders: *Et pone super pulverem munitionem,* "And fix a tower upon the dust;" וּבְצוּר נְחָלִים אוֹפִיר *ubetsur nechalim Ophir, et in petra torrentes Ophir,* "and in the rock, the torrents of Ophir."

The *Vulgate* is widely different: *Dabit pro terra silicem, et pro silice torrentes aureos,* "He will give thee flint for earth: and torrents of gold for flint;" which *Calmet* thus paraphrases: "Instead of brick thou shalt build with solid stone; and for ornaments, instead of stone as formerly, thou shalt have massive gold!"

All the versions are different. Mr. *Good* translates: "Then count thou treasure as dust: then shall he make fountains to gush forth amidst the rocks."

Coverdale is different from all: 𝕳𝖊 𝖘𝖍𝖆𝖑 𝖌𝖎𝖇𝖊 𝖙𝖍𝖊 𝖆𝖚 𝖍𝖆𝖗𝖛𝖊𝖘𝖙, 𝖜𝖍𝖎𝖈𝖍, 𝖎𝖓 𝖕𝖑𝖊𝖓𝖙𝖞 𝖆𝖓𝖉 𝖆𝖇𝖚𝖓𝖉𝖆𝖓𝖈𝖊, 𝖘𝖍𝖆𝖑 𝖊𝖝𝖈𝖊𝖆𝖉𝖊 𝖙𝖍𝖊 𝖉𝖚𝖘𝖙 𝖔𝖋 𝖙𝖍𝖊 𝖊𝖆𝖗𝖙𝖍𝖊, 𝖆𝖓𝖉 𝖙𝖍𝖊 𝖌𝖔𝖑𝖉𝖊 𝖔𝖋 𝕺𝖕𝖍𝖎𝖗 𝖑𝖎𝖐𝖊 𝖗𝖞𝖇𝖊𝖗 𝖘𝖙𝖔𝖓𝖊𝖘.

Verse 25. *Thou shalt have plenty of silver.*] Here again the versions and critics vary. The critics may disagree; but the doctrine of Eliphaz is sufficiently plain: "To those whom God loves best he gives the most earthly good. The rich and the great are his high favorites: the poor and the distressed he holds for his enemies."

In the above verses there seems to be a reference to the mode of obtaining the precious metals: 1. Gold in dust; 2. Gold in streams from the hills and mountains; 3. Silver in mines; כֶּסֶף תּוֹעָפוֹת *keseph toaphoth,* "silver of giddiness;" of mines so deep as to make one giddy by looking into them. See Mr. *Good.*

Verse 26. *For then shalt thou have thy delight*] Thou shalt know, from thy temporal prosperity, that God favours thee; and for his bounty thou shalt be grateful. How different is this doctrine from that of St. Paul and St. John! "Being justified by faith, we have peace with God, through our Lord Jesus." "Because ye are sons, God hath sent forth the Spirit of his Son into your hearts, crying, Abba, Father!" "The Spirit himself beareth witness with our spirits that we are the children of God." "We glory in tribulation also, knowing that tribulation worketh patience; and patience, experience; and experience, hope: and hope maketh not ashamed, because the love of God is shed abroad in our hearts by the Holy Ghost, which is given unto us." "We love him because he first loved us." *Tribulation* itself was often a mark of God's favour.

Verse 27. *Thou shalt make thy prayer unto him*] תַּעְתִּיר *tatir, thou shalt open* or *unbosom thyself.* And when the *heart* prays, God hears; and the person, being blessed, vows fidelity, prays on, is supported, and enabled to pay his vows.

Verse 28. *Thou shalt also decree a thing*] Whatsoever thou purposest in his strength, thou shalt be enabled to accomplish.

Verse 29. *When* men *are cast down*] There is a great difficulty in this verse; the sense, however, is tolerably evident, and the following is nearly a literal version: *When they shall humble themselves, thou shalt say, Be exalted,* or, *there is exaltation: for the down-cast of eye he will save.* The same sentiment as that of our Lord, "He that exalteth himself shall be abased; but he that humbleth himself shall be exalted."

Verse 3. *He shall deliver the island of the innocent*] The word אִי *ai,* which we translate *island,* is most probably the Arabic particle اَيْ *whosoever, whatsoever, any, whosoever he may be,* as اَيْ رَجُل *ai rajuli, whatsoever man he may be.* And it is most probable that both words are Arabic, اَيْ نَقِيّ or تَقَا اَى *any innocent, chaste, pure,* or *holy person;* for the word has the same meaning both in Hebrew and Arabic. The text may therefore be translated, *He shall deliver every innocent person: He,* the innocent person, *shall be delivered by the pureness of thy hands;* i. e., as thou lovest justice, so thou wilt do justice. Instead of כַּפֶּיךָ *cappeyca, thy hands,* the *Vulgate, Syriac,* and *Arabic* have read כַּפָּיו *cappaiv, his* or *their hands.* Mr. *Good* thinks that אִי *ai* signifies *house,* as اَىْ and اَوَىْ in Arabic signify *to reside, to have a home,* &c.; and therefore translates the passage thus: "The house of the innocent shall be delivered; and delivered by the pureness of thy hands." The reader may adopt which he pleases; but the word *island* must be given up, as it cannot make any consistent sense.

THUS ends Eliphaz the Temanite, who began with a tissue of the bitterest charges, continued with the most cruel insinuations, and ended with common-place exhortations to repentance, and promises of secular blessings in consequence:

and from his whole speech scarcely can one new or important maxim be derived. Blessed be God for Moses and the prophets! for Jesus, the evangelists, and the apostles! Their trumpet gives no uncertain sound: but by that of Job's friends who can prepare himself for the battle?

CHAPTER XXIII

Job answers; apologizes for his complaining; wishes to plead his cause in the presence of his Maker, from whom he knows he should receive justice; but regrets that he cannot find him, 1–9. He, however, gives himself and his cause up to God, with the conviction of his own innocence, and God's justice and goodness, 10–14. He is, nevertheless, afraid when he considers the majesty of his Maker, 15–17.

A. M. cir. 2484
B. C. cir. 1520
Ante I. Olymp.
cir. 744
Ante U. C. cir.
767

THEN Job answered and said, 2 Even to-day *is* my complaint bitter: [a]my stroke is heavier than my groaning.

3 [b]O that I knew where I might find him! *that* I might come *even* to his seat!

4 I would order *my* cause before him, and fill my mouth with arguments.

5 I would know the words *which* he would answer me, and understand what he would say unto me.

6 [c]Will he plead against me with *his* great power? No; but he would put *strength* in me.

A. M. cir. 2484
B. C. cir. 1520
Ante I. Olymp.
cir. 744
Ante U. C. cir.
767

7 There the righteous might dispute with him; so should I be delivered for ever from my judge.

8 [d]Behold, I go forward, but he *is* not *there;* and backward, but I cannot perceive him:

9 On the left hand, where he doth work, but

---

[a]Heb. *my hand*——[b]Chap. xiii. 3; xvi. 21

[c]Isa. xxvii. 4, 8; lvii. 16——[d]Chap. ix. 11

NOTES ON CHAP. XXIII

Verse 2. *Even to-day* is *my complaint bitter*] Job goes on to maintain his own innocence, and shows that he has derived neither conviction nor consolation from the discourses of his friends. He grants that his complaint is bitter; but states that, loud as it may be, the affliction which he endures is heavier than his complaints are loud.

Mr. *Good* translates: "And still is my complaint rebellion?" Do ye construe my lamentations over my unparalleled sufferings as rebellion against God? This, in fact, they had done from the beginning: and the original will justify the version of Mr. *Good;* for מרי *meri,* which we translate *bitter,* may be derived from מרה *marah,* "he rebelled."

Verse 3. *O that I knew where I might find him!*] This and the following verse may be read thus: "Who will give me the knowledge of God, that I may find him out? I would come to his establishment; (the place or way in which he has promised to communicate himself;) I would exhibit, in detail, my judgment (the cause I wish to be tried) before his face; and my mouth would I fill with convincing or decisive arguments;" arguments drawn from his common method of saving sinners, which I should prove applied fully to my case. Hence the confidence with which he speaks, ver. 6.

Verse 5. *I would know the words* which *he would answer me*] He would speak nothing but what was true, decree nothing that was not righteous, nor utter any thing that I could not comprehend.

Verse 6. *Will he plead against me*] He would not exhibit his majesty and his sovereign authority to strike me dumb, or so overawe me that I could not speak in my own vindication.

No; but he would put strength *in me.*] On the contrary, he would treat me with tenderness, he would rectify my mistakes, he would show me what was in my favour, and would temper the rigid demands of justice by the mild interpretations of equity; and where *law* could not clear me, *mercy* would conduct all to the most favourable issue.

Verse 7. *There the righteous might dispute with him*] נוכח *nochach,* might *argue* or *plead.* To *dispute with* God sounds very harsh.

So should I be delivered for ever] Mr. *Good* translates: "And triumphantly should I escape from my condemnation." The Hebrew word לנצח *lanetsach* may as well be translated *to victory* as *for ever:* and in this sense the *Vulgate* understood the words: *Proponat æquitatem contra me; et perveniat ad victoriam judicium meum.* "He would set up equity against me; and would lead on my cause to victory." *Coverdale* renders thus:—**But let hym gibe me like power to go to lawe, then am I sure to wynne my matter.** Nothing less than the fullest conviction of his own innocence could have led Job to express himself thus to the Judge of quick and dead!

Verse 8. *Behold, I go forward*] These two verses paint in vivid colours the distress and anxiety of a soul in search of the favour of God. No *means* are left *untried,* no *place unexplored,* in order to find the object of his research. This is a true description of the conduct of a genuine penitent.

Verse 9. *On the left hand, where he doth work*] In these two verses Job mentions the four cardinal points of the heavens: the EAST, by the word קדם *kedem,* which signifies *before;* the WEST, by אחור *achor,* which signifies *after,* or the *back part;* the NORTH, by שמאל *semol,* which signifies the *left;* and the SOUTH, by ימין *yamin,* which signifies the *right.* Such is the situation of the world to a man who faces the

A. M. cir. 2484
B. C. cir. 1520
Ante I. Olymp.
cir. 744
Ante U. S. cir.
767

I cannot behold *him:* he hideth himself on the right hand, that I cannot see *him:*

10 But he [e]knoweth [f]the way that I take: *when* [g]he hath tried me, I shall come forth as gold.

11 [h]My foot hath held his steps, his way have I kept, and not declined.

12 Neither have I gone back from the com-

mandment of his lips; [1] [k]have esteemed the words of his mouth more than [l]my necessary *food.*

A. M. cir. 2484
B. C. cir. 1520
Ante I. Olymp.
cir. 744
Ante U. C. cir.
767

13 But he *is* in one *mind,* and [m]who can turn him? and *what* [n]his soul desireth, even *that* he doeth.

14 For he performeth *the thing that is* [o]appointed for me: and many such *things are* with him.

---

[e]Psa. cxxxix. 1, 2, 3——[f]Heb. *the way* that is *with me*
[g]Psa. xvii. 3; lxvi. 10; James i. 12——[h]Psa. xliv. 18
[1]Heb. *I have hid* or *laid up*

[k]John iv. 32, 34——[l]Or, *my appointed portion*
[m]Chap. ix. 12, 13; xii. 14; Rom. ix. 19——[n]Psa. cxv. 3
[o]1 Thess. iii. 3

---

east; see Gen. xiii. 9, 11, and xxviii. 14. And from this it appears that the Hebrews, Idumeans, and Arabs had the same ideas of these points of the heavens. It is worthy of remark that Job says, He *hideth himself on the right hand,* (the *south,*) *that I cannot see him:* for in fact, the southern point of heaven is not visible in Idumea, where Job was. Hence it comes that when he spake before, chap. ix. 9, of the constellations of the antarctic pole, he terms them the *hidden chambers of the south;* i. e., those compartments of the celestial concave that never appeared above the horizon in that place.—See *Calmet.*

Mr. *Good* translates these verses as follows:—

Behold! I go forward, and he is not there;
And backward, but I cannot perceive him.
On the left hand I feel for him, but trace *him* not:
He enshroudeth the right hand, and I cannot see *him.*

The simple rendering of *Coverdale* is nervous and correct:—

For though I go before, I fynde hym not:
Yf I come behynde, I can get no knowledge of him:
Yf I go on the left syde to pondre his workes,
I cannot atteyne unto them:
Agayne, yf I go on the right syde, he hydeth himself,
That I cannot se him.

Verse 10. *But he knoweth the way that I take*] He *approves* of my conduct; my ways *please* him. He tries me: but, like gold, I shall lose nothing in the fire; I shall come forth more pure and luminous. If that which is reputed to be gold is exposed to the action of a strong fire, if it be genuine, it will lose nothing of its *quality,* nor of its *weight.* If it went into the fire *gold,* it will come out *gold;* the strongest fire will neither alter nor destroy it. So Job: he went into this furnace of affliction an innocent, righteous man; he came out the same. His character lost nothing of its *value,* nothing of its *lustre.*

Verse 11. *My foot hath held his steps, his way have I kept*] I have carefully marked his *providential dealings;* and in his *way*—his pure and undefiled religion—have I walked. I have not only been *generally* but *particularly* religious: I have attended carefully to the *weightier* matters of the law, and have not forgotten its *slightest* injunctions.

Coverdale is curious:—Neverthelesse my fete kepe his path, his hye strete have I holden, and not gone

out of it. The hye strete is *highway,* the *causeway,* or *raised road;* formed, as they anciently were, by stones in the manner of *pavement.* It has its name from the Latin *strata,* paved, *via* being understood: *via lapidibus strata,* "a way paved with stones:" hence *street,* a raised road or pavement either in town or country. And hence the *four grand Roman* or *British roads* which intersected this kingdom: viz. *Watling street, Icknild* or *Ricknild street, Ermin street,* and *Fosse street.* Some say these *streets* or roads were made by *Bellinus,* a British king.

Fosse street began in Cornwall, passed through Devonshire, Somersetshire, and along by Titbury upon Toteswould, beside Coventry, unto Leicester; and thence by the wide plains to Newark and to Lincoln, where it ends.

Watling street begins at Dover, passes through the middle of Kent, over the Thames by London, running near Westminster, and thence to St. Alban's, Dunstable, Stratford, Towcester, Weden, Lilbourn, Atherston, Wreaken by Severn, Worcester, Stratton, through Wales unto Cardigan, and on to the Irish sea.

Ermin, or *Erminage street,* running from St. David's in Wales, to Southampton.

Ricknild, or *Icknild street,* running by Worcester, Wycomb, Birmingham, Lichfield, Derby, Chesterfield, and by York, into Tynemouth. See *Camden, Holinshed,* and *Minshieu.*

Verse 12. *The commandment of his lips*] The written law that proceeded from his own mouth.

I have esteemed the words of his mouth] Mr. *Good* has given a better version of the original: *In my bosom have I stored up the words of his mouth.* The Asiatics carry every thing precious or valuable in their *bosom,* their handkerchiefs, jewels, purses, &c. Job, therefore, intimates that the words of God's mouth were to him a *most precious treasure.*

Verse 13. *But he is in one mind*] The original is והוא באחד *vehu beechad,* and is literally, *But he is in one:* properly rendered by the *Vulgate, Ipse enim solus est, But he is alone.* And not badly rendered by *Coverdale:*—It is he himself alone. He has no partner; his designs are his own, they are formed in his infinite wisdom, and none can turn his determinations aside. It is vain, therefore, for man to contend with his Maker. He designs my happiness, and you cannot prevent its accomplishment.

Verse 14. *For he performeth the thing that is appointed for me*] *Coverdale* translates:— He rewardeth me into my bosome, and many other thinges mo doth he, as he maye by his power. חקי *chukki* may as well be translated *bosom* here as in the 12th verse; but probably it may mean

A. M. cir. 2484
B. C. cir. 1520
Ante I. Olymp.
cir. 744
Ante U. C. cir.
767

15 Therefore am I troubled at his presence: when I consider, I am afraid of him.

16 For God ᵖmaketh my heart soft, and the Almighty troubleth me:

17 Because I was not cut off before the darkness, *neither* hath he covered the darkness from my face.

A. M. cir. 2484
B. C. cir. 1520
Ante I. Olymp.
cir. 744
Ante U. C. cir.
767

ᵖPsalm xxii. 14

---

a *portion, lot, sufficiency: For he hath appointed me my lot; and like these there are multitudes with him.* He diversifies human affairs: scarcely any two men have the same lot; nor has the same person the same portion at all times. He has multitudes of resources, expedients, means, &c., which he employs in governing human affairs.

Verse 15. *Therefore am I troubled*] I do not as yet see an end to my afflictions: he has not exhausted his means of trial; therefore, when I consider this, I am afraid of him.

Verse 16. *For God maketh my heart soft*] Prostrates my *strength*, deprives me of *courage*, so that I sink beneath my burden, and I am troubled at the thought of the Almighty, the self-sufficient and eternal Being.

Verse 17. *Because I was not cut off*] "O, why can I not draw darkness over my face? Why may not thick darkness cover my face?"— Mr. *Good.* This verse should be read in connection with the preceding; and then we shall have the following sense. Ver. 16: "The Lord hath beaten down my strength, and my soul has been terrified by his fear." Ver. 17: "For it is not this deep night in which I am enveloped, nor the evils which I suffer, that have overwhelmed me; I sink only through the fear which the presence of his Majesty inspires. This is my greatest affliction; sufferings, diseases, yea, death itself, are nothing in comparison of the terror which my soul feels in the presence of his tremendous holiness and justice."

NOTHING can humble a pious mind so much as Scriptural apprehensions of the majesty of God. It is easy to contemplate his *goodness, loving-kindness,* and *mercy;* in all these we have an interest, and from them we expect the greatest good: but to consider his *holiness* and *justice,* the infinite *righteousness* of his nature, under the conviction that we have *sinned,* and *broken the laws* prescribed by his *sovereign Majesty,* and to feel ourselves brought as into the presence of his judgment-seat,—who can bear the thought? If cherubim and seraphim veil their faces before his throne, and the *holiest* soul exclaims,

I loathe myself when God I see,
　　And into nothing fall;

what must a *sinner* feel, whose conscience is not yet purged from dead works, and who feels the wrath of God abiding on him? And how, without such a mediator and sacrifice as Jesus Christ is, can any human spirit come into the presence of its Judge? Those who can approach him *without terror,* know little of *his* justice, and nothing of *their* sin. When we approach him in prayer, or in any ordinance, should we not feel more *reverence* than we generally do?

CHAPTER XXIV

Job asserts that there are various transgressors whose wickedness is not visited on them in this life; and particularizes the unjust and oppressive, 1–6; those who are cruel to the poor, 7–13; the murderer, 14; the adulterer, 15; thieves and plunderers, 16, 17. Nevertheless they have an accursed portion, and shall die, and their memory perish, 18–20. He speaks of the abuse of power, and of the punishment of oppressors, 21–24; and asserts that what he has said on these subjects cannot be contradicted, 25.

A. M. cir. 2484
B. C. cir. 1520
Ante I. Olymp.
cir. 744
Ante U. C. cir.
767

WHY, seeing ᵃtimes are not hidden from the Almighty, do they that know him not see his days?

2 *Some* remove the ᵇlandmarks; they violently take away flocks, and ᶜfeed *thereof*.

3 They drive away the ass of

A. M. cir. 2484
B. C. cir. 1520
Ante I. Olymp.
cir. 744
Ante U. C. cir.
767

ᵃActs i. 7——ᵇDeut. xix. 14; xxvii. 17; Prov. xxii. 28; xxiii. 10; Hos. v. 10——ᶜOr, *feed* them

---

NOTES ON CHAP. XXIV

Verse 1. *Why, seeing times are not hidden from the Almighty*] Mr. *Good* translates: "Wherefore are not doomsdays kept by the Almighty, so that his offenders may eye their periods?" *Doomsdays* are here used in the same sense as *term times;* and the wish is, that God

would appoint such times that the falsely accused might look forward to them with comfort; knowing that, on their arrival, they should have a fair hearing, and their innocence be publicly declared; and their detractors, and the unjust in general, meet with their deserts. But God reserves the knowledge of these things to himself. "The holy patriarch," says Mr. *Good*

A. M. cir. 2484
B. C. cir. 1520
Ante I. Olymp.
cir. 744
Ante U. C. cir.
767

the fatherless, they ^dtake the widow's ox for a pledge.

4 They turn the needy out of the way: ^ethe poor of the earth hide themselves together.

5 Behold, *as* wild asses in the desert, go they forth to their work; rising betimes for a prey: the wilderness *yieldeth* food for them *and* for *their* children.

6 They reap *every one* his ^fcorn in the field: and ^gthey gather the vintage of the wicked.

7 They ^hcause the naked to lodge without clothing, that *they have* no covering in the cold.

8 They are wet with the showers of the mountains, and ⁱembrace the rock for want of a shelter.

A. M. cir. 2484
B. C. cir. 1520
Ante I. Olymp.
cir. 744
Ante U. C. cir.
767

---

^dChap. xxii. 6; Deut. xxiv. 6, 10, 12, 17——^eProv. xxviii. 28——^fHeb. *mingled corn* or *dredge*

^gHeb. *the wicked gather the vintage*——^hExod. xxii. 26, 27; Deut. xxiv. 12, 13; chap. xxii. 6——ⁱLam. iv. 5

"has uniformly admitted that in the aggregate scale of Providence the just are rewarded and the wicked punished for their respective deeds, in some period or other of their lives. But he has contended in various places, and especially in chap. xxi. 7-13, that the exceptions to this general rule are numerous: so numerous, as to be sufficient to render the whole scheme of providential *interposition* perfectly mysterious and incomprehensible, chap. xxiii. 8-12; so in the passage before us: if the retribution ye speak of be universal, and which I am ready to admit to a certain extent to be true and unquestionable, I not only ask, Why do the just ever suffer in the midst of their righteousness? but, Why do not the wicked see such retribution displayed before their eyes by stated judgments, so that they may at one and the same time know and tremble?"

Verse 2. Some *remove the landmarks*] Stones or posts were originally set up to ascertain the bounds of particular estates: and this was necessary in open countries, before *hedges* and *fences* were formed. Wicked and covetous men often removed the landmarks or *termini*, and set them *in* on their neighbours' ground, that, by contracting their boundaries, they might enlarge their own. The law of Moses denounces curses on those who remove their neighbours' landmarks. See Deut. xix. 14, xxvii. 17, and the note on the former place, where the subject is considered at large.

They violently take away flocks, and feed thereof.] Mr. *Good* translates יִרְעוּ *yiru, they destroy*, deriving the word, not from רָעָה *raah*, to *feed*, but from רַע *ra*, to *rend*, to *destroy*.

The Septuagint had read רֹעֶה *roeh*, a shepherd; and therefore have translated ποιμνιον συν ποιμενι ἁρπασαντες, "violently carrying off both the flock and the shepherd."

Verse 4. *They turn the needy out of the way*] They will not permit them to go by the accustomed paths; they oblige them to take circuitous routes. When the Marquis of H. was made ranger of Richmond Park, he thought it his duty to shut up a pathway which had existed for a long time; and those who presumed, after this shutting up, to break the fence, and take that path as formerly, were prosecuted. A *cobbler* near the place entered an action against the marquis: the cause was tried, the marquis cast, and the path ordered to be opened, on the ground that it had, time out of mind, been a public undisputed path. When one asked the *cobbler*, "How he could have the boldness to go to law with the Marquis of H.?" he answered, "Because I did not like to leave the world worse than I found it." All tolerated oppression and

voluntary forfeiture of ancient rights, are injurious to society at large, and they who *wink* at them *leave the world worse than they found it.*

Verse 5. *Rising betimes for a prey*] The general sense here seems plain enough. There are some who live a lawless roaming life: make a predatory life their employment; for this purpose, frequent the wilderness, where they seize on and appropriate whatsoever they find, and by this method they and their families are supported.

Mr. *Good* says: "The sense has never yet been understood by any commentator;" and hence he proposes a different division of the words, placing עֲרָבָה *arabah*, the *desert* or *wilderness*, in the first hemistich, thus:—

"Rising early for the pillage of the wilderness;
The bread of themselves *and* of their children."

Others think that the words are spoken solely of the poor under the hand of oppression, who are driven away from their homes, and obliged to seek such support as the wilderness can afford. Such was originally the state of the *Bedouins*, and of the wandering Arab hordes in general: the oppression of the tyrannous governors obliged them to seek refuge in the deserts, where they still live in a roaming predatory life.

Verse 6. *They reap* every one *his corn in the field*] This is perfectly characteristic. These wandering hordes often make sudden irruptions, and carry off the harvest of grain, olives, vines, &c., and plunge with it into the wilderness, where none can follow them. The *Chaldee* gives the same sense: "They reap in a field that is not their own, and cut off the vineyard of the wicked."

Verse 7. *They cause the naked to lodge without clothing*] Or rather, *They spend the night naked, without clothing; and without a covering from the cold:* another characteristic of the wandering Arabs. They are *ill-fed, ill-clothed*, and often miserably off, even for *tents*. They can have little household stuff: as they are plunderers, they are often obliged to fly for their lives, and cannot encumber themselves with what is not absolutely needful.

Verse 8. *They are wet with the showers of the mountains*] Mr. *Good* thinks that *torrents*, not *showers*, is the proper translation of the original זֶרֶם *zerem;* but I think *showers of the mountain* strictly proper. I have seen many of these in mountainous countries, where the tails of *water-spouts* have been intercepted and broken, and the *outpouring* of them would be

A. M. cir. 2484
B. C. cir. 1520
Ante I. Olymp. cir. 744
Ante U. C. cir. 767

9 They pluck the fatherless from the breast, and take a pledge of the poor.

10 They cause *him* to go naked without clothing, and they take away ᵏthe sheaf *from* the hungry;

11 *Which* make oil within their walls, *and* tread *their* wine-presses, and suffer thirst.

A. M. cir. 2484
B. C. cir. 1520
Ante I. Olymp. cir. 744
Ante U. C. cir. 767

12 Men groan from out of the city, and the soul of the wounded crieth out: yet God layeth not folly *to them.*

13 They are of those that rebel against the light; they know not the ways thereof, nor abide in the paths thereof.

ᵏJob chap. xxii. 7

---

incredible to those who have never witnessed similar phenomena. The *rain* fell in *torrents*, and produced torrents on the land, carrying away earth and stones and every thing before them, scooping out great gullies in the sides of the mountains. *Mountain torrents* are not produced but by such extraordinary *outpourings of rain*, formed either by *water-spouts*, or by vast *masses of clouds intercepted* and *broken* to pieces by the mountain tops.

And embrace the rock for want of a shelter.] In such cases as that related above, the *firm rock* is the only shelter which can be found, or safely trusted.

Verse 9. *They pluck the fatherless from the breast*] They forcibly take young children in order that they may bring them up in a state of *slavery*. This verse is the commencement of a new paragraph, and points out the arbitrary dealings of oppressors, under despotic governors.

Take a pledge of the poor.] Oppressive landlords who let out their grounds at an exorbitant rent, which the poor labourers, though using the utmost diligence, are unable at all times to pay; and then the unfeeling wretch *sells them up*, as the phrase here is, or takes their *cow*, their *horse*, their *cart*, or their *bed*, in pledge, that the money shall be paid in such a time. This is one of the crying sins of some countries of Europe.

Verse 10. *They cause* him *to go naked*] These cruel, hard-hearted oppressors seize the *cloth* made for the *family wear*, or the *wool* and *flax* out of which such *clothes* should be made.

And they take away the sheaf] Seize the *grain* as soon as it is reaped, that they may pay themselves the exorbitant rent at which they have leased out their land: and thus the *sheaf* —the *thraves* and *ricks*, by which they should have been supported, are taken away from the hungry.

Verse 11. *Make oil within their walls*] Thus stripped of all that on which they depended for *clothing* and *food*, they are obliged to become *vassals* to their lord, labour in the fields on scanty fare, or *tread their wine-presses*, from the produce of which they are not permitted to quench their *thirst.*

Verse 12. *Men groan from out of the city*] This is a new paragraph. After having shown the oppressions carried on in the *country*, he takes a view of those carried on in the *town*. Here the miseries are too numerous to be detailed. The *poor* in such places are often in the most wretched state; they are not only *badly fed*, and *miserably clothed*, but also most *unwholesomely lodged*. I was once appointed with a benevolent gentleman, J. S., Esq., to visit a district in St. Giles's London, to know the real state of the poor. We took the district in *House*

Row, and found each dwelling full of people, dirt, and wretchedness. Neither old nor young had the appearance of health: some were *sick*, and others lying *dead*, in the same place! Several beds, if they might be called such, on the floor in the same apartment; and, in one single house, *sixty souls!* These were groaning under various evils; *and the soul of the wounded*, wounded in spirit, and *afflicted* in body, *cried out* to God and man for help! It would have required no subtle investigation to have traced all these miseries to the *doors*, the *hands*, the *lips*, and the *hearts*, of ruthless landlords; or to oppressive systems of public expenditure in the support of ruinous wars, and the stagnation of trade and destruction of commerce occasioned by them: to which must be added the enormous taxation to meet this expenditure.

Yet God layeth not folly to them.] He does not impute their calamities to their own folly. Or, according to the *Vulgate, Et Deus inultum abire non patitur;* "And God will not leave (these disorders) unpunished." But the Hebrew may be translated *And God doth not attend to their prayers*. Job's object was to show, in opposition to the mistaken doctrine of his friends, that God did not hastily punish every evil work, nor reward every good one. That *vice* often went long unpunished, and *virtue* unrewarded; and that we must not judge of a man's state either by his *prosperity* or *adversity*. Therefore, there might be cases in which the innocent oppressed poor were crying to God for a redress of their grievances, and were not immediately heard; and in which their oppressors were faring sumptuously every day, without any apparent mark of the Divine displeasure. These sentiments occur frequently.

Verse 13. *They—rebel against the light*] Speaking of wicked men. They rebel against the light of God in their consciences, and his light in his word. They are tyrants *in grain*, and care neither for God nor the poor. *They know not the ways thereof*—they will not learn their duty to God or man. *Nor abide in the paths thereof*—if brought at any time to a better mind, they speedily relapse; and are *steady* only in *cruelty* and *mischief*. This is the character of the oppressors of suffering humanity, and of sinners audacious and hardened.

This whole verse Mr. *Good* translates in the following manner:—

> They are indignant of the light;
> They respect not its progress;
> And will not return to its paths.

They hate good; they regard not its operation; they go out of the way of righteousness, and refuse to return.

A. M. cir. 2484
B. C. cir. 1520
Ante I. Olymp.
cir. 744
Ante U. C. cir.
767

14 [l]The murderer rising with the light killeth the poor and needy, and in the night is as a thief.

15 [m]The eye also of the adulterer waiteth for the twilight, [n]saying, No eye shall see me: and [o]disguiseth *his* face.

16 In the dark they dig through houses, *which* they had marked for themselves in the daytime: they [p]know not the light.

17 For the morning *is* to them even as the shadow of death: if *one* know them, *they are in* the terrors of the shadow of death.

A. M. cir. 2484
B. C. cir. 1520
Ante I. Olymp.
cir. 744
Ante U. C. cir.
767

18 He *is* swift as the waters; their portion is cursed in the earth: he beholdeth not the way of the vineyards.

19 Drought and heat [q]consume the snow-waters: *so doth* the grave *those which* have sinned.

20 The womb shall forget him; the worm shall feed sweetly on him; [r]he shall be no

---

[l]Psalm x. 8——[m]Proverbs vii. 9——[n]Psalm x. 11
[o]Heb. *setteth his face in secret*

[p]John iii. 20——[q]Hebrew, *violently take*
[r]Prov. x. 7

Verse 14. *The murderer rising with the light*] Perhaps the words should be read as Mr. *Good* has done:—

With the daylight ariseth the murderer;
Poor and needy, he sheddeth blood.

This description is suitable to a *highwayman;* one who robs in daylight, and who has been *impelled* by *poverty* and *distress* to use this most unlawful and perilous mode to get bread; and for fear of being discovered or taken, commits murder, and thus adds crime to crime.

In the night is as a thief.] Having been a *highwayman* in the *daytime*, he turns *footpad* or *housebreaker by night;* and thus goes on from sin to sin.

There have been several instances like the case above, where poverty and distress have induced a man to go to the highway and rob, to repair the ruin of himself and family. I shall introduce an *authentic* story of this kind, which the reader may find at the end of this chapter.

Verse 15. *The eye also of the adulterer*] This is another sin particularly of the city. The *adulterer* has made his *assignation;* he has *marked the house* of her into whose good graces he has *insinuated himself*, called *digging through the house;* he *waits* impatiently *for the dusk;* and then goes forth, having *muffled* or *disguised his face*, and spends a criminal night with the faithless wife of another man. The *morning dawns:* but it is to him *as the shadow of death*, lest he should be detected before he can reach his own home. *And if one know him* —if he happen to be *recognized* in coming out of the forbidden house; *the terrors of death* seize upon him, being afraid that the thing shall be brought to light, or that he shall be called to account, a sanguinary account, by the injured husband.

This seems to be the general sense of the very natural picture which Job draws in the 15th, 16th, and 17th verses.

Verse 16. *In the dark they dig through houses*] Thieves in Bengal very frequently dig through the *mud wall* and under the *clay floors* of houses, and, entering unperceived, plunder them while the inhabitants are asleep.

Mr. *Good's* version of this paragraph I shall lay before the reader:—

Ver. 15. For the dark too watcheth the eye of the adulterer;

Exclaiming, No eye shall behold me.
Then putteth he the muffler on his face;

Ver. 16. He wormeth into houses amidst the darkness.
In the daytime they seal themselves up,
They know not the light:

Ver. 17. For, the dawn they reckon to themselves as the death-shade;
The horrors of the death-shade as it returneth.

Verse 18. *He* is *swift as the waters*] Literally, *Light is he on the face of the waters: and cursed shall be their portion on the earth*, which Mr. *Good* translates:—

Miserable is this man on the waters:
Deeply miserable the lot of those on dry land.

He beholdeth not the way of the vineyards.] These no longer flourish or bring forth fruit. The labour of the vintage fails.

Verse 19. *Drought and heat consume the snow-waters*] The public cisterns or large tanks which had been filled with water by the melting of the snow on the mountains, and which water was stored for the irrigation of their lands, had been entirely exhausted by the intensity of the heat, and the long continuance of drought.

So doth the grave those which have sinned.] For this whole paragraph we have only two words in the original; viz., שָׁאוּל חָטָאוּ *sheol chatau*, "the pit, they have sinned;" which Mr. *Good* translates:—"They fall to their lowest depth."

I believe the meaning to be,—even the deepest tanks, which held most water, and retained it longest, had become exhausted; so that expectation and succour were cut off from this as well as from every other quarter.

I have elsewhere shown that שָׁאוּל *sheol* signifies, not only *hell* and the *grave*, but any deep *pit;* and, also, that חָטָא *chata* signifies *to miss the mark*. Mr. *Good*, properly aware of these acceptations of the original words, has translated as above; and it is the only ground on which any consistent meaning can be given to the original.

Verse 20. *The womb shall forget him*] The mother that bare him shall have no affection for him, nor be afflicted at his death. But the word רחם *rechem* signifies *compassion, mercy. Mercy shall be unmindful of him.* How dread-

A. M. cir. 2484
B. C. cir. 1520
Ante I. Olymp.
cir. 744
Ante U. C. cir.
767

more remembered; and wicked- ness shall be broken as a tree.

21 He evil entreateth the barren *that* beareth not: and doeth not good to the widow.

22 He draweth also the mighty with his power: he riseth up, ˢand no *man* is sure of life.

23 *Though* it be given him *to be* in safety,

whereon he resteth; yet ᵗhis eyes *are* upon their ways.

A. M. cir. 2484
B. C. cir. 1520
Ante I. Olymp.
cir. 744
Ante U. C. cir.
767

24 They are exalted for a little while, but ᵘare gone and brought low; they are ᵛtaken out of the way as all *other*, and cut off as the tops of the ears of corn.

25 And if *it be* not *so* now, who will make me a liar, and make my speech nothing worth?

ˢOr, *he trusteth not* his own *life*——ᵗPsa. xi. 4; Prov. xv. 3——ᵘHeb. *are not*——ᵛHeb. *closed up*

---

ful such a state! When mercy itself forgets the sinner, his perdition slumbereth not.

The worm shall feed sweetly on him] The *Chaldee* has, "The cruel, who have neglected to commiserate the poor, shall be sweet to the worms." He shall be brought into a state of the greatest degradation, and shall be no more remembered.

And wickedness shall be broken as a tree.] He shall be as a rotten or decayed tree, easily broken to pieces. If it were clear that עולה *avlah*, here rendered *wickedness*, has the same sense as עלה *aleh*, a *leaf, sucker*, or *shoot*, then we might translate according to the ingenious version of Mr. *Good;* viz., *But the shoot shall be broken off as a tree;* which might, in this case, be supposed to refer to illicit commerce, the *fruit* of the *womb* becoming *abortive*.

Verse 21. *He evil entreateth the barren*] I believe the original word יְעֶה should be translated *he feedeth;* and so the *Vulgate* understood the word: *Pavit enim sterilem*. He has been kind to the barren woman; but he has done no good to the widow. He has shown no mercy to *large families;* he has been an enemy to the procreation of children. Though he may, for particular reasons, have provided for a *barren woman;* yet the *widow* he has not comforted, she being old or infirm, or such as might not suit his purpose.

Verse 22. *He draweth also the mighty*] Calmet gives the following version of the original: "He draws with him guards for his defence; he raises himself up, but he does not feel assured of his life." In the midst even of his guards he is afraid; and dares not put confidence in any person. This is an admirable delineation of the inquietudes and terrors of a tyrant.

Verse 23. Though *it be given him* to be *in safety*] The *Vulgate* gives this verse a singular turn: *Dedit ei Deus locum pœnitentiæ, et ille abutitur eo in superbiam,* "God gave him space for repentance, but he has abused it through pride." This is by no means conformable to the original. I think the words should be translated thus: "He gives *them* (i. e., the guards) to him for security, and he leans upon them; yet his eyes are upon their ways." Though he have taken the guards, mentioned in the preceding verse, for his personal defence, and for this purpose he uses them; yet he is full of diffidence, and he is continually watching them lest they should be plotting his destruction. The true picture of an Eastern tyrant. *Without* are fightings; *within* are fears.

Verse 24. *They are exalted for a little while*] Such tyrants are exalted for a time, for God putteth down one and raiseth up another; but

he turns his hand against them, and they are gone. They are removed by his justice as all of the same character have been and shall be; time and judgment shall mow them down as the grass, and crop them off as the ears of ripe corn. They may flourish for a time, and continue their oppressions; but they shall at last come to an untimely end. Few tyrants ever visit the eternal world *sicca morte*, but by a violent death. All Eastern history is full of this great *fact*.

Verse 25. *And if* it be *not so now*] Job has proved by examples that the righteous are often oppressed; that the wicked often triumph over the just; that the impious are always wretched even in the midst of their greatest prosperity; and he defies his friends to show one flaw in his argument, or an error in his illustration of it; and that existing facts are farther proofs of what he has advanced.

In the preceding chapters we find Job's friends having continual recourse to this assertion, which it is the grand object of all ·their discourses to prove, viz., The righteous are so distinguished in the approbation of God, that they live always in prosperity, and die in peace.

On the other hand, Job contends that the dispensations of Providence are by no means thus equal in this life; that experience shows that the righteous are often in adversity, and the wicked in power and prosperity.

Job's friends had also endeavoured to prove that if a reported good man fell into adversity, it was a proof that his character had been mistaken, that he was an internal sinner and hypocrite; and that God, by these manifest proofs of his disapprobation, unmasked him. Hence they charged Job with hypocrisy and secret sins, because he was now suffering adversity; and that his sins must be of the most heinous nature, because his afflictions were uncommonly great. This Job repels by appeals to numerous facts where there was nothing equivocal in the character; where the *bad* was demonstrably bad, and yet in *prosperity;* and the *good* demonstrably good, and yet in *adversity.* It is strange that none of these could hit on a middle way: viz., The wicked may be in prosperity, but he is ever miserable in his soul: the righteous may be in adversity, but he is ever happy in his God. In these respects, God's ways are always equal.

On ver. 14, I have referred to the case of unfortunate men who, falling into adversity, madly have recourse to plunder to restore their ruined circumstances. The following anecdote is told of the justly celebrated Dr. Sharp, archbishop of York, the grandfather of that highly benevolent, useful, learned, and eminent man, Granville Sharp, Esq., with whom I had for several years the honour of a personal acquaintance.

"Never was any man, as well by the tenderness of his nature as by the impulse of religion, better disposed to succour the distressed, and relieve the necessities of the poor; to which merciful offices he had so strong an inclination that no reasonable solicitations were ever in danger of meeting with a repulse. Nay, he was more prone to seek out proper objects of his bounty, than to reject them when recommended; and so far was his charity from any suspicion of being extorted by importunity, that it appeared rather a delight than uneasiness to him to extend his liberality upon all proper occasions."

For the same reason, a singular anecdote of the archbishop, related in the London Chronicle of Aug. 13, 1785, and always credited by his family, may be thought worth preserving.

"It was his lordship's custom to have a saddle-horse attend his carriage, that in case of fatigue from sitting, he might take the refreshment of a ride. As he was thus going to his episcopal residence, and was got a mile or two before his carriage, a decent, well-looking young man came up with him; and, with a trembling hand and a faltering tongue presented a pistol to his lordship's breast, and demanded his money. The archbishop, with great composure, turned about; and, looking steadfastly at him, desired he would remove that dangerous weapon, and tell him fairly his condition. 'Sir! sir!' with great agitation, cried the youth; 'no words, 'tis not a time; your money instantly.' 'Hear me, young man,' said the archbishop; 'you see I am an old man, and my life is of very little consequence: yours seems far otherwise. I am named Sharp, and am archbishop of York; my carriage and servants are behind. Tell me what money you want, and who you are, and I will not injure you, but prove a friend. Here, take this; and now ingenuously tell me how much you want to make you independent of so destructive a business as you are now engaged in.' 'O sir,' replied the man, 'I detest the business as much as you. I am—but—but—at home there are creditors who will not stay—fifty pounds, my lord, indeed would do what no tongue besides my own can tell.' 'Well, sir, I take it on your word; and, upon my honour, if you will, in a day or two, call on me at ——, what I have now given you shall be made up that sum.' The highwayman looked at him, was silent, and went off; and, at the time appointed, actually waited on the archbishop, and assured his lordship his words had left impressions which nothing could ever destroy.

"Nothing more transpired for a year and a half or more; when one morning a person knocked at his grace's gate, and with peculiar earnestness desired to see him. The archbishop ordered the stranger to be brought in. He entered the room where his lordship was, but had scarce advanced a few steps before his countenance changed, his knees tottered, and he sank almost breathless on the floor. On recovering, he requested an audience in private. The apartment being cleared, 'My lord,' said he, 'you cannot have forgotten the circumstances at such a time and place; gratitude will never suffer them to be obliterated from my mind. In me, my lord, you now behold that once most wretched of mankind; but now, by your inexpressible humanity, rendered equal, perhaps superior, in happiness to millions. O, my lord!' tears for a while preventing his utterance, "tis you, 'tis you that have saved me, body and soul; 'tis you that have saved a dear and much-loved wife, and a little brood of children, whom I tendered dearer than my life. Here are the fifty pounds; but never shall I find language to testify what I feel. Your God is your witness; your deed itself is your glory; and may heaven and all its blessings be your present and everlasting reward! I was the younger son of a wealthy man; your lordship knows him; his name was ——. My marriage alienated his affection; and my brother withdrew his love, and left me to sorrow and penury. A month since my brother died a bachelor and intestate. What was *his*, is become *mine;* and by your astonishing goodness, I am now at once the most penitent, the most grateful, and happiest of my species.' "

See *Prince Hoar's* life of *Granville Sharp, Esq.*, page 13.

I have no doubt there have been several cases of a similar kind, when the *first step* in delinquency was urged by *necessity;* but few of such wretched adventurers have met with an *Archbishop Sharp.* An *early* and *pious education* is the only means under God to prevent such dangerous steps, which generally lead to the most fearful catastrophe. Teach a child, that whom God loveth he chasteneth. Teach him, that God suffers men to hunger, and be in want, that he may try them if they will be faithful, and do them good in their latter end. Teach him, that he who patiently and meekly bears providential afflictions, shall be relieved and exalted in due time. Teach him, that if is no sin to die in the most abject poverty and affliction, brought on in the course of Divine providence; but that any attempts to alter his condition by robbery, knavery, cozening, and fraud, will be distinguished with heavy curses from the Almighty, and necessarily end in perdition and ruin. A child thus educated is not likely to abandon himself to unlawful courses.

CHAPTER XXV

Bildad, the Shuhite, in an irregular speech, shows that God's dominion is supreme, his armies innumerable, and his providence extended over all, 1-3; that man cannot be justified before God; that even the heavenly bodies cannot be reputed pure in his sight; much less man, who is naturally weak and sinful, 4-6.

A. M. cir. 2484
B. C. cir. 1520
Ante I. Olymp.
cir. 744
Ante U. C. cir.
767

THEN answered Bildad the Shuhite, and said,

2 Dominion and fear *are* with him, he maketh peace in his high places.

3 Is there any number of his armies? and upon whom doth not ᵃhis light arise?

4 ᵇHow then can man be justified with God?

or how can he be clean *that is* born of a woman?

5 Behold even to the moon, and it shineth not; yea, the stars are not pure in his sight.

6 How much less man, *that is* ᶜa worm? and the son of man, *which is* a worm?

A. M. cir. 2484
B. C. cir. 1520
Ante I. Olymp.
cir. 744
Ante U. C. cir.
767

ᵃJames i. 17——ᵇChap. iv. 17, &c.; xv. 14,

&c.; Psa. cxxx. 3; cxliii. 2——ᶜPsa. xxii. 6

NOTES ON CHAP. XXV

Verse 1. *Bildad the Shuhite*] This is the last attack on Job; the others felt themselves foiled, though they had not humility enough to acknowledge it, but would not again return to the attack. Bildad has little to say, and that little is very little to the point. He makes a few assertions, particularly in reference to what Job had said in the commencement of the preceding chapter, of his *desire to appear before God, and have his case tried by him, as he had the utmost confidence that his innocence should be fully proved.* For this Bildad reprehends Job with arguments which had been brought forth often in this controversy, and as repeatedly confuted, chap. iv. 18, and xv. 14, 15, 16.

Verse 2. *Dominion and fear are with him*] God is an absolute sovereign; his fear is on all the hosts of heaven; and by his sovereignty he establishes and preserves order in the heavens, and among all the inhabitants of the eternal world: how canst thou, therefore, dare to appeal to him, or desire to appear before him?

Verse 3. *Is there any number of his armies?*] He has *troops* innumerable; he can serve himself of all his creatures; every thing may be a means of *help* or *destruction,* according to his Divine will. When he purposes to save, none can destroy; and when he is determined to destroy, none can save. It is vain to trust in his creatures against himself.

Upon whom doth not his light arise?] That is, his *providence* rules over all; he is universal Lord; he causes his sun to arise on the evil and the good, and sends his rain on the just and unjust.

Verse 4. *How then can man be justified?*] Or, מה umah, With what, shall a man be justified with God? Though this is no conclusion from Bildad's premises, yet the question is of the highest importance to man. Neither Bildad nor any of his fellows could answer it; the doctrine of redemption through the *blood of the cross* was then known only through *types* and *shadows.* We, who live in the Gospel dispensation, can readily answer the question, With what shall *miserable man* (אנוש enosh) be justified with God?—*Ans.* By bringing forward, by *faith,* to the throne of the Divine justice, the *sacrificial offering of the Lord Jesus Christ;* and confiding absolutely in it, as being a full, sufficient, and complete atonement and sacrifice for his sins, and for the salvation of a lost world.

How, or *with what* (ומה umah) shall he be clean that is born of a woman?—*Ans.* By receiving that grace or heavenly influence communicated by the power and energy of the eternal Spirit applying to the heart the efficacy of that blood which cleanses from all unrighteousness.

This, and this only, is the way in which a *sinner,* when truly *penitent,* can be *justified before God:* and in which a *believer,* convinced of indwelling sin, can be *sanctified* and cleansed from all unrighteousness. This is the only means of *justification* and *sanctification,* without which there can be no *glorification.* And these two great works, which constitute the whole of *salvation,* have been procured for a lost world by the incarnation, passion, death, and resurrection of the Lord Jesus Christ, who was delivered for our offences, and rose again for our justification; to whom be glory and dominion now and for evermore, Amen!

Verse 5. *Behold even to the moon, and it shineth not*] It is continually *changing* its appearance. It never appears twice in its whole revolution with the *same face:* it is ever *waxing* or *waning;* and its face is variegated with opaque spots. Its changeableness can never be compared with the unchangeable nature of God.

Yea, the stars are not pure in his sight.] Whatever their excellence may be as stars, it is nothing in comparison with him from whom they have derived their being and splendour. See the notes on chap. iv. 18, and xv. 14-16. The *Targum* reads: "Behold, the moon is as yet spotted in her eastern part; the sun shines not; and the stars are not pure in his sight."

Some think that by *stars* are meant those *angels who kept not their first estate:* this may be so, but I cannot see it in the text. It may, however, mean the *heavenly host,* as it is supposed to do, chap. xxviii. 7; but I still must hesitate on the propriety of such applications.

It is probable this speech of Bildad was delivered in the *night-season,* when clouds interrupted the bright shining of the moon. The third verse seems to refer immediately to the *stars,* which to the naked eye are innumerable. The *sun* is not mentioned, because of his absence.

This speech of Bildad is both confused and inconclusive. His reasoning is absurd, and he draws false conclusions from his premises. In the third verse, he says, "Is there any number of his armies? and upon whom does not his light arise?" But how absurd is the conclusion which he draws from his questions:—"How then can a man be justified with God, or he be clean who is born of a woman?"

This has no relation to the premises; still to us the question is not difficult, and has already been answered in the notes: "A man can be justified with God," through the blood of Christ; and "he can be clean who is born of a woman," through the sanctification of the Spirit.

Verse 6. *How much less man, that is a worm?*] Or as the *Targum:*—"How much more man, who in his life is a reptile; and the son of man, who in his death is a worm." Almost all the *versions* read, "Truly man is corruption, and the son of man a worm." The *original* is degradingly expressive: "Even because אנש *enosh, miserable man*, is רמה *rimmah, a crawling worm;* and the son of Adam, who is תולעה *toleah*, a *worm*, or rather *maggot*, from its eating into and dividing certain substances."—*Parkhurst.*

Thus endeth Bildad the Shuhite, who endeav-oured to speak on a subject which he did not understand; and, having got on bad ground, was soon confounded in his own mind, spoke incoherently, argued inconclusively, and came abruptly and suddenly to an end. Thus, his three friends being confounded, Job was left to pursue his own way; they trouble him no more; and he proceeds in triumph to the end of the thirty-first chapter.

CHAPTER XXVI

Job, perceiving that his friends could no longer support their arguments on the ground they had assumed, sharply reproves them for their want both of wisdom and feeling, 1–4; shows that the power and wisdom of God are manifest in the works of creation and providence; gives several proofs; and then adds that these are a small specimen of his infinite skill and unlimited power, 5–14.

A. M. cir. 2484
B. C. cir. 1520
Ante I. Olymp.
cir. 744
Ante U. C. cir.
767

BUT Job answered and said, 2 How hast thou helped *him that is* [a]without power? *how* savest thou the arm *that* hath [b]no strength?

3 How hast thou counselled *him that hath* no wisdom? and *how* hast thou plentifully declared the thing as it is?

4 To whom hast thou uttered words? and whose spirit came from thee?

5 Dead *things* are formed from under the

A. M. cir. 2484
B. C. cir. 1520
Ante I. Olymp.
cir. 744
Ante U. C. cir.
767

---

[a]Neh. v. 5

[b]1 Sam. ii. 9

NOTES ON CHAP. XXVI

Verse 2. *How hast thou helped* him] This seems a species of irony. How wonderfully hast thou counselled the unskilful and strengthened the weak! Alas for you! ye could not give what ye did not possess! In this way the *Chaldee* understood these verses: "Why hast thou pretended to give succour, when *thou art* without strength? And save, while thy arm is weak? Why hast thou given counsel, when *thou art* without understanding? And supposest that thou hast shown the very essence of wisdom?"

Verse 4. *Whose spirit came from thee?*] Mr. *Good* renders the verse thus: *From whom hast thou pillaged speeches? And whose spirit hath issued forth from thee?* The retort is peculiarly severe; and refers immediately to the proverbial sayings which in several of the preceding answers have been adduced against the irritated sufferer; for which see chap. viii. 11-19, xv. 20-35, some of which he has already complained of, as in chap. xii. 3, and following. I concur most fully therefore with Dr. Stock in regarding the remainder of this chapter as a sample, ironically exhibited by Job, of the harangues on the power and greatness of God which he supposes his friends to have taken out of the mouths of other men, to deck their speeches with borrowed lustre. Only, in descanting on the same subject, he shows how much he himself can go beyond them in eloquence and sublimity.

Job intimates that, whatever *spirit* they had, it was not the Spirit of God, because in their answers falsehood was found.

Verse 5. *Dead* things *are formed from under the waters*] This verse, as it stands in our version, seems to convey no meaning; and the He-brew is obscure; הרפאים *harephaim*, "the Rephaim," certainly means not *dead things;* nor can there be any propriety in saying that *dead things*, or things without life, *are formed under the waters*, for such things are formed everywhere in the earth, and under the earth, as well as under the waters.

The *Vulgate* translates: *Ecce gigantes gemunt sub aquis, et qui habitant cum eis.* "Behold the giants, and those who dwell with them, groan from under the waters."

The *Septuagint:* Μη γιγαντες μαιωθησονται υποκατωθεν υδατος, και των γειτονων αυτου; "Are not the giants formed from under the waters, and their neighbours?"

The *Chaldee:* אפשר דנבריא דמתמזמזין יתברין ואנון מלרע למיא ומשריתהון *eposhar degibraiya demithmazmezin yithbareyan veinnun millera lemaiya umashreiyatehon*, "Can the trembling giants be regenerated, when they and their hosts are under the water?"

The *Syriac* and *Arabic:* "Behold, the giants are slain, and are drawn out of the water." None of these appear to give any sense by which the true meaning can be determined.

There is probably here an allusion to the destruction of the earth by the general deluge. Moses, speaking concerning the state of the earth before the flood, says, Gen. vi. 4, "There were giants נפלים *nephilim*, in the earth in those days." Now it is likely that Job means the same by רפאים *rephaim* as Moses does by the *nephilim;* and that both refer to the antediluvians, who were all, for their exceeding great iniquities, overwhelmed by the waters of the deluge. Can those mighty men and their neighbours, all the sinners who have been gath-

A. M. cir. 2484
B. C. cir. 1520
Ante I. Olymp.
cir. 744
Ante U. C. cir.
767

waters, ᶜand the inhabitants thereof.

6 ᵈHell *is* naked before him, and destruction hath no covering.

7 ᵉHe stretcheth out the north over the empty place, *and* hangeth the earth upon nothing.

8 ᶠHe bindeth up the waters in his thick

clouds; and the cloud is not rent under them.

9 He holdeth back the face of his throne, *and* spreadeth his cloud upon it.

10 ᵍHe hath compassed the waters with bounds, ʰuntil the day and night come to an end.

A. M. cir. 2484
B. C. cir. 1520
Ante I. Olymp.
cir. 744
Ante U. C. cir.
767

ᶜOr, *with the inhabitants*——ᵈPsa. cxxxix. 8, 11; Prov. xv. 11; Hebrews iv. 13——ᵉChap. ix. 8; Psa. xxiv. 2; civ. 2, &c.

ᶠProv. xxx. 4——ᵍChap. xxxviii. 8; Psa. xxxiii. 7; civ. 9; Prov. viii. 29; Jer. v. 22——ʰHeb. *until the end of light with darkness*

---

ered to them since, be rejected from under the waters, by which they were judicially overwhelmed?

Mr. *Good* thinks the shades of the heroes of former times, the gigantic spectres, the mighty or enormous dead, are meant.

I greatly question whether *sea-monsters* be not intended, such as porpoises, sharks, narwals, grampuses, and whales. We know, however, that an opinion anciently prevailed, that the Titans, a race of men of enormous stature, rebelled against the gods, and endeavoured to scale heaven by placing one mountain on the top of another; and that they and their structure were cast down by the thunder of the deities, and buried under the earth and sea; and that their struggles to arise produce the earthquakes which occur in certain countries. Now although this opinion is supported by the most respectable antiquity among the heathens, it is not to be supposed that in the word of God there can be any countenance given to an opinion at once as absurd as it is monstrous. (But still the poet may use the language of the common people.) I must therefore either refer the passage here to the *antediluvians*, or to the vast *sea-monsters* mentioned above.

Verse 6. *Hell is naked before him*] *Sheol*, the place of the dead, or of *separate spirits*, is always in his view. *And there is no covering to Abaddon*—the place of the *destroyer*, where destruction reigns, and where those dwell who are eternally separated from God. The ancients thought that hell or Tartarus was a vast space in the centre, or at the very bottom of the earth. So VIRGIL, *Æn.* lib. vi., ver. 577:—

——————————— Tum Tartarus ipse
Bis patet in præceps tantum, tenditque sub umbras,
Quantus ad æthereum cœli suspectus Olympum
Hic genus antiquum terræ, Titania pubes,
Fulmine dejecti, fundo volvuntur in imo.

"Full twice as deep the dungeon of the fiends,
The huge Tartarean gloomy gulf, descends
Below these regions, as these regions lie
From the bright realms of yon ethereal sky.
Here roar the *Titan race*, th' *enormous birth;*
The ancient offspring of the teeming earth.
Pierced by the *burning bolts* of old they fell,
And still roll bellowing in the depths of hell."
               PITT.

And some have supposed that there is an allusion to this opinion in the above passage, as well as in several others in the Old Testament; but it is not likely that the sacred writers would

countenance an opinion that certainly has nothing in fact or philosophy to support it. Yet still a poet may avail himself of popular opinions.

Verse 7. *He stretcheth out the north over the empty place*] על תהו *al tohu*, to the hollow waste. The same word as is used, Gen. i. 2, *The earth was without form*, תהו *tohu*. The north must here mean the *north pole*, or northern hemisphere; and perhaps what is here stated may refer to the opinion that the earth was a vast extended plain, and the heavens poised upon it, resting on this plain all round the horizon. Of the *south* the inhabitants of Idumea knew nothing; nor could they have any notion of inhabitants in that hemisphere.

Hangeth the earth upon nothing.] The *Chaldee* says: "He lays the earth upon the waters, nothing sustaining it."

Verse 8. *He bindeth up the waters*] Drives the aqueous particles together, which were raised by evaporation, so that, being condensed, they form clouds which float in the atmosphere, till, meeting with strong currents of wind, or by the agency of the electric fluid, they are farther condensed; and then, becoming too heavy to be sustained in the air, fall down in the form of rain, when, in this poetic language, *the cloud is rent under them.*

Verse 9. *He holdeth back the face of his throne*] Though all these are most elegant effects of an omniscient and almighty power, yet the great Agent is not personally discoverable; he dwelleth in light unapproachable, and in mercy hides himself from the view of his creatures. The words, however, may refer to those obscurations of the face of heaven, and the hiding of the body of the sun, when the atmosphere is laden with dense vapours, and the rain begins to be poured down on the earth.

Verse 10. *He hath compassed the waters with bounds*] Perhaps this refers merely to the *circle* of the horizon, the line that terminates light and commences darkness, called here עד

עד תכלית אורעם חשך *ad tachlith or im chosech*, "until the completion of light with darkness." Or, if we take תכלית *tachlith* here to be the same with תכלת *techeleth*, Exod. xxv. 4, and elsewhere, which we translate *blue*, it may mean that sombre sky-blue appearance of the horizon at the time of *twilight*, i. e., between light and darkness; the line where the one is terminating and the other commencing. Or, He so circumscribes the waters, retaining them in their own place, that they shall not be able to overflow the earth until day and night, that is, time itself, come to an end.

A. M. cir. 2484
B. C. cir. 1520
Ante I. Olymp.
cir. 744
Ante U. C. cir.
767

11 The pillars of heaven trem-ble, and are astonished at his reproof.

12 ¹He divideth the sea with his power, and by his understanding he smiteth through ᵏthe proud.

13 ¹By his Spirit he hath gar-nished the heavens; his hand hath formed ᵐthe crooked serpent.

14 Lo, these *are* parts of his ways: but how little a portion is heard of him? but the thunder of his power who can understand?

A. M. cir. 2484
B. C. cir. 1520
Ante I. Olymp.
cir. 744
Ante U. C. cir.
767

---

¹Exod. xiv. 21; Psa. lxxiv. 13; Isa. li. 15; Jer. xxxi. 35

ᵏHeb. *pride*——¹Psa. xxxiii. 6——ᵐIsa. xxvii. 1

Verse 11. *The pillars of heaven tremble*] This is probably a poetical description either of thunder, or of an earthquake:—

"He shakes creation with his nod;
Earth, sea, and heaven, confess him God."

But there may be an allusion to the *high mountains*, which were anciently esteemed by the common people as the *pillars* on which the *heavens rested;* and when these were shaken with earthquakes, it might be said *the pillars of heaven tremble.* Mount *Atlas* was supposed to be one of those pillars, and this gave rise to the fable of Atlas being a man who bore the heavens on his shoulders. The Greek and Roman poets frequently use this image. Thus SILIUS ITALI-CUS, lib. i., ver. 202:—

Atlas subducto tracturus vertice cœlum:
Sidera nubiferum fulcit caput, æthereasque
Erigit æternum compages ardua cervix:
Canet barba gelu, frontemque immanibus umbris
Pinea silva premit; vastant cava tempora venti
Nimbosoque ruunt spumantia flumina rictu.

"Atlas' broad *shoulders* prop th' incumbent *skies:*
Around his cloud-girt *head* the *stars* arise.
His towering *neck* supports th' *ethereal way;*
And o'er his *brow* black *woods* their gloom display.
Hoar is his *beard; winds* round his *temples* roar;
And from his *jaws* the rushing *torrents* pour."
J. B. C.

Verse 12. *He divideth the sea with his power*] Here is a manifest allusion to the passage of the Red Sea by the Israelites, and the overthrow of Pharaoh and his host, according to the opinion of the most eminent critics.
He smiteth through the proud.] רהב *Rahab,* the very name by which Egypt is called Isa. li. 9, and elsewhere. *Calmet* remarks: "This appears to refer only to the passage of the Red Sea, and the destruction of Pharaoh. Were we not pre-possessed with the opinion that Job died before Moses, every person at the first view of the subject must consider it in this light." I am not thus prepossessed. Let *Job* live when he might, I am satisfied the *Book of Job* was writ-ten long after the death of Moses, and not earlier than the days of Solomon, if not later. The farther I go in the work, the more this con-viction is deepened; and the opposite sentiment appears to be perfectly gratuitous.
Verse 13. *By his Spirit he hath garnished the heavens*] See the observations below.
Verse 14. *Lo, these* are *parts of his ways*] קצות *ketsoth,* the *ends* or *extremities,* the out-lines, an *indistinct sketch,* of his eternal power and Godhead.

How little a portion is heard] שמץ *shemets, a mere whisper;* admirably opposed, as Mr. *Good* has well observed, to רעם *raam, the thunder,* mentioned in the next clause. As the *thunder* is to a *whisper,* so are the *tremendous and infinitely varied works* of God to the *faint out-lines* exhibited in the above discourse. Every reader will relish the dignity, propriety, and sense of these expressions. They force them-selves on the observation of even the most heedless.
By his Spirit he hath garnished the heavens. —Numerous are the opinions relative to the true meaning of this verse. Some think it refers to the *clearing of the sky* after a storm, such as appears to be described ver. 11, 12; and suppose *his Spirit* means the *wind,* which he directs to sweep and cleanse the face of the sky, by which the splendour of the day or the lustre of the night is restored: and by the *crooked, flying,* or *aerial serpent,* as it is vari-ously rendered, the *ecliptic* is supposed to be meant, as the sun's apparent course in it ap-pears to be *serpentine,* in his approach to and recession from each of the *tropics.* This *tortu-ous line* may be seen on any terrestrial globe. Many will object to this notion as too refined for the time of Job; but this I could easily admit, as astronomy had a very *early existence* among the *Arabians,* if not its *origin.* But with me the chief objection lies against the *obscurity* of the allusion, if it be one; for it must require no small ingenuity, and almost the spirit of divination, to find out the *sun's oblique path in the zodiac* in the words *His hand hath formed the crooked serpent.* Others have imagined that the allusion is to the *lightning* in that *zigzag form* which it assumes when discharged from one cloud into another during a thunder storm. This is at once a natural and very apparent sense. To *conduct* and *manage* the *lightning* is most certainly a work which requires the *skill* and *omnipotence* of GOD, as much as *garnishing the heavens by his Spirit, dividing the sea by his power,* or causing *the pillars of heaven to tremble by his reproof.* Others think that the *act* of the *creation* of the solar system is in-tended to be expressed, which is in several parts of the sacred writings attributed to the *Spirit of God;* (Gen. i. 2; Psa. xxxiii. 6;) and that the *crooked serpent* means either *Satan,* who de-ceived our first parents, or *huge aquatic ani-mals;* for in Isa. xxvii. 1, we find the *leviathan* and *dragon of the sea* called נחש ברח *nachash bariach,* the very terms that are used by Job in this place: "In that day the Lord with his sore and great and strong sword shall punish leviathan, the piercing serpent, (נחש ברח *nachash bariach,*) even leviathan, that crooked serpent, (נחש עקלתון *nachash akallathon,*) and he shall slay the dragon (התנין *hattannin*) that is in the sea."
And we know that in Gen. i. 21 התנינם הגדלים

hattanninim haggedolim, which we translate *great whales*, includes all *sea-monsters* or *vast aquatic animals. Calmet*, who without hesitation adopts this sentiment, says: "I see no necessity to have recourse to allegory here. After having exhibited the effects of the sovereign power of God in the *heavens*, in the *clouds*, in the vast collection of *waters* in the *sea*, it was natural enough for Job to speak of the production of *fishes*." The intelligent Dr. *Sherlock* gives another interpretation. After strongly expressing his disapprobation of the opinion that Job should descend, after speaking of the *creation of the heavens and their host*, to the *formation of snakes* and *adders*, he supposes "that Job here intended to oppose that grand religious system of *sabæism* which prevailed in his time, and to which, in other parts of this book, he alludes; a system which acknowledged two opposite independent principles by which the universe was governed, and paid Divine adoration to the celestial luminaries. Suppose, therefore, Job to be acquainted with the fall of man, and the part ascribed to the *serpent* of the introduction of evil, see how aptly the parts cohere. In opposition to the idolatrous practice of the time, he asserts God to be the maker of all the host of heaven: *By his Spirit he garnished the heavens:* In opposition to the false notion of two independent principles, he asserts God to be the maker of him who was the author of evil: *His hand hath formed the crooked serpent.* You see how properly the *garnishing of the heavens* and the *forming of the serpent* are joined together. That this is the ancient traditionary explication of this place, we have undeniable evidence from the translation of the *Septuagint*, who render the latter part of this verse, which relates to the serpent, in this manner: Προσταγματι δε εθανατωσε δρακοντα αποστατην. *By a decree he destroyed the apostate dragon.* The *Syriac* and *Arabic* versions are to the same effect: *And his hand slew the flying serpent.*

"These translators apply the place to the *punishment* inflicted on the serpent; and it comes to the same thing, for the *punishing the serpent* is as clear an evidence of God's power over the author of evil as the *creating* him. We need not wonder to see so much concern in this book to maintain the supremacy of God, and to guard it against every false notion; for this was the theme, the business of the author."—Bp. *Sherlock* on Prophecy, Diss. ii.

From the contradictory opinions on this passage, the reader will no doubt feel cautious what mode of interpretation he adopts, and the absolute necessity of admitting no texts of doubtful interpretation as vouchers for the essential doctrines of Christianity. Neither metaphors, allegories, similes, nor figurative expressions of any kind, should ever be adduced or appealed to as proofs of any article in the Christian faith. We have reason to be thankful that this is at present the general opinion of the most rational divines of all sects and parties, and that the *allegory* and *metaphor men* are everywhere vanishing from the meridian and sinking under the horizon of the Church. Scriptural Christianity is prevailing with a strong hand, and going forward with a firm and steady step.

CHAPTER XXVII

Job strongly asserts his innocence; determines to maintain it, and to avoid every evil way, 1–7. Shows his abhorrence of the hypocrite by describing his infamous character, accumulated miseries, and wretched end, 8–23.

A. M. cir. 2484
B. C. cir. 1520
Ante I. Olymp.
cir. 744
Ante U. C. cir.
767

MOREOVER Job [a]continued his parable, and said,

2 *As* God liveth, [b]*who* hath taken away my judgment; and the Almighty, *who* hath [c]vexed my soul;

3 All the while my breath *is* in me, and [d]the spirit of God *is* in my nostrils;

4 My lips shall not speak wickedness, nor my tongue utter deceit.

A. M. cir. 2484
B. C. cir. 1520
Ante I. Olymp.
cir. 744
Ante U. C. cir.
767

---

[a]Hebrew, *added to take up*——[b]Chapter xxxiv. 5
[c]Hebrew, *made my soul bitter*, Ruth i. 20; 2 Kings

iv. 27——[d]That is, *the breath which God gave him*, Gen. ii. 7

NOTES ON CHAP. XXVII

Verse 1. *Continued his parable*] After having delivered the preceding discourse, Job appears to have *paused* to see if any of his friends chose to make any reply; but finding them all silent, he resumed his discourse, which is here called משלו *meshalo*, his *parable*, his *authoritative weighty discourse;* from משל *mashal*, to exercise rule, authority, dominion, or power.—Parkhurst. And it must be granted that in this speech he assumes great boldness, exhibits his own unsullied character, and treats his friends with little ceremony.

Verse 2. *Who hath taken away my judgment*] Who has *turned aside my cause*, and has not permitted it to come to a hearing, where I might have justice done to me, but has abandoned me to the harsh and uncharitable judgment of my enemies? There appears to be a great want of reverence in these words of Job; he speaks with a degree of irritation, if not bitterness, which cannot be justified. No man should speak thus of his Maker.

Verse 3. *All the while my breath is in me*] As Job appears to allude to the *creation of Adam*, whom God made out of the dust of the earth, *and breathed into his nostrils the breath of life*, so that *he became a living soul*, the whole of Job's assertion may be no more than a periphrasis for *As long as I live and have my understanding*. Indeed נשמתי *nishmathi* may be rendered *my mind* or *understanding*, and רוח אלוה *ruach Eloah, the breath of God, the*

A. M. cir. 2484
B. C. cir. 1520
Ante I. Olymp.
cir. 744
Ante U. C. cir.
767

5 God forbid that I should justify you: till I die ^eI will not remove my integrity from me.

6 My righteousness ^fI hold fast, and will not let it go: ^gmy heart shall not reproach *me* ^hso long as I live.

7 Let mine enemy be as the wicked, and he that riseth up against me as the unrighteous.

8 ⁱFor what *is* the hope of the hypocrite, though he hath gained, when God taketh away his soul?

A. M. cir. 2484
B. C. cir. 1520
Ante I. Olymp.
cir. 744
Ante U. C. cir.
767

9 ^kWill God hear his cry when trouble cometh upon him?

10 ^lWill he delight himself in the Almighty? will he always call upon God?

11 I will teach you ^mby the hand of God: *that* which *is* with the Almighty will I not conceal.

---

^eChap. ii. 9; xiii. 15——^fChap. ii. 3——^gActs xxiv. 16
^hHeb. *from my days*——ⁱMatt. xvi. 26; Luke xii. 20
^kChap. xxxv. 12; Psa. xviii. 41; cix. 7.; Prov. i. 28;

xxviii. 9; Isa. i. 15; Jer. xiv. 12; Ezek. viii. 18; Mic. iii. 4; John ix. 31; James iv. 3——^lSee chap. xxii. 26, 27——^mOr, being *in the hand*, &c.

---

principle of animal life, the same that he breathed into Adam; for it is there said, Gen. ii. 7, He breathed into his nostrils, נשמת חיים *nismath chaiyim, the breath of lives,* or that principle from which *animal* and *spiritual* life proceeds; in consequence of which he became לנפש חיה *lenephesh chaiyah, an intelligent* or *rational animal.*

Verse 4. *My lips shall not speak wickedness*] As I have hitherto lived in all good conscience before God, as he knoweth, so will I continue to live.

Verse 5. *God forbid*] חלילה לי *chalilah lli, far be it from me, that I should justify you*—that I should now, by any kind of acknowledgment of wickedness or hypocrisy justify your harsh judgment. You say that God afflicts me for my crimes; I say, and God knows it is truth, that I have not sinned so as to draw down any such judgment upon me. Your judgment, therefore, is pronounced at your own risk.

Verse 6. *My righteousness I hold fast*] I stand firmly on this ground; I have endeavoured to live an upright life, and my afflictions are not the consequence of my sins.

My heart shall not reproach me] I shall take care so to live that I shall have a conscience void of offence before God and man. "Beloved, if our heart condemn us not, then have we confidence toward God;" 1 John iii. 21. This seems to be Job's meaning.

Verse 7. *Let mine enemy be as the wicked*] Let my accuser be proved a lying and perjured man, because he has laid to my charge things which he cannot prove, and which are utterly false.

Verse 8. *What is the hope of the hypocrite*] The word חנף *chaneph,* which we translate, most improperly, *hypocrite,* means a *wicked fellow,* a *defiled, polluted wretch,* a *rascal,* a *knave,* a man who sticks at nothing in order to gain his ends. In this verse it means a *dishonest man,* a *rogue,* who by overreaching, cheating, &c., has amassed a fortune.

When God taketh away his soul?] Could he have had any well-grounded hope of eternal blessedness when he was acquiring earthly property by guilt and deceit? And of what avail will this property be when his soul is summoned before the judgment-seat? A righteous man *yields up* his soul to God; the wicked does not, because he is afraid of God, of death, and of eternity. God therefore takes the soul away—forces it out of the body. Mr. *Blair* gives us

an affecting picture of the death of a wicked man. Though well known, I shall insert it as a striking comment on this passage:—

"How shocking must thy summons be, O death!
To him that is at ease in his possessions;
Who, counting on long years of pleasures here;
Is quite unfurnished for that world to come!
In that dread moment how the frantic soul
Raves round the walls of her clay tenement;
Runs to each avenue, and shrieks for help,
But shrieks in vain! How wishfully she looks
On all she's leaving, now no longer hers!
A little longer, yet a *little* longer,
O, might she stay, to wash away her stains,
And fit her for her passage! Mournful sight!
Her very eyes weep blood; and every groan
She heaves is big with horror. But the foe,
Like a stanch murderer, steady to his purpose,
Pursues her close, through every lane of life,
Nor misses once the track, but presses on;
Till, forced at last to the tremendous verge,
At once she sinks to everlasting ruin."

THE GRAVE.

The *Chaldee* has, *What can the detractor expect who has gathered together* (ממון דשקר) *mamon dishkar, the mammon of unrighteousness*) *when God plucks out his soul?* The *Septuagint:* Τις γαρ εστιν ετι ελπις ασεβει, οτι επεχει; Μη πεποιθως επι Κυριον ει αρα σωθησεται; *"For what is the hope of the ungodly that he should wait for? shall he, by hoping in the Lord, be therefore saved?"* Mr. *Good* translates differently from all the versions:—

"Yet what is the hope of the wicked that he
    should prosper,
That God should keep his soul in quiet?"

I believe our version gives as true a sense as any; and the words appear to have been in the eye of our Lord, when he said, "For what is a man profited if he shall gain the whole world, and lose his own soul? or what shall a man give in exchange for his soul?" Matt xvi. 26.

Verse 11. *I will teach you by the hand of God*] Relying on *Divine* assistance, and not speaking out of my own head, or quoting what *others* have said I will teach you what the mind of the Almighty is, and I will conceal nothing. Job felt that the *good hand of his God was upon him,* and that therefore he should make no mistake in his doctrines. In this way the *Chaldee* understood the words, ביד אל *beyad El, by the*

A. M. cir. 2484
B. C. cir. 1520
Ante I. Olymp.
cir. 744
Ante U. C. cir.
767

12 Behold, all ye yourselves have seen *it;* why then are ye thus altogether vain?

13 ⁿThis *is* the portion of a wicked man with God, and the heritage of oppressors, *which* they shall receive of the Almighty.

14 °If his children be multiplied, *it is* for the sword: and his offspring shall not be satisfied with bread.

A. M. cir. 2484
B. C. cir. 1520
Ante I. Olymp.
cir. 744
Ante U. C. cir.
767

15 Those that remain of him shall be buried in death: and ᴾhis widows shall not weep.

16 Though he heap up silver as the dust, and prepare raiment as the clay;

17 He may prepare *it,* but �q the just shall put *it* on, and the innocent shall divide the silver.

18 He buildeth his house as a moth, and ʳas a booth *that* the keeper maketh.

ⁿChap. xx. 29——°Deut. xxviii. 41; Esther ix. 10; Hos. ix. 13

ᴾPsa. lxxviii. 64——�q Prov. xxviii. 8; Eccles. ii. 26 ʳIsa. i. 8; Lam. ii. 6

---

hand of God, which it translates בנבואת אלהא *binbuath Elaha, by the prophecy of God.* Those who reject the literal meaning, which conveys a very good sense, may adopt the translation of Mr. *Good,* which has much to recommend it: "I will teach you concerning the *dealings of God.*"

Verse 12. *Ye yourselves have seen* it] Your own experience and observation have shown you that the righteous are frequently in affliction, and the wicked in affluence.

Why then are ye thus altogether vain?] The original is very emphatical: הבל תהבלו *hebel tehbalu,* and well expressed by Mr. *Good:* "Why then should ye thus *babble babblings?*" If our language would allow it, we might say *vanitize vanity.*

Verse 13. *This is the portion of a wicked man*] Job now commences his promised teaching; and what follows is a description of the *lot* or *portion* of the *wicked man* and of *tyrants.* And this remuneration shall they have *with God* in general, though the hand of man be not laid upon them. Though he does not at all times show his displeasure against the wicked, by reducing them to a state of poverty and affliction, yet he often does it so that men may see it; and at other times he seems to pass them by, reserving their judgment for *another world,* that men may not forget that there is a day of judgment and perdition for ungodly men, and a future recompense for the righteous.

Verse 14. *If his children be multiplied*] As numerous families were supposed to be a proof of the benediction of the Almighty, Job shows that this is not always the case; for the offspring of the wicked shall be partly cut off by *violent deaths,* and partly reduced to great *poverty.*

Verse 15. *Those that remain of him*] שרידיו *seridaiv, his remains,* whether meaning himself personally, or his family.

Shall be buried in death] Shall come to *utter* and *remediless destruction.* Death shall have his *full conquest* over them, and the *grave* its *complete victory.* These are no common dead. All the *sting,* all the *wound,* and all the *poison* of sin, remains: and so evident are God's judgments in his and their removal, that even *widows* shall not weep for them; the *public* shall not bewail them; for when the wicked perish *there is shouting.*

Mr. *Good,* following the *Chaldee,* translates: *Entombed in corruption,* or *in the pestilence.* But I see no reason why we should desert the literal reading. *Entombed in corruption* gives

no nervous sense in my judgment; for in corruption are the high and the low, the wicked and the good, entombed: but *buried in death* is at once nervous and expressive. Death itself is the *place* where he shall lie; he shall have no redemption, no resurrection to life; death shall ever have dominion over him. The expression is very similar to that in Luke xvi. 22, as found in several *versions* and MSS.: *The rich man died, and was buried in hell; and, lifting up his eyes, being in torment, he saw,* &c. See my note there.

Verse 16. *Though he heap up silver*] Though he amass riches in the greatest abundance, he shall not enjoy them. Unsanctified wealth is a curse to its possessor. *Money,* of all earthly possessions, is the most dangerous, as it is the *readiest* agent to do good or evil. He that *perverts* it is doubly cursed, because it affords him the most immediate means of sinful gratification; and he can sin more in an hour through this, than he can in a day or week by any other kind of property. On the other hand, they who use it *aright* have it in their power to do the most *prompt* and *immediate* good. Almost every kind of want may be speedily relieved by it. Hence, he who uses it as he ought is doubly blessed; while he who *abuses* it is doubly cursed.

Verse 17. *The just shall put it on*] Money is God's property. "The silver is mine, and the gold is mine, saith the Lord;" and though it may be abused for a time by unrighteous hands, God, in the course of his providence, brings it back to its proper use; and often the righteous possess the inheritance of the wicked.

Verse 18. *He buildeth his house as a moth*] With great skill, great pains, and great industry; but the structure, however skilful, shall be dissolved; and the materials, however costly, shall be brought to corruption. To its owner it shall be only a temporary habitation, like that which the *moth* makes in its *larve* or *caterpillar* state, during its change from a *chrysalis* to a winged insect.

As a booth that the keeper maketh.] A *shed* which the *watchman* or *keeper of a vineyard* erects to cover him from the scorching sun, while watching the ripening grapes, that they may be preserved from depredation. Travellers in the East have observed that such *booths* or *sheds* are made of the *lightest* and most *worthless* materials; and after the harvest or vintage is in, they are quite neglected, and by the winter rains, &c., are soon dissolved and destroyed.

A. M. cir. 2484
B. C. cir. 1520
Ante I. Olymp.
cir. 744
Ante U. C. cir.
767

19 The rich man shall lie down, but he shall not be gathered: he openeth his eyes, and he *is* not.

20 *Terrors take hold on him as waters, a tempest stealeth him away in the night.

21 The east wind carrieth him away, and he

departeth: and as a storm hurleth him out of his place.

22 For *God* shall cast upon him, and not spare: ᵗhe would fain flee out of his hand.

23 *Men* shall clap their hands at him, and shall hiss him out of his place.

A. M. cir. 2484
B. C. cir. 1520
Ante I. Olymp.
cir. 744
Ante U. C. cir.
767

ˢChap. xviii. 11

ᵗHeb. *in fleeing he would flee*

Verse 19. *The rich man shall lie down*] In the grave.

But he shall not be gathered] Neither have a respectable burial among men, nor be gathered with the righteous in the kingdom of God. It may be that Job alludes here to an opinion relative to the state of certain persons after death, prevalent in all nations in ancient times, viz., that those whose funeral rites had not been duly performed, wander about as *ghosts*, and find *no rest*.

He openeth his eyes] In the morning of the resurrection.

And he is *not.*] He is utterly lost and undone for ever. This seems to be the plain sense of the passage; and so all the *versions* appear to have understood it; but *Reiske* and some others, by making אסף *yeaseph* an *Arabic* word, signifying, not the idea of *gathering*, but care, anxiety, &c., have quite altered this sense of the passage; and Mr. *Good*, who copies them, translates thus: *Let the rich man lie down, and care not.* I see no manner of occasion to resort to this interpretation, which, in my judgment, gives a sense inferior to that given above, or to the following: *The rich man shall lie down*—go to his rest, fully persuaded that his property is in perfect safety; *but he shall not be gathered*, or *he shall not gather*—make any farther addition to his stores: *he openeth his eyes in the morning, when he is not*—marauders in the night have stripped him of all his property, as in the case of Job himself; a case quite probable, and not unfrequent in Arabia, when a hostile tribe makes a sudden incursion, and carries off an immense booty. But I prefer the first meaning,

as it is obtained without crucifying the text. *Coverdale* translates: 𝕸hen the rich man dyeth, he carieth nothinge with him: he is gone in the twincklinge of an eye.

Verse 20. *Terrors take hold on him as waters*] They come upon him as an irresistible flood; and he is overwhelmed as by a tempest in the night, when darkness partly hides his danger, and deprives him of discerning the way to escape.

Verse 21. *The east wind carrieth him away*] Such as is called by Mr. *Good a levanter*, the *euroclydon*, the *eastern storm* of Acts xxvii. 14.

Verse 22. God *shall cast upon him*] Or, rather, the *storm* mentioned above shall incessantly pelt him, and give him no respite; nor can he by any means escape from its fury.

Verse 23. Men *shall clap their hands at him*] These two verses refer to the storm, which is to sweep away the ungodly; therefore the word *God*, in verse 22, and *men* in this verse, should be omitted. Verse 22: "For it shall fall upon him, and not spare: flying from its power he shall continue to fly. Verse 23. It shall clap its hands against him, and *hiss*, וישרק *veyishrok, shriek,* him out of his place." Here the storm is personified, and the wicked actor is *hissed* and driven by it from off the stage. It seems it was an ancient method to *clap the hands* against and *hiss* a man from any public office, who had acted improperly in it. The populace, in European countries, express their disapprobation of public characters who have not pleased them in the same manner to the present day, by *hisses, groans,* and the like.

CHAPTER XXVIII

Job, in showing the vanity of human pursuits in reference to genuine wisdom, mentions mining for and refining
gold and silver, 1; iron and other minerals, 2; the difficulties of mining, 3, 4; produce of grain for bread from
the earth, and stones of fire from under it, 5. He speaks of precious stones and gold dust, 6; of the instinct
of fowls and wild beasts in finding their way, 7, 8; and of the industry and successful attempts of men in mining
and other operations, 9–11: but shows that with all their industry, skill, and perseverance, they cannot find
out true wisdom, 12; of which he gives the most exalted character, 13–22; and shows that God alone, the foun-
tain of wisdom, knows and can teach it, 23–27; and in what this true wisdom consists, 28.

A. M. cir. 2484
B. C. cir. 1520
Ante I. Olymp.
cir. 744
Ante U. C. cir.
767

SURELY there is ᵃa vein for the silver, and a place for gold *where they fine it*.

2 Iron is taken out of the ᵇearth, and brass *is* molten *out of* the stone.

3 He setteth an end to darkness, and searcheth out all perfection: the ᶜstones of

darkness, and the ᵈshadow of death.

4 The flood breaketh out from the inhabitant; *even the waters* forgotten of the foot: they are dried up, they are gone away from men.

5 *As for* the earth, out of it cometh bread,

A. M. cir. 2484
B. C. cir. 1520
Ante I. Olymp.
cir. 744
Ante U. C. cir.
767

ᵃOr, *a mine*——ᵇOr, *dust*

ᶜVer. 6——ᵈPsa. xxiii. 4

NOTES ON CHAP. XXVIII

Verse 1. *Surely there is a vein for the silver*] This chapter is the oldest and finest piece of *natural history* in the world, and gives us very important information on several curious subjects; and could we ascertain the precise meaning of all the original words, we might, most probably, find out allusions to several useful arts which we are apt to think are of modern, or comparatively modern, invention.

The word מוצא *motsa*, which we here translate *vein*, signifies literally, *a going out;* i. e., a *mine*, or place dug in the earth, whence the silver ore is extracted. And this ore lies generally in *veins* or *loads*, running in certain directions.

A place for gold where *they fine* it.] This should rather be translated, *A place for gold* which *they refine*. Gold ore has also its peculiar mine, and requires to be refined from earthy impurities.

Verse 2. *Iron is taken out of the earth*] This most useful metal is hidden under the earth, and men have found out the method of separating it from its ore.

Brass is molten out of the stone.] As brass is a factitious metal, *copper* must be the meaning of the Hebrew word נחושה *nechusah:* literally, the stone is poured out for brass. If we retain the common translation, perhaps the process of making brass may be that to which Job refers; for this metal is formed from copper melted with the stone *calamine;* and thus *the stone is poured out* to make *brass*.

Verse 3. *He setteth an end to darkness*] As it is likely Job still refers to mining, the words above may be understood as pointing out the persevering industry of man in penetrating into the bowels of the earth, in order to seek for metals and precious stones. Even the stones that lay hidden in the bowels of the earth he has digged for and brought to light, and has penetrated in directions in which the solar light could not be transmitted; so that he appears to have gone to the regions of the shadow of death. Mr. *Good* translates: "*Man* delveth into *the region* of darkness; and examineth, to the uttermost limit, the stones of darkness and death-shade."

Verse 4. *The flood breaketh out from the inhabitant*] This passage is very difficult. Some think it refers to *mining;* others to *navigation*. If it refer to the former, it may be intended to point out the waters that spring up when the miners have sunk down to a considerable depth, so that the mine is drowned, and they are obliged to give it up. Previously to the invention of the steam-engine this was generally the case: hence ancient mines may be reopened and worked to great advantage, because we have the means now to take off the water which the

ancient workers had not. When, therefore, floods break out in those *shafts*, they are abandoned; and thus they are,

Forgotten of the foot] No man treads there any more. The waters increase דלו *dallu, they are elevated*, they rise up to a level with the spring, or till they meet with some fissure by which they can escape; and then מאנש נעו *meenosh nau, they are moved* or carried away *from men;* the stream is lost in the bowels of the earth.

Mr. *Peters* thinks that both this verse, and ver. 26 of chap. ix., refer to navigation, then in a state of infancy; for the *sea* is not so much as mentioned; but נחל *nachal*, a torrent or flood, some river or arm of the sea perhaps of a few leagues over, which, dividing the several nations, must interrupt their hospitality and commerce with each other, unless by the help of navigation. According to this opinion the verse may be translated and paraphrased thus: *The flood*—rivers and arms of the sea—*separateth from the stranger*, מעם גר *meim gar*, divides different nations and peoples: *they are forgotten of the foot*—they cannot walk over these waters, they must embark in vessels; then *they dwindle away*, דלו *dallu*, from the size of men, that is, in proportion to their departure from the land they lessen on the sight; נעו *nau, they are tossed up and down*, namely, by the action of the waves. This receives some countenance from the psalmist's fine description, Psa. cvii. 26, 27, of a ship in a rough sea: *They mount up to heaven; they go down again to the depths: their soul is melted because of trouble. They reel to and fro*, ינועו *yanuu*, (the same word as above,) *they stagger like a drunken man.* Mr. *Good's* translation is singular:—

He breaketh up the veins from the matrice,
Which, though thought nothing of under the foot,
Are drawn forth, are brandished among mankind.

This learned man thinks that it applies solely to *mining*, of which I cannot doubt; and therefore I adopt the first interpretation: but as to agreement among translators, it will be sought in vain. I shall just add *Coverdale:* 𝔚𝔦𝔱𝔥 𝔱𝔥𝔢 𝔯𝔶𝔳𝔢𝔯 𝔬𝔣 𝔴𝔞𝔱𝔢𝔯 𝔭𝔞𝔯𝔱𝔢𝔱𝔥 𝔥𝔢 𝔞 𝔰𝔲𝔫𝔡𝔢𝔯 𝔱𝔥𝔢 𝔰𝔱𝔯𝔞𝔲𝔫𝔤𝔢 𝔭𝔢𝔬𝔭𝔩𝔢, 𝔱𝔥𝔞𝔱 𝔨𝔫𝔬𝔴𝔢𝔱𝔥 𝔫𝔬 𝔤𝔬𝔬𝔡 𝔫𝔢𝔦𝔤𝔥𝔟𝔬𝔲𝔯𝔥𝔢𝔞𝔡𝔢; 𝔰𝔲𝔠𝔥 𝔞𝔰 𝔞𝔯𝔢 𝔯𝔲𝔡𝔢, 𝔲𝔫𝔪𝔞𝔫𝔫𝔢𝔯𝔩𝔶, 𝔞𝔫𝔡 𝔟𝔬𝔶𝔰𝔱𝔢𝔯𝔬𝔲𝔰.

Verse 5. *The earth, out of it cometh bread*] Or the earth, ממנה *mimmennah, from itself*, by its own vegetative power, *it sends out* bread, or the *corn* of which bread is made.

And under it is turned up as it were fire.] It seems as if this referred to some combustible fossil, similar to our stone coal, which was dug up out of the earth in some places of Arabia. The *Chaldee* gives a translation, conformable to

A. M. cir. 2484
B. C. cir. 1520
Ante I. Olymp.
cir. 744
Ante U. C. cir.
767

and under it is turned up as it were fire.

6 The stones of it *are* the place of sapphires: and it hath ᵉdust of gold.

7 *There is* a path which no fowl knoweth, and which the vulture's eye hath not seen:

8 The lion's whelps have not trodden it, nor the fierce lion passed by it.

---

9 He putteth forth his hand upon the ᶠrock; he overturneth the mountains by the roots.

A. M. cir. 2484
B. C. cir. 1520
Ante I. Olymp.
cir. 744
Ante U. C. cir.
767

10 He cutteth out rivers among the rocks; and his eye seeth every precious thing.

11 He bindeth the floods ᵍfrom overflowing; and *the thing that is* hid bringeth he forth to light.

ᵉOr, *gold ore*——ᶠOr, *flint*

ᵍHeb. *from weeping*

---

a very ancient opinion, which supposed the centre of the earth to be a vast *fire*, and the place called *hell*. "The earth from which food proceeds, and under which is gehenna, whose cold snow is converted into the likeness of fire; and the garden of Eden, which is the place whose stones are sapphires," &c. The *Vulgate* has, "The land from which bread has been produced has been destroyed by fire." If this be the meaning of the original, there is probably an allusion to the destruction of Sodom and Gomorrah; and the seventh and eighth verses may be supposed to refer to that catastrophe, there being no place left tangible or visible where those cities once stood: neither *fowl* nor *beast* could discern a *path* there, the whole land being covered with the lake Asphaltites.

Verse 6. *The stones—the place of sapphires*] In the language of mineralogists, the gangue, matrix, or bed in which the sapphire is found. For a description of this stone, see on ver. 16.

Dust of gold] Or rather, *gold dust*.

Verse 7. There is *a path which no fowl knoweth*] The instinct of birds is most surprising. They traverse vast forests, &c., in search of food, at a great distance from the place which they have chosen for their general residence; and return in all weathers, never missing their track: they also find their own nest without ever mistaking another of the same kind for it. Birds of passage, also, after tarrying in a foreign clime for six or seven months, return to their original abode over kingdoms and oceans, without missing their way, or deviating in the least from the proper direction; not having a single object of sight to direct their peregrinations. In such cases even the keen scent of the vulture, and the quick, piercing sight of the eagle, would be of no use. It is possible that Job may here refer to undiscovered mines and minerals; that notwithstanding man had already discovered much, yet much remained undiscovered, especially in the internal structure and contents of the earth. Since his time innumerable discoveries have been made; and yet how little do we know! Our various conflicting and contradictory *theories* of the earth are full proofs of our ignorance, and strong evidences of our folly. The present dogmatical systems of *geology* itself are almost the *ne plus ultra* of brain-sick visionaries, and system-mad mortals. They talk as confidently of the structure of the globe, and the manner and time in which all was formed, as if they had examined every part from the centre to the circumference; though not a soul of man has ever penetrated two miles in perpendicular depth into the bowels of the earth.

And with this scanty, defective knowledge, they pretend to build systems of the universe, and blaspheme the revelation of God! Poor souls! All these things are to them *a path which no fowl knoweth*, which the *vulture's eye hath not seen*, on which the *lion's whelps have not trodden*, and by which the *fierce lion hath not passed*. The *wisdom* necessary to such investigations is out of *their* reach; and they have not simplicity of heart to seek it where it may be found.

One of the *Chaldee Targums* gives a strange turn to this verse:—"The path of the tree of life Sammael, (Satan,) though flying like a bird, hath not known; nor hath the eye of Eve beheld it. The children of men have not walked in it; nor hath the serpent turned towards it."

Verse 9. *He putteth forth his hand upon the rock*] Still there appears to be a reference to *mining*. Man puts his hand upon the rock, he breaks that to pieces, in order to extract the metals which it contains.

He overturneth the mountains] He excavates, undermines, or digs them away, when in search of the metals contained in them: this is not only poetically, but literally, the case in many instances.

Verse 10. *He cutteth out rivers among the rocks*] He cuts canals, adits, &c., in the rocks, and drives levels under ground, in order to discover *loads* or *veins* of ore. These are often continued a great way under ground; and may be poetically compared to rivers, channels, or canals.

His eye seeth every precious thing.] He sinks those *shafts*, and drives those *levels*, in order to discover where the precious minerals lie, of which he is in pursuit.

Verse 11. *He bindeth the floods*] Prevents the risings of springs from drowning the mines; and conducts rivers and streams from their wonted course, in order to *bring forth to light what was hidden under their beds*. The *binding* or *restraining* the *water*, which, at different depths, annoys the miner, is both difficult and expensive: in some cases it may be drawn off by pipes or canals into neighbouring water courses; in others, it is conducted to one receptacle or reservoir, and thence drawn off. In Europe it is generally done by means of *steam-engines*. What method the ancients had in mining countries, we cannot tell; but they *dug deep* in order to find out the riches of the earth. PLINY says, nervously, *Imus in viscera terræ; et in sede manium opes quærimus.* "We descend into the bowels of the earth; and seek for wealth even in the abodes of departed spirits."—The *manes* or ghosts of the dead, or spirits pre-

A. M. cir. 2484
B. C. cir. 1520
Ante I. Olymp.
cir. 744
Ante U. C. cir.
767

12 [h]But where shall wisdom be found? and where *is* the place of understanding?

13 Man knoweth not the [i]price thereof; neither is it found in the land of the living.

14 [k]The depth saith, It *is* not in me: and the sea saith, *It is* not with me.

15 [l]It [m]cannot be gotten for gold, neither shall silver be weighed *for* the price thereof.

A. M. cir. 2484
B. C. cir. 1520
Ante I. Olymp.
cir. 744
Ante U. C. cir.
767

---

[h]Ver. 20; Eccles. vii. 24——[i]Prov. iii. 15——[k]Ver. 22;
Rom. xi. 33, 34

[l]Heb. *fine gold shall not be given for it*——[m]Prov. iii. 13,
14, 15; viii. 10, 11, 19; xvi. 16

---

siding over the dead, were supposed to have their habitation in the centre of the earth; or in the deepest pits and caves. Ovid, speaking of the degeneracy of men in the iron age, *Met.* lib. i., ver. 137, says:—

Nec tantum segetes alimentaque debita dives
Poscebatur humus; sed *itum est in viscera
    terræ:*
Quasque *recondiderat, Stygiisque admoverat
    umbris,*
Effodiuntur opes, irritamenta malorum.
Jamque nocens ferrum, ferroque nocentius
    aurum
Prodierat: prodit bellum, quod pugnat utroque;
Sanguineaque manu crepitantia concutit arma.

"Nor was the ground alone required to bear
 Her annual income to the crooked share:
 But greedy mortals, rummaging her store,
 Digg'd from her entrails first the precious ore;
 And that alluring ill to sight display'd,
 Which, next to hell, the prudent gods had laid.
 Thus cursed *steel*, and more accursed *gold*,
 Gave mischief birth, and made that mischief
     bold;
 And double death did wretched man invade,
 By *steel* assaulted, and by *gold* betray'd."
                                        DRYDEN.

By *binding the floods from overflowing*, some have supposed that there is an allusion to the *flux* and *reflux* of the sea. In its *flowing* it is so *bound*, has its *bounds* assigned by the Most High, that it does not drown the adjacent country; and in its *ebbing* the parts which are ordinarily *covered* with the water are *brought to view.*

Verse 12. *But where shall wisdom be found?*] It is most evident that the terms *wisdom* and *understanding* are used here in a widely different sense from all those arts and sciences which have their relation to man in his animal and social state, and from all that *reason* and *intellect* by which man is distinguished from all other animals. Now as these terms חכמה *chochmah, wisdom,* and בינה *binah, understanding* or *discernment*, are often applied in the sacred writings in their common acceptations, we must have recourse to what Job says of them, to know their meaning in *this place.* In ver. 28, he says, The *fear of the Lord is* WISDOM, *and to depart from evil is* UNDERSTANDING. We know that the *fear of the Lord* is often taken for the whole of that religious reverence and holy obedience which God prescribes to man in his word, and which man owes to his Maker. Hence the *Septuagint* render חכמה *chochmah, wisdom,* by θεοσεβια, *Divine worship;* and as to a *departure from evil*, that is necessarily implied in

a religious life; but it is here properly distinguished, that no man might suppose that a *right faith*, and a proper performance of the rites of religious worship, is the whole of religion. No. They must not only worship God *in the letter,* but also in the *spirit;* they must not only have the *form,* but also the *power* of *godliness:* and this will lead them to worship God in spirit and truth, to walk in his testimonies, and abstain from every appearance of evil; hence they will be truly *happy:* so that *wisdom* is another word for *happiness.* Now these are things which man by study and searching could never find out; they are not of an *earthly* origin. The *spirit of a man,* human understanding, *may know the things of a man*—those which concern him in his animal and social state: *but the Spirit of God* alone *knows the things of God;* and therefore WISDOM—all true religion—must come by Divine revelation, which is the mode of its attainment. *Wisdom* finds out the *thing,* and *understanding* uses and applies the *means;* and then the great *end* is obtained.

Verse 13. *Man knoweth not the price thereof*] It is of infinite value; and is the only science which concerns *both worlds.* Without it, the wisest man is but a beast; with it, the simplest man is next to an angel.

Neither is it found in the land of the living.] The world by wisdom, *its* wisdom, never knew God. True religion came by Divine revelation: that alone gives the true notion of God, his attributes, ways, designs, judgments, providences, &c., whence man came, what is his duty, his nature, and his end. *Literature, science, arts,* &c., &c., can only avail man for the *present life;* nor can they contribute to his true *happiness,* unless tempered and directed by genuine religion.

Verse 14. *The depth saith, It is not in me*] Men may dig into the bowels of the earth, and there find gold, silver, and precious stones; but these will not give them true happiness.

The sea saith, It is not with me.] Men may explore foreign countries, and by navigation connect as it were the most distant parts of the earth, and multiply the comforts and luxuries of life; but every voyage and every enjoyment proclaim, True happiness is not here.

Verse 15. *It cannot be gotten for gold*] Genuine religion and true happiness are not to be acquired by earthly property. Solomon made gold and silver as plentiful as the stones in Jerusalem, and had all the delights of the sons of men, and yet he was not happy; yea, he had *wisdom,* was the wisest of men, but he had not the wisdom of which Job speaks here, and therefore, to him, all was vanity and vexation of spirit. If Solomon, as some suppose, was the author of this book, the sentiments expressed here are such as we might expect from this deeply experienced and wise man.

A. M. cir. 2484
B. C. cir. 1520
Ante I. Olymp.
cir. 744
Ante U. C. cir.
767

16 It cannot be valued with the gold of Ophir, with the precious onyx, or the sapphire.

17 The gold and the crystal cannot equal it: and the exchange of it

shall not be for [n]jewels of fine gold.

18 No mention shall be made of [o]coral, or of pearls: for the price of wisdom *is* above rubies.

A. M. cir. 2484
B. C. cir. 1520
Ante I. Olymp.
cir. 744
Ante U. C. cir.
767

---

[n]Or, *vessels of fine gold*

[o]Or, *Ramoth*

Verse 16. *The gold of Ophir*] Gold is *five* times mentioned in this and verses 17 and 19, and *four* of the times in different words. I shall consider them all at once.

1. סגור SEGOR, from סגר *sagar*, to *shut up. Gold* in the *mine*, or *shut up* in the *ore; native* gold washed by the streams out of the mountains, &c.; *unwrought* gold.

Verse 16. 2. כתם KETHEM, from כתם *catham*, to *sign* or *stamp: gold* made *current* by being *coined*, or *stamped* with its *weight* or *value;* what we would call *standard* or *sterling* gold.

Verse 17. 3. זהב ZAHAB, from זהב *zahab*, to be *clear, bright*, or *resplendent:* the *untarnishing* metal; the only metal that always keeps its lustre. But probably here it means gold *chased*, or that in which precious stones are *set; burnished* gold.

4. פז PAZ, from פז *paz*, to *consolidate*, joined here with כלי *keley, vessels, ornaments, instruments*, &c.: *hammered* or *wrought gold;* gold in the finest *forms*, and most elegant *utensils*. This metal is at once the brightest, most solid, and most precious, of all the *metals* yet discovered, of which we have no less than *forty* in our catalogues.

In these verses there are also *seven* kinds of *precious stones*, &c., mentioned: *onyx, sapphire, crystal, coral, pearls, rubies*, and *topaz*. These I shall also consider in the order of their occurrence.

Verse 16. 1. שהם *shoham*, the ONYX, from ονυξ, *a man's nail, hoof of a horse*, because in *colour* it resembles both. This stone is a species of *chalcedony;* and consists of alternate layers of white and brown *chalcedony*, under which it generally ranges. In the *Vulgate* it is called *sardonyx*, compounded of *sard* and *onyx. Sard* is also a variety of chalcedony, of a deep reddish-brown colour, of which, and alternate layers of *milk-white* chalcedony, the sardonyx consists. A most beautiful block of this mineral sardonyx, from Iceland, now lies before me.

2. ספיר *sappir*, the SAPPHIRE stone, from ספר *saphar*, to *count, number;* probably from the number of *golden spots* with which it is said the *sapphire of the ancients* abounded. PLINY says, *Hist. Nat.* lib. xxxvii., cap. 8: Sapphirus *aureis punctis* collucet: cœruleæ et sapphiri, raraque cum purpura: optimæ apud Medos, nusquam tame perlucidæ. "The sapphire glitters with golden spots. Sapphires are sometimes of an azure, never of a purple colour. Those of Media are the best, but there are none transparent." This may mean the *blood stones;* but see below.

What we call the *sapphire* is a variety of the perfect *corundum;* it is in hardness inferior only to the *diamond*. It is of several colours, and from them it has obtained several names. 1. The transparent or translucent is called the *white* sapphire. 2. The *blue* is called the oriental *sapphire*. 3. The *violet blue*, the oriental *amethyst*. 4. The *yellow*, the oriental *topaz*. 5.

The *green*, the oriental *emerald*. 6. That with *pearly reflections*, the *opalescent* sapphire. 7. When transparent, with a pale, reddish, or bluish reflection, it is called the *girasol* sapphire. 8. A variety which, when polished, shows a *silvery star* of six rays in a direction perpendicular to the axis, is called *asteria*. When the meaning of the Hebrew word is collated with the description given by *Pliny*, it must be evident that a *spotted opaque* stone is meant, and consequently not what is now known by the name *sapphire*. I conjecture, therefore, that *lapis lazuli*, which is of a *blue colour*, with *golden-like spots*, formed by *pyrites* of iron, must be intended. The *lapis lazuli* is that from which the beautiful and unfading colour called *ultramarine* is obtained.

Verse 17. 3. זכוכית *zechuchith*, CRYSTAL, or *glass*, from זכה *zachah*, to be *pure, clear, transparent. Crystal* or *crystal of quartz* is a six-sided prism, terminated by six-sided pyramids. It belongs to the *siliceous* class of minerals: it is exceedingly clear and brilliant, insomuch that this property of it has become proverbial, as *clear as crystal*.

Verse 18. 4. ראמות *ramoth*, CORAL, from ראם *raam*, to be *exalted* or *elevated;* probably from this remarkable property of coral, "it always grows from the tops of marine rocky caverns with the head downwards." *Red coral* is found in the Mediterranean, about the isles of Majorca and Minorca, on the African coast, and in the Ethiopic ocean.

5. גביש *gabish*, PEARLS, from גבש *gabash*, in Arabic, to be *smooth*, to *shave off the hair;* and hence גביש *gabish*, the *pearl*, the *smooth round substance;* and also *hail* or *hailstones*, because of their resemblance to *pearls*. The *pearl* is the production of a shell-fish of the *oyster* kind, found chiefly in the East Indies, and called *berberi;* but pearls are occasionally found in the *common oyster*, as I have myself observed, and in the *muscle* also. They are of a brilliant sparkling white, perfectly round in general, and formed of *coats* in the manner of an *onion*. Out of one oyster I once took *six* pearls. When large, fine, and without spots, they are valuable. I have seen one that formed the whole body of a Hindoo idol, *Creeshna*, more than an inch in length, and valued at 300 guineas.

Verse 18. 6. פנינים *peninim*, RUBIES, from פנה *panah*, he *turned, looked, beheld*. The *oriental ruby* is blood-red, rose-red, or with a tinge of violet. It has occasionally a mixture of *blue*, and is generally in the form of *six-sided prisms*. It is a species of the *sapphire*, and is sometimes *chatoyant* in its appearance, i. e., has a curious kind of reflection, similar to the *cat's eye:* and as this is particularly striking, and *changes* as you *turn* the stone, hence probably the name *peninim*, which you derive from פנה *panah*, to turn, look, behold, &c.

But some learned men are of opinion that the *magnet* or *loadstone* is meant, and it is thus called because of the remarkable property it has

A. M. cir. 2484
B. C. cir. 1520
Ante I. Olymp. cir. 744
Ante U. C. cir. 767

19 The topaz of Ethiopia shall
not equal it, neither shall it be
valued with pure gold.
20 [p]Whence then cometh wis-
dom? and where *is* the place of understanding?
21 Seeing it is hid from the eyes of all living and kept close from the fowls of the [q]air.
22 [r]Destruction and death say, We have
heard the fame thereof with our
ears.
23 God understandeth the way
thereof, and he knoweth the place
thereof.
24 For he looketh to the ends of the earth,
and [s]seeth under the whole heaven;
25 [t]To make the weight for the winds;

[p]Ver. 12——[q]Or, *heaven*——[r]Ver. 14

[s]Prov. xv. 3——[t]Psa. cxxxv. 7

of *turning north* and *south*. And this notion is rendered the more likely, because it agrees with another word in this verse, expressive of a different property of the magnet, viz., its *attractive* influence: for the Hebrew words משך חכמה מפנינים *meshech chochmah mippeninim*, which we render, *The price of wisdom is above rubies*, is literally, *The* ATTRACTION *of wisdom is beyond the peninim*, the *loadstone;* for all the gold, silver, and precious stones, have strong influence on the human heart, attracting all its passions strongly; yet the *attraction of wisdom*—that which insures a man's *happiness* in both worlds—is more powerful and influential, when understood, than all of these, and even than the *loadstone*, for that can only attract *iron;* but, *through desire* of the other, *a man, having separated himself* from all those earthly entanglements, *seeketh and intermeddleth with* ALL WISDOM. The *attractive* property of the loadstone must have been observed from its first discovery; and there is every reason to believe that the *magnet* and its virtues were known in the East long before they were discovered in Europe.

7. פטדה *pitdah, the* TOPAZ. This word occurs only in Exod. xxviii. 17; xxxix. 10; Ezek. xxviii. 13, and in the present place; in all of which, except that of Ezekiel, where the Septuagint is all confusion, the *Septuagint* and *Vulgate* render the word always *τοπαζιον*, *topazius*, *the* TOPAZ. This stone is generally found in a prismatic form, sometimes limpid and nearly transparent, or of various *shades* of *yellow*, *green*, *blue*, *lilac*, and *red*.

I have thus given the best account I can of the stones here mentioned, allowing that they answer to the names by which we translate them. But on this point there is great uncertainty, as I have already had occasion to observe in other parts of this work. Beasts, birds, plants, metals, precious stones, unguents, different kinds of grain, &c., are certainly mentioned in the sacred writings; but whether we know what the different Hebrew terms signify, is more than we can certainly affirm. Of some there is little room to doubt; of others *conjecture* must, in the present state of our knowledge, supply the place of *certainty*. See PHILIP'S *Elementary Introduction* to MINERALOGY; an accurate work, which I feel pleasure in recommending to all students in the science.

Verse 19. *The topaz of Ethiopia*] The country called *Cush*, which we call *Ethiopia*, is supposed to be that which extends from the eastern coast of the Red Sea, and stretches towards Lower Egypt. *Diodorus Siculus* says that the topaz was found in great abundance, as his description intimates, in an island in the Red Sea called *Ophiodes*, or the *isle of serpents*. *Hist.* lib. iii., p. 121. His account is curious, but I greatly doubt its correctness; it seems too much in the form of a legend: yet the reader may consult the place.

Verse 20. *Whence then cometh wisdom?*] Nearly the same words as in verse 12, where see the note.

Verse 22. *Destruction and death say, We have heard the fame thereof*] אבדון ומות *Abaddon vamaveth*, the destroyer, and his offspring death. This is the very name that is given to the *devil* in Greek letters *Αβαδδων*, Rev. ix. 11, and is rendered by the Greek word *Απολλυων*, *Apollyon*, a word exactly of the same meaning. No wonder *death* and the *devil* are brought in here as saying *they had heard the fame of wisdom*, seeing ver. 28 defines it to be *the fear of the Lord, and a departure from evil;* things point blank contrary to the interests of Satan, and the extension of the empire of death.

Verse 23. *God understandeth the way thereof*] It can only be taught by a revelation from himself. Instead of הבין *hebin*, *understandeth*, six MSS. have הכין *hechin*, *disposed* or *established*. This reading is also supported by the *Septuagint;* Ὁ Θεος ευ συνεστησεν αυτης ὁδον, "God hath well established her way:" *falsely* rendered *bene cognovit, hath well known*, in the *Latin version* of the Septuagint in the London Polyglot; but *bene constituit, hath well established*, in the *Complutensian*, *Antwerp*, and *Paris* Polyglots.

Verse 24. *For he looketh to the ends of the earth*] His knowledge is unlimited, and his power infinite.

Verse 25. *To make the weight for the winds*] God has given an atmosphere to the earth, which, possessing a certain degree of *gravity* perfectly suited to the necessities of all animals, plants, vegetables, and fluids, is the cause in his hand of preserving animal and vegetative life through the creation; for by it the *blood* circulates in the veins of animals, and the *juices* in the tubes of vegetables. Without this *pressure* of the atmosphere, there could be no respiration; and the *elasticity* of the particles of air included in animal and vegetable bodies, without this superincumbent pressure, would rupture the vessels in which they are contained, and destroy both kinds of life. So exactly is this *weight of the winds* or *atmospheric air* proportioned to the necessities of the globe, that we find it in the mean neither too *light* to prevent the undue *expansion* of animal and vegetable tubes, nor too *heavy* to *compress* them so as to prevent due circulation. See at the end of the chapter.

A. M. cir. 2484
B. C. cir. 1520
Ante I. Olymp.
cir. 744
Ante U. C. cir.
767

and he weigheth the waters by measure.

26 When he ᵘmade a decree for the rain, and a way for the lightning of the thunder:

27 Then did he see it, and ᵛdeclare it; he

prepared it, yea, and searched it out.

28 And unto man he said, Behold, ʷthe fear of the LORD, that *is* wisdom: and to depart from evil *is* understanding.

A. M. cir. 2484
B. C. cir. 1520
Ante I. Olymp.
cir. 744
Ante U. C. cir.
767

ᵘChap. xxxviii. 25——ᵛOr, *number it*——ʷDeut.

iv. 6; Psa. cxi. 10; Prov. i. 7; ix. 10; Eccles. xii. 13

And he weigheth the waters by measure.] He has exactly proportioned the *aqueous surface* of the earth to the *terrene parts*, so that there shall be an adequate surface to produce, by *evaporation*, moisture sufficient to be treasured up in the atmosphere for the irrigation of the earth, so that it may produce grass for cattle, and corn for the service of man. It has been found, by a pretty exact calculation, that the aqueous surface of the globe is to the terrene parts as *three* to *one*; or, that *three-fourths* of the surface of the globe is *water*, and about *one-fourth earth.* And other experiments on evaporation, or the quantity of vapours which arise from a given space in a given time, show that it requires such a proportion of *aqueous surface* to afford moisture sufficient for the other proportion of *dry land.* Thus God has given the waters by measure, as he has given the due proportion of *weight* to the *winds.*

Verse 26. *When he made a decree for the rain*] When he determined how that should be *generated;* viz., By the *heat* of the sun *evaporation* is produced: the particles of vapour being lighter than the air on the surface, ascend into the atmosphere, till they come to a region where the air is of their own *density;* there they are formed into *thin clouds,* and become suspended. When, by the sudden passages of *lightning,* or by *winds* strongly *agitating* these clouds, the particles are driven together and condensed, so as to be *weightier* than the *air* in which they float, then they fall down in the form of *rain;* the drops being greater or less according to the *force* or *momentum,* or suddenness, of the agitation by which they are driven together, as well as to the degree of *rarity* in the lower regions of the atmosphere through which they fall.

A way for the lightning of the thunder] ודרך לחזיז קולות *vederech lachaziz koloth.* קול *kol* signifies *voice* of any kind; and *koloth* is the plural, and is taken for the frequent *claps* or *rattlings* of thunder. חז *chaz* signifies to *notch, indentate,* or *serrate,* as in the *edges* of the leaves of trees; חזיז *chaziz* must refer to the *zigzag* form which lightning assumes in passing from one cloud into another. We are informed that "this is a frequent occurrence in hot countries." Undoubtedly it is; for it is frequent in *cold countries* also. I have seen this phenomenon in England in the most distinct manner for hours together, with a few seconds of interval between each flash. Nothing can better express this appearance than the original word.

Verse 27. *Then did he see it, and declare it*] When he had finished all his creative operations, and tried and proved his work, חקרה *chakarah,* investigated and found it to be very good; then he gave the needful revelation to man; for,

Verse 28. *Unto man he said*] לאדם *laadam,*

unto man, he said: This probably refers to the revelation of his will which God gave to Adam after his fall. He had before sought for *wisdom* in a *forbidden way.* When he and Eve saw that the tree was pleasant to the eyes, *and a tree to be desired to make one wise,* they took and did eat, Gen. iii. 6. Thus they lost all the *wisdom* that they had, by not setting the *fear of the Lord* before their eyes; and became *foolish, wicked,* and *miserable.* Hear, then, what God prescribes as a proper remedy for this dire disease: The fear of the Lord, that is wisdom; it is thy only wisdom now to set God always before thy eyes, that thou mayest not again transgress.

Depart from evil is *understanding.*] Depart from the evil *within* thee, and the evil *without* thee; for thy own evil, and the evil that is now, through thee, brought into the world, will conspire together to sink thee into ruin and destruction. Therefore, let it be thy constant employment to shun and avoid that evil which is everywhere diffused through the whole moral world by thy offence; and labour to be *reconciled* to him by the righteousness and true holiness, that thou mayest escape the bitter pains of an eternal death. See the note on verse 12.

FROM what has been observed on verses 25, 26, and from the doctrine of the atmosphere in general, I can safely draw the following conclusions:—

1. From the *gravity* and *elasticity* of the air, we learn that it closely invests the earth, and all bodies upon it, and binds them down with a force equal to 2160 pounds on every square foot. Hence it may properly be termed the *belt* or *girdle* of the globe.

2. It prevents the arterial system of animals and plants from being too much distended by the impetus of the circulating juices, or by the elastic power of the air so plenteously contained in the blood, and in the different vessels both of plants and animals.

3. By its gravity it prevents the blood and juices from oozing through the pores of the vessels in which they are contained; which, were it not for this circumstance, would infallibly take place. Persons who ascend high mountains, through want of a sufficiency of pressure in the atmosphere, become relaxed, and spit blood. Animals, under an exhausted receiver, swell, vomit, and discharge their fæces.

4. It promotes the mixture of contiguous fluids; for when the air is extracted from certain mixtures, a separation takes place, by which their properties, when in combination, are essentially changed.

5. To this principle we owe winds in general, so essential to navigation, and so necessary to the purification of the atmosphere. The air is

put into motion by any alteration of its equilibrium.

6. Vegetation depends entirely on the gravity and elasticity of the air. Various experiments amply prove that plants in vacuo never grow.

7. Without air there could be no evaporation from the sea and rivers; and, consequently, no rain; nor could the clouds be suspended, so necessary to accumulate and preserve, and afterwards to distil, these vapours, in the form of dew, rain, snow, and hail, upon the earth.

8. Without air, all the charms of vocal and instrumental sounds would become extinct; and even language itself would cease.

9. Without it heat could not be evolved, nor could fire exist; hence a universal rigour would invest the whole compass of created nature.

10. Without air, animal life could never have had a being; hence God created the firmament or atmosphere before any animal was produced. And without its continual influence animal life cannot be preserved; for it would require only a few moments of a total privation of the benefits of the atmosphere to destroy every living creature under the whole heaven.

11. It has been found, by repeated *experiments*, that a column or rod of *quicksilver*, about *twenty-nine inches and a half high*, and *one inch* in *diameter*, weighs about *fifteen* pounds; and such a column is suspended in an exhausted tube by the weight of the *atmosphere;* hence it necessarily follows, that a column of *air*, one *square inch* in diameter, and as *high as the atmosphere*, weighs about *fifteen pounds* at a medium. Thus it is evident that the atmosphere presses with the weight of *fifteen pounds* on every *square inch;* and, as a *square foot* contains *one hundred and forty-four* square inches, every such foot must sustain a weight of incumbent atmospheric air equal to *two thousand one hundred and sixty pounds*, as has been before stated. And from this it will follow, that a middle-sized man, whose surface is about *fifteen square feet*, constantly sustains a load of air equal to *thirty-two thousand four hundred pounds!* But this is so completely counterbalanced by the air *pressing equally in all directions*, and by the *elasticity* of the air included in the various cavities of the body, that no person in a pure and healthy state of the atmosphere feels any inconvenience from it; so accurately has God *fitted the weight to the winds.*

It has been suggested that my computation of 15 *square* feet for the surface of a *middle-sized man*, is too *much;* I will, therefore, take it at 14 *square* feet. From this computation, which is within the measure, it is evident that every such person sustains *a weight of air* equal, at a medium, to about 30,240 *lbs.* troy, or 24,882½ *lbs.* avoirdupois, which make 1,777 *stone*, 4 *lbs.* equal to *eleven* TONS, *two* HUNDRED and *eighteen pounds* and *a half.*

12. Though it may appear more *curious* than *useful*, yet from the simple fact which I have completely demonstrated myself by experiment, that *the atmosphere presses with the weight of fifteen pounds on every square inch*, we can tell the *quantum of pressure* on the *whole globe*, and weigh the whole atmosphere to a pound!

The *polar* and *equatorial* circumference of the earth is well known. Without, therefore, entering too much into *detail*, I may state that the surface of the terraqueous globe is known to contain about *five thousand, five hundred, and seventy-five* BILLIONS *of square* FEET; hence, allowing *fifteen pounds to each square inch, and two thousand one hundred and sixty pounds to each square foot*, the whole surface must sustain a pressure from the atmosphere equal to *twelve* TRILLIONS *and forty-two thousand billions of* POUNDS! or *six thousand and twenty-one* BILLIONS *of* TONS! And this weight is the *weight of the whole atmosphere* from its contact with every part of the earth's surface to its utmost highest extent!

Experiments also prove that the air presses *equally in all directions, whether upwards, downwards*, or *laterally;* hence the earth is not incommoded with this enormous weight, because its *zenith* and *nadir, north* and *south* pressure, being perfectly equal, *counterbalance* each other! This is also the case with respect to the human body, and to all bodies on the earth's surface.

To make the foregoing calculations more satisfactory, it may be necessary to add the following observations:—

A bulk of atmospheric air, equal to one *quart*, when taken near the level of the sea, at a temperature of 50° Fahrenheit, weighs about 16 *grains*, and the same bulk of *rain water*, taken at the same temperature, weighs about 14,621 *grains:* hence *rain water* is about 914 times specifically heavier than *air.*

I have already shown that the *pressure* of the atmosphere is equal to about 15 *lbs.* troy on every *square inch;* and that this pressure is the same in all directions; and thence shown that on this datum the *whole weight of the atmosphere* may be computed. I shall re-state this from a computation of the earth's surface in *square miles*, which is recommended to me as peculiarly accurate. A square mile contains 27,878,400 square feet. The earth's surface, in round numbers, is 200,000,000, or *two hundred millions*, of square miles. Now, as from the preceding data it appears that there is a pressure of 19,440 *lbs.* troy on every *square yard*, the pressure or *weight* of the *whole atmosphere*, circumfused round the whole surface of the earth, amounts to 12,043,468,800,-000,000,000, or, *twelve* TRILLIONS, *forty-three thousand four hundred and sixty-eight* BILLIONS, *eight hundred thousand* MILLIONS *of pounds.*

Though we cannot tell to what *height* the atmosphere extends, the air growing more and more *rare* as we ascend in it; yet we can ascertain, as above, the quantum of *weight* in the whole of this atmosphere, which the terraqueous globe sustains equally diffused over its surface, as well as over the surfaces of all bodies existing on it. At first view, however, it is difficult for minds not exercised in matters of philosophy to conceive how such an immense pressure can be borne by animal beings. Though this has been already explained, let the reader farther consider that, as *fishes* are surrounded by *water*, and live and move in it, which is a much denser medium than our atmosphere; so all *human beings* and all other animals are surrounded by *air*, and live and move in it. A *fish taken out of the water* will die in a very short time: *a human being*, or any other animal, *taken out of the air*, or put in a place *whence the air is ex-*

tracted, will die in a much shorter time. *Water gravitates* towards the *centre* of the earth, and so does *air*. Hence, as a *fish* is pressed on every side by that fluid, so are all animals on the earth's surface by atmospheric air. And the pressure in both cases, on a given surface, is as has been stated above; the air contained in the vessels and cells of animal bodies being a sufficient counterpoise to the air without.

Having said thus much on the pressure of the atmosphere, as intimated by Job, the reader will permit me to make the following general reflections on the subject, of which he may make what use he may judge best.

It is generally supposed that former times were full of barbaric ignorance; and that the system of philosophy which is at present in repute, and is established by experiments, is quite a modern discovery. But nothing can

be more false than this; as the Bible plainly discovers to an attentive reader that the doctrine of *statics*, the *circulation* of the blood, the *rotundity* of the earth, the *motions* of the celestial bodies, the process of *generation*, &c., were all known long before *Pythagoras*, *Archimedes*, *Copernicus*, or *Newton* were born.

It is very reasonable to suppose that God implanted the first principles of every science in the mind of his first creature; that *Adam* taught them to his posterity, and that *tradition* continued them for many generations with their proper improvements. But many of them were lost in consequence of wars, captivities, &c. Latter ages have re-discovered many of them, principally by the direct or indirect aid of the Holy Scriptures; and others of them continue hidden, notwithstanding the accurate and persevering researches of the moderns.

CHAPTER XXIX

Job laments his present condition, and gives an affecting account of his former prosperity, having property in abundance, being surrounded by a numerous family, an enjoying every mark of the approbation of God, 1–6. Speaks of the respect he had from the young, 7, 8; and from the nobles, 9, 10. Details his conduct as a magistrate and judge in supporting the poor, and repressing the wicked, 11–17; his confidence, general prosperity, and respect, 18–25.

A. M. cir. 2484
B. C. cir. 1520
Ante I. Olymp. cir. 744
Ante U. C. cir. 767

MOREOVER Job [a]continued his parable, and said,

2 O that I were [b]as *in* months past, as *in* the days *when* God preserved me;

3 [c]When his [d]candle shined upon my head, *and when* by his light I walked *through* darkness;

4 As I was in the days of my youth, when

A. M. cir. 2484
B. C. cir. 1520
Ante I. Olymp. cir. 744
Ante U. C. cir. 767

---

[a]Heb. *added to take up*——[b]See chap. vii. 3

[c]Chap. xviii. 6——[d]Or, *lamp;* Psa. xviii. 28

NOTES ON CHAP. XXIX

Verse 2. *O that I were as* in *months past*] Job seems here to make an apology for his complaints, by taking a view of his former prosperity, which was very great, but was now entirely at an end. He shows that it was not removed because of any bad use he had made of it; and describes how he behaved himself before God and man, and how much, for justice, benevolence, and mercy, he was esteemed and honoured by the wise and good.

Preserved me] Kept, guarded, and watched over me.

Verse 3. *When his candle shined upon my head*] Alluding most probably to the custom of illuminating festival or assembly rooms by lamps pendant from the ceiling. These shone literally *on the heads* of the guests.

By his light I walked through *darkness*] His *light*—prosperity and peace—continued to illuminate my way. If adversity came, I had always the light of God to direct me. Almost all the nations of the world have represented their great men as having a *nimbus* or *Divine glory* about their heads, which not only signified the honour they had, but was also an emblem of the inspiration of the Almighty.

Verse 4. *The days of my youth*] The original word rather means *in the days of my winter*, חרפי *charpi*, from חרף *charaph*, "to strip or make bare." Mr. *Harmer* supposes the *rainy season* is intended, when the fields, &c., parched up by long drought, are revived by the *plentiful showers*. Mr. *Good* thinks the word as found in the *Arabic*, which means *top* or *summit*, and which he translates *perfection*, is that which should be preferred. Others think the *autumnal* state is meant, when he was *loaded with prosperity*, as the trees are with *ripe fruit*.

The secret of God was upon *my tabernacle*] בסוד אלוה *besod Eloah*, "the secret assembly of God," meaning probably the same thing that is spoken of in the beginning of this book, *the sons of God, the devout people, presenting themselves before God*. It is not unlikely that such a *secret assembly of God* Job had in his own house; where he tells us, in the next verse, "The Almighty was with him, and his children were about him."

Mr. *Good* translates differently: *When God fortified my tent over me;* supposing that the Hebrew סוד *sod* is the Arabic سود *sud*, "a barrier or fortification." Either will make a good sense.

A. M. cir. 2484 B. C. cir. 1520 Ante I. Olymp. cir. 744 Ante U. C. cir. 767

[e]the secret of God *was* upon my
tabernacle;
5 When the Almighty *was* yet
with me, *when* my children *were*
about me;
6 When [f]I washed my steps with butter,
and [g]the rock poured [h]me out rivers of oil;
7 When I went out to the gate through the
city, *when* I prepared my seat in the street!
8 The young men saw me, and hid themselves: and the aged arose, *and* stood up.
9 The princes refrained talking, and [i]laid
their hand on their mouth.
10 [k]The nobles held their peace, and their
[l]tongue cleaved to the roof of their mouth.
11 When the ear heard *me,* then it blessed me;
and when the eye saw *me,* it gave witness to me:
12 Because [m]I delivered the
poor that cried, and the fatherless, and *him that had* none to
help him.
13 The blessing of him that was ready to
perish came upon me: and I caused the
widow's heart to sing for joy.
14 [n]I put on righteousness, and it clothed
me: my judgment *was* as a robe and a diadem.
15 I was [o]eyes to the blind, and feet *was*
I to the lame.
16 I *was* a father to the poor: and [p]the
cause *which* I knew not I searched out.
17 And I brake [q]the [r]jaws of the wicked,
and [s]plucked the spoil out of his teeth.
18 Then I said, [t]I shall die in my nest, and
I shall multiply *my* days as the sand.

[e]Psa. xxv. 14——[f]Gen. xlix. 11; Deut. xxxii. 13; xxxiii. 24; ch. xx. 17——[g]Psa. lxxxi. 16——[h]Heb. *with me*——[i]Ch. xxi. 5——[k]Heb. *The voice of the nobles was hid*——[l]Psa. cxxxvii. 6——[m]Psa. lxxii. 12; Prov. xxi. 13; xxiv. 11

[n]Deut. xxiv. 13; Psa. cxxxii. 9; Isa. lix. 17; lxi. 10; Ephes. vi. 14, &c.; 1 Thess. v. 8——[o]Num. x. 31
[p]Prov. xxix. 7——[q]Psa. lviii. 6; Prov. xxx. 14——[r]Heb. *the jaw-teeth* or *the grinders*——[s]Heb. *cast*——[t]Psa. xxx. 6

Verse 6. *Washed my steps with butter*] See the note on chap. xx. 17.

Verse 7. *When I went out to the gate*] Courts of justice were held at the gates or entrances of the cities of the East; and Job, being an *emir,* was *supreme magistrate:* and here he speaks of his going to the gate to administer justice.

I prepared my seat in the street] I administered judgment openly, in the most public manner; and none could say that I, in any case, perverted justice. Mr. *Good* translates:—"As I went forth the city rejoiced at me, as I took my seat abroad."

Verse 8. *The young men saw me, and hid themselves*] From all classes of persons I had the most marked respect. The YOUNG, through modesty and bashfulness, shrunk back, and were afraid to meet the eye of their prince; and the AGED *rose from their seats* when I entered the place of judgment. These were the *elders* of the people, who also sat with the judge, and assisted in all legal cases.

Verse 9. *The princes refrained talking*] They never ventured an opinion in opposition to mine; so fully were they persuaded of the justice and integrity of my decision.

Verse 10. *The nobles held their peace*] PRINCES שרים *sarim,* and NOBLES, נגידים *negidim,* must have been *two* different classes of the great men of Idumea. שר *sar,* PRINCE, *director,* or *ruler,* was probably the *head of a township,* or what we would call a *magistrate* of a particular district. נגיד *nagid,* a NOBLE, or one of those who had the privilege of standing *before,* or in the *presence* of, the chief ruler. The participle נגד *neged* is frequently used to signify *before, in the presence of, publicly, openly.* And on this account, it is most likely that the *noun* means one of those nobles or counsellors who were always admitted to the royal presence. Mr. *Good* thinks that *renowned speakers* or *eminent orators* are meant: and others have embraced the same opinion. Job here intimates that his *judgment* was so *sound,* his *decisions* so *accredited,* and his *reasoning power* so *great,* that every person paid him the utmost deference.

Verse 11. *When the ear heard* me] This and the six following verses present us with a fine exhibition of a man full of benevolence and charity, acting up to the highest dictates of those principles, and rendering the miserable of all descriptions happy, by the constant exercise of his unconfined philanthropy.

Verse 12. *Because I delivered the poor that cried*] This appears to be intended as a *refutation* of the charges produced by *Eliphaz,* chap. xxii. 5-10, to confute which Job appeals to *facts,* and to *public testimony.*

Verse 15. *I was eyes to the blind, and feet* was *I to the lame.*] Alluding probably to the difficulty of travelling in the Arabian deserts. *I was eyes to the blind*—those who *did not know the way,* I furnished with *guides. I was feet to the lame*—those who were *worn out,* and *incapable* of walking, I set forward on my *camels,* &c.

Verse 16. *The cause* which *I knew not I searched out.*] When any thing difficult occurred, I did not give it a *slight* consideration; I examined it to the bottom, whatever pain, time, and trouble it cost me, that I might not pronounce a hasty judgment.

Verse 17. *I brake the jaws of the wicked*] A metaphor taken from hunting. A *beast of prey* had entered into the fold, and carried off a *sheep.* "The *huntsman* comes, assails the *wicked* beast, *breaks his jaws,* and *delivers the spoil out of his teeth.* See the case 1 Sam. xvii. 34-37.

Verse 18. *I shall die in my nest*] As I endeavoured to live *soberly* and *temperately, fearing God,* and *departing from evil,* endeavouring *to promote the welfare of all around me,* it was natural for me to conclude that I should live

A. M. cir. 2484
B. C. cir. 1520
Ante I. Olymp.
cir. 744
Ante U. C. cir.
767

19 ^uMy root *was* ^vspread out ^wby the waters, and the dew lay all night upon my branch.

20 My glory *was* ^xfresh in me, and ^ymy bow was ^zrenewed in my hand.

21 Unto me *men* gave ear, and waited, and kept silence at my counsel.

22 After my words they spake not again; and my speech dropped upon them.

23 And they waited for me as for the rain; and they opened their mouth wide, *as* for ^athe latter rain.

A. M. cir. 2484
B. C. cir. 1520
Ante I. Olymp.
cir. 744
Ante U. C. cir.
767

24 *If* I laughed on them, they believed *it* not; and the light of my countenance they cast not down.

25 I chose out their way, and sat chief, and dwelt as a king in the army, as one *that* comforteth the mourners.

---

^uChap. xviii. 16——^vHeb. *opened*——^wPsa. i. 3; Jer. xvii. 8

^xHeb. *new*——^yGen. xlix. 24——^zHeb. *changed*   ^aZech. x. 1

---

long, be very prosperous, and see my posterity multiply as the sands on the seashore.

Verse 19. *My root* was *spread out by the waters*] A metaphor taken from a healthy tree growing beside a rivulet where there is plenty of water; which in consequence flourishes in *all seasons;* its leaf does not *wither,* nor its fruit *fall off.* See Psa. i. 3; Jer. xvii. 8.

Verse 20. *My glory* was *fresh in me*] My *vegetative* power was great; my *glory*—my splendid *blossom,* large and *mellow fruit,* was always in season, and in every season.

My bow was renewed] I was never without means to accomplish all my wishes. I had prosperity everywhere.

Verse 21. *Unto me* men *gave ear*] The same idea as in ver. 9-11.

Verse 22. *My speech dropped upon them.*] It descended as *refreshing dew;* they were encouraged, comforted, and strengthened by it.

Verse 23. *They waited for me as for the rain*] The idea continued. They longed as much to hear me speak, to receive my counsel and my decisions, as the thirsty land does for refreshing waters.

They opened their mouth wide] A metaphor taken from ground *chapped* with long drought.

The latter rain.] The rain that falls a little before *harvest,* in order to *fill* and *perfect* the grain. The *former* rain is that which falls about *seed-time,* or in *spring,* in order to impregnate and *swell* the seed, and *moisten* the earth to produce its nourishment.

Verse 24. *I laughed on them, they believed* it *not*] Similar to that expression in the Gospel, Luke xxiv. 41: *And while they believed not for joy, and wondered, he said* ——. Our version is sufficiently perspicuous, and gives the true sense of the original, only it should be read in the *indicative* and not in the *subjunctive* mood: *I laughed on them—they be-*

lieved *it not.* We have a similar phrase: *The news was too good to be true.*

The light of my countenance] This evidence of my benevolence and regard. A *smile* is, metaphorically, *the light of the countenance.*

They cast not down.] They gave me no occasion to change my sentiments or feelings towards them. I could still smile upon them, and they were *then* worthy of my approbation. Their *change* he refers to in the beginning of the next chapter.

Verse 25. *I chose out their way, and sat chief—as a king in the army*] I cannot see, with some learned men, that our version of the original is wrong. I have not seen it mended, and I am sure I cannot improve it. The whole verse seems to me to point out Job in his *civil, military,* and *domestic* life.

As *supreme magistrate* he *chose out their way,* adjusted their differences, and *sat chief,* presiding in all their civil assemblies.

As *captain general* he *dwelt as a king in the midst of his troops,* preserving order and discipline, and seeing that his fellow soldiers were provided with requisites for their warfare, and the necessaries of life.

As a *man* he did not think himself superior to the meanest offices in domestic life, to relieve or support his fellow creatures; he went about *comforting the mourners*—visiting the sick and afflicted, and ministering to their wants, and seeing that the *wounded* were properly attended. Noble Job! Look at him, ye *nobles* of the earth, ye lieutenants of counties, ye generals of armies, and ye lords of provinces. Look at JOB! Imitate his active benevolence, and be healthy and happy. Be as guardian angels in your particular districts, blessing all by your example and your bounty. Send your *hunting horses* to the plough, your *game cocks* to the *dunghill;* and at last live like *men* and *Christians.*

CHAPTER XXX

Job proceeds to lament the change of his former condition, and the contempt into which his adversity had brought him, 1-15. Pathetically describes the afflictions of his body and mind, 16-31.

A. M. cir. 2484
B. C. cir. 1520
Ante I. Olymp.
cir. 744
Ante U. C. cir.
767

BUT now *they that are* [a]younger than I have me in derision, whose fathers I would have disdained to have set with the dogs of my flock.

2 Yea, whereto *might* the [b]strength of their hands *profit* me, in whom old age was perished?

A. M. cir. 2484
B. C. cir. 1520
Ante I. Olymp.
cir. 744
Ante U. C. cir.
767

3 For want and famine *they* were [c]solitary; fleeing into the wilderness [d]in former time desolate and waste;

4 Who cut up mallows by the bushes, and juniper roots *for* their meat.

5 They were driven forth from among *men,* (they cried after them as *after* a thief;)

---

[a]Heb. *of fewer days than I*——[b]Chap. xii. 21

[c]Or, *dark as the night*——[d]Heb. *yesternight*

NOTES ON CHAP. XXX

Verse 1. *But now* they that are *younger than I have me in derision*] Compare this with chap. xxix. 8, where he speaks of the respect he had from the youth while in the days of his prosperity. Now he is no longer affluent, and they are no longer respectful.

Dogs of my flock.] Persons who were not deemed sufficiently respectable to be trusted with the care of those dogs which were the guardians of my flocks. Not confidential enough to be made shepherds, ass-keepers, or camel-drivers; nor even to have the care of the dogs by which the flocks were guarded. This saying is what we call an expression of *sovereign contempt.*

Verse 2. *The strength of their hands* profit *me*] He is speaking here of the fathers of these young men. What was the strength of their hands to me? Their old age also has perished. The sense of which I believe to be this: I have never esteemed their strength even in their most vigorous youth, nor their conduct nor their counsel even in old age. They were never good for any thing, either young or old. As their youth was without profit, so their old age was without honour. See *Calmet.*

Mr. *Good* contends that the words are Arabic, and should be translated according to the meaning in that language, and the first clause of the third verse joined to the latter clause of the second, without which no good meaning can be elicited so as to keep properly close to the letter. I shall give the Hebrew text, Mr. Good's Arabic, and its translation:—

The Hebrew text is this:—

עלימו אבר כלח
aleymo abad calach

בחסר ובכפן גלמוד:
becheser ubechaphan galmud

The Arabic version this:—

عليهم ابٮ لاح
بعصر و جوع جلمود ﷽

Which he translates thus:—

"With whom crabbed looks are perpetual,
From hunger and flinty famine."

This translation is very little distant from the import of the present Hebrew text, if it may be called *Hebrew,* when the principal words are pure Arabic, and the others constructively so.

Verse 3. *Fleeing into the wilderness*] Seeking something to sustain life even in the barren desert. This shows the extreme of want, when the desert is supposed to be the only place where any thing to sustain life can possibly be found.

Verse 4. *Who cut up mallows by the bushes*] מלוח *malluach,* which we translate *mallows,* comes from מלח *melach, salt;* some herb or shrub of a salt nature, sea-purslane, or the salsaria, salsola, or saltwort. *Bochart* says it is the ἅλιμος of the Greeks, and the *halimus* of the Romans. Some translate it *nettles.* The *Syriac* and *Arabic* omit the whole verse. The halimus, or *atriplex halimus,* grows near the sea in different countries, and is found in Spain, America, England, and Barbary. The *salsaria, salsola,* or *saltwort,* is an extensive genus of plants, several common to Asia, and not a few indigenous to a dry and sandy soil.

And juniper roots for *their meat.*] רתמים *rethamim.* This is variously translated *juniper, broom, furze, gorse,* or *whin.* It is supposed to derive its name from the *toughness* of its twigs, as רתם *ratham* signifies to *bind;* and this answers well enough to the *broom. Genista quoque vinculi usum præstat,* "The broom serves for bands," says PLINY, *Hist. Nat.* lib. xxiv., c. 9. But how can it be said that the roots of this shrub were eaten? I do not find any evidence from Asiatic writers that the roots of the juniper tree were an article of food; and some have supposed, because of this want of evidence, that the word לחמם *lachmam, for their bread,* should be understood thus, *to bake their bread,* because it is well known that the wood of the juniper gives an intense heat, and the coals of it endure a long time; and therefore we find *coals of juniper,* נחלי רתמים *gachaley rethamim,* used Psa. cxx. 4 to express severe and enduring punishment. But that the roots of the juniper were used for food in the *northern countries,* among the *Goths,* we have a positive testimony from Olaus Magnus, himself a Goth, and archbishop of Upsal, in lib. vii., c. 4, of his *Hist. de Gentibus Septentrionalibus.* Speaking of the great number of different trees in their woods, he says: "There is a great plenty of beech trees in all the northern parts, the virtue whereof is this: that, being cut between the bark and the wood, they send forth a juice that is good for drink. The fruit of them in famine serves for *bread,* and their bark for clothing. Likewise also the berries of the juniper, yea, even the roots of this tree are eaten for bread, as holy Job testifies, though it is difficult to come at them by reason of their prickles: in these prickles, or thorns, live coals will last a whole year. If the inhabitants do not quench them, when winds arise they set the woods on fire, and destroy all the circumjacent fields." In this account both the properties of the juniper tree, referred to by Job and David, are mentioned by the Gothic prelate. They use its berries and roots for *food,* and its wood for *fire.*

Verse 5. *They were driven forth*] They

A. M. cir. 2484
B. C. cir. 1520
Ante I. Olymp.
cir. 744
Ante U. C. cir.
767

6 To dwell in the cliffs of the valleys, *in* °caves of the earth, and *in* the rocks.

7 Among the bushes they brayed; under the nettles they were gathered together.

8 *They were* children of fools, yea, children of ᶠbase men: they were viler than the earth.

9 ᵍAnd now am I their song, yea, I am their by-word.

10 They abhor me, they flee far from me, ʰand spare not ⁱto spit in my face.

11 Because he ᵏhath loosed my cord, and

afflicted me, they have also let loose the bridle before me.

A. M. cir. 2484
B. C. cir. 1520
Ante I. Olymp.
cir. 744
Ante U. C. cir.
767

12 Upon *my* right *hand* rise the youth: they push away my feet, and ⁱthey raise up against me the ways of their destruction.

13 They mar my path, they set forward my calamity, they have no helper.

14 They came *upon me* as a wide breaking in *of waters:* in the desolation they rolled themselves *upon me.*

15 Terrors are turned upon me: they pursue ᵐmy soul as the wind; and my welfare passeth away as a cloud.

°Heb. *holes*——ᶠHeb. *men of no name*——ᵍChap. xvii. 6; Psa. xxxv. 15; lxix. 12; Lam. iii. 14, 63——ʰHeb. *and withhold not spittle from my face*

ⁱNum. xii. 14; Deut. xxv. 9; Isa. l. 6; Matt. xxvi. 67; xxvii. 30——ᵏSee chap. xii. 18——ⁱChap. xix. 12 ᵐHeb. *my principal*

---

were persons whom no one would employ; they were driven away from the city; and if any of them appeared, the hue and cry was immediately raised up against them. The last clause Mr. *Good* translates, "They slunk away from them like a thief," instead of "They cried after them," &c.

Verse 6. *To dwell in the cliffs of the valleys*] They were obliged to take shelter in the most dangerous, out-of-the-way, and unfrequented places. This is the meaning.

Verse 7. *Among the bushes they brayed*] They cried out among the bushes, seeking for food, as the wild ass when he is in want of provender. Two MSS. read ינאקו *yinaku, they groaned,* instead of ינהקו *yinhaku, they brayed.*

Under the nettles] חרול *charul,* the *briers* or *brambles,* under the brushwood in the thickest parts of the underwood; they huddled together like wild beasts.

Verse 8. *Children of fools*] *Children of nabal; children without a name;* persons of no consideration, and descendants of such.

Viler than the earth.] Rather, *driven out of the land;* persons not fit for civil society.

Verse 9. *Now am I their song*] I am the subject of their mirth, and serve as a proverb or by-word. They use me with every species of indignity.

Verse 10. *They abhor me*] What a state must civil society be in when such indignities were permitted to be offered to the aged and afflicted!

Verse 11. *Because he hath loosed my cord*] Instead of יתרי *yithri, my cord,* which is the keri or marginal reading, יתרו *yithro, his cord,* is the reading of the text in many copies; and this reading directs us to a metaphor taken from an archer, who, observing his butt, sets his arrow on the string, draws it to a proper degree of tension, levels, and then loosing his hold, the arrow flies at the mark. He hath let loose his arrow against me; it has hit me; and I am wounded. The *Vulgate* understood it in this way: *Pharetram enim suam aperuit.* So also the *Septuagint:* Ανοιξας γαρ φαρετραν αυτου; "He hath opened his quiver."

They have also let loose the bridle] When

they perceived that God had afflicted me, they then threw off all restraints; like headstrong horses, *swallowed the bit,* got the *reins on their own neck,* and *ran off at full speed.*

Verse 12. *Upon my right* hand *rise the youth*] The word פרחח *pirchach,* which we translate *youth,* signifies properly *buds,* or the *buttons* of *trees.* Mr. *Good* has *younglings. Younkers* would be better, were it not too colloquial.

They push away my feet] They trip up my heels, or they in effect trample me under their feet. They rush upon and overwhelm me. They are violently incensed against me. They roll themselves upon me, התגלגלו *hithgalgalu, velut unda impellit undam,* as waves of the sea which wash the sand from under the feet, and then swamp the man to the bottom; see verse 14.

Verse 13. *They mar my path*] They destroy the *way-marks,* so that there is no safety in travelling through the deserts, the *guide-posts* and *way-marks* being gone.

These may be an allusion here to a besieged city: the besiegers strive by every means and way to distress the besieged; *stopping up the fountains, breaking up the road, raising up towers* to project arrows and stones into the city, called here *raising up against it the ways of destruction,* verse 12; preventing all succour and support.

They have no helper.] "There is not an adviser among them."—Mr. *Good.* There is none to give them better instruction.

Verse 14. *They came* upon me *as a wide breaking in*] They *storm* me on every side.

In the desolation they rolled themselves] When they had made the *breach,* they *rolled in* upon me as an *irresistible torrent.* There still appears to be an allusion to a besieged city: the *sap,* the *breach,* the *storm,* the *flight,* the *pursuit,* and the *slaughter.* See the following verse.

Verse 15. *Terrors are turned upon me*] Defence is no longer useful; they have beat down my walls.

They pursue my soul as the wind] I seek safety in flight, my strong holds being no longer tenable; but they pursue me so swiftly, that it

A. M. cir. 2484
B. C. cir. 1520
Ante I. Olymp.
cir. 744
Ante U. C. cir.
767

16 [n]And now my soul is poured out upon me; the days of affliction have taken hold upon me.

17 My bones are pierced in me in the night season: and my sinews take no rest.

18 By the great force *of my disease* is my garment changed: it bindeth me about as the collar of my coat.

19 He hath cast me into the mire, and I am become like dust and ashes.

20 I cry unto thee, and thou dost not hear me: I stand up, and thou regardest me *not.*

21 Thou art [o]become cruel to me: with [p]thy strong hand thou opposest thyself against me.

22 Thou liftest me up to the wind; thou causest me to ride *upon it,* and dissolvest my [q]substance.

A. M. cir. 2484
B. C. cir. 1520
Ante I. Olymp.
cir. 744
Ante U. C. cir.
767

23 For I know *that* thou wilt bring me *to* death and *to* the house [r]appointed for all living.

24 Howbeit he will not stretch out *his* hand to the [s]grave, though they cry in his destruction.

25 [t]Did not I weep [u]for him that was in trouble? was *not* my soul grieved for the poor?

26 [v]When I looked for good, then evil came *unto me:* and when I waited for light, there came darkness.

---

[n]Psa. xlii. 4——[o]Heb. *turned to be cruel*——[p]Heb. *the strength of thy hand*——[q]Or, *wisdom*——[r]Heb. ix. 27

[s]Hebrew, *heap*——[t]Psalm xxxv. 13, 14; Rom. xii. 15 [u]Heb. *for him that was hard of day*——[v]Jer. viii. 15

---

is impossible for me to escape. They follow me like a *whirlwind;* and as *fast* as that drives away the *clouds* before it, so is my prosperity destroyed. The word נדבתי *nedibathi,* which we translate *my soul,* signifies properly *my nobility, my excellence:* they endeavour to destroy both *my reputation* and *my property.*

Verse 18. *Is my garment changed*] There seem to be here plain allusions to the effect of his cruel disease; the whole body being enveloped with a kind of elephantine hide, formed by innumerable incrustations from the ulcerated surface.

It bindeth me about] There is now a new kind of covering to my body, formed by the effects of this disease; and it is not a garment which I can cast off; it is as closely attached to me as the collar of my coat. Or, my disease seizes me as a strong armed man; it *has throttled me, and cast me in the mud.* This is probably an allusion to two persons struggling: the stronger seizes the other by the throat, brings him down, and treads him in the dirt.

Verse 20. *I cry unto thee*] I am persecuted by man, afflicted with sore disease, and apparently forsaken of God.

I stand up] Or, as some translate, "I persevere, and thou lookest upon me." Thou seest my desolate, afflicted state; but thine eye doth not affect thy heart. Thou leavest me unsupported to struggle with my adversities.

Verse 21. *Thou art become cruel to me*] Thou appearest to treat me with cruelty. I cry for mercy, trust in thy goodness, and am still permitted to remain under my afflictions.

Thou opposest thyself] Instead of *helping,* thou opposest me; thou appearest as my *enemy.*

Verse 22. *Thou liftest me up to the wind*] Thou hast so completely stripped me of all my substance, that I am like *chaff* lifted up by the wind; or as a *straw,* the sport of every breeze; and at last carried totally away, being *dissipated* into particles by the continued agitation.

Verse 23. *Thou wilt bring me to death*] This must be the issue of my present affliction: to God alone it is possible that I should survive it.

To the house appointed for all living.] Or to

the house, מועד *moed,* the *rendezvous,* the place of general assembly of human beings: the great devourer in whose jaws all that have lived, now live, and shall live, must necessarily meet.

```
"——————O great man-eater!
Whose every day is carnival; not sated yet!
Unheard of epicure! without a fellow!
The veriest gluttons do not always cram!
Some intervals of abstinence are sought
To edge the appetite: thou seekest none.
Methinks the countless swarms thou hast
      devour'd,
And thousands that each hour thou gobblest
      up,
This, less than this, might gorge thee to the
      full.
But O! rapacious still, thou gap'st for more,
Like one, whole days defrauded of his meals,
On whom lank hunger lays her skinny hand,
And whets to keenest eagerness his cravings;
As if diseases, massacres, and poisons,
Famine, and war, were not thy caterers."
```
                                  THE GRAVE.

Verse 24. *He will not stretch out* his *hand to the grave*] After all that has been said relative to the just *translation* and true *meaning* of this verse, is it not evident that it is in the mouth of Job a *consolatory* reflection? As if he said, Though I suffer *here,* I shall not suffer *hereafter.* Though he add stroke to stroke, so as to destroy my life, yet his displeasure shall not proceed beyond the grave.

Though they cry in his destruction.] Mr. *Good* translates: *Surely there, in its ruin, is freedom.* In the *sepulchre* there is *freedom* from calamity, and rest for the weary.

Verse 25. *Did not I weep for him that was in trouble?*] Mr. *Good* translates much nearer the sense of the original, לקשה יום *liksheh yom.* "Should I not then weep for the *ruthless day?*" May I not lament that my sufferings are only to terminate with my life? Or, Did I not mourn for those who *suffered* by *times of calamity?*

Was not my soul grieved for the poor? Did I not relieve the distressed according to my power; and did I not sympathize with the sufferer?

A. M. cir. 2484
B. C. cir. 1520
Ante I. Olymp. cir. 744
Ante U. C. cir. 767

27 My bowels boiled, and rested not: the days of affliction prevented me.

28 [w]I went mourning without the sun: I stood up, *and* I cried in the congregation.

29 [x]I am a brother to dragons, and a companion to [y]owls.

30 [z]My skin is black upon me, and [a]my bones are burned with heat.

31 My harp also is *turned* to mourning, and my organ into the voice of them that weep.

A. M. cir. 2484
B. C. cir. 1520
Ante I. Olymp. cir. 744
Ante U. C. cir. 767

---

[w]Psa. xxxviii. 6; xlii. 9; xliii. 2——[x]Psa. cii. 6; Mic. i. 8

[y]Or, *ostriches*——[z]Psa. cxix. 83; Lam. iv. 8; v. 10
[a]Psa. cii. 3

Verse 27. *My bowels boiled*] This alludes to the strong commotion in the bowels which every humane person feels at the sight of one in misery.

Verse 28. *I went mourning without the sun*] חמה *chammah*, which we here translate *the sun*, comes from a root of the same letters, which signifies to hide, protect, &c., and may be translated, *I went mourning without a protector* or *guardian;* or, the word may be derived from חם *cham*, to be *hot*, and here it may signify fury, rage, anger; and thus it was understood by the *Vulgate: Mœrens incedebam, sine furore*, I went mourning without anger; or, as *Calmet* translates, *Je marchois tout triste, mais sans me laisser aller a l'emportement;* "I walked in deep sadness, but did not give way to an angry spirit." The *Syriac* and *Arabic* understood it in the same way.

Verse 29. *I am a brother to dragons*] By my mournful and continual cry I resemble חנים *tannim*, the *jackals* or *hyenas*.

And a companion to owls.] בנות יענה *benoth yaanah*, to the *daughters of howling:* generally understood to be the *ostrich;* for both the *jackal* and the *female ostrich* are remarkable for their mournful cry, and for their attachment to desolate places.—*Dodd*.

Verse 30. *My skin is black*] By continual exposure to the open air, and parching influence of the sun.

My bones are burned with heat.] A strong expression, to point out the raging fever that was continually preying upon his vitals.

Verse 31. *My harp also is* turned *to mourning*] Instead of the *harp*, my only music is my own *plaintive cries.*

And my organ] What the ענב *uggab* was, we know not; it was most probably some sort of pipe or *wind instrument*. His *harp*, בנור *kinnor*, and his *pipe*, ענב *uggab*, were equally mute, or only used for mournful ditties.

THIS chapter is full of the most painful and pathetic sorrow; but nevertheless tempered with a calmness and humiliation of spirit, which did not appear in Job's lamentations previously to the time in which he had that remarkable revelation mentioned in the nineteenth chapter. After he was assured that his *Redeemer was the living God*, he submitted to his dispensations, kissed the rod, and mourned not without hope, though in deep distress, occasioned by his unremitting sufferings. If the groaning of Job was great, his stroke was certainly heavy.

CHAPTER XXXI

Job makes a solemn protestation of his chastity and integrity, 1–12; of his humanity, 13–16; of his charity and mercy, 17–23; of his abhorrence of covetousness and idolatry, 24–32; and of his readiness to acknowledge his errors, 33, 34; and wishes for a full investigation of his case, being confident that this would issue in the full manifestation of his innocence, 36–40.

A. M. cir. 2484
B. C. cir. 1520
Ante I. Olymp. cir. 744
Ante U. C. cir. 767

I MADE a covenant with mine [a]eyes; why then should I think upon a maid?

2 For what [b]portion of God is there from above? and what inheritance of the Almighty from on high?

3 *Is* not destruction to the

A. M. cir. 2484
B. C. cir. 1520
Ante I. Olymp. cir. 744
Ante U. C. cir. 767

---

[a]Matt. v. 28

[b]Chap. xx. 29; xxvii. 13

NOTES ON CHAP. XXXI

Verse 1. *I made a covenant with mine eyes*] ברית כרתי לעיני *berith carati leeynai:* "I have cut" or divided "the covenant sacrifice with my eyes." My conscience and my eyes are the contracting parties; God is the Judge; and I am therefore bound not to look upon any thing with a delighted or covetous eye, by which my conscience may be defiled, or my God dishonoured.

Why then should I think upon a maid?]

ומה אתבונן על בתולה *umah ethbonen al bethulah. And why should I set myself to contemplate*, or *think upon, Bethulah?* That *Bethulah* may here signify an *idol*, is very likely. *Sanchoniatho* observes, that *Ouranos* first introduced *Baithulia* when he erected *animated stones*, or rather, as *Bochart* observes, ANOINTED stones, which became representatives of some deity. I suppose that Job purges himself here from this species of idolatry. Probably the *Baithulia* were at first emblems only of the *tabernacle;* בית אלוה *beith Eloah*, "the house

A. M. cir. 2484
B. C. cir. 1520
Ante I. Olymp.
cir. 744
Ante U. C. cir.
767

wicked? and a strange *punish-ment* to the workers of iniquity?

4 [c]Doth not he see my ways, and count all my steps?

5 If I have walked with vanity, or if my foot hath hasted to deceit;

6 [d]Let me be weighed in an even balance, that God may know mine integrity.

7 If my step hath turned out of the way, and [e]mine heart walked after mine eyes, and if any blot hath cleaved to mine hands;

8 *Then* [f]let me sow, and let another eat; yea, let my offspring be rooted out.

9 If mine heart have been deceived by a woman, or *if* I have laid wait at my neighbour's door;

10 *Then* let my wife grind unto [g]another, and let others bow down upon her.

A. M. cir. 2484
B. C. cir. 1520
Ante I. Olymp.
cir. 744
Ante U. C. cir.
767

11 For this *is* a heinous crime; yea, [h]it is an iniquity *to be punished by* the judges.

12 For it *is* a fire *that* consumeth to destruction, and would root out all mine increase.

13 If I did despise the cause of my man servant or of my maid-servant, when they contended with me;

14 What then shall I do when [i]God riseth up? and when he visiteth, what shall I answer him?

---

[c]2 Chron. xvi. 9; chap. xxxiv. 21; Prov. v. 21; xv. 3; Jer. xxxii. 19——[d]Heb. *Let him weigh me in balances of justice*——[e]See Num. xv. 39; Eccles. xi. 9; Ezek. vi. 9; Matt. v. 29

[f]Lev. xxvi. 16; Deut. xxviii. 30, 38, &c.; Mic. vi. 15 [g]2 Sam. xii. 11; Jer. viii. 10; Amos vii. 17——[h]Gen. xxxviii. 24; Lev. xx. 10; Deut. xxii. 22; see ver. 28 [i]Psa. xliv. 21

---

of God;" or of that *pillar* set up by Jacob, Gen. xxviii. 18, which he called בית אלהים *beith Elohim*, or *Bethalim;* for idolatry always supposes a pure and holy worship, of which it is the counterfeit. For more on the subject of the *Baithulia*, see the notes on Gen. xxviii.

Verse 2. *For what portion of God is there from above?*] Though I have not, in this or in any other respect, wickedly departed from God, yet what reward have I received?

Verse 3. *Is not destruction to the wicked?*] If I had been guilty of such secret hypocritical proceedings, professing faith in the *true God* while in *eye* and *heart* an *idolater*, would not such a worker of iniquity be distinguished by a *strange* and unheard-of punishment?

Verse 4. *Doth not he see my ways*] Can I suppose that I could screen myself from the eye of God while guilty of such iniquities?

Verse 5. *If I have walked with vanity*] If I have been guilty of *idolatry*, or the worshipping of a *false god:* for thus שוא *shav*, which we here translate *vanity*, is used Jer. xviii. 15; (compare with Psa. xxxi. 6; Hos. xii. 11; and Jonah ii. 9;) and it seems evident that the whole of Job's discourse here is a vindication of himself from all idolatrous dispositions and practices.

Verse 6. *Mine integrity.*] תמתי *tummathi*, my perfection; the totality of my unblameable life.

Verse 7. *If my step hath turned out of the way*] I am willing to be sifted to the uttermost—for every *step* of my *foot*, for every *thought* of my *heart*, for every *look* of mine *eye*, and for every *act* of my *hands*.

Verse 8. *Let me sow, and let another eat*] Let me be plagued both in my circumstances and in my family.

My offspring be rooted out.] It has already appeared probable that *all* Job's children were not destroyed in the fall of the house mentioned chap. i. 18, 19.

Verse 9. *If mine heart have been deceived by a woman*] The Septuagint add, ανδρος ετερου, *another man's wife.*

Verse 10. *Let my wife grind unto another*] Let her work at the *handmill*, grinding corn; which was the *severe* work of the meanest *slave*. In this sense the passage is understood both by the *Syriac* and *Arabic*. See Exod. xi. 5, and Isa. xlvii. 2; and see at the end of the chapter.

And let others bow down upon her.] Let her be in such a state as to have no command of her own person; her owner disposing of her person as he pleases. In Asiatic countries, slaves were considered so absolutely the property of their owners, that they not only served themselves of them in the way of scortation and concubinage, but they were accustomed to accommodate their guests with them! Job is so conscious of his own innocence, that he is willing it should be put to the utmost proof; and if found guilty, that he may be exposed to the most distressing and humiliating punishment; even to that of being deprived of his goods, bereaved of his children, his wife made a *slave*, and subjected to all indignities in that state.

Verse 11. *For this* is *a heinous crime*] Mr. *Good* translates,

"For this would be a premeditated crime,
And a profligacy of the understanding."

See also ver. 28.
That is, It would not only be a sin against the *individuals* more particularly concerned, but a sin of the first magnitude against *society;* and one of which the *civil magistrate* should take particular cognizance, and punish as justice requires.

Verse 12. *For it* is *a fire*] Nothing is so destructive of domestic peace. Where *jealousy* exists, unmixed misery dwells; and the adulterer and fornicator *waste their substance* on the unlawful objects of their impure affections.

Verse 13. *The cause of my man-servant*] In ancient times *slaves* had no action at law against their owners; they might dispose of them as they did of their cattle, or any other property. The slave might complain; and the owner might hear him if he pleased, but he was not compelled to do so. Job states that he had admitted them to all civil rights; and, far from preventing their case from being heard, he was ready to permit them to complain even against *himself*, if they had a cause of complaint, and to give them all the benefit of the law.

A. M. cir. 2484
B. C. cir. 1520
Ante I. Olymp.
cir. 744
Ante U. C. cir.
767

15 ᵏDid not he that made me in the womb make him? and ˡdid not one fashion us in the womb?

16 If I have withheld the poor from their desire, or have caused the eyes of the widow to fail;

17 Or have eaten my morsel myself alone, and the fatherless hath not eaten thereof;

18 (For from my youth he was brought up

with me, as *with* a father, and I have guided ᵐher from my mother's womb;)

19 ⁿIf I have seen any perish for want of clothing, or any poor without covering;

20 If his loins have not ᵒblessed me, and *if* he were *not* warmed with the fleece of my sheep;

21 If I have lifted up my hand ᵖagainst the fatherless, when I saw my help in the gate:

A. M. cir. 2484
B. C. cir. 1520
Ante I. Olymp.
cir. 744
Ante U. C. cir.
767

ᵏChap. xxxiv. 19; Prov. xiv. 31; xxii. 2; Mal. ii. 10 ˡOr, *did he not fashion us in one womb?*

ᵐThat is, *the widow*——ⁿEzek. xviii. 7, 16; Matt. xxv. 36——ᵒSee Deut. xxiv. 13——ᵖChap. xxii. 9

Verse 15. *Did not he that made me—make him?*] I know that God is the Judge of all; that all shall appear before him in that state where the king and his subject, the master and his slave, shall be on an equal footing, all civil distinctions being abolished for ever. If, then, I had treated my slaves with injustice, how could I stand before the judgment-seat of God? I have treated others as I wish to be treated.

Verse 17. *Or have eaten my morsel myself alone*] Hospitality was a very prominent virtue among the ancients in almost all nations: friends and strangers were equally welcome to the board of the affluent. The supper was their grand meal: it was then that they saw their friends; the business and fatigues of the day being over, they could then enjoy themselves comfortably together. The supper was called *cœna* on this account; or, as *Plutarch* says, Τo μεν γαρ δειπνον φασι κοινα δια την κοινωνιαν καλεισθαι· καθ᾽ ἑαυτους γαρ ηριστων επιεικως οἱ παλαι ᾽Ρωμαιοι, συνδειπνουντες τοις φιλοις. "The ancient Romans named *supper* CŒNA, (κοινα,) which signifies *communion* (κοινωνια) or *fellowship;* for, although they *dined alone,* they *supped with their friends.*"—PLUT. *Symp.* lib. viii., prob. 6, p. 687. But Job speaks here of dividing his bread with the hungry: *Or have eaten my morsel myself alone.* And he is a poor despicable caitiff who would eat it alone, while there was another at hand full as hungry as himself.

Verse 18. This is a very difficult verse, and is variously translated. Take the following instances:—For from his youth *he* (the male orphan) was brought up with me as a father. Yea, I have guided *her* (the female orphan) from her mother's womb.—*Heath.*

Nam a pueris educavit me commiseratio; jam inde ab utero matris meæ illa me deduxit. —*Houbigant.*

"For commiseration educated me from my childhood;
And she brought me up even from my mother's womb."

This is agreeable to the *Vulgate.*

"Behold, from my youth calamity hath quickened me;
Even from my mother's womb have I distributed it."

This is Mr. *Good's* version, and is widely different from the above.

*For mercy grewe up with me fro my youth,
And compassion fro my mother's wombe.*
Coverdale.

᾽Οτι εκ νεοτητος μου εξετρεφον ὡς πατηρ, και εκ γαστρος μητρος μου ὡδηγησα.—*Septuagint.* "For from my youth I nourished them as a father; and I was their guide from my mother's womb." The *Syriac.*—"For from my childhood he educated me in distresses, and from the womb of my mother in groans." The *Arabic* is nearly the same.

The general meaning may be gathered from the above; but who can reconcile such discordant translations?

Verse 20. *If his loins have not blessed me*] This is a very delicate touch: the part that was *cold* and *shivering* is now covered with *warm woollen.* It *feels* the comfort; and by a fine *prosopopœia,* is represented as blessing him who furnished the clothing.

Verse 21. *If I have lifted up my hand against the fatherless*] I have at no time opposed the orphan, nor given, in behalf of the rich and powerful, a decision against the poor, *when I saw my help in the gate*—when I was sitting chief on the throne of judgment, and could have done it without being called to account.

There are sentiments very like these in the poem of *Lebeid,* one of the authors of the *Moallakhat.* I shall quote several verses from the elegant translation of Sir William Jones, in which the character of a charitable and bountiful chief is well described:—

"Oft have I invited a numerous company to the death of a camel bought for slaughter, to be divided with arrows of equal dimensions."

"I invite them to draw lots for a camel without a foal, and for a camel with her young one, whose flesh I distribute to all the neighbours."

"The guest and the stranger admitted to my board seem to have alighted in the sweet vale of *Tebaala,* luxuriant with vernal blossoms."

"The cords of my tent approaches every needy matron, worn with fatigue, like a camel doomed to die at her master's tomb, whose vesture is both scanty and ragged."

"There they crown with meat (while the wintry winds contend with fierce blasts) a dish flowing like a rivulet, into which the famished orphans eagerly plunge."

"He distributes equal shares, he dispenses justice to the tribes, he is indignant when their right is diminished; and, to establish their right, often relinquishes his own."

"He acts with greatness of mind, and nobleness of heart; he sheds the dew of his liberality

A. M. cir. 2484 B. C. cir. 1520 Ante I. Olymp. cir. 744 Ante U. C. cir. 767

22 *Then* let mine arm fall from
my shoulder blade, and mine arm
be broken from [q]the bone.
23 For [r]destruction *from* God
was a terror to me, and by reason of his highness I could not endure.
24 [s]If I have made gold my hope, or have
said to the fine gold, *Thou art* my confidence;
25 [t]If I rejoiced because my wealth *was*
great, and because mine hand had [u]gotten
much;
26 [v]If I beheld [w]the sun when it shined,
or the moon walking [x]*in* brightness;
27 And my heart hath been secretly enticed,
or [y]my mouth hath kissed my hand:
28 This also *were* [z]an iniquity
to be punished by the judge: for
I should have denied the God
that is above.
29 [a]If I rejoiced at the destruction of him
that hated me, or lifted up myself when evil
found him;
30 ([b]Neither have I suffered [c]my mouth to
sin, by wishing a curse to his soul;)
31 If the men of my tabernacle said not, O that
we had of his flesh! we cannot be satisfied.
32 [d]The stranger did not lodge in the street:
but I opened my doors [e]to the traveller.
33 If I covered my transgressions [f]as
[g]Adam, by hiding mine iniquity in my bosom:

A. M. cir. 2484 B. C. cir. 1520 Ante I. Olymp. cir. 744 Ante U. C. cir. 767

---

[q]Or, *the chanelbone*——[r]Isaiah xiii. 6; Joel i. 15——[s]Mark x. 24; 1 Tim. vi. 17——[t]Psa. lxii. 10; Prov. xi. 28——[u]Heb. *found much*——[v]Deut. iv. 19; xi. 16; xvii. 3; Ezek. viii. 16——[w]Heb. *the light*——[x]Heb. *bright*——[y]Heb. *my hand hath kissed my mouth*

[z]Ver. 11——[a]Prov. xvii. 5——[b]Matt. v. 44; Rom. xii. 14——[c]Heb. *my palate*——[d]Gen. xix. 2, 3; Judg. xix. 20, 21; Rom. xii. 13; Heb. xiii. 2; 1 Pet. iv. 9——[e]Or, *to the way*——[f]Or, *after the manner of men*——[g]Gen. iii. 8, 12; Prov. xxviii. 13; Hos. vi. 7

---

on those who need his assistance; he scatters around his own gains and precious spoils, the prizes of his valour."—Ver. 73-80.

Verse 22. *Let mine arm fall*] Mr. *Good*, as a medical man, is at home in the translation of this verse:—

"May my shoulder-bone be shivered at the blade,
And mine arm be broken off at the socket."

Let judgment fall particularly on those parts which have either done wrong, or refused to do right when in their power.

Verse 23. *Destruction* from *God* was *a terror*] I have ever been preserved from outward sin, through the fear of God's judgments; I knew his eye was constantly upon me, and I could

"Never in my Judge's eye my Judge's anger dare."

Verse 24. *Gold my hope*] For the meaning of זהב *zahab*, polished gold, and כתם *kethem*, stamped gold, see on chap. xxviii. 15-17.

Verse 26. *If I beheld the sun when it shined*] In this verse Job clears himself of that idolatrous worship which was the most ancient and most consistent with reason of any species of idolatry; viz., *Sabæism*, the worship of the heavenly bodies; particularly the *sun* and *moon*, *Jupiter* and *Venus;* the two latter being the *morning* and *evening stars*, and the most resplendent of all the heavenly bodies, the sun and moon excepted.

"Job," says *Calmet*, "points out three things here:

"1. The worship of the sun and moon; much used in his time, and very anciently used in every part of the East; and in all probability that from which idolatry took its rise.

"2. The custom of adoring the sun at its rising, and the moon at her change; a superstition which is mentioned in Ezek. viii. 16, and in every part of profane antiquity.

"3. The custom of *kissing the hand;* the form of adoration, and token of sovereign respect."

Adoration, or the religious act of *kissing the hand*, comes to us from the Latin; *ad*, to, and *os*, *oris*, the mouth. The hand lifted to the mouth, and there saluted by the lips.

Verse 28. *For I should have denied the God* that is *above.*] Had I paid Divine adoration to them, I should have thereby denied the God that made them.

Verse 29. *If I rejoiced*] I did not avenge myself on my enemy; and I neither bore malice nor hatred to him.

Verse 30. *Neither have I suffered my mouth to sin*] I have neither *spoken evil* of him, nor *wished evil* to him. How few of those called *Christians* can speak thus concerning their *enemies;* or those who have done them any mischief!

Verse 31. *If the men of my tabernacle said*] I believe the *Targum* gives the best sense here:—"If the men of my tabernacle have not said, Who hath commanded that we should not be satisfied with his flesh?" My domestics have had all kindness shown them; they have lived like my own children, and have been served with the *same viands* as my family. They have never seen *flesh* come to my table, when they have been obliged to live on *pulse.*

Mr. *Good's* translation is nearly to the same sense:—

"If the men of my tabernacle do not exclaim,
Who hath longed for his meat without fulness?"

"Where is the man that has not been satisfied with his flesh?" i. e., fed to the full with the provisions from his table. See Prov. xxiii. 20; Isa. xxiii. 13, and Dan. x. 3.

Verse 32. *The stranger did not lodge in the street*] My kindness did not extend merely to my family, domestics, and friends; the *stranger*—he who was to me perfectly unknown, and the *traveller*—he who was on his journey to some other district, found my doors ever open to receive them, and were refreshed with my *bed* and my *board.*

Verse 33. *If I covered my transgressions as*

A. M. cir. 2484
B. C. cir. 1520
Ante I. Olymp. cir. 744
Ante U. C. cir. 767

34 Did I fear a great [h]multitude, or did the contempt of families terrify me, that I kept silence, *and* went not out of the door?

35 [i]O that one would hear me! [k]behold, my desire is, [l]*that* the Almighty would answer me,

and *that* mine adversary had written a book:

A. M. cir. 2484
B. C. cir. 1520
Ante I. Olymp. cir. 744
Ante U. C. cir. 767

36 Surely I would take it upon my shoulder, *and* bind it *as a* crown to me.

37 I would declare unto him the number of my steps; as a prince would I go near unto him.

---

[h]Exod. xxiii. 2——[i]Ch. xxxiii. 6——[k]Or, *behold my sign*   is that *the Almighty will answer me*——[l]Chap. xiii. 22

Adam] Here is a most evident allusion to the *fall*. Adam *transgressed* the commandment of his Maker, and he endeavoured to *conceal* it; *first*, by *hiding himself* among the trees of the garden: "I heard thy voice, and went and HID myself;" *secondly*, by laying the *blame* on his *wife*: "The woman gave me, and I did eat;" and *thirdly*, by *charging* the whole directly on *God* himself: "The woman which THOU GAVEST ME to be with me, SHE gave me of the tree, and I did eat." And it is very likely that Job refers immediately to the Mosaic account in the Book of *Genesis*. The spirit of this saying is this: When I have departed at any time from the path of rectitude, I have been ready to *acknowledge* my error, and have not sought excuses or palliatives for my sin.

Verse 34. *Did I fear a great multitude*] Was I ever prevented by the voice of the *many* from decreeing and executing what was right? When many *families* or *tribes* espoused a particular cause, which I found, on examination, to be wrong, did they *put me in fear*, so as to prevent me from doing justice to the weak and friendless? Or, in any of these cases, was I ever, *through fear*, self-seeking, or favour, prevented from declaring my mind, or constrained to keep my house, lest I should be obliged to give judgment against my conscience? Mr. *Good* thinks it an imprecation upon himself, if he had done any of the evils which he mentions in the preceding verse. He translates thus:—

"Then let me be confounded before the assembled multitude,
And let the reproach of its families quash me!
Yea, let me be struck dumb! let me never appear abroad!"

I am satisfied that ver. 38, 39, and 40, should come in either here, or immediately after ver. 25; and that Job's words should end with ver. 37, which, if the others were inserted in their proper places, would be ver. 40. See the reasons at the end of the chapter.

Verse 35. *O that one would hear me!*] I wish to have a fair and full hearing: I am grievously accused; and have no proper opportunity of clearing myself, and establishing my own innocence.

Behold, my desire is] Or, הן תוי *hen tavi*, "There is my pledge." I bind myself, on a great penalty, to come into court, and abide the issue.

That *the Almighty would answer me*] That he would call this case immediately *before himself;* and oblige my *adversary* to come into court, to put his accusations into a legal form, that I might have the opportunity of vindicating myself in the presence of a judge who would hear dispassionately my pleadings, and bring the cause to a righteous issue.

And that *mine adversary had written a book*]

That he would not indulge himself in vague accusations, but would draw up a proper *bill of indictment*, that I might know to what I had to plead, and find the accusation in a tangible form.

Verse 36. *Surely I would take it upon my shoulder*] I would be contented to stand before the bar as a criminal, bearing upon my shoulder the *board* to which the *accusation* is affixed. In a book of *Chinese punishments* now before me, containing *drawings* representing various criminals brought *to* trial, *in* trial, and *after* trial, charged with different offences; in almost all of them a *board* appears, on which the *accusation* or *crime* of which they are accused, or for which they suffer, is fairly written. Where the punishment is capital, this board appears fastened to the *instrument*, or stuck near the *place* of *punishment*. In one case a large, heavy plank, through which there is a hole to pass the head,—or rather a *hole* fitting the *neck*, like that in the *pillory*,—with the *crime* written upon it, rests on the *criminal's shoulders;* and this he is obliged to carry about for the *weeks* or *months* during which the punishment lasts. It is probable that Job alludes to something of this kind; which he intimates he would *bear about with him* during the *interim* between *accusation* and the *issue* in judgment; and, far from considering this a disgrace, would clasp it as dearly as he would adjust a crown or diadem to his head; being fully assured, from his *innocence*, and the *evidence* of it, which would infallibly appear on the trial, that he would have the *most honourable acquittal*. There may also be an allusion to the manner of receiving a favour from a superior: it is immediately *placed on the head*, as a mark of respect; and if a piece of *cloth* be given at the *temple*, the receiver not only puts it on his *head*, but *binds* it there.

Verse 37. *I would declare unto him the number of my steps*] I would show this adversary the different *stations* I had been in, and the *offices* which I had filled in life, that he might trace me through the whole of my civil, military, and domestic life, in order to get evidence against me.

As a prince would I go near] Though carrying my own accusation, I would go into the presence of my judge as the נגיד *nagid*, chief, or *sovereign commander* and *judge*, of the people and country, and would not shrink from having my conduct investigated by even the meanest of my subjects.

In these *three* verses we may observe the following particulars:—

1. Job wishes to be *brought to trial*, that he might have the opportunity of vindicating himself: *O that I might have a hearing!*

2. That his *adversary*, Eliphaz and his companions, whom he considers as *one party*, and

A. M. cir. 2484
B. C. cir. 1520
Ante I. Olymp.
cir. 744
Ante U. C. cir.
767

38 If my land cry against me, or that the furrows likewise there- of ^mcomplain;

39 If ⁿI have eaten ^othe fruits thereof without money, or ^phave ^qcaused the owners thereof to lose their life:

A. M. cir. 2484
B. C. cir. 1520
Ante I. Olymp.
cir. 744
Ante U. C. cir.
767

40 Let ^rthistles grow instead of wheat, and ^scockle instead of barley. The words of Job are ended.

---

^mHeb. *weep*——ⁿJames v. 4——^oHeb. *the strength thereof*——^p1 Kings xxi. 19

^qHeb. *caused the soul of the owners thereof to expire* or *breathe out*——^rGen. iii. 18——^sOr, *noisome weed*

---

joined together *in one*, would *reduce* their vague charges *to writing*, that they might come before the court in a legal form: *O that my adversary would write down the charge!*

3. That the Almighty, שַׁדַּי *Shaddai*, the *all-sufficient* GOD, and not *man*, should be the judge, who would not permit his adversaries to attempt, by false evidence, to establish what was false, nor suffer himself to cloak with a hypocritical covering what was iniquitous in his conduct: *O that the Almighty might answer for me*—take notice of or be judge in the cause!

4. To him he purposes cheerfully to confess all his ways, who could at once judge if he prevaricated, or concealed the truth.

5. This would give him the strongest encouragement: he would go *boldly* before him, with the highest persuasion of an honourable acquittal.

Verse 38. *If my land cry*] The most careless reader may see that the introduction of this and the two following verses here, disturbs the connection, and that they are most evidently out of their place. Job seems here to refer to that *law*, Lev. xxv. 1-7, by which the Israelites were obliged to give the *land rest every seventh year*, that the soil might not be too much exhausted by perpetual cultivation, especially in a country which afforded so few advantages to improve the arable ground by manure. He, conscious that he had acted according to this law, states that his *land* could *not cry out against him*, nor its *furrows complain*. He had not broken the law, nor exhausted the soil.

Verse 39. *If I have eaten the fruits thereof without money*] I have never been that *narrow-minded* man who, through a principle of *covetousness*, exhausts his land, putting himself to no *charges*, by *labour* and *manure*, to strengthen it; or defrauds those of their *wages* who were employed under him. *If I have eaten the fruits of it*, I have cultivated it *well* to produce those fruits; and this has not been *without money*, for I have gone to expenses on the soil, and *remunerated* the labourers.

Or have caused the owners thereof to lose their life] Coverdale translates, 𝔇𝔢𝔢 𝔶𝔱 𝔍 𝔥𝔞𝔳𝔢 𝔤𝔯𝔢𝔳𝔢𝔡 𝔞𝔫𝔶 𝔬𝔣 𝔱𝔥𝔢 𝔭𝔩𝔬𝔴𝔪𝔢𝔫. They have not panted in labour without due recompense.

Verse 40. *Let thistles grow instead of wheat*] What the word חוֹחַ *choach* means, which we translate *thistles*, we cannot tell: but as חח *chach* seems to mean *to hold, catch as a hook, to hitch*, it must signify some kind of *hooked thorn*, like the brier; and this is possibly its meaning.

And cockle] בָּאְשָׁה *bashah*, some *fetid* plant, from בָּאַשׁ *baash*, to *stink*. In Isa. v. 2, 4, we translate it *wild grapes;* and Bishop *Lowth*, *poisonous berries:* but *Hasselquist*, a pupil of the famous Linnæus, in his Voyages, p. 289, is inclined to believe that the *solanum incanum*, or *hoary nightshade* is meant, as this is common in Egypt, Palestine, and the East. Others are

of opinion that it means the *aconite*, which بيش *beesh*, in Arabic, denotes: this is a poisonous herb, and grows luxuriantly on the sunny hills among the vineyards, according to *Celsus* in *Hieroboticon*. بيش *beesh* is not only the name of an *Indian poisonous* herb, called the *napellus moysis, but* بيش موش *beesh moosh*, or مارة البيش *farut al beesh*, is the name of an *animal*, resembling a mouse, which lives among the roots of this very plant. "May I have a crop of this instead of barley, if I have acted improperly either by my land or my labourers!"

The words of Job are ended.] That is, his defence of himself against the accusations of his *friends*, as they are called. He spoke afterwards, but never to *them;* he only addresses God, who came to determine the whole controversy.

These words seem very much like an *addition* by a later hand. They are wanting in many of the MSS. of the Vulgate, two in my own possession; and in the *Editio Princeps* of this version.

I suppose that at first they were inserted in *rubric*, by some scribe, and afterwards taken into the text. In a MS. of my own, of the *twelfth* or *thirteenth* century, these words stand in *rubric*, actually *detached from the text;* while in another MS., of the *fourteenth* century, they form a *part of the text.*

In the Hebrew text they are also *detached:* the hemistichs are complete without them; nor indeed can they be incorporated with them. They appear to me as an *addition* of no authority. In the first edition of our Bible, that by Coverdale, 1535, there is a *white line* between these words and the conclusion of the chapter; and they stand, forming no part of the text, thus:—

𝔥𝔢𝔯𝔢 𝔢𝔫𝔡𝔢 𝔱𝔥𝔢 𝔴𝔬𝔯𝔡𝔢𝔰 𝔬𝔣 𝔍𝔬𝔟.

Just as we say, in reading the Scriptures, "Here ends such a chapter;" or, "Here ends the first lesson," &c.

ON the subject of the *transposition*, mentioned above, I have referred to the *reasons* at the end of the chapter.

Dr. Kennicott, on this subject, observes: "Chapters xxix., xxx., and xxxi., contain Job's animated *self-defence*, which was made necessary by the reiterated accusation of his friends. This defence now concludes with six lines (in the Hebrew text) which declare, that if he had enjoyed his estates *covetously*, or procured them *unjustly*, he wished them to prove *barren* and *unprofitable*. This part, therefore, seems naturally to follow ver. 25, where he speaks of his *gold*, and how *much his hand had gotten*. The remainder of the chapter will then consist of these *four* regular parts, viz.,

"1. His *piety to God,* in his freedom from idolatry, ver. 26-28.

"2. His *benevolence to men,* in his charity both of temper and behaviour, 29-32.

"3. His *solemn assurance* that he did not *conceal* his guilt, from fearing either the *violence* of the *poor,* or the *contempt* of the *rich,* ver. 33, 34.

"4. (Which must have been the last article, because conclusive of the work) he infers that, being *thus secured by his integrity,* he may *appeal safely to God himself.* This appeal he therefore makes boldly, and in such words as, when rightly translated, form an image which perhaps has no parallel. For where is there an image so magnificent or so splendid as this? Job, thus conscious of innocence, wishing even God *himself* to draw up his indictment, [rather his *adversary* Eliphaz and companions to draw up this indictment, the *Almighty* to be *judge,*] that very indictment *he would bind round his head;* and with that indictment as *his crown* of glory, he would, with the dignity of a *prince, advance* to his trial! Of this wonderful passage I add a version more just and more intelligible than the present:—

"Ver. 35. O that one would grant me a hearing!
Behold, my desire is that the Almighty would answer me;
And, as plaintiff against me, draw up the indictment.
With what earnestness would I take it on my shoulders!
I would bind it upon me as a diadem.
The number of my steps would I set forth unto Him;
Even as a prince would I approach before Him!"

I have already shown that *Eliphaz* and his *companions,* not GOD, are the *adversary* or *plaintiff* of whom Job speaks. This view makes the whole clear and consistent, and saves Job from the charge of presumptuous rashness. See also Kennicott's Remarks, p. 163.

It would not be right to say that no other interpretation has been given of the first clause of verse 10 than that given above. The manner in which Coverdale has translated the 9th and 10th verses is the way in which they are generally understood: 𝔜𝔣 𝔪𝔶 𝔥𝔢𝔯𝔱 𝔥𝔞𝔱𝔥 𝔩𝔲𝔰𝔱𝔢𝔡 𝔞𝔣𝔱𝔢𝔯 𝔪𝔶 𝔫𝔢𝔤𝔥𝔟𝔬𝔲𝔯'𝔰 𝔴𝔦𝔣𝔢, 𝔬𝔯 𝔶𝔣 𝔍 𝔥𝔞𝔲𝔢 𝔩𝔞𝔶𝔢𝔡 𝔴𝔞𝔶𝔱𝔢 𝔞𝔱 𝔥𝔦𝔰 𝔡𝔬𝔯𝔢; 𝔒 𝔱𝔥𝔢𝔫 𝔩𝔢𝔱 𝔪𝔶 𝔴𝔦𝔣𝔢 𝔟𝔢 𝔞𝔫𝔬𝔱𝔥𝔢𝔯 𝔪𝔞𝔫'𝔰 𝔥𝔞𝔯𝔩𝔬𝔱, 𝔞𝔫𝔡 𝔩𝔢𝔱 𝔬𝔱𝔥𝔢𝔯 𝔩𝔶𝔢 𝔴𝔦𝔱𝔥 𝔥𝔢𝔯.

In this sense the word *grind* is not unfrequently used by the ancients. *Horace* represents the *divine Cato* commending the young men whom he saw frequenting the stews, because they left other men's wives undefiled!

Virtute esto, inquit sententia *dia Catonis,*
Nam simul ac venas inflavit tetra libido,
Huc juvenes *æquum est* descendere, non alienas
Permolere uxores.   SAT. lib. i., s. 2., ver. 32.

"When awful Cato saw a noted spark
From a night cellar stealing in the dark:
'Well done, my friend, if lust thy heart inflame,
Indulge it *here,* and spare the married dame.' "
                                        FRANCIS.

Such were the *morals* of the *holiest state* of heathen Rome; and even of *Cato,* the purest and severest *censor* of the public manners! O tempora! O mores!

I may add from a scholiast:—*Molere* vetus verbum est pro *adulterare, subagitare,* quo verbo in deponenti significatione utitur alibi *Ausonius,* inquiens, Epigr. vii., ver. 6, de crispa impudica et detestabili:—

Deglubit, fellat, *molitur,* per utramque cavernam.

Qui enim coit, quasi *molere* et terere videtur.

Hinc etiam *molitores* dicti sunt, *subactores,* ut apud eundem, Epigr. xc., ver. 3.

Cum dabit uxori *molitor* tuus, et tibi *adulter.*

Thus the *rabbins* understand what is spoken of *Samson grinding* in the prison-house: quod ad ipsum Palæstini certatim suas uxores adduxerunt, suscipiendæ ex eo prolis causa, ob ipsius robur.

In this sense St. *Jerome* understands *Lam.* v. 13: *They took the young men to* GRIND. *Adolescentibus ad impudicitiam sunt abusi,* ad concubitum scilicet nefandum. Concerning *grinding of corn,* by portable *millstones,* or *querns,* and that this was the work of *females* alone, and they the *meanest slaves;* see the note on Exod. xi. 5, and on Judg. xvi. 21.

The *Greeks* use μυλλας to signify a *harlot;* and μυλλω, to *grind,* and also *coeo, ineo,* in the same sense in which *Horace,* as quoted above, *alienas* PERMOLERE *uxores.*

So *Theocritus,* Idyll. iv., ver. 58.

Ειπ' αγε μοι Κορυδων, το γεροντιον η ρ' ετι μυλλει
Τηναν ταν κυανοφρυν ερωτιδα, τας ποτ' εκνισθη·

Dic age mihi, Corydon, senecio ille num adhuc *molit,*
Illud nigro supercilio *scortillum,* quod olim deperibat?

Hence the Greek *paronomasia,* μυλλαδα μυλλειν, *scortam molere.* I need make no apology for leaving the principal part of this note in a foreign tongue. To those for whom it is designed it will be sufficiently plain. If the above were Job's meaning, how dreadful is the wish or imprecation in verse the *tenth!*

CHAPTER XXXII

Elihu comes forward, and expresses his disapprobation both of Job and his three friends—with the one for justifying himself; and with the others for taking up the subject in a wrong point of view, and not answering satisfactorily—and makes a becoming apology for himself, 1-22.

A. M. cir. 2484
B. C. cir. 1520
Ante I. Olymp.
cir. 744
Ante U. C. cir.
767

SO these three men ceased [a]to answer Job, because he *was* [b]righteous in his own eyes.

2 Then was kindled the wrath of Elihu the son of Barachel [c]the Buzite, of the kindred of Ram: against Job was his wrath kindled because he justified [d]himself rather than God.

3 Also against his three friends was his wrath kindled, because they had found no answer, and *yet* had condemned Job.

4 Now Elihu had [e]waited till Job had spoken, because they *were* [f]elder than he.

5 When Elihu saw that *there was* no answer in the mouth of *these* three men, then his wrath was kindled.

A. M. cir. 2484
B. C. cir. 1520
Ante I. Olymp.
cir. 744
Ante U. C. cir.
767

6 And Elihu the son of Barachel the Buzite answered and said, I *am* [g]young, [h]and ye *are* very old; wherefore I was afraid, and [i]durst not show you mine opinion.

7 I said, Days should speak, and multitude of years should teach wisdom.

8 But *there is* a spirit in man; and [k]the inspiration of the Almighty giveth them understanding.

---

[a]Hebrew, *from answering*——[b]Chapter xxxiii. 9 [c]Genesis xxii. 21——[d]Hebrew, *his soul*——[e]Hebrew, *expected Job in words*——[f]Hebrew, *elder for days* [g]Hebrew, *few of days*

[h]Chapter xv. 10——[i]Hebrew, *feared*——[k]1 Kings iii. 12; iv. 29; chapter xxxv. 11; xxxviii. 36; Proverbs ii. 6; Ecclesiastes ii. 26; Daniel i. 17; ii. 21; Matthew xii. 25; James i. 5

NOTES ON CHAP. XXXII

Verse 1. *These three men ceased to answer Job*] They supposed that it was of no use to attempt to reason any longer with a man who justified himself before God. The truth is, they failed to convince Job of any point, because they argued from false principles; and, as we have seen, Job had the continual advantage of them. There were points on which he might have been successfully assailed; but they did not know them. Elihu, better acquainted both with human nature and the nature of the Divine law, and of God's moral government of the world, steps in, and makes the proper discriminations; acquits Job on the ground of their accusations, but condemns him for his too great self-confidence, and his trusting too much in his external righteousness; and, without duly considering his frailty and imperfections, his incautiously arraigning the providence of God of unkindness in its dealings with him. This was the point on which Job was particularly vulnerable, and which Elihu very properly clears up.

Because he was righteous in his own eyes.] The *Septuagint, Syriac, Arabic,* and *Chaldee,* all read, "Because he was righteous in THEIR eyes;" intimating, that they were now convinced that he was a holy man, and that they had charged him foolishly. The reading of these ancient versions is supported by a MS. of the *thirteenth* century, in Dr. *Kennicott's* collections; which, instead of בעיני *beeinaiv,* in HIS *eyes,* has בעיניהם *beeineyhem,* in THEIR *eyes.* This is a reading of considerable importance, but it is not noticed by *De Rossi. Symmachus* translates nearly in the same way: Δια τον αυτον δικαιον φαινεσθαι επ᾽ αυτων; *Because he appeared more righteous than themselves.*

Verse 2. *Then was kindled the wrath*] This means no more than that Elihu was *greatly excited,* and felt a *strong* and *zealous* desire to vindicate the justice and providence of God, against the aspersions of Job and his friends.

Elihu the son of Barachel the Buzite] Buz was the second son of Nahor, the brother of Abram, Gen. xxii. 21.

Of the kindred of Ram] Kemuel was the third son of Nahor; and is called in Genesis (see above) *the father of Aram,* which is the same as *Ram.* A city of the name of *Buz* is found in Jer. xxv. 23, which probably had its name from this family; and, as it is mentioned with Dedan and Tema, we know it must have been a city in *Idumea,* as the others were in that district. Instead of the *kindred of Ram,* the Chaldee has *of the kindred of Abraham.* But still the question has been asked, *Who was Elihu?* I answer, He was "the son of Barachel the Buzite, of the kindred of Ram:" this is all we know of him. But this Scriptural answer will not satisfy those who are determined to find out mysteries where there are none. Some make him a descendant of Judah; St. Jerome, Bede, Lyranus, and some of the rabbins, make him Balaam the son of Beor, the magician; Bishop Warburton makes him Ezra the scribe; and Dr. Hodges makes him the second person in the glorious Trinity, the Lord Jesus Christ, and supposes that the chief scope of this part of the book was to convict Job of self-righteousness, and to show the necessity of the doctrine of justification by faith! When these points are *proved,* they should be *credited.*

Because he justified himself rather than God.] Literally, *he justified his soul,* נפשׁו *naphhso, before God.* He defended, not only the *whole of his conduct,* but also his *motives, thoughts,* &c.

Verse 3. *They had found no answer*] They had condemned Job; and yet could not answer his arguments on the general subject, and in vindication of himself.

Verse 6. *I am young*] How *young* he was, or how *old* they were, we cannot tell; but there was no doubt a great disparity in their ages; and among the Asiatics the *youth* never spoke in the presence of the *elders,* especially on any subject of controversy.

Verse 7. *Days should speak*] That is, men are to be reputed wise and experienced in proportion to the time they have lived. The Easterns were remarkable for treasuring up wise sayings: indeed, the principal part of their boasted wisdom consisted in *proverbs* and *maxims* on different subjects.

Verse 8. *But there is a spirit in man*] Mr. *Good* translates:—

A. M. cir. 2484
B. C. cir. 1520
Ante I. Olymp.
cir. 744
Ante U. C. cir.
767

9 [1]Great men are not *always* wise; neither do the aged understand judgment.

10 Therefore I said, Hearken to me; I also will show mine opinion.

11 Behold, I waited for your words; I gave ear to your [m]reasons, whilst ye searched out [n]what to say.

12 Yea, I attended unto you, and, behold,

there was none of you that convinced Job, *or* that answered his words:

A. M. cir. 2484
B. C. cir. 1520
Ante I. Olymp.
cir. 744
Ante U. C. cir.
767

13 [o]Lest ye should say, We have found out wisdom: God thrusteth him down, not man.

14 Now he hath not [p]directed *his* words against me: neither will I answer him with your speeches.

---

[1]1 Cor. i. 26——[m]Heb. *understandings*——[n]Heb. *words*

[o]Jer. ix. 23; 1 Cor. i. 29——[p]Or, *ordered his words*

"But surely there is an afflation in mankind,
And the inspiration of the Almighty actuateth them."

Coverdale, thus—

𝕰𝖛𝖊𝖗𝖕 man (no doute) hath a mynde; but it is the inspyracion of the Allmightie that gebeth understondinge.

I will now offer my own opinion, but first give the original text: רוח היא באנוש ונשמת שדי תבינם *ruach hi beenosh venishmath shaddai tebinem.* "The spirit itself is in miserable man, and the breath of the Almighty causeth them to understand." How true is it that *in God we live, move, and have our being!* The *spirit itself* is in man as the spring or fountain of his animal existence; and by the afflatus of this spirit he becomes capable of understanding and reason, and consequently of discerning Divine truth. The animal and intellectual lives are here stated to be *from God;* and this appears to be an allusion to man's creation, Gen. ii. 7: "And God breathed into man's nostrils the breath of lives," נשמת חיים *nishmath chaiyim,* i. e., animal and intellectual, and thus he became *a living soul,* נפש חיה *nephesh chaiyah,* a *rational animal.*

When man fell from God, the Spirit of God was grieved, and departed from him; but was restored, as the enlightener and corrector, in virtue of the *purposed* incarnation and atonement of our Lord Jesus; hence, he is "the true Light that lighteth every man that cometh into the world," John i. 9. That afflatus is therefore still continued to אנש *enosh,* man, in his *wretched, fallen state;* and it is by *that Spirit,* the רוח אלהים *Ruach Elohim,* "the Spirit of the merciful or covenant God," that we have any conscience, knowledge of good and evil, judgment in Divine things, and, in a word, *capability of being saved.* And when, through the light of that Spirit, convincing of sin, righteousness, and judgment, the sinner turns to God through Christ, and finds redemption in his blood, the remission of sins; then it is the office of *that same Spirit* to give him *understanding* of the great work that has been done *in* and *for* him; "for *the Spirit itself* (αυτο το Πνευμα, Rom. viii. 16, the same words in *Greek* as the *Hebrew* רוח היא *ruach hi* of Elihu) beareth witness with his spirit that he is a child of God." It is the *same Spirit* which *sanctifies,* the *same Spirit* that *seals,* and the *same Spirit* that *lives* and *works* in the believer, *guiding* him by his *counsel* till it leads

him *into glory.* In this one saying, independently of the above paraphrase, Elihu spoke more sense and sound doctrine than all Job's friends did in the whole of the controversy.

Verse 9. *Great men are not* always *wise*] This is a true saying, which the experience of every age and every country increasingly verifies. And it is most certain that, in the case before us, the aged did not understand judgment; they had a great many wise and good sayings, which they had collected, but showed neither wisdom nor discretion in applying them.

Verse 11. *I waited for your words; I gave ear to your reasons*] Instead of תבונותיכם *tebunotheychem,* your *reasons,* תבונותיכם *techunotheychem,* your *arguments,* is the reading of nine of *Kennicott's* and *De Rossi's* MSS. The sense, however, is nearly the same.

Whilst ye searched out what to say.] עד תחקרון מלין *ad tachkerun millin;* "Whilst ye were searching up and down for words." A fine irony, which they must have felt.

Verse 12. *Yea, I attended unto you*] Instead of עדיכם *veadeychem,* and *unto you,* one MS. reads the above letters with *points* that cause it to signify *and your testimonies;* which is the reading of the *Syriac, Arabic,* and *Septuagint.*

Behold, there was *none of you that convinced Job*] Confuted Job. They spoke multitudes of *words,* but were unable to overthrow his *arguments.*

Verse 13. *We have found out wisdom*] We, by dint of our own wisdom and understanding, have found out the *true system of God's providence;* and have been able to account for all the sufferings and tribulations of Job. Had they been able to *confute* Job, they would have *triumphed* over him in their own self-sufficiency.

God thrusteth him down, not man.] This is no *accidental* thing that has happened to him: he is suffering under the just judgments of God, and therefore he must be the wicked man which we supposed him to be.

Verse 14. *He hath not directed*] I am no *party* in this controversy; I have no party feeling in it: he has not spoken a word against me, therefore I have no cause of irritation. I shall speak for *truth;* not for *conquest* or *revenge. Neither will I answer him with your speeches;* your passions have been inflamed by contradiction, and you have spoken foolishly with your lips.

A. M. cir. 2484
B. C. cir. 1520
Ante I. Olymp.
cir. 744
Ante U. C. cir.
767

15 They were amazed, they answered no more: qthey left off speaking.

16 When I had waited, (for they spake not, but stood still, *and* answered no more;)

17 *I said,* I will answer also my part, I also will show mine opinion.

18 For I am full of rmatter, sthe spirit within me constraineth me.

19 Behold, my belly *is* as wine which thath no vent; it is ready to burst like new bottles.

A. M. cir. 2484
B. C. cir. 1520
Ante I. Olymp.
cir. 744
Ante U. C. cir.
767

20 I will speak, uthat I may be refreshed; I will open my lips, and answer.

21 Let me not, I pray you, vaccept any man's person, neither let me give flattering titles unto man.

22 For I know not to give flattering titles; *in so doing* my Maker would soon take me away.

---

qHebrew, *they removed speeches from themselves*
rHebrew, *words*——sHebrew, *the spirit of my belly*
tHebrew, *is not opened*——uHebrew, *that I may breathe*——vLeviticus xix. 15; Deuteronomy i. 17; xvi. 19; Proverbs xxiv. 23; Matthew xxii. 14; Mark xii. 14; Luke xx. 21

Verse 15. *They were amazed*] Mr. *Good* translates: "They (the *speeches*) are dissipated; they no longer produce effect; the words have flirted away from them." Your words, being without proper reference and point, are scattered into thin air: there is nothing but *sound* in them; they are quite destitute of *sense.* But I prefer the words as spoken of Job's *friends.* They took their several parts in the controversy as long as they could hope to maintain their ground: for a considerable time they had been able to bring nothing *new;* at last, weary of their own *repetitions,* they gave up the contest.

Verse 16. *When I had waited*] I waited to hear if they had any thing to reply to Job; and when I found them in effect speechless, then I ventured to come forward.

Verse 17. *I will answer also my part*] אענה

חלקי *aaneh chelki,* "I will recite my portion." We have already seen that the book of Job is a sort of *drama,* in which several persons have their different *parts* to *recite.* Probably the book was used in this way, in ancient times, for the sake of public instruction. Eliphaz, Zophar, and Bildad, had *recited* their *parts,* and Job had *responded* to each: nothing was brought to issue. Elihu, a bystander, perceiving this, comes forward and takes a *part,* when all the rest had expended their materials: yet Elihu, though he spoke well, was incapable of closing the controversy; and God himself appears, and decides the case.

Verse 18. *I am full of matter*] מלים *millim,* "I am full of WORDS," or *sayings;* i. e., wise sentences, and ancient opinions.

The spirit within me constraineth me.] How similar to the words of St. Paul! *The love of Christ constraineth us.* Elihu considered himself *under the influence of that Spirit of God* which gives understanding, and felt anxiously concerned for the welfare both of Job and his friends.

Verse 19. *My belly* is *as wine which hath no vent*] New wine in a state of effervescence.

Like new bottles.] *Bottles,* or rather *bags,* made of *goat-skins.* The head and shanks being cut off, the animal is *cased* out of the skin. The skin is then properly dressed; the *anus* and four shank holes properly tied up; and an aperture left at the neck or in some other place for the liquor to be poured in, and drawn out. One of these now lies before me, well tanned, and beautifully ornamented, and capable of holding many gallons. They are used, not only to carry wine and water, but for butter, and also for various *dry goods.* I have mentioned this in another place. When the wine is in a state of fermentation, and the skin has no vent, these bottles or *bags* are ready to *burst;* and if they be *old,* the *new wine* destroys them, breaks the old stitching, or rends the old skin. Our Lord makes use of the same figure, Matt. ix. 17; where see the note.

Verse 20. *I will open my lips and answer.*] In the preceding verse Elihu compares himself to a *skin-bottle,* in which the wine was in a state of *fermentation,* and the *bottle* ready to burst for want of *vent.* He carries on the metaphor in this verse: the bottle must be *opened* to save it from bursting; *I will* OPEN *my mouth.*

Verse 21. *Let me not—accept any man's person*] I will speak the truth without fear or favour.

Neither let me give flattering titles] I will not give epithets to any man that are not descriptive of his true state. I will not beguile him by telling him he *is* what he *is not.* אכנה *acanneh,* from כנה *canah,* is generally supposed to signify to *surname,* to put a name *to* or *upon* a name, as the French word *surnom* implies. It means to give proud titles to persons who are worthless. It is well known that the Arabs make court to their superiors by carefully avoiding to address them by their proper names, instead of which they salute them with some title or epithet expressive of respect.—Scott. See below. Titles expressive of *office, ecclesiastical, civil,* or *military,* are always proper, and never forbidden, because they serve for *distinction;* but the Asiatic titles are in general bombastically and sinfully complimentary. The reader will find several specimens at the end of this chapter.

Verse 22. *My Maker would soon take me away.*] Were I to copy this conduct while under the influence which I now feel, God might justly consume me as in a moment. He is my Maker; he made me to *know truth,* to *tell truth,* and to *live* according to *truth;* for he is the *God of truth:* I shall, therefore, through his help, speak *the* TRUTH, *the* WHOLE TRUTH, *and* NOTHING BUT THE TRUTH.

WE find from the above that *vain titles* of ceremony, expressive of the most eminent qualities, were given to *worthless men,* from time immemorial; and no wonder, for *hypocrisy* entered into *man* at the same time that *sin* entered into the *world.*

Of the flattering titles used in the East, I shall give a few specimens from the قواعد

السلطنت شاه جهان *Kooayid us Sultanet* Shah Jehan, or, "The Rules observed during the Reign of the Mogul Emperor Shah Jehan."

Speaking of the emperor, he is entitled, "The Sun which illuminates the firmament in the universe of royalty and dominion; the Moon, which irradiates the sky of monarchy and felicity; the King who in pomp resembles *Gem-sheed.* His hand is boundless as the ocean in bestowing bounties, being the key of the gates of kindness and liberality!" Again:—

"The Sun of the heaven of prosperity and empire, the Shadow of God, the Asylum of the Universe, the splendour of whose instructive front causes light and gladness to the world and to mankind."

"The just and vigilant Monarch; the Asylum of Truth, the Refuge of the World; the Diffuser of Light, the Solver of all human difficulties."

"The Lord of the Age, who is endowed with such perfect excellence, both in internal and external qualifications, that on all occasions he holds fast the thread of good counsel, prudence, and purity of morals."

"The faculty of apprehension is possessed by him in such a degree, that before the matter has scarcely obtained utterance he comprehends the purport, and gives answers with the tongue of inspiration."

Addresses to Persons of Distinction

"Let them convey to the presence of glorious empire, the Sultan, in pomp like Solomon, the centre of the universe, powerful as heaven!"

"Let them who kiss the carpet of the palace, in pomp like heaven, convey this letter to his majesty, whose sight is as creative as alchymy, king of kings, the asylum of the world!"

"To the exalted presence, which gratifies the desires of all people, the most beneficent of the age, the *vizier,* protector of the universe, may the Almighty perpetuate his fortune!"

"May this letter be dignified in the presence of *Naweeb Saheb,* diffuser of benefits, of exalted pomp, the respectable, the discriminator of ranks! May his power increase!"

"Let them convey this to the perusal of his excellency, conversant in realities and mysteries, the support of excellencies, the cream of his contemporaries, and the cherisher of the poor!"

These are a specimen of the *flattering titles* given in the East to persons in eminent stations. Their kings they clothe in all the attributes of the Deity, when both in their public and private character they are corrupt and unholy, rascals in grain, and the ruthless oppressors of suffering humanity.

CHAPTER XXXIII

Elihu offers himself in God's stead to reason with Job in meekness and sincerity, 1–7. Charges Job with irreverent expressions, 8–12. Vindicates the providence of God, and shows the various methods which he uses to bring sinners to himself:—By dreams and visions, 13–15; by secret inspirations, 16–18; by afflictions, 19–22; by messengers of righteousness, 23; and by the great atonement, 24. How and from what God redeems men, and the blessings which he communicates, 25–30. Job is exhorted to listen attentively to Elihu's teaching, 31–33.

A. M. cir. 2484
B. C. cir. 1520
Ante I. Olymp. cir. 744
Ante U. C. cir. 767

WHEREFORE, Job, I pray thee, hear my speeches, and hearken to all my words.

2 Behold, now I have opened my mouth, my tongue hath spoken in ªmy mouth.

3 My words *shall be of* the uprightness of my heart: and my lips shall utter knowledge clearly.

4 ᵇThe Spirit of God hath made me, and the breath of the Almighty hath given me life.

A. M. cir. 2484
B. C. cir. 1520
Ante I. Olymp. cir. 744
Ante U. C. cir. 767

5 If thou canst answer me, set *thy words* in order before me, stand up.

6 ᶜBehold, I *am* ᵈaccording to thy wish in God's stead: I also am ᵉformed out of the clay.

ªHeb. *in my palate*——ᵇGen. ii. 7——ᶜChap. ix. 34, 35; xiii. 20, 21; xxxi. 35

ᵈHeb. *according to thy mouth*——ᵉHeb. *cut out of the clay*

NOTES ON CHAP. XXXIII

Verse 3. *My words shall be of the uprightness*] As God has given me his Spirit, from that Spirit alone will I speak; therefore all my words shall be of uprightness, knowledge, and truth.

Knowledge clearly.] דעת ברור *daath barur,* pure science. I shall lay down no *false positions,* and I shall have no false consequences.

Verse 4. *The Spirit of God hath made me*] Another plain allusion to the account of the *creation of man,* Gen. ii. 7, as the words נשמת *nishmath, the breath* or *breathing* of God, and תחיני *techaiyeni, hath given me life,* prove: "He *breathed* into his nostrils the *breath* of lives, and he became a *living soul.*"

Verse 6. *I am according to thy wish in God's stead: I also am formed out of the clay.*] Mr. *Good,* and before him none other that I have seen, has most probably hit the true meaning:—

"Behold, I am thy fellow.
    I too was formed by God out of the clay."

The word כפיך *kephicha,* which we translate *according to thy wish,* and which, if *Hebrew,* would mean *like to thy mouth;* he considers as pure Arabic, with a Hebrew postfix, كفو *kefoo,* signifying *fellow, equal, like.* Taken in this way, the passage is very plain, only לאל *lael, by* or *through God,* must be added to the *last* clause of the verse instead of the *first,* as Mr. *Good* has properly done.

A. M. cir. 2484
B. C. cir. 1520
Ante I. Olymp. cir. 744
Ante U. C. cir. 767

7 ᶠBehold, my terror shall not make thee afraid, neither shall my hand be heavy upon thee.

8 Surely thou hast spoken ᵍin mine hearing, and I have heard the voice of *thy* words, *saying,*

9 ʰI am clean without transgression, I *am* innocent; neither *is there* iniquity in me.

10 Behold, he findeth occasions against me, ⁱhe counteth me for his enemy.

11 ᵏHe putteth my feet in the stocks, he marketh all my paths.

A. M. cir. 2484
B. C. cir. 1520
Ante I. Olymp. cir. 744
Ante U. C. cir. 767

12 Behold, *in* this thou art not just: I will answer thee, that God is greater than man.

13 Why dost thou ˡstrive against him? for ᵐhe giveth not account of any of his matters.

14 ⁿFor God speaketh once, yea twice, *yet man* perceiveth it not.

15 ᵒIn a dream, in a vision of the night, when deep sleep falleth upon men, in slumberings upon the bed;

16 ᵖThen ᑫhe openeth the ears of men, and sealeth their instruction,

---

ᶠChap. ix. 34; xiii. 21——ᵍHeb. *in mine ears*——ʰCh. ix. 17; x. 7; xi. 4; xvi. 17; xxiii. 10, 11; xxvii. 5; xxix. 14; xxxi. 1——ⁱChap. xiii. 24; xvi. 9; xix. 11——ᵏChap. xiii. 27; xiv. 16; xxxi. 4

ˡIsa. xlv. 9——ᵐHeb. *he answereth not*——ⁿChap. xl. 5; Psalm. lxii. 11——ᵒNumbers xii. 6; chapter iv. 13——ᵖChapter xxxvi. 10, 15——ᑫHebrew, *he revealeth* or *uncovereth*

Verse 7. *My terror shall not make thee afraid*] This is an allusion to what Job had said, chap. ix. 34: "Let him take his rod away from me, and let not his fear terrify me." Being *equal*, no fear can impose upon thee so far as to overawe thee; so that thou shouldst not be able to conduct thy own defence. We are on *equal terms;* now prepare to defend thyself.

Verse 8. *Surely thou hast spoken*] What Elihu speaks here, and in the three following verses, contains, in general, simple quotations from Job's own words, or the obvious sense of them, as the reader may see by referring to the *margin*, and also to the notes on those passages.

Verse 11. *He putteth my feet in the stocks*] See the note on chap. xiii. 27.

Verse 12. *In this thou art not just*] Thou hast laid charges against God's dealings, but thou hast not been able to *justify* those charges; and were there nothing else against thee, these irreverent speeches are so many proofs that thou art not *clear* in the sight of God.

Verse 13. *Why dost thou strive against him?*] Is it not useless to contend with God? Can he do any thing that is *not right?* As to his giving thee *any account* of the *reasons why* he deals *thus and thus* with thee, or any one else, thou needest not expect it; he is sovereign, and is not to be called to the bar of his creatures. It is sufficient for thee to know that "he is too wise to err, and too good to be unkind."

Verse 14. *For God speaketh once*] Though he will not be summoned to the bar of his creatures, nor condescend to detail the reasons of his conduct, which they could not comprehend, yet he so acts, in the main, that the *operation* of his *hand* and the *designs* of his *counsel* may sufficiently appear, provided men had their *eyes* open upon his *ways*, and their *hearts* open to receive his *influence.*

Elihu, having made the general statement that God would not come to the bar of his creatures to give account of his conduct, shows the *general means* which he uses to bring men to an acquaintance with themselves and with him: he states these in the six following *particulars*, which may be collected from ver. 15-24.

Verse 15. I. *In a* DREAM—*when deep sleep falleth upon men*] Many, by such means, have had the most salutary warnings; and to decry *all* such, because there are many *vain dreams*, would be nearly as much wisdom as to deny the Bible, because there are many foolish books, the authors of which supposed they were under a Divine influence while composing them.

II. *In a* VISION *of the night—in slumberings upon the bed*] *Visions* or *images* presented in the *imagination* during slumber, when men are betwixt sleeping and waking, or when, *awake* and in bed, they are wrapt up in deep contemplation, the darkness of the night having shut out all objects from their sight, so that the mind is not diverted by images of earthly things impressed on the senses. Many warnings in this way have come from God; and the impression they made, and the good effect they produced, were the proofs of their Divine origin. To deny this would be to call into doubt the testimony of the best, wisest, and holiest men in all ages of the Church. Of one of these visions we have a remarkable account in chap. iv. of this book, ver. 12-21. And this vision seems to have taken place in the night season, when *Eliphaz* awoke *from a deep sleep.* There is this difference between the accidents of the *dream* and the *vision*: the *former* takes place *when deep sleep falleth upon men;* the *latter*, in the *night*, *in* or *after* slumberings upon the bed.

Verse 16. *Then he openeth the ears of men, and sealeth, &c.*] III. By *secret* INSPIRATIONS. A dream or a vision simply considered is likely to do no good; it is the *opening of the understanding*, and the *pouring in of the light*, that make men wise to salvation. Serious alarms, holy purposes, penitential pangs for past sins, apprehension of death and judgment, discoveries of God's justice, of Christ's love, of the world's vanity, of heaven's excellence, &c., &c., &c., are often used by the Divine Spirit *to withdraw men from their evil purpose, and to hide pride from man*, ver. 17; and of all these openings of the ear of the heart, and sealing instructions upon the conscience, we have numerous examples in the history of the Church, in the experience of good men, and even in the civil and providential history of all nations.

A. M. cir. 2484
B. C. cir. 1520
Ante I. Olymp.
cir. 744
Ante U. C. cir.
767

17 That he may withdraw man *from his* ʳpurpose, and hide pride from man.

18 He keepeth back his soul from the pit, and his life ˢfrom perishing by the sword.

19 He is chastened also with pain upon his bed, and the multitude of his bones with strong *pain:*

20 ᵗSo that his life abhorreth bread, and his soul ᵘdainty meat.

21 His flesh is consumed away, that it cannot be seen; and his bones *that* were not seen stick out.

A. M. cir. 2484
B. C. cir. 1520
Ante I. Olymp.
cir. 744
Ante U. C. cir.
767

22 Yea, his soul draweth near unto the grave, and his life to the destroyer.

23 If there be a messenger with him, an interpreter, one among a thousand, to show unto man his uprightness:

24 Then he is gracious unto him, and saith, Deliver him from going down to the pit: I have found ᵛa ransom.

ʳHebrew, *work*——ˢHebrew, *from passing by the sword*

ᵗPsa. cvii. 18——ᵘHeb. *meat of desire*——ᵛOr, *an atonement*

Verse 18. *He keepeth back his soul from the pit*] By the above means, how many have been snatched from an untimely death! By taking the warning thus given, some have been prevented from perishing by the *pit*—some *sudden accident;* and others from the *sword* of the *assassin* or *nocturnal murderer.* It would be easy to give examples, in all these kinds; but the knowledge of the reader may save this trouble to the commentator.

Verse 19. *He is chastened also with pain upon his bed, &c.*] IV.—AFFLICTIONS are a *fourth* means which God makes use of to awaken and convert sinners. In the hand of God these were the cause of the salvation of *David,* as himself testifies: *Before I was afflicted, I went astray,* Psa. cxix. 67, 71, 75.

The multitude of his bones] By such diseases, especially those of a *rheumatic* kind, when to the patient's apprehension *every bone* is *diseased,* broken, or out of joint.

Some render the passage, *When the multitude of his bones is yet strong;* meaning those sudden afflictions which fall upon men when in a state of great firmness and vigour. The original, ורוב עצמיו אתן *verob atsamaiv ethan,* may be translated, *And the strong multitude of his bones.* Even the strong multitude of his bones is chastened with pain upon his bed; the place of rest and ease affording him no peace, quiet, or comfort.

The *bones* may be well termed *multitudinous,* as there are no less than 10 in the *cranium,* or *skull; upper jaw,* 13; *lower jaw,* 1; *teeth,* 32; *tongue,* 1; *vertebræ,* or *back-bone,* 24; *ribs,* 24; *sternum,* or *breast-bone,* 3; *os innominatum,* 1; *scapula,* or *shoulder-blades,* 2; *arms,* 6; *hands,* 54; *thigh-bones,* 2; *knee-bones,* 2; *legs,* 4; *feet,* 54: in all, not less than 233 bones, without reckoning the *ossa sethamoides;* because, though often numerous, they are found only in hard labourers, or elderly persons.

Verse 20. *His life abhorreth bread*] These expressions strongly and naturally point out that general *nausea,* or *loathing* which sick persons feel in almost every species of disorder.

Verse 21. *His flesh is consumed away*] As in atrophy, marasmus, and consumptive complaints in general.

Verse 22. *His soul draweth near unto the grave*] נפש *nephesh, soul,* is here taken for the *immortal spirit,* as it is distinguished from חיה *chaiyah,* the *animal life.* The former draws near to the pit, שחת *shachath,* corrup-

tion; perhaps he meant dissipation, considering it merely as the *breath.* The latter draws near לממתים *lamemithim,* to the *dead;* i. e., to those who are *already buried.* Mr. *Good* translates it *the Destinies;* and supposes the same is meant among the HEBREWS by the *Memithim,* as among the GREEKS by their Μοιραι; the LATINS, by their *Parcæ;* the GOTHS, by their *Fatal Sisters;* the SCANDINAVIANS, by their goddess *Hela;* and the ARABIANS, by *Azrael,* or the *angel of death.* I think, however, the signification given above is more natural.

Verse 23. *If there be a messenger with him, an interpreter, &c.*] V.—The MESSENGERS of righteousness; this is a FIFTH *method,* אם יש עליו מלאך מליץ *im yesh alaiv malach melits,* "If there be over him an interpreting or mediatorial angel or messenger." *One among a thousand,* אחד מני אלף *echad minni aleph.* "One from the CHIEF, HEAD, or TEACHER."

To show unto man his uprightness] להגיד לאדם ישרו *lehaggid leadam yoshro,* "to manifest or cause to be declared to man his righteousness:" to show unto *Adam—men in general,* the descendants of the first man—his purity and holiness; to convince him of sin, righteousness, and judgment, that he may be prepared for the discovery of what is next to be exhibited.

Verse 24. *Then he is gracious unto him*] He exercises mercy towards fallen man, and gives command for his respite and pardon.

Deliver him from going down to the pit] Let him who is thus instructed, penitent, and afflicted, and comes to me, find a *pardon;* for—

VI. *I have found a ransom.*] כפר *copher, an* atonement. *Pay a ransom for him,* פדעהו *pedaehu,* that he may not go down *to the pit*—to corruption or destruction, for *I have found out an atonement.* It is this that gives efficacy to all the preceding means; without which they would be useless, and the salvation of man impossible. I must think that the *redemption of a lost world,* by *Jesus Christ,* is not obscurely signified in ver. 23, 24.

While the whole world lay in the wicked one, and were all hastening to the *bottomless pit,* God so loved the world that he gave his only-begotten Son, that whosoever believeth on him might not perish, but have everlasting life. Jesus Christ, the great sacrifice, and *head* of the Church, commissions his *messengers*—apostles and their *successors*—to show men the *righteousness of God,* and his displeasure at

A. M. cir. 2484
B. C. cir. 1520
Ante I. Olymp.
cir. 744
Ante U. C. cir.
767

25 His flesh shall be fresher ʷthan a child's: he shall return to the days of his youth:

26 He shall pray unto God, and he will be favourable unto him: and he shall see his face with joy: for he will render unto man his righteousness.

27 ˣHe looketh upon men, and *if any* ʸsay, I have sinned, and perverted *that which was* right, and it ᶻprofited me not:

28 ᵃHe will ᵇdeliver his soul from going into the pit, and his life shall see the light.

29 Lo, all these *things* worketh God ᶜoftentimes with man,

A. M. cir. 2484
B. C. cir. 1520
Ante I. Olymp.
cir. 744
Ante U. C. cir.
767

30 ᵈTo bring back his soul from the pit, to be enlightened with the light of the living.

31 Mark well, O Job, hearken unto me: hold thy peace, and I will speak.

32 If thou hast any thing to say, answer me: speak, for I desire to justify thee.

33 If not, ᵉhearken unto me: hold thy peace, and I shall teach thee wisdom.

ʷHeb. *than childhood*——ˣOr, *He shall look upon men, and say, I have sinned,* &c.——ʸ2 Sam. xii. 13; Prov. xxviii. 13; Luke xv. 21; 1 John i. 9

ᶻRom. vi. 21——ᵃOr, *He hath delivered my soul,* &c.; *and my life*——ᵇIsa. xxxviii. 17——ᶜHeb. *twice* and *thrice*——ᵈVer. 28; Psa. lvi. 13——ᵉPsa. xxxiv. 11

---

sin; and at the same time his infinite love, which commands them to proclaim *deliverance* to the captives, and that they who believe on him shall not perish, shall not *go down to the pit* of destruction, for *he has found out an atonement;* and that whoever comes to him, through Christ, shall have everlasting life, in virtue of that atonement or ransom price.

Should it be objected against my interpretation of אלף *aleph,* that it cannot be translated *chief* or *head,* because it is without the *vau shurek,* אלוף *alluph,* which gives it this signification; I would answer, that this form of the word is not *essential* to the signification given above, as it occurs in several places without the *vau shurek,* where it most certainly signifies a *chief,* a *leader, captain,* &c. e. g., Zech. ix. 7; Jer. xiii. 21, and Gen. xxxvi. 30; in the first of which we translate it *governor;* in the second, *captain;* and in the third, *duke.* And although we translate אלוף *alluph* an *ox* or *beeve,* (and it most certainly has this meaning in several places,) yet in this signification it is written without the *vau shurek* in Prov. xiv. 4; Psa. viii. 7; Isa. xxx. 24; and in Deut. vii. 13; xxviii. 4, 18, 51; which all show that this letter is not absolutely necessary to the above signification.

Verse 25. *His flesh shall be fresher than a child's*] He shall be born a *new creature.*

He shall return to the days of his youth] He shall be *born again,* and become a *child of God,* through faith in Christ Jesus.

Verse 26. *He shall pray unto God*] Being now adopted into the heavenly family, and become a *new creature,* he shall have the *spirit of prayer,* which is indeed the very *breath* and *language* of the *new* or *spiritual life.*

He will be favourable unto him] He shall manifest his good will to him; he shall live under the influences of Divine grace.

He shall see his face with joy] He shall know that God is reconciled to him; and this shall fill him with joy, בתרועה *bithruah, with exultation:* for, "being justified by faith, he has peace with God, through our Lord Jesus Christ, by whom he has received the atonement; and REJOICES in the hope of the glory of God."

He will render unto man his righteousness.] So good and gracious is the Lord, that by his grace he will enable this convert to live to his glory, to bring forth all the fruits of the Spirit,

and then *reward* him for the work, as if it were done by his own might.

Verse 27. *He looketh upon men*] אנשים *anashim,* wretched, fallen men. He *shines into them,* to convince them of sin; and if any, under this convincing light of God, *say, I have sinned* against *heaven* and before thee, *and perverted the right*—abused the powers, faculties, mercies, and advantages, which thou didst give me, by seeking rest and happiness in the creature, *and it profited me not*—it was all *vanity* and *vexation* of spirit; ולא שוה לי *velo shavah li,* "and it was not equal to me," did not *come up* to my expectation, nor supply my wants:—

Verse 28. *He will deliver his soul*] He will do that to every *individual penitent sinner* which he has promised in his word to do for a lost world—he will deliver his soul from going down to the pit of hell.

And his life shall see the light.] He shall walk in the light, as Christ is in the light; always enjoying a clear sense of his acceptance through the blood of the Lamb. See another mode of paraphrasing these verses at the end of the chapter.

Verse 29. *Lo, all these* things *worketh God*] God frequently uses one, or another, or all of these means, to bring *men,* נבר *gaber,* stout-hearted men, who are far from righteousness, to holiness and heaven.

Oftentimes] פעמים שלש *paamayim shalosh,* "three times over;" or as פעמים *paamayim* is by the *points* in the *dual* number, then it signifies *twice three times,* that is, *again* and *again; very frequently.* Blessed be God!

Verse 30. *To bring back his soul from the pit*] Nearly a repetition of the promise in ver. 28.

To be enlightened with the light of the living.] An echo of Psa. lvi. 13: "Thou hast delivered my soul from death, that I may walk before God in the light of the living;" and probably quoted from it.

Verse 31. *Mark well, O Job*] Pay the deepest attention to what I have said, and to what I shall say.

Verse 32. *If thou hast any thing to say*] If thou hast any objection to make against what I have already stated, now answer, now speak freely; for it is my desire that thou shouldst stand clear of all charges.

Verse 33. *If not*] Then I will proceed:

listen carefully, *keep silence*, and *I will teach thee* what true *wisdom* is.

Job was silent; none of his friends chose to intermeddle farther; and in the next chapter Elihu addresses both Job and them.

THERE are some *various readings* in the MSS. and *versions* on certain words in the concluding verses of this chapter, which it will be necessary to mention, as they, if adopted, will lead to a somewhat different paraphrase to that given, especially of verses 26, 27, and 28.

Verse 26. For צדקתו *tsidkatho*, HIS *righteousness*, one MS. and the *Chaldee* have כצדקתו *ketsidkatho*, ACCORDING *to his righteousness*.

Verse 28. For נפשׁו *naphsho*, HIS *soul*, which is the *keri* reading, and that which our translation has followed, נפשׁי MY *soul* is the reading of many MSS., early *editions*, the *Complutensian, Antwerp*, and *London Polyglots*, the *Jerusalem Targum*, the *Chaldee*, the *Vulgate*, and *Coverdale*.

For חיתו *chaiyatho*, HIS *life*, many MSS., early *editions*, the *Complutensian, Antwerp*, and *London Polyglots*, the *Jerusalem Targum, Chaldee, Vulgate*, and *Coverdale*, read חיתי *chaiyathi*, MY *life*. Both of these are properly the *kethib* or *textual* readings in the best editions, but are directed by the *Masora* to be changed for the *keri* readings, or those inserted in the *margin*.

For באור תראה *baor tireh*, SHALL SEE *the light*, six of *Kennicott's* and *De Rossi's* MSS. have תהיה *tihyeh*, and *twenty-one* have כאור *caor*, thus כאור תהיה *caor tihyeh*, SHALL BE AS *the light*. The whole verse, by these various readings, will stand thus:—"He will deliver MY soul from going into the pit, and MY life SHALL BE AS the light." But if, with the *Septuagint, Syriac*, and *Arabic*, we read פדה *padah*, in the *imperative* mood, then the verse will read thus:—"DELIVER THOU MY SOUL from going

down to the pit, and MY life SHALL BE AS the light."

On the 26th, 27th, 28th, and 29th, verses, the following paraphrase has been recommended.

Verse 26. *He* (Jesus Christ, the *head* and *ransom price*) *shall pray unto God*, (shall make *intercession* for the transgressors, for he is the Mediator between God and man.) *And he* (God the Father) *will be favourable*, (ירצהו *yirtsehu*, will manifest his *good will* towards him.) *And he shall see his face* (פניו *panaiv*, his *faces*, God the Father, Son, and Spirit) *with joy*, (בתרעה *bithruah*, with *exultation* or *triumph*,) *for he will render unto man his righteousness*, (ישׁב לאנשׁ צדקתו *yasheb leenosh tsidkatho*, "He will restore to wretched man his righteousness;" i. e., he will create the soul anew, and restore to the fallen spirit that righteousness and true holiness which it has lost, and bring it again to its original state of perfection, through the grand atonement mentioned ver. 24.)

But *when* is it that wretched miserable man shall be brought to this state of salvation? This is answered in

Verse 27. *When God, looking upon men, seeth any of them saying, I have sinned and perverted that which is right, and it hath profited me nothing*—has afforded nothing *equal* to my wishes, and the tribulation which I sustained in seeking happiness in forbidden things. *Redeem my soul from going down to destruction, and my life shall see the light*, or *shall be as the light*. This is the prayer of the penitent, which God has promised to hear.

This is one of the best, the deepest, the most spiritual, and most important chapters which the reader has yet met with in the Book of Job. It is every way important, and full of useful information. It is a grand exhibition of the WAY of salvation as revealed to patriarchs and prophets.

CHAPTER XXXIV

Elihu begins with an exhortation to Job's friends, 1-4; charges Job with accusing God of acting unrighteously, which he shows is impossible, 5-12; points out the power and judgments of the Almighty, 13-30; shows how men should address God, and how irreverently Job has acted, 31-37.

A. M. cir. 2484
B. C. cir. 1520
Ante I. Olymp.
cir. 744
Ante U. C. cir.
767

FURTHERMORE Elihu answered and said,

2 Hear my words, O ye wise *men;* and give ear unto me, ye that have knowledge.

3 [a]For the ear trieth words, as the [b]mouth tasteth meat.

4 Let us choose to us judgment: let us know among ourselves what *is* good.

A. M. cir. 2484
B. C. cir. 1520
Ante I. Olymp.
cir. 744
Ante U. C. cir.
767

---

[a]Chap. vi. 30; xii. 11

[b]Heb. *palate*

NOTES ON CHAP. XXXIV

Verse 3. *The ear trieth words*] I do not think, with *Calmet*, that the *inward ear*, or *judgment*, is meant simply. The Asiatics valued themselves on the *nice and harmonious collection of words*, both in speaking and in writing; and perhaps it will be found here that Elihu labours as much for harmonious versification

as for pious and weighty sentiments. To connect *sense* with *sound* was an object of general pursuit among the *Hebrew, Arabic*, and *Persian* poets; and so fond are the latter of *euphony*, that they often sacrifice both *sense* and *sentiment* to it; and some of the *Greek* poets are not exempt from this fault.

Verse 4. *Let us choose to us judgment*] Let us not seek the applause of men, nor contend

A. M. cir. 2484
B. C. cir. 1520
Ante I. Olymp.
cir. 744
Ante U. C. cir.
767

5 For Job hath said, ᵉI am righteous; and ᵈGod hath taken away my judgment.

6 ᵉShould I lie against my right? ᶠmy wound *is* incurable without transgression.

7 What man *is* like Job, ᵍ*who* drinketh up scorning like water?

8 Which goeth in company with the workers of iniquity, and walketh with wicked men.

9 For ʰhe hath said, It profiteth a man

nothing that he should delight himself with God.

10 Therefore hearken unto me, ye ˡmen of understanding; ᵏfar be it from God, *that he should do* wickedness; and *from* the Almighty, *that he should commit* iniquity.

11 ˡFor the work of a man shall he render unto him, and cause every man to find according to *his* ways.

12 Yea, surely God will not do wickedly,

A. M. cir. 2484
B. C. cir. 1520
Ante I. Olymp.
cir. 744
Ante U. C. cir.
767

ᵉCh. xxxiii. 9——ᵈCh. xxvii. 2——ᵉCh. ix. 17
ᶠHeb. *mine arrow;* ch. vi. 4; xvi. 13——ᵍCh. xv. 16
ʰCh. ix. 22, 23, 30; xxxv. 3; Mal. iii. 14——ˡHeb. *men of heart*——ᵏGen. xviii. 25; Deut. xxxii. 4; 2 Chron. xix. 7;

chap. viii. 3; xxxvi. 23; Psa. xcii. 15; Rom. ix. 14
ˡPsa. lxii. 12; Prov. xxiv. 12; Jer. xxxii. 19; Ezek. xxxiii. 20; Matt. xvi. 27; Romans ii. 6; 2 Cor. v. 10; 1 Peter i. 17; Rev. xxii. 12

---

for victory. Let our aim be to obtain correct views and notions of all things; and let us labour to find out what is good.

Verse 5. *Job hath said, I am righteous*] Job had certainly said the words attributed to him by Elihu, particularly in chap. xxvii. 2, &c., but it was in vindication of his aspersed character that he had asserted his own righteousness, and in a different sense to that in which Elihu appears to take it up. He asserted that he was righteous *quoad* the charges his friends had brought against him. And he never intimated that he had at all times a pure heart, and had never transgressed the laws of his Maker. It is true also that he said, *God hath taken away my judgment;* but he most obviously does not mean to charge God with injustice, but to show that he had dealt with him in a way wholly mysterious, and not according to the ordinary dispensations of his providence; and that he did not interpose in his behalf, while his friends were overwhelming him with obloquy and reproach.

Verse 6. *Should I lie against my right?*] Should I acknowledge myself the sinner which they paint me, and thus lie against my right to assert and maintain my innocence?

My wound is incurable without transgression.] If this translation is correct, the meaning of the place is sufficiently evident. In the tribulation which I endure, I am treated as if I were the worst of culprits; and I labour under incurable maladies and privations, though without any *cause* on my part for such treatment. This was all most perfectly true; it is the testimony which God himself gives of Job, that "he was a perfect and upright man, fearing God and eschewing evil;" and that "Satan had moved the Lord against him, to destroy him, WITHOUT A CAUSE." See chap. i. 1, and ii. 3.

The *Chaldee* translates thus:—

"On account of my judgment, I will make the son of man a liar, who sends forth arrows without sin."

Mr. *Good* thus:—

"Concerning my cause I am slandered;
He hath reversed my lot without a trespass."

The latter clause is the most deficient, אנוש חצי בלי פשע; Miss Smith's translation of which

VOL. III

is the best I have met with: "A man cut off, without transgression." The word חצי *chitstsi,* which we translate *my wound,* signifies more literally,*my arrow;* and if we take it as a contracted noun, חצי *chitstsey* for חצים *chitstsim,* it means *calamities.* אנוש *anush,* which we translate *incurable,* may be the noun *enosh,* wicked, miserable man; and then the whole may be read thus: "A man of calamities without transgression." I suffer the punishment of an enemy to God, while free from transgression of this kind.

Verse 7. *Drinketh up scorning like water?*] This is a repetition of the charge made against Job by *Eliphaz,* chap. xv. 16. It is a proverbial expression, and seems to be formed, as a metaphor, from a *camel drinking,* who takes in a large draught of water, even the most *turbid,* on its setting out on a journey in a caravan, that it may serve it for a long time. Job deals largely in scorning; he fills his heart with it.

Verse 8. *Which goeth in company with the workers of iniquity*] This is an allusion to a *caravan:* all kinds of persons are found there; but yet a holy and respectable man might be found in that part of the company where profligates assembled. But surely this assertion of Elihu was not strictly true; and the words, literally translated, will bear a less evil meaning: "Job makes a *track* ארח *arach,* to *join fellowship,* לחברה *lechebrah,* with the workers of iniquity;" i. e., Job's present mode of reasoning, when he says, "I am righteous, yet God hath taken away my judgment," is according to the assertion of sinners, who say, "There is no profit in serving God; for, if a man be righteous, he is not benefited by it, for God does not vindicate a just man's cause against his oppressors." By adopting so much of their creed, he intimates that Job is taking the *steps* that lead to *fellowship* with them. See ver. 9.

Verse 10. *Far be it from God*] Rather, *Wickedness, far be that from God; and from iniquity, the Almighty.* The sense is sufficiently evident without the *paraphrase* in our version.

Verse 11. *For the work of a man shall he render*] God ever will do *justice;* the righteous shall never be forsaken, nor shall the wicked ultimately prosper.

A. M. cir. 2484
B. C. cir. 1520
Ante I. Olymp. cir. 744
Ante U. C. cir. 767

neither will the Almighty [m]pervert judgment.
13 Who hath given him a charge over the earth? or who
hath disposed [n]the whole world?
14 If he set his heart [o]upon man, *if* he
[p]gather unto himself his spirit and his breath;
15 [q]All flesh shall perish together, and man
shall turn again unto dust.
16 If now *thou hast* understanding, hear
this: hearken to the voice of my words.
17 [r]Shall even he that hateth right [s]govern?
and wilt thou condemn him that is most just?
18 [t]*Is it fit* to say to a king, *Thou art*
wicked? *and* to princes, *Ye are* ungodly?
19 *How much less to him* that [u]accepteth
not the persons of princes, nor regardeth the
rich more than the poor? for
[v]they all *are* the work of his
hands.

A. M. cir. 2484
B. C. cir. 1520
Ante I. Olymp. cir. 744
Ante U. C. cir. 767

20 In a moment shall they die,
and the people shall be troubled [w]at midnight,
and pass away: and [x]the mighty shall be
taken away without hand.
21 [y]For his eyes *are* upon the ways of man,
and he seeth all his goings.
22 [z]*There is* no darkness, nor shadow of
death, where the workers of iniquity may hide
themselves.
23 For he will not lay upon man more *than*
right; that he should [a]enter into judgment
with God.
24 [b]He shall break in pieces mighty men
[c]without number, and set others in their stead.

---

[m]Ch. viii. 3——[n]Heb. *all of it*——[o]Heb. *upon him*——[p]Psa. civ. 29——[q]Gen. iii. 19; Eccles. xii. 7——[r]Gen. xviii. 25; 2 Samuel xxiii. 3——[s]Heb. *bind*——[t]Exodus xxii. 28——[u]Deut. x. 17; 2 Chron. xix. 7; Acts x. 34; Rom. ii. 11; Gal. ii. 6; Ephes. vi. 9; Col. iii. 25; 1 Pet. i. 17

[v]Ch. xxxi. 15——[w]Exod. xii. 29, 30——[x]Heb. *they shall take away the mighty*——[y]2 Chron. xvi. 9; ch. xxxi. 4; Psa. xxxiv. 15; Prov. v. 21; xv. 3; Jer. xvi. 17; xxxii. 19——[z]Psa. cxxxix. 12; Amos ix. 2, 3; Heb. iv. 13——[a]Heb. *go*——[b]Dan. ii. 21——[c]Heb. *without searching out*

Verse 13. *Who hath given him a charge*] *Who* is it that governs the world? Is it not God? Who disposes of all things in it? Is it not the Almighty, by his just and merciful providence? The government of the world shows the care, the justice, and the mercy of God.

Verse 14. *If he set his heart upon man*] I think this and the following verse should be read thus:—"If he set his heart upon man, he will gather his soul and breath to himself; *for* all flesh shall perish together, and man shall turn again unto dust." On whomsoever God *sets his heart*, that is, *his love*, though his body shall perish and turn to dust, like the rest of men, yet his *soul* will God gather to himself.

Verse 17. *Shall—he that hateth right govern?*] Or, *Shall he who hateth judgment, lie under obligation?* It is preposterous to suppose that he who lives by no rule, should impose rules upon others. God, who is the *fountain* of all *justice* and *righteousness, binds* man by his laws; and wilt thou, therefore, *pretend to condemn him who is the sum of righteousness?*

Verse 18. Is it fit *to say to a king,* Thou art *wicked?*] The sentence is very short, and is thus translated by the Vulgate: *Qui dicit regi, Apostata? Qui vocat duces impios?* "Who says to a king, Apostate? Who calls leaders impious?" Literally, *Who calls a king Belial? Who calls princes wicked?* Civil governors should be treated with respect; no man should speak evil of the ruler of the people. This should never be permitted. Even where the *man* cannot be respected, because his *moral conduct* is improper, even there the *office* is sacred, and should be reverenced. He who permits himself to talk against the *man*, would destroy the *office* and *authority*, if he could.

Verse 19. *That accepteth not*] If it be utterly improper to speak against a king or civil governor, how much more so to speak disrespectfully of God, who is not influenced by human caprices or considerations, and who regards the *rich* and the *poor* alike, being equally his creatures, and equally dependent on his providence and mercy for their support and salvation.

Verse 20. *In a moment shall they die*] Both are equally dependent on the Almighty for their breath and being; the *mighty* as well as the *poor*. If the *great men* of the earth have abused their power, he sometimes cuts them off by the most *sudden* and *unexpected death;* and even at midnight, when in security, and least capable of defence, they are cut off by the people whom they have oppressed, or by the *invisible hand* of the angel of death. This appears to be spoken in reference to *Eastern tyrants*, who seldom die a natural death.

Verse 22. There is *no darkness*] In this life; and *no shadow of death* in the other world—no annihilation *in which the workers of iniquity may hide themselves*, or take refuge.

Verse 23. *For he will not lay upon man*] The meaning appears to be this: He will not call man a second time into judgment; he does not try a cause twice; his decisions are just, and his sentence without appeal.

Mr. *Good* translates:—

"Behold, not to man hath he intrusted the time
Of coming into judgment with God."

Man's time is not in his own hand; nor is his lot cast or ruled by his own wisdom and power. When God thinks best, he will judge for him; and, if oppressed or calumniated, he will bring forth his righteousness as the light, and do him justice on his adversaries.

Verse 24. *He shall break in pieces*] In multitudes of cases God depresses the *proud*, and raises up the *humble* and *meek*. Neither their *strength* nor *number* can afford them security.

A. M. cir. 2484
B. C. cir. 1520
Ante I. Olymp.
cir. 744
Ante U. C. cir.
767

25 Therefore he knoweth their works, and he overturneth *them* in the night, so that they are ᵈdestroyed.

26 He striketh them as wicked men ᵉin the open sight of others;

27 Because they ᶠturned back ᵍfrom him, and ʰwould not consider any of his ways:

28 So that they ⁱcause the cry of the poor

to come unto him, and he ᵏheareth the cry of the afflicted.

29 When he giveth quietness, who then can make trouble? and when he hideth *his* face, who then can behold him? whether *it be done* against a nation, or against a man only:

30 That the hypocrite reign not, lest ˡthe people be ensnared.

31 Surely it is meet to be said unto God,

A. M. cir. 2484
B. C. cir. 1520
Ante I. Olymp.
cir. 744
Ante U. C. cir.
767

ᵈHeb. *crushed*——ᵉHeb. *in the place of beholders*
1 Sam. xv. 11——ᵍHeb. *from after him*——ʰPsa. xxviii.

5; Isa. v. 12——ⁱChap. xxxv. 9; James v. 4——ᵏExod.
xxii. 23——ˡ1 Kings xii. 28, 30; 2 Kings xxi. 9

Verse 25. *He knoweth their works*] He knows what they have done, and what they are *plotting* to do.

He overturneth them *in the night*] In the revolution of a single night the plenitude of power on which the day closed is annihilated. See the cases of Belshazzar and Babylon.

Verse 26. *He striketh them as wicked men*] At other times he executes his judgments *more openly;* and they are suddenly destroyed in the *sight of the people.*

Verse 27. *Because they turned back*] This is the reason why he has dealt with them in judgment. They had departed from him in their *hearts,* their *moral conduct,* and their *civil government.* He is speaking of corrupt and tyrannical rulers. And *they did not,* would not, *understand* any of his ways.

Verse 28. *So that they cause the cry of the poor*] They were cruel and oppressive: the poor cried through their distresses, and against their oppressors; and God heard the cry of the poor. Nothing so dreadful appears in the court of heaven against an unfeeling, hard-hearted, and cruel man of power, as the prayers, tears, and groans of the poor.

In times of little liberality, when some men thought they did God service by persecuting those who did not exactly receive *their creed,* nor worship God in *their way,* a certain great man in Scotland grievously persecuted his tenants, because they had religious meetings in private houses out of the order of the establishment; though he never molested them when they spent their time and their money in the alehouse. A holy, simple woman, one of those people, went one morning to the house of the great persecutor, and desired to speak with him. The servant desired to know her message, and he would deliver it; for she could not be admitted. She told him she could deliver her message to none but his master; said it was a matter of great importance, and concerned himself intimately, and alone. The servant having delivered this message, and stated that the woman appeared to have something particular on her mind, his worship condescended to see her. "What is your business with *me?*" said he, in a haughty, overbearing tone. To which she answered, "Sir, we are a hantle o' puir folk at ——, who are strivin' to sairve God accordin' to our ain conscience, and to get our sauls sav'd: yee persecute us; and I am come to beg yee to let us alane; and in ye dinna, we'll pray yee dead." This rhetoric was irresistible. His lordship did not know what influence such people might have in heaven;

he did not like to put such prayers to the proof; wisely took the old woman's advice, and *e'en let them alane.* He was safe; they were satisfied; and God had the glory. When the poor refer their cause to God, he is a terrible avenger. Let the potsherds strive with the potsherds of the earth; but wo to the man that contendeth with his Maker.

Verse 29. *When he giveth quietness, who then can make trouble?*] How beautiful is this sentiment, and how true! He ever acts as a sovereign; but his actions are all wise and just. *If he give quietness, who dares to give trouble?* And if he give to every human being the right to worship himself according to their conscience, for the director of which he gives both his *word* and his *Spirit,* who shall dare to say to another, "Thou shalt worship God in my way, or not at all;" or, through a *pretended liberality,* say, "Thou shalt be *tolerated* to worship him so and so;" and even that toleration be shackled and limited?

Reader, thou hast as much right to tolerate another's mode of worship as he has to tolerate thine: or, in other words, neither of you have any such right at all; the pretension is as absurd as it is wicked.

If, however, there be any thing in the religious practice of any particular people that is inimical, by fair construction, to the peace of the country, then the civil power may interfere, as they ought to do in all cases of *insurrection;* but let no such inference be drawn when not most obviously flowing from the practice of the people, and the principles they profess; and when solemnly disclaimed by the persons in question. Whatever converts sinners from the error of their ways must be good to society and profitable to the state.

Whether it be done *against a nation*] He defends and supports nations or individuals, howsoever weak, against their enemies, howsoever numerous and powerful. He destroys nations or individuals who have filled up the measure of their political or moral iniquity, though all other nations and individuals stand up in their support.

Verse 30. *That the hypocrite reign not*] The *Vulgate* translates, *Who causes a wicked man to reign because of the sins of the people.* This was precisely the defence which Hegiage, the oppressive ruler of the Babylonian Irak, under the caliph Abdul Malec, made when he found the people in a state of insurrection. See at the end of the chapter.

Verse 31. *Surely it is meet to be said unto God*] This is Elihu's exhortation to Job:

A. M. cir. 2484
B. C. cir. 1520
Ante I. Olymp. cir. 744
Ante U. C. cir. 767

[m]I have borne *chastisement,* I will not offend *any more:*

32 *That which* I see not teach thou me: if I have done iniquity, I will do no more.

33 [n]*Should it be* according to thy mind? he will recompense it, whether thou refuse, or whether thou choose; and not I: therefore speak what thou knowest.

34 Let men [o]of understanding tell me, and

let a wise man hearken unto me.

A. M. cir. 2484
B. C. cir. 1520
Ante I. Olymp. cir. 744
Ante U. C. cir. 767

35 [p]Job hath spoken without knowledge, and his words *were* without wisdom.

36 [q]My desire *is that* Job may be tried unto the end, because of *his* answers for wicked men.

37 For he addeth rebellion unto his sin, he [r]clappeth *his hands* among us, and multiplieth his words against God.

---

[m]Dan. ix. 7-14——[n]Heb. Should it be *from with thee?*
[o]Heb. *of heart*

[p]Chapter xxxv. 16——[q]Or, *My father, let Job be tried*
[r]Isa. lv. 12

Humble thyself before God, and say, "I have suffered—*I will not offend.*"
Verse 32. That which *I see not*] "What I do not know, teach thou me; wherein I have done iniquity, I will do so no more."
Verse 33. *According to thy mind? he will recompense it*] Mr. *Good* renders the whole passage thus:—

"Then in the presence of thy tribes,
According as thou art bruised shall he make it whole.
But it is thine to choose, and not mine;
So, what thou determinest, say."

This may at least be considered a paraphrase on the very obscure original. If thou wilt not thus come unto him, he will act according to justice, whether that be *for* or *against* thee. Choose what part thou wilt take, to humble thyself under the mighty hand of God, or still persist in thy supposed integrity. Speak, therefore; the matter concerns thee, not me; but let me know what thou art determined to do.
Verse 34. *Let men of understanding tell me*] I wish to converse with wise men; and by men of wisdom I wish what I have said to be judged.
Verse 35. *Job hath spoken without knowledge*] There is no good in arguing with a self-willed, self-conceited man. Job has spoken like a man destitute of wisdom and discretion.
Verse 36. *My desire* is that *Job may be tried unto the end*] אבי יבחן איוב *abi yibbachen Aiyob,* "My father, let Job be tried." So the VULGATE, *Pater mi, probetur Job.* But it may be as in the common translation, *I wish Job to be tried;* or, as Mr. *Good* renders it, *Verily, let Job be pursued to conquest for replying like wicked men.*
This is a very harsh wish: but the whole chapter is in the same spirit; nearly destitute of mildness and compassion. Who could suppose that such arguings could come out of the mouth of the loving Saviour of mankind? The reader will recollect that a very pious divine has supposed *Elihu* to be *Jesus Christ!*
Verse 37. *He addeth rebellion unto his sin*] An ill-natured, cruel, and unfounded assertion, borne out by nothing which Job had ever said or intended; and indeed, more severe than the most inveterate of his friends (so called) had ever spoken.
Mr. *Good* makes this virulent conclusion still more virulent and uncharitable, by translating thus:—

"For he would add to his transgressions apostasy;
He would clap his hands in the midst of us:
Yea, he would tempest his words up to God."

There was no need of *adding* a caustic here; the words in the tamest translation are tart enough. Though Elihu began well and tolerantly, he soon got into the spirit, and under the mistake, of those who had preceded him in this "tempest of words."

ON ver. 30 I have referred to the case of Hegiage, governor of the Babylonian Irak, under the caliph Abdul Malec. When Hegiage was informed that the people were in a state of mutiny because of his oppressive government, before they broke out into open acts of hostility, he mounted on an eminence, and thus harangued them:—
"God has given me dominion over you; if I exercise it with severity, think not that by putting me to death your condition will be mended. From the manner in which you live you must be always ill-treated, for God has many executors of his justice; and when I am dead he will send you another, who will probably execute his orders against you with more rigour. Do you wish your prince to be moderate and merciful? Then exercise righteousness, and be obedient to the laws. Consider that your own conduct is the cause of the good or evil treatment which you receive from him. A prince may be compared to a *mirror;* all that you see in him is the reflection of the objects which you present before him."
The people immediately dropped their weapons, and quietly returned to their respective avocations. This man was one of the most valiant, eloquent, and cruel rulers of his time; he lived towards the close of the 7th century of the Christian era. He is said to have put to death 120,000 people; and to have had 50,000 in his prisons at the time of his decease.
Yet this man was capable of *generous actions.* The following anecdote is given by the celebrated Persian poet *Jami,* in his *Baharistan:—*
Hegiage, having been separated from his attendants one day in the chase, came to a place where he found an Arab feeding his camels. The camels starting at his sudden approach, the Arab lifted up his head. and seeing a man splendidly arrayed, became incensed, and said, *Who is this who with his fine clothes comes into the desert to frighten my camels? The curse of God light upon him!* The governor,

approaching the Arab, saluted him very civilly, with the *salaam, Peace be unto thee!* The Arab, far from returning the salutation, said, *I wish thee neither peace, nor any other blessing of God.* Hegiage, without seeming to heed what he had said, asked him very civilly "to give him a little water to drink." The Arab, in a surly tone, answered, *If thou desirest to drink, take the pains to alight, and draw for thyself; for I am neither thy companion nor thy slave.* The governor accordingly alighted, and having drank, asked the Arab, "Whom dost thou think the greatest and most excellent of men?" *The prophet sent by God,* said the Arab, *and thou mayest burst with spleen.* "And what thinkest thou of Aaly?" returned Hegiage. *No tongue can declare his excellence,* said the Arab. "What," asked Hegiage, "is thy opinion of the caliph Abdul Malec?" *I believe him to be a very bad prince,* replied the Arab. "For what reason?" said Hegiage. *Because,* said the Arab, *he hath sent us for governor the most execrable wretch under heaven.* Hegiage, finding himself thus characterized, was silent; but his attendants coming up, he rejoined them, and ordered them to bring the Arab with them.

The next day Hegiage ordered him to be set at table with himself, and bade him "eat freely." The Arab, ere he tasted, said his usual grace, *"God grant that the end of this repast may be no worse than the beginning!"* While at meat the governor asked him, "Dost thou recollect the discourse we had together yesterday?" The Arab replied, *God prosper thee in all things! but as to the secret of yesterday, take heed that thou disclose it not to-day.* "I will not," said Hegiage; "but thou must choose one of these two things: either *acknowledge me for thy master,* and I will retain thee about my person; or else *I will send thee to Abdul Malec,* and tell him what thou hast said of him." *There is a third course,* replied the Arab, *preferable to those two.* "Well, what is that?" said the governor. *Why, send me back to the desert, and pray God that we may never see each other's face again.* Cruel and vindictive as Hegiage was, he could not help being pleased with the frankness and courage of the man; and not only forgave him the preceding insults, but ordered him 10,000 pieces of silver, and sent him back to the desert, according to his wish.

CHAPTER XXXV

Elihu accuses Job of impious speeches, 1–4. No man can affect God by his iniquity, nor profit him by his righteousness, 5–8. Many are afflicted and oppressed, but few cry to God for help; and, for want of faith, they continue in affliction, 9–16.

A. M. cir. 2484
B. C. cir. 1520
Ante I. Olymp.
cir. 744
Ante U. C. cir.
767

ELIHU spake moreover, and said,

2 Thinkest thou this to be right, *that* thou saidst, My righteousness *is* more than God's?

3 For [a]thou saidst, What advantage will it be unto thee? *and,* What profit shall I have [b]*if I be cleansed* from my sin?

4 [c]I will answer thee, and [d]thy companions with thee.

5 [e]Look unto the heavens, and see; and behold the clouds *which* are higher than thou.

A. M. cir. 2484
B. C. cir. 1520
Ante I. Olymp.
cir. 744
Ante U. C. cir.
767

6 If thou sinnest, what doest thou [f]against him? or *if* thy transgressions be multiplied, what doest thou unto him?

7 [g]If thou be righteous, what givest thou him? or what receiveth he of thine hand?

8 Thy wickedness *may hurt* a man as thou

---

[a]Ch. xxi. 15; xxxiv. 9——[b]Or, by it *more than by my sin*
[c]Heb. *I will return to thee words*——[d]Chap. xxxiv. 8

[e]Chap. xxii. 12——[f]Prov. viii. 36; Jer. vii. 19——[g]Ch. xxii. 2, 3; Psa. xvi. 2; Prov. ix. 12; Rom. xi. 35

NOTES ON CHAP. XXXV

Verse 2. *My righteousness* is *more than God's?*] This would indeed be a blasphemous saying; but Job never said so, neither directly nor constructively: it would be much better to translate the words צדקי מאל *tsidki meel, I am righteous* BEFORE *God.* And Job's meaning most certainly was, "Whatever I am in *your* sight, I know that in the *sight of God* I am a righteous man;" and he had a right to assume this character, because God himself had given it to him.

Verse 3. *What advantage will it be unto thee?*] As if he had said to God, "My righteousness cannot profit thee, nor do I find that it is of any benefit to myself." Or perhaps Elihu makes here a general assertion, which he afterwards endeavours to exemplify: Thou hast been reasoning *how* it may *profit thee,* and thou hast said, "What profit shall I have in righteousness more than in sin?"

Verse 4. *I will answer thee*] I will show thee the evil of a sinful way, and the benefit of righteousness; and supply what thy friends have omitted in their discourses with thee.

Verse 5. *Look unto the heavens*] These heavens, and their host, God has created: the bare sight of them is sufficient to show thee that God is infinitely beyond thee in wisdom and excellence.

Behold the clouds] שחקים *shechakim,* the *ethers,* (Vulgate, *æthera,*) from שחק *shachak,* to *contend, fight together:* the agitated or conflicting air and light; the strong agitation of these producing both light and heat. Look upon these, consider them deeply, and see and acknowledge the perfections of the Maker.

Verse 6. *If thou sinnest*] God is not benefited by thy righteousness, nor injured by thy iniquity, howsoever multiplied it may be.

Verse 8. *Thy wickedness* may hurt] It is better to translate this literally:

A. M. cir. 2484
B. C. cir. 1520
Ante I. Olymp.
cir. 744
Ante U. C. cir.
767 *art;* and thy righteousness *may* *profit* the son of man.

9 [h]By reason of the multitude of oppressions they make *the oppressed* to cry: they cry out by reason of the arm of the mighty.

10 But none saith, [l]Where *is* God my Maker, [k]who giveth songs in the night;

11 Who [l]teacheth us more than the beasts of the earth, and maketh us wiser than the fowls of heaven?

12 [m]There they cry, but none giveth answer, because of the pride of evil men.

A. M. cir. 2484
B. C. cir. 1520
Ante I. Olymp.
cir. 744
Ante U. C. cir.
767 13 [n]Surely God will not hear vanity, neither will the Almighty regard it.

14 [o]Although thou sayest thou shalt not see him, *yet* judgment *is* before him; therefore [p]trust thou in him.

15 But now, because *it is* not *so,* [q]he hath [r]visited in his anger; yet [s]he knoweth *it* not in great extremity:

16 [t]Therefore doth Job open his mouth in vain; he multiplieth words without knowledge.

---

[h]Exod. ii. 23, 24; iii. 7, 8, 9, 16, 19; v. 4, 5, 6, &c.; Psa. xii. 5; Eccles. v. 8; Isa. v. 7; chap. xxxiv. 28——[i]Isa. li. 13——[k]Psa. xlii. 8; lxxvii. 6; cxlix. 5; Acts xvi. 25 [l]Psa. xciv. 12——[m]Prov. i. 28

[n]Chap. xxvii. 9; Prov. xv. 29; Isa. i. 15; Jer. xi. 11 [o]Chap. ix. 11——[p]Psa. xxxvii. 5, 6——[q]That is, *God* [r]Psa. lxxxix. 32——[s]That is, *Job*——[t]Chap. xxxiv. 35, 37; xxxviii. 2

To a man like thyself is thy wickedness:
And to the son of man, thy righteousness:

That is—

Thou mayest injure thyself and others by thy wickedness,
And thou mayest benefit both by thy righteousness;
But God thou canst neither hurt nor profit.

Verse 9. *By reason of the multitude*] Or rather, "From among the multitude" the oppressed clamour, יזיקן *yaziku: they shout,* ישועו *yeshavveu, because of the mighty.*

The wicked rich oppress the wicked poor; these cry aloud because of their oppressors; but they have no relief, because they call not upon God.

Verse 10. *Where* is *God my Maker*] They have no just apprehension of his *being;* they do not consider themselves his *creatures,* or that he who created them still *preserves* them, and would make them *happy* if they would pray unto him.

Who giveth songs in the night] This is variously translated. "Before whom the high angels give praise in the night."—CHALDEE.

"Who sets the night-watches."—SEPTUAGINT.

"Gives meditations in the night."—SYRIAC and ARABIC.

"And that shyneth upon us that we might prayse him in the night."—COVERDALE.

A holy soul has continual communion with God: night and day its happiness is great; and God, from whom it comes, is the continual subject of its songs of praise.

Verse 11. *Who teacheth us more than the beasts*] "The ox knoweth his owner, and the ass his master's crib; but Israel doth not know me, my people do not consider;" Isa. i. 3. *Beasts, birds, fowls,* and in many cases *pond-fishes,* know and seem thankful to the hand that feeds them; while man, made much more noble than they, gifted with the greatest powers, privileged with the most important benefits, considers not the Lord, nor discerns the opera-

tion of his hand. Quadrupeds, reptiles, and fowls, have more gratitude to their masters than man has to his God.

Verse 12. *There they cry*] They bewail their calamities, but sorrow not for the *cause* of them; they cry against their *oppressors,* but they call not upon God.

Because of the pride of evil men.] Or מפני *mippeney,* from the face, presence, or influence, of the pride of wicked men. They cry for deliverance from the pride of wicked men; but they are not heard, because they cry not to God.

Verse 13. *Surely God will not hear vanity*] He will not attend to such vain cries; they cry *from* their oppressions, but they cry not *to* God.

Verse 14. *Thou sayest thou shalt not see* HIM] Several MSS. have "Thou shalt not see *me,*" and the Septuagint, and *one* other, "Thou shalt not see *us;*" but without the points, תשורנו, the original may be read *see* HIM or *see* US, the third person singular, or the first person plural.

Yet *judgment is before him*] Rest assured that God has not forgotten either to *punish* or to *save;* therefore trust in him; choose to be a *monument* of his *mercy,* rather than of his *justice.*

Verse 15. *But—because* it is *not* so] Rather, "But now, because he visiteth not in his anger." This is more literal than the versions generally proposed; and the sense of the place appears to be this: Because vengeance is not speedily executed on an evil work, therefore are the hearts of the children of men set in them to do iniquity. This is, in effect, the charge which Elihu brings against Job.

Verse 16. *Therefore doth Job open his mouth in vain*] God will execute vengeance when it may best serve the ends of his justice, providence, and mercy. The delay of judgment is not proof that it shall not be executed; nor is the deferring of mercy any proof that God has forgotten to be gracious.

He multiplieth words without knowledge] However this may apply to Job, it most certainly applies very strongly and generally to the words, not only of Job's three friends, but to those also of Elihu himself. The contest is frequently a *strife of words.*

CHAPTER XXXVI

Elihu vindicates God's justice, and his providential and gracious dealings with men, 1–9. Promises of God to the obedient, and threatenings to the disobedient; also promises to the poor and afflicted, 10–16. Sundry proofs of God's mercy, with suitable exhortations and cautions, 17–33.

A. M. cir. 2484
B. C. cir. 1520
Ante I. Olymp.
cir. 744
Ante U. C. cir.
767

ELIHU also proceeded, and said,

2 Suffer me a little, and I will show thee that ªI have yet to speak on God's behalf.

3 I will fetch my knowledge from afar, and will ascribe righteousness to my Maker.

4 For truly my words *shall* not *be* false:

he that is perfect in knowledge *is* with thee.

5 Behold, God *is* mighty, and despiseth not *any:* ᵇ*he is* mighty in strength *and* ᶜwisdom.

6 He preserveth not the life of the wicked: but giveth right to the ᵈpoor.

7 ᵉHe withdraweth not his eyes from the

A. M. cir. 2484
B. C. cir. 1520
Ante I. Olymp.
cir. 744
Ante U. C. cir.
767

ªHeb. *that* there are *yet words for God*——ᵇChap. ix. 4; xii. 13, 16; xxxvii. 23; Psa. xcix. 4

ᶜHeb. *heart*——ᵈOr, *afflicted*——ᵉPsa. xxxiii. 18; xxxiv. 15

NOTES ON CHAP. XXXVI

Verse 1. *Elihu also proceeded*] Mr. *Heath* gives a good summary of this chapter. Elihu goes on to lay before Job the impropriety of his behaviour towards God, and desires him to consider how vain it will prove. That God Almighty will never yield the point; that he will administer impartial justice to all men, ver. 2-6. That the general course of his providence is to favour the righteous: and that though he may sometimes correct them in love, yet if they submit patiently to his fatherly corrections, they shall enjoy all manner of prosperity; but if they be stubborn, and will not submit, they will only draw down greater proofs of his displeasure, ver. 7-16. He tells him that, had he followed the former course, he had probably, before now, been restored to his former condition; whereas, by persisting in the latter course, he was in a fair way of becoming a signal example of Divine justice, ver. 17, 18. He therefore warns him to use the present opportunity, lest God should cut him off while he was in a state of rebellion against him; for with God neither wealth, power, nor any other argument that he could use, would be of any avail, ver. 18-26. That God was infinitely powerful; there was no resisting him: and infinitely wise, as sufficiently appeared by his works; there was, therefore, no escaping out of his hands. That his purity was so great that the sun, in his presence, was more dim than the smallest ray of light when compared to that grand luminary; that his holiness was manifest by his aversion to iniquity; and his goodness, in supplying the wants of his creatures.

Verse 2. *That I have yet to speak on God's behalf.*] I have other proofs to allege in behalf of God's justice and providence.

Verse 3. *I will fetch my knowledge from afar*] מרחוק *lemerachok*, "from the distant place," meaning probably both *remote antiquity* and *heaven;* see below. I will show thee that all antiquity and experience are on my side. I can bring proofs from the remotest ages and from the most distant countries to demonstrate that God is infinitely WISE, and can do nothing *foolish* or *erroneous;* that he is infinitely POWERFUL, and can bring all the *purposes* of his

wisdom to *effect;* that he is infinitely GOOD, and can will nothing, and can do nothing that is not *good* in itself, and well calculated to do *good* to his creatures. And I shall show that his operations in the *heavens* and on the *earth* prove and demonstrate the whole.

And will ascribe righteousness to my Maker.] By proving the above points, the righteous conduct of God, and his gracious government of the world, will be fully established.

That Elihu brings his knowledge *from afar* —from *every part* of the *creation*, as well as from the *Divine nature*—is evident from the end of the chapter. 1. The *omnipotence* of God;—*God is great.* 2. The *eternity* of God;— *We know him not, the number of his years cannot be found out*, ver. 26. 3. From the *economy* of God in the atmosphere, in *dews, rain, vapour*, and the *irrigation* of the earth;—*He maketh small the drops*, &c., ver. 27, 28. 4. In the *thunder* and *lightning*, by which he performs such wonders in the atmosphere, and executes such judgments in the world;—*Also who can understand the noise of his tabernacle? He spreadeth his light upon it. He judgeth the people*, &c., ver. 29-33.

Verse 4. *My words shall not be false*] My words shall be truth without falsity.

He that is perfect in knowledge is with thee.] "The perfection of knowledge is with thee." Thou art a sensible, well-informed man, and will be able to judge of what I say.

Verse 5. *God is mighty, and despiseth not any*] He reproaches no man for his want of knowledge. *If any man lack wisdom, he may come to God, who giveth liberally, and upbraideth not.* I prefer this to the *passive* sense, *will not be despised.*

He is mighty] Literally, "He is mighty in strength of heart;" he can never be terrified nor alarmed.

Verse 6. *He preserveth not the life*] He will not give *life* to the wicked; all such forfeit life by their transgressions.

But giveth right] Justice will he give to the afflicted or *humble*, עניים *aniyim.*

Verse 7. *He withdraweth not his eyes*] Exactly similar to those words of David, Psa. xxxiv. 15: "The eyes of the Lord are upon the righteous."

But with kings are they on the throne] I think the words should be read thus:—"But

A. M. cir. 2484
B. C. cir. 1520
Ante I. Olymp. cir. 744
Ante U. C. cir. 767

righteous: but [f]with kings *are* they on the throne; yea, he doth establish them for ever, and they are exalted.

8 And [g]if *they be* bound in fetters, *and* be holden in cords of affliction;

9 Then he showeth them their work, and their transgressions that they have exceeded.

10 [h]He openeth also their ear to discipline, and commandeth that they return from iniquity.

11 If they obey and serve *him,* they shall [i]spend their days in prosperity, and their years in pleasures.

12 But if they obey not, [k]they shall perish

by the sword, and they shall die without knowledge.

A. M. cir. 2484
B. C. cir. 1520
Ante I. Olymp. cir. 744
Ante U. C. cir. 767

13 But the hypocrites in heart [l]heap up wrath: they cry not when he bindeth them.

14 [m]They [n]die in youth, and their life *is* among the [o]unclean.

15 He delivereth the [p]poor in his affliction, and openeth their ears in oppression.

16 Even so would he have removed thee out of the strait [q]*into* a broad place, where *there is* no straitness; and [r]that [s]which should be set on thy table *should be* full of [t]fatness.

17 But thou hast fulfilled the judgment of

---

[f]Psa. cxiii. 8——[g]Psa. cvii. 10——[h]Ch. xxxiii. 16, 23 [i]Ch. xxi. 13; Isa. i. 19, 20——[k]Heb. *they shall pass away by the sword*——[l]Rom. ii. 5——[m]Chap. xv. 32; xxii. 16; Psa. lv. 23

[n]Heb. *their soul dieth*——[o]Or, *sodomites;* Deut. xxiii. 17——[p]Or, *afflicted*——[q]Psa. xviii. 19; xxxi. 8; cxviii. 5 [r]Heb. *the rest of thy table*——[s]Psalm xxiii. 5——[t]Psalm xxxvi. 8

---

with kings upon the throne shall he place them; and they shall be exalted for ever." The word וישיבם *vaiyeshibem,* he will *establish* or *place them,* should be added to the first clause, as I have done; and then the sense becomes much clearer. Instead of לנצח *lanetsach, for ever,* perhaps *to victory* would be a better sense: "But with kings upon the throne will he place them; and they shall be exalted or triumph to victory." This is precisely the same idea, and conveyed in nearly the same words, as that of our Lord:—"To him that overcometh will I grant to sit with me in my throne, even as I also overcame, and am set down with my Father in his throne;" Rev. iii. 21. "Unto him that loved us, and washed us from our sins in his own blood, and hath made us kings and priests unto God and his Father, to him be glory," &c.; Rev. i. 5, 6.

Verse 8. *And if* they be *bound in fetters*] These are *means* which God uses, not of *punishment,* but of *correction.*

Verse 9. *He showeth them their work*] He shows them the exceeding sinfulness of sin.

That they have exceeded.] יתגברו *yithgabbaru,* "that they have strengthened themselves," and did not trust in the living God; and therefore they would not help themselves when trouble came.

Verse 10. *He openeth also their ear*] He gives them to *understand* the reason why they are thus corrected, and commands them to *return* from those iniquities which have induced him to visit them with afflictions and distresses.

Verse 11. *If they obey and serve* him] There may appear in the course of Providence to be some exceptions to this *general rule;* but it is most true, that this is literally or spiritually fulfilled to all the genuine followers of God. Every man is happy, in whatsoever circumstances, whose heart is unreservedly dedicated to his Maker.

Verse 12. *But if they obey not*] This also is a *general rule,* from which, in the course of Providence, there are only few, and those only *apparent,* deviations. Instead of *they shall perish by the sword,* the meaning of the Hebrew

בשלח יעברו *beshelach yaaboru,* is, "By a dart they shall pass by." They shall be in *continual dangers,* and often *fall* before they have lived out half their days. Mr. *Good* translates: *They pass by as an arrow.* The VULGATE: *Transibunt per gladium.* "They shall pass away by the sword."

Verse 13. *But the hypocrites in heart*] חנפי *chanphey, the profligates, the impious,* those who have neither the *form* nor the *power* of godliness. The *hypocrite* is he who has the *form* but not the *power,* though he wishes to be thought as *inwardly* righteous as he is *outwardly* correct; and he takes up the profession of religion only to serve secular ends. This is not the meaning of the word in the book of Job, where it frequently occurs.

They cry not] "Though he binds them, yet they cry not." They are too *obstinate* to humble themselves even under the *mighty hand of God.*

Verse 14. *They die in youth*] Exactly what the psalmist says, "Bloody and deceitful men shall not live out *half their days,*" Psa. lv. 23. Literally, the words of Elihu are, "They shall die in the youth of their soul."

Their life is *among the unclean.*] בקדשים *bakedeshim,* among the whores, harlots, prostitutes, and sodomites. In this sense the word is used, though it also signifies *consecrated persons;* but we know that in idolatry characters of this kind were consecrated to Baal and Ashtaroth, Venus, Priapus, &c. Mr. *Good* translates, *the rabble.* The *Septuagint: Their life shall be wounded by the angels.*

Verse 15. *And openeth their ears in oppression.*] He will let them know for what end they are afflicted, and *why* he permits them to be oppressed. The word ינל *yigel* might be translated *he shall make them exult,* or *sing with joy,* in oppression; like the three Hebrews in the burning fiery furnace.

Verse 16. *Even so would he have removed thee*] If thou hadst turned to, obeyed, and served him, thy present state would have been widely different from what it is.

Verse 17. *But thou hast fulfilled the judg-*

A. M. cir. 2484
B. C. cir. 1520
Ante I. Olymp.
cir. 744
Ante U. C. cir.
767

the wicked: [u]judgment and justice take hold *on thee.*

18 Because *there is* wrath, *beware* lest he take thee away with *his* stroke: then [v]a great ransom cannot [w]deliver thee.

19 [x]Will he esteem thy riches? *no,* not gold, nor all the forces of strength.

20 Desire not the night, when the people are cut off in their place.

21 Take heed, [y]regard not iniquity: for [z]this hast thou chosen rather than affliction.

22 Behold, God exalteth by his power: [a]who teacheth like him?

23 [b]Who hath enjoined him his way? or [c]who can say, Thou hast wrought iniquity?

24 Remember that thou [d]magnify his work, which men behold.

25 Every man may see it; man may behold *it* afar off.

26 Behold, God *is* great, and we [e]know *him* not, [f]neither can the number of his years be searched out.

27 For he [g]maketh small the drops of water:

A. M. cir. 2484
B. C. cir. 1520
Ante I. Olymp.
cir. 744
Ante U. C. cir.
767

---

[u]Or, *judgment and justice should uphold* thee——[v]Psa. xlix. 7——[w]Heb. *turn thee aside*——[x]Prov. xi. 4 [y]Psa. lxvi. 18——[z]See Heb. xi. 25——[a]Isa. xl. 13, 14; Rom. xi. 34; 1 Cor. ii. 16

[b]Chapter xxxiv. 13——[c]Chapter xxxiv. 10——[d]Psa. xcii. 5; Revelation xv. 3——[e]1 Corinthians xiii. 12 [f]Psalm xc. 2; cii. 24, 27; Hebrews i. 12——[g]Psalm cxlvii. 8

---

ment of the wicked] As thou art acting like the wicked, so God deals with thee as he deals with them.

Elihu is not a whit behind Job's other friends. None of them seems to have known any thing of the permission given by God to Satan to afflict and torment an innocent man.

Verse 18. *Because* there is *wrath*] This is a time in which God is punishing the wicked; take heed lest thou be cut off in a moment. Redeem the time; the days are evil.

Then a great ransom] When he determines to *destroy,* who can *save?*

Verse 20. *Desire not the night*] Thou hast wished for *death;* (here called *night;*) desire it not; leave that with God. If he hear thee, and send *death,* thou mayest be cut off in a way at which thy soul would shudder.

Verse 21. *Regard not iniquity*] It is sinful to entertain such wishes; it is an insult to the providence of God. *He* sends affliction; he knows this to be best for thee: but *thou* hast preferred *death* to *affliction,* thereby setting thy wisdom against the wisdom of God. Many in affliction, long for death; and yet they are not prepared to appear before God! What madness is this! If he takes them at their wish, they are ruined for ever. Affliction may be the means of their salvation; the wished-for death, of their eternal destruction.

Verse 22. *God exalteth by his power*] He has brought thee low, but he can raise thee up. Thou art not yet out of the reach of his mercy. Thy affliction is a proof that he acts towards thee as a merciful Parent. He knows what is best to be done; he teaches thee how thou shouldst suffer and improve. Why sin against his kindness? *Who can teach like him?*

Verse 23. *Who hath enjoined him his way*] Has God taken instructions from any man how he shall govern the world?

Thou hast wrought iniquity?] Who can prove, in the whole compass of the creation, that there is one thing *imperfect, superabundant,* or *out of its place?* Who can show that there is, in the course of the Divine providence, one *unrighteous,* cruel, or unwise *act?* All the cunning and wickedness of man have never been able to find out the *smallest flaw* in the work of God.

Verse 24. *Remember that thou magnify his work*] Take this into consideration; instead of fretting against the dispensations of Divine providence, and quarrelling with thy Maker, attentively survey his works; consider the operation of his hands; and see the proofs of his *wisdom* in the *plan* of all, of his *power* in the *production* and *support* of all, and of his *goodness* in the *end* for which all have been made, and to which every operation in *nature* most obviously tends; and then *magnify his work.* Speak of him as thou shalt find; let the visible works of thy Maker prove to thee his eternal power and Godhead, and let *nature* lead thee to the Creator.

Verse 25. *Every man may see it*] He who says he can examine the earth with a philosophic eye, and the heavens with the eye of an astronomer, and yet says he cannot see in them a system of infinite skill and contrivance, must be ignorant of science, or lie against his conscience, and be utterly unworthy of confidence or respect.

Verse 26. *God is great*] He is *omnipotent.*

We know him *not*] He is *unsearchable.*

Neither can the number of his years be searched out.] He is *eternal.*

These three propositions are an ample foundation for endless disquisition. As to paraphrase and comment, they need none in this place; they are too profound, comprehensive, and sublime.

Verse 27. *He maketh small the drops of water*] This appears simply to refer to *evaporation,* and perhaps it would be better to translate יגרע *yegara,* "he exhales;" detaches the smallest particles of the aqueous mass from the surface in order to form *clouds,* as *reservoirs* for the purpose of furnishing *rain* for the watering of the earth. God is seen in *little* things, as well as *great things;* and the *inconceivably little,* as well as the *stupendously great,* are equally the work of *Omnipotence.*

They pour down rain] These exceedingly minute drops or *vapour* become collected in *clouds;* and then, when *agitated by winds,* &c., many particles being united, they become *too heavy* to be sustained by the air in which they before were suspended, and so *fall down* in rain, which is either a *mist,* a *drizzle,* a *shower,*

A. M. cir. 2484
B. C. cir. 1520
Ante I. Olymp.
cir. 744
Ante U. C. cir.
767

they pour down rain according to the vapour thereof:

28 [h]Which the clouds do drop *and* distil upon man abundantly.

29 Also can *any* understand the spreadings of the clouds, *or* the noise of his tabernacle?

30 Behold, he [i]spreadeth his light upon it, and covereth [k]the bottom of the sea.

31 For [l]by them judgeth he the people; he [m]giveth meat in abundance.

A. M. cir. 2484
B. C. cir. 1520
Ante I. Olymp.
cir. 744
Ante U. C. cir.
767

---

[h]Prov. iii. 20——[i]Chap. xxxvii. 3——[k]Heb. *the roots*
[l]Chap. xxxvii. 13; xxxviii. 23

[m]Psalm cxxxvi. 25; Acts
xiv. 17

---

a *storm*, or a *waterspout*, according to the influence of different *winds*, or the presence and quantum of the *electric fluid*. And all this is proportioned, לאדו *le-edo*, "to its vapour," to the *quantity of the fluid evaporated* and condensed into clouds.

Verse 28. *Which the clouds do drop*] In proportion to the *evaporation* will be the *clouds* or *masses of volatilized* and *suspended vapour;* and in proportion to this will be the quantum of *rain* which in different forms will fall upon the earth.

There is a remarkable addition to this verse in the *Septuagint*. I shall insert the whole verse: Ῥυησονται παλαιωματα, εσκιασε δε νεφη επι αμυθητῳ βροτῳ· ωραν εθετο κτηνεσιν, οιδασι δε κοιτης ταξιν· επι τουτοις πασιν ουκ εξισταται σου ἡ διανοια, ουδε διαλλασσεται σου ἡ καρδια απο σωματος; "The rains descend, and the clouds cover with their shadows multitudes of men: he hath appointed to animals to know the order of their dwellings. At the contemplation of these things is not thy mind transported, and thy heart ready to part from thy body?"

Verse 29. *Can any understand the spreadings of the clouds*] Though the *vapour* appear to be fortuitously raised, and subject, when suspended in the atmosphere, to innumerable *accidents*, to different winds and currents which might drive it all to the *sandy deserts*, or direct its course so that it should fall again into the *great deep* from which it has been exhaled, without watering and refreshing the earth; yet so does the good and wise providence of God manage this matter, that every part of the arable terrene surface receives an ample supply; and in every place, where requisite, it may be truly said that "The rain cometh down, and the snow from heaven, and water the earth, and cause it to bring forth and bud, that it may minister seed to the sower, and bread to the eater."

In *Egypt*, where there is *little or no rain*, the earth is watered by the annual *inundation of the Nile;* there, because this system of *evaporation* is not necessary, it does not exist. Who can account for this economy? How are these clouds so judiciously and effectually *spread through the atmosphere*, so as to supply the wants of the earth, of men, and of cattle? I ask, with Elihu, "Who can understand the spreadings of these clouds?" And I should like to see that volunteer in the solution of paradoxes who would step forward and say, *I am the man.*

The noise of his tabernacle?] By the *tabernacle* we may understand the whole *firmament* or *atmospheric expansion;* the place where the Almighty seems more particularly to dwell; whence he sends forth the *rain of his strength*, and the *thunder of his power*.

The *noise* must refer to the blowing of winds and tempests, or to the claps, peals, and rattling of thunder, by means of the electric fluid.

Verse 30. *He spreadeth his light upon it*] Or, as Mr. *Good* translates, "He throweth forth from it his flash." These two verses may both have an allusion to the sudden rarefaction of that part of the atmosphere whence the thunder proceeds, by the agency of the electric fluid; the *rushing in of the air* on each side to restore the equilibrium, which the passage of the fire had before destroyed. The noise produced by this sudden rushing in of the air, as well as that occasioned by the *ignition* of the *hydrogen gas*, which is one of the constituents of water, is *the thunder of his tabernacle*, viz., the *atmosphere*, where God appears, in such cases, to be manifesting his presence and his power.

Elihu says that *God spreadeth his light upon it*. This is spoken in reference to the *flashes* and *coruscations* of *lightning* in the time of thunder storms, when, even in a dark night, a *sudden flash* illuminates for a moment the surface of the earth under that place.

And covereth the bottom of the sea.] He doth whatsoever it pleaseth him in the heavens above, in the earth beneath, in the sea, and in all deep places. Yea, the depths of the sea are as much under his control and influence as the atmosphere, and its whole collection of vapours, meteors, and galvanic and electric fluids.

Verse 31. *By them judgeth he the people*] He makes storms, tempests, winds, hurricanes, tornadoes, thunder and lightning, drought and inundation, the instruments of his justice, to punish rebellious nations.

He giveth meat in abundance.] Though by these he punishes offenders, yet through the same, as instruments, he provides for the wants of men and animals in general. Storms, tempests, and hurricanes, agitate the lower regions of the atmosphere, disperse noxious vapours, and thus render it fit for *respiration;* and without these it would soon become a stagnant, putrid, and deadly mass, in which neither animals could live, nor vegetables thrive. And by *dews, rains, snows, frosts, winds, cold*, and *heat*, he fructifies the earth, and causes it to bring forth abundantly, so that every thing living is filled with plenteousness.

Some critics translate this latter clause thus:—*He passeth sentence amain.* I cannot see this meaning in the original words. Not one of the versions has so understood them; nor does this translation, supposing even that the Hebrew would bear it, give so fine and so elegant an idea as that of the common version. I always feel reluctant to give a sense in any case that is not supported in some of its parts by any of the ancient versions, and more especially when it is contrary to the whole of them; and still more particularly when opposed to the *Arabic*, which in the *Book of Job*, contain-

A. M. cir. 2484
B. C. cir. 1520
Ante I. Olymp. cir. 744
Ante U. C. cir. 767

32 ⁿWith clouds he covereth the light; and commandeth it not to *shine* by *the cloud* that cometh betwixt.

33 ^oThe noise thereof showeth concerning it, the cattle also concerning ^pthe vapour.

A. M. cir. 2484
B. C. cir. 1520
Ante I. Olymp. cir. 744
Ante U. C. cir. 767

ⁿPsa. cxlvii. 8——^o1 Kings xviii. 41, 45

^pHeb. *that which goeth up*

---

ing so many *Arabisms*, I consider to be of very great importance.

Verse 32. *With clouds he covereth the light.*]
This is an extraordinary saying, על כפים כסה אור *al cappayim kissah or*, which Mr. *Good* translates, "He brandisheth the blaze athwart the concave." The *Vulgate*, with which all the other *versions* less or more agree, has, *In manibus abscondit lucem*, "In his hands he hideth the light;" or, more literally, "By the hollow of his hands (כפים *cappayim*) he concealeth the light, (אור *or*,") the *fountain of light*, i. e., the SUN.

And commandeth it not to shine *by* the cloud *that cometh betwixt.*] I am afraid this is no translation of the original. Old *Coverdale* is better:—𝔄𝔫𝔡 𝔞𝔱 𝔥𝔦𝔰 𝔠𝔬𝔪𝔪𝔞𝔫𝔡𝔢𝔪𝔢𝔫𝔱 𝔦𝔱 𝔠𝔬𝔪𝔪𝔢𝔱𝔥 𝔞𝔤𝔞𝔶𝔫𝔢; which is a near copy of the *Vulgate*. Here again Mr. *Good* departs from all the versions, both ancient and modern, by translating thus:—"And launcheth his penetrating bolt." Dr. *Stock*, in my opinion, comes nearer the original and the versions in his translation:—

"And giveth charge as to what it shall meet."

The mending of the text by conjecture, to which we should only recur in desperate necessity, has furnished Mr. *Good* and *Reiske* with the above translation. For my own part, I must acknowledge an extreme difficulty both here and in the concluding verse, on which I am unwilling to lay a correcting hand. I think something of the doctrine of *eclipses* is here referred to; the *defect of the solar light*, by the *interposition* of the *moon*. So in the time of an eclipse God is represented as *covering the body of the sun with the hollow of his hand*, and thus obscuring the solar light, and then removing his hand so as to permit it to re-illuminate the earth.

Mr. *Good* gets his translation by dividing the words in a different manner from the present text. I shall give both:—

Hebrew: ויצו עליה במפגיע
Vayetsav aleyha bemaphgia

Mr. Good: ויצו ליהב מפגיע
Veyezvo liahbe mapegio.

Of which he learnedly contends, "And launcheth his penetrating bolt," is the literal sense. The change here made, to produce the above meaning, is not a violent one; and I must leave the reader to judge of its importance.

Verse 33. *The noise thereof showeth concerning it, the cattle also concerning the vapour.*] I think this translation very unhappy. I shall give each hemistich in the original:—

יגיד עליו רעו
Yaggid alaiv reo

מקנה אף על עולה
Mikneh aph al oleh.

I think this may be translated without any violence to any word in the text:—

Its loud noise (or his thunder) shall proclaim concerning him;
A magazine of wrath against iniquity.

This is literal, and gives, in my opinion, a proper meaning of the passage, and one in strict connection with the context. And it is worthy of remark that every wicked man trembles at the *noise of thunder* and the *flash of lightning*, and considers this a *treasury of Divine wrath*, emphatically called among us *the artillery of the skies;* and whenever the noise is heard, it is considered *the voice of God.* Thus the thunder *declares concerning him.* The next chapter, which is a continuation of the subject here, confirms and illustrates this meaning. For יניד *yaggid*, Houbigant reads יניד *yanid;* and for מקנה *mikneh*, מקנאת *mikkinath;* and translates thus: "He agitates with himself his thunder, from the indignation of his wrath against iniquity."

CHAPTER XXXVII

Elihu continues to set forth the wisdom and omnipotence of God, as manifested in the thunder and lightning, 1–5; in the snows and frosts, 6–8; in various meteors; and shows the end for which they are sent, 9–13. Job is exhorted to consider the wondrous works of God in the light, in the clouds, in the winds, in heat and cold, in the formation of the heavens, and in the changes of the atmosphere, 14–22. The perfections of God, and how he should be reverenced by his creatures, 23, 24.

A. M. cir. 2484
B. C. cir. 1520
Ante I. Olymp.
cir. 744
Ante U. C. cir.
767

AT this also my heart trembleth, and is moved out of his place.

2 [a]Hear attentively the noise of his voice, and the sound *that* goeth out of his mouth.

3 He directeth it under the whole heaven, and his [b]lightning unto the [c]ends of the earth.

A. M. cir. 2484
B. C. cir. 1520
Ante I. Olymp.
cir. 744
Ante U. C. cir.
767

4 After it [d]a voice roareth: he thundereth with the voice of his excellency; and he will not stay them when his voice is heard.

---

[a]Heb. *Hear in hearing*——[b]Heb. *light*

[c]Heb. *wings of the earth*——[d]Psa. xxix. 3; lxviii. 33

NOTES ON CHAP. XXXVII

Verse 1. *My heart trembleth*] This is what the *Septuagint* has anticipated; see under ver. 28 of the preceding chapter. A proper consideration of God's majesty in the *thunder* and *lightning* is enough to appal the stoutest heart, confound the wisest mind, and fill all with humility and devotion. This, to the middle of ver. 5, should be added to the preceding chapter, as it is a continuation of the account of the thunder and lightning given at the conclusion of that chapter. Our present division is as absurd as it is unfortunate.

Verse 2. *Hear attentively*] "Hear with hearing." The words seem to intimate that there was *actually at that time* a violent storm of thunder and lightning, and that the successive peals were now breaking over the house, and the lightning flashing before their eyes. The storm *continued* till Elihu had finished, and out of *that* storm the Almighty spoke. See the beginning of the succeeding chapter.

The noise of his voice] The sudden *clap*.

And the sound that *goeth out*.] The *peal* or *continued rattling, pounding,* and *thumping,* to the end of the peal. The whole is represented as the *voice of God* himself, and the *thunder* is immediately *issuing from his mouth*.

Verse 3. *He directeth it under the whole heaven*] He directeth it (*the lightning*) under the whole heaven, in the twinkling of an eye from east to west; *and its light*—the reflection of the flash, not the *lightning, unto the ends of the earth,* so that a whole hemisphere seems to see it at the same instant.

Verse 4. *After it a voice roareth*] After the flash has been seen, the peal is heard; and this will be more or fewer seconds after the peal, in proportion to the distance of the thunder cloud from the ear. Lightning traverses any space without any perceivable succession of time; nothing seems to be any obstacle to its progress. A multitude of persons taking hands, the first and the last connected with the electric machine, all feel the shock in the same instant; and were there a chain as conductor to go round the globe, the last would feel the shock in the same moment as the first. But as *sound* depends on the undulations of the air for its propagation, and is known to travel at the rate of only 1142 feet in a second; consequently, if the flash were only 1142 feet from the spectator, it would be seen in one second, or one swing of the pendulum, *before* the sound could reach the *ear*, though the clap and the flash take place in the same instant, and if twice this distance, two seconds, and so on. It is of some consequence to know that lightning, at a considerable distance, suppose six or eight seconds of time, is never known to burn, kill, or do injury. When the flash and the clap immediately succeed each other, then there is strong ground for apprehension, as the thunder cloud is *near*. If the thunder cloud be a *mile and a half* distant, it is, I believe, never known to kill man or beast, or to do any damage to buildings, either by throwing them down or burning them. Now its distance may be easily known by means of a pendulum clock, or watch that has seconds. When the *flash* is *seen*, count the *seconds* till the *clap* is *heard*. Then compute: If only one second is counted, then the thunder cloud is within 1142 feet, or about 380 yards; if two seconds, then its distance is 2284 feet, or 761 yards; if three seconds, then 3426 feet, or 1142 yards; if four seconds, then the cloud is distant 4568 feet, or 1522 yards; if five seconds, then the distance is 5710 feet, or 1903 yards; if six seconds, then the distance is 6852 feet, or 2284 yards, one mile and nearly one-third; if seven seconds, then the distance of the cloud is 7994 feet, or 2665 yards, or one mile and a half, and 25 yards. Beyond this distance lightning has not been known to do any damage, the fluid being too much diffused, and partially absorbed, in its passage over *electric* bodies, i. e., those which are not fully impregnated with the electric matter, and which receive their full charge when they come within the electric attraction of the lightning. For more on the rain produced by thunder storms, see on chap. xxxviii. 25. This scale may be carried on at pleasure, by adding to the last sum for every second 1142 feet, and reducing to yards and miles as above, allowing 1760 yards to one mile.

He thundereth with the voice of his excellency] גאונו *geono, of his majesty:* nor is there a sound in nature more descriptive of, or more becoming, the majesty of God, than that of THUNDER. We hear the *breeze* in its *rustling,* the *rain* in its *pattering,* the *hail* in its *rattling,* the *wind* in its *hollow howlings,* the *cataract* in its *dash,* the *bull* in his *bellowing,* the *lion* in his *roar;* but we hear GOD, the Almighty, the Omnipresent, in the continuous peal of THUNDER! This sound, and this sound only, becomes the majesty of Jehovah.

And he will not stay them] ולא יעקבם *velo yeahkebem,* and he hath not *limited* or *circumscribed* them. His lightnings light the world; literally, the whole world. The electric fluid is diffused through all nature, and everywhere art can exhibit it to view. To his thunder and lightning, therefore, he has assigned no limits. And when his voice soundeth, when the lightning goes forth, who shall assign its limits, and who can stop its progress? It is, like God, IRRESISTIBLE.

A. M. cir. 2484
B. C. cir. 1520
Ante I. Olymp.
cir. 744
Ante U. C. cir.
767

5 God thundereth marvellously with his voice; ^egreat things doeth he, which we cannot comprehend.

6 For ^fhe saith to the snow, Be thou *on*

the earth; ^glikewise to the small rain, and to the great rain of his strength.

7 He sealeth up the hand of every man: ^hthat all men may know his work.

A. M. cir. 2484
B. C. cir. 1520
Ante I. Olymp.
cir. 744
Ante U. C. cir.
767

---

^eChap. v. 9; ix. 10; xxxvi. 26; Rev. xv. 3—— ^fPsa. cxlvii. 16, 17

^gHeb. *and to the showers of rain, and to the showers of rain of his strength*——^hPsa. cix. 27

Verse 5. *God thundereth marvellously with his voice*] This is the conclusion of Elihu's description of the lightning and thunder: and here only should chap. xxxvi. have ended. He began, chap. xxxvi. 29, with the *noise of God's tabernacle;* and he ends here with the *marvellous thundering* of Jehovah. Probably the writer of the book of Job had seen the description of a similar thunder storm as given by the psalmist, Psa. lxxvii. 16, 17, 18, 19:—

Ver. 16. The waters saw thee, O God!
The waters saw thee, and were afraid.
Yea, the deeps were affrighted!
Ver. 17. The clouds poured out water;
The ethers sent forth a sound;
Yea, thine arrows went abroad.
Ver. 18. The voice of thy thunder was through the expanse:
The lightnings illumined the globe;
The earth trembled and shook!
Ver. 19. Thy way is in the sea,
And thy paths on many waters;
But thy footsteps are not known.

Great things doeth he] This is the beginning of a new paragraph; and relates particularly to the phenomena which are afterwards mentioned. All of them wondrous things; and, in many respects, to us incomprehensible.

Verse 6. *For he saith to the snow, Be thou on the earth*] Snow is generally defined, "A well-known meteor, formed by the freezing of the vapours in the atmosphere." We may consider the formation of snow thus:—A cloud of vapours being condensed into drops, these drops, becoming too heavy to be suspended in the atmosphere, descend; and, meeting with a *cold region* of the air, they are frozen, each drop shooting into several points. These still continuing their descent, and meeting with some intermitting gales of a warmer air, are a little thawed, blunted, and again, by falling into colder air, frozen into clusters, or so entangled with each other as to fall down in what we call *flakes.*

Snow differs from *hail* and *hoar-frost* in being *crystallized:* this appears on examining a flake of snow with a magnifying glass; when the whole of it will appear to be composed of fine *spicula* or points diverging like rays from a centre. I have often observed the particles of snow to be of a regular figure, for the most part beautiful stars of *six points* as clear and transparent as ice. On each of these points are other collateral points, set at the same angles as the main points themselves, though some are irregular, the points broken, and some are formed of the fragments of other regular stars. I have observed snow to fall sometimes entirely in the form of separate regular *six-pointed stars,* without either clusters or flakes, and each so large as to be the eighth of an inch in diameter.

The *lightness* of snow is owing to the excess of its *surface,* when compared with the *matter* contained under it.

Its *whiteness* is owing to the small particles into which it is divided: for take *ice,* opaque almost as *blackness,* and pound it fine, and it becomes as white as snow.

The immediate cause of the formation of snow is not well understood: it has been attributed to *electricity;* and *hail* is supposed to owe its more compact form to a more intense electricity, which unites the particles of *hail* more closely than the moderate electricity does those of *snow.* But rain, snow, hail, frost, ice, &c., have all one common origin; they are formed out of the *vapours* which have been exhaled by heat from the surface of the waters.

Snow, in northern countries, is an especial blessing of Providence; for, by covering the earth, it prevents corn and other vegetables from being destroyed by the intense cold of the air in the winter months; and especially preserves them from cold piercing winds. It is not a fact that it possesses in itself any fertilizing quality, such as *nitrous salts,* according to vulgar opinion: its whole use is covering the vegetables from intense cold, and thus preventing the natural heat of the earth from escaping, so that the intense cold cannot freeze the juices in the tender tubes of vegetables, which would *rupture* those tubes, and so destroy the plant.

Mr. *Good* alters the *punctuation* of this verse, and translates thus:—

Behold, he saith to the snow, Be!
On earth then falleth it.
To the rain,—and it falleth:
The rains of his might.

By the *small rain,* we may understand *drizzling showers:* by the *rain of his strength,* sudden *thunder storms,* when the rain descends in *torrents:* or violent rain from dissipating waterspouts.

Verse 7. *He sealeth up the hand of every man*] After all that has been said, and much of it most learnedly, on this verse, I think that the act of *freezing* is probably intended; that when the earth is bound up by intense frost, *the hand,* ׳ד *yad,* labour, of *every man is sealed up;* he can do no more labour in the field, till the *south wind* blow, by which a *thaw* takes place. While the earth is in this state of rigidity, *the beasts go into their dens, and remain in their places,* ver. 8, some of them sleeping out the winter in a state of torpor, and others of them feeding on the stores which they had collected in *autumn.* However, the passage may mean no more than by the severity of the rains beasts are drawn to their covers; and man is obliged to intermit all his labours. The mighty rains are past. Who would have thought that on this verse, as its *Scriptural* foundation, the doctrine of *chiromancy* is built! God has

A. M. cir. 2484
B. C. cir. 1520
Ante I. Olymp.
cir. 744
Ante U. C. cir.
767

8 Then the beasts ¹go into dens, and remain in their places.

9 ᵏOut of the south cometh the whirlwind: and cold out of the ¹north.

10 ᵐBy the breath of God frost is given: and the breadth of the waters is straitened.

11 Also by watering he wearieth the thick

cloud: he scattereth ⁿhis bright cloud:

12 And it is turned round about by his counsels: that they may °do whatsoever he commandeth them upon the face of the world in the earth.

13 ᵖHe causeth it to come, whether for ᑫcorrection, or ʳfor his land, or ˢfor mercy.

A. M. cir. 2484
B. C. cir. 1520
Ante I. Olymp.
cir. 744
Ante U. C. cir.
767

ⁱPsa. civ. 22——ᵏHeb. *out of the chamber*——ˡHeb. *scattering* winds——ᵐChap. xxxviii. 29, 30; Psa. cxlvii. 17, 18——ⁿHeb. *the cloud of his light*——°Psa. cxlviii. 8

ᵖExod. ix. 18, 23; 1 Sam. xii. 18, 19; Ezra x. 9; chap. xxxvi. 31——ᑫHeb. *a rod*——ʳChap. xxxviii. 26, 27 ˢ2 Sam. xxi. 10; 1 Kings xviii. 45

---

so *marked the hand* of every man by the *lines* thereon exhibited, that they tell all the good or bad fortune they shall have during life; and he has done this that all men, by a judicious examination of their hands, *may know his work!* On this *John Taisnier*, a famous mathematician, lawyer, musician, and poet laureate of Cologne, has written a large folio volume, with more *hands* in it than fell to the lot of *Briareus:*—printed at Cologne, 1683.

Verse 9. *Out of the south cometh the whirlwind*] See the note on chap. ix. 9. What is rendered *south* here, is there rendered *chambers.* Mr. *Good* translates here, *the utmost zone.* The *Chaldee:*—"From the supreme chamber the commotion shall come; and from the cataracts of Arcturus the cold." What the *whirlwind*, סופה *suphah,* is, we know not. It might have been a wind peculiar to that district; and it is very possible that it was a scorching wind, something like the *simoom.*

Verse 10. *By the breath of God frost is given*] The *freezing* of water, though it is generally allowed to be the effect of *cold*, and has been carefully examined by the most eminent philosophers, is still involved in much mystery; and is a very proper subject to be produced among the *great things which God doeth*, and which *we cannot comprehend*, ver. 5. Water, when frozen, becomes *solid*, and increases considerably in *bulk.* The expansive power in freezing is so great, that, if water be confined in a *gun-barrel*, it will split the solid metal throughout its whole length. Bombshells have been filled with water, and plugged tight, and exposed to cold air, when they have been rent, though the shell has been nearly two inches thick! Attempts have been made to account for this; but they have not, as yet, been generally successful. The *breath of God freezes the waters;* and that *breath thaws them.* It is the work of Omnipotence, and there, for the present, we must *leave it.*

The breadth of the waters is straitened.] This has been variously translated; מוצק *mutsak,* which we here render *straitened*, we translate ver. 18 *melted.* Mr. *Good* thinks that the idea of a mirror is implied, or something *molten;* and on this ground it may be descriptive of the state of water formed into *ice.* He therefore translates:—

By the blast of God the frost congealeth,
And the expanse of the waters into a mirror.

I have only to observe, that in the act of freezing wind or air is necessary; for it has been observed that water which lay low in

ponds did not freeze till some slight current of air fell on and ruffled the surface, when it instantly shot into ice.

Verse 11. *By watering he wearieth the thick cloud*] Perhaps it would be better to say, *The brightness* ברי *beri,* dissipates the cloud; or, if we follow our version, *By watering the earth he wearieth*, wearieth out or emptieth, *the thick cloud*—causes it to pour down all its contents upon the earth, that they may cause it to bring forth and bud. The *Vulgate* understood it differently: *Frumentum desiderat nubes; et nubes spargunt lumen suum.* "The grain desireth the clouds; and the clouds scatter abroad their light."

Verse 12. *And it is turned round about by his counsels*] The original is difficult: והוא מסבות מתהפך בתחבולתו *vehu mesibboth mithhappech bethachbulothav;* which has been thus paraphrased: *And he*—the sun, *makes revolutions*—causes the heavenly bodies to revolve round him, *turning round himself*—turning round his own axis, *by his attachments*—his *attractive* and *repulsive* influences, by which the heavenly bodies revolve round him, and by which, as if strongly *tied* to their *centre*, בחבל *bechebel,* with a *cable* or *rope*, they are projected to their proper distances, and prevented from *coming too near*, or *flying off too far.*

That they may do whatsoever he commandeth them] That men may perform his will, availing themselves of the influences of the sun, moon, times, seasons, &c., to cultivate the earth for the sustenance of themselves and their cattle.

Upon the face of the world in the earth.] אל פני תבל ארצה *al peney thebel aretsah,* over the surface of the habitable world. Perhaps the above exposition may appear to be too far-fetched; and possibly the passage refers only to the *revolutions of the seasons*, and the operations connected with them.

Verse 13. *He causeth it to come*] The *Vulgate* translates the text thus: *Sive in una tribu, sive in terra sua, sive in quocunque loco misericordiæ suæ eas jusserit inveniri.* "Whether in one tribe, or whether in his own land, or in whatsoever place of his mercy he has commanded them to come." In the preceding verse it is said that God conducts the clouds according to the orders of his counsels, whithersoever he pleases: and here it is added that, when he designs to heap *favours* upon any land, he commands the clouds to go thither, and pour out on it their fertilizing showers. See *Calmet.*

The *Vulgate* certainly gives a good sense, and our *common version* is also clear and intelligi-

A. M. cir. 2484
B. C. cir. 1520
Ante I. Olymp.
cir. 744
Ante U. C. cir.
767

14 Hearken unto this, O Job: stand still, and ᵗconsider the wondrous works of God.

15 Dost thou know when God disposed them, and caused the light of his cloud to shine?

16 ᵘDost thou know the balancings of the clouds, the wondrous works of ᵛhim which is perfect in knowledge?

ᵗPsa. cxi. 2——ᵘChap. xxxvi. 29

---

17 How thy garments *are* warm, when he quieteth the earth by the south *wind?*

18 Hast thou with him ʷspread out the sky, *which is* strong, *and* as a molten looking-glass?

19 Teach us what we shall say unto him? *for* we cannot order *our speech* by reason of darkness.

A. M. cir. 2484
B. C. cir. 1520
Ante I. Olymp.
cir. 744
Ante U. C. cir.
767

ᵛChap. xxxvi. 4——ʷGen. i. 6; Isa. xliv. 24

---

ble; but there are doubts whether the *Hebrew* will bear this meaning. Here it is stated that God sends the rain either *for correction,* לשבט *leshebet,* which signifies *rod, staff, tribe,* and is here taken as the symbol of *correction;* he sends rain sometimes as a *judgment,* inundating certain lands, and sweeping away their produce by irresistible floods: or *for his land,* לארצו *leartso,* his own land, *Palestine,* the place of his favoured people: or *for mercy,* לחסד *lechesed;* when a particular district has been devoured by *locusts,* or cursed with *drought,* God, in his mercy, sends fertilizing rains to such places to restore the ears which the caterpillars have eaten, and to make the desert blossom like the garden of the Lord. Some think that Job refers to the curse brought upon the *old world* by the *waters of the deluge.* Now, although God has promised that there shall no more be a flood of waters to destroy the whole earth; yet we know he can, very consistently with his promise, inundate any particular district; or, by a superabundance of rain, render the toil of the husbandman in any place vain. Therefore, still his rain may come for judgment, for mercy, or for the especial help of his people or Church.

Verse 14. *Hearken unto this*] Hear what I say on the part of God.

Stand still] Enter into deep contemplation on the subject.

And consider] Weigh every thing; examine separately and collectively; and draw right conclusions from the whole.

The wondrous works of God.] *Endless* in their *variety; stupendous* in their *structure; complicated* in their *parts; indescribable* in their *relations* and *connections;* and *incomprehensible* in the *mode* of their *formation,* in the *cohesion* of their parts, and in the *ends* of their creation.

Verse 15. *Dost thou know when God disposed them*] Dost thou know the laws by which they are governed; and the causes which produce such and such phenomena?

And caused the light of his cloud to shine?] Almost every critic of note understands this of the *rainbow,* which God gave as a sign that the earth should no more be destroyed by water. See Gen. ix. 13, and the note there.

Verse 16. *Dost thou know the balancings of the clouds*] How are the clouds suspended in the atmosphere? Art thou so well acquainted with the nature of *evaporation,* and the *gravity* of the *air* at different heights, to support different *weights* of aqueous vapour, so as to keep them floating for a certain portion of time, and then let them down to water the earth; dost

thou know these things so as to determine the laws by which they are regulated?

Wondrous works of him which is perfect in knowledge?] This is a paraphrase. Mr. *Good's* translation is much better:—

"Wonders, perfections of wisdom!"

Verse 17. *How thy garments* are *warm*] What are *warmth* and *cold?* How difficult this. question! Is *heat* incontestably a *substance,* and is *cold* none? I am afraid we are in the dark on both these subjects. The existence of *caloric,* as a substance, is supposed to be demonstrated. Much, satisfactorily, has been said on this subject; but is it yet beyond doubt? I fear not. But supposing this question to be set at rest, is it demonstrated that *cold* is only a *quality,* the mere *absence* of *heat?* If it be demonstrated that there is such a substance as *caloric,* is it equally certain that there is *no such substance* as *frigoric?* But *how do our garments keep us warm?* By preventing the too great dissipation of the natural heat. And why is it that certain substances, worked into clothing, keep us warmer than others? Because they are bad conductors of caloric. Some substances conduct off the caloric or natural heat from the body; others do not conduct it at all, or imperfectly; hence those keep us warmest which, being bad conductors of caloric, do not permit the natural heat to be thrown off. In these things we know but little, after endless cares, anxieties, and experiments!

But is the question yet satisfactorily answered, why the north wind brings cold, and the south wind heat? If it be so to my *readers,* it is not so to *me;* yet I know the *reasons* which are alleged.

Verse 18. *Hast thou with him spread out the sky*] Wert thou with him when he made the expanse; fitted the weight to the winds; proportioned the aqueous to the terrene surface of the globe; the solar attraction to the quantum of vapours necessary to be stored up in the clouds, in order to be occasionally deposited in fertilizing showers upon the earth? and then dost thou know how gravity and elasticity should be such essential properties of atmospheric air, that without them and their due proportions, we should neither have animal nor vegetable life?

Strong—as a molten looking-glass?] Like a *molten mirror.* The whole concave of heaven, in a clear day or brilliant night, being like a mass of polished metal, reflecting or transmitting innumerable images.

Verse 19. *Teach us what we shall say unto him?*] Thou pretendest to be so very wise, and to know every thing about God, pray make

A. M. cir. 2484
B. C. cir. 1520
Ante I. Olymp. cir. 744
Ante U. C. cir. 767

20 Shall it be told him that I speak? If a man speak, surely he shall be swallowed up.

21 And now *men* see not the bright light which *is* in the clouds: but the wind passeth, and cleanseth them.

22 [x]Fair weather cometh out of the north: with God *is* terrible majesty.

23 *Touching* the Almighty, [y]we cannot find him out: [z]he *is* excellent in power, and in judgment, and in plenty of justice: he will not afflict.

A. M. cir. 2484
B. C. cir. 1520
Ante I. Olymp. cir. 744
Ante U. C. cir. 767

24 Men do therefore [a]fear him: he respecteth not any *that are* [b]wise of heart.

---

[x]Heb. *Gold*——[y]1 Tim. vi. 16——[z]Chap. xxxvi. 5

[a]Matt. x. 28——[b]Matt. xi. 25; 1 Cor. i. 26

---

us as wise as thyself, that we may be able to approach with thy boldness the Sovereign of the world; and maintain our cause with thy confidence before him. As for our parts, we are ignorant; and, on all these subjects, are enveloped with darkness. Mr. *Good* translates:—

"Teach us how we may address him,
When arrayed in robes of darkness."

It is a strong and biting *irony*, however we take it.

Verse 20. *Shall it be told him that I speak?*] Shall I dare to whisper even before God? And suppose any one were to *accuse* me before him for what I have spoken of him, though that has been well intended, how should I be able to stand in his presence? I should be swallowed up in consternation, and consumed with the splendour of his majesty.

But in what state art *thou?* What hast *thou* been doing? *Thou* hast arraigned God for his government of the world; *thou* hast found fault with the dispensations of his providence; *thou* hast even charged him with *cruelty!* What will become of THEE?

Verse 21. *And now* men *see not the bright light*] Mr. *Good* gives the sense clearer:—

"Even now we cannot look at the light
When it is resplendent in the heavens,
And a wind from the north hath passed
along and cleared them."

Elihu seems to refer to the insufferable brightness of the *sun.* Can any man look at the sun shining in his strength, when a clear and strong wind has purged the sky from clouds and vapours? Much less can any gaze on the majesty of God. Every creature must sink before him. What execrably dangerous folly in man to attempt to arraign His conduct!

Verse 22. *Fair weather cometh out of the north*] Is this any version of the original מצפון זהב יאתה *mitstsaphon zahab yeetheh?* which is rendered by almost every version, ancient and modern, thus, or to this effect: "From the north cometh gold." Calmet justly remarks, that in the time of Moses. Job, and Solomon, and for a long time after, gold was obtained from Colchis, Armenia, Phasis, and the land of Ophir, which were all north of Judea and Idumea; and are in the Scriptures ordinarily termed the north country. "But what relation can there be between, *Gold cometh out of the north*, and, *With God is terrible majesty?*" Answer: Each thing has its properties, and proper characteristics, which distinguish it; and each country has its advantages. *Gold*, for instance, comes from the *northern countries;* so praises offered to the Supreme God should be accom-

panied with fear and trembling: and as this metal is from the north, and northern countries are the places whence it must be procured; so terrible majesty belongs to God, and in him alone such majesty is eternally resident.

As זהב *zahob*, which we translate *gold*, (see chap. xxviii. 16,) comes from a root that signifies to be *clear, bright, resplendent, &c.*; Mr. *Good* avails himself of the radical idea, and translates it *splendour:*—

"Splendour itself is with God;
Insufferable majesty."

But he alters the text a little to get this meaning, particularly in the word יאתה *yeetheh*, which we translate *cometh*, and which he contends is the pronoun אתה *itself;* the י *yod*, as a performative, here being, as he thinks, an *interpolation.* This makes a very good sense; but none of the ancient versions understood the place thus, and none of the MSS. countenance this very learned critic's emendation.

Verse 23. *Touching the Almighty, we cannot find him out*] This is a very abrupt exclamation, and highly descriptive of the state of mind in which Elihu was at this time; full of solemnity, wonder, and astonishment, at his own contemplation of this "great First Cause, least understood." The ALMIGHTY! we cannot find him out.

Excellent in power and in judgment] We must not pretend to comprehend his being, the mode of his existence, the wisdom of his counsels, nor the mysteries of his conduct.

He will not afflict.] לא יענה *la yeanneh*, he *will not* ANSWER. He will give account of none of his matters to us. We cannot comprehend his *motives*, nor the *ends* he has in view.

Verse 24. *Men do therefore*] Therefore men, אנשים *anashim*, wretched, miserable, ignorant, sinful men, *should fear him.*

He respecteth not any] No man is valuable in his sight on account of his wisdom; for what is his wisdom when compared with that of the *Omniscient?* Whatever good is in man, God alone is the author of it. Let him, therefore, that glorieth, glory in the Lord.

THUS ends the speech of *Elihu;* a speech of a widely different description, on the whole, from that of the three friends of Job who had spoken so largely before him. In the speeches of Eliphaz, Zophar, and Bildad, there is little besides a tissue of borrowed *wise sayings*, and *ancient proverbs* and *maxims*, relative to the nature of God, and his moral government of the world. In the speech of Elihu every thing appears to be *original;* he speaks from a deep and comprehensive mind, that had profoundly studied the subjects on which he discoursed.

His descriptions of the Divine attributes, and of the wonderful works of God, are correct, splendid, impressive, and inimitable. Elihu, having now come nearly to a close, and knowing that the Almighty would appear and speak for himself, judiciously prepares for and announces his coming by the thunder and lightning of which he has given so terrific and majestic a description in this and the preceding chapter. The evidences of the Divine presence throng on his eyes and mind; the incomprehensible glory and excellency of God confound all his powers of reasoning and description; he cannot arrange his words by reason of darkness; and he concludes with stating, that to poor weak man God must for ever be incomprehensible, and to him a subject of deep religious fear and reverence. Just then the terrible majesty of the Lord appears! Elihu is silent! The rushing mighty wind, for which the description of the thunder and lightning had prepared poor, confounded, astonished Job, proclaims the presence of Jehovah: and out of this whirlwind God answers for and proclaims himself! Reader, canst thou not conceive something of what these men felt? Art thou not astonished, perplexed, confounded, in reading over these descriptions of the thunder of God's power? Prepare, then, to hear the voice of God himself out of this whirlwind.

CHAPTER XXXVIII

The Lord answers Job out of a whirlwind, and challenges him to answer, 1–3. He convinces him of ignorance and weakness, by an enumeration of some of his mighty works; particularly of the creation of the earth, 4–7. The sea and the deeps, 8–18. The light, 19–21. Snow, hail, thunder, lightning, rain, dew, ice, and hoarfrost, 22–30. Different constellations, and the ordinances of heaven influencing the earth, 31–33. Shows his own power and wisdom in the atmosphere, particularly in the thunder, lightnings, and rain, 34–38. His providence in reference to the brute creation, 39–41.

A. M. cir. 2484
B. C. cir. 1520
Ante I. Olymp.
cir. 744
Ante U. C. cir.
767

THEN the LORD answered Job [a]out of the whirlwind, and said,

2 [b]Who *is* this that darkeneth counsel by [c]words without knowledge?

3 [d]Gird up now thy loins like a man; for I will demand of thee, and [e]answer thou me.

4 [f]Where wast thou when I laid the foundations of the earth? declare, [g]if thou hast understanding.

5 Who hath laid the measures thereof, if thou knowest? or who hath stretched the line upon it?

6 Whereupon are the [h]foundations thereof

A. M. cir. 2484
B. C. cir. 1520
Ante I. Olymp.
cir. 744
Ante U. C. cir.
767

---

[a]So Exod. xix. 16, 18; 1 Kings xix. 11; Ezek. i. 4; Nah. i. 3——[b]Chap. xxxiv. 35; xlii. 3——[c]1 Tim. i. 7 [d]Chap. xl. 7

[e]Heb. *make me know*——[f]Psa. civ. 5; Prov. viii. 29; xxx. 4——[g]Hebrew, *if thou knowest understanding* [h]Heb. *sockets*

NOTES ON CHAP. XXXVIII

Verse 1. *The Lord answered Job out of the whirlwind*] It is not סופה *suphah*, as in the preceding chapter, ver. 9; but סערה *searah*, which signifies something turbulent, tumultuous, or violently agitated; and here may signify what we call a *tempest*, and was intended to fill Job's mind with solemnity, and an awful sense of the majesty of God. The *Chaldee* has, a *whirlwind of grief*, making the whole rather *allegorical* than *real;* impressing the scene on Job's *imagination*.

Verse 2. *Who is this that darkeneth counsel*] As if he had said, Who art *thou* who pretendest to speak on the deep things of God, and the administration of his justice and providence, which thou canst not comprehend; and leavest my counsels and designs the darker for thy explanation?

Verse 3. *Gird up now thy loins*] I will not confound thee with my terrors; dismiss all fearful apprehensions from thy mind; now act like a man, כגבר *kegeber*, like a hero: stand and vindicate thyself. *For I will demand of thee*—I will ask thee a series of questions more easy of solution than those which thou hast affected to discuss already; and then thou shalt have the opportunity of answering for thyself.

The most impressive and convincing manner of arguing is allowed to be that by *interrogation*, which the Almighty here adopts. The best orations delivered by the ancients were formed after this manner. That celebrated oration of Cicero against Catiline, which is allowed to be his masterpiece, begins with a multitude of short questions, closely pressed upon each other. See the end of the chapter.

Verse 4. *Where wast thou when I laid the foundations of the earth?*] Thou hast a limited and derived being; thou art only of *yesterday;* what canst thou know? Didst thou see me create the world?

Verse 5. *Who hath laid the measures thereof*] Who hath adjusted its polar and equatorial distances from the centre?

Who hath stretched the line] Who hath formed its zones and its great circles, and adjusted the whole of its *magnitude* and *gravity* to the *orbit* in which it was to move, as well as its *distance* from that great centre about which it was to revolve? These questions show the difficulty of the subject; and that there was an unfathomable depth of counsel and design in the formation of the earth.

Verse 6. *Whereupon are the foundations thereof fastened?*] How does it continue to revolve in the immensity of space? What *supports* it? Has it foundations like a *building*,

A. M. cir. 2484
B. C. cir. 1520
Ante I. Olymp.
cir. 744
Ante U. C. cir.
767

¹fastened? or who laid the corner-stone thereof;

7 When the morning stars sang together, and all ᵏthe sons of God shouted for joy?

8 ¹Or *who* shut up the sea with doors, when it brake forth, *as if* it had issued out of the womb?

9 When I made the cloud the garment thereof, and thick darkness a swaddlingband for it,

10 And ᵐbrake ⁿup for it my decreed *place,* and set bars and doors,

11 And said, Hitherto shalt thou come, but no farther: and here shall °thy proud waves ᵖbe stayed?

A. M. cir. 2484
B. C. cir. 1520
Ante I. Olymp.
cir. 744
Ante U. C. cir.
767

---

¹Heb. *made to sink*——ᵏChap. i. 6——¹Gen. i. 9; Psa. xxxiii. 7; civ. 9; Prov. viii. 29; Jer. v. 22

ᵐOr, *establish my decree upon it*——ⁿCh. xxvi. 10 °Heb. *the pride of thy waves*——ᵖPsa. lxxxix. 9; xciii. 4

---

and is it fastened with a *key-stone,* to keep the mighty fabric in union?

Verse 7. *When the morning stars sang together*] This must refer to some intelligent beings who existed before the creation of the visible heavens and earth: and it is supposed that this and the following clause refer to the same beings; that by the *sons of God,* and the *morning stars,* the angelic host is meant; as they are supposed to be *first,* though perhaps not *chief,* in the order of creation.

For the latter clause the *Chaldee* has, "All the troops of angels." Perhaps their creation may be included in the term *heavens,* Gen. i. 1: "In the beginning God created the heavens and the earth." These witnessed the progress of the creation; and, when God had finished his work, celebrated his wisdom and power in the highest strains.

Verse 8. *Who shut up the sea with doors*] Who *gathered the waters together into one place,* and fixed the sea its limits, so that it cannot overpass them to inundate the earth?

When it brake forth, as if it had issued out of the womb?] This is a very fine metaphor. The sea is represented as a newly born infant issuing from the womb of the void and formless chaos; and the delicate circumstance of the *liquor amnii,* which bursts out previously to the birth of the fœtus, alluded to. The allusion to the birth of a child is carried on in the next verse.

Verse 9. *When I made the cloud the garment*] Alluding to the cloth in which the new-born infant is first received. The *cloud* was the same to the newly raised *vapour,* as the above recipient to the new-born child.

And thick darkness a swaddlingband for it] Here is also an allusion to the first dressings of the new-born child: it is *swathed* in order to support the body, too tender to bear even careful handling without some medium between the hand of the nurse and the flesh of the child. "The image," says Mr. *Good,* "is exquisitely maintained: the new-born ocean is represented as issuing from the womb of chaos; and its dress is that of the new-born infant."

There is here an allusion also to the creation, as described in Gen. i. *Darkness* is there said to be *on the face of the* DEEP. Here it is said, the *thick darkness* was a *swaddlingband* for the new-born SEA.

Verse 10. *And brake up for it my decreed* place] This refers to the decree, Gen. i. 9: "Let the waters under the heavens be gathered together unto one place."

And set bars and doors] *And let the dry land appear.* This formed the *bars* and *doors* of the sea; the land being everywhere a barrier against the encroachments and inundations of the sea; and great rivers, bays, creeks, &c., the doors by which it passes into the interior of continents, &c.

Verse 11. *Hitherto shalt thou come*] Thus far shall thy flux and reflux extend. The *tides* are marvellously limited and regulated, not only by the *lunar* and *solar attractions,* but by the quantum of *time* also which is required to remove any part of the earth's surface from under the immediate attractive influence of the sun and moon. And this regulation takes place by means of the *rotation* of the earth round its own axis, which causes *one thousand and forty-two* miles of its equator to pass from under any given point in the heavens in one hour; and about *five hundred and eighty* miles in the latitude of London: so that the *attracted fluid parts* are every moment passing from under the direct attractive influence, and thus the tides cannot generally be raised to any extraordinary height. The attraction of the sun and moon, and the gravitation of its own parts to its own centre, which prevent too great a *flux* on the one hand, and too great a *reflux* on the other; or, in other words, too *high* a tide, and too *deep* an ebb, are also some of those *bars* and *doors* by which its *proud waves are stayed,* and prevented from *coming farther;* all being regulated by these laws of attraction by the sun and moon, the gravitation of its own parts from the sun and moon, and the diurnal motion round its own axis, by which the fluid parts, easily yielding to the above attraction, are continually moving from under the direct attractive influence. Here a world of wisdom and management was necessary, in order to proportion all these things to each other, so as to procure the great benefits which result from the flux and reflux of the sea, and prevent the evils that must take place, at least occasionally, were not those *bars* and *doors* provided. It is well known that the spring-tides happen at the *change* and *full* of the moon, at which time she is in *conjunction* with and *opposition* to the sun. As these *retire* from their conjunction, the tides *neap* till about three days after the *first quadrature,* when the tides begin again to be more and more elevated, and arrive at their *maximum* about the *third* day after the *opposition.* From this time the tides *neap* as before till the *third* day after the *last quadrature;* and afterwards their daily elevations are continually increased till about the *third* day after the *conjunction,* when they recommence their *neaping;* the principal phenomena of the tides always taking place *at or near the same points* of every *lunar synodic* revolution.

A. M. cir. 2484
B. C. cir. 1520
Ante I. Olymp.
cir. 744
Ante U. C. cir.
767

12 Hast thou �q commanded the morning since thy days; *and* caused the dayspring to know his place;

13 That it might take hold of the ʳ ends of the earth, that ˢ the wicked might be shaken out of it?

14 It is turned as clay *to* the seal; and they stand as a garment.

A. M. cir. 2484
B. C. cir. 1520
Ante I. Olymp.
cir. 744
Ante U. C. cir.
767

15 And from the wicked their ᵗ light is withholden, and ᵘ the high arm shall be broken.

16 Hast thou ᵛ entered into the springs of the

---

q Psa. lxxiv. 16; cxlviii. 5——ʳ Heb. *wings*——ˢ Psa. civ.

35——ᵗ Ch. xviii. 5——ᵘ Psa. x. 15——ᵛ Psa. lxxvii. 19

Verse 12. *Hast thou commanded the morning*] This refers to *dawn* or *morning twilight*, occasioned by the *refraction* of the *solar rays* by means of the *atmosphere;* so that we receive the light by *degrees*, which would otherwise burst at once upon our eyes, and injure, if not destroy, our sight; and by which even the body of the sun himself becomes evident several minutes before he rises above the horizon.

Caused the dayspring to know his place] This seems to refer to the different *points* in which *daybreak* appears during the *course of the earth's revolution in its orbit;* and which variety of *points of appearing* depends on this annual revolution. For, as the earth goes round the sun every year in the ecliptic, one half of which is on the north side of the equinoctial, and the other half on its south side, the sun appears to change his place every day. These are matters which the wisdom of God alone could plan, and which his power alone could execute.

It may be just necessary to observe that the dawn does not appear, nor the sun rise exactly in the same point of the horizon, two successive days in the whole year, as he declines *forty-three* degrees north, and *forty-three* degrees south, of east; beginning on the 21st of March, and ending on the 22d of December; which variations not only produce the *places* of *rising* and *setting*, but also the *length of day and night*. And by this declination north and south, or approach to and recession from the tropics of Cancer and Capricorn, the solar light *takes hold of the ends of the earth*, ver. 13,— enlightens the arctic and antarctic circles in such a way as it would not do were it always on the equinoctial line; these tropics taking the sun *twenty-three and a half* degrees north, and as many south, of this line.

Verse 13. *That the wicked might be shaken out of it?*] The meaning appears to be this: as soon as the light begins to dawn upon the earth, thieves, assassins, murderers, and adulterers, who all hate and shun the light, fly like ferocious beasts to their several dens and hiding places; for such do not dare to *come to the light, lest their works be manifest*, which *are not wrought in God*. To this verse the *fifteenth* appears to belong, as it connects immediately with it, which connection the introduction of the *fourteenth* verse disturbs. "And from the wicked," such as are mentioned above, "their light is withholden;" they love darkness rather than light, because their deeds are evil; and as they prowl after their prey in the night-season, they are obliged to *sleep in the day*, and thus its "light is withholden" from them. "And the high arm shall be broken;" or, as Mr. *Good* translates, "The roving of wickedness is

broken off." They can no longer pursue their predatory and injurious excursions.

Verse 14. *It is turned as clay to the seal*] The earth, like *soft clay*, is capable of modifying itself in endless ways, and assuming infinite forms. As a proof of this, see the astonishing variety of plants, flowers, and fruits, and the infinitely diversified hues, odours, tastes, consistency, and properties, of its vegetable productions.

There seems to be an allusion here to the *sealing of clay*, which I believe *has been*, and is now, frequent in the East. *Six* of those *Eastern seals* for *sealing clay*, made of brass, the *figures* and *characters* all in *relief*, the interstices being entirely perforated and cut out, so that the upper side of the seal is the same as the lower, now lie before me. They seem to have been used for stamping *pottery*, as some of the fine clay still appears in the interstices.

And they stand as a garment.] The earth receiving these *impressions* from the solar light and heat, plants and flowers spring up, and *decorate* its surface as the most beautiful *stamped garment* does the person of the most sumptuously dressed female.

Mr. *Good* translates the whole verse thus:—
"Canst thou cause them to bend round as clay to the mould, so that they are made to sit like a garment?"

He supposes that reference is here made to the *rays of light;* but take his own words: "The image, as it appears to me, is taken directly from the art of pottery, an image of very frequent recurrence in Scripture; and in the present instance admirably forcible in painting the ductility with which the new light of the morning bends round like clay to the mould, and accompanies the earth in every part of its shape so as to fit it, as we are expressly told in the ensuing metaphor, like a garment, as the clay fits the mould itself." Mr. *Good* supposes that a *mould* in which the pottery is *formed*, not a *seal* by which it is *impressed*, is referred to here. In this sense I do not see the metaphor consistent, nor the allusion happy. It is well known that the rays of light never *bend*. They may be reflected at particular angles, but they never go out of a *straight course*. A gun might as well be expected to shoot round a corner, as a ray of light to go out of a straight line, or to follow the sinuous or angular windings of a tube, canal, or adit. But if we take in the sun as he advances in his diurnal voyage, or rather the earth, as it turns round its own axis from west to east, the metaphor of Mr. *Good* will be correct enough; but we must leave out *bending* and *ductility*, as every part of the earth's surface will be at least successively *invested* with the light.

Verse 16. *Hast thou entered into the springs*

A. M. cir. 2484
B. C. cir. 1520
Ante I. Olymp.
cir. 744
Ante U. C. cir.
767
sea? or hast thou walked in the search of the depth?

17 Have ʷthe gates of death been opened unto thee? or hast thou seen the doors of the shadow of death?

18 Hast thou perceived the breadth of the earth? declare if thou knowest it all.

19 Where *is* the way *where* light dwelleth? and *as for* darkness, where *is* the place thereof,

20 That thou shouldest take it ˣto the bound thereof, and that thou shouldest know the paths *to* the house thereof?

A. M. cir. 2484
B. C. cir. 1520
Ante I. Olymp.
cir. 744
Ante U. C. cir.
767

21 Knowest thou *it,* because thou wast then born? or *because* the number of thy days *is* great?

22 Hast thou entered into ʸthe treasures of the snow? or hast thou seen the treasures of the hail,

---

ʷPsa. ix. 13——ˣOr, *at*　　　　ʸPsa. cxxxv. 7

---

of the sea? Of these *springs, inlets,* or *outlets* of the sea, we know just as much as Job. There was prevalent among philosophers an opinion, that through a *porous bottom* fresh matter was constantly oozing by which the sea was supplied with new materials. But through such pores these materials might as well ooze *out* as ooze *in.*

Walked in the search of the depth?] Hast thou walked from the shallow beach through the great ocean's bed, till thou hast arrived at its profoundest depths? In other words, Dost thou know the depths of the sea? Job, we may presume, did not. No man since him has found them out. In multitudes of places they are unfathomed by any means hitherto used by man.

Verse 17. *Have the gates of death been opened unto thee?* Dost thou know in what the article of *death* consists? This is as inexplicable as the question, What is animal *life?*

The doors of the shadow of death?] צלמות *tsalmaveth, the intermediate state, the openings into the place of separate spirits.* Here two places are distinguished: מות *maveth, death,* and צלמות *tsalmaveth, the shadow of death.* It will not do to say, *death* is the *privation of life,* for what then would be the *shadow* of that *privation?*

Verse 18. *The breadth of the earth?*] At that time the circumference of the globe was not known, because the earth itself was supposed to be a vast *extended plain,* bordered all round with the ocean and the sky.

Verse 19. *Where light dwelleth*] What is the *source of light?* Yea, what is *light* itself? It is not in the *sun,* for *light* was before the *sun;* but *what* is *light?* It is no doubt a *substance;* but of what kind? and of what are its *particles?* As to *darkness,* what is IT? Is it philosophical to say, it is the mere *privation of light?* I shall think philosophy has made some advances to general accuracy and perfection when it proves to us what *cold* is, and what *darkness* is, leaving *mere privations* out of the question.

Verse 20. *Shouldest take it to the bound thereof?*] Or, as Mr. *Good,* translates, "That thou shouldest lay hold of it in its boundary." That thou shouldest go to the very spot where *light* commences, and where *darkness* ends; and see the *house* where each dwells. Here *darkness* and *light* are *personified,* each as a real intelligent being, having a separate existence and local dwelling. But poetry animates everything. It is the region of fictitious existence.

I believe this verse should be translated thus:—"For thou canst take us to its boundary; for thou knowest the paths to its house." This is a strong irony, and there are several others in this Divine speech. Job had valued himself too much on his knowledge; and a chief object of this august speech is to humble his "knowing pride," and to cause him to seek true wisdom and humility where they are to be found.

Verse 21. *Knowest thou*] This is another strong and biting irony, and the literal translation proves it: "Thou knowest, because thou was then born; and the number of thy days is great," or *multitudinous,* רבים *rabbim, multitudes.*

Verse 22. *The treasures of the snow*] The places where *snow* is formed, and the cause of that formation. See on chap. xxxvii. 6.

Treasures of the hail] It is more easy to account for the formation of *snow* than of *hail.* Hail, however, is generally supposed to be drops of rain frozen in their passage through cold regions of the air; and the hail is always in proportion to the *size of the raindrop* from which it was formed. But this meteor does not appear to be formed from a *single drop of water,* as it is found to be composed of *many small spherules* frozen together, the centre sometimes *soft* like snow, and at other times formed of a *hard nucleus,* which in some cases has been of a *brown* colour, capable of ignition and explosion. In the description given of snow, chap. xxxvii. 6, it has been stated that both *snow* and *hail* owe their formation to electricity; the hail being formed in the higher regions of the air, where the cold is intense, and the electric matter abundant. By this agency it is supposed that a great number of aqueous particles are brought together and frozen, and in their descent collect other particles, so that the *density* of the substance of the hailstone grows less and less from the centre, this being formed *first* in the higher regions, and the surface being collected in the lower. This theory is not in all cases supported by fact, as in some instances the *centre* has been found *soft* and *snow-like,* when the *surface* has been *hard.*

Hail is the only meteor of this kind, from which no apparent good is derived. *Rain* and *dew* invigorate and give life to the whole vegetable world; *frost,* by expanding the water contained in the earth, pulverizes and renders the soil fertile; *snow* covers and defends vegetables from being destroyed by too severe a frost; but *hail* does none of these. It not only does *no good,* but often *much harm*—always

A. M. cir. 2484
B. C. cir. 1520
Ante I. Olymp.
cir. 744
Ante U. C. cir.
767

23 ˢWhich I have reserved against the time of trouble, against the day of battle and war?

24 By what way is the light parted, *which* scattereth the east wind upon the earth?

25 Who ᵃhath divided a water-course for

the overflowing of waters, or a way for the lightning of thunder;

A. M. cir. 2484
B. C. cir. 1520
Ante I. Olymp.
cir. 744
Ante U. C. cir.
767

26 To cause it to rain on the earth, *where* no man *is; on* the wilderness, wherein *there is* no man;

27 ᵇTo satisfy the desolate and waste

ˢExod. ix. 18; Josh. x. 11; Isa. xxx. 30; Ezek. xiii. 11, 13; Rev. xvi. 21——ᵃChap. xxviii. 26——ᵇPsa. cvii. 35

---

some. It has a chilling, blasting effect in spring and summer, and cuts the tender plants so as to injure or totally destroy them. In short, the *treasures* of hail are not well known; and its *use* in the creation has not yet been ascertained. But *frost* is God's universal *plough*, by which he cultivates the whole earth.

Verse 23. *Reserved against the time of trouble*] צָר לְעֵת *leeth tsar,* "to the season of strictness," i. e., the season when the earth is *constringed* or *bound* by the frost.

Against the day of battle and war?] Hailstones being often employed as instruments of God's displeasure against his enemies, and the enemies of his people. There is probably an allusion here to the *plague of hail* sent on the Egyptians. See Exod. ix. 23, and the notes there, for more particulars concerning *hailstones*, remarkable showers of them, &c. There may be also a reference to Josh. x. 10, 11, where a destructive shower of what are called *hailstones* fell upon the Canaanitish kings who fought against Israel. See the note there also.

Verse 24. *By what way is the light parted*] Who can accurately describe the *cause* and *operation* of a *thunder cloud*, the cause, nature, and mode of operation of the *lightning* itself? Is it a *simple element* or *compound substance?* What is its *velocity?* and why not *conductible* by *every kind* of *substance*, as it is known to exist in *all*, and, indeed, to be diffused through every portion of nature? How *is it parted?* How does it take its *zigzag* form? This is the curious, indescribable, and unknown *parting*. Are all the *causes* of *positive* and *negative* electricity found out? What are *its particles*, and how do they *cohere*, and in what *order* are they propagated? Much has been said on all these points, and how little of that much satisfactorily!

Scattereth the east wind upon the earth?] קָדִים *kadim,* the *eastern storm, euroclydon,* or *levanter.*

Verse 25. *Divided a water-course*] The original תְּעָלָה *tealah,* from עָלָה *alah, to ascend,* may signify rather a *cloud*, or *clouds* in general, where the waters are *stored up.* I cannot see how the *overflowings* or *torrents* of water can be said to *ascend* any other way than by *evaporation;* and it is by this Divine contrivance that the earth is not only *irrigated*, but even *dried;* and by this means too much moisture is not permitted to lie upon the ground, which would not only be injurious to vegetation, but even destroy it. But *query*, may not a *waterspout* be intended?

A way for the lightning of thunder] "A path for the bolt of thunder." God is represented as directing the course even of the *lightning;* he launches the bolt, and makes the

path in which it is to run. To grasp, manage, and dart the thunderbolt or lightning, was a work which heathenism gave to Jupiter, its supreme god. None of the inferior deities were capable of this. But who can thunder with a voice like the Almighty? He is THE THUNDERER.

Verse 26. *To cause it to rain on the earth*] It is well known that *rain* falls copiously in thunder-storms. The *flash* is first seen, the *clap* is next heard, and last the *rain* descends. The *lightning* travels all lengths in no perceivable *succession* of time. *Sound* is propagated at the rate of 1142 feet in a second. *Rain* travels still more slowly, and will be seen *sooner* or *later* according to the weight of the drops, and the *distance* of the cloud from the place of the spectator. Now the *flash*, the *clap*, and the *rain*, take place all in the same moment, but are discernible by us in the *succession* already mentioned, and for the reasons given above; and more at large in the note on chap. xxxvi. 29, &c.

But how are these things formed? The *lightning* is represented as coming immediately from the hand of God. The *clap* is the effect of the *lightning*, which causes a vacuum in that part of the atmosphere through which it passes; the air rushing in to restore the equilibrium may cause much of the noise that is heard in the clap. An easy experiment on the airpump illustrates this: Take a glass receiver open at both ends, over one end tie a piece of sheep's bladder wet, and let it stand till thoroughly dry. Then place the open end on the plate of the airpump, and exhaust the air slowly from under it. The bladder soon becomes *concave*, owing to the pressure of the atmospheric air on it, the supporting air in the receiver being partly thrown out. Carry on the exhaustion, and the air presses at the rate of *fifteen pounds* on every square inch; see on chap. xxviii. The fibres of the bladder, being no longer capable of bearing the pressure of the atmospheric column upon the receiver, are torn to pieces, with a noise equal to the report of a musket, which is occasioned by the air rushing in to restore the equilibrium. Imagine a rapid succession of such experiments, and you have the *peal* of thunder, the rupture of the first bladder being the *clap*. But the *explosion* of the gases (oxygen and hydrogen) of which water is composed will also account for the noise. See below.

But how does the thunder cause rain? By the most accurate and incontestable experiments it is proved that *water* is a composition of *two elastic airs* or *gases* as they are called, *oxygen* and *hydrogen*. In 100 parts of water there are 88¼ of *oxygen*, and 11¾ of *hydrogen*. Pass a succession of electric sparks through

A. M. cir. 2484
B. C. cir. 1520
Ante I. Olymp.
cir. 744
Ante U. C. cir.
767
ground; and to cause the bud of the tender herb to spring forth? 28 ^cHath the rain a father? or who hath begotten the drops of dew?

29 Out of whose womb came the ice? and the ^dhoary frost of heaven, who hath gendered it?

30 The waters are hid as *with* a stone, and the face of the deep ^eis ^ffrozen.

A. M. cir. 2484
B. C. cir. 1520
Ante I. Olymp.
cir. 744
Ante U. C. cir.
767

---

^cJer. xiv. 22; Psa. cxlvii. 8——^dPsa. cxlvii. 16

^eHeb. *is taken*——^fChap. xxxvii. 10

---

water by means of a proper apparatus, and the two gases are produced in the proportions mentioned above.

To decompose water by *galvanism:*—Take a narrow glass tube *three* or *four inches* long; fit *each* end with a cork penetrated by a piece of slender iron wire, and fill the tube with water. Let the ends of the two wires within the tube be distant from each other about *three quarters of an inch,* and let one be made to communicate with the *top,* the other with the bottom of a *galvanic pile* in action. On making this communication, bubbles of air will be formed, and ascend to the top of the tube, the water decreasing as it is decomposed.

The oxygen and hydrogen formed by this experiment may be *recomposed* into the same weight of *water.* Take any quantity of the oxygen and hydrogen gases in the proportions already mentioned; ignite them by the electric spark, and they produce a quantity of *water* equal in weight to the gases employed. Thus, then, we can convert *water* into air, and reconvert this air into water; and the proportions hold as above. I have repeatedly seen this done, and assisted in doing it, but cannot, in this place, describe every thing in detail.

Now to the purpose of this note: the *rain* descending after the *flash* and the *peal.* The electric spark or matter of lightning, passing through the atmosphere, ignites and decomposes the *oxygen* and *hydrogen,* which *explode,* and the *water* which was formed of these two falls down in the form of *rain.* The explosion of the gases, as well as the rushing in of the circumambient air to restore the equilibrium, will account for the *clap* and *peal:* as the *decomposition* and *ignition* of them will account for the *water* or *rain* which is the attendant of a thunder storm. Thus by the *lightning of thunder* God *causes it to rain on the earth.* How marvellous and instructive are his ways!

Verse 27. *To satisfy the desolate and waste*] The thunder cloud not only explodes over *inhabited* countries, that the air may be purified, and the rain sent down to fertilize the earth, but it is conducted over *deserts* where there is no human inhabitant; and this to *cause the bud of the tender herb to spring forth:* for there are beasts, fowls, and insects, that inhabit the desert and the wilderness, and must be nourished by the productions of the ground. Every tribe of animals was made by the hand of God, and even the lowest of them is supported by his kind providence.

Verse 28. *Hath the rain a father?*] Or, *Who is the father of the rain?* We have seen above one part of the apparatus by which God produces it; other causes have been mentioned on chap. xxxvi. 27, &c.

The drops of dew?] אגלי *egley,* the sphericles, the small round drops or *globules. Dew* is a dense moist vapour, found on the earth in spring and summer mornings, in the form of a mizzling rain. Dr. *Hutton* defines it, "a thin, light, insensible mist or rain, descending with

a slow motion, and falling while the sun is below the horizon. It appears to differ from *rain* as *less* from *more.* Its origin and matter are doubtless from the *vapours* and *exhalations* that rise from the earth and water." Various experiments have been instituted to ascertain whether dew *arises* from the *earth,* or *descends* from the *atmosphere;* and those *pro* and *con* have alternately *preponderated.* The question is not yet decided; and we cannot yet tell any more than Job *which hath begotten* the *drops of dew,* the *atmosphere* or the *earth.* Is it *water* deposited from the atmosphere, *when the surface of the ground is colder than the air?*

Verse 29. *Out of whose womb came the ice?*] ICE is a solid, transparent, and brittle body, formed of water by means of cold. Some philosophers suppose that ice is only the re-establishment of water in its *natural state;* that the mere absence of *fire* is sufficient to account for this re-establishment; and that the *fluidity of water* is a *real fusion,* like that of *metals* exposed to the action of *fire;* and differing only in this, that a greater portion of fire is necessary to one than the other. *Ice,* therefore, is supposed to be the *natural state of water;* so that in its natural state water is *solid,* and becomes fluid only by the action of fire, as solid metallic bodies are brought into a state of fusion by the same means.

Ice is *lighter* than water, its specific gravity being to that of water as *eight* to *nine.* This *rarefaction* of ice is supposed to be owing to the *air-bubbles* produced in water by *freezing,* and which, being considerably larger in proportion to the water frozen, render the body so much specifically lighter; hence *ice* always *floats* on water. The air-bubbles, during their production, acquire a great expansive power, so as to burst the containing vessels, be they ever so strong. See examples in the note on chap. xxxvii. 10.

The hoary frost of heaven, who hath gendered it?] *Hoar-frost* is the congelation of *dew,* in frosty mornings, on the grass. It consists of an assemblage of little crystals of ice, which are of various figures, according to the different disposition of the vapours when met and condensed by the cold. Its production is owing to some laws with which we are not yet acquainted. Of this subject, after the lapse and experience of between *two* and *three* thousand years, we know about as much as Job did. And the question, *What hath engendered the hoar-frost of heaven?* is, to this hour, nearly as inexplicable to *us* as it was to *him!* Is it enough to say that hoar-frost is water deposited from the atmosphere at a low temperature, so as to produce *congelation?*

Verse 30. *The waters are hid as* with *a stone*] Here is a reference to *freezing* in the winter, as we may learn from some of the constellations mentioned below, which arise above our horizon, in the winter months.

The word יתחבאו *yithchabbau* is understood by the versions in general as implying *harden-*

A. M. cir. 2484
B. C. cir. 1520
Ante I. Olymp.
cir. 744
Ante U. C. cir.
767

31 Canst thou bind the sweet influences of[g] [h]Pleiades, [i]or loose the bands of [k]Orion?

32 Canst thou bring forth [l]Mazzaroth in his season? or canst thou [m]guide Arcturus with his sons?

33 Knowest thou [n]the ordinances of heaven? canst thou set the dominion thereof in the earth?

34 Canst thou lift up thy voice to the clouds, that abundance of waters may cover thee?

A. M. cir. 2484
B. C. cir. 1520
Ante I. Olymp.
cir. 744
Ante U. C. cir.
767

35 Canst thou send lightnings, that they may go, and say unto thee, [o]Here we *are?*

36 [p]Who hath put wisdom in the inward parts? or who hath given understanding to the heart?

---

[g]Chap. ix. 9; Amos v. 8——[h]Or, *the seven stars*——[i]Heb.
Cimah——[k]Heb. *Cesil*——[l]Or, *the twelve signs*

[m]Heb. *guide them*——[n]Jer. xxxi. 35——[o]Heb. *Behold us*
[p]Chap. xxxii. 8; Psa. li. 6; Eccles. ii. 26

---

ing or *congelation;* and we know in some intense frosts the ice becomes as *hard as a stone;* and even the *face of the deep*—the very *seas* themselves, not only in the polar circles, but even in northern countries, *Norway, Sweden, Denmark, Holland,* and parts of *Germany,* are really frozen, and locked up from all the purposes of navigation for several months in winter.

Verse 31. *Canst thou bind the sweet influences of Pleiades*] The *Pleiades* are a constellation in the sign *Taurus.* They consist of *six stars* visible to the naked eye; to a good eye, in a clear night, *seven* are discernible; but with a *telescope* ten times the number may be readily counted. They make their appearance in the *spring. Orion* may be seen in the morning, towards the end of *October,* and is visible through *November, December,* and *January;* and hence, says Mr. *Good,* it becomes a correct and elegant synecdoche for the winter at large. The *Pleiades* are elegantly opposed to *Orion,* as the *vernal* renovation of nature is opposed to its *wintry* destruction; the mild and open benignity of *spring,* to the severe and icy inactivity of *winter.*

I have already expressed my mind on these supposed constellations, and must refer to my notes on chap. ix. 9, &c., and to the learned notes of Doctor *Hales* and Mr. *Mason Good* on these texts. They appear certain, where I am obliged to doubt; and, from their view of the subject, make very useful and important deductions. I find reluctance in departing from the ancient versions. In this case, these learned men follow them; I cannot, because I do not see the evidence of the groundwork; and I dare not draw conclusions from premises which seem to me precarious, or which I do not understand. I wish, therefore, the reader to examine and judge for himself.

Coverdale renders the 31st and 32d verses thus:

𝕳ast thou brought the 𝖁𝕴𝕴 starres together? 𝕺r, 𝕬rt thou able to breake the circle of heaven? 𝕮anst thou bringe forth the mornynge starre, or the evenynge starre, at convenient tyme, and conveye them home agayne?

Verse 32. *Mazzaroth in his season?*] This is generally understood to mean the *signs of the zodiac.* מזרות *Mazzaroth,* according to Parkhurst, comes from מזר *mazar,* to *corrupt;* and he supposes it to mean that *pestilential* wind in Arabia, called *simoom,* the *season* of which is the *summer heats.*

Verse 33. *Knowest thou the ordinances of heaven?*] Art thou a thorough astronomer? Art thou acquainted with all the laws of the plane-

tary system? Canst thou account for the difference of their motions, and the influence by which they are retained and revolve in their o, bits? And canst thou tell what influence or *dominion* they exercise *on the earth?* Sir Isaac Newton has given us much light on many of these things; but to his system, which is most probably the true one, *gravity* is essential; and yet what this *gravity* is he could neither explain nor comprehend; and his followers are not one whit wiser than he. No man has ever yet fully *found out the ordinances of heaven, and the dominion thereof on the earth.*

Verse 34. *Canst thou lift up thy voice to the clouds*] Canst thou produce *lightning* and *thunder,* that water may be formed, and poured down upon the earth?

Thunder is called קלות *koloth,* voices; for it is considered the voice of God: here then *Job's voice,* קולך *kolecha,* is opposed to the *voice of* JEHOVAH!

Verse 35. *Canst thou send lightnings*] We have already seen that the lightning is supposed to be immediately in the *hand* and under th *management* of God. The great god of the heathen, *Jupiter Brontes,* is represented with the forked lightnings and thunderbolt in his hand. He seems so to grasp the bickering flame that, though it struggles for liberty, it cannot escape from his hold. *Lightnings*—How much like the sound of thunder is the original word: ברקים *Berakim!* Here are both *sense* and *sound.*

Here we are?] Will the winged lightnings be thy messengers, as they are mine?

Verse 36. *Who hath put wisdom in the inward parts?*] Who has given לשכוי *lasechvi,* to the *contemplative* person, *understanding?* Even the most sedulous attention to a subject, and the deepest contemplation, are not sufficient to investigate truth, without the inspiration of the Almighty, which alone can give understanding. But who has given man the *power* to conceive and understand? A power which he knows he has, but which he cannot comprehend. Man knows nothing of his own *mind,* nor of the *mode* of its *operations.* This mind we possess, these operations we perform;—and of either do we know any thing? If we know not *our own spirit,* how can we comprehend that SPIRIT which is *infinite* and *eternal?*

Mr. *Good* thinks that this verse is a continuation of the subject above, relative to the *lightnings,* and therefore translates thus:—

Who putteth understanding into the vollies?
And who giveth to the shafts discernment?

A. M. cir. 2484
B. C. cir. 1520
Ante I. Olymp.
cir. 744
Ante U. C. cir.
767

37 Who can number the clouds in wisdom? or [q]who can stay the bottles of heaven,

38 [r]When the dust[s]groweth into hardness, and the clods cleave fast together?

39 [t]Wilt thou hunt the prey for the lion? or fill [u]the appetite of the young lions,

40 When they [v]couch in *their* dens, *and* abide in the covert to lie in wait?

A. M. cir. 2484
B. C. cir. 1520
Ante I. Olymp.
cir. 744
Ante U. C. cir.
767

41 [w]Who provideth for the raven his food? when his young ones cry unto God, they wander for lack of meat.

---

[q]Heb. *who can cause to lie down*——[r]Or, *When the dust is turned into mire*——[s]Heb. *is poured*

[t]Psa. civ. 21; cxlv. 15——[u]Heb. *the life*——[v]Gen. xlix. 9
[w]Psa. cxlvii. 9; Matt. vi. 26

All the *versions*, except the *Septuagint*, which trifles here, understand the place as we do. Either makes a good sense. The *Septuagint* has, "Who hath given the knowledge of weaving to women; or the science of embroidery?" Instead of *understanding to the heart*, the *Vulgate* has, *understanding to the cock;* that it might be able to distinguish and proclaim the watches of the night.

Verse 37. *Who can number the clouds*] Perhaps the word ספר *saphar*, which is commonly rendered to *number*, may here mean, as in Arabic, to *irradiate*, as Mr. *Good* contends; and may refer to those celestial and inimitable tinges which we sometimes behold in the sky.

Bottles of heaven] The clouds: it is an allusion to the *girbahs*, or bottles made of skin, in which they are accustomed to carry their water from *wells* and *tanks*.

Verse 38. *When the dust groweth into hardness*] That is, Who knows how the *dust*—the *elementary particles* of matter, were concreted; and how the *clods*—the several parts of the earth, continue to cohere? What is the principle of *cohesion* among the different particles of matter, in all *metals* and *minerals?* Even *water*, in a solid form, constitutes a part of several gems, called thence *water of crystallization*. Who can solve this question? How is it that 90 parts of *alumine*, 7 of *silex*, and 1.2 of *oxide* of *iron*, constitute the *oriental ruby?* and that 90 parts of *silex*, and 19 of *water*, form the *precious opal?* And how can 46 parts of *silex*, 14 of *alumine*, 28 of *carbonate of lime*, 6.5 of *sulphate of lime*, 3 of *oxide of iron*, and 2 of *water*, enter into the constitution, and form the substance, of the *lapis lazuli?* How do these solids and fluids of such differing natures *grow into hardness*, and form this curious mineral?

Take another example from that beautiful precious stone, the emerald. Its analysis shows it to be composed of *glucine* 13, *silex* 64.5, *alumine* 16, *lime* 1.6, and *oxide of chrome* 3.25. Now how can these *dusts*, utterly worthless in themselves, *grow into hardness*, combine, and form one of the most beautiful, and, next to the *diamond*, the most precious, of all the *gems?* The almighty and infinitely wise God has done this in a way only known to and comprehensible by himself.

Verse 39. *Wilt thou hunt the prey for the lion?*] Rather the *lioness*, or *strong lion*. Hast thou his instinct? Dost thou know the *habits* and *haunts* of such animals as he seeks for his food? Thou hast neither his *strength*, his *instinct* nor his *cunning*.

In the best Hebrew Bibles, the *thirty-ninth* chapter begins with this verse, and begins properly, as a new subject now commences, relating to the *natural history* of the *earth*, or

the animal kingdom; as the preceding chapter does to *astronomy* and *meteorology*.

Verse 40. *When they couch in* their *dens*] Before they are capable of trusting themselves abroad.

Abide in the covert] Before they are able to hunt down the prey by running. It is a fact that the *young lions*, before they have acquired sufficient strength and swiftness, *lie under cover*, in order to surprise those animals which they have not fleetness enough to overtake in the forest; and from this circumstance the כפירים *kephirim*, "young lions, or lions' whelps," have their name: the root is כפר *caphar*, to *cover* or *hide*. See the note on chap. iv. 11, where *six* different names are given to the lion, all expressing some distinct quality or state.

Verse 41. *Who provideth for the raven*] This bird is chosen, perhaps, for his voracious appetite, and general hunger for prey, beyond most other fowls. He makes a continual cry, and the cry is that of hunger. He dares not frequent the habitations of men, as he is considered a bird of ill omen, and hated by all. This verse is finely paraphrased by Dr. YOUNG:—

"Fond man! the vision of a moment made!
Dream of a dream, and shadow of a shade!
What worlds hast thou produced, what creatures framed,
What insects cherish'd, that thy God is blamed?
When pain'd with hunger, the wild *raven's* brood
Calls upon God, importunate for food,
Who hears their cry? Who grants their hoarse request,
And stills the clamours of the craving nest?"

On which he has this note:—"The reason given why the raven is particularly mentioned as the care of Providence is, because by her *clamorous* and *importunate voice* she particularly seems always calling upon it; thence κορασσω, α κοραξ, is *to ask earnestly.*—*Ælian.* lib. ii., c. 48. And since there were ravens on the banks of the Nile, more clamorous than the rest of that species, those probably are meant in this place."

THE commencement of Cicero's oration against Catiline, to which I have referred on ver. 3, is the following:—

Quousque tandem abutere, Catilina, patientia **nostra?** Quamdiu etiam furor iste tuus nos eludet? Quem ad finem sese effrenata jactabit audacia? Nihilne te nocturnum præsidium palatii,—nihil urbis vigiliæ,—nihil timor populi,—nihil concursus bonorum omnium,—nihil hic munitissimus habendi senatus locus—nihil horum ora, vultusque moverunt? Patere tua consilia non sentis? Constrictam jam omnium horum conscientia teneri conjurationem tuam non vides? Quid proxima, quid superiore nocte egeris,—ubi fueris,—quos convocaveris,—quid consilii ceperis, quem nostrum ignorare arbitraris? O tempora! O mores! Senatus hæc intelligit,—consul videt; hic tamen vivit! Vivit? immo vero eitam in senatum venit; fit publici consilii particeps; notat et designat oculis ad cædem unumquemque nostrum! Nos autem, viri fortes, satisfacere reipublicæ videmur, si istius furorem ac tela vitemus!

"How long wilt thou, O Catiline, abuse our patience? How long shall thy madness outbrave our justice? To what extremities art thou resolved to push thy unbridled insolence of guilt? Canst thou behold the nocturnal arms that watch the palatium,—the guards of the city,—the consternation of the citizens,—all the wise and worthy clustering into consultation,—the impregnable situation of the seat of the senate,—and the reproachful looks of the fathers of Rome? Canst thou behold all this, and yet remain undaunted and unabashed? Art thou insensible that thy measures are detected? Art thou insensible that this senate, now thoroughly informed, comprehend the whole extent of thy guilt? Show me the senator ignorant of thy practices during the last and preceding night, of the place where you met, the company you summoned, and the crime you concerted. The senate is conscious,—the consul is witness to all this; yet, O how mean and degenerate! the traitor lives! Lives? he mixes with the senate; he shares in our counsels; with a steady eye he surveys us; he anticipates his guilt; he enjoys the murderous thought, and coolly marks us to bleed! Yet we, boldly passive in our country's cause, think we act like Romans, if we can escape his frantic rage!"

The reader will perceive how finely Cicero rushes into this invective, as if the danger had been too immediate to give him leisure for the formality of address and introduction. See *Guthrie's* Orations of Cicero.

Here is eloquence! Here is nature! And in thus speaking her language, the true orator pierces with his lightnings the deepest recesses of the heart. The success of this species of oratory is infallible in the *pulpit*, when the preacher understands how to manage it.

CHAPTER XXXIX

Several animals described: the wild goats and hinds, 1–4. The wild ass, 5–8. The unicorn, 9–12. The peacock and ostrich, 13–18. The war-horse, 19–25. The hawk, 26. And the eagle and her brood, 27–30.

A. M. cir. 2484
B. C. cir. 1520
Ante I. Olymp. cir. 744
Ante U. C. cir. 767

KNOWEST thou the time when the wild goats of the [a]rock bring forth? *or* canst thou mark when [b]the hinds do calve?

2 Canst thou number the months *that* they fulfil? or knowest thou the time when they bring forth?

A. M. cir. 2484
B. C. cir. 1520
Ante I. Olymp. cir. 744
Ante U. C. cir. 767

---

[a]1 Sam. xxiv. 2; Psa. civ. 18

[b]Psa. xxix. 9

NOTES ON CHAP. XXXIX

Verse 1. *Knowest thou the time*] To know *time*, &c., only, was easy, and has nothing extraordinary in it; but the meaning of these questions is, to know the *circumstances*, which have something peculiarly expressive of God's providence, and make the questions proper in this place. *Pliny* observes, that the *hind* with young is by instinct directed to a certain herb, named *seselis*, which facilitates the birth. *Thunder*, also, which looks like the more immediate hand of Providence, has the same effect. Psa. xxix. 9: "The VOICE of the Lord maketh the HINDS to CALVE." See Dr. YOUNG. What is called the *wild goat*, יעל *yael*, from עלה *alah, to ascend, go* or *mount up*, is generally understood to be the *ibex* or *mountain goat*, called *yael*, from the wonderful manner in which it *mounts* to the *tops* of the *highest* rocks. It is certain, says *Johnston*, there is no crag of the mountains so *high, prominent* or *steep*, but this animal will *mount* it in a number of *leaps*, provided only it be rough, and have protuberances large enough to receive its hoofs in leaping. This animal is indigenous to Arabia, is of amazing strength and agility, and considerably larger than the common goat. Its *horns* are very long, and often bend back over the whole body of the animal; and it is said to throw itself from the tops of rocks or towers, and light upon its horns, without receiving any damage. It goes five months with young.

When the hinds do calve?] The *hind* is the *female* of the *stag*, or *cervus elaphus*, and goes *eight months* with young. They live to *thirty-five* or *forty* years. Incredible *longevity* has been attributed to some stags. One was taken by Charles VI., in the forest of Senlis, about whose neck was a collar with this inscription, *Cæsar hoc mihi donavit*, which led some to believe that this animal had lived from the days of some one of the *twelve Cæsars*, emperors of Rome.

I have seen the following form of this inscription:

Tempore quo Cæsar Roma dominatus in alta
Aureolo jussit collum signare monili;
Ne depascentem quisquis me gramina lædat.
Cæsaris heu! caussa perituræ parcere vitæ!

Which has been long public in the old English ballad strain, thus:—

"When Julius Cæsar reigned king,
About my neck he put this ring;
That whosoever should me take
Would save my life for Cæsar's sake."

A. M. cir. 2484
B. C. cir. 1520
Ante I. Olymp.
cir. 744
Ante U. C. cir.
767

3 They bow themselves, they bring forth their young ones, they cast out their sorrows.

4 Their young ones are in good liking, they grow up with corn; they go forth, and return not unto them.

5 Who hath sent out the wild ass free? or who hath loosed the bands of the wild ass?

6 °Whose house I have made the wilderness, and the ᵈbarren land his dwellings.

7 He scorneth the multitude of the city,

neither regardeth he the crying ᵉof the driver.

8 The range of the mountains *is* his pasture, and he searcheth after every green thing.

9 Will the ᶠunicorn be willing to serve thee, or abide by thy crib?

10 Canst thou bind the unicorn with his band in the furrow? or will he harrow the valleys after thee?

11 Wilt thou trust him, because his strength

A. M. cir. 2484
B. C. cir. 1520
Ante I. Olymp.
cir. 744
Ante U. C. cir.
767

°Chap. xxiv. 5; Jeremiah ii. 24; Hos. viii. 9——ᵈHeb. *salt places*

ᵉHeb. *of the exactor*, chap. iii. 18——ᶠNum. xxiii. 22; Deut. xxxiii. 17

Aristotle mentions the longevity of the stag, but thinks it *fabulous*.

Verse 3. *They bow themselves*] In order to bring forth their young ones.

They cast out their sorrows.] חבליהם *chebleyhem;* the *placenta, afterbirth,* or umbilical cord. So this word has been understood.

Verse 4. *In good liking*] After the fawns have sucked for some time, the dam leads them to the pastures, where they feed on different kinds of herbage; but not *on corn*, for they are not born before harvest-time in Arabia and Palestine, and the stag does not feed on corn, but on grass, moss, and the shoots of the *fir, beech,* and other trees: therefore the word בר *bar,* here translated *corn,* should be translated the *open field* or *country.* See *Parkhurst. Their nurslings bound away.*—Mr. *Good.* In a short time they become independent of the mother, leave her, *and return no more.* The spirit of the *questions* in these verses appears to be the following:—Understandest thou the cause of breeding of the mountain goats, &c.? Art thou acquainted with the course and progress of the parturition, and the manner in which the bones grow, and acquire solidity in the womb? See Mr. *Good's* observations.

Houbigant's version appears very correct: (Knowest thou) "how their young ones grow up, increase in the fields, and once departing, return to them no more?"

Verse 5. *Who hath sent out the wild ass free?*] פרא *pere,* which we translate *wild ass,* is the same as the ονος αγριος of the Greeks, and the *onager* of the Latins; which must not, says *Buffon,* be confounded with the *zebra,* for this is an animal of a different species from the *ass.* The *wild ass* is not *striped* like the *zebra,* nor so elegantly shaped. There are many of those animals in the deserts of Libya and Numidia: they are of a gray colour; and run so swiftly that no horse but the Arab *barbs* can overtake them. *Wild asses* are found in considerable numbers in East and South Tartary, in Persia, Syria, the islands of the Archipelago, and throughout Mauritania. They differ from *tame* asses only in their independence and liberty, and in their being stronger and more nimble: but in their shape they are the same. See on chap. vi. 5.

The bands of the wild ass?] ערוד *arod,* the *brayer,* the same animal, but called thus because of the frequent and peculiar noise he makes. But Mr. *Good* supposes this to be ⸱ different

animal from the wild ass, (the *jichta* or *equus hemionus,*) which is distinguished by having solid hoofs, a uniform colour, no cross on the back, and the tail hairy only at the tip. The ears and tail resemble those of the *zebra;* the hoofs and body, those of the *ass;* and the limbs, those of the *horse.* It inhabits Arabia, China, Siberia, and Tartary, in grassy *saline plains* or *salt wastes,* as mentioned in the following verse.

Verse 6. *Whose house*] Habitation, or place of resort.

The barren land] מלחה *melechah,* the *salt land,* or *salt places,* as in the margin. See above.

Verse 7. *He scorneth the multitude*] He is so swift that he cannot be run or hunted down. See the description in ver. 5.

Verse 8. *The range of the mountains*] The mountains and desert places are his peculiar places of pasture; and he lives on any thing that is *green,* or any kind of *vegetable* production.

Verse 9. *Will the unicorn be willing to serve thee?*] The "fine elegant animal like a horse, with one long rich curled horn growing out of his forehead," commonly called the *unicorn,* must be given up as fabulous. The *heralds* must claim him as their own; place him in their armorial bearings as they please, to indicate the unreal actions, fictitious virtues, and unfought martial exploits of mispraised men. It is not to the honour of the royal arms of Great Britain that this fabulous animal should be one of their *supporters.*

The animal in question, called רים *reim,* is undoubtedly the *rhinoceros,* who has the latter name from the *horn* that grows on his *nose.* The rhinoceros is known by the name of *reim* in Arabia to the present day. He is allowed to be a savage animal, showing nothing of the intellect of the elephant. His *horn* enables him to combat the latter with great success; for, by putting his nose under the elephant's belly, he can rip him up. His *skin* is like armour, and so very hard as to resist sabres, javelins, lances, and even musket-balls; the only penetrable parts being the belly, the eyes, and about the ears.

Or abide by thy crib?] These and several of the following expressions are intended to point out his *savage, untameable* nature.

Verse 10. *Canst thou bind the unicorn—in the furrow?*] He will not plough, nor draw in the yoke *with another?* nor canst thou use him singly, to harrow the ground.

A. M. cir. 2484
B. C. cir. 1520
Ante I. Olymp.
cir. 744
Ante U. C. cir.
767

is great? or wilt thou leave thy labour to him?

12 Wilt thou believe him, that he will bring home thy seed, and gather *it into* thy barn?

13 *Gavest thou* the goodly wings unto the peacocks? or [g]wings and feathers unto the ostrich?

14 Which leaveth her eggs in the earth,

and warmeth them in the dust,

A. M. cir. 2484
B. C. cir. 1520
Ante I. Olymp.
cir. 744
Ante U. C. cir.
767

15 And forgetteth that the foot may crush them, or that the wild beast may break them.

16 She is [h]hardened against her young ones, as though *they were* not hers: her [i]labour is in vain without fear;

17 Because God hath deprived her of wis-

---

[g]Or, *the feathers of the stork and ostrich*

[h]Lam. iv. 3——[i]Ver. 17

Verse 12. *That he will bring home thy seed*]
Thou canst make no domestic nor agricultural use of him.

Verse 13. *The goodly wings unto the peacocks?*] I believe *peacocks* are not intended here; and the Hebrew word רננים *renanim* should be translated *ostriches;* and the term חסידה *chasidah*, which we translate *ostrich*, should be, as it is elsewhere translated, *stork;* and perhaps the word נצה *notsah*, rendered here *feathers*, should be translated *hawk*, or *pelican*.

The *Vulgate* has, *Penna struthionis similis est pennis herodii et accipitris;* "the feather of the ostrich is like to that of the stork and the hawk." The *Chaldee* has, "The wing of the wild cock, who crows and claps his wings, is like to the wing of the stork and the hawk." The *Septuagint*, not knowing what to make of these different terms, have left them all untranslated, so as to make a sentence without sense. Mr. *Good* has come nearest both to the *original* and to the meaning, by translating thus:—

"The wing of the ostrich tribe is for flapping;
But of the stork and falcon for flight."

Though the wings of the ostrich, says he, cannot raise it from the ground; yet by the motion here alluded to, by a *perpetual vibration*, or *flapping*—by perpetually catching or *drinking in* the wind, (as the term נעלסה *neelasah* implies, which we render *goodly*,) they give it a rapidity of running beyond that possessed by any other animal in the world. *Adanson* informs us, that when he was at the factory in Padore, he was in possession of two tame ostriches; and to try their strength, says he, "I made a full-grown negro mount the smallest, and two others the largest. This burden did not seem at all disproportioned to their strength. At first they went a pretty high trot; and, when they were heated a little, they expanded their wings, as if it were *to catch the wind*, and they moved with such fleetness as to seem to be off the ground. And I am satisfied that those ostriches would have distanced the fleetest race-horses that were ever bred in England."

As to נצה *notsah*, here translated *falcon*, Mr. *Good* observes, that the term ناز *naz* is used generally by the Arabian writers to signify both *falcon* and *hawk;* and there can be little doubt that such is the real meaning of the Hebrew word; and that it imports various species of the falcon family, as *jer-falcon*, *gos-hawk*, and *sparrow-hawk*.

"The argument drawn from natural history advances from *quadrupeds* to *birds;* and of

birds, those only are selected for description which are most common to the country in which the scene lies, and at the same time are most singular in their properties. Thus the *ostrich* is admirably contrasted with the *stork* and the *eagle*, as affording us an instance of a winged animal totally incapable of flight, but endued with an unrivalled rapidity of running, compared with birds whose flight is proverbially fleet, powerful, and persevering. Let man, in the pride of his wisdom, explain or arraign this difference of construction.

"Again, the *ostrich* is peculiarly opposed to the *stork* and to some species of the *eagle* in another sense, and a sense adverted to in the verses immediately ensuing; for the *ostrich* is well known to take *little* or *no care* of its *eggs*, or of its *young;* while the *stork* ever has been, and ever deserves to be, held in proverbial repute for its *parental tenderness*. The Hebrew word חסידה *chasidah*, imports kindness or affection; and our own term *stork*, if derived from the Greek στοργη, *storgé*, as some pretend, has the same original meaning."—GOOD'S JOB.

Verse 14. *Which leaveth her eggs in the earth*] This want of parental affection in the *ostrich* is almost universally acknowledged. Mr. *Jackson*, in his *Account of Morocco*, observes: "The ostrich, having laid her eggs, goes away, *forgetting* or *forsaking* them: and if some other ostrich discover them, she hatches them as if they were her own, *forgetting* probably whether they are or are not; so deficient is the recollection of this bird." This illustrates verse 15: "And forgetteth that the foot may crush them, or that the wild beast may break them." The poet seems well acquainted with every part of the subject on which he writes; and facts incontestable confirm all he says. For farther illustration, see the account from Dr. *Shaw* at the end of the chapter.

Verse 16. *She is hardened against her young*] See before, and the extracts from Dr. *Shaw* at the end of the chapter. She neglects her little ones, which are often found half starved, straggling, and moaning about, like so many deserted orphans, for their mother.

Verse 17. *God hath deprived her of wisdom*] Of this foolishness we have an account from the ancients; and here follow two instances: "1. It covers its head in the reeds, and thinks itself all out of sight because itself cannot see. So *Claudian:*—

——————'Stat lumine clauso
Ridendum revoluta caput: creditque latere
Quæ non ipsa videt.'

"2. They who hunt them draw the skin of an ostrich's neck on one hand, which proves a suffi-

A. M. cir. 2484
B. C. cir. 1520
Ante I. Olymp.
cir. 744
Ante U. C. cir.
767

dom, neither hath he [k]imparted to her understanding.

18 What time she lifteth up herself on high, she scorneth the horse and his rider.

19 Hast thou given the horse strength?

hast thou clothed his neck with thunder?

A. M. cir. 2484
B. C. cir. 1520
Ante I. Olymp.
cir. 744
Ante U. C. cir.
767

20 Canst thou make him afraid as a grasshopper? the glory of his nostrils [l]is terrible.

21 [m]He paweth in the valley, and rejoiceth

---

[k]Chap. xxxv. 11——[l]Heb. *terrors*

[m]Or, His feet *dig*

---

cient lure to take them with the other. They have so little brain that Heliogabalus had *six hundred* heads for his supper. Here we may observe, that our judicious as well as sublime author just touches the great points of distinction in each creature, and then hastens to another. A description is exact when you cannot add but what is common to another thing; nor withdraw, but something peculiarly belonging to the thing described. A likeness is lost in too much description, as a meaning is often in too much illustration."—Dr. YOUNG.

Verse 18. *She lifteth up herself*] *When she raiseth up herself to run away.* Proofs of the fleetness of this bird have already been given. It neither flies nor runs distinctly, but has a motion composed of both; and, using its wings as sails, makes great speed. So *Claudian:*—
Vasta velut Libyæ venantum vocibus ales
Cum premitur, calidas cursu transmittit arenas,
Inque modum veli sinuatis flamine pennis
Pulverulenta volat.

"*Xenophon* says, *Cyrus* had horses that could overtake the goat and the wild ass; but none that could reach this creature. A thousand golden ducats, or a *hundred* camels, was the stated price of a horse that could equal their speed."—Dr. YOUNG.

Verse 19. *Hast thou given the horse strength?*] Before I proceed to any observations, I shall give Mr. *Good's* version of this, perhaps inimitable, description:—

Ver. 19. Hast thou bestowed on the horse mettle?
     Hast thou clothed his neck with the thunder flash?
Ver. 20. Hast thou given him to launch forth as an arrow?
     Terrible is the pomp of his nostrils.
Ver. 21. He paweth in the valley, and exulteth.
     Boldly he advanceth against the clashing host:
Ver. 22. He mocketh at fear, and trembleth not:
     Nor turneth he back from the sword.
Ver. 23. Against him rattleth the quiver,
     The glittering spear, and the shield:
Ver. 24. With rage and fury he devoureth the ground;
     And is impatient when the trumpet soundeth.
Ver. 25. He exclaimeth among the trumpets, Aha!
     And scenteth the battle afar off,
     The thunder of the chieftains, and the shouting.

In the year 1713, a letter was sent to the GUARDIAN, which makes No. 86 of that work, containing a critique on this description, compared with similar descriptions of *Homer* and *Virgil*. I shall give the substance of it here:—
The great Creator, who accommodated himself to those to whom he vouchsafed to speak, hath put into the mouths of his prophets such sublime sentiments and exalted language as must abash the pride and wisdom of man. In the book of Job, the most ancient poem in the world, we have such paintings and descriptions as I have spoken of in great variety. I shall at present make some remarks on the celebrated description of the *horse*, in that holy book; and compare it with those drawn by *Homer* and *Virgil.*

Homer hath the following similitude of a *horse* twice over in the *Iliad*, which *Virgil* hath copied from him; at least he hath deviated less from *Homer* than Mr. *Dryden* hath from him:—

'Ως δ' ότε τις στατος ιππος, ακοστησας επι φατνη,
Δεσμον απορρηξας θειει πεδιοιο κροαινων,
Ειωθως λουεσθαι εϋρρειος ποταμοιο,
Κυδιοων· υψου δε καρη εχει, αμφι δε χαιται
Ωμοις αϊσσονται· ό δ' αγλαϊηφι πεποιθως
'Ριμφα έ γουνα φερει μετα τ' ηθεα και νομον ιππων.

HOM. Il. lib. vi., ver. 506; and lib. xv., ver. 263.

Freed from his keepers, thus with broken reins
The wanton courser prances o'er the plains,
Or in the pride of youth o'erleaps the mound,
And snuffs the female in forbidden ground;
Or seeks his watering in the well-known flood,
To quench his thirst, and cool his fiery blood;
He swims luxuriant in the liquid plain,
And o'er his shoulders flows his waving mane;
He neighs, he snorts, he bears his head on high;
Before his ample chest the frothy waters fly.

Virgil's description is much fuller than the foregoing, which, as I said, is only a simile; whereas *Virgil* professes to treat of the *nature* of the *horse:*—

—— Tum, si qua sonum procul arma dedere,
Stare loco nescit: micat auribus, et tremit artus
Collectumque premens volvit sub naribus ignem:
Densa juba, et dextro jactata recumbit in armo.
At duplex agitur per lumbos spina, cavatque
Tellurem, et solido graviter sonat ungula cornu.
VIRG. Georg. lib. iii., ver. 83.

Which is thus admirably translated:—

The fiery courser, when he hears from far
The sprightly trumpets, and the shouts of war,
Pricks up his ears; and, trembling with delight,
Shifts pace, and paws, and hopes the promised fight.
On his right shoulder his thick mane reclined,
Ruffles at speed, and dances in the wind.
His horny hoofs are jetty black and round;
His chin is double: starting with a bound,
He turns the turf, and shakes the solid ground.
Fire from his eyes, clouds from his nostrils flow;
He bears his rider headlong on the foe.

Now follows that in the *Book of Job*, which, under all the disadvantages of having been written in a language little understood, of being expressed in phrases peculiar to a part of

A. M. cir. 2484
B. C. cir. 1520
Ante I. Olymp.
cir. 744
Ante U. C. cir.
767

in *his* strength: [n]he goeth on to meet the °armed men.

22 He mocketh at fear, and is not affrighted: neither turneth he back from the sword.

---

[n]Jer. viii. 6

---

the world whose manner of thinking and speaking seems to us very uncouth; and, above all, of appearing in a *prose* translation; is nevertheless so transcendently above the heathen descriptions, that hereby we may perceive how faint and languid the images are which are formed by human authors, when compared with those which are figured, as it were, just as they appear in the eye of the Creator. God, speaking to Job, asks him:—

[To do our translators as much justice as possible, and to help the critic, I shall throw it in the hemistich form, in which it appears in the Hebrew, and in which all Hebrew poetry is written.]

Ver. 19. Hast thou given to the HORSE strength?
     Hast thou clothed his neck with thunder?

Ver. 20. Canst thou make him afraid as a grasshopper?
     The glory of his nostrils is terrible!

Ver. 21. He paweth in the valley, and rejoiceth in strength:
     He goeth on to meet the armed men.

Ver. 22. He mocketh at fear, and is not affrighted:
     Neither turneth he back from the sword.

Ver. 23. Against him rattleth the quiver,
     The glittering spear and the shield.

Ver. 24. He swalloweth the ground with rage and fierceness:
     Nor doth he believe that it is the sound of the trumpet.

Ver. 25. He saith among the trumpets, Heach!
     And from afar he scenteth the battle,
     The thunder of the captains, and the shouting.

Here are all the great and sprightly images that thought can form of this generous beast, expressed in such force and vigour of style as would have given the great wits of antiquity new laws for the sublime, had they been acquainted with these writings.

I cannot but particularly observe that whereas the classical poets chiefly endeavour to paint the *outward figure, lineaments, and motions,* the *sacred poet* makes all the beauties to flow from an *inward principle* in the creature he describes; and thereby gives great spirit and vivacity to his description. The following phrases and circumstances are singularly remarkable:—

Ver. 19. *Hast thou clothed his neck with thunder?*

Homer and *Virgil* mention nothing about the neck of the horse but his mane. The sacred author, by the bold figure of *thunder,* not only expresses the *shaking* of that remarkable beauty in the horse, and the *flakes of hair,* which naturally suggest the idea of *lightning;* but likewise the *violent agitation* and force of the neck, which in the oriental tongues had been

A. M. cir. 2484
B. C. cir. 1520
Ante I. Olymp.
cir. 744
Ante U. C. cir.
767

23 The quiver rattleth against him, the glittering spear and the shield.

24 He swalloweth the ground with fierceness and rage: neither believeth

---

°Heb. *the armour*

---

flatly expressed by a metaphor less bold than this.

Ver. 20. *Canst thou make him afraid as a grasshopper?*—There is a twofold beauty in this expression, which not only marks the courage of this beast, by asking if he can be *scared;* but likewise raises a noble image of his *swiftness,* by insinuating that, if he could be frightened, he would *bound away* with the *nimbleness* of a *grasshopper.*

The glory of his nostrils is terrible.] This is more strong and concise than that of Virgil, which yet is the noblest line that was ever written without inspiration:—

Collectumque premens volvit sub naribus ignem.

And in his nostrils rolls collected fire.
GEOR. iii., ver. 85.

Ver. 21. He rejoiceth in his strength.
Ver. 22. He mocketh at fear.
Ver. 24. Neither believeth he that it is the sound of the trumpet.
Ver. 25. He saith among the trumpets, Ha! ha!

These are signs of courage, as I said before, flowing from *an inward principle.* There is a peculiar beauty in his *not believing it is the sound of the trumpet:* that is, he cannot believe it for joy; but when he is sure of it, and is *among the trumpets,* he saith, Ha! ha! He neighs, he rejoices.

His docility is elegantly painted in his being *unmoved at the rattling quiver, the glittering spear, and the shield,* ver. 23, and is well imitated by Oppian,—who undoubtedly read Job, as Virgil did,—in his Poem on Hunting:—

Πως μεν γαρ τε μαχαισιν αρηϊος εκλυεν ἱππος
Ηχον εγερσιμοθον δολιχων πολεμηϊον αυλων;
Η πως αντα δεδορκεν ασκαρδαμυκτοισιν οπωπαις
Αιζηοισι λοχον πεπυκασμενον ὁπλιτῃσι;
Και χαλκον σελαγευντα, και αστραπτοντα σιδηρον;
Και μαθεν ευτε μενειν χρειω, ποτε δ' αυτις ορουειν.
OPPIAN CYNEGET, lib. i., ver. 206.

Now firm the managed war-horse keeps his ground,
Nor breaks his order though the trumpet sound!
With fearless eye the glittering host surveys,
And glares directly at the helmet's blaze.
The master's word, the laws of war, he knows;
And when to stop, and when to charge the foes.

He swalloweth the ground, ver. 24, is an expression for *prodigious swiftness* in use among the Arabians, Job's countrymen, to the present day. The Latins have something like it:—

Latumque fuga *consumere campum.*
NEMESIAN.

In flight the extended champaign to consume.

Carpere prata fuga.
VIRG. GEORG. iii., ver. 142.

In flight to crop the meads.

A. M. cir. 2484
B. C. cir. 1520
Ante I. Olymp.
cir. 744
Ante U. C. cir.
767
he that it is ᴾthe sound of the trumpet.

25 He saith among the trumpets, Ha, ha; and he smelleth

the battle afar off, the thunder of the captains, and the ۹shouting.

26 Doth the hawk fly by thy
A. M. cir. 2484
B. C. cir. 1520
Ante I. Olymp.
cir. 744
Ante U. C. cir.
767

ᴾ2 Sam. vi. 15; xv. 10

۹Amos i. 14

————Campumque volatu
Cum rapuere, pedum vestigia quæras.

When, in their flight, the champaign they have snatch'd,
No track is left behind.

It is indeed the boldest and noblest of images for swiftness; nor have I met with any thing that comes so near it as Mr. Pope's, in *Windsor Forest:*—

Th' impatient courser pants in every vein,
And pawing, seems to beat the distant plain;
Hills, vales, and floods, appear already cross'd;
And ere he starts, a thousand steps are lost.

He smelleth the battle afar off, and what follows about the *shouting,* is a circumstance expressed with great spirit by *Lucan:*—

So when the ring with joyful shouts resounds,
With rage and pride th' imprison'd courser bounds;
He frets, he foams, he rends his idle rein,
Springs o'er the fence, and headlong seeks the plain.

This judicious and excellent critique has left me little to say on this sublime description of the horse: I shall add some cursory notes only. In verse 19 we have the singular image, *clothed his neck with thunder.* How *thunder* and the *horse's neck* can be well assimilated to each other, I confess I cannot see. The author of the preceding critique seems to think that the principal part of the allusion belongs to the *shaking* of this remarkable beauty (the *mane*) in a horse; and the *flakes* of hair, which naturally suggest the idea of *lightning.* I am satisfied that the *floating mane* is here meant. The original is רעמה *ramah,* which *Bochart* and other learned men translate as above. How much the *mane* of a horse *shaking* and *waving* in the wind adds to his beauty and stateliness, every one is sensible; and the Greek and Latin poets, in their description of the horse, take notice of it. Thus Homer:—

———— Ἀμφι δε χαιται
Ὡμοις ἀἴσσονται.   ILIAD vi., ver. 509.

"His *mane dishevell'd* o'er his shoulders *flies.*"

And Virgil:—

Luduntque per colla, per armos.
ÆN. xi., ver. 497.

The verb רעם *raam* signifies to *toss,* to *agitate;* and may very properly be applied to the *mane,* for reasons obvious to all. *Virgil* has seized this characteristic in his fine line, Georg. iii. ver. 86:—

Densa juba, et dextro jactata recumbit in armo.

"His *toss'd* thick mane on his right shoulder falls."

Naturally, the horse is one of the most *timid* of animals; and this may be at once accounted for

from his *small quantity of brain.* Perhaps there is no animal of his size that has *so little.* He acquires *courage* only from *discipline;* for naturally he starts with terror and affright at any sudden noise. It requires much discipline to bring him to hear the *noise of drums* and *trumpets,* and especially to bear a pair of kettle drums placed on each side his neck, and beaten there, with the most alarming variety of sounds. Query, Does the sacred text allude to *any thing of this kind?* I have been led to form this thought from the following circumstance. In some ancient MSS. of the *Shah Nameh,* a most eminent heroic poem, by the poet *Ferdoosy,* the Homer of India, in my own collection, adorned with paintings, representing regal interviews, animals, battles, &c., there appear in some places representations of *elephants, horses,* and *camels,* with a pair of drums, something like our kettle drums, hanging on each side of the animal's neck, and beaten, by a person on the saddle, with two plectrums or drumsticks; the *neck* itself being literally *clothed* with the *drums* and the *housings* on which they are fixed. Who is it then that has *framed* the *disposition* of such a *timid* animal, that by proper *discipline* it can bear those *thundering* sounds, which at first would have scared it to the uttermost of distraction? The *capacity* to receive *discipline* and *instruction* is as great a *display* of the *wisdom* of God as the *formation* of the *bodies* of the largest, smallest, or most complex animals is of his *power.* I leave this observation without laying any stress upon it. On such difficult subjects *conjecture* has a lawful range.

Verse 21. *He paweth in the valley*] יחפרו *yachperu,* "they *dig* in the valley," i. e., in his violent galloping, in every pitch of his body, he scoops up sods out of the earth. *Virgil* has seized this idea also, in his *cavat tellurem;* "he scoops out the ground." See before.

Verse 25. *He saith among the trumpets, Ha, ha*] The original is peculiarly emphatical: האח *Heach!* a strong, partly *nasal,* partly *guttural* sound, exactly resembling the first note which the horse emits in *neighing.* The strong, guttural sounds in this hemistich are exceedingly expressive: האח ומרחק יריח מלחמה *Heach! umerachok yariach milchamah;* "Heach, for from afar he scenteth the battle."

The reader will perceive that Mr. *Good* has given a very different meaning to ver. 20 from that in the present text, *Canst thou make him afraid as a grasshopper?* by translating the Hebrew thus:—

"Hast thou given him to launch forth as an arrow?"

The word ארבה *arbeh,* which we translate *locust* or *grasshopper,* and which he derives from רבה *rabah,* the א *aleph* being merely formative, he says, "may as well mean an *arrow* as it does in chap. xvi. 13, רבין *rabbaiv,* 'His arrows fly around me.'" The verb רעש *raash* in the word התרעישנו *hatharishennu,* "Canst thou make him

A. M. cir. 2484
B. C. cir. 1520
Ante I. Olymp.
cir. 744
Ante U. C. cir.
767

wisdom, *and* stretch her wings toward the south?

27 Doth the eagle mount up ʳat thy command, and ˢmake her nest on high?

28 She dwelleth and abideth on the rock,

upon the crag of the rock, and the strong place.

29 From thence she seeketh ᵗthe prey, *and* her eyes behold afar off.

30 Her young ones also suck up blood: and ᵘwhere the slain *are,* there *is* she.

A. M. cir. 2484
B. C. cir. 1520
Ante I. Olymp.
cir. 744
Ante U. C. cir.
767

ʳHeb. *by thy mouth*——ˢJer. xlix. 16; Obad. 4

ᵗChap. ix. 26——ᵘMatt. xxiv. 28; Luke xvii. 37

---

afraid?" he contends, "signifies to *tremble, quiver, rush, launch, dart forth;* and, taken in this sense, it seems to unite the two ideas of *rapidity* and *coruscation.*" This is the *principal* alteration which this learned man has made in the text.

I shall conclude on this subject by giving *Coverdale's* translation: 𝔥𝔞𝔰𝔱 𝔱𝔥𝔬𝔲 𝔤𝔢𝔟𝔢𝔫 𝔱𝔥𝔢 𝔥𝔬𝔯𝔰𝔢 𝔥𝔦𝔰 𝔰𝔱𝔯𝔢𝔫𝔤𝔱𝔥, or lerned him to bow down his neck with feare; that he letteth himself be dryven forth like a greshopper, where as the stout nevenge that he maketh is fearfull? He breaketh the grounde with the hoffes of his fete chearfully in his strength, and runneth to mete the harnest men. He layeth aside all feare, his stomack is not abated, neither starteth he aback for eny swerde. Though the qvbers rattle upon him, though the speare and shilde glistre: yet russheth he in fearsley, and beateth upon the grounde. He feareth not the noise of the trompettes, but as soone as he heareth the shawmes blowe, Tush (sayeth he) for he smelleth the batell afarre of, the noyse, the captaynes, and the shoutinge. This is wonderfully nervous, and at the same time accurate.

Verse 26. Doth the hawk fly by thy wisdom] The *hawk* is called נץ *nets,* from its swiftness in darting down upon its prey; hence its *Latin* name, *nisus,* which is almost the same as the *Hebrew.* It may very probably mean the *falcon,* oberves Dr. *Shaw.* The flight of a strong falcon is wonderfully swift. A falcon belonging to the Duke of Cleves flew out of Westphalia into Prussia in one day; and in the county of Norfolk, a hawk has made a flight at a woodcock of near *thirty miles* in an *hour. Thuanus* says, "A hawk flew from London to Paris in one night." It was owing to its *swiftness* that the Egyptians in their hieroglyphics made it the emblem of the *wind.*

Stretch her wings toward the south?] Most of the *falcon* tribe pass their spring and summer in cold climates; and wing their way toward warmer regions on the approach of winter. This is what is here meant by *stretching her wings toward the south.* Is it through thy teaching that *this* or any other *bird of passage* knows the precise time for taking flight, and the direction in which she is to go in order to come to a warmer climate? There is much of the *wisdom* and *providence* of God to be seen in the migration of *birds of passage.* This has been remarked before. There is a beautiful passage in *Jeremiah,* chap. viii. 7, on the same subject: "The stork in the heavens knoweth her appointed times; and the turtle, and the crane, and the swallow, observe the time of their coming: but my people know not the judgment of the Lord."

Verse 27. Doth the eagle mount up] The eagle is said to be of so acute a sight, that when she is so high in the air that men cannot see her, she can discern a small fish in the water! See on ver. 29.

Verse 28. Upon the crag of the rock] שן סלע

shen sela, the *tooth of the rock,* i. e., some *projecting* part, whither *adventurous man* himself dares not follow her.

And the strong place.] ומצודה *umetsudah.* Mr. *Good* translates this word *ravine,* and joins it to ver. 29, thus: "And thence espieth the ravine: her eyes trace the prey afar off."

Verse 29. Her eyes behold afar off.] The *eagle* was proverbial for her strong and clear sight. So *Horace,* lib. i., sat. iii., ver 25:—

Cum tua pervideas oculis mala lippus inunctis,
Cur in amicorum vitiis tam cernis acutum,
Quam aut aquila, aut serpens Epidaurius?

"For wherefore while you carelessly pass by
Your own worst vices with unheeding eye,
Why so sharp-sighted in another's fame,
Strong as an *eagle's ken,* or dragon's beam?"
                        FRANCIS.

So *Ælian,* lib. i., cap. 42. And *Homer,* Iliad xvii., calls the eagle οξυτατον ὑπουρανιων πετεηνων, "The most quick-sighted of all fowls under heaven."

Verse 30. Her young ones also suck up blood] The eagle does not feed her young with *carrion,* but with prey *newly* slain, so that they may *suck up blood.*

Where the slain are, *there* is *she.*] These words are quoted by our Lord. "Wheresoever the carcass is, there will the eagles be gathered together," Matt. xxiv. 28. It is likely, however, that this was a proverbial mode of expression; and our Lord adapts it to the circumstances of the Jewish people, who were about to fall a prey to the Romans. See the notes there.

IN the preceding notes I have referred to Dr. *Shaw's* account of the *ostrich* as the most accurate and authentic yet published. With the following description I am sure every intelligent reader will be pleased.

"In commenting therefore upon these texts it may be observed, that when the *ostrich* is full grown, the neck, particularly of the male, which before was almost naked, is now very beautifully covered with red feathers. The plumage likewise upon the shoulders, the back, and some parts of the wings, from being hitherto of a dark grayish colour, becomes now as black as jet, whilst the rest of the feathers retain an exquisite whiteness. They are, as described ver. 13, *the very feathers and plumage of the stork,* i. e., they consist of such black and white feathers as the *stork,* called from thence חסידה *chasidah,* is known to have. But the belly, the thighs, and the breast, do not partake of this covering, being usually naked, and when touched are of the same warmth as the flesh of *quadrupeds.*

"Under the joint of the great pinion, and sometimes under the less, there is a strong pointed excrescence like a cock's spur, with which it is said to prick and stimulate itself, and thereby acquire fresh strength and vigour whenever it is pursued. But nature seems rather to have intended that, in order to prevent the suffocating effects of too great a *plethora*, a loss of blood should be consequent thereupon, especially as the *ostrich* appears to be of a hot constitution, with lungs always confined, and consequently liable to be preternaturally inflamed upon these occasions.

"When these birds are surprised by coming suddenly upon them whilst they are feeding in some valley, or behind some rocky or sandy eminence in the deserts, they will not stay to be curiously viewed and examined. Neither are the *Arabs* ever dexterous enough to overtake them, even when they are mounted upon their *jinse*, or horses, as they are called, of family. *They, when they raise themselves up for flight,* (ver. 18,) *laugh at the horse and his rider.* They afford him an opportunity only of admiring at a distance the extraordinary agility and the stateliness of their motions, the richness of their plumage, and the great propriety there was of ascribing to them (ver. 13) *an expanded quivering wing.* Nothing, certainly, can be more beautiful and entertaining than such a sight! The wings, by their repeated though unwearied vibrations, equally serving them for sails and oars; whilst their feet, no less assisting in conveying them out of sight, are in no degree sensible of fatigue.

"By the repeated accounts which I often had from my conductors, as well as from *Arabs* of different places, I have been informed that the *ostrich* lays from thirty to fifty eggs. *Ælian* mentions more than eighty, but I never heard of so large a number. The first egg is deposited in the centre; the rest are placed as conveniently as possible round about it. In this manner it is said to lay—deposit or thrust (ver. 14)—*her eggs in* THE EARTH, and *to warm them in the sand, and forgetteth,* as they are not placed, like those of some other birds, upon trees or in the clefts of rocks, &c., *that the foot of the traveller may crush them, or that the wild beasts may break them.*

"Yet notwithstanding the ample provision which is hereby made for a numerous offspring, scarce one quarter of these eggs are ever supposed to be hatched; and of those that are, no small share of the young ones may perish with hunger, from being left too early by their dams to shift for themselves. For in these the most barren and desolate recesses of the *Sahara*, where the *ostrich* chooses to make her nest, it would not be enough to lay eggs and hatch them, unless some proper food was near at hand, and already prepared for their nourishment. And accordingly we are not to consider this large collection of eggs as if they were all intended for a brood; they are, the greatest part of them, reserved for food, which the dam breaks and disposes of according to the number and the cravings of her young ones.

"But yet, for all this, a very little share of that στοργη, or natural affection, which so strongly exerts itself in most other creatures, is observable in the *ostrich.* For, upon the least distant noise or trivial occasion, she forsakes her eggs, or her young ones, to which perhaps she never returns; or if she do, it may be too late either to restore life to the one, or to preserve the lives of the other. Agreeably to this account, the *Arabs* meet sometimes with whole

nests of these eggs undisturbed; some of which are sweet and good, others are addle and corrupted, others again have their young ones of different growths, according to the time it may be presumed they have been forsaken by the dam. They oftener meet a few of the little ones, no bigger than well-grown pullets, half starved, straggling, and moaning about, like so many distressed orphans, for their mother. And in this manner the *ostrich* may be said (ver. 16) *to be hardened against her young ones, as though they were not hers; her labour* in hatching and attending them so far *being vain without fear,* or the least concern of what becomes of them afterwards. This want of affection is also recorded, Lam. iv. 3: *The daughter of my people,* says the prophet, *is cruel, like the ostriches in the wilderness.*

"Neither is this the only reproach that may be due to the *ostrich;* she is likewise inconsiderate and foolish in her private capacity; particularly in the choice of food, which is frequently highly detrimental and pernicious to her; for she swallows every thing greedily and indiscriminately, whether it be pieces of rags, leather, wood, stone, or iron. When I was at *Oram,* I saw one of these birds swallow, without any seeming uneasiness or inconveniency, several leaden bullets, as they were thrown upon the floor, scorching hot from the mould; the inner coats of the *œsophagus* and *stomach* being probably better stocked with glands and juices than in other animals with shorter necks. They are particularly fond of their own excrement, which they greedily eat up as soon as it is voided. No less fond are they of the dung of hens and other poultry. It seems as if their *optic* as well as *olfactory* nerves were less adequate and conducive to their safety and preservation than in other creatures. The *Divine providence in this,* no less than in other respects, (ver. 17,) *having deprived them of wisdom, neither hath it imparted to them understanding.*

"Those parts of the *Sahara* which these birds chiefly frequent are destitute of all manner of food and herbage, except it be some few tufts of coarse grass, or else a few other solitary plants of the *laureola, apocynum,* and some other kinds; each of which is equally destitute of nourishment; and, in the *psalmist's* phrase, (Psa. cxxix. 6,) *even withereth afore it groweth up.* Yet these herbs, notwithstanding their dryness, and want of moisture in their temperature, will sometimes have both their leaves and their stalks studded all over with a great variety of *land snails,* which may afford them some little refreshment. It is very probable, likewise, that they may sometimes seize upon *lizards, serpents,* together with *insects* and *reptiles* of various kinds. Yet still, considering th great voracity and size of this *camel-bird,* it is wonderful, not only how the little ones, after they are weaned from the provisions I have mentioned, should be brought up and nourished, but even how those of fuller growth and much better qualified to look out for themselves, are able to subsist.

"Their organs of digestion, and particularly the gizzards, which, by their strong friction, will wear away iron itself, show them indeed to be *granivorous;* but yet they have scarce ever an opportunity to exercise them in this way, unless when they chance to stray, which is very seldom, towards those parts of the country which are sown and cultivated. For these, as they are much frequented by the *Arabs* at the several seasons of grazing, ploughing, and gathering in the harvest; so they are little visited by, as indeed they would be an improper abode for, this shy, timorous bird; φιλερημος, *a lover of the deserts.* This last circumstance in the behaviour of the *ostrich* is frequently alluded to in the Holy Scriptures; particularly Isa. xiii. 21, and xxxiv. 13, and xliii. 20; Jer. l. 39; where the word, יענה *yaanah*, instead of being rendered the *ostrich*, as it is rightly put in the margin, is called the *owl;* a word used likewise instead of *yaanah* or the *ostrich*, Lev. xi. 16, and Deut. xiv. 15.

"Whilst I was abroad, I had several opportunities of amusing myself with the actions and behaviour of the *ostrich.* It was very diverting to observe with what dexterity and *equipoise* of body it would play and frisk about on all occasions. In the heat of the day, particularly, it would strut along the sunny side of the house with great majesty. It would be perpetually fanning and priding itself with its *quivering expanded wings;* and seem at every turn to admire and be in love with its shadow. Even at other times whether walking about, or resting itself upon the ground, the wings would continue these fanning vibrating motions, as if they were designed to mitigate and assuage that extraordinary heat wherewith their bodies seem to be naturally affected.

"Notwithstanding these *birds* appear tame and tractable to such persons of the family as were more known and familiar to them, yet they were often very rude and fierce to strangers, especially the poorer sort, whom they would not only endeavour to push down by running furiously upon them; but would not cease to peck at them violently with their bills, and to strike them with their feet; whereby they were frequently very mischievous. For the inward claw, or hoof rather as we may call it, of this *avis bisulca*, being exceedingly strong pointed and angular, I once saw an unfortunate person who had his belly ripped open by one of these strokes. Whilst they are engaged in these combats and assaults, they sometimes make a fierce, angry, and hissing noise, with their throats inflated, and their mouths open; at other times, when less resistance is made, they have a chuckling or cackling voice, as in the poultry kind; and thereby seem to rejoice and laugh as it were at the timorousness of their adversary. But during the lonesome part of the night, as if their organs of voice had then attained a quite different tone, they often made a very doleful and hideous noise; which would be sometimes like the roaring of a *lion;* at other times it would bear a near resemblance to the hoarser voices of other *quadrupeds*, particularly of the *bull* and the *ox.* I have often heard them groan, as if they were in the greatest agonies; an action beautifully alluded to by the Prophet *Micah*, i. 8, where it is said, *I will make a mourning like the yaanah* or *ostrich. Yaanah*, therefore, and רננים *renanim*, the names by which the *ostrich* is known in the Holy Scriptures, may very properly be deduced from ענה *anah*, and רנן *ranan*, words which the *lexicographi* explain by *exclamare* or *clamare fortiter;* for the noise made by the *ostrich* being loud and sonorous, *exclamare* or *clamare fortiter* may, with propriety enough, be attributed to it; especially as those words do not seem to denote any certain or determined mode of voice or sound peculiar to any one particular *species* of animals, but such as may be applicable to them all, to *birds* as well as to *quadrupeds* and other creatures."

Shaw's Travels, p. 541, edit. 4to. 1757.

The subjects in this chapter have been so various and important, that I have been obliged to extend the notes and observations to an unusual length; and yet much is left unnoticed which I wished to have inserted. I have made the best selection I could, and must request those readers who wish for more information to consult *zoological* writers.

CHAPTER XL

Job humbles himself before the Lord, 1–5. And God again challenges him by a display of his power and judgments, 6–14. A description of behemoth, 15–24.

A. M. cir. 2484
B. C. cir. 1520
Ante I. Olymp.
cir. 744
Ante U. C. cir.
767

MOREOVER the LORD answered Job, and said,

2 Shall he that [a]contendeth with the Almighty instruct *him?*

he that reproveth God, let him answer it.

3 Then Job answered the LORD, and said,

A. M. cir. 2484
B. C. cir. 1520
Ante I. Olymp.
cir. 744
Ante U. C. cir.
767

---

[a]Chap. xxxiii. 13

NOTES ON CHAP. XL

Verse 1. *Moreover the Lord answered*] That is, the Lord continued his discourse with Job. *Answered* does not refer to any thing *said* by Job, or any *question* asked.

I think it very likely that this whole piece, from the beginning of this *first* verse to the end of the *fourteenth*, was originally the *ending* of the poem. Mr. *Heath* has noticed this,

and I shall lay his words before the reader: "The former part of this chapter is evidently the conclusion of the poem; the latter part whereof seems to be in great disorder; whether it has happened from the carelessness of the transcriber, or, which appears most probable, from the skins of parchment composing the roll having by some accident changed their places. It is plain from the *seventh* verse of the *forty-second* chapter that Jehovah is the *last* speaker

A. M. cir. 2484
B. C. cir. 1520
Ante I. Olymp.
cir. 744
Ante U. C. cir.
767

4 [b]Behold, I am vile; what shall I answer thee? [c]I will lay mine hand upon my mouth.

5 Once have I spoken; but I will not answer; yea, twice; but I will proceed no farther.

6 [d]Then answered the LORD unto Job out of the whirlwind, and said,

7 [e]Gird up thy loins now like a man: [f]I will demand of thee, and declare thou unto me.

8 [g]Wilt thou also disannul my judgment? wilt thou condemn me, that thou mayest be righteous?

9 Hast thou an arm like God? or canst thou thunder with [h]a voice like him?

10 [i]Deck thyself now *with* majesty and excellency; and array thyself with glory and beauty.

A. M. cir. 2484
B. C. cir. 1520
Ante I. Olymp.
cir. 744
Ante U. C. cir.
767

11 Cast abroad the rage of thy wrath: and behold every one *that is* proud, and abase him.

12 Look on every one *that is* [k]proud, *and* bring him low; and tread down the wicked in their place.

13 Hide them in the dust together; *and* bind their faces in secret.

14 Then will I also confess unto thee that thine own right hand can save thee.

---

[b]Ezra ix. 6; chapter xlii. 6; Psalm li. 4——[c]Chapter xxix. 9; Psalm xxxix. 9——[d]Chapter xxxviii. 1——[e]Ch. xxxviii. 3

[f]Chapter xlii. 4——[g]Psalm li. 4; Romans iii. 4 [h]Chapter xxxvii. 4; Psalm xxix. 3, 4——[i]Psalm xciii. 1; civ. 1——[k]Isaiah ii. 12; Daniel iv. 37

---

in the poem. If, then, immediately after the end of the *thirty-ninth* chapter, we subjoin the *fifteenth* verse of the *forty-second* chapter, and place the *fourteen* first verses of the *fortieth* chapter immediately after the *sixth* verse of the *forty-second* chapter, and by that means make them the conclusion of the poem, all will be right; and this *seventh* verse of the *forty-second* chapter will be in its natural order. The action will be complete by the judgment of the Almighty; and the catastrophe of the poem will be grand and solemn." To these reasons of Mr. *Heath*, Dr. *Kennicott* has added others, which the reader may find at the end of the chapter. Without taking any farther notice of the transposition in this place, I will continue the notes in the present order of the verses.

Verse 2. *He that reproveth God, let him answer it.*] Let the man who has made so free with God and his government, answer to what he has now heard.

Verse 4. *Behold, I am vile*] I acknowledge my inward defilement. I cannot answer thee.

I will lay mine hand upon my mouth.] I cannot excuse myself, and I must be dumb before thee.

Verse 5. *Once have I spoken*] See on chap. xlii. 3, &c.

I will proceed no farther.] I shall attempt to justify myself no longer; I have spoken repeatedly; and am confounded at my want of respect for my Maker, and at the high thoughts which I have entertained of my own righteousness. All is impurity in the presence of thy Majesty.

Verse 7. *Gird up thy loins*] See chap. xxxviii. 1-3. Some think that this and the preceding verse have been repeated here from chap. xxxviii. 1-3, and that several of the words *there*, *here*, and chap. xlii. 3, have been repeated, in after times, to connect some false gatherings of the sheets of parchment, on which the end of this poem was originally written. See on ver. 1, and at the end of the chapter.

Verse 8. *Wilt thou condemn me*] Rather than submit to be thought in the wrong, wilt thou condemn MY conduct, in order to justify

thyself? Some men will never acknowledge themselves in the wrong. "God may err, but we cannot," seems to be their impious maxim. Unwillingness to acknowledge a fault frequently leads men, directly or indirectly, to this sort of blasphemy. There are *three* words most difficult to be pronounced in all languages,—I AM WRONG.

Verse 9. *Hast thou an arm like God?*] Every word, from this to the end of verse 14, has a wonderful tendency to humble the soul; and it is no wonder that at the conclusion of these sayings Job fell in the dust confounded, and ascribed righteousness to his Maker.

Verse 10. *Deck thyself now* with *majesty*] Act like God, seeing thou hast been assuming to thyself perfections that belong to him alone.

Verse 13. *Hide them in the dust together*] Blend the high and the low, the rich and the poor, in one common ruin. Show them that thou art supreme, and canst do whatsoever thou pleasest.

Bind their faces in secret.] This seems to refer to the custom of preserving *mummies:* the whole body is wrapped round with strong swathings of linen or cotton cloth. Not only the limbs, but the very *head, face*, and all, are rolled round with strong filleting, so that not *one feature* can be seen, not even the protuberance of the nose. On the outside of these involutions a human face is ordinarily *painted;* but as to the *real face* itself, it is emphatically *bound in secret*, for those rollers are never intended to be removed.

Verse 14. *Thine own right hand can save thee.*] It is the prerogative of God alone to save the human soul. Nothing less than unlimited power, exerted under the direction and impulse of unbounded mercy, can save a sinner. This is most clearly asserted in this speech of Jehovah: When thou canst extend an arm like God, i. e., an uncontrollable power—when thou canst arm thyself with the lightning of heaven, and thunder with a voice like God—when thou canst deck thyself with the ineffable glory, beauty, and splendour of the supreme majesty of Jehovah—when thou canst dispense thy judgments over all the earth, to abase the proud, and tread down the wicked—when thou

A. M. cir. 2484
B. C. cir. 1520
Ante I. Olymp. cir. 744
Ante U. C. cir. 767

15 Behold now ¹behemoth, which I made with thee; he eateth grass as an ox.

16 Lo now, his strength *is* in

his loins, and his force *is* in the navel of his belly.

17 ᵐHe moveth his tail like a cedar: the sinews of

A. M. cir. 2484
B. C. cir. 1520
Ante I. Olymp. cir. 744
Ante U. C. cir. 767

---

¹Or, *the elephant*, as some think

ᵐOr, *He setteth up*

---

canst as having the keys of hell and death, blend the high and the low in the dust together; then I will acknowledge to thee that thy own right hand can save thee. In other words: Salvation belongeth unto the Lord; no man can save his own soul by works of righteousness which he *has* done, *is* doing, or *can* possibly do, to all eternity. Without Jesus every human spirit must have perished everlastingly. Glory be to God for his unspeakable gift!

Verse 15. *Behold now behemoth*] The word בהמות *behemoth* is the plural of בהמה *behemah*, which signifies *cattle* in general, or *graminivorous* animals, as distinguished from חיתו *chayetho*, all *wild* or *carnivorous* animals. See Gen. i. 24. The former seems to mean kine, horses, asses, sheep, &c., and all employed in domestic or agricultural matters; the latter, all wild and savage beasts, such as lions, bears, tigers, &c.: but the words are not always taken in these senses.

In this place it has been supposed to mean some animal of the *beeve* kind. The *Vulgate* retains the *Hebrew* name; so do the *Syriac* and *Arabic*. The *Chaldee* is indefinite, translating *creature* or *animal*. And the *Septuagint* is not more explicit, translating by θηρια, *beasts* or *wild beasts;* and old *Coverdale*, **the cruell beaste,** perhaps as near to the truth as any of them. From the *name*, therefore, or the understanding had of it by the ancient *versions*, we can derive no assistance relative to the individuality of the animal in question; and can only hope to find what it is by the characteristics it bears in the description here given of it.

These, having been carefully considered and deeply investigated both by critics and naturalists, have led to the conclusion that either the *elephant*, or the *hippopotamus* or *riverhorse*, is the animal in question; and on comparing the characteristics between these two, the balance is considerably in favour of the *hippopotamus*. But even here there are still some difficulties, as there are some parts of the description which do not well suit even the *hippopotamus;* and therefore I have my doubts whether *either* of the animals above is that in question, or whether any animal now in existence be that described by the Almighty.

Mr. *Good* supposes, and I am of the same opinion, that the animal here described is now *extinct*. The *skeletons* of three lost genera have actually been found out: these have been termed *palæotherium, anoplotherium,* and *mastodon* or *mammoth*. From an actual examination of a part of the skeleton of what is termed the *mammoth*, I have described it in my note on Gen. i. 24.

As I do not believe that either the *elephant* or the *river-horse* is intended here, I shall not take up the reader's time with any detailed description. The elephant is well known; and, though not an inhabitant of these countries, has been so often imported in a tame state, and so frequently occurs in exhibitions of wild

beasts, that multitudes, even of the common people, have seen this tremendous, docile, and sagacious animal. Of the *hippopotamus* or *river-horse*, little is generally known but by description, as the habits of this animal will not permit him to be tamed. His amphibious nature prevents his becoming a constant resident on dry land.

The *hippopotamus* inhabits the rivers of *Africa* and the lakes of *Ethiopia:* feeds generally by night; wanders only a few miles from water; feeds on vegetables and roots of trees, but never on *fish;* lays waste whole plantations of the sugar-cane, rice, and other grain. When irritated or wounded, it will attack boats and men with much fury. It moves slowly and heavily: swims dexterously; walks deliberately and leisurely over head into the water; and pursues his way, even on all fours, on the bottom; but cannot remain long under the water without rising to take in air. It sleeps in reedy places; has a tremendous voice, between the *lowing* of an *ox* and the *roaring* of the *elephant*. Its head is large; its mouth, very wide; its skin, thick and almost devoid of hair; and its tail, naked and about a foot long. It is nearly as large as the elephant, and some have been found *seventeen feet* long. Mr. *Good* observes: "Both the *elephant* and *hippopotamus* are naturally quiet animals; and never interfere with the grazing of others of different kinds unless they be irritated. The *behemoth*, on the contrary, is represented as a quadruped of a ferocious nature, and formed for tyranny, if not rapacity; equally lord of the floods and of the mountains; rushing with rapidity of foot, instead of slowness or stateliness; and possessing a rigid and enormous *tail*, like a cedar tree, instead of a short naked tail of about a *foot* long, as the hippopotamus; or a weak, slender, hog-shaped tail, as the elephant."

The *mammoth*, for size, will answer the description in this place, especially ver. 19: *He is the chief of the ways of God*. That to which the part of a skeleton belonged which I examined, must have been, by computation, not less than *twenty-five* feet high, and *sixty* feet in length! The bones of *one toe* I measured, and found them *three feet* in length! One of the very smallest grinders of an animal of this extinct species, full of processes on the surface more than an inch in depth, which shows that the animal had lived on *flesh*, I have just now weighed, and found it, in its very dry state, *four pounds eight ounces*, avoirdupois: the same grinder of an *elephant* I have weighed also, and found it just *two pounds*. The mammoth, therefore, from this proportion, must have been as large as two *elephants* and a quarter. We may judge by this of its size: *elephants* are frequently *ten* and *eleven* feet high; this will make the mammoth at least *twenty-five* or *twenty-six* feet high; and as it appears to have been a *many-toed* animal, the *springs* which such a creature could make must have been almost incredible: nothing by *swift-*

A. M. cir. 2484
B. C. cir. 1520
Ante I. Olymp.
cir. 744
Ante U. C. cir.
767

his stones are wrapped to-gether.

18 His bones *are as* strong pieces of brass; his bones *are* like bars of [n]iron.

19 He *is* the chief of the ways of God: he that made him can make his sword to approach *unto him*.

20 Surely the mountains [o]bring him forth food, where all the beasts of the field play.

---

21 He lieth under the shady trees, in the covert of the reed, and fens.

A. M. cir. 2484
B. C. cir. 1520
Ante I. Olymp.
cir. 744
Ante U. C. cir.
767

22 The shady trees cover him *with* their shadow, the willows of the brook compass him about.

23 Behold, [p]he drinketh up a river, *and* hasteth not: he trusteth that he can draw up Jordan into his mouth.

24 [q]He taketh it with his eyes: *his* nose pierceth through snares.

---

[n]Daniel ii. 40——[o]Psalm civ. 14——[p]Hebrew, *he oppresseth*

[q]Or, *Will* any *take him in his sight*, or bore his *nose with a gin?* chap. xli. 1, 2

---

ness could have escaped its pursuit. God seems to have made it as the proof of his power; and had it been prolific, and not become extinct, it would have depopulated the earth. Creatures of this kind must have been living in the days of Job; the behemoth is referred to here, as if perfectly and commonly known.

He eateth grass as an ox.] This seems to be mentioned as something *remarkable* in this animal: that though from the form of his *teeth* he must have been *carnivorous*, yet he *ate grass as an ox;* he lived both on animal and vegetable food.

Verse 16. *His strength* is *in his loins*] This refers to his great *agility*, notwithstanding his *bulk;* by the *strength of his loins* he was able to take vast *springs*, and make astonishing bounds.

Verse 17. *He moveth his tail like a cedar*] Therefore it was neither the *elephant*, who has a *tail* like that of the *hog*, nor the *hippopotamus*, whose tail is only about a *foot* long.

The sinews of his stones] I translate with Mr. *Good*, and for the same reasons, *the sinews of his haunches*, which is still more characteristic; as the animal must have excelled in *leaping*.

Verse 18. *His bones* are as *strong pieces of brass—bars of iron.*] The tusk I have mentioned above is uncommonly *hard, solid,* and *weighty* for its size.

Verse 19. *He is the chief of the ways of God*] The *largest, strongest,* and *swiftest* quadruped that God has formed.

He that made him] No power of *man* or *beast* can overcome him. God alone can overcome him, and God alone could *make his sword* (of *extinction*) *approach* to him.

Verse 20. *The mountains bring him forth food*] It cannot therefore be the *hippopotamus*, as he is seldom found far from the rivers where he has his chief residence.

Where all the beasts of the field play.] He frequents those places where he can have most *prey*. He makes a mock of all the beasts of the field. They can neither resist his *power*, nor escape from his *agility*. All this answers to what we know of the *mammoth*, but not at all to the *hippopotamus*.

Verse 21. *He lieth under the shady trees*] This and the following verses refer to certain *habits* of the *behemoth*, with which we are and must be unacquainted.

Verse 22. *The willows of the brook compass him*] This would agree well enough with the hippopotamus.

Verse 23. *Behold, he drinketh up a river*] A similar mode of expression, and of precisely the same meaning, as that in chap. xxxix. 24: "He swalloweth the ground with fierceness." No river can stop his course: he wades through all; stems every tide and torrent; and *hurries not* as though he were in danger.

He trusteth that he can draw up Jordan] Even when the river overflows its banks, it is no stoppage to him: though the whole impetuosity of its stream rush against his mouth, he is not afraid. Mr. *Good* has seized the true idea in his translation of this verse:—

"If the stream rage, he revileth not:
He is unmoved, though Jordan rush against his mouth."

From this mention of Jordan it is probable that the behemoth was once an *inhabitant* of the mountains, marshes, and woods, of the land of Palestine.

Verse 24. *He taketh it with his eyes*] He looks at the sweeping tide, and *defies* it.

His *nose pierceth through snares.*] If *fences* of *strong stakes* be made in order to restrain him, or prevent him from passing certain boundaries, he tears them in pieces with his teeth; or, by pressing his nose against them, breaks them off. If other parts of the description would answer, this might well apply to the elephant, the *nose* here meaning the *proboscis*, with which he can *split trees*, or even *tear them up from the roots!*

Thus ends the description of the *behemoth;* what I suppose to be the *mastodon* or *mammoth*, or some creature of this kind, that God made as *the chief of his works*, exhibited in various countries for a time, cut them off from the earth, but by his providence preserved many of their skeletons, that succeeding ages might behold the *mighty power* which produced this *chief of the ways of God*, and admire the *providence* that rendered that race extinct which would otherwise, in all probability, have extinguished every other race of animals!

I am not unapprized of the strong arguments produced by learned men to prove, on the one hand, that *behemoth* is the *elephant;* and, on the other, that he is the *hippopotamus* or *river-horse;* and I have carefully read all that *Bochart*, that chief of learned men, has said on the subject. But I am convinced that an animal now *extinct*, probably of the kind already mentioned, is the creature pointed out and described by the inspiration of God in this chapter.

ON ver. 30 of the preceding chapter we have seen, from Mr. *Heath's* remarks, that the *fourteen* first verses were probably transposed. In the following observations Dr. Kennicott appears to prove the point.

"It will be here objected, that the poem could not possibly end with this question from *Job;* and, among other reasons, for this in particular; because we read in the very next verse, *That after the Lord had spoken these words unto Job,* &c. If, therefore, the last speaker was not *Job,* but *the Lord,* Job could not originally have concluded this poem, as he does at present.

"This objection I hold to be exceedingly important; and, indeed, to prove decisively that the poem must have ended at first with some speech from God.

"And this remark leads directly to a very interesting inquiry: *What* was at first *the conclusion* of this poem? This may, I presume, be pointed out and determined, not by the alteration of any one word, but only by allowing a *dislocation* of the *fourteen* verses which now begin the *fortieth* chapter. Chapters xxxviii., xxxix., xl., and xli., contain a magnificent display of the Divine power and wisdom in the works of the Creator; specifying the *lion, raven, wild goat, wild ass, unicorn, peacock, ostrich, horse, hawk, eagle, behemoth,* and *leviathan.*

"Now, it must have surprised most readers to find that the description of these creatures is strangely *interrupted* at chap. xl. 1, and as strangely *resumed* afterwards at chap. xl. 15; and therefore, if these *fourteen* verses will connect with and regularly follow what now *ends* the poem, we cannot much doubt that these *fourteen verses* have again found their true station, and should be restored to it.

"The greatness of the supposed transposition is no objection: because so *many verses* as would fill *one piece of vellum* in an ancient roll, might be easily sewed in *before* or *after* its proper place. In the case before us, the *twenty-five lines* in the *first fourteen* verses of chapter xl. seem to have been sewed in improperly after chap. xxxix. 30, instead of after chap. xlii. 6. That such large parts have been transposed in rolls, to make which the parts are sewed together, is absolutely certain; and

that this has been the case here, is still more probable for the following reason:—

"The lines here supposed to be out of place are *twenty-five*, and contain *ninety-two words;* which might be written on *one piece* or *page* of *vellum.* But the MS. in which these *twenty-five lines* made *one page*, must be supposed to have the same, or nearly the same, number of lines in *each of the pages adjoining.* And it would greatly strengthen this presumption if these *twenty-five* lines would fall in regularly at the end of any other set of lines, nearly of the same number; if they would fall in after the *next* set of *twenty-five*, or the *second* set, or the *third*, or the *fourth*, &c. Now, *this is actually the case here;* for the lines after these *twenty-five*, being *one hundred* or *one hundred and one*, make just *four times twenty-five.* And, therefore, if we consider these *one hundred and twenty-five lines* as written on *five equal pieces* of vellum, it follows that the *fifth* piece *might be* carelessly sewed up *before* the other *four.*

"Let us also observe that present *disorder* of the speeches, which is this. In chapters xxxviii. and xxxix., *God* first speaks to Job. The end of chap. xxxix. is followed by, 'And the Lord answered Job and said,' whilst yet Job had *not* replied. At chap. xl. 3-5, Job answers; but he says, *he had* then *spoken* TWICE, and *he would add no more;* whereas, this was his *first* reply, and he speaks afterwards. From chap. xl. 15 to xli. 34 are now the description of behemoth and leviathan, which would regularly follow the descriptions of the horse, hawk, and eagle. And from chap. xlii. 1 to xlii. 6 is now *Job's* speech, after which we read in ver. 7, 'After the Lord had spoken these words unto Job!'

"Now, all these confusions are removed at once if we only allow that a piece of vellum containing the *twenty-five lines*, (chap. xl. 1-14,) originally followed chap. xlii. 6. For then, after God's *first speech,* ending with *leviathan*, Job replies: then God, to whom Job replies the *second* time, when he *added no more;* and then God addresses him the *third*, when Job is silent, and the *poem* concludes: upon which the *narrative* opens regularly, with saying, 'After the Lord had spoken these words unto Job,' &c.; chap. xlii. 7."—*Kennicott's* Remarks, p. 161.

The reader will find much more satisfaction if he read the places as above directed. Having ended chap. xxxix., proceed immediately to ver. 15 of chap. xl.; go on regularly to the end of ver. 6 of chap. xlii., and immediately after that, add the first *fourteen* verses of chap. xl. We shall find then that the poem has a consistent and proper ending, and that the concluding speech was spoken by JEHOVAH.

CHAPTER XLI

God's great power in the leviathan, of which creature he gives a very circumstantial description, 1-34.

A. M. cir. 2484
B. C. cir. 1520

CANST thou draw out ªleviathan ᵇwith a hook? or his tongue with a cord ᶜ*which* thou lettest down?

A. M. cir. 2484
B. C. cir. 1520

ªThat is, *a whale* or *a whirlpool*——ᵇPsa. civ. 26;   Isa. xxvii. 1——ᶜHeb. which *thou drownest*

NOTES ON CHAP. XLI

Verse 1. *Canst thou draw out leviathan*] We come now to a subject not less perplexing

than that over which we have passed, and a subject on which learned men are less agreed than on the preceding. What is *leviathan?* The Hebrew word לִוְיָתָן *livyathan* is retained by

A. M. cir. 2484
B. C. cir. 1520
Ante I. Olymp. cir. 744
Ante U. C. cir. 767

2 Canst thou [d]put a hook into
his nose? or bore his jaw through
with a thorn?
3 Will he make many suppli-
cations unto thee? will he speak soft *words*
unto thee?
4 Will he make a covenant with thee? wilt
thou take him for [e]a servant for ever?
5 Wilt thou [f]play with him as *with* a bird?
or wilt thou bind him for thy
maidens?
6 Shall thy companions make
a banquet of him? shall they part
him among the merchants?
7 Canst thou fill his skin with barbed irons?
or his head with fish spears?
8 Lay thine hand upon him, remember the
battle, do no more.

[d]Isa. xxxvii. 29——[e]Exod. xxi. 1, &c.

[f]Psa. civ. 26

the Vulgate and the Chaldee. The Septuagint have, Αξεις δε δρακοντα; "*Canst* thou draw out the DRAGON?" The Syriac and Arabic have the same. A species of *whale* has been supposed to be the creature in question; but the description suits no animal but the *crocodile* or alligator; and it is not necessary to seek elsewhere. The crocodile is a natural inhabitant of the Nile, and other Asiatic and African rivers. It is a creature of enormous voracity and strength, as well as fleetness in swimming. He will attack the largest animals, and even men, with the most daring impetuosity. In proportion to his size he has the largest mouth of all monsters. The upper jaw is armed with *forty* sharp strong teeth, and the under jaw with *thirty-eight*. He is clothed with such a coat of mail as cannot be pierced, and can in every direction resist a musket-ball. The Hebrew לוי *levi* תן *ten* signifies the *coupled dragon;* but what this is we know not, unless the crocodile be meant.

With a hook] That crocodiles were caught with a *baited hook*, at least one species of crocodile, we have the testimony of *Herodotus*, lib. ii., c. 70: Επεαν νωτον συος δελεασῃ περι αγκιστρον, μετιει ες μεσον τον ποταμον, κ. τ. λ. "They take the back or chine of a swine, and bait a hook with it, and throw it into the midst of the river; and the fisherman stands at some distance on the shore holding a young pig, which he irritates, in order to make it squeak. When the crocodile hears this he immediately makes towards the sound; and, finding the baited hook in his way, swallows it, and is then drawn to land, when they dash mud into his eyes, and blind him; after which he is soon despatched." In this way it seems *leviathan* was *drawn out by a hook:* but it was undoubtedly both *a difficult* and *dangerous* work, and but barely practicable in the way in which *Herodotus* relates the matter.

Or his tongue with a cord] It is probable that, when the animal was taken, they had some method of casting a noose round his *tongue*, when opening his mouth; or piercing it with some barbed instrument. *Thevenot* says that in order to take the crocodile they dig holes on the banks of the river, and cover them with sticks. The crocodiles fall into these, and cannot get out. They leave them there for several days without food, and then let down nooses which they pitch on their jaws, and thus draw them out. This is probably what is meant here.

Verse 2. *Canst thou put a hook into his nose?*] Canst thou put a ring in his nose, and lead him about as thou dost thine ox? In the East they frequently lead the oxen and buffaloes with a ring in their noses. So they do *bulls* and *oxen* in this country.

Bore his jaw through with a thorn?] Some have thought that this means, Canst thou deal with him as with one of those little fish which thou stringest on a rush by means of the thorn at its end? Or perhaps it may refer to those *ornaments* with which they sometimes adorned their horses, mules, camels, &c.

Verse 3. *Will he make many supplications*] There are several allusions in these verses to matters of which we know nothing.

Verse 4. *Will he make a covenant*] Canst thou *hire* him as thou wouldst a servant, who is to be so *attached* to thy family as to have *his ear bored*, that he may abide in thy house for ever? Is not this an allusion to the law, Exod. xxi. 1-6?

Verse 5. *Wilt thou play with him*] Is he such a creature as thou canst tame; and of which thou canst make a *pet*, and give as a plaything to thy little girls? נערותיך *naarotheycha;* probably alluding to the custom of catching birds, tying a string to their legs, and giving them to children to play with; a custom execrable as ancient, and disgraceful as modern.

Verse 6. *Shall thy companions make a banquet*] Canst thou and thy friends feast on him as ye were wont to do on a camel sacrificed for this purpose? Or, canst thou dispose of his flesh to the *merchants*—to buyers, as thou wouldst do that of a camel or an ox? It is certain, according to *Herodotus*, lib. ii. c. 70, that they killed and ate crocodiles at *Apollonople* and *Elephantis*, in Egypt.

Verse 7. *Canst thou fill his skin with barbed irons?*] This refers to some kind of harpoon work, similar to that employed in taking *whales*, and which they might use for some other kinds of animals; for the skin of the crocodile could not be pierced. *Herrera* says that he saw a crocodile defend itself against *thirty* men; and that they fired six balls at it without being able to wound it. It can only be wounded under his belly.

Verse 8. *Lay thine hand upon him?*] Mr. *Heath* translates, "Be sure thou strike home. Mind thy blow: rely not upon a second stroke." Mr. *Good* translates:—

> "Make ready thy hand against him.
> Dare the contest: be firm."

He is a dangerous animal; when thou attackest him, be sure of thy advantage; if thou miss, thou art ruined. Depend not on other advantages, if thou miss the first. Kill him at once, or he will kill thee.

A. M. cir. 2484
B. C. cir. 1520
Ante I. Olymp.
cir. 744
Ante U. C. cir.
767

9 Behold, the hope of him is in vain: shall not *one* be cast down even at the sight of him?

10 None *is* so fierce that dare stir him up: who then is able to stand before me?

11 ᵍWho hath prevented me, that I should repay *him?* ʰ*whatsoever is* under the whole heaven is mine.

12 I will not conceal his parts, nor his power, nor his comely proportion.

13 Who can discover the face of his garment? *or* who can come *to him* ˡwith his double bridle?

14 Who can open the doors of his face? his teeth *are* terrible round about.

15 *His* ᵏscales *are his* pride, shut up together *as with* a close seal.

A. M. cir. 2484
B. C. cir. 1520
Ante I. Olymp.
cir. 744
Ante U. C. cir.
767

16 One is so near to another, that no air can come between them.

17 They are joined one to another, they stick together, that they cannot be sundered.

18 By his neesings a light doth shine, and his eyes *are* like the eyelids of the morning.

19 Out of his mouth go burning lamps, *and* sparks of fire leap out.

20 Out of his nostrils goeth smoke, as *out* of a seething pot or caldron.

21 His breath kindleth coals, and a flame goeth out of his mouth.

ᵍRom. xi. 35——ʰExod. xix. 5; Deut. x. 14; Psa. xxiv. 1; l. 12; 1 Cor. x. 26, 28

ˡOr, *within*——ᵏHebrew, *strong pieces of shields*

Verse 9. *Behold, the hope*] If thou miss thy first advantage, there is no hope afterwards: the very sight of this terrible monster would dissipate thy spirit, if thou hadst not a positive advantage against *his life,* or a place of sure retreat to save *thine own.*

Verse 10. *None is so fierce that dare stir him up*] The most courageous of men dare not provoke the crocodile to fight, or even attempt to rouse him, when, sated with fish, he takes his repose among the reeds. The strongest of men cannot match him.

Who then is able] If thou canst not stand against the *crocodile,* one of the *creatures* of my hand, how canst thou resist me, who am his Maker? This is the use which God makes of the formidable description which he has thus far given of this terrible animal.

Verse 11. *Who hath prevented me*] Who is it that hath laid me under obligation to him? Do I need my creatures? All under the heavens is my property.

Verse 12. *I will not conceal his parts*] This is most certainly no just translation of the original. The *Vulgate* is to this effect: *I will not spare him:* nor yield to his *powerful words,* framed for the purpose of entreaty. Mr. *Good* applies it to leviathan:—

"I cannot be confounded at his limbs and violence;
The strength and structure of his frame."

The Creator cannot be intimidated at the most formidable of his own works: *man* may and should tremble; Gᴏᴅ cannot.

Verse 13. *Who can discover the face of his garment?*] Who can rip up the hide of this terrible monster? Who can take away his covering, in order to pierce his vitals?

Verse 14. *The doors of his face?*] His jaws; which are most tremendous.

Verse 15. *His scales are his pride*] They are impenetrable, as we have already seen.

Verse 16. *One is so near to another*] It has already been stated, that a musket-ball fired at him in *any direction* cannot make a passage through his scales.

Verse 18. *By his neesings a light doth shine*] It is very likely that this may be taken *literally.* When he spurts up the water out of his nostrils, the drops form a sort of *iris* or *rainbow.* We have seen this effect produced when, in certain situations and state of the atmosphere, water was thrown up forcibly, so as to be broken into small drops, which has occasioned an appearance like the *rainbow.*

The eyelids of the morning.] It is said that, under the water, the eyes of the crocodile are exceedingly *dull;* but when he lifts his head above water they *sparkle* with the greatest vivacity. Hence the Egyptians, in their hieroglyphics, made the *eyes* of the *crocodile* the emblem of the *morning.* Ανατολην λεγοντες δυο οφθαλμους κροκοδειλου ζωογραφουσι.—Hᴏʀᴀᴘᴘ. Egypt. Ieroglyph., lib. i., c. 65. This is a most remarkable circumstance, casts light on ancient history, and shows the rigid correctness of the picture drawn above.

The same figure is employed by the Greek poets.

Χρυσεας ἡμερας βλεφαρον.

"The *eyelid* of the golden day."
Soph. Antig. ver. 103.

Νυκτος αφεγγες βλεφαρον.

"The darksome *eyelid* of the night."
Eurip. Phœniss. ver. 553.

Verse 19. *Out of his mouth go burning lamps*] Dr. *Young,* in his paraphrase, has a sensible note on this passage:—"This is nearer the truth than at first view may be imagined. The crocodile, according to naturalists, lying long under water, and being there forced to hold its breath, when it emerges, the breath long repressed is hot, and bursts out so violently, that it resembles fire and smoke. The *horse* does not repress his breath by any means so long, neither is he so fierce and animated; yet the most correct of poets ventures to use the same metaphor concerning him, *volvit sub naribus ignem.* By this I would caution against a false opinion of the boldness of Eastern metaphors, from passages ill understood."

A. M. cir. 2484
B. C. cir. 1520
Ante I. Olymp.
cir. 744
Ante U. C. cir.
767

22 In his neck remaineth strength, and [1]sorrow is turned into joy before him.

23 [m]The flakes of his flesh are joined together: they are firm in themselves: they cannot be moved.

24 His heart is as firm as a stone; yea, as hard as a piece of the nether *millstone.*

25 When he raiseth up himself, the mighty are afraid; by reason of breakings they purify themselves.

26 The sword of him that layeth at him cannot hold: the spear, the dart, nor the [n]habergeon.

27 He esteemeth iron as straw, *and* brass as rotten wood.

28 The arrow cannot make him flee: sling-stones are turned with him into stubble.

29 Darts are counted as stubble: he laugheth at the shaking of a spear.

30 [o]Sharp stones *are* under him: he spreadeth sharp-pointed things upon the mire.

31 He maketh the deep to boil like a pot: he maketh the sea like a pot of ointment.

32 He maketh a path to shine after him; *one* would think the deep *to be* hoary.

33 Upon earth there is not his like, [p]who is made without fear.

34 He beholdeth all high *things:* he *is* a king over all the children of pride.

A. M. cir. 2484
B. C. cir. 1520
Ante I. Olymp.
cir. 744
Ante U. C. cir.
767

---

[1]Heb. *sorrow rejoiceth*——[m]Heb. *The fallings*——[n]Or, *breastplate*

[o]Heb. *Sharp pieces of potsherd*——[p]Or, *who behave themselves without fear*

Verse 22. *In his neck remaineth strength*] Literally, "strength has its dwelling in his neck." The *neck* is the seat of strength of most animals; but the *head* and *shoulders* must be here meant, as the crocodile has *no neck*, being shaped nearly like a *lizard.*

And sorrow is turned into joy before him.]

ולפניו תדוץ דאבה *ulephanaiv taduts deabah;* "And *destruction* exulteth before him." This is as fine an image as can well be conceived. It is in the true spirit of poetry, the legitimate offspring of the *genie createur.* Our translation is simply *insignificant.*

Verse 23. *The flakes of his flesh*] His muscles are strongly and firmly compacted.

Verse 24. *Hard as a piece of the nether* millstone.] Which is required to be harder than that which runs above.

Verse 25. *By reason of breakings they purify themselves.*] No version, either ancient or modern, appears to have understood this verse; nor is its true sense known. The *Septuagint* have, "When he turns himself, he terrifies all the quadrupeds on the earth." The original is short and obscure: משברים יתחטאו *mishshebarim yithchattau.* Mr. *Good* takes the plural termination ים *im*, from the first word, of which he makes the noun ים *yam, the sea,* and thus translates it, "They are confounded at the tumult of the sea." In this I can find no more light than in our own. Mr. *Heath* has, "For very terror they fall to the ground." The translations of it are as unsatisfactory as they are various. I shall give both the verses from *Coverdale:*——

His herte is as harde as a stone; and as fast as the stythye (anvil) that the hammer man smyteth upon: when he goeth the mightiest off all are afrayed, and the waibes heby. The dull swell in the waters proclaims his advance; and when this is perceived, the stout-hearted tremble.

Verse 26. *Habergeon.*] The hauberk, the Norman armour for the head, neck, and breast, formed of rings. See on Neh. iv. 16.

Verse 29. *Darts are counted as stubble*] All these verses state that he cannot be *wounded*

by any kind of *weapon,* and that he cannot be *resisted* by any human *strength.*

A young crocodile, seen by M. *Maillet, twelve* feet long, and which had not eaten a morsel for *thirty-five* days, its mouth having been tied all that time, was nevertheless so strong, that with a blow of its tail it overturned a bale of coffee, and five or six men, with the utmost imaginable ease! What power then must lodge in one *twenty* feet long, well fed, and in health!

Verse 30. *Sharp stones are under him*] So hard and impenetrable are his scales, that splinters of flint are the same to him as the softest reeds.

Verse 31. *He maketh the deep to boil like a pot*] This is occasioned by strongly agitating the waters at or near the bottom; and the froth which arises to the top from this agitation may have the appearance of *ointment.* But several travellers say that the crocodile has a very strong scent of musk, and that he even imparts this *smell* to the *water* through which he passes, and therefore the text may be taken literally. This property of the crocodile has been noticed by several writers.

Verse 32. *He maketh a path to shine after him*] In certain states of the weather a rapid motion through the water disengages many sparks of phosphoric fire. I have seen this at sea; once particularly, on a fine clear night, with a good breeze, in a fast-sailing vessel, I leaned over the stern, and watched this phenomenon for hours. The *wake* of the vessel was like a stream of fire; millions of particles of fire were disengaged by the ship's swift motion through the water, nearly in the same way as by the electric cushion and cylinder; and all continued to be absorbed at a short distance from the vessel. Whether this phenomenon takes place in *fresh water* or in the *Nile,* I have had no opportunity of observing.

The deep to be *hoary.*] By the *frost* and *foam* raised by the rapid passage of the animal through the water.

Verse 33. *Upon earth there is not his like*] There is no creature among terrestrial animals so thoroughly dangerous, so exceedingly strong, and so difficult to be wounded or slain.

Who is made without fear.] Perhaps there is no creature who is at all acquainted with *man*, so totally destitute of fear as the crocodile.

Verse 34. *He is a king over all the children of pride.*] There is no animal in the waters that does not fear and fly from him. Hence the *Chaldee* renders it, *all the offspring of* FISHES.

Calmet says, that by *the children of pride* the Egyptians are meant; that the crocodile is called their *king*, because he was one of their principal divinities; that the kings of Egypt were called *Pharaoh,* which signifies a *crocodile;* and that the Egyptians were proverbial for their *pride,* as may be seen in Ezek. xxxii. 12. And it is very natural to say that Job, wishing to point out a cruel animal, adored by the Egyptians, and considered by them as their chief divinity, should describe him under the name of *king of all the children of pride.*

Houbigant considers the לויתן *livyathan,* the *coupled dragon,* to be emblematical of *Satan:* "He lifts his proud look to God, and aspires to the high heavens; and is king over all the sons of pride." He is, in effect, the governor of every proud, haughty, impious man. What a king! What laws! What subjects!

Others think that MEN are intended by *the sons of pride;* and that it is with the design

to abate their pride, and confound them in the high notions they have of their own importance, that God produces and describes an animal of whom they are all afraid, and whom none of them can conquer.

AFTER all, what is *leviathan?* I have strong doubts whether either *whale* or *crocodile* be meant. I think even the *crocodile* overrated by this description. He is too great, too powerful, too important, in this representation. No beast, terrestrial or aquatic, deserves the high character here given, though that character only considers him as unconquerably strong, ferociously cruel, and wonderfully made. Perhaps *leviathan* was some extinct *mammoth* of the *waters,* as *behemoth* was of the *land.* However, I have followed the general opinion by treating him as the *crocodile* throughout these notes; but could not finish without stating my doubts on the subject, though I have nothing better to offer in the place of the animal in behalf of which almost all learned men and critics argue, and concerning which they generally agree. As to its being an emblem either of *Pharaoh* or the *devil,* I can say little more than, *I doubt.* The description is extremely dignified; and were we sure of the animal, I have no doubt we should find it in every instance correct. But after all that has been said, we have yet to learn what leviathan is!

CHAPTER XLII

Job humbles himself before God, 1–6. God accepts him; censures his three friends; and commands Job to offer sacrifices for them, that he might pardon and accept them, as they had not spoken what was right concerning their Maker, 7–9. The Lord turns Job's captivity; and his friends visit him, and bring him presents, 10, 11. Job's affluence becomes double to what it was before, 12. His family is also increased, 13–15. Having lived one hundred and forty years after his calamities, he dies, 16, 17.

A. M. cir. 2484
B. C. cir. 1520
Ante I. Olymp.
cir. 744
Ante U. C. cir.
767

THEN Job answered the LORD, and said,

2 I know that thou ªcanst do every *thing,* and *that* ᵇnothought can be withholden from thee.

3 ᶜWho *is* he that hideth counsel without knowledge? therefore have I uttered that I

understood not; ᵈthings too wonderful for me, which I knew not.

4 Hear, I beseech thee, and I will speak: ᵉI will demand of thee, and declare thou unto me.

5 I have heard of thee by the hearing of the ear; but now mine eye seeth thee:

A. M. cir. 2484
B. C. cir. 1520
Ante I. Olymp.
cir. 744
Ante U. C. cir.
767

ªGen. xviii. 14; Matt. xix. 26; Mark x. 27; xiv. 36; Luke xviii. 27——ᵇOr, *no thought of thine can be hindered*

ᶜChap. xxxviii. 2——ᵈPsa. xl. 5; cxxxi. 1; cxxxix. 6 ᵉChap. xxxviii. 3; xl. 7

NOTES ON CHAP. XLII

Verse 2. *I know that thou canst do every* thing] Thy power is unlimited; thy wisdom infinite.

Verse 3. *Who is he that hideth counsel*] These are the words of Job, and they are a repetition of what Jehovah said, chap. xxxviii. 2: "Who is this that darkeneth counsel by words without knowledge?" Job now having heard the Almighty's speech, and having received his reproof, echoes back his words: "Who is he that hideth counsel without knowledge?" Alas, *I* am the man; *I have uttered what I understood not; things too wonderful for me, that I knew not.*

God had said, chap. xxxviii. 3: "Gird up now thy loins like a man; I will demand of thee,

and answer thou me." In allusion to this, Job exclaims to his Maker, ver. 4: "Hear, I beseech thee, and I will speak: I will ask of THEE, and declare THOU unto ME." I acknowledge my ignorance; I confess my foolishness and presumption; I am ashamed of my conduct; I lament my imperfections; I implore thy mercy; and beg thee to show me thy will, that I may ever think, speak, and do, what is pleasing in thy sight.

Things too wonderful] I have spoken of thy judgments, which I did not comprehend.

Verse 5. *I have heard of thee*] I have now such a discovery of thee as I have never had before. I have only heard of thee by tradition, or from imperfect information; now the eye of my mind clearly perceives thee; and in seeing *thee,* I see *myself;* for the light that discovers

A. M. cir. 2484
B. C. cir. 1520
Ante I. Olymp. cir. 744
Ante U. C. cir. 767

6 Wherefore I [f]abhor *myself,* and repent in dust and ashes.

7 And it was *so,* that after the LORD had spoken these words unto Job, the LORD said to Eliphaz the Temanite, My wrath is kindled against thee, and against thy two friends: for ye have not spoken of me *the thing that is* right, as my servant Job *hath.*

8 Therefore take unto you now [g]seven bullocks and seven rams, and [h]go to my servant Job, and offer up for yourselves a burnt-offer-

ing; and my servant Job shall [i]pray for you: for [k]him will I accept: lest I deal with you *after* your folly, in that ye have not spoken of me *the thing which is* right, like my servant Job.

A. M. cir. 2484
B. C. cir. 1520
Ante I. Olymp. cir. 744
Ante U. C. cir. 767

9 So Eliphaz the Temanite and Bildad the Shuhite *and* Zophar the Naamathite went, and did according as the LORD commanded them; the LORD also accepted [l]Job.

10 [m]And the LORD turned the captivity of Job, when he prayed for his friends: also the

[f]Ezra ix. 6; chap. xl. 4——[g]Num. xxiii. 1——[h]Matt. v. 24——[i]Gen. xx. 17; James v. 15, 16; 1 John v. 16

[k]Heb. *his face* or *person;* 1 Sam. xxv. 35; Mal. i. 8
[l]Heb. *the face of Job*——[m]Psa. xiv. 7; cxxvi. 1

thy glory and excellence, discovers my meanness and vileness.

Verse 6. *I abhor* myself] Compared with thine, my strength is weakness; my wisdom, folly; and my righteousness, impurity.

"I loathe myself when thee I see;
And into nothing fall."

Repent] I am deeply distressed on account of the *imaginations* of my heart, the *words* of my tongue, and the *acts* of my life. I roll myself in the *dust,* and sprinkle *ashes* upon my head. Job is now sufficiently humbled at the feet of Jehovah; and having earnestly and piously prayed for instruction, the Lord, in a finishing speech, which appears to be contained in the *first fourteen verses* of chap. xl., perfects his teaching on the subject of the late controversy, which is concluded with, "When thou canst act like the Almighty," which is, in effect, what the questions and commands amount to in the preceding verses of that chapter, "then will I also confess unto thee, that thy own right hand can save thee." In the *fifth* verse of the *fortieth* chapter, Job says, "ONCE have I spoken." This must refer to the declaration above, in the beginning of this chapter, (xlii.) And he goes on to state, chap. xl. 5: "Yea, TWICE; but I will proceed no farther." This *second* time is that in which he uses these words: after which he spoke no more; and the Lord concluded with the remaining part of these *fourteen* verses, viz., from ver. 7 to 14, inclusive. Then the thread of the story, in the form of a *narration* is resumed in this chapter (xlii.) at ver. 7.

Verse 7. *After the Lord had spoken these words*] Those recorded at chap. xl. 7-14; he said to Eliphaz, who was the eldest of the three friends, and chief speaker: *Ye have not spoken of me—right.* Mr. *Peters* observes, "It will be difficult to find any thing in the speeches of Eliphaz and his companions which should make the difference here supposed, if we set aside the doctrine of a *future state;* for in this view the others would speak more worthily of God than Job, by endeavouring to vindicate his providence in the exact distribution of good and evil in this life: whereas Job's assertion, chap. ix. 22, 'This is one thing, therefore I said it, *He destroyeth the perfect and the wicked,'* which is the argument on which he all along insists, would, upon this supposition, be directly charging God that he made no distinction between

the good and the bad. But now, take the other life into the account, and the thing will appear in quite a contrary light; and we shall easily see the reason why God approves of the sentiments of *Job,* and condemns those of his *friends.* For supposing the friends of Job to argue that the *righteous* are never afflicted *without remedy* here, nor the *wicked prosperous on the whole* in this life, which is a wrong representation of God's providence; and Job to argue, on the other hand, that the righteous are sometimes afflicted here, and that *without remedy,* but shall be *rewarded in the life to come;* and that the *wicked prosper* here, but shall be *punished hereafter,* which is the true representation of the Divine proceedings; and here is a very apparent difference in the drift of the one's discourse, and of the others'. For Job, in this view, speaks worthily of God, and the rest unworthily. The best moral argument that mankind have ever had to believe in *a life to come,* is that which Job insists on—that *good* and *evil* are, for the most part, dealt out *here* promiscuously. On the contrary, the topic urged by his friends, and which they push a great deal too far, that God rewards and punishes in this world, tends, in its consequences, like that other opinion which was held by the stoics in after times, that *virtue is its own reward,* to sap the very foundation of that proof we have, from reason, of another life. No wonder, therefore, that the sentiments of the one are approved, and those of the other condemned."

Verse 8. *Take—seven bullocks and seven rams*] From this it appears that Job was considered a *priest,* not only in his own family, but also for others. For his children he offered burnt-offerings, chap. i. 5; and now he is to make the same kind of *offerings,* accompanied with *intercession,* in behalf of his three friends. This is a full proof of the innocence and integrity of Job: a more decided one could not be given, that the accusations of his friends, and their bitter speeches, were as *untrue* as they were *malevolent.* God thus clears *his* character, and confounds *their* devices.

Verse 10. *The Lord turned the captivity of Job*] The *Vulgate* has: Dominus quoque conversus est ad pœnitentiam Job; "And the LORD turned Job to repentance." The *Chaldee:* "The WORD of the Lord (מימרא דייי *meymera dayai*) turned the captivity of Job." There is a remark which these words suggest, which has been

A. M. cir. 2484
B. C. cir. 1520
Ante I. Olymp.
cir. 744
Ante U. C. cir.
767

LORD ⁿgave Job °twice as much as he had before.

11 Then came there unto him ᴾall his brethren, and all his sisters, and all they that had been of his acquaintance before, and did eat bread with him in his house: and they bemoaned him, and comforted him over all the evil that the LORD had brought upon him: every man also gave him a piece of money, and every one an earring of gold.

12 So the LORD blessed qthe latter end of Job more than his beginning: for he had ʳfourteen thousand sheep, and six thousand camels, and a thousand yoke of oxen, and a thousand she-asses.

A. M. cir. 2484
B. C. cir. 1520
Ante I. Olymp.
cir. 744
Ante U. C. cir.
767

13 ˢHe had also seven sons and three daughters.

14 And he called the name of the first, Jemima; and the name of the second, Kezia; and the name of the third, Keren-happuch.

ⁿHeb. *added all that* had been *to Job unto the double*
°Isa. xl. 2——ᴾSee chap. xix. 13

qChap. viii. 7; James v. 11——ʳSee chap. i. 3——ˢChap.
i. 2

---

rarely, if at all, noticed. It is said that *the Lord turned the captivity of Job* WHEN HE PRAYED FOR HIS FRIENDS. He had suffered much through the unkindness of these friends; they had criticised his conduct without *feeling* or *mercy;* and he had just cause to be irritated against them: and that he had such a feeling towards *them,* several parts of his discourses sufficiently prove. God was now about to show Job his *mercy;* but *mercy* can be shown only to the *merciful;* Job must *forgive* his unfeeling friends, if he would be *forgiven* by the *Lord;* he directs him, therefore, to *pray for them,* ver. 8. He who can *pray* for another cannot entertain *enmity* against him: Job did so; and *when* he prayed for his friends, God turned the captivity of Job. "Forgive, and ye shall be forgiven."

Some suppose that Job, being miraculously restored, armed his servants and remaining friends, and fell upon those who had spoiled him; and not only recovered his own property, but also spoiled the spoilers, and thus his substance became double what it was before. Of this I do not see any intimation in the sacred text.

Verse 11. *Then came there unto him all his brethren*] "Job being restored to his former health and fortunes, the author," says Mr. Heath, "presents us with a striking view of *human friendship.* His *brethren,* who, in the time of his affliction, *kept at a distance* from him; his *kinsfolk,* who *ceased to know him;* his *familiar friends,* who had *forgotten* him; and his *acquaintance,* who had *made themselves perfect strangers* to him; those to whom he had *showed kindness,* and who yet had *ungratefully* neglected him, on the return of his prosperity now come and condole with him, desirous of renewing former familiarity; and, according to the custom of the Eastern countries, where there is no approaching a great man without a *present,* each brings him a *kesitah,* each a jewel of gold." See ver. 12.

A piece of money] קשיטה *kesitah* signifies a *lamb;* and it is supposed that this piece of money had a *lamb* stamped on it, as that quantity of gold was generally the current value for a lamb. See my note on Gen. xxxiii. 19, where the subject is largely considered. The *Vulgate, Chaldee, Septuagint, Arabic,* and *Syriac,* have *one lamb* or *sheep;* so it appears that they did not understand the *kesitah* as implying a *piece of money* of any kind, but a *sheep* or a *lamb.*

Earring of gold] Literally, a *nose-jewel.* The *Septuagint* translate, τετραδραχμον χρυσου, a tetradrachm of gold, or *golden daric;* but by adding και ασημον, *unstamped,* they intimate that it was four drachms of uncoined gold.

Verse 12. *The Lord blessed the latter end of Job*] Was it not in consequence of his friends bringing him a *lamb, sheep,* or other kind of *cattle,* and the *quantity of gold* mentioned, that his stock of *sheep* was increased so speedily to 14,000, his *camels* to 6000, his *oxen* to 2000, and his *she-asses* to 1000?

Mr. *Heath* takes the story of the conduct of Job's friends by the worst handle; see ver. 11. Is it not likely that they themselves were the *cause* of his sudden accumulation of property? and that they did not visit him, nor seek his familiarity *because* he *was now prosperous;* but because they saw that *God had turned his captivity,* and miraculously healed him? This gave them full proof of his *innocence,* and they no longer considered him an *anathema,* or *devoted person,* whom they should avoid and detest, but one who had been suffering under a strange dispensation of Divine Providence, and who was now no longer a suspicious character, but a favourite of heaven, to whom they should show every possible kindness. They therefore joined hands with God to make the poor man live, and their *presents* were the cause, under God, of his restoration to *affluence.* This takes the subject by the other handle; and I think, as far as the text is concerned, by the *right* one.

He had fourteen thousand sheep] The reader, by referring to chap. i. 3, will perceive that the whole of Job's property was exactly *doubled.*

Verse 13. *Seven sons and three daughters.*] This was the *same number* as before; and so the Vulgate, Septuagint, Syriac, and Arabic read: but the Chaldee *doubles* the sons, "And he had *fourteen* sons, and three daughters."

Verse 14. *The name of the first Jemima*] ימימה *yemimah, days upon days.*

Kezia] קציעה *ketsiah, cassia,* a well-known aromatic plant. And,

Keren-happuch.] קרן הפוך *keren happuch,* the *inverted* or *flowing horn, cornucopiæ,* the *horn of plenty.* The Chaldee will not permit these names to pass without a *comment,* to show the reason of their imposition: "He called the first *Jemimah,* because she was as *fair* as the *day;* the second *Ketsiah,* because she was as precious as *cassia;* the third *Keren-happuch,* because her face was as splendid as the *emerald.*" Cardmarden's Bible, 1566, has the Hebrew names.

A. M. cir. 2484
B. C. cir. 1520
Ante I. Olymp. cir. 744
Ante U. C. cir. 767

15 And in all the land were no women found *so* fair as the daughters of Job: and their father gave them inheritance among their brethren.

16 After this ᵗlived Job a hundred and forty years, and saw his sons, and his sons' sons, *even* four generations.

A. M. cir. 2484
B. C. cir. 1520
Ante I. Olymp. cir. 744
Ante U. C. cir. 767

17 So Job died, *being* old and ᵘfull of days.

ᵗChap. v. 28; Prov. iii. 16

ᵘGen. xxv. 8

The Vulgate has, "He called the name of one *Day*, of the second *Cassia*, and of the third *The Horn of Antimony*."

The versions in general preserve these names, only the Septuagint, Syriac, and Arabic translate *Jemimah*, DAY; and the former for *Keren-happuch* has Αμαλθαιας κερας, the *horn of Amalthea*. This refers to an ancient fable. *Amalthea* was the nurse of Jupiter, and fed him with goat's milk when he was young. The goat having by accident her *horn* struck off, Jupiter translated the animal to the heavens, and gave her a place among the *constellations*, which she still holds; and made the *horn* the emblem of *plenty:* hence it is always pictured or described as filled with *fruits, flowers,* and the *necessaries* and *luxuries* of life. It is very strange how this fable got into the Septuagint.

Coverdale is singular: 𝕿𝖍𝖊 𝖋𝖎𝖗𝖘𝖙 𝖍𝖊 𝖈𝖆𝖑𝖑𝖊𝖉 𝕯𝖆𝖞𝖊, 𝖙𝖍𝖊 𝖘𝖊𝖈𝖔𝖓𝖉𝖊 𝕻𝖔𝖇𝖊𝖗𝖙𝖊, 𝖙𝖍𝖊 𝖙𝖍𝖎𝖗𝖉𝖊, 𝕬𝖑𝖑 𝖕𝖑𝖊𝖓𝖙𝖊𝖔𝖚𝖘𝖓𝖊𝖘.

Verse 15. *Gave them inheritance among their brethren.*] This seems to refer to the history of the daughters of *Zelophehad*, given Num. xxviii. 1-8, who appear to have been the *first* who were allowed an *inheritance among their brethren.*

Verse 16. *After this lived Job a hundred and forty years*] How *long* he *had* lived before his afflictions, we cannot tell. If we could rely on the *Septuagint*, all would be plain, who add here, Τα δε παντα ετη εζησεν, διακοσια τεσσαρακοντα; "And all the years that Job lived were two hundred and forty." This makes him *one hundred years of age* when his trial commenced. *Coverdale* has, 𝕬𝖋𝖙𝖊𝖗 𝖙𝖍𝖎𝖘 𝖑𝖞𝖇𝖊𝖉 𝕵𝖔𝖇 𝖋𝖔𝖗𝖙𝖞 𝖞𝖊𝖆𝖗𝖊𝖘, omitting the *hundred*. So also in *Becke's* Bible, 1549. From the age, as marked down in the *Hebrew text*, we can infer nothing relative to the *time* when Job lived. See the subscription at the end of the Arabic.

Verse 17. *Job died,* being *old and full of days.*] He had seen life in all its varieties; he had *risen higher* than all the men of the East, and *sunk lower* in affliction, poverty, and distress, than any other human being that had existed before, or has lived since. He died when he was *satisfied with this life;* this the word שבע *seba* implies. He knew the *worst* and the *best* of human life; and in himself the whole *history of Providence* was exemplified and illustrated, and many of its *mysteries* unfolded.

We have now seen the end of the *life of Job,* and the *end* or *design* which God had in view by his afflictions and trials, in which he has shown us that he is *very pitiful, and of tender mercy,* James v. 11; and to discern this *end of the Lord* should be the object of every person who reads or studies it. *Laus in excelsis Deo!*

Both in the *Arabic* and *Septuagint* there is a considerable and important addition at the end of the *seventeenth* verse, which extends to many lines; of this, with its variations, I have given a translation in the PREFACE.

At the end of the *Syriac* version we have the following subscription:—

"The Book of the righteous and renowned Job is finished, and contains 2553 verses."

At the end of the *Arabic* is the following:—

"It is completed by the assistance of the Most High God. The author of this copy would record that this book has been translated into Arabic from the Syriac language." "Glory be to God, the giver of understanding!" "The Book of Job is completed; and his age was *two hundred and forty* years." "Praise be to God for ever!"

So closely does the *Arabic* translator copy the *Syriac,* that in the Polyglots one *Latin* version serves for both, with the exception of a few marginal readings at the bottom of the column to show where the *Syriac* varies.

Masoretic Notes

Number of verses, *one thousand and seventy. Middle* verse, chap. xxii. 16. *Sections, eight.*

AT the close of a book I have usually endeavoured to give some account of the *author,* or of him who was its chief *subject.* But the Book of Job is so *unique* in its subject and circumstances, that it is almost impossible to say any thing satisfactorily upon it, except in the way of *notes* on the *text.* There has been so much controversy on the *person* and *era* of Job, that he has almost been reduced to an *ideal* being, and the book itself considered rather as a *splendid poem* on an *ethic* subject than a *real history* of the man whose name it bears.

The *author,* as we have already seen in the *preface,* is not known. It has been attributed to *Job* himself; to *Elihu,* one of his friends; to *Moses;* to some *ancient Hebrew,* whose name is unknown; to *Solomon;* to *Isaiah* the prophet; and to *Ezra* the scribe.

The *time* is involved in equal darkness: *before* Moses, in the *time* of the *exodus,* or a *little after;* in the *days of Solomon;* during the *Babylonish captivity,* or even *later;* have all been mentioned as probable *eras.*

How it was originally *written,* and in what *language,* have also been questions on which great and learned men have divided. Some think it was originally written in *prose,* and afterwards reduced to *poetry,* and *the substance* of the different speeches being retained, but much *added* by way of *embellishment.* *Theodore,* bishop of *Mopsuestia* in *Cilicia,* a writer of the *fourth* century, distinguishes between *Job* and the *author* of the *book* that goes under his name, whom he accuses of a vain ostentation of profane sciences; ˙of writing a *fabulous* and *poetical* history; of making Job speak things inconsistent with his religion and piety, and more proper to give offence than to edify. As *Theodore* had only seen the Book of Job in the *Greek version,* it must be owned that he had too much ground for his severe criticism, as there are in that version several allusions to the *mythology* of the Greeks, some of which are cursorily mentioned in the *notes*. Among these may be reckoned the names of *constellations* in chapters ix. and xxxviii., and the naming one of Job's daughters *Keren-happuch*, the *horn of Amalthea*, chap. xlii. 14.

We need not confound the *time* of Job and the *time* of the *author* of the book that goes under his name. Job may have been the same as *Jobab*, 1 Chron. i. 35-44, and the *fifth* in descent from Abraham; while the *author* or *poet*, who reduced the memoirs into verse, may have lived as late as the *Babylonish captivity*.

As to the *language*, though nervous and elevated, it is rather a *compound* of *dialects* than a *regular language*. Though Hebrew be the basis, yet many of the *words*, and frequently the *idiom*, are pure Arabic, and a Chaldee phraseology is in many places apparent.

Whoever was the *author*, and in whatsoever *time* it may have been written, the Jewish and Christian Church have ever received it as a *canonical book*, recommended by the *inspiration* of the Almighty. It is in many respects an obscure book, because it refers to all the *wisdom of the East*. If we understood all its allusions, I have little doubt that the best judges would not hesitate to declare it *the Idumean Encyclopædia*. It most obviously makes continual references to *sciences* the most exalted and useful, and to *arts* the most difficult and ornamental. Of these the notes have produced frequent proofs.

The *author* was well acquainted with all the wisdom and learning of the ancient world, and of his own times; and as a *poet* he stands next to David and Isaiah: and as his subjects have been more varied than theirs, he knew well how to avail himself of this circumstance; and has pressed into his service all the influence and beauty of his art, to make the four persons, whom he brings upon the stage, keep up each his proper character, and maintain the opinions which they respectively undertook to defend. "The *history*," says *Calmet*, "as to the *substance* and circumstances, is exactly true. The *sentiments*, *reasons*, and *arguments* of the several persons, are very faithfully expressed; but it is very probable that the *terms* and *turns of expression* are the *poet's*, or the *writer's*, whosoever he may be."

The *authority* of this book has been as much acknowledged as its *Divine inspiration*. The Prophet *Ezekiel* is the first who quotes it, chap. xiv. 14-20, where he mentions Job with Noah and Daniel, in such a way as makes his *identity* equal with *theirs*; and of *their* personal existence no one ever doubted.

The Apostle *James*, chap. v. 11, mentions him also, and celebrates his *patience*, and refers so particularly to the termination and happy issue of his trials, as leaves us no room to doubt that he had seen his history, as here stated, in the book that bears his name.

St. *Paul* seems also to quote him. Compare Rom. ii. 11, "For there is no respect of persons with God," with Job xxxiv. 19, "God accepteth not the person of princes, nor regardeth the rich more than the poor; for they are all the work of his hands."

1 Tim. vi. 7: "For we brought nothing into this world; and it is certain we can carry nothing out." Job i. 21: "Naked came I out of my mother's womb; and naked shall I return thither."

Heb. xii. 5: "My son, despise not thou the chastening of the Lord, nor faint when thou art rebuked of him." Job v. 17: "Happy is the man whom God correcteth; therefore despise not thou the chastening of the Almighty." A similar saying is found Prov. iii. 11, probably all coming from the same source. See the comparisons from the writings of Solomon, in the *preface*.

Job is to be found in the ancient *martyrologies*, with the title of *prophet*, *saint*, and *martyr;* and the *Greek Church* celebrates a festival in his honour on the *fifth* of May; and the corrupt Churches of *Arabia*, *Egypt*, *Ethiopia*, *Russia*, and *Muscovy*, follow it in their worship of *Saint Job!*

But no Church has proceeded so far both to *honour* and *disgrace* this excellent man as the *Church of Rome*. I shall quote the words of *Dom. Calmet*, one of the most learned and judicious divines that Church could ever boast of. "The *Latins* keep his festival on the *tenth* of May. This, next to the *Maccabees*, brothers and martyrs, is the first saint to whom the western Church has decreed public and religious honours, and we know not of any saint among the patriarchs and prophets to whom *churches* have been consecrated, or *chapels* dedicated in *greater number*, than to this holy man. We see abundance of them, particularly in *Spain* and *Italy*. And he is invoked principally against the *leprosy*, *itch*, *foul disease*, and other distempers which relate to *these*." See *Baillie's* Lives of the Saints.

Calmet goes on to say that "there are several reputable *commentators* who maintain that Job was afflicted with this *scandalous disease;* among whom are *Vatablus*, *Cyprian Cisterc. Bolducius*, and *Pineda*, in their commentaries on Job; and *Desganges* in *Epist. Medicin. Hist. De Lue Venerea*. The *Latin Church* invokes Saint Job in diseases of this nature; and lazarettos and hospitals, wherein care is taken of persons who have this *scandalous distemper* upon them, are for the most part dedicated to him." See *Calmet's Dissertation sur la maladie de Job*, and his Dictionary, under the article JOB.

The conduct of this Church, relative to this holy man, forms one of the foulest calumnies ever inflicted on the character of either saint or sinner; and to make him the *patron* of every diseased prostitute and debauchee through the whole extent of the papal dominions and influence, is a conduct the most execrable, and little short of blasphemy against the *holiness* of God. As to their *lazarettos*, *hospitals*, and *chapels*, dedicated to this eminent man on these scandalous grounds, better raze them from their foundations, carry their materials to an unclean place, or transport them to *the valley of the son of Hinnom*, and consume them there; and then openly build others dedicated *ad fornicantem Jovem*, in conjunction with *Baal Peor* and *Ashtaroth*, the *Priapus* and *Venus* of their predecessors!

If those of that communion should think these reflections severe, let them know that the *stroke* is heavier than the *groan;* and let them put away from among them what is a dishonour to God, a disgrace to his saints, and their own ineffable reproach.

Of the *disease* under which Job laboured, enough has been said in the notes. On this head many writers have run into great extravagance. *Bartholinus* and *Calmet* state that he was afflicted with *twelve* several diseases; the latter specifies them. *Pineda* enumerates *thirty-one* or *thirty-two;* and St. *Chrysostom* says he was afflicted with all the maladies of which the human body is capable; that he suffered them in their *utmost extremities;* and, in a word, that on his one body all the maladies of the world were accumulated! How true is the saying, "*Over*-doing is *un*-doing!" It is enough to say, that this great man was afflicted in his *property, family, body,* and *soul;* and perhaps none, before or since his time, to a greater degree in all these kinds.

On Job's *character* his own words are the best comment. Were we to believe his mistaken and uncharitable *friends,* he, by *assertion* and *inuendo,* was guilty of almost every species of crime; but every charge of this kind is rebutted by his own *defence,* and the character given to him by the God whom he worshipped, frees him from even the *suspicion* of guilt.

His *patience, resignation,* and *submission* to the Divine will, are the most prominent parts of his character which are presented to our view. He bore the loss of every thing which a worldly man values without one unsanctified feeling or murmuring word. And it is in this respect that he is recommended to our notice and to our *imitation.* His *wailings* relative to the *mental* agonies through which he passed, do not at all affect this part of his character. He bore the loss of his goods, the total ruin of his extensive and invaluable establishment, and the destruction of his hopes in the awful death of his children, without uttering a reprehensible word, or indulging an irreligious feeling.

If however we carefully examine our translation of this poem, we shall find many things in Job's *speeches* that appear to be blemishes in his *character.* Even his own concessions appear to be heavy taxes on the high reputation he has had for *patience* and humble submission to the Divine will. In several cases these apparent *blemishes* are so contrasted with declarations of the highest *integrity* and *innocence* that they amount nearly to *contradictions.* Dr. *Kennicott* has examined this subject closely, and has thought deeply upon it, and strongly asserts that this *apparent inconsistency* arises from a misapprehension of Job's words in some cases, and mistranslation of them in others.

I shall take a large quotation on this subject from his "Remarks on Select Passages of Scripture."

"The *integrity* or *righteousness* of Job's character being resolutely maintained by Job himself, and the whole poem turning on the *multiplied miseries* of a man *eminently good,* the grand difficulty through the poem seems to be, how these positions can consist with the several passages where Job is now made to own himself *a very grievous sinner.* This matter, as being of great moment, should be carefully examined.

"In chap. vii. 20, 21, he says, 'I have sinned; What shall I do unto thee, O thou Preserver of men? Why dost thou not pardon my transgression, and take away mine iniquity?'

"In chap. ix. 20: 'If I justify myself, mine own mouth shall condemn me: If I say, I am perfect, it shall also prove me perverse. I know that thou wilt not hold me innocent.' 30, 31: 'If I wash myself with snow-water, yet shalt thou plunge me in the ditch, and my own

clothes shall abhor me.' Lastly, in xlii. 6: 'I abhor myself, and repent in dust and ashes.'

"Whereas he says, in chap. x. 7, 'Thou knowest that I am not wicked.' xiii. 15: 'I will maintain my own ways before him.' 18. 'I know that I shall be justified.' xxiii. 10: 'He knoweth the way that I take; when he hath tried me, I shall come forth as gold.' 11: 'My foot hath held his steps; his way have I kept, and not declined.' And lastly, in chap. xxvii. 5: 'Till I die I will not remove my integrity from me.' 6: 'My righteousness I hold fast; I will not let it go: my heart shall not reproach me so long as I live.'

"And now if any one, ascribing these contrarieties to Job's inconsistency with himself, should pronounce him *right* in owning himself a *great sinner,* and *wrong* in pleading his own *integrity,* he will soon see it necessary to infer the contrary. Had Job really been, and owned himself to be, a *great sinner,* his *great sufferings* had been then accounted for, agreeably to the maxims of his friends, and all difficulty and dispute had been at an end. But as the whole poem turns on Job's uncommon *goodness,* and yet uncommon *misery,* so this *goodness* or *innocence,* this *righteousness* or *integrity,* is not only insisted upon by Job, but expressly admitted by God himself, both in the beginning of this book and at the end of it. See chap. i. 8, 21; ii. 3; and xlii. 7, 8.

"That *Job* did not here plead *guilty,* or contradict the asseveration of his *innocence,* appears farther from the subsequent speeches. So *Bildad,* who spoke next, understood him, chap. viii. 6. So *Zophar* understood him, chap. xi. 4. So *Eliphaz,* to whom he spoke the former words, understood him likewise, chap. xv. 13, 14. And, lastly, *Elihu,* after hearing all the replies of Job to his friends, tells him, (chap. xxxiii. 8, 9,) 'Surely, thou hast spoken in mine hearing, and I have heard the voice of thy words, saying, I am clean, without transgression; I am innocent, neither is there iniquity in me.'

"If therefore this inconsistency in Job's declaration concerning himself cannot have obtained in this book at first, it must arise from some *misrepresentation* of the true sense. And as it relates to Job's *confession of guilt,* expressed in the three chapters, vii., ix., and xlii., on these passages I shall make a few remarks, in hopes of removing one of the greatest general difficulties which now attend this poem.

"As to the first instance, Job appears, at least from our English version of chap. vii. 20, to be confessing his sins to *God,* whereas he is really speaking there in reply to *Eliphaz;* and it is obvious that the same words, applied thus differently, must carry very different ideas. Who does not see the *humility* and *sorrow* with which Job would say, 'I have sinned against thee, O God?' and yet see the resentment and force with which he would say to *Eliphaz, I have sinned,* you say; but, granting this, What is it to YOU? *to* (or against) *thee, O Eliphaz, what crime have I committed?* That Job, in other places, *repeats* ironically, and confutes by *quoting* the sayings of his friends, will appear hereafter.

"*Eliphaz* had been attempting to terrify him by the recital of a *vision,* and the long speech of a *spirit,* chap. iv. 12-21. Job in reply, (chap. vi. 15-27,) complains of the cruel treatment he had begun to experience from his nominal friends, and false brethren; and (chap. vii. 14) particularly complains that he (*Eliphaz*) had terrified him with *dreams* and *visions*, Job then goes on, (chap. vii. 17, &c.,) *What is a miserable man,* like myself, *that thou makest so much of him?* 1 Sam. xxvi. 24: *That thou settest thy heart upon him? that,* with such officious affection, *thou visitest him every morning, and art trying him every moment? How long will it be till thou depart from me; and leave me at liberty to* breathe, and even *swallow down my spittle?* You say, I *must have been a sinner;* what then? I have not sinned against THEE. *O thou spy upon mankind! Why hast thou set up me* as a butt or *mark to shoot at? Why am I become a burden unto thee?* Why not rather *overlook my transgression,* and *pass by mine iniquity? I am now sinking to the dust; to-morrow, perhaps, I shall be sought in vain.*

"As the first part of this difficulty arose from Job's first reply to *Eliphaz,* the second part of the same difficulty arises from Job's first reply to *Bildad,* in chap. ix., when Job is now made to say as follows, (ver. 2 and 4:) 'How shouldst thou be just with God? Who hath hardened himself against him and prospered?' Ver. 20: 'If I justify myself, my own mouth shall condemn me;' with many other self-accusatory observations, which have been already quoted from verses 28, 30, and 31. Now this chapter, which in our present version of it is very unintelligible, will perhaps recover its original meaning, and prove beautifully consistent, upon these two principles: That from ver. 2 to ver. 24, Job is really *exposing his friends,* by ironically quoting some of *their absurd maxims;* and that in verses 28 and 31 he is speaking, *not to God,* but in reply to *Bildad.*

"Thus, in ver. 2, 'I know it is so of a truth;' i. e., Verily I perceive that *with you* the matter stands thus, as, *How shall man be just with God;* and again, *God is omnipotent;* which is granted and enlarged upon.

"Verses 15 and 16 strongly confirm the idea of Job's *irony* on the maxims of his friends, thus: Whom (God) *I am not to answer,* you say, *even though I were righteous; but I am to make supplication to my Judge.* Nay; *If I have called to God, and he hath really answered me, I am not to believe that he hath heard my voice, Because, &c.* So again, as to verses 20-22: *If I justify myself,* then you say, *My own mouth proves me wicked! If I say, I am perfect,* then *it proves me perverse.* And even supposing that *I am perfect and upright, yet am I not to know it.* In short, *my soul loatheth my very life;* i. e., I am almost tired to death with such nonsense.

"Whereas the *one* sole true conclusion is *this,* which, therefore, I resolutely *maintain:* 'God destroyeth the perfect and the wicked.' And as to verses 28 and 31, the whole embarrassment attending them is removed when we consider them as directed to *Bildad;* who, by the vehemence of his speech, hath shown that he would continue to insist upon Job's guilt: 'If I wash myself in snow-water, and make my hands ever so clean; yet wilt thou (Bildad) plunge me in the ditch,' &c.

"Let us proceed, therefore, to the third and last part of this general difficulty, which arises at present from Job's confession in chap. xlii. 5: 'I abhor myself, and repent in dust and ashes.' But *repent* of what? and why *abhor himself?* He was at that instant in the very situation he had been earnestly wishing and

often praying for: and was it possible for him not to seize that favourable moment? What he had so often wished was, that God would appear, and permit him to ask the reason for his uncommon sufferings. See chap. x. 2; xiii. 3, and 18 to 23; xix. 7; xxiii. 3-10; xxxi. 35-37, &c. And now when *God* does appear, we see that Job, immediately attentive to this matter, resolves to put the question, and declares this resolution: 'Hear, I beseech thee, and I will speak; I will demand of thee, and declare thou unto me. I have heard of thee by the hearing of the ear; but now mine eye seeth thee.' What now becomes of Job's *question?* Does he put any? Far, at present, are the next words from any such meaning, at least in our present version; for there the verse expresses nothing but *sorrow for sin,* which sets the poem at variance with itself. It also loses all sight of the *question,* for which the poem had been preparing, and which Job himself declares he would now put. Add, that in the first of these two lines the verb does not signify, *I abhor myself;* that the first hemistich is evidently too short, and that the second is not properly IN *dust,* but עַל *al,* UPON *dust* and *ashes.*"

"It is therefore submitted to the learned, whether the restoration of *two letters,* which, at the same time that they lengthen the line, will remove the inconsistency, and give the very question here wanted, be not strongly and effectually recommended by *the exigence of the place.* As עַל כֵּן *al ken,* is properly *therefore,* and עַל מָה *al mah* (x. 2) is *wherefore,* מָה *mah* was easily dropped before כֵּן *ken;* it not being recollected that כֵּן *ken* here is connected, not with the preposition before it, but with the verb after it, and signifies *hoc modo.* The true reading, therefore, and the true sense I humbly conceive to stand thus:—

Hear, I beseech thee, and I will speak;
I will demand of thee, and declare thou unto
    me.
I have heard of thee by the hearing of the ear;
But now mine eye seeth thee.

WHEREFORE (עַל מָה) am I thus become loathsome
And scorched up, upon dust and ashes?

"See chap. vii. 5: 'My flesh is clothed with worms, and clods of dust; my skin is broken (יִמָּאֵס) and *become loathsome.*' See also chap. xxx. 30: 'My skin is black upon me, and my bones are *burnt with heat;*' and ii. 8, x. 2, xvi. 15."

So far Dr. *Kennicott* in vindication of Job; and the reader will do justice to his learning and ingenuity. Allowing his general positions to be true, he has, in my opinion, pushed his consequences too far. Job certainly was not a *grievous sinner,* but a most *upright man.* This point is sufficiently proved; but that he accuses himself of *nothing* wrong, of *no inward* evil, is certainly not correct. He thought too highly of himself; he presumed too much on what was without; but when God shone upon his heart, he saw that he was vile, and therefore might most properly *loathe himself.* There are multitudes who are decent and correct in their outward behaviour, whose hearts may be deceitful and desperately wicked. Even the Pharisees made clean the outside of the cup and platter. Job was a very righteous and upright man; but at the time in question, he was not cleansed from all inward sin. This removes all contradiction from what he *asserts*, and from what he *concedes*. With this abatement, Dr. *Kennicott's* criticism may fairly stand. When a man sees himself in the light of God, he sees what, by his own discernment, wisdom, and reason, he had never seen before. His mind might have been previously deeply imbued with the principles of justice, righteousness, and truth, his whole conduct be regulated by them, and he be conscious to himself that he had not wickedly departed from the laws imposed on him by these principles. But when the *light that maketh manifest* shines through the inmost recesses of the heart, and vibrates through the soul, then *spiritual wickedness* becomes evident, and the deceitfulness of the heart is discovered. That light refers every thing to the Divine *standard*, the *holiness of God;* and the man's own righteousness in this comparison is found to be imperfection itself, and little short of impurity. Job appears to have been in this state: he thought himself *rich and increased in goods*, and *to have need of nothing;* but when God shone in upon his heart, he found himself to be *wretched*, and *miserable*, and *poor*, and *blind*, and *naked;* and he was now as ready to confess his great vileness, as he was before to assert and vindicate the unimpeachable righteousness of his *conduct*. Here was no *contradiction*. His friends attacked him on the ground of his being a bad and wicked man: this charge he repels with indignation, and dared them to the proof. They had nothing to allege but their *system* and

their *suspicions:* but he who suffers must have sinned. Job, being conscious that this was false as applied to him, knowing his own innocence, boldly requires on their ground to know *why* God contended with him? God answers for himself; humbles the self-confident yet upright man; shines into his heart, and then he sees that he is *vile*. When a beam of the solar light is admitted into an apartment we see ten thousand atoms or motes dancing in that beam. These are no particles of *light*, nor did the light bring them there; they were there before, but there was not light sufficient to make them manifest. Just so when the light of God visits the soul of a sincere man, who has been labouring in all his outward conduct to stand approved of God; he is astonished at his inward impurity, loathes himself, and is ready to think that many devils have *suddenly* entered into him. No: all the evils thou seest were there before, but thou hadst not light sufficient to make them manifest. Shall it be said after this, that the conduct of Divine Providence cannot be vindicated in suffering an upright man to become a butt for the malice of Satan for so long a time, and for no purpose? The greatest, the most important purposes were accomplished by this trial. Job became a much better man than he ever was before; the dispensations of God's providence were illustrated and justified; Satan's devices unmasked; patience crowned and rewarded; and the Church of God greatly enriched by having bequeathed to it the vast treasury of Divine truth which is found in the BOOK OF JOB.

Corrected for a new edition, March 1st, 1829.—A. C.

INTRODUCTION

TO THE

BOOK OF PSALMS

SECTION I.—ON THE NAMES GIVEN TO THIS BOOK

THIS book is termed in Hebrew ספר תהלים *Sepher Tehillim*, which some learned men derive from הל *hal* or הלל *halal*, to *move briskly, irradiate, shine;* and translate, The Book of the Shinings forth, Irradiations, Manifestations, or Displays, namely, of Divine wisdom and love exhibited in God's dealing with his chosen people, or with particular persons, as *figures, for the time being*, of what should be accomplished either in the person of Christ, or in his mystical body the Church. But as *halal* signifies also *to praise*, and praise arises from a sense of gratitude, is the expression of inward joy, and was often exhibited by brisk notes, sprightly music, &c., it may be well denominated *The Book of Praises*, as the major part of the Psalms have for their subject the praises of the Lord.

That the Psalms were sung in the Jewish service, and frequently accompanied by musical instruments, there is no doubt, for the fact is repeatedly mentioned; and hence the most ancient translation we have of the Psalms, viz., the Septuagint, as it stands in what is called the Codex Alexandrinus, is called Ψαλτηριον, *The Psaltery*, which is a species of musical instrument resembling the *harp*, according to the accounts given of it by some of the ancients. From this term came the *Psalterium* of the *Vulgate*, and our word *Psalter*, all of which are deduced from the verb ψαλλω, *to sing*, as the voice no doubt always accompanied this instrument, and by it the key was preserved and the voice sustained.

A *Psalm* is called in Hebrew מזמור *mizmor*, from זמר *zamar, to cut off*, because in singing each word was separated into its component syllables, each syllable answering to a note in the music.

SECTION II.—GENERAL DIVISION OF THE BOOK

The Hebrews divide the Psalms into *five books*, and this division is noticed by several of the primitive fathers. The origin of this division is not easily ascertained; but as it was considered a book of great excellence, and compared for its importance to the Pentateuch itself, it was probably divided into five books, as the law was contained in so many volumes. But where the divisions should take place the ancients are not agreed; and some of them divide into *three fifties* rather than into *five parts;* and for all these divisions they assign certain allegorical reasons which merit little attention.

The division of the Hebrews is as follows:—

Book I. From Psalm i. to Psalm xli. inclusive.
Book II. From Psalm xlii. to Psalm lxxii. inclusive.
Book III. From Psalm lxxiii. to Psalm lxxxix. inclusive.
Book IV. From Psalm xc. to Psalm cvi. inclusive.
Book V. From Psalm cvii. to Psalm cl. inclusive.

The *First, Second*, and *Third* Books end with *Amen and Amen;* the *Fourth*, with *Amen and Hallelujah;* the *Fifth*, with *Hallelujah*.

But the Psalms themselves are differently divided in all the VERSIONS, and in many MSS. This is often very embarrassing to the reader, not only in consulting the Polyglots, but also in referring to theological works, whether of the Greek or Latin Church, where the Psalms are quoted; the Greek ecclesiastical writers following the *Septuagint;* and those of the Latin Church, the *Vulgate*. I shall lay a proper table of these variations before the reader, remarking first, that though they differ so much in the division of the Psalms, they all agree in the *number one hundred and fifty*.

A Table of the Differences in dividing the Psalms between the *Hebrew* text and the ancient VERSIONS, *Syriac, Septuagint, Chaldee, Arabic, Æthiopic,* and *Vulgate.*

In the above versions Psalm ix. and x. make only Psalm ix. Hence there is one Psalm *less* in the reckoning as you proceed to

Psalm cxiv., cxv., which make Psalm cxiii. in all those versions. Hence two Psalms are *lost* in the reckoning.

Psalm cxvi. is divided at verse 9, the versions beginning Psalm cxv. at verse 10. Hence one Psalm is *gained* on the above reckoning.

Psalm cxix. makes Psalm cxviii. in all the versions.

Psalm cxlvii. they divide at verse 11, and begin Psalm cxlvii. with verse 12. Here then the reckoning becomes equal, and all end alike with Psalm cl.

In the Syriac, Septuagint, Æthiopic, and Arabic, there is what they call an *extra-numeral* Psalm, said to have been composed by David after his victory over Goliath. A translation of this will be found at the close of these notes.

The Hebrew MSS. agree often with the *versions* in uniting Psalms which the common *Hebrew* text has separated, and thus often support the ancient *versions*. These things shall be considered in the course of the notes.

SECTION III.—ON THE COMPILATION OF THE BOOK, AND THE AUTHORS TO WHOM THE PSALMS HAVE BEEN ATTRIBUTED

After having said so much on the *name* and ancient *divisions* of this important book, it may be necessary to say something in answer to the question, "Who was the author of the Book of Psalms?" If we were to follow the popular opinion, we should rather be surprised at the question, and immediately answer, DAVID, king of Israel! That many of them were composed by *him*, there is no doubt; that several were written long after his time, there is internal evidence to prove; and that many of them were written even by his *contemporaries*, there is much reason to believe.

That the *collection*, as it now stands, was made long after David's death, is a general opinion among learned men; and that *Ezra* was the collector and compiler is commonly believed. Indeed all antiquity is nearly unanimous in giving Ezra the honour of collecting the different writings of Moses and the prophets, and reducing them into that form in which they are now found in the Holy Bible, and consequently the *Psalms* among the rest. See this subject treated at large in the *preface to Ezra*, &c.

In making this collection it does not appear that the compiler paid any attention to *chronological arrangement*. As he was an inspired man, he could judge of the pieces which came by Divine inspiration, and were proper for the general edification of the Church of God.

The writer of the SYNOPSIS, attributed to St. *Athanasius*, says that the friends of King Hezekiah chose *one hundred and fifty* Psalms out of the number of *three thousand* which David had composed, and that they suppressed the rest: he says farther, that this is written in the *Chronicles;* but it is not found in the *Chronicles* which we now have, though it might have been in other Chronicles which that author had seen.

That some Scriptural collections were made under the influence and by the order of Hezekiah, we learn from Prov. xxv. 1: "These are also proverbs of Solomon, which the men of Hezekiah, king of Judah, copied out." But whether these were employed on the writings of the *father*, as they were on those of the *son*, we cannot tell. The above authority is too slender to support any building of magnitude.

The only method we have of judging is from the internal evidence afforded by several of the Psalms themselves, and from the *inscriptions* which many of them bear. As far as *time* and *facts* are concerned, many of them can be traced to the days of David, and the *transactions* which then occurred, and in which he bore so eminent a part. But there are others in which we find no *note* of *time*, and no reference to the *transactions* of David's reign.

As to the *inscriptions*, they are of slender authority; several of them do not agree with the subject of the Psalm to which they are prefixed, and not a few of them appear to be out of their places.

In one of the prologues attributed to St. *Jerome*, but probably of Eusebius, at the end of

Vol. II. of St. Jerome's Works by *Martinay,* we find a *table* in which the whole Book of Psalms is dissected, showing those which have *inscriptions,* those which have *none,* and those to which the *name* of a particular *person,* as author, is prefixed. I shall give these in gross, and then in detail: Psalms without any name prefixed, 17; Psalms with an inscription, 133; in all 150.

These are afterwards divided into those which bear *different kinds* of *titles, without names;* and those which have *names* prefixed. I shall give these from the *Quincuplex Psalterium,* fol. *Paris,* 1513, as being more correct than in the edition of Jerome, by *Martinay.*

Psalms which have no inscription *of any kind:* Psa. i., ii., xxxii., xlii., lxx., xc., xcii., xciii., xciv., xcv., xcvi., xcvii., xcviii., xcix., ciii., cxv., cxxxvi., cxlvii 18

Psalms to which David's *name is prefixed:* Psa. iii., iv., v., vi., vii., viii., ix., x., xi., xii., xiii., xiv., xv., xvi., xvii., xviii., xix., xx., xxi., xxii., xxiii., xxiv., xxv., xxvi., xxvii., xxviii., xxix., xxx., xxxi., xxxiii., xxxiv., xxxv., xxxvi., xxxvii., xxxviii., xxxix., xl., l., li., lii., liii., liv., lv., lvi., lvii., lviii., lix., lx., lxi., lxii., lxiii., lxiv., lxvii., lxviii., lxix., lxxxv., c., cii., cvii., cviii., cix., cxxxiii., cxxxvii., cxxxviii., cxxxix., cxl., cxli., cxlii., cxliii., cxliv., 70

Psalms attributed to Solomon: Psa. lxxi., cxxvi 2

Psalms attributed to the sons of Korah: Psa. xli., xliii., xliv., xlv., xlvi., xlvii., xlviii., lxxxiii., lxxxiv., lxxxvi 10

Psalms with the name of Asaph *prefixed:* Psa. xlix., lxxii., lxxiii., lxxiv., lxxv., xxvi., lxxvii., lxxviii., lxxix., lxxx., lxxxi., lxxxii 12

A Psalm to which the name of Heman *is prefixed:* Psa. lxxxvii 1

A Psalm to which the name of Ethan *is prefixed:* Psa. lxxxviii 1

A Psalm to which the name of Moses *is prefixed:* Psa. lxxxix 1

Psalms with titles without any name *specified:* A Song or Psalm, lxv. A Song or Psalm, lxvi. A Psalm or Song, xci. A Prayer of the Afflicted, ci 4

Hallelujah *Psalms:* Psa. civ., cv., cvi., cx., cxi., cxii., cxiii., cxiv., cxvi., cxvii., cxviii., cxxxiv., cxxxv., cxlv., cxlvi., cxlviii., cxlix., cl 18

Psalms or Songs of Degrees: Psa. cxix., cxx., cxxi., cxxii., cxxiii., cxxiv., cxxv., cxxvii., cxxviii., cxxix., cxxx., cxxxi., cxxxii 13

Sum total of all kinds: Psalms having no inscription, 18. David's, 70. Solomon's, 2. Sons of Korah, 10. Asaph, 12. Heman, 1. Ethan, 1. Moses, 1. Psalms and Songs, 3. Prayer, 1. Hallelujah, 18. Psalms of Degrees, 13.

Grand total 150

Supposing that the *persons* already mentioned are the authors of those Psalms to which their names are prefixed, there are still *fifty-three,* which, as bearing *no proper name,* must be attributed to uncertain authors, though it is very probable that several of them were made by David.

The reader will observe that as the preceding enumeration is taken from the *Vulgate,* consequently it is not exactly the same with ours: but the rules already given at page 200, will enable him to accommodate this division to that in our common Bibles, which is the same with that in the *Hebrew* text.

In order to make the preceding table as correct as possible, I have carefully collated that in the Benedictine edition of St. Jerome's WORKS, with professedly the same table in the Quincuplex Psalter, in both of which there are several errors. In the *Works,* though all the numbers are given at large, as *primus, decimus, centesimus,* &c., yet the sum total, under each head, rarely agrees with the items above it. This was so notoriously the case in the table in Jerome's Works, that I thought best to follow that in the *Psalter* above mentioned, which had been carefully corrected by Henry Stephens.

After all, this table gives but small satisfaction, when we come to collate it with the Psalms in the Hebrew text, or as they stand in our common English Bibles. That nothing might be wanting, I have made an analysis of the whole from our present text, collating this with the Hebrew where I was in doubt; and by this the reader will see how greatly these tables differ from each other; and that many Psalms must now come under a different arrangement, because of their different titles, from that which they had in St. Jerome's time. For instance, in St. Jerome's time there were *seventy*, or, as in some copies, *seventy-two* Psalms that had the name of David in the inscriptions; at present there are *seventy-three* thus inscribed in the Hebrew text.

SECTION IV.—CLASSIFICATION OF THE PSALMS AS THEY STAND IN OUR COMMON VERSION

Jerome gave two editions of the Latin Psalter, one from the Hebrew, and the other corrected from the Septuagint. Both of these may be found in his WORKS, and in the Quincuplex Psalter mentioned above. I shall now add a table, on a similar plan with the above, taken from our present authorized text.

A Classified Table of the Psalms taken from the text in common use

Psalms which have no inscription *of any kind:* Psa. i., ii., x., xxxiii., xliii., lxxi., xci., xciii., xciv., xcv., xcvi., xcvii., xcix., civ., cv., cvii., cxiv., cxv., cxvi., cxvii., cxviii., cxix., cxxxvi., cxxxvii. 24

Psalms to which David's *name is prefixed:* Psa. iii., iv., v., vi., vii., viii., ix., xi., xii., xiii., xiv., xv., xvi., xvii., xviii., xix., xx., xxi., xxii., xxiii., xxiv., xxv., xxvi., xxvii., xxviii., xxix., xxx., xxxi., xxxii., xxxiv., xxxv., xxxvi., xxxvii., xxxviii., xxxix., xl., xli., li., lii., liii., liv., lv., lvi., lvii., lviii., lix., lx., lxi., lxii., lxiii., lxiv., lxv., lxviii., lxix., lxx., lxxxvi., ci., ciii., cviii., cix., cx., cxxii., cxxiv., cxxxi., cxxxiii., cxxxviii., cxxxix., cxl., cxli., cxlii., cxliii., cxliv., cxlv. 73

Psalms attributed to Solomon: Psa. lxxii., cxxvii. 2

Psalms attributed to the sons of Korah: Psa. xlii., xliv., xlv., xlvi., xlvii., xlviii., xlix., lxxxiv., lxxxv., lxxxvii. 10

Psalms with the name of Asaph *prefixed:* Psa. l., lxxiii., lxxiv., lxxv., lxxvi., lxxvii., lxxviii., lxxix., lxxx., lxxxi., lxxxii., lxxxiii. 12

A Psalm to which the name of Heman *is prefixed:* Psa. lxxxix. 1

A Psalm to which the name of Ethan *is prefixed:* Psa. lxxxix. 1

A Psalm to which the name of Moses *is prefixed:* Psa. xc. 1

Psalms with titles without any name *specified:* A Song or Psalm, lxvi. A Psalm or Song, lxvii. A Psalm or Song for the Sabbath day, xcii. A Psalm or Song, xcviii. A Psalm or Song, c. A Prayer of the Afflicted, cii. 6

Hallelujah *Psalms:* Psa. cvi., cxi., cxii., cxiii., cxxxv., cxlvi., cxlvii., cxlviii., cxlix., cl. 10

Psalms or Songs of Degrees: Psa. cxx., cxxi., cxxiii., cxxv., cxxvi., cxxviii., cxxix., cxxx., cxxxii., cxxxiv. 10

Sum total of all kinds: Psalms having no *inscription*, 24. Psalms having David's name prefixed, 73. Psalms having Solomon's name, 2. Ditto, sons of Korah, 10. Ditto, Asaph, 12. Ditto, Heman, 1. Ditto, Ethan, 1. Psalms and Songs, 6. Hallelujah Psalms, 10. Psalms of Degrees, 10.

Grand total 150

After all that has been done to assign each Psalm to its author, there are few of which we can say positively, *These were composed by David.*

Most commentators, as well as historians of the life and reign of David, have taken great pains to throw some light upon this subject, particularly *Calmet, Delaney, Chandler,* and *Venema.* The former has made *seven divisions* of them, to ascertain the *order* of *time* in which they were written. I shall adopt this plan, and accommodate it to the Psalms as they stand in our present authorized version, after simply remarking that there are several Psalms which appear to be ill-divided, some making *two* or *three*, which in all probability made originally but one; and others, which formerly made *two* or more, now improperly connected.

This has been already noticed in comparing the differences of the numeration between the *versions* and the *Hebrew* text. See p. 201; see also at the end of the following table.

SECTION V.—CHRONOLOGICAL ARRANGEMENT OF THE BOOK OF PSALMS

1. PSALMS *which contain* no Note *or* Indication *of the* Time *when written*

Psalm i. "Blessed is the man," &c. This is generally considered as **a** *Preface* to the whole book; supposed by some to have been written by *David:* but others attribute it to *Ezra*, who collected the book of Psalms.

Psalm iv. "Hear me when I call." The evening prayer of a *pious man.*

Psalm viii. "O Lord our Lord." The *privileges* and *dignity* of man.

Psalm xix. "The heavens declare the glory of God." God's glory in the *creation.* The excellence, perfection, and use of the Divine *law.*

Psalm lxxxi. "Sing aloud unto God." Supposed to be a Psalm usually sung at the *Feast of Trumpets*, or the beginning of the *year;* and at the *Feast of Tabernacles.*

Psalm xci. "He that dwelleth in the secret place." The *happiness* of those who trust in the Lord. This Psalm might be placed during or after the *Captivity.*

Psalm cx. "The Lord said unto my Lord." The advent, birth, passion, priesthood, and kingdom of Christ. Probably composed by *David.*

Psalm cxxxix. "O Lord, thou hast searched me." On the *wisdom* and *providence* of God.

Psalm cxlv. "I will extol thee, my God, O King." Thanksgiving for the *general benefits* bestowed by God.

In none of these is there any distinct notation of time.

II. PSALMS *composed by* David *while* persecuted *by* Saul

Psalm xi. "In the Lord put I my trust." Composed by David when in the court of Saul, his friends exhorting him to escape for his life from the jealousy and cruelty of Saul.

Psalm xxxi. "In thee, O Lord, do I put my trust." Composed when David was proscribed, and obliged to flee from Saul's court.

Psalm xxxiv. "I will bless the Lord at all times." Supposed to have been composed by David, when, by feigning himself to be mad, he escaped from the court of Achish, king of Gath.

Psalm lvi. "Be merciful unto me, O God." Composed in the *cave* of *Adullam*, after his escape from Achish.

Psalm xvi. "Preserve me, O God." David persecuted by Saul, and obliged to take refuge among the *Moabites* and *Philistines.*

Psalm liv. "Save me, O God, by thy name." David, betrayed by the *Ziphims*, escapes from the hands of Saul.

Psalm lii. "Why boastest thou thyself in mischief." Composed by David when *Doeg* betrayed him to Saul, who, not finding him, slew the priests at *Nob.*

Psalm cix. "Hold not thy peace, O God." An invective against *Doeg*, and the rest of his *enemies.*

Psalm xvii. "Hear the right, O Lord." When Saul carried his persecution to the highest pitch.

Psalm xxii. "My God, my God, why hast thou forsaken me." *Saul's* persecution of *David* an emblem of the persecutions of *Christ* by the *Jews.*

Psalm xxxv. "Plead my cause, O Lord." Against *Saul* and his *courtiers*, who plotted his destruction.

Psalm lvii. "Be merciful unto me, O God." While shut up in the cave of *En-gedi;* 1 Sam. xxiv. 4.

Psalm lviii. "Do ye indeed speak righteousness." Against the wicked *counsellors* of Saul.

Psalm cxiii. "I cried unto the Lord with my voice." David in the cave of *En-gedi*, 1 Sam. xxiv.

Psalm cxl. "Deliver me, O Lord." Under the same persecutions praying for Divine succour.

Psalm cxli. "Lord, I cry unto thee." Same as the preceding.

Psalm vii. "O Lord my God, in thee do I put my trust." When violently persecuted by Saul.

III. PSALMS *composed after the Commencement of the reign of* David, *and after the Death of* Saul

Psalm ii. "Why do the heathen rage." Written by David after he had established his throne at Jerusalem, notwithstanding the envy and malice of his enemies. A prophecy of the reign of Christ.

Psalm ix. "I will praise thee, O Lord, with my whole heart." Sung by David on bringing the ark from the house of *Obed-edom*.

Psalm xxiv. "The earth is the Lord's, and the fulness thereof." Sung on the same occasion.

Psalm lxviii. "Let God arise, let his enemies be scattered." Sung on bringing the ark from *Kirjath-jearim* to Jerusalem.

Psalm ci. "I will sing of mercy and judgment." David describes the manner in which he will form his court, his ministers, and confidential servants.

Psalm xxix. "Give unto the Lord, O ye mighty." Composed after the *dearth* which fell on the land because of Saul's unjust persecution of the *Gibeonites;* 2 Sam. xxi.

Psalm xx. "The Lord hear thee in the day of trouble." Composed when David was about to march against the *Ammonites* and *Syrians;* 2 Sam. x. 16.

Psalm xxi. "The king shall joy in thy strength." Thanksgiving to God for the victory over the *Ammonites*, &c.; a continuation of the subject in the preceding.

Psalm xxxviii. "O Lord, rebuke me not in thy wrath." Composed during the time of a grievous *affliction*, after his transgression with *Bath-sheba*. See Psa. vi.

Psalm xxxix. "I said, I will take heed to my ways." A continuation of the same subject.

Psalm xl. "I waited patiently for the Lord." Thanksgiving for his *recovery*.

Psalm xli. "Blessed is he who considereth the poor." A continuation of the preceding subject.

Psalm vi. "O Lord, rebuke me not in thine anger." Supposed to be written in a time of *sickness* after his sin with *Bath-sheba*. See Psa. xxxviii.

Psalm li. "Have mercy upon me, O God." Written after he received the reproof by *Nathan* the prophet; 2 Sam. xii.

Psalm xxxii. "Blessed is he whose transgression is forgiven." Written about the same time, and on the same subject.

Psalm xxxiii. "Rejoice in the Lord, O ye righteous." A continuation of the preceding Psalm.

IV. PSALMS *composed during the* rebellion *of* Absalom

Psalm iii. "Lord, how are they increased that trouble me?" When David was driven from Jerusalem by Absalom.

Psalm iv. "Hear me when I call." Composed at the same time.

Psalm lv. "Give ear to my prayer." When he was flying from Jerusalem before Absalom.

Psalm lxii. "Truly my soul waiteth upon God." Exercising faith and patience during Absalom's rebellion.

Psalm lxx. "Make haste, O God, to deliver me." During the same.

Psalm lxxi. "In thee, O Lord, do I put my trust." Continuation of the preceding.

Psalm cxliii. "Hear my prayer, O Lord." Written during the *war* with *Absalom*.

Psalm cxliv. "Blessed be the Lord my strength." Written after the overthrow of *Absalom*, *Sheba*, and other rebels.

V. Psalms *written between the* Rebellion *of* Absalom, *and the* Babylonish Captivity

Psalm xviii. "I will love thee, O Lord, my strength." Thanksgivings for all the benefits which David had received from God. See 2 Sam. xxii.

Psalm xxx. "I will extol thee, O Lord." Composed at the dedication of the *threshing-floor* of *Ornan;* 2 Sam. xxiv. 25.

Psalm lxxii. "Give the king thy judgments." Composed by David when he invested *Solomon* with the kingdom.

Psalm xlv. "My heart is inditing a good matter." Written by the sons of Korah, for *Solomon's marriage*.

Psalm lxxviii. "Give ear, O my people." Sung by the choir of *Asaph*, on the *victory* gained by *Asa* over *Baasha* king of Israel; 2 Chron. xvi. 4, &c.

Psalm lxxxii. "God standeth in the congregation." Instructions given to the *judges* in the days of *Jehoshaphat*, king of Judah.

Psalm lxxxiii. "Keep not thou silence, O God." Thanksgiving for the *victories* of *Jehoshaphat*, king of Judah, over the *Ammonites*, *Idumeans*, and others. See 2 Chron. xx. 1, &c.

Psalm lxxvi. "In Judah is God known." Sung by the choir of *Asaph* after the victory over *Sennacherib*.

Psalm lxxiv. "O God, why hast thou cast us off?" Lamentation over the temple destroyed by *Nebuchadnezzar*.

Psalm lxxix. "O God, the heathen are come." On the same subject; composed probably during the captivity.

VI. Psalms *composed during the* Captivity

Psalm x. "Why standeth thou afar off?" Lamentation of the Jews during the captivity.

Psalm xii. "Help, Lord, for the godly man ceaseth." Composed by the captive Jews showing the wickedness of the *Babylonians*.

Psalm xiii. "How long wilt thou forget me." Continuation of the preceding.

Psalm xiv. "The fool hath said in his heart." A prayer of the poor captives for deliverance from their captivity.

Psalm liii. "The fool hath said in his heart, There is no God." This Psalm is almost verbatim with Psalm xiv., and, like it, describes the wickedness of the *Babylonians*, both having been composed during the captivity.

Psalm xv. "Lord, who shall abide in thy tabernacle?" This Psalm was probably intended to point out the *character* of *those* who might expect to return to their own land, and join in the temple service.

Psalm xxv. "Unto thee, O Lord, do I lift up my soul." A prayer of the captives for deliverance.

Psalm xxvi. "Judge me, O Lord." Continuation of the same.

Psalm xxvii. "The Lord is my light and my salvation." The *captives* express their confidence in God.

Psalm xxviii. "Unto thee will I cry." Prayers and thanksgivings of the *captives*.

Psalm xxxvi. "The transgression of the wicked." Complaints of the captives against the Babylonians.

Psalm xxxvii. "Fret not thyself." A Psalm of consolation for the *captives*.

Psalm xlii. "As the hart panteth." Composed by the sons of *Korah* during the *captivity*.

Psalm xliii. "Judge me, O God." Continuation of the same.

Psalm xliv. "We have heard with our ears." Same subject.

Psalm xlix. "Hear this, all ye people." By the sons of *Korah:* comfort for the *captives*.

Psalm l. "The mighty God, even the Lord, hath spoken." God's reprehension of the Jews, showing them the *cause* of their *captivity*.

Psalm lx. "O God, thou hast cast us off." The *captives* express their hope of a speedy restoration.

Psalm lxiv. "Hear my voice, O God." The captives complain of their *oppression* under the *Babylonians*.

Psalm lxix. "Save me, O God." The captive *Levites* complain of the *cruelty* of the *Babylonians*.

Psalm lxxiii. "Truly God is good to Israel." *Asaph* warns the captives against the bad *example* of the *Babylonians*, and against being *envious* at the *prosperity* of the *wicked*. Compare this with Psalm xxxvii.

Psalm lxxv. "Unto thee, O God, do we give thanks." *Asaph* prays for the deliverance of the people.

Psalm lxxvii. "I cried unto God with my voice." *Jeduthun* and *Asaph* complain of the long duration of the *captivity*.

Psalm lxxx. "Give ear, O Shepherd of Israel." *Asaph* prays for the deliverance of the people.

Psalm lxxxiv. "How amiable are thy tabernacles." The sons of *Korah* pray for their release.

Psalm lxxxvi. "Bow down thine ear." The same subject.

Psalm lxxxviii. "O Lord God of my salvation." The same subject.

Psalm lxxxix. "I will sing of the mercies of the Lord." *Ethan* prays for the deliverance of the captive Jews.

Psalm xc. "Lord, thou hast been our dwelling." The *Levites*, the *descendants of Moses*, request their return from captivity.

Psalm xcii. "It is a good thing to give thanks." The same subject, and by the same persons.

Psalm xciii. "The Lord reigneth." The same, by the same persons.

Psalm xcv. "O come, let us sing unto the Lord." The same.

Psalm cxix. "Blessed are the undefiled in the way." A Psalm supposed to have been made by *Daniel*, or some other *captive prophet*, for the instruction of the people.

Psalm cxx. "In my distress I cried." The captives pray for deliverance.

Psalm cxxi. "I will lift up mine eyes." The same subject.

Psalm cxxx. "Out of the depths have I cried." The same.

Psalm cxxxi. "Lord, my heart is not haughty." The *heads* of the *people* pray for their return.

Psalm cxxxii. "Lord, remember David." A prayer of the captive Jews in behalf of the *house of David*.

VII. *Psalms written* after *the Jews were permitted by the edict of* Cyrus *to return to their own land*

Psalm cxxii. "I was glad when they said." A Psalm of thanksgiving when they heard of the *edict of Cyrus*, permitting their return.

Psalm lxi. "Hear my cry, O God." Thanksgivings when the Jews were about to return to Jerusalem.

Psalm lxiii. "O God, thou art my God." A Psalm of the people, now on their return to Judea.

Psalm cxxiv. "If it had not been the Lord, who was on our side." On the same subject.

Psalm xxiii. "The Lord is my shepherd." Thanksgiving to God for their *redemption* from *captivity*.

Psalm lxxxvii. "His foundation is in the holy mountains." Thanksgivings by the sons of Korah for their return from captivity.

Psalm lxxxv. "Lord, thou hast been favourable unto thy land." Thanksgivings for their return.

Psalm xlvi. "God is our refuge and strength." Sung by the sons of *Korah* at the *dedication of the second temple*.

Psalm xlvii. "O clap your hands, all ye people." The same.

Psalm xlviii. "Great is the Lord." A continuation of the preceding.

Psalm xcvi. "O sing unto the Lord a new song." This and the three preceding all sung at the *dedication of the second temple*.

Psalm xcvii. "The Lord reigneth; let the earth rejoice." Thanksgivings of the Jews for their deliverance; sung at the *dedication of the second temple*.

Psalm xcviii. "O sing unto the Lord a new song; for he hath done marvellous things." A continuation of the above.

Psalm xcix. "The Lord reigneth; let the people tremble." Sung on the same occasion.

Psalm c. "Make a joyful noise." On the same occasion.

Psalm cii. "Hear my prayer, O Lord." A description of the *sufferings* of the *captives* while in *Babylon;* and thanksgivings for their *deliverance*.

Psalm ciii. "Bless the Lord, O my soul." On the same subject.

Psalm civ. "Bless the Lord, O my soul. O Lord my God." On the same.

Psalm cv. "O give thanks unto the Lord." Thanksgivings for deliverance from Babylon.

Psalm cvi. "Praise ye the Lord. O give thanks unto the Lord." On the same subject. A recapitulation of what God did for their fathers in *Egypt* and in the *wilderness*.

Psalm cvii. "O give thanks—his mercy endureth for ever." A fine poetical description of the *miseries of the captivity*.

Psalm cviii. "O God, my heart is fixed." The Jews, delivered from captivity, pray for their brethren yet beyond the *Euphrates*.

Psalm cxi. "Praise ye the Lord. I will praise the Lord with my whole heart." Thanksgivings of the Jews *after* their *captivity.*

Psalm cxii. "Praise ye the Lord. Blessed is the man that feareth." A continuation of the same subject.

Psalm cxiii. "Praise ye the Lord. Praise, O ye servants." A continuation of the above.

Psalm cxiv. "When Israel went out of Egypt." The same subject.

Psalm cxvi. "I love the Lord." The same subject.

Psalm cxvii. "O praise the Lord, all ye nations." The same subject.

Psalm cxxvi. "When the Lord turned again our captivity." A prayer for the remnant *still remaining in captivity.*

Psalm cxxxiii. "Behold, how good and how pleasant." Happy union of the *priests* and *Levites* in the service of God, after the *captivity.*

Psalm cxxxiv. "Behold, bless ye the Lord." An exhortation to the priests and Levites properly to discharge their duties in the temple, after they had returned from their captivity.

Psalm cxxxv. "Praise ye the Lord. Praise ye the name of the Lord." Same as the preceding.

Psalm cxxxvi. "O give thanks unto the Lord." Same as before.

Psalm cxxxvii. "By the rivers of Babylon, there we sat down." The Levites on their return, relate how they were insulted in their captivity.

Psalm cxlviii. "Praise ye the Lord. Praise ye the Lord from the heavens." Thanksgiving for deliverance from the captivity; and an invitation to all creatures to celebrate the praise of the Lord.

Psalm cxlix. "Praise ye the Lord. Sing unto the Lord a new song." On the same subject.

Psalm cl. "Praise ye the Lord. Praise God in his sanctuary." A continuation of the preceding Psalms.

Psalm cxlvi. "Praise ye the Lord. Praise the Lord, O my soul." Supposed to have been composed by *Haggai,* and *Zechariah,* to comfort the people when the edict of Cyrus was *revoked.* See the notes on this Psalm.

Psalm cxlvii. "Praise ye the Lord: for it is good." Thanksgiving of the same *prophets* after the long *dearth* mentioned by *Haggai,* chap. i. In the *Vulgate* this Psalm is divided at ver. 12, "Praise the Lord, O Jerusalem;" and is supposed by *Calmet* to have been sung at the dedication of the walls of Jerusalem. The *whole* Psalm is suitable to the occasions mentioned above.

Psalm lix. "Deliver me from mine enemies." Probably sung about the same time. See Neh. iv. and following chapters.

Psalm lxv. "Praise waiteth for thee, O God." Composed by *Haggai* and *Zechariah,* after the Lord had sent the *rain promised by Haggai,* chap. i.; and when they had begun the *repairs* of the *temple.* See Psalm cxlvii.

Psalm lxvi. "Make a joyful noise." A continuation of the above.

Psalm lxvii. "God be merciful unto us." The same subject.

Psalm cxviii. "O give thanks unto the Lord; for he is good." A song of praise after the death of *Cambyses,* or probably after the *dedication of the walls of Jerusalem.* Supposed to have been written by *Nehemiah.*

Psalm cxxv. "They that trust in the Lord." The Jews encouraging each other to resist *Sanballat* and *Tobiah,* and their other enemies.

Psalm cxxvii. "Except the Lord build the house." Composed to encourage the people to labour at the rebuilding of the walls of Jerusalem; and to put their confidence in the Lord.

Psalm cxxviii. "Blessed is every one that feareth the Lord." A continuation of the preceding.

Psalm cxxix. "Many a time have they afflicted me." A description of the peace and comfort enjoyed by the Jews under the reign of Darius.

Psalm cxxxviii. "I will praise thee with my whole heart." A continuation of the same subject.

For the *reasons* of the above *chronological arrangement* the reader may refer to the notes, and see also another table, page 214. This arrangement is better than none; and I hope will in the main be found as correct as can reasonably be expected, and a great help to a proper understanding of the Psalms.

Section VI. General Observations on the great Difference of Character between the Hebrew Poets, and those of Greece and Italy

The *Hebrew Psalter* is the most ancient collection of poems in the world; and was composed long before those in which ancient Greece and Rome have gloried. Among all the *heathen* nations *Greece* had the honour of producing not only the *first*, but also the most sublime, of poets: but the subjects on which they employed their talents had, in general, but little tendency to meliorate the moral condition of men. Their subjects were either a *fabulous theology*, a *false and ridiculous religion*, *chimerical wars*, *absurd heroism*, *impure love*, *agriculture*, *national sports*, or *hymns in honour of gods* more corrupt than the most profligate of men. Their writings served only to render vice amiable, to honour superstition, to favour the most dangerous and most degrading passions of men, such as impure love, ambition, pride, and impiety. What is said of the *Greek poets* may be spoken with equal truth of their successors and imitators, the *Latin poets;* out of the whole of whose writings it would be difficult to extract even the *common maxims* of a *decent morality*. I am well aware that fine sentiments, strong and terse expressions, and luminous thoughts, may be found in different parts of their writings; but compared with what is of a different kind, it may be well said of these,—

"Apparent rari nantes in gurgite vasto."

The Hebrew poets, on the contrary, justly boast the highest antiquity: they were men inspired of God, holy in their lives, pure in their hearts, labouring for the good of mankind; proclaiming by their incomparable compositions the infinite perfections, attributes, and unity of the Divine nature; laying down and illustrating the purest rules of the most refined morality, and the most exalted piety. God, his attributes, his works, and the religion which he has given to man, were the grand subjects of their Divinely inspired muse. By their wonderful art, they not only embellished the history of their own people, because connected intimately with the history of God's providence, but they also, by the light of the Spirit of God that was within them, foretold future events of the most unlikely occurrence, at the distance of many hundreds of years, with such exact circumstantiality as has been the wonder and astonishment of considerate minds in all succeeding generations; a fact which, taken in its connection with the holiness and sublimity of their doctrine; the grandeur, boldness, and truth of their imagery; demonstrates minds under the immediate inspiration of that God whose nature is ineffable, who exists in all points of time, and whose wisdom is infinite.

Some of the greatest both of the Greek and Roman poets, were men obscure in their birth, desperate in their fortunes, and of profligate manners; a fact at once proved both by their history and by their works. But the Hebrew poets were among the greatest men of their nation: and among them were found kings of the highest character, judges of the greatest integrity, heroes the most renowned, and lawgivers whose fame has reached every nation of the earth. By means of these men the lamp of true religion has been lighted in the earth; and wherever there is a ray of truth among the sons of men, it is an emanation immediately taken, or indirectly borrowed, from the prophets, poets, and statesmen, of the sons of Jacob.

The chief of the Hebrew *poets* were *Moses, David, Solomon, Job,* or whoever was the author of the book so called, *Isaiah, Jeremiah,* and most of the *minor prophets*. Solomon himself wrote *one thousand and five* hymns and poems: yet we know not that we have any of his poetical works, except the *Canticles*, though there may be some *Psalms* of his composition in the book before us.

Several of the *fathers*, both Greek and Latin, maintain that David is the author of the *whole book of Psalms*. And although they allow that several of them speak of times most obviously *posterior* to the days of David, yet they assert that he is the author of these also, and that he spoke of those events by the *spirit of prophecy!* The rabbins assert that the book of Psalms was composed by *ten* different authors, viz. *Adam, Melchizedek, Abraham, Moses,* the *sons of Korah, David, Solomon, Asaph, Jeduthun,* and *Ethan.* But this opinion is slenderly supported.

SECTION VII. OBSERVATIONS ON THE MANNER IN WHICH SEVERAL OF THE PSALMS APPEAR TO HAVE BEEN COMPOSED

That there were *several authors,* and that the Psalms were composed at *different times,* is sufficiently evident from the compositions themselves. The *occasions* also on which they were written are frequently pointed out by their contents; and these things have been kept constantly in view, in the construction of the preceding table.

There is a difficulty which should not be overlooked, and with which almost every reader is puzzled, viz., How is it that in the *same Psalm* we find so many *different states* of mind and circumstances pointed out? These could not be the experience of *one* and the *same person,* at the *same time.* The answer that is commonly given is this: Such Psalms were composed *after* the full termination of the *events* which they celebrate. For instance, David had fallen into distress—his sorrows became multiplied—he was filled with torturing fears. He called earnestly on the Lord for help; he was heard after a long night and fight of afflictions; and he most feelingly and sublimely praises God for his deliverance. Now all these different circumstances he describes *as if then existing,* though considerably *distant* in point of time; *beginning* the Psalm with the language of the *deepest penitential distress,* almost bordering on despair; and *ending* it with the *strongest confidence in God,* and thanksgiving for his *deliverance.* The thirtieth Psalm is a case in point; to the *notes* on which the reader is referred. Now it is possible that the psalmist, having obtained deliverance from sore and oppressive evils, might sit down to compose a hymn of thanksgiving to celebrate God's mercies; and in order to do this the more effectually, might describe the different circumstances enumerated above, as if he *were then passing through them.*

But I own that, to me, this is not a satisfactory solution. I rather suppose that such Psalms, and perhaps most of those called *acrostic,* were composed from *diaries* or *memoranda;* and in forming a Psalm, materials out of *different days,* having little congruity with each other as to the time in which they happened, would necessarily enter into the composition. This supposition will, in my opinion, account for all anomalies of this kind, which we perceive in the book of Psalms.

On this rule we can account for apparent contradictions in several Psalms: taken as metrical compositions formed from memoranda of religious experience for different days, they may well express different states; as the state of the author's mind was not likely to be precisely the same in all those times on which he made the memoranda. I can illustrate what I mean by the following extract from the *Spiritual Diary of Doctor John Rutty:*—

"*Seventh month,* 1768, 3d day: Amidst our palpable desolations, matter of some comfort appeared. An inward voice of thanksgiving to God for the gift of his Son, the Lord Jesus Christ, to us Gentiles; the mystery hid from ages, adorable, incomprehensible, unutterable, and unmerited; and if the sweet singer of Israel had occasion to say, 'Awake, sackbut, psaltery, and harp, and praise the Lord;' so had I, so had we, so had every one whose eyes the god of this world had not blinded.

"My native fierceness seemed, in the clear vision, to be the chief sin of my bosom, not yet wholly subdued: good Lord, and God of love, subdue it!

"7th. Soul, awake! the everlasting antitypal Sabbath I trust is at hand, the end of all labours, sufferings, and sins; see and prepare for it by letting the earth now enjoy its Sabbaths, even in a gradual relaxation and holy carelessness in all the special concerns of flesh and blood.

"8th. Protracted my vesper beyond the usual time, by reason of a sweet inspired song of thanksgiving to a gracious and ever adorable Providence.

"10th. Thy work is not yet done; the war in the members is still felt. Patience hath not yet had its perfect work. O my poverty! Lord, help me!

"11th. In the midst of various discouragements I was induced, even from observation, to believe that our late labour had not been wholly in vain; yea, on the 15th and 20th, I was a witness to some effects thereof.

"19th. A silent meeting with a loaded atmosphere; great heaviness, and the holy fire almost but not quite out.

"22d. I am a wonder of God's mercy and bounty. He is, as it were, renewing my youth, and giving, in old age, to enjoy and sweetly apply the labours of my youth, whilst multitudes of my equals and associates are dropping into eternity, or else various ways distressed. Awake, soul, and work; for the eleventh hour is come!

"23d. In a religious view, suffering is my portion. Lord, sustain!

"25th. A sweet song of thanksgiving.

"31st. The tenor of the drawing or proper steerage this day was, to keep carefully the holy medium between a criminal remissness in temporals on the one hand, and an anxiety about them on the other." *Spiritual Diary*, vol. ii, p. 235.

One sentence excepted, which is not relevant, here are the whole memoranda of the eminent man's religious experience for one month, in which we find the following states distinctly marked:

1. Mourning over the small progress of religion in the place where he dwelt, yet receiving encouragement from other quarters, day 3d. 2. Exulting in God for redemption by Christ Jesus, ditto. 3. Humbled on a view of his natural fierceness of spirit, ditto. 4. Rejoicing at the prospect of being soon released from earth, day 7th. 5. Thanksgiving for providential blessings, day 8th. 6. Fighting against inward sin, day 10th. 7. Encouraged in the performance of his duty, days 11th, 15th, 20th. 8. Mourning over the heavenly flame, almost extinct, day 19th. 9. Triumphing in a restoration of mental and bodily vigour, day 22d. 10. Complaining of his suffering lot, day 23d. 11. Happy in his soul, and giving praise to God, day 25th. 12. Forming holy resolutions for the government of his future life, day 31st.

Let us compare this with Psalm xxx., to which I have already referred in this introduction.

The Psalm begins with "I will extol thee, O Lord." And we find in it *seven* different states distinctly marked:

1. He had been in great distress, and nearly overwhelmed by his enemies; implied in ver. 1. 2. He extols God for having lifted him up, and preserved him from his adversaries, ver. 1, 3. 3. He is brought into great prosperity, trusts in what he had received, and forgets to depend wholly on the Lord, ver. 4–6. 4. The Lord hides his face from him, and he is brought into great distress, ver. 7: "Thou didst hide thy face, and I was troubled." 5. He makes earnest prayer and supplication, and pleads strongly with the Lord, ver. 8–10. 6. He is restored to the Divine favour, and filled with joy, ver. 11. 7. He purposes to glory in God alone, and trust in him forever, ver. 12.

Now it is impossible that David could have been in all these states when he penned this Psalm: suppose them to be the *memoranda* taken from one week's journal, and dressed in this poetic form; for it is possible that he might have passed through all these states in one *week*. Let us examine the *month's* experience, extracted from the diary of *Dr. Rutty;* and let an able hand clothe that in a poetic dress; and we shall find it as apparently contradictory as the xxxth Psalm. Suppose both formed from *memoranda* of a *diary*, and all is plain.

I have spent the more time on this subject, because it is important to have some *general rule* by which we may account for the apparent inconsistencies often occurring in the same Psalm.

There is another class of Psalms to which this mode of interpretation is not applicable: I mean those composed in the *dialogue* form. There are several of this kind; and as the several interlocutors are not distinguished, it requires considerable attention to find out the different parts which belong to the speakers. I shall give an example of this class.

The *ninety-first* Psalm contains, in general, a description of the happiness of those who trust in the Lord: but is evidently divided among *three* speakers: the *psalmist;* another whom we may call his *friend;* and thirdly, *Jehovah.* I shall endeavour to assign to each his part.

The *psalmist* begins with asserting, in general terms, the happiness of the godly: "He that dwelleth in the secret place of the Most High shall abide under the shadow of the Almighty," ver. 1.

His *friend* states his own experience, and replies, "I will say of the Lord, He is my refuge," &c., ver. 2.

The psalmist answers: "Surely he shall deliver thee," &c., ver. 3; and goes on to enumerate the great privileges of the godly, to ver. 8.

The *friend* then resumes, and shows how blessed the psalmist must be, who has an interest in the same God; and enters into a detail of his privileges, ver. 9–13.

This speech concluded, *Jehovah* speaks, confirms what was said concerning the blessedness of the godly; and to such persons he promises the highest spiritual honours, long life, and endless salvation, ver. 14–16.

Other Psalms of this class, such as the xxth and xxxth, &c., will be particularly pointed out in the course of the notes on this subject.

Section VIII.—On the Use made of the Psalms in the New Testament

Some have imagined that the book of Psalms is to be understood mystically, in reference to the Christian system; and, indeed, on this plan they have been interpreted and applied by many *fathers*, both ancient and modern. To this opinion I cannot subscribe: and therefore cannot frame a commentary in this way. That several of them are quoted, both by our Lord and his apostles, we have the fullest proof; and where they have shown the way, we may safely follow. Bishop *Horne*, who contends for the spiritual sense of this book, gives an interesting view of the principal passages that have been *quoted* in the *New Testament;* and from his *preface* I shall select a few paragraphs on this part of the subject: "No sooner," says he, "have we opened the book, than the *second* Psalm presents itself, to all appearance, as an inauguration hymn composed by David, the anointed of Jehovah; when by him crowned with victory, and placed triumphant on the sacred hill of Sion. But let us turn to Acts iv. 25, and there we find the apostles declaring the Psalm to be descriptive of the exaltation of Jesus Christ, and of the opposition raised against his Gospel, both by Jew and Gentile.

"In the *eighth* Psalm we may imagine the writer to be setting forth the pre-eminence of man in general above the rest of the creation: but by Heb. ii. 6, we are informed that the supremacy conferred on the second Adam, the man Christ Jesus, over all things in heaven and earth, is the subject there treated of.

"St. Peter stands up, Acts ii. 25, and preaches the resurrection of Jesus from the latter part of the *sixteenth* Psalm; and, lo, *three thousand* souls are converted by the sermon.

"Of the *eighteenth* Psalm we are told in the course of the sacred history, 2 Sam. xxii., that 'David spake unto the Lord the words of this song in the day that the Lord had delivered him out of the hand of all his enemies, and out of the hand of Saul:' yet, in Rom. xv. 9, the *ninth* verse of that Psalm is adduced as a proof that the Gentiles should glorify God for his mercy in Christ Jesus: 'As it is written, For this cause I will confess to thee among the Gentiles, and sing unto thy name.'

"In the *nineteenth* Psalm David seems to be speaking of the material heavens and their operations only, when he says: 'Their sound is gone out into all the earth, and their words into the ends of the world.' But St. Paul, Rom. x. 18, quotes the passage to show that the Gospel had been universally published by the apostles.

"The *twenty-second* Psalm Christ appropriated to himself, by beginning it in the midst of his sufferings on the cross: 'My God, my God, why hast thou forsaken me?' Three other verses of it are also applied to him; and the words of the *eighth* verse were actually used by the chief priests when they reviled him: 'He trusted in God,' &c., Matt. xxvii. 43.

"When David says, in the *fortieth* Psalm, 'Sacrifice and offering thou didst not desire— Lo, I come—to do thy will;' we might suppose him only to declare, in his own person, that obedience is better than sacrifice; but, from Heb. x. 5, we learn that Messiah in that place speaks of his advent in the flesh to abolish the legal sacrifices, and to do away sin by the oblation of himself, once for all.

"That tender and pathetic complaint in the *forty-first* Psalm: 'Mine own familiar friend, in whom I trusted, which did eat of my bread, hath lifted up his heel against me,' undoubtedly might be, and probably was, originally uttered by David upon the revolt of his old friend and counsellor Ahithophel, to the party of his rebellious son Absalom. But we are certain, from John xiii. 18, that this scripture was fulfilled when Christ was betrayed by his apostate disciple: 'I speak not of you all; I know whom I have chosen: but that the scripture may be fulfilled, He that eateth bread with me hath lifted up his heel against me.'

"The *forty-fourth* Psalm we must suppose to have been written on occasion of a persecution under which the Church at that time laboured; but a verse of it is cited, Rom. viii. 36, as expressive of what Christians were to suffer on their blessed Master's account: 'As it is written, For thy sake we are killed all the day long; we are accounted as sheep for the slaughter.'

"A quotation from the *forty-fifth* Psalm in Heb. i. 3, certifies us that the whole is addressed to the Son of God, and therefore celebrates his spiritual union with the Church, and the happy fruits of it.

"The *sixty-eighth* Psalm, though apparently conversant about Israelitish victories, the translation of the ark to Sion, and the services of the tabernacle; yet does, under those figures, treat of Christ's resurrection; his going up on high leading captivity captive, pouring out the gifts of the Spirit, erecting his Church in the world, and enlarging it by the accession of the nations to the faith; as will be evident to any one who considers the force and consequence of the apostle's citation from it, Eph. iv. 7, 8: 'Unto every one of us is given grace according to the measure of the gift of Christ. Wherefore he saith, When he ascended up on high, he led captivity captive, and gave gifts unto men.'

"The *sixty-ninth* Psalm is *five* times referred to in the Gospels, as being uttered by the prophet in the person of the Messiah. The *imprecations*, or rather *predictions*, at the latter end of it, are applied, Rom. xi. 9, 10, to the Jews; and to Judas, Acts i. 20, where the *hundred and ninth* Psalm is also cited as prophetical of the sore judgments which should befall that arch traitor, and the wretched nation of which he was an epitome.

"St. Matthew, informing us, chap. xiii. 35, that Jesus spake to the multitude in parables, gives it as one reason why he did so: 'That it might be fulfilled which was spoken by the prophet, Psa. lxxiii. 2, I will utter things which have been kept secret from the foundation of the world.

"The *ninety-first* Psalm was applied by the tempter to the Messiah; nor did our Lord object to the application, but only to the false inference which his adversary suggested from it; Matt. iv. 6, 7.

"The *ninety-fifth* Psalm is explained at large in Heb. iii. and iv., as relative to the state and trials of Christians in the world, and to their attainment of the heavenly rest.

"The *hundred and tenth* Psalm is cited by Christ himself, Matt. xxii. 44, as treating of his exaltation, kingdom, and priesthood.

"The *hundred and seventeenth* Psalm, consisting only of *two verses*, is employed, Rom. xv. 11, to prove that the Gentiles were one day to praise God for the mercies of redemption.

"The twenty-second verse of the *hundred and eighteenth* Psalm: 'The stone which the builders refused,' &c., is quoted *six* different times as spoken of our Saviour. See Matt. xxi. 42; Mark xii. 10; Luke xx. 17; Acts iv. 11.

"And *lastly:* 'the fruit of David's body,' which God is said in the *hundred and thirty-second* Psalm to have promised that he would place upon his *throne*, is asserted, Acts ii. 30, to be 'Jesus Christ.' " Bishop Horne on the Psalms, preface, p. xi.

That several of the above quotations are directly *prophetic*, and were intended to announce and describe the Redeemer of the world and the Gospel state, there is not the slightest reason to doubt; that others of them are *accommodated* to the above subjects, their own historical meaning being different, may be innocently credited: but let it always be remembered, that these accommodations are made by the same Spirit by which the Psalms were originally given; that this Spirit has a right to extend his own meaning, and to adapt his own words to subjects, transactions, and times, to which, from similarity of circumstances, they may be applicable. Many passages of the Old Testament seem to be thus quoted in the New; and often the words a *little altered*, and the meaning *extended*, to make them suitable to existing circumstances. Every writer is at perfect liberty thus to employ his own words, which he might have already used on very different occasions. I need not tell the learned reader that the finest, as well as the oldest, of the heathen writers, *Homer*, is full of quotations *from himself;* and *Virgil*, his imitator, has not unfrequently followed his steps. But still there is a great and weighty difference as the subject respects the Holy Spirit; to his infinite wisdom and knowledge all times and circumstances, whether *past* or *future*, are always laid open; and, as it is one of the perfections of the work of God to produce the *greatest* and most *numerous effects* by the *fewest* and *simplest means*, so it is one of the perfections of the Holy Scriptures to represent things that are not as though they were; and to make the facts which then existed the representatives of those which should afterwards take place. Thus, the Holy Scriptures contain an infinity of meaning: the Old Testament, as it were, included and referred to in the New; as the New refers *back* to the Old, by which it was adumbrated; and refers *forward*, not only to all times and great occurrences during this mortal state, but also to the endless states of the just and the unjust in the eternal world.

Section IX.—On the Subject Matter of the Psalms, and the Method of
applying them

The late learned Bishop *Horsley*, in his *preface* to the book of Psalms, says: "It is true that many of the Psalms are commemorative of the miraculous interpositions of God in behalf of his chosen people; for, indeed, the history of the Jews is a fundamental part of revealed religion. Many were probably composed upon the occasion of remarkable passages in David's life, his dangers, his afflictions, his deliverances. But of those which relate to the public history of the natural Israel, there are few in which the fortunes of the mystical Israel, the Christian Church, are not adumbrated; and of those which allude to the life of David, there are none in which the *Son of David* is not the principal and immediate subject.

"David's complaints against his enemies are Messiah's complaints, first of the unbelieving Jews, then of the heathen persecutors and the apostate faction in the latter ages. David's afflictions are the Messiah's sufferings; David's penitential supplications are the supplications of Messiah in agony; David's songs of triumph and thanksgiving are Messiah's songs of triumph and thanksgiving for his victory over sin, and death, and hell. In a word, there is not a page of this book of Psalms in which the pious reader will not find his *Saviour*, if he read with a view of finding him; and it was but a just encomium of it (the book of Psalms) that came from the pen of one of the early fathers, that '*it is a complete system of divinity for the use and edification of the common people of the Christian Church.*' "

Of the compilation of this book the above learned writer speaks thus: "The Psalms appear to be compositions of various authors, in various ages; some much more ancient than the time of King David, some of a much later age. Of many, David himself was undoubtedly the author; and that those of *his* composition were *prophetic*, we have David's own authority; for thus King David, at the close of his life, describes himself and his sacred songs: "David the son of Jesse said, and the man who was raised up on high, the anointed of the God of Jacob, and the sweet psalmist of Israel, said, The Spirit of Jehovah spake by me, and his word was in my tongue." It was the word, therefore, of *Jehovah's Spirit* which was uttered by David's tongue.

"The Psalms are all poems of the lyric kind, that is, adapted to music, but with great variety in the style of composition. Some are simply odes. An *ode* is a dignified sort of song, narrative of the facts either of public history or private life, in a highly adorned and figurative style. Some are of the kind called elegiac, which are pathetic compositions upon mournful subjects. Some are ethic, delivering grave maxims of life or the precepts of religion in solemn, but for the most part simple, strains. Some are enigmatic, delivering the doctrines of religion in *enigmas* contrived to strike the imagination forcibly, and yet easy to be understood. In all these the author delivers the whole matter in his own person. But a very great, I believe the far greater, part are a sort of dramatic odes, consisting of *dialogues* between persons sustaining certain characters. In these dialogue Psalms the persons are frequently the *psalmist* himself, or the *chorus of priests and Levites*, or the *leader* of the

Levitical band, opening the ode with a proem, declarative of the subject, and very often closing the whole with a solemn admonition drawn from what the other persons say. The other persons are JEHOVAH, sometimes as one, sometimes as another of the *Three Persons;* CHRIST in his incarnate state sometimes *before,* sometimes *after,* his resurrection; the *human soul* of Christ as distinguished from the *Divine essence.* Christ, in his incarnate state, is personated sometimes as a *Priest,* sometimes as a *King,* sometimes as a *Conqueror.* The resemblance is very remarkable between this *Conqueror* in the book of *Psalms,* and the *Warrior* on the *white horse* in the book of *Revelation,* who goes forth with a *crown* on his head, and a *bow* in his hand, conquering and to conquer. And the conquest in the *Psalms* is followed, like the conquest in the Revelation, by the *marriage* of the Conqueror. These are circumstances of similitude which, to any one versed in the *prophetic style,* prove beyond a doubt that the *mystical Conqueror* is the same personage in both."

There is an opinion relative to the construction of this book, which, though to myself it appear as fanciful as it is singular, yet deserves to be mentioned, especially as so great a man as Dr. *Horsley* supposes, that if it were kept in view, it would conduce much to a right understanding of the book.

The whole collection of the Psalms forms a sort of HEROIC TRAGEDY. The *redemption of man* and the *destruction of Satan,* is the PLOT. The PERSONS OF THE DRAMA are the *Persons* of the GODHEAD; *Christ* united to one of them: *Satan, Judas,* the *apostate Jews,* the *heathen persecutors,* the *apostates of latter times.* The ATTENDANTS: *believers, unbelievers,* *angels.* The SCENES: *heaven, earth, hell.* The TIME of the *action:* from the *fall* to the final overthrow of the *apostate faction,* and the *general judgment.*

SECTION X.—ON THE PARTICULAR SUBJECT AND USE OF EACH PSALM

I have already given different tables relative to the division, chronological arrangement, and supposed authors and occasions on which they were composed. There have been some others made, in which they have been classed according to their subjects, and their uses for the godly and the Christian Church. The most circumstantial that I have seen is that in the *Quintuplex Psalterium,* printed in 1508, already noticed in the beginning of this introduction. The following, from Bishop *Horsley,* may be probably of most general use:—

Services of the Festivals *of the Jewish Church*

For the SABBATH, Psa. xix., civ., and cxviii. For the PASSOVER, Psa. lxxviii., cv., cxiv. For PENTECOST, Psa. cxi., cxxxv., cxxxvi. For the FEAST OF TRUMPETS, Psa. lxxxi. For the FEAST OF TABERNACLES, Psa. lxv., lxvii.

A war song, Psa. cxlix. Thanksgiving for national deliverances, or successful war, Psa. xlviii., lxvi., lxxvi., cxv., cxxiv., cxxv., cxliv. Thanksgiving after a storm, hurricane, or earthquake, Psa. xxix., xlvi. Upon placing the ark in Solomon's temple, Psa. cxxxii. Prayers in seasons of national calamity, Psa. lxxix. Prayers for help in war, Psa. xliv., lx., lxi. Thanksgiving for Hezekiah's recovery, Psa. xxx., cxvi. Prayers in the time of Manasseh's captivity, Psa. lxxix., lxxx. Thanksgiving for Manasseh's return, Psa. lxxxv. Prayers, lamentations, and confessions of the captives, Psa. lxxiv., lxxvii., cii., cvi., cxxxvii. Songs of triumph and thanksgiving of the returned captives, Psa. cvii., cxxvi., cxlvi., cxlvii. A king of Judah's inauguration vow, Psa. ci. Grand chorus for all the voices and all the instruments, Psa. cl. The blessedness of the righteous, and the final perdition of the opposite faction, Psa. i., xxxvi., xxxvii., cxii. The extermination of the religious faction, Psa. xiv., liii. True godliness described as distinct from the ritual, Psa. xv., 1. The believer's scruples arising from the prosperity of the wicked, removed by revealed religion, and the consideration of their latter end, Psa. lxxiii. The pleasures of devotion, Psa. lxxxiv. Divine ænigmata; the subject, the Redeemer's divinity, the immortality of the soul, and a future retribution, Psa. xlix. A mystical prayer of David in the character of the high priest, Psa. xvi. Prayers of believers for protection against the atheistical conspiracy, Psa. iii., iv., x., xii., xiii., xvii., xliii., liv., cxx., cxxiii., cxl. The believer's penitential confessions and deprecations, Psa. vi., xxxii., xxxviii., xxxix., li. Believer's prayer for the promised redemption, Psa. cxxx., cxliii.

Believers lament their afflicted state in this short and evil life, and pray for the resurrection, Psa. xc. Prayers for grace and mercy, Psa. v., xxv., xxvi., cxxxi. Songs of triumph in prospect of the establishment of God's universal kingdom, Psa. xlvii., lxvii., xciii. A believer's general praises and thanksgivings, Psa. viii., xix., xxiii., ciii., cxix. A believer's thanksgiving for the final extirpation of iniquity, and the idolatrous religions and persecuting power, Psa. ix., xi., lii., lxvi. The Church prays for preservation from corruptions, Psa. xxviii., cxli.; for deliverance from the persecution of her enemies, Psa. vii., latter part of xxvii., from ver. 7 to the end, and xxxi., lix.; for Messiah's deliverance and success, Psa. xx. The Church gives thanks for Messiah's victory, Psa. xxi.; for her own final deliverance, Psa. xviii.; for the final extirpation of iniquity and idolatry, Psa. xcii. Messiah's prayers, Psa. xxii., xxxv., xli., lvi., lvii., lxi., lxii., lxiii., lxxxvi., lxxxviii.; in agony. When taken and deserted, Psa. cxlii.; thanksgivings, Psa. xl., cxvii., and cxviii., one Psa. cxxxviii; accusation of the impenitent Jews, his enemies, Psa. lv., lxiv., lxix.; prophetic malediction of the Jewish nation, Psa. cix.; exaltation, Psa. ii., xxiv., xlv., xcv., xcvi., xcvii., xcviii., xcix., c., cx.; comforts of the afflicted Israelites with the promise of the final excision of the idolatrous faction, Psa. xciv., exhorts to holiness and trust in God by the example of his own deliverance, Psa. xxxiv.; predicts the final judgment, Psa. lxxv. God promises the Messiah protection and glory, Psa. xci. God's just judgment foretold upon the unjust judges of our Lord, Psa. lviii., lxxxii. The reign of the king's son, Psa. lxxii. Salvation is of the Jews, Psa. lxxxvii.

Of the Psalms, *six* are alphabetical, xxv., xxxiv., xxxvii., cxi., cxii., cxlv.

Forty-five of the Psalms are called by the Masoretes *Mizmor*, iii., iv., v., vi., viii., ix., xii., xiii., xv., xix., xx., xxi., xxii., xxiii., xxiv., xxix., xxxi., xxxviii., xxxix., xl., xli., xlvii., xlix., l., li., lii., liii., liv., lv., lxxiii., lxxvii., lxxix., lxxx., lxxxii., lxxxiv., lxxxv., xcviii., c., ci., cix., cx., cxxxix., cxl., cxli., cxliii.

Six are called *Michtam*, xvi., lvi., lvii., lviii., lix., lx.

Thirteen are called *Maschil*, xxxii., xlii., xliv., xlv., lii., liii., liv., lv., lxxiv., lxxviii., lxxxviii., lxxxix., cxlii.

Seven are called *Mizmor Shir*, xxxi., lxv., lxvii., lxviii., lxxv., lxxvii., xcii.

Five are called *Shir Mizmor*, xlviii., lxvi., lxxxiii., lxxxviii., cviii.

One is called *Shir*, xlvi.

Four are called *Tephillah*, xvii., lxxxvi., xc., cii.

One is called *Tehillah*, cxlv.; one, *Shiggaion*, vii.; one, *Lehazchir*, lxx.

Fifteen are called *Shir Hammaaloth*, or *Songs of Steps*, cxx.–cxxxiv.

SECTION XI.—ON THE GENERAL USE OF THE PSALMS IN THE CHRISTIAN CHURCH

That our blessed Lord used the book of Psalms as he did other books of Scripture, and quoted from it, we have already seen; this stamps it with the highest authority: and that he and his disciples used it as a book of *devotion*, we learn from their singing the *Hillel* at his last supper, which we know was composed of Psalms cxiii., cxiv., cxv., cxvi., cxvii., and cxviii.; see Matt. xxvi. 30, and the notes there: and that they were used by the Christian Church from the earliest times in devotional exercises, especially in praising God, we have the most ample proof. At first what was called *singing* was no more than a *recitativo* or solemn mode of reading or repeating, which in the Jewish Church was accompanied by *instruments of music*, of the nature of which we know nothing. The Christian religion, which delights in *simplicity*, while it retained the Psalms as a book Divinely inspired, and a book of devotion, omitted the instrumental music, which, however, in after times, with other corruptions, crept into the Church, and is continued in many places, with small benefit to the godly, and little edification to the multitude. What good there might have been derived from it has been lost in consequence of the improper persons who generally compose what is commonly called the *choir of singers*. Those whose peculiar office it is to direct and lead the singing in Divine worship, should have clean hands and pure hearts. To see this part of public worship performed by unthinking if not profligate youths of both sexes, fills the serious with pain, and the ungodly with contempt. He who sings not with the *spirit* as well as the *understanding*, offers a sacrifice to God as acceptable as the dog's head and swine's blood would have been under the Mosaic law.

I shall not enter into the question whether the *Psalms of David*, or *hymns* formed on New Testament subjects, be the most proper for Christian congregations; *both* I think may be profitably used. Nor will I take up the controversy relative to the adapting the Psalms to express an evangelical meaning in every place. I need only give my opinion, that I consider this a difficult, if not a dangerous, work. Where the Psalms evidently relate to the *Gospel dispensation*, the matter is plain; there it is proper and necessary to give them their full direction and meaning; but to turn those in this way that evidently have no such reference, I consider a temerarious undertaking, and wholly unwarrantable.

But the most difficult task is, throwing them into a *modern poetic form*, especially into *metre;* as in such cases many things are introduced for the sake of the poetry, and the final jingle, which were never spoken by the inspired penman; and it is an awful thing to add to or detract from the word of God, either in *poetry* or *prose*. And how frequently this is done in most metrical versions of the Psalms, need not be pointed out here. Perhaps one of the most faultless in this respect is an almost obsolete one in our own language, viz., that by *Sternhold* and *Hopkins*. Because of its uncouth form, this version has been unjustly vilified, while others, by far its inferiors, have been as unreasonably extolled. The authors of this *version* (for it has been taken directly from the Hebrew text) have sacrificed every thing to the literal sense and meaning. The others, and especially that of *Tate* and *Brady*, which is no version from the original, sacrifice often the literal and true sense to sound and smoothness of numbers; in which, however, they are not always successful.

I shall add only one word on the subject of this very ancient version. I can sing almost every Psalm in the version of *Sternhold* and *Hopkins* as the *Psalms of David;* I can sing those of the *new version* as the Psalms of Dr. *Brady* and *Nahum Tate*. Either let one equally *literal*, with a better *versification*, be made; or restore to the people that form of sound words of which they have too long been deprived. But, to serve the purposes of devotion, we want a better translation of the Psalms; a translation in which the *hemistich*, or Hebrew poetic form, shall be carefully preserved; and with a very few expletives, (which should be distinguished by *italics*, or otherwise, in the printing, to bring the lines into those forms, to which our versification or musical measures may extend,) we might sing the whole, without singing any thing in sense or meaning which was not *David's*. Indeed a species of *recitativo* singing would be the most proper for these sacred odes; as it would answer much better the solemn purposes of devotion, than the great mass of those tunes which are commonly employed in Church music, in which the style of singing is rarely adapted to the grand and melting compositions of *the sweet singer of Israel*. Let the plan be copied which is adopted from the Hebrew MSS. in Dr. *Kennicott's* edition; let them be translated line for line, as Dr. *Lowth* has done his version of Isaiah; let a dignified recitativo music be adapted to the words; attend to metre, and be regardless of rhyme; and then the Psalms will be a mighty help to devotion, and truly religious people will sing with the spirit and the understanding also. Were a version of this kind made and substituted for that most inaccurate version in the *Prayerbook*, a stumbling-block would be taken out of the way of some sincere minds, who are pained to find, not only important differences, but even contradictions, between the Psalms which they read in their authorized version, and those which are used in the public service of the Church.

As many persons are greatly at a loss to account for the strange varieties between these two versions, (that in the *Bible*, and that in the Prayerbook,) it may be necessary to give them some information on this head. Properly speaking, the *Psalms* in the *Prayerbook*, called the *reading Psalms*, are rather a *paraphrase* than a *version*. It was never taken immediately from the *Hebrew*, with which it disagrees in places innumerable. In the main it follows the *Septuagint* and the *Vulgate*, but often differs from *them*, even where they *differ* from the *Hebrew*, and yet without following the *latter*. And there are many *words, turns of thought*, and varieties of *mood, tense*, and *person*, in it which do not appear in any of the above.

In the *prose Psalms* in our *authorized version* our translators have acted very conscientiously, as they have done in all other cases where they have *added* any thing, even the smallest particle, in order to fill up the sense, or accommodate the *Hebrew idiom* to that of the *English;* they have shown this by putting the *expletive* or *supplied* word in the *italic* letter. Thousands of such expletives, many of them utterly unnecessary, are found in the *prose Psalms* in the *Prayerbook;* but they have no such distinguishing mark, and are all printed as if they were the words of the Holy Spirit!

There are some things in this version that are *contradictory* to what is found in the Hebrew text. I shall give one example.

In Psalm cxxv. 3 we have the following words in the Hebrew text: כי לא ינוח שבט הרשע על גורל הצדיקים *ki lo yanuach shebet haresha al goral hatstsaddikim,* which is faithfully translated in our common version, "For the rod of the wicked (*wickedness,* marg.) shall not rest upon the lot of the righteous:" this is rendered in the *prose Psalms* in the *Prayerbook* thus: "For the rod of the ungodly cometh not into the lot of the righteous."

"This," say the objectors, "is neither *Scripture* nor *truth.* 1. It is not *Scripture:* the *Hebrew* is, as our authorized version hath it: 'The rod of the wicked shall not rest.' But your version saith, 'The rod of the ungodly cometh not.' 2. It is not *truth:* 'The rod of the wicked *often* cometh *into* the lot of the righteous;' but here is the difference: though it *may come,* and often *doth come, into the lot of the righteous,* yet God never permitteth it to *rest* there. Here therefore your reading Psalms contradict both *Scripture* and *fact.*"

It may be asked, From what source is this objectionable reading derived? It evidently cannot be derived from the *Hebrew text,* as the reader will at once perceive. It is not in the *Vulgate,* which reads, Quia non relinquet Dominus virgam peccatorum super sortem justorum. "For the Lord will not leave the rod of sinners upon the lot of the righteous." It is not in the *Septuagint,* Ὁτι ουκ αφησει Κυριος την ραβδον των ἁμαρτωλων επι τον κληρον των δικαιων, which is precisely the same as the *Vulgate.* Nor does this strange version receive any support from either the *Chaldee, Syriac, Æthiopic,* or *Arabic.*

To attempt to vindicate such a translation will neither serve the interests of the *Church,* nor those of Christianity, especially when we have one so very different and so very faithful put into the hands of the people by the *authority of the Church and the state.* That in the *Prayerbook* should be immediately suppressed, and replaced by that in our *authorized version,* that the people may not have a different version put into their hands on the *Lord's day,* and in times of *public devotion,* from that which they find in their *Bible;* in consequence of which they are often confounded with discrepancies which it is out of their power to reconcile. It is passing strange that the rulers of the Church have slumbered so long over a subject of such vast magnitude and importance.

To be fully satisfied on this subject, I have collated this *Prayerbook version* in many places with the *Hebrew text,* the *Septuagint,* the *Vulgate,* the old *Itala* or *Antehieronymian,* and the *oriental* versions in general; and find much cause of complaint against its general looseness, and frequent inaccuracy; and would give that advice to the rulers of our Church, that the prophet did to the rulers of the Jewish Church, on a subject in which the best interests of the people were concerned: "Go through, go through the *gates;* cast up, cast up the *highway; take up* the *stumbling-block* out of the way of my people; lift up a *standard* for the people;" Isa. lvii. 14; lxii. 10.

With respect to *helps,* I may say in general that I have occasionally consulted, 1. The *Critici Sacri.* 2. *Venema;* whom I should have been glad to have used more particularly, but his plan would have led me into such an extent of comment, as would have far surpassed my limits. 3. *Rosenmüller's* collections were of more use; but neither did his plan quadrate with mine. 4. *Calmet* afforded me most assistance, as he is, in almost all respects, the most judicious of all the commentators. 5. Could I have wholly agreed with the plan of the truly pious *Bishop Horne,* I might have enriched my work with many of those spiritual remarks with which his *commentary* abounds. Where I differ from *his plan* will best appear in a preceding part of this *introduction,* to which I must refer the reader. 6. From the very learned *Bishop Horsley* I have borrowed several useful *notes,* particularly of a critical kind. 7. But the work which I think may be of most use to masters of families, and ministers in general, is that excellent and judicious one by *Dr. Wm. Nicolson,* formerly *bishop of Gloucester,* with the quaint but expressive title, "DAVID'S HARP STRUNG AND TUNED; or an easy ANALYSIS of the whole *book of Psalms,* cast into such method, that the sum of every Psalm may quickly be collected and remembered." In many places I have introduced the whole of the *analysis,* with some corrections, leaving out the *prayers* at the *end of each Psalm;* which, though very useful for the *family,* or for the *closet,* could not properly have a place in a *comment.* This work was *finished* by the author, October 22, 1658. 8. From an old folio MS. on vellum in my own collection, I have extracted some curious notes and renderings. It contains the Vulgate, or more properly the Antehieronymian version, with a translation after each verse in the ancient Scottish dialect, and after that a paraphrase in same language. I have given the eighth Psalm as it stands in this ancient MS., after my notes on that Psalm. Most of my readers will find this at least an *edifying curiosity.* Extracts from it will appear in different parts of the work. I know nothing like the book of Psalms: it contains all the lengths, breadths, depths, and heights of the patriarchal, Mosaic, and Christian dispensations. It is the most useful book in the Bible, and is every way worthy of the wisdom of God.

Reader, may the Spirit of the ever blessed God make this most singular, most excellent, and most exalted of all his works, a present and eternal blessing to thy soul!—Amen.

ADAM CLARKE.

THE BOOK

OF

PSALMS

Chronological Notes relative to the Psalms written by David, upon the supposition that they were all composed in a period of about forty-seven years. See the Introduction.

Year from the Creation, 2942–2989.—Year before the birth of Christ, 1058–1011.—Year before the vulgar era of Christ's nativity, 1062–1015.—Year since the Deluge, according to Archbishop Usher, and the English Bible, 1286–1333.—Year from the destruction of Troy, according to Dionysius of Halicarnassus, 123–170.—Year before the first Olympiad, 286–239.—Year before the building of Rome, 309–262.—Year of the Julian Period, 3652–3699.—Year of the Dionysian Period, 460–507.

PSALM I

The blessedness of the righteous shown, in his avoiding every appearance of evil, 1. In his godly use of the law of the Lord, 2. This farther pointed out under the metaphor of a good tree planted in a good well-watered soil, 3. The opposite state of the ungodly pointed out, under the metaphor of chaff driven away by the wind, 4. The miserable end of sinners, and the final happiness of the godly, 5, 6.

I. DAY. MORNING PRAYER

BLESSED [b]*is* the man that walketh not in the counsel of the [c]ungodly, nor stand-eth in the way of sinners, [d]nor sitteth in the seat of the scornful.

2 But [e]his delight *is* in the law of the LORD;

---

[a]Luke xx. 42; Acts i. 20——[b]Prov. iv. 14, 15
[c]Or, *wicked*

[d]Psa. xxvi. 4; Jer. xv. 17——[e]Psa. cxix. 35, 47, 92

NOTES ON PSALM I

Verse 1. *Blessed is the man*] This Psalm has no *title*, and has been generally considered, but without especial reason, as a *preface* or *introduction* to the whole book.

The word אשרי *ashrey*, which we translate *blessed*, is properly in the *plural* form, *blessednesses;* or may be considered as an *exclamation* produced by contemplating the state of the man who has taken God for his portion; *O the blessedness of the man!* And the word האיש *haish*, is emphatic: THAT *man;* that *one* among a *thousand* who lives for the accomplishment of the end for which God created him. 1. God made man for happiness. 2. Every man feels a desire to be happy. 3. All human beings abhor misery. 4. Happiness is the grand object of pursuit among all men. 5. But so perverted is the human heart, that it seeks happiness where it cannot be found; and in things which are naturally and morally unfit to communicate it. 6. The true way of obtaining it is here laid down.

That walketh not in the counsel of the ungodly] There is a double CLIMAX in this verse, which it will be proper to note:—

1. There are here *three* characters, each *exceeding* the other in sinfulness. 1. The UN-GODLY רשעים *reshaim*, from רשע *rasha*, to be *unjust;* rendering to none his due; withholding from God, society, and himself, what belongs to each. *Ungodly*—he who has not God in him; who is without God in the world. 2. SINNERS, חטאים *chattaim*, from חטא *chata*, "to miss the mark," "to pass over the prohibited limits," "to transgress." This man not only does *no good*, but he *does evil*. The former was *without God*, but not *desperately wicked*. The latter adds *outward transgression* to the *sinfulness* of his heart. 3. SCORNFUL, לצים *letsim*, from לצה *latsah*, "to mock, deride." He who has no religion; lives in the open breach of God's laws; and turns *revelation*, the *immortality of the soul*, and the existence of an *invisible world*, into ridicule. He is at least a *deist*, and endeavours to *dissolve*, as much as he can, the *bonds* of moral obligation in civil society. As the *sinner* exceeds the *ungodly*, so the *scornful* exceeds *both*.

The *second climax* is found in the words, 1. *Walk;* 2. *Stand;* 3. *Sit:* which mark *three different degrees* of evil in the *conduct* of those persons.

Observe, 1. The *ungodly* man—one uninfluenced by God. 2. The *sinner*—he who adds to *ungodliness transgression*. 3. The *scornful*—the deist, atheist, &c., who make a mock of every thing sacred. The UNGODLY man *walks*, the SINNER *stands, and the* SCORNFUL man *sits down* in the way of iniquity.

Mark certain circumstances of their differing characters and conduct. 1. The *ungodly*

and ᶠin his law doth he meditate day and night.

3 And he shall be like a tree ᵍplanted by the rivers of water, that bringeth forth his fruit in his season : his leaf also shall not ʰwither; and whatsoever he doeth shall ⁱprosper.

ᶠJosh. i. 8; Psa. cxix. 1, 97——ᵍJer. xvii. 8; Ezek. xlvii. 12

ʰHeb. *fade*——ⁱGen. xxxix. 3, 23; Psa. cxxviii. 2; Isa. iii. 10

---

man has his *counsel;* 2. The *sinner* has his *way;* and, 3. The *scorner* has his *seat.*

The *ungodly man* is unconcerned about religion; he is neither zealous for his own salvation, nor for that of others: and he *counsels* and *advises* those with whom he converses to adopt his plan, and not trouble themselves about praying, reading, repenting, &c., &c.; there is no need for such things; live an honest life, make no fuss about religion, and you will fare well enough at last. Now, "blessed is the man who walks not in this man's counsel;" who does not come into his measures, nor act according to his plan.

The *sinner* has his particular *way* of transgressing; one is a *drunkard,* another *dishonest,* another *unclean.* Few are given to every species of vice. There are many *covetous men* who abhor *drunkenness;* many *drunkards* who abhor *covetousness;* and so of others. Each has his *easily besetting sin;* therefore, says the prophet, *let the wicked* forsake HIS WAY. Now, *blessed is he who stands not in such a man's* WAY.

The *scorner* has brought, in reference to himself, all religion and moral feeling to an end. He has *sat down*—is utterly confirmed in impiety, and makes a mock at sin. His conscience is seared; and he is a believer in all unbelief. Now, *blessed is the man who sits not down in his* SEAT.

See the *correspondent relations* in this account. 1. He who *walks* according to the *counsel* of the *ungodly* will soon, 2. *Stand* to look on the *way* of *sinners;* and thus, being off his guard, he will soon be a partaker in their evil deeds. 3. He who has abandoned himself to transgression will, in all probability, soon become hardened by the deceitfulness of sin; and *sit down* with the *scorner,* and endeavour to turn religion into ridicule.

The last correspondency we find is:—1. The *seat* answers to the *sitting* of the *scornful.* 2. The *way* answers to the *standing* of the *sinner;* and 3, the *counsel* answers to the *walking* of the *ungodly.*

The great lesson to be learned from the whole is, sin is *progressive;* one evil propensity or act leads to another. He who acts by *bad counsel* may soon do *evil deeds;* and he who abandons himself to *evil doings* may end his life in *total apostasy* from God. "When lust has conceived, it brings forth sin; and when sin is finished, it brings forth death." Solomon, the son of David, adds a profitable advice to those words of his father: "Enter not into the path of the wicked, and go not in the way of evil *men;* avoid it, pass not by it, turn from it, and pass away;" Prov. iv. 14, 15.

As the *blessedness* of the man is great who avoids the ways and the workers of iniquity, so his *wretchedness* is great who acts on the *contrary:* to him we must reverse the words of David: "Cursed is the man who walketh in the counsel of the ungodly; who standeth in the way of sinners; and who sitteth in the seat of the scornful." Let him that readeth understand.

Verse 2. *But his delight is in the law of the Lord*] חפצו *chephtso,* his will, desire, affection, every *motive* in his heart, and every *moving principle* in his soul, are on the side of God and his *truth.* He takes up *the law of the Lord* as the *rule of his life;* he brings all his actions and affections to this holy *standard.* He looketh into the perfect law of liberty; and is not a forgetful hearer, but a doer of the word; and is therefore blessed in his deed. He not only *reads* to gain knowledge from the Divine oracles, but he *meditates* on what he has read, feeds on it; and thus receiving *the sincere milk of the word,* he grows thereby unto eternal life. This is not an *occasional* study to him; it is his work *day and night.* As his *heart* is in it, the *employment* must be *frequent,* and the *disposition* to it *perpetual.*

Verse 3. *Like a tree planted*] Not like one growing wild, however strong or luxuriant it may appear; but one that has been carefully *cultivated;* and for the proper growth of which all the advantages of soil and situation have been chosen. If a child be brought up in the discipline and admonition of the Lord, we have both reason and revelation to encourage us to expect a godly and useful life. Where religious education is neglected, alas! what fruits of righteousness can be expected? An *uncultivated soul* is like an *uncultivated field,* all overgrown with briers, thorns, and thistles.

By the rivers of water] פלגי מים *palgey mayim,* the streams or divisions of the waters. Alluding to the custom of *irrigation* in the eastern countries, where streams are conducted from a canal or river to different parts of the ground, and turned *off* or *on* at pleasure; the person having no more to do than by *his foot* to turn a sod from the side of one stream, to cause it to share its waters with the other parts to which he wishes to direct his course. This is called "watering the land with the foot," Deut. xi. 10, where see the note.

His fruit in his season] In such a case expectation is never disappointed. Fruit is expected, fruit is borne; and it comes also in the time in which it should come. A godly education, under the influences of the Divine Spirit, which can never be withheld where they are earnestly sought, is sure to produce the fruits of righteousness; and he who reads, prays, and meditates, will ever *see* the *work* which God has given him to do; the *power* by which he is to perform it; and the *times, places,* and *opportunities* for doing those things by which God can obtain most glory, his own soul most good, and his neighbour most edification.

His leaf also shall not wither] His *profession* of true religion shall always be regular and unsullied; and his *faith* be ever shown by his *works.* As the *leaves* and the *fruit* are the evidences of the vegetative perfection of the tree; so a zealous religious profession, accompanied with good works, are the evidences of

4 The ungodly *are* not so : but *are*
ᵏlike the chaff which the wind driveth
away.

5 Therefore the ungodly ¹shall not stand in

the judgment, nor sinners in the congregation
of the righteous.

6 For ᵐthe LORD knoweth the way of the righteous : but the way of the ungodly shall perish.

ᵏJob xxi. 18; Psa. xxxv. 5; Isa. xvii. 13; xxix. 5; Hos.
xiii. 3

¹Wisd. v. 1——ᵐPsa. xxxvii. 18; Nah. i. 7; John x. 14;
2 Tim. ii. 19

---

the soundness of faith in the Christian man.
Rabbi Solomon Jarchi gives a curious turn to
this expression: he considers the *leaves* as expressing those matters of the law that seem to
be of no real use, to be quite unimportant, and
that apparently neither add nor diminish. But
even these things are parts of the Divine revelation, and *all have their use;* so even the apparently indifferent actions or sayings of a
truly holy man have their use; and from the
manner and *spirit* in which they are done or
said, have the tendency to bear the observer to
something great and good.

Whatsoever he doeth shall prosper] It is
always healthy; it is extending its roots, increasing its woody fibres, circulating its nutritive juices, putting forth fruitbuds, blossoms,
leaves, or fruit; and all these operations go on,
in a healthy tree, in their proper seasons. So
the godly man; he is ever taking deeper root,
growing stronger in the grace he has already
received, increasing in heavenly desires, and,
under the continual influence of the Divine
Spirit, forming those purposes from which
much fruit to the glory and praise of God shall
be produced.

Verse 4. *The ungodly* are *not so*] The *Vulgate* and *Septuagint*, and the versions made
from them, such as the *Æthiopic* and *Arabic*,
double the last negation, and add a clause to
the end of the verse, "Not so the ungodly, *not
so;* they shall be like the dust which the wind
scatters away *from the face of the earth.*"
There is nothing solid in the men; there is
nothing good in their ways. They are not of
God's planting; they are not good grain; they
are only *chaff*, and a chaff that shall be separated from the good grain when the fan or
shovel of God's power throws them up to the
wind of his judgments. The manner of *winnowing* in the eastern countries is nearly the
same with that practised in various parts of
these kingdoms before the invention of *winnowing machines.* They either throw it up in
a place out of doors by a large wooden shovel
against the wind; or with their *weights* or
winnowing fans shake it down leisurely in the
wind. The grain falls down nearly perpendicularly; and the chaff, through its lightness, is
blown away to a distance from the grain.

An ungodly man is never steady; his purposes are abortive; his conversation light, trifling, and foolish; his professions, friendships,
&c., frothy, hollow, and insincere; and both he
and his works are carried away to destruction
by the wind of God's judgments.

Verse 5. *Therefore the ungodly shall not
stand*] This refers to the *winnowing* mentioned in the preceding verse. Some of the
versions have, *The ungodly shall not arise in
the judgment*—they shall have *no resurrection*,
except to shame and everlasting contempt. But
probably the meaning is, When they come to be
judged, they shall be condemned. They shall
have nothing to plead in their behalf. That

the impious were never to have any resurrection, but be annihilated, was the opinion of
several among the Jews, and of some among
Christians. The former believe that only the
true Israelites shall be raised again; and that
the souls of all others, the Christians not excepted, die with their bodies. Such unfounded
opinions are unworthy of refutation.

Verse 6. *The Lord knoweth*] יֹדֵעַ *yodea*,
approveth the way, **aloweth the way,** *Coverdale*,
of the righteous, צַדִּיקִים *tsaddikim*, from צדק
tsadak, to *give even weight;* the men who give
to all their *due;* opposed to רשׁעים *reshaim*, ver.
1, they who withhold *right* from all; see above.
Such holy men are under the continual eye of
God's *providence;* he *knows* the way that they
take; *approves* of their motives, purposes, and
works, because they are all wrought through
himself. He *provides* for them in all exigencies,
and *defends* them both in body and soul.

The way of the ungodly shall perish.] Their
projects, designs, and operations, shall perish;
God's curse shall be on all that they *have, do,*
and *are.* And in the day of judgment they
shall be condemned to everlasting fire in the
perdition of ungodly men. *The wicked shall
perish at the presence of the Lord.* Reader,
take warning!

ANALYSIS OF THE FIRST PSALM

The το κρινομενον in this Psalm is, *Who is the
happy man?* or, *What may make a man happy?*
I. This question the prophet resolves in the
first two verses: 1. *Negatively.* It is he, 1.
"That walks not in the counsel of the ungodly."
2. "That stands not in the way of sinners." 3.
"That sits not in the seat of the scornful." 2.
Positively. It is he. 1. "Whose delight is in
the law of the Lord." 2. "Who doth meditate
in the law day and night."

II. This happiness of the good man is illustrated two ways: 1. By a similitude. 2. By
comparing him with a wicked man.

1. The similitude he makes choice of is that
of a *tree;* not every *tree* neither, but that which
hath these eminences: 1. It is "planted;" it
grows not of itself, neither is wild. 2. "Planted
by the rivers of water;" it wants not moisture
to fructify. 3. It doth fructify; "it brings forth
fruit;" it is no *barren* tree. 4. The fruit it
brings is seasonable; "it brings forth fruit in
its season." 5. It is always green, winter and
summer; "the leaves wither not." Clearly,
without any trope, *Whatsoever* this good man
doth, or takes in hand, "it shall prosper."

2. He shows this good man's happiness by
comparing him with a wicked man, in whom
you shall find all the contrary.

1. In general. *Not so.* As for the ungodly,
it is not so with them: *not so* in the planta-
tion; in the place; in the seasonable fruit; in
the greenness; in the prosperity. So far from
being like a *tree*, that they are like, 1. *Chaff*,
a light and empty thing. 2. *Chaff* which the
wind whiffles up and down. 3. *Chaff* which the

wind scatters or *driveth away.* 4. And never leaves scattering, till it has driven it from the face of the earth. So the *Vulgate, Septuagint,* and *Arabic.*

2. And that no man may think that their punishment shall extend only to this life; in plain terms he threatens to them, 1. Damnation at the great day: "They shall not stand in judgment;" though some refer this clause to this life. When he is judged by men, *causa cadet,*

he shall be condemned. 2. Exclusion from the company of the just: "Sinners shall not stand in the congregation of the righteous."

III. In the close he shows the cause why the godly is happy, the wicked unhappy: 1. Because "the way of the righteous is known to God;" approved by him, and defended. 2. But the way, studies, plots, "counsels of the wicked, shall perish."—DAVID'S HARP STRUNG AND TUNED. See the introduction.

PSALM II

This Psalm treats of the opposition raised, both by Jew and Gentile, against the kingdom of Christ, 1–3. Christ's victory, and the confusion of his enemies, 4–6. The promulgation of the Gospel after his resurrection, 7–9. A call to all the potentates and judges of the earth to accept it, because of the destruction that shall fall on those who reject it, 10–12.

A. M. cir. 2957
B. C. cir. 1047
Ante I. Ol. 271
Anno Davidis,
Regis
Israelitarum, 9

WHY [a]do the heathen [b]rage, and the people [c]imagine a vain thing?

2 The kings of the earth set themselves, and the rulers take counsel together, against the LORD, and against his [d]anointed, *saying,*

3 [e]Let us break their bands asunder, and cast away their cords from us.

4 [f]He that sitteth in the heavens [g]shall laugh: the LORD shall have them in derision.

5 Then shall he speak unto them in his

A. M. cir. 2957
B. C. cir. 1047
Ante I. Ol. 271
Anno Davidis,
Regis
Israelitarum, 9

---

[a]Psa. xlvi. 6; Acts iv. 25, 26——[b]Or, *tumultuously assemble*——[c]Heb. *meditate*

[d]Psa. xlv. 7; John i. 41——[e]Jer. v. 5; Luke xix. 14
[f]Psa. xi. 4——[g]Psa. xxxvii. 13; lix. 8; Prov. i. 26

NOTES ON PSALM II

Verse 1. *Why do the heathen rage*] It has been supposed that David composed this Psalm after he had taken Jerusalem from the Jebusites, and made it the head of the kingdom; 2 Sam. v. 7-9. The Philistines, hearing this, encamped in the valley of Rephaim, nigh to Jerusalem, and Josephus, Antiq. lib. vii. c. 4, says that all Syria, Phœnicia, and the other circumjacent warlike people, united their armies to those of the Philistines, in order to destroy David before he had strengthened himself in the kingdom. David, having consulted the Lord, 2 Sam. v. 17-19, gave them battle, and totally overthrew the whole of his enemies. In the *first* place, therefore, we may suppose that this Psalm was written to celebrate the taking of Jerusalem, and the overthrow of all the kings and chiefs of the neighbouring nations. In the *second* place we find, from the use made of this Psalm by the apostles, Acts iv. 27, that David typified Jesus Christ; and that the Psalm celebrates the victories of the Gospel over the *Philistine Jews,* and all the confederate power of the *heathen governors* of the Roman empire.

The heathen, נוים *goyim,* the nations; those who are commonly called *the Gentiles.*

Rage, רנשו *rageshu;* the gnashing of teeth, and tumultuously rushing together, of those indignant and cruel people, are well expressed by the *sound* as well as the *meaning* of the original word. *A vain thing.* Vain indeed to prevent the spread of the Gospel in the world. To prevent Jesus Christ, the King of kings, and Lord of lords, from having the empire of his own earth. So vain were their endeavours that

every effort only tended to open and enlarge the way for the all-conquering sway of the sceptre of righteousness.

Verse 2. *Against his anointed*] על משיחיה *al Meshichiah,* "Against his *Messiah.*"—*Chaldee.* But as this signifies the *anointed* person, it may refer first to *David,* as it does secondly to *Christ.*

Verse 3. *Let us break their bands*] These are the words of the confederate heathen powers; and here, as Bishop Horne well remarks, "we may see the ground of opposition; namely, the unwillingness of rebellious nature to submit to the obligations of Divine laws, which cross the interests, and lay a restraint on the desires of men. Corrupt affections are the most inveterate enemies of Christ, and their language is, We will not have this man to reign over us. Doctrines would be readily believed if they involved in them no precepts; and the Church may be tolerated in the world if she will only give up her discipline."

Verse 4. *He that sitteth in the heavens*] Whose kingdom ruleth over all, and is *above* all might and power, human and diabolical. *Shall laugh.* Words spoken after the manner of men; shall utterly contemn their puny efforts; shall beat down their pride, assuage their malice, and confound their devices.

Verse 5. *Then shall he speak unto them in his wrath*] He did so to the Jews who rejected the Gospel, and vexed and ruined them by the Roman armies; he did so with the opposing Roman emperors, destroying all the contending factions, till he brought the empire under the dominion of one, and him he converted to Christianity viz., *Constantine* the Great.

A. M. cir. 2957
B. C. cir. 1047
Ante I. Ol. 271
Anno Davidis,
    Regis
Israelitarum, 9

wrath, and [h]vex them in his sore displeasure.

6 Yet have I [i]set my king [k]upon [l]my holy hill of Zion.

7 I will declare [m]the decree: the LORD

hath said unto me, [n]Thou *art* my Son; this day have I begotten thee.

8 [o]Ask of me, and I shall give *thee* the heathen *for* thine inheritance,

A. M. cir. 2957
B. C. cir. 1047
Ante I. Ol. 271
Anno Davidis,
    Regis
Israelitarum, 9

---

[b]Or, *trouble*——[i]Heb. *anointed*——[k]Heb. *upon Zion the hill of my holiness*——[l]2 Sam. v. 7——[m]Or, *for a decree*

[n]Acts xiii. 33; Heb. i. 5; v. 5——[o]Psa. xxii. 27; lxxii. 8; lxxxix. 27; Dan. vii. 13, 14; see John xvii. 4, 5; xix. 15

Verse 6. *I set my king upon my holy hill of Zion.*] Here the Gospel shall be first preached; here the kingdom of Christ shall be founded; and from hence shall the doctrine of the Lord go out into all the earth.

Verse 7. *I will declare the decree*] These words are supposed to have been spoken by the Messiah. I will declare to the world the decree, the purpose of God to redeem them by my blood, and to sanctify them by my Spirit. My death shall prove that the required *atonement* has been made; my *resurrection* shall prove that this atonement has been *accepted*.

Thou art my Son] Made man, born of a woman by the creative energy of the Holy Ghost, that thou mightest feel and suffer for man, and be the first-born of many brethren.

This day have I begotten thee.] By thy *resurrection* thou art declared to be the Son of God, εν δυναμει, *by miraculous power*, being raised from the dead. Thus by thy wondrous and supernatural *nativity*, most extraordinary *death*, and miraculous *resurrection*, thou art declared to be the Son of God. And as in that Son dwelt all the fulness of the Godhead bodily, all the sufferings and the death of that human nature were stamped with an infinitely meritorious efficacy. We have St. Paul's authority for applying to the *resurrection* of our Lord these words, "Thou art my Son; this day have I begotten thee;"—see Acts xiii. 33; see also Heb. v. 5;—and the man must indeed be a bold interpreter of the Scriptures who would give a different gloss to that of the apostle. It is well known that the words, "Thou art my Son; this day have I begotten thee," have been produced by many as a proof of the *eternal generation of the Son of God*. On the subject itself I have already given my opinion in my note on Luke i. 35, from which I recede not one hair's breadth. Still however it is necessary to spend a few moments on the clause before us. The word היום *haiyom*, TO-DAY, is in no part of the sacred writings used to express *eternity*, or any thing in reference to it; nor can it have any such signification. *To-day* is an absolute designation of the *present*, and equally excludes *time past* and *time future;* and never can, by any figure, or allowable latitude of construction, be applied to express *eternity*. But why then does the Divine Spirit use the word *begotten* in reference to the declaration of the inauguration of the Messiah to his kingdom, and his being seated at the right hand of God? Plainly to show both to Jews and Gentiles that this Man of sorrows, this Outcast from society, this Person who was prosecuted as a blasphemer of God, and crucified as an enemy to the public peace and a traitor to the government, is no less than that *eternal Word*, who *was in the beginning with God*, who *was God*, and *in whom dwelt all the fulness of the Godhead bodily:* that this rejected Person was he for whom in

the fulness of time a body was prepared, *begotten* by the exclusive *power* of the *Most High* in the womb of an *unspotted virgin*, which body he gave unto death as a *sin-offering* for the redemption of the world; and having raised it from death, *declared* it to be that *miraculously-begotten Son of God*, and now gave farther proof of this by raising the God-man to *his right hand.*

The word ילדתי *yalidti*, "I have begotten," is here taken in the sense of *manifesting, exhibiting,* or *declaring;* and to this sense of it St. Paul (Rom. i. 3, 4) evidently alludes when speaking of "Jesus Christ, who was made of the seed of David according to the flesh, του ορισθεντος Υιου Θεου εν δυναμει, κατα Πνευμα αγιωσυνης, εξ αναστασεως νεκρων; *and declared* (exhibited or determined) *to be the Son of God with power,* according to the Spirit of holiness." This very rejected Person I this day, by raising him from the dead, and placing him at my right hand, giving to him all power in heaven and earth, declare to be my Son, the beloved one in whom I am well pleased. Therefore hear *him*, believe on *him*, and obey *him;* for there is no redemption but through *his* blood; no salvation but in *his* name; no resurrection unto eternal life but through *his* resurrection, ascension, and powerful intercession at my right hand. *Thou art my Son; this day have I declared and manifested thee to be such.* It was absolutely necessary to the salvation of men, and the credibility of the Gospel, that the *supernatural* origin of the *humanity* of Jesus Christ should be manifested and demonstrated. Hence we find the inspired writers taking pains to show that he was born of a *woman*, and of that woman by the *sovereign power of the everlasting God.* This vindicated the character of the blessed virgin, showed the human nature of Christ to be immaculate, and that, even in respect to this nature, he was every way qualified to be a proper atoning sacrifice and Mediator between God and man. I need not tell the learned reader that the Hebrew verb ילד *yalad, to beget,* is frequently used in reference to *inanimate* things, to signify their *production,* or the *exhibition* of the things produced. In Gen. ii. 4: *These are the generations,* תולדות *toledoth,* of the heavens and the earth; this is the order in which God produced and exhibited them. See *Heb.* and *Eng. Concord., Venema,* &c.

Verse 8. *Ask of me, and I shall give* thee] Here a *second* branch of Christ's office as Saviour of the world is referred to; viz., his *mediatorial* office. Having died as an *atoning sacrifice,* and *risen again* from the dead, he was now to *make intercession* for mankind; and in virtue and on account of what he had done and suffered, he was, *at his request,* to have the *nations for his inheritance, and the uttermost parts of the earth for his possession.* He was to become supreme Lord in the mediatorial

A. M. cir. 2957
B. C. cir. 1047
Ante I. Ol. 271
Anno Davidis, Regis
Israelitarum, 9

and the uttermost parts of the earth *for* thy possession.

9 ᵖThou shalt break them with a rod of iron; thou shalt dash them in pieces like a potter's vessel.

10 Be wise now therefore, O ye kings: be instructed, ye judges of the earth.

ᵖPsa. lxxxix. 23; Rev. ii. 27; xii. 5——ᑫHeb. xii. 28——ʳPhil. ii. 12——ˢGen. xli. 40; 1 Sam. x. 1; John v. 23

11 ᑫServe the LORD with fear, and rejoice ʳwith trembling.

12 ˢKiss the Son, lest he be angry, and ye perish *from* the way, when ᵗhis wrath is kindled but a little. ᵘBlessed *are* all they that put their trust in him.

A. M. cir. 2957
B. C. cir. 1047
Ante I. Ol. 271
Anno Davidis, Regis
Israelitarum, 9

ᵗRev. vi. 16, 17——ᵘPsa. xxxiv. 8; lxxxiv. 12; Prov. xvi. 20; Isa. xxx. 18; Jer. xvii. 7; Rom. ix. 33; x. 11; 1 Pet. ii. 6

kingdom; in consequence of which he sent his apostles throughout the habitable globe to preach the Gospel to every man.

Verse 9. Thou shalt break them with a rod of iron] This may refer to the *Jewish nation*, whose final rejection of the Gospel was foreseen, and in whose place the *Gentiles* or *heathen* were brought into the Church of Christ. They were dispossessed of their land, their *city* was razed to its foundations, their *temple* was burnt with fire, and upwards of a *million of themselves* were slaughtered by the Romans! So heavily did the *iron rod* of God's judgments fall upon them for their obstinate unbelief.

Verse 10. Be wise—O ye kings] An exhortation of the Gospel to the rulers of all kingdoms, nations, and states, to whom it may be sent. All these should listen to its maxims, be governed by its precepts, and rule their subjects according to its dictates.

Be instructed, ye judges] Rather, *Be ye reformed*—cast away all your idolatrous maxims; and receive the Gospel as the law, or the *basis* of the law, of the land.

Verse 11. Serve the Lord with fear] A general direction to all men. *Fear God* with that *reverence* which is due to his supreme *majesty*. *Serve* him as *subjects* should their *sovereign*, and as *servants* should their *master*.

Rejoice with trembling.] If ye serve God aright, ye cannot but be *happy;* but let a *continual filial fear* moderate all your joys. Ye must all stand at last before the judgment-seat of God; watch, pray, believe, work, and keep humble.

Verse 12. Kiss the Son, lest he be angry] It is remarkable that the word *son* (בר *bar*, a Chaldee word) is not found in any of the versions except the *Syriac*, nor indeed any thing equivalent to it.

The *Chaldee, Vulgate, Septuagint, Arabic*, and *Æthiopic*, have a term which signifies *doctrine* or *discipline:* "Embrace discipline, lest the Lord be angry with you," &c. This is a remarkable case, and especially that in so pure a piece of Hebrew as this poem is, a *Chaldee* word should have been found; בר *bar*, instead of בן *ben*, which adds nothing to the strength of the expression or the elegance of the poetry. I know it is supposed that בר *bar* is also pure Hebrew, as well as Chaldee; but as it is taken in the former language in the sense of *purifying*, the versions probably understood it so here. *Embrace that which is pure;* namely, the *doctrine* of God.

As all *judgment* is committed to the *Son*, the Jews and others are exhorted to *submit* to him, to be *reconciled* to him, that they might be received into his family, and be acknowledged

as his adopted children. Kissing was the token of *subjection* and *friendship.*

Is kindled but a little.] The *slightest stroke* of the *iron rod* of Christ's justice is sufficient to break in pieces a whole rebel world. Every sinner, not yet reconciled to God through Christ, should receive this as a most solemn warning.

Blessed are *all they*] He is only the *inexorable Judge* to them who harden their hearts in their iniquity, and will not come unto him that they may have life. But all they who *trust in him*—who repose all their trust and confidence in him as their *atonement* and as their *Lord*, shall be blessed with *innumerable blessings.* For as the word is the same here as in Psa. i. 1, אשרי *ashrey*, it may be translated the same. "O the blessedness of all them who trust in him!"

This Psalm is remarkable, not only for its subject—the future kingdom of the *Messiah*, its *rise, opposition*, and *gradual extent*, but also for the elegant *change of person.* In the first verse the *prophet* speaks; in the third, the *adversaries;* in the fourth and fifth, the *prophet answers;* in the sixth, *Jehovah* speaks; in the seventh, the *Messiah;* in the eighth and ninth, *Jehovah answers;* and in the tenth to the twelfth, the *prophet* exhorts the *opponents* to submission and obedience.—Dr. *A. Bayly.*

ANALYSIS OF THE SECOND PSALM

The prime subject of this Psalm is CHRIST; the type, DAVID. The persons we are chiefly to reflect on are *three*, and which make *three parts* of the Psalm: I. The enemies of Christ; II. Christ the Lord; III. The princes and judges of the earth.

I. The enemies of Christ are great men, who are described here, partly from their *wickedness*, and partly from their *weakness.*

First, Their *wickedness* is apparent. 1. They *furiously rage.* 2. They *tumultuously assemble.* 3. They *set themselves*—stand up, *and take counsel, against the Lord and against his anointed.* 4. They encourage themselves in mischief, saying, "Come, and let us cast away their cords from us." All which is sharpened by the interrogatory *Why?*

Secondly, Their *weakness;* in that they shall never be able to bring their plots and conspiracies against Christ and his kingdom to pass; for, 1. What *they imagine is but a vain thing.* 2. "He that sits in heaven shall laugh, and have them in derision." 3. "He shall speak unto them in his wrath, and vex them in his sore displeasure." 4. For, maugre all their plots, "God hath set up his king upon his holy hill of Zion."

II. At ver. 6 begins the exaltation of Christ

to his kingdom, which is the SECOND PART of the Psalm; in which the prophet, by a προσωποποιΐα, or personification, brings in God the Father speaking, and the Son answering.

First, The words of the Father are, "I have set my king;" where we have the inauguration of Christ, or his vocation to the crown.

Secondly, The answer of the Son, "I will preach the law;" which sets forth his willing obedience to publish and proclaim the laws of the kingdom; of which the chief is, "Thou art my Son, this day have I begotten thee."

Thirdly, The reply of the Father, containing the reward that Christ was to have upon the publication of the Gospel; which was, 1. An addition to his empire by the conversion and accession of the Gentiles: "Ask of me, and I will give thee the heathen for thine inheritance," &c. 2. And the confusion of his enemies: "Thou shalt break them," who would not have thee reign, that did rage and stand up against thee, "with a rod of iron; and break them in pieces as a potter's vessel."

III. In the *third part* the prophet descends to his exhortation and admonition, and that very aptly; for, Is Christ a King? Is he a King anointed by God? Is he a great King, a powerful King? So great that the nations are his subjects? So powerful that he will break and batter to pieces his enemies? Besides, Is he the only begotten Son of God? Be wise, therefore, O ye kings. In this we find,

First, The persons to whom this *caveat* is given: *kings* and *judges.*

Secondly, What they are taught. 1. To *know* their duty: "Be wise; be learned." 2. To *do* their duty: "Serve the Lord with fear; rejoice with trembling; kiss the Son."

Thirdly, The time when this is to be done; even *now.* The reason double: 1. Drawn from his wrath, and the consequent punishment: "Lest he be angry, and ye perish from the right way, when his wrath is kindled but a little." 2. From the happy condition of those who learn to know, and fear, and serve, and adore him: "Blessed are all they that put their trust in him." There must be no delay; this is the time of wrath, and the day of salvation.

PSALM III

David complains, in great distress, of the number of his enemies, and the reproaches they cast on him, as one forsaken of God, 1, 2; is confident, notwithstanding, that God will be his protector, 3; mentions his prayers and supplications, and how God heard him, 4, 5; derides the impotent malice of his adversaries, and foretells their destruction, 6, 7; and ascribes salvation to God, 8.

A Psalm of David, ᵃwhen he fled from Absalom his son

A. M. 2981
B. C. 1023
Anno Davidis,
Regis
Israelitarum,
33

LORD, ᵇhow are they increased that trouble me? many *are* they that rise up against me.

2 Many *there be* which say of my soul, ᶜ*There is* no help for him in God. Selah.

3 But thou, O LORD, *art* ᵈa shield ᵉfor me; my glory, and ᶠthe lifter up of mine head.

A. M. 2981
B. C. 1023
Anno Davidis,
Regis
Israelitarum,
33

ᵃ2 Sam. xv., xvi., xvii., xviii.——ᵇ2 Sam. xv. 12; xvi. 15
ᶜ2 Sam. xvi. 8; Psa. lxxi. 11

ᵈGen. xv. 1; Psa. xxviii. 7; cxix. 114——ᵉOr, *about*
ᶠPsa. xxvii. 6

NOTES ON PSALM III

This is said to be *A Psalm of David, when he fled from Absalom his son.*] See the account, 2 Sam. xv. 1, &c. And David is supposed to have composed it when obliged to leave Jerusalem, passing by the mount of Olives, weeping, with his clothes rent, and with dust upon his head. This Psalm is suitable enough to these circumstances; and they mutually cast light on each other. If the inscription be correct, this Psalm is a proof that the Psalms are not placed in any chronological order.

The word *Psalm,* מזמור *mizmor,* comes from זמר *zamar,* to *cut,* whether that means to *cut into syllables,* for the purpose of its being adapted to musical tones, or whether its being *cut on wood,* &c., for the direction of the singers; what we would call a Psalm in *score.* This last opinion, however, seems too technical.

Verse 1. *Lord, how are they increased that trouble me?*] We are told that *the hearts of all Israel went after Absalom,* 2 Sam. xv. 13; and David is astonished to find such a *sudden* and *general* revolt. Not only the *common people,* but his *counsellors* also, and many of his chief *captains.* How *publicly* does God take vengeance for the sins which David committed so *privately!* In the horrible rebellion of Absalom we see the adultery of Bath-sheba, and the murder of Uriah. Now the words of Nathan begin to be fulfilled: "The sword shall not depart from thy house."

Verse 2. *No help for him in God.*] These were some of the *reproaches* of his enemies, *Shimei* and others: "He is now down, and he shall never be able to rise. God alone can save him from these his enemies; but God has visibly cast him off." These reproaches deeply affected his heart; and he mentions them with that *note* which so frequently occurs in the Psalms, and which occurs here for the *first* time, סלה *selah.* Much has been said on the meaning of this word; and we have nothing but conjecture to guide us. The *Septuagint* always translate it by Διάψαλμα *diapsalma,* "a pause in the Psalm." The *Chaldee* sometimes translates it by לעלמין *lealmin,* "for ever." The rest of the versions leave it unnoticed. It either comes

A. M. 2981
B. C. 1023
Anno Davidis,
Regis
Israelitarum,
33

4 I cried unto the Lord with my voice, and ᵍhe heard me out of his ʰholy hill. Selah.

5 ˡI laid me down and slept; I awaked; for the Lord sustained me.

6 ᵏI will not be afraid of ten thousands of people, that have set *themselves* against me round about.

ᵍPsalm xxxiv. 4——ʰPsalm ii. 6; xliii. 3; xcix. 9
ˡLeviticus xxvi. 6; Psalm iv. 8; Prov. iii. 24——ᵏPsalm
xxvii. 3——ˡJob xvi. 10; xxix. 17; Psalm lviii. 6;

---

from סל *sal*, to *raise* or *elevate*, and may denote a particular *elevation* in the voices of the performers, which is very observable in the Jewish singing to the present day; or it may come from סלה *salah*, to *strew* or *spread out*, intimating that the subject to which the word is attached should be *spread out, meditated on,* and *attentively considered* by the reader. *Fenwick, Parkhurst,* and *Dodd,* contend for this meaning; and think "it confirmed by Psa. ix. 16, where the word *higgaion* is put before *selah*, at the end of the verse." Now higgaion certainly signifies *meditation*, or a fit subject for meditation; and so shows *selah* to be really a *nota bene, attend to* or *mind this*.

Verse 3. *Thou, O Lord,* art *a shield*] As a *shield* covers and defends the body from the strokes of an adversary, so wilt thou cover and defend me from them that rise up against me.

The lifter up of mine head.] Thou wilt restore me to the *state* from which my enemies have cast me down. This is the meaning of the phrase; and this he speaks *prophetically.* He was satisfied that the deliverance would take place, hence his confidence in prayer; so that we find him, with comparative unconcern, laying himself down in his bed, expecting the sure protection of the Almighty.

Verse 4. *I cried unto the Lord with my voice*] He was exposed to much danger, and therefore he had need of *fervour.*

He heard me] Notwithstanding my enemies said, and my friends feared, that there *was no help for me in my God; yet he heard me out of his holy hill. Selah: mark this*, and take encouragement from it. God never forsakes those who trust in him. He never shuts out the prayer of the distressed.

Verse 5. *I laid me down and slept*] He who knows that he has God for his Protector may go quietly and confidently to his bed, not fearing the *violence of the fire,* the *edge of the sword,* the *designs of wicked men,* nor the *influence of malevolent spirits.*

I awaked] Though humanly speaking there was reason to fear I should have been murdered in my bed, as my most confidential servants had been corrupted by my rebellious son; yet God, my shield, protected me. I both slept and awaked; and my life is still whole in me.

Verse 6. *I will not be afraid of ten thousands*] Strength and numbers are nothing against the omnipotence of God. He who has made God his refuge certainly has no cause to fear.

Verse 7. *Arise, O Lord*] Though he knew that God had undertaken his defence, yet he knew that his continued protection depended

7 Arise, O Lord; save me, O my God: ˡfor thou hast smitten all mine enemies *upon* the cheek bone; thou hast broken the teeth of the ungodly.

8 ᵐSalvation *belongeth* unto the Lord: thy blessing *is* upon thy people. Selah.

A. M. 2981
B. C. 1023
Anno Davidis,
Regis
Israelitarum,
33

ˡLamentations iii. 30——ᵐProverbs xxi. 31; Isaiah xliii.
11; Jeremiah iii. 23; Hosea xiii. 4; Jonah ii. 9; Rev.
vii. 10; xix. 1

---

on his continual prayer and faith. God never ceases to help as long as we pray. When our hands hang down, and we restrain prayer before him, we may then justly fear that our enemies will prevail.

Thou hast smitten] That is, Thou *wilt* smite. He speaks in full confidence of God's interference; and knows as surely that he shall have the victory, as if he had it already. *Breaking the jaws* and *the teeth* are expressions which imply, confounding and destroying an adversary; treating him with extreme contempt; *using him like a dog,* &c.

Verse 8. *Salvation* belongeth *unto the Lord*] It is God alone who saves. He is the fountain whence help and salvation come; and to him alone the praise of all saved souls is due. His blessing is upon his people. Those who are saved from the power and the guilt of sin are his people. His mercy saved them; and it is by his *blessing* being continually upon them, that they continue to be saved. David adds his *selah* here also: *mark this!* 1. Salvation comes from God. 2. Salvation is continued by God. These are great truths; *mark them!*

ANALYSIS OF THE THIRD PSALM

The occasion of this Psalm was Absalom's rebellion. David being deserted by his subjects, railed on by Shimei, pursued for his crown and life by his ungracious son, and not finding to whom to make his moan, betakes himself to his God; and before him he expostulates his wrong, confesses his faith, and makes his prayer.

There are *three* strains of this accurate Psalm: I. His complaint. II. The confession of his confidence. III. His petition.

I. He begins with a sad and bitter complaint, amplified,

1. By the number and multitude of his enemies. They were many, very many; they were multiplied and increased: "All Israel was gathered together from Dan to Beer-sheba, as the sand of the sea for multitude;" 2 Sam. xvii. 11.

2. From their malice they came together to do him mischief. They rose up, not *for* him, but *against* him; not to *honour,* but to *trouble* him; not to *defend* him as they ought, but to take away his *crown* and *life;* 2 Sam. xvii. 2.

3. From their insults and sarcasm. It was not *Shimei* only, but many, that said it: "Many —say there is no help for him in his God."

II. The *second* part of the Psalm sets forth David's confidence:—

1. To their *multitude,* he opposeth ONE GOD. But THOU, O LORD!

2. To their malicious insurrection, Jehovah;

who, he believed, 1. Would be a *buckler* to receive all the arrows shot against him. 2. His *glory*, to honour, though they went about to dishonour, him. 3. The *lifter up of his head*, which they wished to lay low enough.

3. To their vain boast of desertion, *There is no help for him in his God*, he opposeth his own experience, "I cried unto the Lord, and he heard me."

4. By whose protection being sustained and secured, he deposes all care and fear, all anxiety and distraction. 1. He sleeps with a quiet mind: "I laid me down and slept; I awoke." 2. He sings a *requiem:* "I will not be afraid of ten thousands of the people, that have set themselves against me round about."

III. In the close, or *third* part, he petitions and prays, notwithstanding his security: "Arise, O Lord; save me, O my God!" To move God to grant his request, he thankfully reminds him of what he had done before:—

1. "Arise and save me, for thou hast smitten all mine enemies." Thou art the same God: do then the same work; be as good to thy servant as ever thou hast been.

2. He inserts an excellent maxim: *Salvation* belongeth *unto the Lord.* As if he had said, It is thy property and prerogative to save. If thou save not, I expect it from none other.

3. Lastly, as a good king should, in his prayers he remembers his subjects. He prayed for those who were using him despitefully: *Thy blessing be upon thy people!* To the same sense, *Coverdale,* in his translation.

PSALM IV

David prays to be heard, 1; expostulates with the ungodly, 2; exhorts them to turn to God, and make their peace with him, 3–5; shows the vain pursuits of men in search of happiness, which he asserts exists only in the approbation of God, 6, 7; commends himself to the Lord, and then quietly takes his repose, 8.

To the ^achief Musician on Neginoth, A Psalm of David

A. M. cir. 2981
B. C. cir. 1023
Anno Davidis,
Regis
Israelitarum,
33

HEAR me when I call, O God of my righteousness: thou hast enlarged me *when I was* in distress; ^bhave mercy upon me, and hear my prayer.

2 O ye sons of men, how long *will ye turn* my glory into shame? *how long* will ye love vanity, *and* seek after leasing? Selah.

A. M. cir. 2981
B. C. cir. 1023
Anno Davidis,
Regis
Israelitarum,
33

3 But know that the ^cLord hath set apart him that is godly for himself: the

---

^aOr, *overseer*, Hab. iii. 19——^bOr, *be gracious*　　　*unto me*——^c2 Tim. ii. 19; 2 Pet. ii. 9

NOTES ON PSALM IV

This Psalm seems to have been composed on the same occasion with the preceding, viz., *Absalom's rebellion.* It appears to have been an *evening* hymn, sung by David and his company previously to their going to rest. It is inscribed *to the chief Musician upon Neginoth,* למנצח בנגינות *lamnatstseach binginoth.* Probably the first word comes from נצח *natsach,* to be *over,* or *preside;* and may refer to the *precentor* in the choir. Some suppose that it refers to the *Lord Jesus,* who is the Supreme Governor, or victorious Person; the Giver of *victory. Neginoth* seems to come from נגן *nagan,* to strike; and probably may signify some such instruments as the *cymbal, drum,* &c., and *stringed instruments* in general. But there is no certainty in these things. What they *mean,* or what they *were,* is known to no man.

Verse 1. *Hear me when I call*] No man has a right to expect God to hear him if he do not call. Indeed, how shall he be heard if he *speak* not? There are multitudes who expect the blessings of God as confidently as if they had prayed for them most fervently; and yet such people pray not at all!

God of my righteousness] Whatever pardon, peace, holiness, or truth I possess, has come entirely from thyself. Thou art the *God of my salvation,* as thou art the *God of my life.*

Thou hast enlarged me] I was in *prison;* and thou hast brought me forth *abroad.* Have mercy on me—continue to act in the same way. I shall always *need* thy *help;* I shall never *deserve* to have it; let me have it in the way of *mere mercy,* as thou hast hitherto done.

Verse 2. *O ye sons of men*] בני איש *beney ish,* ye *powerful men*—ye who are now at the head of affairs, or who are leaders of the multitude.

Love vanity] The poor, empty, shallow-brained, pretty-faced Absalom; whose prospects are all *vain,* and whose promises are all *empty!*

Seek after leasing?] This is a Saxon word, from leasunge. *falsehood,* from lejian, *to lie. Cardmarden* has adopted this word in his translation, Rouen, 1566. It is in none of the Bibles *previously* to that time, nor in any *after,* as far as my own collection affords me evidence; and appears to have been borrowed by King James's translators from the above.

Selah.] Mark this! See what the end will be!

Verse 3. *The Lord hath set apart him that is godly*] חסיד *chasid,* the pious, benevolent man. He has marked such, and put them aside as his own property. "This merciful man, this feeling, tender-hearted man, is my own property; touch not a hair of his head!"

A. M. cir. 2981
B. C. cir. 1023
Anno Davidis,
Regis
Israelitarum,
33

LORD will hear when I call unto him.

4 ^dStand in awe, and sin not: ^ecommune with your own heart upon your bed, and be still. Selah.

5 Offer ^fthe sacrifices of righteousness, and ^gput your trust in the LORD.

6 *There be* many that say, Who will show us

---

^dEph. iv. 26——^ePsalm lxxvii. 6; 2 Cor. xiii. 5
^fDeut. xxxiii. 19; Psa. l. 14; li. 19; 2 Sam. xv. 12
^gPsa. xxxvii. 3; lxii. 8

---

any good? ^hLORD, lift thou up the light of thy countenance upon us.

7 Thou hast put ⁱgladness in my heart, more than in the time *that* their corn and their wine increased.

8 ^kI will both lay me down in peace, and sleep: ^lfor thou, LORD, only makest me dwell in safety.

A. M. cir. 2981
B. C. cir. 1023
Anno Davidis,
Regis
Israelitarum,
33

---

^hNum. vi. 26; Psa. lxxx. 3, 7, 19; cxix. 135——ⁱIsa. ix. 3——^kJob xi. 18, 19; Psa. iii. 5——^lLev. xxv. 18, 19; xxvi. 5; Deut. xii. 10

Verse 4. *Stand in awe, and sin not*] The *Septuagint*, which is copied by St. *Paul*, Eph. iv. 26, translate this clause, Οργιζεσθε, και μη αμαρτανετε; *Be ye angry, and sin not.* The *Vulgate*, *Syriac*, *Æthiopic*, and *Arabic*, give the same reading; and thus the original רגזו *rigzu* might be translated: If ye be angry, and if ye think ye have cause to be angry; do not let your disaffection carry you to acts of rebellion against both God and your king. Consider the subject deeply before you attempt to act. Do nothing rashly; do not justify one evil act by another: sleep on the business; converse *with your own heart upon your bed;* consult your pillow.

And be still.] ודמו *vedommu*, "and be *dumb*." Hold your peace; fear lest ye be found fighting against God. *Selah. Mark this!*

Verse 5. *Offer the sacrifices of righteousness*] Do not attempt to offer a sacrifice to God for prosperity in your present rebellious conduct. Such a sacrifice would be a sin. Turn to God from whom you have revolted; and offer to him a *righteous sacrifice,* such as the *law* prescribes, and such as *he* can receive. Let all hear and consider this saying. No *sacrifice*—no performance of religious duty, will avail any man, if his heart be not right with God. And let all know, that under the Gospel dispensation no sacrifice of any kind will be received but through the all-atoning sacrifice made by Christ.

Because of sin, justice has *stopped every man's mouth;* so that none can have access to God, but through the Mediator. By him only can the *mouth* of a sinner be *opened* to plead with God. Hear this, ye who trust in *yourselves,* and hope for heaven without either faith or dependence on the vicarious sacrifice of Christ.

Verse 6. *Who will show us* any *good?*] This is not a fair translation. The word *any* is not in the text, nor any thing equivalent to it; and not a few have quoted *it,* and preached upon the text, placing the principal emphasis on this illegitimate word.

The place is sufficiently emphatic without this. There are *multitudes who say, Who will show us good?* Man wants *good;* he hates *evil* as evil, because he has *pain, suffering,* and *death* through it; and he wishes to find that *supreme good* which will content his heart, and save him from evil. But men mistake this good. They look for a good that is to gratify their *passions;* they have no notion of any happiness that does not come to them through the *medium of their senses.* Therefore they reject *spiritual good,* and they reject the Supreme God, by whom alone all the powers of the soul of man can be gratified.

Lift thou up the light of thy countenance] This alone, the *light of thy countenance*—thy peace and *approbation,* constitute the *supreme good.* This is what we want, wish, and pray for. The *first* is the *wish* of the *worldling,* the *latter* the wish of the *godly.*

Verse 7. *Thou hast put gladness in my heart*] Thou hast given my soul what it wanted and wished for. I find now a happiness which earthly things could not produce. I have peace of conscience, and joy in the Holy Ghost; such inward happiness as they cannot boast who have got the highest increase of *corn* and *wine;* those TWO THINGS in the abundance of which many suppose happiness to be found.

To *corn* and *wine* all the versions, except the *Chaldee,* add *oil;* for *corn, wine,* and *oil,* were considered the highest blessings of a temporal kind that man could possess.

Verse 8. *I will both lay me down in peace, and sleep*] Most men lie down, and most sleep, daily, for without *rest* and *sleep* life could not be preserved; but alas! how few lie down in *peace!* peace with their own consciences, and peace with God! David had then two great blessings, *rest* by *sleep,* and *peace* in his *soul.* He had a happy soul; and when he lay down on his bed, his body soon enjoyed its repose, as the *conscience* was in *peace.* And he had a *third* blessing, a *confidence* that he should sleep in *safety.* And it was so. No fearful *dreams* disturbed his repose, for he had a mind *tranquillized* by the peace of God. As to his *body,* that enjoyed its due rest, for he had not overloaded *nature* either with *dainties* or *superfluities.* Reader, are not many of thy sleepless hours to be attributed to thy disordered soul—to a sense of guilt on thy conscience, or to a fear of death and hell?

Pray incessantly till thou get the *light of God's countenance,* till his Spirit bear witness with thine that thou art a child of God. Then thy repose will do thee good: and even in thy sleep thy happy soul will be getting forward to heaven.

ANALYSIS OF THE FOURTH PSALM

There are THREE parts in this Psalm:—

I. An entrance, or petition for audience, ver. 1.

II. An *apostrophe* to his enemies, which is, 1. Reprehensive, ver. 2, 3. 2. Admonitory, ver. 4, 5.

III. A *petition* for himself and God's people, ver. 6, 7, 8.

I. He proposes his request and suit for audience. "Hear me when I call;" and this he founds on *four* arguments: 1. God has *promised* to hear me when I call: "Call upon me in

---

trouble, and I will hear thee." I call; hear me, therefore, when I call. 2. His own *innocence:* "Hear me, O God of my righteousness." 3. He requests no more than what God had done for him at other times: *Thou hast enlarged me in trouble,* and why not now? 4. It was *mercy* and *favour* to answer him then; it will be the same to do it again: "Have mercy on me, and hear."

II. His *petition* being thus proposed and ended, he proceeds to the *doctrinal* part; and, turning himself to his enemies, 1. He sharply reproves them; 2. Then warns them, and gives them good counsel.

1. He turns his speech from God to men; the chief but the worst of men. בני איש *beney ish,* "ye eminent men." Not plebeians, but nobles. The charge he lays to them, 1. They "turned his glory into shame." They endeavoured to dishonour him whom God had called and anointed to the kingdom. 2. "They loved vanity." A vain attempt they were in love with. 3. "They sought after falsity." They pursued that which would deceive them; they would find at last that treachery and iniquity lied to itself. 4. That this charge might have the more weight, he figures it with a stinging interrogation, *How long?* Their sin had *malice* and *pertinacity* in it; and he asks them *how long* they intended to act thus.

And that they might, if possible, be drawn from their attempts, he sends them a *noverint, know ye,* which has two clauses: 1. Let them *know* that God hath set apart him that is godly for himself. 2. That God *will hear,* when either he or any good man calls upon him.

2. The reproof being ended, he gives them *good counsel:—*

1. That though they be *angry,* they ought not to let the sun go down upon their wrath.

2. That they *commune with their own hearts* —their conscience. That they do this on their

beds, when secluded from all company, when passion and self-interest did not rule; and then they would be the better able to judge whether they were not in an *error,* whether their anger were not *causeless,* and their persecution *unjust?*

3. That they *offer the sacrifice of righteousness*—that they serve and worship God with an honest, sincere, and contrite heart.

4. That they *put their trust in the Lord;* trusting no more to their lies, nor loving their vanities, but relying on God's promises.

III. The *third* part begins with this question, *Who will show us any good?* 1. Who will show us that good which will make us happy? To which David, in effect, returns this answer, that it is not *bona animi,* intellectual gifts; nor *bona fortunæ,* earthly blessings; nor *bona corporis,* corporeal endowments: but *the light of God's countenance.* 2. Therefore he prefers his petition: "Lord, lift thou up the light of thy countenance upon us." God's countenance is his *grace,* his *favour,* his *love;* and the *light of his countenance,* the *exhibition* and *expression* of this grace, favour, and love; in which alone lies all the happiness of man. Of this David expresses two effects, *gladness* and *security:—*

1. *Gladness* and *joy* far beyond that which may be had from any temporal blessings: "Thou hast put gladness in my heart more than in the time that their corn, and wine, and oil increased; gladness beyond the joy in harvest; and this joy is from the *light of God's countenance. Thou puttest.* THOU, by way of eminence.

2. *Security,* expressed under the metaphor of *sleep:* "I will lay me down in peace, and sleep;" just as in a *time of peace,* as if there were no *war* nor preparation for *battle.*

3. To which he adds the reason: "For thou, Lord, alone makest me to dwell in safety." I am safe, because I enjoy the light of thy countenance.

PSALM V

David continues instant in prayer, 1, 2; makes early application to God, 3; and shows the hatred which God bears to the workers of iniquity, 4–6. His determination to worship God, and to implore direction and support, 7, 8. He points out the wickedness of his enemies, 9, and the destruction they may expect, 10; and then shows the happiness of those who trust in the Lord, 11, 12.

To the chief Musician upon Nehiloth, A Psalm of David

GIVE ear to my words, O LORD, consider my meditation.

2 Hearken unto the [a]voice of my cry, my King, and my God: [b]for unto thee will I pray.

[a]Psa. iii. 4

[b]Psa. lxv. 2

NOTES ON PSALM V

This Psalm is inscribed *to the chief Musician upon Nehiloth, A Psalm of David.* As *neginoth* may signify all kinds of instruments struck with a *plectrum,* stringed instruments, those like the drum, cymbals, &c.; so *nechiloth,* from לח *chal,* to be *hollow,* to *bore through,* may signify any kind of *wind* instruments, such as the horn, trumpet, flute, &c. See on the title to the preceding Psalm. The *Septuagint* have, Εἰς τὸ τέλος, ὑπὲρ τῆς κληρονομούσης, "In favour of

her who obtains the inheritance." The *Vulgate* and *Arabic* have a similar reading. The word נחילות *nechiloth* they have derived from נחל *nachal,* to *inherit.* This may either refer to the Israelites who obtained the inheritance of the promised land, or to the Church of Christ which obtains through him, by faith and prayer, the inheritance among the saints in light. This Psalm is, especially, for the whole Church of God.

Verse 1. *Give ear to my words*] This is properly a *morning hymn,* as the preceding was

3 ᶜMy voice shalt thou hear in the morning, O LORD; in the morning will I direct *my prayer* unto thee, and will look up.

4 For thou *art* not a God that hath pleasure in wickedness: neither shall evil dwell with thee.

5 ᵈThe foolish shall not stand ᵉin thy sight: thou hatest all workers of iniquity.

6 ᶠThou shalt destroy them that speak leasing: ᵍthe LORD will abhor ʰthe bloody and deceitful man.

7 But as for me, I will come *into* thy house

ᶜPsa. xxx. 5; lxxxviii. 13; cxxx. 6——ᵈHab. i. 13
    ᵉHeb. *before thine eyes*

ᶠRev. xxi. 8——ᵍPsa. lv. 23——ʰHeb. *the man of blood and deceit*

---

an *evening hymn.* We have seen from the conclusion of the last Psalm that David was very happy, and lay down and slept in the peace and love of his God. When he opens his eyes on the following morning, he not only remembers but feels the happiness of which he spoke; and with his first recollections he *meditates* on the goodness and mercy of God, and the glorious state of salvation into which he had been brought. He calls on God *to give ear to his words;* probably words of God's *promises* which he had been pleading.

Verse 2. *Hearken unto the voice of my cry*] We may easily find the process through which David's mind was now passing: 1. We have seen from the preceding Psalm that he lay down in a very happy frame of mind, and that he had enjoyed profound repose. 2. As soon as he awakes in the morning, his heart, having a right direction, resumes its work. 3. He meditates on God's goodness, and on his own happy state, though pursued by enemies, and only safe as long as God preserved him by an almighty hand and especial providence. 4. This shows him the need he has of the *continual protection* of the Most High; and therefore he begins to form his *meditation* and the *desires* of his heart into *words,* to which he entreats the Lord to *give ear.* 5. As he was accustomed to have answers to his prayers, he feels the necessity of being *importunate,* and therefore lifts up his voice. 6. Seeing the *workers of iniquity, liars,* and *blood-thirsty* men strong to accomplish their own purposes in the destruction of the godly, he becomes greatly in earnest, and *cries* unto the Lord: "Hearken unto the voice of my cry." 7. He knows that, in order to have a *right answer,* he must have a proper *disposition of mind.* He feels his subjection to the supreme authority of the Most High, and is ready to *do his will* and *obey his laws;* therefore he prays to God as his *King:* "Hearken, my King and my God." I have not only taken thee for my GOD, to *save, defend,* and make me *happy;* but I have taken thee for my KING, to *govern, direct,* and *rule* over me. 8. Knowing the necessity and success of prayer, he purposes to continue in the spirit and practice of it: "Unto thee will I pray." R. S. Jarchi gives this a pretty and pious turn: "When I have power to pray, and to ask for the things I need, then, O Lord, give ear to my *words;* but when I have no power to plead with thee, and fear seizes on my heart, then, O Lord, consider my *meditation!*"

Verse 3. *My voice shalt thou hear in the morning*] We find from this that he had not prayed in vain. He had received a blessed answer; God had *lifted upon him the light of his countenance;* and he therefore determines to be an early applicant at the throne of grace: "My voice shalt thou hear in the morning." He

finds it good to *begin* the day with God; to let Divine things occupy the first place in his waking thoughts; as that which first occupies the mind on awaking is most likely to keep possession of the *heart* all the day through.

In the morning will I direct my prayer] Here seems to be a metaphor taken from an archer. He *sees* his *mark;* puts his *arrow in his bow; directs* his shaft to the mark, i. e., takes his aim; lets fly; and then *looks up,* to see if he have hit his mark. Prayers that have a right aim, will have a prompt answer; and he who sends up his petitions to God through Christ, from a warm, affectionate heart, may confidently *look up* for an answer, for it will come. If an immediate answer be not given, let not the upright heart suppose that the prayer is not heard. It has found its way to the throne; and *there* it is registered.

Verse 4. *Neither shall evil dwell with thee.*] As thou art holy, so thou hast pleasure only in holiness; and as to *evil men,* they shall never enter into thy glory; לֹא יְגֻרְךָ רָע *lo yegurecha ra,* "the evil man shall not even *sojourn* with thee."

Verse 5. *The foolish shall not stand*] He is a fool and a madman who is running himself out of breath for no prize, who is fighting against the Almighty; this every wicked man does; therefore is every *wicked* man a *fool* and a *madman.*

Thou hatest all workers of iniquity] Some sin *now* and *then,* others *generally;* some *constantly,* and some *labour* in it with all their might. These are the WORKERS *of iniquity.* Such even the God of infinite love and mercy *hates.* Alas! what a *portion* have the workers of iniquity! the hatred of God Almighty!

Verse 6. *That speak leasing*] Falsity, from the Anglo-Saxon leasunge *leasunge, a lie, falsity, deceit;* from leas *leas,* lie, which is from the verb leasian *leasian, to lie.* See on Psa. iv. 2.

The Lord will abhor the bloody and deceitful man.] אִישׁ דָּמִים *ish damim,* the man of bloods; for he who has the *spirit* of a murderer, will rarely end with *one* bloodshedding. So the Jews, who clamoured for the blood of our Lord, added to that, as far and as long as they could, the blood of his disciples.

Verse 7. *In the multitude of thy mercy*] David considered it an inexpressible privilege to be permitted to attend *public worship;* and he knew that it was only through the *multitude of God's mercy* that he, or any man else, could enjoy such a privilege. He knew farther that, from the *multitude of this mercy,* he might receive *innumerable blessings* in his house. In this spirit, and with this dependence, he went to the house of the Lord. He who takes David's views of this subject will never, willingly, be absent from the means of grace.

in the multitude of thy mercy: *and* in thy fear will I worship ¹toward ᵏthy holy temple.

8 ¹Lead me, O Lord, in thy righteousness, because of ᵐmine enemies; make ⁿthy way straight before my face.

9 For *there is* no °faithfulness ᵖin their mouth; their inward part *is* ۹very wickedness; ʳtheir throat *is* an open sepulchre; ˢthey flatter with their tongue.

10 ᵗDestroy thou them, O God; ᵘlet them

fall ᵛby their own counsels; cast them out in the multitude of their transgressions; for they have rebelled against thee.

11 But let all those that put their trust in thee ʷrejoice: let them ever shout for joy, because ˣthou defendest them: let them also that love thy name be joyful in thee.

12 For thou, Lord, ʸwilt bless the righteous; with favour wilt thou ᶻcompass him as *with* a shield.

---

¹1 Kings viii. 29, 30, 35, 38; Psa. xxviii. 2; cxxxii. 7; cxxxviii. 2——ᵏHeb. *the temple of thy holiness*——¹Psa. xxv. 5——ᵐHeb. *those which observe me;* Psa. xxvii. 11 ⁿPsa. xxv. 4; xxvii. 11——°Or, *steadfast*——ᵖHeb. *in his mouth,* that is, *in the mouth of any of them*

۹Heb. *wickedness*——ʳLuke xi. 44; Rom. iii. 13 ˢPsa. lxii. 4——ᵗOr, *Make them guilty*——ᵘ2 Sam. xv. 31; xvii. 14, 23——ᵛOr, *from their counsels*——ʷIsa. lxv. 13——ˣHeb. *thou coverest over,* or *protectest them* ʸPsa. cxv. 13——ᶻHeb. *crown him*

In thy fear] Duly considering the infinite holiness of thy majesty, will I worship, אשתחוה *eshtachaveh,* will I bow and prostrate myself in the deepest self-abasement and humility.

Toward thy holy temple.] If David was the author of this Psalm, as is generally agreed, the *temple* was not built at this time: only the *tabernacle* then existed; and in the preceding clause he speaks of coming into the *house,* by which he must mean the *tabernacle.* But *temple* here may signify the *holy of holies, before* which David might prostrate himself while in the *house,* i. e., the court of the tabernacle. Even *in* the *house of God,* there is the *temple of God;* the *place* where the Divine Shechinah dwells. God was in Christ reconciling the world to himself. In him dwelt all the fulness of the Godhead bodily. In all ages and dispensations, Jesus was ever the *temple* where the Supreme Deity was met with and worshipped. The human nature of Jesus was the real temple of the Deity. Nowhere else can God be found.

Verse 8. *Lead me, O Lord, in thy righteousness*] When entered into the *house,* and prostrated before the *temple,* he knew that, unless God continued to *lead* and direct, he was not likely to profit even by such great advantages. We need God not only to bring us to his house, but to keep our feet while we are there.

Because of mine enemies] His conduct was marked; his enemies looked upon and watched him with an evil eye. They would have been glad of his *halting,* that they might have brought a reproach on the good cause which he had espoused. O how cautiously should those walk who make a profession of living to God, of knowing themselves to be in his favour, and of being delivered from all sin in this life!

Make thy way straight] Show me that I must go *right on;* and let thy light always shine on my path, that I may see how to proceed.

Verse 9. *No faithfulness in their mouth*] They make professions of friendship; but all is hollow and deceitful: "They flatter with their tongue."

Very wickedness] Their *heart* is full of all kinds of depravity.

Their throat is an open sepulchre] It is continually gaping for the dead; and sends forth effluvia destructive to the living. I fear that this is too true a picture of the whole human race; totally corrupt within, and abominable without. The heart is the *centre* and *spring*

of this corruption; and the *words* and *actions* of men, which proceed from this source, will send out incessant streams of various impurity; and thus they continue till the grace of God changes and purifies the heart.

Verse 10. *Destroy thou them, O God*] All these apparently *imprecatory* declarations should be translated in the *future* tense, to which they belong; and which shows them to be *prophetic.* Thou wilt destroy them; thou wilt cast them out, &c.

Verse 11. *Let all those that put their trust in thee rejoice*] Such expressions as these should be translated in the same way, *declaratively* and *prophetically:* "All those who put their trust in thee shall rejoice,—shall ever shout for joy."

Verse 12. *For thou, Lord, wilt bless the righteous*] A righteous soul is a peculiar object of God's affectionate regards; and therefore will be a subject of continual blessing.

With favour] Literally, *Like a shield, thy favour will crown him.* God loves such; and this love is their defence. In all places, times, and circumstances, it will preserve them. "Keep yourselves," says the apostle, "in the love of God." He who abides in this love need not fear the face of any adversary. Thus ended the morning's devotion of this excellent man: a model by which every Christian may frame his own.

Analysis of the Fifth Psalm

This Psalm consists of five *parts:*—

I. An introduction, in which he petitions to be heard; professes his earnestness about it, ver. 1, 2, 3; and his confidence of audience.

II. He delivers his petition, ver. 8; and the reason of it—his *enemies.*

III. These enemies he circumstantially describes, ver. 9.

IV. He prophesies that God will destroy them, ver. 10.

V. He prays for the Church, that God would preserve it, ver. 11, 12.

I. 1. In the entrance he prays very earnestly for audience; he shows that he meant to be serious and fervent in it; and he chooses a variety of *words* to express the *same thing,* which rise by degrees in the description: 1. He rises from *meditation;* 2. To *words;* 3. From words to a *voice;* 4. From a voice to a *cry.* Then he desires God, 1. To *consider.* 2. To *give ear.* 3.

To *hearken*. 1. He *considers*, who weighs the justice of the cause. 2. He *gives ear*, who would understand what the suppliant means. 3. He attends and *hearkens*, who intends to satisfy the petitioner.

2. The reasons he uses here to beget audience are very considerable:—

1. The relation that was between him and his God: "Thou art my King and my God."

2. That he would sue to none other: "To thee will I pray;" which he illustrates. 1. From the *time*. It is a morning petition. 2. It was a well composed and ordered prayer. 3. He would *lift up his eyes* with it; that is, have all his hope and expectation exercised in it. "My voice shalt thou hear in the morning; I will direct my prayer unto thee, and look up."

3. The *third* reason is taken from the nature of God: whom he *will* and whom he *will not hear*. 1. Persevering sinners God will not regard. 2. To the upright he is ready to look. The sinners whom God will not hear he thus describes: 1. Men who *delighted in wickedness, evil, foolish, workers of iniquity—liars—bloodthirsty* and *deceitful*. Now it was not likely that God should hear such: "For thou art not a God who hast pleasure in wickedness, neither shall evil dwell with thee." These it is said he *hated;* these he would *destroy;* these he did *abhor*. 2. But on the contrary, he who was *faithful;* who *relied on God;* who *feared the Lord;* who *attended the ordinances of his house;* who *worshipped towards his temple;* and who came, not *trusting to himself*, but in the *multitude of God's mercies;* him he would hear.

II. David, having petitioned for audience, and delivered the grounds of his confidence, brings forth his petition that his lif) may be *holy* and *innocent:—*

1. "Lead me in thy righteousness."

2. "Make thy way straight before me." For which he gives this reason: "Because of mine enemies."

III. These his enemies he circumstantially describes:—

1. By their MOUTH: "There is no faithfulness in their mouth."

2. By their HEART: "Their inward parts are very wickedness."

3. By their THROAT: "Their throat is an open sepulchre."

4. By their TONGUE: "They flatter with their tongue."

IV. Then he proceeds to prophesy against these enemies:—

1. God will *destroy them*.

2. They shall *fall by their own counsels*.

3. They shall *be cast out in the multitude of their transgressions*. For which predictions he gives this reason: *They are rebels*. For *they have rebelled against thee*. Rebels, not against *David*, but against *God*. They have not rejected *me*, but they have rejected *thee*.

V. The *conclusion* contains his prayer for God's people, whom he here describes: 1. They are *righteous*. 2. They *put their trust in God*. 3. They *love his name*.

And he prays for them, that, 1. They may be happy; that they may *shout for joy*. 2. They may be *joyful in God*.

And he expects an answer; because, 1. God *defends them*. 2. He will continue to *bless them*. 3. He will with his *favour compass them as with a shield*.

PSALM VI

This Psalm contains a deprecation of eternal vengeance, 1; a petition to God for mercy, 2. This is enforced from a consideration of the psalmist's sufferings, 3; from that of the Divine mercy, 4; from that of the praise and glory which God would fail to receive if man were destroyed, 5; from that of his humiliation and contrition, 6, 7. Being successful in his supplication, he exults in God, 8, 9; and predicts the downfall of all his enemies, 10.

I. DAY. EVENING PRAYER

To the chief Musician on Neginoth [a]upon [b]Sheminith, A Psalm of David

A. M. cir. 2970
B. C. cir. 1034
Davidis, Regis
Israelitarum,
cir. annum
22

O [c]LORD, rebuke me not in thine anger, neither chasten me in thy hot displeasure.

2 [d]Have mercy upon me, O LORD, for I *am* weak: O LORD, [e]heal me; for my bones are vexed.

A. M. cir. 2970
B. C. cir. 1034
Davidis, Regis
Israelitarum,
cir. annum
22

3 My soul is also sore vexed: but thou, O LORD, [f]how long?

4 Return, O LORD, deliver my soul: O save me for thy mercies' sake.

---

[a]Or, *upon the eighth;* see 1 Chron. xv. 21——[b]Psa. xii. title

[c]Psa. xxxviii 1; Jer. x. 24; xlvi. 28——[d]Psa. xli. 4 [e]Hos. vi. 1——[f]Psa. xc. 13

NOTES ON PSALM VI

This Psalm has the following inscription: *To the chief Musician, upon Sheminith, A Psalm of David;* which the *Chaldee* translates, "To be sung on neginoth, a harp of eight strings." The various interpretations given to this inscription, both by ancients and moderns, show us that nothing is known concerning it. We have already seen that *neginoth* probably signifies all instruments which emitted sounds by *strokes*, or *stringed instruments* in general. This Psalm was to be accompanied with such instruments; but *one* of a particular kind is specified, viz., *sheminith;* so called from its having *eight* strings. The *chief musician* is directed to accompany the recital of this Psalm with the above instrument.

Verse 1. *O Lord, rebuke me not*] This Psalm, which is one of the *seven Penitential Psalms*, is

A. M. cir. 2970
B. C. cir. 1034
Davidis, Regis
Israelitarum,
cir. annum
22

5 ᵍFor in death *there is* no remembrance of thee: in the grave who shall give thee thanks?

6 I am weary with my groaning; ʰall the night make I my bed to swim; I water my couch with my tears.

7 ¹Mine eye is consumed because of grief; it waxeth old because of all mine enemies.

8 ᵏDepart from me, all ye workers of iniquity; for the LORD hath ¹heard the voice of my weeping.

A. M. cir. 2970
B. C. cir. 1034
Davidis, Regis
Israelitarum,
cir. annum
22

9 The LORD hath heard my supplication; the LORD will receive my prayer.

10 Let all mine enemies be ashamed and sore vexed: let them return *and* be ashamed suddenly.

ᵍPsa. xxx. 9; lxxxviii. 11; cxv. 17; cxviii. 17; Isa. xxxviii. 18——ʰOr, *every night*——ⁱJob xvii. 7; Psa. xxxi. 9; xxxviii. 10; lxxxviii. 9; Lam. v. 17——ᵏPsa. cxix. 115; Matt. vii. 23; xxv. 41; Luke xiii. 27——ˡPsa. iii. 4

---

supposed to have been written during some grievous disease with which David was afflicted after his transgression with Bath-sheba. It argues a deep consciousness of sin, and apprehension of the just displeasure of God. It is the very language of a true penitent who is looking around for help, and who sees, as *Bishop Horne* well expresses it, "*above*, an angry God, ready to take vengeance; *beneath*, the fiery gulf, ready to receive him; *without*, a world in flames; *within*, the gnawing worm." Of all these, none so dreadful as an angry God; his wrath he particularly deprecates. God rebukes and chastens him, and he submits; but he prays not to be rebuked *in anger*, nor chastened in *hot displeasure*, because he knows that these must bring him down to total and final *destruction*.

Verse 2. *Have mercy*] I have no *merit*. I deserve all I feel and all I fear.

O Lord, heal me] No earthly physician can cure my malady. *Body* and *soul* are both diseased, and only God can help me.

I am weak] אמלל *umlal*. I am *exceedingly weak;* I cannot take nourishment, and my strength is exhausted.

My bones are vexed.] The disease hath entered into my bones.

Verse 3. *How long?*] How long shall I continue under this malady? How long will it be before thou speak peace to my troubled heart?

Verse 4. *Return, O Lord*] Once I had the light of thy countenance; by sin I have forfeited this; I have provoked thee to depart: O Lord, return! It is an awful thing to be obliged to say, *Return, O Lord,* for this supposes *backsliding;* and yet what a mercy it is that a *backslider may* RETURN to God, with the expectation that *God* will *return* to *him!*

Verse 5. *In death* there is *no remembrance of thee*] Man is to glorify thee on earth. The end for which he was born cannot be accomplished in the grave; heal my body, and heal my soul, that I may be rendered capable of loving and serving thee here below. A dead body in the grave can do no good to men, nor bring any glory to thy name!

Verse 7. *Mine eye is consumed*] עששה *asheshah*, is blasted, withered, sunk in my head.

Verse 8. *Depart from me, all ye workers of iniquity*] It seems that while he was suffering grievously through the disease, his enemies had insulted and mocked him;—upbraided him with his transgressions, not to increase his *penitence*, but to cast him into *despair.*

The Lord hath heard the voice of my weep-

ing.] The Lord pitifully beheld the sorrows of his heart, and mercifully forgave his sins.

Verse 10. *Ashamed and sore vexed*] May they as deeply deplore their transgressions as I have done mine! May *they return;* may they be *suddenly converted!* The original will bear this meaning, and it is the most congenial to Christian principles.

ANALYSIS OF THE SIXTH PSALM

The parts of this Psalm are TWO, in general:—

I. A *petition* to God for himself, contained in the first *seven* verses.

II. The account of his *restoration*, contained in the *three* last.

I. The *petition* consists of *two* parts: 1. Deprecation of *evil;* 2. Petition for *good.*

1. He prays to God to *avert* his *wrath:* "O Lord, rebuke me not," &c.

2. He entreats to be partaker of *God's favour:* "Have mercy upon me," &c. 1. To his BODY: "Heal me, O Lord." 2. To his SOUL: "Deliver my soul: O save me!"

He enforces his petition by divers weighty reasons:

1. From the *quantity* and *degrees* of his *calamity,* which he shows to be great from the *effects.* 1. In *general;* he was in a languishing disease: "I am weak." 2. In *particular;* 1. Pains in his *bones:* "My bones are vexed." 2. Trouble in his *soul:* "My *soul* also is troubled."

2. From the *continuance* of it. It was a *long* disease; a lingering sickness; and he found no ease, no, not from his God. The pain I could the better bear if I had comfort from heaven. "But thou, O Lord, how long?" Long hast thou withdrawn the light of thy countenance from thy servant.

3. From the *consequence* that was likely to follow; *death,* and the *event* upon it. It is my intention to celebrate and praise thy name; the *living* only can do this: therefore, let *me live;* for *in death there is no remembrance of thee; in the grave who shall give thee thanks?*

4. And that he was brought now to the *gates of death,* he shows by *three apparent symptoms:* 1. *Sighs* and *groans,* which had almost broken his heart; the companions of a perpetual grief: "I am weary of my groaning." 2. The abundance of his *tears* had dried and wasted his body: "He made his bed to swim, and watered his couch with his tears." 3. His *eyes* also *melted away,* and *grew dim,* so that he seemed *old* before his time: "My eye is consumed because of grief; it waxeth old."

5. That which added to his sorrow was, *he had many ill-wishers* who insulted over him:

"Mine eye is waxen old because of mine enemies."

II. But at last receiving comfort and joy, he is enabled to look up; and then he turns upon his enemies, who were longing for his destruction: "Depart from me, all ye workers of iniquity."

He magnifies God's mercy; and mentions its manifestation *thrice* distinctly: 1. "The Lord hath heard the voice of my weeping." 2. "The Lord hath heard my supplication." 3. "The Lord will receive my prayer."

Then follows his prophetic declaration concerning them: 1. Shame and confusion to see their hope frustrated: "They shall be confounded." 2. Vexation, to see the object of their envy restored to health and prosperity: "They shall be sore vexed." 3. They shall return to their companions with *shame*, because their wishes and plots have miscarried. 4. He intimates that this shame and confusion shall be *speedy*: "They shall return, and be ashamed suddenly." Or, possibly, this may be a wish for their conversion, יָשֻׁבוּ *yashubu*, let *them be* CONVERTED, רָגַע *raga*, *suddenly*, lest sudden destruction from the Lord should fall upon them. Thus the genuine follower of God prays, "That it may please thee to have mercy upon our enemies, persecutors, and slanderers; and to TURN their HEARTS." A *Christian* should take up every thing of this kind in a *Christian* sense.

PSALM VII

The psalmist prays against the malice of his enemies, 1, 2; protests his own innocence, 3-5; prays to God that he would vindicate him, for the edification of his people, 6-8; prays against the wickedness of his enemies, 9; expresses strong confidence in God, 10; threatens transgressors with God's judgments, 11-13; shows the conduct and end of the ungodly, 14-16; and exults in the mercy and lovingkindness of his Maker, 17.

ᵃShiggaion of David, which he sang unto the Lord, ᵇconcerning the ᶜwords of Cush the Benjamite

A. M. cir. 2943
B. C. cir. 1061
Sauli, Regis
Israelitarum,
cir. annum
35

O LORD my God, in thee do I put my trust: ᵈsave me from all them that persecute me, and deliver me:

2 ᵉLest he tear my soul like a lion, ᶠrending *it* in pieces, while *there is* ᵍnone to deliver.

3 O LORD my God, ʰif I have done this; if there be ⁱiniquity in my hands;

A. M. cir. 2943
B. C. cir. 1061
Sauli, Regis
Israelitarum,
cir. annum
35

ᵃHab. iii. 1——ᵇ2 Samuel xvi.——ᶜOr, *business* ᵈPsa. xxxi. 15

ᵉIsa. xxxviii. 13——ᶠPsa. l. 22——ᵍHebrew, *not a deliverer*——ʰ2 Sam. xvi. 7, 8——ⁱ1 Sam. xxiv. 11

This Psalm is entitled, *Shiggaion of David, which he sang unto the Lord, concerning the words of Cush the Benjamite*. The word שִׁגָּיוֹן *shiggayon* comes from שָׁגָה *shagah*, to *wander*, a wandering song; i. e., a Psalm composed by David in his wanderings, when he was obliged to hide himself from the fury of Saul.

Bishop *Horsley* thinks it may have its name, a *wandering ode*, from its being in different parts, taking up different subjects, in different styles of composition. But he has sometimes thought that *shiggaion* might be an *unpremeditated* song; an *improviso*.

As to *Cush the Benjamite*, he is a person unknown in the Jewish history; the name is probably a name of *disguise*; and by it he may covertly mean *Saul* himself, the *son of Kish*, who was of the *tribe* of *Benjamin*. The subject of the Psalm will better answer to Saul's unjust persecution and David's innocence, than to any other subject in the history of David.

Verse 1. *O Lord my God*] יהוה אלהי *Yehovah Elohai*, words expressive of the strongest confidence the soul can have in the Supreme Being. Thou self-existent, incomprehensible, almighty, and eternal Being, who neither needest nor hatest any thing that thou hast made; thou art my God: God in *covenant* with thy creature man; and my God and portion particularly. Therefore, *in thee do I put my trust*—I repose all my confidence *in thee*, and expect all my good *from thee*.

Save me] Shield me from my persecutors; abate their pride, assuage their malice, and confound their devices!

Deliver me] From the counsels which they have devised, and from the snares and gins they have laid in my path.

Verse 2. *Lest he tear my soul like a lion*] These words seem to answer well to *Saul*. As the *lion* is king in the forest; so was *Saul* king over the land. As the *lion*, in his fierceness, seizes at once, and tears his prey in pieces; so David expected to be seized and suddenly destroyed by *Saul*. He had already, in his rage, thrown his javelin at him, intending to have pierced him to the wall with it. As from the *power of the lion* no beast in the forest could deliver any thing; so David knew that *Saul's power* was irresistible, and that none of his friends or well-wishers could save or deliver him out of such hands. "Lest he tear my soul (my life) like a lion, rending it in pieces, while there is none to deliver." All this answers to *Saul*, and to none else.

Verse 3. *If I have done this*] David was accused by Saul of *affecting the kingdom;* and of *waiting* for an opportunity to *take away the life of his king, his patron, and his friend*. In his application to God he refers to these charges; meets them with indignation; and clears himself by a strong appeal to his Judge; and an imprecation that, if he had meditated or designed any such thing, he might meet with

A. M. cir. 2943
B. C. cir. 1061
Sauli, Regis
Israelitarum,
cir. annum
35

4 If I have rewarded evil unto him that was at peace with me; (yea, kI have delivered him that without cause is mine enemy:)

5 Let the enemy persecute my soul, and take *it;* yea, let him tread down my life upon the earth, and lay mine honour in the dust. Selah.

6 Arise, O LORD, in thine anger, llift up thyself because of the rage of mine enemies: and mawake for me *to* the judgment *that* thou hast commanded.

7 So shall the congregation of the people com-

pass thee about: for their sakes therefore return thou on high.

8 The LORD shall judge the people: judge me, O LORD, nac-cording to my righteousness, and according to mine integrity *that is* in me.

9 O let the wickedness of the wicked come to an end; but establish the just: ofor the righteous God trieth the hearts and reins.

10 PMy defence *is* of God, which saveth the qupright in heart.

11 rGod judgeth the righteous, and God is angry *with the wicked* every day.

A. M. cir. 2943
B. C. cir. 1061
Sauli, Regis
Israelitarum,
cir. annum
35

---

k1 Samuel xxiv. 7; xxvi. 9——lPsa. xciv. 2——mPsa. xliv. 23——nPsalm xviii. 20; xxxv. 24——o1 Samuel xvi. 7; 1 Chronicles xxviii. 9; Psalm cxxxix. 1; Jeremiah xi. 20; xvii. 10; xx. 12; Revelation ii. 23——pHebrew, *My buckler* is *upon God*——qPsalm cxxv. 4——rOr, *God is a righteous Judge*

---

nothing but curse and calamity either from God or man.

Verse 4. *Yea, I have delivered him*] When, in the course of thy providence, thou didst put his life in my hand in the *cave,* I contented myself with cutting off his skirt, merely to show him the danger he had been in, and the spirit of the man whom he accused of designs against his life; and yet even for this my heart smote me, because it appeared to be an indignity offered to him who was the *Lord's anointed.* This fact, and my venturing my life frequently for his good and the safety of the state, sufficiently show the falsity of such accusations, and the innocence of my life.

Verse 5. *Let the enemy persecute my soul*] If I have been guilty of the things laid to my charge, let the worst evils fall upon me.

Verse 6. *Arise, O Lord, in thine anger*] To thee I commit my cause; arise, and sit on the throne of thy judgment in my behalf.

Verse 7. *For their sakes therefore return thou on high.*] Thy own people who compass thy altar, the faithful of the land, are full of gloomy apprehensions. They hear the charges against me; and see how I am persecuted. Their minds are divided; they know not what to think. For *their sakes, return thou on high*—ascend the judgment-seat; and let them see, by the dispensations of thy providence, *who* is *innocent* and *who is guilty.* David feared not to make this appeal to God; for the consciousness of his innocence showed him at once how the discrimination would be made.

Verse 8. *The Lord shall judge the people*] He will execute justice and maintain truth among them. They shall not be as sheep without a shepherd.

Judge me, O Lord] Let my innocence be brought to the light, and my just dealing made clear as the noonday.

Verse 9. *The wickedness of the wicked*] The iniquity of *Saul's* conduct.

But establish the just] Show the people *my* uprightness.

Verse 10. *My defence is of God*] I now leave my cause in the hands of my Judge. I have no uneasy or fearful apprehensions, because I know God will save the upright in heart.

Verse 11. *God is angry* with the wicked *every*

day.] The *Hebrew* for this sentence is the following: וְאֵל זֹעֵם בְּכָל יוֹם *veel zoem becol yom;* which, according to the *points,* is, *And God is angry every day.* Our translation seems to have been borrowed from the *Chaldee,* where the whole verse is as follows: אלהא דינא זכאה ובתקוף רגיז על רשיעי כל יומא: *elaha daiyana zaccaah ubithkoph rageiz al reshiey col yoma:* "God is a righteous Judge; and in strength he is angry against the wicked every day."

The VULGATE: *Deus Judex justus, fortis, et patiens; numquid irascitur per singulos dies?* "God is a Judge righteous, strong, and patient; —will he be angry every day?"

The SEPTUAGINT: Ὁ Θεος Κριτης δικαιος, και ισχυρος, και μακροθυμος, μη οργην επαγων καθ᾽ ἑκαστην ἡμεραν; "God is a righteous Judge, strong and longsuffering; not bringing forth his anger every day."

SYRIAC: "God is the Judge of righteousness; he is not angry every day."

The ARABIC is the same as the *Septuagint.*

The ÆTHIOPIC: "God is a just Judge, and strong and longsuffering; he will not bring forth tribulation daily."

COVERDALE: God is a righteous judge, and God is ever threateninge.

KING EDWARD'S Bible by *Becke* 1549, follows this reading.

CARDMARDEN: God is a righteous judge, [strong and patient] and God is provoked every day. *Card-marden* has borrowed *strong and patient* from the *Vulgate* or *Septuagint;* but as he found nothing in the *Hebrew* to express them, he put the words in a *smaller letter,* and included them in *brackets.* This is followed by the *prose version* in our *Prayer Book.*

The GENEVAN *version,* printed by *Barker,* the king's printer, 1615, translates thus: "God judgeth the righteous, and him that contemneth God every day." On which there is this marginal note: "He doth continually call the wicked to repentance, by some signs of his judgments."

My ancient *Scotico-English* MS. *Psalter* only begins with the conclusion of this Psalm.

I have judged it of consequence to trace this verse through all the ancient versions in order to be able to ascertain what is the *true reading,* where the evidence on one side amounts to a

A. M. cir. 2943
B. C. cir. 1061
Sauli, Regis
Israelitarum,
cir. annum
35

12 If he turn not, he will ⁸whet his sword; he hath bent his bow, and made it ready.

13 He hath also prepared for him the instruments of death; ᵗhe ordaineth his arrows against the persecutors.

14 ᵘBehold, he travaileth with iniquity, and hath conceived mischief, and brought forth falsehood.

15 ᵛHe made a pit, and digged it, ʷand is fallen into the ditch *which* he made.

A. M. cir. 2943
B. C. cir. 1061
Sauli, Regis
Israelitarum,
cir. annum
35

16 ˣHis mischief shall return upon his own head, and his violent dealing shall come down upon his own pate.

17 I will praise the ʸLORD according to his righteousness: and will sing praise to the name of the LORD most high.

ˢDeut. xxxii. 41——ᵗDeut. xxxii. 23, 42; Psa. lxix. 7
ᵘJob xv. 35; Isa. xxxiii. 11; lix. 4; James i. 15——ᵛHeb.
He hath digged a pit——ʷEsth. vii. 10; Job iv. 8; Psa. ix.
15; x. 2; xxxv. 8; xciv. 23; cxli. 10; Prov. v. 22; xxvi.

27; Eccles. x. 8——ˣ1 Kings ii. 32; Esth. ix. 25
ʸPsa. ix. 1; xxii. 22; xxviii. 7; xxxv. 18; xliii. 4; lii. 9;
liv. 6; lvi. 4; lvii. 9; lxix. 30; lxxi. 22; lxxxvi. 12; cviii.
3; cix. 30; cxi. 1, &c.

---

positive *affirmation*, "God IS angry every day;" and, on the other side, to as positive a *negation*, "He is NOT angry every day." The mass of evidence supports the latter reading. The *Chaldee* first corrupted the text by making the addition, *with the wicked*, which our translators have followed, though they have put the words into *italics*, as not being in the Hebrew text. In the MSS. collated by *Kennicott* and *De Rossi* there is no various reading on this text.

The true sense may be restored thus:—

אֵל *el*, with the vowel point *tsere*, signifies GOD: אַל *al*, the same letters, with the point *pathach*, signifies *not*. Several of the versions have read it in this way: "God judgeth the righteous, and is NOT angry every day." He is not always chiding, nor is he daily punishing, notwithstanding the continual wickedness of men: hence, the ideas of *patience* and *long-suffering* which several of the versions introduce. Were I to take any of the translations in preference to the above, I should feel most inclined to adopt that of *Coverdale*.

Verse 12. *If he turn not*] This clause the *Syriac* adds to the preceding verse. Most of the versions read, "If ye return not." Some contend, and not without a great show of probability, that the two verses should be read in connection, thus: "God is a just Judge; a God who is provoked every day. If (the sinner) turn not, he will whet his sword; he hath bent his bow, and made it ready." This, no doubt, gives the sense of both.

Verse 13. *He hath also prepared for him the instruments of death*] This appears to be all a prophecy of the tragical death of *Saul*. He was wounded by the *arrows* of the *Philistines;* and his own *keen sword*, on which he fell, terminated his woful days!

Verse 14. *He travaileth with iniquity*] All these terms show the pitch of envy, wrath, and malevolence, to which Saul had carried his opposition against David. He *conceived mischief;* he *travailed* with *iniquity;* he *brought forth falsehood*—all his expectations were blasted.

Verse 15. *He made a pit*] He determined the destruction of David. He laid his plans with much artifice; he executed them with zeal and diligence; and when he had, as he supposed, the grave of David digged, he fell into it himself! The metaphor is taken from pits dug in the earth, and slightly covered over with reeds, &c., so as not to be discerned from the solid ground; but the animal steps on them, the surface breaks, and he falls into the pit and is

taken. "All the world agrees to acknowledge the equity of that sentence, which inflicts upon the *guilty* the punishment intended by them for the *innocent*."—*Horne*.

Verse 16. *Shall come down upon his own pate.*] Upon his *scalp*, קָדְקֹד *kodkod*, the top of the head. It may refer to *knocking the criminal on the head*, in order to deprive him of life. Had *scalping* been known in those days, I should have thought the reference might be to that barbarous custom.

Verse 17. *I will praise the Lord according to his righteousness*] I shall celebrate both his justice and his mercy. I will sing praise to the name of the Lord Most High. The *name* of God is often put for his *perfections*. So here, שֵׁם יְהוָה עֶלְיוֹן *shem Yehovah Elyon;* "The perfections of Jehovah, who is above all." My old *Scotico-English* MS., mentioned as the conclusion of the *introduction*, begins at this verse, where are the following words by way of paraphrase: 𝔖ang falles til iop; and he that synges well that name, his iop es mare than i kan tell. Those who are happy may sing; and he who can duly celebrate the name of God, who knows it to be a strong tower into which he can run and find safety, has inexpressible happiness. That is the sense of the above.

ANALYSIS OF THE SEVENTH PSALM

I. His appeal to God by way of *petition*, ver. 1, 2, 6.

II. The *reasons* of this appeal,—set down through the whole Psalm.

III. His doxology or thanksgiving, ver. 17.

I. He begins his appeal with a petition for deliverance from his persecutors: "Save me, and deliver me," ver. 1. In which he desires God to be,

1. *Attentive* to him: 1. Because of the relation between them. For he was *the Lord his God.* 2. He trusted in him: "O Lord my God, I trust in thee," ver. 1.

2. *Benevolent* to him. For he was now in danger of death. He had, 1. Enemies. 2. Many enemies. 3. Persecuting enemies. 4. But one above the rest, a *lion ready to rend him in pieces;* so that if God forsook him, he would do it. "Save me from those that persecute me," &c., ver. 2.

II. And then he gives his reasons why he doth appeal to his God, which are: 1. His own *innocence.* 2. God's *justice.*

1. He makes a protestation of his innocence. He was accused that he lay in wait, and plotted

for Saul's life and kingdom; but he clears himself, shows the impossibility of it, and that with a fearful imprecation. 1. *O Lord—if I have done* any such thing as they object; *if I have rewarded evil to him that was at peace with me*, ver. 3, 4, which was indeed an impossible matter. *For I have delivered him—*as Saul in the *cave*, 1 Sam. xxiv. 2. His imprecation— *Then let mine enemy persecute me—*let him take both my life and my honour, kingdom, property, and whatever thou hast promised me.

2. And, which is the second reason of this appeal, being innocent, he calls for justice. "Arise, O Lord—lift up thyself—awake for me to judgment." For, 1. The rage of my enemies is great. 2. The judgment was thine that chose me to be king of thy people. Awake for me. 3. This will be for thy honour, and the edification of thy Church. "The congregation of thy people shall compass thee about. For their sakes return thou on high." Ascend the tribunal, and do justice.

Now, upon this argument of God's justice, he dwells and insists to the last verse of the Psalm.

1. He avows God to be his Judge.

2. He prays for justice to be done to *him* and to the *wicked*. 1. To *him*, an innocent person: "Judge me, O Lord, according to my righteousness." 2. To the *wicked:* "O let the wickedness of the wicked come to an end!"

3. He prays not only for *himself*, but for all *good men:* "Establish the just." And adds this reason, that as "God trieth the hearts and reins," he is fittest to be judge, in whom is required *knowledge* and *prudence.*

4. The other two properties of a judge are, to *save*, and to *punish;* and the triumph of his faith is, that he knows He will do both. 1. *He will save the just and upright in heart*, and therefore his *defence is in God.* 2. He will *punish the wicked*, for he is *angry with them every day;* and yet even to them he shows much clemency and forbearance. He waits for their conversion. He whets, binds on, and sharpens his instruments of death; but he shoots not till there is no remedy. But, *If they will not return he will whet his sword*, &c.

5. But the Lord's longsuffering had no good effect upon Saul; he grew worse and worse: *He travailed with mischief; conceived iniquity; brought forth falsehood;* and *digged a pit* for his innocent neighbour, into which he fell himself. Thus the righteous God *executed judgment* and *vindicated innocence.*

III. The close of the Psalm is a *doxology.* Thanks that a good and merciful God would judge for the righteous, save those who are true of heart, *establish the just*, and take vengeance upon the wicked. For this, saith David, "I will praise the Lord according to his righteousness, and I will sing praise to the name of the Lord the Most High."

The righteous may be oppressed, but they shall not be forsaken: nor can they lose even by their afflictions, for they shall be turned to their advantage. Every occurrence helps a good man, whether prosperous or adverse; but to the wicked every thing is a curse. By his wickedness, even his blessings are turned to a bane.

PSALM VIII

The glory and excellence of God manifested by his works, 1, 2; *particularly in the starry heavens*, 3; *in man*, 4; *in his formation*, 5; *and in the dominion which God has given him over the earth, the air, the sea, and their inhabitants*, 6, 7, 8: *in consequence of which God's name is celebrated over all the earth*, 9.

To the chief Musician [a]upon Gittith, A Psalm of David

O LORD our Lord, how [b]excellent *is* thy name in all the earth! who [c]hast set thy glory above the heavens.

2 [d]Out of the mouth of babes and sucklings hast thou [e]ordained strength because of thine enemies, that thou mightest still [f]the enemy and the avenger.

---

[a]Psa. lxxxi., lxxxiv., title——[b]Psa. cxlviii. 13——[c]Psa. cxiii. 4

[d]See Matt. xi. 25; xxi. 16; 1 Cor. i. 27——[e]Heb. *founded* [f]Psa. xliv. 16

NOTES ON PSALM VIII

The inscription to this Psalm is the following: *To the chief Musician upon Gittith, A Psalm of David.* This has been metaphrased, "To the conqueror, concerning the winepresses;" and has been supposed to be a Psalm intended for the time of *vintage:* and as that happened about the time of the year in which it is supposed the world was created, hence there is a general celebration of those works, and of the creation, and the high privileges of man. The *Chaldee* gives it a different turn: "A Psalm of David, to be sung upon the harp, which he brought out of Gath." That the Psalm

has respect to our Lord and the time of the Gospel, is evident from the reference made to ver. 2, in Matt. xi. 25, the express quotation of it in Matt. xxi. 16, and another reference to it in 1 Cor. i. 27. The *fourth* and *sixth* verses are quoted Heb. ii. 6-9. See also 1 Cor. xv. 27, and Eph. i. 22. The *first* and *second* ADAM are both referred to, and the first and second creation also; and the glory which God has received, and is to receive, through both. It relates simply to Christ and redemption.

Verse 1. *O Lord our Lord*] יהוה אדנינו *Yehovah Adoneynu; O Jehovah our Prop, our Stay*, or *Support.* אדני *Adonai* is frequently used: sometimes, indeed often, for the word

3 When I ^gconsider thy heavens, the work of thy fingers, the moon and the stars, which thou hast ordained;

4 ^hWhat is man, that thou art mindful of him? and the son of man, that thou visitest him?

---

^gPsa. cxi. 2

^hJob vii. 17; Psa. cxliv. 3; Heb. ii. 6

יהוה *Yehovah* itself. The root דן *dan* signifies *to direct, rule, judge, support.* So *Adonai* is the Director, Ruler, Judge, Supporter of men. It is well joined with *Jehovah;* this showing what God is *in himself;* that, what God is *to man;* and may here very properly refer to our Lord Jesus.

How excellent is thy name in all the earth!] How illustrious is the name of Jesus throughout the world! His incarnation, birth, humble and obscure life, preaching, miracles, passion, death, resurrection, and ascension, are celebrated through the whole world. His religion, the gifts and graces of his Spirit, his people—Christians—his Gospel and the preachers of it, are everywhere spoken of. No name is so universal, no power and influence so generally felt, as those of the Saviour of mankind. Amen.

Thy glory above the heavens.] The *heavens* are glorious, the most glorious of all the works of God which the eye of man can reach; but the *glory of God* is infinitely *above* even these. The words also seem to intimate that no power, earthly or diabolical, can *lessen* or injure that glory. The glory and honour which God has by the Gospel shall last through time, and through eternity; and of that glory none shall be able to rob him, to whom majesty and dominion are eternally due. This has been applied by some to the *resurrection* of our Lord. He *rose* from the dead, and *ascended* above all heavens; and by these his glory was sealed, his mission accomplished, and the last proof given to his preceding miracles.

Verse 2. *Out of the mouth of babes and sucklings*] We have seen how our Lord applied this passage to the Jewish children, who, seeing his miracles, cried out in the temple, "Hosanna to the Son of David!" Matt. xxi. 16. And we have seen how the *enemy* and *the avenger*—the *chief priests* and the *scribes*—were offended because of these things; and as the Psalm wholly concerns Jesus Christ, it is most probable that in this act of the Jewish children the prophecy had its *primary* fulfilment; and was left to the Jews as a witness and a sign of the Messiah, which they should have acknowledged when our Lord directed their attention to it.

There is also a very *obvious sense* in which the *mouths of babes and sucklings show forth the praises of God;* viz., the means by which they derive their first nourishment. In order to extract the milk from the breasts of their mothers, they are obliged to *empty their own mouths entirely of air,* that the eternal air, pressing on the breast, may force the milk through its proper canals into the mouth of the child, where there is no resistance, the child having extracted all air from its own mouth, which in this case resembles a perfectly *exhausted receiver* on the plate of an *airpump;* and the *action* of *sucking* is performed on the same principle that the receiver is exhausted by the working of the airpump. Of this curious pneumatic action the child is capable the moment it breathes; and, its strength considered, performs it as perfectly the first hour as it does in any other period of its childhood or infancy. What does all this argue? Why *instinct.* And pray what is *instinct?* You cannot tell. But here is an operation by which the pure *Boylean vacuum* is made; and this by an infant *without any previous teaching!* Do you suppose that this is an *easy operation,* and that it requires little *skill?* You are mistaken. You have done this yourself while an infant, under the sole guidance of God. Can you do it *now?* You are startled! Shall I tell you what appears to you a secret? There is not one in ten thousand *adults,* who have had their first nourishment from the breasts of their mothers, who can perform the same operation again! And those who have had occasion to practise it have found great difficulty *to learn that art* which, in the first moment of their birth, they performed to perfection! Here is the finger of God; and here, *out of the mouths of babes and sucklings, he has ordained* such a *strength* of *evidence* and *argument* in favour of his being, his providence, and his goodness, as is sufficient to *still* and *confound* every infidel and atheist in the universe, all the *enemies* of righteousness, and all the *vindicators* of desperate and hopeless causes and systems.

The words may also be applied to the *apostles* and *primitive preachers* of the Gospel; to the *simple* and *comparatively unlearned* followers of Christ, who, through his teaching, were able to confound the *wise* among the *Jews,* and the *mighty* among the *heathens:* and in this sense our Lord uses the term *babes,* Matt. xi. 25: "I thank thee, O Father—because thou hast hid these things from the *wise* and *prudent,* and hast revealed them to *babes.*"

We may also witness, in the *experience* of multitudes of simple people who have been, by the preaching of the Gospel, converted from the error of their ways, such a strength of *testimony* in favour of the work of God in the *heart,* and his effectual teaching in the *mind,* as is calculated to *still,* or reduce to silence, every thing but *bigotry* and *prejudice,* neither of which has either *eyes* or *ears.* This *teaching,* and these *changing* or *converting* influences, come from God. They are not acquired by human *learning;* and those who put this in the place of the Divine teaching never grow wise to salvation. To enter into the kingdom *of* heaven, a MAN must become as a *little child.*

Verse 3. *When I consider thy heavens*] כי אראה *ki ereh; because I will see.* He had often seen the heavens with astonishment, and he purposes to make them frequent subjects of contemplation; and he could not behold them without being affected with the skill, contrivance, and power, manifested in their formation.

The work of thy fingers] What a view does this give of the majesty of God! The *earth* is nearly *eight thousand* English miles in diameter: but to form an adequate conception of its magnitude, we must consider it in its *superficial* and *solid contents.* Upon the supposition

5 For thou hast made him a little lower than the angels, and hast crowned him with glory and honour.

6 ⁱThou madest him to have dominion over the works of thy hands; ᵏthou hast put all *things* under his feet:

ⁱGen. i. 26, 28

ᵏ1 Cor. xv. 27; Heb. ii. 8

---

that the earth's *polar* diameter is *seven thousand nine hundred and forty* miles, and its *equatorial, seven thousand nine hundred and seventy-seven,* (estimates considered to very near approximations to the truth,) the whole superficies of the terraqueous globe will amount to about *one hundred and ninety-eight millions, nine hundred and eighty thousand, seven hundred* square miles; and its solid contents, in *cubic miles,* will be expressed by the following figures: 264,544,857,944, i. e., *two hundred and sixty-four thousand five hundred and forty-four millions, eight hundred and fifty-seven thousand, nine hundred and forty-four.* Great as we have shown the *bulk* of the earth to be, from the most accurate estimates of its diameter, it is but small when compared with the bulks of some of the other bodies in the solar system. The planet *Herschel,* or *Georgium Sidus,* known on the continent of Europe by the name of *Uranus,* is *eighty times and a half* greater than the earth; *Saturn, nine hundred and ninety-five* times greater; *Jupiter, one thousand two hundred and eighty-one* times greater; and the *sun,* the most prodigious body in the system, *one million three hundred and eighty-four thousand, four hundred and sixty-two* times greater. The *circumference* of the sun contains not *fewer* than *two millions seven hundred and seventy-seven thousand* English miles; and a degree of latitude, which on the earth amounts only to *sixty-nine* miles and a *half,* will on the sun (the circle being supposed in both instances to be divided into *three hundred and sixty degrees*) contain not less than about *seven thousand seven hundred* and *forty miles,* a quantity almost equal to the terrestrial axis. But the immense *volume* (in cubic miles) which the solar surface includes amounts to the following most inconceivable quantity: 366,252,-303,118,866,128, i. e., *three hundred and sixty-six thousand two hundred and fifty-two billions, three hundred and three thousand one hundred and eighteen millions, eight hundred and sixty-six thousand, one hundred and twenty-eight.* Notwithstanding the amazing magnitude of the sun, we have abundant reason to believe that some of the fixed stars are much larger; and yet we are told they are *the work of* God's FINGERS! What a *hand,* to move, form, and launch these globes! This expression is much more *sublime* than even that of the prophet: "Who hath measured the waters in the hollow of his hand, and meted out the heavens with a span, and comprehended the dust of the earth in a measure; and weighed the mountains in scales, and the hills in a balance!" Isa. xl. 12. This is *grand;* but the *heavens* being the work of God's FINGERS is yet more sublime.

The moon and the stars] The sun is not mentioned, because the heavens—the moon, planets, and stars—could not have appeared, had *he* been present. Those he wished to introduce because of their immense variety, and astonishing splendour; and, therefore, he skilfully leaves out the sun, which would have afforded him but one object, and one idea. To

have mentioned him with the others would have been as ridiculous in *astronomy,* as the exhibition of the top and bottom of a vessel would be in *perspective.* Various critics have endeavoured to restore the *sun* to this place: and even Bishop *Horsley* says, "It is certainly strange that the sun should be omitted, when the moon and the stars are so particularly mentioned." But with great deference to him, and to Dr. *Kennicott,* who both show how the text may be *mended,* I say, it would be most strange had the psalmist introduced the *sun,* for the reasons already assigned. The *Spirit* of God is always right; our *heads* sometimes, our *hearts* seldom so.

Which thou hast ordained] כוננתה *conantah,* which thou hast prepared and established. Made their respective spheres, and fitted them for their places. Space to matter, and matter to space; all adjusted in number, weight, and measure.

Verse 4. *What is man*] מה אנוש *mah enosh,* what is wretched, miserable man; man in his fallen state, full of infirmity, ignorance, and sin?

That thou art mindful of him?] That thou settest thy heart upon him, keepest him continually in thy merciful view.

And the son of man] ובן אדם *uben Adam,* and the son of Adam, the first great rebel; the fallen child of a fallen parent. See the note on Job vii. 17. Some think eminent men are here intended. What is *man* in *common;* what the *most eminent men;* that thou shouldst be mindful of them, or deign to visit them?

That thou visitest him?] By sending thy Holy Spirit to convince him of *sin, righteousness,* and *judgment.* It is by these *visits* that man is preserved in a salvable state. Were God to withhold them, there would be nothing in the soul of man but sin, darkness, hardness, corruption, and death.

Verse 5. *Thou hast made him a little lower than the angels*] The original is certainly very emphatic: ותחסרהו מעט מאלהים *vattechasserchu meat meelohim,* Thou hast lessened him for a little time from God. Or, Thou hast made him less than God for a little time. See these passages explained at large in the notes on Heb. ii. 6, &c., which I need not repeat here.

Verse 6. *Thou madest him to have dominion*] Jesus Christ, who, being in the form of God, and equal with God, *for a time* emptied himself, and made himself of no reputation; was afterwards *highly exalted,* and had a name above every name. See the notes referred to above, and those on Phil. ii. 6-9.

Thou hast put all things *under his feet*] Though the whole of the brute creation was made subject to Adam in his state of innocence; yet it could never be literally said of him, that God had put all things under his feet, or that he had dominion over the work of God's hands; but all this is most literally true of our Lord Jesus; and to him the apostle, Heb. ii. 6, &c., applies all these passages.

7 ¹All sheep and oxen, yea, and the beasts

of the field ;

8 The fowl of the air, and the fish of the sea,

and whatsoever passeth through the paths of the seas.

9 ᵐO Lᴏʀᴅ our Lord, how excellent *is* thy name in all the earth !

---

¹Heb. *Flocks and oxen all of them*

ᵐVer. 1

Verse 7. *All sheep and oxen*] All *domestic* animals, and those to be employed in *agriculture.*
  Beasts of the field] All *wild beasts*, and inhabitants of the *forest.*
  Verse 8. *The fowl of the air*] All these were given to man in the beginning; and he has still a general dominion over them; for thus saith the Lord: "The fear of you, and the dread of you, shall be upon every ʙᴇᴀsᴛ of the ᴇᴀʀᴛʜ, and upon every ꜰᴏᴡʟ of the ᴀɪʀ, and upon all that ᴍᴏᴠᴇᴛʜ upon the ᴇᴀʀᴛʜ, and upon all the ꜰɪsʜᴇs of the sᴇᴀ; into your hand are they delivered;" Gen. ix. 2. To this passage the psalmist most obviously refers.
  Verse 9. *O Lord our Lord*] The psalmist concludes as he began. Jehovah, our prop and support! his name is excellent in all the earth. The name of Jᴇsᴜs is celebrated in almost every part of the habitable globe; for his Gospel has been preached, or is in the progress of being preached, through the whole world. *Bibles* and *missionaries* are now carrying his name, and proclaiming his fame, to the utmost nations of the earth.
  The whole of this Psalm, and *the seventh and eighth* verses in particular, have been the subject of much *spiritualization* in ancient and modern times. I shall give two examples: one from the pious Bishop *Horne;* the other from the ancient *Latino-Scotico-English* Psalter, mentioned before.
  That of Bishop *Horne*, on the 7th and 8th verses, is as follows: "Adam, upon his creation, was invested with sovereign dominion over the creatures, in words of the same import with these, Gen. i. 28, which are therefore here used, and the creatures particularized, to inform us that what the first Adam lost by transgression, the second Adam gained by obedience. That glory which was set above the heavens could not but be over all things on the earth; and accordingly we hear our Lord saying, after his resurrection, 'All power is given unto me in heaven and earth,' Matt. xxviii. 18. Nor is it a speculation unpleasing or unprofitable to consider that he who rules over the material world is Lord also of the intellectual or spiritual creation represented thereby.
  "The souls of the faithful, lowly, and harmless, are the *sheep* of his pasture; those who, like *oxen*, are strong to labour in the Church, and who by expounding the word of life tread out the corn for the nourishment of the people, own him for their kind and beneficent Master. Nay, tempers fierce and untractable as the *wild beasts* of the desert, are yet subject to his will. Spirits of the angelic kind, that, like the *birds of the air*, traverse freely the superior region, move at his command; and these evil ones, whose habitation is in the *deep abyss*, even to the great *leviathan* himself, all, all are put under the feet of the King Messiah; who, because he humbled himself, and became obedient to death, was therefore highly exalted, and had a name given him above every name; that at

the name of Jesus every knee should bow, whether of things in heaven, or things on earth, or things under the earth; and that every tongue should confess that Jesus is Lord, to the glory of God the Father; Phil. ii. 8, &c." Thus far the pious bishop.
  I shall now give, as a singular curiosity, the whole Psalm, with its translation and paraphrase, from the ancient MS. already mentioned; inserting first the *Latin text;* next, the *translation;* and, thirdly, the *paraphrase.* The Latin text seems to be the old *Itala*, or *Ante-hieronymian;* at least it has readings which have been thought peculiar to that version.

PSALM VIII

Ver. 1. Domine Deus noster, quoniam admirabile est nomen tuum in universa terra.
  Trans. 𝕷ord our 𝕷ord, qᴡat thi name es ᴡonderfull in al the 𝕰rde.
  Par. The prophete in louing, bygynnes and says: Lord of al, thow ert specialy our Lord that dredes the, loves the. *Thi name* that es the ioy and the fame of thi name Ihesu: for the creaturs that thu hes made and bought qwat it es wonderful. Als so say withouten end: for nane suffis for to knaw al creaturs: in qwilk wonder of the, and that in al the Erd, nought in a party anely.
  Quoniam elevata est magnificencia tua super Celos.
  Trans. 𝔍or lyfted es thi ᴡorchyp aboᴠen heᴠens.
  Par. That es at say, thu ert mare worthy to be loued and wirchepyd than any Aungel or haly Saule may thynk.
  Verse 2. Ex ore infancium et lactencium perfecisti laudem, propter inimicos tuos, ut destruas inimicum et ultorem.
  Trans. 𝕺f the mouth of nought spekand, and sowkand, thou has made louping, for thin enmys, that thou destroye the enmy and the venger.
  Par. Nought anely thow ert loued of perfite men, bot of the mouthe of barnes that spekes nought: Zit there er tha that kan nought speke the wisdom of this werld: and of soukand, the qwilk gladdely resayves the lare of haly Kyrk theare moder. Thow has made thi luf thug perfyte for thin enmys: fals cristen men, to schame and to schende for thai er wer than er haythen men. That thu destruy the enmy; that es, he that es wyse in his awen eghen; and wil nought be underloute til thi wil: *and the venger:* that es he that defends his Syn; and sais that he synnes nought; or that his syn es les than other mennes.
  Ver. 3. Quoniam videbo celos tuos, et opera digitorum tuorum, lunam et stellas quas tu fundasti.
  Trans. 𝔍or 𝕴 sal se thi heᴠens ᴡerkes of thi fyngers the mone and the 𝕾ternys the qᴡilk thoᴡ groundid.
  Par. Thow destrues al that es contrariand til the; bot i in al thying confourom me to do thi wil; for thi i sal se in lyf withouten end. *Thi hevens*, that es Aungels and Apostels the qwilk er werkes of thi fingers: that es, thai er mode

perfyte thurgh the Haly Gost, of qwam es seven gyftes. Of he be bot a Spirit, als mani fyngers er in a hand. And i sal see the *Mone*, that es haly Kyrk: and the sternes that es ilk a ryghtwise man by hym selfe, the qwilk thu groundid in charite.

Ver. 4. Quid est homo quod memor es ejus; aut filius hominis, quoniam visitas eum?

Trans. 𝕼wat es man that thu ert menand of hym: or son of man for thou bisites hym?

Par. Als it war with despyte, he sais *man*, erdely and synful, qwat es he, that thu has mynd of hym. Als fer sett fra the; at the lest gyfand hym hele and ese of body. Or *son of man:* that es, he that es gastely, and beres the ymage of heven. Qwat es he, for thou visits hym. Als present the qwilk es nere the for clennes of lyf. Or *son of man* he calles Crist, thrugh qwam he visits mannes kynd.

Ver. 5. Minuisti eum paullo minus ab angelis: gloria et honore coronasti eum; et constituisti eum super opera manuum tuarum.

Trans. 𝕿how lessed hym a littil fra aungels; with ioy and honour thu coround hym: and thu sett him aboven the werkes of thi hend.

Par. Crist was *lessed fra aungels*, for he was dedely, and mught suffer pyne; but a littel; for in other thyng, es he abouen aungels, thair Kyng and Sychthu thou coround hym with ioy, that es with brighthede of body, na mare sufferand pyne; and honour, for he es honourable til al: and thou sett hym abouen aungels and al creatures.

Ver. 6, 7. Omnia subjecisti sub pedibus ejus: oves et boves insuper et pecora campi.

Trans. 𝕬l thynges thu underkest undyr his fete: schepe and oxen al ouer that, and the bestes of the feld.

Par. That undyr hys Lordschyp and hys myght, in has cestyn al thyng: tha er *schepe* that er innocentes, als well aungels als men. *And oxen*, tha er, traveland men gastely, in haly Kyrk, *over that;* and the *bestes of the feld;* thai er lufers of this werld, wonnand, in the feld of fleschly lusts; noght in hillis of vertus; and so be the brode way thai ga til hell.

Ver. 8. Volucres celi et pisces maris qui perambulant semitas maris.

Trans. 𝕱owls of heven and fysche of the see, that gas the wayes of the see.

Par. Fowls of heven, er prowde men that wald hee thair setil abouen al other. *Fysches of the see*, er covaytus men, the qwilk in the ground of the werld, sekes erthdly gudes, that all stretes in the see, sone wither oway. Al thir sal be underlout til Crist onther herts in grace, or thare in pine.

Ver. 9. Domine Deus noster, quam admirabile est nomen tuum in universa terra.

Trans. 𝕷ard our 𝕷ard qwat thi name is wonderful in al the erth.

Par. Als he bigan swa he endes, schewand that bygyning and endyng of al gode, is of Gode; and til his louing agh i for to-be done.

The reader will no doubt be struck with the remarkable agreement between the pious bishop of Norwich and this ancient translator and paraphrast, particularly on the 7th and 8th verses. The language also is in several respects singular. The participle of the present tense, which we terminate with *ing*, is here almost always terminated with *and*. So *Spekand*, *sowkand*, *gyfand*, *sufferand*, *traveland*, for speaking, sucking, giving, suffering, travelling, &c.

As the participle signifies the *continuance* of

the action, the termination *and* seems much more proper than *ing; speak-and*, i. e., *continuing* to speak; *give-and, continuing* to give; *suffer-and*, suffer more; *travel-and*, travel on, &c. There are some words in this ancient MS. which I have met nowhere else.

ANALYSIS OF THE EIGHTH PSALM

This Psalm begins and ends with a general proposition, figured by an exclamation, which contains an admiration; for he admires what he cannot perfectly comprehend. "O Lord our Lord, how excellent is thy name in all the earth! who hast set thy glory above the heavens." Such is the glory of thy divinity, power, and goodness, that it fills not only the earth, but transcends the very heavens, in which angels and blessed spirits, though they know much more than we on earth, yet cannot comprehend thy Majesty, which fills all and exceeds all.

This general proposition being premised, the prophet descends to some *particular instances*, in which the excellence of God's name particularly appears; and he mentions *three:* I. *Infants*. II. The *heavens*, with the *moon* and *stars*. III. *Man* himself.

I. The excellence of God's power, divinity, and goodness, appears in infants: "Out of the mouth of babes and sucklings thou hast ordained strength." 1. The sucking of babes, and speaking of young children, are evident demonstrations of God's excellent name; for who taught the babe to suck, or the dumb infant to speak, but the *Lord our Governor?* 2. The children that cried "Hosanna!" in the temple, struck with the miracles of our Lord; while the priests, through *envy*, were *dumb*. 3. Or by *babes* may be meant such as the worldlywise repute no better than *children* and *fools*. By simple *prophets*, ignorant *fishermen*, humble *confessors*, and faithful *martyrs*, hath he *stilled the enemy* and the *avenger;* confounded the wisest philosophers, and stopped the mouths of devils.

II. The next instance in which the glory and excellence of God's name appears is the *heavens*, the *moon* and the *stars:* these are the works of his *fingers*, and therefore called *Thy heavens;* whose amplitude is great, order and orbs wonderful, beauty admirable, matter durable, and motions various yet stable; together with the *stars*, whose multitude is innumerable, magnitude vast and various, order admirable, and influences secret and wonderful. The varying, yet regular and constant course of the *moon*, her changes, phases, and influences on the earth and the waters, on men and other animals. All these have been *ordained* by the all-wise God; and the earth and its inhabitants are receiving continual benefits from them.

When I *consider* these things, then I say to myself:

III. "What is man, that thou art mindful of him? or the son of man, that thou visitest him?" This is the psalmist's *third* instance to manifest the excellence of God's providence and government of the world, in which he reflects upon man in his *baseness* and in his *dignity*.

1. In his baseness, vileness, and misery, signified by the question, *What is man?* As if he should say, What a poor creature? how miserable! What except dust and ashes, as to his body, when he was at the best; for he was *taken from the dust of the ground*, even when his soul was formed *in the image of God*. But now

miserable dust while he lives, and to dust he shall return when he dies. What then is this miserable creature, of what worth, that thou, so great, and so glorious a Being, who art higher than the heavens, shouldst *visit* and *take care* of him!

2. This is his dignity; he can know, love, serve, and enjoy thee for ever; and thou settest thy love upon him above all other creatures. This thou hast showed in the following ways:—

1. In *visiting* him, and in being *mindful* of him: 1. Thou visitest him by conferring on him many temporal blessings. 2. In illuminating his mind by thy Holy Spirit. 3. In sending him thy *law* and thy *Gospel*, by *prophets* and

apostles. 4. In giving thy *Son* to take upon himself human nature, and to die, the just for the unjust, that thou mightest bring him to thyself, through whom he is to receive remission of sins, and an eternal inheritance among the saints in light. 5. In making him, fallen and wretched as he is, lord of thy creatures; giving him all sheep and oxen, the beasts of the field, the fowls of heaven, and the fish of the sea. 6. But this universal dominion belongs principally to the Lord Jesus, *through* whom and *by* whom all good comes to man, and *to* whom all glory should be given, world without end. Let God's excellent name be exalted throughout all the earth!

PSALM IX

David praises God for the benefits which he has granted to Israel in general, and to himself in particular, 1–6. He encourages himself in the Lord, knowing that he will ever judge righteously, and be a refuge for the distressed, 7–10. He exhorts the people to praise God for his judgments, 11, 12; prays for mercy and support; and thanks God for his judgments executed upon the heathen, 13–16. He foretells the destruction of the ungodly, 17; prays for the poor and needy, and against their oppressors, 18–20.

II. DAY. MORNING PRAYER

To the chief Musician upon Muth-labben, A Psalm of David

A. M. cir. 2962
B. C. cir. 1042
Davidis, Regis
Israelitarum,
cir. annum
14

I WILL praise *thee*, O LORD, with my whole heart; I will show forth all thy marvellous works.

2 I will be glad and [a]rejoice in thee: I will sing praise to thy name, O [b]thou Most High.

3 When mine enemies are turned back, they shall fall and perish at thy presence.

A. M. cir. 2962
B. C. cir. 1042
Davidis, Regis
Israelitarum,
cir. annum
14

[a]Psa. v. 11

[b]Psa. lvi. 2; lxxxiii. 18

NOTES ON PSALM IX

The inscription to this Psalm in the HEBREW text is, *To the chief Musician upon Muth-labben, A Psalm of David.* The CHALDEE has, "A Song of David, to be sung concerning the Death of the Strong Man, (or *champion*, דנברא *degabra*,) who went out between the Camps;" that is, Goliath, on account of whose defeat this Psalm has been supposed by many to have been composed. The date in the margin is several years posterior to the death of Goliath. See the *introduction*.

The VULGATE: "A Psalm of David, for the end; concerning the secrets of the Son."

The SEPTUAGINT and ÆTHIOPIC are the same with the *Vulgate*.

The SYRIAC: "A Psalm of David concerning Christ's receiving the throne and the kingdom, and defeating his enemies."

The ARABIC: "Concerning the mysteries of the Son, as to the glory of Christ, his resurrection, and kingdom, and the destruction of all the disobedient."

Houbigant causes the Hebrew title to agree with the *Vulgate*, *Septuagint*, and *Æthiopic*, by uniting על מות *al muth*, "concerning the death," into the word עלמות *alamoth*, which signifies *secrets* or hidden things. "To the chief musician, or conqueror; secrets concerning the Son: A Psalm of David."

About a hundred MSS. and printed editions unite the words as above. Some translate עלמות *alamoth*, "concerning the youth or infancy; the infancy of the Son." Several of the *fathers* have on this ground interpreted it, "concerning the *incarnation* of our Lord." Indeed, the title and the Psalm have been so variously understood, that it would be as painful as it would be useless to follow the different commentators, both ancient and modern, through all their conjectures.

Verse 1. *I will praise* thee, O Lord, with my *whole heart*] And it is only when the *whole heart* is employed in the work that God can look upon it with acceptance.

I will show forth] אספרה *asapperah*, "I will *number out*, or *reckon up*;" a very difficult task, נפלאותיך *niphleotheycha*, "thy miracles;" supernatural interventions of thy power and goodness. He whose eye is attentive to the operation of God's hand will find many of these. In the Vulgate this Psalm begins with *Confitebor tibi, Domine*, "I will confess unto thee, O Lord," which my old MS. above quoted translates thus: *J sal schrife Lard, til þe, in al my hert, J sal tel al þi wonders.* On which we find the following curious *paraphrase:* "Here the prophete spekes agaynes that grucches with ese of il men: and the travel and anguis of gude men. *I sal schrife til the Lard;* that is, I sal lufe the in al my hert, hally gederant it til þi luf: and gyfand

A. M. cir. 2962
B. C. cir. 1042
Davidis, Regis
Israelitarum,
cir. annum
14

4 For ^cthou hast maintained my right and my cause; thou sattest in the throne judging ^dright.

5 Thou hast rebuked the heathen, thou hast destroyed the wicked, thou hast ^eput out their name for ever and ever.

6 ^fO thou enemy, destructions are come to a perpetual end: and thou hast destroyed cities; their memorial is perished with them.

7 ^gBut the LORD shall endure for ever: he hath prepared his throne for judgment.

8 And ^hhe shall judge the world in righteousness, he shall minister judgment to the people in uprightness.

A. M. cir. 2962
B. C. cir. 1042
Davidis, Regis
Israelitarum,
cir. annum
14

9 ⁱThe LORD also will be ^ka refuge for the oppressed, a refuge in times of trouble.

10 And they that ^lknow thy name will put their trust in thee: for thou, LORD, hast not forsaken them that seek thee.

11 Sing praises to the LORD, which dwelleth in Zion: ^mdeclare among the people his doings.

12 ⁿWhen he maketh inquisition for blood, he remembereth them: he forgetteth not the cry of the ^ohumble.

13 Have mercy upon me, O LORD; consider my trouble *which I suffer* of them that hate me, thou that liftest me up from the gates of death:

---

^cHeb. *thou hast made my judgment*——^dHeb. *in righteousness*——^eDeut. ix. 14; Prov. x. 7——^fOr, *the destructions of the enemy are come to a perpetual end; and their cities hast thou destroyed,* &c.

^gPsa. cii. 12, 26; Heb. i. 11——^hPsa. xcvi. 13; xcviii. 9 ⁱPsa. xxxii. 7; xxxvii. 39; xlvi. 1; xci. 2——^kHeb. *a high place*——^lPsa. xci. 14——^mPsa. cvii. 22——ⁿGen. ix. 5——^oOr, *afflicted*

---

na party tharof tyl errour, na to covatyse: ne til fleschly luf. A vile errour it is that some men says, that God dose unrightwisly in mani thinges in erthe: for tham thynk that tay sold noght be done. Als I hard say noght lang sythem, of a man of religyon, and of grete fame, that qwen he was in the see, in poynte to peryshe, he said tyl Gode: Lard thu dos unryghtwysly if thou sofyr us to perysch here. God myght haf answered and said, My rightwysnes reches to sofer a beter man than thou ert to perisse here: for I hope, had he ben a ryghtwyse man, he had noght sayd swa: for al ar unryghtwyse, that hopes that any unrightwysnes may be in Godes wylle. Bot I sal luf the in al thi workes; and tel al thy wonders; that is, bathe that er sene, and that ar noght sene; visibels and invisibels."

Verse 2. *I will be glad and rejoice in thee*] I am glad that thou hast heard my prayer, and showed me mercy; and I will rejoice in thee, in having thee as my portion, dwelling and working in my heart.

Verse 3. *When mine enemies are turned back*] It is a sure sign of a nearly approaching complete conquest over sin, when, by resistance to its influences, it begins to lose its power. That is the time to *follow on to know the Lord*.

Verse 5. *Thou hast rebuked the heathen*] We know not what this particularly refers to, but it is most probably to the Canaanitish nations, which God destroyed from off the face of the earth; hence it is said, *Thou hast put out their name for ever and ever,* עד לעולם *leolam vaed, endlessly.* Here עולם *olam* has its proper signification, *without end.* He who contends it means only *a limited time,* let him tell us *where* the Hivites, Perizzites, Jebusites, &c., now dwell; and *when* it is likely they are to be restored to Canaan.

Verse 6. *Destructions are come to a perpetual end*] Rather, "The enemy is desolated for ever; for thou hast destroyed their cities, and their memory is perished with them." Multitudes of the cities of the Canaanites have perished so

utterly that neither name nor vestige remains of them.

Verse 7. *But the Lord shall endure*] All things shall have an end but God and holy spirits.

Verse 8. *He shall judge the world in righteousness*] All the dispensations of God's providence are founded in righteousness and truth.

Verse 9. *A refuge*] משגב *misgab, a high place,* where their enemies can neither *reach* nor *see* them. He who has God for his portion has all safety in him.

Verse 10. *They that know thy name*] Who have an experimental acquaintance with thy mercy, *will put their trust in thee,* from the conviction that *thou never hast forsaken,* and *never will forsake, them that trust in thee.*

Verse 11. *Declare among the people his doings.*] It is the duty of all those who have received the salvation of God, to recommend him and his salvation to the whole circle of their acquaintance, Christians, so called, when they meet, seldom speak about God! Why is this? Because they have nothing to say.

Verse 12. *When he maketh inquisition for blood*] This not only applies to the *Canaanites, Moabites, Ammonites,* and *Philistines,* who shed the blood of God's people unjustly, but to all the nations of the earth who, to enlarge their territory, increase their wealth, or extend their commerce, have made destructive wars. For the blood which such nations have shed, their blood shall be shed. If *man* should make no inquisition for this iniquitously spilt blood, GOD will do it, for he *remembers them;* and the *cry of the humbled,* distressed people, driven to distraction and ruin by such wars, *is not forgotten before him.*

Verse 13. *Have mercy upon me, O Lord*] David, having laid down the preceding maxims, now claims his part in their truth. I also am in trouble through the unjust dealings of my enemies; I am brought to the *gates of death;* have mercy on *me,* and lift *me* up, that, being saved from the *gates of death,* I may show forth thy praise in *the gates of the daughter of Zion.*

A. M. cir. 2962
B. C. cir. 1042
Davidis, Regis
Israelitarum,
cir. annum
14

14 That I may show forth all thy praise in the gates of the daughter of Zion: I will [p]rejoice in thy salvation.

15 [q]The heathen are sunk down in the pit *that* they made: in the net which they hid is their own foot taken.

16 The LORD is [r]known *by* the judgment *which* he executeth: the wicked is snared in the work of his own hands. [s]Higgaion.[t] Selah.

17 The wicked shall be turned into hell, *and* all the nations [u]that forget God.

A. M. cir. 2962
B. C. cir. 1042
Davidis, Regis
Israelitarum,
cir. annum
14

18 [v]For the needy shall not always be forgotten: [w]the expectation of the poor shall *not* perish for ever.

19 Arise, O LORD; let not man prevail: let the heathen be judged in thy sight.

20 Put them in fear, O LORD: *that* the nations may know themselves *to be but* men. Selah.

---

[p]Psa. xiii. 5; xx. 5; xxxv. 9——[q]Psa. vii. 15, 16; xxxv. 8; vii. 6; xciv. 23; Prov. v. 22; xxii. 8; xxvi. 27——[r]Exod. vii. 5; xiv. 4, 10, 31

[s]That is, *meditation*——[t]Psa. xix. 14; xcii. 3——[u]Job viii. 13; Psa. l. 22——[v]Ver. 12; Psa. xii. 5——[w]Prov. xxiii. 18; xxiv. 14

The gates of death—an *open grave*, leading to a *yawning hell*. *The gates of the daughter of Zion*—all the *ordinances* of God, by which the soul is helped forward to heaven.

Verse 15. *The heathen are sunk down in the pit*] See on Psa. vii. 15.

Verse 16. *The Lord is known* by *the judgment*] It is not every *casualty* that can properly be called a *judgment of God*. Judgment is his strange work; but when he executes it, his mind is plainly to be seen. There are no natural causes to which such calamities can be legally attributed.

The wicked is snared in the work of his own hands.] There is nothing that a wicked man does that is not against his own interest. He is continually doing himself harm, and takes more pains to destroy his soul than the righteous man does to get his saved unto eternal life. This is a weighty truth; and the psalmist adds: *Higgaion; Selah*. Meditate on this; mark it well. See on Psa. iii. 3. Some think that it is a direction to the musicians, something like our *Presto*, *Largo*, *Vivace*, *Allegro*, "Play briskly and boldly; beat away; and let *sense* and *sound* accompany each other."

Verse 17. *The wicked shall be turned into hell*] לשאולה *lisholah, headlong into hell, down into hell*. The original is very emphatic.

All the nations that forget God.] They will not live in his fear. There are both *nations* and *individuals* who, though they *know* God, *forget* him, that is, are *unmindful* of him, do not *acknowledge* him in their designs, ways, and works. These are all to *be thrust down into hell*. Reader, art thou forgetful of thy *Maker*, and of HIM who *died* for thee?

Verse 18. *The needy shall not alway be forgotten*] The needy, and the poor, whose expectation is from the Lord, are never forgotten, though sometimes their deliverance is delayed for the greater confusion of their enemies, the greater manifestation of God's mercy, and the greater benefit to themselves.

Verse 19. *Arise, O Lord*] Let this be the time in which thou wilt deliver thy poor people under oppression and persecution.

Verse 20. *Put them in fear*] שיתה יהוה מורה להם *shithah Yehovah morah lahem*, "O Lord, place a teacher among them," that they may know they also are accountable creatures, grow wise unto salvation, and be prepared for a state of blessedness. Several MSS. read מורא *morre, fear;* but *teacher* or *legislator* is the reading of all the *versions* except the *Chaldee*. *Coverdale* has hit the sense, translating thus: **O Lorde, set a Scholemaster over them**; and the old Psalter, **Sett Lord a brynger of Law abouen tham.**

That *the nations may know themselves* to be but *men*] אנוש *enosh;* Let the Gentiles be taught by the preaching of thy Gospel that they are *weak* and *helpless*, and stand in need of the salvation which Christ has provided for them. This may be the spirit of the petition. And this is marked by the extraordinary note *Selah;* Mark well, take notice. So the term may be understood.

"This whole Psalm," says Dr. Horsley, "seems naturally to divide into three parts. The first *ten* verses make the FIRST part; the *six* following, the SECOND; and the remaining *four* the THIRD.

"The FIRST part is prophetic of the utter extermination of the irreligious persecuting faction. The prophecy is delivered in the form of an Επινικιον, or song of victory, occasioned by the promise given in the *fifteenth* verse of the *tenth* Psalm; and through the whole of this song the psalmist, in the height of a prophetic enthusiasm, speaks of the threatened vengeance as accomplished.

"The SECOND part opens with an exhortation to the people of God to praise him as the Avenger of their wrongs, and the watchful Guardian of the helpless, and, as if the flame of the prophetic joy which the oracular voice had lighted in the psalmist's mind was beginning to die away, the strain is gradually lowered, and the notes of triumph are mixed with supplication and complaint, as if the mind of the psalmist were fluttering between things present and to come, and made itself alternately present to his actual condition and his future hope.

"In the THIRD part the psalmist seems quite returned from the prophetic enthusiasm to his natural state, and closes the whole song with explicit but cool assertions of the future destruction of the wicked, and the deliverance of the persecuted saints, praying for the event."

ANALYSIS OF THE NINTH PSALM

This Psalm consists of *five* chief parts:—

I. David's thanksgiving, ver. 1, 2, amplified and continued till the *tenth* verse.

II. An exhortation to others to do the like, ver. 11, and the reason of it, ver. 12.

III. A petition for himself, ver. 13, and the reason of it, ver. 14.

IV. A remembrance of God's mercy in the overthrow of his enemies, for which he sings a song of triumph, from ver. 15-19.

V. A prayer in the conclusion against the prevalence of the heathen, ver. 19, 20.

I. His profession of praise is set down in the two first verses, in which we may perceive,—

1. The matter of it, with the extent: *All the marvellous works of God.*

2. That he varies the synonyms. *I will praise thee; I will show forth; I will be glad and rejoice in thee; I will sing praise to thy name, O thou Most High!* in which there is a *climax.*

3. The principle whence this praise flowed: 1. Not from the *lips,* but from the *heart.* 2. From the *whole heart:* "I will praise thee with my whole heart."

This he amplifies from the cause, which is double:

1. That which outwardly moved him, and gave him a just occasion to do so; the overthrow of his enemies: "When my enemies are turned back;" who were not overcome by strength or valour, but by the presence and power of God.

2. They shall fall and perish at thy presence. Thou wast the chief cause of this victory; and, therefore, deservest the thanks. Of this the prophet makes a full narrative in the two next verses, setting God as it were upon the bench, and doing the office of Judge. 1. "Thou maintainest my right, and my cause." 2. "Thou sattest on the throne judging right." 3. "Thou hast rebuked the heathen." 4. "Thou hast destroyed the wicked; thou hast put out their name for ever." In a word, Thou art a just Judge, and defendest the innocent, and punishest their oppressors; and *therefore I will praise thee.*

3. And then, upon the confidence of God's justice and power, he exults over his enemies. *O thou enemy, destructions are come to a perpetual end.* Thy power of hurting and destroying is taken away; the fortified cities in which thou dwellest are overthrown; and their memory and thine are perished.

4. Next, to make his assertion clearer; to the enemies' power he opposes that of God; his kingdom to their kingdom. But the Lord, in the administration of his kingdom, is, 1. Eternal: "The Lord shall endure for ever." 2. His office to be Judge: "He hath prepared his throne for judgment." 3. He is a universal Judge: "He shall judge the whole world." 4. He is a just Judge: "He shall judge in righteousness; he shall minister judgment to the people in uprightness." 5. He is a merciful Judge: "For the Lord will be a refuge for the oppressed; a refuge in times of trouble."

5. The effect of this execution of justice. His people are encouraged: who are here described, 1. By their *knowing* him: "They that know thy name." 2. By *trusting* in him: "Will put their trust in thee." 3. By their *seeking* him: "For

thou, Lord, hast not forsaken them that seek thee."

II. An exhortation to others to praise God: "Sing praises to the Lord." The reason of this, 1. He *dwells* in Zion. 2. He *works* graciously there: "Sing praises to the Lord that DWELLS in Zion: declare among the people his DOINGS.' 3. That will destroy their oppressors, and avenge their blood: "When he maketh inquisition for blood, he remembereth them; he forgetteth not the cry of the humble."

III. A petition for himself: "Have mercy on me, O Lord; consider my trouble," &c.; for which he gives these reasons:—

1. That "I may show forth thy praise."

2. "ALL thy praise."

3. "In the gates of the daughter of Zion."

4. That I may do it with joyful lips.

5. Which I will do: "I WILL rejoice in thy salvation."

IV. Then he sings forth his song of triumph over his enemies:—

1. The "heathen are sunk down in the pit they have made."

2. "In the net which they hid are their own feet taken."

3. This is the Lord's work. Though wicked men did doubt before of his providence and justice; yet now "the Lord was known by the judgment which he executed."

4. For "the wicked was snared in the work of his own hands. Higgaion, Selah." Which is a thing exceedingly to be meditated upon, and not forgotten.

5. "The wicked shall be turned into hell, and all the people that forget God." 1. Their breath is in their nostrils, and die they must. 2. If they repent not, they shall suffer eternal punishment. 3. However this may be, God's goodness shall be manifested to the innocent: "The expectation of the poor shall not perish for ever."

V. A prayer in the conclusion against the prevalence of the heathen, in which he shows great earnestness and faith:—

1. "Arise, O Lord; let not man prevail."

2. "Let the heathen be judged in thy sight."

3. "Put them in fear, O Lord!" Now they fear nothing, being in their height of prosperity. They are insolent and proud; manifest thy Divine presence to their terror.

4. For then they will know themselves to be but *men*—infirm and mortal creatures; and not insult over thy people, nor glory in their own strength and prosperity.

The original word has been translated *teacher, lawgiver, governor.* Then send them, 1. A *teacher,* who may make them wise unto salvation. 2. A *lawgiver,* who shall rule them in thy fear. 3. A *governor,* that shall tame and reduce to order their fierce and savage nature. Let the nations be converted unto thee. This will be the noblest triumph. Let their hearts be conquered by thy mercy. And thus the Psalm will conclude as it began, *To the Conqueror,* on whose vesture and thigh is the name written, KING OF KINGS, AND LORD OF LORDS.

PSALM X

The psalmist complains to God of the oppressions which the poor suffer from the wicked man, whom he describes as the hater of the poor, 1, 2; proud, 3; one who will not seek God, 4; and is regardless of his judgments, 5; self-confident, 6; blasphemous and deceitful, 7; strives by subtlety and treachery to destroy the poor, 8–10; and supposes that God is regardless of his conduct, 11. The psalmist calls earnestly on God to preserve the poor and humble, and cast down the oppressor, 12–15. He foresees that his prayer is heard; that judgment will be executed, and the poor delivered, 16–18.

A. M. cir. 3559
B. C. cir. 445
Artaxerxis,
R. Persarum,
cir. annum
20

WHY standest thou afar off, O LORD? *why* hidest thou *thyself* in times of trouble?

2 [a]The wicked in *his* pride doth persecute the poor: [b]let them be taken in the devices that they have imagined.

3 For the wicked [c]boasteth of his [d]heart's desire, and [e]blesseth [f]the covetous, *whom* the LORD abhorreth.

4 The wicked, through the pride of his countenance, [g]will not seek *after God:* [h]God *is* not in all his [i]thoughts.

5 His ways are always grievous: [k]thy judg-ments *are* far above out of his sight: *as for* all his enemies, [l]he puffeth at them.

6 [m]He hath said in his heart, I shall not be moved: [n]for *I shall* [o]never *be* in adversity.

7 [p]His mouth is full of cursing, and [q]deceit, and fraud: [r]under his tongue *is* mischief [s]and [t]vanity.

8 He sitteth in the lurking places of the villages: [u]in the secret places doth he murder the innocent: [v]his eyes are [w]privily set against the poor.

A. M. cir. 3559
B. C. cir. 445
Artaxerxis,
R. Persarum,
cir. annum
20

---

[a]Hebrew, *In the pride of the wicked he doth persecute* [b]Psalm vii. 16; ix. 15, 16; Proverbs v. 22——[c]Psalm xciv. 4——[d]Heb. *souls*——[e]Prov. xxviii. 4; Rom. i. 32 [f]Or, *the coveteous blesseth* himself, *he abhorreth the LORD*——[g]Psa. xiv. 2——[h]Or, *all his thoughts are* There is *no God*——[i]Psa. xiv. 1; lxxiii. 1

[k]Prov. xxiv. 1; Isa. xxvi. 11——[l]Psa. xii. 5——[m]Psa. xxx. 6; Eccles. viii. 11; Isa. lvi. 12——[n]Rev. xviii. 7 [o]Heb. *unto generation and generation*——[p]Rom. iii. 14 [q]Heb. *deceits*——[r]Job xx. 12——[s]Psa. xii. 2——[t]Or, *iniquity*——[u]Hab. iii. 14——[v]Psa. xvii. 11——[w]Heb. *hide themselves*

NOTES ON PSALM X

Verse 1. *Why standest thou afar off, O Lord?*] This Psalm makes a part of the preceding in the *Vulgate* and *Septuagint;* and in four of *Kennicott's* and *De Rossi's* MSS. It seems to belong to the time of the *captivity,* or the *return* of the captives. It was probably made in reference to *Sanballat,* and the other enemies of the Jews. There is a great similarity between this and Psalms xiii., xiv., xxxv., and liii. In these, as *Calmet* remarks, we find the same complaints, the same sentiments, and almost the same expressions.

God is represented here as standing at some distance, beholding the oppression of his people, and yet apparently disregarding it.

Verse 2. *The wicked in his pride*] On no principle of *nature* or *reason* can we account for a *wicked* man persecuting a *humble follower of God* because of his *religion.* The devil hates godliness; and the wicked man hates it also, because the devil is in his heart.

Verse 3. *Boasteth of his heart's desire*] Boasts among his fellows how often he has gratified such and such passions, in such and such circumstances. This shows the excess of a depraved and imbruted spirit. He who can boast of his iniquity, is in the broad road to perdition. Should such a one repent and turn to God, it would be equal to any miracle.

Blesseth the covetous, whom the Lord abhorreth.] Or, *he blesseth the covetous, he abhorreth the Lord.* Those who are like himself he commends, and with them he associates; and *they abhor the Lord*—they have a mortal hatred against every thing that is holy; and they are under the full influence of that *carnal mind* which is *enmity* to the Lord.

Verse 4. *Will not seek after God*] He is too proud to bend his knee before his Judge; he is too haughty to put on sackcloth, and lay himself in the dust; though without deep repentance and humiliation he must without doubt perish everlastingly.

Verse 5. *His ways are always grievous*] Or, *He is travailing in pain to bring forth iniquity at all times.* He is full of lust, or *irregular* and *unholy desires;* he *conceives* and *brings forth sin;* and sin being finished, time, place, and opportunity concurring, *death* is *soon brought forth.*

Thy judgments are far above out of his sight] He is so blinded with sin, that he cannot see the operations of God's hand.

He puffeth at them.] He whistles at them; insults God, and despises men. He overthrows them with his *breath;* he has only to give orders, and they are destroyed. "Bring me the head of Giaffer," said an Asiatic despot. The head was immediately brought! No trial, no judge, no jury; but the despot's will and caprice.

Verse 6. *I shall not be moved*] I have whatever I covet. I hold whatsoever I have gotten. I have money and goods to procure me every gratification.

Verse 7. *His mouth is full of cursing, and deceit, and fraud*] What a finished character! A blasphemer, a deceitful man, and a knave!

Verse 8. *He sitteth in the lurking places*] In this and the following verse there appears to be an allusion to *espionage,* or setting of *spies* on a man's conduct; or to the conduct of an assassin or private murderer. He sitteth in *lurking* places—in *secret* places; his *eyes*—spies—are *privily set;* he lieth in *wait secretly:* he doth *catch* the poor, when he draweth him into his *net.* He is like a hunter that lays his

A. M. cir. 3559
B. C. cir. 445
Artaxerxis,
R. Persarum,
cir. annum
20

9 He ˣlieth in wait ʸsecretly as a lion in his den: he lieth in wait to catch the poor: he doth catch the poor, when he draweth him into his net.

10 ᶻHe croucheth, *and* humbleth himself, that the poor may fall ᵃby his strong ones.

11 He hath said in his heart, God hath forgotten: ᵇhe hideth his face; he will never see *it*.

12 Arise, O Lᴏʀᴅ; O God, ᶜlift up thine hand: forget not the ᵈhumble.

13 Wherefore doth the wicked contemn God? he hath said in his heart, Thou wilt not require *it*.

14 Thou hast seen *it;* for thou beholdest mischief and spite, to requite *it* with thy hand: the poor ᵉcommitteth ᶠhimself unto thee; ᵍthou art the helper of the fatherless.

15 ʰBreak thou the arm of the wicked and the evil *man*: seek out his wickedness *till* thou find none.

16 ⁱThe Lᴏʀᴅ *is* King for ever and ever: the heathen are perished out of his land.

17 Lᴏʀᴅ, thou hast heard the desire of the humble: thou wilt ᵏprepare ˡtheir heart, thou wilt cause thine ear to hear:

18 To ᵐjudge the fatherless and the oppressed, that the man of the earth may no more ⁿoppress.

A. M. cir. 3559
B. C. cir. 445
Artaxerxis,
R. Persarum,
cir. annum
20

ˣPsa. xvii. 12; Mic. vii. 2——ʸHeb. *in the secret places*——ᶻHeb. *he breaketh himself*——ᵃOr, *into his strong parts*——ᵇJob xxii. 13; Psalm. lxxiii. 11; xciv. 7; Ezekiel viii. 12; ix. 9——ᶜMicah v. 9——ᵈOr, *afflicted* ᵉHebrew, *cleaveth*

ᶠ2 Tim. i. 12; 1 Pet. iv. 19——ᵍPsa. lxviii. 5; Hos. xiv. 3——ʰPsa. xxxvii. 17——ⁱPsa. xxix. 10; cxlv. 13; cxlvi. 10; Jer. x. 10; Lam. v. 19; Dan. iv. 34; vi. 26; 1 Tim. i. 17——ᵏOr, *establish*——ˡ1 Chron. xxix. 18 ᵐPsa. lxxxii. 3; Isa. xi. 4——ⁿOr, *terrify*

---

traps and gins, digs his pits, sets his nets; and when the prey falls into them, he destroys its life.

Verse 10. *He croucheth*] Of the scoffing, mocking, insulting, and *insidious* conduct of *Sanballat, Tobiah,* and *Geshem,* the fourth and sixth chapters of *Nehemiah* give abundant proof; and possibly the allusion is to them. The lion squats down and gathers himself together, that he may make the greater spring.

Verse 11. *God hath forgotten*] He hath cast off this people, and he will never more re-establish them. So *Sanballat* thought.

Verse 12. *Arise, O Lord*] Hear their reproaches see their guile, consider thy oppressed people. "Lift up thine hand," *threaten* them, that they may desist and repent. If they repent not let them be punished.

Verse 13. *Wherefore doth the wicked contemn God?*] How is it that the Lord permits such persons to triumph in their iniquity? The longsuffering of God leadeth them to repentance.

Verse 14. *Thou hast seen* it] Nothing can escape thy notice. Thou hast not forgotten thy justice, though judgment is not speedily executed on an evil work. But thou *wilt requite it with thy hand.* By thy *power* thou wilt cast down and destroy the wicked.

The poor committeth himself unto thee] To thee he has given up his body, his soul, and his cause; with the full conviction that thou who art the *helper of fatherless,* will not forget *him.*

Verse 15. *Break thou the arm*] Destroy his *power,* deprive him of his *influence,* that he may be no longer able to oppress.

Seek out his wickedness till *thou find none.*] All his public haunts and private ways shall be investigated; thou wilt bring all his villanies to light, and continue to inflict punishment, while there is a crime to punish. Or, "Continue to judge and punish transgressors, till not one is to be found." This agrees with the following verse.

Verse 16. *The Lord* is *king for ever*] He has, and ever will have, the supreme power.

The heathen are perished out of his land.] They are all either cut off or *converted.* This may refer to the *Canaanites.* What a mercy that we can say this of our own country! Once it was entirely heathen; now not one heathen family in the whole land.

Verse 17. *Lord, thou hast heard*] Thou hast not permitted thy tempted and afflicted followers to pray in vain.

Thou wilt prepare their heart] See the economy of the grace of God: 1. God *prepares* the *heart;* 2. *Suggests the prayer;* 3. *Hears* what is prayed; 4. *Answers* the petition. He who has got a cry in his heart after God, may rest assured that that cry proceeded from a Divine preparation, and that an answer will soon arrive. No man ever had a cry in his heart after salvation, but from God. He who continues to cry shall infallibly be heard.

Verse 18. *That the man of the earth may no more oppress.*] I believe the Hebrew will be better translated thus: "That he may not add any more to drive away the wretched man from the land." Destroy the influence of the tyrant; and let him not have it again in his power to add even one additional act of oppression to those which he has already committed.

How many for the sake of their religion, and because they would serve God with a pure conscience, have, by wicked *lords,* proud and arrogant *land owners,* been driven off their farms, turned out of their houses, deprived of their employments, and exposed to wretchedness! While they served the devil, and were regardless of their souls, they had quiet and peaceable possession; but when they turned to the Lord, and became *sober* and *industrious,* attended the means of grace, read their Bible, and were frequent in prayer, then the *vile man of the earth* drove them from their dwellings! In the sight of such Philistines, piety towards God is the highest of crimes. What a dreadful account must these give *to the Judge of the fatherless and the oppressed!*

ANALYSIS OF THE TENTH PSALM

This Psalm divides itself into three parts:—
I. A complaint against the enemies of the godly.
II. A narration of the enemies' malice.
III. A petition to be delivered from them.

I. 1. He complains of God's absence, which is quickened by the question, 1. "Why standest thou afar off?" 2. "Why hidest thou myself in times of trouble?" ver. 1.

II. He complains of the enemies: "The wicked in his pride doth persecute the poor."

These he describes by *eight* characters:—

1. *Insolence*, pride, and the effect, persecution of good men. Having acquired dignity, places of honour, and riches, they become persecutors, they conspire to oppress good men. "Let them be taken in their own devices," ver. 2. Amen.

2. The wicked man *glories in mischief*, which is a sign of extreme malice: "The wicked boasteth of his heart's desire," ver. 3.

3. He *applauds* and *encourages* others in their *rapine* and *spoil*, to which they are moved by their *covetousness:* "He blesseth the covetous," ver. 3.

4. He *contemns God* and *man*. 1. MAN. He never thinks of being called to an account: God's "judgments are out of his sight, and he puffs at his enemies." 2. GOD. Him he reverences not: "He will not seek after God; neither is he in all his thoughts," 4, 5.

5. He lives in *profane security:* "He saith in his heart, I shall never be moved; I shall never be in adversity;" I am elevated beyond the reach of misfortune, ver. 6.

6. He is full of falsehood and deceit: "His mouth is full of cursing, deceit, and fraud." He will not stick at an *oath*. He will curse himself; and take God to witness in his exactions, that he is doing nothing but what is right, ver. 7.

7. He is *cruel*. See the 9th and 10th verses, where he is compared to a *thief*, an *archer*, an *assassin*, a *lion*, &c. He is bad in heart, ver. 6;

in *tongue*, ver. 7; in *work*, ver. 8, 10:—he is altogether bad.

8. He is a close atheist: "He hath said in his heart, God hath forgotten; he hideth his face, and will never see it:" which is the cause of his cruelty, falsehood, security, &c., ver. 11.

III. The THIRD part is a *petition* to be freed from the wicked man: "Arise, O Lord, lift up thy hand, forget not the humble," ver. 12. To induce God thus to act, he uses two arguments:—

1. That thereby God would assert his own glory. For why should the wicked be suffered thus to blaspheme? "Wherefore doth the wicked contemn God? He hath said in his heart, Thou wilt not require it," ver. 13.

2. The *second* argument is taken from God's *nature* and *work*. 1. In punishing wicked men. 2. In defending the helpless. "Surely thou hast seen it; for thou beholdest michief and spite to requite it," &c., ver. 14.

Then he returns to his prayer, and enforces his *second* argument taken from the *justice* and *office* of God:

1. That he would deprive the wicked of his power and strength: "Break thou the arm of the wicked—seek out his wickedness till thou find none," ver. 15. Let none escape—let them appear no more.

2. That he would *hear* and defend the righteous. Be to thy people what thou hast been in times past. 1. "The Lord is King for ever and ever." 2. He *had expelled the Canaanites* before them: "The heathen are perished out of the land." 3. "Thou hast heard the desire of the humble," ver. 16, 17.

Upon which he concludes with profession of strong confidence:—

1. "Thou wilt prepare the heart of the humble."

2. "Thou wilt cause thine ear to hear." 1. To the safety of the oppressed: "To judge the fatherless and the poor," ver. 18. 2. To the ruin of the oppressor: "That the man of the earth may no more oppress;" that he may have neither power nor influence left by which he may be a plague to the upright, or a supporter of infidelity, ver. 18.

PSALM XI

David's friends advise him to flee to the wilderness from Saul's fury, 1–3. He answers that, having put his trust in God, knowing that he forsakes not those who confide in him, and that he will punish the ungodly, he is perfectly satisfied that he shall be in safety, 4–7.

To the chief Musician, *A Psalm* of David

A. M. cir. 2942
B. C. cir. 1062
Sauli, Regis
Israelitarum,
cir. annum
34

[a]IN the LORD put I my trust: [b]how say ye to my soul, Flee *as* a bird to your mountain?

2 For, lo, [c]the wicked bend *their* bow, [d]they make ready their arrow upon the string, that they may [e]privily shoot at the upright in heart.

A. M. cir. 2942
B. C. cir. 1062
Sauli, Regis
Israelitarum,
cir. annum
34

---

[a]Psa. lvi. 11——[b]See 1 Sam. xxvi. 19, 20——[c]Psa. lxiv. 3, 4——[d]Psa. xxi. 12——[e]Heb. *in darkness*

NOTES ON PSALM XI

The inscription is, *To the chief Musician, A Psalm of David*. By the *chief musician* we may understand the *master-singer;* the *leader of the band;* the *person who directed the choir:* but

we know that the word has been translated, *To the Conqueror;* and some deep and mystical senses have been attributed to it, with which I believe the text has nothing to do.

Verse 1. *In the Lord put I my trust: how say ye*] Some of David's friends seem to have

A. M. cir. 2942
B. C. cir. 1062
Sauli, Regis
Israelitarum,
cir. annum
34

3 'If the foundations be destroyed, what can the righteous do?

4 ^gThe LORD *is* in his holy temple, the LORD's ^hthrone *is* in heaven: ⁱhis eyes behold, his eyelids try, the children of men.

5 The LORD ^ktrieth the righteous: but the

wicked and him that loveth violence his soul hateth.

6 ^lUpon the wicked he shall rain ^msnares, fire, and brimstone, and ⁿa horrible tempest: ^o*this shall be* the portion of their cup.

7 For the righteous LORD ^ploveth righteousness; ^qhis countenance doth behold the upright.

A. M. cir. 2942
B. C. cir. 1062
Sauli, Regis
Israelitarum,
cir. annum
34

---

^fPsa. lxxxii. 5——^gHeb. ii. 20——^hPsa. ii. 4; Isa. lxvi. 1; Matt. v. 34; xxiii. 22; Acts vii. 49; Rev. iv. 2——ⁱPsa. xxxiii. 13; xxxiv. 15, 16; lxvi. 7——^kGen. xxii. 1; James i. 12——^lGen. xix. 24; Ezek. xxxviii. 22

^mOr, *quick burning coals*——ⁿOr, *a burning tempest*
^oSee Gen. xliii. 34; 1 Sam. i. 4; ix. 23; Psa. lxxv. 8
^pPsa. xlv. 7; cxlvi. 8——^qJob xxxvi. 7; Psa. xxxiii. 18; xxxiv. 15; 1 Pet. iii. 12

---

given him this advice when they saw Saul bent on his destruction: "Flee *as* a bird to your mountain;" you have not a moment to lose; your ruin is determined; escape for your life; get off as *swiftly* as possible to the hill-country, to some of those inaccessible fortresses best known to yourself; and hide yourself there from the cruelty of Saul. To which advice he answers, "In the Lord put I my trust;" shall I act as if I were conscious of evil, and that my wicked deeds were likely to be discovered? Or shall I act as one who believes he is forsaken of the protection of the Almighty? No: I put my trust in him, and I am sure I shall never be confounded.

Verse 2. *For, lo, the wicked bend their bow*] Perhaps these are more of the words of his advisers: Every thing is ready for thy destruction: the arrow that is to pierce thy heart is already set on the bow-string; and the person who hopes to despatch thee is concealed in ambush.

Verse 3. *If the foundations be destroyed*] If Saul, who is the vicegerent of God, has cast aside his fear, and now regards neither truth nor justice, a righteous man has no security for his life. This is at present thy case; therefore flee! They have utterly destroyed the foundations; (of truth and equity;) what can righteousness now effect? *Kimchi* supposes this refers to the *priests* who were murdered by Doeg, at the command of Saul. The priests are destroyed, the preservers of knowledge and truth; the Divine worship is overthrown; and what can the righteous man work? These I think to be also the words of David's advisers. To all of which he answers:—

Verse 4. *The Lord is in his holy temple*] He is still to be sought and found in the place where he has registered his name. Though the priests be destroyed, the God in whose worship they were employed still lives, and is to be found in his temple by his upright worshippers. And he tries the heart and the reins of both sinners and saints. Nothing can pass without his notice. I may expect his presence in the *temple;* he has not promised to meet me in the *mountain*.

Verse 5. *The Lord trieth the righteous*] He does not abandon them; he tries them to show their faithfulness, and he afflicts them for their good.

His soul hateth.] The *wicked* man must ever be abhorred of the Lord; and the *violent* man—the destroyer and murderer—*his soul hateth;* an expression of uncommon strength and energy: all the perfections of the Divine nature have such in abomination.

Verse 6. *Upon the wicked he shall rain*] This is a manifest allusion to the destruction of Sodom and Gomorrah.

Snares] Judgments shall fall upon them *suddenly* and *unawares*.

Fire] Such as shall come immediately from God, and be *inextinguishable*.

Brimstone] Melted by the fire, for their *drink!* This shall be the portion of their *cup*.

A horrible tempest] רוח זלעפות *ruach zila-photh*, "the spirit of terrors." Suffering much, and being threatened with more, they shall be filled with confusion and dismay. My old MS. has **gost of stormis**. See at the end. Or, *the blast of destructions*. This may refer to the horribly suffocating Arabian wind, called رسموم *Smum*.

Mohammed, in describing his *hell*, says, "The wicked shall drink nothing there but hot stinking water; breathe nothing but burning winds; and eat nothing but the fruit of the tree *zakon*, which shall be in their bellies like *burning pitch*." Hell enough!

The portion of their cup.] *Cup* is sometimes put for *plenty*, for *abundance;* but here it seems to be used to express the *quantum* of *sorrow* and *misery* which the *wicked* shall have on the earth. See Psa. lxxv. 8; Isa. li. 17, 21, 22, 23; Jer. xxv. 15, xlix. 12; Lam. iv. 21, 22. It is also used in reference to the afflictions of the *righteous*, Matt. xx. 22, xxvi. 39, 42; John xviii. 11.

We find a similar metaphor among the heathens. The following, from *Homer*, Il. **xxiv.**, ver. 525, is in point:—

Ὡς γαρ επεκλωσαντο θεοι δειλοισι βροτοισι,
Ζωειν αχνυμενους· αυτοι δε τ᾽ ακηδεες εισι.
Δοιοι γαρ τε πιθοι κατακειαται εν Διος ουδει
Δωρων, οια διδωσι, κακων· ετερος δε εαων·
Ὡ μεν καμμιξας δῳη Ζευς τερπικεραυνος,
Αλλοτε μεν τε κακῳ ὁγε κυρεται, αλλοτε δ᾽ εσθλῳ.

Such is, alas! the god's severe decree,
They, only they are *bless'd*, and only free.
Two urns by Jove's high throne have ever stood,
The source of *evil* one, and one of *good*.
From thence the CUP of mortal man he fills:
Blessings to *these;* to *those* distributes *ills*.
To most he mingles *both:* the wretch decreed
To taste the bad *unmix'd*, is curs'd indeed.
　　　　　　　　　　　　　　　—POPE.

Verse 7. *The righteous Lord loveth righteousness*] He loves that which resembles himself. *His countenance*—his face—is ever open and unclouded to the upright. They always enjoy his salvation, and know that he is pleased with them.

The preceding verse my old MS. translates and paraphrases thus:—

𝔚e sal rayne on synful, snares, fyre, brimstane, and gost of stormis.

Par.—He sal rayne on synful in this werld, *snares*, that es wiked Lare: *fyre* is covatyse: *brunstane*, that es stynk of il werkes: and *gost of stormis*, that es a stormy though that es withoutyn rest in Ihesu Crist, and ay es traveld with the wynd of the devel. Or *the gast of stormys*, es the last departyng of synful fra ryghtwis men, and there fyre, brunston, storm, er part of the chalyie of thaim: that es, thai ar thair part in pyne. He cals thair pyne a *Cop*, for ilk dampned man sal drynk of the sorow of Hel, eftir the mesure of hys Syn. Behald the pynes of wikid men: fyrst, God raynes upon thaim *snares*, that es qwen he suffers fals prophetes that comes in clathing of mekenes; and withinnen er wers than wolves, to desayf thaim thurgh errour. Sythen the fyre of lychery, and covatys wastes al the gude that thai haf done: eftirward for stynk of il werkes thai er castyn fra Crist, and al his Halows, and then er in sentence of dome; as in a grete storme, dryven in til a pitte of Hel, to bryn in fyre withoutyn ende. This es the entent of this wers.

Verse 7. 𝔉or ryghtwis es 𝔏ord; and he lufes rryghtwisnes; evennes saw the face of hym] Yf ge ask qwy oure lorde yelded pyne to synful? lo here an answere; for he es rightwis. Als so if ge wil witt qwy he gifes ioy til gude men? Lo here an answere; for he lufed ryghtwisnes: that es, ryghtwis men, in the qwilk er many ryghtwisnesses: thof ane be the ryghtwisnes of God, in the qwilk al ryghtwise men or parcenel. *Evenes saw his face:* that es, evenes es sene in his knawyng inence, both the partys of gud and il. This es ogayne wryches at sais, If God saf me noght, I dar say he es unryghtwis: bot thof thai say it now, qwen he suffris wryched men errour in thought, and worde and dede; thai sal noght be so hardy to speke a worde qwen he comes to dampne thaire errour. Bot who so lufes here and haldes that na unevenes may be in hym, qwam so he dampnes, or qwam so he saves, he sal have thaire myght to stand and to speke gude space. Now er swilk in a wonderful wodenes, that wenes for grete wordes to get ought of God.

The former part of this Psalm, *Flee as a bird*, &c., this ancient author considers as the voice of *heresy* inviting the *true Church* to go away into error; and intimates that those who were separating from *haly kyrk* were very pure, and unblameable in all their conduct; and that *mountain* or *hill*, as he translates it, signifies *eminent virtues*, of which they had an apparently good stock. So it appears that those called *heretics* lived then a holier life than those called *halows* or saints.

ANALYSIS OF THE ELEVENTH PSALM

This Psalm is composed dialoguewise, betwixt David and those of his counsellors that per-suaded him to fly to some place of safety from Saul's fury; which, if he did not, he was in a desperate condition. The Psalm has *two* parts.

I. He relates his counsellors' words, ver. 1, 2, 3.

II. To which he returns his answer, ver. 1, and confirms it, ver. 4-7.

I. You, my counsellors, whether of good or bad will I know not, tempt me, that, giving up all hope of the kingdom, I go into perpetual banishment. Such, you say, is Saul's fury against me. Thus, then, ye advise, "Flee *as* a bird to your mountain:" and your arguments are,

1. The greatness of the danger I am in: "For, lo, the wicked bend *their* bow."

2. The want of aid; there is no hope of help. For *the foundations are cast down.* Saul has broken all the leagues and covenants he has made with you. He has slain the priests with the sword, has taken thy fortresses, laws sub-verted. If thou stay, perish thou must: some righteous men, it is true, are left; but *what can the righteous do?*

II. To these their arguments and counsel, David returns his answer in a sharp repre-hension. I tell you,

1. "I trust in God: how say you then to my soul." And he gives his reasons for it from the sufficiency and efficiency of God.

1. You say *the foundations are cast down;* yet I despair not, for God is sufficient.

1. *Present in his holy temple;* he can defend.

2. He is a great King, and *his throne is in heaven.*

3. Nothing is hidden from him: "His eyes behold, and his eyelids," &c.

4. He is a just God, and this is seen in his proceedings both to the just and unjust. 1. *He trieth the righteous*, by a fatherly and gentle correction. 2. "But the wicked, and him that loveth violence, his soul hateth."

These two last propositions he expounds sev-erally, and begins with the *wicked*.

1. "Upon the wicked he shall rain snares, fire and brimstone," &c. 1. He shall rain upon them when they least think of it, even in the midst of their jollity, as rain falls on a fair day. 2. Or, he shall *rain down* the vengeance when he sees good, for it *rains not always.* Though he defer it, yet it *will* rain. 3. The punishment shall come to their utter subversion, as the fire on Sodom, &c. 4. This is the portion of their cup, that which they must expect from him.

2. But he does good to the just: "For the righteous Lord loveth righteousness; his coun-tenance doth behold the upright." He bears him good will, and is careful to defend him.

On the whole the Psalm shows, 1. That David had the strongest conviction of his own upright-ness. 2. That he had the fullest persuasion that God would protect him from all his enemies, and give him a happy issue out of all his dis-tresses.

PSALM XII

The psalmist, destitute of human comfort, craves help from God, 1; gives the character of those who surrounded him, and denounces God's judgments against them, 2-5; confides in the promises of God, and in his protection of him and all good men, 6-8.

To the chief Musician ᵃupon ᵇSheminith, A Psalm of David

HELP, ᶜLORD; for the ᵈgodly man ceaseth; for the faithful fail from among the children of men.

2 ᵉThey speak vanity every one with his neighbour: ᶠ*with* flattering lips, *and* with ᵍa double heart do they speak.

3 The LORD shall cut off all flattering lips, *and* the tongue that speaketh ʰproud ⁱthings:

4 Who have said, With our tongue will we prevail; our lips ᵏ*are* our own: who *is* lord over us?

5 For the oppression of the poor, for the sighing of the needy, ˡnow will I arise, saith the LORD; I will set *him* in safety *from him that* ᵐpuffeth ⁿat him.

6 The words of the LORD *are* ᵒpure words: *as* silver tried in a furnace of earth, purified seven times.

ᵃOr, *upon the eighth*——ᵇPsalm vi. title——ᶜOr, *Save*——ᵈIsaiah lvii. 1; Micah vii. 2——ᵉPsalm x. 7——ᶠPsalm xxviii. 3; lxii. 4; Jeremiah ix. 8; Romans xvi. 18——ᵍHebrew, *a heart and a heart;* 1 Chronicles xii. 33——ʰ1 Samuel ii. 3; Psalm xvii. 10; Daniel vii. 8, 25——ⁱHebrew, *great things*——ᵏHebrew, are *with us*——ˡExodus iii. 7, 8; Isaiah xxxiii. 10 ᵐOr, *would ensnare him*——ⁿPsalm x. 5——ᵒ2 Samuel xxii. 31; Psalm xviii. 30; xix. 8; cxix. 140; Proverbs xxx. 5

NOTES ON PSALM XII

The inscription to this Psalm is: *To the chief Musician upon Sheminith, A Psalm of David.* See on the title of Psa. vi. The *Arabic* has "Concerning the end (of the world which shall happen) on the eighth day. A prophecy relative to the Advent of the Messiah."

Some think that this Psalm was made when Doeg and the Ziphites betrayed David to Saul, see 1 Sam. xxii. and xxiii.; but it is most likely that was written during the Babylonish captivity.

Verse 1. *Help, Lord*] Save me, O Lord; for merciful men fail, and faithful men have passed away from the sons of Adam. 𝔐𝔞𝔨𝔢 𝔰𝔞𝔣𝔢 𝔪𝔢, 𝔏𝔬𝔯𝔡; 𝔣𝔬𝔯 𝔥𝔞𝔩𝔭 𝔣𝔞𝔦𝔩𝔢𝔡, 𝔣𝔬𝔯 𝔩𝔢𝔰𝔰𝔢𝔡 𝔢𝔰 𝔰𝔬𝔱𝔥𝔣𝔞𝔰𝔱𝔫𝔢𝔰 𝔣𝔯𝔞 𝔰𝔬𝔫𝔰 𝔬𝔣 𝔪𝔢𝔫. OLD MS.

Verse 2. *They speak vanity every one with his neighbour*] They are false and hollow; they say one thing while they mean another; there is no trusting to what they say.

Flattering lips, and *with a double heart do they speak*] בלב ולב *beleb valeb*, "With a heart and a heart." They seem to have *two hearts;* one to speak fair words, and the *other* to invent mischief. The old MS. both translates and paraphrases curiously.

Trans. 𝔇𝔞𝔶𝔫 𝔰𝔭𝔞𝔨 𝔦𝔩𝔨𝔞𝔫 𝔱𝔦𝔩 𝔥𝔦𝔰 𝔫𝔢𝔤𝔥𝔟𝔲𝔯: 𝔰𝔱𝔴𝔭𝔨𝔦𝔩 𝔩𝔦𝔭𝔭𝔦𝔰 𝔦𝔫 𝔥𝔢𝔯𝔱, 𝔞𝔫𝔡 𝔱𝔥𝔲𝔯𝔤𝔥 𝔥𝔢𝔯𝔱 𝔱𝔥𝔞𝔦 𝔰𝔭𝔞𝔨.

Par.—Sothfastnes es lessed, and falsed waxes: and al sa vayn spak ilkone to bygyle his neghbur: and many spendes thair tyme in vayne speche withoutyn profyte and gastely frute. And thai er *swyku lippis;* that er jangelers berkand ogaynes sothfastnes. And *swykel,* for *thai speke in hert and thurgh hert;* that es in dubil hert, qwen a fals man thynkes ane, and sais another, to desaif hym that he spekes with. This homely comment cannot be mended.

Verse 3. *Proud things*] נדלות *gedoloth, great things;* great swelling words, both in their *promises* and in their *commendations.*

Verse 4. *Our lips* are *our own*] Many think, because they have the faculty of speaking, that therefore they may speak what they please.

Old MS.—The qwilk sayd, our toung we sal wyrchip, our lippes er of us, qwas our Lorde? Tha Ypocrites worchepes thair toung; for thai hee tham self janglyng and settes in thaire pouste to do mykil thyng and grete: and thai rose tham that thair lippes that es thair facund and thair wyls er of tham self, nought of God, ne of haly menes lare; for thi thai say *qua es our Lord?* that es, qwat es he to qwas rewle and conversacioun we sal be undir lout? and confourme us til? Als so to say, Thar es none.

Verse 5. *For the oppression of the poor*] This seems to refer best to the tribulations which the poor Israelites suffered while captives in Babylon. The Lord represents himself as looking on and seeing their affliction; and, hearing their cry, he determines to come forward to their help.

Now will I arise] I alone delivered them into the hands of their enemies, because of their transgressions; I alone can and will deliver them from the hands of their enemies; and the manner of their deliverance shall show the power and influence of their God.

From him that *puffeth at him.*] Here is much *interpolation* to make out a sense. Several of the *versions* read, "I will give him an open salvation." My work shall be manifest.

Verse 6. *The words of the Lord* are *pure words*] None of his promises shall fall to the ground; the salvation which he has promised shall be communicated.

Silver tried in a furnace of earth] A reference to the purification of silver by the *cupel.* This is a sort of instrument used in the purification of silver. It may be formed out of a strong iron ring or hoop, adjusted in width and depth to the quantum of silver to be purified, and rammed full of well pulverized calcined bone. The metal to be purified must be mingled with *lead,* and laid on the cupel, and exposed to a strong heat in an air furnace. The impurities of the metal will be partly absorbed, and partly

7 Thou shalt keep them, O Lord, thou shalt preserve [p]them from this generation for ever.

8 The wicked walk on every side, when [q]the vilest men are exalted.

---

[p]Heb. *him;* that is, *every one of them*

[q]Heb. *the vilest of the sons of men are exalted*

---

thrown off in fume. The metal will continue in a state of agitation till all the impurities are thrown off; it will then become perfectly *still,* no more *motion* appearing, which is the token that the process is completed, or, according to the words of the text, is *seven times,* that is, perfectly *purified.*

Verse 7. *Thou shalt keep them—thou shalt preserve them*] Instead of the pronoun *them* in these clauses, several MSS., with the *Septuagint,* the *Vulgate,* and the *Arabic,* have *us.* The sense is equally good in both readings. God did bring forth the Israelites from Babylon, according to his word; he separated them from *that generation,* and reinstated them in their own land, according to his word; and most certainly he has *preserved them from generation to generation* to the present day, in a most remarkable manner.

Verse 8. *The wicked walk on every side*] The land is full of them. *When the vilest men are exalted;* rather, *As villany gains ground among the sons of Adam.* See the Hebrew. The *Vulgate* has, "In circuito impii ambulant; secundum altitudinem tuam multiplicasti filios hominum;" which is thus translated and paraphrased in my old MS.:—

Trans. **In umgang wiked gos: eftir thy heenes thu has multiplied the sons of man.**

Par. Us thu kepes; bot wiked gas in umgang; that es, in covatyng of erdley gudes, that turnes with the whele of seven daies: in the qwilk covatys, thai ryn ay aboute; for thai sett nane endyng of thaire syn: and tharfor settes God na terme of thair pyne, but sons of men that lyfs skilwisly and in ryghtwisnes, thu has multiplied, aftir thi heghnes in vertus; aftir the heghnes of thi consayll, thou hast multiplied men bath il and gude; for na man may perfitely witt in erd, qwy God makes so many men, the qwilk he wote well sal be dampned: bot it es the privete of his counsayle, so ryghtwis, that no thyng may be ryghtwiser.

In this we find a number of singular expressions, which, while they elucidate the text, will not be uninteresting to the antiquary. Here, for instance, we see the true etymology of the words *righteous* and *righteousness,* i. e., *right wise* and *right wiseness.* For we have it above as a *noun,* **ryghtwisnes**; as an *adjective,* **ryghtwis**; and as an *adjective* in the *comparative* degree, **rightwiser**: and we should have had it as an *adverb, ryghtwisely,* had not the word **skilwisly** occurred to the author.

Righteousness is *right wiseness,* or that which is according to *true wisdom.* A *righteous* man is one who is *right wise;* properly instructed in *Divine wisdom,* and *acts* according to its dictates; and among them who act *rightwisely,* there are some who act *rightwiser* than others; and nothing can be *rightwiser* than ever to *think* and *act* according to the *principles* of that *wisdom* which comes from above.

Right, ꞃehꞇ rectus, *straight,* is opposed to *wrong,* from ƿꞃænᵹ, *injury,* and that from ƿꞃanᵹen, to *twist.* As ꞃehꞇan *rehtan* signifies to *direct,* so ƿꞃanᵹen *wrangen* signifies to *twist,* or *turn* out of a *straight* or *direct* line. *Right* is *straight,* and *wrong, crooked.* Hence the *righteous* man is one who goes *straight forward,* acts and walks by *line* and *rule;* and the *unrighteous* is he who walks in *crooked paths,* does what is *wrong,* and is never guided by true *wisdom.* Such a person is sometimes termed *wicked,* from the Anglo-Saxon ƿiccian, to act by *witch*-craft, (hence ƿicca, *wicca,* a *witch,*) that is to renounce God and righteousness, and to give one's self to the devil, which is the true character of a *wicked* man. Let him that readeth understand.

The vilest men are exalted] Were we to take this in its obvious sense, it would signify that at that time wickedness was the way to preferment, and that good men were the objects of persecution.

Analysis of the Twelfth Psalm

There are *four* parts in this Psalm:—

I. A *prayer,* and the reason of it; ver. 1, 2.

II. A *prophecy* of the fall of the wicked, ver. 3, whose arrogance he describes, ver. 4.

III. God's *answer* to the petition, with a promise full of comfort, ver. 5; ratified, ver. 6.

IV. A *petitory,* or *affirmative conclusion: Keep them;* or a confident affirmation that God will keep them from the contagion of the wicked, ver. 7, of which there were too many, ver. 8.

I. The *prayer,* which is very short, for he breaks in upon God with one word, הושעה *Hoshiah! Help! Save, Lord!* ver. 1. For which he gives two reasons:—

1. The scarcity of good men: "For the godly man ceaseth," &c. There is neither piety nor fidelity among men.

2. The great abundance of the wicked; the licentious times; the perfidiousness, hypocrisy, and dissimulation of the men among whom he lived. "They speak vanity every one with his neighbour," &c.; ver. 2. They take no care to perform what they promise.

II. The *prophecy.* This shows the end of their dissembling: "The Lord shall cut off all flattering lips;" ver. 3. These are described,

1. As proud boasters: "With our tongues will we prevail," &c.

2. As persons restrained by no authority: "Who is the Lord over us?" ver. 4.

III. God's *answer* to the petition, *Help, Lord!* is it so that the wicked are so numerous, so tyrannous, so proud, and so arrogant?

1. "I will arise, saith the Lord."

2. I will not delay: "Now I will arise;" ver. 5.

3. "I will set him in safety (my followers) from him that puffeth," &c.

4. I am moved to it by his sighs and groans: "For the oppression of the poor, for the sighing of the needy," &c.; ver. 5.

5. And of this let no man doubt: "The words of the Lord are pure words." There is no more fallacy in the words of God than there is impurity in silver seven times refined; ver. 6.

IV. A petitory, or affirmative conclusion: *Thou shalt keep them, O Lord;* or, *O keep them!* The overflowings of wickedness are great.

1. *Keep them.* For unless God keep them they will be infected.

2. *Keep them from this generation.* **For they are a generation of vipers.**

3. *Keep them for ever.* For unless thou enable them to *persevere*, they will fall.

4. *And keep them.* For the power, pride, and influence of these impious men are very great. 1. "The wicked walk on every side." As wolves they seek whom they may devour. 2. And wickedness is the way to preferment: "The vilest men are exalted;" ver. 8.

Thy people call on thee for help; they know thou canst help, and therefore are they confident that thou wilt help, because they know that thou art good.

PSALM XIII

This Psalm contains the sentiments of an afflicted soul that earnestly desires succour from the Lord. The psalmist complains of delay, 1–3; prays for light and comfort, because he finds himself on the brink of death, 3; dreads the revilings of his enemies, 4; anticipates a favourable answer, and promises thanksgiving, 5, 6.

To the ªchief Musician, A Psalm of David

A. M. cir. 3464
B. C. cir. 540
Ante U. C. cir.
214
Olymp. LX.
cir. ann. prim.

HOW long wilt thou forget me, O LORD? for ever? ᵇhow long wilt thou hide thy face from me?

2 How long shall I take counsel in my soul, *having* sorrow in my heart daily? how long shall mine enemy be exalted over me?

3 Consider *and* hear me, O LORD my God:

ᶜlighten mine eyes, ᵈlest I sleep the *sleep of* death;

4 ᵉLest mine enemy say, I have prevailed against him: *and* those that trouble me, rejoice when I am moved.

5 But I have ᶠtrusted in thy mercy; my heart shall rejoice in thy salvation.

6 I will sing unto the LORD, because he hath ᵍdealt bountifully with me.

A. M. cir. 3464
B. C. cir. 540
Ante U. C. cir.
214
Olymp. LX.
cir. ann. prim.

ªOr, *overseer*——ᵇDeut. xxxi. 17; Job xiii. 24; Psa. xliv. 24; lxxxviii. 14; lxxxix. 46; Isa. lix. 2

ᶜEzra ix. 8——ᵈJer. li. 39——ᵉPsa. xxv. 2; xxxv. 19; xxxviii. 16——ᶠPsa. xxxiii. 21——ᵍPsa. cxvi. 7; cxix. 17

NOTES ON PSALM XIII

There is nothing particular in the inscription. The Psalm is supposed to have been written during the captivity, and to contain the prayers and supplications of the distressed Israelites, worn out with their long and oppressive bondage.

Verse 1. *How long wilt thou forget me*] The words עד אנה *ad anah, to what length, to what time,* translated here *how long?* are *four* times repeated in the two first verses, and point out at once great dejection and extreme earnestness of soul.

Hide thy face from me?] How long shall I be destitute of a clear sense of thy *approbation?*

Verse 2. *Take counsel in my soul*] I am continually framing ways and means of deliverance; but they all come to naught, because thou comest not to my deliverance. When a soul feels the burden and guilt of sin, it tries innumerable schemes of self-recovery; but they are all useless. None but God can speak peace to a guilty conscience.

Mine enemy be exalted] Satan appears to triumph while the soul lies under the curse of a broken law.

Verse 3. *Consider and hear me*] Rather, *answer me.* I have prayed; I am seeking thy face; I am lost without thee; I am in darkness; my life draws nigh to destruction; if I die unforgiven, I die eternally. O Lord my God, *consider* this; hear and answer, for thy name's sake.

Verse 4. *Let mine enemy say*] Satan's ordinary method in temptation is to excite strongly to sin, to blind the understanding and inflame the passions; and when he succeeds, he triumphs by insults and reproaches. None so ready then to tell the poor soul how deeply, disgracefully, and ungratefully it has sinned! Reader, take heed.

When I am moved.] When moved from my steadfastness and overcome by sin. O what desolation is made by the fall of a righteous soul! Itself covered with darkness and desolation, infidels filled with scoffing, the Church clad in mourning, the Spirit of God grieved, and Jesus crucified afresh, and put to an open shame! O God, save the pious reader from such wreck and ruin!

Verse 5. *But I have trusted in thy mercy*] Thou wilt not suffer me to fall; or if I have fallen, wilt thou not, for his sake who died for sinners, once more lift up the light of thy countenance upon me? Wilt thou not cover my sin?

My heart shall rejoice in thy salvation.] There is no true joy but of the heart; and the heart cannot rejoice till all guilt is taken away from the conscience.

Verse 6. *I will sing unto the Lord*] That heart is turned to God's praise which has a clear sense of God's favour.

Because he hath dealt bountifully with me.]

כי נמל עלי *ki gamel alai, because he hath recompensed me.* My sorrows were deep, long continued, and oppressive, but in thy favour is life. A moment of this spiritual joy is worth a year of sorrow! O, to what blessedness has this godly sorrow led! He has given me the oil of joy for the spirit of heaviness, and the garments of praise for mourning.

The old MS. Psalter, which I have so frequently mentioned and quoted, was written at least *four hundred* years ago, and written probably in Scotland, as it is in the Scottish dialect. That the writer was not merely a commentator, but a truly religious man, who was well acquainted with the travail of the soul, and that faith in the Lord Jesus Christ which brings peace to the troubled heart, is manifested from various portions of his comment. To prove this I shall, I think I may say, favour the reader with another extract from this Psalm on the words, "How long wilt thou forget me," &c., ver. 1. I have only to observe that with this commentator a true penitent, one who is deeply in earnest for his salvation, is called a *perfyte man;* i. e., one wholly given up to God.

𝕳𝖔𝖜 𝖑𝖆𝖓𝖌 𝖑𝖔𝖗𝖉 𝖋𝖔𝖗 𝖌𝖊𝖙𝖊𝖘 𝖙𝖍𝖚 𝖒𝖊 𝖎𝖓 𝖙𝖍𝖊 𝖊𝖓𝖉𝖞𝖓𝖌? How long o way turnes thou thi face fro me? The voice of haly men that covaytes and yernes the comyng of Iehu Crist, that thai might lyf with hym in ioy; and pleynaund tham of delaying. And sais, *Lord how lang for getes thu me in the endyng?* That I covayte to haf and hald. That es how lang delayes thu me fra the syght of Iehu Crist, that es ryght endyng of myn entent. And how lang turnes thu thi face fra me? that es, qwen wil thu gif me perfyte Knawing of the? This wordes may nane say sothly, bot a perfyte man or woman, that has gedyrd to gydir al the desyres of thair Saule, and with the nayle of luf fested tham in Iehu Crist. Sa tham thynk one hour of the day war our lang to dwel fra hym; for tham langes ay til hym; bot tha that lufs noght so, has no langyng that he come: for thair conscience sais thaim, that thai haf noght lufed hym als thai suld have done.

The language of true Christian experience has been the same in all times and nations. "But he that loveth not knoweth not God; for God is love;" and to such this is strange language.

ANALYSIS OF THE THIRTEENTH PSALM

"This Psalm," says Bishop Nicolson, "is a fit prayer for a soul that is sensible of God's desertion."

It has *three* parts:—

I. A heavy and bitter complaint of God's absence, ver. 1, 2.

II. An earnest petition for God's return, ver. 3. The reason, ver. 4.

III. A profession of faith and confidence, with joy in God, accompanied with thanksgiving, ver. 5, 6.

I. He bitterly complains, and aggravates it.

1. That God had forgotten him: "Wilt thou forget me?"

2. That he hid his face from him: "Wilt thou hide thy face?"

3. That he was distracted with many cares, what way to take, and what counsel to follow, to recover God's favour: "I take counsel in my soul, having sorrow in my heart."

4. In the meantime, his *enemy was exalted, triumphed* and *insulted over him.*

5. And, lastly, he complains of the delay, which is quickened by the *erotesis,* (interrogation,) and *anaphora,* (beginning several sentences with the same words,) *How long? How long? How long? What! for ever?*

II. His petition, ver. 3. Of which there are three degrees opposed to the parts of his complaint, ver. 1, 2.

1. *Look upon me,* or *consider me.* Thou hast hitherto seemed to turn away thy face; but once behold me, and give me a proof of thy love.

2. *Hear me.* Thou hast seemed to have forgotten; but now, I pray thee, remember me; and show that thou dost not neglect my prayer.

3. *Lighten my eyes.* I have been vexed in my soul, and agitated various counsels to recover thy favour; but do thou instruct me, and illuminate me, as to what course I shall take.

That his petition might be the sooner heard, he urges many arguments:—

1. From that relation that was between him and God: "O Lord my God, hear me!"

2. From a bitter event that was likely to follow, if God heard him not: "Lest I sleep the sleep of death."

3. From another afflictive consequence—the boasting and insult of his adversaries: "Lest my enemy say, I have prevailed against him; and those that trouble me rejoice when I am moved."

But although the answer was delayed, yet he does not despair—for,

III. In the conclusion, he professes faith, joy, and thankfulness:—

1. His *faith:* "I have trusted in thy mercy."

2. His *joy:* "My heart shall rejoice in thy salvation."

3. His *thankfulness:* "I will sing unto the Lord, because he hath dealt bountifully with me."

According to this scale, this Psalm can neither be read nor paraphrased without profit.

PSALM XIV

The sentiments of atheists and deists, who deny the doctrine of a Divine providence. Their character: they are corrupt, foolish, abominable, and cruel, 1–4. God fills them with terror, 5; reproaches them for their oppression of the poor, 6. The psalmist prays for the restoration of Israel, 7.

To the chief Musician, *A Psalm* of David

A. M. cir. 3440
B. C. cir. 564
Ante U. C. cir.
190
Olymp. LIV.
cir. ann. prim.

THE [a]fool hath said in his heart, *There is* no God. [b]They are corrupt, they have done abominable works, *there is* none that doeth good.

2 [c]The LORD looked down from heaven upon the children of men, to see if there were any that did understand, *and* seek God.

3 [d]They are all gone aside, they are *all* together become [e]filthy: *there is* none that doeth good, no, not one.

A. M. cir. 3440
B. C. cir. 564
Ante U. C. cir.
190
Olymp. LIV.
cir. ann. prim.

4 Have all the workers of iniquity no knowledge? who [f]eat up my people *as* they eat bread, and [g]call not upon the LORD.

5 There [h]were they in great fear: for God *is* in the generation of the righteous.

6 Ye have shamed the counsel of the

---

[a]Psa. x. 4; liii. 1, &c.——[b]Gen. vi. 11, 12; Rom. iii. 10, &c.——[c]Psa. xxxiii. 13; cii. 19——[d]Rom. iii. 10, 11, 12——[e]Heb. *stinking*

[f]Jeremiah x. 25; Amos iii. 4; Micah iii. 3——[g]Psalm lxxix. 6; Isaiah lxiv. 7——[h]Hebrew, *they feared a fear;* Psalm liii. 5

NOTES ON PSALM XIV

There is nothing particular in the *title;* only it is probable that the word לדוד *ledavid, of David,* is improperly prefixed, as it is sufficiently evident, from the construction of the Psalm, that it speaks of the *Babylonish captivity.* The author, whoever he was, (some say Haggai, others Daniel, &c.,) probably lived beyond the Euphrates. He describes here, in fervid colours, the iniquity of the Chaldeans. He predicts their terror and destruction; he consoles himself with the prospect of a speedy return from his exile; and hopes soon to witness the reunion of the tribes of Israel and Judah. It may be applied to *unbelievers* in general.

Verse 1. *The fool hath said in his heart, There is no God.*] נבל *nabal,* which we render *fool,* signifies an *empty fellow,* a *contemptible person,* a *villain.* One who has a muddy head and an unclean heart; and, in his darkness and folly, says in his heart, "There is no God." "And none," says one, "but a *fool* would say so." The word is not to be taken in the strict sense in which we use the term *atheist,* that is, one who denies the *being of a God,* or confounds him with *matter.* 1. There have been some, not many, who have denied the existence of God. 2. There are others who, without absolutely denying the Divine existence, deny his *providence;* that is, they acknowledge a Being of infinite power, &c., but give him nothing to do, and no world to govern. 3. There are others, and they are very numerous, who, while they profess to acknowledge both, deny them in their heart, and live as if they were persuaded there was no God either to punish or reward.

They are corrupt] They are in a state of *putrescency;* and *they have done abominable works*—the corruption of their *hearts* extends itself through all the actions of their *lives.* They are a plague of the most deadly kind; propagate nothing but destruction; and, like their father the devil, spread far and wide the contagion of sin and death. Not *one of them does good.* He cannot, for he has no Divine influence, and he denies that such can be received.

Verse 2. *The Lord looked down from heaven*] Words spoken after the manner of men. From this glorious eminence God is represented as looking down upon the habitable globe, *to see if there were any that did understand* that there was a Supreme Being, the governor and judge of men; and, in consequence, *seek God* for his mercy, support, and defence.

Verse 3. *They are all gone aside*] They will not walk in the *straight* path. They seek *crooked* ways; and they have departed from *truth,* and the God of truth.

They are all *together become filthy*] נאלחו *neelachu.* They are become *sour* and *rancid;* a metaphor taken from milk that has fermented, and turned sour, rancid, and worthless.

There is *none that doeth good, no, not one.*] This is not only the state of heathen Babylon, but the state of the *whole inhabitants of the earth,* till the grace of God changes their heart. By *nature,* and from nature, by *practice,* every man is sinful and corrupt. He *feels* no good; he is *disposed* to no good; he *does* no good. And even God himself, who cannot be deceived, cannot find a single exception to this! Lord, what is man?

The *Vulgate,* the Roman copy of the *Septuagint,* the *Æthiopic,* and the *Arabic,* add those six verses here which are quoted by St. Paul, Rom. iii. 13-18. See the notes on those passages, and see the *observations* at the end of this Psalm.

Verse 4. *Have all the workers of iniquity no knowledge?*] Is there not one of them who takes this dreadful subject into consideration? To their deeply fallen state they add cruelty; they oppress and destroy the poor, without either interest or reason.

Who eat up my people as they eat bread] Ye make them an easy and unresisting prey. They have no power to oppose you, and therefore you destroy them. That this is the meaning of the expression, is plain from the speech of Joshua and Caleb relative to the Canaanites. Num. xiv. 9: "Neither fear ye the people of the land; for they are bread for us."

And call not upon the Lord.] They have no *defence,* for they *invoke not* the Lord. They are all either *atheists* or *idolaters.*

Verse 5. *There were they in great fear*] This is a manifest allusion to the history of the *Canaanitish nations;* they were struck with terror at the sight of the Israelites, and by this allusion the psalmist shows that a destruction similar to that which fell upon them, should fall on the Babylonians. Several of the versions add, from Psa. liii. 5, "Where no fear was." They were struck with terror, where no real cause of terror existed. Their fears had magnified their danger.

For God is in the generation] They feared the Israelites, because they knew that the Almighty God was among them.

Verse 6. *Ye have shamed the counsel of the*

A. M. cir. 3440
B. C. cir. 564
Ante U. C. cir.
190
Olymp. LIV.
cir. ann. prim.

poor, because the LORD *is* his
¹refuge.

7 ᵏO ¹that the salvation of
Israel *were come* out of Zion!

ᵐwhen the LORD bringeth back
the captivity of his people, Jacob
shall rejoice, *and* Israel shall be
glad.

A. M. cir. 3440
B. C. cir. 564
Ante U. C. cir.
190
Olymp. LIV.
cir. ann. prim.

ⁱPsa. ix. 9; cxlii. 5——ᵏHeb. *Who will give*, &c.; see Rom.   xi. 26——¹Psa. liii. 6——ᵐJob xlii. 10; Psa. cxxvi. 1

---

poor] Instead of תבישו *tabishu*, "Ye have
shamed," Bishop *Horsley* proposes to read תבישם
tabishem, and translates the clause thus: "The
counsel of the helpless man shall put *them* to
shame." But this is not authorized by MS. or
version. There is no need for any change: the
psalmist refers to the *confidence* which the
afflicted people professed to have in God for
their deliverance, which confidence the Babylonians turned into *ridicule*. The poor people
took counsel together to expect help from God,
and to wait patiently for it; and this counsel
ye derided, because ye did not *know*—did not
consider, that God was in the congregation of
the righteous.

Verse 7. *O that the salvation*] Or, more
literally, *Who will give from Zion salvation to
Israel?* From Zion the deliverance must come;
for God alone can deliver them; but *whom* will
he make his instruments?

When the Lord bringeth back] For it is Jehovah alone who can do it. *Jacob shall rejoice,*
and *Israel shall be glad.* That is, according to
Calmet, the remains of the kingdom of Israel,
and those of Judah, shall be rejoined, to their
mutual satisfaction, and become one people,
worshipping the same God; and he has endeavoured to prove, in a dissertation on the
subject, that this actually took place after the
return from the Babylonish captivity.

Many of the fathers have understood this
verse as referring to the *salvation of mankind
by Jesus Christ;* and so it is understood by
my old MS. Psalter, as the following paraphrase
will show: 𝔔wa sal gyf of 𝔖yon hele til 𝔍srael?
qwen 𝔏ord has turned o way the captyfte of his folk,
glad sal 𝔍acob, and fayne be 𝔍srael. Qwa bot Crist
that ge despyse, qwen ge wil nout do his coun-
saile of Syon fra heven, sal gyf hele til Israel?
that es, sal saf al trew cristen men; noght als
ge er that lufs noght God. And qwen our Lord
has turned o way the captyfte of his folk: that
es, qwen he has dampned the devel, and al his
Servaundes, the qwilk tourmentes gude men,
and makes tham captyfs in pyne. *Then glade
sal Jacob;* that es, al that wirstils o gayns vices
and actyf: *and fayne sal be Israel:* that es, al
that with the clene egh of thair hert, sees God
in contemplatyf lyf. For *Jacob* es als mikil
at say als, *Wrestler*, or *suplanter* of *Syn*. Israel
es, *man seand God*.

Of the two chief opinions relative to the
design of this Psalm: 1. That it refers to *Absalom's rebellion*. 2. That it is a complaint of
the *captives in Babylon;* I incline to the latter,
as by far the most probable.

I have referred, in the note on ver. 3, to that
remarkable addition of no less than *six verses*,
which is found here in the *Vulgate*, the Vatican
copy of the *Septuagint*, the *Æthiopic*, and the
Arabic, and also in St. *Paul's* Epistle to the
Romans, chap. iii. 13-18, which he is supposed
to have quoted from this Psalm as it then stood
in the Hebrew text; or in the version of the
Seventy, from which it has been generally

thought he borrowed them. That they are not
interpolations in the *New Testament* is evident
from this, that they are not wanting in any MS.
yet discovered; and they exist in all the ancient
versions, the *Vulgate*, *Syriac*, *Æthiopic*, and
Arabic. Yet it has been contended, particularly
by St. *Jerome*, that St. Paul did not quote them
from this Psalm; but, being intent on showing
the corruption and misery of man, he collected
from *different parts* several passages that bore
upon the subject, and united them here, with
his quotation from Psa. xiv. 3, as if they had
all belonged to that place: and that succeeding
copyists, finding them in *Romans*, as quoted
from that Psalm, inserted them into the *Septuagint*, from which it was presumed they had
been lost. It does not appear that they made
a part of this Psalm in *Origen's Hexapla*. In
the portions that still exist of this Psalm there
is not a word of these additional verses referred
to in that collection, neither here nor in the
parallel Psalm liii.

The places from which *Jerome* and others
say St. Paul borrowed them are the following:—

Rom. iii. 13: "Their mouth is an open sepulchre; with their tongues they have used deceit."
Borrowed from Psa. v. 10.

"The poison of asps is under their lips."
From Psa. cxl. 3.

Verse 14: "Whose mouth is full of cursing
and bitterness." From Psa. x. 7.

Verse 15: "Their feet are swift to shed blood."
From Prov. i. 16, or Isa. lix. 7.

Verses 16, 17, 18: "Destruction and misery
are in their ways, the way of peace they have
not known, and there is no fear of God before
their eyes." From Isa. lix. 7, 8.

When the reader has collated all these passages in the *original*, he will probably feel
little satisfaction relative to the probability of
the hypothesis they are summoned to support.

These verses are not found in the best copies
of the *Vulgate*, though it appears they were in
the old *Itala* or *Antehieronymain* version. They
are not in the *Codex Alexandrinus* of the *Septuagint;* nor are they in either the *Greek* or
Latin text of the *Complutensian* Polyglot. They
are wanting also in the *Antwerp* and *Parisian*
Polyglots. They are neither in the *Chaldee* nor
Syriac versions. They are not acknowledged
as a part of this Psalm by *Theodoret*, *Chrysostom*, *Euthymius*, *Arnobius*, *Apollinaris*, the
Greek Catena, *Eusebius*, of Cæsarea, nor *Jerome*.
The latter, however, acknowledges that they
were in his time *read in the churches*. I have
seen no Latin MS. without them; and they are
quoted by *Justin Martyr* and *Augustine*. They
are also in the *Editio Princeps* of the *Vulgate*,
and in all the ancient *Psalters* known. They
are in that *Psalter* which I have frequently
quoted, both in the *Latino-Scotico-English* version and paraphrase.

Of this version the following is a faithful
copy, beginning with the *third* verse of the
fourteenth Psalm:—

Al tha helddid togyder ; thai er made unprofytable :
Thar es none that dos gude ; thar es none til one.
A grave oppnnand, es the throte of tham.
With thaire tunges trycherusly thai wroght
Venym of snakes undir the lippis of tham.
Qwhas mouth es ful of weryng and bitternes :
Swyft thaire fete to spil blode.
Brekyng and wikednes in thair waies :
And the way of pees thai knew noght :
The drede of God es noght byfore the eghen of thaim.

There is a good deal of difference between this, and that *version* attributed to *Wiclif*, as it stands in my large MS. Bible, quoted in different parts of the New Testament, particularly in 1 Cor. xiii. 1, &c. I shall give it here line for line with the above.

Alle boweden atweye to gydre ; thei ben maad unprofitable :
Ther is not that doith good thing, ther is not til to oon.
A Sepulcre opnyng is the throote of hem :
With her tungis thei diden gylinly ; or trecherously :
The venym of eddris, that is clepid Aspis, under her lippis :
The mouth of whom is ful of cursing, or worrying and bittrenesse :
The feet of hem ben swift for to schede out blood :
Contricioun or defouling to God, and infelicite or cursidnesse, the wayes of hem ;
And thei knewen not the weyes of pees ;
The dreed of God is not bifore her ygen.

The words underlined in the above are added by the translator as explanatory of the preceding terms. It is worthy of remark that *Coverdale* inserts the whole of the addition in this Psalm; and *Cardmarden* has inserted it in his Bible, but in a letter different from the text.

It is now time to state what has been deemed of considerable importance to the authenticity of these verses; viz., that they are found in a *Hebrew* MS., numbered by *Kennicott* in his catalogue 649. It is in the public library at *Leyden;* contains the *Psalms* with a *Latin version* and *Scholia;* and appears to have been written about the end of the *fourteenth* century, and probably by some *Christian*. I shall give the text with a literal *translation*, as it stands in this MS., line for line with the preceding:—

קבר פתוח גרונם
An open sepulchre is their throat;

לשונם יחליקיון
With their tongues they flatter;

חמת עכשוב תחת לשונם
The venom of the asp is under their tongue;

אשר פיהם אלה ומרמה מלא
Whose mouth of cursing and bitterness is full;

קלו רגליהם לשפוך דם :
Swift are their feet to shed blood;

מזל רע ופגע רע בדרכיהם
An evil aspect, and an evil event, in their ways:

ודרך שלום לא ידעו
And the way of peace they know not.

אין פחד אלהים לנגר עיניהם :
No fear of God before their eyes.

It would be easy to criticise upon the Hebrew in this long quotation. I shall content myself with what *Calmet*, who received his informa-

tion from others that had inspected the Leyden MS., says of this *addition:* "Les sçavans, qui ont examiné ce manuscrit, y ont remarqué un Hebreu barbare en cet endroit; et des façons de parler, qui ne sentent point les siecles où la langue Hebraïque etoit en usage." "Learned men, who have examined this MS., have remarked a barbarous Hebraism in this place, and modes of speech which savour not of those ages in which the Hebrew language was in use."

If this be an interpolation in the Psalm, it is *very ancient;* as we have the testimony of *Jerome*, who was prejudiced against it, that it was read in all the churches in his time, and how long before we cannot tell. And that these verses are a valuable portion of Divine revelation, as they stand in Rom. iii. 13-18, none can successfully deny. See *Rosenmüller, Kennicott,* and *De Rossi.*

ANALYSIS OF THE FOURTEENTH PSALM

This Psalm is the practical atheist's character, and has TWO parts:—
I. The description of the practical atheist, from ver. 1 to 7.
II. A petition for the Church, ver. 7.
1. 1. The atheist is here noted to us by different characters:—
1. From his *name,* נבל *nabal,* a *fool,* or rather a *churl;* no natural fool, but a sinful: a *fool* in that in which he should be wise.
2. His hypocrisy or cunning; *he saith,* but he will not have it known, it is to himself, "He saith in his heart." He is a close, politic *fool.*
3. His saying, or his chief and prime principle: "There is no God."
4. From his practice; confessing God in his words for some political advantages, yet in his works denying him. For, 1. His heart is wicked and unregenerate: "They are corrupt." 2. He is a sinner in a high practical degree: "They have done abominable works." 3. He performs no duty: "There is none that doeth good." He *commits* sin; he *omits* duty.
2. The psalmist demonstrates what he said *three* ways; and convinces them,—
1. By the testimony of *God* himself; he is a witness against them. He is, 1. An eyewitness: *he looks on.* 2. He is in heaven, and they are continually under his notice: "He looked down from heaven." 3. He sees *the children of men,* their *hearts* and their *works.* 4. And the object of his looking is to inquire after their *religion:* "To see if there were any that did understand and seek God."
2. And then he gives his testimony in these general terms: "They are all gone aside, they are all together become filthy: there is none that doeth good, no, not one."
3. Next he accuses them of *two sins* of which they were especially guilty. 1. *Injustice:* "They eat up my people as bread." 2. *Impiety:* "They call not upon the Lord."
4. And that his testimony is true, he convinces them, 1. By the light of their own *conscience:* "Have all the workers of iniquity no knowledge?" Does not their own conscience tell them that all this is true? Do they not *know* this? 2. By *fear* and *terror*, the effects of an evil conscience: "There were they in great fear." They said, *There is no God;* but their conscience told them that *God was in the congregation of the righteous,* and that they should grievously answer for their *injustice* and *impiety.* 3. By the *hardness* of their *heart,* and contempt of the good counsels of the godly.

If *he* reproved, *they* mocked. If he said *God was his refuge*, they laughed him to scorn. "Ye have shamed the counsel of the poor, because the Lord is his refuge."

II. The second part of the Psalm contains a petition for the Church:—

1. He prays that God would *send salvation to his people*.

2. That it might be *out of Zion;* because

Christ was anointed and set a King upon the holy hill of Zion: "O that the salvation of Israel were come out of Zion!"

3. For then the consequence would be the great joy and happiness of all his people for their deliverance from captivity, *spiritual* and *temporal:* "When the Lord bringeth back the captivity of his people, Jacob shall rejoice, and Israel shall be glad."

PSALM XV

The important question answered, Who is a proper member of the Church militant? *and who shall finally join the* Church triumphant?   *Ver. 1 contains the question; ver. 2–5, the answer.*

A Psalm of David

L ORD, ªwho shall ᵇabide in thy tabernacle? who shall dwell in ᶜthy holy hill?

2 ᵈHe that walketh uprightly, and worketh righteousness, and ᵉspeaketh the truth in his heart.

ªPsa. xxiv. 3, &c.——ᵇHeb. *sojourn*——ᶜPsa. ii. 6; iii. 4

ᵈIsa. xxxiii. 15——ᵉZech. viii. 16; Eph. iv. 25

NOTES ON PSALM XV

The *title*, לדוד מזמור *mizmor ledavid, a Psalm of David*, has nothing in it particularly worthy of notice. If it were a Psalm composed during the captivity, relating to their return and settlement in their own land, with the restoration of their temple service and all the ordinances of God, and a description of the persons who should then be considered Israelites indeed, the name of *David* is improperly prefixed. But the subject is of the most general utility, and demands the most solemn and serious attention of all men who profess to believe in the immortality of the soul.

Verse 1. *Lord, who shall abide in thy tabernacle?*] The literal translation of this verse is, "Lord, who shall sojourn in thy tabernacle? who shall dwell in the mountain of thy holiness?" For the proper understanding of this question we must note the following particulars:—

1. The *tabernacle*, which was a kind of *moveable temple*, was a type of the *Church militant*, or the state of the people of God in this world.

2. *Mount Zion*, the *holy mount*, where the temple was built, was the type of the *kingdom of heaven*. There the ark became *stationary*, and was no longer carried about from place to place; and the whole was typical of the *rest* that remains for the people of God.

3. The TABERNACLE was a temporary and frequently-removed building, carried about from place to place, and not long in any one place. Concerning this it is said ינור מי *mi yagur*, "Who shall *lodge*, or *sojourn*," there? It is not a *residence*, or *dwelling-place*, but a place to *lodge* in for a time.

4. The TEMPLE was a *fixed* and *permanent* building; and here it is inquired, ישכן מי *mi yiscon*, "Who shall *dwell*, *abide*," or have his *permanent residence*, there?

5. The *tabernacle* being a migratory temple, carried about on the shoulders of the priests and Levites, there was no *dwelling* there for any; they could but *lodge* or *sojourn*.

6. The *temple* being *fixed*, the priests, Levites, &c., became *permanent occupiers*. There was no *lodging* or *sojourning*, but *permanent residence* for all connected with it.

7. The *tabernacle* is, therefore, a proper type of the *Church militant*, wandering up and down, tossed by various storms and tempests; the followers of God, having here *no continuing city; sojourning* only on earth to get a preparation for eternal glory.

8. The *temple* is also a proper type or emblem of the *Church triumphant* in heaven. "Here the wicked cease from troubling, and the weary are at rest." It is the *dwelling-place*, the *eternal residence*, of all who are faithful unto death, who are made *pillars in that temple of God, to go no more out for ever*.

The questions therefore are,

1. Who can be considered a fit member of the Church of Christ here below? and,

2. Who shall be made partakers of an endless glory? In answer to these questions, the character of what we may term a *true Israelite*, or a *good Christian*, is given in the following particulars:—

Verse 2. *He that walketh uprightly*] הולך תמים *holech tamim*, 1. *He walks perfectly*. Who sets God before his eyes, takes his word for the rule of his conduct, considers himself a *sojourner* on earth, and is continually *walking* to the kingdom of God. He acts according to the *perfections* of God's law; he has respect to all its parts, and feels the weight and importance of all its injunctions.

And worketh righteousness] 2. He is not

3 ¹*He that* backbiteth not with his tongue, nor doeth evil to his neighbour, ᵍnor ʰtaketh up a reproach against his neighbour.

4 ¹In whose eyes a vile person is contemned; but he honoureth them that fear the Lᴏʀᴅ.

ᶦLev. xix. 16; Psalm xxxiv. 13——ᵍExod. xxiii. 1
ʰOr, *receiveth, or, endureth*——ᶦEsther iii. 2——ᵏJudges xi. 35

He that ᵏsweareth to *his own* hurt, and changeth not.

5 ¹*He that* putteth not out his money to usury, ᵐnor taketh reward against the innocent. He that doeth these *things* ⁿshall never be moved.

ᶦExod. xxii. 25; Lev. xxv. 36; Deut. xxiii. 19; Ezek. xviii. 8; xxii. 12——ᵐExod. xxiii. 8; Deut. xvi. 19 ⁿPsa. xvi. 8; 2 Pet. i. 10

---

satisfied with a *contemplative* life; he has *duties* to perform. The law of *righteousness* has placed him in certain *relations*, and each of these relations has its peculiar duties. פֹּעֵל צֶדֶק *poel tsedek*, the words here used, signify to *give just weight*, to *render* to all their *dues*. 1. As he is the *creature* of Gᴏᴅ, he has duties to perform to *him*. He owes God his heart: *My son, give me thy heart;* and should love him with all his heart, soul, mind, and strength. This is giving Gᴏᴅ *his due*. 2. As a *member of civil society*, he has various duties to perform to his fellows, as they have to him. He is to love them as himself, and do unto all men as he would they should do unto him. 3. There are duties which he owes to *himself*. That his *body* may be in health, vigour, and activity, he should avoid every thing by which it might be injured, particularly all excesses in eating, drinking, sleeping, &c. That his *soul* may be saved, he should avoid all sin; all irregular and disorderly passions. He owes it to his soul to apply to God for that grace which produces repentance, faith, and holiness; and in order to get all these blessings, he should *read, watch, pray, hear the word preached,* and diligently use all the *ordinances of God.* He who acts not thus, *defrauds both his body and soul:* but the person in the text works righteousness—*gives to all their due;* and thus keeps a conscience void of offence, both towards God and man.

And speaketh the truth in his heart.] 3. He is a *true* man; in him there is no *false way.* He is no man of *pretences; speaking one thing,* and *meaning another.* He *professes* nothing but what he *feels* and *intends;* with him there are no *hollow friendships, vain compliments,* nor *empty professions of esteem, love, regard,* or *friendship.* His *mouth* speaks nothing but what his *heart* dictates. His *heart,* his *tongue,* and his *hand,* are all in unison. *Hypocrisy, guile,* and *deceit,* have no place in his soul.

Verse 3. He that *backbiteth not with his tongue*] לֹא רָגַל עַל לְשֹׁנוֹ *lo ragal al leshono*, "he foots not upon his tongue." 4. He is one who treats his neighbour with respect. He says nothing that might injure him in his *character, person,* or *property; he forgets* no calumny, he is *author* of no slander, he *insinuates* nothing by which his neighbour may be injured. The *tongue,* because of its slanderous conversation, is represented in the nervous original as *kicking about* the character of an absent person; a very common vice, and as destructive as it is common: but the man who expects to see God abhors it, and *backbites not with his tongue.* The words *backbite* and *backbiter* come from the Anglo-Saxon bac, *the back,* and bɪᴄᴀɴ, *to bite.* How it came to be used in the sense it has in our language, seems at first view unaccountable; but it was intended to convey the treble sense of *knavishness, cowardice,*

and *brutality.* He is a *knave,* who would rob you of your *good name;* he is a *coward,* that would speak of you in your *absence* what he dared not to do in your *presence;* and only an ill-conditioned *dog* would fly at and *bite* your *back* when your *face* was *turned.* All these *three ideas* are included in the term; and they all meet in the *detractor* and *calumniator.* His tongue is the tongue of a *knave,* a *coward,* and a *dog.* Such a person, of course, has no right to the privileges of the *Church militant,* and none of his disposition can ever see God.

Nor doeth evil to his neighbour] 5. He not only avoids *evil speaking,* but he avoids also *evil acting* towards his neighbour. He *speaks* no *evil* of him; he *does* no *evil* to him; he does him no *harm;* he occasions him no *wrong.* On the contrary, he *gives him his due.* See under the second particular.

Nor taketh up a reproach against his neighbour.] 6. The word חֶרְפָּה *cherpah,* which we here translate *a reproach,* comes from חָרַף *charaph, to strip,* or *make bare,* to *deprive one of his garments;* hence חֹרֶף *choreph,* the *winter,* because it *strips the fields* of their *clothing,* and the *trees* of their *foliage.* By this, nature appears to be *dishonoured* and *disgraced.* The application is easy: a man, for instance, of a *good character* is reported to have done something wrong: the tale is spread, and the slanderers and *backbiters* carry it about; and thus the man is *stripped* of his *fair character,* of his *clothing of righteousness, truth,* and *honesty.* All may be *false;* or the man, in an hour of the power of darkness, may have been tempted and *overcome;* may have been wounded in the cloudy and dark day, and deeply mourns his fall before God. Who that has not the heart of a devil would not strive rather to *cover* than *make bare* the fault? Those *who feed,* as the proverb says, *like the flies, passing over all a man's whole parts to light upon his wounds,* will take up the tale, *and carry it about.* Such, in the course of their diabolic work, carry the story of scandal to the righteous man; to him who loves his God and his neighbour. But what reception has the tale-bearer? The good man *taketh it not up;* לֹא נָשָׂא *lo nasa,* he will not *bear* it; it shall not be propagated from him. He cannot prevent the detractor from *laying it down;* but it is in his power not to *take it up:* and thus the progress of the slander may be arrested. *He taketh not up a reproach against his neighbour;* and the tale-bearer is probably discouraged from carrying it to another door. Reader, drive the slanderer of your neighbour far away from you: ever remembering that in the law of God, as well as in the law of the land, "the *receiver* is as bad as the *thief.*"

Verse 4. *In whose eyes a vile person is contemned*] 7. This man judges of others by their conduct; he tries no man's heart. He knows men only by the *fruits* they bear; and thus he gains knowledge of the *principle* from which they proceed. *A vile person,* נמאס *nimas,* the *reprobate,* one abandoned to sin; is *despised,* נבזה *nibzeh,* is *loathsome,* as if he were covered with the *elephantiasis* or *leprosy,* for so the word implies. He may be *rich,* he may be *learned,* he may be a *great man* and *honourable* with his master, in high offices in the state; but if he be a spiritual *leper,* an *infidel,* a *profligate,* the righteous man must despise him, and hold him, because he is an enemy to God and to man, in sovereign contempt. If he be in power, he will not treat him as if *worthy* of his dignity; while he *respects* the *office* he will *detest* the *man.* And this is quite right; for the popular odium should ever be pointed against vice.

Aben Ezra gives a curious turn to this clause, which he translates thus: "He is mean and contemptible in his own eyes;" and it is certain that the original, נבזה בעיניו נמאס *nibzeh beeynaiv nimas,* will bear this translation. His *paraphrase* on it is beautiful: "A pious man, whatever good he may have done, and however concordant to the Divine law he may have walked, considers all this of no worth, compared with what it was his duty to do for the glory of his Creator." A sentiment very like that of our Lord, Luke xvii. 10: "So likewise ye, when ye shall have done all those things which are commanded you, say, We are unprofitable servants; we have done that which was our duty to do."

Taken in this sense, the words intimate, that the man who is truly pious, who is a proper member of the Church *militant,* and is going straight to the *Church triumphant,* is truly *humble;* he knows he *has nothing but what he has received,* he has no *merit,* he trusts not in himself, but in the living God. He renounces his *own righteousness,* and trusts in the *eternal mercy of God* through the *infinitely meritorious atonement* made by Jesus Christ. The language of his heart is,—

> "I loathe myself when God I see,
> And into nothing fall;
> Content that thou exalted be,
> And Christ be all in all."

He honoureth them that fear the Lord] 8. This cause is a proof, however just the sentiment, that *Aben Ezra* has mistaken the meaning of the preceding clause. The truly pious man, while he has in contempt the *honourable* and *right honourable* profligate, yet *honours them that fear the Lord,* though found in the most abject poverty; though, with *Job,* on the *dunghill,* or, with *Lazarus,* covered with *sores* at the rich man's gate. Character is the object of his attention; persons and circumstances are of minor importance.

The fear of the Lord is often taken for the *whole of religion;* and sometimes for that *reverence* which a man feels for the *majesty* and *holiness of God,* that induces him to hate and depart from evil. Here it may signify the lowest degree of religion, *repentance whereby we forsake sin.*

Sweareth to his own *hurt, and changeth not.*] 9. If at any time he have bound himself by a solemn engagement to do so and so, and he finds afterwards that to keep his *oath* will be greatly to his *damage;* yet such reverence has he for *God* and for *truth,* that he will not *change,* be the consequences what they may.

He is faithful also to his *promises;* his bare word will bind him equally with an *oath.* He that will not be honest *without* an oath will not be honest *with* one.

The *Hebrew* might be thus translated: "He sweareth to afflict himself, and does not change;" and thus the *Chaldee* has rendered this clause. He has promised to the Lord to keep his body under, and bring it into subjection; to deny himself that he may not pamper the flesh, and have the more to give to the poor.

Verse 5. *Putteth not out his money to usury*] 10. As *usury* signifies *unlawful interest,* or that which is got by *taking advantage of the necessity of a distressed neighbour,* no man that fears God can be guilty of it. The word נשך *neshech,* which we translate *usury,* comes from *nashach,* to *bite as a serpent;* and here must signify that *biting* or *devouring usury,* which ruins the man who has it to pay. "The *increase of usury* is called נשך *neshech,* because it resembles the *biting of a serpent.* For as this is so small at first, as scarcely to be perceptible, but the *venom* soon spreads and diffuses itself till it reaches the vitals; so the *increase* of usury, which at first is not perceived nor felt, at length grows so much as by degrees to *devour* another's substance." *Middoch's* edition of *Leigh's* Critica Sacra, sub voce נשך.

The Jews ever were, and are still, remarkable for *usury* and *usurious contracts;* and a Jew that is saved from it is in the fair way, charity would suppose, to the kingdom of heaven. The Roman laws condemned the *usurer* to the forfeiture of *four times the sum.* Cato de Rust., lib. i.

Nor taketh reward against the innocent.] 11. He neither gives nor receives a *bribe* in order to pervert justice or injure an innocent man in his cause. The lawyer, who sees a poor man opposed by a rich man, who, though he is convinced in his conscience that the poor man has justice and right on his side, yet takes the *larger fee* from the *rich* man to plead against the poor man, has in fact taken a *bribe against the innocent,* and without the most signal interposition of the mercy of God, is as sure of hell as if he were already there.

He that doeth these things] He in whose character all these excellences meet, though still much more is necessary under the *Christian dispensation, shall never be moved*—he shall stand fast for ever. He is an upright, honest man, and God will ever be his support.

Now we have the important question answered, Who shall go to heaven? The man who to *faith in Christ Jesus* adds those *eleven* moral excellences which have been already enumerated. And only such a character is fit for a place in the Church of Christ.

On this verse there is a singular reading in my old MS. *Psalter,* which I must notice. The clause, *Qui pecuniam suam non dedit ad usuram,* "who putteth not out his money to usury," is thus translated: ꝯe tʜat gaf nout ʜis catel til oʜer. Now this intimates that the author had either read *pecudem,* CATTLE, for *pecuniam,* MONEY; or that *catel* was the only *money* current in his time and country. And indeed it has long been the case, that the *Scottish* peasantry paid their rents *in kind;* so many *cows* or *sheep* given to the laird for the usufruct of the ground. That this is no mistake in the *translation* is evident enough from the *paraphrase,* where he repeats the words, with his gloss upon them: 𝔥𝔢 𝔱𝔥𝔞𝔱 𝔤𝔞𝔣 𝔫𝔬𝔲𝔱 𝔥𝔦𝔰 ℭ𝔞𝔱𝔢𝔩 𝔱𝔦𝔩𝔩 𝔬𝔨𝔢𝔯 bodly als covaytus men dos gastly: that he seke naght for his gude dede, na mede of this werld, bot anely of heven.

The very unusual word *oker* signifies *produce* of any kind, whether of *cattle, land, money,* or even the human *offspring*. It is found in the *Anglo-Saxon,* the *Gothic,* the *German,* and the *Danish;* in all which languages it signifies *produce, fruit, offspring, usury,* and the like. Dr. *Jameson* does not show the word in any of its forms, though it is evident that it existed in the ancient *Scottish* language.

The word *catel* may be used here for *chattels, substance* of any kind, moveable or immoveable; but this word itself was originally derived from *cattle,* which were from the beginning the *principal substance* or *riches* of the inhabitants of the country. Indeed the word *pecunia, money,* was derived from *pecus, cattle,* which were no longer used as a medium of commerce when silver and gold came into use. There is a passage in *Chaucer* where *cattel catching* seems to be used for *getting money*. Speaking of the wicked priests of his time, he says:—

𝔖𝔬𝔪𝔢 𝔬𝔫 𝔥𝔢𝔯 𝔠𝔥𝔲𝔯𝔠𝔥𝔢𝔰 𝔡𝔴𝔢𝔩𝔩
𝔄𝔭𝔭𝔞𝔯𝔞𝔦𝔩𝔩𝔢𝔡 𝔭𝔬𝔬𝔯𝔢𝔩𝔶 𝔭𝔯𝔬𝔲𝔡 𝔬𝔣 𝔭𝔬𝔯𝔱𝔢;
𝔗𝔥𝔢 𝔰𝔢𝔟𝔢𝔫 𝔖𝔞𝔠𝔯𝔞𝔪𝔢𝔫𝔱𝔢𝔰 𝔱𝔥𝔢𝔦 𝔡𝔬𝔢𝔫 𝔰𝔢𝔩𝔩,
𝔍𝔫 ℭ𝔞𝔱𝔱𝔢𝔩 𝔠𝔞𝔱𝔠𝔥𝔦𝔫𝔤 𝔦𝔰 𝔥𝔢𝔯 𝔠𝔬𝔪𝔣𝔬𝔯𝔱.
𝔒𝔣 𝔢𝔞𝔠𝔥 𝔪𝔞𝔱𝔱𝔢𝔯 𝔱𝔥𝔢𝔦 𝔴𝔬𝔩𝔩𝔢𝔫 𝔪𝔢𝔩𝔩;
𝔄𝔫𝔡 𝔡𝔬𝔢𝔫 𝔥𝔢𝔪 𝔴𝔯𝔬𝔫𝔤 𝔦𝔰 𝔥𝔢𝔯 𝔡𝔦𝔰𝔭𝔬𝔯𝔱.
𝔗𝔬 𝔞𝔣𝔣𝔯𝔞𝔦𝔢 𝔱𝔥𝔢 𝔭𝔢𝔬𝔭𝔩𝔢 𝔱𝔥𝔢𝔦 𝔟𝔢𝔢𝔫 𝔣𝔢𝔩𝔩
𝔄𝔫𝔡 𝔥𝔬𝔩𝔡 𝔥𝔢𝔪 𝔩𝔬𝔴𝔢𝔯 𝔱𝔥𝔞𝔫 𝔡𝔬𝔢𝔱𝔥 𝔱𝔥𝔢 𝔏𝔬𝔯𝔡𝔢.
Plowmanne's Tale, 3d part.

ANALYSIS OF THE FIFTEENTH PSALM

A Psalm of doctrine, consisting of *two* parts, in which we have the character of a sound Christian, (rather, an upright Jew.)

I. The *first* part is delivered in the form of a *dialogue* between God and the prophet, from ver. 1-5.

II. The *second* is the *epiphonema,* or moral reflection, in the close of the last verse.

I. 1. The question proposed by the psalmist to God,

1. "Lord, who shall sojourn in thy holy tabernacle?"

2. "Who shall rest upon thy holy hill?" That is, because all are not *Israel* which are *of Israel,* therefore the psalmist asks of God, Who shall *sojourn* as a true member in the *Church militant?* And who shall *rest* in the *Church triumphant?*

2. To which God returns the following answer, containing very remarkable notes of the true character of a member of the Church:—

1. In *general,* he is a man, who is, 1. *Upright* in *thought;* he is an honest man: "He that walketh uprightly." 2. *Just* in his *deed:* "He works righteousness." 3. *True* in his *word:* "He speaks the truth in his heart."

2. In *particular,* he is a man who avoids evil.

1. In himself he is no slanderer: "He backbites not with his tongue."

2. He is no wrong-doer: "Nor doeth evil to his neighbour."

3. He is no reviler, tale-bearer, nor tale-hearer: "He takes not up a reproach against his neighbour."

4. He is no favourer of sin: "In whose eyes an evil person is contemned."

5. He is no oppressor nor extortioner: *He puts not his money* to his poor brother *to usury.*

6. No briber: "He takes no reward against the innocent."

3. Such a man is he who *honours them that fear the Lord.*

4. "He sweareth to his own hurt, and changeth not." He will surely keep his word; his character is composed of piety and charity.

II. The *epiphonema,* or moral reflection has these *two* parts:—

1. The *party* to whom this privilege belongs: "He that doeth these things;" for the *doers,* not the *hearers,* of the law shall be justified.

2. The *promise* made to him: "He shall never be moved." The life of grace is the way to the life of glory. See the preceding notes.

PSALM XVI

The contents of this Psalm are usually given in the following manner: David, sojourning among idolaters, and being obliged to leave his own country through Saul's persecution, cries to God for help; expresses his abhorrence of idolatry, and his desire to be again united to God's people, 1–4; and declares his strong confidence in God, who had dealt bountifully with him, 5–7. Then follows a remarkable prophecy of the resurrection of Christ, 8–11.

ᵃMichtam ᵇof David

A. M. cir. 2946
B. C. cir. 1058
Sauli, Regis
Israelitarum,
cir. annum
38

PRESERVE me, O God: ᶜfor in thee do I put my trust. 2 O my soul, thou hast said unto the LORD, Thou *art* my

LORD; ᵈmy goodness *extendeth* not to thee;

3 *But* to the saints that *are* in the earth, and *to* the excellent, in whom *is* all my delight.

A. M. cir. 2946
B. C. cir. 1058
Sauli, Regis
Israelitarum,
cir. annum
38

ᵃOr, *A golden* Psalm *of David*——ᵇSo Psa. lvi., lvii., lviii., lix., lx.

ᶜPsa. xxv. 20——ᵈJob xxii. 2, 3; xxxv. 7, 8; Psa. l. 9; Rom. xi. 35

NOTES ON PSALM XVI

The *title* of this Psalm in the Hebrew is מכתם לדוד *michtam ledavid;* which the *Chaldee* translates, "A straight sculpture of David." The *Septuagint*, Στηλογραφια τῳ Δαυιδ, "The inscription on a pillar to David;" as if the Psalm had been inscribed on a pillar, to keep it in remembrance. As כתם *catham* signifies to *engrave* or *stamp*, this has given rise to the above inscription. מכתם *michtam* also means *pure* or *stamped gold;* and hence it has been supposed that this title was given to it on account of its *excellence:* a *golden* Psalm, or a Psalm worthy to be *written in letters of gold;* as some of the verses of *Pythagoras* were called *the golden verses*, because of their *excellence*. Gold being the most *excellent* and *precious* of all metals, it has been used to express metaphorically *excellence* and *perfection* of *every* kind. Thus a *golden tongue* or *mouth*, the most *excellent eloquence;* so *Chrysostom* means, this eminent man having had his name from his eloquence;—a *golden book*, one of the *choicest* and *most valuable* of its kind, &c. But I have already sufficiently expressed my doubts concerning the meanings given to these titles. See the note on the title of Psalm lx.

That David was the author there can be no doubt. It is most pointedly attributed to him by St. Peter, Acts ii. 25-31. That its principal parts might have some relation to his circumstances is also probable; but that Jesus Christ is its main scope, not only appears from quotations made by the apostle as above, but from the circumstance that some parts of it never did and never could apply to David. From the most serious and attentive consideration of the whole Psalm, I am convinced that every verse of it belongs to Jesus Christ, and none other: and this, on reference, I find to be the view taken of it by my ancient Psalter. But as he is referred to here as the Redeemer of the world, consequently, as God manifested in the flesh, there are several portions of the Psalm, as well as in the New Testament, where the *Divine* and *human* natures are spoken of *separately:* and if this *distinction* be properly regarded, we shall find, not only no inconsistency, but a beautiful harmony through the whole.

Verse 1. *Preserve me, O God: for in thee do I put my trust.*] On the mode of interpretation which I have hinted at above, I consider this a prayer of the *man* Christ Jesus on his entering on his great atoning work, particularly his *passion* in the garden of Gethsemane. In that passion, Jesus Christ most evidently speaks as *man;* and with the strictest propriety, as it was the *manhood*, not the *Godhead*, that was engaged in the *suffering*.

שמרני *shomreni, keep me—preserve, sustain,* this feeble *humanity*, now about to bear the load of that punishment due to the whole of the human race. *For in thee*, חסיתי *chasithi, have I hoped*. No *human* fortitude, or animal courage, can avail in my circumstances. These are no *common* sufferings; they are not of a *natural* kind; they are not *proportioned* to the strength of a *human* body, or the *energy* of a human spirit; and my *immaculate humanity*, which is subjected to these sufferings, must be dissolved by them, if not upheld by thee, the strong God. It is worthy of remark, that our Lord here uses the term, אל *El*, which signifies the *strong God*, an expression remarkably suited to the *frailty* of that *human nature*, which was now entering upon its vicarious sufferings. It will be seen with what admirable propriety the *Messiah varies the appellations* of the Divine Being in this address; a circumstance which no translation without paraphrase can express.

Verse 2. *Thou hast said unto the Lord, Thou art my Lord*] Thou hast said ליהוה *layhovah*, to Jehovah, the supreme, self-existing, and eternal Being; *Thou* art *my Lord*, אדני אתה *adonai attah*, Thou art my *prop, stay*, or *support*. As the Messiah, or Son of God, Jesus derived his being and support from Jehovah; and the man Christ was supported by the eternal Divinity that dwelt within him, without which he could not have sustained the sufferings which he passed through, nor have made an atonement for the sin of the world; it is the suffering Messiah, or the Messiah in prospect of his sufferings, who here speaks.

My goodness extendeth not to thee] There are almost endless explanations of this clause; no man can read them without being confounded by them. The SEPTUAGINT read οτι των αγαθων μου ου χρειαν εχεις; *Because thou dost not need my goods*. The VULGATE follows the *Septuagint*. The CHALDEE: *My good is given only by thyself*. So the SYRIAC: *My good is from thee*. The ARABIC: *Thou dost not need my good works*. And in this sense, with shades of difference, it has been understood by most commentators and critics.

Bishop *Horsley* translates, *Thou art my good —not besides thee*. Dr. *Kennicott*, *My goodness is not without thee*.

I think the words should be understood of what the Messiah was doing for men. My goodness, טובתי *tobathi*, "my bounty," is not to thee. What I am doing can add nothing to thy divinity; thou art not providing this astonishing sacrifice because thou canst derive any excellence from it: but this bounty extends *to the saints*—to all the spirits of just men made perfect, whose bodies are still in the earth; and to the excellent, אדירי *addirey*, "the noble or supereminent ones," those who through faith and patience inherit the promises. The saints and illustrious ones not only taste of my goodness, but enjoy my salvation. Perhaps *angels*

A. M. cir. 2946
B. C. cir. 1058
Sauli, Regis
Israelitarum,
cir. annum
38

4 Their sorrows shall be multiplied *that* ᵉhasten *after* another *god:* their drink-offerings of blood will I not offer, ᶠnor take up their names into my lips.

5 ᵍThe LORD *is* the portion of ʰmine inheritance ˡand ᵏof

A. M. cir. 2946
B. C. cir. 1058
Sauli, Regis
Israelitarum,
cir. annum
38

ᵉOr, *give gifts to another*——ᶠExodus xxiii. 13; Joshua xxiii. 7; Hosea ii. 16, 17——ᵍDeut. xxxii. 9; Psa. lxxiii. 26; cxix. 57; cxlii. 5; Jeremiah x. 16; Lamentations iii. 24——ʰHebrew, *of my part*——ˡNumbers xvi. 14; Deuteronomy ix. 29——ᵏPsalm xi. 6; xxiii. 5; cxvi. 13

---

themselves may be intended; they are not uninterested in the incarnation, passion, death, and resurrection of our Lord. They *desire to look into these things;* and the victories of the cross in the conversion of sinners cause joy among the angels of God.

The קדושים *kedoshim,* "saints," or consecrated persons, may refer to the *first planters of Christianity, evangelists, apostles,* &c., who were separated from all others, and *consecrated* to the great important work of preaching among the Gentiles the unsearchable riches of Christ. With these was all the *desire,* חפץ *chephets,* the *good will* and *delight* of Christ. In all their ministrations he was both *with* them and *in* them.

The passage, taken as referring to David, intimates that he abhorred the company of the profane and worthless, and delighted to associate with them that excelled in virtue.

On these two verses the translation and paraphrase of my old Psalter must not be forgotten:—

Verse 1. Conserva me, Domine, &c.

Trans. 𝕶epe me Lord, for 𝕴 hoped in the; 𝕴 said til Lord, my God thou ert; for, of my gudes thu has na nede.

Par.—The voice of Crist in his manhede; prayand til the fader, and sayand: Lord, fader, kepe me imang peplis, for I hoped in the, noght in me. I said til the, my God, thu ert in that, that I am man; for thu has no nede of my godes; bot I haf of the, al that I haf; here is the wil pride of men confounded; that evenes that thai haf ought of tham self bot syn.

Verse 2. Sanctis qui sunt in terra, &c.

Trans. 𝕿il halowes the qwilk er in his land, he selcouthed all my willes in tham.

Par.—Noght til wiked, bot til halows clene in saule, and depertid fra erdly bysynes, the qwilk er in his land: that es, thai haf fested thair hope in the land of heven; and rotyd in luf: the qwilk hope es als anker in stremys of this werld. He selcouthed al my willes, that of wondirful, he made my willes, of dying and rysing, sett and fulfilled in tham: that es, in thair profete, qware in thai feled qwat it profeted tham my mekenes that wild dye, and my myght to rise.

Verse 4. *Their sorrows shall be multiplied that hasten after another* god] The Chaldee has: "They multiply their idols, and afterwards hasten that they may offer their gifts." In the Hebrew text there is no word for *God,* and therefore *Messiah* or *Saviour* might be as well substituted; and then the whole will refer to the unbelieving Jews. They would not have the true Christ; they have sought, and are seeking, another Messiah; and how amply fulfilled has the prophetic declaration been in them! Their *sorrows have been multiplied* for more than 1800 years.

The *Vulgate* and *Septuagint,* and after them the *Æthiopic* and *Arabic,* have given this clause a widely different turn: "their afflictions have been multiplied, and afterwards they have run swiftly;" referring to the suffering saints: the more they were afflicted and persecuted, the more fervent and prosperous they became.

Their drink-offerings of blood will I not offer] נסך *nesech* is a *libation,* whether of *wine* or *water,* poured out on the sacrifice. A *drink-offering of blood* is not a correct form of expression; it is rather the *libation on the blood of the sacrifice* already made. Coverdale translates the same; but *Mathewes,* who reformed his text in a few places, has 𝕿heir brente offeringes of bloude, without much mending the text; though by this the exceptionable idea of a *drink-offering of blood* is avoided. As applicable to our Lord, here is an intimation that their libations and sacrifices should cease. None of these should exist under the Christian dispensation; Jesus Christ's offering upon the cross being the accomplishment and termination of all such sacrifices.

Nor take up their names into my lips.] None of those sacrifices shall be mentioned with any kind of respect after the *end* of their institution shall have been accomplished; for sacrifice, offering, burnt-offering, and sacrifice for sin, such as are offered according to the law, God would no longer receive; therefore Jesus said; "Lo, I come to do thy will; a body hast thou prepared me." Since that time all these sacrifices have ceased. The old *Psalter* is curious:—

Verse 4. Multiplicate sunt infirmitates eorum; postea acceleraverunt.

Trans. 𝕸anyfalded er thair sekenes: and sythen thai hasted thaim.

Par.—That es at say; thai knew that thai war ful seke in body and saule, and sythen thai hasted tham til the Leche; for he that feles him seke, he sekes remedy. Il men wenes that thai er noght seke for thi thai dye in thair syn.

Non congregabo conventicula eroum de sanguinibus, &c.

Trans. 𝕴 sal noght gadyr the coventes of tha of blodes; ne 𝕴 sal be menand of their names thurgh my lippis.

Par. That est at say, by the coventes of haly men, my servaundes sal nout fleschely, but gastly: for *blode* bytakyns syn and unclenes that thai er in, that folous thair flesche, and the vanites of thair blode; that er comen of grete kyn. Ne I sal by menand of thair names; for thai er chaunged fra syn till ryghtwisnes on domesday, qwen I sal speke thrugh my lippes til thaim that haldes the name of wykednes: sa ye weryed til fyer with outen end.

Verse 5. *The Lord* is *the portion of mine inheritance*] The Messiah speaks. Jehovah is the portion of mine inheritance; I seek no earthly good; I desire to do the will of God, and that only. It is God who has given me this lot—to redeem mankind—to have them for

A. M. cir. 2946
B. C. cir. 1058
Sauli, Regis
Israelitarum,
cir. annum
38
my cup: thou maintainest my lot.

6 The lines are fallen unto me in pleasant *places;* yea, I have a goodly heritage.

7 I will bless the LORD, who hath given me counsel: [l]my reins also instruct me in the night seasons.

8 [m]I have set the LORD always before me: because [n]*he is* at my right hand, [o]I shall not be moved. A. M. cir. 2946
B. C. cir. 1058
Sauli, Regis
Israelitarum,
cir. annum
38

9 Therefore my heart is glad, [p]and my glory rejoiceth: my flesh also shall [q]rest in hope.

10 [r]For thou wilt not leave [s]my soul in

---

[l]Psa. xvii. 3——[m]Acts ii. 25, &c.——[n]Psa. lxxiii. 23; cx. 5; cxxi. 5——[o]Psa. xv. 5——[p]Psa. xxx. 12; lvii. 8

[q]Heb. *dwell confidently*——[r]Psa. xlix. 15; Acts ii. 27, 31; xiii. 35——[s]Lev. xix. 28; Num. vi. 6

---

mine inheritance. From him I have received the *cup of suffering,* which I shall drink for their sake, through which I shall impart to them the *cup of consolation.* He, by the grace of God, has *tasted death for every man;* and he has instituted the *cup of blessing* to commemorate his passion and death.

Verse 6. *The lines are fallen unto me in pleasant* places] Here is an allusion to the ancient division of the land by lot among the Israelites, the breadth and length being ascertained by lines which were used in measuring. I have got a rich inheritance of immortal spirits; and I myself, as man, shall have a name above every name, and be raised to thy throne, on which I shall sit, and be admired in my saints to all eternity.

I have a goodly heritage.] A Church, an innumerable multitude of saints, partakers of the Divine nature, and filled with all the fulness of God. And these shall dwell with me in the heaven of heavens to all eternity. The old *Psalter:*—

Verse 5. Dominus pars hereditatis mee et calicis mei, &c.

Trans. 𝕷𝖔𝖗𝖉 𝖊𝖘 𝖕𝖆𝖗𝖙 𝖔𝖋 𝖒𝖞𝖓 𝖍𝖊𝖗𝖞𝖙𝖆𝖌𝖊 𝖆𝖓𝖉 𝖔𝖋 𝖒𝖞 𝖈𝖍𝖆𝖑𝖞𝖈𝖊; 𝖙𝖍𝖔𝖜 𝖊𝖗𝖙 𝖙𝖍𝖆𝖙 𝖘𝖆𝖑 𝖗𝖊𝖘𝖙𝖔𝖗𝖊 𝖒𝖞𝖓 𝖍𝖊𝖗𝖞𝖙𝖆𝖌𝖊 𝖙𝖎𝖑 𝖒𝖊.

Par. Lord the fader es part, that es, he es porcioun and mede of myn herytage; that es of haly men, qwam I weld in herytage. Other men cheses tham what tham lyst: my part es God, and he es part of my chalyce: that es, he es my copp of al my delyte and joy. Wereldys men drynkes the venemus lustes, and the drubly delytes of lychery and covatys: I in my halows sal drynk God; for thu ert fadyr that sal restore till me, that es, til my men, myn herytage, that thai lost in Adam: that es thu restores til tham the knawyng of my bryghthede.

Verse 6. Punes ceciderunt michi in preclaris, &c.

Trans. 𝕾𝖙𝖗𝖞𝖓𝖌𝖊𝖘 𝖋𝖊𝖑 𝖙𝖔 𝖒𝖊 𝖎𝖓 𝖋𝖚𝖑 𝖇𝖗𝖞𝖌𝖍𝖙: 𝖋𝖔𝖗 𝖖𝖜𝖞, 𝖒𝖞𝖓 𝖍𝖊𝖗𝖞𝖙𝖆𝖌𝖊 𝖎𝖘 𝖋𝖚𝖑 𝖇𝖗𝖞𝖌𝖍𝖙 𝖙𝖎𝖑 𝖒𝖊.

Par. Strynges, that er merkes of my possessioun, in thi bryghtnes, fel als with cutte; als the possessioun of prestes and dekens in the alde law, was God; for qwy myn herytage, that es haly men es bryght til me of thai seme layth and aute castyng til some of the werld, til me thai er fairer and bryght.

Verse 7. *Who hath given me counsel*] Jesus, as *man,* received all his knowledge and wisdom from God; Luke ii. 40-52. And in him were hidden all the treasures of wisdom and knowledge.

My reins also instruct me] כליותי *kilyothai, reins* or *kidneys,* which from their *retired*

situation in the body, says *Parkhurst,* and being *hidden* in fat, are often used in Scripture for the most *secret workings* and *affections of the heart.*

The *kidneys* and their *fat* were always to be burnt in sacrifice, to indicate that the most secret purposes and affections of the soul are to be devoted to God.

In the night seasons.] That is, in the time of my *passion,* my secret purposes and determinations concerning the redemption of man support me. "For the joy that was set before him he endured the cross, despising the shame;" Heb. xii. 2.

Verse 8. *I have set the Lord always before me*] This verse, and all to the end of ver. 11, are applied by St. Peter to the *death and resurrection of Christ.* Acts ii. 25, &c.

In all that our Lord *did, said,* or *suffered,* he kept the glory of the Father and the accomplishment of his purpose constantly in view. He tells us that he did not come down from heaven to do his own will, but the will of the Father who had sent him. See John xvii. 4.

He is at my right hand] That is, I have his constant presence, approbation, and support. All this is spoken by Christ as *man.*

I shall not be moved.] Nothing can swerve me from my purpose; nothing can prevent me from fulfilling the Divine counsel, in reference to the salvation of men.

Verse 9. *Therefore my heart is glad*] Unutterably happy in God; always full of the Divine presence; because whatsoever I do pleaseth him. The *man* Christ Jesus must be constantly in communion with God, because he was without spot and blemish.

My glory rejoiceth] My *tongue,* so called by the Hebrews, (see Psa. lvii. 8; xxx. 12,) because it was bestowed on us to glorify God, and because it is our *glory,* being the instrument of expressing our thoughts by words. *See Dodd.* But *soul* bids as fair to be the meaning. See the notes on Acts ii. 25, &c.

My flesh also shall rest in hope.] There is no sense in which these and the following words can be spoken of David. Jesus, even on the cross, and breathing out his soul with his life, saw that his rest in the grave would be very short: just a sufficiency of time to prove the *reality* of his death, but not *long enough* to produce *corruption;* and this is well argued by St. Peter, Acts ii. 31.

Verse 10. *Thine Holy One*] This is in the plural number, חסידיך *chasideycha, thy Holy Ones;* but none of the *versions* translate it in the *plural;* and as it is in the singular number, חסידך *chasidecha,* in several *ancient*

A. M. cir. 2946
B. C. cir. 1058
Sauli, Regis
Israelitarum,
cir. annum
38

hell; neither wilt thou suffer thine Holy One to see corruption.

11 Thou wilt show me the 'path of life: ^uin thy presence *is* fulness of joy; ^vat thy right hand *there are* pleasures for evermore.

A. M. cir. 2946
B. C. cir. 1058
Sauli, Regis
Israelitarum,
cir. annum
38

---

^tMatt. vii. 14——^uPsa. xvii. 15; xxi. 6; Matt. v. 8; 1 Cor. xiii. 12; 1 John. iii. 2——^vPsa. xxxvi. 8

---

editions, among which is the *Complutensian Polyglot*, and no less than *two hundred and sixty-four* of *Kennicott's* and *De Rossi's* MSS., and in the quotation by St. *Peter*, in Acts ii. 27; xiii. 35, we may take it for granted that the present reading is a corruption; or that חסידיך is an emphatic singular.

As to *leaving the soul in hell*, it can only mean permitting the *life* of the Messiah to *continue* under the power of *death;* for שׁאוֹל *sheol* signifies a *pit*, a *ditch*, the *grave*, or *state of the dead*. See the notes on the parallel places, Acts ii. 25, &c.

See corruption.] All human beings see corruption, because born in sin, and liable to the curse. The human body of Jesus Christ, as being without sin, saw no corruption.

Verse 11. *Thou wilt show me the path of life*] I first shall find the *way out of the regions of death*, to *die no more*. Thus Christ was the *first fruits* of them that slept. Several had before risen from the dead, but they *died again*. Jesus rose from the dead, and is alive for evermore. Jesus Christ's resurrection from the dead was the first entrance out of the grave to eternal life or lives, חיים *chaiyim*, for the word is in the *plural*, and with great propriety too, as this resurrection implies the *life* of the *body*, and the *life* of the *rational soul* also.

In thy presence] פניך *paneycha, thy faces*. Every holy soul has, throughout eternity, the *beatific vision*, i. e., "it sees God as he is," because it is *like him;* 1 John iii. 2. It drinks in beatification from the presence of the Eternal TRINITY.

Thy right hand] The place of honour and dignity; repeatedly used in this sense in the Scriptures.

Pleasures for evermore.] נצח *netzach, onwardly; perpetually, continually*, well expressed by our translation, *ever* and *more;* an eternal progression. Think of *duration* in the most extended and unlimited manner, and there is still *more;* more to be suffered in hell, and more to be enjoyed in heaven. Great God! grant that my readers may have this beatific sight; this eternal progression in unadulterated, unchangeable, and unlimited happiness! Hear this prayer for His sake, who found out the path of life, and who by his blood purchased an entrance into the holiest! Amen and Amen.

For the application of the whole Psalm to David, see the analysis at the end, which is a little altered from *David's Harp Strung and Tuned*.

The remains of this Psalm in the old *Psalter* are worthy to be inserted:—

Verse 7. Benedicam Dominum qui tribuit michi intellectum, &c.

Trans. 𝕴 sal blis the Lord that gaf til me undirstandyng; and over that til the nyght, supled me my neres.

Par. That es I sal luf the fader that hafs gyfen undyrstandyng til my servauntes, thurgh the qwilk the herytage of heven may be sene

and welded; and over that undyrstandyng, in the qwilk I saw, sais Crist, al sothefast thynges and haly. Of that I sal lof him that my nerys that es the Jewis of qwas kynd I toke flesch, that es my kyn snybbed me in wranges and temptaciounis, and passiouns, til the nyght, that es al the dede thai missaid hym, als so oure nerys; that es our fleschely delytes makes us worthy snybbyng til our dede; for perfytely may we noght be with outen syn, qwyles we lyf.

Verse 8. Providebam Dominum in conspectu meo, &c.

Trans. 𝕴 pervaide God ay in my syght; for he es at the ryght hand til me, that 𝕴 be nout styrred.

Par. And in al thys anguys I for gatt nout God: bot I pervayde hym ay in my syght; that es, I comande o mang passand thynges: I toke nout my nee fra hym that ay es; bot I fested it in hym, so that he was ay in my sight, and he es nout fyled in synnes that assyduely with the ee of his thoght, byhaldes God, for he es at the ryght hand of me: that I be noght styred; that es, he helps me in desyre of endless gudes, that I last stabil in hym, and for thi nane il thyng may haf mayster of me.

Verse 9. Propter hoc, elatum, est cor meum, et exultavit lingua mea, &c.

Trans. Thar fore gladded es my hert, and my toung joyed over that, and my flesch sal rest in hope.

Par. This es ful joy that in hert es resayved and with toung schewed, and over that joy in hert and mouth, my flesch sal rest in hope of rysyng.

Verse 10. Quoniam non derelinques in Inferno animam meam, &c.

Trans. For thow sal noght lefe my Saule in hell; ne thu sal noght gyf thi Halow to se corrupcioun.

Par. That es at say, the Saule that I haf als veray man, sal noght be left in hell; and my body that thu haloued, sal noght rote. Here men may knaw that this es goddes word; for other mens bodis rotes.

Verse 11. Notas michi fecisti vias vite, &c.

Trans. Knawen thu maked til me, the wayes of lyf: thou sal ful fil me of joy with thi face, delytynges in thi ryghth and in til the end.

Par. Knawen thu maked thurgh me till myne, the wayes of lyf, that es the wayes of mekenes and charite, that men came til heven thurgh mekenes, fra qwethyn thai fel thurgh Pryde: and thow sal ful fil me; that es, my servaundes, of joy with thi face; that es, in the syght of the, apertly; so that thai desyre nothing over, qwen thai af sene the, face til face, and ay til than delytynges til tham in way of this lyf. In thi ryght hand; that es thi favoure, and thi mercy the qwilk delytyngs ledys tham intil the ende; that es, in til perfectioun of endeles Blisfulhede.

I have given the whole of the translation and comment of this Psalm from this ancient Psalter, as a curious specimen of the doctrine and language of our northern neighbours in the *thirteenth* or *fourteenth* century.

ANALYSIS OF THE SIXTEENTH PSALM

Michtam David: David's precious jewel, or Psalm of gold; literally to be understood of David, but primarily and principally of Christ, Acts ii., whom he calls חסיד *chasid*, God's Holy One, ver. 10. And foretells his passion, resurrection, and ascension, ver. 9, 10, 11.

This Psalm has *two* parts: I. *Petition*, ver. 1. II. *Thanksgiving*, ver. 7.

I. The *petition* begins the Psalm. It is for *preservation:* "Preserve me, O God." Keep me to the kingdom both temporal and eternal that thou hast promised. Guard me; guide me; keep me. To induce the Lord to do this, he produces his reasons:—

1. His *confidence:* "For in thee I trust." This is a powerful plea; for to trust God is the highest honour we can do him; it acknowledges him as Sovereign.

2. His *relation:* "O my soul, thou hast said unto the Lord, Thou art my God."

3. For this I would show myself thankful, and return the best of my best. But what can I give, save τα σα εκ των σων, "thy own things from thy own property?" *My goods* or goodness, my beneficence or bounty, *is nothing unto thee.* Sacrifice thou needest not, Psa. l. 8, nor art delighted in them: but mercy thou requirest, Hosea, vi. 6.

4. Then I will seek out thy *receivers:* "Thy saints that are in the earth." The family of the saints were the object of David's bounty, and his delight. But my liberality and charity shall extend *to the saints that are in the earth,* and unto such as are excellent; "in whom is all my delight."

5. But as for the *wicked* men and idolaters, I have no delight in them.

These he points out by two characteristics:—

1. They "hasten after another god," or *endow another god.* They spare no cost, but are lavish in endowing their gods: "Israel, part with thy jewels," &c.

2. They offer their children to Molech: "Their drink-offerings of BLOOD will I not offer." On these accounts:—

1. "Their sorrows shall be multiplied." They shall be grievously punished.

2. I will not participate with them: "Their offerings I will not offer."

3. They are objects of my detestation: "I will not take up their names into my lips."

6. He gives another reason why he should show himself so thankful to God and bountiful to his saints—God's great bounty and liberality to him.

1. That God had given him a satisfactory portion: "The Lord is the portion of mine inheritance, and of my cup."

2. That God defended him in it: "Thou maintainest my lot."

3. That it was a fair portion: "The lines are fallen to me in pleasant places," &c.

II. The *second* part of this Psalm is David's THANKSGIVING. It begins with, "I will bless the Lord," ver. 7, not only for the temporal blessings mentioned before, but for the following spiritual blessings:—

1. For the illumination of his mind; that I may understand the thing that is right: "The Lord hath given me counsel."

2. For the sanctifying influence on his heart: "My reins instruct me in the night seasons." When he was most retired he seemed to hear a voice within him, saying, "This is the way; walk in it."

3. For his *confidence and watchfulness:* "I have set the Lord always before me." I do not forget my God; and he does not forget me.

4. For the *consciousness* he had of the Divine *presence:* "The Lord is at my right hand;" always ready to help and support me.

5. For his *power to preserve:* "I shall not be moved." Satan may stand at my right hand to resist and trouble me; Zech. iii. 1; but God is on my right hand to assist and comfort me; therefore, "I shall not be moved." While David prays and trusts, God supports; and while God supports, Satan cannot conquer.

6. For his *inward* happiness: "Therefore, my heart is glad." Wicked men rejoice in *appearance;* but David rejoiced in *heart.* He was all happy. His heart, glory, flesh, spirit, soul, body—all were overjoyed; and the reason was the prospect of his *resurrection.*

1. "My flesh shall rest or dwell in hope." 1. In this world, as in an *inn;* 2. In the *grave,* as in a *repository;* 3. In *heaven,* as in an endless *mansion.*

2. "Thou wilt not leave my soul in hell." Thou wilt not suffer death to have a final triumph; my flesh shall revive.

3. "Neither wilt thou suffer thy HOLY ONE to see corruption;" meaning the *Messiah,* who should descend from his family. Christ's resurrection is the cause and pledge of ours.

7. He is thankful for the promise of a future life, which is here illustrated:—

1. From the *quantity:* "Fulness of joy."

2. From the *quality:* "Pleasures."

3. From the *honour:* "At thy right hand."

4. From the *perpetuity:* "For evermore."

5. From the *cause:* "Thy presence." The sight of God, the beatific vision. "Thou wilt show me the path of life: in thy presence is fulness of joy; at thy right hand there are pleasures for evermore."

For the application of the whole Psalm to *Christ* alone, see the preceding notes.

PSALM XVII

David implores the succour of God against his enemies; and professes his integrity and determination to live to God's glory, 1. He prays for support, and expresses strong confidence in God, 5–9; describes the malice and cruelty of his enemies, and prays against them, 10–14; receives a strong persuasion of support and final victory, 15.

A. M. cir. 2946
B. C. cir. 1058
Sauli, Regis
Israelitarum,
cir. annum
38

A Prayer of David

HEAR [a]the right, O LORD, attend unto my cry, give ear unto my prayer, *that goeth* [b]not out of feigned lips.

2 Let my sentence come forth from thy presence; let thine eyes behold the things that are equal.

3 Thou hast proved mine heart; [c]thou hast visited *me* in the night; [d]thou hast tried me,

and shalt find nothing: I am purposed *that* my mouth shall not transgress.

4 Concerning the works of men, by the word of thy lips I have kept *me from* the paths of the destroyer.

5 [e]Hold up my goings in thy paths, *that* my footsteps [f]slip not.

6 [g]I have called upon thee, for thou wilt

A. M. cir. 2946
B. C. cir. 1058
Sauli, Regis
Israelitarum,
cir. annum
38

---

[a]Heb. *justice*——[b]Heb. *without lips of deceit*——[c]Psa. xvi. 7——[d]Job xxiii. 10; Psa. xxvi. 2; lxvi. 10; cxxxix. 2; Zech. xiii. 9; Mal. iii. 2, 3; 1 Pet. i. 7——[e]Psa. cxix. 133 [f]Heb. *be not moved*——[g]Psa. cxvi. 2

NOTES ON PSALM XVII

The title is, *A prayer of David;* in which there is nothing that requires explanation. David was most probably the author of this Psalm; and it appears to have been written about the time in which Saul had carried his persecution against him to the highest pitch. See 1 Sam. xxvii. The Arabic calls it "A prayer of a perfect man, of Christ himself, or of any one redeemed by him." Dr. *Delaney*, in his life of David, supposes that this poem was written just after parting with Jonathan, when David went into exile.

Verse 1. *Hear the right*] Attend to the justice of my cause, יהוה צדק *Yehovah tsedek,* righteous Jehovah. "O righteous Jehovah, attend unto my cry."

Goeth *not out of feigned lips.*] My supplication is sincere: and the desire of my heart accompanies the words of my lips.

Verse 2. *My sentence come forth from thy presence*] Thou knowest my heart, and my ways; judge me as thou shalt find; let me not fall under the judgment of man.

Let thine eyes behold the things that are equal.] Thou knowest whether I render to all their due, and whether others act justly by me. Thou canst not be deceived: do justice between me and my adversaries.

Verse 3. *Thou hast proved mine heart*] Thou well knowest whether there be any evil way in me. Thou hast given me to see many and sore trials; and yet, through thy mercy, I have preserved my integrity both to thee and to my king. Thou hast seen me in my most *secret* retirements, and knowest whether I have *plotted* mischief against him who now wishes to take away my life.

Thou hast tried me] צרפתני *tseraphtani;* Thou *hast put me to the test,* as they do *metals,* in order to detect their *alloy,* and to *purify* them: well expressed by the *Vulgate, Igne me examinasti,* "Thou hast tried me by fire;" and well paraphrased in my old *Psalter,—Thu examynd* me the lykkenyng of the fournas, that purges metal, *and imang* al this, wykednes

es nout funden in me: that es, *I am funden clene of syn,* and so ryghtwis.—He who is saved from his sin is *right wise;* he has found the *true wisdom.*

My mouth shall not transgress.] This clause is added to the following verse by the *Vulgate* and *Septuagint:* "That my mouth may not speak according to the works of men, I have observed difficult ways because of the words of thy lips." That is, So far from doing any improper *action,* I have even refrained from all *words* that might be counted inflammatory or seditious by my adversaries; for I took thy word for the regulation of my conduct, and prescribed to myself the most painful duties, in order that I might, in every respect, avoid what would give offence either to thee or to man. Among the genuine followers of God, plots and civil broils are never found.

Verse 4. *The paths of the destroyer.*] Some render, *hard* or *difficult paths,* the sense of which is given above. But the passage is exceedingly obscure. My old *Psalter* translates and paraphrases as follows:—

Trans. **That my mouthe speke noght the werkes of men, for the wordes of thi lippes I haf keped hard wayse.**

Par. That es, that nothing passe of my mouthe bot at falles to the louyng of *the; noght til werkes of men,* that dos o gaynes thy wil; als to say, I spak *noght* bot gude; and *for the wordes of thi lippes,* that es, to ful fil the *wordes* that thi prophetes saide; *I kepe hard waies* of verteus and of *tribulacioun,* the qwilk men thynk hard; and for thi thai leve the *hard* way til heven, and takes the soft way til hel; but it es ful hard *at the* end.

Verse 5. *Hold up my goings in thy paths*] David walked in God's ways; but, without Divine assistance, he could not walk *steadily,* even in them. The *words of God's lips* had shown him the steps he was to take, and he implores the strength of God's grace to enable him to walk in those steps. He had been kept from the *paths of the destroyer;* but this was not sufficient; he must *walk in God's paths*— must spend his life in *obedience* to the Divine

A. M. cir. 2946
B. C. cir. 1058
Sauli, Regis
Israelitarum,
cir. annum
38
hear me, O God: incline thine ear unto me, *and hear* my speech.

7 hShow thy marvellous lovingkindness, O thou ithat savest by thy right hand them which put their trust *in thee* from those that rise up *against them.*

8 kKeep me as the apple of the eye, lhide me under the shadow of thy wings,

9 From the wicked mthat oppress me, *from* nmy deadly enemies, *who* compass me about.

10 oThey are enclosed in their own fat:

with their mouth they pspeak proudly.

11 They have now qcompassed us in our steps: rthey have set their eyes bowing down to the earth;

12 sLike as a lion *that* is greedy of his prey, and as it were a young lion tlurking in secret places.

13 Arise, O LORD, udisappoint him, cast him down: deliver my soul from the wicked, vwhich is wthy sword;

A. M. cir. 2946
B. C. cir. 1058
Sauli, Regis
Israelitarum,
cir. annum
38

---

hPsa. xxxi. 21——iOr, *that savest them which trust* in thee *from those that rise up against thy right hand* kDeut. xxxii. 10; Zech. ii. 8——lRuth ii. 12; Psa. xxxvi. 7; lvii. 1; lxi. 4; lxiii. 7; xci. 1, 4; Matt. xxiii. 37 mHeb. *that waste me*——nHeb. *my enemies against the soul*

oDeut. xxxii. 15; Job xv. 27; Psa. lxxiii. 7; cxix. 70 p1 Sam. ii. 3; Psa. xxxi. 18——q1 Sam. xxiii. 26——rPsa. x. 8, 9, 10——sHeb. *The likeness of him* (that is, *of every one of them*) is *as a lion* that *desireth to ravin*——tHeb. *sitting*——uHeb. *prevent his face*——vIsa. x. 5——wOr, *by thy sword*

---

will. Negative holiness can save no man. "Every tree that bringeth not forth good fruit is hewn down, and cast into the fire."

Verse 6. Incline thine ear unto me] David prayed from a conviction that God would hear: but he could not be satisfied unless he received an answer. In a believer's mind the petition and the answer should not be separated.

Verse 7. Show thy marvellous lovingkindness] David was now exposed to imminent danger; common interpositions of Providence could not save him; if God did not work *miracles* for him, he must fall by the hand of Saul. Yet he lays no *claim* to such miraculous interpositions; he expects all from God's *lovingkindness.*

The common reading here is הפלה חסדיך *haphleh chasadeycha,* "distinguish thy holy ones;" but הפלא *haphle,* "do wonders," is the reading of about *seventy* MSS., some ancient editions, with the *Septuagint, Vulgate, Chaldee, Syriac,* and *Arabic.* The marginal reading of this verse is nearer the original than that of the text.

Verse 8. Keep me as the apple of the eye] Or, *as the black of the daughter of eye.* Take as much care to preserve me now by *Divine* influence, as thou hast to preserve my *eye* by thy *good* providence. Thou hast entrenched it deeply in the skull; hast ramparted it with the forehead and cheek-bones; defended it by the eyebrow, eyelids, and eyelashes; and placed it in that situation where the hands can best protect it.

Hide me under the shadow of thy wings] This is a metaphor taken from the *hen* and her *chickens.* See it explained at large in the note on Matt. xxiii. 37. The Lord says of his followers, Zech. ii. 8: "He that toucheth you, toucheth the apple of mine eye." How dear are our eyes to us! how dear must his followers be to God!

Verse 9. From my deadly enemies, who compass me about.] This is a metaphor taken from huntsmen, who spread themselves around a large track of forest, driving in the deer from every part of the circumference, till they are forced into the nets or traps which they have set for them in some particular narrow passage. The metaphor is carried on in the following verses.

Verse 10. They are enclosed in their own fat] Dr. *Kennicott,* Bishop *Horsley, Houbigant,* and others, read the passage thus: עלי חבלמו סגרו *alai chablamo sageru,* "They have closed their net upon me." This continues the metaphor which was introduced in the preceding verse, and which is continued in the two following: and requires only that עלי *ali,* "upon me," should *begin* this verse instead of *end* the preceding; and that חלב *cheleb,* which signifies *fat,* should be read חבל *chebel,* which signifies *rope, cable,* or *net.* This important reading requires only the *interchange of two letters.* The *Syriac* translates it, *shut their mouth:* but the above emendation is most likely to be true.

They speak proudly.] Having compassed the mountain on which I had taken refuge, they now exult, being assured that they will soon be in possession of their prey.

Verse 11. They have now compassed us in our steps] Instead of אשרנו *ashshurenu,* "our steps," Dr. *Kennicott* and others recommend אשרינו *ashreynu,* "O lucky we, at last we have compassed him." He cannot now escape; he is sure to fall into our hands.

They have set their eyes bowing down to the earth] All the commentators and critics have missed the very expressive and elegant metaphor contained in this clause. *Kennicott* says, *They drove the hart into toils, and then shot him.* Bishop *Horsley* says, on the clause, *They have set their eyes bowing down to the earth:* "This is the attitude of huntsmen, taking aim at an animal upon the ground." No, it is the attitude of the huntsmen looking for the *slot,* or track of the hart's, hind's, or antelope's foot on the ground. See at the conclusion of the Psalm.

Verse 12. Like as a lion that is greedy of his prey] I believe the word *lion* is here used to express *Saul* in his strength, kingly power, and fierce rapacity. See the observations at the end of the Psalm.

Verse 13. Arise, O Lord, disappoint him] When *he* arises to spring upon and tear me to pieces, arise *thou,* O Lord; disappoint him of his prey; seize him, and cast him down.

Deliver my soul] Save my life.

From the wicked, which is *thy sword*] Saul

A. M. cir. 2946
B. C. cir. 1058
Sauli, Regis
Israelitarum,
cir. annum
38

14 ˣFrom men *which are* thy hand, O Lord, from men of the world, ʸ*which have* their portion in *this* life, and whose belly thou fillest with thy hid *treasure:* ᶻthey are full of

children, and leave the rest of their *substance* to their babes.

15 As for me, ᵃI will behold thy face in righteousness: ᵇI shall be satisfied, when I awake, with thy likeness.

A. M. cir. 2946
B. C. cir. 1058
Sauli, Regis
Israelitarum,
cir. annum
38

ˣOr, *From men* by *thine hand*——ʸPsa. lxxiii. 12; Luke xvi. 25; James v. 5

ᶻOr, *their children are full*——ᵃ1 John iii. 2——ᵇPsa. iv. 6, 7; xvi. 11; lxv. 4

---

is still meant, and we may understand the words as either implying the *sword*, the *civil power*, with which God had intrusted him, and which he was now grievously abusing; or, it may mean, *deliver me by* thy *sword*—cut him off who wishes to cut me off. On this ground the next verse should be read *from men*, by *thy hand*. So the margin. The hand of God not only meaning his *power*, but his *providence*.

Verse 14. *From men of the world*, which have] ממתים מחלד *mimethim mecheled, from mortal men of time;* temporizers; men who shift with the times; who have no fixed principle but one, that of securing their own secular interest: and this agrees with what follows— which have *their portion in this life;* who never seek after any thing *spiritual;* who have bartered heaven for earth, and have got the *portion* they desired; for thou *fillest their belly with thy hid treasure.* Their *belly*—their *sensual appetites*—is their *god;* and, when their animal desires are satisfied, they take their rest without consideration, like the beasts that perish.

Their portion in this *life*] בחיים *bachaiyim, in lives*, probably meaning *heritable lands* and *estates;* for they leave them to their children, they *descend* to *posterity*, and every one has his *life portion* in them. They are *lands of lives.*

They are full of children] Have a numerous offspring, whom they educate in the same principles, and to whom they leave a large earthly patrimony, and who spend it as their fathers have done, and perhaps even more dissolutely. Often *covetous* fathers lay up riches, which *profligate* sons scatter to all the winds of heaven. I have seen many instances of this.

Verse 15. *As for me*] I cannot be satisfied with such a portion.

I will behold thy face] Nothing but an evidence of thy *approbation* can content my soul.

In righteousness] I cannot have thy approbation unless I am *conformed* to thy *will.* I must be *righteous* in order that my *heart* and *life* may please thee.

I shall be satisfied, when I awake, with thy likeness.] Nothing but God can satisfy the wishes of an immortal spirit. He made it with infinite capacities and desires; and he alone, the infinite Good, can meet and gratify these desires, and fill this all-capacious mind. No soul was ever satisfied but by God; and he satisfies the soul only by restoring it to his image, which, by the *fall*, it has lost.

I think there is an allusion here to the *creation of Adam.* When God breathed into him the *breath of lives*, and *he became a living soul*, he would appear as one *suddenly awaked from sleep.* The first object that met his eyes was his *glorious Creator;* and being *made* in his *image* and in his *likeness*, he could converse with him face to face—was capable of the

most intimate union with him, because he was filled with holiness and moral perfection. Thus was he *satisfied;* the God of infinite perfection and purity filling all the powers and faculties of his soul. David sees this in the light of the Divine Spirit, and knows that his happiness depends on being *restored to this image* and *likeness;* and he longs for the time when he shall completely arise out of the *sleep* and *death* of sin, and be *created anew after the image of God, in righteousness and true holiness.* I do not think that he refers to the *resurrection* of the *body*, but to the resurrection of the *soul* in this life; to the regaining the image which Adam lost.

The paraphrase in my old *Psalter* understands the whole of this Psalm as referring to the persecution, passion, death, and resurrection of Christ; and so did several of the primitive fathers, particularly St. Jerome and St. Augustine. I shall give a specimen from ver. 11:—

Projicientes me, nunc circumdederunt me: oculos suos statuerunt declinare in terram.

Trans. 𝔉orth cast𝔞n𝔡 me no𝔴, thai haf umgyfen me: thair eghen thai sette to heel𝔡e in the er𝔡e.

Par.—Forth kasten me out of the cite, als the stede had bene fyled of me: now thai haf umgyfen me in the cros hyngand, als folk that gedyrs til a somer gamen: for thai sett thair eghen, that es the entent of thaire hert to heeld in the erde; that es, in erdly thynges to covayte tham, and haf tham. And thai wende qwen thai slew Crist that he had suffird al the ill, and thai nane.

Perhaps some of my readers may think that this needs translating, so far does our present differ from our ancient tongue.

Text.—They have now cast me forth; they have surrounded me: their eyes they set down to the earth.

Par.—They have cast me out of the city, as if the state were to be defiled by me: now they have surrounded me hanging on the cross, as people gathered together at summer games. For they set their eyes, that is, the intent of their heart, down to the earth; that is, earthly things, to covet them and to have them: and they thought, when they slew Christ, that *he* had suffered all the ill, and *they* none.

By the *slot* or track of the hart on the ground, referred to in ver. 11, experienced huntsmen can discern whether there have been a hart *there*, whether he has been there *lately*, whether the *slot* they see be the track of a *hart* or a *hind*, and whether the animal be *young* or *old*. All these can be discerned by the *slot.* And if the reader have that *scarce book* at hand, *Tuberville on Hunting*, 4to, 1575 or 1611, he will find all this information in chap. xxii., p. 63, entitled, *The Judgment and Knowledge by the Slot of a Hart;* and on the same page a wood-cut, representing a huntsman with *his eyes set, bowing down to the earth*, examining *three slots* which he had just found. The cut is a fine illustration of this clause. Saul and his men were hunting David, and curiously searching every place to find out any *track, mark*, or *footstep*, by which they might learn whether he *had been in such a place*, and whether he had been *there lately*. Nothing can more fully display the accuracy and intensity of this search than the metaphor contained in the above clause. He who has been his late Majesty's huntsmen looking for the slot in Windsor Forest will see the strength and propriety of the figure used by the psalmist.

Verse 12. *Like as a lion* that *is greedy of his prey.*—This is the picture of Saul. While his huntsmen were beating every bush, prying into every cave and crevice, and examining every foot of ground to find out a *track*, Saul is ready, whenever the game is started, to spring upon, seize, and destroy it. The metaphors are well connected, well sustained, and strongly expressive of the whole process of this persecution.

In the *ninth* verse the huntsmen beat the forest to raise and drive in the game. In the *tenth* they set their nets, and speak confidently of the expected success. In the *eleventh*, they felicitate themselves on having found the *slot*, the certain indication of the prey being at hand. And in the *twelfth*, the king of the sport is represented as just ready to spring upon the prey; or, as having his bow bent, and his arrow on the string, ready to let fly the moment the prey appears. It is worthy of remark, that *kings* and *queens* were frequently present, and were the *chiefs of the sport;* and it was they who, when he had been killed, *broke up* the deer: 1. Slitting down the brisket with their knife or sword; and, 2. Cutting off the head. And, as *Tuberville* published the first edition of his book in the reign of Queen *Elizabeth*, he gives a large wood-cut, p. 133, representing this princess just alighted from her horse—the stag stretched upon the ground—the huntsman kneeling, holding the fore foot of the animal with his left hand, and with his right presenting a knife to the queen for the purpose of the *breaking up*. As the second edition was published in the reign of *James the First*, the image of the *queen* is taken out and a *whole length of James* introduced in the place.

The same appears in *Tuberville's* Book of *Falconrie*, connected with the above. In p. 81, edition 1575, where the *flight of the hawk at the heron* is represented, the queen is seated on her charger: but in the edition of 1611 King James is placed on the same charger, the queen being removed.

The *lion* is the *monarch of the forest;* and is used successfully here to represent *Saul, king of Israel*, endeavouring to *hunt down David; hemming him in* on *every side; searching* for *his footsteps;* and ready to *spring upon him, shoot him* with his *bow*, or *pierce* him with his *javelin*, as soon as he should be obliged to flee from his *last cover*. The whole is finely imagined, and beautifully described.

ANALYSIS OF THE SEVENTEENTH PSALM

David's appeal to God in justification of himself; and his petition for defence against his enemies.

There are THREE parts in this Psalm:—

I. A *petition*. 1. For audience, ver. 1 and 6.

2. For perseverance in good, ver. 5. 3. For special favour, ver. 7, 8. 4. For immediate deliverance, ver. 13, 14.

II. A *narration;* in which we meet with, 1. His appeal to God, and his own justification, ver. 2, 3, 4. 2. The reasons of it; his enemies and their character, ver. 9 to 14.

III. A *conclusion;* which has two parts. 1. One belonging to this life; and, 2. One belonging to the life to come, ver. 15.

I. 1. He begins with *petition* for audience. And he urges it for two reasons: 1. The justness of his cause: "Hear the right, O Lord." 2. The sincerity of his heart: "That goeth not out of feigned lips."

2. Again, there were other reasons why he desired to be heard: 1. He felt himself prone to slip, and fall from God: "Hold up my goings," &c. 2. He was in great danger, and nothing but a miracle could save him: "Show thy marvellous lovingkindness." 3. His enemies were insolent and mighty, and God's sword only could prevail against them: "Arise, O Lord," ver. 13, 14.

II. A *narration:* His appeal to God. Since a verdict must pass upon him, he desired that God should pronounce it: "Let my sentence come forth from thy presence." I know that thou art a righteous Judge, and canst not be swayed by prejudice: "Let thine eyes behold the thing that is equal," and then I know it must go well with me: "Thou hast proved my heart. Thou hast tried me before on this business, and hast *found nothing*.

1. *Nothing* in my HEART: "Thou hast proved my heart."

2. *Nothing* in my TONGUE: "For I am purposed that my mouth shall not offend."

3. *Nothing* in my HAND: "For, concerning the works of men," which are mischievous; *by the words of thy lips*, I have had so great a regard to thy commandments that "I have kept myself from the paths of the wicked;" of him who, to satisfy his own desires, breaks all laws.

4. He confesses that he was poor and weak, and liable to fall, unless sustained by the grace of God: "Hold up my goings in thy paths."

And this first petition he renews, and takes courage from the assurance that he shall be heard: "I will call upon thee, for thou wilt hear me." And he puts in a special petition, which has two parts:—

1. "Show thy marvellous lovingkindness;" let me have more than ordinary help. And this he urges from the consideration that *God saves them who trust in him from those who rise up against them.*

2. That he would save him with the greatest care and vigilance, as a man would preserve the apple of his eye, or as a hen would guard her young: "Keep me as the apple of the eye; hide me," &c.

And to prevail in this *special petition*, he brings his arguments from his present necessity. He was encompassed with enemies, whom he describes:—

1. They were capital enemies; they hemmed him in on every side.

2. They were powerful, proud, and rich: "Men enclosed in their own fat, speaking proudly with their tongues," ver. 10.

3. Their counsels were fixed, and bent to ruin him: "They set their eyes, bowing down to the earth," ver. 11.

4. They were such enemies as prospered in

their designs, ver. 14. 1. Men of the world. 2. They had their portion in this life, and sought for none other. 3. They fed themselves without fear: "Their bellies were full." 4. They had a numerous offspring, and therefore more to be dreaded because of their family connections. 5. They left much substance behind them, so that their plans might be all continued and brought to effect,

III. The *conclusion,* containing the expectation of David, opposed to his enemies' felicity.
1. In this life: "As for me, I will behold thy face in righteousness."
2. In the life to come: "When I awake," rise from the dead, "after thy likeness, I shall be satisfied with it."
On each of these divisions the reader is referred to the notes.

PSALM XVIII

David's address of thanks to Jehovah, 1–3. A relation of sufferings undergone, and prayers made for assistance, 4–6. A magnificent description of Divine interposition in behalf of the sufferer, 7–15; and of the deliverance wrought for him, 16–19. That this deliverance was in consideration of his righteousness, 20–24; and according to the tenor of God's equitable proceedings, 25–28. To Jehovah is ascribed the glory of the victory, 29–36; which is represented as complete by the destruction of all his opponents, 37–42. On these events the heathen submit, 43–45. And for all these things God is glorified, 46–50.

III. DAY. EVENING PRAYER

To the chief Musician, *A Psalm* of David, ᵃthe servant of the LORD, who spake unto the LORD the words of ᵇthis song in the day *that* the LORD delivered him from the hand of all his enemies, and from the hand of Saul: And he said,

A. M. cir. 2986
B. C. cir. 1018
Davidis, Regis
Israelitarum,
cir. annum
38

I ᶜWILL love thee, O LORD, my strength.

2 The LORD *is* my rock, and my fortress, and my deliverer;

my God, ᵈmy strength, ᵉin whom I will trust; my buckler, and the horn of my salvation, *and* my high tower.

A. M. cir. 2986
B. C. cir. 1018
Davidis, Regis
Israelitarum,
cir. annum
38

3 I will call upon the LORD, ᶠ*who is worthy* to be praised: so shall I be saved from mine enemies.

4 ᵍThe sorrows of death compassed me, and

ᵃPsa. xxxvi. title——ᵇ2 Sam. xxii——ᶜPsa. cxliv. 1
ᵈHeb. *my rock*

ᵉHebrews ii. 13——ᶠPsalm lxxvi. 4——ᵍPsalm cxvi. 3

NOTES ON PSALM XVIII

The title: "To the chief Musician, *A Psalm* of David, the servant of the LORD, who spake unto the LORD the words of this song in the day *that* the LORD delivered him from the hand of all his enemies, and from the hand of Saul."

Except the first clause, this title is taken from 2 Sam. xxii. 1. The reader is requested to turn to the notes on 2 Sam. xxii. 1, for some curious information on this Psalm, particularly what is extracted from Dr. *Kennicott.* This learned writer supposes the whole to be a song of the Messiah, and divides it into *five parts,* which he thus introduces:—

"The Messiah's sublime thanksgivings, composed by David when his wars were at an end, towards the conclusion of his life. And in this sacred song the goodness of God is celebrated, 1. For Messiah's resurrection from the dead, with the wonders attending that awful event, and soon following it. 2. For the punishment inflicted on the Jews; particularly by the destruction of Jerusalem. And, 3. For the obedience of the Gentile nations. See Rom. xv. 9; Heb. ii. 13; and Matt. xxviii. 2-4; with xxiv. 7, and 29."

And that the title now prefixed to this hymn here and in 2 Sam. xxii. 1, describes only the *time* of its composition, seems evident; for who can ascribe to David *himself* as the subject, verses 5, 6, 8-17, 21-26, 30, 42, 44, &c.?

In Dr. *Kennicott's* remarks there is a new translation of the whole Psalm, p. 178, &c.

The strong current of commentators and critics apply this Psalm to Christ; and to op-

pose a whole host of both ancients and moderns would argue great self-confidence. In the *main* I am of the same mind; and on this principle chiefly I shall proceed to its illustration; still however considering that there are many things in it which concern David, and him only. Drs. *Chandler* and *Delaney* have been very successful in their illustration of various passages in it; all the best critics have brought their strongest powers to bear on it; and most of the commentators have laboured it with great success; and Bishop *Horne* has applied the whole of it to Christ. My old Psalter speaks highly in its praise: "This Psalme contenes the sacrement of al chosyn men, the qwilk doand the law of God thurgh the seven fald grace of the Haly Gast fra al temptaciouns, and the pouste of dede and of the devel lesid: this sang thai syng til God; and thankes him and says, *I sal luf the Lord,* noght a day or twa, bot ever mare: *my strength,* thurgh quam I am stalworth in thoght."

Verse 1. *I will love thee*] Love always subsists on motive and reason. The verb רחם *racham* signifies to *love with all the tender feelings of nature.* "From my inmost bowels will I love thee, O Lord!" Why should he love Jehovah? Not merely because he was infinitely great and good, possessed of all possible perfections, but because he was *good to him:* and he here enumerates some of the many blessings he received from him.

My strength.] 1. Thou who hast given me *power* over my adversaries, and hast enabled me to avoid evil and do good.

Verse 2. *The Lord is my rock*] 2. I stand

A. M. cir. 2986
B. C. cir. 1018
Davidis, Regis
Israelitarum,
cir. annum
38

the floods of [h]ungodly men made me afraid.

5 The [i]sorrows of hell compassed me about: the [k]snares of death prevented me.

6 In my distress I called upon the Lord,

and cried unto my God: he heard my voice out of his temple, and my cry came before him, *even* into his ears.

7 [l]Then the earth shook and trembled; the foundations also of the hills moved and

A. M. cir. 2986
B. C. cir. 1018
Davidis, Regis
Israelitarum,
cir. annum
38

---

[h]Heb. *Belial*——[i]Or, *cords*——[k]2 Sam. xxii. 6; Prov. xiii. 14; xiv. 27——[l]Acts iv. 31

---

on him as my *foundation*, and derive every good from him who is the source of good. The word סֶלַע *sela* signifies those craggy precipices which afford shelter to men and wild animals; where the *bees* often made their nests, and whence honey was collected in great abundance. "He made him to suck honey out of the rock," Deut. xxxii. 13. 3. He was his *fortress;* a place of *strength* and *safety*, fortified by *nature* and *art*, where he could be safe from his enemies. He refers to those inaccessible heights in the rocky, mountainous country of Judea, where he had often found refuge from the pursuit of Saul. What these have been to my body, such has the Lord been to my soul.

Deliverer] 4. מְפַלְטִי *mephalleti*, he who causes me to *escape*. This refers to his preservation in straits and difficulties. He was often *almost* surrounded and taken, but still the Lord *made a way for his escape*—made a *way out* as his enemies *got in;* so that, while they got in at one side of his strong hold, he got out of the other, and so *escaped* with his life. These escapes were so narrow and so unlikely that he plainly saw the hand of the Lord was in them. 5. *My God*, אֵלִי *Eli*, my *strong God*, not only the object of my adoration, but he who puts strength in my soul. 6. *My strength*, צוּרִי *tsuri*. This is a different word from that in the first verse. *Rabbi Maimon* has observed that צוּר *tsur*, when applied to God, signifies *fountain, source, origin*, &c. God is not only the *source* whence my *being* was *derived*, but he is the *fountain* whence I *derive* all my *good; in whom*, says David, *I will trust*. And why? Because he knew him to be an eternal and *inexhaustible fountain* of goodness. This fine idea is lost in our translation; for we render two Hebrew words of widely different meaning, by the same term in English, *strength*. 7. *My buckler*, מָגִנִּי *maginni*, my *shield*, my *defender*, he who covers my head and my heart, so that I am neither slain nor wounded by the darts of my adversaries. 8. *Horn of my salvation*. *Horn* was the emblem of power, and power in exercise. This has been already explained; see on 1 Sam. ii. 1. The *horn of salvation* means a *powerful*, an *efficient salvation*. 9. *My high tower;* not only a place of defence, but one from which I can discern the country round about, and always be able to discover danger before it approaches me.

Verse 3. *I will call upon the Lord*] When he was conscious that the object of his worship was such as he has pointed out in the above *nine* particulars, it is no wonder that he resolves to *call upon him;* and no wonder that he expects, in consequence, to be saved from his enemies; for who can destroy him whom such a God undertakes to save?

Verse 4. *The sorrows of death compassed me*] חֶבְלֵי מָוֶת *chebley maveth*, the *cables* or *cords of death*. He was almost taken in those *nets* or *stratagems*, by which, if he had been entangled, he would have lost his life. The stratagems to which he refers were those that were intended for his destruction; hence called *the cables* or *cords of death*.

The floods of ungodly men] Troops of wicked men were rushing upon him like an irresistible torrent; or like the waves of the sea, one impelling another forward in successive ranks; so that, thinking he must be overwhelmed by them, he was for the moment *affrighted;* but God turned the torrent aside, and he escaped.

Verse 5. *The sorrows of hell*] חֶבְלֵי שְׁאוֹל *chebley sheol*, the *cables* or *cords of the grave*. Is not this a reference to the *cords* or *ropes* with which they *lowered the corpse into the grave?* or the bandages by which the dead were swathed? He was as good as dead.

The snares of death prevented me.] I was just on the point of dropping into the pit which they had digged for me. In short, I was all but a dead man; and nothing less than the immediate *interference* of God could have saved my life.

Verse 6. *In my distress I called*] His enemies had no hope of his destruction unless God should abandon him. They hoped that this was the case, and that therefore they should prevail. But God *heard his cry and came down* to his help; and this interference is most majestically described in the 7th and following verses. Dr. *Dodd* has collected some excellent observations on these verses from *Chandler*, *Delaney*, and others, which I shall transcribe, as I know not that any thing better can be offered on the subject.

Verse 7. *Then the earth shook and trembled*] "In this and the following verses David describes, by the sublimest expressions and grandest terms, the majesty of God, and the awful manner in which he came to his assistance. The representation of the storm in these verses must be allowed by all skilful and impartial judges to be truly sublime and noble, and in the genuine spirit of poetry. The majesty of God, and the manner in which he is represented as coming to the aid of his favourite king, surrounded with all the powers of nature as his attendants and ministers, and arming (as it were) heaven and earth to fight his battles, and execute his vengeance, is described in the loftiest and most striking terms. The *shaking of the* earth; the *trembling of the* mountains and pillars of heaven; the *smoke* that drove out of his nostrils; the *flames* of devouring fire that flashed from his mouth; the *heavens bending* down to convey him to the battle; his *riding upon a cherub*, and rapidly

A. M. cir. 2986
B. C. cir. 1018
Davidis, Regis
Israelitarum,
cir. annum
38

were shaken, because he was wroth.

8 There went up a smoke ᵐout of his nostrils, and fire out of his mouth devoured: coals were kindled by it.

9 ⁿHe bowed the heavens also, and came down: and darkness *was* under his feet.

10 ᵒAnd he rode upon a cherub, and did fly: yea, ᵖhe did fly upon the wings of the wind.

A. M. cir. 2986
B. C. cir. 1018
Davidis, Regis
Israelitarum,
cir. annum
38

ᵐHeb. *by his*——ⁿPsa. cxliv. 5

ᵒPsa. xcix. 1——ᵖPsa. civ. 3

---

flying on the *wings of a whirlwind;* his concealing his majesty in the *thick clouds* of heaven; the bursting of the *lightnings* from the *horrid darkness; the uttering of his voice* in *peals* of *thunder;* the *storm* of *fiery hail;* the *melting of the heavens,* and their dissolving into floods of *tempestuous rain;* the *cleaving of the earth,* and disclosing of the bottom of the hills, and the subterraneous channels or torrents of water, by the very breath of the nostrils of the Almighty; are all of them circumstances which create admiration, excite a kind of horror, and exceed every thing of this nature that is to be found in any of the remains of heathen antiquity. See *Longinus* on the Sublime, sec. 9, and *Hesiod's* description of Jupiter fighting against the Titans, which is one of the grandest things in all pagan antiquity; though upon comparison it will be found infinitely short of this description of the *psalmist's;* throughout the whole of which God is represented as a mighty warrior going forth to fight the battles of David, and highly incensed at the opposition his enemies made to his power and authority.

"When he descended to the engagement the very heavens bowed down to render his descent more awful; his *military tent* was *substantial darkness; the voice* of his *thunder* was the *warlike alarm* which sounded to the *battle;* the *chariot* in which he rode was the *thick clouds* of heaven, conducted by *cherubs,* and carried on by the irresistible force and rapid wings of an *impetuous tempest;* and the darts and weapons he employed were *thunderbolts, lightnings, fiery hail, deluging rains,* and *stormy winds!*

"No wonder that when God thus arose, all his enemies should be scattered, and those who hated him should flee before him.

"It does not appear from any part of David's history that there was any such storm as is here described, which proved destructive to his enemies, and salutary to himself. There might, indeed, have been such a one, though there is no particular mention of it: unless it may be thought that something of this nature is intimated in the account given of David's second battle with the Philistines, 2 Sam. v. 23, 24. It is undoubted, however, that the storm is represented as real; though David, in describing it, has heightened and embellished it with all the ornaments of poetry. See Chandler, Delaney, and Lowth's ninth Prelection.

"Verse 8. *There went up a smoke out of his nostrils*—Or, 'There ascended into his nostrils a smoke,' as the words, literally rendered, signify. The ancients placed the seat of anger in the *nose,* or nostrils; because when the passions are warm and violent, it discovers itself by the heated vehement breath which proceeds from them. Hence the physiognomists con-

sidered open wide nostrils as a sign of an angry, fiery disposition.

"This description of a *smoke* arising into and a *fire* breaking forth from the nostrils of God, denotes, by a poetical figure, the greatness of his anger and indignation.

"*Fire out of his mouth devoured*—means that consuming fire issued out of his mouth. *Coals were kindled by it,* thus we render the next clause; but the words do not mean that fire proceeding from God kindled coals, but that burning coals issued from his mouth; and it should be rendered 'living coals from his mouth burned, and consumed around him.'—*Chandler.*

"Verse 9. *He bowed the heavens also, and came down*—He made the heavens bend under him when he descended to take vengeance on his enemies. The psalmist seems here to express the appearance of the Divine majesty in a glorious cloud, descending from heaven, which underneath was substantially dark, but above, bright, and shining with exceeding lustre; and which, by its gradual approach to the earth, would appear as though the heavens themselves were bending down and approaching towards us.

"Verse 10. *He rode upon a cherub, and did fly*—That is, as it is immediately explained, *Yea, he did fly upon the wings of the wind.* God was in the storm, and by the ministry of angels guided the course of it, and drove it on with such an impetuous force as nothing could withstand. He 'rides in the whirlwind and directs the storm.' Angels are in a peculiar sense the attendants and messengers of the Almighty, whom he employs as his ministers in effecting many of those great events which take place in the administration of his providence; and particularly such as manifest his immediate interposition in the extraordinary judgments which he inflicts for the punishment of sinful nations. See Psa. ciii. 20, civ. 4. The *cherub* is particularly mentioned as an emblem of the Divine presence, and especially as employed in supporting and conveying the chariot of the Almighty, when he is represented as riding in his majesty through the firmament of heaven:—

——Forth rush'd with whirlwind sound
The chariot of paternal Deity;
Flashing thick flames, wheel within wheel undrawn,
Itself instinct with spirit, but convey'd
By four cherubic shapes.
                 Par. Lost, lib. vi."

This seems to be the image intended to be conveyed in the place before us. "He rode upon a cherub, and did fly; he flew on the wings of the wind," i. e., the cherub supported and led on the tempest, in which the Almighty rode as in his chariot. This is agreeable to the office elsewhere ascribed to the cherubim. **Thus**

A. M. cir. 2986
B. C. cir. 1018
Davidis, Regis
Israelitarum,
cir. annum
38

11 He made darkness his secret place; qhis pavilion round about him *were* dark waters *and* thick clouds of the skies.

12 rAt the brightness *that was* before him his thick clouds passed; hail-*stones* and coals of fire.

13 The LORD also thundered in the heavens,

---

and the Highest gave shis voice; hail-*stones* and coals of fire.

A. M. cir. 2986
B. C. cir. 1018
Davidis, Regis
Israelitarum,
cir. annum
38

14 tYea, he sent out his arrows, and scattered them; and he shot out lightnings, and discomfited them.

15 uThen the channels of waters were seen, and the foundations of the world were discov-

---

qPsa. xcvii. 3——rPsa. xcvii. 3——sPsalm xxix. 3

tJosh. x. 10; Psa. cxliv. 6; Isa. xxx. 30——uExod. xv. 8; Psa. cvi. 9

---

they supported the mercy-seat, which was peculiarly the throne of God under the Jewish economy. God is expressly said to "make the clouds his chariot," Psa. civ. 3; and to "ride upon a swift cloud," Isa. xix. 1: so that "riding upon a cherub," and "riding upon a swift cloud," is riding in the cloud as his chariot, supported and guided by the ministry of the cherubim. The next clause in the parallel place of Samuel is, "He was seen on the wings of the wind;" ירא *yera*, he *was seen*, being used for ידא *yede*, he *flew*, ר *daleth* being changed into ר *resh*. Either of them may be the true reading, for the MSS. are greatly divided on these places; but on the whole וירא *vaiyera* appears to be the better reading: "And he was *seen* on the wings of the wind."

As the original has been supposed by adequate judges to exhibit a fine specimen of that poetry which, in the choice of its terms, conveys both *sense* and *sound*, I will again lay it before the reader, as I have done in the parallel place, 2 Sam. xxii. 2. The words in *italic* to be read from right to left.

ויעף   כרוב   על   וירכב
vaiyaoph   *kerub*   *al*   *waiyirkab*
And he rode upon a cherub, and did fly!

רוח   כנפי   על   וידא
ruach   *canphey*   *al*   *waiyede*
Yea, he flew on the wings of the wind!

The word רוח *ruach*, in the last line, should be pronounced, not *ruak*, which is no Hebrew word: but as a Scottish man would pronounce it, were it written *ruagh*. With this observation, how astonishingly is the *rushing of the wind* heard in the last word of each hemistich! *Sternhold* and *Hopkins* have succeeded in their version of this place, not only beyond all *they* ever did, but beyond every ancient and modern poet on a similar subject:—

"On cherub and on cherubin
 Full royally he rode;
 And on the wings of mighty winds
 Came flying all abroad."

Even the old *Anglo-Scottish Psalter* has not done amiss:—

𝕬nd he steygh aboben cherubyn and he flotv;
𝕳e flotv aboben the fethers of wyndes.

Verse 11. *He made darkness his secret place*] God is represented as dwelling in the *thick darkness*, Deut. iv. 11, Psa. xcvii. 2. This representation in the place before us is peculiarly proper; as thick heavy clouds deeply charged, and with lowering aspects, are always the forerunners and attendants of a tempest, and

---

greatly heighten the horrors of the appearance: and the representation of them, spread about the Almighty as a tent, is truly grand and poetic.

Dark waters] The vapours strongly condensed into clouds; which, by the stroke of the lightning, are about to be precipitated in torrents of rain. See the next verse.

Verse 12. *At the brightness that was before him his thick clouds passed*] The word נגה *nogah* signifies the *lightning*. This *goes before him*; the *flash* is seen before the *thunder* is heard, and before the *rain* descends; and then the *thick cloud passes*. Its contents are precipitated on the earth, and the cloud is entirely dissipated.

Hail-stones and coals of fire.] This was the storm that followed the *flash* and the *peal*; for it is immediately added—

Verse 13. *The Lord also thundered in the heavens, and the Highest gave his voice*] And then followed the *hail and coals of fire*. The former verse mentioned the *lightning*, with its effects; this gives us the report of the *thunder*, and the increasing *storm of hail and fire* that attended it. Some think the words *hail-stones and coals of fire* are entered here by some careless transcribers from the preceding verse; and it is true that they are wanting in the Septuagint and the Arabic, in the parallel place in 2 Samuel, and in *five of Kennicott's* and *De Rossi's* MSS. I should rather, with Bishop *Horsley*, suppose them to be an interpolation in the preceding verse: or in that to have been borrowed from this; for this most certainly is their true place.

Verse 14. *He sent out his arrows—he shot out lightnings*] I believe the latter clause to be an illustration of the former. *He sent out his arrows*—that is, he shot out *lightnings*; for lightnings are the *arrows* of the Lord, and there is something very like the *arrowhead* apparent in the *zigzag* lightning. *Sense* and *sound* are wonderfully combined in the Hebrew of this last clause: וברקים רב ויהמם *uberakim rab vaihummem*, "and thunderings he multiplied and confounded them." Who does not hear the *bursting*, *brattling*, and *pounding* of thunder in these words? See *Delaney?*

Verse 15. *The channels of water were seen*] This must refer to an *earthquake*; for in such cases, the ground being rent, water frequently gushes out at the fissures, and often rises to a tremendous height. Whole rivers were poured out of the chasms made by the earthquake in Jamaica, A. D. 1694; and new lakes of water were formed, covering a *thousand* acres of land!

A. M. cir. 2986
B. C. cir. 1018
Davidis, Regis
Israelitarum,
cir. annum
38
ered at thy rebuke, O Lord, at the blast of the breath of thy nostrils.

16 ᵛHe sent from above, he took me, he drew me out of ʷmany waters.

17 He delivered me from my strong enemy, and from them which hated me: for they were too strong for me.

18 They prevented me in the day of my calamity: but the Lord was my stay.

19 ˣHe brought me forth also into a large place; he delivered me, because he delighted in me.

20 ʸThe Lord rewarded me according to my righteousness; according to the cleanness of my hands hath he recompensed me.

21 For I have kept the ways of the Lord, and have not wickedly departed from my God. A. M. cir. 2986
B. C. cir. 1018
Davidis, Regis
Israelitarum,
cir. annum
38

22 For all his judgments *were* before me, and I did not put away his statutes from me.

23 I was also upright ᶻbefore him, and I kept myself from mine iniquity.

24 ᵃTherefore hath the Lord recompensed me according to my righteousness, according to the cleanness of my hands ᵇin his eyesight.

25 ᶜWith the merciful thou wilt show thyself merciful; with an upright man thou wilt show thyself upright;

26 With the pure thou wilt show thyself

ᵛPsa. cxliv. 7——ʷOr, *great waters*——ˣPsa. xxxi. 8; cxviii. 5——ʸ1 Sam. xxiv. 20

ᶻHeb. *with*——ᵃ1 Sam. xxvi. 23——ᵇHeb. *before his eyes* ᶜ1 Kings viii. 32

Verse 16. *He drew me out of many waters.*] Here the allusion is still carried on. The waters thus poured out were sweeping the people away; but God, by a miraculous interference, sent and drew David out. Sometimes *waters* are used to denote *multitudes of people;* and here the word may have that reference; multitudes were gathered together against David, but God delivered him from them all. This seems to be countenanced by the following verse.

Verse 17. *He delivered me from my strong enemy*] Does not this refer to his conflict with Ishbi-benob? "And Ishbi-benob, which *was* of the sons of the giant—thought to have slain David. But Abishai the son of Zeruiah succoured him, and smote the Philistine, and killed him. Then the men of David sware unto him, saying, Thou shalt go no more out with us to battle, that thou quench not the light of Israel;" 2 Sam. xxi. 16, 17. It appears that at this time he was in the most imminent danger of his life, and that he must have fallen by the hands of the giant, if God had not sent Abishai to his assistance. *They were too strong for me.* He was nearly overpowered by the Philistines; and his escape was such as evidently to show it to be supernatural.

Verse 18. *They prevented me in the day of my calamity*] They took advantage of the time in which I was least able to make head against them, and their attack was sudden and powerful. I should have been overthrown, *but the Lord was my stay.* He had been nearly exhausted by the fatigue of the day, when the giant availed himself of this advantage.

Verse 19. *He brought me forth also into a large place*] He enabled me to clear the country of my foes, who had before cooped me up in holes and corners. This appears to be the allusion.

Verse 20. *The Lord rewarded me*] David proceeds to give the reasons why God had so marvellously interposed in his behalf.

According to my righteousness] Instead of being an enemy to Saul, I was his friend. I dealt *righteously* with him while he dealt *unrighteously* with me.

Verse 21. *I have kept the ways of the Lord*] I was neither an *infidel* nor a *profligate;* I trusted in God, and carefully observed all the ordinances of his religion.

Verse 22. *All his judgments* were *before me*] I kept his law before my eyes, that I might see my duty and know how to walk and please God.

Verse 23. *I was also upright*] The times in which David was most afflicted were the times of his greatest uprightness. *Adversity* was always to him a time of spiritual prosperity.

Mine iniquity.] Probably meaning what is generally termed *the easily-besetting sin; the sin of his constitution,* or that to which the *temperament* of his body most powerfully disposed him. What this was, is a subject of useless conjecture.

Verse 25. *With the merciful thou wilt show thyself merciful*] Thou wilt deal with men as they deal with each other. This is the general tenor of God's providential conduct towards mankind; well expressed by Mr. *Pope* in his universal prayer:—

> "Teach me to feel another's wo;
>   To hide the fault I see:
> The mercy I to others show,
>   That mercy show to me."

It is in reference to this that our Lord teaches us to pray: "Forgive us our trespasses, as we forgive them that trespass against us." If we act *feelingly* and *mercifully* towards our fellow creatures, God will act *tenderly* and *compassionately* towards us. The merciful, the upright, and the pure, will ever have the God of mercy, uprightness, and purity, to defend and support them.

Verse 26. *With the froward*] עקש *ikkesh, the perverse man;* he that is crooked in his tempers and ways.

Thou wilt show thyself froward.] תתפתל *tithpattal,* thou wilt set thyself to twist, twine, and wrestle. If *he* contend, *thou* wilt contend with him. Thou wilt follow him through all his windings; thou wilt trace him through all his crooked ways; untwist him in all his cun-

A. M. cir. 2986
B. C. cir. 1018
Davidis, Regis
Israelitarum,
cir. annum
38

pure; and [d]with the froward thou wilt [e]show thyself froward.

27 For thou wilt save the afflicted people; but wilt bring down [f]high looks.

28 [g]For thou wilt light my [h]candle: the LORD my God will enlighten my darkness.

29 For by thee I have [i]run through a troop; and by my God have I leaped over a wall.

30 *As for* God, [k]his way *is* perfect: [l]the word of the LORD is [m]tried: he *is* a buckler

[n]to all those that trust in him.

31 [o]For who *is* God save the LORD? or who *is* a rock save our God?

32 *It is* God that [p]girdeth me with strength and maketh my way perfect.

33 [q]He maketh my feet like hinds' *feet,* and [r]setteth me upon my high places.

34 [s]He teacheth my hands to war, so that a bow of steel is broken by mine arms.

35 Thou hast also given me the shield of

A. M. cir. 2986
B. C. cir. 1018
Davidis, Regis
Israelitarum,
cir. annum
38

[d]Lev. xxvi. 23, 24, 27, 28; Prov. iii. 34——[e]Or, *wrestle*——[f]Psa. ci. 5; Prov. vi. 17——[g]Job xviii. 6 [h]Or, *lamp*, Job xxix. 3——[i]Or, *broken*——[k]Deut. xxxii. 4; Dan. iv. 37; Rev. xv. 3——[l]Psa. xii. 6; cxix. 140; Prov. xxx. 5

[m]Or, *refined*——[n]Psalm xvii. 7——[o]Deuteronomy xxxii. 31, 39; 1 Sam. ii. 2; Psa. lxxxvi. 8; Isa. xlv. 5 [p]Psalm xci. 2——[q]2 Samuel ii. 18; Habakkuk iii. 19——[r]Deuteronomy xxxii. 13; xxxiii. 29——[s]Psalm cxliv. 1

ning wiles; and defeat all his schemes of stubbornness, fraud, overreaching, and deceit.

My old *Psalter* has, **With the wicked thou sal be wike.** Here the term *wicked* is taken in its *true original* sense, *crooked,* or *perverse.* With the **wiked,** the *perverse,* thou wilt show thyself **wike,** i. e., *perverse;* from **piccan,** to *draw back,* to *slide.* As *he draws back* from thee, thou wilt *draw back* from him. It may, as before intimated, come from **piccian,** to seek for *enchantments; leaving God,* and *going to devils;* to act like a *witch:* but *here* it must *mean* as above. The plain import is, "If thou perversely oppose thy Maker, he will oppose thee: no work or project shall prosper that is not begun in his name, and conducted in his fear."

Verse 27. *For thou wilt save the afflicted*] The afflicted are the *humble;* and those thou hast ever befriended.

Verse 28. *For thou wilt light my candle*] Thou wilt restore me to prosperity, and give me a happy issue out of all my afflictions. By the *lamp of David* the *Messiah* may be meant: thou wilt not suffer my family to become extinct, nor the kingdom which thou hast promised me utterly to fail.

Verse 29. *I have run through a troop*] This may relate to some remarkable victory; and the taking of some fortified place, possibly *Zion,* from the Jebusites. See the account 2 Sam. v. 6-8.

Verse 30. *God, his way is perfect*] His conduct is like his nature, absolutely pure.

The word of the Lord is tried] Literally *tried in the fire.* It has stood all tests; and has never failed those who pleaded it before its author.

He is a buckler] A sure protection to every simple believing soul. We cannot believe his word too *implicitly;* nor trust too *confidently* in him.

Verse 31. *For who is God save the Lord?*] "For who is Eloah, except Jehovah?" None is worthy of adoration but the self-existent, eternal, infinitely perfect, and all-merciful Being.

Or who is a rock] A *fountain* emitting continual supplies of grace and goodness.

Verse 32. *God—girdeth me with strength*] The girdle was a necessary part of the East-

ern dress; it *strengthened* and *supported* the loins; served to *confine* the *garments* close to the body; and in it they tucked them up when journeying. The *strength* of God was to his *soul* what the *girdle* was to the *body.* I need not add, that the *girdle* was also an *ornamental* part of the dress, and from it the sword was suspended.

And maketh my way perfect.] He directs me so that I do not go astray; he blesses me in my undertakings; and by him the issue of my labours is crowned with prosperity.

Verse 33. *My feet like hinds' feet*] Swiftness, or *speed of foot,* was a necessary qualification of an ancient hero. This was of great advantage in pursuing, combating, or escaping from a fallen foe. Ποδας ωκυς Αχιλλευς, "the swift-footed Achilles," is frequently given by *Homer* as a most honourable qualification of his hero.

Upon my high places.] In allusion to the *hinds, antelopes, mountain goats,* &c., which frequented such places, and in which they found both *food* and *safety.* God frequently preserved the life of David by means of these.

Verse 34. *He teacheth my hands to war*] The success which I have had in my military exercises I owe to the Divine help. How few of the conquerors of mankind can say so! And how few among those who call themselves *Christian warriors* dare to say so! *War* is as contrary to the spirit of Christianity as murder. Nothing can justify Christian nations in shedding each other's blood! All men *should* live in peace; all men *might* live in peace; and the nation that is *first* to break it is under a heavy curse.

A bow of steel is broken by mine arms.] All the *versions* render this: "Thou hast made my arm like a brazen bow." A bow of *steel* is out of the question. In the days of David it is not likely that the method of making *steel* was known. The method of making *brass* out of *copper* was known at a very early period of the world; and the ancients had the art of *hardening* it, so as to work it into the most efficient swords. From his own account David was *swift, courageous,* and *strong.*

Verse 35. *The shield of thy salvation*] In all battles and dangers God defended him. He was constantly safe because he possessed the

A. M. cir. 2986
B. C. cir. 1018
Davidis, Regis
Israelitarum,
cir. annum
38

thy salvation: and thy right hand hath holden me up, and [t]thy gentleness hath made me great.

36 Thou hast enlarged my steps under me, [u]that [v]my feet did not slip.

37 I have pursued mine enemies, and overtaken them; neither did I turn again till they were consumed.

38 I have wounded them that they were not able to rise: they are fallen under my feet.

39 For thou hast girded me with strength unto the battle: thou hast [w]subdued under me those that rose up against me.

40 Thou hast also given me the necks of mine enemies; that I might destroy them that hate me.

41 They cried, but *there was* none to save *them:* [x]*even* unto the LORD, but he answered them not.

A. M. cir. 2986
B. C. cir. 1018
Davidis, Regis
Israelitarum,
cir. annum
38

42 Then did I beat them small as the dust before the wind: I did [y]cast them out as the dirt in the streets.

43 [z]Thou hast delivered me from the strivings of the people; *and* [a]thou hast made me the head of the heathen: [b]a people *whom* I have not known shall serve me.

44 [c]As soon as they hear of me, they shall obey me: [d]the strangers [e]shall [f]submit [g]themselves unto me.

45 [h]The strangers shall fade away, and be afraid out of their close places.

---

[t]Or, *with thy meekness thou hast multiplied me* [u]Prov. iv. 12——[v]Heb. *mine ankles*——[w]Heb. *caused to bow*——[x]Job xxvii. 9; xxxv. 12; Prov. i. 28; Isa. i. 15; Jer. xi. 11; xiv. 12; Ezek. viii. 18; Mic. iii. 4; Zech. vii. 13——[y]Zech. x. 5

[z]2 Sam. ii. 9, 10; iii. 1——[a]2 Sam. viii——[b]Isa. lii. 15; lv. 5——[c]Heb. *At the hearing of the ear*——[d]Heb. *the sons of the stranger*——[e]Deut. xxxiii. 29; Psa. lxvi. 3; lxxxi. 15——[f]Or, *yield feigned obedience*——[g]Heb. *lie* [h]Mic. vii. 17

---

salvation of God. Everywhere God protected him. *Thy gentleness,* ענותך *anvathecha,* thy *meekness* or *humility.* Thou hast enabled me to bear and forbear; to behave with courage in adversity, and with humility in prosperity; and thus I am become *great.* By these means thou hast *multiplied* me. The *Vulgate* reads, *Disciplina tua ipsa me docebit;* "And thy discipline itself shall teach me." In this sense it was understood by most of the *versions.* The old *Psalter* paraphrases thus: Thi chastying suffers me noght to erre fra the end to com.

Verse 36. *Enlarged my steps*] See on ver. 19. From the hand of God he had continual prosperity; and while he walked with God no enemy was able to prevail against him. He details his successes in the following verses.

Verse 40. *The necks of mine enemies*] Thou hast made me a complete conqueror. *Treading on the neck* of an enemy was the triumph of the conqueror, and the utmost disgrace of the vanquished.

Verse 41. *They cried*] The Philistines called upon their gods, but there was none to save them.

E*ven unto the Lord*] Such as Saul, Ishbosheth, Absalom, &c., who, professing to worship the true God, *called on him* while in their opposition to David; but God no more heard *them* than their *idols* heard the Philistines.

Verse 42. *Then did I beat them*] God was with *him,* and *they* had only an arm of flesh. No wonder then that his enemies were destroyed.

Small as the dust before the wind] This well expresses the manner in which he treated the Moabites, Ammonites, and the people of Rabbah: "He put them under saws, and under harrows of iron, and under axes of iron; and made them pass through the brick-kiln," &c. See 2 Sam. xii. 31, and the notes there.

Verse 43. *The strivings of the people*] Disaffections and insurrections among my own subjects, as in the revolt of *Absalom,* the civil *war of Abner* in favour of *Ish-bosheth,* &c.

The head of the heathen] ראש גוים *rosh goyim,* "the chief," or "governor," of the nations;" all the circumjacent heathen people; all these were subdued by David, and brought under tribute.

A people whom I have not known] The people whom he *knew* were those of the *twelve tribes;* those whom he did not *know* were the Syrians, Philistines, Idumeans, &c. All these *served him,* that is, paid him *tribute.*

Verse 44. *As soon as they hear of me*] His victories were so rapid and splendid over powerful enemies, that they struck a general terror among the people, and several submitted without a contest.

Strangers shall submit themselves unto me.] Some translate this: "The children of the foreign woman have lied unto me." This has been understood *two* ways: My own people, who have sworn fealty to me, have broken their obligation, and followed my rebellious son. Or, The heathens, who have been brought under my yoke, have promised the most cordial obedience, and flattered me with their tongues, while their hearts felt enmity against me and my government. Nevertheless, even in this unwilling subjection I was secure, my police being so efficient, and my kingdom so strong.

Verse 45. *The strangers shall fade away*] בני נכר *beney nechar,* the same persons mentioned above. They shall not be able to effect any thing against me; יבלו *yibbolu,* "they shall fall as the leaves fall off the trees in winter."

And be afraid out of their close places.] Those who have formed themselves into *banditti,* and have taken possession of *rocks* and *fortified places,* shall be so afraid when they hear of my successes, that they shall surrender at discretion, without standing a siege. Perhaps all these verbs should be understood in the *perfect* tense, for David is here evidently speaking of a kingdom at rest, all enemies having *been subdued;* or, as the *title* is, *when the Lord* HAD *delivered him from all his enemies.*

A. M. cir. 2986
B. C. cir. 1018
Davidis, Regis
Israelitarum,
cir. annum
38

46 The LORD liveth, and bless-ed *be* my Rock: and let the God of my salvation be exalted.

47 *It is* God that [1]avengeth me, [k]and [l]subdueth the people under me.

48 He delivereth me from mine enemies: yea, [m]thou liftest me up above those that rise up against me: thou hast deliver-ed me from the [n]violent man.

A. M. cir. 2986
B. C. cir. 1018
Davidis, Regis
Israelitarum,
cir. annum
38

49 [o]Therefore will I [p]give thanks unto thee, O LORD, among the heathen, and sing praises unto thy name.

50 [q]Great deliverance giveth he to his king; and showeth mercy to his anointed, to David, and to his seed [r]for evermore.

---

[1]Heb. *giveth avengements for me*——[k]Psa. xlvii. 3
[l]Or, *destroyeth*——[m]Psa. lix. 1

[n]Heb. *man of violence*——[o]Rom. xv. 9——[p]Or, *confess*
[q]Psa. cxliv. 10——[r]2 Sam. vii. 13

Verse 46. *The Lord liveth*] By him alone I have gained all my victories; and he *continueth*, and will be my *Rock*, the *Source* whence I may at all times derive help and salvation. May his name be blessed! May his kingdom be exalted!

Verse 47. *God that avengeth me*] The way that I took was after his own heart; therefore he sustained me in it, and did me justice over my enemies.

Subdueth the people under me.] He keeps down the spirits of the disaffected, and weakens their hands. They are subdued, and they continue under me; and this is the Lord's doing.

Verse 48. *He delivereth me*] That is, he *hath delivered* me, and continues to deliver me, from all that rise up against me.

The violent man.] Saul; this applies particularly to him.

Verse 49. *Will I give thanks unto thee—among the heathen*] Quoted by St. Paul, Rom. xv. 9, to prove that the *calling of the Gentiles* was predicted, and that what then took place was the fulfilment of that prediction.

But there is a sense in which it applies particularly to David, well observed by *Theodoret:* "We see," says he, "evidently the fulfilment of this prophecy; for even to the present day David praises the Lord among the Gentiles by the mouth of true believers; seeing there is not a town, village, hamlet, country, nor even a desert, where Christians dwell, in which God is not praised by their singing the Psalms of David."

Verse 50. *Great deliverance giveth he to his king*] David was a king of God's appointment, and was peculiarly favoured by him. Literally, *He is magnifying the salvations of his king.* He not only delivers, but follows up those deliverances with innumerable blessings.

Showeth mercy—to David] I have no *claim* upon his bounty. I *deserve* nothing from him, but he continues to show *mercy.*

To his seed] His *posterity.* So the words עֶרַז *zera* and σπερμα, in the Old and New Testament, should be universally translated. The common translation is totally improper, and *now* more so than formerly, when *anatomy* was less understood.

For evermore.] עַד עוֹלָם *ad olam, for ever;* through all duration of created worlds. And *more*—the eternity that is beyond time. This shows that another *David* is meant, with another kind of *posterity*, and another sort of *kingdom.* From the *family of David* came the man, Christ Jesus; his *posterity* are the *genuine Christians;* his *kingdom*, in which they are *subjects*, is *spiritual.* This *government* shall last through all time, for Christianity will

continue to prevail till the *end of the world:* and it will be extended through *eternity;* for that is the kingdom of glory in which Jesus reigns on the throne of his Father, and in which his followers shall reign with him for ever and ever.

It has already been remarked that this whole Psalm has been understood as relating to the *passion* and *victories* of CHRIST, and the *success of the Gospel in the earth.* In this way Bishop *Horne* has understood and paraphrased it; and in the same way it is considered by the ancient *Psalter,* so often mentioned. Many of the primitive *fathers* and modern *interpreters* have taken the same view of it. Those passages which I judged to have this meaning I have pointed out, and have only to add that, as David was a *type of Christ,* many things spoken of him *primarily,* refer to our Lord *ultimately;* but much judgment and caution are required in their application. To apply the whole Psalm in this way appears to me very injudicious, and often derogatory from the majesty of Christ. Let this be my excuse for not following the same track in which many of my predecessors have gone.

ANALYSIS OF THE EIGHTEENTH PSALM

David's Επινικιον, or song of triumph after his conquest of all his enemies.

This Psalm may be divided into *four* parts:—

I. David shows what God is to his servants, and the effect it wrought upon him, ver. 1, 2, 3.

II. The great danger in which he was from the power and multitude of his enemies, ver. 4-28.

III. His glorious victories, and their consequences, ver. 29-45.

IV. His thanksgiving for those victories, ver. 46-50.

I. What God is to his servants, and to him especially. 1. *Strength.* 2. *Rock.* 3. *Fortress.* 4. *Deliverer.* 5. *Tower.* 6. *Buckler.* 7. *Horn* of *salvation.* 8. *High tower,* ver. 1, 2. (See the *notes.*)

The *effect* it wrought in him. It produced, 1. *Love:* "I will love the Lord." 2. *Confidence:* "In him will I trust." 3. The *spirit* of *prayer:* "I will call on the Lord." The fruit of all which was his *safety:* "So shall I be saved from mine enemies," ver. 3.

II. The great dangers in which he was, and of his escape.

1. His danger was great; for, 1. He was *encompassed with the sorrows of death.* 2. Was *terrified* with the *floods of ungodly men.* 3. *Surrounded* by the *sorrows of hell.* And, 4. *Prevented* by the *snares of death,* ver. 4, 5.

2. He shows how he *behaved* in these dangers, and from whom he sought for help: 1. "He called upon the Lord." 2. "He cried unto his God."

3. He shows the *goodness* of God to him, and his readiness to help him: 1. "He heard me out of his holy temple." 2. "My cry came into his ears."

4. The *cause* of his escape was the immediate hand of God, who testified his presence by many supernatural signs. 1. EARTHQUAKES: "The earth shook and trembled." 2. HILLS and *mountains* were *moved* from their places: "The hills moved," &c., ver. 7. 3. SMOKE came out of his nostrils. 4. A consuming FIRE came out of his mouth; and became permanent, for *coals were kindled* by it, ver. 8. 5. A THICK DARKNESS announced his presence; and the atmosphere was greatly confused: "He bowed the heavens; darkness was under his feet," ver. 9. 6. There were *mighty winds* and *tempests:* "He flew on the wings of the wind," ver. 10. 7. There were violent inundations, with blackness of the atmosphere, dark waters, thick clouds of the sky, ver. 11. 8. Great THUNDERS: "The Lord thundered; the Highest gave his voice." 9. There was great HAIL, and FIERY METEORS: "Hailstones and coals of fire," ver. 12, 13. 10. *Tremendous* LIGHTNINGS, and *fearful* CHASMS opened in the earth: "He sent out," &c., ver. 14, 15.

5. He reckons up his *deliverances*, with the *manner* and *causes:*—

1. "He took, he drew me out of many waters," ver. 16.

2. He did this in a supernatural way: "He sent from above," ib.

6. He describes his enemies from whom God delivered him. 1. They were very *numerous*, compared to *many waters*, ver. 16: "He drew me out of many waters." 2. They were very *strong*. 3. Full of *malice*. 4. Too *strong for him*. 5. INSIDIOUS and CRUEL: "They prevented me in the day of my calamity," ver. 17, 18.

7. But God was his STAY: and the *causes* which moved God to help him were, 1. His own *good will:* "Because he delighted in me." 2. David's *innocence;* which he declares from ver. 20 to ver. 25.

8. And then, *ab hypothesi*, from his own particular case, he takes occasion to discourse *in thesi*, that this is not only true in David's person, but shall be verified in all that are upright as he was: which he proves from the nature and usual manner of God's proceedings with good and bad men, from ver. 25 to 28.

III. David's *glorious* VICTORIES, and their CONSEQUENCES, from ver. 28 to 46.

1. His victory he expresses and amplifies many ways:—

1. From the opposition which he conquered. Nor *troops* nor *walls* hindered, ver. 29.

2. From God's singular *protection*. He was his *Buckler, his Rock*.

3. From his *armour*. He was made *fleet;* and had military *knowledge, strength*, and *defence*, from God, ver. 33.

4. From his *safety*. He was not wounded in the battle.

5. From his *success*. He routed his enemies; they fled, and he pursued, ver. 37.

6. From the *greatness* of the *victory*. It was a complete conquest; for his enemies were *taken*, or *consumed*, or *wounded*, so as to be *unable* to *rally*. They *fell under his feet;* their *necks* were *brought down*, ver. 38 to 42.

7. From the *cause*. All was of God; he takes nothing to himself. THOU *hast girded me*. THOU *hast subdued*. THOU *hast given me*, &c.

2. The *consequences* of these victories were the propagation and enlargement of David's kingdom:—

1. Before these victories there were murmurings and insurrections among his people: but now, being conqueror, they are all quiet: "Thou hast delivered me from the strivings of the people," ver. 43.

2. He was exalted to be *head of the heathen:* Moabites, Ammonites, &c., *served him*, ver. 44.

3. People whom he had *not known* became tributary to him: "Aliens shall serve me," ver. 44.

4. This, it is true, they did out of *fear*, not *affection*. They *dissembled* in their fidelity; and several *fell off:* but still they were obliged to *submit*, ver. 45.

IV. David's THANKSGIVING. This is the main scope of the Psalm; to celebrate and extol the name and mercy of God for his victories. This has *two* parts: 1. His *present* thanksgiving. 2. His profession for the *future*.

1. He magnifies God: "The Lord liveth; and blessed be my Rock; and let the God of my salvation be exalted;" ver. 46. And to this end, in the two next verses, he makes mention again of his victories, and attributes the whole success to God, ver. 47, 48.

2. He professes still to do it; he will not cease even among the heathen: "Therefore will I give thanks," ver. 49.

3. And he shows how much reason he had to do so: because, 1. He had *great deliverances*. 2. He was the man of God's *choice; his king—his anointed*. 3. This goodness was to survive him, and go to his *posterity:* "To David, and to his seed." 4. It was to have *no end:* it was to be *for evermore*, ver. 50.

Here the *true David* and the *spiritual seed* are referred to; and for this the reader is requested to examine the notes, and the remark before this *analysis*.

PSALM XIX

The heavens and their host proclaim the majesty of God, 2–6; the excellence and perfection of the Divine law, 7–10; its usefulness, 11. The psalmist prays for pardon and preservation from sin, 12, 13; and that his words and thoughts may be holy, 14.

IV. DAY. MORNING PRAYER

To the chief Musician, A Psalm of David

THE [a]heavens declare the glory of God; and the firmament showeth his handy-work.

2 Day unto day uttereth speech, and night unto night showeth knowledge.

3 *There is* no speech nor language [b]*where* [c]their voice is not heard.

4 [d]Their [e]line is gone out through all the

---

[a]Gen. i. 6; Isa. xl. 22; Rom. i. 19, 20——[b]Or, *without these their voice is heard*

[c]Heb. *without their voice heard*——[d]Rom. x. 18——[e]Or, *Their rule* or *direction*

NOTES ON PSALM XIX

The *title* of this Psalm has nothing particular in it; but it is not very clear that it was written by David, to whom it is attributed; though some think that he composed it in the wilderness, while persecuted by Saul. For this opinion, however, there is no solid ground. There is no note in the Psalm itself to lead us to know *when, where,* or *by whom* it was written. It is a highly finished and beautiful ode.

Verse 1. *The heavens declare the glory of God*] Literally, *The heavens number out the glory of the strong God.* A first view of the starry heavens strikes every beholder with astonishment at the *power* by which they were made, and by which they are supported. To find out the *wisdom* and *skill* displayed in their contrivance requires a measure of *science:* but when the vast *magnitude* of the celestial bodies is considered, we feel increasing astonishment at these works of the *strong God.*

The firmament] The whole *visible expanse;* not only containing the *celestial bodies* above referred to, but also the *air, light, rains, dews,* &c., &c. And when the composition of these principles is examined, and their great utility to the earth and its inhabitants properly understood, they afford matter of astonishment to the wisest mind, and of adoration and gratitude even to the most unfeeling heart.

Verse 2. *Day unto day uttereth speech*] Each day is represented as teaching another relative to some new excellence discovered in these *manifold works* of God. The *nights* also, by the same figure, are represented as giving information to each other of the increase of knowledge already gained.

"The labours of these our instructers know no intermission; but they continue incessantly to lecture us in the science of Divine wisdom. There is one glory of the sun, which shines forth by day; and there are other glories of the moon and of the stars, which become visible by night. And because *day* and *night* interchangeably divide the world between them, they are therefore represented as transmitting, in succession, each to other, the task enjoined them, like the two parts of a choir, chanting forth alternately the praises of God."—*Bishop Horne.*

Verse 3. There is *no speech nor language* where *their voice is not heard.*] Leave out the expletives here, which pervert the sense; and what remains is a tolerable translation of the original:—

אין אמר ואין דברים בלי נשמע קולם:

Ein omer veein debarim, beli nishma kolam.

"No speech, and no words; their voice without hearing."

בכל הארץ יצא קום ובקצה תבל מליהם

Bechol haarets yatsa kavvam: Ubiktsey thebel milleyhem.

"Into all the earth hath gone out their sound; and to the extremity of the habitable world, their eloquence."

The word קו *kav,* which we translate *line,* is rendered *sonus, by the Vulgate, and* φθογγος, sound, *by the Septuagint;* and St. Paul, Rom. x. 18, uses the same term. Perhaps the idea here is taken from a *stretched cord,* that emits a *sound* on being struck; and hence both ideas may be included in the same word; and קום *kavvam* may be either *their line,* or *cord,* or *their sound.* But I rather think that the Hebrew word originally meant *sound* or *noise;* for in Arabic the verb قَبَا *kavaha* signifies *he called out, cried, clamavit.* The sense of the whole is this, as Bishop *Horne* has well expressed it:—

"Although the heavens are thus appointed to teach, yet it is not by *articulate sounds* that they do it. They are not endowed, like man, with the faculty of speech; but they address themselves to the mind of the intelligent beholder in another way, and that, when understood, a no less forcible way, the way of picture or representation. The instruction which the heavens spread abroad is as universal as their substance, which extends itself in lines, or *rays.* By this means their words, or rather their *significant actions* or operations, מליהם, are everywhere present; and thereby they preach to all the nations the power and wisdom, the mercy and lovingkindness, of the Lord."

St. Paul applies this as a prophecy relative to the universal spread of the Gospel of Christ, Rom. x. 18; for God designed that the light of the Gospel should be diffused wheresoever the light of the celestial luminaries shone; and be as useful and beneficent, in a *moral* point of view, as that is in a *natural.* All the inhabitants of the earth shall benefit by the Gospel of Christ, as they all benefit by the *solar, lunar,* and *stellar light.* And, indeed, all have thus benefited, even where the *words* are not yet come. "Jesus is the true Light that lighteth every man that cometh into the world." His *light,* and the *voice* of his *Spirit,* have already gone through the earth; and his *words,* and the *words of his apostles,* are by means of the *Bible* and *missionaries* going out to all the extremities of the habitable globe.

On these words I shall conclude with the translation of my old *Psalter:*—

Verse 1. 𝔥ebens telles the joy of 𝔊od; and the werkes of his handes schewis the firmament.

Verse 2. Day til day riftes word; and nyght til nyght schewes conyng.

Verse 3. Na speches er, ne na wordes, of the qwilk the voyces of thaim be noght herd.

earth, and their words to the end of the world. In them hath he set a tabernacle for the sun,

5 Which *is* as a bridegroom coming out of his chamber, ᶠ*and* rejoiceth as a strong man to run a race.

6 His going forth *is* from the end of the heaven, and his circuit unto the ends of it: and there is nothing hid from the heat thereof.

7 ᵍThe ʰlaw of the Lord *is* perfect, ⁱconverting the soul: the testimony of the Lord *is* sure, making wise the simple.

ᶠEccles. i. 5——ᵍPsa. cxi. 7

ʰOr, *doctrine*——ⁱOr, *restoring*

Verse 4. Jn al the land yede the soune of tham; and in endes of the wereld thair wordes.

Verse 5. Jn the Soun he sett his tabernacle; and he as a spouse comand forth of his chaumber: he joyed als geaunt at ryn the way.

Verse 6. Fra heest heben the gangyng of hym: and his gayne rase til the heest of hym: nane es that hym may hyde fra his hete.

All the *versions*, except the *Chaldee*, render the last clause of the *fourth* verse thus: "In the sun he hath placed his tabernacle;" as the old *Psalter* likewise does. They supposed that if the Supreme Being had a *local* dwelling, this must be it; as it was to all human appearances the fittest place. But the Hebrew is, "Among them hath he set a tabernacle for the sun." He is the *centre* of the *universe;* all the other heavenly bodies appear to serve him. He is like a *general* in his pavilion, surrounded by his troops, to whom he gives his orders, and by whom he is obeyed. So, the solar influence gives motion, activity, light, and heat to all the planets. To none of the other heavenly bodies does the psalmist assign a *tabernacle*, none is said to have a *fixed dwelling*, but the sun.

Verse 5. *Which is as a bridegroom, &c.*] This is a reference to the *rising of the sun*, as the following verse is to the *setting*. He makes his appearance above the horizon with splendour and majesty; every creature seems to rejoice at his approach; and during the whole of his course, through his whole circuit, his apparent revolution from east to west, and from one tropic to the same again, no part of the earth is deprived of its proper proportion of light and heat. The sun is compared to a *bridegroom* in his *ornaments*, because of the *glory* and *splendour* of his *rays;* and to a *giant* or *strong man* running a race, because of the *power* of his *light* and *heat*. The apparent motion of the sun, in his *diurnal* and *annual* progress, are here both referred to. Yet both of these have been demonstrated to be *mere* appearances. The sun's *diurnal* motion arises from the earth's rotation on its axis from west to east in *twenty-three hours, fifty-six minutes*, and *four seconds*, the *mean* or *equal* time which elapses between the two consecutive meridian-transits of the same fixed star. But on account of the sun's apparent ecliptic motion in the *same* direction, the earth must make about the *three hundred and sixty-fifth* part of a *second* revolution on its axis before any given point of the earth's surface can be *again* brought into the same direction with the sun as before: so that the length of a natural day is *twenty-four hours* at a mean rate. The apparent revolution of the sun through the *twelve* constellations of the zodiac in a *sidereal* year, is caused by the earth's making one *complete* revolution in its orbit in the same time. And as the earth's axis makes an angle with the axis of the ecliptic of about *twenty-three degrees* and *twenty-*

eight minutes, and always maintains its parallelism, i. e., is always directed to the same point of the starry firmament; from these circumstances are produced the regular *change* of the seasons, and continually differing *lengths* of the days and nights in all parts of the terraqueous globe, except at the *poles* and on the *equator*. When we say that the earth's axis is always directed to the *same* point of the heavens, we mean to be understood only in a *general* sense; for, owing to a *very slow* deviation of the terrestrial axis from its *parallelism*, named the *precession of the equinoctial points*, which becomes sensible in the lapse of some years, and which did not escape the observation of the ancient astronomers, who clearly perceived that it was occasioned by a slow revolution of the celestial poles around the poles of the ecliptic, the complete revolution of the earth in its orbit is *longer* than the *natural* year, or the earth's *tropical* revolution, by a little more than *twenty* minutes; so that in *twenty-five thousand seven hundred and sixty-three* entire terrestrial revolutions round the sun, the seasons will be renewed *twenty-five thousand seven hundred and sixty-four* times. And in *half* this period of *twelve thousand eight hundred and eighty-two* natural years, the points which are *now* the north and south poles of the heavens, around which the whole starry firmament appears to revolve, will describe circles about the *then* north and south poles of the heavens, the semi-diameters of which will be upwards of *forty-seven* degrees.

Coming out of his chamber] מחפתו *mechuppatho*, from under his veil. It was a sort of canopy erected on four poles, which four Jews held over the bridegroom's head.

Verse 7. *The law of the Lord*] And here are *two books* of Divine Revelation: 1. The *visible* heavens, and the *works of creation* in general. 2. The Bible, or Divinely inspired writings contained in the *Old* and *New Testaments*. These may all be called the law of the *Lord;* תורה *torah*, from ירה *yarah*, to *instruct, direct,* put *straight, guide*. It is God's system of *instruction*, by which men are *taught* the knowledge of God and themselves, *directed* how to walk so as to please God, redeemed from *crooked* paths, and *guided* in the way everlasting. Some think that תורה *torah* means the *preceptive* part of Revelation. Some of the primitive fathers have mentioned *three* laws given by God to man: 1. The *law of nature*, which teaches the knowledge of God, as to his eternal power and Deity, by the visible creation. 2. The *law* given to *Moses* and the *prophets*, which teaches more perfectly the knowledge of God, his *nature*, his *will* and our *duty*. 3. The *law of grace* given by Christ Jesus, which shows the doctrine of the *atonement*, of *purification*, and of the *resurrection* of the body. The *first* is written in *hieroglyphics* in the heavens and the earth.

8 The statutes of the LORD *are* right, rejoicing the heart: ᵏthe commandment of the LORD *is* pure, ˡenlightening the eyes.

9 The fear of the LORD *is* clean, enduring for ever: the judgments of the LORD *are* ᵐtrue *and* righteous altogether.

10 More to be desired *are they* than gold, ⁿyea, than much fine gold: °sweeter also than honey, and ᵖthe honey-comb.

11 Moreover, by them is thy servant warned: and qin keeping of them *there is* great reward.

ᵏPsa. xii. 6——ˡPsa. xiii. 3——ᵐHeb. *truth*——ⁿPsa. cxix. 72, 127; Prov. viii. 10, 11, 19

°Psa. cxix. 103——ᵖHeb. *the dropping of honey-combs*——qProv. xxix. 18

The *second* was written on *tables* of *stone*, and in many *rites* and *ceremonies*. The *third* is to be written on the *heart* by the *power* of the *Holy Ghost*.

Is perfect] תמימה *temimah*, it is perfection. it is perfect in itself as a law, and requires *perfection* in the *hearts* and *lives* of men. This is ITS *character*.

Converting the soul] Turning it back to God. Restoring it to right reason, or to a sound mind; teaching it its own interest in reference to both worlds. This is ITS *use*.

The testimony of the Lord] עדות *eduth*, from עד *ad*, beyond, forward. The various types and appointments of the law, which *refer* to something *beyond* themselves, and *point forward* to the Lamb of God who takes away the sin of the world. Some understand, the *doctrinal* parts of the law.

Is sure] נאמנה *neemanah*, are *faithful;* they point out the things *beyond* them *fairly*, *truly*, and *fully*, and make no vain or *false* report. They all bear testimony to the great atonement. This is THEIR *character*.

Making wise the simple.] The simple is he who has but *one end* in view: who is concerned about his soul, and earnestly inquires, "What shall I do to be saved?" These testimonies point to the atonement, and thus the *simple-hearted* is made wise unto salvation. This is THEIR *use*.

Verse 8. *The statutes of the Lord*] פקודים *pikkudim*, from פקד *pakad*, he visited, cared, took notice of, appointed to a charge. The *appointments*, or *charge delivered* by God to man for his regard and observance.

Are right] ישרים *yesharim*, from ישר *yashar*, to make *straight*, *smooth*, *right*, *upright*, opposed to *crookedness* in mind or conduct; showing what the man should be, both *within* and *without*. This is THEIR *character*.

Rejoicing the heart] As they show a man what he is to observe and keep in charge, and how he is to please God, and the Divine help he is to receive from the *visitations* of God, they contribute greatly to the *happiness* of the upright—they *rejoice the heart*. This is THEIR *use*.

The commandment] מצוה *mitsvah*, from צוה *tsavah*, to command, give orders, ordain. What God has *ordered* man to do, or not to do. What he has *commanded*, and what he has *prohibited*.

Is pure] From ברה *barah*, to clear, *cleanse*, *purify*. All God's commandments lead to *purity*, enjoin purity, and *point out* that *sacrificial offering* by which *cleansing* and *purification* are acquired. This is ITS *character*.

Enlightening the eyes.] Showing men what they should *do*, and what they should *avoid*. It is by God's commandments that we *see* the exceeding *sinfulness of sin*, and the *necessity*

of redemption, so that we may love the Lord with all our heart, and our neighbour as ourselves. For this is the end of the commandment, and thus to *enlighten the eyes* is ITS *use*.

Verse 9. The fear of the Lord] יראה *yirah*, from ירא *yara*, to *fear*, to *venerate;* often put for the whole of Divine worship. The reverence we owe to the Supreme Being.

Is clean] טהורה *tehorah*, from טהר *tahar*, to be *pure, clean;* not differing much from ברה *barah*, (see above,) to be *clean* and *bright* as the *heavens;* as purified SILVER. Its object is to purge away all *defilement*, to make a *spotless character*.

Enduring for ever] עומדת לעד *omedeth laad*, standing up to PERPETUITY. The *fear* that prevents us from offending God, that causes us to *reverence* him, and is the *beginning* as it is the safeguard of *wisdom*, must be carried all through life. No soul can be safe for a moment without it. It prevents departure from God, and keeps that clean which God has purified. This is ITS *use*.

The judgments of the Lord] משפטים *mishpatim*, from שפט *shaphat*, he *judged, regulated, disposed*, All God's *regulations*, all his *decisions;* what he has *pronounced* to be *right* and proper.

Are true] אמת *emeth*, *truth*, from אם *am*, to support, confirm, make stable, and certain. This is the *character* of God's *judgments*. They shall all *stand*. All dispensations in providence and grace *confirm* them; they are *certain*, and have a *fixed character*.

And righteous altogether.] They are not only according to *truth;* but they are *righteous*, צדקו *tsadeku*, they give to *all their due*. They show what belongs to *God*, to *man*, and to *ourselves*. And hence the word *altogether*, יחדו *yachdav*, *equally*, is added; or *truth and righteousness united*.

Verse 10. *More to be desired are they than gold*] This is strictly true; but who believes it? By most men *gold* is preferred both to *God* and his *judgments;* and they will barter every heavenly portion for gold and silver!

Sweeter also than honey] To those whose mental taste is rectified, who have a spiritual discernment.

Honey-comb.] Honey is *sweet;* but honey just out of the *comb* has a sweetness, richness, and flavour, far beyond what it has after it becomes exposed to the *air*. Only those who have eaten of honey from the comb can feel the force of the psalmist's comparison: *it is better than gold*, yea, than *fine gold* in the greatest quantity; it is *sweeter* than *honey*, yea, than *honey* from the *comb*.

Verse 11. *By them is thy servant warned*] נזהר *nizhar*, from זהר *zahar*, to be *clear*, pellucid. By these laws, testimonies, &c., thy ser-

12 ʳWho can understand *his* errors? ˢcleanse thou me from ᵗsecret *faults*.

13 ᵘKeep back thy servant also from presumptuous *sins:* ᵛlet them not have dominion over me: then shall I be upright,

and I shall be innocent from ʷthe great transgression.

14 ˣLet the words of my mouth, and the meditation of my heart, be acceptable in thy sight, O LORD, ʸmy strength, and my ᶻredeemer.

ʳPsalm xl. 12——ˢLev. iv. 2, &c.- —ᵗPsa. xc. 8——ᵘGen. xx. 6; 1 Sam. xxv. 32, 33, 34, 39——ᵛPsa. cxix. 133; Rom. vi. 12, 14

ʷOr, *much*——ˣPsa. li. 15——ʸHeb. *my rock;* Psa. xviii. 1——ᶻIsa. xliii. 14; xliv. 6; xlvii. 4; 1 Thess. i. 10

---

vant is *fully instructed; he sees all clearly;* and he *discerns* that in *keeping of them there is great reward:* every man is wise, holy, and happy, who observes them. All Christian experience confirms this truth. Reader, what says *thine?*

Verse 12. *Who can understand his errors?*] It is not possible, without much of the Divine light, to understand all our *deviations* from, not only the *letter,* but the *spirituality,* of the Divine law. Frequent self-examination, and walking in the light, are essentially necessary to the requisite degree of spiritual perfection.

Cleanse thou me from secret faults.] From those which I have committed, and have forgotten; from those for which I have not repented; from those which have been committed in my heart, but have not been brought to act in my life; from those which I have committed without knowing that they were sins, sins of *ignorance;* and from those which I have committed in private, for which I should blush and be confounded were they to be made public.

Verse 13. *From presumptuous* sins] Sins committed not through *frailty* or *surprise,* but those which are the offspring of *thought, purpose,* and *deliberation.* Sins against judgment, light, and conscience. The words might be translated, *Preserve thy servant also from the proud;* from tyrannical governors, i. e., from evil spirits.—Bishop *Horsley.* So most of the *versions* understand the place.

Let them not have dominion over me] Let me never be brought into a *habit* of sinning. He who sins *presumptuously* will soon be *hardened* through the deceitfulness of sin.

Then shall I be upright] Let me be preserved from all the evil that the craft and malice of the devil or man work against me, then shall I continue to walk *uprightly,* and shall be *innocent from the great transgression*—from habitual sinning, from *apostasy,* from my *easily-besetting sin.* He who would be innocent from the great transgression, must take care that he indulge not himself in any. See Bishop *Horne.* Most men have committed some particular sin which they ought to deplore as long as they breathe, and on account of the enormity of which they should for ever be humbled.

Verse 14. *Let the words of my mouth*] He has prayed against practical sin, the sins of the *body;* now, against the *sins* of the *mouth* and of the *heart.* Let my *mouth* speak nothing but what is *true, kind,* and *profitable;* and my *heart* meditate nothing but what is *holy, pure,* and *chaste.*

Acceptable in thy sight] Like a *sacrifice* without spot or blemish, offered up with a perfect heart to God.

O Lord, my strength] צוּרִי *tsuri,* "my fountain, my origin."

My redeemer.] גֹּאֲלִי *goali,* my *kinsman,* he

VOL. III

whose right it is to redeem the forfeited inheritance; for so was the word used under the old law. This prayer is properly concluded! he was *weak,* he felt the need of God's *strength.* He had *sinned* and *lost all title to the heavenly inheritance,* and therefore needed the interference of the *Divine kinsman;* of HIM who, because the children were partakers of flesh and blood, also partook of the same. No prayer can be *acceptable* before God which is not offered up in his *strength;* through HIM who took our nature upon him, that he might redeem us unto God, and restore the long-lost inheritance. 𝕷𝖔𝖗𝖉 𝖒𝖞 𝖍𝖊𝖑𝖕𝖆𝖗 𝖆𝖓𝖉 𝖒𝖞 𝖇𝖞𝖊𝖗.—Old *Psalter.* He who is my only *help,* and he that *bought* me with his blood. This prayer is often, with great propriety, uttered by pious people when they enter a place of worship.

ANALYSIS OF THE NINETEENTH PSALM

I. There are TWO parts in this Psalm. The *first* is *doctrinal;* the second, *penitential.* The doctrinal part has two members:—

1. The first teaches us to know God by *natural reason,* from the *book of creation,* from ver. 1 to ver. 7.

2. But because this way is insufficient to save a soul, therefore in the *second* part we have a better way prescribed, which is the *book of the Scriptures;* the excellences of which are described from ver. 7 to ver. 11.

II. The *penitential* part begins at the *twelfth* verse, for since the reward to be expected proceeds from the keeping of God's law, and David's heart told him he had not kept it, therefore, he begs *pardon* and *grace,* ver. 12 to ver. 14.

I. "The heavens declare," &c. By the *glory of God* we are to understand his goodness, wisdom, power; in a word, all his attributes, of which we have a double declaration:—

1. A testimony from the *creatures,* but especially the *heavens,* whose magnitude, beauty, order, variety, perpetual motion, light, influences, &c., declare that there is an omnipotent, wise, good, and gracious God, who is their Creator; with this David begins: "The heavens declare the glory of God, and the firmament showeth forth," &c.

2. The vicissitude of day and night, proceeding from their motions, declares this also: "Day unto day uttereth speech," &c. 1. The heavens are *diligent* preachers; for they *preach all day* and *all night,* without intermission. 2. They are *learned* preachers, for they preach in all tongues: "There is no speech—where their voice is not heard." 3. They are *universal preachers,* for they preach to the whole world: "Their sound is gone through all the earth," &c.

3. But among all these creatures the SUN, for which God in heaven has set a *throne,*

makes the fairest and clearest evidence, and that in the three following ways:—

1. By his *splendour*, light, and beauty; he riseth as gloriously as a bridegroom coming from under his canopy.

2. By his *wonderful celerity*, not only in revolving round his own axis, which revolution, although he is *one million three hundred and eighty-four thousand four hundred and sixty-two* times bigger than the earth, he performs in *twenty-five* days *fourteen* hours of our time, but also in the *swiftness* with which his light comes to the earth. It travels at the rate of *one hundred and ninety-four thousand one hundred and eighty-eight* miles in a *second* of time; and reaches our earth in *eight minutes* and about *twelve seconds*, a distance of *ninety-five millions five hundred and thirteen thousand seven hundred and ninety-four* English miles, at a mean rate.

3. His strange and miraculous *heat*, from which nothing is *hidden*, and by which every thing is *benefited*.

II. But as the declaration, even from the most glorious of creatures, is not sufficient to make men wise and happy, he has been pleased to declare himself by his WRITTEN WORD, called here the LAW generally; and is commended to us by the following reasons:—

1. From the *author:* It is the "law of Jehovah."

2. From its *sufficiency:* It is "perfect."

3. From its *utility:* "It converts the soul:— gives wisdom to the simple."

4. From its *infallibility:* "The testimony of the Lord is sure."

5. From its *perspicuity:* "The statutes of the Lord are right."

6. From the *effects* it works on the *soul:* "They rejoice the heart." They quiet the troubled conscience; "being justified by faith, we have peace with God."

7. From its *purity:* "The commandment of the Lord is pure." It is opposed to all *bad opinions* and *evil practices.*

8. From its *effects in the understanding:* "It enlightens the eyes." It dispels all darkness and ignorance, all doubts and fears, diffidence, carnal security, false worship, &c., and gives us to see our own *deformities.*

9. From its *uncorruptness:* "The fear of the Lord is clean." Other religions are *polluted* with human inventions, strange ceremonies, uncommanded sacrifices, false gods, &c.

10. From its *perpetuity:* "It endureth for ever." It is an endless law, and an everlasting Gospel.

11. From its *truth and equity:* "It is altogether true and righteous."

From all which David concludes, that it is both *precious* and *delightful.*

1. The *price* of it is beyond the best gold: "More to be desired than gold; yea, than much fine gold."

2. It is *delightful:* "Sweeter than honey and the honey-comb."

3. This he knew by his own *experience:* "Moreover, by them is thy servant illuminated."

4. It is *profitable* to observe them: "For in keeping of them there is, 1. A *reward.* 2. A *great reward.*"

III. But this last consideration sent David to the throne of mercy. What! a reward, a great reward! and only to those who *keep God's law?* My conscience tells me that the reward is not for *me; I* cannot plead this *observance.* David had public sins, secret faults and errors, to deplore. But he had at hand *three* means of help: 1. *Confession of sin.* 2. *Petition* for *grace.* 3. *Faith* in the Divine *mercy,* through the great *Redeemer.*

1. He knew he was an *offender,* but he *knew not how greatly* he had *offended.* He saw that he was *guilty,* and asked *pardon.* He felt that he was *impure,* and asked *cleansing:* "Who can understand his errors? cleanse thou me from my secret faults."

2. He prays that he may be preserved from *presumptuous sins;* that he might not be hardened in transgression: "Keep back also thy servant from presumptuous sins." For which he gives *two* reasons: 1. If he were not *kept back* from them, sin would get the *dominion* over him. Sin would become a king, who would command, rule, and enslave him. 2. If thus kept back, he would be *innocent from the great transgression;* for he that gets under the strong habit of sin may at last deny God himself, renounce the blood of the covenant, and become a castaway.

3. Lastly, that his prayer may be heard, he prays for his prayer: "Let the words of my mouth and the meditation of my heart be acceptable in thy sight." This is *pleading,* or *supplication.*

That prayer and supplication may be successful he acts *faith* in God, whom he,

1. Claims as his *strength;* literally, his *rock,* by whom alone he could resist and overcome.

2. His *redeemer,* through whom alone he could get pardon for the past, and grace to help him in time of need. To this word he adds nothing, as it includes every thing necessary to saint and sinner. See the *notes.*

PSALM XX

A prayer for the king in his enterprises, that his prayers may be heard, his offerings accepted, and his wishes fulfilled, 1–4. Confidence of victory expressed, 5, 6. Vain hopes exposed; and supplication made for the king.

A. M. cir. 2968
B. C. cir. 1036
Davidis, Regis
Israelitarum,
cir. annum
20

To the chief Musician, A Psalm of David

THE LORD hear thee in the day of trouble; [a]the name of the God of Jacob [b]defend thee.

2 Send [c]thee help from [d]the sanctuary, and [e]strengthen thee out of Zion.

3 Remember all thy offerings, and [f]accept thy [g]burnt sacrifice. Selah.

4 [h]Grant thee according to thine own heart, and fulfil all thy counsel.

A. M. cir. 2968
B. C. cir. 1036
Davidis, Regis
Israelitarum,
cir. annum
20

5 We will [i]rejoice in thy salvation, and [k]in the name of our God we will set up *our* banners: the LORD fulfil all thy petitions.

6 Now know I that the LORD saveth [l]his anointed; he will hear him [m]from his holy heaven [n]with the saving strength of his right hand.

---

[a]Prov. xviii. 10——[b]Heb. *set thee on a high place*
[c]Heb. *thy help*——[d]1 Kings vi. 16; 2 Chron. xx. 8; Psa.
lxxiii. 17——[e]Heb. *support thee*——[f]Heb. *turn to ashes*;
or, *make fat*——[g]Exod. xxx. 9; Lev. i. 9; Num. xxiii. 6;
Deut. xxxiii. 10; 2 Sam. xxiv. 22——[h]Psa. xxi. 2
[i]Psa. xix. 4——[k]Exod. xvii. 15; Psa. lx. 4——[l]Psa. ii. 2
[m]Heb. *from the heaven of his holiness*——[n]Heb. *by the strength of the salvation of his right hand*

NOTES ON PSALM XX

It is most likely that this Psalm was penned on the occasion of David's going to war; and most probably with the Ammonites and Syrians, who came with great numbers of *horses* and *chariots* to fight with him. See 2 Sam. x. 6-8; 1 Chron. xix. 7. It is one of the *Dialogue Psalms*, and appears to be thus divided: Previously to his undertaking the war, David comes to the tabernacle to offer sacrifice. This being done, the *people*, in the king's behalf, offer up their prayers; these are included in the *three* first verses: the fourth was probably spoken by the *high priest;* the *fifth*, by *David* and his *attendants;* the last clause, by the high priest; the *sixth*, by the *high priest*, after the victim was consumed; the *seventh* and *eighth*, by *David* and his *men;* and the *ninth*, as a *chorus* by all the *congregation*.

Verse 1. *The Lord hear thee*] David had already offered the *sacrifice* and *prayed*. The *people* implore God to succour him in the day of trouble; of both *personal* and *national* danger.

The name of the God of Jacob] This refers to Jacob's wrestling with the Angel; Gen. xxxii. 24, &c. And who was this Angel? Evidently none other than the *Angel of the Covenant*, the Lord Jesus, in whom was the *name of God*, the *fulness of the Godhead bodily*. He was the *God of Jacob*, who *blessed* Jacob, and gave him a *new name* and a *new nature*. See the *notes* on the above place in Genesis.

Verse 2. *Send thee help from the sanctuary*] This was the *place* where God recorded his name; the place where he was to be sought, and the place where he manifested himself. He dwelt between the *cherubim* over the *mercy-seat*. He is now in Christ, reconciling the world to himself. This is the true sanctuary where God must be sought.

Strengthen thee out of Zion] The *temple* or *tabernacle* where his prayers and sacrifices were to be offered.

Verse 3. *Remember all thy offerings*] The *minchah*, which is here mentioned, was a *gratitude-offering*. It is rarely used to signify a bloody sacrifice.

Burnt sacrifice] The *olah* here mentioned was a *bloody sacrifice*. The blood of the victim was spilt at the altar, and the flesh consumed. One of these offerings implied a *consciousness* of *sin* in the offerer; and this sacrifice he

brought as an *atonement:* the other implied a sense of *mercies* already *received*, and was offered in the way of *gratitude*.

David presents himself before the Lord with offerings of both kinds.

This prayer of the *people* is concluded with *Selah*, which we have taken up in the general sense of *so be it. Hear and answer. It will and must be so*, &c.

Verse 4. *Grant thee according to thine own heart*] May God give thee whatsoever thou art setting thy heart upon, and accomplish all *thy desires!* This was probably the prayer of the *high priest*.

Verse 5. *We will rejoice in thy salvation*] We expect help from thee alone; it is in thy cause we engage; and to *thee*, as our war is a just one, we consecrate our banners, inscribed with thy name. It is said that the *Maccabees* had their name from the inscription on their banners; which was taken from Exod. xv. 11,

מי כמכה באלם יהוה *mi camochah baelim Yehovah*, "Who is like unto thee, O Lord, among the gods?" The word being formed from the *initial* letters מ M, כ C, ב B, י I, מכבי *Ma Ca B I*, whence *Maccabeus* and *Maccabees*.

The words of this verse were spoken by David and his officers; immediately after which I suppose the high priest to have added, *The Lord fulfil all thy petitions!*

Verse 6. *Now know I that the Lord saveth his anointed*] These are probably the words of the *priest* after the victim had been consumed; and those *signs* had accompanied the offering, which were proofs of God's *acceptance* of the sacrifice; and, consequently, that the campaign would have a successful issue. David is God's *anointed;* therefore, he is under his especial care. *He will hear him.* David must continue to *pray*, and to *depend* on God; else he cannot expect continual salvation. David has vast multitudes of enemies against him; he, therefore, requires supernatural help. Because of this, *God will hear him with the saving strength of his right hand.*

The HAND of God is his *power;* the RIGHT hand, his *almighty power;* the STRENGTH *of his right hand*, his almighty power in *action;* the SAVING strength *of his right hand*, the miraculous *effects* wrought by his almighty power brought into *action*. This is what David was to expect; and it was the prospect of this that caused him and his officers to exult as they do in the following verse.

A. M. cir. 2968
B. C. cir. 1036
Davidis, Regis
Israelitarum,
cir. annum
20

7 °Some *trust* in chariots, and some in horses: Pbut we will remember the name of the LORD our God.

8 They are brought down and fallen: but

we are risen, and stand upright.

9 Save, LORD: let the king hear us when we call.

A. M. cir. 2968
B. C. cir. 1036
Davidis, Regis
Israelitarum,
cir. annum
20

°Psa. xxxiii. 16, 17; Prov. xxi. 31; Isa. xxxi. 1

P2 Chron. xxxii. 8

Verse 7. *Some* trust *in chariots*] The words of the original are short and emphatic: *These in chariots; and these in horses; but we will record in the name of Jehovah our God.* Or, as the *Septuagint*, μεγαλυνθησομεθα, "we shall be magnified." Or, as the *Vulgate*, *invocabimus*, "we shall invoke the name of the Lord." This and the following verse I suppose to be the words of David and his officers. And the mention of *chariots* and *horses* makes it likely that the war with the *Ammonites* and *Syrians* is that to which reference is made here; for they came against him with vast multitudes of *horsemen* and *chariots*. See 2 Sam. x. 6-8. According to the law, David could neither have chariots nor horses; and those who came against him with cavalry must have a very great advantage; but he saw that Jehovah his God was more than a match for all his foes, and in him he trusts with implicit confidence.

Verse 8. *They are brought down and fallen*] They were so confident of victory that they looked upon it as *already gained.* They who trusted in their *horses* and *chariots* are *bowed down*, and prostrated on the earth: they are all overthrown.

But we are risen] We who have trusted in the *name of Jehovah* are *raised up* from all despondency; and we *stand upright*—we shall conquer, and go on to conquer.

Verse 9. *Save, Lord*] This verse was spoken by all the *congregation*, and was the *chorus* and *conclusion* of the piece.

The verse may be read, *Lord, save the king! He will hear us in the day of our calling.* The *Vulgate, Septuagint, Æthiopic, Arabic, Anglo-Saxon*, read the verse thus: *Lord, save the king! and hear us whensoever we shall call upon thee.* The *Syriac* reads differently: *The Lord will save us: and our king will hear us in the day in which we shall call upon him.* This refers all to GOD; while the others refer the latter clause *to* DAVID. *Lord, save David; and David will save us.* "If thou preservest *him*, he will be thy minister for good to *us*." This appears to be the easiest sense of the place, and harmonizes with all the rest.

ANALYSIS OF THE TWENTIETH PSALM

This Psalm is a form of prayer delivered by David to the people, to be used by them for the king, when he went out to battle against his enemies.

In this Psalm there are the following parts:—

I. A benediction of the people for their king, ver. 1-4.

II. A congratulation or triumph of the people after the victory, supposed to be already obtained, ver. 5-8.

III. A petition, ver. 9.

I. The benediction directed to David's person. The particulars; that he may have,

1. *Audience* in his necessity: "The Lord hear thee in the day of trouble."

2. *Protection:* "The name of the God of Jacob defend thee," ver. 1.

3. *Help* and *strength* in battle: "Send thee help—strengthen thee;" which is amplified, 1. By the *place:* "Help from the sanctuary;" 2. "Strength out of Zion."

4. *Acceptance* of his *person;* testified by the acceptance of his offerings and sacrifices, ver. 3.

5. *Answers* to his *petitions:* "Grant thee according to thy own heart, and fulfil all thy counsel," ver. 4; which is plainly set down in the next verse: "The Lord fulfil all thy petitions," ver. 5.

This benediction being ended, they persuade themselves that the prayer of it shall be granted, because it will redound to God's glory; and they will be thankful, and honour him for the victory.

1. "We will rejoice in thy salvation." Or, Do this, "that we may rejoice."

2. "In the name of our God will we set up our banners." We will enter the city joyfully, with displayed banners, which we will erect as trophies to the honour of God.

II. Now follow the congratulation and triumph of their faith: for they give thanks as for a victory already obtained; as to their faith it was certain. *Before* they prayed for *audience* and *protection: here* they testify they are certain and secure of both.

1. Of *protection:* "Now know I that the Lord will save," &c.

2. Of *audience:* "He will hear from his holy heaven."

3. Of *help:* "With the saving strength of his right hand," ver. 6.

The certainty they had of this victory proceeded solely from their confidence in God. And this they illustrate by an argument drawn *a dissimili:* they were *not like* others who trust more to their *arms* than to their *prayers;* more to their *numbers* than to *God.*

1. "Some trust in chariots, and some in horses;" as the Ammonites, 2 Sam. x. 6.

2. But we do not so: "We will remember the name of the Lord our God; the Lord of hosts, mighty in battle." Arms may be used by good or bad men; but the difference lies in the *object*, the *end*, and the *confidence.* A bad cause cannot have God's concurrence: a good cause will have his countenance and support.

3. And therefore the *success* was according to the confidence. 1. They who trusted in their arms, &c., *are brought down, and fallen.* 2. We who trusted in the Lord our God, are *risen, and stand upright*, ver. 8.

III. The third part contains a short ejaculation, and is the sum of the Psalm.

1. "Save, Lord!" *Thou* alone canst save us: in *thee*, and in none other, do we put our trust.

2. "Let the king hear us." We propose to continue in prayer and faith; therefore, when we call, *let the king*, the *Messiah*, which *thou hast set on thy holy hill.* Psa. ii. 6, hear us.

Or, according to another arrangement of the words: 1. *Lord, save our king.* Make him wise and good, preserve his person, and prosper his government; that we may have peace in our time, and secular prosperity. 2. Hear thou us when we call. Let us have also spiritual prosperity, that we may perfectly love thee, and worthily magnify thy name.—Ᵹala ðu ðriht, ᵹehalne ðo cyninᵹe. "O thou Lord, health give the king."—*Anglo-Saxon.*

PSALM XXI

The psalmist returns thanks to God for giving him the victory over his enemies; which victory he had earnestly requested, 1, 2. He enters into a detail of the blessings that in consequence of the victory he had obtained, 3–7. He predicts the destruction of all those who may hereafter rise up against him, 8–12; and concludes with praising the power of Jehovah, 13.

To the chief Musician. A Psalm of David

A. M. cir. 2968
B. C. cir. 1036
Davidis, Regis
Israelitarum,
cir. annum
20

THE king shall joy in thy strength, O LORD; and ᵃin thy salvation how greatly shall he rejoice!

2 ᵇThou hast given him his heart's desire, and hast not withholden the request of his lips. Selah.

3 For thou preventest him with the blessings of goodness: thou ᶜsettest a crown of pure gold on his head.

A. M. cir. 2968
B. C. cir. 1036
Davidis, Regis
Israelitarum,
cir. annum
20

4 ᵈHe asked life of thee, *and* thou gavest *it* him, ᵉ*even* length of days for ever and ever.

5 His glory *is* great in thy salvation: honour and majesty hast thou laid upon him.

ᵃPsa. xx. 5, 6——ᵇPsa. xx. 4, 5——ᶜ2 Sam. xii. 30; 1 Chron. xx. 2

ᵈPsalm lxi. 5, 6——ᵉ2 Samuel vii. 19; Psa. xci. 16

NOTES ON PSALM XXI

In the *title* of this Psalm there is nothing particularly worthy of remark. The *occasion* of it is variously understood. Some think it was composed to celebrate the victory obtained over *Sennacherib;* others, that it was made on the recovery of *Hezekiah*, and the grant of *fifteen* years of longer life; see ver. 4. Others, and they with most appearance of propriety, consider it a song of rejoicing composed by David for his victory over the *Ammonites*, which ended in the capture of the royal city of *Rabbah*, the crown of whose king David put on his own head, see ver. 3, and to procure which victory David offered the prayers and sacrifices mentioned in the preceding Psalm. Lastly, many think that it is to be wholly referred to the *victories of the Messiah;* and it must be owned that there are several expressions in it which apply better to our Lord than to David, or to any other person; and to him the *Targum* applies it, as does likewise my old *Anglo-Scottish Psalter* in paraphrasing the text.

Verse 1. *The king shall joy*] מלך משיחא *melech Meshicha,* "the King Messiah."—*Targum.* What a difference between ancient and modern heroes! The former acknowledged all to be of God, because they took care to have their quarrel *rightly founded;* the latter sing a *Te Deum,* pro forma, because they well know that their battle is *not* of the Lord. Their own vicious conduct sufficiently proves that they looked no higher than the arm of human strength. God suffers such for a time, but in the end he confounds and brings them to naught.

Verse 2. *Thou hast given him his heart's desire*] This seems to refer to the prayers offered in the preceding Psalm; see especially verses 1–4.

Verse 3. *Thou preventest him*] To *prevent,* from *prævenio,* literally signifies *to go before.* Hence that prayer in the *communion service* of our public Liturgy, "Prevent us, O Lord, in all our doings, with thy most gracious favour!" That is, "*Go before us* in thy mercy, make our way plain, and enable us to perform what is right in thy sight!" And this sense of *prevent* is a literal version of the original word תקדמנו *tekademennu.* "For thou shalt go before him with the blessings of goodness."

Our ancestors used *God before* in this sense. So in Henry V.'s speech to the French herald previously to the battle of *Agincourt:*—

"Go therefore; tell thy master, here I am.
My ransom is this frail and worthless trunk;
My army, but a weak and sickly guard:
Yet, *God before,* tell him we will come on,
Though France himself, and such another neighbour,
Stand in our way."

A crown of pure gold] Probably alluding to the crown of the king of Rabbah, which, on the taking of the city, David took and put on his own head. See the history, 2 Sam. xii. 26-30.

Verse 4. *He asked life of thee*] This verse has caused some interpreters to understand the Psalm of *Hezekiah's sickness, recovery,* and the promised *addition to his life* of fifteen *years;* but it may be more literally understood of the *Messiah,* of whom David was the *type,* and in several respects the *representative.*

Verse 5. *His glory is great*] But great as

A. M. cir. 2968
B. C. cir. 1036
Davidis, Regis
Israelitarum,
cir. annum
20

6 For thou hast made [f]him most blessed for ever: [g]thou hast [h]made him exceeding glad with thy countenance.

7 For the king trusteth in the Lord, and through the mercy of the Most High he [i]shall not be moved.

8 Thine hand shall [k]find out all thine enemies: thy right hand shall find out those that hate thee.

9 [l]Thou shalt make them as a fiery oven in the time of thine anger: the Lord shall [m]swallow them up in his wrath, [n]and the fire shall devour them.

10 [o]Their fruit shalt thou destroy from the earth, and their seed from among the children of men.

11 For they intended evil against thee: they [p]imagined a mischievous device, *which* they are not able *to perform*.

12 Therefore [q]shalt thou make them turn their [r]back, *when* thou shalt make ready *thine arrows* upon thy strings against the face of them.

13 Be thou exalted, Lord, in thine own strength: *so* will we sing and praise thy power.

A. M. cir. 2968
B. C. cir. 1036
Davidis, Regis
Israelitarum,
cir. annum
20

---

[f]Heb. *set him* to be *blessings;* Gen. xii. 2; Psa. lxxii. 17 [g]Psa. xvi. 11; xlv. 7; Acts ii. 28——[h]Heb. *gladded him with joy*——[i]Psa. xvi. 8——[k]1 Sam. xxxi. 3——[l]Mal. iv. 1——[m]Psa. lvi. 1, 2

[n]Psa. xviii. 8; Isa. xxvi. 11——[o]1 Kings xiii. 34; Job xviii. 16, 17, 19; Psa. xxxvii. 28; cix. 13; Isa. xiv. 20 [p]Psa. ii. 1——[q]Or, *thou shalt set them* as *a butt;* see Job vii. 20; xvi. 12; Lam. iii. 12——[r]Heb. *shoulder*

---

his glory was, it had its greatness from *God's salvation.* There is no true *nobility* but of the soul, and the soul has none but what it receives from the *grace* and *salvation* of God.

Verse 6. *Thou hast made him most blessed for ever*] Literally, "Thou hast set him for blessings for ever." Thou hast made the Messiah the *Source* whence all blessings for time and for eternity shall be derived. He is the Mediator between God and man.

Thou hast made him exceeding glad] Jesus, as Messiah, *for the joy that was set before him,* of redeeming a lost world by his death, *endured the cross, and despised the shame,* and is for ever set down on the right hand of God.

Verse 7. *The king trusteth in the Lord*] It was not by my *skill* or *valour* that I have gained this victory, but by *faith* in the *strong, protecting, and conquering arm of* Jehovah.

He shall not be moved.] Perhaps this may be best understood of him who was David's *prototype.* His throne, kingdom, and government, shall remain for ever.

Verse 8. *Thine hand shall find out*] Thy uncontrollable *power* shall find out all thine enemies, wheresoever *hidden* or howsoever *secret.* God knows the secret sinner, and where the workers of iniquity hide themselves.

Verse 9. *Thou shalt make them as a fiery oven*] By thy wrath they shall be burnt up, and they shall be the means of consuming others. One class of sinners shall, in God's judgments, be the means of destroying another class; and at last themselves shall be destroyed.

Verse 10. *Their fruit shalt thou destroy*] Even their *posterity* shall be cut off, and thus their *memorial* shall perish.

Verse 11. *For they intended evil*] Sinners shall not be permitted to do all that *is in their power* against the godly; much less shall they be able to perform all that they *wish.*

Verse 12. *Therefore shalt thou make them turn their back*] God can in a moment strike the most powerful and numerous army, even in the moment of victory, with *panic;* and then even the *lame,* the army which they had

nearly routed, shall take the prey, and divide the spoil.

Against the face of them.] Thou shalt cause them to turn their backs and fly, as if a volley of arrows had been discharged in their faces. This seems to be the *sense* of this difficult verse.

Verse 13. *Be thou exalted*] *Exalt thyself, O Lord*—thy creatures cannot exalt thee. *Lift thyself up,* and discomfit thy foes by thine own strength! Thou canst give a victory to thy people over the most formidable enemies, though they strike not one blow in their own defence. God's right hand has often given the victory to his followers, while they stood still to see the salvation of God. How little can the strength of man avail when the Lord *raiseth up himself* to the battle! His children, therefore, may safely trust in him, for the name of the Lord is a strong tower; the righteous flee into it, and are safe.

Praise thy power.] God is to receive praise in reference to that attribute which he has *exhibited* most in the defence or salvation of his followers. Sometimes he *manifests* his *power,* his *mercy,* his *wisdom,* his *longsuffering,* his *fatherly care,* his *good providence,* his *holiness,* his *justice,* his *truth,* &c. Whatever attribute or perfection he exhibits most, *that* should be the chief subject of his children's *praise.* One wants *teaching,* prays for it, and is deeply instructed: he will naturally celebrate the *wisdom* of God. Another feels himself beset with the most *powerful* adversaries, with the *weakest* of whom he is not *able* to cope: he cries to the Almighty God for *strength;* he is heard, and strengthened with strength in his soul. He therefore will naturally magnify the all-conquering *power* of the Lord. Another feels himself lost, condemned, on the brink of hell; he calls for *mercy,* is heard and saved: *mercy,* therefore, will be the *chief subject* of his praise, and the *burden of his song.*

The old Anglo-Scottish Psalter says, We sal make knowen thi wordes in gude wil and gude werk, for he synges well that wirkes well. For thi, sais he twise, we sal syng; ane tyme for the luf of hert; another, for the schewyng of ryghtwisness, til ensampil.

ANALYSIS OF THE TWENTY-FIRST PSALM

This is the people's Επινικιον, or *triumphal song*, after the victory which they prayed for in the former Psalm, when David went out to war. In this they praise God for the conquest which he gave him over his enemies, and for the singular mercies bestowed on himself. It consists of *three* parts:—

I. The general proposition, ver. 1.

II. The narration, which is twofold, from ver. 1-4. 1. An enumeration of the blessings bestowed on David, from ver. 1 to 6. 2. An account how God would deal with his enemies, from ver. 6 to 12.

III. A vow, or acclamation, ver. 13, which is the *epilogue* of the piece.

I. The *sum of the Psalm* is contained in the *first verse:* "The king shall joy; the king shall be exceeding glad." Joy is the affection with which the king and people were transported; for all that follows shows but the rise and causes of it.

I. The rise and object of it: "The strength of God; the salvation of God." 1. His *strength*, by which he subdued his enemies, and contemned dangers. 2. His *salvation*, by which he escaped dangers, and fell not in battle.

II. 1. The *narration* of the goodness of God to David's person, the particulars of which are the following:—

1. God granted to him what his *heart* desired: "Thou hast given him his heart's desire;" and what his *lips* requested: "and hast not withholden the request of his lips."

2. He granted him more than he asked: "Thou preventest him with the blessings of goodness."

3. He chose him to be *king:* "Thou hast set a crown of pure gold upon his head." In which God prevented him, and chose him when he thought not of it.

4. When David went to war, "he asked life, and thou gavest him even length of days for ever and ever:" which is most true of Christ, the Son of David. In him his life and kingdom are immortal.

5. A great accession of *glory, honour,* and *majesty.* Though his glory was great, it was *in God's salvation:* "Honour and majesty did God lay upon him."

All which are summed up under the word *blessing* in the next verse. "For thou hast made him most blessed for ever;" and God had added the *crown* of all, a *heart to rejoice* in it: "Thou hast made him exceeding glad with thy countenance."

6. The *continuance* of these blessings, which is *another* favour, with the *cause* of it: "For the king trusteth in the Lord, and through the mercy of the Most High he shall not be moved." Thus far the *first part* of the *narrative*, which concerned David's person particularly.

2. The *effects* of God's goodness to David in *outward* things, and to the whole kingdom, in the overthrow of his enemies, (for without God's protection what kingdom is safe?) form the *second part.*

1. God would make David his *instrument* in delivering Israel by the overthrow of his enemies: "Thine hand."

2. He would certainly do it, for he could *find them out* wheresoever they were: "Thine hand shall find out thine enemies."

3. This was easy to be done, as easy as for fire to consume stubble: "Thou shalt make them as a fiery oven."

4. This destruction should be universal; it should reach even to their *posterity:* "Their fruit shalt thou destroy, and their seed."

5. Their judgment should be fearful and unavoidable. God would set them up as a *mark to shoot at:* "Thou shalt make them turn their back, when thou shalt make ready thine arrows."

At last the *cause* is added for these judgments; of the succour he will afford his afflicted, oppressed people; and the revenge he will take upon their enemies: "They intended evil against thee; they imagined a mischievous device."

III. The vow or acclamation. This is properly the *epilogue*, and has *two parts:* 1. A petition—"Save the king and the people." 2. A profession: "And we will give thanks to thee."

1. "Be thou exalted, O Lord, in thine own strength." Show thyself more powerful in defending thy Church than men and devils are in their attempts to destroy it.

2. We will be a thankful people; we will show that we have not received this grace of God in vain: "So will we sing, and praise thy power."

PSALM XXII

Under great affliction and distress, the psalmist prays unto God, 1-3; appeals to God's wonted kindness in behalf of his people, 4, 5; relates the insults that he received, 6-8; mentions the goodness of God to him in his youth, as a reason why he should expect help now, 9-11; details his sufferings, and the indignities offered to him, 12-18; prays with the confidence of being heard and delivered, 19-24; praises God. and foretells the conversion of the nations to the true religion, 25-31.

IV. DAY. EVENING PRAYER

To the chief Musician upon ªAijeleth Shahar, A Psalm of David

A. M. cir. 2946
B. C. cir. 1058
Sauli Regis
Israelitarum,
cir. annum
38

MY ᵇGod, my God, why hast thou forsaken me? *why art thou so* far ᶜfrom helping me, *and from* ᵈthe words of my roaring?

2 O my God, I cry in the day-time, but thou hearest not; and in the night-season, and ᵉam not silent.

A. M. cir. 2946
B. C. cir. 1058
Sauli, Regis
Israelitarum,
cir. annum
38

3 But thou *art* holy, O *thou* that inhabitest the ᶠpraises of Israel.

ªOr, *the hind of the morning*——ᵇMatt. xxvii. 46; Mark xv. 34——ᶜHeb. *from my salvation*

ᵈHeb. v. 7——ᵉHeb. there is *no silence to me*——ᶠDeut. x. 21

NOTES ON PSALM XXII

The title of this Psalm, *To the chief Musician upon Aijeleth Shahar, A Psalm of David*, has given rise to many conjectures. The words אילת השחר *aiyeleth hashshachar* are translated in the margin, "the hind of the morning;" but what was this? Was it the name of a *musical instrument?* or of a tune? or of a *band of music?* *Calmet* argues for the last, and translates "A Psalm of David, addressed to the Musicmaster who presides over the Band called the Morning Hind." This is more likely than any of the other conjectures I have seen. But *aiyeleth hashshachar* may be the name of the *Psalm* itself, for it was customary among the Asiatics to give names to their poetic compositions which often bore no relation to the subject itself. Mr. *Harmer* and others have collected a few instances from *D'Herbelot's* Bibliotheque Orientale. I could add many more from MSS. in my own collection:—thus *Saady* calls a famous miscellaneous work of his *Gulistan*, "The Country of Roses," or, "The Rose Garden:" and yet there is nothing relative to such a *country*, nor concerning *roses* nor *rose gardens*, in the book. Another is called *Negaristan*, "The Gallery of Pictures;" yet no *picture gallery* is mentioned. Another *Beharistan*, "The Spring Season;" *Bostan*, "The Garden;" *Anvar Soheely*, "The Light of Canopus;" *Bahar Danush*, "The Garden of Knowledge;" *Tuhfit Almumeneen*, "The Gift of the Faithful," a treatise on *medicine; Kemeea Isadut*, "The Alchymy of Life;" *Mukhzeen ul Asrar*, "The Magazine of Secrets;" *Sulselet al Zahab*, "The Golden Chain;" *Zuhfit al Abrar*, "The Rosary of the Pious;" *Merat ul Asrar*, "The Mirror of Secrets;" *Durj ul Durar*, "The most precious Jewels;" *Deru Majlis*, "The Jewel of the Assembly;" *Al Bordah*, "The Variegated Garment;" a poem written by *Al Basiree*, in praise of the *Mohammedan* religion, in gratitude for a cure which he believed he received from the prophet who appeared to him in a dream. The poem is written in *one hundred and sixty-two couplets*, each of which ends with م *mim*, the *first letter* in the name of *Mohammed*.

Scarcely one of the above *titles*, and their number might be easily trebled, bears any relation to the *subject* of the work to which it is prefixed, no more than *Aijeleth Shahar* bears to the matter contained in the twenty-second Psalm. Such *titles* are of very little importance *in themselves;* and of no farther use to us than as they serve to distinguish the different *books, poems,* or *Psalms*, to which they are prefixed. To me, many seem to have spent their time uselessly in the investigation of such subjects. See my note on 2 Sam. i. 18.

On the *subject* of the Psalm itself, there is considerable diversity of opinion: 1. Some referring it all to David; 2. Others referring it all to Christ; and, 3. Some, because of the application of several verses of it to our Lord in his sufferings, take a middle way, and apply it *primarily* to David, and in a *secondary* or *accommodated* sense, to *Christ*. Of this opinion was *Theodore* of *Mopsuestia*, who gave a very rational account of his own plan of interpretation; for which he was condemned by the *second* council of Constantinople or *fifth* Œcumenic council. *Grotius* and others have nearly copied his plan; and I think, with a little correction, it is the only safe one. That several parts of it relate to *David, primarily*, there is very little reason to doubt; that several passages may be applied by way of *accommodation* to our *Lord*, though *originally* belonging to and expressing the state of *David*, may be piously believed; and that it contains portions which are *direct prophecies* of our Lord's passion, death, and victory, appears too evident to be safely denied. On this plan I propose to treat it in the following paraphrase; keeping it as near to the Gospel standard as I can. Dr. *Delaney* supposes the Psalm to have been written by David when he was at *Mahaniam*, the very place where God appeared to Jacob in his distress. See Gen. xxii. And on this supposition the *third, fourth,* and *fifth* verses may be easily and strikingly illustrated: *Our fathers trusted in thee; why may not I? Thou didst deliver* THEM; *why may not I* expect deliverance also? THEY *cried unto thee, trusted in thee, and were not confounded; I* cry unto thee, trust in thee; and why should *I* be confounded? For thou art the same God, thou changest not; and with thee there is no respect of persons. Thus David encouraged himself in the Lord; and these considerations helped to sustain him in his painful exercises and heavy distresses.

Verse 1. *My God, my God, why hast thou forsaken me?*] Show me the cause why thou hast abandoned me to my enemies; and why thou seemest to disregard my prayers and cries? For a full illustration of this passage, I beg the reader to refer to my note on Matt. xxvii. 46.

The words of my roaring?] שאגתי *shaagathi*, The *Vulgate, Septuagint, Syriac, Æthiopic,* and *Arabic*, with the *Anglo-Saxon*, make use of terms which may be thus translated: "My sins (or foolishness) are the cause why deliverance is so far from me." It appears that these versions have read שגגתי *shegagathi*, "my sin of ignorance," instead of שאגתי *shaagathi*, "my roaring:" but no MS. extant supports this reading.

Verse 2. *I cry in the day-time, and in the night-season*] This seems to be David's own experience; and the words seem to refer to his own case alone. Though I am not heard, and

A. M. cir. 2946
B. C. cir. 1058
Sauli, Regis
Israelitarum,
cir. annum
38

4 Our fathers ᵍtrusted in thee: they trusted, and thou didst deliver them.

5 They cried unto thee, and were delivered: ʰthey trusted in thee, and were not confounded.

6 But I *am* ⁱa worm, and no man; ᵏa reproach of men, and despised of the people.

7 ¹All they that see me laugh me to scorn: they ᵐshoot out the lip, ⁿthey shake the head, *saying,*

8 ᵒHe ᵖtrusted on the LORD *that* he would deliver him: �q let him deliver him, ʳseeing he delighted in him.

9 ˢBut thou *art* he that took me out of the womb: thou ᵗdidst make me hope *when I was* upon my mother's breasts.

A. M. cir. 2946
B. C. cir. 1058
Sauli, Regis
Israelitarum,
cir. annum
38

10 I was cast upon thee from the womb: ᵘthou *art* my God from my mother's belly.

11 Be not far from me; for trouble *is* near; for *there is* ᵛnone to help.

12 ʷMany bulls have compassed me: strong *bulls* of Bashan have beset me round.

13 ˣThey ʸgaped upon me *with* their mouths, *as* a ravening and a roaring lion.

14 I am poured out like water, ᶻand all my bones are ᵃout of joint: ᵇmy heart is like

---

ᵍ2 Kings xviii. 5; Psa. xiii. 5; Dan. iii. 28; Eph. i. 12, 13——ʰPsa. xxv. 2, 3; xxxi. 1; lxxi. 1; Isa. xlix. 23; Rom. ix. 33——ⁱJob xxv. 6; Isa. xli. 14——ᵏIsa. liii. 3 ¹Matt. xxvii. 39; Mark xv. 29; Luke xxiii. 35——ᵐHeb. *open*——ⁿJob xvi. 4; Psa. cxix. 25——ᵒMatt. xxvii. 43——ᵖHeb. *He rolled* himself *on the LORD*——�q Psa. xci. 14

ʳOr, *if he delight in him*——ˢPsa. lxxi. 6——ᵗOr, *kept-est me in safety*——ᵘIsa. xlvi 3; xlix. 1——ᵛHeb. *not a helper*——ʷDeut. xxxii. 14; Psa. lxviii. 30; Ezek. xxxix. 18; Amos iv. 1——ˣJob xvi. 10; Psa. xxxv. 21; Lam. ii. 16; iii. 46——ʸHeb. *opened their mouths against me* ᶻDan. v. 6——ᵃOr, *sundered*——ᵇJosh. vii. 5; Job xxiii. 16

---

thou appearest to forget or abandon me; yet I continue to cry both day and night after thy salvation.

Verse 3. But thou art holy] Though I be not heard, even while I cry earnestly, yet I cannot impute any fault or unkindness to my Maker; for *thou art holy,* and canst do nothing but what is *right.* This is the language of profound resignation, in trials the most difficult to be borne.

Inhabitest the praises of Israel.] Thou dwellest in the *sanctuary* where the praises, thanksgivings, and sacrifices of thy people are continually offered.

Verse 4. Our fathers trusted in thee] David is supposed to have been, at the time of composing this Psalm, at *Mahanaim,* where Jacob was once in such great distress; where he wrestled with the angel, and was so signally blessed. David might well allude to this circumstance in order to strengthen his faith in God. I am now in the place where God so signally blessed the *head* and *father* of our tribes. I *wrestle* with God, as he did; may I not expect similar success?

Verse 5. They cried unto thee] So do *I.* THEY *were delivered;* so may *I.* THEY *trusted in thee; I* also trust in thee. *And were not confounded;* and is it likely that *I* shall be put to confusion?

Verse 6. But I am *a worm, and no man*] I can see no sense in which our Lord could use these terms. David might well use them to express his vileness and worthlessness. The old Psalter gives this a remarkable turn: **J am a worme,** that es, I am borne of the mayden with outen manseede; **anb nout man** anely, bot god als so: and nevir the latter, **J am reprobe of men,** In spitting, buffetyng, and punging with the thornes **anb outkasting of folk;** for thai chesed Barraban the thefe, and nought me.

Verse 7. Laugh me to scorn] They utterly despised me; set me at naught; treated me with the utmost contempt. *Laugh to scorn* is so completely antiquated that it should be no longer used; *derided, despised, treated with*

contempt, are much more expressive and are still in common use.

They shoot out the lip, they shake the head] This is applied by St. Matthew, chap. xxvii. 39, to the conduct of the Jews towards our Lord, when he hung upon the cross; as is also the following verse. But both are primarily true of the insults which David suffered from Shimei and others during the rebellion of Absalom; and, as the cases were so similar, the evangelist thought proper to express a similar conduct to Jesus Christ by the same expressions. These insults our Lord literally received; no doubt David received the same.

Verse 9. But thou art *he that took me out of the womb*] Thou hast made me; and hast guided and defended me from my earliest infancy.

Verse 11. Be not far from me; for trouble is near] A present God is a present blessing. We always need the Divine help; but more especially when troubles and trials are at hand.

Verse 12. Many bulls have compassed me] The *bull* is the emblem of brutal strength, that gores and tramples down all before it. Such was Absalom, Ahithophel, and others, who rose up in rebellion against David; and such were the Jewish rulers who conspired against Christ.

Strong bulls of Bashan] Bashan was a district beyond Jordan, very fertile, where they were accustomed to fatten cattle, which became, in consequence of the excellent pasture, the largest, as well as the fattest, in the country. See *Calmet.* All in whose hands were the chief power and influence became David's enemies; for Absalom had stolen away the hearts of all Israel. Against Christ, the chiefs both of Jews and Gentiles were united.

Verse 13. They gaped upon me] They were fiercely and madly bent on my destruction.

Verse 14. I am poured out like water] That is, as the old *Psalter:* **Thai rougbt na mare to sla me than to spil water.**

The images in this verse are strongly descriptive of a person in the deepest distress:

A. M. cir. 2946
B. C. cir. 1058
Sauli, Regis
Israelitarum,
cir. annum
38

wax; it is melted in the midst of my bowels.

15 ^cMy strength is dried up like a potsherd; and ^dmy tongue cleaveth to my jaws; and thou hast brought me into the dust of death.

16 For ^edogs have compassed me: the assembly of the wicked have enclosed me: ^fthey pierced my hands and my feet.

17 I may tell all my bones: ^gthey look *and* stare upon me.

18 ^hThey part my garments among them, and cast lots upon my vesture.

19 But be ⁱnot thou far from me, O LORD: O my strength, haste thee to help me.

20 Deliver my soul from the sword; ^kmy ^ldarling ^mfrom the power of the ⁿdog.

A. M. cir. 2946
B. C. cir. 1058
Sauli, Regis
Israelitarum,
cir. annum
38

---

cProv. xvii. 22——dJob xxix. 10; Lam. iv. 4; John xix. 28——eRev. xxii. 15——fMatt. xxvii. 35; Mark xv. 24; Luke xxiii. 33; John xix. 23, 37; xx. 25

gLuke xxiii. 27, 35——hLuke xxiii. 34; John xiv. 23, 24——iVer. 11; Psa. x. 1——kPsa. xxxv. 17——lHeb. *my only one*——mHeb. *from the hand*——nVer. 16

---

whose strength, courage, hope, and expectation of succour and relief, had entirely failed.

Our Lord's sufferings were extreme; but I cannot think there is any sound theologic sense in which these things can be spoken of Christ, either in his agony in the garden, or his death upon the cross.

Verse 15. *My strength is dried up*] All these expressions mark a most distressed and hopeless case.

Into the dust of death.] This means only that he was *apparently* brought nigh to the grave, and consequent *corruption;* this latter David saw; but Jesus Christ never saw corruption.

Verse 16. *For dogs have compassed me*] This may refer to the *Gentiles,* the Roman soldiers, and others by whom our Lord was surrounded in his trial, and at his cross.

They pierced my hands and my feet] The other sufferings David, as a type of our Lord, might pass through; but the *piercing of the hands and feet* was peculiar to our Lord; therefore, this verse may pass for a *direct revelation.* Our Lord's hands and feet were pierced when he was nailed to the cross, David's never were pierced.

But there is a various reading here which is of great importance. Instead of כארו *caaru,* they pierced, which is what is called the *kethib,* or *marginal* reading, and which our translators have followed; the *keri* or textual reading is כארי *caari, as a lion.* In support of each reading there are both MSS. and eminent critics. The *Chaldee* has, "Biting as a lion my hands and my feet;" but the *Syriac, Vulgate, Septuagint, Æthiopic,* and *Arabic* read, "they pierced or *digged;*" and in the *Anglo-Saxon* the words are, hí bulpon hanbe mine anb pet mine; "*They dalve* (digged) *hands mine, and feet mine.*"

The *Complutensian* Polyglot has כארו *caaru,* they digged or pierced, in the *text;* for which it gives כרה *carah,* to *cut, dig,* or *penetrate,* in the margin, as the root whence כארו is derived. But the Polyglots of *Potken, Antwerp, Paris,* and *London,* have כארי *caari* in the text; and כארו *caaru* is referred to in the *margin;* and this is the case with the most correct Hebrew Bibles. The whole difference here lies between י *yod* and ו *vau,* which might easily be mistaken for each other; the former making *like a lion;* the latter, *they pierced.* The latter is to me most evidently the true reading.

Verse 17. *I may tell all my bones*] This may refer to the violent *extension* of his body when the whole of its weight hung upon the nails which attached his hands to the transverse

beam of the cross. The body being thus extended, the principal bones became prominent, and easily discernible.

Verse 18. *They part my garments*] This could be true in *no sense* of David. The fact took place at the crucifixion of our Lord. The soldiers divided his *upper garment* into four parts, each soldier taking a part; but his *tunic* or *inward vestment* being without seam, woven in one entire piece, they agreed not to divide, but to cast lots *whose* the *whole* should be. Of this scripture the Roman soldiers knew nothing; but they fulfilled it to the letter. This was foreseen by the Spirit of God; and this is a direct revelation concerning Jesus Christ, which impresses the whole account with the broad seal of eternal truth.

Verse 19. *Be not thou far from me*] In the first verse he asks, *Why hast thou forsaken me?* Or, as if astonished at their wickedness, *Into what hands hast thou permitted me to fall?* Now he prays, *Be not far from me.* St. *Jerome* observes here, that it is the *humanity* of our blessed Lord which speaks to his *divinity.* Jesus was *perfect man;* and as *man* he suffered and died. But this *perfect* and *sinless man* could not have sustained those sufferings so as to make them expiatory had he not been supported by the *Divine* nature. All the expressions in this Psalm that indicate any *weakness,* as far as it relates to Christ, (and indeed it relates *principally* to him,) are to be understood of the *human nature;* for, that in him *God* and *man* were united, but not confounded, the whole New Testament to me bears evidence, the *manhood* being a perfect man, the *Godhead* dwelling bodily in that manhood. Jesus, as MAN, was conceived, born, grew up, increased in wisdom, stature, and favour with God and man; hungered, thirsted, suffered, and died. Jesus, as GOD, knew all things, was from the beginning with God, healed the diseased, cleansed the lepers, and raised the dead; calmed the raging of the sea, and laid the tempest by a word; quickened the human nature, raised it from the dead, took it up into heaven, where as the Lamb newly slain, it ever appears in the presence of God for us. These are all Scripture facts. The *man* Christ Jesus could not work those miracles; the *God* in that man could not have *suffered* those sufferings. Yet *one person* appears to do and suffer all; here then is GOD *manifested in the* FLESH.

O my strength] The *divinity* being the power by which the *humanity* was sustained in this dreadful conflict.

Verse 20. *Deliver my soul from the sword*]

A. M. cir. 2946
B. C. cir. 1058
Sauli, Regis
Israelitarum,
cir. annum
38

21 °Save me from the lion's mouth: Pfor thou hast heard me from the horns of the unicorns.

22 qI will declare thy name unto rmy brethren: in the midst of the congregation will I praise thee.

23 sYe that fear the LORD, praise him; all ye the seed of Jacob, glorify him; and fear him, all ye the seed of Israel.

24 For he hath not despised nor abhorred the affliction of the afflicted; neither hath he hid his face from him; but twhen he cried unto him, he heard.

25 uMy praise *shall be* of thee in the great congregation: vI will pay my vows before them that fear him.

26 wThe meek shall eat and be satisfied: they shall praise the LORD that seek him: your heart xshall live for ever.

27 yAll the ends of the world shall remember and turn unto the LORD: zand all the kindreds of the nations shall worship before thee.

28 aFor the kingdom *is* the LORD's: and he *is* the governor among the nations.

29 bAll *they that be* fat upon earth shall

A. M. cir. 2946
B. C. cir. 1058
Sauli, Regis
Israelitarum,
cir. annum
38

°2 Tim. iv. 17——PIsa. xxxiv. 7; Acts iv. 27——qHeb. ii. 12; Psa. xl. 9——rJohn xx. 17; Rom. viii. 29——sPsa. cxxxv. 19, 20——tHeb. v. 7——uPsa. xxxv. 18; xl. 9, 10; cxi. 1——vPsa. lxvi. 13; cxvi. 14; Eccles. v. 4

wLev. vii. 11, 12, 15, 16; Psa. lxix. 32; Isa. lxv. 13
xJohn vi. 51——yPsa. ii. 9; lxxii. 11; lxxxvi. 3; xcviii. 3; Isa. xlix. 6——zPsa. xcvi. 7——aPsa. xlvii. 8; Obad. 21; Zech. xiv. 9; Matt. vi. 13——bPsa. xlv. 12

Deliver נפשי *naphshi, my life;* save me alive, or raise me again.

My darling] יחידתי *yechidathi, my only one.* The only human being that was ever produced since the creation, even by the power of God himself, without the agency of man. ADAM the *first* was created out of the dust of the earth; that was his *mother;* God was the *framer.* ADAM the *second* was produced in the womb of the *virgin;* that was his mother. But that which was conceived in her was by the *power of the Holy Ghost;* hence the man Christ Jesus is the ONLY Son of God; God is his Father, and he is his ONLY ONE.

Verse 21. *Save me from the lion's mouth*] Probably our Lord here includes his *Church* with himself. The *lion* may then mean the *Jews;* the *unicorns,* רמים *remim,* (probably the *rhinoceros,*) the *Gentiles.* For the *unicorn,* see the note on Num. xxiii. 22. There is no quadruped or *land animal* with one horn only, except the rhinoceros; but there is a *marine* animal, the *narwall* or *monodon,* a species of *whale,* that has a very fine curled ivory horn, which projects from its snout. One in my own museum measures *seven feet four inches,* and is very beautiful. Some of these animals have struck their horn through the side of a ship; and with it they easily transfix the whale, or any such animal. The old Psalter says, "The unicorn es ane of the prudest best that es, so that he wil dye for dedeyn if he be haldyn ogayn his wil."

Verse 22. *I will declare thy name unto my brethren*] I will make a complete revelation concerning the God of justice and love, to my *disciples;* and I will announce to the Jewish *people* thy merciful design in sending me to be the Saviour of the world.

Verse 23. *Ye that fear the Lord*] This is an exhortation to the *Jews* particularly, to profit by the preaching of the Gospel. Perhaps, by *them that fear him,* the *Gentiles,* and particularly the *proselytes,* may be intended. The *Jews* are mentioned by name: *Glorify him, all ye seed of Jacob; fear him, all ye seed of Israel.*

Verse 24. *For he hath not despised*] It is his property to help and save the poor and the humble; and he rejects not the sighings of a con-

trite heart. Perhaps it may mean, Though ye have despised *me* in my humiliation, yet God has graciously received me in the character of a sufferer on account of sin; as by that humiliation unto death the great atonement was made for the sin of the world.

Verse 25. *The great congregation*] In ver. 22 he declares that he will *praise God in the midst of the congregation.* Here the *Jews* seem to be intended. In this verse he says *he will praise him in the* GREAT CONGREGATION. Here the *Gentiles* are probably meant. The Jewish nation was but a *small number* in comparison of the *Gentile* world. And those of the former who received the Gospel were very few when compared with those among the Gentiles who received the Divine testimony. The one *was* (for there is scarcely a converted Jew *now*) קהל *kahal,* an *assembly;* the other *was, is,* and *will be* increasingly, קהל רב *kahal rab,* a GREAT ASSEMBLY. Salvation *was* of the Jews, it is now of the *Gentiles.*

Verse 26. *The meek shall eat*] ענוים *anavim,* the POOR, shall eat. In the true only Sacrifice there shall be such a provision for all believers, that they shall have a fulness of joy. Those who offered the sacrifice, fed on what they offered. Jesus, the true Sacrifice, is the bread that came down from heaven; they who eat of this bread shall never die.

Verse 27. *All the ends of the world*] The Gospel shall be preached to every nation under heaven; and *all the kindred of nations,* משפחות *mishpechoth.* the *families* of the nations: not only the *nations* of the world shall receive the Gospel as a *revelation* from God, but *each family* shall embrace it for their own salvation. *They shall worship before* Jesus the Saviour, and through him shall all their praises be offered unto God.

Verse 28. *The kingdom is the Lord's*] That universal sway of the Gospel which in the New Testament is called *the kingdom of God;* in which all men shall be God's subjects; and righteousness, peace, and joy in the Holy Ghost, be *universally* diffused.

Verse 29. *All they that be fat upon earth*] The *rich,* the *great,* the *mighty,* even *princes,*

A. M. cir. 2946
B. C. cir. 1058
Sauli, Regis
Israelitarum,
cir. annum
38

eat and worship: c all they that go down to the dust shall bow before him: and none can keep alive his own soul.

30 A seed shall serve him; d it shall be ac-

counted to the LORD for a gene-ration.

31 e They shall come, and shall declare his righteousness unto a people that shall be born, that he hath done this.

A. M. cir. 2946
B. C. cir. 1058
Sauli, Regis
Israelitarum,
cir. annum
38

---

c Isa. xxvi. 10; Phil. ii. 19——d Psa. lxxxvii. 6——e Psa. lxxviii. 6; lxxxvi. 9; cii. 18; Isa. lx. 3; see Rom. iii. 21, 22

---

governors, and kings, shall embrace the Gospel. They shall count it their greatest honour to be called Christian; to join in the assemblies of his people, to commemorate his sacrificial death, to dispense the word of life, to discourage vice, and to encourage the profession and practice of pure and undefiled religion.

That go down to the dust] Every *dying man* shall put his trust in Christ, and shall expect glory only through the great Saviour of mankind.

None can keep alive his own soul.] The *Vulgate* has: Et anima mea illi vivet, et semen meum serviet ipsi; "and my soul shall live to him, and my seed shall serve him." And with this agree the *Syriac, Septuagint, Æthiopic, Arabic,* and *Anglo-Saxon.* The old *Psalter* follows them closely: And my saule sal lyf til him; and my sede til hym sal serve. I believe this to be the true reading. Instead of נפשו *naphsho,* HIS *soul,* some MSS., in accordance with the above ancient versions, have נפשי *naphshi,* MY *soul.*

And instead of לא *lo, not,* two MSS., with the versions, have לו *lo, to* HIM. And for חיה *chiyah,* shall *vivify,* some have יחיה *yichyeh,* shall *live.* The text, therefore, should be read,

My soul (נפשי *napshi*) *shall live* (לו *lo*) *to him: my seed* (וזרעי *zari*) *shall serve him.* These may be the words of *David* himself: "I will live to this Saviour while I live; and my spiritual posterity shall serve him through all generations."

Verse 30. *Shall be accounted to the Lord for a generation.*] They shall be called *Christians* after the name of Christ.

Verse 31. *Unto a people that shall be born*] That is, one generation shall continue to announce unto another the true religion of the Lord Jesus; so that it shall be for ever propagated in the earth. Of his kingdom there shall be no end.

ANALYSIS OF THE TWENTY-SECOND PSALM

This Psalm concerns the Messiah, his passion, and his kingdom. Though, in some sense, it, may be applied to David as a *type,* yet *Christ* is the *thing signified,* and therefore it is primarily and principally verified of and in him; for he is brought in here, speaking,

First, Of his *dereliction;* then showing his *passion,* and the *cruelty* of his enemies.

Secondly, Entreating ease and *deliverance* from his sufferings.

Thirdly, Promising thanks to God; foretelling the preaching of the Gospel, and the enlargement of his kingdom by the accession of all nations.

There are *three* chief parts in this Psalm:—
I. Our Saviour's *complaint,* and the *causes* of it: prophetically expressing his sufferings nearly throughout the whole Psalm.

II. His *petition* and *prayer* that God would

not absent himself, but deliver and save him, ver. 3, 4, 5, 9, 10, 11, 19, 20, 21.

III. His *thanksgiving* and *prophetic declaration* concerning the conversion of the Gentiles; from ver. 22 to the end.

I. He begins with a heavy complaint of dereliction in his extremity; and that he was not heard, though he prayed with strong crying and tears: "My God, my God, why hast thou forsaken me?" &c. The words are *repeated* to show the deep anguish of his heart.

2. He shows how well-grounded his complaint was: for God had dealt with him contrary to his usual method; for when his saints called upon him, he heard *them* in *their* distress. Martyres si non eripuit, tum non deseruit. "If he did not deliver the martyrs, yet he did not desert them in their sufferings." His case was more grievous than any that had gone before. Of this he speaks particularly in the three succeeding verses, 3, 4, and 5, by which he reminds God of his promise: "Call on me in the time of trouble, and I will deliver thee." Of this they who went before had experience: and as he was the same God still, why should *this Sufferer* only be deserted? for *they* were heard and comforted.

1. "Thou art holy," propitious and benevolent. "Thou dwellest in the praises of Israel;" thou art continually helping them, and they are continually praising thee for this help.

To prove all this he brings the *example* of the *fathers:*—

2. "Our fathers trusted in thee, and thou didst deliver them."

3. "They cried unto thee—and were not confounded."

But my case is worse than any other: "I am a worm, and am no man."

He then details his sufferings:—

1. The scoffs and scorns cast upon him: "I am become the reproach of men, and the despised among the people."

2. Their contempt is expressed both by *words* and *gestures:* "All they that see me laugh me to scorn: they shoot out the lip—and shake the head."

3. They laboured to deprive him of his God. They uttered this insulting sarcasm: "He trusted in the Lord that he would deliver him; let him deliver him, since he delighted in him."

II. He now breaks off the narration of his sufferings, has immediate recourse to God, refutes their irony, shows his confidence in God, and prays for assistance. This he strengthens by *three arguments* drawn from God's goodness towards him:—

1. His *generation* and *birth:* "Thou—tookest me out of my mother's womb."

2. His *sustenance* and support ever since: "Thou didst make me hope when I was upon my mother's breasts;—thou art my God from my mother's belly." In a word, he was his *Saviour, Protector,* and *Preserver.*

3. Trouble is near, and there is none to help. Therefore, "Be not far from me."

Now he returns to the *narration* of his passion, in which he sets forth the *despite, cruelty,* and *rage* of the Jews towards him, whom he compares to *bulls, lions, dogs,* &c., ver. 16.

1. They apprehended him: "Many bulls have compassed me;" &c.

2. They longed to condemn and devour him: "They gaped on me with their mouths, as a ravening and roaring lion."

3. This was the cruelty of the *lions* and *bulls,* the *chief rulers,* and *chief priests;* and now follows the ravin of the *dogs,* the "multitude of the people:" they were the "assembly of the wicked;" and being stirred up by the *priests* and *rulers,* "they compassed him round about."

4. They crucify him. And his passion is foretold, with what he should suffer in body and soul.

1 "I am poured out like water." My blood is poured out freely; and no more account taken of it, than if it were water spilt on the ground.

2. "All my bones (when hung on the cross) are out of joint."

3. "My heart (at the sense of God's hatred to sin) is dissolved *and melted* like wax."

4. "My strength (my animal spirits and muscular energy) is dried up like a potsherd;" or like a *pot,* whose *fluid* is *evaporated* by hanging long over a fierce fire.

5. "My tongue (for thirst) cleaveth to my jaws."

6. "Thou hast brought me to death—to the dust of death:" to the grave.

7. "They pierced my hands and my feet." I am crucified also, and die upon the cross.

8. By my long hanging upon the cross, my bones are so disjointed that they may be easily told: "I may tell all my bones."

9. "They look and stare upon me." They feel no *compassion,* but take pleasure in my agonies. This is an affection which is characteristic only of a devil.

10. "They part my garments among them." They delighted in his destruction for the sake of his *spoils.*

Having thus far described his *sufferings,* and the *malice* of his enemies, he begins again to *pray;* which is, in effect, the same with that ejaculation with which Christ gave up the ghost: "Into thy hands, O Lord, I commend my spirit." "Be not thou far from me, O Lord." "Deliver my soul from the sword, my darling from the power of the dog." "Save me from the lion's mouth," &c.

III. This part, which is a *profession of thanks* for deliverance, contains a clear prophecy of the resurrection of Christ; that, having conquered death and Satan, he was to reign and gather a Church out of all nations, which was to continue for ever. This is amplified,

First, By a public profession of the benefit received from God: "I will declare thy name in the midst of the congregation, I will pay my vows." In which we have,

1. The *propagation, proclamation,* and *preaching* of the *Gospel:* "I will declare thy name;" which is amplified,

(1.) By the notation of the *objects* to whom preached, honoured here by the name of, 1. *Brethren.* 2. Those that *fear the Lord.* 3. The *seed of Jacob,* the *seed of Israel.* 4. The *meek* or *poor.* 5. The *fat*—rich, great, or eminent of the earth. 6. They that go down to the dust.

(2.) By the *place:* "The midst of the congregation"—the *great* congregation, i. e., both among the *Jews* and among the *Gentiles.*

(3.) By the *worship* they were to pay: 1. *Praise.* 2. *Paying of vows.* 3. *Fear,* or religious reverence.

2. An *exhortation* to his brethren, &c., to do this duty; and they must be fit for it, for every one is not fit to take God's name in his mouth. It is, *Ye that fear the Lord—the seed of Jacob— the seed of Israel,* fear him, serve the Lord in fear, rejoice before him with reverence. Give him both external and internal worship.

3. And to *engage* them to this, he gives *two reasons:*

Reason 1. Drawn from God's *goodness,* his acceptance of our worship, hearing our prayers, and affording help when we call: "For the Lord hath not despised nor abhorred the affliction of the afflicted. When he cried to him, he heard him."

Reason 2. The great *good* that should happen to them who would believe and accept the Gospel; whom he calls here *the meek,* that is, the humble, broken-hearted, the penitent, the heavy laden; those who are oppressed with the burden of their sins, and astonished at a sense of God's wrath. To them are made *three* promises of comfort:—

1. "They shall eat, and be satisfied." They shall be fed with the word and ordinances of God.

2. "They shall praise the Lord for his mercy;" seeking his favour in his ordinances, which, under the Gospel, are generally *eucharistical.*

3. "Their heart shall live for ever;" their conscience being quieted and pacified, and freed from a sense of God's wrath.

Secondly, The prophet proceeds, and shows us the amplitude of these benefits; that they belong, not only to the Jews but to the Gentiles, by whose conversion the kingdom of Christ is to be enlarged.

1. "All the ends of the world," being warned, by the preaching of the Gospel, and allured by these promises, shall remember—consider the lamentable condition in which they are, and deplore their former estate, impiety, and idolatry. And the mercy of God being now manifested to them—

2. They shall cast away their gods, *turn* from their evil ways, and seek that God from whom they have been alienated. And being converted—

3. They shall embrace a new form of religion under the Gospel: "All the kindreds of the nations shall worship before thee."

4. Of which the reason is, because Christ is advanced to the throne; all power is given to him: "For the kingdom is the Lord's, and he is governor among the people."

5. He then shows the *two kinds* of *people* who should become subjects of the kingdom; in effect, *rich* and *poor.*

1. "The fat upon the earth." The wealthy, the mighty; kings, princes, great men, are to be called into the kingdom, that they may be partakers of its grace: "All *they that be* fat upon the earth," &c.

2. "They also that go down to the dust." That is, the *poor,* the neglected, who draw out their life in misery, and sit, as it were, in the dust; those who are perpetual mourners, and have, as it were, perpetual dust and ashes upon their heads: "These shall bow before him."

Lastly. He amplifies the greatness of this

benefit by the *perpetuity* of Christ's kingdom. It was not a feast of one hour, it was to continue.

1. "A seed shall serve him." But this and the preceding clause may signify the psalmist's resolution to live to God himself, and to show others the same way. See the *notes*.

This *seed*, however, shall be accounted to the Lord for a generation. It shall be a peculiar people, a royal priesthood, a holy nation, and called by Christ's own name—CHRISTIANS.

2. When *one* generation is past, *another* shall

come up to perform this duty, being instructed by their fathers: "They shall come and declare his righteousness to a people that shall be born." *Manebit semper ecclesia;* "the Church is immortal."

3. He concludes with the *cause* of all. Why called, justified, sanctified, saved. He hath done it; the GOD, the Author of all; the Fountain of all grace; the Giver of Jesus Christ, and eternal life through him. For by him, and of him, and through him, are all things; and to him be glory and dominion for ever and ever!

PSALM XXIII

The Lord is the Pastor of his people; therefore it may be inferred that they shall not want, 1. How he guides, feeds, and protects them, 2, 3. Even in the greatest dangers they may be confident of his support, 4. His abundant provision for them, 5. The confidence they may have of his continual mercy, and their eternal happiness.

A Psalm of David

A. M. cir. 3468
B. C. cir. 536
Cyri,
R. Persarum,
cir. annum
primum.

THE LORD *is* [a]my shepherd; [b]I shall not want.

2 [c]He maketh me to lie down in [d]green pastures; [e]he lead-

eth me beside the [f]still waters.

3 He restoreth my soul: [g]he leadeth me in the paths of righteousness for his name's sake.

A. M. cir. 3468
B. C. cir. 536
Cyri,
R. Persarum,
cir. annum
primum.

---

[a]Isa. xl. 11; Jer. xxiii. 4; Ezek. xxxiv. 11, 12, 23; John x. 11; 1 Peter ii. 25; Revelation vii. 17——[b]Phil. iv. 19 [c]Ezek. xxxiv. 14

[d]Hebrew, *pastures of tender grass*——[e]Revelation vii. 17——[f]Hebrew, *waters of quietness*——[g]Psalm v. 8; xxxi. 3; Prov. viii. 20

NOTES ON PSALM XXIII

There is nothing particular in the *title;* it is simply attributed to *David;* but as it appears to be a thanksgiving of the Israelites for their *redemption from the Babylonish captivity,* it cannot with propriety be attributed to David. Some think it was written by David in his *exile,* which is not likely; others, that he penned it when he was *finally delivered from the persecution of Saul.* I rather incline to the opinion that it was written *after the captivity.* The *Chaldee* seems to suppose that it was written to celebrate the goodness of God to the *Israelites in the desert.* It is a truly beautiful Psalm. Supposing it to have been written *after the captivity,* we see, 1. The redeemed captives giving thanks to God for their liberty. 2. Acknowledging that God had brought back their lives from the grave. 3. They represent themselves in Judea as a flock in an excellent pasture. 4. They declare that from the dangers they have passed through, and from which God had delivered them, they can have no fear of any enemy. 5. They conclude, from what God has done for them, that his goodness and mercy shall follow them all their days. And, 6. That they shall no more be deprived of God's worship, but shall all their days have access to his temple.

Verse 1. *The Lord is my shepherd*] There **are** two *allegories* in this Psalm which are ad-

mirably well adapted to the purpose for which they are produced, and supported both with *art* and *elegance.* The *first* is that of a *shepherd;* the *second,* that of a *great feast,* set out by a *host* the most kind and the most liberal. As a *flock,* they have the most excellent *pasture;* as *guests,* they have the most nutritive and abundant *fare.* God condescends to call himself the *Shepherd* of his people, and his followers are considered as a *flock* under his guidance and direction. 1. He leads them out and in, so that they find pasture and safety. 2. He knows where to feed them, and in the course of his grace and providence leads them in the way in which they should go. 3. He watches over them, and keeps them from being destroyed by ravenous beasts. 4. If any have strayed, he brings them back. 5. He brings them to the *shade* in times of scorching heat; in times of persecution and affliction, he finds out an asylum for them. 6. He takes care that they shall lack no manner of thing that is good.

But who are his flock? All real penitents, all true believers; all who obediently *follow* his example, abstaining from every appearance of evil, and in a holy life and conversation showing forth the virtues of Him who called them from darkness into his marvellous light. "My sheep hear my voice, and follow me."

But who are not his flock! Neither the backslider in heart, nor the vile Antinomian, who thinks the more he sins, the more the grace of

A. M. cir. 3468
B. C. cir. 536
  Cyri,
R. Persarum,
cir. annum
  primum

4 Yea, though I walk through the valley of ^hthe shadow of death, ⁱI will fear no evil: ^kfor thou *art* with me; thy rod and thy staff they comfort me.

5 ^lThou preparest a table before me in the presence of mine enemies: thou ^manointest ⁿmy head with oil; my cup runneth over.

6 Surely goodness and mercy shall follow me all the days of my life: and I will dwell in the house of the LORD ^ofor ever.

A. M. cir. 3468
B. C. cir. 536
  Cyri,
R. Persarum,
cir. annum
  primum.

---

^hJob iii. 5; x. 21, 22; xxiv. 17; Psa. xliv. 19——ⁱPsa. iii. 6; xxvii. 1; cxviii. 6——^kIsa. xliii. 2

^lPsa. civ. 15——^mHeb. *makest fat*——ⁿPsa. xcii. 10   ^oHeb. *to length of days*

God shall be magnified in saving him; nor those who fondly suppose they are covered with the righteousness of Christ while living in sin; nor the crowd of the *indifferent* and the *careless*, nor the immense herd of *Laodicean loiterers;* nor the fiery bigots who would exclude all from heaven but themselves, and the party who believe as they do. These the Scripture resembles to *swine, dogs, wandering stars, foxes, lions, wells without water*, &c., &c. Let not any of these come forward to *feed on this pasture*, or take of the *children's bread.* Jesus Christ is the *good Shepherd;* the Shepherd who, to save his flock, laid down his own life.

I shall not want.] How can they? He who is their Shepherd has all power in heaven and earth; therefore he *can protect them.* The silver and gold are his, and the cattle on a *thousand* hills; and therefore he can *sustain* them. He has all that they need, and his heart is full of love to mankind; and therefore he will withhold from them no manner of thing that is good. The old *Psalter* both translates and paraphrases this clause well: 𝔏𝔬𝔯𝔡 𝔤𝔬𝔟𝔢𝔯𝔫𝔰 𝔪𝔢, 𝔞𝔫𝔡 𝔫𝔞𝔱𝔥𝔦𝔫𝔤 𝔰𝔞𝔩 𝔴𝔞𝔫𝔱 𝔱𝔬 𝔪𝔢. 𝔍𝔫 𝔰𝔱𝔢𝔡𝔢 𝔬𝔣 𝔭𝔞𝔰𝔱𝔬𝔲𝔯 𝔱𝔥𝔞𝔯𝔢 𝔥𝔢 𝔪𝔢 𝔰𝔢𝔱𝔱. "The voice of a rightwis man: 𝔏𝔬𝔯𝔡 𝔠𝔯𝔦𝔰𝔱 𝔢𝔰 𝔪𝔶 𝔨𝔶𝔫𝔤, and for thi (therefore) 𝔫𝔞𝔱𝔥𝔶𝔫𝔤 𝔰𝔞𝔩 𝔪𝔢 𝔴𝔞𝔫𝔱: that es, in hym I sal be siker, and suffisand, for I hope in hymn gastly gude and endles. 𝔄𝔫𝔡 𝔥𝔢 𝔩𝔢𝔡𝔢𝔰 𝔪𝔢 𝔦𝔫 𝔰𝔱𝔢𝔡𝔢 𝔬𝔣 𝔭𝔞𝔰𝔱𝔬𝔲𝔯𝔢, that es, understandyng of his worde, and delyte in his luf. Qwar I am siker to be fild, thar in that stede (place) he sett me, to be nurysht til perfcctioun." Who can say more, who need say less, than this?

Verse 2. He maketh me to lie down in green pastures] בִנְאוֹת דֶשֶׁא *binoth deshe*, not *green pastures*, but *cottages of turf* or *sods*, such as the shepherds had in open champaign countries; places in which themselves could repose safely; and *pens* thus constructed where the flock might be safe all the night. They were enclosures, and enclosures where they had *grass* or provender to eat.

Beside the still waters.] *Deep waters*, that the strongest heat could not exhale; not by a *rippling current*, which argues a *shallow* stream. Or perhaps he may here refer to the waters of *Siloam*, or *Shiloah, that go softly*, Isa. viii. 6, compared with the *strong current* of the *Euphrates.* Thou hast brought us from the land of our captivity, from beyond this mighty and turbulent river, to our own country streams, wells, and fountains, where we enjoy peace, tranquillity, and rest.

The old *Psalter gives this a beautiful turn:* 𝔒𝔫 𝔱𝔥𝔢 𝔴𝔞𝔱𝔢𝔯 𝔬𝔣 𝔯𝔢𝔥𝔢𝔱𝔶𝔫𝔤 𝔣𝔬𝔯𝔱𝔥 𝔥𝔢 𝔪𝔢 𝔟𝔯𝔬𝔤𝔥𝔱. On the water of grace er we broght forth, that makes to recover our strengthe that we lost in syn. 𝔄𝔫𝔡 𝔯𝔢𝔥𝔢𝔱𝔢𝔦𝔰 (strengthens) us to do gude workes. 𝔐𝔶 𝔰𝔞𝔲𝔩𝔢 𝔥𝔢 𝔱𝔲𝔯𝔫𝔢𝔡, that es, of a synful wreche, he made it ryghtwis, and waxyng of luf in mekeness. First he turnes our saules til hym; and then he ledes and fedes it. Ten graces he telles in this psalme, the qwilk God gyfs til his lufers, (i. e., them that love him.)

Verse 3. He restoreth my soul] Brings back my life from destruction; and converts my soul from sin, that it may not eternally perish. Or, after it has *backslidden* from him, heals its backslidings, and restores it to his favour. See the old paraphrase on this clause in the preceding note.

In the paths of righteousness] בְמַעְגְלֵי צֶדֶק *bemageley tsedek*, "in the circuits" or "orbits of righteousness." In many places of Scripture man appears to be represented under the notion of a *secondary planet moving round its primary;* or as a planet revolving round the sun, from whom it receives its *power* of *revolving*, with all its *light* and *heat.* Thus man stands in reference to the *Sun of righteousness;* by *his power* alone is he enabled to *walk uprightly;* by his *light* he is *enlightened;* and by his *heat* he is *vivified*, and enabled to bring forth *good fruit.* When he keeps in his proper *orbit*, having the *light* of the glory of God reflected from the face of Jesus Christ, he is enabled to *enlighten* and *strengthen* others. He that is enlightened may enlighten; he that is fed may feed.

For his name's sake.] To display the glory of his grace, and not on account of any *merit* in me. God's motives of conduct towards the children of men are derived from the perfections and goodness of his own nature.

Verse 4. Yea, though I walk through the valley of the shadow of death] The reference is still to the *shepherd.* Though I, as one of the *flock*, should walk through the most dismal valley, in the dead of the night, exposed to pitfalls, precipices, devouring beasts, &c., I should fear no evil under the guidance and protection of such a Shepherd. He knows all the *passes*, dangerous defiles, hidden pits, and abrupt precipices in the way; and he will guide me around, about, and through them. See the phrase *shadow of death* explained on Matt. iv. 16. "Thof I ward well and imang tha, that nouther has knowyng of God, ne luf or in myddis of this lyf, that es schadow of ded; for it es blak for myrkenes of syn; and it ledes til dede and il men, imang qwam gude men wones:—I sal nout drede il, pryve nor apert; for thu ert with me in my hert, qwar I fele thu so, that eftir the schadow of dede, I be with the in thi vera lyf."—Old *Psalter.*

For thou art with me] He who has his God for a companion need fear no danger; for he can neither *mistake* his way, nor be *injured.*

Thy rod and thy staff] שִׁבְטֶךָ *shibtecha*, thy *sceptre, rod, ensign* of a *tribe, staff of office;* for so שֵׁבֶט *shebet* signifies in Scripture. *And thy staff,* וּמִשְׁעַנְתֶּךָ *umishantecha,* thy *prop* or support. The former may signify the shepherd's crook; the latter, some sort of *rest* or *support,* similar to our *camp stool,* which the shepherds might carry with them as an occasional seat, when the earth was *too wet* to be sat on with safety. With the *rod* or *crook* the shepherd could *defend* his sheep, and with it lay *hold of their horns* or legs to pull them out of *thickets, bogs, pits,* or *waters.* We are not to suppose that by the rod *correction* is meant: there is no idea of this kind either in the text, or in the original word; nor has it this meaning in any part of Scripture. Besides, *correction* and *chastisement* do not *comfort;* they are not, at least for the present, joyous, but grievous; nor can any person look forward to them with *comfort.* They abuse the text who paraphrase *rod* correction, &c. The other term שָׁעַן *shaan* signifies *support,* something *to rest on,* as a *staff, crutch, stave,* or the like. The *Chaldee* translates thus: "Even though I should walk in captivity, in the valley of the shadow of death, I will not fear evil. Seeing thy WORD (מֵימְרָךְ *meymerach,* thy personal Word) is my Assistant or Support; thy right word and thy law console me." Here we find that the WORD, מֵימַר *meymar,* is distinguished from any *thing spoken,* and even from the *law* itself. I cannot withhold the paraphrase of the *old Psalter,* though it considers the *rod* as signifying correction: "Sothly I sal drede na nylle; for þþ þwanðe, that es thi lyght disciplyne, that chasties me as thi son: anð þþi staf, that es thi stalworth help, that I lene me til, and haldes me uppe; thai have comforthed me; lerand (*learning, teaching*) me qwat I suld do; and haldand my thoght in the, that es my comforth."

Verse 5. Thou preparest a table before me] Here the *second allegory* begins. A magnificent banquet is provided by a most liberal and benevolent host; who has not only the *bounty* to feed me, but *power* to protect me; and, though surrounded by *enemies,* I sit down to this table with confidence, knowing that I shall feast in perfect security. This may refer to the favour God gave the poor captive Israelites in the sight of the Chaldeans who had grievously treated them for *seventy* years; and whose king, Cyrus, had not only permitted them now to return to their own land, but had also furnished them with every thing requisite for their passage, and for repairing the walls of Jerusalem, and rebuilding the temple of the Lord, where the sacrifices were offered as usual, and the people of God *feasted* on them.

Thou anointest my head with oil] Perfumed oil was poured on the heads of distinguished guests, when at the feasts of great personages. The woman in the Gospel, who poured the box of ointment of spikenard on the head of our Lord, (see Matt. xxvi. 6, 7; Mark xiv. 8; Luke vii. 46,) only acted according to the custom of her own country, which the host, who invited our Lord, had shamefully neglected.

My cup runneth over.] Thou hast not only given me abundance of *food,* but hast filled my *cup* with the best *wine.*

Verse 6. Goodness and mercy shall follow me] As I pass on through the vale of life, thy goodness and mercy shall follow my every step; as I proceed, so shall they. There seems to be an allusion here to the waters of the rock smitten by the rod of Moses, which followed the Is-

raelites all the way through the wilderness, till they came to the Promised Land. God never leaves his true followers; providential mercies, gracious influences, and miraculous interferences, shall never be wanting when they are necessary. *I will dwell in the house,* וְשַׁבְתִּי *veshabti,* "and I shall RETURN to the house of the Lord," *for ever,* לְאֹרֶךְ יָמִים *leorech yamim,* "for length of days." During the rest of my life, I shall not be separated from God's house, nor from God's ordinances; and shall at last dwell with him in glory. These two last verses seem to be the language of a priest returned from captivity to live in the temple, and to serve God the rest of his life.

ANALYSIS OF THE TWENTY-THIRD PSALM

The scope of this Psalm is to show the happiness of that man who has God for his protector, and is under his care and tuition.

To illustrate this protection, &c., David proposes *two allegories:* the one of a *shepherd;* the other of a *free-hearted man* given to *hospitality,* and *entertaining* his guests bountifully. It has *two* parts: the *first* sets forth, 1. God's care in providing him with all necessaries, ver. 1-4. 2. His liberality in supplying him with all that he needed, ver. 5.

The *second* part shows his confidence in God's grace, and his thankfulness, ver. 6.

I. He begins the first with this position, "God is my shepherd;" and upon it infers, "Therefore I shall not want." He will do for me what a good shepherd will do for his sheep.

1. He will feed me in *green pastures,* ver. 2.

2. He will there provide for my safety: "He makes me to lie down."

3. He will provide waters of comfort for me.

4. These waters shall be gently-flowing streams, *still waters*—not turbulent and violent.

5. He will take care to preserve me in health; if sick, he will *restore me.*

6. He goes before and leads me, that I may not mistake my way: "He leads me in paths of righteousness," which is his love; for it is "for his name's sake."

7. He *restores.* If I err and go astray, and *walk through the valley of the shadow of death,* (for a sheep is a straggling creature,) *I will fear no evil: for his rod and staff comfort me;* his *law* and his *Gospel* both contribute to my correction and support.

Thus, as a good Shepherd, he supplies me with *necessaries,* that I want nothing: but over and above, as a *bountiful Lord,* he has furnished me *copiously* with *varieties* which may be both for *ornament* and *honour.*

1. He *has prepared a table for me*—and that *in the presence of my enemies.*

2. He *hath anointed my head with oil,* to refresh my spirits, and cheer my countenance.

3. And *my cup runneth over*—with the choicest wine he gladdens my heart.

II. The last verse, 1. Sets out David's confidence that it shall be no worse with him: "Surely goodness and mercy shall follow me all the days of my life."

2. Then he expresses his *thankfulness:* "I will dwell in the house of the Lord for ever." In thy house, among the faithful, I will praise thy name as long as I live.

On each point in this analysis the reader is requested to consult the *notes.*

PSALM XXIV

The Lord is Sovereign Ruler of the universe, 1, 2. The great question, Who is fit to minister to the Lord in his own temple? 3–6. The glory of God in his entrance into his temple, 7–10.

V. DAY. MORNING PRAYER

A Psalm of David

A. M. cir. 2962
B. C. cir. 1042
Davidis, Regis
Israelitarum,
cir. annum
14

THE ᵃearth *is* the LORD's, and the fulness thereof; the world, and they that dwell therein.

2 ᵇFor he hath founded it upon the seas, and established it upon the floods.

3 ᶜWho shall ascend into the hill of the LORD? or who shall stand in his holy place?

4 ᵈHe ᵉthat hath ᶠclean hands, and ᵍa pure heart; who hath not lifted up his soul unto vanity, nor ʰsworn deceitfully.

A. M. cir. 2962
B. C. cir. 1042
Davidis, Regis
Israelitarum,
cir. annum
14

5 He shall receive the blessing from the LORD, and righteousness from the God of his salvation.

6 This *is* the generation of them that seek him, that ⁱseek thy face, ᵏO Jacob. Selah.

7 ˡLift up your heads, O ye gates; ᵐand be

ᵃExod. ix. 29; xix. 5; Deut. x. 14; Job xli. 11; Psa. l. 12; 1 Cor. x. 26, 28——ᵇGen. i. 9; Job xxxviii. 6; Psa. civ. 5; cxxxvi. 6; 2 Peter iii. 5——ᶜPsa. xv. 1——ᵈIsaiah xxxiii. 15, 16

ᵉHebrew, *the clean of hands*——ᶠJob xvii. 9; 1 Tim. ii. 8——ᵍMatt. v. 8——ʰPsa. xv. 4——ⁱPsa. xxvii. 8; cv. 4——ᵏOr, O God of *Jacob*——ˡIsa. xxvi. 2——ᵐPsa. xcvii. 6; Hag. ii. 7; Mal. iii. 1; 1 Cor. ii. 8

NOTES ON PSALM XXIV

It is probable that this Psalm was composed on occasion of bringing the ark from the house of Obed-edom to Mount Sion, and the questions may respect the fitness of the persons who were to minister before this ark: the last verses may refer to the opening of the city gates in order to admit it. As many of the expressions here are nearly the same with those in Psalm xv., I must refer to that place for their particular illustration; though it is most likely that the two Psalms were composed on very different occasions. The first contains a *general question* relative to *who shall be saved?* This is more particular; and refers to the temple and tabernacle service, and who is fit to minister there.

Verse 1. *The earth* is *the Lord's*] He is the Creator and Governor of it; it is his own property. Men may claim districts and kingdoms of it as *their* property, but God is Lord of the soil.

The fulness thereof] "All its creatures."— *Targum.* Every tree, plant, and shrub; the silver and the gold, and the cattle on a thousand hills.

They that dwell therein.] All *human beings.*

Verse 2. *He hath founded it upon the seas*] He not only created the vast *mass*, but separated the land from the waters, so that the mountains, &c., being elevated above the waters, appear to be founded on them, and notwithstanding all the tossings and ragings of the ocean, these waters cannot prevail. It is established upon the floods, and cannot be shaken.

Verse 3. *Who shall ascend*] Who is sufficiently holy to wait in his temple? Who is fit to minister in the holy place?

Verse 4. He that *hath clean hands*] He whose conscience is irreproachable; whose heart is without deceit and uninfluenced by unholy passions.

Who hath not lifted up his soul] Who has no *idolatrous* inclination; whose faith is pure, and who conscientiously fulfils his promises and engagements.

Verse 5. *He shall receive the blessing*] Perhaps alluding to Obed-edom, at whose house the ark had been lodged, and on whom God had poured out especial blessings.

And righteousness] Mercy: every kind of necessary good. It is the mercy of God that crowns the *obedience* and *fidelity* of good men. For what made them *good* and *faithful?* God's mercy. What crowns their fidelity? God's mercy.

Verse 6. *This* is *the generation*] This is the description of people who are such as God can approve of, and delight in.

That seek thy face, O Jacob.] It is most certain that אֱלֹהֵי *Elohey, O God,* has been lost out of the *Hebrew* text in most MSS., but it is preserved in two of *Kennicott's* MSS., and also in the *Syriac, Vulgate, Septuagint, Æthiopic, Arabic,* and *Anglo-Saxon.* "Who seek thy face, O God of Jacob."

Selah.] That is, It is confirmed; it is true. The persons who abstain from every appearance of evil, and seek the approbation of God, are those in whom God will delight.

Verse 7. *Lift up your heads, O ye gates*] The address of those who preceded the ark, the gates being addressed instead of the *keepers* of the gates. Allusion is here made to the triumphal entry of a victorious general into the imperial city.

In the hymn of *Callimachus* to Apollo, there are two lines very much like those in the text; they convey the very same sentiments. The poet represents the god coming into his temple, and calls upon the priests to open the doors, &c.

Αυτοι νυν κατοχηες ανακλινεσθε πυλαων,
Αυται δε κληιδες· ὁ γαρ Θεος ουκ ετι μακραν;

"Fall back, ye bolts; ye pond'rous doors, give way;
For not far distant is the god of day."

             Callim. Hymn in Apol., ver. 6, 7.

The whole of this hymn contains excellent sentiments even on the subject of the Psalms.

A. M. cir. 2962
B. C. cir. 1042
Davidis, Regis
Israelitarum,
cir. annum
14

ye lift up, ye everlasting doors; and the King of glory shall come in.

8 Who *is* this King of glory? The LORD strong and mighty, the LORD mighty in battle.

9 Lift up your heads, O ye gates: even lift *them* up, ye everlasting doors: and the King of glory shall come in.

A. M. cir. 2962
B. C. cir. 1042
Davidis, Regis
Israelitarum,
cir. annum
14

10 Who is this King of glory? The LORD of hosts, he *is* the King of glory. Selah.

Everlasting doors] There seems to be a reference here to something like our *portcullis*, which hangs by pullies *above* the gate, and can be let down at any time so as to prevent the gate from being forced. In the case to which the psalmist refers, the portcullis is let down, and the persons preceding the ark order it to be raised. When it is lifted up, and appears above the head or top of the gate, then the folding doors are addressed: "Be ye lift up, ye everlasting doors;" let there be no obstruction; and the mighty Conqueror, the King of glory, whose presence is with the ark, and in which the symbol of his glory appears, shall enter. Make due preparations to admit so august and glorious a Personage.

Verse 8. *Who is this King of glory?*] This is the answer of those who are *within*. Who is this glorious King, for whom ye demand entrance? To which they reply:—

The Lord strong and mighty, the Lord mighty in battle.] It is *Jehovah*, who is come to set up his abode in his imperial city: He who has conquered his enemies, and brought salvation to Israel. To make the matter still more solemn, and give those *without* an opportunity of describing more particularly this glorious Personage, those *within* hesitate to obey the first summons: and then it is *repeated*, ver. 9—

Lift up your heads, O ye gates; even lift them *up, ye everlasting doors; and the King of glory shall come in.*] To which a more particular question is proposed:—*Who is* HE, THIS *King of glory?* To which an answer is given that admitted of no reply. *The Lord of hosts*— he who is coming with innumerable armies, *He is this King of glory.* On which, we may suppose, the portcullis was lifted up, the gates thrown open, and the whole cavalcade admitted. This verse seems to have been spoken before the ark appeared: Who is this (זה *zeh*) King of glory? when its coming was merely announced. In the *tenth* verse the form is a little altered, because the ark, the symbol of the Divine Presence, had then arrived. Who is He, (מי הוא *mi hu*,) this King of glory? Here He is, to answer for himself. "The Lord is in his holy temple; let all the earth keep silence before him."

Though this Psalm has all the appearance of being an *unfinished piece*, yet there is a vast deal of dignity and majesty in it; and the *demands* from *without*, the *questions* from those *within*, and the *answers* to those questions, partake of the true sublime; where nature, dignity, and simplicity, are very judiciously mingled together. The whole procedure is *natural*, the *language dignified*, and the *questions* and *answers* full of *simplicity* and elevated sentiments.

Several, both among ancients and moderns, have thought this Psalm speaks of the *resurrection of our Lord*, and is thus to be understood. It is easy to apply it in this way: Jesus has conquered sin, Satan, and death, by dying. He now rises from the dead; and, as a mighty Conqueror, claims an entrance into the realms of glory, the kingdom which he has purchased by his blood; there to appear ever in the presence of God for us, to which he purposes to raise finally the innumerable *hosts* of his followers; for in reference to these, He is *the Lord of hosts;* and, in reference to his victory, He is *the Lord mighty in battle.*

ANALYSIS OF THE TWENTY-FOURTH PSALM

The subject of this Psalm is Christ, called the King of glory, ver. 7, and it has *two* parts:—

I. The first concerns Christ's lordship, which is, in general, over the whole world, ver. 1, 2; but in particular, over the Church, ver. 3 to 7.

II. An exhortation to all men to receive Christ for their King.

I. The first part of this Psalm shows that God is King of all the world; but in this kingdom he has two kinds of subjects:—

1. Either all men in general: "For the earth is the Lord's, and all that therein is; the compass of the world, and they that dwell therein." And for this he gives a reason, from the creation of it. He ought to have the dominion of it, and all in it: "For he hath founded it upon the seas, and established it upon the floods."

2. But all are not his subjects in the same way. There are a people whom he has called to be his subjects in another manner. There is a mountain which he hath sanctified and chosen above all other hills to make the seat of his kingdom, viz., the *Church;* and over them that live in it he is in a more peculiar manner said to be *Lord*, than of the whole earth; and these are more properly called his servants and subjects. And yet among these there is a difference too, for some only profess to be his servants, and call him *Lord*, as hypocrites; there are some others that are his servants really and truly. And that this difference may be taken notice of, the prophet asks, *Quis?* "WHO shall ascend into the hill of the Lord?" And "WHO shall stand in his holy place?" As if he should say, Not *quisquis;* it is not *every one;* for infidels are not so much as *in* the Church. Hypocrites, howsoever in the Church, are not true members of the mystical Church; and some who come to the hill of the Lord, yet stand not in his holy place; *for many believe only for a season, and few continue faithful unto death.*

3. That it may then be truly known who they are over whom he is truly *Rex gloriæ*, "the King of glory," the prophet gives us their character, and sets down three distinctive notes by which they may be known:—

1. *Cleanness of hands:* "He that hath clean hands;" *à cæde furto, &c.;* is free from all external wicked actions. For the hand is οργανον οργανων, the organ of the organs.

2. *Purity of heart.* For external purity is not enough, except the heart, the fountain of our actions, be clean.

3. *Truth of the tongue.* Is not guilty of lies and perjuries. "He that hath clean hands and

a pure heart; who hath not lifted up his soul unto vanity, nor sworn deceitfully." After the prophet has given the character by which you may know the man, he assigns his reward, and ends with an acclamation. 1. This is he that "shall receive the blessing from the Lord, and righteousness (i. e., justification) from the God of his salvation." 2. "This is the generation of them that seek thee;" that is, these are the people of God: let others boast themselves, and please themselves as they list, yet these are the godly party; these are they "that seek thy face, O God of Jacob."

II. The second part is considered by some as an *exhortation* to all men, especially princes, nobles, and magistrates, that they receive, acknowledge, and worship Christ, as King.

1. *Lift up your heads, O ye gates;* that is, as some understand it—O ye princes that sit in the *gates,* lift up your *heads* and *hearts* to him, that the King of glory may come in.

2. To which good counsel the prophet brings in the princes asking this question: "Who is this King of glory!" to which he answers, "The Lord strong and mighty, the Lord mighty in battle." One who is able to bruise you to atoms with his iron rod, and will do so if you reject him. And that the exhortation may pierce the deeper, he doubles both it and the answer.

After all, the most natural meaning is that which is given in the notes: from which we may infer:—

1. That the regal city is in no state of safety, if it have not the *ark of the Lord.*

2. That the *ark*—even the purest form of sound words in devotion, is nothing, unless they who minister and worship have *clean hands* and *pure hearts,* endeavouring to worship God in spirit and in truth.

3. That where the right faith is professed, and the worshippers act according to its dictates, *there* is the presence and the continual indwelling of God: "Lift up your heads, O ye gates—and the King of glory shall come in."

PSALM XXV

The psalmist, in great distress, calls upon God frequently, 1–5; prays for pardon with the strong confidence of being heard, 6–11; shows the blessedness of the righteous, 12–14; again earnestly implores the Divine mercy; and prays for the restoration of Israel, 15–22.

A Psalm of David

A. M. cir. 3426
B. C. cir. 578
A. U. C. cir. 176
Olymp. L.
cir. annum
tertium

UNTO [a]thee, O Lord, do I lift up my soul.

2 O my God, I [b]trust in thee: let me not be ashamed, [c]let not mine enemies triumph over me.

3 Yea, let none that wait on thee be ashamed: let them be ashamed which transgress without cause.

A. M. cir. 3426
B. C. cir. 578
A.U. C. cir. 176
Olymp. L.
cir. annum
tertium

---

[a]Psalm lxxxvi. 4; cxliii. 8; Lamentations iii. 41

[b]Psa. xxii. 5; xxxi. 1; xxxiv. 8; Isa. xxviii. 16; xlix. 23; Rom. x. 11——[c]Psa. xiii. 4

NOTES ON PSALM XXV

This Psalm seems to refer to the case of the captives in Babylon, who complain of oppression from their enemies, and earnestly beg the help and mercy of God.

It is the first of those called acrostic Psalms, i. e., Psalms each line of which begins with a several letter of the Hebrew alphabet in their common order. Of acrostic Psalms there are *seven,* viz., xxv., xxxiv., xxxvii., cxi., cxii., cxix., and cxlv. It is fashionable to be violent in encomiums on the Jews for the very *faithful manner* in which they have preserved the Hebrew Scriptures; but these encomiums are, in general, ill placed. Even this Psalm is a proof with what *carelessness* they have watched over the sacred deposit committed to their trust. The letter ו *vau* is wanting in the *fifth* verse, and ק *koph* in the *eighteenth;* the letter ר *resh* being twice inserted, once instead of ק *koph;*

and a whole line added at the end, entirely out of the alphabetical series.

Verse 1. *Do I lift up my soul.*] His soul was *cast down,* and by *prayer* and *faith* he endeavours to *lift it up* to God.

Verse 2. *I trust in thee*] I depend upon thy infinite goodness and mercy for my support and salvation.

Let me not be ashamed] Hide my iniquity, and forgive my guilt.

Verse 3. *Let none that wait on thee be ashamed*] Though he had burden enough of *his own,* he felt for *others* in similar circumstances, and became an intercessor in their behalf.

Transgress without cause.] Perhaps בוגדים *bogedim* may here mean *idolatrous persons.* "Let not them that wait upon and worship thee be ashamed: but they shall be ashamed who vainly worship, or trust in false gods." See Mal. ii. 11-16. The Chaldeans have evil en-

A. M. cir. 3426
B. C. cir. 578
A. U. C. cir. 176
Olymp. L.
cir. annum
tertium

4 ᵈShow me thy ways, O LORD; teach me thy paths.

5 Lead me in thy truth, and teach me: for thou *art* the God of my salvation; on thee do I wait all the day.

6 Remember, O LORD, ᵉthy ᶠtender mercies and thy loving-kindnesses; for they *have been* ever of old.

7 Remember not ᵍthe sins of my youth, nor my transgressions: ʰaccording to thy mercy remember thou me for thy goodness' sake, O LORD.

8 ¹Good and upright *is* the LORD: therefore will he teach sinners in the way.

A. M. cir. 3426
B. C. cir. 578
A. U. C. cir. 176
Olymp. L.
cir. annum
tertium

9 The meek will he guide in judgment: and the meek will he teach his way.

10 All the paths of the LORD *are* mercy and truth unto such as keep his covenant and his testimonies.

11 ᵏFor thy name's sake, O LORD, pardon mine iniquity; ˡfor it *is* great.

12 What man *is* he that feareth the LORD?

ᵈExod. xxxiii. 13; Psa. v. 1; xxvii. 11; lxxxvi. 11; cxix. cxliii. 8, 10——ᵉPsa. ciii. 17; cvi. 1; cvii. 1; Isa. lxiii. 15; Jer. xxxiii. 11——ᶠHeb. *thy bowels*

ᵍJob xiii. 26; xx. 11; Jer. iii. 25——ʰPsa. li. 1——¹Psa lii. 9; liv. 6; lxxiii. 1, &c.——ᵏPsa. xxxi. 3; lxxix. 9; cix. 21; cxliii. 11——ˡSee Rom. v. 20

---

treated us, and oppressed us: they trust in their idols, let them see the vanity of their idolatry.

Verse 4. *Show me thy ways*] The psalmist wishes to *know* God's *way*, to be taught his *path*, and to be led into his *truth*. He cannot discern this *way* unless God *show* it; he cannot *learn* the *path* unless God *teach* it; and he cannot *walk* in God's *truth* unless God *lead* him: and even then, unless God *continue* to *teach*, he shall never *fully* learn the lessons of his salvation; therefore he adds, "Lead me in thy truth, and teach me;" ver. 5.

That he may get this *showing, teaching*, and *leading*, he comes to God, as the "God of his salvation;" and that he may not lose his labour, he "waits on him all the day." Many lose the benefit of their earnest prayers, because they do not *persevere* in them. They pray for *a time;* get remiss or discouraged; restrain prayer; and thus lose all that was already wrought for and in them.

Verse 5. *On thee do I wait*] This is the line in which ו *vau*, the sixth letter in the order of the alphabet, is lost; for the line begins with א *aleph*, אותך *othecha*, "on thee." But four of *Kennicott's* and *De Rossi's* MSS. have ואותך *veothecha*, "AND upon thee." This restores the lost ו *vau*, which signifies "and." The *Septuagint, Syriac, Vulgate, Arabic, Æthiopic*, and *Anglo-Saxon*, preserve it.

Verse 6. *Remember, O Lord, thy tender mercies, and thy loving-kindness*] The word רחמים *rachamim*, means the *commiseration* that a man feels in his bowels at the sight of distress. The second word, חסדים *chasadim*, signifies those *kindnesses* which are the offspring of a *profusion of benevolence*.

They have been *ever of old*.] Thou wert ever wont to display thyself as a ceaseless fountain of good to all thy creatures.

Verse 7. *Remember not the sins of my youth*] Those which I have committed through *inconsiderateness*, and *heat of passion*.

According to thy mercy] As it is *worthy of thy mercy* to act according to the measure, the greatness, and general practice of thy mercy; so give me an *abundant pardon, a plentiful salvation*.

For thy goodness' sake] Goodness is the nature of God; *mercy* flows from that *goodness*.

Verse 8. *Good and upright* is *the Lord*] He is *good* in his *nature*, and *righteous* in his *conduct*.

Therefore will he teach sinners] Because he is good, he will teach sinners, though they deserve nothing but destruction: and because he is *right*, he will *teach* them the *true way*.

Verse 9. *The meek will he guide*] עניים *anavim*, the *poor*, the *distressed; he will lead in judgment*—he will direct them in their cause, and bring it to a happy issue, for he will show them the *way* in which they should go.

Verse 10. *All the paths of the Lord*] ארחות *orchoth* signifies the *tracks* or *ruts* made by the *wheels of wagons* by often passing over the same ground. *Mercy* and *truth* are the *paths* in which God *constantly walks* in reference to the children of men; and so *frequently* does he show them *mercy*, and so frequently does he fulfil his *truth*, that his paths are earnestly discerned. How frequent, how deeply indented, and how multiplied are those *tracks* to every *family* and *individual!* Wherever we go, we see that God's mercy and truth have *been there* by the *deep tracks* they have left behind them. But he is more abundantly merciful to those who *keep his covenant and his testimonies;* i. e., those who are conformed, not only to the letter, but to the spirit of his pure religion.

Verse 11. *For thy name's sake, O Lord, pardon*] I have sinned; I need mercy; there is no reason why thou shouldst show it, but what thou drawest from the goodness of thy own nature.

Verse 12. *That feareth the Lord*] Who has a proper apprehension of *his* holiness, justice, and truth; and who, at the same time, sees *himself* a fallen spirit, and a transgressor of God's holy law, and consequently under the curse. That is the person that truly and reverently fears God.

Him shall he teach] Such a person has a *teachable spirit*.

The way that *he shall choose*.] The way that in the course of Providence he has chosen, as the way in which he is to gain things honest in the sight of all men; God will bless him in it, and give him as much earthly prosperity as may be useful to his soul in his secular *vocation*.

A. M. cir. 3426
B. C. cir. 578
A. U. C. cir. 176
Olymp. L.
cir. annum
tertium

^mhim shall he teach in the way *that* he shall choose.

13 ⁿHis soul ^oshall dwell at ease; and ^phis seed shall inherit the earth.

14 ^qThe secret of the Lord *is* with them that fear him; ^rand he will show them his covenant.

15 ^sMine eyes *are* ever toward the Lord; for he shall ^tpluck my feet out of the net.

16 ^uTurn thee unto me, and have mercy upon me; for I *am* desolate and afflicted.

17 The troubles of my heart are enlarged:

O bring thou me out of my distresses.

A. M. cir. 3426
B. C. cir. 578
A. U. C. cir. 176
Olymp. L.
cir. annum
tertium

18 ^vLook upon mine affliction and my pain; and forgive all my sins.

19 Consider mine enemies; for they are many; and they hate me with ^wcruel hatred.

20 O keep my soul, and deliver me: ^xlet me not be ashamed; for I put my trust in thee.

21 Let integrity and uprightness preserve me; for I wait on thee.

22 ^yRedeem Israel, O God, out of all his troubles.

---

^mPsalm xxxvii. 23——ⁿProverbs xix. 23——^oHebrew, *shall lodge in goodness*——^pPsalm xxxvii. 11, 22, 29——^qProverbs iii. 32; see John vii. 17; xv. 15

^rOr, *and his covenant to make them know it*——^sPsa. cxli. 8——^tHeb. *bring forth*——^uPsa. lxix. 16; lxxxvi. 16 ^v2 Sam. xvi. 12——^wHeb. *hatred of violence*——^xVer. 2 ^yPsa. cxxx. 8

Verse 13. *His soul shall dwell at ease*] בטוב תלין *betob talin*, "shall lodge in goodness;" this is the *marginal* reading in our version; and is preferable to that in the text.

His seed shall inherit] His *posterity* shall be blessed. For them many prayers have been sent up to God by their pious fathers; and God has registered these prayers in their behalf.

Verse 14. *The secret of the Lord* is *with them*] סוד *sod*, the *secret assembly* of the Lord is with them that fear him; many of them have a Church in their own house.

He will show them his covenant.] He will let them see how great blessings he has provided for them that love him. Some refer this to the covenant of redemption by Christ Jesus.

Verse 15. *Mine eyes* are *ever toward the Lord*] All my expectation is from him alone. If I get at any time entangled, he will pluck my feet out of the net.

Verse 16. *Turn thee unto me*] Probably the prayer of the poor captives in Bablyon, which is continued through this and the remaining verses.

Verse 17. *The troubles of my heart are enlarged*] The evils of our captive state, instead of lessening, seem to multiply, and each to be extended.

Verse 18. *Look upon mine affliction*] See my distressed condition, and thy eye will affect thy heart.

Forgive all my sins.] My sins are the *cause* of all my sufferings; forgive these.

This is the verse which should begin with the letter ק *koph;* but, instead of it, we have ר *resh* both here, where it should *not* be, and in the next verse where it should be. Dr. *Kennicott* reads קומה *kumah*, "arise," and *Houbigant*, קצר *ketsar*, "cut short." The word which began with ק *koph* has been long lost out of the verse, as every *version* seems to have read that which now stands in the Hebrew text.

Verse 19. *Consider mine enemies*] Look upon them, and thou wilt see how impossible it is that I should be able to resist and overcome them. They are many, they hate me, and their hatred drives them to acts of *cruelty* against me.

Verse 20. *O keep my soul*] Save me from sin, and keep me alive.

Let me not be ashamed] He ends as he began; see verse 2: "Let me not be confounded, for I put my trust in thee."

Verse 21. *Let integrity and uprightness*] I wish to have a *perfect heart*, and an *upright life*. This seems to be the meaning of these two words.

Verse 22. *Redeem Israel, O God*] The people are prayed for in the preceding verses as if *one person;* now he includes the whole, lest his own personal necessities should narrow his heart, and cause him to forget his fellow sufferers.

This verse stands out of the order of the Psalm; and does not appear to have formed a part of the *alphabetical* arrangement. It is a general prayer for the redemption of Israel from captivity; and may well be applied to those of the true Israel who are seeking for complete redemption from the power, the guilt, and the pollution of sin; and from all the *troubles* that spring from it. And let it be ever known, that God alone can redeem Israel.

ANALYSIS OF THE TWENTY-FIFTH PSALM

This Psalm is a continued earnest prayer of a man or a people pressed with danger and enemies, and sensible of God's heavy displeasure against sin. It consists of *five petitions*.

I. His *first* petition is, that his "enemies may not triumph over him," ver. 2, 3.

II. His *second* is for *instruction*, ver. 4, 5, which he urges, ver. 8, 9, 10, 12, 13, 14.

III. His *third* is for *mercy* and *forgiveness*, ver. 6, 7, 11.

IV. His *fourth* is a renewal of his first, ver. 15, 16, 17, &c., with many arguments.

V. His *fifth* is for Israel in general, ver. 22.

I. He begins with the profession of his faith and confidence in God, without which there can be no prayer: "Unto thee, O Lord," &c.; he relies not on, nor seeks after, any human help. And upon this living hope, he prays—

1. For this life, that it shame him not, as it does where a man hopes, and is frustrated: "Let me not be ashamed." Make it appear that I hope not in thee in vain.

2. "Let not mine enemies triumph over me." Glorying that I am deserted. This petition he urges by this argument: The example may prove dangerous, if thou send me no help; but it will be to thy glory, if I be relieved. If he were delivered, the faith and hope of others would be confirmed; if deserted, the good would faint and fail, the wicked triumph: therefore he prays, O, let none that wait on thee be ashamed; but let them be ashamed who transgress, that is, they that do me wrong *maliciously, without any cause* being given by *myself*.

II. He petitions for *instruction*, that he may be always guided and governed by the word of God, that he sink not under the cross, but rely on God's promises.

1. "Show me thy ways, and teach me thy paths." Show me that thou often dealest severely with thy best servants: bringest down, before thou exaltest; mortifiest, before thou quickenest; and settest the cross before the crown. *Teach me*—show me, that this is *thy way*.

2. "Lead me in thy truth, and teach me." Cause me to remember that thy promises are firm and true; *yea* and *amen* to those who trust in thee. This makes me hope still: "Thou art the God of my salvation."

III. His third petition is for *mercy*. He prays for mercy, and the removal of the sin that obstructs it.

1. "Remember, O Lord, thy tender mercies, &c., which have been ever of old;" i. e., deal mercifully with me as thou hast ever done with those who flee to thee in their extremity.

2. He prays for the *remission* of the *sins* of his *youth:* "Remember not the sins of my youth." This petition he repeats, ver. 11: "For thy name's sake pardon mine iniquity;" and upon this confession: "For it is great."

The psalmist here breaks off prayer; and, to confirm his confidence, speaks of the nature and person of God. It is necessary sometimes, even in the midst of our prayers, to call to mind the nature of God, and his ways with his people, lest, through a sense of our unworthiness or great unfaithfulness, we should be discouraged. And this course David takes; he says,

1. "Good and upright is the Lord." 1. *Good*, for he receives sinners *gratis*. 2. *Upright*—constant and true in his promises; therefore he will teach sinners in the way.

2. "The meek will he guide in judgment." He will not suffer them to be tempted above their strength; will teach them what to answer; and will not proceed with rigour, but will interpret all in the most favourable sense.

3. In a word, "All the ways of the Lord are mercy and truth." 1. *Mercy*, in that he freely offers the remission of sins, the graces of his Spirit, support in distresses, and at last eternal life, to those who by faith and a good conscience walk before him: "Keep his covenant and his testimonies;" for the words of the *covenant* are: "I will be thy God, and the God of thy seed;" upon which follows: "Walk before me, and be thou perfect."

4. Upon the confidence of which promises and covenant the psalmist repeats his prayer: "O Lord, pardon mine iniquity; for it is great," ver. 11.

The psalmist now admires the happiness of him who trusts in God: "What man is he that feareth the Lord!" This happiness he sets forth by the fruits that follow his piety:—

1. The *first* fruit he shall gather is instruction and direction in his vocation, and private life: "Him shall he teach in the way," &c.

2. The *second* is, that his happiness shall not be *momentary*, but firm and lasting: "His soul shall dwell at ease."

3. The *third* is, that he shall be happy in his *posterity:* "His seed shall inherit the land."

4. The *fourth* is, that the redemption of mankind by Christ Jesus, with all the effects of it, pardon, holiness, &c., which is a secret unknown to the world, shall be revealed and applied to him: "The secret of the Lord is with them that fear him; and he will show them his covenant."

IV. Being confirmed by these promises, and cheered with these fruits, he,

1. Testifies his faith in God for deliverance: "My eyes are ever toward the Lord; he will pluck my feet out of the net."

2. He then renews his former prayer, it being nearly the same as that with which he began. It is conceived in several clauses: 1. "Turn thee unto me." 2. "Have mercy upon me." 3. "O bring me out of my distresses." 4. "Look upon my affliction and trouble, and forgive me all my sins." 5. "Consider mine enemies." 6. "O keep my soul, and deliver me." 7. "Let me not be ashamed." 8. "Let integrity and uprightness preserve me."

Petitioners, and men in misery, think they can never say enough. This makes him often *repeat* the same thing. The sum is, that God would hear and grant him defence and deliverance in his dangers; remission of sins which caused them; and protect, direct, and govern him in his troubles.

3. That he might prevail in his suit, like an excellent orator, he uses many arguments to induce God to be propitious to him:—

1. His faith and trust in his promises: "Mine eyes are ever towards the Lord."

2. The danger he was now in: "His feet were in the net."

3. He was oppressed, alone, and had none to help him: "I am desolate and afflicted."

4. His inward afflictions and pain were grievous: "The troubles of my heart are enlarged."

5. His enemies were many, powerful, merciless, cruel: "Mine enemies are many—and hate me with cruel hatred."

6. And yet I am innocent, and desire to be so; and am thy servant: "Let integrity and uprightness preserve me; for I wait upon thee."

V. The psalmist having thus, through the Psalm, prayed for himself, at last offers up a short but earnest petition for the whole Church; which proceeds from that *fellowship* or *communion* which ought to be among all saints: "Redeem Israel, O God, out of all his troubles!" Turn our captivity, and forgive the sins which have occasioned it.

PSALM XXVI

The psalmist appeals to God for his integrity, and desires to be brought to the Divine test in order to have his innocence proved, 1–3; shows that he had avoided all fellowship with the wicked, and associated with the upright, 4–8; prays that he may not have his final lot with the workers of iniquity, 9, 10; purposes to walk uprightly before God, 11, 12.

A Psalm of David

A. M. cir. 3426
B. C. cir. 578
A. U. C. cir. 176
Olymp. L.
cir. annum
tertium

JUDGE ^ame, O LORD; for I have ^bwalked in mine integrity: ^cI have trusted also in the LORD; *therefore* I shall not slide.

2 ^dExamine me, O LORD, and prove me; try my reins and my heart.

3 For thy ^eloving-kindness *is* before mine eyes: and ^fI have walked in thy truth.

4 ^gI have not sat with vain persons, nei-

ther will I go in with dissem-blers.

5 I have ^hhated the congregation of evil doers; ⁱand will not sit with the wicked.

6 ^kI will wash mine hands in innocency: so will I compass thine altar, O LORD:

7 That I may publish with the voice of thanksgiving, and tell of all thy wondrous works.

8 LORD, ^lI have loved the habitation of thy

A. M. cir. 3426
B. C. cir. 578
A. U. C. cir. 176
Olymp. L.
cir. annum
tertium

---

^aPsalm vii. 8——^bVerse 11; 2 Kings xx. 3; Proverbs xx. 7——^cPsalm xxviii. 7; xxxi. 14; Proverbs xxix. 25 ^dPsalm vii. 9; xvii. 3; lxvi. 10; cxxxix. 23; Zechariah xiii. 9——^ePsalm xvii. 7; xxxvi. 7; xl. 10, 11; li. 1,

&c.——^f2 Kings xx. 3——^gPsalm i. 1; Jeremiah xv. 17 ^hPsalm xxxi. 6; cxxxix. 21, 22——ⁱPsalm i. 1——^kSee Exodus xxx. 19, 20; Psalm lxxiii. 13; 1 Timothy ii. 8 ^lPsa. xxvii. 4

NOTES ON PSALM XXVI

This Psalm, and the two following, are supposed by *Calmet* to be all parts of one ode, and to relate to the time of the captivity, containing the prayers, supplications, complaints, and resolutions of the Israelites in Babylon. This is probable; but we have not evidence enough to authorize us to be nice on such points. See on the following verse.

Verse 1. *Judge me, O Lord*] There are so many strong assertions in this Psalm concerning the innocence and uprightness of its author, that many suppose he wrote it to vindicate himself from some severe reflections on his conduct, or accusations relative to plots, conspiracies, &c. This seems to render the opinion probable that attributes it to David during his exile, when all manner of false accusations were brought against him at the court of Saul.

I have walked in mine integrity] I have never plotted against the life nor property of any man; I have neither coveted nor endeavoured to possess myself of Saul's crown.

I have trusted] Had I acted otherwise, I could not have been prosperous; for thou wouldst not have worked miracles for the preservation of a wicked man.

I shall not slide.] I shall be preserved from swerving from the paths of righteousness and truth.

Verse 2. *Examine me, O Lord*] To thee I appeal; and feel no hesitation in wishing to have all the motives of my heart dissected and exposed to thy view, and to that of the world.

Verse 3. *For thy loving-kindness*] A sense of thy favour and approbation was more to my heart than thrones and sceptres; and in order to retain this blessing, *I have walked in thy truth.*

Verse 4. *I have not sat with vain persons*] מְתֵי שָׁוְא *methey shav, men of lies, dissemblers, backbiters,* &c.

Neither will I go in with dissemblers] נַעֲלָמִים *naalamim,* the *hidden ones,* the *dark designers,* the *secret plotters* and conspirators in the state.

Verse 5. *I have hated the congregation of evil doers*] I have never made one in the crowds of discontented persons; persons who,

under pretence of rectifying what was wrong in the *state,* strove to subvert it, to breed general confusion, to overturn the laws, seize on private property, and enrich themselves by the spoils of the country.

Verse 6. *I will wash mine hands in innocency*] Washing the hands was frequent among the Jews, and was sometimes an action by which a man declared his innocence of any base or wicked transaction. This *Pilate* did, to protest his innocence of the mal-treatment and death of Christ. I will maintain that innocence of life in which I have hitherto walked; and take care that nothing shall be found in my heart or life that would prevent me from using the most holy ordinance, or worshipping thee in spirit and truth.

So will I compass thine altar] It is a mark of respect among the Hindoos to *walk* several times *round* a *superior,* and round a *temple.*

Verse 7. *That I may publish*] I have endeavoured to act so as always to keep a conscience void of offence towards thee and towards man. I have made a profession of faith in thee, and salvation from thee, and my *practice* gives no lie to my *profession.*

Verse 8. *Lord, I have loved the habitation of thy house*] I have carefully used thine ordinances, that I might obtain more grace to help me to persevere. And I have not been attentive to those duties, merely because they were *incumbent* on me; but *I have loved the place where thine honour dwelleth;* and my delight in thy ordinances has made my attendance as pleasant as it was profitable. This verse would be better translated, *Jehovah, I have loved the habitation of thy house, and the place of the tabernacle of thy glory.* The *habitation* must mean the *holy of holies,* where the Divine Presence was manifest; and the *place of the tabernacle* must refer to the *mercy-seat,* or the place where the *glory of the Lord* appeared between the cherubim, upon the lid or cover of the ark of the covenant. From his dwelling there, מִשְׁכָּן *mishcan,* the *place* and the *appearance* were called שְׁכִינָה *shechinah;* the dwelling of Jehovah, or that glorious appearance which was the symbol of the Divine Presence.

A. M. cir. 3426
B. C. cir. 578
A. U. C. cir. 176
Olymp. L.
cir. annum
tertium

house, and the place ^mwhere thine honour dwelleth.

9 ⁿGather^o not my soul with sinners, nor my life with ^pbloody men:

10 In whose hands *is* mischief, and their right hand is ^qfull of ^rbribes.

11 But as for me, I will walk ^sin mine integrity: redeem me and be merciful unto me.

A. M. cir. 3426
B. C. cir. 578
A. U. C. cir. 176
Olymp. L.
cir. annum
tertium

12 ^tMy foot standeth in an ^ueven place: ^vin the congregations will I bless the LORD.

---

^mHeb. *of the tabernacle of thy honour*——ⁿOr, *Take not away*——^oSee 1 Sam. xxv. 29; Psa. xxviii. 3 ^pHeb. *men of blood*——^qHeb. *filled with*

^rExod. xxiii. 8; Deut. xvi. 19; 1 Sam. viii. 3; Isa. xxxiii. 15——^sVer. 1——^tPsa. xl. 2——^uPsa. xxvii. 11 ^vPsa. xxii. 22; cvii. 32; cxi. 1

Verse 9. *Gather not my soul with sinners*] As I have never loved their company, nor followed their practice, let not my eternal lot be cast with them! I neither love them nor their ways; may I never be doomed to spend an eternity with them!

Verse 10. *Their right hand is full of bribes*] He speaks of persons in office, who took bribes to pervert judgment and justice.

Verse 11. *But as for me, I will walk in mine integrity*] Whatever I may have to do with public affairs, shall be done with the strictest attention to truth, justice, and mercy.

Redeem me] From all snares and plots laid against my life and my soul.

And be merciful unto me.] I *deserve* no good, but thou art merciful; deal with me ever in thy mercy.

Verse 12. *My foot standeth in an even place*] On the above principles I have taken my stand: to abhor evil; to cleave to that which is good; to avoid the company of wicked men; to frequent the ordinances of God; to be true and just in all my dealings with men; and to depend for my support and final salvation on the mere mercy of God. He who acts in this way, *his feet stand in an even place.*

I will bless the Lord.] In all my transactions with men, and in all my assemblings with holy people, I will speak good of the name of the Lord, having nothing but good to speak of that name.

ANALYSIS OF THE TWENTY-SIXTH PSALM

There are *four* general parts in this Psalm:—
I. An appeal of David to God to be his Judge, ver. 1, 2.
II. The causes that induced him to make the appeal. His conscious innocence, integrity, &c.
III. A petition, ver. 9, 11.
IV. His gratitude, ver. 12.

I. He begins with his appeal to God, whom he knew to be a *just Judge;* and therefore desires to be dealt with according to law: "Judge me; examine me; prove me; try me; even my reins and my heart."

II. Then he assigns two causes of it; his *integrity* and his *faith.*
1. His *faith* and confidence in God were such that he knew that the Judge of all the world would do him right. "I have trusted in the Lord; therefore, I shall not slide." I will not change my religion, though powerfully tempted to do so.
2. His *integrity:* "I have walked in my integrity." For which he assigns the cause: "Thy loving-kindness is before my eyes; I have walked in thy truth." I follow thy *word,* and the principle it lays down.

Next he sets down his integrity by an in-

junction of parts, which were two: 1. How he carried himself to men; 2. How he conducted himself towards God.

1. He abstained from all society, confederacy, counsels, and intimacy with wicked men; he did hate and abominate their ways: "I have not sat in counsel with vain persons, neither will I go in with dissemblers. I have hated the congregation of evil doers, and will not sit with the wicked."

2. The other degree of his *integrity* was, his *piety:* "I will wash my hands in innocence," i. e., I will worship thee; and for this end he would keep his hands from blood, oppression, &c., in order that he "might publish with the voice of thanksgiving, and tell of all the wondrous works of the Lord."

3. He mentions a second act of his piety, his *love to God's house,* and the service done in it: "O Lord, I have loved the habitation of thy house, and the place where thy honour dwelleth."

III. Upon which conscientiousness of his integrity he falls to prayer, that God would not suffer him to be polluted with the conversation of wicked men, nor involved in their punishment: "Gather not my soul with sinners." Observe the many titles he gives to wicked men:—

1. They are *vain persons;* void of the fear of God; irreligious, ver. 4.
2. *Deep, dark men;* saying one thing with their mouth, and another with their heart, ver. 4.
3. *Malignant;* doing all for their own ends, ver. 5.
4. *Impious;* regardless of God and religion, ver. 5.
5. *Sinners;* traders in wickedness, ver. 9.
6. *Blood-thirsty* men; cruel and revengeful. ver. 9.
7. *Mischievous;* ready to execute with their *hands* what they had plotted in their *heart.* ver. 10.
8. *Lovers of bribes;* perverting judgment for the sake of money, ver. 10.

With such David will have nothing to do: "But as for me, I will walk in my integrity." *Redeem me* from such people, *and be merciful to me.*

IV. Lastly. He shows his gratitude. "My foot stands in an even place;" hitherto I am sure I am in the good way. I will *therefore praise the Lord in the congregation;* not only privately, but publicly.

My foot hath hitherto been kept right by thy grace and mercy; therefore, when thou shalt bring me back again to thy temple, I will not be ungrateful, but will sing praises to thy name in and with the great congregation. Amen.

PSALM XXVII

The righteous man's confidence in God, 1–3; his ardent desire to have the spiritual privilege of worshipping God in his temple, because of the spiritual blessings which he expects to enjoy there, 4–6; his prayer to God for continual light and salvation, 7–9; his confidence that, though even his own parents might forsake him, yet God would not, 10. Therefore he begs to be taught the right way to be delivered from all his enemies, and to see the goodness of the Lord in the land of the living, 11–13; he exhorts others to trust in God; to be of good courage; and to expect strength for their hearts, 14.

V. DAY. EVENING PRAYER

A Psalm of David

A. M. cir. 3426
B. C. cir. 578
A. U. C. cir. 176
Olymp. L.
cir. annum
tertium

THE LORD *is* ᵃmy light and ᵇmy salvation; whom shall I fear? ᶜthe LORD *is* the strength of my life; of whom shall I be afraid?

2 When the wicked, *even* mine enemies and my foes, ᵈcame upon me to ᵉeat up my flesh, they stumbled and fell.

3 ᶠThough a host should encamp against me, my heart shall not fear: though war should rise against me, in this *will* I *be* confident.

A. M. cir. 3426
B. C. cir. 578
A. U. C. cir. 176
Olymp. L.
cir. annum
tertium

4 ᵍOne *thing* have I desired of the LORD, that will I seek after; that I may ʰdwell in the house of the LORD all the days of my life, to behold ⁱthe ᵏbeauty of the LORD, and to inquire in his temple.

5 For ˡin the time of trouble he shall hide

ᵃPsa. lxxxiv. 11; Isa. lx. 19, 20; Mic. vii. 8——ᵇExod. xv. 2——ᶜPsa. lxii. 2, 6; cxviii. 14, 21; Isa. xii. 2 ᵈHeb. *approached against me*——ᵉPsa. xiv. 4

ᶠPsa. iii. 6——ᵍPsa. xxvi. 8——ʰPsa. lxv. 4; Luke ii. 37——ⁱOr, *the delight*——ᵏPsa. xc. 17——ˡPsa. xxxi. 20; lxxxiii. 3; xci. 1; Isa. iv. 6

NOTES ON PSALM XXVII

In the *Hebrew* and *Chaldee* this Psalm has no other title than simply לדוד *ledavid: To* or *For David.* In the *Syriac:* "For David; on account of an infirmity which fell upon him." In the *Vulgate, Septuagint, Arabic,* and *Æthiopic,* it has this title: "A Psalm of David, before he was anointed." The *Anglo-Saxon* omits all the titles. For this title there is no authority in fact. However, it may be just necessary to state that David appears to have received the royal unction three times: 1. In Bethlehem, from the hand of Samuel, in the house of his father Jesse; 1 Sam. xvi. 13. 2. At Hebron, after the death of Saul, by the men of Judah; 2 Sam. ii. 4. 3. By the elders of Israel, at Hebron, after the death of Ishbosheth, when he was acknowledged king over all the tribes; 2 Sam. v. 3. At which of these anointings the Psalm was written, or whether before any of them, we know not; nor is the question to be decided. Some commentators say that it is a Psalm belonging to the *captivity,* and upon that system it may be well interpreted. And lastly, it has been contended that it was written by David after he had been in danger of losing his life by the hand of a gigantic Philistine, and must have perished had he not been succoured by Abishai; see the account 2 Sam. xxi. 17; and was counselled by his subjects not to go out to battle any more, *lest he should extinguish the light of Israel.* To these advisers he is supposed to make the following reply:—

Verse 1. *The Lord* is *my light and my salvation*] This light can never be extinguished by man; the Lord is my salvation, my safeguard, my shield, and my defence; of whom then should I be afraid?

Verse 2. *When the wicked—came upon me*] Near as I appeared to you to be in danger of losing my life, I was safe enough in the hands of the Lord; and those who thought to *have eaten me up, stumbled,* failed of their purpose, and *fell;* the Philistine lost his own life.

Verse 3. *Though a host should encamp against me*] I am so confident of the Almighty's protection, that were I *alone,* and encompassed by a host, I would not fear. I am in the hand of God; and while in that hand, I am safe.

Verse 4. *One* thing *have I desired*] If I am grown too old, and from that circumstance unable to serve my country, I shall then prefer a retirement to the tabernacle, there to serve God the rest of my days. There I shall behold his glory, and there I may *inquire* and get important answers respecting Israel.

But though these words may be thus interpreted, on the above supposition, that David penned the Psalm on the occasion of his escape from the Philistine, and the desire expressed by his subjects that he should go no more out to war; yet it appears that they more naturally belong to the *captivity,* and that this verse especially shows the earnest longing of the captives to return to their own land, that they might enjoy the benefit of Divine worship.

Verse 5. *He shall hide me in his pavilion*] בסכה *besuccoh, in his tabernacle.* I would make his temple my residence; I would dwell with God, and be in continual safety. *Pavilion* comes from *papilio* and παπιλων, a *butterfly.* It signifies a *tent* made of cloth stretched out on poles, which in form resembles in some measure the insect above named.

In the secret of his tabernacle] Were there no other place, he would put me in the *holy of holies,* so that an enemy would not dare to approach me.

He shall set me upon a rock.] He shall so *strengthen* and *establish* me, that my enemies shall not be able to prevail against me. He shall hide me where they cannot find me, or put me out of the reach of the fiery darts of the wicked. He who lives *nearest to God* suffers least from temptation. "Draw nigh to God, and he will draw nigh to thee: resist the devil, and he will flee from thee."

A. M. cir. 3426
B. C. cir. 578
A. U. C. cir. 176
Olymp. L.
cir. annum
tertium

me in his pavilion: in the secret
of his tabernacle shall he hide
me; he shall [m]set me upon a rock.
6 And now shall [n]mine head
be lifted up above mine enemies round about
me; therefore will I offer in his tabernacle
sacrifices [o]of joy; I will sing, yea, I will sing
praises unto the LORD.

7 Hear, O LORD, *when* I cry
with my voice: have mercy also
upon me, and answer me.
8 [p]*When thou saidst,* [q]Seek
ye my face; my heart said unto thee, Thy
face, LORD, will I seek.
9 [r]Hide not thy face *far* from me; put not
thy servant away in anger: thou hast been [s]my

[m]Psa. xl. 2——[n]Psa. iii. 3——[o]Heb. *of shouting*——[p]Or, *My heart said unto thee, Let my face seek thy face, &c.*

[q]Psa. xxiv. 6; cv. 4——[r]Psa. lxix. 17; cxliii. 7——[s]Psa. xl. 7; lxiii. 7; lxx. 5

Verse 6. *Now shall mine head be lifted up*] We shall most assuredly be redeemed from this captivity, and restored to our own land, and to the worship of our God in his own temple. There shall we offer sacrifices of joy; we will sing praises unto the Lord, and acknowledge that it is by his might and mercy alone that we have been delivered.

Verse 7. *Hear, O Lord,* when *I cry*] This is the utmost that any man of common sense can expect—*to be heard when he cries.* But there are multitudes who suppose God will bless them whether they *cry or not;* and there are others, and not a few, who although they *listlessly pray* and *cry* not, yet imagine God must and will hear them! God will answer them that *pray and cry;* those who do *not* are most likely to be without the blessings which they so much need.

Verse 8. When thou saidst, *Seek ye my face*] How much labour and skill have been employed to make sense of this verse as it stands in our translation! The original words are the following, from which our Version has been forcibly extracted:—

לך אמר לבי בקשו פני את פניך יהוה אבקש *lecha amar libbi bakkeshu panai; eth paneycha, Yehovah, abakkesh;* of which I believe the true rendering to be as follows: "Unto thee, my heart, he hath said, Seek ye my face. Thy face, O Jehovah, I will seek. O my heart, God hath commanded thee to seek his face." Then, *his face I will seek.* Which may be paraphrased thus: *Unto thee,* his Church, God *hath said, Seek ye,* all who compose it, *my face.* To which *I,* his Church, have answered, *Thy face, O Jehovah, I will seek.* On referring to Archbishop *Secker,* I find that he, and indeed Bishop *Horsley,* are of the same mind.

I had formerly proposed another method of reading this difficult verse. Suspecting that some *error* had got into the text, for בקשו פני *bakkeshu panay,* "seek ye my face," I had substituted אבקש פניך *abakkesh paneycha,* "I will seek thy face;" or with the *Vulgate* and *Septuagint,* בקשתי פניך *bakkesti paneycha,* "I have sought thy face," *exquisivit te facies mea,* Εξεζητησα το προσωπον σου. And this small alteration seemed to make a good sense: "My heart said unto thee, I have sought thy face, (or, I will seek thy face,) and thy face, O Lord, I will seek." I have not only *done* what it was my duty and interest to do, but I will *continue to do* it. Some have proposed to *mend* the text thus: לך לך אמר לבי *lech lecha, amar libbi,* "Go to, saith my heart," נבקש פני יהוה *nebakkesh peney Yehovah,* "Let us seek the face of Jehovah." This is rather a violent emendation, and is supported by neither MSS. nor *Versions.* The whole verse is wanting in one of Dr. Kennicott's MSS. On the whole I prefer what is first proposed, and which requires no alteration in the text; next, that of the *Vulgate* and *Septuagint.*

The old *Psalter* paraphrases thus: **Til the saide my hert, the my face soght: thy face, lord, I sal seke.** "The gernyng of my hert that spekes til god, and he anely heres: saide **til the my face,** that es my presence soght the and na nother thyng. And fra now I sal seke thy face lastandly, til my dede; and that I fynd my sekyng:" i. e., To thee, said my heart; thee my face sought: thy face, O Lord, I shall seek. "**The gerning of my hert,** that spekes til God, and he anely heres, **til the my face;** that es, my presence soght the and no nother thyng: **and fra now I sal seke thy face** lastandly, til my dede, and that I fynd my sekyng:" i. e., The yearning strong desire of my heart, which speaks to God, and he alone hears; my face is to thee; that is, myself sought thee, and none other thing, and from now I shall seek thee lastingly till my death, and till that I find what I seek.

Verse 9. *Hide not thy face—from me*] As my face is towards thee wheresoever I am, so let thy face be turned towards me. In a Persian MS. poem entitled شاه وگدا *Shah we Gudda,* "The King and the Beggar," I have found a remarkable couplet, most strangely and artificially involved, which expresses exactly the same sentiment:—

روي ما سوي تست از همه رو
سوي ما روي تست از همه سو

One meaning of which is—

OUR *face is towards* THEE in all our ways;
THY *face is towards* US in all our intentions.

Something similar, though not the same sentiment is in *Hafiz,* lib. i., gaz. v., cap. 2:—

با مريدان روبسوي كعبه چون اريم چون
روبسوي خانه خمار دارد پير ما

How can we with the disciples *turn our face towards* the kaaba,
When our spiritual instructer *turns his face towards* the wine-cellar?

I shall subjoin a higher authority than either:—

Ὁτι οφθαλμοι Κυριου επι δικαιους,
Και ωτα αυτου εις δεησιν αυτων·
Προσωπον δε Κυριου επι ποιουντας κακα.
1 Pet. iii. 12.

A. M. cir. 3426
B. C. cir. 578
A. U.C.cir.176
Olymp. L.
cir. annum
tertium

help; leave me not, neither forsake me, O God of my salvation.

10 ᵗWhen my father and my mother forsake me, then the LORD ᵘwill take me up.

11 ᵛTeach me thy way, O LORD, and lead me in a ʷplain path, because of ˣmine enemies.

12 ʸDeliver me not over unto the will of mine

---

enemies: for ᶻfalse witnesses are risen up against me, and such as ᵃbreathe out cruelty.

A. M. cir. 3426
B. C. cir. 578
A. U.C.cir.176
Olymp. L.
cir. annum
tertium

13 *I had fainted,* unless I had believed to see the goodness of the LORD ᵇin the land of the living.

14 ᶜWait on the LORD: be of good courage, and he shall strengthen thine heart: wait, I say, on the LORD.

ᵗIsa. xlix. 15——ᵘHeb. *will gather me;* Isa. xl. 11
ᵛPsa. xxv. 4; lxxxvi. 11; cxix.——ʷHeb. *a way of plainness;* Psa. xxvi. 12——ˣHeb. *those which observe me;* Psa. v. 8; liv. 5——ʸPsa. xxxv. 25

ᶻ1 Sam. xxii. 9; 2 Sam. xvi. 7, 8; Psa. xxxv. 11
ᵃActs ix. 1——ᵇPsa. lvi. 13; cxvi. 9; cxlii. 5; Jer. xi. 19;
Ezek. xxvi. 20——ᶜPsa. xxxi. 24; lxii. 1, 5; cxxx. 5;
Isa. xxv. 9; Hab. ii. 3

For the *eyes of the Lord* are *upon* the righteous;
And *his ears* to their supplication:
And the *face of the Lord* is *upon* the workers
  of evil.

Verse 10. *When my father and my mother forsake me*] Or, more literally, "For my father and my mother have forsaken me; but the Lord hath gathered me up." My parents were my protectors *for a time;* but the Lord has been my Protector *always.* There is no time in which I do not fall under his merciful regards.

Verse 11. *Teach me thy way*] Let me know the gracious designs of thy providence towards me, that my heart may submit to thy will.

And lead me in a plain path] In the path of righteousness, because of mine enemies, who watch for my halting.

Verse 12. *Deliver me not over unto the will of mine enemies*] *To their soul* בנפש *benephesh;* their whole soul thirsts for my destruction. Let them not be gratified. They have suborned witnesses against me, but they are false witnesses: unmask their wickedness, and confound their counsels.

Verse 13. I had fainted, *unless I had believed*] The words in italics are supplied by our translators; but, far from being necessary, they injure the sense. Throw out the words *I had fainted,* and leave a *break* after the verse, and the elegant figure of the psalmist will be preserved: "Unless I had believed to see the goodness of the Lord in the land of the living" ———What! what, alas! should have become of me!

Dr. *Hammond* has observed that there is a remarkable elegance in the original, which, by the use of the beautiful figure *aposiopesis,* makes an abrupt breaking off in the midst of a speech. He compares it to the speech of *Neptune* to the winds that had raised the tempest to drown the fleet of Æneas.—*Æneid.* lib. i., ver. 131.

Eurum ad se zephyrumque vocat: dehinc talia
  fatur;
Tantane vos generis tenuit fiducia vestri?
Jam cœlum terramque, meo sine numine, venti,
Miscere, et tantas audetis tollere moles?
Quos ego—sed motos præstat componere fluctus.

To Eurus and the western blast he cried,
Does your high birth inspire this boundless
  pride?
Audacious winds! without a power from me,
To raise at will such mountains on the sea?

Thus to confound heaven, earth, the air, and
  main;
Whom I———but, first, I'll calm the waves
  again.   PITTS.

Verse 14. *Wait on the Lord*] All ye who are in distress, *wait on the Lord.* Take me for an example. I waited on him, and *he strengthened my heart;* wait ye on him, and he *will strengthen your heart.* You cannot be unsuccessful; fear not. *Wait, I say, on the Lord;* wait for his succour in doing his will. *Age viriliter,* says the *Vulgate;* act like a man, *hope, believe, work,* and *fear not.*

ANALYSIS OF THE TWENTY-SEVENTH PSALM

There are *four* general *parts* in this Psalm. David shows,

I. How free he is from fear in any danger; and he shows also the cause of his confidence, ver. 1, 2, 3.

II. He expresses his love to God's house and his religion, ver. 4, 5, 6.

III. He prays for succour and support, ver. 7, &c.

IV. He exhorts others to dependence on the Lord, ver. 14.

I. It is possible (independently of the reason given in the notes) that some person, friend or foe, might ask David how he felt during the persecutions raised against him by Saul? To whom he may be supposed to return this answer: "I was never disheartened, never in despair; and the reason was, God was my *Light* to guide me, my *Rock* to save me, and my *Strength* to sustain and support me: 'The Lord is my light,' &c." And this he amplifies in the next two verses: 1. By *experience:* he had already found this true: "When the wicked, even mine enemies, came upon me to eat up my flesh, they stumbled and fell." 2. He puts a *case:* "Though a host should encamp against me, my heart shall not fear; though war should rise against me, in this will I be confident."

The arguments for his confidence were, 1. God's *goodness,* ver. 1. 2. His own *experience,* ver. 2. To which he adds, 3. What *God would do for him.*

1. He would hide him in his tabernacle, ver. 5.

2. That though his father and mother should forsake him, God would take him up, ver. 10.

3. That he should see the *goodness* of God in the land of the living, ver. 13.

II. He expresses his great love and affection to the house of God: "One thing I have desired," and in this he was constant. "THAT (emphatically) I will seek after; that I may dwell in the house of the Lord all the days of my life." For *three* ends:—

1. "To behold the beauty of the Lord." To taste how good and gracious he is.

2. "To inquire in his temple." There to search the mind of God.

3. "To offer in his temple sacrifices of joy, and to sing praises to the Lord."

And this was another argument of his security: "For in the time of trouble he will hide me in his pavilion—he shall set me upon a rock, and my head shall be lifted up." And—

III. He prays for succour and support.

1. For *audience*, and an *answer:* "Hear, O Lord, when I cry; have mercy upon me, and answer me."

2. The *ground* of his prayer; his having willingly received the commandment of God: "He hath said, Seek ye my face. Thy face, O Lord, will I seek."

3. The *matter* of his prayer in *general:* "Hide not thy face from me; put not thy servant away in anger." In which he had good hope of success from former experience. "Thou hast been my help;" be to me now as thou hast been: "Leave me not, nor forsake me, O God of my salvation," &c.

4. The *matter* of his prayer in *particular:* "Teach me thy way, O God; lead me in a plain path." That is, teach me what to do that I may please thee, and "lead me in a plain path," that I may escape the snares of my enemies. "Deliver me not over to their will," for they seek my ruin. 1. They are perjured men: "False witnesses have risen up again me." 2. They are mischievously bent: "They breathe out cruelty."

5. And their cruelty and falsehood are so great that "unless I had believed to see the goodness of the Lord in the land of the living," what would have become of me!

IV. He concludes with an *exhortation* that all others would consider his example, and in their greatest extremities be courageous, and put their trust in God as he did: "Wait on the Lord, be of good courage, and he shall strengthen thy heart; wait, I say, on the Lord." Be an expectant; for he that has promised to come will come, and will not tarry. But wait *actively;* be not *idle.* Use the *means* of grace; *read, hear, pray, believe, work.* Acknowledge him in all thy ways, and he will direct thy steps. They that wait upon the Lord shall never be confounded.

PSALM XXVIII

A righteous man in affliction makes supplication to God, and complains of the malice of his enemies, 1–4; whom he describes as impious, and whose destruction he predicts, 5. He blesses God for hearing his prayers, and for filling him with consolation, 6, 7; then prays for God's people, 8, 9.

A Psalm of David

A. M. cir. 3426
B. C. cir. 578
A. U. C. cir. 176
Olymp. L. cir. annum tertium

UNTO thee will I cry, O LORD my rock; [a]be not silent [b]to me: [c]lest, *if* thou be silent to me, I become like them that go down into the pit.

2 Hear the voice of my supplications, when I cry unto thee, [d]when I lift up my hands [e]toward [f]thy holy oracle.

A. M. cir. 3426
B. C. cir. 578
A. U. C. cir. 176
Olymp. L. cir. annum tertium

---

[a]Psa. lxxxiii. 1——[b]Heb. *from me*——[c]Psa. lxxxiv. 4; cxliii. 7——[d]1 Kings vi. 22, 23; viii. 28, 29; Psa. v. 7

[e]Or, *toward the oracle of thy sanctuary*——[f]Psalm cxxxviii. 2

NOTES ON PSALM XXVIII

This Psalm is of the same complexion with the two preceding; and belongs most probably to the times of the captivity, though some have referred it to David in his persecutions. In the *five* first verses the author prays for support against his enemies, who appear to have acted treacherously against him. In the *sixth* and *seventh* he is supposed to have gained the victory, and returns with songs of triumph. The *eighth* is a chorus of the people sung to their conquering *king.* The *ninth* is the prayer of the king for his people.

Verse 1. *O Lord my rock*] צורי *tsuri* not only means *my rock,* but *my fountain,* and the *origin* of all the good I possess.

If *thou be silent*] If thou do not answer in such a way as to leave no doubt that thou hast heard me, I shall be as a dead man. It is a modern refinement in theology which teaches that no man *can know* when God hears and answers his prayers, but by an *induction of particulars,* and

by an *inference* from his *promises.* And, on this ground, how can any man fairly presume that he is heard or answered at all? May not his *inductions* be no other than the *common occurrences* of *providence?* And may not *providence* be no more than the *necessary occurrence of events?* And is it not possible, on this skeptic ground, that there is *no God* to hear or answer? True religion knows nothing of these abominations; it teaches its votaries to pray to God, to expect an answer from him, and to look for the Holy Spirit to bear witness with their spirits that they are the sons and daughters of God.

Verse 2. *Toward thy holy oracle.*] דביר קדשך *debir kodshecha; debir* properly means that place in the holy of holies from which God gave oracular answers to the high priest. This is a presumptive proof that there was a *temple* now standing; and the custom of stretching out the hands in prayer *towards the temple,* when the Jews were at a distance from it, is here referred to.

A. M. cir. 3426
B. C. cir. 578
A. U.C. cir. 176
Olymp. L.
cir. annum
tertium

3 ^gDraw me not away with the wicked, and with the workers of iniquity, ^hwhich speak peace to their neighbours, but mischief *is* in their hearts.

4 ⁱGive them according to their deeds, and according to the wickedness of their endeavours: give them after the work of their hands; render to them their desert.

5 Because ^kthey regard not the works of the LORD, nor the operation of his hands, he shall destroy them, and not build them up.

6 Blessed *be* the LORD, because he hath heard the voice of my supplications.

7 The LORD *is* ^lmy strength and my shield; my heart ^mtrusted in him, and I am helped: therefore my heart greatly rejoiceth; and with my song will I praise him.

8 The LORD *is* ⁿtheir strength, and he *is* the ^osaving ^pstrength of his anointed.

9 Save thy people, and bless ^qthine inheritance: ^rfeed them also, ^sand lift them up for ever.

A. M. cir. 3426
B. C. cir. 578
A. U.C. cir. 176
Olymp. L.
cir. annum
tertium

---

^gPsa. xxvi. 9——^hPsa. xii. 2; lv. 21; lxii. 4; Jer. ix. 8
ⁱ2 Tim. iv. 14; Rev. xviii. 6——^kJob xxxiv. 27; Isa. v. 12
^lPsa. xviii. 2——^mPsa. xiii. 5; xxii. 4

ⁿOr, *his strength*——^oHeb. *strength of salvations*
^pPsa. xx. 6——^qDeut. ix. 29; 1 Kings viii. 51, 53
^rOr, *rule;* Psa. lxxviii. 71——^sEzra i. 4

Verse 3. *Draw me not away*] Let me not be involved in the punishment of the wicked.

Verse 4. *Give them*] Is the same as *thou wilt give them;* a prophetic declaration of what their lot will be.

Verse 5. *They regard not the works of the Lord*] They have no knowledge of the true God, either as to his *nature,* or as to his *works.*

He shall destroy them, and not build them up.] This is a remarkable prophecy, and was literally fulfilled: the Babylonian empire was destroyed by Cyrus, and never built up again; for he founded the Persian empire on its ruins. Even the place where Babylon stood is now no longer known.

Verse 7. *The Lord is my strength*] I have the fullest persuasion that he hears, will answer, and will save me.

Verse 8. *The Lord is their strength*] Instead of לָמוֹ *lamo, to them,* eight MSS. of *Kennicott* and *De Rossi* have לְעַמּוֹ *leammo, to his people;* and this reading is confirmed by the *Septuagint, Syriac, Vulgate, Æthiopic, Arabic,* and *Anglo-Saxon.* This makes the passage more precise and intelligible; and of the truth of the reading there can be no reasonable doubt. "The Lord is the strength of his PEOPLE, and the saving strength of his anointed." Both *king* and *people* are protected, upheld, and saved by him.

Verse 9. *Save thy people*] Continue to preserve them from all their enemies; from idolatry, and from sin of every kind.

Bless thine inheritance] They have taken thee for their God; thou hast taken them for thy people.

Feed them] רְעֵה *raah* signifies both to *feed* and to *govern. Feed them,* as a *shepherd* does his *flock; rule them,* as a *father* does his *children.*

Lift them up for ever.] Maintain thy true Church; let no enemy prevail against it. Preserve and magnify them for ever. *Lift them up:* as hell is the bottomless pit in which damned spirits sink down for ever; or, as Chaucer says, *downe all downe;* so heaven is an endless height of glory, in which there is an eternal rising or exaltation. Down, all down; up, all up; for ever and ever.

ANALYSIS OF THE TWENTY-EIGHTH PSALM

There are *three* parts in this Psalm:—
I. A prayer, ver. 1-6.

II. A thanksgiving, ver. 6-9.
III. A prayer for the Church, ver. 9.

I. The first part is a prayer to God; in which he first requests audience, ver. 2: "Hear me." And his prayer is so described, that it sets forth most of the conditions requisite in one that prays:—

1. The *object*—GOD: "Unto thee, O Lord, do I cry."

2. His *faith:* "To thee I cry, who art my rock."

3. His *fervour:* It was an ardent and vehement prayer: "I cry."

4. *Humility;* it was a supplication: "Hear the voice of my supplication."

5. His *gesture:* "I lift up my hands."

6. According to God's ORDER: "Towards thy holy temple."

1. The argument he uses to procure an audience; the danger he was in: "Lest, if thou be silent, I become like them that go down to the pit."

2. Then he expresses what he prays for, which is, that either

1. He might not be corrupted by the fair persuasions of hypocrites:

2. Or that he might not be partaker of their punishments: "Draw me not away with the wicked." Upon whom he sets this mark: "Who speak peace—but mischief is in their hearts."

3. Against whom he uses this imprecation, which is the second part of his prayer: "Give them according to their own deeds," &c.

4. For which he gives this reason: They were enemies to God and to his religion; far from repentance, and any hope of amendment: "They regard not the words of the Lord, nor the operation of his hands; therefore he shall destroy them, and not build them up."

II. Then follows an excellent form of thanksgiving, which he begins with "Blessed be the Lord;" and assigns the reasons, which express the chief parts of thanksgiving.

1. That God heard him: "He hath heard the voice of my supplication."

2. That he would be his Protector: "The Lord is my strength and my shield."

3. For his grace of confidence: "My heart trusted in him."

4. That from him he had relief: "I am helped."

5. The testification and annunciation of this gratitude: "Therefore my heart greatly re-

joiceth; and with my song will I praise him." He remembers the indenture: "I will DELIVER THEE,—thou shalt PRAISE ME." And, therefore, with heart and tongue he gives thanks.

6. And that God might have all the honour, he repeats what he said before: "The Lord is their strength," &c., that is, of all them that were with him.

III. He concludes with a prayer, in which he commends the whole Church to God's care and tuition.

1. "Save thy people," in the midst of these tumults and distractions.

2. "Bless thine inheritance;" that they increase in knowledge, piety, and secular prosperity.

3. "Feed them:" Give them a godly king.

4. "Lift them up for ever:" Make their name famous among the Gentiles; let them increase and multiply till thy Church embraces all nations, and kindreds, and people, and tongues. This hath the Lord promised.

PSALM XXIX

The psalmist calls upon the great and mighty to give thanks unto God, and to worship him in the beauty of holiness, on account of a tempest that had taken place, 1, 2. He shows the wonders produced by a thunderstorm, which he calls the voice of God, *3–9. Speaks of the majesty of God, 10; and points out the good he will do to his people, 11.*

A Psalm of David

A. M. cir. 2985
B. C. cir. 1019
Davidis, Regis
Israelitarum,
cir. annum
37

GIVE ªunto the LORD, O ᵇye mighty, give unto the LORD glory and strength.

2 Give unto the LORD ᶜthe glory due unto his name; worship the LORD ᵈin ᵉthe beauty of holiness.

3 The voice of the LORD *is* upon the waters: ᶠthe God of glory thundereth: the LORD *is* upon ᵍmany waters.

A. M. cir. 2985
B. C. cir. 1019
Davidis, Regis
Israelitarum,
cir. annum
37

4 The voice of the LORD *is* ʰpowerful; the voice of the LORD *is* ⁱfull of majesty.

5 The voice of the LORD breaketh the ce-

ª1 Chron. xvi. 28, 29; Psa. xcvi. 7, 8, 9——ᵇHeb. *ye sons of the mighty*——ᶜHeb. *the honour of his name*——ᵈOr, *in* his *glorious sanctuary*

ᵉ2 Chronicles xx. 21——ᶠJob xxxvii. 4, 5 ᵍOr, *great waters*——ʰHeb. *in power*——ⁱHeb. *in majesty*

NOTES ON PSALM XXIX

In the Hebrew, this is called *A Psalm for David.* The *Vulgate* says, "A Psalm of David, when the tabernacle was completed." The *Septuagint* says: "A Psalm of David, at the going out or exodus of the tabernacle." The *Arabic* states it to be "A prophecy concerning the incarnation; and concerning the ark and the tent." Num. v. 12. The *Syriac*, "A Psalm of David, concerning oblation." The Psalm was probably written to commemorate the abundant rain which fell in the days of David, after the heavens had been shut up for three years; 2 Sam. xxi. 1-10.

Verse 1. *O ye mighty*] אלים בני *beney elim,* "sons of the strong ones," or "sons of rams." The *Chaldee* has, "Ye hosts of angels, sons of God." The *Vulgate* has, "Offer to the Lord, ye sons of God; offer to the Lord the sons of rams;" in this rendering agree the *Septuagint, Æthiopic, Arabic,* and *Anglo-Saxon.* The old Psalter has, 𝔅𝔯𝔦𝔫𝔤𝔢𝔰 𝔱𝔦𝔩 𝔏𝔬𝔯𝔡 𝔶𝔢 𝔤𝔬𝔡𝔡𝔢𝔰 𝔰𝔬𝔫𝔫𝔢𝔰; 𝔟𝔯𝔶𝔫𝔤𝔢𝔰 𝔱𝔦𝔩 𝔏𝔬𝔯𝔡 𝔰𝔬𝔫𝔫𝔢𝔰 𝔬𝔣 𝔴𝔢𝔱𝔥𝔢𝔯: which it paraphrases thus: that es, yourself, sonnes of apostles, that war leders of goddes folk; qwam ye study to folow.

Glory and strength.] Ascribe all excellence and might to him.

The whole Psalm is employed in describing the effects produced by a thunder-storm which had lately taken place.

Verse 2. *The glory due unto his name*] Rather, *the glory of his name.* His name is *Mercy;* his nature is *love.* Ascribe *mercy, love,*

power, and *wisdom* to him. All these are implied in the name *Jehovah.*

In the beauty of holiness.] קדש בהדרת *behadrath kodesh,* "the beautiful garments of holiness." Let the priests and Levites put on their best and cleanest apparel; and let the whole service be conducted in such a way as to be no dishonour to the Divine Majesty. The *Vulgate* and others read, *In the palace of his holiness.* Let all go to the temple, and return thanks to God for their preservation during this dreadful storm. See on ver. 9.

Verse 3. *The voice of the Lord*] THUNDER, so called, Exod. ix. 23, 28, 29; Job xxxvii. 4; Psa. xviii. 13; Isa. xxx. 30. On this subject see the note on Job xxxvii. 4, where there is a particular description of the nature and generation of thunder; and of the *lightning, clap, rain,* and other *phenomena* which accompany it.

Upon many waters.] The clouds, which Moses calls the waters which are above the firmament.

Verse 4. Is *powerful*] There is no agent in universal nature so powerful as the electric fluid. It destroys life, tears castles and towers to pieces, rends the strongest oaks, and cleaves the most solid rocks: universal animate nature is awed and terrified by it. To several of these effects the psalmist here refers; and for the illustration of the whole I must refer to the above notes on Job.

Full of majesty.] No sound in nature is so tremendous and majestic as that of *thunder;* it is the most fit to represent the voice of God.

Verse 5. *Breaketh the cedars*] Very tall trees attract the lightning from the clouds, by which

A. M. cir. 2985
B. C. cir. 1019
Davidis, Regis
Israelitarum,
cir. annum
37

dars; yea, the LORD breaketh ᵏthe cedars of Lebanon.

6 ¹He maketh them also to skip like a calf; Lebanon and ᵐSirion like a young unicorn.

7 The voice of the LORD ⁿdivideth the flames of fire.

8 The voice of the LORD shaketh the wilderness; the LORD shaketh the wilderness of ᵒKadesh.

9 The voice of the LORD maketh ᵖthe hinds ᑫto calve, and discovereth the forests: and in his temple ʳdoth every one speak of *his* glory.

10 The LORD ˢsitteth upon the flood; yea, ᵗthe LORD sitteth King for ever.

11 ᵘThe LORD will give strength unto his people; the LORD will bless his people with peace.

A. M. cir. 2985
B. C. cir. 1019
Davidis, Regis
Israelitarum,
cir. annum
37

ᵏIsa. ii. 13——¹Psa. cxiv. 4——ᵐDeut. iii. 9——ⁿHeb. *cutteth out*——ᵒNum. xiii. 26——ᵖJob xxxix. 1, 2, 3——ᑫOr, *to be in pain*——ʳOr, *every whit of it uttereth,* &c.——ˢGen. vi. 17; Job xxxviii. 8, 25——ᵗPsa. x. 16——ᵘPsa. xxviii. 8

---

they are often torn to pieces. *Woods* and *forests* give dreadful proof of this after a thunderstorm.

Verse 7. *Divideth the flames of fire.*] The forked zigzag lightning is the cause of *thunder;* and in a thunder-storm these lightnings are variously dispersed, smiting houses, towers, trees, men, and cattle, in different places.

Verse 8. *The wilderness of Kadesh.*] This was on the frontiers of Idumea and Paran. There may be a reference to some terrible thunder-storm and earthquake which had occurred in that place.

Verse 9. *Maketh the hinds to calve*] Strikes terror through all the tribes of animals; which sometimes occasions those which are pregnant to cast their young. This, I believe, to be the whole that is meant by the text. I meddle not with the *fables* which have been published on this subject both by *ancients* and *moderns.*

Discovereth the forests] Makes them sometimes evident in the darkest night, by the sudden flash; and often by setting them on fire.

And in his temple] Does this refer to the effect which a dreadful thunder-storm often produces? Multitudes run to places of worship as asylums in order to find safety, and pray to God. See on ver. 2.

Verse 10. *The Lord sitteth upon the flood*] יהוה למבול ישב *Yehovah lammabbul yashab,* "Jehovah sat upon the deluge." It was Jehovah that commanded those waters to be upon the earth. He directed the storm; and is here represented, after all the confusion and tempest, as sitting on the floods, appeasing the fury of the jarring elements; and reducing all things, by his governing influence, to regularity and order.

Sitteth king for ever.] He governs universal nature; whatsoever he wills he does, in the heavens above, in the earth beneath, and in all deep places. Every phenomenon is under his government and control. There is something very like this in Virgil's description of Neptune appeasing the storm raised by Juno for the destruction of the fleet of Æneas. See at the end of this Psalm.

Verse 11. *The Lord will give strength*] Prosperity in our secular affairs; success in our enterprises; and his blessing upon our fields and cattle.

The Lord will bless his people with peace.] Give them victory over their enemies, and cause the nations to be at peace with them; so that they shall enjoy uninterrupted prosperity. The

plentiful rain which God has now sent is a foretaste of his future blessings and abundant mercies.

In the note on ver. 10 I have referred to the following description taken from Virgil. Did he borrow some of the chief ideas in it from the 29th Psalm? The reader will observe several coincidences.

Interea magno misceri murmure pontum,
Emissamque hyemem sensit Neptunus, et imis
Stagna refusa vadis: graviter commotus, et alto
Prospiciens, summa placidum caput extulit unda.
Disjectam Æneæ toto videt æquore classem,
Fluctibus oppressos Troas, cœlique ruina.

    ＊   ＊   ＊   ＊   ＊

Eurum ad se zephyrumque vocat: dehinc talia fatur

    ＊   ＊   ＊   ＊   ＊

Sic ait: et dicto citius tumida æquora placat,
Collectasque fugat nubes, solemque reducit.
Cymothoë simul, et Triton adnixus acuto
Detrudunt naves scopulo; levat ipse tridenti;
Et vastas aperit syrtes, et temperat æquor,
Atque rotis summas levibus perlabitur undas.

    ＊   ＊   ＊   ＊   ＊

Sic cunctus pelagi cecidit fragor, æquora postquam
Prospiciens genitor, cæloque invectus aperto,
Flectit equos, curruque volans dat lora secundo.
          Æn. lib. i., ver. 124.

"Mean time, imperial Neptune heard the sound
Of raging billows breaking on the ground.
Displeased, and fearing for his watery reign,
He rears his awful head above the main,
Serene in majesty; then rolled his eyes
Around the space of earth, of seas, and skies.
He saw the Trojan fleet dispersed, distressed,
By stormy winds and wintry heaven oppressed.

    ＊   ＊   ＊   ＊   ＊

He summoned Eurus and the Western Blast,
And first an angry glance on both he cast;
Then thus rebuked.

    ＊   ＊   ＊   ＊   ＊

He spoke; and while he spoke, he soothed the sea,
Dispelled the darkness, and restored the day.
Cymothoë, Triton, and the sea-green train
Of beauteous nymphs, and daughters of the main,

Clear from the rocks the vessels with their
    hands;
The god himself with ready trident stands,
And opes the deep, and spreads the moving
    sands;
Then heaves them off the shoals: where'er he
    guides
His finny coursers, and in triumph rides,
The waves unruffle, and the sea subsides.

   *   *   *   *   *

So when the father of the flood appears,
And o'er the seas his sovereign trident rears,
Their fury fails: he skims the liquid plains
High on his chariot; and with loosened reins,
Majestic moves along, and awful peace main-
    tains.
                               DRYDEN.

Our God, Jehovah, sitteth upon the flood: yea,
Jehovah sitteth King for ever.

The heathen god is drawn by his *sea-horse*,
and *assisted* in his work by *subaltern deities:*
Jehovah sits on the flood an everlasting Governor, ruling all things by his *will*, maintaining
order, and dispensing strength and peace to his
people. The description of the Roman poet is
fine; that of the Hebrew poet, majestic and
sublime.

ANALYSIS OF THE TWENTY-NINTH PSALM

There are two *parts* in this Psalm:—
I. The *exhortation* itself, ver. 1, 2.
II. The *reasons* on which it is founded. These
are drawn,
  1. From his *power*, ver. 3, to ver. 11.
  2. From the *protection* he affords to his people, ver. 11.
  I. The *exhortation*, which is singular. It proceeds from a king, and not from a common
man; a prince, a great prince; and reminds
princes and great men that there is *One greater
than they;* and that, therefore, they should yield
unto him his *due honour and worship.*
  1. That they *freely* yield and *give* it up: for
which he is very earnest, as appears from the
urged *repetition, give, give, give.*
  2. That in *giving* this, they must understand
they are giving him no more than *his due:*
"Give him the honour due to his name."
  3. *What* they are to give: *glory* and *strength.*
1. They must make his *name to be glorious.* 2.
They must attribute their *strength* to him.
  4. That they *bow before* and *adore* him.
  5. That they *exhibit* this honour in the proper
PLACE: "In his temple; and in the beauty of
holiness."
  II. And that they may be more easily persuaded to give the Lord the honour due to his

name, he proposes *two reasons* to be considered:—
  First. His *power;* for although *they* be *mighty
ones*, his power is infinitely beyond theirs;
which is seen in his *works of nature;* but, omitting many others, he makes choice of the
thunder, and the *effects* it produces.
  1. From its *nature:* for howsoever philosophers may assign it to *natural causes*, yet religious men will look higher; and, when they
hear those fearful noises in the air, will confess, with the psalmist, that it is *the voice of
the Lord*, which he repeats here *seven* times;
and this voice has affrighted the stoutest-hearted
sinners, and the mightiest of tyrants.
  2. From the *place* where this voice is given:
"The voice of the Lord is upon the waters;
upon many waters."
  3. From its *force* and *power.* They are not
vain and empty noises, but strike a terror: "The
voice of the Lord is powerful; the voice of the
Lord is full of majesty."
  4. From its *effects;* which he explains by an
induction:—
  1. Upon the strong TREES, *the cedars of Lebanon:* "The voice of the Lord breaks the cedars,"
&c.
  2. Upon the *firmest* MOUNTAINS, even *Lebanon*
and *Sirion;* for sometimes the thunder is accompanied with an *earthquake*, and the mountains *skip like a calf.*
  3. Upon the *air;* which is, to common minds,
no small wonder; for, as nothing is more contrary to *fire* than *water*, it is next to miraculous
how, out of a *watery* cloud, such *flames* of *fire*
should be darted. "The voice of the Lord
divideth the flames of fire."
  4. In the *brute creation;* for it makes them
fear and leave their caves, dens, and woods;
yea, makes some of them cast their young: "The
voice of the Lord shaketh the wilderness," &c.;
"it maketh the hinds to calve."
  5. In the mighty *rains* which follow upon it;
when the cataracts of heaven are opened, and
such floods of water follow that a man might
fear that the earth was about to be overwhelmed by a *second inundation.* Out of all
which he draws this conclusion: "The Lord
sitteth upon the flood; the Lord sitteth a King
for ever;" therefore, the earth is not destroyed.
  Secondly. His *second* reason is drawn from
the *works of grace.* 1. When He moves men to
acknowledge his voice, and to give him glory
in his temple: "In his temple doth every man
speak of his honour." 2. By the *security* He
gives to his people, even in the time when he
utters his voice, and *speaks in thunder;* whereas
the *wicked* then tremble and quake: "The Lord
will give strength unto his people; the Lord
will bless his people with peace," i. e., bodily
security, and peace of conscience.

PSALM XXX

*The psalmist returns thanks to God for deliverance from great danger, 1–3. He calls upon the saints to give
thanks to God at the remembrance of his holiness, because of his readiness to save, 4, 5. He relates how his
mind stood affected before this great trial, and how soon an unexpected change took place, 6, 7; mentions how,
and in what terms, he prayed for mercy, 8–10; shows how God heard and delivered him, and the effect it had
upon his mind, 11, 12.*

VI. DAY. MORNING PRAYER

A Psalm *and* Song ᵃ*at the dedication of the house of David*

A. M. cir. 2987
B. C. cir. 1017
Davidis, Regis
Israelitarum,
cir. annum
39

I WILL extol thee, O LORD; for thou hast ᵇlifted me up, and hast not made my foes to ᶜrejoice over me.

2 O LORD my God, I cried unto thee, and thou hast ᵈhealed me.

ᵃDeuteronomy xx. 5; 2 Samuel v. 11; vi. 20——ᵇPsa. xxviii. 9——ᶜPsalm xxv. 2; xxxv. 19, 24——ᵈPsalm vi. 2; ciii. 3——ᵉPsalm lxxxvi. 13——ᶠPsalm xxviii 1——ᵍPsa. xl. 2; lv. 23; lxxxviii. 4, 6; cxliii. 7; Prov. i. 12

---

3 O LORD, ᵉthou hast brought up my soul from the grave: thou hast kept me alive, that I should not ᶠgo down to the ᵍpit.

A. M. cir. 2987
B. C. cir. 1017
Davidis, Regis
Israelitarum,
cir. annum
39

4 ʰSing unto the LORD, O ye saints of his, and give thanks ⁱat the remembrance of his holiness.

5 For ᵏhis ˡanger *endureth but* a moment;

ʰ1 Chron. xvi. 4; Psa. xcvii. 12——ⁱOr, *to the memorial*——ᵏPsalm ciii. 9; Isaiah xxvi. 20; liv. 7, 8; 2 Corinthians iv. 17——ˡHebrew, there is but *a moment in his anger*

NOTES ON PSALM XXX

This *Psalm* or *song* is said to have been made or used *at the dedication of the house* of David, or rather the dedication of a house or temple; for the word *David* refers not to הבית *habbayith,* the *house,* but to מזמור *mizmor,* a *Psalm.* But what temple or house could this be? Some say, the *temple* built by *Solomon;* others refer it to the *dedication* of the *second temple* under Zerubbabel; and some think it intended for the dedication of a *third* temple, which is to be built in the days of the Messiah. There are others who confine it to the *dedication of the house which David built* for himself on Mount Sion, after he had taken Jerusalem from the Jebusites; or to the purgation and re-dedication of his own house, that had been defiled by the wicked conduct of his own son Absalom. *Calmet* supposes it to have been made by David on the dedication of the place which he built on the threshing floor of Araunah, after the grievous *plague* which had so nearly desolated the kingdom, 2 Sam. xxiv. 25; 1 Chron. xxi. 26. All the parts of the Psalm agree to this: and they agree to this so well, and to no other hypothesis, that I feel myself justified in modelling the comment on this principle alone.

Verse 1. *I will extol thee—for thou hast lifted me up*] I will lift thee up, for thou hast lifted me up. Thou hast made me blessed, and I will make thee glorious. Thou hast magnified me in thy mercy; and I will show forth thy praise, and speak good of thy name.

I have made some remarks on this Psalm in the Introduction.

In this Psalm we find *seven* different states of mind distinctly marked:—

1. It is implied, in the *first verse,* that David had been in great distress, and nearly overwhelmed by his enemies.

2. He extols God for having lifted him up, and having preserved him from the cruelty of his adversaries, ver. 1-3.

3. He is brought into great prosperity, trusts in what he had received, and forgets to depend wholly on the Lord, ver. 4-6.

4. The Lord hides his face from him, and he is brought into great distress, ver. 7.

5. He feels his loss, and makes earnest prayer and supplication, ver. 8-10.

6. He is restored to the Divine favour, and filled with joy, ver. 11.

7. He purposes to glory in God alone, and to trust in him for ever, ver. 12.

As it is impossible for any man to have passed through *all these states* at the same time; it is supposed that the Psalm, like many others of the same complexion, has been formed out of the *memoranda of a diary.* See this point illustrated in the Introduction.

Thou hast lifted me up] Out of the pit into which I had fallen: the vain curiosity, and want of trust in God, that induced me to number the people. Bishop *Horsley* translates, *Because thou hast depressed me.* I thank God for my humiliation and afflictions, because they have been the means of teaching me lessons of great profit and importance.

Verse 2. *Thou hast healed me.*] Thou hast removed the plague from my people by which they were perishing in *thousands* before my eyes.

Verse 3. *Thou hast brought up my soul from the grave*] I and my people were both about to be cut off; but thou hast spared us in mercy, and given us a most glorious respite.

Verse 4. *Sing unto the Lord, O ye saints of his*] Ye *priests,* who wait upon him in his sanctuary, and whose business it is to offer prayers and sacrifices for the people, magnify him for the mercy he has now showed in staying this most destructive plague.

Give thanks at the remembrance of his holiness.] "Be ye holy," saith the Lord, "for I am holy." He who can give thanks at the *remembrance* of his holiness, is one who *loves holiness;* who *hates sin;* who longs to be saved from it; and takes encouragement at the recollection of God's holiness, as he sees in this the *holy nature* which *he* is to share, and the *perfection* which he is *here* to attain. But most who call themselves Christians hate the doctrine of holiness; never hear it inculcated without pain; and the principal part of their studies, and those of their pastors, is to find out *with how little holiness they can rationally expect to enter into the kingdom of God.* O fatal and soul-destroying delusion! How long will a holy God suffer such abominable doctrines to pollute his Church, and destroy the souls of men?

Verse 5. *For his anger* endureth but *a moment*] There is an elegant abruptness in these words in the Hebrew text. This is the literal translation: "For a moment in his anger. Lives in his favour. In the evening weeping may lodge: but in the morning exultation." So good is God, that he cannot delight in either the depression or ruin of his creatures. When he afflicts, it is for our advantage, that we may be partakers of his holiness, and be not condemned with the world. If he be *angry* with us, it is but for a *moment;* but when we have recourse to him, and seek his face, his *favour*

A. M. cir. 2987
B. C. cir. 1017
Davidis, Regis
Israelitarum,
cir. annum
39

[m]in his favour *is* life: weeping may endure [n]for a night, but [o]joy [p]*cometh* in the morning.

6 And [q]in my prosperity I said, I shall never be moved.

7 LORD, by thy favour thou hast [r]made my mountain to stand strong: [s]thou didst hide thy face, *and* I was troubled.

8 I cried to thee, O LORD; and unto the LORD I made supplication.

9 What profit *is there* in my blood, when I go down to the pit? [t]Shall the dust praise thee? shall it declare thy truth?

10 Hear, O LORD, and have mercy upon me: LORD, be thou my helper.

11 [u]Thou hast turned for me my mourning into dancing: thou hast put off my sackcloth, and girded me with [v]gladness;

12 To the end that [w]*my* glory may sing praise to thee, and not be silent. O LORD my God, I will give thanks unto thee for ever.

A. M. cir. 2987
B. C. cir. 1017
Davidis, Regis
Israelitarum,
cir. annum
39

---

[m]Psalm lxiii. 3——[n]Hebrew, *in the evening*——[o]Psa. cxxvi. 5——[p]Hebrew, *singing*——[q]Job xxix. 18 [r]Hebrew, *settled strength for my mountain*——[s]Psalm civ. 29——[t]Psalm vi. 5; lxxxviii. 11; cxv. 17; cxviii.

17; Isaiah xxxviii. 18——[u]2 Samuel vi. 14; Isaiah lxi. 3; Jeremiah xxxi. 4——[v]Psalm iv. 7; xlv. 15; cv. 43; Isaiah xxx. 29——[w]That is, my *tongue,* or my *soul;* see Gen. xlix. 6; Psa. xvi. 9; lvii. 8

---

is soon obtained, and there are *lives* in that favour—the *life* that *now is,* and the *life* that is *to come.* When *weeping* comes, it is only to *lodge* for the *evening;* but *singing* will surely come in the *morning.* This description of God's slowness to anger, and readiness to save, is given by a man long and deeply acquainted with God as his *Judge* and as his *Father.*

Verse 6. *In my prosperity I said, I shall never be moved.*] Peace and prosperity had seduced the heart of David, and led him to suppose that *his mountain*—his dominion, *stood so strong,* that adversity could never affect him. He wished to know the physical and political strength of his kingdom; and, forgetting to depend upon God, he desired Joab to make a *census* of the people; which God punished in the manner related in 2 Sam. xxiv., and which he in this place appears to acknowledge.

Verse 7. *Thou didst hide thy face*] Thou didst show thyself displeased with me for my pride and forgetfulness of thee: and then I found how vainly I had trusted in an arm of flesh.

Verse 8. *I cried to thee, O Lord*] I found no help but *in him* against whom I had sinned. See his confession and prayer, 2 Sam. xxiv. 17.

Made supplication.] Continued to urge my suit; was instant in prayer.

Verse 9. *What profit is there in my blood*] My being cut off will not magnify thy mercy. Let not the sword, therefore, come against me. If spared and pardoned, I will declare thy truth; I will tell to all men what a merciful and gracious Lord I have found. *Hear,* therefore, *O Lord;* ver. 10.

Verse 11. *Thou hast turned—my mourning into dancing*] Rather *into piping.* I have not prayed in vain. Though I deserved to be cut off from the land of the living, yet thou hast spared me, and the remnant of my people. Thou hast *taken away my sackcloth,* the emblem of my distress and misery, and *girded me with gladness,* when thou didst say to the destroying angel, when he stood over Jerusalem ready to destroy it: "It is enough, stay now thy hand;" 2 Sam. xxiv. 16.

Verse 12. *To the end that* my *glory may sing*] The word כבוד *cabod,* which we here translate *glory,* is sometimes taken to signify the *liver.* Here it is supposed to mean the *tongue;* why not the *heart?* But does not David mean, by

his glory, the *state* of *exaltation* and *honour* to which God had raised him, and in which he had before too much trusted; forgetting that he held it in a state of dependence on God? Now he was disciplined into a better sentiment. My *glory* before had sung praise to myself; *in* it I had rested; *on* it I had presumed; and intoxicated with my success, I sent Joab to number the people. Now my *glory* shall be employed for *another purpose;* it shall give thanks to God, and *never be silent.* I shall *confess* to all the world that all the good, the greatness, the honour, the wealth, prosperity, and excellence I possess, came from God alone; and that I hold them on his mere good pleasure. It is so; therefore, "O Lord my God, I will give thanks unto thee for ever."

The old *Psalter* translates and paraphrases the last verse thus:—𝕿𝖍𝖆𝖙 𝖒𝖞 𝖏𝖔𝖞 𝖘𝖕𝖓𝖌 𝖙𝖎𝖑 𝖙𝖍𝖊, 𝖆𝖓𝖉 𝕴 𝖇𝖊 𝖓𝖔𝖌𝖍𝖙 𝖘𝖙𝖆𝖓𝖌𝖊𝖉: 𝕷𝖔𝖗𝖉 𝖒𝖞 𝕲𝖔𝖉 𝖜𝖎𝖙𝖍𝖔𝖚𝖙𝖊𝖓 𝖊𝖓𝖉𝖊 𝕴 𝖘𝖆𝖑 𝖘𝖈𝖍𝖗𝖞𝖋 𝖙𝖎𝖑 𝖙𝖍𝖊. The dede and the sorrow of oure syn God turnes in til joy of remission; and scheres oway oure sekk—(drives away our distress) and umgyfs (surrounds) qwen we dye, with gladness. 𝕿𝖍𝖆𝖙 𝖔𝖚𝖗𝖊 𝖏𝖔𝖞 𝖘𝖕𝖓𝖌 𝖙𝖎𝖑 𝖍𝖞𝖒, that has gyfen us that joy; for we be 𝖓𝖔 𝖒𝖔𝖗𝖊 𝖘𝖙𝖆𝖓𝖌𝖊𝖉 (stung) with conscience of syn: na drede of dede or of dome; bot 𝖜𝖎𝖙𝖍𝖔𝖚𝖙𝖊𝖓 𝖊𝖓𝖉𝖊 we sal loue (praise) him. Na tunge may telle na herte may thynk the mykelnes of joy that es in louing [praising] of hym in gast, and in sothfastnes, i. e., *spirit* and *truth.*

ANALYSIS OF THE THIRTIETH PSALM

There are *two* parts in this Psalm:—

I. The *giving of thanks* for delivery from a great danger, 1, 2, 3.

II. An *exhortation* to others to follow his example, and thus acknowledge God's merciful dealings with them, ver. 4-12.

I. He begins with thanksgiving: "I will extol thee, O Lord;" and adds the *causes.*

1. "Thou hast lifted me up," as one out of a deep dark pit.

2. "Thou hast not made my foes to triumph over me;" but rather turned their mirth into sadness.

3. "Thou hast healed me;"—both in body and mind.

4. "Thou hast brought up my soul from the grave;" restored me to life, when apparently condemned to death.

5. He earnestly sought these blessings: "O Lord my God, I cried unto thee," and thou didst for me all that I have mentioned.

II. After having given thanks, he calls on the saints to acknowledge and celebrate the goodness of God to him and to others: "Sing unto the Lord," &c. And to induce them to do this, he gives the instance in himself, that God was angry with him, but soon appeased.

1. He was angry, but his anger *endured but a moment;* but *life,* and a continuance of it, are from his favour.

2. And justly angry he was for his sin and carnal confidence: "In my prosperity I said, I shall never be moved."

3. The *effect* of his anger was: "He hid his face, and I was troubled."

This is the example that he sets before the saints, that they be not secure when the world goes well with them; lest they have experience of God's displeasure, as he had.

Next he shows the *means* he used to avert God's wrath; and this he proposes as a pattern for all to follow in like cases.

1. He betook himself to *prayer.* 2. He sets down the *form* he used.

1. He that is ill sends for the physician—so did I. This was the fruit of my chastisement; I cried unto thee, O Lord; and unto the Lord I made supplication.

2. And the *form* he used was this:—I earnestly pleaded with God thus: 1. "What profit is there in my blood when I go down to the pit?" 2. "Shall the dust praise thee? shall it declare thy truth?" 3. Can a dead man praise thee, or canst thou make good thy promises to the dead? 4. And he concluded with, "Hear, O Lord, and have mercy upon me; O Lord, be thou my helper."

3. He shows the effect of his prayer: "Thou hast turned my mourning into dancing, thou hast put off my sackcloth, and girded me with gladness."

4. For what end God did this: "That my glory may sing praise to thee, and not be silent. O Lord my God, I will give thanks to thee for ever."

Now, O ye saints, 1. You see my case; 2. You see what course I took; 3. You see the effect; 4. You see the end why God was so good to me, that I should praise him. To you, who are in my state, I propose my example. Betake yourselves to God in your necessities; and, having obtained deliverance by earnest prayer and faith, remember to return praise to God for his ineffable goodness.

PSALM XXXI

The psalmist, with strong confidence in God, in a time of distress prays earnestly for deliverance, 1–5. He expresses his abhorrence of evil, 6; gratefully mentions former interpositions of God, 7, 8; continues to detail the miseries of his case, 9–18; points out the privileges of them that fear God, 19, 20; shows that God had heard his prayers, notwithstanding he had given himself over for lost, 21, 22; calls on the saints to love God, and to have confidence in him, because he preserves the faithful, and plentifully rewards the proud doer, 23, 24.

To the chief Musician, A Psalm of David

A. M. cir. 2942
B. C. cir. 1062
Sauli, Regis
Israelitarum,
cir. annum
34

IN [a]thee, O LORD, do I put my trust; let me never be ashamed: [b]deliver me in thy righteousness.

2 [c]Bow down thine ear to me; deliver me speedily: be thou [d]my strong rock, for a house of defence to save me.

3 [e]For thou *art* my rock and my fortress; therefore [f]for thy name's sake lead me, and guide me.

A. M. cir. 2942
B. C. cir. 1062
Sauli, Regis
Israelitarum,
cir. annum
34

---

[a]Psa. xxii. 5; xxv. 2; lxxi. 1; Isa. xlix. 23——[b]Psa. cxliii. 1——[c]Psa. lxxi. 2

[d]Heb. *to me for a rock of strength*——[e]Psa. xviii. 1
[f]Psa. xxiii. 3; xxv. 11; cix. 21; cxliii. 11; Jer. xiv. 7

NOTES ON PSALM XXXI

This Psalm contains no notes of *time* or *place,* to help us to ascertain *when, where,* or on *what account* it was written. Nor have we any certain evidence relative to the *author:* it might have been written by *David* during his persecution by Saul. Some think *Jeremiah* to have been the author: the *thirteenth* verse begins exactly with the same words as Jer. xx. 10. There are several other apparent references to passages in the book of Jeremiah, which shall be produced in the notes.

Verse 1. *In thee, O Lord, do I put my trust*]

I confide in thee for every good I need: *let me not be confounded* by not receiving the end of my faith, the supply of my wants, and the salvation of my soul.

Verse 2. *Bow down thine ear*] Listen to my complaint. Put thy ear to my lips, that thou mayest hear all that my *feebleness* is capable of uttering. We generally put our ear near to the lips of the sick and dying, that we may hear what they say. To this the text appears to allude.

Strong rock] Rocks, rocky places, or caves in the rocks, were often *strong places* in the land of Judea. To such natural fortifications

A. M. cir. 2942
B. C. cir. 1062
Sauli, Regis
Israelitarum,
cir. annum
34

4 Pull me out of the net that they have laid privily for me: for thou *art* my strength.

5 gInto thine hand I commit my spirit: thou hast hredeemed me, O Lord God of truth.

6 I have hated them ithat regard lying vanities: but I trust in the Lord.

7 I will be glad and rejoice in thy mercy: for thou hast considered my trouble; thou hast kknown my soul in adversities;

8 And hast not lshut me up into the hand of the enemy: mthou hast set my foot in a large room.

9 Have mercy upon me, O Lord, for I am in trouble: nmine eye is consumed with grief, *yea,* my soul and my belly.

10 For my life is spent with grief, and my years with sighing: my strength faileth because of mine iniquity, and omy bones are consumed.

A. M. cir. 2942
B. C. cir. 1062
Sauli, Regis
Israelitarum,
cir. annum
34

---

gLuke xxiii. 46; Acts vii. 59——hExod. xv. 13; Deut. xiii. 5; xxi. 8——iJonah ii. 8——kJohn x. 27

lDeut. xxxii. 30; 1 Sam. xvii. 46; xxiv. 18——mPsa. iv. 1; xviii. 19——nPsa. vi. 7——oPsa. xxxii. 3; cii. 3

---

allusions are repeatedly made by the Hebrew poetic writers.

Verse 4. *Pull me out of the net*] They have hemmed me in on every side, and I cannot escape but by miracle.

Verse 5. *Into thine hand I commit my spirit*] These words, as they stand in the *Vulgate,* were in the highest credit among our ancestors; by whom they were used in all dangers, difficulties, and in the article of death. *In manus tuas, Domine, commendo spiritum meum,* was used by the sick when about to expire, if they were sensible; and if not, the priest said it in their behalf. In *forms of prayer* for sick and dying persons, these words were frequently inserted in Latin, though all the rest of the prayer was English; for it was supposed there was something sovereign in the *language* itself. But let not the abuse of such words hinder their usefulness. For an ejaculation nothing can be better; and when the pious or the tempted with confidence use them, nothing can exceed their effect. "Into thy hands I commend my spirit; for thou hast redeemed me, O Lord God of truth." I give my soul to thee, for it is thine: thou hast redeemed it by thy blood; it is safe nowhere but in thy hand. Thou hast promised to save them that trust in thee; thou art the *God of truth,* and canst not deny thyself. But these words are particularly sanctified, or *set apart* for this purpose, by the use made of them by our blessed Lord just before he expired on the cross. "And when Jesus had cried with a loud voice, he said, Πατερ, εις χειρας σου παρατιθεμαι το πνευμα μου· 'Father, into thy hands I commend my spirit,'" Luke xxiii. 46. The rest of the verse was not *suitable* to the Saviour of the world, and therefore he omits it; but it is suitable to us who have been redeemed by that sacrificial death. St. Stephen uses nearly the same words, and they were the last that he uttered. Acts vii. 59.

Verse 6. *I have hated them*] That is, I have abominated their ways. *Idolaters* are the persons of whom David speaks.

I trust in the Lord.] While *they* trust in *vanities, vain things;* (for *an idol is nothing in the world;*) and in *lying* vanities; (for much is *promised* and nothing *given;*) I trust in Jehovah, who is God all-sufficient, and is my Shepherd, and therefore I shall lack no good thing.

Verse 7. *Thou hast known my soul in adversities*] When all forsook me; when none could help me; when I could not save my own

life; when my enemies were sure that I could not escape; then I found *thee* to be my Friend and Supporter. When *friend,* so called, finds it convenient not to know his friend in affliction and poverty, then thou didst acknowledge me as thine own, all worthless as I was. Human friendships may fail; but the Friend of sinners never fails. Cicero defines a real friend, *Amicus certus in re incerta cernitur:* "A friend in need is a friend indeed." Reader, such a Friend is the *Lord.*

Verse 8. *Thou hast set my foot in a large room.*] Many hair-breadth escapes David had for his life; at that time especially when, playing before Saul, the furious king took a spear and endeavoured to pierce him through the body, but he escaped and got to the deserts. Here God, who had saved his life, set his *feet in a large room.* The seventh and eighth verses speak of what God had done previously for him.

Verse 9. *Mine eye is consumed*] He now returns, and speaks of his present situation. Grief had brought many tears from his eyes, many agonies into his soul, and many distressful feelings into his whole frame.

My soul and my belly.] The *belly* is often taken for the whole body. But the term *belly* or *bowels,* in such as case as this, may be the most proper; for in distress and misery, the *bowels* being the most tender part, and in fact the very *seat of compassion,* they are often most affected. In Greek the word σπλαγχνον signifies a *bowel,* and σπλαγχνιζομαι signifies *to be moved with compassion;* to feel misery in the bowels at the sight of a person in pain and distress.

Verse 10. *My life is spent with grief*] My life is a life of suffering and distress, and by grief my days are shortened. *Grief* disturbs the functions of life, prevents the due concoction of food, injures the digestive organs, destroys appetite, impairs the nervous system, relaxes the muscles, induces morbid action in the animal economy, and hastens death. These effects are well expressed in the verse itself.

My years with sighing] אנחה anachah. This is a mere *natural* expression of grief; the very *sounds* which proceed from a distressed mind; *an-ach-ah!* common, with little variation, to all nations, and nearly the same in all languages. The *och-och-on* of the Irish is precisely the same sound, and the same sense. Thousands of beauties of this kind are to be found in the sacred language.

A. M. cir. 2942
B. C. cir. 1062
Sauli, Regis
Israelitarum,
cir. annum
34

11 ᴾI was a reproach among all mine enemies, but �qespecially among my neighbours, and a fear to mine acquaintance: ʳthey that did see me without fled from me.

12 ˢI am forgotten as a dead man out of mind: I am like ᵗa broken vessel.

13 ᵘFor I have heard the slander of many: ᵛfear *was* on every side: while they ʷtook counsel together against me, they devised to take away my life.

14 But I trusted in thee, O LORD: I said, Thou *art* my God.

15 My times *are* in thy hand: deliver me from the hand of mine enemies, and from them that persecute me.

16 ˣMake thy face to shine upon thy servant: save me for thy mercies' sake.

17 ʸLet me not be ashamed, O LORD; for I have called upon thee: let the wicked be ashamed, *and* ᶻlet ᵃthem be silent in the grave.

A. M. cir. 2942
B. C. cir. 1062
Sauli, Regis
Israelitarum,
cir. annum
34

18 ᵇLet the lying lips be put to silence; which ᶜspeak ᵈgrievous things proudly and contemptuously against the righteous.

19 ᵉO how great *is* thy goodness, which thou hast laid up for them that fear thee; *which* thou hast wrought for them that trust in thee before the sons of men!

20 ᶠThou shalt hide them in the secret of thy presence from the pride of man: ᵍthou shalt keep them secretly in a pavilion from the strife of tongues.

21 Blessed *be* the LORD: for he ʰhath showed me his marvellous kindnessⁱ in a ᵏstrong city.

ᴾPsa. xli. 8; Isa. liii. 4——�q Job xix. 13; Psa. xxxviii. 11; lxxxviii. 8, 18——ʳPsa. lxiv. 8——ˢPsa. lxxxviii. 4, 5 ᵗHeb. *a vessel that perisheth*——ᵘJer. xx. 10——ᵛJer. vi. 25; xx. 3; Lam. ii. 22——ʷMatt. xxvii. 1——ˣNum. vi. 25, 26; Psa. iv. 6; lxvii. 1——ʸPsa. xxv. 2

ᶻ1 Sam. ii. 9; Psa. cxv. 17——ᵃOr, *let them be cut off for the grave*——ᵇPsa. xii. 3——ᶜ1 Sam. ii. 3; Psa. xciv. 4; Jude 15——ᵈHeb. *a hard thing*——ᵉIsa. lxiv. 4; 1 Cor. ii. 9——ᶠPsa. xxvii. 5; xxxii. 7——ᵍJob v. 21 ʰPsa. xvii. 7——ⁱ1 Sam. xxiii. 7——ᵏOr, *fenced city*

Verse 11. *I was a reproach*] When proscribed at the court of Saul, my *enemies* triumphed, and loaded me with execrations; my *neighbours* considered me as a dangerous man, now deservedly driven from society; my *acquaintance*, who knew me best, were afraid to hold any communication with me; and *they* who *saw* me in *my exile* avoided me as if affected with a contagious disorder.

Verse 12. *I am forgotten as a dead man*] I am considered as a person adjudged to death. *I am like a broken vessel*—like a thing totally useless.

Verse 13. *I have heard the slander of many*] To this and the two foregoing verses the reader may find several parallels; Jer. xviii. 18 to the end of chap. xix., and ten first verses of chap. xx. This has caused several to suppose that Jeremiah was the author of this Psalm.

Verse 14. *But I trusted in thee*] Hitherto thou hast been my Helper, and thou art my God; I have taken thee for my eternal portion.

Verse 15. *My times* are *in thy hand*] The events of my life are under thy control. No danger can happen to me without thy foresight; thou seest what is prepared for or meditated against me; thou canst therefore deliver me from mine enemies.

Verse 16. *Make thy face to shine upon thy servant*] Only let me know that thou art reconciled to and pleased with me, and then, come what will, all must be well.

Save me for thy mercies' sake.] Literally, *Save me in thy mercy.*

Verse 17. *Let the wicked be ashamed*] Those who traduce my character and lay snares for my life; let them be confounded.

Verse 18. *Let the lying lips be put to silence*] As to my enemies, persecutors, and slanderers, abate their pride, assuage their malice, and confound their devices. See Jer. xviii. 18.

Verse 19. *O how great* is *thy goodness*] God's goodness is infinite; there is enough for *all*, enough for *each*, enough for *evermore*. It is laid up where neither devils nor men can reach it, and it is laid up for *them that fear the Lord;* therefore every one who trembles at his word, may expect all he needs from this Fountain that can never be dried up.

Which thou hast wrought] Thou hast already prepared it; it is the work of thy own hands; thou hast provided it and proportioned it to the necessities of men, and all who trust in thee shall have it. And for them especially it is prepared *who trust in thee before men*—who boldly confess thee amidst a crooked and perverse generation.

Verse 20. *Thou shalt hide them in the secret of thy presence*] בסתר פניך *besether paneycha*, "With the covering of thy countenance." Their life shall be so hidden with Christ in God, that their enemies shall not be able to find them out. To such a hiding-place Satan himself dare not approach. There *the pride of man* cannot come.

Thou shalt keep them secretly in a pavilion] Thou shalt put them in the innermost part of thy tent. This implies that they shall have much communion and union with God; that they shall be transformed into his likeness, and have his highest approbation.

Verse 21. *In a strong city.*] If this Psalm was written by David, this must refer to his taking refuge with *Achish, king of Gath*, who gave him *Ziklag*, a fortified city, to secure himself and followers in. See 1 Sam. xxvii. 6. This is more likely than that it was *Keilah*, where he only had intimation of the traitorous design of the inhabitants to deliver him up to Saul; so that the place was no refuge to him, howsoever fortified. Perhaps the passage may mean that, under the protection of God, he was as safe as if he had been in a fortified city.

A. M. cir. 2942
B. C. cir. 1062
Sauli, Regis
Israelitarum,
cir. annum
34

22 For [1]I said in my haste, [m]I am cut off from before thine eyes: nevertheless thou heardest the voice of my supplications when I cried unto thee.

23 [n]O love the LORD, all ye his saints: *for*

the LORD preserveth the faithful, and plentifully rewardeth the proud doer.

24 [o]Be of good courage, and he shall strengthen your heart, all ye that hope in the LORD.

A. M. cir. 2942
B. C. cir. 1062
Sauli, Regis
Israelitarum,
cir. annum
34

---

[1]1 Sam. xxiii. 26; Psa. cxvi. 11——[m]Isa.
[n]Psalm xxxiv. 9

xxxviii. 11, 12; Lam. iii. 54; Jonah ii. 4
[o]Psalm xxvii. 14

Verse 22. *I said in my haste*] Not duly adverting to the promise of God, I was led to conclude that my enemies were so strong, so numerous, and had so many advantages against me, that I must necessarily fall into and by their hands; however, I continued to pray, and thou didst hear the voice of my supplication.

Verse 23. *O love the Lord, all ye his saints*] It is only the *saints* that can love God, as they only are made partakers of the Divine nature. *Holy spirits* can love God, who is the fountain of their holiness; and the *saints* should love him.

Preserveth the faithful] Those who, being filled with the love of God, bring forth the fruits of that love—universal obedience to the will of God; for to such persons his commands are not grievous, their *duty* is their *delight;* while a man is *faithful* to the grace he has received, that is, uses and improves the talents with which God has intrusted him, God's service is perfect freedom.

The proud doer.] The man of the proud heart, haughty and supercilious carriage, and insulting and outrageous conduct. A *proud man* is peculiarly odious in the sight of God; and in the sight of reason how absurd! A sinner, a fallen spirit, an heir of wretchedness and corruption—proud! Proud of what? Of an indwelling devil! Well; such persons shall be *plentifully rewarded.* They shall get their *due*, their *whole due*, and *nothing but their due.*

Verse 24. *Be of good courage, and he shall strengthen your heart*] In 1 Cor. xvi. 13, St. Paul says, "Watch ye, stand fast in the faith; quit you like men; be strong:" Γρηγορειτε, στηκετε εν τη πιστει, ανδριζεσθε, κραταιουσθε. The latter words he seems to have borrowed from the *Septuagint*, who translate, "Be of good courage, and he shall strengthen your heart," by Ανδριζεσθε και κραταιουσθω ἡ καρδια ὑμων· "Act like men, and your hearts shall be strengthened."

They that hope in God, and are endeavouring to walk carefully before him, may take courage at all times, and expect the fulness of the blessing of the Gospel of peace.

ANALYSIS OF THE THIRTY-FIRST PSALM

This Psalm is composed and mixed of divers affections; for David sometimes prays, sometimes gives thanks; now he complains, now he hopes; at one time fears, at another exults. This vicissitude of affection is *six-fold*, and it may very well divide the Psalm.

I. With great confidence he prays to God; ver. 1-6.

II. He exults for mercy and help received; ver. 7, 8.

III. He grievously complains of the misery he was in; ver. 9-14.

IV. He prays again, upon the strength of God's goodness; ver. 15-18.

V. He admires, exults in, and proclaims God's goodness; ver. 19-22.

VI. He exhorts others to love God, and be courageous; ver. 23, 24.

I. In the six first verses he prays to God, and shows his reasons:—

1. That he be never ashamed in his hope: "Let me never be ashamed."

2. That he be delivered, "speedily delivered."

3. That God would be "his rock, and a house of defence, to save him."

4. That God would lead and guide him: "Lead me, and guide me."

5. That God would "pull his feet out of the net which they had laid for him."

The *reasons* on which he founds his prayer and expectations:—

1. His faith and confidence: "In thee, O Lord, I put my trust."

2. The reason of his faith: "Thou art my ROCK and FORTRESS."

3. His deliverance would be to the honour of God: "For thy name's sake."

4. Thou art my strength; exert it in my behalf.

5. I rely upon thee: "Into thy hands I commit my spirit."

6. I expect thee to do for me as thou hast ever done: "Thou hast redeemed me."

7. I rely on thee alone, I seek no vain helps: "I have hated them that regard lying vanities; but I trust in the Lord."

His *petition* and his *reasons* are in effect the same; his confidence in God to be his *Deliverer, Fortress, Rock, Redeemer*, &c.

II. He exults for mercy and help already received, and by the experience of that, doubts the less in this: "I will be glad and rejoice in thy mercy." And his reason follows from his experience: 1. "For thou hast considered my trouble." 2. "Thou hast known my soul in adversity." 3. "Thou hast not shut me up into the hand of the enemy." 4. But "hast set my feet in a large room."

III. He prays, and grievously complains of what he suffered *within* and *without*.

1. He *prays:* "Have mercy upon me, O Lord."

2. Then he *complains*, and his complaint shows the reason of his prayer.

1. *Within*—at home, he was in a distressed state: "I am in trouble; my eye is consumed with grief; my years with sighing; my strength faileth; my bones are consumed."

2. *Without*—I have no comfort either from friends or enemies.

1. "I was a reproach among all my enemies."

2. My *friends* stand afar off: "I was a reproach, especially among my neighbours." "A fear to my acquaintance." "They that did see me without fled from me."

3. He shows the greatness of his grief, and the scorn he endured: "I am forgotten as a

dead man;" "I am as a broken vessel," vile and useless.

4. I am mocked by the people: "I have heard the slander of many."

5. And the consequence was mischievous. 1. "Fear is on every side." 2. While they conspired, or "took counsel against my life." 3. And their counsel was, "to take away my life." What more could my enemies do, or my friends permit?

IV. After his complaint he comforts himself with his chief reason, *the goodness of God.* I have trusted in thee, O Lord, and said, Thou art my God. Let them conspire, take counsel, and devise what they can; yet I know, except thou permit them, they are not able to do it. "My times are in thy hand," not in *theirs.*

He then begins to pray again, and his prayer consists of *three* parts: 1. Deprecation. 2. Supplication. 3. Imprecation.

1. A *deprecation:* "Deliver me from the hands of my enemies," &c.

2. A *supplication:* "Make thy face to shine upon thy servant; save me." "Let me not be ashamed, for I have called upon thee."

3. An *imprecation:* 1. "Let the wicked be ashamed, and be silent in the grave." 2. "Let the lying lips be put to silence, which speak grievous things," &c.

In this imprecation *four arguments* are used to enforce it:—

1. The *quality* of their persons: "They are wicked, impious men."

2. There is *no truth* in them: "They have lying lips." 1. Their *words* are false. 2. Their *actions* are worse: *They speak grievous things,* and that *against the righteous.* 3. But their *intention* is worst of all, for they do it *proudly, contemptuously, disdainfully, despitefully;* all proceeding from a *bad heart.*

V. In the *fifth* part he sets out the *abundant goodness of the Lord* to his people, and exclaims, in holy rapture, "O how great is thy goodness which thou hast laid up for them that fear thee—which thou hast wrought for them that trust in thee before the sons of men!"

This goodness of God is always treasured up, and to be had at all times. But observe: 1. It is *laid up* for none, nor *wrought* for any one, but *them that fear the Lord.* 2. And for those *who put their trust in him,* and acknowledge him, his cause, his people, and his cross, *before the sons of men.* And the acts of his goodness are here specified:—

1. "Thou shalt hide them in the secret of thy presence from the pride of man."

2. "Thou shalt keep them secretly in a pavilion from the strife of tongues." Upon which consideration he breaks out into praise: 1. "Blessed be the Lord, for he hath showed me his marvellous kindness." 2. He *corrects* his error, and former mistake: "I said in my haste, (rashly, imprudently,) I am cut off from before thine eyes; nevertheless thou heardest the voice of my supplication."

VI. The last part is an *exhortation to the saints:* 1. That they *love God.* 2. That they be of *good courage;* for he was the same God still, and would be as good to others as he was to him.

1. That they *love God,* and that for two reasons:—1. Because the "Lord preserveth the faithful." This is his *mercy.* 2. That he "plentifully rewardeth the proud doer." This is his *justice.*

2. That they *be of good courage;* for then "he shall strengthen your heart, all ye that hope in the Lord." They were not to despair, but keep their hearts firmly fixed in the profession of the truth, which would be a seal of their *hope.*

PSALM XXXII

True blessedness consists in remission of sin, and purification of the heart, 1, 2. What the psalmist felt in seeking these blessings, 3–5. How they should be sought, 6, 7. The necessity of humility and teachableness, 8, 9. The misery of the wicked, 10. The blessedness of the righteous, 11.

VI. DAY. EVENING PRAYER

ᵃ*A Psalm* of David, Maschil

A. M. cir. 2970
B. C. cir. 1034
Davidis, Regis
Israelitarum,
cir. annum
22

BLESSED *is he whose* ᵇtransgression *is* forgiven, *whose* sin *is* covered.

2 Blessed *is* the man unto whom the LORD ᶜimputeth not iniquity, and ᵈin whose spirit *there is* no guile.

3 When I kept silence, my bones waxed old through my roaring all the day long.

A. M. cir. 2970
B. C. cir. 1034
Davidis, Regis
Israelitarum,
cir. annum
22

ᵃOr, A Psalm *of David giving instruction*——ᵇPsa. lxxxv.

2; Rom. iv. 6, 7, 8——ᶜ2 Cor. v. 19——ᵈJohn i. 47

NOTES ON PSALM XXXII

The *title* of this Psalm is significant, לדוד משכיל *ledavid maskil,* A Psalm *of David, giving instruction, an instructive Psalm;* so called by way of eminence, because it is calculated to give the highest instruction relative to the guilt of sin, and the blessedness of pardon and holiness, or *justification* and *sanctification.* It is supposed to have been composed after David's transgression with Bath-sheba, and subsequently to his obtaining pardon. The *Syriac* entitles it, "A Psalm of David concerning the sin of Adam, who dared and transgressed; and a prophecy concerning Christ, because through him we are to be delivered from hell." The

A. M. cir. 2970
B. C. cir. 1034
Davidis, Regis
Israelitarum,
cir. annum
22

4 For day and night thy [e]hand was heavy upon me: my moisture is turned into the drought of summer. Selah.

5 I acknowledge my sin unto thee, and mine iniquity have I not hid. [f]I said, I will confess my transgressions unto the LORD; and thou forgavest the iniquity of my sin. Selah.

6 [g]For this shall every one that is godly [h]pray unto thee [i]in a time when thou mayest be found: surely in the floods of great waters they shall not come nigh unto him.

7 [k]Thou *art* my hiding place; thou shalt preserve me from trouble; thou shalt compass me about with [l]songs of deliverance. Selah.

8 I will instruct thee and teach thee in the way which thou shalt go: [m]I will guide thee with mine eye.

A. M. cir. 2970
B. C. cir. 1034
Davidis, Regis
Israelitarum,
cir. annum
22

---

[e]1 Sam. v. 6, 11; Job xxxiii. 7; Psa. xxxviii. 2
[f]Prov. xxviii. 13; Isa. lxv. 24; Luke xv. 18, 21 &c.;
1 John i. 9——[g]1 Tim. i. 16——[h]Isa. lv. 6; John
vii. 34

[i]Heb. *in a time of finding*——[k]Psa. ix. 9; xxvii. 5; xxxi.
20; cxix. 114——[l]Exod. xv. 1; Judg. v. 1; 2 Sam. xxii.
1——[m]Heb. *I will counsel* thee, *mine eye* shall be *upon
thee*

Arabic says, "David spoke this Psalm prophetically concerning the redemption." The *Vulgate, Septuagint,* and *Æthiopic,* are the same in meaning as the *Hebrew.*

Verse 1. *Blessed* is he whose *transgression* is *forgiven*] In this and the following verse *four* evils are mentioned: 1. *Transgression,* פשע *pesha.* 2. *Sin,* חטאה *chataah.* 3. *Iniquity,* עון *avon.* 4. *Guile,* רמיה *remiyah.* The *first* signifies the *passing over a boundary, doing what is prohibited.* The *second* signifies the *missing of a mark,* not doing what was commanded; but is often taken to express *sinfulness,* or sin in the future, producing transgression in the life. The *third* signifies *what is turned out of its proper course or situation;* any thing *morally distorted* or *perverted. Iniquity,* what is contrary to *equity* or *justice.* The *fourth* signifies *fraud, deceit, guile,* &c. To remove these evils, *three* acts are mentioned: *forgiving, covering,* and not *imputing.* 1. TRANSGRESSION, פשע *pesha,* must be *forgiven,* נשוי *nesui,* borne away, i. e., by a vicarious sacrifice; for *bearing sin,* or *bearing away sin,* always implies this. 2. SIN, חטאה *chataah,* must be *covered,* כסוי *kesui,* hidden from the sight. It is odious and abominable, and must be put out of sight. 3. INIQUITY, עון *avon,* which is *perverse* or *distorted,* must not be imputed, לא יחשב *lo yachshob,* must *not be reckoned to his account.* 4. GUILE, רמיה *remiyah,* must be annihilated from the soul: *In whose spirit there is no* GUILE. The man whose *transgression* is forgiven; whose *sin* is hidden, God having cast it as a millstone into the depths of the sea; whose iniquity and perversion is not reckoned to his account; and whose *guile,* the deceitful and desperately wicked heart, is annihilated, being emptied of sin and filled with righteousness, is necessarily a happy man.

The old *Psalter* translates these two verses thus: 𝖡𝔩𝔦𝔰𝔰𝔦𝔡 𝔮𝔴𝔞𝔰 𝔴𝔦𝔨𝔢𝔡𝔫𝔢𝔰 𝔢𝔰 𝔣𝔬𝔯 𝔤𝔭𝔟𝔢𝔫, 𝔞𝔫𝔟 𝔮𝔴𝔞𝔰 𝔰𝔶𝔫𝔫𝔢𝔰 𝔦𝔰 𝔥𝔶𝔩𝔢𝔡 (covered.) 𝖡𝔩𝔦𝔰𝔣𝔲𝔩 𝔪𝔞𝔫 𝔱𝔦𝔩 𝔮𝔴𝔞𝔪 𝕷𝔬𝔯𝔡 𝔯𝔢𝔱𝔱𝔢𝔡 (reckoneth) 𝔫𝔬𝔤𝔥𝔱 𝕾𝔶𝔫: 𝔫𝔢 𝔫𝔞 𝔱𝔯𝔢𝔰𝔬𝔫 𝔢𝔰 𝔦𝔫 𝔥𝔦𝔰 𝔤𝔞𝔰𝔱 (spirit.) In vain does any man look for or expect happiness while the *power* of sin remains, its *guilt unpardoned,* and its *impurity* not *purged away.* To the person who has got such blessings, we may say as the psalmist said, אשרי *ashrey, O the blessedness of that man, whose transgression is forgiven!* &c.

St. Paul quotes this passage, Rom. iv. 6, 7, to illustrate the doctrine of *justification by faith;* where see the notes.

Verse 3. *When I kept silence*] Before I humbled myself, and confessed my sin, my soul was under the deepest horror. "I roared all the day long;" and felt the hand of God heavy upon my soul.

Verse 5. *I acknowledged my sin*] When this confession was made thoroughly and sincerely, and I ceased to *cover* and *extenuate my offence,* then thou didst forgive the iniquity of my sin. I felt the hardness of heart: I felt the deep distress of soul; I felt power to confess and abhor my sin; I felt confidence in the mercy of the Lord; and I felt the forgiveness of the iniquity of my sin.

Selah.] This is all true; I *know* it; I *felt* it; I *feel* it.

Verse 6. *For this shall every one that is godly*] Because thou art merciful; because thou hast shown mercy to all who have truly turned to thee, and believed in thee; every one who fears thee, and hears of this, *shall pray unto thee* in an acceptable time, *when thou mayest be found;* in the time of finding. When the heart is softened and the conscience alarmed, that is a time of finding. God is ever ready; men are not so. Who can pray with a hard heart and a dark mind? While you feel relentings, pray.

Surely in the floods] In violent trials, afflictions, and temptations; when the rains descend, the winds blow, and the floods beat against that godly man who prays and trusts in God; "they shall not come nigh him," so as to weaken his confidence or destroy his soul. His *house* is founded on a *rock.*

Verse 7. *Thou* art *my hiding place*] An allusion, probably, to the *city of refuge:* "Thou shalt preserve me from trouble." The avenger of blood shall not be able to overtake me. And being encompassed with an impregnable wall, I shall feel myself *encompassed with songs of deliverance*—I shall know that I am safe.

Verse 8. *I will instruct thee*] These are probably the Lord's words to David. Seeing thou art now sensible of the mercy thou hast received from me, and art purposing to live to my glory, I will give thee all the assistance requisite. I will become thy *Instructor,* "and will teach thee," in all occurrences, "the way thou shouldst go." I will keep *mine eyes* upon thee, and thou shalt keep thine upon me: as I go, thou must follow me; and I will continually watch for thy good.

A. M. cir. 2970
B. C. cir. 1034
Davidis, Regis
Israelitarum,
cir. annum
22

9 ⁿBe ye not as the horse, *or* as the mule, *which* have °no understanding: whose mouth must be held in with bit and bridle, lest they come near unto thee.

10 ᵖMany sorrows *shall be* to the wicked:

but �q he that trusteth in the Lord, mercy shall compass him about.

11 ʳBe glad in the Lord, and rejoice, ye righteous: and shout for joy, all *ye that are* upright in heart.

A. M. cir. 2970
B. C. cir. 1034
Davidis, Regis
Israelitarum,
cir. annum.
22

ⁿProv. xxvi. 3; James iii. 3——°Job xxxv. 11——ᵖProv. xiii. 21; Rom. ii. 9

�q Psa. xxxiv. 8; lxxxiv. 12; Prov. xvi. 20; Jer. xvii. 7
ʳPsa. lxiv. 10; lxviii. 3

Verse 9. *Be ye not as the horse* or *as the mule*] They will only act by *force* and *constraint;* be not like *them;* give a *willing service* to your Maker. "They have no understanding;" you have a *rational soul*, made to be guided and influenced by *reason*. The service of your God is a *reasonable service;* act, therefore, as a *rational being*. The horse and the mule are turned with difficulty; they must be constrained with *bit* and *bridle*. Do not *be like them;* do not oblige your Maker to have continual recourse to afflictions, trials, and severe dispensations of providence, to keep you in the way, or to recover you after you have gone out of it.

Verse 10. *Many sorrows shall be to the wicked*] Every *wicked* man is a *miserable* man. God has wedded sin and misery as strongly as he has holiness and happiness. God hath joined them together; none can put them asunder.

But he that trusteth in the Lord] Such a person is both safe and happy.

Verse 11. *Be glad—and rejoice*] Let every *righteous soul* rejoice and glory, but let it be *in the Lord*. Man was made for *happiness*, but his happiness must be founded on holiness: and holiness, as it comes from God, must be retained by continual union with him. Probably this verse belongs to the next Psalm, and was originally its first verse.

ANALYSIS OF THE THIRTY-SECOND PSALM

This Psalm is *doctrinal*, and shows the happiness of the man whose sin is pardoned, and who is himself restored to the favour and image of God. It is called *maschil*, or *instruction;* and the reason of this is shown at the *eighth* verse: "I will instruct thee, and teach thee." In it we have instruction, especially on these *three* points, which divide the Psalm:—

I. The happy state of a justified person, ver. 1, 2.

II. The unhappy condition of that man who is not assured that he is justified and reconciled to God, ver. 3, 4. And the way is prescribed how to gain this assurance, ver. 5.

III. A lesson given for obedience after a man is brought into that state, ver. 8, 9.

I. The prophet first instructs us in what *justification* consists:—

I. It is a *free remission*, a *covering of sin;* a *nonimputation of iniquities*. 2. In what state a person must be in order to obtain it. He must be honest, sincere, and upright in heart; deeply penitent, feeling the guilt of sin, and acknowledging its enormity. He must avoid *guile* or deceit; and not excuse, palliate, or extenuate his sin, but confess it.

II. This he proves by his own experience: he hid his sin, he confessed it not; and was, in consequence, miserable.

1. I held my peace I confessed not. I did not ask pardon: "When I kept silence," &c.

2. I was wounded with the sting of a guilty conscience; fears, horrors, troubles of soul, came upon me: "My bones waxed old through my roaring."

3. And then he shows the *way* he took to *regain* happiness; it was a *contrary course* to that above; he concealed his sin no longer. 1. "I acknowledged my sin unto thee, and mine iniquity I have not hidden." 2. "I said, I will confess my transgressions to the Lord."

Of which the effects were various:—

1. Upon *himself*. He recovered his happiness in being justified: "Thou forgavest the iniquity of my sin."

2. On the *whole Church:* "For this shall every one that is godly pray unto thee."

3. *Comfort* in *extremities*, and safety in the greatest danger: "Surely in the floods of great waters," in an inundation of calamities, *they*—the troubles—*shall not come nigh him* who depends upon God's goodness and mercy, and is reconciled to him. And he shows the reason from his own experience. God was his *Protector:* 1. "Thou art my hiding place: thou shalt preserve me from trouble." 2. "Thou shalt compass me about with songs of deliverance."

III. And now David sets down the duty of a justified person; that he is, after his pardon, obedient to God; and that not out of compulsion, but *freely* and *willingly*. In order to this, God condescends to be his *Instructor*.

1. "I will instruct;" give thee general counsel.

2. "I will guide thee with mine eye." A good servant needs no *stripes;* he will observe *nutum*, the nod, or *nictum heri*, the *wink of the master*. As my eye is always over you, carefully to instruct; so be you as ready to observe it.

3. Be not like *beasts:* the HORSE, *headlong;* the MULE, *headstrong;* "whose mouths must be held in with bit and bridle," lest they fling, kick, hurt, or kill thee. *Constrained obedience* is for a *beast;* free and *voluntary obedience*, for a *man.*

4. Besides, to quicken your obedience, I will teach you two reasons. 1. From inconvenience and loss: "Many sorrows shall be to the wicked:" their griefs, troubles and punishments, are many and grievous. Be not, therefore, disobedient like the wicked. 2. From the *gain*. Your obedience shall be rewarded, and that amply: "He that trusteth in the Lord, mercy shall compass him round about." It shall be like the *girdle* with which he *is girded*. God will be present with him in his troubles. He shall perceive that he is in favour with God, that his sins are pardoned, and that he is an heir of eternal life.

Upon which he concludes with this exhortation: "Be glad in the Lord, and rejoice, ye righteous; and shout for joy, all ye that are up-right in heart." For this rejoicing there is great cause; for this doctrine of free remission of sin can alone quiet a guilty conscience. And this pardon can only be obtained by faith in Christ Jesus.

PSALM XXXIII

The Lord is praised for his works of creation, 1–9; and for the stability of his own counsels, 10, 11. The blessed-ness of the people who have the knowledge of the true God, his grace, and providence, 12–15. The vanity of all earthly dependence, 16, 17. The happiness of them that fear God, and trust in his mercy, 18–22.

REJOICE ᵃin the Lord, O ye righteous: *for* ᵇpraise is comely for the upright.

2 Praise the Lord with harp: sing unto him with the psaltery ᶜ*and* an instrument of ten strings.

3 ᵈSing unto him a new song; play skil-fully with a loud noise.

4 For the word of the Lord *is* right; and all his works *are done* in truth.

5 ᵉHe loveth righteousness and judgment: ᶠthe earth is full of the ᵍgoodness of the Lord.

6 ʰBy the word of the Lord were the hea-vens made, and ⁱall the host of them ᵏby the breath of his mouth.

7 ˡHe gathereth the waters of the sea to-gether as a heap: he layeth up the depth in storehouses.

ᵃPsa. xxxii. 11; xcvii. 12——ᵇPsa. cxlvii. 1——ᶜPsa. xcii. 3; cxliv. 9——ᵈPsa. xcvi. 1; xcviii. 1; cxliv. 9; cxlix. 1; Isa. xlii. 10; Rev. v. 9——ᵉPsa. xi. 7; xlv. 7

ᶠPsa. cxix. 64——ᵍOr, *mercy*——ʰGen. i. 6, 7; Heb. xi. 3; 2 Pet. iii. 5——ⁱGen. ii. 1——ᵏJob xxvi. 13 ˡGen. i. 9; Job xxvi. 10; xxxviii. 8

NOTES ON PSALM XXXIII

This Psalm has no *title* in the Hebrew and it was probably written on no particular occasion, but was intended as a hymn of praise in order to celebrate the power, wisdom, and mercy of God. Creation and providence are its principal subjects; and these lead the psalmist to glance at different parts of the ancient Jewish history. In eight of *Kennicott's* MSS., this Psalm is writ-ten as a part of the preceding.

Verse 1. *Rejoice in the Lord*] It is very likely that the *last* verse of the preceding Psalm was formerly the *first* verse of this. As this Psalm has no *title*, the verse was the more easily separated. In the preceding Psalm we have an account of the happiness of the justified man: in this, such are taught how to glorify God, and to praise him for the great things he had done for them.

Praise is comely for the upright.] It is *right* they should give thanks to Him, who is the fountain whence they have received all the good they possess and thankfulness becomes the lips of the upright.

Verse 2. *Praise the Lord with harp*] כנור *kinnor;* probably something like our *harp:* but Calmet thinks it the ancient *testudo,* or lyre with three strings.

The psalter] נבל *nebel.* Our translation seems to make a *third* instrument in this place, by rendering עשור*asor, an instrument of ten strings;* whereas they should both be joined together, for נבל עשור *nebel-asor* signifies the *nebal,* or *nabla,* with ten strings, or holes. Calmet sup-poses this to have resembled our *harp.* In one of *Kennicott's* MSS., this Psalm begins with the second verse.

Verse 3. *Sing unto him a new song*] Do not wear out the old forms: fresh mercies call for new songs of praise and gratitude.

Play skilfully with a loud noise.] Let *sense* and *sound* accompany each other; let the style of the music be suited to the words. This *skill* is possessed by few singers. They can make a *loud noise,* but they cannot adapt *sound* to *sense.*

Verse 4. *The word of the Lord is right*] He is infinitely wise, and can make no mistakes; and all his works are done in truth. All the words, laws, promises, and threatenings of God are perfectly true and just. The dispensations of his providence and mercy are equally so. When he *rewards* or *punishes,* it is according to *truth* and *justice.*

Verse 5. *He loveth righteousness*] What he delights in himself, he loves to see in his fol-lowers.

The earth is full of the goodness of the Lord.] To hear its worthless inhabitants complain, one would think that God dispensed *evil,* not *good.* To examine the operation of his hand, every thing is marked with mercy and there is no place where his goodness does not appear. The *overflowing kindness* of God fills the earth. Even the iniquities of men are rarely a bar to his goodness: he causes his sun to rise on the evil and the good, and sends his rain upon the *just* and the *unjust.*

Verse 6. *By the word of the Lord were the heavens made*] This is illustrated in the 9th verse: "He spake, and it was done; he com-manded, and it stood fast." This evidently refers to the account of the creation, as it stands in the first chapter of Genesis.

Verse 7. *He gathereth the waters of the sea together*] He separated the *water* from the *earth* and, while the latter was collected into continents, islands, mountains, hills, and valleys, the former was collected into *one place,* and

8 Let all the earth fear the LORD: let all the inhabitants of the world stand in awe of him.

9 For [m]he spake, and it was *done;* he commanded, and it stood fast.

10 [n]The LORD [o]bringeth the counsel of the heathen to naught: he maketh the devices of the people of none effect.

11 [p]The counsel of the LORD standeth for ever, the thoughts of his heart [q]to all generations.

12 [r]Blessed *is* the nation whose God *is* the LORD; *and* the people *whom* he hath [s]chosen for his own inheritance.

13 [t]The LORD looketh from heaven; he beholdeth all the sons of men.

14 From the place of his habitation he looketh upon all the inhabitants of the earth.

15 He fashioneth their hearts alike; he [u]considereth all their works.

16 [v]There is no king saved by the multitude of a host: a mighty man is not delivered by much strength.

17 [w]A horse *is* a vain thing for safety: neither shall he deliver *any* by his great strength.

18 [x]Behold, the eye of the LORD *is* [y]upon them that fear him, upon them that hope in his mercy;

---

[m]Gen. i. 3; Psa. cxlviii. 5——[n]Isa. viii. 10; xix. 3 [o]Heb. *maketh frustrate*——[p]Job xxiii. 13; Prov. xix. 21; Isaiah xlvi. 10——[q]Hebrew, *to generation and generation*——[r]Psalm lxv. 4; cxliv. 15——[s]Exodus xix. 5; Deuteronomy vii. 6

[t]2 Chron. xvi. 9; Job xxviii. 24; Psa. xi. 4; xiv. 2; Prov. xv. 3——[u]Job xxxiv. 21; Jer. xxxii. 19——[v]Psa. xliv. 6——[w]Psalm xx. 7; cxlvii. 10; Proverbs xxi. 31 [x]Job xxxvi. 7; Psalm xxxiv. 15; 1 Peter iii. 12——[y]Psalm cxlvii. 11

---

called *seas;* and by his all-controlling power and providence the waters have been retained in their place, so that they have not returned to drown the earth: and he has so adapted the *solar* and *lunar influence* exerted on the waters, that the tides are only raised to certain heights, so that they cannot overflow the shores, nor become dissipated in the atmospheric regions. In this one economy there is a whole circle of science. The quantity of matter in the sun, moon, and in the earth, are all adjusted to each other in this astonishing provision: the *course of the moon,* and the *diurnal* and *annual revolutions of the earth,* are all concerned here; and so concerned, that it requires some of the nicest of the Newtonian calculations to ascertain the laws by which the whole is affected.

Verse 8. *Let all the earth fear the Lord*] He who has thus *bound,* can *unloose;* he who has *created,* can *destroy.* He has promised life and prosperity *only* to the *godly;* let the *ungodly* stand in awe of him.

Verse 10. *The counsel of the heathen to naught*] This appears to be similar to what is mentioned in the second *Psalm;* the useless attempts of the Gentiles to prevent the extension of the kingdom of Christ in the earth: and it may refer to similar attempts of ungodly nations or men to prevent the promulgation of the Gospel, and the universal dissemination of truth in the world.

Verse 11. *The counsel of the Lord*] What he has determined shall be done. He determined to make a world, and he made it; to create man, and he created him. He determined that at a certain period God should be manifested in the flesh, and it was so; that he should taste death for every man, and he did so; that his Gospel should be preached in all the world; and behold it has already nearly overrun the whole earth. All his other counsels and thoughts, which refer to the *future,* shall be accomplished in their times.

Verse 12. *Blessed* is *the nation*] O how happy is that nation which has יהוה *Jehovah* for its אלהים *Elohim;* the self-existent and eternal Lord for its covenant God; one who should

unite himself to it by connections and ties the most powerful and endearing! The word אלהים *Elohim,* which we translate GOD, refers to that economy in which God is manifested in the flesh.

The people whom *he hath chosen*] The *Jews,* who were *elected* to be his *heritage,* whom he preserved as such for two thousand years, and whom he has *reprobated* because of their unbelief and rebellion, and elected the Gentiles in their place.

Verse 13. *The Lord looketh from heaven*] This and the following verse seem to refer to God's *providence.* He sees all that is done in the earth, and his eye is on all the children of men.

Verse 15. *He fashioneth their hearts alike*] He forms their hearts in unity; he has formed them *alike;* they are all the *works of his hands:* and he has formed them with the same powers, faculties, passions, &c.; body and spirit having the same essential properties in every human being.

Verse 16. *There is no king saved by the multitude of a host*] Even in the midst of the most *powerful* and *numerous army,* no *king* is in *safety* unless he have God's protection. A king is but a *man,* and may as easily lose his life as one of his common soldiers.

A mighty man is not delivered by much strength.] There are times in which his might can be of no avail to him: and unless the *mighty,* the *wise,* the *honourable,* &c., have the protection of God, there is no time in which their *might* may not be turned into *weakness,* their *wisdom* into *folly,* and their *dignity* into *disgrace.*

Verse 17. *A horse is a vain thing for safety*] Even the horse, with all his fleetness, is no sure means of escape from danger: the *lion* or the *tiger* can overtake him or he may stumble, fall, and destroy his rider.

Verse 18. *Behold, the eye of the Lord*] Though all the above are unavailing, yet here is one thing that can never fail; "the eye of the Lord"—the watchful providence of the Most High, "is upon them that fear him, upon them that hope in his mercy."

19 To deliver their soul from death, and ᶻto keep them alive in famine.

20 ᵃOur soul waiteth for the Lᴏʀᴅ: ᵇhe *is* our help and our shield.

ᵃJob v. 20; Psa. xxxvii. 19——ᵃPsa. lxii. 1, 5; cxxx. 6

Verse 19. *To deliver their soul from death*] To watch over and protect them in all sudden dangers and emergencies, so that they shall not lose their ʟɪᴠᴇꜱ *by any accident.*

And to keep them alive in famine.] Not only prevent *sudden death* by an instantaneous interposition of my power, but keep them from a lingering death, by *extraordinary* supplies granted them in an *extraordinary manner;* because I am all in all, and all everywhere.

Verse 20. *Our soul waiteth*] Our whole life is employed in this blessed work; we *trust* in nothing but him; neither in multitudes of armed men, nor in natural strength, nor in the fleetest animals, nor in any thing human: we trust in Him alone "who is our help and our shield."

Verse 21. *For our heart shall rejoice in him*] Here is the fruit of our confidence: our *souls are always happy*, because we have taken God for our *portion.*

Verse 22. *Let thy mercy, O Lord, be upon us*] We cannot abide in this state unless upheld by thee; and, as we disclaim all *merit*, we seek for a continuance of thy *mercy;* and this we cannot expect but in a continual dependence on thee. "Let thy mercy, O Lord be upon us, according as we hope in thee."

Analysis of the Thirty-third Psalm

This Psalm is *eucharistic:* the contents are—
I. An *exhortation* to *praise* God, ver. 1, 2, 3.
II. The *arguments* he uses to enforce the duty, 4-19.
III. The *confidence* of God's people in his name. Their happiness, and petition, 20-22.
I. In the three first verses he exhorts men to praise God: but whom?
1. The *upright;* those who are not upright, cannot praise God.
2. That it be done with *zeal* and *affection;* with *singing*, with *voice*, and the *instruments* then in use; with some *new song*, composed on the occasion, for some new mercy; and that the whole be *skilfully* expressed.
II. This he urges on several good grounds:—
1. The first *argument*, in general drawn from the *truth*, the *faithfulness*, the *justice*, and *goodness* of God: 1. "For the word of the Lord is right." 2. "All his works are done in truth." 3. "He loveth righteousness and judgment." 4. "The earth is full of his goodness."
2. His *second argument* is drawn from God's power in the creation of all things, and that by his word alone, ver. 6, 7, 9; and upon it introduces, "Let all the earth fear the Lord; let all the inhabitants of the world stand in awe of him."
3. His *third argument* is drawn from God's *providence* in governing the world, which may easily be discerned by those who will diligently

consider his ways and proceedings, both to other people and to his Church.
1. He makes void all enterprises undertaken against his will, not only of single men, but of whole nations. "The Lord bringeth the counsel of the heathen to naught; he maketh the devices of the people of none effect."
2. Whereas, on the contrary, what he hath decreed shall be done. "The counsel of the Lord standeth for ever; the thoughts of his heart to all generations." On the consideration of which he breaks out into this *epiphonema*, or joyous reflection: "Blessed is the nation whose God is the Lord! and the people whom he hath chosen for his own inheritance!"
After which he returns to his discourse on God's *providence*, and by a *hypotyposis*, or splendid imagery, amplifies his former argument. For he sets God before us, as some great king on his throne, providing for all the parts of his empire, examining all causes, and doing justice to every one.
1. "The Lord looks from heaven, and beholds all the sons of men."
2. "From the place of his habitation he looks upon all the inhabitants of the earth."
3. And he is not an *idle spectator:* "He sees and considers their hearts and their works."
And he sees in what they *put their confidence;* in their *armies*, their *strength*, their *horse*, but not in *him*. But all in vain; for "there is no king saved by the multitude of a host: a mighty man is not delivered by much strength. A horse is a vain thing for safety." Multitude, strength, &c., without God, are useless.
Hitherto he had given a proof of God's providence towards *all men*, but now he descends to a particular proof of it, by his care over his *Church*, which he wonderfully guides, defends, and protects, in all dangers and assaults: and that notice may be taken of it, he begins with, *Behold!*
1. "Behold, the eye of the Lord," his tenderest care, "is over them that fear him, upon them that hope in his mercy."
2. "To deliver their soul from death, and keep them alive in famine."
III. The three last verses contain the acclamation of God's people, who place all their hope and trust in him; for, being stimulated by the former arguments, they do *three* things:—
1. They profess and express their *faith* and *dependence* on God: "Our soul waiteth on God, he is our help and our shield."
2. They declare the *hope* by which they are upheld, and how *comforted:* "For our heart shall rejoice in him, because we have trusted in his holy name."
3. Upon this hope they commend themselves by prayer to God; "Let thy mercy, O Lord, be upon us, according as we hope in thee."

PSALM XXXIV

David praises God, and exhorts others to do the same, 1–3; shows how he sought the Lord, and how he was found of him, 4–6. All are exhorted to taste and see the goodness of God; with the assurance of support and comfort, 7–10. He shows the way to attain happiness and long life, 11–16; the privileges of the righteous, and of all who sincerely seek God, 17–22.

A *Psalm* of David, when he changed his behaviour before ᵃAbimelech; who drove him away, and he departed

A. M. cir. 2942
B. C. cir. 1062
Sauli, Regis
Israelitarum,
cir. annum
34

I WILL ᵇbless the LORD at all times: his praise *shall* continually *be* in my mouth.

2 My soul shall make her ᶜboast in the LORD: ᵈthe humble shall hear *thereof,* and be glad.

3 O ᵉmagnify the LORD with me, and let us exalt his name together.

4 I ᶠsought the LORD, and he heard me, and delivered me from all my fears.

5 ᵍThey looked unto him, and were lightened; and their faces were not ashamed.

A. M. cir. 2942
B. C. cir. 1062
Sauli, Regis
Israelitarum,
cir. annum
34

ᵃOr, *Achish;* 1 Samuel xxi. 13——ᵇEphesians v. 20; 1 Thessalonians v. 18; 2 Thessalonians i. 3; ii. 13 ᶜJer. ix. 24; 1 Cor. i. 31; 2 Cor. x. 17

ᵈPsa. cxix. 74; cxlii. 7——ᵉPsa. lxix. 30; Luke i. 46 ᶠMatt. vii. 7; Luke xi. 9——ᵍOr, *They flowed* unto him

---

NOTES ON PSALM XXXIV

The *title* states that this is "A Psalm of David, when he changed his behaviour before Abimelech; who drove him away, and he departed." The history of this transaction may be found in 1 Sam. xxi.; on which chapter see the notes. But *Abimelech* is not the person there mentioned; it was *Achish*, king of Gath, called here *Abimelech*, because that was a common name of the Philistine kings. Neither MS. nor version reads *Achish* in this place; and all the versions agree in the title as it stands in our version, except the *Syriac*, which states it to be "A Psalm of David, when he went to the house of the Lord, that he might give the first-fruits to the priests."

Of the *occasion* of this Psalm, as stated here, I have given my opinion in the notes on 1 Sam. xxi., to which I have nothing to add. On the whole I prefer the view taken of it by the *Septuagint*, which intimates that "David fell into an epileptic fit; that he frothed at the mouth, fell against the doorposts, and gave such unequivocal evidences of being subject to epileptic fits, and during the time his intellect became so much impaired, that *Achish Abimelech* dismissed him from his court." This saves the character of David; and if it cannot be vindicated in this way, then let it fall under reproach as to this thing; for hypocrisy, deceit, and falsehood, can never be right in the sight of God, whatever men may ingeniously say to excuse them.

This is the *second* of the *acrostic* or *alphabetical Psalms*, each verse beginning with a consecutive letter of the Hebrew alphabet. But in this Psalm some derangement has taken place. The verse which begins with ו *vau*, and which should come in between the *fifth* and *sixth*, is totally wanting; and the *twenty-second* verse is entirely out of the series; it is, however, my opinion that this verse (the *twenty-second*) which now begins with פ *phe*, פודה *podeh*, redeemeth, was originally written ופודה *vepodeh* or with פדה *padah*, as more than a hundred of Dr. *Kennicott's* MSS. read it, thus making ופדה *vepodah*, "*and* will redeem" and this reads

admirably in the above connection. I shall here place the verses at one view, and the reader shall judge for himself:

Ver. 5. "They looked unto him, and were enlightened: and their faces were not ashamed."
Ver. 22. "AND the Lord will redeem the soul of his servants, and none of them that trust in him shall be desolate."
Ver. 6. "This poor man cried, and the Lord heard *him*, and saved him out of all his troubles."
Ver. 7. "The angel of the Lord encampeth round about them that fear him, and delivereth them."

Thus we find the connection complete, with the above emendation.

Verse 1. *I will bless the Lord at all times*] He has laid me under endless obligation to him, and I will praise him while I have a being.

Verse 2. *My soul shall make her boast*] Shall set *itself* to praise the Lord—shall consider this its chief work.

The humble] עניים *anavim*, the afflicted, such as *David* had been.

Verse 3. *Magnify the Lord with me*] נגדלו ליהוה *gaddelu layhovah*, "make greatness to Jehovah;" show his greatness; and let "us exalt his name," let us show how *high* and *glorious* it is.

Verse 4. *I sought the Lord*] This is the *reason* and *cause* of his gratitude. I sought the Lord, and he heard me, and delivered me out of all my fears. This answers to the history; for when David heard what the servants of Achish said concerning him, "he laid up the words in his heart, and was greatly afraid," 1 Sam. xxi. 13. To save him, God caused the epileptic fit to seize him; and, in consequence, he was dismissed by Achish, as one whose defection from his master, and union with the Philistines, could be of no use, and thus David's life and honour were preserved. The reader will see that I proceed on the ground laid down by the *Septuagint*. See before, verse 1.

Verse 5. *They looked unto him*] Instead of הביטו *hibbitu*, they *looked*, several of Dr. *Kennicott's* and *De Rossi's* MSS. have הביטו *habbitu*, with the point *pathach*, "Look ye."

And their faces were not ashamed.] Some

A. M. cir. 2942
B. C. cir. 1062
Sauli, Regis
Israelitarum,
cir. annum
34

6 [h]This poor man cried, and the LORD heard *him,* and [i]saved him out of all his troubles.

7 [k]The angel of the LORD [l]encampeth round about them that fear him, and delivereth them.

8 O [m]taste and see that the LORD *is* good: [n]blessed is the man *that* trusteth in him.

9 [o]O fear the LORD, ye his saints: for *there is* no want to them that fear him.

10 [p]The young lions do lack, and suffer hunger: [q]but they that seek the LORD shall not want any good *thing.*

11 Come, ye children, hearken unto me: [r]I will teach you the fear of the LORD.

A. M. cir. 2942
B. C. cir. 1062
Sauli, Regis
Israelitarum,
cir. annum
34

12 [s]What man *is he that* desireth life, *and* loveth many days, that he may see good?

13 Keep thy tongue from evil, and thy lips from [t]speaking guile.

14 [u]Depart from evil, and do good; [v]seek peace, and pursue it.

15 [w]The eyes of the LORD *are* upon the righteous, and his ears *are open* unto their [x]cry.

16 [y]The face of the LORD *is* against them that do evil, [z]to cut off the remembrance of them from the earth.

17 *The righteous* cry, and [a]the LORD hear-

---

[h]Psa. iii. 4——[i]Ver. 17, 19; 2 Sam. xxii. 1——[k]Dan. vi. 22; Heb. i. 14——[l]See Gen. xxxii. 1, 2; 2 Kings vi. 17; Zech. ix. 8——[m]1 Pet. ii. 3——[n]Psa. ii. 12——[o]Psa. xxxi. 23——[p]Job iv. 10, 11——[q]Psa. lxxxiv. 11——[r]Psa. xxxii. 8——[s]1 Pet. iii. 10, 11

[t]1 Pet. ii. 22——[u]Psa. xxxvii. 27; Isa. i. 16, 17——[v]Rom. xii. 18; Heb. xii. 14——[w]Job xxxvi. 7; Psa. xxxiii. 18; 1 Pet. iii. 12——[x]Ver. 6, 17——[y]Lev. xvii. 10; Jer. xliv. 11; Amos ix. 4——[z]Proverbs x. 7——[a]Verse 6, 15, 19; Psa. cxlv. 19, 20

MSS., and the *Complutensian Polyglot,* make this clause the beginning of a new verse and as it begins with a *vau,* ופניהם *upheneyhem,* "*and their faces,*" they make it supply the place of the verse which appears to be lost; but see what is said in the introduction before the *first* verse.

Verse 6. *This poor man cried*] זה עני *zeh ani,* "This *afflicted* man," David.

Verse 7. *The angel of the Lord encampeth round*] I should rather consider this angel in the light of a *watchman going round his circuit,* and having for the objects of his especial care such as *fear the Lord.*

Verse 8. *O taste and see that the Lord is good*] Apply to him by faith and prayer; plead his *promises,* he will fulfil them; and you shall know in consequence, that *the Lord is good.* God has put it in the power of every man to *know* whether the religion of the Bible be true or false. The *promises* relative to enjoyments in this life are the grand tests of Divine revelation. These must be fulfilled to all them who with deep repentance and true faith turn unto the Lord, if the revelation which contains them be of God. Let any man in this spirit approach his Maker, and plead the *promises* that are suited to his case, and he will soon know whether the doctrine be of God. He shall *taste,* and then *see, that the Lord is good,* and that the *man is blessed who trusts in him.* This is what is called *experimental religion;* the living, operative knowledge that a true believer has that he is passed from death unto life; that his sins are forgiven him for Christ's sake, the Spirit himself bearing witness with his spirit that he is a child of God. And, as long as he is faithful, he carries about with him the testimony of the Holy Ghost; and he knows that he is of God, by the Spirit which God has given him.

Verse 9. There is no *want to them that fear him.*] He who truly *fears* God *loves* him; and he who *loves* God *obeys* him, and to him who *fears, loves,* and obeys God, there can be no want of things essential to his happiness, whether spiritual or temporal, for this life or

for that which is to come. This verse is wanting in the *Syriac.*

Verse 10. *The young lions do lack*] Instead of כפירים *kephirim,* the young lions, one of *Kennicott's* MSS. has כבירים *cabbirim,* "powerful men." The *Vulgate, Septuagint, Æthiopic, Syriac, Arabic,* and *Anglo-Saxon* have the same reading. *Houbigant* approves of this; and indeed the sense and connection seem to require it. My old *Psalter* reads:—𝔗𝔥𝔢 𝔯𝔶𝔠𝔥𝔢 𝔥𝔞𝔡 𝔫𝔢𝔡𝔢; 𝔞𝔫𝔡 𝔱𝔥𝔞𝔦 𝔥𝔲𝔫𝔤𝔢𝔯𝔡: 𝔟𝔲𝔱 𝔰𝔢𝔨𝔞𝔫𝔡 𝔏𝔞𝔯𝔡 𝔰𝔞𝔩 𝔫𝔬𝔤𝔥𝔱 𝔟𝔢 𝔩𝔢𝔰𝔰𝔢𝔡 𝔬𝔣 𝔞𝔩𝔩𝔢 𝔤𝔬𝔡𝔢. That es, says the paraphrase, with outen lessyng thai sal have God; that es alle gode; for in God is al gode.

Verse 11. *Come, ye children*] All ye that are of an *humble, teachable* spirit.

I will teach you the fear of the Lord.] I shall introduce the *translation* and *paraphrase* from my old Psalter; and the rather because I believe there is a reference to that very improper and unholy method of teaching youth the system of heathen mythology before they are taught one sound lesson of true divinity, till at last their *minds* are *imbued* with *heathenism,* and the vicious conduct of gods, goddesses, and heroes, here very properly called *tyrants,* becomes the model of their own; and they are as heathenish *without* as they are heathenish *within.*

Trans. 𝔠𝔲𝔪𝔪𝔢𝔰 𝔰𝔬𝔫𝔢𝔰 𝔥𝔢𝔯𝔢𝔰 𝔪𝔢: 𝔡𝔯𝔢𝔡 𝔬𝔣 𝔏𝔞𝔯𝔡 𝔍 𝔰𝔞𝔩 𝔤𝔬𝔲 𝔩𝔢𝔯𝔢.

Par. 𝔠𝔲𝔪𝔪𝔢𝔰 with trauth and luf: 𝔰𝔬𝔫𝔢𝔰, qwam I gette in haly lere: 𝔥𝔢𝔯𝔢𝔰 𝔪𝔢. With eres of hert. 𝔍 𝔰𝔞𝔩 𝔩𝔢𝔯𝔢 𝔭𝔬𝔲, noght the fabyls of poetes; na the storys of tyrauntz; bot the dred of oure Larde, that wyl bryng you til the felaghschippe of aungels; and thar in is lyfe." I need not paraphrase this paraphrase, as it is plain enough.

Verse 12. *What man* is he that *desireth life*] He who wishes to live long and to live happily, let him act according to the following directions. For a comment upon this and the *four* ensuing verses, see the notes on 1 Peter iii. 10-12.

Verse 17. The righteous *cry*] There is no

A. M. cir. 2942
B. C. cir. 1062
Sauli, Regis
Israelitarum,
cir. annum
34

eth, and delivereth them out of all their troubles.

18 [b]The LORD *is* nigh [c]unto [d]them that are of a broken heart; and saveth [e]such as be of a contrite spirit.

19 [f]Many *are* the afflictions of the righteous: [g]but the LORD delivereth him out of them all.

20 He keepeth all his bones: [h]not one of them is broken.

21 [i]Evil shall slay the wicked: and they that hate the righteous [k]shall be desolate.

22 The LORD [l]redeemeth the soul of his servants: and none of them that trust in him shall be desolate.

A. M. cir. 2942
B. C. cir. 1062
Sauli, Regis
Israelitarum,
cir. annum
34

---

[b]Psa. cxlv. 18——[c]Psa. li. 17; Isa. lvii. 15; lxi. 1; lxvi. 2——[d]Heb. *to the broken of heart*——[e]Heb. *contrite of spirit*——[f]Prov. xxiv. 16; 2 Tim. iii. 11, 12

[g]Ver. 6, 17——[h]John xix. 36——[i]Psa. xciv. 23
[k]Or, *shall be guilty*——[l]2 Sam. iv. 9; 1 Kings i. 29; Psa. lxxi. 23; ciii. 4; Lam. iii. 58

---

word in the present *Hebrew* text for righteous; but all the *versions* preserve it. I suppose it was lost through its similitude to the word צעקו *tsaaku*, they cry צעקו צדיקים *tsaaku tsaddikim*, the righteous cry.

Verse 18. *A broken heart*] נשברי לב *nishberey leb*, the heart *broken to shivers*.

A contrite spirit.] דכאי רוח *dakkeey ruach*, "the beaten-out spirit." In both words the *hammer* is necessarily implied; in breaking to pieces the ore first, and then plating out the metal when it has been separated from the ore. This will call to the reader's remembrance Jer. xxiii. 29: "Is not my word like as a fire, saith the Lord? And like a *hammer* that breaketh the *rock* in pieces?" The *breaking to shivers*, and *beating out*, are metaphorical expressions: so are the *hammer* and the *rock*. What the large *hammer* struck on a rock by a powerful hand would do, so does the word of the Lord when struck on the sinner's heart by the power of the Holy Spirit. The *broken heart*, and the *contrite spirit*, are two essential characteristics of true repentance.

Verse 19. *Many* are *the afflictions of the righteous*] No commander would do justice to a brave and skilful soldier, by refusing him opportunities to put his skill and bravery to proof by combating with the adversary; or by preventing him from taking the *post of danger* when necessity required it. The righteous are God's soldiers. He suffers them to be tried, and sometimes to enter into the hottest of the battle and in their victory the power and influence of the grace of God is shown, as well as their faithfulness.

Delivereth him out of them all.] He may well combat heartily, who knows that if he fight in the Lord, he shall necessarily be the conqueror.

Verse 20. *He keepeth all his bones*] He takes care of his life; and if he have *scars*, they are honourable ones.

Verse 21. *Evil shall slay the wicked*] The very thing in which they delight shall become their bane and their ruin.

They that hate the righteous] All persecutors of God's people shall be followed by the chilling blast of God's displeasure in this world; and if they repent not, shall perish everlastingly.

Verse 22. *The Lord redeemeth*] Both the *life* and *soul* of God's followers are ever in danger, but God is continually redeeming both.

Shall be desolate.] Literally, *shall be guilty*. They shall be preserved from sin, and neither forfeit *life* nor soul. This verse probably should come in after the fifth. See the introduction to this Psalm.

ANALYSIS OF THE THIRTY-FOURTH PSALM

This Psalm is composed with great art, and this must be attended to by those who would analyze it. The scope of it is to praise God, and to instruct in his fear. Its parts are, in general, the following:—

I. He praises God himself, and calls upon others to follow his example, 1-8.

II. He assumes the office of a teacher, and instructs both young and old in the fear of the Lord, 9-22.

1. He praises God, and expresses himself thus:—1. I will bless the Lord. 2. His praise shall be in my mouth. 3. It shall be in my mouth continually. 4. It shall be expressed by a *tongue* affected by the *heart:* "My soul shall make her boast in the Lord." 5. And so long would he continue it till others should be moved to do the like: "The humble shall hear thereof, and be glad."

2. Upon which he calls upon others to join with him: "O magnify the Lord with me, and let us exalt his name together." And to encourage them he proposes his own example: "I sought the Lord," &c. Should it be said this was a singular mercy shown to David which others are not to expect, he in effect replies, No; a mercy it is, but it belongs to all that seek God: "They looked unto him," &c. But should not this satisfy, and should they rejoin, This poor man (David) cried, and the Lord heard him, but David was in the Divine favour; he may be supposed to reply by this general maxim: "The angel of the Lord encampeth round about them that fear him;" and be they who they may, *if they fear God*, this is their privilege.

II. Now he assumes the chair of the teacher; and the lessons are *two:*—

1. That they make a trial of God's goodness: "O taste and see that the Lord is good."

2. That they become his servants: "O fear ye the Lord, for there is no want," &c.

And this he illustrates by a comparison: "The young lions (or, the rich and the powerful) may lack and suffer hunger," but they *that seek the Lord* shall not.

These promises and blessings belong only to them that fear the Lord and lest some should imagine they had this fear, and were entitled to the promise, he shows them what this fear is. He calls an assembly, and thus addresses them: "Come, ye children, and hearken unto me and I will teach you the fear of the Lord." That fear of the Lord which, if a man be desirous of life, and to see many days, shall satisfy him; and if he be ambitious to see good, the peace of a quiet *soul* and a good conscience shall lodge with him.

1. Let him be sure to take care of his tongue: "keep thy tongue from evil, and thy lips that they speak no guile."

2. Let him act according to justice: "Depart from evil."

3. Let him be charitable, ready to do good works: "Do good."

4. Let him be peaceable: "Seek peace, and pursue it."

These are the characteristics of those who fear the Lord, and seek him; and they shall want no manner of thing that is good.

It may be objected: The righteous are exposed to afflictions, &c., and ungodly men have power and prosperity; to which it may be answered: Afflictions do not make the godly *miserable*, nor does prosperity make the wicked *happy*. 1. As to the righteous, they are always objects of God's merciful regards: "For the eyes of the Lord are upon the righteous, and his ears are open to their prayers." But, 2. "The face of the Lord is against those who do evil," &c.

These points he illustrates:—

1. The righteous cries, and the Lord heareth him, and delivereth him out of all his troubles; either, 1. By taking *them* from *him* or, 2. By taking *him* from *them*.

2. "The Lord is nigh to them that are of a broken heart," &c. Thus he comforts, confirms, and strengthens.

3. Although the afflictions of the righteous are many, yet the Lord delivers him out of them all; makes him patient, constant, cheerful in all, superior to all.

4. "He keeps all his bones." He permits him to suffer no essential hurt.

But as to the ungodly, it is not so with them; the very root of their perdition is their malice, which they show, 1. To God; 2. To good men.

1. "Evil shall slay the wicked."

2. "And they that hate the righteous shall be desolate."

And then David concludes the Psalm with this excellent sentiment; Though God may suffer his servants to come into trouble, yet he delivers them from it. For it belongs to redemption to free one from misery; for no man can be redeemed who is under no hardship. This shall be done, says David. The "Lord redeemeth the souls of his servants, and none of them that trust in him shall be desolate." The Lord redeems from *trouble* and *affliction*, as well as from *sin*. He knows how to deliver the godly *from* temptation; and he knows how to preserve them *in* it. But it is his *servants* that he redeems, not his *enemies*. The *servant* may confidently look to his *master* for support.

PSALM XXXV

The psalmist, in great straits, prays for his personal safety, 1–3; and for the confusion of his enemies, 4–8; expresses his confidence in God, 9, 10; mentions his kindness to those who had rewarded him evil for his good, 11–16; appeals to God against them, 17–26; prays for those who befriended him; and praises God for his goodness, 27, 28.

VII. DAY. MORNING PRAYER

A Psalm of David

A. M. cir. 2943
B. C. cir. 1061
Sauli, Regis
Israelitarum,
cir. annum
35

PLEAD ^a*my cause,* O LORD, with them that strive with me: ^bfight against them that fight against me.

2 ^cTake hold of shield and buckler, and stand up for mine help.

3 Draw out also the spear, and stop *the way* against them that persecute me: say unto my soul, I *am* thy salvation.

A. M. cir. 2943
B. C. cir. 1061
Sauli, Regis
Israelitarum,
cir. annum
35

4 ^dLet them be confounded and put to shame that seek after my soul: let them be ^eturned back and brought to confusion that devise my hurt.

---

^aPsa. xliii. 1; cxix. 154; Lam. iii. 58——^bExod. xiv. 25
^cIsa. xlii. 13

^dVerse 26; Psalm xl. 14, 15; lxx. 2, 3——^ePsalm cxxix. 5

NOTES ON PSALM XXXV

There is nothing in the *title* worthy of remark. The Psalm is simply attributed to David, and was most probably of his composing; and refers to the time of his persecution by Saul and his courtiers. The *Syriac* says it was composed when the Idumeans attacked David. The Arabic says it is a prophecy concerning the incarnation, and concerning the things practised against Jeremiah by the *people*. Some think that our Lord's sufferings are particularly pointed out here; and Bishop *Horsley* thinks that verses 11 to 16 apply more literally and exactly to Christ than to any other whomsoever.

Verse 1. *Plead* my cause, *O Lord*] Literally, *Contend, Lord, with them that contend with*

me. The word is often used in a *forensic* or *law* sense.

Verse 2. *Take hold of shield and buckler*] Let them be discomfited in battle who are striving to destroy my life. It is by the *shield* and *buckler* of *others*, not any of his *own*, that God overthrows the enemies of his people. This is spoken merely after the manner of men.

Verse 3. *Say unto my soul, I am thy salvation.*] Give me an assurance that thou wilt defend both body and soul against my adversaries.

Verse 4. *Let them be confounded*] Let none of their projects or devices against me succeed. Blast all their designs.

The *imprecations* in these verses against enemies are all *legitimate*. They are not against the *souls* or *eternal welfare* of those sinners,

A. M. cir. 2943
B. C. cir. 1061
Sauli, Regis
Israelitarum,
cir. annum
35

5 [f]Let them be as chaff before the wind: and let the angel of the LORD chase *them*.

6 Let their way be [g]dark [h]and slippery: and let the angel of the LORD persecute them.

7 For without cause have they [i]hid for me their net *in* a pit, *which* without cause they have digged for my soul.

8 Let [k]destruction come upon him [l]at unawares; and [m]let his net that he hath hid catch himself: into that very destruction let him fall.

9 And my soul shall be joyful in the LORD: [n]it shall rejoice in his salvation.

10 [o]All my bones shall say, LORD, [p]who *is* like unto thee, which deliverest the poor from him

A. M. cir. 2943
B. C. cir. 1061
Sauli, Regis
Israelitarum,
cir. annum
35

that is too strong for him, yea, the poor and the needy from him that spoileth him?

11 [q]False [r]witnesses did rise up: [s]they laid to my charge *things* that I knew not.

12 [t]They rewarded me evil for good *to* the [u]spoiling of my soul.

13 But as for me, [v]when they were sick, my clothing *was* sackcloth: I [w]humbled my soul with fasting; [x]and my prayer returned into mine own bosom.

14 I [y]behaved myself [z]as though *he had been* my friend *or* brother: I bowed down heavily, as one that mourneth *for his* mother.

15 But in mine [a]adversity they rejoiced,

---

[f]Job. xxi. 18; Psa. i. 4; lxxxiii. 13; Isa. xxix. 5; Hos. xiii. 3——[g]Heb. *darkness and slipperiness*——[h]Psa. lxxiii. 18; Jer. xxiii. 12——[i]Psa. ix. 15——[k]1 Thess. v. 3 [l]Heb. *which he knoweth not of*——[m]Psa. vii. 15, 16; lvii. 6; cxli. 9, 10; Prov. v. 22——[n]Psa. xiii. 5——[o]See Psa. li. 8 [p]Exod. xv. 11; Psa. lxxi. 19

[q]Hebrew, *Witnesses of wrong*——[r]Psalm xxvii. 12 [s]Heb. *they asked me*——[t]Psa. xxxviii. 20; cix. 3, 4, 5; Jer. xviii. 20; John x. 32——[u]Heb. *depriving*——[v]Job xxx. 25; Psa. lxix. 10, 11——[w]Or, *afflicted*——[x]Matt. x. 13; Luke x. 6——[y]Heb. *walked*——[z]Heb. *as a friend, as a brother to me*——[a]Heb. *halting*; Psalm xxxviii. 17

---

but against their *schemes* and *plans* for *destroying the life of an innocent man;* and the holiest Christian may offer up such prayers against his adversaries. If a man aim a blow at another with a design to take away his life, and the blow would infallibly be mortal if it took place, and the person about to be slain see that by breaking the arm of his adversary he may prevent his own death, and thus save his enemy from *actual* murder; it is his duty to prevent this double evil by breaking the arm of the blood-thirsty man. It is on this principle that David prays against his adversaries in the first eight verses of this Psalm.

Verse 5. *Let the angel of the Lord chase them.*] By *angel* we may either understand one of those *spirits*, whether good or bad, commonly thus denominated, or *any thing* used by God himself as the instrument of their confusion.

Verse 6. *Let their way be dark*] Let them lose their way, be entangled in morasses and thickets, and be confounded in all their attempts to injure me. All these phrases are *military;* and relate to *ambushes, hidden snares, forced marches* in order to *surprise*, and *stratagems* of different kinds.

Verse 7. *For without cause have they hid for me their net in a pit*] The word שחת *shachath*, a *pit*, belongs to the second member of this verse; and the whole should be read thus: For without a cause they have hidden for me their net, without a cause they have digged a *pit* for my life. They have used every degree and species of cunning and deceit to ruin me.

Verse 8. *Let his net that he hath hid*] See the notes on Psa. vii. 15 and 16.

Verse 9. *My soul*] My life, thus saved—
Shall be joyful in the Lord] I am so circumstanced at present as to be in the utmost danger of being destroyed by my foes; if I escape, it must be by the strong arm of the Lord; and to him shall the glory be given.

Verse 10. *All my bones shall say*] My life being preserved, all the members of my body shall magnify thy saving mercy.
Deliverest the poor] This is a general maxim: God is peculiarly mindful of the poor. Where secular advantages are withheld, there is the more need for spiritual help. God considers this, and his kind providence works accordingly.

Verse 11. *False witnesses did rise up*] There is no doubt that several of this kind were found to depose against the life of David; and we know that the wicked Jews employed such against the life of Christ. See Matt. xxvi. 59, 60.
They laid to my charge things that I knew not.] They produced the most unfounded charges; things of which I had never before heard.

Verse 12. *To the spoiling of my soul*] *To destroy my life;* so נפש *nephesh* should be translated in a multitude of places, where our translators have used the word *soul.*

Verse 13. *When they were sick*] This might refer to the case of Absalom, who was much beloved of his father, and for whose life and prosperity he no doubt often prayed, wept, and fasted.
My prayer returned into mine own bosom.] Though from the wayward and profligate life they led, they did not profit by my prayers, yet God did not permit me to pray in vain. They were like alms given to the miserable for God's sake, who takes care to return to the merciful man tenfold into his bosom. The *bosom* is not only the place where the Asiatics carry their purses, but also where they carry any thing that is given to them.

Verse 14. *Mourneth for his mother.*] כאבל אם *caabel em*, as a mourning mother. How expressive is this word!

Verse 15. *But in mine adversity they rejoiced*] How David was mocked and insulted

A. M. cir. 2943
B. C. cir. 1061
Sauli, Regis
Israelitarum,
cir. annum
35

and gathered themselves to-gether: *yea,* ^bthe abjects gath-ered themselves together against me, and I knew *it* not; they did ^ctear *me,* and ceased not:

16 With hypocritical mockers in feasts, ^dthey gnashed upon me with their teeth.

17 LORD, how long wilt thou ^elook on? rescue my soul from their destructions, ^fmy^g darling from the lions.

18 ^hI will give thee thanks in the great con-gregation: I will praise thee among ⁱmuch people.

19 ^kLet not them that are mine enemies ^lwrongfully rejoice over me: *neither* ^mlet them wink with the eye ⁿthat hate me without a cause.

20 For they speak not peace: but they de-vise deceitful matters against *them that are* quiet in the land.

21 Yea, they ^oopened their mouth wide against me, *and* said, ^pAha, aha, our eye hath seen *it.*

22 *This* thou hast ^qseen, O LORD: ^rkeep not silence: O LORD, be not ^sfar from me.

23 ^tStir up thyself, and awake to my judgment, *even* unto my cause, my God and my Lord.

24 ^uJudge me, O LORD, my God, ^vaccording to thy righteousness; and ^wlet them not re-joice over me.

25 ^xLet them not say in their hearts, ^yAh, so would we have it: let them not say, ^zWe have swallowed him up.

26 ^aLet them be ashamed and brought to confusion together that rejoice at mine hurt: let them be ^bclothed with shame and dis-honour that ^cmagnify *themselves* against me.

27 ^dLet them shout for joy, and be glad, that favour ^emy righteous cause: yea, let them ^fsay continually, Let the LORD be magnified, ^gwhich hath pleasure in the prosperity of his servant.

28 ^hAnd my tongue shall speak of thy right-eousness *and* of thy praise all the day long.

A. M. cir. 2943
B. C. cir. 1061
Sauli, Regis
Israelitarum,
cir. annum
35

^bJob xxx. 1, 8, 12——^cJob xvi. 9——^dJob xvi. 9; Psa. xxxvii. 12; Lam. ii. 16——^eHab. i. 13——^fHeb. *my only one*——^gPsa. xxii. 20——^hPsa. xxii. 25, 31; xl. 9, 10; cxi. 1——ⁱHeb. *strong*——^kPsa. xiii. 4; xxv. 2; xxxviii. 16——^lHeb. *falsely*; Psa. xxxviii. 19——^mJob xv. 12; Prov. vi. 13; x. 10——ⁿPsa. lxix. 4; cix. 3; cxix. 161; Lam. iii. 52; John xv. 25——^oPsa. xxii. 13——^pPsa. xl. 15; liv. 7; lxx. 3——^qExod. iii. 7; Acts vii. 34

^rPsa. xxviii. 1; lxxxiii. 1——^sPsa. x. 1; xxii. 11, 19; xxxviii. 21; lxxi. 12——^tPsa. xliv. 23; lxxx. 2——^uPsa. xxvi. 1——^v2 Thess. i. 6——^wVer. 19——^xPsa. xxvii. 12; lxx. 3; cxl. 8——^yHeb. *Ah, ah, our soul*——^zLam. ii. 16——^aVer. 4; Psa. xl. 14——^bPsa. cix. 29; cxxxii. 18 ^cPsa. xxxviii. 16——^dRom. xii. 15; 1 Cor. xii. 26 ^eHeb. *my righteousness;* Prov. viii. 18——^fPsa. lxx. 4 ^gPsa. cxlix. 4——^hPsa. l. 15; li. 14; lxxi. 24

in the case of Absalom's rebellion by Shimei and others, is well known.

The abjects] נכים *nechim,* the *smiters,* prob-ably hired assassins. They were everywhere lying in wait, to take away my life.

Verse 16. *With hypocritical mockers in feasts*] These verses seem to be prophetic of the treatment of Christ. *They did tear me, and I knew it not.* They blindfolded and buffeted him; they placed him in such circumstances as not to be able to discern who insulted him, ex-cept by a supernatural knowledge. *With hypo-critical mockers in feasts* may also relate pro-phetically to our Lord's sufferings. Herod clothed him in a purple robe, put a *reed* in his hand for a *sceptre,* bowed the knee before him, and set him at nought. Here their hypocritical conduct (pretending one thing while they meant another) was manifest, and possibly this occurred at one of Herod's *feasts.*

Verse 17. *My darling*] יחידתי *yechidathi, my only one,* Psa. xxii. 20. *My united one,* or *He that is alone.* Perhaps this may relate to Christ. See the note on Psa. xxii. 20.

Verse 18. *I will give thee thanks in the great congregation*] I hope to be able to attend at the tabernacle with thy followers, and there pub-licly express my gratitude for the deliverance thou hast given me.

Verse 19. *That are mine enemies*] Saul and his courtiers.

Verse 21. *They opened their mouth wide*] Gaped upon me to express their contempt.

And *said, Aha, aha, our eye hath seen* it.] They said, האח האח *heach, heach,* the last sylla-ble in each word being a protracted strongly gut-tural sound, marking insult and triumph at the same time. It is the word which we translate *Ah,* ver. 25.

Verse 22. This *thou hast seen*] I have no need to adduce evidences of these wrongs; thou, to whom I appeal, hast seen them. Therefore,

Verse 23. *Stir up thyself, and awake to my judgment*] I have delivered my cause into thy hand, and appeal to thee as my Judge; and by thy decision I am most willing to abide.

Verse 24. *Judge me, O Lord my God*] The manner of his appeal shows the strong confi-dence he had in his own innocence.

Verse 25. *Swallowed him up.*] בלענוהו *bil-laanuhu, we have gulped him down.*

Verse 26. *Let them be ashamed*] This may be a prophetic declaration against Saul and his courtiers. They were ashamed, confounded, clothed with shame, and dishonoured. All these took place in Saul's last battle with the Philis-tines, where he lost his crown and his life, and came to a most dishonourable end.

Verse 27. *Let them shout for joy and be glad*] While my enemies are confounded, let my friends exult in the Lord; and let them all praise him for his marvellous kindness to me.

Verse 28. *And my tongue shall speak*] I, who am chiefly concerned, and who have received most, am under the greatest obligation; and it will require the constant gratitude and obedience of my whole life to discharge the mighty debt I owe.

ANALYSIS OF THE THIRTY-FIFTH PSALM

This Psalm may be divided into *three* parts:—

I. A prayer for defence against his enemies. In which he prays, 1. For protection, ver. 1, 2, 3, 17, 19, 22, 23, 24, 25. And, 2. Imprecates evil to fall on their counsels and designs.

II. A bitter complaint against the malice of his enemies, which he pours out into the ears of God as motives to plead his cause, ver. 7, 11, 12, 13, 14, 15, 16, 19, 20, 21.

III. An expression of his trust and confidence in God for help and deliverance; his joy in it, ver. 9, 10; his thanks for it, ver. 18, 28; and a motive to others to do the like, ver. 27.

1. In the courts of men and princes innocent persons are often oppressed by false accusations and calumnies, persecuted and overborne by power.

He then, *first*, prays to God to be his Advocate, his Patron, and his Protector: 1. "Plead my cause, O Lord, with them that strive against me." 2. "Fight against them that fight against me," &c. 3. "Say unto my soul, I am thy salvation." Assure me of thy favour.

He *secondly*, begins an imprecation against his enemies: 1. "Let them be confounded and put to shame," ver. 4. 2. "Let them be as chaff before the wind," ver. 5. 3. "Let their way be dark and slippery," ver. 6. 4. "Let destruction come upon him unawares," ver. 8.

And here he inserts some reasons for his *petition* and *imprecation:*—

1. From the *justice* of *his* cause, and *their injustice:* "Without cause they hid for me their net," ver. 7.

2. From his gratitude; that, being delivered, he would be thankful: "And my soul shall be joyful in the Lord," &c., ver. 9, 10.

3. From his enemies' dealings with him, ver. 11-17.

II. He then enters upon his complaint; and lays to their charge,

1. *Perfidiousness*, extreme malice, and perjury: "False witnesses did rise," &c.

2. *Ingratitude.* They rewarded me evil for good. Good he did to them; for, when they were afflicted, he fasted and prayed for them.

3. They were *cruel* to him: "In my adversity they rejoiced."

4. They *mocked* him and made him their cruel sport: "The abjects gathered themselves together against me," &c.

5. And a *conspiracy* in all, ver. 20, 21.

Then he returns again to his petition; and expostulates with God, wondering that he should be so patient with them: "Lord, how long wilt thou look on? Rescue my soul from destruction," &c.

And, to move God the sooner to do it, he repeats his former reason, ver. 9, engaging himself to be thankful: "I will give thee thanks in the great congregation; I will praise thee among much people."

He continues his suit to the end of the Psalm; sometimes *praying*, at others *imprecating.*

1. He deprecates: "Let not my enemies wrongfully rejoice over me, neither let them wink with the eye," &c. And that God may be the readier to hear him, and stay their joy and triumph, he subjoins these reasons: 1. "For they speak not peace." 2. "They devise deceitful matters against them that are quiet in the land." 3. They are impudent, lying people: "Yea, they opened their mouth wide against me," &c. This is a truth; this is not hidden from thee: "This thou hast seen," and from them to thee I turn my eyes; and thus renew my prayer:—

1. "Keep not silence." Do not appear to neglect my cause; nor to let them pass on with impunity.

2. "Stir up thyself, and awake to my judgment," &c. Defend me, and confound them:—

3. "Judge me according to thy righteousness," which suffers not the just to be always oppressed.

4. "Let them not rejoice over me," and, in me, over the truth, and over a just cause.

5. "Let them not say in their hearts, So would we have it," &c.

6. But rather let that befall them which I have prayed for: "Let them be ashamed,—brought to confusion,—and clothed with shame and dishonour, that magnify themselves against me."

III. In the conclusion he expresses his trust and confidence in God; and intimates that if he be heard, then he, and the whole Church, and all good men, will rejoice together.

1. To them he first directs his speech: "Let them shout for joy that favour my righteous cause; yea, let them say continually; Let the Lord be magnified, which hath pleasure in the prosperity of his servant."

2. He then declares what effect this will have upon him in particular: "My tongue shall speak of thy righteousness and of thy praise all the day long."

PSALM XXXVI

The miserable state of the wicked, 1–4. The excellence of God's mercy in itself, and to his followers, 5–9. He prays for the upright, 10; for himself, that he may be saved from pride and violence, 11; and shows the end of the workers of iniquity, 12.

To the chief Musician, *A Psalm* of David the servant of the
LORD

THE transgression of the wicked saith within my heart, *that* [a]*there is* no fear of God before his eyes.

2 For [b]he flattereth himself in his own eyes, [c]until his iniquity be found to be hateful.

3 The words of his mouth *are* iniquity and

[d]deceit: [e]he hath left off to be wise, *and* to do good.

4 [f]He deviseth [g]mischief upon his bed; he setteth himself [h]in a way *that is* not good; he abhorreth not evil.

5 [i]Thy mercy, O LORD, *is* in the heavens; *and* thy faithfulness *reacheth* unto the clouds.

---

[a]Rom. iii. 18——[b]Deut. xxix. 19; Psalm x. 3; xlix. 18
[c]Heb. *to find his iniquity to hate*——[d]Psa. xii. 2

[e]Jer. iv. 22——[f]Prov. iv. 16; Mic. ii. 1——[g]Or, *vanity*
[h]Isa. lxv. 2——[i]Psa. lvii. 10; cviii. 4

NOTES ON PSALM XXXVI

The *title* in the Hebrew is, *To the conqueror, to the servant of Jehovah, to David.* The *Syriac* and *Arabic* suppose it to have been composed on occasion of Saul's persecution of David. *Calmet* supposes, on good grounds, that it was written during the Babylonish captivity. It is one of the finest Psalms in the whole collection.

Verse 1. *The transgression of the wicked saith within my heart*] It is difficult to make any sense of this line as it now stands. How can *the transgression of the wicked speak within my heart?* But instead of לבי *libbi*, MY *heart*, four of *Kennicott's* and *De Rossi's* MSS. have לבו *libbo*, HIS *heart.* "The speech of transgression to the wicked is in the midst of his heart." "There is no fear of God before his eyes." It is not by *example* that such a person sins; the *fountain* that sends forth the impure streams is *in his own heart.* There the spirit of transgression lives and reigns; and, as he has no *knowledge* of God, so he has no *fear of God;* therefore, there is no check to his wicked propensities: all come to full effect. Lust is conceived, sin is brought forth vigorously, and transgression is multiplied. The reading above proposed, and which should be adopted, is supported by the *Vulgate, Septuagint, Syriac, Æthiopic, Arabic,* and *Anglo-Saxon.* This latter reads the sentence thus: Iꞅpeð ꞅe unꞃiȝhtƿyꞃa pƿꞇ he aȝꞅꞇce oa him ꞃylꞃum: niꞃ eȝe ȝoðeꞃ ƿꞇꞃoꞃan eȝan hiꞃ; which I shall give as nearly as possible in the order of the original. "Quoth the unrightwise, that he do guilt in himself: is not fear God's at fore eyes his." That is, The unrighteous man saith in himself that he will sin: God's fear is not before his eyes. The old *Psalter,* in *language* as well as *meaning,* comes very near to the Anglo-Saxon: Ꞇhe unrightwis saide that he trespas in hym self: the drede of God es noght before his een. And thus it paraphrases the passage: Ꞇhe unryghtwis, that es the kynde [the whole generation] of wyked men; saide in hym self, qwar man sees noght; that he trespas, that es, he synne at his wil, als [as if] God roght noght [did not care] qwat he did; and so it es sene, that the drede of God es noght by fore his een; for if he dred God, he durst noght so say."

I believe these *versions* give the true sense of the passage. The psalmist here paints the true state of the *Babylonians:* they were *idolaters* of the grossest kind, and worked iniquity with greediness. The account we have in the book of *Daniel* of this people, exhibits them in the worst light; and profane history confirms the account. Bishop *Horsley* thinks that the word פשע *pesha*, which we render *transgression,* signifies the apostate or *devil.* The devil says to

the *wicked, within his heart, There is no fear;* i. e., no cause of fear: "God is not before his eyes." Placing the colon after *fear* takes away all ambiguity in connection with the reading, HIS *heart,* already contended for. The *principle of transgression, sin in the heart,* says, or suggests to every *sinner, there is no cause for fear:* go on, do not fear, for there is no danger. He obeys this suggestion, goes on, and acts wickedly, as "God is not before his eyes."

Verse 2. *For he flattereth himself*] He is ruled by the suggestion already mentioned; endeavours to persuade himself that he may safely follow the propensities of his own heart, *until his iniquity be found to be hateful.* He sins so boldly, that at last he becomes detestable. Some think the words should be thus understood: "He smootheth over in his own eyes with respect to the finding out of his iniquity, to hate it. That is, he sets such a false gloss in his own eyes upon his worst actions, that he never finds out the blackness of his iniquity; which, were it perceived by him, would be hateful even to himself."—Bishop *Horsley.*

Verse 3. *The words of his mouth* are *iniquity*] In the principle; *and deceit* calculated to pervert others, and lead them astray.

He hath left off to be wise, and to do good.] His heart is become foolish, and his actions wicked. He has cut off the connection between himself and all righteousness.

Verse 4. *He deviseth mischief upon his bed*] He seeks the silent and undisturbed watches of the night, in order to fix his plans of wickedness.

He setteth himself] Having laid his *plans,* he fixes his *purpose* to do what is bad; and he does it without any checks of conscience or abhorrence of evil. He is bent only on mischief, and lost to all sense of God and goodness. A finished character of a perfect sinner.

Verse 5. *Thy mercy, O Lord, is in the heavens*] That is, thou art abundant, infinite in thy mercy; else such transgressors must be immediately cut off; but thy long-suffering is intended to lead them to repentance.

Thy faithfulness reacheth *unto the clouds*] עד שחקים *ad shechakim,* to the eternal regions; above all visible space. God's *faithfulness* binds him to fulfil the *promises* and *covenants* made by his mercy. Blessings from the *heavens,* from the *clouds,* from the *earth,* are promised by God to his followers; and his *faithfulness* is in all those places, to distribute to his followers the mercies he has promised.

Verse 6. *Thy righteousness* is *like the great mountains.*] כהררי אל *keharerey El,* like the *mountains of God;* exceeding high mountains; what, in the present language of *geology,* would

6 Thy righteousness *is* like [k]the great mountains; [l]thy judgments *are* a great deep: O
LORD, [m]thou preservest man and beast.
7 [n]How [o]excellent *is* thy loving-kindness,
O God! therefore the children of men
[p]put their trust under the shadow of thy
wings.
8 [q]They shall be [r]abundantly satisfied
with the fatness of thy house; and thou shalt
make them drink of [s]the river [t]of thy
pleasures.
9 [u]For with thee *is* the fountain of life: [v]in
thy light shall we see light.
10 O [w]continue thy loving-kindness [x]unto
them that know thee; and thy righteousness
to the [y]upright in heart.

---

[k]Heb. *the mountains of God*——[l]Job xi. 8; Psa. lxxvii. 19; Rom. xi. 33——[m]Job vii. 20; Psalm cxlv. 9; 1 Tim. iv. 10——[n]Psalm xxxi. 19——[o]Hebrew, *precious* [p]Ruth ii. 12; Psa. xvii. 8; xci. 4——[q]Psa. lxv. 4

[r]Heb. *watered*——[s]Job xx. 17; Rev. xxii. 1——[t]Psa. xvi. 11——[u]Jer. ii. 13; John iv. 10, 14——[v]1 Pet. ii. 9 [w]Heb. *draw out at length*——[x]Jer. xxii. 16——[y]Psa. vii. 10; xciv. 15; xcvii. 11

---

be called *primitive mountains*, those that were formed at the beginning; and are not the effects of *earthquakes* or *inundations*, as *secondary* and *alluvial mountains* are supposed to be.

Thy judgments are *a great deep*] תהום רבה *tehom rabbah, the great abyss;* as incomprehensible as the *great chaos*, or first matter of all things which God created in the beginning, and which is mentioned Gen. i. 2, *and darkness was on the face*, תהום *tehom, of the deep*, the vast profound, or what is *below all* conjecturable *profundity*. How astonishing are the thoughts in these two verses! What an idea do they give us of the mercy, truth, righteousness, and judgments of God!

The old *Psalter*, in paraphrasing *mountains of God*, says, **Thi ryghtwisnes**, that es, ryghtwis men, er gastly hilles of God; for thai er hee in contemplacioun, and soner resayves the lyght of Crist. Here is a metaphor taken from the *tops* of *mountains* and *high hills* first catching the *rays of the rising sun*. "Righteous men are spiritual hills of God; for they are *high* in contemplation, and *sooner* receive the *light of Christ*." It is really a very fine thought; and much beyond the rudeness of the times in which this Psalter was written.

Man and beast.] Doth God take care of cattle? Yes, he appoints the lions their food, and hears the cry of the young ravens; and will he not provide for the poor, especially the poor of his people? He will. So infinitely and intensely good is the nature of God, that it is his delight to make all his creatures happy. He preserves the *man*, and he preserves the *beast;* and it is his providence which supplies the *man*, when his propensities and actions level him with the *beasts* that perish.

Verse 7. *How excellent* is *thy loving-kindness*] He asks the question in the way of admiration; but expects no answer from angels or men. It is indescribably excellent, abundant, and free; and, "therefore, the children of Adam put their trust under the shadow of thy wings." They trust in thy good *providence* for the supply of their *bodies;* they trust in thy *mercy* for the salvation of their *souls*. These, speaking after the *figure*, are the *two wings* of the Divine goodness, under which the children of men take refuge. The allusion may be to the *wings of the cherubim*, above the mercy-seat.

Verse 8. *They shall be abundantly satisfied*] ירוין *yirveyun*, they *shall be saturated*, as a thirsty field is by showers from heaven. *Inebriaduntur*, they shall be inebriated.—*Vulgate*. **That sal be drunken of the plenteuoste of thi house.**—Old *Psalter*. This refers to the joyous expectation they had of being restored to their own land, and to the ordinances of the temple.

Of the river of thy pleasures.] נחל אדניך *nachal adaneycha*, (or עדנך *edencha*, as in four MSS.,) *the river of thy Eden*. They shall be restored to their paradisaical estate; for here is a reference to the *river* that ran through the *garden of Eden, and watered it;* Gen. ii. 10. Or the *temple*, and under it the *Christian Church*, may be compared to this *Eden;* and the *gracious influences of God* to be had in his *ordinances*, to the *streams* by which that *garden* was *watered*, and its fertility promoted.

Verse 9. *For with thee* is *the fountain of life*] This, in Scripture phrase, may signify a *spring of water;* for such was called among the Jews *living water*, to distinguish it from *ponds, tanks*, and *reservoirs*, that were supplied by water either received from the *clouds*, or conducted into them by *pipes* and *streams* from other quarters. But there seems to be a higher allusion in the sacred text. כי עמך מקור חיים *ki immecha mekor chaiyim*, "For with thee is the vein of lives." Does not this allude to the great *aorta*, which, receiving the blood from the heart, distributes it by the arteries to every part of the human body, whence it is conducted back to the heart by means of the *veins*. *As* the *heart*, by means of the great *aorta*, distributes the blood to the remotest parts of the body; so, GOD, by Christ Jesus, conveys the life-giving streams of his providential goodness to all the worlds and beings he has created, and the influences of his grace and mercy to every soul that has sinned. All spiritual and temporal good comes *from* Him, the FATHER, *through* Him, the SON, to every part of the creation of God.

In thy light shall we see light.] No man can illuminate his own soul; all understanding must come from above. Here the metaphor is changed, and God is compared to the *sun* in the firmament of heaven, that gives light to all the *planets* and their *inhabitants*. "God said, Let there be light; and there was light;" by that light the eye of man was enabled to behold the various works of God, and the beauties of creation: so, when God speaks light into the dark heart of man, he not only beholds his own deformity and need of the salvation of God, but he beholds the "light of the glory of God in the face of Jesus Christ;" "God, in Christ, reconciling the world to himself." "In thy light shall we see light." This is literally true, both in a spiritual and philosophical sense.

Verse 10. *O continue thy loving-kindness*]

11 Let not the foot of pride come against me, and let not the hand of the wicked remove me.

12 There are the workers of iniquity fallen: they are cast down, ᶻand shall not be able to rise.

ᵃPsa. i. 5

Literally, "Draw out thy mercy." The allusion to the *spring* is still kept up.

Unto them that know thee] To them who *acknowledge thee* in the midst of a crooked and perverse generation.

And thy righteousness] That *grace* which *justifies the ungodly*, and *sanctifies the unholy*.

To the upright in heart.] לישרי לב *leyishrey leb, to the straight of heart;* to those who have but *one end* in view, and *one aim* to that *end*. This is true of every genuine *penitent*, and of every true *believer*.

Verse 11. *Let not the foot of pride come against me*] Let me not be trampled under foot by proud and haughty men.

Let not the hand of the wicked remove me.] תנדני *tenideni, shake me,* or *cause me to wander*. Both these verses may have immediate respect to the captives in Babylon. The Jews were, when compared with the Babylonians, *the people that knew God;* for *in Jewry was God known*, Psa. lxxvi. 1; and the psalmist prays against the treatment which the Jews had received from the proud and insolent Babylonians during the *seventy* years of their captivity: "Restore us to our own land; and let not the proud foot or the violent hand ever *remove us from our country* and its *blessings;* the *temple, and its ordinances.*"

Verse 12. *There are the workers of iniquity fallen*] THERE, in Babylon, are the workers of iniquity fallen, and so *cast down that they shall not be able to rise*. A prophecy of the destruction of the Babylonish empire by Cyrus. That it was destroyed, is an historical fact; that they were never able to recover their liberty, is also a fact; and that Babylon itself is now blotted out of the map of the universe, so that the site of it is no longer known, is confirmed by every traveller who has passed over those regions.

The word שם *sham*, THERE, has been applied by many of the fathers to the *pride* spoken of in the preceding verse. *There*, in or by pride, says *Augustine*, do all sinners perish. *There*, in heaven, have the evil angels fallen through pride, says St. *Jerome*. *There*, in paradise, have our first parents fallen, through pride and disobedience. *There*, in hell, have the proud and disobedient angels been precipitated.—*Eusebius, &c.* THERE, by pride, have the *persecutors* brought God's judgments upon themselves. See *Calmet*. But the first interpretation is the best.

ANALYSIS OF THE THIRTY-SIXTH PSALM

The object of this Psalm is to implore God, out of his goodness, that he would deliver the upright from the pride and malice of the wicked.

I. The psalmist sets down the character of a wicked man, and his fearful state, 1-5.

II. He makes a narrative in commendation of God's mercy, 6-10.

III. He prays for a continuance of God's goodness to his people, petitions against his proud enemy, and exults at his fall, 10-12.—

I. The character of a wicked man:—

1. "There is no fear of God before his eyes;"

and from this, as an evil root, all the other evils spring: and thus he enters on an induction of particulars.

2. "He flattereth himself in his own eyes." A great sin, in his eyes, is no sin: vice is virtue; falsehood, truth.

3. In this he continues, "until his iniquity be found to be hateful;"—till God, by some heavy judgment, has passed his sentence against it.

4. He is full of hypocrisy and deceit; "the words of his mouth are iniquity and deceit;" he gives goodly words, but evil is in his heart.

5. He has renounced all wisdom and goodness: "He hath left off to be wise, and to do good."

6. He enters deliberately and coolly into evil plans and designs: 1. "He deviseth mischief upon his bed." 2. "He sets himself (of firm purpose) in the way that is not good." 3. "He abhors not evil." He invents wickedness; he labours to perfect it; yea, though it be of the deepest stain, he abhors it not.

II. How comes it that such wicked men are permitted to live? How is it that God can bear patiently with such workers of iniquity? The psalmist answers this question by pointing out God's mercy, from which this long-suffering proceeds; which he considers in a *twofold* point of view: 1. *Absolute* and *general*, extending to all. 2. *Particular*, which is exhibited to the faithful only.

1. *General*. God is good to all; which is seen in his bountifulness, fidelity, justice; and in his preservation of all things: 1. "Thy mercy, O Lord, is in the heavens." Thou preservest them. Thy *faithfulness* reacheth *unto the clouds*. They water the earth, as thou hast promised. 3. "Thy righteousness is like the great mountains." Immovable. 4. "Thy judgments are a great deep." Unsearchable, and past finding out. 5. "Thou, Lord, preservest man and beast." In thee we live, move, and have our being.

2. In *particular*. He is especially careful of his followers. The providence by which he sustains them is, 1. A precious thing: "O, how excellent (quam pretiosa) how precious is thy loving-kindness, O Lord!" The operation of which, in behalf of the faithful, is hope, confidence, and comfort in distress: "Therefore the children of men shall put their trust under the shadow," &c. 2. The effects of this, the plenty of all good things prepared for them: 1. "They shall be abundantly satisfied with the goodness of thy house." 2. "Thou shalt make them drink of the river of thy pleasures." To which he adds the cause: "For with thee is the fountain of life; in thy light we shall see light."

III. He concludes with a *prayer*, 1. For all God's people. 2. For himself.

1. He prays that this excellent and precious mercy may light on all those who serve God sincerely: "O continue thy loving-kindness to them that know thee."

2. He *prays* for himself; that he may be defended from the pride and violence of wicked

men: "Let not the foot of pride come against me; and let not the hand of the wicked remove me."

3. Lastly, he closes all with this *exultation:* "There are the workers of iniquity fallen!"

There, when they promised themselves peace and security, and said, Tush! no harm shall happen to us; *there* and *then* are they fallen: "They are cast down, and shall not be able to rise."

PSALM XXXVII

Godly directions for those who are in adversity not to envy the prosperity of the wicked, because it is superficial, and of short duration, 1–22; to put their confidence in God, and live to his glory, as this is the sure way to be happy in this life, and in that which is to come, 23–40.

VII. DAY. EVENING PRAYER

A Psalm of David

FRET ᵃnot thyself because of evil-doers, neither be thou envious against the workers of iniquity.

2 For they shall soon be cut down ᵇlike the grass, and wither as the green herb.

3 Trust in the LORD, and do good; *so* shalt thou dwell in the land, and ᶜverily thou shalt be fed.

ᵃVer. 7; Psa. lxxiii. 3; Prov. xxiii. 17; xxiv. 1, 19

ᵇPsa. xc. 5, 6——ᶜHeb. *in truth* or *stableness*

NOTES ON PSALM XXXVII

In the *title* this Psalm is attributed to *David* by the *Hebrew*, and by most of the *Versions:* but it is more likely it was intended as an instructive and consoling ode for the captives in Babylon, who might feel themselves severely tempted when they saw those idolaters in prosperity; and themselves, who worshipped the true God, in affliction and slavery. They are comforted with the prospect of speedy deliverance; and their return to their own land is predicted in not less than *ten* different places in this Psalm.

This Psalm is one of the *acrostic* or *alphabetical* kind: but it differs from those we have already seen, in having *two* verses under each letter; the first only exhibiting the *alphabetical letter* consecutively. There are a few anomalies in the Psalm. The *hemistich*, which should begin with the letter ע *ain*, has now a ל *lamed* prefixed to the word with which it begins, לעולם *leolam;* and the hemistich which should begin with ת *tau* (ver. 39) has now a ו *vau* prefixed, ותשועת *utheshuath.* It appears also that the letters ד *daleth*, כ *caph*, and ק *koph*, have each lost a hemistich; and ע *ain*, half a one. The manner in which this Psalm is printed in Dr. *Kennicott's* Hebrew Bible gives a full view of all these particulars. To the English reader some slighter differences may appear; but it should be observed, that the verses in our English Bibles are not always divided as those in the Hebrew. In all the Psalms that have a *title*, the *title* forms the *first* verse in the Hebrew; but our translation does not acknowledge any of those titles as a *part* of the Psalm, and very properly leaves them out of the enumeration of the verses.

Verse 1. *Fret not thyself because of evil doers*] It is as foolish as it is wicked to repine or be envious at the prosperity of others. Whether they are godly or ungodly, it is God who is the dispenser of the *bounty* they enjoy;

and, most assuredly, he has a right to do what he will with his own. To be envious in such a case, is to arraign the providence of God. And it is no small condescension in the Almighty to reason with such persons as he does in this Psalm.

Verse 2. *For they shall soon be cut down*] They have their portion in this life; and their enjoyment of it cannot be long, for their breath is but a vapour that speedily vanishes away. They fall before death, as the *greensward* does before the *scythe* of the *mower*.

Verse 3. *Dwell in the land*] Do not flee to foreign climes to escape from that providence which, for thy own good, denies thee affluence in thy own country.

And verily thou shalt be fed.] God will provide for thee the *necessaries* of life: its *conveniences* might damp thy intellect in its *inventions*, and lead thee into *idleness;* and its *superfluities* would induce thee to pamper thy *passions* till the concerns of thy *soul* would be absorbed in those of the *flesh* and, after having lived an *animal* life, thou mightest die without God, and perish everlastingly.

The original, ורעה אמונה *ureeh emunah*, might be translated, "and feed by faith." The *Septuagint* has καὶ ποιμανθήσῃ ἐπὶ τῷ πλούτῳ αὑτῆς, *and thou shalt feed upon its riches.* The *Vulgate, Æthiopic*, and *Arabic*, are the same. The *Syriac, seek faith.* The *Chaldee, be strong in the faith.* The *Anglo-Saxon*, ꝼ þu biꞃꞇ ꞃeꝺeꝺ on ꝼelum hiꞃ, *and feeded thou shalt be in its welfare.* Old *Psalter*, anꝺ þu ſal be feꝺ in ꞃꝣcheſ of it. But it is probable that אמונה *emunah* here signifies *security. And thou shalt be fed in security.*

Dr. *Delaney* supposed that the Psalm might have been written by David in the behalf of *Mephibosheth*, who, being falsely accused by his servant *Ziba*, had formed the resolution to *leave a land* where he had met with such bad treatment. David, being convinced of his innocence,

4 [d]Delight thyself also in the LORD; and he shall give thee the desires of thine heart.

5 [e]Commit[f] thy way unto the LORD; trust also in him, and he shall bring *it* to pass.

6 [g]And he shall bring forth thy righteousness as the light, and thy judgment as the noonday.

7 [h]Rest[i] in the LORD, [k]and wait patiently for him: [l]fret not thyself because of him who prospereth in his way, because of the man who bringeth wicked devices to pass.

8 Cease from anger, and forsake wrath: [m]fret not thyself in any wise to do evil.

9 [n]For evil doers shall be cut off: but those that wait upon the LORD, they shall [o]inherit the earth.

10 For [p]yet a little while, and the wicked *shall* not *be:* yea, [q]thou shalt diligently consider his place, and it *shall* not *be.*

11 [r]But the meek shall inherit the earth; and shall delight themselves in the abundance of peace.

12 The wicked [s]plotteth against the just, [t]and gnasheth upon him with his teeth.

13 [u]The LORD shall laugh at him: for he seeth that [v]his day is coming.

14 The wicked have drawn out the sword, and have bent their bow, to cast down the poor and needy, *and* to slay [w]such as be of upright conversation.

15 [x]Their sword shall enter into their own heart, and their bows shall be broken.

---

[d]Isa. lviii. 14——[e]Heb. *Roll thy way upon the LORD*——[f]Psa. lv. 22; Prov. xvi. 3; Matt. vi. 25; Luke xii. 22; 1 Pet. v. 7——[g]Job xi. 17; Mic. vii. 9——[h]Psa. lxii. 1——[i]Heb. *Be silent to the LORD*——[k]Psa. lxii. 5; Isa. xxx. 15; Jer. xiv. 22; Lam. iii. 25, 26; 1 Thess. i. 10

[l]Ver. 1, 8; Jer. xii. 1——[m]Psa. lxxiii. 3; Eph. iv. 26——[n]Job xxvii. 13, 14——[o]Ver. 11, 22, 29; Isa. lvii. 13——[p]Heb. x. 36, 37——[q]Job vii. 10; xx. 9——[r]Matt. v. 5——[s]Or, *practiseth*——[t]Psa. xxxv. 16——[u]Psa. ii. 4——[v]1 Sam. xxvi. 10——[w]Heb. *the upright of way*——[x]Mic. v. 6

---

entreats him to dwell in the land, with the assurance of *plenty* and *protection.* It is more likely that it is addressed to the *captives in Babylon;* and contains the promise that they shall return to their own land, and again enjoy *peace* and *plenty.*

Verse 4. *Delight thyself also in the Lord*] Expect all thy happiness *from* him, and seek it *in* him.

The desires of thine heart.] משאלות *mishaloth,* the *petitions.* The godly man never indulges a *desire* which he cannot form into a *prayer* to God.

Verse 5. *Commit thy way unto the Lord*] גול על יהוה *gol al Yehovah,* ROLL *thy way upon the Lord:* probably, a metaphor taken from the *camel,* who lies down till his load be *rolled* upon him.

He shall bring it *to pass.*] יעשה *yaaseh,* "He will *work.*" Trust God, and he will work for thee.

Verse 6. *Thy righteousness as the light*] As God said in the beginning, "Let there be light, and there was light;" so he shall say, Let thy innocence appear, and it will appear as suddenly and as evident as the *light* was at the beginning.

Verse 7. *Rest in the Lord*] דום *dom,* "be silent, be *dumb.*" Do not find fault with thy Maker; he does all things well for others, he will do all things well for thee.

And wait patiently for him] והתחולל לו *vehithcholel lo,* and *set thyself* to expect him; and be *determined* to expect, or wait for him. Such is the import of a verb in the *hithpoel* conjugation.

A heathen gives good advice on a similar subject:—

Nil ergo optabunt homines? Si consilium vis,
Permittes ipsis expendere Numinibus, quid
Conveniat nobis, rebusque sit utile nostris.
Nam pro jucundis aptissima quæque dabunt Di.
Carior est illis homo, quam sibi.
JUV. *Sat.* x. 346.

"What then remains? Are we deprived of will?
Must we not wish, for fear of wishing ill?
Receive my counsel, and securely move;
Intrust thy pastime to the powers above.
Leave them to manage for thee, and to grant
What their unerring wisdom sees thee want.
In goodness, as in greatness, they excel:
Ah, that we loved ourselves but half so well!"
DRYDEN.

Verse 9. *They shall inherit the earth.*] The word ארץ *arets,* throughout this Psalm, should be translated *land,* not *earth;* for it is most probable that it refers to the *land of Judea;* and in this verse there is a promise of their *return* thither.

Verse 10. *For yet a little while, and the wicked* shall *not* be] A prediction of the destruction of Babylon. This empire was now in its splendour; and the captives lived to see it totally overturned by Cyrus, so that even the shadow of its power did not remain.

Thou shalt diligently consider his place] ואיננו *veeynennu, and he is not.* The ruler is killed; the city is taken; and the whole empire is overthrown, in one night! And now even the place where Babylon stood cannot be ascertained.

Verse 11. *But the meek*] ענוים *anavim,* the *afflicted,* the poor Jewish captives.

Shall inherit the earth] ארץ *arets,* the *land* of *Judea,* given by God himself as an *inheritance* to their fathers, and to their posterity for ever. See ver. 9.

Verse 13. *He seeth that his day is coming.*] The utter desolation of your oppressors is at hand. All this may be said of every *wicked man.*

Verse 14. *The wicked have drawn out the sword*] There is an irreconcilable enmity in the souls of sinners against the godly; and there is much evidence that the idolatrous Babylonians *whetted their tongue like a sword, and shot out their arrows, even bitter words,* to malign the poor captives, and to insult them in every possible way.

Verse 15. *Their sword shall enter into their*

16 ʸA little that a righteous man hath *is* better than the riches of many wicked.

17 For ᶻthe arms of the wicked shall be broken: but the Lord upholdeth the righteous.

18 The Lord ᵃknoweth the days of the upright: and their inheritance shall be ᵇfor ever.

19 They shall not be ashamed in the evil time: and ᶜin the days of famine they shall be satisfied.

20 But the wicked shall perish, and the enemies of the Lord *shall be* as ᵈthe fat of lambs: they shall consume; ᵉinto smoke shall they consume away.

21 The wicked borroweth and payeth not

again: but the ᶠrighteous showeth mercy, and giveth.

22 ᵍFor *such as be* blessed of him shall inherit the earth; and *they that be* cursed of him ʰshall be cut off.

23 ¹The steps of a *good* man are ᵏordered by the Lord: and he delighteth in his way.

24 ˡThough he fall, he shall not be utterly cast down; for the Lord upholdeth *him with* his hand.

25 I have been young, and *now* am old; yet have I not seen the righteous forsaken, nor his seed ᵐbegging bread.

ʸProv. xv. 16; xvi. 8; 1 Tim. vi. 6——ᶻJob xxxviii. 15; Psa. x. 15; Ezek. xxx. 21, &c.——ᵃPsa. i. 6——ᵇIsa. lx. 21——ᶜJob v. 20; Psa. xxxiii. 19——ᵈHeb. *the preciousness of lambs*——ᵉPsa. cii. 3

ᶠPsa. cxii. 5, 9——ᵍProv. iii. 33——ʰVer. 9——ⁱ1 Sam. ii. 9; Prov. xvi. 9——ᵏOr, *established*——ˡPsa. xxxiv. 19, 20; xl. 2; xci. 12; Prov. xxiv. 16; Mic. vii. 8; 2 Cor. iv. 9——ᵐJob xv. 23; Psa. lix. 15; cix. 10

---

own heart] All their execrations and maledictions shall fall upon themselves, and their power to do mischief shall be *broken*.

Verse 16. *A little that a righteous man hath*] This is a solid *maxim*. Whatever a good man has, has God's blessing in it; even the *blessings* of the wicked are *cursed*.

Verse 17. *The arms of the wicked*] Their power to do evil. Of this they are often deprived. *Talents* lent and abused shall be resumed, and the misuser called to a severe account by the Lord of the talents.

Verse 18. *The Lord knoweth the days of the upright*] He is acquainted with all his *circumstances, sufferings,* and *ability* to bear them; and he will either *shorten his trials* or *increase his power*. The Lord also *approves* of the man and his concerns; and his *inheritance shall be for ever*. He shall have God for his portion, here and hereafter. This is probably another indirect promise to the captives that they shall be restored to their own land. See ver. 11.

Verse 19. *They shall not be ashamed*] They have expressed strong confidence in the Lord; and he shall so work in their behalf that their enemies shall never be able to say, "Ye have trusted in your God, and yet your enemies have prevailed over you." No; for even *in the days of famine they shall be satisfied*.

Verse 20. *The enemies of the Lord shall be as the fat of lambs*] This verse has given the critics some trouble. Several of the Versions read thus: "But the enemies of the Lord, as soon as they are exalted to honour, shall vanish; like smoke they vanish." If we follow the *Hebrew*, it intimates that *they shall consume as the fat of lambs*. That is, as the *fat* is *wholly consumed* in sacrifices by the fire on the altar, so shall they consume away in the fire of God's wrath.

Verse 21. *The wicked borroweth*] Is often reduced to *penury*, and is obliged to become debtor to those whom he before despised.

And payeth not again] May *refuse* to do it, because he is a *wicked man;* or be *unable* to do it, because he is reduced to *beggary*.

But the righteous showeth mercy] Because he has received mercy from God, therefore he

shows mercy to men. And even to his enemies *he showeth mercy, and giveth;* his *heart* being disposed to it by the influence of *Divine grace,* and his hand being enabled to do it by the blessing of God's *providence*.

Verse 22. *Shall inherit the earth*] ארץ *arets,* the *land,* as before. See ver. 11.

Shall be cut off.] A *wicked Jew* shall meet with the same fate as a *wicked Babylonian;* and a *wicked Christian* shall fare no better.

Verse 23. *The steps of a* good *man are ordered by the Lord*] There is nothing for *good* in the text. נבר *geber* is the original word, and it properly signifies *a strong man,* a *conqueror* or *hero;* and it appears to be used here to show, that even the *most powerful* must be supported by the Lord, otherwise their strength and courage will be of little avail.

And he delighteth in his way.] When *his steps are ordered by the Lord, he delighteth in his way,* because it is that into which his own good Spirit has directed him. Or, the *man delights in God's way*—in the *law* and *testimonies* of his Maker.

Verse 24. *Though he fall, he shall not be utterly cast down*] The original is short and emphatic כי יפל לא יוטל *ki yippol, lo yutal,* which the *Chaldee* translates, "Though he should fall into sickness, he shall not die;" for which the reason is given, because *the Lord sustains by his hand*. Though he may for a time fall under the power of his adversaries, as the Jews have done under the Babylonish captivity, he shall not be forsaken. The right hand of God shall sustain him in his afflictions and distresses; and at last God will give him a happy issue out of them all. Neither the *text* nor any of the *Versions* intimate that a *falling into sin* is meant; but a falling into *trouble, difficulty, &c.*

Verse 25. *I have been young, and now am old*] I believe this to be literally true in all cases. I am now grey-headed myself; I have travelled in different countries, and have had many opportunities of seeing and conversing with religious people in all situations in life; and I have not, to my knowledge, seen one instance to the contrary. I have seen no *righteous man forsaken,* nor any *children* of the righteous *begging their*

26 [n]*He is* [o]ever merciful, and lendeth; and his seed *is* blessed.

27 [p]Depart from evil, and do good; and dwell for evermore.

28 For the LORD [q]loveth judgment, and forsaketh not his saints; they are preserved for ever: [r]but the seed of the wicked shall be cut off.

29 [s]The righteous shall inherit the land, and dwell therein for ever.

30 [t]The mouth of the righteous speaketh wisdom, and his tongue talketh of judgment.

31 [u]The law of his God *is* in his heart; none of his [v]steps shall slide.

32 The wicked [w]watcheth the righteous, and seeketh to slay him.

33 The LORD [x]will not leave him in his hand, nor [y]condemn him when he is judged.

34 [z]Wait on the LORD, and keep his way, and he shall exalt thee to inherit the land: [a]when the wicked are cut off, thou shalt see *it.*

35 [b]I have seen the wicked in great power, and spreading himself like [c]a green bay-tree.

36 Yet he [d]passed away, and, lo, he *was* not:

[n]Deut. xv. 8, 10; Psa. cxii. 5, 9——[o]Heb. *all the day* [p]Psa. xxxiv. 14; Isa. i. 16, 17——[q]Psa. xi. 7——[r]Psa. xxi. 10; Prov. ii. 22; Isa. xiv. 20——[s]Prov. ii. 21 [t]Matt. xii. 35——[u]Deut. vi. 6; Psa. xl. 8; cxix. 98; Isa. ii. 7

[v]Or, *goings*——[w]Psalm x. 8——[x]2 Peter ii. 9 [y]Psalm cix. 31——[z]Verse 9; Psalm xxvii. 14; Proverbs xx. 22——[a]Psalm lii. 5, 6; xci. 8——[b]Job v. 3——[c]Or, *a green tree that groweth in his own soil*——[d]Job xx. 5, &c.

bread. God puts this honour upon all that fear him; and thus careful is he of *them,* and of their *posterity.*

Verse 26. He is *ever merciful, and lendeth*] כל היום חונן *kol haiyom chonen,* "all the day he is compassionate." He is confirmed in the habit of godliness: he feels for the distresses of men, and is ready to divide and distribute to all that are in necessity.

And his seed is *blessed.*] The preceding words were not spoken casually; *his seed,* his *posterity, is blessed;* therefore they are not abandoned *to beg their bread.*

Verse 27. *Depart from evil, and do good*] Seeing the above is so, *depart from all evil*—avoid all sin; and let not this be sufficient, *do good.* The grace of God ever gives this *twofold power* to all who receive it; strength to *overcome evil,* and strength to *do that which is right.*

Dwell for evermore.] Be for ever an inhabitant of God's house. This may be also a promise of return to their own land, and of permanent residence there. See ver. 9, 11, &c.

Verse 28. *Forsaketh not his saints*] את חסידיו *eth chasidaiv,* his *merciful* or *compassionate ones;* those who, through love to him and all mankind, are ever ready to give of their substance to the poor.

But the seed of the wicked shall be cut off.] The children who follow the wicked steps of wicked parents shall, like their parents, be cut off. God's *judgments descend to posterity,* as well as his *mercies.*

Verse 29. *The righteous shall inherit the land*] If this be not another promise of return to their own land, from that of their captivity, it must be spiritually understood, and refer to their eternal dwelling with God in glory.

Verse 30. *The mouth of the righteous speaketh wisdom*] Foolish and corrupt conversation cannot come out of their mouth. They are taught of God, and they speak according to the wisdom that is from above.

Verse 31. *The law of his God* is *in his heart*] The Lord promised that a time should come in which he would make a *new covenant* with the house of Israel; he would put his laws in their minds, and in their hearts he would write them. This is fulfilled in the case above.

None of his steps shall slide.] His holy heart always dictates to his *eyes,* his *mouth,* his *hands,* and his *feet.* The precepts which direct his conduct are not only *written in his Bible,* but also *in his heart.*

Verse 32. *The wicked watcheth the righteous, and seeketh to slay him.*] Similar to what is said ver. 8: "The wicked plotteth against the righteous." But it is added, ver. 33: "The Lord will not leave him in his hands;" he will confound his devices, and save his own servants.

Verse 34. *Wait on the Lord, and keep his way*] This is the *true mode of waiting on God* which the Scripture recommends; *keeping God's way*—using all his ordinances, and living in the spirit of obedience. He who *waits* thus is sure to have the farther blessings of which he is in pursuit. קוה *kavah,* to *wait,* implies the *extension of a right line from one point to another.* The first *point* is the human *heart;* the *line* is its *intense desire;* and the *last point* is GOD, *to* whom this *heart* extends this *straight line* of *earnest desire* to be filled with the fulness of the blessing of the Gospel of peace.

And he shall exalt thee to inherit the land] If ye keep his way, and be faithful to him in your exile, he will *exalt you, lift you up* from your present abject state, to inherit the land of your fathers. See before, ver. 9, 11, &c.

When the wicked are cut off, thou shalt see it.] They did see the destruction of the Babylonish king, *Belshazzar,* and his empire; and it was in consequence of that destruction that they were enlarged.

Verse 35. *I have seen the wicked in great power, and spreading himself like a green bay-tree.*] Does not this refer to Nebuchadnezzar, king of Babylon, and to the *vision* he had of the *great tree which was in the midst of the earth, the head of which reached up to heaven?* See Dan. iv. 10, &c.

Verse 36. *Yet he passed away*] Both *Nebuchadnezzar* and his wicked successor, *Belshazzar;* and on the destruction of the latter, when God had *weighed him in the balance, and found him wanting, numbered his days,* and consigned him to death, his *kingdom was delivered to the Medes and Persians;* and thus the Babylonian empire was destroyed.

yea, I sought him, but he could not be found.

37 Mark the perfect *man,* and behold the upright: for [e]the end of *that* man *is* peace.

38 [f]But the transgressors shall be destroyed together: the end of the wicked shall be cut off.

---

[e]Isa. xxxii. 17; lvii. 2——[f]Psa. i. 4; lii. 5——[g]Psa. iii. 8
[h]Psa. ix. 9

Verse 37. *Mark the perfect man*] Him who is described above. Take notice of him: he is *perfect in his soul,* God having saved him from all sin, and filled him with his own *love* and *image.* And he is *upright* in his *conduct;* and his *end,* die when he may or where he may, is peace, quietness, and assurance for ever.

Almost all the *Versions* translate the *Hebrew* after this manner: *Preserve innocence, and keep equity in view; for the man of peace shall leave a* numerous *posterity.*

Bishop *Horsley* thus translates: "Keep (thy) loyalty, and look well to (thy) integrity; for a posterity is (appointed) for the perfect man." He comes nearer to the original in his *note* on this verse: "Keep innocency, and regard uprightness; for the perfect man hath a posterity:" "but the rebellious shall be destroyed together; the posterity of the wicked shall be cut off," ver. 38.

Dr. *Kennicott's* note is, "אחרית *acharith,* which we render *latter end,* is *posterity,* Psa. cix. 13. The *wicked* and all his race to be destroyed, the *pious man* to have a numerous progeny, see his sons' sons to the *third* and *fourth* generation. See Job viii. 19, xviii, 13-20."

I think the original cannot possibly bear *our translation.* I shall produce it here, with the literal version of *Montanus:*——

<small>pax   viro   novissimum quia; rectum vide et, integrum custodi</small>

שמר תם וראה ישר כי אחרית לאיש שלום

The nearest translation to this is that of the *Septuagint* and *Vulgate: Φυλασσε ακακιαν, και ιδε ευθυτητα, ὁτι εστιν εγκαταλειμμα ανθρωπῳ ειρηνικῳ.* Custodi innocentiam, et vide æquitatem; quoniam, sunt reliquiæ homini pacifico. "Preserve innocence, and behold equity; seeing there is a posterity to the pacific man." The *Syriac* says, "Observe simplicity, and choose rectitude; seeing there is a good end to the man of peace." The reader may choose. Our common version, in my opinion, cannot be sustained. The 38th verse seems to confirm the translation of the *Septuagint* and the *Vulgate,* which are precisely the same in meaning; therefore I have given one translation for both.

The old *Psalter* deserves a place also: **Kepe unnopandnes, and se ebenhebe; for tha relpkes er til** *ꝓ* **pesful man.**

Verse 39. *The salvation of the righteous* is *of the Lord*] It is the Lord who made them *righteous,* by blotting out their sins, and infusing his Holy Spirit into their hearts; and it is by his grace they are continually sustained, and finally brought to the kingdom of glory: "He is their strength in the time of trouble."

Verse 40. *The Lord—shall deliver them*] For they are always exposed to trials, and liable to fall.

39 But [g]the salvation of the righteous *is* of the LORD: *he is* their strength [h]in the time of trouble.

40 And [i]the LORD shall help them, and deliver them: he shall deliver them from the wicked, and save them, [k]because they trust in him.

---

[i]Isa. xxxi. 5——[k]1 Chron. v. 20; Dan. iii. 17, 28; vi. 23

Because they trust in him.] They keep faith, prayer, love, and obedience in continual exercise. They continue to *believe* in, *love,* and *obey God;* and he continues to *save them.*

ANALYSIS OF THE THIRTY-SEVENTH PSALM

What is here delivered may be reduced to these two general heads:——

I. He sets down the duty of a good man, which is to be patient, and put his confidence in God when he sees the wicked prosper and flourish.

II. He gives many reasons to prove the propriety of such conduct.

I. He begins with an interdict, and then descends to give some directions.

1. His interdict is, "Fret not thyself," &c. Be not angry nor envious; to which he adds this reason, that their prosperity is but short: "For they shall be cut down," &c.

2. Then he sets down some directions and rules to prevent *fretting* and *anger.*

1. The first is a perpetual rule for our whole life: "Trust in the Lord." Rely not on human helps, friends, riches, &c.

2. "Be good." Increase not thy state by evil arts or means.

3. "Dwell in the land." Desert not thy station.

4. "And verily thou shalt be fed." Enjoy quietly what thou hast at present.

5. "Delight thyself in the Lord." Be pleased with his way.

6. "Commit thy way unto the Lord." Labour in an honest vocation, and leave the rest to him; for "he will work for thee."

7. "Rest in the Lord." Acquiesce in his will and the dispensations of his providence; wait patiently for him; his time is the best. And then he repeats his interdict: "Fret not thyself."

II. Then he resumes his *former* reason, mentioned ver. 2, and amplifies it by an *antithesis,* viz., that it shall be well with the good, ill with the wicked, ver. 9, 10, 11; and so it falls out for the *most part,* but not always; which is enough for temporal blessings.

1. "Evil doers shall be cut off; but those who wait on the Lord shall inherit the land."

2. "Yet a little while, and the wicked shall not be," &c.

To this he adds a *second* reason, taken from the providence of God:——

1. In protecting the righteous, and confounding their enemies.

2. In blessing the little they have; in which he seems to remove a double objection: the first, about the tyranny of the wicked over the righteous; the second, that they are commonly in want and poverty.

The first temptation, by which many pious souls are troubled, is the power, the cruelty, and the implacable hatred of wicked men: "The wicked plotteth against the just, and gnasheth upon him." To which the psalmist answers, "The Lord shall laugh at him; for he seeth that his day of *punishment* is coming." Yea, "but the wicked have drawn out their sword, and bent their bow," which is beyond plotting and derision, "to cast down the poor, and slay such as are of an upright conversation." To which he answers, Be it so: "Their sword shall enter into their own heart, and their bow shall be broken."

The other temptation is beggary and poverty, than which nothing is more afflictive. The ungodly swim in wealth; but the godly are commonly poor, and therefore exposed to contempt; for poverty reckons up no reputable genealogy. To this he answers: "A little that the righteous hath is better than the riches of many wicked." *Better*, because used better; *better*, because possessed with contentment; *better*, because it has God's blessing upon it. And this he proves by many reasons:—

1. "For the arms of the wicked (their riches) shall be broken; but the Lord upholdeth the righteous."

2. "The Lord knoweth the days (good or bad) of the upright." He loves them, and they are his care; and "their inheritance shall be for ever," firm and stable.

3. "They shall not be ashamed in the evil time," nor destitute, nor forsaken of necessaries; for "in the days of famine they shall be satisfied."

But with rich wicked men it is not so. Though they abound in wealth, yet they shall insensibly consume and perish, "as the fat of lambs," burnt upon the altar, "vanisheth into smoke and passeth away."

4. And yet there is another blessing on the good man's little: he has often over and above, and something to spare to *give*, whereas the wicked is a borrower, with this bad quality, that *he payeth not again*. "But the righteous showeth mercy, and giveth."

Of which he gives this reason: for "such as God blesseth shall possess the earth;" and "they that be cursed of him shall be cut off." They may *have*, but not *enjoy*, the goods of this life.

And thus much the psalmist proved by his own experience: "I have been young, and now am old; yet have I not seen the righteous forsaken, nor his seed begging their bread." His liberality was the cause of it; "He is ever merciful, and lendeth; and his seed is blessed."

A third reason of God's protection is, that God upholds him: "The steps of a good man are ordered of the Lord;" and should he by infirmity fall into error, or get into trouble or affliction, "he shall not be utterly cast down, for the Lord upholdeth him with his hand." He shall have his judgment corrected by God's teaching, and no disease shall be able to remove him till God's work be done *in him*, and *by him*.

In the rest of the Psalm he makes a repetition of all that went before: he repeats his chief rule, his promises, his comforts, and his threatenings.

He begins with this rule, ver. 3: "Depart from evil and do good, and dwell for evermore." In which he exhorts to obedience, and in both parts brings instances of repentance, mortification, and vivification, which he fortifies with a double reason, as before.

1. A promise to the godly: "For the Lord loveth righteousness; he forsaketh not his saints; they are preserved for ever."

2. A threatening to the wicked: "But the seed of the wicked shall be cut off." These two reasons he resumes, amplifies, and illustrates.

First, That of the righteous: "The righteous shall inherit the land," &c.; and that you may know whom he means by the righteous, he sets down his character.

1. He is one whose mouth speaks wisdom. He speaks reverently of God's justice and providence.

2. One *whose mouth talks of judgment;* i. e., of that only which is just and right.

3. "The law of God is in his heart;" not in his tongue alone, or in his brain.

4. "None of his steps shall slide." He keeps on his right way, and will not be seduced. Yet this righteous man has his enemies, ver. 13-15: "For the wicked watcheth the righteous, and seeketh to slay him."

But although he has his enemies, yet has he also his protector: "The Lord will not leave him in his hand," &c.; therefore "wait on the Lord, and keep his way, and he shall exalt thee. When the wicked are cut off, thou shalt see it."

Secondly, For they shall be cut off, as was said before, ver. 28; and this he knew from his own experience: "I have seen the wicked in great power, and flourishing like a green baytree; yet I passed by, and lo, he was gone; I sought him, but he could not be found."

And what he observed, others, if attentive and diligent, may observe also, both in respect of the righteous and the wicked. 1. For "mark the perfect man, and behold the upright; for the end of that man is peace." 2. "But the transgressors shall be destroyed together; the end of the wicked shall be cut off."

Should the cause be inquired why God does these things, it is added, that this sums up all the doctrine of the Psalm:—

1. "The salvation of the righteous is of the Lord; he will save them because they trust in him."

2. On the contrary, "the wicked shall be cut off and perish, because they trust not in him."

PSALM XXXVIII

David prays God to have mercy upon him, and gives a most affecting account of his miserable state, 1–10; complains of his being forsaken by his friends, and cruelly persecuted by his enemies, 11–16; confesses his sin; and earnestly implores help, 17–22.

VIII. DAY. MORNING PRAYER

A Psalm of David, ^ato bring to remembrance

A. M. cir. 2970
B. C. cir. 1034
Davidis, Regis
Israelitarum,
cir. annum
22

O ^bLORD, rebuke me not in thy wrath: neither chasten me in thy hot displeasure.

2 For ^cthine arrows stick fast in me, and ^dthy hand presseth me sore.

3 *There is* no soundness in my flesh because of thine anger; ^eneither *is there any* ^frest in my bones because of my sin.

4 For ^gmine iniquities are gone over mine head: as a heavy burden they are too ^hheavy for me.

5 My wounds stink *and* are corrupt because of my foolishness.

6 I am ⁱtroubled; ^kI am bowed down greatly; ^lI go mourning all the day long.

7 For my loins are filled with a ^mloathsome *disease:* and *there is* ⁿno soundness in my flesh.

8 I am feeble and sore broken: ^oI have roared by reason of the disquietness of my heart.

9 LORD, all my desire *is* before thee; and my groaning is not hid from thee.

A. M. cir. 2970
B. C. cir. 1034
Davidis, Regis
Israelitarum,
cir. annum
22

---

^aPsa. lxx. title——^bPsa. vi. 1——^cJob vi. 4——^dPsa. xxxii. 4——^ePsalm vi. 2——^fHebrew, *peace* or *health* ^gEzra ix. 6; Psa. xl. 12——^hMatt. xi. 28

ⁱHeb. *wried*——^kPsa. xxxv. 14——^lJob xxx. 28; Psa. xlii. 9; xliii. 2——^mJob vii. 5——ⁿVer. 3——^oJob iii. 24; Psa. xxii. 1; Isa. lix. 11

NOTES ON PSALM XXXVIII

The title in the HEBREW states this to be *A Psalm of David, to bring to remembrance.* The CHALDEE; "A Psalm of David for a good memorial to Israel." The VULGATE, SEPTUAGINT, and ÆTHIOPIC: "A Psalm of David, for a commemoration concerning the Sabbath." The ARABIC: "A Psalm in which mention is made of the Sabbath; besides, it is a thanksgiving and a prophecy." Never was a title more misplaced or less expressive of the contents. There is no mention of the *Sabbath* in it; there is no *thanksgiving* in it, for it is deeply *penitential;* and I do not see that it contains any *prophecy.* The SYRIAC: "A Psalm of David, when they said to the Philistine king, Achish, This is David, who killed Goliath; we will not have him to go with us against Saul. Besides, it is a form of confession for us." It does not appear that, out of all the titles, we can gather the true intent of the Psalm.

Several conjectures have been made relative to the *occasion* on which this Psalm was composed; and the most likely is, that it was in reference to some severe affliction which David had after his illicit commerce with Bath-sheba; but of what nature we are left to conjecture from the *third, fifth,* and *seventh* verses. Whatever it was, he deeply repents for it, asks pardon, and earnestly entreats support from God.

Verse 1. *O Lord, rebuke me not*] He was sensible that he was suffering under the displeasure of God; and he prays that the chastisement may be in *mercy,* and not in *judgment.*

Verse 2. *Thine arrows stick fast in me*] This, no doubt, refers to the *acute pains* which he endured; each appearing to his feeling as if an arrow were shot into his body.

Verse 3. *No soundness in my flesh*] This seems to refer to some *disorder* which so affected the *muscles* as to produce *sores* and *ulcers;* and so affected his *bones* as to leave him no peace nor rest. In short, he was completely and thoroughly diseased; and all this he attributes to his sin, either as being its natural consequence, or as being inflicted by the Lord as a punishment on its account.

Verse 4. *Mine iniquities are gone over mine head*] He represents himself as one sinking in deep *waters,* or as one oppressed by a *burden* to which his strength was unequal.

Verse 5. *My wounds stink* and *are corrupt*] Taking this in connection with the rest of the Psalm, I do not see that we can understand the word in any *figurative* or *metaphorical* way. I believe they refer to *some disease* with which he was at this time afflicted; but whether the *leprosy,* the *small pox,* or some other disorder that had attacked the whole system, and showed its virulence on different parts of the outer surface, cannot be absolutely determined.

Because of my foolishness.] This may either signify *sin* as the cause of his present affliction, or it may import an affliction which was the consequence of that *foolish levity* which prefers the momentary gratification of an irregular passion to health of body and peace of mind.

Verse 6. *I am troubled*] In mind. *I am bowed down*—in body. I am altogether afflicted, and full of distress.

Verse 7. *For my loins are filled with a loathsome disease*] Or rather, a *burning;* נקלה *nikleh,* from קלה *kalah,* to *fry,* *scorch,* &c., hence נקלה *nikleh,* a *burning,* or *strongly feverish disease.*

There is *no soundness in my flesh.*] All *without* and all *within* bears evidence that the whole of my solids and fluids are corrupt.

Verse 8. *I am feeble and sore broken*] I am so exhausted with my disease that I feel as if on the brink of the grave, and unfit to appear before God; therefore "have I roared for the disquietness of my heart."

That David describes a *natural disease* here cannot reasonably be doubted; but what that disease was, who shall attempt to say? However, this is evident, that whatever it was, he most deeply deplored the cause of it; and as he worthily lamented it, so he found mercy at the hand of God. It would be easy to show a disease of which what he here enumerates are the very general symptoms; but I forbear, because in this I might attribute to one what, perhaps, in Judea would be more especially descriptive of another.

Verse 9. *Lord, all my desire is before thee*] I long for nothing so much as thy favour; and for this my heart is continually going out after

A. M. cir. 2970
B. C. cir. 1034
Davidis, Regis
Israelitarum,
cir. annum
22

10 My heart panteth, my strength faileth me: as for [p]the light of mine eyes, it also [q]is gone from me.

11 [r]My lovers and my friends [s]stand aloof from my [t]sore; and [u]my kinsmen [v]stand afar off.

12 They also that seek after my life [w]lay snares *for me:* and they that seek my hurt [x]speak mischievous things, and [y]imagine deceits all the day long.

13 But [z]I, as a deaf *man,* heard not; [a]and *I was* as a dumb man *that* openeth not his mouth.

14 Thus I was a man that heareth not, and in whose mouth *are* no reproofs.

15 For [b]in thee, O LORD, [c]do I hope: thou wilt [d]hear, O LORD my God.

16 For I said, *Hear me,* [e]lest *otherwise* they should rejoice over me: when my [f]foot slippeth, they [g]magnify *themselves* against me.

A. M. cir. 2970
B. C. cir. 1034
Davidis, Regis
Israelitarum,
cir. annum
22

17 For I *am* ready [h]to halt, and my sorrow *is* continually before me.

18 For I will [i]declare mine iniquity; I will be [k]sorry for my sin.

19 But mine enemies [l]*are* lively, *and* they are strong: and they that [m]hate me wrongfully are multiplied.

20 They also [n]that render evil for good are mine adversaries; [o]because I follow *the thing that* good *is.*

21 Forsake me not, O LORD: O my God, [p]be not far from me.

22 Make haste [q]to help me, O LORD [r]my salvation.

---

[p]Psa. vi. 7; lxxxviii. 9——[q]Heb. is *not with me*——[r]Psa. xxxi. 11——[s]Luke x. 31, 32——[t]Heb. *stroke*——[u]Or, *my neighbours*——[v]Luke xxiii. 49——[w]2 Sam. xvii. 1, 2, 3——[x]2 Sam. xvi. 7, 8——[y]Psa. xxxv. 20——[z]See 2 Sam. xvi. 10——[a]Psa. xxxix. 2, 9——[b]Or, *thee do I wait for*——[c]2 Sam. xvi. 12; Psa. xxxix. 7——[d]Or, *answer*

[e]Psalm xiii. 4——[f]Deut. xxxii. 35——[g]Psa. xxxv. 26——[h]Heb. *for halting;* Psa. xxxv. 15——[i]Psa. xxxii. 5; Prov. xxviii. 13——[k]2 Cor. vii. 9, 10——[l]Heb. being *living, are strong*——[m]Psalm xxxv. 19——[n]Psalm xxxv. 12——[o]See 1 John iii. 12; 1 Peter iii. 13——[p]Psalm xxxv. 22——[q]Heb. *for my help*——[r]Psalm xxvii. 1; lxii. 2, 6; Isa. xii. 2

---

thee. Instead of אדני *Adonai, Lord,* several of Dr. *Kennicott's* MSS. have יהוה *Yehovah.*

Verse 10. *My heart panteth*] סחרחר *secharchar, flutters, palpitates,* through fear and alarm.

My strength faileth] Not being able to take nourishment.

The light of mine eyes—is gone] I can scarcely discern any thing through the general decay of my health and vigour, particularly affecting my sight.

Verse 11. *My lovers*] Those who professed much affection for me; my friends, רעי *reai,* my *companions,* who never before left my company, *stand aloof.*

My kinsmen] קרובי *kerobai,* my *neighbours,* stand afar off. I am deserted by all, and they stand off because of נגעי *nigi,* my *plague.* They considered me as suffering *under a Divine judgment;* and, thinking me an *accursed being,* they avoided me lest they should be infected by my disease.

Verse 12. *They also that seek after my life*] They act towards me as *huntsmen* after their prey; *they lay snares to take away my life.* Perhaps this means only that they *wished* for his death, and would have been glad to have had it in their power to end his days. Others *spoke all manner of evil of him,* and *told falsities* against him *all the day long.*

Verse 13. *But I, as a deaf* man] I was conscious of my guilt; I could not vindicate myself; and I was obliged in silence to bear their insults.

Verse 14. *No reproofs.*] תוכחות *tochachoth, arguments* or *vindications;* a forensic term. I was as a man accused in open court, and I could make no *defence.*

Verse 15. *In thee, O Lord, do I hope*] I have no helper but thee.

Thou wilt hear, O Lord my God.] Thou art eternal in thy compassions, and wilt hear the prayer of a penitent soul. In the printed copies of the Hebrew text we have אדני אלהי *Adonai Elohai, Lord my God;* but, instead of אדני *Adonai,* one hundred and two of *Kennicott's* and *De Rossi's* MSS. read יהוה *Yehovah.* As this word is never pronounced by the Jews, and they consider it dreadfully sacred, in reading, wherever it occurs, they pronounce אדני *Adonai;* and we may well suppose that Jewish scribes, in writing out copies of the sacred Scriptures, would as naturally write *Adonai* for *Yehovah,* as they would in reading supply the *former* for the *latter.*

Verse 16. *When my foot slippeth*] They watched for my halting; and when my foot slipped, they rejoiced that I had fallen into sin!

Verse 17. *For I* am *ready to halt*] Literally, *I am prepared to halt.* So completely infirm is my soul, that it is impossible for me to take one right step in the way of righteousness, unless strengthened by thee.

Verse 18. *I will declare mine iniquity*] I will confess it with the deepest humiliation and self-abasement.

Verse 19. *But mine enemies* are *lively*] Instead of חיים *chaiyim, lively,* I would read חינם *chinam, without cause;* a change made by the half of one letter, a נ *nun* for a י *yod.* See the parallel places, Psa. xxxv. 19; lxxix. 5. See also the Preliminary Dissertation to Dr. *Lowth's* Isaiah, p. 40: "But without cause my enemies have strengthened themselves; and they who wrongfully hate me are multiplied." Here the one member of the verse answers to the other.

Verse 20. *Because I follow* the thing that *good* is.] The translation is as bad as the sentence is awkward. תחת רדופי טוב *tachath rodpi tob, because I follow goodness.* There is a remarkable addition to this verse in the Arabic: "They have rejected me, the beloved one, as an abominable dead carcass; they have pierced my body with nails." I suppose the Arabic translator meant to refer this to Christ.

None of the other Versions have any thing like this addition; only the Æthiopic adds, "They rejected their brethren as an unclean carcass." St. Ambrose says this reading was found in some Greek and Latin copies in his time; and Theodoret has nearly the same reading with the Arabic: Και απερριψαν με τον αγαπητον, ως νεκρον εβδελυγμενον· "And they cast me, the beloved, out, as an abominable dead carcass." Whence this reading came I cannot conjecture.

Verse 21. *Forsake me not, O Lord*] Though all have forsaken me, do not thou.

Be not far from me] Though my friends keep aloof, be thou near to help me.

Verse 22. *Make haste to help me*] I am dying; save, Lord, or I perish. Whoever carefully reads over this Psalm will see what a grievous and bitter thing it is to sin against the Lord, and especially to sin after having known his mercy, and after having escaped from the corruption that is in the world. Reader, be on thy guard; a life of righteousness may be lost by giving way to a moment's temptation, and a fair character sullied for ever! Let him that most assuredly standeth take heed lest he fall.

'Tis but a grain of sweet that one can sow,
To reap a harvest of wide-wasting wo.

ANALYSIS OF THE THIRTY-EIGHTH PSALM

This Psalm may be divided into *two* parts:—
I. A *deprecation;* begun ver. 1, and continued in ver. 21, 22.

II. A *grievous complaint* of sin, disease, misery, God's anger, the ingratitude of his friends, coldness of his acquaintances, and cruelty of his enemies; all which he uses as arguments to induce God to help him; continued from ver. 2 to ver. 20.

I. In the first part he deprecates God's anger, and entreats a mitigation of it; though rebuked, let it not be in wrath; if corrected, let it not be in rigour: "O Lord, rebuke me not in thy wrath," &c.

II. His *complaint,* on which he falls instantly, and amplifies in a variety of ways.

1. From the prime cause, GOD: "Thine arrows stick fast in me," &c.

2. From the impulsive cause: "His *sin,* his *iniquities,*" ver. 4; "His *foolishness,*" ver. 5.

3. From the *weight* of his afflictions, which were, in general, "the arrows of God which stuck in him; the hand of God, by which he was pressed;" which were so grievous "that there was no soundness in his flesh—no rest in his bones."

4. By an induction of particulars, where he declares many effects of the disease:—

1. Putrefaction of his flesh: "My wounds stink, and are corrupt."

2. The *uncomfortable posture* of his *body:* "I am troubled, I am bowed down greatly."

3. Torment in his bowels, &c.: "My loins are filled with a loathsome disease."

4. Diseases through the whole system: "There is no soundness in my flesh."

5. Debility and grievous plague: "I am feeble," &c.

6. Anguish that forced him to cry out: "I have roared," &c.

7. His heart was disquieted: "The disquietness of my heart." But that it might appear that he had not lost his hold of his hope and his confidence in God, he directs his speech to him, and says: "Lord, all my desire is before thee, and my groaning is not hidden from thee."

8. He had a palpitation or trembling of heart: "My heart pants."

9. His strength decayed: "My strength fails."

10. A defect of sight: "The sight of my eyes is gone from me."

All these calamities David suffered from within. He was tormented in body and mind; but had he any comfort from without? Not any.

1. None from his friends: "My lovers and my friends stand aloof." 2. As for his enemies, they even then added to his affliction: "They also that seek after my life lay snares for me." In purpose, word, and deed, they sought to undo him.

He next shows his behaviour in these sufferings; he murmured not, but was silent and patient. "I was as a deaf man;—I was as a dumb man." He made no defence.

This he uses as an argument to induce the Lord to mitigate his sufferings; and of his patience he gives the following reasons:—

1. His reliance on God for audience and redress: "For in thee, O Lord, do I hope; thou wilt hear me."

2. For this he petitions; for to God he was not silent, though deaf and dumb to man. For *I said, Hear me!* and the assurance that he should be heard made him patient; for if not heard, his enemies would triumph: "Hear me, lest otherwise they should rejoice over me."

3. He was thus patient when his grief was extreme: "For I am ready to halt, and my sorrow is continually before me." I am under a bitter cross; and I know that if I be thy servant, I must bear my cross; therefore, I take it up, and suffer patiently.

4. This cross I have deserved to bear; it comes on account of mine iniquity, and I will not conceal it: "I will declare mine iniquity; I will be sorry for my sin." I suffer *justly,* and therefore have reason to be patient.

He complains again of his enemies. Though he suffered justly, yet this was no excuse for their cruelty; he complains of their strength, their number, and their hatred. My enemies are *living,* while I am at *death's door;* they are *multiplied* while I am *minished;* they render me *evil* for the *good* I have done *them.*

Then he concludes with a petition to God, in which he begs *three* things:—

1. God's presence: "Forsake me not, O Lord; my God, be not far from me."

2. He begs for help: "Help me, O Lord."

3. And prays that this help may come speedily: "Make haste to help me."

And these three petitions are directed to the Most High, as the God of his salvation: "O Lord, my salvation;" my deliverer from sin, guilt, pain, death, and hell.

In this Psalm, deeply descriptive of the anguish of a penitent soul, most persons, who feel distress on account of sin, may meet with something suitable to their case.

PSALM XXXIX

The psalmist's care and watchfulness over his thoughts, tongue, and actions, 1–3. He considers the brevity and uncertainty of human life, 4–7; prays for deliverance from sin, 8–11; and that he may be protected and spared till he is fitted for another world, 12, 13.

To the chief Musician, *even* to ªJeduthun, A Psalm of David

A. M. cir. 2970
B. C. cir. 1034
Davidis, Regis
Israelitarum,
cir. annum
22

I SAID, I will ᵇtake heed to my ways, that I sin not with my tongue: I will keep ᶜmyᵈ mouth with a bridle, ᵉwhile the wicked is before me.

2 ᶠI was dumb with silence, I held my peace, *even* from good; and my sorrow was ᵍstirred.

3 My heart was hot within me, while I was

musing ʰthe fire burned: *then* spake I with my tongue.

A. M. cir. 2970
B. C. cir. 1034
Davidis, Regis
Israelitarum,
cir. annum
22

4 LORD, ⁱmake me to know mine end, and the measure of my days, what it *is; that* I may know ᵏhow frail I *am*.

5 Behold, thou hast made my days *as* a handbreadth; and ˡmine age *is* as nothing before thee: ᵐverily every man ⁿat his best state *is* altogether vanity. Selah.

6 Surely every man walketh in ᵒa ᵖvain

ª1 Chron. xvi. 41; xxv. 1; Psa. lxii., lxxvii. title ᵇ1 Kings ii. 4; 2 Kings x. 31——ᶜHeb. *a bridle* or *muzzle for my mouth*——ᵈPsa. cxli. 3; James iii. 2——ᵉCol. iv. 5——ᶠPsa. xxxviii. 13——ᵍHeb. *troubled*

ʰJer. xx. 9——ⁱPsa. xc. 12; cxix. 84——ᵏOr, *what time I have here*——ˡPsa. xc. 4——ᵐVer. 11; Psa. lxii. 9; cxliv. 4——ⁿHeb. *settled*——ᵒHeb. *an image*——ᵖ1 Cor. vii. 31; James iv. 14

NOTES ON PSALM XXXIX

The *title* says, *To the chief Musician, Jeduthun himself, A Psalm of David.* It is supposed that this *Jeduthun* is the same with *Ethan,* 1 Chron. vi. 44, compared with 1 Chron. xvi. 41; and is there numbered among the sons of *Merari.* And he is supposed to have been one of the *four masters of music,* or *leaders of bands,* belonging to the temple. And it is thought that David, having composed this Psalm, gave it to *Jeduthun and his company* to sing. But several have supposed that *Jeduthun* himself was the author. It is very likely that this Psalm was written on the same occasion with the preceding. It relates to a grievous malady by which David was afflicted after his transgression with Bath-sheba. See what has been said on the foregoing Psalm.

Verse 1. *I said, I will take heed to my ways*] I must be *cautious* because of my *enemies;* I must be *patient* because of my *afflictions;* I must be *watchful* over my tongue, lest I offend my GOD, or give my *adversaries* any cause to speak evil of me.

Verse 2. *I held my peace, even from good*] "I ceased from the words of the law," says the *Chaldee.* I spoke nothing, *either good or bad.* I did not even defend myself.

My sorrow was stirred.] My afflictions increased, and I had an exacerbation of pain. It is a hard thing to be denied the benefit of *complaint* in sufferings, as it has a tendency to relieve the mind, and indeed, in some sort, to call off the attention from the *place* of actual suffering: and yet undue and extravagant *complaining* enervates the mind, so that it becomes a double prey to its sufferings. On both sides there are *extremes:* David seems to have steered clear of them on the right hand and on the left.

Verse 3. *My heart was hot within me*] A natural feeling of repressed grief.

While I was musing] What was at first a simple sensation of *heat* produced a *flame;* the *fire broke out* that had long been *smothered.*

It is a metaphor taken from vegetables, which, being heaped together, begin to heat and ferment, if not scattered and exposed to the air; and will soon produce a *flame,* and consume themselves and every thing within their reach.

Verse 4. *Lord, make me to know mine end*] I am weary of life; I wish to know *the measure of my days,* that I may see how long I have to suffer, and *how frail* I am. I wish to know what is *wanting* to make up the number of the days I have to live.

Verse 5. *My days as a handbreadth*] My life is but a *span; σπιθαμη του βιου.*

And mine age is as nothing] כאין *keein,* as *if it were not before thee.* All *time* is swallowed up in thy *eternity.*

Verily every man at his best state] כל אדם נצב *col adam nitstab,* "every man that *exists,* is vanity." All his projects, plans, schemes, &c., soon come to nothing. His body also moulders with the dust, and shortly passes both from the *sight* and *remembrance* of men.

Verse 6. *Walketh in a vain show*] בצלם *betselem,* in a *shadow.* He is but the *semblance* of being: he *appears* for a while, and then *vanisheth* away. Some of the fathers read, "Although every man walketh in the image of God, yet they are disquieted in vain."

He heapeth up riches, *and knoweth not who shall gather them.*] He *raketh together.* This is a metaphor taken from *agriculture:* the husbandman rakes the corn, &c., together in the field, and yet, so uncertain is life, that he knows not who shall gather them into the granary!

Verse 7. *And now, Lord, what wait I for?*] Have I any object of pursuit in life, but to regain thy *favour* and thine *image.*

Verse 8. *Deliver me from all my transgressions*] I seek the pardon of my sins; I expect it from thy *mercy.* Grant it, "that I be not the reproach of the foolish," (the godless and the profane,) who deride my expectation, and say no such blessings can be had. Let them know, by thy saving me, that there is a God who hear-

A. M. cir. 2970
B. C. cir. 1034
Davidis, Regis
Israelitarum,
cir. annum
22

show; surely they are disquieted in vain: qhe heapeth up *riches,* and knoweth not who shall gather them.

7 And now, LORD, what wait I for? rmy hope *is* in thee.

8 Deliver me from all my transgressions: make me not sthe reproach of the foolish.

9 tI was dumb, I opened not my mouth; because uthou didst *it.*

10 vRemove thy stroke away from me: I am consumed by the wblow of thine hand.

11 When thou with rebukes dost correct man for iniquity, thou makest xhis beauty yto consume away like a moth: zsurely every man *is* vanity. Selah.

12 Hear my prayer, O LORD, and give ear unto my cry; hold not thy peace at my tears: afor I *am* a stranger with thee, *and* a sojourner, bas all my fathers *were.*

13 cO spare me, that I may recover strength, before I go hence, and dbe no more.

A. M. cir. 2970
B. C. cir. 1034
Davidis, Regis
Israelitarum,
cir. annum
22

---

qJob xxvii. 17; Eccles. ii. 18, 21, 26; v. 14; Luke xii. 20, 21——rPsa. xxxviii. 15——sPsa. xliv. 13; lxxix. 4 tLev. x. 3; Job xl. 4, 5; Psa. xxxviii. 13——u2 Sam. xvi. 10; Job ii. 10——vJob ix. 34; xiii. 21——wHeb. *conflict* xHeb. *that which is to be desired in him to melt away*

yJob iv. 19; xiii. 28; Isa. l. 9; Hos. v. 12——zVer. 5——aLev. xxv. 23; 1 Chron. xxix. 15; Psa. cxix. 19; 2 Corinthians v. 6; Hebrews xi. 13; 1 Pet. i. 17; ii. 11 bGenesis xlvii. 9——cJob x. 20, 21; xiv. 5, 6——dJob xiv. 10, 11, 12

---

eth prayer, and giveth his Holy Spirit to all them that ask him.

Verse 10. Remove thy stroke away from me] This seems to be a figure taken from *gladiators,* or persons *contending in single combat.* One is wounded so as to be able to maintain the fight no longer: he therefore *gives in,* and prays his adversary to spare his life. I am conquered; I can hold the contest no longer: thou art too powerful for me. He cries what our ancestors used to term *craven;* the word spoken by him who was conquered in the battle *ordeal,* or *trial by combat.*

Verse 11. When thou with rebukes dost correct man] תוכחות *tochachoth* signifies a *vindication of proceedings in a court of law,* a *legal defence.* When God comes to maintain the credit and authority of his law against a sinner, he "causes his beauty to consume away:" a metaphor taken from the case of a culprit, who, by the arguments of counsel, and the unimpeachable evidence of witnesses, has the facts all proved against him, grows pale, looks terrified; his fortitude forsakes him, and he faints in court.

Surely every man is vanity.] He is incapable of resistance; he falls before his Maker; and none can deliver him but his *Sovereign* and *Judge,* against whom he has offended.

Selah.] This is a true saying, an everlasting truth.

Verse 12. Hear my prayer] Therefore, O Lord, show that mercy upon me which I so much need, and without which I must perish everlastingly.

I am a stranger with thee] I have not made this earth my home; I have not trusted in any arm but thine. Though I have sinned, I have never denied thee, and never cast thy words behind my back. I knew that *here* I had no continuing city. *Like my fathers,* I looked for a city that has permanent foundations, in a better state of being.

Verse 13. O spare me] Take me not from this *state* of *probation* till I have a thorough preparation for a *state* of *blessedness.* This he terms *recovering his strength*—being restored to the *favour* and *image* of God, from which he had fallen. This should be the daily cry of every human spirit: Restore me to thine image,

guide me by thy counsel, and then receive me to thy glory!

ANALYSIS OF THE THIRTY-NINTH PSALM

This Psalm was apparently written on the same occasion as the preceding. The psalmist is still suffering as before, yet is silent and patient; but the suffering at last becoming very sharp, he could hold his peace no longer: then he spoke. And we have reason to be thankful that he broke silence, as whoever considers the weighty truths which he spoke must allow.

There are *three* parts in this Psalm:—

I. His own account of his resolution to keep silence, ver. 1, and the consequences of it, ver. 2, 3.

II. His expostulation with God on the shortness, uncertainty, and frailty of life, ver. 4, 5, 6.

III. His petition to have his sin pardoned, ver. 8; to be saved from punishment, ver. 10; and for farther grace and respite, ver. 12, 13.

I. David acquaints us with his resolution: *I said*—I fully purposed to keep silence.

1. "I said, I will take heed to my ways, that I sin not with my tongue."

2. This resolution he kept for a while: "I was dumb; I held my peace even from good," even from making a just defence.

3. But in this I found great difficulty, nay, impossibility.

1. For all the time "my sorrow was stirred." My pain was increased by silence.

2. "My heart was hot." I was strongly incited to utter my mind.

3. "And, while thus musing, the fire burned;" what was within I saw should not be longer concealed: "Then spake I with my tongue."

II. He expostulates with God: and, being greatly oppressed both in body and mind, prays to know how long he is to live; or, rather, how soon he may get rid of his maladies, false friends, and deceitful enemies. Many considerations render his life uncomfortable.

1. It is very brittle and frail: "Make me to know how frail I am."

2. It is very *short:* "Behold, thou hast made my days as a handbreadth."

3. Yea, when carefully considered, it was

even less, of no consideration: "Mine age is as nothing before thee."

4. It was full of vanity: "Verily, every man at his best estate (in his strength, riches, power) is altogether vanity." His labours promise much, perform little.

5. It is unstable and uncertain, as a *shadow*. "Surely, every man walketh in a vain shadow."

6. It is full of trouble and inquietude: "Surely, they are disquieted in vain."

7. Man labours for he knows not whom: "He heapeth up riches, and knoweth not who shall gather them."

Notwithstanding all this, he finds that even here God is a sufficient Portion for them that trust in him. Let others toil for riches; admire dignities, empires, pleasures; let them be proud of these, and complain that their life is too short to enjoy them; I have a stronger hold; I am persuaded that the Lord will have mercy upon me, and be my Support in all the troubles and uncertainties of life: "And now, Lord, what wait I for? My hope is in thee."

III. On this confidence he again begins to pray,—

1. For remission of sin: "Deliver me from all my transgressions."

2. For defence against malicious tongues: "Make me not a reproach to the foolish."

3. For submission under Divine chastisement: "I was dumb, because thou didst it."

4. For a removal of his punishment: "Take away thy plague from me."

1. And he adds the cause;—either remove thy hand, or I must needs perish: "I am even consumed by the blow of thy hand."

2. This he amplifies by the similitude of a moth; and adds a second reason: "When thou with rebukes dost correct man, thou makest his beauty to consume away like the moth," which frets and destroys a garment. And, for confirmation, delivers his former opinion, which is to be considered as an incontrovertible maxim: "Surely, every man is vanity. Selah." Mark that!

3. To which he adds a *third*—the consideration of our present condition in this life. We and all our fathers are but pilgrims in this life: "I am a stranger with thee, and a sojourner, as all my fathers were." Therefore, spare me.

Faith has always to struggle with difficulties. Though he was confident, ver. 7, that God was his hope; yet his calamities, his sickness, his enemies, the brevity, fugacity, and troubles of life, come ever into his memory; and, therefore, he prays again for them. And this rises by a climax or gradation:—

1. He prays for audience: "Hear my prayer, O Lord!"

2. That his *cry*, for such it was, be heard: "Give ear unto my cry."

3. For admission of his tears: "Hold not thy peace at my tears. The reason, as *a stranger*. Thy grace, thy favour.

4. For some relaxation and ease: "O spare me, that I may recover strength;" which he urges with this motive, "before I go hence, and be no more." Restore me to thy favour in *this life*. Hereafter, it will be too late to expect it. Let me not die *unsaved!*

PSALM XL

The benefit of confidence in God, 1–3. The blessedness of those who trust in God, 4, 5. The termination of the Jewish sacrifices in that of Christ, 6–8. The psalmist's resolution to publish God's goodness, 9, 10: he prays to be delivered from evils, 11–13; against his enemies, 14, 15; and in behalf of those who are destitute, 16, 17.

To the chief Musician, A Psalm of David

A. M. cir. 2971
B. C. cir. 1033
Davidis, Regis
Israelitarum,
cir. annum
23

I [a]WAITED [b]patiently for the Lord; and he inclined unto me, and heard my cry.

2 He brought me up also out of [c]a horrible pit, out of [d]the miry clay, and [e]set my feet upon a rock, *and* [f]established my goings.

A. M. cir. 2971
B. C. cir. 1033
Davidis, Regis
Israelitarum,
cir. annum
23

3 [g]And he hath put a new song in my mouth,

---

[a]Heb. *In waiting I waited*——[b]Psa. xxvii. 14; xxxvii. 7
[c]Heb. *a pit of noise*

[d]Psa. lxix. 2, 14.——[e]Psa. xxvii. 5——[f]Psa. xxxvii. 23
[g]Psa. xxxiii. 3

NOTES ON PSALM XL

The TITLE, "To the chief Musician," we have already seen, and it contains nothing worthy of particular remark. Concerning the *occasion* and *author* of this Psalm there has been a strange and numerous diversity of opinions. I shall not trouble the reader with sentiments which I believe to be ill founded; as I am satisfied the Psalm was composed by *David*, and about the same time and on the *same occasion* as the two preceding; with this difference, that *here* he magnifies God for having bestowed

the mercy which he sought *there*. It is, therefore, a *thanksgiving* for his recovery from the *sore disease* by which he was afflicted in his body, and for his restoration to the Divine favour. The *sixth, seventh,* and *eighth* verses contain a remarkable prophecy of the incarnation and sacrificial offering of Jesus Christ. From the *eleventh* to the end contains a new subject, and appears to have belonged to an *other Psalm*. It is the same as the *seventieth* Psalm; only it wants the two first verses.

Verse 1. *I waited patiently for the Lord*] The two preceding Psalms are proofs of the

A. M. cir. 2971
B. C. cir. 1033
Davidis, Regis
Israelitarum,
cir. annum
23

even praise unto our God:
[h]many shall see *it,* and fear,
and shall trust in the LORD.

4 [i]Blessed *is* that man that
maketh the LORD his trust, and [k]respecteth
not the proud, nor such as [l]turn aside to
lies.

5 [m]Many, O LORD my God, *are* thy wonderful works *which* thou hast done, [n]and thy

thoughts *which are* to us-ward: [o]they cannot be reckoned up in
order unto thee: *if* I would declare and speak *of them,* they
are more than can be numbered.

A. M. cir. 2971
B. C. cir. 1033
Davidis, Regis
Israelitarum,
cir. annum
23

6 [p]Sacrifice and offering thou didst not desire; mine ears hast thou [q]opened: burnt-offering and sin-offering hast thou not required.

---

[h]Psalm lii. 6——[i]Psalm xxxiv. 8; Jeremiah xvii. 7
[k]Psalm ci. 3, 7——[l]Psalm cxxv. 5——[m]Exod. xi. 15;
Job v. 9; ix. 10; Psalm lxxi. 15; xcii. 5; cxxxix. 6, 17
[n]Isaiah lv. 8——[o]Or, *none can order them unto thee*

[p]1 Sam. xv. 22; Psa. xl. 6; l. 8; li. 16; Proverbs xxi. 3;
Eccles. v. 1; Isaiah i. 11; lxvi. 3; Hosea vi. 6; Matthew
ix. 13; xii. 7; Hebrews x. 5——[q]Hebrew, *digged;* Exodus
xxi. 6

---

patience and *resignation* with which David waited for the mercy of God. The reader is requested to consult the notes on them.

And heard my cry.] The two preceding Psalms show how he *prayed* and *waited; this* shows how he *succeeded.*

Verse 2. A horrible pit] Literally, the *sounding pit;* where nothing was heard except the howlings of wild beasts, or the hollow sounds of winds reverberated and broken from the craggy sides and roof.

The miry clay] Where the longer I stayed the deeper I sank, and was utterly unable to save myself. The *Syriac* and *Arabic* translate, "The pit of perdition, and the mud of corruption." These are figurative expressions to point out the dreary, dismal, ruinous state of sin and guilt, and the utter inability of a condemned sinner to save himself either from the guilt of his conscience, or the corruption of his heart.

Set my feet upon a rock] Thou hast changed my state from *guilt* to *pardon;* from *corruption* to *holiness;* in consequence of which *my goings are established.* I have now power over all sin, and can walk steadily in the way that leads to God's kingdom.

Verse 3. A new song] Cheerfulness and joy had long been strangers to him. He seemed to live to utter the most doleful complaints, and be a prey to suffering and wretchedness. *Praise* for a sense of God's favour was a *new* song to him. The word is often used to signify *excellence:* I will sing a most *excellent* and *eminent* song.

Many shall see it] I will publish it abroad; *and fear*—to sin against the Lord, knowing by my example what a grievous and bitter thing it is.

And shall trust in the Lord.] Even the worst of sinners shall not despair of mercy, being penitent, when they see that I have found favour in his sight.

Verse 4. Blessed is that man] The man must be blessed and happy who casts his soul, with all its burden of sin and wretchedness, at the footstool of God's mercy; for he will save all who come to him through the Son of his love.

Verse 5. Many—are thy wonderful works] The psalmist seems here astonished and confounded at the *counsels, loving-kindnesses,* and *marvellous works* of the Lord, not in *nature,* but in *grace;* for it was the mercy of God towards himself that he had now particularly in view.

Verse 6. *Sacrifice and offering*] The apostle, Heb. x. 5, &c., quoting this and the two following verses, says, *When he* (the Messiah) *cometh into the world*—was about to be incarnated, *He saith*—to God the Father, *Sacrifice and offering thou wouldst not*—it was never thy *will* and design that the sacrifices under thy own law should be considered as making atonement for sin; they were only designed to point out my incarnation and consequent sacrificial death: and therefore *a body hast thou prepared me,* by a miraculous conception in the womb of a virgin; according to thy word, *The seed of the woman shall bruise the head of the serpent.*

A body hast thou prepared me.—The quotation of this and the two following verses by the apostle, Heb. x. 5, &c., is taken from the *Septuagint,* with scarcely any variety of reading: but, although the general meaning is the same, they are widely different in verbal expression in the Hebrew. David's words are אזנים כרית לי *oznayim caritha lli,* which we translate, *My ears hast thou opened;* but they might be more properly rendered, *My ears hast thou bored;* that is, Thou hast made me *thy servant for ever,* to dwell in thine own house: for the allusion is evidently to the custom mentioned Exod. xxi. 2, &c.: "If thou buy a Hebrew servant, six years he shall serve, and in the seventh he shall go out free: but if the servant shall positively say, I love my master, &c., I will not go out free; then his master shall bring him to the doorpost, and shall bore his ear through with an awl, and he shall serve him for ever."

But how is it possible that the Septuagint and the apostle should take a meaning so totally different from the sense of the Hebrew? Dr. Kennicott has a very ingenious conjecture here: he supposes that the Septuagint and apostle express the meaning of the words as they stood in the copy from which the Greek translation was made; and that the present Hebrew text is corrupted in the word אזנים *oznayim,* ears, which has been written through carelessness for אז גוה *az gevah,* THEN, a BODY. The first syllable, אז *az,* THEN, is the same in both; and the latter, נים, which, joined to אז makes אזנים *oznayim,* might have been easily mistaken for גוה *gevah,* BODY; נ *nun* being very like ג *gimel;* י *yod* like ו *vau;* and ה *he* like final ם *mem;* especially if the line on which the letters were written in the MS. hap-

A. M. cir. 2971
B. C. cir. 1033
Davidis, Regis
Israelitarum,
cir. annum
23

7 Then said I, Lo, I come: in the volume of the book *it is* ^rwritten of me,

8 ^sI delight to do thy will, O my God: yea, thy law *is* ^twithin ^umy heart.

9 ^vI have preached righteousness in the great

congregation: lo, ^wI have not refrained my lips, O LORD, ^xthou knowest.

10 ^yI have not hid thy righteousness within my heart; I have declared thy faithfulness and thy salvation: I have not con-

A. M. cir. 2971
B. C. cir. 1033
Davidis, Regis
Israelitarum,
cir. annum
23

---

^rLuke xxiv. 44——^sPsalm cxix. 16, 24, 47, 92; John iv. 34; Romans vii. 22——^tHebrew, *in the midst of my bowels*——^uPsalm xxxvii. 31; Jeremiah xxxi. 33; 2 Corinthians iii. 3——^vPsalm xxii. 22, 25; xxxv. 18——^wPsalm cxix. 13——^xPsalm cxxxix. 2 ^yActs xx. 20, 27

---

pened to be blacker than ordinary, which has often been a cause of mistake, it might then have been easily taken for the under-stroke of the *mem*, and thus give rise to a corrupt reading; add to this, the root כרה *carah* signifies as well to *prepare*, as to *open*, *bore*, &c. On this supposition the ancient copy translated by the Septuagint, and followed by the apostle, must have read the text thus: אז גוה כרית לי *az gevah charitha lli; Σωμα δε κατηρτισω μοι·* Then *a body thou hast prepared me:* thus the Hebrew text, the version of the Septuagint, and the apostle, will agree in what is known to be an indisputable fact in Christianity; namely, that Christ was *incarnated* for the sin of the world.

The *Æthiopic* has nearly the same reading: the *Arabic* has both, "A body hast thou prepared me, and mine ears thou hast opened." But the *Syriac*, the *Chaldee*, and the *Vulgate*, agree with the present Hebrew text; and none of the MSS. collated by *Kennicott* and *De Rossi* have any various reading on the disputed words.

It is remarkable, that all the offerings and sacrifices which were considered to be of an atoning or cleansing nature, offered under the law, are here enumerated by the psalmist and the apostle, to show that *none* of them, nor *all* of them, could take away sin; and that the grand sacrifice of Christ was that alone which could do it.

Four kinds are here specified, both by the psalmist and the apostle: viz. SACRIFICE, זבח *zebach*, θυσια; OFFERING, מנחה *minchah*, προσφορα; BURNT-OFFERING, עולה *olah*, ὁλοκαυτωμα; SIN-OFFERING, חטאה *chataah*, περι ἁμαρτιας. Of all these we may say, with the apostle, it was impossible that the blood of bulls and goats, &c. should take away sin.

Thou hast had no pleasure.—Thou couldst never be pleased with the victims under the law; thou couldst never consider them as atonements for sin, as they could never satisfy thy justice, nor make thy law honourable.

Verse 7. *In the volume of the book*] במגלת ספר *bimegillath sepher*, "in the *roll* of the book." Anciently, books were written on skins, and rolled up. Among the Romans, these were called *volumina*, from *volvo*, *I roll;* and the Pentateuch in the Jewish synagogues is still written in this way. There are two wooden rollers; on one they roll *on*, on the other they roll *off*, as they proceed in reading. One now lying before me, written on vellum, is *two feet two inches* in *breadth*, and *one hundred and two feet long*. To roll and unroll such a MS. was no easy task; and to be managed must lie flat on a table. This contains the Pentateuch only, and is without *points*, or any other Ma-

soretic distinction. The *book* mentioned here must be the *Pentateuch*, or five books of Moses; for, in David's time no other part of Divine revelation had been committed to writing. This whole book speaks about Christ, and his accomplishing the *will* of God, not only in "the seed of the woman shall bruise the head of the serpent," and "in thy seed shall all the nations of the earth be blessed;" but in all the *sacrifices* and sacrificial rites mentioned in the law.

Verse 8. *To do thy will*] God *willed* not the sacrifices under the law, but he *willed* that a human victim of infinite merit should be offered for the redemption of mankind. That there might be *such a victim*, a *body* was prepared for the eternal Logos, and in that body *he came* to do the *will of God;* that is, to suffer and die for the sins of the world.

1. Hence we see that the sovereign WILL of God is that Jesus should be incarnated; that he should suffer and die; or, in the apostle's words, *taste death for every man;* that all should believe on him, and be saved from their sins; for this is the WILL of God, our *sanctification.*

2. And as the apostle grounds this on the words of the Psalm, we see that it is the WILL of *God* that that system shall end; for as the essence of it is contained in its *sacrifices*, and God says he *will* not have these, and has appointed the *Messiah* to do his will, i. e., to *die for men*, hence it necessarily follows, from the psalmist himself, that the introduction of the Messiah into the world is the abolition of the law; and that his sacrifice is that which shall last for ever.

Verse 9. *I have preached righteousness*] I think it best to refer these words to Christ and his apostles. In consequence of his having become a sacrifice for sin, the Jewish sacrificial system being ended, the middle wall of partition was broken down, and the door of faith, the doctrine of justification by faith, opened to the Gentiles. Hence the Gospel was preached in all the world, and the mercy of God made known to the Gentiles; and thus *righteousness* —justification by faith, was preached *in the great congregation*—to Jews and Gentiles, throughout the Roman empire.

The great congregation, both in this and the following verse, I think, means the Gentiles, contradistinguished from the Jews.

The word *righteousness* means the plan or method of salvation by Jesus Christ—God's method of justifying sinners by faith, without the deeds of the law. See Rom. iii. 25, 26, and the notes there.

Verse 10. *Thy faithfulness*] This means the exact fulfilment of the promises made by the prophets relative to the incarnation of Christ,

A. M. cir. 2971
B. C. cir. 1033
Davidis, Regis
Israelitarum,
cir. annum
23

cealed thy loving-kindness and thy truth from the great congregation.

11 Withhold not thou thy tender mercies from me, O LORD: [z]let thy loving-kindness and thy truth continually preserve me.

12 For innumerable evils have compassed me about: [a]mine iniquities have taken hold upon me, so that I am not able to look up; they are more than the hairs of mine head: therefore [b]my heart [c]faileth me.

13 [d]Be pleased, O LORD, to deliver me: O LORD, make haste to help me.

14 [e]Let them be ashamed and confounded together that seek after my soul to destroy it; let them be driven backward and put to shame that wish me evil.

A. M. cir. 2971
B. C. cir. 1033
Davidis, Regis
Israelitarum,
cir. annum
23

15 [f]Let them be [g]desolate for a reward of their shame that say unto me, Aha, aha.

16 [h]Let all those that seek thee rejoice and be glad in thee: let such as love thy salvation [i]say continually, The LORD be magnified.

17 [k]But I *am* poor and needy; *yet* [l]the LORD thinketh upon me: thou *art* my help and my deliverer; make no tarrying, O my God.

---

[z]Psalm xliii. 3; lvii. 3; lxi. 7——[a]Psalm xxxviii. 4
[b]Psalm lxxiii. 26——[c]Hebrew, *forsaketh*——[d]Psalm
lxx. 1, &c.——[e]Psalm xxxv. 4, 26; lxx. 2, 3; lxxi. 13

[f]Psalm lxx. 3——[g]Psalm lxxiii. 19——[h]Psalm lxx. 4
[i]Psalm xxxv. 27——[k]Psalm lxx. 5——[l]1 Peter
5, 7

---

and the opening of the door of faith to the *Gentiles.*

Loving-kindness] Shows the gift itself to Jesus Christ, the highest proof that God could give to a lost world of his *mercy, kindness,* and *loving-kindness.*

Verse 11. *Thy tender mercies*] רחמיך *rachameycha,* such propensities and feelings as a mother bears to her child; or animals in general to their young.

Let thy loving-kindness] חסדך *chasdecha,* thy overflowing and superabundant mercy.

And thy truth] What is revealed in thy word: *continually preserve me. Mercy* to help me, *truth* to direct me; and, by the operation of both, I shall be continually preserved from sin and evil.

Verse 12. *Innumerable evils have compassed me about*] This part does not comport with the preceding; and either argues a former experience, or must be considered a part of another Psalm, written at a different time, and on another occasion, and, were we to prefix the two first verses of the *seventieth* Psalm to it we should find it to be a Psalm as complete in itself as that is.

They are more than the hairs of mine head] This could not be said by any person who was exulting in the pardoning mercy of God, as David was at the time he penned the commencement of this Psalm.

Verse 15. *That say unto me, Aha, aha.*] האח האח *heach, heach.* See on Psa. xxxv. 21.

Verse 16. *Let all those that seek thee—be glad*] In making prayer and supplication to thee, let them ever find thee, that they may magnify thee for the blessings they receive.

Love thy salvation] Who earnestly desire to be saved from sin: saved in thy *own way,* and on thy *own terms.*

The Lord be magnified.] Let God be praised continually for the continual blessings he pours down.

Verse 17. *But I* am *poor*] עני *ani,* afflicted, greatly depressed.

And needy] אביון *ebyon,* a *beggar.* One utterly destitute, and seeking help.

The Lord thinketh upon me] The words are very emphatic; אדני *Adonai,* my prop, my support, *thinketh,* ישב *yachshab,* meditateth, *upon*

me. On which he concludes: "Thou art my help and deliverer." Seeing that my miserable state occupies thy *heart,* it will soon *employ* thy *hand.* Thou, who meditatest upon me, wilt deliver me.

Make no tarrying] Seeing thou art *disposed to help,* and I am in such *great necessity,* delay not, but come speedily to my assistance. The old *Psalter* speaks to this effect: "Let us not be so long under distress and misery that we lose our patience, or our love to thee."

ANALYSIS OF THE FORTIETH PSALM

There are *two* main parts in this Psalm:—

I. A *thanksgiving,* ver. 1-11.

II. A *prayer,* from ver. 12 to the end.

Thankfulness consists in the exercise of two virtues, *truth* and *justice.*

1. Truth calls upon us to acknowledge the *benefit,* and *him* from whom we receive it.

2. Justice obliges us to be grateful, and to perform some duties as evidences of our thankful minds; and both these we meet with in the first part.

I. David begins with a profession of thankfulness; shows his *confidence:* "I waited patiently for the Lord;" then shows the success, or what God did for him.

1. "He inclined his ear, and heard my cry."

2. "He brought me out of the horrible pit, and out of the miry clay."

3. "He set my feet upon a rock." Being redeemed from danger, he set me in a safe place.

4. "He established my goings." He confirmed my steps, so that I slipped and slided no more.

5. And he hath moved me to be thankful: "He hath put a new song in my mouth." The deliverance was not common, and therefore the praise should not be common, but expressed by a new and exquisite song.

And in this he supposed his example would be a common document. Many shall see my deliverance and my thanksgiving, and shall fear God, and acknowledge his *grace,* his *providence,* and *protection;* and be led thereby to put their trust in him. And then he produces his *form* of *thanksgiving:*—

First, He pronounces the man blessed who relies on God. 1. "Blessed is the man that maketh the Lord his trust." 2. "And blessed is he who respects not the proud;" men proud of their wealth and power, or such as turn aside to lies.

Secondly, Then by exclamation admires God's *mercies,* and goodness to his people. 1. For their grandeur and multitude: "Many, O Lord my God, are thy works." 2. For their supernatural appearance: "Thy wonderful works." 3. For the incomparable wisdom by which they are ordered: "Many, O Lord, are thy wondrous works; and thy thoughts to us-ward, they cannot be reckoned up," &c.

And having acknowledged his thankfulness, he speaks of the other part, his gratitude; to which, in equity, he thought himself bound, viz., to be obedient to God's voice, which is, indeed, the best sacrifice, and far beyond all those that are offered by the law; as is apparent in *Christ,* to whom these words and the obedience contained in them are principally attributed: by way of accommodation, they belong to every one of his members who means to be thankful for his redemption.

And, first, he tells us that outward worship is of little worth, if sincerity and true piety be wanting: "Sacrifice and offering thou didst not require." Not these absolutely, but as subservient to the true piety, and significative of the obedience of Christ unto death.

2. To this end "mine ears hast thou opened;" bored, made docile, and taken me for thy servant.

3. And I will be thy voluntary and obedient servant: "Then said I, Lo, I come!" I am ready to hear thy commands.

4. He describes his ready obedience:—

1. That he performed it cheerfully: "I delight to do thy will."

2. That he did it heartily: "Thy law is in my heart." The obedience of eyes, hands, and feet may be hypocritical; that which is of the heart cannot. The heart thou requirest, and the heart thou shalt have; and to that purpose "I have put thy law in my heart."

3. He did this for the benefit of others: he published the Gospel. 1. "I have preached righteousness in the great congregation." 2. "I have not refrained my lips; that thou knowest." 3. "I have not hid thy righteousness within my heart." 4. "I have declared thy faithfulness and thy salvation." 5. "I have not concealed thy loving-kindness and truth from the great congregation."

In this verse we have the commendation of the Gospel, that it is *righteousness.* Jesus, who is the sum and substance of it, *justifies* and *sanctifies.* It is God's *truth* and *faithfulness,* for in it his promises are performed. It is our *salvation,* freeing us from sin, death, the curse of the law, and hell-fire. It must, as such, be preached in the great congregation. And to it *obedience* must be yielded; and to this *four things* are necessary:—

1. The help of God's Spirit: "Thou hast opened mine ears."

2. A ready and willing mind: "Then said I, Lo, I come."

3. A ready performance in the work: "I delight to do thy will."

4. That respect be had to God's law: "Thy law is within my heart."

But all that is here spoken must be considered as resting on the sacrificial offering which Christ made; for we must be justified by his blood; and through him alone can we have remission of sins, the help of God's Spirit, or any power to do any kind of good.

II. This second part of the Psalm appears rather to be a part of another, or a Psalm of itself, as it relates to a different subject.

In the *first* part of the following prayer we have the sorrowful sighing of a distressed heart, vented in the most earnest petitions on account of the greatness of its sins, and the evils by which it was surrounded. A fear of being cut off causes the penitent to pray, "Withhold not thou thy mercy from me, O Lord." 1. "For innumerable evils have compassed me," &c. 2. "My iniquities have taken fast hold upon me," &c. 3. "Therefore my heart faileth me." My agony is great, my vital spirit fails; and therefore he prays again, 4. "Be pleased, O Lord, to deliver me! make haste to help me!"

The *second* part of his prayer is for the confusion of his *wicked enemies:* "Let them be ashamed and confounded together, that say, Aha! aha!"

The *third* part of the prayer is for *all good men.* Let all those who seek thee be joyful and glad in thee; let them say, "The Lord be magnified."

In the *close* he prays for *himself;* and to move Divine mercy the sooner,—

1. He puts himself in the number of the poor and afflicted. He boasts not that he is a king, a prophet, a great man; but "I am poor and needy."

2. He shows his hope and confidence: "Yet the Lord thinketh upon me."

3. He casts himself wholly upon God: "Thou art my help and my deliverer."

4. Therefore delay not: "Make no tarrying, O my God!"

PSALM XLI

The blessedness of the man who is merciful to the poor, 1–3. The psalmist complains of his enemies, and prays for support, 4–10; and blesses God for having heard his prayer, and preserved him from his adversaries, 11, 12. A fine doxology closes the Psalm, 13.

To the chief Musician, A Psalm of David

A. M. cir. 2971
B. C. cir. 1033
Davidis, Regis
Israelitarum,
cir. annum
23

BLESSED ᵃ*is* he that considereth ᵇthe poor: the LORD
will deliver him ᶜin time of
trouble.

2 The LORD will preserve him, and keep him
alive: *and* he shall be blessed upon the earth:
ᵈand ᵉthou wilt not deliver him unto the will
of his enemies.

3 The LORD will strengthen him upon the
bed of languishing: thou wilt ᶠmake all his
bed in his sickness.

ᵃProverbs xiv. 21——ᵇOr, *the weak or sick*——ᶜHebrew, *in the day of evil*——ᵈPsalm xxvii. 12——ᵉOr,
do not thou deliver——ᶠHeb. *turn*

NOTES ON PSALM XLI

The *title* as before. The *Syriac* says it was
"A Psalm of David, when he appointed over-
seers to take care of the poor." The *Arabic*
says, "It is a prophecy concerning the incarnation; and also of the salutation of Judas." It
appears to me to have been written on the same
occasion as the three former, and to relate to
David's malady and cure, and the evil treatment he had from his enemies during his affliction. Our Lord, by accommodation, applies the
ninth verse to the treachery of Judas, John xiii.
18; but as to any other direct reference to
Christ, or his history, I believe the Psalm has
none.

Verse 1. *Blessed is he that considereth*] God
is *merciful;* he will have man to *resemble* him:
as far as he is *merciful*, feels a *compassionate
heart*, and uses a *benevolent hand*, he *resembles*
his Maker; and the mercy he shows to others
God will show to him. But it is not a *sudden
impression* at the sight of a person in distress,
which obliges a man to give something for the
relief of the sufferer, that constitutes the *merciful character*. It is he *who considers the poor;*
who endeavours to find them out; who looks
into their circumstances; who is in the habit
of doing so; and actually, according to his
power and means, *goes about to do good;* that
is the merciful man, of whom God speaks with
such high approbation, and to whom he
promises a rich reward.

Verse 2. *The Lord will preserve him, and
keep him alive*] It is worthy of remark, that
benevolent persons, who *consider* the *poor*, and
especially the *sick poor;* who *search cellars,
garrets, back lanes,* and *such abodes of misery,*
to find them out, (even in the places where contagion keeps its seat,) very seldom fall a prey
to their own benevolence. The Lord, in an especial manner, keeps them *alive*, and preserves
them; while many, who endeavour to keep far
from the contagion, are assailed by it, and fall
victims to it. God loves the merciful man.

Verse 3. *The Lord will strengthen him*]
Good, benevolent, and merciful as he is, he must
also die: but he shall not die as other men; he
shall have peculiar consolations, refreshment,
and support, while passing *through the valley
of the shadow of death.*

4 I said, LORD, be merciful
unto me: ᵍheal my soul; for I
have sinned against thee.

A. M. cir. 2971
B. C. cir. 1033
Davidis, Regis
Israelitarum,
cir. annum
23

5 Mine enemies speak evil of
me, When shall he die, and his name perish?

6 And if he come to see *me,* he ʰspeaketh
vanity: his heart gathereth iniquity to itself;
when he goeth abroad, he telleth *it.*

7 All that hate me whisper together against
me: against me do they devise ⁱmy hurt.

8 ᵏAn evil disease, *say they,* cleaveth fast
unto him: and *now* that he lieth he shall
rise up no more.

ᵍ2 Chron. xxx. 20; Psa. vi. 2; cxlvii. 3——ʰPsa.
xii. 2; Prov. xxvi. 24, 25, 26——ⁱHeb. *evil to me*——ᵏHebrew, *A thing of Belial*

Thou wilt make all his bed] הפכת *haphachta,*
thou hast *turned up, tossed,* and *shaken* it; and
thou wilt do so to *all his bed*—thou wilt not
leave one *uneasy place* in it—not one *lump*, or
any *unevenness*, to prevent him from sleeping.
Thou wilt do every thing, consistently with the
accomplishment of the great decree, "Unto dust
thou shalt return," to give him ease, refreshment, and rest. We may sum up the privileges
of the merciful man: 1. He is generally *blessed*,
ver. 1. 2. He will be *delivered in the time of
trouble*, ver. 1. 3. He will be *preserved* by a
particular providence, ver. 2. 4. He shall be
kept alive amidst infection and danger, ver. 2.
5. He *shall be blessed on the earth* in his temporal concerns, ver. 2. 6. His *enemies* shall not
be able to spoil or destroy him, ver. 2. 7. He
shall be *strengthened on a bed of languishing*,
to enable him to bear his afflictions, ver. 3. 8.
He shall have *ease, comfort,* and *support* in his
last hours, ver. 3.

Verse 4. *I said, Lord, be merciful unto me*] I
need thy mercy especially, because I have
sinned against thee, and my sin is a *deadly
wound* to my soul; therefore *heal* my soul, *for
it has sinned against thee.*

Verse 5. *Mine enemies speak evil*] It is often
a good man's lot to be evil spoken of; to have
his *motives*, and even his most *benevolent acts*,
misconstrued.

Verse 6. *And if he come to see* me] This may
relate to *Ahithophel;* but it is more likely that
it was to some other person who was his secret
enemy, who pretended to come and inquire after
his health, but with the secret design to see
whether death was *despatching his work.*

When *he goeth abroad, he telleth* it.] He
makes several observations on my dying state;
intimates that I am suffering deep remorse for
secret crimes; that God is showing his displeasure against me, and that I am full of sorrow at the approach of death.

Verse 7. *All that hate me whisper together
against me*] This is in consequence of the *information* given by the *hypocritical friend,*
who came to him with the *lying tongue,* and
whose *heart gathereth iniquity to itself,* which,
when *he went abroad,* he told to others as ill-
minded as himself, and they also drew their
wicked inferences.

Verse 8. *An evil disease, say they, cleaveth*

A. M. cir. 2971
B. C. cir. 1033
Davidis, Regis
Israelitarum,
cir. annum
23

9 [1]Yea, [m]mine own familiar friend, in whom I trusted, [n]which did eat of my bread, hath [o]lifted up *his* heel against me.

10 But thou, O Lord, be merciful unto me, and raise me up, that I may requite them.

11 By this I know that thou favourest me,

because mine enemy doth not triumph over me.

A. M. cir. 2971
B. C. cir. 1033
Davidis, Regis
Israelitarum,
cir. annum
23

12 And as for me, thou upholdest me in mine integrity, and [p]settest me before thy face for ever.

13 [q]Blessed *be* the Lord God of Israel from everlasting, and to everlasting. Amen, and Amen.

---

[1]2 Sam. xv. 12; Job xix. 19; Psa. lv. 12, 13, 20; Jer. xx. 10 [m]Heb. *the man of my peace*

[n]Obad. 7; John xiii. 18——[o]Heb. *magnified*——[p]Job xxxvi. 7; Psa. xxxiv. 15——[q]Psa. cvi. 48

---

fast unto him] דבר בליעל יצוק בו *debar beliyaal yatsuk bo,* a *thing, word,* or *pestilence of Belial, is poured out upon him.* His disease is of no common sort; it is a *diabolical* malady.

He shall rise up no more.] His disease is incurable without a miracle; and he is too much hated of God to have one wrought for him. Some apply this to the death and resurrection of Christ; he *lieth*—he is *dead* and buried; he shall never *rise again* from the dead.

Verse 9. *Mine own familiar friend*] This is either a direct prophecy of the treachery of Judas, or it is a fact in David's distresses which our Lord found so similar to the falsity of his treacherous disciple, that he applies it to him, John xiii. 18. What we translate *mine own familiar friend,* איש שלומי *ish shelomi,* is *the man of my peace.* The man who, with the שלום לך *shalom lecha, peace be to thee!* kissed me; and thus gave the agreed-on signal to my murderers that I was the person whom they should seize, hold fast, and carry away.

Did eat of my bread] Was an *inmate in my house.* Applied by our Lord to Judas, when eating with him out of the same dish. See John xiii. 18, 26. Possibly it may refer to *Ahithophel,* his counsellor, the *man of his peace,* his prime minister; who, we know, was the strength of Absalom's conspiracy.

Verse 10. *Raise me up*] Restore me from this sickness, *that I may requite them.* This has also been applied to our Lord; who, knowing that he *must die,* prays that he *may rise again,* and thus disappoint the malice of his enemies.

Verse 11. *By this I know that thou favorest me*] If thou hadst not been on my side, I had perished by this disease; and then my enemies would have had cause to triumph.

This also has been applied to our Lord; and *Calmet* says it is the greatest proof we have of the divinity of Christ, that he did not permit the malice of the Jews, nor the rage of the devil, to prevail against him. They might persecute, blaspheme, mock, insult, crucify, and slay him; but his *resurrection* confounded them; and by it he gained the victory over sin, death, and hell.

Verse 12. *Thou upholdest me*] I am still enabled to show that my heart was upright before God.

Settest me before thy face for ever.] Thou showest that thou dost *approve* of me: that I stand *in thy presence,* under the smiles of thy approbation.

This also has been applied to our Lord, and considered as pointing out his *mediatorial office* at the right hand of God.

Verse 13. *Blessed be the Lord God of Israel*]

By all these circumstances and events glory shall redound to the name of God for ever; for the *record* of these things shall never perish, but be published from one generation to another; and it has been so.

From everlasting, and to everlasting.] מהעולם ועד העולם *mehaolam vead haolam; From the hidden time to the hidden time;* from that which had no beginning to that which has no end.

To which he subscribes, *Amen and Amen. Fiat, fiat.—Vulgate.* Γένοιτο, γένοιτο.—*Septuagint.* The *Chaldee* says, "And let the righteous say, Amen, and Amen." ᚱᚷᛖᛒᛚᛖᛏᚱᚩᛟ ᚩᚾᛁᚻᛏᛖᚾ ᚷᚩᚩ ᛁᚱᚾᚪᚻᛖᛚᚪ ᚱᚾᚪᛗ ᛈᚩᛈᚢᛚᚩᛟ ᚷ ᚩᚾ ᛈᚩᛈᚢᛚᚩᛟ. ᛒᛖᚩᚻᛁᚳ ᚱᚣᚻᛁᚳᚱᛈᚪ. "Be blessed, Lord God of Israel, from world, and in world. Be it! So be it!"—*Anglo-Saxon.* To which the Old *Psalter* approaches very nearly: 𝔅𝔩𝔶𝔰𝔰𝔢𝔡 𝔏𝔬𝔯𝔡 𝔊𝔬𝔡 𝔬𝔣 𝔍𝔰𝔯𝔢𝔩, 𝔣𝔯𝔞 𝔴𝔢𝔯𝔩𝔡, 𝔞𝔫𝔡 𝔦𝔫 𝔴𝔢𝔯𝔩𝔡: 𝔅𝔢 𝔦𝔱 𝔡𝔬𝔫𝔢! 𝔟𝔢 𝔦𝔱 𝔡𝔬𝔫𝔢. Thus illustrated by the same, 𝔉𝔯𝔞 𝔴𝔢𝔯𝔩𝔡 𝔦𝔫 𝔴𝔢𝔯𝔩𝔡; that es, fra the bygynnyng of this wereld, in til wereld that lastes ay. 𝔅𝔢 𝔦𝔱 𝔡𝔬𝔫𝔢, 𝔟𝔢 𝔦𝔱 𝔡𝔬𝔫𝔢. This dubblying schews that it es at do of al men. In *Latyn,* it es, *fiat, fiat!* in *Ebru, Amen Amen* es writyn: tharfore that *Aquila* translated *vere,* vel *fideliter,* that es, *sothfastly* or *trew.*

Thus ends what the Hebrews call the *first book* of Psalms; for the reader will recollect that this book is divided by the Jews into *five* books, the first of which ends with this Psalm.

This *doxology,* Dr. *Kennicott* supposes, may have been added by the collector of this book; and he thinks that the division into *books* is *not arbitrary;* and that the Psalms were collected at different times by different persons. See the *Introduction.* There is certainly a considerable *variety* in the *style* of the several books; in the examination of which the Hebrew critic will not lose his labour.

ANALYSIS OF THE FORTY-FIRST PSALM

In this Psalm David shows how men should, and how commonly they do, carry themselves towards men in affliction and trouble.

I. They should behave compassionately and kindly, which would tend to their own happiness, and cause them to find mercy from God, ver. 1-4.

II. But they commonly behave unkindly, and afflict the afflicted, ver. 4-10.

III. On which unkindness he flies to God, and prays for mercy, ver. 11; shows his hope and confidence in God, ver. 11, 12.

I. He begins with an excellent grave sentence: "Blessed is he who considereth the poor;" that is, any man in trouble and want, &c. This is a happy man. His particular comforts and privileges are *six:*—

1. "The Lord will deliver him in the time of trouble."

2. The Lord will *preserve* him, "that he faint not in his troubles."

3. The Lord will *keep him alive.* Prolong his life and days.

4. "He shall be blessed upon earth:" God shall enrich him, and bless his substance.

5. He shall not be delivered unto the will of his enemies,—never to their full desires, though often into their hands.

6. "The Lord will strengthen him upon a bed of languishing," and make all his bed in his *sickness:* he shall have comfort and assurance of God's favour.

II. He begins the second part with an ejaculation:—

1. "I said, The Lord be merciful unto me!" pardon my sin.

2. "Heal my soul:" extract the sting of sin, and all inward corruption.

3. He prays thus, because he is sensible that he "has sinned against the Lord."

The complaint against himself being ended, he begins to complain of others.

1. Of their hatred and malice: "Mine enemies speak evil of me."

2. Of their cruelty; they longed for his death: "When shall he die, and his name perish?" they would have even his memorial cut off.

3. Their perfidious dealing and dissimulation. They came to visit him: but it was fraudulently to search out his counsels, and to entrap him in his words; and then to detail them abroad: "If he come to see me," &c.

4. Of their plots and conspiracies: "All they that hate me whisper," &c.

5. Their exultation at his misery: "An evil disease, say they, cleaveth unto him," &c.

6. Of the perfidiousness of some particular friend, perhaps Ahithophel: "Yea, mine own familiar friend hath lifted up his heel against me."

III. And then, against all these evils, and in his own defence, he prays: "But thou, O Lord, be merciful unto me, and raise me up." For which he gives these reasons:—

1. That thereby, as a king, he should have power to do justice on traitors: "That I may requite them."

2. By this he should have experience of God's favour: "By this I know thou favourest me," &c.

3. It will be a testimony unto me that thou favourest not only my person, but my cause: "As for me, thou upholdest me in mine integrity, and settest me before thy face for ever."

The Psalm, and with it the *first book* of the Psalms, according to the Jewish division, is closed with a doxology to God: "Blessed be the Lord God of Israel, from everlasting to everlasting. Amen and Amen."

PSALM XLII

The psalmist earnestly longs for the ordinances of the Lord's house, 1–4; describes his deep distress, 5–7; endeavours to take comfort from the consideration that the Lord would appear in his behalf, 8, 9; speaks of the insults of his enemies, 10; and again takes encouragement, 11.

To the chief Musician, [a]Maschil, for the sons of Korah

A S the hart [b]panteth after the water brooks, so panteth my soul after thee, O God.

2 [c]My soul thirsteth for God, for [d]the living God: when shall I come and appear before God?

---

[a]Or, A Psalm *giving instruction of the sons,* &c.; see 1 Chron. vi. 33, 37; xxv. 5

[b]Heb. *brayeth*——[c]Psa. lxiii. 1; lxxxiv. 2; John vii. 37
[d]1 Thess. i. 9

NOTES ON PSALM XLII

The *title, To the chief Musician, giving instruction to the sons of Korah.* This is the first of the Psalms that has this title prefixed, and it is probable that such Psalms were composed by the *descendants of Korah* during the Babylonish captivity, or by some eminent person among those descendants, and that they were used by the Israelites during their long captivity, as means of consolation: and, indeed, most of the Psalms which bear this inscription are of the *consoling* kind and the sentiments appear to belong to that period of the Jewish history, and to none other. The word משכיל *maskil,* from שכל *sakal,* signifies to *make wise,* to *direct wisely,* to *give instruction;* and here is so understood by our translators, who have left this signification in the *margin;* and so the *Versions* in general.

The *Syriac* says, "It is a Psalm which David sung when he was an exile, and desired to return to Jerusalem." The *Arabic* says: "A Psalm for the backsliding Jews."

Verse 1. *As the hart panteth after the water brooks*] The *hart* is not only fond of feeding near some water for the benefit of *drinking,* "but when he is hard hunted, and nearly spent, he will take to some river or brook, in which," says *Tuberville,* "he will keep as long as his breath will suffer him. Understand that when a hart is spent and sore run, his last refuge is to the water; and he will commonly descend down the streame and swimme in the very middest thereof; for he will take as good heede as he can to touch no boughes or twygges that grow upon the sides of the river, for feare lest the hounds should there take sent of him. And sometimes the hart *will lye under the water,* all but *his very nose;* and I have seene divers lye so until the hounds have been upon

3 [e]My tears have been my meat day and night, while [f]they continually say unto me, Where *is* thy God?

4 When I remember these *things*, [g]I pour out my soul in me: for I had gone with the multitude, [h]I went with them to the house of God, with the voice of joy and praise, with a multitude that kept holyday.

5 [i]Why art thou [k]cast down, O my soul? and *why* art thou disquieted in me? [l]hope thou

in God: for I shall yet [m]praise him [n]*for* the help of his countenance.

6 O my God, my soul is cast down within me: therefore will I remember thee from the land of Jordan, and of the Hermonites, from [o]the hill Mizar.

7 [p]Deep calleth unto deep at the noise of thy waterspouts: [q]all thy waves and thy billows are gone over me.

8 Yet the LORD will [r]command his loving-

---

[e]Psa. lxxx. 5; cii. 9——[f]Ver. 10; Psa. lxxix. 10; cxv. 2 [g]Job xxx. 16; Psa. lxii. 8——[h]Isa. xxx. 29——[i]Ver. 11; Psa. xliii. 5——[k]Heb. *bowed down*——[l]Lam. iii. 24 [m]Or, *give thanks*

[n]Or, *his presence* is *salvation*——[o]Or, *the little hill;* Psa. cxxxiii. 3——[p]Jer. iv. 20; Ezek. vii. 26——[q]Psa. lxxxviii. 7; Jonah ii. 3——[r]Lev. xxv. 21; Deut. xxviii. 8; Psa. cxxxiii. 3

---

them, before they would rise; for *they are constrayned to take the water as their last refuge.*"—*Tuberville's* Art of Venerie, chap. xl. Lond. 4to., 1611.

The above extracts will give a fine illustration of this passage. The hart feels himself almost entirely spent; he is nearly hunted down; the dogs are in full pursuit; he is parched with thirst; and in a burning heat pants after the water, and when he comes to the river, plunges in *as his last refuge.* Thus pursued, spent, and nearly ready to give up the ghost, the psalmist *pants for God,* for the *living God!* for him who can give *life,* and save from *death.*

Verse 2. *When shall I come*] When, when shall I have the privilege of appearing in his courts *before God?* In the mouth of a *Christian* these words would import: "*When* shall I see my heavenly country? *When* shall I come to God, the Judge of all, and to Jesus, the Mediator of the new covenant?" He who is a *stranger* and a *pilgrim* here below, and feels a heart full of piety to God, may use these words in this sense; but he who feels himself here at home, whose soul is not spiritual, wishes the earth to be eternal, and himself eternal on it—feels no panting after the *living God.*

Verse 3. *My tears have been my meat day and night*] My longing has been so intense after spiritual blessings, that I have forgotten to take my necessary food; and my sorrow has been so great, that I have had no appetite for any. I feel more for the honour of my God and his truth than for myself, when the idolaters, who have thy people in captivity, insultingly cry, *Where is thy God?*

Verse 4. *When I remember these* things] Or, *these things I shall remember.* They often occur to me, and sharpen my distressful feelings. My soul is dissolved, becomes weak as water, when I reflect on what I have had, and on what I have lost. Or, *I pour out my soul to myself* in deep regrets and complaints, when reflecting on these things. I once enjoyed all the ordinances of God, and now I have none. I once had the joyous communion of saints in God's ordinances; but that communion no longer exists, for there are no ordinances to support it. There was a *multitude* to worship God in public; with these *I often went:* but, alas, this is no more; now there are found only a few *solitary individuals* who sigh for the desolations of Zion. *There* we had our holy

days, our appointed *feasts,* to commemorate the wonderful works of the Lord; now there are no processions, no festivals, no joyous assemblies; all is desolation in Zion, and all is mourning in our captivity. I have endeavoured to give a general sense to this verse, but there are several difficulties in it; and different commentators and critics have given it a great variety of translations, and as many different meanings. My plan will not permit me to follow them. Much may be seen in Dr. *Horsley's* work on this verse.

Verse 5. *Why art thou cast down, O my soul?*] Bad as the times are, desolate as Jerusalem is, insulting as are our enemies, hopeless as in the sight of man our condition may be, yet there is no room for *despair.* All things are possible to God. We have a promise of restoration; he is as good as he is powerful; hope therefore in him.

I shall yet praise him] For my restoration from this captivity. He is the health of my soul. I shall have the *light and help of his countenance,* his approbation, and a glorious deliverance wrought by his right hand.

Verse 6. *O my God, my soul is cast down*] It is impossible for me to lighten this load; I am full of discouragements, notwithstanding I labour to hope in thee.

Therefore will I remember thee from the land of Jordan] That is, from Judea, this being the chief river of that country.

And of the Hermonites] הרמונים the *Hermons,* used in the *plural* because Hermon has a *double* ridge joining in an angle, and rising in many summits. The river *Jordan,* and the mountains of *Hermon,* were the most striking features of the holy land.

From the hill Mizar.] מהר מצער *mehar mitsar, from the little hill,* as in the *margin.* The *little hill* probably means *Sion,* which was little in comparison of the Hermons.—Bishop *Horsley.* No such hill as Mizar is known in India.

Verse 7. *Deep calleth unto deep*] One wave of sorrow rolls on me, impelled by another. There is something *dismal* in the sound of the original; תהום אל תהום קורא *tehom el tehom kore;* something like "And hollow howlings hung in air." *Thompson's Ellenore.* Or like *Homer's* well known verse:—

Βη δ' ακεων παρα θινα πολυφλοισβοιο θαλασσης.

kindness in the daytime, and ˢin the night his song *shall be* with me, *and* my prayer unto the God of my life.

9 I will say unto God my rock, Why hast thou forgotten me? ᵗwhy go I mourning because of the oppression of the enemy?

10 *As* with a ᵘsword in my bones, mine enemies reproach me; ᵛwhile they say daily unto me, Where *is* thy God?

11 ʷWhy art thou cast down, O my soul? and why art thou disquieted within me? hope thou in God: for I shall yet praise him, *who is* the health of my countenance, and my God.

ˢJob xxxv. 10; Psa. xxxii. 7; lxiii. 6; cxlix. 5——ᵗPsa. xxxviii. 6; xliii. 2

ᵘOr, *killing*——ᵛVerse 3; Joel ii. 17; Mic. vii. 10 ʷVer. 5; Psa. xliii. 5

"He went silently along the shore of the vastly-sounding sea."   Il. i., ver. 34.

The rolling up of the waves into a swell, and the break of the top of the swell, and its *dash* upon the shore, are surprisingly represented in the sound of the two last words.

The psalmist seems to represent himself as cast away at sea; and by wave impelling wave, is carried to a rock, around which the surges dash in all directions, forming *hollow* sounds in the creeks and caverns. At last, several waves breaking over him, tear him away from that rock to which he clung, and where he had a little before found a resting-place, and, apparently, an escape from danger. "All thy waves and thy billows are gone over me;" he is then whelmed in the deep, and God alone can save him.

Waterspouts] A large tube formed of clouds by means of the electric fluid, the base being uppermost, and the point of the tube let down perpendicularly from the clouds. This tube has a particular kind of *circular motion* at the point; and being hollow within, attracts vast quantities of water, which it pours down in torrents upon the earth. These spouts are frequent on the coast of Syria; and Dr. *Shaw* has often seen them at *Mount Carmel.* No doubt the psalmist had often seen them also, and the ravages made by them. I have seen vast gullies cut out of the sides of mountains by the fall of *waterspouts*, and have seen many of them in their fullest activity.

Verse 8. *The Lord will command*] Every day the Lord will give an especial commission to his loving-kindness to visit me. During the night I shall sing of his mercy and goodness; and alternately mingle my *singing* with *prayer* for a continuance of his mercy, and for power to make the best use of these visitations.

Verse 9. *I will say unto God my rock*] God, my Fortress and Support.

Why hast thou forgotten me?] This and the following verse is badly pointed in our Bibles: "Why go I mourning as with a sword in my bones because of the oppression of the enemy? Mine enemies reproach me daily, while they say unto me, Where is thy God?" See on ver. 3. Their reproaches are to my soul as cutting and severe as a sword thrust into my body, and separating between my bones; because these reproaches are intended to fall on thee, my God, as if thou hadst not power to save us from the hands of our oppressors.

Verse 11. *Why art thou cast down*] There is no reason why thou shouldst despair. God will appear and release thee and thy brother captives and soon thy sighing and sorrowing shall flee away.

Who is the health of my countenance] As a healthy state of the constitution shows itself in the appearance of the face; God will so rejoice thy heart, heal all thy spiritual maladies, that thy face shall testify the happiness that is within thee.

There is a curious gloss on the first verse of this Psalm in my old *Psalter*, which I cannot withhold from the reader. The author translates and paraphrases the verse thus:—

Trans. Als þe Hert ȝernes til þe welles of waters; so my saule ȝernes til þe God.

Par. This Psalm es al of perfite men, that er brinnand in the flamme of Goddes luf, and passes in til the contemplatyf lif: and tharfore it es sungen in the office of the dede men: for than haf thai, that thai yearned; that es, the syght of God. Far thi, sais he, *als the Hert that has eten the nedder, gretely yernes to com til the welles of waters for to drynk and wax yong ogayne:* so destroyed in me vices and unclennes, my saule desyres with brinnand yernyng, to come til the God.

Ælian, Appian, Aristotle, Nicander, and *Pliny,* all inform us that one cause why the hart thirsts for the waters is, that *they eat serpents,* and that the *poison* of them diffused through their entrails produces a *burning heat* and *fever,* to ease and cure themselves of which they have recourse to *water.* Many of the *fathers* tell the same tale, and from them the paraphrast in the old Psalter has borrowed what is inserted above: "Like as the hart, which has eaten the adder, greatly longs to come to the fountains of water to drink, that he may grow young again." The hart is undoubtedly a *cunning* animal; but it would be as difficult to believe that he *eats serpents* as it would be to believe that he seeks for and eats the *fresh water crab* or *cray fish,* in order to cure and make him grow young again, as *Eusebius, Didymus, Theodoret, Jerome, Epiphanius, Gregory Nyssen,* and others of the primitive fathers gravely inform us.

ANALYSIS OF THE FORTY-SECOND PSALM

The psalmist, driven from the assemblies of God's people, complains; and as men overwhelmed with troubles are also oppressed with grief, so is he; and as they abruptly express their thoughts, so does he; for sometimes he *expostulates,* sometimes he *complains,* sometimes he *corrects* and *checks* himself for his weakness. One while he opens his *doubts,* and presently again sets forth his *confidence* in God. It is difficult on this account to analyze this Psalm; but it may be reduced to these *four heads:*—

I. The zeal of the psalmist to serve God in God's own house; ver. 1, 2, 4, 6.

II. His complaint and expressions of grief for

his absence, for his affliction, and his enemies' insults on that ground; ver. 3, 4, 7, 10.

III. His expostulation with his soul for its diffidence, ver. 5, 6; and again with God for his desertion, ver. 9.

IV. His faith and confidence in God's promises; ver. 5, 8, 11.

I. 1. He begins with an expression of his grief for his exile from the ordinances of God, and the assemblies of his people. And he sets forth his zeal and longing desire under the expressive similitude of a hard-hunted and thirsty stag: "As the hart panteth," &c.; ver. 1, 2.

2. He shows the state he was in. 1. "My tears have been my meat day and night;" ver. 3. 2. And the cause was the bitter sarcasm of his enemies: "Where is now thy God?" Where is thy Protector? him in whom thou trustest?

II. That which added to his grief was that which gave occasion to this sarcasm, his banishment from the sanctuary.

1. When I remember these things, my absence, their insults, I pour out my heart to myself; *tear* follows *tear*, and one complaint succeeds to another.

2. And much reason I have to grieve when I compare my present with my former condition. Formerly "I went with the multitude to the house of God,—with the voice of joy and praise," &c. I had *gone; now I cannot* and *must not go.*

III. Hitherto he had expressed his zeal, his sorrow, and his complaints, with their causes. These put his soul in a sad condition; and thus he expostulates with himself:—

1. Blaming himself for his weakness and diffidence: "Why art thou cast down, O my soul," &c.

2. Then presently fortifies himself in God's promises: "Hope thou in God, for I shall yet praise him," &c.

In all which is described the combat that a good man has when he is in heaviness through manifold temptation, and finds great difficulty to struggle between hope and despair; but at last conquers by faith, and inherits the promises.

3. But his conflict is not yet over; he exclaims again, and still more affectingly, "O my God, my soul is cast down." Of which he assigns two causes:—

1. That though he was ready to remember and serve God, yet he was forced to do it in an improper place. He remembered the pleasant *land of Palestine*, the stately *mountains of Hermon*, and the *little hill of Sion:* but *there* he could not worship; he was in an enemy's country, and in captivity in that country.

2. The greatness and continual succession of his troubles: "Deep calleth unto deep." Calamity on calamity, one trial on the heels of another; so that he might well say, "All thy waves and thy billows are gone over me."

3. And yet he despairs not, he encourages himself in the Lord: "Yet the Lord will command his loving-kindness," &c. 1. "His song shall be with me." 2. "And my prayer unto the God of my life."

IV. On which he grows more confident and courageous, and again expostulates, not now with his *soul*, as before, but with his GOD: "I will say unto God my rock."

1. "Why hast thou forgotten me?"

2. "Why go I mourning because of the oppression of the enemy?"

3. Why am I wounded with grief, "as with a sword in my bones," while they use the sarcasm, "Where is now thy God?"

But in the conclusion, after all his complaints and expostulations, he gains a full assurance of God's favour and protection.

1. Chiding himself for his discontent and diffidence, "Why art thou cast down?"

2. Then he encourages his heart in God's goodness and faithfulness: "Hope thou in God, for I shall yet praise him, who is the health of my countenance, and my God."

The *forty-third* is most probably a part of this Psalm: they should be read and expounded together, as the subject is not complete in either, taken as separate Psalms. See, therefore, on the following.

PSALM XLIII

The psalmist begs God to take his part against his enemies, 1, 2; to send his light and truth to guide him to the tabernacle, 3; promises, if brought thither, to be faithful in the Divine service, 4; chides himself for despondency, and takes courage, 5.

JUDGE [a]me, O God, and [b]plead my cause against an [c]ungodly nation: O deliver me [d]from the deceitful and unjust man.

2 For thou *art* the God of [e]my strength: why dost thou cast me off? [f]why go I mourning because of the oppression of the enemy?

---

[a]Psalm xxvi. 1; xxxv. 24——[b]Psalm xxxv. 1——[c]Or, *unmerciful*

[d]Heb. *from a man of deceit and iniquity*——[e]Psalm xxviii. 7——[f]Psa. xlii. 9

NOTES ON PSALM XLIII

There is no *title* to this Psalm in the *Hebrew*, nor in the *Chaldee*. The *Syriac* says it was composed "by David when Jonathan told him that Saul intended to slay him." The *Arabic* says of this, as of the preceding, that it is a *prayer for the backsliding Jews.* It is most evidently on the same subject with the *forty-* second Psalm, had the same author or authors, and contains the remaining part of the complaint of the captive Jews in Babylon. It is written as a part of the *forty-second* Psalm in *forty-six* of *Kennicott's* and *De Rossi's* MSS.

Verse 1. *Judge me, O God, and plead my cause*] ריבה ריבי *ribah ribi*, a forensic term, properly enough translated, *plead my cause, be my counsellor and advocate.*

3 ᵍO send out thy light and thy truth: let them lead me; let them bring me unto ʰthy holy hill, and to thy tabernacles.

4 Then will I go unto the altar of God, unto God ˡmy exceeding joy: yea, upon the harp will I praise thee, O God **my** God.

5 ᵏWhy art thou cast down, O my soul? and why art thou disquieted within me? hope in God: for I shall yet praise him, *who is* the health of my countenance, and my God.

ᵍPsa. xl. 11; lvii. 3——ʰPsa. iii. 4

ˡHeb. *the gladness of my joy*——ᵏPsa. xlii. 5, 11

Ungodly nation] The Babylonians; the impious, perfidious, wicked, and deceitful Babylonians.

The deceitful and unjust man.] Nebuchadnezzar.

Verse 2. *For thou* art *the God of my strength*] The psalmist speaks here, as in other places, in the person of the whole Israelitish people then captive in Babylon. We still acknowledge thee for our God. *Why are we cast off?* Now that we are humbled and penitent, why are we not enlarged? Why are we not saved from this oppression of the Babylonians?

Verse 3. *O send out thy light and thy truth*] We are in *darkness* and *distress*, O send *light* and *prosperity;* we look for the fulfilment of thy *promises;* O send forth thy *truth.* Let thy *light* guide me to thy *holy hill*, to the country of my fathers; let thy *truth* lead me to thy tabernacles, there to worship thee in *spirit* and in *truth.*

Verse 4. *Then will I go unto the altar*] When thy *light*—a *favourable turn in our affairs*, leads us to the land of our fathers, and thy *truth*—the *fulfilment of thy gracious promises*, has placed us again at the door of thy tabernacles, then will we go to *thy altar,* and joyfully offer those sacrifices and offerings which thy law requires, and rejoice in thee with exceeding great joy.

Verse 5. *Why art thou cast down*] Though our deliverance be delayed, God has not forgotten to be gracious. The vision, the prophetic declaration relative to our captivity, was for an appointed time. Though it appear to tarry, we must wait for it. In the end it will come, and will not tarry; why then should we be discouraged? Let us still continue to trust in God, for we *shall yet praise him* for the fullest proofs of his approbation in a great outpouring of his benedictions.

ANALYSIS OF THE FORTY-THIRD PSALM

This Psalm, which is of the same nature with the former, and properly a part or continuation of it, contains *two chief* things:—

I. A *petition*, which is double. 1. One in the *first* verse. 2. The other in the *fourth* verse.

II. A *comfortable apostrophe* to his own soul, ver. 5.

First, He petitions God,—

1. That, being *righteous*, he would be his Judge: "Judge me, O Lord."

2. That, being *merciful*, he would plead his cause: "Plead my cause."

3. That, being *almighty*, he would deliver him: "Deliver me," ver. 1.

For this petition he assigns *two* reasons:—

1. The unmerciful disposition of his enemies. 1. They were a factious, bloody, inhuman people: "Plead my cause against an ungodly nation," גוי לא חסיד *goi lo chasid*, "a people without mercy." 2. They were men of deceit and iniquity: "Deliver me from the deceitful and unjust man," ver. 1.

2. The other reason he draws from the nature of God, and his relation to him: "For thou art the God of my strength." Thou hast promised to defend me. On this he expostulates: 1. "Why hast thou cast me off?" For so, to the eye of sense, it at present appears. 2. "Why go I mourning, because of the oppression of the enemy?" ver. 2.

Secondly, The second part of his petition is, that he may be restored to God's favour, and brought back to his own country, ver. 3.

1. "O send forth thy light and thy truth," the light of thy favour and countenance, and make thy promises true to me: "Let them lead me," ver. 3.

2. "Let them guide me;"—whither? To dignity and honours? No, I ask not those: I ask to be guided to thy holy hill and tabernacles, where I may enjoy the exercises of piety in thy pure worship, ver. 3.

Thirdly, That he might the better move God to hear his petition, he does as good as *vow* that he would be thankful, and make it known how good God had been to him.

1. "Then will I go unto the altar of God, my exceeding joy." The joy and content he would take in this should not be of an ordinary kind.

2. "Yea, upon the harp will I praise thee, O God." His joy should be expressed outwardly by a Psalm, doubtless composed for the occasion; the singing of which should be accompanied by the *harp*, or such instruments of music as were *then* commonly used in the Divine worship.

The petitions being ended, and now confident of audience and favour, he thus addresses his heavy and mournful heart, as in the former Psalm: 1. Chiding himself. 2. Encouraging himself.

1. "Why art thou cast down, O my soul? and why art thou disquieted within me?" Chiding.

2. "Hope in God: for I shall yet praise him, who is the health of my countenance, and my God." Encouraging. See notes and analysis of the preceding Psalm.

PSALM XLIV

The psalmist recounts the mercies of God; shows to his people how God in ancient times gave them the victory over all their enemies, 1–8; points out their present miserable state, 9–16; asserts that they have not apostatized, and appeals to God for the truth of his assertion, 17–22; and calls upon the Lord for deliverance from their enemies, 23–26.

IX. DAY. MORNING PRAYER

To the chief Musician for the sons of Korah, Maschil

WE have heard with our ears, O God, [a]our fathers have told us, *what* work thou didst in their days, in the times of old.

2 *How* [b]thou didst drive out the heathen with thy hand, and plantedst them: *how* thou didst afflict the people, and cast them out.

3 For [c]they got not the land in possession by their own sword, neither did their own arm save them: but thy right hand, and thine arm, and the light of thy countenance, [d]because thou hadst a favour unto them.

4 [e]Thou art my King, O God: command deliverances for Jacob.

5 Through thee [f]will we push down our enemies: through thy name will we tread them under that rise up against us.

6 For [g]I will not trust in my bow, neither shall my sword save me.

7 But thou hast saved us from our enemies, and [h]hast put them to shame that hated us.

8 [i]In God we boast all the day long, and praise thy name for ever.   Selah.

9 But [k]thou hast cast off, and put us to shame; and goest not forth with our armies.

10 Thou makest us to [l]turn back from the enemy: and they which hate us spoil for themselves.

11 [m]Thou hast given us [n]like sheep *appointed* for meat; and hast [o]scattered us among the heathen.

---

[a]Exod. xii. 26, 27; Psa. lxxviii. 3——[b]Exod. xv. 17; Deut. vii. 1; Psa. lxxviii. 55; lxxx. 8——[c]Deut. viii. 17; Josh. xxiv. 12——[d]Deut. iv. 37; vii. 7, 8——[e]Psa. lxxiv. 12——[f]Dan. viii. 4——[g]Psa. xxxiii. 16; Hos. i. 7 [h]Psa. xl. 14

[i]Psa. xxxiv. 2; Jer. ix. 24; Rom. ii. 17——[k]Psa. lx. 1, 10; lxxiv. 1; lxxxviii. 14; lxxxix. 38; cviii. 11——[l]Lev. xxvi. 17; Deut. xxviii. 25; Josh. vii. 8, 12——[m]Rom. viii. 36——[n]Heb. *as sheep of meat*——[o]Deut. iv. 27; xxviii. 64; Psa. lx. 1

NOTES ON PSALM XLIV

The *title* here is the same as that in Psa. xlii.; which see.   The *Syriac* says it was "A Psalm of the sons of Korah, which the people and Moses sung at Horeb." Such titles are fancies to which no credit should be attached. Like the preceding, it appears to belong to the time of the *captivity.*

Verse 1. *We have heard with our ears*] The psalmist begins with recounting the marvellous interpositions of God in behalf of the Jewish people, that he might the better strengthen his confidence, and form a ground on which to build his expectation of additional help.

Verse 2. *Thou didst drive out the heathen*] The Canaanites were as a bad tree planted in a good soil, and bringing forth bad fruit with great luxuriance. God plucked up this bad tree from the roots, and in its place planted the Hebrews as a good tree, a good vine, and caused them to take root, and fill the land.

Verse 3. *For they got not the land*] Neither by their valour, nor cunning, nor for their merit; yet, they were obliged to fight.   But how did they conquer?   By the right hand of the Lord, and by his arm; by his strength alone, and the *light of his countenance*—his favour most manifestly shown unto them.

Verse 4. *Thou art my king*]   What thou wert to *them,* be to *us.* We believe in thee as they did; we have sinned and are in captivity, but we repent and turn unto thee; command, therefore, deliverances to Jacob, for we are the descendants of him in whose behalf thou hast wrought such wonders.

Verse 5. *Through thee will we push down*] *Through thy* WORD, במימרא *bemeimra,* "Thy substantial Word."—*Chaldee.* If thou be with us, who can be successfully against us?   Literally, "We will toss them in the air with our horn;" a metaphor taken from an ox or bull tossing the dogs into the air which attack him.

Through thy name]   Jehovah; the infinite, the omnipotent, the eternal Being; whose power none is able to resist.

Verse 6. *I will not trust in my bow*]   As he is speaking of what God had already done for his forefathers, these words should be read in the *past* tense: "We have not trusted," &c.

Verse 8. *In God we boast*]   We have told the heathen how great and powerful our God is.   If thou do not deliver us by thy mighty power, they will not believe our report, but consider that we are held in bondage by the superior strength of their gods.

Verse 9. *But thou hast cast off*]   Our enemies have dominion over us.

And goest not forth with our armies.]   Were we to attempt to muster our several tribes, and form a *host,* like our fathers when they came out of Egypt, thou wouldst not accompany us as thou didst them: the horses and chariots of the Babylonians would soon overtake and destroy us.

Verse 10. *Thou makest us to turn back*]   This thou didst: and our enemies, profiting by the occasion, finding our strength was departed from us, made us an easy prey, captivated our persons, and spoiled us of our property.

Verse 11. *And hast scattered us among the heathen.*]   This most evidently alludes to the

12 [p]Thou sellest thy people [q]for nought, and dost not increase *thy wealth* by their price.

13 [r]Thou makest us a reproach to our neighbours, a scorn and a derision to them that are round about us.

14 [s]Thou makest us a byword among the heathen, [t]a shaking of the head among the people.

15 My confusion *is* continually before me, and the shame of my face hath covered me,

16 For the voice of him that reproacheth and blasphemeth; [u]by reason of the enemy and avenger.

17 [v]All this is come upon us; yet have we not forgotten thee, neither have we dealt falsely in thy covenant.

18 Our heart is not turned back, [w]neither have our [x]steps declined from thy way.

19 Though thou hast sore broken us in [y]the place of dragons, and covered us [z]with the shadow of death.

20 If we have forgotten the name of our God, or [a]stretched out our hands to a strange god;

21 [b]Shall not God search this out? for he knoweth the secrets of the heart.

22 [c]Yea, for thy sake are we killed all the day long; we are counted as sheep for the slaughter.

23 [d]Awake, why sleepest thou, O LORD? arise, [e]cast *us* not off for ever.

24 [f]Wherefore hidest thou thy face, *and* forgettest our affliction and our oppression?

[p]Isa. lii. 3, 4; Jer. xv. 13——[q]Heb. *without riches* [r]Deut. xxviii. 37; Psa. lxxix. 4; lxxx. 6——[s]Jer. xxiv. 9——[t]2 Kings xix. 21; Job xvi. 4; Psa. xxii. 7——[u]Psa. viii. 2——[v]Dan. ix. 13——[w]Job xxiii. 11; Psalm cxix. 51, 157——[x]Or, *goings*

[y]Isa. xxxiv. 13; xxxv. 7——[z]Psa. xxiii. 4——[a]Job xi. 13; Psa. lxviii. 31——[b]Job xxxi. 14; Psa. cxxxix. 1; Jer. xvii. 10——[c]Rom. viii. 36——[d]Psa. vii. 6; xxxv. 23; lix. 4, 5; lxxviii. 65——[e]Ver. 9——[f]Job xiii. 24; Psa. xiii. 1; lxxxviii. 14

captivity. From the successful wars of the kings of Assyria and Chaldea against the kings of Israel and Judah, and the dispersion of the tribes under Tiglath-pileser, Shalmaneser, and Nebuchadnezzar, Jews have been found in every province of the east; there they settled, and there their successors may be found to the present day.

Verse 12. *Thou sellest thy people for nought*] An allusion to the mode of disposing of slaves by their proprietors or sovereigns. Instead of seeking profit, thou hast made us a present to our enemies.

Verse 14. *Thou makest us a byword*] We are evidently abandoned by thee, and are become so very miserable in consequence, that we are a proverb among the people: "See the Hebrews! *see their misery and wretchedness! see how low the wrath of God has brought down an offending people!*" And the worst curse that can be imprecated against a wicked nation is: "*Mayest thou become as wretched as the Jews;*" or as the old *Psalter:* "**Thou has seet us reprobe til our neghburs: scornyng and hethyng til tha that er in our umgang.** That es, gref, tourment that es of our neghburs, and that hethyng es noght sone gave or passand, that we suffer of tha, that er al aboute us. When men sais *so byfal ye, als byfel him.*"

Verse 17. *Yet have we not forgotten thee*] These are bold words; but they must be understood in a qualified sense. We have not *apostatized* from thee; we have not *fallen into idolatry.* And this was strictly true: the charge of idolatry could never be brought against the Jewish nation from the time of the captivity, with sufficient evidence to support it.

Verse 19. *Thou hast sore broken us in the place of dragons*] Thou hast delivered us into the hands of a fierce, cruel, and murderous people. We, as a people, are in a similar state to one who has strayed into a wilderness, where there are no human inhabitants; who hears nothing round about him but the hissing of serpents, the howling of beasts of prey, and the terrible roaring of the lion; and who expects every moment to be devoured.

Verse 20. *If we have forgotten the name of our God*] *That name,* יהוה *Yehovah,* by which the true God was particularly distinguished, and which implied the exclusion of all other objects of adoration.

Or stretched out our hands] Made supplication; offered prayer or adoration to any *strange god*—a god that we had not known, nor had been acknowledged by our fathers. It has already been remarked, that from the time of the Babylonish captivity the Jews never relapsed into idolatry.

It was customary among the ancients, while praying, to *stretch out their hands* towards the *heavens,* or the *image* they were worshipping, as if they expected to *receive* the favour they were asking.

Verse 21. *Shall not God search this out?*] We confidently appeal to the true God, the searcher of hearts, for the truth of this statement.

Verse 22. *For thy sake are we killed all the day long*] Because of our attachment to thee and to thy religion, we are exposed to continual death; and some of us fall a daily sacrifice to the persecuting spirit of our enemies, and we all carry our lives continually in our hands. In the same state were the primitive Christians; and St. Paul applies these words to their case, Rom. viii. 36.

Verse 23. *Awake, why sleepest thou, O Lord?*] That is, Why dost thou appear as one asleep, who is regardless of the safety of his friends. This is a *freedom of speech* which can only be allowed to inspired men; and in their mouths it is always to be *figuratively* understood.

Verse 24. *Wherefore hidest thou thy face*] Show us the cause why thou withdrawest from us the testimony of thy approbation.

25 For ^gour soul is bowed down to the dust: our belly cleaveth unto the earth.

26 Arise ^hfor our help, and redeem us for thy mercies' sake.

---

^gPsa. cxix. 25

^hHeb. *a help for us*

Verse 25. *Our soul is bowed down*] Our life is drawing near to the grave. If thou delay to help us, we shall become extinct.

Verse 26. *Arise for our help*] Show forth thy power in delivering us from the hands of our enemies.

Redeem us] Ransom us from our thraldom.

For thy mercies' sake.] לְמַעַן חַסְדֶּךָ *lemaan chasdecha, On account of thy mercy.* That we may have that proper view of thy mercy which we should have, and that we may magnify it as we ought to do, redeem us. The Vulgate has, Redime nos, propter nomen tuum, "Redeem us on account of thy name;" which the old *Psalter* thus paraphrases: "Help us in ryghtwysness, and by us (buy,) that es, delyver us, that we be withouten drede; and al this for thi name Jehsu; noght for oure merite."

ANALYSIS OF THE FORTY-FOURTH PSALM

In this Psalm are livelily expressed the sufferings, the complaints, the assurances, the petitions which are offered to God by good men, who suffer, together with others, in the common afflictions that God brings on his people.

The parts are *two:*—

I. A *petition* from ver. 24 to the end.

II. The *arguments* by which the petition is quickened, from ver. 1 to 24.

First, He begins with the *arguments*, of which the first is drawn from God's goodness, of which he gives in particular, his benefits and miracles done for their fathers; as if he had said, "This thou didst for them; why art thou so estranged from us?"

I. "We have heard with our ears, O God, and our fathers have told us what works thou didst in their days, and in the times of old." The particulars of which are,—

1. "How thou didst drive out the heathen," namely, the Canaanites.

2. "How thou plantedst them."

3. "How thou didst afflict the people, and cast them out," ver. 2.

II. This we acknowledge to be thy word; expressed thus:—

1. "How thou didst drive out the heathen;" negatively, by remotion of what some might imagine: "They got not the land in possession by their own sword, neither was it their own arm that helped them," ver. 3. "Not unto us, O Lord, not unto us, but unto thy name be the praise."

2. "How thou plantedst them;" positively: "For it was thy right hand and thy arm, and the light of thy countenance." A mere *gratuito*: "because thou hadst a favour unto them;" no other reason can be assigned but that, ver. 3.

3. Upon this consideration, by an apostrophe, he turns his speech to God, and sings a song of triumph, of which the strains are,—

1. An open confession: "Thou art my king, O God."

2. A petition: "Send help unto Jacob," ver. 4.

3. A confident persuasion of future victory; but still with God's help and assistance, ver. 5, 6, 7. 1. "Through thee will we push down our

enemies." 2. "Through thee will we tread them under that rise up against us." All through thee; *in thy name, by thy power.*

4. An abrenunciation of his own power or arm: "For I will not trust in my bow, neither shall my sword save me."

5. A reiteration, or a second ascription of the whole victory to God: "But thou hast saved us from our enemies; thou hast put them to shame that hated us," ver. 7.

6. A grateful return of thanks; which is indeed the tribute God expects, and which we are to pay upon our deliverance: "In God we boast all the day long, and praise thy name for ever."

Secondly, The second argument by which he wings his petition is drawn from the condition which, for the present, God's people were in, before he had done wonders for their deliverance; but now he had delivered them to the will of their enemies. This would move a man to think that his good will was changed toward them: "But thou hast cast us off, and put us to shame, and goest not forth with our armies."

Of which the consequences are many and grievous, although we acknowledge that all is from thee, and comes from thy hand and permission.

1. The *first* is: "Thou makest us to turn back from the enemy," ver. 10.

2. The *second*, We become a prey: "They which hate us spoil for themselves," ver. 10.

3. The *third*, We are devoured: "Thou hast given us as sheep appointed for meat;" killed cruelly, and when they please, ver. 11.

4. The *fourth*, We are driven from our country, and made to dwell where they will plant us: "Thou hast scattered us among the heathen;" (inter gentes,) and that is a great discomfort, to live among people *without God in the world*.

5. The *fifth*, We are become slaves, sold and bought as beasts; and that for any price, upon any exchange: "Thou sellest thy people for nought, and dost not increase thy wealth by their price," ver. 12; puts them off as worthless things.

6. The *sixth*, We are made a scorn, a mock; and to whom? To our enemies: but that might be borne; but even to our friends and neighbours: "Thou makest us a reproach to our neighbours, a scorn and derision to them that are round about us."

And this he amplifies,—

1. From the circumstance that they are a proverb of reproach: "Thou makest us a byword among the heathen."

That in scorn any one that would used a scornful gesture toward them: "We are become a shaking of the head among the people."

3. That this insulting is continual: "My confusion is daily before me."

4. It is superlative; shame so great that he had not what to say to it: "The shame of my face hath covered me."

5. It is public; their words and gestures are not concealed; they speak out what they please: "Ashamed I am for the voice of him that reproacheth and blasphemeth; for the enemy and avenger."

Thirdly, And yet he useth a third argument, that the petition may be the more grateful, and more easily granted; drawn from the constancy and perseverance of God's people in the profession of the truth, notwithstanding this heavy loss, persecution, and affliction: "All this is come upon us;"—thus we are oppressed, devoured, banished, sold, derided; *yet* we continue to be thy servants still, we retain our faith, hope, service.

1. *We have not forgotten thee*, not forgotten thou art our God. We acknowledge no idols.

2. *We have not dealt falsely in thy covenant.* We have not juggled in thy service, dealing with any side for our advantage, renouncing our integrity.

3. *Our heart is not turned back.* Our heart is upright, not turned back to the idols our fathers worshipped.

4. *Our steps are not gone out of thy way.* Slip we may, but not revolt; no, not though great calamities are come upon us. 1. *Broken.* 2. *Broken in the place of dragons*, i. e., enemies fierce as dragons. 3. *Though covered with the shadow of death.* Now, that all this is true we call our God to witness, who knoweth the very secrets of the heart, and is able to revenge it: "We have not forgotten the name of our God, or stretched out our hands," &c. "Shall not God search it out? for he knows the very secret of the heart."

Fourthly. But the last argument is more pressing than the other three. It is not for any thing we have done to those that oppress us, that we are thus persecuted by them; it is for

thee, it is because we profess thy name, and rise up in defence of thy truth: "Yea, for thy sake are we killed all the day long; for thy sake are we counted as sheep for the slaughter." The sum then is: Since thou hast been a good God to our fathers; since we suffered great things under bitter tyrants; since, notwithstanding all our sufferings, we are constant to thy truth; since these our sufferings are for thee, *for thy sake*, thy truth; therefore *awake, arise, help us*, for upon these grounds he commences his petition.

II. This is the *second* part of the Psalm, which begins at ver. 23, and continues to the end, in which petition there are these degrees:—

1. That God, who to flesh and blood, in the calamities of his Church, seems to sleep, would awake and put an end to their trouble: "Awake, why sleepest thou, O Lord," ver. 23.

2. That he would arise and judge their cause, and not seem to neglect them as abjects: "Arise, cast us not off for ever," ver. 23.

3. That he would show them some favour, and not seem to forget their miseries: "Wherefore hidest thou thy face, and forgettest our affliction and oppression?"

4. *Lastly*, That he would be their helper, and actually deliver them: "Arise for our help, and redeem us for thy mercies' sake."

And that this petition might be the sooner and more readily granted, he briefly repeats the second argument: "For our soul is bowed down to the dust, our belly cleaveth to the earth," ver. 25. Brought we are as low as low may be, even to the dust, to death, to the grave.

PSALM XLV

The contents of this Psalm are generally summed up thus: The majesty and grace of Christ's kingdom; or an epithalamium of Jesus Christ and the Christian Church; the duty of this Church, and its privileges. The Psalm contains a magnificent description of the beauty, ornaments, valour, justice, and truth of the Divine Bridegroom; the beauty, magnificence, and riches of the bride, who was to become mother of a numerous and powerful posterity. The preamble is found in the title and verse 1. The description and character of the Bridegroom, 2–9. The address to the bride by her companions, 10–15. A prediction of her numerous and glorious descendants, 16, 17.

To the chief Musician [a]upon Shoshannim, for the sons of Korah, [b]Maschil,

A Song of loves

A. M. cir. 2996
B. C. cir. 1008
Salomonis, Reg.
Israelitarum,
cir. annum
8

MY heart [c]is inditing a good matter: I speak of the things which I have made touching the king: my

tongue *is* the pen of a ready writer.

2 Thou art fairer than the children of men: [d]grace is poured into thy lips: therefore God hath blessed thee for ever.

A. M. cir. 2996
B. C. cir. 1008
Salomonis, Reg.
Israelitarum,
cir. annum
8

---

[a]Psa. lxix., lxxx. title——[b]Or, *of instruction*

[c]Heb. *boileth* or *bubbleth up*——[d]Luke iv. 22

NOTES ON PSALM XLV

The title is nearly the same with that of Psalm lxix. and lxxx. "To the chief musician, *or master of the band of those who played* on the six-stringed instruments, giving instruction, for the sons of Korah; a song of loves, *or amatory ode;* or a song of the beloved maids." The *Vulgate* and *Septuagint* have, *For those who shall be changed*, or brought into another

state, which some have interpreted as relating to the *resurrection of the just;* but if I could persuade myself that the title came by Divine inspiration, I would say it more properly belonged to the calling and conversion of the Gentiles, and bringing them over from idolatry to the worship of the true God. By some the word שׁשׁנּים *shoshannim*, is translated *lilies;* and a world of labour has been spent to prove that these *lilies* mean the saints, Jesus Christ

A. M. cir. 2996
B. C. cir. 1008
Salomonis, Reg.
Israelitarum,
cir. annum
8

3 Gird thy °sword upon *thy* thigh, 'O *most* mighty, with thy glory and thy majesty.

4 ᵍAnd in thy majesty ʰride

prosperously because of truth and meekness *and* righteousness; and thy right hand shall teach thee terrible things.

A. M. cir. 2996
B. C. cir. 1008
Salomonis, Reg.
Israelitarum,
cir. annum
8

°Isa. xlix. 2; Heb. iv. 12; Rev. i. 16; xix. 15——'Isa. ix. 6——ᵍRev. vi. 2——ʰHeb. *prosper thou, ride thou*

---

himself, and the Divine light which is a banner to them that fear him. I cannot believe that any such meaning is intended, and, consequently, I cannot attempt to interpret the Psalm after this model. I believe it to be an epithalamium, or nuptial song, which primarily respected Solomon's marriage with the daughter of Pharaoh; and that it probably has a prophetic reference to the conversion of the Gentiles, and the final aggrandisement of the Christian Church.

Verse 1. *My heart is inditing a good matter*] רחש *rachash*, boileth or bubbleth up, as in the margin. It is a metaphor taken from a fountain that sends up its waters from the earth in this way. The Vulgate has *eructavit*, which is most literally translated by the old Psalter: 𝔐i 𝔥ert rpfteb gube 𝔴orb. Bealcetteb 𝔥eopte min. *My heart belcheth.*—Anglo-Saxon.

I speak of the things which I have made touching the king] אמר אני מעשי למלך, literally, "I dedicate my work unto the king." Or, as the *Psalter*, 𝕴 𝔰ap mp 𝔴erkes til t𝔥e 𝔨png. This was the general custom of the Asiatic poets. They repeated their works before princes and honourable men; and especially those parts in which there was either a direct or constructive compliment to the great man. Virgil is reported to have a part of his Æneid before Augustus, who was so pleased with it that he ordered *ten sestertia* to be given him for every line. And the famous Persian poet Ferdusi read a part of his Shah Nameh before Sultan Mahmoud, who promised him *thirty thousand* denars for the poem.

My tongue is the pen of a ready writer.] I shall compose and speak as fluently the Divine matter which is now in my heart, as the most expert scribe can write from my recitation. 𝔐p tung of maister s𝔴iftlp 𝔴rptanb. "That es, my tung is pen of the Haly Gast; and nout but als his instrument, wham he ledis als he wil. For I speke noght bot that he settis on my tung; als the pen dos noght withouten the writer. 𝔖𝔴pttlp 𝔴rptanb, for the vertu of goddes inspiracioun is noght for to thynk with mons study, that he schewes til other of the purete of heven; that es some for to com that he wrytes."—Old *Psalter*.

Verse 2. *Thou art fairer than the children of men*] By whom are these words spoken? As this is a regular epithalamium, we are to consider that the bride and bridegroom have compliments paid them by those called the friends of the bridegroom, and the companions or maids of the bride. But it seems that the whole Psalm, except the first verse, was spoken by those who are called in the title ידידת *yedidoth*, the *beloved maids*, or *female companions*, who begin with his perfections, and then describe hers. And afterwards there is a prophetical declaration concerning his issue. We may, therefore, consider that what is spoken here is spoken by companions of the bride, or what are called *yedidoth* in the *title*. It would be unauthenticated to say Solomon was the most

beautiful man in the universe; but to the perfections of the Lord Jesus they may be safely applied.

Grace is poured into thy lips] This probably refers to his speech, or the gracious words which he spoke. Solomon was renowned for wisdom, and especially the wisdom of his conversation. The queen of Sheba came from the uttermost parts of the land to hear the wisdom of Solomon; and so far did she find him exceeding all his fame, that she said *one half had not been told her:* but behold, *a greater than Solomon is here. No man ever spoke like this man,* his enemies themselves being judges.

God hath blessed thee for ever.] This, I am afraid, could in no sense be ever spoken of Solomon; but of the man Christ Jesus it is strictly true.

Verse 3. *Gird thy sword upon thy thigh, O most mighty*] This clause should be translated, *O hero, gird thy sword upon thy thigh!* This, I think, cannot be spoken of Solomon. He was not a warlike prince: he never did any feats of arms. It has been said he would have been a warrior, if he had had enemies; it might have been so: but the words more properly apply to Christ, who is King of kings, and Lord of lords; whose sword with two edges, proceeding from his mouth, cuts all his adversaries to pieces.

With thy glory and thy majesty.] Be as warlike as thou art glorious and majestic. Solomon's court was splendid, and his person was majestic. These words may be well said of him. But the majesty and glory of Christ are above all: he is higher than all the kings of the earth; and has a name above every name; and at it every knee shall bend, and every tongue confess.

Verse 4. *In thy majesty ride prosperously*] These words cannot be spoken of Solomon; they are true only of Christ. His *riding* is the prosperous progress of his Gospel over the earth. He uses no sword but the sword of the Spirit; and what religion, system of truth, pretended or real, ever made such progress as the religion of Christ has done, without one sword being ever drawn to propagate it from the first introduction of Christianity to the present time? His Gospel is TRUTH, proclaiming HUMILITY, ענוה *anvah*, and RIGHTEOUSNESS. This, indeed, is the *sum* of the Gospel; and an *epitome* of its operations in the hearts of men. 1. The Gospel is a revelation of *eternal* TRUTH, in opposition to all *false* systems of religion, and to all *figurative* and *ceremonial representations* of the true religion. It is *truth* concerning GOD, his NATURE, and his WORKS. It is *truth* concerning MAN, his ORIGIN, his INTENTS, his DUTIES, and his END. It is truth in what it says concerning the *natural*, the *moral*, and the *invisible world*. 2. It teaches the doctrine of *meekness* or HUMILITY; opposes *pride* and *vain glory;* strips man of his *assumed merits;* proclaims and enforces the *necessity* of humiliation or repentance because of sin, *humiliation* under the

A. M. cir. 2996
B. C. cir. 1008
Salomonis, Reg.
Israelitarum,
cir. annum
8
5 Thine ¹arrows *are* sharp in the heart of the king's enemies; *whereby* the people fall under thee.

6 ᵏThy throne, O God, *is* for ever and ever: the sceptre of thy kingdom *is* a right sceptre.

7 ¹Thou lovest righteousness, and hatest wickedness; therefore ᵐGod, ⁿthy God, °hath anointed thee with the oil ᵖof gladness above thy fellows.

8 qAll thy garments *smell* of myrrh, and aloes, *and* cassia, out of the ivory palaces, whereby they have made thee glad.
A. M. cir. 2996
B. C. cir. 1008
Salomonis, Reg.
Israelitarum,
cir. annum
8

---

iNum. xxiv. 8; 2 Sam. xxii. 15; Job vi. 4——kPsa. xciii. 2; Heb. i. 8——lPsa. xxxiii. 5

mOr, *O God*——ⁿIsa. lxi. 1——o1 Kings i. 39, 40 ᵖPsa. xxi. 6——qCant. i. 3

---

providential hand of God, and *humility* in imitation of the character of the Lord Jesus Christ throughout life. 3. The Gospel teaches RIGHTEOUSNESS: shows the nature of *sin, wrong, injustice, transgression,* &c.; works *righteousness* in the *heart;* and *directs* and *influences* to the *practice* of it in all the *actions of life.* The Gospel leads him who is under its influences to *give to all their due;* to GOD, to his *neighbour,* to *himself.* And it is by the propagation of *truth, humility,* and *righteousness,* that the earth has become so far *blessed,* and the kingdom of Christ become extended among men.

And thy right hand shall teach thee terrible things.] The *Chaldee* is different: "And the Lord will teach thee to perform terrible things by thy right hand." The *Arabic:* "And with admiration shall thy right hand direct thee." The *Septuagint:* "And thy right hand shall lead thee wonderfully." To the same purpose are the *Vulgate, Anglo-Saxon,* and the old *Psalter.* The meaning is, Nothing shall be able to resist thee, and the judgments which thou shalt inflict on thine enemies shall be terrible.

Verse 5. *Thine arrows* are *sharp*] The arrows here may mean the convictions produced in the hearts of men by the preaching of the Gospel. The King is God himself; his enemies are sinners of all sorts. The people, the Jews, thousands of whom were pricked in their hearts under the preaching of *Peter* and others. All *fall* before Christ; those who received the word rose again by repentance and faith; those who did not, fell down—all down!

Verse 6. *Thy throne, O God, is for ever*] כסאך אלהים עולם ועד *kisacha Elohim olam vaed.* "O God, thy throne is for ever, and eternal!" The word *Elohim* here is the very *first* term or *name* by which the Supreme God has made himself known to the children of men. See Gen. i. 1; and this very verse the apostle, Heb. i. 8, has applied to Jesus Christ. On this I shall make a very short remark, but it shall be conclusive: If the apostle did not believe Jesus Christ to be the true and eternal God, he has utterly misapplied this Scripture.

The translation in the old Psalter, and the paraphrase will, on this controverted text, be considered of some importance: Thi settil God in werld of werlde: wande of rȝghtyng wande of thi kyngedome. Here he loues [celebrates] God Crist of dome. Thi settil of demyng and of kynges pouste. God es werld of werld for al that he demes es noȝht chaunged and that byfalles the, for the wande that es ceptre and the governyng of thi kyngdom es wande of rȝghtyng, that ryghtes croked men this es the wand of goddes evenes that ay es ryght and never croked that reules ryghtwis men and smytes wiked men. The reader will observe a blank

space between the word Crist and of dome: it is the same in the original. A word has been so carefully erased with the *scalpel* in the above place, that not a vestige of a letter is left. From the following words I should suspect it to have been kynge or lard. *Here he praises God, Christ, king of judgment.* However this may be, it is evident that this ancient commentator understood the word *God* to be applied to Christ. I have given the sentence as it is *pointed* in the original.

Verse 7. *Oil of gladness*] As an evidence that all causes of *mourning, sorrow,* and *death,* were at an end; as in the state of mourning the ancients did not anoint themselves.

I have mentioned above that the author of the Epistle to the Hebrews, chap. i. 8, 9, quotes verses 6, 7, of this Psalm. I shall subjoin the substance of what I have written on these verses in that place:—

"Verse 8. *Thy throne, O God, is for ever and ever.*—If this be said of the Son of God, i. e., Jesus Christ, then Jesus Christ must be God; and indeed the design of the apostle is to prove this. The words here quoted are taken from Psa. xlv. 6, 7, which the ancient Chaldee paraphrast, and the most intelligent rabbins, refer to the Messiah. On the third verse of this Psalm, 'Thou art fairer than the children of men,' the *Targum* says: 'Thy beauty,מלכא משיחא *malca Meshicha, O King Messiah,* is greater than the children of men.' *Aben Ezra* says: 'This Psalm speaks of David, or rather of his Son the *Messiah,* for this is his name, Ezek. xxxiv. 24: *And David my servant shall be a prince over them for ever.*' Other rabbins confirm this opinion.

"This verse is very properly considered a proof, and indeed a strong one, of the divinity of Christ; but some late versions of the New Testament have endeavoured to avoid the evidence of this proof by translating the word thus: 'God is thy throne for ever and ever;' and if this version be correct, it is certain that the text can be no proof of the doctrine. Mr. Wakefield vindicates this translation at large in his *History of Opinions;* and ὁ Θεος being the *nominative* case is supposed to be sufficient justification of this version. In answer to this it may be stated that the *nominative* case is often used for the *vocative,* particularly by the Attics, and the whole scope of the place requires it should be so used here; and with due deference to all of a contrary opinion, the original Hebrew cannot be consistently translated any other way; כסאך אלהים עולם ועד *kisacha Elohim olam vaed,* 'Thy throne, O God, is for ever, and to eternity.' It is in both worlds, and extends over all time, and will exist through all endless duration. To this our Lord seems to

A. M. cir. 2996
B. C. cir. 1008
Salomonis, Reg.
Israelitarum,
cir. annum
8

9 ʳKings' daughters *were* among thy honourable women: ˢupon thy right hand did stand the queen in gold of Ophir.

10 Hearken, O daughter, and consider, and incline thine ear; ᵗforget also thine own people, and thy father's house;

A. M. cir. 2996
B. C. cir. 1008
Salomonis, Reg.
Israelitarum,
cir. annum
8

ʳCant. vi. 8

ˢSee 1 Kings ii. 9——ᵗSee Deut. xxi. 13

---

refer, Matt. xxviii. 18: 'All power is given unto me, both in HEAVEN and EARTH.' My *throne*, i. e., my *dominion*, extends from the creation to the consummation of all things. These I have made, and these I uphold; and from the end of the world, throughout eternity, I shall have the same *glory*—sovereign unlimited power and authority, which I had with the Father before the world began; John xvii. 5. I may add that none of the ancient Versions has understood it in the way contended for by those who deny the Godhead of Christ, either in the Psalm from which it is taken, or in this place where it is quoted. Aquila translates אלהים *Elohim*, by Θεε, *O God*, in the vocative case; and the Arabic adds the sign of the vocative ی *ya*, reading the place thus: كرسي يا الله الي ابد الابد *korsee yallaho ila abadilabada*, the same as in our Version. And even allowing that ὁ Θεος here is to be used as the *nominative* case, it will not make the sense contended for without adding εστι to it, a reading which is not countenanced by any *Version*, nor by any MS. yet discovered. Wiclif, Coverdale, and others, understood it as the nominative, and translated it so; and yet it is evident that this nominative has the power of the vocative: 𝔉orsoþe to þe ſone God þi troone into þe world of world: a gerde of equite þe gerde of þi reume. I give this, pointing and all, as it stands in my old MS. Bible. *Wiclif* is nearly the same, but is evidently of a more modern cast: 𝔅ut to þe ſone he ſeith, God þy trone is into þe world of world, a gherd of equyte is þe gherd of þi reume. *Coverdale* translates it thus: 'But unto the sonne he sayeth: God, thi seate endureth for ever and ever: the cepter of thy kyngdome is a right cepter.' *Tindal* and others follow in the same way, all reading it in the *nominative* case, with the force of the *vocative;* for none of them has inserted the word εστι, *is*, because not authorized by the original; a word which the opposers of the Divinity of our Lord are obliged to *beg*, in order to support their interpretation.

"*A sceptre of righteousness.*—The sceptre, which was a sort of staff or instrument of various forms, was the ensign of government, and is here used for government itself. This the ancient Jewish writers understand also of the Messiah.

"Verse 9. *Thou hast loved righteousness.*—This is the characteristic of a just governor; he abhors and suppresses iniquity; he countenances and supports righteousness and truth.

"*Therefore God, even thy God.*—The original, δια τουτου εχρισε δε, ὁ Θεος, ὁ Θεος σου, may be thus translated: 'Therefore, O God, thy God hath anointed thee.' The form of speech is nearly the same with that in the preceding verse; but the sense is sufficiently clear if we read: 'Therefore God, thy God, hath anointed thee,' &c.

"*With the oil of gladness.*—We have often had occasion to remark that anciently *kings*, *priests*, and *prophets*, were consecrated to their several offices by anointing, and that this signified the gifts and influences of the Divine Spirit. Christ, ὁ χριστος, signifies *The anointed*

One, the same as the Hebrew Messiah; and he is here said to be 'anointed with the oil of gladness above his fellows.' None was ever constituted *prophet*, *priest*, and *king*, but himself: some were kings only, prophets only, and priests only; others were kings and priests, or priests and prophets, or kings and prophets; but none had ever the *three offices* in his own person but Jesus Christ; and none but himself can be a King over the universe, a Prophet to all intelligent beings, and a Priest to the whole human race. Thus he is infinitely exalted *beyond his fellows*—all that had ever borne the regal, prophetic, or sacerdotal offices.

"Some think that the word μετοχους, *fellows*, refers to *believers* who are made partakers of the same Spirit, but cannot have its infinite plenitude. The first sense seems the best. *Gladness* is used to express the *festivities* which took place on the inauguration of kings," &c.

Verse 8. *All thy garments smell of myrrh*] The Asiatics are very partial to perfumes; every thing with them is perfumed, and especially their garments. And the *ivory palaces* mentioned are the *wardrobes* inlaid with ivory, in which their numerous changes of raiment were deposited. *Myrrh* and *aloes* are well known; *cassia* is probably the bark or wood of the *cinnamon* tree. These with *frankincense*, *galbanum* and other odoriferous drugs, were and are frequently used in the perfumes of the Asiatic nations.

Whereby they have made thee glad.] Referring to the effect of strong perfumes refreshing and exhilarating the spirits.

Verse 9. *Kings' daughters were among*] Applied to Solomon, these words have no difficulty. We know he had *seven hundred* wives, *princesses;* and the mention of those here may be intended only to show how highly respected he was among the neighbouring sovereigns, when they cheerfully gave him their daughters to constitute his harem. If we apply it to Solomon's marriage with the daughter of the king of Egypt, it may signify no more than the *princesses* and *ladies* of *honour* who accompanied her to the Israelitish court. Applied to *Christ*, it may signify that the Gospel, though preached particularly to the *poor*, became also the means of salvation to many of the *kings*, *queens*, and *nobles*, of the earth. The *Chaldee* interprets the *queen standing at his right hand*, by the *law;* and the *honourable women*, by the different *regions* and *countries* coming to *receive that law from his right hand.* Perhaps by *kings' daughters* may be meant different regions and countries, which are represented as constituting the *families* of potentates. Whole nations shall be converted to the Christian faith; and the *queen*—the Christian Church, shall be most elegantly adorned with all the graces and good works which at once constitute and adorn the Christian character.

Verse 10. *Hearken, O daughter, and consider*] This is the beginning of the address by the *companions of the bride* to their mistress; after

A. M. cir. 2996
B. C. cir. 1008
Salomonis, Reg.
Israelitarum,
cir. annum
8

11 So shall the king greatly desire thy beauty: [u]for he *is* thy LORD; and worship thou him.

12 And the daughter of Tyre *shall be there* with a gift; *even* [v]the rich among the people shall entreat [w]thy favour.

13 [x]The king's daughter *is* all glorious within: her clothing *is* of wrought gold.

14 [y]She shall be brought unto the king in raiment of needlework: the virgins her com-panions that follow her shall be brought unto thee.

15 With gladness and rejoicing shall they be brought: they shall enter into the king's palace.

16 Instead of thy fathers shall be thy chil-dren, [z]whom thou mayest make princes in all the earth.

17 [a]I will make thy name to be remem-bered in all generations: therefore shall the people praise thee for ever and ever.

A. M. cir. 2996
B. C. cir. 1008
Salomonis, Reg.
Israelitarum,
cir. annum
8

---

[u]Psa. xcv. 6; Isa. liv. 5——[v]Psa. xxii. 29; lxxii. 10; Isa. xlix. 23; lx. 3

[w]Heb. *thy face*——[x]Rev. xix. 7, 8——[y]Cant. i. 4——[z]1 Pet. ii. 9; Rev. i. 6; v. 10; xx. 6——[a]Mal. i. 11

---

having, in the preceding verses, addressed the bridegroom; or, rather, given a description of his person, qualities, and magnificence. Sup-pose the daughter of Pharaoh to be intended, the words import: Thou art now become the spouse of the most magnificent monarch in the universe. To thee he must be all in all. *For-get* therefore *thy own people*—the Egyptians, and take the Israelites in their place. *Forget* also *thy father's house;* thou art now united to a new family. *So shall the king*—Solomon, *greatly desire thy beauty*—thou wilt be, in all respects, pleasing to him. And it is right thou shouldst act so; for he is now become *thy lord* —thy supreme governor. *And worship thou him*—submit thyself reverently and affection-ately to all his commands.

Taken in reference to *Christ* and the *Gospel,* this is an address to the Gentiles to forsake their idolatrous customs and connexions, to em-brace Christ and his Gospel in the spirit of reverence and obedience, with the promise that, if beautified with the graces of his Spirit, Christ will delight in them, and take them for his peculiar people; which has been done.

Verse 12. *The daughter of Tyre shall be there with a gift*] The Tyrians shall pay tribute to thy spouse, and assist him in all his grand and magnificent operations.

As, at this time, Tyre was the greatest mari-time and commercial city in the world, it may be here taken as representing those places which lay on the coasts of the sea, and carried on much traffic; such as parts of Syria, Egypt, Asia Minor, Greece, Italy, France, the British Isles, &c., which first received the Gospel of Christ and were the instruments of sending it to all the other nations of the earth.

Rich among the people] The most powerful and opulent empires, kingdoms, and states, shall embrace Christianity, and entreat the *favour* of its Author.

Verse 13. *The king's daughter is all glorious within*] This, in some sense, may be spoken of Solomon's bride, the daughter of the king of Egypt; and then the expression may refer either to the cultivation of her mind, or the ornaments and splendour of her palace. The Asiatic queens, sultanas, and begums, scarcely ever appear in public. They abide in the harem in the greatest luxury and splendour; and to this, as its literal meaning, the text may pos-sibly refer.

Her clothing is of wrought gold.] Of the most costly embroidery: her palace, and her person, are decorated in the very highest state of elegance and magnificence.

Spiritually, the *king's daughter* may mean the *Christian Church* filled with the mind that was in Christ, and adorned with the graces of the Holy Spirit; while the whole of its outward conduct is pure and holy, ornamented with the works of faith and love, and always bringing forth the fruits of the Spirit.

Verse 14. *She shall be brought unto the king*] When an Asiatic princess is brought to her spouse, she is inclosed in a *palakee,* and no part of her person is visible. She is attended by her principal friends and companions, who *follow* the palakee, and the ceremony is accompanied with great *rejoicing;* and thus they *enter into* the *palace of the king.*

This part of this parabolical Psalm may refer to the glories of a future state. The Christian Church shall be brought to the KING eternal in the *great day,* adorned with the graces of the Divine Spirit; and thus shall all the redeemed of the Lord enter *into the king's palace*—into the everlasting joy of their Lord.

Verse 16. *Instead of thy fathers shall be thy children*] This is the *third* part, or prophetic declaration relative to the numerous and power-ful issue of this marriage. Instead of the kin-dred, which thou hast left behind in Egypt, thou shalt have numerous children. This cannot refer either to Solomon, or to the daughter of Pharaoh; for there is no evidence that he ever had a child by Pharaoh's daughter; and it is very certain that Rehoboam, Solomon's suc-cessor, was not son to the daughter of Pharaoh; nor did any princes of that line ever occupy a foreign throne; nor by successive generations ever continue the remembrance of Solomon and his Egyptian queen. The *children* mentioned here are generally supposed to mean the *apostles* and their *successors in the Christian ministry;* founding Churches all over the world, by whom the Christian name becomes a me-morial through all the earth.

Verse 17. *Therefore shall the people praise thee*] They shall magnify the heavenly Bride-groom, and sing the wonderful displays of his love to the Church, his spouse. And the con-stant use of this Psalm in the Christian Church is a literal fulfilment of the prophecy.

ANALYSIS OF THE FORTY-FIFTH PSALM

The type of the *Messiah* is *Solomon;* of the *Church,* especially of the *Gentiles* to be espoused, *Pharaoh's daughter.*

There are *three* parts in this Psalm:—

I. A preface, ver. 1, 2.

II. The body of this Psalm contains two commendations,—

1. Of the bridegroom, from ver. 3 to 9.

2. Of the bride, from ver. 10 to 15.

III. The conclusion promissory and laudatory, ver. 16 to 17.

I. In the preface the prophet commends the subject he is to treat of,—

1. Signifying that it is *a good thing; good,* as speaking of the Son of God, who is the *chief good.*

2. And *good* for us; for, on our union with the Church, and Christ's union with that, depends our eternal good.

That the author of this Psalm, and the subject of it, is God: the psalmist was but the pen to write, for he was full of the Holy Ghost. Therefore, his heart was inditing, and his tongue followed the dictate of his heart, and presently became the instrument of a ready writer, viz., of the Holy Spirit: "My tongue is the pen of a ready writer."

Thus, having endeavoured to gain over his auditory, 1. By the commendation of the matter of which he is to treat, viz., that it is *good.* 2. That it tends to a good end, viz., the *honour of the King,* that is, Christ, the King of the Church: he then enters on the main business, which has two particulars.

II. 1. He turns his speech to Christ, the King, and commends him for many eminent and excellent endowments:—

1. His beauty: "Thou art fairer than the children of men."

2. His elocution: "Grace is poured into thy lips."

3. For his valour: "O hero, gird thy sword upon thy thigh."

4. For his prosperity in his kingdom: "In thy majesty ride prosperously."

5. For his just administration of public affairs. "Ride on, because of truth, meekness, and righteousness."

6. For his battles and conquests: "Thy right hand shall teach thee terrible things. Thy arrows are sharp in the hearts of the king's enemies, whereby the people shall fall under thee."

7. For the stability and eternity of his power: "Thy throne, O God, is for ever and ever."

8. For his justice and equity: "The sceptre of thy kingdom is a right sceptre. Thou lovest righteousness, and hatest iniquity."

9. For the fulness of his gifts and graces, beyond all others: "Therefore God—hath anointed thee with the oil of gladness above thy fellows."

10. For the splendour of his apparel and buildings. "All thy garments smell of myrrh, &c., out of the ivory palaces." There is nothing we can call good, great, or excellent; nothing praiseworthy in a prince; that may not be found in this king.

2. From the bridegroom he proceeds to the bride, which here means the universal Church; whom he sets forth:—

1. By her attendants; no mean persons: *kings' daughters* and *honourable women.*

2. By her name, title, and dignity: a *queen.*

3. By her place: she *stood on the right hand,* the place of confidence and respect.

4. By her attire and vesture: *she stood in a vesture of gold of Ophir.*

In the midst of this great *encomium* he breaks off and, by an *apostrophe,* turns his speech to the Church lest she should forget herself in the height of her honour; giving her this good counsel:—

1. "Hearken, O daughter!" mark what Christ saith unto thee.

2. "Consider." Look about, and see what is done for thee.

3. "Incline thine ear." Be obedient.

4. "Forget thine own people, and thy father's house." Leave all for Christ; leave thy old way, old opinions, and old companions.

5. The consequence of which will be, "The king shall greatly desire thy beauty."

6. And there is the utmost reason that thou shouldst hear, and be obedient, and conformable to his will. 1. For, "He is the Lord thy God, and thou shalt worship him." 2. This will promote thy interest: "Tyre shall be there with a gift, and the rich among the people shall entreat thy favour."

This counsel and admonition being ended, he returns again to the encomium of the spouse, and commends her,—

1. For her inward virtues and endearments: "The king's daughter (that is, the Church) is all glorious within."

2. For her externals; whether doctrine, morals, offices, which are, as it were, her clothing: "It is of wrought gold."

3. For her rites and ceremonies,—they are a *needlework* of divers colours, in divers Churches.

4. Her maids of honour, *virgins;* holy and sincere souls. Believers, pure in heart, life, and doctrine, living in every particular Church. These, *her companions, shall follow her:* 1. These shall be brought to thee (the Church) from all nations. 2. They shall be brought with joy and gladness, and enter into the king's palace. Gladly and willingly, shall they enter her courts here below, and afterwards be received to mansions in heaven.

5. For her fruitfulness. She shall have many children, good, and great. For the fathers, patriarchs, prophets, and priests, under the *Old Law;* apostles, evangelists, and their successors, under the *New;* that they may be made princes in all lands. Her officers are not contemptible.

III. The conclusion which is gratulatory. For this honour the Church would,

1. Set up a memorial to the honour of the Bridegroom: "I will make thy name to be remembered in all generations."

2. The praise of the heavenly Bridegroom shall be ever perpetuated: "Therefore, shall the people praise thee for ever and ever."

The Christian Church shall ever proclaim the name of Jesus, as the name alone in which salvation is to be found; and as the eternal Fountain of all blessings.

PSALM XLVI

The confidence of believers in God, 1–3. The privileges of the Church, 4, 5; her enemies, and her helper, 6, 7. God's judgments in the earth, 8, 9. He will be exalted among the heathen, and throughout the earth, 10, 11.

To the chief Musician ªfor the sons of Korah, ᵇa Song upon ᶜAlamoth

A. M. 3485
B. C. 519
A. U. C. 235
Anno Darii
I., Regis
Persarum, 6

GOD *is* our ᵈrefuge and strength, ᵉa very present help in trouble.

2 Therefore will not we fear, though the earth be removed, and though the mountains be carried into ᶠthe midst of the sea;

3 ᵍ*Though* the waters thereof roar *and* be troubled, *though* the mountains shake with the swelling thereof. Selah.

A. M. 3485
B. C. 519
A. U. C. 235
Anno Darii
I., Regis
Persarum, 6

4 *There is* ʰa river, the streams whereof shall make glad ⁱthe city of God, the holy *place* of the tabernacles of the Most High.

5 God *is* ᵏin the midst of her; she shall not be moved: God shall help her, ˡ*and that* right early.

6 ᵐThe heathen raged, the kingdoms were

ªOr, *of*——ᵇPsa. xlviii., lxvi——ᶜ1 Chron. xv. 20 ᵈPsa. lxii. 7, 8; xci. 2; cxlii. 5——ᵉDeut. iv. 7; Psa. cxlv. 18——ᶠHeb. *the heart of the seas*——ᵍPsa. xciii. 3, 4; Jer. v. 22; Matt. vii. 25——ʰSee Isa. viii. 7——ⁱPsa. xlviii. 1, 8; Isa. lx. 14

ᵏDeut. xxiii. 14; Isa. xii. 6; Ezek. xliii. 7, 9; Hos. xi. 9; Joel ii. 27; Zeph. iii. 15; Zech. ii. 5, 10, 11; viii. 3 ˡHeb. *when the morning appeareth;* see Exod. xiv. 24, 27; 2 Chronicles xx. 20; Psalm xxx. 5; cxliii. 8——ᵐPsa. ii. 1

NOTES ON PSALM XLVI

The *title* in the *Hebrew* is, "To the chief musician for the sons of Korah; an ode upon *Alamoth, or concerning the virgins.*" possibly meaning a choir of *singing girls.* Some translate the word *secrets* or *mysteries;* and explain it accordingly. *Calmet* thinks it was composed by the descendants of Korah, on their return from the Babylonian captivity, when they had once more got peaceably settled in Jerusalem; and that the disturbances to which it refers were those which took place in the *Persian empire* after the death of *Cambyses,* when the *Magi* usurped the government. Many other interpretations and conjectures are given of the occasion of this fine ode. *Houbigant* thinks it was made on occasion of an *earthquake,* which he supposes took place on the *night* that all Sennacherib's army was destroyed. Dr. *Kennicott* thinks that *alamoth* means a musical instrument. All I can pretend to say about it is, that it is a very *sublime ode;* contains much consolation for the Church of God; and was given by the inspiration of his Holy Spirit.

Verse 1. God is our refuge] It begins abruptly, but nobly; ye may trust in whom and in what ye please: but GOD (ELOHIM) *is our refuge and strength.*

A very present help] A help found to be very powerful and effectual in straits and difficulties. The words are very emphatic: עזרה בצרות נמצא מאד *ezerah betsaroth nimtsa meod,* "He is found an exceeding, or superlative help in difficulties." Such we have found him, and therefore celebrate his praise.

Verse 2. Therefore will not we fear] Let what commotions will take place in the earth, we will trust in the all-powerful arm of God. Probably the *earthquake* referred to, here means *political commotions,* such as those mentioned under the title; and by *mountains,* kings or secular states may be intended.

Verse 3. Though the waters thereof roar]

Waters, in prophetic language, signify people; and, generally, people in a state of political commotion, here signified by the term *roar.* And by these strong agitations of the people, the *mountains*—the secular rulers, *shake with the swelling thereof*—tremble, for fear that these popular tumults should terminate in the subversion of the state. This very people had seen all Asia in a state of war. The Persians had overturned Asia Minor, and destroyed the Babylonian empire: they had seen Babylon itself sacked and entered by the Persians; and Cyrus, its conqueror, had behaved to them as a father and deliverer. While their oppressors were destroyed, themselves were preserved, and permitted to return to their own land.

Verse 4. There is *a river, the streams whereof*] The Chaldee understands the *river,* and its *streams* or *divisions,* as pointing out various peoples who should be converted to the faith, and thus make glad the city of God, Jerusalem, by their flowing together to the worship of the true God.

But the *river* may refer to the vast Medo-Persian army and its divisions: those branches which took Babylon; and, instead of ruining and destroying the poor Jews, preserved them alive, and gave them their liberty; and thus the city of God, and the tabernacle of the Most High, were gladdened.

Verse 5. *God is in the midst of her*] God will not abandon them that trust in him; he will maintain his own cause; and, if his Church should at any time be attacked, he will help her, *and that right early*—with the utmost speed. As soon as the onset is made, God is there to resist. As by the day-break the shadows and darkness are dissipated; so by the bright rising of Jehovah, the darkness of adversity shall be scattered.

Verse 6. *The heathen raged*] There had been terrible wars on all hands, and mighty states were crushed, when the poor Jews were, by the especial favour of God, kept in peace and safety.

A. M. 3485 B. C. 519 A. U. C. 235 Anno Darii I., Regis Persarum, 6

moved: he uttered his voice,
[n]the earth melted.
7 [o]The LORD of hosts *is* with
us; the God of Jacob *is* [p]our
refuge. Selah.
8 [q]Come, behold the works of the LORD,
what desolations he hath made in the earth.
9 [r]He maketh wars to cease unto the end of
the earth; [s]he breaketh the bow,
and cutteth the spear in sunder;
[t]he burneth the chariot in the fire.
10 Be still, and know that I
am God: [u]I will be exalted among the heathen,
I will be exalted in the earth.
11 [v]The LORD of hosts *is* with us; the
God of Jacob *is* our refuge. Selah.

[n]Josh. ii. 9, 24——[o]Ver. 11; Num. xiv. 9; 2 Chron. xiii. 12——[p]Heb. *a high place for us;* Psa. ix. 9

[q]Psa. lxvi. 5——[r]Isa. ii. 4——[s]Psa. lxxvi. 3——[t]Ezek. xxxix. 9——[u]Isa. ii. 11, 17——[v]Ver. 7

Kingdoms were moved while they were preserved.

He uttered his voice] These words seem to refer to thunder, lightning, and earthquake. The expressions, however, may be figurative, and refer to the wars and desolations already mentioned. God gave the command; and one empire was cast down, and another was raised up.

Verse 7. *The Lord of hosts* is *with us*] We, feeble Jews, were but a handful of men; but the *Lord of hosts*—the God of armies, was on our side. Him none could attack with hope of success, and his legions could not be overthrown.

The God of Jacob] The God who appeared to Jacob in his distress, and saved him out of all his troubles, appeared also for us his descendants, and has amply proved to us that he has not forgotten his covenant.

Verse 8. *Come, behold the works of the Lord*] See empires destroyed and regenerated; and in such a way as to show that a supernatural agency has been at work. By the hand of God alone could these great changes be effected.

Verse 9. *He maketh wars to cease*] By the death of Cambyses, and setting Darius, son of Hystaspes, upon the Persian throne, he has tranquillized the whole empire. That same God who for our unfaithfulness has delivered us into the hands of our enemies, and subjected us to a long and grievous captivity and affliction, has now turned our captivity, and raised us up the most powerful friends and protectors in the very place in which we have been enduring so great a fight of afflictions.

He breaketh the bow] He has rendered useless all the implements of war; and so profound and secure is the general tranquillity, that the *bow* may be safely *broken*, the *spear snapped asunder*, and the *chariot burnt in the fire*.

Verse 10. *Be still, and know that I* am *God*] הרפו *harpu*, *Cease* from your provocations of the Divine justice; cease from murmuring against the dispensations of his providence; cease from your labour for a season, that ye may deeply reflect on the severity and goodness of God—severity to those who are brought down and destroyed; goodness to you who are raised up and exalted:—cease from sin and rebellion against your God; let that disgrace you no more, that we may no more be brought into distress and desolation.

Know that I am *God*] Understand that I am the Fountain of power, wisdom, justice, goodness, and truth.

I will be exalted among the heathen] By the dispensation of punishments, the heathen shall know me to be the God of justice; by the publication of my Gospel among them, they shall know me to be the God of goodness.

I will be exalted in the earth.] I will have my salvation proclaimed in every nation, among every people, and in every tongue.

Verse 11. *The Lord of hosts* is *with us*] Having heard these declarations of God, the people cry out with joy and exultation, The Lord of hosts, the God of armies, is with us; we will not fear what man can do unto us.

The God of Jacob is *our refuge.*] He who saved our fathers will save us, and will never abandon his people in distress.

Selah.] This is a firm, lasting, unshaken, well-tried truth.

ANALYSIS OF THE FORTY-SIXTH PSALM

Two things especially are to be considered in this Psalm:—

I. The confidence the Church has in God, ver. 1-8.

II. The exhortation to consider him as the Lord of hosts, the Punisher of the refractory and disobedient nations, often by means of *war;* and the only Giver of peace and tranquillity, ver. 8-10.

I. He begins with a maxim which is the ground of all the confidence which the people of God can have. God is our *Asylum*, or place of *refuge* to fly to; our *Strength, Stay, Munition*, on which to rely: "A very present help to deliver us in time of trouble."

From which maxim this conclusion is drawn: "therefore will we not fear;" not even in the greatest calamities, nor in the midst of the most numerous adversaries. This he expresses, first, *metaphorically;* next, in *plain terms:*—

1. Though the earth on which the Church is seated be moved or removed.

2. "Though the mountains be carried into the midst of the sea;" that is, the greatest and strongest empires and kingdoms should be ruined and overwhelmed.

3. "Though the waters roar and be troubled." Though multitudes of people threaten, and join their forces to ruin the Church.

4. "Though the mountains (i. e., kingdoms) shake with the swelling thereof." *Waters* mean people, Rev. xvii.

More plainly, for we have the interpretation of these metaphors, ver. 6: "Though the heathen raged, and the kingdoms were moved," yet we were not afraid, nor will we fear. We have a fine illustration of this bold feeling (from a consciousness of rectitude, and consequently Divine protection) from the pen of a heathen poet:—

Justum et tenacem propositi virum
Non civium ardor prava jubentium,
Non vultus instantis tyranni,
Mente quatit solida: Neque Auster,
Dux inquieti turbidus Adriæ,
Nec fulminantis magna Jovis manus.
Si fractus illabatur orbis,
Impavidum ferient ruinæ.

         Hor. Car. lib. iii., od. 3.

"The man, in conscious virtue bold,
   Who dares his secret purpose hold,
Unshaken hears the crowd's tumultuous cries;
And the impetuous tyrant's angry brow defies.
   Let the wild winds that rule the seas,
   Tempestuous all their horrors raise;
Let Jove's dread arm with thunders rend the
     spheres;
Beneath the crush of worlds, undaunted he
     appears."

         FRANCIS.

2. Of this undaunted state of mind he next descends to show the *reasons:*—

1. "There is a river," &c. The *city of God* was *Jerusalem,* the type of the *Church;* and the *holy place* of *the tabernacles* was the *temple.* The little *Shiloh,* that ran softly, watered *Jerusalem;* and the *promises* of the Gospel, that shall always flow in the Church, shall *make glad* the hearts of God's people.

2. "God is in the midst of her," to keep, to defend her; "therefore she shall not be moved," i. e., utterly removed, but "shall remain for ever."

3. "God shall help her and deliver her;" *right early*—in the proper season.

4. "He uttered his voice, and the earth melted." The hearts of the men of the earth, that exalted themselves against his Church, at the least word uttered from his mouth, *melted*—were struck with fear and terror.

5. "The Lord of hosts is with us." And even the armies of our *enemies* are at *his* command, and will fight for us whenever he pleases: "He is the Lord of all hosts."

6. "The God of Jacob is our refuge." He is our *Asylum,* and he will save us, ver. 7, 11.

II. The *second* part contains *two exhortations:*—

1. He calls on all to *behold the works of the Lord;* and he produces *two* instances worthy of observation: 1. JUDGMENT is his work, and he afflicts refractory and sinful nations by WAR: "See what desolations he hath made in the earth!" 2. PEACE is his work: "He maketh war to cease to the end of the earth."

2. Then, in the person of God, he exhorts the enemies of the Church to be quiet; for their endeavours are vain, and their rage is to no purpose: "Be still, and know that I am God."

3. And he concludes with a gracious promise, of being celebrated *among the heathen, and through the whole earth.*

PSALM XLVII

The Gentiles are invited to celebrate the praises of God as the Sovereign of the world, 1, 2. *The Jews exult in his kindness to them,* 3, 4. *All then join to celebrate his Majesty, as reigning over the heathen, and gathering the dispersed Jews and Gentiles together into one Church,* 5–9.

IX. DAY. EVENING PRAYER

To the chief Musician, A Psalm [a]for the sons of Korah

A. M. 3485
B. C. 519
A. U. C. 235
Anno Darii
   I., Regis
Persarum, 6

O [b]CLAP your hands, all ye people; shout unto God with the voice of triumph.

2 For the LORD most high *is* [c]terrible; [d]*he is* a great King over all the earth.

A. M. 3485
B. C. 519
A. U. C. 235
Anno Darii
   I., Regis
Persarum, 6

3 [e]He shall subdue the people under us, and the nations under our feet.

4 He shall choose our [f]inheritance for us,

---

[a]Or, *of*——[b]Isa. lv. 12——[c]Deut. vii. 21; Neh. i. 5; Psa. lxxvi. 12——[d]Mal. i. 14——[e]Psa. xviii. 47——[f]1 Pet. i. 4

NOTES ON PSALM XLVII

The *title,* "A Psalm for the sons of Korah," has nothing remarkable in it. The Psalm was probably written about the same time with the preceding, and relates to the happy state of the Jews when returned to their own land. They renewed their praises and promises of obedience, and celebrate him for the deliverance they had received. See the *introduction* to the preceding Psalm. In a spiritual sense, it appears to relate to the *calling of the Gentiles* to be made partakers of the blessings of the Gospel with the converted Jews.

Verse 1. *O clap your hands, all ye people*] Let both Jews and Gentiles magnify the Lord: the Jews, for being *delivered* from the *Babylonish captivity;* the *Gentiles,* for being called

to enter into the glorious liberty of the children of God.

Verse 2. *For the Lord most high is terrible*] He has insufferable majesty, and is *a great King* —the mightiest of all emperors, for he is Sovereign over the whole earth.

Verse 3. *He shall subdue the people under us*] He shall do again for us what he had done for our forefathers—give us dominion over our enemies, and establish us in our own land. I would rather read this in the *past tense,* relative to what God did for their fathers in destroying the Canaanites, and giving them the promised land for their possession, and taking the people for his own inheritance. This is also applied to the *conversion of the Gentiles,* who, on the rejection of the Jews, have become his inheritance; and whom he has chosen to

A. M. 3485
B. C. 519
A. U. C. 235
Anno Darii
I., Regis
Persarum, 6

the excellency of Jacob whom he loved. Selah.

5 ᵍGod is gone up with a shout, the LORD with the sound of a trumpet.

6 Sing praises to God, sing praises: sing praises unto our King, sing praises.

7 ʰFor God *is* the King of all the earth: ⁱsing ye praises ᵏwith understanding.

---

8 ˡGod reigneth over the heathen: God sitteth upon the throne of his holiness.

9 ᵐThe princes of the people are gathered together, ⁿ*even* the people of the God of Abraham: ᵒfor the shields of the earth *belong* unto God: he is ᵖgreatly exalted.

A. M. 3485
B. C. 519
A. U. C. 235
Anno Darii
I., Regis
Persarum, 6

ᵍPsa. lxviii. 24, 25——ʰZech. xiv. 9——ⁱ1 Cor. xiv. 15, 16——ᵏOr, every one *that hath understanding* ˡ1 Chron. xvi. 31; Psa. xciii. 1; xcvi. 10; xcvii. 1; xcix. 1; Rev. xix. 6

ᵐOr, *The voluntary of the people are gathered* into *the people of the God of Abraham*——ⁿRom. iv. 11, 12 ᵒPsa. lxxxix. 18——ᵖPsa. cxii. 9; Isa. ii. 11, 17; xxxiii. 10; Phil. ii. 9

---

inherit all those spiritual blessings typified by the sacrifices and other significant rites and ceremonies of the Jewish Church.

Verse 5. *God is gone up with a shout*] Primarily, this may refer to the rejoicing and sounding of trumpets, when the ark was lifted up to be carried on the shoulders of the Levites. But it is generally understood as a *prophetic declaration* of the *ascension of our Lord Jesus Christ;* and the *shout* may refer to the exultation of the evangelists and apostles in preaching Christ crucified, buried, risen from the dead, and ascended to heaven, ever to appear in the presence of God for us. This was the *triumph of the apostles;* and the conversion of multitudes of souls by this preaching was the *triumph of the cross of Christ.*

Verse 6. *Sing praises*] זמרו *zammeru:* this word is *four* times repeated in this short verse, and shows at once the *earnestness* and *happiness* of the people. They are the words of *exultation* and *triumph.* Feel your obligation to God; express it in thanksgiving: be thankful, be eternally thankful, to God your King.

Verse 7. *For God* is *the King of all the earth*] He is not *your* King only, but the King of the *universe.* He has no *limited power,* no *confined* dominion.

Sing ye praises with understanding] זמרו משכיל *zammeru maskil, sing an instructive song.* Let *sense* and *sound* go together. Let your *hearts* and *heads* go with your *voices. Understand* what you *sing;* and *feel* what you *understand;* and let the *song* be what will *give instruction in righteousness* to them that hear it. ᵽᵧᵑᵹᵃ⁶ ᵽᵢᵽˡᶦᶜᵉ, *Sing wisely.*—Anglo-Saxon. Multitudes *sing foolishly.*

Verse 8. *God reigneth over the heathen*] Though this is literally true in God's universal dominion, yet *more* is here meant. God *reigns over the heathen* when, by the preaching of the Gospel, they are brought into the Church of Christ.

God sitteth upon the throne of his holiness.] He is a holy God; he proclaims holiness. His laws are holy, he requires holiness, and his genuine *people* are all holy. The *throne of his holiness* is the *heaven of heavens;* also the *temple* at Jerusalem; and, lastly, the *hearts of the faithful.*

Verse 9. *The princes of the people are gathered together*] נדיבי עמים *nedibey ammim.* The *voluntary people*—the *princely, noble,* or *free-willed people;* those who gladly receive the word of life; those who, like the *Bereans,* were of a *noble* or *liberal disposition;* and, when they

heard the Gospel, searched the Scriptures to see whether these things were so. It is a similar word which is used Psa. cx. 3; and I believe both texts speak of the same people—the *Gentiles who gladly come unto his light,* and present themselves a *free-will offering* to the Lord.

The people of the God of Abraham] Who were Abraham's people? Not the *Jews;* the covenant was made with him while yet in *uncircumcision.* Properly speaking, the *Gentiles* are those whom he *represented;* for the covenant was made with him while yet a *Gentile;* and in his seed all the *nations*—the *Gentiles,* of the earth were to be *blessed.* The *people of the God of Abraham* are the *Gentiles,* who, receiving the Gospel, are made partakers of the *faith of Abraham,* and are his *spiritual children.* The God of Abraham has Abraham's spiritual posterity, the believing Gentiles, for his own people.

The shields of the earth belong *unto God.*] The *Septuagint* translate this οἱ κραταιοί, *the strong ones of the earth.* The *Vulgate* reads, Quoniam dii fortes terræ vehementer elevati sunt; "Because the strong gods of the earth are exceedingly exalted." These are supposed to mean *kings* and *rulers of provinces* which were present at the dedication of the temple; (for some suppose the Psalm to have been composed for this solemnity;) and that they are said here to be *greatly exalted,* because they exercised a very high degree of power over their respective districts. The words refer to something by which the inhabitants of the earth are defended; God's providence, guardian angels, &c., &c.

He is greatly exalted.] Great as secular rulers are, God is greater, and is above all; King of kings and Lord of lords; and the hearts of kings and governors are in his hand; and he turns them whithersoever he pleases.

ANALYSIS OF THE FORTY-SEVENTH PSALM

This Psalm, under the figure of the ark being brought into the temple, foretells the ascension of Christ to heaven; who was the true ark of the covenant, and the propitiatory or mercy-seat. It contains a prophecy of Christ's kingdom, and has *two* especial parts:—

First, An invitation to sing praises to Christ.

Secondly, The reasons why we should do it.

1. The ascension of Christ is typified under the ark's ascension, ver. 1: "God is gone up with a shout; the Lord with the sound of a trumpet."

2. On which he invites the people to do now what was then done, "that we clap our hands,

and sing praises." This should be done, 1. Cheerfully: "Clap your hands;" for this is a sign of inward joy, Nah. iii. 19. 2. Universally: "O clap your hands, all ye people." 3. Vocally: "Shout unto God with the voice of triumph." 4. Frequently: "Sing praises—sing praises—sing praises—sing praises," ver. 6, and again "sing praises," ver. 7. It cannot be done too frequently. 5. Knowingly and discreetly: "Sing ye praises with understanding;" know the reason why ye are to praise him.

3. Now these reasons are drawn from his *greatness* and from his *goodness*.

1. He is GREAT. 1. He is the Lord Most High; 2. He is terrible; 3. He is a great King over all the earth. All power, at his ascension, was given unto him in heaven and earth.

2. He is GOOD. 1. In collecting his Church by subduing the nations, not by the *sword*, but by his word and Spirit, by which he would subdue their iniquities, the iniquity of the *Jew* first, and then of the *Gentile;* for the law was to come out of Zion, and the word of the Lord from Jerusalem. To the discipline of that religion both were to submit; and therefore both might well be said "to be subdued to us, and brought under our feet."

2. In honouring and rewarding his Church: "He shall choose out our inheritance for us, the excellency of Jacob whom he loved."

1. His Church was his *choice:* "It is a chosen generation, a peculiar people."

2. His *heritage;* for he will dwell among them, and provide an inheritance for them; blessings on earth and glory in heaven.

3. This is "the excellency of Jacob;" of Jacob after the Spirit; the kingdom, priesthood, and all the promises made unto Jacob and the fathers being theirs.

4. The cause: "His love only—he chose—the excellency of Jacob whom he loved."

3. In the increase and amplification of his Church: "God is *now* the king of all the earth;" not of the *Jews* only, for he "reigns over the heathen" also. He "sits upon a throne of holiness;" rules by his holy word and Spirit. 1. Making them holy who were unholy. 2. They are "a willing people" also. For the princes—the volunteers, among the people, are gathered together; even the people of the God of Abraham—the Gentiles, converted and reconciled to God.

4. In protecting his Church; whether by himself, or by the *princes* he raises up; by his *providence*, or his *angels*, or all together. For the "shields of the earth belong *unto* God." Secular rulers, and ecclesiastical governors, are shields of the Church. But God is the *Head* of it, and the *Chief:* "He is greatly exalted."

PSALM XLVIII

The ornaments and the privileges of the Church, 1–8. The duty of God's people, 9–14.

A Song *and* Psalm ᵃfor the sons of Korah

A. M. 3485
B. C. 519
A. U. C. 235
Anno Darii
I., Regis
Persarum, 6

GREAT *is* the LORD, and greatly to be praised ᵇin the city of our God, *in* the ᶜmountain of his holiness.

2 ᵈBeautiful for situation, ᵉthe joy of the whole earth, *is* Mount Zion, ᶠon the sides of the north, ᵍthe city of the great King.

A. M. 3485
B. C. 519
A. U. C. 235
Anno Darii
I., Regis
Persarum, 6

ᵃOr. *of*——ᵇPsa. xlvi. 4; lxxxvii. 3——ᶜIsa. ii. 2, 3; Mic. iv. 1; Zech. viii. 3

ᵈPsa. l. 2; Jer. iii. 19; Lam. ii. 15; Dan. viii. 9; xi. 16 ᵉEzek. xx. 6——ᶠIsa. xiv. 13——ᵍMatt. v. 35

NOTES ON PSALM XLVIII

The *title: A Song* and *Psalm for the sons of Korah.* To which the *Vulgate, Septuagint, Æthiopic,* and *Arabic* add, *for the second day of the week;* for which I believe it would be difficult to find a meaning. It is evidently of the same complexion with the two preceding, and refers to the Jews returned from captivity; and perhaps was sung at the dedication of the second temple, in order to return thanks to the Lord for the restoration of their political state, and the reestablishment of their worship.

Verse 1. *Great is the Lord*] This verse should be joined to the last verse of the preceding Psalm, as it is a continuation of the same subject; and indeed in some of *Kennicott's* MSS. it is written as a part of the foregoing. *That* concluded with *He is greatly exalted; this* begins with *Great is the Lord, and greatly to be praised;* i. e., He should be praised according to his greatness; no common praise is suited to the nature and dignity of the Supreme God.

In the city of our God] That is, in the tem-

ple; or in Jerusalem, where the temple was situated.

The mountain of his holiness.] Mount Moriah, on which the temple was built. The ancient city of Jerusalem, which David took from the Jebusites, was on the *south* of Mount Zion, on which the temple was built, though it might be said to be more properly on Mount *Moriah*, which is one of the *hills* of which Mount Zion is composed. The temple therefore was to the *north* of the city, as the psalmist here states, ver. 2: "Beautiful for situation, the joy of the whole earth, is Mount Zion, on the sides of the north, the city of the great King." But some think that it is the *city* that is said to be on the *north*, and *Reland* contends that the temple was on the *south* of the city.

Verse 2. *The joy of the whole earth*] Commentators have been greatly puzzled to show in what sense Zion, or the temple, could be said to be the *joy of the whole earth*. If we take the earth here for the *habitable* globe, there is no sense in which it ever was the joy of the whole earth; but if we take כל הארץ *col haarets*, as

A. M. 3485
B. C. 519
A. U. C. 235
Anno Darii
I., Regis
Persarum, 6

3 God is known in her palaces for a refuge.

4 For, lo, [h]the kings were assembled, they passed by together.

5 They saw *it, and* so they marvelled; they were troubled, *and* hasted away.

6 Fear [i]took hold upon them there, [k]*and* pain, as of a woman in travail.

7 Thou [l]breakest the ships of Tarshish [m]with an east wind.

8 As we have heard, so have we seen in [n]the city of the LORD of hosts, in the city of our God: God will [o]establish it for ever. Selah.

9 We have thought of [p]thy loving-kindness,

O God, in the midst of thy temple.

10 According to [q]thy name, O God, so *is* thy praise unto the ends of the earth: thy right hand is full of righteousness.

11 Let Mount Zion rejoice, let the daughters of Judah be glad, because of thy judgments.

12 Walk about Zion, and go round about her: tell the towers thereof.

13 [r]Mark ye well her bulwarks, [s]consider her palaces; that ye may tell *it* to the generation following.

14 For this God *is* [t]our God for ever and ever: he will [u]be our guide *even* unto death.

A. M. 3485
B. C. 519
A. U. C. 235
Anno Darii
I., Regis
Persarum, 6

---

[h]2 Samuel x. 6, 14, 16, 18, 19——[i]Exod. xv. 15 [k]Hos. xiii. 13——[l]Ezek. xxvii. 26——[m]Jer. xviii. 17 [n]Ver. 1, 2——[o]Isa. ii. 2; Mic. iv. 1——[p]Psa. xxvi. 3; xl. 10

[q]Deut. xxviii. 58; Joshua vii. 9; Psalm cxiii. 3; Mal. i. 11, 14——[r]Hebrew, *Set your heart to her bulwarks*——[s]Or, *raise up*——[t]Psa. xlviii. 14; lxxvii. 13; xcv. 7——[u]Isa. lviii. 11

---

signifying the *whole of this land*, (and it has no other meaning,) the assertion is plain and easy to be understood, for the temple was considered the *ornament* and *glory* of the whole *land* of Judea.

Verse 3. *God is known in her palaces for a refuge.*] All those who worship there in spirit and truth, find God for their refuge. But the words may be understood: God is known for the defence of her palaces; and with this view of the subject agree *the three* following verses.

Verse 4. *For, lo, the kings were assembled*] Many of the neighbouring potentates, at different times, envied the prosperity of the Jewish nation, and coveted the riches of the temple; but they had no power against it till the cup of Jewish transgression was full. In vain did they *assemble*—confederate, and invade the land. *Saw it*—reconnoitered the place; *marvelled* at its excellence and strength, for *they were troubled*—struck with fear; *hasted away* for fear of destruction, for *fear took hold on them* as pains seize on a *woman in travail.* Those who came to destroy were glad to make their own escape.

Verse 7. *Thou breakest the ships of Tarshish*] *Calmet* thinks this may refer to the discomfiture of *Cambyses*, who came to destroy the land of Judea. "This is apparently," says he, "the same *tempest* which struck dismay into the land-forces of Cambyses, and wrecked his fleet which was on the coasts of the Mediterranean sea, opposite to his army near the port of *Acco*, or the *Ptolemais;* for Cambyses had his quarters at *Ecbatana*, at the foot of Mount Carmel; and his army was encamped in the valley of Jezreel." *Ships of Tarshish* he conjectures to have been large stout vessels, capable of making the voyage of *Tarsus*, in Cilicia.

Verse 8. *As we have heard, so have we seen*] Our fathers have declared what mighty works thou didst in their time; and we have seen the same. God has often interposed and afforded us a most miraculous defence. So it was when they were invaded by the Assyrians, Syrians, Egyptians, Babylonians, Persians and the Greeks under Alexander.

The city of the Lord of hosts] His *hosts* de-

fended the city, and it was known to be *the city of the great King.*

God will establish it for ever.] This must refer to the true temple, the Christian Church, of which the Jewish Church was a type. The *type* perished, but the *antitype* remained, and will remain till time shall be no more.

Selah.] So be it; and so it will be for evermore.

Verse 9. *We have thought of thy loving-kindness*] We went to thy temple to worship thee; we meditated on thy goodness; we waited for a display of it; and the panic that in the first instance struck *us*, was transferred to our *enemies;* and *fear took hold upon them, they marvelled, were troubled,* and *hasted away.*

Verse 10. *According to thy name*] As far as thou art known, so far art thou praised; and where thou art known, thou *wilt* have praise to the end of the earth. And why? "Thy right hand is full of righteousness." Thou art continually dispensing thy blessings to the children of men.

Verse 11. *Let Mount Zion rejoice*] The temple is restored in majesty, which was threatened with total destruction; it is again repaired.

Let the daughters of Judah be glad] That thou hast turned her captivity, and poured out thy judgments upon her oppressors.

Verse 12. *Walk about Zion*] Consider the beauty and magnificence of the temple, count the towers by which it is fortified.

Verse 13. *Mark ye well her bulwarks*] See the *redoubts* by which she is defended.

Consider her palaces] See her *courts, chambers, altars,* &c., &c.; make an exact register of the whole, that ye may have to tell to your children how Jerusalem was built in troublesome times; how God restored you; and how he put it into the hearts of the heathen to assist to build, beautify, and adorn the temple of our God.

Verse 14. *For this God*] Who did all these wonderful things,—

Is our God] He is our portion, and he has taken us for his people.

He will be our guide] Through all the snares and difficulties of life,—

Even unto death] He will never leave us;

and we, by his grace, will never abandon him. He is just such a God as we need; infinite in *mercy, goodness,* and *truth.* He is *our Father,* and we are the *sons and daughters* of God Almighty. Even unto and in death, he will be our portion.

ANALYSIS OF THE FORTY-EIGHTH PSALM

Under the type of Jerusalem is set down the happiness of the Church, which is always protected by the Divine favour. There are *three* parts in this Psalm:—

I. The excellences and privileges of the city of God, ver. 1-3.

II. A narration of a miraculous deliverance she obtained, and the terror that fell upon her enemies, ver. 4-8.

III. An exhortation to consider it, and to praise God, ver. 9-14.

I. The psalmist begins with a *maxim:* "Great is the Lord, and greatly to be praised." Great in himself; and greatly to be praised for *all things,* in *all places;* but especially in the *city of our God,* in the *mountain of holiness.*

Then he descends to set forth the excellences and ornaments of the Church.

1. It is "the city of God," built and governed by him, and in it he resides.

2. "It is a holy mountain:" The *religion* in it is holy; the *people,* a holy people.

3. "It is beautiful for situation:" God has put his beauty upon it.

4. "The joy of the whole earth is Mount Zion:" The joy and ornament of all the land of Judea then, and afterwards of the whole world, because the law was to come out of Zion.

5. "It is the city of the great King," i. e., God. He founded, and rules in it.

6. "God is known in her palaces:" In her is the knowledge of God; yea, and by an experimental knowledge, he is found to be an asylum, a *sure refuge.*

II. And it is well that it is so; for Jerusalem, i. e., the Church, has many and great enemies, which (ver. 5) the prophet begins to describe; and desires that notice may be taken of them, for he points them out with "Lo! or Behold!"

1. They are many and powerful. They were "kings," a plurality of them.

2. Confederate kings: "The kings were assembled." United power is the more effectual.

But all the endeavours of those kings, those confederate kings, came to nothing.

1. "They passed by together:" together they came, together they vanished.

2. "They saw—they marvelled:" They saw the strength of this city, and wondered how it could be so strangely delivered out of their hands.

3. On this they were troubled, they trembled, and hasted away. *Fear* took hold upon them; which the prophet illustrates by a double similitude: 1. By a travailing woman; "Fear took hold upon them, and pain, as of a woman in travail." 2. By the fear of mariners at sea, when euroclydon threatens to destroy their ship; their amazement was such "as when thou breakest the ships of Tarshish with an east wind."

III. In this third part of the Psalm there are *two* especial points:—

A grateful acknowledgment of God's protection of his Church: "As we have heard, so have we seen in the city of our God." We have heard that he will protect this city, and we see that he hath done it; and persuaded we are that he will always do it: "God will establish it for ever."

2. And this shall never be forgotten by us: "We have thought of thy loving-kindness in the midst of thy temple."

3. And so thought of it as to praise thee for it: "According to thy name so is thy praise; thy right hand is full of righteousness." All the earth shall know that thou dost help with thy powerful hand thy afflicted and oppressed people. Thou wilt punish their adversaries, "for thy right hand is full of righteousness—and justice."

The second point of this third part is an exhortation to God's people.

1. That they exult and rejoice for what God does for them: "Let Mount Zion rejoice, let the daughters of Judah be glad, because of thy judgments," in defending thy Church, and punishing their enemies.

2. That they take especial notice of his miraculous deliverance of Jerusalem; that, notwithstanding the army was great that lay against it, yet no harm was done: "Walk about Zion, tell the towers thereof; mark well her bulwarks, and her palaces." See whether they be not all standing and entire.

3. And do it for this end: "That you may tell it to the generation following." Leave it on record how miraculously God hath delivered you.

4. For this there are *two* strong reasons: 1. "For this God," who protects and defends us, "is our God for ever." 2. "He will be our guide unto death." He will not leave us when all the world leaves us. In the time in which we need him most, we shall find him most powerfully present to help us. Therefore, exult, rejoice, mark it; and make it known to the generations to come.

PSALM XLIX

All men are invited to attend to lessons of wisdom relative to the insufficiency of earthly good to save or prolong life; to secure the resurrection from the dead, 1–9. Death is inevitable, 10. The vain expectations of rich men, 11–13. Death renders all alike, 14. The psalmist encourages and fortifies himself against envying the apparently prosperous state of the wicked, who are brutish, and die like beasts, 15–20.

To the chief Musician, A Psalm ᵃfor the sons of Korah

HEAR this, all *ye* people; give ear, all *ye* inhabitants of the world:

2 Both ᵇlow and high, rich and poor, together.

3 My mouth shall speak of wisdom; and the meditation of my heart *shall be* of understanding.

4 ᶜI will incline mine ear to a parable: I will open my dark saying upon the harp.

5 Wherefore should I fear in the days of evil: *when* ᵈthe iniquity of my heels shall compass me about?

6 They that ᵉtrust in their wealth, and boast themselves in the multitude of their riches;

7 None *of them* can by any means redeem his brother, nor ᶠgive to God a ransom for him:

8 (For ᵍthe redemption of their soul *is* precious, and it ceaseth for ever:)

9 That he should still live for ever, *and* ʰnot see corruption.

10 For he seeth *that* ⁱwise men die, likewise the fool and the brutish person perish, ᵏand leave their wealth to others.

11 Their inward thought *is, that* their

ᵃOr, *of*——ᵇPsa. lxii. 9——ᶜPsa. lxxviii. 2; Matt. xiii. 35——ᵈPsa. xxxviii. 4——ᵉJob xxxi. 24, 25; Psa. lii. 7; lxii. 10; Mark x. 24; 1 Tim. vi. 17

ᶠMatt. xvi. 26——ᵍJob xxxvi. 18, 19——ʰPsa. lxxxix. 48——ⁱEccles. ii. 16——ᵏProv. xi. 4; Eccles. ii. 18, 21

NOTES ON PSALM XLIX

The *title, To the chief Musician, A Psalm for the sons of Korah,* has nothing particular in it; and the *Versions* say little about it. One of the descendants of the children of Korah might have been the author of it; but *when* or on *what occasion* it was made, cannot now be discovered. The author aimed to be *obscure,* and has succeeded; for it is very difficult to make out his meaning. It is so much in the style of the Book of Job, that one might believe they had the same author; and that this Psalm might have made originally a part of that book. "It seems," says Dr. *Dodd,* "to be a meditation on the vanity of riches, and the usual haughtiness of those who possess them. As a remedy for this, he sets before them the near prospect of death, *from* which no riches can save, *in* which no riches can avail. The author considers the subject he is treating as a kind of wisdom concealed from the world; a mystery, an occult science with respect to the generality of mankind." Dr. *Kennicott* has given an excellent translation of this Psalm, which is very literal, simple, and elegant; and by it the reader will be convinced that a good translation of a difficult passage is often better than a comment.

Verse 1. *Hear this, all ye people*] The four first verses contain the author's exordium or introduction, delivered in a very pompous style, and promising the deepest lessons of wisdom and instruction. But what was *rare* then is *common-place* now.

Verse 4. *I will incline mine ear to a parable*] This was the general method of conveying instruction among the Asiatics. They used much figure and metaphor in order to induce the reader to study deeply in order to find out the meaning. This had its use; it obliged men to *think* and *reflect* deeply; and thus in some measure taught them the use, government, and management of their *minds.*

My dark saying upon the harp.] Music was sometimes used to soothe the animal spirits, and thus prepare the mind for the prophetic influx.

Verse 5. *The iniquity of my heels*] Perhaps עקבי *akebai,* which we translate *my heels,* should be considered the contracted plural of עקבים *akebim, supplanters.* The verse would

then read thus: "Wherefore should I fear in the days of evil, though the iniquity of my supplanters should compass me about." The *Syriac* and *Arabic* have taken a similar view of the passage: "Why should I fear in the evil day, when the iniquity of my enemies compasses me about." And so Dr. *Kennicott* translates it.

Verse 7. *None* of them *can by any means redeem his brother*] Wealth cannot save from death; brother, however rich, cannot save his brother; nor will God accept *riches* as a ransom for the *life* or *soul* of any transgressor. To procure health of body, peace of mind, redemption from death, and eternal glory, riches are sought for and applied in vain.

Verse 8. *For the redemption of their soul* is *precious*] It is of too high a price to be redeemed with corruptible things, such as *silver* or *gold,* and has required the sacrificial death of Christ.

And it ceaseth for ever] This is very obscure, and may apply to the *ransom* which *riches* could produce. That ransom must be for ever unavailable, because of the *value of the soul.* Or this clause should be added to the following verse, and read thus: "And though he cease to be, (וחדל *vechadal,*) during the hidden time, (לעולם *leolam;*) yet he shall live on through eternity, (ויחי עוד לנצח *vichi od lanetsach,*) and not see corruption." This is probably the *dark saying* which it was the design of the author to utter in a parable, and leave it to the ingenuity of posterity to find it out. The verb חדל *chadal* signifies a *cessation of being* or *action,* and עולם *olam* often signifies *hidden time,* that which is not *defined,* and the *end* of which is not *ascertained,* though it is frequently used to express *endless duration.* This translation requires no alteration of the original text, and conveys a precise and consistent meaning.

Verse 10. *For he seeth that wise men die*] Though they may be rich, and their wisdom teach them the best method of managing their riches so as to derive all the good from them they can possibly produce, yet *they* die as well as the *fool* and the poor ignorant man; and their wealth is left to others who will be equally disappointed in their expectation from it.

Verse 11. *Their inward thought* is, that *their*

houses *shall continue* for ever, *and* their
dwelling places [l]to all generations; they [m]call
their lands after their own names.
12 Nevertheless [n]man *being* in honour abideth not: he is like the beasts *that* perish.
13 This their way *is* their [o]folly: yet their
posterity [p]approve their sayings. Selah.
14 Like sheep they are laid in the grave;
death shall feed on them; and [q]the upright
shall have dominion over them in the morning; [r]and their [s]beauty shall consume [t]in the
grave from their dwelling.
15 But God [u]will redeem my soul [v]from
the power of [w]the grave: for he shall receive
me. Selah.
16 Be not thou afraid when one is made rich,
when the glory of his house is increased;
17 [x]For when he dieth he shall carry nothing
away: his glory shall not descend after him.
18 Though [y]while he lived [z]he blessed his
soul: and *men* will praise thee, when thou
doest well to thyself.
19 [a]He shall [b]go to the generation of his
fathers; they shall never see [c]light.
20 [d]Man *that is* in honour, and understandeth not, [e]is like the beasts *that* perish.

---

[l]Heb. *to generation and generation*——[m]Gen. iv. 17 [n]Ver. 20; Psa. xxxix. 5; lxxxii. 7——[o]Luke xii. 20 [p]Heb. *delight in their mouth*——[q]Psa. xlvii. 3; Dan. vii. 22; Mal. iv. 3; Luke xxii. 30; 1 Cor. vi. 2; Rev. ii. 26; xx. 4——[r]Job iv. 21; Psalm xxxix. 11——[s]Or, *strength* [t]Or, *the grave* being *a habitation to every one of them*

[u]Psalm lvi. 13; Hosea xiii. 14——[v]Hebrew, *from the hand of the grave*——[w]Or, *hell*——[x]Job xxvii. 19 [y]Hebrew, *in his life*——[z]Deuteronomy xxix. 19; Luke xii. 19——[a]Hebrew, The soul *shall go*——[b]Gen xv. 15——[c]Job xxxiii. 30; Psalm lvi. 13——[d]Verse 12 [e]Eccles. iii. 19

---

houses shall continue *for ever*] Thus, by interpolation, we have endeavoured to patch up a sense to this clause. Instead of קרבם *kirbam*, their *inward part*, the *Septuagint* appear to have used a copy in which the second and third letters have been transposed קברם *kibram, their sepulchres;* for they translate: Και οἱ ταφοι αυτων οικιαι αυτων εις τον αιωνα· "For their graves are their dwellings for ever." So six or seven feet long, and two or three wide, is sufficient to hold the greatest conqueror in the universe! What a small house for the quondam possessor of numerous palaces and potent kingdoms!

They call their *lands after their own names.*] There would have been no evil in this if it had not been done on an infidel principle. They expected no state but the *present;* and if they could not continue themselves, yet they took as much pains as possible to perpetuate their *memorial.*

Verse 12. *Man* being *in honour abideth not*] However rich, wise, or honourable, they must die; and if they die not with a sure hope of eternal life, they die like beasts. See on ver. 20.

Verse 13. *Their posterity approve their sayings.*] Go the same way; adopt their maxims.

Verse 14. *Like sheep they are laid in the grave*] לשאול *lishol, into sheol,* the place of *separate* spirits.

Death shall feed on them מות ירעם *maveth yirem,* "Death shall feed them!" What an astonishing change! All the good things of life were once their portion, and they lived only to eat and drink; and now they *live in sheol,* and *Death himself feeds them!* and with what? Damnation. *Houbigant* reads the verse thus: "Like sheep they shall be laid in the place of the dead; death shall feed on them; their morning shepherds rule over them; and their flesh is to be consumed. Destruction is to them in their folds."

Verse 15. *But God will redeem my soul from the power of the grave*] מיד שאול *miyad sheol,* "from the hand of sheol." That is, by the plainest construction, I shall have a resurrection from the dead, and an entrance into his glory; and death shall have no dominion over me.

Verse 16. *Be not thou afraid when one is made rich*] Do not be envious; do not grieve: it will do you no harm; it will do him no good. All he gets will be left behind; he can carry nothing with him. Even his glory must stay behind; he shall mingle with the common earth.

Verse 18. *He blessed his soul*] He did all he could to procure himself animal gratifications, and he was applauded for it; for it is the custom of the world to praise them who pay most attention to their secular interest; and he who attends most to the concerns of his soul is deemed weak and foolish, and is often persecuted by an ungodly world.

Verse 19. *They shall never see light.*] Rise again they shall; but they shall never see the light of glory, for there is prepared for them the *blackness of darkness* for ever.

Verse 20. *Man* that is *in honour*] The rich and honourable man who has no spiritual understanding, is a *beast* in the sight of God. The spirit of this maxim is, A man who is in a dignified official situation, but destitute of learning and sound sense, is like a beast. The important place which he occupies reflects no honour upon him, but is disgraced by him. Who has not read the fable of the beautifully carved head? It was every thing that it should be, but had no *brains.*

This verse has been often quoted as a proof of the *fall of man;* and from ילין *yalin,* (in ver. 12,) which signifies *to lodge for a night,* it has been inferred that Adam fell on the same day on which he was created, and that he did not spend a single night in the terrestrial paradise. Adam, who was in a state of glory, did not remain in it one night, but became stupid and ignorant as the beasts which perish. But we may rest assured this is no meaning of the text.

Analysis of the Forty-ninth Psalm

The doctrine taught by this Psalm is the following: That rich men be not proud of their wealth, nor poor men dejected nor humbled at their mean estate, since all men are mortal; and it is not the wealth of the one can make them happy, nor the poverty of the others can make them unhappy, there being another life by which the condition of both is to be judged.

The Psalm has *three* parts:—

I. An *exordium* or *preface:* ver. 1-4.

II. The *matter* proposed, debated, and argued, from ver. 5 to 16.

III. The *advice* or *admonition* given, from. ver. 16 to 20.

I. In the *exordium,*—

1. He calls together his auditory: "All people, all nations, low, high, rich, and poor;" because what he speaks concerns all.

2. Then he calls them to be attentive. "Hear, give ear."

3. He labours to make them teachable, by commending the matter of which he treats; they are not frivolous, but weighty and important things: 1. "My mouth shall speak of wisdom," &c. I will speak of what I know, and speak so that others may understand. 2. "I will incline my ear." I will teach you nothing but what I teach myself. 3. It is a *parable* which I am about to deliver, and will require all your attention. 4. That it may be brought to your ear with more delight, I shall accompany it with the *harp:* "I will open my dark saying upon the harp."

II. Having now assembled his congregation; endeavoured to make them attentive, docile, and well-disposed, lest any should suppose that he was envious at the prosperity of the wicked, or had so little trust in God that he lived in terror of his adversaries; he says, "Wherefore should I fear in the days of evil, though the iniquity of my supplanters surrounds me?" He had no reason thus to fear; but the wealthy and ambitious had. And this he demonstrates *two ways:* for he takes away happiness from the *one*, ver. 6-15, and places happiness in the other, ver. 16.

1. They that trust in their wealth, and boast themselves in the multitude of their riches, are not happy, ver. 6. For wealth will not deliver in the evil day.

1. It will save no man's life: "None of them (the rich men) can redeem his brother, nor give to God a ransom for him." God will not be bribed to save any man's life.

2. It will save no man's soul. The ransom required for that is more valuable than any thing the earth can produce.

3. Suppose he was wise, and a long-lived man, yet he must die at last: "For he seeth that wise men die; likewise the fool, and the brutish."

4. Which sufficiently shows the vanity of their riches: 1. They leave them. 2. They leave these great riches. 3. They leave them to others; sometimes to children, but often to strangers, such as they thought never would have entered into their labours.

5. "Their thoughts are vain." For, 1. "Their inward thoughts are that their houses shall continue," &c. 2. To this end, "They call their lands after their own names;" they not only study to be *rich*, but they are *vain-glorious* also. But their study is, 1. Vanity. 2. Folly.

1. *Vanity:* "Nevertheless, man being in honour, abideth not;" a change there will be, and the most glorious man will be *like the beasts that perish.*

2. *Folly:* "This their way is their foolishness." A great foolery to place their chief good in riches; yet their posterity act in the same

way, tread in their steps, and pant after riches and honours.

To correct this propensity, he lays before them certain considerations relative to their future condition:—

1. "Like sheep they are laid in the grave." That is their common condition; like sheep they are fatted for slaughter.

2. "Death shall feed on them." The second death; for, like *Dives*, they *shall be burned in hell;* and the *fire that cannot be extinguished* shall feed upon their souls and bodies.

3. In the morning of the resurrection, the "upright shall have power over them." The *righteous* shall shine like the sun, when *they* shall be Christ's footstool. The *godly* shall be placed on the right hand, and seated on thrones to judge them; when *they* shall be seated on the left, and be condemned.

4. "Their beauty shall consume in the grave." Their riches, power, and glory, shall wax old as doth a garment: "For the figure of this world passeth away." Therefore the *rich* of this world, and the *possessors of great glory, are not happy.* He therefore sets down the *happy man:* the man who trusts in God, and lives to him, he is happy in life, notwithstanding his afflictions, and he shall be happy for ever. Therefore he says, "God will redeem my soul from the power of the grave," &c.

1. He shall redeem me. All good men's souls.

2. Not from the grave, for die we must; but from the *hand*, that is, the dominion and power, of death: "Death shall not reign over them."

3. The reason is, For *he shall receive me*— adopt me into his family, and make me a partaker of the Divine nature.

III. On these considerations, relative to good and bad men, and their different conditions, he admonishes the good that they be not troubled at the prosperity of the wicked: "Be not thou afraid," &c.

1. Not at the great wealth of the rich: "Be not afraid when one is made rich."

2. Not at the glory and honour of the mighty: "Nor when the glory of his house is increased."

And he repeats the former reason: "For when he dieth, he shall carry nothing away; his glory shall not descend after him." Their happiness, such as it was, was only momentary.

This he amplifies: Be it granted that they flattered themselves, and were flattered by others.

1. "Though while he lived he blessed his own soul." "Soul, take thy ease," &c.

2. Though men will praise thee, and sound in thy ears, Well done! "so long as thou doest well to thyself,"—heapest up riches, and followest after honour.

1. A mortal thou art, short-lived as all that went before thee: "He shall go to the generation of his fathers." And,

2. If wicked, be cast into utter darkness: "They shall never see the light."

3. Surely any man, however rich, however great, who understands not thus much, must be a beast; and with this sentiment concludes the Psalm; and it is doubled that it may be remembered: "Man, who is in honour, and understandeth not, is like the beasts that perish." Even while he lives, without this understanding, his life is little more than the life of the beast.

PSALM L

God, the Sovereign Judge, cites before his throne all his people, and the priests and the judges, 1–6; and reproaches them for their vain confidence in the sacrifices they had offered, 7–13; and shows them the worship he requires, 14, 15; and then enters into a particular detail of their hypocrisy, injustice, and union with scandalous transgressors; all of whom he threatens with heavy judgments, 16–22. The blessedness of him who worships God aright, and walks unblamably, 23.

X. DAY. MORNING PRAYER

A Psalm of ᵃAsaph

THE ᵇmighty God, *even* the LORD, hath spoken, and called the earth from the rising of the sun unto the going down thereof.

2 Out of Zion, ᶜthe perfection of beauty, ᵈGod hath shined.

3 Our God shall come, and shall not keep silence: a ᵉfire shall devour before him, and it shall be very tempestuous round about him.

4 ᶠHe shall call to the heavens from above, and to the earth, that he may judge his people.

5 Gather ᵍmy saints together unto me; ʰthose that have made a covenant with me by sacrifice.

6 And ⁱthe heavens shall declare his

ᵃOr, *for Asaph;* see 1 Chron. xv. 17; xxv. 2; 2 Chron. xxix. 30——ᵇNeh. ix. 32; Isa. ix. 6; Jer. xxxii. 18 ᶜPsa. xlviii. 2——ᵈDeut. xxxiii. 2; Psa. lxxx. 1——ᵉLev. x. 2; Num. xvi. 35; Psa. xcvii. 3; Dan. vii. 10——ᶠDeut. iv. 26; xxxi. 28; xxxii. 1; Isa. i. 2; Mic. vi. 1, 2——ᵍDeut. xxxiii. 3; Isa. xiii. 3——ʰExod. xxiv. 7——ⁱPsa. xcvii. 6

NOTES ON PSALM L

In the *title* this is said to be *A Psalm of Asaph.* There are *twelve* that go under his name; and most probably he was author of each, for he was of high repute in the days of David, and is mentioned *second* to him as a composer of psalms: *Moreover Hezekiah the king, and the princes, commanded the Levites to sing praise unto the Lord, with the* WORDS *of* DAVID, *and of* ASAPH *the* SEER. His band, sons or companions, were also eminent in the days of David, as we learn from 1 Chron. xxv., &c. *Asaph* himself was one of the *musicians* who *sounded with cymbals of brass,* 1 Chron. xv. 19. And he is mentioned with great respect, Neh. xii. 46: *And in the days of* DAVID *and* ASAPH *of old* there were CHIEF *of the* SINGERS, *and* SONGS *of* PRAISE *and* THANKSGIVING *unto God.* He was certainly a *prophetic* man: he is called a *seer*—one on whom the *Spirit of God rested;* and seems from this, his education, and natural talent, to be well qualified to *compose* hymns or psalms in the honour of God. Persons capable of judging, on a comparison of those Psalms attributed to *Asaph* with those known to be of *David,* have found a remarkable *difference* in the *style.* The style of David is more *polished, flowing, correct,* and *majestic,* than that of Asaph, which is more *stiff* and *obscure.* He has been compared to *Persius* and to *Horace;* he is *keen, full of reprehensions,* and his subjects are generally of the *doleful* kind; which was probably caused by his living in times in which there was great corruption of manners, and much of the displeasure of God either *theatened* or *manifested.* It is not known on what particular *occasion* this Psalm was written; but at most times it was suitable to the state of the Jewish Church.

Verse 1. *The mighty God, even the Lord, hath spoken*] Here the *essential names of God* are used: אל אלהים יהוה EL, ELOHIM, YEHOVAH, *hath spoken.* The *six first verses* of this Psalm seem to contain a description of the *great judgment:* to any minor consideration or fact it seems impossible, with any propriety, to re-strain them. In this light I shall consider this part of the Psalm, and show,—

First, The preparatives to the coming of the great Judge. *El Elohim Jehovah hath spoken, and called the earth*—all the children of men, *from the rising of the sun unto the going down thereof. Out of Zion, the perfection of beauty,* (מכלל יפי michlal yophi, the beauty where all perfection is comprised,) *God hath shined,* ver. 1, 2. 1. He has sent his Spirit to convince men of sin, righteousness, and judgment. 2. He has sent his WORD; has made a revelation of himself; and has declared both his law and his Gospel to mankind: "Out of Zion, the perfection of beauty, God hath shined," ver. 2. For out of Zion the law was to go forth, and the word of the Lord from Jerusalem. Isa. ii. 3.

Secondly, The accompaniments. 1. His approach is proclaimed, ver. 3: "Our God shall come." 2. The trumpet proclaims his approach: "He shall not keep silence." 3. Universal nature shall be shaken, and the earth and its works be burnt up: "A fire shall devour before him, and it shall be very tempestuous round about him," ver. 3.

Thirdly, The witnesses are summoned and collected, and collected from all quarters; some frcm heaven, and some from earth. 1. Guardian angels. 2. Human associates: "He shall call to the heavens from above, and to the earth, that he may judge his people," ver. 4.

Fourthly, The procedure. As far as it respects the righteous, orders are issued: "Gather my saints," those who are saved from their sins and made holy, "together unto me." And that the word *saints* might not be misunderstood, it is explained by "those that have made a covenant with me by sacrifice;" those who have entered into union with God, through the sacrificial offering of the Lord Jesus Christ. All the rest are passed over in silence. We are told who they are that shall enter into the joy of their Lord, viz., only the *saints,* those who have made a covenant with God by sacrifice. All, therefore, who do not answer this description are excluded from glory.

Fifthly, The final issue: all the angelic host,

righteousness: for [k]God *is* judge himself. Selah.

7 [l]Hear, O my people, and I will speak; O Israel, and I will testify against thee: [m]I *am* God, *even* thy God.

8 [n]I will not reprove thee [o]for thy sacrifices or thy burnt-offerings, *to have been* continually before me.

9 [p]I will take no bullock out of thy house, *nor* he-goats out of thy folds.

10 For every beast of the forest *is* mine, *and* the cattle upon a thousand hills.

11 I know all the fowls of the mountains: and the wild beasts of the field *are* [q]mine.

12 If I were hungry, I would not tell thee: [r]for the world *is* mine, and the fulness thereof.

13 Will I eat the flesh of bulls, or drink the blood of goats?

14 [s]Offer unto God thanksgiving; and [t]pay thy vows unto the Most High:

15 And [u]call upon me in the day of trouble: I will deliver thee, and thou shalt [v]glorify me.

16 But unto the wicked God saith, What

---

[k]Psa. lxxv. 7——[l]Psa. lxxxi. 8——[m]Exod. xx. 2 [n]Isa. i. 11; Jer. vii. 22——[o]Hos. vi. 6——[p]Mic. vi. 6; Acts xvii. 25——[q]Heb. *with me*——[r]Exod. xix. 5; Deut. x. 14; Job xli. 11; Psa. xxiv. 1; 1 Cor. x. 26, 28

[s]Hos. xiv. 2; Heb. xiii. 15——[t]Deut. xxiii. 21; Job xxii. 27; Psa. lxxvi. 11; Eccles v. 4, 5——[u]Job xxii. 27; Psa. xci. 15; cvii. 6, 13, 19, 28; Zech. xiii. 9——[v]Ver. 23; Psa. xxii. 23

---

and all the redeemed of the Lord, join in applauding acclamation at the decision of the Supreme Judge. The heavens (for the earth is no more, it is burnt up) shall declare his righteousness, the exact justice of the whole procedure, where justice alone has been done without partiality, and without severity; nor could it be otherwise, *for God is Judge himself.* Thus the assembly is dissolved; the righteous are received into everlasting glory, and the wicked turned into hell, with all those who forget God. Some think that the sentence against the wicked is that which is contained from ver. 16 to ver. 22. See the *analysis* at the end, and particularly on the six first verses, in which a somewhat different view of the subject is taken.

Verse 7. *Hear, O my people*] As they were now amply informed concerning the nature and certainty of the general judgment, and were still in a state of probation, Asaph proceeds to show them the danger to which they were exposed, and the necessity of repentance and amendment, that when that great day should arrive, they might be found among those who had made a covenant with God by sacrifice. And he shows them that the sacrifice with which God would be well pleased was quite different from the bullocks, he-goats, &c., which they were in the habit of offering. In short, he shows here that God has intended to abrogate those sacrifices, as being no longer of any service: for when the people began to trust in them, without looking to the thing signified, it was time to put them away. When the people began to pay Divine honours to the *brazen serpent*, though it was originally an ordinance of God's appointment for the healing of the Israelites, it was ordered to be taken away; called *nehushtan*, a bit of brass; and broken to pieces. The sacrifices under the Jewish law were of God's appointment; but now that the people began to put their trust in them, God despised them.

Verse 8. *I will not reprove thee*] I do not mean to find fault with you for not offering sacrifices; you have offered them, they *have been continually before me:* but you have not offered them in the proper way.

Verse 10. *Every beast of the forest* is mine] Can ye suppose that ye are laying me under *obligation* to you, when ye present me with a part of my own property?

Verse 12. *The world* is *mine, and the fulness thereof.*] Ye cannot, therefore, give me any thing that is not my own.

Verse 13. *Will I eat the flesh of bulls*] Can ye be so simple as to suppose that I appointed such sacrifices for my own gratification? All these were significative of a spiritual worship, and of the sacrifice of that Lamb of God which, in the fulness of time, was to take away, in an *atoning manner*, the sin of the world.

Verse 14. *Offer unto God thanksgiving; and pay thy vows unto the Most High*] זבח *zebach*, "sacrifice unto God, אלהים *Elohim*, the תודה *todah, thank-offering*," which was the same as the *sin-offering*, viz. *a bullock, or a ram, without blemish;* only there were, in addition, "unleavened cakes mingled with oil, and unleavened wafers anointed with oil; and cakes of fine flour mingled with oil and fried," Lev. vii. 12.

And pay thy vows] נדריך *nedareycha*, "thy vow-offering, to the Most High." The *neder* or *vow-offering* was *a male without blemish, taken from among the beeves, the sheep, or the goats.* Compare Lev. xxii. 19 with ver. 22. Now these were offerings, in their spiritual and proper meaning, which God required of the people: and as the sacrificial system was established for an especial end—to show the *sinfulness of sin*, and the *purity of Jehovah*, and to show how sin could be *atoned for, forgiven*, and *removed;* this system was now to end in the thing that it signified,—the grand sacrifice of Christ, which was to make *atonement, feed, nourish*, and *save* the souls of believers unto eternal life; to excite their praise and thanksgiving; *bind* them to God Almighty by the most solemn *vows* to live to him in the spirit of *gratitude* and *obedience* all the days of their life. And, in order that they might be able to hold fast faith and a good conscience, they were to make continual *prayer to God*, who promised to hear and deliver them, that they might glorify him, ver. 15.

From the 16th to the 22nd verse Asaph appears to refer to the final rejection of the Jews from having any part in the true *covenant sacrifice.*

Verse 16. *But unto the wicked*] The bloodthirsty priests, proud Pharisees, and ignorant scribes of the Jewish people.

hast thou to do to declare my statutes, or *that* thou shouldest take my covenant in thy mouth?

17 ᵂSeeing thou hatest instruction, and ˣcastest my words behind thee.

18 When thou sawest a thief, then thou ʸconsentedst with him, and ᶻhast been ᵃpartaker with adulterers.

19 ᵇThou givest thy mouth to evil, and ᶜthy tongue frameth deceit.

20 Thou sittest *and* speakest against thy brother; thou slanderest thine own mother's son.

21 These *things* hast thou done, ᵈand I kept silence; ᵉthou thoughtest that I was altogether *such an one* as thyself: *but* ᶠI will reprove thee, and set *them* in order before thine eyes.

22 Now consider this, ye that ᵍforget God, lest I tear *you* in pieces, and *there be* none to deliver.

23 ʰWhoso offereth praise glorifieth me: and ⁱto him ᵏthat ordereth *his* conversation *aright* will I show the salvation of God.

ᵂRom. ii. 21, 22——ˣNeh. ix. 26——ʸRom. i. 32 ᶻHeb. *thy portion* was *with adulterers*——ᵃ1 Tim. v. 22 ᵇHeb. *Thou sendest*——ᶜPsa. lii. 2——ᵈEccles. viii. 11,

12; Isa. xxvi. 10; lvii. 11——ᵉSee Rom. ii. 4——ᶠPsa. xc. 8 ᵍJob viii. 13; Psa. ix.17; Isa. li. 13——ʰPsa. xxvii. 6; Rom. xii.1 ——ⁱGal. vi. 16——ᵏHeb. *that disposeth* his *way*

Verse 17. *Seeing thou hatest instruction*] All these rejected the counsel of God against themselves; and refused to receive the instructions of Christ.

Verse 18. *When thou sawest a thief*] Rapine, adulteries, and adulterous *divines*, were common among the Jews in our Lord's time. The Gospels give full proof of this.

Verse 21. *These* things *hast thou done*] My eye has been continually upon you, though my judgments have not been poured out: and because I was *silent*, thou didst suppose *I was such as thyself*; *but I will reprove thee*, &c. I will visit for these things.

Verse 22. *Now consider this*] Ye have forgotten your God, and sinned against him. He has marked down all your iniquities, and has them *in order* to exhibit against you. Beware, therefore, *lest he tear you to pieces, when there is none to deliver;* for none can deliver you but the *Christ* you reject. And how can ye escape, if ye neglect so great a salvation?

Verse 23. *Whoso offereth praise*] These are the very same words as those in ver. 14, זבח תודה; and should be read the same way independently of the *points, zebach todah*, "sacrifice the thank-offering." JESUS is the great *eucharistic sacrifice;* offer him up to God in your faith and prayers. By this sacrifice is God *glorified*, for in him is God *well pleased;* and it was by the *grace* or *good pleasure of God* that he *tasted death for every man.*

Ordereth his *conversation*] שׂם דרך *sam derech*, DISPOSETH his *way.—Margin. Has his way* THERE, שׂם דרך *sham derech*, as many MSS. and old editions have it; or *makes that his custom.*

Will I show the salvation of God.] אראנו *arennu*, I will cause him to see בישׁע *beyesha*, into the salvation of God; into God's method of saving sinners by Christ. He shall witness my saving power even to the uttermost; such a salvation as it became a God to bestow, and as a fallen soul needs to receive; the salvation from all sin, which Christ has purchased by his death. **I sall scheu til him, the hele of God**; that es JESHU, that he se him in the fairehed of his majeste.—*Old Psalter.*

ANALYSIS OF THE FIFTIETH PSALM

The prophet, by a *prosopopœia*, brings in God prescribing rules for his own worship. The point in debate is: *How God will be honoured in his own Church?* And as none can teach this but God, he brings him in speaking to his people.

The Psalm has *two* general parts:—

I. The *majesty* and *authority* of the person who is to judge this debate, ver. 1-6.

II. The *sentence* which he pronounces, ver. 7-23.

The prophet begins with calling an *assize.* He summons a *court*, presents us with a *judge*, produces *witnesses*, cites those who are to *answer*, and, having seated the Judge on his throne, gives forth his *charge.*

I. *First.* He *presents*, 1. The *Judge*, in authority and majesty: "The mighty God, even the Lord, hath spoken," ver. 1.

2. The *place* to which he comes to hold his court—the *Church:* "Out of Zion, the perfection of beauty; God hath shined." To Zion the *law* was given; and *out of* Zion the law was to come, by which he would judge; and therefore it was rightly said, "Out of Zion the Lord hath shined."

3. His *appearance*, which is *terrible.* It was so when he gave his *law* on Mount *Sinai;* and it will be so when he comes to require it: "Our God shall come, and shall not keep silence; a fire shall devour before him, and it shall be very tempestuous round about him." See 2 Pet. iii. 10; Luke xxi. 25, 26.

Secondly. Those who are *cited* to appear before him—his *saints*—those who had undertaken to worship him as he had appointed: "Gather my saints together; those who have made a covenant with me by sacrifice."

Thirdly. Against these he produces his *witnesses*, whom he collects, 1. From *heaven;* 2. From *earth.* "He shall call the heavens from above, and the earth, that he may judge his people." Including the inhabitants of the whole earth, "from the rising of the sun until the going down thereof." And his *award* shall be universally approved: "The heavens shall declare his righteousness—his just method of procedure; for God himself is Judge."

II. Next follows the *charge* given by God himself the Judge; and, to engage attention, he proclaims: "Hear, O my people, and I will speak," &c.

1. "I am God;" therefore, worship and obedience are due to me from all creatures.

2. "I am thy God; and thou art my people;" therefore, due from thee especially.

3. "I will speak." I will judge and determine this controversy about my worship.

4. "I will testify against thee," and convict thee of what thou hast done amiss.

There is a *twofold worship:* 1. *Ceremonial* and external. 2. *Spiritual* and moral. And I will *speak* and *testify* of both.

It was the *duty* of the people to bring the sacrifice, and perform the ceremonies appointed by the law: but God is not pleased with the outward act merely; nothing pleases him where the heart and affections are wanting.

1. "I will not reprove thee for thy sacrifices." These thou bringest, and these I accept. But in this I reprove thee, because thou thinkest that I must be pleased with the *external service,* howsoever performed; and that thou hast a right to expect pardon and all other blessings.

2. Unless the heart be penitent, and the offerings be made in faith, I will not accept them: "I will take no bullock out of thy house, nor he-goat," &c. And this for *two* reasons:—

1. I do not need them: "Every beast of the forest is mine—the cattle on a thousand hills—the fowls of the mountain—the wild beasts of the field—the world and its fulness."

2. My perfection is such that I could not use them: "Thinkest thou that I will eat the flesh of bulls, or drink the blood of goats?"

The heathen priests taught the people that the gods *fed* on the *odour* of the sacrifices; and they represented them as complaining of being *starved,* when they were withheld!

For these reasons the sacrifices, as you have performed them, do not please me; but I shall acquaint you with those that do please me; *thanksgiving* and *prayer* or *invocation.*

1. *Thankfulness:* "Offer unto God thanksgiving, and pay thy vows," &c.

2. *Invocation:* "Call upon me in the day of trouble."

Which being done, he makes an *indenture* with us:

1. On *his* part, that he will *save us:* "I will deliver thee."

2. On *our* part, that we give him the *glory* of our *salvation:* "Thou shalt glorify me."

3. And yet he makes an *exception* to some

men's *prayers* and *praises,* hypocrites and impious men. *Praise is not comely in the mouth of a sinner,* and petitions offered by the *profane* shall not be heard.

1. "To the wicked God saith, What hast thou to do to declare my statutes," &c.

2. The reason is: Thou professest to love me, but in works thou deniest me: for thou hatest instruction, and hast cast my words behind thee: how then can I be pleased with thee? I shall now prove this against thee.

1. Thou hast broken the *eighth* commandment: "Thou sawest the thief, and consentedst to him,"—joinedst with him to carry off the spoil; or, when he *stole,* thou didst *receive.*

2. Thou hast broken the *seventh* commandment. "Thou hast been a partaker with the adulterers."

3. And the *ninth:* "Thou givest thy mouth to evil, and thy tongue frameth deceit;—thou sittest and speakest against thy brother, and slanderest thy own mother's son." Thou didst do all this deliberately. Thou didst *sit* and *speak.*

4. Thou hast broken the *first* commandment. Because I did not execute judgment upon thy evil works, "thou thoughtest that I was altogether such a one as thyself;" or, in a word, that there was *no God,* or none worthy of fear and reverence.

This wickedness I will not suffer to go unpunished; for the day will come when "I will reprove thee,—set thy sins in order before thee, and punish the wickedness which thou hast attempted to hide. Yet in *judgment* God remembers *mercy;* he gives warning to the wicked, and threatens that he may spare, and that they may repent and perish not.

1. *Now,* while you have respite, *consider this,* that God is not pleased with outward rites and formalities, and that they who trust in merely having performed them are far from being in a safe state. They do the outward work, and *forget God.* Take heed, lest as a lion he rush out upon you, and *tear you to pieces.*

2. To the pure and spiritual worshippers he makes a gracious promise of *defence, help,* and *salvation. He who sacrifices the thank-offering,* with an humble, believing heart, *glorifies me;* and to him who *places his feet in that path,* and THERE determinately abides, going the right way which God's word directs, *I will show the salvation of God*—he shall be saved; and shall know that he worships not God in vain. See the preceding *notes* on this Psalm.

PSALM LI

The psalmist, with a deeply penitent heart, prays for remission of sins, 1–4; which he confesses, and deeply deplores, 5–14; states his willingness to offer sacrifice, but is convinced that God prefers a broken heart to all kinds of oblations, 15–17; prays for the restoration of the walls of Jerusalem, and promises that then the Lord's sacrifice shall be properly performed, 18, 19.

To the chief Musician, A Psalm of David, [a]when Nathan the prophet came unto him, after he had gone in to Bath-sheba

A. M. cir. 2971
B. C. cir. 1033
Davidis, Regis
Israelitarum,
cir. annum
23

HAVE mercy upon me, O God, according to thy loving-kindness: according unto the multitude of thy tender mercies, [b]blot out my transgressions.

2 [c]Wash me throughly from mine iniquity, and cleanse me from my sin.

A. M. cir. 2971
B. C. cir. 1033
Davidis, Regis
Israelitarum,
cir. annum
23

3 For [d]I acknowledge my transgressions: and my sin *is* ever before me.

4 [e]Against thee, thee only, have I sinned, and done *this* evil [f]in thy sight: [g]that thou might-

---

[a]2 Sam. xii. 1; xi. 2, 4——[b]Ver. 9; Isa. xliii. 25; xliv. 22; Col. ii. 14——[c]Hebrews ix. 14; 1 John i. 7, 9; Rev. 1. 5

[d]Psa. xxxii. 5; xxxviii. 18——[e]Gen. xx. 6; xxxix. 9; Lev. v. 19; vi. 2; 2 Sam. xii. 13——[f]Luke xv. 21 [g]Rom. iii. 4

NOTES ON PSALM LI

The *title* is long: "To the chief Musician, A Psalm of David, when Nathan the prophet came unto him, after he had gone in to Bath-sheba." The propriety of this title has been greatly suspected, says Bishop *Horsley:* "That this Psalm was not written on the occasion to which the title refers, is evident from the 4th and 18th verses. The 4th verse ill suits the case of David, who laid a successful plot against Uriah's life, after he had defiled his bed: and the 18th verse refers the Psalm to the time of the captivity, when Jerusalem lay in ruins." Dr. *Kennicott* is of the same mind. He says: "The title is misplaced; that it was written during the *captivity,* and the cessation of the temple worship; the author under great depression of mind, arising from the guilt of some crime, probably some compliance with heathen idolatry, not *murder* nor *adultery; is plain* from the 4th verse, "Against THEE ONLY have I sinned."

The crime mentioned in the *title* was not only against God, but against the whole order of civil society; against the life of the noble and valiant captain whose wife Bath-sheba was, and against every thing sacred in friendship and hospitality. It was a congeries of sins against God and society. Were it not for the 4th, 18th, and 19th verses, the rest of the Psalm would accord well enough with the *title,* and the deep penitence it expresses would be suitable enough to David's state. But see on verses 4, 18, 19.

Verse 1. Have mercy upon me, O God] Without mercy I am totally, finally ruined and undone.

According to thy loving-kindness] Mark the gradation in the sense of these three words, *Have* MERCY *on me,* חנני *chonneni; thy* LOVING-KINDNESS, חסדך *chasdecha;—thy* TENDER MERCIES, רחמיך *rachameycha,* here used to express the Divine compassion. The propriety of the order in which they are placed deserves particular observation.

The *first,* rendered *have mercy* or *pity,* denotes that kind of affection which is expressed by moaning over an object we love and pity; that natural affection and tenderness which even the brute creation show to their young by the several noises they respectively make over them.

The *second,* rendered *loving-kindness,* denotes a strong proneness, a ready, large, and liberal disposition, to goodness and compassion, powerfully prompting to all instances of *kindness* and bounty; flowing as freely as waters from a perpetual fountain. This denotes a higher degree of goodness than the former.

The *third,* rendered *tender mercies,* denotes

what the Greeks called σπλαγχνἰζεσθαι, that *most tender pity* which we signify by the moving of the heart and bowels, which argues the highest degree of compassion of which nature is susceptible. See *Chandler.*

Blot out my transgressions] מחה *mecheh, wipe out.* There is a reference here to an *indictment:* the psalmist knows what it contains; he pleads guilty, but begs that the writing may be *defaced;* that a proper fluid may be applied to the parchment, *to discharge the ink,* that no record of it may ever appear against him: and this only the *mercy, loving-kindness,* and *tender compassions* of the Lord can do.

Verse 2. *Wash me throughly]* הרבה כבסני *harbeh cabbeseni,* "Wash me again and again, —cause my washings to be multiplied." My stain is deep; ordinary purgation will not be sufficient.

Verse 3. *For I acknowledge my transgressions]* I know, I feel, I confess that I have sinned.

My sin is ever before me.] A true, deep, and unsophisticated mark of a genuine penitent. Wherever he turns his face, he sees his sin, and through it the eye of an angry God.

Verse 4. *Against thee, thee only, have I sinned]* This verse is supposed to show the impropriety of affixing the above *title* to this Psalm. It could not have been composed on account of the matter with Bath-sheba and the murder of Uriah; for, surely, these sins could not be said to have been committed against God ONLY, if we take the words of this verse in their common acceptation. That was a *public* sin, grievous, and against society at large, as well as against the peace, honour, comfort, and *life* of an innocent, brave, and patriotic man. This is readily granted: but see below.

That thou mightest be justified when thou speakest] Perhaps, to save the propriety of the *title,* we might understand the verse thus: David, being *king,* was not liable to be called to account by any of his *subjects;* nor was there any *authority* in the land by which he could be *judged* and *punished.* In this respect, God ALONE was *greater than the king;* and to *him* ALONE, as king, he was responsible. *Nam quando rex deliquit,* SOLI DEO *reus est; quia hominem non habet qui ejus facta dijudicet,* says *Cassiodorus.* "For when a king transgresses, he is accountable to GOD ONLY; for there is no person who has authority to take cognizance of his conduct." On this very maxim, which is a maxim in all countries, David might say, *Against thee only have I sinned.* "I cannot be called to the bar of my subjects; but I arraign myself before thy bar. They can neither judge nor condemn me; but thou canst: and such are my crimes that thou wilt be justified in the

A. M. cir. 2971
B. C. cir. 1033
Davidis, Regis
Israelitarum,
cir. annum
23

est be justified when thou speak-est, *and* be clear when thou judgest.

5 [h]Behold, I was shapen in ini-quity; [i]and in sin did my mother[k]conceive me.

6 Behold, thou desirest truth [l]in the inward parts; and in the hidden *part* thou shalt make me to know wisdom.

7 [m]Purge me with hyssop, and I shall be clean: wash me, and I shall be [n]whiter than snow.

A. M. cir. 2971
B. C. cir. 1033
Davidis, Regis
Israelitarum,
cir. annum
23

8 Make me to hear joy and gladness; *that* the bones *which* thou hast broken [o]may rejoice.

9 [p]Hide thy face from my sins, and [q]blot out all mine iniquities.

10 [r]Create in me a clean heart, O God; and renew [s]a right spirit within me.

11 Cast me not away [t]from thy pre-sence; and take not thy [u]Holy Spirit from me.

---

[h]Job xiv. 4; Psa. lviii. 3; John. iii. 6; Rom. v. 12; Eph. ii. 3——[i]Job xiv. 4——[k]Heb. *warm me*——[l]Job xxxviii. 36——[m]Lev. xiv. 4, 6, 49; Num. xix. 18; Heb. ix. 19

[n]Isa. i. 18——[o]Matt. v. 4——[p]Jer. xvi. 17——[q]Ver. 1 [r]Acts xv. 9; Eph. ii. 10——[s]Or, *a constant spirit* [t]Gen. iv. 14; 2 Kings xiii. 23——[u]Rom. viii. 9; Eph. iv. 30

---

eyes of all men, and cleared of all *severity*, shouldst thou inflict upon me the heaviest pun-ishment." This view of the subject will recon-cile the Psalm to the *title*. As to the eighteenth and nineteenth verses, we shall consider them in their own place; and probably find that the objection taken from *them* has not much weight.

Verse 5. *Behold, I was shapen in iniquity*] A genuine penitent will hide nothing of his state; he sees and bewails, not only the *acts* of sin which he has committed, but the *dis-position* that led to those acts. He deplores, not only the *transgression*, but the *carnal mind*, which is enmity against God. The light that shines into his soul shows him the very source whence transgression proceeds; he sees his fallen nature, as well as his sinful life; he asks *pardon* for his transgressions, and he asks *washing* and *cleansing* for his inward defile-ment. Notwithstanding all that *Grotius* and others have said to the contrary, I believe David to speak here of what is commonly called *origi-nal sin;* the propensity to evil which every man brings into the world with him, and which is the fruitful source whence all transgression pro-ceeds. The word חוללתי *cholalti*, which we translate *shapen*, means more properly, *I was brought forth from the womb;* and יחמתני *yechemathni* rather signifies *made me warm*, alluding to the whole process of the formation of the *fetus in utero*, the formative heat which is necessary to develope the parts of all embryo animals; to incubate the *ova* in the female, after having been impregnated by the male; and to bring the whole into such a state of maturity and perfection as to render it capable of subsisting and growing up by aliment re-ceived from *without*. "As my parts were developed in the womb, the sinful principle diffused itself through the whole, so that body and mind grew up in a state of corruption and moral imperfection."

Verse 6. *Behold, thou desirest truth*] I am the very reverse of what I should be. *Thou desirest truth in the heart;* but in me there is nothing but sin and falsity.

Thou shalt make me to know wisdom.] Thou wilt teach me to restrain every inordinate pro-pensity, and to act according to the dictates of sound wisdom, the rest of my life.

Verse 7. *Purge me with hyssop*] תחטאני *techatteeni*, "thou shalt make a sin-offering for me;" probably alluding to the cleansing of the

leper: Lev. xiv. 1, &c. The priest took two clean birds, cedar-wood, scarlet, and hyssop; one of the birds was killed; and the living bird, with the scarlet, cedar, and hyssop, dipped in the blood of the bird that had been killed, and then sprinkled over the person who had been infected. But it is worthy of remark that this ceremony was not performed till the plague of the leprosy had *been healed* in the leper; (Lev. xiv. 3;) and the ceremony above mentioned was for the purpose of *declaring* to the people that the man was healed, that he might be restored to his place in society, having been healed of a disease that the finger of God alone could remove. This David seems to have full in view; hence he requests the *Lord* to *make the sin-offering for him*, and to show to the people that he had accepted him, and cleansed him from his sin.

Verse 8. *Make me to hear joy*] Let me have a full testimony of my reconciliation to thee; that the soul, which is so deeply distressed by a sense of thy displeasure, may be healed by a sense of thy pardoning mercy.

Verse 9. *Hide thy face from my sins*] The sentiment here is nearly the same as that in ver. 3: *His sin was ever before his own face;* and he knew that the eye of God was constantly upon him, and that his purity and justice must be highly incensed on the account. He there-fore, with a just horror of his transgressions, begs God to *turn away his face from them*, and to blot them out, so that they may never more be seen. See the note on ver. 1.

Verse 10. *Create in me a clean heart*] Mend-*ing* will not avail; my heart is altogether cor-rupted; it must be *new made*, made as it was in the beginning. This is exactly the sentiment of St. Paul: *Neither circumcision availeth any thing, nor uncircumcision, but a new creation;* and the salvation given under the Gospel dis-pensation is called a *being created anew in Christ Jesus.*

A right spirit within me.] רוח נכון *ruach nachon*, a constant, steady, determined spirit; called ver. 12, רוח נדיבה *ruach nedibah*, a noble spirit, a *free, generous, princely* spirit; cheer-fully giving up itself to thee; no longer *bound* and *degraded* by the sinfulness of sin.

Verse 11. *Cast me not away from thy pres-ence*] Banish me not from thy house and ordi-nances.

Take not thy Holy Spirit from me.] I know I

A. M. cir. 2971
B. C. cir. 1033
Davidis, Regis
Israelitarum,
cir. annum
23

12 Restore unto me the joy of thy salvation; and uphold me *with thy* ᵛfree spirit.

13 *Then* will I teach transgressors thy ways; and sinners shall be converted unto thee.

14 Deliver me from ʷblood-guiltiness, ˣO God, thou God of my salvation: *and* ʸmy tongue shall sing aloud of thy righteousness.

15 O LORD, open thou my lips; and my mouth shall show forth thy praise.

16 For ᶻthou desirest not sacrifice; ᵃelse

would I give *it:* thou delightest not in burnt-offering.

17 ᵇThe sacrifices of God *are* a broken spirit: a broken and a contrite heart, O God, thou wilt not despise.

18 Do good in thy good pleasure unto Zion: build thou the walls of Jerusalem.

19 Then shalt thou be pleased with ᶜthe sacrifices of righteousness, with burnt-offering and whole burnt-offering; then shall they offer bullocks upon thine altar.

A. M. cir. 2971
B. C. cir. 1033
Davidis, Regis
Israelitarum,
cir. annum
23

ᵛ2 Corinthians iii. 17——ʷHebrew, *bloods*——ˣ2 Samuel xi. 17; xii. 9——ʸPsalm xxxv. 28——ᶻNumbers xv. 27, 30; Psalm xl. 6; l. 8; Isaiah i. 11; Jeremiah vii. 22; Hosea vi. 6——ᵃOr, *that I should give it*——ᵇPsa. xxxiv. 18; Isaiah lvii. 15; lxvi. 2——ᶜPsalm iv. 5; Mal. iii. 3

---

have sufficiently grieved it to justify its departure for ever; in consequence of which I should be consigned to the blackness of darkness,—either to utter despair, or to a hard heart and seared conscience; and so work iniquity with greediness, till I fell into the pit of perdition. While the Spirit stays, painfully convincing of sin, righteousness, and judgment, there is hope of salvation; when it departs, then the hope of redemption is gone. But while there is any *godly sorrow*, any *feeling* of regret for having sinned against God, any *desire* to seek mercy, then the case is not hopeless; for these things prove that the light of the Spirit is not withdrawn.

Verse 12. *Restore unto me the joy of thy salvation*] This is an awful prayer. And why? Because it shows he *once* HAD *the joy of God's salvation; and had* LOST *it by sin!*

Uphold me with thy *free spirit.*] Prop me up; support me with a princely spirit, one that will not stoop to a mean or base act. See on ver. 10.

Verse 13. Then *will I teach transgressors*] I will show myself to be grateful; I will testify of thy loving-kindness; I will call on transgressors to consider the error of their ways; and shall set before them so forcibly thy *justice* and *mercy*, that sinners shall be converted unto thee. With a little change I can adopt the language of Dr. *Delaney* on this place: "Who can confide in his own strength, when he sees David fall? Who can despair of Divine mercy when he sees *him* forgiven? Sad triumph of sin over all that is great or excellent in man! Glorious triumph of grace over all that is shameful and dreadful in sin!"

Verse 14. *Deliver me from blood-guiltiness*] This is one of the expressions that gives most colour to the propriety of the title affixed to this Psalm. Here he may have in view the *death of Uriah*, and consider that *his blood* cries for vengeance against him; and nothing but the mere mercy of God can wipe this blood from his conscience. The prayer here is earnest and energetic: *O God! thou God of my salvation! deliver me!* The *Chaldee* reads, "Deliver me (מדין קטול *middin ketol*) from the judgment of slaughter."

My tongue shall sing aloud] My tongue shall praise thy righteousness. I shall testify to all that thou hast the highest displeasure against

sin, and wilt excuse it in no person; and that so merciful art thou, that if a sinner turn to thee with a deeply penitent and broken heart, thou wilt forgive his iniquities. None, from my case, *can* ever *presume;* none, from my case, *need* ever *despair.*

Verse 15. *O Lord, open thou my lips*] My heart is believing unto righteousness; give me thy peace, that my tongue may make confession unto salvation. He could not praise God for pardon till he felt that God had pardoned him; then his lips would be opened, and his tongue would show forth the praise of his Redeemer.

Verse 16. *For thou desirest not sacrifice*] This is the same sentiment which he delivers in Psa. xl. 6, &c., where see the notes. There may be here, however, a farther meaning: Crimes, like mine, are not to be expiated by any sacrifices that the law requires; nor hast thou appointed in the law any sacrifices to atone for deliberate murder and adultery: if thou hadst, I would cheerfully have given them to thee. The matter is before thee as Judge.

Verse 17. *The sacrifices of God* are *a broken spirit*] As my crimes are such as admit of no legal atonement, so thou hast reserved them to be punished by exemplary acts of justice, or to be pardoned by a sovereign act of mercy: but in order to find this mercy, thou requirest that the heart and soul should deeply feel the transgression, and turn to thee with the fullest compunction and remorse. This thou hast enabled me to do. I have the broken spirit, רוח נשברה *ruach nishbarah;* and the broken and contrite heart, לב נשבר ונדכה *leb nishbar venidkeh.* These words are very expressive. שבר *shabar* signifies exactly the same as our word *shiver*, to *break into pieces*, to *reduce into splinters;* and דכה *dakah*, signifies to *beat out thin*,—to beat out masses of metal, &c., *into laminæ* or *thin plates.* The spirit broken all to pieces, and the heart broken all to pieces, stamped and beaten out, are the sacrifices which, in such cases, thou requirest; and these "thou wilt not despise." We may now suppose that God had shone upon his soul, healed his broken spirit, and renewed and removed his broken and distracted heart; and that he had now received the answer to the preceding prayers. And here the Psalm properly ends; as, in the two following verses, there is nothing similar to what we find in the rest of this very nervous and most important composition.

Verse 18. *Do good in thy good pleasure unto Zion*] This and the following verse most evidently refer to the time of the *captivity*, when the *walls of Jerusalem were broken down*, and the *temple service entirely discontinued;* and, consequently, are long posterior to the times of David. Hence it has been concluded that the Psalm was not composed by David, nor in his time and that the *title* must be that of some other Psalm inadvertently affixed to this. The fourth verse has also been considered as decisive against this *title:* but the note on that verse has considerably weakened, if not destroyed, that objection. I have been long of opinion that, whether the *title* be properly or improperly affixed to this Psalm, these *two verses* make no part of it: the subject is totally dissimilar; and there is no rule of analogy by which it can be interpreted as belonging to the *Psalm*, to the *subject*, or to the *person.* I think they originally made a Psalm of themselves, a kind of *ejaculatory prayer* for the *redemption of the captives from Babylon*, the *rebuilding of Jerusalem*, and *the restoration of the temple worship.* And, taken in this light, they are very proper and very expressive.

The cxviith Psalm contains only *two verses;* and is an *ejaculation of praise from the captives who had just then returned from Babylon.* And it is a fact that this Psalm is written as a *part* of the cxviith in no less than *thirty-two* of *Kennicott's* and *De Rossi's* MSS.; and in some early editions. Again, because of its smallness, it has been absorbed by the cxviiith, of which it makes the *commencement*, in *twenty-eight* of *Kennicott's* and *De Rossi's* MSS. In a similar way I suppose the two last verses of this Psalm to have been absorbed by the preceding, which originally made a complete Psalm of themselves; and this absorption was the more easy, because, like the cxviith it has no *title.* I cannot allege a similar evidence relative to these two verses, as ever having made a distinct Psalm; but of the fact I can have no doubt, for the reasons assigned above. And I still think that Psalm is too dignified, too energetic, and too elegant, to have been the composition of any but David. It was not Asaph; it was not any of the sons of Korah; it was not Heman or Jeduthun: the hand and mind of a greater master are here.

ANALYSIS OF THE FIFTY-FIRST PSALM

In general the Psalm contains David's prayer,—
I. For himself, ver. 1-12.
II. Three vows or promises, ver. 13-18.
III. For the Church, ver. 18, 19.

I. David being in deep distress on account of his sins, prays to God for *mercy:* and while he feels that he is unworthy of the name of *king*, or *God's anointed*, of *his son*, or of *his servant*, he uses *no plea of his* own *merit*, but, —1. Of the loving-kindness of God: "According to thy loving-kindness." 2. Of the compassion of God: "According to the multitude of thy tender mercies."

The general petition for mercy being offered, next he offers *three* particular petitions:—

First. He prays for *forgiveness of sins.* The fact was past, but the guilt remained: therefore, he earnestly petitions: "Put away mine

iniquities;" my sin is a deep stain: "Wash me throughly from mine iniquities, and cleanse me from my sin," *multiply* washing; my sin is a *deep* defilement.

To this petition he joins *confession of sin;* from which we may learn the conditions requisite in a genuine confession:—

He considers the *nature* of his sin; he feels the *weight* of it, the *burden*, and the *anguish* of it; and *abhors* it.

1. "I know mine iniquity." It is no longer hidden from me.

2. "It is ever before me;" and the sight breaks my heart.

3. He uses different *epithets* for it, in order to aggravate the guilt, and deepen the repentance. 1. It is *transgression*, פשע *pesha*, rebellion. 2. It is *iniquity*, עון *avon*, crooked dealing. 3. It is *sin*, חטאת *chattath*, error and wandering.

Then he begins his earnest *confession:* "I have sinned." And this he aggravates by several circumstances:—

1. Of the *person.* It is "against thee;" a good and gracious God, who of a *shepherd* made me a *king* over thy own people. *Against thee*, the great and terrible God. The people are my *subjects*, and they cannot judge me: it is against *thee* I have sinned, and to *thee* I must give account, and by *thee* be judged and punished.

2. Of the *manner.* It was an *impudent* sin; not committed by *surprise*, but done openly: "In thy sight." Therefore, the threatenings by thy prophet are all right. Whatever punishment thou mayest inflict upon me, both thy justice and mercy will stand clear: "That thou mightest be justified," &c.

3. He shows from what *root* his sin sprang; from his *original corruption:* "Behold, I was shapen in iniquity, and in sin did my mother conceive me." I am all corruption *within*, and defilement *without.* The evil fountain hath sent forth bitter waters.

4. Another aggravation of his sin was, that he was in *principle* devoid of that which God *loves:* "Thou desirest truth in the inward parts."

5. The greatest aggravation of all was, his having sinned against light and knowledge. God had endued him with *wisdom in the hidden part*, by the motions of his own Spirit; but he had permitted his passions to obscure that light, and had quenched the Spirit.

Having made this general confession, he names the *particular sin* that lay heaviest on his conscience: "Deliver me from blood-guiltiness." And then renews his petition for *pardon* under a *type* then in use, and a *metaphor.* The type, *hyssop;* the metaphor, *wash me.*

1. "Purge me with hyssop." With a bunch of hyssop, dipped in the blood of the paschal lamb, the Israelites sprinkled their doors. It was also used in the sprinkling of the *leper*, and in the *sacrifice for sin:* and the *blood* and *sprinkling* were a *type of Christ's blood*, and the pardon and holiness that came through it. Sprinkled with this, David knew he must be clean; "for the blood of Christ cleanseth from all sin;" and it is "the blood of Christ that justifies."

2. *Sanctified* also he wishes to be; and there, he says, *Wash me.* And this is done by the influence of God's Spirit: "I will sprinkle clean water upon you, and you shall be clean," Ezek. xxxvi. 25.

Secondly. David, having ended his *petitions for pardon*, proceeds,—

1. To pray that the *evil effects* which had been produced by his sin might be removed: "Make me to hear joy and gladness," &c.

2. That his *body*, which was in a pining condition, might be restored: "That the bones which thou hast broken may rejoice."

3. A *third* evil effect of his sin was, that God's face, that is, his favour, was turned away from him: he therefore begs,—

(1) "Hide thy face from my sins." Remember them not against me.

(2) "And blot out mine iniquities." I know there is a long and black catalogue in thy book against me; blot it out; blot out the handwriting of ordinances that is against me.

Thirdly. Now follows David's *last* petition; in which he again craves more particularly the grace of *sanctification*. He first prayed for *remission;* next for *reconciliation;* and now for *renovation*, which he asks of God in the *three* following verses: 1. "Create in me a clean heart." 2. "Renew a right spirit within me." 3. "Cast me not away from thy presence." 4. "Take not thy Holy Spirit from me." 5. "Restore unto me the joy of thy salvation." 6. "Uphold me with thy free spirit." In which petitions we are to consider,—

1. The *subject* on which the work is to be done. The *heart,—the spirit.* For as the heart is that part that first lives in nature; so it is the first that lives in grace. The work must begin *within*, else *outward* renovation will be to little purpose.

2. The *work* itself, which is,—

1. A *creation.* Sin had reduced David's heart to *nothing* in respect to heavenly affections and things; and to bring it into a state in which it would answer the *end of its creation;* was to bring *something* out of *nothing;* which, in all cases, is the work of Almighty God: "Create in me, O God," &c.

2. It is a *renovation.* All in David was the *old man*, nothing left of the *new man*. He prays, therefore, to be renewed in the spirit of his mind: "Renew a right spirit within me."

3. *Reconciliation* and *restitution.* Cast me not away—as a dead man; nor take away thy Spirit from me, by which I live: "Cast me not away;—take not thy Holy Spirit from me."

4. A *confirmation* in what was good. *Uphold*—*confirm me.*

3. Who was to do this work? Not *himself;* God alone. Therefore, he prays: "O God, create;—O Lord, renew;—uphold by thy Spirit."

4. The *quality* of this. A *cleansing*—implied in these remarkable words:—a *right spirit,*—a *holy spirit,*—a *free spirit;* in which some have thought they saw the *mystery of the* Holy Trinity.

1. A *right spirit.* He felt that he might easily go *wrong;* a *crooked* and *perverse* spirit had prevailed within him, which had led him out of the *right way* to salvation: "Renew in me a right spirit."

2. A *holy spirit;* one opposed to the *carnal spirit* that was *enmity* against God, the motions and desires of which were from the flesh, and tended only to its gratification: "Take not thy Holy Spirit from me." It is God's Holy Spirit that makes the spirit of man *holy. Holiness of heart* depends on the indwelling of the *Holy Ghost.*

3. A *free spirit.* A *noble*, a *princely* spirit. Ever since his fall he felt he did nothing good; but by *constraint*, he was in *bondage* to corruption. There was no *dignity* in his mind, sin had *debased* it. "Ennoble me by a birth from above," and by thy *noble Spirit uphold me!*

II. He had now presented his *three petitions*, and now he makes his *vows:* 1. To teach others; 2. To praise God; and, 3. To offer him such a sacrifice as he could perform.

His *first* vow. 1. *Then*, after pardon obtained, "I shall teach;" for a man under guilt is not able to declare *pardon* to others.

2. "I will teach thy way to sinners;" viz.: that to the *stubborn* thou wilt show thyself *froward;* but to the *penitent* thou wilt show *mercy.*

The *effect* of which will be: "Sinners shall be converted unto thee." They who hear of thy *justice* and *mercy*, as manifested in my case, will *fear*, and turn from *sin;* have *faith*, and turn to THEE.

His *second* vow and promise is to *praise God:* "My tongue shall sing aloud of thy righteousness." But to this he was 1. *Unapt;* and must be so till received into *favour*. And, 2. *Unable*, till he received the healthful Spirit of the grace of God. Therefore he prays for a capacity to do both: 1. "Deliver me from blood-guiltiness, O God; then my tongue shall sing." 2. "O Lord, open my lips—and my mouth shall show forth thy praise."

His *third* promise is about a *sacrifice*, not of any *animal*, but of a "broken spirit; a broken and contrite heart," which he knew God would not despise. 1. "Thou desirest no sacrifice, else I would give it thee." No *outward* sacrifice can be of any avail if the *heart* be not offered. 2. Nor will the *heart* be accepted if it be not *sacrificed.* "The broken spirit and contrite heart," this sacrifice he vowed to bring.

III. Having finished his *prayers* and *vows* for himself, he forgets not *Jerusalem.* He petitions for God's Church; and the reason might be, that he was afraid Jerusalem would suffer because of his sins; for *peccant reges, plectuntur Achivi*, "the king sins, the people suffer." This was the case when he sinned against God by numbering the people.

His *method* and his *charity* in this are both instructive.

1. His *method.* 1. To be reconciled to God himself; and then, 2. To pray for others. "The prayers of the righteous avail much."

2. His *charity;* for we are always bound "to remember the afflictions of Joseph, and pray for the peace of Jerusalem." He prays,

1. That God, who out of his good pleasure did choose a Church, would out of his mere good will *do it good*, and preserve it: "Do good, in thy good pleasure, to Zion."

2. That he would have a special favour, even to the *building:* "Build thou the walls of Jerusalem;" for these fall not alone; religion and the service of God fall, when the people permit their churches and chapels to be dilapidated or get out of repair. Of this there are multitudes of proofs.

3. For the consequence of Jerusalem's prosperity would be this, that "religion would flourish with it;" then there would be *sacrifices, burnt-offerings*, and *holocausts:* "Then they shall offer bullocks upon thine altar."

4. And, what is yet *more* and *better, we* shall offer, and THOU wilt accept: "Then thou shalt

be pleased with the sacrifices of righteousness." Being reconciled to thee, justified, and sanctified; and righteous in all our conduct; all our

sacrifices, springing from thy own grace and love in us, shall find a gracious acceptance. See the note on ver. 18.

PSALM LII

The psalmist points out the malevolence of a powerful enemy, and predicts his destruction, 1–5. At which destruction the righteous should rejoice, 6, 7. The psalmist's confidence in God, 8, 9.

To the chief Musician, Maschil, *A Psalm* of David, ᵃwhen Doeg the Edomite came and ᵇtold Saul, and said unto him, David is come to the house of Ahimelech

A. M. cir. 2942
B. C. cir. 1062
Sauli, Regis
Israelitarum,
cir. annum
34

WHY boastest thou thyself in mischief, O ᶜmighty man? the goodness of God *endureth* continually.

2 ᵈThy tongue deviseth mischief; ᵉlike a sharp razor, working deceitfully.

3 Thou lovest evil more than good; *and*

ᶠlying rather than to speak righteousness. ᵍSelah.

A. M. cir. 2942
B. C. cir. 1062
Sauli, Regis
Israelitarum,
cir. annum
34

4 Thou lovest all devouring words, ʰO *thou* deceitful tongue.

5 God shall likewise ⁱdestroy thee for ever, he shall take thee away, and pluck thee out of *thy* dwelling place, and ᵏroot thee out of the land of the living. Selah.

ᵃ1 Sam. xxii. 9——ᵇEzek. xxii. 9——ᶜ1 Sam. xxi. 7
ᵈPsa. l. 19——ᵉPsa. lvii. 4; lix. 7; lxiv. 3——ᶠJer. ix. 4, 5

ᵍPsa. iii. 2, 4, 8; iv. 2, 4; vii. 5; ix. 16, &c.——ʰOr, *and the deceitful tongue*——ⁱHeb. *beat thee down*——ᵏProv. ii. 22

NOTES ON PSALM LII

The *title* is, "To the chief Musician, an instructive Psalm of David, when Doeg the Edomite came and informed Saul, and said to him, David is come to the house of Ahimelech." The history to which this alludes is the following: David, having learned that Saul was determined to destroy him, went to take refuge with Achish, king of Gath: in his journey he passed by *Nob*, where the tabernacle then was, and took thence the sword of Goliath; and, being spent with hunger, took some of the shewbread. *Doeg*, an Edomite, one of the domestics of Saul, being there, went to Saul, and informed him of these transactions. Saul immediately ordered Ahimelech into his presence, upbraided him for being a partisan of David, and ordered Doeg to slay him and all the priests. Doeg did so, and there fell by his hand eighty-five persons. And Saul sent and destroyed *Nob* and all its inhabitants, old and young, with all their property; none escaping but *Abiathar*, the son of Ahimelech, who immediately joined himself to David. The account may be found 1 Sam. xxi. 1-7, xxii. 9-23. All the Versions agree in this title except the *Syriac*, which speaks of it as a Psalm directed against vice in general, with a prediction of the destruction of evil.

Though the Psalm be evidently an invective against some great, wicked, and tyrannical man, yet I think it too mild in its composition for a transaction the most barbarous on record, and the most flagrant vice in the whole character of Saul.

Verse 1. *Why boastest thou thyself*] It is thought that Doeg *boasted* of his loyalty to Saul in making the above discovery; but the information was aggravated by circumstances of falsehood that tended greatly to inflame and irritate the mind of Saul. Exaggeration and lying are common to all informers.

O mighty man?] This character scarcely com-

ports with Doeg, who was only *chief of the herdsmen of Saul*, 1 Sam. xxi. 7; but I grant this is not decisive evidence that the Psalm may not have Doeg in view, for the chief *herdsman* may have been a man of credit and authority.

Verse 2. *Deviseth mischiefs*] Lies and slanders proceeding from the tongue argue the desperate wickedness of the heart.

Like a sharp razor, working deceitfully.] Which instead of taking off the beard, cuts and wounds the flesh; or as the operator who, when pretending to trim the beard, cuts the throat.

Verse 3. *Thou lovest evil*] This was a finished character. Let us note the particulars:—1. He boasted in the power to do evil. 2. His tongue devised, studied, planned, and spoke mischiefs. 3. He was a deceitful worker. 4. He loved evil and not good. 5. He loved lying; his delight was in falsity. 6. Every word that tended to the destruction of others he loved. 7. His tongue was deceitful; he pretended friendship while his heart was full of enmity, ver. 1-4. Now behold the *punishment:*—

Verse 5. *God shall likewise destroy thee*] 1. God shall *set himself* to destroy thee; יתצך *yittotscha*, "he will pull down thy building;" he shall unroof it, dilapidate, and dig up thy foundation. 2. He shall bruise or break thee to pieces for ever; thou shalt have neither strength, consistence, nor support. 3. He will mow thee down, and sweep thee away like dust or chaff, or light hay in a whirlwind, so that thou shalt be scattered to all the winds of heaven. Thou shalt have no residence, no tabernacle: *that* shall be entirely destroyed. Thou shalt be rooted out for ever from the land of the living. The bad fruit which it has borne shall bring God's curse upon the tree; it shall not merely wither, or die, but it shall be plucked up from the roots, intimating that such a sinner shall die a violent death. *Selah.* So it shall be, and so it ought to be.

A. M. cir. 2942
B. C. cir. 1062
Sauli, Regis
Israelitarum,
cir. annum
34

6 ¹The righteous also shall see, and fear, ᵐand shall laugh at him:

7 Lo, *this is* the man *that* made not God his strength; but ⁿtrusted in the abundance of his riches, *and* strengthened himself in his °wickedness.

ᴵJob xxii. 19; Psa. xxxvii. 34; xl. 3; lxiv. 9; Mal. i. 5
ᵐPsa. lviii. 10

8 But I *am* ᴾlike a green olive-tree in the house of God: I trust in the mercy of God for ever and ever.

9 I will praise thee for ever, because thou hast done *it:* and I will wait on thy name; �q for *it is* good before thy saints.

A. M. cir. 2942
B. C. cir. 1062
Sauli, Regis
Israelitarum,
cir. annum
34

ⁿPsa. xlix. 6——°Or, *substance*——ᴾJer. xi. 16; Hos. xiv. 6——qPsa. liv. 6

Verse 6. *The righteous also shall see, and fear*] The thing shall be done in the sight of the saints; they shall see God's judgments on the workers of iniquity; and they shall *fear* a God so holy and just, and feel the necessity of being doubly on their guard lest they fall into the same condemnation. But instead of ויראו *veyirau*, "and they shall fear," three of *Kennicott's* and *De Rossi's* MSS., with the *Syriac*, have וישמחו *veyismachu*, "and shall rejoice;" and, from the following words, "and shall laugh at him," this appears to be the true reading, for *laughing* may be either the consequence or accompaniment of *rejoicing*.

Verse 7. *Made not God his strength*] Did not make God his *portion*.

In the abundance of his riches] Literally, in the *multiplication of his riches*. He had got much, he hoped to get more, and expected that his *happiness* would *multiply* as his *riches* multiplied. And this is the case with most rich men.

Strengthened himself in his wickedness.] Loved money instead of God; and thus his depravity, being increased, was *strengthened*.

Crescit amor nummi, quantum ipsa pecunia crescit.

"In proportion to the increase of wealth, so is the love of it."

Where is the religious man, in whose hands money has multiplied, who has not lost the spirit of piety in the same ratio? To prevent this, and the perdition to which it leads, there is no way but opening both hands to the *poor*.

Verse 8. *But I* am *like a green olive-tree in the house of God*] I shall be in the house of *God*, full of spiritual vigour, bringing forth evergreen leaves and annual fruit, as the *olive* does when planted in a proper soil and good situation. It does not mean that there were *olive-trees* planted *in* God's house; but *he* was in God's house, as the olive was in *its* proper place and soil.

I trust in the mercy of God] The *wicked man* trusts in his riches: *I* trust in my God. *He*, like a bad tree, bringing forth poisonous fruit, shall be cursed, and pulled up from the roots; *I*, like a healthy olive in a good soil, shall, under the influence of God's mercy, bring forth fruit to his glory. As the olive is ever green, so shall I flourish in the mercy of God for *ever and ever*.

Verse 9. *I will praise thee for ever*] Because I know that all my good comes from thee; therefore, will I ever praise thee for that good.

I will wait on thy name] I will expect all my blessings from the all-sufficient *Jehovah*, who is *eternal* and *unchangeable*.

It is good before thy saints.] It is right that I should expect a continuation of thy blessings by *uniting with thy saints in using thy ordinances.* Thus I shall *wait*.

ANALYSIS OF THE FIFTY-SECOND PSALM

There are *three* parts in this Psalm:—
I. An *invective* against Doeg, and a *prediction* of his fall, ver. 1-5.
II. The *comfort* which God's people should take in this, ver. 6, 7.
III. The *security* and *flourishing* state of those who trust in God, and the psalmist's thanks for it, ver. 8, 9.

I. David begins with an abrupt *apostrophe* to Doeg: "Why boastest thou thyself in mischief, thou mighty man?" And answers that this boasting was but vain; because *the goodness of God* endureth *continually*. This was sufficient to quiet all those who might be afraid of his *boasting*. Having given a *general character* of this man, as having a *delight* in *mischief*, he enters into *particulars;* and especially he considers the bad use he made of his *tongue*.

1. *Thy tongue deviseth mischief, like a razor working deceitfully.* Perhaps there may be here a reference to a case where a man, employed to take off or trim the beard, took that opportunity to cut the throat of his employer. In this manner had Doeg often acted; while pretending by his *tongue* to favour, he used it in a deceitful way to ruin the character of another.

2. "Thou lovest evil more than good:" his wickedness was *habitual;* he *loved* it.

3. "Thou lovest lying more than righteousness:" he was an *enemy* to the *truth*, and by lies and flatteries a destroyer of *good men*.

4. This is expressed more fully in the next verse: "Thou lovest all deceitful words, O thou false tongue!" he was all *tongue;* a *man of words:* and these the most deceitful and injurious.

This is his character; and now David foretells his fall and destruction, which he amplifies by a congeries of words. 1. "God shall likewise destroy thee for ever." 2. "He shall take thee away." 3. "He shall pluck thee out of thy dwelling place." 4. "He shall root thee out of the land of the living." See the notes.

II. Then follows how God's people should be affected by Doeg's fall.

1. "The righteous shall see it and fear:" they shall reverence God more than formerly, as taking vengeance on this singularly wicked man.

2. They shall *laugh at him*, using this bitter sarcasm, "Lo, this is the man that made not God his strength," &c.; he trusted in his *gold* more than in his *God*.

III. But such a fearful end shall not fall on any good man: while the wicked is plucked up from the roots, the righteous shall flourish like a healthy olive-tree.

1. "As for me, I am like the green olive-tree;" ever fruitful and flourishing.

2. I am planted in the house of the Lord; and derive all my nourishment from him, through his ordinances.

3. The olive is perhaps one of the most useful trees in the world. Its *fruit* and its *oil* are of great use to the inhabitants of those countries where the olive is cultivated; and are transported to most parts of the world, where the culture of the olive is unknown.

4. The reason why he shall be like the olive: his faith in God: "I trust in the mercy of God for ever."

Hence, the psalmist's *conclusion* is full of confidence:—

1. "I will praise thee for ever, because thou hast done it."

2. "I will wait on thy name:" I will continue to use those means by which thou communicatest thy grace to the soul.

3. I shall do this because it is my duty, and because it is right in the sight of thy people: "For it is good before thy saints."

PSALM LIII

The sentiments of atheists and deists, who deny Divine Providence; their character: they are corrupt, foolish, abominable, and cruel, 1–4; God fills them with terror, 5; reproaches them for their oppression of the poor, 5. The psalmist prays for the restoration of Israel, 6.

X. DAY. EVENING PRAYER

To the chief Musician upon Mahalath, Maschil, *A Psalm* of David

THE [a]fool hath said in his heart, *There is* no God. Corrupt are they, and have done abominable iniquity: [b]*there is* none that doeth good.

2 God [c]looked down from heaven upon the children of men, to see if there were *any* that did understand, that did [d]seek God.

3 Every one of them is gone back: they are altogether become filthy; *there is* none that doeth good, no, not one.

4 Have the workers of iniquity [e]no knowledge? who eat up my people *as* they eat bread: they have not called upon God.

5 [f]There [g]were they in great fear, *where* no fear was: for God hath [h]scattered the bones of him that encampeth *against* thee: thou hast put *them* to shame, because God hath despised them.

6 [i]O [k]that the salvation of Israel *were* come out of Zion! When God bringeth back the captivity of his people, Jacob shall rejoice, *and* Israel shall be glad.

---

[a]Psalm x. 4; xiv. 1, &c.——[b]Romans iii. 10——[c]Psa. xxxiii. 13——[d]2 Chronicles xv. 2; xix. 3——[e]Jeremiah iv. 22——[f]Leviticus xxvi. 17, 36; Proverbs

xxviii. 1——[g]Hebrew, *they feared a fear;* Psalm xiv. 5——[h]Ezekiel vi. 5——[i]Psalm xiv. 7——[k]Heb. *who will give salvations,* &c.

NOTES ON PSALM LIII

The *title, To the chief Musician upon Mahalath, an instructive Psalm of David.* The word מחלת *machalath,* some translate the *president;* others, the *master or leader of the dance;* others, *hollow instruments;* others, *the chorus.* A *flute pipe,* or *wind instrument* with *holes,* appears to be what is intended. "To the chief player on the flute;" or, "To the master of the band of pipers."

Verse 1. *The fool hath said in his heart*] The whole of this Psalm, except a few inconsiderable differences, is the same as the *fourteenth;* and, therefore, the same *notes* and *analysis* may be applied to it; or, by referring to the *fourteenth,* the reader will find the subject of it amply explained. I shall add a few short notes.

Have done abominable iniquity] Instead of עול *avel, evil* or *iniquity,* eight of *Kennicott's* and *De Rossi's* MSS. have עלילה *alilah, work,* which is nearly the same as in Psa. xiv.

Verse 4. *Have the workers of iniquity*] For פעלי *poaley, workers* seventy-two of *Kennicott's* and *De Rossi's* MSS., with several ancient

editions, the *Chaldee,* though not noticed in the Latin translation in the *London Polyglot,* the *Syriac, Vulgate, Septuagint, Æthiopic,* and the *Arabic,* with the *Anglo-Saxon,* add the word כל *col, all,*—ALL *the workers of iniquity;* which is the reading in the parallel place in Psa. xiv. It may be necessary to observe, that the *Chaldee,* in the *Antwerp* and *Paris Polyglots,* and in that of *Justinianus,* has not the word כל *col,* ALL.

Have not called upon God] אלהים *Elohim;* but many MSS. have יהוה *Yehovah,* LORD.

Verse 5. *For God hath scattered the bones of him that encampeth against thee: thou hast put them to shame, because God hath despised them.*] The reader will see, on comparing this with the fifth and sixth verses of Psa. xiv., that the words above are mostly *added* here to what is said *there;* and appear to be levelled against the *Babylonians,* who sacked and ruined Jerusalem, and who were now sacked and ruined in their turn. The sixth verse of Psa. xiv., "Ye have shamed the counsel of the poor, because the Lord is his refuge," is added here by more than twenty of *Kennicott's* and *De Rossi's* MSS.

Verse 6. *O that the salvation of Israel* were come *out of Zion!*] I have already shown that the proper translation is, "Who shall give from Zion salvation to Israel?" The word *salvation* is in the *plural* here, *deliverances:* but many MSS., with the *Septuagint, Vulgate, Arabic,* and *Anglo-Saxon,* have it in the *singular.*

When God bringeth back] *When Jehovah bringeth back,* is the reading of more than twenty of *Kennicott's* and *De Rossi's* MSS., with the *Septuagint, Syriac,* and *Chaldee,* and *Justinianus'* Polyglot Psalter.

For larger notes and an analysis, the reader is requested to refer to Psa. xiv.; and for a comparison of the two Psalms he may consult Dr. *Kennicott's* Hebrew Bible, where, under Psa. xiv., in the lower margin, the variations are exhibited at one view.

PSALM LIV

The psalmist complains that strangers were risen up against him to take away his life, 1-3; expresses his confidence in God that he will uphold him, and punish his enemies, 4, 5; on which he promises to sacrifice to God, 6; he speaks of his deliverance, 7.

To the chief Musician on Neginoth, Maschil, *A Psalm* of David, [a]when the Ziphims came and said to Saul, Doth not David hide himself with us?

A. M. cir. 2943
B. C. cir. 1061
Sauli, Regis
Israelitarum,
cir. annum
35

SAVE me, O God, by thy name, and judge me by thy strength.

2 Hear my prayer, O God; give ear to the words of my mouth.

3 For [b]strangers are risen up against me, and oppressors seek after my soul; they have not set God before them. Selah.

A. M. cir. 2943
B. C. cir. 1061
Sauli, Regis
Israelitarum,
cir. annum
35

4 Behold, God *is* mine helper: [c]the LORD *is* with them that uphold my soul.

5 He shall reward evil unto [d]mine enemies: cut them off [e]in thy truth.

6 I will freely sacrifice unto thee: I will praise thy name, O LORD; [f]for *it is* good.

7 For he hath delivered me out of all trouble: [g]and mine eye hath seen *his desire* upon mine enemies.

---

[a]1 Samuel xxiii. 19; xxvi. 1——[b]Psalm lxxxvi. 14 [c]Psalm cxviii. 7——[d]Hebrew, *those that observe me;* Psa. v. 8

[e]Psa. lxxxix. 49——[f]Psa. lii. 9; c. 5; cvi. 1; cvii. 1; cxviii. 1, 29; cxxxv. 3; cxxxvi. 1; cxlv. 9——[g]Psa. lix. 10; xcii. 11

NOTES ON PSALM LIV

The title is, "To the chief Musician upon Neginoth, an instructive Psalm of David, when the Ziphites came to Saul, and said, Doth not David conceal himself among us?"

Ziph was a village in the southern part of Palestine. David having taken refuge in the mountains of that country, the Ziphites went to Saul, and informed him of the fact. Saul, with his army, immediately went thither, and was on one side of a mountain while David was on the other. Just when he was about to fall into the hands of his merciless pursuer, an express came to Saul that the Philistines had invaded Israel, on which he gave up the pursuit, and returned to save his country, and David escaped to En-gedi. See the account in 1 Sam. xxiii. 19-29. It is supposed to have been after this deliverance that he composed this Psalm. *Neginoth,* from נגן *nagan,* to *strike* or *play* on some kind of instrument, probably signifies *stringed instruments,* such as were played on with a *plectrum.*

Verse 1. *Save me, O God, by thy name*] Save me by *thyself* alone; so *name* here may be understood. The *name of God* is often *God himself.* David was now in such imminent danger of being taken and destroyed, that no human means were left for his escape; if God therefore had not interfered, he must have been destroyed. See the *introduction* above.

Verse 2. *Hear my prayer*] In his straits he had recourse to God; for from him alone, for the reasons alleged above, his deliverance must proceed.

Verse 3. *Strangers are risen up against me*] The *Ziphites.*

And oppressors] Saul, his courtiers, and his army.

They have not set God before them.] It is on *no religious account,* nor is it to accomplish any *end,* on which they can ask the *blessing* of God.

Selah.] This is true.

Verse 4. *Behold, God is mine helper*] This would naturally occur to him when he saw that Saul was obliged to leave the pursuit, and go to defend his territories, when he was on the very point of seizing him. God, whose providence is ever watchful, had foreseen this danger, and stirred up the Philistines to make this inroad just at the time in which Saul and his army were about to lay hands on David. Well might he then say, "Behold, God is mine helper."

Is with them that uphold my soul.] נפשי *naphshi,* my *life.* This may even refer to the *Philistines,* who had at this time made an inroad on Israel. God was even with his own enemies, by making them instruments to save the life of his servant.

Verse 5. *He shall reward evil*] Saul and his courtiers, instead of having God's approbation, shall have his curse.

Cut them off in thy truth.] Thou hast *promised* to save me; these have purposed to destroy me. Thy *truth* is engaged in my defence; they will destroy me if permitted to *live:* to save *thy truth,* and to accomplish its *promises,* thou must cut them *off.*

Verse 6. *I will freely sacrifice unto thee*] Or, *I will sacrifice nobly unto thee.* Not only with a *willing mind*, but with a *liberal hand* will I bring sacrifice unto thee.

For it is *good*] Thy *name* is *good;* it is descriptive of thy nature; full of goodness and mercy to man. And *it is good* to be employed in such a work: whoever worships thee in sincerity is sure to be a gainer. To him who orders his conversation aright, thou dost show thy salvation.

Verse 7. *For he hath delivered me*] Saul had now decamped; and was returned to save his territories; and David in the meanwhile escaped to En-gedi. God was most evidently the author of this deliverance.

Mine eye hath seen his desire *upon mine enemies.*] It is not likely that this Psalm was written after the *death of Saul;* and therefore David could not say that *he had seen his desire.* But there is nothing in the text for *his desire;* and the words might be translated, *My eye hath seen my enemies*—they have been *so near* that I could plainly discover them. Thus almost all the *Versions* have understood the text. *I have seen them,* and yet they were not permitted to approach me. God has been my Deliverer.

ANALYSIS OF THE FIFTY-FOURTH PSALM

There are *three parts* in this Psalm:—

I. David's prayer for help and salvation, ver. 1-3.

II. His confidence that he should have help, ver. 4, 5.

III. His *gratitude* and *obedience*, ver. 6, 7.

1. David's petition: 1. "Save me." 2. "Plead my cause." 3. "Hear my prayer." 4. "Give ear to my words." He is much in earnest; and yet does not desire his prayer to be heard unless his *cause be just.* If just, then let *God plead it.*

2. He produces *two* grounds upon which he petitions: 1. God's *name.* 2. God's *strength.* 1. He that calls on the name of the Lord shall be saved; I call: "Save me in thy name!" 2. Thou art a *powerful* God, able to do it: "Save me in thy strength."

The greatness of his danger causes him to urge his prayer.

1. His enemies were *strangers;* from whom no favour could be expected.

2. They were *violent oppressors*—formidable, cruel tyrants, from whom he could expect no mercy.

3. They were such as could be satisfied with nothing less than his blood: "They rise to seek after my life."

4. They had no *fear of God:* "They have not set God before them."

II. Notwithstanding they are all that I have already stated; and, humanly speaking, I have nothing but destruction to expect; yet I will not fear: because, 1. God is *with me.* 2. He is *against them.*

1. "God is my helper:" as he has promised, so he has done, and will do, to me.

2. "God is with them also who uphold my soul. Selah." *Behold this!*

But he opposes them who oppose me; is an enemy to them who are mine enemies.

1. "He shall reward evil" to such: of this being assured, he proceeds to imprecate.

2. Destroy thou them: "Cut them off in thy truth." Thou hast promised that it *shall be well with the righteous;* and that *snares, fire, and brimstone, shall be rained on the wicked.* Let God be true: *Fiat justitia; ruat cœlum, pereat mundus.* They *must be cut off.*

III. For such a mercy David promises not to be unthankful.

1. For this he would offer a *princely sacrifice:* "I will freely sacrifice."

2. He would praise the name of the Lord: "I will praise thy name."

For this he gives *two* reasons:—

1. That which *internally* moved him: "For it is good."

2. That which was *outwardly impulsive;* his *deliverance.* 1. His deliverance was great and effectual: "Thou hast delivered me out of all my trouble." 2. His danger was so *imminent* that, humanly speaking, there was no escape. The enemy was within sight who was bent on his destruction; yet *he* was delivered; and *they* were confounded. On these accounts it was right that he should sing praise, and offer sacrifice. To the grateful God is bountiful.

PSALM LV

David, in great danger and distress from the implacable malice of his enemies, calls on God for mercy, 1-5; wishes he had the wings of a dove, that he might flee away, and be at rest, 6-8; prays against his enemies, and describes their wickedness, 9-11; speaks of a false friend, who had been the principal cause of all his distresses, 12-14; again prays against his enemies, 15; expresses his confidence in God, 16-18; gives a farther description of the deceitful friend, 19-21; encourages himself in the Lord, and foretells the destruction of his foes, 22, 23.

To the chief Musician on Neginoth, Maschil, *A Psalm* of David

A. M. cir. 2981
B. C. cir. 1023
Davidis, Regis
Israelitarum,
cir. annum
33

GIVE ear to my prayer, O God; and hide not thyself from my supplication.

2 Attend unto me, and hear me : I ᵃmourn in my complaint, and make a noise;

3 Because of the voice of the enemy, because of the oppression of the wicked : ᵇfor they cast iniquity upon me, and in wrath they hate me.

4 ᶜMy heart is sore pained within me : and the terrors of death are fallen upon me.

5 Fearfulness and trembling are come upon me, and horror hath ᵈoverwhelmed me.

6 And I said, O that I had wings like a dove! *for then* would I fly away, and be at rest.

A. M. cir. 2981
B. C. cir. 1023
Davidis, Regis
Israelitarum,
cir. annum
33

7 Lo, *then* would I wander far off, *and* remain in the wilderness. Selah.

8 I would hasten my escape from the windy storm *and* tempest.

9 Destroy, O LORD, *and* divide their tongues : for I have seen ᵉviolence and strife in the city.

10 Day and night they go about it upon the walls thereof : mischief also and sorrow *are* in the midst of it.

ᵃIsaiah xxxviii. 14——ᵇ2 Samuel xvi. 7, 8; xix. 19

ᶜPsalm cxvi. 3——ᵈHebrew, *covered me*——ᵉJeremiah vi. 7

NOTES ON PSALM LV

The *title*, "To the chief Musician upon Neginoth, *A Psalm* of David, giving instruction." This is the same as the preceding, which see.

Verse 1. *Give ear to my prayer*] The frequency of such petitions shows the great earnestness of David's soul. If God did not hear and help, he knew he could not succeed elsewhere; therefore he continues to knock at the gate of God's mercy.

Verse 2. *I mourn in my complaint*] בשיחי *besichi*, in my *sighing;* a strong *guttural* sound, expressive of the natural accents of sorrow.

And make a noise] I am in a *tumult*—I am strongly *agitated.*

Verse 3. *They cast iniquity upon me*] To give a colourable pretence to their rebellion, they charge me with horrible crimes; as if they had said: Down with such a wretch; he is not fit to reign. Clamour against the person of the sovereign is always the watch-word of *insurrection*, in reference to *rebellion*.

Verse 4. *The terrors of death are fallen upon me.*] I am in hourly expectation of being massacred.

Verse 5. *Fearfulness*] How natural is this description! He is in *distress;*—he *mourns;*—makes a *noise;*—sobs and *sighs;*—his *heart is wounded;*—he expects nothing but *death;*—this produces *fear;*—this produces *tremor*, which terminates in that *deep apprehension* of *approaching* and *inevitable ruin* that overwhelms him with *horror*. No man ever described a wounded heart like David.

Verse 6. *O that I had wings like a dove!*] He was so surrounded, so hemmed in on every side by his adversaries, that he could see no way for his escape unless he had wings, and could take flight. The *dove* is a bird of very rapid wing; and some of them passing before his eyes at the time, might have suggested the idea expressed here.

And be at rest.] Get a *habitation*.

Verse 7. *Would I wander far off*] He did escape; and yet his enemies were *so near*, as to *throw stones at him:* but he escaped beyond Jordan. 2 Sam. xvii. 22, 23.

A passage in the *Octavia* of SENECA has been referred to as being parallel to this of David.

It is in the answer of *Octavia* to the *Chorus*, Acts v., ver. 914-923.

*Quis mea digne deflere potest
Mala? Quæ lacrymis nostris quæstus
Reddet Aedon? cujus pennas
Utinam miseræ mihi fata darent!
Fugerem luctus ablata meos
Penna volucri, procul et cœtus
Hominum tristes sedemque feram.
Sola in vacuo nemore, et tenui
Ramo pendens, querulo possem
Gutture mœstum fundere murmur.*

My woes who enough can bewail?
O what notes can my sorrows express?
Sweet Philomel's self e'en would fail
To respond with her plaintive distress.
O had I her wings I would fly
To where sorrows I ne'er should feel more,
Upborne on her plumes through the sky,
Regions far from mankind would explore.
In a grove where sad silence should reign,
On a spray would I seat me alone;
In shrill lamentations complain,
And in wailings would pour forth my moan.

            J. B. CLARKE.

Verse 8. *The windy storm*] From the sweeping wind and tempest—Absalom and his party and the mutinous people in general.

Verse 9. *Destroy, O Lord*] *Swallow them up*—confound them.

Divide their tongues] Let his counsellors give opposite advice. Let them never agree, and let their devices be confounded. And the prayer was heard. Hushai and Ahithophel gave opposite counsel. Absalom followed that of *Hushai;* and *Ahithophel*, knowing that the steps advised by Hushai would bring Absalom's affairs to ruin, went and hanged himself. See 2 Sam. xv., xvi., and xvii.

Violence and strife in the city.] They have been concerting violent measures; and thus are full of contention.

Verse 10. *Day and night they go about*] This and the following verse show the state of Jerusalem at this time. Indeed, they exhibit a fair view of the state of any city in the beginning of an *insurrection*. The leaders are plotting continually; going about to strengthen their party, and to sow new dissensions by misrepresentation, hypocrisy, calumny, and lies.

A. M. cir. 2981
B. C. cir. 1023
Davidis, Regis
Israelitarum,
cir. annum
33

11 Wickedness *is* in the midst thereof: deceit and guile depart not from her streets.

12 ᶠFor *it was* not an enemy *that* reproached me; then I could have borne *it:* neither *was it* he that hated me *that* did ᵍmagnify *himself* against me; then I would have hid myself from him.

13 But *it was* thou, ʰa man mine equal, ⁱmy guide, and mine acquaintance.

14 ᵏWe took sweet counsel together, *and* ˡwalked unto the house of God in company.

15 Let death seize upon them, *and* let them ᵐgo down quick into ⁿhell: for wickedness *is* in their dwellings, *and* among them.

16 As for me, I will call upon

God; and the Lᴏʀᴅ shall save me.

A. M. cir. 2981
B. C. cir. 1023
Davidis, Regis
Israelitarum,
cir. annum
33

17 ᵒEvening, and morning, and at noon, will I pray, and cry aloud: and he shall hear my voice.

18 He hath delivered my soul in peace from the battle *that was* against me: for ᵖthere were many with me.

19 God shall hear, and afflict them, ᑫeven he that abideth oᵈ old. Selah. ʳBecause they have no changes, therefore they fear not God.

20 He hath ˢput forth his hands against such as ᵗbe at peace with him: ᵘhe hath broken his covenant.

21 ᵛ*The words* of his mouth were smoother

ᶠPsa. xli. 9——ᵍPsa. xxxv. 26; xxxviii. 16——ʰHeb. *a man according to my rank*——ⁱ2 Sam. xv. 12; xvi. 23; Psa. xli. 9; Jer. ix. 4——ᵏHeb. *Who sweetened counsel*——ˡPsa. xlii. 4——ᵐNum. xvi. 30——ⁿOr, *the grave*——ᵒDan. vi. 10; Luke xviii. 1; Acts iii. 1; x. 3, 9, 30; 1 Thess. v. 17——ᵖ2 Chron. xxxii. 7, 8——ᑫDeut. xxxiii. 27——ʳOr, *with whom* also there be *no changes, yet they fear not God*——ˢActs xii. 1——ᵗPsalm vii. 4 ᵘHebrew, *he hath profaned*——ᵛPsalm xxviii. 3; lvii. 4; lxii. 4; lxiv. 3; Prov. v. 3, 4; xii. 18

Verse 12. It was *not an enemy*] It is likely that in all these *three* verses Ahithophel is meant, who, it appears, had been at the bottom of the conspiracy from the beginning; and probably was the first mover of the vain mind of Absalom to do what he did.

Verse 14. *Walked unto the house of God in company.*] Or with haste; for the rabbins teach that we should walk *hastily* ᴛᴏ the temple, but *slowly* ꜰʀᴏᴍ it.

Verse 15. *Let death seize upon them*] This is a prediction of the sudden destruction which should fall on the ringleaders in this rebellion. And it was so. *Ahithophel*, seeing his counsel rejected, *hanged* himself. *Absalom* was defeated; and, fleeing away, he was suspended by the hair in a tree, under which his mule had passed; and being found thus by Joab, he was despatched with *three darts;* and the *people* who espoused his interests were almost all cut off. They fell by the sword, or perished in the woods. See 2 Sam. xviii. 8.

Let them go down quick into hell] Let them go down alive into the pit. Let the earth swallow them up! And something of this kind actually took place. Absalom and his army were defeated; *twenty thousand* of the rebels were slain on the field; and *the wood devoured more people that day than the sword devoured*, 2 Sam. xviii. 7, 8. The words might be rendered, "Death shall exact upon them; they shall descend alive into sheol." And death did *exact* his debt upon them, as we have seen above.

Verse 16. *I will call upon God*] He foresaw his deliverance, and the defeat of his enemies, and therefore speaks confidently, "The Lord shall save me;" or, as the *Targum*, "The Wᴏʀᴅ of the Lord shall redeem me."

Verse 17. *Evening, and morning, and at noon, will I pray*] This was the custom of the pious Hebrews. See Dan. vi. 10. The Hebrews began their day in the *evening*, and hence David mentions the *evening* first. The rabbins say, Men should pray three times each day,

because the day changes three times. This was observed in the primitive Church; but the times, in different places, were various. The old *Psalter* gives this a curious turn: "At *even* I sall tel his louing (*praise*) what tim Crist was on the Crosse: and at *morn* I sall schew his louing, what tim he ros fra dede. And sua he sall here my voyce at *mid day*, that is sitand at the right hand of his fader, wheder he stegh (*ascended*) at mid day."

Verse 18. *He hath delivered my soul*] My *life* he has preserved in perfect safety from the sword; *for there were many with me:* "for in many afflictions his Wᴏʀᴅ was my support."— *Targum.* Or David may refer to the *supernatural assistance* which was afforded him when his enemies were so completely discomfited.

Verse 19. *Because they have no changes*] At first Absalom, Ahithophel, and their party, carried all before them. There seemed to be a very general defection of the people; and as in their first attempts they suffered no *reverses*, therefore they feared not God. Most of those who have few or no afflictions and trials in life, have but little religion. They become sufficient to themselves, and call not upon God.

Verse 20. *He hath put forth his hands*] A farther description of Ahithophel. He betrayed his friends, and he broke his covenant with his king. He had agreed to serve David for his own emolument, and a stipulation was made accordingly; but while receiving the king's pay, he was endeavouring to subvert the kingdom, and destroy the life of his sovereign.

Verse 21. *Were smoother than butter*] He was a complete courtier, and a deep, designing hypocrite besides. His words *were as soft as butter, and as smooth as oil*, while he meditated war; and the fair words which were intended to *deceive*, were intended also to *destroy:* they *were drawn swords*. This is a literal description of the words and conduct of Absalom, as we learn from the inspired historian, 2 Sam.

A. M. cir. 2981
B. C. cir. 1023
Davidis, Regis
Israelitarum,
cir. annum
33

than butter, but war *was* in his heart: his words were softer than oil, yet *were* they drawn swords.

22 ʷCast thy ˣburden upon the Lord, and he shall sustain thee: ʸhe shall never

---

ʷPsa. xxxvii. 5; Matt. vi. 25; Luke xii. 22; 1 Pet. v. 7
ˣOr, *gift*——ʸPsa. xxxvii. 24——ᶻPsa. v. 6

---

xv. 2, &c. He was accustomed to wait at the gate; question the persons who came for justice and judgment; throw out broad hints that the king was negligent of the affairs of his kingdom, and had not provided an effective magistracy to administer justice among the people; and added that if he were appointed judge in the land, justice should be done to all. He bowed also to the people, and kissed them; and thus *he stole the hearts of the men of Israel.* See the passages referred to above.

Verse 22. *Cast thy burden upon the Lord*] Whatever cares, afflictions, trials, &c., they may be with which thou art oppressed, lay them upon him.

And he shall sustain thee] He shall bear both thee and thy burden. What a glorious promise to a tempted and afflicted soul! God will carry both *thee* and thy *load.* Then cast *thyself* and *it* upon *him.*

He shall never suffer the righteous to be moved.] While a man is righteous, trusts in and depends upon God, he will never suffer him to be shaken. *While he trusts in God, and works righteousness,* he is as safe as if he were in heaven.

Verse 23. *But thou, O God, shalt bring them down into the pit of destruction*] The *Chaldee* is emphatic: "And thou, O Lord, by thy Word (במימרך *bemeymerach*) shalt thrust them into the deep gehenna, the bottomless pit, whence they shall never come out; the *pit of destruction,* where all is amazement, horror, anguish, dismay, ruin, endless loss, and endless suffering."

Bloody and deceitful men shall not live out half their days] So we find, if there be an appointed time to man upon earth, beyond which he cannot pass; yet he may so live as to provoke the justice of God to cut him off *before* he arrives at that period; yea, before he has reached *half way* to that limit. According to the decree of God, he might have lived the *other half;* but he has not done it.

But I will trust in thee.] Therefore I shall not be moved, and shall live out all the days of *my* appointed time.

The fathers in general apply the principal passages of this Psalm to our Lord's sufferings, the treason of Judas, and the wickedness of the Jews; but these things do not appear to me fairly deducible from the text. It seems to refer plainly enough to the rebellion of Absalom. "The consternation and distress expressed in verses 4, 5, 6, 7, and 8, describe the king's state of mind when he fled from Jerusalem, and marched up the mount of Olives, weeping. The *iniquity cast upon the psalmist* answers to the complaints artfully laid against the king by his son of a negligent administration of justice: and to the reproach of *cruelty* cast upon him by Shimei, 2 Sam. xv. 2, 4; xvi. 7, 8.

suffer the righteous to be moved.

23 But thou, O God, shalt bring them down into the pit of destruction: ᶻbloody ᵃand deceitful men ᵇshall ᶜnot live out half their days; but I will trust in thee.

A. M. cir. 2981
B. C. cir. 1023
Davidis, Regis
Israelitarum,
cir. annum
33

ᵃHeb. *men of bloods and deceit*——ᵇHeb. *shall not half their days*——ᶜJob xv. 32; Prov. x. 27; Eccles. vii. 17

The *equal,* the *guide,* and the *familiar friend,* we find in *Ahithophel,* the confidential counsellor, first of David, afterwards of his son Absalom. The *buttery mouth* and *oily words* describe the insidious character of *Absalom,* as it is delineated, 2 Sam. xv. 5-9. Still the believer, accustomed to the double edge of the prophetic style, in reading this Psalm, notwithstanding its agreement with the occurrences of David's life, will be led to think of David's great descendant, who endured a bitter agony, and was the victim of a baser treachery, in the same spot where David is supposed to have uttered these complaints."—*Bishop Horsley.*

Analysis of the Fifty-fifth Psalm

There are *five* general parts in this *Psalm:*—
I. The psalmist entreats God to hear his prayer, ver. 1, 2.
II. He complains of his trouble, ver. 3-8.
II. He prays against his enemies, and shows the causes, ver. 8-15.
IV. He takes courage upon assurance of God's help, and his enemies' overthrow, ver. 15-21.
V. An epilogue, in which he exhorts all men to rely upon God, ver. 22, 23.

I. He begs audience.
1. "Give ear—hide not thyself—attend—hear me."
2. "My prayer—supplication—that I mourn—complain—make a noise." Affected he was with the sense of what he prayed for, and he was therefore earnest in it.

II. This in general; but next, in particular, he mentions the causes of his complaint, and earnestness to God, that he might be heard both in regard of his enemies, and the condition he was now in. The danger he was in was very great; escape he could not without God's help, for his enemies persecuted him very sore.
1. They slandered and calumniated him, and threatened him: "Because of the voice," &c.
2. They vexed, pressed upon him, and oppressed him: "Because of the oppression of the wicked."
3. They plotted his ruin, devolved, and *cast iniquity upon him*—charged him home.
4. They were implacable, angry, and hated him: "In wrath they hate me."
Then, as to his own person, he was in a sad, heavy, doleful condition.
1. "My heart is sore pained within me." His grief was inward.
2. "The terrors of death are fallen upon me." He saw nothing but death before him.
3. "Fearfulness and trembling are come upon me." Which are the outward effects of fear.
4. "And a horrible dread within hath overwhelmed me." Amazement followed his fear.
And he illustrates this his condition by the counsel he took with his own heart. Upon the

deliberation the result was, that he would speedily fly away, fly into the wilderness, as if he might be safer among beasts than such men.

1. "And I said." That was the result upon his debate with himself.

2. "O that I had wings like a dove!" It is a fearful creature of a swift wing. In fear he was, and he would fly as fast and as far as the dove from the eagle.

3. As far, even to some remote land, where I should have rest from these wicked men.

And he amplifies and explains himself again:—

1. That he would fly far away, even to some desolate place out of their reach: "Lo, then would I wander far off, and remain in the wilderness."

2. That he would do it with speed: "I would hasten my escape from the windy storm and tempest." Such turbulent and impetuous creatures his enemies were that threw down all before them, as a wind, storm, and tempest.

III. To his prayer he adds an imprecation:—

1. "Destroy them, O Lord; destroy them in their own counsels."

2. Or else, "divide their tongue." Let them not agree in their counsels.

Of this he gives the reason in the following words: viz., that they were a band of violent, contentious, ungodly, troublesome, crafty, and fraudulent people.

1. Violent they were, and litigious: "I have seen violence and strife in the city."

2. Ungodly, and workers of iniquity they were; and incessant in it: "Day and night they go about it upon the walls thereof: mischief also and sorrow are in the midst of it."

3. Crafty and fraudulent also: "Deceit and guile depart not from her streets." It was then a city, a corporation, a society of evil doers.

And of this he produces an instance, which whether it were some bosom friend of *David* who stole out of the city of *Keilah*, and betrayed his counsels to *Saul;* or else *Ahithophel*, who, being formerly his great favourite and counsellor, fell to *Absalom*, it is uncertain. Whoever it was, such a treacherous person there was, and of him he complains: and well he might; for ουδεν μειζον ελκος η φιλος αδικων, "there is not a greater sore than a treacherous friend." This treachery he exaggerates most eloquently by an incrementum and apostrophe, drawing his aggravation from the laws of friendship, which he had broken. Had it been an enemy, he could have borne it; but that it was a friend was intolerable, and also inexcusable. Thus the climax stands:—

1. "For it was not an enemy that reproached me; then I could have borne it."

2. "Neither was it he that hated me that did magnify himself," that is, arise and insult me; "then I would have hid myself from him," never admitted him to my bosom.

But mark this emphatic adversative, for now he turns his speech to the man:—

1. "It was thou," emphatically *thou*, principally and beyond all others. None *but thou*.

2. "A man," according to my own rank, mine equal; my guide or counsellor; my acquaintance, my own familiar friend.

3. "We took sweet counsel together." One to whom I communicated my secrets.

4. "And walked unto the house of God in company." Professors we were of the same religion.

Now all these circumstances much heighten

and aggravate the treachery: that thou, my equal, my director, my familiar friend, one whom I made the master of all my secrets, one who was a great professor of the same religion with me, that *thou* shouldst betray me, even break my heart. Συ τεκνον; *Judas—betrayest thou?*

Being thus much wronged and moved, as he had just reason, he begins again with an imprecation, not only on him, but on all who believed him, even upon the whole faction: "Let death seize upon them, and let them go down quick into hell," have *Korah, Dathan,* and *Abiram's* wages. And he adds the reason. They are signally and incorrigibly wicked: "For wickedness is in their dwellings, and among them."

IV. Hitherto hath *David* prayed, complained, imprecated; but now he shows how he recovered courage again, being certain of God's help, and a revenge to be taken on his enemies.

1. "As for me, I will call upon God fervently, and the Lord shall save me."

2. "Evening, and morning, and at noon-day," incessantly, "will I pray and cry aloud; and he shall hear me."

3. And I pray in faith; experience I have of his deliverance; he hath done it, and he will do it again. "He hath redeemed my soul in peace from the battle which was against me." Even in the midst of the battle, I was as safe as in a time of peace; miraculously delivered, as if there had been no danger.

4. "For there were many with me." *Many enemies,* say some; others, *many angels.* Those refer it to the danger; these, to the protection. Many enemies round about me, and then it is a wonder I should be delivered. Many angels press to help me, and then it was no wonder that my life was saved. But as for the ungodly, it was not so with them; for this *verse* is opposed to the former.

1. "God shall hear," viz., me and my prayers, and the wrongs they do me.

2. "And shall afflict them," i. e., my enemies.

3. "Even he that abideth of old. Selah." Mark that, for He is immutable. His power and strength is the same, and his care and love to his people; therefore, he will afflict them.

And, besides, there are those who will provoke him to it,—

1. Because "they have no changes." Obstinate they are, impertinent, and change not their ways. Or else they prosper, they have perpetual success, and meet with no alteration; this makes them secure and proud.

2. "They fear not God." They ask, "Who is the Lord, that we should let Israel go?"

3. They are truce-breakers, violators of oaths, leagues, covenants, articles of war. "He (that is, some chief commander among them) hath put forth his hands, made war, imbrued his hands in blood, against such as are at peace with him." He hath broken and profaned his covenant—his oath.

4. He is a gross hypocrite; his deeds answer not to his words: "The words of his mouth were smoother than butter, but war was in his heart; his words were softer than oil, yet they were drawn swords."

V. In the *epilogue* of the Psalm he exhorts good men to rely upon God: "Cast thy burden (the cares, troubles, &c., with which thou art loaded) on the Lord;" and he fits it to his present purpose, both as it concerns the godly and the ungodly.

1. To the godly he gives this comfort: 1. "He (that is, God) shall sustain thee." He will uphold thee, and give thee strength under the heaviest burdens. "Come unto me, all ye that are heavy laden." 2. "He shall never suffer the righteous to be moved." With the temptation he will also give the issue; pressed they may be, but not oppressed so as finally to be overthrown.

2. To the ungodly. 1. Overthrown they shall be, and utterly destroyed: "Thou, O God, shalt bring them down into the pit of destruction;"

the grave—hell. 2. "Bloody and deceitful men shall not live out half their days." They come commonly to some untimely death, as *Absalom* and *Ahithophel,* concerning whom the Psalm was composed.

He concludes with the use he would make of it; as if he had said: Let these bloody and deceitful men repose their confidence in their armies, in their violence, in their crafty and subtle ways; I will take another course: "But I will trust in thee."

PSALM LVI

David prays for support against his enemies, whose wickedness he describes, 1–6; and foretells their destruction, 7; expresses his confidence in God's mercy, expects deliverance, and promises thanksgiving and obedience, 8–13.

XI. DAY. MORNING PRAYER

To the chief Musician upon Jonath-elem-rechokim, [a]Michtam of David, when the [b]Philistines took him in Gath

A. M. cir. 2942
B. C. cir. 1062
Sauli, Regis
Israelitarum,
cir. annum
34

BE [c]merciful unto me, O God; for man would swallow me up: he fighting daily oppresseth me.

2 [d]Mine enemies would daily [e]swallow *me* up: for *they be* many that fight against me, O thou Most High.

A. M. cir. 2942
B. C. cir. 1062
Sauli, Regis
Israelitarum,
cir. annum
34

3 What time I am afraid, I will trust in thee.

4 [f]In God I will praise his word, in [g]God

---

[a]Or, *a golden* Psalm *of David;* so Psa. xvi.——[b]1 Sam. xxi. 11——[c]Psa. lvii. 1

[d]Heb. *Mine observers;* Psa. liv. 5——[e]Psa. lvii. 3 [f]Ver. 10, 11——[g]1 Chron. v. 20; Psa. v. 11; vii. 1; ix. 10

NOTES ON PSALM LVI

The *title* of this Psalm is very long: "To the conqueror, concerning the dumb dove in foreign places: golden Psalm of David." The *Vulgate* translates the original thus: "to the end. For the people who were afar off from holy things." "This inscription David placed here for a title when the Philistines took him in Gath;" so the *Septuagint* and *Æthiopic.* The *Chaldee* is profuse: "To praise, for the congregation of Israel, which are compared to the silence of a dove, when they were afar off from their cities; but being returned, they praise the Lord of the world; like David, contrite and upright, when the Philistines kept him in Gath." The *Syriac:* "A thanksgiving of the righteous man, because he was delivered from his enemy, and from the hand of Saul. Also concerning the Jews and Christ." *Bochart* translates, "To the tune of the dove in the remote woods."

If the title be at all authentic, David may mean himself and his companions by it, when he escaped from the hands of the Philistines; particularly from the hands of Achish, king of Gath. אלם *elem* signifies to *compress* or *bind together;* also, a *small band* or *body of men:* and יונת *yonath,* from ינה *yanah,* to *oppress* or *afflict,* is properly applied to the *dove,* because of its being so *defenceless,* and often becoming the *prey* of ravenous birds. It is possible, therefore, that the title may imply no more than— "A prayer to God in behalf of himself and the *oppressed band* that followed him, and shared his misfortunes in *distant places.*"

Others will have it to mean a simple direction "To the master of the band, to be sung to

the time of a well-known ode, called 'The dumb dove, in distant places.'" There is no end to conjectures, and all the *titles* in the whole book are not worth one hour's labour. Perhaps there is not one of them *authentic.* They may have been *notices* that such a Psalm was to be sung to *such and such a tune;* giving the *catch-words* of some well-known song or ode: a custom that prevails much among us in songs and hymns, and is to be found even among the Asiatics.

Verse 1. *Be merciful unto me*] I am assailed both at home and abroad. I can go nowhere without meeting with enemies: unless thou, who art the Fountain of mercy and the *Most High,* stand up in my behalf, my enemies will most undoubtedly prevail against me. *They fight against me continually,* and I am in the utmost danger of *being swallowed up* by them.

Verse 2. *O thou Most High.*] מרום *marom.* I do not think that this word expresses any attribute of God, or indeed is at all addressed to him. It signifies, literally, *from on high,* or *from a high* or *elevated place:* "For the multitudes fight against me from the high or elevated place;" the place of *authority*—the court and cabinet of Saul.

Most of the *Versions* begin the next verse with this word: "From the light of the day, though I fear, yet will I trust in thee." From the time that *persecution waxes hot against me,* though I often am seized with fear, yet I am enabled to maintain my trust in thee. Dr. *Kennicott* thinks there is a corruption here, and proposes to read: "I look upwards all the day long."

Verse 4. *In God I will praise his word*] באלהים *belohim* may mean here, *through God,*

A. M. cir. 2942
B. C. cir. 1062
Sauli, Regis
Israelitarum,
cir. annum
34
I have put my trust; [h]I will not fear what flesh can do unto me.

5 Every day they wrest my words: all their thoughts *are* against me for evil.

6 [i]They gather themselves together, they hide themselves, they mark my steps, [k]when they wait for my soul.

7 Shall they escape by iniquity? in *thine* anger cast down the people, O God.

8 Thou tellest my wanderings: put thou my tears into thy bottle: [l]*are they* not in thy book?

9 When I cry *unto thee,* then shall mine enemies turn back: this I know; for [m]God *is* for me.
A. M. cir. 2942
B. C. cir. 1062
Sauli, Regis
Israelitarum,
cir. annum
34

10 [n]In God will I praise *his* word: in the LORD will I praise *his* word.

11 In God have I put my trust: I will not be afraid what man can do unto me.

12 Thy vows *are* upon me, O God: I will render praises unto thee.

13 For [o]thou hast delivered my soul from death: *wilt* not *thou deliver* my feet from falling, that I may walk before God in [p]the light of the living?

---

[h]Psa. cxviii. 6; Isa. xxxi. 3; Heb. xiii. 6——[i]Psa. lix. 3; cxl. 2——[k]Psa. lxxi. 10

[l]Mal. iii. 16——[m]Rom. viii. 31——[n]Ver. 4——[o]Psa. cxvi. 8——[p]Job xxxiii. 30

---

or *by the help of God, I will praise his word.* And, that he should have cause to do it, he says, "In God I have put my trust," and therefore he says, "I will not fear what flesh can do unto me." Man is but FLESH, *weak* and *perishing;* God is an infinite SPIRIT, *almighty* and *eternal.* He repeats this sentiment in the *tenth* and *eleventh* verses.

Verse 5. *Every day they wrest my words*] They have been spies on my conduct continually; they collected all my sayings, and wrested my words out of their proper sense and meaning, to make them, by *inuendos,* speak treason against Saul. They are full of evil purposes against me.

Verse 6. *They gather themselves together*] They form cabals; have secret meetings and consultations how they may most effectually destroy me, under the pretence of justice and safety to the state.

They hide themselves] They do all secretly.

They mark my steps] They are constantly at my heels.

They wait for my soul.] They lie in wait for my *life.* Our translators have missed the meaning of נֶפֶשׁ *nephesh* and ψυχέ,—which generally signify the *animal life,* not the immortal spirit, —more than any other words in the Old or New Testament.

Verse 7. *Shall they escape by iniquity?*] Shall such conduct go unpunished? Shall their address, their dexterity in working iniquity, be the means of their escape? No. "In anger, O God, wilt thou cast down the people."

Verse 8. *Thou tellest my wanderings*] Thou seest how often I am obliged to *shift the place* of my *retreat.* I am hunted every where; but thou *numberest* all my *hiding-places,* and seest how often I am in danger of losing my life.

Put thou my tears into thy bottle] Here is an allusion to a very ancient custom, which we know long obtained among the *Greeks* and *Romans,* of putting the tears which were shed for the death of any person into small phials, called *lacrymatories* or *urnæ lacrymales* and offering them on the tomb of the deceased. Some of these were of *glass,* some of *pottery,* and some of *agate, sardonyx,* &c. A small one in my own collection is of *hard baked clay.*

Are they *not in thy book?*] Thou hast taken an exact account of all the tears I have shed in relation to this business; and thou wilt call my enemies to account for *every tear.*

Verse 9. *When I cry* unto thee, *then shall mine enemies turn back*] As soon as they know that I call upon thee, then, knowing that thou wilt hear and save, my enemies will immediately take flight. The cry of faith and prayer to God is more dreadful to our spiritual foes than the war-whoop of the Indian is to his surprised brother savages.

This I know] I have often had experience of the Divine interposition; and I know it will be so now, *for God is with me.* He who has *God* WITH *him* need not fear the face of any adversary.

Verses 10, 11. See on ver. 4, where the same words occur.

Verse 12. *Thy vows* are *upon me*] I have promised in the most solemn manner to be thy servant; to give my whole life to thee; and to offer for my preservation sacrifices of praise and thanksgiving.

Reader, what hast *thou vowed* to God? To renounce the devil and all his works, the pomps and vanities of this wicked world, and all the sinful desires of the flesh; to keep God's holy word and commandment, and to walk before him all the days of thy life. These things hast *thou vowed;* and these *vows* are *upon thee.* Wilt thou *pay* them?

Verse 13. *Thou hast delivered my soul from death*] My *life* from the *grave,* and my *soul* from *endless perdition.*

My feet from falling] Thou hast preserved me from taking any false way, and keepest me steady in my godly course; and so supportest me that I may continue to *walk before thee in the light of the living,* ever avoiding that which is evil, and moving towards that which is good; letting my light shine before men, that they may see my good works, and glorify my Father which is in heaven. *To walk before God* is to please him; the *light of the living* signifies the whole course of human life, with all its *comforts* and *advantages.*

ANALYSIS OF THE FIFTY-SIXTH PSALM

David, in banishment among the Philistines, and being then in great danger of his life, complains, and professes his confidence in God.

The contents of this Psalm are the following:—

I. David's *prayer*, ver. 1, 7, 8.

II. The *cause;* the fear of his enemies, whom he describes, ver. 1, 2, 5, 6.

III. His *confidence* in God's word, ver. 3, 4, 9, 10, 11.

IV. His *thankfulness*, ver. 4, 10, 12, 13.

I. He begins with a prayer for mercy. Little was he likely to find from man; from his God he expected it; and therefore he prays: "Be merciful unto me, O God."

II. And then presently he subjoins the *cause;* the danger he was in by his bloody and cruel enemies, whom he begins to describe:—

1. From their *insatiable rapacity.* Like a wolf they would *swallow me up.* Enemies at home and abroad would swallow me up.

2. From the *time.* Daily they would do it; without intermission.

3. From their *number:* "Many there be that fight against me."

Of these he gives us a farther description in the fifth and sixth verses:—

1. From their *incessant malice:* "Every day they wrest my words. All their thoughts are against me for evil."

2. From their *secret treachery, craft,* and *vigilance:* "They gather themselves together, they hide themselves;" their counsels lying, as it were, in ambush for me. "They mark my steps." Go where I will, they are at my heels.

3. From their *implacable hatred;* nothing could satisfy them but his blood: "They lay wait for my soul."

In the very midst of this complaint, he inserts his courage and confidence.

1. "What time I am afraid, I will trust in thee."

2. "I will not fear." He rises higher: even when he fears, he will not fear. His word, his

promise, is passed to me for protection; and I will trust in it: "In God will I praise his word; in God have I put my trust, I will not fear what flesh, (for the proudest, the mightiest enemy I have, is but flesh, *and all flesh is grass,*) I will not then fear what flesh can do unto me."

This *reason* he repeats again, ver. 10, 11.

1. "In God I will praise his word; in the Lord I will praise his word."

2. "In God have I put my trust, I will not fear what man can do to me."

III. And this, his *confidence*, he quickens and animates,—

1. From his assurance that God would punish and bring down his enemies: "Shall they escape for their iniquity?" No, no; "in thine anger thou wilt cast them down."

2. From his *assurance* of God's *tutelage*, and paternal eye over him in all his dangers, griefs, complaints, petitions, and banishment.

Men think God does not meddle with little things: he knew otherwise.

1. "Thou tellest," and hast upon account, "my wanderings;" my flights, exile.

2. "Thou puttest my tears into thy bottle;" preservest them as rich wine.

3. Thou keepest a record for them: "Are they not in thy book?"

4. Thou puttest my enemies to flight: "When I cry unto thee, then I know mine enemies shall be turned back; for God is with me."

IV. And therefore, at last, he concludes with thanks, to which he holds himself bound by *vow.*

1. "Thy vows are upon me:" I owe thee thanks by vow, and I will pay them. "I will render praises unto thee."

2. The *reason* is, "For thou hast delivered my soul from death."

3. Thou wilt deliver me: "Wilt not thou deliver my feet from falling?"

4. The end is, "That I may walk before God in the light of the living." That I may live awhile, and walk as before thy eye; as in thy sight, uprightly, sincerely, and prosperously. That in me men may behold how powerfully thou hast saved both my body and soul.

PSALM LVII

David cries to God for mercy, with the strongest confidence of being heard, 1–3; he describes his enemies as lions, 4; thanks God for his deliverance, 5; and purposes to publish the praises of the Lord among his people, 6–11.

To the chief Musician, [a]Al-taschith, Michtam of David, [b]when he fled from Saul in the cave

A. M. cir. 2943
B. C. cir. 1061
Sauli, Regis
Israelitarum,
cir. annum
35

BE [c]merciful unto me, O God, be merciful unto me: for my soul trusteth in thee: [d]yea, in the shadow of thy wings will I make my refuge, [e]until *these* calamities be overpast.

2 I will cry unto God most high; unto God [f]that performeth *all things* for me.

3 [g]He shall send from heaven, and save me [h]*from* the reproach of him that would [1]swal-

low me up. Selah. God [k]shall send forth his mercy and his truth.

A. M. cir. 2943
B. C. cir. 1061
Sauli, Regis
Israelitarum,
cir. annum
35

4 My soul *is* among lions: *and* I lie *even among* them that are set on fire, *even* the sons of men, [1]whose teeth *are* spears and arrows, and [m]their tongue a sharp sword.

5 [n]Be thou exalted, O God, above the heavens; *let* thy glory *be* above all the earth.

6 [o]They have prepared a net for my steps; my soul is bowed down: they have digged a

---

[a]Or, *Destroy not, A golden* Psalm——[b]1 Sam. xxii. 1; xxiv. 3; Psa. cxlii. title——[c]Psa. lvi. 1——[d]Psa. xvii. 8; lxiii. 7——[e]Isa. xxvi. 20——[f]Psa. cxxxviii. 8 [g]Psa. cxliv. 5, 7

[h]Or, *he reproacheth him that would swallow me up* [i]Psa. lvi. 1——[k]Psa. xl. 11; xliii. 3; lxi. 7——[l]Prov. xxx. 14——[m]Psa. lv. 21; lxiv. 3——[n]Ver. 11; Psa. cviii. 5——[o]Psa. vii. 15, 16; ix. 15

NOTES ON PSALM LVII

The *title* is, *To the chief Musician, Al-taschith,* (destroy not,) *a golden Psalm of David,* (or one to be engraven,) *when he fled from Saul in the cave.* It is very likely that this Psalm was made to commemorate his escape from Saul in the cave of *En-gedi,* where Saul had entered without knowing that David was there, and David cut off the skirt of his garment. And it is not improbable that, when he found that Saul was providentially delivered into his hand, he might have formed the hasty resolution to take away his life, as his companions counselled him to do; and in that moment the Divine monition came, אל תשחת *al tascheth! Destroy not! lift not up thy hand against the Lord's anointed!* Instead, therefore, of taking away his *life,* he contented himself with taking away his *skirt,* to show him that he had been in his power. When, afterwards, he composed the Psalm, he gave it for *title* the words which he received as a Divine warning. See the history, 1 Sam. xxiv. See also my note upon the *fourth* verse of that chapter.

Verse 1. *Be merciful unto me*] To show David's deep earnestness, he repeats this *twice;* he was in great danger, surrounded by implacable enemies, and he knew that God alone could deliver him.

My soul trusteth in thee] I put my *life* into thy hand; and my *immortal spirit* knows no other portion than thyself.

In the shadow of thy wings] A metaphor taken from the brood of a hen taking shelter under her wings when they see a bird of prey; and there they continue to *hide themselves* till their *enemy disappears.* In a *storm,* or *tempest of rain,* the mother covers them with her wings to afford them shelter and defence. This the psalmist has particularly in view, as the following words show: "Until these calamities be overpast."

Verse 2. *I will cry unto God most high*] He is the *Most High;* and therefore far above all my enemies, though the *prince of the power of the air* be at their head.

Unto God, לאל *lael,* unto the *strong God,* one against whom no human or diabolic might can prevail. David felt his own *weakness,* and he

knew the *strength* of his adversaries; and therefore he views God under those *attributes* and *characters* which were suited to his state. This is a great *secret* in the Christian life; few pray to God *wisely;* though they may do it *fervently.*

That performeth all things *for me.*] Who *works* for me; גמר *gomer,* he who *completes* for me, and will bring all to a happy issue.

Verse 3. *He shall send from heaven, and save me*] Were there no human agents or earthly means that he could employ, he would send his angels from heaven to rescue me from my enemies. Or, He will give his command from heaven that this may be done on earth.

Selah] I think this word should be at the *end* of the verse.

God shall send forth his mercy and his truth.] Here *mercy* and *truth* are personified. They are the *messengers* that God will send from heaven to save me. His *mercy* ever inclines him to help and save the distressed. This he has *promised* to do; and his *truth* binds him to fulfil the promises or engagements his mercy has made, both to saints and sinners.

Verse 4. *My soul* is *among lions*] בתוך לבאם *bethoch lebaim.* I agree with Dr. *Kennicott* that this should be translated, "My soul dwells in *parched places,*" from לאב *laab,* he thirsted. And thus the *Chaldee* seems to have understood the place, though it be not explicit.

I lie even among them that are set on fire] I seem to be among *coals.* It is no ordinary rage and malice by which I am pursued: each of my enemies seems determined to have my life.

Verse 5. *Be thou exalted, O God, above the heavens*] Let the glory of thy mercy and truth be seen in the heavens above, and in the earth beneath. Several of the fathers apply what is said above to the *passion* of our Lord, and what is said here to his *resurrection.*

Verse 6. *They have prepared a net for my steps*] A gin or springe, such as huntsmen put in the places which they know the prey they seek frequents: such, also, as they place in *passages in hedges,* &c., through which the game creeps.

They have digged a pit] Another method of catching game and wild beasts. They dig a pit, cover it over with weak sticks and turf.

A. M. cir. 2943
B. C. cir. 1061
Sauli, Regis
Israelitarum,
cir. annum
35
pit before me, into the midst whereof they are fallen *them-selves*. Selah.

7 ᵖMy heart is ᑫfixed, O God, my heart is fixed: I will sing and give praise.

8 Awake up, ʳmy glory: awake, psaltery and harp: I *myself* will awake early.

ᵖPsa. cviii. 1, &c.——ᑫOr, *prepared*——ʳPsa. xvi. 9; xxx. 12; cviii. 1, 2

The beasts, not suspecting danger where none appears, in attempting to walk over it, fall through, and are taken. Saul digged a pit, laid snares for the life of David; and fell into one of them himself, particularly at the cave of *En-gedi;* for he entered into the very pit or cave where David and his men were hidden, and his life lay at the generosity of the very man whose life he was seeking! The rabbins tell a curious and instructive tale concerning this: "God sent a spider to weave her web at the mouth of the cave in which David and his men lay hid. When Saul saw the spider's web over the cave's mouth, he very naturally conjectured that it could neither be the haunt of *men* nor *wild beasts;* and therefore went in with confidence to repose." The *spider* here, a vile and contemptible animal, became the instrument in the hand of God of saving David's life, and of confounding Saul in his policy and malice. This may be a *fable;* but it shows by what apparently insignificant *means* God, the universal ruler, can accomplish the greatest and most beneficent *ends.* Saul continued to dig pits to entrap David; and at last fell a prey to his own obstinacy. We have a proverb to the same effect: *Harm watch, harm catch.* The *Greeks* have one also: Ἡ τε κακη βουλη τῳ βουλευσαντι κακιστη, "An evil advice often becomes most ruinous to the adviser." The *Romans* have one to the same effect:—

Neque enim lex justior ulla est
Quam necis artificem arte perire sua.

"There is no law more just than that which condemns a man to suffer death by the instrument which he has invented to take away the life of others."

Verse 7. *My heart is fixed*] My heart is *prepared* to do and suffer thy will. It is *fixed*— it has made the *firmest purpose* through his strength by which I can do all things.

Verse 8. *Awake up, my glory*] Instead of כבודי *kebodi,* "my glory," one MS., and the *Syriac,* have כנורי *kinnori,* "my harp." Dr. Kennicott reads כבורי *kebori,* which he supposes to be some instrument of music; and adds that the instrument used in church-music by the Ethiopians is now called כבר *kaber.* I think the *Syriac* likely to be the true reading: "Awake up, my harp; awake, psaltery and harp: I will awake early." Such *repetitions* are frequent in the Hebrew poets. If we read *my glory,* it may refer either to his *tongue;* or, which is more likely, to his *skill in composition,* and in *playing on different instruments.* The *five* last verses of this Psalm are nearly the same with the *five* first verses of

9 ˢI will praise thee, O Lord, among the people: I will sing unto thee among the nations.

A. M. cir. 2943
B. C. cir. 1061
Sauli, Regis
Israelitarum,
cir. annum
35

10 ᵗFor thy mercy *is* great unto the heavens, and thy truth unto the clouds.

11 ᵘBe thou exalted, O God, above the heavens: *let* thy glory *be* above all the earth.

ˢPsa. cviii. 3——ᵗPsa. xxxvi. 5; lxxi. 19; ciii. 11; cviii. 4
ᵘVer. 5

Psa. cviii. The reason of this may be, the *notes* or *memoranda* from the *psalmist's diary* were probably, through mistake, twice copied. The insertion at the beginning of the cviiith Psalm seems to bear no relation to the rest of that ode.

Rabbi Solomon Jarchi tells us that *David had a harp at his bed's head, which played of itself when the north wind blew on it; and then David arose to give praise to God.* This account has been treated as a *ridiculous fable* by grave Christian writers. I would however hesitate, and ask one question: Does not the account itself point out an instrument then well known, similar to the comparatively lately discovered *Æolian harp?* Was not *this* the instrument hung at David's bed's head, which, when the night breeze (which probably blew at a certain time) began to act upon the cords, sent forth those dulcet, those heavenly sounds, for which the Æolian harp is remarkable? "Awake, my harp, at the *due time:* I will not wait for thee *now,* I have the strongest cause for gratitude; I will awake earlier than usual to sing the praises of my God."

Verse 9. *Among the people*] The *Israelites. Among the nations.*] The *Gentiles* at large. A prophecy either relating to the Gospel times, Christ being considered as the Speaker: or a prediction that these Divine compositions should be sung, both in synagogues and in Christian churches, in all the nations of the earth. And it is so: wherever the name of Christ is known, there is David's known also.

Verse 10. *Thy mercy* is *great unto the heavens*] It is as far above all human description and comprehension as the heavens are above the earth. See the notes on Psa. xxxvi. 5, 6, where nearly the same words occur.

Verse 11. *Be thou exalted, O God, above the heavens*] The same sentiments and words which occur in verse 5. See the note there.

David was not only in a happy state of mind when he wrote this Psalm, but in what is called a state of *triumph.* His confidence in God was unbounded; though encompassed by the most ferocious enemies, and having all things against him except God and his innocence. David will seldom be found in a more blessed state than he here describes. Similar faith in God will bring the same blessings to every true Christian in similar circumstances.

ANALYSIS OF THE FIFTY-SEVENTH PSALM

The contents of this Psalm are,—
I. David's *petition,* ver. 1.
II. The *reasons* which induced him to offer it, ver. 2-6.

III. His *resolution* to give God due praise, ver. 5, 7-11.

I. His *petition* is ardent. The *repetition* shows this: it is for grace and protection: "Be merciful unto me, be merciful unto me, O God!"

II. He adduces his *reasons* to persuade the Lord to be merciful.

First reason. The faith and confidence he had in God: "My soul trusteth in thee; and under the shadow of thy wings," as the chicken does under those of the hen, "shall be my refuge until these calamities be overpast."

Second reason. The sufficiency and efficiency of God: "I will call upon God."

1. He is the *Most High;* then he is sufficient and able to deliver me.

2. He will perform all things for me: therefore he will effect this.

In the following verse he insists on this argument.

"He shall send from heaven." He will do it in a miraculous way, if there be no other way: "He will send from heaven, and save me. He will send forth his mercy and his truth;" he will *perform* his *word,* and *graciously* save me.

The *third reason* of his petition is the extreme danger he was then in by a cruel and merciless enemy.

1. "My soul is among the lions," a ravenous, strong, and bloody creature.

2. "I lie even among those who are set on fire." Their anger and hatred to me are implacable.

3. Even among those whose "teeth are spears and arrows, and their tongue a sharp sword." They wound by calumniating me. A *spear* wounds near; an *arrow,* afar off; a *sword,* at hand: *near* or *far off,* they spare not to disgrace me.

He now brings another *argument,* stronger than all the rest, viz., *God's glory.* It will be to his glory to be merciful, to save, and to deliver; and therefore he prays: "Be thou exalted, O God, above the heavens, and let thy glory," &c. That is, Let not the wicked triumph; but display thy power, and assert thy glory; which, if thou do, thy glory will be conspicuous *above*—in the heavens, and *below*—over all the earth.

He then begins his complaint, describing the practices of his enemies:—

1. "They have prepared a net for my feet." They lay *snares* as fowlers do.

2. Through which "my soul is bowed down." My life is in extreme danger.

3. "They have digged a pit before me;" intending to take me like some wild beast; but, praised be God I foresee the event. "They are fallen into the pit themselves."

III. In confidence of this David gives thanks, which may be considered a *fourth* argument; for there is no such way to procure a new favour as to be *thankful.* Our thanksgiving should consist of *two* especial points: 1. Commemoration; 2. Declaration.

1. He that will be thankful should treasure up in his *heart* and *memory* the kindness that is done to him. This David had done: "My heart is fixed, my heart is fixed."

2. After he remembers it, he should be *affected* by it, and *resolve* on it. So does David. My heart is *ready, prepared, fixed. I will* be thankful. I am *determined.*

3. It is not enough that a man have a thankful heart; he must *declare* it, and make publicly known what God has done for him: "I will sing, and give praise."

4. He should use all means in his power to make it known; *tongue, psaltery, harp,* are all little enough. To these he addresses himself: "Awake, tongue, lute, harp," &c.

5. He must not do it carelessly: "Awake! Awake! Myself will awake."

6. He must take the first opportunity, and not delay it: "I will awake EARLY."

7. He should do it in such a way as most tends to God's glory: "I will praise thee among the people—I will sing of thee among the nations."

That all this may be done, David gives a sufficient reason,—God's *mercy* and *truth.* His infinite *mercy* in *promising,* his *truth* in *performing:* "Thy mercy is great unto the heavens; thy truth unto the clouds."

And then he concludes with a repetition of the *fifth* verse: "Be thou exalted above the heavens, and thy truth unto the clouds." Let all give thee the glory due to thy name.

PSALM LVIII

David reproves wicked counsellors and judges, who pervert justice, and stir up the strong against the weak and innocent, 1-5. He foretells their destruction, and describes the nature of it, 6-9. The righteous, seeing this, will magnify God's justice and providence, 10, 11.

To the chief Musician, ªAl-taschith, ᵇMichtam of David

A. M. cir. 2943 B. C. cir. 1061 Sauli, Regis Israelitarum, cir. annum 35

DO ye indeed speak righteousness, O congregation? do ye judge uprightly, O ye sons of men?

2 Yea, in heart ye work wickedness; ᶜye weigh the violence of your hands in the earth.

A. M. cir. 2943 B. C. cir. 1061 Sauli, Regis Israelitarum, cir. annum 35

3 ᵈThe wicked are estranged from the

ªOr, *Destroy not, A golden* Psalm *of David*——ᵇPsa. lvii. title

ᶜPsa. xciv. 20; Isaiah x. 1——ᵈPsalm li. 5; Isa. xliii. 8

NOTES ON PSALM LVIII

The *title* seems to have no reference to the subject of the Psalm. See the introduction to

the preceding. Saul having attempted the life of David, the latter was obliged to flee from the court, and take refuge in the deserts of Judea. Saul, missing him, is supposed by Bishop

A. M. cir. 2943
B. C. cir. 1061
Sauli, Regis
Israelitarum,
cir. annum
35

womb: they go astray °as soon as they be born, speaking lies.

4 ʳTheir poison *is* ᵍlike the poison of a serpent: *they are* like ʰthe

deaf ˡadder *that* stoppeth her ear;

5 Which will not hearken to the voice of charmers, ᵏcharming never so wisely.

A. M. cir. 2943
B. C. cir. 1061
Sauli, Regis
Israelitarum,
cir. annum
35

°Heb. *from the belly*——ʳPsa. cxl. 3; Eccles. x. 11
ᵍHeb. *according to the likeness*

ʰJer. viii. 17——ˡOr, *asp*——ᵏOr, *be the charmer never so cunning*

Patrick to have called a council, when they, to ingratiate themselves with the monarch, adjudged David to be guilty of treason in aspiring to the throne of Israel. This being made known to David was the cause of this Psalm. It is a good lesson to all kings, judges, and civil magistrates; and from it they obtain maxims to regulate their conduct and influence their decisions; and at the same time they may discern the awful account they must give to God, and the dreadful punishment *they* shall incur who prostitute justice to serve sinister ends.

Verse 1. *Do ye indeed speak righteousness*] Or, O cabinet, seeing ye profess to act according to the principles of justice, why do ye not give righteous counsels and just decisions, ye sons of men? Or, it may be an irony: What excellent judges you are! well do ye judge according to law and justice, when ye give decisions not founded on any law, nor supported by any principle of justice! To please your master, ye pervert judgment; and take part against the innocent, in order to retain your places and their emoluments. Saul's counsellors appear to have done so, though in their consciences they must have been satisfied of David's innocence.

Verse 2. *Yea, in heart ye work wickedness*] With their *tongues* they had spoken maliciously, and given evil counsel. In their *hearts* they meditated nothing but wickedness. And though in their *hands* they held the *scales of justice*, yet in their use of them they were *balances of injustice and violence*. This is the *fact* to which the psalmist alludes, and the *figure* which he uses is that of *justice with her scales* or *balances*, which, though it might be the emblem of the court, yet it did not prevail in the *practice* of these magistrates and counsellors.

Verse 3. *The wicked are estranged from the womb*] "This," says Dr. *Kennicott*, "and the next *two* verses, I take to be the answer of Jehovah to the question in the *two* first verses, as the 6th, 7th, and 8th, are the answer of the psalmist, and the remainder contains the decree of Jehovah." He calls these *wicked* men, men who had been always wicked, originally and naturally bad, and brought up in falsehood, flattery, and lying. The part they acted now was quite in character.

Verse 4. *Their poison* is *like the poison of a serpent*] When they bite, they convey poison into the wound, as the serpent does. They not only injure you by outward acts, but by their malevolence they poison your reputation. They do you as much evil as they can, and propagate the worst reports that others may have you in abhorrence, treat you as a bad and dangerous man; and thus, as the poison from the bite of the serpent is conveyed into the whole mass of blood, and circulates with it through all the system, carrying death every where; so their

injurious speeches and vile insinuations circulate through society, and poison and blast your reputation in every place. Such is the *slanderer*, and such his influence in society. *From* such no reputation is safe; *with* such no character is sacred; and *against* such there is no defence. God alone can shield the innocent from the envenomed tongue and lying lips of such inward monsters in the shape of men.

Like the deaf adder that *stoppeth her ear*] It is a fact that cannot be disputed with any show of reason, that in ancient times there were persons that charmed, lulled to inactivity, or professed to charm, serpents, so as to prevent them from biting. See Eccles. x. 11; Jer. viii. 17. The prince of Roman poets states the fact, VIRG. Ecl. viii., ver. 71.

Frigidus in prati *cantando* rumpitur anguis.

"In the meadows the cold snake is burst by incantation."

The same author, Æn. vii., ver. 750, gives us the following account of the skill of Umbro, a priest of the Marrubians:—

Quin et *Marrubia* venit de gente sacerdos,
Fronde super galeam, et felici comptus oliva,
Archippi regis missu, fortissimus *Umbro;*
Vipereo generi, et graviter spirantibus *hydris*,
Spargere qui *somnos cantuque* manuque solebat,
Mulcebatque iras, et morsus arte levabat.

"*Umbro*, the brave *Marubian* priest, was there,
Sent by the *Marsian monarch* to the war.
The smiling olive with her verdant boughs
Shades his bright helmet, and adorns his brows.
His *charms* in peace the furious serpent *keep*,
And *lull the envenomed viper's race to sleep:*
His healing hand allayed the raging pain;
And at his touch the poisons fled again."
                                        PITT.

There is a particular sect of the Hindoos who profess to bring serpents into subjection, and deprive them of their poison, by *incantation*. See at the end of this Psalm.

Verse 5. *Which will not hearken to the voice of charmers*] The old Psalter translates and paraphrases these two verses curiously:—

Vulg. Furor illis secundum similitudinem serpentis; sicut aspidis surdæ et obturantis aures suas: Quæ non exaudiet vocem incantantium et venefici incantantis sapienter.

Trans. 𝔚𝔬𝔡𝔫𝔢𝔰 (madness) til thaim aftir the liking of the neddir, as of the snake doumb and stoppand her eres.

Paraph. Right calles he tham wod, (*mad,*) for thai hafe na witte to se whider thai ga: for thai louke thair eghen, and rennys till the are thaire wodness til clumsthed that wil noght be turned as of the snake that festis (*fastens*)

A. M. cir. 2943
B. C. cir. 1061
Sauli, Regis
Israelitarum,
cir. annum
35

6 [1]Break their teeth, O God, in their mouth: break out the great teeth of the young lions, O LORD.

7 [m]Let them melt away as waters *which* run continually: *when* he bendeth *his bow to shoot* his arrows, let them be as cut in pieces.

8 As a snail *which* melteth, let *every one of them* pass away; [n]*like* the untimely birth of a woman, *that* they may not see the sun.

9 Before your pots can feel the thorns, he shall take them away [o]as with a whirlwind, [p]both living, and in *his* wrath.

10 [q]The righteous shall rejoice when he seeth the vengeance: [r]he shall wash his feet in the blood of the wicked.

11 [s]So that a man shall say, Verily *there is* [t]a reward for the righteous: verily he is a God that [u]judgeth in the earth.

A. M. cir. 2943
B. C. cir. 1061
Sauli, Regis
Israelitarum,
cir. annum
35

---

[1]Job iv. 10; Psa. iii. 7——[m]Josh. vii. 5; Psa. cxii. 10 [n]Job iii. 16; Eccles. vi. 3——[o]Prov. x. 25——[p]Heb. *as living as wrath*

[q]Psa. lii. 6; lxiv. 10; cvii. 42——[r]Psa. lxviii. 23 [s]Psa. xcii. 15——[t]Heb. *fruit of the,* &c.; Isa. iii. 10 [u]Psa. lxvii. 4; xcvi. 13; xcviii. 9

---

the ta ere til the erth, and the tother ere stoppis with hir taile: Sua do thai that thai here not Godis word; thai stope thair eris with luf of erthli thing that thai delite thaim in; and with thair taile, that es with all synnes, that thai will noght amend.

Trans. 𝔗𝔥𝔢 𝔴𝔥𝔦𝔩𝔨 𝔰𝔞𝔩𝔩𝔢 𝔫𝔬𝔤𝔥𝔱 𝔥𝔢𝔯𝔢 𝔱𝔥𝔢 𝔟𝔬𝔶𝔠𝔢 𝔬𝔣 𝔠𝔥𝔞𝔯𝔪𝔞𝔫𝔡, 𝔞𝔫𝔡 𝔬𝔣 𝔱𝔥𝔢 𝔟𝔢𝔫𝔦𝔪 𝔦𝔫 𝔞𝔨𝔞𝔯𝔢 𝔬𝔣 𝔠𝔥𝔞𝔯𝔪𝔞𝔫𝔡 𝔴𝔦𝔰𝔩𝔦.

Paraph. This snake stopis hir eres that she be noght broth to light; for if she herd it, she come forth sone, he charmes swa wysli in his craft. Swa the wikkid men wil noght here the voyce of Crist and his lufers that are wys charmes; for thi wild (*would*) bring them till light of heven. Wyt ye well (*know*) that he (i. e., *Christ*) lufes noght charmars and venim makers but be (*by*) vices of bestes, he takes lickening of vices of men.

It seems as if there were a species of *snake* or *adder* that is *nearly deaf;* and as their instinct informs them that if they listen to the sounds which charmers use they shall become a prey; therefore they stop their ears to prevent the little hearing they have from being the means of their destruction. To this the *Old Psalter* refers. We have also an account of a species of *snake*, which, if it cast its eye on the charmer, feels itself obliged to come out of its hole; it therefore keeps close, and takes care neither to *see* nor be *seen*. To this also the Old Psalter alludes; and of this *fact*, if it be one, he makes a good use.

Verse 6. *Break their teeth*] He still compares Saul, his captains, and his courtiers, to *lions;* and as a lion's power of doing mischief is greatly lessened if all his teeth be broken, so he prays that God may take away their power and means of pursuing their bloody purpose. But he may probably have the serpents in view, of which he speaks in the preceding verse: *break their teeth—destroy the fangs* of these serpents, in which *their poison* is contained. This will amount to the same meaning as above. Save me from the *adders*—the sly and poisonous slanderers: save me also from the *lions*—the tyrannical and blood-thirsty men.

Verse 7. *Let them melt away as waters*] Let them be minished away like the waters which sometimes run in the desert, but are soon evaporated by the *sun*, or absorbed by the *sand*.

When *he bendeth* his bow] When my adversaries aim their envenomed shafts against me, let their arrows not only fall short of the mark,

but he broken to pieces in the flight. Some apply this to GOD. When he bends his bow against them, they shall all be exterminated.

Verse 8. *As a snail* which *melteth*] The *Chaldee* reads the verse thus: "They shall melt away in their sins as water flows off; as the creeping snail that smears its track; as the untimely birth and the blind mole, which do not see the sun."

The original word שבלול *shablul,* a snail, is either from שביל *shebil,* a *path,* because it leaves a *shining path* after it by emitting a portion of *slime,* and thus *glaring* the ground; and therefore might be emphatically called the *path-maker;* or from ישב *yashab* to *dwell,* ב *be, in,* לול *lul,* a *winding* or *spiral shell,* which is well known to be its house, and which it always *inhabits;* for when it is not coiled up within this shell, it carries it with it wheresoever it goes. See *Bochart.* These figures need no farther explanation.

Verse 9. *Before your pots can feel the thorns*] Ye shall be destroyed with a sudden destruction. From the time that the fire of God's wrath is kindled about you, it will be but as a moment before ye be entirely consumed by it: so very short will be the time, that it may be likened to the heat of the first blaze of dry thorns under a pot, that has not as yet been able to penetrate the metal, and warm what is contained in it.

A whirlwind] Or the suffocating *simoom* that destroys life in an instant, without previous warning: so, without *pining sickness*—while ye are *living*—lively and active, the whirlwind of God's wrath shall sweep you away.

Verse 10. *The righteous shall rejoice when he seeth the vengeance*] He shall have a strong proof of the Divine providence, of God's hatred against sinners, and his continual care of his followers.

He shall wash his feet in the blood of the wicked.] This can only mean that the slaughter would be so great, and at the same time so very nigh to the dwelling of the righteous, that he could not go out without dipping his feet in the blood of the wicked. The *Syriac, Vulgate, Septuagint, Æthiopic, Arabic,* and *Anglo-Saxon,* read *hands* instead of *feet.* Every thing that is *vindictive* in the Psalms must be considered as totally alien from the spirit of the Gospel, and not at all, under our dispensation, to be imitated. If the passage above be *really* vindictive, and it certainly will admit of the interpretation given above, it is to be considered as not belonging to that state in which the Son of man is come, not to *destroy* men's lives, but to *save.*

Verse 11. *So that a man shall say*] That is, people, seeing these just judgments of God, shall say, There is a reward (פְּרִי *peri, fruit*) to the righteous man. He has not sown his seed in vain; he has not planted and watered in vain: he has the fruit of his labours, he eats the fruit of his doings. But wo to the wicked, it is ill with him; for the reward of his hands has been given him.

He is a God that judgeth in the earth] There is a God who does not entirely defer judgment till the judgment-day; but executes judgment now, even in this earth; and thus continues to give such a proof of his hatred to sin and love to his followers, that every considerate mind is convinced of it. And hence arise the indisputable maxims: "There is, even *here,* a reward for the righteous;" "There is a God who, even *now,* judgeth in the earth."

I have seen Indian priests who professed to charm, not only serpents, but the most ferocious wild beasts; even the enraged elephant, and the royal tiger! Two priests of *Budhoo,* educated under my own care, repeated the *Sanscrit incantations* to me, and solemnly asserted that they had seen the power of them repeatedly and successfully put to the test. I have mislaid these incantations, else I should insert them as a curiosity; for to *charms* of the same nature the psalmist most undoubtedly alludes.

The term חוֹבֵר *chober,* which we translate *charmer,* comes from חָבַר *to join,* or *put together;* i. e., certain unintelligible words or sentences, which formed the *spell.*

I once met with a man who professed to remove diseases by pronouncing an unintelligible jingling jargon of words oddly tacked together. I met with him one morning proceeding to the cure of a horse affected with the *farcin.* With a very grave countenance he stood before the diseased animal, and, taking off his hat, devoutly muttered the following words; which, as a matter of peculiar favour, he afterwards taught me, well knowing that *I* could never use them successfully, *because not taught me by a woman;* "for," said he, "to use them with success, a *man* must be taught them by a *woman,* and a *woman* by a *man.*" What the genuine orthography may be I cannot pretend to say, as I am entirely ignorant of the language, if the words belong to any language: but the following words exactly express his sounds:—

> Murry fin a liff cree
> Murry fin a liss cree
> Ard fin deriv dhoo
> Murry fin firey fu
> Murry fin elph yew.

When he had repeated these words *nine* times, he put on his hat and walked off; but he was to return the next morning, and so on for *nine* mornings successively, always *before he had broken his fast.* The *mother* of the above person, a very old woman, and by many reputed a *witch,* professed to do miracles by pronouncing, or rather *muttering,* certain *words* or *sounds,* and by *measuring* with a cord the diseased parts of the sick person. I saw her

practise twice: 1st, on a person afflicted with a violent headache, or rather the effects of a *coup de soleil;* and, 2ndly, on one who had got a dangerous mote or splinter in his eye. In the *first* case she began to measure the head, round the temples, marking the length; then from the vertex, under the chin, and so up to the vertex again, marking that length. Then, by observing the dimensions, passed judgment on the *want of proportion* in the two admeasurements, and said the brain was compressed by the sinking down of the skull. She then began her incantations, *muttering* under her breath a supplication to certain divine and angelic beings, *to come and lift up the bones, that they might no longer compress the brain.* She then repeated her admeasurements, and showed how much was gained towards a restoration of the *proportions* from the *spell* already *muttered.* The spell was again muttered, the *measurements* repeated, and at each time a comparison of the first measurement was made with the succeeding, till at last she said she had the due proportions; that the disease, or rather the *cause* of it, was removed; and that the operations were no longer necessary.

In the case of the *diseased eye,* her manner was different. She took a cup of clean pure water, and washed her mouth well. Having done so, she filled her mouth with the same water, and walked to and fro in the apartment (the patient sitting in the midst of the floor) *muttering* her *spell,* of which nothing could be heard but a *grumbling noise.* She then emptied her mouth into a clean white bason, and showed the motes which had been conveyed out of the patient's eye into the water in her mouth, while engaged in *muttering the incantation!* She proffered to teach me her wonder-working words; but the sounds were so very uncouth, if not barbarous, that I know no combination of letters by which I could convey the pronunciation.

Ridiculous as all this may appear, it shows that this incantation work is conducted in the present day, both in *Asia* and *Europe,* where it is professed, in precisely the same manner in which it was conducted formerly, by pronouncing, or rather *muttering certain words* or *sounds,* to which they attach *supernatural power* and *efficiency.* And from this came the term *spell:* Anglo-Saxon ꞃpell. a *word,* a *charm,* composed of such supposed *powerful words;* and ꝥꞃᶜᵃⁿ ꞃpell *wyrkan spell* signified among our ancestors *to use enchantments.*

ANALYSIS OF THE FIFTY-EIGHTH PSALM

David deprecates the danger that hung over his head from Saul and his council.

The Psalm is divided into *three* parts:—

I. A sharp invective, or reprehension of his enemies, ver. 1.

II. An imprecation, or denunciation of God's judgment on them, ver. 6-9.

III. The benefits that from thence redound to the righteous, ver. 10, 11.

I. 1. David begins with an apostrophe, and figures it with an *erotesis,* which makes his reproof the sharper. 1. "O congregation;" O ye counsel of Saul. 2. "Do you indeed speak righteously?" 3. "Do ye judge uprightly, O ye sons of men?" By which he intimates that indeed they do neither.

2. Which in the next verse he affirms in plain terms, and brings home to their charge: "Yea, in heart you work wickedness; you weigh the violence of your hands in the earth?" heart and hand are bent to do evil, which the words, well considered, do exaggerate. 1. They were iniquities, a plurality of them. 2. It was their work. 3. Their hearty work. 4. Their handy work. 5. Weighed out by their scale of justice. 6. Which, indeed, under the colour of justice, was but violence. 7. And it was in this earth—in *Israel*, where no such thing was to be done.

3. This, their wickedness, he amplifies, both from their origin and progress:—

1. The root of it was very old; brought into the world with them: 1. "The wicked are estranged from the womb:" from God and all goodness. 2. "They go astray:" from their cradle they take the wrong way. 3. "As soon as they be born, speaking lies:" from their birth inclined to falsehood.

2. And in this their falsehood they are malicious and obstinate. 1. *Malicious.* The poison of their tongue is like the poison of a serpent, innate, deadly. 2. *Obstinate.* For they will not be reclaimed by any counsel or admonition: They are like the deaf adder that stoppeth her ear, which refuseth to hear the voice of the charmer, "charm he never so wisely."

II. Their wickedness, malice, and obstinacy, being so great, he now prays against and devotes them to God's judgment. He prays, in general, for their ruin, esteeming them no better than lions. Saul, the *old lion;* and his council, *lions' whelps.*

1. To God he turns his speech; and prays against their means to hurt, whether near or afar off.

2. And thence, against their persons: "O God, break their teeth in their mouth; break out the great teeth of the lions." O Lord, remove their strength; their nearest instruments to hurt, to destroy: "O God, when they purpose to harm us, let it be in vain; when he bends his bow to shoot his arrows, let them be as cut in pieces."

Thus let it fall to their arms: but as for their persons,—

1. "Let them melt away as waters." Great brooks, that run with great force from the mountains, and overrun for a little while the valleys; but run quickly into the channels, and thence to the sea, and are swallowed up.

2. Let them be *as a snail* that melts in her passage, and leaves a slimy track behind, which yet quickly passeth away. So let them be like a snail, which, when its shell is taken off, grows cold and dies.

3. Let them be "like the untimely fruit of a woman, that they may not see the sun."

4. "Before your pots can feel the thorns"—ere they do mischief, "He shall take them away as with a whirlwind, both living and in his wrath."

III. The *benefits* which, from his judgment upon the wicked, shall flow to the righteous.

1. Joyfulness: "The righteous shall rejoice when he seeth the vengeance."

2. Amendment. Being warned thus, "He shall wash his footsteps in their blood." Their slaughter shall be great; and he shall be near it, yet unhurt.

3. Confirmation of their faith, and giving glory to God: "So that a man shall say, Verily, there is a reward for the righteous: doubtless, there is a God that judgeth in the earth."

PSALM LIX

The psalmist prays for deliverance from his enemies, whose desperate wickedness he describes, 1-7; professes strong confidence in God, 8-10; speaks of the destruction of his enemies, 11-15; praises God for benefits already received; and determines to trust in him, 16, 17.

XI. DAY. EVENING PRAYER

To the chief Musician, ᵃAl-taschith, ᵇMichtam of David; ᶜwhen Saul sent, and they watched the house to kill him

A. M. cir. 3559
B. C. cir. 445
Artaxerxis I.,
R. Persarum,
cir. annum
20

DELIVER ᵈme from mine enemies, O my God: ᵉdefend me from them that rise up against me.

2 Deliver me from the workers of iniquity, and save me from bloody men.

A. M. cir. 3559
B. C. cir. 445
Artaxerxis I.,
R. Persarum,
cir. annum
20

3 For, lo, they lie in wait for my soul: ᶠthe mighty are gathered against me; ᵍnot *for* my transgression, nor *for* my sin, O LORD.

ᵃOr, *Destroy not, A golden* Psalm *of David*——ᵇPsa. lvii. title——ᶜ1 Sam. xix. 11

ᵈPsa. xviii. 48——ᵉHeb. *set me on high*——ᶠPsa. lvi. 6
ᵍ1 Sam. cxiv. 11

NOTES ON PSALM LIX

The *title*, "To the chief Musician, Al-taschith, Michtam of David," has already occurred: and

perhaps means no more than that the present Psalm is to be sung as Psa. lvii., the *first* which bears this title. But there is here added the supposed occasion on which David made this

A. M. cir. 3559
B. C. cir. 445
Artaxerxis I.,
R. Persarum,
cir. annum
20

4 They run and prepare themselves without *my* fault: [h]awake [i]to help me, and behold.

5 Thou therefore, O LORD God of hosts, the God of Israel, awake to visit all the heathen: be not merciful to any wicked transgressors. Selah.

6 [k]They return at evening; they make a noise like a dog, and go round about the city.

7 Behold, they belch out with their mouth:

[l]swords *are* in their lips: for [m]who, *say they*, doth hear?

8 But [n]thou, O LORD, shalt laugh at them: thou shalt have all the heathen in derision.

9 *Because of* his strength will I wait upon thee: [o]for God *is* [p]my defence.

10 The God of my mercy shall [q]prevent me: God shall let me see [r]*my desire* upon [s]mine enemies.

A. M. cir. 3559
B. C. cir. 445
Artaxerxis I.,
R. Persarum,
cir. annum
20

---

[h]Psa. xxxv. 23; xliv. 23——[i]Heb. *to meet me*——[k]Ver. 14——[l]Psa. lvii. 4; Prov. xii. 18——[m]Psa. x. 11, 13; lxiv. 5; lxxiii. 11; xciv. 7——[n]1 Sam. xix. 16; Psa. ii. 4

[o]Verse 17; Psalm lxii. 2——[p]Heb. *my high place* [q]Psa. xxi. 3——[r]Psa. liv. 7; xcii. 11; cxii. 8——[s]Heb. *mine observers;* Psa. lvi. 2

Psalm: it was, "when Saul sent, and they watched the house to kill him." When the reader considers the whole of this Psalm carefully, he will be convinced that the *title* does not correspond to the contents. There is scarcely any thing in it that can apply to the circumstances of Saul's sending his guards by night to keep the avenues to the house of David, that when the morning came they might seize and slay him; and of his being saved through the information given him by his wife Michal, in consequence of which he was let down through a window, and so escaped. See 1 Sam. xix. 10, 11. There is not in the whole Psalm any positive allusion to this history; and there are many things in it which show it to be utterly inconsistent with the facts of that history. The Psalm most evidently agrees to the time of Nehemiah, when he was endeavouring to rebuild the walls of Jerusalem, when the enterprise was first mocked; then opposed by Sanballat the Horonite, Tobiah the Ammonite, and Geshem the Arabian, who watched day and night that they might cause the work to cease; and laid ambuscades for the life of Nehemiah himself. Every part of the Psalm agrees to this: and I am therefore of *Calmet's* opinion, that the Psalm was composed in that time, and probably by *Nehemiah*, or by *Esdras*.

Verse 1. *Deliver me from mine enemies, O my God*] A very proper prayer in the mouth of Nehemiah, when resisted in his attempts to rebuild the walls of Jerusalem by Sanballat, Tobiah, and Geshem, who opposed the work, and endeavoured to take away the life of the person whom God had raised up to restore and rebuild Jerusalem. I conceive the Psalm to have been made on this occasion; and on this hypothesis alone I think it capable of consistent explanation.

Verse 2. *The workers of iniquity*] Principally Sanballat the Horonite, Tobiah the Ammonite, and Geshem the Arabian; who were the chief enemies of the poor returned captives.

Bloody men.] The above, who sought the destruction of the Israelites; and particularly, that of Nehemiah, whom *four* several times they endeavoured to bring into an ambush, that they might take away his life. See Neh. vi. 1-4.

Verse 3. *For, lo, they lie in wait for my soul*] For my *life*. See the passages referred to above.

Verse 4. *They run and prepare themselves*] They leave no stone unturned that they may effect my destruction and prevent the building.

Verse 5. *O Lord God of hosts*] This was a

proper view to take of God, when Israel, a *handful* of poor distressed captives were surrounded and oppressed by the heathen chiefs above mentioned, and their several tribes. But Jehovah, *God of hosts,* was the *God of Israel;* and hence Israel had little to fear.

Be not merciful to any wicked transgressors.] Do not favour the cause of these wicked men. They are בגדי און *bogedey aven,* "changers of iniquity:" they go through the whole round of evil; find out and exercise themselves in all the *varieties of transgression.* How exactly does this apply to Nehemiah's foes! They sought, by open attack, wiles, flattery, foul speeches, fair speeches, threats, and ambuscades, to take away his life. Do not show them favour, that they may not succeed in their wicked designs. The prayer here is exactly the same in sentiment with that of Nehemiah, chap. iv. 4, 5. Hear, our God, for we are despised; turn their reproach upon their own heads;—cover not their iniquity, "and let not their sin be blotted out."

Verse 6. *They return at evening*] When the beasts of prey leave their dens, and go prowling about the cities and villages to get offal, and entrap domestic animals, these come about the city to see if they may get an entrance, destroy the work, and those engaged in it.

Verse 7. *They belch out with their mouth*] They use the lowest insult, the basest abuse. They deal in sarcasm, ridicule, slander, and lies.

Verse 8. *Thou, O Lord, shalt laugh at them*] They have mocked us; God will turn them and their schemes into ridicule and contempt: "Thou shalt have all these heathenish nations in derision."

Verse 9. Because of *his strength will I wait upon thee*] With this reading, I can make no sense of the passage. But instead of עזו *uzzo,* his strength," עזי *uzzi,* "my strength," is the reading of *fourteen* of *Kennicott's* and *De Rossi's* MSS., of the *Vulgate, Septuagint, Chaldee,* and, in effect, of the *Æthiopic, Syriac,* and *Arabic;* and also of the *Anglo-Saxon. To thee I commit all* MY *strength;* all I have I derive from thee, and all the good I possess I attribute to thee. The old Psalter translates, 𝖬𝖞 𝖘𝖙𝖗𝖊𝖓𝖌𝖍𝖙 𝖎 𝖘𝖍𝖆𝖑𝖑 𝖐𝖊𝖕𝖊 𝖙𝖎𝖑𝖑 𝖙𝖍𝖊, 𝖋𝖔𝖗 𝖒𝖞𝖓 𝖚𝖕𝖙𝖆𝖐𝖊𝖗 𝖙𝖍𝖔𝖚 𝖆𝖗𝖙. See on ver. 17.

Verse 10. *The God of my mercy shall prevent me*] The mercy of God shall go before me, and thus help me in all my doings.

God shall let me see my desire] The sentence is short. *God will let me see concerning my enemies,* i. e., how he will treat them.

A. M. cir. 3559
B. C. cir. 445
Artaxerxis I.,
R. Persarum,
cir. annum
20

11 [t]Slay them not, lest my people forget: scatter them by thy power; and bring them down, O LORD our shield.

12 [u]*For* the sin of their mouth *and* the words of their lips let them even be taken in their pride: and for cursing and lying *which* they speak.

13 [v]Consume *them* in wrath, consume *them,* that they *may* not *be:* and [w]let them know that God ruleth in Jacob unto the ends of the earth. Selah.

14 And [x]at evening let them return; *and* let them make a noise like a dog, and go round about the city.

A. M. cir. 3559
B. C. cir. 445
Artaxerxis I.,
R. Persarum,
cir. annum
20

15 Let them [y]wander up and down [z]for meat, [a]and grudge if they be not satisfied.

16 But I will sing of thy power; yea, I will sing aloud of thy mercy in the morning: for thou hast been my defence and refuge in the day of my trouble.

17 Unto thee, [b]O my strength, will I sing: [c]for God *is* my defence, *and* the God of my mercy.

---

[t]So Genesis iv. 12, 15——[u]Proverbs xii. 13; xviii. 7 [v]Psa. vii. 9——[w]Psa. lxxxiii. 18——[x]Ver. 6——[y]Job xv. 23; Psa. cix. 10

[z]Hebrew, *to eat*——[a]Or, *If they be not satisfied, then they will stay all night*——[b]Psalm xviii. 1——[c]Verses 9, 10

Verse 11. *Slay them not, lest my people forget*] I believe the Chaldee gives the true sense of this verse: "Do not slay them suddenly, lest my people should forget. Drive them from their habitations by thy power, and reduce them to poverty *by the loss* of their property." Preserve them long in a state of chastisement, that Israel may see thou hast undertaken for them: that thy hand is on the wicked for evil, and on them for good. The Canaanites were not suddenly destroyed; they were left to be pricks in the eyes and thorns in the sides of the Israelites. It is in a sense somewhat similar that the words are used here.

Verse 12. *For the sin of their mouth*] This verse has puzzled all the commentators. If we take חטאת *chattath* for *sin-offering* instead of *sin*, we shall get a better sense. Some of Nehemiah's enemies made a profession of the Jewish religion. Tobiah and his son were allied by marriage to the Jews; for Eliashib the priest had married his grandson to the daughter of *Sanballat;* and this produced a connexion with *Tobiah,* the fast friend of Sanballat. Besides, this very priest had given Tobiah one of the *great chambers in the house of the Lord,* where formerly the *meat-offerings, the frankincense, the vessels,* and *the tithe of the corn* and *wine* and *oil* were kept; Neh. xiii. 4, 5, 7, 8, 9. And there were *children of Tobiah* (probably the same family) who professed to be of the *Levites, Nethinim,* or *children of Solomon's servants;* but as they could not show *their father's house and their seed,* whether they were of Israel; these, and others which were children of the priests, were put out of the priesthood, and out of the sacred service, as polluted; as having sprung from intermarriages with heathens. See Ezra ii. 59, 60, 61, 62. Tobiah was expelled from the house of the Lord by Nehemiah, and all his household stuff thrown out of doors: Neh. xiii. 7, 8. And this was doubtless one ground of the enmity of Tobiah to Nehemiah; and in this verse of the Psalm he may allude particularly to his occupancy of the chamber of offerings, which offerings, instead of being given to the Levites, were consumed by Tobiah and his household. This may be fairly gathered from Neh. xiii. 5, 10, 11. Here then we have the *sin of their mouth;* their *eating* the offerings that belonged to the Levites; so that the temple service was deserted, the Levites being obliged to go and till the ground in order to obtain the means of life. And if we take חטאת *chattath* for *sin-offering,* it may refer to *promises* of sacrifice and offering which Tobiah and his family made, but never performed. They ate instead of offering them; and here was the *sin of their mouth,* in connexion with the *words of their lips,* and their *cursing and lying which they spake,* for which the psalmist calls upon the Lord *to consume them, that they may not* be, ver. 13.

Verse 14. *At evening let them return*] He had mentioned before, ver. 6, that these persons came like beasts of prey round the city striving to get in, that they might take possession. Now, being fully assured of God's protection, and that they shall soon be made a public example, he says, *Let them return and make a noise like a dog,* &c., like dogs, jackals, and other famished creatures, who come howling about the city-walls for something to eat, and wander up and down for meat, grumbling because they are not satisfied, ver. 15. Nehemiah had made up all the breaches; and had the city guarded so well day and night, by watches who continually relieved each other, that there was no longer any fear of being taken by surprise: and now they must feel like the hungry beasts who were disappointed of their prey.

Verse 16. *I will sing of thy power*] For it was because thy *hand* was upon me for good, that I have thus succeeded in my enterprises.

Yea, I will sing aloud of thy mercy] I shall publish abroad what thou hast done; and done not for *my worthiness,* nor for the *worthiness* of the *people;* but for thy own *mercy's* sake.

In the day of my trouble.] When I came with small means and feeble help, and had the force and fraud of many enemies to contend with, besides the corruption and unfaithfulness of my own people; *thou* wast then *my defence;* and in all attacks, whether *open* or *covered, my* sure *refuge.* I will, therefore, *sing of thy mercy in the morning*—I will *hasten* to acquit myself of a duty I owe to thee for such singular interpositions of mercy and power.

Verse 17. *Unto thee, O my strength*] A similar sentiment to that expressed, ver. 9. But the words are very emphatic: *God is my strength; God is my elevation. My God is my mercy.* I have nothing good but what I have from God. And all springs from his dwelling in me. God, therefore, shall have all the glory, both now and for ever.

As many persons may still think that the inscription to this Psalm is correct, the following analysis may be applied in that way; or considered as containing a general resolution of the Psalm, without referring it to any particular occasion.

ANALYSIS OF THE FIFTY-NINTH PSALM

The contents of this Psalm are:—

I. The psalmist's prayer for deliverance, ver. 1, 2, and against his foes, ver. 5.

II. He complains of and expresses his enemies' cruelty and improbity, ver. 3-8.

III. He comforts himself, being confident of his own preservation, ver. 8-10.

1. And of their punishment, for which he prays, ver. 14.

2. And of their vain endeavours, for which he insults over them, ver. 14, 15.

IV. He concludes with thanks, ver. 16, 17.

I. He begins with a petition for deliverance, defence, salvation; and urges it from the qualities of his enemies.

1. "Deliver me, defend me from mine enemies:" 1. "Them that rise up against me." 2. "From the workers of iniquity." 3. "From bloody men." These considerations make him pray, "O my God, deliver," &c.

2. And yet, more particularly, he expresses their cruelty and treachery; to aggravate which he pleads his innocence towards them.

II. 1. Their cruelty: "Lo, they lie in wait for my soul."

2. Their treachery: "The mighty are gathered against me." They run and prepare themselves.

3. 1. They are diligent about it: "They return at evening." 2. *Mad*, and set to do it: "They make a noise like a dog," and threaten boldly. 3. Unwearied and obdurate in their purpose: "They go round about the city." 4. Impudent, and brag what they will do to me: "Behold, they belch out with their mouth." 5. And their words are bloody: "Swords are in their lips."

4. And the cause of this is, that they are proud and atheistical. *Who*, say they, *doth hear?* They think themselves secure, supposing they may contemn God and man; neither regarding what is done or becomes of poor *David*.

5. In the midst of which aggravations he asserts his own innocence: "They gather themselves together, not for my transgression, nor for my sin, O Lord."

Then he renews his petition:—

1. Awake to help me, and behold: "Thou, therefore, the Lord God of hosts, the God of Israel." 1. The Lord God of hosts; therefore, powerful. 2. The God of Israel; therefore, merciful.

2. "Awake to visit all the heathen," *i, e.*, punish the heathen; and the Israelites, in this no better.

3. And be not merciful to any wicked transgressors, *i. e.*, obstinate nations.

III. To this rage and implacable hatred of his enemies he now begins to oppose the comfort he had in God's promises. This I know,—

1. "Thou, O Lord, shalt laugh at them." As it were in sport, destroy them, be their power never so great: "Thou wilt laugh them to scorn."

2. Them and all that are like them: "Thou shalt have all the heathen in derision."

3. I confess that Saul's strength is great; but my Protector is greater: "Because of his strength will I wait upon thee, for God is my defence."

4. This I am assured also, "that the God of my mercy," that hath hitherto showed me mercy, "shall prevent me," come in season to my help. "And God shall let me see my desire upon mine enemies."

And to the 16th verse he expresses what his desires were:—

1. Negatively; he would not have them slain and eradicated; and he gives his reason for it: "Slay them not, lest my people forget;" for a dead man is quickly out of mind, and his punishment also, and few the better for it.

2. Positively; the first degree of which is dispersion, vagrancy, banishment. *Scatter them*, which however severe a judgment, let *the Jews* witness.

2. Humiliation: "Bring them down, O Lord, our shield." Bring them from their power, command, honour, to a low degree, which is no small heart-breaking to a great spirit. *Fuimus Troes*, is never remembered without a groan.

And now he assigns the cause why he would have them scattered, and brought low; that their blasphemies and lies may never be forgotten, but stand as a terror to all liars and blasphemers.

1. "For the sin of their mouth, and the words of their lips, let them even be taken in their pride;" the Jews cried Beelzebub, *nolumus hunc;* and they were taken.

2. "And for cursing and lying which they speak." They cursed themselves: "His blood be upon us;" and upon them, indeed, it was.

3. He goes on in his desires. "Consume them, O Lord," emphatically, "consume them in wrath, that they may not be;" which, at first sight, appears contrary to the first desire, "Slay them not:" but he speaks not of their life as if he would have it consumed; but he desires only a consumption of their power, royalty, command. And so these words are a farther explication of his second desire, "Bring them down." He would have them brought down in their strength, dignity, command, wealth, riches, which made them proud; that they might never be able to oppose God any more, hurt his people, trample upon religion and his Church; but he would have them live.

4. And shows the end why he would have them live, and still remain—that they might know by their calamities and miseries, that "it is God that ruleth in Jacob, and unto the ends of the earth;" that he doth wonderfully govern and preserve his Church that is scattered over all the earth.

5. And now by a bitter *epitrope*, or rather *synchoresis*, he insults over them. In the sixth verse he showed their double diligence to do mischief.

1. "They return at evening." Well, *esto;* be it so; "At evening let them return."

2. "They make a noise like a dog." Well; "let them make a noise like a dog."

3. "And go round about the city." Well; "let them go round about the city."

They know that they shall be in a miserable poor mean condition:—

1. "Let them wander up and down for meat." Let them find no settled habitation, but seek necessary food in a strange nation.

2. "And grudge if they be not satisfied." Let them be always grudging, if they have not con-

tent. If they be not satisfied, they will stay all night; be importunate and unmannerly beggars.

IV. The conclusion is a doxology, and contains David's thanks that *God is his defence*, his refuge, his strength. Of him, therefore, he makes his song.

1. "I will sing of thy power."

2. "I will sing of thy mercy." 1. "Aloud." 2. "In the morning."

3. The reason he gives: "For thou hast been my refuge and defence in the day of my trouble."

Both he repeats again:—

1. "Unto thee, O my strength, will I sing."

2. The reason: "For God is my defence, and the God of my mercy."

And he joins these two attributes, *strength* and *mercy*. Take away *strength* from him, and he cannot, remove *mercy*, and he will not, protect. Both must go together; *power* that he can, *mercy* that he will; otherwise it is in vain that we hope for help from him. David found God to be both, and for both he extols him.

PSALM LX

The psalmist complains of the desolations which had fallen on the land; prays for deliverance, 1–5; and promises himself victory over Shechem, Succoth, Gilead, Ephraim, Moab, Idumea, and the Philistines, by the special help and assistance of God, 6–12.

To the chief Musician [a]upon Shushan-eduth, [b]Michtam of David, to teach; [c]when he strove with Aram-naharaim and with Aram-zobah, when Joab returned, and smote of Edom in the valley of salt twelve thousand

A. M. cir. 3464
B. C. cir. 540
Olymp. LX.
cir. annum
primum
A. U. C. cir. 214

O GOD, [d]thou hast cast us off, thou hast [e]scattered us, thou hast been displeased: O turn thyself to us again.

2 Thou hast made the earth to tremble; thou hast broken it: [f]heal the breaches thereof; for it shaketh.

3 [g]Thou hast showed thy people hard things: [h]thou hast made us to drink the wine of astonishment.

A. M. cir. 3464
B. C. cir. 540
Olymp. LX.
cir. annum
primum
A. U. C. cir. 214

---

[a]Psa. lxxx. *title*——[b]Or, *A golden* Psalm——[c]2 Sam. viii. 3, 13; 1 Chron. xviii. 3, 12——[d]Psa. xliv. 9

[e]Heb. *broken*——[f]2 Chron. vii. 14——[g]Psa. lxxi. 20 [h]Isa. li. 17, 22; Jer. xxv. 15

NOTES ON PSALM LX

The title, "To the chief Musician upon the *hexachord*, or *lily of the testimony*, a golden Psalm of David, for instruction; when he strove with Aram Naharaim, Syria of the two rivers (Mesopotamia) and Aram-Zobah, Syria of the watchmen, (Cœlosyria,) when Joab returned, and smote twelve thousand Edomites in the Valley of Salt." I have only to remark here that there is nothing in the contents of this Psalm that bears any relation to this title. According to the title it should be a *song of victory and triumph;* instead of which the first part of it is a tissue of *complaints* of disaster and *defeat*, caused by the Divine desertion. Besides, it was not *Joab* that slew *twelve thousand* men in the *Valley of Salt;* it was *Abishai*, the brother of Joab; and the number *twelve thousand* here is not correct; for there were *eighteen thousand* slain in that battle, as we learn from 1 Chron. xviii. 12. The *valley of salt* or *salt pits* is in Idumea. To reconcile the difference between the numbers, various expedients have been hit on; but still the insuperable objection remains; the *contents* of this Psalm and this *title* are in opposition to each other. That the Psalm deplores a *defeat*, is evident from the three first and two last verses. And the *Targumist* seems to have viewed it in this light, perhaps the proper one, by expressing the title thus: "To give praise for the ancient testimony, (אהדותא *sahadutha,*) of the sons of Jacob and Laban, (see Gen. xxxi. 47,) an ex-

emplar by the hand of David, to give instruction when he gathered together the people, and passed by the *heap of testimony,* (אינר סהדותא *ayegar sahadutha,*) and set the battle in array against Aram, which is by the Euphrates; and against Aram, which is by Izobah. And after this Joab returned and smote the Idumeans in the Valley of Salt; and of the armies of David and Joab there fell *twelve thousand* men." The Psalm, therefore, seems to deplore this disastrous event; for although they had the victory at last, *twelve thousand* of the troops of Israel were justly considered too great a sacrifice for such a conquest, and a proof that God had not afforded them that succour which they had long been in the habit of receiving. The latter part of the Psalm seems to be intended to put God in remembrance of his ancient promise of putting Israel in possession of the whole land by driving out the ancient iniquitous inhabitants. Others consider the Psalm as descriptive of the distracted state of the land after the fatal battle of Gilboa, till David was anointed king of the whole at Hebron.

This is the *last* of the *six Psalms* to which מכתם *michtam* is prefixed; the others are Psa. xvi., lvi., lvii., lviii., and lix. I have said something relative to this word in the introduction to Psa. xvi.; but some *observations* of Mr. Harmer lead me to consider the subject more at large. It is well known that there were *seven* most eminent Arabic *poets* who flourished *before* and at the commencement of the career of *Mohammed:* their names were *Amriolkais,*

A. M. cir. 3464
B. C. cir. 540
Olymp. LX.
cir. annum
primum
A. U. C. cir. 214

4 ¹Thou hast given a banner to them that feared thee, that it may be displayed because of the truth. Selah.

5 ᵏThat thy beloved may be delivered; save *with* thy right hand, and hear me.

6 God hath ¹spoken in his holi-

A. M. cir. 3464
B. C. cir. 540
Olymp. LX.
cir. annum
primum
A. U. C. cir. 214

---

¹Psa. xx. 5——ᵏPsa. cviii. 6, &c.

¹Psa. lxxxix. 35

Amru, Hareth, Tharafah, Zohair, Lebeid, and *Antarah.* These poets produced *each a poem,* which because of its excellence was deemed worthy to be *suspended* on the walls of the *temple* of *Mecca;* and hence the collection of the seven poems was termed Al Moallakat, *The Suspended;* and Al Modhahebat, *The Gilded* or *Golden,* because they were written in *letters of gold* upon the Egyptian papyrus. The six *michtams* of David might have this title for the same reason; they might have been *written in letters of gold,* or on *gilded vellum,* or the *Egyptian papyrus;* for the word מכתם *michtam* is generally supposed to signify *golden,* and כתם *kethem* is used to signify *gold,* probably *stamped* or *engraven* with *figures* or *letters.* That the *Moallakat* were written in this way, there can be no question; and that the works of men of great eminence in Asiatic countries are still thus written, my own library affords ample evidence. Copies of the following works are written on paper all *powdered with gold, with gold borders, and highly illuminated anwans or titles:* The Misnavi of *Jelaluddeen Raumy;* The Deevan of *Zuheer Faryabi;* The Hadikatusani, or *Garden of Praise;* The Suh-bet al Abrar; The Deevan of *Hafiz;* Gulistan of *Saady;* Deevan of *Shahy,* with many more, all works of eminent authors, written in the finest manner, ruled with gold borders, &c.

Copies of the *Koran* are often done in the same manner: one in 12mo., so thickly *powdered over with gold* that the *ground* on which the text is written appears to be almost *totally gilded;* another large *octavo, all powdered with gold,* and *golden flowers* down every margin; another small *octavo,* that might be almost called the *Codex Aureus,* with rich *golden borders* on every page. And, lastly, one in large *folio,* which besides superbly illuminated *anwans,* has *three gold lines in every page;* one at the *top,* one in the *middle,* and one at the *bottom.* To the above may be added a small *folio,* that opens out about *eleven feet,* every page of which is like a plate of solid gold, with the characters engraven on it. It is a *collection of elegant extracts.* Another of the *same kind,* large folio, opens out *sixty-two feet,* on which every page is finished in the same manner, with a vast variety of borders, sprigs, and flowers. And to close the whole, a copy of the *Borda,* supposed to be the most elegant MS. in Europe, entirely covered with *gold flowers* and *lines,* the writing the most perfect I ever saw; so that of this MS. it might be truly said, splendid as it is, *materiam superabit opus.*

As Mr. Harmer has alluded to accounts which he has collected from other writers in order to illustrate the *michtams* of David, I have above produced a number of *evidences* to bear witness to the *fact* that such is and such was the custom in the east, to write the works of the most eminent authors in *letters of gold,* or *on a page highly ornamented with the utmost profusion of golden lines, figures, flowers,* &c. In this way these Psalms might have been written, and

from this circumstance they may have derived their name. I may just add, that I think these *titles* were made long after the Psalms were composed.

Verse 1. *O God, thou hast cast us off*] Instead of being our *general* in the battle, thou hast left us to ourselves; and then there was only the *arm of flesh* against the *arm of flesh,* numbers and physical power were left to decide the contest. We have been scattered, our ranks have been broken before the enemy, and thou hast caused the whole land to tremble at our bad success; the people are become divided and seditious. "Thou hast made the land to tremble, even the breaches of it, for it shaketh, it is all in commotion," ver. 2.

Verse 3. *Thou hast made us to drink the wine of astonishment*] We reel as *drunken* men; we are *giddy,* like those who have drank too much wine; but *our giddiness* has been occasioned by the *astonishment* and *dismay* that have taken place in consequence of the prevalence of our enemies, and the unsettled state of the land. It has been remarked that the *three first* verses of this Psalm do not agree with the rest, and it also appears that the *three first* verses of Psa. lxxxv. do not agree with the rest of *that* Psalm. But let them change places, and the three first verses of this be set instead of the three first verses of Psa. lxxxv., and let those be placed here instead of these, and then the whole of each Psalm will be consistent. This was first suggested by Bishop *Hare,* and the supposition seems to be well founded. Some imagine that the whole of the Psalm refers to the distracted state of the land after the death of Saul till the time that David was anointed king over all Israel, at Hebron; others, to the disastrous war with the *Syrians.* See before.

Verse 4. *Thou hast given a banner*] נס *nes,* a *sign,* something that was capable of being fixed on a pole.

That it may be displayed] להתנוסס *lehithno-ses, that it may be unfurled.*

Because of the truth.] מפני קשט *mippeney koshet, from the face of truth;* which has been thus paraphrased: If we have displayed the *ensign of Israel,* and gone forth against these our enemies, who have now made such a terrible breach among us, (ver. 1-3,) it was *because of thy truth*—the *promises* of victory which we supposed would attend us at all times.

Mr. *Mudge,* thus: "Thou givest to them that fear thee a signal to be displayed before the truth. That thy favoured ones may be delivered, clothe thy right arm with victory, and answer us. God speaketh in his sanctuary, I will exult; I shall portion out Shechem, and measure the valley of Succoth." The *fourth* verse seems to mean that God had appointed for the consolation of his people a certain *signal* of favour, with which therefore he prays him to answer them. This, accordingly, he does. *God speaketh in his sanctuary,* called דביר *debir* or *oracle* for that very reason. What he desires

A. M. cir. 3464
B. C. cir. 540
Olymp. LX.
cir. annum primum
A. U. C. cir. 214

ness; I will rejoice, I will
[m]divide [n]Shechem, and mete
out [o]the valley of Succoth.
7 Gilead *is* mine, and Manasseh *is* mine; [p]Ephraim also *is* the strength
of mine head; [q]Judah *is* my lawgiver:
8 [r]Moab *is* my washpot; [s]over Edom will
I cast out my shoe: [t]Philistia, [u]triumph thou
because of me.
9 Who will bring me *into* the [v]strong
city? who will lead me into
Edom?
10 *Wilt* not thou, O God, *which*
[w]hadst cast us off? and *thou,* O
God, *which* didst [x]not go out with our armies?
11 Give us help from trouble: for [y]vain *is*
the [z]help of man.
12 Through God [a]we shall do valiantly:
for he *it is that* shall [b]tread down our
enemies.

A. M. cir. 3464
B. C. cir. 540
Olymp. LX.
cir. annum primum
A. U. C. cir. 214

[m]Josh. i. 6——[n]Gen. xii. 6——[o]Josh. xiii. 27——[p]See Deut. xxxiii. 17——[q]Gen. xlix. 10——[r]2 Sam. viii. 2 [s]Psa. cviii. 9; 2 Sam. viii. 14——[t]2 Sam. viii. 1——[u]Or, *triumph thou over me;* (by an irony;) see Psa. cviii. 10

[v]Heb. *city of strength;* 2 Sam. xi. 1; xii. 26——[w]Ver. 1; Psa. xliv. 9; cviii. 11——[x]Josh. vii. 12——[y]Psa. cxi. 8; cxlvi. 3——[z]Heb. *salvation*——[a]Num. xxiv. 18; 1 Chron. xix. 13——[b]Isa. lxiii. 3

then, as he stands imploring the mercy of God before the oracle, is, that he may see the *usual signal of favour* proceed from it; a *voice,* perhaps joined with some *luminous emanation,* whence the phrase of *the light of God's countenance.* The expression in the *sixth* verse seems to be proverbial, and means, "I shall divide the spoils of my enemies with as much ease as the sons of Jacob portioned out Shechem, and measured out for their tents the valley of Succoth." Mr. *Harmer* gives a very ingenious illustration of the *giving the banner.* "*Albertus Aquensis* informs us that when Jerusalem was taken in 1099 by the crusaders, about *three hundred* Saracens got on the roof of a very high building, and earnestly begged for quarter; but could not be induced by any *promises* of safety to come down, till they had received the *banner of Tancred,* one of the crusade generals, as *a pledge of life.* The event showed the faithlessness of these zealots, they put the whole to the sword. But the Saracens surrendering themselves upon the *delivering of a standard* to them, proves in how strong a light they looked upon the *giving a banner,* since it induced them to trust *it,* when they would not trust *any promises.* Perhaps the *delivery of a banner* was anciently esteemed in like manner an obligation to *protect;* and the psalmist might here consider it in this light when he says, *Thou hast shown thy people hard things;* but *thou hast given a banner to them that fear thee.* Though thou didst for a time give up thy Israel into the hands of their enemies, thou hast now given them an assurance of thy having received them under thy protection. Thus God *gave them a banner* or standard that it might be displayed, or *lifted up;* or rather, *that they may lift up a banner to themselves,* or encourage themselves with the confident persuasion that they are under the protection of God: *because of the truth*—the word of promise, which is an *assurance of protection*—like *the giving me and my people a banner,* the surest of pledges."—*Harmer's* Observations. See at the end of the chapter.

Verse 6. *God hath spoken*] Judah shall not only be re-established in Jerusalem, but shall possess Samaria, where *Shechem is,* and the country beyond Jordan, in which is situated the *valley of Succoth. Dividing* and *meting* out signify *possession.*

Verse 7. *Gilead* is *mine*] This country was also beyond Jordan, and *Manasseh* and *Ephraim* are put for the *tribes* that formed the kingdom of Israel. All these, after the return from the captivity, formed but one people, the Jews and Israelites being united.

The strength of mine head] It shall be the principal support of the new-found kingdom, when all distinctions shall be buried.

Judah is *my lawgiver*] This tribe was chief of all those who returned from the captivity; and *Zerubbabel,* who was their leader, was *chief of that tribe,* and of the *family of David.* As this part of the Psalm appears to relate to the return of the captives from Babylon, and their repossession of their own land, the psalmist may refer, not only to the promises of their restoration, but also to the principal person under whose superintendence they returned.

Verse 8. *Moab* is *my washpot*] The Moabites shall be reduced to the *meanest* slavery.

Over Edom will I cast out my shoe] I will make a complete conquest of Idumea, and subject the Edomites to the meanest offices, as well as the Moabites.

Philistia, triumph thou because of me.] John *Hyrcanus* subdued the Idumeans, and caused them to receive circumcision, and profess the Jewish religion. The words here seem to predict their entire subjugation.

In an essay for a new translation of the Bible, there is what appears to me a correct paraphrase of the *seventh* and *eighth* verses: "Gilead and Manasseh have submitted unto me; Ephraim furnishes me with valiant men, and Judah with men of prudence and wisdom. I will reduce the Moabites to servitude; I will triumph over the Edomites, and make them my slaves; and the Philistines shall add to my triumph."

Verse 9. *Who will bring me* into *the strong city?*] If this part of the Psalm, from the *sixth* to the *twelfth* verse, refer to *the return of the captives from Babylon,* as I think probable; then the *strong city* may mean either *Petra,* the capital of *Idumea; Bozra,* in Arabia, near the mountains of Gilead; *Rabba,* the capital of the Ammonites; or *Tyre,* according to the *Chaldee,* the capital of Phœnicia; or *Jerusalem* itself, which, although dismantled, had long been one of the strongest cities of the east. Or it may imply, Who shall give me the dominion over the countries already mentioned? who will lead me into Edom? who will give me the dominion over that people?

Verse 10. Wilt *not thou, O God*] It is God alone from whom we can expect our enlargement. He who has cast us off, and has abandoned us in battle; it is that very God alone from whom we expect complete enlargement, the repossession of our own land, and the subduction of the surrounding nations; and we expect this, because he has graciously *promised* these mercies.

Verse 11. *Give us help from trouble: for vain is the help of man.*] We have done all we can do, and have trusted too much in ourselves; now, Lord, undertake for us.

Verse 12. *Through God we shall do valiantly*] Through thee *alone* shall we do valiantly; thou *alone* canst tread down our enemies; and to thee *alone* we look for conquest.

THE author to whom *Harmer* refers in the note on the *fourth* verse, is one of the writers in a work entitled *Gesta dei per Francos*, fol. Hanoviæ, 1611, 2 vols. And the places quoted by *Harmer* may be found in vol. i., p. 282; and as the passage is singular, and a good use has been made of it for the illustration of a difficult passage, I shall lay the words of the original before the reader: "Proxima ab hinc die sabbati clarescente, quidam Sarracenorum spe vitæ in summitatem tecti domus præcelsæ Solomonis ab armis elapsi, circiter trecenti, confugerant. Qui multa prece pro vita flagitantes, in mortis articulo positi, nullius fiducia aut promissione audebant descendere, *quousque vexillum Tankradi in signum protectionis vivendi susceperunt*. Sed minime misellis profuit. Nam plurimis super hoc indignantibus, et Christianis furore commotis, ne unus quidem illorum evasit."

It is very properly added by *Albertus*, that the noble spirit of *Tancred* was filled with indignation at this most horrible breach of faith; and he was about to take a summary revenge on the instigators and perpetrators of this unprincipled butchery, when the *chiefs* interposed, and not only maintained the expediency of the massacre that had already been committed, *but the necessity of putting all the inhabitants to the sword.* On this the savage fiends, called *Christians*, flew to arms, and made a universal slaughter of all that remained of the inhabitants. They drew out the prisoners, chopped off their heads, stabbed all they met with in the streets, and—but I can translate no farther; it is too horrible. I shall give my author's words, who was an ecclesiastic, and wrote down the account from eye-witnesses: "Concilio hoc accepto, (the determination of the *chiefs* to put all to the sword,) tertio die post victoriam egressa est sententia a *majoribus*: et ecce universi arma rapiunt, et miserabili cæde in omne vulgus Gentilium, quod adhuc erat residuum, exsurgunt, alios producentes e vinculis et decollantes: alios per vicos et plateas civitatis inventos trucidantes, quibus antea causa pecuniæ, aut humana pietate pepercerunt. Puellas vero, mulieres, matronas nobiles, et fætas cum puellis tenellis detruncabant, aut lapidibus obruebant, in nullis aliquam considerantes ætatem. E contra, puellæ, mulieres, matronæ, metu momentaneæ mortis angustiatæ et horrore gravissimæ necis concussæ Christianos in jugulum utriusque sexus debacchantes ac sævientes, medios pro liberanda vita amplexabantur, quædam pedibus eorum advolvebantur, de vita et salute sua illos nimium miserando fletu et ejulatu solicitantes. Pueri vero quinquennes aut triennes matrum patrumque crudelem casum intuentes, una miserum clamorem et fletum multiplicabant. Sed frustra

hæc pietatis et misericordiæ signa fiebant: nam Christiani sic neci totum laxaverunt animum, ut non lugens masculus aut fæmina, nedum infans unius anni vivens, manum percussoris evaderet. Unde plateæ totius civitatis *Jerusalem* corporibus extinctis virorum et mulierum, lacerisque membris infantium, adeo stratæ et opertæ fuisse referuntur, ut non solum in vicis, soliis et palatiis, sed etiam in locis desertæ solitudinis copia occisorum reperiretur innumerabilis." GESTA DEI Vol. I., p. 283.

This is one specimen of the spirit of the crusaders, and is it any wonder that God did not shine on such villanous measures! No wonder that the Mohammedans have so long hated the name of *Christian*, when they had no other specimen of Christianity than what the conduct of these ferocious brutes exhibited; and these were called *Gesta Dei*, the *transactions* of God!

There are many difficulties in this Psalm; whether they are in general removed by the preceding notes, the reader must judge. The following analysis is constructed on the supposition that the Psalm speaks of the distracted state of the kingdom from the fatal battle of Gilboa, in which Saul fell, to the death of Ish-bosheth, when the whole kingdom was united under David.

ANALYSIS OF THE SIXTIETH PSALM

Before David's time, and in the beginning of his reign, Israel was in a distressed condition; he composed and quieted the whole. Edom only was not vanquished. In this Psalm he gives thanks for his victories, and prays for assistance for the conquest of Edom.

There are *three* general parts in this Psalm:—

I. A commemoration of the former lamentably distracted condition of the Israelites, ver. 1, 2, 3.

II. The condition of it under his reign much better, ver. 4-9.

III. His thankfulness in ascribing all his victories to God, ver. 9-12.

I. In the first he shows that God was angry with Israel. On which he laments the effects of his anger. 2. And then prays for the aversion: 1. "O Lord, thou hast (or hadst) cast us off." 2. "Thou hast scattered us abroad; thou hast been displeased." 3. "Thou hast made the earth to tremble." 4. "Thou hast broken it." 5. "Thou hast showed thy people hard things." 6. "Thou hast given us to drink the wine of astonishment." Every syllable of which *congeries* will appear to be most true when we examine the history of the Israelites before *Saul's* reign, under his government, and upon his death; and the first entrance of *David* upon his reign; his wars with the house of *Saul*, until *Ish-bosheth* was taken out of the way.

All which wars, civil and external, with the calamities that flowed from them, he imputes to God's anger: "Thou hast been displeased," ver. 1.

2. And upon it he prays: "O turn thee to us again." Let us again enjoy thy countenance. 2. "Heal the breaches of the land." Close the wounds made by these contentions: they were not closed; for it adds, "It shaketh."

II. And now the condition of it was much

better; all being brought under one king, and he victorious over his foreign enemies.

1. "Thou hast now given a banner to them that fear thee." All *Israel*—all those that are thy servants, are brought to acknowledge thee, and fight under one standard; in effect, have received me as their sole king, their factions and parties being quieted.

2. "That it may be displayed." Set up, that Israel may know under whom to fight, and whose part to take.

3. "Because of thy truth." Who by this hast made it appear that it was no fiction nor ambition of mine to set up this standard; but a *truth* that I was by *Samuel*, by thy special appointment, anointed to be king; and I am now invested with the crown for the performance of thy truth and promise.

4. And the end is especially, that I should bring deliverance to thy servants: it was that "thy beloved may be delivered." That the godly and good men, and those that fear thee, living hitherto oppressed, and in these distractions kept low, might be delivered.

5. Which, that it may be done, he inserts a short ejaculation for himself and them: "Save with thy right hand, and hear thou me." And now he begins to commemorate the *particulars* that God had done for him, and the several victories he had obtained; also, in what manner he ruled this people. All which he prefaces with this *oracle:*—

"God hath spoken in his holiness." He certainly and *truly* hath promised to save us: "I will be glad and rejoice in it." With much joy and gladness I will enter upon the kingdom, being confirmed by his promise, which I will administer in a different manner; my government shall be *paternal* to the *Israelites*, which are his people; but more severe to the *Moabites*, *Ammonites*, *Edomites*, and *Syrians*, because they are aliens to the commonwealth of *Israel*.

1. "I will divide Shechem, and mete out the valley of Succoth." I will bring under my power those places of Israel; and, as a true lord of them, I will *divide* and *measure out* what portions I shall think fit to the inhabitants.

2. "Gilead also is mine, and Manasseh is mine." The Israelites that followed the house of *Saul* are come into my power, and I will divide and apportion them also. Yet, as being mine, I will deal mildly with them.

3. Of *Ephraim* I shall make reckoning. Ephraim "shall be the strength of my head." As this tribe had more *men* than any other, so they were great *soldiers;* and these he esteemed as his *life-guard*.

4. "Judah is my lawgiver." His chief counsel were of this tribe, in whom, with himself, was the legislative power, according to the prophecy

of Jacob: "The sceptre shall not depart from Judah, nor a lawgiver from between his feet, till Shiloh come." And thus, having showed his kingdom, and the administration over the Israelites, he passes to the *strangers* whom he had conquered, over whom he would carry a severe hand, putting them into a slavish subjection, and to base offices.

1. "Moab is my washpot." A servant to hold the bason, and to wash my feet.

2. "Over Edom I will cast my shoe." Trample on their necks.

3. "Philistia, triumph thou because of me:" which is either spoken ironically, as if he would say: "O Philistine, whom I have subdued, go, go triumph because I have conquered thee." Or else, "Triumph thou in the triumph I shall celebrate for my conquest; bear among the rest thy part, though unwillingly. Follow the train with acclamations, and proclaim me thy king."

III. After the enumerations of his victories, and form of government, that no man should take this for a vain boast of his own strength, he thankfully ascribes all the glory to God, both of which he had done, and what he was yet to do. One people he had yet to conquer; and that could not be done except that God, who had hitherto gone out with his armies, would again vouchsafe to lead them; and, therefore, he asks,—

1. "Who will bring me into the strong city? who will lead me into Edom?" No question, had *Joab*, *Abishai*, &c., or any of his worthies, been by, they would have striven who should have performed this service. Every one would have said, "I will be the man."

2. But he prevents them all; and returns this answer to himself, that none but God should do it, and that he was persuaded that he would do it; even that God who was formerly displeased with them, had cast them off, but was now reconciled: "Wilt not thou, O God, lead us into the strong city which hadst cast us off? and thou, O God, bring us into Edom, which didst not go forth with our armies."

3. And to that purpose he prays, "Give us help from trouble." And he adds his reason, that nothing can be well done without God's assistance; for the strength, power, prudence, and skill of man, without God, are to little purpose: "Vain is the help of man."

And he concludes all with this *epiphonema:* "In God we shall do great or valiant acts; for he it is that shall tread down our enemies." In war these two must be joined, and indeed in all actions. HE, *we;* GOD and *man*.

1. "We shall do valiantly," for God helps not remiss, or cowardly, or negligent men.

2. And yet, that being done, the work is *his:* "He shall tread down;" the blow and overthrow are not to be attributed to *us*, but to HIM.

PSALM LXI

The psalmist's prayer for those who were banished from their own land, and from the ordinances of God, 1, 2. He praises God for his past mercies, 3; purposes to devote himself entirely to his service, 4, 5. He prays for the king, 6, 7; and promises to perform his vow to the Lord daily, 8.

To the chief Musician upon Neginah, *A Psalm* of David

A. M. cir. 3468
B. C. cir. 536
Olymp. LXI.
cir. annum
primum
A. U. C. cir. 218

HEAR ᵃmy cry, O God; attend unto my prayer.

2 From the end of the earth will I cry unto thee, when my heart is overwhelmed: lead me to the rock *that* is higher than I.

3 For thou hast been a shelter for me, *and* ᵇa strong tower from the enemy.

4 ᶜI will abide in thy tabernacle for ever: ᵈI will ᵉtrust in the covert of thy wings. Selah.

5 For thou, O God, hast heard my vows: thou hast given *me* the heritage of those that fear thy name.

A. M. cir. 3468
B. C. cir. 536
Olymp. LXI.
cir. annum
primum
A. U. C. cir. 218

6 ᶠThou ᵍwilt prolong the king's life: *and* his years ʰas many generations.

7 He shall abide before God for ever: O prepare mercy ⁱand truth, *which* may preserve him.

8 So will I sing praise unto thy name for ever, that I may daily perform my vows.

ᵃ1 Kings xviii. 37——ᵇProv. xviii. 10——ᶜPsa. xxvii. 4——ᵈPsa. xvii. 8; lvii. 1; xci. 4——ᵉOr, *make my refuge*——ᶠPsa. xxi. 4

ᵍHeb. *thou shalt add days to the days of the king* ʰHeb. *as generation and generation*——ⁱPsa. xl. 11; Prov. xx. 28

NOTES ON PSALM LXI

The *title, To the chief Musician upon Neginath,* נגינת. The verb נגן *nagan* signifies to *strike* or *play on a musical instrument,* especially one of the *stringed* kind; but the נגינות *neginoth,* as it is written in about *thirty* MSS., may signify either the *players* on the instruments or the *instruments* themselves. The Psalm appears to have been written about the close of the captivity; and the most judicious interpreters refer it to that period. On this supposition the notes are formed.

Verse 1. *Hear my cry, O God*] In the midst of a long and painful captivity, oppressed with suffering, encompassed with cruel enemies and isolent masters, I address my humble prayer to THEE, *O my God.*

Verse 2. *From the end of the earth*] ארץ *arets* should be here translated *land,* not *earth,* and so it should be in numerous places besides. But here it seems to mean the *country beyond the Euphrates;* as it is thought to do, Psa. lxv. 5, 8, called there also *the ends of the earth* or *land.* It may be remarked that the Jews were always more pious and devoted to God in their afflictions and captivities, than when in their own land, in ease and affluence. But who can bear prosperity? How many hearts filled with heavenly *ardour* in affliction and persecution have grown *cold* under the beams of the sun of prosperity!

Lead me to the rock that *is higher than I.*] Direct me to a place of refuge and safety. It is a metaphorical expression; and *Calmet* interprets it of the liberty granted to the Jews by Cyrus to return to their own land. This was a privilege far *higher* than any thing they could expect. The fathers think Jesus Christ is meant by this *high rock.*

Verse 3. *Thou hast been a shelter for me*] During the whole duration of the captivity God marvellously dealt with the poor Jews; so that, although they were cast down, they were not utterly forsaken.

Verse 4. *I will abide in thy tabernacle*] The

greater portion of those Psalms which were composed during and after the captivity, says *Calmet,* had *Levites* and *priests* for their authors. Hence we find the ardent desire so frequently expressed of seeing the *temple;* of *praising God there;* of spending their lives in that place, performing the functions of their sacred office. There I *shall sojourn;*—there I *shall dwell,*—be *at rest,*—be *in safety,*—be *covered with thy wings,* as a bird in its nest is covered with the wings of its mother. These simple comparisons, drawn from rural affairs and ordinary occurrences, are more pleasing and consolatory in the circumstances in question, than allegories derived from subjects the most noble and sublime.

Verse 5. *Hast heard my vows*] Often have I purposed to be wholly thine,—to serve thee alone,—to give up my whole life to thy service: and thou hast heard me, and taken me at my word; and given me that heritage, the privilege of enjoying thee in thy ordinances, which is the lot of them that *fear thy name.* The Psalm seems to have been composed either after the captivity, or at the time that Cyrus published his decree in their favour, as has been remarked before.

Verse 6. *Thou wilt prolong the king's life*] The words are very emphatic, and can refer to no ordinary person. Literally, "Days upon days thou wilt add to the king; and his years shall be like the generations of this world, and the generations of the world to come." This is precisely the paraphrase I had given to this text before I had looked into the *Chaldee Version;* and to which I need add nothing, as I am persuaded no earthly king is intended: and it is Christ, as *Mediator,* that "shall abide before God for ever," ver. 7. Neither to David, nor to any earthly sovereign, can these words be applied.

Verse 7. *He shall abide before God for ever*] Literally, "He shall sit for ever before the faces of God." He shall ever appear in the presence of God for us. And he ever *sits at the right hand of the Majesty on high;* for he undertook this office after having, by his sacrificial offering, made atonement for our sins.

Prepare mercy and truth, which may preserve him.] As *Mediator*, his attendants will ever be *mercy* and *truth*. He will dispense the *mercy* of God, and thus fulfil the *truth* of the various promises and predictions which had preceded his incarnation. There is an obscurity in this clause, חסד ואמת מן ינצרהו *chesed veemeth man yintseruhu*, owing to the particle מן *man*, which some translate *who* or *what;* and others, *number thou*, from מנה *manah*, to count. *Houbigant*, and he is followed by Bishop *Lowth*, would read מיהוה *miyehovah*, *Mercy and truth from Jehovah shall preserve him.* The *Anglo-Saxon* has, mildheoᵽtnyᵹᵹe ᴊ soᵬᵽæᵱtnyᵹᵹo hiᵱ, hᵽilc ᵱecep? Mildheartedness, and soothfastness his, who seeketh? which is nearly the rendering of the old Psalter: Mercy anꝺ soþſaſtnes of him, wha ſall ſeke? Dr. *Kennicott* says, מן *man* is a *Syriasm;* and should be translated *quæsoutinam*, I beseech thee,—I wish,—O that! On this very ground *Coverdale* appears to have translated, ⊕ let thy lovynge mercy anꝺ faithfulnes preſerve him! The sense I have given above I conceive to be the true one.

Verse 8. *So will I sing praise unto thy name for ever*] For the benefits which I have received, and hope to receive endlessly from thee, I will to all perpetuity praise thee.

That I may daily perform my vows.] While I live, I shall יום יום *yom, yom*, "day by day," each day as it succeeds, render to thee my vows—act according to what I have often *purposed*, and as often *promised*. The Chaldee ends remarkably: "Thus I will praise thy name for ever, when I shall perform my vows in the day of the redemption of Israel; and in the day in which the King Messiah shall be anointed, that he may reign."

The *ancient Jews* were full of the expectation of the Messiah; the *Jews of the present day* have given up their *hope*.

ANALYSIS OF THE SIXTY-FIRST PSALM

The author of this Psalm prays and vows perpetual service to God. It is composed of *two* parts:—

I. His prayer, ver. 1, 2, 3.

II. His vow, ver. 4-8.

He begins with a prayer, in which he begs,—

1. Audience: "Hear my cry, O God; attend unto my prayer," ver. 1.

2. The reason to enforce it.

1. He was in banishment, in the farther part of the land of Judah: "From the end of the earth will I cry unto thee."

2. He was in extremity: "When my heart is overwhelmed."

3. For defence: "Lead me to the rock that is higher than I;" that is, To some safe and defenced place to which my enemies may have no access, whither without thy help I cannot ascend.

And he adds a reason to this part of his prayer drawn from his own experience: "For thou hast been a shelter for me, and a strong tower from the enemy."

His faith now presents him as delivered; and, therefore, he *vows*,—

1. "I will abide in thy tabernacle for ever." I will return, and adore thee in thy temple.

2. "I will trust in the covert of thy wings." He alludes to the cherubim, whose wings cover the ark.

And for this he assigns many reasons also:—

1. "For thou, O God, hast heard my vows," i. e., my prayers.

2. "Thou hast given me the heritage of those that fear thy name;" made me king over thy people, and more fully performed to me the promise made to *Abraham*, in the land of Canaan.

3. "Thou wilt prolong the king's life."

4. "And his years," i. e., in his posterity, "as many generations;" of which the beginning of the next verse is the prediction. "He shall abide before God for ever."

And now David, assuring himself of the crown, and that his posterity should inherit it, puts forth an earnest vote for that which should establish it: "O prepare mercy and truth, which may preserve him; i. e., me thy king;" for these two *virtues*, *mercy*, i. e., *clemency*, and *truth*, do commend a king, and make him dear to his subjects; for in the practice of these it is not possible that his government should be harsh, unjust, or tyrannical.

Which if it please God to bestow upon him, then he makes a new vow: "So will I sing praise unto thy name for ever."

Though here this appears to be a new vow, yet he had vowed it before, and engaged to discharge; for in singing praise to God's name, he should but pay what by vow he had often undertaken: "I will sing praise unto thy name for ever, that I may daily perform my vows."

PSALM LXII

David, in imminent danger, flees to God for help and safety, 1, 2; points out the designs of his adversaries, 3, 4; encourages his soul to wait on God, 5–8; shows the vanity of trusting in man, and of trusting in riches, 9, 10; and concludes with asserting that power and mercy belong to God, and that he will give to every man according to his works, 11, 12.

To the chief Musician, to ªJeduthun, A Psalm of David

A. M. cir. 2981
B. C. cir. 1023
Davidis, Regis
Israelitarum,
cir. annum
33

ᵇTRULY ᶜmy soul ᵈwaiteth upon God: from him com*eth* my salvation.

2 ᵉHe only *is* my rock and my salvation; *he is* my ᶠdefence; ᵍI shall not be greatly moved.

3 How long will ye imagine mischief against a man? ye shall be slain all of you: ʰas a bowing wall *shall ye be, and as* a tottering fence.

4 They only consult to cast *him* down from

his excellency: they delight in lies: ⁱthey bless with their mouth, but they curse ᵏinwardly. Selah.

A. M. cir. 2981
B. C. cir. 1023
Davidis, Regis
Israelitarum,
cir. annum
33

5 ˡMy soul, wait thou only upon God; for my expectation *is* from him.

6 He only *is* my rock and my salvation: *he is* my defence; I shall not be moved.

7 ᵐIn God *is* my salvation and my glory: the rock of my strength, *and* my refuge, *is* in God.

8 Trust in him at all times; ye people, ⁿpour out your heart before him: God *is* ᵒa refuge for us. Selah.

ª1 Chron. xxv. 1, 3——ᵇOr, *Only*——ᶜPsa. xxxiii. 20 ᵈHeb. *is silent;* Psa. lxv. 1——ᵉVer. 6——ᶠHeb. *high place;* Psa. lix. 9, 17——ᵍPsa. xxxvii. 24——ʰIsa. xxx.13

ⁱPsalm xxviii. 3——ᵏHebrew, *in their inward parts* ˡVer. 1, 2——ᵐJer. iii. 23——ⁿ1 Sam. i. 15; Psa. xlii. 4; Lam. ii. 19——ᵒPsa. xviii. 2

NOTES ON PSALM LXII

The *title*, "To the chief Musician, to Jeduthun," may mean that the Psalm was sent to him who was the chief or leader of the band of the family of Jeduthun. It appears that *Asaph, Jeduthun,* and *Heman,* were chief singers in the time of David; that they, with their families, presided over different departments of the vocal and instrumental worship in the tabernacle, 1 Chron. xxv. 1, &c.; that they were holy men, full of the Divine Spirit, (a thing very rare among singers and performers in these latter days,) and that *they prophesied with harps, with psalteries, and with cymbals;* that Jeduthun had *six* sons thus employed; that himself prophesied with a harp to give thanks and praise to God, ver. 3; and that the sons of Jeduthun were appointed by *lot* to the different courses. The *eighth* course fell to his son *Jeshaiah,* ver. 15; the *twelfth,* to *Hashabiah,* ver. 19; and the *fourteenth,* to *Mattithiah,* ver. 21.

Will our modern performers on instruments of music in churches and chapels, pretend to the *prophetic influence?* If they do not, and cannot, how dare they quote such passages in vindication of their practice, which can be no better than a dulcet noise without its original meaning, and alien from its primary use? Do they indeed *prophesy* with *harps,* and *psalteries,* and *cymbals?* or with their *play-house aggregate* of fiddles and flutes, bass-viols and bassoons, clarionets and kettle-drums? Away with such trumpery and pollution from the worship and Churcb or Christ!

Though it is not very clear from the Psalm itself on what occasion it was composed, yet it is most likely it was during the rebellion of Absalom; and perhaps at the particular time when David was obliged to flee from Jerusalem.

Verse 1. *Truly my soul waiteth upon God*] I do not think that the original will warrant this translation, אַךְ אֶל אֱלֹהִים דּוּמִיָּה נַפְשִׁי *ak el Elohim dumiyah naphshi,* "Surely to God only is my soul dumb." I am subject to God Almighty. He has a right to lay on me what he pleases; and what he lays on me is much less than I deserve: therefore am I *dumb* before God. The *Vulgate,* and almost all the Versions,

have understood it in this sense: Nonne Deo subjecta erit anima mea? Shall not my soul be subject to God? In other words, God alone has a right to dispose of my *life* as he pleases.

Verse 2. *I shall not be greatly moved.*] Having God for my *rock*—strong fortified place, for my *salvation*—continual safety, and my *defence* —my elevated tower, which places me out of the reach of my enemies; *I shall not be greatly moved*—I may be *shaken,* but cannot be *cast down.*

Verse 3. *How long will ye imagine mischief*] The original word, תְּהוֹתְתוּ *tehothethu,* has been translated variously; *rush upon, rage against, stir yourselves up, thrust against:* the root is התת *hathath* or התה *hathah, to rush violently upon, to assault.* It points out the disorderly riotous manner in which this rebellion was conducted.

As a bowing wall—a tottering fence.] Ye are just ready to fall upon others, and destroy them; and in that fall yourselves shall be destroyed: "Ye shall be slain the whole of you."

Verse 4. *To cast* him *down from his excellency*] They are consulting to dethrone me, and use treachery and falsehood in order to bring it about: "They delight in lies."

They bless with their mouth] Probably alluding to Absalom's blandishments of the people. He flattered them in order to get the sovereign rule. Or it may refer to the people of Jerusalem, whose perfidy he saw, while they were full of professions of loyalty, &c.; but he could not trust them, and therefore retired from Jerusalem.

Verse 5. *Wait thou only upon God*] There is none but him in whom thou canst safely trust; and to get his help, resign thyself into his hands; be subject to him, and be silent before him; thou hast what thou hast deserved. See on ver. 1.

Verse 7. *In God* is *my salvation*] עַל אֱלֹהִים *al Elohim,* "Upon God is my salvation;" he has taken it *upon himself. And my glory*—the preservation of my *state,* and the safety of my *kingdom.*

Verse 8. *Trust in him—ye people*] All ye who are faithful to your king, continue to trust in God. The usurper will soon be cast down, and your rightful sovereign restored to his

A. M. cir. 2981
B. C. cir. 1023
Davidis, Regis
Israelitarum,
cir. annum
33

9 PSurely men of low degree *are* vanity, *and* men of high degree *are* a lie: to be laid in the balance, they *are* qaltogether *lighter* than vanity.

10 Trust not in oppression, and become not vain in robbery: rif riches increase, set not your heart *upon them.*

PPsa. xxxix. 5, 11; Isa. xl. 15, 17; Rom. iii. 4——qOr, *alike*——rJob xxxi. 25; Psa. lii. 7; Luke xii. 15; 1 Tim. vi. 17——sJob xxxiii. 14——tRev. xix. 1——uOr, *strength*

---

11 God hath spoken sonce; twice have I heard this; that tpower ubelongeth unto God.

12 Also unto thee, O LORD, *belongeth* vmercy: for wthou renderest to every man according to his work.

A. M. cir. 2981
B. C. cir. 1023
Davidis, Regis
Israelitarum,
cir. annum
33

---

vPsa. lxxxvi. 15; ciii. 8; Dan. ix. 9——wJob xxxiv. 11; Prov. xxiv. 12; Jer. xxxii. 19; Ezek. vii. 27; xxxiii. 20; Matt. xvi. 27; Rom. ii. 6; 1 Cor. iii. 8; 2 Cor. v. 10; Eph. vi. 8; Col. iii. 25; 1 Pet. i. 17; Rev. xxii. 12

---

government. Fear not the threatenings of my enemies, for *God will be a refuge for us.*

Verse 9. *Men of low degree* are *vanity*] בני אדם *beney Adam*, which we here translate *men of low degree*, literally, *sons of Adam*, are put in opposition to בני איש *beney ish, men of high degree*, literally, the *sons of substance*, or children of substantial men. *Adam* was the name of the first man when formed out of the *earth; Ish* was his name when united to his wife, and they became one flesh. *Before*, he was the *incomplete* man; *after*, he was the *complete* man; for it seems, in the sight of God, it requires the male and female to make one *complete human being.* אנוש *enosh* is another name given to man; but this concerns him in his low, fallen, wretched estate: it properly signifies *weak, poor, afflicted, wretched man.*

Common men can give no help. They are *vanity*, and it is folly to trust in them; for although they may be *willing*, yet they have no *ability* to help you: "Rich men are a lie." They promise much, but perform nothing; they cause you to *hope*, but mock your *expectation.*

To be laid in the balance] במאזנים לעלות *bemozenayim laaloth, In the balances they ascend*: exactly answerable to our phrase, *they kick the beam.*

They are *altogether* lighter *than vanity*.] Literally, *Both of them united are vanity*, המה מהבל יחד *hemmah mehebel yachad.* Put both together in one scale, and *truth* in the opposite, and both will kick the beam. They weigh nothing, they avail nothing.

Verse 10. *Trust not in oppression*] Do not suppose that my unnatural son and his partisans can succeed.

Become not vain in robbery] If ye have laid your hands on the spoils of my house, do not imagine that these ill-gotten riches will prosper. God will soon scatter them to all the winds of heaven. All oppressors come to an untimely end; and all property acquired by injustice has God's curse on it.

Verse 11. *God hath spoken once*] God has *once* addressed his people in giving the law on Mount Sinai. The *Chaldee* translates the whole passage thus: "God hath spoken one law, and twice have we heard this from the mouth of Moses the great scribe, that strength is before God: and it becomes thee, O God, to show mercy to the righteous; for thou renderest to man according to his works."

Twice have I heard this] Except some of the *ancient* Versions, almost every version, translation, and commentary has missed the sense

and meaning of this verse. I shall set down the text: אחת דבר אלהים שתים זו שמעתי *achath dibber Elohim; shetayim zu shamati;* of which the true version is this: *Once hath God spoken; these two things have I heard.* Now what are the *two things* he had heard? 1. כי עז לאלהים *ki oz lelohim,* "That strength is the Lord's;" that is, He is the *Origin* of power. 2. ולך אדני חסד *ulecha Adonai, chased;* "and to thee, Lord, is mercy;" that is, He is the *Fountain* of mercy. These, then, are the *two* grand truths that the *law*, yea, the whole *revelation* of God, declares through every page. He is the *Almighty;* he is the *most merciful;* and hence the *inference:* The powerful, just, and holy Lord, the most merciful and compassionate Lord, *will* by and by *judge the world*, and *will render to man according to his works.* How this beautiful meaning should have been unseen by almost every interpreter, is hard to say: these verses contain one of the most instructive truths in the Bible.

ANALYSIS OF THE SIXTY-SECOND PSALM

The intent of this Psalm is to teach men to trust in God; and not to trust in wealth, or strength, nor in the power or promise of men.

It may be divided into the *five* following parts:—

I. David's confidence in God, ver. 1, 2.

II. The mischievous but vain attempts of his enemies, ver. 3, 4.

III. He encourages himself and others in the same confidence, ver. 5-9.

IV. That no trust is to be put in men, nor riches, ver. 9, 10.

V. The grounds of our confidence in God, ver. 11, 12.

I. In the first verses David expresses, or rather labours to express, as appears by his frequent repetition of the same thing in divers words, his trust, hope, and confidence in God:—

1. "Truly, my soul waiteth upon God." I acquiesce in his will.

2. "From him comes my salvation." If I be *safe* in my greatest troubles, it is from him.

3. "He only is my rock, and my salvation; he is my defence so that I shall not greatly be moved." He is to me what a rock or tower of defence is to such as flee to them.

II. And upon this he infers that the mischievous attempts of his bitterest adversaries are but vain; with them he expostulates; them he checks, and over them he insults.

1. "How long will ye imagine mischief against a man?" i. e., *me*. He chides their obstinacy.

2. "Ye shall be slain all of you;" and their ruin he declares by a double similitude; "Ye shall be as a bowing wall;" whence when some stones begin to start out or fall, the rest follow: or *as a tottering fence*, that is easily thrown down.

Next, by the description of their manners, he intimates the cause of their ruin.

1. "They only consult to cast him down from his excellency;" their counsel is to destroy David.

2. "They delight in lies;" invent lies and tales to destroy him.

3. Flatterers and dissemblers are they: "They bless with their mouth but they curse inwardly;" no wonder then, if destined to the slaughter, "if they be as a broken wall," &c.

III. And lest his heart faint and fail through the multitude of temptations, he first encourages himself to be confident still. Secondly, persuades others to do so.

1. He encourages himself, making use of the words of the first and second verses for reasons: "My soul, wait thou only upon God; for my expectation is from him: he only is my rock, and my salvation; he is my defence, I shall not be moved. In God is my salvation, and my glory; the rock of my strength, and my refuge, is in God."

2. He exhorts others to do the like: "Trust in him, ye people," which he amplifies:—

1. By assignation of the time: "Trust in him at all times:" in prosperity, that he be not secure; in adversity, that he be not heartless.

2. And in our saddest occasions he shows what is to be done, that we bring our grievances and complaints before God, and with an honest heart open them: "Pour out your heart (that is, the griefs of your hearts) before him."

3. Adding this reason: "God is a refuge for us."

IV. So are not other things; whether, 1. *Men*. 2. *Wealth*, especially unjustly got.

1. Not men; there is no credit or trust to be put in them of *any degree*. 1. "Surely men of low degree are vanity," 2. "And men of high degree are a lie." The *low* are not *able;* the *high deceive* our hopes.

"Put them into the balance; they are altogether lighter than vanity." Make trial of them, as of things in a scale, and you shall find them so vain and light that they carry no proportion to what is weighty, but ascend as an empty scale.

2. Nor *wealth*, nor *riches;* especially if unjustly heaped together: "Trust not in oppression, and become not vain in robbery: if riches increase, set not your heart upon them."

V. In the *close*, he sets down the grounds of his confidence, taken upon God's word: "God hath spoken; twice have I heard the same;" or, "I have heard these two things:"—

1. "That power belongs to God;" and therefore he is to be trusted.

2. "That mercy belongs to God;" and therefore, also, you may have the utmost confidence in him.

The consequence of both is, "Thou renderest to every one according to his works," *bonis vera, malis mala:* rely upon him. *Bad* work cannot have *good* wages; *good* work cannot have *bad* wages. "What a man soweth, that shall he also reap." "The righteous shall inherit glory, but shame shall be the promotion of fools." A man may deserve hell by a wicked life; but he cannot merit heaven by a good life because he cannot do good but through the grace of God, and the merit of the work belongs to the grace by which it was wrought. Reader, hear God's sentence on this subject: "The *wages* of sin is death." This is desert. "But the *gift* of God is eternal life." Here is no desert, for it is "by Jesus Christ our Lord." To him be glory for ever. Amen.

PSALM LXIII

David's soul thirsts after God, while absent from the sanctuary, and longs to be restored to the Divine ordinances, 1, 2. He expresses strong confidence in the Most High, and praises him for his goodness, 3–8; shows the misery of those who do not seek God, 9, 10; and his own safety as king of the people, 11.

A Psalm of David, [a]when he was in the wilderness of Judah

A. M. cir. 2943
B. C. cir. 1061
Sauli, Regis
Israelitarum,
cir. annum
35

O GOD, thou *art* my God; early will I seek thee: [b]my soul thirsteth for thee, my flesh longeth for thee in a dry and [c]thirsty land, [d]where no water is;

2 To see [e]thy power and thy glory, so *as* I have seen thee in the sanctuary.

A. M. cir. 2943
B. C. cir. 1061
Sauli, Regis
Israelitarum,
cir. annum
35

[a]1 Sam. xxii. 5; xxiii. 14, 15, 16——[b]Psa. xlii. 2; lxxxiv. 2; cxliii. 6——[c]Heb. *weary*

[d]Heb. *without water*——[e]See 1 Sam. iv. 21; 1 Chron. xvi. 11; Psa. xxvii. 4; lxxviii. 61

NOTES ON PSALM LXIII

The *title* of this Psalm is, *A Psalm of David, when he was in the wilderness of Judea;* but instead of *Judea*, the *Vulgate, Septuagint, Æthiopic, Arabic*, several of the ancient Latin

Psalters, and several of the *Latin fathers*, read *Idumea*, or *Edom;* still there is no evidence that David had ever taken refuge in the *deserts of Idumea*. The *Hebrew* text is that which should be preferred; and all the MSS. are in its favour. The *Syriac* has, "Of David, when he

A. M. cir. 2943
B. C. cir. 1061
Sauli, Regis
Israelitarum,
cir. annum
35

3 ᶠBecause thy loving-kindness *is* better than life, my lips shall praise thee.

4 Thus will I bless thee ᵍwhile I live: I will lift up my hands in thy name.

5 My soul shall be ʰsatisfied as *with* ⁱmarrow and fatness; and my mouth shall praise *thee* with joyful lips:

6 When ᵏI remember thee upon my bed, *and* meditate on thee in the *night* watches.

7 Because thou hast been my help, therefore ˡin the shadow of thy wings will I rejoice.

8 My soul followeth hard after thee: thy right hand upholdeth me.

A. M. cir. 2943
B. C. cir. 1061
Sauli, Regis
Israelitarum,
cir. annum
35

ᶠPsa. xxx. 5——ᵍPsa. civ. 33; cxlvi. 2——ʰPsa. xxxvi. 8
ⁱHeb. *fatness*

ᵏPsa. xlii. 8; cxix. 55; cxlix. 5——ˡPsa. xvii. 8; xxxvi. 7;
lvii. 1; lxi. 4; xci. 4

---

said to the king of Moab, My father and mother fled to thee from the face of Saul; and I also take refuge with thee." It is most probable that the Psalm was written when David took refuge in the forest of *Hareth*, in the wilderness of Ziph, when he fled from the court of Achish. But Calmet understands it as a prayer by the captives in Babylon.

Verse 1. *O God, thou art my God*] He who can say so, and feels what he says, need not fear the face of any adversary. He has God, and all sufficiency in him.

Early will I seek thee] From the dawn of day. *De luce*, from the light, *Vulgate;* as soon as day breaks; and often before this, for his eyes prevented the night-watches; and he longed and watched for God more than they who watched for the morning. The old Psalter says, **God my God, til the fram light J wake**; and paraphrases thus: God of all, thurgh myght; thu is my God, thurgh lufe and devocion; speciali till the I wak. **Fra light**, that is, fra thy tym that the light of thi grace be in me, that excites fra night of sine. And makes me wak till the in delite of luf, and swetnes in saul. Thai **wak** till God, that setes all thar thoght on God, and for getns the werld. Thai **slep** till God, that settis thair hert on ani creatur.—I **wak** till the, and that gars me thirst in saule and body.

What first lays hold of the heart in the morning is likely to occupy the place all the day. First impressions are the most durable, because there is not a multitude of ideas to drive them out, or prevent them from being deeply fixed in the moral feeling.

In a dry and thirsty land] בארץ *beerets*, IN a land: but several MSS. have כארץ *keerets*, AS a dry and thirsty land, &c.

Verse 2. *To see thy power and thy glory—in the sanctuary.*] In his public ordinances God had often showed his *power* in the judgments he executed, in the terror he impressed, and in awakening the sinful; and his glory in delivering the tempted, succouring the distressed, and diffusing peace and pardon through the hearts of his followers. God shows his *power* and *glory* in his *ordinances;* therefore *public worship* should never be neglected. *We must see God*, says the old Psalter, *that he may see us.* In his temple he dispenses his choicest blessings.

Verse 3. *Thy loving-kindness* is *better than life*] This is the language of every regenerate soul. But O how few prefer the approbation of God to the blessings of life, or even to life itself in *any circumstances!* But the psalmist says, *Thy loving-kindness,* חסדך *chasdecha*, thy effu-

sive mercy, is better מחיים *mechaiyim*, than LIVES: *it is better than*, or *good beyond,* countless *ages of human existence.*

My lips shall praise thee.] Men praise, or speak *well*, of power, glory, honour, riches, worldly prospects and pleasures; but the truly religious *speak well* of GOD, in whom they find infinitely more satisfaction and happiness than worldly men can find in the possession of all *earthly good.*

Verse 4. *I will lift up my hands in thy name.*] I will take God for my portion. I will dedicate myself to him, and will take him to witness that I am upright in what I profess and do. Pious Jews, in every place of their dispersion, in all their prayers, praises, contracts, &c., *stretched out their hands towards Jerusalem,* where the true God had his temple, and where he manifested his presence.

Verse 5. *My soul shall be satisfied*] I shall have, in the true worshipping of thee, as complete a sensation of spiritual sufficiency and happiness, so that no desire shall be left unsatisfied, as any man can have who enjoys health of body, and a fulness of all the necessaries, conveniences, and comforts of life.

Verse 6. *When I remember thee upon my bed*] I will lie down in thy fear and love; that I may sleep soundly under thy protection, and awake with a sense of thy presence and approbation; and when I awake in the *night watches*, or be awakened by them, I will spend the waking moments in meditation upon thee.

Verse 7. *Therefore in the shadow of thy wings*] I will get into the very secret of thy presence, into the holy of holies, to the *mercy-seat*, over which the *cherubs extend their wings*. If the psalmist does not allude to the *overshadowing* of the *mercy-seat* by the *extended wings of the cherubim*, he may have in view, as a metaphor, the young of fowls, seeking shelter, protection, and warmth under the wings of their mothers. See the same metaphor, Psa. lxi. 4. When a bird of prey appears, the chickens will, by natural instinct, run under the wings of their mothers for protection.

The old *Psalter* translates, **And in hiling of thi wenges J sall joy**. The paraphrase is curious. "Thou art my helper, in perels; and I can joy in gode dedes in thi hiling, (covering,) for I am thi bride, (bird,) and if thou hil (cover) me noght, the glede (kite) will rawis me, (carry me away.")

Verse 8. *My soul followeth hard after thee*] דבקה נפשי אחריך *dabekah naphshi achareycha*, "My soul cleaves (or) is glued after thee." This phrase not only shows the *diligence* of the pursuit, and the *nearness* of the attainment,

A. M. cir. 2943
B. C. cir. 1061
Sauli, Regis
Israelitarum,
cir. annum
35

9 But those *that* seek my soul, to destroy *it,* shall go into the lower parts of the earth.

10 ᵐThey ⁿshall fall by the sword: they shall be a portion for foxes.

11 But the king shall rejoice in God; °every one that sweareth by him shall glory: but the mouth of them that speak lies shall be stopped.

A. M. cir. 2943
B. C. cir. 1061
Sauli, Regis
Israelitarum,
cir. annum
35

ᵐHeb. *They shall make him run out* like water *by the hands of the sword*

ⁿEzek. xxxv. 5——°Deut. vi. 13; Isa. xlv. 23; lxv. 16; Zeph. i. 5

---

but also the *fast hold* he had got of the mercy of his God.

Verse 9. *Lower parts of the earth.*] They are appointed, in the just judgment of God, to destruction; they shall be slain and buried in the earth, and shall be seen no more. Some understand the passage as referring to the punishment of *hell;* which many supposed to be in the *centre of the earth.* So the old *Psalter,—Thai sall entir in till lagher pine of hell. Lagher* or *laigher,* lower, undermost.

Verse 10. *They shall fall by the sword*] *They shall be poured out by the hand of the sword,* Heb. That is, their life's blood shall be shed either in war, or by the hand of justice.

They shall be a portion for foxes.] They shall be left *unburied,* and the *jackals* shall feed upon their dead bodies. Or, being all cut off by utter destruction, their *inheritance* shall be left for the *wild beasts.* That which was their *portion* shall shortly be the *portion* of the wild beasts of the forest. If he here refers to the destruction of the *Babylonians,* the prediction has been literally fulfilled. Where ancient Babylon stood, as far as it can be ascertained, is now the *hold of dangerous reptiles and ferocious beasts.* The *jackal,* or *chokal,* is a very ravenous beast, and fond of *human flesh.* It devours dead bodies, steals infants out of the lap of their mothers, devours alive the *sick* who are left by the side of the *Ganges,* and even in the streets of Calcutta has been known to eat persons who were in a state of intoxication. WARD's *Customs.*

Verse 11. *But the king shall rejoice*] David shall come to the kingdom according to the promise of God. Or, if it refer to the *captivity,* the *blood royal* shall be preserved in and by *Zerubbabel* till the *Messiah* come, who shall be David's spiritual successor in the kingdom for ever.

That sweareth by him] It was customary to swear *by the life* of the king. The *Egyptians* swore *by the life of Pharaoh;* and *Joseph* conforms to this custom, as may be seen in the book of *Genesis,* chap. xlii. 15, 16. See also 1 Sam. i. 26, and xvii. 55, and Judith xi. 7. But here it may refer to GOD. He is THE KING, and *swearing by his name* signifies *binding* themselves by his *authority, acknowledging* his *supremacy,* and *devoting* themselves to his *glory* and *service* alone.

The *Chaldee* has: "And the King shall rejoice במימר אלהא *bemeymar Eloha,* in the WORD of God;" or, in the WORD GOD; *Meymar,* WORD, being taken here *substantially,* as in many other places, by the Targumist.

The mouth of them that speak lies] The mouth of those who acknowledge *lying vanities,* that worship *false gods,* shall be *stopped.* All false religions shall be destroyed by the prevalence of the truth. For he, CHRIST, shall *reign* till all his enemies are put under his feet.

"Thy kingdom come, and hell's o'erpower: and to thy sceptre all subdue." Amen and Amen.

ANALYSIS OF THE SIXTY-THIRD PSALM

The *contents* are,—

I. David's ardent desire to be in the assembly of the saints, ver. 1. And the *reasons* on which this desire was founded, ver. 2, 3, 4, 5.

II. That though *absent* from God's ordinances, yet he forgot not his Maker, ver. 6, 7, 8.

III. A double *prophecy.* 1. What should befall his enemies, ver. 9, 10. And, 2. What should come to himself, ver. 11.

I. 1. In the *first part* he states his confidence in God, as the foundation of his desires, contemplations, meditations, invocations, and consolations: "O God, thou art my God," ver. 1.

2. Then he expresses his fervent desire and ardent affection. 1. "Early will I seek thee." THEE, not other things. 2. "My soul thirsteth for thee," &c. There is no doubt that he wanted many things in this barren thirsty land; but of this he does not complain, but of his want of God in the sanctuary.

And so he expresses himself in the following verse: He *was about to see the power and glory of God in the sanctuary, as he had formerly done.* He gives the *reason* of this: "Because thy loving-kindness is better than life," ver. 3. To see thy goodness in the use of thy ordinances, I count far beyond all the *blessings of life;* and could I again be admitted there, these effects would follow:—

1. Praise: "My lips shall praise," &c., ver. 4.

2. Invocation and prayer: "I will lift up my hands," &c., ver. 4.

3. The satisfaction he should receive from these: "My mouth shall be satisfied as with marrow and fatness," &c., ver. 5.

II. Though David is now in the wilderness, he does not forget his duty.

1. Even there he remembered God upon his bed; and meditated, &c., ver. 6.

2. "Because thou hast been my help; therefore," &c., ver. 7.

3. "My soul followeth hard after thee," &c., ver. 8. It is evident, therefore, that even here David was not without comfort; for, 1. He meditates, and remembers what God had done for him. 2. He remembers that he had been his help; and therefore he rejoices. 3. He still adheres to him, and *follows hard after him* for help still.

III. And now, being secure of God's protection, he foretells, 1. What would befall his enemies; and, 2. What would come to himself.

1. To his *enemies,* ruin: "Those who seek after my soul, they shall go (some) into the lower parts of the earth," the grave or hell.

Others should "fall by the sword," lie unburied, and be devoured by wild beasts.

——————'Ελωρια τευχε κυνεσσιν,

Οιωνοισι τε πασι.   Il., I. ver. 4.

"Whose limbs, unburied on the naked shore,
Devouring dogs and hungry vultures tore."
POPE.

2. To *himself*, honour and a crown: "But the king (David) shall rejoice in God." The reason is,—

1. "Every one that swears by him," that is who worships and fears God, an oath being put

by *synecdoche* for the whole worship of God. See the notes.

2. "The mouth of them that speak lies," utter blasphemies, curses, and perjuries, or pray and confess to strange gods, "shall be stopped;" they shall be ashamed and confounded, and an end be put to their iniquity by a sudden and violent death. The *mouth of God's people* shall *glory;* but the *mouth of the wicked* shall be *stopped*, and be silent in the dust.

PSALM LXIV

The psalmist prays for preservation from the wicked, 1, 2; whom he describes, 3–6; shows their punishment, 7, 8; and the effect that this should have on the godly, 9, 10.

To the chief Musician, A Psalm of David

A. M. cir. 3436
B. C. cir. 568
A. U. C. cir. 186
Olymp. LIII.
cir. annum
primum

HEAR my voice, O God, in my prayer: preserve my life from fear of the enemy.

2 Hide me from the secret counsel of the wicked; from the insurrection of the workers of iniquity:

3 ªWho whet their tongue like a sword, ᵇ*and* bend *their bows to shoot* their arrows, *even* bitter words:

4 That they may shoot in secret at the perfect: suddenly do they shoot at him, and fear not.

A. M. cir. 3436
B. C. cir. 568
A. U. C. cir. 186
Olymp. LIII.
cir. annum
primum

5 ᶜThey encourage themselves *in* an evil ᵈmatter: they commune ᵉof laying snares privily; ᶠthey say, Who shall see them?

6 They search out iniquities; ᵍthey accomplish ʰa diligent search: both the inward *thought* of every one *of them,* and the heart *is* deep.

ªPsa. xi. 2; lvii. 4——ᵇPsa. lviii. 7; Jer. ix. 3——ᶜSee Prov. i. 11——ᵈOr, *speech*——ᵉHeb. *to hide snares*

ᶠPsa. x. 11; lix. 7——ᵍOr, *we are consumed by that which they have throughly searched*——ʰHeb. *a search searched*

NOTES ON PSALM LXIV

The *title*, To the chief Musician, or *conqueror, A Psalm of David.* The *Syriac* says, "composed by David when warned by Gad the prophet, who said, Stay not in Masrob, because Saul seeks thy life." Some think it was composed by David when he was persecuted by Saul; or during the rebellion of Absalom. But *Calmet* thinks it is a complaint of the captives in Babylon.

Verse 1. *Hear my voice*] The psalmist feared for his life, and the lives of his fellow-captives; and he sought help of God. He *prayed*, and he lifted up his *voice;* and thus showed his *earnestness*.

Verse 2. *Hide me from the secret counsel*] They *plotted* his destruction, and then formed *insurrections* in order to accomplish it.

Workers of iniquity] Those who made *sin* their *labour*, their daily employment; it was their *occupation* and *trade*. It is supposed that by this title the Babylonians are intended. See Psa. vi. 3; xiv. 4; xxxvi. 12; liii. 4; lix. 2.

Verse 3. *Who whet their tongue like a sword*] They *devise* the evil they shall speak, and meditate on the most provoking, injurious, and *defamatory words;* as the soldier *whets* his sword that he may thereby the better cut down his enemies.

Their arrows—bitter words] Their defamatory sayings are here represented as deadly as *poisoned arrows;* for to such is the allusion here made.

Verse 4. *That they may shoot in secret*] They *lurk*, that they may take their aim the more surely, and not miss their mark.

Suddenly] When there is no fear apprehended, because none is seen.

Verse 5. *They commune of laying snares*] They lay snares to *entrap* those whom they cannot slay by *open* attack or private *ambush*.

Verse 6. *They search out iniquities; they accomplish a diligent search*] The word חפש *chaphash*, which is used *three* times, as a noun and a verb, in this sentence, signifies *to strip off the clothes*. "They investigate iniquities; they perfectly investigate an investigation." Most energetically translated by the old *Psalter:* Thai ransaked wickednesses; thai failled ransakand in ransaking. To *ransack* signifies to search every corner, to examine things part by part, to turn over every leaf, to leave no hole or cranny unexplored. But the word *investigate* fully expresses the meaning of the term, as it comes either from *in*, taken privately, and *vestire*, to *clothe*, *stripping the man bare*, that he may be exposed to all shame, and be the more easily wounded; or from the word *investigo*, which may be derived from *in*, *intensive*, and *vestigium*, the *footstep* or *track* of man or beast. A metaphor from hunting the stag; as the *slot*, or *mark of his foot*, is diligently sought out, in order to find whither he is gone, and whether he is *old* or *young*, for huntsmen can determine the age by the *slot*. *Tuberville*, in his Treatise on *Hunting*, gives rules to form this judgment. To this the next verse seems to refer.

A. M. cir. 3436
B. C. cir. 568
A. U. C. cir. 186
Olymp. LIII.
cir. annum
primum

7 [l]But God shall shoot at them *with* an arrow; suddenly [k]shall they be wounded.

8 So they shall make [l]their own tongue to fall upon themselves: [m]all that see them shall flee away.

9 [n]And all men shall fear, and shall [o]declare

the work of God; for they shall wisely consider of his doing.

A. M. cir. 3436
B. C. cir. 568
A. U. C. cir. 186
Olymp. LIII.
cir. annum
primum

10 [p]The righteous shall be glad in the Lord, and shall trust in him; and all the upright in heart shall glory.

---

[l]Psa. vii. 12, 13——[k]Heb. *their wound shall be*——[l]Prov. xii. 13; xviii. 7

[m]Psa. xxxi. 11; lii. 6——[n]Psa. xl. 3——[o]Jer. l. 28; li. 10
[p]Psa. xxxii. 11; lviii. 10; lxviii. 3

Verse 7. *But God shall shoot at them* with *an arrow*] They endeavour to *trace* me out, that they may shoot me; but God will *shoot at them.* This, if the Psalm refer to the times of David, seems to be prophetic of Saul's death. The *archers* pressed upon him, and sorely wounded him with their arrows. 1 Sam. xxxi. 3.

Verse 8. *Their own tongue to fall upon themselves*] All the plottings, counsels, and curses, they have formed against me, shall come upon themselves.

Verse 9. *And all men shall fear*] They endeavoured to *hide* their mischief; but God shall so punish them that all shall *see it,* and shall acknowledge in their chastisement the just judgment of God. The wicked, in consequence, *shall fear,* and,

Verse 10. *The righteous shall be glad*] They shall see that God does not abandon his followers to the malice of bad men. The rod of the wicked may *come into the heritage of the just;* but *there* it shall not *rest.* *Calmet* thinks that this is a prediction of the destruction of the Chaldeans, in consequence of which the Jewish people became highly respected by all the surrounding nations. But it may be applied more *generally* to the enmity of the wicked against the righteous, and how God counterworks their devices, and vindicates and supports his own followers.

ANALYSIS OF THE SIXTY-FOURTH PSALM

I. The psalmist, in danger, commends his cause to God, ver. 1, 2.
II. Complains of his enemies, who are described by their inward devices, and outward conduct, ver. 3-6.
III. He foretells their ruin, and the consequences, ver. 7-10.
I. 1. He prays in general: "Hear my voice."
2. Then in special, that his life may be safe: "Hide me from the secret counsel," &c., ver. 2.
He describes his enemies, generally:—
1. They were wicked men.
2. They were workers of iniquity.
3. They worked secret counsels against him.
4. They acted according to their counsels.

II. After this general character, he particularly describes their villany.
1. They were calumniators; no *sword* sharper than their tongue, no *arrow* swifter than their accusations.
They were *diligent* and *active* to wound his credit; and the evil of their conduct was aggravated by *two* circumstances: 1. It was in *secret;* 2. It was against the *innocent* and *upright:* "They whet their sword; and bend their bow, to shoot their arrows," &c.
2. They were *obstinate* and *confirmed* in mischief:—1. "They encourage themselves in an evil thing." 2. "They commune," lay their heads together how to lay snares, &c.
3. They are *impudent* and *atheistical:* "They say, Who shall see them?"
4. They are *indefatigable*—they are carried on with an earnest desire to do mischief; they invent all crafty ways to circumvent the righteous.
5. All this they do *subtly, craftily:* "Both the inward thought and heart of them is deep;" it is not easy to find out their snares.
III. Now he foretells, 1. Their *punishment;* and, 2. The *event.*
1. Their *punishment* was to be hasty, sharp, deadly, and very just. 1. "God shall shoot at them with an arrow; suddenly shall they be wounded." 2. Most just. For they shall "make their own tongues fall upon themselves." By their *tongues* did they *mischief;* by their *tongues* shall they *fall.*
2. The *event* shall be *double:* 1. In *general,* to *all;* 2. In *particular,* to the *righteous.*
1. Universally: "All that see them shall flee away,"—fear, desert, forsake them.
2. All men "shall see and declare the work of the Lord, and consider it as his doing."
The *effect* it shall have on the righteous. They shall acknowledge God's justice; and farther,—
1. They *shall be glad* in the Lord—in the judgments he has shown.
2. They shall *trust in him*—that he will always protect and deliver them.
3. They *shall glory*—make their *boast* in God, and tell to all the wonders which in his justice and his mercy he has wrought for them.

PSALM LXV

God is praised for the fulfilment of his promises, and for his mercy in forgiving sins, 1–3. He is praised for the wonders that he works in nature, which all mankind must acknowledge, 4–8; for the fertilizing showers which he sends upon the earth, and the abundance thereby produced both for men and cattle, 9–13.

XII. DAY. EVENING PRAYER

To the chief Musician, A Psalm *and* Song of David

A. M. cir. 3484
B. C. cir. 520
A. U. C. cir. 234
Darii I., R. Per.
cir. annum
secundum

PRAISE [a]waiteth for thee, O God, in Sion: and unto thee shall the vow be performed.

2 O thou that hearest prayer, [b]unto thee shall all flesh come.

3 [c]Iniquities [d]prevail against me: *as for*

our transgressions, thou shalt [e]purge them away.

4 [f]Blessed *is the man whom* thou [g]choosest, and causest to approach *unto thee, that* he may dwell in thy courts: [h]we shall be satisfied with the goodness of thy house, *even* of thy holy temple.

5 *By* terrible things in righteousness wilt

A. M. cir. 3484
B. C. cir. 520
A. U. C. cir. 234
Darii I., R. Per.
cir. annum
secundum

---

[a]Heb. *is silent;* Psa. lxii. 1——[b]Isa. lxvi. 23——[c]Psa. xxxviii. 4; xl. 12——[d]Hebrew, *Words* or *Matters of iniquities*

[e]Psa. li. 2; lxxix. 9; Isa. vi. 7; Heb. ix. 14; 1 John i. 7, 9 [f]Psa. xxxiii. 12; lxxxiv. 4——[g]Psa. iv. 3——[h]Psa. xxxvi. 8

NOTES ON PSALM LXV

The *title,* "To the chief Musician or conqueror, a Psalm and Song of David." So the *Hebrew;* and, in effect, the *Chaldee, Æthiopic,* and best copies of the *Septuagint.* The *Arabic* has, "A Psalm of David concerning the transmigration of the people."

The *Vulgate* is singular: "A Psalm of David. A hymn of Jeremiah and Ezekiel for the people of the transmigration, when they began to go out," from Babylon, understood. This title is of no authority; it neither accords with the *subject* of the Psalm, nor with the *truth of history. Calmet* has very properly remarked that *Jeremiah* and *Ezekiel* were never found together, to compose this Psalm, neither *before, at,* nor *after* the captivity. It should therefore be utterly rejected. In the *Complutensian* edition *Haggai* is added to *Jeremiah* and *Ezekiel,* all with equal propriety.

It is supposed to have been written after a great drought, when God had sent a plentiful rain on the land. I rather think that there was no direct drought or rain in the prophet's view, but a celebration of the praises of God for his giving rain and fruitful seasons, and filling men's mouths with food, and their hearts with gladness. There is a particular providence manifested in the quantity of rain that falls upon the earth, which can neither be too much admired nor praised.

Verse 1. *Praise waiteth for thee*] Praise is silent or *dumb* for thee. *Thou* alone art worthy of praise; all other perfections are lost in thine; and he who considers *thee* aright can have no other subject of adoration.

Unto thee shall the vow be performed.] All offerings and sacrifices should be made to thee. All human spirits are under obligation to live to and serve thee. All Jews and Christians, by circumcision and baptism, belong to thee; and they are all bound to *pay the vow* of their respective *covenants* to thee alone; and the spirit of this *vow* is, to love thee with all their powers, and to serve thee with a perfect heart and willing mind, all the days of their life.

Verse 2. *Unto thee shall all flesh come.*] All *human beings* should pray to God; and from him alone the sufficient portion of human spirits is to be derived. It is supposed to be a prediction of the calling of the Gentiles to the faith of the Gospel of Christ. A minister, immensely *corpulent,* began his address to God in the pulpit with these words: "O thou that hearest prayer, unto thee shall all flesh come!" and most unluckily laid a strong *emphasis* on ALL FLESH. The coincidence was ominous; and

I need not say, the people were not edified, for the effect was ludicrous. I mention this fact, which fell under my own notice, to warn those who minister in righteousness to avoid expressions which may be capable, from a similar circumstance, of a ludicrous application. I have known many good men who, to their no small grief, have been encumbered with a preternatural load of muscles; an evil to be deprecated and deplored.

Verse 3. *Iniquities prevail against me*] This is no just rendering of the original, דברי עונת גברו מני *dibrey avonoth gaberu menni;* "iniquitous words have prevailed against me," or, "The words of iniquity are strong against me." All kinds of calumnies, lies, and slanders have been propagated, to shake my confidence, and ruin my credit.

Our transgressions, thou shalt purge them away.] Whatsoever offences we have committed against thee, thou wilt pardon; תכפרם *tecapperem,* thou wilt make *atonement* for them, when with hearty repentance and true faith we turn unto thee. This verse has been abused to favour Antinomian licentiousness. The true and correct translation of the former clause will prevent this.

The old Scottish Version of this verse, in their *singing Psalms,* is most execrable:—

> "Iniquities, I must confess,
>   Prevail against me do:
> And as for our trans-gres-si-ons,
>   Them purge away wilt thou."

O David, if thou art capable of hearing such abominable doggerel substituted for the nervous words thou didst compose by the inspiration of the Holy Ghost, what must thou feel, if chagrin can affect the inhabitants of heaven!

Verse 4. *Blessed is the man whom thou choosest*] This is spoken in reference to the *priests* who were *chosen of God* to minister at the tabernacle; and who were permitted *to approach, draw nigh,* to the Divine Majesty by the various offerings and sacrifices which they presented.

We shall be satisfied with the goodness of thy house] Though *we* are not priests, and have not the great felicity to minister before thee in holy things; yet *we* can worship at thy temple, feel the outpouring of thy Spirit, and be made happy with the blessings which thou dispensest there to thy true worshippers.

Verse 5. *By terrible things in righteousness*] The *Vulgate* joins this clause to the preceding verse: "Thy holy temple is wonderful in righteousness: thou wilt hear us, O God of our salvation." But the psalmist may refer to those

A. M. cir. 3484
B. C. cir. 520
A.U.C. cir. 234
Darii I., R. Per.
cir. annum
secundum

thou answer us, O God of our salvation; *who art* the confidence of ¹all the ends of the earth, and of them that are afar off *upon* the sea:

6 Which by his strength setteth fast the mountains; ᵏ*being* girded with power:

7 ¹Which stilleth the noise of the seas, the noise of their waves, ᵐand the tumult of the people.

8 They also that dwell in the uttermost parts are afraid at thy tokens: thou makest the outgoings of the morning and evening ⁿto rejoice.

9 Thou °visitest the earth, and ᵖwaterest�q

it: thou greatly enrichest it ʳwith the river of God, *which* is full of water: thou preparest them corn, when thou hast so provided for it.

A. M. cir. 3484
B. C. cir. 520
A. U.C. cir. 234
Darii I., R. Per.
cir. annum
secundum

10 Thou waterest the ridges thereof abundantly: ˢthou settlest the furrows thereof: ᵗthou makest it soft with showers: thou blessest the springing thereof.

11 Thou crownest ᵘthe year with thy goodness; and thy paths drop fatness.

12 They drop *upon* the pastures of the wilderness: and the little hills ᵛrejoice on every side.

13 The pastures are clothed with flocks; ʷthe valleys also are covered over with corn; they shout for joy, they also sing.

ⁱPsalm xxii. 27——ᵏPsalm xciii. 1——ˡPsa. lxxxix. 9; cvii. 29; Matthew viii. 26——ᵐPsalm lxxvi. 10; Isa. xvii. 12, 13——ⁿOr, *to sing*——°Deut. xi. 12——ᵖOr, *after thou hadst made it to desire* rain——qGen. ii. 6; Leviticus xxvi. 4; Deuteronomy xi. 14; 1 Kings xviii.

44, 45; Psalm lxviii. 9, 10; civ. 13; Jeremiah v. 24; Matthew v. 45——ʳPsalm xlvi. 4——ˢOr, *thou causest* rain *to descend* into *the furrows thereof*——ᵗHeb. *thou dissolvest it*——ᵘHebrew, *the year of thy goodness* ᵛHeb. *are girded with joy*——ʷIsa. lv. 12

---

wonderful displays of God's providence in the change of seasons, and fertilization of the earth; and, consequently, in the sustenance of all animal beings.

The confidence of all the ends of the earth] Thou art the hope of thy people scattered through different parts of the world, and through the isles of the sea. This passage is also understood of the vocation of the Gentiles.

Verse 6. *Setteth fast the mountains*] It is by thy strength they have been raised, and by thy power they are girded about or preserved. He represents the mountains as being formed and pitched into their proper places by the mighty hand of God; and shows that they are preserved from splitting, falling down, or mouldering away, as it were, by a girdle by which they are surrounded. The image is very fine. They were hooped about by the Divine power.

Verse 7. *Stilleth the noise of the seas*] Thou art Sovereign over all the operation of sea and land. Earthquakes are under thy control: so are the flux and reflux of the sea; and all storms and tempests by which the great deep is agitated. Even the *headstrong multitude* is under thy control; for thou stillest the madness of the people.

Verse 8. *Are afraid at thy tokens*] Thunder and lightning, storms and tempests, eclipses and meteors, tornadoes and earthquakes, are proofs to all who dwell even in the remotest parts of the earth, that there is a Supreme Being who is wonderful and terrible in his acts. By these things an eternal power and Godhead become manifest even to the most barbarous. From this verse to the end of the Psalm there is a series of the finest poetic imagery in the world.

The outgoings of the morning, &c.] The *rising* and *setting* sun, the morning and evening twilight, the invariable succession of day and night, are all ordained by thee, and contribute to the happiness and continuance of man and beast. Or, All that fear thee praise thee in the *morning*, when they go to their work, and in the *evening*, when they return home, for thy

great goodness manifested in the continuance of their strength, and the success of their labour.

Verse 9. *Thou visitest the earth*] God is represented as going through the whole globe, and examining the wants of every part, and directing the *clouds* how and where to deposit their fertilizing showers, and the *rivers* where to direct their beneficial courses.

The river of God] Some think the *Jordan* is meant; and the visiting and watering refer to rain after a long drought. But the *clouds* may be thus denominated, which properly are the origin of rivers.

Thou preparest them corn] Or, Thou wilt prepare them corn, because "thou hast provided for it." Thou hast made all necessary provision for the fertilization of the earth. Thou hast endued the ground with a vegetative power. Rains, dews, and the genial heat of the sun enable it to put forth that power in providing grass for cattle, and corn for the service of man.

Verse 10. *Thou waterest the ridges*] In seed-time thou sendest that measure of rain that is necessary, in order to prepare the earth for the plough; and then, when the *ridges* are thrown into *furrows*, thou makest them *soft* with showers, so as to prepare them for the expansion of the seed, and the vegetation and developement of the embryo plant.

Thou blessest the springing thereof.] Literally, *Thou wilt bless its germinations—its springing buds.* Thou watchest over the young sprouts; and it is by thy tender, wise, and provident care that the *ear* is formed; and by thy bountiful goodness that *mature grains* fill the *ear;* and that *one* produces *thirty, sixty,* or a *hundred* or a *thousand* fold.

Verse 11. *Thou crownest the year*] A full and *plentiful harvest* is the *crown* of the year; and this springs from the unmerited *goodness* of God. This is the *diadem* of the earth. עטרת *ittarta, Thou encirclest,* as with a *diadem.* A most elegant expression, to show the progress of the sun through the *twelve* signs of the zodiac, producing the seasons, and giving a sufficiency of light and heat alternately to all places on the surface of the globe, by its north and south declination (amounting to 23° 28' at the solstices) on each side of the equator. A more beautiful image could not have been chosen; and the very appearance of the *space* termed the *zodiac* on a celestial globe, shows with what propriety the idea of a *circle* or *diadem* was conceived by this inimitable poet.

Thy paths drop fatness.] מַעְגָּלֶיךָ *magaleycha*, "thy orbits." The various planets, which all have their revolutions within the zodiacal space, are represented as contributing their part to the general fructification of the year. Or perhaps the solar revolution through the *twelve* signs, dividing the year into *twelve* parts or months, may be here intended; the *rains* of *November* and *February*, the *frosts* and *snows* of *December* and *January*, being as necessary for the fructification of the soil, as the gentle *showers* of *spring*, the warmth of *summer*, and the *heat* and *drought* of *autumn*. The earth's diurnal rotation on its axis, its annual revolution in its orbit, and the moon's course in accompanying the earth, are all *wheels* or *orbits* of God, which drop fatness, or produce fertility in the earth.

Verse 12. *The pastures of the wilderness*] Even the places which are not cultivated have their *sufficiency of moisture*, so as to render them proper places of pasturage for cattle. The terms *wilderness* and *desert*, in the Sacred Writings, mean, in general, places *not inhabited* and *uncultivated*, though abounding with timber, bushes, and herbage.

The little hills rejoice] Literally, *The hills gird themselves with exultation.* The metaphor appears to be taken from the frisking of lambs, bounding of kids, and dancing of shepherds and shepherdesses, in the joy-inspiring summer season.

Verse 13. *The pastures are clothed with flocks*] Cattle are seen in every plain, avenue, and vista, feeding abundantly; and the *valleys* are *clothed*, and wave with the richest *harvests;* and transports of joy are heard every where in the cheerful songs of the peasantry, the singing of the birds, the neighing of the horse, the lowing of the ox, and the bleating of the sheep. Claudian uses the same image:—

Viridis amictus montium.

"The green vesture of the mountains."

Shout for joy, they also sing.] They are not loud and unmeaning sounds, they are both music and harmony in their different notes; all together form one great concert, and the *bounty of God* is the subject which they all celebrate. What an inimitable description! And yet the nervous Hebrew is not half expressed, even by the amended translation and paraphrase above.

Analysis of the Sixty-fifth Psalm

This is wholly a poem of thanksgiving; and teaches us *how*, and for *what*, we are to praise God. 1. For *spiritual;* 2. For *temporal* blessings; and, 3. This *publicly; in Zion*—in his *Church*.

It has *two* general parts:—

I. Praise to God for his blessings to his followers, ver. 1-5.

II. His common benefits to all mankind, ver. 6-13.

I. He sets forth God's grace to his followers, of which he reckons several particulars:—

1. He has established a public ministry among them, and *an atoning sacrifice*.

2. He directs and hears their prayers; and to him by sacrifice, prayer, and praise, may all human beings come.

3. Though evil tongues may prevail against them for a time, yet he will deliver them.

4. The *transgressions* committed against him he will accept an *atonement for*, and *pardon*, ver. 1-4. See the notes.

5. All that truly worship him in his ordinances shall be made partakers of spiritual blessedness: "We shall be satisfied with the goodness of thy house," ver. 4.

6. He works powerfully and terribly, but righteously, in behalf of his followers, against their enemies: "By terrible things in righteousness," ver. 5. 1. He *answers* them when they call. 2. By *terrible* things,—as in *Egypt*, the *wilderness*, &c. 3. And the *motive* to it is, his *justice* or *righteousness*, by which he punishes his enemies, and gives retribution to his people.

All this he concludes with a double *eulogy* of God:

1. Showing what he is *peculiarly* to his people: "O God of our salvation."

2. What he is to ALL; "the confidence of all the ends of the earth," for he sustains all, be they where they may.

II. He descends from his *peculiar providence*, —the care he takes of, and the benefits he bestows on, his *Church*,—to his *general providence*, his ordering and sustaining the whole *world;* which he amplifies:—

1. "By his strength he setteth fast the mountains," &c., which is true literally: but, *tropologically*, it may mean *kingdoms* and *states*.

2. He stilleth the noise of the sea,—and of the waves,—for to them he sets bounds: "And the tumult of the people." He stills devils, tyrants, armies, seditions, &c.

3. He does this so, that even those who are in the *uttermost parts of the sea* are afraid at his tokens. They see from the phenomena of nature how powerful and fearful God is.

4. The *sun, moon, planets*, and *stars* are under his guidance. *Day* and *night* are ordered by him: "Thou makest the outgoings of the morning and evening to rejoice."

5. The earth and its inhabitants are his peculiar care: "Thou visitest the earth," &c., ver. 9-11.

In all which the prophet shows God's mercy, 1. In the *rain*. 2. In the *rivers*. 3. In the *growing of the corn*. 4. In *providing grass for cattle*. 5. In providing *store* in the *summer* and *autumn*. 6. His *clouds* drop fatness upon the earth, and all nature rejoices. The meaning of all is, Man may plough, sow, dig, manure, prune, watch, fence, &c.; but it is God that gives the increase.

For an account of the *imagery* here employed, see the notes. The Psalm is grand beyond description, and can never be sufficiently admired.

PSALM LXVI

The psalmist exhorts all to praise God for the wonders he has wrought, 1–4; calls on Israel to consider his mighty acts in behalf of their fathers, 5–7; his goodness in their own behalf, 8–12; he resolves to pay his vows to God, and offer his promised sacrifices, 13–15; calls on all to hear what God had done for his soul, 15–20.

To the chief Musician, A Song *or* Psalm

A. M. cir. 3484
B. C. cir. 520
Darii I.,
R. Persarum,
cir. annum
secundum

MAKE [a]a joyful noise unto God, [b]all ye lands:

2 Sing forth the honour of his name: make his praise glorious.

3 Say unto God, How [c]terrible *art thou in* thy works! [d]through the greatness of thy power shall thine enemies [e]submit[f] themselves unto thee.

4 [g]All the earth shall worship thee, and [h]shall sing unto thee; they shall sing *to* thy name. Selah.

5 [i]Come and see the works of God: *he is* terrible *in his* doing toward the children of men.

6 [k]He turned the sea into dry land: [l]they went through the flood on foot: there did we rejoice in him.

A. M. cir. 3484
B. C. cir. 520
Darii I.,
R. Persarum,
cir. annum
secundum

7 He ruleth by his power for ever; [m]his eyes behold the nations: let not the rebellious exalt themselves. Selah.

8 O bless our God, ye people, and make the voice of his praise to be heard:

9 Which [n]holdeth our soul in life, and [o]suffereth not our feet to be moved.

10 For [p]thou, O God, hast proved us: [q]thou hast tried us, as silver is tried.

---

[a]Psa. c. 1——[b]Heb. *all the earth*——[c]Psa. lxv. 5
[d]Psa. xviii. 44——[e]Or, *yield feigned obedience;* Psa.
xviii. 44; lxxxi. 15——[f]Heb. *lie*——[g]Psa. xxii. 27; lxvii.
3; cxvii. 1——[h]Psa. xcvi. 1, 2

[i]Psa. xlvi. 8——[k]Exod. xiv. 21——[l]Josh. iii. 14, 16
[m]Psalm xi. 4——[n]Hebrew, *putteth*——[o]Psalm cxxi. 3
[p]Psalm xvii. 3; Isaiah xlviii. 10——[q]Zech. xiii. 9;
1 Pet. i. 6, 7

NOTES ON PSALM LXVI

There is nothing particular in the *title* of the Psalm. It is not attributed to *David* either by the *Hebrew, Chaldee, Syriac, Septuagint, Vulgate,* or *Æthiopic.* The *Arabic* alone prefixes the name of *David.* The *Vulgate, Septuagint, Æthiopic,* and *Arabic,* call it a *psalm of the resurrection:* but for this there is no authority. By many of the ancients it is supposed to be a celebration of the restoration from the Babylonish captivity. Others think it commemorates the deliverance of Israel from Egypt, their introduction into the Promised Land, and the establishment of the worship of God in Jerusalem.

Verse 1. *Make a joyful noise*] Sing aloud to God, *all ye lands*—all ye people who, from different parts of the Babylonish empire, are now on return to your own land.

Verse 2. *The honour of his name*] Let his glorious and merciful acts be the *subject* of your songs.

Verse 3. *How terrible* art thou] Consider the plagues with which he afflicted Egypt before he brought your fathers from their captivity, which obliged all his enemies to submit.

Thine enemies submit themselves] Literally, *lie unto thee.* This was remarkably the case with *Pharaoh* and the *Egyptians.* They promised again and again to let the people go, when the hand of the Lord was upon them: and they as frequently falsified their word.

Verse 4. *All the earth*] The whole land shall worship *thee.* There shall no more an *idol* be found among the tribes of Israel. This was literally true. After the Babylonish captivity the Israelites never relapsed into idolatry.

Selah.] Remark it: this is a well attested truth.

Verse 5. *Come and see the works of God*] Let every man lay God's wonderful dealings

with us to heart; and compare our deliverance from *Babylon* to that of our fathers from *Egypt.*

Verse 6. *He turned the sea into dry land*] This was a plain miracle: no human art or contrivance could do this. Even in the bed of the waters THEY *did rejoice in him.* WE have not less cause to praise and be thankful.

Verse 7. *He ruleth by his power*] His *omnipotence* is employed to support his followers, and cast down his enemies.

His eyes behold the nations] He sees what they purpose, what they intend to do; and what they will do, if he restrain them not.

Let not the rebellious exalt themselves.] They shall not succeed in their designs: they have their own aggrandizement in view, but thou wilt disappoint and cast them down.

Selah.] Mark this. It is true.

Verse 8. *O bless our God*] Who have so much cause as you to sing praises to the Lord? Hear what he has done for you:

Verse 9. *Which holdeth our soul in life*] Literally, "he who placeth our soul בחיים *bachaiyim,* in lives." We are preserved *alive,* have *health* of body, and feel the *life* of God in our hearts.

And suffereth not her feet to be moved.] Keeps us steadfast in his testimonies. We have our *life,* our *liberty,* and our *religion.* O, what hath the Lord wrought for us! "Make, therefore, the voice of his praise to be heard." Let God and man know you are thankful.

Verse 10. *For thou, O God, hast proved us*] This is a metaphor taken from *melting* and *refining metals;* afflictions and trials of various kinds are represented as a *furnace* where *ore* is melted, and a *crucible* where it is *refined.* And this metaphor is used especially to represent cases where there is *doubt* concerning the purity of the metal, the quantity of alloy, or even the nature or kind of metal subjected to the trial. So God is said to *try the Israelites*

A. M. cir. 3484
B. C. cir. 520
Darii I.,
R. Persarum,
cir. annum
secundum

11 ʳThou broughtest us into the net; thou laidest affliction upon our loins.

12 ˢThou hast caused men to ride over our heads; ᵗwe went through fire and through water: but thou broughtest us out into a ᵘwealthy *place*.

13 ᵛI will go into thy house with burnt-offerings; ʷI will pay thee my vows,

14 Which my lips have ˣuttered, and my mouth hath spoken, when I was in trouble.

15 I will offer unto thee burnt sacrifices of ʸfatlings, with the incense of rams; I will

offer bullocks with goats. Selah.

A. M. cir. 3484
B. C. cir. 520
Darii I.,
R. Persarum,
cir. annum
secundum

16 ᶻCome *and* hear, all ye that fear God, and I will declare what he hath done for my soul.

17 I cried unto him with my mouth, and he was extolled with my tongue.

18 ᵃIf I regard iniquity in my heart, the LORD will not hear *me:*

19 *But* verily God ᵇhath heard *me;* he hath attended to the voice of my prayer.

20 Blessed *be* God, which hath not turned away my prayer, nor his mercy from me.

ʳLam. i. 13——ˢIsa. li. 23——ᵗIsa. xliii. 2——ᵘHeb. *moist*——ᵛPsa. c. 4; cxvi. 14, 17, 18, 19——ʷEccles. v. 4——ˣHeb. *opened*

ʸHeb. *marrow*——ᶻPsa. xxxiv. 11——ᵃJob xxvii. 9; Prov. xv. 29; xxviii. 9; Isa. i. 15; John ix. 31; James iv. 3——ᵇPsa. cxvi. 1, 2

---

that he *might know what was in them;* and *whether they would keep his testimonies:* and then, according to the issue, his conduct towards them would appear to be founded on reason and justice.

Verse 11. *Thou broughtest us into the net*] This refers well to the case of the Israelites, when, in their departure from Egypt, pursued by the Egyptians, having the Red Sea before them, and no method of escape, Pharaoh said, "The wilderness hath shut them in,—they are entangled;" comparing their state to that of a *wild beast* in a *net.*

Affliction upon our loins.] Perhaps this alludes to that sharp *pain in the back and loins* which is generally felt on the apprehension of *sudden* and *destructive danger.*

Verse 12. *Thou hast caused men to ride over our heads*] Thou hast permitted us to fall under the dominion of our enemies; who have treated us as broken infantry are when the cavalry dashes among their disordered ranks, treading all under the horses' feet.

We went through fire and through water] Through afflictions of the most torturing and *overwhelming* nature. To represent such, the metaphors of *fire* and *water* are often used in Scripture. The old *Psalter* considers these trials as a proof of the uprightness of those who were tried—𝖂𝖊 𝖕𝖆𝖘𝖘𝖎𝖉 𝖙𝖍𝖚𝖗𝖌𝖍 𝖋𝖎𝖗𝖊 𝖆𝖓𝖉 𝖜𝖆𝖙𝖎𝖗: that is, thurgh wa and wele, as a man that leves noght his waye for hete na for kald, for dry na for wette; 𝖆𝖓𝖉 𝖙𝖍𝖔𝖚 𝖔𝖚𝖙 𝖑𝖊𝖉𝖊 𝖚𝖘 fra tribulacyon 𝖎𝖓𝖙𝖎𝖑𝖑 𝖐𝖔𝖑𝖎𝖓𝖌 (cooling) that is, in till endles riste, that we hope to hafe after this travell.

Wealthy place.] *Well watered* place, to wit, the land of *Judea.*

Verse 13. *I will go into thy house with burnt-offerings*] Now that thou hast restored us to our own land, and established us in it, we will establish thy worship, and offer all the various kinds of sacrifices required by thy law.

I will pay thee my vows] We often *vowed*, if thou wouldst deliver us from our bondage, to worship and *serve thee alone:* now thou hast heard our prayers, and hast delivered us; therefore will we fulfil our engagements to thee. The old *Psalter* gives this a pious turn:—𝕴 𝖘𝖆𝖑𝖑 𝖕𝖊𝖑𝖉𝖊 𝖙𝖎𝖑𝖑 𝖙𝖍𝖊 𝖒𝖞 𝖜𝖔𝖚𝖊𝖘, that is, the vowes of louying (praising) the; whilk vowes my lipes divisid sayand, that I am noght, and thou arte

all: and I hafe nede of the, noght thou of me. This is a right distinction—It is certainly a *good distinction*, and it is strictly true. The all-*sufficient* God needs not his *creatures.*

Verse 14. *When I was in trouble.*] This is generally the time when good resolutions are formed, and vows made; but how often are these forgotten when affliction and calamity are removed!

Verse 15. *I will offer, &c.*] Thou shalt have the best of the herd and of the fold; the lame and the blind shall never be given to thee for sacrifice.

The incense of rams] The fine effluvia arising from the burning of the pure fat.

Verse 16. *Come* and *hear, all ye that fear God*] While in captivity, the psalmist had sought the Lord with frequent prayer for his own personal salvation, and for the deliverance of the people; and God blessed him, heard his prayer, and turned the captivity. Now that he is returned in safety, he is determined to perform his vows to the Lord; and calls on all them that fear their Maker, who have any religious reverence for him, to attend to his account of the Lord's gracious dealings with him. He proposes to tell them his spiritual experience, what he needed, what he earnestly prayed for, and what God has done for him. Thus he intended to teach them by *example*, more powerful always than *precept*, however weighty in itself, and impressively delivered.

Verse 17. *I cried unto him with my mouth*] My prayer was fervent; he heard and answered; and my tongue celebrated his mercies; and he as graciously received my *thanksgiving*, as he compassionately heard my *prayer.*

Verse 18. *If I regard iniquity in my heart*] "If I have seen (ראיתי *raithi*) iniquity in my heart," if I have known it was there, and *encouraged* it; if I *pretended* to be what I *was not;* if I *loved iniquity*, while I *professed to pray* and be *sorry* for *my sin; the Lord,* אדני *Adonai*, my Prop, Stay, and Supporter, would not have heard, and I should have been left without *help* or *support.*

Verse 19. *Verily God hath heard me*] A sure proof that my prayer was upright, and my heart honest, before him.

Verse 20. *Blessed be God*] I therefore praise God, who has not turned aside my prayer, and who has not withheld his mercy from me. Thus he told them what God had done for his soul.

ANALYSIS OF THE SIXTY-SIXTH PSALM

There are *five parts* in this Psalm:—

I. An *invitation*.

1. To praise God, ver. 1-4.

2. To consider his works, ver. 5-7.

II. A *repetition* of the *invitation*, ver. 8, for the benefit and deliverance lately received, ver. 9-12.

III. A *protestation* and *vow* for himself, that he would serve the Lord, ver. 13-15.

IV. A *declaration* of *God's goodness* to him, which he invites all to come and hear, ver. 16-19.

V. A *doxology*, with which he concludes, ver. 20.

I. The invitation to praise God affectionately and heartily.

1. "Make a joyful song." 2. "Sing the honour of his name." 3. "Make his praise glorious." 4. "Say unto God," &c. Where he prescribes the *form* in which God shall be praised.

He calls all men to *consider his works*, and the double effect:—1. On God's *enemies*. 2. On his *people*.

1. On his enemies, a *feigned obedience*, ver. 3. See the note.

2. On his people, a *willing service*, ver. 4.

He calls on them again, ver. 5, to consider God's works, specially in delivering his people: 1. At the *Red Sea*. 2. In *passing Jordan* on foot, ver. 6.

He calls them to *behold God's power* and providence. 1. His *power* in ruling. 2. His *providence* in beholding, and, 3. His *justice* in punishing the rebellious, ver. 7.

II. He again invites them to praise God for some *special* mercy, without which they would have been destroyed, ver. 8. 1. He kept them *alive*. 2. *Suffered not their feet* to *slip*, ver. 9. 3. He *tried*, that he might purify, them.

He illustrates this trial by *five* similes taken, —1. From *silver*. 2. From a *net*. 3. From a *burden* laid on the loins. 4. From *bondage and slavery*—men rode over us. 5. From *fire and water;* useful *servants*, but cruel *masters*, ver. 10-12.

But the *issue* of all these trials was good:— they were brought *through* all, and profited by *each.*

III. For this he gives thanks, and purposes to *pay his vows*.

1. He would attend God's worship: "I will go into thy house," ver. 13.

2. He would there present his offerings, ver. 14.

3. These should be of the *best kind*, ver. 15.

IV. He declares God's *goodness*, and *invites all that fear God to hear what he has got to say.* Not of what he was *to offer* to God, but of what God *had done for him.*

1. He cried to God, and he heard him.

2. He took care to *avoid iniquity*, that his prayers might not be cast out: "For God heareth not sinners."

V. He closes the Psalm with a doxology, blessing God that, not through his *merit*, but his own *mercy*, he had heard and answered him. He attributes nothing to himself, but all mercy to his God, ver. 20.

PSALM LXVII

The psalmist prays for the enlargement of God's kingdom, 1, 2; calls upon all nations to serve him, because he judges and governs righteously, 3-5; promises prosperity to the faithful and obedient, 6, 7.

To the chief Musician on Neginoth, A Psalm or Song

A. M. cir. 3484
B. C. cir. 520
Darii I.,
R. Persarum,
cir. annum
secundum

GOD be merciful unto us, and bless us; *and* ªcause his face to shine ᵇupon us. Selah.

2 That ᶜthy way may be known upon earth, ᵈthy saving health among all nations.

3 ᵉLet the people praise thee, O God; let all the people praise thee.

A. M. cir. 3484
B. C. cir. 520
Darii I.,
R. Persarum,
cir. annum
secundum

Num. vi. 25; Psa. iv. 6; xxxi. 16; lxxx. 3, 7, 19; cxix. 135
ᵇHeb. *with us*

ᶜActs xviii. 25——ᵈLuke ii. 30, 31; Tit. ii. 11——ᵉPsa. lxvi. 4

NOTES ON PSALM LXVII

The *title* here is the same with that of Psalm iv., where see the notes. It is supposed to have been written at the return from the Babylonish captivity, and to foretell the conversion of the Gentiles to the Christian religion. The prayer for their salvation is very energetic.

Verse 1. *God be merciful unto us*] Show the Jewish people thy mercy, bless them in their bodies and souls and give a full evidence of thy

approbation. This is nearly the same form of blessing as that used Num. vi. 25, where see the notes.

Verse 2. *That thy way may be known*] That thy will, thy gracious designs towards the children of men, thy way of reconciling them to thyself, of justifying the ungodly, and sanctifying the unholy, may be known to all the nations upon the earth! God's *way* is God's *religion;* what *he walks in* before men; and in which men must *walk* before him. A man's religion

A. M. cir. 3484
B. C. cir. 520
Darii I.,
R. Persarum,
cir. annum
secundum

4 O let the nations be glad and sing for joy: for ᶠthou shalt judge the people righteously, and ᵍgovern the nations upon earth. Selah.

5 Let the people praise thee, O God; let all the people praise thee.

6 ʰ*Then* shall the earth yield her increase; *and* God, *even* our own God, shall bless us.

A. M. cir. 3484
B. C. cir. 520
Darii I.,
R. Persarum,
cir. annum
secundum

7 God shall bless us, and ¹all the ends of the earth shall fear him.

ᶠPsa. xcvi. 10, 13; xcviii. 9——ᵍHeb. *lead*——ʰLev.

xxvi. 4; Psa. lxxxv. 12; Ezek. xxxiv. 27——¹Psa. xxii. 27

---

is his *way* of worshipping God, and going to heaven. The whole Gospel is called *this way*, Acts xix. 9.

Thy saving health] ישועתך *yeshuathecha*, "thy salvation." The great *work* which is performed in God's *way*, in destroying the power, pardoning the guilt, cleansing from the infection, of all sin; and filling the soul with holiness, with the mind that was in Christ. Let *all nations*—the whole Gentile world, know that *way*, and this *salvation!*

Verse 3. *Let the people praise thee*] When this is done, the *people*—the Gentiles, will praise thee; all will give thanks to God for his unspeakable gift.

Verse 4. *Glad and sing for joy*] They shall be made happy in thy salvation. Even their political state shall be greatly meliorated; for God will be acknowledged the supreme Judge; *their laws* shall be founded on *his word;* and the nations of the earth shall be *governed* according to judgment, justice, and equity.

Selah.] This is true. There are innumerable facts to confirm it. All the nations who have received the Gospel of Christ have been benefited *politically*, as well as *spiritually*, by it.

Verse 5. *Let the people praise thee*] Seeing the abundance of the blessings which the Gentiles were to receive, he calls again and again upon them to magnify God for such mercies.

Verse 6. *The earth yield her increase*] As the ground was *cursed* for the sin of man, and the *curse* was to be *removed* by *Jesus Christ*, the fertility of the ground should be influenced by the preaching of the Gospel; for as the people's minds would become enlightened by the truth, they would, in consequence, become capable of making the most *beneficial discoveries* in *arts* and *sciences;* and there should be an especial blessing on the toil of the pious husbandman. Whenever true religion prevails, every thing partakes of its beneficent influence.

Verse 7. *God shall bless us*] He shall ever be *speaking good* to us, and ever showering down good things upon us.

The last clause of the *sixth verse* should be joined to the *seventh*, as it is in several of the *Versions*, and should be in all. Many of the *fathers*, and several *commentators*, have thought that there is a reference to the *Holy Trinity* in the triple repetition of the word GOD: "God, our God, shall bless us; God shall bless us;" thus paraphrased in the old *Psalter:* "Blis us God the Fader: and our God the sone: and blis us and multipli us God the Hali Gast; that swa drede him God, all the endis of erth; for he wil comme to deme rightwysly that unrightwysly was demed. He that kan drede him, he cesses noght to lufe him."

When or by *whom* this Psalm was written cannot be ascertained. It seems to be simply a prophecy concerning the calling of the Gentiles,

the preaching of the apostles, and the diffusion and influence of Christianity in the world. It is a fine piece of devotion; and it would be nearly impossible to read or repeat it with a cold and unaffected heart.

ANALYSIS OF THE SIXTY-SEVENTH PSALM

This Psalm may be divided into *three* parts:—

I. A general *prayer*, ver. 1. And the *reason* of it, ver. 2.

II. A double *vow*, ver. 3, 4. With the *reason*. The vow repeated, ver. 6.

III. The *effects* that were to follow, ver. 6, 7.

1. The first part, a *prayer for mercy:* "God be merciful to us!" for *God's mercy* is the fountain of all our blessings.

2. Then *bless us* through that mercy with *temporal* and *spiritual* good.

3. "Cause his face to shine." Give us a sense of thy *approbation*.

4. Let these blessings be extended *to all men*. For this reason: 1. "That thy way," thy will, word, worship, &c., "may be known upon earth." 2. "Thy saving health," the redemption by Christ, "to all nations."

II. Then shall God be honoured; one will readily flow from the other; for *mercy* brings *knowledge* of God and his goodness, and this knowledge brings *praise*. This verse is emphatic:—

1. In respect of the object; "Thee," not strange gods.

2. ALL *shall praise*—not *mutter* or *meditate* praise, but make it illustrious.

3. This should be done *frequently*, an example of which we have in this Psalm.

4. It should be done *cheerfully*, with a glad heart; not *words* merely, but *affections* of praise.

For this also he gives a *reason* which is twofold:—

1. His *equity* in judging: "Thou shalt judge the people righteously."

2. His *wisdom* in governing. Thou shalt *lead them*, תנחם *tanchem*, thy government shall be full of *wise teaching:* "Wisdom and knowledge shall be the stability of his times."

III. The *effects* of his blessing, and our praise.

1. "The earth shall yield her increase:" the *people* shall be *multiplied;* the *harvests* shall be *ample*, and the *Church* shall *overflow* with converts.

2. God shall *bless this increase;* for, without this, temporal blessings may become a curse. He doubles this that it may not be forgotten.

3. The last and finest effect is, that God shall be worshipped over all the earth: "All the ends of the earth shall fear him." Amen. The *fear of God* is frequently ⁿsed to express the whole of his worship.

PSALM LXVIII

The psalmist calls upon God to arise, bless his people, and scatter his enemies, 1–3; exhorts them to praise him for his greatness, tenderness, compassion, and judgments, 4–6; describes the grandeur of his march when he went forth in the redemption of his people, 7, 8; how he dispensed his blessings, 9, 10; what he will still continue to do in their behalf, 11–13; the effects produced by the manifestation of God's majesty, 14–18; he is praised for his goodness, 19, 20; for his judgments, 21–23; he tells in what manner the Divine worship was conducted, 24–27; how God is to be honoured, 28–31; all are invited to sing his praises, and extol his greatness, 32–35.

XIII. DAY. MORNING PRAYER

To the chief Musician, A Psalm *or* Song of David

A. M. cir. 2962
B. C. cir. 1042
Dav. Reg. Isr.
cir. annum 14

LET ᵃGod arise, let his enemies be scattered; let them also that hate him flee ᵇbefore him.

2 ᶜAs smoke is driven away, *so* drive *them* away: ᵈas wax melteth before the fire, *so* let the wicked perish in the presence of God.

3 But ᵉlet the righteous be glad; let them rejoice before God: yea, let them ᶠexceedingly rejoice.

4 ᵍSing unto God, sing praises to his name: ʰextol him that rideth upon the heavens ⁱby his name JAH, and rejoice before him.

A. M. cir. 2962
B. C. cir. 1042
Davidis, Regis
Israelitarum,
cir. annum
14

5 ᵏA father of the fatherless, and a judge of the widows, *is* God in his holy habitation.

6 ˡGod setteth the solitary ᵐin families: ⁿhe bringeth out those which are bound with chains: but ᵒthe rebellious dwell in a dry *land.*

7 O God, ᵖwhen thou wentest forth before

ᵃNumbers x. 35; Isaiah xxxiii. 3——ᵇHebrew, *from his face*——ᶜIsaiah ix. 18; Hosea xiii. 3——ᵈPsa. xcvii. 5; Micah i. 4——ᵉPsalm xxxii. 11; lviii. 10; lxiv. 10——ᶠHebrew, *rejoice with gladness*——ᵍPsalm lxvi. 4

ʰDeut. xxxiii. 26; ver. 33——ⁱExod. vi. 3——ᵏPsa. x. 14, 18; cxlvi. 9——ˡ1 Sam. ii. 5; Psa. cxiii. 9 ᵐHeb. *in a house*——ⁿPsa. cvii. 10, 14; cxlvi. 7; Acts xii. 6, &c.——ᵒPsa. cvii. 34, 40——ᵖExod. xiii. 21; Judg. iv. 14; Hab. iii. 13

NOTES ON PSALM LXVIII

In the *title* of this Psalm there is nothing particular to be remarked. It is probable that this Psalm, or a part of it at least, might have been composed by Moses, to be recited when the Israelites journeyed. See Num. x. 35; and that David, on the same model, constructed this Psalm. It might have been sung also in the ceremony of transporting the ark from Kirjath-jearim, to Jerusalem; or from the house of Obed-edom to the tabernacle erected at Sion.

I know not how to undertake a comment on this Psalm: it is the most difficult in the whole Psalter; and I cannot help adopting the opinion of *Simon De Muis:* In hoc Psalmo tot ferme scopuli, tot labyrinthi, quot versus, quot verba. Non immerito crux ingeniorum, et interpretum opprobrium dici potest. "In this Psalm there are as many precipices and labyrinths as there are verses or words. It may not be improperly termed, the torture of critics, and the reproach of commentators." To attempt any thing *new* on it would be dangerous; and to say what has been so often said would be unsatisfactory. I am truly afraid to fall over one of those *precipices,* or be endlessly entangled and lost in one of these *labyrinths.* There are customs here referred to which I do not fully understand; there are *words* whose meaning I cannot, to my own satisfaction, ascertain; and allusions which are to me inexplicable. Yet of the composition itself I have the highest opinion: it is sublime beyond all comparison; it is constructed with an art truly admirable; it possesses all the dignity of the sacred language; none but David could have composed it; and, at this lapse of time, it would require no small influence of the Spirit that was upon him, to give its true interpretation. I shall subjoin a few notes, chiefly philological; and beg leave to refer the reader to those who have written

profusely and *laboriously* on this sublime Psalm, particularly *Venema, Calmet, Dr. Chandler,* and the writers in the *Critici Sacri.*

Verse 1. *Let God arise*] This was sung when the Levites took up the ark upon their shoulders; see Num. x. 35, 36, and the notes there.

Verse 4. *Extol him that rideth upon the heavens by his name JAH*] "Extol him who sitteth on the throne of glory, in the ninth heaven; YAH is his name; and rejoice before him."—*Targum.*

בערבות *baaraboth,* which we render *in the high heavens,* is *here* of doubtful signification. As it comes from the root ערב *arab,* to mingle, (hence *ereb* the evening or *twilight,* because it appears to be formed of an *equal mixture of light and darkness;* the *Septuagint* translate it δυσμων, the *west,* or *setting* of the sun; so does the *Vulgate* and others;) probably it may mean the *gloomy desert,* through which God, in the chariot of his glory, led the Israelites. If this interpretation do not please, then let it be referred to the *darkness* in which God is said to dwell, through which the *rays of his power and love,* in the various dispensations of his power and mercy, shine forth for the comfort and instruction of mankind.

By his name Jah] יה *Yah,* probably a contraction of the word יהוה *Yehovah;* at least, so the ancient Versions understood it. It is used but in a few places in the sacred writings. It might be translated *The Self existent.*

Verse 6. *The solitary in families*] יחדים *yechidim,* the *single persons.* Is not the meaning, God is the Author of marriage; and children, the legal fruit of it, are an inheritance from him?

Verse 7. *O God, when thou wentest forth*] This and the following verse most manifestly refer to the passage of the Israelites through the wilderness.

A. M. cir. 2962
B. C. cir. 1042
Davidis, Regis
Israelitarum,
cir. annum
14

thy people, when thou didst march through the wilderness; Selah:

8 qThe earth shook, the heavens also dropped at the presence of God: *even* Sinai itself *was moved* at the presence of God, the God of Israel.

9 rThou, O God, didst ssend a plentiful rain, whereby thou didst tconfirm thine inheritance, when it was weary.

10 Thy congregation hath dwelt therein: uthou, O God, hast prepared of thy goodness for the poor.

11 The Lord gave the word: great *was* the vcompany of those that published *it*.

12 wKings of armies xdid flee apace: and she that tarried at home divided the spoil.

A. M. cir. 2962
B. C. cir. 1042
Davidis, Regis
Israelitarum,
cir. annum
14

13 yThough ye have lien among the pots, zyet shall ye be as the wings of a dove covered with silver, and her feathers with yellow gold.

14 aWhen the Almighty scattered kings bin it, it was *white* as snow in Salmon.

15 The hill of God *is as* the hill of Bashan; a high hill *as* the hill of Bashan.

16 cWhy leap ye, ye high hills? d*this is* the hill *which* God desireth to dwell in; yea, the Lord will dwell *in it* for ever.

---

qExod. xix. 16, 18; Judg. v. 4; Isa. lxiv. 1, 3——rDeut xi. 11, 12; Ezek. xxxiv. 26——sHeb. *shake out*——tHeb. *confirm it*——uDeut. xxvi. 5, 9; Psa. lxxiv. 19——vHeb. *army*——wNum. xxxi. 8, 9, 54; Josh. x. 16; xii. 8

xHeb. *did flee, did flee*——yPsa. lxxxi. 6——zPsa. cv. 37——aNum. xxi. 3; Josh. x. 10; xii. 1, &c.——bOr, *for her, she was*——cPsa. cxiv. 4, 6——dDeut. xii. 5, 11; 1 Kings ix. 3; Psa. lxxxvii. 1, 2; cxxxii. 13, 14

Verse 9. *Didst send a plentiful rain*] נשם נדבות *geshem nedaboth*, a *shower of liberality*. I believe this to refer to the *manna* by which God refreshed and preserved alive the weary and hungry Israelites.

Verse 10. *Thy congregation hath dwelt therein*] חיתך *chaiyathecha, thy living creature;* τα ζωα, *Septuagint; animalia, Vulgate;* so all the Versions. Does not this refer to the *quails* that were brought to the camp of the Israelites, and *dwelt*, as it were, *round about it?* And was not *this*, with the *manna* and the *refreshing rock*, that *goodness which God had provided for the poor*—the needy Israelites?

Verse 11. *Great* was *the company of those that published* it.] המבשרות צבא רב *hammebasseroth tsaba rab;* "Of the female preachers there was a great host." Such is the literal translation of this passage; the reader may make of it what he pleases. Some think it refers to the *women* who, with music, songs, and dances, celebrated the victories of the Israelites over their enemies. But the publication of *good news*, or of any *joyful event*, belonged to the *women*. It was they who announced it to the people at large; and to this universal custom, which prevails to the *present day*, the psalmist alludes. See this established in the note on Isa. xl. 9.

Verse 12. *Kings of armies did flee*] *Jabin* and the kings of the Canaanites, who united their forces to overwhelm the Israelites.

And she] Deborah the prophetess, a *woman* accustomed to *tarry at home*, and take care of the family; she divided the spoils, and vanquished their kings.

Verse 13. *Though ye have lien among the pots*] The prophet is supposed here to address the tribes of *Reuben* and *Gad*, who remained in their *inheritances*, occupied with *agricultural, maritime,* and *domestic affairs*, when the other tribes were obliged to go against *Jabin*, and the other Canaanitish kings. Ye have been thus occupied, while your brethren sustained a desperate campaign; but while you are inglorious, they obtained the most splendid victory, and dwell under those rich tents which they have taken from the enemy; coverings of the most beautiful colours, adorned with gold and silver. The words בירקרק חרוץ *birakrak charuts, native gold,* so exceedingly and splendidly *yellow* as to approach to *greenness*—from ירק *yarak, to be green;* and the doubling of the last syllable denotes an excess in the denomination—*excessively green—glistering green*. The *Targum* gives us a curious paraphrase of this and the following verse: "If ye, ♁ ye kings, slept among your halls, the congregation of Israel, which is like a dove covered with the clouds of glory, divided the prey of the Egyptians, purified silver, and coffers full of the finest gold. And when it stretched out its hands in prayer over the sea, the Almighty cast down kingdoms; and for its sake cooled hell like snow, and snatched it from the shadow of death." Perhaps the Romanists got some idea of purgatory here. For the sake of the righteous, the flames of hell are extinguished!

Verse 15. *The hill of God* is as *the hill of Bashan*] This and the following verse should be read thus: "Is Mount Bashan the craggy mount, Mount Bashan, the mount of God? Why envy ye, ye craggy mounts? This is the mount of God in which he has desired to dwell." The *Targum* countenances this translation: Mount *Moriah*, the place where our fathers of old worshipped God, is chosen to build on it the house of the sanctuary, and Mount *Sinai* for the giving of the law. Mount *Bashan*, Mount *Tabor*, and *Carmel* are rejected; they are made as Mount *Bashan*."

Verse 16. *Why leap ye, ye high hills?*] "God said, Why leap ye, ye high hills? It is not pleasing to me to give my law upon high and towering hills. Behold, Mount Sinai is low; and the WORD of the Lord has desired to place on it the Divine majesty. Moreover, the Lord dwells for ever in the heaven of heavens."—*Targum.*

The psalmist is speaking particularly of the mountains of Judea, and those of Gilead; the former were occupied by the Canaanites, and the others by Og, king of Bashan, and Sihon, king of the Amorites, whom Moses defeated.

A. M. cir. 2962
B. C. cir. 1042
Davidis, Regis
Israelitarum,
cir. annum
14

17 ^eThe chariots of God *are* twenty thousand, ^f*even* thousands of angels: the LORD *is* among them, *as in* Sinai, in the holy *place.*

18 ^gThou hast ascended on high, ^hthou hast led captivity captive: ⁱthou hast received gifts ^kfor men; yea, *for* ^lthe rebellious also, ^mthat the LORD God might dwell *among them.*

19 Blessed *be* the LORD, *who* daily loadeth us *with benefits, even* the God of our salvation. Selah.

20 *He that is* our God *is* the God of salvation; and ⁿunto God the LORD *belong* the issues from death.

21 But ^oGod shall wound the head of his enemies, ^p*and* the hairy scalp of such a one as goeth on still in his trespasses.

22 The LORD said, I will bring ^qagain from Bashan, I will bring *my people* again ^rfrom the depths of the sea:

23 ^sThat thy foot may be ^tdipped in the blood of *thine* enemies, ^u*and* the tongue of thy dogs in the same.

24 They have seen thy goings, O God; *even* the goings of my God, my King, in the sanctuary.

25 ^vThe singers went before, the players on instruments *followed* after; among *them were* the damsels playing with timbrels.

26 Bless ye God in the congregations, *even*

A. M. cir. 2962
B. C. cir. 1042
Davidis, Regis
Israelitarum,
cir. annum
14

---

^eDeut. xxxiii. 2; 2 Kings vi. 16, 17; Dan. vii. 10; Heb. xii. 22; Rev. ix. 16——^fOr, even *many thousands* ^gActs i. 9; Eph. iv. 8——^hJudg. v. 12——ⁱActs ii. 4, 33 ^kHeb. *in the man*——^l1 Tim. i. 13——^mPsa. lxxviii. 60

ⁿDeut. xxxii. 39; Prov. iv. 23; Rev. i. 18; xx. 1 ^oPsa. cx. 6; Hab. iii. 13——^pPsa. lv. 23——^qNum. xxi. 33——^rExod. xiv. 22——^sPsa. lviii. 10——^tOr, *red* ^u1 Kings xxi. 19——^v1 Chron. xiii. 8; xv. 16; Psa. xlvii. 5

Verse 17. *The chariots of God* are *twenty thousand*] רבתים אלפי שנאן *ribbothayim alpey shinan,* "two myriads of thousands doubled." Does not this mean simply *forty thousand?* A myriad is 10,000; two myriads, 20,000; these doubled, 40,000. Or thus: 10,000+10,000+20,-000=40,000. The Targum says, "The chariots of God are two myriads; *two thousand* angels draw them; the majesty of God rests upon them in holiness on Mount Sinai." But what does this mean? We must die to know.

Verse 18. *Thou hast ascended on high*] When the ark had reached the top of Sion, and was deposited in the place assigned for it, the singers joined in the following chorus. This seems to be an allusion to a *military triumph.* The conqueror was placed on a very elevated chariot.

Led captivity captive] The conquered kings and generals were usually tied behind the chariot of the conqueror—bound to it, bound together, and walked after it, to grace the triumph of the victor.

Thou hast received gifts for men] "And *gave* gifts *unto* men;" Eph. iv. 8. At such times the conqueror threw money among the crowd. *Thou hast received gifts among men,* באדם *baadam,* IN MAN, in human nature; and *God manifest in the flesh* dwells among mortals! Thanks be to God for his unspeakable GIFT! By establishing his *abode among the rebellious,* the prophet may refer to the conquest of the land of Canaan, and the country beyond Jordan.

Yea, for the rebellious also] Even to the rebellious. Those who were his enemies, who traduced his character and operations, and those who fought against him now submit to him, and share his munificence; for it is the property of a hero to be generous.

That the Lord God might dwell among them.]

יה אלהים *yah Elohim,* the *self-existing God;* see on ver. 4. The conqueror now coming to fix his abode among the conquered people to organize them under his laws, to govern and dispense justice among them. The whole of this is very properly applied by St. Paul, Eph. iv. 5, to the *resurrection and glory of Christ;*

where the reader is requested to consult the note.

Verse 19. *Blessed be the Lord, who daily loadeth us*] With benefits is not in the text. Perhaps it would be better to translate the clause thus: "Blessed be Adonai, our Prop day by day, who supports us." Or, "Blessed be the Lord, who supports us day by day." Or as the *Vulgate, Septuagint,* and *Arabic:* "Blessed be the Lord daily, our God who makes our journey prosperous; even the God of our salvation." The *Syriac,* "Blessed be the Lord daily, who hath chosen our inheritance." The word עמם *amas,* which we translate *to load,* signifies to *lift, bear up, support,* or *to bear a burden for another.* Hence it would not be going far from the ideal meaning to translate: "Blessed be the Lord day by day, who bears our burdens for us." But *loadeth us with benefits* is neither a *translation* nor *meaning.*

Verse 20. *The issues from death.*] The *going out* or *exodus* from *death*—from the land of Egypt and house of bondage. Or the expression may mean, Life and death are in the hand of God. "He can create, and he destroy."

Verse 21. *The hairy scalp*] קדקד שער *kodkod sear.* Does this mean any thing like the Indian *scalping?* Or does it refer to a *crest* on a *helmet* or *headcap?* I suppose the latter.

Verse 22. *From the depths of the sea*] All this seems to speak of the defeat of the Egyptians, and the miraculous passage of the Red Sea.

Verse 23. *That thy foot may be dipped in the blood*] God will make such a slaughter among his enemies, the Amorites, that thou shalt walk over their dead bodies; and beasts of prey shall feed upon them.

Verse 24. *They have seen thy goings*] These kings of the Amorites have seen thy terrible majesty in their discomfiture, and the slaughter of their subjects.

Verse 25. *The singers went before*] This verse appears to be a description of the procession.

Verse 26. *Bless ye God*] This is what they sung.

A. M. cir. 2962
B. C. cir. 1042
Davidis, Regis
Israelitarum,
cir. annum
14
the Lord, [w]from [x]the fountain of Israel.

27 There is [y]little Benjamin *with* their ruler, the princes of Judah [z]*and* their council, the princes of Zebulun, *and* the princes of Naphtali.

28 Thy God hath [a]commanded thy strength: strengthen, O God, that which thou hast wrought for us.

29 Because of thy temple at Jerusalem [b]shall kings bring presents unto thee.

30 Rebuke [c]the company of spearmen, [d]the multitude of the bulls, with the calves of the people, *till every one* [e]submit himself with pieces of silver: [f]scatter thou the people *that* delight in war.

A. M. cir. 2962
B. C. cir. 1042
Davidis, Regis
Israelitarum,
cir. annum
14
31 [g]Princes shall come out of Egypt; [h]Ethiopia shall soon [i]stretch out her hands unto God.

32 Sing unto God, ye kingdoms of the earth; O sing praises unto the LORD; Selah:

33 To him [k]that rideth upon the heavens of heavens, *which were* of old; lo, [l]he doth [m]send out his voice, *and that* a mighty voice.

34 [n]Ascribe ye strength unto God: his excellency *is* over Israel, and his strength *is* in the [o]clouds.

35 O God, [p]*thou art* terrible out of thy holy places: the God of Israel *is* he that giveth strength and power unto *his* people. Blessed *be* God.

---

[w]Or, ye that are *of the fountain of Israel*——[x]Deut. xxxiii. 28; Isa. xlviii. 1——[y]1 Sam. ix. 21——[z]Or, with *their company*——[a]So Psa. xlii. 8——[b]1 Kings x. 10, 24, 25; 2 Chron. xxxii. 23; Psa. lxxii. 10; lxxvi. 11; Isa. lx. 16, 17——[c]Or, *the beast of the reeds;* Jer. li. 32, 33 [d]Psa. xxii. 12

[e]2 Sam. viii. 2, 6——[f]Or, *he scattereth*——[g]Isa. xix. 19, 21——[h]Psa. lxxii. 9; Isa. xlv. 14; Zeph. iii. 10 Acts viii. 27——[i]Psa. xliv. 20——[k]Psa. xviii. 10. civ. 3; ver. 4——[l]Psa. xxix. 3, &c.——[m]Heb. *give* [n]Psa. xxix. 1——[o]Or, *heavens*——[p]Psa. xlv. 4; lxv. 5; lxvi. 3; lxxvi. 12

Verse 27. *There is little Benjamin*] This is a description of another part of the procession.

Verse 28. *Thy God hath commanded*] This and the following verses is what they sung.

Verse 30. *Rebuke the company of spearmen*] חית קנה *chaiyath kaneh, the wild beast of the reed*—the crocodile or hippopotamus, the emblem of Pharaoh and the Egyptians: thus all the *Versions*. Our translators have mistaken the meaning; but they have put the true sense in the *margin*.

Verse 31. *Ethiopia shall soon stretch out her hands unto God.*] This verse had its literal fulfilment under Solomon, when Egypt formed an alliance with that king by his marriage with Pharaoh's daughter; and when the queen of Sheba came to Jerusalem to hear the wisdom of Solomon. But as this may be a *prophetic declaration* of the spread of Christianity, it was literally fulfilled after the resurrection of our Lord. There were *Egyptians* at Jerusalem on the day of Pentecost, who, St. Hilary tells us, on their return to their own country proclaimed what they had seen, and became in that country the ambassadors of Christ. The *Ethiopian eunuch* was one of the first among the Gentiles who received the Gospel. Thus *princes* or *chief men came out of Egypt*, and *Ethiopia stretched out her hands to God*. The words themselves refer to the sending ambassadors, and making alliances. The Hebrew is very emphatic: כוש תריץ ידיו לאלהים *cush tarits yadaiv lelohim; Cush will cause her hands to run out to God*. She will, with great *alacrity* and delight, surrender her *power* and *influence* unto God. The *Chaldee* paraphrases well: "The sons of Cush will run, that they may spread out their hands in prayer before God."

Verse 32. *Sing unto God*] All the inhabitants of the earth are invited to sing unto God, to acknowledge him as their God, and give him the praise due to his name.

Verse 33. *Rideth upon the heavens*] He who manages the heavens, directing their course

and influence, he formed every orb, ascertained its motion, proportioned its solid contents to the orbit in which it was to revolve, and the other bodies which belong to the same system. As an able and skilful rider manages his horse, so does God the sun, moon, planets, and all the hosts of heaven.

He doth send out his voice] At his *word of command* they run, shed, or reflect their light; and without the smallest deviations obey his will.

Mighty voice.] He thunders in the heavens, and men tremble before him.

Verse 34. *His strength is in the clouds.*] This refers to the bursting, rattling, and pounding of thunder and lightning; for all nations have observed that this is an irresistible agent; and even the most enlightened have looked on it as an especial manifestation of the power and sovereignty of God.

Verse 35. *O God, thou art terrible out of thy holy places*] The sanctuary and heaven. Out of the former he had often shone forth with consuming splendour; see the case of Korah and his company: out of the latter he had often appeared in terrible majesty in storms, thunder, lightning, &c.

He that giveth strength and power unto his people.] Therefore that people must be invincible who have this strong and irresistible God for their support.

Blessed be God.] He alone is worthy to be worshipped. Without him nothing is wise, nothing holy, nothing strong; and from him, as the inexhaustible Fountain, all good must be derived. His *mercy* over his creatures is equal to his *majesty* in the universe; and as he has all good in his possession, so is he willing to deal it out, to supply the utmost necessities of his creatures. Blessed be God! The *Arabic* adds, *Alleluiah!*

The best *analysis* I find of this Psalm is that by Bishop Nicholson. I shall give it at large, begging the reader to refer particularly to those passages on which the preceding notes are written, as in some of them the analysis gives a different view of the subject. The old Psalter gives the whole Psalm a spiritual and mystical interpretation. And this is commonly the case in the commentaries of the *fathers*.

ANALYSIS OF THE SIXTY-EIGHTH PSALM

There are many conjectures as to the occasion of the composing of this Psalm; but the most probable is, that it was composed by *David* when he brought up the ark of God, which was the type of the Church and symbol of God's presence, to Jerusalem. After the ark was sent home by the Philistines, it rested first in the obscure lodge of *Aminadab;* it then for a time stayed with Obed-edom, nearly sixty years in both places. It was David's care to provide a fit room for it in the head of the tribes, even in his own city; and to express his joy, and honour the solemnity, David led the way, dancing with all his might in a linen ephod; and all the house of *Israel* followed with shouts and instruments of music in a triumphant manner. Now, that the choir might not want to know how to express their joyful affections, the sweet singer of Israel made this anthem, beginning the verse himself, as was commanded at the removal of the ark, Num. x. 35. The Psalm has *six* parts:—

I. The entrance, or exordium, ver. 1-4.

II. The invitation to praise God, ver. 4.

III. The confirmation of it by many arguments, ver. 4-24.

IV. A lively description of triumph, or pomp of the ark's deportation, ver. 24-28.

V. A petition, which has three parts, ver. 28-31.

VI. An exhortation to all nations to praise God, ver. 31 to the end.

I. "Let God arise" is either a prayer or acclamation; a prayer that he would, or an acclamation that he does, show his power and presence. Of which the consequence would be double:—

1. Towards his enemies, destruction; for he prays, "Let his enemies be scattered; let those that hate him fly before him."

He illustrates it by a twofold comparison:—

(1) "As smoke (when it is at the highest) is driven away, so drive them away."

(2) "As wax melteth before the fire, so let the wicked perish in the presence of God."

2. Towards good men, his servants; which is quite contrary to the other: "Let the righteous be glad; let them rejoice before God; yea, let them exceedingly rejoice." Thus it happened; for when the *ark* was taken by the *Philistines*, the glory was departed from *Israel*, and there was nothing but sadness and sorrow: but with the return of the *ark* the glory returned and all was joy and gladness.

II. And so, by an apostrophe, he turns his speech to all good men, and exhorts them to praise God.

1. "Sing unto God." Let it be done with your voice publicly.

2. *Psallite:* "Sing praises to his name," with instruments of music."

3. "Extol him." Show his way, as in a triumph. Thus, when our Saviour rode into Jerusalem they cut down branches, and strewed their garments in the way.

III. And so David enters upon his confirmation, producing his reasons why they should praise God.

1. Drawn from his majesty: "He rideth upon the heavens;" that is, he rules in the heavens.

2. From the essence: "By his name Jah," the contraction of Jehovah, *I am.* He gives essence to all things; therefore, "rejoice before him."

3. From his general providence and goodness towards his Church.

(1) "He is the father of the fatherless." Loves, cares, and provides an inheritance for them.

(2) "A judge of the widows." He cares for his people when deserted, and for whom no man cares, and when exposed to injury. Such is God in his holy habitation; whose presence is represented by this ark.

(3) "God setteth the solitary in families." He makes the barren woman to keep house, and to be the joyful mother of children. As also the barren woman—the Gentile Church that had no husband, to bring forth children to God.

(4) He brings forth those which are bound with chains; as Joseph, Jeremiah, Daniel, Peter, Paul.

4. On the contrary: "But the rebellious dwell in a dry land;" perish with want and hunger.

IV. From his special providence toward his people *Israel*, which he introduces by an elegant apostrophe: "O God, when thou wentest forth before thy people;" thus amplified:—

1. God's going before them, and marching along with them in *Egypt*, in the wilderness. These signs manifested his presence: "The earth shook, the heavens also dropped at the presence of God: even Sinai itself was moved at the presence of God, the God of Israel."

2. God's provision for them after he gave them the possession of the good land. He fed, sustained them there, counted them his inheritance, and gave them rain and fruitful seasons: "Thou, O God, didst send a plentiful rain, whereby thou didst confirm thine inheritance, when it was weary. The congregation hath dwelt therein: thou, O God, hast prepared of thy goodness for the poor."

3. The victories he gave them over their enemies, ver. 12, which he prefaces by imitation of the song of the victory, sung usually by the women and damsels of those times, ver. 11: "The Lord gave the word," that is, either the *word of war, or* else the *song;* and then "Great was the company of those that published it." As Miriam, Deborah, &c. And in these songs they sang, "Kings of armies did flee apace; and she that tarried at home divided the spoil." So great was the prey.

4. The deliverance he sends from troubles, and the joy he gives after them. "Though ye have lien among the pots," that is, cast aside as some useless or broken pot, the offscouring of all things; "yet shall ye be as the wings of a dove

covered with silver, and her feathers with yellow gold;" i. e., shining and glorious. The allusion seems to be taken from some standard, whose portraiture and device was a dove so overlaid. The Babylonian ensign was a dove. But see the note on this passage.

And this he farther declares by another similitude: "When the Almighty scattered kings in it:" or *for her, i. e.,* his Church, *it was white*—glittering, glorious, to be seen afar off; "it was white as snow in Salmon," with which it is generally covered.

5. From God's especial presence among them, which, that he might make it more evident, David enters upon the commendation of the hill of Sion to which the ark was at this time brought, comparing it with other hills, especially with *Bashan.* That is a hill of God; a high, plentiful, and fertile hill. As if he had said, So much I grant. But, "why leap ye, ye high hills?" Why are ye so proud? Why do ye boast your vines, your fruits, your pastures, your cattle? Sion has the pre-eminence of you all in two respects:—

1. For God's continual habitation and common presence is there: "This is the hill which God desireth to dwell in; yea, the Lord will dwell in it for ever."

2. For his defence of it. "The chariots of God are twenty thousand, even thousands of angels:" and these are for the defence of Sion, his Church; "for God is among them as in Sinai, in the holy place;" in glory and majesty, in Sinai, and in Sion.

And yet he goes on to persuade us to praise God, 1. For his strange and wonderful works. 2. For the performance of his promises. Among his great works there was none so glorious as the ascension of our Saviour, of which the ark's ascension to Jerusalem at this time was a type.

First. 1. Before the ark David and the people used this acclamation: "Thou hast ascended on high." Thou, O God, whose presence is shadowed out by the ark, hast ascended from an obscure house to a kingly palace, *Sion.*

2. "Thou hast led captivity captive;" those that led us captives being captives themselves, and now led in *triumph.*

3. "Thou hast received gifts for men;" spoils and gifts from the conquered kings; or who may become homagers unto him, and redeem their peace.

4. "Yea, for the rebellious also:" Formerly so, but now tributaries.

5. "That the Lord God might dwell among them;" might have a certain place to dwell in; and the ark not be carried, as before, from place to place.

This is the literal sense; but the mystical refers to our Saviour's ascension. St. Paul says, Eph. iv. 8:

1. "Thou hast ascended on high:" when the cloud carried him from earth to heaven.

2. "Thou hast led captivity," those who captured us, "captive;" death, the devil, sin, the power of hell, the curse of the law.

3. "He received, and gave gifts to men:" The

apostles, *evangelists, prophets, doctors,* and *teachers,* were these gifts—graces, gifts of the Spirit.

4. "Yea, for the rebellious also:" Paul, a persecutor; Austin, a Manichæan.

5. "That the Lord God might dwell among them:" for to that end St. Paul says these gifts were given, "to the work of the ministry, to the edification of the Church, to the building up of the body of Christ." Eph. iv. 12, &c.

The two effects of his ascension then were, one towards his enemies, the other for his friends: "When thou ascendest up on high,"—

1. "Thou leddest captivity captive:" this was the consequence to his enemies.

2. "Thou receivedst, and gavest gifts:" This for his friends. For which he sings, "Blessed be God;" for he comes over both again:—

1. The gifts to his friends: "Blessed be the Lord, who daily loadeth us with benefits, even the God of our salvation." "He that is our God is the God of salvation; and unto God the Lord belong the issues from death." He knows many ways to deliver in death itself, when there is no hope.

2. The conquest of his enemies; for such he counts obstinate impenitent sinners; those he will destroy: "God shall wound the head of his enemies, and the hairy scalp of such a one as goeth on still in his trespasses."

Secondly, His last argument is, God's performance of his promise to save them. When you were in the wilderness; when you fought with *Og,* king of *Bashan;* when at the Red Sea, I delivered you. The Lord saith still to his people:—

1. "I will bring again from Bashan;" from equally great dangers.

2. "I will bring my people again from the depths of the sea:" when there is no hope.

3. And for thy enemies, they shall be destroyed by a great effusion of blood: "That thy foot may be dipped in the blood of thine enemies, and the tongue of thy dogs in the same;" thou shalt waste, and make a great slaughter.

4. And now he descends to set before our eyes the pomp and show which was used in the ascent and bringing back of the *ark,* and the proceeding of it.

1. The people were present to witness it: "They have seen thy goings, O God; even the goings of my God, my King, in the sanctuary."

2. The manner of the pomp: "The singers went before, the players on instruments followed after; among them were the damsels playing with timbrels."

3. In the pomp they were not silent; and that they be not, he exhorts them: "Bless ye God in the congregations, even the Lord, from the fountain of Israel,"—Jacob's posterity.

4. And he gives in the catalogue of the tribes that were present, but these especially,—

1. "There is little Benjamin," Jacob's youngest son, or now the least, wasted with war, "with their ruler," the chief prince of their tribe.

2. "The princes of Judah, and their council."

3. "The princes of Zebulun, and the princes of Naphtali;" the farthest tribes, therefore the nearest.

V. And in the midst of the pomp he makes a prayer which has three vows, before which he prefixes the acknowledgment that all the power and strength of *Israel* was from God: "Thy God hath commanded thy strength." He then prays,—

1. For the confirmation, establishment, and continuance of this strength: "Strengthen, O God, that which thou hast wrought for us;" and let this be evinced "by the kings and tributaries that shall bring gifts. Because of thy temple at Jerusalem shall kings bring presents unto thee."

2. For the conquest and subduing of the enemy, until they become tributaries, and do homage: "Rebuke the company of spearmen, the multitude of the bulls, with the calves of the people;" kings, princes, and their potent subjects; "till every one submit himself with pieces of silver: scatter thou the people that delight in war." See the note.

3. For the increase of Christ's kingdom, of which David was but a type, by the access of the *Gentiles*. "Princes shall come out of Egypt; Ethiopia shall soon stretch out her hands unto God." These, by a *synecdoche*, being put for all nations.

VI. This excellent Psalm draws now towards a conclusion; and it is a resumption of that which he principally intended; that is, that God be blessed, honoured, praised. He first exhorts, then shows the reasons for it.

1. He exhorts all nations to perform this duty: at first, the Jews, but now all universally: "Sing unto God, ye kingdoms of the earth; O sing praises unto the Lord."

2. His reasons to induce them to do it.
The majesty of God testified,—

1. By his works: "To him that rideth upon the heaven of heavens, which were of old."

2. His power, in his thunder, in his word: "He doth send out his voice, and that a mighty voice."

3. His wise protection of and providence over his people: "Ascribe ye strength unto God: his excellency is over Israel, and his strength is in the clouds."

4. His communication of himself to his Church in particular: 1. "O God, thou art terrible out of thy holy places." 2. "The God of Israel is he that giveth strength and power unto his people." 3. "Blessed be God." With this *epiphonema* he concludes.

PSALM LXIX

The psalmist describes his afflicted state, and the wickedness of his adversaries, 1–21; he declares the miseries that should come upon his enemies, 22–28; enlarges on his afflicted state, and expresses his confidence in God, 29–34; prophesies the restoration of the Jews to their own land and temple, 35, 36.

XIII. DAY. EVENING PRAYER

To the chief Musician ªupon Shoshannim, *A Psalm* of David

SAVE me, O God; for ᵇthe waters are come in unto *my* soul.

2 ᶜI sink in ᵈdeep mire, where *there is* no standing: I am come into ᵉdeep waters, where the floods overflow me.

3 ᶠI am weary of my crying: my throat is dried: ᵍmine eyes fail while I wait for my God.

4 They that ʰhate me without a cause are more than the hairs of mine head: they that would destroy me, *being* mine enemies wrongfully, are mighty: then I restored *that* which I took not away.

ªPsa. xlv. title——ᵇVer. 2, 14, 15; Jonah ii. 5——ᶜPsa. xl. 2——ᵈHeb. *the mire of depth*

ᵉHeb. *depth of waters*——ᶠPsa. vi. 6——ᵍPsa. cxix. 82, 123; Isa. xxxviii. 14——ʰPsa. xxxv. 19; John xv. 25

NOTES ON PSALM LXIX

The *title* is: "To the chief Musician upon Shoshannim, *A Psalm* of David." See this title explained on Psalm xlv.

The Psalm is supposed to have been written *during the captivity*, and to have been the work of some Levite Divinely inspired. It is a very fine composition, equal to most in the Psalter. Several portions of it seem to have a reference to our Lord; to his advent, passion, resurrection, the vocation of the Gentiles, the establishment of the Christian Church, and the reprobation of the Jews. The *ninth* verse is quoted by St. John, chap. ii. 17. The *twenty-first* verse is quoted by St. *Matthew*, chap. xxvii. 34, 48; by St. *Mark*, chap. xv. 23; by St. *John*, chap. xix. 29; and applied to the sufferings of our Lord, in the treatment he received from the Jews. St. *Paul* quotes the *twenty-second* as a prophecy of the wickedness of the Jews, and the punishment they were to receive. He quotes the *twenty-third* verse in the same way. See the marginal references. Those portions which the writers of the New Testament apply to our Lord, we may apply also; of others we should be careful.

Verse 1. *The waters are come in unto* my *soul.*] I am in the deepest distress. The waters have broken their dikes, and are just ready to sweep me away! Save me, Lord! In such circumstances I can have no other help.

In the *first, second, third, fourteenth,* and *fifteenth* verses, the psalmist, speaking in the person of the captives in Babylon, compares their captivity to an *abyss of waters*, breaking all bounds, and ready to swallow them up; to a *deep mire*, in which there was no solid bottom, and no *standing*; and to a *pit*, in which they were about to *be inclosed* for ever. This is strongly figurative, and very expressive.

Verse 3. *I am weary of my crying*] A pathetic description of the state of the poor captives for about *seventy* years.

Verse 4. *Then I restored* that *which I took not away.*] I think, with Calmet, that this is

5 O God, thou knowest my foolishness; and my ¹sins are not hid from thee.

6 Let not them that wait on thee, O Lord God of hosts, be ashamed for my sake: let not those that seek thee be confounded for my sake, O God of Israel.

7 Because for thy sake I have borne reproach; shame hath covered my face.

8 ᵏI am become a stranger unto my brethren, and an alien unto my mother's children.

9 ˡFor the zeal of thine house hath eaten me up: ᵐand the reproaches of them that reproached thee are fallen upon me.

10 ⁿWhen I wept, *and chastened* my soul with fasting, that was to my reproach.

11 I made sackcloth also my garment; ᵒand I became a proverb to them.

12 They that sit in the gate speak against me; and ᵖI *was* the song of the ᑫdrunkards.

13 But as for me, my prayer *is* unto thee, O Lord, ʳ*in* an acceptable time; O God, in the multitude of thy mercy hear me, in the truth of thy salvation.

14 Deliver me out of the mire, and let me not sink: ˢlet me be delivered from them that hate me, and out of ᵗthe deep waters.

15 Let not the waterflood overflow me, neither let the deep swallow me up, and let not the pit ᵘshut her mouth upon me.

16 Hear me, O Lord; ᵛfor thy loving-kindness *is* good: ʷturn unto me according to the multitude of thy tender mercies.

17 And ˣhide not thy face from thy servant; for I am in trouble: ʸhear me speedily.

ˡHeb. *guiltiness*——ᵏPsa. xxxi. 11; Isa. liii. 3; John i. 11; vii. 5——ˡPsa. cxix. 139; John ii. 17——ᵐSee Psa. lxxxix. 50, 51; Rom. xv. 3——ⁿPsa. xxxv. 13, 14——ᵒ1 Kings ix. 7; Jer. xxiv. 9——ᵖJob xxx. 9; Psa. xxxv.15, 16

ᑫHeb. *drinkers of strong drink*——ʳIsa. xlix. 8; lv. 6; 2 Cor. vi. 2——ˢPsa. cxliv. 7——ᵗVer. 1, 2, 15——ᵘNum. xvi. 33——ᵛPsa. lxiii. 3——ʷPsa. xxv. 16; lxxxvi. 16 ˣPsa. xxvii. 9; cii. 2——ʸHeb. *make haste to hear me*

---

a sort of *proverbial* expression, like such as these, "Those who suffered the wrong, pay the costs." Delirant reges, plectuntur Achivi. "Kings sin, and the people are punished." "The fathers have eaten sour grapes, and the children's teeth are set on edge." Our fathers have grievously sinned against the Lord, and we their posterity suffer for it. See on verse 12. Some have applied it to our Lord. I restored, by my suffering and death, that image of God and the Divine favour, which I took not away. That is, In my *human nature* I expiated the crime that *human beings* had committed against God. But such applications are very gratuitous.

Verse 5. *Thou knowest my foolishness*] Though we have been brought into captivity in consequence of the crimes of our fathers, yet we have guilt enough of our own to merit a continuation of our miseries. How can such words as are in this verse be attributed to our blessed Lord, however they may be twisted or turned?

Verse 6. *Be ashamed for my sake*] The sins of the Jews were a great stumbling-block in the way of the conversion of the Gentiles. They had been the *peculiar people* of the Lord. "How," say the Gentiles, "can a pure and holy Being love such people?" They were now *punished* for their crimes. "How," say the Gentiles, "can God deal so hardly with those whom he professes to love?" The pious among the captives felt keenly, because this reproach seemed to fall upon their gracious and merciful God.

Verse 7. *For thy sake I have borne reproach*] The Gentiles have said, "Why such an obstinate attachment to the *worship* of a Being who treats you so rigorously, and who interests not himself in your comfort and deliverance?" And in these cutting reproaches some of the ungodly *Jews* took a part: "I am an alien to my mother's children."

Verse 9. *The zeal of thine house hath eaten me up*] The strong desire to promote thy glory

has absorbed all others. All the desires of my *body* and *soul* are wrapped up in this. This verse is very properly applied to our Lord, John ii. 17, who *went about doing good;* and gave up his life, not only for the redemption of man, but to "magnify the law, and make it honourable."

Verse 12. *They that sit in the gate*] At the gates were the courts for public justice; *there* were complaints lodged, and causes heard. No doubt many vexatious complaints were made against the poor captives; and false accusations, through which they grievously suffered; so that, literally, they were often "obliged to restore that which they had not taken away." See ver. 4.

The song of the drunkards.] These poor miserable people were exposed to all sorts of indignities. Though the conduct is base, the exultation over a fallen enemy is frequent. How miserable was this lot! Forsaken by friends, scorned by enemies, insulted by inferiors; the scoff of libertines, and the song of drunkards; besides hard travail of body, miserably lodged and fed; with the burning crown of all, a deep load of guilt upon the conscience. To such a life any death was preferable.

Verse 13. *My prayer is unto thee, O Lord,* in *an acceptable time*] This seems to refer to the *end of the captivity,* which Jeremiah had said should last *seventy years,* Jer. xxv. 11, 12: "The whole land shall be a desolation, and an astonishment; and these nations shall serve the king of Babylon seventy years. And it shall come to pass, when seventy years are accomplished, that I will punish the king of Babylon," &c. The conclusion of this period was the *accepted time* of which the psalmist speaks. *Now,* they incessantly pray for the fulfilment of the promise made by Jeremiah: and to hear them, would be the *truth* of God's *salvation;* it would show the promise to be *true,* because 'the *salvation*—the *deliverance,* was granted.

Verse 16. *Thy loving-kindness is good*] The

18 Draw nigh unto my soul, *and* redeem it: deliver me because of mine enemies.

19 Thou hast known ^zmy reproach, and my shame, and my dishonour: mine adversaries *are* all before thee.

20 Reproach hath broken my heart; and I am full of heaviness: and I ^alooked *for some* ^bto take pity, but *there was* none; and for ^ccomforters, but I found none.

21 They gave me also gall for my meat; ^dand in my thirst they gave me vinegar to drink.

22 ^eLet their table become a snare before them: and *that which should have been* for *their* welfare, *let it become* a trap.

23 ^fLet their eyes be darkened, that they see not; and make their loins continually to shake.

24 ^gPour out thine indignation upon them, and let thy wrathful anger take hold of them.

25 ^hLet ⁱtheir habitation be desolate; *and* ^klet none dwell in their tents.

26 For ^lthey persecute ^m*him* whom thou hast smitten; and they talk to the grief of ⁿthose whom thou hast wounded.

27 ^oAdd ^piniquity unto their iniquity: ^qand let them not come into thy righteousness.

28 Let them ^rbe blotted out of the book of the living, ^sand not be written with the righteous.

29 But I *am* poor and sorrowful: let thy salvation, O God, set me up on high.

30 ^tI will praise the name of God with a song, and will magnify him with thanksgiving.

31 ^u*This* also shall please the LORD better than an ox *or* bullock that hath horns and hoofs.

---

^zPsa. xxii. 6, 7; Isa. liii. 3; Heb. xii. 2——^aPsa. cxlii. 4; Isa. lxiii. 5——^bHeb. *to lament* with me——^cJob xvi. 2——^dMatt. xxvii. 34, 48; Mark xv. 23; John xix. 29 ^eRom. xi. 9, 10——^fIsa. vi. 9, 10; John xii. 39, 40; Rom. xi. 10; 2 Cor. iii. 14——^g1 Thess. ii. 16——^hMatt. xxiii. 38; Acts i. 20——ⁱHeb. *their palace*——^kHeb. *let there*

not be a dweller——^lSee 2 Chron. xxviii. 9; Zech. i. 15 ^mIsa. liii. 4——ⁿHeb. *thy wounded*——^oRom. i. 28 ^pOr, *punishment of iniquity*——^qIsa. xxvi. 10; Rom. ix. 31——^rExod. xxxii. 32; Phil. iv. 3; Rev. iii. 5; xiii. 8——^sEzek. i. 39; Luke x. 20; Heb. xii. 23——^tPsa. xxviii. 7——^uPsa. l.13, 14, 23

---

word חסד *chesed* signifies *exuberance of kindness;* and the word רחמים *rachamim*, which we translate *tender mercies*, signifies such *affection* as *mothers* bear to their *young:* and in God, there is רב *rob*, a *multitude*, of such tender *mercies* towards the children of men!

Verse 18. *Deliver me because of mine enemies.*] Probably they now began to think that the redemption of these captives was not an impossible thing; that it was not far off; and therefore they had great rage, because they found their time was but short.

Verse 19. *Thou hast known my reproach*] This is one of the most forcible appeals to mercy and compassion that was ever made. The language of these two verses is inimitable; and the sentiment cannot be mended. I can devise no comment that would not lessen their effect.

Verse 21. *They gave me also gall for my meat*] Even the *food*, necessary to preserve us in their slavery, was frequently mingled with what rendered it unpleasant and disgusting, though not absolutely unwholesome. And vinegar, sour small wines, was given us for our beverage. This is applied to our Lord, Matt. xxvii. 34, where the reader is requested to consult the notes.

Verse 22. *Let their table become a snare*] The execrations here and in the following verses should be read in the *future* tense, because they are *predictive;* and not in the *imperative* mood, as if they were the offspring of the psalmist's resentment: "Their table SHALL become a snare;—their eyes SHALL be darkened; —thou WILT pour out thine indignation upon them;—thy wrathful anger SHALL take hold of them;—their habitation SHALL be desolate,— and none SHALL dwell in their tents."

The psalmist *prophesies* that the evils which

they had inflicted on the Israelites should be visited on themselves; that as they had made them *eat, drink, labour,* and *suffer,* so God should in his judgment treat them.

Verse 27. *Add iniquity unto their iniquity*]

תנה עון על עונם *tenah avon al avonam; give iniquity,* that is, the *reward* of it, *upon* or *for their iniquity.* Or, as the original signifies *perverseness,* treat their *perverseness* with *perverseness:* act, in thy judgments, as *crookedly* towards them as they dealt *crookedly* towards thee. They shall get, in the way of punishment, what they have dealt out in the way of oppression.

Verse 28. *Let them be blotted out*] They *shall* be blotted out from the land of the living. They shall *be cut off from life,* which they have forfeited by their cruelty and oppression. The psalmist is speaking of *retributive* justice; and in this sense all these passages are to be understood.

And not be written with the righteous.] They shall have no title to that *long life* which God has promised to his followers.

Verse 29. *I am poor and sorrowful*] Literally, *I am laid low, and full of pain* or *grief.* Hence the prayer, "Let thy salvation, O God, set me on high!" My oppression has laid me *low;* thy salvation shall make me *high!*

Verse 31. *An ox or bullock that hath horns and hoofs.*] Oxen offered in sacrifice had their horns and hoofs *gilded;* and the psalmist might mention these parts of the victim more particularly, because they were more *conspicuous.* Others think that *full-grown* animals are intended, those that had perfect *horns,* in opposition to *calves* or *steers.* I think the first the preferable sense; for the horns, &c., of consecrated animals are thus ornamented in the east to the present day.

32 ⱽThe ʷhumble shall see *this, and* be glad: and ˣyour heart shall live that seek God.

33 For the LORD heareth the poor, and despiseth not ʸhis prisoners.

34 ᶻLet the heaven and earth praise him, the seas, ᵃand every thing that ᵇmoveth therein.

35 ᶜFor God will save Zion, and will build the cities of Judah: that they may dwell there, and have it in possession.

36 ᵈThe seed also of his servants shall inherit it: and they that love his name shall dwell therein.

ⱽPsalm xxxiv. 2——ʷOr, *meek*——ˣPsa. xxii. 26 ʸEph. iii. 1——ᶻPsa. xcvi. 11; cxlviii. 1; Isa. xliv. 23;

xlix. 13——ᵃIsa. lv. 12——ᵇHeb. *creepeth*——ᶜPsa. li. 18; Isa. xliv. 26——ᵈPsa. cii. 28

Verse 32. *The humble shall see* this, *and be glad*] Those who are *low*, pressed down by misfortune or cruelty, shall see this and take courage; expecting that thou wilt lift *them* up also; and thus the heart of those who seek the Lord shall be *revived*.

Verse 33. *For the Lord heareth the poor*] אביונים *cbyonim, of the beggars.* He perhaps refers here to the case of the captives, many of whom were reduced to the most abject state, so as to be obliged to beg bread from their heathen oppressors.

His prisoners.] The captives, shut up by his judgments in Chaldea, without any civil liberty, like culprits in a prison.

Verse 34. *Let the heaven and earth praise him*] The psalmist has the fullest confidence that God will turn their captivity, and therefore calls upon all creatures to magnify him for his mercy.

Verse 35. *God will save Zion*] This fixes the Psalm to the time of the captivity. There was no *Zion* belonging to the Jews in the time of *Saul*, when those suppose the Psalm to be written who make David the author; for David, after he came to the throne, won the stronghold of Zion from the Jebusites. 2. Sam. v. 7; 1 Chron. xi. 5.

Will build the cities of Judah] This refers to the return from the captivity, when all the destroyed cities should be rebuilt, and the Jews repossess their forfeited heritages. Some apply this to the redemption of the human race; and suppose that *Zion* is the type of the Christian Church into which the Gentiles were to be called. What evangelists and apostles apply to our Lord, we safely may. What others see so clearly in this Psalm relative to Gospel matters, I cannot discern.

ANALYSIS OF THE SIXTY-NINTH PSALM

There are *three* parts in this Psalm:—

I. The psalmist's *prayer*, and the *reasons* for it, ver. 1-21.

II. *Declaration* of God's *judgments* against his enemies, ver. 22-28.

III. His *profession of thanks*, ver. 29-36.

I. His *prayer:* "Save me, O God!" And then his reasons.

1. His present condition: "The waters are come in unto my soul."

2. "I sink in deep mire."

3. "I am come into deep waters."

4. "I am weary of my crying."

5. "My throat is dried" with calling on thee.

6. "Mine eyes fail while I wait for my God."

When he considered his enemies, he found reason to cry. They were,

1. *Malicious:* "They hate me without a cause."

2. *Numerous:* "More than the hairs of my head."

3. *Powerful:* "My enemies are mighty," ver. 1-4.

1. He declares his innocence with respect to their accusations, and the oppression he suffered: "I restored that which I took not away."

2. Begs to be heard, lest he should be confounded before his enemies.

3. Shows that he *suffers* for God's *cause.*

4. He was *zealous* for the Divine worship.

5. He was a deep *penitent.*

On which account he was a subject of reproach:—

1. To the *high*—those who sat in the gate.

2. To the *low* and *base:* "I was the song of the drunkards."

He renews his *petition,* and presses on God to hear him:—

1. Because of his being *ready to sink,* ver. 13-15.

2. Because of *God's goodness, mercy,* and *truth:* "In the multitude of thy mercies," &c.

3. Because he was *God's servant,* and would not desert his Master.

4. Because of his *enemies,* who would have a sinful triumph if he was not delivered.

And he pleads their *ill usage* as a reason why God should help him.

1. They were *scorners,* and God knew it: "They are all before thee," ver. 19.

2. *Reproach* had almost *broken his heart.*

3. His *friends* had *abandoned* him, ver. 20.

4. His *enemies* were *inhuman:* "They gave me gall," &c., ver. 22.

II. *Prophetic declaration of God's judgments* against them:—

1. Their "table should be a snare to them," ver. 22.

2. They should be given up to judicial *blindness,* ver. 23.

3. They should be *enfeebled in their bodies:* "Make their loins shake," ver. 23.

4. God's "wrath should be poured out upon them," ver. 24.

5. Their *country* should be *wasted,* ver. 25.

6. They should have the *punishment* due to their *iniquity,* ver. 27.

7. They should come to an *untimely* death: "Let them be blotted out," ver. 28.

III. His *profession* of *thanks.* Having spoken of his own condition, that he was *poor* and sorrowful, he now breaks out into praise:—

1. "I will praise the name of God," ver. 30.

2. This will be the most *acceptable sacrifice*, ver. 31.

The *effect* of his *deliverance* would be *double:*—

1. It would "gladden the poor," ver. 32, 33.

2. All "creatures would take an interest in it," ver. 34. All shall praise God.

And for this he gives the following *reasons:*—

1. God's *goodness* to his Church: "He will save Zion."

2. He will *confirm his kingdom* among them: "He will build," &c.

3. They shall have peace and security: "That they may dwell there, and have it in possession," ver. 35.

4. All that *love his name* should have it *perpetually*, ver. 36.

The cruel, the oppressor, the scorner, the irreligious, the hypocrite, shall have nothing of God's approbation here, and shall be excluded from his heavenly kingdom for ever.

PSALM LXX

The psalmist prays for speedy deliverance, 1; prays against those who sought his life, 2, 3; and for the blessedness of those who sought God, 4; urges his speedy deliverance, 5.

To the chief Musician, *A Psalm* of David, ªto bring to remembrance

A. M. cir. 2981
B. C. cir. 1023
Davidis, Regis
Israelitarum,
cir. annum
33

MAKE *haste,* ᵇO God, to deliver me; make haste ᶜto help me, O Lord.

2 ᵈLet them be ashamed and confounded that seek after my soul: let them be turned backward, and put to confusion, that desire my hurt.

3 ᵉLet them be turned back for a reward of their shame that say, Aha, aha.

4 Let all those that seek thee rejoice and be glad in thee: and let such as love thy salvation say continually, Let God be magnified.

5 ᶠBut I *am* poor and needy: ᵍmake haste unto me, O God: thou *art* my help and my deliverer; O Lord, make no tarrying.

A. M. cir. 2981
B. C. cir. 1023
Davidis, Regis
Israelitarum,
cir. annum
33

ªPsalm xxxviii. title——ᵇPsalm xl. 13, &c.; lxxi. 12
ᶜHeb. *to my help*

ᵈPsa. xxxv. 4, 26; lxxi. 13——ᵉPsa. xl. 15——ᶠPsa. xl. 17——ᵍPsa. cxli. 1

NOTES ON PSALM LXX

The *title* in the *Hebrew* is, *To the chief Musician, A Psalm of David, to bring to remembrance.* There seems little sense in this title. It seems to intimate that the Psalm was written as a memorial that David had been in sore affliction, and that God had delivered him. So the *Vulgate, Septuagint, Æthiopic,* and *Arabic.* It is almost word for word the same with *the five last verses of* Psalm xl., to the notes on which the reader is referred.

Verse 1. *Make haste to help me*] I am in extreme distress, and the most imminent danger. *Haste to help me, or I am lost.*

Verse 2. *Let them be turned backward*] They are coming in a *body* against me. Lord, stop their progress!

Verse 3. *That say, Aha, aha.*] האח האח *heach! heach!* a note of supreme contempt. See on Psa. xl. 15.

Verse 4. *Let God be magnified.*] Let his glory, mercy, and kindness, continually appear in the *increase* of his own work in the souls of his followers!

Verse 5. *But I* am *poor and needy*] עני ואביון *ani veebyon,* I am a poor man, and a beggar— an *afflicted beggar;* a sense of my poverty causes me to beg.

Thou art *my help*] I know thou hast enough, and to spare; and therefore I come to *thee.*

Make no tarrying.] My wants are many, my danger great, my time short. O God, delay not!

ANALYSIS OF THE SEVENTIETH PSALM

The contents of this Psalm are the following:—

I. The prayer of David for himself, that he may be freed from his enemies, ver. 1, repeated ver. 5.

II. For the speedy overthrow of the wicked, ver. 2, 3.

III. For the prosperity of the godly, ver. 4.

IV. The arguments he uses to induce God to answer his prayer.

1. His miserable condition: "I am poor and needy."

2. God's office: "Thou art my Helper and Redeemer."

For a farther analysis, see at the end of the *fortieth* Psalm.

PSALM LXXI

The prophet, in confidence, prays for God's favour, 1-5; recounts God's kindness to him from youth to old age, 6-9; shows what his adversaries plot against him, and prays for their confusion, 10-13; promises fidelity, and determines to be a diligent preacher of righteousness even in old age, 14-19; takes encouragement in God's mercy, and foresees the confusion of all his adversaries, 20-24.

A. M. cir. 2981
B. C. cir. 1023
Davidis, Regis
Israelitarum,
cir. annum
33

IN [a]thee, O LORD, do I put my trust: let me never be put to confusion.

2 [b]Deliver me in thy righteousness, and cause me to escape: [c]incline thine ear unto me, and save me.

3 [d]Be [e]thou my strong habitation, whereunto I may continually resort: thou hast given [f]commandment to save me; for thou *art* my rock and my fortress.

4 [g]Deliver me, O my God, out of the hand of the wicked, out of the hand of the unrighteous and cruel man.

5 For thou *art* [h]my hope, O Lord GOD: *thou art* my trust from my youth.

6 [i]By thee have I been holden up from the womb: thou art he that took me out of my mother's bowels: my praise *shall be* continually of thee.

7 [k]I am as a wonder unto many; but thou *art* my strong refuge.

A. M. cir. 2981
B. C. cir. 1023
Davidis, Regis
Israelitarum,
cir. annum
33

8 Let [l]my mouth be filled *with* thy praise *and with* thy honour all the day.

9 [m]Cast me not off in the time of old age; forsake me not when my strength faileth.

10 For mine enemies speak against me; and they that [n]lay wait for my soul [o]take counsel together,

11 Saying, God hath forsaken him: persecute and take him; for *there is* none to deliver *him*.

12 [p]O God, be not far from me: O my God, [q]make haste for my help.

13 [r]Let them be confounded *and* consumed that are adversaries to my soul: let them be covered *with* reproach and dishonour that seek my hurt.

14 But I will hope continually, and will yet praise thee more and more.

---

[a]Psalm xxv. 2, 3; xxxi. 1——[b]Psalm xxxi. 1——[c]Psa. xvii. 6——[d]Psalm xxxi. 2, 3——[e]Hebrew, *Be thou to me for a rock of habitation*——[f]Psalm xliv. 4——[g]Psa. cxl. 1, 4——[h]Jer. xvii. 7, 17——[i]Psa. xxii. 9, 10; Isaiah xlvi. 3

[k]Isa. viii. 18; Zech. iii. 8; 1 Cor. iv. 9——[l]Psa. xxxv. 28——[m]Ver. 18——[n]Heb. *watch*, or *observe*——[o]2 Sam. xvii. 1; Matt. xxvii. 1——[p]Psa. xxii. 11, 19; xxxv. 22; xxxviii. 21, 22——[q]Psa. lxx. 1——[r]Ver. 24; Psa. xxxv. 4, 26; xl. 14; lxx. 2

NOTES ON PSALM LXXI

There is no *title* to this Psalm either in the *Hebrew* or *Chaldee;* and the reason is, it was written as a part of the preceding Psalm, as appears by about *twenty-seven* of *Kennicott's* and *De Rossi's* MSS. The *Vulgate, Septuagint, Æthiopic,* and *Arabic,* have, "A Psalm of David for the sons of Jonadab, and the first of those who were led captives." For the *first, second,* and *third* verses, see the notes on their parallels, Psa. xxxi. 1-3.

Verse 3. *Be thou my strong habitation*] Instead of מעון *maon, habitation,* many of *Kennicott's* and *De Rossi's* MSS. read מעוז *maoz, munition* or *defence.* Be thou my rock of defence.

Thou hast given commandment to save me] Thou hast determined my escape, and hast ordered thy angels to guard me. See Psa. xci. 11, 12.

Verse 4. *Out of the hand of the wicked*] Probably his unnatural son *Absalom,* called here רשע *rasha,* the WICKED, because he had violated all laws, human and Divine.

The unrighteous and cruel man.] Probably *Ahithophel* who was the iniquitous counsellor of a wicked and rebellious son.

Verse 5. *My trust from my youth.*] When I was born into the world, thou didst receive me, and thou tookest me under thy especial care. "My praise *shall be* continually of thee." Rather, *I have always made thee my boast.*

Verse 7. *I am as a wonder unto many*] I am כמופת *kemopheth,* "as a portent," or "type:" I am a *typical person;* and many of the things that happen to *me* are to be considered in reference to *him* of whom I am a type. But he may mean, I am a *continual prodigy.* My low estate, my slaying the lion and the bear, conquering

the Philistine, escaping the fury of Saul, and being raised to the throne of Israel, are all so many *wonders* of thy providence, and effects of thy power and grace.

Verse 9. *Cast me not off in the time of old age*] The original might be translated and paraphrased thus: "Thou wilt not cast me off till the time of old age; and according to the failure of my flesh, thou wilt not forsake me." My expectation of rest and happiness will not be deferred till the time that I shall be an aged man. Thou wilt not withdraw thy presence from me as my flesh decays, and as my natural strength abates; but, on the contrary, as my outward man decays, my inward man shall be renewed day by day. It was in David's *old age* that the rebellion of Absalom took place.

Verse 10. *Lay wait for my soul*] They seek to destroy my *life.*

Verse 11. *God hath forsaken him*] "God, who has been his special help all through life, and who has guarded him so that no hand could be raised successfully against him, has now cast him off; therefore we shall easily prevail against him. His present adversity shows that God is no longer his friend." Thus *men* judge. "Secular prosperity is a proof of God's favour: adversity is a proof of his displeasure." But this is not God's way, except in especial judgments, &c. He never manifests his pleasure or displeasure by secular good or ill.

Verse 13. *Let them be confounded*] They *shall* be confounded: these are *prophetic* denunciations.

Verse 14. *I will hope continually*] I shall expect deliverance after deliverance, and blessing after blessing; and, in consequence, I will praise thee more and more. As thy blessings abound, so shall my praises.

A. M. cir. 2981
B. C. cir. 1023
Davidis, Regis
Israelitarum,
cir. annum
33

15 ⁸My mouth shall show forth thy righteousness *and* thy salvation all the day; for ᵗI know not the numbers *thereof.*

16 I will go in the strength of the Lord GOD: I will make mention of thy righteousness, *even* of thine only.

17 O God, thou hast taught me from my youth: and hitherto have I declared thy wondrous works.

18 ᵘNow also ᵛwhen I am old and greyheaded, O God, forsake me not; until I have showed ʷthy strength unto *this* generation, *and* thy power to every one *that* is to come.

19 ˣThy righteousness also, O God, *is* very high, who hast done great things: ʸO God, who *is* like unto thee!

20 ᶻ*Thou,* which hast showed me great and sore troubles, ᵃshalt quicken me again, and shalt bring me up again from the depths of the earth.

21 Thou shalt increase my greatness, and comfort me on every side.

22 I will also praise thee ᵇwith ᶜthe psaltery, *even* thy truth, O my God: unto thee will I sing with the harp, O thou ᵈHoly One of Israel.

23 My lips shall greatly rejoice when I sing unto thee; and ᵉmy soul, which thou hast redeemed.

24 ᶠMy tongue also shall talk of thy righteousness all the day long: for ᵍthey are confounded, for they are brought unto shame, that seek my hurt.

A. M. cir. 2981
B. C. cir. 1023
Davidis, Regis
Israelitarum,
cir. annum
33

ᵃVer. 8, 24; Psa. xxxv. 28——ᵗPsa. xl. 5; cxxxix. 17, 18 ᵘVer. 9——ᵛHeb. *unto old age and grey hairs*——ʷHeb. *thine arm*——ˣPsa. lvii. 10——ʸPsa. xxxv. 10; lxxxvi. 8; lxxxix. 6, 8

ᶻPsa. lx. 5——ᵃHos. vi. 1, 2——ᵇHeb. *with the instrument of psaltery*——ᶜPsa. xcii. 1, 2, 3; cl. 3 ᵈ2 Kings xix. 22; Isa. lx. 9——ᵉPsa. ciii. 4——ᶠVer. 8, 15——ᵍVer. 13

Verse 15. *I know not the numbers*] I must be continually in the spirit of gratitude, praise, and obedience; for thy blessings to me are innumerable.

Verse 16. *I will go*] אבוא *abo,* I will enter, i. e., into the tabernacle, in the strength or *mightinesses of Adonai Jehovah,* the supreme God, who is my *Prop, Stay,* and *Support.*

I will make mention of thy righteousness] I will continually record and celebrate the *acts of thy mercy and goodness.* They are without number, (verse 15,) and of these alone will I speak.

Verse 17. *Thou hast taught me from my youth*] I have had thee for my continual instructor: and thou didst begin to teach me thy fear and love from my tenderest infancy. Those are well taught whom God instructs; and when he teaches, there is no delay in learning.

Verse 18. *Old and grey-headed*] In the *ninth* verse he mentioned the circumstance of *old age;* here he *repeats* it, with the addition of *hoary-headedness,* which, humanly speaking, was calculated to make a deeper impression in his favour. Though all these things are well known to God, and he needs not our information, yet he is pleased to say, "Come now, and let us *reason* together." And when his children plead and reason with him, they are acting precisely as he has commanded.

Verse 19. *Thy righteousness—is very high*] עד מרום *ad marom*—is up to the exalted place, reaches *up* to heaven. The mercy of God fills all *space* and *place.* It crowns in the heavens what it governed upon earth.

Who hast done great things] נדלות *gedoloth.* Thou hast worked *miracles,* and displayed the *greatest acts of power.*

Who is like unto thee!] מי כמוך *mi camocha.* God is alone,—who can resemble him? He is eternal. He can have none *before,* and there can be none *after;* for in the infinite *unity* of his *trinity* he is that eternal, unlimited, impartible, incomprehensible, and uncompounded ineffable Being, whose *essence* is hidden from all created intelligences, and whose *counsels* cannot be fathomed by any creature that even his own hand can form. WHO IS LIKE UNTO THEE! will excite the wonder, amazement, praise, and adoration of angels and men to all eternity.

Verse 20. Thou, *which hast showed me great and sore troubles*] *Multiplied straits* and difficulties. And thou hast only *showed* them. Hadst thou permitted them to have *fallen upon me* with all their own energy and natural consequences, they would have destroyed me. As it was, I was nearly buried under them.

Shalt quicken me again] Shalt revive me—put new life in me. This has been applied to the passion of our Lord, and his resurrection; for it is added, Thou

Shalt bring me up again from the depths of the earth.] Death shall not prey upon my body; thy Holy One can see no corruption. As applicable to David, it might mean his being almost overwhelmed with afflictions; and his deliverance was like a life from the dead.

Verse 21. *Thou shalt increase my greatness*] Thou wilt restore me to my throne and kingdom; and it shall be done in such a way that all shall see it was the hand of God; and I shall have the more honour on the account.

Comfort me on every side.] I shall have friends in all quarters; and the *tribes* on all sides will support me.

Verse 22. *I will also praise thee with the psaltery*] בכלי נבל *bichli nebel,* with the instrument *nebel.* Unto thee will I sing with the harp; בכנור *bechinnor,* with the *kinnor.* Both were *stringed instruments,* and the principal used in the Jewish worship; and with which, or any thing like them, in Divine worship, *we,* as *Christians,* have nothing to do.

Verse 23. *My lips shall greatly rejoice—and my soul*] My *lips* shall use words expressive of my *soul's* happiness and gratitude. Thou hast *redeemed* me; and thou shalt have the eternal praise.

Verse 24. *Talk of thy righteousness*] The *righteousness of God* is frequently used in this

Psalm, and in other places, to signify his justice, judgments, faithfulness, truth, mercy, &c. There are few words of more *general* import in the Bible.

They are confounded] The counsel of Ahithophel is *confounded*, and turned to foolishness; and he was so *ashamed* that he went and hanged himself. As to the vain and wicked Absalom, he met with the fate that he had meditated against his father. Though not yet done, David sees all these things as actually accomplished; for he had got a Divine assurance that God would bring them to pass.

ANALYSIS OF THE SEVENTY-FIRST PSALM

The *parts* of this Psalm, generally, are these *two:*—

I. A *prayer* that God would help and deliver him, which he urges by many arguments, ver. 1-21.

II. His *vow of thanksgiving*, ver. 22 to the end.

I. 1. His petition in general: "Let me never be put to confusion."

2. He intimates the *cause:* "I put my trust in thee," &c., ver. 2.

To induce the Lord to hear, he uses many *arguments*, drawn,—

1. From his *justice* and *equity:* "Deliver me in thy righteousness."

2. From his *word* and *promise:* "Thou hast given commandment," &c.

3. From his *power:* "Thou art my rock," &c.

4. From his *relation* to him: "My God, my hope."

5. From the *qualities* of his *adversaries:* "They were wicked, unrighteous, and cruel."

6. From his *confidence:* "Thou art my hope."

7. From his *gracious providence:* "By thee have I been holden up," &c.

8. From his *thankful heart:* "My praise shall be continually," &c.

9. He had *none to trust to* but GOD: "Thou art my refuge."

3. He resumes his *prayer:* "Cast me not off in the time of old age," &c.

He describes his enemies:—

1. They were continual *calumniators:* "Mine enemies speak against me."

2. They *laboured* to take away his *life.*

3. They *studied mischief* against him: "They take counsel together."

4. Their *words* were *cruel:* "God hath forsaken him; persecute," &c.

4. He resumes his prayer, and predicts his enemies' downfall: "O my God, be not far from me; make haste for my help."

He prays against his enemies,—

1. "Let them be confounded," &c.: they shall be confounded.

2. He expresses his hope: "I will hope continually."

3. And his purpose of *gratitude:* "I will praise thee more and more."

4. He pleads from his *past experience* of God's mercy to him.

1. God had "taught him from his youth" both by his word and Spirit.

2. Hitherto he had "declared God's wondrous works."

3. Therefore, "forsake me not now that I am old and grey-headed."

4. I have still *much to do:* "Until I have showed thy strength," &c.

From all these considerations he feels gratitude, and praises God.

1. Thy righteousness is very high. There is nothing like IT.

2. God is wonderful: "There is none like HIM."

Of all this he had full and satisfactory proof.

1. Thou *hast showed me troubles*—"sore troubles."

2. Yet thou *shalt revive me.*

3. Thou "shalt bring me from the depths of the earth."

4. "Thou shalt increase my greatness."

5. "Thou shalt support me on every side."

II. The SECOND part contains David's *thanksgiving.*

1. He will praise the *truth* of the "Holy One of Israel:" not only with *nebel* and *kinnor*—instruments of music then used,—

2. But with his *lips* and *soul; heart* and *mouth* going together.

3. With his *tongue;* speaking of God's goodness to *others.*

4. And for this reason, "They are confounded, for they are brought to shame that seek my hurt."

PSALM LXXII

David prays to God for Solomon, 1; prescribes Solomon's work, 2; the effects of his administration, 3-7; the extent of his dominion, 8-11; his mercy and kindness to the poor, and the perpetuity of his praise, 12-17. God is blessed for his power and goodness; and the psalmist prays that the whole earth may be filled with his glory, 18-20.

A Psalm ªfor ᵇSolomon

A. M. 2989
B. C. 1015
Davidis, Regis
Israelitarum,
cir. annum
40

GIVE the king thy judgments, O God, and thy righteousness unto the king's son.

2 ᶜHe shall judge thy people with righteousness, and thy poor with judgment.

3 ᵈThe mountains shall bring peace to the people, and the little hills, by righteousness.

4 ᵉHe shall judge the poor of the people, he shall save the children of the needy, and shall break in pieces the oppressor.

A. M. 2989
B. C. 1015
Davidis, Regis
Israelitarum,
cir. annum
40

5 They shall fear thee ᶠas long as the sun and moon endure, throughout all generations.

6 ᵍHe shall come down like rain upon the mown grass: as showers *that* water the earth.

ªOr, *of*——ᵇPsa. cxxvii. title——ᶜIsa. xi. 2, 3, 4; xxxii. 1
ᵈPsa. lxxxv. 10; Isa. xxxii. 17; lii. 7

ᵉIsa. xi. 4——ᶠVer. 7, 17; Psa. lxxxix. 36, 37——ᵍ2 Sam. xxiii. 4; Hos. vi. 3

NOTES ON PSALM LXXII

The *title* לשלמה *lishelomoh*, we translate, *A Psalm for Solomon.* The *Chaldee* says, "By the hand of Solomon, spoken prophetically." The *Syriac*, "A Psalm of David, when he had constituted Solomon king." All the other *Versions* attribute it to *Solomon* himself. But in the conclusion of the Psalm it appears to be attributed to *David.* "The prayers of David the son of Jesse are ended." It is most probably a Psalm of David, composed in his last days, when he had set this beloved son on the throne of the kingdom. "Then," says *Calmet*, "transported with joy and gratitude, he addressed this Psalm to God, in which he prays him to pour out his blessings on the young king, and upon the people. He then, wrapped up in a Divine enthusiasm, ascends to a higher subject; and sings the glory of the Messiah, and the magnificence of his reign. Hence it is that we may see in this Psalm a great number of expressions which cannot relate to Solomon, unless in a hyperbolical and figurative sense; but, applied to Christ, they are literally and rigorously exact."

Verse 1. *Give the king thy judgments*] Let Solomon receive *thy law*, as the civil and ecclesiastical code by which he is to govern the kingdom.

And thy righteousness unto the king's son.] *Righteousness* may signify *equity.* Let him not only rule according to the *strict letter of thy law*, that being the *base* on which all his decisions shall be founded; but let him rule also according to *equity*, that *rigorous justice* may never become *oppressive.* Solomon is called here *the king*, because now set upon the Jewish throne; and he is called *the king's son*, to signify his *right* to that throne on which he now sat.

Verse 2. *He shall judge thy people with righteousness*] With justice and mercy mixed, or according to *equity.*

And thy poor with judgment.] Every one according to the *law* which thou hast *appointed;* but with especial tenderness to the *poor* and *afflicted.*

Verse 3. *The mountains shall bring peace*] Perhaps *mountains* and *hills* are here taken in their *figurative* sense, to signify *princes* and *petty governors;* and it is a prediction that all governors of provinces and magistrates should administer equal justice in their several departments and jurisdictions; so that universal *peace* should be preserved, and the people be every where *prosperous;* for שלום *shalom* signi-

fies both peace and prosperity, for without the former the latter never existed.

But what is the meaning of "the little hills by righteousness?" Why, it has no meaning: and it has none, because it is a false division of the verse. The word בצדקה *bitsedakah, in righteousness*, at the end of verse 3, should begin verse 4, and then the sense will be plain. Ver. 3: "The mountains and the hills shall bring prosperity to the people." Ver. 4: "In righteousness he shall judge the poor of the people: he shall save the children of the needy, and shall break in pieces the oppressor."

The *effects*, mentioned in the *fourth* verse, show that King Solomon should act according to the law of his God; and that all officers, magistrates, and governors, should minister equal rights through every part of the land. The *Septuagint* has the true division: Αναλαβετω τα ορη ειρηνην τω λαω σου, και οἱ βουνοι· Εν δικαιοσυνη κρινει τους πτωχους του λαου, κ. τ. λ. "The mountains shall bring peace to thy people, and the hills: In righteousness shall he judge the poor of thy people," &c.

Verse 5. *They shall fear thee*] There is no sense in which this can be spoken of *Solomon*, nor indeed of any other man· it belongs to *Jesus Christ*, and to him alone. He is the *Prince of peace*, who shall be *feared* and *reverenced* "through all generations, and as long as the sun and moon endure."

Verse 6. *He shall come down like rain upon the mown grass*] The word גז *gez*, which we translate *mown grass*, more properly means *pastured grass* or *pastured land;* for the *dew* of the night is intended to restore the grass which has been eaten in the course of the day. This very idea the *Chaldee* has seized, and renders the place thus: "He shall descend gently, like rain upon the grass which has been eaten by the locust." But there seems to be a reference to the *thick night dews* which in summer fall on the pasturages, and become the means of restoring the grass consumed in the day-time by the cattle. This is finely expressed by the most accomplished of all poets and agriculturists:—

Et quantum longis carpent armenta diebus,
Exigua tantum gelidus ros nocte reponet.

VIRG. Geor. ii., ver. 201.

"For what the day devours, the nightly dew
Shall to the morn by pearly drops renew."

DRYDEN.

Or to leave *poetry*, which always says *too much* or *too little*, the plain prose is:—

A. M. 2989
B. C. 1015
Davidis, Regis
Israelitarum,
cir. annum
40

7 In his days shall the right-eous flourish; [h]and abundance of peace [i]so long as the moon endureth.

8 [k]He shall have dominion also from sea to sea, and from the river unto the ends of the earth.

9 [l]They that dwell in the wilderness shall bow before him; [m]and his enemies shall lick the dust.

10 [n]The kings of Tarshish and of the isles shall bring presents: the kings of Sheba and Seba shall offer gifts.

A. M. 2989
B. C. 1015
Davidis, Regis
Israelitarum,
cir. annum
40

11 [o]Yea, all kings shall fall down before him: all nations shall serve him.

12 For he [p]shall deliver the needy when he crieth; the poor also, and *him* that hath no helper.

13 He shall spare the poor and needy, and shall save the souls of the needy.

14 He shall redeem their soul from deceit

---

[h]Isa. ii. 4; Dan. ii. 44; Luke i. 33——[i]Heb. *till there be no moon*——[k]See Exod. xxiii. 31; 1 Kings iv. 21, 24; Psa. ii. 8; lxxx. 11; lxxxix. 25; Zech. ix. 10

[l]Psa. lxxiv. 14——[m]Isa. xlix. 23; Mic. vii. 17——[n]2 Chron. ix. 21; Psa. xlv. 12; lxviii. 29; Isa. xlix. 7; lx. 6, 9 [o]Isa. xlix. 22, 23——[p]Job xxix. 12

"And as much as the flocks crop in the long days,
So much shall the cold dew restore in one short night."

As showers that *water the earth.*] The influence of the *doctrine* and *Spirit* of Christ on the soul of man shall be as *grateful*, as *refreshing*, and as *fructifying*, as the nightly dews on the cropped fields, and the *vernal showers* on the cultivated lands. Without his influence all tillage is vain; without him there can neither be seed nor fruit.

Verse 7. *In his days shall the righteous flourish*] There was nothing but peace and prosperity all the days of Solomon: for, "In his days Judah and Israel dwelt safely; every man under his vine and under his fig-tree, from Dan even to Beersheba;" 1 Kings iv. 25.

So long as the moon endureth] עד בלי ירח *ad beli yareach*, "Till there be no more moon."

Verse 8. *He shall have dominion also from sea to sea*] The best comment on this, as it refers to Solomon, may be found in 1 Kings iv. 21, 24: "And Solomon reigned over all kingdoms, from the river unto the land of the Philistines, and unto the border of Egypt; for he had dominion over all on this side the river, from Tiphsah even to Azzah, over all the kings on this side the river; and he had peace on all sides round about him."

Solomon, it appears, reigned over all the provinces from the river *Euphrates* to the land of the *Philistines*, even to the frontiers of *Egypt*. The *Euphrates* was on the *east* of Solomon's dominions; the *Philistines* were *westward*, on the *Mediterranean sea;* and *Egypt* was on the *south*. Solomon had therefore, as tributaries, the kingdoms of *Syria, Damascus, Moab*, and *Ammon*, which lay between the *Euphrates* and the *Mediterranean*. Thus he appears to have possessed all the land which God covenanted with Abraham to give to his posterity.

Unto the ends of the earth.] Or *land*, must mean the tract of country along the *Mediterranean sea*, which was the *boundary of the land* on that side: but, as the words may refer to Christ, every thing may be taken in its utmost latitude and extent.

Verse 9. *They that dwell in the wilderness*] The ציים *tsiyim*, termed *Ethiopians* by the *Vulgate, Septuagint, Æthiopic*, and *Arabic*. The *Syriac* terms them *the islands*. But it is likely that those who dwell by the sea-coasts, and support themselves by navigation and fishing, are here intended.

His enemies shall lick the dust.] Shall be so completely subdued, that they shall be reduced to the most abject state of vassalage, till they shall become proselytes to the Jewish faith.

Verse 10. *The kings of Tarshish and of the isles shall bring presents*] Though Solomon did not reign over *Cilicia*, of which *Tarsus* was the capital, yet he might receive *gifts*, not in the sense of *tribute;* for מנחה *minchah*, the word here used, signifies a *gratitude* or *friendly offering*.

The kings of Sheba and Seba] Both countries of Arabia. From the former came the *queen of Sheba*, to hear the wisdom of Solomon. And she brought exceeding great *presents* or *gifts*, but not in the way of *tribute*, for Solomon had no jurisdiction in her country. And certainly many sovereigns, to obtain his *friendship*, sent him various presents of the choicest produce of their respective countries; and no doubt he did with them as with the queen of Sheba, gave them gifts in return. Hence the word אשכר *eshcar* is used, which signifies "a *compensative present*, made on account of benefits received."

Verse 11. *All kings shall fall down before*] They shall reverence him on account of his great wisdom, riches, &c.

All nations shall serve him.] All the surrounding nations. This and the preceding verses are fully explained by 1 Kings x. 23-25: "King Solomon exceeded all the kings of the earth for riches and for wisdom. And all the earth sought unto Solomon to hear his wisdom. And they brought every man his present, vessels of silver, and vessels of gold, and garments, and armour, and spices, horses and mules, a rate year by year." If we take these expressions to mean literally *all the habitable globe*, then they cannot be applied to Solomon; but if we take them as *they are most evidently used by the sacred writer*, then they are literally true. When all the earth shall be brought to receive the Gospel of Christ, then they may be applied to *him*.

Verse 12. *He shall deliver the needy when he crieth*] The poor and the rich shall, in the administration of justice, be equally respected; and the strong shall not be permitted to oppress the weak.

Verse 14. *From deceit and violence*] Be-

A. M. 2989
B. C. 1015
Davidis, Regis
Israelitarum,
cir. annum
40
and violence: and ^qprecious shall their blood be in his sight.

15 And he shall live, and to him ^rshall be given of the gold of Sheba: prayer also shall be made for him continually; *and* daily shall he be praised.

16 There shall be a handful of corn in the earth upon the top of the mountains; the fruit thereof shall shake like Lebanon: ^sand *they* of the city shall flourish like grass of the earth.

17 ^tHis name ^ushall endure for ever: ^vhis

name shall be continued as long as the sun: and ^w*men* shall be blessed in him: ^xall nations shall call him blessed.

A. M. 2989
B. C. 1015
Davidis, Regis
Israelitarum,
cir. annum
40

18 ^yBlessed *be* the Lord God, the God of Israel, ^zwho only doeth wondrous things.

19 And ^ablessed *be* his glorious name for ever: ^band let the whole earth be filled *with* his glory; Amen, and Amen.

20 The prayers of David the son of Jesse are ended.

---

^qPsalm cxvi. 15——^rHebrew, one *shall give*——^s1 Kings iv. 20——^tPsalm lxxxix. 36——^uHebrew, *shall be* ^vHeb. *shall be as a son to continue his father's name for ever*

^wGen. xii. 13; xxii. 18——^xLuke i. 48——^y1 Chron. xxix. 10; Psa. xli. 13; cvi. 48——^zExod. xv. 11; Psa. lxxvii. 14; cxxxvi. 4——^aNeh. ix. 5——^bNum. xiv. 21; Zech. xiv. 9

---

cause they are poor and uneducated, they are liable to be *deceived;* and because they are *helpless,* they are liable to *oppression;* but his equal justice shall duly consider these cases; and no man shall suffer because he is deceived, though the *letter of the law* may be against him.

And precious shall their blood be] If the blood or life of such a person shall have been spilt by the hand of violence, he shall seek it out, and visit it on the murderer, though he were the chief in the land. He shall not be screened, though he were of the blood royal, if he have wilfully taken away the life of a man.

Verse 15. *To him shall be given of the gold of Sheba*] The Arabians shall pay him tribute.

Prayer also shall be made for him continually] In all conquered countries *two* things marked the subjection of the people: 1. Their money was stamped with the name of the conqueror. 2. They were obliged to pray for him in their acts of public worship.

Daily shall he be praised.] He shall not act by the conquered like conquerors in general: he shall treat them with benignity; and shall give them the same laws and privileges as his natural subjects, and therefore "he shall be daily praised." All shall speak well of him.

Verse 16. *There shall be a handful of corn*] The earth shall be exceedingly fruitful. Even a handful of corn sown on the top of a mountain shall grow up strong and vigorous; and it shall be, in reference to *crops* in *other times,* as the *cedars of Lebanon* are to *common trees* or *shrubs:* and as the earth will bring forth in handfuls, so the *people* shall be *multiplied* who are to consume this great produce.

And they *of the city shall flourish like grass of the earth.*] There have been many puzzling criticisms concerning this verse. What I have given I believe to be the *sense.*

Verse 17. *His name shall endure for ever*] Hitherto this has been literally fulfilled. Solomon is celebrated in the *east* and in the *west,* in the *north* and in the *south;* his writings still remain, and are received, both by *Jews* and by *Gentiles,* as a revelation from God; and it is not likely that the name of the author shall ever perish out of the records of the world.

All nations shall call him blessed.] Because of the extraordinary manner in which he was *favoured* by the Most High. I well know that all these things are thought to belong properly

to Jesus Christ; and, in reference to him, they are all true, and *ten thousand* times more than these. But I believe they are all properly applicable to Solomon: and it is the business of the commentator to find out the literal sense, and historical fact, and not seek for allegories and mysteries where there is no certain evidence of their presence. Where the sacred writers of the New Testament quote passages from the Old, and apply them to our Lord, we not only *may* but *should* follow them. And I am ready to grant there may be many other passages equally applicable to him with those they have quoted, which are not thus applied. Indeed, HE is the sum and substance of the whole Scripture. HE spoke by his Spirit in the prophets; and *himself* was the subject of their declarations. See our Lord's saying, Luke xxiv. 44.

Verse 18. *Blessed be the Lord God*] David foresaw all Solomon's *grandeur;* his *justice, equity,* and the *happiness* of the *subjects* under his government; and his soul has, in consequence, sensations of pleasure and gratitude to God, which even his own wondrous pen cannot describe. But it is worthy of remark, that God did not reveal to him the *apostasy* of this beloved son. He did not foresee that this once holy, happy, wise, and prosperous man would be the means of debasing the Divine worship, and establishing the grossest idolatry in Israel. God hid *this* from his eyes, that his heart might not be grieved, and that he might die in peace. Besides, there was still much *contingency* in the business. God would not predict a thing as *absolutely certain,* which was still poised between a *possibility of being and not being;* the scale of which he had left, as he does all contingencies, to the free-will of his creature to turn.

Who only doeth wondrous things.] God alone works *miracles:* wherever there is a *miracle,* there is God. *No creature* can *invert* or *suspend* the *course* and *laws* of *nature;* this is properly the work of God. Jesus Christ, most incontrovertibly, wrought such miracles; therefore, most demonstrably, Jesus Christ is God.

Verse 19. *Let the whole earth be filled* with *his glory*] Let the Gospel—the light, the Spirit, and power of Christ, fill the world.

Amen] So *let* it be.

And Amen.] So it *shall be.* Hallelujah!

Verse 20. *The prayers of David the son of*

Jesse are ended.] This was most probably the *last Psalm* he ever wrote. There may be several in the after part of this book which were written by him; but they were probably composed in a former period of his life, for this was the *end* of the *poetic prayers of David the son of Jesse.* Those that were found afterwards have got out of their proper connexion.

ANALYSIS OF THE SEVENTY-SECOND PSALM

David being near his death, makes his prayer for his son Solomon, that he may be a just, peaceable, and great king, and his subjects happy under his government. But this is but the *shell* of the Psalm: the *kernel* is Christ and his kingdom, under whom righteousness, peace, and felicity shall flourish, and *unto whom all nations shall do homage for ever and ever.*

The parts of this Psalm are the following, viz.:—

I. The petition, ver. 1.
II. The general declaration of the qualities of this kingdom, ver. 2, 3, 4.
III. The particular unfolding of these in their effects, ver. 4-18.
IV. The doxology, ver. 18-20.

I. David, being taught by experience how hard a matter it is to govern a kingdom well, prays God to assist his son *Solomon*, to whom, being near death, he was to leave his crown and sceptre.

1. "Give the king thy judgments, O God;" the true knowledge of thy law.

2. "And thy righteousness unto the king's son;" that he may not decline to the right or left hand, but administer by justice, judge for God.

II. For then this will follow:—

1. Justice will flourish in his kingdom: "He shall judge thy people with righteousness, and thy poor with judgment."

2. And peace also, and prosperity: "The mountains," that is, the chief magistrates; "and the little hills,"—the lesser officers, shall bring peace to the people: but "by righteousness," for justice upholds the world.

III. And now he proceeds to unfold himself upon the two former generals: first, *justice;* then, *peace.*

Of justice he assigns two effects:—

1. The defence of good men: "He shall judge the poor of the people; he shall save the children of the needy."

2. The punishment of the wicked: "He shall break in pieces the oppressor."

The consequences of peace are,—

1. Fear, and reverence, and the service of God: "They shall fear thee as long as the sun and moon endure, throughout all generations."

2. Plenty and abundance: "He shall come down like rain upon the mown grass; as showers that water the earth."

3. Prosperity of good men: "In his days shall the righteous flourish; and abundance of peace so long as the moon endureth."

Now he shows the greatness and amplitude of this kingdom, which will not be so true of *Solomon* as of *Christ* and his kingdom.

1. His kingdom will be very large: "He shall have dominion from sea to sea, and from the river unto the ends of the earth."

2. His subjects shall be many. Some willingly, others against their will, shall obey him: "They that dwell in the wilderness shall bow before him. His enemies shall lick the dust,"—crouch at his feet.

3. Homage shall be done to him by Asiatic, European, and Arabian princes. 1. "The kings of Tarshish and of the isles shall bring presents, the kings of Sheba and Seba shall offer gifts." 2. "Yea, all kings shall fall down before him; all nations shall serve him."

He sets down many excellent qualities of this king:

1. He should be ready to do good; a gracious lord to the meanest subject: "For he shall deliver the needy when he crieth; the poor also, and him that hath no helper."

2. He should be far from loading his subjects with exactions: "He shall spare the poor and shall save the souls of the needy."

3. Far from all tyranny: "He shall redeem their soul from deceit and violence."

4. Far from shedding innocent blood: "And precious shall their blood be in his sight."

And as he shall be kind and loving to his subjects, so shall his subjects show great love and affection to him.

1. They shall pray for his life: "He shall live."

2. And they shall offer him presents: "And to him shall be given of the gold of Arabia."

3. They shall pray for him: "Prayer also shall be made for him continually."

4. They shall speak well of him: "Daily shall he be praised."

And that which would induce them to it might be, that besides the equity and justice, love and kindness he showed to all, they find that under him they enjoy great plenty and abundance of all things.

1. For the earth brought forth corn, and the mountains afforded them an ample harvest: "There shall be a handful of corn in the earth, upon the top (the highest part) of the mountains; the fruit thereof shall shake (stand so thick that the ears shall brush one against another) as the trees in Lebanon."

2. The kingdom shall abound in people: "They of the city shall flourish like grass of the earth," which is thick and green. In a word, the king shall be dear to his people; and they shall love his name when living, and honour him when dead, and continue it to all posterities.

1. "His name shall endure for ever: his name shall be continued as long as the sun."

2. "Men shall be blessed in him." God shall bless thee, as he did Solomon.

3. "All nations shall call him blessed." Acknowledge his happiness, and wish a blessing to themselves after Solomon's example.

IV. In the close of the Psalm, as usual, he gives thanks for taking into consideration the happiness that was to accrue to his people under such a king, even when he was laid in the grave. He breaks forth,

1. "Blessed be the Lord God, the God of Israel, who only doeth wondrous things;" for indeed such a king is a wonder, and it is the grace of God must make him such.

2. And again: "Blessed be his glorious name for ever."

3. And that not in Judea alone, but in all the world: "And let the whole world be filled with his glory. Amen, amen."

"The prayers of David the son of Jesse are ended." Of which some, indeed most, judge this was the last prayer David made. See the notes at the end of the Psalm.

With the *seventy-second* Psalm the SECOND BOOK of the Psalter ends, according to the division of the Jewish Masoretes. The THIRD BOOK commences with a series, chiefly composed by other inspired writers.

THE following poetical version of some of the principal passages of the foregoing Psalm was made and kindly given me by my much respected friend, *James Montgomery*, Esq., of Sheffield. I need not tell the intelligent reader that he has seized the spirit, and exhibited some of the principal beauties, of the Hebrew bard; though, to use his own words in his letter to me, his "hand trembled to touch the harp of Zion." I take the liberty here to register a wish, which I have strongly expressed to himself, that he would favour the Church of God with a metrical version of the whole book.

> Hail to the Lord's Anointed,
>   Great David's greater Son!
> Hail! In the time appointed,
>   His reign on earth begun!
> He comes to break oppression,
>   To let the captive free,
> To take away transgression,
>   And reign in equity.
>
> He comes with succour speedy
>   To those who suffer wrong;
> To help the poor and needy,
>   And bid the weak be strong;
> To give them songs for sighing,
>   Their darkness turn to light,
> Whose souls, in misery dying,
>   Were precious in his sight.

> By such shall he be feared
>   While sun and moon endure,
> Beloved, adored, revered,
>   For he shall judge the poor,
> Through changing generations,
>   With justice, mercy, truth,
> While stars maintain their stations,
>   And moons renew their youth.
>
> He shall come down like showers
>   Upon the fruitful earth,
> And joy, and hope, like flowers,
>   Spring in his path to birth:
> Before him, on the mountains,
>   Shall Peace, the herald, go,
> And righteousness, in fountains,
>   From hill to valley flow.
>
> Arabia's desert-ranger
>   To him shall bow the knee;
> The Æthiopian stranger
>   His glory come to see:
> With offerings of devotion,
>   Ships from the isles shall meet
> To pour the wealth of ocean
>   In tribute at his feet.
>
> Kings shall fall down before him,
>   And gold and incense bring;
> All nations shall adore him,
>   His praise all people sing:
> For he shall have dominion
>   O'er river, sea, and shore,
> Far as the eagle's pinion,
>   Or dove's light wing, can soar.
>
> For him shall prayer unceasing,
>   And daily vows, ascend;
> His kingdom still increasing,—
>   A kingdom without end;
> The mountain-dews shall nourish
>   A need in weakness sown,
> Whose fruit shall spread and flourish
>   And shake like Lebanon.
>
> O'er every foe victorious,
>   He on his throne shall rest,
> From age to age more glorious,—
>   All-blessing, and all-blest:
> The tide of time shall never
>   His covenant remove;
> His name shall stand for ever,
>   His name—what is it?—LOVE.

PSALM LXXIII

The psalmist speaks of God's goodness to his people, 1; shows how much he was stumbled at the prosperity of the wicked, and describes their state, 2–12; details the process of the temptation, and the pain he suffered in consequence, 13–16; shows how he was delivered, and the dismal reverse of the state of the once prosperous ungodly man, by which his own false views were corrected, 17–22; his great confidence in God, and the good consequences of it, 23–28.

XIV. ᴅᴀɪ. EVENING PRAYER
ᵃ*A Psalm of* ᵇAsaph

TRULY ᶜGod *is* good to Israel, *even* to such as are ᵈof a clean heart.

2 But as for me, my feet were almost gone; my steps had well nigh slipped.

3 ᵉFor I was envious at the foolish, *when* I saw the prosperity of the wicked.

4 For *there are* no bands in their death: but their strength *is* ᶠfirm.

5 ᵍThey *are* not ʰin trouble *as other* men; neither are they plagued ⁱlike *other* men.

6 Therefore pride compasseth them about as a chain; violence covereth them ᵏ*as* a garment.

7 ˡTheir eyes stand out with fatness: ᵐthey have more than heart could wish.

8 ⁿThey are corrupt, and ᵒspeak wickedly *concerning* oppression: they ᵖspeak loftily.

ᵃOr, *A Psalm for Asaph*——ᵇPsa. l. title——ᶜOr, *Yet* ᵈHeb. *clean of heart*——ᵉJob xxi. 7; Psa. xxxvii. 1; Jer. xii. 1——ᶠHeb. *fat*——ᵍJob xxi. 6——ʰHeb. *in the trouble of* other *men*——ⁱHeb. *with*

ᵏSo Psa. cix. 18——ˡJob xv. 27; Psa. xvii. 10; cxix. 70; Jer. v. 28——ᵐHeb. *they pass the thoughts of the heart* ⁿPsa. liii. 1——ᵒHos. vii. 16——ᵖ2 Pet. ii. 18; Jude 16

NOTES ON PSALM LXXIII

THIS is the commencement of the THIRD BOOK of the *Psalter;* and the Psalm before us has for title, *A Psalm of Asaph;* or, as the *margin* has it, *A Psalm for Asaph.* The title in the Hebrew is מזמור לאסף *mizmor leasaph;* "A Psalm of Asaph:" and it is likely that this *Asaph* was the composer of it; that he lived under the Babylonish captivity; and that he published this Psalm to console the Israelites under bondage, who were greatly tried to find themselves in such outward distress and misery, while a people much more wicked and corrupt than they, were in great prosperity, and held them in bondage.

Verse 1. *Truly God is good to Israel*] Captives as they were, they still had many blessings from God; and they had promises of deliverance, which must be fulfilled in due time.

Such as are of a clean heart.] Those who have a clean heart must have inward happiness: and, because they resemble God, they can never be forsaken by him.

Verse 2. *My feet were almost gone*] I had nearly given up my confidence. I was ready to find fault with the dispensations of providence; and thought the Judge of all the earth did not do right.

Verse 3. *I was envious at the foolish*] I saw persons who *worshipped not* the true God, and others who were *abandoned to all vices,* in possession of every temporal comfort, while the godly were in straits, difficulties, and affliction. I began then to doubt whether there was a wise providence; and my mind became *irritated.* It seems to have been a maxim among the ancient heathens, Θεου ονειδος τους κακους ευδαιμονειν, "The prosperity of the wicked is a reproach to the gods." But they had no just conception of a state of future rewards and punishments. Besides, man could not bear prosperity. If men had uninterrupted comforts here, perhaps not one soul would ever seek a preparation for heaven. Human trials and afflictions, the *general warfare of human life,* are the highest proof of a providence as benevolent as it is wise. Were the state of human affairs different from what it is, hell would be more thickly peopled; and there would be fewer inhabitants in glory. There is reason to doubt whether there would be *any religion* upon earth had we

nothing but temporal prosperity. Indeed, all the following verses are proofs of it.

Verse 4. *No bands in their death*] Many of the godly have sore conflicts at their death. Their enemy then thrusts sore at them that they may fall; or that their confidence in their God may be shaken. But of this the ungodly know nothing. Satan will not molest *them;* he is sure of his prey; they are entangled, and cannot now break their nets; their consciences are seared, they have no sense of guilt. If they think at all of another world, they presume on that mercy which they never sought, and of which they have no distinct notion. Perhaps, "they die without a sigh or a groan; and thus go off as quiet as a lamb"—to the slaughter.

Verse 6. *Pride compasseth them about as a chain*] Perhaps there is an allusion here to the office which some of them bore. *Chains of gold,* and *golden rings,* were ensigns of magistracy and civil power. As these chains encompassed their necks, or the rings their wrists and fingers, as the signs of the *offices* in virtue of which they acted; so חמס *chamas,* violence, oppressive conduct, encompassed them. They made no other use of their great power, than to oppress the poor and the needy; and to drive things to extremities. The *Chaldee,* instead of *a chain,* represents this as a crown or diadem, which they had formed out of the plunder of the poor and defenceless.

Verse 7. *Their eyes stand out with fatness*] "Their countenance is changed because of fatness."—*Chaldee.* By fatness, or corpulency, the natural lines of the face are *changed,* or rather *obliterated.* The characteristic distinctions are gone; and we see little remaining besides the *human hog.*

They have more than heart could wish.] I doubt this translation. *Whose heart* ever said, *I have enough,* which had not its portion with God? It would be more literal to say, "They surpass the thoughts of their heart." They have *more* than they *expected,* though *not more* than they *wish.*

Verse 8. *They are corrupt*] ימיקו *yamiku,* they *mock, act dissolutely.*

And speak wickedly concerning oppression] They vindicate excessive acts of government: they push justice to its rigour. They neither show equity, lenity, nor mercy; they are cruel, and they *vindicate* their proceedings.

9 They set their mouth ᑫagainst the heavens, and their tongue walketh through the earth.

10 Therefore his people return hither: ʳand waters of a full *cup* are wrung out to them.

11 And they say, ˢHow doth God know? and is there knowledge in the Most High?

12 Behold, these *are* the ungodly, who ᵗprosper in the world; they increase *in* riches.

13 ᵘVerily I have cleansed my heart *in* vain, and ᵛwashed my hands in innocency.

14 For all the day long have I been plagued, and ʷchastened every morning.

15 If I say, I will speak thus; behold I should offend *against* the generation of thy children.

16 ˣWhen I thought to know this, ʸit *was* too painful for me,

17 Until ᶻI went into the sanctuary of God; *then* understood I ᵃtheir end.

ᑫRev. xiii. 6——ʳPsa. lxxv. 8——ˢJob xxii. 13; Psa. x. 11; xciv. 7——ᵗVer. 3——ᵘJob xxi. 15; xxxiv. 9; xxxv. 3; Mal. iii. 14——ᵛPsa. xxvi. 6

ʷHeb. *my chastisement* was——ˣEccles. viii. 17. ʸHeb. *it* was *labour in mine eyes*——ᶻPsa. lxxvii. 13 ᵃPsa. xxxvii. 38

Verse 9. *Set their mouth against the heavens*] They blaspheme God, ridicule religion, mock at Providence, and laugh at a future state.

Their tongue walketh through the earth.] They find fault with every thing; they traduce the memory of the just in heaven, and ridicule the saints that are upon earth. They criticise every dispensation of God.

Verse 10. *Therefore his people return hither*] There are very few verses in the Bible that have been more variously translated than this; and, like the man in the fable, they have blown the *hot* to *cool* it, and the *cold* to *warm* it. It has been translated, "Therefore God's people fall off to them; and thence they reap no small advantage." And, "Therefore let his people come before them; and waters in full measure would be wrung out from them." That is, "Should God's people come before them, they would squeeze them to the utmost; they would wring out all the juice in their bodies." The *Chaldee* has, "Therefore, are they turned against the people of the Lord, that they may bruise and beat them with mallets; that they may pour out to them abundance of tears." The *Vulgate,* "Therefore shall my people return here, and days of abundance shall be found by them." The *Septuagint* is the same. The *Æthiopic, Arabic,* and *Syriac,* nearly the same.

The *Hebrew* text is, לכן ישוב עמו הלם ומי מלא ימצו למו *lachen yashub ammo* (עמי *ammi*) *halom; umey male yimmatsu lamo;* "Therefore shall my people be converted, where they shall find abundance of waters." That is, The people, seeing the iniquity of the Babylonians, and feeling their oppressive hand, shall be converted to me; and I shall bring them to their own land, where they shall find an abundance of all the necessaries of life. I believe this to be the meaning; and thus we find their afflictions were sanctified to them; for they obliged them *to return to God,* and then God caused them to return to their own land. The *Vulgate* translates ומי מלא *umey male,* "abundance of waters," by *et dies pleni,* "and days of plenty;" for it has read ימי *yemey, days,* for ומי *umey, and waters.* Almost all the *Versions* support this reading; but it is not acknowledged by any MS. The old *Psalter* is here mutilated.

Verse 11. *They say, How doth God know?*] My people are so stumbled with the prosperity of the wicked, that they are ready in their temptation to say, "Surely, God cannot know these things, or he would never dispense his favours thus." Others consider these words as the saying of the *wicked:* "We may oppress these people as we please, and live as we list; God knows nothing about it."

Verse 12. *These are the ungodly*] The people still speak. It is the ungodly that prosper, the irreligious and profane.

Verse 13. *I have cleansed my heart in vain*] It is no advantage to us to worship the true God, to walk according to the law of righteousness, and keep the ordinances of the Most High.

Verse 14. *For all the day long have I been plagued*] Far from enjoying worldly prosperity, we are not only *poor,* but we are *afflicted* also; and every *succeeding day* brings with it some new trouble.

Verse 15. *If I say, I will speak thus*] I have at last discovered that I have reasoned incorrectly; and that I have the uniform testimony of all thy children against me. From generation to generation they have testified that the Judge of all the earth does right; they have trusted in thee, and were never confounded. They also met with afflictions and sore trials, but thou didst bring them safely through all, didst sustain them in the worst, and sanctifiedst the whole to their eternal good.

Verse 16. *When I thought to know this*] When I reviewed the history of our fathers, I saw that, though thou hadst from time to time hidden thy face because of their sins, yet thou hadst never utterly abandoned them to their adversaries; and it was not reasonable to conclude that thou wouldst do now what thou hadst never done before; and yet the continuance of our captivity, the oppressive hardships which we suffer, and the small prospect there is of release, puzzle me again. These things have been very *painful* to me.

Verse 17. *Until I went into the sanctuary*] Until, in the use of thy ordinances, I entered into a deep consideration of thy secret counsels, and considered the future state of the righteous and the wicked; that the unequal distribution of temporal good and evil argued a future judgment; that the present is a state of trial; and that God exercises his followers according to his godly wisdom and tender mercy. Then light sprang up in my mind, and I was assured that all these exercises were for our benefit, and that the prosperity of the wicked here was

18 Surely ᵇthou didst set them in slippery places: thou castedst them down into destruction.

19 How are they *brought* into desolation, as in a moment! they are utterly consumed with terrors.

20 ᶜAs a dream when *one* awaketh; *so,* O LORD, ᵈwhen thou awakest, thou shalt despise their image.

21 Thus my heart was ᵉgrieved, and I was pricked in my reins.

22 ᶠSo foolish *was* I, and ᵍignorant: I was *as* a beast ʰbefore thee.

23 Nevertheless I *am* continually with thee: thou hast holden *me* by my right hand.

24 ⁱThou shalt guide me with thy counsel, and afterward receive me *to* glory.

25 ᵏWhom have I in heaven *but thee?* and *there is* none upon earth *that* I desire beside thee.

26 ˡMy flesh and my heart faileth: *but* God

ᵇPsa. xxxv. 6——ᶜJob xx. 8; Psa. xc. 5; Isa. xxix. 7, 8
ᵈPsa. lxxviii. 65——ᵉVer. 3——ᶠPsa. xcii. 6; Prov. xxx. 2

ᵍHeb. *I knew not*——ʰHeb. *with thee*——ⁱPsa. xxxii. 8; Isa. lviii. 8——ᵏPhil. iii. 8——ˡPsa. lxxxiv. 2; cxix. 81

---

a prelude to their destruction. And this I saw to be their *end.*

That this Psalm was written during the *captivity,* there is little room to doubt. How then can ⸴he psalmist speak of the *sanctuary?* There was none at Babylon; and at Jerusalem it had been long since destroyed? There is no way to solve this difficulty but by considering that מקדשי *mikdeshey* may be taken in the sense of *holy places*—places set apart for prayer and meditation. And that the captives had such places in their captivity, there can be no doubt; and the place that is set apart to meet God in, for prayer, supplication, confession of sin, and meditation, is *holy* unto the Lord; and is, therefore, his *sanctuary,* whether a *house* or the open *field. Calmet* thinks by holy meditations a view of the Divine secrets, to which he refers, ver. 24, is here meant.

Verse 18. *Thou didst set them in slippery places*] Affluence is a slippery path; few have ever walked in it without *falling.* It is possible to be *faithful* in the *unrighteous mammon,* but it is very *difficult.* No man should *desire riches;* for they bring with them so many cares and temptations as to be almost *unmanageable.* Rich men, even when pious, are seldom happy; they do not enjoy the consolations of religion. A good man, possessed of very extensive estates, unblamable in his whole deportment, once said to me: "There must be some strange malignity in riches thus to keep me in continual bondage, and deprive me of the consolations of the Gospel." Perhaps to a person to whom his estates are a snare, the words of our Lord may be *literally* applicable: "Sell what thou hast, and give to the poor; and thou shalt have treasure in heaven: and come, take up thy cross, and follow me." But he went away sorrowful, for he had great possessions! May we not then say with the psalmist, *Surely thou didst set them in slippery places,* &c.?

Verse 19. *Are they* brought *into desolation*] This is often a literal fact. I have known several cases where persons, very rich, have by sudden losses been brought into desolation as in a moment; in consequence of which *they were utterly consumed in terrors.*

Verse 20. *As a dream when* one *awaketh*] So their goods fled away. Their *possession* was a *dream*—their *privation,* real.

Thou shalt despise their image.] While destitute of true religion, whatever appearance they had of greatness, nobility, honour, and happiness; yet in the sight of God they had no more

than the *ghost* or *shade* of excellence, which God is said here to *despise.* Who would be rich at such risk and dishonour?

Verse 21. *Thus my heart was grieved*] The different views which I got of this subject quite confounded me; I was equally astonished at their sudden overthrow and my own ignorance. I felt as if I were a *beast* in stupidity. I permitted my mind to be wholly occupied with *sensible things,* like the beasts that perish, and did not look into a future state; nor did I consider, nor submit to, the wise designs of an unerring Providence.

Verse 23. *I am continually with thee*] I now see that myself and my people are under thy guardian care; that we are continually upheld by thee; and while in thy *right hand,* we shall not be utterly cast down.

Verse 24. *Thou shalt guide me with thy counsel*] After we have suffered awhile, receiving directions and consolations from thy good Spirit, by means of thy prophets, who are in the same captivity with ourselves; thou wilt grant us deliverance, restore us to our own land, and crown us with honour and happiness. Any sincere follower of God may use these words in reference to this and the coming world. *Thy counsel*—thy WORD and SPIRIT, shall *guide me* through life; and when I have done and suffered thy righteous will, thou wilt *receive me into thy* eternal *glory.*

Verse 25. *Whom have I in heaven but thee?*] The original is more emphatic: מי לי בשמים ועמך לא חפצתי בארץ *mi li bashshamayim; veimmecha lo chaphatsti baarets.* "Who is there to me in the heavens? And with thee I have desired nothing in the earth." No man can say this who has not taken God for his portion in reference to both worlds.

Verse 26. *My flesh—faileth*] I shall soon die: *and my heart*—even my natural courage, will fail; and no support but what is *supernatural* will then be available. Therefore, he adds,—

God is the strength of my heart] Literally, *the rock of my heart.*

And my portion] Allusion is here made to the division of the promised land. I ask no inheritance below; I look for one above. I do not look for this in the possession of any *place;* it is GOD alone that can content the desires and wishes of an immortal spirit. And even this would not satisfy, had I not the prospect of its being *for ever,* לעולם *leolam,* "to eternity!"

is the [m]strength of my heart, and [n]my portion for ever.

27 For, lo, [o]they that are far from thee shall perish: thou hast destroyed all them that [p]go a whoring from thee.

28 But *it is* good for me to [q]draw near to God: I have put my trust in the Lord GOD, that I may [r]declare all thy works.

[m]Heb. *rock*——[n]Psa. xvi. 5; cxix. 57——[o]Psa. cxix. 155

[p]Exod. xxxiv. 15; Num. xv. 39; James iv. 4——[q]Heb. x. 22——[r]Psa. cvii. 22; cxviii. 17

Verse 27. *They that are far from thee shall perish*] The term perish is generally used to signify a *coming to nothing*, being *annihilated;* and by some it is thus applied to the *finally impenitent*, they shall all be *annihilated.* But where is this to be found in the Scriptures? In no part, properly understood. In the new heavens and the new earth none of the wicked shall be found; for therein dwells righteousness —nothing but God and righteous spirits; but at the same time the wicked shall be in their own place. And to suppose that they shall be *annihilated,* is as great a heresy, though scarcely so absurd, as to believe that the pains of damnation are *emendatory*, and that *hell-fire* shall burn out. There is presumptive evidence from Scripture to lead us to the conclusion, that if there be not eternal punishment, glory will not be eternal; as the same terms are used to express the duration of both. No human spirit that is not *united* to God can be saved. *Those who are* FAR FROM THEE *shall perish*—they shall be *lost, undone, ruined;* and that without remedy. Being *separated from God* by sin, they shall never be *rejoined;* the great gulf must be between them and their Maker *eternally.*

All them that go a whoring from thee.] That is, all that worship false gods; all idolaters. This is the only meaning of the word in such a connexion. I have explained this elsewhere.

Verse 28. It is *good for me to draw near*] We have already seen that those who are *far off* shall perish; therefore, it is *ill for them.* Those who *draw near*—who come in the true *spirit of sacrifice*, and with the only available offering, the Lord Jesus, shall be finally saved; therefore, it is *good* for *them.*

I have put my trust in the Lord God] I confide in *Jehovah, my Prop and Stay.* I have taken him for my portion.

That I may declare all thy works.] That I may testify to all how good it is to *draw nigh to God;* and what a *sufficient portion* he is to the soul of man.

The *Vulgate, Septuagint, Æthiopic,* and *Arabic,* add, *in the gates of the daughter of Sion.* These words appear to make a better finish; but they are not acknowledged by any Hebrew MS.

ANALYSIS OF THE SEVENTY-THIRD PSALM

The prophet shows the grief that many good men feel at the prosperity of the wicked, and the distresses of the godly; but at last, consulting the will of God, he finds that the felicity of the wicked ends in wretchedness, and the crosses of the godly are the way to happiness; and, with this consideration, he gains quiet to his troubled mind. Let the question be, Who is the *happy man?* The *godly* or *ungodly?* And then the parts of the Psalm will be as follows:—

I. The arguments produced for the happiness of the wicked, ver. 1-9.

II. The impression these arguments make in carnal minds, ver. 2, 3, 10-14.

III. The rejection of these doubts and impressions, ver. 15-17.

IV. The refutation of the former arguments, ver. 18-20.

V. The psalmist's censure of himself for his precipitate judgment, ver. 21, 22.

VI. His full resolution of the doubt, after the full examination of the reasons on both sides. That true happiness consists in *union with God;* and therefore the wicked, who are *far from him*, however they flourish, are unhappy, ver. 23-28.

But, more particularly, the Psalm is divisible into the following parts:—

I. There is, *first*, an assertion: "Certainly, God is good to Israel, to such as are of a clean heart," ver. 1. But can this comport with their present afflicted state? With this he was greatly harassed, ver. 2. He saw the wicked in prosperity, which he states in several particulars.

II. What carnal minds think of them.

1. They have no conflicts in their death, ver. 4.

2. They are not troubled like other men, ver. 5.

3. They are proud and haughty, ver. 6, and yet are not punished.

4. They are oppressive tyrants: "Violence covereth them."

5. They feed luxuriously, ver. 7.

6. They speak evil against the poor, ver. 8.

7. They even speak against God, and all the dispensations of his providence: "Their tongue walketh through the earth," ver. 9.

8. They assert that he takes no cognizance of their ways, ver. 10, 11.

III. The evil conclusion formed from these premises refuted.

1. It is the ungodly that prosper in the earth, ver. 12.

2. If so, then of what avail are my religious observances and sufferings, &c.? ver. 13, 14.

He resolves the question,—

1. From *the testimony of* ALL *the godly,* ver. 15.

2. He tried to solve it by *reason*, but did not succeed, ver. 16.

3. He *consults with God,* and the whole is made plain, ver. 17.

From him he learns,—

1. That the happiness of the wicked is *unstable*, ver. 18.

2. They stand on a *precipice*, and are *cast down*, ver. 19.

3. Their desolation comes *suddenly* and *unexpectedly*, ver. 19.

4. Their ruin is *fearful:* "They are consumed with terrors."

5. Thus it is demonstrated that their happiness was vain, empty, as unsubstantial as a *dream*, ver. 20.

IV. He now acknowledges that he had formed

an erroneous judgment. 1. That he gave way to *animosity*. 2. That he acted rather like a *beast* than a *man*, in looking only to the present life, ver. 21, 22. He now receives instruction and encouragement.

1. The godly are not neglected: "They are continually with God," ver. 23.

2. They are tenderly *led* as by *the hand* of a loving father, ver. 23.

3. They are directed by the *word* and *Spirit* of God, ver. 24.

4. They are often *crowned* with signal marks of God's esteem, even in this life, ver. 24.

V. His resolution to live to God, as he sees that such alone are happy.

1. He expects nothing in *heaven* but God: "Whom have I in heaven," &c.

2. He will seek no other portion on *earth:* "There is none on earth," ver. 25.

3. I will cleave to him in life and death: "When my flesh and my heart fail."

4. My confidence in him shall be unshaken, ver. 26.

VI. He draws two conclusions from what he had learned:—

1. They that are far from God *perish*.

2. They that *draw nigh* to him are saved, ver. 27.

Therefore, I will so trust in God that I shall be able to declare his works, ver. 28.

PSALM LXXIV

The psalmist complains of the desolations of the sanctuary, and pleads with God, 1–3; shows the insolence and wickedness of their enemies, 4–8; prays to God to act for them as he had done for their fathers, whom, by his miraculous power, he had saved, 9–17; begs God to arise, and vindicate his own honour against his enemies, and the enemies of his people, 18–23.

[a]Maschil of Asaph

O GOD, why hast thou [b]cast *us* off for ever? *why* doth thine anger [c]smoke against [d]the sheep of thy pasture?

2 Remember thy congregation, [e]*which* thou hast purchased of old; the [f]rod [g]of thine inheritance, *which* thou hast redeemed; this Mount Zion, wherein thou hast dwelt.

3 Lift up thy feet unto the perpetual desolations; *even* all *that* the enemy hath done wickedly in the sanctuary.

4 [h]Thine enemies roar in the midst of thy congregations; [i]they set up their ensigns *for* signs.

5 *A man* was famous according as he had lifted up axes upon the thick trees.

6 But now they break down [k]the carved work thereof at once with axes and hammers.

7 [l]They [m]have cast fire into thy sanctuary, they have defiled [n]*by casting down* the dwelling-place of thy name to the ground.

---

[a]Or, A Psalm *for Asaph to give instruction*——[b]Psa. xliv. 9, 23; lx. 1, 10; lxxvii. 7; Jer. xxxi. 37; xxxiii. 24 [c]Deut. xxix. 20——[d]Psa. xcv. 7; c. 3——[e]Exod. xv. 16; Deut. ix. 29

[f]Or, *tribe*——[g]Deut. xxxii. 9; Jer. x. 16——[h]Lam. ii. 7——[i]Dan. vi. 27——[k]1 Kings vi. 18, 29, 32, 35 [l]2 Kings xxv. 9——[m]Heb. *They have sent thy sanctuary into the fire*——[n]Psa. lxxxix. 39

NOTES ON PSALM LXXIV

The *title* is, *Maschil of Asaph*, or, "A Psalm of Asaph, to give instruction." That this Psalm was written at a time when the *temple* was ruined, *Jerusalem* burnt, and the prophets scattered or destroyed, is evident. But it is not so clear whether the desolations here refer to the days of *Nebuchadnezzar*, or to the desolation that took place under the *Romans* about the *seventieth* year of the Christian era. *Calmet* inclines to the former opinion; and supposes the Psalm to be a lamentation over the *temple* destroyed by Nebuchadnezzar.

Verse 1. *O God, why hast thou cast* us *off for ever?*] Hast thou determined that we shall never more be thy people? Are we never to see an end to our calamities?

Verse 2. *Remember thy congregation, which thou hast purchased of old*] We are the descendants of that people whom thou didst take unto thyself; the children of Abraham, Isaac, and Jacob. Wilt thou never more be reconciled to us?

Verse 3. *Lift up thy feet*] Arise, and return to us; our desolations still continue. Thy sanctuary is profaned by thine and our enemies.

Verse 4. *Thine enemies roar*] Thy people, who were formerly a distinct and separate peo-

ple, and who would not even touch a Gentile, are now obliged to mingle with the most profane. Their boisterous mirth, their cruel mockings, their insulting commands, are heard every where in all our assemblies.

They set up their ensigns for signs.] שמו אותחם אתות *samu othotham othoth*, they set up their standards in the place of ours. All the ensigns and trophies were those of our enemies; our own were no longer to be seen.

The *fifth, sixth,* and *seventh* verses give a correct historical account of the ravages committed by the Babylonians, as we may see from 2 Kings xxv. 4, 7, 8, 9, and Jer. lii. 7, 18, 19: "And the city was broken up, and all the men fled by night by the way of the gate. They took Zedekiah, and slew his sons before his eyes; and put out his eyes, and bound him with fetters of brass, and carried him to Babylon. And on the *second* day of the *fifth* month of the *nineteenth* year of Nebuchadnezzar, Nebuzaradan, the captain of the guard, came unto Jerusalem; and he burnt the house of the Lord, and the king's house, and every great man's house; and all the houses of Jerusalem burnt he with fire. And they broke down the walls of Jerusalem round about. And the pillars of brass, and the bases, and the brazen sea, they broke in pieces, and carried the brass to Babylon.

8 [o]They said in their hearts, Let us [p]destroy them together: they have burned up all the synagogues of God in the land.

9 We see not our signs: [q]*there is* no more any prophet: neither *is there* among us any that knoweth how long.

10 O God, how long shall the adversary reproach? shall the enemy blaspheme thy name for ever?

11 [r]Why withdrawest thou thy hand, even thy right hand? pluck *it* out of thy bosom.

12 For [s]God *is* my King of old, working salvation in the midst of the earth.

13 [t]Thou didst [u]divide the sea by thy strength: [v]thou brakest the heads of the [w]dragons in the waters.

14 Thou brakest the heads of leviathan in

[o]Psa. lxxxiii. 4——[p]Heb. *break*——[q]1 Sam. iii. 1; Amos viii. 11; 1 Mac. iv. 46——[r]Lam. ii. 3

[s]Psa. xliv. 4——[t]Exod. xiv. 21——[u]Heb. *break*——[v]Isa. li. 9, 10; Ezek. xxix. 3; xxxii. 2——[w]Or, *whales*

And the pots, shovels, snuffers and spoons, and the fire pans and bowls, and such things as were of gold and silver, they took away." Thus they broke down, and carried away, and destroyed this beautiful house; and in the true barbarian spirit, neither sanctity, beauty, symmetry, nor elegance of workmanship, was any thing in their eyes. What *hammers* and *axes* could ruin, was ruined; Jerusalem was totally destroyed, and its walls laid level with the ground. Well might the psalmist sigh over such a desolation.

Verse 8. *Let us destroy them*] Their object was totally to annihilate the political existence of the Jewish people.

They have burned up all the synagogues of God in the land.] It is supposed that there were no *synagogues* in the land till after the Babylonish captivity. How then could the Chaldeans burn up any in Judea? The word מועדי *moadey*, which we translate *synagogues*, may be taken in a more general sense, and mean *any places* where *religious assemblies* were held: and that such places and assemblies did exist long *before* the Babylonish captivity, is pretty evident from different parts of Scripture. It appears that Elisha kept such at his house on the *sabbaths* and *new moons*. See 2 Kings iv. 23. And perhaps to such St. James may refer, Acts xv. 23, a species of *synagogues*, where *the law was read of old, in every city of the land.* And it appears that such religious meetings were held at the house of the Prophet *Ezekiel*, chap. xxxiii. 31. And perhaps every prophet's house was such. This is the only place in the *Old Testament* where we have the word *synagogue*. Indeed, wherever there was a *place* in which God met with *patriarch* or *prophet*, and any memorial of it was *preserved*, there was a מועד *moed*, or place of religious meeting; and all such places the Chaldeans would destroy, pursuant to their design to extinguish the Jewish religion, and blot out all its memorials from the earth. And this was certainly the most likely means to effect their purpose. How soon would Christianity be destroyed in England if all the churches, chapels, and places of worship were destroyed, and only the poor of the people left in the land; who, from their circumstances, could not build a place for the worship of God! After such desolation, what a miracle was the restoration of the Jews!

Verse 9. *We see not our signs*] "They have taken away all our trophies, and have left us no memorial that God has been among us. Even thou thyself hast left us destitute of all those *supernatural evidences* that have so often convinced us that thou wert among us of a truth." But we may say that they were not totally destitute even of these. The preservation of Daniel in the lion's den, and of the three Hebrews in the fiery furnace; the metamorphosis of Nebuchadnezzar; the handwriting that appeared to Belshazzar; were all so many prodigies and evidences that God had not left them without proofs of his *being* and his *regard*.

There is *no more any prophet*] There was not one among them in that place that could tell them *how long* that captivity was yet to endure. But there were prophets in the captivity. *Daniel* was one; but his prophecies were confined to one place. *Ezekiel* was another, but he was among those captives who were by the river *Chebar*. They had not, as usual, prophets who went *to* and *fro* through the land, preaching repentance and remission of sins.

Verse 11. *Why withdrawest thou thy hand*] It has been remarked, that as the outward habit of the easterns had no sleeves, the hands and arms were frequently covered with the folds of the robe; and in order to do any thing, the hand must be disentangled and drawn out. The literal version of the *Hebrew* is: "To what time wilt thou draw back thy hand; yea, thy right hand, from within thy bosom?" *Consume;* that is, manifest thy power, and *destroy* thy adversaries. I have, in the *introduction* to the book of Psalms, spoken of the old metrical version by *Sternhold* and *Hopkins*, and have stated that it was formed from the original text. A proof of this may be seen by the learned reader in this and the preceding verse; where, though their version is harsh, and some of their expressions quaint almost to ridicule, yet they have hit the true meaning which our prose translators have missed:—

Ver. 10. When wilt thou once, Lord, end this shame,
And cease thine en'mies strong?
Shall they always blaspheme thy name,
And rail on thee so long?

Ver. 11. Why dost thou draw thy hand aback,
And hide it in thy lap?
O pluck it out, and be not slack
To give thy foes a rap!

Verse 12. *For God* is *my King of old*] We have always acknowledged thee as our sovereign; and thou hast reigned as a king in the midst of our land, dispensing salvation and deliverance from the *centre* to every part of the *circumference*.

Verse 13. *Thou didst divide the sea*] When our fathers came from Egypt.

Thou brakest the heads of the dragons in the

pieces, *and* gavest him [x]*to be* meat [y]to the people inhabiting the wilderness.

15 [z]Thou didst cleave the fountain and the flood: [a]thou driedst up [b]mighty rivers.

16 The day *is* thine, the night also *is* thine: [c]thou hast prepared the light and the sun.

17 Thou hast [d]set all the borders of the earth: [e]thou hast [f]made summer and winter.

18 [g]Remember this, *that* the enemy hath reproached, O LORD, and *that* [h]the foolish people have blasphemed thy name.

19 O deliver not the soul [i]of thy turtle-dove unto the multitude *of the wicked:* [k]forget not the congregation of thy poor for ever.

20 [l]Have respect unto the covenant: for the dark places of the earth are full of the habitations of cruelty.

21 O let not the oppressed return ashamed: let the poor and needy praise thy name.

22 Arise, O God, plead thine own cause: [m]remember how the foolish man reproacheth thee daily.

23 Forget not the voice of thine enemies: the tumult of those that rise up against thee [n]increaseth continually.

---

[x]Num. xiv. 9——[y]Psa. lxxii. 9——[z]Exod. xvii. 5, 6; Num. xx. 11; Psa. cv. 41; Isa. xlviii. 21——[a]Josh. iii. 13, &c.——[b]Heb. *rivers of strength*——[c]Gen. i. 14, &c. [d]Acts xvii. 26——[e]Gen. viii. 22

[f]Heb. *made them*——[g]Ver. 22; Rev. xvi. 19——[h]Psa. xxxix. 8——[i]Cant. ii. 14——[k]Psa. lxviii. 10——[l]Gen. xvii. 7, 8; Lev. xxvi. 44, 45; Psa. cvi. 45; Jer. xxxiii. 21 [m]Ver. 18; Psa. lxxxix. 51——[n]Heb. *ascendeth;* Jonah i. 2

---

waters.] Pharaoh, his captains, and all his hosts were drowned in the Red Sea, when attempting to pursue them.

Verse 14. *The heads of leviathan*] Leviathan might be intended here as a personification of the *Egyptian government;* and its *heads,* Pharaoh and his chief captains.

To the people inhabiting the wilderness.] Probably meaning the *birds and beasts of prey.* These were the people of the wilderness, which fed on the dead bodies of the Egyptians, which the tides had cast ashore. The *Vulgate, Septuagint, Æthiopic,* and *Arabic* read, "Thou hast given him for meat to the Ethiopians," or Abyssinians.

Verse 15. *Thou didst cleave the fountain*] Thou didst cleave the *rock* in the wilderness, of which all the congregation drank.

Thou driedst up mighty rivers.] Does not this refer to the cutting off the waters of the Jordan, so that the people passed over dry-shod?

Verse 16. *The day* is *thine, the night also* is *thine*] Thou art the Author of light, and of the sun, which is the means of dispensing it.

Verse 17. *Thou hast set all the borders of the earth*] Thou alone art the Author of all its grand *geographical* divisions.

Thou hast made summer and winter.] Thou hast appointed that peculiarity in the poise and rotation of the earth, by which the *seasons* are produced.

Verse 18. *Remember this*] The heathen not only deny these things, but give the honour of them to their false gods, and thus blaspheme thy name.

Verse 19. *Deliver not the soul of thy turtle-dove*] Thy people Israel are helpless, defenceless, miserable, and afflicted: O deliver them no longer into the power of their brutal adversaries.

Verse 20. *Have respect unto the covenant*]

הבט לברית *habbet labberith.* Pay attention to the *covenant sacrifice;* to that offered by Abraham, Gen. xv. 9, &c., when the contracting parties, God and Abram, passed through between the separated parts of the covenant sacrifice. An indisputable type of Jesus Christ; and of God and man meeting in his sacrificed humanity.

The dark places of the earth] The caves, dens, woods, &c., of the *land* are full of robbers, cut-throats, and murderers, who are continually destroying thy people, so that the holy seed seems as if it would be entirely cut off and the *covenant* promise thus be rendered void.

The words may either apply to *Chaldea* or *Judea.* Judea was at this time little else than a den of robbers, its own natural inhabitants being removed. Chaldea was infested with hordes of banditti also.

Verse 21. *Let not the oppressed return ashamed*] Do not permit thy people to be so diminished, that when, according to thy promise, they are restored to their own land, they may appear to be but a handful of men.

Verse 22. *Plead thine own cause*] Thy honour is concerned, as well as our safety and salvation. *The fool*—the idolater, *reproacheth thee daily*—he boasts of the superiority of his idols, by whose power, he asserts, we are brought under their domination.

Verse 23. *Forget not the voice*] While we pray to thee for our own salvation, we call upon thee to vindicate thy injured honour: and let all the nations see that thou lovest thy followers, and hatest those who are thy enemies. Let not man prevail against thee or thine.

ANALYSIS OF THE SEVENTY-FOURTH PSALM

This Psalm divides itself into *two* parts:—
I. The Psalmist's complaint, ver. 1-10.
II. His prayer, ver. 10-23.
Both the complaint and petition are summarily comprised in the *three* first verses; and afterwards amplified throughout the Psalm.

I. He expostulates with God about their calamity.
1. From the author of it: "Thou, O God."
2. From the extremity of it: "Cast us not off."
3. From the duration of it: "For ever."
4. From the cause: "Thy anger smokes against us."
5. From the object of it: "The sheep of thy pasture."

To his complaint he subjoins his *petition;* in which every word has the strength of an argument.
1. "Remember thy congregation:" Thy chosen people.

2. "Whom thou hast purchased:" By a mighty hand from Pharaoh.

3. "Of old:" Thy people ever since thy covenant with Abraham.

4. "The rod of thine inheritance;" dwelling in that land which thou didst *measure* out to them.

5. "Whom thou hast redeemed:" From the Canaanites, &c.

6. "This Mount Zion, wherein thou hast dwelt:" Where we gave thee the worship which belonged to the true God; and thou wert pleased with our sacrifices and services. *Remember* this people, and all these engagements; and "cast us not off for ever."

7. "Lift up thy feet:" Consider thy *own dishonour;* they are *thy enemies* as well as ours. See what they have done against thee, thy *temple,* thy *ordinances.* Look at their *blasphemies,* and avenge the quarrel of thy *covenant,* ver. 3-11.

Consider what thou hast done for our forefathers.

1. Thou hast been long *our King* and Deliverer. See the proofs, ver. 12-15.

2. Thy general *providence* respects all men. Thou hast given them *light;* the *sun* and *moon,* the *vicissitude of seasons,* &c., ver. 16, 17.

II. The psalmist's *prayer:*—

1. That God would *remember* the *reproaches* of his *enemies,* ver. 18.

2. That he would *deliver the souls* of his *children,* ver. 19.

3. That he would not forget "the congregation of the poor," ver. 19.

4. That he *would remember his covenant* with Abram, to make them an innumerable people, and a blessing to all mankind, ver. 20.

5. That, when they did return, they might not be a diminished people; for their enemies were determined to destroy them, ver. 21.

6. That they might be led from all considerations to *praise his name,* ver. 21.

At the conclusion he urges his petition:—

1. "Arise,—plead thine own cause."

2. "Remember the foolish."

3. "Forget not thine enemies."

4. They make a *tumult,* and their partisans *daily increase,* ver. 22, 23.

PSALM LXXV

The psalmist praises God for present mercies, 1; the Lord answers, and promises to judge the people righteously, 2, 3; rebukes the proud and haughty, 4, 5; shows that all authority comes from himself, 4–7; that he will punish the wicked, 8; the psalmist resolves to praise God, 9; and the Most High promises to cast down the wicked, and raise up the righteous, 9, 10.

XV. DAY. MORNING PRAYER

To the chief Musician, ᵃAl-taschith, ᵇA Psalm *or* Song ᶜof Asaph

UNTO thee, O God, do we give thanks, unto *thee* do we give thanks: for *that* thy name is near thy wondrous works declare.

2 ᵈWhen I shall receive the congregation I will judge uprightly.

3 The earth and all the inhabitants thereof are dissolved: I bear up the pillars of it. Selah.

4 I said unto the fools, Deal not fool-

ᵃOr, *Destroy not*——ᵇPsa. lvii. title

ᶜOr, *for Asaph*——ᵈOr, *When I shall take a set time*

NOTES ON PSALM LXXV

The *title* is, "To the chief Musician, or conqueror, *Al-taschith,* destroy not, *A Psalm* or *Song of Asaph.*" See this title Al-taschith explained Psa. lvii. The *Chaldee* supposes that this Psalm was composed at the time of the pestilence, when David prayed the Lord *not to destroy the people.* Some of the Jews suppose that *Al-taschith* is the beginning of a Psalm, to the air of which this Psalm was to be set and sung. The Psalm seems to have been composed during the captivity; and appears to be a continuation of the subject in the preceding.

Verse 1. *Unto thee, O God, do we give thanks*] Thou canst not forget thy people. The numerous manifestations of thy providence and mercy show that thou art not far off, but near: this

Thy wondrous works declare.] These words would make a proper conclusion to the preceding Psalm, which seems to end very abruptly. The *second* verse is the commencement of the Divine answer to the prayer of *Asaph.*

Verse 2. *When I shall receive the congregation*] When the proper time is come that the congregation, my people of Israel, should be brought out of captivity, and received back into favour, I shall not only enlarge them, but punish their enemies. They shall be cut off and

cast out, and become a more miserable people than those whom they now insult. I will destroy them as a nation, so that they shall never more be numbered among the empires of the earth.

Verse 3. *The earth and all the inhabitants thereof are dissolved*] They all depend on me; and whenever I withdraw the power by which they exist and live, they are immediately dissolved.

I bear up the pillars of it.] By the word of my power all things are upheld; and without me nothing can subsist. Those who consider this Psalm to have been written by David before he was anointed king over ALL *Israel,* understand the words thus: "All is at present in a state of confusion; violence and injustice reign: but when 'I shall receive the *whole* congregation,' when all the tribes shall acknowledge me as *king,* I will reorganize the whole constitution. It is true that the *land* and *all its inhabitants are dissolved*—unsettled and unconnected by the bands of civil interest. The whole system is disorganized: 'I bear up the pillars of it;' the expectation of the *chief people* is placed upon *me;* and it is the hope they have of my coming speedily to the throne of all Israel that prevents them from breaking out into actual rebellion."

Verse 4. *I said unto the fools*] I have given

ishly: and to the wicked, [e]Lift not up the horn:

5 Lift not up your horn on high: speak *not with* a stiff neck.

6 For promotion *cometh* neither from the east, nor from the west, nor from the [f]south.

7 But [g]God *is* the Judge: [h]he putteth down one, and setteth up another.

8 For [i]in the hand of the LORD *there is* a

cup, and the wine is red; it is [k]full of mixture: and he poureth out of the same: [l]but the dregs thereof, all the wicked of the earth shall wring *them* out, *and* drink *them.*

9 But I will declare for ever; I will sing praises to the God of Jacob.

10 [m]All the horns of the wicked also will I cut off; *but* [n]the horns of the righteous shall be exalted.

---

[e]Zechariah i. 21——[f]Hebrew, *desert*——[g]Psalm l. 6; lviii. 11——[h]1 Samuel ii. 7; Daniel ii. 21——[i]Job xxi. 20; Psa. lx. 3; Jeremiah xxv. 15; Revelation xiv. 10; xvi. 19——[k]Proverbs xxiii. 30——[l]Psalm lxxiii. 10 [m]Psalm ci. 8; Jeremiah xlviii. 25——[n]Psalm lxxxix. 17; cxlviii. 14

---

the idolatrous Chaldeans sufficient warning to abandon their idols, and worship the true God; but they would not. I have also charged the wicked, to whom for a season I have delivered you because of your transgressions, not to *lift up their horn*—not to use their *power* to oppress and destroy. They have, notwithstanding, abused their power in the persecutions with which they have afflicted you. For all these things they shall shortly be brought to an awful account. On the term *horn*, see the note on Luke i. 69.

Verse 5. *Speak* not with *a stiff neck.*] Mr. *Bruce* has observed that the Abyssinian kings have a *horn* on their *diadem;* and that the keeping it erect, or in a projecting form, makes them appear as if they had a *stiff neck;* and refers to this passage for the antiquity of the usage, and the *appearance* also.

Verse 6. *For promotion* cometh *neither from the east, &c.*] As if the Lord had said, speaking to the Babylonians, None of all the surrounding powers shall be able to help you; none shall pluck you out of my hand. I am the *Judge:* I will pull you down, and set my afflicted people up, ver. 7.

Calmet has observed that the Babylonians had Media, Armenia, and Mesopotamia on the EAST; and thence came Darius the Mede: that it had Arabia, Phœnicia, and Egypt on the WEST; thence came Cyrus, who overthrew the empire of the Chaldeans. And by the *mountains of the desert*, מדבר הרים *midbar harim*, which we translate SOUTH, Persia, may be meant; which government was established on the ruins of the Babylonish empire. No help came from any of those powers to the sinful Babylonians; they were obliged to drink the *cup of the red wine* of God's judgment, even to the very *dregs.* They were to receive no *other* punishment; this one was to *annihilate* them as a people for ever.

Verse 8. *It is full of mixture*] Alluding to that mingled potion of stupifying drugs given to criminals to drink previously to their execution. See a parallel passage to this, Jer. xxv. 15-26.

Verse 9. *I will sing praises to the God of Jacob.*] These are the words of the psalmist, who magnifies the Lord for the promise of deliverance from their enemies.

Verse 10. *All the horns of the wicked*] All their *power* and *influence*, will I cut off; and will exalt and extend the *power* of the righteous. The psalmist is said to *do these things*, because he is as the *mouth* of God to *denounce* them. All was punctually fulfilled: the *wicked* —the Babylonians, were all cut off; the *right-*

eous—the Jews, called so from the holy covenant, *which required righteousness*, were delivered and *exalted.*

ANALYSIS OF THE SEVENTY-FIFTH PSALM

Bishop *Nicholson* supposes that *David* was the author of this Psalm; and that he composed it on his inauguration or entrance upon the kingdom; and by it he gives us an example of a good king.

There are *three* chief parts in this Psalm:—
I. A doxology, ver. 1; repeated, ver. 9.
II. His profession how to perform the regal office, ver. 2, 3, 10.
III. His rebuke of foolish men for mistakes occasioned,—
1. Partly by their *pride* when they rise to great places, ver. 4, 5.
2. That they do not consider whence their preferment comes, ver. 6, 7.
3. That they judge not rightly of afflictions, ver. 8.

I. The doxology or thanksgiving.
1. He *doubles* it to show that it should be *frequently* done: "Unto thee do we give thanks; unto thee," &c.
2. His reason for it: "For that thy name is near,"—thy help is always at hand. "The Lord is nigh to all that call upon him."
3. Of which he had experience in his exaltation to the kingdom, which he calls God's "wondrous works."

II. How the office of a good king is to be discharged.
1. I will judge uprightly.
2. To rectify disorders. They had need of a just and upright king. 1. The land and its inhabitants were disorganized. 2. He was the only stay and support of the state: "I bear up the pillars."

III. His rebuke of bad men.
1. They were *fools*, and dealt unjustly.
2. *Wicked*, and vaunted their wealth and power.
3. They used their *power* to oppress.
4. They were *obstinate* in their oppression of the poor. He refers to their false judgments.
1. They supposed that their authority and influence came by their own *merit;* and for them they were accountable to none.
2. They did not consider that *God* was the author of power, &c.
3. Their third mistake was, they imputed afflictions to a wrong cause, and did not consider that they came from God.
To show this, the Psalmist uses an elegant comparison, comparing God to the master of a

feast, who invites and entertains all kinds of men at his table; who has a cup of mixed wine in his hand, by which he represents the *miseries* of this life. To all God reaches this cup; and *every one drinks* of it, some more, some less.

1. "In the hand of the Lord there is a cup." He apportions the afflictions of men.
2. "The wine is red." The high-coloured feculent wine, i. e., *afflictions*.
3. "It is full of mixture;" not all *sour*, nor *sweet*, nor *bitter*. The strength of it is tempered by God to the circumstances of his creatures.
4. "He poureth out of the same." He gives to all, some even to his own children. ALL *must drink of this cup.*
5. But the *lees* or *dregs* of it "all the wicked of the earth shall wring out." Those who are incorrigible have afflictions without benefit; they wring the dregs out. On them God's judgments fall without mitigation.

He concludes the Psalm with—
1. A repetition of his thanks: "I will declare for ever; I will sing praises to the God of Jacob."

2. A protestation of his duty: 1. "I will cut off the horns of the wicked." 2. "I will exalt the horns of the righteous." Those who exalt themselves shall be abased: those who humble themselves shall be exalted.

Tu regere imperio populos, Romane, memento,
(Hæ tibi erunt artes) pacisque imponere morem;
Parcere subjectis, et debellare superbos.
VIRG. Æn. lib. vi., ver. 851.

"But, Rome, 'tis thine alone, with awful sway,
To rule mankind, and make the world obey,
Disposing peace and war thy own majestic way:
To tame the proud, the fettered slave to free:
These are imperial arts, and worthy thee."
DRYDEN.

These lines of the Roman poet contain precisely the same sentiment that is expressed in the *tenth* verse of the Psalm. And thus God acts in the government of the world, dealing with nations as they have dealt with others: so the conquerors are conquered; the oppressed, raised to honour and dominion.

PSALM LXXVI

The true God known in Judah, Israel, Salem, and Zion, 1, 2. A description of his defeat of the enemies of his people, 3–6. How God is to be worshipped, 7–9. He should be considered as the chief Ruler: all the potentates of the earth are subject to him, 10–12.

To the chief Musician on Neginoth, A Psalm *or* Song ᵃof Asaph

A. M. cir. 3294
B. C. cir. 710
Ezechiæ, Regis
Judææ,
cir. annum
17

IN ᵇJudah *is* God known: his name *is* great in Israel.

2 In Salem also is his tabernacle, and his dwelling place in Zion.

3 ᶜThere brake he the arrows of the bow, the shield, and the sword, and the battle. Selah.

A. M. cir. 3294
B. C. cir. 710
Ezechiæ, Regis
Judææ,
cir. annum
17

4 Thou *art* more glorious *and* excellent ᵈthan the mountains of prey.

ᵃOr, *for Asaph*——ᵇPsa. xlviii. 1, &c.——ᶜPsa. xlvi. 9;

Ezek. xxxix. 9——ᵈEzek. xxxviii. 12, 13; xxxix. 4

NOTES ON PSALM LXXVI

The *title*, "To the chief Musician on Neginoth, a Psalm *or* Song of Asaph." See the titles to Psalms iv. and vi. The *Vulgate, Septuagint,* and others have, "A Psalm for the Assyrians;" and it is supposed to be a thanksgiving for the defeat of the Assyrians. The Syriac says it is a thanksgiving for the taking of Rabbah, belonging to the children of Ammon. It is considered by some of the best commentators to have been composed after the defeat of Sennacherib. That it was composed after the death of David, and after the two kingdoms of Israel and Judah were separated, is evident from the first verse. If *Asaph* was its author, it could not be the *Asaph* that flourished in the days of David but some other gifted and Divinely inspired man of the same name, by whom several others of the Psalms appear to have been composed during the captivity.

Verse 1. *In Judah is God known*] The true God revealed himself to the *Jews*. The *Israelites*, after the separation of the tribes, had the same knowledge, but they greatly corrupted the Divine worship; though still God was *great*, even in Israel.

Verse 2. *In Salem also is his tabernacle*] *Salem* was the ancient name of *Jebus*, afterward called *Jerusalem*. Here was the *tabernacle* set up; but afterwards, when the *temple* was built on *Mount Zion*, there was his *habitation*. The Psalm was evidently composed after the building of Solomon's temple.

Verse 3. *There brake he the arrows of the bow*] רשפי *rishphey*, the *fiery arrows*. Arrows, round the heads of which inflammable matter was rolled, and then ignited, were used by the ancients, and shot into towns to set them on fire; and were discharged among the towers and wooden works of besiegers. The Romans called them *phalaricæ;* and we find them mentioned by Virgil, Æn. lib. ix., ver. 705:—

Sed magnum stridens contorta phalarica venit,
Fulminis acta modo.

On this passage *Servius* describes the *phalarica* as a dart or spear with a spherical leaden head to which fire was attached. Thrown by a strong hand, it killed those whom it hit, and set fire to buildings, &c. It was called *phalarica* from the towers called *phalæ* from which it was generally projected. In allusion to these St. Paul speaks of the *fiery darts of the devil*, Eph. vi.

A. M. cir. 3294
B. C. cir. 710
Ezechiæ, Regis
Judææ,
cir. annum
17

5 [e]The stout-hearted are spoiled, [f]they have slept their sleep: and none of the men of might have found their hands.

6 [g]At thy rebuke, O God of Jacob, both the chariot and horse are cast into a dead sleep.

7 Thou, *even* thou, *art* to be feared: and [h]who may stand in thy sight when once thou art angry?

8 [i]Thou didst cause judgment to be heard from heaven; [k]the earth feared, and was still,

A. M. cir. 3294
B. C. cir. 710
Ezechiæ, Regis
Judææ,
cir. annum
17

9 When God [l]arose to judgment, to save all the meek of the earth. Selah.

10 [m]Surely the wrath of man shall praise thee: the remainder of wrath shalt thou restrain.

---

[e]Isa. xlvi. 12——[f]Psa. xiii. 3; Jer. li. 39——[g]Exod. xv. 1, 21; Ezek. xxxix. 20; Nah. ii. 13; Zech. xii. 4 [h]Nah. i. 6

[i]Ezek. xxxviii. 20——[k]2 Chron. xx. 29, 30——[l]Psa. ix. 7, 8, 9; lxxii. 4——[m]See Exod. ix. 16; xviii. 11; Psa. lxv. 7

16, to the note on which the reader is requested to refer.

The shield and the sword] If this refers to the destruction of Sennacherib's army, it may be truly said that God rendered useless all their warlike instruments, his angel having destroyed 185,000 of them in one night.

Verse 4. *Than the mountains of prey.*] This is an address to Mount *Zion*. Thou art more illustrious and excellent than all the mountains of prey, i. e., where wild beasts wander, and prey on those that are more helpless than themselves. Zion was the place where GOD *dwelt;* the other mountains were the *abode of wild beasts.*

Verse 5. *The stout-hearted are spoiled*] The boasting blasphemers, such as Rab-shakeh, and his master Sennacherib, the king of Assyria.

They have slept their sleep] They were asleep in their tent when the destroying angel, the suffocating wind, destroyed the whole; they over whom it passed never more awoke.

None of the men of might] Is not this a strong irony? Where are your mighty men? their boasted armour, &c.?

Verse 6. *At thy rebuke*] It was not by any human means that this immense army was overthrown; it was by the power of God alone. Not only *infantry* was destroyed, but the *cavalry* also.

The chariot and horse] That is, the chariot horses, as well as the men, were

Cast into a dead sleep.] Were all suffocated in the same night. On the destruction of this mighty host, the reader is requested to refer to the notes on 2 Kings xix.

Verse 7. *Thou, even thou, art to be feared*] The Hebrew is simple, but very emphatic: אתה נורא אתה *attah nora attah,* "Thou art terrible; thou art." The repetition of the *pronoun* deepens the sense.

When once thou art angry?] Literally, *From the time thou art angry.* In the moment thy wrath is kindled, in that moment judgment is executed. How awful is this consideration! If *one hundred and eighty-five thousand* men were in one moment destroyed by the wrath of God, canst *thou,* thou poor, miserable, feeble sinner, resist his will, and turn aside his thunder!

Verse 8. *Thou didst cause judgment to be heard*] When God declared by his prophet that the enemy should not prevail, but on the contrary be destroyed, *the earth*—the *land,* and by *metonymy* the *inhabitants* of the land, were struck with astonishment and terror, so as not to be able to move. The great boaster Sen-

nacherib, who carried terror, dismay, and desolation every where, was now struck with dumb amazement; and the angel of the Almighty, in a moment, stopped the breath of those hosts in which he confided.

Verse 9. *The meek of the earth.*] The *humbled* or *oppressed people of the land.* The poor *Jews,* now utterly helpless, and calling upon the Lord for succour.

Verse 10. *Surely the wrath of man shall praise thee*] The rage of Sennacherib shall only serve to manifest thy glory. The stronger he is, and the more he threatens, and the weaker thy people, the more shall thy majesty and mercy appear in his destruction and their support.

The remainder of wrath shalt thou restrain.] The Hebrew gives rather a different sense: "Thou shalt gird thyself with the remainder of wrath." Even after thou hast sent this signal destruction upon Sennacherib and his army, thou wilt continue to pursue the *remnant* of the persecutors of thy people; their wrath shall be the cause of the excitement of thy justice to destroy them. As a man *girds* himself with his girdle, that he may the better perform his work, so thou wilt gird thyself *with wrath,* that thou mayest destroy thy enemies. A good maxim has been taken from this verse: "God often so *counterworks* the evil designs of men against his cause and followers, that it turns out to their advantage and his glory; nor does he permit them to go to the extent of what they have *purposed,* and of what they are *able* to perform. He *suffers* them to do *some mischief,* but not *all* they *would* or *can* do." But how different is the reading of the *Vulgate! Quoniam cogitatio hominis confitebitur tibi: et reliquiæ cogitationis diem festum agent tibi:* "The thought of man shall praise thee; and the remains of thought shall celebrate a feast day to thee." The *Septuagint* and the *Æthiopic* have understood the text in the same way. Some translate thus: "Certainly, the ferocity of the man (Sennacherib) shall praise thee: and thou shalt gird thyself with the spoils of the furious." The spoils of this great army shall be a booty for thy people. Probably this is the true notion of the place. The old *Psalter* renders it thus: For thoght of man sal schrie (confess) to the, and levyngs (remains) of thoght a feste day till the sal wirk. The paraphrase is curious, of which this is the substance: "When man forsakes perfitly his synne, and sithen (afterwards) rightwisness werks; it is a feste day; whenne the conscience is clered, and makes feste with the swetnes of goddes

A. M. cir. 3294
B. C. cir. 710
Ezechiæ, Regis
Judææ,
cir. annum
17

11 ⁿVow, and pay unto the LORD your God: ᵒlet all that be round about him bring presents ᵖunto him that ought to be feared.

12 He shall cut off the spirit of princes: �q*he is* terrible to the kings of the earth.

A. M. cir. 3294
B. C. cir. 710
Ezechiæ, Regis
Judææ,
cir. annum
17

ⁿEccles. v. 4, 5, 6——ᵒ2 Chron. xxxii. 22, 23; Psa. lxviii.

29; lxxxix. 7——ᵖHeb. *to fear*——qPsa. lxviii. 35

---

lufe, restand fra besynes of any creatur in erth: Than is God at hame with his spouse dwelland."

Verse 11. *Vow, and pay unto the Lord*] *Bind* yourselves to him, and forget not your *obligations.*

Let all that be round about him] All the neighbouring nations, who shall see God's judgments against his enemies, should

Bring presents unto him] Give him that homage which is due unto him.

That ought to be feared.] למורא *lammora,* "to the terrible One;" lest they be consumed as the Assyrians have been.

Verse 12. *He shall cut off the spirit of princes*] Even in the midst of their conquests, he can fill them with terror and dismay, or cut them off in their career of victory.

He is terrible to the kings of the earth.] "He is the only Ruler of princes;" to him they must account. And a terrible account most of them will have to give to the great God; especially those who, instigated by the desire of dominion, have, in the lust of conquest which it generates, laid countries waste by fire and sword, making widows and orphans without number, and extending the empire of desolation and death.

Thus *all* are under his dominion, and are accountable to him. Even those whom *man* cannot bring to justice, God will; and to judge *them* is one grand use of a *final judgment-day.*

ANALYSIS OF THE SEVENTY-SIXTH PSALM

In this Psalm there are *three* parts:—

I. The prerogative of Judah and Israel, ver. 1, 2.

II. A narration of God's majesty in the Church, ver. 3-11.

III. An exhortation to worship and serve God.

I. The prerogatives of the Jews above all other nations.

1. God was *known* among them: "In Judah is God known."

2. His *name* was *great* in *Israel.* Illustrious for his manifold deliverances.

3. At *Salem* was his tabernacle,—his *seat of worship,* his peculiar presence.

4. His dwelling in *Zion,*—his constant habitation.

II. A narration of God's power and majesty.

He was *glorious* among good men; *more glorious than the mountains of prey*—kingdoms acquired by violence, murder, and robbery.

And this *glory* was manifest in the following particulars:—

1. They who came to *spoil* were *spoiled,* ver. 5.

2. They were *slain:* "They have slept their sleep," ver. 5.

3. They could make no head against their destroyer, though they were both *numerous* and *strong:* "None of the men of might have found their hands," ver. 5.

The cause of their consternation:—

1. The *rebuke* of God, ver. 6.

2. He was *terrible:* "None could stand in his sight," ver. 7.

3. He was *determinate:* "Judgment was heard from heaven," ver. 8. Sennacherib and his host were destroyed.

The *effects* produced by this were,

1. Praise from the wicked: "They shall acknowledge this as the hand of God." ver. 10.

2. Victory; though they rally, and return again to the battle, they shall be routed: "The remainder of wrath shalt thou restrain," ver. 10. See the notes.

III. He exhorts all to praise him:—1. "Vow, and pay." 2. "Fear and submit to him," ver. 11.

This exhortation he founds on the following REASONS:—

1. "He shall cut off the spirit of princes;" take away from tyrants their prudence and courage.

2. "He is terrible to the kings of the earth." They also shall know that he is God.

PSALM LXXVII

The psalmist's ardent prayer to God in the time of distress, 1-4. The means he used to excite his confidence, 5-12. God's wonderful works in behalf of his people, 13-20.

To the chief Musician, ᵃto Jeduthun, A Psalm ᵇof Asaph

I ᶜCRIED unto God with my voice, *even* unto God with my voice; and he gave ear unto me.

2 ᵈIn the day of my trouble I ᵉsought the LORD: ᶠmy sore ran in the night, and ceased not: my soul refused to be comforted.

ᵃPsa. xxxix., lxii., title——ᵇOr, *for Asaph*——ᶜPsa. iii. 4

ᵈPsa. l. 15——ᵉIsa. xxvi. 9, 16——ᶠHeb. *my hand*

NOTES ON PSALM LXXVII

The *title,* "To the chief Musician, (or conqueror,) to Jeduthun, A Psalm of Asaph." On this title we may observe that both *Asaph* and *Jeduthun* were celebrated singers in the time

of David, and no doubt were masters or leaders of bands which long after their times were called by their names. Hence Psalms composed during and after the captivity have these names prefixed to them. But there is reason to believe also, that there was a person of the name

3 I remembered God, and was troubled: I complained, and ^gmy spirit was overwhelmed. Selah.

4 Thou holdest mine eyes waking: I am so troubled that I cannot speak.

5 ^hI have considered the days of old, the years of ancient times.

6 I call to remembrance ⁱmy song in the night: ^kI commune with mine own heart: and my spirit made diligent search.

7 ^lWill the LORD cast off for ever? and will he ^mbe favourable no more?

8 Is his mercy clean gone for ever? doth ⁿhis promise fail ^ofor evermore?

9 Hath God ^pforgotten to be gracious? hath he in anger shut up his tender mercies? Selah.

10 And I said, This *is* ^qmy infirmity: *but I will remember* the years of the right hand of the Most High.

---

^gPsa. cxlii. 3; cxliii. 4——^hDeut. xxxii. 7; Psa. cxliii. 5; Isa. li. 9——ⁱPsa. xlii. 8——^kPsa. iv. 4——^lPsa. lxxiv. 1

^mPsalm lxxxv. 1——ⁿRomans ix. 6——^oHebrew, *to generation and generation*——^pIsaiah xlix. 15——^qPsa. xiii. 22

---

of *Asaph* in the captivity at Babylon. The author must be considered as speaking in the persons of the captive Israelites. It may however be adapted to the case of any individual in spiritual distress through strong temptation, or from a sense of the Divine displeasure in consequence of backsliding.

Verse 1. *I cried unto God*] The *repetition* here marks the earnestness of the psalmist's soul; and the word *voice* shows that the Psalm was not the issue of private *meditation*, but of deep mental trouble, which forced him to *speak* his griefs *aloud*.

Verse 2. *My sore ran in the night, and ceased not*] This is a most unaccountable translation; the literal meaning of ידי נגרה *yadi niggerah*, which we translate *my sore ran*, is, *my hand was stretched out*, i. e., in prayer. He continued during the whole night with his voice and hands lifted up to God, *and ceased not*, even in the midst of great discouragements.

Verse 3. *My spirit was overwhelmed.*] As the verb is in the *hithpael* conjugation, the word must mean *my spirit was overpowered in itself*. It purposed to involve itself in this calamity. I felt exquisitely for my poor suffering countrymen.

"The generous mind is not confined at home;
It spreads itself abroad through all the public,
And feels for every member of the land."

Verse 4. *Thou holdest mine eyes waking*] Literally, *thou keepest the watches of mine eyes*—my grief is so great that I cannot sleep.

I am so troubled that I cannot speak.] This shows an *increase* of sorrow and anguish. At *first* he felt his misery, and *called aloud*. He receives more light, sees and feels his deep wretchedness, and then his words are swallowed by excessive distress. His woes are too big for utterance. "Small troubles are loquacious; the great are dumb." Curæ leves loquuntur; ingentes stupent.

Verse 5. *I have considered the days of old*] חשבתי *chishshabti*, I have counted up; I have reckoned up the various dispensations of thy mercy in behalf of the distressed, marked down in the history of our fathers.

Verse 6. *I call to remembrance my song in the night*] I do not think that נגינתי *neginathi* means *my song*. We know that נגינת *neginath* signifies some *stringed* musical instrument that was struck with a *plectrum;* but here it possibly might be applied to the *Psalm* that was played on it. But it appears to me rather that

the psalmist here speaks of the circumstances of composing the short ode contained in the *seventh, eighth*, and *ninth verses;* which it is probable he sung to his harp as a kind of dirge, if indeed he had a harp in that distressful captivity.

My spirit made diligent search.] The verb חפש *chaphas* signifies such an investigation as a man makes who is obliged to *strip himself* in order to do it; or, to *lift up coverings*, to search fold by fold, or in our phrase, to *leave no stone unturned*. The Vulgate translates: "Et scopebam spiritum meum." As *scopebam* is no pure Latin word, it may probably be taken from the Greek σκοπεω *scopeo*, "to look about, to consider attentively." It is however used by no author but St. Jerome; and by him only here and in Isa. xiv. 23: *And I will sweep it with the besom of destruction;* scopabo eam in scopa terens. Hence we see that he has formed a verb from a noun *scopæ*, a *sweeping brush* or *besom;* and this sense my old Psalter follows in this place, translating the passage thus: **And I sweped my gast;** which is thus paraphrased: "And swa I sweped my gaste, (I swept my soul,) that is, I purged it of all fylth."

Verse 7. *Will the Lord cast off for ever?*] Will there be no end to this captivity? Has he not said, "Turn, ye backsliders; for I am married unto you: I will heal your backsliding, and love you freely." *Will he* then be *favourable no more?* Thus the psalmist pleads and reasons with his Maker.

Verse 8. *For evermore?*] לדר ודר *ledor vador*, "to generation and generation." From race to race. Shall no mercy be shown even to the remotest generation of the children of the offenders?

Verse 9. *Hath God—in anger shut up his tender mercies?*] The *tender mercies* of God are the *source* whence all his kindness to the children of men flows. The metaphor here is taken from a *spring*, the mouth of which is closed, so that its waters can no longer run in the same channel; but, being confined, break out, and take some other course. Wilt thou take thy mercy from the Israelites, and give it to some other people? This he most certainly did. He took it from the *Jews*, and gave it to the *Gentiles*.

Verse 10. *And I said, This is my infirmity*] The Hebrew is very obscure, and has been differently translated: ואמר חלותי היא שנות ימין עליון *vaomar challothi hi shenoth yemin elyon;* "And I said, Is this my weakness? Years the right

11 ʳI will remember the works of the Lᴏʀᴅ: surely I will remember thy wonders of old.

12 I will meditate also of all thy work, and talk of thy doings.

13 ˢThy way, O God, *is* in the sanctuary: ᵗwho *is* so great a God as *our* God?

14 Thou *art* the God that doest wonders: thou hast declared thy strength among the people.

15 ᵘThou hast with *thine* arm redeemed thy people, the sons of Jacob and Joseph. Selah.

16 ᵛThe waters saw thee, O God, the waters

saw thee; they were afraid: the depths also were troubled.

17 ʷThe clouds poured out water: the skies sent out a sound: ˣthine arrows also went abroad.

18 The voice of thy thunder *was* in the heaven: ʸthe lightnings lightened the world: ᶻthe earth trembled and shook.

19 ᵃThy way *is* in the sea, and thy path in the great waters, ᵇand thy footsteps are not known.

20 ᶜThou leddest thy people like a flock by the hand of Moses and Aaron.

ʳPsa. cxliii. 5——ˢPsa. lxxiii. 17——ᵗExod. xv. 11
ᵘExod. vi. 6; Deut. ix. 29——ᵛExod. xiv. 21; Josh. iii.
15, 16; Psa. cxiv. 3; Hab. iii. 8, &c.——ʷHeb. *The
clouds were poured forth with water*

ˣ2 Sam. xxii. 15; Hab. iii. 11——ʸPsa. xcvii. 4
ᶻ2 Sam. xxii. 8——ᵃHab. iii. 15——ᵇExod. xiv. 28
ᶜExod. xiii. 21; xiv. 19; Psa. lxxviii. 52; lxxx. 1; Isa.
lxiii. 11, 12; Hos. xii. 13

---

hand of the Most High." If חלּותי *challothi* comes from חלה *chalah*, and signifies to *pray*, as *De Dieu* has thought, then his translation may be proper: Precari hoc meum est; mutare dextram Altissimi. "To pray, this my business; to change the right hand of the Most High." I can do nothing else than pray; God is the Ruler of events. Mr. *N. M. Berlin* translates, "Dolere meum hoc *est;* mutare *est* dextra Altissimi." *To grieve is my portion; to change* (my condition) *belongs to the right hand of the Most High.* Here שׁנות *shenoth*, which we translate *years*, is derived from שׁנה *shanah*, to *change*. This latter appears to me the better translation; the sum of the meaning is, "I am in deep distress; the Most High alone can change my condition." The old Psalter, following the *Vulgate*,—Et dixi, Nunc cœpi: hæc mutatio dexteræ Excelsi,—translates: 𝔄𝔫𝔡 𝔍 𝔰𝔞𝔦𝔡, 𝔑𝔬𝔴 𝔍 𝔟𝔢𝔤𝔞𝔫 𝔱𝔥𝔦𝔰 𝔠𝔥𝔞𝔲𝔫𝔠𝔥𝔶𝔫𝔤 𝔬𝔣 𝔯𝔶𝔤𝔥𝔱 𝔥𝔞𝔫𝔡 𝔬𝔣 𝔥𝔦𝔥𝔢𝔤𝔥 (highest) Alswa say, God sal noght kast al man kynde fra his sigt with outen ende: for nowe I began to understand the syker; (the truth;) that man sal be brogt to endles; and thar fore, now I said, that this chaunchyng fra wreth to mercy, is thrugh Ihu Criste that chaunges me fra ill to gude, fra noy to gladnes.

Once more, *Coverdale*, who is followed by Matthews and Becke, takes the passage by storm: "At last I came to this poynte, that I thought; O why art thou so foolish? The right hande of the Most Hyest can chaunge all."

Verse 11. *I will remember the works of the Lord*] I endeavour to recollect what thou hast done in behalf of our fathers in past times; in no case hast thou cast them off, when, with humbled hearts, they sought thy mercy.

Verse 13. *Thy way—is in the sanctuary*] See Psa. lxxiii. 17. I must go to the sanctuary now to get *comfort*, as I went before to get *instruction*. What a mercy to have the privilege of drawing near to God in his ordinances! How many doubts have been solved, fears dissipated, hearts comforted, darknesses dispelled, and snares broken, while waiting on God in the means of grace!

Some understand the words, *Thy way is in holiness*—all thy dispensations, words, and works are holy, just and true. And as is thy majesty, so is thy mercy. O, who is so great a God as our God?

Verse 14. *Thou—doest wonders*] Every act of God, whether in nature or grace, in creation or providence, is wondrous; surpasses all *power* but his own; and can be comprehended only by his own *wisdom*. To the *general observer*, his *strength* is most apparent; to the *investigator of nature*, his *wisdom;* and to the genuine *Christian*, his *mercy* and *love*.

Verse 15. *The sons of Jacob and Joseph.*] "The sons which Jacob begat and Joseph nourished." says the *Chaldee*. The Israelites are properly called the sons of Joseph as well as of Jacob, seeing *Ephraim* and *Manasseh*, his sons, were taken into the number of the tribes. All the latter part of this Psalm refers to the deliverance of the Israelites from Egypt; and the psalmist uses this as an argument to excite the expectation of the captives. As God delivered *our fathers* from *Egypt*, so we may expect him to deliver *us* from *Chaldea*. It required his *arm* to do the former, and that arm is not shortened that it cannot save.

Verse 16. *The waters saw thee*] What a fine image! He represents God approaching the Red Sea; and the waters, seeing him, took fright, and ran off before him, dividing to the right and left to let him pass. I have not found any thing more majestic than this.

The depths also were troubled.] Every thing appears here to have *life* and *perception*. The *waters* see the Almighty, do not wait his coming, but in terror flee away! The deeps, uncovered, are astonished at the circumstance; and as they cannot fly, they are filled with trouble and dismay. Under the hand of such a poet, *inanimate nature* springs into *life;* all *thinks, speaks, acts;* all is in motion, and the dismay is general.

Verse 17. *The clouds poured out water*] It appears from this that there was a violent *tempest* at the time of the passage of the Red Sea. There was a violent storm of *thunder, lightning,* and *rain.* These *three* things are distinctly marked here. 1. "The skies sent out a sound:" the ᴛʜᴜɴᴅᴇʀ. 2. "Thine arrows went abroad:" the ʟɪɢʜᴛɴɪɴɢ. 3. "The clouds poured out water:" the ʀᴀɪɴ. In the next verse we have, 4. An ᴇᴀʀᴛʜQᴜᴀᴋᴇ: "The earth trembled and shook," ver. 18.

Verse 19. *Thy way* is *in the sea*] Thou didst walk through the sea, thy path was through a multitude of waters.

Thy footsteps are not known.] It was evident from the *effects* that God was there: but his *track* could not be discovered; still he is the Infinite Spirit, without parts, limits, or passions. No object of sense.

Verse 20. *Thou leddest thy people like a flock*] This may refer to the *pillar of cloud and fire.* It went before them, and they followed it. So, in the eastern countries, the shepherd does not *drive,* but *leads,* his flock. He goes *before* them to find them pasture, and they regularly *follow* him.

By the hand of Moses and Aaron.] They were God's agents; and acted, in *civil* and *sacred* things, just as directed by the Most High.

ANALYSIS OF THE SEVENTY-SEVENTH PSALM

In this Psalm the prophet shows the bitter agony which a troubled spirit undergoes from a sense of God's displeasure; and the comfort which it afterwards receives through faith in his promises.

There are *two* parts in this Psalm:—

I. The psalmist sets forth the strife between the flesh and the spirit; and how the flesh tempts the spirit to despair, and calls in question the goodness of God, ver. 1-10.

II. Next, he shows the victory of the spirit over the flesh; being raised, encouraged, and confirmed by the nature, promises, and works of God, ver. 11-20.

This is an excellent Psalm, and of great use in spiritual desertion.

I. The *strife.* The prophet betakes himself to God. 1. He prays. 2. Prays often. 3. Prays earnestly. 4. And with a troubled soul. The Psalm is, therefore, not the expression of a *despairing* soul, but of one that has a great conflict with temptation.

Though he complains, yet he despairs not.

I. His complaint is bitter, and he sets down how he was exercised.

1. He found no intermission; day and night he was in distress. His voice was continually lifted up, and his hands constantly stretched out to God in prayer. When no man saw him, ne prayed. His complaint was in *secret,* and far from *hypocrisy,* which always loves to have *witnesses.*

2. He refused to be comforted, ver. 2.

3. Even the "remembrance of God troubled him," ver. 3.

4. His *soul* was *overwhelmed,* ver. 3.

5. He became at last *speechless* through grief, ver. 4.

6. All *sleep* departed from him, ver. 4.

II. He shows that his grief was aggravated by a consideration of the happiness he once enjoyed, but had lost.

1. He had considered the days of old, ver. 5.

2. He could rejoice in and praise God, ver. 6.

3. But now, on diligent search, all good is gone, ver. 6.

4. His debate between hope and despair, which leads him to break out in the following interrogations: 1. Will the Lord cast off for ever? 2. Will he be favourable no more? 3. Is his mercy clean gone? 4. Doth his promise fail? 5. Hath God forgotten to be gracious? 6. Hath he in anger shut up his tender mercies? ver. 7-9.

II. How he is restored.

1. He begins with a correction of himself: "I said, This is my infirmity," ver. 10.

2. Takes encouragement from a remembrance,—

(1) Of God's *ways:* "I will remember—the right hand of the Most High," ver. 10.

(2) Of his WORKS: "I will remember thy wonders of old," ver. 11.

3. On these he will *meditate* and *discourse,* ver. 12.

(1) He then addresses his speech to God; who he understands is to be sought in his *sanctuary,* ver. 13.

(2) And who is "infinitely great and good," ver. 13.

(3) Who has declared his strength among the people, ver. 14.

(4) And particularly to the descendants of Jacob, ver. 15.

III. He amplifies the story of their deliverance from Egypt by several instances of God's power.

1. In the RED SEA: "The waters saw thee," ver. 16.

2. In the HEAVENS: "The clouds poured out water, ver. 17.

3. In the EARTH: "The earth trembled and shook," ver. 18.

IV. The final cause of all was that he might lead his people out of their bondage, and destroy their enemies, ver. 19, 20.

PSALM LXXVIII

An enumeration of the principal effects of the goodness of God to his people, 1–16; of their rebellions and punishment, 17–33; their feigned repentance, 34–37; God's compassion towards them, 38, 39; their backsliding, and forgetfulness of his mercy, 40–42; the plagues which he brought upon the Egyptians, 43–51; the deliverance of his own people, and their repeated ingratitude and disobedience, 52–58; their punishment, 59–64; God's wrath against their adversaries, 65, 66; his rejection of the tribes of Israel and his choice of the tribe of Judah, and of David to be king over his people, 67–72.

XV. DAY.　EVENING PRAYER

[a]Maschil [b]of Asaph

A. M. cir. 3074
B. C. cir. 930
Assæ, Regis
Judææ,
cir. annum
26

GIVE [c]ear, O my people, *to* my law: incline your ears to the words of my mouth.

2 [d]I will open my mouth in a parable: I will utter dark sayings of old:

3 [e]Which we have heard and known, and our fathers have told us.

4 [f]We will not hide *them* from their children, [g]showing to the generation to come the praises of the LORD, and his strength, and his wonderful works that he hath done.

5 For [h]he established a testimony in Jacob, and appointed a law in Israel, which he commanded our fathers, that [i]they should make them known to their children:

6 [k]That the generation to come might know

them, even the children which should be born; who should arise and declare them to their children:

A. M. cir. 3074
B. C. cir. 930
Assæ, Regis
Judææ,
cir. annum
26

7 That they might set their hope in God, and not forget the works of God, but keep his commandments:

8 And [l]might not be as their fathers, [m]a stubborn and rebellious generation; a generation [n]*that* [o]set not their heart aright, and whose spirit was not steadfast with God.

9 The children of Ephraim, *being* armed, *and* [p]carrying bows, turned back in the day of battle.

10 [q]They kept not the covenant of God, and refused to walk in his law;

11 And [r]forgat his works, and his wonders that he had showed them.

---

[a]Psa. lxxiv. title——[b]Or, A Psalm *for Asaph to give instruction*——[c]Isa. li. 4——[d]Psa. xlix. 4; Matt. xiii. 35 [e]Psa. xliv. 1——[f]Deut. iv. 9; vi. 7; Joel i. 3——[g]Exod. xii. 26, 27; xiii. 8, 14; Josh. iv. 6, 7——[h]Psa. cxlvii. 19 [i]Deut. iv. 9; vi. 7; xi. 19

[k]Psa. cii. 18——[l]2 Kings xvii. 14; Ezek. xx. 18 [m]Exod. xxxii. 9; xxxiii. 3; xxxiv. 9; Deut. ix. 6, 13; xxxi. 27; Psa. lxviii. 6——[n]Heb. that *prepared not their heart* [o]Ver. 37; 2 Chron. xx. 33——[p]Heb. *throwing forth* [q]2 Kings xviii. 15——[r]Psa. cvi. 13

NOTES ON PSALM LXXVIII

The *title, Maschil of Asaph;* or, according to the *margin,* A Psalm *for Asaph to give instruction;* contains nothing particular. The *Arabic* has, "A sermon from Asaph to the people." The Psalm was probably not written by David, but *after* the separation of the *ten* tribes of Israel, and *after* the days of Rehoboam, and *before* the Babylonish captivity, for the *temple* was still standing, ver. 69. *Calmet* supposes that it was written in the days of *Asa,* who had gained, by the aid of the Syrians, a great victory over the Israelites; and brought back to the pure worship of God many out of the tribes of *Ephraim, Manasseh,* and *Simeon.* See 2 Chron. xv. and xvi.

Verse 1. *Give ear, O my people*] This is the *exordium* of this very pathetic and instructive discourse.

Verse 2. *In a parable*] Or, I will give you *instruction* by numerous *examples;* see Psa. xlix. 1-4, which bears a great similarity to this; and see the notes there. The term *parable,* in its various acceptations, has already been sufficiently explained; but משל *mashal* may here mean *example,* as opposed to תורה *torah, law* or *precept,* ver. 1.

Verse 3. *Which we have heard and known*] We have heard the *law,* and known the *facts.*

Verse 4. *We will not hide* them] In those ancient times there was very *little reading,* because *books* were exceedingly scarce; *tradition* was therefore the only, or nearly the only, means of preserving the memory of past events. They were handed down from father to son by *parables* or *pithy sayings,* and by *chronological poems.* This very Psalm is of this kind, and must have been very useful to the Israelites, as giving instructions concerning their ancient history, and recounting the wonderful deeds of the Almighty in their behalf.

Verse 5. *A testimony in Jacob*] This may

signify the various *ordinances, rites,* and *ceremonies* prescribed by the law; and the word *law* may mean the *moral* law, or system of religious *instruction,* teaching them their duty to God, to their neighbour, and to themselves. These were commanded to the *fathers*—the *patriarchs* and *primitive Hebrews,* that they should make them known to their children, who should make them known to the generation that was to come, whose children should also be instructed that they might declare them to their children; to the end that their hope might be in God, that they might not forget his works, and might keep his commandments: that they might not be as their fathers, but have their heart right and their spirit steadfast with God, ver. 6-8. *Five* generations appear to be mentioned above: 1. Fathers; 2. Their children; 3. The generation to come; 4. And their children; 5. And their children. They were never to lose sight of their history throughout all their generations. Some think the *testimony* here may mean the *tabernacle.*

Verse 9. *The children of Ephraim—turned back*] This refers to some defeat of the Ephraimites; and some think to that by the *men of Gath,* mentioned 1 Chron. vii. 21. R. D. *Kimchi* says this defeat of the Ephraimites was in the desert; and although the story be not mentioned in the law, yet it is written in the Books of the Chronicles, where we read, on the occasion of "Zabad the Ephraimite, and Shuthelah, &c., whom the men of Gath, who were born in the land, slew; and Ephraim their father mourned many days, and his brethren came to comfort him," 1 Chron. vii. 20-22: but to what defeat of the Ephraimites this refers is not certainly known; probably the *Israelites* after the division of the two kingdoms are intended.

Verse 10. *They kept not the covenant of God*] They abandoned his worship, both *moral* and *ritual.* They acted like the Ephraimites in

A. M. cir. 3074
B. C. cir. 930
Assæ, Regis
Judææ,
cir. annum
26

12 ^sMarvellous things did he in the sight of their fathers, in the land of Egypt, ^t*in* the field of Zoan.

13 ^uHe divided the sea, and caused them to pass through; and ^vhe made the waters to stand as a heap.

14 ^wIn the daytime also he led them with a cloud, and all the night with a light of fire.

15 ^xHe clave the rocks in the wilderness, and gave *them* drink as *out of* the great depths.

16 He brought ^ystreams also out of the rock, and caused waters to run down like rivers.

17 And they sinned yet more against him by ^zprovoking the Most High in the wilderness.

18 And ^athey tempted God in their heart by asking meat for their lust.

19 ^bYea, they spake against God; they said, Can God ^cfurnish a table in the wilderness?

20 ^dBehold, he smote the rock, that the waters gushed out, and the streams overflowed; can he give bread also? can he provide flesh for his people?

21 Therefore the LORD heard *this,* and ^ewas

wroth: so a fire was kindled against Jacob, and anger also came up against Israel;

A. M. cir. 3074
B. C. cir. 930
Assæ, Regis
Judææ,
cir. annum
26

22 Because they ^fbelieved not in God, and trusted not in his salvation:

23 Though he had commanded the clouds from above, ^gand opened the doors of heaven,

24 ^hAnd had rained down manna upon them to eat, and had given them of the corn of heaven.

25 ⁱMan did eat angels' food: he sent them meat to the full.

26 ^kHe caused an east wind ^lto blow in the heaven: and by his power he brought in the south wind.

27 He rained flesh also upon them as dust, and ^mfeathered fowls like as the sand of the sea:

28 And he let *it* fall in the midst of their camp, round about their habitations.

29 ⁿSo they did eat, and were well filled: for he gave them their own desire;

30 They were not estranged from their lust. But ^owhile their meat *was* yet in their mouths,

---

^sExod. vii., viii., ix., x., xi., xii.——^tGen. xxxii. 3; Num. xiii. 22; ver. 43; Isa. xix. 11, 13; Ezek. xxx. 14 ^uExod. xiv. 21——^vExod. xv. 8; Psa. xxxiii. 7 ^wExod. xiii. 21; xiv. 24; Psa. cv. 39——^xExod. xvii. 6; Num. xx. 11; Psa. cv. 41; 1 Cor. x. 4——^yDeut. ix. 21; Psa. cv. 41——^zDeut. ix. 22; Psa. xcv. 8; Heb. iii. 16 ^aExod. xvi. 2——^bNum. xi. 4

^cHebrew, *order*——^dExod. xvii. 6; Num. xx. 11 ^eNum. xi. 1, 10——^fHeb. iii. 18; Jude 5——^gGen. vii. 11; Mal. iii. 10——^hExod. xvi. 4, 14; Psa. cv. 40; John vi. 31; 1 Cor. x. 3——ⁱOr, *Every one did eat the bread of the mighty;* Psa. ciii. 20——^kNum. xi. 31 ^lHeb. *to go*——^mHebrew, *fowl of wing*——ⁿNumbers xi. 20——^oNumbers xi. 33

---

the above case, who threw down their bows and arrows, and ran away.

Verse 12. *The field of Zoan.*] "In campo Taneos," *Vulgate. Tanis* was the capital of Pharaoh, where Moses wrought so many miracles. It was situated in the *Delta,* on one of the most easterly branches of the *Nile.* It was afterwards called *Thanis;* and from *it* the district was called the *Thanitic Canton.* See *Calmet.* Dr. *Shaw* thinks *Zoan* was intended to signify *Egypt* in general.

Verse 13. *He divided the sea, and caused them to pass through*] The reader is requested to consult the notes on the parallel passages marked in the margin on this verse and verses 14, 15, 16, 17, &c., where all these miracles are largely explained.

Verse 18. *By asking meat for their lust.*] לנפשם *lenaphsham,* "for their souls," i. e., *for their lives;* for they said in their hearts that the *light bread,* the *manna,* was not sufficient to sustain their natural force, and preserve their lives. It seems, however, from the expression, that they were wholly *carnal;* that they had no *spirituality* of mind: they were *earthly, animal,* and *devilish.*

Verse 22. *They believed not in God*] After all the miracles they had seen, they were not convinced that there was a Supreme Being! and, consequently, they did *not trust in his salvation*—did not expect the *glorious rest*

which he had promised them. Their descendants in the present day are precisely in this state. Multitudes of them disbelieve the Divine origin of their *law,* and have given up all hopes of a *Messiah.*

Verse 24. *The corn of heaven.*] The *manna.* It fell about their camp in the form of seeds; and as it appeared to come down from the clouds, it was not improperly termed *heavenly corn,* or *heavenly grain,* דגן שמים *degan shamayim.* The word *shamayim* is frequently taken to express the *atmosphere.*

Verse 25. *Man did eat angels' food*] לחם אבירים אכל איש *lechem abbirim achal ish,* "Man did eat the bread of the mighty ones;" or, *each person ate,* &c. They ate such bread as could only be expected at the tables of the *rich* and *great;* the best, the most delicate food. How little did this gross people know of the sublime excellence of that which they called *light bread,* and which they said their *soul loathed;* Num. xxi. 5! It was a type of Jesus Christ, for so says St. Paul: "They all ate the same spiritual meat, and drank the same spiritual drink," &c., 1 Cor. x. 3, 4. And our Lord calls himself "the bread that came down from heaven, that giveth life unto the world," John vi. 31-35: but a Jew sees nothing but with the eyes of *flesh.* It is true their doctors or rabbins are full of allegories, mysteries, and conceits; but they are, in general, such as would disgrace

A. M. cir. 3074
B. C. cir. 930
Assæ, Regis
Judææ,
cir. annum
26

31 The wrath of God came upon them, and slew the fattest of them, and ᵖsmote down the �q chosen *men* of Israel.

32 For all this ʳthey sinned still, and ˢbelieved not for his wondrous works.

33 ᵗTherefore their days did he consume in vanity, and their years in trouble.

34 ᵘWhen he slew them, then they sought him: and they returned and inquired early after God.

35 And they remembered that ᵛGod *was* their rock, and the high God ʷtheir Redeemer.

36 Nevertheless they did ˣflatter him with their mouth, and they lied unto him with their tongues.

A. M. cir. 3074
B. C. cir. 930
Assæ, Regis
Judææ,
cir. annum
26

37 For ʸtheir heart was not right with him, neither were they steadfast in his covenant.

38 ᶻBut he, *being* full of compassion, forgave *their* iniquity, and destroyed *them* not: yea, many a time ᵃturned he his anger away, and ᵇdid not stir up all his wrath.

39 For ᶜhe remembered ᵈthat they *were but* flesh; ᵉa wind that passeth away, and cometh not again.

ᵖHeb. *made to bow*——�q Or, *young men*——ʳNum. xiv., xvi., xvii.——ˢVer. 22——ᵗNum. xiv. 29, 35; xxvi. 64, 65——ᵘSee Hos. v. 15——ᵛDeut. xxxii. 4, 15, 31 ʷExod. xv. 13; Deut. vii. 8; Isa. xli. 14; xliv. 6; lxiii. 9

ˣEzek. xxxiii. 31——ʸVer. 8——ᶻNum. xiv. 18 20——ᵃIsa. xlviii. 9——ᵇ2 Kings xxi. 29——ᶜPsa. ciii. 14, 16——ᵈGen. vi. 3; John iii. 6——ᵉJob vii. 7, 16; James iv. 14

---

the *Cabinet des Fees*, and would not be tolerated in the *nursery*. O, how thick a veil hangs over their *gross* and *hardened hearts*.

Verse 26. *He caused an east wind to blow*] See the note on Num. xi. 31.

Verse 32. *For all this they sinned still*] How astonishing is this! They were neither *drawn* by *mercies*, nor *awed* by *judgments!* But we shall cease to wonder at this, if we have a thorough acquaintance with our own hearts.

Verse 33. *Their days did he consume in vanity*] By causing them to wander forty years in the wilderness, *vainly expecting* an end to their labour, and the enjoyment of the promised rest, which, by their rebellions, they had forfeited.

Verse 34. *When he slew them*] While his judgments were upon them, then they began to humble themselves, and deprecate his wrath. When they saw some fall, the rest began to tremble.

Verse 35. *That God was their rock*] They recollected in their affliction that Jehovah was their *Creator*, and their *Father;* the *Rock*, the *Source*, not only of their *being*, but of all their *blessings;* or, that he was their sole *Protector*.

And the high God their Redeemer.] ואל עליון

גאלם *veel elyon goalam*, "And the strong God, the Most High, their kinsman." That one who possessed the *right of redemption;* the *nearest akin* to him who had *forfeited* his *inheritance;* so the word originally means, and hence it is often used for a *redeemer*. The Hebrew word גאל *goel* answers to the Greek σωτηρ, a *saviour;* and is given to the *Lord Jesus Christ*, the *strong God*, the *Most High*, the *Redeemer of a lost world*. After this verse there is the following Masoretic note: חצי הספר *chatsi hassepher*, "The middle of the book." And thus the reader has arrived at the *middle of the Psalter*, a book for excellence unparalleled.

Verse 36. *Nevertheless they did flatter him with their mouth*] What idea could such people have of God, whom they supposed they could thus deceive? They promised well, they called him their God, and their fathers' God; and told him how good, and kind, and merciful he had been to them. Thus, *their mouth flattered him*. And they said that, whatever the Lord their

God commanded them to *do*, they would perform.

And they lied unto him.] I think the *Vulgate* gives the true sense of the Hebrew: Dilexerunt eum in ore suo; et lingua sua mentiti sunt ei,— "They loved him with their mouth; and they lied unto him with their tongue." "That is," says the old *Psalter*, "thai sayde thai lufed God, bot thai lighed, als thair dedes schewes; for thai do noght als thai hight; for when God ceses to make men rad; than cese thai to do wele."

Verse 37. *Their heart was not right*] When the *heart* is *wrong*, the *life* is *wrong;* and because their heart was not right with God, therefore they were not faithful in his covenant.

Verse 38. *But he, being full of compassion*] Feeling for them as a *father* for his children.

Forgave their iniquity] יכפר *yechapper*, made an *atonement* for their iniquity.

And did not stir up all his wrath.] Though they often grieved his Spirit, and rebelled against him, yet he seldom punished them; and when he did chastise them, it was as a tender and merciful Father. *He did not stir up all his wrath*—the punishment was much less than the iniquity deserved.

Verse 39. *He remembered that they* were but *flesh*] Weak mortals. He took their feeble perishing state always into *consideration*, and knew how much they needed the whole of their state of *probation;* and therefore he bore with them to the uttermost. How merciful is God!

A wind that passeth away, and cometh not again.] I believe this to be a bad translation, and may be productive of error; as if when a man dies his being were ended, and death were an eternal sleep. The original is, רוח הולך ולא ישוב *ruach holech velo yashub:* and the translation *should* be, "The spirit goeth away, and it doth not return." The present life is the state of probation; when therefore the *flesh*— the *body*, fails, the *spirit* goeth away into the eternal world, and returneth not hither again. Now God, being full of compassion, spared them, that their salvation might be accomplished before they went into that state where there is no *change;* where the pure are pure still, and the defiled are defiled still. All the *Versions* are right; but the polyglot translator of the *Syriac*, ܪܘܚܐ *rocho*, has falsely put

A. M. cir. 3074
B. C. cir. 930
Assæ, Regis
Judææ,
cir. annum
26

40 How oft did they 'provoke[g] him in the wilderness, *and* grieve him in the desert!

41 Yea, [h]they turned back and tempted God, and [i]limited the Holy One of Israel.

42 They remembered not his hand, *nor* the day when he delivered them [k]from the enemy.

43 How [l]he had [m]wrought his signs in Egypt, and his wonders in the field of Zoan:

44 [n]And had turned their rivers into blood; and their floods, that they could not drink.

45 [o]He sent divers sorts of flies among them, which devoured them; and [p]frogs, which destroyed them.

46 [q]He gave also their increase unto the caterpillar, and their labour unto the locust.

47 [r]He [s]destroyed their vines with hail, and their sycamore-trees with [t]frost.

48 [u]He [v]gave up their cattle also to the hail, and their flocks to [w]hot thunderbolts.

49 He cast upon them the fierceness of his anger, wrath, and indignation, and trouble, by sending evil angels *among them.*

50 [x]He made a way to his anger; he spared not their soul from death, but gave [y]their life over to the pestilence;

51 [z]And smote all the first-born in Egypt; the chief of *their* strength in [a]the tabernacles of Ham:

A. M. cir. 3074
B. C. cir. 930
Assæ, Regis
Judææ,
cir. annum
26

[f]Or, *rebel against him*——[g]Ver. 17; Psa. xcv. 9, 10; Isaiah vii. 13; lxiii. 10; Eph. iv. 30; Heb. iii. 16, 17 [h]Num. xiv. 22; Deut. vi. 16——[i]Ver. 20——[k]Or, *from affliction*——[l]Ver. 12; Psa. cv. 27, &c.——[m]Heb. *set* [n]Exod. vii. 20; Psa. cv. 29——[o]Exod. viii. 24; Psa. cv. 31——[p]Exod. viii. 6; Psa. cv. 30

[q]Exod. x. 13, 15; Psa. cv. 34, 35——[r]Exod. ix. 23, 25; Psa. cv. 33——[s]Heb. *killed*——[t]Or, *great hail stones* [u]Exod. ix. 23, 24, 25; Psa. cv. 32——[v]Heb. *He shut up* [w]Or, *lightnings*——[x]Heb. *He weighed a path*——[y]Or, *their beasts to the murrain;* Exod. ix. 3, 6——[z]Exod. xii. 29; Psa. cv. 36; cxxxvi. 10——[a]Psa. cvi. 22

ventus, wind, instead of *spiritus,* soul or spirit. The *Arabic* takes away all ambiguity:

خرج لم يعد بمد ﮑﮧ ذكرانہم لحم وروح اذا

"He remembered that they were flesh; and a spirit which, when it departs, does not again return." The human being is composed of flesh and spirit, or body and soul; these are easily separated, and, when separated, the body turns to dust, and the spirit returns no more to animate it in a state of probation. *Homer* has a saying very like that of the psalmist:—

Ανδρος δε ψυχη παλιν ελθειν ουτε ληιστη,
Ουθ' ελετη, επει αρ κεν αμειψεται ἑρκος οδοντων.
Il. ix., ver., 408.

"But the soul of man returns no more; nor can it be acquired nor caught after it has passed over the barrier of the teeth."

Pope has scarcely given the passage its genuine meaning:—

"But from our lips the vital spirit fled, Returns no more to wake the silent dead."

And the *Ossian-like* version of *Macpherson* is but little better: "But the life of man returns no more; nor acquired nor regained is the soul which once *takes its flight on the wind.*" What has the *wind* to do with the ἑρκος οδοντων of the Greek poet?

Several similar sayings may be found among the Greek poets; but they all suppose the *materiality* of the soul.

Verse 41. *Limited the Holy One of Israel.*] The *Chaldee* translates, "And the Holy One of Israel they signed with a sign." The Hebrew word התוו *hithvu* is supposed to come from the root תוה *tavah*, which signifies to *mark;* and hence the letter ת *tau*, which in the ancient Hebrew character had the form of a cross X, had its name probably because it was used as a *mark.* Mr. *Bate* observes that in *hithpael* it

signifies to *challenge* or *accuse;* as one who gives his *mark* or *pledge* upon a trial, and causes his adversary to do the same. Here it most obviously means an insult offered to God.

Verse 44. *Turned their rivers into blood*] See on Exod. vii. 20.

Verse 45. *He sent—flies—and frogs*] See on Exod. viii. 6, 24.

Verse 46. *The caterpillar, and—the locust.*] See on Exod. x. 13.

Verse 47. *He destroyed their vines with hail*] Though the *vine* was never plentiful in Egypt, yet they have some; and the wine made in that country is among the most delicious. The *leaf* of the vine is often used by the Egyptians of the present day for wrapping up their mincemeat, which they lay leaf upon leaf, season it after their fashion, and so cook it, making it a most exquisite sort of food, according to Mr. *Maillet.*

And their sycamore-trees] This tree was very useful to the ancient Egyptians, as all their *coffins* are made of this wood; and to the modern, as their barques are made of it. Besides, it produces a kind of *fig,* on which the common people in general live; and Mr. *Norden* observes that "they think themselves well regaled when they have a piece of bread, a couple of sycamore figs, and a pitcher of water from the Nile." The loss therefore of their *vines* and *sycamore-trees* must have been very distressing to the Egyptians.

Verse 48. *He gave up their cattle*] See on Exod. ix. 23.

Verse 49. *By sending evil angels*] This is the first mention we have of *evil angels.* There is no mention of them in the account we have of the plagues of Egypt in the Book of Exodus, and what they were we cannot tell: but by what the psalmist says here of their operations, they were the sorest plague that God had sent; they were marks of the *fierceness of his anger, wrath, indignation, and trouble.* Some think the *destroying angel* that slew all the first-born

A. M. cir. 3074
B. C. cir. 930
Assæ, Regis
Judææ,
cir. annum
26

52 But [b]made his own people to go forth like sheep, and guided them in the wilderness like a flock.

53 And he [c]led them on safely, so that they feared not: but the sea [d]overwhelmed [e]their enemies.

54 And he brought them to the border of his [f]sanctuary, *even to* this mountain, [g]*which* his right hand had purchased.

55 [h]He cast out the heathen also before them, and [i]divided them an inheritance by line, and made the tribes of Israel to dwell in their tents.

56 [k]Yet they tempted and provoked the most high God, and kept not his testimonies:

57 But [l]turned back, and dealt unfaithfully like their fathers: they were turned aside [m]like a deceitful bow.

58 [n]For they provoked him to anger with their [o]high places, and moved him to jealousy with their graven images.

59 When God heard *this,* he was wroth, and greatly abhorred Israel:

60 [p]So that he forsook the tabernacle of Shiloh, the tent *which* he placed among men;

61 [q]And delivered his strength into captivity, and his glory into the enemy's hand.

62 [r]He gave his people over also unto the sword; and was wroth with his inheritance.

63 The fire consumed their young men; and

A. M. cir. 3074
B. C. cir. 930
Assæ, Regis
Judææ,
cir. annum
26

---

[b]Psa. lxxvii. 20——[c]Exod. xiv. 19, 20——[d]Exod. xiv. 27, 28; xv. 10——[e]Heb. *covered*——[f]Exod. xv. 17 [g]Psa. xliv. 3——[h]Psa. xliv. 2——[i]Josh. xiii. 7; xix. 51; Psa. cxxxvi. 21, 22——[k]Judg. ii. 11, 12——[l]Ver. 41; Ezek. xx. 27, 28

[m]Hosea vii. 16——[n]Deut. xxxii. 16, 21; Judg. ii. 12, 20; Ezek. xx. 28——[o]Deut. xii. 2, 4; 1 Kings xi. 7; xii. 31——[p]1 Samuel iv. 11; Jeremiah vii. 12, 14; xxvi. 6, 9——[q]Judges xviii. 30——[r]1 Samuel xiv. 10

---

is what is here intended; but this is distinctly mentioned in ver. 51. An *angel* or *messenger* may be either *animate* or *inanimate;* a *disembodied spirit* or *human being;* any *thing* or *being* that is an instrument *sent of God* for the punishment or support of mankind.

Verse 54. *The border of his sanctuary*] קדשו *kodsho,* "of his holy place," that is, the *land of Canaan,* called afterwards *the mountain* which *his right hand had purchased;* because it was a *mountainous country,* widely differing from Egypt, which was a long, continued, and almost perfect *level.*

Verse 57. *They were turned aside like a deceitful bow.*] The eastern bow, which when at rest is in the form of a ◯, must be *recurved,* or *turned the contrary way,* in order to be what is called *bent* and *strung.* If a person who is unskilful or weak attempt to *recurve* and string one of these bows, if he take not great heed it will spring back and regain its quiescent position, and perhaps break his arm. And sometimes I have known it, when bent, to *start aside,* and regain its quiescent position, to my no small danger, and in one or two cases to my injury. This image is frequently used in the sacred writings; but no person has understood it, not being acquainted with the eastern *bow* ◯, which must be *recurved,* or bent the contrary way, ⌒ in order to be proper for use. If not well made, they will fly back in discharging the arrow. It is said of the *bow* of Jonathan, *it turned not back,* 2 Sam. i. 22, לא נשוג אחור *lo nasog achor,* "did not twist itself backward." It was a good bow, one on which he could depend. Hosea, chap. vii. 16, compares the unfaithful Israelites to a *deceitful bow;* one that, when bent, would suddenly start aside and recover its former position. We may find the same passage in Jer. ix. 3. And this is precisely the kind of bow mentioned by *Homer,* Odyss. xxi., which none of Penelope's suitors could bend, called καμπυλα τοξα and αγκυλα τοξα, the *crooked bow* in the state of rest; but τοξον παλιντονον, the *recurved bow* when prepared for use. And of this trial of *strength* and *skill* in the bending of the bow of Ulysses, none of the critics and commentators have been able to make any thing, because they knew not the instrument in question. On the τοξου θησις of *Homer,* I have written a dissertation elsewhere. The image is very correct; these Israelites, when brought out of their natural bent, soon recoiled, and relapsed into their former state.

Verse 60. *He forsook the tabernacle of Shiloh*] The Lord, offended with the people, and principally with the *priests,* who had profaned his holy worship, gave up his ark into the hands of the Philistines. And so true it is that he *forsook the tabernacle of Shiloh,* that he never returned to it again. See 1 Sam. vi. 1; 2 Sam. vi.; 1 Kings viii. 1; where the several removals of the ark are spoken of, and which explain the remaining part of this Psalm. Because God suffered the Philistines to take the ark, it is said, ver. 61: "He delivered his strength into captivity, and his glory into the enemy's hand;" and ver. 67, that "he refused the tabernacle of Joseph, and chose not the tribe of Ephraim;" for *Shiloh* was in the tribe of *Ephraim* the son of Joseph; and God did not suffer his ark to return thither, but to go to *Kirjath-jearim,* which was in the tribe of *Benjamin;* from thence to the house of *Obed-edom:* and so to *Zion* in the tribe of *Judah,* as it follows, ver. 68.

The *tabernacle* which Moses had constructed in the wilderness remained at Shiloh, even after the *ark* was taken by the Philistines, and afterwards sent to Kirjath-jearim. From Shiloh it was transported to *Nob;* afterwards to Gibeon, apparently under the reign of Saul; and it was there at the commencement of Solomon's reign, for this prince went thither to offer sacrifices, 1 Kings iii. 4. From the time in which the temple was built, we know not what became of the tabernacle of Moses: it was probably laid up in some of the chambers of the temple. See *Calmet.*

Verse 63. *Their maidens were not given to*

A. M. cir. 3074
B. C. cir. 930
Assæ, Regis
Judææ,
cir. annum
26

[s]their maidens were not [t]given to marriage.

64 [u]Their priests fell by the sword; and [v]their widows made no lamentation.

65 Then the LORD [w]awaked as one out of sleep, *and* [x]like a mighty man that shouteth by reason of wine.

66 And [y]he smote his enemies in the hinder part: he put them to a perpetual reproach.

67 Moreover he refused the tabernacle of Joseph, and chose not the tribe of Ephraim:

68 But chose the tribe of Judah, the Mount Zion [z]which he loved.

69 And he [a]built his sanctuary like high *palaces,* like the earth which he hath [b]established for ever.

70 [c]He chose David also his servant, and took him from the sheepfolds:

71 [d]From following the [e]ewes great with young he brought him [f]to feed Jacob his people, and Israel his inheritance.

72 So he fed them according to the [g]integrity of his heart; and guided them by the skilfulness of his hands.

A. M. cir. 3074
B. B. cir. 930
Assæ, Regis
Judææ,
cir. annum
26

---

[s]Jer. vii. 34; xvi. 9; xxv. 10——[t]Heb. *praised*——[u]1 Sam. iv. 11; xxii. 18——[v]Job xxvii. 15; Ezek. xxiv. 23 [w]Psa. xliv. 23——[x]Isa. xlii. 13——[y]1 Sam. v. 6, 12; vi. 4——[z]Psa. lxxxvii. 2

[a]1 Kings vi——[b]Heb. *founded*——[c]1 Sam. xvi. 11, 12; 2 Sam. vii. 8——[d]Heb. *from after*——[e]Gen. xxxiii. 13; Isa. xl. 11——[f]2 Sam. v. 2; 1 Chron. xi. 2——[g]1 Kings ix. 4

---

marriage.] הוללו *hullalu,* were not celebrated with marriage songs. It is considered a calamity in the east if a maiden arrives at the age of *twelve years* without being *sought* or *given in marriage.*

Verse 64. *Their priests fell by the sword*] Hophni and Phinehas, who were slain in that unfortunate battle against the Philistines in which the ark of the Lord was taken, 1 Sam. iv. 11.

A Chaldee *Targum* on this passage says, "In the time in which the ark of the Lord was taken by the Philistines, Hophni and Phinehas, the two priests, fell by the sword at Shiloh; and when the news was brought, their wives made no lamentation, for they both died the same day."

Verse 65. *Then the Lord awaked*] He seemed as if he had totally disregarded what was done to his people, and the reproach that seemed to fall on himself and his worship by the capture of the ark.

Like a mighty man] כגבור *kegibbor, like a hero that shouteth by reason of wine.* One who, going forth to meet his enemy, having taken a sufficiency of wine to refresh himself, and become a proper stimulus to his animal spirits, *shouts*—gives the *war-signal* for the *onset;* impatient to meet the foe, and sure of victory. The idea is not taken from the case of a *drunken man.* A person in such a state would be very unfit to meet his enemy, and could have little prospect of conquest.

Verse 66. *He smote his enemies in the hinder part*] This refers to the *hemorrhoids* with which he afflicted the Philistines. See the note on 1 Sam. v. 6-10.

Verse 67. *He refused the tabernacle of Joseph*] See the note on ver. 60.

Verse 69. *He built his sanctuary like high palaces*] כמו רמים *kemo ramim,* which several of the *Versions* understand of the *monoceros* or *rhinoceros.* The temple of God at Jerusalem was the *only one* in the land, and stood as *prominent* on Mount Zion as the horn of the unicorn or rhinoceros does upon his snout. And there *he established* his ark, to go no more out as long as the temple should last. Before this time it was frequently in a migratory state, not only in the wilderness, but afterwards in the promised land. See the notes on ver. 60.

Verse 70. *He chose David*] See the account, 1 Sam. xvi. 11, &c.

Verse 71. *From following the ewes*] Instances of this kind are not unfrequent in the ancient Greek and Roman history. *Crœsus* said that *Gyges,* who was the first of his race, was a *slave,* and rose to *sovereignty,* succeeding his predecessor, *of whose sheep he had been the pastor.*

Verse 72. *So he fed them*] Here David is mentioned as *having terminated his reign.* He *had* fed the people, *according to the integrity of his heart,* for that was ever disposed to do the will of God in the administration of the kingdom: and his *hand* being *skilful* in war, he always led them out to victory against their enemies.

ANALYSIS OF THE SEVENTY-EIGHTH PSALM

The psalmist, considering that it is God's command that his works be not forgotten, but that the father should deliver his former doings to posterity, that they might be to them both *comfort* and *instruction, deter them from sin, and persuade them to fear God,* gives in this Psalm a long catalogue of God's dealings with his people, even from their coming out of Egypt to the conclusion of the reign of David.

There are *three* principal parts in this Psalm:—

I. A *preface,* in which the psalmist exhorts men to learn and declare the way of God, ver. 1-9.

II. A *continued narrative* of God's administration among the people, and their *stubbornness, disobedience,* and *contumacy;* together with the *punishments* which God inflicted upon them, ver. 9-67.

III. His *mercy,* manifested in the midst of judgment; that he did not cut them off, but, after the rejection of Ephraim, (Israel,) made choice of Judah, Zion, and David.

I. In the PREFACE or *exordium* he labours to gain attention: "Give ear, O my people," ver. 1.

1. Shows that he is about to deliver doctrines and precepts from heaven. It is God's law, and

it should be heard: 1. For its excellence, ver. 2. 2. For its certainty, ver. 3.

2. He shows the *end*, which is another argument for attention. 1. It must not be hidden from their children, that God might be praised, ver. 4. 2. And his power magnified; and 3. His people edified, ver. 5.

Then follow the *duties* of their *children*, which are *three:* 1. That they might *know* God, his law, his works, ver. 6. 2. That they might *trust* in him, ver. 7. 3. That they might be *obedient*, ver. 8.

II. The NARRATION. Their fathers were stubborn and rebellious, of which he gives several examples:—

1. In *Ephraim:* "They turned back in the day of battle," ver. 9.

2. They kept not the *covenant* of God, ver. 10.

3. They *forgat his works* in Egypt, ver. 11.

The psalmist extends this narrative, and shows, 1. God's goodness; 2. Israel's obstinacy; 3. Their punishment.

I. His *goodness* in bringing them out of Egypt in such a marvellous way, ver. 12. 1. He divided the Red Sea, ver. 13. 2. He made the waters to stand on a heap, ver. 13.

1. His *care* in guiding them: 1. In the daytime by a *cloud*, ver. 14. 2. In the night by *fire*, ver. 14.

2. His *love* in providing for them. 1. He clave the rock that they might have water, ver. 15. 2. He caused these waters to follow them as rivers, ver. 16. 3. And thus they had an abundant supply, ver. 16.

II. *Israel's* obstinacy. 1. They sinned. 2. More and more. 3. Provoked the Holy One of Israel, ver. 17, 18.

They were *incredulous*.

1. They *tempted* God by desiring *other supplies* than his providence had designed. He gave them *manna;* they would have *flesh*.

2. They questioned his *power*, ver. 19.

3. They were foolishly *impatient*, and must have immediately whatever they thought proper, else they murmured. They said, 1. He smote the rock, and the *water* gushed out. 2. But can he give *bread* also? ver. 20.

III. Their *punishment*. 1. The Lord was wroth, ver. 21. 2. A *fire was kindled*. 3. Because they *believed him not*, nor trusted in his salvation, ver. 22.

He provided *manna* for them; an especial blessing, on various considerations.

1. It came from heaven, ver. 23.

2. It came abundantly. He "rained it down," ver. 24.

3. It was *most excellent:* "Man did eat angels' food," ver. 25.

Weary of this, they desired *flesh*. In this also God heard them. 1. He brought *quails*. 2. In abundance. 3. Brought them to and about the *camp*, so that they had no labour to find them, ver. 25, 26, 28. 4. They were all *gratified* with them, ver. 29.

See God's *justice* in their punishment, and the cause of it. 1. They were "not estranged from their lust," ver. 30. 2. His *wrath* came

upon them. 3. It came *suddenly*. 4. It *slew* them. 5. Even the *chief* of them, ver. 31.

See their *sin* notwithstanding. 1. For all this, they sinned yet more. 2. They were incredulous, ver. 32. 3. He caused them to consume their days in vanity. 4. And their years (forty long years) in trouble, ver. 33.

They began apparently to relent. 1. They sought him. 2. They returned. 3. They sought after God. 4. They remembered that he was their Rock. 5. And the Most High their Redeemer, ver. 34, 35.

But in this, their *apparent* amendment, they were guilty—1. Of *hypocrisy*, ver. 36. 2. Of *insincerity*, ver. 37. 3. Of *instability:* "They were not steadfast in his covenant," ver. 37.

On a review of this, the prophet extols the *goodness* of God that bore with such a people.

1. He opened to them the *fountain of mercy:* "He being full of compassion."

2. He displayed an *act* of this mercy: "He forgave their iniquity."

3. Though he punished *in a measure*, yet he restrained his vindictive justice, and destroyed them not, ver. 38.

His motives for this tenderness: 1. He remembered that they were but *flesh*. 2. That, their *probation* once ended, their state was fixed for ever, ver. 39. See the note.

He proceeds with the story of their *rebellions*. 1. They provoked him often in the wilderness. 2. They grieved him in the desert, ver. 40. 3. They *returned to sin*, tempted him. 4. Insulted him. 5. And forgat all his past mercies, ver. 41-43. More particularly, 1. They remembered not his hand, ver. 42. 2. Nor his signs in Egypt, ver. 44.

The wonders which he wrought in Egypt. *Five* of the plagues mentioned:—

First plague. He turned their *rivers into blood*, ver. 44.

Fourth plague. He sent *divers flies*, ver. 45.

Second plague. The *frogs* destroyed them, ver. 45.

Eighth plague. The *locusts*, ver. 46.

Seventh plague. Their *vines*, &c. were destroyed, ver. 47.

1. He cast upon them the fierceness of his wrath. 2. Sent evil angels among them. 3. And made a *path for his anger*, ver. 49.

The *first plague*. He gave their life to the pestilence, ver. 50.

The *last* plague. He slew their first-born, ver. 51.

He now gives a recital of God's mercy in the following particulars:

1. He brought his people through the Red Sea, ver. 52.

2. He guided them as a flock.

3. He kept them in safety, ver. 53.

4. He did not suffer them still to wander, but brought them,—1. To the border of his sanctuary. 2. Even to Mount Zion. 3. Cast out the heathen before them. 4. And divided them an inheritance by lot, ver. 54, 55.

Yet still, 1. "They tempted and provoked him." 2. "Kept not his testimonies." 3.

"Turned aside" from his worship. 4. Were *un-faithful*. 5. And *idolatrous*, ver. 55-58.

For this,—1. God's wrath grows more hot against the people. 2. He greatly abhorred Israel. 3. Forsook the tabernacle. 4. Delivered up the ark. 5. Gave the people to the sword. 6. Gave up the priests to death. 7. And brought upon them general desolation, ver. 59-64.

Once more, God—1. Remembers them in mercy. 2. Fixes his *tabernacle* among them. 3. Chooses *David* to be their king. 4. During the whole of whose days they had prosperity in all things, ver. 65-72.

Behold here the goodness and severity of God. Reader, learn wisdom by what those have suffered.

PSALM LXXIX

The psalmist complains of the cruelty of his enemies and the desolations of Jerusalem, and prays against them, 1–7. He prays for the pardon and restoration of his people, and promises gratitude and obedience, 8–13.

XVI. DAY. MORNING PRAYER

A Psalm of [a]Asaph

O GOD, the heathen are come into [b]thine inheritance; [c]thy holy temple have they defiled; [d]they have laid Jerusalem on heaps.

2 [e]The dead bodies of thy servants have they given *to be* meat unto the fowls of the heaven, the flesh of thy saints unto the beasts of the earth.

3 Their blood have they shed like water round about Jerusalem; [f]and *there was* none to bury *them*.

4 [g]We are become a reproach to our neigh-bours, a scorn and derision to them that are round about us.

5 [h]How long, LORD? wilt thou be angry for ever? shall thy [i]jealousy burn like fire?

6 [k]Pour out thy wrath upon the heathen that [l]have not known thee, and upon the kingdoms that have [m]not called upon thy name.

7 For they have devoured Jacob, and laid waste his dwelling-place.

8 [n]O remember not against us [o]former iniquities: let thy tender mercies speedily prevent us: for we are [p]brought very low.

---

[a]Or, *for Asaph*——[b]Exod. xv. 17; Psa. lxxiv. 2 [c]Psa. lxxiv. 7; 1 Mac. i. 31, 39——[d]2 Kings xxv. 9, 10; 2 Chron. xxxvi. 19; Mic. iii. 12——[e]Jer. vii. 33; xvi. 4; xxxiv. 20; 1 Mac. vii. 17——[f]Psa. cxli. 7; Jer. xiv. 16; xvi. 4; Rev. xi. 9——[g]Psa. xliv. 13; lxxx. 6

[h]Psa. lxxiv. 1, 9, 10; lxxxv. 5; lxxxix. 46——[i]Zeph. i. 18; iii. 8——[k]Jer. x. 25; Rev. xvi. 1——[l]Isa. xlv. 4, 5; 2 Thess. i. 8——[m]Psa. liii. 4——[n]Isa. lxiv. 9——[o]Or, *the iniquities of them that were before us*——[p]Deut. xxviii. 43; Psa. cxlii. 6

NOTES ON PSALM LXXIX

The *title, A Psalm of Asaph,* must be understood as either applying to a person of the name of *Asaph* who lived under the captivity; or else to the *family of Asaph;* or to a *band of singers* still bearing the name of that *Asaph* who flourished in the days of *David;* for most undoubtedly the Psalm was composed during the Babylonish captivity, when the city of Jerusalem lay in heaps, the temple was defiled, and the people were in a state of captivity. *David* could not be its author. Some think it was composed by *Jeremiah;* and it is certain that the *sixth* and *seventh* verses are exactly the same with Jer. x. 25: "Pour out thy fury upon the heathen that know thee not, and upon the families that call not on thy name: for they have eaten up Jacob, and devoured him, and consumed him; and have made his habitation desolate."

Verse 1. *The heathen are come into thine inheritance*] Thou didst cast them *out,* and take thy people *in;* they have cast *us* out, and now taken possession of the land that belongs to *thee.* They have defiled the temple, and reduced Jerusalem to a heap of ruins; and made a general slaughter of thy people.

Verse 2. *The dead bodies of thy servants*] It appears that in the destruction of Jerusalem the Chaldeans did not bury the bodies of the slain, but left them to be devoured by birds and beasts of prey. This was the grossest inhumanity.

Verse 3. *There was none to bury* them.] The Chaldeans would not; and the Jews who were not slain were carried into captivity.

Verse 4. *We are become a reproach to our neighbours*] The Idumeans, Philistines, Phœnicians, Ammonites, and Moabites, all gloried in the subjugation of this people; and their insults to them were mixed with blasphemies against God.

Verse 5. *How long, Lord?*] Wilt thou continue thine anger against us; and suffer us to be insulted, and thyself blasphemed?

Verse 6. *Pour out thy wrath*] Bad as we are, we are yet less wicked than they. We, it is true, have been unfaithful; but they never knew thy name, and are totally abandoned to idolatry.

Verse 7. *Laid waste his dwelling-place.*] The *Chaldee* understands this of the *temple.* This, by way of eminence, was Jacob's *place.* I have already remarked that these two verses are almost similar to Jer. x. 25, which has led many to believe that *Jeremiah* was the author of this Psalm.

Verse 8. *Remember not against us former*

9 ᑫHelp us, O God of our salvation, for the glory of thy name: and deliver us, and purge away our sins, ʳfor thy name's sake.

10 ˢWherefore should the heathen say, Where *is* their God? let him be known among the heathen in our sight *by* the ᵗrevenging of the blood of thy servants *which is* shed.

11 Let ᵘthe sighing of the prisoner come before thee; according to the greatness of ᵛthy

power ʷpreserve thou those that are **appointed** to die;

12 And render unto our neighbours ˣsevenfold into their bosom ʸtheir reproach, wherewith they have reproached thee, **O** Lord.

13 So ᶻwe thy people and sheep of **thy** pasture will give thee thanks for ever: ᵃwe will show forth thy praise ᵇto all generations.

ᑫ2 Chron. xiv. 11——ʳJer. xiv. 7, 21——ˢPsa. xlii. 10; cxv. 2——ᵗHeb. *vengeance*——ᵘPsa. cii. 20——ᵛHeb. *thine arm*——ʷHeb. *reserve the children of death*

ˣGen. iv. 15; Isa. lxv. 6, 7; Jer. xxxii. 18; Luke vi. 38——ʸPsa. lxxiv. 18, 22; xcv. 7——ᶻPsa. lxxiv.1; c. 3 ᵃIsa. xliii. 21——ᵇHeb. *to generation and generation*

---

iniquities] Visit us not for the sins of our forefathers.

Speedily prevent us] Let them *go before us*, and turn us out of the path of destruction; for there is no help for us but in *thee*.

We are brought very low.] Literally, "We are greatly thinned." Few of us remain.

Verse 9. *Purge away our sins*] כפר *capper*, be propitiated, or *receive an atonement* (על חטאתינו *al chattotheynu*) *on account of our sins*.

Verse 10. *Where* is *their God?*] Show *where* thou art by rising up for our redemption, and the infliction of deserved punishment upon our enemies.

Verse 11. *The sighing of the prisoner*] The poor captive Israelites in Babylon, who sigh and cry because of their bondage.

Those that are appointed to die] בני תמותה *beney themuthah*, "sons of death." Either those who were condemned to death because of their crimes, or condemned to be destroyed by their oppressors. Both these senses apply to the Israelites: they were sons of death, i. e., worthy of death because of their sins against God; they were condemned to death or utter destruction, by their Babylonish enemies.

Verse 12. *Sevenfold into their bosom*] That is, Let them get in this world what they deserve for the cruelties they have inflicted on us. Let them suffer in captivity, who now have us in bondage. Probably this is a *prediction*.

Verse 13. *We thy people*] Whom thou hast chosen from among all the people of the earth.

And sheep of thy pasture] Of whom thou thyself art the *Shepherd*. Let us not be destroyed by those who are thy enemies; and we, in all our generations, will give thanks unto thee for ever.

ANALYSIS OF THE SEVENTY-NINTH PSALM

This Psalm contains the *four* following parts:—

I. A complaint for the desolation of Jerusalem, ver. 1-5.

II. A deprecation of God's anger, ver. 5.

III. A twofold petition:—

1. Against the enemies of God's people, ver. 6, 7, 10-12.

2. For the people, ver. 8, 9.

IV. A doxology, ver. 13.

I. The complaint is bitter, and is amplified by a *climax*,—

1. "The heathen are come into thine inheritance," ver. 1.

2. "The holy temple they have defiled," ver. 1.

3. "They have laid Jerusalem in heaps," ver. 2.

4. They have exercised cruelty towards the dead.

5. "They have shed blood like water," ver. 3.

6. They have not even buried those whom they slaughtered.

7. "We are become a reproach, a scorn, and a derision," ver. 4.

II. Next comes the cause of their calamity.

1. God's anger was kindled because of their sins, ver. 5.

2. This anger he deprecates, ver. 5.

III. The twofold prayer,—

1. Against the enemy: 1. Pour out thy wrath on *them*, not on *us*, ver. 6; 2. He adds the reason: "They have devoured Jacob." ver. 7.

2. The second part of the prayer is in behalf of the people: 1. "Remember not against us former offences," ver. 8. 2. "Let thy mercy prevent us." The reasons: "We are brought very low." 3. His prayer is directed for help to the God of salvation. 4. For deliverance and pardon of sin, ver. 9.

His arguments to prevail with God:—

1. The blasphemy of the heathen, ver. 10.

2. The misery of the people, ver. 11. And another prayer against the enemy, ver. 12.

IV. The doxology.

1. We, who are thy people, will be thankful.

2. We will leave a record of thy mercy to all generations, ver. 13.

PSALM LXXX

A prayer for the captives, 1-3. A description of their miseries, 4-7. Israel compared to a vineyard, 8-14. Its desolate state, and a prayer for its restoration, 15-19.

To the chief Musician [a]upon Shoshannim-Eduth, A Psalm [b]of Asaph

GIVE ear, O Shepherd of Israel, thou that leadest Joseph [c]like a flock; [d]thou that dwellest *between* the cherubims, [e]shine forth.

2 [f]Before Ephraim and Benjamin and Manasseh stir up thy strength, and [g]come *and* save us.

3 [h]Turn us again, O God, [i]and cause thy face to shine; and we shall be saved.

4 O LORD God of hosts, how long [k]wilt thou be angry against the prayer of thy people?

5 [l]Thou feedest them with the bread of tears; and givest them tears to drink in great measure.

6 [m]Thou makest us a strife unto our neighbours: and our enemies laugh among themselves.

7 [n]Turn us again, O God of hosts, and cause thy face to shine; and we shall be saved.

8 Thou hast brought [o]a vine out of Egypt; [p]thou hast cast out the heathen, and planted it.

9 Thou [q]preparedst *room* before it, and didst cause it to take deep root, and it filled the land.

---

[a]Psa. xlv., lxix. title——[b]Or, *for Asaph*——[c]Psa. lxxvii. 20——[d]Exod. xxv. 20, 22; 1 Sam. iv. 4; 2 Sam. vi. 2; Psa. xcix. 1——[e]Deut. xxxiii. 2; Psa. l. 2; xciv. 1 [f]Num. ii. 18–23——[g]Heb. *come for salvation to us* [h]Ver. 7, 19; Lam. v. 21

[i]Num. vi. 25; Psa. iv. 6; lxvii. 1——[k]Heb. *wilt thou smoke;* Psa. lxxiv. 1——[l]Psa. xlii. 3; cii. 9; Isa. xxx. 20 [m]Psa. xliv. 13; lxxix. 4——[n]Ver. 3, 19——[o]Isa. v. 1, 7; Jer. ii. 21; Ezek. xv. 6; xvii. 6; xix. 10——[p]Psa. xliv. 2; lxxviii. 55——[q]Exod. xxiii. 28; Josh. xxiv. 12

NOTES ON PSALM LXXX

The *title:* see Psa. xlv., lx., and lxix., where every thing material is explained. This Psalm seems to have been written on the same occasion with the former. One ancient MS. in the public library in Cambridge writes the *eightieth* and the *seventy-ninth* all as one Psalm; the subject-matter is precisely the same—was made on the same occasion, and probably by the same author.

Verse 1. *O Shepherd of Israel*] The subject continued from the last verse of the preceding Psalm.

Leadest Joseph] *Israel* and *Joseph* mean here the whole of the Jewish tribes; all were at this time in captivity; all had been the people of the Lord; all, no doubt, made supplication unto him now that his chastening hand was upon them; and for all the psalmist makes supplication.

That dwellest between the cherubims] It was between the cherubim, over the *cover* of the ark, called the *propitiatory* or *mercy-seat*, that the glory of the Lord, or symbol of the Divine Presence, appeared. It is on this account that the Lord is so often said *to dwell between the cherubim*. Of these symbolical beings there is a long and painful account, or system of conjectures, in *Parkhurst's* Hebrew Lexicon, of about twenty quarto pages, under the word כרב *carab*.

Shine forth.] Restore thy worship; and give us such evidences of thy presence *now*, as our fathers had under the first tabernacle, and afterwards in the temple built by Solomon.

Verse 2. *Before Ephraim and Benjamin and Manasseh*] It is supposed that these three tribes represent the whole, Benjamin being incorporated with Judah, Manasseh comprehending the country beyond Jordan, and Ephraim all the rest.—*Dodd.*

Verse 3. *Turn us again*] השיבנו *hashibenu*, *convert* or *restore us*. There are *four* parts in this Psalm, *three* of which end with the above words; see the *third, seventh*, and *nineteenth* verses; and *one* with words similar, ver. 14.

Verse 5. *Thou feedest them with the bread of tears*] They have no peace, no comfort, nothing but continual sorrow.

In great measure.] שליש *shalish, threefold.* Some think it was a certain *measure* used by the Chaldeans, the real capacity of which is not known. Others think it signifies *abundance* or *abundantly.*

Verse 6. *Thou makest us a strife*] The neighbouring districts have a controversy about us; we are a subject of contention to them. A people so wonderfully preserved, and so wonderfully punished, is a mystery to them. They see in us both the *goodness* and *severity* of God. Or, all the neighbouring nations join together to malign and execrate us. We are hated by all; derided and cursed by all.

Verse 8. *Thou hast brought a vine out of Egypt*] This is a most elegant metaphor, and every where well supported. The same similitude is used by Isaiah, chap. v. 1, &c.; by Jeremiah, chap. ii. 21; by Ezekiel, chap. xvii. 5, 6; by Hosea, chap. x. 1; by Joel, chap. i. 7; by Moses, Deut. xxxii. 32, 33; and often by our Lord himself, Matt. xx. 1, &c.; xxi. 33, &c.; Mark xii. 1, &c. And this was the ordinary figure to represent the Jewish Church. We may remark several analogies here:—

1. This vine was brought out of Egypt that it might be planted in a better and more favourable soil. The Israelites were brought out of their Egyptian bondage that they might be established in the land of Canaan, where they might grow and flourish, and worship the true God.

2. When the husbandman has marked out a proper place for his vineyard, he hews down and roots up all other trees; gathers out the stones, brambles, &c., that might choke the young vines, and prevent them from being fruitful. So God cast out the *heathen nations* from the land of Canaan, that his pure worship might be established, and that there might not remain there any incitements to idolatry.

Verse 9. *Thou preparedst—before it*] 3. When the ground is properly cleared, then it is well digged and manured, and the vines are placed in the ground at proper distances, &c. So when God had cast out the heathen, he caused the land to be divided by lot to the different tribes, and then to the several families of which these tribes were composed.

And didst cause it to take deep root] 4. By sheltering, propping up, and loosening the

10 The hills were covered with the shadow of it, and the boughs thereof *were like* ʳthe goodly cedars.

11 She sent out her boughs unto the sea, and her branches ˢunto the river.

12 Why hast thou *then* ᵗbroken down her hedges, so that all they which pass by the way do pluck her?

13 The boar out of the wood doth waste it, and the wild beast of the field doth devour it.

14 Return, we beseech thee, O God of hosts: ᵘlook down from heaven, and behold, and visit this vine;

15 And the vineyard which thy right hand hath planted, and the branch *that* thou madest ᵛstrong for thyself.

16 *It is* burned with fire, *it is* cut down: ʷthey perish at the rebuke of thy countenance.

17 ˣLet thy hand be upon the man of thy right hand, upon the son of man *whom* thou madest strong for thyself.

18 So will not we go back from thee: quicken us, and we will call upon thy name.

19 ʸTurn us again, O LORD God of hosts, cause thy face to shine; and we shall be saved.

ʳHeb. *the cedars of God*——ˢPsa. lxxii. 8——ᵗPsa. lxxxix. 40, 41; Isa. v. 5; Nah. ii. 2——ᵘIsa. lxiii. 15

ᵛIsa. xlix. 5——ʷPsa. xxxix. 11; lxxvi. 7——ˣPsa. lxxxix. 21——ʸVer. 3, 7

---

ground about the tender plants, they are caused to take a deep and firm rooting in the ground. Thus did God, by especial manifestations of his kind providence, support and protect the Israelites in Canaan; and by various religious ordinances, and civil institutions, he established them in the land; and, by the ministry of priests and prophets, did every thing necessary to make them *morally fruitful*.

It filled the land.] 5. To multiply vines, the gardener cuts off a shoot from the old tree, leaving a joint or knob both at top and bottom; then plants it in proper soil; the lower knob furnishes the *roots*, and the upper the *shoot*, which should be carefully trained as it grows, in order to form another vine. By these means one tree will soon form a complete vineyard, and multiply itself to any given quantity. Thus God so carefully, tenderly, and abundantly blessed the Israelites, that they increased and multiplied; and, in process of time, filled the whole land of Canaan. Vines are propagated, not only by *cuttings*, but by *layers, seed, grafting,* and *inoculation*.

Verse 10. *The hills were covered*] 6. The vine, carefully cultivated in a suitable soil, may be spread to any extent. In the land of Judea it formed shades under which the people not only sheltered and refreshed themselves in times of sultry heats; but it is said they even ate, drank, and dwelt under the shelter of their vines. See 1 Kings iv. 25; Mic. iv. 4; 1 Mac. xiv. 12. God so blessed the Jews, particularly in the days of David and Solomon, that all the neighbouring nations were subdued—the Syrians, Idumeans, Philistines, Moabites, and Ammonites.

Verse 11. *She sent out her boughs unto the sea, and her branches unto the river.*] The Israelitish empire extended from the River *Euphrates* on the east to the *Mediterranean Sea* on the west, and from the same Euphrates on the north of the promised land to its farthest extent on the south; Syria bounding the north, and Arabia and Egypt the south. And this was according to the promises which God had made to the fathers, Exod. xxiii. 31; Deut. xi. 24.

Verse 12. *Why hast thou broken down*] 7. When a vineyard is planted, it is properly *fenced* to preserve it from being trodden down, or otherwise injured by beasts; and to protect

the fruit from being taken by the unprincipled passenger. So God protected Jerusalem and his temple by his own almighty arm; and none of their enemies could molest them as long as they had that protection. As it was *now spoiled*, it was a proof that that protection had been withdrawn; therefore the psalmist addresses the Lord with, "Why hast thou broken down her hedges?" Had God continued his protection, Jerusalem would not have been destroyed.

Verse 13. *The boar out of the wood*] Nebuchadnezzar, king of Babylon, who was a fierce and cruel sovereign. The allusion is plain. The wild *hogs* and *buffaloes* make sad havoc in the *fields* of the *Hindoos*, and in their *orchards*: to keep them out, men are placed at night on covered stages in the fields.

Verse 14. *Return—O God of hosts*] Thou hast *abandoned* us, and therefore our enemies have us in captivity. *Come back* to us, and we shall again be restored.

Behold, and visit this vine] Consider the state of thy own people, thy own worship, thy own temple. Look down! Let thine eye affect thy heart.

Verse 15. *The vineyard which thy right hand hath planted*] Thy holy and pure worship, which thy Almighty power had established in this city.

And the branch—thou madest strong for thyself.] The original is בן על veal ben, "and upon the SON whom thou hast strengthened for thyself." Many have thought that the *Lord Jesus* is meant. And so the *Chaldee* understood it, as it translates the passage thus: מלכא ועל משיחא veal MALCA MESHICHA, "And upon the King Messiah, whom thou hast strengthened for thyself." The Syriac, Vulgate, Septuagint, Æthiopic, and Arabic, have, "the Son of man," as in the *seventeenth* verse. *Eighteen* of Kennicott's and *De Rossi's* MSS. have בן אדם *ben Adam*, "Son of man;" and as the *Versions* have all the same reading, it was probably that of the original copies. As *Christ* seems here to be intended, this is the *first place* in the Old Testament where the title *Son of man* is applied to him. The old Psalter understands this of *setting Christ at the right hand of God*.

Verse 17. *The man of thy right hand*] The

only person who can be said to be at the right hand of God as intercessor, is JESUS the MESSIAH. Let him become our Deliverer: appoint him for this purpose, and let his strength be manifested in our weakness! By whom are the Jews to be restored, if indeed they ever be restored to their own land, but by JESUS CHRIST? By HIM alone can they find mercy; through HIM *alone* can they ever be reconciled to God.

Verse 18. *So will not we go back from thee*] We shall no more become *idolaters:* and it is allowed on all hands that the Jews were never guilty of idolatry after their return from the Babylonish captivity.

Quicken us] Make us *alive,* for we are nearly as good as *dead.*

We will call upon thy name.] We will invoke thee. Thou shalt be for ever the object of our adoration, and the centre of all our hopes.

Verse 19. *Turn us again*] Redeem us from this captivity.

O Lord God of hosts] Thou who hast all power in heaven and earth, the innumerable *hosts* of both worlds being at thy command.

Cause thy face to shine] Let us know that thou art *reconciled* to us. Let us once more enjoy thy *approbation.* Smile upon thy poor rebels, weary of their sins, and prostrate at thy feet, imploring mercy.

And we shall be saved.] From the power and oppression of the Chaldeans, from the guilt and condemnation of our sins, and from thy wrath and everlasting displeasure. Thus, O God, *save us!*

ANALYSIS OF THE EIGHTIETH PSALM

The parts of this Psalm are the following:—
I. A prayer, ver. 1-3.
II. A complaint by way of expostulation, ver. 4-7.
III. In the *twelve* last verses, to move God's mercy, he, 1. Shows God's love to Israel under the allegory of a vine, ver. 8-12. 2. Deplores the waste made upon it, ver. 12, 13. 3. Prays for its restoration, ver. 13-18.
IV. He makes a vow of perpetual service, ver. 19.
I. The *first* part, his *petition,* ver. 1. 1. For

audience, ver. 2. 2. For assistance, ver. 3. 3. For grace to amend, ver. 3.

The arguments he uses to induce the Lord to hear. 1. He was formerly their Shepherd. 2. He sat between the cherubim, on the *mercy-seat.* 3. He has only to *shine forth,* and show himself; and they shall be saved.

II. The *second* part, his complaint. He complains, 1. That God was angry with them. 2. That the people were in the most distressed circumstances, ver. 5. 3. Of what they suffered from their neighbours, ver. 6.

On which he redoubles his prayer. 1. Turn us. 2. Cause thy face to shine. And, 3. Then we shall be saved, ver. 7.

III. The *third* part: what God *had done* for his people. 1. He brought the vine out of Egypt, ver. 8. 2. He cast out the heathen, ver. 8. 3. He planted it. 4. He prepared the soil for it. 5. He caused it to take deep root. 6. And it filled the land, from the *river* Euphrates to the Mediterranean Sea, ver. 9-11.

He deplores the *waste* made upon it. 1. The fence was broken down. 2. It was spoiled by those who passed by, and by the wild beasts.

Then he prays, 1. Look down from heaven. 2. Visit this vine. 3. It is cut down. 4. It is burnt with fire. 5. Let thy power in its behalf be shown by the Man of thy right hand. See the notes.

Some think *Zerubbabel* is meant; others think the *Jewish nation* is thus called *the son of man,* and the *man of God's right hand.*

IV. The *last* part of the Psalm: gratitude and obedience are promised. 1. We will backslide no more, ver. 18. 2. We are nearly dead; quicken us, and we will live to thee. 3. We will invoke thy name. We will serve thee alone, and never more bow down to any strange god, ver. 18.

All these things considered, he thinks he has good ground for his prayer; and therefore confidently *repeats* what he had twice before said: "Turn us again, O Lord God of hosts, cause thy face to shine," &c.

PSALM LXXXI

An exhortation to the people to praise God for his benefits, 1–7; and to attend to what he had prescribed, 8–10; their disobedience lamented, 11; the miseries brought on themselves by their transgressions, 12–16.

To the chief Musician [a]upon Gittith, *A Psalm* [b]of Asaph

SING aloud unto God our strength: make a joyful noise unto the God of Jacob.

2 Take a psalm, and bring hither the timbrel, the pleasant harp with the psaltery.

3 Blow up the trumpet in the new moon

---

[a]Psa. viii. title

[b]Or, *for Asaph*

NOTES ON PSALM LXXXI

The *title* is the same as to Psalm viii, which see. There are various opinions concerning the *occasion* and *time* of this Psalm: but it is pretty generally agreed that it was either written *for* or used *at* the celebration of the Feast

of Trumpets, (see on Lev. xxiii. 24,) which was held on the first day of the month *Tisri,* which was the beginning of the Jewish year; and on that day it is still used in the Jewish worship. According to Jewish tradition, credited by many learned Christians, the world was created in *Tisri,* which answers to our *September.* The

in the time appointed, on our solemn feast
day.
4 For [c]this *was* a statute for Israel, *and* a
law of the God of Jacob.
5 This he ordained in Joseph *for* a testimony, when he went out [d]through the land of
Egypt: [e]*where* I heard a language *that* I
understood not.
6 [f]I removed his shoulder from the burden:
his hands [g]were delivered from [h]the pots.
7 [i]Thou calledst in trouble, and I delivered
thee; [k]I answered thee in the secret place of
thunder: I [l]proved thee at the waters of
[m]Meribah. Selah.
8 [n]Hear, O my people, and I will testify
unto thee: O Israel, if thou wilt hearken unto
me;
9 [o]There shall no [p]strange god be in thee;
neither shalt thou worship any strange god.
10 [q]I *am* the LORD thy God, which brought
thee out of the land of Egypt: [r]open thy
mouth wide, and I will fill it.
11 But my people would not hearken to my
voice; and Israel would [s]none of me.

---

[c]Lev. xxiii. 24; Num. x. 10——[d]Or, *against*——[e]Psa. cxiv. 1——[f]Isa. ix. 4; x. 27——[g]Heb. *passed away* [h]Exodus i. 14——[i]Exodus ii. 23; xiv. 10; Psa. l. 15 [k]Exod. xix. 19——[l]Exod. xvii. 6, 7; Num. xx. 13

[m]Or, *strife*——[n]Psalm l. 7——[o]Exodus xx. 3, 5 [p]Deut. xxxii. 12; Isa. xliii. 12——[q]Exod. xx. 2——[r]Psa. xxxvii. 3, 4; John xv. 7; Eph. iii. 20——[s]Exod. xxxii. 1; Deut. xxxii. 15, 18

Psalm may have been used in celebrating the Feast of Trumpets on the first day of Tisri, the Feast of Tabernacles on the *fifteenth* of the same month, the *creation* of the world, the Feasts of the New Moons, and the deliverance of the Israelites from Egypt; to all which circumstances it appears to refer.

Verse 1. *Sing aloud unto God our strength*] There is much *meaning* here: as God is our *strength*, let that strength be devoted to his service; therefore, sing *aloud!* This is principally addressed to the *priests* and *Levites*.

Verse 2. *Take a psalm*] זמרה *zimrah*. I rather think that this was the name of a *musical instrument*.

***Bring hither the timbrel*] תף *toph;* some kind of *drum* or *tom tom*.**

***The pleasant harp*] כנור *kinnor*. Probably a *sistrum*, or something like it. A STRINGED instrument.**

***With the psaltery.*] נבל *nebel*, the *nabla*. The *cithara, Septuagint*.**

Verse 3. *Blow up the trumpet*] שופר *shophar*, a species of *horn*. Certainly a *wind* instrument, as the two last were *stringed* instruments. Perhaps some chanted a *psalm* in *recitativo*, while all these *instruments* were used as *accompaniments*. In a *representative* system of religion, such as the Jewish, there must have been much *outside* work, all emblematical of better things: no proof that such things should be continued under the Gospel dispensation, where outsides have disappeared, shadows flown away, and the *substance* alone is presented to the *hearts* of mankind. He must be ill off for proofs in favour of instrumental music in the Church of Christ, who has recourse to practices under the Jewish ritual.

The feast of the *new moon* was always proclaimed by sound of trumpet. Of the ceremonies on this occasion I have given a full account in my *Discourse on the Eucharist*. For want of astronomical knowledge, the poor Jews were put to sad shifts to know the real time of the new moon. They generally sent persons to the top of some hill or mountain about the time which, according to their supputations, the new moon should appear. The first who saw it was to give immediate notice to the Sanhedrin; they closely examined the reporter as to his credibility, and whether his information agreed with their calculations. If all was found satisfactory, the president proclaimed the new moon by shouting out מקדש *mikkodesh! "It is consecrated."* This word was repeated *twice* aloud by the people; and was then proclaimed every where by *blowing of horns*, or what is called the sound of *trumpets*. Among the Hindoos some feasts are announced by the sound of the *conch* or *sacred shell*.

Verse 4. *This* was *a statute for Israel*] See the statute, Num. x. 10, and Lev. xxiii. 24.

Verse 5. *I heard a language I understood not.*] This passage is difficult. *Who* heard? And *what* was heard? All the *Versions*, except the *Chaldee*, read the pronoun in the *third* person, instead of the *first*. "*He* heard a language that *he* understood not." And to the Versions *Kennicott* reforms the text, שפת לא ידעה ישמע *sephath lo yadah yisma;* "a language which *he* did not understand *he* heard." But what was that *language?* Some say the *Egyptian;* others, who take *Joseph* to signify the *children of Israel* in general, say it was the declaration of God by Moses, that Jehovah was the true God, that he would deliver their *shoulder from their burdens, and their hands from the pots*—the moulds and furnaces in which they formed and baked their brick.

Verse 7. *Thou calledst in trouble*] They had *cried* by reason of their burdens, and the cruelty of their task-masters; and God heard that cry, and delivered them. See Exod. iii. 7, &c.

***In the secret place of thunder*] On Mount Sinai; where God was *heard*, but not *seen*. They heard a *voice*, but they saw no *shape*.**

***At the waters of Meribah.*] See this transaction, Exod. xvii. 1, &c.**

Verse 8. *Hear, O my people*] These are nearly the same words with those spoken at the giving of the law, Exod. xx. 2.

Verse 10. *Open thy mouth wide*] Let thy desires be ever so extensive, I will gratify them if thou wilt be faithful to me. Thou shalt lack no manner of thing that is good.

Verse 11. *Israel would none of me.*] לא אבה לי *lo abah li*, They willed me not, they would not have me for their God.

12 ^tSo I gave them up ^uunto their own hearts' lust: *and* they walked in their own counsels.

13 ^vO that my people had hearkened unto me, *and* Israel had walked in my ways;

14 I should soon have subdued their enemies, and turned my hand against their adversaries.

ᵗActs vii. 42; xiv. 16; Rom. i. 24, 28——ᵘOr, *to the hardness of their hearts*, or *imaginations*——ᵛDeut. v. 29; x. 12, 13; xxxii. 29; Isa. xlviii. 18——ʷPsa. xviii. 45; Rom. i. 30

Verse 12. *Unto their own hearts' lust*] To the *obstinate wickedness* of their heart.

In their own counsels.] God withdrew his restraining grace, which they had abused; and then they fulfilled the inventions of their wicked hearts.

Verse 13. *O that my people had hearkened unto me,—Israel had walked in my ways*] Nothing can be more plaintive than the original; *sense* and *sound* are surprisingly united. I scruple not to say to him who understands the Hebrew, however learned, he has never found in any poet, Greek or Latin, a finer example of deep-seated grief, unable to express itself in appropriate words without frequent interruptions of sighs and sobs, terminated with a mournful cry.

לו עמי שמע לי
ישראל בדרכי יהלכו

Lo ammi shomea li
Yishrael bidrachi yehallechu!

He who can give the proper guttural pronunciation to the letter ע *ain;* and gives the ו *vau,* and the י *yod,* their full Asiatic sound, not pinching them to death by a compressed and worthless European enunciation; will at once be convinced of the propriety of this remark.

Verse 14. *I should soon have subdued*] If God's promise appeared to fail in behalf of his people, it was because they rejected his counsel, and walked in their own. While they were faithful, they prospered; and not one jot or tittle of God's word failed to them.

Verse 15. *Their time should have endured for ever.*] That is, Their *prosperity* should have known no end.

Verse 16. *With the finest of the wheat*] מחלב חטה *mecheleb chittah;* literally, *with the fat of wheat,* as in the *margin.*

Honey out of the rock] And he fed thaim of the grese of whete: And of the hony stane he thaim filled. Old *Psalter.* Thus paraphrased: "He fed thaim with the body of Criste and gastely understandyng; and of hony that ran of the stane, that is, of the wisedome that is swete to the hert."

ˣOr, *yielded feigned obedience;* Psa. xviii. 44; lxvi. 3——ʸHebrew, *lied*——ᶻDeuteronomy xxxii. 13, 14; Psalm cxlvii. 14——ᵃHebrew, *with the fat of wheat* ᵇJob xxix. 6

15 ^wThe haters of the Lord should have ^xsubmitted ^ythemselves unto him: but their time should have endured for ever.

16 He should ^zhave fed them also ^awith the finest of the wheat: and with honey ^bout of the rock should I have satisfied thee.

Several of the fathers understand this place of Christ.

Analysis of the Eighty-first Psalm

The contents of this Psalm are the following:—

I. The psalmist exhorts them to celebrate God's name in their festivals, ver. 1-4.

II. The reasons why they should do this: God's benefits conferred on Israel, ver. 5-10.

III. Israel's ingratitude, and its consequences, ver. 11, 12.

IV. God's love and call to amendment, with the reasons for obedience, ver. 13-16.

I. He exhorts them to rejoice: but this must be, 1. *In God,* ver. 1. 2. At his *festivals,* ver. 2, 3.

II. The reasons. 1. It was God's command, ver. 4. 2. It was an ancient ordinance, ver. 5. 3. Their deliverance from base servitude, ver. 6. 4. When in deep affliction, ver. 7. 5. In a miraculous manner, ver. 7. 6. His mercy shown at the waters of Meribah, ver. 7. 7. His giving them his law, ver. 8, 9.

He then inculcates obedience, for which he gives *three* reasons: 1. "I am the Lord thy God," ver. 10. 2. Who *redeemed* thee from bondage, ver. 10. 3. He will make thee *truly happy:* "Open thy mouth wide, and I will fill it," ver. 10.

III. Israel's ingratitude, and its consequences. 1. God gave them up; left them to themselves, ver. 12. 2. They walked in their own counsels, ver. 12. And came to ruin.

IV. God's love and call, &c.

He calls them to repentance, ver. 13. The fruits of which would be *three* great benefits. 1. The subjugation of their enemies, ver. 14. 2. A long uninterrupted prosperity. 3. An abundance of all temporal and spiritual blessings, ver. 15, 16.

Under the emblems of the *finest wheat,* and the *purest honey* from the hives of bees in the rocks, where they abounded in Judea, he shows them that his followers should have so much of earthly and spiritual blessings, that they should be *satisfied,* and say, It is enough. But, alas! Israel would not be obedient; and, therefore, Israel is under the curse.

PSALM LXXXII

A warning to corrupt judges, 1, 2; an exhortation to them to dispense justice without respect of persons, 3-5; they are threatened with the judgments of the Lord, 6-8.

XVI. DAY. EVENING PRAYER

A Psalm ᵃof Asaph

A. M. cir. 3092
B. C. cir. 912
Josaphati, Regis
Judææ,
cir. annum
3

GOD ᵇstandeth in the congregation of the mighty; he judgeth among ᶜthe gods.

2 How long will ye judge unjustly, and ᵈaccept the persons of the wicked? Selah.

3 ᵉDefend the poor and fatherless: ᶠdo justice to the afflicted and needy.

4 ᵍDeliver the poor and needy: rid *them* out of the hand of the wicked.

5 They ʰknow not, neither will they understand; they walk on in darkness: ¹all the foundations of the earth are ᵏout of course.

A. M. cir. 3092
B. C. cir. 912
Josaphati, Regis
Judææ,
cir. annum
3

6 ¹I have said, Ye *are* gods; and all of you *are* children of the Most High.

7 But ᵐye shall die like men, and fall like one of the princes.

8 ⁿArise, O God, judge the earth: ᵒfor thou shalt inherit all nations.

ᵃOr, *for Asaph*——ᵇ2 Chron. xix. 6; Eccles. v. 8 ᶜExod. xxi. 6; xxii. 28——ᵈDeut. i. 17; 2 Chron. xix. 7; Prov. xviii. 5——ᵉHeb. *Judge*——ᶠJer. xxii. 3——ᵍJob xxix. 12; Prov. xxiv. 11

ʰMic. iii. 1——ⁱPsa. xi. 3; lxxv. 3——ᵏHeb. *moved* ¹Exod. xxii. 9, 28; ver. 1; John x. 34——ᵐJob xxi. 32; Psa. xlix. 12; Ezek. xxxi. 14——ⁿMic. vii. 2, 7——ᵒPsa. ii. 8; Rev. xi. 15

NOTES ON PSALM LXXXII

This Psalm, which, in the *title*, is attributed to *Asaph*, was probably composed in the time when *Jehoshaphat* reformed the courts of justice throughout his states; see 2 Chron. xix. 6, 7, where he uses nearly the same words as in the beginning of this Psalm.

Verse 1. *God standeth in the congregation of the mighty*] The Hebrew should be translated, "God standeth in the assembly of God." God is among his people; and he presides especially in those courts of justice which himself has established. The *Court of King's Bench* is properly the place where the *king presides*, and where he is supposed to be always present. But the kings of England seldom make their appearance there. King James I. sometimes attended: at such times it might be said, "The *king* is in the *king's* court." I believe the case above to be similar. Judges! beware what you do! God is in his court, and in the midst (of the assembly) God will judge. See *Parkhurst* under אלה.

Verse 2. *Accept the persons of the wicked?*] "Lift up their faces," encourage them in their oppressions.

Selah.] "Mark this:" ye *do* it, and sorely shall ye *suffer* for it.

Verse 3. *Defend the poor*] You are their natural *protectors* under God. They are *oppressed: punish* their *oppressors*, however rich or powerful: and *deliver them*.

Verse 5. *They know not*] The judges are not acquainted with the law of God, on which all their decisions should be founded.

Neither will they understand] They are ignorant, and do not wish to be instructed. They will not learn; they cannot teach. Happy England! How different from Judea, even in the days of Jehoshaphat! All thy judges are learned, righteous, and impartial. Never did greater men in their profession dignify any land or country.—(1822.)

All the foundations of the earth] "All the civil institutions of the land totter." Justice is at the *head* of all the institutions in a well regulated state: when that gets poisoned or perverted, every evil, political and domestic, must prevail; even *religion* itself ceases to have any influence.

Verse 6. *Ye are gods*] Or, with the prefix

of כ *ke,* the particle of *similitude,* כאלהים *keelohim,* "like God." Ye are my *representatives,* and are clothed with my power and authority to dispense judgment and justice, therefore *all of them* are said to be *children of the Most High.*

Verse 7. *But ye shall die like men*] כאדם *keadam,* "ye shall die like *Adam,*" who fell from his high perfection and dignity as ye have done. Your high office cannot secure you an immortality.

And fall like one of the princes.] *Justice* shall pursue you, and *judgment* shall overtake you; and you shall be executed like public *state criminals.* You shall not, in the course of nature, fall into the grave; but your life shall be brought to an end by a *legal sentence,* or a *particular judgment* of God.

Verse 8. *Arise, O God, judge the earth*] Justice is perverted in the land: take the sceptre, and rule thyself.

For thou shalt inherit all nations.] Does not this last verse contain a prophecy of our Lord, the calling of the Gentiles, and the prevalence of Christianity over the earth? Thus several of the *fathers* have understood the passage. It is only by the universal spread of Christianity over the world, that the reign of righteousness and justice is to be established: and of whom can it be said that *he shall inherit all nations,* but of *Jesus Christ?*

ANALYSIS OF THE EIGHTY-SECOND PSALM

There are *three* parts in this Psalm:—

I. The prophet's proclamation, ver. 1.

II. God's controversy with the judges of the land, ver. 2-7.

III. The prophet's prayer that God would rise and judge, ver. 8.

I. God's presence proclaimed in court. At an assize the judge sits in the midst of the justices: "God standeth in the congregation," &c., ver. 1.

II. 1. He *reproves* them, ver. 2. 1. For their unjust judgment: "Ye judge unjustly." 2. For their obstinate continuance in it: "How long will ye," &c. Ye have not done it once, but often. 3. For their partiality: "they accepted persons," ver. 2.

2. He *exhorts* them to do their duty. 1. "Defend the poor and fatherless." Do right to

every man. 2. "Deliver the poor and needy," ver. 3.

3. He acquaints them with the events that shall follow where justice is not done: all is out of order; and the judges are the cause of it. 1. Through ignorance: "They know not the law," ver. 5. 2. Through obstinacy: "They will not learn it," ver. 5. 3. Through their determination to walk in their own way, ver. 5: "They walk on in darkness." 4. They shall in consequence be brought, 1. To an untimely death: "Ye shall die like men." 2. To a shameful death: "Ye shall fall like one

of the princes," ye shall have a mighty fall, ver. 7.

III. The prophet's prayer. Since judgment and justice have failed in the land, he says, 1. "Arise, O Lord!" He does not say, Arise, O people, and put down those unjust judges. No; their function is from God, and God alone is to *reform*, or *strip*, or *punish* them. 2. "Judge the earth." Take the state of all people into thy consideration: there is much injustice in the earth. 3. For this petition he gives a reason: "For thou shalt inherit all nations," ver. 8. Publish thy own laws, appoint thy own officers, and let them in thy name dispense righteousness and true holiness throughout the world.

PSALM LXXXIII

The psalmist calls upon God for immediate help against a multitude of confederate enemies who had risen up against Judah, 1–5. He mentions them by name, 6–8; shows how they were to be punished, 9–17; and that this was to be done for the glory of God, 18.

A Song *or* Psalm [a]of Asaph

A. M. vir. 3108
B. C. cir. 896
Josaphati,Regis
Judææ,
cir. annum
19

KEEP [b]not thou silence, O God: hold not thy peace, and be not still, O God.

2 For, lo, [c]thine enemies make a tumult: and they that [d]hate thee have lifted up the head.

3 They have taken crafty counsel against thy

people, and consulted [e]against thy hidden ones.

A. M. cir. 3108
B. C. cir. 896
Josaphati,Regis
Judææ,
cir. annum
19

4 They have said, Come, and [f]let us cut them off from *being* a nation; that the name of Israel may be no more in remembrance.

5 For they have consulted together with one [g]consent: they are confederate against thee:

---

[a]Or, *for Asaph*——[b]Psa. xxviii. 1; xxxv. 22; cix. 1 [c]Psa. ii. 1; Acts iv. 25——[d]Psa. lxxi. 15

[e]Psa. xxvii. 5; xxxi. 20——[f]See Esth. iii. 6, 9; Jer. xi. 19; xxxi. 36——[g]Heb. *heart*

NOTES ON PSALM LXXXIII

The title, *A Song* or *Psalm of Asaph*, contains nothing particular. Among a multitude of conjectures relative to the *time* and *occasion* of this Psalm, that which refers it to the confederacy against *Jehoshaphat*, king of Judah, mentioned 2 Chron. xx., is the most likely. The following reasons make it probable: 1. The children of *Ammon*, that is, the *Ammonites* and *Moabites*, were the principal movers in the war. 2. The *Idumeans* came to their assistance, 2 Chron. xx. 22; with certain *Ammonites* or *Meonians*, referred to here in ver. 8, and in 2 Chron. xx. 1. 3. There were also in this confederacy many *strangers* of Syria, and from beyond the sea, most likely the Dead Sea, which seems to indicate the *Assyrians, Hagaranes*, and *Ishmaelites*, designed expressly here, ver. 7, 8. 4. In that transaction there was a prophet of the race of *Asaph*, named *Jahaziel*, who foretold to *Jehoshaphat* their total overthrow, 2 Chron. xx. 14, &c., and probably this *Jahaziel* is the same with *Asaph*, the author of this Psalm. In the course of the notes we shall see other circumstances relative to the war of the *Moabites* and *Ammonites* against *Jehoshaphat*, which illustrates several particulars in this Psalm. See *Calmet*.

Verse 1. *Keep not thou silence*] A strong appeal to God just as the confederacy was discovered. Do not be inactive; do not be neuter. Thy honour and our existence are both at stake.

Verse 2. *Thine enemies make a tumult*] They are not merely the enemies of *thy people*, but they are the enemies of *thyself*, thy worship, ordinances, and laws: "They make a tumult," they *throng* together.

They—have lifted up the head.] They have made an irruption into the land of Judea, and encamped at *En-gedi*, by the Dead Sea, 2 Chron. xx. 1, 2.

Verse 3. *Consulted against thy hidden ones.*] צפוניך *tsephuneycha*, Thy hidden things; *places; persons.* "The hidden things in thy treasures."—CHALDEE. "Thy holy ones."—SYRIAC. "Thy saints."—VULGATE and SEPTUAGINT; and so the *Æthiopic* and *Arabic.* The *people of Israel* are probably meant. Or perhaps the *temple*, the *ark*, and the *treasures of the temple*, are intended.

Verse 4. *Let us cut them off*] Let us exterminate the whole race, that there may not be a record of them on the face of the earth. And their scheme was well laid: *eight* or *ten* different nations united themselves in a firm bond to do this; and they had kept their purpose so secret that the king of Judah does not appear to have heard of it till his territories were actually invaded, and the different bodies of this coalition had assembled at En-gedi. Never was Judah before in greater danger.

Verse 5. *They have consulted together with one consent*] With a united heart, לב יחדו *leb yachdav*. Their heart and soul are in the work.

They are confederate against thee] "They

A. M. cir. 3108 B. C. cir. 896 Josaphati, Regis Judææ, cir. annum 19

6 [h]The tabernacles of Edom, and the Ishmaelites; of Moab, and the Hagarenes;

7 Gebal, and Ammon, and Amalek; the Philistines with the inhabitants of Tyre;

8 Assur also is joined with them: [i]they have holpen the children of Lot. Selah.

9 Do unto them as *unto* the [k]Midianites; as *to* [l]Sisera, as *to* Jabin, at the brook of Kison:

10 *Which* perished at En-dor: [m]they became *as* dung for the earth.

A. M. cir. 3108 B. C. cir. 896 Josaphati, Regis Judææ, cir. annum 19

11 Make their nobles like [n]Oreb, and like Zeeb: yea, all their princes as [o]Zebah, and as Zalmunna:

12 Who said, Let us take to ourselves the houses of God in possession.

13 [p]O my God, make them like a wheel; [q]as the stubble before the wind.

[h]See 2 Chron. xx. 1, 10, 11——[i]Heb. *they have been an arm to the children of Lot*——[k]Numbers xxxi. 7; Judg. vii. 22

[l]Judg. iv. 15, 24; v. 21——[m]2 Kings ix. 37; Zeph. i. 17——[n]Judg. vii. 25——[o]Judg. vii. 12, 21——[p]Isa. xvii. 13, 14——[q]Psa. xxxv. 5

have made a covenant," ברית יכריתו *berith yachrithu*, "they have cut the covenant sacrifice." They have slain an animal, divided him in twain, and passed between the pieces of the victim; and have thus bound themselves to accomplish their purpose.

Verse 6. *The tabernacles of Edom*] The *tents* of these different people are seen in the grand encampment. *Tents* are probably mentioned because it was the custom of some of these people, particularly the *Ishmaelites*, to live a migratory or wandering life; having no fixed habitation, but always abiding in tents. Their posterity remain to the present day, and act and live in the same manner.

Hagarenes] These people dwelt on the east of *Gilead;* and were nearly destroyed in the days of Saul, being totally expelled from their country, 1 Chron. v. 10, but afterwards recovered some strength and consequence; but *where* they dwelt after their expulsion by the Israelites is not known.

Verse 7. *Gebal*] The *Giblites*, who were probably the persons here designed, were a tribe of the ancient inhabitants of the land of Canaan, and are mentioned as unconquered at the death of Joshua, chap. xiii. 5. They are called *stone-squarers* or *Giblites*, 1 Kings v. 18, and were of considerable assistance to Hiram, king of Tyre, in preparing timber and stones for the building of the temple. They appear to have been eminent in the days of Ezekiel, who terms them the "ancients of Gebal, and the wise men thereof," who were ship-builders, chap. xxvii. 3. What is now called *Gibyle*, a place on the Mediterranean Sea, between Tripoli and Sidon, is supposed to be the remains of the city of the *Giblites*.

Ammon and *Moab* were the descendants of the children of *Lot*. Their bad origin is sufficiently known. See Gen. xix. 30, &c. Calmet supposes that *Ammon* is put here for *Men* or *Maon*, the *Meonians*, a people who lived in the neighbourhood of the Amalekites and Idumeans. See the notes on 2 Chron. xx. 1; xxvi. 7.

Amalek] The Amalekites are well known as the ancient and inveterate enemies of the Israelites. They were neighbours to the Idumeans.

The Philistines] These were tributaries to Jehoshaphat, 2 Chron. xvii. 11; but it seems they took advantage of the present times, to join in the great confederacy against him.

The inhabitants of Tyre] These probably joined the confederacy in hopes of making conquests, and extending their territory on the *main land*.

Verse 8. *Assur also is joined*] The *Ammonites* might have got those auxiliaries from beyond the Euphrates, against Jehosphaphat, as formerly they were brought against David. See 2 Sam. x. 16.

They have holpen the children of Lot.] The Ammonites, who appear to have been the chief instigators in this war.

Verse 9. *Do unto them as* unto *the Midianites*] Who were utterly defeated by *Gideon*, Judg. vii. 21, 22.

As to *Sisera*] Captain of the army of *Jabin*, king of Canaan, who was totally defeated by *Deborah* and *Barak*, near Mount *Tabor*, by the river *Kishon;* and himself, after having fled from the battle, slain by *Jael*, the wife of *Heber*, the Kenite. See Judg. iv. 15, &c.

Verse 10. *Perished at En-dor*] This refers to the defeat of the *Midianites* by *Gideon*, who were encamped in the valley of *Jezreel*, at the foot of Mount *Gilboa*, and near to *Tabor*, Judg. vi. 33, vii. 1, and consequently in the environs of *En-dor*. There *Gideon* attacked and defeated them; and, in various places during their flight, they were destroyed, and left to rot upon the earth. Judg. vii. 22-25.

Verse 11. *Make their nobles like Oreb, and like Zeeb*] They were two of the chiefs, or generals, of the Midianites; and were slain in the pursuit of the Midianites, by the men of Ephraim; and their heads brought to *Gideon* on the other side of Jordan. Judg. vii. 24, 25.

Yea, all their princes as Zebah, and as Zalmunna] These were kings of *Midian*, who were encamped at *Karkor* with *fifteen thoussand* men, whom Gideon attacked there, and defeated, and took the kings prisoners; and finding that they had killed his own brothers slew them both. See Judg. viii 10-21. Of the Midianites there fell at this time *one hundred and twenty thousand* men.

Verse 12. *Let us take to ourselves the houses of God in possession.*] Nearly the words spoken by the confederates when they came to attack Jehoshaphat. *They come* (says the king in address to God) *to cast us out of thy possession, which thou hast given us to inherit.* See 2 Chron. xx. 11.

Verse 13. *O my God, make them like a wheel*] Alluding to the manner of threshing corn in the east. A *large broad wheel* was rolled over the grain on a threshing-floor, which was generally in the open air; and the grain being thrown up by a shovel against the wind the chaff was thus separated from it, in the place where it was threshed.

A. M. cir. 3108
B. C. cir. 896
Josaphati,Regis
Judææ,
cir. annum
19

14 As the fire burneth a wood, and as the flame ʳsetteth the mountains on fire;

15 So persecute them ˢwith thy tempest, and make them afraid with thy storm.

16 ᵗFill their faces with shame; that they may seek thy name, O Lᴏʀᴅ.

17 Let them be confounded and troubled for ever; yea, let them be put to shame, and perish:

A. M. cir. 3108
B. C. cir. 896
Josaphati,Regis
Judææ,
cir. annum
19

18 ᵘThat *men* may know that thou, whose ᵛname alone *is* JEHOVAH, *art* ʷthe Most High over all the earth.

ʳDeut. xxxii. 22——ˢJob ix. 17——ᵗPsa. xxxv. 4, 26

ᵘ Psa. lix. 13——ᵛExod. vi. 3——ʷPsa. xcii. 8

Verse 14. *The flame setteth the mountains on fire*] This may refer to the burning of the straw and chaff, after the grain was threshed and winnowed. And as their threshing-floors were situated often on the *hills* or *mountains*, to take the advantage of the wind, the *setting the mountains on fire* may refer to the burning of the *chaff*, &c., in those places. Let them be like *stubble* driven away by the *wind*, and burnt by the *fire*.

Verse 15. *So persecute them*] In this and the two following verses we find several awful execrations; and all this seems to be done in reference to that ancient custom, "pouring execrations on an enemy previously to battle." Of this I have already given specimens in this work; and the reader is particularly requested to refer to the case of Balaam being hired by the king of Moab to curse Israel previously to his intended attack: see the note on Num. xxii. 6, where the subject is treated at large.

This custom prevailed much among the *Romans*, and the ancient *Druids* of *Britain*. In all cases the *priests* were employed to utter the execrations, as they were supposed to have the greatest influence with the gods, in whose name the curses were uttered.

Verse 16. *That they may seek thy name*] Let them be confounded in all their attempts on Israel; and see, so manifestly, that thou hast done it, that they may invoke thy name, and be converted to thee.

Verse 17. *Let them—perish*] That is, in their present attempts. Some have objected to the execrations in this Psalm, without due consideration. None of these execrations refer either to their *souls* or to their *eternal state*; but merely to their *discomfiture in their present attempts*. Suppose the continental powers should join together to subjugate Britain, and destroy the Protestant religion; is there a Christian in the land that would not be justified in meeting them with the same or similar execrations? On the knees of my soul would I offer every one of them to God against such invaders. Selah.—A. C.

Verse 18. *That* men *may know*] That they may acknowledge, and be converted to thee. Here is no *malice;* all is *self-defence*.

ᴀɴᴀʟʏsɪs ᴏꜰ ᴛʜᴇ Eɪɢʜᴛʏ-ᴛʜɪʀᴅ Psᴀʟᴍ

This Psalm divides itself into *four* parts:—
I. A short ejaculation, ver. 1.
II. A complaint against God's enemies, which is the reason of this prayer, ver. 2-10.
III. A fearful imprecation against them, ver. 12-17.
IV. The charitable ends proposed, ver. 18.
I. The *ejaculation* or prayer: "Keep not thou

silence—be not still." Thy enemies are *loud* in their threatenings, and *active* in their endeavours, to destroy thy *people* and *thy worship:* "Hold not thy peace!"

II. He complains—These are enemies, 1. To thy people, ver. 2. 2. To God himself, ver. 5. Then he describes them, ver. 6-8.

1. They were banditti—spoilers: They "make a tumult," ver. 2.

2. Proud and arrogant: "They have lifted up the head," ver. 2.

3. They were subtle and crafty: "They have taken crafty counsel," ver. 3.

4. They carried their cunning counsel into acts of aggression: "Come, and let us cut them off," &c., ver. 4.

5. They were conspirators,—1. Against God. 2. Against his people. All the world against God and his Church! Not an uncommon case.

6. He gives us a *catalogue* of these conspirators, ver. 6-8: *Edom,* &c.

III. *He prays to God against them.* In which there are *four* particulars: 1. Their fall and ruin. 2. Their persecution. 3. Their terror. 4. Their disgrace.

These he illustrates by *five* similitudes: 1. Of a *wheel* that, running on, crushes all under it successively. 2. Of *stubble* or *chaff,* easily driven away by the *wind,* ver. 13. 3. Of a *wood* or *forest* in a state of general *conflagration,* ver. 14. 4. Of a *flame* that even consumes the *mountains,* ver. 14.

Their fall and ruin he wished to be—
1. *Speedy* and *perpetual:* "Do unto them as unto the Midianites," &c., ver. 9-13.
2. *Sudden* and *violent:* "As fire," ver. 13.
3. *Terrible* and *shameful:* "Fill their faces with shame," ver. 15, 16.

There are here *three* particulars of their punishment: 1. *Flight.* 2. *Terror.* 3. *Shame* and *ignominy.*

IV. The charitable ends proposed. These were *two:*—
1. That they might *seek after God,* be converted to him, ver. 16.
2. That they might *know him to be Jehovah,* the only true God, that they might be saved from all idolatry, ver. 18.

The spirit of this prayer is, 1. If they will not *seek* thee, and be converted, let them be *confounded* in their attempts against thy people. 2. If they will not *acknowledge* thee, let them be utterly *routed and overthrown:* "Let them be put to shame, and perish!"

PSALM LXXXIV

The psalmist longs for communion with God in the sanctuary, 1–3. The blessedness of those who enjoy God's ordinances, 4–7. With confidence in God, he prays for restoration to his house and worship, 8–12.

To the chief Musician ªupon Gittith, A Psalm ᵇfor the sons of Korah

HOW ᶜamiable *are* thy tabernacles, O LORD of hosts!

2 ᵈMy soul longeth, yea, even fainteth for the courts of the LORD: my heart and my flesh crieth out for the living God.

3 Yea, the sparrow hath found a house, and the swallow a nest for herself, where she may lay her young, *even* thine altars, O LORD of hosts, my King and my God.

4 ᵉBlessed *are* they that dwell in thy house; they will be still praising thee. Selah.

5 Blessed *is* the man whose strength *is* in thee; in whose heart *are* the ways *of them:*

6 *Who* passing through the valley ᶠofᵍ Baca make it a well; the rain also ʰfilleth the pools.

ªPsa. viii. title——ᵇOr, *of*——ᶜPsa. xxvii. 4——ᵈPsa. xlii. 1, 2; lxiii. 1; lxxiii. 26; cxix. 20——ᵉPsa. lxv. 4

ᶠOr, *of mulberry trees make him a well,* &c.——ᵍ2 Sam. v. 22, 23——ʰHeb. *covereth*

NOTES ON PSALM LXXXIV

The *title* here is the same as that of Psalm lxxxi., only that was for *Asaph*, this *for the sons of Korah.* This person was one of the chief rebels against Moses and Aaron; there were *three, Korah, Dathan,* and *Abiram,* who made an insurrection; and the earth opened, and swallowed them and their partisans up, Num. xvi. The children of Dathan and Abiram perished with their fathers; but by a particular dispensation of Providence, the children of *Korah* were *spared.* See Num. xxvi. 11, and the *note* there. The family of *Korah* was continued in Israel; and it appears from 1 Chron. xxvi. 1-19 that they were still employed about the temple, and were *porters* or *keepers of the doors.* They were also *singers* in the temple; see 2 Chron. xx. 19. This Psalm might have been sent to them to be sung, or one of themselves might have been its author.

Verse 1. *How amiable* are *thy tabernacles*] In this *plural* noun he appears to include all the *places* in or near the temple where acts of Divine worship were performed. The holy of holies, the holy place, the altar of incense, the altar of burnt-offering, &c., &c.; all called here God's *tabernacles* or *dwelling-places;* for wherever God was worshipped, there he was supposed to dwell.

Verse 2. *My soul longeth*] It is a Levite that speaks, who ardently longs to regain his place in the temple, and his part in the sacred services.

My heart and my flesh] All the desires of my *soul* and *body;* every *appetite* and *wish,* both *animal* and *spiritual,* long for thy service.

Verse 3. *Yea, the sparrow hath found a house*] It is very unlikely that sparrows and swallows, or birds of any kind, should be permitted to build their nests, and hatch their young, in or about altars which were kept in a state of the *greatest purity;* and where *perpetual fires* were kept up for the purpose of sacrifice, burning incense, &c. Without altering the text, if the clause be read in a parenthesis, the absurdity will be avoided, and the sense be good. "My heart crieth out for the living God, (even the sparrow hath found a house, and the swallow דרור *deror,* the *ring-dove,* a nest for herself, where she may lay her young,) for thine altars. O Lord of hosts!" Or, read the

parenthesis last: "My heart crieth out for the living God; for thine altars, O Lord of hosts, my King and my God. Even the sparrow hath found out a house, and the swallow (ring-dove) a nest for herself, where she may lay her young;" but I have no place, either of rest or worship, understood. The *Chaldee* translates thus: "Even the pigeon hath found a house, and the turtle-dove hath a nest, because their young may be offered lawfully upon thine altars, O Lord of hosts, my King and my God." Or, as a *comparison* seems to be here intended, the following may best express the meaning: "Even as the sparrow finds out (seeks) a house, and the swallow her nest in which she may hatch her young; so I, thine altars, O Lord of hosts, my King and my God."

Verse 4. *Blessed* are *they that dwell in thy house*] They who have such a constant habitation in thy temple as the sparrow or the swallow has in the house wherein it has built its nest.

They will be still praising thee.] They will find it good to draw nigh unto God, as he always pours out his Spirit on his sincere worshippers.

Verse 5. *The man whose strength* is *in thee*]

"Who life and strength from thee derives;
And by thee moves and in thee lives."

In whose heart are *the ways* of them] This is no sense. The original, however, is obscure: מסלות בלבבם *mesilloth bilebabam,* "the high ways are in their hearts;" that is, the roads winding to thy temple. Perhaps there is a reference here to the *high roads* leading to the *cities of refuge.* We wish to escape from the hands and dominion of these murderers, and the roads that lead to Jerusalem and the temple we think on with delight; our hearts are with them, we long to be travelling on them.

Verse 6. *Passing through the valley of Baca make it a well*] Instead of בכא *bacha,* a *mulberry-tree,* seven MSS. have בכה *becheh, mourning.* I believe *Baca* to be the same here as *Bochim,* Judg. ii. 1-5, called *The Valley of Weeping.* Though they pass through this barren and desert place, they would not fear evil, knowing that thou wouldst supply all their wants; and even in the sandy desert cause them to find pools of water, in consequence of

7 They go [i]from [k]strength to strength, *every*
one of them in Zion [l]appeareth before God.
8 O LORD God of hosts, hear my prayer:
give ear, O God of Jacob. Selah.
9 [m]Behold, O God our shield, and look
upon the face of thine anointed.
10 For a day in thy courts *is* better than a
thousand. [n]I had rather be a doorkeeper in
the house of my God, than to dwell in the
tents of wickedness.
11 For the LORD God *is* a [o]sun and [p]shield:
the LORD will give grace and glory: [q]no good
thing will he withhold from them that walk
uprightly.
12 O LORD of hosts, [r]blessed *is* the man
that trusteth in thee.

---

[i]Or, *from company to company*——[k]Prov. iv. 18; 2 Cor. iii. 18——[l]Deut. xvi. 16; Zech. xiv. 16——[m]Gen. xv. 1; ver. 11

[n]Heb. *I would choose rather to sit at the threshold*——[o]Isa. lx. 19——[p]Gen. xv. 1; ver. 9; Psa. cxv. 9, 10, 11; cxix. 114; Prov. ii. 7——[q]Psa. xxxiv. 9, 10——[r]Psa. ii. 12

---

which they shall advance with renewed strength, and shall meet with the God of Israel in Zion.

The rain also filleth the pools.] The *Hebrew* may be translated differently, and has been differently understood by all the *Versions.* גם ברכות יעטה מורה *gam berachoth yaateh moreh;* "Yea, the instructor is covered or clothed with blessings." While the followers of God are passing through the *wilderness* of this world, God *opens* for them *fountains* in the *wilderness, and springs in the dry places.* They *drink* of the *well-spring of salvation;* they are not destitute of their *pastors.* God takes care to give his followers *teachers* after his own heart, that shall feed them with knowledge; and while they are watering the people they are watered themselves; for God *loads them with his benefits,* and the people *cover* them with their *blessings.*

Verse 7. *They go from strength to strength*] They proceed from one degree of grace to another, gaining Divine virtue through all the steps of their probation.

Every one of them *in Zion appeareth before God.*] This is a paraphrase, and a bad one, but no translation. They shall proceed from strength to strength, יראה אל אלהים בציון *yeraeh el Elohim betsiyon,* "The God of gods shall be seen in Zion." God shall appear in their behalf, as often as they shall seek him; in consequence of which they shall increase in spiritual strength.

Some think there is a reference here to *companies* of people going up to Jerusalem from different parts of the land, blending together as they go on, so that the crowd is continually increasing. This meaning our translators have put in the *margin.*

Verse 8. *Hear my prayer*] Let us be restored to thy sanctuary, and to thy worship.

Verse 9. *Behold, O God, our shield*] We have no Protector but thee. Thou seest the deadly blows that are aimed at us; cover our souls; protect our lives!

Look upon the face of thine anointed.] Consider the supplications sent up by him whom thou hast appointed to be Mediator between thee and man—thy *Christ.* But some apply this to *David,* to *Zerubbabel,* to the *people of Israel;* and each has his reasons.

Verse 10. *A day in thy courts* is *better than a thousand.*] Not only better than *one thousand* in captivity, as the *Chaldee* states, but any where else. For in God's courts we meet with God the King, and are sure to have what petitions we offer unto him through his Christ.

I had rather be a doorkeeper] O what a strong desire does this express for the ordinances of God! Who *now* prefers the worship of God to genteel, gay, honourable, and noble company, to mirthful feasts, public entertainments, the stage, the oratorio, or the ball! Reader, wouldst thou rather be in thy *closet,* wrestling in prayer, or reading the Scriptures on thy knees, than be at any of the above places? How often hast thou sacrificed thy *amusement,* and *carnal delight,* and *pleasures,* for the benefit of a pious heart-searching sermon? Let conscience speak, and it will tell thee.

Verse 11. *For the Lord God* is *a sun and shield*] To *illuminate, invigorate,* and *warm;* to *protect* and *defend* all such as prefer him and his worship to every thing the earth can produce.

It is remarkable that not one of the *Versions* understand the שמש *shemesh,* as signifying *sun,* as we do. They generally concur in the following translation: "For the Lord loveth mercy and truth, and he will give grace and glory." The *Chaldee* says, "The Lord is as a high wall and a strong shield; grace and glory will the Lord give, and will not deprive those of blessedness who walk in perfection." Critics in general take the word as signifying a *defence* or a *guard.* Instead of שמש *shemesh, sun, Houbigant* reads שמר *shemer,* a *keeper* or *guardian,* and says that to represent God as the *sun* is without example in the sacred writings. But is not Mal. iv. 2, a parallel passage to this place? "Unto you that fear my name shall the *Sun of righteousness arise with healing in his wings.*" No MS. countenances the alteration of *Houbigant.*

The Lord will give grace] To pardon, purify, and save the soul from sin: and then he will *give glory* to the *sanctified* in his eternal kingdom; and even *here* he withholds no good thing from them that walk uprightly. Well, therefore, might the psalmist say, verse 12, "O Lord of hosts, blessed is the man that trusteth in thee."

ANALYSIS OF THE EIGHTY-FOURTH PSALM

This Psalm may be divided into the following parts:—

I. The psalmist, absent from the public worship of God, shows his love to the house of God, and his desire to be present in it, ver. 1-3.

II. The happiness of those who continue in that assembly, ver. 4-7.

III. He prays for restoration to it, and sets down the causes, ver. 8-11.

IV. The blessedness of the man who trusts in God, ver. 12.

I. 1. He begins with the pathetical exclamation, "How amiable are thy tabernacles!" A mode of expression which intimates *there is none equal to them*.

2. He expresses his ardent affection to the house of God:—1. "My soul longeth," &c. 2. "My heart and flesh cry out," &c.

3. He laments his absence from God's house. The *sparrows* and *swallows* have their respective houses, where they may be present, build, hatch their young, &c., but he could have no access to God's house. And this he expresses in an affecting appeal to God to move his pity:—1. "O Lord of hosts!" I acknowledge thee as my *Leader*. 2. "My King." I acknowledge myself as thy *subject*. 3. "My God." Whom I serve, and have taken for my portion.

II. The happiness of those who have liberty to worship God in his temple.

1. "Blessed are they." They enjoy thy ordinances, and have blessings in all.

2. "Who dwell:" Who continue in union with God, ever prizing his ordinances.

3. "They will be still praising thee:" As being continually happy in thy presence.

"Blessed is the man whose strength is in thee:" Who knows his own weakness, and depends upon thee for his continual support.

This is the happiness of those who are near God's house: but there is a happiness for those also whose hearts are there, though their bodies are detained at a distance from it.

1. Blessed are they in whose hearts are the ways of them, ver. 5.

2. Even when they are passing through desert and inhospitable countries, ver. 6.

3. "They go from strength to strength:" 1. They get from one place of protection to another. 2. They increase in the Divine light and life. 3. They get many companions on the way.

III. His prayer. 1. He begs to be heard. 2. He remembers God, who succoured *Jacob* in weakness and distress. 3. He considers himself as the *anointed* of God, and under his especial care, ver. 8. He wishes to be employed, even in the meanest offices, in the house of God, which he illustrates by an opposition of *time, place,* and *persons*.

1. *Time*. One day in thy courts is better than a *thousand out of it*.

2. *Place*. God's house, to the *tents* of wickedness.

3. *Persons*. A doorkeeper, a Korahite at the temple, rather than an emperor in his palace.

For this he gives *five* reasons:—

1. "The Lord is a sun:" He dispels darkness, comforts, warms, gives life.

2. He is a *shield:* The Defender and Protector of his followers.

3. He *gives grace*, to prepare for heaven.

4. *Glory*, to crown that grace.

5. He is all-sufficient. "He will withhold no good thing."

But sinners and hypocrites need not expect these blessings; they are for them that walk uprightly.

1. They must *walk*—go on, be constant, abide in the way.

2. They must be *upright*—truly sincere and obedient.

IV. The blessedness of the man who trusts in God. "O Lord of hosts, blessed is the man that trusts in thee!" This acclamation may be intended to answer an objection: "If those be blessed who dwell in thy temple, then those must be wretched who are exiled from it." No, says the psalmist; though there be many advantages enjoyed by those who can attend the ordinances of God, and some may attend them without profit; yet he who trusts in God can never be confounded. Faith in God will always be crowned; and, when absent through necessity, every place is a temple.

"Though fate command me to the farthest verge
Of the green earth————————————————
Yet God is ever present, ever felt,
In the wide waste as in the city full;
And where he vital breathes, there must be joy.

PSALM LXXXV

Thanksgiving to God for restoration to the Divine favour, 1–3; prayer for farther mercies, 4–7; the psalmist waits for a gracious answer in full confidence of receiving it, 8. He receives the assurance of the greatest blessings, and exults in the prospect, 9–13.

To the chief Musician, A Psalm ᵃfor ᵇthe sons of Korah

A. M. cir. 3468
B. C. cir. 536
Cyri,
R. Persarum,
cir. annum
primum

LORD, thou hast been ᶜfavourable unto thy land: thou hast ᵈbrought back the captivity of Jacob.

2 ᵉThou hast forgiven the iniquity of thy people, thou hast covered all their sin. Selah.

A. M. cir. 3468
B. C. cir. 536
Cyri,
R. Persarum,
cir. annum
primum

3 Thou hast taken away all thy wrath:

ᵃPsa. xlii. title——ᵇOr, *of*——ᶜOr, *well pleased;* Psa. lxxvii. 7

ᵈEzra i. 11; ii. 1; Psa. xiv. 7; Jer. xxx. 18; xxxi. 23; Ezek. xxxix. 25; Joel iii. 1——ᵉPsa. xxxii. 1

NOTES ON PSALM LXXXV

The *title* of this Psalm we have seen before, Psa. xlii. As to the *time*, it seems to have been written during, or even after, the return from the Babylonish captivity. In the *three* first verses the psalmist acknowledges the goodness of God in bringing the people back to their own land; he next prays to God to restore them to their ancient prosperity. In the spirit of prophecy, he waits on God, and hears him promise to do it; and then exults in the prospect of so great a good. The whole Psalm seems also to have a reference to the redemption of the world by Jesus Christ.

Verse 1. *Lord, thou hast been favourable*] Literally, *Thou hast been well pleased with thy land*.

A. M. cir. 3468
B. C. cir. 536
Cyri,
R. Persarum,
cir. annum
primum

[f]thou hast turned *thyself* from the fierceness of thine anger.

4 [g]Turn us, O God of our salvation, and cause thine anger toward us to cease.

5 [h]Wilt thou be angry with us for ever? wilt thou draw out thine anger to all generations?

6 Wilt thou not [i]revive us again: that thy people may rejoice in thee?

7 Show us thy mercy, O Lord, and grant us thy salvation.

8 [k]I will hear what God the Lord will speak: for [l]he will speak peace unto his people, and to his saints: but let them not [m]turn again to folly.

9 Surely [n]his salvation *is* nigh them that fear him; [o]that glory may dwell in our land.

10 Mercy and truth are met together; [p]righteousness and peace have kissed *each other*.

A. M. cir. 3468
B. C. cir. 536
Cyri,
R. Persarum,
cir. annum
primum

---

[f]Or, *thou hast turned thine anger from waxing hot;* Deut. xiii. 17——[g]Psa. lxxx. 7——[h]Psa. lxxiv. 1; lxxix 5; lxxx. 4——[i]Hab. iii. 2——[k]Hab. ii. 1

[l]Zech. ix. 10——[m]2 Pet. ii. 20, 21——[n]Isa. xlvi. 13 [o]Zech. ii. 5; John i. 14——[p]Psa. lxxii. 3; Isa. xxxii. 17; Luke ii. 14

Thou hast brought back the captivity] This seems to fix the *time* of the Psalm to be after the return of the Jews from Babylon.

Verse 2. *Thou hast forgiven the iniquity*] נשאת עון *nasatha avon, Thou hast borne,* or *carried away, the iniquity.* An allusion to the ceremony of the *scapegoat.*

Thou hast covered all their sin.] As thou hast freely *forgiven* it, its offensiveness and abominable nature no longer *appear.* The whole is put *out of sight;* and, as we are restored from our captivity, the *consequences* no longer *appear.*

Selah.] This is true. Our return to our own land is the full proof.

Verse 3. *Thou hast taken away*] אספת *asaphta,* "Thou hast *gathered up* all thy wrath." This carries on the *metaphor* in the *second* verse: "Thou hast *collected* all thy wrath, and *carried it away* with all our iniquities."

Verse 4. *Turn us, O God of our salvation*] Thou hast turned our captivity; now convert our souls. And they find a *reason* for their prayer in an attribute of their God; *the God of their salvation.* And as his work was to *save,* they beg that *his* anger towards them might *cease.* The Israelites were not restored from their captivity *all at once.* A few returned with *Zerubbabel;* some more with *Ezra* and *Nehemiah;* but a great number still remained in *Babylonia, Media, Assyria, Egypt,* and other *parts.* The request of the psalmist is, to have a complete restoration of all the Israelites from all places of their dispersion.

Verse 5. *Wilt thou draw out thine anger*] We have already suffered much and long; our fathers have suffered, and we have succeeded to their distresses. Draw not out thy anger against us from generation to generation.

Verse 6. *Wilt thou not revive us*] We have long had the sentence of death in ourselves; and have feared an utter extinction. Shall not our nation yet live before thee? Shall we not become once more numerous, pious, and powerful; that

Thy people may rejoice in thee?] As the Source of all our mercies; and give thee the glory due to thy name?

Verse 7. *Show us thy mercy*] Blot out all our sins.

And grant us thy salvation.] Give us such a complete deliverance as is worthy of thy *majesty* and *mercy* to bestow!

Verse 8. *I will hear what God the Lord will speak*] The psalmist goes as a prophet to consult the Lord; and, having made his request,

waits an answer from the spirit of prophecy. He is satisfied that the answer will be gracious; and having received it he relates it to the people.

He will speak peace] He will give *prosperity* to *the people* in general; and to *his saints*—his followers, in particular.

But let them not turn again to folly.] Let them not abuse the mercy of their God, by sinning any more against him.

Verse 9. *Surely his salvation is nigh*] To him who *fears* God, and trembles at his word, his salvation is nigh at hand.

That glory may dwell in our land.] That thy worship may be restored, the temple rebuilt, and the Divine shechinah, or symbol of the presence of God, resume its place. The pure and undefiled religion of God preached, professed, and experienced in a nation, is the *glory* of that land. The Prophet *Haggai* had said that *the glory of the latter house*—the temple built after their return from Babylon, *should be greater than the glory of the former,* viz., of that built by Solomon: but, as a building, it was far inferior to the former; yet it had a *superior* glory in being visited by Jesus Christ. This was the glory that excelled.

Verse 10. *Mercy and truth are met together*] It would be more simple to translate the original,—

חסד ואמת נפגשו
צדק ושלום נשקו

Chesed veemeth niphgashu;
Tsedek veshalom nashaku,—

"Mercy and truth have met on the way;
Righteousness and peace have embraced."

This is a remarkable text, and much has been said on it: but there is a beauty in it which, I think, has not been noticed.

Mercy and *peace* are on one side; *truth* and *righteousness* on the other. *Truth* requires *righteousness; mercy* calls for *peace.*

They meet together on the way; one going to make inquisition for sin, the other to plead for reconciliation. Having met, their differences on certain considerations, not here particularly mentioned, are adjusted; and their mutual claims are blended together in one common interest; on which *peace* and *righteousness* immediately embrace. Thus, *righteousness* is given to *truth,* and *peace* is given to *mercy.*

Now, *Where* did these meet? In Christ Jesus. *When* were they reconciled? When he poured out his life on Calvary.

A. M. cir. 3468
B. C. cir. 536
Cyri,
R. Persarum,
cir. annum
primum

11 �q Truth shall spring out of the earth; and righteousness shall look down from heaven.

12 ʳYea, the Lord shall give *that which is* good; and ˢour land shall yield her increase.

13 ᵗRighteousness shall go before him; and shall set *us* in the way of his steps.

A. M. cir. 3468
B. C. cir. 536
Cyri,
R. Persarum,
cir. annum
primum

---

qIsa. xlv. 8——rPsa. lxxxiv. 11; James i. 17

sPsa. lxvii. 6——tPsa. lxxxix. 14

Verse 11. *Truth shall spring out of the earth*] In consequence of this wonderful *reconciliation,* the truth of God shall prevail among men. The *seeds* of it shall be so plentifully sown by the preaching of Christ and his apostles that true religion shall be diffused over the world.

And righteousness shall look down from heaven.] And be delighted with the reformation of the sons of Adam; and shall be so satisfied with the glorious work which is carried forward, that,

Verse 12. *The Lord shall give—good*] הטוב *hattob,* THE GOOD *thing*—what is the supreme good, the *summum bonum,* for which man has searched in vain through all his generations. Those who are reconciled to him through the Son of his love shall enjoy the *favour* of their God; to have which is the supreme happiness of man.

Our land shall yield her increase.] There shall be neither *dearth* nor *barrenness;* for *truth,* that *springs out of the earth,* shall yield an abundant harvest, in the conversion of all nations to the faith of our Lord Jesus Christ.

Verse 13. *Righteousness shall go before him*] Perhaps this verse may receive its best solution from Rom. iii. 25: "Whom God hath set for a propitiation through faith in his blood, to declare his RIGHTEOUSNESS for the remission of sins that are past." This term the apostle uses to point out *God's method of justifying* or *saving mankind.* And this, in the preaching of the pure Gospel, is ever *going before* to point out the Lord Jesus, and the redemption that is in his blood. And thus going before him, the sinner, who feels his need of salvation, is *Set—in the way of his steps;* as Bartimeus sat by the way-side begging, by which way Jesus walked; and when he came where he was, heard his prayer, and restored him his sight. Or, *righteousness*—the pure and holy law of God, must be proclaimed as broken by sinners, and calling aloud for vengeance, before they can see and feel their need of Christ crucified. By the preaching of the law they are prepared to receive the grace of the Gospel.

ANALYSIS OF THE EIGHTY-FIFTH PSALM

Mystically, this Psalm may be considered as treating of the redemption of the world by Jesus Christ. It has the *three* following parts:—

I. An acknowledgment of God's former mercies, ver. 1-3.

II. A petition on that ground that he would repeat them, ver. 4-7.

III. A profession of obedience, and an advice to continue in it, ver. 8. That men may be partakers of the promises, both *spiritual,* ver. 9, 10, 11; and *temporal,* ver. 12, which shall be fulfilled to those who keep in the ways of God, ver. 13.

I. In the *three* first verses, the psalmist commemorates God's mercies to his people; of which his *good will* or *favour* is the Fountain. These mercies are, 1. *Temporal:* "Thou hast been favourable unto thy land," &c., ver. 1. 2. *Spiritual:* 1. "Thou hast forgiven the iniquities of thy people:" Justification. 2. "Thou hast taken away all thy wrath:" Reconciliation.

II. Upon this he founds a prayer: "Turn us, O God."

1. Thou hast turned away the captivity. Restore and convert us.

2. Thou hast brought us back. Revive our hearts, that they may rejoice in thee.

3. Thou hast been reconciled to our *fathers.* Be reconciled to *us.*

4. Thou hast forgiven the iniquity of thy people. Save us.

III. He promises obedience: "I will hear what God will speak;" and I shall hear nothing from him but what is for his own glory, and his people's good.

1. "He will speak peace:" He will turn all their sufferings to their advantage.

2. But they must hear, and be steady. They must "not turn again to folly;" let them remember this.

3. To such his promise is sure: "His salvation is nigh them."

4. And it comes, that "glory may dwell in our land;" that it may be crowned with peace and plenty.

In this prosperity of theirs, there shall be a combination of *mercy, truth, justice,* and *peace.*

1. "Justice and peace shall embrace;" for there is such a league between these two, that where *peace* is made without *justice,* it cannot long continue: and *mercy* and *truth* must; for it is inconsistent with mercy to be in concord with falsehood.

2. "Truth shall spring out of the earth." Men shall observe it in all their transactions, contracts, and promises.

3. "Righteousness shall look down from heaven." God will smile on this state of things, and pour out upon them the continual dew of his blessing.

4. In a word, 1. They shall enjoy all *spiritual* blessings; for the "Lord shall give that which is good." 2. And all *temporal;* "for the land shall yield her increase."

For these mercies he sets down our duty:—

1. "Righteousness shall go before him." All his saints shall walk before him in righteousness and true holiness.

"And this righteousness shall set them in the

way of his steps." It shall teach them to walk constantly and steadily in the way of his commandments all the days of their life.

By many of the ancients and moderns the whole of this Psalm has been applied to Christ, and his salvation. See the preceding notes.

PSALM LXXXVI

The psalmist prays to God for support, from a conviction that he is merciful, good, ready to forgive, and that there is none like him, 1–8; all nations shall bow before him because of his wondrous works, 9, 10; he prays to be instructed, and promises to praise God for his great mercy, 11–13; describes his enemies, and appeals to God, 14–16; begs a token for God, that his enemies may be confounded, 17.

XVII. DAY. MORNING PRAYER

ᵃA Prayer of David

BOW down thine ear, O LORD, hear me: for I *am* poor and needy.

2 Preserve my soul; for I *am* ᵇholy: O thou my God, save thy servant ᶜthat trusteth in thee.

3 ᵈBe merciful unto me, O LORD: for I cry unto thee ᵉdaily.

4 Rejoice the soul of thy servant: ᶠfor unto thee, O LORD, do I lift up my soul.

5 ᵍFor thou, LORD, *art* good, and ready to forgive; and plenteous in mercy unto all them that call upon thee.

6 Give ear, O LORD, unto my prayer; and attend to the voice of my supplications.

7 ʰIn the day of my trouble I will call upon thee: for thou wilt answer me.

8 ⁱAmong the gods *there is* none like unto thee, O LORD; ᵏneither *are there any works* like unto thy works.

9 ˡAll nations whom thou hast made shall come and worship before thee, O LORD; and shall glorify thy name.

10 For thou *art* great, and ᵐdoest wondrous things: ⁿthou *art* God alone.

ᵃOr, *A Prayer,* being a Psalm *of David*——ᵇOr, *one whom thou favourest*——ᶜIsa. xxvi. 3——ᵈPsa. lvi. 1; lvii. 1——ᵉOr, *all the day*——ᶠPsa. xxv. 1; cxliii. 8 ᵍVer. 15; Psa. cxxx. 7; cxlv. 9; Joel ii. 13——ʰPsa. l 15

ⁱExodus xv. 11; Psalm lxxxix. 6——ᵏDeut. iii. 24 ˡPsa. xxii. 31; cii. 18; Isa. xliii. 7; Rev. xv. 4——ᵐExod. xv. 11; Psa. lxxii. 18; lxxvii. 15——ⁿDeut. vi. 3; xxxii. 39; Isa. xxxvii. 16; xliv. 6; Mark xii. 29; 1 Cor. viii. 4; Eph. iv. 6

NOTES ON PSALM LXXXVI

The *title* attributes this Psalm to *David;* and in this all the *Versions* agree: but in its structure it is the same with those attributed to the *sons of Korah;* and was probably made during the captivity. It is a very suitable prayer for a person labouring under affliction from persecution or calumny.

Verse 1. *Bow down thine ear*] Spoken after the manner of men: I am so *low,* and so *weak,* that, unless thou *stoop to me,* my voice cannot reach thee.

Poor and needy.] I am afflicted, and destitute of the necessaries of life.

Verse 2. *Preserve my soul*] Keep it as in a strong place.

For I am holy] כי חסיד אני *ki chasid ani,* for I am merciful. The spirit of this prayer is,

"The mercy I to others show,
That mercy show to me!"

Save thy servant] I have long taken thee as my *Master* and *Lord;* I receive the word from thy mouth, and *obey* thee.

Verse 3. *Be merciful unto me*] I have no *merit;* I plead none, but trust in thee alone.

I cry unto thee daily.] My state deeply affects me; and I incessantly cry for thy salvation.

Verse 4. *Rejoice the soul of thy servant*] I want spiritual blessings; I want such consolations as thou dost impart to them that love thee; I present that soul to thee which I wish thee to console.

Verse 5. *For thou, Lord, art good*] I found my expectations of help on thy own goodness, through which thou art always ready to forgive. And I found it also on thy well-known character, to which all thy followers bear testimony, viz., that "thou art plenteous in mercy unto all them that call upon thee."

Verse 6. *Give ear, O Lord*] Attend to *me.* Millions call upon thee for help and mercy; but who has more need than myself? That the psalmist was deeply in earnest, his conduct shows. 1. He *prayed.* 2. His prayer was vehement; he lifted up his *voice.* 3. He continued in prayer; he abounded in *supplications.*

Verse 7. *Thou wilt answer me.*] Because thou art good, merciful, and ready to forgive; and I call upon thee fervently, and seek thee in thy own way.

Verse 8. *Among the gods there is none like unto thee, O Lord*] None that trusted in an idol ever had help in time of need; none that prayed to any of them ever had an answer to his petitions. *Thou* savest; *they* cannot; thou *upholdest;* they must be *upheld* by their foolish worshippers. *Thou art my Director,* אדני *Adonai;* but they cannot *direct* nor *teach;* they have mouths, but they speak not.

Verse 9. *All nations*] Thy word shall be proclaimed among all the Gentiles: they *shall* receive thy testimony, and worship thee as the only true and living God.

Verse 10. *For thou* art *great*] Almighty, infinite, eternal.

And doest wondrous things] ועשה נפלאות *veoseh niphlaoth;* thou art the *Worker of mir-*

11 [o]Teach me thy way, O LORD; I will walk
in thy truth: unite my heart to fear thy
name.
12 I will praise thee, O LORD my God,
with all my heart: and I will glorify thy name
for evermore.
13 For great *is* thy mercy toward me: and
thou hast [p]delivered my soul from the lowest
[q]hell.
14 O God, [r]the proud are risen against me,
and the assemblies of [s]violent *men* have sought
after my soul; and have not set thee before
them.
15 [t]But thou, O LORD, *art* a God full of
compassion, and gracious, long suffering, and
plenteous in mercy and truth.
16 O [u]turn unto me, and have mercy upon
me; give thy strength unto thy servant, and
save [v]the son of thine handmaid.
17 Show me a token for good; that they
which hate me may see *it*, and be ashamed:
because thou, LORD, hast holpen me, [w]and
comforted me.

---

[o]Psa. xxv. 4; xxvii. 11; cxix. 33; cxliii. 8——[p]Psa. lvi. 13; cxvi. 8——[q]Or, *grave*——[r]Psa. liv. 3——[s]Heb. *terrible*——[t]Exod. xxxiv. 6; Num. xiv. 18; Neh. ix. 17; ver. 5; Psa. ciii. 8; cxi. 4; cxxx. 4, 7; cxlv. 8; Joel ii. 13——[u]Psa. xxv. 16; lxix. 16——[v]Psa. cxvi. 16; Luke i. 38, 48 [w]Isa. xlix. 13; li. 12; Matt. v. 4

---

acles. This thou hast done in numerous instances, and thereby showed thy infinite power and wisdom.

This appears to be a prophecy of the calling of the Gentiles to the faith of Christ, and the evidence to be given to his Divine mission by the *miracles* which he should work.

Thou art *God alone.*] Συ ει ὁ Θεος μονος ὁ μεγας.—*Sept. Thou art the only,* THE GREAT *God.* In this the *Æthiopic* and *Arabic* agree.

Verse 11. *Teach me thy way*] Instruct me in the steps I should take; for without thy teaching I must go astray.

Unite my heart] יחד לבבי *yached lebabi, join* all the purposes, resolutions, and affections of my heart *together,* to fear and to glorify thy name. This is a most important prayer. A *divided* heart is a great curse; *scattered* affections are a miserable plague. When the *heart* is not at *unity* with itself, the work of religion cannot go on. *Indecision* of *mind* and *division* of *affections* mar any work. The *heart* must be *one,* that the *work* may be *one.* If this be wanting, all is wrong. This is a prayer which becomes the mouth of every Christian.

Verse 12. *I will praise thee—with all my heart*] When my *heart* is *united* to fear thy name, then shall I praise thee with my *whole heart.*

Verse 13. *Thou hast delivered my soul from the lowest hell.*] This must mean more than the *grave;* a *hell below hell*—a place of perdition for the soul, as the grave is a place of corruption for the *body.*

Verse 14. *The assemblies of violent* men] עדת עריצים *adath aritsim,* the *congregation of the terrible ones.* Men of violent passions, violent counsels, and violent acts; and, because they have power, *terrible* to all.

Have not set thee before them.] Who sins that sets God before his eyes? Who does not sin that has no consciousness of the Divine presence?

Verse 15. *But thou, O Lord*] What a wonderful character of God is given in this verse! אדני *Adonai,* the Director, Judge, and Support;—but instead of אדני *Adonai, thirty-four* of Kennicott's MSS. have יהוה *Yehovah,* the self-existent and eternal Being;—אל *El,* the strong God; רחום *rachum,* tenderly compassionate; חנון *channun,* the Dispenser of grace or favour; ארך אפים *erech appayim,* suffering long, not easily provoked; רב חסד *rab chesed,* abundant in blessings; and אמת *emeth,* faithful and true. Such is the God who has made himself more particularly known to us in Christ. The scanty language of our ancestors was not adequate to a full rendering of the original words: **⁊ ðu driht god gemildsiend ⁊ mildheort, geþyldig, ⁊ mucel mildheortnysse ⁊ soþfæst.** "And thu driht God gemildsiend, and mildheort, gethyldig and mucel mildheortnysse and sothfæst.—And thou, Lord God, art mild, and mildhearted, patient, and of much mildheartedness, and soothfast,"—steady in truth.

In the old *Psalter* the language is but little improved: **And thou Lorde God mercier, and mercyful, sufferand, and of mykel mercy, and sothefast.**

The word **mercier** is interpreted, *doand dede of mercy.*

Verse 16. *O turn unto me*] He represents himself as following after God; but he cannot overtake him; and then he prays that he would *turn* and meet him through pity; or give him *strength* that he might be able to hold on his race.

Give thy strength unto thy servant] The *Vulgate* renders, Da imperium tuum puero tuo, "Give thy empire to thy child." The old *Psalter:* **Gyf empyre to thi barne, and make safe the son of thi hand mayden.** *Thi barne*—thy tender child. **cnapan** or **cnapan þinum,** Anglo-Saxon; *thy knave;* signifying either a *serving man* or a *male child.* As many *servants* were found to be purloiners of their masters' property, hence the word **cnapan,** and **cnapan,** and *knave,* became the title of an unprincipled servant. The term *fur,* which signifies a *thief* in Latin, for the same reason became the appellative of a *dishonest servant.*

Quid domini facient, audent cum talia FURES?

When servants (*thieves*) do such things, what may not be expected from the masters?
VIRG. Ecl. iii. 16.

So PLAUTUS, speaking of a *servant,* Aulul. ii. 46, says: Homo es trium literarum, "Thou art a man of *three* letters," i. e., FUR, a *thief.* The word *knave* is still in use, but is always taken in a bad sense. The *paraphrase* in the old *Psalter* states the *handmaid* to be the *kirk,* and the *son* of this *handmaid* to be a *true believer.*

Verse 17. *Show me a token for good*] עשה

עמי אות *aseh immi oth*, "*Make* with me a sign." Fix the honourable mark of thy name upon me, that I may be known to be thy servant. There seems to be an allusion here to the *marking of a slave*, to ascertain whose property he was. The *Anglo-Saxon*, **do mid me tacn** on **gode**, "do with me a token in good." Old *Psalter:* **Do with me signe in gude.** From **tacn** *tacn* we have our word *token*, which signifies a *sign*, *mark*, or *remembrancer* of something beyond itself; a *pledge* that something, then specified, shall be *done* or *given*. Give me, from the influence of thy Spirit in my heart, a *pledge* that the blessings which I now ask shall be given in due time. But he wished for such a sign as his enemies might see; that they might know God to be his helper, and be confounded when they sought his destruction.

ANALYSIS OF THE EIGHTY-SIXTH PSALM

This Psalm is a continued prayer, and may be divided into *four* parts:—

I. The *first* part is a petition for safety, drawn from *his own person*, ver. 1-4.

II. The *second*, a quickening of the same petition, drawn from the *person* and *nature* of *God*, ver. 5-13.

III. The *third*, taken from the *quality* of his *adversaries*, ver. 14.

IV. The *fourth*, a conjunction of all these *three;* the *first*, ver. 15; the *second*, ver. 16; the *third*, ver. 17.

I. The reasons of his petition, drawn from *himself*.

1. "Bow down thine ear." Reason: "I am poor and needy," ver. 1.

2. "Preserve my soul." Reason: "I am holy," or merciful, ver. 2.

3. "Save thy servant." Reason: "He puts his trust in thee," ver. 3.

4. "Be merciful unto me." Reason: "I cry unto thee daily," ver. 4.

5. "Rejoice the soul of thy servant." Reason: "For unto thee do I lift up my soul," ver. 4.

II. A quickening of the petition, drawn from the *nature of God*.

1. "For thou, Lord, art good," &c., ver. 5, 6.

2. "I will call upon thee: for thou wilt answer me," ver. 7.

3. "There is none like unto thee," ver. 8.

4. "Nor any works like unto thy works," ver. 8. This shall be amply proved: for

5. "All nations," **now** worshipping idols, "shall be converted to thee," ver. 9.

6. "Because thou art great, and doest wondrous things," ver. 10.

On this reason, that there is none like God,—

1. He begs to be governed by his word and Spirit, ver. 11.

2. Promises to praise him for his great mercy, ver. 12, 13.

III. He presses another argument taken from his *enemies*.

1. They were *proud:* "The proud are risen against me."

2. They were *powerful:* "The assemblies of violent men."

3. They were *ungodly:* "They did not set thee before them," ver. 14.

IV. He amplifies his former argument.

1. From the *nature of God:* "Thou art full of compassion," &c., ver. 15.

2. From his *own condition:* "Turn unto me, and have mercy upon me," ver. 16.

3. From the *quality of his adversaries:* "Show me a token—that they which hate me may be ashamed," ver. 17.

PSALM LXXXVII

The nature and glorious privileges of Zion and Jerusalem, 1–3. *No other city to be compared to this*, 4. *The privilege of being born in it*, 5, 6. *Its praises celebrated*, 7.

A Psalm *or* Song [a]for the sons of Korah

A. M. cir. 3468
B. C. cir. 536
Cyri,
R. Persarum,
cir. annum
primum

HIS foundation *is* [b]in the holy
mountains.
2 [c]The LORD loveth the gates
of Zion more than all the dwellings of Jacob.
3 [d]Glorious things are spoken
of thee, O city of God. Selah.
4 I will make mention [e]of Rahab and Babylon to them that
know me: behold Philistia, and Tyre, with
Ethiopia; this *man* was born there.

A. M. cir. 3468
B. C. cir. 536
Cyri,
R. Persarum,
cir. annum
primum

[a]Or, *of*——[b]Psa. xlviii. 1——[c]Psa. lxxviii. 67, 68

[d]See Isa. lx.——[e]Psa. lxxxix. 10; Isa. li. 9

NOTES ON PSALM LXXXVII

The *title*, *A Psalm* or *Song for the sons of Korah*, gives us no light into the *author* or *meaning* of this Psalm. It begins and ends so abruptly that many have thought it to be only a *fragment* of a larger Psalm. This opinion is very likely. Those who suppose it to have been made when Jerusalem was rebuilt and fortified, imagine it to have been an exclamation of the author on beholding its beauty, and contemplating its privileges. If this opinion be allowed, it will account for the apparent abruptness in the beginning and end. As to its general design it seems to have been written in praise of Jerusalem; and those who are for *mystic* meanings, think that it refers to the Christian Church; and, on this supposition it is interpreted by several writers, both ancient and modern. To pretend to have found out the true meaning would be very absurd. I have done the best I could to give its *literal* sense.

Verse 1. *His foundation* is *in the holy mountains.*] Jerusalem was founded on the mountains or hills of *Zion* and *Moriah*. The after increase of the population obliged the inhabitants to inclose all the contiguous hills; but *Zion* and *Moriah* were the principal. We know that ancient Rome was built on *seven hills*.

Verse 2. *The Lord loveth the gates of Zion*

A. M. cir. 3468
B. C. cir. 536
Cyri,
R. Persarum,
cir. annum
primum

5 And of Zion it shall be said,
This and that man was born in
her; and the Highest himself
shall establish her.

6 ᶠThe Lord shall count, when he ᵍwriteth

up the people, *that* this *man* was
born there. Selah.

7 As well the singers as the
players on instruments *shall be
there:* all my springs *are* in thee.

A. M. cir. 3468
B. C. cir. 536
Cyri,
R. Persarum,
cir. annum
primum

ᶠPsa. xxii. 30

ᵍEzek. xiii. 9

---

more than all the dwellings of Jacob.] That is,
he preferred Zion for his habitation, to be the
place of his temple and sanctuary, before any
other place in the promised land. Mystically,
the Lord prefers the Christian Church to the
Jewish: the latter was only a type of the
former; and had no glory by reason of the
glory that excelleth. To this position no exception can be made.

Verse 3. *Glorious things are spoken of thee*]
Or, there are glorious words or doctrines in
thee. Does this refer to the glorious doctrines
of the Christian Church? These are glorious
sayings indeed.

Verse 4. *I will make mention of Rahab*]
The meaning seems to be, *Rahab*, i. e., *Egypt,
Babylon, Tyre, Philistia,* and *Ethiopia* are not
so honourable as *Jerusalem.* To be born in any
of them is no privilege when compared with
being a native of Jerusalem: their cities are
but heads of villages; Jerusalem alone is a
city. I have met with a very similar sentiment
in a Persian work, of which I know not the
author:

چه مصر و چه شام و چه بر و بحر
همه رستاي اند و شيرازي شهر

Tche Mesr, o tche Sham, o tche Birr o Buhr.
Hemè rustaee and, we Sheerazee Shuhr.

What celebrity can *Egypt* or *Syria,* or any thing
  on *earth* or on the *sea,* pretend to?
"When compared to *Sheeraz,* those are but *villages,* but this alone is a city."

The meaning seems to be the same in both
the *Hebrew* and *Persian* poet.

Verse 5. *This and that man was born in her*]
It will be an honour to any person to have been
born in Zion. But how great is the honour to
be *born from above,* and be a citizen of the
Jerusalem that is from above! To be children
of God, by faith in Christ Jesus! The *Targum*
has, "David the king, and Solomon his son,
were brought up here."

The Highest himself shall establish her.] The
Christian Church is built on the foundation of
the prophets and apostles; Jesus Christ himself being the Cornerstone.

Verse 6. *The Lord shall count, when he
writeth up the people*] בכתוב עמים *bichthob
ammim,* in the register of the people. When
he takes account of those who dwell in Jerusalem, he will particularly note those who were
born in Zion.

This has an easy spiritual meaning. When
God takes an account of all *professing Christians,* he will set apart those for inhabitants of
the New Jerusalem who were born in Zion, who
were born again, received a new nature, and
were fitted for heaven.

Verse 7. *As well the singers, &c.*] Perhaps,
this may mean no more than, The burden of
the songs of all the singers and choristers shall

be, "All my fountains (ancestors and posterity)
are in thee;" and consequently, entitled to all
thy privileges and immunities. Instead of שרים
sharim, "singers," many MSS. and early
printed editions have, *sarim,* "princes." Some
for מעיני *mayenai,* "my fountains," would read
with several of the *Versions,* מעוני *meoney,*
"habitations;" but no MS. yet discovered supports this reading.

It would be a very natural cause of exultation, when considering the great privileges of
this royal city, to know that all his friends,
family, and children, were citizens of this city,
were entered in God's register, and were entitled to his protection and favour. Applied to
the Christian Church, the privileges are still
higher: born of God, enrolled among the living
in Jerusalem, having their hearts purified by
faith, and being washed and made clean
through the blood of the covenant, and sealed
by the Holy Spirit of promise, such have a
right to the inheritance among the saints in
light. I need not add that *springs, wells, fountains,* and *cisterns,* and *waters* are used metaphorically in the sacred writings for children,
posterity, fruitful women, people, &c.; see
among others Prov. v. 15, 16; Psa. lxviii. 26;
Isa. xlviii. 1; and Rev. xvii. 15. The old *Psalter* understands the whole as relating to Gospel times; and interprets it accordingly. Bishop Horne takes it in the same sense. The
whole Psalm is obscure and difficult. I will
venture a literal version of the whole, with a
few explanatory interpolations, instead of
notes, in order to cast a little more light upon
it.

1. A Psalm *to be sung* by the posterity of
Korah. A *prophetic* song.

2. "Jehovah loves his foundation, the city
built by him on holy mountains. He loves the
gates of Zion more than all the habitations of
Jacob."

3. "Honourable things are declared of thee,
O city of God. Selah."

4. "I will number Egypt and Babylon among
my worshippers; behold Philistia and Tyre!
They shall be born in the same place." They
shall be considered as born in the city of God.

5. "But of Zion it shall be said, This one, and
that one," persons of different nations, "was
born in it, and the Most High shall establish
it."

6. "Jehovah shall reckon in the registers of
the people, This one was born there."

7. "The people shall sing, as in leading up a
choir, All my fountains," the springs of my
happiness, "are in thee."

I have nearly followed here the version of
Mr. *N. M. Berlin,* who wonders that there
should be any doubt concerning this translation
of the last verse, when *Symmachus* and *Aquila,*
who must have well known the sense of the
Masoretic text, have translated: Καὶ ᾀδοντης ως
χοροι πασαι πηγαι εν σοι· "And they shall sing,
as in leading up a dance, *All my fountains are*

in thee." The translation cannot be far from the meaning.

ANALYSIS OF THE EIGHTY-SEVENTH PSALM

This Psalm contains marks of the beauty and perfection of the Church.

1. Its *foundation.* The author is GOD, it is *his foundation;* not laid in the *sand,* but upon the *mountains;* not common, but *holy mountains,* ver. 1.

2. The *Lord loveth his Church*—this assembly, beyond all others: "The Lord loveth," &c., ver. 2.

3. All the prophets have spoken *glorious things* concerning it, and have considered it as the "city of God," ver. 3.

4. One of the *glorious things* spoken of it was the *conversion* of the *Gentiles* to it. So here *Egyptians, Babylonians, Tyrians, Ethiopians,* &c., are to be gathered into it by regeneration. They shall all be brought to *know* the true God; and shall be classed in the multitude of those *who know him,* i. e., who offer him a pure and holy worship, ver. 4.

5. By having the word of God in this true Church, they shall be converted to God; so that it may be said, "This and that man were born to God in it," ver. 5.

6. All other cities shall decay and perish; but the Church of God, the city of the Great King, shall be *established for ever,* the gates of hell shall never prevail against it, ver. 5.

7. The converted Gentiles shall have equal privileges with the converted Jews; and in the Christian Church they shall all *be enrolled* without difference or precedence, ver. 6.

8. They shall *enjoy a perpetual solemnity.* They shall ever have cause to *sing* and *rejoice,* ver. 7.

9. The highest privilege is that in God's Church he opens the *fountains of living water;* in his ordinances God dispenses every blessing; every sincere and upright soul rejoices in opportunities to wait on God in his ordinances. Such a one can sing, "All my springs are in thee." All other *fountains* are *muddy;* this alone is as *clear as crystal.* Worldly springs yield no pure delight; all there are mixed and turbulent: all here are refreshing, satisfying, delightful.

PSALM LXXXVIII

The earnest prayer of a person in deep distress, abandoned by his friends and neighbours, and apparently forsaken of God, 1–18.

A Song *or* Psalm ᵃfor the sons of Korah, to the chief Musician upon Mahalath ᵇLeannoth, ᶜMaschil of ᵈHeman the Ezrahite

O LORD ᵉGod of my salvation, I have ᶠcried day *and* night before thee:

2 Let my prayer come before thee: incline thine ear unto my cry;

3 For my soul is full of troubles; and my life ᵍdraweth nigh unto the grave.

ᵃOr, *of*——ᵇThat is, *To humble*——ᶜOr, A Psalm *of Heman the Ezrahite, giving instruction*

ᵈ1 Kings iv. 31; 1 Chron. ii. 6——ᵉPsa. xxvii. 9; li. 14
ᶠLuke xviii. 7——ᵍPsa. cvii. 18

NOTES ON PSALM LXXXVIII

Perhaps the *title* of this Psalm, which is difficult enough, might be thus translated: "A Poem to be sung to the conqueror, by the sons of Korah, responsively, in behalf of a distressed person; to give instruction to Heman the Ezrahite." *Kennicott* says this Psalm has *three* titles, but the last only belongs to it; and supposes it to be the prayer of a person shut up in a separate house, because of the leprosy, who seems to have been in the last stages of that distemper; this disease, under the Mosaic dispensation, being supposed to come from the immediate stroke of God. *Calmet* supposes it to refer to the captivity; the Israelitish nation being represented here under the figure of a person greatly afflicted through the whole course of his life. By some *Heman* is supposed to have been the author; but who he was is not easy to be determined. *Heman* and *Ethan,* whose names are separately prefixed to this and the following Psalm, are mentioned as the grandsons of Judah by his daughter-in-law Tamar, 1 Chron. ii. 6, for they were the sons of Zerah, his immediate son by the above. "And Tamar, his daughter-in-law, bare him Pharez and Zerah," ver. 4. "And the sons of Zerah, Zimri, and Ethan, and Heman, and Calcol, and Dara, (or Darda,") ver. 6. If these were the same persons mentioned 1 Kings iv. 31, they

were *eminent in wisdom;* for it is there said that Solomon's wisdom "excelled the wisdom of all the children of the east country, and all the wisdom of Egypt. For he was wiser than all men; than Ethan the Ezrahite, and Heman, and Chalcol, and Darda, the sons of Mahol," ver. 30, 31. Probably *Zerah* was also called *Mahol.* If the Psalms in question were written by these men, they are the *oldest* poetical compositions extant; and the *most ancient part of Divine revelation,* as these persons lived at least *one hundred and seventy* years before Moses. This may be true of the *seventy-eighth* Psalm; but certainly not of the following, as it speaks of transactions that took place long afterwards, at least as late as the days of *David,* who is particularly mentioned in it. Were we sure of Heman as the author, there would be no difficulty in applying the whole of the Psalm to the state of the Hebrews in Egypt, persecuted and oppressed by Pharaoh. But to seek *or* labour to reconcile matters contained in the *titles* to the Psalms, is treating them with too much respect, as many of them are wrongly placed, and none of them Divinely inspired.

Verse 1. *O Lord God of my salvation*] This is only the *continuation of prayers and supplications* already often sent up to the throne of grace.

Verse 2. *Let my prayer come before thee*]

4 ʰI am counted with them that go down into the pit: ¹I am as a man *that hath* no strength:

5 Free among the dead, like the slain that lie in the grave, whom thou rememberest no more: and they are ᵏcut off ¹from thy hand.

6 Thou hast laid me in the lowest pit, in darkness, in the deeps.

ʰPsa. xxviii. 1——¹Psa. xxxi. 12

ᵏIsa. liii. 8——¹Or, *by thy hand*

It is weak and helpless, though fervent and sincere: take all hinderances out of its way, and let it have a free passage to thy throne. One of the finest thoughts in the Iliad of *Homer* concerns *prayer;* I shall transcribe a principal part of this incomparable passage—incomparable when we consider its origin:—

Και γαρ τε Λιται εισι Διος κουραι μεγαλοιο,
Χωλαι τε, ρυσσαι τε, παραβλωπες τ' οφθαλμω·
Αἱ ῥα τε και μετοπισθ' Ατης αλεγουσι κιουσαι·
'Η δ' Ατη σθεναρη τε και αρτιπος· ουνεκα πασας
Πολλον ὑπεκπροθεει, φθανει δε τε πασαν επ' αιαν,
Βλαπτους' ανθρωπους· αἱ δ' εξακεονται οπισσω·
'Ος μεν τ' αιδεσεται κουρας Διος, ασσον ιουσας,
Τονδε μεγ' ωνησαν, και τ' εκλυον ευξαμενοιο.
'Ος δε κ' ανηνηται, και τε στερεως αποειπη,
Λισσονται δ' αρα ταιγε Δια Κρονιωνα κιουσαι,
Τῳ Ατην αμ' επεσθαι, ἱνα βλαφθεις αποτιση.
Αλλ', Αχιλευ, πορε και συ Διος κουρησιν επεσθαι
Τιμην, ἡτ' αλλων περ επιγναμπτει φρενας εσθλων.
Iliad., ix. 498-510.

Prayers are Jove's daughters; wrinkled, lame, slant-eyed,
Which, though far distant, yet with constant pace
Follow *offence.* Offence, robust of limb,
And treading firm the ground, outstrips them all,
And over all the earth, before them runs
Hurtful to man: *they,* following, heal the hurt.
Received respectfully when they approach,
They yield us aid, and listen when we pray.
But if we slight, and with obdurate heart
Resist them, to Saturnian Jove they cry.
Against, us supplicating, that *offence*
May cleave to us for vengeance of the wrong.
Thou, therefore, O Achilles! honour yield
To *Jove's own daughters,* vanquished as the brave
Have ofttimes been, by honour paid to thee.
COWPER.

On this allegory the translator makes the following remarks: "*Wrinkled,* because the countenance of a man, driven to prayer by a consciousness of guilt, is sorrowful and dejected. *Lame,* because it is a remedy to which men recur late, and with reluctance. *Slant-eyed,* either because in that state of humiliation they fear to lift up their eyes to heaven, or are employed in taking a retrospect of their past misconduct. The whole allegory, considering *when* and *where* it was composed, forms a very striking passage."

Prayer to God for mercy must have the qualifications marked above. *Prayer comes from God.* He *desires* to save us: this desire is impressed on our hearts by his Spirit, and *reflected* back to himself. Thus says the allegory, "Prayers are the daughters of Jupiter." But they are *lame,* as *reflected light* is much *less intense* and *vivid* than *light direct.* The desire of the heart is afraid to go into the presence of God, because the man knows, *feels,* that he has sinned against goodness and mercy. They are *wrinkled*—dried up and withered, with incessant longing: even the *tears* that refresh the soul are dried up and exhausted. They are *slant-eyed;* look aside through shame and confusion; dare not look God in the face. But *transgression* is strong, bold, impudent, and destructive: it treads with a *firm step* over the earth, bringing down curses on mankind. *Prayer and repentance follow,* but generally at a *distance.* The heart, being hardened by the deceitfulness of sin, does not *speedily* relent. They, however, *follow:* and when, with humility and contrition, they approach the throne of grace, they are *respectfully received.* God acknowledges them *as his offspring,* and *heals* the *wounds* made by *transgression.* If the heart remain *obdurate,* and the man *will not humble himself* before his God, then his *transgression cleaves to him,* and the heartless, lifeless prayers which he may offer in that state, presuming on God's mercy, will turn against him; and to such a one the sacrificial death and mediation of Christ are in vain. And this will be the case especially with the person who, having received an offence from another, *refuses to forgive.* This latter circumstance is that to which the poet particularly refers. See the whole passage, with its context.

Verse 4. *I am counted with them, &c.*] I am as good as dead; nearly destitute of life and hope.

Verse 5. *Free among the dead*] במתים חפשי *bammethim chophshi,* I rather think, means *stripped among the dead.* Both the *fourth* and *fifth* verses seem to allude to a *field of battle:* the *slain* and the *wounded,* are found scattered over the plain; the *spoilers* come among them, and strip, not only the *dead,* but those also who appear to be *mortally wounded,* and cannot recover, and are so feeble as not to be able to *resist.* Hence the psalmist says, "I am counted with them that go down into the pit; I am as a man that hath no strength," ver. 4. And I am stripped among the dead, like the mortally wounded (חללים *chalalim*) that lie in the grave. "Free among the dead," *inter mortuos liber,* has been applied by the fathers to our Lord's voluntary death: all others were *obliged* to die; he alone *gave up his life,* and could take it again, John x. 18. He went into the grave, and came out when he *chose.* The dead are *bound* in the grave; *he was free,* and not obliged to continue in that state as *they* were.

They are cut off from thy hand.] An allusion to the roll in which the general has the names of all that compose his army under their respective officers. And when one is killed, he is erased from this register, and *remembered no more,* as belonging to the army; but his name is entered among those who are dead, in a separate book. This latter is termed the *black book,* or the *book of death;* the other is called the *book of life,* or the *book* where the *living*

7 Thy wrath lieth hard upon me, and
[m]thou hast afflicted *me* with all thy waves.
Selah.
8 [n]Thou hast put away mine acquaintance
far from me; thou hast made me an abomination
unto them: *I am* shut up, and I cannot
come forth.
9 [o]Mine eye mourneth by reason of affliction:
LORD, I have called daily upon thee, [p]I have
stretched out my hands unto thee.
10 [q]Wilt thou show wonders to the dead?
shall the dead arise *and* praise thee? Selah.
11 Shall thy loving-kindness be declared in
the grave? *or* thy faithfulness in destruction?
12 [r]Shall thy wonders be known in the
dark? [s]and thy righteousness in the land of
forgetfulness?
13 But unto thee have I cried, O LORD; and
[t]in the morning shall my prayer prevent
thee.
14 LORD, why castest thou off my soul?
why hidest thou thy face from me?
15 I *am* afflicted and ready to die from *my*
youth up: *while* [u]I suffer thy terrors I am distracted.
16 Thy fierce wrath goeth over me; thy
terrors have cut me off.
17 They came round about me [v]daily like
water; they compassed me about together.
18 [w]Lover and friend hast thou put far from
me, *and* mine acquaintance into darkness.

---

[m]Psa. xlii. 7——[n]Job xix. 13; Psa. xxxi. 11; cxlii. 4——[o]Psa. xxxviii. 10——[p]Job xi. 13; Psa. cxliii. 6——[q]Psa. vi. 5; xxx. 9; cxv. 17; cxviii. 17; Isa. xxxviii. 18

[r]Job x. 21; Psa. cxliii. 3——[s]Psa. xxxi. 12——[t]Psa. v. 3——[u]Job vi. 4——[v]Or, *all the day*——[w]Psalm xxxi. 11; xxxviii. 11

---

are enrolled. From this circumstance, expressed in different parts of the sacred writings, the doctrine of unconditional reprobation and election has been derived. How wonderful!

Verse 7. *Thou hast afflicted* me *with all thy waves.*] The figures in this verse seem to be taken from a tempest at sea. The storm is fierce, and the waves cover the ship.

Verse 8. *Thou hast made me an abomination*] This verse has been supposed to express the *state of a leper*, who, because of the infectious nature of his disease, is *separated* from his *family*—is *abominable* to all, and at last *shut up* in a *separate house*, whence he does not *come out* to mingle with society.

Verse 10. *Wilt thou show wonders to the dead?*] מתים *methim, dead men.*

Shall the dead] רפאים *rephaim*, "the manes or departed spirits."

Arise and *praise thee?*] Any more in this life? The *interrogations* in this and the two following verses imply the strongest *negations.*

Verse 11. Or *thy faithfulness in destruction?*] *Faithfulness* in God refers as well to his *fulfilling his threatenings* as to his *keeping his promises.* The wicked are threatened with such *punishments* as their crimes have deserved; but *annihilation* is no *punishment.* God therefore does not intend to *annihilate* the wicked; their *destruction* cannot declare the *faithfulness of God.*

Verse 12. *The land of forgetfulness?*] The place of *separate spirits*, or the *invisible world.* The heathens had some notion of this state. They feigned a river in the invisible world, called *Lethe*, Ληθη, which signifies *oblivion*, and that those who drank of it remembered no more any thing relative to their former state.

————Animæ, quibus altera fato
Corpora debentur, *lethæi* ad *fluminis undam*
Securos latices et *longa oblivia potant.*
VIRG. Æn. vi. 713.

To all those souls who round the river wait
New mortal bodies are decreed by fate;
To yon *dark stream* the gliding ghosts repair,
And quaff *deep draughts* of *long oblivion* there.

Verse 13. *Shall my prayer prevent thee.*] It shall get *before* thee; I will not wait till the accustomed time to offer my morning sacrifice, I shall call on thee long before others come to offer their devotions.

Verse 14. *Why castest thou off my soul?*] Instead of *my soul*, several of the ancient *Versions* have *my prayer.* Why dost thou refuse to *hear* me, and thus abandon me to *death?*

Verse 15. *From* my *youth up.*] I have always been a child of sorrow, afflicted in my body, and distressed in my mind. There are still found in the Church of God persons in similar circumstances; persons who are continually mourning for themselves and for the desolations of Zion. A disposition of this kind is sure to produce an unhealthy body; and indeed a weak constitution may often produce an enfeebled mind; but where the *terrors of the Lord* prevail, there is neither health of *body* nor peace of *mind.*

Verse 16. *Thy fierce wrath goeth over me.*] It is a mighty flood by which I am overwhelmed.

Verse 17. *They came round about me daily like water*] Besides his spiritual conflicts, he had many enemies to grapple with. The waves of God's displeasure broke over him, and his enemies came around him like water, increasing more and more, rising higher and higher, till he was at last on the point of being submerged in the flood.

Verse 18. *Lover and friend*] I have no comfort, and neither *friend* nor *neighbour* to sympathize with me.

Mine acquaintance into darkness.] All have forsaken me; or מידעי מחשך *meyuddai machsach*, "Darkness is my companion." Perhaps he may refer to the *death* of his acquaintances; all were gone; there was none left to console him! That man has a dismal lot who has outlived all his old friends and acquaintances; well may such complain. In the removal of their friends they see little else than the triumphs of death. *Khosroo*, an eminent Persian poet, handles this painful subject with great delicacy and beauty in the following lines:—

رفتم سوي خطيره بكريستيم بزار
از هجره دوستان كه اسير فنا شدند
گفتم ايشان كجا شدند و خطر
داد از صدا جواب ايشان كجا

Ruftem sauee khuteereh bekerestem bezar
Az Hijereh Doostan ke aseer fana shudend:
Guftem *Eeshah Kuja shudend?* ve Khatyr
Dad az sada jouab *Eeshan Kuja!*

"Weeping, I passed the place where lay my
    friends
Captured by death; in accents wild I cried,
Where are they? And stern Fate, by Echo's
    voice,
Returned in solemn sound the sad *Where are
    they?*"   J. B. C.

ANALYSIS OF THE EIGHTY-EIGHTH PSALM

There are *four* parts in this Psalm:—

I. A petition, ver. 1, 2.

II. The cause of this petition, his misery, which he describes, ver. 3-9.

III. The effects produced by this miserable condition: 1. A special prayer, ver. 10-12; 2. An expostulation with God for deliverance, ver. 10-12.

IV. A grievous complaint, ver. 14-18.

The psalmist offers his petition; but before he begins, he lays down four arguments why it should be admitted,—

1. His confidence and reliance on God: "O Lord God of my salvation."

2. His earnestness to prevail: "I have cried."

3. His assiduity: "Day and night."

4. His sincerity: "I have cried before thee."

And then he tenders his request for audience: "Let my prayer come before thee, incline thine ear unto my cry."

II. And then next he sets forth the pitiful condition he was in, that hereby he might move God to take compassion, which he amplifies several ways:—

1. From the weight and variety of his troubles; many they were, and pressed him to death. "For my soul is full of troubles, and my life draweth nigh to the grave."

2. From the danger of death in which he was. Which is illustrated by three degrees:—

1. That he was *moribundus, dying,* no hope of life in him even by the estimate of all men: "I am counted with them that go down to the pit; I am as a man that hath no strength."

2. That he was *plane mortuus, nearly dead;* but as a dead man, "free among the dead;" freed from all the business of this life; as far separate from them as a dead man.

3. Yea, dead and buried: "Like the slain that lie in the grave; whom thou rememberedst no more;" i. e., to care for in this life; and "they are cut off from thy hand," i. e., thy providence, thy custody, as touching matter of this life.

And yet he farther amplifies his sad condition by two similitudes:—

1. Of a man in some deep dark dungeon: "Thou hast laid me in the lowest pit, in darkness, in the deeps;" as was Jeremiah, chap. xxxvii.

2. Of a man in a wreck at sea, that is com-

passed with the waves, to which he compares God's anger: "Thy wrath lieth hard upon me, and thou hast afflicted me with all thy waves." One wave impels another. The recurrence of his troubles was perpetual; one no sooner gone but another succeeded.

And, to add to this his sorrow, his friends, whose visits in extremity used to alleviate the grief of a troubled soul, even these proved perfidious, and came not to him; he had no comfort with them; which was also God's doing, and thus augmented his grief.

The *auxesis* or *augmentation* is here very elegant:

1. "Thou hast put away mine acquaintance from me." THOU.

2. "Thou hast made me an abomination to them." No less; *an abomination.*

3. "I am shut up, I cannot come forth." As a man in prison, I cannot come at them, and they will not come to me.

III. The effect of which grievous affliction was threefold: 1. An internal grief and wasting of the body; 2. An ardent affection in God; and, 3. An expostulation with God.

1. "My eye mourns by reason of affliction." An evidence that I am troubled and grieved to the heart, that my eye droops and fails; for when the animal and vital spirits suffer a decay, the eye will quickly, by her dimness, deadness, and dulness, discover it.

2. It produced an ardent affection, a continuance and assiduity in prayer, which is here made evident by the adjuncts.

1. His *voice:* "I have called daily upon thee." It was, 1. A cry; 2. It was continual.

2. By the extension of his hands: "I have stretched out my hands to thee." Men used to do so when they expected help; when they looked to receive; whence we sometimes say, Lend me thy hand.

3. The third effect was, an expostulation with God, in which he presseth to spare his life from the inconvenience that might thereby happen, viz., that he should be disabled to praise God, and celebrate his name, as he was bound and desired to do, among the living: an argument used before, Psa. vi. 3. This argument, though it savours too much of human frailty, yet he thought by it to move God, who above all things is jealous of his own glory, which by his death he imagines will suffer loss; and therefore he asks,—

1. "Wilt thou show wonders among the dead?" That is, thy desire is to set forth thy honour, which cannot be done if I go to the grave, except by some miracle I should be raised from thence.

2. "Shall the dead arise again and praise thee?" It is the living that shall show forth thy praise, thy power, and goodness; thy fidelity in keeping thy promises to the sons of men. The dead, as dead, cannot do this; and they return not from the grave, except by miracle.

3. "Shall thy lovingkindness be declared in the grave, or thy faithfulness in destruction? shall thy wonders be known in the dark, or thy righteousness in the land of forgetfulness?" Such is the grave, a place of oblivion; for *Abraham* is ignorant of us. The goodness and faithfulness of God, which he makes known to us in this life, are not known nor can be declared by the dead: the living see them; they have experience of them; and therefore he desires that his life may be spared to that end, lest if he die now that faculty should be taken from him; **he**

should no longer be able to resound the praise of God, which is the end for which men ought to desire life.

IV. He returns to his complaint; and again repeats what he had said before, and almost in the same words, and gives *three* instances:—

1. In his prayer: "But unto thee have I cried, O Lord; and in the morning shall my prayer prevent thee." He prayed earnestly, early, not drowsily; for he did prevent God: he prayed, and would continue in prayer; and yet all in vain.

2. For God seems to be inexorable, of which he complains: "Lord, why castest thou off my soul? why hidest thou thy face from me?" Even the best of God's servants have sometimes been brought to that strait, that they have not had a clear sense of God's favour, but conceived themselves neglected and deserted by him, and discountenanced.

His *second* instance is, his present affliction, mentioned before, ver. 4, 5, 6, 7: "I am afflicted and ready to die," which he here exaggerates:—

1. From the time and continuance of it; for he had borne it "even from his youth up."

2. From the cause. It did not proceed from any outward or human cause; that might have

been borne and helped: but it was an affliction sent from God: "Thy terrors have I suffered;" it came from a sense of God's wrath.

3. From an uncomfortable effect. It wrought in his soul amazement, unrest, a perpetual trouble and astonishment: "Thy terrors have I suffered with a troubled mind: "I am distracted with them."

He amplifies this wrath by the former similes, ver. 7; waves•and water.

1. "Thy fierce wrath goes over me;" as waves over a man's head at sea. "Thy terrors have cut me off;" as a weaver's thrum.

2. "They came round about me like water; daily like water."

3. "They compassed me about together," as if they conspired my ruin: "all thy waves," ver. 7.

His *third* instance, which is the same, ver. 8. The perfidiousness and desertion of friends: a loving friend is some comfort in distress; but this he found not: "Lover and friend hast thou put far from me, and mine acquaintance into darkness." They appear no more to me to give me any counsel, help, or comfort, than if they were hidden in perpetual darkness. His case, therefore, was most deplorable.

PSALM LXXXIX

The psalmist shows God's great mercy to the house of David, and the promises which he had given to it of support and perpetuity, 1–37; complains that, notwithstanding these promises, the kingdom of Judah is overthrown, and the royal family nearly ruined, 38–45; and earnestly prays for their restoration, 46–52.

XVII. DAY. EVENING PRAYER
ᵃMaschil of ᵇEthan the Ezrahite

ᶜI WILL sing of the mercies of the LORD for ever: with my mouth will I make known thy faithfulness ᵈto all generations.

2 For I have said, Mercy shall be built up for ever: ᵉthy faithfulness shalt thou establish in the very heavens.

3 ᶠI have made a covenant with my chosen, I have ᵍsworn unto David my servant,

---

ᵃOr, A Psalm *for Ethan the Ezrahite, to give instruction*
ᵇ1 Kings iv. 31; 1 Chron. ii. 6——ᶜPsa. ci. 1

ᵈHeb. *to generation and generation;* so ver. 4——ᵉPsa. cxix. 89——ᶠ1 Kings viii. 16——ᵍ2 Sam. vii. 11, &c.

NOTES ON PSALM LXXXIX

It is most probable that this Psalm was composed during the captivity. Of *Ethan* and *Heman* we have already seen something in the introduction to the preceding Psalm; see also the parallel places in the margin. The *title* should probably be translated,—*To give instruction to Ethan the Ezrahite.* The *Chaldee* has, "A good instruction, delivered by Abraham, who came from the east country." The *Septuagint* and *Æthiopic* have *Ethan the Israelite;* the *Arabic* has *Nathan the Israelite.*

The Psalm divides itself into *two* grand parts; the first extends from ver. 1 to 37, in which the psalmist shows God's mercy to the house of David, and the promises which he has given to it of support and perpetuity. The *second* part begins with ver. 38, and ends with the Psalm; and in it the author complains that, notwithstanding these promises, the kingdom of Judah is overthrown and the royal family ruined; and he entreats the Lord to remember

his covenant made with that family, and restore them from their captivity.

Verse 1. I will sing of the mercies of the Lord] I will celebrate the mercy of God to the house of Jacob; the mercy that has been shown to our fathers from time *immemorial.*

To all generations] What I say concerning thy mercy and goodness, being inspired by thy Spirit, is not only *true*, but shall be *preserved* by the Divine providence for ever.

Verse 2. Mercy shall be built up for ever] God's *goodness* is the *foundation* on which his *mercy rests;* and from that source, and on that foundation, acts of mercy shall flow and be built up for ever and ever.

Thy faithfulness shalt thou establish] What thou hast promised to do to the children of men on earth, thou dost register in heaven; and thy promise shall never fail.

Verse 3. I have made a covenant with my chosen] I have made a covenant with Abraham, Isaac, and Jacob; and renewed it with Moses and Joshua in reference to the Israelites

4 [h]Thy seed will I establish for ever, and build up thy throne [i]to all generations. Selah.

5 And [k]the heavens shall praise thy wonders, O LORD: thy faithfulness also in the congregation of the saints.

6 [l]For who in the heaven can be compared unto the LORD? *who* among the sons of the mighty can be likened unto the LORD?

7 [m]God is greatly to be feared in the assembly of the saints, and to be had in reverence of all *them that are* about him.

8 O LORD God of hosts, who *is* a strong LORD [n]like unto thee? or to thy faithfulness round about thee?

9 [o]Thou rulest the raging of the sea: when the waves thereof arise, thou stillest them.

10 [p]Thou hast broken [q]Rahab in pieces, as one that is slain; thou hast scattered thine enemies [r]with thy strong arm.

---

[h]Ver. 29, 36——[i]See ver. 1——[k]Psa. xix. 1——[l]Psa. xl. 5; lxxi. 19; lxxxvi. 8; cxiii. 5——[m]Psa. lxxvi. 7, 11 [n]Exod. xv. 11; 1 Sam. ii. 2; Psa. xxxv. 10; lxxi. 19

[o]Psa. lxv. 7; xciii. 3, 4; cvii. 29——[p]Exod. xiv. 26, 27, 28; Psa. lxxxvii. 4; Isa. xxx. 7; li. 9——[q]Or, *Egypt* [r]Heb. *with the arm of thy strength*

---

in general: but I have made one with David in especial relation to himself and posterity, of whom, according to the flesh, the Christ is to come. And this is the covenant with David:—

Verse 4. *Thy seed will I establish for ever, and build up thy throne to all generations.*] And this covenant had most incontestably Jesus Christ in view. This is the *seed*, or posterity, that should sit on the throne, and reign for ever and ever. David and his family are long since become extinct; none of his race has sat on the Jewish throne for more than *two thousand* years: but the Christ has reigned invariably since that time, and will reign till all his enemies are put under his feet; and to this the psalmist says *Selah*. It will be so; it is so; and it cannot be otherwise; for the Lord hath *sworn* that he shall have an *everlasting kingdom*, as he has an *everlasting priesthood*.

Verse 5. *The heavens shall praise thy wonders*] The works that shall be wrought by this descendant of David shall be so plainly miraculous as shall prove their origin to be Divine: and both saints and angels shall join to celebrate his praises.

Thy faithfulness also] All thy promises shall be fulfilled; and particularly and supereminently those which respect the *congregation of the saints*—the assemblies of Christian believers.

Verse 6. *For who in the heaven*] שׁחק *shachak* signifies the ethereal regions, all visible or unbounded space; the universe. Who is like Jesus? Even in his *human nature* none of *the sons of the mighty* can be compared with him. He atones for the sin of the world, and saves to the uttermost all who come unto God through him.

This may also be considered a reproof to idolaters. Is there any among the heavenly hosts like to God? Even the most glorious of them were made by his hands. Can the stars, or the more distant planets, or the moon, or the sun, be likened unto God most high?

Who *among the sons of the mighty*] Instead of אלים *elim, mighty ones*, four of *Kennicott's* and *De Rossi's* MSS. have איל *eil, strength:*— sons of strength, strong persons. Several of the *Versions* seem to have read אלהים *Elohim*, GOD, instead of אלים *elim*, strong ones. So my old Psalter, following the *Vulgate:*—ﬀor wha in the clowdes sal be euened to Lorde; like sal be to God in sons of God! which it paraphrases thus: "Emang al haly men nane may be evened to

Ihu Crist: and nane may be like to hym in God's sons: for he is God's son be kynde, and thai thrugh grace."

Verse 7. *God is greatly to be feared*] In all religious assemblies the deepest reverence for God should rest upon the people. Where this does not prevail, there is no true worship. While some come with a proper Scriptural boldness to the throne of grace, there are others who come into the presence of God with a reprehensible, if not sinful, boldness.

Verse 8. *O Lord God of hosts*] Thou who hast all armies at thy command, and canst serve thyself by every part of thy creation, whether animate or inanimate.

Who is a strong Lord] See ver. 6.

Thy faithfulness round about thee?] Or, more properly, *thy faithfulness is round about thee*. Thou still keepest thy promises *in view*. God's *truth* leads him to fulfil his promises: they stand round his throne as the faithful servants of an eastern monarch stand round their master, waiting for the moment of their dismission to perform his will.

Verse 9. *Thou rulest the raging of the sea*] Whoever has seen the sea in a storm, when its waves run what is called *mountain high*, must acknowledge that nothing but omnipotent power could rule its raging.

When the waves thereof arise, thou stillest them.] Thou governest both its *flux* and *reflux*. Thou art the Author of *storms* and *calms*. There may be a reference here to the passage of the Red Sea, and the strong wind that agitated its waves at that time; as the next verse seems to indicate.

Verse 10. *Thou hast broken Rahab*] Thou hast destroyed the power of *Egypt*, having overthrown the king and its people when they endeavoured to prevent thy people from regaining their liberty.

As one that is slain] The whole clause in the original is, אתה דכאת כחלל רהב *attah dikkitha kechalal Rahab,* "Thou, like a hero, hast broken down Egypt." Dr. *Kennicott* has largely proved that חלל *chalal*, which we render *wounded, slain, &c.*, means a *soldier, warrior, hero;* and it is certain that this sense agrees better with it than the other in a great number of places. Mr. *Berlin* translates, Tu contrivisti ut cadaver Ægyptum; "Thou hast bruised down Egypt like a dead carcass." The whole strength of Egypt could avail nothing against thee. Thou didst trample them down as easily as if they had all been dead carcasses.

11 ˢThe heavens *are* thine, the earth also *is* thine: *as for* the world and the fulness thereof, thou hast founded them.

12 ᵗThe north and the south thou hast created them: ᵘTabor and ᵛHermon shall rejoice in thy name.

13 Thou hast ʷa mighty arm: strong is thy hand, *and* high is thy right hand.

14 ˣJustice and judgment *are* the ʸhabitation of thy throne: ᶻmercy and truth shall go before thy face.

15 Blessed *is* the people that know the

ᵃjoyful sound: they shall walk, O LORD, in the ᵇlight of thy countenance.

16 In thy name shall they rejoice all the day: and in thy righteousness shall they be exalted.

17 For thou *art* the glory of their strength: ᶜand in thy favour our horn shall be exalted.

18 For ᵈthe LORD *is* our defence; and the Holy One of Israel *is* our King.

19 Then thou spakest in vision to thy Holy One, and saidst, I have laid help upon *one that is* mighty; I have exalted *one* ᵉchosen out of the people.

ˢGen. i. 1; 1 Chron. xxix. 11; Psa. xxiv. 1, 2; l. 12
ᵗJob xxvi. 7——ᵘJosh. xix. 12, 22; Judg. iv. 6, 12, 14;
viii. 18; 1 Sam. x. 3; 1 Chron. vi. 17; Jer. xlvi. 18; Hos.
v. 1——ᵛJosh. xii. 1——ʷHebrew, *an arm with might*
ˣPsalm xcvii. 2

ʸOr, *establishment*——ᶻPsa. lxxxv. 13——ᵃNum. x.
10; xxiii. 21; Psa. xcviii. 6——ᵇPsa. iv. 6; xliv. 3
ᶜVer. 24; Psa. lxxv. 10; xcii. 10; cxxxii. 17——ᵈOr, *our shield* is *of the LORD, and our king* is *of the Holy One of Israel;* Psa. xlvii. 9——ᵉVer. 3; 1 Kings xi. 34

Verse 11. *The heavens* are *thine*] Thou art the Governor of all things, and the Disposer of all events.

The world] The terraqueous globe.

And the fulness] All the generations of men. *Thou hast founded them*—thou hast *made* them, and dost *sustain* them.

After this verse, the *Editio Princeps* of the Hebrew Bible, printed at Soncini, 1488, adds:—

לך יום אף לך לילה

lailah lecha aph yom lecha

אתה הכינות מאור ושמש

vashamesh maor hachinotha attah

To thee is the day; also to thee is the night: Thou hast prepared the light and the sun.

But these same words are found in Psa. lxxiv. 16.

Verse 12. *The north and the south*] It is generally supposed that by these *four* terms all the four quarters of the globe are intended. *Tabor,* a mountain of Galilee, was on the *west* of Mount *Hermon,* which was beyond Jordan, to the *east* of the source of that river.

Verse 14. *Justice and judgment* are *the habitation of thy throne*] The throne—the government, of God, is founded in *righteousness* and *judgment.* He knows what is right; he sees what is right; he does what is right; and his *judgments* are ever according to righteousness. His decisions are all *oracles;* no one of them is ever reversed.

Mercy and truth shall go before thy face.] These shall be the *heralds* that shall announce the coming of the Judge. His *truth* binds him to fulfil all his declarations; and his *mercy* shall be shown to all those who have fled for refuge to the hope that is set before them in the Gospel. See the notes on Psa. lxxxv. 10, 11.

Verse 15. *Blessed* is *the people*] "O the blessednesses of that people (אשרי העם *ashrey haam*) that know the joyful sound;" that are spared to hear the sound of the trumpet on the morning of the *jubilee,* which proclaims deliverance to the captives, and the restoration of all their forfeited estates. "They shall walk vigorously (יהלכון *yehallechun*) in the light of thy countenance" (באור פניך *beor paneycha*)—the

full persuasion of the approbation of God their *Father, Redeemer,* and *Sanctifier.*

Verse 16. *In thy name shall they rejoice*] Or, "greatly exult," יגילון *yegilun;* "all that day," היום *haiyom,* the jubilee, referred to above.

And in thy righteousness] In the declaration of thy righteousness for the remission of sins that are past, Rom. iii. 25, 26.

Shall they be exalted.] They shall be justified freely from all things, be purified from all unrighteousness, grow in grace, and in the knowledge of Jesus Christ here below, and at last be exalted to his right hand to reign with him for ever. The jubilee was a type of the Gospel, and under that type the psalmist here speaks of the glorious advent of the Lord Jesus, and the great happiness of believers in him. Let it be observed that the letters in the above Hebrew words called *paragogic,* as ן *nun* in יהלכון *yehallechuɴ,* and יגילון *yegiluɴ,* always increase and deepen the meaning of the words to which they are attached.

Verse 17. *For thou* art *the glory of their strength*] They are strong in faith, and give glory to thee, because they know that their strength cometh from the Lord of hosts.

And in thy favour our horn shall be exalted.] Instead of תרום *tarum,* "shall be exalted," תרים *tarim,* "thou shalt exalt," is the reading of several MSS.: but תרום *tarum,* "shall be exalted," is supported by *forty-four* of *Kennicott's* MSS., and *sixty* of *De Rossi's,* as well as by several ancient editions, with the *Septuagint, Syriac, Vulgate,* and *Arabic* Versions. In the enjoyment of the Divine favour they shall grow more *wise,* more *holy,* more *powerful,* and, consequently, more *happy.*

Verse 19. *Then thou spakest in vision to thy holy one*] Instead of חסידך *chasidecha,* "thy holy one," חסידיך *chasideycha,* "thy holy ones," is the reading of *sixty-three* of *Kennicott's* and *seventy-one* of *De Rossi's* MSS., and a great number of *editions* besides.

If we take it in the *singular,* it most probably means *Samuel,* and refers to the *revelation* God gave to him relative to his appointment of *David* to be king in the stead of Saul. If we take it in the *plural,* it may mean not only *Samuel,* but also *Nathan* and *Gad.*

20 [f]I have found David my servant; with
my holy oil have I anointed him:
21 [g]With whom my hand shall be established: mine arm also shall strengthen
him.
22 [h]The enemy shall not exact upon him;
nor the son of wickedness afflict him.
23 [i]And I will beat down his foes before
his face, and plague them that hate him.
24 But [k]my faithfulness and my mercy *shall be* with him: and [l]in my name shall his horn
be exalted.
25 [m]I will set his hand also in the sea, and
his right hand in the rivers.
26 He shall cry unto me, Thou *art* [n]my
father, my God, and [o]the rock of my salvation.
27 Also I will make him [p]*my* first-born,
[q]higher than the kings of the earth.
28 [r]My mercy will I keep for him for evermore, and [s]my covenant shall stand fast with
him.
29 [t]His seed also will I make *to endure* for
ever, [u]and his throne [v]as the days of heaven.
30 [w]If his children [x]forsake my law, and
walk not in my judgments;
31 If they [y]break my statutes, and keep not
my commandments;
32 Then [z]will I visit their transgression
with the rod, and their iniquity with stripes.

---

[f]1 Sam. xvi. 1, 12——[g]Psa. lxxx. 17——[h]2 Sam. vii. 10——[i]2 Sam. vii. 9——[k]Psa. lxi. 7——[l]Ver. 17 [m]Psa. lxxii. 8; lxxx. 11——[n]2 Sam. vii. 14; 1 Chron. xxii. 10——[o]2 Sam. xxii. 47——[p]Psa. ii. 7; Col. i. 15, 18 [q]Num. xxiv. 7——[r]Isa. lv. 3——[s]Ver. 34——[t]Ver. 4, 36 [u]Ver. 4; Isa. ix. 7; Jer. xxxiii. 17——[v]Deut. xi. 21 [w]2 Sam. vii. 14——[x]Psa. cxix. 53; Jer. ix. 13——[y]Heb. *profane my statutes*——[z]2 Sam. vii. 14; 1 Kings xi. 31

For what God revealed to *Samuel* relative to David, see 2 Sam. vii. 5, &c.; 1 Chron. xi. 2, 3; and for what he said to *Nathan* on the same subject, see 1 Chron. xvii. 3, 7-15. All the *Versions* have the word in the *plural.*

Verse 20. *I have found David my servant*] This is the sum of what God had said in prophetic *visions* to his *saints* or holy persons, *Samuel, Nathan,* and *Gad;* see the parallel places in the *margin.* Here the psalmist begins to reason with God relative to David, his posterity, and the perpetuity of his kingdom; which promises appear now to have utterly failed, as the throne had been overturned, and all the people carried into captivity. But all these things may have reference to *Christ* and his kingdom; for we are assured that David was a type of the Messiah.

Verse 22. *The enemy shall not exact upon him*] None of his enemies shall be able to prevail against him. It is worthy of remark that David was never overthrown; he finally conquered every foe that rose up against him. Saul's persecution, Absalom's revolt, Sheba's conspiracy, and the struggle made by the partisans of the house of Saul after his death, only tended to call forth David's skill, courage, and prowess, and to seat him more firmly on his throne. The Philistines, the Ammonites, the Syrians, &c., united all their forces to crush him, but in vain: "God beat down all his foes before his face," and variously *plagued* those who opposed him, ver. 23.

Verse 25. *I will set his hand also in the sea*] This was literally fulfilled in David. *Hand* signifies power or authority; he set his hand on the sea in *conquering* the Philistines, and extending his empire along the coast of the Mediterranean Sea, from Tyre to Pelusium. All the coasts of the Red Sea, the Persian Gulf, and the Arabic Ocean, might be said to have been under his *government,* for they all paid tribute to *him* or his son Solomon.

His right hand in the rivers] First, the Euphrates: he subjected all Syria, and even a part of Mesopotamia; 2 Sam. viii. 3; 1 Chron. xviii. 3. He also took Damascus, and consequently had his *hand* or authority over the river Chrysorrhoes, or Baraddi; and in his conquest of all Syria his hand must have been on the *Orontes* and other rivers in that region. But if this be considered as referring to the typical David, we see that *He* was never conquered; he never lost a battle; the hosts of hell pursued him in vain. Satan was discomfited, and all his enemies bruised under his feet. Even over *death* he triumphed; and as to his dominion, it has spread and is spreading over all the isles of the sea, and the continents of the world.

Verse 27. *I will make him* my *first-born*] I will deal with him as a father by his *first-born son,* to whom a double portion of possessions and honours belong. *First-born* is not always to be understood *literally* in Scripture. It often signifies simply a *well-beloved,* or *best-beloved son;* one preferred to all the rest, and distinguished by some eminent prerogative. Thus God calls Israel *his son,* his *first-born,* Exod. iv. 22. See also Ecclus. xxxvi. 12. And even Ephraim is called God's *first-born,* Jer. xxxi. 9. In the same sense it is sometimes applied even to *Jesus Christ himself,* to signify his supereminent dignity; not the *eternal Sonship* of his *Divine nature,* as inveterate prejudice and superficial thinking have supposed.

Verse 29. *His seed also will I make* to endure *for ever*] This can apply only to the spiritual David. The posterity of David are long since extinct, or so blended with the remaining Jews as to be utterly indiscernible; but Jesus ever liveth, and his seed (*Christians*) are spread, and are spreading over all nations; and *his* throne is eternal. As to his *manhood,* he is of the house and lineage of David; the government is upon his shoulders, and of its increase there shall be no end, upon the throne of David and on his kingdom to order it and to establish it with judgment and justice, from henceforth even for ever. Isa. ix. 7.

Verse 30. *If his children forsake my law*] See the notes on 2 Sam. vii. 13, where this

33 ^aNevertheless my lovingkindness ^bwill I not utterly take from him, nor suffer my faithfulness ^cto fail.

34 My covenant will I not break, nor alter the thing that is gone out of my lips.

35 Once have I sworn ^dby my holiness ^ethat I will not lie unto David.

36 ^fHis seed shall endure for ever, and his throne ^gas the sun before me.

37 It shall be established for ever as the moon, and *as* a faithful witness in heaven. Selah.

38 But thou hast ^hcast off and ⁱabhorred, thou hast been wroth with thine anointed.

39 Thou hast made void the covenant of thy servant; ^kthou hast profaned his crown *by casting it* to the ground.

40 ^lThou hast broken down all his hedges; thou hast brought his strong holds to ruin.

41 All that pass by the way spoil him: he is ^ma reproach to his neighbours.

42 Thou hast set up the right hand of his adversaries; thou hast made all his enemies to rejoice.

43 Thou hast also turned the edge of his sword, and hast not made him to stand in the battle.

44 Thou hast made his ⁿglory to cease, and ^ocast his throne down to the ground.

45 The days of his youth hast thou shortened: thou hast covered him with shame. Selah.

---

^a2 Sam. vii. 13——^bHeb. *I will not make void from him* ^cHeb. *to lie*——^dAmos iv. 2——^eHeb. *If I lie*——^f2 Sam. vii. 16; Luke i. 33; John xii. 34; ver. 4, 29 ^gPsa. lxxii. 5, 17; Jer. xxxiii. 20

^h1 Chron. xxviii. 9; Psa. xliv. 9; lx. 1, 10——ⁱDeut. xxxii. 19; Psa. lxxviii. 59——^kPsa. lxxiv. 7; Lam. v. 16——^lPsa. lxxx. 12——^mPsa. xliv. 13; lxxix. 4 ⁿHeb. *brightness*——^oVerse 39

---

and some of the following verses are explained.

Verse 34. *My covenant will I not break*] My determination to establish a spiritual kingdom, the head of which shall be Jesus, the son of David, shall never fail. My prophets have declared this, and I will not alter the thing that is gone out of my mouth.

Verse 35. *Once have I sworn*] I have made one determination on this head, and have bound myself by my holiness; it is impossible that I should change, and there needs no second oath, the one already made is of endless obligation.

Verse 36. *His throne as the sun*] Splendid and glorious! dispensing light, heat, life, and salvation to all mankind.

Verse 37. *As the moon, and* as *a faithful witness in heaven.*] That is, as long as the sun and moon shall endure, as long as *time* shall last, his kingdom shall last among men. The moon appears to be termed *a faithful witness* here, because by her particularly *time* is measured. Her *decrease* and *increase* are especially observed by every nation, and by these time is generally estimated, especially among the eastern nations. *So many moons is a man old; so many moons since such an event happened;* and even their years are reckoned by *lunations.* This is the case with the Mohammedans to the present day. Or the *rainbow* may be intended; that sign which God has established in the cloud; that faithful witness of his that the earth shall no more be destroyed by water. As long therefore as the *sun*, the *moon*, and the *rainbow* appear in the heavens, so long shall the spiritual David reign, and his seed prosper and increase.

Selah.] It is confirmed; it shall not fail.

Verse 38. *But thou hast cast off*] Hitherto the psalmist has spoken of the *covenant of God with David* and his family, which led them to expect all manner of prosperity, and a perpetuity of the Jewish throne; now he shows what appears to him a failure of the promise, and what he calls in the next verse the *making void the covenant of his servant.* God cannot

lie to David; how is it then that his *crown is profaned,* that it is cast *down to the ground;* the land being possessed by strangers, and the twelve tribes in the most disgraceful and oppressive captivity?

Verse 40. *Thou hast broken down all his hedges*] Thou hast permitted the land to be stripped of all defence; there is not even one strong place in the hands of thy people.

Verse 41. *All that pass by the way spoil him.*] The land is in the condition of a vineyard, the hedge of which is broken down, so that they who pass by may pull the grapes, and dismantle or tear down the vines. The *Chaldeans* and the *Assyrians* began the ravage; the *Samaritans* on the one hand, and the *Idumeans* on the other, have completed it.

Verse 42. *Thou hast set up the right hand of his adversaries*] Thou hast given them that *strength* which thou didst formerly give to thy own people; therefore *these* are depressed, *those* exalted.

Verse 43. *Thou hast also turned the edge of his sword.*] The arms and military prowess of thy people are no longer of any use to them; THOU art *against* them, and therefore they are fallen. In what a perilous and hopeless situation must that soldier be who, while defending his life against his mortal foe, has his sword *broken,* or its *edge turned;* or, in modern warfare, whose *gun misses fire!* The *Gauls,* when invaded by the Romans, had no method of *hardening iron;* at every blow their swords *bended,* so that they were obliged, before they could strike again, to put them under their foot or over their knee, to straighten them; and in most cases, before this could be done, their better armed foe had taken away their life! The edge of their sword was turned, so that they could not stand in battle; and hence the *Gauls* were conquered by the Romans.

Verse 44. *Thou hast made his glory to cease*] The kingly dignity is destroyed, and there is neither *king* nor *throne* remaining.

Verse 45. *The days of his youth hast thou shortened*] Our kings have not reigned half

46 [p]How long, LORD? wilt thou hide thyself for ever? [q]shall thy wrath burn like fire?

47 [r]Remember how short my time is: wherefore hast thou made all men in vain?

48 [s]What man *is he that* liveth, and shall not [t]see death? shall he deliver his soul from the hand of the grave? Selah.

49 LORD, where *are* thy former lovingkindnesses, *which* thou [u]swarest unto David [v]in thy truth?

50 Remember, LORD, the reproach of thy servants; [w]*how* I do bear in my bosom *the reproach of* all the mighty people;

51 [x]Wherewith thine enemies have reproached, O LORD; wherewith they have reproached the footsteps of thine anointed.

52 [y]Blessed *be* the LORD for evermore. Amen, and Amen.

---

[p]Psa. lxxix. 5——[q]Psa. lxxviii. 63——[r]Job vii. 7; x. 9; xiv. 1; Psa. xxxix. 5; cxix. 84——[s]Psa. xlix. 9

[t]Heb. xi. 5——[u]2 Sam. vii. 15; Isa. lv. 3——[v]Psa. liv. 5 [w]Psa. lxix. 9, 19——[x]Psa. lxxiv. 22——[y]Psa. xli. 13

---

their days, nor lived out half their lives. The *four* last kings of Judea reigned but a short time, and either died by the sword or in captivity.

Jehoahaz reigned only *three months*, and was led captive to Egypt, where he *died*. *Jehoiakim* reigned only *eleven years*, and was tributary to the Chaldeans, who *put him to death*, and cast his body into the common sewer. *Jehoiachin* reigned *three months* and *ten days*, and was led *captive* to Babylon, where he continued in prison to the time of Evilmerodach, who, though he loosed him from prison, never invested him with any power. *Zedekiah*, the last of all, had reigned only *eleven years* when he was taken, *his eyes put out*, was *loaded with chains*, and thus carried to Babylon. Most of these kings died a violent and *premature* death. Thus the *days of their youth*—of their power, dignity, and life, *were shortened*, and they themselves *covered with shame. Selah;* so it most incontestably is.

Verse 46. *How long, Lord?*] The promise cannot utterly fail. When then, O Lord, wilt thou restore the kingdom to Israel?

Verse 47. *How short my time is*] If thou deliver not speedily, none of the present generations shall see thy salvation. Are all the remnants of our tribes created in vain? shall they never see happiness?

Verse 48. *What man* is he that *liveth*] All men are mortal, and death is uncertain and no man, by wisdom, might, or riches, can deliver his life from the *hand*—the power, of death and the grave.

Verse 49. *Lord, where* are *thy former lovingkindnesses*] Wilt thou not deal with *us* as thou didst with our *fathers?* Didst thou not swear unto David that thou wouldst distinguish *him* as thou didst *them?*

Verse 50. *I do bear in my bosom*] Our enemies, knowing our confidence, having often heard our boast in thee, and now seeing our low and hopeless estate, mock us for our confidence, and blaspheme *thee*. This wounds my soul; I cannot bear to hear thy name blasphemed among the heathen. *All these mighty people* blaspheme the God of Jacob.

Verse 51. *They have reproached the footsteps of thine anointed.*] They search into the whole history of thy people; they trace it up to the earliest times; and they find we have been disobedient and rebellious; and on this account we suffer much, alas, *deserved* reproach. The *Chaldee* gives this clause a singular turn: "Thy enemies have reproached the slowness of the footsteps of the feet of thy Messiah, O Lord. We have trusted in him as our great Deliverer, and have been daily in expectation of his coming: but there is no deliverer, and our enemies mock our confidence." This expectation seems *now* wholly abandoned by the Jews: they have rejected the *true Messiah*, and the ground of their expectation of *another* is now cut off. When will they turn unto the Lord? When shall the veil be taken away from their hearts?

"Bend by thy grace, O *bend* or *break*
The *iron sinew* in their neck!"

Verse 52. *Blessed* be *the Lord for evermore.*] Let him treat us as he will, his name deserves eternal praises: our affliction, though great, is less than we have deserved.

This verse concludes the THIRD BOOK of the PSALTER; and, I think, has been added by a later hand, in order to make this *distinction*, as every *Masoretic* Bible has something of this kind at the end of each book. The verse is wanting in one of *Kennicott's* and one of *De Rossi's* MSS.; in *another* it is written without points, to show that it does not belong to the text, and in *three* others it is written *separately* from the text. It is found, however, in all the ancient *Versions*. The *Chaldee* finishes thus: "Blessed be the name of the Lord in this world. Amen and Amen. Blessed be the name of the Lord in the world to come. Amen and Amen." And the reader will find no difficulty to subscribe his Amen, so be it.

ANALYSIS OF THE EIGHTY-NINTH PSALM

In this Psalm the stability and perpetuity of Christ's kingdom, of which the kingdom of David was but a type, are excellently described and foretold.

The *parts* of this Psalm are these:—

I. The *argument* and *sum* of the whole; the loving-kindness and the truth of God, ver. 1, 2.

II. The *particular instance* of God's goodness and truth in making a covenant with David, ver. 3, 4.

III. A *doxology* in which God is praised for his wonders, faithfulness, power, providence, justice, judgment, mercy, and truth, ver. 3-15

IV. The *happy state* of God's people, ver. 15-19.

V. A *special example* of God's goodness towards his Church, *exemplified* in David, but *verified* in Christ, ver. 20-28.

VI. How David's *posterity should be dealt with*, on their disobedience, ver. 29-38.

VII. An *expostulation* on the contrary events, where the psalmist deplores the ruined state of the Jewish kingdom, ver. 38-47.

VIII. A *petition* for mercy and restoration, ver. 48-51.

IX. The *conclusion*, in which the psalmist blesseth God for the hope he has in his favour, in all states, ver. 52.

I. The *argument* or *sum* of the Psalm set down in the *first verse*, and amplified by the reason in the *second*.

1. "I will sing." I will set this forth in a song; because, 1. It is the fittest way to express joy for any thing. 2. It will be best inculcated in this way. 3. It will be more easily remembered; and, 4. More easily delivered to others, in order to be remembered. Many ancient histories had not been preserved at all, had they not been delivered in *poetry*.

2. "Of thy mercies." Plurally, for they are many; and a song of this kind should be of *all*.

3. "For ever." Intentionally, not in himself, not actually; for as a wicked man, could he live always, would sin always; so a good man, could he live here for ever, would sing for ever of the mercies of the Lord.

4. "With my mouth will I make known," &c. While I live I will make them known, and when I am dead they shall be known by the record which I leave behind. His reason for it is, because God's mercy is everlasting; it is therefore proper to be the subject of everlasting song.

1. "For I have said." This is an indubitable truth.

2. "Mercy shall be built up for ever." It is not exhausted in one age, but, as a house built on a strong foundation, it shall be firm, and last from age to age.

3. "Thy faithfulness shalt thou establish." As is thy *mercy*, so is thy faithfulness, perpetual as the heavens.

II. For the proof of God's goodness and truth he produces the instance of the covenant made with David, where he brings in God speaking:—

1. "I have made a covenant with my chosen." I have made this covenant through my mere mercy, not on account of their merits. I have chosen David, not because he *deserved* it, but because he is fit for it.

2. "I have sworn." In compassion to the weakness of men, I have condescended to bind myself by an oath; and the covenant and the oath are extant. 2 Sam. vii. 11.

3. The tenor of the covenant is, "Thy seed will I establish for ever, and build up thy throne to all generations." *Thy seed*—this is true of Christ only, who was of the seed of David, and of whose kingdom there shall be no end. The words are not to be understood of David's earthly kingdom, but of Christ's spiritual kingdom, for that alone will be established for ever.

III. A Doxology. What the psalmist undertook in the *first* part he now performs, and thus he begins: "The heavens shall praise." By these some understand the Church, and the preachers in the Church; others, the *angels:* both are true. GOD's *followers* and his *angels* praise him; and the subject of their praise is:—

1. God's *wondrous works*, and his *truth*. 2. The manner in which he showed his works and his truth, in promising the Messiah, and in so faithfully keeping that promise.

And now he sings praise to his majesty, setting forth his power in *three* respects:—

1. By way of comparison; there is nothing in heaven or earth equal to it, ver. 6-8.

2. By his agency in governing the world: as, for example, the *sea*, Thou stillest the raging of it, &c.

3. The creation of all things; the world and its fulness.

The other part of the praise, sung both by the prophets and the angels, is taken from his attributes, summed up in ver. 14: "Justice and judgment are the habitation of thy throne; mercy and truth shall go before thy face."

He represents God as a great King sitting in his throne; the *basis* of which is, 1. *Justice* and *Judgment*. 2. The *attendants* are *mercy* and *truth*.

1. Justice, which defends his subjects, and does every one right.

2. Judgment, which restrains rebels, and keeps off injuries.

3. Mercy, which shows compassion, pardons, supports the weak.

4. Truth, that performs whatsoever he promiseth.

IV. And in regard that God is powerful, just, merciful, faithful, he takes an occasion to set out the happy condition of God's people, who live under this King.

"Blessed are the people that know the joyful sound:" that is, do know that God is present with them, and his kingly Majesty is at hand to protect them. The phrase is taken from *Moses.* For the law was given by sound of trumpet. The calling of the feasts was by sound of trumpet: at that sound they removed; at that sound they assembled. *Balaam* said, "The sound of a king is among them." Happy, then, are the people that know the joyful sound. God presents their King speaking, ruling, defending, pardoning them. Or it may refer to the year of jubilee, (see the notes.) That they are happy, the effects do evince; which are:—

1. "They shall walk in the light of thy countenance," i. e., though beset with troubles, yet they shall walk confidently, being assured of God's favour.

2. "In thy name shall they rejoice all the day long." Their joy is firm.

3. "In thy righteousness shall they be exalted." They shall get a name, strength. In their union and communion with God they shall be happy.

Confident, yea, joyful and strong they are in all temptations; which yet they have not from themselves. All is from God. For "thou art the glory of their strength, and in thy favour our horn shall be exalted. For the Lord is our defence, the Holy One of Israel is our King."

V. The doxology being now ended, and the happiness of God's people expressed and proved, the prophet now enlarges himself upon the covenant formerly mentioned, ver. 4, 5, exemplified in *David*, but truly verified in *Christ*. Which he continues to verse 30.

1. "Then," i. e., when *David* was chosen to be king, and invested with the regal robe.

2. "Thou spakest in vision to thy Holy One." To *Samuel* for his anointing; and saidst,

3. "I have laid help upon one that is mighty; I have exalted one chosen out of the people." That is, *David* in type, but *Christ* in the antitype. So explained, "I have found *David* my servant; with my holy oil have I anointed him."

To which there follow the promises made to him:—

1. For his establishment and confirmation in the throne: "With whom my hand shall be established; mine arm also shall strengthen him."

2. For protection against his enemies: "The enemy shall not exact upon him, nor the son of wickedness afflict him."

3. A conquest over his enemies: "And will beat down his foes before his face, and plague them that hate him."

4. And that there be no doubt of the performance of these ample promises, nor yet those that follow, the prophet interposes the cause, viz., the faithfulness and mercy of God. In mercy he said it, and it should so come to pass: "But my faithfulness and mercy shall be with him." And now he goes on:—

5. "His horn shall be exalted." His power shall be greatly increased.

And this his exaltation appears:—

1. In the dilatation of his empire: "I will set his hand also in the sea, and his right hand in the rivers," i. e., from the sea to *Euphrates*, 2 Sam. viii.

2. In the honour done him, to call GOD Father, his God, his Rock: "He shall call to me, Thou art my Father, my God, and the Rock of my salvation."

3. Then that God asserts and fixes this prerogative upon him, acknowledging him to be his Son; his first-born Son: "Also I will make him my first-born, higher than the kings of the earth."

4. In the perpetuity of his kingdom, which is rightly attributed to God's mercy; as ver. 25: "My mercy will I keep for him for evermore, and my covenant shall stand fast with him."

5. In the promise made to his seed: "His seed also will I make to endure for ever, and his throne as the days of heaven."

VI. And next the prophet puts a case, and answers it: But what, if *David's* seed transgress God's covenant, break his laws, violate his statutes, become rebels and disobedient; will God then *keep covenant with them? shall his seed endure for ever? and his throne as the days of heaven?* To this doubt God answers, from ver. 30 to 38; showing us how David's seed, if they transgress, shall be dealt with.

1. "If his children forsake my law;" that is, my whole doctrine of worship, religion, faith, &c.

2. "And walk not in my judgments;" i. e., in those laws which set out rewards and punishments.

3. "If they break my statutes." Those statutes I have set down for my service, the rites, ceremonies, new moons, Sabbaths, sacrifices, circumcision, passover, &c.

4. "And keep not my commandments;" that is, the decalogue and moral law. In a word, if they become vicious in their morals, and profane, and rebels in my worship and religion. This then shall happen unto them,—escape they shall not, but shall soundly smart for it. They shall feel,—1. *The rod;* and, 2. *The scourge.* Then,

1. "I will visit (that is, punish) their transgression with the rod."

2. "And their iniquity with stripes." Which was often done by the *Babylonians, Antiochus,* &c. And yet in judgment I will remember mercy. I will remember my covenant, my promise, my word, my oath, and will make that

good. I will not totally cast off David's seed; which I mean not after the flesh, for that is long since cast off, but after the Spirit. *Christ,* which was of the seed of *David,* and those which are his seed, viz., the Church, shall enjoy the benefit of my covenant and oath for ever: "Nevertheless, my loving-kindness will I not utterly take from him, nor suffer my faithfulness to fail. My covenant will I not break, nor alter the thing gone out of my lips."

And that there be no doubt of this, he brings in God repeating his oath and covenant.

1. His oath: "Once have I sworn by my holiness;" that is, by myself, who am holy.

2. His covenant: "That I will not lie unto David; for his seed shall endure for ever, and his throne as the sun before me. It shall be established for ever as the moon, and as a faithful witness in heaven." As the sun and moon are not liable to any ruinous mutations, no more is this covenant: they must endure to the end of the world; and so must this covenant. They are faithful witnesses in heaven; and so we are to seek for the performance of this covenant in heaven; not in the earth, the covenant being about a heavenly kingdom, not an earthly; it being evident that the kingdom of *David* on earth has failed many ages since: but that of *Christ* shall never fail.

VII. Now that *David's* kingdom did fail, or at least was brought to a low ebb, is the complaint in the following words, which flesh and blood considering, gave a wrong judgment upon it, as if God did nothing less than perform his oath and covenant. This is what the prophet lays to God's charge: "But thou hast cut off and abhorred, thou hast been wroth with thine anointed." Both king and people are cast aside, than which nothing seems more contrary to thy covenant.

Thou hast made void the covenant of thy servant, of which there are many lamentable consequences:—

1. "His crown is cast to the ground." The glory of his kingdom trampled upon.

2. "His hedges broken down." His strongholds brought to ruin.

3. "All that pass by the way spoil him." He is exposed to all rapine and plunder.

4. "He is a reproach to his neighbour." Exposed to all contumely and disgrace.

5. "Thou hast set up the right hand of his enemies, and made all his adversaries to rejoice." Thou seemest to take part with the enemy against him, and makest him to exult and rejoice in oppressing him.

6. "Thou hast also turned the edge of his sword, (blunted his sword that was wont to slay,) and hast not made him to stand in the battle," but to fly and turn his back.

7. "Thou hast made his glory (the glory, dignity, authority of his kingdom) to cease, and cast his crown to the ground."

8. "The days of his youth hast thou shortened;" cut him off in the prime and strength of his years. "Thou hast covered him with shame;" made his opulent, glorious kingdom ignominious; which was true in divers of *David's* posterity, especially *Jehoiakim.*

These were the sad complaints which the prophet pours out; but he quickly recovers and recalls his thoughts; and that he may move God to help, he falls to prayer, which is very pathetic.

VIII. He considers the nature of God as kind, loving, merciful, slow to anger; and asks,—

1. "How long, Lord? wilt thou hide thyself for ever?" Hide thy favour?

2. "Shall thy wrath burn like fire?" An element that hath no mercy.

He then uses other arguments, pathetically expressed, to move God to pity:—

1. Drawn from the brevity of man's life: "Remember how short my time is."

2. From the end for which man was created; not in vain, but to be an object of God's goodness and favour.

3. From the weakness and disability of man. His life is short; and can he lengthen it? "What man is he that liveth, and shall not see death?" Yea, though he live long, yet he is a mortal creature: "Shall he deliver his soul from the grave?"

4. From the covenant, of which he puts God in mind: "Lord, where are thy former lovingkindnesses, which thou swarest to David in thy truth?"

5. From the ignominy, scorns, sarcasms, by enemies cast upon them, which he desires God to look upon. 1. "Remember, Lord, the reproach of thy servant." 2. "And how I do bear in my bosom." Not spoken afar off, but in my hearing, and to my face, as if poured and emptied into my bosom; the *rebukes* not of this or that man, but of *many people.*

6. And lastly, that these reproaches, in effect, fall upon God. For they who reproach God's servants are his enemies: "Remember the reproaches"—1. "Wherewith thine enemies have reproached, O Lord." 2. "Wherewith they have reproached the footsteps of thine anointed," i. e., either whatsoever he says or does; or else by *footsteps* is to be understood the latter end of *David's* kingdom, which was indeed subject to reproach. 3. But the *Chaldee* paraphrast by *footsteps* understands the coming of the Messiah in the flesh; which, because it was long promised and men saw not performed, many derided, mocked, and reproached, as vain.

IX. The close of this long Psalm is a *benediction,* by which the prophet, after his combat with flesh and blood about the performance of the covenant, composes his troubled soul, and acquiesces in God; blessing him for whatever falls out, breaking forth into:—

1. "Blessed be the Lord for evermore:" Blessed be his name, who does and orders all things for the best of his people, although in the midst of calamities and troubles he seems to desert them.

2. And that we may know that he did this from his heart, he seals it with a double Amen. "Amen, Amen." So I wish it; so be it.

PSALM XC

The eternity of God, 1, 2; the frailty of the state of man, 3-9; the general limits of human life, 10; the danger of displeasing God, 11; the necessity of considering the shortness of life, and of regaining the favour of the Almighty, 12; earnest prayer for the restoration of Israel, 13-17.

XVIII. DAY. MORNING PRAYER

[a]A Prayer [b]of Moses the man of God

L ORD, [c]thou hast been our dwelling-place [d]in all generations.

2 [e]Before the mountains were brought forth, or ever thou hadst formed the earth and the world, even from everlasting to everlasting, thou *art* God.

[a]Or, *A Prayer* being a Psalm *of Moses*——[b]Deut. xxxiii. 1——[c]Deut. xxxiii. 27; Ezek. xi. 16

[d]Hebrew, *in generation and generation*——[e]Proverbs viii. 25, 26

NOTES ON PSALM XC

The *title* of this Psalm is, *A Prayer of Moses the man of God.* The *Chaldee* has, "A prayer which Moses the prophet of the Lord prayed when the people of Israel had sinned in the wilderness." All the *Versions* ascribe it to Moses; but that it could not be of Moses the *lawgiver* is evident from this consideration, that the age of man was not then *seventy* or *eighty years,* which is here stated to be its almost universal limit, for Joshua lived *one hundred and ten* years, and Moses himself *one hundred and twenty;* Miriam his sister, *one hundred and thirty;* Aaron his brother, *one hundred and twenty-three;* Caleb, *four-score and five* years; and their contemporaries lived in the same proportion. See the note on ver. 4. Therefore the Psalm cannot at all refer to such *ancient* times. If the *title* be at all authentic, it must refer to some *other person* of that name; and indeed אִישׁ אֱלֹהִים *ish Elohim,* a man of God, a divinely inspired man, agrees to the times of

the prophets, who were thus denominated. The Psalm was doubtless composed during or after the captivity; and most probably on their return, when they were engaged in rebuilding the temple; and this, as Dr. *Kennicott* conjectures, may be *the work of their hands,* which they pray God to *bless* and *prosper.*

Verse 1. *Lord, thou hast been our dwelling-place*] מָעוֹן *maon;* but instead of this several MSS. have מָעוּז *maoz,* "place of defence," or "refuge," which is the reading of the *Vulgate, Septuagint, Arabic,* and *Anglo-Saxon.* Ever since thy covenant with Abraham thou hast been the Resting-place, Refuge, and Defence of thy people Israel. Thy mercy has been lengthened out from generation to generation.

Verse 2. *Before the mountains were brought forth*] The mountains and hills *appear* to have been everlasting; but as they were *brought forth* out of the womb of eternity, there was a *time* when *they were not:* but THOU hast been *ab æternitate a parte ante, ad æternitatem a parte post;* from the eternity that is past, be-

3 Thou turnest man to destruction; and sayest, [f]Return, ye children of men.

4 [g]For a thousand years in thy sight *are but* as yesterday [h]when it is past, and *as* a watch in the night.

5 Thou carriest them away as with a flood; [i]they are *as* a sleep; in the morning [k]*they are* like grass *which* [l]groweth up.

6 [m]In the morning it flourisheth, and groweth up; in the evening it is cut down, and withereth.

7 For we are consumed by thine anger, and by thy wrath are we troubled.

8 [n]Thou hast set our iniquities before thee, our [o]secret *sins* in the light of thy countenance.

9 For all our days are [p]passed away in thy wrath: we spend our years [q]as a tale *that is told.*

10 [r]The days of our years *are* threescore years and ten; and if by reason of strength *they be* fourscore years, yet *is* their strength

[f]Genesis iii. 19; Eccles. xii. 7——[g]Ecclus. xviii. 10; 2 Peter iii. 8——[h]Or, *when he hath passed* them——[i]Psa. lxxiii. 20——[k]Psalm ciii. 15; Isaiah xl. 6——[l]Or, *is changed*——[m]Psalm xcii. 7; Job xiv. 2——[n]Psalm l. 21; Jeremiah xvi. 17——[o]Psalm xix. 12——[p]Heb. *turned away*——[q]Hebrew, Or, *as a meditation*——[r]Hebrew, As for *the days of our years, in them* are *seventy years*

fore time began; to the eternity that is after, when time shall have an end. This is the highest description of the *eternity* of God to which human language can reach.

Verse 3. *Thou turnest man to destruction*] Literally, Thou shalt turn dying man, אנוש *enosh*, to the small dust, דכא *dacca* but thou wilt say, Return, ye children of Adam. This appears to be a clear and strong promise of the *resurrection* of the human body, after it has long slept, mingled with the *dust of the earth.*

Verse 4. *For a thousand years in thy sight*] As if he had said, Though the resurrection of the body may be a *thousand* (or any indefinite number of) years distant; yet, when these are past, they are *but as yesterday*, or a single *watch of the night.* They pass through the mind in a moment, and appear no longer in their duration than the time required by the mind to reflect them by thought. But, short as they appear to the eye of the mind, they are *nothing* when compared with the *eternity* of God! The author probably has in view also that economy of Divine justice and providence by which the life of man has been shortened from *one thousand years* to *threescore years and ten*, or *fourscore.*

Verse 5. *Thou carriest them away as with a flood*] Life is compared to a *stream*, ever *gliding away;* but sometimes it is as a *mighty torrent*, when by reason of *plague*, *famine*, or *war*, thousands are swept away daily. In particular cases it is a *rapid stream*, when the *young* are suddenly carried off by consumptions, fevers, &c.; this is the *flower that flourisheth* in the *morning*, and in the *evening* is *cut down* and *withered.* The whole of life is like a *sleep* or as a *dream.* The eternal world is *real;* all *here* is either *shadowy* or *representative.* On the whole, *life* is represented as a *stream; youth*, as *morning; decline of life*, or *old age*, as *evening; death*, as *sleep;* and the *resurrection* as the *return of the flowers* in *spring.* All these images appear in these curious and striking verses, 3, 4, 5, and 6.

Verse 7. *We are consumed by thine anger*] *Death* had not entered into the world, if men had not fallen from God.

By thy wrath are we troubled] Pain, disease, and sickness are so many proofs of our defection from original rectitude. The *anger* and *wrath* of God are moved against all *sinners.* Even in protracted life we *consume away*, and only seem to live in order to die.

"Our wasting lives grow shorter still,
As days and months increase;
And every beating pulse we tell
Leaves but the number less."

Verse 8. *Thou hast set our iniquities before thee*] Every one of our transgressions is *set before thee;* noted and minuted down in thy awful register!

Our secret sins] Those committed in darkness and privacy are easily discovered by thee, being shown by the splendours of thy face shining upon them. Thus we light a candle, and bring it into a dark place to discover its contents. O, what can be hidden from the all-seeing eye of God? Darkness is no darkness to him; wherever he comes there is a profusion of light—for God is light!

Verse 9. *We spend our years as a tale*] The *Vulgate* has: Anni nostri sicut aranea meditabuntur; "Our years pass away like those of the spider." Our *plans* and *operations* are like the *spider's web;* life is as *frail*, and the *thread* of it as *brittle*, as one of those that constitute the well-wrought and curious, but *fragile*, habitation of that insect. All the *Versions* have the word *spider;* but it neither appears in the *Hebrew*, nor in any of its MSS. which have been collated.

My old *Psalter* has a curious paraphrase here: "Als the iran (spider) makes vayne webe for to take flese (flies) with gile, swa our yeres ere ockupide in ydel and swikel castes about erthly thynges; and passes with outen frute of gude werks, and waste in ydel thynkyns." This is *too true* a picture of most lives.

But the *Hebrew* is different from all the *Versions.* "We consume our years (כמו הגה *kemo hegeh*) like a groan." We live a dying, whining, complaining life, and at last a *groan* is its termination! How amazingly expressive!

Verse 10. *Threescore years and ten*] See the note on the *title* of this Psalm. This Psalm could not have been written by *Moses*, because the *term* of human life was much more *extended* when he flourished than *eighty* years at the most. Even in *David's* time many lived *one hundred* years, and the author of *Ecclesiasticus*, who lived after the captivity, fixed this term at *one hundred* years at the most (chap. xviii. 9;)

labour and sorrow; for it is soon cut off, and we fly away.

11 Who knoweth the power of thine anger? even according to thy fear, *so is* thy wrath.

12 [s]So teach *us* to number our days, that we may [t]apply *our* hearts unto [u]wisdom.

13 Return, O LORD, how long? and let it [v]repent thee concerning thy servants.

14 O satisfy us early with thy mercy; [w]that we may rejoice and be glad all our days.

15 Make us glad according to the days *wherein* thou hast afflicted us, *and* the years *wherein* we have seen evil.

16 [x]Let thy work appear unto thy servants, and thy glory unto their children.

17 [y]And let the beauty of the LORD our God be upon us: and [z]establish thou the work of our hands upon us; yea, the work of our hands establish thou it.

---

[s]Psa. xxxix. 4——[t]Heb. *cause to come*——[u]Job xxviii. 28; Psa. cxi. 10; Prov. ix. 10

[v]Deut. xxxii. 36; Psa. cxxxv. 14——[w]Psa. lxxxv. 6; cxlix 2——[x]Heb. iii. 2——[y]Psa. xxvii. 4——[z]Isa. xxvi. 12

---

but this was merely a general average, for even in our country we have many who exceed *a hundred years.*

Yet is their strength labour and *sorrow*] This refers to the infirmities of old age, which, to those well advanced in life, produce *labour* and *sorrow.*

It is soon cut off] *It*—the *body*, is soon cut off.

And we fly away.] The *immortal spirit* wings its way into the eternal world.

Verse 11. *Who knoweth the power of thine anger?*] The afflictions of *this life* are not to be compared to the *miseries* which await them who live and die without being reconciled to God, and saved from their sins.

Verse 12. *So teach us to number our days*] Let us deeply consider our own frailty, and the shortness and uncertainty of life, that we may live for eternity, acquaint ourselves with thee, and be at peace; that we may die in thy favour, and live and reign with thee eternally.

Verse 13. *Return, O Lord, how long?*] Wilt thou continue angry with us for ever?

Let it repent thee] הנחם *hinnachem*, be *comforted*, rejoice over them to do them good. Be glorified rather in our salvation than in our destruction.

Verse 14. *O satisfy us early*] Let us have thy mercy soon, (literally, *in the morning.*) Let it now shine upon us, and it shall seem as the morning of our days, and we shall exult in thee all the days of our life.

Verse 15. *Make us glad according to the days*] Let thy people have as many years of *prosperity* as they have had of *adversity.* We have now suffered *seventy* years of a most distressful captivity.

Verse 16. *Let thy work appear unto thy servants*] That thou art working for us we know; but O, let thy work *appear!* Let us *now see*, in our deliverance, that thy thoughts towards us were mercy and love.

And thy glory] Thy pure worship be established among our *children* for ever.

Verse 17. *And let the beauty of the Lord*] Let us have thy *presence, blessing*, and *approbation*, as our fathers had.

Establish thou the work of our hands] This is supposed, we have already seen, to relate to their *rebuilding the temple*, which the surrounding heathens and Samaritans wished to hinder. We have begun, do not let them demolish our work; let the top-stone be brought on with shouting, *Grace, grace* unto it.

Yea, the work of our hands] This repetition is **wanting in** *three* of Kennicott's MSS., in the

Targum, in the *Septuagint*, and in the *Æthiopic.* If the repetition be genuine, it may be considered as marking great earnestness; and this earnestness was to get the temple of God rebuilt, and his pure worship restored. The pious Jews had this more at heart than their own restoration; it was their highest grief that the temple was destroyed and God's ordinances suspended; that his enemies insulted them, and blasphemed the worthy name by which they were called. Every truly pious man feels more for God's glory than his own temporal felicity, and rejoices more in the prosperity of God's work than in the increase of his own worldly goods.

A FEW INSTANCES OF MODERN LONGEVITY

In the year 1790 I knew a woman in the city of Bristol, Mrs. *Somerhill*, then in the 106th year of her age. She read the smallest print without spectacles, and never had used any helps to decayed sight. When she could not go any longer to a place of worship, through the weakness of her limbs, she was accustomed to read over the whole service of the Church for each day of the year as it occurred, with all the *Lessons, Psalms*, &c. She had been from its commencement a member of the Methodist Society; heard Mr. *John Wesley* the first sermon he preached when he visited Bristol in 1739; and was so struck with his clear manner of preaching the doctrine of *justification through faith*, that, for the benefit of hearing *one more sermon* from this apostolic man, she followed him *on foot* to Portsmouth, a journey of *one hundred and twenty-five* miles! On my last visit to her in the above year, I was admitted by a *very old decrepit woman*, then a widow of *seventy-five* years of age, and the *youngest daughter* of Mrs. Somerhill. I found the aged woman's faculties strong and vigorous, and her eyesight unimpaired, though she was then confined to her bed, and was hard of hearing. She died rejoicing in God, the following year.

Agnes Shuner is another instance. She lived at Camberwell in Surrey; her husband, *Richard Shuner*, died in 1407, whom she survived *ninety-two* years. She died in 1499, aged *one hundred and nineteen* years.

The *Countess of Desmond* in Ireland. On the ruin of the house of Desmond, she was obliged at the age of *one hundred and forty* to travel from Bristol to London, to solicit relief from the court, being then reduced to *poverty.* She renewed her teeth *two* or *three* times, and died in 1612, aged *one hundred and forty-five* years.

Thomas Parr, of Winnington, in Shropshire, far outlived the term as set down in the Psalm. At the age of *eighty-eight* he married his first wife, by whom he had *two* children. At the age of *one hundred and two* he fell in love with *Catharine Milton*, by whom he had an illegitimate child, and for which he did penance in the Church! At the age of *one hundred and twenty*, he married a widow woman; and when he was *one hundred and thirty* could perform any operation of husbandry. He died at the age of *one hundred and fifty-two*, A. D. 1635. He had seen *ten* kings and queens of England.

Thomas Damme, of Leighton, near Minshul in Cheshire, lived *one hundred and fifty-four* years, and died A. D. 1648.

Henry Jenkins, of Ellerton upon Swale, in Yorkshire, was sent, when a boy of about *twelve* years of age, with a *cart load of arrows* to Northallerton, to be employed in the battle of *Flodden Field*, which was fought September 9, 1513. He was a *fisherman;* and often *swam* in the rivers when he was more than *one hundred* years of age! He died A. D. 1670, being then *one hundred and sixty-nine* years of age!

I shall add one foreigner, *Peter Toston*, a peasant of Temiswar, in Hungary. The remarkable longevity of this man exceeds the age of *Isaac five* years; of *Abraham, ten;* falls short of *Terah's*, Abraham's father, *twenty;* and exceeds that of *Nahor*, Abraham's grandfather, *thirty-seven* years. He died A. D. 1724, at the extraordinary age of *one hundred and eighty-five!*

ANALYSIS OF THE NINETIETH PSALM

There are four parts in this Psalm:—

I. An ingenuous acknowledgment of God's protection of the people, ver. 1, 2.

II. A lively narration of the mortality of man, the fragility and brevity of his life, together with the misery of it, ver. 2-7.

III. The causes: man's rebellion and God's anger for it, ver. 7-12.

IV. A petition, which is double: 1. That God would instruct man to know his fragility. 2. That he would return, and restore him to his favour, ver. 12-17.

I. In the beginning the psalmist freely acknowledges what God had always been unto his people. What he is in himself, and his own nature.

1. To his people he had always been a refuge, as it were, a dwelling-place: though they had been pilgrims and sojourners in a strange land for many years, yet he had been, nay dwelt, among them; and no doubt he alludes to the tabernacle of God that was pitched among them as an evidence of his presence and protection: "Lord, thou hast been our dwelling-place (a secure place to rest in) in all generations," Deut. xxxiii. 1-6.

2. But in himself he was from everlasting: other creatures had a beginning, and their creation and ornaments from him. He, the Eternal Being, "Before the mountains were brought forth, or ever thou hadst formed the earth, and the world, even from everlasting to everlasting thou art God." Not like man, then, whose mutability, fragility, mortality, brevity, he next describes.

II. "Thou turnest man to destruction." Though framed according to thy own image, yet he is but an earthen vessel; to that pass thou bringest him, till he be broken to pieces, broken as a potter's vessel. To him thou sayest, "Return, ye children of men, (of Adam,) return; for dust thou art, and to dust shalt thou return." The mortality of man may not be then attributed to diseases, chance, fortune, &c., but to God's decree, pronounced on man upon his disobedience. First, then, let the sons of *Adam* remember that they are mortal; next, that their life is but very short. Suppose a man should live the longest life, and somewhat longer than the oldest patriarch, a thousand years; yet, let it be compared with eternity, it is as nothing: "A thousand years in thy sight are but as yesterday, when it is past;" but as a day which is short, as a day which is past and forgotten; which the *prophet* farther illustrates by elegant similitudes.

1. "And as a watch in the night." A time of three hours' continuance, which is but the eighth part of a natural day, and so far less than he said before. The flower of our youth, our constant age, and our old age, may well be the three hours of this watch; and wise they are that observe their stations in either of them.

2. "Thou carriest them away as with a flood." As a sudden inundation of waters our life passeth; we swell and fall. Or, As all waters come from the sea, and return thither; so from the earth we came, and thither return. Or, We are as water spilt on the earth, which cannot be gathered up again.

3. "They are as a sleep," or rather a dream; all our happiness a dream of felicity. In our dreams many pleasant, many fearful things are presented; we pass half our time in sleep; drowsily, it is certain, for our life is σκιας οναρ, *the shadow of a dream.*—Pindar.

4. Or we are like grass: "In the morning they are like grass that groweth up: in the morning it flourisheth and groweth up, in the evening it is cut down and withereth." The herb hath its morning and evening, and its mid-day, and so hath our life; *naturally* it fades, or *violently* it is cut off.

III. After he had spoken of and explained our mortality, the brevity, the misery of our life, he next descends to examine the causes of it, which are two. 1. God's anger; and that which brought it upon us, our own iniquities.

1. God's anger: "We consume away by thine anger; and by thy wrath are we troubled." The cause, then, of death and disease is not the decay of the radical moisture, or defect of natural heat; but that which brought these defects upon us, *God's wrath* because of *sin.*

2. Our own sin: For this anger of God was not raised without a just cause; he is a just Judge, and proceeds not to punishment, but upon due examination and trial; and to that end he takes an account, not only of our open sins, but even of our secret faults, such as are not known to ourselves, or such as we labour to conceal from others.

1. "Thou hast set our iniquities before thee."

2. "And our secret sins in the light of thy countenance." No hypocrisy, no contempt, can escape thine eye: all to thee is revealed, and clear as the light.

3. And then he repeats the effect, together with the cause: "Therefore all our days (viz., the *forty* years in the wilderness and the *seventy* in captivity) are passed away in thy wrath." 2. "We spend our days as a tale that is told;" *et fabula fies*, the tale ended, it vanisheth, and is thought of no more.

4. And as for our age, it is of no great

length: "The days of our years are threescore years and ten." To that time some men may be said to live, because the faculties of their souls are tolerably vigorous, and their bodies proportionately able to execute the offices of life.

But allow that it so happen, which happens not to many, "that by reason of strength," some excellent natural constitution, "a man arrive to fourscore years," yet our life is encumbered with these *three* inconveniences, labour, sorrow, and brevity.

1. It is laborious, even labour itself. One is desirous to be rich, another wise; this man potent, another prudent, or at least to seem so; and this will not be without labour: "All is affliction of spirit."

2. Sorrow; for our life is only the shadow of real life.

3. Short; for it is soon cut off, and we flee away: *Avolat umbra.* 1. God's anger for sin is not laid to heart; and of this the *prophet* in the next verse sadly complains: "Who knows the power of thy anger?" Thine anger is great for sin; the power of it fearful and terrible. Thou canst and wilt cast sinners into hell-fire; but who regards it? Thy threats to men seem to be old wives' fables. 2. "Even according to thy fear, so is thy wrath;" but be it that this stupidity possess men, yet this is certain, that thy wrath is great; and it shall be executed according to thy fear, in such proportion as men have stood in fear of thee. They that have in a reverential fear stood in awe of thee shall escape it; they that have contemned and slighted thy wrath shall feel it to the uttermost.

IV. Upon all the former considerations the psalmist converts his words to a prayer, in which he implores God's mercy, that he would turn, 1. The stupidity of men into wisdom. 2. Our calamity into felicity. 3. His wrath into compassion. And, 4. Our sorrow into joy. For the first he begins thus:—

1. "So teach us to number our days," to cast up the labour, the sorrow, the brevity, the fugacity; thy anger, our sin, that caused it.

2. "That we may apply our hearts unto wisdom;" be no more stupid and secure, but wise; wise, to avoid thy anger, wise to set a true estimate on this life, and wise in time to provide for another.

3. "So teach us;" for God must teach it, or it will not be learned: this wisdom comes from above.

Secondly, he deprecates God's anger: "Return, O Lord, how long? and let it repent thee concerning thy servants."

Thirdly, he begs restoration to God's favour; and what will follow upon it, peace of conscience.

1. "O satisfy us with thy mercy." We hunger for it as men do for meat.

2. Early let it be done, quickly, before our sorrows grow too high, and overwhelm us.

3. With thy mercy; not with wealth, delights, &c.

4. And with a perpetual joy of heart: "That we may be glad and rejoice all our days."

5. And let our joy bear proportion to our sorrows: "Make us glad according to the days wherein thou hast afflicted us, and the years wherein we have seen evil."

6. This is the work he calls God's work; for as to punish is his strange work, Isa. xxviii., so to have pity and mercy is his own proper work; and this he desires that it should be made manifest: "Let thy work appear unto thy servants, and thy glory unto their children."

Fourthly, he begs for success in all their work and labours.

1. "Let the beauty of the Lord our God be upon us;" for no action of ours is beautiful, except the beauty of God be stamped upon it; done by his direction, his rule, his word, and to his glory.

2. And therefore he prays, and repeats this prayer: "Establish thou the work of our hands upon us; yea, the work of our hands establish thou it." There must be *opus*, our work; for God blesseth not the idle. 2. And *opus manuum*, a laborious work. 3. God's direction, his word the rule. 4. A good end in it, for that is his beauty upon it. 5. So it will be established, confirmed, ratified. 6. And, lastly, know that there is no blessing to be expected without prayer; and therefore he prays, "Let the beauty of the Lord our God be upon us." See the notes on this Psalm.

PSALM XCI

The safety of the godly man, and his confidence, 1, 2. How he is defended and preserved, 3–10. The angels of God are his servants, 11, 12; and he shall tread on the necks of his adversaries, 13. What God says of, and promises to, such a person, 14–16.

HE [a]that dwelleth in the secret place of the Most High shall [b]abide [c]under the shadow of the Almighty.

2 [d]I will say of the LORD, *He is* my refuge and my fortress: my God; in him will I trust.

---

[a]Psa. xxvii. 5; xxxi. 20; xxxii. 7——[b]Heb. *lodge*

[c]Psa. xvii. 8——[d]Psa. cxlii. 5

NOTES ON PSALM XCI

This Psalm has no *title* in the Hebrew; nor can it be determined on what occasion or by whom it was composed. It is most likely by the author of the preceding; and is written as a *part* of it, by *fifteen* of *Kennicott's* and De

Rossi's MSS., commencing before the *repetition* of the four last words of the *ninetieth*. It is allowed to be one of the finest Psalms in the whole collection. Of it *Simon de Muis* has said: "It is one of the most excellent works of this kind which has ever appeared. It is impossible to imagine any thing more solid, more

3 Surely °he shall deliver thee from the snare of the fowler, *and* from the noisome pestilence.

4 ᶠHe shall cover thee with his feathers, and under his wings shalt thou trust: his truth *shall be thy* shield and buckler.

5 ᵍThou shalt not be afraid for the terror by night; *nor* for the arrow *that* flieth by day;

6 *Nor* for the pestilence *that* walketh in darkness; *nor* for the destruction *that* wasteth at noonday.

°Psa. cxxiv. 7——ᶠPsa. xvii. 8; lvii. 1; lxi. 4——ᵍJob v.

19, &c.; Psa. cxii. 7; cxxi. 6; Prov. iii. 23, 24; Isa. xliii. 2

---

beautiful, more profound, or more ornamented. Could the Latin or any modern languages express thoroughly all the beauties and elegancies as well of the *words* as of the *sentences*, it would not be difficult to persuade the reader that we have no poem, either in *Greek* or *Latin*, comparable to this Hebrew ode."

Verse 1. *He that dwelleth in the secret place*] The *Targum* intimates that this is a *dialogue* between *David, Solomon*, and *Jehovah*. Suppose we admit this,—then

DAVID asserts: "He who dwelleth in the secret place of the Most High shall abide under the shadow of the Almighty," ver. 1.

SOLOMON answers: "I will say of the Lord, He is my refuge and my fortress; my God, in him will I trust," ver. 2.

DAVID replies, and tells him what blessings he shall receive from God if he abide faithful, ver. 3-13.

Then the SUPREME BEING is introduced, and confirms all that *David* had spoken concerning *Solomon*, ver. 14-16: and thus this sacred and instructive dialogue ends.

In the secret place of the Most High] Spoken probably in reference to the *Holy of holies*. He who enters legitimately there shall be covered with the cloud of God's glory—the protection of the all-sufficient God. This was the privilege of the *high priest* only, under the law: but under the new covenant all believers in Christ *have boldness to enter into the holiest by the blood of Jesus;* and those who thus enter are safe from every evil.

Verse 2. *I will say of the Lord*] This is my experience: "He is my fortress, and in him will I continually trust."

Verse 3. *Surely he shall deliver thee*] If thou wilt act thus, then the God in whom thou trustest will deliver thee from the snare of the fowler, from all the devices of Satan, and from all dangerous maladies. As the original word, דבר *dabar*, signifies a *word spoken*, and *deber*, the same *letters*, signifies *pestilence;* so some translate one way, and some another: he shall deliver thee from the evil and *slanderous word;* he shall deliver thee from the *noisome pestilence*—all blasting and injurious *winds, effluvia,* &c.

Verse 4. *He shall cover thee with his feathers*] He shall act towards thee as the hen does to her brood,—take thee under his wings when birds of prey appear, and also shelter thee from chilling blasts. This is a frequent metaphor in the sacred writings; see the parallel texts in the *margin*, and the notes on them. The *Septuagint* has Εν τοις μεταφρενοις αυτου επισκιασει σοι· *He will overshadow thee between his shoulders;* alluding to the custom of parents carrying their weak or sick children on their backs, and having them covered even there with a mantle. Thus the Lord is represented carrying the Israelites in the wilderness.

See Deut. xxxii. 11, 12, where the metaphor is taken from the *eagle*.

His truth shall be thy *shield and buckler*] His revelation; his Bible. That truth contains promises for all times and circumstances; and these will be invariably fulfilled to him that trusts in the Lord. The fulfilment of a promise relative to defence and support is to the soul what the best shield is to the body.

Verse 5. *The terror by night*] Night is a time of terrors, because it is a time of treasons, plunder, robbery, and murder. The godly man lies down in peace, and sleeps quietly, for he trusts his body, soul, and substance, in the hand of God; and he knows that he who keepeth Israel neither slumbers nor sleeps. It may also mean all *spiritual foes,—the rulers of the darkness of this world.* I have heard the following petition in an evening family prayer: "Blessed Lord, take us into thy protection this night; and preserve us from disease, from sudden death, from the violence of fire, from the edge of the sword, from the designs of wicked men, and from the influence of malicious spirits!"

Nor *for the arrow*] The *Chaldee* translates this verse, "Thou shalt not fear the demons that walk by night; nor the arrow of the angel of death which is shot in the day time." Thou needest not to fear a sudden and unprovided-for death.

Verse 6. Nor *for the pestilence that walketh in darkness; nor for the destruction* that *wasteth at noonday.*] The rabbins supposed that the empire of death was under two demons, one of which ruled by *day*, the other by *night*. The *Vulgate* and *Septuagint* have—the *noonday devil*. The ancients thought that there were some demons who had the power to injure particularly at *noonday*. To this *Theocritus* refers, Id. i. ver. 15:—

Ου θεμις, ω ποιμαν, το μεσαμβρινον, ου θεμις αμμιν
Συρισδεν· τον Πανα δεδοικαμες· η γαρ απ' αγρας
Τανικα κεκμακως αμπανεται, εντι γε πικρος,
Και οι αει δριμεια χολα ποτι ρινι καθηται.

"It is not lawful, it is not lawful, O shepherd, to play on the flute at *noonday:* we fear Pan, who at that hour goes to sleep in order to rest himself after the fatigues of the chase; *then he is dangerous*, and his wrath easily kindled."

Lucan, in the horrible account he gives us of a grove sacred to some barbarous power, worshipped with the most horrid rites, refers to the same superstition:—

Lucus erat longo nunquam violatus ab ævo,
Non illum cultu populi propiore frequentant,
Sed cessere deis: *medio* cum *Phœbus in axe est*,
Aut *cœlum nox atra tenet*, pavet ipse sacerdos
Accessus, dominumque timet deprendere luci.
LUCAN. lib. iii., ver. 399.

7 A thousand shall fall at thy side, and ten thousand at thy right hand; *but* it shall not come nigh thee.

8 Only ʰwith thine eyes shalt thou behold and see the reward of the wicked.

9 Because thou hast made the LORD *which is* ⁱmy refuge, *even* the Most High, ᵏthy habitation;

10 ˡThere shall no evil befall thee, neither shall any plague come nigh thy dwelling.

11 ᵐFor he shall give his angels charge over thee, to keep thee in all thy ways.

12 They shall bear thee up in *their* hands, ⁿlest thou dash thy foot against a stone.

13 Thou shalt tread upon the lion and °adder: the young lion and the dragon shalt thou trample under feet.

14 Because he hath set his love upon me,

ʰPsa. xxxvii. 34; Mal. i. 5——ⁱVer. 2——ᵏPsa. lxxi. 3; xc. 1——ˡProv. xii. 21——ᵐPsa. xxxiv. 7; lxxi. 3;

Matt. iv. 6; Luke iv. 10, 11; Heb. i. 14——ⁿJob v. 23; Psa. xxxvii. 24——°Or, *asp*

"Not far away, for ages past, had stood
An old inviolated sacred wood:—
The pious worshippers approach not near,
But shun their gods, and kneel with distant fear:
The *priest* himself, when, or the *day* or *night*
Rolling have reached their full *meridian* height,
Refrains the gloomy paths with wary feet,
Dreading the *demon* of the grove *to meet;*
Who, terrible to sight, at *that fixed hour*
Still treads the round about this dreary bower."   ROWE.

It has been stated among the heathens that the gods should be worshipped *at all times,* but the *demons* should be worshipped at *midday:* probably because these demons, having been employed during the *night,* required *rest at noonday;* and that was the most proper time to appease them. See *Calmet* on this place. Both the *Vulgate* and *Septuagint* seem to have reference to this superstition.

The *Syriac* understands the passage of a *pestilential wind,* that *blows at noonday.* *Aquila* translates, *of the bite of the noonday demon.*

Verse 7. *A thousand shall fall at thy side*] *Calmet* thinks this place should be translated thus: "A thousand enemies may fall upon thee on one side, and ten thousand may fall upon thee on thy right hand: but they shall not come nigh thee to take away thy life." It is a promise of perfect protection, and the utmost safety.

Verse 8. *The reward of the wicked.*] Thou shalt not only be safe thyself, but thou shalt see all thy enemies discomfited and cast down.

Verse 9. *Because thou hast made the Lord*] Seeing thou hast taken Jehovah, the Most High, for thy portion and thy refuge, *no evil shall come nigh thy dwelling;* thou shalt be safe in thy soul, body, household, and property, ver. 10. Every pious man may expect such protection from his *God* and *Father.*

Verse 11. *He shall give his angels charge over thee*] Evil spirits may attempt to injure thee; but they shall not be able. The *angels of God* shall have an especial charge to accompany, defend, and preserve thee; and against their power, the influence of evil spirits cannot prevail. These will, when necessary, turn thy steps out of the way of danger; ward it off when it comes in thy ordinary path; suggest to thy mind prudent counsels, profitable designs, and pious purposes; and thus minister to thee as a child of God, and an heir of salvation.

To keep thee in all thy ways.] The path of duty is the way of safety. Thou canst not reasonably expect protection if thou walk not in the way of obedience. *Thy ways* are the paths of duty, which God's word and providence have marked out for thee. The *way of sin* is not *thy way*—thy duty, thy interest. Keep in *thy own ways,* not in those of *sin,* Satan, the *world,* and the *flesh;* and God will take care of thee.

Verse 12. *They shall bear thee up in* their *hands*] Take the same care of thee as a *nurse* does of a weak and tender child; lead thee,—teach thee to walk,—lift thee up out of the way of danger, "lest thou shouldst dash thy foot against a stone," receive any kind of injury, or be prevented from pursuing thy path with safety and comfort.

Let us remember that it is GOD, whose these angels are; HE gives them charge—from HIM they receive their commission,—to HIM they are responsible for their charge. From God thou art to expect them; and for their help he alone is to receive the praise. It is expressly said, *He shall give his angels charge;* to show that they are not to be *prayed to* nor *praised;* but GOD *alone,* whose *servants* they are. See the note on Matt. iv. 6.

Verse 13. *Thou shalt tread upon the lion and adder*] Even the king of the forest shall not be able to injure thee; should one of these attack thee, the angels whom God sends will give thee an easy victory over him. And even the *asp,* (פתן *pethen,*) one of the most venomous of serpents, shall not be able to injure thee.

The asp is a very small serpent, and peculiar to Egypt and Libya. Its poison kills without the possibility of a remedy. Those who are bitten by it die in about from three to eight hours; and it is said they die by sleep, without any kind of *pain.* Lord *Bacon* says the asp is less painful than all the other instruments of death. He supposes it to have an affinity to *opium,* but to be less disagreeable in its operation. It was probably on this account that *Cleopatra,* queen of Egypt, chose to die by the asp, as she was determined to prevent the designs of *Augustus,* who intended to have carried her captive to Rome to grace his *triumph.*

The dragon shalt thou trample] The תנין *tannin,* which we translate *dragon,* means often any large aquatic animal; and perhaps here the *crocodile* or *alligator.*

Verse 14. *Because he hath set his love upon me*] Here the *Most High* is introduced as confirming the word of his servant. He has fixed his *love*—his heart and soul, on me.

therefore will I deliver him: I will set
him on high, because he hath [p]known my
name.
15 [q]He shall call upon me, and I will answer
him: [r]I *will be* with him in trouble; I will
deliver him and [s]honour him.
16 With [t]long life will I satisfy him, and
show him my salvation.

---

[p]Psa. ix. 10——[q]Psa. l. 15——[r]Isa. xliii. 2

[s]1 Sam. ii. 30——[t]Heb. *length of days;* Prov. iii. 2

Therefore will I deliver him] I will save him in all troubles, temptations, and evils of every kind.

I will set him on high] I will place him *out of the reach* of all his enemies. I will *honour* and *ennoble* him, *because he hath known my name*—because he has loved, honoured, and served me, and rendered me that worship which is my due. He has *known* me to be the God of infinite mercy and love.

Verse 15. *He shall call upon me*] He must *continue to pray;* all his blessings *must come in this way;* when he *calls*, I will *answer* him—I will give him whatever is best for him.

I will be *with him in trouble*] Literally, *I am with him.* עמו אנכי *immo anochi;* as soon as the trouble comes, *I am there.*

I will deliver him] For his good I may permit him to be exercised for a time, but *delivered* he shall be.

And honour him] אכבדהו *acabbedehu*, "I will glorify him." I will *load* him with *honour;* that honour that comes from God. I will even show to men how highly I prize such.

Verse 16. *With long life*] Literally, *With length of days will I fill him up.* He shall neither live a useless life, nor die before his time. He shall live happy and die happy.

And show him my salvation.] ואראהו בישועתי *vearehu bishuathi*, "I will make him see (or contemplate) in my salvation." He shall discover infinite lengths, breadths, depths, and heights, in my salvation. He shall feel boundless desires, and shall discover that I have provided boundless gratifications for them. He shall dwell in my glory, and throughout eternity increase in his resemblance to and enjoyment of me. Thus shall it be done to the man whom the Lord delighteth to honour; and he delights to honour that man who *places his love on him.* In a word, he shall have *a long life* in this world, and an *eternity of blessedness* in the world to come.

Analysis of the Ninety-first Psalm

The full intent and purpose of this Psalm is to encourage and exhort the godly in all extremities, pressures, troubles, temptations, afflictions, assaults, inward or outward; in a word, in all dangers to put their trust and confidence in God, and to rely upon his protection.

There are *two* parts in this Psalm:—

I. A general proposition, in which is given an assurance of help and protection to every godly man, ver. 1: "He that dwelleth," &c.

II. The proof of this by three witnesses:—

1. Of the just man, in whose person the *psalmist* speaks, ver. 2: "I will say of the Lord," &c.

2. Of the prophet, ver. 3: "Surely he shall deliver thee from the snare," &c.; which he amplifies by an enumeration of the dangers, God's assistance, and the angels' protection, ver. 3-14.

3. Of God himself, whom he brings in speaking to the same purpose, ver. 14-16.

I. The first part or verse is a universal proposition, in which is contained a comfortable and excellent promise made by the Holy Ghost of security, viz., that God's help shall never be wanting to those who truly put their hope and trust in him: "He that dwelleth in the secret place of the Most High shall abide (or lodge) under the shadow of the Almighty."

1. *He,*—be he who he will, rich or poor, king or people; God is no respecter of persons.

2. "That dwells." For that he must be sure to do, constantly, daily, firmly, rest and acquiesce in God, to persevere in the faith of his promise, and carry that about him, else he cannot be assured by this promise.

3. "In the secret place." For his aid and defence is not as some strong-hold or castle which is visible; it is a secret and invisible fortress, known only to a faithful soul. In that he may repose his hope, as a means and secondary defence; but he dwells, relies, rests in that help of God which is secret, and is not seen except by the eye of faith.

4. "Of the Most High." And upon this he relies, because he is the *Most High. Above* he is, and sees all; nothing is hid from him. And again, *above* he is, sits in the highest throne, and rules all. All things are under his feet; he can therefore deliver his people from all troubles and dangers. Yea, he will do it for this faithful man; he that relies and trusts in him shall never be frustrated of his hope; protected he shall be; he shall be safe. 1. "He dwells, therefore he shall abide." He shall lodge quietly—securely. 2. "He dwells in the secret place, therefore he shall abide under the shadow." In the cool, the favour, the cover from the heat. 3. "He dwelleth in the secret place of the Most High, therefore he shall abide under the shadow of the Almighty;" i. e., of the all-powerful God, of the God of heaven; of that God whose name is Shaddai, All-sufficient; by which name he made his promise to Abraham, Gen. xvii. 1.

II. This proposition being most certainly true, in the next place the psalmist explains it. And that no man may doubt of it, descends to prove it by three witnesses: first, of a just man; secondly, of the prophet; thirdly, of God himself.

He brings in the just man thus speaking in his own person: "I will say unto the Lord, He is my refuge, my fortress, my God; in him will I trust." Is it so? "Shall he that dwells in the secret of the Most High, abide under the shadow of the Almighty?" Therefore I will say, in the person of all just men, to the Lord, that hath no superior, that hath no peer; to that Lord to whose command all things are subject, and who can be commanded by none; I will say to him,—

1. "Thou art my refuge." If pursued, I will flee to thee as a sanctuary.

2. "Thou art my fortress." If set upon, I will betake myself to thee as a strong tower.

3. "Thou art my God." If assaulted by men or devils, thou, the Most High; thou, Almighty,

art a God able to defend me, and therefore "I will hope in thee;" I will dwell, trust, rely upon thee and this thy promise, in every temptation and danger.

Next, to assert the truth of this, he brings in the attestation of the prophet; for, being moved by the Holy Ghost, he saith as much, "Surely he shall deliver thee;" and then falls upon the particulars, from which the godly man shall be delivered, set down in many metaphors.

1. "He shall deliver thee from the snare of the fowler;" the deceits of evil men or devils.

2. "From the noisome pestilence," all danger to which we are incident, by plague, war, or famine.

Again, when thou art little in thine own eyes,—

1. "He shall cover thee," as the hen does her young, "with his feathers; and under his wings shalt thou trust," secured from the rain, the storm, the heat of the sun, and the birds of prey.

2. When thou art grown up, and able to encounter an enemy in the field, he shall help thee to a shield and buckler, and that shall be his truth, his veracity, thy faith in it; and which is yet more,—

Thou shalt not be afraid,—

1. "For the terror by night;" any hidden secret temptation, danger, treachery, detraction, conspiracy.

2. "Nor for the arrow that flies by day;" any open persecution, calamity, fraud, assault, invasion.

3. "Nor for the pestilence that walks in darkness;" the machinations of wicked men hatched in the dark.

4. "Nor for the destruction that wasteth at noon-day;" the bold threats and decrees of tyrants and persecutors.

Moller observes rightly that the promises of deliverance here made do not belong to one or other kind of evil, but to all kinds of calamities, open or secret, and so may be applicable to any; some of which steal upon us, as in the night secretly; others overwhelm as in the day, openly. But the promise is general, as Bellarmine well observes; whether the danger come by day or night, those who trust in God are armed with his shield of truth against it. "For if God be for us, who can be against us?" Rom. viii.

The prophet goes on, and confirms the godly in their security by the dissimilarity or unlike condition of wicked men. When thou shalt be safe, they shall fall.

1. "A thousand shall fall at thy side, on thy left hand," overcome by adversity.

2. "Ten thousand on thy right hand," flattered into sin by prosperity. "But neither the fear by night, nor the arrow by day, shall come nigh thee."

3. And, which is another cause of comfort and pleasure: "Only with thine eyes shalt thou behold, and see the reward of the wicked;" which sometimes falls out in this life, as the *Israelites* saw the Egyptians dead upon the sea-shore; *Moses* and *Aaron* saw *Dathan* and *Abiram* swallowed up quick, &c. But it shall be amply fulfilled at the last judgment, Matt. xxv. Of which security, comfort, content, the *prophet* in the next verse gives the reason; the danger shall not come nigh thee; when they fall thou shalt see it, and consider it with content. "Because thou hast made the Lord, which is my refuge, even the Most High, thy habitation;" thou trustest in him as I do; and therefore

shalt have the like protection, deliverance, comfort, that I by his promise have. Farther, "there shall no evil befall thee, neither shall any plague come nigh thy dwelling." But the just man may say, I am secure that no evil shall befall me; I desire to know how I may be kept so, that I fall not among thieves. This *objection* the *prophet prevents*, saying, in effect, Fear not, "for he shall give his angels charge over thee, to keep thee in all thy ways; they shall bear thee up in their hands, lest thou dash thy foot against a stone."

In which verses consider,—

1. That the good man is protected by angels; many angels have a care of one poor man.

2. That they are commanded by God to do it; for are not they ministering spirits sent by God to that end? Heb. i. 14.

3. That it is a particular administration, a charge given to the poorest, the meanest saint.

4. That they are to keep, to look to, defend thee, and what is thine; thou hast an invisible guard.

5. But then mark the limitation and restriction; it is in "all thy ways," in the walk of thy vocation to which God hath called thee; either walk in them, or the angels have no charge to keep thee.

6. Lastly, "In all thy ways;" not in *one* but *all;* for the ways of men are many, and in *all* he needs the custody of angels: 1. The law is a way, and the way of the law is manifold. 2. Our works and operations are manifold; which are our way too. 3. Our life is a way, and there be many parts and conditions of our life, various ages, manifold states; and in all these ways we need a guardian, for we may slip in every law, in every operation, in every age, in every state of life.

Which that it be not done, God hath given his angels charge over us: to keep us only; nay, which is more,—

1. "They shall bear thee," as kind mothers and nurses do their children.

2. "They shall bear thee in their hands;" the will, understanding, wisdom, and power are, as it were, the angels' hand; with all these they will bear us.

3. "That thou dash not thy foot;" that is, thy affections, which carry the soul to good or bad.

4. "Against a stone;" which are all difficulties and obstacles.

And, which is yet more, under their custody we shall tread under foot Satan, and all his accomplices; him, a roaring lion, an old serpent, a fierce dragon, and all his associates, tyrants, persecutors, and hypocrites; for such is the promise; "Thou shalt tread upon the lion and adder; the young lion and dragon shalt thou trample under feet."

5. "In the mouth of two or three witnesses shall every word stand, saith God;" and here we find the law strictly observed: it was to be proved, that all who truly trust in God were to be protected by God; of which one witness was the *just man*, ver. 2; another, the testimony of the Spirit by the *prophet*, from verse 3 to this verse; to which a third, we have here even GOD himself; for in these three last verses the *prophet* brings Him, God himself, testifying this great and comfortable truth with his own mouth:—

1. "Because he hath set his love upon me," pleased me, loved me, adhered to me, hoped in me, trusted to me with a filial love and adherence.

2. "Because he hath known my name," acknowledged my power, wisdom, goodness; these are the causes and conditions presupposed in the protected.

3. "He shall call upon me." Invocation is necessary also. "Therefore I will deliver him, I will answer him, I will be with him in trouble, I will honour him. I will glorify him, or set him on high;" and the second, "I will deliver him; with long life will I satisfy him, and show him my salvation."

1. "I will deliver him," by the shield, by my angels, by other ways, directly or indirectly, yet so that it be remembered that I do it; for these shall not deliver without me.

2. "I will answer him;" answer his desires, answer his prayers, so they be *cries.*

3. "I will be with him in trouble;" join myself close to him, go into prison with him as it were, suffer with him, and think myself pursued when he is persecuted, give him comfort even then; they sung in prison; he neither delivers the martyrs from death, nor does he forsake them.

4. "I will honour him:" for the names of those who suffered for his sake are honourable; "precious in the sight of the Lord is the death of his saints."

These promises may belong to this life; those that follow to the other.

1. "I will deliver him." For the just by death are freed from the present and all future miseries: "Blessed are the dead, for they rest from their labours."

2. "I will glorify him." As if it were not enough to deliver him; such a thing in this life may fall out, as it happened to Joseph, Job, David, Daniel; but the true glory no question must be, "when the righteous shall shine like the sun, be set upon their thrones, and judge the twelve tribes of Israel."

3. "With long life will I satisfy him," i. e., with eternal felicity, with a continuance in bliss, which shall be eternal; for without eternity even length of days cannot satisfy; as appears by old men, who yet have complained of a short life.

4. And that the *prophet* speaks of this eternal felicity is more than probable, because he adds, "I will show him my salvation;" I will show him Jesus, my salvation; that is, I will bring to pass, that when through his whole life I have given him sufficient evidences of my fatherly affection, I will at last translate him to a place where he shall no longer live by faith, but shall see, and experimentally feel, what he hath believed.

PSALM XCII

The psalmist shows the duty and advantage of praising God, 1–3; speaks of the grandeur of God's works, 4–6; the fall of the wicked, 7–9; the happiness of the righteous, 10–14; and all this founded on the perfections of God.

A Psalm *or* Song for the Sabbath day

*I*T is a ᵃgood *thing* to give thanks unto the Lord, and to sing praises unto thy name, O Most High:

2 To ᵇshow forth thy loving-kindness in the morning, and thy faithfulness ᶜevery night.

3 ᵈUpon an instrument of ten strings, and

ᵃPsa. cxlvii. 1——ᵇPsa. lxxxix. 1——ᶜHeb. *in the nights*——ᵈ2 Chron. xxiii. 5; Psa. xxxiii. 2

NOTES ON PSALM XCII

The *title, A Psalm* or *Song for the Sabbath,* gives no information concerning the *time, occasion,* or *author.* The *Chaldee,* has "Praise, and a song which the first man spoke concerning the Sabbath:" but this is an idle conceit; and, though entertained by some *rabbins,* has been followed by none of the *Versions. Calmet* supposes the Psalm to have been composed by some of the Levites during or near the close of the Babylonish captivity, acknowledging the mercy of God, and foreseeing the desolation of their enemies, and their own return to Jerusalem, and their temple service.

Verse 1. It is a *good* thing *to give thanks*] This Psalm begins very *abruptly. Good to confess unto the Lord.* He *had been* acknowledging God's goodness, and praising him for his mercy; and now he breaks out and tells how good he felt this employment to be.

Verse 2. *To show forth thy loving-kindness*] חסדך *chasdecha,* thy abundant mercy, *in the morning*—that has preserved me throughout

the night, and brought me to the beginning of a new day: *and thy faithfulness in the night,* that has so amply fulfilled the promise of preservation during the course of the day. This verse contains a general plan for morning and evening prayer.

Verse 3. *Upon an instrument of ten strings*] Eusebius, in his comment on this Psalm, says: Ψαλτηριον δε δεκαχορδον, ἡ του Ἁγιου Πνευματος δια των αισθητηριων πεντε μεν του σωματος, ισαριθμων δε της ψυχης δυναμεων, επιτελουμενη λατρεια· "The *Psaltery of ten strings* is the worship of the Holy Spirit, performed by means of the *five* senses of the body, and by the *five* powers of the soul." And, to confirm this interpretation, he quotes the apostle, 1 Cor. xiv. 15: "I will pray with the spirit, and with the understanding also; I will sing with the spirit, and with the understanding also." "As the mind has its influence by which it moves the body, so the spirit has its own influence by which it moves the soul." Whatever may be thought of this gloss, one thing is pretty evident from it, that *instrumental music* was not in use in the Church of Christ in the time of Eusebius, which was near

upon the psaltery; [e]upon the harp with [f]a solemn sound.

4 For thou, LORD, hast made me glad through thy work: I will triumph in the works of thy hands.

5 [g]O LORD, how great are thy works! *and* [h]thy thoughts are very deep.

6 [i]A brutish man knoweth not; neither doth a fool understand this.

7 When [k]the wicked spring as the grass, and when all the workers of iniquity do flourish; *it is* that they shall be destroyed for ever:

8 [l]But thou, LORD, *art most* high for ever more.

9 For, lo, thine enemies, O LORD, for, lo, thine enemies shall perish; all the workers of iniquity shall [m]be scattered.

10 But [n]my horn shalt thou exalt like *the horn of* an unicorn: I shall be [o]anointed with fresh oil.

11 [p]Mine eye also shall see *my desire* on mine enemies, *and* mine ears shall hear *my desire* of the wicked that rise up against me.

12 The [q]righteous shall flourish like the

---

[e]Or, *upon the solemn sound with the harp*——[f]Heb. *Higgaion;* Psa. ix. 16——[g]Psa. xl. 5; cxxxix. 17——[h]Isa. xxviii. 29; Rom. xi. 33, 34——[i]Psa. lxxiii. 22; xciv. 8——[k]Job xii. 6; xxi. 7; Psa. xxxvii. 1, 2, 35, 38;

Jer. xii. 1, 2; Mal. iii. 15——[l]Psa. lvi. 2; lxxxiii. 18 [m]Psa. lxviii. 1; lxxxix. 10——[n]Psa. lxxxix. 17, 24 [o]Psa. xxiii. 5——[p]Psa. liv. 7; lix. 10; cxii. 8——[q]Psa. lii. 8; Isa. lxv. 22; Hos. xiv. 5, 6

---

the middle of the *fourth* century. Had any such thing then existed in the Christian Church, he would have doubtless alluded to or spiritualized it; or, as he quoted the words of the apostle above, would have shown that *carnal usages* were substituted for *spiritual exercises.* I believe the whole verse should be translated thus: *Upon the asur, upon the nebel, upon the higgayon, with the kinnor.* Thus it stands in the Hebrew.

Verse 4. *For thou, Lord, hast made me glad through thy work*] I am delighted with thy conduct towards me; with the work of thy *providence,* the works of thy *grace,* and thy works of *creation.*

Verse 5. *How great are thy works!*] They are multitudinous, stupendous, and splendid: *and thy thoughts*—thy designs and counsels, *from* which, *by* which, and *in reference* to which, they have been formed; *are very deep*— so profound as not to be fathomed by the comprehension of man.

Verse 6. *A brutish man knoweth not*] איש בער *ish baar,* the human hog—the stupid bear—the *boor;* the man who is all flesh; in whom *spirit* or *intellect* neither seems to work nor exist. The *brutish man,* who never attempts to see God in his works.

Neither doth a fool understand this.] כסיל *kesil,* the fool, is different from בער *baar,* the brutish man; the latter *has mind,* but it is buried in flesh; the former has *no mind,* and his stupidity is unavoidable.

Verse 7. *When the wicked spring as the grass*] This is a lesson which is frequently inculcated in the sacred writings. The favour of God towards man is not to be known by outward prosperity; nor is his disapprobation to be known by the adverse circumstances in which any person may be found. When, however, we see the wicked flourish, we may take for granted that their *abuse* of God's mercies will cause him to cut them off as cumberers of the ground; and, dying in their sins, *they are destroyed for ever.*

Verse 8. *High for evermore.*] *They* are brought down and destroyed; but the Lord is exalted eternally, both for his judgments and his mercies.

Verse 10. *Like* the horn of *a unicorn.*] ראים *reeym,* perhaps here, the *oryx* or *buffalo.* But

the *rhinoceros* seems to be the real *monoceros* of the Scriptures.

I shall be anointed with fresh oil.] Perhaps the allusion is here not to any *sacramental* anointing, but to such anointings as were frequent among the Asiatics, especially after bathing, for the purpose of health and activity.

Verse 11. *Mine eye also shall see,*—and *mine ears shall hear*] Even in my own times my enemies shall be destroyed; and of this destruction I shall either be an *eye-witness* or have authentic *information.*

Verse 12. *The righteous shall flourish like the palm-tree*] Very different from the wicked, ver. 7, who are likened to *grass.* These shall have a *short duration;* but those shall have a long and useful life. They are compared also to the *cedar of Lebanon,* an incorruptible wood, and extremely long-lived. Mr. *Maundrell,* who visited those trees in 1697, describes them thus: "These noble trees grow among the snow, near the highest part of Lebanon. Some are very old, and of prodigious bulk. I measured one of the largest, and found it *twelve* yards *six* inches in girt, and yet sound; and *thirty-seven* yards in the spread of its boughs. At about *five* or *six* yards from the ground, it was divided into *five* limbs, each of which was equal to a large tree." Some of these trees are supposed to have lived upwards of *one thousand* years! The figure of the *palm-tree* gives us the idea of *grandeur* and *usefulness.* The *fruit* of the palm-tree makes a great part of the *diet* of the people of *Arabia,* part of *Persia,* and *Upper Egypt.* The *stones* are ground down for the camels; the *leaves* are made into *baskets;* the *hard boughs,* or rather *strong leaves,* some being *six* or *eight* feet in length, make *fences;* the *juice* makes *arrack;* the *threads* of the web-like integument between the leaves make *ropes,* and the rigging of small vessels; and the *wood* serves for slighter buildings and fire-wood. In short, the *palm* or *date tree,* and the *olive,* are two of the most excellent and useful productions of the forest or the field.

The *cedar* gives us the idea of *majesty, stability, durableness,* and *incorruptibility.* To these *two* trees, for the most obvious reasons, are the righteous compared. *William Lithgow,* who travelled through the *holy land* about A. D. 1600, describes the cedars of Mount *Leba-*

palm-tree: he shall grow like a cedar in Lebanon.

13 Those that be planted in the house of the LORD shall flourish ʳin the courts of our God.

14 They shall still bring forth fruit in old age; they shall be fat and ˢflourishing;

15 To show that the LORD *is* upright: ᵗ*he is* my rock, and ᵘ*there is* no unrighteousness in him.

ʳPsa. c. 4; cxxxv. 2——ˢHeb. *green*

ᵗDeut. xxxii. 4——ᵘRom. ix. 14

---

non as "being in number twenty-four, growing after the manner of oaks, but a great deal taller, straighter, and thicker, and the branches growing so straight, and interlocking, as though they were kept by art: and yet from the root to the top they bear no boughs, but grow straight and upwards like to a palm-tree. Their circle-spread tops do kiss or embrace the lower clouds, making their grandeur overlook the highest bodies of all other aspiring trees. The nature of this tree is, that it is always green, yielding an odoriferous smell, and an excellent kind of fruit, like unto apples, but of a sweeter taste, and more wholesome. The roots of some of these cedars are almost destroyed by the shepherds, who have made fires thereat, and holes where they sleep; yet nevertheless they flourish green above, in the tops and branches."—Lithgow's 17 years' Travels, 4to., London, 1640.

Verse 13. *Those that be planted in the house of the Lord*] I believe the *Chaldee* has the true meaning here: "His children shall be planted in the house of the sanctuary of the Lord, and shall flourish in the courts of our God." As these trees flourish in their respective soils and climates, so shall the *righteous* in the ordinances of God. I do not think there is any allusion to either *palm-trees* or *cedars*, planted near the tabernacle or temple.

Verse 14. *They shall still bring forth fruit in old age*] They shall continue to grow in grace, and be fruitful to the end of their lives. It is a rare case to find a man in old age full of faith, love, and spiritual activity.

Verse 15. *To show that the Lord is upright*] Such persons show how faithful God is to his promises, how true to his word, how kind to them who trust in him. He is the *Rock*, the *Fountain*, whence all good comes.

There is no unrighteousness in him.] He does nothing *evil*, nothing *unwise*, nothing *unkind*. He is both *just* and *merciful*.

ANALYSIS OF THE NINETY-SECOND PSALM

I. A general proposition, ver. 1: "It is good to give thanks to the Lord," &c.; which is explained ver. 2, 3, and applied ver. 4.

II. A particular narration of such works, in which the goodness and faithfulness of God do especially consist, viz., the creation and government of the world, ver. 4, 5. And of the last he gives two instances:—

1. One in wicked men; of their stupidity, ver. 6. Then of their sudden extirpation, ver. 7, 8, 9.

2. Another in the godly, whose prosperity is great, ver. 10-14, and security certain, ver. 15.

I. He begins with a maxim: 1. "It is good," i. e., just, profitable, pleasant, and commendable, "to give thanks to the Lord." 2. "And to sing praises (with heart and tongue) to thy glorious name, O thou Most High."

And both parts he explains. 1. That we give thanks at all times, morning and evening, in prosperity and in adversity; and in our praises

especially to remember his loving-kindness and faithfulness. These must be the matter of our thanksgiving: "It is good to show forth thy loving-kindness in the morning, and thy faithfulness every night," ver. 2; and by all manner of means, ver. 3.

And thus the maxim being proposed and explained, he applies it to himself, and shows his own practice, and the reason of it: "For thou, Lord, hast made me glad through thy work; I will triumph in the works of thy hands," ver. 4.

1. "Thou hast made me glad." He was first delighted and affected with God's work.

2. And then he exults and triumphs in it. The heart must be first truly affected with the work of God before a man shall take any true content or delight in it.

II. He had made mention of the works of God; and now he farther opens what they are: First, The creation of the universe; Secondly, His especial providence in ordering the things of this world, particularly about man.

1. First, he begins with the work of creation, upon which he enters, not with less than an admiration: "O Lord, how great are thy works! and thy thoughts are very deep." As if he said, I cannot be satisfied in the contemplation of them. There is such a depth in them, that I cannot attain to it, nor comprehend it.

2. And he ends it, not without an indignation, that the wise men of the world, who yet in his judgment, for their disregard of it, are but fools, should not consider it. In the creature they look after nothing but profit and pleasure, in which regard they are but fools. *For this brutish man knows not* how great are his works; *this fool understands not* how deep are his cogitations.

And that he may illustrate their folly the more, from the work of creation he comes to God's work of governance of the world; and shows, that as they who would be and are reputed wise, are mistaken in the one, so also they are mistaken in the other; for they think the ungodly, and such as flourish in power and wealth, happy, and that the righteous men, sometimes oppressed, are unhappy: and upon these two instances he insists to the end of the Psalm. First, he instances the ungodly: *When the wicked spring up*—rise on a sudden, (for such a time there is,) *as the grass*, that grows insensibly and in a night; *and when all the workers of iniquity do flourish*—become very conspicuous, exalted in power and pride, and abound in wealth; who would not now take them for happy men? No, saith our prophet, it is not so.

1. This their felicity is the greatest infelicity: It is, "that they may perish," be destroyed.

2. "That they may perish for ever." Remember the rich man in the Gospel.

3. And this their destruction is from God, that sits on the throne, and is immutable in his decrees and ways. They flourish and are exalted; but it is but for a moment: "But thou,

Lord, art most high for evermore." And thou wilt execute thy decree upon them.

4. Which the prophet fully opens in the next verse, which the *epizeuxis* makes more emphatical: "For, lo, thine enemies, O Lord, for, lo, thine enemies shall perish; and all the workers of iniquity shall be scattered."

1. Behold, they were green, they *flourished:* but the change shall be sudden.

2. They were *enemies, thy enemies, workers of iniquity;* therefore cursed with a curse.

3. "They shall perish, they shall be scattered;" they rose, they flourished as grass, and they shall be scattered as dry grass, which the wind blows from the face of the earth.

His second instance is the godly, whose happy condition he demonstrates, 1. In *hypothesi,* or in himself, ver. 10, 11; and, 2. In *thesi;* in all others that be true members of the mystical Church of Christ, ver. 12-15.

He instanceth in himself, that his condition is not like the ungodly. He shot not up as the fading grass, but his strength and power should be as a unicorn.

1. "But my horn shalt thou exalt as the horn of a unicorn;" that is, my power, and glory, and felicity shall still mount higher.

2. "And I shall be anointed with fresh oil." Anointed to be king over *Israel,* by *Samuel,* with a horn of oil;—by God, with the gracious oil of his Spirit.

3. And that which adds to my flourishing estate: "My eye shall see my desire upon my enemies, and my ears shall hear my desire of the wicked that rise up against me;" which David lived to see and hear in the ruin of *Saul* and his house.

And that which the prophet said of himself he now transfers to all just and righteous men, whom he compares to the *palm* and *cedar.*

1. "The righteous shall flourish like a palmtree." So a good Christian; the greater weight he carries, the more he flourishes.

2. "He shall grow like a cedar in Lebanon." Cedar-wood is not consumed by worms or time; nor the Church by antiquity nor persecution. The gates of hell shall not prevail against it, nor any true member of it.

Of which the reason is, because these *palms* and *cedars*—these righteous men, are planted, set by faith, watered by the word and sacraments, rooted by charity in the Church, which is the house of the Lord; and therefore they *shall flourish*—be green and vigorous, *in the courts of our God.*

Nay, which is yet more, they shall be full of sap and laden with fruit.

1. "They shall bring forth fruit in their old age." It shall be contrary to them, as with other trees. Those grow fruitless, and bear not when they grow old; these are then most laden with the fruits of grace.

2. "They shall be fat and flourishing." Other trees, when old, are hard and dry; these then are fat in juice, and flourish in good works.

3. And the reason of this vigour, of the continuance of this radical and vital moisture to old age, is, that they bring forth fruit, which is specified in the last verse: "That they might show forth God's faithfulness, praise him for that," as it is in the second verse. 1. "That they might show that the Lord is upright,"—just and righteous in himself. 2. "That he is a Rock,"—a sure, stable foundation to trust to. 3. "And that there is no unrighteousness in him,"—no injustice; though for a time he suffer the wicked to flourish, and the just to be under the cross. For in his good time he will show his justice in rewarding the just, and punishing the unjust.

PSALM XCIII

The universal government of God, 1, 2; the opposition to that government, 3, 4; the truth of God's testimonies, 5.

XVIII. DAY. EVENING PRAYER

A. M. cir. 3468
B. C. cir. 536
Cyri,
R. Persarum,
cir. annum
primum

THE [a]Lord reigneth, [b]he is clothed with majesty; the Lord is clothed with strength, [c]wherewith he hath girded him-self: [d]the world also is established, that it cannot be moved.

2 [e]Thy throne *is* established[f] of old: thou *art* from everlasting.

A. M. cir. 3468
B. C. cir. 536
Cyri,
R. Persarum,
cir. annum
primum

---

[a]Psa. xcvi. 10; xcvii. 1; xcix. 1; Isa. lii. 7; Rev. xix. 6
[b]Psa. civ. 1——[c]Psa. lxv. 6

[d]Psa. xcvi. 10——[e]Psa. xlv. 6; Prov. viii. 22, &c.
[f]Heb. *from them*

NOTES ON PSALM XCIII

This Psalm has no *title* either in the Hebrew or Chaldee. The *Vulgate, Septuagint, Æthiopic,* and *Arabic,* state it to be "A song of praise of David for the day preceding the Sabbath, when the earth was founded;" but in such a title there is no information on which any man can rely. This Psalm is written as a part of the

preceding in *twelve* of *Kennicott's* and *De Rossi's* MSS. It was probably written at the close of the captivity by the *Levites,* descendants of Moses.

Verse 1. *The Lord reigneth*] He continues to govern every thing he has created; and he is every way qualified to govern all things, for *he is clothed with majesty and with strength*—dominion is his, and he has supreme power to

A. M. cir. 3468
B. C. cir. 536
Cyri,
R. Persarum,
cir. annum
primum

3 The floods have lifted up, O Lord, the floods have lifted up their voice; the floods lift up their waves.

4 ᵍThe Lord on high *is* mightier than the noise of many waters, *yea, than* the mighty waves of the sea.

5 Thy testimonies are very sure: holiness becometh thine house, O Lord, ʰfor ever.

A. M. cir. 3468
B. C. cir. 536
Cyri,
R. Persarum,
cir. annum
primum

ᵍPsa. lxv. 7; lxxxix. 9

ʰHeb. *to length of days*

---

exercise it; and *he has so established the world* that nothing can be driven out of order; all is ruled by him. *Nature* is his agent: or rather, nature is the sum of the laws of his government; the operations carried on by the Divine energy, and the effects resulting from those operations.

He hath girded himself] The *girding with strength* refers to the *girding* in order to *strengthen the loins, arms, knees, &c.* When a Hindoo is about to set off on a journey, to lift a burden, or to do something that requires exertion, he *binds firmly* his loose upper garment round his loins.—WARD.

Verse 2. *Thy throne is established of old*] There never was a time in which God did not reign, in which he was not a supreme and absolute Monarch; for he is from *everlasting*. There never was a time in which he was not; there never can be a period in which he shall cease to exist.

Verse 3. *The floods have lifted up*] Multitudes of people have confederated against thy people; and troop succeeds troop as the waves of the sea succeed each other.

Verse 4. *The Lord—is mightier than the noise of many waters*] Greater in strength than all the *peoples* and *nations* that can rise up against him.

Mighty waves of the sea.] Even the most powerful empires can prevail nothing against him; therefore those who trust in him have nothing to fear.

Verse 5. *Thy testimonies are very sure*] Thou wilt as surely fulfil thy word as thou wilt keep possession of thy throne.

Holiness becometh thine house] Thy *nature* is holy, all thy *works* are holy, and thy *word* is holy; therefore, thy *house*—thy *Church*, should be holy. The *building* itself should be *sanctified*—should be so *consecrated* to thy worship alone, that it shall never be employed in any other service. The *ministers* of this Church should be holy, the *members* holy, the *ordinances* holy; its *faith*, its *discipline*, and its *practice* holy. And this at all times, and in all circumstances; for holiness becometh thine house—for ever," לארך ימים *le-orech yamim*, for length of days. During the whole lapse of time; till the sun and moon shall be no more. The old *Psalter* says the house of God is *man's saule;* and of this house holiness is נָאוָה *naavah,* "the *ornament;*" it produces that meek and quiet spirit which is in the sight of God of great price. No decoration of person nor simplicity of dress can supply the place of this heavenly clothing.

ANALYSIS OF THE NINETY-THIRD PSALM

In this Psalm it is the purpose of the prophet to comfort the Church, oppressed by tyrants and persecutors; and yet she shall not utterly fail. The gates of hell shall not prevail against her; because Christ sits in his Church as *King.* The sum of it is,—

I. The magnificence and power of Christ our eternal King, ver. 1, 2.

II. That he defends his Church in the day of a storm, ver. 3, 4.

III. That his laws are holy, and his Church also, ver. 5.

I. The prophet in the first verse describes our King:

First. From his office:—

1. "He reigns." He is the great and chief Monarch; he is no idle spectator of things below; but wisely, and justly, and powerfully administers all things.

2. He is a glorious King: "He is clothed with majesty."

3. He is a potent King: "The Lord is clothed with strength."

4. He is a warlike King: "He hath girded himself," buckled his sword upon his armour; for offence towards his enemies, for defence of his kingdom.

Secondly. From his kingdom:—

1. It is universal: "The world."

2. It is fixed, firm, and stable: "The world is also established, and cannot be moved."

3. It is an everlasting kingdom: "From everlasting to everlasting; thy throne is established of old: thou art from everlasting."

II. But in this his kingdom there are those who raise tumults, commotions, and rebellions. These he compares to swelling waters and foaming waves.

1. "The floods," that is, tyrants, persecutors, &c., "have lifted up, O Lord, the floods have lifted up their voice; the floods lift up their waves." The Church dwells in the sea; and the waves of tyranny, ambition, and malice, beat furiously upon it.

2. Well, be it so; yet "the Lord on high is mightier than the noise of many waters; yea, than the mighty waves of the sea." He wonderfully and strangely hath showed his might in getting himself the victory over all persecutors, and propagating and enlarging his kingdom over all the earth in despite of his enemies.

III. 1. And as his kingdom is immovable, so are the laws by which it is governed fixed and unalterable also: "Thy testimonies are very sure." The Gospel is an eternal Gospel; the doctrine thereof is holy and inviolable; by which God hath declared his good will to man, and what he requires of all his loving subjects; which is, that they be a holy people. For,

2. "Holiness becomes thy house for ever." The temple, the priests, the people, must be a holy nation; for ever correspondent to the holiness of his law and testimonies: "Be ye holy, for I am holy." "Holiness becomes thy house, O Lord, for ever."

PSALM XCIV

An appeal to God against oppressors, 1–7. Expostulations with the workers of iniquity, 8–11. God's merciful dealings with his followers, 12–15; and their confidence in him, 16–19. The punishment of the wicked foretold, 20–23.

O LORD ᵃGod, ᵇto whom vengeance belongeth; O God, to whom vengeance belongeth, ᶜshow thyself.

2 ᵈLift up thyself, thou ᵉJudge of the earth: render a reward to the proud.

3 LORD, ᶠhow long shall the wicked, how long shall the wicked triumph?

4 *How long* shall they ᵍutter *and* speak hard things? *and* all ʰthe workers of iniquity boast themselves?

5 They break in pieces thy people, O LORD, and afflict thine heritage.

6 They slay the widow and the stranger, and murder the fatherless.

7 ¹Yet they say, The LORD shall not see, neither shall the God of Jacob regard *it*.

8 ᵏUnderstand, ye brutish among the people: and *ye* fools, when will ye be wise?

9 ˡHe that planted the ear, shall he not hear? he that formed the eye, shall he not see?

10 He that chastiseth the heathen, shall not he correct? he that ᵐteacheth man knowledge, *shall not he know?*

ᵃHeb. *God of revenges*——ᵇDeut. xxxii. 35; Nah. i. 2——ᶜHebrew, *shine forth;* Psa. lxxx. 1——ᵈPsa. vii. 6 ᵉGen. xviii. 25——ᶠJob xx. 5——ᵍPsalm xxxi. 18; Jude 15

ʰJob xxxi. 3; xxxiv. 8, 22; Prov. x. 29; Luke xiii. 27 ¹Psalm x. 11, 13; lix. 7——ᵏPsalm lxxiii. 22; xcii. 6 ˡExod. iv. 11; Prov. xx. 12——ᵐJob xxxv. 11; Isa. xxviii. 26; 1 Cor. ii. 13; 1 John ii. 27

NOTES ON PSALM XCIV

This Psalm has no *title* either in the *Hebrew* or *Chaldee.* The *Vulgate, Septuagint, Æthiopic,* and *Arabic,* have "A Psalm of David, for the fourth day of the week;" but this gives us no information on which we can rely. In *three* of *Kennicott's* MSS. it is written as a *part* of the preceding. It is probably a prayer of the captives in Babylon for deliverance; and was written by the descendants of Moses, to whom some of the preceding Psalms have been attributed. It contains a description of an iniquitous and oppressive government, such as that under which the Israelites lived in Babylon.

Verse 1. *O Lord God, to whom vengeance belongeth*] God is the author of *retributive justice,* as well as of *mercy.* This retributive justice is what we often term *vengeance,* but perhaps improperly; for vengeance with us signifies an excitement of *angry passions,* in order to *gratify* a *vindictive spirit,* which supposes itself to have received some real injury; whereas what is here referred to is that simple act of justice which gives to all their due.

Verse 2. *Lift up thyself*] Exert thy power.

Render a reward to the proud.] To the Babylonians, who oppress and insult us.

Verse 3. *How long shall the wicked triumph?*] The wicked are often in prosperity; and this only shows us of how little worth riches are in the sight of God, when he bestows them on the most contemptible of mortals. But their time and prosperity have their *bounds.*

Verse 4. *They utter and speak*] יביאו *yabbiu,* their hearts *get full* of pride and insolence; and then, from the abundance of such vile hearts, the mouth *speaks;* and the speech is of *hard things, threatenings* which they are determined to execute, *boastings* of their power, authority, &c.

Verse 5. *They break in pieces thy people*] This was true of the Babylonians. Nebuchad-

nezzar slew many; carried the rest into captivity; ruined Jerusalem; overturned the temple; sacked, pillaged, and destroyed all the country.

Verse 6. *They slay the widow*] Nebuchadnezzar carried on his wars with great cruelty. He carried fire and sword every where; spared neither *age, sex,* nor *condition.* The *widow,* the *orphan,* and the *stranger,* persons in the most desolate condition of life, were not distinguished from others by his ruthless sword.

Verse 7. *The Lord shall not see*] This was either the language of *infidelity* or *insult.* Indeed, what could the Babylonians know of the true God? They might consider him as the God of a *district* or *province,* who knew nothing and did nothing out of his own territories.

Verse 8. *Understand, ye brutish*] These are the same expressions as in Psa. xcii. 6, on which see the note.

Verse 9. *He that planted the ear, shall he not hear?*] This is allowed to be an unanswerable mode of argumentation. Whatever is found of excellence in the *creature,* must be derived from the *Creator,* and exist in him in the plenitude of infinite excellence. God, says St. Jerome, is all *eye,* because he sees all; he is all *hand,* because he does all things; he is all *foot,* for he is every where present. The psalmist does not say, He that planted the ear, *hath he not an ear?* He that formed the eye, *hath he not eyes?* No; but, Shall he not *hear?* Shall he not *see?* And why does he say so? To prevent the error of humanizing God, of attributing members or corporeal parts to the infinite Spirit. See *Calmet.*

Verse 10. *He that chastiseth the heathen, shall not he correct?*] YOU, who are heathens, and heathens of the most abandoned kind.

He that teacheth man knowledge] We here supply *shall not he know?* But this is not acknowledged by the *original,* nor by any of the *Versions.* Indeed it is not necessary; for either the words contain a simple proposition, "It is

11 ⁿThe Lord knoweth the thoughts of man, that they *are* vanity.

12 ᵒBlessed *is* the man whom thou chastenest, O Lord, and teachest him out of thy law;

13 That thou mayest give him rest from the days of adversity, until the pit be digged for the wicked.

14 ᵖFor the Lord will not cast off his people, neither will he forsake his inheritance.

15 But judgment shall return unto righteousness: and all the upright in heart ᑫshall follow it.

16 Who will rise up for me against the evil-doers? *or* who will stand up for me against the workers of iniquity?

17 ʳUnless the Lord *had been* my help, my soul had ˢalmost dwelt in silence.

18 When I said, ᵗMy foot slippeth; thy mercy, O Lord, held me up.

19 In the multitude of my thoughts within me thy comforts delight my soul.

20 Shall ᵘthe throne of iniquity have fellowship with thee, which ᵛframeth mischief by a law?

21 ʷThey gather themselves together against

ⁿ1 Cor. iii. 20——ᵒJob v. 17; Prov. iii. 11; 1 Cor. xi. 32; Hebrews xii. 5, &c.——ᵖ1 Samuel xii. 22; Romans xi. 1, 2

ᑫHeb. shall be *after it*——ʳPsa. cxxiv. 1, 2——ˢOr, *quickly*——ᵗPsa. xxxviii. 16——ᵘAmos vi. 3——ᵛPsa. lviii. 2; Isa. x. 1——ʷMatt. xxvii. 1

---

he who teacheth man knowledge," or this clause should be read in connexion with ver. 11: "Jehovah, who teacheth man knowledge, knoweth the devices of man, that they are vanity." As he teaches *knowledge* to man, must he not *know* all the reasonings and devices of the human heart?

Verse 12. *Blessed* is *the man whom thou chastenest*] תיסרנו *teyasserennu*, whom thou *instructest; and teachest him out of thy law.* *Two* points here are worthy of our most serious regard: 1. God gives *knowledge* to man: gives him *understanding* and *reason.* 2. He gives him a *revelation* of himself; he places before that *reason* and *understanding* his *Divine law.* This is God's system of teaching; and the human intellect is his gift, which enables man to understand this teaching. We perhaps may add a *third* thing here; that as by sin the understanding is darkened, he gives the Holy Spirit to dispel this darkness from the intellect, in order that his word may be properly apprehended and understood. But he gives no *new faculty;* he removes the impediments from the old, and invigorates it by his Divine energy.

Verse 13. *That thou mayest give him rest*] He whom God instructs is made wise unto salvation; and he who is thus taught has rest in his soul, and peace and confidence in adversity.

Verse 14. *The Lord will not cast off his people*] Though they are now suffering under a grievous and oppressive captivity, yet the Lord hath not utterly cast them off. They are his inheritance, and he will again restore them to their own land.

Verse 15. *But judgment shall return unto righteousness*] If we read יושב *yosheb, shall sit,* for ישוב *yashub, shall return,* which is only placing the ו *vau* before the ש *shin* instead of after it, we have the following sense: *Until the just one shall sit in judgment, and after him all the upright in heart.* Cyrus has the epithet צדק *tsedek,* the *just one,* in different places in the Prophet Isaiah. See Isa. xli. 2, 10; xlv. 8; li. 5. It was Cyrus who gave liberty to the Jews; who appeared as their deliverer and conductor to their own land, and they are all represented as *following* in his *train.*

Verse 16. *Who will rise up for me*] Who is he that shall be the deliverer of thy people?

Who will come to our assistance against these wicked Babylonians?

Verse 17. *Unless the Lord* had been *my help*] Had not God in a strange manner supported us while under his chastising hand, we had been utterly cut off.

My soul had almost dwelt in silence.] The *Vulgate* has *in inferno,* in *hell* or the *infernal world;* the *Septuagint,* τῳ ᾅδῃ, in *the invisible world.*

Verse 18. *When I said, My foot slippeth*] When I found myself so weak and my enemy so strong, that I got *first* off my guard, and then off my *centre* of *gravity,* and my fall appeared inevitable,—

Thy mercy, O Lord, held me up.] יסעדני *yisadeni, propped me.* It is a metaphor taken from any thing *falling,* that is *propped, shored up,* or *buttressed.* How often does the *mercy* of God thus prevent the ruin of weak believers, and of those who have been unfaithful!

Verse 19. *In the multitude of my thoughts*] Of my griefs, (*dolorum,* Vulgate;) my sorrows, (ὀδυνων, Septuagint.) According to the multitude of my trials and distresses, have been the consolations which thou hast afforded me. Or, While I have been deeply *meditating* on thy wondrous grace and mercy, Divine light has broken in upon my soul, and I have been filled with delight.

Verse 20. *Shall the throne of iniquity*] No wicked king, judge, or magistrate shall ever stand in thy presence. No countenance shall such have from thy grace or providence.

Which frameth mischief] Devise, plan, and execute, as if they acted by a positive law, and were strictly enjoined to do what they so much delighted in.

Verse 21. *They gather themselves together*] In every thing that is *evil,* they are in *unity.* The devil, his angels, and his children, all join and draw together when they have for their object the destruction of the works of the Lord. But this was particularly the case with respect to the poor Jews among the Babylonians: they were objects of their continual hatred, and they laboured for their destruction.

This and the following verses have been applied to our Lord, and the treatment he met with both from his own countrymen and from

the soul of the righteous, and [x]condemn the innocent blood.

22 But the LORD is [y]my defence; and my God *is* the rock of my refuge.

23 And [z]he shall bring upon them their own iniquity, and shall cut them off in their own wickedness; *yea,* the LORD our God shall cut them off.

---

[x]Exod. xxiii. 7; Prov. xvii. 15——[y]Psa. lix. 9; lxii. 2, 6——[z]Psa. vii. 16; Prov. ii. 22; v. 22

---

the Romans. They pretended to "judge him according to the law, and framed mischief against him;" they "assembled together against the life of the righteous one," and "condemned innocent blood;" but God evidently interposed, and "brought upon them their own iniquity," according to their horrible imprecation: "His blood be upon us and upon our children!" God "cut them off in their own iniquity." All this had, in reference to him, a most literal fulfilment.

Verse 22. *The rock of my refuge.*] Alluding to those natural fortifications among rocks, which are frequent in the land of Judea.

Verse 23. *Shall cut them off*] This is *repeated,* to show that the destruction of the Babylonians was fixed and indubitable: and in reference to the Jews, the persecutors and murderers of our Lord and his apostles, it was not less so. *Babylon* is totally destroyed; not even a *vestige* of it remains. The *Jews* are no longer a nation; they are scattered throughout the world, and have no certain place of abode. They do not possess even one *village* on the face of the earth.

The last verse is thus translated and paraphrased in the old Psalter:—

Trans. And he sal yelde to thaim thair wickednes, and in thair malice he sall skater thaim : skater thaim sal Lorde oure God.

Par. Alswa say efter thair il entent, that thai wil do gude men harme; he sall yelde thaim pyne, and in thair malice thai sal be sundred fra the hali courte of hevene, and skatred emang the wiked fendes of hell.

For different views of several parts of this Psalm, see the *Analysis.*

ANALYSIS OF THE NINETY-FOURTH PSALM

In this Psalm the parts are,—

I. A petition for vengeance upon the wicked, ver. 1, 2.

II. A pitiful complaint, with the causes of it, which were two:—

1. The delay of God's judgments on them, ver. 3, 4.

2. Their insolence, oppression of the poor, and blasphemy against God, ver. 4-7.

III. A sharp reprehension of their blasphemy and atheism, and the refutation of it.

IV. A consolation to all good men, that God will punish the wicked and defend the righteous, ver. 12-23. Which is confirmed,—

1. From God's faithfulness, who hath promised, and will perform it, ver. 14.

2. From David's own experience, ver. 16-20.

3. From God's hatred of injustice, tyranny, and oppression, ver. 20, 21. 1. Which will cause him to be a rock and defence to his people, ver. 22. 2. A severe revenger to the oppressors, ver. 23.

1. He begins with a petition that God would take vengeance of the oppressors of his people: "O Lord God, to whom vengeance belongs, to whom vengeance belongs;" as if he had said, Thou art the most powerful Lord, a God of justice and power, and hast vengeance in thine own hand. Therefore now—

1. "Show thyself." Appear, shine forth evidently, and apparently show thy justice, ver. 1.

2. "Lift up thyself, thou Judge of the earth." Do thy office of judicature; ascend thy throne and tribunal, as judges use to do when they give judgment.

3. "Render a reward unto the proud." For the proud humble themselves not unto thee; they repent not.

II. And now the prophet begins to complain that, by the delay of God's judgment, wicked men were hardened in their impiety, and gloried in their villany.

1. "How long? how long?" This thy forbearance seems tedious; especially since the wicked grow worse and worse by it, and insult over us the more.

2. "For they triumph in their strength." They glory in their prosperity, and in their wickedness.

3. "They utter and speak hard things." Boldly, rashly, proudly, they threaten ruin to thy Church.

4. "They are workers of iniquity, and they boast themselves." It is not sufficient for them to do ill, but they boast of it.

Now to what end do they make use of all these? The consequence is lamentable—the event sad. The effects are lamentable, for in their fury and injustice—

1. "They break in pieces thy people, O Lord." The people dedicated to thee.

2. "They afflict thine heritage." The people that thou hast chosen for thy possession.

3. "They slay the widow," destitute of the comfort of a husband;—1. "And the stranger." A man far from his friends and country. 2. "And murder the fatherless." All which thou hast taken into thy protection, and commanded that they be not wronged. Exod. xxii.; Deut. xxiv. Yet such is their fury, that they spare neither sex, nor age, nor any condition of men.

"Yet they say, The Lord shall not see, neither shall the God of Jacob regard it." This is their impiety; this is their blasphemy; this is the true cause of all their injustice, tyranny, cruelty, and oppression.

III. Now our prophet sets himself seriously to reprehend and confute this. By an *apostrophe* he turns to them, and calls them fools; and proves by a manifest argument that they are fools; demonstrating, from the cause to the effect, that God is neither deaf nor blind, as they presumed and conceived: and urgeth them emphatically,—

1. "Understand, ye brutish among the people. O ye fools, when will ye be wise?" What! will ye be brutish always? will ye never have common sense in your heads?

2. "He planted the ear," caused you to hear; "and shall he not then hear?"

3. *He formed the eye* with all the tunicles, and put into it the faculty of vision by which you see; "and shall he not see?" To say the

contrary, is as if you should affirm that the fountain that sends forth the stream had no water in it; or the sun that enlightens the world had no light; or the fire that warms, no heat. Are these affirmations fit for wise men? Neither is it, that the God of Jacob doth not hear nor see.

4. "He chastiseth the heathen," as *Sodom, Gomorrah,* &c.; or he chastises them by the checks of their own conscience; "and shall not he then correct you," who go under the name of his people, and yet so impiously blaspheme?

5. "He that teacheth man knowledge"—hath endued him with a reasonable soul, and made him capable of all arts and sciences; is he stupid? is he without understanding? "Shall not he know?" He looks into your hearts, and knows your thoughts and counsels, and findeth them all vain: "The Lord knows the thoughts of man, that they are but vanity." With which he concludes his reprehension.

IV. And so from them he comes to the good man, and shows his happiness, whom he labours to comfort in his extremities, pronouncing him *blessed:* "Blessed is the man." And his blessedness lies in three things:—

1. In his sufferings; because when he is punished, he is but chastised, and his chastisements are from the Lord: "Blessed is the man whom thou chastenest."

2. In his teaching; for when he is chastised, he is but taught obedience to the law of God, taught *out of thy law.*

3. In consideration of the end; that he feel not, but bear more moderately, the injuries of the wicked; for the end why God chastiseth and teacheth thee out of his law is: *That he may give thee rest*—a quiet and even soul, *from the days of adversity;* and that thou shouldst expect with patience, *till the pit be digged up for the ungodly.* Such a day there is, and the day will come. Hell is as ready to receive the sinner, as a grave digged up for a dead body. Expect, therefore, their punishment and thy deliverance with a quiet mind. For which he gives *three* reasons:—

The *first* reason is, that though God for a time seem to be angry, and suffer his people to be afflicted, yet he will not utterly neglect and forsake them:—

1. "For the Lord will not cast off his people, neither will he forsake his inheritance."

2. A day of judgment and execution of justice shall come, "when judgment shall return unto righteousness."

A *second* confirmation of the comfort he gave to the Church in affliction is drawn from his own experience, ver. 16-20.

1. Object. Yea, but this time of judgment may be long; in the meanwhile it is necessary to have some helper and help against the persecutions and injuries of cruel men. Who will arise for me, and labour to protect me in so great a concourse of devils or mischievous men? "Who will stand up for me, and defend me against the workers of iniquity?"

Resp. Even he that then stood up for me. No man, but God alone. He did it; and "unless the Lord had been my help, my soul had almost dwelt in silence;" I had been laid in the grave among the dead, saith David, ver. 17.

2. *If I said,* and complained to him, that I was in any danger, *my foot slips*—I was tempted and ready to fall, *thy mercy, O Lord, held me up;* in mercy he lent me his hand, and sustained me.

3. "In the multitude of my thoughts within me thy comforts delight my soul:"—

(1) The *thoughts within me* were sorrows of heart, and many they were, occasioned from within, from without; *a multitude of them.*

(2) "Thy comforts delight my soul." As were the troubles in the flesh, so were comforts in my soul.

His *third* reason, to comfort the Church in affliction, is drawn from the nature of God, to whom all iniquity is hateful.

1. "Shall the throne of iniquity have fellowship with thee?" Thou art a just God, and wilt thou have any thing to do, any society, with those that sit upon thrones and seats of justice, and execute injustice?

2. "Which frame mischief by a law," i. e., frame wicked laws; or, under the colour of law and justice, oppress the innocent. With those who do injustice by the sword of justice, God will have no fellowship.

3. And yet there is a third pretence of wicked men to colour their proceedings against innocent men. The first was their *throne,* the second was the *law,* and the third is their *council,* and consultations in them. These they call to that end. They meet by troops as thieves; they assemble, they convene in synods; "they gather themselves together," and that to a most wicked end:—

1. "Against the soul of the righteous." Θηρευσαι, To hunt.—*Septuagint.*

2. "To condemn the innocent blood." Their laws are *Draco's* laws. Now what shall the poor innocent do in such a case? How shall he be comforted? Help he must not expect from man; from man it cannot come; it must come from heaven; and therefore let him say with *David,* Though my enemies rage as they list, and exercise all cruelties towards me, under a pretence of zeal, piety, and legal justice; yet

1. "The Lord is my defence," so that their treachery and plots shall not hurt me.

2. "My God is the rock of my refuge," on whom my hope shall safely rely.

3. "I am fully assured, for I have his word and his promise engaged for it."

1. "That he shall bring upon them their own iniquity;" that is, that the iniquity of the wicked man shall return upon his own head.

2. "And shall cut them off in their own wickedness;" not so much for their sin as for the malice of it.

3. Which for assurance of it he repeats, and explains who it is that shall do it: "Yea, the Lord our God shall cut them off;" the Lord, whose providence they derided; "our God," the God of Jacob, whom they contemned, ver. 7, he "shall cut them off;" they shall have no part with his people.

PSALM XCV

An invitation to praise God, 1, 2. The reason on which this is founded, the majesty and dominion of God, 3–5. An invitation to pray to God, 6. And the reasons on which that is founded, 7. Exhortation not to act as their fathers had done, who rebelled against God, and were cast out of his favour, 8–11.

XIX. DAY. MORNING PRAYER

O COME, let us sing unto the LORD: [a]let us make a joyful noise to [b]the rock of our salvation.

2 Let us [c]come before his presence with thanksgiving, and make a joyful noise unto him with psalms.

3 For [d]the Lord *is* a great God, and a great King above all gods.

4 [e]In his hand *are* the deep places of the earth; [f]the strength of the hills *is* his also.

5 [g]The [h]sea is *his,* and he made it: and his hands formed the dry *land.*

6 O come, let us worship and bow down: let [i]us kneel before the LORD our Maker.

7 For he *is* our God; and [k]we *are* the people of his pasture, and the sheep of

---

[a]Psa. c. 1——[b]Deut. xxxii. '15; 2 Sam. xxii. 47 [c]Heb. *prevent his face*——[d]Psa. xcvi. 4; xcvii. 9; cxxxv. 5 [e]Heb. *in whose*

[f]Or, *the heights of the hills* are *his*——[g]Heb. *Whose the sea is*——[h]Gen. i. 9, 10——[i]1 Cor. vi. 20——[k]Psa. lxxix. 13; lxxx. 1; c. 3

NOTES ON PSALM XCV

This Psalm is also without a *title,* both in the *Hebrew* and *Chaldee:* but is attributed to *David* by the *Vulgate, Septuagint, Æthiopic, Arabic,* and *Syriac;* and by the *author* of the Epistle to the Hebrews, chap. iv. 3-7. *Calmet* and other eminent critics believe that it was composed during the time of the *captivity,* and that the apostle only followed the *common opinion* in quoting it as the production of *David,* because in general the Psalter was attributed to him.

The Psalm is a solemn invitation to the people, when assembled for public worship, to praise God from a sense of his great goodness; and to be attentive to the instructions they were about to receive from the reading and expounding of the law; and or these accounts it has been long used in the Christian Church, at the commencement of public service, to prepare the people's minds to worship God in spirit and in truth.

Houbigant, and other learned divines, consider this Psalm as composed of *three* parts. 1, The part of the *people,* ver. 1 to the middle of ver. 7. 2. The part of the *priest* or *prophet,* from the middle of ver. 7 to the end of ver. 8. 3. The part of *Jehovah,* ver. 9-11. It is written as a part of the preceding Psalm by *nine* of *Kennicott's* and *De Rossi's* MSS.; but certainly it must have been originally an ode by itself, as the subject is widely different from that in the foregoing.

Verse 1. *O come, let us sing*] Let us *praise* God, not only with the most joyful accents which can be uttered by the *voice;* but let us also praise him with *hearts* tuned to gratitude, from a full sense of the manifold benefits we have already received.

The rock of our salvation.] The strong *Fortress* in which we have always found *safety,* and the *Source* whence we have always derived *help* for our souls. In both these senses the word *rock,* as applied to God, is used in the Scriptures.

Verse 2. *Let us come before his presence*] פניו *panaiv,* his faces, with thanksgiving, בתודה *bethodah,* with *confession,* or *with the confes-*

sion-*offering. Praise* him for what he has already done, and *confess* your unworthiness of any of his blessings. The *confession-offering,* the great *atoning sacrifice,* can alone render your *acknowledgment of sin* and *thanksgiving* acceptable to a *holy* and *just* God.

Verse 3. *For the Lord is a great God*] Or, "A great God is Jehovah, and a great King above all gods;" or, "God is a great King over all." The Supreme Being has *three* names here: אל EL, יהוה JEHOVAH, אלהים ELOHIM, and we should apply none of them to *false* gods. The *first* implies his *strength;* the *second* his *being* and *essence;* the *third,* his *covenant relation* to mankind. In public worship these are the views we should entertain of the Divine Being.

Verse 4. *In his hand are the deep places of the earth*] The greatest deeps are *fathomed by him.*

The strength of the hills is his also.] And to him the *greatest heights* are *accessible.*

Verse 5. *The sea is his*] The sea and the dry land are equally his, for he has formed them both, and they are his property. He governs and disposes of them as he sees good. He is the absolute Master of universal nature. Therefore there is no other object of worship nor of confidence.

Verse 6. *O come, let us worship*] Three distinct words are used here to express *three different acts of adoration:* 1. *Let us worship,* נשתחוה *nishtachaveh,* let us *prostrate* ourselves; the highest act of adoration by which the *supremacy* of God is acknowledged. 2. *Let us bow down,* נכרעה *nichrah,* let us *crouch* or *cower down, bending the legs under,* as a dog in the presence of his master, which solicitously waits to receive his commands. 3. *Let us kneel,* נברכה *nibrachah, let us put our knees to the ground,* and thus put ourselves in the *posture* of those who *supplicate.* And let us consider that all this should be done in the *presence* of HIM who is *Jehovah our Creator.*

Verse 7. *For he is our God*] Here is the reason for this service. He has condescended to enter into a *covenant* with us, and he has taken us for his own; therefore—

We are the people of his pasture] Or, rather,

his hand. [1]To-day if ye will hear his voice,

8 Harden not your heart, [m]as in the [n]provocation, *and* as *in* the day of temptation in the wilderness:

9 When [o]your fathers tempted me, proved me, and [p]saw my work.

---

[1]Heb. iii. 7, 15; iv. 7——[m]Exod. xvii. 2, 7; Num. xiv. 22, &c.; xx. 13; Deut. vi. 16——[n]Heb. *contention* [o]Psa. lxxviii. 18, 40, 56; 1 Cor. x. 9

as the *Chaldee, Syriac, Vulgate,* and *Æthiopic* read, "We are his people, and the sheep of the pasture of his hand." We are his own; he feeds and governs us, and his powerful *hand* protects us.

To-day if ye will hear his voice] To-day— you have no time to lose; *to-morrow* may be too late. God calls to-day; to-morrow he may be silent. This should commence the eighth verse, as it begins what is supposed to be the part of the *priest* or *prophet* who now exhorts the people; as if he had said: Seeing you are in so good a spirit, do not forget your own resolutions, and harden not your hearts, "as your fathers did in Meribah and Massah, in the wilderness;" the *same fact* and the *same names* as are mentioned Exod. xvii. 7; when the people murmured at *Rephidim,* because they had no water; hence it was called *Meribah,* contention or provocation, and *Massah,* temptation.

Verse 9. When your fathers tempted me] *Tried* me, by their insolence, unbelief, and blasphemy. They *proved* me—they had full proof of my power to save and to destroy. There *they saw my works*—they saw that nothing was too hard for God.

Verse 10. Forty years long] They did nothing but murmur, disbelieve, and rebel, from the time they began their journey at the *Red Sea* till they passed over Jordan, a period of *forty* years. During all this time God was *grieved* by *that generation;* yet he seldom showed forth that *judgment* which they most righteously had deserved.

It is a people that do err in their heart] Or, according to the *Chaldee,* These are *a people whose idols are in their hearts.* At any rate they had not Gᴏᴅ there.

They have not known my ways] The verb יָדַע *yada, to know,* is used here, as in many other parts of Scripture, to express *approbation.* They knew God's ways well enough; but they did not *like* them; and would not walk in them. "These wretched men," says the old Psalter, "were gifnen to the lufe of this lyfe: knewe noght my ways of mekenes, and charite: for thi in my wreth I sware to thaim; that es, I sett stabely that if thai sall entre in till my rest;" that is, they shall not enter into my rest.

This ungrateful people did not approve of God's ways—they did not enter into his designs —they did not conform to his commands—they paid no attention to his miracles—and did not acknowledge the benefits which they received from his hands; therefore God determined that they should not enter into the *rest* which he had promised to them on condition that, if they were obedient, they should inherit the promised land. So none of those who came out of Egypt, except *Joshua* and *Caleb,* entered into Canaan;

10 [q]Forty years long was I grieved with *this* generation, and said, It *is* a people that do err in their heart, and they have not known my ways:

11 Unto whom [r]I sware in my wrath [s]that they should not enter into my rest.

---

[p]Num. xiv. 22——[q]Heb. iii. 10, 17——[r]Num. xiv. 23, 28, 30; Heb. iii. 11, 18; iv. 3, 5——[s]Heb. *if they enter into my rest*

all the rest died in the wilderness, wherein, because of their disobedience, God caused them to wander *forty* years.

It is well known that the land of Canaan was a type of heaven, where, after all his toils, the good and faithful servant is to enter into the joy of his Lord. And as those Israelites in the wilderness were not permitted to enter into the land of Canaan because of their unbelief, their distrust of God's providence, and consequent disobedience, St. Paul hence takes occasion to exhort the Jews, Heb. iv. 2-11, to accept readily the terms offered to them by the Gospel. He shows that the words of the present Psalm are applicable to the state of Christianity; and intimates to them that, if they persisted in obstinate refusal of those gracious offers, *they* likewise would fall according to the same example of unbelief.—*Dodd.*

ANALYSIS OF THE NINETY-FIFTH PSALM

This Psalm contains *two* parts:—

I. An exhortation to praise God, to adore, worship, kneel, ver. 1, 2, 6.

II. Reasons to persuade to it.

1. God's mercies, ver. 3, 4, 5, 7.

2. His judgments in punishing his own people *Israel* for neglect of this duty.

I. The psalmist begins this *Psalm* with an earnest invitation, including himself; saying,—

1. "O come, let us;" come along with me. Though a king, he thought not himself exempted.

2. And the assembly being come together, he acquaints them what they came for:—

1. "To sing to the Lord." 1. Heartily, joyfully: "Let us make a joyful noise;" make a *jubilee* of it. 2. Openly, and with a loud voice: "Let us make a joyful noise with Psalms." 3. Reverently, as being in his eye, "his presence." 4. Gratefully: "Let us come before his presence with thanksgiving."

2. "To worship, to bow down, to kneel," ver. 6. Adoration, humble adoration; outward worship—that of the body, as well as inward—that of the soul, is his due; and that for these reasons:—

II. 1. Because he is "the Rock of our salvation;" whether temporal or spiritual. So long as we rely on him as a Rock, we are safe from the tyranny of men, from the wrath of God, from the power of the devil, death, and hell.

2. Because he is "a great God, and a great King above all gods," JEHOVAH, a God whose name is *I am,* an incommunicable name to any other; for his essence is from himself, and immutable; all others derivative and mutable; and the *great* JEHOVAH, great in power, majesty, and glory; for he "is above all gods."

3. The whole orb of the earth is under his

power and dominion: "In his hands are all the corners of the earth; the strength of the hills is his also." The globe in all its extensions is subject to him.

4. And no wonder, for he is the Creator of both, which is another argument: "The sea is his, and he made it; and his hands formed the dry land."

5. "He is our Maker," the Creator and Lord of men also.

6. *Our Lord God* in particular, for he hath called us to be his inheritance: "For we are the people of his pasture, and the sheep of his hand."

In which duty, if we fail, he proposeth what is to be expected by the example of the *Israelites*.

I. God gave them a day, and he gives it to you; it is the *hodie*, to-day, of your life.

2. In this day he speaks, he utters his voice: outwardly he speaks by his word; inwardly, by his Spirit.

3. This you are bound to hear, to obey.

4. And it is your own fault if you hear it not, for you may hear it if you will; to that purpose he hath given you a day: "To-day if you will hear his voice."

5. Suppose you hear it not; the cause is, the hardness of your hearts: and take heed of it; "harden not your hearts."

For then it will be with you as it was with the Israelites.

1. "As in the day of temptation in the wilderness," at *Meribah* and *Massah*.

2. "When your fathers," the Israelites that then lived, "tempted me and proved me." They asked whether God was among them or not? They questioned my power, whether I was able to give them bread and water, and flesh?

3. And they found that I was able to do it: "They saw my works;" for I brought them water out of the rock, and gave them bread from heaven, and flesh also.

Their stubbornness was of long continuance, and often repeated, for it lasted *forty* years: "Forty years was I grieved with this generation;" which drew God to pass this censure and verdict upon them:—

1. His censure was, that they were an obstinate perverse people, "a people that do always err in their hearts;" that were led by their own desires, which caused them to err; the way of God they would not go in; they knew it not, that is, they liked it not.

2. This verdict upon them: "Unto whom I sware in my wrath, that they should not enter into my rest;" i, e., literally, into the land of *Canaan* that I promised them. The oath is extant, Num. xiv: "As I live, saith the Lord, your carcasses shall fall in the wilderness;" and in the wilderness they did fall, every one, except *Caleb* and *Joshua*, a fearful example against stubbornness and disobedience. Let him that readeth understand.

PSALM XCVI

All the inhabitants of the earth are invited to praise the Lord, 1–3. His supreme majesty, 3–6. The tribes of Israel are invited to glorify him, 7–9; and to proclaim him among the heathen, 10. The heavens and the earth are commanded to rejoice in him, 11–13.

A. M. 3489
B. C. 515
A. U. C. 239
Darii I.,
R. Persarum,
anno sexto

O ^aSING unto the Lord a new song: sing unto the Lord, all the earth.

2 Sing unto the Lord, bless his name; show forth his salvation from day to day.

3 Declare his glory among the heathen, his wonders among all people.

A. M. 3489
B. C. 515
A. U. C. 239
Darii I.,
R. Persarum,
anno sexto

^a1 Chron. xvi. 23–33;   Psa. xxxiii. 3

NOTES ON PSALM XCVI

This Psalm has no *title*, either in the *Hebrew* or *Chaldee*. The *Syriac:* "Of David. A prophecy of the advent of Christ, and the calling of the Gentiles to believe in him." The *Vulgate, Septuagint, Æthiopic,* and *Arabic* have, "A Song of David, when the House was built after the Captivity." We have seen in 1 Chron. xvi. 23-33 a Psalm nearly like this, composed by David, on bringing the ark to Sion, from the house of Obed-edom. See the notes on the above place. But the Psalm, as it stands in the *Chronicles,* has *thirty* verses; and this is only a section of it, from the *twenty-third* to the *thirty-third*. It is very likely that this part was taken from the Psalm above mentioned, to be used at the dedication of the *second temple*. The one hundred and fifth Psalm is almost the same as that in Chronicles, but much more extensive. Where they are in the *main* the same, there are differences for which it is not easy to account.

Verse 1. *Sing unto the Lord a new song*] A song of peculiar excellence, for in this sense the term *new* is repeatedly taken in the Scriptures. He has done extraordinary things for us, and we should *excel* in praise and thanksgiving.

Verse 2. *Show forth his salvation from day to day*.] The original is very emphatic, בשרו מיום ליום ישועתו *basseru miyom leyom yeshuatho,* "Preach the Gospel of his salvation from day to day." To the same effect the Septuagint, Ευαγγελιζεσθε ημεραν εξ ημερας το σωτηριον αυτου, "Evangelize his salvation from day to day."

Verse 3. *Declare his glory among the heathen*.] The heathen do not know the true God: as his being and attributes are at the foundation of all religion, these are the first subjects of instruction for the Gentile world. *Declare,* ספרו *sapperu, detail, number out* his *glory,* כבודו *kebodo,* his *splendour* and *excellence.*

His wonders among all people.] Declare also to the *Jews* his wonders, נפלאותיו *niphleothaiv, his miracles.* Dwell on the works which he

A. M. 3489
B. C. 515
A. U. C. 239
Darii I.,
R. Persarum,
anno sexto

4 For ^bthe LORD *is* great, and ^cgreatly to be praised: ^dhe *is* to be feared above all gods.

5 For ^eall the gods of the nations *are* idols: ^fbut the LORD made the heavens.

6 Honour and majesty *are* before him: strength and ^gbeauty *are* in his sanctuary.

7 ^hGive unto the LORD, O ye kindreds of the people, give unto the LORD glory and strength.

8 Give unto the LORD the glory ⁱ*due unto* his name: bring an offering, and come into his courts.

9 O worship the LORD ^kin ^lthe beauty of holiness: fear before him, all the earth.

A. M. 3489
B. C. 515
A. U. C. 239
Darii I.,
R. Persarum,
anno sexto

10 Say among the heathen *that* ^mthe LORD reigneth: the world also shall be established that it shall not be moved: ⁿhe shall judge the people righteously.

11 ^oLet the heavens rejoice, and let the earth be glad; ^plet the sea roar, and the fulness thereof.

12 Let the field be joyful, and all that *is* therein: then shall all the trees of the wood rejoice

13 Before the LORD: for he cometh, for he cometh to judge the earth: ^qhe shall judge the world with righteousness, and the people with his truth.

---

^bPsa. cxlv. 3——^cPsa. xviii. 3——^dPsa. xcv. 3 ^eSee Jer. x. 11, 12——^fPsa. cxv. 15; Isa. xlii. 5——^gPsa. xxix. 2——^hPsa. xxix. 1, 2——ⁱHeb. *of his name* ^kPsa. xxix. 2; cx. 3

^lOr, *in the glorious sanctuary*——^mPsa. xciii. 1; xcvii. 1; Rev. xi. 15; xix. 6——ⁿVer. 13; Psa. lxvii. 4; xcviii. 9 ^oPsa. lxix. 34——^pPsa. xcviii. 7, &c.——^qPsa. lxvii. 4; Rev. xix. 11

---

shall perform in Judea. The miracles which Christ wrought among the Jews were full proof that he was not only the *Messiah*, but the *mighty power of God.*

Verse 4. *He is to be feared above all gods.*] I think the two clauses of this verse should be read thus:—

Jehovah is great, and greatly to be praised.
Elohim is to be feared above all.

I doubt whether the word אלהים *Elohim* is ever, by fair construction, applied to false gods or idols. The *contracted* form in the following verse appears to have this meaning.

Verse 5. *All the gods of the nations* are *idols*]
אלהי *elohey.* All those reputed or worshipped as gods among the heathens are אלילים *elilim, vanities, emptinesses, things of nought.* Instead of being *Elohim*, they are *elilim;* they are not only not GOD, but they are *nothing."* "Jehovah made the heavens." He who is the Creator is alone worthy of adoration.

Verse 6. *Honour and majesty* are *before him*] Does this refer to the cloud of his glory that preceded the ark in their journeying through the wilderness? The words *strength* and *beauty*, and *glory and strength*, ver. 7, are those by which the ark is described, Psa. lxxviii. 61.

Verse 7. *Ye kindreds of the people*] Ye families, all the *tribes* of Israel in your respective *divisions.*

8. *Come into his courts.*] Probably referring to the *second temple.* The reference must be either to the *tabernacle* or *temple.*

Verse 9. *Worship the Lord in the beauty of holiness*] I think בהדרת קדש *behadrath kodesh*, signifies *holy ornaments,* such as the high priest wore in his ministrations. These were given him for *glory* and *beauty;* and the psalmist calls on him to put on his sacerdotal garments, to bring his offering, מנחה *minchah,* and come into the courts of the Lord, and perform his functions, and make intercession for the people.

Verse 10. *Say among the heathen* that *the*

Lord reigneth] *Justin Martyr*, in his dialogue with *Trypho* the Jew, quotes this passage thus: Ειπατε εν τοις εθνεσι, ὁ Κυριος εβασιλευσε απο του ξυλου, "Say among the nations, the Lord ruleth *by the wood,*" meaning the *cross;* and accuses the Jews of having blotted this word out of their Bibles, because of the evidence it gave of the truth of Christianity. It appears that this reading did exist anciently in the *Septuagint,* or at least in some ancient copies of that work, for the reading has been quoted by *Tertullian, Lactantius, Arnobius, Augustine, Cassiodorus, Pope Leo, Gregory of Tours,* and others. The reading is still extant in the ancient *Roman* Psalter, *Dominus regnavit a ligno,* and in some others. In an ancient MS. copy of the Psalter before me, while the text exhibits the commonly received reading, the margin has the following gloss: *Regnavit a ligno crucis,* "The Lord reigns by the wood of the cross." My old *Scotico-Latin* Psalter has not a *ligno* in the text, but seems to refer to it in the paraphrase: **ꝼor Criſte regneꝺ efter þe ꝺeꝺe on þe croſſe.** It is necessary, however, to add, that no such words exist in any copy of the Hebrew text now extant, nor in any MS. yet collated, nor in any of the ancient Versions. Neither *Eusebius* nor *Jerome* even refer to it, who wrote comments on the Psalms; nor is it mentioned by any *Greek* writer except *Justin Martyr.*

The world also shall be established] The word תבל *tebel* signifies the *habitable globe,* and may be a metonymy here, the container put for the contained. And many think that by it the *Church* is intended; as the *Lord,* who is announced to the heathen as reigning, is understood to be Jesus Christ; and *his judging among the people,* his establishing the holy Gospel among them, and governing the nations by its laws.

Verse 11. *Let the heavens rejoice*] The publication of the Gospel is here represented as a universal blessing; the *heavens,* the *earth,* the *sea,* and its *inhabitants,* the *field,* the *grass,* and the *trees* of the *wood,* are all called to rejoice at this glorious event. This verse is well and harmoniously translated in the old Psalter:—

> ffayne be hebenes,—anb the erth glab;
> Stprbe be the see,—anb the fulnes of it;
> Joy sal felbes,—anb al that ere in thaim.

And the paraphrase is at least curious:—

> Hebens, haly men. Erthe, meke men that receyves lare (learning.) ffelbes, that is even men, mylde and softe: they shall joy in Criste. Anb all that is in thaim, that es, strengh, wyttes & skill."

I shall give the remaining part of this ancient paraphrase, which is an echo of the opinion of most of the Latin fathers.

Verse 12. **Thou sal glab al the trese of woobes.**—**Thou,** that is in another lyfe. **Trese of woobes.**—Synful men that were fyrst withouten frut, and sithen taken into God's temple.

Verse 13. **ffor he coms, he coms. He coms,** fyrste to be man.—Sythen he comes to deme the erth.

He sal deme in ebenes the erth:—anb folk in his sothfastnes. Nothing is evener, or sothfaster, than that he geder with hym perfyte men; to deme and to deperte to the rig hande (thaim) that did mercy:—pase to the lefte hande (thaim) that did it nogt.

The psalmist here in the true spirit of poetry, gives life and intelligence to universal nature, producing them all as exulting in the reign of the Messiah, and the happiness which should take place in the earth when the Gospel should be universally preached. These predictions seem to be on the eve of complete fulfilment. Lord, hasten the time! For a fuller explanation see the following analysis.

ANALYSIS OF THE NINETY-SIXTH PSALM

Although this Psalm was composed by David at the bringing back of the ark, yet most ancient and modern Christian expositors acknowledge it a prophecy of Christ's kingdom, to be enlarged by the accession of all the Gentiles, and finally, his coming to judgment.

There are *two* parts in this Psalm:—

I. A general exhortation to both Jews and Gentiles to praise God, ver. 1-3.

II. A prophecy of Christ's kingdom, described by its greatness, ver. 4, 5; the honours and glory, ver. 6; of the majesty of the King, ver. 7, 8.

1. The amplitude of this kingdom, ver. 10.
2. His judicature in it, ver. 11-13.

I. 1. The invitation to praise God for the benefits conferred on the whole earth by Christ, ver. 1-3. That the praise be full, he thrice repeats, "O sing, sing, sing;" to the honour of the Trinity, says *Bellarmine*, obscurely intimated in the Old, but plainly to be preached in the New, Testament. 2. "Show forth." Give praise by thanks and singing. 3. "Declare." Carry good news—the Gospel of glad tidings.

2. The song to be sung must be new: "Sing unto the Lord a new song." New, for a new benefit; new, to be sung by new people; new, as being on a most excellent subject.

3. It was to be sung "by the whole earth." By new men, and all the world over; for God was not now to be known in *Judea* only, but by all nations.

4. It must be continually sung, from day to day, without cessation; for as one day succeeds another, so should there be a continual succession in his praise.

Afterwards he expresses the benefits for

which the whole earth is to praise him, which is for the redemption of the world by his Son.

1. He shows forth his salvation, which he has conferred on mankind by Christ.

2. "Declare his glory among the heathen, his wonders among all people." Salvation was a glorious work, full of wonders. And this was to be evangelized, as before to the *Jews* by the *prophets*, so now to *all people* by the *apostles*.

II. And that this exhortation might appear more reasonable, he presents God as a king, and sets down the greatness, amplitude, and equity of his kingdom.

1. "Sing to the Lord all the earth, for he is Lord of the whole earth." 1. "The Lord is great." Great in power, wisdom, goodness, mercy, dominion, riches; great in every way of greatness. 2. "He is greatly to be praised," or worthy of all praise, for his innumerable benefits. He bestows them, spiritually and temporally, in his creation, redemption, and preservation of the world. What is praiseworthy in any king may be found superlatively in him.

2. "He is to be feared above all gods;" for he can cast body and soul into hell. They, though called gods, can do neither good nor hurt; the devils, who set them up, believe that he is above them, and they tremble. Sing to him then, for the supremacy is his; he is above all gods. If there be other gods, show their works; produce the heavens they have made, or the earth they have framed. It is our God alone who "made the heavens, and all things that are in them;" fear him, and not them.

The prophet elegantly derides the heathenish gods, and the heathen for fearing them.

1. For the multitude of them, for they were many; which is contrary to the nature of God, who must be but one, for there can be but one Supreme.

2. For their division: one of the *Ammonites; another* of the *Moabites;* one of the *Philistines;* many of the *Assyrians, Egyptians, Greeks, Romans:* their gods were according to the number of their cities; three hundred Jupiters, thirty thousand deities.

3. They were *elilim, Dii minores. Moloch* had the rule of the *sun; Astarte,* of the *moon; Ceres,* of *corn; Pluto,* of *hell; Neptune,* of the *sea,* &c. Their power was not universal, as the power of God ought to be.

4. Lastly, in the opposition, which plainly shows the difference between God and idols. They are but the work of men's hands. Our God is a creator; he made the heavens, and all that is contained in and under them. He then is terrible, and to be feared; not those diminutive, vain, unprofitable gods of the nations.

And so, having removed out of his way all the gods of the nations, he returns to our God and King. Having said "he was great, greatly to be feared, and praised above all gods," he now sets forth his majesty to the eye of the subject and stranger: *Honour, majesty, strength, beauty;* so says our prophet: "Honour and majesty are before him, strength and beauty are in his sanctuary." God is invisible; but his honour and majesty, strength and beauty, may be easily observed in his ordering, governing, and preserving the whole world and his Church; both which may be justly called his sanctuary, and the last *his holy place.*

He has proved God to be a universal King, and now he endeavours to persuade his subjects, all kindreds of people, to return to their king his tribute, his honour and worship, which he comprehends in these words: *Give—bring an offering—worship—fear—proclaim him to be King.*

1. "Give unto the Lord;" and again, "Give unto the Lord glory and strength." Give freely to him, and alone attribute to him the glory of your being and well-being, that he made and redeemed you, and that by the strength of his right hand he has plucked you out of the hands of your enemies. This was the glorious work of his mercy and power.

2. "Give unto the Lord the honour due to his name." It is a debt; and a debt, in equity, must be paid. The honour due to his name is to acknowledge him to be holy, just, true, powerful: "The Lord, the faithful God,"—"good, merciful, long-suffering," &c. Defraud not his name of the least honour.

3. "Bring an offering, and come into his courts." *Appear not before the Lord empty*, as the *Jews* were commanded; to which the prophet alludes. "They had their sacrifices, and we also have our spiritual sacrifices, acceptable to God through Jesus Christ," to bring; 1 Peter ii. 5. These are the sacrifices of a contrite heart. Bring these when you enter into his courts, and into his house of prayer.

4. "O worship the Lord in the beauty of holiness." They who enter into the presence of a king presently fall on their knees in token of submission and homage; in the presence of your King do the same. *Adore*, and remember to do it in the beauty of holiness; referred to the material temple, it is by relation a *holy place*, and should not be profaned; a beautiful place, and should not be defaced, but kept beautiful. If referred to the spiritual temple, the temple of the Holy Ghost is to be beautiful with holiness; a holy life, holy virtues, beautiful garments, righteousness and true holiness.

5. "Fear before him, all the earth." Join fear to your worship, for a man may be bold in the presence of his king. "Serve the Lord with fear, and rejoice with reverence." There is a fear which arises out, of an apprehension of greatness and excellency in the person, together with our dependence on and our submission to him, which in body and mind makes us step back, and keep at a distance. This kind of fear produces reverence and adoration, and this the prophet here means.

6. "Say among the heathen, the Lord reigns;" or, as some say: "The Lord reigns among the heathen." Be heralds; and proclaim, with the sound of the trumpet, *God reigns, God is King.*

The prophet begins to set forth the amplitude of Christ's kingdom:—

1. Before, it was confined to Judea, but is now enlarged: "All nations are become his subjects; he reigns among the heathen."

2. Its stability: "The world shall be established, that it shall not be moved." The laws of this kingdom are not to be altered, as were the laws of Moses, but fixed and established for ever. The Gospel is an eternal Gospel, a standing law.

3. The equity to be observed in it: "He shall judge the people righteously," for he shall give to those who observe his laws, rewards; to those who despise them, break them, and say, "We will not have this man to reign over us," condign punishment.

4. The prophet, having described the King, and the state of his kingdom, exults in spirit, as if he had seen him coming to sit upon the throne. He calls, not the *Gentiles* only, whom it did very nearly concern, but all creatures, to rejoice in him; *heaven, earth, sea, trees, fields*, &c. Although there are who by *heaven* understand *angels; by the earth, men; by the sea, troublesome spirits;* by *trees* and *fields*, the *Gentiles* who were to believe; yet this need not be thought strange, because such *prosopopœias* are frequent in Scripture. The meaning is, that as the salvation was universal, so he would have the joy to be universal: "Let the heavens rejoice, and let the earth be glad; let the sea roar, and the fulness thereof. Let the field be joyful, and all that is therein: then shall the trees of the wood rejoice before the Lord."

He incites all creatures to rejoice for Christ's coming, both for the first and for the second: for the first, in which he consecrated all things; for the second, in which he will free all things from corruption, Rom. viii. 19-22.

1. "For he cometh, for he cometh to judge the earth."—Which first part of the verse the fathers refer to his first coming, when he was incarnate, and came to redeem the world by his death: and was to the end to judge, that is to rule and govern, the world by his word, ordinances, and Spirit.

2. And again: "He shall come to judge the world with righteousness, and the people with his truth:" which coming, though terrible to the wicked, will be joyful and comfortable to the righteous. For, says our Lord, "Lift up your heads, for your redemption draweth near;" and to comfort them, and terrify the wicked, he tells them he will judge with equity, that is, in justice and in truth, according to his word and promise. He will accept no man's person, but render to every man according to his works.

PSALM XCVII

A. M. 3489
B. C. 515
A. U. C. 239
Darii I.,
R. Persarum,
anno sexto

T HE ᵃLᴏʀᴅ reigneth; let
  the earth rejoice; let the
ᵇmultitude of ᶜisles be glad
thereof.

2 ᵈClouds and darkness *are*
round about him: ᵉrighteous-
ness and judgment *are* the ᶠha-
bitation of his throne.

A. M. 3489
B. C. 515
A. U. C. 239
Darii I.,
R. Persarum,
anno sexto

ᵃPsa. xcvi. 10——ᵇHeb. *many* or *great isles*——ᶜIsa.
lx. 9

ᵈ1 Kings viii. 12; Psa. xviii. 11——ᵉPsa. lxxxix. 14
ᶠOr, *establishment*

NOTES ON PSALM XCVII

This Psalm has no *title* either in the *Hebrew*
or *Chaldee; and in fourteen* of *Kennicott's* and
De Rossi's MSS. it is written as a part of the
preceding. In the *Vulgate* it is thus entitled,
Psalmus David, quando terra ejus restituta est.
"A Psalm of David when his land was restored;" the meaning of which I suppose to be,
after he had obtained possession of the kingdom of Israel and Judah, and became king over
all the tribes; or perhaps, after he had gained
possession of all those countries which were
originally granted to the Israelites in the Divine promise. See 1 Chron. xviii. 1, 2. The
Septuagint is nearly to the same purpose, ὅτι
ἡ γη αυτου καθισταται, "when his land was established:" so the *Æthiopic* and *Arabic.* The
Syriac has, "A Psalm of David, in which he
predicts the advent of Christ, (i. e., in the
flesh,) and through it his last appearing, (i. e.,
to judgment.") The author of the Epistle to
the Hebrews, chap. i. 6, quotes a part of the
seventh verse of this Psalm, and applies it to
Christ. Who the author was is uncertain: it is
much in the spirit of David's finest compositions; and yet many learned men suppose it
was written to celebrate the Lord's power and
goodness in the restoration of the Jews from
the *Babylonish captivity.*

Verse 1. *The Lord reigneth*] Here is a simple proposition, which is a self-evident axiom,
and requires no proof: Jᴇʜᴏᴠᴀʜ is *infinite* and
eternal; is possessed of *unlimited power* and
unerring wisdom; as he is the *Maker,* so he
must be the *Governor,* of all things. His authority is absolute, and his government therefore universal. In all places, on all occasions,
and in all times, Jehovah reigns.

But this supreme King is not only called
יהוה Yᴇʜᴏᴠᴀʜ, which signifies his infinite and
eternal being, unlimited power, and unerring
wisdom; and, as Creator, his *universal government;* but he is also אדני Aᴅᴏɴᴀɪ, the *Director*
and *Judge.* He *directs* human actions by his
word, Spirit, and *Providence.* Hence are his
laws and *revelation* in general; for the governed should know their governor, and should
be acquainted with his laws, and the reasons
on which *obedience* is founded. As *Adonai* or
Director, he shows them the difference between
good and evil; and their duty to their God,
their neighbours, and themselves: and he finally
becomes the *Judge* of their actions. But as his
law is holy, and his commandment holy, just,
and good, and man is in a fallen, sinful state;
hence he *reveals* himself as אלהים Eʟᴏʜɪᴍ,
God, entering into a *gracious* covenant with
mankind, to enlighten his darkness, and help
his infirmities; that he may see what is *just,*
and be *able* to do it. But as this will not can-
cel the sins *already committed,* hence the necessity of a Saviour, an atonement; and hence the
incarnation, passion, death, and resurrection of
our Lord Jesus. This is the *provision* made by

the great God for the more effectual administration of his kingdom upon earth. *Jehovah,
Adonai, Elohim* reigneth; *et his animadversis,*
and these points considered, it is no wonder
that the psalmist should add,

*Let the earth rejoice; let the multitude of
isles be glad*] The *earth,* the *terraqueous globe;*
especially, here, the *vast continents,* over every
part of which God's dominion extends. But it
is not confined to *them;* it takes in the *islands*
of the sea; all the *multitude* of those islands,
even to the smallest inhabited rock; which are
as much the objects of his care, the number of
their inhabitants considered, as the vastest continents on which are founded the mightiest empires. All this government springs from his
holiness, righteousness, and *benignity;* and is
exercised in what we call *providence,* from *pro,*
for, before, and *video,* to see, which word is
well defined and applied by Cɪᴄᴇʀᴏ: *Providentia
est, per quam futurum aliquid videtur, antequam
factum sit.* "Providence is that by which any
thing future is seen before it takes place." *De
Invent.* c. 53. And, in reference to a *Divine*
providence, he took up the general opinion, viz.,
*Esse deos, et eorum providentia mundum ad-
ministrari. De Divinat.* c. 51, *ad finem.* "There
are gods; and by their providence the affairs
of the world are administered."

This providence is not only *general,* taking
in the *earth* and its *inhabitants, en masse;* giving and establishing *laws* by which all things
shall be governed; but it is also *particular;*
it takes in the multitudes of the *isles,* as well
as the vast *continents;* the different *species* as
well as the *genera;* the *individual,* as well as
the *family.* As every *whole* is composed of its
parts, without the smallest of which it could
not be a whole; so all *generals* are composed
of *particulars.* And by the *particular* providence of God, the *general* providence is formed;
he takes care of each *individual;* and, consequently, he takes care of the *whole.* Therefore,
on the *particular* providence of God, the *general*
providence is built; and the *general* providence
could not exist without the *particular,* any
more than a *whole* could subsist independently
of its *parts.* It is by this particular providence
that God governs *the multitude of the isles,*
notices the *fall of a sparrow, bottles* the *tears*
of the mourner, and *numbers the hairs* of his
followers. Now, as God is an infinitely *wise*
and *good* Being, and governs the world in *wisdom* and *goodness,* the *earth* may well *rejoice,*
and *the multitude of the isles be glad.*

Verse 2. *Clouds and darkness are round
about him*] It is granted that this is a subject
which cannot be comprehended. And why?
Because God is *infinite;* he acts from his own
counsels, which are *infinite;* in reference to *ends*
which are also *infinite:* therefore, the *reasons*
of his government cannot be comprehended by
the feeble, limited powers of man. There must
be *clouds and darkness*—an impenetrable obscurity, round about him; and we can no more

A. M. 3489
B. C. 515
A. U. C. 239
Darii I.,
R. Persarum,
anno sexto

3 gA fire goeth before him, and burneth up his enemies round about.

4 hHis lightnings enlightened the world: the earth saw, and trembled.

5 iThe hills melted like wax at the presence of the LORD, at the presence of the LORD of the whole earth.

6 kThe heavens declare his righteousness, and all the people see his glory.

7 lConfounded be all they that serve graven

A. M. 3489
B. C. 515
A. U. C. 239
Darii I.,
R. Persarum,
anno sexto

---

gPsa. xviii. 8; l. 3, Dan. vii. 10; Hab. iii. 5——hExod. xix. 18; Psa. lxxvii. 18; civ. 32

iJudg. v. 5; Mic. i. 4; Nah. i. 5——kPsa. xix. 1; l. 6
lExod. xx. 4; Lev. xxvi. 1; Deut. v. 8; xxvii. 15

---

comprehend him in what is called *æternitas a parte ante*—the eternity that passed before *time* commenced, than we can in the *æternitas a parte post*—the eternity that is to come, when time shall be no more. Yet such a Being cannot but *see* all things *clearly*, and *do* all things *well;* therefore the psalmist properly asserts,—

Righteousness and judgment are *the habitation of his throne.*] *Righteousness*, צדק *tsedek*, the principle that acts according to *justice* and *equity;* that gives to all their *due*, and ever holds in all things an *even balance. And judgment*, משפט *mishpat*, the principle that *discerns*, *orders*, *directs*, and *determines* every thing according to truth and justice: these form *the habitation of his throne;* that is, his government and management of the world are according to these; and though we cannot see the *springs*, the *secret counsels*, and the *times*, which this *omniscient* and *almighty* FATHER must ever have in his own power, yet we may rest assured that all his administration is wise, just, holy, good, and kind. For, although his counsels be inscrutable, and the dispensations of his providence be sometimes apparently unequal, yet righteousness and judgment are the habitation of his throne.

In this most sublime description the psalmist, by the *figure* termed *prosopopœia*, or personification, gives *vitality* and *thought* to all the subjects he employs; here, the very *throne* of God is *animated;* righteousness and judgment are two *intellectual* beings who support it. The *fire*, the *lightnings*, the *earth*, the *heavens* themselves, are all intellectual beings, which either accompany, go before him, or proclaim his majesty.

Verse 3. *A fire goeth before him*] Literally, this and the following verse may refer to the electric fluid, or to manifestations of the Divine displeasure, in which, by means of *ethereal fire*, God consumed his enemies. But *fire* is generally represented as an accompaniment of the appearances of the Supreme Being. He appeared on *Mount Sinai* in the midst of *fire*, *thunder*, and *lightnings*, Exod. xix. 16-18. Daniel, chap. vii. 9, 10, represents the Sovereign Judge as being on a throne which was a *fiery flame*, and the *wheels* of his chariot like *burning fire;* and a *fiery stream* issuing from it, and coming forth from before him. St. *Paul* tells us (2 Thess. i. 8) that the Lord Jesus shall be revealed from heaven with his mighty angels, in *flaming fire;* and St. *Peter*, (2 Epist. iii. 7, 10, 11,) that when the Lord shall come to judgment the heavens and the earth shall be destroyed by *fire*, the heavens shall pass away with a *great noise*, the *elements melt with fervent heat*, and the *earth* and its works be *burnt up.* Here then, will appear,—

"Our God in grandeur, and our world on fire."

Burneth up his enemies round about.] The fire is his pioneer which destroys all the hinderances in his way, and makes him a plain passage.

Verse 4. *His lightnings enlightened the world*] Though this be no more than a majestic description of the coming of the Lord, to confound his enemies and succour his followers, yet *some spiritualize* the passage, and say, the *lightnings* signify the *apostles*, who *enlightened* the world by their heavenly doctrine.

The earth saw, and trembled.] The earth is represented as a sentient being. It saw the terrible majesty of God; and trembled through terror, fearing it should be destroyed on account of the wickedness of its inhabitants.

Verse 5. *The hills melted like wax*] The fire of God seized on and liquefied them, so that they no longer opposed his march; and the mountains before him became a plain.

The Lord of the whole earth.] ארון כל הארץ *adon col haarets*, the Director, Stay, and Support of the whole earth. The universal Governor, whose jurisdiction is not confined to any one place; but who, having created all, governs all that he has made.

Verse 6. *The heavens declare his righteousness*] They also, in this poetic description, become *intelligent* beings, and proclaim the majesty and the mercy of the Most High. Metaphorically, they may be said to declare his glory. Their magnitude, number, revolutions, order, influence, and harmony, proclaim the wondrous skill, matchless wisdom, and unlimited power of the Sovereign of the universe. See the notes on Psalm xix.

And all the people see his glory.] Whatsoever God has made proclaims his eternal power and Godhead; and who, from a contemplation of the work of his hands, can be ignorant of his being and providence?

Verse 7. *Confounded be all they*] Rather, *They shall be confounded that boast themselves in idols.* There is a remarkable play on the letters here, המתהללים *hammithhalelim*, who move like madmen; referring to the violent gestures practised in idolatrous rites.

Of idols] באלילים *baelilim*, in vanities, emptinesses; who "make much ado about nothing," and take a *mad* and *painful* pleasure in *ridiculous* and *unprofitable* ceremonies of religion.

Worship him] WHO? JESUS: so says the apostle, Heb. i. 6. Who will dare to dispute his authority?

All ye gods.] Οἱ αγγελοι αυτου, *his angels:* so the *Septuagint* and the *apostle:* "Let all the angels of God worship him:" and the words are most certainly applied to the Saviour of the world by the author of the Epistle to the Hebrews; see the note there. The *Chaldee* says: "All nations who worship idols shall adore him."

A. M. 3489
B. C. 515
A. U. C. 239
Darii I.,
R. Persarum,
anno sexto
images, that boast themselves of idols: ᵐworship him, all *ye* gods.

8 Zion heard, and was glad; and the daughters of Judah rejoiced because of thy judgments, O LORD.

9 For thou, LORD, *art* ⁿhigh above all the earth: ᵒthou art exalted far above all gods.

10 Ye that love the LORD, ᵖhate evil: �qhe preserveth the souls of his saints; ʳhe delivereth them out of the hand of the wicked.

A. M. 3489
B. C. 515
A. U. C. 239
Darii I.,
R. Persarum,
anno sexto

11 ˢLight is sown for the righteous, and gladness for the upright in heart.

12 ᵗRejoice in the LORD, ye righteous; ᵘand give thanks ᵛat the remembrance of his holiness.

---

mHeb. i. 6——ⁿPsa. lxxxiii. 18——ᵒExod. xviii. 11; Psa. xcv. 4; xcvi. 5——ᵖPsa. xxxiv. 14; xxxvii. 27; ci. 3; Amos v. 15; Rom. xii. 9——qPsa. xxxi. 23; xxxvii. 28; cxlv. 20; Prov. ii. 8

ʳPsalm xxxvii. 39, 40; Daniel iii. 28; vi. 22, 27 ˢJob xxii. 28; Psalm cxii. 4; Proverbs iv. 18——ᵗPsalm xxxiii. 1——ᵘPsalm xxx. 4——ᵛOr, *to the memorial*

Verse 8. *Zion heard, and was glad*] All the land of *Israel*, long desolated, heard of the judgments which God had shown among the enemies of his people.

And the daughters of Judah] All the villages of the land—*Zion* as the mother, and all the *villages* in the country as her *daughters*, rejoice in the deliverance of God's people.

Verse 9. *For thou, Lord,* art *high*] Thou art infinitely exalted above *men* and *angels*.

Verse 10. *Ye that love the Lord, hate evil*] Because it is inconsistent with his love to you, as well as your love to him.

He preserveth the souls of his saints] The *saints,* חסידיו *chasidaiv, his merciful people:* their *souls*—lives, are precious in his sight. He *preserves* them; keeps them from every evil, and every enemy.

Out of the hand of the wicked.] From his *power* and influence.

Verse 11. *Light is sown for the righteous*] The Divine light in the soul of man is a seed which takes root, and springs up and increases *thirty, sixty,* and *a hundred* fold. *Gladness* is also a seed: it is *sown,* and, if carefully improved and cultivated, will also multiply itself into *thousands.* Every grace of God is a *seed,* which he intends should produce a *thousand* fold in the hearts of genuine believers. We do not so much require *more* grace from God, as the *cultivation* of what we have received. God will not give more, unless we improve what we have got. Remember *the parable of the talents.* Let the *light* and *gladness* be faithfully cultivated, and they will multiply themselves till the whole body shall be full of light, and the whole soul full of happiness. But it is the *righteous* only for whom the *light* is sown; and the *upright in heart* alone for whom the *gladness* is sown.

The words may also signify that, however *distressed* or *persecuted* the *righteous* and the *upright* may be, it shall not be always so. As surely as the *grain* that is sown in the earth shall vegetate, and bring forth its proper fruit in its season, so surely shall *light*—prosperity, and *gladness*—comfort and peace, be communicated to them. They also will *spring up* in due time.

Verse 12. *Rejoice in the Lord, ye righteous*] It is your privilege to be *happy.* Exult in him through whom ye have received the atonement. *Rejoice;* but let it be *in the Lord.* All other joy is the *mirth of fools,* which is as the *crackling of thorns under a pot*—it is a luminous blaze for a moment, and leaves nothing but smoke and ashes behind.

At the remembrance of his holiness.] But

why should you give thanks at the remembrance that God is holy? Because he has said, *Be ye holy; for I am holy:* and in *holiness* alone true *happiness* is to be found. *As he, therefore, who hath called you is holy; so be ye holy in all manner of conversation.* False Christians hate the doctrine of Christian holiness; they are willing to be holy in another, but not holy in themselves. There is too much cross-bearing and self-denial in the doctrine of holiness for them. A perfect heart they neither expect nor wish.

The analysis considers the whole Psalm as relating to Jesus Christ and the last judgment: so it was understood by several of the ancient fathers. The reader may take it in either sense.

ANALYSIS OF THE NINETY-SEVENTH PSALM

There are *three* parts in this Psalm, if we interpret it as referring to our blessed Lord:—

I. A *prophetical* description of his power and glory, especially at the *day of judgment,* ver. 1-6.

II. A manifest difference between the states of idolaters and the people of God, ver. 7-9.

III. An exhortation to love God and hate evil; and the reason on which it is founded: a two-fold gracious reward, ver. 10-12.

I. The psalmist begins with a solemn acclamation: "The Lord reigneth." He is the supreme King; and he will use his kingly power both now and in the day of judgment. 1. For the good of his subjects. 2. For the confusion of his enemies.

1. For "clouds and darkness are round about him," as when he gave the law on Mount Sinai. 2. "Righteousness and judgment are the habitation of his throne;" and therefore a just sentence shall come forth *against* his *enemies,* and in *behalf* of his *friends,* ver. 2-5. 3. His appearance shall be very glorious; for the "heavens shall declare it, and all people shall see it," ver. 6.

II. The difference between the state of idolaters and the people of God.

1. *Confusion* and a *curse* shall fall upon the *former:* "They shall be confounded," &c., ver. 7.

2. He exhorts all in power, men—*magistrates,* &c., and all who excel in strength—*angels,* to worship him: "Worship him, all ye gods," ver. 7. All confidence should be reposed in him.

3. God's people rejoice when they find that it is their own Lord who is coming to judgment:

"Zion heard, and was glad; the daughters of Judah rejoiced," ver. 8.

4. And they rejoiced chiefly in knowing that their God "was high above all the earth, and exalted far above all gods," ver. 9.

III. The *expostulation*, which gives us the *character* by which God's people may be known. He exhorts them to *love God, and to hate evil.* Hence we see that the true followers of God, 1. Love him; 2. Hate evil, as the infallible consequence of loving him, ver. 10.

He shows them the gracious reward which God promises.

1. "He preserveth the souls of his saints." Often their *lives*, in an especial manner, are *preserved* by him; but always their *souls.* The accuser of the brethren shall not hurt them.

2. "He delivereth them out of the hands of the wicked." Sometimes out of their hand, that they fall not into it; and sometimes out of their hand, when they are in it. This is their *first* reward, ver. 10.

A *second* reward is in the next verse: that in their miseries they shall be filled with spiritual happiness, when perhaps they little expect it: "Light is sown for the righteous, and gladness for the upright in heart," ver. 11.

1. By *light* we may understand a peculiar manifestation of God's favour; comfort, peace, and joy; or deliverance from their spiritual and temporal oppressors.

2. This is *sown* as a seed. For the light of comfort, of peace of conscience, and joy in the Holy Spirit, though it may be clouded in times of heaviness, through manifold temptations, yet it will spring forth again, like the corn, which, after it is sown, lies hidden for some time, under the clods of the earth; yet all that time it is *vegetating* and coming forth to public view. And deliverance from their enemies, though slow, will come; though the rod of the wicked *come* into the lot of the just, it shall not *rest* there.

3. From these premises the psalmist draws this conclusion: Since God is preparing those blessings for you that fear and love him, then, 1. "Rejoice in the Lord;" glory in him as the Fountain of your blessedness. 2. "Give thanks at the remembrance of his holiness." Remember the good he has done you, the grace he has bestowed on you, and the holiness you may yet receive from him; and rejoice in the encouragement, and give thanks. Rejoice that ye may be *holy*, for in that your *happiness* consists.

PSALM XCVIII

God is celebrated for his wondrous works, 1, 2; for the exact fulfilment of his gracious promises, 3. The manner in which he is to be praised, 4–6. Inanimate creation called to bear a part in this concert, 7, 8. The justice of his judgments, 9.

XIX. DAY. EVENING PRAYER

A Psalm

A. M. 3489
B. C. 515
A. U. C. 239
Darii I.,
R. Persarum,
anno sexto

O ªSING unto the Lord a new song, for ᵇhe hath done marvellous things: ᶜhis right hand, and his holy arm hath gotten him the victory.

2 ᵈThe Lord hath made known his salva-tion: ᵉhis righteousness hath he ᶠopenly showed in the sight of the heathen.

3 He hath ᵍremembered his mercy and his truth toward the house of Israel: ʰall the ends of the earth have seen the salvation of our God.

4 ¹Make a joyful noise unto the Lord, all

A. M. 3489
B. C. 515
A. U. C. 239
Darii I.,
R. Persarum,
anno sexto

ªPsa. xxxiii. 3; xcvi. 1; Isa. xlii. 10——ᵇExod. xv. 11; Psa. lxxvii. 16; lxxxvi. 10; cv. 5; cxxxvi. 4; cxxxix. 14 ᶜExod. xv. 6; Isa. lix. 16; lxiii. 5——ᵈIsa. lii. 10; Luke ii. 30, 31

ᵉIsaiah lxii. 2; Romans iii. 25, 26——ᶠOr, *revealed* ᵍLuke i. 54, 55, 72——ʰIsa. xlix. 6; lii. 10; Luke ii. 30, 31; iii. 6; Acts xiii. 47; xxviii. 28——¹Psalm xcv. 1; c. 1

NOTES ON PSALM XCVIII

In the *Hebrew* this is simply termed מזמור *mizmor*, a Psalm. In the *Chaldee, A prophetic Psalm.* In the *Vulgate, Septuagint, Æthiopic, A Psalm of David.* In the *Syriac* it is attributed to *David*, and stated to be composed concerning the "Restoration of the Israelites from Egypt; but is to be understood spiritually of the advent of the Messiah, and the vocation of the Gentiles to the Christian faith."

The Psalm in its subject is very like the *ninety-sixth.* It was probably written to celebrate the deliverance from the Babylonish captivity; but is to be understood prophetically of the redemption of the world by Jesus Christ.

Verse 1. *A new song*] A song of *excellence.* Give him the *highest* praise. See on Psa. xcvi. 1.

Hath done marvellous things] נפלאות *niphlaoth*, "miracles;" the same word as in Psa. xcvi. 3, where we translate it *wonders.*

His holy arm] His Almighty power,—

Hath gotten him the victory.] הושיעה לו *hoshiah llo*, "hath made salvation to himself."

Verse 2. *Made known his salvation*] He has delivered his people in such a way as to show that it was supernatural, and that their confidence in the unseen God was not in vain.

Verse 3. *He hath remembered his mercy*] His gracious promises to their forefathers.

A. M. 3489
B. C. 515
A. U. C. 239
Darii I.,
R. Persarum,
anno sexto

the earth: make a loud noise, and rejoice, and sing praise.

5 Sing unto the LORD with the harp; with the harp, and the voice of a psalm.

6 ᵏWith trumpets, and sound of cornet, make a joyful noise before the LORD the King.

7 ¹Let the sea roar, and the fulness thereof; the world, and they that dwell therein.

8 Let the floods ᵐclap *their* hands: let the hills be joyful together.

9 Before the LORD; ⁿfor he cometh to judge the earth: with righteousness shall he judge the world, and the people with equity.

A. M. 3489
B. C. 515
A. U. C. 239
Darii I.,
R. Persarum,
anno sexto

ᵏNumbers x. 10; 1 Chronicles xv. 28; 2 Chronicles xxix. 27

¹Psalm xcvi. 11, &c.——ᵐIsaiah lv. 12——ⁿPsalm xcvi. 10, 13

And his truth] Faithfully accomplishing what he had promised. All this was fulfilled under the Gospel.

Verse 5. *With—the voice of a Psalm.*] I think זמרה *zimrah*, which we translate *Psalm*, means either a *musical instrument*, or a *species of ode* modulated by different voices.

Verse 6. *With trumpets*] חצצרות *chatsotseroth*. Some kind of tubular instruments, of the form and management of which we know nothing.

And sound of cornet] שופר *shophar*, the word commonly used for what we call *trumpet*.

Verse 7. *Let the sea roar*] These are either fine poetic images; or, if we take them as referring to the promulgation of the Gospel, by the *sea* all maritime countries and commercial nations may be intended.

Verse 8. *Let the floods clap their hands*] נהרות *neharoth*, properly *the rivers*—possibly meaning immense *continents*, where only *large rivers* are found; thus including *inland* people, as well as *maritime nations*, and those on the sea-coasts generally; as in those early times little more than the *coasts* of the sea were known. The Gospel shall be preached in the most secluded nations of the world.

Let the hills be joyful] All the inhabitants of *rocky* and *mountainous* countries.

Verse 9. *For he cometh to judge the earth*] He comes to make known his salvation, and show his merciful designs to all the children of men.

With righteousness shall he judge the world] His word shall not be confined; all shall know him, from the least to the greatest: he shall show that he is loving to every man, and hateth nothing that he hath made. See the notes on Psa. xcvi. There is a very great similarity between this Psalm and the Song or *Magnificat* of the Blessed Virgin. I shall note some of the parallels, chiefly from Bishop Nicholson.

This Psalm is an evident prophecy of Christ's coming to save the world; and what is here *foretold* by David is, in the Blessed *Virgin's* song, chanted forth as being *accomplished.* David is the *Voice*, and Mary is the *Echo.*

1. DAVID. "O sing unto the Lord a new song." (The *Voice.*)
    MARY. "My soul doth magnify the Lord." (The *Echo.*)
2. DAVID. "He hath done marvellous things." (The *Voice.*)
    MARY. "He that is mighty hath done great things." (The *Echo.*)
3. DAVID. "With his own right hand and holy arm hath he gotten himself the victory." (The *Voice.*)

    MARY. "He hath showed strength with his arm and scattered the proud in the imagination of their hearts." (The *Echo.*)
4. DAVID. "The Lord hath made known his salvation; his righteousness hath he openly showed," &c. (The *Voice.*)
    MARY. "His mercy is on them that fear him, from generation to generation." (The *Echo.*)
5. DAVID. "He hath remembered his mercy and his truth toward the house of Israel." (The *Voice.*)
    MARY. "He hath holpen his servant Israel, in remembrance of his mercy." (The *Echo.*)

These parallels are very striking; and it seems as if Mary had this Psalm in her eye when she composed her song of triumph. And this is a farther argument that the whole Psalm, whether it record the deliverance of Israel from Egypt, or the Jews from the Babylonish captivity, is yet to be ultimately understood of the redemption of the world by Jesus Christ, and the proclamation of his Gospel through all the nations of the earth: and taken in this view, no language can be too strong, nor poetic imagery too high, to point out the unsearchable riches of Christ.

ANALYSIS OF THE NINETY-EIGHTH PSALM

This Psalm has the *two* following parts:—

I. An *exhortation* to sing to the Lord, and the *reasons* of it, ver. 1-3.

II. A *new invitation* to praise him, and that it be *universal*, ver. 4-9.

I. He calls upon them to praise God: 1. *Sing*—a *song* or hymn, to *the Lord*—and to none other. A *new song*—a song of excellency.

For this exhortation and command he gives the reasons. His work was a work of power and holiness.

1. "He hath done marvellous things." He has opened his greatness and goodness in the work of redemption. What *marvels* has not Christ done? 1. He was conceived by the Holy Ghost. 2. Born of a virgin. 3. Healed all manner of diseases. 4. Fed thousands with a few loaves and fishes. 5. Raised the dead. 6. And what was more *marvellous*, died himself. 7. Rose again by his own power. 8. Ascended to heaven. 9. Sent down the Holy Ghost. 10. And made his apostles and their testimony the instruments of enlightening, and ultimately converting, the world.

2. "His right hand and his holy arm hath got him the victory." 1. It was all *his own work*, whatever were the *instruments;* for without his energy they could do nothing. 2. It was his *holy arm*—no *bloody sword*, but a *holy hand*, to do a *holy work*. 3. "He got himself the victory" over *sin, Satan, death,* and *hell*.

3. This salvation was *made known:*—1. By *himself* to the *Jews*. 2. By his *apostles* to *all nations*.

4. This salvation has been *applied*. 1. He hath showed his *righteousness*—his method of *justifying sinners* through his own blood, and *sanctifying* them by his own Spirit. 2. This he hath *openly* showed, plainly revealing the whole in his Gospel. 3. He has done this in the *sight of the heathen*, calling them to be partakers of the same salvation promised to Abraham and to his posterity, both *Jews* and *Gentiles*.

5. That which moved him to do this; his *mercy*, and *truth:* 1. "He hath remembered his mercy." This mercy was to the *house of Israel*, and through them to the *Gentiles;* for the Gentiles were the *first* in the promise and covenant. There was no *Jew* when the covenant was made with Abraham: it was made with him while he was yet in uncircumcision; consequently the *Gentiles*, the *whole human race*, were originally included in that covenant. The descendants of Jacob were made depositaries of it for a season; but they, not having benefited by it, were rejected, and the salvation of Christ was given to the Gentiles, for whom it was originally intended, and who have kept the faith, and are daily profiting by it. 2. It is called *mercy;* for it was the merest mercy that said: "The seed of the woman shall bruise the serpent's head." 3. He *remembered* this; it was never out of the Divine mind; "Jesus was the Lamb slain from the foundation of the world." 4. As this mercy was intended for every human soul; so it is here *prophetically* said: "All the ends of the earth have seen the salvation of our God." This Gospel has been preached, is now in the course of being preached, and shortly will be preached to every people under heaven.

II. A new invitation to praise God; and to do this in every possible way.

1. "Make a joyful noise." Jump for joy, because of this most glorious news.

2. As *all* are interested in it, so let *all* do it: "All the earth."

3. In all possible ways. With *harp, psaltery, trumpet, cornet;* with *vocal, chordal,* and *pneumatic* music. But it is the *joyful* music, the *heart* music, which the Lord seeks.

4. "Before the Lord." In his immediate presence. Let all be sincere, pure, and holy. Remember the eye of the Lord is upon you: do not draw near with your *lips, pipes,* or *stringed* instruments, while your *hearts* are far from him.

5. And to make the music full, as if the inanimate creation had *ears* and *hands* to give an *applause* at the relation, and *feet* to *dance* because of it, he says: "Let the sea roar, the floods clap their hands, and the hills be joyful together."

And for all this he gives a reason, with which he concludes: "For he cometh to judge the earth;" which may be referred to his *first* and *second* coming.

1. If to the *first*, then the sense is—Let all creatures rejoice because he comes to *judge*, that is, to enlighten, order, and govern the world. For this purpose he was incarnated, suffered, died, and rose again for the redemption of mankind; and has sent his holy *Gospel* to enlighten the world, and his *Spirit* to apply its truths to the hearts of men.

2. If we consider this as referring to his *last coming*, then let all men rejoice, as he comes to destroy evil, to root out incorrigible sinners, and to make a new heaven and a new earth.

3. All this shall be done with that rectitude of judgment, that there shall be nothing crooked, oblique, or savouring of iniquity in it: "For he shall judge the world, and the people with equity."

PSALM XCIX

The empire of God in the world and the Church, 1, 2. He ought to be praised, 3. Justice and judgment are his chief glory, 4. He should be worshipped as among the saints of old, whom he graciously answered and saved, 5–8. Exalt him because he is holy, 9.

A. M. cir. 3489
B. C. cir. 515
A. U. C. 239
Darii I.,
R. Persarum,
anno sexto

THE [a]LORD reigneth; let the people tremble: [b]he sitteth *between* the cherubims; let the earth [c]be moved.

2 The LORD *is* great in Zion; and he *is* [d]high above all the people.

A. M. 3489
B. C. 515
A. U. C. 239
Darii I.,
R. Persarum,
anno sexto

3 Let them praise [e]thy great

---

[a]Psalm xciii. 1——[b]Exodus xxv. 22; Psalm xviii. 10; lxxx. 1

[c]Heb. *stagger*——[d]Psa. xcvii. 9——[e]Deut. xxviii. 58; Rev. xv. 4

NOTES ON PSALM XCIX

The *Hebrew* and *Chaldee* have no *title;* all the *versions* but the *Chaldee* attribute it to *David*. The *Syriac* says it concerns "the slaughter of the Midianites which Moses and the children of Israel had taken captive; and is a prophecy concerning the glory of the kingdom of Christ." But the mention of *Samuel* shows that it cannot be referred to the time of *Moses*. *Calmet* thinks that it was sung at the dedication of the city, or of the second temple, after the return from the Babylonish captivity. Eight of *Kennicott's* and *De Rossi's* MSS. join it to the preceding psalm.

Verse 1. The Lord reigneth] See the note on Psa. xcvii. 1.

Let the people tremble] He will establish his kingdom in spite of his enemies; let those who oppose him tremble for the consequences.

He sitteth between *the cherubims*] This is in reference to the *ark*, at each end of which was a

A. M. 3489
B. C. 515
A. U. C. 239
Darii I.,
R. Persarum,
anno sexto

and terrible name; *for it is* holy.

4 [t]The king's strength also loveth judgment; thou dost establish equity, thou executest judgment and righteousness in Jacob.

5 [g]Exalt ye the LORD our God, and worship at [h]his footstool; *for* [i]he [k]*is* holy.

6 [l]Moses and Aaron among his priests, and Samuel among them that call upon his name;

they [m]called upon the LORD, and he answered them.

7 [n]He spake unto them in the cloudy pillar: they kept his testimonies, and the ordinance *that* he gave them.

8 Thou answeredst them, O LORD our God: [o]thou wast a God that forgavest them, though [p]thou tookest vengeance of their inventions.

9 [q]Exalt the LORD our God, and worship at his holy hill; for the LORD our God *is* [r]holy.

A. M. 3489
B. C. 515
A. U. C. 239
Darii I.,
R. Persarum,
anno sexto

---

[t]Job xxxvi. 5, 6, 7——[g]Verse 9——[h]1 Chronicles xxviii. 2; Psalm cxxxii. 7——[i]Or, *it is holy*——[k]Leviticus xix. 2——[l]Exodus xvii. 4; 1 Samuel vii. 9; Jeremiah xv. 1——[m]Exodus xiv. 15; xv. 25; 1 Samuel vii. 9; xii. 18——[n]Exodus xxxiii. 9

[o]Num. xiv. 20; Jer. xlvi. 28; Zeph. iii. 7——[p]See Exod. xxxii. 2, &c.; Num. xx. 12, 24; Deut. ix. 20 [q]Ver. 5; Exod. xv. 2; Psa. xxxiv. 3; cxviii. 28——[r]Lev. xxi. 8; 1 Sam. ii. 2; Psa. xxii. 3; cxlv. 17; Isa. vi. 3; John xvii. 11

---

cherub of glory; and the *shechinah*, or symbol of the Divine Presence, appeared on the lid of the ark, called also the *mercy-seat*, between the cherubim. *Sitting between the cherubim* implies God's *graciousness* and *mercy*. While then, in his reign, he was terrible to sinners, he is on the *throne of grace* to all who fear, love, and obey him. Though this *symbol* were not in the *second* temple, yet the Divine Being might very well be thus denominated, because it had become one of his titles, he having thus appeared under the *tabernacle* and *first temple*.

Verse 2. *The Lord is great in Zion*] It is among his own worshippers that he has manifested his *power* and *glory* in an especial manner. *There* he is known, and *there* he is worthily magnified.

Verse 3. *Let them praise thy great and terrible name*] Let them confess thee to be great and terrible: let them tremble before thee.

For *it is holy*.] קדוש הוא *kadosh hu*. As this not only ends this verse but the *fifth* also, and in effect the *ninth*, it seems to be a species of *chorus* which was sung in a very solemn manner at the conclusion of each of these parts. His *holiness*—the immaculate purity of his nature, was the reason why he should be exalted, praised, and worshipped.

Verse 4. *The king's strength*] If this Psalm were written by David, he must mean by it that he was God's *vicegerent* or *deputy*, and that, even as king, God was *his* strength, and the *pattern* according to which equity, judgment, and righteousness should be executed in Jacob.

Verse 5. *Worship at his footstool*] Probably meaning the *ark* on which the Divine glory was manifested. Sometimes the *earth* is called God's *footstool*, Matt. v. 35, Isa. lxvi. 1; sometimes *Jerusalem;* sometimes the *temple*, Lam. ii. 1; sometimes the *tabernacle*, Psa. xxxii. 7; and sometimes the *ark*, 1 Chron. xxviii. 2. The Israelites, when they worshipped, turned their faces toward the *ark*, because that was the place where was the symbol of the Divine Presence.

For *he is holy*.] The burden chanted by the *chorus*.

Verse 6. *Moses and Aaron*] As Moses and Aaron among the priests, and as Samuel among the prophets, worshipped God in humility, gratitude, and the spirit of obedience, and received the strongest tokens of the Divine favour; so worship ye the Lord, that he may bless, support, and save you. Moses was properly the priest

of the Hebrews before Aaron and his family were appointed to that office.

Verse 7. *He spake unto them in the cloudy pillar*] That is, he directed all their operations, marchings, and encampments by this cloudy pillar. See Exod. xxxiii. 9.

They kept his testimonies] Do ye the same, and God will be *your* portion as he was *theirs*.

Verse 8. *Thou—forgavest them*] When the people had sinned, and wrath was about to descend on them, Moses and Aaron interceded for them, and they were not destroyed.

Tookest vengeance of their inventions.] God spared them, but showed his displeasure at their misdoings. He chastised, but did not consume them. This is amply proved in the history of this people.

Verse 9. *Worship at his holy hill*] Worship him *publicly* in the *temple*.

For the Lord our God is holy.] The words of the *chorus;* as in the *third* and *fifth* verses.

ANALYSIS OF THE NINETY-NINTH PSALM

There are *two* parts in this Psalm:—

I. A description of the kingdom of God.

1. From the *majesty* and *terror* of it against his enemies, ver. 1-3.

2. From its *equity* in the execution of *judgment* and *justice*, ver. 4.

3. From his *patience* and *clemency* in giving audience to his servants, ver. 6-8.

II. A demand of praise and honour of all that acknowledge him for their King, begun at the *third* verse, repeated at the *fifth*, and continued in the *last*. The Psalm contains a prophecy of the kingdom of Christ, and its glory.

I. 1. The terror, power, and majesty of this kingdom: "The Lord reigneth." 1. He bids defiance to his enemies: "Let the people tremble." 2. "He sitteth between the cherubim." He is always present with his people; they need not fear, though *the earth be moved*. 3. "He is great in Zion." More potent and higher than all people. 4. "His name is great and terrible." His *enemies* have every thing to *fear*, while his *friends* have every thing to *hope*.

2. The psalmist describes this kingdom, from its *justice* and *equity*. 1. "He loveth judgment." This is one of his perfections. 2. "He establishes equity." Gives just and equal laws to all. 3. "He executes judgment in Jacob." None of his followers shall live without law; they are obedient children, living according to his will. 4. And therefore he requires them to *exalt and*

adore him. 5. They are to *worship at his footstool*—all their approaches are to be made in the *deepest reverence*, with the *truest self-abasement*. 6. "For he is holy;" and he requires all his followers to be holy also.

3. He describes it from the *mercy* and *clemency* of the ruler. 1. He showed his mercy and kindness to *Moses, Aaron*, and *Samuel*, as intercessors for the people. "They called upon God," for themselves and for the people; "and he answered them." 1. See the intercession of Moses, Exod. xxxii. 31; 2. Of *Aaron*, Num. xvi. 46-48. 3. Of *Samuel*, 1 Sam. vii. 5, 9, 10. 4. He spake to *Moses*, Exod. xxxiii. 8, 9, 11; and to *Aaron*, Num. xii. 5-8.

And now he adds the *reason* why he heard them:—
1. "They kept his testimonies." Those precepts that were common to all others.
2. "And the ordinances that he gave them." As public persons who were to rule in Church and state.

And that it was a great mercy that the Lord heard them, the prophet acknowledges by this *apostrophe*—
1. "Thou answeredst them, O Lord our God." Which the history shows.

2. "Thou forgavest them;" that is, the *people* for whom they prayed: for in Hebrew the *relative* is often put without an *antecedent*.
3. "Thou tookest vengeance of their inventions." The *golden calf* was broken to pieces, Exod. xxxii.; and the *false gods* were put away, 1 Sam. vii. The people were not consumed, though their sin was in a certain manner visited upon them. See Num. xiv. 23, 30, and xx. 12.

II. The psalmist concludes with a *demand of praise* to this kind God.
1. "Exalt the Lord." Show that he is high, holy, just, good, and kind.
2. "Worship at his holy hill." Attend his public worship, and show a godly example in this way to all others. He who is indifferent about the *public worship* of God is generally not less so in *private devotion*.
3. The reason for all this is: "The Lord our God is holy." He requires this worship because it is a chief *means* by which he communicates *his holiness* to his followers. Without this holiness there is no happiness here, and without it none shall ever see God. Get *holiness*, that you may get happiness *here*, and heaven *hereafter*.

PSALM C

All nations are exhorted to praise the Lord, 1, 2; to acknowledge him to be the Sovereign God and their Creator, and that they are his people and the flock of his pasture, 3; to worship him publicly, and be grateful for his mercies, 4. The reasons on which this is founded; his own goodness, his everlasting mercy, and his ever-during truth, 5.

[a]A Psalm of [b]Praise

A. M. 3489
B. C. 515
A. U. C. 239
Darii I.,
R. Persarum,
anno sexto

MAKE [c]a joyful noise unto the LORD, [d]all ye lands.

2 Serve the LORD with gladness: come before his presence with singing.

3 Know ye that the LORD he *is* God: [e]*it is* he *that* hath made us, [f]and. not we ourselves; [g]*we are* his peo-

A. M. 3489
B. C. 515
A. U. C. 239
Darii I.,
R. Persarum,
anno sexto

[a]Psa. cxlv. title——[b]Or, *thanksgiving*——[c]Psa. xcv. 1; xcviii. 4——[d]Heb. *all the earth*

[e]Psa. cxix. 73; cxxxix. 13, &c.; cxlix. 2; Eph. ii. 10
[f]Or, *and his we are*——[g]Psa. xcv. 7; Ezek. xxxiv. 30, 31

NOTES ON PSALM C

This Psalm is entitled in the Hebrew מזמור לתודה *mizmor lethodah*, not "A Psalm of Praise," as we have it, but "A Psalm for the confession, or *for the confession-offering*," very properly translated by the Chaldee: שבחא על קורבן תודתא *shibcha al kurban todetha*, "Praise for the sacrifice (or *offering*) of confession." The *Vulgate, Septuagint*, and *Æthiopic* have followed this sense. The Arabic attributes it to *David*. The Syriac has the following prefixed: "Without a name. Concerning Joshua the son of Nun, when he had ended the war with the Ammonites: but in the new covenant it relates to the conversion of the Gentiles to the faith." It is likely that it was composed after the captivity, as a form of thanksgiving to God for that great deliverance, as well as an inducement to the people to consecrate themselves to him, and to be exact in the performance of the acts of public worship.

Verse 1. *Make a joyful noise*] הריעו *hariu*, exult, triumph, leap for joy.

All ye lands.] Not only Jews, but Gentiles,

for the Lord bestows his benefits on all with a liberal hand.

Verse 2. *Serve the Lord with gladness*] It is your privilege and duty to be happy in your religious worship. The religion of the true God is intended to remove human misery, and to make mankind happy. He whom the religion of Christ has not made happy does not understand that religion, or does not make a proper use of it.

Verse 3. *Know ye that the Lord he is God*] Acknowledge in every possible way, both in public and private, that Jehovah, the uncreated, self-existent, and eternal Being, is *Elohim*, the God who is in covenant with man, to instruct, redeem, love, and make him finally happy.

It is *he that hath made us*] He is our *Creator* and has consequently the only right in and over us.

And not we ourselves] ולא אנחנו *velo anachnu*. I can never think that this is the true reading, though found in the present Hebrew text, in the *Vulgate, Septuagint, Æthiopic*, and *Syriac*. Was there ever a people on earth, however grossly heathenish, that did believe, or could believe, that *they had made themselves?*

A. M. 3489
B. C. 515
A. U. C. 239
Darii I.,
R. Persarum,
anno sexto

ple, and the sheep of his pasture.

4 [h]Enter into his gates with thanksgiving, *and* into his courts with praise: be thankful unto him, *and* bless his name.

5 For the LORD *is* good; [i]his mercy *is* everlasting; and his truth endureth [k]to all generations.

A. M. 3489
B. C. 515
A. U. C. 239
Darii I.,
R. Persarum,
anno sexto

---

[h]Psa. lxvi. 13; cxvi. 17, 18, 19——[i]Psa. cxxxvi. 1, &c.

[k]Heb. *to generation and generation;* Psa. lxxxix. 1

In *twenty-six* of *Kennicott's* and *De Rossi's* MSS. we have ולו אנחנו *velo anachnu,* "and HIS we are;" לו *lo,* the pronoun, being put for לא *lo,* the *negative* particle. This is the reading of the *Targum,* or Chaldee paraphrase, ודיליה אנחנא *vedileyh anachna,* "and his we are," and is the reading of the text in the Complutensian Polyglot, of both the Psalters which were printed in 1477, and is the *keri,* or marginal reading in most Masoretic Bibles. Every person must see, from the nature of the subject that it is the genuine reading. The position is founded on the maxim that what a man invents, constructs out of his own materials, without assistance in genius, materials or execution from any other person, is HIS OWN; and to it, its use, and produce, he has the only right. *God made us;* therefore *we are* HIS: we are his people, and should acknowledge him for our God; we are the sheep of his pasture, and should devote the lives to him constantly which he continually supports.

Verse 4. *Enter into his gates with thanksgiving*] Publicly worship God; and when ye come to the house of prayer, be thankful that you have such a privilege; and when you *enter his courts,* praise him for the permission. The word בתודה *bethodah,* which we render *with thanksgiving,* is properly *with the confession-offering* or *sacrifice.* See on the *title.*

Bless his name.] Bless *Jehovah,* that he is your *Elohim;* see ver. 3. In our liturgic service we say, "Speak good of his name;" we cannot do otherwise; we have nothing *but good* to speak of our God.

Verse 5. *For the Lord is good*] GOODNESS, the perfect, eternal opposition to all *badness* and *evil,* is essential to God. *Mercy* and *compassion* are modifications of his *goodness;* and as his *nature* is *eternal,* so his *mercy,* springing from his *goodness,* must be *everlasting.* And as TRUTH is an essential characteristic of an infinitely intelligent and perfect nature; therefore *God's truth* must endure *from generation to generation.* Whatsoever he has *promised* must be fulfilled, through all the successive generations of men, as long as sun and moon shall last.

As this is a very important Psalm, and has long made a part of our *public worship,* I shall lay it before the reader in the oldest vernacular Versions I have hitherto met with,—the *Anglo-Saxon* and the *Anglo-Scottish,* with a literal interlineary translation of the former.

The Anglo-Saxon Hundredth Psalm

Rhyme ye the Lord all earth, serve the Lord in
1. Iꝺꞃymeꝺ ꝺꞃihtne, eall eoꞃꝺe, ꝺeoꝼiaꝺ ꝺꞃihtne on

bliss;
bliꞃꞃe;

Infare in sight his in blithness;
2. Inꝼanaꝺ on ᵹeꞃyhꝺe hyꞃ on bliꝺnyꞃꞃe;

Wit ye, for that Lord he is God, he did us
3. Wiꞇaꝺᵹe ꝼoꝛꝺonꝺe ꝺꞃihꞇen he iꞃ Loꝺ, he ꝺyꝺe Uꞃ, *& not self we;*
ꞡ na ꞃelꝼe ꝼe;

Folk his & sheep leeseway his; fare into gates his in
4. Folc hiꞃ ꞡ ꞃceap læꞃꝼe hiꞃ, inꝼanaꝺ ᵹaꞇu hiꞃ on *confession, into courts is in hymns, confess*
anꝺeꞇnyꞃꞃe. on caꝼenꞇunaꞃ, hiꞃ on ymnum anꝺeꞇꞇaꝺ *him.*
him;

Praise name his, for that winsom is; Lord thro'
5. Ꝺeꞃiaꝺ naman hiꞃ ꝼoꝛꝺonꝺe ꝼinꞃom iꞃ; ꝺꞃihꞇ on *eternity mildheartedness his, & unto on kindred & kindred*
ecnyꞃꞃe milꝺheoꞃꞇnyꞃꞃa hiꞃ ꞡ oꝺ on cynꝼine ꞡ cynꝼine *sothfastnes his*
ꞃoꝺꝼæꞃꞇnyꞃ hiꞃ.

The reader will see that, in order to make this translation as literal as possible, I have preserved some old English words which we had from the Anglo-Saxon, and which have nearly become obsolete: e. g., *Infare,* "to go in;" *blithness,* "joy, exultation;" *wit ye,* "know ye;" *did,* the preterite of *to do,* "made, created," the literal translation of the Hebrew, עשה *asah, he made; leeseway,* "pasturage on a common;" *winsom,* "cheerful, merry;" *mildheartedness,* "tenderness of heart, compassion;" *sothfastness,* "steady to the sooth or truth, fast to truth."

I might have noticed some various readings in Anglo-Saxon MSS.; e. g., ver. 1. for ꞃꝺꞃymeꝺ *idrymeth,* "rhyme ye;" ꝼinꞃumiaꝺ *winsumiath,* "be winsom, be joyful." And ver. 5, for ꝼinꞃum *winsom,* "cheerful;" ꞃꝼeꞇe, *swete,* "sweet."

Anglo-Scottish Version of the Hundredth Psalm

1. Joyes to God al þe erth; serves to Lord in gladnes.
2. Enters in his sight with joying.
3. Wittes for Lorde he is God; he made us and nogt we;
4. Folke of hym, and schepe of his pasture; enters þe gates of him in schrift; hys Halles in ympnys; schryves to hym.
5. Loues his name, for soft is Lorde; withouten end in his mercy; and in generation and generation þe sothfastnes of hym.

Thus our forefathers *said* and *sung* in heart and mouth and with their tongues made confession to salvation. There are but few words here which require explanation: Ver. 3, *Wittes,* "wot ye, know ye." Ver. 4, *Schrift,* "confession;" *schryves,* "confess ye." Ver. 5, *Loues,* "praise ye, laud ye." *Sothfastness,* as above, steadfastness in the truth.

ANALYSIS OF THE HUNDREDTH PSALM

There are *two* parts in this Psalm:—
I. An *exhortation* to praise God, and the manner in which it is to be done, ver. 1-4.

II. The *reasons* on which this is founded, ver. 3-5.

I. In his exhortation to praise God it is required,—

1. That the praise be *universal:* "All ye lands."

2. That it be *hearty:* "Make a joyful noise." Let the soul be cheerful in the work.

3. That it be not *partial* nor restrained: "Make a joyful noise—serve—be glad—sing—be thankful—give praise—bless his name." The various expressions show the completeness of this blessed word.

4. That it be sincere—done in *his presence.*

5. That it be an *intelligent* service: "Know ye."

6. That it be *frequent* and *public:* "Enter his gates—go into his courts."

7. That *gratitude* shall be a part of it: "With thanksgiving."

II. The *reasons* on which this is grounded; they are,—

1. Drawn from the *nature* of God: "Know ye that Jehovah is Elohim," the true God; therefore, alone worthy to be worshipped.

2. Drawn from the *benefits* bestowed on us:

1. "He has made us"—capable of knowing him, and being eternally happy with him. 2. He has called upon us by his *grace* to be "his people, and the sheep of his pasture." He both *governs* and *feeds* us.

And that we may be the more cheerful in this work he puts us in mind of the Divine *attributes* engaged in our redemption, *goodness, mercy,* and *truth.*

1. "He is good." This is his very *nature.*

2. "He is merciful." This *flows* from his *goodness.*

3. "He is true;" keeping covenant for ever with them that fear him; and *fulfilling* all his *promises* to the believing and obedient.

And that we may have the more confidence,

1. "His mercy is everlasting." It *continues* through all the changes and chances of this life to them who trust in him; and extends through all the generations of men.

2. His truth is like his mercy, it is pledged to fulfil his promises. "God is not man that he should lie;" he has promised, and will save to the uttermost all who come to him through Christ Jesus: "Be therefore thankful to him, and speak good of his name."

PSALM CI

The subject proposed, mercy and judgment, 1. The psalmist's resolution in respect to his private conduct, 2. He will put away evil, inward and outward, 3. No evil person shall stand in his presence, 4; nor any slanderer of his neighbour, 4, 5. He will encourage the faithful and upright, 6; but the deceitful, the liars, and the profligate, he will cast out of the city of God, 7, 8.

A Psalm of David

A. M. cir. 2949
B. C. cir. 1055
Ante I. Ol. 279
Ante Urbem
Conditam
302

I [a]WILL sing of mercy and judgment: unto thee, O LORD, will I sing.

2 I will [b]behave myself wisely in a perfect way. O when wilt thou come unto me? I will [c]walk within my house with a perfect heart.

3 I will set no [d]wicked thing before mine

A. M. cir. 2949
B. C. cir. 1055
Ante I. Ol. 279
Ante Urbem
Conditam
302

---

[a]Psa. lxxxix. 1——[b]1 Sam. xviii. 14   [c]1 Kings ix. 4; xi. 4——[d]Heb. *thing of Belial*

NOTES ON PSALM CI

The *Hebrew* and all the *Versions* attribute this Psalm to *David.* It shows us the resolutions he formed when he came to the throne; and it is a perfect model according to which a wise prince should regulate his conduct and his government.

Verse 1. *I will sing of mercy and judgment*] David might say, Adverse and prosperous providences have been of the utmost use to my soul; therefore, I will thank God for *both.* Or, as he was probably now called to the government of *all the tribes,* he might make a resolution that he would show חסד *chesed,* incessant benevolence, to the upright; and משפט *mishpat,* the execution of judgment, to the wicked; and would make the conduct of God the model of his own.

Verse 2. *I will behave myself wisely*] God's law prescribes a perfect way of life; in this perfect way I have professed to walk, and I must act *wisely* in order to walk in it.

When wilt thou come unto me?] I can neither walk in this way, nor grow *wise* unto salvation, unless *thou come unto me* by thy grace and Spirit; for without thee I can do nothing.

I will walk within my house] It is easier for most men to walk with a perfect heart in the *Church,* or even in the *world,* than in their *own families.* How many are as meek as lambs among *others,* when at *home* they are *wasps* or *tigers!* The man who, in the midst of family provocations, maintains a Christian character, *being meek, gentle,* and *long-suffering* to his *wife,* his *children,* and his *servants,* has got a *perfect heart,* and adorns the doctrine of God his Saviour in all things.

The original is very emphatic: אתהלך *ethhallech.* "I will set myself to walk," I will make it a determined point thus to walk. I will bear and forbear with children, servants, &c., not speaking rashly, nor giving way to bad tempers. Through various motives a man will behave with propriety and decorum among others; but none of these motives operate in his own house, where he feels himself *master,* and consequently under no restraint.

A. M. cir. 2949
B. C. cir. 1055
Ante I. Ol. 279
Ante Urbem
Conditam
302

eyes: ᵉI hate the work of them ᶠthat turn aside; *it* shall not cleave to me.

4 A froward heart shall depart from me: I will not ᵍknow a wicked *person*.

5 Whoso privily slandereth his neighbour, him will I cut off: ʰhim that hath a high look and a proud heart will not I suffer.

6 Mine eyes *shall be* upon the faithful of the land, that they may dwell with me: he that walketh ⁱin a perfect way, he shall serve me.

7 He that worketh deceit shall not dwell within my house: he that telleth lies ᵏshall not tarry in my sight.

8 I will ˡearly destroy all the wicked of the land; that I may cut off all wicked doers ᵐfrom the city of the LORD.

A. M. cir. 2949
B. C. cir. 1055
Ante I. Ol. 279
Ante Urbem
Conditam
302

ᵉPsa. xcvii. 10——ᶠJosh. xxiii. 6; 1 Sam. xii. 20, 21; Psa. xl. 4; cxxv. 5——ᵍMatt. vii. 23; 2 Tim. ii. 19 ʰPsa. xviii. 27; Prov. vi. 17

ⁱOr, *perfect in the way;* Psalm cxix. 1——ᵏHebrew, *shall not be established*——ˡPsa. lxxv. 10; Jer. xxi. 12 ᵐPsalm xlviii. 2, 8

Verse 3. *I will set no wicked thing before mine eyes*] I will undertake no unjust wars; will enter into no sinful alliances; will not oppress my subjects by excessive taxation, to support extravagance in my court. I will not look favourably on *things* or *words of Belial.* What is *good for nothing* or evil in its operation, what is wicked in its principle, and what would lead me away from righteousness and truth, I will never set before my eyes.

Them that turn aside] I shall particularly abominate the conduct of those who apostatize from the true religion, and those who deny its Divine authority, and who live without having their conduct governed by its influence, such shall never be put in a place of political trust or confidence by me.

Verse 4. *A froward heart*] Rash and headstrong men shall not be employed by me.

I will not know a wicked person.] I will give no countenance to sinners of any kind; and whatever is *evil* shall be an object of my abhorrence.

Verse 5. *Whoso privily slandereth his neighbour*] All flatterers and time-servers, and those who by insinuations and false accusations endeavour to supplant the upright, that they may obtain their offices for themselves or their dependants, will I consider as enemies to the state, I will abominate, and expel them from my court.

The Chaldee gives a remarkable meaning to the Hebrew, מלשני בסתר רעהו *melasheni bassether reehu,* which we translate, *Whoso privily slandereth his neighbour,* and which it renders thus, דמשתעי לישן תליתי על חבריה *demishtaey lishan telitai al chabreyah:* "He who speaks with the *triple tongue* against his neighbour." That is, the tongue by which he slays *three* persons, viz., 1. The *man* whom he slanders; 2. *Him* to whom he *communicates* the slander; and, 3. *Himself,* the slanderer. Every slanderer has his *triple tongue,* and by every slander inflicts those *three* deadly wounds. Such a person deserves to be *cut off.* On this subject St. Jerome speaks nearly in the same way: Ille qui detrahit, et se, et illum qui audit, demergit; "He who slanders ruins both himself and him who hears him;" he might have added, *and him who is slandered,* for this is often the case; the *innocent* are ruined by detraction.

A high look and a proud heart] One who is seeking preferment; who sticks at nothing to gain it; and one who behaves himself haughtily and insolently in his office.

Will not I suffer.] לא אוכל *lo uchal,* I cannot

away with. These persons especially will I drive from my presence, and from all state employments.

Verse 6. *Mine eyes*] My approbation.

Upon the faithful] The humble, upright followers of God.

That they may dwell with me] Be my confidants and privy counsellors. No irreligious or wicked man, whatever his abilities may be, shall be countenanced or supported by me. I will purify my court from the base, the irreligious, the avaricious, the venal, the profligate, and the wicked.

He that walketh in a perfect way] He that is truly religious.

He shall serve me.] Shall be my prime minister, and the chief officer in my army, and over my finances.

Verse 7. *He that worketh deceit—that telleth lies*] I will expel from my court all sycophants and flatterers. *Tiberius* encouraged flatterers; *Titus* burned some, *banished* several others, and *sold* many for *slaves.*

Verse 8. *I will early destroy*] I will take the first opportunity of destroying all the wicked of the land. I will purify my court, purge Jerusalem, and cleanse the whole land of every abomination and abominable person; so that the city of my God, where *holiness* alone should dwell, shall indeed become *the Holy City;* that the *state* may be made *prosperous,* and the *people* happy. Such an administration must have been a good one, where such pious caution was used in choosing all the officers of the state.

ANALYSIS OF THE HUNDRED AND FIRST PSALM

There are *two* parts of this Psalm:—

I. The *sum,* with the dedication of it, ver. 1.

II. The full explanation of *mercy* and *judgment,* and how practised:—

1. Towards *himself,* ver. 2-5.

2. Towards *ungodly* men, ver. 4, 5, 7, 8.

3. Towards all *good* men, ver. 6.

I. The sum of the Psalm, *mercy* and *judgment,* the two great virtues of a king.

1. *Mercy* in countenancing, giving audience, judging, and rewarding the good.

2. *Judgment* in discountenancing, being a terror to and punishing the evil doers.

II. He begins with his *own* reformation and that of his *house,* that he may set a godly example to his *kingdom.*

1. "I will behave myself wisely:" most act *foolishly;* I shall be guided by Divine wisdom.

2. "I am in a perfect way:" I have professed to believe in the God of Israel, and I must walk suitably to this profession.

3. "When wilt thou come unto me?" I am sincere in my resolves; but without thee I can do nothing. Stand by me, and I will walk uprightly.

In his house he resolves, "I will walk within my house with a perfect heart."

1. "I will walk:" it shall be my constant employment.

2. "I will walk in my house:" I will see that my *family* fear God.

3. "I will walk with a perfect heart:" I shall do nothing for *show;* all shall be sincere and pious.

In order to walk in this perfect way, he promises,—

1. "I will set no wicked thing before my eyes:" evil desires enter more frequently into the soul by the *eye* than by any of the other senses.

2. "I hate the work of them that turn aside:" he that would leave sin must hate and abhor it: he that *leaves God* is an object of abhorrence.

3. "It shall not cleave to me:" it will cleave to him who cleaves to it. He who does not *hate* it, will *cleave* to it.

He shows what he will be towards the *ungodly.*

1. "A froward heart shall depart from me:" the headstrong, stubborn, and refractory.

2. "I will not know the wicked:" I shall not only not approve of such, but I will cultivate no acquaintance with them.

These wicked persons he particularizes. They are,

1. *Slanderers:* "Him that slandereth his neighbour I will cut off."

2. *The ambitious:* "Him that hath a high look," who wants influence and honour.

3. The *proud:* the haughty, who thinks all born to be his vassals.

How he will treat the *godly.*

1. "His eye shall be upon the faithful." Of them he will take especial care; he shall dwell with me.

2. The truly religious, "he that walks in a perfect way," shall be employed by himself. "He shall serve me."

He farther states what he will do in reference to the *ungodly.*

1. No fraudulent person shall dwell in his house: "He that worketh deceit," &c.

2. *Liars shall be banished out of his sight.*

In this work he tells us how he would proceed.

1. "I will early destroy." I will make *despatch,* that the *land* be not polluted.

2. The *end,* in reference to the Church: "I will cut off the wicked from the city of the Lord." The city, the seat of government, the place of God's *altars,* must be kept pure. There must be a thorough, a radical reform. No corruption or abuse, either in things *political,* *domestic,* or *religious,* shall be tolerated. All must be holy, as he who has called us is holy. This was a reformation according to God's word; not according to the caprice of the multitude.

PSALM CII

The complaint and miserable state of the poor captives, 1–11; the expectation of deliverance, 12–14; the conversion of the heathen, 15–18; the termination of the captivity, 19–22; the great frailty of man, 23, 24; the unchangeableness of God, 25–27; the permanence of the Church, 28.

XX. DAY. MORNING PRAYER

A Prayer *a*of the afflicted, *b*when he is overwhelmed, and poureth out his complaint before the LORD

HEAR my prayer, O LORD, and let my cry *c*come unto thee.

2 *d*Hide not thy face from me in the day *when* I am in trouble; *e*incline thine ear unto me: in the day *when* I call answer me speedily.

3 *f*For my days are consumed *g*like smoke, and *h*my bones are burned as a hearth.

4 My heart is smitten, and *i*withered like grass; so that I forget to eat my bread.

---

*a*Or, *for*——*b*Psa. lxi. 2; cxlii. 2——*c*Exod. ii. 23; 1 Sam. ix. 16; Psa. xviii. 6——*d*Psa. xxvii. 9; lxix. 17 *e*Psa. lxxi. 2; lxxxviii. 2

*f*Psa. cxix. 83; James iv. 14——*g*Or, (as some read,) *into smoke*——*h*Job xxx. 30; Psa. xxxi. 10; Lam. i. 13 *i*Psa. xxxvii. 2; ver. 11

NOTES ON PSALM CII

The *Hebrew,* and nearly all the *Versions,* give the following *title* to this Psalm: *A prayer of the afflicted, when he is overwhelmed, and pours out his sighing before the Lord.* There seems to be little doubt that this is the prayer of the captives in Babylon, when, towards the end of the captivity, they were almost worn out with oppression, cruelty, and distress. The Psalm has been attributed to *Daniel,* to *Jeremiah,* to *Nehemiah,* or to some of the other *prophets* who flourished during the time of the captivity. The author of the Epistle to the Hebrews has applied the *twenty-fifth, twenty-sixth,* and *twenty-seventh* verses to our Lord, and the perpetuity of his kingdom.

Verse 1. *Hear my prayer*] The chief parts of the Psalm answer well to the title: it is the *language of the deepest distress,* and well directed to *Him* from whom alone help can come.

Verse 3. *My days are consumed like smoke*] He represents himself (for the psalmist speaks in the name of the people) under the notion of a *pile of combustible matter,* placed upon a *fire,* which soon consumes it; part flying away in *smoke,* and the residue lying on the hearth in the form of *charred coal* and *ashes.* The *Chaldeans* were the *fire,* and the *captive Jews* the *fuel,* thus converted into *smoke* and *ashes.*

Verse 4. *My heart is smitten, and withered like grass*] The metaphor here is taken from

5 By reason of the voice of my groaning [k]my bones cleave to my [l]skin.

6 [m]I am like [n]a pelican of the wilderness: I am like an owl of the desert.

7 I [o]watch, and am as a sparrow [p]alone upon the house-top.

8 Mine enemies reproach me all the day; *and* they that are [q]mad against me are [r]sworn against me.

9 For I have eaten ashes like bread, and [s]mingled my drink with weeping,

10 Because of thine indignation and thy wrath: for [t]thou hast lifted me up, and cast me down.

11 [u]My days *are* like a shadow that

declineth; and [v]I am withered like grass.

12 But [w]thou, O Lord, shalt endure for ever; and [x]thy remembrance unto all generations.

13 Thou shalt arise, *and* [y]have mercy upon Zion: for the time to favour her, yea, the [z]set time is come.

14 For thy servants take pleasure in [a]her stones, and favour the dust thereof.

15 So the heathen shall [b]fear the name of the Lord, and all the kings of the earth thy glory.

16 When the Lord shall build up Zion, [c]he shall appear in his glory.

---

[k]Job xix. 20; Lam. iv. 8——[l]Or, *flesh*——[m]Job xxx. 29——[n]Isaiah xxxiv. 11; Zephaniah ii. 14——[o]Psa. lxxvii. 4——[p]Psalm xxxviii. 11——[q]Acts xxvi. 11 [r]Acts xxiii. 12——[s]Psalm xlii. 3; lxxx. 5——[t]Psalm xxx. 7——[u]Job xiv. 2; Psalm cix. 23; cxliv. 4; Eccles.

vi. 12——[v]Verse 4; Isaiah xl. 6, 7, 8; James i. 10 [w]Verse 26; Psalm ix. 7; Lamentations v. 19——[x]Psalm cxxxv. 13——[y]Isaiah lx. 10; Zechariah i. 12——[z]Isaiah xl. 2——[a]Psalm lxxix. 1——[b]1 Kings viii. 43; Psalm cxxxviii. 4; Isa. lx. 3——[c]Isa. lx. 1, 2

---

grass cut down in the meadow. It is first *smitten* with the *scythe*, and then *withered* by the *sun*. Thus the Jews were smitten with the judgments of God; and they were now withered under the fire of the *Chaldeans*.

Verse 6. *I am like a pelican of the wilderness*] It may be the *pelican* or the *bittern*. The original, קאת *kaath*, is mentioned Lev. xi. 18, and is there described. See the note.

Owl of the desert.] כוס *cos*, some species of *owl;* probably the night raven. See the notes referred to above.

Verse 7. *As a sparrow alone*] צפור *tsippor*, seems to be often used for any small bird, such as the *swallow, sparrow*, or the like. *Bochart* supposes the *screech owl* is intended.

Verse 8. *They that are mad against me are sworn against me.*] The Chaldeans are determined to destroy us; and they have bound themselves *by oath* to do it. See a similar case related Acts xxiii. 12-14, where a number of Jews had bound themselves by an *oath* neither to eat nor drink till they had slain Paul.

Verse 9. *I have eaten ashes like bread*] Fearful of what they might do, we all humbled ourselves before thee, and sought thy protection; well knowing that, unless we were supernaturally assisted, we must all have perished; our enemies having sworn our destruction.

Verse 10. *For thou hast lifted me up, and cast me down.*] Thou hast lifted me on high, that thou mightest dash me down with the *greater force*. We were *exalted* in thy *favour* beyond any people, and now thou hast made us the *lowest* and most *abject* of the children of men.

Verse 11. *My days are like a shadow that declineth*] Or rather, *My days decline like the shadow*. I have passed my *meridian*, and the sun of my prosperity is about to set for ever. There may be here an allusion to the declination of the sun towards the south, which, by shortening their days, would greatly lengthen their nights. Similar to the exclamation of a contemporary prophet, Jer. viii. 20: "The harvest is past, the summer is ended, and we are

not saved." There is now scarcely any human hope of our deliverance.

Verse 12. *But thou, O Lord, shalt endure for ever*] Our life is a shadow; we can scarcely be called *beings* when compared with thee, for thou art *eternal*. Have mercy upon us, *creatures of a day*, and thy kindness shall be a *memorial* in all our *generations*.

Verse 13. *Thou shalt arise, and have mercy upon Zion*] While he is humbled at the footstool of mercy, and earnestly praying for mercy, an answer of peace is given; he is assured, not only that they *shall be delivered*, but that the time of deliverance is *at hand*. The *set time*— the *seventy* years predicted by Jeremiah, was ended; and God gave him to see that he was ever mindful of his promises.

Verse 14. *Thy servants take pleasure in her stones*] Though Jerusalem was at this time in a heap of ruins, yet even her rubbish was sacred in the eyes of the pious; for this had been *the city of the great King*.

Verse 15. *So the heathen shall fear the name of the Lord*] It is granted that after the edict of Cyrus to restore and rebuild Jerusalem, which was about *four hundred and ninety* years before Christ, the name of the true God was more generally known among the heathen; and the translating the Sacred Writings into Greek, by the command of Ptolemy Philadelphus, king of Egypt, about *two hundred and eighty-five* years before the Christian era, spread a measure of the light of God in the Gentile world which they had not before seen. Add to this, the dispersion of the Jews into different parts of the Roman empire, after Judea became a Roman province, which took place about *sixty* years before the advent of our Lord; and we may consider these as so many preparatory steps to the conversion of the heathen by the Gospel of our Lord Jesus Christ. And to this last general illumination of the Gentile world the psalmist must allude here, when he speaks of "the heathen fearing God's name, and all the kings of the earth his glory."

Verse 16. *When the Lord shall build up Zion*]

17 [d]He will regard the prayer of the destitute, and not despise their prayer.

18 This shall be [e]written for the generation to come: and [f]the people which shall be created shall praise the LORD.

19 For he hath [g]looked down from the height of his sanctuary; from heaven did the LORD behold the earth;

20 [h]To hear the groaning of the prisoner; to loose [i]those that are appointed to death;

21 To [k]declare the name of the LORD in Zion, and his praise in Jerusalem;

22 When the people are gathered together, and the kingdoms, to serve the LORD.

23 He [l]weakened my strength in the way; he [m]shortened my days.

24 [n]I said, O My God, take me not away in the midst of my days: [o]thy years *are* throughout all generations.

25 [p]Of old hast thou laid the foundation of the earth: and the heavens *are* the work of thy hands.

26 [q]They shall perish, but [r]thou shalt [s]endure: yea, all of them shall wax old like a garment; as a vesture shalt thou change them, and they shall be changed:

27 But [t]thou *art* the same, and thy years shall have no end.

28 [u]The children of thy servants shall continue, and their seed shall be established before thee.

---

[d]Neh. i. 6, 11; ii. 8——[e]Rom. xv. 4; 1 Cor. x. 11 [f]Psa. xxii. 31; Isa. xliii. 21——[g]Deut. xxvi. 15; Psa. xiv. 2; xxxiii. 13, 14——[h]Psa. lxxix. 11——[i]Heb. *the children of death*——[k]Psa. xxii. 22——[l]Heb. *afflicted* [m]Job xxi. 21

[n]Isa. xxxviii. 10——[o]Psa. xc. 2; Hab. i. 12——[p]Gen. i. 1; ii. 1; Heb. i. 10——[q]Isa. xxxiv. 4; li. 6; lxv. 17; lxvi. 22; Rom. viii. 20; 2 Pet. iii. 7, 10, 11, 12——[r]Ver. 12——[s]Heb. *stand*——[t]Mal. iii. 6; Heb. xiii. 8; James i. 17——[u]Psa. lxix. 36

It is such a difficult thing, so wholly improbable, so far out of the reach of human power, that when God does it, he must manifest his power and glory in a most extraordinary manner.

Verse 17. *The prayer of the destitute*] הערער *haarar* of him who is laid in utter ruin, who is entirely wasted.

Verse 18. *The people which shall be created*] "The Gentiles, who shall be brought to the knowledge of salvation by Christ," as the *Syriac* states in its inscription to this Psalm: how often the conversion of the soul to God is represented as a *new creation*, no reader of the New Testament need be told. See Eph. ii. 10, iv. 24; 2 Cor. v. 17; Gal vi. 15. Even the publication of the Gospel, and its influence among men, is represented under the notion of "creating a new heaven and a new earth," Isa. lxv. 17, 18.

Verse 19. *For he hath looked down*] This, with the three following verses, seems to me to contain a glorious prophecy of the incarnation of Christ, and the gathering in of the Jews and the Gentiles to him. *The Lord looks down from heaven*, and sees the whole earth groaning and travailing in pain; his eye affects his heart, and he purposes their salvation.

Verse 20. *To hear the groaning*] By sin, all the inhabitants of the earth are *miserable*. They have broken the Divine laws, are under the arrest of judgment, and all cast into *prison*. They have been tried, *found guilty*, and *appointed to die;* they *groan* under their chains, are alarmed at the prospect of death, and implore mercy.

Verse 21. *To declare the name of the Lord*] To publish that Messenger of the Covenant in whom the name of the Lord is, that Messiah in whom the fulness of the Godhead dwelt; and to commence at *Jerusalem*, that the first offers of mercy might be made to the Jews, from whom the word of reconciliation was to go out to all the ends of the earth.

Verse 22. *When the people are gathered together*] When all the *Gentiles* are enlightened, and the kings of the earth brought to pay homage to the King of kings.

Verse 23. *He weakened my strength in the way*] We are brought so low in our captivity by oppression, by every species of hard usage, and by death, that there is now no hope of our restoration by any efforts of our own.

Verse 24. *I said, O my God*] This and the following verses seem to be the *form of prayer* which the captives used previously to their deliverance.

Thy years are throughout all generations.] This was a frequent argument used to induce God to hear prayer. We are *frail* and *perishing;* thou art *everlasting*: deliver us, and we will glorify thee.

Verse 25. *Of old hast thou laid the foundation*] None taught of God ever imagined the world to have been *eternal. Of old*, לפנים *lephanim*, before there were any *faces* or *appearances*, thou didst lay the foundations of the earth. It was created by thee; it did not grow by *accretion* or *aggregation* from a *pre-existent nucleus*. There was *nothing;* and thou didst produce *being—substance* or *matter*. Out of that created matter thou didst make the *earth* and the *heavens*.

Verse 26. *They shall perish*] Nothing can be eternal *a parte ante*, or *a parte post*, but thyself. Even that which thou hast created, because not necessarily *eternal*, must be perishable; necessary *duration* belongs to God only; and it is by his will and energy alone that universal nature is preserved in existence, and preserved from running into speedy disorder, decay, and ruin.

Yea, all of them shall wax old] Every thing must *deteriorate*, unless *preserved* by thy *renewing* and *invigorating energy*. Even the *heavens* and the *earth* are subject to this law; for that which is not, from the infinite perfection of its own nature, ETERNAL, must be perishable; therefore the heavens and the earth must necessarily come to an end. They contain the seeds of their own dissolution. It is true that in sublunary things, the *vicissitudes of seasons* is a sort of check to the principle of dissolution; but it only partially corrects this tendency. Even the productions of the earth *wear out* or *deteriorate.* Plant the same seed or grain for several years consecutively, and it degenerates so as at last not to be worth the labour of tillage, however expensively the soil may be manured in which it is planted. I may instance in *wheat* and in the *potatoe,* the two grand supporters of life in European countries. All other seeds and plants, as far as they have fallen under my observation, are subject to the same law.

Verse 27. *But thou* art *the same*] ואתה הוא *veattah* HU, *but thou art* HE, that is, *The* ETERNAL; and, consequently, he who only has *immortality.*

Thy years shall have no end.] לא יתמו *lo yit-tammu,* "they shall not be completed." Every thing has its revolution—its conception, growth, perfection, decay, dissolution, and death, or corruption. It may be said that *regeneration* restores all these substances; and so it does in a measure, but not without *deterioration.* The *breed of animals,* as well as *vegetables, wears out;* but God's eternal round has *no completion.* I repeat it,—what is *necessarily eternal* is unchangeable and imperishable; all created beings are perishable and mutable, because not eternal. God alone is eternal; therefore God alone is imperishable and immutable.

Verse 28. *The children of thy servants shall continue*] Thy *Church* shall be permanent, because founded *on thee;* it shall live throughout all the revolutions of time. And as thy followers are made *partakers of the Divine nature,* they shall live in *union with God* in the other world, deriving *eternal duration* from the *inexhaustible Fountain* of *being.* Nothing can be permanent but by God's supporting and renewing influence.

ANALYSIS OF THE ONE HUNDRED AND SECOND PSALM

There are *two* general parts in this Psalm:—
I. A description of the calamities of the Church, under the person of an afflicted man, ver. 1-11.
II. The consolation afforded in these calamities, and the ground of it, ver. 12-28.
I. The description, &c., is formed into a *prayer* proposed in the *two first verses:*—
1. "Hear my prayer."
2. "Hide not thy face."
In this prayer he complains, and shows his wretched state by various metaphors or figures.
1. A consumption of strength: "My days are consumed."
2. From continual *weeping:* "My bones cleave to my skin."
3. From his *solitude:* "Like a pelican in the wilderness."
4. From his continual *watching:* "I watch, and am like a sparrow," &c.
5. From the *reproach* of his enemies. "Mine enemies reproach me."
6. From his *sadness:* "I have eaten ashes like bread."
All these increased, from a *sense of God's displeasure.*

VOL. III

1. "Because of thine indignation."
2. Because of his *sufferings:* "Thou hast lifted me up, and hast cast me down."
3. And the *effect* produced: "My days are as a shadow."
II. He comforts himself in the promises of God:—
1. "I am withered like grass: but thou shalt endure for ever."
2. I shall soon be forgotten; "but thy remembrance is unto all generations."
3. Thou seemest to take no heed: but "thou wilt arise."
He was the more confident,—
1. Because the *set time* to favour Zion was come.
2. This he saw more clearly from the *concern* with which God had filled the hearts of the people: "Thy servants take pleasure in her stones."
3. He consoled himself in the prospect of the *conversion of the heathen* themselves: "So the heathen shall fear thy name."
4. For this he gives a particular reason: Because "the Lord shall build up Zion."
5. And he will do this, because of the *prayers of the people:* "He will regard the prayer," &c.
This should be done in such a *manner,* that,—
1. *Record* should be made of it: "This shall be written."
2. And it should be a blessing to those that were unborn: "The people which shall be created shall praise the Lord."
And for this he assigns the *proper reasons.*
1. "The Lord looked down from heaven."
2. "He heard the groans of the prisoners."
These mercies call for *gratitude* and *obedience:*—
1. They should "declare the name of the Lord."
2. And this will take place "when the people are gathered together," &c.
The psalmist fears that he shall *not live* to see this deliverance:—
1. "For he weakened my strength in the way,—he shortened my days."
2. Yet he earnestly desires to see it: "Take me not away."
To strengthen this petition, he pleads God's *unchangeableness;* and he proves God to be *eternal,* because he is *immutable.*
1. Not so the *earth,* for it had a *beginning:* "Of old thou hast laid," &c.
2. Not so the *heavens;* for they are "the work of thy hands."
3. Neither shall they continue: "They shall perish," &c.
But God is *always the same.* Every thing that is *mutable* acquires by its change some *property, quality, form* or *accident,* which *it had not before:* but God, being an infinite Spirit, and infinitely perfect, can suffer no loss, can have no addition. For as he *wants nothing,* nothing can be *added* to him; as he *inhabits eternity,* nothing can be *taken from him.* In him, therefore, there is no possibility of *change;* and, consequently, none of *decay* or *perishing.*

From these considerations the psalmist draws this comfortable conclusion:—

1. His Church and servants shall continue also: "The children of thy servants,"—the apostles, with the patriarchs, shall dwell in thy kingdom—in the new Jerusalem.

2. "And their seed;" as many as are begotten by the Gospel, if they remain in the faith that works by love, "shall be established,"—persevere, remain, continue *before thee*—live in thy presence for ever. As thou art eternal, so thou wilt unite them to thyself and make *them* eternally happy.

PSALM CIII

God is praised for his benefits to his people, 1, 2; he forgives their iniquities, and heals their diseases, 3; redeems their lives, crowns them with loving-kindness, 4; satisfies them with good things, renews their youth, 5; he helps the oppressed, makes his ways known, is merciful and gracious, and keeps not his anger for ever, 6–9; his forbearance, and pardoning mercy, 10–12; he is a tender and considerate Father, 13, 14; the frail state of man, 15, 16; God's everlasting mercy, and universal dominion, 17–19; all his angels, his hosts, and his works, are invited to praise him, 20–22.

A Psalm of David

A. M. cir. 3468
B. C. cir. 536
Cyri,
R. Persarum,
cir. annum
primum

BLESS [a]the Lord, O my soul: and all that is within me, *bless* his holy name.

2 Bless the Lord, O my soul, and forget not all his benefits:

3 [b]Who forgiveth all thine iniquities; who [c]healeth all thy diseases;

4 Who [d]redeemeth thy life from destruction; [e]who crowneth thee with loving-kindness and tender mercies;

5 Who satisfieth thy mouth with good *things;* so that [f]thy youth is renewed like the eagle's.

A. M. cir. 3468
B. C. cir. 536
Cyri,
R. Persarum,
cir. annum
primum

---

[a]Ver. 22; Psa. civ. 1; cxlvi. 1——[b]Psa. cxxx. 8; Isa. xxxiii. 24; Matt. ix. 2, 6; Mark ii. 5, 10, 11; Luke vii. 47

[c]Exod. xv. 26; Psa. cxlvii. 3; Jer. xvii. 14——[d]Psa. xxxiv. 22; lvi. 13——[e]Psa. v. 12——[f]Isa. xl. 31

NOTES ON PSALM CIII

The *inscription* in the *Hebrew*, and in all the *Versions*, gives this Psalm to *David;* and yet many of the ancients believed it to refer to the times of the captivity, or rather to its *conclusion*, in which the redeemed Jews give thanks to God for their restoration. It is a Psalm of inimitable sweetness and excellence; contains the most affectionate sentiments of gratitude to God for his mercies; and the most consoling motives to continue to trust in God, and be obedient to him.

Verse 1. *Bless the Lord*] He calls on his soul, and all its faculties and powers, to magnify God for his mercies. Under such a weight of obligation the *lips* can do little; the soul and all its powers must be engaged.

Verse 2. *Forget not all his benefits*] Call them into recollection; particularize the chief of them; and here record them for an everlasting memorial.

Verse 3. *Who forgiveth*] The benefits are the following, 1. Forgiveness of sin. 2. Restoration of health: "Who healeth all thy diseases."

Verse 4. *Who redeemeth*] 3. Preservation from destruction. הגואל *haggoel*, properly, *redemption of life by the kinsman;* possibly looking forward, in the spirit of prophecy, to him who became partaker of our flesh and blood, that he might have the right to redeem our souls from death by dying in our stead. 4. Changing and ennobling his state; weaving a crown for him out of *loving-kindness* and *tender mercies*.

Verse 5. *Who satisfieth thy mouth*] 5. For continual communications of spiritual and temporal good; so that the vigour of his mind was constantly supported and increased.

Thy youth is renewed like the eagle's.] There is such a vast variety of the eagle, or genus *Falco*, that it is not easy to determine which is meant here. The Hebrew נשר *neser* is a general name for such as were known in the land of Judea; which were probably such as belong to the genus *Aquila*, comprehending *forty-one* species and *seven* varieties.

There are as many *legends* of the *eagle* among the ancient writers, as there are of some saints in the calendar; and all *equally true*. Even among *modern divines, Bible Dictionary* men, and such like, the most ridiculous tales concerning this bird continue to be propagated; and no small portion of them have been crowded into comments on this very verse. One specimen my *old Psalter* affords, which, for its curiosity, I shall lay before the reader:—

Trans. Renewed sal be als of arren þi youþed.

Par. The arne when he is greved with grete elde, his neb waxis so gretely, that he may nogt open his mouth and take mete: bot then he smytes his neb to the stane, and has away the solgh, and than he gaes til mete, and be commes yong a gayne. Swa Criste duse a way fra us oure elde of syn and mortalite, that settes us to ete oure brede in hevene, and newes us in hym.

The plain English of all this is:—

"When the arne [*eagle*, from the Anglo-Saxon earn, a word which Dr. Jamieson has not entered in his dictionary] is oppressed with old age, his bill grows so much that he cannot open his mouth in order to take meat. He then smites his bill against a stone, and breaks off the slough—the excrescence that prevented him from eating; and then he goes to his ordinary food, and becomes young again. So Christ takes away from us our old age of sin and death, and gives us to eat that bread which comes down

A. M. cir. 3468
B. C. cir. 536
Cyri,
R. Persarum,
cir. annum
primum

6 ᵍThe LORD executeth righteousness and judgment for all that are oppressed.

7 ʰHe made known his ways unto Moses, his acts unto the children of Israel.

8 ¹The LORD is merciful and gracious, slow to anger, and ᵏplenteous in mercy.

9 ¹He will not always chide: neither will he keep *his anger* for ever.

10 ᵐHe hath not dealt with us after our sins;

nor rewarded us according to our iniquities.

11 ⁿFor ᵒas the heaven is high above the earth, *so* great is his mercy toward them that fear him.

12 As far as the east is from the west *so* far hath he ᵖremoved our transgressions from us.

13 ᵠLike as a father pitieth *his* children, *so* the LORD pitieth them that fear him.

14 For he knoweth our frame; ʳhe remembereth that we *are* dust.

A. M. cir. 3468
B. C. cir. 536
Cyri,
R. Persarum,
cir. annum
primum

ᵍPsalm cxlvi. 7——ʰPsalm cxlvii. 19——¹Exod. xxxiv. 6, 7; Numbers xiv. 18; Deuteronomy v. 10; Nehemiah ix. 17; Psalm lxxxvi. 15; Jeremiah xxxii. 18 ᵏHebrew, *great of mercy*——¹Psalm xxx. 5; Isaiah lvii.

16; Jeremiah iii. 5; Micah vii. 18——ᵐEzra ix. 13 ⁿPsalm lvii. 10; Ephesians iii. 18——ᵒHebrew, *according to the height of the heaven*——ᵖIsaiah xliii. 25; Mic. vii. 18——ᵠMal. iii. 17——ʳPsa. lxxviii. 39

---

from heaven: and thus gives us a new life in himself."

I believe the meaning of the psalmist is much more simple: he refers to the *moulting* of birds, which, in most, takes place annually, in which they cast their old feathers and get a new plumage. To express this, he might as well have chosen any bird, as this is common to all the feathered race; but he chose the *king of the birds*, because of his bulk, his strength, and vivacity.

The *long life* of the eagle might have induced the psalmist to give it the preference. An eagle was nine years in the possession of *Owen Holland*, Esq., of Conway, in Wales, and had lived *thirty-two* years in the possession of the gentleman who made it a present to him: but of its previous age, for it came from Ireland, we are not informed. *Keysler* relates that an eagle died at Vienna, after a confinement of *one hundred and four* years!

The *eagle* can subsist a long time without food. That first mentioned above, through the neglect of a servant, was *twenty-one* days without food, and yet survived this long fast.

The meaning and moral of the psalmist are not difficult of comprehension. The Israelites, when redeemed from their captivity, should be so blessed by their God that they should reacquire their political strength and vigour; and should be so quickened by the Divine Spirit, that old things should be passed away, and all things become new.

Verse 6. *The Lord executeth*] This shall be done because the Lord will avenge his elect who have cried unto him day and night for his deliverance: "He is slow to anger;" but he will punish. "He is plenteous in mercy," and he will save. The persevering sinner shall be destroyed; the humble penitent shall be saved.

Verse 7. *He made known his ways unto Moses*] From the earliest part of our history he has been our protector and defence. His wonderful *acts* in behalf of the *children of Israel* are so many *proofs* of his *mercy*, power, and goodness; and so many *reasons* why *we* should now trust in him.

Verse 8. *The Lord is merciful*] See the note on Psa. lxxxvi. 15.

Verse 9. *He will not always chide*] He will not contend with us continually. He has often reproved, often punished us; but his mercy ever rejoiced over judgment.

Verse 10. *He has not dealt with us after our sins*] He has never apportioned our *punishment* to our *sins*, nor has he regulated the exercise of his *mercy* by our *merits*.

Verse 11. *For as the heaven is high above the earth*] Great and provoking as our crimes may have been, yet his mercies have, in their magnitude and number, surpassed these, as far as the heavens are elevated beyond the earth.

Verse 12. *As far as the east is from the west*] As the east and the west can never meet in one point, but be for ever at the same distance from each other, so our sins and their decreed punishment are removed to an eternal distance by his mercy.

Verse 13. *Like as a father pitieth his children*] This is a very emphatic verse, and may be thus translated: "As the tender compassions of a father towards his children; so the tender compassions of Jehovah towards them that fear him." Nothing can place the tenderness and concern of God for his creatures in a stronger light than this. What yearnings of bowels does a *father* feel toward the *disobedient child*, who, sensible of his ingratitude and disobedience, falls at his parent's feet, covered with confusion and melted into tears, with, "Father, I have sinned against heaven, and before thee, and am not worthy to be called thy son!" The same in *kind*, but infinitely more exquisite, does God feel when the penitent falls at his feet, and implores his mercy through Christ crucified.

Verse 14. *For he knoweth our frame*] יצרנו *yitsrenu*, "our formation;" the *manner* in which we are constructed, and the *materials* of which we are made. He knows we cannot contend with him, and if he uses his power against us, we must be crushed to destruction. In all his conduct towards us he considers the frailty of our nature, the untowardness of our circumstances, the strength and subtlety of temptation, and the sure party (till the heart is renewed) that the tempter has within us. Though all these things are against us, yet it must ever be said, whatever use we make of it, "the grace of God is sufficient for us." But alas! alas! who makes use of that sufficient grace? Here, then, is cause for condemnation. But, O amazing mercy! if any man sin, we have an advocate with the Father, Jesus Christ the righteous. And like as a father pitieth his children, so the Lord pitieth them that fear him; for he knoweth our frame, he remembereth that we are but

A. M. cir. 3468
B. C. cir. 536
Cyri,
R. Persarum,
cir. annum
primum

15 *As for* man, ªhis days *are* as grass: ᵗas a flower of the field, so he flourisheth.

16 For the wind passeth over it, and ᵘit is gone; and ᵛthe place thereof shall know it no more.

17 But the mercy of the LORD *is* from everlasting to everlasting upon them that fear him, and his righteousness unto ʷchildren's children;

18 ˣTo such as keep his covenant, and to those that remember his commandments to do them.

19 The LORD hath prepared his ʸthrone in the heavens; and ᶻhis kingdom ruleth over all.

A. M. cir. 3468
B. C. cir. 536
Cyri,
R. Persarum,
cir. annum
primum

20 ªBless the LORD, ye his angels, ᵇthat excel in strength, that ᶜdo his commandments, hearkening unto the voice of his word.

21 Bless ye the LORD, all *ye* ᵈhis hosts; ᵉye ministers of his, that do his pleasure.

22 ᶠBless the LORD, all his works in all places of his dominion: ᵍbless the LORD, O my soul.

ªPsa. xc. 5, 6; 1 Pet. i. 24——ᵗJob xiv. 1, 2; James i. 10, 11——ᵘHebrew, *it is not*——ᵛJob vii. 10; xx. 9 ʷExod. xx. 6——ˣDeut. vii. 9——ʸPsa. xi. 4——ᶻPsa. xlvii. 2; Dan. iv. 25, 34, 35

ªPsa. cxlviii. 2——ᵇHeb. *mighty in strength*; see Psa. lxxviii. 25——ᶜMatt. vi. 10; Heb. i. 14——ᵈGen. xxxii. 2; Josh. v. 14; Psa. lxviii. 17——ᵉDan. vii. 9, 10; Heb. i. 14——ᶠPsa. cxlv. 10——ᵍVer. 1

---

dust. The man who can say, in the face of these Scriptures, *Let us sin that grace may abound*, is a brute and demon, who has neither lot nor part in this thing.

Verse 15. *His days are as grass*] See the note on Psa. xc. 5.

Verse 16. *The wind passeth over it*] Referring perhaps to some blasting pestilential wind.

Verse 17. *The mercy of the Lord is from everlasting to everlasting*] חסד *chesed* signifies more particularly the *exuberant goodness of God.* This is an attribute of his nature, and must be from everlasting to everlasting; and hence, his righteousness (צדקת *tsidketh*)—his merciful *mode of justifying the ungodly*, is extended from one generation to another.

Unto children's children.] It is still in force, and the doctrine of reconciliation through Christ shall continue to be preached till the conclusion of time.

Verse 18. *To such as keep his convenant*] The spirit of which was, *I will be your* GOD; WE *will be thy* PEOPLE. From the covenant came the *commandments*, and their obligation *to remember and do them;* and on such *keepers* of the covenant, and *doers* of the commandments, God promises to pour out his mercy through all generations.

Verse 19. *The Lord hath prepared his throne in the heavens*] There he is Sovereign; but his dominion extends equally over all the earth; for his *kingdom*—regal government, influence, and sway, *ruleth over all.*

Verse 20. *Bless the Lord, ye his angels*] Every person who has a sense of God's goodness to his soul feels his own powers inadequate to the praise which he ought to offer; and therefore naturally calls upon the holiest of men, and the supreme angels, to assist him in this work.

That excel in strength] Some take נברי כח *gibborey coach* the *mighty in strength*, for another class of the hierarchy,—*they that do his commandments, hearkening to his words;* and consider them to be that order of beings who are particularly employed in operations among and for the children of men; probably such as are called *powers* in the New Testament.

Verse 21. *All ye his hosts; ye ministers of his*] We know almost nothing of the economy of the heavenly host; and, therefore, cannot tell what is the difference between *angels, mighty*

powers, hosts, and *ministers* who do his pleasure. All owe their being and all its blessings to God; all depend upon his bounty; and without him they can do nothing; therefore, all should praise him.

Verse 22. *Bless the Lord, all his works*] Let every thing he has done be so considered as to show forth his praise.

Bless the Lord, O my soul.] Let *me* never forget my obligation to his mercy; for with tender mercies and loving-kindness has he crowned me. I will therefore be thankful unto him, and speak good of his name.

ANALYSIS OF THE ONE HUNDRED AND THIRD PSALM

There are *three* parts in this Psalm:—

I. The *exordium*, in which the psalmist invites his own soul to praise the Lord, ver. 1, 2.

II. The *narration*, being a declaration of God's benefits conferred on him and others, and the causes of those benefits, ver. 3-19.

III. The *conclusion*, in which he calls on all creatures to assist him in praising the Lord, ver. 20-22.

I. The *exordium*,—

1. Bless God. Think on the benefit, and praise the Benefactor.

2. Let the *soul* join in this. Let it be done heartily; *lip-labour* is little worth.

3. "All that is within me." Every faculty,—understanding, will, memory, judgment, affections, desires, &c.

4. "Bless Jehovah," who gave thee thy being, and all thy blessings.

5. "Forget not his benefits." Most forget their obligations both to God and man; but *ingratitude*, which is the source of *forgetfulness*, is abominable.

6. "All his benefits." Thou hast already forgotten many; forget no more. The word גמולי *gemuley*, signifies, literally, *retributions* or *recompenses*, as the *Vulgate* has well expressed it. And of what kind are these *recompenses?* Invariably *good for evil;* nor hast thou ever offered him one accent of praise that he has not compensated with a *blessing of infinite value.*

II. The *narration*. A declaration of benefits. 1. To *himself*. 2. To the *Church*. These were,—1. *Spiritual;* 2. *Temporal* benefits.

First spiritual benefit—*justification:* "He forgiveth all thine iniquities."

Second spiritual benefit—*regeneration* or *sanctification:* "Healeth all thy diseases."

Third spiritual benefit—*redemption* from the first and second death, in consequence of being thus justified and sanctified.

Fourth spiritual benefit—*glorification* anticipated: "Who crowneth thee with loving-kindness and tender mercy." The *crown* comes from the *loving-kindness* and *tender mercy* of God; not from any *merit* in man.

The *temporal* benefits are,—

1. Abundance of the necessaries of life: "Who satisfieth thy mouth with good things."

2. Health and long life: "Thy youth is renewed like the eagle's." See the note on this passage.

The benefits to the whole *Church are,*—

1. *Defence* and *deliverance:* "The Lord executes judgment."

2. *Manifestation* of *his will:* "He made known his ways," &c.

All these spring from the *four attributes* mentioned below,—

1. "He is *merciful*," רחום *rachum*, bearing a paternal affection to his intelligent creatures, especially to those who fear him.

2. "*Gracious*," חנון *channun*, the Giver of grace and favour; for he who has a fatherly heart will *give*.

3. "*Slow to anger*," ארך אפים *erech appayim*, *long in nostrils*, not hasty; not *apt to be angry*.

4. "*Plenteous in mercy*," רב חסד *rab chesed*, *multiplying kindness*. Gives abundantly from his own *bounty*, not according to our *merit*.

The effects of all these are,—

1. Because he is *merciful:* "He will not always chide."

2. Because he is *gracious:* "He deals not with us after our sin."

3. Because he is *slow to anger:* "He will not keep his anger forever."

4. Because he is *plenteous in mercies:* His mercies surpass our sins as much as heaven surpasses the earth.

5. Because he is *like a father:* He "pities his children;" considers their frame, and makes all the allowance that *justice* mingled with *mercy* can make.

6. And as he is *righteous*—true, and faithful in performing his covenant, his mercy is everlasting to those that fear him.

But let it be remembered who they are that have a right to expect such blessings:—

1. "Those who fear him."

2. "Those who keep his covenant."

3. "Those who remember his commandments, and do them."

That he is *able* to do all that he has promised, the psalmist marks his *dominion:*—

1. It is not circumscribed: "His throne is in heaven."

2. It takes in all *places* and all *nations*. For "his kingdom ruleth over all;" he is King of kings, and Lord of lords.

III. The *conclusion*. For these benefits he invites all creatures to praise the Lord.

1. The *angels*, whom he describes,—1. From their *excellence:* "Ye that excel in strength." 2. From their *obedience:* "Ye that do his commandments." 3. From their *readiness and cheerfulness* in it: "Ye that hearken to the voice of his words,"—who are ever ready, at the slightest intimation, to perform his will.

2. All the *hosts* or *armies* of God,—archangels, principalities, dominions, powers, thrones, &c.

3. He invites all the creatures of God to praise him, whether *animate* or *inanimate:* "All creatures, in all places of his dominion." This extends throughout immensity. For this there is the strongest reason—he *made* all—*rules* over all—"is in all places" *with* all—*preserves* all—*moves* all.

4. To show that he who calls upon others will not be backward himself to praise God; as he began, so he concludes, with "Bless the Lord, O my soul!" Thus he had the high praises of God continually in his mouth.

And thus finishes this most excellent and inimitable Psalm. The *old Psalter* concludes thus: "Blysses to Lorde al his werks in ilk stede of his Lordschip: blisse my saule to Lorde. When men well lyfes, al thair werks blysses God. Fra blyssyng we cum forth to blyssyngs, gawe agayne, and therein dwell we."

The more we praise God, the more occasion we shall see to praise him, and the more spiritually minded we shall become. *Praise* proceeds from *gratitude;* gratitude from a sense of *obligation;* and both *praise* and *gratitude* will be in *proportion* to the *weight* of that obligation; and the *weight* will be in proportion to the *sense* we have of God's *great goodness* and our own *unworthiness*. As the reader's heart may be in a heavenly frame, I shall help him to express his feelings by the following *inimitable verses*, which express the substance of the preceding Psalm:—

From all that dwell below the skies
Let the Creator's praise arise!
Let the Redeemer's grace be sung
In every land, by every tongue!

Eternal are thy mercies, Lord!
Eternal truth attends thy word!
Thy praise shall sound from shore to shore,
Till sun shall rise and set no more.

Praise GOD, from whom all blessings flow!
Praise Him, all creatures here below!
Praise Him above, ye heavenly host!
Praise FATHER, SON, and HOLY GHOST!
              Amen and Amen.

PSALM CIV

The majesty and power of God manifested in the creation of the heavens and the atmosphere, 1–3; of the earth and sea, 4–9; of the springs, fountains, and rivers, 10–13; of vegetables and trees, 14–18; of the sun and moon, 19; of day and night, and their uses, 20–23; of the riches of the earth, 24; of the sea, its inhabitants, and its uses, 25, 26; of God's general providence in providing food for all kinds of animals, 27–31; of earthquakes and volcanoes, 32. God is praised for his majesty, and the instruction which his works afford, 33, 34. Sinners shall be destroyed, 35.

A. M. cir. 3468
B. C. cir. 536
Cyri,
R. Persarum,
cir. annum
primum

XX. DAY. EVENING PRAYER

BLESS ªthe LORD, O my soul. O LORD my God, thou art very great; ᵇthou art clothed with honour and majesty.

2 ᶜWho coverest *thyself* with light as *with* a garment: ᵈwho stretchest out the heavens like a curtain:

3 ᵉWho layeth the beams of his chambers

A. M. cir. 3468
B. C. cir. 536
Cyri,
R. Persarum,
cir. annum
primum

ªPsa. ciii. 1; ver. 35——ᵇPsa. xciii. 1

ᶜDan. vii. 9——ᵈIsa. xl. 22; xlv. 12——ᵉAmos ix. 6

NOTES ON PSALM CIV

This Psalm has no title either in the Hebrew or Chaldee; but it is attributed to David by the Vulgate, Septuagint, Æthiopic, Arabic, and Syriac. It has the following title in the Septuagint, as it stands in the Complutensian Polyglot: Ψαλμος τῳ Δαυιδ ὑπερ της του κοσμου συστασεως· "A Psalm of David concerning the formation of the world." The Syriac says it is "A Psalm of David when he went with the priests to adore the Lord before the ark." It seems a continuation of the preceding Psalm; and it is written as a part of it in *nine* of Kennicott's and De Rossi's MSS. It is properly a poem on the works of God in the creation and government of the world; and some have considered it a sort of epitome of the history of the creation, as given in the book of Genesis.

Verse 1. *O Lord my God, thou art very great*] The works of God, which are the subject of this Psalm, particularly show the grandeur and majesty of God. The strongest proofs of the being of God, for common understandings, are derived from the works of creation, their magnitude, variety, number, economy, and use. And a proper consideration of those works presents a greater number of the attributes of the Divine nature than we can learn from any other source. Revelation alone is superior.

Verse 2. *Who coverest* thyself *with light*] Light, insufferable splendour, is the robe of the Divine Majesty. *Light* and *fire* are generally the accompaniments of the Supreme Being, when he manifests his presence to his creatures. He appeared thus to *Abraham* when he made a covenant with him, Gen. xv. 17; and to *Moses* when he appointed him to bring the people out of Egypt, Exod. iii. 2; and when he gave him his law on Sinai, Exod. xix. 18. Moses calls *God a consuming fire*, Deut. iv. 24. When *Christ* was transfigured on the mount, his face shone like the sun, and his garment was white as the light, Matt. xvii. 2. And when the Lord manifests himself to the prophets, he is always surrounded with *fire*, and the most brilliant *light*.

Bishop *Lowth* has some fine remarks on the *imagery* and *metaphors* of this Psalm. The *exordium*, says he, is peculiarly magnificent, wherein the majesty of God is described, so far as we can investigate and comprehend it, from the admirable construction of nature; in which passage, as it was for the most part necessary to use translatitious images, the sacred poet has principally applied those which would be esteemed by the Hebrews the most elevated, and

worthy such an argument; for they all, as it seems to me, are taken from the *tabernacle*. We will give these passages verbally, with a short illustration:—

הוד והדר לבשת *hod vehadar labashta.*

"Thou hast put on honour and majesty."

The original, לבשת, is frequently used when speaking of the *clothing* or *dress* of the *priests*.

Verse 2. עטה אור כשלמה *oteh or cassalmah.*

"Covering thyself with light as with a garment."

A manifest symbol of the Divine Presence; the light conspicuous in the holiest is pointed out under the same idea; and from this single example a simile is educed to express the ineffable glory of God generally and universally.

נוטה שמים כיריעה *noteh shamayim kayeriah.*

"Stretching out the heavens like a curtain."

The word יריעה, rendered here *curtain*, is that which denotes the *curtains* or *uncovering* of the whole *tabernacle*. This may also be an allusion to those curtains or awnings, stretched over an area, under which companies sit at weddings, feasts, religious festivals, curiously *painted under*, to give them the appearance of the visible heavens in the night-season.

Verse 3. המקרה במים עליותיו *hamekareh bammayim aliyothaiv.*

"Laying the beams of his chambers in the waters."

The sacred writer expresses the wonderful nature of the *air* aptly, and regularly constructed, from various and flux elements, into one continued and stable series, by a metaphor drawn from the singular formation of the *tabernacle*, which, consisting of many and different parts, and easily reparable when there was need, was kept together by a perpetual juncture and contignation of them all together. The poet goes on:—

השם עבים רכובו *hassem abim rechubo,*
המהלך על כנפי רוח *hamehallech al canphey ruach.*

"Making the clouds his chariot,
Walking upon the wings of the wind."

He had first expressed an image of the Divine Majesty, such as it resided in the holy of holies, discernible by a certain investiture of the most splendid light; he now denotes the same from

A. M. cir. 3468
B. C. cir. 536
Cyri,
R. Persarum,
cir. annum
primum
in the waters: 'who maketh the clouds his chariot: ᵍwho walketh upon the wings of the wind:

4 ʰWho maketh his angels spirits; ⁱhis ministers a flaming fire:

5 ᵏ*Who* ˡlaid the foundations of the earth, *that* it should not be removed for ever.

6 ᵐThou coveredst it with the deep as *with*

a garment: the waters stood above the mountains.

7 ⁿAt thy rebuke they fled; at the voice of thy thunder they hasted away.

8 ᵒThey ᵖgo up by the mountains; they go down by the valleys unto ᑫthe place which thou hast founded for them.

9 ʳThou hast set a bound that they may

A. M. cir. 3468
B. C. cir. 536
Cyri,
R. Persarum,
cir. annum
primum

ᶠIsa. xix. 1——ᵍPsa. xviii. 10——ʰHeb. i. 7——ⁱ2 Kings ii. 11; vi. 17——ᵏHeb. *He hath founded the earth upon her bases*——ˡJob xxvi. 7; xxxviii. 4, 6; Psa. xxiv. 2; cxxxvi. 6; Eccles. i. 4

ᵐGenesis vii. 19——ⁿGenesis viii. 1——ᵒOr, *The mountains ascend, the valleys descend*——ᵖGenesis viii. 5——ᑫJob xxxviii. 10, 11——ʳJob xxvi. 10; Psalm xxxiii. 7; Jer. v. 22

---

that light of itself which the Divine Majesty exhibited, when it moved together with the ark, sitting on a circumambient cloud, and carried on high through the air. That seat of the Divine Presence is even called by the sacred historians, as its proper name, המרכבה *hammercabah*, THE CHARIOT.

Verse 4. עשה מלאכיו רחות *oseh malachaiv ruchoth,*

משרתיו אש להט *mesharethaiv esh lohet.*

The elements are described as prompt and expedite to perform the Divine commands, like angels or ministers serving in the tabernacle; the Hebrew word משרתיו *mesharethaiv* being a word most common in the sacred ministrations.

Verse 5. יסד ארץ על מכוניה *yasad erets al mechoneyha,*

בל תמוט עולם ועד *bal tammot olam vaed.*

"Laying the earth upon its foundations,
That it should not be shaken for evermore."

This image Bishop Lowth thinks evidently taken from the *tabernacle*, which was so laid upon its foundations that nothing could move it, and the dispensation to which it was attached, till the end purposed by the secret counsel of God was accomplished: and thus the *earth* is established, till the end of its creation shall be fully answered; and then it and its works shall be burnt up. On the above ground, the stability of the sanctuary and the stability of the earth are sometimes mentioned in the same words.

Verse 6. *Thou coveredst it with the deep*] This seems to be spoken in allusion to the creation of the earth, when it was without form and void, and darkness was upon the face of the deep, and the waters invested the whole, till God separated the dry land from them; thus forming the seas and the terraqueous globe. The poet Ovid has nearly the same idea:—

Densior his tellus, elementaque grandia traxit,
Et pressa est gravitate sua; circumfluus humor
Ultima possedit, solidumque coercuit orbem.
             Met. lib. i., ver. 29.

Earth sinks beneath, and draws a numerous throng
Of ponderous, thick, unwieldy seeds along:
About her coasts unruly waters roar;
And, rising on a ridge, insult the shore.
             DRYDEN.

Verse 7. *At thy rebuke they fled*] When God separated the *waters which were above the firmament* from those *below*, and caused the *dry land to appear.* He commanded the separation to take place; and the waters, as if instinct with life, hastened to obey.

At the voice of thy thunder] It is very likely God employed the *electric fluid* as an agent in this separation.

Verse 8. *They go up by the mountains; they go down by the valleys*] Taking the words as they stand here, *springs* seem to be what are intended. But it is difficult to conceive how the water could ascend, through the fissures of mountains, to their tops, and then come down their sides so as to form rivulets to water the valleys. Most probably all the springs in mountains and hills are formed from waters which fall on their tops in the form of rain, or from clouds that, passing over them, are arrested, and precipitate their contents, which, sinking down, are stopped by some solid strata, till, forcing their way at some aperture at their sides, they form springs and fountains. Possibly, however, *vapours* and *exhalations* are understood; these by *evaporation* ascend to the tops of mountains, where they are condensed and precipitated. Thus the vapours ascend, and then come down to the valleys, forming fountains and rivulets in those places which the providence of God has allotted them; that is, continuous valleys, with such a degree of *inclination* as determines their waters to run in that direction till they reach another river, or fall into the ocean.

Some have thought there is a reference to the *breaking up of the fountains of the great deep*, at the time of the flood; while the protrusion of the waters would raise the circumambient crust, so as to form mountains, the other parts, falling in to fill up the vacuum occasioned by the waters which were thrown up from the central abyss, would constitute *valleys*.

Ovid seems to paraphrase this verse:—

Jussit et extendi campos, subsidere valles,
Fronde tegi sylvas, lapidosos surgere montes.
             Met. lib. i., ver. 43.

"He shades the woods, the valleys he restrains
With rocky mountains, and extends the plains."
             DRYDEN.

Verse 9. *Thou hast set a bound that they may not pass*] And what is this *bound*? The *flux*

A. M. cir. 3468
B. C. cir. 536
Cyri,
R. Persarum,
cir. annum
primum

not pass over; [a]that they turn not again to cover the earth.

10 [t]He sendeth the springs into the valleys, *which* [u]run among the hills.

11 They give drink to every beast of the field: the wild asses [v]quench their thirst.

12 By them shall the fowls of the heaven have their habitation, *which* [w]sing among the branches.

13 [x]He watereth the hills from his cham-

bers: [y]the earth is satisfied with [z]the fruit of thy works.

14 [a]He causeth the grass to grow for the cattle, and herb for the service of man: that he may bring forth [b]food out of the earth;

15 And [c]wine *that* maketh glad the heart of man, *and* [d]oil to make *his* face to shine, and bread *which* strengtheneth man's heart.

16 The trees of the LORD are full of *sap;* the cedars of Lebanon, [e]which he hath planted;

A. M. cir. 3468
B. C. cir. 536
Cyri,
R. Persarum,
cir. annum
primum

---

[a]Genesis ix. 11, 15——[t]Heb. *Who sendeth*——[u]Heb. *walk*——[v]Hebrew, *break*——[w]Hebrew, *give a voice* [x]Psalm cxlvii. 8——[y]Psalm lxv. 9, 10——[z]Jeremiah x. 13; xiv. 22——[a]Genesis i. 29, 30; iii. 18; ix. 3; Psalm

cxlvii. 8——[b]Psalm cxxxvi. 25; cxlvii. 9; Job xxviii. 5 [c]Judges ix. 13; Psalm xxiii. 5; Proverbs xxxi. 6, 7 [d]Hebrew, *to make* his *face shine with oil,* or *more than oil*——[e]Num. xxiv. 6

---

and *reflux* of the sea, occasioned by the solar and lunar *attraction,* the *rotation* of the earth on its own axis, and the *gravitation* of the waters to the centre of the earth. And what is the *cause* of all these? The will and energy of God. Thus the sea is prevented from drowning the earth equally where there are *flat shores* as where the sea seems hemmed in by huge mounds of land and mountains. The *above,* not *these,* are the *bounds which it cannot pass, so that they cannot turn again to cover the earth.*

Verse 10. *He sendeth the springs into the valleys*] *Evaporation* is guided and regulated by Divine Providence. The sun has a certain power to raise a certain portion of vapours from a given space. God has apportioned the *aqueous* to the *terrene surface,* and the solar attraction to both. There is just as much *aqueous surface* as affords a sufficiency of vapours to be raised by the solar attraction to water the *earthy surface.* Experiments have been instituted which prove that it requires a given space of aqueous surface to provide vapours for a given space of terrene surface; and the proportion appears ordinarily to be *seventeen of water* to *three of earth;* and this is the proportion that the aqueous bears to the terrene surface of the globe. See Ray's three Physico-theological Discourses.

Verse 11. *The wild asses quench their thirst.*] The פֶּרֶא *pere, onager* or *wild ass,* differs in nothing from the *tame ass,* only it has not a broken spirit, and is consequently more lively and active. It is so very swift that no horse except the Arab barb can overtake it. It is a gregarious animal, and they go in troops to feed and to drink. It is very timid, or rather jealous of its liberty, and therefore retires deep into the desert; yet even there the providence of God regards it; springs are provided, and it has the instinct to find them out.

Verse 12. *By them shall the fowls of the heaven have their habitation*] All fowls love verdure, and have their residence where they can find wood and water.

Verse 13. *From his chambers*] The *clouds,* as in ver. 3.

The earth is satisfied] The inhabitants of it.

Verse 14. *He causeth the grass to grow for the cattle*] Doth God care for oxen? Yes, and there is not a beast of the field that does not share his merciful regards.

And herb for the service of man] Plants,

esculent herbs, and nutritive grain in general; and thus *he brings forth food* (לֶחֶם *lechem, bread) out of the earth.* In the germination and growth of a grain of wheat there is a profusion of miracles. God takes care of man, and of all those animals which are so necessary to the convenience and comfort of man.

Verse 15. *And wine*] Wine, in moderate quantity, has a wondrous tendency to revive and invigorate the human being. *Ardent spirits* exhilarate, but they *exhaust* the strength; and every dose leaves man the worse. Unadulterated wine, on the contrary, *exhilarates* and *invigorates:* it makes him cheerful, and provides for the continuance of that cheerfulness by *strengthening* the *muscles,* and *bracing* the *nerves.* This is its *use.* Those who continue drinking till wine inflames them, *abuse* this mercy of God.

Oil to make his *face to shine*] That is, to anoint the body; and particularly those parts most exposed to the sun and weather. This is of high importance in all arid lands and sultry climates. By it the pores are kept open, and perspiration maintained.

Bread which *strengtheneth man's heart.*] In hunger not only the *strength* is prostrated, but the *natural courage* is also abated. *Hunger* has no enterprise, emulation, nor courage. But when, in such circumstances, a little bread is received into the stomach, even before concoction can have time to prepare it for nutriment, the *strength* is restored, and the *spirits* revived. This is a surprising effect; and it has not yet been satisfactorily accounted for.

Three of the choicest and most important articles of life are here mentioned: WINE, for the support of the vital and intellectual spirits; BREAD, for the support of the nervous and muscular system; and OIL, as a seasoner of food, and for those *unctions* so necessary for the maintenance of health. Where *wine, oil,* and *bread* can be had in sufficient quantities, there *animal food,* ardent spirits, and all high-seasoned aliments, may be well dispensed with. Heavy taxes on these necessaries of life are taxes on *life,* itself; and infallibly lead to adulteration of the articles themselves; especially *wine* and *oil,* which, in countries where they are highly taxed, are no longer to be found pure.

Verse 16. *The trees of the Lord are full of sap*] יִשְׂבְּעוּ *yisbeu,* "are saturated."

A. M. cir. 3468
B. C. cir. 536
Cyri,
R. Persarum,
cir. annum
primum

17 Where the birds make their nests: *as for* the stork, the fir-trees *are* her house.

18 The high hills *are* a refuge for the wild goats; *and* the rocks for ʳthe conies.

19 ᵍHe appointed the moon for seasons: the sun ʰknoweth his going down.

20 ⁱThou makest darkness, and it is night; wherein ᵏall the beasts of the forests do creep *forth*.

21 ˡThe young lions roar after their prey, and seek their meat from God.

22 The sun ariseth, they gather themselves together, and lay them down in their dens.

23 Man goeth forth unto ᵐhis work and to his labour until the evening.

24 ⁿO Lord, how manifold are thy works! in wisdom hast thou made them all: the earth is full of thy riches.

25 *So is* this great and wide sea, wherein *are* things creeping innumerable, both small and great beasts.

26 There go the ships: *there is* that ᵒleviathan, *whom* thou hast ᵖmade to play therein.

A. M. cir. 3468
B. C. cir. 536
Cyri,
R. Persarum,
cir. annum
primum

ᶠProv. xxx. 26——ᵍGen. i. 14——ʰJob xxxviii. 12
ⁱIsa. xlv. 7——ᵏHeb. *all the beasts thereof do trample on*

the forest——ˡJob xxxviii. 39; Joel i. 20——ᵐGen. iii. 19
ⁿProv. iii. 19——ᵒJob xli. 1——ᵖHeb. *formed*

The cedars of Lebanon] God's providence not only extends to *men* and *cattle*, but also to the *trees* of the field and forest. Many of these are not only sustained, but *planted* by his providence. Who ever planted the seeds of the cedars of Lebanon, or of the thousands of woods and forests on the globe? God himself sowed those seeds, and they have sprung up and flourished without the care of man.

Verse 17. *Where the birds make their nests*] צפרים *tsipporim* signifies *swallows, sparrows,* and *small birds* in general; here opposed to the חסידה *chasidah* or *stork*. Perhaps the *heron* may be understood, which is said to be the first of all birds to build her nest, and she builds it on the very highest trees. The general meaning is, that God has provided shelter and support for the greatest and smallest birds; they are all objects of his providential regard.

Verse 18. *The high hills* are *a refuge*] The barren tops of the highest hills, and the craggy abrupt precipices of the most stupendous rocks, are not without their uses: they afford protection, refuge, and food, for creatures whose dispositions and habits are suited to such places; and thus no part of the creation is useless. The creatures who are their inhabitants are necessary *links* in the great *chain* of animated beings, and show the wisdom and providence of God.

For a description of the *coney*, see Lev. xi. 5. The יעל *yael*, translated here the *wild goat*, is no doubt a creature of the *stag* or *deer* kind; the *ibex, chamois, antelope,* &c.

Verse 19. *He appointed the moon for seasons*] The heathens thought that the *sun* and *moon* were gods, and worshipped them as such. The psalmist shows, 1. That they are creatures dependent on God for their being and continuance; and, 2. That they were made for the use of man. See what has been said on these luminaries in the notes on Gen. i.

Verse 20. *Thou makest darkness*] It is not the design of God that there should be either constant *darkness* or constant *light*. That man may *labour*, he gives him, by means of the *sun*, the *light of the day;* and that he may *rest* from his labour, and get his strength recruited, he gives him *night*, and comparative *darkness*. And as it would not be convenient for man and the wild beasts of the forest to collect their food

at the same time, he has given the *night* to them as the proper time to procure their prey, and the *day* to rest in. When MAN *labours*, THEY *rest; when* MAN *rests*, THEY *labour*.

Verse 21. *The young lions roar after their prey*] It is said of the lion, that his *roaring* is so terrible as to astonish and quite unnerve the beast which he pursues; so that, though fleeter than himself, it falls down and becomes an easy prey.

Verse 22. *The sun ariseth*] The dawn of day is the warning for *man* to arise and betake himself to his work; and is the warning to *them* to retire to their dens.

Verse 24. *O Lord, how manifold are thy works*] In this verse there are *three* propositions: 1. The works of the Lord are multitudinous and varied. 2. They are so constructed as to show the most consummate wisdom in their *design*, and in the *end* for which they are formed. 3. They are all God's *property*, and should be used only in reference to the end for which they were created. All *abuse* and *waste* of God's creatures are spoil and robbery on the property of the Creator. On this verse Mr. *Ray* has published an excellent work, entitled, "The Wisdom of God in the Creation," which the reader will do well, not only to consult, but carefully to read over and study.

Verse 25. *This great and wide sea*] The original is very emphatic: זה הים גדול ורחב ידים *zeh haiyam gadol urechab yadayim*, "This very sea, great and extensive of hands." Its waters, like *arms*, encompassing all the terrene parts of the globe. I suppose the psalmist was within sight of the Mediterranean when he wrote these words.

Verse 26. *There go the ships*] By means of navigation countries the most remote are connected, and all the inhabitants of the earth become known to each other. He appears at this time to have seen the ships under sail.

That leviathan] This may mean the *whale*, or any of the large marine animals. The *Septuagint* and *Vulgate* call it *dragon*. Sometimes the *crocodile* is intended by the original word.

To play therein.] Dreadful and tempestuous as the sea may appear, and uncontrollable in its billows and surges, it is only the field of *sport*, the *play-ground*, the *bowling-green* to those huge marine monsters.

A. M. cir. 3468
B. C. cir. 536
Cyri,
R. Persarum,
cir. annum
primum

27 �q These wait all upon thee; that thou mayest give *them* their meat in due season.

28 *That* thou givest them they gather: thou openest thine hand, they are filled with good.

29 Thou hidest thy face, they are troubled: ʳthou takest away their breath, they die, and return to their dust.

30 ˢThou sendest forth thy spirit, they are created: and thou renewest the face of the earth.

31 The glory of the LORD ᵗshall endure for ever: the LORD ᵘshall rejoice in his works.

A. M. cir. 3468
B. C. cir. 536
Cyri,
R. Persarum,
cir. annum
primum

32 He looketh on the earth, and it ᵛtrembleth: ʷhe toucheth the hills, and they smoke.

33 ˣI will sing unto the LORD as long as I live: I will sing praise to my God while I have my being.

34 My meditation of him shall be sweet: I will be glad in the LORD.

35 Let ʸthe sinners be consumed out of the earth, and let the wicked be no more. ᶻBless thou the LORD, O my soul. Praise ye the LORD.

---

qPsa. cxxxvi. 25; cxlv. 15; cxlvii. 9——rJob xxxiv. 14, 15; Psa. cxlvi. 4; Eccles. xii. 7——sIsa. xxxii. 15; Ezek. xxxvii. 9

tHeb. *shall be*——uGen. i. 31——vHab. iii. 10 wPsa. cxliv. 5——xPsa. lxiii. 4; cxlvi. 2——yPsa. xxxvii. 38; Prov. ii. 22——zVer. 1

Verse 27. *These wait all upon thee*] The innumerable *fry* of the smaller aquatic animals, as well as *whales, dolphins, porpoises,* and *sharks,* all have their meat from God. He has in his gracious providence furnished that sort of food which is suitable to all. And this provision is *various;* not only for *every kind* of fish does God provide food, but a *different kind* of aliment for each in its different *periods* of *growth.* Here are displayed the goodness and infinitely varied providence of God: "He giveth them their meat in due season."

Verse 28. That *thou givest them they gather*] All creatures are formed with such and such digestive organs, and the food proper for them is provided. Infinitely varied as are living creatures in their habits and internal economy, so are the aliments which God has caused the *air,* the *earth,* and the *waters* to produce.

Thou openest thine hand] An allusion to the act of scattering grain among fowls.

Verse 29. *Thou hidest thy face*] If thou bring dearth or famine on the *land,* contagion in the *air,* or any destruction on the provision made by the *waters,* then beasts, fowl, and fish die, and are dissolved.

Verse 30. *Thou sendest forth thy spirit, they are created*] יבראון *yibbareun,* "They are created again."

And thou renewest the face of the earth.] Do not these words plainly imply a *resurrection* of the bodies which have died, been dissolved, or turned to dust? And is not the brute creation principally intended here? Is it not on this account it is said, ver. 31, "the glory of the Lord shall endure for ever, (לעולם *leolam,*)" to be manifest in those *times* which are *secret,* when *Jehovah* himself *shall rejoice in his works;* when the brute creation shall be delivered from the bondage of its corruption? See the notes on Rom. viii. 19-23.

Verse 32. *He looketh on the earth*] Even the look of God terrifies all created nature!

He toucheth the hills] So easy is it for God to burn up the earth and the works thereof, that even his *touch* kindles the mountains into flames! See *Etna, Vesuvius, Stromboli,* &c.; these are *ignited* by the touch of God. How majestic are these figures!

The renewal of the earth, and re-creation of deceased animals, shall take place when he shall shake terribly the heavens and the earth; when they shall be wrapped together as a scroll, and the earth and its works be dissolved, that is, after the general *convulsion* and *conflagration* of the world.

Verse 33. *I will sing unto the Lord*] The psalmist exulting in the glorious prospect of the renovation of all things, breaks out in triumphant anticipation of the great event, and says, I will sing unto the Lord בחיי *bechaiyai,* with my *lives,* the life that I *now* have, and the *life* that I *shall have* hereafter.

I will sing praise to my God] בעודי *beodi,* "in my eternity;" my going on, my endless progression. What astonishing ideas! But then, how shall this great work be brought about? and how shall the new earth be inhabited with righteous spirits only? The answer is,

Verse 35. *Let the sinners be consumed out of the earth, and let the wicked be no more.*] Or, He shall consume the wicked and ungodly, till no more of them be found. Then the wicked shall be turned into hell, with all the nations that forget God. No wonder, with these prospects before his eyes, he cries out, "Bless Jehovah, O my soul! Hallelujah!" And *ye* that hear of these things, *bless the Lord* also.

ANALYSIS OF THE HUNDRED AND FOURTH PSALM

The scope of this Psalm is the same with that of the former, i. e., to excite them to praise God in consideration of his benefits; but yet on a different ground. In the former, for the benefits of grace conferred upon his Church; in this, for the gifts of nature bestowed in general upon all. Those flow immediately from his mercy; these, from his power, wisdom, and goodness, and depend upon his providence, and are manifest in the creation, governance, and preservation of all things. The creature then is the subject of this Psalm, relative to which we have a long but very methodical narration.

I. The exhortation proposed briefly, ver. 1.

II. The exhortation urged by the inspection of the fabric, the beauty, order, and government of the world, ver. 1-33.

III. The duty practised by himself, ver. 33, 34.

IV. An imprecation on them that neglect the duty, ver. 35.

I. He begins with a double apostrophe:—

1. To his own soul, to praise God: "Bless the Lord, O my soul;" which was the conclusion of the former Psalm.

2. To his God: "O Lord my God," whom he describes to be great and glorious. That he may set forth his majesty and glory, borrowing his figure from the person of some great king, presenting himself very glorious to his people in his robes, in his pavilion, with a glittering canopy extended over his throne; sometimes in his chariot, drawn by the swiftest horses, with his nobles, ministers, and servants, waiting on his pleasure.

In this way he describes the majesty of God in the works of the first and second day, for by that order he proceeds in setting forth God's works, that in which they were made.

1. His robe is the light, the work of the first day, which is the purest, the most illustrious and cheerful of all God's creatures. With this "he is clothed as with a garment," for he is light, John i. 1; and he dwells in that inaccessible light that no man hath seen, nor can see, 1 Tim. vi. 16.

2. His pavilion stretched round about him is the heavens, the work of the second day. These are as the hangings and curtains of his chamber of presence, by his fiat and power stretched out as we now see them: "He stretched out the heavens as a curtain."

3. His palace built in a most miraculous manner. The beams are laid, not as usual on a solid body, but upon that which is most fluent: "He lays the beams of his chambers in the waters." In Gen. i. 7 we read of the "waters above the firmament," which were a part of the second day's work; and of these the prophet surely speaks.

4. His chariot, the clouds: "Who makes the clouds his chariot." Upon these he rides in a most wonderful manner, in all places he pleases; which are now in this place, and then instantly removed to another.

5. The horses that draw it, the *winds*, *alipedes*, as the poets feigned the horses who drew the chariot of the sun. The psalmist intends to show that by the power of God they are brought upon the face of heaven, and removed at his pleasure.

6. His attendants, angels: "He maketh his angels spirits, his ministers a flaming fire." No creature of greater quickness and agility than a *spirit*, no element more active than *fire*. These blessed spirits he sends forth as he pleases, to defend his servants; and as a flame of fire to consume and burn up his enemies: in which appears his might and majesty.

II. Next, the prophet descends from the heavens, and out of the air, and speaks of the work of the third day; and begins with the earth, that element which is best known to us, in which he shows the power and wisdom of God many ways.

1. In the foundation of it upon its centre.

Strange it is that so great and heavy a body should remain in the midst of it and not sink; this the prophet attributes to the power and providence of God: "Who laid the foundations of the earth that it should not be removed for ever."

2. Another part of his providence about the *earth* was, that the water, being the lighter element, covered the earth, and thus rendered it useless. God, either by taking some parts of the upper superficies out of the earth in some places, made it more hollow, and putting them in others, made it convex; or in other words, by raising some and depressing others, made room for the sea; this was the work of God's word, and the prophet speaks of this in the three following verses.

1. He shows in what condition the *earth* was in the first creation; it was covered, and under water: "Thou coveredst it with the deep as with a garment; the waters stood above the mountains."

2. He shows that the earth became uncovered by the voice, power, and fiat of God: "Let the waters be gathered together into one place, and let the dry land appear." This the psalmist here calls the rebuke of God, the voice of thunder; for God no sooner spake than it was done: "At thy rebuke they fled, at the voice of thy thunder they were afraid."

3. And so there became a new world. The mountains and valleys take the lower place; the mists and vapours *go up by the mountains*.

4. There they inclose them: "Thou hast set a bound," &c. Yet not violently kept there, but restrained by an ordinary law of nature, it being natural for water to descend to the lower places.

III. He next speaks of the rivers and springs, and shows God's wonderful providence over them:—

1. "He sendeth the springs," the streams of water, from the hills "into the valleys."

2. "The end of this infinitely declares God's providence; it is for the sustenance of beasts and fowls, or they must perish for thirst: "The springs and rivers give drink to every beast of the field, the wild asses," &c.

IV. But the springs and rivers cannot water all parts of the earth; therefore, his wisdom devised the rain and the clouds.

"He watereth the hills from his chambers." The effect of which is,—

1. In general, the satisfaction of the earth, which, being thirsty, gapes for rain: "The earth is satisfied with the fruit of thy works."

2. In particular, the effects and consequences of the dews. 1. Grass for the cattle: "He causeth the grass to grow for the cattle." 2. Herbs for meat and medicine: "And herbs for the service of man." 3. All kinds of food: "And that he may bring forth food." 4. "And wine that makes glad the heart of man," lawfully used. 5. "And oil to make his face to shine." Oil supplies and strengthens the nerves, and keeps the flesh smooth, fresh, and youthful. 6. "And bread which strengtheneth man's heart;"

for it is always the chief and necessary part of the service.

V. Neither hath the God of providence forgotten to provide us trees for shade, building, and fuel, as well as to yield us fruit.

1. "The trees of the Lord also." His trees, because he first made them, and now causes them to grow. "They are full of sap," which is another effect of the rain.

2. "Where the birds make their nests."

3. Other creatures are not forgotten; not the goats nor the conies: "For the high hills," &c.

The psalmist next mentions the work of the fourth day; the creation of the two great luminaries, the sun and the moon.

1. "God appointed the moon for certain seasons."

2. "And the sun knoweth his going down."

And in this division of time, the providence of God is admirable: "Thou makest darkness, and it is night."

1. For the good of the beasts, even the wildest, that they be sustained. 1. The night comes, and the beasts of the forest creep forth: "The young lions," &c. 2. Again, the day appears: "The sun ariseth, and they appear not," &c.

2. For the good of man: "Man goeth forth to his labour." Labour he must all day, and then take rest: "Labour till the evening."

Upon the consideration of all which the prophet exclaims: "O God, how manifold are thy works! in wisdom hast thou made them all: the earth is full of thy riches."

1. "How manifold are thy works." How great, how excellent, how worthy of praise! such that I cannot express them.

2. "In wisdom hast thou made them all." Nothing is done by chance or rashness, but with great reason; neither too much nor too little.

3. "All the earth is full of thy riches." No place, no part of it, but thy works proclaim that thou art a bountiful and most wise Creator; an open handed and liberal bestower of riches.

The prophet has hitherto set forth God's wisdom in his works; in the heavens, air, the earth; and now he descends into the sea.

1. In the amplitude of it: It is the *great and wide sea.*

2. In the abundance of the fish, the work of the fifth day: "Wherein are things creeping innumerable."

3. In the useful art of navigation, which God taught by Noah's ark: "There go the ships."

4. In the whale: "There is that leviathan."

And the conservation of the creature now follows, from verse 27 to 30; where their dependence is shown upon the providence of God, both for their meat, life, and continuation of their *species.*

1. "These all wait upon thee;" they expect till thou givest.

2. "That thou mayest give them their meat." Meat fit for every season of the year, and when they want it.

3. "That thou givest them they gather." That, and no more nor less: and his power and blessing must co-operate with the second causes.

4. This he farther explains: "Thou openest thine hand, and they are filled with good."

Farther, life and death are in thy power. Death, and the forerunner of it; trouble.

1. "Thou hidest thy face;" seemest displeased, and withdrawest help and assistance; "and they are troubled."

2. "Thou takest away their breath; they die." And life also.

1. "Thou sendest forth thy spirit," a vital spirit, by restoring new individuals to every species.

2. And by this "thou renewest the face of the earth;" which, if not done, the whole would fail in an age.

Now, after this long catalogue of the creatures, and God's power, wisdom, and goodness made most manifest in the creation, governance, and sustentation of them, he descends, ver. 32.

1. "Let the glory of the Lord," his glory, for his wisdom, and goodness and power, "endure for ever." Hallowed be his name!

2. "The Lord shall rejoice in his works." Let man be so careful to use them well, that by the abuse he grieve not God, and cause him to repent that he made them.

3. Which if it happen, it would be remembered that he is a God, and able to punish the ungrateful person: "For if he looketh on the earth with a threatening brow, it trembleth."

He makes then an open profession of his own practice.

1. "I will sing unto the Lord as long as I live," &c.

2. And this he would do with delight: "My meditation of him shall be sweet," &c.

3. And he concludes with an imprecation against unthankful and negligent persons, who regard not the works of God, and will not see his glory, power, wisdom, and goodness, in his creating, governing, and sustaining this universe; and therefore very little praise him. Against these he prays that they may be confounded or converted.

"But, O my soul," be not thou like to them,— "bless the Lord. Hallelujah."

PSALM CV

An exhortation to praise God for his wondrous works, 1–5; his goodness to Abraham, Isaac, and Jacob, 6–16; to Joseph in Egypt, 17–22; to Israel in Egypt, 23–25; to Moses in the same land, 26; the plagues sent on the Egyptians, 27–36; the deliverance of the Israelites out of Egypt, 37, 38; how he supported them in the wilderness, 39–43; and brought them into Canaan, 44, 45.

A. M. cir. 3468
B. C. cir. 536
Cyri,
R. Persarum,
cir. annum
primum

O ᵃGIVE thanks unto the LORD; call upon his name: ᵇmake known his deeds among the people.

2 Sing unto him, sing psalms unto him: ᶜtalk ye of all his wondrous works.

3 Glory ye in his holy name: let the heart of them rejoice that seek the LORD.

4 Seek the LORD, and his strength: ᵈseek his face evermore.

5 ᵉRemember his marvellous works that he hath done; his wonders, and the judgments of his mouth;

6 O ye seed of Abraham his servant, ye children of Jacob his chosen.

7 He *is* the LORD our God: ᶠhis judgments *are* in all the earth.

8 He has ᵍremembered his covenant for ever,

the word *which* he commanded to a thousand generations.

A. M. cir. 3468
B. C. cir. 536
Cyri,
R. Persarum,
cir. annum
primum

9 ʰWhich *covenant* he made with Abraham, and his oath unto Isaac;

10 And confirmed the same unto Jacob for a law, *and.* to Israel *for* an everlasting covenant:

11 Saying, ⁱUnto thee will I give the land of Canaan, ᵏthe lot of your inheritance:

12 ˡWhen there were *but* a few men in number; yea, very few, ᵐand strangers in it.

13 When they went from one nation to another, from *one* kingdom to another people;

14 ⁿHe suffered no man to do them wrong: yea, ᵒhe reproved kings for their sakes;

15 *Saying,* Touch not mine anointed, and do my prophets no harm.

16 Moreover ᵖhe called for a famine upon

ᵃ1 Chron. xvi. 8–22; Isa. xii. 4——ᵇPsa. cxlv, 4. 5, 11 ᶜPsa. lxxvii. 12; cxix. 27——ᵈPsa. xxvii. 8——ᵉPsa. lxxvii. 11——ᶠIsa. xxvi. 9——ᵍLuke i. 72——ʰGen. xvii. 2; xxii. 16, &c.; xxvi. 3; xxviii. 13; xxxv. 11; Luke

i. 73; Heb. vi. 17——ⁱGen. xiii. 15; xv. 18——ᵏHeb. *the cord*——ˡGen. xxxiv. 30; Deut. vii. 7; xxvi. 5——ᵐHeb. xi. 9——ⁿGen. xxxv. 5——ᵒGen. xii. 17; xx. 3, 7 ᵖGen. xli. 54

NOTES ON PSALM CV

We find several verses of this Psalm in 1 Chron. xvi., from which it is evident that David was the author of the principal part of it: but it was probably enlarged and sung at the restoration of the people from the Babylonish captivity. The *hallelujah* which terminates the preceding Psalm, is made the *title* of this by the *Vulgate, Septuagint, Æthiopic,* and *Arabic:* but it has no title either in the *Hebrew* or *Chaldee.* The Syriac considers it a paraphrase on the words, "Fear not, Jacob, to go down into Egypt; and teach us spiritually not to fear when we are obliged to contend with devils; for God is our shield, and will fight for us." The Psalm is a history of God's dealings with Abraham and his posterity, till their settlement in the promised land.

Verse 1. *O give thanks*] He had been meditating on God's gracious dealings with their fathers; and he calls upon himself and all others to magnify God for his mercies.

Verse 2. *Talk ye of all his wondrous works.*]

נפלאתיו *niphleothaiv,* "of his miracles." Who have so many of these to boast of as Christians! Christianity is a tissue of miracles; and every part of the work of grace on the soul is a miracle. Genuine Christian converts may talk of miracles from morning to night; and they *should talk of them,* and recommend to others their miracle-working God and Saviour.

Verse 3. *Glory ye in his holy name*] Show the name Jesus: exult in it—praise it. His name was called *Jesus;* because he came to save his people from their sins.

Let the heart of them rejoice] That is, the heart of those *shall* rejoice who seek the Lord: therefore it is added,—

Verse 4. *Seek the Lord*] Worship the one

only Supreme Being, as the only and all-sufficient good for the soul of man.

And his strength] Man is *weak;* and needs connexion with the *strong* God that he may be enabled to avoid evil and do good.

Seek his face] Reconciliation to him. Live not without a sense of his favour.

Evermore.] Let this be thy chief business. In and above all thy seeking, seek this.

Verse 5. *Remember his marvellous works*] Keep up communion with thy Maker, that thou mayest neither forget him nor his works.

The judgments of his mouth] Whatsoever he has spoken concerning good or evil. His commands, promises, threatenings; and particularly what he has foretold, and what he has done.

Verse 6. *O ye seed of Abraham*] Ye Jews especially, who have been the peculiar objects of the Divine favour.

Verse 7. *He is the Lord our God*] He is *Jehovah,* the self-existent and eternal God. He is *our God,* he is our portion; has taken us for his people, and makes us happy in his love.

The following abstract of the history of the Israelites presents but few difficulties. See the notes on Psalm lxxviii.

Verse 12. But *a few men*] When all appearances were against them, and nothing but the arm of God could have brought them through their difficulties, and given them a settlement in the promised land.

Verse 13. *When they went from one nation to another*] From several circumstances in the history of the travels of the ancient Hebrews, we find that the wilderness through which they then passed was well peopled.

Verse 15. *Touch not mine anointed*] It is supposed that the *patriarchs* are here intended; but the whole people of Israel may be meant. They were a kingdom of *priests* and *kings*

A. M. cir. 3468
B. C. cir. 536
Cyri,
R. Persarum,
cir. annum
primum

the land: he brake the whole qstaff of bread.

17 rHe sent a man before them, *even* Joseph, *who* swas sold for a servant:

18 tWhose feet they hurt with fetters: uhe was laid in iron:

19 Until the time that his word came: vthe word of the LORD tried him.

20 wThe king sent and loosed him; *even* the ruler of the people, and let him go free.

21 xHe made him lord of his house, and ruler of all his ysubstance:

22 To bind his princes at his pleasure; and teach his senators wisdom.

23 zIsrael also came into Egypt; and Jacob sojourned ain the land of Ham.

24 And bhe increased his people greatly; and made them stronger than their enemies.

25 cHe turned their heart to hate his people, to deal subtilly with his servants.

26 dHe sent Moses his servant; *and* Aaron ewhom he had chosen.

27 fThey showed ghis signs among them, hand wonders in the land of Ham.

28 iHe sent darkness, and made it dark; and kthey rebelled not against his word.

29 lHe turned their waters into blood, and slew their fish.

30 mTheir land brought forth frogs in abundance, in the chambers of their kings.

31 nHe spake, and there came divers sorts of flies, *and* lice in all their coasts.

32 oHe pgave them hail for rain, *and* flaming fire in their land.

33 qHe smote their vines also and their fig-trees; and brake the trees of their coasts.

34 rHe spake, and the locusts came, and caterpillars, and that without number,

35 And did eat up all the herbs in their land, and devoured the fruit of their ground.

36 sHe smote also all the first-born in their land, tthe chief of all their strength.

37 uHe brought them forth also with silver and gold: and *there was* not one feeble *person* among their tribes.

38 vEgypt was glad when they departed: for the fear of them fell upon them.

39 wHe spread a cloud for a covering; and fire to give light in the night.

40 x*The people* asked, and he brought quails and ysatisfied them with the bread of heaven.

41 zHe opened the rock, and the waters

A. M. cir. 3468
B. C. cir. 536
Cyri,
R. Persarum,
cir. annum
primum

---

qLev. xxvi. 26; Isa. iii. 1; Ezek. iv. 16——rGen. xlv. 5; l. 20——sGen. xxxvii. 28, 36——tGen. xxxix. 20; xl. 15 uHeb. *his soul came into iron*——vGen. xli. 25——wGen. xli. 14——xGen. xli. 40——yHeb. *possession*——zGen. xlvi. 6——aPsa. lxxviii. 51; cvi. 22——bExod. i. 7 cExod. i. 8, &c.——dExod. iii. 10; iv. 12, 14——eNum. xvi. 5; xvii. 5——fExod. vii., viii., ix., x., xi., xii.; Psa. lxxviii. 43, &c.——gHeb. *words of his signs*——hPsa. cvi. 22——iExod. x. 22——kPsa. xcix. 7

lExod. vii. 20; Psa. lxxviii. 44——mExod. viii. 6; Psa. lxxviii. 45——nExod. viii. 17, 24; Psa. lxxviii. 45 oExod. ix. 23, 25; Psa. lxxviii. 48——pHeb. *He gave their rain hail*——qPsa. lxxviii. 47——rExod. x. 4, 13, 14; Psa. lxxviii. 46——sExod. xii. 29; Psa. lxxviii. 51 tGen. xlix. 3——uExod. xii. 35——vExod. xii. 33 wExod. xiii. 21; Neh. ix. 12——xExod. xvi. 12, &c.; Psa. lxxviii. 18, 27——yPsa. lxxviii. 24, 25——zExod. xvii. 6; Num. xx. 11; Psa. lxxviii. 15, 16; 1 Cor. x. 4

---

unto God; and *prophets, priests,* and *kings* were always *anointed.*

Verse 19. *Until the time that his word came*] This appears to refer to the completion of Joseph's interpretation of the dreams of the chief butler and baker.

The word of the Lord tried him.] This seems to refer to the interpretation of Pharaoh's dreams, called אמרת יהוה *imrath Yehovah*, "the oracle of the Lord," because sent by him to Pharaoh. See Gen. xli. 25, and *Kennicott in loco.*

Verse 25. *He turned their heart*] "Their heart was turned." So the *Syriac* and *Arabic.* After befriending the Hebrews on Joseph's account, to whom they were so deeply indebted, finding them to multiply greatly in the land, and at last to become more powerful than the Egyptians themselves, they turned their attention to the adoption of measures, in order to prevent the Hebrews from possessing themselves of the government of the whole land; they curtailed them of their privileges, and endeavoured to depress them by all possible means, and by a variety of legal enactments. This appears to be the sole meaning of the

phrase, "He turned their heart;" or, "their heart was turned."

Verse 27. *They showed his signs*] Here is a reference to the *plagues* with which God afflicted the Egyptians. See the places in the margin, and the notes on them.

Verse 28. *They rebelled not against his word.*] Instead of ולא מרו *velo maru,* "they rebelled," some think that a ש *shin* has been lost from before the word, and that it should be read ולא שמרו *velo shamru,* "they did not observe *or* keep his word." Or the words may be spoken of *Moses* and *Aaron;* they received the commandment of God, and they did not rebel against it. They believed what he had spoken, and acted according to his orders. It could not be spoken of the *Egyptians;* for they rebelled against his words through the whole course of the transactions.

Verse 33. *He smote their vines also, and their fig trees*] This is not mentioned in Exodus; but we have had it before, Psalm lxxviii. 47.

Verse 41. *He opened the rock, and the waters gushed out*] See the note on Exod. xvii. 6, to

A. M. cir. 3468
[B. C. cir. 536
Cyri,
R. Persarum,
cir. annum
primum

gushed out; they ran in the dry places *like* a river.

42 For he remembered ^ahis holy promise, *and* Abraham his servant.

43 And he brought forth his people with joy, *and* his chosen with ^bgladness:

44 ^cAnd gave them the lands of the heathen: and they inherited the labour of the people;

45 ^dThat they might observe his statutes, and keep his laws. ^ePraise ye the LORD.

A. M. cir. 3468
B. C. cir. 536
Cyri,
R. Persarum,
cir. annum
primum

---

^aGenesis xv. 14——^bHebrew, *singing*——^cDeuteronomy vi. 10, 11; Joshua xiii. 7, &c.; Psalm lxxviii.

55——^dDeuteronomy iv. 1, 40; vi. 21-25——^eHebrew, *Hallelujah*

---

which I can now add, that a piece of this rock, broken off by the hand of my nephew, E. S. A. Clarke, in the course of the present year [1822,] now lies before me. It is fine *granite;* and so well distinguished as a granite, that the *feldt-spar*, the *mica*, and the *quartz*, of which granite is composed, appear very distinctly. It is worthy of remark, that, as *granite* is supposed, in the most accredited *systems of geology*, to be the very *basis* of the *earth*, the *original rock*, and all other substances to be superimpositions upon it, and as the decompositions of the *feldt-spar* produce pure vegetable earth, this rock should be used for this purpose, and should be an emblem of Jesus Christ, the Creator and Redeemer of the human race; and that it should signify him who is the *basis of all things;* who upholds all by the word of his power; without whom nothing is *stable*, nothing *fruitful;* from whom alone the *water of life* proceeds; and in whose name only is salvation. *And that rock* (in the wilderness) *was Christ!* and it is the only *remaining emblem* of him in creation.

Verse 45. *That they might observe his statutes*] That they might be properly *instructed*, and properly *disciplined*. This is the end proposed by Divine revelation: men are to be made wise unto salvation, and then to be brought under the yoke of obedience. He who is not conformed to God's word shall not enter into Christ's kingdom.

ANALYSIS OF THE HUNDRED AND FIFTH PSALM

The *title* of this Psalm is *Hallelujah*, as are also the two following; and the first fifteen verses of it were sung at the bringing up of the ark by *David*, 1 Chron. xvi.

The scope of it is the same with the two former Psalms, "that we praise God;" but yet with this difference: in the hundred and third, that he be magnified "for his benefits of redemption;" in the hundred and fourth, "for the manifestation of his power and providence in creating, governing, and sustaining the world;" but in this, "for the gracious covenant he made with Abraham, and, in him, with his whole Church."

I. An exhortation to praise God, ver. 1-7.

II. An enumeration of the favours God bestowed to persuade to it, from ver. 7 to the end.

I. He that loves his prince truly desires also that others should magnify and honour him. This was David's case; he was a true lover of his God, and set a true estimate upon him. He honoured and praised God himself, and desired that others should do the same outwardly and inwardly, with heart and tongue: he thought

all too little, and therefore, he repeats the duty often, and shows how it is to be done.

1. By giving of thanks: "O give thanks unto the Lord."

2. By invocation: "Call upon his name."

3. By communication: "Make known his deeds among the people."

4. By voices, psalms, and hymns: "Sing unto him; sing psalms unto him."

5. By frequent colloquies of his works: "Talk ye of all his wondrous works."

6. By boasting of him: "Glory ye in his holy name." Profess that you are happy men, that God's holy name was ever made known to you. "He that glories, let him glory in the Lord;" 2 Cor. xi.

He invites all outwardly to exhibit praise; and now he advises that it be done inwardly also, with exultation and gladness of heart.

1. "Let the heart of them rejoice." The Holy Spirit does not sing but out of a joyous heart.

2. "Let them seek the Lord." For, indeed, they only who seek him rejoice heartily: they can acquiesce in God, in his promises of grace, pardon, and acceptance; which is so necessary to every one who will make his approaches to the throne of grace, and have his praise rendered acceptable, that the prophet seriously urges the duty:—

(1) "Seek the Lord." Cast all impiety and wickedness away: seek him.

(2) "Seek his strength." Which at that time was the ark, it being the symbol of his presence. Seek him in his Church.

(3) "Seek his face evermore." His favour, and grace, and reconciliation; seek them in his word and sacraments, &c.

(4) "Evermore seek him." Now and then is too little; it must be our constant work.

Having thus spoken of the heart, he comes to the memory: "Remember, forget not." And the things to be remembered are, 1. *His marvellous works*. 2. *His wonders*. 3. *His judgments;* which three are the substance of this whole Psalm, and are explained according to their heads. They ought to be particularly remembered by the Israelites, the posterity of Abraham, and the sons of Jacob.

"Remember his marvellous works," &c. "O ye seed of Abraham, his servant; ye children of Jacob, his chosen." Remember that he made *Abraham* and chose *Jacob* to be his servants, gave you laws, and showed you with what rites he would be worshipped. Forget them not.

II. But at the *seventh* verse the prophet begins his narration; and tells the *Israelites*, and in them us, what marvellous works God had done for his people, all which he presses as arguments to his people that they should praise, honour, worship, and obey him. There is much reason for it.

1. "He is the Lord our God." The same argument prefaces the commandments: "I am the Lord thy God."

2. "His judgments are in all the earth." He is a mighty Monarch, and has all nature under his empire.

And if neither of these move, yet there is another, drawn from his many and infinite favours: "On you Israelites," and all mankind as well; for on the fall of man his covenant was, *That the seed of the woman should bruise the serpent's head;* and this he forgot not: "He hath remembered his covenant," &c.

1. "Which covenant he made with Abraham," and confirmed it by sacrifice, Gen. xv. 13.

2. "His oath unto Isaac," Gen. xxvi. 3, 4.

3. "And confirmed the same unto Jacob for a law," &c.; Gen. xxviii. 13, 14, 15.

4. The form of the covenant recited: "Saying, Unto thee will I give," &c.; for it was divided to the tribes by lots.

Which covenant God made with their fathers and them, not out of any merit that could be in them; Deut. viii. 4, 5, 6; Josh. xxiv. 2.

1. "When there were but a few men," and humble; "yea, very few."

2. And they "strangers" in the land. For the patriarchs only sojourned in *Canaan.*

3. Yea, "when they went from one nation to another," &c.

Now when they were in this condition, *very few, strangers, sojourners,* and *pilgrims,* God protected and defended them.

1. "He suffered no man to do them wrong," &c.; no, not the greatest, for "he reproved even kings for their sakes."

2. For he gave the command: "Touch not mine anointed,"—*Abraham, Isaac,* and *Jacob,* who were anointed with the Holy Ghost, though not with material oil; "and do my prophets no harm," i. e., the same men, for they were prophets. *Abraham* foresaw the bondage of his seed in *Egypt; Isaac* foretold what should befall *Esau's* posterity, Gen. xxvii.; and *Jacob,* by a prophetical spirit, gave his blessings, Gen. xlix. Of *Abraham* it is expressly said, "He is a prophet, and he shall pray for thee," Gen. xx. 7.

Two of these mercies, the covenant and protection, are already named; and now he goes on and insists upon the third, verses 16-23, for which there was infinite matter of praise for the wonderful wisdom of God, that brought out of the greatest evils the chiefest good, by preserving their lives in *Egypt* in the midst of famine, Gen. xxxvii.

1. "Moreover he called for a famine upon the land." It came not by chance.

2. "He brake the whole staff of bread," the upholder of our lives; and this he brake when he ordered that there should be no ploughing, sowing, nor harvest, Gen. xlv.

3. By this famine the patriarchs were to suffer; yet God provided for their subsistence: "He sent a man, (a wise man,) before them,"— Joseph.

4. This Joseph was sold by the envy and cruelty of his brethren.

And now he comes, 1. To his base usage. 2. His advancement.

1. By the false accusation of *Potiphar's* wife, who turned her base love into hatred: "His feet were hurt with fetters of iron."

2. "He was laid in iron;" or, as some read,

"the iron entered into his soul." Grief that he should lie under foul aspersions.

There he lay: "Until the time that his word came." So long then he lay in prison, and no longer.

1. "Until the time that his word came:" his word—God's word for his deliverance. Or, as others: "Joseph's word to the butler."

2. "The word of the Lord tried him." God tried his patience: or the interpretation of the dreams proved that by the Lord he spake.

And now follows his honour and advancement:—

1. *Pharaoh,* by his *butler,* hearing of *Joseph's* wisdom: "He sent," &c.

2. "Even the ruler of the people let him go free." A work fit for a king.

And his advancement follows:—

1. "He made him lord of his house."

2. "A ruler of all his substance." A viceroy, a grand vizier.

The king's end in it; not only in the famine to provide bread for their bodies, but for the good of their souls.

1. To punish the rebellious: "To bind his princes at his pleasure."

2. To instruct his counsellors in wisdom, arts, sciences, religion. It is supposed that all the learning in which the Egyptians excelled was first taught them by *Joseph.*

The fourth benefit follows of God towards his people, ver. 22-37, which was their nourishment, increase in Egypt, their oppression, and deliverance.

1. He begins with Jacob's descent thither: 1. "Israel also, Joseph's father, went down into Egypt," Gen. xlvi. 2. "And Jacob with all his family," &c.

2. He proceeds with their strange increase there; for it is wonderful that in so short a time they should grow into such a multitude, Exod. i. 7. At their going out they were six hundred thousand, besides children, Exod. xii. 37: "And he increased his people greatly, and made them stronger than their enemies," Exod. i. 9.

This was the occasion of their afflictions, bondage, and sufferings; for,—

1. "He turned the Egyptians' hearts to hate his people." He suffered them to be turned: "For there arose another king," &c.

2. "And to deal subtilly with his people. Come on, say they," &c.

"To set over them taskmasters," &c.; Exod. i. 11. But when they saw "that the more they afflicted them, the more they multiplied," ver. 12, then they ordered "that all the male children should be strangled by the midwives," ver. 16. And when even this would not do, then *Pharaoh* charged "that every son that was born," &c., ver. 22. Thus subtilly they dealt; but it did not hinder their multiplication. There is no counsel against God.

Now God, seeing their affliction, and hearing their groans, sent them a deliverer.

1. "He sent Moses his servant, and Aaron whom he had chosen."

2. "They showed his signs among them." 1. To the Israelites; 2. "And wonders in the land of Ham."

The catalogue follows:—

1. "He sent darkness," &c.

2. "He turned their waters into blood," &c.

3. "The land brought forth frogs," &c.

4. "He spake, and there came divers sorts of flies," &c.

5. "He gave them hail for rain," &c.

6. "He smote the vines also, and the fig-trees," &c.

7. "He spake, and the locusts came," &c.

8. "He smote also the first-born of their land," &c.

These were the wonders that God wrought in Egypt by the hand of *Moses* and *Aaron* for the deliverance of his people, which the psalmist briefly records that they might remember—be thankful, and praise him.

The fifth benefit that the psalmist records is, that God brought not out his people beggars, but enriched them with the spoils of Egypt.

1. "He brought them forth with silver and gold." For they were sent by God to ask jewels: and when the Jews pretend by their example to rob more honest men than themselves, when they can show an immediate commission from God to do it, I am content that they borrow, and never restore; rob and spoil whom they please. Till this be shown, they are thieves and sacrilegious persons.

2. Farther, they left the *Egyptians* afflicted with some strange disease, of which their first-born had died; yet they were healthy: "There was not one, no, not one feeble person, among them."

The terror of them was so great, and the fear of death so instant, that, regarding not their jewels, they urged them to be gone—they thrust them out; which the prophet expresses: "Egypt was glad when they departed."

The sixth benefit follows after their departure, which was "the pillar of cloud by day, and of fire by night. He spread a cloud for a covering," &c.; which most interpret as if the cloud kept off the heat of the sun; and therefore the prophet says: "He spread it for a covering."

The seventh benefit was *quails* and *manna:*—

1. "The people asked, and he brought quails." Those given Exod. xvi.

2. "And satisfied them with the bread of heaven"—*manna*, because it was made of the sweet dew descending from the air, and therefore called heavenly bread; the earth having nothing to do with its production.

The eighth benefit was the water out of the rock; "for they travelled through a dry wilderness."

1. "He opened the rock." He did not turn the rock into water, but opened a passage for the fountain he had made.

2. *For the waters gushed out* upon the passage being made for them.

3. "And they ran in dry places."

Now here he inserts the reason both of the former and latter benefits, which was his covenant and promise to Abraham: "For he remembered his holy promise," &c.

The ninth benefit was, he brought them not only out of Egypt; but that too in such a manner that they had reason to exult and triumph, Exod. xv.: "And he brought forth his people with joy," &c.

And to make the number of his benefits complete, he adds a tenth, which was the exact fulfilling of his promise, his introduction of them into *Canaan*, ejection of the inhabitants, and the donation of their inheritances to his people, which they afterwards possessed.

"He gave them the lands of the heathen," &c. The houses they built not, the vines they planted not, the lands they tilled not, fell to them.

For which benefits God requires no more than their obedience: this he requires as his due and tribute. He bestowed so many benefits on them for one end only: "That they might observe his statutes, and keep his laws." Hallelujah! "Let *your* light so shine before men, that they may glorify your Father who is in heaven."

PSALM CVI

God is praised for his manifold mercies, 1–3. The prophet prays for himself, 4, 5. A recapitulation of the history of the Hebrew people: of God's mercies toward them, and their rebellions, 6–39. The judgments and afflictions which their transgressions brought upon them, 40–42. God's mercy to them notwithstanding their transgressions, 43–46. He prays for their restoration, 47, 48.

XXI. DAY. EVENING PRAYER

P RAISE [a]ye the LORD. [b]O [c]give thanks unto the LORD; for *he is* good: for his mercy *endureth* for ever.

2 [d]Who can utter the mighty acts of the LORD? *who* can show forth all his praise?

3 Blessed *are* they that keep judgment, *and* he that [e]doeth righteousness at [f]all times.

---

[a]Heb. *Hallelujah*——[b]1 Chron. xvi. 34——[c]Psa. cvii. 1; cxviii. 1; cxxxvi. 1

[d]Psa. xl. 5——[e]Psa. xv. 2——[f]Acts xxiv. 16; Gal. vi. 9

NOTES ON PSALM CVI

As a part of the preceding Psalm is found in 1 Chron. xvi., so the first and two last verses of *this* are found in the same place, (ver. 34-36,) and yet it is supposed by eminent commentators to be a prayer of the captives in Babylon, who acknowledge the mercies of God, confess their own sins, and those of their forefathers, and implore the Lord to gather them from among the heathen, and restore them to their own country. In none of the *Versions* except the *Syriac* has it any title, except HALLELUJAH, *Praise ye the Lord*, the word with which the original commences. The *Syriac* gives us a sort of table of its contents; or rather shows us the subjects to which it may be *applied*, and the uses we should make of it. After stating that it has *no* title, it says, "It calls upon men to observe the Divine precepts, and teaches us that the

4 ᵍRemember me, O Lord, with the favour *that thou bearest unto* thy people: O visit me with thy salvation;

5 That I may see the good of thy chosen, that I may rejoice in the gladness of thy nation, that I may glory with thine inheritance.

6 ʰWe have sinned with our fathers, we have committed iniquity, we have done wickedly.

7 Our fathers understood not thy wonders in Egypt; they remembered not the multitude of thy mercies; ⁱbut provoked *him* at the sea, *even* at the Red Sea.

8 Nevertheless he saved them ᵏfor his name's sake, ˡthat he might make his mighty power to be known.

9 ᵐHe rebuked the Red Sea also, and it was

ᵍPsa. cxix. 132——ʰLev. xxvi. 40; 1 Kings viii. 47; Dan. ix. 5——ⁱExod. xiv. 11, 12

ᵏEzek. xx. 14——ˡExod. ix. 16——ᵐExod. xiv. 21; Psa. xviii. 15; Nah. i. 4

---

more the Jews transgressed, the more we should fear. That we should not talk together in the Church, nor ever contend with our brethren on any account; and especially when we assist in the celebration of the Divine mysteries and in prayer: and that when we sin we should repent." All this is very good: but it would be difficult to find these subjects in the Psalm, or any thing on which they could be rationally founded. But it shows us that the Scriptures were very easily *accommodated* to particular uses, not originally intended: and hence arose much of the practice of *spiritualizing* and *allegorizing;* which, to say the least of it, has been of no use to the Church of Christ.

Verse 1. *Praise ye the Lord*] This, which is a sort of *title,* is wanting in several MSS., and in the Syriac Version.

O give thanks unto the Lord; for he is good] Ye who live by his bounty should praise his mercy. God is the good Being, and of all kinds of good he is the Author and Dispenser. That the term *God* among our Anglo-Saxon ancestors, expressed both the Supreme Being and *good* or *goodness,* is evident from the Anglo-Saxon version of this clause: anꝺettaꝺ ꝺrihtne ꝼonꝺon ᵹoꝺ, ꝼonꝺon on populꝺa milꝺheortnyrra. "Confess Lord for that God, (or good,) for that on world mildheartness his." Which the old Psalter thus translates and paraphrases:—

Trans. 𝔖chriſes to 𝔏orꝺe for ϸe iſ ᵹuꝺe; for in worlꝺe ϸe mercy of ϸim.

Par. Schryfes synes, and louyngs to God. for he is gude of kynde, that nane do bot aske his mercy; for it lastes to the worlds ende in wriches whame it comfortes and delyvers: and the blysfulhede that is gyfen thrugh mercy is endles. That is:—

Confess your sins, and give praise to God, for he is good in his nature to all that ask his mercy; for it lasts to the world's end in comforting and delivering the wretched: and the blessedness that is given through mercy is endless.

Verse 2. *Who can utter the mighty acts of the Lord?*] His acts are all acts of *might;* and particularly those in behalf of his followers.

Verse 3. *Blessed* are *they that keep judgment, and he that doeth righteousness at all times.*] How near do the *Anglo-Saxon,* the ancient *Scottish Version,* and the *present translation,* approach to each other!

Anglo-Saxon. eaꝺiᵹ ϸaꝺe healꝺaꝺ ꝺom, ⁊ ꝺoϸ rihtꝼiᵹnyrre on ælcеɲе tiꝺе. "Blessed they that holdeth doom, and doth righteousness in ilkere tide."

Anglo-Scottish. Blisful tha that kepes dome, and duse rightwisnes in ilk tyme.

Those are truly blessed, or happy, whose

hearts are devoted to God, and who live in the habit of obedience. Those, the general tenor of whose life is not conformed to the will of God, have no true happiness.

Verse 4. *Remember me*] This and the following clauses are read in the plural by several MSS.: *Remember* us—*that* we *may rejoice,*—*that* we *may glory,* &c.: and thus *all the Versions* except the *Chaldee;* and this is more agreeable to the context.

Verse 5. *That I may see the good of thy chosen*] That I may *enjoy* the good, for so the word *see* is understood among the Hebrews. "Blessed are the pure in heart, for they shall *see* God,"—they shall *enjoy* him, possess his favour, and be made like unto him.

Verse 6. *We have sinned*] Here the confession begins; what preceded was only the *introduction* to what follows: *Our forefathers sinned,* and suffered; we, like them, have sinned, and do suffer.

Verse 7. *Our fathers understood not*] They did not regard the operation of God's hands; and therefore they understood neither his designs nor their own interest.

At the sea, even at the Red Sea.] Some of the rabbins suppose that the repetition of the words point out *two* faults of the Israelites at the Red Sea. 1. They murmured against Moses for bringing them out of Egypt, when they saw the sea before them, and Pharaoh behind them. 2. When the waters were divided, they were afraid to enter in, lest they sould stick in the mud which appeared at the bottom. The word seems to be added by way of explanation, and perhaps may refer to the above: *they provoked* עַל יָם *al yam,* "at the sea;" בְּיַם סוּף *beyam suph,* "in the sea *Suph,*" or *Red Sea.* They provoked him *at* it and *in* it.

Verse 8. *He saved them for his name's sake*] לְמַעַן שְׁמוֹ *lemaan shemo,* "on account of his name;" to manifest his own power, goodness, and perfections. There was nothing which he could draw from them as a reason why he should save them; therefore he drew the reason from himself. There is a singular gloss in the old *Psalter* on this verse: "Whan thai cam oute of Egypt to the rede Se, whare thai were closed on a syde with a hylle that na man mygt passe: on another side was the rede See: behynde tham was men of Egypt foluand; and for this thai began to gruch, forgetand Gods mygt: bot than he safed tham, depertand the Se in twelfe, to ilk kynde of Isrel a passage." It seems as if this author thought there were *twelve* passages made through the Red Sea, that each tribe should have a passage to itself.

Verse 9. *He rebuked the Red Sea*] In the

dried up: so [n]he led them through the depths, as through the wilderness.

10 And he [o]saved them from the hand of him that hated *them,* and redeemed them from the hand of the enemy.

11 [p]And the waters covered their enemies: there was not one of them left.

12 [q]Then believed they his words; they sang his praise.

13 [r]They [s]soon forgat his works; they waited not for his counsel:

14 [t]But [u]lusted exceedingly in the wilderness, and tempted God in the desert.

15 [v]And he gave them their request; but [w]sent leanness into their soul.

16 [x]They envied Moses also in the camp, *and* Aaron the saint of the LORD.

17 [y]The earth opened and swallowed up Dathan, and covered the company of Abiram.

18 [z]And a fire was kindled in their company; the flame burned up the wicked.

19 [a]They made a calf in Horeb and worshipped the molten image.

20 Thus [b]they changed their glory into the similitude of an ox that eateth grass.

21 They [c]forgat God their Saviour, which had done great things in Egypt;

22 Wondrous works in [d]the land of Ham, *and* terrible things by the Red Sea.

23 [e]Therefore he said that he would destroy them, had not Moses his chosen [f]stood before him in the breach, to turn away his wrath, lest he should destroy *them.*

24 Yea, they despised [g]the [h]pleasant land, they [i]believed not his word:

25 [k]But murmured in their tents, *and* hearkened not unto the voice of the LORD.

26 [l]Therefore he [m]lifted up his hand against them, to overthrow them in the wilderness:

27 [n]To [o]overthrow their seed also among the nations, and to scatter them in the lands.

28 [p]They joined themselves also unto Baalpeor, and ate the sacrifices of the dead.

29 Thus they provoked *him* to anger with their inventions: and the plague brake in upon them.

30 [q]Then stood up Phinehas, and executed judgment: and *so* the plague was stayed.

31 And that was counted unto him [r]for righteousness unto all generations for evermore.

32 [s]They angered *him* also at the waters of strife, [t]so that it went ill with Moses for their sakes:

---

[n]Isa. lxiii. 11, 12, 13, 14——[o]Exod. xiv. 30——[p]Exod. xiv. 27, 28; xv. 5——[q]Exod. xiv. 31; xv. 1——[r]Exod. xv. 24; xvi. 2; xvii. 2; Psa. lxxviii. 11——[s]Heb. *They made haste, they forgat*——[t]Num. xi. 4, 33; Psa. lxxviii. 18; 1 Cor. x. 6——[u]Heb. *lusted a lust*——[v]Num. xi. 31; Psa. lxxviii. 29——[w]Isa. x. 16——[x]Num. xvi. 1, &c. [y]Num. xvi. 31, 32; Deut. xi. 6——[z]Num. xvi. 35, 46 [a]Exod. xxxii. 4——[b]Jer. ii. 11; Rom. i. 23——[c]Psa. lxxviii. 11, 12——[d]Psa. lxxviii. 51; cv. 23, 27——[e]Exod. xxxii. 10, 11, 32; Deut. ix. 19, 25; x. 10; Ezek. xx. 13

[f]Ezek. xiii. 5; xxii. 30——[g]Deut. viii. 7; Jer. iii. 19. Ezek. xx. 6——[h]Heb. *a land of desire*——[i]Heb. iii. 18 [k]Num. xiv. 2, 27——[l]Num. xiv. 28, &c.; Psa. xcv. 11; Ezek. xx. 15; Heb. iii. 11, 18——[m]Exod. vi. 8; Deut. xxxii. 40——[n]Heb. *To make them fall*——[o]Lev. xxvi. 33; Psa. xliv. 11; Ezek. xx. 23——[p]Num. xxv. 2, 3; xxxi. 16; Deut. iv. 3; xxxii. 17; Hos. ix. 10; Wisd. xiv. 15; Rev. ii. 14——[q]Num. xxv. 7, 8——[r]Num. xxv. 11, 12, 13 [s]Num. xx. 3, 13; Psa. lxxxi. 7——[t]Num. xx. 12; Deut. i. 37; iii. 26

---

descriptions of the psalmist *every thing has life.* The *sea* is an *animated being,* behaves itself proudly, is rebuked, and retires in confusion.

Verse 10. *The hand of him that hated* them] Pharaoh.

Verse 12. *Then believed they*] Just while the miracle was before their eyes.

Verse 13. *They soon forgat his works*] Three days afterwards, at the waters of Marah, Exod. xv. 24.

They waited not for his counsel] They were impatient, and would not wait till God should in his own way fulfil his own designs.

Verse 15. *Sent leanness*] They despised the manna, and called it *light,* that is, *innutritive, bread.* God gave *flesh* as they desired, but gave no blessing with it; and in consequence they did not fatten, but grew *lean* upon it. Their souls also suffered want.

Verse 16. *They envied Moses*] A reference to the case of *Korah* and his company.

Aaron the saint.] The *anointed,* the *high priest* of the Lord.

Verse 20. *Thus they changed their glory*]

That is, their God, who was their glory; and they worshipped an ox in his stead. See the use St Paul makes of this, Rom. i. 23; see also the note there. The incorruptible God was thus served by all the heathen world.

Verse 22. *Wondrous works in the land of Ham*] The plagues inflicted on the *Egyptians.* Egypt is called the *Land of Ham* or *Cham,* because it was peopled by *Misraim* the son of *Cham.*

Verse 23. *Moses his chosen*] Or elect; (Vulgate, *electus ejus; Septuagint, ὁ εκλεκτος αυτου;*) the person that he had *appointed* for this work. It would be very difficult to show that this word in any part of the Old Testament refers to the *eternal state* of any man, much less to the doctrine of *unconditional election* and *reprobation.*

Verse 28. *They joined themselves also unto Baalpeor*] The *Vulgate, Septuagint,* and others, have *Belphegor; the Syriac* and *Arabic,* the *idol Phegor,* or *Phaaur;* the ע *ain* in the word being pronounced as *gh.*

Ate the sacrifices of the dead] מתים *methim,*

33 [u]Because they provoked his spirit, so that he spake unadvisedly with his lips.

34 [v]They did not destroy the nations [w]concerning whom the LORD commanded them:

35 [x]But were mingled among the heathen, and learned their works.

36 And [y]they served their idols: [z]which were a snare unto them.

37 Yea, [a]they sacrificed their sons and their daughters unto [b]devils.

38 And shed innocent blood, *even* the blood of their sons and of their daughters, whom they sacrificed unto the idols of Canaan: and [c]the land was polluted with blood.

39 Thus were they [d]defiled with their own works, and [e]went a whoring with their own inventions.

40 Therefore [f]was the wrath of the LORD

kindled against his people, insomuch that he abhorred [g]his own inheritance.

41 And [h]he gave them into the hand of the heathen; and they that hated them ruled over them.

42 Their enemies also oppressed them, and they were brought into subjection under their hand.

43 [i]Many times did he deliver them; but they provoked *him* with their counsel, and were [k]brought low for their iniquity.

44 Nevertheless he regarded their affliction, when [l]he heard their cry:

45 [m]And he remembered for them his covenant, and [n]repented [o]according to the multitude of his mercies.

46 [p]He made them also to be pitied of all those that carried them captives.

47 [q]Save us, O LORD our God, and gather

---

[u]Numbers xx. 10——[v]Judges i. 21, 27, 28, 29, &c.——[w]Deuteronomy vii. 2, 16; Judges ii. 2——[x]Judges ii. 2; iii. 5, 6; Isa. ii. 6; 1 Cor. v. 6——[y]Judges ii. 12, 13, 17, 19; iii. 6, 7——[z]Exodus xxiii. 33; Deuteronomy vii. 16; Judges ii. 3, 14, 15——[a]2 Kings xvi. 3; Isaiah lvii. 5; Ezekiel xvi. 20; xx. 26——[b]Leviticus xvii. 7; Deut. xxxii. 17; 2 Chron. xi. 15; 1 Cor. x. 20——[c]Num. xxxv. 33——[d]Ezek. xx. 18, 30, 31

[e]Lev. xvii. 7; Num. xv. 39; Ezek. xx. 30——[f]Judg. ii. 14, &c.; Psalm lxxviii. 59, 62——[g]Deut. ix. 29 [h]Judg. ii. 14; Neh. ix. 27, &c.——[i]Judg. ii. 16; Neh. ix. 27, &c.——[k]Or, *impoverished,* or *weakened*——[l]Judg. iii. 9; iv. 3; vi. 7; x. 10; Neh. ix. 27, &c.——[m]Lev. xxvi. 41, 42——[n]Judg. ii. 18——[o]Psa. li. 1; lxix. 16; Isa. lxiii. 7; Lam. iii. 32——[p]Ezra ix. 9; Jer. xlii. 12——[q]1 Chron. xvi. 35, 36

---

of *dead men*. Most of the heathen idols were *men*, who had been deified after their death; many of whom had been execrated during their life.

Verse 33. *They provoked his spirit*] המרו *himru*, from מרה *marah, to rebel:* they brought it into a rebellious state; he was soured and irritated, and was off his guard.

So that he spake unadvisedly with his lips.] For this *sentence* we have only these *two words* in the Hebrew, ויבטא בשפתיו *vayebatte bisephathaiv, he stuttered* or *stammered with his lips,* indicating that he was transported with anger. See the notes on Num. xx. 10-12.

Verse 36. *They served their idols*] עצביהם *atsabbeyhem,* their *labours* or *griefs*—idols, so called because of the *pains* taken in *forming* them, the *labor* in *worshipping* them, and the *grief* occasioned by the *Divine judgments* against the people for their idolatry.

Verse 37. *They sacrificed their sons and their daughters unto devils.*] See the places referred to in the margin. That *causing their sons and their daughters to pass through the fire to Moloch* did not always mean they *burnt them to death* in the flames, is very probable. But all the heathen had *human sacrifices;* of this their history is full. *Unto devils,* לשדים *lashshedim, to demons. Devil* is never in Scripture used in the *plural;* there is but ONE *devil,* though there are MANY *demons.*

Verse 39. *And went a whoring.*] By *fornication, whoredom,* and *idolatry,* the Scripture often expresses *idolatry and idolatrous acts.* I have given the reason of this in other places. Besides being false to the true God, to whom they are represented as *betrothed* and *married,*

(and their acts of idolatry were breaches of this solemn engagement,) the *worship of idols* was frequently accompanied with various acts of *impurity.*

The translation in the *Anglo-Saxon* is very remarkable: ꝺ hi ꝼyꝛenliȝeꞃeꝺon, *and they fornicated.* In *Anglo-Saxon,* ꝼyꞃen signifies to *fire, to ignite;* ꝼyꞃenan, to *commit adultery.* So ꝼyꞃenhicȝenꝺ is a *prostitute,* a *whore;* and ꝼyꞃen liȝnenian is to *go a whoring,* to *fornicate;* probably from ꝼyꞃ, or ꝼyꞃen, to *fire,* and liȝan, to *lie,* or liccena, a *glutton;*—one *who lies with fire,* who is *ignited* by it, who is *greedily intent* upon the act by which he is *inflamed.* And do not the words themselves show that in former times whoredom was punished, as it is now, by a disease which produces the *sensation of burning* in the unhappy prostitutes, whether male or female? And to this meaning the following seems particularly to be *applicable.*

Verse 40. *Therefore was the wrath of the Lord kindled*] God *kindled a fire* in his judgments for those who by their flagitious conduct had *inflamed* themselves with their idols, and the *impure rites* with which they were worshipped.

Verse 43. *Many times did he deliver them*] See the Book of *Judges;* it is a history of the rebellions and deliverances of the Israelites.

Verse 46. *He made them also to be pitied*] This was particularly true as to the Babylonish captivity; for *Cyrus* gave them their liberty; *Darius* favoured them, and granted them several privileges; and *Artaxerxes* sent back Nehemiah, and helped him to rebuild Jerusalem and the temple. See the Books of Ezra and Nehemiah; and see *Calmet.*

Verse 47. *Save us, O Lord—and gather us*]

us from among the heathen, to give thanks unto thy holy name, *and* to triumph in thy praise.

48 [r]Blessed *be* the LORD God of Israel from everlasting to everlasting: and let all the people say, Amen. [s]Praise ye the LORD.

---

[r]Psa. xli. 13

[s]Heb. *Hallelujah*

These words, says *Calmet*, are found in the hymn that was sung at the ceremony of bringing the ark to Jerusalem, 1 Chron. xvi.; but it is supposed they were added by Ezra or some other prophet: here they are in their natural place. The author of the Psalm begs the Lord to gather the Israelites who were dispersed through different countries; for at the dedication of the second temple, under Nehemiah, (where it is probable this Psalm, with the cvth and the cviith, was sung,) there were very few Jews who had as yet returned from their captivity.

Verse 48. *Blessed* be *the Lord God of Israel*] Here both *gratitude* and *confidence* are expressed; *gratitude* for what God had already wrought, and *confidence* that he would finish the great work of their restoration.

From everlasting to everlasting] מן האולם ועד העולם *min haolam vead haolam*, "from the hidden term to the hidden term," from the beginning of time to the end of time, from eternity and on to eternity. **ꝼꞃam ƿoꞃulꝺ ⁊ oꝺ ƿoꞃulꝺe**, *Anglo-Saxon.* **Fra worlde and into worlde**, *old Psalter;* which it paraphrases thus: Fra with outen beginning, & withouten endyng.

And let all the people say, Amen.] Let the people join in the prayer and in the thanksgiving, that God may hear and answer. *Anglo-Saxon:* **⁊ cƿeðe eall ꝼolc, beo hit beo hit;** "And, quoth all folk, be it, be it." *Hallelujah*—Praise ye Jehovah! Let his name be eternally magnified! Amen.

This is the end of the *fourth book* of the Psalms.

ANALYSIS OF THE ONE HUNDRED AND SIXTH PSALM

The intention of the prophet in this Psalm is to express God's long-suffering in bearing with rebellious sinners, and yet in pardoning them upon the confession of their sins, and turning to him; both which he exemplifies by a long narration of Israel's rebellions, repentance, and turning to God, and God's dealing with them, which gave him just occasion to praise God, and to pray for his Church and people.

I. An exhortation to praise God, with the reasons in general, ver. 1; and who are fit to perform this duty, ver. 2, 3.

II. A petition and prayer directed to God in his own person for the whole Church, and the end of it, ver. 4, 5.

III. A confession of sin, particularly of the Israelites', together with God's patience with them, and their repentance, ver. 646.

IV. His prayer that God would collect his Church out of all nations, that they might meet and praise him, ver. 47, 48.

I. "Praise ye the Lord, O give thanks unto the Lord." To this the prophet invites, for two reasons:—

1. "Because he is good." He is beforehand with us, and prevents men with many benefits.

2. "Because his mercy endures for ever." It is everlasting, and far exceeds our sins and miseries; for after men have offended him, and deserve no mercy, yet he receives the penitent offenders. But who is sufficient for these things? Who is fit to praise him, and set forth his mercies? "Who can utter the mighty acts of the Lord?" That is, the infinite benefits exhibited to his people. Or, Who can show forth all his praise in preserving, pardoning, and propagating his Church?

They alone are happy men "who keep judgment, and do righteousness at all times."

1. They are happy in prosperity and adversity, they dwell in the house of God, under his protection.

2. "They keep his judgments." Follow in their lives the strict rules of the Divine law, by which they judge all their actions, and so keep faith and a good conscience.

3. "They do righteousness at all times." They approve that which is right, true, and just; condemn, hate, and punish what is unjust: such are fit to praise God with their tongues, because they praise him in their lives.

II. After the prophet had invited men to praise God, and showed who were fit to do it, he begins his petition, which he proposes in his own person for the whole Church.

1. "Remember me." Me; but not me alone, rather thy whole Church. By what we suffer, thou hast seemed to forget thy covenant and promise; but now call it to mind again.

2. Which I expect, not for any desert of mine, but merely from thy good will: "Remember me with the favour," &c.

3. "O visit me;" but not in wrath, for such a visitation there is; but in mercy and grace.

4. "With thy salvation." Save me at this time from my sins, and from my present calamities.

And to this end I desire thy favour, thy salvation.

1. "That I may see the good of thy chosen." Be a partaker of and in their happiness.

2. "That I may rejoice in the gladness of thy nation." Partake of it.

3. "That I may glory with thine inheritance." Glorify thee with them.

But observe here the three eminent titles given to God's Church:—

1. They are a "chosen" people; which is a glorious and gracious title, and intimates favour.

2. They are his "nation," his peculiar people.

3. They are his "inheritance."

III. In the following part of the Psalm, from ver. 7 to 46, he makes use of a new argument to move God to mercy. He represents not the present condition the people of God are in, not their captivity, miseries, and afflictions, but ingenuously confesses how they had offended God, and how justly they suffered.

1. "We have sinned with our fathers." Trodden in their steps, and filled up the measure of their sins.

2. "We have committed iniquity." Not only from infirmity, but choice.

3. "We have done wickedly." The intent and purpose in it was evil. And by these three steps he exaggerates the sin; the *act*, the *frequency*, the *intent;* as every true confessionist to God ought never to extenuate, but to aggravate the offence against himself.

And because he had mentioned their fathers at large, now he instances their rebellions: "Our fathers understood not thy wonders in Egypt;" that is, they laid them not to heart.

1. "They remembered not the multitude of thy mercies," &c. When they saw Pharaoh's army on one side, and the sea on the other, they grew heartless, diffident, and murmured.

2. This was their sin at that time; but God was then merciful to them: "Nevertheless he saved them."

For which he assigns two reasons:—

1. "For his name's sake." To advance his glory and honour.

2. "That he might make his mighty power to be known." Pharaoh and the Egyptians might have taken notice of it by the plagues he had already brought upon them.

In the following verses, by a distribution, he shows the manner of their deliverance.

1. By God's rebuke, and drying up of the sea: "He rebuked the Red Sea also," &c.

2. By the unheard-of way: "He led them through the depths as through the wilderness;" there was no more water there to offend them than in the sands of Arabia.

3. By the consequence of it: "And he saved them by the hand of him," &c.

4. "And the waters covered their enemies," &c.

The effect was, for the present,

1. It extorted from them a confession that God was true in his promises: "Then believed they his words."

2. It excited them to praise him: "They sang his praise," Exod. xv. But these very men who were forced to confess his power and sing his praises for the overthrow of Pharaoh in the Red Sea, were scarcely departed from those banks, when they, for want of a little bread and water, grew as impatient and distrustful as they were before.

1. They made haste to forget: "They soon forgot;" which aggravates their sin.

2. They forgot his omnipotence, his providence.

3. "They waited not for his council." With patience they expected not the end, why God in his wisdom suffered them now to wait, which was, to prove their faith, hope, and love.

4. And what they did at this time they did also at others: "For they lusted exceedingly in the wilderness."

Now God yielded to these desires of the people: "He gave them bread, flesh, and water."

1. And he gave them their request, Exod. xvi. 12.

2. "But he sent leanness into their souls." Which certainly has reference to the quails in Num. xi. 20 and 33, where the people ate, and died of plague.

Another rebellion the prophet now touches, which was, when they rose up against the king and the priest.

1. "They envied also Moses in the camp;" objecting that he had usurped a power over them, and taken it upon his own head.

2. "And Aaron, the saint of the Lord." He whom God had chosen, anointed, and sanctified to the priest's office.

The punishment follows, Num. xvi.

1. "The earth opened, and swallowed up Dathan, and covered the congregation of Abiram."

2. "And a fire was kindled in their company; the flame burned up the wicked." That is, the *two hundred and fifty* men that presumed to offer incense; and presently after the *fourteen thousand seven hundred* that murmured, and objected to *Moses* and *Aaron* that they had killed the people of the Lord.

Still the prophet goes on in his story of Israel's stubbornness and rebellion; and comes to their grand sin, their idolatry in erecting the golden calf, Exod. xxxii.

1. "They made a calf in Horeb," &c., contrary to God's command.

2. "Thus they changed their glory." That is, the true God, who was indeed their glory, "into the similitude of an ox," a brute beast, "that eateth grass," a base creature, which much aggravates their sin.

3. But the *prophet* aggravates their stupidity and folly: "They forgat God," &c.

In the following verse are expressed God's just anger and mercy,—

1. His anger against their sins: "Therefore he saith," &c. Pronounced his will to destroy them.

2. His mercy, in that he spared them at the intercession of Moses: "Had not Moses his chosen stood before him in the breach." The breach and division which this sin had made between God and his people, like that in the wall of a besieged town, in which some valiant captain stands, and opposes himself against the assault of the enemy; so did Moses.

For his object was the same, it was "to turn away his wrath lest he should destroy;" and the end was answered—it was turned away.

Farther yet, he calls to mind a new rebellion, which fell out upon the report of the spies sent to search the land, Num. xiii. 26, &c., and xiv.

1. "They despised the pleasant land," and wished to return into Egypt, Num. xiv. 1-5.

2. "They believed not his word;" for they said, "Hath the Lord brought us," &c.

3. "But murmured in their tents, and hearkened not," &c., Num. xiv. "Therefore he lifted up his hand against them," &c. As their sin, so their punishment, is extant; Num. xiv. 29: "Your carcasses shall fall in the wilderness; ye shall not come into the land."

This punishment fell upon the murmurers themselves; but if their children should be guilty of the like rebellion, they should not escape, for they too should be *overthrown;* which is fully brought to pass.

The prophet joins to that of the golden calf another piece of idolatry in the wilderness, to which there was joined fornication also, by the counsel of *Balaam* and the policy of Balak. This caused them to eat and sacrifice to their god, Num. xxv., which the prophet next insists upon,—

1. "They joined themselves to Baal-peor," because the idol was set up upon that mountain.

2. "And ate the offerings of the dead." They left the sacrifice of the living God, and ate those meats which were offered to dead idols.

Upon which there followed God's wrath and their own punishment:—

1. God was angry: "For they provoked him to wrath."

"And the plague brake in upon them" like mighty waters, or as an army into a city at a breach; for there died of it *twenty-four thousand*, Num. xxv. 9.

In the former idolatry God's anger was averted by the intercession of *Moses;* in this, by the execution of judgment by *Phinehas;* for—

1. "There stood up Phinehas;" moved, no question, with a zeal for God's honour.

2. "And he executed judgment upon Zimri and Cozbi;" for which (let men conceive as they please—I see nothing to the contrary) he had his commission from Moses, or rather God; Num. xxv. 4, 5.

3. The event was, the plague was stayed; the execution of offenders pacifies the anger of God.

Which zeal of his was well rewarded: "This was accounted to him for righteousness," &c. This act was an act of righteousness, and an ample reward he had for it; for God established the dignity of the high priesthood in *Phinehas* and his posterity, as long as the Jewish commonwealth continued.

The prophet comes to another remarkable sin of the Jews, Num. xx., where the people chid Moses for want of water:—

1. "They angered him also at the waters of strife," when they contradicted *Moses.*

2. "So that it went ill with Moses for their sakes;" for, being disturbed with choler, "he spake unadvisedly with his lips,"—"Hear now, ye rebels," &c.; and he smote the rock. By their murmuring they so provoked his spirit to bitterness, that he who at other times was cheerful, and ready to obey God's commands, now acted with reluctance.

Hitherto the prophet has set down several rebellions of the Jews during their abode in the wilderness; and now he shows how they behaved themselves after they came into the land of *Canaan.* Better, a man would think, they should be after God had fulfilled his word to them; but an Ethiopian cannot change his skin, nor they their manners; disobedient, stubborn, and rebellious they remained.

1. God had expressly commanded that the nations of *Canaan* should be destroyed, Deut. vii. 1, 2, 3: "But they did not destroy the nations," &c.

2. "But they mingled among the heathen:" in leagues and marriages, Judg. ii. and iii.

3. "And learned their works:" many superstitious and evil customs.

But, beyond all, they learned to be idolaters; forsook God for the devil.

1. "They served their idols, which was a snare unto them," for that they became their slaves, Judg. ii., &c.

2. "Yea, they sacrificed their sons," &c., to Moloch.

3. With inhuman sin, they "shed innocent blood;" the blood of innocent children, &c.

The consequences of which are double. First, A double pollution. Secondly, A heavy punishment.

1. A pollution of the land: "The land was defiled with blood."

2. A pollution of their own souls: "Thus were they defiled with their own works."

The judgment, or punishment, now follows; and a signification whence it proceeded; it came not by chance, but by God's order and anger.

1. "Therefore was the wrath of the Lord kindled," &c. For their idolatry, murder, whoredom; so that he was not only angry, but his anger was kindled to a flame.

2. Insomuch "that he abhorred his own inheritance."

And the punishment he inflicted on them was very just,—

1. "He gave them into the hand," that is, the power, "of the heathen." God had given the heathen into their hands to destroy them; which, because they did not, but learned their works, therefore God gave them into the hands of the heathen.

2. He made them their lords; and hard masters they were, as plainly appears from the Book of Judges, and 1 Samuel.

And *little* they; for the prophet in the next verse adds,

1. "Their enemies oppressed them:" tyrants, oppressors they were. Read the Book of Judges, &c.

2. "They were brought into subjection," &c., under the Philistines, Moabites, Ammonites, &c.

In which condition God did not forget them, for "many times did he deliver them;" not once only, but often, as by *Gideon, Jephthah, Deborah, Samson,* and others. But, O the ingratitde of a sinful nation! instead of serving God, "they provoked him with their counsel," that is, by following the dictates of their own hearts.

And so were very justly brought into the same case they were before; for "they were brought low for their iniquity."

And now the prophet adds, which indeed he infers through the whole Psalm, the wonderful and immutable good will of God to them. Though he forgave and delivered them upon their repentance, and they in a short time provoked him again; yet he received them to grace, even after their relapses. And the causes that moved him to this were external and internal.

The cause that outwardly and occasionally moved him to it was their affliction and cry: "He regarded their affliction," &c.

But the cause that inwardly swayed him was his word passed to them, and his mercy.

1. His word and his promise were passed to "Abraham, to be their God;" and he would not break it. "And he remembered for them his covenant."

2. His tender affection that he bare them; this caused him to repent, and grieve that they should be in misery. "He repented," &c.

3. And the effect which all these causes had was beneficial to them even in their bondage and captivity; for even their very enemies' hearts were often turned to do them good, as is evident in *Jeremiah, David, Daniel, Ezra, Zerubbabel, Mordecai,* and indeed the whole nation under the *Babylonian, Philistian, Egyptian,* and *Persian* kings, which the prophet sets down, ver. 46: "He made them also to be pitied of all those that carried them captives." According to the saying of the wise man: "When a man's ways please God, he will make his very enemies to be at peace with him," Prov. xvi. 7.

4. And this sense makes the way plainer to what follows, the petition and the doxology; for if God showed himself merciful in the time of his anger, and made it apparent even to the

very view of their enemies, encouragement they might have,—

1. To pray: "Save us, O Lord our God, and gather us from among the heathen," &c.

2. Then to give thanks: 1. "Blessed be the Lord God of Israel from everlasting to everlasting. 2. And for it let the people do their duty; that is, the solemn and necessary forms: "Let all the people say, Amen. Hallelujah."

PSALM CVII

A thanksgiving of the people for deliverance from difficulties and dangers; their state compared to a journey through a frightful wilderness, 1–9; to confinement in a dreary dungeon, 10–16; to a dangerous malady, 17–22; to a tempest at sea, 23–32. The psalmist calls on men to praise God for the merciful dispensations of his providence, in giving rain and fruitful seasons, after affliction by drought and famine, 33–38; for supporting the poor in affliction, and bringing down the oppressors, 39–41. The use which the righteous should make of these providences, 42; and the advantage to be derived from a due consideration of God's merciful providence, 43.

XXII. DAY. MORNING PRAYER

O ᵃGIVE thanks unto the Lᴏʀᴅ, for ᵇ*he is* good : for his mercy *endureth* for ever.

ᵃPsa. cvi. 1; cxviii. 1; cxxxvi. 1

2 Let the redeemed of the Lᴏʀᴅ say *so,* ᶜwhom he hath redeemed from the hand of the enemy;

ᵇPsa. cxix. 68; Matt. xix. 17——ᶜPsa. cvi. 10

NOTES ON PSALM CVII

This Psalm has no title, either in the Hebrew, or any of the Versions; the word "Hallelujah," which is prefixed to some of the latter, is no title, but was most probably borrowed from the conclusion of the preceding Psalm. The author is unknown; but it was probably like Psalms cv. and cvi., made and sung at the dedication of the second temple. The three Psalms seem to be on the same subject. In them the author has comprised the marvellous acts of the Lord towards his people; the transgressions of this people against God; the captivities and miseries they endured in consequence; and finally God's merciful kindness to them in their restoration from captivity, and re-establishment in their own land.

This Psalm seems to have been sung in parts: the 8th, 15th, 21st, and 31st verses, with the 6th, 13th, 19th, and 28th, forming what may be called the burden of the song. In singing of which the whole chorus joined.

We may easily perceive that the Psalm must have been sung in alternate parts, having a double burden, or *intercalary* verse often recurring, and another immediately following, giving a reason for the former. See the 8th and 9th, the 15th and 16th, the 21st and 22nd, the 31st and 32nd, and the 42nd and 43rd, which may be reckoned under the same denomination.

Dr. Lowth, in his 29th prelection, has made some excellent remarks on this Psalm. "It is observable," says he, "that after each of the intercalary verses one is added, expressive of deliverance or praise. I would farther observe, that if the Psalm be supposed to be made with a view to the *alternate* response of one side of the choir to the other, then it may be considered as if it were written exactly after the method of the ancient *pastorals*, where, be the subject of their verse what it will, each swain endeavours to excel the other; and one may perceive their thoughts and expressions gradually to *arise* upon each other; and hence a manifest beauty may be discovered in this Divine pastoral. We will suppose, then, that the author composed it for the use of his brethren the Jews, when, in the joy of their hearts, they were assembled after their return from captivity. At such a time, what theme could be so proper for the subject of his poem, as the manifest goodness of Almighty God? The first performers, therefore, invite the whole nation to praise God for this; a great instance of it being their late return from captivity. At ver. 10, the other side take the subject, and rightly observe that the return of their great men, who were actually in chains, was a more remarkable instance of God's mercy to them, than the return of the people in general, who were only dispersed, we may suppose, up and down the open country. Then the first performers beautifully compare this unexpected deliverance to that which God sometimes vouchsafes to the languishing dying man, when he recalls, as it were, the sentence of death, and restores him to his former vigour. The others again compare it, with still greater strength and expression, to God's delivering the affrighted *mariner* from all the dreadful horrors of the ungovernable and arbitrary ocean. But the *first*, still resolved to outdo the rest, recur to that series of wonderful works which God had vouchsafed to their nation, ver. 32, and of which they had so lately such a convincing proof. Wherefore at last, as in a common chorus, they all conclude with exhorting each other to a serious consideration of these things, and to make a proper return to Almighty God for them.

"No doubt the composition of this Psalm is admirable throughout; and the descriptive part of it adds at least its share of beauty to the whole; but what is most to be admired is its *conciseness*, and withal the expressiveness of the diction, which strikes the imagination with inimitable elegance. The *weary* and *bewildered traveller*, the miserable *captive* in the hideous dungeon, the sick and dying man, the *seaman foundering* in a storm, are described in so affecting a manner, that they far exceed any thing of the kind, though never so much laboured." I

3 And [d]gathered them out of the lands, from the east, and from the west, from the north, and [e]from the south.

4 They [f]wandered in [g]the wilderness in a solitary way; they found no city to dwell in.

5 Hungry and thirsty, their soul fainted in them.

6 [h]Then they cried unto the LORD in their trouble, *and* he delivered them out of their distresses.

7 And he led them forth by the [i]right way, that they might go to a city of habitation.

8 [k]O that *men* would praise the LORD *for* his goodness, and *for* his wonderful works to the children of men!

9 For [l]he satisfieth the longing soul, and filleth the hungry soul with goodness.

10 Such as [m]sit in darkness and in the shadow of death, *being* [n]bound in affliction and iron;

11 Because they [o]rebelled against the words of God, and contemned [p]the counsel of the Most High:

12 Therefore he brought down their heart with labour; they fell down, and *there was* [q]none to help.

[d]Psa. cvi. 47; Isa. xliii. 5, 6; Jer. xxix. 14; xxxi. 8, 10; Ezek. xxxix. 27, 28——[e]Heb. *from the sea*——[f]Ver. 40 [g]Deut. xxxii. 10——[h]Ver. 13, 19, 28; Psa. l. 15; Hos. v. 15——[i]Ezra viii. 21

[k]Ver. 15, 21, 31——[l]Psa. xxxiv. 10; Luke i. 53 [m]Luke i. 79——[n]Job xxxvi. 8——[o]Lam. iii. 42——[p]Psa. lxxiii. 24; cxix. 24; Luke vii. 30; Acts xx. 27——[q]Psa. xxii. 11; Isa. lxiii. 5

may add that had such an *Idyl* appeared in *Theocritus* or *Virgil*, or had it been found as a scene in any of the *Greek tragedians*, even in *Æschylus* himself, it would have been praised up to the heavens, and probably been produced as their master-piece.

Verse 1. *O give thanks*] Here is a duty prescribed; and the reasons of it are immediately laid down. 1. He is *good*. This is his nature. 2. *His mercy* endureth *for ever*. This is the *stream* that flows from the *fountain* of his goodness.

Verse 2. *Let the redeemed of the Lord say so*] For they have had the fullest proof of this goodness, in being saved by the continuing stream of his mercy.

Verse 3. *And gathered them out of the lands*] Though many Jews returned into Jerusalem from various parts of the world, under the reigns of *Darius Hystaspes*, *Artaxerxes*, and *Alexander the Great;* yet this prophecy has its completion only under the Gospel, when all the ends of the earth hear the salvation of God.

Verse 4. *They wandered in the wilderness*] Here begins the FIRST *comparison:* the Israelites in captivity are compared to *a traveller in a dreary, uninhabited, and barren desert*, spent with hunger and thirst, as well as by the fatigues of the journey, ver. 5.

Verse 6. *Then they cried unto the Lord*] When the Israelites began to pray heartily, and the eyes of all the tribes were as the eyes of one man turned unto the Lord, then he delivered them out of their distresses.

Verse 7. *That they might go to a city of habitation.*] God stirred up the heart of *Cyrus* to give them liberty to return to their own land: and *Zerubbabel*, *Ezra*, and *Nehemiah*, at different times, brought many of them back to Judea.

Verse 8. *O that* men *would praise the Lord*] This is what is called the *intercalary verse*, or *burden* of each *part* of this *responsive song:* see the *introduction*. God should be praised because he is *good*. We naturally speak highly of those who are eminent. God is infinitely excellent, and should be celebrated for his *perfections*. But *he does wonders for the children of men;* and, therefore, men should *praise the Lord*. And he is the more to be praised, because these wonders, נפלאות *niphlaoth*, miracles of mercy and grace, are done for the *undeserving*. They are done לבני אדם *libney Adam*, for the children of *Adam*, the corrupt descendants of a rebel father.

Verse 9. *For he satisfieth the longing soul*] This is the reason which the psalmist gives for the *duty* of thankfulness which he prescribes. *The longing soul*, נפש שוקקה *nephesh shokekah*, *the soul that pushes forward in eager desire* after salvation.

Verse 10. *Such as sit in darkness*] Here begins the SECOND *similitude*, which he uses to illustrate the state of the captives in Babylon, viz., that of *a prisoner in a dreary dungeon*. 1. *They sit in* or *inhabit darkness*. They have no light, no peace, no prosperity. 2. "In the shadow of death." The place where death reigns, over which he has projected his shadow; those against whom the sentence of death has been pronounced. 3. They are *bound* in this darkness, have no liberty to revisit the light, and cannot escape from their executioners. 4. They are *afflicted*, not only by want and privation in general, but they are tortured in the prison, עני *oni*, afflicted, humbled, distressed. 5. Their fetters are such as they cannot break; they are *iron*. The reason of their being in this wretched state is given.

Verse 11. *Because they rebelled against the words of God*] 1. God showed them their duty and their interest, and commanded them to obey his word; but they cast off all subjection to his authority, acted as if they were independent of heaven and earth, and broke out into open rebellion against him. 2. He *counselled* and exhorted them to return to him: but they contemned his advice, and turned his counsel into ridicule. 3. As lenient means were ineffectual, he visited them in judgment: hence it is added,

Verse 12. *He brought down their heart with labour*] He delivered them into the hands of their enemies. and, as they would not be under subjection to GOD, he delivered them into slavery to wicked men: "So they fell down, and there was none to help;" God had forsaken them because they had forsaken him.

13 [r]Then they cried unto the LORD in their trouble, *and* he saved them out of their distresses.

14 [s]He brought them out of darkness, and the shadow of death, and brake their bands in sunder.

15 [t]O that *men* would praise the LORD *for* his goodness, and *for* his wonderful works to the children of men!

16 For he hath [u]broken the gates of brass, and cut the bars of iron in sunder.

17 Fools [v]because of their transgression, and because of their iniquities, are afflicted.

18 [w]Their soul abhorreth all manner of meat; and they [x]draw near unto the gates of death.

19 [y]Then they cry unto the LORD in their trouble, *and* he saveth them out of their distresses.

20 [z]He sent his word, and [a]healed them, and [b]delivered *them* from their destructions.

21 [c]O that *men* would praise the LORD *for* his goodness, and *for* his wonderful works to the children of men!

22 And [d]let them sacrifice the sacrifices of thanksgiving, and [e]declare his works with [f]rejoicing.

23 They that go down to the sea in ships, that do business in great waters;

24 These see the works of the LORD, and his wonders in the deep.

25 For he commandeth, and [g]raiseth [h]the stormy wind, which lifteth up the waves thereof.

26 They mount up to the heaven, they go down again to the depths: [i]their soul is melted because of trouble.

27 They reel to and fro, and stagger like

---

[r]Ver. 6, 19, 28——[s]Psa. lxviii. 6; cxlvi. 7; Acts xii. 7, &c.; xvi. 26, &c.——[t]Ver. 8, 21, 31——[u]Isa. xlv. 2 [v]Lam. iii. 39——[w]Job xxxiii. 20——[x]Job xxxiii. 22; Psa. ix. 13; lxxxviii. 3——[y]Ver. 6, 13, 28——[z]2 Kings xx. 4, 5; Psa. cxlvii. 15, 18; Matt. viii. 8

[a]Psa. xxx. 2; ciii. 3——[b]Job xxxiii. 28, 30; Psa. xxx. 3; xlix. 15; lvi. 13; ciii. 4——[c]Ver. 8, 15, 31——[d]Lev. vii. 12; Psa. l. 14; cxvi. 17; Heb. xiii. 15——[e]Psa. ix. 11; lxxiii. 28; cxviii. 17——[f]Heb. *singing*——[g]Heb. *maketh to stand* [h]Jonah i. 4——[i]Psa. xxii. 14; cxix. 28; Nah. ii. 10

Verse 13. *Then they cried unto the Lord in their trouble*] This was the salutary effect which their afflictions produced: they began to cry to God for mercy and help; and God mercifully heard their prayer, and reversed their state; for,

Verse 14. *He brought them out of darkness*] 1. Gave them again peace and prosperity. 2. Repealed the *sentence of death.* 3. "Unbound the poor prisoners." 4. Broke their iron bonds in sunder.

Verse 15. *O that* men, *&c.*] This is the *intercalary verse*, or *burden*, of the *second* part, as it was of the *first*. See verse 8.

Verse 16. *For he hath broken*] This is the *reason* given for thanks to God for his deliverance of the captives. It was not a simple deliverance; it was done so as to manifest the *irresistible* power of God. He tore the prison in pieces, and cut the bars of iron asunder.

Verse 17. *Fools because of their transgression*] This is the THIRD *comparison;* the captivity being compared to *a person in a dangerous malady.* Our Version does not express this clause well: *Fools* מדרך פשעם *midderech pisham, because of the way of their transgressions, are afflicted.* Most human maladies are the fruits of sin; *misery* and *sin* are married together in bonds that can never be broken.

Verse 18. *Their soul abhorreth all manner of meat*] A natural description of a sick man: appetite is gone, and all desire for food fails; nutriment is no longer necessary, for death has seized upon the whole frame. See a similar image, Job xxxiii. 20.

Verse 10. *Then they cry*] The effect produced by affliction as before.

Verse 20. *He sent his word, and healed them*] He spoke: "Be thou clean, be thou whole;" and immediately the disease departed; and thus they were *delivered from the destructions* that awaited them.

Verse 21. *O that* men, *&c.*] The *intercalary* verse, or *burden*, as before.

Verse 22. *And let them sacrifice*] For their *healing* they should bring a *sacrifice;* and they should offer the *life* of the innocent animal unto God, as he has spared their *lives;* and let them thus *confess* that God has spared *them* when they deserved to die; and let them *declare* also "his works with rejoicing;" for who will not rejoice when he is delivered from *death?*

Verse 23. *They that go down to the sea in ships*] This is the FOURTH *comparison.* Their captivity was as dangerous and alarming as a dreadful tempest at sea to a weather-beaten mariner.

Verse 24. *These see the works of the Lord*] Splendid, Divinely impressive, and glorious in *fine weather.*

His wonders in the deep.] Awfully terrible in a *tempest.*

Verse 25. *For he commandeth*] And what less than the command of God can raise up such winds as seem to heave old Ocean from his bed?

Verse 26. *They mount up to the heaven*] This is a most natural and striking description of the state of a ship at sea in a storm: when the *sea* appears to *run mountains high,* and the vessel seems for a moment to stand on the sharp ridge of one most stupendous, with a valley of *a frightful depth* between it and a similar mountain, which appears to be flying in the midst of heaven, that it may submerge the hapless bark, when she descends into the valley of death below. This is a sight the most terrific that can be imagined: nor can any man conceive or form an adequate idea of it, who has not himself been at sea in such a storm.

Their soul is melted because of trouble.] This

a drunken man, and ^kare at their wit's end.

28 ^lThen they cry unto the LORD in their trouble, and he bringeth them out of their distresses.

29 ^mHe maketh the storm a calm, so that the waves thereof are still.

30 Then are they glad because they be quiet; so he bringeth them unto their desired haven.

31 ⁿO that *men* would praise the LORD *for* his goodness, and *for* his wonderful works to the children of men!

32 Let them exalt him also ^oin the congre-

---

^kHebrew, *all their wisdom is swallowed up*——^lVerse 6, 13, 19

^mPsa. lxxxix. 9; Matt. viii. 26——ⁿVer. 8, 15, 21 ^oPsa. xxii. 22, 25; cxi. 1

---

is not less expressive than it is *descriptive*. The action of raising the vessel to the clouds, and precipitating her into the abyss, seems to dissolve the very soul: the whole mind seems to melt away, so that neither feeling, reflection, nor impression remains, nothing but the apprehension of inevitable destruction! When the ship is buffeted between conflicting waves, which threaten either to tear her asunder or crush her together; when she *reels to and fro, and staggers like a drunken man*, not being able to hold any certain course; when *sails* and *masts* are an incumbrance, and the *helm* of no use; when all *hope of safety* is taken away; and when the experienced *captain*, the skilful *pilot*, and the hardy *sailors*, cry out, with a voice more terrible than the cry of fire at midnight, *We are* ALL *lost! we are all* LOST! then, indeed, are they *at their wit's end;* or, as the inimitable original expresses it, וכל חכמתם תתבלע *vechol chochmatham tithballa*, "and all their skill is swallowed up,"—seems to be gulped down by the frightful abyss into which the ship is about to be precipitated. Then, indeed, can the hand of God alone "bring them out of their distresses." Then, a cry to the Almighty (and in such circumstances it is few that can lift up such a cry) is the only means that can be used to save the perishing wreck! Reader, dost thou ask why I paint thus, and from whose authority I describe? I answer: Not from any books describing storms, tempests, and shipwrecks; not from the relations of shipwrecked marines; not from viewing from the shore a tempest at sea, and seeing a vessel beat to pieces, and all its crew, one excepted, perish. Descriptions of this kind I have read, with the shipwrecked mariner I have conversed, the last scene mentioned above I have witnessed: but none of these could give the fearful impressions, the tremendous and soul-melting apprehensions, described above. "*Where* then have you had them?" I answer, From the great deep. I have been at sea in the storm, and in the circumstances I describe; and, having *cried to the Lord in my trouble*, I am spared to describe the storm, and recount the tale of his mercy. None but either a man inspired by God, who, in describing, will show things *as they are*, or one who has been actually in these circumstances, can tell you with what propriety the psalmist speaks, or utter the thousandth part of the dangers and fearful apprehensions of those concerned in a tempest at sea, where all the winds of heaven seem collected to urge an already crazy vessel among the most tremendous rocks upon a lee shore! God save the reader from such circumstances!

When, in the visitation of the winds,
He takes the ruffian billows by the top,

Curling their monstrous heads, and hanging them,
With deafening clamours, on the slippery clouds,
That with the hurly death itself awakes!
                                      HENRY IV.

A storm at sea—*the lifting the vessel to the clouds*—her *sinking into the vast marine valleys*—the *melting of the soul*—and *being at their wit's end*, are well touched by several of the ancient poets. See particularly Virgil's description of the storm that dispersed the fleet of Æneas, who was himself not unacquainted with the dangers of the sea:—

Tollimur in cœlum curvato gurgite, et idem
Subducta ad manes imos descendimus unda.
                                      ÆN. iii., 364.

Now on a towering arch of waves we rise,
Heaved on the bounding billows to the skies.
Then, as the roaring surge retreating fell,
We shoot down headlong to the gates of hell.
                                      PITT.

Rector in incerto est, nec quid fugiatve, petatve,
Invenit: ambiguis ars stupet ipsa malis.

"The pilot himself is in doubt what danger to shun; or whither to steer for safety he knows not: his skill is nonplussed by the choice of the difficulties before him."

See more in the analysis.

Verse 29. *He maketh the storm a calm*] He causes the storm to stand *dumb*, and *hushes* the waves. See the original, where *sense* and *sound* emphatically meet:—

גליהם   ויחשו   לדממה   סערה   יקם
galleyhem vaiyecheshu lidemamah secrah yakem

He shall cause the whirlwind to stand *dumb*, and he shall *hush* their billows.

Verse 30. *Then are they glad because they be quiet*] The turbulence of the sea being hushed, and the waves still, they rejoice to see an end to the tempest; and thus, having fine weather, a smooth sea, and fair wind, they are speedily brought to the *desired haven*.

Verse 31. *O that men*] The *intercalary* verse, or *burden*, as before. See ver. 8.

Verse 32. *Let them exalt him also in the congregation*] Their deliverance from such imminent danger, and in a way which clearly showed the Divine interposition, demands, not only gratitude of heart and the song of praise at the end of the storm, but when they come to *shore* that they *publicly* acknowledge it in the congregation of God's people. I have been often pleased, when in sea-port towns, to see and hear notes sent to the minister from pious sailors, returning thanks to the Almighty for preservation from shipwreck, and, in general, from the

gation of the people, and praise him in the assembly of the elders.

33 He [p]turneth rivers into a wilderness, and the watersprings into dry ground;

34 A [q]fruitful land into [r]barrenness, for the wickedness of them that dwell therein.

35 [s]He turneth the wilderness into a standing water, and dry ground into watersprings.

36 And there he maketh the hungry to dwell, that they may prepare a city for habitation;

37 And sow the fields, and plant vineyards, which may yield fruits of increase.

38 [t]He blesseth them also, so that they [u]are multiplied greatly; and suffereth not their cattle to decrease.

39 Again, they are [v]minished and brought low through oppression, affliction, and sorrow.

40 [w]He poureth contempt upon princes, and causeth them to wander in the [x]wilderness, *where there is* no way.

41 [y]Yet setteth he the poor on high, [z]from affliction, and [a]maketh *him* families like a flock.

42 [b]The righteous shall see *it,* and rejoice: and all [c]iniquity shall stop her mouth.

43 [d]Whoso *is* wise, and will observe these *things,* even they shall understand the lovingkindness of the LORD.

---

[p]1 Kings xvii. 1, 7——[q]Gen. xiii. 10; xiv. 3; xix. 25 [r]Heb. *saltness*——[s]Psa. cxiv. 8; Isa. xli. 18——[t]Gen. xii. 2; xvii. 16, 20——[u]Exod. i. 7——[v]2 Kings x. 32 [w]Job xii. 21, 24——[x]Or, *void place*

[y]1 Sam. ii. 8; Psa. cxiii. 7, 8——[z]Or, *after*——[a]Psa. lxxviii. 52——[b]Job xxii. 19; Psa. lii. 6; lviii. 10——[c]Job v. 16; Psa. lxiii. 11; Prov. x. 11; Rom. iii. 19——[d]Psa. lxiv. 9; Jer. ix. 12; Hos. xiv. 9

---

dangers of the sea; and for bringing them back in safety to their own port. Thus "they exalt the Lord in the congregation, and praise him in the assembly of the elders." And is it not something of this kind that the psalmist requires?

Verse 33. *He turneth rivers into a wilderness*] After having, as above, illustrated the state of the Jews in their captivity, and the deliverance which God wrought for them, he now turns to the general conduct of God in reference to the poor and needy; and his gracious interpositions in their behalf, the providential supply of their wants, and his opposition to their oppressors. *On account of the wickedness of men,* he sometimes changes a *fruitful land into a desert.* See the general state of Egypt in the present time: once a fertile land; now an arid, sandy wilderness. Again, by his blessing on honest industry, he has changed deserts into highly fertile ground. And, as for the wickedness of their inhabitants, many lands are cursed and rendered barren; so, when a people acknowledge him in all their ways, he blesses their toil, gives them rain and fruitful seasons, and fills their hearts with joy and gladness.

Verse 26. *And there he maketh the hungry to dwell*] All this seems to apply admirably to the first colonists of any place. They flee from a land of want, an *ingrata terra* that did not repay their toil, and they seek the wilderness where the land wants only cultivation to make it produce all the necessaries of life. He, by his providence, so guides their steps as to lead them to *rivers* which they can navigate, and from which they can procure plenty of fish, and shows them *wells* or *springs* which they have not digged. The *hungry dwell there;* and jointly agree, for convenience and defence, *to build them a city for habitation.* They sow the fields which they have cleared; and plant vineyards, and orchards which yield them increasing fruits, ver. 37, and he multiplies their cattle greatly, and does not suffer them to decrease, ver. 38. What a fine picture is this of the first peopling and planting of *America,* and of the multiplication and extension of that people; of the Divine blessing on their industry, and the general and astonishing prosperity of their country! May they never again know what is spoken in the following verse:

Verse 39. *Again, they are minished*] Sometimes by war, or pestilence, or famine. How minished and brought low was the country already spoken of, by the long and destructive war which began in 1775, and was not ended till 1783! And what desolations, minishings, and ruin have been brought on the fertile empires of Europe by the war which commenced in 1792, and did not end till 1814! And how many millions of lives have been sacrificed in it, and souls sent unprepared into the eternal world! When God makes inquisition for blood, on whose heads will he find the blood of these slaughtered millions? Alas! O, alas!

Verse 40. *He poureth contempt upon princes*] How many have lately been raised from *nothing,* and set upon thrones! And how many have been cast down from thrones, and reduced to nothing! And where are now those mighty troublers of the earth? On both sides they are in general gone to give an account of themselves to God. And what an account!

Where there is *no way.*] Who can consider the fate of the late emperor of the French, *Napoleon,* without seeing the *hand of God* in his downfall! All the powers of Europe were leagued against him in vain; they were as stubble to his bow. "HE *came,* HE *saw,* and HE *conquered*" almost every where, till God, by a *Russian* FROST, destroyed his tens of thousands of veteran troops. And afterwards his armies of *raw conscripts* would have overmatched the world had not a particular providence intervened at *Waterloo,* when all the *skill* and *valour* of his opponents had been nearly reduced to nothing. How terrible art thou, O Lord, in thy judgments! Thou art fearful in praises, doing wonders.

The dreary rock of St. Helena, where there was no way, saw a period to the mighty conqueror, who had *strode* over all the countries of Europe!

Verse 41. *Yet setteth he the poor on high*] This probably refers to the case of the *Israelites* and their restoration from captivity. But these are incidents which frequently occur, and mark the superintendence of a *benign Providence,* and the hand of a just *God;* and are applicable to a multitude of cases.

Verse 42. *The righteous shall see it*] The wicked are as inconsiderate as they are obstinate and headstrong.

And rejoice] To have such ample proofs that God ruleth in the earth, and that none that trust in him shall be desolate.

All iniquity shall stop her mouth.] God's judgments and mercies are so evident, and so distinctly marked, that atheism, infidelity, and irreligion are confounded, and the cause of error and falsehood has become hopeless. It was only the *mouth* that could do any thing; and that only by *lies, calumnies,* and *blasphemies:* but God *closes this mouth,* pours contempt upon the *head* and *judgment* upon the *heart.* This may also be applied to the case of the *Israelites* and the *Babylonians.* The former, when they turned to God, became *righteous; the* latter were a personification of *all iniquity.*

Verse 43. *Whoso is wise*] That is, He that is wise, he that fears God, and regards the operation of his hand *will observe*—lay up and keep, *these things.* He will hide them in his heart, that he sin not against Jehovah. He will encourage himself in the Lord, because he finds that he is a *never-failing spring of goodness* to the righteous.

They shall understand the loving-kindness of the Lord] חסדי יהוה *chasdey Yehovah,* the *exuberant goodness of Jehovah.* This is his peculiar and most prominent characteristic among men; for "judgment is his strange work." What a wonderful discourse on Divine Providence, and God's management of the world, does this inimitable Psalm contain! The *ignorant* cannot read it without profit; and by the study of it, the *wise man* will become yet wiser.

ANALYSIS OF THE ONE HUNDRED AND SEVENTH PSALM

The title of this Psalm is *Hallelujah,* because it sets forth the praises of God for delivering such as are oppressed from four common miseries; after each of which is expressed those intercalary verses: "O that men would praise the Lord," &c.; "They cried unto the Lord in their trouble." It also praises God for his providence in its effects.

I. A preface in which he exhorts all to praise God, especially the redeemed, ver. 1, 2.

II. A declaration of his goodness in particular.

I. To the travellers and strangers, famished, ver. 3-9.

2. To the prisoners and captives, ver. 10-16.

3. To the sick, ver. 16-23.

4. To the mariners, ver. 23-32.

III. A praise of God's power and providence. which is evidently seen in the changes and varieties in the world, of which he gives many instances, that prove him to be the sole Disposer and Governor of the universe, ver. 33-42.

IV. The conclusion, which sets forth the use we are to make of it, ver. 42, 43.

I. 1. This Psalm, like the former, begins: "That we celebrate and set forth God's praise," and for the same reasons. "O give thanks unto the Lord;" 1. "For he is good;" 2. And merciful: "For his mercy endureth for ever."

2. And those whom he invites to perform this duty are all who are sensible that they have received any mercy or goodness from him in either soul or body, whom he calls the redeemed of the Lord; that men may know, when they are freed from any evil, that it is not by chance or their wisdom: God's hand is in it; he is the First Cause; the rest are only his instruments.

1. "Let the redeemed of the Lord say," i. e., that he is good and merciful.

2. "They say so whom he hath redeemed," &c. If the Holy Ghost means, when he speaks of our redemption by Christ, *the enemy,* the devil, or some tyrant, tribulation, &c.; then a corporeal and temporal redemption is meant. The next verse seems to refer to their banishment.

3. "And gathered them out of the lands," &c. Which is yet as true of our spiritual redemption. Matt. viii. 11; John x. 16; and xi. 52.

II. Most expositors begin the *second* part at the second verse, but some at the fourth; but it is not material. In those two there was mention made of God's goodness in their deliverance, in their collection from all lands. But the following is a declaration of what they suffered during their absence from their country. And this is the misery which the prophet first instances in this place, then shows the course the travellers took, and lastly acquaints us with the manner of their deliverance. Their misery was—

1. "That they wandered." No small discomfort for an ingenious native to go from place to place as a vagrant. God's people were for a time pilgrims; "few and evil were their days."

2. The place adds to their misery. Travellers are not confined always to solitary places, they occasionally have company; but these "wandered in the wilderness in a solitary place," &c. Literally it was fulfilled in the *Israelites,* while they travelled through the wilderness.

3. "Hungry and thirsty." Men may wander and be solitary; and yet have a sufficient supply of food; but God's people sometimes fast, as *Elijah, David,* &c.

4. And the famine was so great "that their soul," that is, their life, "was ready to faint." This is the *incrementum* that the prophet uses to aggravate the misery of the travellers, and the several steps by which it rises.

The prophet shows the course which these travellers and hungry souls took for ease and help; and that it did not fail them, nor any one else who has tried it.

1. "Then in their trouble." God let them be brought into trouble to bring them back to himself.

2. "They cried." In their petition they were very earnest; it was no cold prayer, which froze on the way before it got to heaven; but fervent. *A cry.*

3. "And they cried." Not to any false god, but *unto the Lord.*

The success was answerable to their desire.

1. In general, "He delivered them out of their distresses."

2. But in particular, the deliverance was every way fit.

1. "They wandered in the wilderness," &c., ver. 4. "But he led them forth, that they might go to a city of habitation."

2. "They were hungry, and thirsty," &c. But "he filled the hungry soul," &c.

And upon this he concludes his exhortation to praise God, which he is so earnest for them to do, that he inserts the exhortation between each mention of the mercies.

1. The Lord delivered: "The Lord led them forth." Praise him then.

2. Of his mere mercy, not of desert. "For he is good."

3. And the effects of his goodness were seen in his works; let his praise then be as public as his works: "O that men," &c.

The *second* corporeal misery to which men are subject is captivity and imprisonment; he then shows the course the captives took, and God's mercy in their deliverance.

1. Captives; they were taken by the enemy, put in dungeons and prisons, where they were debarred the comfort of the sun: "For they sat in darkness," &c., and in fear of death.

2. Besides, in this place "they were fast bound with affliction," &c., because of their rebellion against the Lord: "The iron entered into their soul." "He brought them low;" but they sought help of the Lord.

"They cried unto the Lord in their trouble." "And found the same favour as the travellers did. "And he saved them out of their distresses."

The manner was suitable to their distress.

1. "For they sat in darkness," &c. "But he brought them out," &c.

2. "They were bound in affliction and iron," &c. The prison was not so strong but he was stronger, and delivered them from captivity. Now the psalmist interposes his thanksgiving: "O that men," &c.

The *third* misery is some great sickness or pining away of the body under some grievous disease, such as when stung by fiery serpents, as the Israelites. 1. He describes the danger under which they languished. 2. Shows the method they took for their recovery.

1. The appellation he fastens on the diseased persons, *fools;* not but that, generally speaking, they were wise enough; but in that they sinned with a high hand against God, "they are fools."

2. Now such *fools* God often smites with an incurable disease: "Fools, because of their transgression," &c. Not but that all sickness is from sin; but this that the prophet speaks of was their general apostasy, rebellion, and contempt of God's will and commandment.

The effect was lamentable and double.

1. "Their soul abhorred all manner of meat." Meat, with which the life of man is sustained, became loathsome to them, the disease was so grievous.

2. And deadly too; no art of the physician could cure them. "For they drew near to the gates of death," that is, the grave, where Death exercises his power, as the judges of Israel did in the gates.

But these, being but dead men in the eye of man, took the same course as they did before.

1. "They cried unto the Lord in their trouble."

2. And by God's blessing they recovered; God was alone their Physician.

3. This was the manner of their cure. "He saved them out of their distress."

1. "He sent his word, and healed them." He said the word only, and they were made whole. Or if any medicine were made use of, it was his word which made it medicinal, as in the case of the bunch of figs, and therefore the prophet uses an apt word to put them in mind. "He sent his word," as a great prince sends forth his ambassadors to do his commands. Most probably the centurion had this in his mind

when he said, "Say the word only, and my servant shall be whole."

2. "And he delivered them from their destructions," which are opposed to their previous danger. "They drew nigh," &c.

3. But he exhorts the saved to be thankful: "O that men," &c.

And he adds,

1. "Let them sacrifice their sacrifices."

2. But with these conditions and limitations: 1. That it be with a thankful heart, for an outward sacrifice is nothing. 2. That with the sacrifice there go an annunciation; that men *declare* and *publish* that the cure came from God. 3. That it be done with rejoicing; that we have an experience of God's presence, favour, and mercy, for which the heart ought to rejoice more than for the cure of the body.

The *fourth* misery arises from the danger at sea.

1. He describes.

2. Shows the course they take in a storm.

3. And the event following upon their prayers.

Upon which he calls upon them, as upon the three before, to praise God.

1. "They that go down to the sea in ships." For the sea is lower than the earth.

2. "That do business in great waters." As merchants, mariners, &c.

3. "These men see the works of the Lord," &c. Others hear of them by relation, but these see them: they see the great whales, innumerable kinds of fish, and monsters; islands dispersed and safe in the waves; whirlpools, quicksands, rocks; and have experience of the virtue of the loadstone. They discover many stars we know not; and they behold the vast workings of the sea, which fill the most valiant with fear.

4. "For he commandeth," &c.

Now he describes the tempest:—

1. From the cause. God speaks the word.

2. By it "he raiseth the stormy wind."

3. Which, inspired by his word, "lifts up the waves thereof."

———Fluctus ad sidera tollit.

"The waves arise to heaven."

4. "They" (that is, the passengers) "mount up to heaven," &c.

Hi summo in fluctu pendent, his unda dehiscens.

"They hung upon the wave; the sea yawns under them; and the bottom seems to be laid bare between the surges."

5. "Their soul is melted because of trouble." Their spirit fails.

Extemplo Æneæ solvuntur frigora membra.

"The limbs of the hero himself dissolve with terror."

6. "They reel to and fro." Tossed this way and that way.

Tres Eurus ab alto in brevia, et syrtes urget.

"They are dashed against the shoals and quicksands."

7. "They stagger and totter," &c. An apt simile.

Cui dubii stantque labantque pedes.

"They cannot keep their feet."

8. "And are at their wit's end." Omnis sapientia eorum absorbetur.—"Their judgment roves; their art fails; their skill is at an end."

Et meminisse viæ media Palinurus in unda.

"Even the pilot loses his way in the troubled deep."

Hitherto the prophet has poetically described the tempest and storm; and now he gives an account of the course they took to save their lives. "Then they cried unto the Lord," &c. An old proverb says: Qui nescit orare, discat navigare. "He who knows not how to pray, let him learn to be a sailor."

And the consequence of their praying was:

"And he brings them out," &c. In this manner:—

1. " He makes the storm a calm."

————Dicto citius tumida æquora placat.

"By his word the swelling sea becomes calm."

2. "So that the waves thereof are still." Et cunctus pelagi cecidit fragor. "And the noise of it is hushed to silence."

3. "Then they are glad," &c., no more reeling to and fro; whence arises their joy.

————Læto testantur gaudia plausu.

"The clapping of hands expresses their joy."

4. And to increase it: "So he brings them to their desired haven."

————Magno telluris amore,
Egressi optata nautæ potiuntur arena,
Et sale tabentes artus in littore ponunt.

"The weather-beaten marines having reached the shore, in an ecstacy of joy kiss the sand, and lay themselves down upon the beach."

And now, in the last place, he calls upon them to pay their tribute of thankful duty for the miracle done them in their preservation: "O that men would praise the Lord," &c.

And probably in their danger they might have made a vow, which is frequently done in such cases. Read the Life of *Nazianzen*. This vow the prophet would have them pay openly.

1. "Let them exalt him also in the congregation," &c.

2. And that not only before the promiscuous multitude; but " let them praise him in the assembly of the elders," &c. Sua tabula sacer votiva paries indicat, uvida suspendisse potenti vestimenta maris Deo. "Let them here suspend their votive tablet; and hang their wet clothes against a wall, as a grateful offering to him who rules the seas."

III. The prophet had exalted God's mercies in freeing men from these four miseries and calamities; these travellers through the wilderness, captivity, sickness, shipwreck; and now he manifests his power, providence, and wisdom, in the vicissitudes we meet with below. In the earth we see strange mutations; in kingdoms, wonderful revolutions; yet we must go higher,

and not rest short of the hand which governs all.

The prophet first instances the earth's changes.

1. "He turns rivers into a wilderness," &c. The fertility of any land arises from its rivers, as is apparent in Egypt from the overflowing of the *Nile*. And when Elisha would free the soil from barrenness, he first healed the waters. The drying up of rivers produces famine, and when the channels are directed from their courses, the fruitful land becomes a wilderness.

2. And the cause of this is: "The iniquity of them that dwell therein."

On the contrary, God illustrates his mercy by sometimes changing the wilderness into a fruitful and abundant place.

1. "He turneth the wilderness into a standing water," &c. They shall be fruitful for man's sake.

2. "For there he makes the hungry to dwell." God puts it into men's minds to plant colonies in some newly found and good land, where the hungry find plenty and are satisfied.

3. And to build houses: "That they may prepare a city," &c.

Pars aptare locum tecto, pars ducere muros.

"Some dig out the foundations, others raise the walls."

4. The endeavours of the colonists are: 1. "To sow fields." 2. "To plant vineyards." Which was the first trade in the world.

5. And God's blessing on those endeavours: "God blessed them also." 1. In children: "So that they multiplied greatly." 2. In cattle: "And suffered not their cattle to decrease."

But there is nothing in this world perpetual and stable: even those whom God had sometimes blessed and enriched continued not at one stay.

1. These are "minished, and brought low."

2. These are "worn out by oppression," &c. By some public calamity, war, famine, invasion, &c.

Even monarchs are subject to changes.

1. "He pours contempt upon princes." It is a heavy judgment for princes, civil or ecclesiastical, to become contemptible; for then the reins of discipline are let loose, confusion follows, and all things grow worse. And this *for the iniquity of those*, &c.

2. "He causeth them to wander in the wilderness," &c., which clause is subject to a double interpretation.

Either that he suffers princes to err in their counsels, lives, and example; or they enact unjust laws, favour wicked men, or oppress the good. But in the following verse there is some comfort.

"Yet setteth he the poor man on high," &c. Delivers him from all affliction.

"And maketh him families like a flock." Becomes his shepherd, and governs him by his special providence.

IV. He concludes the Psalm with an *epiphonema*, in which he persuades good men to consider the former promises, and lay them to heart; to observe the whole course of God's providence, that they impute not the changes of the world to chance or fortune, but bless God for all his dispensations.

1. "The righteous shall see it," &c. Consider, meditate upon it.

2. "And rejoice." When they are assured that God is their Guardian, and that all he lays upon them is for their real good.

"And all iniquity shall stop her mouth." By the observation of the event, at last evil doers shall not have cause to laugh and blaspheme, but to confess that all is justly and wisely done by God.

And this consideration is that of the wise man who looks afar off.

1. "Who is wise," &c., so as to mark these changes in the world properly.

2. "And they shall understand the loving-kindness of the Lord." It shall be seen by them how ineffable is his mercy towards those who truly fear him, and call upon his name: but our life is hid with Christ in God.

PSALM CVIII

The psalmist encourages himself to praise the Lord for mercies he had received, 1–5. He prays for the Divine succour, 6; and encourages the people to expect their restoration, and the enjoyment of all their former privileges and possessions, 7–13.

XXII. DAY. EVENING PRAYER

A Song *or* Psalm of David

O ªGOD, my heart is fixed; I will sing and give praise, even with my glory.

2 ᵇAwake, psaltery and harp: I *myself* will awake early.

3 I will praise thee, O Lord, among the people: and I will sing praises unto thee among the nations.

4 For thy mercy *is* great above the heavens: and thy truth *reacheth* unto the ᶜclouds.

5 ᵈBe thou exalted, O God, above the heavens: and thy glory above all the earth;

6 ᵉThat thy beloved may be delivered: save *with* thy right hand, and answer me.

7 God hath spoken in his holiness; I will rejoice, I will divide Shechem, and mete out the valley of Succoth.

8 Gilead *is* mine; Manasseh *is* mine; Ephraim also *is* the strength of mine head; ᶠJudah *is* my lawgiver;

9 Moab *is* my washpot; over Edom will I cast out my shoe; over Philistia will I triumph.

10 ᵍWho will bring me into the strong city? who will lead me into Edom?

11 *Wilt* not *thou,* O God, *who* hast cast us off? and wilt not thou, O God, go forth with our hosts?

12 Give us help from trouble: for vain *is* the help of man.

13 ʰThrough God we shall do valiantly: for he *it is that* shall tread down our enemies.

ªPsa. lvii. 7——ᵇPsa. lvii. 8–11——ᶜOr, *skies*——ᵈPsa. lvii. 5, 11

ᵉPsa. lx. 5, &c.——ᶠGen. xlix. 10——ᵍPsa. lx. 9 ʰPsa. lx. 12

NOTES ON PSALM CVIII

This Psalm is compounded of *two Psalms* which we have had already under review. The 1st, 2nd, 3rd, 4th, and 5th verses, are the same with the 7th, 8th, 9th, 10th, and 11th verses of Psalm lvii. And the 6th, 7th, 8th, 9th, 10th, 11th, 12th, and 13th, are the same with the 5th, 6th, 7th, 8th, 9th, 10th, 11th, and 12th of Psalm lx. The *variations* are few, and of little moment, and the explanation may be seen in the notes on the preceding Psalms, which need not be repeated here. That the Psalms referred to were made by *David,* and were applicable to the *then* state of his affairs, has been the opinion of many; and it is probable that the captives in Babylon composed *this* out of two above, and applied it to the state of their affairs. Their captivity being now ended, or nearly at an end, they look and pray for their restoration to their own land, as amply as it was possessed in the most prosperous days of *David.* The *Syriac* considers it as a prophecy of the vocation of the Gentiles. The *Hebrew* and all the *Versions* attribute it to *David.*

Verse 1. *Even with my glory.*] My greatest glory shall be in publishing thy praise. Some make the *glory* here to mean the Lord himself; some, the Ark of the *covenant;* some, the soul of the *psalmist;* others, his tongue; some, the gift of prophecy; and some, the psalmist's spirit or vein of *poetry.* See the notes on Psalm lvii. 8.

Verse 3. *Among the people*] The *Jews.*

Among the nations.] The *Gentiles.* Wherever this Psalm is sung or read, either among *Jews* or *Gentiles, David* may be said to sing praise to God.

Verse 7. *God hath spoken in his holiness*] בקדשו *bekodsho;* some think this means *in his Holy One,* referring to the *Prophet Jeremiah,* who predicted the captivity, its duration of *seventy* years, and the deliverance from it.

Verse 10. *The strong city*] The possession of the *metropolis* is a sure proof of the subjugation of the country.

Verse 13. *Through God we shall do valiantly*]

From him we derive our courage, from him our strength, and by him our success.

[For the ANALYSIS, see the Psalms from which our is composed.]

PSALM CIX

The psalmist speaks against his inveterate enemies, 1–5. He prays against them, and denounces God's judgments, 6–15. The reason on which this is grounded, 16–20. He prays for his own safety and salvation, using many arguments to induce God to have mercy upon him.

To the chief Musician, A Psalm of David

A. M. cir. 2981
B. C. cir. 1023
Davidis, Regis
Israelitarum,
cir. annum
33

HOLD ᵃnot thy peace, O God of my praise;

2 For the mouth of the wicked and the ᵇmouth of the deceitful ᶜare opened against me: they have spoken against me with a lying tongue.

3 They compassed me about also with words of hatred; and fought against me ᵈwithout a cause.

A. M. cir. 2981
B. C. cir. 1023
Davidis, Regis
Israelitarum,
cir. annum
33

4 For my love they are my adversaries: but I *give myself unto* prayer.

5 And ᵉthey have rewarded me evil for good, and hatred for my love.

6 Set thou a wicked man over him: and

ᵃPsa. lxxxiii. 1——ᵇHeb. *mouth of deceit*——ᶜHeb. *have opened* themselves

ᵈPsa. xxxv. 7; lxix. 4; John xv. 25——ᵉPsa. xxxv. 7, 12 xxxviii. 20

NOTES ON PSALMS CIX

The *title* of this Psalm, *To the chief Musician, A Psalm of David*, has already often occurred, and on it the *Versions* offer nothing new. The *Syriac* says it is "a Psalm of David, when the people, without his knowledge, made *Absalom* king; on which account he was slain: but to us (Christians) he details the passion of Christ." That it contains a prophecy against *Judas* and the enemies of our Lord, is evident from Acts i. 20. Probably, in its primary meaning, (for such a meaning it certainly has,) it may refer to *Ahithophel*. The execrations in it should be rendered in the *future* tense, as they are mere prophetic denunciations of God's displeasure against sinners. Taken in this light, it cannot be a stumbling-block to any person. God has a right to denounce those judgments which he will inflict on the workers of iniquity. But perhaps the whole may be the execrations of *David's* enemies against himself. See on ver. 20. *Ahithophel*, who gave evil counsel against *David*, and being frustrated hanged himself, was no mean prototype of *Judas* the traitor; it was probably on this account that *St.* Peter, Acts i. 20, applied it to the case of *Judas*, as a prophetic declaration concerning him, or at least a subject that might be accommodated to his case.

Verse 1. *Hold not thy peace*] Be not silent; arise and defend my cause.

Verse 2. *The mouth of the wicked and—the deceitful are opened against me*] Many persons are continually uttering calumnies against me. Thou knowest my heart and its innocence; vindicate my uprightness against these calumniators.

Verse 4. *For my love they are my adversaries*] In their behalf I have performed many acts of kindness, and they are my adversaries notwithstanding; this shows principles the most vicious, and hearts the most corrupt. Many

of the fathers and commentators have understood the principal part of the things spoken here as referring to our Lord, and the treatment he received from the Jews; and whatever the original intention was, they may safely be applied to this case, as the 2nd, 3rd, 4th, and 5th verses are highly illustrative of the conduct of the Jewish rulers towards our Lord as the following verses are of the conduct of Judas; but allowing these passages to be prophetic, it is the *Jewish state* rather than an *individual*, against which these awful denunciations are made, as it seems to be represented here under the person and character of an extremely hardened and wicked man; unless we consider the curses to be those of *David's* enemies. See the note on verse 20.

But I give myself unto prayer] ואני תפלה *vaani thephillah;* "And I prayer." The *Chaldee:* ואנא אצלי *vaana atsalley*, "but I pray." This gives a good sense, which is followed by the *Vulgate, Septuagint, Æthiopic, Arabic*, and *Anglo-Saxon.* The *Syriac*, "I will pray for them." This, not so correctly; as dreadful *imprecations*, not *prayers*, follow. But probably the whole ought to be interpreted according to the mode laid down, verse 20. The translation and paraphrase in the old Psalter are very simple:—

Trans. ﬀor that thyng that thai sulde hate lufed me, thai bakbited me; bot I prayed.

Par. That is, thai sulde haf lufed me for I was godson, and thai bakbited me sayande, in Belzebub he castes oute fendes; bot I prayed for thaim.

Verse 6. *Let Satan stand at his right hand.*] As the word שטן *satan* means an *adversary* simply, though sometimes it is used to express the evil spirit *Satan*, I think it best to preserve here its grammatical meaning: "Let an *adversary* stand at his right hand:" i. e., Let him be *opposed* and *thwarted* in all his purposes.

All the *Versions* have *devil*, or some equivocal word. The ARABIC has ابليس *eblees.* the chief

A. M. cir. 2981
B. C. cir. 1023
Davidis, Regis
Israelitarum,
cir. annum
33

let [f]Satan [g]stand at his right hand.

7 When he shall be judged, let him [h]be condemned : and [i]let his prayer become sin.

8 Let his days be few; *and* [k]let another take his [l]office.

9 [m]Let his children be fatherless, and his wife a widow.

10 Let his children be continually vagabonds, and beg : let them seek *their bread* also out of their desolate places.

11 [n]Let the extortioner catch all that he hath; and let the strangers spoil his labour.

12 Let there be none to extend mercy unto him : neither let there be any to favour his fatherless children.

A. M. cir. 2981
B. C. cir. 1023
Davidis, Regis
Israelitarum,
cir. annum
33

---

[f]Zech. iii. 1——[g]Or, *an adversary*——[h]Heb. *go out guilty*, or *wicked*——[i]Prov. xxviii. 9

[k]Ac s 1. 20——[l]Or, *charge*——[m]Exod. xxii. 24——[n]Job v. 5; xviii. 9

---

of the apostate spirits; but the name is probably corrupted from the GREEK διαβολος *diabolos;* from which the LATIN *diabolus*, the ITALIAN *diavolo*, the SPANISH *diablo*, the FRENCH *diable*, the IRISH or CELTIC *diabal*, the DUTCH *duivel*, the GERMAN *teufel*, the ANGLO-SAXON *deofal*, and the ENGLISH *devil*, are all derived. The original, διαβολος, comes from δια βαλλειν, to *shoot* or *pierce through*.

Verse 7. *Let him be condemned*] יצא רשע *yetse rasha.* "Let him come out a wicked man;" that is let his wickedness be made manifest.

Let his prayer become sin.] Thus paraphrased by Calmet: "Let him be accused, convicted, and condemned, and let the *defence* which he brings for his justification only serve to deepen his guilt, and hasten his condemnation." I once more apprise the reader, that if these are not the words of *David's* enemies against himself, (see on verse 20,) they are *prophetic denunciations* against a rebellious and apostate person or people, hardened in crime, and refusing to return to God.

Verse 8. *Let another take his office.*] The original is פקדתו *pekuddatho*, which the margin translates *charge*, and which literally means *superintendance, oversight, inspection* from actual *visitations.* The translation in our common Version is too technical. *His bishopric,* following the *Septuagint*, επισκοπην, and *Vulgate, episcopatum*, and has given cause to some light people to be *witty*, who have said, "The first bishop we read of was bishop Judas." But it would be easy to convict this witticism of blasphemy, as the word is used in many parts of the sacred writings, from Genesis downward, to signify offices and officers, appointed either by God immediately, or in the course of his providence, for the accomplishment of the most important purposes. It is applied to the patriarch *Joseph,* Gen. xxxix. 4, ויפקדהו *vaiyaphkidehu, he made him bishop*, alias *overseer;* therefore it might be as *wisely* said, and much more correctly, "The first bishop we read of was bishop Joseph;" and many such bishops there were of God's making long before Judas was born. After all, Judas was no *traitor* when he was appointed to what is called his *bishopric, office*, or *charge* in the apostolate. Such witticisms as these amount to no argument, and serve no cause that is worthy of defence.

Our common Version, however, was not the first to use the word: it stands in the *Anglo-Saxon* ꞇ bïꞃhophæꝺ hïꞃ, oꞃꝩo oꝺeꞃ, "and his episcopacy let take other." The old Psalter is nearly the same; I shall give the whole verse: ꝼa be mabe ḣis baẏs, anb ḣis bẏsshoprẏk another take.

"For Mathai was sett in stede of Judas; and his days was ꝼa that hynged himself."

Verse 9. *Let his children be fatherless, &c.*] It is said that Judas was a married man, against whom this verse, as well as the preceding is supposed to be spoken; and that it was to support them that he stole from the bag in which the property of the apostles was put, and of which he was the treasurer.

Verse 10. *Let his children—beg*] The father having lost his *office*, the children must necessarily be destitute; and this is the hardest lot to which any can become subject, after having been born to the expectation of an ample fortune.

Verse 11. *Let the strangers spoil his labour.*] Many of these execrations were literally fulfilled in the case of the miserable Jews, after the death of our Lord. They were not only expelled from their own country, after the destruction of Jerusalem, but they were prohibited from returning; and so taxed by the Roman government, that they were reduced to the lowest degree of poverty. *Domitian* expelled them from Rome; and they were obliged to take up their habitation without the gate Capena, in a wood contiguous to the city, for which they were obliged to pay a rent, and where the whole of their property was only a *basket and a little hay.* See JUVENAL, Sat. ver. 11:—

Substitit ad veteres arcus, madidamque Capenam:
Hic ubi nocturnæ Numa constituebat amicæ,
Nunc sacri fontis nemus, et delubra locantur
Judæis: quorum cophinus, fœnumque supellex:
Omnis enim populo mercedem pendere jussa est
Arbor, et ejectis mendicat silva Camœnis.

He stopped a little at the conduit gate,
Where Numa modelled once the Roman state;
In nightly councils with his nymph retired:
Though now the sacred shades and founts are hired
By banished Jews, who their whole wealth can lay
In a small basket, on a wisp of hay.
Yet such our avarice is, that every tree
Pays for his head; nor sleep itself is free;
Nor place nor persons now are sacred held,
From their own grove the Muses are expelled.
DRYDEN.

The same poet refers again to this wretched state of the Jews, Sat. vi., ver. 541; and shows to what vile extremities they were reduced in order to get a morsel of bread:—

A. M. cir. 2981
B. C. cir. 1023
Davidis, Regis
Israelitarum,
cir. annum
33

13 [o]Let his posterity be cut off; *and* in the generation following let their [p]name be blotted out.

14 [q]Let the inquity of his fathers be remembered with the LORD; and let not the sin of his mother [r]be blotted out.

15 Let them be before the LORD continually, that he may [s]cut off the memory of them from the earth.

16 Because that he remembered not to show mercy, but persecuted the poor and needy man, that he might even slay the [t]broken in heart.

17 [u]As he loved cursing, so let it come unto him: as he delighted not in blessing, so let it be far from him.

A. M. cir. 2981
B. C. cir. 1023
Davidis, Regis
Israelitarum,
cir. annum
33

18 As he clothed himself with cursing like as with his garment, so let it [v]come [w]into his bowels like water, and like oil into his bones.

19 Let it be unto him as the garment *which* covereth him, and for a girdle wherewith he is girded continually.

20 *Let* this *be* the reward of mine adversaries from the LORD, and of them that speak evil against my soul.

21 But do thou for me, O GOD the Lord,

---

[o]Job xviii. 19; Psalm xxxvii. 28——[p]Prov. x. 7——[q]Exod. xx. 5——[r]Neh. iv. 5; Jer. xviii. 23——[s]Job xviii. 17; Psa. xxxiv. 16——[t]Psa. xxxiv. 18——[u]Prov. xiv. 14; Ezek. xxxv. 6——[v]Num. v. 22——[w]Heb. *within him*

Cum dedit ille locum, cophino fœnoque relicto,
Arcanam Judæa tremens mendicat in aurem,
Interpres legum Solymarum, et magna sacerdos
Arboris, ac summi fida internuncia cœli.
Implet et illa manum, sed parcius, ære minuto.
Qualia cunque voles Judæi somnia vendunt.

Here a *Jewess* is represented as coming from the wood mentioned above, to gain a few *oboli* by fortune-telling; and, trembling lest she should be discovered, she leaves her *basket* and *hay*, and whispers lowly in the ear of some female, from whom she hopes employment in her line. She is here called by the poet the *interpretess of the laws of Solymae*, or Jerusalem, and the *priestess of a tree*, because obliged, with the rest of her nation, to lodge in a *wood;* so that she and her countrymen might be said *to seek their bread out of desolate places, the stranger having spoiled their labour.* Perhaps the whole of the Psalm relates to their infidelities, rebellions, and the miseries inflicted on them from the crucifixion of our Lord till the present time. I should prefer this sense, if what is said on ver. 20 be not considered a better mode of interpretation.

Verse 13. *Let his posterity be cut off*] It is a fact that the *distinction* among the Jewish tribes in entirely lost. Not a Jew in the world knows from what tribe he is sprung; and as to the royal family, it remains nowhere but in the person of Jesus the Messiah. He *alone* is the Lion of the tribe of Judah. Except as it exists in him, *the name is blotted out.*

Verse 16. *Persecuted the poor and needy man*] In the case of Jesus Christ all the dictates of justice and mercy were destroyed, and they persecuted this poor man unto death. They acted from a diabolical malice. On common principles, their opposition to Christ cannot be accounted for.

Verse 17. *As he loved cursing, so let it come unto him*] The Jews said, when crucifying our Lord, *His blood be upon us and our children!* Never was an imprecation more dreadfully fulfilled.

Verse 18. *Let it come into his bowels like water*] Houbigant thinks this is an allusion to the *waters of jealousy;* and he is probably right,—the bitter waters that produce the curse. See Num. v. 18.

Verse 19. *And for a girdle*] Let the curse *cleave* to him throughout life: as the girdle binds all the clothes to the body, let the curse of God bind all mischiefs and maladies to his body and soul.

The *Hindoos, Budhists*, and others often wear a *gold* or *silver chain* about their waist. One of those chains, once the ornament of a *Moudeliar* in the island of Ceylon, lies now before me: it is silver, and curiously wrought.

Verse 20. Let *this* be *the reward of mine adversaries from the Lord, and of them that speak evil against my soul.*] Following the mode of interpretation already adopted, this may mean: All these maledictions shall be fulfilled on my enemies; they shall have them for their reward. So all the opposition made by the Jews against our Lord, and the obloquies and execrations wherewith they have loaded him and his religion, have fallen upon themselves; and they are awful examples of the wrath of God abiding on *them* that believe not.

But is not this verse a *key to* all that preceded it? The original, fairly interpreted, will lead us to a somewhat different meaning: זאת פעלת שטני מאת יהוה והדברים רע על נפשי *zoth peullath soteney meeth Yehovah, vehaddoberim ra al naphshi.* "This is the work of my adversaries before the Lord, and of those who speak evil against my soul," or *life.* That is, all that is said from the *sixth* to the *twentieth* verse consists of the evil words and imprecations of my enemies against my soul, laboring to set the Lord, by imprecations, against me, that their curses may take effect. This, which is a reasonable interpretation, frees the whole Psalm from *every difficulty.* Surely, the curses contained in it are more like those which proceed from the mouth of the wicked, than from one inspired by the Spirit of the living God. Taking the words in this sense, which I am persuaded is the best, and which the *original* will well bear and several of the *Versions* countenance, then our translation may stand just as it is; only let the reader remember that at the *sixth* verse David begins to tell *how his enemies cursed* HIM, *while he prayed for* THEM.

Verse 21. *But do thou for me*] While they

A. M. cir. 2981
B. C. cir. 1023
Davidis, Regis
Israelitarum,
cir. annum
33

for thy name's sake: because thy mercy *is* good, deliver thou me,

22 For I *am* poor and needy, and my heart is wounded within me.

23 I am gone ˣlike the shadow when it declineth: I am tossed up and down as the locust.

24 My ʸknees are weak through fasting; and my flesh faileth of fatness.

25 I became also ᶻa reproach unto them: *when* they looked upon me ᵃthey shaked their heads.

26 Help me, O LORD my God: O save me according to thy mercy:

27 ᵇThat they may know that this *is* thy hand; *that* thou, LORD, hast done it.

28 ᶜLet them curse, but bless thou: when they arise, let them be ashamed; but let ᵈthy servant rejoice.

29 ᵉLet mine adversaries be clothed with shame, and let them cover themselves with their own confusion, as with a mantle.

30 I will greatly praise the LORD with my mouth; yea, ᶠI will praise him among the multitude.

31 For ᵍhe shall stand at the right hand of the poor, to save *him* ʰfrom those that condemn his soul.

A. M. cir. 2981
B. C. cir. 1023
Davidis, Regis
Israelitarum,
cir. annum
33

ˣPsa. cii. 11; cxliv. 4——ʸHeb. xii. 12——ᶻPsa. xxii. 6, 7——ᵃMatt. xxvii. 39——ᵇJob xxxvii. 7——ᶜ2 Sam. xvi. 11, 12——ᵈIsa. lxv. 14

ᵉPsa. xxxv. 26; cxxxii. 18——ᶠPsa. xxxv. 18; cxi. 1 ᵍPsa. xvi. 8; lxxiii. 23; cx. 5; cxxi. 5——ʰHeb. *from the judges of his soul*

---

use horrible imprecations against me, and load me with their curses, *act thou for me*, and *deliver me* from their maledictions. While they *curse*, do thou *bless*. This verse is a farther proof of the correctness of the interpretation given above.

Verse 22. *I am poor and needy*] I am *afflicted* and *impoverished; and my heart is wounded*—my very *life* is sinking through distress.

Verse 23. *I am gone like the shadow*] "I have walked like the declining shadow,"—I have passed my meridian of health and life; and as the sun is going below the horizon, so am I about to go under the earth.

I am tossed up and down as the locust.] When swarms of locusts take wing, and infest the countries in the east, if the wind happen to blow *briskly*, the swarms are agitated and driven upon each other, so as to appear to be heaved to and fro, or tossed up and down. Dr. *Shaw*, who has seen this, says it gives a lively idea of the comparisons of the psalmist.

Verse 24. *My knees are weak through fasting*] That *hunger* is as soon felt in *weakening the knees*, as in producing an *uneasy sensation in the stomach*, is known by all who have ever felt it. Writers in all countries have referred to this effect of hunger. Thus *Tryphioderus*, Il. Excid. ver. 155:—

Τειρομενου βαρυθειεν ατερπει γουνατα λιμῳ.

"Their knees might fail, by hunger's force subdued;
And sink, unable to sustain their load."
MERRICK.

So PLAUTUS, Curcul, act. ii., scen. 3:—

Tenebræ oboriuntur, genua inedia succidunt.

"My eyes grow dim; my knees are weak with hunger."

And LUCRETIUS, lib. iv. ver. 950:—

Brachia, palpebræque cadunt, poplitesque procumbunt.

"The arms, the eyelids fall; the knees give way."

Both the *knees* and the *sight* are particularly affected by hunger.

Verse 25. When *they looked upon me they shaked their heads.*] Thus was David treated by *Shimei*, 2 Sam. xvi. 5, 6, and our blessed Lord by the *Jews*, Matt. xxvii. 39.

Verse 27. *That they may know that this is thy hand*] Let thy help be so manifest in my behalf, that they may see it is thy hand, and that thou hast undertaken for me. Or, if the words refer to the passion of our Lord, Let them see that I suffer not on my own account; "for the transgression of my people am I smitten."

Verse 28. *Let them curse, but bless thou*] See on ver. 20: Of the mode of interpretation recommended there, this verse gives additional proof.

Verse 29. *Let them cover themselves*] He here retorts their own curse, ver. 18.

Verse 30. *I will greatly praise the Lord*] I have the fullest prospect of deliverance, and a plenary vindication of my innocence.

Verse 31. *He shall stand at the right hand of the poor*] Even if Satan himself be the accuser, God will vindicate the innocence of his servant. Pilate and the Jews condemned our Lord to death as a malefactor; God showed his immaculate innocence by his resurrection from the dead.

The whole of this Psalm is understood by many as referring solely to *Christ*, the traitor *Judas*, and the *wicked Jews*. This is the view taken of it in the analysis.

ANALYSIS OF THE HUNDRED AND NINTH PSALM

The later expositors expound this Psalm of *Doeg Ahithophel*, and other persecutors of *David;* and so it may be understood in the type; but the ancient fathers apply it to *Judas*, and the Jews who put Christ to death; which opinion, being more probable, and because Peter (Acts i. 20) applies a passage out of ver. 8 to *Judas*, I shall expound the Psalm as of Christ, whom David personated, and of *Judas*, and the malicious *Jews*, as understood in the persons of his wicked and slanderous enemies.

The Psalm has four parts:—

I. A short ejaculation, ver. 1, and the reasons expressed in a complaint of the fraud and malice of his enemies, ver. 6.

II. A bitter imprecation against their fury, ver. 6-21.

III. A supplication presented to God for himself, and the reasons, ver. 21-30.

IV. A profession of thanks.

I. He begins with an ejaculation: "Hold not thy peace, O God of my praise."

1. Either actively, that is, "O God, whom I praise," even in the greatest calamities.

2. Or passively; "Who art my praise:" The Witness and Advocate of my innocency when I am condemned by malicious tongues; which sense appears best for this place.

"Hold not thy peace." *Tacere*, to be silent, in Scripture, when referred to God, is to connive, to rest, to appear not to regard; and, on the contrary, *loqui*, to speak, to do something for revenge or deliverance; it is what David here asks, that, when the malice of his enemies arrived at its height, God should not suffer them, but show his displeasure.

Then by way of complaint, he describes their malicious nature, which he aggravates by an elegant gradation. "For the mouth of the wicked:" and they were, 1. Impious. 2. Deceitful. 3. Liars.

1. "For the mouth of the wicked:" *Caiaphas, Judas, the priests, Jews,* &c.

2. "And the mouth of the deceitful," &c. *They sought to entrap him in his words.*

3. "They have spoken against me," &c. "He casteth out devils through Beelzebub," &c.

And yet the mischief rises higher, even to hatred and malice.

1. "They compassed me about," &c. Manifesting in plain words the malice they carried in their hearts. "This man is not of God," &c.

2. "They hated me without a cause:" Wantonly, idly. They were not only evil, deceitful, and malicious; but very ungrateful. "He went about doing good;" and "How often would I have gathered you," &c.; and for this love they returned hatred.

1. "For my love, they are my adversaries:" But, nevertheless,

2. "I give myself to prayer:" "Father, forgive them; they know not," &c. Which base ingratitude of theirs he opens in fuller words. "They have rewarded me evil." And Theognis truly says,

'Η χαρις αλλαξαι την φυσιν ου δυναται.

No kindness can invert an evil nature:

A Jew will ever be a Jew.

II. The prophet, having complained of the malice, spiteful usage, and ingratitude of his nation, their crafty dealing with him, and their lies against him, proceeds to pray against them, and that in most bitter and fearful imprecations. Enemies he foresaw they would be to the flourishing state of Christ's Church, and that nothing had power to restrain or amend them; and therefore he curses them with a curse the most bitter that ever fell from the lips of man. In particular *Judas,* who was guide to them who took Jesus, is pointed out; but, as Augustine observes, he represented the person of the whole synagogue; therefore, it is involved necessarily. But some understanding these curses as uttered by the Jews against *David.* See the note on ver. 20.

1. "Set thou a wicked man over him," &c.: A fearful imprecation. Subject him to the will of some impious and wicked man, to whose lust and violence he may be no better than a slave. Others understand by *a wicked man* a false teacher, who may seduce him by false doctrines.

2. "Let Satan stand at his right hand:" Have full power over him. Let him stand; which signifies a perpetual endeavour to urge him forward till he effect his intended mischief. And so it was with *Judas* and the *Jews;* Satan was their guide, and they followed him.

The second is, "When he shall be judged, let him be condemned;"—find no mercy, no favour, at the judge's hands; thus, when *Judas,* accused and condemned by his own conscience, went to the high priest, who had bribed him, he would not acquit him; and *Judas,* in despair and grief for his sin, "went out and hanged himself."

The third, "Let his prayer become sin:" He turned his ear from hearing God, why then should God hear him? No prayer is acceptable to God but through Christ, and that out of a sincere heart; any other prayers become sin.

The fourth is the shortening of their life and honour.

1. "Let his days be few:" Length of days is promised only to the obedient, and is a blessing: but the prayer is that this man's life be a short one, and so Judas's was.

2. "And let another take his office:" Which must be applied to *Judas,* since St. Peter (Acts i. 20) so interprets it; and it is at this day as true of the Jews, for they have no high priest. Another, after the order of *Melchizedek,* has succeeded Aaron's priesthood.

The fifth is—

1. "Let his children be fatherless," &c.: Which follows on the former curse.

2. "Let his children be continually vagabonds, and beg:" And such the Jews are to this day; and beggars they were for a long time after the overthrow of Jerusalem.

The sixth execration is upon his goods.

1. "Let the extortioner catch all that he hath:" Probably the publicans.

2. "And let the strangers spoil his labour:" Which was verified by the soldiers of *Titus,* who ripped up the bellies of the captive *Jews* to see if they had swallowed gold.

But the prophet again returns to his children.

1. "Let there be none to extend mercy unto him," &c.: To beg, or to want, is a misery; but there is some comfort in it when beggars meet with some to relieve it. But the prophet says, Let there be none to pity him, or his. *Judas* found none to pity him.

2. Men, because they must die themselves, desire, if possible, to be immortal in their issue. *Bellarmine* observes that *Judas* had no issue; for that *Matthias,* who came in his place, did not derive his office from him. Though a posterity of the *Jews* remained after the flesh, yet, in the next generation, their ecclesiastical and civil polity was at an end; and since their dispersion they are without king, without priest, without sacrifice, without altar, without ephod, and without teraphim, as foretold by *Hosea.*

3. "Let the iniquity of his fathers be remembered," &c.: This imprecation answers God's threat: "I will visit the iniquity of the fathers upon the children." And this curse has come upon the Jews to the uttermost; they are self-

devoted: "Let his blood be upon us, and upon our children." The guilt of his blood is yet upon them; the iniquity of their fathers is yet remembered; and the sin of their mother, the synagogue, is not yet done away.

He repeats again the sin of their fathers, and the sin of the synagogue; this verse being but the exposition of the former.

1. "Let them be before the Lord continually:" The sin their father and mother committed, never let it be forgotten by God.

2. "That he may cut off the memory," &c.: Except it be in contempt.

The prophet having now finished his execrations, acquaints us with the causes of them.

1. Their want of pity to them in distress: "Have ye no regard, all ye that pass by?" Lam. i. 12. It is but just then "that they find judgment without mercy, that would show no mercy."

2. So far from that, "that he persecuted the poor and needy man," &c., which is the second cause; the inhumanity of *Judas* and the Jews against Christ, who is here called—1. *Poor*, because, "when he was rich, for our sakes he became poor, that we through his poverty might be rich;" 2 Cor. ix. 2. *The needy man:* "For the foxes have holes," &c.; Luke ix. 58. 3. *The broken in heart.* For he was in agony, and his soul was troubled, when he sweated great drops of blood; when he cried, "My God, my God!" not with compunction or contrition for any fault he had committed, but from a sense of pain, and his solicitude for the salvation of mankind.

In this verse there is noted the extreme cruelty and inhumanity of the *Jews;* for whoever persecutes a man for his life is inclined to it either from some real or supposed injury, or else through envy: but Christ was humble and lowly in heart; he went about doing good, and yet they persecuted him.

But, thirdly, he complains: "He loved cursing;" therefore, it is but reason that he should have what he loved: "As he clothed himself with cursing—so let it come," &c. No man can love a curse or hate a blessing, if it be proposed to the will under the form of a curse or blessing: but a man is said to love a curse when he follows a wicked course, and avoids the blessing of a good life. This *Judas* and the *Jews* did: *Judas*, by loving money more than his Master; the Jews, by—"Let his blood," &c.

Neque enim lex justior ulla est, &c.

It is just that a man should suffer for his own wicked inventions. But the prophet adds, Let it sit close to him as a garment; let it be converted into his substance: let him carry it perpetually, &c.

1. "As he clothed himself with cursing," &c. As in clothes he delights in.

2. "So let it come as waters," &c. As the stomach concocts and turns every thing into the very flesh of the animal; so let his curse be converted into his nature and manners.

3. "Let it come as oil into his bones," &c. Oil will pierce the bones; water will not.

This curse must be of great efficacy; he must always carry it.

1. "Let it be unto him," &c. Stick close as a garment.

2. "And for a girdle," &c. Compass him round about.

For a garment some read *pallium;* a cloak that a man puts off at home, and calls for when he goes abroad: thus let God set an out-

ward mark upon him; let him be known as a cast-away.

If *Doeg* were the type of *Judas*, as most agree, in this Psalm, then by the girdle might be understood *cingulum militare*, the military girdle, which, while they were of that profession, they cast not off: and he, *Doeg*, being a military man, the curse was to cleave to him, and compass him as his girdle.

The prophet concludes this part of the Psalm with an exclamation, as being persuaded his curses were not in vain.

"Let this be the reward of mine adversaries," &c., who say that I am a deceiver, and deny me to be the Saviour of the world.

III. The prophet now turns from curses to prayer: and in the person of Christ, directs it to God for protection and deliverance both of himself and the whole Church.

1. "But do thou for me," &c. He asks help against his persecutors on these three grounds: 1. Because his Lord was *Jehovah*, the fountain of all being and power. 2. Because it would be for his honour: "Do it for thy name's sake." Thy faithfulness and goodness to the Church, and justice in executing vengeance on her enemies. 3. Do it, *because thy mercy is good*—easily inclined to succour the miserable.

2. "Deliver me," may have reference to Christ's prayer, "Father, save me from this hour," &c.

1. "Deliver me," for I am destitute of all human help.

2. "Deliver me," for my heart is wounded within me.

And to these he adds many other reasons; and uses two similes, the one drawn from the shadow of the evening, the other from the *locust.*

1. "I am gone like a shadow:" &c. Which passes away in a moment silently: so was Christ led away as a prisoner, without any murmur: "He was led as a lamb," &c.; Isa. liii. Thus the apostles and martyrs died patiently.

2. "I am tossed up and down as the locust." From one tribunal to another, as the locust carried from place to place, Exod. x. 12, 19.

Secondly, he reasons from his bodily debility.

1. "My knees are weak through fasting." The little sustenance Christ took before his passion, and his watching in prayer all night.

2. "And my flesh faileth of fatness," through the excess of his fatigue, and the anguish of his Spirit: thus he could not bear his cross.

3. A third reason why God should pity and deliver is drawn from the opprobrious usage and the scorn they put upon him, than which there is nothing more painful to an ingenuous and noble nature: "I am become also a reproach unto them," &c. The *four* Gospels are an ample comment upon this verse.

· The second part of his prayer is for a speedy resurrection: "Help me, O Lord my God: O save me," &c. And he supports his petition with a strong reason, drawn from the final cause: "Save me, that they may know," &c. That all men, the Jews especially, may be convinced by my rising again, in despite of the watch and the seal, that it was not their malice and power that brought me to this ignominious death, but that my passion, suffering, and death proceeded from thy hand: "By his resurrection he was declared," Rom. i. 4. And in the close of his prayer he sings a triumph over his enemies, the *devil, Judas*, the *Jews*, those bitter enemies to him and his Church.

1. "Let them curse." Speak evil of me and my followers.

2. "But bless thou." Bless all nations that have faith in me.

3. "When they arise." For, 1. Arise they will, and endeavour by every means to destroy my kingdom; 2. But "let them be ashamed." Confounded that their wishes are frustrated.

4. "But let thy servant (which condition Christ took upon himself) rejoice;" because thy name is thereby glorified.

And he continues his exercrations by way of explanation. "Let mine adversaries," &c, be confounded at the last day, for their ingratitude and malice, before angels and men.

IV. He closes all with thanks, which he opposes to the confusion of the wicked.

1. "I will greatly praise the Lord." With affection and a great jubilee.

2. "I will praise him among the multitude." Before all the world.

For which he assigns this reason,—

1. "He shall stand at the right hand of the poor." That is, such as are *poor in spirit*, who ask and find mercy from God: to such I will be as a shield and buckler.

2. "I will stand at the right hand of the poor, to save him," &c. From the devil and all his instruments. Christ is the all-covering shield of his Church: "He hath blotted out the handwriting of ordinances," &c. So that, cum a mundo damnamur, a Christo ab solvemur. "When we are condemned by the world, we are absolved by Christ."

PSALM CX

The Messiah sits in his kingdom at the right hand of God, his enemies being subdued under him, 1, 2. The nature and extent of his government, 3. His everlasting priesthood, 4. His execution of justice and judgment, 5, 6. The reason on which all this is founded, his passion and exaltation, 7.

XXIII. DAY. MORNING PRAYER

A Psalm of David

A. M. cir. 2989
B. C. cir. 1015
Davidis, Regis
Israelitarum,
cir. annum
40

THE [a]LORD said unto my Lord, Sit thou at my right hand, until I make thine enemies thy footstool.

2 The LORD shall send the rod of thy strength out of Zion: rule thou in the midst of thine enemies.

A. M. cir. 2989
B. C. cir. 1015
Davidis, Regis
Israelitarum,
cir. annum
40

3 [b]Thy people *shall be* willing in the day of thy power, [c]in the beauties of holiness [d]from

---

[a]Matt. xxii. 44; Mark xii. 36; Luke xx. 42; Acts ii. 34; 1 Cor. xv. 25; Heb. i. 13; 1 Pet. iii. 22; see Psa. xlv. 6, 7

[b]Judg. v. 2——[c]Psa. xcvi. 9——[d]Or, *more than the womb of the morning; thou shalt have*, &c.

NOTES ON PSALM CX

The *Hebrew*, and all the *Versions*, except the *Arabic*, attribute this Psalm to *David:* nor can this be doubted, as it is thus attributed in the New Testament; see the places in the margin. We have in it the celebration of some great potentate's accession to the crown; but the subject is so grand, the expressions so noble, and the object raised so far above what can be called *human*, that no history has ever mentioned a prince to whom a literal application of this Psalm can be made. To Jesus Christ alone, to his everlasting priesthood and government, as King of kings and Lord of lords, can it be applied.

The *Jews*, aware of the advantage which the Christian religion must derive from this Psalm, have laboured hard and in vain to give it a contrary sense. Some have attributed it to *Eliezer*, the servant or steward of Abraham; and state that he composed it on the occasion of his master's victory over the *four* kings at the valley of *Shaveh*, Gen. xiv. Others say it was done by *David*, in commemoration of his victory over the Philistines. Others make *Solomon* the author. Some refer it to *Hezekiah*, and others to *Zerubbabel*, &c.: but the bare reading of the Psalm will show the vanity of these pretensions. A King is described here who is *David's* Lord, and sits at the right hand of God; a conqueror, reigning at Jerusalem,

King from all eternity—having an everlasting priesthood, Judge of all nations, triumphing over all potentates, indefatigable in all his operations, and successful in all his enterprises. Where has there ever appeared a prince in whom all these characters met? There never was one, nor is it possible that there ever can be one such, the Person excepted to whom the Psalm is applied by the authority of the Holy Spirit himself. That the Jews who lived in the time of our Lord believed this Psalm to have been written by David, and that it spoke of the Messiah alone, is evident from this, that when our Lord quoted it, and drew arguments from it in favour of his mission, Matt. xxii. 42, they did not attempt to gainsay it. St. *Peter*, Acts ii. 34, and St. *Paul*, 1 Cor. xv. 25; Heb. i. 13, v. 6, 10, vii. 17, x. 12, 13, apply it to show that Jesus is the Messiah. Nor was there any attempt to contradict them; not even an intimation that they had misapplied it, or mistaken its meaning. Many of the later Jews also have granted that it applied to the *Messiah*, though they dispute its application to Jesus of Nazareth. All the critics and commentators whom I have consulted apply it to our Lord; nor does it appear to me to be capable of interpretation on any other ground. Before I proceed to take a general view of it, I shall set down the chief of the *various readings* found in the MSS. on this Psalm.

Verse 1. *Said unto my Lord.* Instead of לאדני

A. M. cir. 2989
B. C. cir. 1015
Davidis, Regis
Israelitarum,
cir. annum
40

the womb of the morning: thou hast the dew of thy youth.

4 The LORD hath sworn, and ⁱwill not repent, ᶠThou *art* a priest for ever after the order of Melchizedek.

5 The LORD ᵍat thy right hand shall strike through kings ʰin the day of his wrath.

6 He shall judge among the heathen, he shall fill *the places* with the dead bodies; ⁱhe shall wound the heads over ᵏmany countries.

7 ˡHe shall drink of the brook in the way: ᵐtherefore shall he lift up the head.

A. M. cir. 2989
B. C. cir. 1015
Davidis, Regis
Israelitarum,
cir. annum
40

ⁱNum. xxiii. 19——ᶠHeb. v. 6; vi. 20; vii. 17, 21; see Zech. vi. 13——ᵍPsa. xvi. 8——ʰPsa. ii. 5, 12; Rom. ii. 5; Rev. xi. 18——ⁱPsa. lxviii. 21; Hab. iii. 13——ᵏOr, *great*——ˡJudg. vii. 5, 6——ᵐIsa. liii. 12

---

ladoni, "my Lord," one MS. seems to have read ליהוה *layhovah*, "Jehovah said unto Jehovah, 'Sit thou on my right hand,'" &c. See *De Rossi*.

Thy footstool. הדם לרגליך *hadom leragleycha*, "the footstool to thy feet." But *eight* MSS. drop the prefix ל *le;* and read the word in the *genitive* case, with the *Septuagint, Vulgate,* and *Arabic*. Many also read the word in the *singular* number.

Ver. 3. Instead of בהדרי קדש *behadrey kodesh*, "in the beauties of holiness," בהררי קדש *beharerey kodesh*, "in the mountains of holiness," is the reading of *thirty-four* of *Kennicott's* MSS., and *fifty-three* of those of *De Rossi*, and also of several printed editions.

Instead of ילדתך *yalduthECA*, "of thy youth," ילדתיך *yaladticha*, "I have begotten thee," is the reading, as to the *consonants*, of *sixty-two* of *Kennicott's* and *twenty-three* of *De Rossi's* MSS., and of some ancient editions, with the *Septuagint, Arabic,* and *Anglo-Saxon*.

Ver. 4. *After the order*, על דברתי *al dibrathi*, דברתו *dibratho*, "HIS order," is the reading of *twelve* of *Kennicott's* and *De Rossi's* MSS.

Ver. 5. *The Lord*, אדני *adonai:* but יהוה *Yehovah* is the reading of a great number of the MSS. in the above collections.

Ver. 6. Instead of בגוים *baggoyim*, "among the heathens" or *nations*, גוים *goyim*, "he shall judge the *heathen*," is the reading of one ancient MS.

Instead of ראש *rosh*, "the head," ראשי *rashey*, "the heads," is the reading of one MS., with the *Chaldee, Septuagint, Vulgate,* and *Anglo-Saxon*.

Ver. 7. For ירים *yarim*, "he shall lift up," ירום *yarom*, "shall be lifted up," is the reading of *six* MSS. and the *Syriac*.

Instead of ראש *rosh*, "THE head," ראשו *rosho*, "HIS head," is the reading of *two* MSS. and the *Syriac*.

A few add הללו יה *halelu Yah*, "Praise ye Jehovah;" but this was probably taken from the beginning of the following Psalm.

The learned *Venema* has taken great pains to expound this Psalm: he considers it a Divine oracle, partly relating to David's Lord, and partly to David himself.

1. David's Lord is here inducted to the highest honour, regal and sacerdotal, with the promise of a most flourishing kingdom, founded in Zion, but extending *every where*, till every enemy should be subdued.

2. David is here promised God's protection; that his enemies shall never prevail against him; but he must go through many sufferings in order to reach a state of glory.

3. The time in which this oracle or prophecy was delivered was probably a little after the time when David had brought home the ark, and before he had his wars with the neighbouring idolatrous nations. The kingdom was *confirmed* in his hand; but it was not yet *extended* over the neighbouring nations.

Verse 1. *The Lord said unto my Lord*] *Jehovah* said unto my *Adoni*. That David's Lord is the Messiah, is confirmed by our Lord himself and by the apostles Peter and Paul, as we have already seen.

Sit thou at my right hand] This implies the possession of the utmost confidence, power, and preeminence.

Until I make thine enemies] Jesus shall reign till all his enemies are subdued under him. Jesus Christ, as GOD, ever dwelt in the fulness of the Godhead; but it was as *God-man* that, after his resurrection, he was raised to the *right hand of the Majesty on high*, ever to appear in the presence of God for us.

Verse 2. *The rod of thy strength*] The Gospel—the *doctrine of Christ crucified;* which is the powerful sceptre of the Lord that bought us; is *quick and powerful, sharper than any two-edged sword;* and is the power of God to salvation to all them that believe.

The kingdom of our Lord was to be founded in Zion; and thence, by gradual conquests, to be extended over the whole earth. It was in Zion the preaching of the Gospel first began; and it is by the Gospel that Christ *rules*, even *in the midst of his enemies;* for the Gospel extends a moralizing influence over multitudes who do not receive it to their salvation.

Verse 3. *Thy people* shall be *willing in the day of thy power*] This verse has been wofully perverted. It has been supposed to point out the irresistible operation of the grace of God on the souls of the elect, thereby making them willing to receive Christ as their Saviour. Now, whether this doctrine be true or false, it is not in this text, nor can it receive the smallest countenance from it. There has been much spoken against the doctrine of what is called *free will* by persons who seem not to have understood the term. *Will* is a free principle. *Free will* is as absurd as *bound will;* it is not *will* if it be *not free;* and if it be *bound* it is no *will*. *Volition* is essential to the being of the soul, and to all rational and intellectual beings. This is the most essential discrimination between *matter* and *spirit*. MATTER can have no *choice;* SPIRIT has. Ratiocination is essential to intellect; and from these *volition* is inseparable. God uniformly treats *man* as a *free agent;* and on this principle the whole of Divine revelation is constructed, as is also the doctrine of future rewards and punishments. If man be *forced* to believe, *he* believes not at all; it is the *forcing power* that believes, not the *machine* forced.

If he be forced to *obey*, it is the forcing power that *obeys;* and he, as a machine, shows only the effect of this irresistible force. If man be incapable of *willing good*, and *nilling evil*, he is incapable of being *saved* as a rational being; and if he acts only under an *overwhelming compulsion*, he is as incapable of being damned. In short, this doctrine reduces him either to a *punctum stans*, which by the *vis inertiæ* is incapable of being moved but as acted upon by foreign influence; or, as an intellectual being, to nonentity. "But, if the text supports the doctrine laid upon it, vain are all these reasonings." *Granted.* Let us examine the text. The Hebrew words are the following: עמך נרבת

ביום חילך *ammecha nedaboth beyom cheylecha*, which literally translated are, *Thy princely people*, or *free people*, *in the day of thy power;* and are thus paraphrased by the *Chaldee:* "Thy people, O house of Israel, who willingly labour in the law, thou shalt be helped by them in the day that thou goest to battle."

The *Syriac* has: "This praiseworthy people in the day of thy power."

The *Vulgate:* "With thee is the principle or origin (principium) in the day of thy power." And this is referred, by its interpreters, to the Godhead of Christ; and they illustrate it by John i. 1: *In principio erat Verbum*, "In the beginning was the Word."

The *Septuagint* is the same; and they use the word as St. John has it in the Greek text: Μετα σου η αρχη εν ημερα της δυναμεως σου· "With thee is the Arche, or principle, in the day of thy power."

The *Æthiopic* is the same; and the *Arabic* nearly so, but rather more express: "The government, اسیۍ *riasat*, exists with thee in the day of thy power."

The *Anglo-Saxon*, ᵹᴉꝛ ᵹᴇ ꝼꞃuma on ᴆæᵹe mæᵹnᴀꝛ þᴉneꞃ. "With thee the principle in day of thy greatness."

The old *Psalter*, With the begynnyngs in day of thi vertu. Which it thus paraphrases: "I, the fader begynnyng with the, begynnyng I and thou, an begynnyng of al thyng in day of thi vertu."

Coverdale thus: "In the day of thy power shal my people offre the free-will offringes with a holy worship." So *Tindal, Cardmarden, Beck*, and the *Liturgic Version.*

The *Bible* printed by *Barker*, the king's printer, 4to. Lond. 1615, renders the whole verse thus: "Thy people *shall come* willingly at the time *of assembling* thine army in the holy beauty; the youth of thy womb *shall be* as the morning dew."

By the authors of the *Universal History*, vol. iii., p. 223, the whole passage is thus explained: "The Lord shall send the rod, or sceptre, of thy power out of Sion," i. e., out of the tribe of Judah: compare Gen. xlix. 20, and Psa. lxxviii. 68. "Rule thou over thy free-will people;" for none but such are fit to be Christ's subjects: see Matt. xi. 29. "In the midst of thine enemies," Jews and heathens; or, in a spiritual sense, the world, the flesh, and the devil. "In the day of thy power," i. e., when all power shall be given him, both in heaven and earth; Matt. xxviii. 18. "In the beauties of holiness," which is the peculiar characteristic of Christ's reign, and of his religion.

None of the *ancient Versions*, nor of our *modern translations*, give any sense to the words that countenances the doctrine above re-

ferred to; it merely expresses the character of the people who shall constitute the kingdom of Christ. נרב *nadab* signifies to be *free, liberal, willing, noble;* and especially *liberality in bringing offerings to the Lord*, Exod. xxv. 2; xxxv. 21, 29. And נריב *nadib* signifies a *nobleman*, a *prince*, Job xxi. 8; and also *liberality.* נרבה *nedabah* signifies a *free-will offering*—an offering made by superabundant gratitude; one *not commanded:* see Exod. xxxvi. 3; Lev. vii. 16, and elsewhere. Now the עם נרבות *am nedaboth* is the people of liberality—the princely, noble, and generous people; Christ's real subjects; his own children, who form his Church, and are the salt of the world; the bountiful people, who live only to get good from God that they may do good to man. Is there, has there ever been, any religion under heaven that has produced the *liberality*, the *kindness*, the *charity*, that characterize *Christianity?* Well may the followers of Christ be termed the *am nedaboth*—the cheerfully beneficent people. They *hear* his call, come *freely*, stay *willingly*, act *nobly*, live *purely*, and obey *cheerfully.*

The *day of Christ's* power is the time of the Gospel, the reign of the Holy Spirit in the souls of his people. *Whenever* and *wherever* the Gospel is preached in sincerity and purity, *then* and *there* is the day or time of Christ's power. It is the time of his exaltation. The days of his *flesh* were the days of his *weakness;* the time of his *exaltation* is the day of his *power.*

In the beauties of holiness] בהדרי קדש *behadrey kodesh*, "In the splendid garments of holiness." An allusion to the beautiful garments of the high priest. Whatever is intended or expressed by superb garments, they possess, in holiness of heart and life, indicative of their Divine birth, noble dispositions, courage, &c. Their garb is such as becomes the children of so great a King. Or, They shall appear on *the mountains of holiness*, bringing glad tidings to Zion.

From the womb of the morning] As the dew flows from the womb of the morning, so shall all the godly from thee. They are *the dew of thy youth;* they are the *offspring* of thy own *nativity.* As the human nature of our Lord was begotten by the creative energy of God in the womb of the Virgin; so the followers of God are born, not of blood, nor of the will of the flesh, but by the Divine Spirit.

Youth may be put here, not only for *young men*, but for *soldiers;*—so the *Trojana juventus* "the Trojan troops," or *soldiers*, in Virgil, Æn. i. ver. 467;—and for persons, courageous, heroic, strong, active, and vigorous. Such were the apostles, and first preachers of the Gospel; and, indeed, all genuine Christians. They may be fully compared to *dew*, for the following reasons:—

1. Like dew, they had their origin from heaven.

2. Like dew, they fructified the earth.

3. Like dew, they were innumerable.

4. Like dew, they were diffused over the earth.

5. Like dew, they came from the morning; the *dawn*, the *beginning* of the *Gospel day* of salvation.

1. As the morning arises in the EAST, and the *sun*, which produces it, proceeds to the WEST; so was the coming of the Son of man, and of his disciples and apostles.

2. They began in the EAST—Asia Proper and

Asia Minor; and shone unto the West—Europe, America, &c. Scarcely any part of the world has been hidden from the bright and enlivening power of the Sun of Righteousness; and *now* this glorious sun is walking in the greatness of its strength.

> Saw ye not the cloud arise,
> Little as a human hand?
> Now it spreads along the skies,
> Hangs o'er all the thirsty land.
> Lo, the promise of a *shower*
> *Drops* already from above;
> But the Lord will shortly pour
> All the spirit of his love.

The heavenly dew is dropping every where from the womb of the morning; and all the ends of the earth are about to see the salvation of God.

Verse 4. *The Lord hath sworn*] Has most firmly purposed, and will most certainly perform it, feeling himself bound by his *purpose*, as an *honest man* would by his *oath*.

And will not repent] Will never change this purpose; it is perfectly without condition, and without contingency. Nothing is left here to the will of man or angel. Christ shall be incarnated, and the Gospel of his salvation shall be preached over the whole earth. This is an *irresistible decree* of that God who loves mankind.

Thou art *a priest for ever*] The word כהן *cohen* signifies, not only a *priest*, but also a *prince;* as, in the patriarchal times, most heads of families had and exercised both *political* and *sacerdotal authority* over all their descendants. Every priest had a *threefold* office: 1. He was an *instructor* of the family or tribe over which he presided. 2. He *offered sacrifices* for the sins of the people, to reconcile them to God, and give them access to his presence. 3. He was their *mediator*, and interceded for them. So is Christ, the grand, the universal *Instructor*, by his word and Spirit; the *Lamb of God*, who, by his *sacrificial offering* of himself, takes away the sin of the world, and still continues to exhibit himself before the throne in his sacrificial character; and also the great *Mediator* between God and man: and in these characters he is a Priest *for ever*. He will instruct, apply the sacrificial offering, and intercede for man, till time shall be no more.

After the order of Melchizedek.] For the elucidation of this point, the reader is requested to refer to the notes on Gen. xiv. 18, 19, and to the *observations* at the end of that chapter, where the subject, relative to the *person, name*, and *office* of this ancient king, is fully discussed; and it will be necessary to read that note, &c., as if appended to this place.

Melchizedek was *king of Salem*, that is, *king of Jerusalem;* for *Salem* was its ancient name: but שלם *salem* signifies *peace*, and צדק *tsedek*, *righteousness*. Christ is styled the *Prince of peace;* and he is the *king* that rules in the empire of righteousness; and all *peace* and *righteousness* proceed from him, Heb. vii. 2.

He is *priest after the order of Melchizedek*—after his *pattern;* in the same kind or manner of way in which this ancient king was priest.

Calmet properly observes that there were *three orders of priesthood.* 1. That of *royalty*. All ancient kings being, in virtue of their office, *priests* also. This seems to have been considered as the *natural right* of royalty, as it obtained in almost every nation of the earth, from the beginning of the world down to the end of the Roman empire. 2. That of the *first-born*. This right appertained naturally to Reuben, as the first-born in the family of Jacob. 3. That of the *Levites*, instituted by God himself, and taken from *Reuben*, because of his transgression. The Levitical *priesthood* ended with the *Jewish polity;* and that also of the *first-born*, which had been absorbed in it. This *order*, therefore, was not perpetual; it was intended to last only for a time. But that of *royalty* is perpetual, though not now in general use, because founded in what is called *natural right*. It is, therefore, according to this most ancient order, that Christ is a Priest for ever. The kings of England as *heads of the Church*, appointing all bishops, continue to assume, in a certain way, this original right.

Melchizedek is said to be "without father, without mother, without beginning of days, or end of life." We have no account of his *parents;* nothing of his *birth;* nothing of his *death*. Christ, as to his Divine nature, is without father or mother, and without beginning of days; nor can he have any end. Other priests could not continue by reason of death; but he is the Eternal, he cannot die, and therefore can have no successor: "*He is a priest* FOR EVER." Therefore, as Melchizedek was a priest and a king, and had no successor, so shall Christ be: of the increase and government of his kingdom there shall be no end.

Melchizedek was *priest of the Most High God;* and consequently not of *one people* or *nation*, but of the *universe*. Aaron was priest of *one people*, and for a *time* only; Jesus is priest of *all mankind*, and *for ever*. He tasted death for every man; he is the King eternal; he has the keys of hell and of death. As God is the King and Governor of all human beings, Christ, being the *priest of the Most High God*, must also be the *priest for* and *over* all whom this most high God made and governs; and therefore he is the priest, the atoning sacrifice, of the *whole human race*. In this the main similitude consists between the *order of Melchizedek* and *that of Christ*.

Verse 5. *The Lord at thy right hand*] Here *Venema* thinks the Psalm speaks of *David*. As Jesus is at the right hand of God, so he will be at thy hand, giving thee all the support and comfort requisite.

Shall strike through kings] As he did in the case of Abraham, Gen. xiv. 1-16, (for to this there seems to be an allusion,) where he smote *four kings*, and *filled the pits* with the *dead bodies* of their troops. That the allusion is to the above transaction seems the most probable; because in the same chapter, where the *defeat of the four kings* is mentioned, we have the account of *Melchizedek coming to meet Abraham*, and receiving the *tenth of the spoils*.

Verse 6. *He shall judge among the heathen*] David shall greatly extend his dominion, and rule over the *Idumeans, Moabites, Philistines*, &c.

He shall fill—with the dead bodies] He shall fill pits—make heaps of slain; there shall be an immense slaughter among his enemies.

He shall wound the heads] He shall so bring down the power of all the neighbouring kings, as to cause them to acknowledge him as their lord, and pay him tribute.

Verse 7. *He shall drink of the brook in the way*] He shall have sore travail, and but little ease and refreshment: but he shall still go *on* from conquering to conquer.

Therefore shall he lift up the head.] Or *his head*. He shall succeed in all his enterprises, and at last be peaceably settled in his ample dominions.

But these verses, as well as the former, may be applied to our Lord. The fifth verse may be an address to Jehovah: *Adonai at thy right hand*, O Jehovah, *shall smite kings*—bring down all powers hostile to his empire, *in the day of his wrath*—when, after having borne long, he arises and shakes terribly the rulers of the earth.

Ver. 6. *He shall judge*, give laws, *among the heathen*—send his Gospel to the whole *Gentile world*. He shall *fill* the field of battle with the dead bodies of the slain, who had resisted his empire, and would not have him to reign over them.

He shall wound the heads over many countries.—This must be spoken against some *person* possessing a very extensive sway. Perhaps Antichrist is meant; he who has so *many countries* under his *spiritual domination*. Christ shall destroy every person, and every thing, which opposes the universal spread of his own empire. He will be a *King*, as well as a *Priest* for ever.

Ver. 7. *He shall drink of the brook*—he shall suffer sorely, and even *die* in the struggle: but in that death his enemies shall all perish; and *he shall lift up the head*—he shall rise again from the dead, possessing all power in heaven and earth, *ascend* to the throne of glory, and reign till time shall be no more. He must suffer and die, in order to have the *triumphs* already mentioned.

While all have acknowledged that this Psalm is of the utmost importance, and that it speaks of Christ's *priesthood* and *victories*, it is amazing how various the interpretations are which are given of different passages. I have endeavoured to give the general sense in the preceding notes, and to explain all the particular expressions that have been thought most *difficult:* and by giving the *various readings* from the MSS., have left it to the learned reader to make farther improvements.

It has, however, long appeared to me that there is a *key* by which all the difficulties in the Psalm may be unlocked. As this has not been suggested by any other, as far as I know, I shall without apology lay it before the reader:—

The hundred and tenth Psalm is a WAR SONG, and every phrase and term in it is MILITARY.

1. In the *first* place may be considered here the *proclamation* of the *Divine purpose* relative to the *sacerdotal, prophetic,* and *regal offices* of the LORD JESUS CHRIST: "*Jehovah said unto my Lord,* SIT THOU ON MY RIGHT HAND."

2. A grievous *battle*, and consequent *victory* over the enemy, foretold: I WILL MAKE THINE ENEMIES THE FOOTSTOOL TO THY FEET, ver. 1.

3. The *ensign* displayed: "THE LORD SHALL SEND FORTH THE ROD OF THY STRENGTH;" the *pole* on which the banner shall be *displayed*, at the *head* of his *strength*—his numerous and *powerful forces*.

4. The *inscription, device,* or *motto* on this *ensign:* "RULE THOU IN THE MIDST OF THINE ENEMIES," ver. 2.

5. The *muster* of the troops. A host of bold, spirited *volunteers;* not *mercenaries,* neither *kidnapped* nor *impressed;* but עם נדבות *am nedaboth,* a volunteer people; high-born, loyal

subjects; veteran soldiers; every man *bringing gifts* to his General and King.

6. The *regimentals* or *uniform* in which they shall appear: "THE BEAUTIES OF HOLINESS;" הדרי קדש *hadrey kodesh, the splendid garments of holiness*. The apparel showing the *richness* of the *King*, and the *worth* and *order* of the *soldiers;* every man being determined to do his duty, and feeling assured of conquest. The Lacedæmonian soldiers were clothed in *scarlet;* and never went to battle without *crowns* and *garlands* upon their heads, being always sure of victory. *Potter's Ant.,* vol. ii., p. 55.

7. The *number* of the troops: THEY SHALL BE AS THE DROPS OF DEW AT BREAK OF DAY:—*innumerable;* and this shall be in consequence ילדתך *yalduthecha,* of *thy nativity*—the *manifestation of Jesus*. THOU shalt be born unto *men;* THEY shall be born of *thy Spirit,* ver. 3.

8. The *title* of the *commander:* "THOU ART A PRIEST," כהן *cohen* a *Priest* and a *Prince.* So was *Agamemnon* in *Homer,* and *Æneas* in *Virgil.* Both were *princes;* both were *priests* and both were *heroes.*

9. The *perpetuity* of this office: "FOR EVER;" לעולם *leolam,* for *futurity*—for *all time*—till the earth and the heavens are no more.

10. The *resolution* of *setting* up such a *Priest* and *King,* and *levying* such an *army:* ACCORDING TO THE ORDER OF MELCHIZEDEK. The *Commander, muster,* and *establishment* of the *corps* shall be according to the *plan* of that *ancient king* and *priest;* or, translating the words literally, על דברתי מלכי צדק *al dabarti malki tsedek,* all shall be executed as *I have spoken to my righteous king;* I have sworn, and will not change my purpose. All my purposes shall be fulfilled. This *speaking* may refer to the *purpose,* ver. 1, confirmed by an *oath,* ver. 4.

11. *Victory* gained: ADONAI AT THY RIGHT HAND HATH TRANSFIXED (מחץ *machats*) KINGS IN THE DAY OF HIS WRATH, i. e., of *battle* and *victory.* Jesus, the Almighty King and Conqueror, fights and gains his battles, while *sitting* at the *right hand* of the *Majesty on high,* ver. 5.

12. *Judgment* instituted and executed: "HE SHALL JUDGE AMONG THE HEATHEN," בגוים *baggoyim, among the nations.* He shall bring forth, judge, and condemn his enemies; and he shall *fill pits with the bodies* of executed criminals, ver. 6.

13. *False religion,* supporting itself by the *secular arm,* under the name of *true religion,* shall be destroyed. מחץ ראש על ארץ רבה *machats rosh al erets rabbah;* "He smites the head that is over an extensive land" or country. The *priesthood* that is not according to the *order of Melchizedek* shall be destroyed; and all *government* that is not according to him who is the eternal King and Priest, shall be brought down and annihilated. Who is this great HEAD? this *usurping power?* this *antichristian authority?* Let the Italian archbishop answer, ver. 6.

14. *Refreshment* and *rest,* the fruits of the victories which have been gained: "HE SHALL DRINK OF THE BROOK IN THE WAY; THEREFORE, SHALL HE LIFT UP THE HEAD." He and his victorious army, having defeated and pursued his enemies, and being spent with fatigue and thirst, are refreshed by drinking from a rivulet providentially met with in the way. But the rout being now complete and final,

15. The emperor is proclaimed and *triumphs:*

God lifts up the HEAD,—ראש *rosh*, the CHIEF, the CAPTAIN; as the word often means. Jesus, the *Captain of our salvation*, has a complete *triumph;* eternal peace and tranquillity are established. The *Messiah* is all in all—the last enemy, *Death*, is destroyed. Jesus, having overcome, has sat down with the Father upon his throne; and his *soldiers*, having also overcome through the blood of the Lamb, seated with him on the same throne, are for ever with the Lord. They *see him as he is;* and eternally contemplate and enjoy his glory:—

"Far from a world of grief and sin,
With God eternally shut in."

Hallelujah! The Lord God Omnipotent reigneth! Amen, Amen.

ANALYSIS OF THE ONE HUNDRED AND TENTH PSALM

This Psalm is short in appearance, but deep and copious in mysteries. The subject, without doubt, is *Christ;* since both *St. Peter* (Acts ii. 34) and *St. Paul* (Heb. i. 13) expound it of Christ; and in Matt. xxii. 44 Christ applies it to himself.

In this Psalm Christ is described as a Priest and a King.

I. Christ's kingdom, in the three first verses.

II. His priesthood, from the fourth to the seventh.

I. In reference to his kingdom the prophet acquaints us, 1. With his person; 2. With his power, and the acquisition of it; 3. The continuance of it; 4. The execution of it—First, Over his enemies; Secondly, Over his own people, which is the sum of the three first verses.

1. The person who was to reign was David's Lord; his son according to the flesh, but his Lord as equal to God; Phil. ii. 6, 7. As made flesh, and born of a virgin, the son of David; but as *Immanuel*, the Lord of David, which the Jews not understanding could not reply to Christ's question, Matt. xxii. 45.

2. As to his power, the Author of it was God: "The Lord said to my Lord," &c. Decreed it from everlasting. And again, "The Seed of the woman," &c.

3. And of his kingdom. He took possession, when the Lord said unto him, "Sit thou on my right hand." Christ, as the Son of God, was ever at God's right hand, equal to him in might and majesty; but, as man, was exalted to honour, not before his glorious ascension, Acts ii. 34; Ephes. i. 20; Phil. ii. 9.

4. For the continuance of it. It is to be UNTIL, which notes, not a portion of time, but a perpetuity. "Sit TILL *I* make," &c. Sit at God's right hand, that is, in power and glory, till he shall say to all the wicked, "Depart from me," Matt. xxv., but not so as to be then dethroned. But when once all his enemies shall be made his footstool, then he shall visibly rule, "sitting at his Father's right hand for evermore;" go on to reign, neither desist to propagate and enlarge thy kingdom, till all men bow the knee to thy name, till all opponents be overthrown.

The beginning of this kingdom was in Zion: "The Lord shall send," &c.

1. The rod of his power was his sceptre; that is, "His word, the Gospel, the wisdom of God," 1 Thess. ii. 13; "The sword of the Spirit," Ephes. vi. 17; "The mighty power of God," &c., Rom. i. 16.

2. And this was to be sent out of *Zion*, Isa. xxiii. "It behoved Christ to suffer," &c., Luke xxiv. 46. The sound of the apostle's words went into all lands; but Zion must first hear, Acts xiii. 46.

And now the prophet comes to the execution of his power: "Rule thou in the midst," &c. Converting all such as believe his Gospel, and confounding those who will not have him to reign over them. Now these enemies are the most in number; for the Church however greatly increased, is still surrounded by Turks, Jews, &c. *Rule* thou; be thou Ruler; go on, and set up thy standard universally; for believers are easily dealt with; they love thy government.

1. "For thy people shall be willing." Not forced by compulsion; "they shall flow together as water," Isa. ii.

2. But not before thy grace has brought down their hearts: "In the day of thy power," that is, in the days of thy solemn assemblies, when the Gospel light shall be sent forth, and the apostles and messengers go abroad to preach thy truth.

3. The third quality of this good people is, "that they be holy." For some read the words thus: "They shall offer freewill-offerings with a holy worship." Our last translators point it, "Thy people shall be willing in the day of thy power." Here they pause, and read on thus: "In the beauty of holiness from the womb of the morning." The *Vulgate, In splendoribus sanctorum*, "In the splendour of the saints," and stops there; but let the reading be as it will, all expositors are agreed that holiness must be the ornament of Christ's Church:—

4. Which sanctity these good people have not from themselves, but by the influence of the Holy Spirit, for "they shall worship in the beauty," &c. This is a very difficult place, and the rendering of it is so various, so perplexed by the several modes of pointing it, that the difficulty is increased. But see the notes. The fathers expound this passage of Christ himself, and the later divines, of his people, which is most probable. By their *youth* they understand their regeneration; by the *dews*, the graces bestowed on them; which come immediately from God. The prophet phrases it, "From the womb of the morning." As if the Holy Ghost had said, "The preaching of thy word shall bring forth a great and good people, plentiful as the drops of the morning dew. As the secret and refreshing dews come from heaven to refresh the earth, so thy power, regenerating the hearts of men by the secret operation of thy Holy Spirit, shall produce an immortal seed, children begotten to God. 'Thou hast the dew,' the grace of God, to beautify thy youth, and to make them holy by the direct influence of thy Spirit, to produce entire regeneration."

II. The prophet, having foretold Christ's kingdom, now predicts his priesthood, under which his prophetical office may be implied. That Messiah was to be a priest at his coming, God sware:—

1. "The Lord sware." His word of assurance was given with his oath. In the priesthood of Christ lies the main weight of our redemption; therefore God swears that he shall be a priest to offer himself, and to intercede for us, without which he had in vain been our Prophet and our King.

2. "And will not repent." This is also added for our greater assurance. God is sometimes represented as repenting, as in the case of *Nineveh;* but now that he was to save the world by this Priest, his Son, he takes an oath to do it, and he will not repent. His sentence for judgment is ever conditional; but his decree for mercy is absolute. "He will not repent," &c.

The matter of the oath follows: "Thou art a priest for ever, after the order of Melchizedek."

1. *Thou* is emphatical: *Thou—David's* Lord, art a Priest, and none such a Priest as *thou.*

2. *Art;* for this priest was the *I am;* therefore, justly said, *Thou art.*

3. *A Priest;* whose office the apostle describes, Heb. v. 1.

4. *For ever*—Not as Aaron and his successors, who were priests, &c., Heb. vii. 23, 24.

5. *After the order*—The right, the law, the custom, the rites. See the notes.

6. *Of Melchizedek.*—Which is opposed to the order of *Aaron.* He was not then to be a priest after the order of *Aaron* but by a former and higher order.

The difference lies in this:—

1. In the constitution of him to the priesthood. He was made with an oath; and so were not any of Aaron's order, Heb. vii. 20, 21.

2. In the succession. In Aaron's priesthood, the high priest, being mortal, died, and another succeeded; but this priest, as *Melchizedek,* "had neither beginning of days nor end of life," Heb. vii.

3. *Melchizedek* was priest and king: so was Christ. *Aaron* was only a priest.

4. "Aaron and his sons offered up oxen," &c., Lev. xvi. 6. "But Christ, being holy," &c., offered no sacrifice for *himself,* but for *our* sins, Isa. liii. 9.

5. "Aaron was a local priest; but Christ an universal priest," John iv. 22.

6. "Aaron was anointed with material oil; Christ, with the Holy Ghost," Luke iv. 18, 21.

7. "Aaron's priesthood was temporary; Christ's for ever."

A priest is to be,—

1. A person taken from among men, but select, fit for the office; thus was Christ a perfect man.

2. A priest must be ordained by God: "For no man," &c. "So Christ glorified not himself to be made a high priest." "Thou art my Son," &c.

3. The high priest was ordained of men in things pertaining to God, to be their advocate, mediator, interpreter, and reconciler, in all those things in which men make their addresses to God, or God is to signify his will to them; and so was Christ, for he is the Advocate, the Mediator for his people; he reconciles them to God, he interprets his will to us by preaching his Gospel to the poor.

4. The high priest was ordained that he might offer gifts and sacrifices for sin. Their sacrifices were the blood of bulls, &c.; but Christ was most infinitely precious, even *his own blood,* Eph. v. 2; Heb. ix. 26, x. 10-12.

5. The high priest must have compassion on the ignorant, and those who are out of the way; such was Christ: "For we have not," &c., Heb. iv. 15.

6. Lastly, the high priest was compassed with infirmities; and so was Christ: "In all things it became him," &c. "He took our infirmities," &c.

It remains now to show,—

1. How he is "a priest for ever?"

2. How a priest "after the order of Melchizedek?"

He is "a priest for ever," in respect to his person, office, and effect.

1. In respect of his person and office. For he succeeded no priest, his vocation being immediate. Neither is any to succeed him in this priesthood; "for he lives for ever," and therefore needs not, as the priests under the old law, any successor to continue his priesthood.

2. A priest he is for ever in respect of the effect: because by that sacrifice which he once offered on the cross he purchased the inestimable effects of redemption and eternal salvation, in which sense the priesthood is eternal.

"That Christ is a priest for ever" is evident; but it remains to be shown how he is *a priest after the order*—the rite, the manner, the word, and power given and prescribed to *Melchizedek.*

1. This *Melchizedek* was king of *Salem,* and priest of the most high God, Gen. xiv.; so was Christ a King of *Jerusalem* above, God's own city, and a priest, "offering himself a sacrifice for sin."

2. *Melchizedek* is by interpretation *king of righteousness;* so is Christ *the Lord our righteousness,* Jer. xxiii. 6; 1 Cor. i. 30.

3. *Melchizedek is king of Salem,* i. e., peace; so Christ is the Prince of peace, Isa. ix. 6.

4. "Melchizedek was without father or mother;" so was this our priest, as revealed by God to us, "without beginning of days or end of life," as touching his Godhead.

5. "Melchizedek blessed Abraham;" so Christ us "in turning every one of us away from his iniquities."

6. "Melchizedek brought forth bread and wine to refresh Abraham's army;" so Christ instituted the sacrament, set forth in bread and wine, to refresh the hungry and thirsty souls of his genuine followers.

After the prophet had said "that the Messiah shall be a priest," &c., he intimates in this verse that, notwithstanding all opposition that shall be made against him, yet his priesthood should be eternal; for,

1. "The Lord is on thy right hand." Giving thee power in defence of his Church.

2. "And this thy Lord shall strike through kings," &c. The greatest of thy enemies.

3. "In the day of his wrath." For such a day there is, and it will come, when the proudest tyrant shall not escape.

In the following verse Christ is described as a valiant conqueror.

1. "He shall rule and judge." Not only the Jews, but all people.

2. "He shall fill the places," &c. Make such a slaughter among his enemies, as enraged soldiers do in the storming of a city, when they fill the trenches with the dead bodies.

"He shall wound the heads," &c. Even kings and monarchs, those in the greatest power and authority.

The prophet, through the whole of the Psalm, had spoken of Christ's exaltation: that he was set at God's right hand; by oath was made a priest; and that, in defence of his kingdom and priesthood, he would subdue, conquer, and break to pieces his enemies. In this last verse he tells us by what means he came to this honour: his cross was the way to the crown; his passion and humiliation, to his exaltation: "He," saith David, "shall drink of the brook by the way; therefore, shall he lift up his head;" as if he had said, with the apostle: "He humbled himself, and became obedient to death," &c.

1. "He shall drink." To drink, is to be afflicted, Jer. xlix. 12.

2. "He shall drink of the brook," נחל *nachal*, of the torrent; and that is more than of the cup, for a cup contains but a certain portion of sorrows, but a torrent, a whole flood of miseries. In a cup, that which is drunk may be clear and clean; but in a torrent, a man can expect nothing but muddy and troubled water. Thus the prophet intimates here that the drink offered him should be much and troubled. And in his passion he descended into the depth of the torrent, and drank deep of it.

3. "In the way." On his journey that preceded his resurrection and ascension.

But *claritas humilitatis præmium,* "glory is the reward of humility." Because he thus humbled himself and willingly underwent his death and passion, for the glory of his Father, and the salvation of man; therefore shall God "lift up his head." He shall ascend into heaven; sit on his right hand, and be constituted the Judge of quick and dead. He shall rise from the dead and have all power committed to him in heaven and earth.

PSALM CXI

The psalmist praises the Lord, and extols his works as great, honourable, glorious, and magnificent, 1–4; his providence and kindness to his followers, 5–8; the redemption he has granted to his people, 9. The fear of the Lord is the beginning of wisdom, 10.

A. M. cir. 3469
B. C. cir. 535
Cyri,
R. Persarum,
cir. annum
secundum

PRAISE [a]ye the Lord. [b]I will praise the Lord with *my* whole heart, in the assembly of the upright, and *in* the congregation.

2 [c]The works of the Lord *are* great, [d]sought out of all them that have pleasure therein.

3 His work *is* [e]honourable and glorious; and his righteousness endureth for ever.

A. M. cir. 3469
B. C. cir. 535
Cyri,
R. Persarum,
cir. annum
secundum

---

[a]Heb. *Hallelujah*——[b]Psa. xxxv. 18; lxxxix. 5; cvii. 32; cix. 30; cxlix. 1

[c]Job xxxviii., xxxix., xl., xli.; Psa. xcii. 5; cxxxix. 14; Rev. xv. 3——[d]Psa. cxliii. 5——[e]Psa. cxlv. 4, 5, 10

NOTES ON PSALM CXI

This is one of the *alphabetical* or *acrostic* Psalms: but it is rather different from those we have already seen, as the first *eight* verses contain each *two members;* and each member commences with a consecutive letter of the Hebrew alphabet. But the two last verses are composed of *three members* each, characterized the same way, making *twenty-two members* or hemistichs in the whole, to each of which a consecutive letter of the alphabet is prefixed. But this division is not proper: it should follow the arrangement in the Hebrew poetry, where every hemistich stands by itself, and each contains a complete sense. The Psalm has no *title* in the Hebrew, unless the word *Hallelujah* be considered as such; and the thanksgivings which it contains were probably composed for the benefit of the Jews after their return from captivity.

Verse 1. *I will praise the Lord with* my *whole heart*] If we profess to "sing to the praise and glory of God," the *heart*, and the *whole heart*, without division and distraction, must be employed in the work.

In the assembly] בסוד *besod,* in the *secret assembly*—the *private religious meetings* for the *communion of saints. And in the congregation,* עדה *edah,* the *general assembly*—the *public congregation.* There were such meetings as the former ever since God had a Church on the earth; and to convey general information, there must be *public assemblies.*

Verse 2. *The works of the Lord are great*] גדלים *gedolim, vast* in *magnitude; as* רבים *rabbim* signifies their *multitude* and *variety.*

A. M. cir. 3469
B. C. cir. 535
Cyri,
R. Persarum,
cir. annum
secundum

4 He hath made his wonderful works to be remembered: [f]the LORD *is* gracious and full of compassion.

5 He hath given [g]meat [h]unto them that fear him: he will ever be mindful of his covenant.

6 He hath showed his people the power of his works, that he may give them the heritage of the heathen.

7 The works of his hands *are* [i]verity and judgment; [k]all his commandments *are* sure.

8 [l]They [m]stand fast for ever and ever, *and are* [n]done in truth and uprightness.

A. M. cir. 3469
B. C. cir. 535
Cyri,
R. Persarum,
cir. annum
secundum

9 [o]He sent redemption unto his people: he hath commanded his covenant for ever: [p]holy and reverend *is* his name.

10 [q]The fear of the LORD *is* the beginning of wisdom: [r]a good understanding have all they that [s]do *his commandments:* his praise endureth for ever.

---

[f]Psa. lxxxvi. 5; ciii. 8——[g]Heb. *prey*——[h]Matt. vi. 26, 33——[i]Rev. xv. 3——[k]Psa. xix. 7——[l]Isa. xl. 8; Matt. v. 18——[m]Heb. are *established*——[n]Psa. xix. 9; Rev. xv. 3

[o]Matt. i. 21; Luke i. 68——[p]Luke i. 49——[q]Deut. iv. 6; Job xxviii. 28; Prov. i. 7; ix. 10; Eccles. xii. 13; Ecclus. i. 16——[r]Or, *good success;* Prov. iii. 4——[s]Heb. *that do them*

Sought out] Investigated, carefully examined.

Of all them that have pleasure therein.] By all that delight in them: by every genuine philosopher; every lover of nature; he who traces out the great First Cause by means of his works. And the man that does so will be astonished at the perfections of the Creator, and admire all the operations of his hands.

Verse 3. *His work* is *honourable, &c.*] He has done nothing in *nature* or *grace* that does not redound to his own honour and glory; and because all is done in *righteousness*, it *endureth for ever.*

Verse 4. *He hath made his wonderful works*] He who seeks them out will never *forget* them; and every thing of God's framing is done in such a way, as to strike the imagination, interest the senses, and charm and edify the intellect. But the psalmist may here intend principally the works of God in behalf of the Jewish people; and particularly in their deliverance from the Babylonish captivity, which this Psalm is supposed to celebrate.

Verse 5. *He hath given meat*] טרף *tereph*, PREY. This may allude to the *quails* in the wilderness. The word signifies what is taken in *hunting*—wild beasts, venison, or *fowls* of any kind; particularly such as were proper for food. It also signifies *spoil* taken from enemies. And he may also refer to the wondrous manner in which they were fed and supported during their captivity; and by his support he proved that he was mindful of his covenant. He had promised such blessings; he was faithful to his promises.

Verse 6. *The power of his works*] They have seen that these things did not arrive in the common course of nature; it was not by might nor by power, but by the Spirit of the Lord of hosts they were done. And it required a display of the power of God to give them the heritage of the heathen.

Verse 7. *Verity and judgment*] His works are *verity* or *truth*, because they were wrought for the fulfilment of the promises he made to their fathers. And they were *just;* for their punishment was in consequence of their infidelities: and the punishment of the Babylonians was only in consequence of their gross iniquities; and in both respects he had proved his work to be according to justice and judgment.

Verse 8. *They stand fast for ever*] סמוכים *semuchim*, they are *propped up, buttressed, for ever.* They can never fail; for God's power supports his works, and his providence preserves the record of what he has done.

Verse 9. *He sent redemption*] He sent Moses to redeem them out of Egypt; various *judges* to deliver them out of the hands of their oppressors; Ezra, Nehemiah, and Zerubbabel, to deliver them from Babylon; and the Lord Jesus to redeem a whole lost world from sin, misery, and death.

Holy and reverend is *his name.*] The word *reverend* comes to us from the Latins, *reverendus*, and is compounded of *re*, intensive, and *vereor*, to be *feared;* and *most* or *right* reverend, *reverendissimus*, signifies *to be greatly feared.* These terms are now only titles of ecclesiastical respect, especially in the *Protestant* ministry; but there was a time in which these were no empty titles. Such was the power of the clergy, that, when they walked not in the fear of the Lord, they caused the *people to fear*, and *they themselves* were to *be feared;* but, when the *secular power* was added to the *spiritual*, they were then truly *reverendi* and *reverendissimi, to be feared* and *greatly to be feared.* But *reverend* is not applied to God in this way; nor does the word נורא *nora* bear this signification; it rather means *terrible: Holy and terrible*, or *holy and tremendous, is his name.* This title belongs not to *man;* nor does any minister, in assuming the title *reverend*, assume *this.* Indeed, the word *reverend*, as now used, gives us a very imperfect conception of the original term. *Holy and tremendous is God's name.* He is glorious in holiness, fearful in praises, doing wonders, both in the way of judgment and in the way of mercy.

Verse 10. *The fear of the Lord* is *the beginning of wisdom*] The original stands thus: ראשית חכמה יראת יהוה *reshith chokmah, yirath Yehovah, The beginning of wisdom* is *the fear of Jehovah. Wisdom* itself begins with this *fear;* true *wisdom* has this for its commencement. It is the first ingredient in it, and is an essential part of it. In vain does any man pretend to be *wise* who does *not fear the Lord;* and he who fears the Lord departs from evil: he who lives in sin neither fears God, nor is wise.

A good understanding have all they that do his commandments] These last words we add as necessary to make up the sense; but there is no need of this expedient, as the words of the original literally read thus: "The beginning of wisdom is the fear of Jehovah; good discernment to the doers." That is, They who act according to the dictates of wisdom, the commencement of which is the fear of Jehovah, have a sound understanding, discern their duty and their interest, and live to secure their own peace, their neighbour's good, and God's glory.

ANALYSIS OF THE HUNDRED AND ELEVENTH PSALM

It is supposed that this hymn was set by the author to be sung at the passover; and that it might be the more readily learned and remembered, the colons are in number as many as, and arranged in the order of, the letters of the Hebrew alphabet. It is an exhortation to praise God for his wonderful benefits bestowed on the world at large, and especially on Israel and the Church.

There are *three* parts in this Psalm:—

I. A resolution of the psalmist to praise God; the manner in which he would do so; and the company with whom he would do it, ver. 1.

II. An expression of the reasons which moved him to praise God, viz., his admirable benefits, special and general, ver. 2-9.

III. An inference from the premises by way of sentiment in which he commends the fear of God, ver. 10.

I. The title of this Psalm is, "Hallelujah, praise ye the Lord;" and he adds,—

1. "I will praise the Lord." And shows how it should be done.

2. Not hypocritically; not with the lips only, but "with the heart."

3. "With the whole heart."

4. Not only secretly, but also "in the assembly of the upright," &c. 1. Both in the assembly, where these good and upright men are. 2. And also in a mixed multitude, and secretly among good men.

II. And, having made a pious confession of his readiness to practise the duty, he next sets down the ground and matter of his praise.

First. His works of *power*, in the creation and conservation of the world, or the favours shown to the Church: "And these works of the Lord are great." 1. *Great*, not only for variety and beauty, but also in base creatures his wisdom is admirable, and to be admired. 2. *Great*; for it was great to take to himself a people out of another people, to make a covenant with them, and to reveal his promises, and give them a law, to settle among them a policy for Church and state. 3. Fools and impious men, indeed, but little consider these works; they think not of their Author: but in the eyes of all wise men "they are sought out," &c.

Secondly. His works of wisdom, in governing the creatures he has created, and in guiding and collecting his Church. 1. It is *honourable;* and much more so its Author. 2. And *glorious;* far above the works of princes. 3. And *righteous:* "He is a righteous God, and his righteousness endureth for ever." For he never departs from the exact rule of justice.

Which record must be kept:—

"He hath made his wonderful works," &c. As in the Jewish hosts.

Thirdly. His works of *mercy.* They proceed from mere mercy: "For the Lord is gracious," &c. 1. "Gracious," in doing these works. 2. "Full of compassion," as a father towards his children.

Of these the prophet gives several instances:—

1. "He hath given meat," &c. He nourished his people for forty years in the wilderness, giving them meat from heaven.

2. "He will ever be mindful," &c. Notwithstanding their provocations.

3. "He hath showed his people," &c. As in the turning of *Jordan* backwards, overthrowing *Jericho*, staying the sun and moon, &c.

4. "That he might give them," &c. By the expulsion of the Canaanites: "The works of the Lord are great," &c.

He now uses an acclamation: "The works of his hands are,"—

1. *Verity.* Making good his promise to *Abraham.*

2. *Judgment.* Executed on idolaters and profane persons.

And shows unto all the world that,—

1. "All his commandments are sure." That his laws, especially his moral laws, are of everlasting obligation on all.

2. That these commands "stand fast for ever;" for they are established in truth, equity, justice, and reason.

The prophet next speaks of a mercy far exceeding all the rest, the work of human redemption by Christ. This may be thus expounded, and better than in reference to the redemption of Israel out of Egypt.

1. "He sent redemption," &c. A Redeemer so long promised.

2. "He hath commanded his covenant," &c. Which is still extant.

III. The prophet, having enumerated many of God's works of power, wisdom, and mercy, concludes the Psalm with three acclamations.

"Holy and reverend," &c. Either in his service, or whenever he is signified.

1. *Holy*—unpolluted by hypocrisy. The command is, "Be ye holy, for I am holy."

2. *Reverend*—not rashly or negligently performed. Or, as some read it, *terrible;* and it is a fearful thing to fall into the hands of the living God.

The second acclamation follows upon the preceding:—

1. This fear "is the beginning of wisdom." For these men begin to be wise; "to eschew evil, and do good."

2. This fear, if it be right, will be practical: "For a good understanding," &c.

The third acclamation is, "His praise endureth for ever." Which some refer to God, others to man; but both are true. For the praise must continue for ever: "His power, mercy," &c.

If referred to man then the sense will be,—

1. "His praise." For "they that dwell in thy house," &c.; Psa. lxxxiv. 4.

2. Or "His praise." The commendation of a good man "will be had in everlasting remembrance," Psa. cxii. 6. "The name of the wicked shall rot," &c.; Prov. x. 7. "Well done, thou good and faithful servant," &c.; Matt. xxv. 21. His praise is in this world lasting, but in the world to come everlasting.

PSALM CXII

The blessedness of the man that fears the Lord, both as it regards himself and his family, 1–3; his conduct to his family, his neighbours, and the poor, 4–9; the envy of the wicked at his prosperity, 10.

A. M. cir. 3469
B. C. cir. 535
Cyri,
R. Persarum,
cir. annum
secundum

P RAISE ᵃye the LORD. ᵇBlessed *is* the man *that* feareth the LORD, *that* ᶜdelighteth greatly in his commandments.

2 ᵈHis seed shall be mighty upon earth: the generation of the upright shall be blessed.

3 ᵉWealth and riches *shall be* in his house: and his righteousness endureth for ever.

4 ᶠUnto the upright there ariseth light in the darkness: *he is* gracious, and full of compassion, and righteous.

5 ᵍA good man showeth favour, and lendeth: he will guide his affairs ʰwith ⁱdiscretion.

6 Surely ᵏhe shall not be moved for ever: ˡthe righteous shall be in everlasting remembrance.

7 ᵐHe shall not be afraid of evil tidings: his ⁿheart is fixed, ᵒtrusting in the LORD.

8 His heart *is* established, ᵖhe shall not be afraid until he ᑫsee *his desire* upon his enemies.

9 ʳHe hath dispersed, he hath given to the poor, ˢhis righteousness endureth for ever; his ᵗhorn shall be exalted with honour.

10 ᵘThe wicked shall see *it,* and be grieved; ᵛhe shall gnash with his teeth, and ᵂmelt away: ˣthe desire of the wicked shall perish.

A. M. cir. 3469
B. C. cir. 535
Cyri,
R. Persarum,
cir. annum
secundum

ᵃHeb. *Hallelujah*——ᵇPsa. cxxviii. 1——ᶜPsa. cxix. 16, 35, 47, 70, 143——ᵈPsa. xxv. 13; xxxvii. 26; cii. 28 ᵉMatt. vi. 33——ᶠJob xi. 17; Psa. xcvii. 11——ᵍPsa. xxxvii. 26; Luke vi. 35——ʰEph. v. 15; Col. iv. 5 ⁱHeb. *judgment*——ᵏPsa. xv. 5——ˡProv. x. 7

ᵐProv. i. 33——ⁿPsa. lvii. 7——ᵒPsa. lxiv. 10 ᵖProv. iii. 33——ᑫPsa. lix. 10; cxviii. 7——ʳ2 Cor. ix. 9 ˢDeut. xxiv. 13; ver. 3——ᵗPsa. lxxv. 10——ᵘSee Luke xiii. 28——ᵛPsalm xxxvii. 12——ᵂPsalm lviii. 7, 8 ˣProv. x. 28; xi. 7

NOTES ON PSALM CXII

This is another of the acrostic or alphabetical Psalms, under the title *Hallelujah.* It is formed exactly as the preceding in the division of its verses. It has *ten* verses in the whole: the first eight contain each two hemistichs, beginning with a consecutive letter of the alphabet; the *ninth* and *tenth* verses, three each, making twenty-two in the whole. It is understood to have been written after the captivity, and probably by Zechariah and Haggai: to them it is ascribed by the Vulgate.

Verse 1. *Blessed* is *the man* that *feareth the Lord*] This seems to be the continuation of the preceding Psalm: *there* it was asserted that the *beginning of wisdom was the fear of the Lord;* and *here* the blessedness of the man who *thus fears* is stated.

That *delighteth greatly*] It is not enough to *fear God,* we must also *love him: fear* will deter us from *evil; love* will lead us to *obedience.* And the more a man fears and loves God, the more obedient will he be; till at last he *will delight greatly in the commandments* of his Maker.

Verse 2. *His seed shall be mighty*] זרעו *zaro,* his *posterity.* So the word should always be understood in this connection.

Verse 3. *Wealth and riches* shall be in *his house*] This is often the case: a godly man must save both *time* and *money.* Before he was converted he lost much time, and squandered his money. All this he now saves, and therefore wealth and riches must be in his house; and if he do not distribute to the necessities of the poor, they will continue to accumulate till they be his curse; or God will, by his providence, sweep them away. Both צדקה *tsedakah* and δικαιοσυνη are often used to signify, not only *justice* and *righteousness,* but also *beneficence*

and *almsgiving;* and this is most probably the meaning here. See ver. 9.

Verse 4. *There ariseth light in the darkness*] The upright are always happy; and when tribulations come, God lifts up the light of his countenance upon him, and causes all occurences to work together for his good.

He is *gracious, and full of compassion, and righteous.*] He enjoys the *favour* of God; that *grace* makes him *compassionate;* and in the general tenor of his conduct he is righteous. From these principles he *shows favour* (ver. 5) to him that *needs* it; that is, to the real poor he *gives* of his substance; and others he obliges by *lending,* they not being utterly in want, but standing in need only of a little *present help.* But he takes heed to *whom* he *gives* and to *whom* he *lends;* that in the first case his bounty may be well applied, and in the second he may not oblige the person who only seeks, under the notion of a *loan,* to appropriate the money *borrowed.* To prevent evils of this kind he acts prudently, and *guides his affairs with discretion,* ver. 5.

Verse 7. *He shall not be afraid of evil tidings*] He knows that God governs the world, therefore he fears not for futurity. And as to the *calumnies* of men, he fears *them* not, because *his heart is fixed*—determined to walk in the path of duty, whatever persecutions he may suffer, for *he trusts in the Lord.*

Verse 8. *His heart* is *established*] סמוך לבו *samuch libbo,* "his heart is propped up;" he is *buttressed up* by the strength of his Maker.

Verse 9. *He hath dispersed*] He has scattered abroad his munificence; he has given particularly to the *poor;* his *righteousness*—his almsgiving, his charity, *remaineth for ever.* See on ver. 3.

His horn] His power and authority *shall be exalted with honour.* He shall rise to influence only through his own worth, and not by extortion or flattery.

Verse 10. *The wicked shall see* it] רשע *rasha*, the *wicked one*. Some think *Satan* is meant. It is distinguished from רשעים *reshaim*, *wicked men*, in the conclusion of the verse.

Shall gnash with his teeth] Through spite and ill will.

And melt away] Through envy and hopeless expectation of similar good; for *his desire* in reference to *himself*, and in reference to him who is the object of his *envy, shall perish*— shall come to nothing.

Analysis of the Hundred and Twelfth Psalm

The psalmist, having put it down for an infallible maxim, in the close of the former Psalm, "that the fear of the Lord is the beginning of wisdom," in this sets down the felicity of that man who fears God, in several particulars.

There are two parts in this Psalm:—

I. A general proposition, that he is blessed.

II. An enumeration of particulars in which that blessedness consists, from ver. 2 to the end.

I. To the first part he prefixes a hallelujah, "praise the Lord," which is the intent and scope of the Psalm; that he be praised for those rewards of piety he bestows on such as fear him.

He delivers this one general proposition to persuade them to piety: "Blessed is the man," &c., that believes, honours, and serves him.

For fear a man should mistake, supposing he fears the Lord when he really does not, he adds these three restrictions to his proposition:—

1. "Keep his commandments." An obedient fear.

2. "He delights in them," &c. Is pleased with their equity, and loves them.

3. "He delights greatly," &c. It must be a thankful and ready fear, performed with alacrity and earnestness, done with all the heart.

II. In the rest of the Psalm he insists on what this blessedness consists in:—

1. That the righteous shall have temporal goods, and that they shall be blessings.

2. That though they shall enjoy them, they are not exempted from crosses, 2 Tim. iii. 12.

3. That God distributes these temporal blessings not equally, but most profitably for him. This being premised, he enumerates the blessings here promised:—

1. "His seed shall be mighty," &c. Which was verified in Abraham and his posterity: "I will show mercy to thousands," &c.

2. "Wealth and riches," &c. That is, abundance of all things *shall be in his house,* and remain in it for his just dealing; and content-ment preserves his well obtained goods to his posterity.

3. "Unto the upright there ariseth light," &c. The light of counsel and consolation, in the midst of doubts, tribulations, and afflictions, which the prophet ascribes to God's mercy and goodness.

4. He hath bowels of compassion, of which he shows two effects: 1. "A good man showeth favour," &c. Easily forgives an injury. 2. Imagines he is not born for himself, but to do good to others.

5. "He will guide his affairs with discretion." Discern between truth and falsehood; be no accepter of persons, but in all things just and upright.

6. He is patient and constant. Troubles and dangers may increase; but in the midst of all he looks to heaven, and remains firm in his principles.

7. "The righteous shall be had," &c. His name is written in the book of life, and it is precious in the Church, such as those of the martyrs; while the wicked are detested, such as Judas, Cain, Pilate. At the last day the one shall have "Come, ye blessed;" the other, "Go, ye cursed."

8. "He shall not be afraid of evil tidings." Scandals may arise; but he remembers "the servant is not above his lord," therefore he bears all patiently, and for these reasons: 1. "Because his heart is fixed," &c. He has a sure rock; God will clear his innocency. 2. "His heart is established," &c. He knows God will take care of him.

9. The ninth felicity to the righteous is, God has given him a charitable heart. 1. "He hath dispersed," acts liberally, that others as well as himself may reap. 2. He does it freely, without looking for any thing again: "He gives." 3. "He hath given to the poor." To those who need his kindness.

For this liberality he is a great gainer in two respects:—

1. "The good work he hath done," &c. His charity and piety are increased by it.

2. "His horn," &c. His power, honour, dignity, and glory.

His last felicity is,

1. "The wicked shall see it," and be grieved at his felicity.

2. "He shall gnash his teeth" as a mad dog, and seek his ruin.

3. But shall not be able to harm him: "The desire of the wicked shall perish." He that fears God is a happy man; he that fears him not, most unhappy. Reader, in what state art thou? Happy or unhappy?

PSALM CXIII

An exhortation to bless God for his own excellencies, 1–6; and for his great mercy to the poor and necessitous, 7–9.

A. M. cir. 3469
B. C. cir. 535
Cyri,
R. Persarum,
cir. annum
secundum

PRAISE [a]ye the LORD. [b]Praise, O ye servants of the LORD, praise the name of the LORD.

2 [c]Blessed be the name of the LORD from this time forth and for evermore.

3 [d]From the rising of the sun unto the going down of the same the LORD'S name is to be praised.

4 The LORD *is* [e]high above all nations, *and* [f]his glory above the heavens.

5 [g]Who *is* like unto the LORD our God, who [h]dwelleth on high.

A. M. cir. 3469
B. C. cir. 535
Cyri,
R. Persarum,
cir. annum
secundum

6 [i]Who humbleth *himself* to behold *the things that are* in heaven, and in the earth!

7 [k]He raiseth up the poor out of the dust, *and* lifteth the needy out of the dunghill;

8 That he may [l]set *him* with princes, *even* with the princes of his people.

9 [m]He maketh the barren woman [n]to keep house, *and to be* a joyful mother of children. Praise ye the LORD.

---

[a]Heb. *Hallelujah*——[b]Psa. cxxxv. 1——[c]Dan. ii. 20 [d]Isa. lix. 19; Mal. i. 11——[e]Psa. xcvii. 9; xcix. 2 [f]Psa. viii. 1——[g]Psa. lxxxix. 6——[h]Heb. *exalteth* himself *to dwell*

[i]Psa. xi. 4; cxxxviii. 6; Isa. lvii. 15——[k]1 Sam. ii. 8; Psa. cvii. 41——[l]Job xxxvi. 7——[m]1 Sam. ii. 5; Psa. lxviii. 6; Isa. liv. 1; Gal. iv. 27——[n]Heb. *to dwell in a house*

NOTES ON PSALM CXIII

Psalms cxiii., cxiv., cxv., cxvi., cxvii., and cxviii., form the great *Hallel*, and were sung by the Jews on their most solemn festivals, and particularly at the *passover*. To these reference is made by the *evangelists*, Matt. xxvi. 30, and Mark xiv. 26, there called the *hymn* which Jesus and his disciples sung at the passover, for the whole of the Psalms were considered as one grand hymn or thanksgiving. It was probably composed after the return from the captivity. It has no title but *Hallelujah* in the *Hebrew* and ancient *Versions*.

Verse 1. *Praise, O ye servants*] Probably an address to the Levites. The Anglo-Saxon has ᏥᏁᏝᏁᏓ ᏟᏁᏗᏁᏗᏁ ᏥᎤᏝᏗᎮ, *praise the Lord, ye knaves.* Knapa or knave signified among our ancestors a *servant;* sometimes a *male, a young man.*

Verse 3. *From the rising of the sun*] From morning to evening be always employed in the work. Or it may be a call on *all mankind* to praise God for his innumerable mercies to the *human race.* Praise him from *one end of the world unto the other.* And therefore the psalmist adds,

Verse 4. *The Lord is high above all nations*] He governs all, he provides for all; therefore let all give him praise.

Verse 5. *Who is like unto the Lord*] Those who are highly exalted are generally unapproachable; they are proud and overbearing; or so surrounded with *magnificence* and *flatterers*, that to them the poor have no access; but *God, though infinitely* exalted, *humbleth himself to behold* even *heaven* itself, and much more does he *humble himself* when he condescends to behold *earth* and her inhabitants; (ver. 6.) But so does he love his creatures that he rejoices over even the meanest of them to do them good.

Verse 7. *He raiseth up the poor*] The poorest man, in the meanest and most abject circumstances, is an object of his merciful regards. He may here allude to the wretched state of the captives in Babylon, whom God raised up out of that dust and dunghill. Others apply it to the resurrection of the dead.

Verse 8. *With the princes*] נדיבים *nedebim* very properly translated by the Anglo-Saxon ᏋᎯᏝᏛᏅᎷᏗᏅᏅᏛᏋ, the aldermen, the most respectable of his people.

Verse 9. *He maketh the barren woman to keep house*] This is a figure to point out the *desolate, decreasing state* of the captives in Babylon, and the happy change which took place on their return to their own land. These are nearly the words of Hannah, 1 Sam. ii. 5.

ANALYSIS OF THE HUNDRED AND THIRTEENTH PSALM

The scope of this Psalm is the same with those that went before, that is, to excite men to praise God.

This Psalm contains three parts:—

I. An exhortation to God's servants to praise him.

II. A form set down how and where to praise him, ver. 2, 3.

III. The reasons to persuade us to it. 1. By his infinite power, ver. 4, 5. 2. His providence, as displayed in heaven and earth, ver. 6.

I. The prophet exhorts men "to praise the Lord;" and,

1. He doubles and trebles his exhortation, that it be not coldly but zealously done, or else to show that he alone is worthy of praise.

2. "Praise the Lord, O ye servants," &c.: They are to praise him, for he is their Lord; praise him likewise with a pure heart.

II. The manner of praising him. Say,

1. "Blessed be the name of the Lord." Job i.

2. "From this time forth," &c.: In prosperity or adversity, in this life or the future.

3. "From the rising of the sun," &c.: In all places, even over all the world.

III: And now follow the reasons to persuade men to praise God.

1. Because of his majesty, infinite power, and glory, which extend not to earth alone, but heaven also: "The Lord is high above," &c.

2. Because of his providence, benignity, and bounty, which being united with so much majesty, appear the more admirable. "Who is like the Lord," &c. None in heaven or on earth are to be compared to him. "Yet he

humbleth himself," &c. He is present with the highest angels, and with the poorest of his creatures, to help them.

In "humbling himself to behold the things on earth" he gives two instances: 1. In states and kingdoms. 2. In private families.

1. In states: "He raiseth up the poor," &c.: Let then no man say, that God does not regard

them that are of low estate; he raiseth up the poor, to the end "that he may set him with the princes," &c.

2. In private families: "He maketh the barren woman," &c. "Children are a heritage of the Lord." Some expositors refer the meaning of this last verse to the Church of the *Gentiles:* "Rejoice, O barren," &c. Isa. liv. 1.

PSALM CXIV

Miracles wrought at the exodus of the Israelites from Egypt, at the Red Sea, and at Jordan, 1–6; and at the rock of Horeb, 7, 8.

XXIII. DAY. EVENING PRAYER

A. M. cir. 3469
B. C. cir. 535
Cyri,
R. Persarum,
cir. annum
secundum

WHEN ªIsrael went out of Egypt, the house of Jacob ᵇfrom a people of strange language;

2 ᶜJudah was his sanctuary, *and* Israel his dominion.

3 ᵈThe sea saw *it,* and fled: ᵉJordan was driven back.

4 ᶠThe mountains skipped like rams, *and* the little hills like lambs.

5 ᵍWhat *ailed* thee, O thou sea, that thou fleddest? thou Jordan, *that* thou wast driven back?

A. M. cir. 3469
B. C. cir. 535
Cyri,
R. Persarum,
cir. annum
secundum

6 Ye mountains, *that* ye skipped like rams; *and* ye little hills, like lambs?

7 Tremble, thou earth, at the presence of the LORD, at the presence of the God of Jacob;

8 ʰWhich turned the rock *into* a standing water, the flint into a fountain of waters.

ªExodus xiii. 3——ᵇPsalm lxxxi. 5——ᶜExodus vi. 7; xix. 6; xxv. 8; xxix. 45, 46; Deuteronomy xxvii. 9 ᵈExodus xiv. 21; Psalm lxxvii. 16

ᵉJoshua iii. 13, 16——ᶠPsalm xxix. 6; lxviii. 16 ᵍHab. iii. 8 ʰExodus xvii. 6; Numbers xx. 11; Psalm cvii. 35

NOTES ON PSALM CXIV

This Psalm has no *title.* The word *Hallelujah* is prefixed in all the Versions except the *Chaldee* and *Syriac.* It seems like a fragment, or a part of another Psalm. In many MSS. it is only the *beginning* of the following; both making but one Psalm in all the Versions, except the *Chaldee.* It is elegantly and energetically composed; but begins and ends very abruptly, if we separate it from the following. As to the *author* of this Psalm, there have been various opinions; some have given the honour of it to *Shadrach, Meshech,* and *Abed-nego;* others to *Esther;* and others, to *Mordecai.*

Verse 1. *A people of strange language*] This may mean no more than a *barbarous* people; a people whom they did not know, and who did not worship their God. But it is a fact that the language of the Egyptians in the time of Joseph was so different from that of the Hebrews that they could not understand each other. See Psa. lxxxi. 5; Gen. xlii. 23.

The *Chaldee* has here מעמי ברבראי *meammey barbarey,* which gives reason to believe that the word is *Chaldee,* or more properly *Phœnician.* See this word fully explained in the note on Acts xxviii. 2. My old *Psalter* understood the word as referring to the *religious* state of the Egyptians: **In gangyng of Isrel oute of Egipt, of þe house of Jacob fra heþen folke.**

Verse 2. *Judah was his sanctuary*] He set up his true worship among the Jews, and took them for his peculiar people.

And *Israel his dominion.*] These words are a proof, were there none other, that this Psalm was composed *after* the days of David, and *after* the division of the tribes, for then the distinction of *Israel* and *Judah* took place.

Verse 3. *The sea saw* it, *and fled*] Mr. Addison has properly observed (see Spect. No. 461) that the author of this Psalm designedly works for effect, in pointing out the miraculous driving back the Red Sea and the river Jordan, and the commotion of the hills and mountains, without mentioning any *agent.* At last, when the reader sees the sea rapidly retiring from the shore, Jordan retreating to its source, and the mountains and hills running away like a flock of affrighted sheep, that the passage of the Israelites might be every where uninterrupted; then the *cause* of all is suddenly introduced, and the *presence of God* in his grandeur solves every difficulty.

Verse 5. *What* ailed *thee, O thou sea*] The original is very abrupt; and the *prosopopœia,* or personification very fine and expressive:—

What to thee, O sea, that thou fleddest away!
O Jordan, that thou didst roll back!
Ye mountains, that ye leaped like rams!
And ye hills, like the young of the fold!

After these very sublime interrogations, God appears; and the psalmist proceeds as if answering his own questions:—

At the appearance of the Lord, O earth, thou didst tremble;
At the appearance of the strong God of Jacob.
Converting the rock into a pool of waters;
The granite into water springs.

I know the present Hebrew text reads חולי *chuli,* "tremble thou," in the *imperative;* but almost all the *Versions* understood the word in *past* tense, and read as if the psalmist was answering his own questions, as stated in the

translation above. "Tremble thou, O earth."
As if he had said, Thou mayest well tremble, O
earth, at the presence of the Lord, at the
presence of the God of Jacob.

Verse 8. *The flint*] I have translated חלמיש
challamish, GRANITE; for such is the rock of
Horeb, a piece of which now lies before me.

This short and apparently imperfect Psalm,
for elegance and sublimity, yields to few in the
whole book.

It is so well translated in the old *Psalter*, that
I think I shall gratify the reader by laying it
before him.

Ver. 1. Jn gangyng of Jsrel oute of Egipt,
     Of the house of Jacob fra hethen folke.
Ver. 2. Made is Jude his halawyng
     Jsrel might of hym.
Ver. 3. The se sawe and fled,
     Jurdan turned is agayne;
Ver. 4. Hawes gladed als wethers,
     And hilles als lambes of schepe.
Ver. 5. What is to the se, that thou fled?
     And thou Jordane that thou ert turned
     agayne?
Ver. 6. Hawes gladded als wethers?
     And hils als lambs of schepe.
Ver. 7. Fra the face of Lorde styrde is the erth,
     Fra the face of God of Jacob;
Ver. 8. That turnes the stane in stank of waters,
     And roche in wels of waters.

And, as a still more ancient specimen of our
language, I shall insert the Anglo-Saxon, with
a literal reading, line for line, as near to the
Saxon as possible, merely to show the affinity
of the languages.

Ver. 1. On utᵹanᵹe Iꞃnael oꝛ Eᵹyptan;
     huꞃ Iacob oꝛ ꝛolce ælðeoðiᵹum.
Ver. 2. ᵹepoꝛðen iꞃ Iuðea halᵹune hiꞃ,
     Iꞃnael anðpealð hiꞃ.
Ver. 3. Sæ ᵹeꞃeah Ɡ ꝛleah
     Ioꞃðan ᵹeciꞃpeð iꞃ unðeꞃbæc.
Ver. 4. ꟃuntaꞃ hi ꝛæᵹnoðon ꞃpa ꞃammaꞃ
     Ɡ beoꞃᵹaꞃ ꞃpa ꞃpa lamb ꞃceap.
Ver. 5. Hpæt iꞃ ðe ꞃæ ꝥ ꝧu ꝛluᵹe
     Ɡ ꝧu ea, ꞃoꞃðon ᵹeciꞃpeð iꞃ unðeꞃbæc?
Ver. 6. ꟃuntaꞃ ᵹeꞃæᵹnoðon ꞃpa ꞃpa ꞃammaꞃ
     Ɡ hylla ꞃpa ꞃpa lambꞃa ꞃceapa.
Ver. 7. ꝛꞃam anꞃine ðꞃihtneꞃ aꞃtyꞃoð iꞃ eoꞃðe
     ꝛꞃam anꞃine ᵹoðeꞃ Iacob
Ver. 8. Seðe ᵹecyꞃðe ꞃtan on meꞃe pæteꞃa
     Ɡ cluðaꞃ on pyllan pæteꞃa.

Ver. 1. On outgang Israel of Egypt,
     House Jacob of folk foreigners;
Ver. 2. Made is Jacob holyness his;
     Israel andweald (government) his.
Ver. 3. Sea saw, and flew!
     Jordan turned underback!
Ver. 4. Mounts they fain (rejoiced) so (as)
     rams,
     And burghs (hillocks) so (as) lamb-
     sheep.
Ver. 5. What is the sea, that thou flew?
     And thou river for that thou turned
     is underback?
Ver. 6. Mounts ye fained (rejoiced) so so
     rams;
     And hills so so lambs-sheep.
Ver. 7. From sight Lord's stirred is earth;
     From sight God of Jacob.
Ver. 8. Who turned stone in mere waters;
     And cliffs in wells waters.

I have retained some words above in nearly
their Saxon form, because they still exist in our
old writers; or, with little variation, in those
of the present day:—

Ver. 2. *Andweald*, government. Hence *weal*
and *wealth*, *commonweal* or *wealth;* the
general government, that which produces the
welfare of the country.

Ver. 4. *Fægnodon*, fained—desired fervently,
felt delight in expectation.

Ver 4. *Burgh*, a hill—a mound or heap of
earth, such as was raised up over the dead.
Hence a *barrow;* and hence the word *bury*, to
inhume the dead.

Ver. 8. *Mere*, or meer, a large pool of water,
a lake, a *lough*, still in use in the north of
England. Gentlemen's ponds, or large sheets
of water so called; and hence *Winander-mere*,
a large lake in Westmoreland. Mere also signifies *limit* or *boundary;* hence the *Mersey*, the
river which divides Lancashire from Cheshire,
and serves as a *boundary* to both counties. The
mere that spreads itself out to the *sea*.

Instead of *cludas*, which signifies *rocks*, one
MS. has **clyꝛ** *clyf*, which signifies *a craggy
mountain* or *broken rock*.

The reader will see from this specimen how
much of our ancient language still remains in
the present; and perhaps also how much, in
his opinion, we have amplified and improved
our mother tongue.

ANALYSIS OF THE HUNDRED AND FOURTEENTH PSALM

David in this Psalm chants forth the wonderful works and miracles that God wrought, when
he brought forth Israel out of Egypt.

This Psalm has *two* parts:—

I. A narration of Israel's deliverance, amplified by the state they were in, ver. 1; the state
to which they were brought, ver. 2; the miracles
then done, ver. 3; and the law given, ver. 4.

II. A *prosopopœia* set down by way of dialogue: 1. The prophet asks the sea and *Jordan* why they fled, ver. 5, 6. 2. To which
the answer is, that "the earth trembled," &c.,
ver. 7, 8.

I. In the narration, Israel's condition is set
down by way of comparison, in order that their
deliverance might make the deeper impression.
We must recollect that *Jacob* and *Judah* in this
place signify the whole nation of the Israelites
that descended out of Jacob's loins; but of the
house of *Jacob* there is made particular mention, because with him they came into *Egypt;*
and of *Judah*, because from him they were
called *Jews*. This being premised. 1. We are
presented with the condition of the Jews *before*
their deliverance; before they were formed into
a state or Church; they were among "a people
of a strange language."

2. The condition of the Jews *after* their deliverance: "When Israel went out of Egypt,"
&c., then "Judah was his sanctuary," &c. 1.
"His sanctuary:" A people sanctified and
adopted by him, consecrated to his worship as
holy temples and sanctuaries, and having a
holy priest to govern them in points of piety.
2. "His dominion:" In which he reigned as
King by his laws and Spirit, and appointed
godly magistrates to rule them in matters of
policy; for the government was a theocracy,
till they cast it off by choosing a king.

The prophet explains the manner of their

deliverance, which was by miracles and signs; and gives us these instances:—

1. "The sea saw it, and fled," as the people advanced to it. "At the presence of the Lord it turned back all night," Exod. xiv. In a poetical strain he attributes this to the sense of the sea. "The sea saw," &c.

2. "Jordan was driven back," &c. Forty years after, when they were entering the promised land, then Jordan suffered a long reflux, Josh. iv.

3. At *Sinai,* when the law was given, then the mountains and hills quaked: "The mountains skipped like rams," &c.

II. This Psalm abounds with poetical imagery; and having related the wonderful deliverances wrought for God's people, the psalmist expostulates with the sea and mountains, and interrogates them as to what so strangely altered their course. "What ailed thee, O thou sea, &c.?—Ye mountains that ye skipped like rams," &c.

To which, in the person of the earth speaking to herself, the prophet answers; thus making both a *prosopopœia* and an *apostrophe.*

1. "Tremble, thou earth, at the presence of the Lord," &c. As if it had been said, Would you know the reason why we fly? The cause is, the Lord has appeared and showed his force and power, and laid his commands upon us; and therefore, not abiding his presence, the mountains are moved, &c.

2. Of his power this miracle is sufficient for an instance: "Which turned the rock into a standing water, the flint into a fountain of waters." Causing not only waters to flow from thence, but turning the very substance of a flint, which is apter to yield fire than water, into that fluid element, Num. xx. [See the note on ver. 8.]

PSALM CXV

God alone is to be glorified, 1–3. The vanity of idols, 4–8. Israel, the house of Aaron, and all that fear God, are exhorted to trust in the Lord, 9–11. The Lord's goodness to his people, and his gracious promises, 12–16. As the dead cannot praise him, the living should, 17, 18.

A. M. cir. 3469
B. C. cir. 535
Cyri,
R. Persarum,
cir. annum
secundum

NOT [a]unto us, O LORD, not unto us, but unto thy name give glory, for thy mercy, *and* for thy truth's sake.

2 Wherefore should the heathen say, [b]Where *is* now their God?

3 [c]But our God *is* in the heavens: he hath done whatsoever he hath pleased.

4 [d]Their idols *are* silver and gold, the work of men's hands.

5 They have mouths, but they speak not:

A. M. cir. 3469
B. C. cir. 535
Cyri,
R. Persarum,
cir. annum
secundum

---

[a]See Isa. xlviii. 11; Ezek. xxxvi. 32——[b]Psa. xlii. 3, 10; lxxix. 10; Joel ii. 17

[c]1 Chron. xvi. 26; Psa. cxxxv. 6; Dan. iv. 35——[d]Deut. iv. 28; Psa. cxxxv. 15, 16, 17; Jer. x. 3, &c.

NOTES ON PSALM CXV

This Psalm is written as a part of the preceding by *eighteen* of *Kennicott's* and *fifty-three* of *De Rossi's* MSS.; by some ancient editions the *Septuagint,* the *Syriac,* the *Vulgate,* the *Æthiopic,* the *Arabic,* and the *Anglo-Saxon.* The old *Anglo-Scottish* Psalter reads it consecutively with the foregoing. Who the author of both was, we know not, nor on what occasion it was written. It seems to be an *epinikion* or triumphal song, in which the victory gained is entirely ascribed to Jehovah.

Verse 1. Not unto us, O Lord] We take no merit to ourselves; as thine is the kingdom, and the power in that kingdom, so is thy glory.

For thy mercy, and *for thy truth's sake.*] Thy mercy gave thy promise, thy truth fulfilled it.

Verse 2. Wherefore should the heathen say] This appears to refer to a time in which the Israelites had suffered some sad reverses, so as to be brought very low, and to be marked by the heathen.

Verse 3. He hath done whatsover he hath pleased.] There was too much cause for his abandoning us to our enemies; yet he still lives and rules in heaven and in earth.

Verse 4. Their idols are *silver,* &c.] They are metal, stone, and wood. They are generally made in the form of man, but can neither see, hear, smell, feel, walk, nor speak. How brutish to trust in such! And next to these, in stupidity

and inanity, must they be who form them, with the expectation of deriving any good from them. So obviously vain was the whole system of idolatry, that the more serious heathens ridiculed it, and it was a butt for the jests of their freethinkers and buffoons. How keen are those words of Juvenal!—

——Audis,
Jupiter, hæc? nec labra moves, cum mittere vocem.
Debueras, vel marmoreus vel aheneus? aut cur
In carbone tuo charta pia thura soluta
Ponimus, et sectum vituli jecur, albaque porci
Omenta? ut video, nullum discrimen habendum est
Effigies inter vestras, statuamque Bathylli.
SAT. xiii., ver. 113.

"Dost thou hear, O Jupiter, these things? nor move thy lips when thou oughtest to speak out, whether thou art of marble or of bronze? Or, why do we put the sacred incense on thy altar from the opened paper, and the extracted liver of a calf, and the white caul of a hog? As far as I can discern there is no difference between thy statue and that of Bathyllus."

This irony will appear the keener, when it is known that Bathyllus was a fiddler and player, whose image by the order of Polycrates, was erected in the temple of Juno at Samos. See

A. M. cir. 3469
B. C. cir. 535
Cyri,
R. Persarum,
cir. annum
secundum eyes have they, but they see not:

6 They have ears, but they hear not: noses have they, but they smell not:

7 They have hands, but they handle not: feet have they, but they walk not: neither speak they through their throat.

8 ᵉThey that make them are like unto them; *so is* every one that trusteth in them.

9 ᶠO Israel, trust thou in the Lᴏʀᴅ: ᵍhe *is* their help and their shield.

10 O house of Aaron, trust in the Lᴏʀᴅ: he *is* their help and their shield.

11 Ye that fear the Lᴏʀᴅ, trust in the Lᴏʀᴅ: he *is* their help and their shield.

12 The Lᴏʀᴅ hath been mindful of us: he

will bless *us;* he will bless the house of Israel; he will bless the house of Aaron.

13 ʰHe will bless them that fear the Lᴏʀᴅ, *both* small ⁱand great.

14 The Lᴏʀᴅ shall increase you more and more, you and your children.

15 Ye *are* ᵏblessed of the Lᴏʀᴅ ˡwhich made heaven and earth.

16 The heaven, *even* the heavens, *are* the Lᴏʀᴅ's: but the earth hath he given to the children of men.

17 ᵐThe dead praise not the Lᴏʀᴅ, neither any that go down into silence.

18 ⁿBut we will bless the Lᴏʀᴅ from this time forth and for evermore. Praise the Lᴏʀᴅ.

A. M. cir. 3469
B. C. cir. 535
Cyri,
R. Persarum,
cir. annum
secundum

ᵉPsa. cxxxv. 18; Isa. xliv. 9, 10, 11; Jonah ii. 8; Hab. ii. 18, 19——ᶠSee Psa. cxviii. 2, 3, 4; cxxxv. 19, 20 ᵍPsa. xxxiii. 20; Prov. xxx. 5

ʰPsa. cxxviii. 1, 4——ⁱHeb. *with*——ᵏGen. xiv. 19 ˡGen. i. 1; Psa. xcvi. 5——ᵐPsa. vi. 5; lxxxviii. 10, 11, 12; Isa. xxxviii. 18——ⁿPsa. cxiii. 2; Dan. ii. 20

Isa. xli. 1. &c.; xlvi. 7; Jer. x. 4, 5, &c.; and Psa. cxxxv. 15, 16.

Verse 9. *O Israel*] The body of the Jewish people.

Verse 10. *O house of Aaron*] All the different classes of the priesthood.

Verse 11. *Ye that fear the Lord*] All real penitents, and sincere believers, *trust in the Lord*, in the almighty, omniscient, and infinitely good Jehovah.

He is their help and shield] He is the succour, support, guardian, and defence of all who put their confidence in him.

Verse 12. *The Lord hath been mindful*] He has never yet wholly abandoned us to our enemies.

He will bless the house of Israel] He will bless the people as a nation; he will bless the priesthood and Levites; he will bless all of them who fear him, great and small, in whatsoever station or circumstances found. There is a great deal of emphasis in this verse: several words are redoubled to make the subject the more affecting. I give a literal translation:—

Ver. 12: "The Lord has been mindful of us; he will bless the house of Israel; he will bless the house of Aaron. Ver. 13: He will bless them that fear Jehovah, the small with the great. Ver. 14: Jehovah will add upon you, upon you and upon all your children. Ver. 15: Blessed are ye of the Lord, the Maker of heaven and earth. Ver. 16: The heavens of heavens are the Lord's: but the earth he hath given to the sons of Adam."

Jehovah is absolute Master of the universe. He has made the heavens of heavens, and also the earth; and this he gives to the children of Adam. When he exiled him from *paradise*, he turned him out into the *earth*, and gave it to him and his sons for ever, that they might dress, till, and eat of its produce all their days.

Verse 17. *The dead praise not the Lord*] המתים *hammethim*, those dead men who worshipped as gods dumb idols, dying in their

sins, worship not Jehovah; nor can any of those who *go down into silence* praise thee: earth is the place in which to praise the Lord for his mercies, and get a preparation for his glory.

Verse 18. *But we will bless the Lord*] Our fathers, who received so much from thy bounty, are *dead;* their *tongues* are *silent* in the *grave;* we are in their place, and wish to magnify thy name, for thou hast dealt bountifully with us. But grant us those farther blessings before we die which we so much need; and we will praise thee as *living* monuments of thy mercy, and the praise we begin *now* shall continue for ever and ever.

The *Targum*, for "neither any that go down into silence," has "nor any that descend into the house of earthly sepulture," that is, the *tomb*. The Anglo-Saxon: ꝺ na ealle þaꞇe nyꝺenꝼꞇꝭꝺ on helle, *neither all they that go down into hell.* Noꝼþ þe ꝺeꝺe ꝼal loue þe Loꝛꝺe, ne al þaꞇ lꝩꝫhꞇeꝼ in hell. Old Psalter. The word *hell* among our ancestors meant originally the *covered*, or *hidden obscure* place, from helan, to *cover* or *conceal:* it now expresses only the *place of endless torment.*

ANALYSIS OF THE HUNDRED AND FIFTEENTH PSALM

The prophet, being zealous of God's honour, which the heathens were solicitous to give to their idols, earnestly beseeches God to manifest that power which belongs to him alone, and which he will not give to another.

This Psalm, has *four* parts:—

I. His petition for God's honour, ver. 1; which belongs to no idol, ver. 3-9.

II. An exhortation to praise God, and hope in him, ver. 10-12.

III. The benefit that will arise from it; a blessing, ver. 12-16.

IV. A profession, that for the blessing they will bless God, ver. 17, 18.

1. Some join this Psalm to the former, conceiving that the prophet, having expressed the

goodness of God in the deliverance of his people from *Egypt*, would not have any of the glory attributed to *Moses* or *Aaron*, but wholly to God. Therefore he begins:—

1. "Not unto us," &c. Or any leader among us.

2. "But unto thy name," &c. We seek it not; take it wholly to thyself.

And this, for these reasons, he desires might always be shown to his people.

1. "Give glory to thy name," &c. For the manifestation of his mercy.

2. "Do it for thy truth's sake." As a promise-keeping God.

3. "Wherefore should the heathen say," &c. Give them not occasion to blaspheme, as if thou hadst forsaken thy people. Should the heathen ask, we can answer: "As for our God, he is in the heavens, which his miracles testify. He can deliver or afflict his people as he pleases."

But where are their gods?

1. "Their idols are silver and gold." The mere productions of the earth.

2. "The work of men's hands." Works, and not makers of works.

3. They are of no use or power, though formed like men: "For they have mouths," &c. "They have hands, but they handle not," &c. They have not the power of articulating sounds; they are lower than even the beasts that perish.

The prophet, having thus described the idols, now notices their makers.

1. "They that make them," &c. Quite senseless people.

2. "So is every one that puts his trust," &c. Christ says, "Having eyes," &c. Mark viii.

II. The prophet, having passed this sarcasm upon the idols and idolaters, leaves them, and exhorts the *Israelites*.

1. "O Israel, trust thou," &c. You are God's servants; and to encourage them he adds, "He is their help," &c. The protector of the whole nation.

2. "O house of Levi," &c. You are the leaders and guides in religion; and therefore, you ought especially to trust in him who is the shield of your tribe.

3. "Ye that fear the Lord," &c. In whatever nation you live; for all who fear him, and do righteously, are accepted of him.

III. That this exhortation might be the deeper rooted, he puts them in mind that God "hath been mindful of us," by his special providence.

1. "He will bless the house of Israel" as a nation.

2. "He will bless the house of Aaron" as the priesthood.

3. "He will bless them that fear the Lord," &c., without distinction.

The prophet, taking his example from God, pours his blessing upon them also, and upon their children.

1. "The Lord shall increase you," &c.

2. "Ye are the blessed of the Lord," &c. Though the world speak evil of you.

3. "The Lord which made heaven and earth." Which words are added that they may be assured that their blessings are real, and come forth from his hand directly and alone.

4. They come from one able to bless; for, 1. *The heaven*, even *the heavens*, &c. In them he especially shows his presence, majesty, and glory; but sends his dews and rain upon the earth. 2. As for the earth, *he hath given it*, &c., that by his blessing upon their labours they might have food and raiment; therefore praise him.

IV. For this is the true end of their being: which he illustrates by an antithesis.

1. "For the dead praise not the Lord," &c. These temporal blessings are not felt by the dead—they need them not: but the living should render continual thanks for them to God their author.

2. But we that are upon earth enjoy his protection and temporal care of us; and besides we have his far richer spiritual blessings; therefore, "we will bless the Lord," &c., by ourselves while we live, and aim by our instructions and prayers that our posterity may do the same when we are gone down into silence.

3. However, ye that are alive this day, "praise ye the Lord."

PSALM CXVI

The psalmist praises God for his deliverance from thraldom, which he compares to death and the grave, 1-9. The exercises through which he had passed, 10, 11. His gratitude for these mercies, and resolution to live to God's glory, 12-19.

XXIV. DAY. MORNING PRAYER

A. M. cir. 3489
B. C. cir. 515
Darii I.,
R. Persarum,
cir. annum
sextum

I [a]LOVE the LORD, because he hath heard my voice *and* my supplications.

2 Because he hath inclined his ear unto me, therefore will I call upon *him* [b]as long as I live.

A. M. cir. 3489
B. C. cir. 515
Darii I.,
R. Persarum,
cir. annum
sextum

3 [c]The sorrows of death compassed me, and the pains of hell [d]gat hold upon me: I found trouble and sorrow.

---

[a]Psa. xviii. 1——[b]Heb. *in my days*   [c]Psa. xviii. 4, 5, 6——[d]Heb. *found me*

NOTES ON PSALM CXVI

This Psalm is also without a *title*, and its *author* is unknown. It appears to have been written after the captivity, and to be a thanksgiving to God for that glorious event. The psalmist compares this captivity to *death* and the *grave;* and shows the happy return to the promised land, called here *The land of the living*. The people recollect the vows of God

A. M. cir. 3489
B. C. cir. 515
Darii I.,
R. Persarum,
cir. annum
sextum

4 Then called I upon the name of the Lord; O Lord, I beseech thee, deliver my soul.

5 ᵉGracious *is* the Lord, and ᶠrighteous; yea, our God *is* merciful.

6 The Lord preserveth the simple: I was brought low, and he helped me.

7 Return unto thy ᵍrest, O my soul: for ʰthe Lord hath dealt bountifully with thee.

8 ⁱFor thou hast delivered my soul from death, mine eyes from tears, *and* my feet from falling.

9 I will walk before the Lord ᵏin the land of the living.

A. M. cir. 3489
B. C. cir. 515
Darii I.,
R. Persarum,
cir. annum
sextum

ᵉPsa. ciii. 8——ᶠEzra ix. 15; Neh. ix. 8; Psa. cxix. 137; cxlv. 17

ᵍJer. vi. 16; Matt. xi. 29——ʰPsa. xiii. 6; cxix. 17 ⁱPsa. lvi. 13——ᵏPsa. xxvii. 13

---

which were upon them, and purpose to fulfil them. They exhult at being enabled to worship God in the temple at Jerusalem.

The *Syriac*, which abounds in conjectural prefaces, supposes this Psalm to have been written on the occasion of Saul coming to the mouth of the cave in which David lay hidden; but spiritually taken, it relates to the bringing of a new people, the Gentiles, to the Christian faith. In a few MSS. this Psalm is joined to the preceding. Many think it relates wholly to the passion, death, and triumph of Christ. Most of the fathers were of this opinion.

Verse 1. *I love the Lord because he hath heard*] How vain and foolish is the *talk*, "To love God for his benefits to us is mercenary, and cannot be pure love!" Whether pure or impure, there is no other love that can flow from the heart of the creature to its Creator. *We love him*, said the holiest of Christ's disciples, *because he first loved us;* and the increase of our love and filial obedience is in proportion to the increased sense we have of our obligation to him. We love him for the benefits bestowed on us. *Love begets love.*

Verse 2. *Because he hath inclined his ear*] The psalmist represents himself to be so sick and weak, that he could scarcely speak. The Lord, in condescension to this weakness, is here considered as *bowing down his ear to the mouth of the feeble suppliant*, that he may receive every word of his prayer.

Therefore will I call upon him] I have had such blessed success in my application to him, that I purpose to invoke him as long as I shall live. He th. t prays much will be emboldened to pray more, because none can supplicate the throne of grace in vain.

Verse 3. *The sorrows of death*] חבלי מות *chebley maveth*, the *cables* or *cords of death;* alluding to their bonds and fetters during their captivity; or to the cords by which a criminal is bound, who is about to be led out to execution; or to the bandages in which the dead were enveloped, when head, arms, body, and limbs were all *laced down* together.

The pains of hell] מצרי שאול *metsarey sheol*, the *straitnesses of the grave.* So little expectation was there of life, that he speaks as if he were condemned, executed, and *closed* up in the tomb. Or, he may refer here to the *small niches* in cemeteries, where the coffins of the dead were placed.

Because this Psalm has been used in the thanksgiving of women after safe delivery, it has been supposed that the pain suffered in the act of parturition was equal for the time to the torments of the damned. But this supposition is shockingly absurd; the utmost power of

human nature could not, for a moment, endure the wrath of God, the deathless worm, and the unquenchable fire. The body must die, be decomposed, and be built up on indestructible principles, before this punishment can be borne.

Verse 5. *Gracious* is *the Lord*] In his own nature.

And righteous] In all his dealings with men. *Our God* is *merciful.*] Of tender compassion to all penitents.

Verse 6. *The Lord preserveth the simple*] פתאים *pethaim*, which all the Versions render *little ones.* Those who are meek and lowly of heart, who feel the spirit of little children, these he preserves, as he does little children; and he mentions this circumstance, because the Lord has a peculiar regard for these *young ones*, and gives his angels charge concerning them. Were it otherwise, children are exposed to so many dangers and deaths, that most of them would fall victims to accidents in their infancy.

Verse 7. *Return unto thy rest, O my soul*] God is the *centre* to which all immortal spirits tend, and in connexion with which alone they can find *rest.* Every thing *separated* from its *centre* is in a state of *violence;* and, if intelligent, cannot be happy. All human souls, while separated from God by sin, are in a state of violence, agitation, and misery. From God all spirits come; to him all must return, in order to be finally happy. This is true in the general case; though, probably, the *rest* spoken of here means the *promised land*, into which they were now *returning.*

A proof of the late origin of this Psalm is exhibited in this verse, in the words למנוחיבי *limenuchaichi*, "to thy rest," and עליבי *alaichi*, "to thee," which are both *Chaldaisms.*

Verse 8. *Thou hast delivered my soul from death*] Thou hast rescued my *life* from the *destruction* to which it was exposed.

Mine eyes from tears] Thou hast turned my *sorrow* into *joy.*

My feet from falling.] Thou hast taken me out of the land of *snares* and *pitfalls*, and brought me into a *plain path.* How very near does our ancient mother tongue come to this:— forþon he nerode raþle mine of þeaðe, eagan mine of teapum, fet mine of sliþe. *For thou he nerode sawle mine of deathe, eagan mine of tearum; fet mine of slide.* And this language is but a little improved in the old Psalter:—

ffor he toke my saule fra bede; my eghen fra teres; my fete fra slippyng.

Verse 9. *I will walk before the Lord*] אתהלך *ethhallech*, I will *set myself to walk.* I am *determined to walk;* my eyes are now bright-

A. M. cir. 3489
B. C. cir. 515
Darii I.,
R. Persarum,
cir. annum
sextum

10 [1]I believed, therefore have I spoken: I was greatly afflicted: 11 [m]I said in my haste, [n]All men *are* liars.

12 What shall I render unto the LORD *for* all his benefits toward me?

13 I will take the cup of salvation, and

call upon the name of the LORD.

A. M. cir. 3489
B. C. cir. 515
Darii I.,
R. Persarum,
cir. annum
sextum

14 [o]I will pay my vows unto the LORD now in the presence of all his people.

15 [p]Precious in the sight of the LORD *is* the death of his saints.

---

[1]2 Cor. iv. 13——[m]Psa. xxxi. 22——[n]Rom. iii. 4

[o]Ver. 18; Psa. xxii. 25; Jonah ii. 9——[p]Psa. lxxii. 14

---

ened, so that I can *see;* my feet are *strengthened,* so that I can *walk;* and my *soul* is *alive,* so that I can *walk* with the *living.*

The *Vulgate,* the *Septuagint,* the *Æthiopic,* the *Arabic,* and the *Anglo-Saxon* end this Psalm here, which is numbered the cxivth; and begin with the *tenth* verse another Psalm, which they number cxvth; but this division is not acknowledged by the *Hebrew, Chaldee,* and *Syriac.*

Verse 10. *I believed, therefore have I spoken*] Distressed and afflicted as I was, I ever believed thy promises to be true; but I had great struggles to maintain my confidence; for my afflictions were great, oppressive, and of long standing.

It is scarcely worth observing that the letters called *heemantic* by the Hebrew grammarians, and which are used in forming the *derivatives* from the *roots,* are taken from the *first* word in this verse, האמנתי *heemanti,* "I have believed;" as the *prefixes* in that language are found in the technical words משה וכלב *Mosheh vecaleb,* "Moses and Caleb;" and the *formatives* of the *future* are found in the word איתן *eythan,* "strength."

Verse 11. *I said in my haste*] This is variously translated: *I said in my flight,* CHALDEE. In my *excess,* or ecstasy, VULGATE. In my *ecstasy,* εκστασει, SEPTUAGINT. فى تهايرى *fi tahayury,* in my *giddiness,* ARABIC. In my *fear* or *tremor,* SYRIAC. ܠܩ ܣ̈ܦ܊ *on uczange mnum, I quoth in outgoing mine,* when I was *beside* myself, ANGLO-SAXON. In mȳn oute passyng, *old Psalter.* When passion got the better of my reason, when I looked not at God, but at my afflictions, and the impossibility of human relief.

All men are liars.] כל האדם כזב *col haadam cozeb,* "the whole of man is a lie." Falsity is diffused through his nature; deception proceeds from his tongue; his actions are often counterfeit. He is imposed on by others, and imposes in his turn; and on none is there any dependence till God converts their heart.

> "O what a thing were man, if his *attires*
> Should *alter* with his *mind,*
> And, like a *dolphin's skin,*
> His *clothes* combine with his desires!
> Surely if each one saw another's heart,
> There would be no commerce;
> All would disperse,
> And live apart."   HERBERT.

To the same purpose I shall give the following Italian proverb:—

> Con arte e con inganno,
> Si vive mezzo l'anno.

Con inganno e con arte
Si vive l' altro parti.

> "Men live half the year by deceit and by art;
> By art and deceit men live the other part."

Who gives this bad character of mankind? MAN.

Verse 12. *What shall I render*] מה אשיב *mah ashib,* "What shall I return?"

For his benefits] תגמולוהי *tagmulohi,* "His retributions," the returns he had made to my prayers and faith.

Verse 13. *I will take the cup of salvation*] Literally, *The cup of salvation,* or *deliverance, will I lift up.* Alluding to the action in taking the *cup of blessing* among the Jews, which, when the person or master of the family *lifted up,* he said these words, "Blessed be the Lord, the Maker of the world, who has created the fruit of the vine!"

But it may probably allude to the libation-offering, Num. xxviii. 7; for the *three* last verses seem to intimate that the psalmist was now at the temple, offering the meat-offering, drink-offering, and sacrifices to the Lord. *Cup* is often used by the Hebrews to denote *plenty* or *abundance.* So, *the cup of trembling,* an abundance of *misery; the cup of salvation,* an abundance of *happiness.*

And call upon the name of the Lord.] I will *invoke* his name, that I may get more of the same blessings; for the only *return* that God requires is, that we ask for *more.* Who is like GOD? One reason why we should never more come to a fellow-mortal for a favour is, we have received so many already. A strong reason why we should claim the utmost salvation of God is, because we are already *so much in debt* to his mercy. Now this is the only way we have of discharging our debts to God; and yet, strange to tell, every such attempt to discharge the debt only serves to *increase* it! Yet, notwithstanding, the debtor and creditor are represented as both *pleased,* both *profited,* and both *happy* in each other! Reader, pray to him, invoke his name; receive the cup—accept the *abundance of salvation* which he has provided thee, that thou mayest love and serve him with a perfect heart.

Verse 14. *I will pay my vows unto the Lord now in the presence of all his people.*] He was probably now bringing his offering to the temple. These words are repeated, ver. 18.

Verse 15. *Precious in the sight of the Lord*] Many have understood this verse as meaning, "the saints are too precious in the Lord's sight, lightly to give them over to death:" and this, *Calmet* contends, is the true sense of the text. Though they have many enemies, their lives are precious in his sight, and their foes shall not prevail against them.

A. M. cir. 3489
B. C. cir. 515
Darii I.,
R. Persarum,
cir. annum
sextum
16 O Lord, truly qI *am* thy servant; I *am* thy servant, *and* rthe son of thine handmaid: thou hast loosed my bonds.

17 I will offer to thee sthe sacrifice of thanksgiving, and will call upon the name of the Lord.

18 tI will pay my vows unto the Lord now in the presence of all his people,

19 In the ucourts of the Lord's house, in the midst of thee, O Jerusalem. Praise ye the Lord.

A. M. cir. 3489
B. C. cir. 515
Darii I.,
R. Persarum,
cir. annum
sextum

---

qPsalm cxix. 125; cxliii. 12——rPsalm lxxxvi. 16

sLev. vii. 12; Psa. l. 14; cvii. 22——tVer. 14——uPsa. xcvi. 8; c. 4; cxxxv. 2

Verse 16. *I am thy servant*] Thou hast preserved me alive. I live *with, for,* and *to* Thee. I am thy *willing domestic, the son of thine handmaid*—like one born in thy house of a woman already thy property. I am a *servant,* son of *thy servant,* made free by thy kindness; but, refusing *to go out,* I have had my *ear bored to thy door-post,* and am to continue by *free choice* in thy house for ever. He alludes here to the case of the servant who, in the year of jubilee being entitled to his liberty, refused to leave his master's house; and suffered his ear to be bored to the door-post, as a proof that by his own consent he agreed to continue in his master's house for ever.

Verse 17. *I will offer to thee*] As it is most probable that this Psalm celebrates the *deliverance from Babylon,* it is no wonder that we find the psalmist so intent on performing the *rites* of his religion in the temple at Jerusalem, which had been burnt with fire, and was now reviving out of its ruins, the temple service having been wholly interrupted for nearly fourscore years.

Verse 19. *In the midst of thee, O Jerusalem.*] He speaks as if present in the city, offering his vowed *sacrifices* in the temple to the Lord.

Most of this Psalm has been applied to *our Lord* and his *Church;* and in this way it has been considered as *prophetic;* and, taken thus, it is innocently accommodated, and is very edifying. This is the interpretation given of the whole by the *old Psalter.*

ANALYSIS OF THE HUNDRED AND SIXTEENTH PSALM

This Psalm is gratulatory; for it shows how great straits the psalmist was brought into, from which God delivered him.

This Psalm has *three* parts:—

I. The psalmist makes profession of his love, and shows the reasons of it: God's goodness in hearing and delivering him from his low and sad condition, ver. 1-9.

II. He professes his duty and faith, ver. 9-11.

III. He promises to be thankful, and in what manner, ver. 12-19.

I. He begins with the expression of his content and love: "I love the Lord." And he gives these reasons:—

1. "Because he hath heard," &c. This is reason enough why I should love him.

2. "Because he hath inclined," &c. An evidence that he was heard. Upon which experience that he was heard he adds: "Therefore will I call," &c.

Another reason which moved him to love God was, that he heard him in the extremity of his deep distress; for,—

1. "The sorrows of death," &c. Death is the king of fear.

2. "The pains of hell," &c. He feared the anger of God for his sins.

3. "I found trouble and sorrow." The psalmist was sensible of his condition: though others might suppose him compassed with prosperity, yet he knew himself distressed.

But he prayed to the Lord.

1. "Then." In these troubles and pangs.

2. "I called upon," &c. Invocation to God was his sole refuge.

3. "O Lord, I beseech thee," &c. He sets down the very words of his prayer.

And then, that he might show that he prayed to God in faith and hope, he points out the attributes of God for the encouragement of others.

1. "God is gracious." It is he who inspires prayer and repentance, remits sin, and pardons those who fly in faith to him for mercy.

2. "And righteous and just." He will perform what he has promised.

3. "Yea, our God is merciful." He mingles mercy with his justice; he corrects with a father's hand, and loves to forgive rather than to punish. Of which David gives an instance in himself: "I was brought low, and he helped me." And all others may find the same who come in the way that I did to him for pardon.

Another reason he gives for loving God was, the tranquillity of soul he found after this storm was over: "Therefore, return unto thy rest, O my soul." Hitherto thou hast been tossed up and down on the waves of sorrow, finding no port or haven: now faith has opened to thee a harbour where thou mayest be safe: "For the Lord hath dealt," &c.: but of his infinite mercy he has given thee joy for sadness.

He attributes to him the whole of his work.

1. "Thou hast delivered," &c. Turned my heaviness into joy, by removing all fear of death.

2. "Thou hast delivered my eyes," &c. Made me joyful.

3. "Thou hast delivered my feet," &c. When my infirmity is great, the devil takes advantage of me that I might fall; but now thou hast settled my feet—made me able to resist him. And this God does for all who call upon him, and trust in him.

II. The psalmist, having expressed his sorrows and God's goodness, now professes his dutiful attachment, 1. By his obedience; 2. By a faithful confession of his errors, and future confidence.

1. "I will walk before the Lord," &c. Be careful to please God, by walking. not after the flesh, but after the Spirit.

He professes his faith, on which he will evermore rely.

1. "I believed, and therefore," &c. Which confidence came from faith.

2. "I was greatly afflicted," &c.; but I became

docile and humble to the Spirit of God. When David was tossed between hope and despair, he found those sorrows were not easily quieted; for "I said in my haste," &c.

Which clause is differently understood by commentators.

1. Some suppose it to be an amplification of his former grief. I was so amazed, and overwhelmed with sorrow, that if any one reminded me of God's promises, "I said in my haste, All men are liars." I will not believe God; he hath no care for me.

2. Others again refer this clause to the preceding: They talk of happiness and felicity, but none is to be found in the land of the living.

3. Some again refer it to *Absalom*, who deceived *David* by his vow at *Hebron;* or to *Ahithophel*, who revolted from him.

4. Again, others suppose that he taxed even *Samuel* himself that he spoke not by God's Spirit, when he anointed him king over Israel; because, during Saul's persecution, there appeared so little hope of it. But the first sense is the most cogent.

III. Henceforth, to the end of the Psalm, David declares his gratitude: "What shall I render to the Lord," &c. As if he had said, I acknowledge the benefits God has bestowed upon me; but in what way can I best evince my gratitude?

1. "I will take the cup of salvation." Here interpreters vary as to what is to be understood by the *cup of salvation*. 1. Some refer it to the ucharistical sacrifices of the old law, in which, when a man offered a sacrifice to God for some deliverance, he made a feast to the people, as did David, 1 Chron. i., ii., iii. 2. The fathers understood it of the cup of patience and affliction, which is often in Scripture called a cup, Matt. xx. 22. 3. But here it seems to signify plenty, abundance, &c. See the note.

2. "I will pay my vows," &c. It was usual in God's service to make vows, or to confess his name in an open assembly. God cares for all his people, however circumstanced; for *precious in the sight of the Lord* is *the death of his saints.* The servants of God trouble themselves in vain when they distrust him; for in life he is with them, and in death he will not forsake them.

The psalmist does not become proud upon God's favours; but in all humility, though a king, he exclaims,—

1. "O Lord, truly I *am* thy servant," &c.

2. And yet no slave, but a willing servant: "Thou hast loosed my bonds,"—taken from my neck the bonds of fear: thou hast made me thy servant through love.

3. And therefore will I do what thy servants ought to do.

Showing his earnestness he repeats again, "I will offer to thee the sacrifice of thanksgiving, and will call upon the name of the Lord. I will pay my vows unto the Lord now in the presence of all his people, in the courts of the Lord's house, in the midst of thee, O Jerusalem. Praise ye the Lord." *Within* the Church, and at all times, he would praise and do him worship. What is not done according to God's word and Spirit is of little service. He who neglects *public worship* is not very likely to keep up private devotion, either in his *family* or in his *closet.* "I will pay my vows in the midst of thee, O Jerusalem."

PSALM CXVII

The psalmist calls upon the nations of the world to praise the Lord for his mercy and kindness, and for the fulfilment of his promises, 1, 2.

A. M. cir. 3489
B. C. cir. 515
Darii I.,
R. Persarum,
cir. annum
sextum

O ª PRAISE the Lord, all ye nations: praise him, all ye people.

2 For his merciful kindness is great toward us: and the ᵇtruth of the Lord *endureth* for ever. Praise ye the Lord.

A. M. cir. 3489
B. C. cir. 515
Darii I.,
R. Persarum,
cir. annum
sextum

ª Rom. xv. 11

ᵇ Psa. c. 5

NOTES ON PSALM CXVII

This is the shortest Psalm in the whole collection; it is written as a part of the preceding in thirty-two of *Kennicott's* and *De Rossi's* MSS. and is found thus printed in some ancient editions. The whole Psalm is omitted in one of *Kennicott's* and in two of *De Rossi's* MSS. It celebrates the redemption from the Babylonish captivity, the grand type of the redemption of the world by our Lord Jesus.

The *Syriac* says: "It was spoken concerning Ananias and his followers when they came out of the furnace; but it also foretells the vocation of the Gentiles by the preaching of the Gospel." In this way St. Paul applies it, Rom. xv. 11.

Verse 1. *O praise the Lord, all ye nations*]

Let all the *Gentiles* praise him, for he provides for their eternal salvation.

Praise him, all ye people.] All ye *Jews*, praise him; for ye have long been his peculiar people. And while he sends his Son to be *a light to the Gentiles*, he sends him also to be *the glory of his people Israel.*

Verse 2. *For his merciful kindness is great*] נבר *gabar*, is *strong:* it is not only *great* in *bulk* or *number*, but it is *powerful;* it *prevails* over *sin, Satan, death*, and *hell.*

And the truth of the Lord endureth for ever.] Whatsoever he has *promised*, that he will most infallibly *fulfil.* He has promised to *send his Son into the world*, and thus he *has done.* He his promised that he should *die for transgressors*, and this he *did.* He has promised to *receive all who come unto him* through Christ

Jesus, and this he invariably *does*. He has promised that his *Gospel shall be preached in every nation*, and this he *is doing;* the truth of the Lord remaineth for ever. Therefore, *Praise ye the Lord!*

ANALYSIS OF THE HUNDRED AND SEVENTEENTH PSALM

This Psalm contains a *doxology* to God for his *mercy* and *truth;* and it is *prophetical,* having reference to the calling of the Gentiles; Rom. xv. 11.

It contains two parts:—

I. An *exhortation* to praise God.

II. The *reason* for it.

I. 1. He speaks to the *Gentiles:* "Praise the Lord, all ye nations." Praise him for the *promise* of salvation; and then, when fulfilled, praise him for the *enjoyment* of this salvation,—for the *remission* of sins, and gift *of the Holy Ghost.*

2. He speaks to the converted *Jews,* whom he notes under the name of *people,* as they are

called Psa. ii. 1; Acts iv. 25. As they and the *Gentiles* are intended to make *one Church,* so they should join in the praise of him *of whom the whole family in heaven and earth is named.*

II. The *reason* given:—

1. Because *his mercy is great.* It is strong; *confirmed* toward us, in sending his Son to save both Jews and Gentiles from their sins.

2. Because the truth of his promises is *fulfilled.* The promised Messiah *is come,* and *has performed* all that was prophesied of him.

3. Because this truth is *forever.* His *promises* and their *fulfilment* belong to *all generations.* There will never be another Messiah; Jesus is the true one: he tasted death for every man; he forgives iniquity, transgression, and sin; and his blood cleanses from all unrighteousness. Now, for all this, "Praise ye the Lord!"

[*N. B.* Proclaiming the eternal mercy of God in Christ is more likely to persuade sinners to return to their Maker than all the fire of hell.]

PSALM CXVIII

A general exhortation to praise God for his mercy, 1–4. *The psalmist, by his own experience, encourages the people to trust in God, and shows them the advantage of it,* 5–9; *then describes his enemies, and shows how God enabled him to destroy them,* 10–13. *The people rejoice on the account,* 15, 16. *He speaks again of the help he received from the Lord; and desires admission into the temple, that he may enter and praise the Lord,* 17–19. *The gate is opened,* 20. *He offers praise,* 21. *The priests, &c., acknowledge the hand of the Lord in the deliverance wrought,* 22–24. *The psalmist prays for prosperity,* 25. *The priest performs his office, blesses the people, and* all *join in praise,* 26, 27. *The* psalmist *expresses his confidence,* 28. *The* general doxology, *or chorus,* 29.

O ªGIVE thanks unto the LORD; for *he is* good : because his mercy *endureth* for ever.

2 ᵇLet Israel now say, that his mercy *endureth* for ever.

ª1 Chron. xvi. 8, 24; Psa. cvi. 1; cvii. 1; cxxxvi. 1

ᵇSee Psa. cxv. 9, &c.

NOTES ON PSALM CXVIII

Most probably David was the author of this Psalm, though many think it was written after the captivity. It partakes of David's spirit, and every where shows the hand of a *master.* The *style* is grand and noble; the *subject,* majestic.

Dr. *Kennicott,* who joins this and the *hundred and seventeenth* Psalm together, considers the whole as a *dialogue,* and divides it accordingly. The whole of the *hundred and seventeenth* he gives to the *psalmist* as part the *first,* with the first four verses of the *hundred and eighteenth.* The *second part,* which is from the *fifth* verse to the *twenty-first* inclusive, he gives to the *Messiah.* The *third part,* from the *twenty-second* verse to the *twenty-seventh,* he gives to the *chorus.* And the *fourth part,* the *twenty-eighth* and *twenty-ninth* verses, he gives to the *psalmist.* Of the whole he has given an improved version.

Bishop *Horsley* is still different. He considers the *hundred and seventeenth* Psalm as only the exordium of this. The whole poem, he states, is a triumphant processional song. The scene passes at the front gate of the temple. A con-

queror with his train appears before it; he demands admittance to return thanks for his deliverance and final success, in an expedition of great difficulty and danger. The *conqueror* and his *train* sing the *hundred and seventeenth* Psalm, and the first four verses of the *hundred and eighteenth,* as they advance to the gate of the temple, in this manner.—The *hundred and seventeenth* Psalm, *Chorus of the whole procession.* The *first* verse of the *hundred and eighteenth* Psalm, A *single voice.* The *second,* Another *single voice.* The *third,* A third *single voice.* The *fourth, Chorus of the whole procession.* Arrived at the temple gate, the *conqueror alone* sings the *fifth, sixth,* and *seventh* verses. The *eighth* and *ninth* are sung by his *train* in *chorus.* The *conqueror,* again *alone,* sings the *tenth, eleventh, twelfth, thirteenth,* and *fourteenth* verses. His *train,* in *chorus,* sing the *fifteenth* and *sixteenth.* The *conqueror alone* sings the *seventeenth, eighteenth,* and *nineteenth* verses. The *twentieth* is sung by the *priests* and *Levites* within, in *chorus.* The *twenty-fifth* by the *conqueror alone* within the gates. The *twenty-sixth,* by the *priests* and *Levites* in *chorus.* The *twenty-seventh,* by the

3 Let the house of Aaron now say, that his mercy *endureth* for ever.

4 Let them now that fear the Lord say, that his mercy *endureth* for ever.

5 [c]I called upon the Lord [d]in distress: the Lord answered me, *and* [e]*set* me in a large place.

6 [f]The Lord *is* [g]on my side; I will not fear: what can man do unto me?

7 [h]The Lord taketh my part with them that help me: therefore shall [i]I see *my desire* upon them that hate me.

8 [k]*It is* better to trust in the Lord than to put confidence in man.

9 [l]*It is* better to trust in the Lord than to put confidence in princes.

10 All nations compassed me about: but in the name of the Lord will I [m]destroy them.

11 They [n]compassed me about; yea, they compassed me about: but in the name of the Lord I will destroy them.

12 They compassed me about [o]like bees; they are quenched [p]as the fire of thorns: for in the name of the Lord I will [q]destroy them.

---

[c]Psa. cxx. 1——[d]Heb. *out of distress*——[e]Psa. xviii. 19——[f]Psa. xxvii. 1; lvi. 4, 11; cxlvi. 5; Isa. li. 12; Heb. xiii. 6——[g]Heb. *for me*——[h]Psa. liv. 4——[i]Psa. lix. 10

[k]Psa. xl. 4; lxii. 8, 9; Jer. xvii. 5, 7——[l]Psa. cxlvi. 3 [m]Heb. *cut them off*——[n]Psa. lxxxviii. 17——[o]Deut. i. 44 [p]Eccles. vii. 6; Nah. i. 10——[q]Heb. *cut down*

---

conqueror's train in *chorus.* The *twenty-eighth,* by the *conqueror alone.* The *twenty-ninth,* by the *united chorus* of *priests* and *Levites,* and the *conqueror's train,* all within the gates. "Now," the learned bishop adds, "the *Jewish temple* was a type of *heaven; the priests* within represent the *angelic host* attending round the throne of God in heaven; the *Conqueror* is *Messiah;* and his *train,* the *redeemed.*" On this distribution the bishop has given a new version. The simple distribution into parts, which I have given in the *contents,* is, in my opinion, the best. Ingenious as Dr. *Kennicott* and Bishop *Horsley* are, they seem to me too *mechanical.* This is the last of those Psalms which form the great *hallel,* which the Jews sung at the end of the *passover.*

Verse 2. *Let Israel now say*] Seeing the hand of the Lord so visibly, and the deliverance gained, that *God's mercy endureth for ever.*

Verse 3. *The house of Aaron*] The priesthood is still preserved, and the temple worship restored.

Verse 4. *That fear the Lord*] All sincere penitents and genuine believers. See the notes on Psa. cxv. 9-11.

Verse 5. *I called upon the Lord*] I am a standing proof and living witness of God's mercy. Take encouragement from me.

Verse 7. *The Lord taketh my part with them that help me*] Literally, *The Lord is to me among my helpers. Therefore shall I see* my desire *upon them that hate me.* Literally, *And I shall look among them that hate me.* As God is on my side, I fear not to look the whole of them in the face. I shall see them defeated.

Verse 8. *Better to trust in the Lord*] Man is feeble, ignorant, fickle, and capricious; it is better to trust in Jehovah than in such.

Verse 9. *In princes.*] Men of high estate are generally *proud, vain-glorious, self-confident,* and *rash:* it is better to trust in God than in them. Often they *cannot* deliver, and often they *will not* when they *can.* However, in the concerns of our *salvation,* and in matters which belong to *Providence,* they can do nothing.

Verse 10. *All nations compassed me about*] This is by some supposed to relate to David, at the commencement of his reign, when all the neighbouring Philistine nations endeavoured to prevent him from establishing himself in the kingdom. Others suppose it may refer to the

Samaritans, Idumeans, *Ammonites,* and others, who endeavoured to prevent the Jews from rebuilding their city and their temple after their return from captivity in Babylon.

But in the name of the Lord will I destroy them.] Dr. *Kennicott* renders אֲסִימִלָם *amilam,* "I shall *disappoint them;*" Bishop *Horsley,* "I cut them to pieces;" Mr. *N. Berlin, repuli eas,* "I have *repelled* them." "I will *cut them off;*" *Chaldee. Ultus sum in eos,* "I am *avenged* on them;" *Vulgate.* So the *Septuagint.*

Verse 12. *They compassed me about like bees; they are quenched as the fire of thorns*] I shall refer to Dr. *Delaney's* note on this passage. The reader has here in miniature two of the finest images in Homer; which, if his curiosity demands to be gratified, he will find illustrated and enlarged, Iliad ii., ver. 86.

—— Επεσσευοντο δε λαοι.

Ηὔτε εθνεα εισι μελισσαων αδιναων,
Πετρης εκ γλαφυρης αιει νεον ερχομεναων,
Βοτρυδον δε πετονται επ' ανθεσιν ειαρινοισιν,
Αἱ μεν τ' ενθα ἁλις πεποτηαται, αι δε τε ενθα·
'Ὡς των εθνεα πολλα νεων απο και κλισιαων
Ηϊονος προπαροιθε βαθειης εστιχοωντο
Ιλαδον εις αγορην.

———— The following host,
Poured forth by thousands, darkens all the coast.
As from some rocky cleft the shepherd sees,
Clustering in heaps on heaps, the driving bees,
Rolling and blackening, swarms succeeding swarms,
With deeper murmurs and more hoarse alarms:
Dusky they spread a close embodied crowd,
And o'er the vale descends the living cloud;
So from the tents and ships a lengthening train
Spreads all the beach, and wide o'ershades the plain;
Along the region runs a deafening sound;
Beneath their footsteps groans the trembling ground.   POPE.

The other image, *the fire consuming the thorns,* we find in the same book, ver. 455:—

Ηὔτε πυρ αἴδηλον επιφλεγει ασπετον ὑλην,
Ουρεος εν κορυφης· ἑκαθεν δε τε φαινεται αυγη·
'Ὡς των ερχομενων, απο χαλκου θεσπεσιοιο
Αιγλη παμφανοωσα δι' αιθερος ουρανον ἱκεν,

13 Thou hast thrust sore at me that I might fall: but the LORD helped me.

14 ʳThe LORD *is* my strength and song, and is become my salvation.

15 The voice of rejoicing and salvation *is* in the tabernacles of the righteous: the right hand of the LORD doeth valiantly.

16 ˢThe right hand of the LORD is exalted: the right hand of the LORD doeth valiantly.

17 ᵗI shall not die, but live, and ᵘdeclare the works of the LORD.

18 The LORD hath ᵛchastened me sore: but he hath not given me over unto death.

19 ʷOpen to me the gates of righteousness: I will go in to them, *and* I will praise the LORD:

20 ˣThis gate of the LORD, ʸinto which the righteous shall enter.

21 I will praise thee: for thou hast ᶻheard me, and ᵃart become my salvation.

22 ᵇThe stone *which* the builders refused is become the head *stone* of the corner.

23 ᶜThis is the LORD'S doing: it *is* marvellous in our eyes.

24 This *is* the day *which* the LORD hath made; we will rejoice and be glad in it.

25 Save now, I beseech thee, O LORD: O LORD, I beseech thee, send now prosperity.

26 ᵈBlessed *be* he that cometh in the name of the LORD: we have blessed you out of the house of the LORD.

27 God *is* the LORD, which hath showed us ᵉlight: bind the sacrifice with cords, *even* unto the horns of the altar.

28 Thou *art* my God, and I will praise thee: ᶠ*thou art* my God, I will exalt thee.

29 ᵍO give thanks unto the LORD, for *he is* good: for his mercy *endureth* for ever.

ʳExod. xv. 2; Isa. xii. 2——ˢExod. xv. 6——ᵗPsa. vi. 5; Hab. i. 12——ᵘPsa. lxxiii. 28——ᵛ2 Cor. vi. 9 ʷIsa. xxvi. 2——ˣPsa. xxiv. 7——ʸIsa. xxxv. 8; Rev. xxi. 27; xxii. 14, 15——ᶻPsa. cxvi. 1——ᵃVer. 14 ᵇMatt. xxi. 42; Mark xii. 10; Luke xx. 17; Acts iv. 11;

Ephesians ii. 20; 1 Peter ii. 4, 7——ᵉHebrew, *This is from the LORD*——ᵈMatthew xxi. 9; xxiii. 39; Mark xi. 9; Luke xix. 38; see Zechariah iv. 7——ᵉEsther viii. 16; 1 Peter ii. 9——ᶠExodus xv. 2; Isaiah xxv. 1 ᵍVer. 1

As on some mountain, through the lofty grove,
The crackling flames ascend and blaze above;
The fires expanding, as the winds arise,
Shoot their long beams, and kindle half the skies;
So, from the polished arms, and brazen shields,
A gleamy splendour flashed along the fields.
POPE.

The arms resembling a gleaming *fire* is common both to the psalmist and Homer; but the idea of that fire being *quenched* when the army was *conquered*, is peculiar to the psalmist.

Verse 13. *Thou hast thrust sore at me*] In pushing thou hast pushed me that I might fall.

But the Lord helped me.] Though he possessed skill, courage, and strength, yet these could not have prevailed had not God been his *helper;* and to him he gives the glory of the victory.

Verse 15. *The voice of rejoicing*] Formerly there was nothing but wailings; but *now* there is universal joy because of the *salvation*—the deliverance, which God has wrought for us.

Verse 16. *The right hand of the Lord is exalted*] Jehovah *lifted up* his right hand, and with it performed prodigies of power.

Verse 17. *I shall not die*] I was nigh unto death; but I am preserved,—preserved to publish the wondrous works of the Lord.

Verse 19. *Open to me the gates*] Throw open the doors of the temple, that I may enter and perform my vows unto the Lord.

Verse 20. *This gate of the Lord*] Supposed to be the answer of the Levites to the request of the king.

Verse 21. *I will praise thee*] He is now got within the gates, and breaks out into thanksgivings for the mercies he had received. *He is become my salvation*—he himself hath saved me from all mine enemies.

Verses 22, 23. *The stone* which *the builders*

refused] See a full elucidation of these two verses in the notes on Matt. xxi. 42.

Verse 24. *This* is *the day* which *the Lord hath made*] As the Lord hath called me to triumph, this is the day which he hath appointed for that purpose. This is a *gracious opportunity;* I will improve it to his glory.

Verse 25. *Save now, I beseech thee*] These words were sung by the Jews on the feast of tabernacles, when carrying green branches in their hands; and from the הושיעה נא *hoshiah nna*, we have the word *hosanna*. This was sung by the Jewish children when Christ made his public entry into Jerusalem. See Matt. xxi. 9, and see the note there, in which the word and the circumstance are both explained.

Verse 26. *We have blessed you*] The answer of the Levites to the king.

Verse 27. *God* is *the Lord*] Rather אל יהוה *El Yehovah*, the strong God Jehovah.

Which hath showed us light] ויאר לנו *vaiyaer lanu*, "And he will illuminate us." Perhaps at this time a Divine splendour shone upon the whole procession; a proof of God's approbation.

Bind the sacrifice with cords] The *Chaldee* paraphrases this verse thus: "Samuel the prophet said, Bind the little one with chains for a solemn sacrifice, until ye have sacrificed him and sprinkled his blood on the horns of the altar." It is supposed that the words refer to the feast of tabernacles, and חג *chag* here means the *festival victim.* Several translate the original "keep the festival with thick boughs of the horns of the altar." In this sense the *Vulgate* and *Septuagint* understood the passage. David in this entry into the temple was a type of our blessed Lord, who made a similar entry, as related Matt. xxi. 8-10.

Verse 29. *O give thanks unto the Lord*] This is the general doxology or chorus. All join in thanksgiving, and they *end* as they began: "His mercy endureth for ever." It began at the creation of man; it will continue till the earth is burnt up.

ANALYSIS OF THE HUNDRED AND EIGHTEENTH PSALM

The parts of this Psalm are the following:—
I. An exhortation to praise God for his mercy, ver. 1-5.
II. A persuasion to trust in God, and that from the psalmist's own example, who called upon God, and was delivered from trouble, ver. 5-14.
III. The exultation of the Church for it, ver. 15-18.
IV. A solemn thanksgiving kept for it, and in what manner it was celebrated, ver. 19-27.
V. A short doxology.
1. The psalmist invites all to praise God: "O give thanks," &c., and adds his reasons:—
1. "For he is good." How briefly and powerfully spoken! He is absolutely good.
2. "He is good, and ever good." To us he is a merciful God, which flows from his goodness; his mercy created, redeemed, protects, and will crown. us. Thus his mercy extends especially to his people; therefore,—
1. "Let Israel now say," &c. The whole nation.
2. "Let the house of Aaron," &c. That whole consecrated tribe.
3. "Let them now that fear the Lord," &c. Proselytes, &c.
II. And thus, having given a general recommendation of his mercy, he descends to instance in what it consists; that is, God's great deliverance of him.
1. "I was in distress,' &c. A frequent case with God's people, as well as with David.
2. "I called upon the lord," &c. I fled to him, not trusting in myself, and found mercy.
3. "The Lord answered me, and set me in a large place." This was the issue.
Upon which experience the psalmist exults, and attributes it to God's mercy.
1. "The Lord is my helper," &c. The Lord is for me, therefore I shall not suffer.
2. "The Lord takes my part," &c. I shall be in safety, while my enemies will be cast down, and the Church freed.
From which he deduces a third inference:—
1. "It is better to trust in the Lord," &c.— He is both able and willing to help.
2. "It is better to trust in the Lord than to put confidence in princes." *David* found this in the case of *Achish,* king of *Gath.*
In a song of triumph he acquaints us in what dangers he was, and from which God delivered him. It is good then to trust in the Lord.
1. "All nations compassed me about," &c., but to no purpose.
2. "They compassed me about; yea, they compassed me about," &c.
3. "They compassed me about like bees," &c. Angry, and armed with stings; but my trust is alone in the Lord. In his name, and by his help, "I will destroy them."

He told us of a multitude of enemies; and for the overthrow of these he sang his triumph.
1. "Thou hast thrust sore at me," &c. I was in great danger; there was little hope of escape.
2. "But the Lord helped me." No help was in myself, but the Lord.
In the next verse he fully acknowledges the Lord as his strength.
1. "My strength." By which I resist my enemies.
2. "My salvation." To deliver me from my enemies.
3. "My song." Him whom I joyfully sing after my deliverance.
III. And that this song might be fuller, he calls for the whole choir to sing with him. His delivery concerned the whole Church, and therefore it must be sung by the whole Church; and so it was kept as a jubilee, a day of thanksgiving.
1. "The voice of rejoicing," &c. They congratulate their own safety in mine.
2. "The right hand of the Lord," &c. This anthem the whole choir sang.
Now this anthem was no sooner ended by the choir, than the psalmist took his harp again; and, exulting over his enemies, sings, "I shall not die," &c. Not be heart-broken, but "declare the works of the Lord."
And among his works this is one:—
1. "The Lord hath chastened me sore," &c. Within have I struggled hard with sin; without have I been assaulted with bitter enemies.
2. "But he hath not given me over," &c. I acknowledge in this his fatherly affection.
IV. It is supposed that this Psalm was composed by *David,* in order that it might be sung when the people and the priests were assembled before the Lord, for the purpose of thanksgiving; we may, with *Junius,* form it into a dialogue.
1. David speaks of the *priests* and *Levites* who had the care of the tabernacle: "Open to me the gates," &c., that is, the Lord's house; "for I will go in to them," &c.
2. To this the priests reply, "This is the gate," &c. The sole gate of justice that leads to him.
David replies, showing in brief his reason: "I will praise thee," &c.; and to the *twenty-eighth* verse, he shows how God had settled him in his kingdom, making him "the head of the corner;" which words, though they refer to David, there is no doubt of their having reference also to Christ, of whom David was a type; and of Christ then I shall rather interpret them.
"The stone which the builders refused," &c.
1. The Church is sometimes in Scripture called a building; the saints are the living stones, and Christ is "the chief Corner-stone."
2. But the *Jews,* the priests, to whom belonged the office of building the Church, refused this stone: "We will not have this man," &c.
3. But "he is become the head of the corner." And whoever is not connected with him cannot be saved. 1. "This was the Lord's doing," &c.

That Christ became our salvation. 2. "And it is marvellous in our eyes." And so it ever must be, that Christ should die, the just for the unjust, to bring us to God.

In commemoration of so great a work, a day should be set apart.

1. "This is the day," &c. Which without doubt was the day of the resurrection; the Lord making it a high and holy day.

2. "We will be glad and rejoice," &c. Adam's fall was a doleful day. On the day of Christ's resurrection we will be glad.

3. In the midst of our rejoicing we will pray, and sound forth Hosanna to the Son of David. This was done by the people on the entering of Christ into *Jerusalem.* It was the opinion of the Jews that this form of acclamation would be used before the *Messiah.*

The whole prophecy of Christ's coming, riding into Jerusalem in triumph, rejection, passion, &c., being thus explained, the prophet puts this into the mouths of the priests:—

"We have blessed you." All true happiness is under this King.

2. "Out of the house of the Lord," &c. From out of the Church.

3. "God is the Lord," &c. Revealed unto us his Son as the Light of the world.

4. "Bind the sacrifice with cords," &c. Be thankful to him, and meet in the Church to celebrate your thanksgivings.

V. The prophet concludes with a doxology.

1. "Thou art my God," I have taken thee for my portion.

2. "And I will praise thee;" which he doubles: "Thou art my God, and I will exalt thee." Which repetition shows his ardent desire of evincing his gratitude.

And thus the psalmist concludes with the same exhortation with which he began the Psalm.

"O give thanks unto the Lord, for he is good; for his mercy endureth for ever." And let him that readeth, and him that heareth, say, Amen!

THIS is an uncommonly fine Psalm, and among the many noble ones it is one of the most noble. Its beauties are so many and so prominent that every reader, whose mind is at all influenced by spiritual things, must see, feel, and admire them.

The 22nd verse, "The stone which the builders rejected is become the head stone of the corner," must have been a *proverbial* expression; but what gave birth to it I cannot find; but, like all other proverbs, it doubtless had its origin from some *fact.* One thing is evident from the Jewish doctors. The most enlightened of them understand this as a prophecy of the *Messiah;* and it was this general opinion, as well as the knowledge that the Spirit of prophecy thus intended it, that caused our Lord to apply it to himself, Matt. xxi. 42; nor did any of them attempt to dispute the propriety of the application.

PSALM CXIX

The various excellencies and important uses of the law or revelation of God.

א ALEPH

BLESSED *are* the [a]undefiled in the way, [b]who walk in the law of the LORD.

2 Blessed *are* they that keep his testimonies, *and that* seek him with the whole heart.

3 [c]They also do no iniquity: they walk in his ways.

[a]Or, *perfect* or *sincere*——[b]Psa. cxxviii. 4

[c]1 John iii. 9; v. 18

NOTES ON PSALM CXIX

This is another of the *alphabetical* or *acrostic* Psalms. It is divided into *twenty-two* parts, answering to the *number* of letters in the *Hebrew alphabet.* Every *part* is divided into *eight verses;* and each verse begins with that letter of the alphabet which forms the *title* of the part, *e. g.:* The *eight* first verses have א *aleph* prefixed, the second *eight* ב *beth,* each of the *eight* verses beginning with *that* letter; and so of the rest. All *connexion,* as might be naturally expected, is sacrificed to this artificial and methodical arrangement.

It is not easy to give any general *Analysis* of this Psalm; it is enough to say that it treats in general on the privileges and happiness of those who observe the law of the Lord. That law is exhibited by various names and epithets tending to show its various excellences. Earnest prayers are offered to God for wisdom to understand it, and for grace to observe it faithfully. These particulars may be collected from the *whole* composition, and appear less or more in *every part.*

The words which express that *revelation* which God had then given to men, or some *particular characteristic* of it, are generally reckoned to be the *ten* following: 1. *Testimonies;* 2. *Commandments;* 3. *Precepts;* 4. *Word;* 5. *Law;* 6. *Ways;* 7. *Truth;* 8. *Judgments*; 9. *Righteousness;* 10. *Statutes.* To these some add the following: 1. *Faithfulness;* 2. *Judgment;* 3. *Name;* but these are not used in the sense of the other *ten* words. I believe it is almost universally asserted that in *every verse* of this Psalm one or other of those *ten* words is used, except in ver. 122; but on a closer inspection we shall find that none of them is used in the above sense in the 84th, 90th, 121st, 122nd, and 132nd. See the notes on these verses.

To save myself unnecessary repetition, and the reader time and trouble, I shall here, once for all, explain the above words, which the reader will do well to keep in remembrance.

1. The LAW, תורה TORAH, from ירה *yarah,* to

4 Thou hast commanded *us* to [d]keep thy precepts diligently.

5 O that my ways were directed to [e]keep thy statutes!

---

[d]Exod. xv. 26; Isa. xxviii. 10, 13——[e]Lev. xviii. 5, 26; xix.

19; xx. 8, 22; Deut. iv. 20; vi. 2; xxvi. 17; xxviii. 45; xxx. 10

---

direct, guide, teach, make straight, or *even, point forward;* because it *guides, directs,* and *instructs* in the way of righteousness; makes our path *straight,* shows what is *even* and *right,* and points us *onward* to peace, truth, and happiness. It is even our *school-master* to bring us to Christ, that we may be justified through faith; and by it is the knowledge of sin.

II. STATUTES, חקים CHUKKIM, *from* חק *chak,* to *mark, trace out, describe,* and *ordain;* because they *mark out* our way, describe the line of conduct we are to pursue, and *order* or *ordain* what we are to observe.

III. PRECEPTS, פקודים PIKKUDIM, *from* פקד *pakad,* to *take notice* or *care* of a thing, to *attend,* have *respect to, appoint,* to *visit;* because they take *notice* of our way, have *respect* to the whole of our life and conversation, *superintend, overlook,* and *visit* us in all the concerns and duties of life.

IV. COMMANDMENTS, מצות MITSVOTH, from צוה *tasvah* to *command, order, ordain;* because they show us what we should do, and what we should leave undone, and exact our obedience.

V. TESTIMONIES, עדות EDOTH, from עד *ad,* denoting *beyond, farther, all along,* to *bear witness,* or *testimony.* The rites and ceremonies of the law; because they point out matters *beyond* themselves, being *types* and *representations* of the good things that were to come.

VI. JUDGMENTS, משפטים MISHPATIM, from שפט *shaphat,* to *judge, determine, regulate, order,* and *discern,* because they *judge* concerning our words and works; show the *rules* by which they should be *regulated;* and cause us to *discern* what is *right* and *wrong,* and *decide* accordingly.

VII. TRUTH, אמונה EMUNAH, from אמן *aman,* to *make steady, constant,* to *settle, trust, believe.* The *law* that is established, steady, confirmed, and ordered in all things, and sure; which should be *believed* on the authority of God, and *trusted* to as an infallible *testimony* from Him who cannot *lie* nor deceive.

VIII. WORD, דבר *dabar,* from the same root, to *discourse, utter one's sentiments, speak consecutively* and *intelligibly;* in which it appears to differ from מלל *malal,* to *utter articulate sounds.* Any *prophecy* or immediate communication from heaven, as well as the whole body of Divine revelation, is emphatically called דבר יהוה *debar Yehovah, the word of Jehovah.* On the same ground we call the whole *Old and New Testament* THE WORD OF THE LORD, as we term the volume in which they are contained THE BIBLE—THE BOOK. In his revelation God speaks to man; shows him, in a clear, concise, intelligible, and rational way, his interest, his duty, his privileges; and, in a word, the reasonable service that he requires of him.

IX. WAY, דרך DERECH, from the same root, to *proceed, go on, walk, tread.* The *way* in which God goes in order to instruct and save man; the *way* in which man must tread in order to be safe, holy, and happy. *God's man-*

ner of *acting* or *proceeding* in providence and grace; and the *way* that man should take in order to answer the end of his creation and redemption.

X. RIGHTEOUSNESS, צדקה TSEDAKAH, from צדק *tsadak,* to *do justice,* to *give full weight.* That which teaches a man to give to all their *due;* to give GOD his *due,* MAN his *due,* and HIMSELF his *due;* for every man has duties to God, his *neighbor,* and *himself,* to perform. This word is applied to God's *judgments, testimonies,* and *commandments;* they are all *righteous,* give to all their *due,* and require what is due from every one.

The *three* words, which some *add* here, are, 1. FAITHFULNESS, אמונה EMUNAH: but see this under No. VII.; nor does it appear in ver. 90, where it occurs, to be used as a characteristic of God's *law,* but rather his exact fulfilment of his *promises* to man.

The *second* is JUDGMENT, משפט *mishpat.* See this under No. VI.: it occurs in ver. 84 and 121: "When wilt thou execute judgment," &c.; but is not used in those places as one of the *ten words.*

The *third* is NAME, שם *shem,* see ver. 132: but this is no characteristic of God's law; it refers here simply to himself. *Those that love thy* NAME is the same as *those that love* THEE. Bishop *Nicholson* inserts *promises* among the *ten* words: but this occurs no where in the Psalm.

We might, and with much more propriety, add a *fourth,* אמרה IMRAH, from אמר *amar,* to *branch out, spread,* or *diffuse itself,* as the *branches of a tree;* and which is often used for a *word spoken, a speech.* This often occurs in the Psalm: and we regularly translate it *word,* and put no difference or distinction between it and דבר *dabar,* No. VIII.: but it is not exactly the *same;* דבר *dabar* may apply more properly to *history, relation, description,* and such like; while, אמרתך *imrathecha, thy word,* may mean an *immediate oracle,* delivered solemnly from God to his prophet for the instruction of men. But the two words appear often indifferently used; and it would not be easy to ascertain the different shades of meaning between these two roots.

Having thus far introduced the Psalm to the reader's attention, I should probably speak at large of the *elegance* of its composition, and the *importance* and *utility* of its matter. Like all other portions of Divine revelation, it is elegant, important, and useful; and while I admire the fecundity of the psalmist's genius, the unabating flow of his poetic vein, his numerous synonyms, and his *copia verborum,* by which he is enabled to expand, diversify, and illustrate the same idea; presenting it to his reader in all possible points of view, so as to render it pleasing, instructive, and impressive; I cannot rob the rest of the book of its just praise by setting this, as many have done, above all the pieces it contains. It is by far the largest, the most artificial, and most diversified; yet, in proportion to its length, it contains the fewest ideas of any Psalm in the Book.

6 ᶠThen shall I not be ashamed, when I have respect unto all thy commandments.

7 ᵍI will praise thee with uprightness of

heart, when I shall have learned ʰthy righteous judgments.

8 I will keep thy statutes: O forsake me not utterly.

ᶠJob xxii. 26; 1 John ii. 28——ᵍVer. 171

ʰHeb. *judgments of thy righteousness*

Several of the ancients, particularly the *Greek fathers*, have considered it as an abridgement of David's life; in which he expresses all the states through which he had passed; the trials, persecutions, succours, and encouragements he had received. The *Latin fathers* perceive in it all the morality of the Gospel, and rules for a man's conduct in every situation of life. Cassiodorus asserts that it contains the sentiments of the prophets, apostles, martyrs, and all the saints. In the introduction to the Book of Psalms I have conjectured that many of them were composed from notes taken at different times, and in widely different circumstances; hence the different states described in the same Psalm, which could not have been at one and the same time the experience of the same person. It is most likely that this Psalm was composed in this way; and this, as well as its *acrostical* arrangement, will account for its general want of connexion.

Though the most judicious interpreters assign it to the times of the Babylonish captivity; yet there are so many things in it descriptive of David's state, experience, and affairs, that I am led to think it might have come from his pen; or if composed at or under the captivity, was formed out of his notes and *memoranda.*

I shall now make short remarks on the principal subjects in each part; and, at the end of each, endeavour by the *Analysis* to show the *connexion* which the *eight* verses of each have among themselves, and the use which the reader should make of them. In all the *Versions* except the *Chaldee* this Psalm is numbered cxviii.

LETTER א ALEPH.—*First Division*

Verse 1. *Blessed are the undefiled in the way*] אשרי תמימי דרך *ashrey temimey darech*, "O the blessedness of the perfect ones in the way." This Psalm begins something like the *first*, where see the notes. By the *perfect*, which is the proper meaning of the original word, we are to undertsand those who sincerely believe what God has spoken, religiously observe all the rules and ceremonies of his religion, and have their lives and hearts regulated by the spirit of love, fear, and obedience. This is farther stated in the *second* verse.

Verse 3. *They also do no iniquity*] They avoid all idolatry, injustice, and wrong; and they walk in God's ways, not in those ways to which an evil heart might entice them, nor those in which the thoughtless and the profligate tread.

Verse 4. *Thy precepts diligently.*] מאד *meod*, "superlatively, to the uttermost." God has never given a commandment, the observance of which he knew to be *impossible.* And to whatsoever he has commanded he requires *obedience; and his grace is sufficient for us.* We must not trifle with God.

Verse 5. *O that my ways were directed*] "I

wish that my way may be *confirmed* to *keep thy statutes.*" Without thee I can do nothing; my soul is *unstable* and *fickle;* and it will continue *weak* and *uncertain* till thou *strengthen* and establish it.

Verse 6. *Then shall I not be ashamed*] Every act of transgression in the wicked man tends to *harden his heart;* and render it *callous.* If a man who fears God is so unhappy as to fall into sin, his conscience reproaches him, and he is *ashamed* before God and man. This is a full proof that God's Spirit has not utterly departed from him, and that he may repent, believe and be *healed.*

Unto all thy commandments.] God requires *universal obedience*, and all things are possible to him whom Christ strengthens; and all things are possible to him that believes. *Allow* that *any* of God's commandments *may* be transgressed, and we shall soon have the whole decalogue set aside.

Verse 8. *O forsake me not utterly.*] עד מאד *ad meod*, "to utter dereliction;" never leave me to my own strength, nor to my own heart!

ANALYSIS OF LETTER ALEPH.—*First Division*

I. In this first *octonary* the prophet commends to us the law of God, and persuades us to practise it by two arguments: 1. Happiness, ver. 1, 2. 2. The excellence of the Lawgiver, ver. 4.

II. He shows his affection to this law, desiring grace to keep it, ver. 5.

On which he knew there would follow two effects:

1. Peace of conscience: "He should not be ashamed," &c.

2. Thankfulness to God for his teaching, ver. 7.

"Blessed are they who are undefiled in the way," &c.

"Blessed are they who keep his testimonies," &c.

"They also do no iniquity," &c.

I. The *first argument* used by the prophet to persuade men to obedience is *blessedness.* He that would be happy must be obedient; and his obedience, if true, may be thus discerned:—

1. "He must be undefiled in the way." Keep himself from sin.

2. "He must walk in the law of the Lord," &c. Which is the *rule* of our faith, life, and worship.

3. "He must keep his testimonies." Search them out in God's word.

4. "He must seek him with a whole heart." With sincerity search his law to the utmost, both what it *bids*, and what it *forbids*, in order to know the mind of the Lawgiver.

5. "They also do no iniquity." They work no iniquity with 1. Purpose of heart; 2. Delight; 3. With perseverance; 4. Nor at all, when the heart is fully sanctified unto God; Christ dwelling in it by faith.

6. *They walk in his way*, which the wicked

ב BETH

9 Wherewithal shall a young man cleanse his way? by taking heed *thereto* according to thy word.

10 With my whole heart have I ¹sought thee: O let me not ᵏwander from thy commandments.

ⁱ2 Chron. xv. 15——ᵏVer. 21, 118——ˡPsa. xxxvii. 31; Luke ii. 19, 51

---

do not: but the righteous have taken it for their path through life; and should they at any time swerve from it, they come back by repentance and confession to God.

The prophet's *second argument* to persuade to obedience is the authority of the Lawgiver. All disobedience proceeds either from contempt of God's laws, or rebellion against them: but David brings to our mind the authority of the Lawgiver, from a consideration of *who* he is who commands our obedience as his servants: "Thou hast commanded that we keep," &c.

1. *Thou*, who knowest when we err, and wilt punish us.

2. *Hast commanded*—absolutely enjoined.

3. *That we keep*, &c.—they cannot be dispensed with.

4. *Diligently*, &c. Not negligently or lazily, or Satan will take advantage of us.

II. The blessedness promised to the keepers of God's law moved the prophet to send forth this ardent prayer, "O that my ways," &c.

1. *David* was a great king, and yet desires to be obedient.

2. He answers God's *command* by a *prayer*, to be enabled to perform it by his grace.

3. "O that my ways," &c. My counsels, actions, &c., were conformable to the straitness and regularity of thy law.

4. He knew he could not be too closely united to God, and therefore he prays to be directed.

Which prayer he knew God would hear; and that the effect would be quietness of soul, and boldness at a throne of grace.

1. "Then shall I not be confounded," &c. If his heart were right with God, he should not fly from him, as did *Adam:* that was the effect of disobedience.

2. If God *directed his ways* to the keeping of his commandments, he should find no amazement in his conscience, but holy boldness.

And this effect will produce another fruit, a thankful heart.

1. "I will praise thee." Give thee thanks for they grace and assistance.

2. "With uprightness of heart." Not with his tongue only, but with an honest and upright heart.

3. But this could not be done till God had taught him: "I will praise thee when I shall have learned," &c. Not to know them only with my *understanding*, but to make them the *rule of my life*, which cannot be but by the *influence* of the *Spirit* of GOD.

And what follows upon this will be a firm purpose of heart to be obedient to God's laws.

1. "I will keep thy statutes." So am I fully resolved and decreed with myself. And it is a great help to godliness to *resolve to live a godly life;* for how shall that be *performed* which is not purposed.

11 ¹Thy word have I hid in mine heart, that I might not sin against thee.

12 Blessed *art* thou, O Lord: ᵐteach me thy statutes.

13 With my lips have I ⁿdeclared all the judgments of thy mouth.

ᵐVer. 26, 33, 64, 68, 108, 124, 135; Psa. xxv. 4——ⁿPsa. xxxiv. 11

---

2. And yet this purpose or conclusion he makes in *God's strength;* and therefore constantly prays: "O forsake me not utterly." Without thy aid I can do nothing: but if at any time in thy just judgment thou desert me, that I may know and feel my own weakness, and learn the better to fly to thee, let it not be an utter desertion. Forsake me not, neither too much nor too long.

Letter ב Beth—*Second Division*

Verse 9. *A young man cleanse his way*] ארח *orach*, which we translate *way* here, signifies a *track*, a *rut*, such as is made by the wheel of a cart or chariot. A *young sinner* has no *broad beaten* path; he has his *private ways* of offence, his *secret pollutions:* and how shall he *be cleansed* from these? how can he be saved from what will destroy mind, body, and soul? Let him hear what follows; the description is from God.

1. He is to *consider* that his way is *impure;* and how abominable this must make him appear in the sight of God.

2. He must examine it *according to God's word*, and carefully hear what God has said concerning *him* and *it*.

3. He must *take heed* to it, לשׁמר *lishmor*, to *keep guard*, and *preserve his way*—his general course of life, from all defilement.

Verse 10. *With my whole heart have I sought thee*] 4. He must *seek God;* make *earnest prayer* and *supplication* to him for Divine *light*, for a *tender conscience*, and for *strength* to walk uprightly. 5. His *whole heart;* all his affections must be engaged here, or he cannot succeed. If he keep any affection for the idol or abomination; if his *heart* do not give it before the Lord, he may make many prayers, but God will answer none of them. 6. He must *take care to keep in the path of duty*, of abstinence and self-denial; not permitting either his *eye*, his *hand*, or his *heart* to *wander* from the *commandments* of his Maker.

Verse 11. *Thy word have I hid in my heart*] 7. He must *treasure* up those portions of *God's word* in his mind and heart which speak against uncleanness of every kind; and that recommend purity, chastity, and holiness. The word of Christ should dwell *richly* in him. If God's word be only in his *Bible*, and not also in his *heart*, he may soon and easily be surprised into his *besetting* sin.

Verse 12. *Blessed* art *thou*] 8. He must *acknowledge the mercy of God*, in so far preserving him from all the *consequences* of his sin. 9. He should beg of him to become his *teacher*, that his heart and conscience might be *instructed* in the *spirituality* of his statutes.

Verse 13. *With my lips have I declared*] **10.**

14 I have rejoiced in the way of thy testimonies, as *much as* in all riches.

15 I will °meditate in thy precepts, and have respect unto thy ways.

16 I will ᴾdelight myself in thy statutes: I will not forget thy word.

ג GIMEL

17 ᑫDeal bountifully with thy servant, *that* I may live, and keep thy word.

18 ʳOpen thou mine eyes, that I may behold wondrous things out of thy law.

19 ˢI *am* a stranger in the earth: hide not thy commandments from me.

20 ᵗMy soul breaketh for the longing *that it hath* unto thy judgments at all times.

21 Thou hast rebuked the proud *that are* cursed, which do ᵘerr from thy commandments.

°Psalm i. 2; verse 23, 48, 78——ᴾPsalm i. 2; verse 35, 47, 70, 77——ᑫPsalm cxvi. 7.——ʳHebrew, *reveal* ˢGenesis xlvii. 9; 1 Chronicles xxix. 15; Psalm xxxix.

12; 2 Corinthians v. 6; Hebrew xi. 13——ᵗPsalm cxlii. 1, 2; lxiii. 1; lxxxiv. 2; verse 40, 131——ᵘVer. 10, 110, 118

He should *declare* to his own heart, and to all his *companions in iniquity*, God's *judgments* against himself and them; that if his *long-suffering mercy* have not made a proper impression on their hearts, they may tremble at his approaching *judgments*.

Verse 14. *I have rejoiced*] 11. He must consider it his *chief happiness* to be found in the *path of obedience*, giving his whole heart and strength to God; and when enabled to do it, he should rejoice more in it than if he had gained thousands of gold and silver. O how great is the treasure of a tender and approving conscience!

Verse 15. *I will meditate*] 12. He should encourage self-examination and reflection; and meditate frequently on God's words, works, and ways; and especially on his gracious dealings towards him. 13. He should *keep his eye* upon *God's steps;* setting the example of his Saviour before his eyes, going *where* he would *go*, and *nowhere* else; *doing* what he would *do*, and *nothing* else; keeping the *company* that he would *keep*, and *none* else; and doing every thing in reference to the *final judgment*.

Verse 16. *I will delight myself*] The word is very emphatical: אשתעשע *eshtaasha, I will skip about and jump for joy.* 14. He must exult in God's word as his treasure, live in the spirit of obedience as his work, and ever glory in God, who has called him to such a *state* of salvation. 15. He must never forget what God has *done for* him, *done in* him, and promised *farther to do;* and he must not *forget the promises* he had made, and the *vows* of the Lord that are upon him. Any young man who attends to these *fifteen* particulars will get his impure way cleansed; victory over his sin; and, if he abide faithful to the Lord that bought him, an eternal heaven at last among them that are *sanctified*.

ANALYSIS OF LETTER BETH.—*Second Division*

In the first part the psalmist, having commended God's law, from its Author—God, and its end—happiness, shows us in the *second* part the efficacy and utility of it to a *holy life*, without which there can be no *happiness*. And in order to show this effect, he chooses the most unlikely *subject*.

I. A *young man*, in whom the law of the members is most strong; he wants experience; he is headstrong, and generally under the government, not of reason nor religion, but of his own passions.

II. The psalmist shows that, to cleanse the

way of such, he must "take heed to them," watch over them, and "remember his Creator in the days of his youth."

As a man must become *holy* in order to be *happy*, he shows how this holiness is to be attained, and adduces his own experience.

1. Seek God with thy "whole heart." Be truly sensible of your wants.

2. Keep and remember what God says: "Thy words have I hidden," &c.

3. Reduce all this to practice: "That I might not sin against thee."

4. Bless God for what he has given: "Blessed art thou," &c.

5. Ask more: "Teach me thy statutes."

6. Be ready to communicate his knowledge to others: "With my lips have I declared."

7. Let it have a due effect on thy own heart: "I have rejoiced," &c.

8. Meditate frequently upon them: "I will meditate," &c.

9. Deeply reflect on them: "I will have respect," &c. As food undigested will not nourish the body, so the word of God not considered with deep meditation and reflection will not feed the soul.

10. Having pursued the above course, he should continue in it, and then his happiness would be secured: "I will not forget thy word. I will (in consequence) delight myself in thy statutes."

LETTER ג GIMEL.—*Third Division*

Verse 17. *Deal bountifully*] גמל *gemol, reward* thy servant. Let him have the return of his faith and prayers, that the Divine *life* may be preserved in his soul! Then he will keep thy word. From גמל *gamal*, to reward, &c., comes the name of ג *gimel*, the *third* letter in the Hebrew alphabet, which is prefixed to every verse in this *part*, and commences it with its own name. This is a stroke of the psalmist's *art* and *ingenuity*.

Verse 18. *Open thou mine eyes*] גל עיני *gal eynai, reveal my eyes*, illuminate my understanding, take away the veil that is on my heart, and then shall I see wonders in thy law. The Holy Scriptures are plain enough; but the heart of man is *darkened* by sin. The *Bible* does not so much need a *comment*, as the *soul* does the *light of the Holy Spirit*. Were it not for the darkness of the human intellect, the things relative to salvation would be easily apprehended.

22 ᵛRemove from me reproach and contempt; for I have kept thy testimonies.

23 Princes also did sit *and* speak against me: *but* thy servant did ʷmeditate in thy statutes.

24 ˣThy testimonies also *are* my delight *and* ʸmy counsellors.

ד DALETH

25 ᶻMy soul cleaveth unto the dust: ᵃquicken thou me according to thy word.

ᵛPsa. xxxix. 8——ʷVer. 15——ˣVer. 77, 92——ʸHeb. *men of counsel*——ᶻPsa. xliv. 25——ᵃVer. 40; Psa.

Verse 19. *I am a stranger in the earth*] In the *land.* Being obliged to wander about from place to place, I am like a *stranger* even in my *own country.* If it refer to the *captives* in *Babylon,* it may mean that they felt themselves there as in a state of *exile;* for, although they had been *seventy* years in it, they still felt it as a *strange* land, because they considered Palestine their *home.*

Verse 20. *My soul breaketh*] We have a similar expression: *It broke my heart, That is heart-breaking, She died of a broken heart.* It expresses excessive longing, grievous disappointment, hopeless love, accumulated sorrow. By this we may see the *hungering* and *thirsting* which the psalmist had after righteousness, often mingled with much *despondency.*

Verse 21. *Thou hast rebuked the proud*] This was done often in the case of David; and was true also in reference to the Babylonians, who held the Israelites in subjection, and whose kings were among the proudest of human beings. Instead of זדים *zedim,* the *proud,* some MSS. read זרים *zarim, strangers,* and one reads גוים *goyim,* the *heathen;* and so the *Syriac.*

Verse 22. *Remove from me reproach and contempt*] Of these the captives in Babylon had a more than ordinary load.

Verse 23. *Princes also did sit*] It is very likely that the *nobles* of Babylon did often, by wicked misrepresentations, render the minds of the kings of the empire evil affected towards the Jews.

Verse 24. *Thy testimonies also are—my counsellors.*] אנשי עצתי *anshey atsathi,* "the men of my counsel." I sit with them; and I consider every testimony thou hast given as a particular counsellor; one whose advice I especially need.

The Analysis will farther explain the particular uses of this part.

ANALYSIS OF LETTER GIMEL.—*Third Division*

In this division the psalmist—

I. Reckons up the *impediments* he may meet with in endeavouring to keep God's law.

II. Prays God to remove them.

First impediment. A *dead soul* and a *dull heart;* and therefore he prays for grace that he may *live* and keep *God's word.*

Second impediment. Blindness of understanding: "Open my eyes, that I may see wonders in thy law." The wonderful equity, wisdom, and profit of it.

26 I have declared my ways, and thou heardest me: ᵇteach me thy statutes.

27 Make me to understand the way of thy precepts: so ᶜshall I talk of thy wondrous works.

28 ᵈMy soul ᵉmelteth for heaviness; strengthen thou me according unto thy word.

29 Remove from me the way of lying: and grant me thy law graciously.

30 I have chosen the way of truth: thy judgments have I laid *before me.*

---

cxliii. 11——ᵇVer. 12; Psa. xxv. 4; xxvii. 11; lxxxvi. 11 ᶜPsa. cxlv. 5, 6——ᵈPsa. cvii. 26——ᵉHeb. *dropped*

Third impediment. His *wayfaring* and *uncertain situation:* I am a "stranger upon the earth;" therefore, "hide not thy commandments from me." Should I be frequently destitute of thy ordinances, leave me not without thy Spirit's teaching.

Fourth impediment. His *infirmity* and *imperfection:* "My soul breaks," &c. I wish to be at *all times,* what I am *sometimes,* full of desire, fervour, zeal, prayer, and faith. Then shall I be what I should be, when my heart is *steady* in seeking his salvation.

Fifth impediment. Pride of heart. This he saw in *others,* and was afraid that it might take place in himself; and he knew if it did, he should *wander from the commandment,* and come under a *curse.*

Sixth impediment. The *reproach* and *contempt* he met with in consequence of his endeavours to live a godly life. Against this he prays as a grievous temptation: "Remove from me reproach and contempt."

Seventh impediment. The *rulers of the people plotted against his life;* they even met in council about it: "Princes did also sit and speak against me." It is difficult to bear reproach even for Christ's sake; though it should be a matter of glorying: but he must be strong in the faith, who can stand against *keen raillery,* and *state persecution.*

But what effect had all this upon the psalmist?

1. He cleaved to God's *testimonies,* and conscientiously *observed* them.

2. He made them his *counsellors*—drew all his wisdom from them; and he was amply rewarded, for they became *his delight.* Every man profits who is faithful to his God.

LETTER ד DALETH.—*Fourth Division*

Verse 25. *My soul cleaveth unto the dust*] It would be best to translate נפשי *naphshi, my life;* and then *cleaving to the dust* may imply an apprehension of *approaching death;* and this agrees best with the petition.

Quicken thou me] חיני *chaiyeni,* "make me alive." Keep me from going down into the dust.

Verse 26. *I have declared my ways*] ספרתי *sipparti,* "I have numbered my ways;" I have searched them out; I have investigated them. And that he had earnestly *prayed* for pardon of what was wrong in them, is evident; for he adds, "Thou heardest me."

Verse 28. *My soul melteth*] דלף *dalaph* sig-

31 I have stuck unto thy testimonies: O LORD, put me not to shame.

32 I will run the way of thy commandments, when thou shalt [f]enlarge my heart.

XXV. DAY. MORNING PRAYER

ה HE

33 [g]Teach me, O LORD, the way of thy statutes; and I shall keep it [h]*unto* the end.

34 [i]Give me understanding, and I shall keep thy law; yea, I shall observe it with *my* whole heart.

35 Make me to go in the path of thy commandments; for therein do I [k]delight.

36 Incline my heart unto thy testimonies, and not to [l]covetousness.

37 [m]Turn [n]away mine eyes from [o]beholding vanity; *and* [p]quicken thou me in thy way.

---

[f]1 Kings iv. 29; Isa. lx. 5; 2 Cor. vi. 11——[g]Ver. 12 [h]Ver. 112; Matt. x. 22; Rev. ii. 26——[i]Ver. 73; Prov. ii. 6; James i. 5——[k]Ver. 16

[l]Ezek. xxxiii. 31; Mark vii. 21, 22; Luke xii. 15; 1 Tim. vi. 10; Heb. xiii. 5——[m]Isa. xxxiii. 15——[n]Heb. *make to pass*——[o]Prov. xxiii. 5——[p]Ver. 40

---

nifies *to distil,* to *drop* as *tears from the eye.* As my distresses cause the *tears* to *distil* from my eyes, so the overwhelming load of my afflictions causes my life to *ebb* and *leak* out.

Verse 29. *The way of lying*] The propensity to *falsity* and *prevarication;* whatsoever is contrary to *truth. Remove me* from its solicitations, and *remove* it from *me.* "Grant me thy law graciously;" give it to me as a rule of moral conduct; but give it to me graciously through the *Gospel;* and then it will not be the letter that killeth, but will be sanctified to me, so as to become to me holy, just, and GOOD.

Verse 30. *I have chosen the way of truth*] And that I may continue in it, "remove from me the way of lying." See above.

Verse 31. *I have stuck*] דבקתי *dabakti,* I have *cleaved* to, been *glued* to, them: the same word as in ver. 25. My *soul cleaves* as much to *thy testimonies,* as my *life* has *cleaved* to the *dust.*

O Lord, put me not to shame.] Let my sins and follies be blotted out by thy mercy; and so *hide* and *cover* them that they shall never appear, either in *this* or the *coming world,* to my *shame* and *confusion!* How many need to be importunate with God in this prayer!

Verse 32. *I will run*] The particle כי, which we translate *when,* should be translated *because: Because thou shalt enlarge,* or dilate, *my heart;* make plain my path by cleansing me from my impurity, and taking the hinderances out of my way. I *will* then *run* without dread of stumbling, and every day make sensible progress.

ANALYSIS OF LETTER DALETH.—*Fourth Division*

The psalmist—

I. Sets down the state of an *imperfect* man.

II. *Confesses* it.

III. *Asks grace and mercy.*

IV. *Professes* what in consequence he would do.

I. 1. "My soul cleaveth unto the dust:" His affections cleaved to things below, instead of being set on things above.

2. "Quicken thou me:" Give me a life *according to thy law.* By cleaving to the earth, he was earthly; by cleaving to the flesh, he was carnal; but by living according to the spiritual law, he was to become one spirit with God.

II. He *confesses* his imperfections.

1. "I have declared my ways." I acknowledge all my wanderings, sins, follies, and unfaithfulness; I have hidden nothing from thee.

2. Thou didst *hear me;* forgavest me out of thy mere mercy.

3. Do the like now: "Teach me thy statutes." These two things should be sought together: *mercy* to pardon, and *grace* to assist and renew.

III. He proceeds in this *prayer.*

1. "Make me to understand:" Where the *mind* is *darkened,* the *heart* cannot be *well ordered.*

2. He that asks *good things* from God should ask them for a *good end:* "Make me to understand; so shall I talk," &c.

3. He would show *God's wondrous works:* I shall talk of thy wondrous *law,*—thy wondrous *Gospel,*—thy wondrous *mercy* in saving sinners, —the wondrous *means* thou usest, &c.

IV. He returns to his confession, and states what he *purposes to do.*

1. "My soul melts:" I am full of trouble and distress.

2. "Strengthen thou me:" Give me the grace thou hast promised.

3. "Remove from me the way of lying:" Give me power to avoid all sin.

4. "Grant me thy law graciously:" Print the matter of it in my heart, and abolish my corruption.

5. He *chooses* the *truth.*

6. He *adheres* to it.

7. He will *continue* in it.

8. Yea, and with *greater diligence* than ever. To make up for lost time, he will now *run:* and, while running, keep in God's way. Some run, but they run *out* of it.

LETTER ה HE.—*Fifth Division*

Verse 33. *Teach me, O Lord, the way of thy statutes*] To understand the spiritual reference of all the statutes, &c., under the law, required a teaching which could only come from God.

I shall keep it unto *the end.*] Here is a *good thing* asked for a good *end.* He wishes for heavenly teaching; not to make a parade of it, but to enable him to discern his duty, that he might act accordingly.

Verse 34. *With my whole heart.*] I will not trifle with my God, I will not divide my affections with the world; God shall have all.

Verse 36. *Not to covetousness.*] Let me have no inordinate love for gain of any kind, nor for any thing that may grieve thy Spirit, or induce me to seek my happiness here *below.*

Verse 37. *From beholding vanity*] An idol,

38 qStablish thy word unto thy servant, who *is devoted* to thy fear.

39 Turn away my reproach, which I fear: for thy judgments *are* good.

40 Behold, I have rlonged after thy precepts: squicken me in thy righteousness.

١ VAU

41 tLet thy mercies come also unto me, O LORD, *even* thy salvation, according to thy word.

42 uSo shall I have wherewith to answer him that reproacheth me: for I trust in thy word.

43 And take not the word of truth utterly out of my mouth; for I have hoped in thy judgments.

44 So shall I keep thy law continually for ever and ever.

45 And I will walk vat liberty: for I seek thy precepts.

---

q2 Sam. vii. 25——rVer. 20——sVer. 25, 37, 88, 107, 149, 156, 159——tPsa. cvi. 4; ver. 77

uOr, *So shall I answer him that reproacheth me in a thing* vHeb. *at large*

---

worldly pleasure, beauty, finery; any thing that is vain, empty, or transitory. Let me not *behold* it; let me not *dwell upon* it. Let me remember *Achan:* he *saw,*—he *coveted,*—he *took,*—he *hid* his theft, and was *slain* for his sin.

Verse 38. *Stablish thy word*] Fulfil the promises thou hast made to me.

Verse 39. *Turn away my reproach, which I fear*] This may be understood of the reproach which a man may meet with in consequence of living a godly life, for such a life was never *fashionable* in any *time* or *country*. But I have found the following note on the passage: "I have done a *secret evil; my* soul is sorry for it: if it become *public*, it will be a heavy reproach to me. O God, turn it away, and let it never meet the eye of man!"—*Anon*.

Verse 40. *Behold, I have longed*] Thou searchest the heart; thou knowest that I have long desired thy salvation; thou seest that this desire still remains. Behold it! it is thy work; and through thy mercy I breathe after thy mercy.

Quicken me] I am *dying;* O give me the spirit of life in Christ Jesus!

ANALYSIS OF LETTER HE.—*Fifth Division*

In this part, which is wholly *precatory*, the psalmist prays,—

I. That God would *illuminate* his mind.

II. That he would *remove all those hinderances* which might prevent him from doing his duty.

I. 1. The first petition is for illumination: "Teach me;" point me out *what* I am to *learn*, and *how* I am to learn it.

2. The second is, "Give me understanding." Let me *comprehend*, that I may *profit* by this teaching.

3. The *end* for which he asks,—that he "may keep the law."

He specifies the manner: 1. He will be no *temporizer;* he will keep it "to the end." 2. He will be no *hypocrite;* he will keep it "with his whole heart."

1. He prays for *power:* "Make me to go." Without thy Spirit's help I can do nothing: I do not know the way without thy *teaching;* I cannot walk in it without thy *help*.

2. He wishes to go in *the path;* the way in which all God's followers have walked.

3. It is a *path*, not a public road; a path where no *beast* goes, and *men* seldom.

4. He gives a *reason* why his petition should be granted: "Therein do I delight."

II. He prays to have all impediments removed.

1. "Incline my heart." Bind it down to a willing obedience.

2. "Not to covetousness." Keep me from the *love* of *money*, the *world*, the *creature*.

3. He prays against the *desire of the eye:* "Turn away mine eyes." Let the eye of my body be turned away *from* vanity; the eye of my mind turned away *to* thee.

4. Let me find the benefit of this turning: "Stablish thy word,"—make good thy word; give me grace to stand.

5. For which he gives this reason: "I am thy servant, and am devoted to thy fear."

6. He is afraid of the consequences if he be not faithful: "Turn away my reproach." Let it not be said, at the day of judgment, "I was hungry, and you gave me no meat," &c.

7. He knows if God condemns it must be justly: "For thy judgments are good." *Man* may *condemn* where *thou approvest; he* may *approve* where *thou condemnest. Thy judgments* alone *are* good.

8. He concludes, desiring the Lord to look on the state of his heart: "Behold!" 1. Is not my heart right before thee? 2. If so, *quicken me; make me alive*, and *keep me alive!* Without the *latter*, the *former* will answer no end.

LETTER ١ VAU.—*Sixth Division*

Verse 41. *Let thy mercies come*] Let me speedily see the accomplishment of all my prayers! Let me have *thy salvation*—such a deliverance as it becomes thy greatness and goodness to impart. Let it be *according to thy word*—thy exceeding great and precious promises.

Verse 42. *So shall I have wherewith to answer*] Many say, "My hope in thy mercy is vain;" but when thou fulfillest thy promises to me, then shall I answer to the confusion of their infidelity.

Verse 43. *Take not the word of truth*] Grant that the assurances which thy prophets have given to the people of approaching deliverance may not fall to the ground; let it appear that *they* have spoken *thy mind*, and that *thou* hast fulfilled *their word*.

Verse 45. *I will walk at liberty*] When freed from the present bondage, we shall rejoice in obedience to thy testimonies; we shall *delight* to keep all thy ordinances.

46 ʷI will speak of thy testimonies also before kings, and will not be ashamed.

47 And I will ˣdelight myself in thy commandments, which I have loved.

48 My hands also will I lift up unto thy commandments, which I have loved; and I will ʸmeditate in thy statutes.

⁊ ZAIN

49 Remember the word unto thy servant, upon which thou hast caused me to ᶻhope.

50 This *is* my ᵃcomfort in my affliction: for thy word hath quickened me.

51 The proud have had me greatly ᵇin derision: *yet* have I not ᶜdeclined from thy law.

52 I remembered thy judgments of old, O LORD; and have comforted myself.

53 ᵈHorror hath taken hold upon me, because of the wicked that forsake thy law.

54 Thy statutes have been my songs in the house of my pilgrimage.

ʷPsa. cxxxviii. 1; Matt. x. 18, 19; Acts xxvi. 1, 2 ——ˣVer. 16——ʸVer. 15——ᶻVer. 74, 81, 147

ᵃRom. xv. 4——ᵇJer. xx. 7——ᶜJob xxiii. 11; Psa. xliv. 18; ver. 157——ᵈEzra ix. 3

Verse 46. *I will speak—before kings*] Dr. *Delaney* supposes that this is spoken in reference to *Achish, king of Gath,* whom David had instructed in the Jewish religion; but we have already seen that it is most likely that the Psalm was compiled under the Babylonish captivity. But the words may with more propriety be referred to the case of *Daniel,* and other bold and faithful Israelites, who spoke courageously before *Nebuchadnezzar, Belshazzar,* and *Darius.* See the books of *Daniel, Ezra,* and *Nehemiah.*

Verse 47. *Thy commandments, which I have loved.*] O shame to Christians who feel so little affection to the *Gospel of Christ,* when we see such cordial, conscientious, and inviolate attachment in a Jew to the laws and ordinances of Moses, that did not afford a thousandth part of the privileges!

Verse 48. *My hands also will I lift up*] I will present every victim and sacrifice which the law requires. I will make prayer and supplication before thee, lifting up holy hands without wrath and doubting.

ANALYSIS OF LETTER VAU.—*Sixth Division*

The psalmist prays for *mercy,* and promises to show his *thankfulness two ways:*—

I. By a bold confession of God's law.

II. By holy obedience to it.

The whole section consists of two petitions and six promises.

I. ɪ. *First petition.* "Let thy mercies come also unto me—even thy salvation." He joins these two, *mercy* and *salvation,* as *cause* and *effect;* for God's *mercy* can alone bring *salvation.*

This being granted, he vows to be thankful and courageous.

1. He vows to confess God's law, and answer any adversary who may say, "It is vain for him to hope in the Lord," by showing that God has fulfilled his word.

2. That he *will put his trust in God;* because he is omnipotent and merciful.

ɪɪ. The *second petition* is, "Take not the word of truth utterly out of my mouth." For which he gives a reason: "I have hoped in thy judgments."

1. "Take not thy word," in which I boast and glory before my adversaries.

2. "Take not the word out of my mouth," so that I dare not speak nor openly profess it.

3. "Take it not away utterly." If for my un-

faithfulness thou shouldst shut my mouth for a time, restore thy favour to me, that I may again make confession unto salvation.

4. For which he gives this reason: "I have hoped," &c. I trust in thy fidelity and justice, that thou wilt accomplish, in *promises* and *threatenings,* whatsoever thou hast engaged to perform.

II. Now he shows his *thankfulness* by determining to make confession of God's mercy in a holy life; serving God.

1. With a *free heart:* "I will walk at liberty;" sin shall have no dominion over me.

2. *With a loosened tongue:* "I will speak of thy testimonies also before kings." It is a difficult thing to speak to great men concerning their salvation; it requires great boldness, and equal *humility. Rudeness,* under the guise of *zeal,* spoils every good.

3. With *hearty affection:* "I will delight myself." He who can *delight* in his *duty* has made considerable progress in *piety.*

4. With *corresponding practice:* "My hands will I lift up." My life shall declare that I have not received the grace of God in vain.

5. With a *considerate mind:* "I will meditate in thy statutes." My understanding shall frequently examine them, approve of them, and turn them over to a heart full of fervent affection.

6. This was a work to which he *was accustomed:* "I have loved thy commandments and statutes." Love feels no loads, and habit is a second nature.

LETTER ⁊ ZAIN.—*Seventh Division*

Verse 49. *Remember the word*] Thou hast *promised* to redeem us from our captivity; on that *word* we have built our *hope. Remember* that thou hast thus promised, and *see* that we thus *hope.*

Verse 50. *This* is *my comfort*] While enduring our harsh captivity, we anticipated our enlargement; and thy *word of promise* was the *means* of keeping our souls *alive.*

Verse 51. *The proud have had me*] We have been treated, not only with oppressive *cruelty,* but also with *contempt,* because we still professed to *trust in thee,* the living God, who because of our transgressions hadst been greatly displeased with us; *yet we have not declined from thy law.*

Verse 52. *I remembered thy judgments of*

55 eI have remembered thy name, O LORD, in the night, and have kept thy law.

56 This I had, because I kept thy precepts.

ח CHETH

57 *fThou art* my portion, O LORD: I have said that I would keep thy words.

58 I entreated thy gfavour with *my* whole heart: be merciful unto me haccording to thy word.

59 I ithought on my ways, and turned my feet unto thy testimonies.

60 I made haste, and delayed not to keep thy commandments.

---

ePsa. lxiii. 6——fPsa. xvi. 5; Jer. x. 16; Lam. — iii. 24

gHeb. *face;* Job xi. 19——hVer. 41——iLuke xv. 17, 18

---

old] The word *judgments* is here taken for *providential dealing;* and indeed *kind treatment;* that which God showed to the Hebrews in bearing with and blessing them. And it was the recollection of *these judgments* that caused him to *comfort* himself.

Verse 53. *Horror hath taken hold upon me*] The word וְלֶעְפָה *zilaphah*, which we render *horror*, is thought to signify the pestilential burning wind called by the Arabs *simoom*. Here it strongly marks the idea that the psalmist had of the destructive nature of *sin;* it is pestilential; it is corrupting, mortal.

Verse 54. *Thy statutes have been my songs*] During our captivity all our consolation was derived from singing thy praises, and chanting among our fellow-captives portions of thy law, and the precepts it contains.

Verse 55. *I have remembered thy name*] Thou art *Jehovah;* and as *our God* thou hast made thyself known unto us. In the deepest *night* of our affliction this has consoled me.

Verse 56. *This I had, because I kept thy precepts.*] Though thou didst leave us under the power of our enemies, yet thou hast not left us without the consolations of thy Spirit.

ANALYSIS OF LETTER ZAIN.—*Seventh Division*

In this part the psalmist—

I. Prays.
II. Shows his trust in God, notwithstanding his discouragements.
III. Commends the word of God, by showing what blessed effects it had produced in him.

I. 1. He prays: "Remember;" accomplish and perfect thy promise. God's promises are made to prayer and faith; if men do not exert these, God will not fulfil the others.

2. "Made to thy servant:" The promises are made to the *obedient*. It is in vain to desire God to remember *his* promises made to *us*, if we make no conscience to perform *our* promises made to *him*.

3. "Wherein thou hast caused me to put my trust:" This is a forcible argument to induce God to fulfil his promises. They are thy promises; thou hast made them to us; and thou hast caused us to hope, because made by thee, that they shall be fulfilled.

II. He shows that the hope he had in God made him steady, even in afflictions.

1. "This is my comfort in affliction:" That is, God's word and promise.

2. "Thy word hath quickened me;" brought me *life, strength,* and *courage.*

3. He mentions his afflictions. 1. The proud have had me in derision. 2. Yet I have not declined from thy law. 3. For in my afflictions

I remembered thy judgments; his casting down the proud and exalting the humble. And, 4. From these considerations he derived comfort.

III. His knowledge of God's purity and judgments caused him to commiserate the state of the wicked.

1. "Horror hath taken hold upon me:" For those who trampled under foot God's word, and persecuted the righteous, he grieved; not because of the evil they did him, but of the evil they did themselves. He describes those men.

2. They forsook God's laws. Probably *apostate* Israelites.

3. He was not without consolation, though much afflicted and harassed. He took delight in God's law, and made his *songs* of it.

4. And this was a source of joy to him both day and night.

5. He concludes with this acclamation: "This I had;" I had this spirit, this power, this comfort, "because I kept thy precepts." While I suffered *for* God, I was enabled to rejoice *in* God. As I made him my portion, so he has been my praise.

LETTER ח CHETH.—*Eighth Division*

Verse 57. Thou art *my portion, O Lord*] From the *fifty-seventh* to the *sixtieth* verse may be seen the *progress* of the work of grace on the human heart, from the first dawn of heavenly light till the soul is filled with the fulness of God. But as I consider this Psalm as *notes* selected from *diaries* of past experience, formed at different times; and that the author has been obliged, for the support of his *acrostic* plan, to interchange circumstances, putting that sometimes *behind* which in the order of grace comes *before;* because, to put it in its right place, the *letters* would not accord with the *alphabetical arrangement;* I shall therefore follow what I conceive to be its *order* in the connexion *of grace*, and not in the *order* in which the words are here laid down.

Verse 59. FIRST.—*I thought on my ways*] חשבתי *chashabti*, I deeply pondered them; I turned them upside down; I viewed my conduct on all sides. The word, as used here, is a metaphor taken from *embroidering*, where the *figure* must appear the *same* on the *one side* as it does on the *other;* therefore, the cloth must be turned on each side every time the needle is set in, to see that the stitch be fairly set. Thus narrowly and scrupulously did the psalmist examine his conduct; and the result was, a deep conviction that he had departed from the way of God and truth.

SECONDLY.—*And turned my feet unto thy testimonies.*] Having made the above discovery, and finding himself under the displeas-

61 The ᵏbands of the wicked have robbed me: *but* I have not forgotten thy law.

62 ¹At midnight I will rise to give thanks unto thee, because of thy righteous judgments.

63 I *am* a companion of all *them* that fear thee, and of them that keep thy precepts.

64 ᵐThe earth, O Lᴏʀᴅ, is full of thy mercy: ⁿteach me thy statutes.

ᵏOr, *companies*——¹Acts xvi. 25

ᵐPsa. xxxiii. 5——ⁿVer. 12, 26

---

ure of God, he abandoned every evil way, took God's word for his directory, and set out fairly in the way of life and salvation.

Verse 60. Tʜɪʀᴅʟʏ.—*I made haste, and delayed not*] He did this with the utmost *speed;* and did not trifle with his convictions, nor seek to drown the voice of conscience.

The original word, which we translate *delayed not*, is amazingly emphatical. ולא התמהמהתי *velo hithmahmahti*, I did not stand *what-what-whating;* or, as we used to express the same sentiment, *shilly-shallying* with myself: I was *determined*, and so set out. The *Hebrew* word, as well as the *English*, strongly marks indecision of mind, positive action being suspended, because the mind is so unfixed as not to be able to make a choice.

Verse 58. Fᴏᴜʀᴛʜʟʏ.—Being determined in his heart, he tells us, *I entreated thy favour with* my *whole heart.* He found he had sinned; that he needed *mercy;* that he had no time to lose; that he must be importunate; and therefore he sought that mercy *with all his soul.*

Fɪꜰᴛʜʟʏ.—Feeling that he *deserved* nothing but wrath, that he had no *right* to any good, he cries for *mercy* in the way that God had promised to convey it: "Be merciful unto me!" And to this he is encouraged only by the *promise* of God; and therefore prays, "Be merciful unto me ᴀᴄᴄᴏʀᴅɪɴɢ to thy ᴡᴏʀᴅ."

Verse 57. Sɪxᴛʜʟʏ.—To keep himself firm in his present resolutions, he binds himself unto the Lord. "I have said that I would keep thy words." Thy vows are upon me, and I must not add to my guilt by breaking them.

Sᴇᴠᴇɴᴛʜʟʏ.—He did not seek in vain; God reveals himself in the fulness of blessedness to him, so that he is enabled to exclaim, *Thou art my portion, O Lord!* My whole soul trusts in thee; my spirit rests supremely satisfied with thee. I have no other inheritance, nor do I desire any. Here then is the *way to seek*, the *way to find*, and the *way to be happy.* Other effects of this conversion may be seen below.

Verse 61. *The bands of the wicked have robbed me*] חבלי *chebley*, the *cables, cords,* or *snares* of the wicked. They have *hunted* us like wild beasts; many they have taken for prey, and many they have destroyed.

Verse 62. *At midnight I will rise*] We are so overpowered with a sense of thy goodness, that in season and out of season we will return thee thanks.

Verse 63. *I am a companion*] This was the natural consequence of his own conversion; he abandoned the workers of iniquity, and associated with them that feared the Lord.

Verse 64. *The earth is full of thy mercy*] What an astonishing operation has the grace of God! In the midst of want, poverty, affliction, and bondage, it makes those who possess it happy! When Christ dwells in the heart by faith, we have nothing but *goodness* around us. Others may complain; but to us even the earth appears full of the mercy of the Lord.

Aɴᴀʟʏsɪs ᴏꜰ Lᴇᴛᴛᴇʀ Cʜᴇᴛʜ.—*Eighth Division*

In this part we have—

I. The assertion of the psalmist, that *God* was his *portion;* and his resolution upon it to keep God's law.

II. His *prayer* for grace to enable him to do it.

III. His *profession* of *duty* and a *holy life.*

IV. His *concluding* acclamation and *prayer.*

I. "Thou art my portion:" Let others choose as they please, *thou* art sufficient for *me;* I ask no more.

1. And on this I resolve to be thy *obedient servant:* "I have said, that I would keep thy words."

2. But thou knowest I am unable without thy grace to do this; therefore I must entreat thy favour: "Be merciful unto me." There are three helps to a godly life, all which we meet here, viz.:—

1. *Determination.* This makes a man *begin* well: "I have said."

2. *Supplication.* This makes a man *continue* well: "I entreated."

3. *Consideration.* This makes a man, when he *errs, come back* to the way again.

II. He was ready to co-operate with grace: "I have thought on my ways." If we be not workers with God, vain are our prayers. *Two things* are required of us: 1. *Aversion* from evil. 2. *Conversion* to good. Both must meet together.

1. Aversion from evil: "I thought on my ways." But he did not rest here.

2. Conversion to good: "I turned my feet unto thy testimonies."

III. And his sincerity is shown many ways:—

1. By his *readiness* and *zeal:* "I made haste, and delayed not."

2. By his *courage* and *constancy.* Though he was *plundered*, for his adherence to God, *by the bands of the wicked*, yet he *did not forget God's law.*

3. By his *fervour* about it. He was always employed in the work; and would rather take something from his natural rest, than not gratify his hunger and thirst after righteousness: "At midnight I will rise to give thanks."

4. By *selecting his company.* "He who walks with the lame will learn to limp:" therefore, avoiding the society of the wicked, he seeks the company of them *that fear the Lord* and *keep his precepts.*

IV. He concludes with an *acclamation* and *prayer.*

1. "The earth, O Lord, is full of thy mercy." There is not a creature that is not a partaker of thy goodness; let *me* have my portion in it.

2. "Teach me thy statutes." That is, continue to instruct me. I need constant teaching, line upon line, and precept upon precept. Teach thou, and I will learn; and as I learn from thy teaching, I will practise by thy grace.

ט TETH

65 Thou hast dealt well with thy servant, O LORD, according unto thy word.

66 Teach me good judgment and knowledge: for I have believed thy commandments.

67 °Before I was afflicted I went astray: but now have I kept thy word.

68 Thou *art* ᴾgood, and doest good; ᑫteach me thy statutes.

69 The proud have ʳforged a lie against me: *but* I will keep thy precepts with *my* whole heart.

70 ˢTheir heart is as fat as grease; *but* I ᵗdelight in thy law.

71 ᵘ*It is* good for me that I have been afflicted; that I might learn thy statutes.

72 ᵛThe law of thy mouth *is* better unto me than thousands of gold and silver.

°Ver. 71; Jer. xxxi. 18, 19; Heb. xii. 11——ᴾPsa. cvi. 1; cvii. 1; Matt. xix. 17——ᑫVer. 12, 26——ʳJob xiii. 4; Psa. cix. 2

ˢPsa. xvii. 10; Isa. vi. 10; Acts xxviii. 27——ᵗVer. 35 ᵘVer. 67; Heb. xii. 10, 11——ᵛVer. 127; Psa. xix. 10; Prov. viii. 10, 11, 19

LETTER ט TETH.—*Ninth Division*

Verse 65. *Thou hast dealt well with thy servant*] Whatsoever thy word has promised, thou hast fulfilled. Every *servant* of God can testify that God has done him nothing but *good*, and therefore he can speak *good* of his name.

Verse 66. *Teach me good judgment and knowledge*] טוב טעם ודעת למדני *tob taam vedaath lammedeni. Teach me* (to have) *a good taste and discernment.* Let me see and know the importance of Divine things, and give me a *relish* for them.

Verse 67. *Before I was afflicted I went astray*] Many have been humbled under affliction, and taught to know themselves and humble themselves before God, that probably without this could never have been saved; after this, they have been serious and faithful. *Affliction* sanctified is a great blessing; unsanctified, it is an additional curse.

Verse 68. *Thou* art *good*] And because thou art good, *thou doest good;* and because thou delightest to do good, *teach me thy statutes.*

Verse 69. *The proud have forged a lie*] The poor captives in Babylon had their conduct and motives continually misrepresented, and themselves belied and calumniated.

Verse 70. *Their heart is as fat as grease*] They are egregiously stupid, they have fed themselves without fear; they are become *flesh —brutalized*, and given over to vile affections, and have no kind of *spiritual relish*: but *I delight in thy law*—I have, through thy goodness, a *spiritual feeling* and a spiritual appetite.

Verse 71. It is *good for me that I have been afflicted*] See on ver. 67.

Verse 72. *The law of thy mouth* is *better*] Who can say this? Who *prefers* the law of his God, the Christ that bought him, and the heaven to which he hopes to go, when he can live no longer upon earth, *to thousands of gold and silver?* Yea, how many are there who, like Judas, *sell their Saviour* even for *thirty* pieces of silver? Hear this, ye lovers of the world and of money!

As the letter ט *teth* begins but few words, not forty, in the Hebrew language, there is less *variety* under this division than under any of the preceding.

ANALYSIS OF LETTER TETH.—*Ninth Division*

The psalmist, having been afflicted, shows,—
I. How graciously God dealt with him, in bringing him profitably through it.

II. Prays for a right judgment and knowledge.

III. Expresses his love to God's law, and the value he set upon it.

I. The psalmist gives thanks for mercy granted in affliction.

1. "Thou hast dealt graciously with thy servant." Graciously in afflicting him, and graciously in relieving him.

2. And this thou hast done "according to thy word." Thou hast fulfilled thy *promise*.

II. He prays to be taught of God:—

1. "Teach me good judgment." Many judge badly; for they think that affliction is a sign of God's displeasure. Let me have that *good judgment* that receives it as a fatherly correction from thee.

2. He asks for *science* and *knowledge*. A spiritual perception, and taste for heavenly things.

3. For this he gives his reason: "I have believed thy commandments." If we believe not God, we cannot profit by his word.

4. There is something remarkable in the *manner* of asking: 1. A good or *sound judgment*. 2. *Knowledge;* for without a *sound judgment, knowledge* is of no use.

III. He acknowledges that God's *chastisements* had done him *good*.

1. "Before I was afflicted." Prosperity is often the mother or error.

2. "Now I have kept thy word." Schola crucis, schola lucis, "The school of the cross is the school of light."

3. He acknowledges that the *good God* had done him *good*. To have a right notion of God is a great blessing.

IV. Much of the psalmist's *affliction* proceeded from *wicked men*. These he describes:—

1. They were *proud*. Pride is the mother of *rebellion*, both against *God* and *man*.

2. They were *liars*. Evil speaking and calumny are the first weapons of persecutors.

3. They *forged* these lies; they invented them. There was none *ready* to their hand, so they framed some to serve their purpose.

4. The psalmist opposes them with *humility* and *truth:* "I will keep thy precepts."

5. He shows more particularly their *moral character:* "Their heart was as fat as grease;" they were *stupid, brutish, hoggish*. Their *god* was their *belly*. 1. Because they abounded in *wealth*, they were *proud*. 2. Because they *pampered* themselves, they were *stupid*, and incapable of *moral feeling*. The *fat* is the least *sensible* part of the animal system.

' YOD

73 ʷThy hands have made me and fashioned me : ˣgive me understanding, that I may learn thy commandments.

74 ʸThey that fear thee will be glad when they see me ; because ᶻI have hoped in thy word.

75 I know, O Lᴏʀᴅ, that thy judgments *are* ᵃright, and ᵇ*that* thou in faithfulness hast afflicted me.

76 Let, I pray thee, thy merciful kindness

be ᶜfor my comfort, according to thy word unto thy servant.

77 ᵈLet thy tender mercies come unto me, that I may live : for ᵉthy law *is* my delight.

78 Let the proud ᶠbe ashamed ; ᵍfor they dealt perversely with me without a cause : *but* I will ʰmeditate in thy precepts.

79 Let those that fear thee turn unto me, and those that have known thy testimonies.

80 Let my heart be sound in thy statutes ; that I be not ashamed.

ʷJob x. 8; Psa. c. 3; cxxxviii. 8; cxxxix. 14——ˣVer. 34, 144——ʸPsa. xxxiv. 2——ᶻVer. 49, 147——ᵃHeb. *righteousness*

ᵇHeb. xii. 10——ᶜHeb. *to comfort me*——ᵈVerse 41 ᵉVerse 24, 47, 174——ᶠPsalm xxv. 3——ᵍVerse 86 ʰVerse 23

V. He shows the *condition* of the godly.
1. They see God's hand in their afflictions.
2. They learn his statutes.
3. They prefer his word to all earthly treasures; and,
4. They persevere in this heavenly disposition, because they continue to depend on God.

Lᴇᴛᴛᴇʀ ' Yᴏᴅ.—*Tenth Division*

Verse 73. *Thy hands have made me*] Thou hast formed the *mass* out of which I was made; and *fashioned me*—thou hast given me that particular *form* that distinguishes me from all thy other creatures.

Give me understanding] As thou hast raised me above the beasts that perish in my *form* and *mode of life, teach me* that I may live for a higher and nobler end, in loving, serving, and enjoying thee for ever. Show me that I was made for *heaven*, not for *earth*.

Verse 74. *They that fear thee*] They who are truly religious *will be glad*—will rejoice, at this farther proof of the saving power of God.

Verse 75. *I know—that thy judgments* are *right*] All the dispensations of thy providence are laid in *wisdom*, and executed in *mercy:* let me see that it is through this wisdom and mercy that I have been afflicted.

Verse 76. *Thy merciful kindness*] Let me derive my comfort and happiness from a diffusion of thy love and mercy, חסדך *chasdecha,* thy exuberant goodness, through my soul.

Verse 77. *Let thy tender mercies*] רחמיך *rachameycha,* thy *fatherly and affectionate feelings.*

Verse 78. *Let the proud be ashamed*] To reduce a *proud man* to *shame,* is to humble him indeed. Let them be *confounded. Without cause*—without any colourable pretext, have they persecuted me.

Verse 79. *Let those that fear thee*] The truly pious.

Turn unto me] Seeing thy work upon me, they shall acknowledge me as a *brand plucked from the burning.*

Verse 80. *Let my heart be sound in thy statutes*] Let it be *perfect*—all given up to thee, and all possessed by thee.

Aɴᴀʟʏꜱɪꜱ ᴏꜰ Lᴇᴛᴛᴇʀ Yᴏᴅ.—*Tenth Division*

I. In the first place the psalmist prays for understanding, *comfort*, and *mercy;* and uses

this argument, I am thy creature: "Thy hands have fashioned me."

II. He prays for *understanding:* Give me *heavenly light* and *influence.*

III. He prays for this that he may *learn God's commandments.* This was his *end.*

1. He endeavours to persuade God to this by the *benefit* that others would receive from seeing his *conversion:* "They that fear thee will be glad," &c.

2. He acknowledges that, if he was at any time *deserted*, it was because he was unfaithful, and that it was in very faithfulness that God had corrected him; therefore God's judgments were right.

3. He prays that God's *merciful kindness* may be extended to him. But this prayer he would not presume to have offered, had he not been authorized and encouraged by God's word: "According to thy word." When God gives a *promise*, he *binds* himself to *fulfil* it.

4. He desires to be treated as a *child* in the *heavenly family;* and therefore prays for God's *fatherly mercies*—his *bowels of compassion.*

5. And he prays for them for this *end*, "that he may live." And here also he adds a reason why he should be heard: "Thy law is my delight."

6. He puts up another petition for his enemies, if they will take timely warning: "Let the proud be ashamed;" let them see their unprincipled conduct and *blush* that they have been persecuting and calumniating innocent people.

7. He next expresses his own resolution: "I will meditate on thy statutes." Howsoever they deal with me, I will cleave unto my God.

8. He prays that he may be acknowledged by the *godly:* "Let them that fear thee turn unto me." God's Church is a communion of saints, and to them has God so distributed his graces that one stands in need of another. Where one *doubts*, the light of another may *solve his difficulty.* One *grieves;* another may *comfort* him. One is *tempted;* another may uphold and restore him. This company the psalmist would have joined to him for these ends.

9. He prays that he may be *sound in the faith*, for without this he could not be *steady* in his *obedience.* Though an *orthodox creed* does not constitute true religion, yet it is the basis of it, and it is a great blessing to have it; and *sound-*

כ CAPH

81 [i]My soul fainteth for thy salvation: *but* [k]I hope in thy word.

82 [l]Mine eyes fail for thy word, saying, When wilt thou comfort me?

83 For [m]I am become like a bottle in the smoke; *yet* do I not forget thy statutes.

84 [n]How many *are* the days of thy servant? [o]when wilt thou execute judgment on them that persecute me?

85 [p]The proud have digged pits for me, which *are* not after thy law.

86 All thy commandments *are* [q]faithful: [r]they persecute me [s]wrongfully; help thou me.

87 They had almost consumed me upon earth; but I forsook not thy precepts.

88 [t]Quicken me after thy loving-kindness; so shall I keep the testimony of thy mouth.

---

[i]Psalm lxxiii. 26; lxxxiv. 2——[k]Ver. 74, 114——[l]Ver. 123; Psalm lxix. 3——[m]Job xxx. 30——[n]Psalm xxxix. 4——[o]Revelation vi. 10

[p]Psalm xxxv. 7; Proverbs xvi. 27——[q]Hebrew, *faithfulness*——[r]Ver. 78——[s]Psalm xxxv. 19; xxxviii. 19 [t]Ver. 40

---

ness of mind is a strong help to the retention of a sound creed.

Finally, he shows the *end* for which he desires this blessing, that "he may not be ashamed." That he may continue sincere and upright, have dominion over all sin, give no place to secret iniquities, and that he may never be put to the blush before God or man. Reader, beg of God to enable *thee* to lay these things profitably to heart.

LETTER כ CAPH.—*Eleventh Division*

Verse 81. *My soul fainteth for thy salvation*] I have longed so incessantly after *thy salvation* —the complete purification and restoration of my soul, that my very spirits are exhausted.

" My heartstrings groan with deep complaint;
   My soul lies panting, Lord, for thee;
And every limb and every joint
   Stretches for perfect purity."

Verse 82. *Mine eyes fail*] With *looking up* for the fulfilment of thy promise, as my heart fails in longing after thy presence.

Verse 83. *Like a bottle in the smoke*] In the eastern countries their *bottles* are made of *skins;* one of these hung in the smoke must soon be *parched* and *shrivelled up.* This represents the exhausted state of his body and mind by long bodily affliction and mental distress.

Verse 84. *How many* are *the days of thy servants*] Dost thou not know that I have few to live, and they are full of trouble?

When wilt thou execute judgment on them that persecute me?] Shall not the pride of the Chaldeans be brought down, the arm of their strength broken, and thy people delivered? In this verse there is none of the *ten* words used in reference to God's law.

Verse 85. *The proud have digged pits*] The *Vulgate, Septuagint, Æthiopic,* and *Arabic,* translate this verse thus: "They have recited to me unholy fables, which are not according to thy law." They wish us to receive their *system of idolatry,* and the *tales* concerning their *gods;* but these *are not according to thy law.* The *Anglo-Saxon* is the same:ɲı cyδon meþa unɲıtɲıɲa ɲpellunᵹa ac na ɲɲa ɲɲa ꝺ þın; *They quothed me the unrightwise spells; but no so so law thine.*

Verse 87. *They had almost consumed me*] Had it not been for thy mercy, we had all been destroyed under this oppressive captivity.

Verse 88. *Quicken me*] Make and keep me *alive.*

So shall I keep] Without the spiritual *life* there is no *obedience;* we must therefore rise from the *dead,* and be *quickened* by the Spirit of Christ.

ANALYSIS OF LETTER CAPH.—*Eleventh Division*

I. In this section the psalmist laments his being grieved with some inward anguish.

II. Complains of his enemies.

III. Expresses his hope and constancy; and,

IV. Prays to God for comfort and grace.

I. 1. He begins with a sad complaint: "My soul fainteth." As the body will fail if it want natural food, so will the soul if it get not the bread of life.

2. His eyes also failed with *looking up.* The blessing was long delayed.

3. Yet *he hoped in God's word.* He knew that it would not fail.

4. He made complaint: "When wilt thou comfort me?"

5. His state was most deplorable; his body *dried* and *shrivelled up* through long *fasting* and *affliction,* so that it resembled a leathern bottle hung up in the smoke.

6. Yet still he continued faithful: "I do not forget thy statutes."

II. He complains against his enemies.

1. How long he should be obliged to suffer them.

2. He inquires "when the Lord will execute judgments."

He describes these enemies from their *qualities:*—

1. They were *proud.* They would not bow down to nor acknowledge God.

2. They were *treacherous.* They *digged pits for him*—used every kind of means in order to destroy him; cruel, treacherous, and cowardly.

3. They were *impious.* In heart and conduct they were not "according to God's law."

4. They acted without a *shadow of justice; wrongfully* against *law and justice.*

III. He prays for *succour:* "Help thou me." Here are three things of especial note: 1. O THOU, who art infinite. 2. *Help;* for thou hast all power in heaven and in earth. 3. *Me,* who cannot stand against my enemies; but "I trust in thee."

IV. 1. He closes with a frequent petition: "Quicken thou me—make me alive." All true religion consists in the LIFE *of* God in the SOUL *of man.*

ל LAMED

89 [u]For ever, O Lord, thy word is settled in heaven.

90 Thy faithfulness *is* [v]unto all generations: thou hast established the earth, and it [w]abideth.

91 They continue this day according to [x]thine ordinances: for all *are* thy servants.

92 Unless [y]thy law *had been* my delights,

I should then have perished in mine affliction.

93 I will never forget thy precepts: for with them thou hast quickened me.

94 I *am* thine, save me; for I have sought thy precepts.

95 The wicked have waited for me to destroy me: *but* I will consider thy testimonies.

96 [z]I have seen an end of all perfection: *but* thy commandment *is* exceeding broad.

---

[u]Psa. lxxxix. 2; Matt. xxiv. 34, 35; 1 Pet. i. 25——[v]Hebrew, *to generation and generation;* Psa. lxxxix. 1

[w]Hebrew, *standeth*——[x]Jer. xxxiii. 25——[y]Ver. 24
[z]Matt. v. 18; xxiv. 35

---

2. The *manner* in which he wishes to be quickened: "After thy loving-kindness." He wishes not to be raised from the *death of sin* by *God's thunder*, but by the *loving voice* of a *tender Father.*
3. The *effect* it should have upon him: "So shall I keep the testimony of thy mouth." Whatever thou *speakest* I will *hear, receive, love,* and *obey.*

LETTER ל LAMED.—*Twelfth Division*

Verse 89. *For ever, O Lord, thy word is settled in heaven.*] Thy purposes are all settled above, and they shall all be fulfilled below.

Verse 90. *Thy faithfulness*] That which binds thee to accomplish the promise made. And this shall be, not for an age merely, but from generation to generation; for thy promises refer to the whole duration of time.

Thou hast established the earth] Thou hast given it its appointed place in the system, and there it abideth.

Verse 91. *They continue this day*] This verse should be thus read: *All are thy servants; therefore, they continue this day according to thy ordinances.* "All the celestial bodies are governed by thy power. Thou hast given an ordinance or appointment to each, and each fulfils thy will in the place thou hast assigned it."

Verse 92. *Unless thy law* had been *my delights*] Had we not had the consolations of religion, we should long ago have died of a broken heart.

Verse 93. *I will never forget thy precepts*] How can I? It is by them I *live.*

Verse 94. *I am thine, save me*] He who can say this need fear no evil. In all trials, temptations, dangers, afflictions, persecutions, I am thine. Thy enemies wish to destroy me! Lord, look to thy servant; thy servant looks to thee. O how sovereign is such a word against all the evils of life! *I am* THINE! therefore *save thine* OWN!

Verse 96. *I have seen an end of all perfection*] Literally, "Of all consummations I have seen the end:" as if one should say, Every thing of human origin has its limits and end, howsoever extensive, noble, and excellent. All arts and sciences, languages, inventions, have their respective principles, have their limits and ends; as they came from man and relate to man, they shall end with man: but thy law, thy revelation, which is a picture of thy own mind, an external manifestation of thy own perfections, conceived in thy infinite ideas, in

reference to eternal objects, is exceeding broad; transcends the limits of creation; and extends illimitably into eternity! This has been explained as if it meant: All the real or pretended perfection that men can arrive at in this life is nothing when compared with what the law of God requires. This saying is *false* in itself, and is no *meaning* of the text. Whatever God requires of man he can, by his grace, work in man.

ANALYSIS OF LETTER LAMED.—*Twelfth Division*

This section contains an *encomium* of the WORD of GOD; of its perfection and immutability; and of the *comfort* the psalmist received from it.

I. In the *three* first verses the psalmist shows that God's word is *immutable*, by an instance in the *creatures.*
1. In the HEAVENS. They *continue* to *this day* as he made them in the beginning.
2. In the EARTH. As it was *established* in the beginning, so it *abideth.*
3. So also of the other heavenly bodies. *They* also *abide* as they were created; and answer still, most exactly, the ends for which they were made.
4. The *reason* of which is, "All are God's servants," made to *obey* his will: and from obedience they never swerve.

II. He shows the *excellence* of this word by a *rare effect* it had on himself: "Unless thy law had been my delight, I should have perished." No such comfort in trouble as God's word and promise. This he remembers with gratitude.
1. "I will never forget thy precepts." Only those forget them who reap no good from them.
2. This word had *quickened* him, i. e., God speaking and working by that word.
3. He will therefore be the *Lord's servant* for ever: "I am thine."
4. He knows he cannot continue so, but by *Divine help:* "Save me!"
5. He shows his love to God's word: "He seeks his precepts," that he may obey them.

III. He needed the help of God, because he had *inveterate enemies.* These he describes:
1. By their *diligence:* "The wicked have waited for me."
2. By their *cruelty:* "They waited to destroy me."
3. His *defence* against them. I will consider אתבונן *ethbonen,* I will set myself to consider. I will use all proper means to enable me to understand them.

ל MEM

97 O how love I thy law! ᵃit *is* my meditation all the day.

98 Thou through thy commandments hast
made me ᵇwiser than mine enemies: for ᶜthey
are ever with me.

99 I have more understanding than all my
teachers: ᵈfor thy testimonies *are* my meditation.

100 ᵉI understand more than the ancients
because I keep thy precepts.

101 I have ᶠrefrained my feet from every
evil way, that I might keep thy word.

102 I have not departed from thy judgments: for thou hast taught me.

103 ᵍHow sweet are thy words unto my
ʰtaste! *yea, sweeter* than honey to my mouth!

104 Through thy precepts I get understanding: therefore ⁱI hate every false way.

ᵃPsa. i. 2——ᵇDeut. iv. 6, 8——ᶜHeb. *it is ever with me*
ᵈ2 Tim. iii. 15——ᵉJob xxxii. 7, 8, 9

ᶠProv. i. 15——ᵍPsa. xix. 10; Prov. viii. 11——ʰHeb.
palate——ⁱVer. 128

IV. Having shown the perfection of God's
word,—
1. In *establishing* and *upholding* the *frame
of the world.*
2. In bringing comfort to the soul. In the
close,
3. He compares it to all other things which
we esteem as *excellent* and *perfect,—riches,
honours, crowns, sceptres, kingdoms,* &c.,
over which the word of God has still the
pre-eminence; they perish, but it endures
for ever: "I have seen an end of all
perfection." Jonah's *gourd* was smitten by
a *worm;* the *golden head* had *feet* of *clay;*
the most *beautiful form* shall dissolve
into *dust; Babylon,* the wonder of the world,
has *perished* from the face of the earth; the
fairest day is succeeded by *midnight;* and so
of other things: "but the commandment is exceeding broad:" all the principles of justice are
contained in it; no just notion of God without
it; all the rules of a holy life, and all the promises of life eternal, are found in it. It is the
word of God, and it endureth for ever. When
the heavens and the earth are no more, this
word shall stand up and flourish.

LETTER ל MEM.—*Thirteenth Division*

Verse 97. *O how love I thy law*] This is one
of the strongest marks of a gracious and pious
heart, cast in the mould of obedience. Such
love the precepts of Christ: in his commandments they delight; and this delight is shown
by their making them frequent subjects of their
meditation.
Verse 98. *Wiser than mine enemies*] Some
have thought that this Psalm was composed by
Daniel, and that he speaks of himself in these
verses. Being instructed by God, he was found
to have more *knowledge* than any of the
Chaldeans, magicians, soothsayers, &c., &c.; and
his wisdom soon appeared to the whole nation
vastly superior to theirs.
Verse 99. *I have more understanding than
all my teachers*] As he had entered into the
spiritual nature of the law of God, and saw into
the exceeding breadth of the commandment, he
soon became wiser than any of the *priests* or
even *prophets* who instructed him.
Verse 100. *I understand more than the
ancients*] God had revealed to him more of
that *hidden wisdom* which was in his law than
he had done to any of his predecessors. And
this was most literally true of *David,* who
spoke more fully about *Christ* than any who
had gone before him; or, indeed, followed after

him. His compositions are, I had almost said,
a *sublime Gospel.*
Verse 101. *I have refrained my feet*] By
avoiding all sin, the spirit of wisdom still continues to rest upon me.
Verse 103. Sweeter *than honey to my
mouth!*] What deep communion must this
man have had with his Maker! These expressions show a soul filled with God. O
Christians, how vastly *superior* are our privileges! and alas! how vastly *inferior* in
general, are our consolations, our communion
with God, and our heavenly-mindedness!
Verse 104. *Through thy precepts I get understanding*] Spiritual knowledge increases while
we tread in the path of *obedience.* Obedience
is the grand means of *growth* and *instruction.*
Obedience trades with the talent of grace, and
thus grace becomes multiplied.

ANALYSIS OF LETTER MEM.—*Thirteenth Division*

In this division we see,—
I. The affection of the psalmist to the law of
God.
II. The great benefits he derived from it.
I. 1. "O how I love thy law." God alone
knows how great that love is which I feel.
2. As true love always seeks opportunities
of conversing with the beloved object, the
psalmist shows his in *meditation* on God's law
by day and night.
He gives us several *encomiums* on God's
word:—
1. The *wisdom* he derived from it. It made
him *wiser than his enemies.* It taught him
how to conduct himself towards them, so as to
disappoint many of their plans, and always
insure his own peace.
2. It made him *wiser than his teachers.*
Many, even of the *Jewish teachers,* took upon
them to *teach* that to others which they had
never learned themselves. He must have been
wiser than these. Many in the present day
take upon themselves the character of *ministers
of Jesus Christ,* who have never felt his Gospel
to be the power of God to their salvation. A
simple woman, who is converted to God, and
feels the *witness of his Spirit* that she is his
child, has *a thousand* times more true wisdom
than such persons, though they may have
learned many languages and many sciences.
3. It made him *wiser than the ancients*—
than any of the *Jewish elders,* who had not
made that word the subject of their deep study
and meditation.
A *second encomium.* God's word *gives power*

נ NUN

105 [k]Thy word *is* a [l]lamp unto my feet, and a light unto my path.

106 [m]I have sworn, and I will perform *it,* that I will keep thy righteous judgments.

107 I am afflicted very much: [n]quicken me, O LORD, according unto thy word.

108 Accept, I beseech thee, [o]the freewill-offerings of my mouth, O LORD, [p]and teach me thy judgments.

109 [q]My soul *is* continually in my hand: yet do I not forget thy law.

110 [r]The wicked have laid a snare for me: yet I [s]erred not from thy precepts.

111 [t]Thy testimonies have I taken as a heritage for ever: for [u]they *are* the rejoicing of my heart.

112 I have inclined mine heart [v]to perform thy statutes alway, [w]*even unto* the end.

---

[k]Proverbs vi. 23——[l]Or, *candle*——[m]Neh. x. 29 [n]Ver. 88——[o]Hos. xiv. 2; Heb. xiii. 15——[p]Ver. 12, 26 [q]Job xiii. 14

[r]Psalm cxl. 5; cxli. 9——[s]Verse 10, 21——[t]Deuteronomy xxxiii. 4——[u]Verse 77, 92, 174——[v]Hebrew, *to do*——[w]Ver. 33

---

over sin: "I have refrained:" and the psalmist was no *speculatist;* he was in every respect a *practical* man.

A *third encomium* is, the more a man resists evil forbidden by that law, and practices righteousness commanded by it, the stronger he grows. The psalmist *refrained from every evil way,* that he might *keep God's word.*

Lest any one should think that he pretends to have acquired all these excellencies by his own *study* and *industry,* he asserts that he had nothing but what he had received: "I have not departed," &c.; "for THOU hast taught me."

A *fourth encomium* is, that God's law gives indescribable *happiness* to them who love and obey it: "How sweet are thy words," &c.

II. In the last verse he proves all that he said by the blessed effects of God's word upon himself.

1. He got *understanding* by it. He became learned, wise, and prudent.

2. He was enabled to *hate every false way*— false religion, lying vanities, empty pleasures; and every thing that did not tend to and prepare for an eternity of blessedness.

LETTER נ NUN.—*Fourteenth Division*

Verse 105. *Thy word* is *a lamp*] This is illustrated thus by *Solomon,* Prov. vi. 23: "The *commandment* is a *lamp;* and the *law* is *light;* and *reproofs of instruction* are the *way* of *life.*" God's word is a *candle* which may be held in the hand to give us light in every *dark place* and *chamber;* and it is a *general light* shining upon all *his works,* and upon all *our ways.*

Verse 106. *I have sworn*] Perhaps this means no more than that he had renewed his *covenant* with God; he had *bound* himself to love and serve him only.

Verse 107. *I am afflicted very much*] עד מאד *ad meod,* "to extremity, excessively." We are in the most oppressive captivity.

Quicken me] Deliver us from our bondage.

Verse 108. *The freewill-offerings of my mouth*] נדבות פי *nidboth pi.* the *voluntary offerings which I have promised.* Or, As we are in *captivity,* and cannot sacrifice to thee, but *would* if we *could;* accept the *praises* of our mouth, and the *purposes* of our *hearts,* instead of the sacrifices and offerings which we *would* bring to thy altar, but *cannot.*

Verse 109. *My soul* is *continually in my hand*] נפשי *naphshi, my life;* that is, it is in *constant danger* every hour I am on the confines of death. The expression signifies to be in *continual danger.* So *Xenarchus* in Athenæus, lib. xiii., c. 4: Εν τη χειρι την ψυχην εχοντα, "having the life in the hand;" which signifies continual danger and jeopardy. There is something like this in the speech of *Achilles* to *Ulysses,* HOM. Il. ix., ver. 322:—

Αιει εμην ψυχην παραβαλλομενος πολεμιζειν·

"Always presenting my life to the dangers of the fight."

My soul is in thy hand, is the reading of the *Syriac, Septuagint, Æthiopic,* and *Arabic;* but this is a *conjectural* and *useless* emendation.

Verse 110. *The wicked have laid a snare*] Thus their lives were continually exposed to danger.

Verse 111. *As a heritage*] In ver. 57 he says, God *is my portion,* חלקי *chelki.* In this he says, *Thy testimonies have I taken as a heritage,* נחל *nachal.* To these he was *heir;* he had *inherited* them from his fathers, and he was determined to leave them to his *family* for ever. If a man can leave nothing to his child but a *Bible,* in that he bequeaths him the greatest treasure in the universe.

Verse 112. *I have inclined mine heart*] I used the power God gave me, and turned to his testimonies with all mine heart. When we *work with God,* we can *do all things.*

ANALYSIS OF LETTER NUN.—*Fourteenth Division*

In this division the psalmist points out farther excellencies of God's word, in the use of it. 1. God's word was a *lamp to his feet* to guide him through every dark place. 2. It was a *light to his path,* ever showing him generally the way in which he should walk.

1. He therefore resolves to keep it, and binds himself to fulfil his resolution. As the lamp was going before, and the light was shining, it was necessary that he should walk while the light shone. He therefore, 1. Binds himself by an *oath* or vow: "I have sworn." 2. He will be *faithful* to his oath: "I will perform it." 3. Not merely to admire, but to *keep* God's word. 4. Not its *promises* merely, but its *righteous judgments.*

2. And this he will do in all circumstances, even in *extreme affliction.* Then he requests *two* things from the Lord. 1. That he would "accept the freewill-offerings of his mouth."

ס SAMECH

113 I hate *vain* thoughts: but thy law do I love.

114 ˣThou *art* my hiding place and my shield: ʸI hope in thy word.

115 ᶻDepart from me, ye evil doers: for I will keep the commandments of my God.

116 Uphold me according unto thy word, that I may live: and let me not ᵃbe ashamed of my hope.

117 Hold thou me up, and I shall be safe:

and I will have respect unto thy statutes continually.

118 Thou hast trodden down all them that ᵇerr from thy statutes: for their deceit *is* falsehood.

119 Thou ᶜputtest away all the wicked of the earth ᵈ*like* dross: therefore I love thy testimonies.

120 ᵉMy flesh trembleth for fear of thee; and I am afraid of thy judgments.

ˣPsa. xxxii. 7; xci. 1——ʸVer. 81——ᶻPsa. vi. 8; cxxxix. 19; Matt. vii. 23——ᵃPsa. xxv. 2; Rom. v. 5; ix. 33; x. 11——ᵇVer. 21——ᶜHeb. *causest to cease* ᵈEzek. xxii. 18——ᵉHab. iii. 16

All his praises, thanksgivings, and vows. 2. That he would "teach him his judgments," that he might perform what he had vowed.

3. He shows the difficulties he was in: 1. "My soul is continually in my hand." I am in continual danger. He had got the *sword of the Spirit*, and his life depended on the use he made of it: if the soldier, whose life depends on his *drawn sword*, does not use it well, his enemy kills him. 2. Hence he says, "I do not forget thy law." I am making a proper use of my sword. 3. And that I have need of it is evident, for "the wicked have laid a snare for me." 4. This did not intimidate him: he did not leave the *path of duty* for fear of a *snare* being in that path: "I erred not from thy precepts." I did not *go about* to seek a *safer* way.

4. He keeps his resolution, and vows still. 1. He preferred God's testimonies even to the land of Canaan, to riches and crowns: "I have taken them for my heritage." 2. He delighted in them: "They are the rejoicing of my heart."

5. In this work he was determined to *continue:* 1. "I have inclined my heart." The counsel of the soul is like a balance; and the mind, which hath the commanding power over the affections, inclines the balance to that which it judges best. 2. It was to *perform it*, that he thus *inclined his heart*. 3. And this, not for a *time*, or on some *particular occasion*, but *always*, and unto *the end*. Then the *end of life* would be the *beginning of glory.*

LETTER ס SAMECH.—*Fifteenth Division*

Verse 113. *I hate* vain *thoughts*] I have hated סעפים *seaphim*, "tumultuous, violent men." I abominate all *mobs* and *insurrections*, and troublers of the public peace.

Verse 114. *My hiding place*] My asylum.

And my shield] There is a time in which I may be called to *suffer in secret;* then thou *hidest me.* There may be a time in which thou callest me to *fight;* then thou art my *Shield* and *Protector.*

Verse 115. *Depart from me*] *Odi profanum vulgus, etarceo,* I abominate the profane, and will have no communion with them. I drive them away from my presence.

Verse 116. *Uphold me*] סמכני *sammecheni*, prop me up; give me thyself to *lean upon.*

Verse 117. *Hold thou me up*] I shall grow weary and faint in the way, if not strengthened and *supported* by thee.

And I shall be safe] No soul can be *safe*, unless upheld by thee.

Verse 118. *Thou hast trodden down*] All thy

enemies will be finally trodden down under thy feet.

Their deceit is *falsehood.*] Their elevation is a *lie.* The wicked often become *rich* and *great*, and affect to be *happy*, but it is all *false;* they have neither a *clean* nor *approving* conscience. Nor can they have *thy* approbation; and, consequently, no true *blessedness.*

Verse 119. *Thou* puttest away all the wicked *of the earth* like *dross*] There is no *true metal* in them: when they are tried by the *refining fire*, they are burnt up; they fly off in fumes, and come to no amount. There is probably an allusion here to the *scum* or *scoriæ* at the surface of melting metals, which is swept off previously to casting the metal into the mould.

Therefore I love thy testimonies.] Thy *testimonies* will stand; and thy *people* will stand; because thou who didst give the one, and who upholdest the other, art *pure, immovable,* and *eternal.*

Verse 120. *My flesh trembleth for fear of thee*] I know thou art a just and holy God: I know thou requirest truth in the inner parts. I know that thou art a Spirit, and that they who worship thee must worship thee in spirit and in truth; and I am often *alarmed* lest I *fall short.* It is only an assurance of my interest in thy mercy that can save me from *distressing fears and harassing doubts.* It is our privilege to know we are in God's favour; and it is not less so to maintain a continual filial fear of offending him. A true conception of God's justice and mercy begets reverence.

ANALYSIS OF LETTER SAMECH.—*Fifteenth Division*

In this section the psalmist—

I. Declares his hatred to wickedness, and his detestation of wicked men.

II. Expresses his love to God's law.

III. Prays for grace to sustain him in the observance of it.

IV. Foretells the destruction of the wicked.

I. "I hate vain thoughts;" not only *evil* itself, but the *thought* that leads to it.

II. 1. "Thy law do I love:" I strive to keep every *affection* exercised on its *proper object.*

2. This is my privilege: for thou art, 1. "My hiding-place," that public evils may not reach me; and 2. "My shield," to ward off the fiery darts of the wicked one.

3. To God, therefore, and his word, he would adhere in all extremities; and would have no communion with the wicked. 1. These he would *drive away* as the pests of piety: "Depart from

ע AIN

121 I have done judgment and justice: leave me not to mine oppressors.

122 Be ᶠsurety for thy servant for good: let not the proud oppress me.

123 ᵍMine eyes fail for thy salvation, and for the word of thy righteousness.

124 Deal with thy servant according unto thy mercy, and ʰteach me thy statutes.

125 ᶦI *am* thy servant; give me understanding, that I may know thy testimonies.

126 *It is* time for *thee,* LORD, to work: *for* they have made void thy law.

127 ᵏTherefore I love thy commandments above gold; yea, above fine gold.

128 Therefore I esteem all *thy* precepts *concerning* all *things to be* right; *and* I ˡhate every false way.

ᶠHeb. vii. 22——ᵍVer. 81, 82——ʰVer. 12——ᶦPsa. cxvi. 16

ᵏVerse 72; Psalm xix. 10; Proverbs viii. 11
ˡVerse 104

---

me." 2. Because he would "*keep* the commandments of God," while the others were bent on *breaking* them.

III. He prays for the grace of God to sustain him.

1. "Uphold me:" if thou do not, I *fall.*

2. "Hold thou me up:" for I am *falling.* One part of this prayer is against the *occurrence* of evil; the other, against evil as *actually taking place.*

IV. He foretells the destruction of wicked men.

1. "Thou hast trodden down:" they who *tread thy commandments* under *their feet* shall be *trodden down* under *thy feet.* The *first* treading shall bring on the *second.*

2. They *deceive* themselves in supposing thou wilt not resent this. This is a *deception,* and a dangerous one too, for it is against the most positive declarations of thy *truth,* therefore it is *falsehood.*

3. This is most certain, for "thou puttest away all the wicked of the earth like dross;" they are utterly vile, and of no account in thy sight.

4. "Therefore I love thy testimonies." And for this, among other reasons, that I may avoid their *judgments.*

5. Foreseeing the *judgments* to fall on the wicked, it was necessary that he should be filled with a salutary *fear.* 1. "My flesh trembleth." Happy is he who by other men's harms learns to be wise. 2. We should work out our salvation with fear and trembling. God is *holy* and *just* as well as *merciful;* therefore we should fear before him. 3. Because he saw those judgments coming on the wicked, he desired to be *established in God's holy fear.* In all cases the old proverb is true: "Too much familiarity breeds contempt."

LETTER ע AIN.—*Sixteenth Division*

Verse 121. *I have done judgment and justice*] I have given the best *decision* possible on every case that came before me; and I have endeavoured to *render* to all their *due.*

Verse 122. *Be surety for thy servant*] ערב *arob,* give a pledge or token that thou wilt help me in times of necessity. Or, *Be bail for thy servant.* What a word is this! Pledge thyself for me, that thou wilt produce me *safely* at the judgment of the great day. Then sustain and keep me blameless till the coming of Christ. Neither of these two verses has any of the *ten words* in reference to God's *law* or *attributes.* The *judgment* and the *justice* refer to the psalmist's own conduct in ver. 121. The hun-

dred and twenty-second has no word of the kind.

Verse 123. *Mine eyes fail*] See on ver. 82.

Verse 125. *I am thy servant*] See on ver. 94.

Verse 126. It is *time for* thee, *Lord, to work*] The *time* is fulfilled in which thou hast promised deliverance to thy people. *They*—the Babylonians,

Have made void thy law.] They have filled up the measure of their iniquities.

Verse 127. *Therefore I love thy commandments*] I see thou wilt do all things well. I will trust in thee.

Above gold] מזהב *mizzahab,* more than resplendent gold; gold without any stain or rust.

Yea, above fine gold.] ומפז *umippaz,* above solid gold; gold separated from the dross, perfectly *refined.*

Verse 128. *All thy precepts* concerning *all* things to be *right*] There are too many *supplied* words here to leave the text unsuspected. All the ancient versions, except the *Chaldec,* seem to have omitted the second כל *col,* ALL, and read the text thus: "Therefore I have walked straight in all thy precepts." I go straight on in all thy precepts, hating every false way. I neither turn to the right hand nor to the left; the *false ways* are *crooked;* thy *way* is *straight.* I am going to heaven, and that way lies *straight before me.* To walk in the way of *falsity* I cannot, because I *hate* it; and I hate such ways because God hates them.

ANALYSIS OF LETTER AIN.—*Sixteenth Division*

In this part the psalmist,

I. Makes a profession of his integrity.

II. Prays for protection against his enemies.

III. Resolves to walk in the right way.

I. He makes a profession of his integrity:—

1. "I have done judgment and justice."

2. Though he had done so, yet he was not free from calumny and oppression. He commends, therefore, his righteous cause to God: "Leave me not to mine oppressors."

3. "Be surety for thy servant:" give me an assurance that thou wilt stand by me.

4. "Let not the proud oppress me." For miserable are the destitute when they fall into such hands.

II. He shows us how he had prayed against his enemies, and for God's salvation.

"Mine eyes fail." My faith is almost gone, and the eye of my mind become dim.

2. It was the *salvation* of God he had in view: "For thy salvation."

3. The ground on which he prayed was *the word of God's righteousness.*

פ PE

129 Thy testimonies *are* wonderful: therefore doth my soul keep them.

130 The entrance of thy words giveth light; ᵐit giveth understanding unto the simple.

131 I opened my mouth, and panted: for I ⁿlonged for thy commandments.

132 ᵒLook thou upon me, and be merciful unto me, ᵖas ᑫthou usest to do unto those that love thy name.

ᵐPsa. xix. 7; Prov. i. 4——ⁿVer. 20——ᵒPsa. cvi. 4 ᵖ2 Thess. i. 6, 7——ᑫHeb. *according to the custom toward those, &c.*

He proceeds in his prayer; and begs God to deal with him as a needy *servant*, and also an *ignorant scholar.*
1. "Deal with thy servant." I am ready to do thy will; but treat me in thy *mercy.*
2. "Teach me thy statutes." I wish to learn what thy will is; and when I know it, faithfully to do it.
He urges the same request, with nearly the same reasons for it: "I am thy servant." I am no *stranger* to thee. I have frequently come to thee to get grace to enable me to serve thee. I am one of thy domestics, a member of thy Church.
He comes now with his complaint.
1. "It is time for thee to work." Thy *enemies* are *strong*, and thy *people weak.*
2. "They have made void thy law." They have entirely trampled it under foot.
III. The zeal of the psalmist increased as the love of many waxed cold.
1. "Therefore," because they despise thy word, ordinances, and people.
2. "I love thy commandments." As they hate, so I love. When we love God's commandments, it is a sign that we have not received the grace of God in vain.
3. To show the greatness of his love, he says, I love thy commandments "above gold; yea, above fine gold." My love is greater to thy *law*, than that of the miser is to his bags.
4. He received all God's precepts to be right; and he takes not some, but the whole of them.
5. Whatever gain *idolatry* and *time-serving* might hold out to him, he abominated it, because he *hated every false way.* His love of God, his law, and holiness, was greater than his love of life.

Letter פ Pe.—*Seventeenth Division*

Verse 129. *Thy testimonies* are *wonderful*] There is a height, length, depth, and breadth in thy word and testimonies that are truly astonishing; and on this account my soul loves them, and I deeply study them. The more I study, the more light and salvation I obtain.
Verse 130. *The entrance of thy words giveth light*] פתח *pethach*, the *opening* of it: when I open my Bible to read, light springs up in my mind. Every sermon, every prayer, every act of faith, is an *opening* by which light is let into the seeking soul.
Verse 131. *I opened my mouth, and panted*] A metaphor taken from an animal exhausted in the chase. He runs, open-mouthed, to take in the cooling air; the heart beating high, and the

133 ʳOrder my steps in thy word: and ˢlet not any iniquity have dominion over me.

134 ᵗDeliver me from the oppression of man: so will I keep thy precepts.

135 ᵘMake thy face to shine upon thy servant; and ᵛteach me thy statutes.

136 ʷRivers of waters run down mine eyes, because they keep not thy law.

ʳPsa. xvii. 5——ˢPsa. xix. 13; Rom. vi. 12——ᵗLuke i. 74——ᵘPsa. iv. 6——ᵛVer. 12, 26——ʷJer. ix. 1; xiv. 17; see Ezek. ix. 4

---

muscular force nearly expended through fatigue. The psalmist sought for salvation, as he would run from a ferocious beast for his life. Nothing can show his earnestness in a stronger point of view.
Verse 132. *As thou usest to do*] Treat me as thy mercy has induced thee to treat others in my circumstances. Deal with me as thou dealest with thy *friends.*
Verse 133. *Order my steps*] הכן *hachen*, make them *firm;* let me not walk with a halting or unsteady step.
Have dominion over me.] בי *bi*, IN me. Let me have no governor but God; let the throne of my heart be filled by him, and none other.
Verse 135. *Make thy face to shine*] Give me a sense of thy approbation. Let me know, by the testimony of thy Spirit in my conscience, that thou art reconciled to me. The godly in all ages derived their happiness from a consciousness of the Divine favour. The witness of God's spirit in the souls of believers was an essential principle in religion from the foundation of the world.
Verse 136. *Rivers of waters run down mine eyes*] How much had this blessed man the honour of God and the salvation of souls at heart! O for more of that spirit which mourns for the transgressions of the land! But we are not properly convinced of the exceeding sinfulness of sin.

Analysis of Letter Pe.—*Seventeenth Division*

In this division the psalmist—
I. Praises God's word.
II. Shows his affection to it.
III. Prays for grace to keep it.
IV. Mourns for those who do not.
1. The eulogy he gives to God's word here is from a *new quality* not mentioned before. "Thy testimonies are wonderful;" wondrous mysteries are contained in the Divine oracles.
1. The *ceremonial* law is wonderful, because the mystery of our redemption by the blood of Christ is pointed out in it.
2. The *prophecies* are wonderful, as predicting things, humanly speaking, so uncertain, and at such great distance of time, with so much accuracy.
3. The *decalogue* is wonderful, as containing in a very few words all the principles of justice and charity.
4. Were we to go to the *New Testament*, here wonders rise on wonders! All is astonishing; but the psalmist could not have had this in view.

צ TSADDI

137 [x]Righteous *art* thou, O LORD, and upright *are* thy judgments.

138 [y]Thy testimonies *that* thou hast commanded *are* [z]righteous and very [a]faithful.

139 [b]My zeal hath [c]consumed me, because mine enemies have forgotten thy words.

140 [d]Thy word *is* very [e]pure: therefore thy servant loveth it.

141 I *am* small and despised: *yet* do not I forget thy precepts.

142 Thy righteousness *is* an everlasting righteousness, and thy law *is* [f]the truth.

143 Trouble and anguish have [g]taken hold on me: *yet* thy commandments *are* [h]my delights.

144 The righteousness of thy testimonies *is* everlasting: [i]give me understanding, and I shall live.

---

[x]Ezra ix. 15; Neh. ix. 33; Jer. xii. 1; Dan. ix. 7
[y]Psa. xix. 7, 8, 9——[z]Heb. *righteousness*——[a]Heb. *faithfulness*——[b]Psa. lxix. 9; John ii. 17——[c]Heb. *cut me off*

[d]Psa. xii. 6; xviii. 30; xix. 8; Prov. xxx. 5——[e]Heb. *tried* or *refined*——[f]Ver. 151; Psa. xix. 9; John xvii. 17——[g]Heb. *found me*——[h]Verse 77——[i]Verse 34, 73, 169

The second eulogy is, that God's law is *the dispenser of light.*

1. The entrance of it, the first chapter of Genesis; what light does that pour on the mind of man! What knowledge of the most important things, which we should never have known without it!

2. *It gives light to the simple*—to those who are not *double;* who have but *one end* in view, and one *aim* to that end.

3. Of those *simple ones* or *babes* our Lord speaks, Matt. xi. 25, and St. Paul, 1 Cor. i. 25, 26, &c.

II. The psalmist shows that he was one of those *simple* ones.

1. "He opened his mouth" by prayer, and sought the spirit of light and piety.

2. He *panted* after it as men do that want *vreath*, and are longing to get fresh air.

3. And this he did because "he longed for God's commandments;" had a vehement desire to know and keep them.

III. He now betakes himself to prayer, and acquaints us with the petitions he had offered.

1. He said, "Look upon me." Consider thy poor, dependent, helpless creature.

2. "Have mercy upon me." Look, not with the indignation which I deserve, but with the mercy which thou knowest I need.

3. "As thou usest to do." Act by me as thou dost by them that love thee.

4. "Order my steps." Give me grace to be obedient. Many look for *mercy to pardon their sin*, but do not look for *grace* to enable them to be *obedient*.

5. "Let not any iniquity have dominion over me." Let me be saved from all my spiritual captivity.

6. "Deliver me from the oppression of men." Let neither wicked men nor wicked spirits rule over me.

7. "Make thy face to shine upon me!" Let me have thy light, thy peace, and thy *approbation.*

8. "And teach me thy statutes." Keep me at thy feet, under continual instruction.

IV. He concludes by telling how he grieved for the wickedness of others and the dishonour of God. If we grieve not for others, their sin may become ours. See Ezek. ix. 8; 1 Cor. v. 2.

LETTER צ TSADDI.—*Eighteenth Division*

Verse 137. *Righteous art thou*] Thou art infinitely holy in thy nature; and therefore thou art *upright in thy judgments*—all thy dispensations to men.

Verse 138. *Thy testimonies*] Every thing that proceeds from thee partakes of the perfections of thy nature.

Verse 139. *My zeal hath consumed me*] My earnest desire to promote thy glory, and the pain I feel at seeing transgressions multiplied, have worn down both my flesh and spirits.

Verse 140. *Thy word is very pure*] צרופה *tseruphah*, it is *purification*. It is not a *purified thing*, but a *thing* that *purifies*. "Now ye are *clean*," said Christ, "by the *word* I have spoken unto you." God's word is a *fire* to *purify* as well as a *hammer* to *break.*

Verse 141. *I am small and despised*] And on these accounts have every thing to *fear*. Being *small*, I cannot *resist;* being *despised*, I am in *danger;* but even all this does not induce me to start aside, or through the fear of man to be unfaithful to thee.

Verse 142. *Thy righteousness is an everlasting righteousness*] The word צדק *tsedek* is a word of very extensive meaning in the Bible. It signifies, not only God's inherent righteousness and perfection of nature, but also his method of treating others; his plan of redemption; *his method of saving others.* And the word δικαιοσυνη, which answers to it, in the *Septuagint* and in the *New Testament*, is used with the same latitude of meaning, and in the same sense; particularly in that remarkable passage, Rom. iii. 25, 26, where see the notes. Thy merciful method of dealing with sinners and justifying the ungodly will last as long as the earth lasts; and thy *law* that witnesses this, in all its pages, is *the truth.*

Verse 143. *Trouble and anguish*] I am exercised with various trials from men and devils.

Have taken hold on me] But still I cleave to my God, and am *delighted* with his law.

Verse 144. *The righteousness of thy testimonies is everlasting*] Thy *moral law* was not made for *one people*, or for one *particular time;* it is as imperishable as thy *nature*, and of *endless obligation.* It is that law by which all the children of Adam shall be judged.

Give me understanding] To know and practise it.

And I shall live.] Shall glorify thee, and live eternally; not for the *merit* of having done it, but because thou didst fulfil the work of the law in my heart, having saved me from condemnation by it.

ק KOPH

145 I cried with *my* whole heart; hear me, O Lord: I will keep thy statutes.

146 I cried unto thee; save me, [k]and I shall keep thy testimonies.

147 [l]I prevented the dawning of the morning, and cried: [m]I hoped in thy word.

148 [n]Mine eyes prevent the *night* watches, that I might meditate in thy word.

149 Hear my voice according unto thy loving-kindness: O Lord, [o]quicken me according to thy judgment.

150 They draw nigh that follow after mischief: they are far from thy law.

151 Thou *art* [p]near, O Lord; [q]and all thy commandments *are* truth.

152 Concerning thy testimonies, I have known of old that thou hast founded them [r]for ever.

---

[k]Or, *that I may keep*——[l]Psa. v. 3; lxxxviii. 13; cxxx. 6 [m]Ver. 74——[n]Psa. lxiii. 1, 6

[o]Ver. 40, 154——[p]Psa. cxlv. 18——[q]Ver. 86, 143, 172 [r]Luke xxi. 33

ANALYSIS OF LETTER TSADDI.—*Eighteenth Division*

In this division the psalmist—
I. Commends the law of God, from its Author, its equity, its purity, and its perpetuity.
II. A consideration of which led him to love and delight in it, though opposed by many enemies.
I. 1. "Righteous art thou." Thou *alterest* not with *times*, thou *changest* not with *persons*, thou art *ever the same*.
2. Thy *judgments*, in giving rewards and dispensing punishments, are upright.
3. Thy *testimonies*, that declare this, are *righteous* and *faithful*.
He consequently felt an ardent *zeal* for God's glory.
1. This "zeal consumed him," and he expresses the cause.
2. Men "forgot God's words." He pined away for grief on this account. He turns to another *character* of God's law.
"Thy word is very pure."
1. It is *pure* in itself, and the *purifier* of the heart.
2. On this account he *loved* it; and we know that "love is the fulfilling of the law."
A *third* effect was a careful remembrance of it, though tried by his enemies.
1. "I am small." Of no weight nor authority; have no secular power.
2. "Despised." Have no credit nor respect.
3. "Yet do I not forget thy precepts." Nothing can move me while upheld by thee; and thou wilt uphold me while I cleave unto thee.
A *fourth* commendation of God's law is its *immutability*.
1. It is immutable, and can never be dispensed with. It is a *righteousness* that is everlasting.
2. It is the *truth:* 1. It has priority of all laws; 2. Contains no falsehood.
3. Its promises and threatenings shall all be punctually fulfilled.
II. He *loved* and *delighted* in it, notwithstanding he had *trouble* and *anguish*.
1. *Trouble* and *anguish*. The righteous are often under the cross.
2. Yet "thy commandments are my delights." While faithful to thee, all my afflictions are sanctified to me, so that I can *rejoice* while I suffer.
He speaks again about the *immutability* of God's word.

1. "The righteousness of thy testimonies," Thy word is like thyself, for it comes from thee.
2. "Give me understanding." I always stand in need of *teaching*.
3. "And I shall live." All is *death* without thee. Live in *me*, that I may live *by* thee.

LETTER ק KOPH.—*Nineteenth Division*
Verse 145. *I cried with* my *whole heart*] The whole soul of the psalmist was engaged in this good work. He whose *whole heart* cries to God will never rise from the throne of grace without a blessing.
Verse 147. *I prevented the dawning*] קדמתי *kiddamti,* "I went before the dawn or twilight."
Verse 148. *Mine eyes prevent*] קדמו *kiddemu,* "go before the watches." Before the watchman proclaims the hour, I am awake, meditating on thy words. The Jews divided the night into three watches, which began at what we call six o'clock in the evening, and consisted each of four hours. The Romans taught them afterwards to divide it into four watches of three hours each; and to divide the day and night into twelve hours each; wherein different guards of soldiers were appointed to watch. At the proclaiming of each watch the psalmist appears to have risen and performed some act of devotion. For a remarkable custom of our Saxon ancestors, see the note on ver. 164.
Verse 150. *They draw nigh*] They are just at hand who seek to destroy me.
They are far from thy law.] They are *near* to all *evil*, but *far* from *thee.*
Verse 151. *Thou* art *near*] As they are *near* to destroy, so art thou *near* to *save*. When the enemy comes in as a flood, the Spirit of the Lord lifts up a standard against him.
Verse 152. *Concerning thy testimonies, I have known of old*] קדם ידעתי *kedem yedati,* "Long ago I have known concerning thy testimonies. Thou hast designed that thy testimonies should bear reference to, and evidence of, those glorious things which thou hast provided for the salvation of men; and that this should be an everlasting testimony. They continue, and Christ is come.

ANALYSIS OF LETTER KOPH.—*Nineteenth Division*

I. The psalmist is earnest in his prayers for deliverance.
II. He shows the *end* for which he desires it.

ר RESH

153 ˢConsider mine affliction, and deliver me: for I do not forget thy law.

154 ᵗPlead my cause, and deliver me: ᵘquicken me according to thy word.

155 ᵛSalvation *is* far from the wicked: for they seek not thy statutes.

156 ʷGreat *are* thy tender mercies, O LORD: ˣquicken me according to thy judgments.

157 Many *are* my persecutors and mine

enemies; *yet* do I not ʸdecline from thy testimonies.

158 I beheld the transgressors, and ᶻwas grieved; because they kept not thy word.

159 Consider how I love thy precepts: ᵃquicken me, O LORD, according to thy lovingkindness.

160 ᵇThy word *is* true *from* the beginning: and every one of thy righteous judgments *endureth* for ever.

ˢPsa. ix. 13; Lam. v. 1——ᵗ1 Sam. xxiv. 15; Psa. xxxv. 1; Mic. vii. 9——ᵘVer. 40——ᵛJob v. 4——ʷOr, *Many*——ˣVer. 149

ʸPsa. xliv. 18; ver. 51——ᶻVer. 136; Ezek. ix. 4 ᵃVer. 25, 37, 40, 88, 107, 149, 154, 156; Psa. cxliii. 11 ᵇHeb. *The beginning of thy word* is true

III. The *necessity* of its being speedy, as his enemies were at hand.

I. 1. His prayer was *earnest;* it was a *cry,* rather than a *petition.*

2. It was *sincere:* "I cried with my whole heart." There was no hypocrisy in it.

3. It was *in season:* "I prevented the dawning of the morning."

4. It was *out of season:* "Mine eyes prevent the night-watches."

What he prayed for,—

1. *Audience:* "Hear me, O Lord."

2. *Deliverance:* "Save me."

3. *Increase of grace:* "Quicken me."

II. The *end* for which he prayed.

1. That he might *keep God's statutes.*

2. That he might keep *his testimonies.* See the explanation of these words at the beginning of this Psalm.

3. That he might *meditate* on God's word.

4. That he might *increase* in the *life* of God.

The *arguments* he uses:—

1. His *faith* and *hope.* I cried, because I *waited* and *hoped* in thy word.

2. *God's mercy.* According to thy lovingkindness.

3. The *danger* he was in from his *pursuing enemies.*—1. *They draw nigh.* 2. They are *mischievously* bent. 3. They are most *impious* men. *Far from the law of God;* they despised and hated it.

III. Near as they may be to *destroy,* thou art nearer to *save.*

1. "Thou art near:" They cannot come where thou art not.

2. "All thy commandments are truth:" And thou hast commanded us to *trust in thee;* and therefore we shall not fear evil. Thou wilt *support* thy *servants,* and *destroy* thine *enemies.*

He concludes with an *acclamation:*—

1. "Concerning thy testimonies:" Thy *will,* which thou hast testified in thy word.

2. "I have known of old:" Ever since I looked into them, began to study and practice them.

3. "That thou hast founded them for ever:" They are of eternal truth, immutable and indispensable. And this is the anchor of our souls, that we may not be carried away by trials and temptations. Not one tittle of God's truth has ever failed any of his sincere followers. No one promise of his that has been sought by faith in Christ has ever been unfulfilled. Blessed be God!

LETTER ר RESH.—*Twentieth Division*

Verse 153. *Consider mine affliction*] See *mine affliction* or *humiliation:* but the *eye of the Lord affects his heart;* and therefore he never *sees* the distresses of his followers without *considering* their situation, and *affording* them help.

Verse 154. *Plead my cause*] ריבה ריבי *ribah ribi.* "Be my Advocate in my suit." Contend for us against the Babylonians, and bring us out of our bondage.

According to thy word.] Spoken by thy prophets for our comfort and encouragement.

Verse 155. *Salvation* is *far from the wicked*] There is no hope of their conversion.

For they seek not thy statutes.] And they who *do not seek,* shall not *find.*

Verse 156. *Great* are *thy tender mercies*] They are רבים *rabbim, multitudes.* They extend to *all* the *wretchednesses* of *all* men.

Verse 158. *I beheld the transgressors, and was grieved*] Literally, *I was affected with anguish.*

Verse 160. *Thy word* is *true from the beginning*] ראש *rosh,* the *head* or *beginning* of thy word, is *true.* Does he refer to the *first word* in the Book of *Genesis,* בראשית *bereshith,* "in the beginning?" The learned reader knows that ראש *rash,* or *raash,* is the *root* in that word. Every word thou hast spoken from the first in *Bereshith* (Genesis) to the end of the law and prophets, and all thou wilt yet speak, as flowing from the *fountain of truth,* must be true; and all shall have in due time, their fulfilment. And all these, thy words endure *for ever.* They are *true,* and *ever will be true.*

ANALYSIS OF LETTER RESH.—*Twentieth Division*

I. 1. The psalmist begins with a petition: "Consider my affliction."

2. Begs that God would help him: "Deliver me."

3. The reason for both: "I do not forget thy law."

4. He begs God to be his Advocate: 1. "Plead my cause." At the bar of men a just cause often miscarries for want of an able advocate, and is borne down by an unjust judge. Be *thou* my Advocate, and I shall not fail. 2. "Quicken me:" Revive my hopes, give *new life* to my soul.

II. He believes he shall be heard, because—

1. "Salvation is far from the wicked:" But he does not *forget* God's law.

שׁ SCHIN

161 ^cPrinces have persecuted me without a cause: but my heart standeth in awe of thy word.

162 I rejoice at thy word, as one that findeth great spoil.

163 I hate and abhor lying: *but* thy law do I love.

164 Seven times a day do I praise thee, because of thy righteous judgments.

---

^c1 Sam. xxiv. 11, 14; xxvi. 18; ver. 23

---

2. "They seek not God's statutes:" But he *meditates* in God's law *day* and *night*.

III. If he ever miscarries, or comes short, he flees to God for mercy.

1. On God's mercies he bestows two epithets: 1. They are *great* or *many*, and they *endure for ever.* 2. They are *tender;* they are *misericordiæ*, q. d., *miseria cordis*, feelings which occasion *pain* and *distress* to the *heart*. רחמים *rachamim*, such as *affect* and *flow* from the *tender yearnings* of the *bowels*. The word signifies what a *mother* feels for the *infant* that lay in her *womb*, and hangs on her *breast*.

2. He prays to be *quickened*. Let me not *die*, but *live*.

IV. He complains of his adversaries:—

1. They are *many*: Many *devils*, many *men;* many *visible*, more *invisible*.

2. Yet he continued steadfast: "I do not decline," &c.

3. They were "transgressors:" Not simple *sinners*, but *workers of iniquity*.

4. He was greatly distressed on their account: "I beheld them, and was grieved."

V. He brings this as a proof of his attachment to God.

1. "Consider how I love:" No man dare say to God, "Look upon *me*," but he who is persuaded that when God looks upon him *he will like him*. This was a sure proof of the psalmist's sincerity.

2. He loves not merely the *blessings* he receives from God, but he loves God's *law;* and none will love this, who does not delight in *obedience*. And how few are there of this character, even in the Church of God!

3. And because he loves he prays to be *quickened*. The soul only which is spiritually *alive*, can *obey*.

VI. He concludes with a commendation of God's word.

1. "Thy word is true," in its *principle* and in all its details, from Adam to Moses; from Moses to Christ; from Christ to the present time; and from the present time to the end of the world.

2. For it "endures for ever:" All other things wear out or decay; lose their *testimony*, and become *obsolete*. But God will ever bear testimony to his own *word*, and continue to support its veracity by fulfilling it to all successive generations.

LETTER שׁ SCHIN.—*Twenty-first Division*

Verse 161. *Princes have persecuted me*] This may refer to what was done by *prime ministers*, and the rulers of provinces, to sour the king against the *unfortunate Jews*, in order still to detain them in bondage. In reference to *David*, the plotting against him in Saul's court, and the dangers he ran in consequence of the jealousies of the Philistine lords while he sojourned among them, are well known.

My heart standeth in awe] They had probably offers made them of enlargement or melioration of condition, providing they submitted to some idolatrous conditions; but they knew they had to do with a jealous God; their hearts *stood in awe*, and they were thereby kept from sin.

Verse 162. *As one that findeth great spoil.*]

שלל רב *shalal rab*. This appears to refer to such *spoil* as is acquired by *stripping the dead* in a field of battle, taking the rich garments of the slain chiefs; or it may refer to *plunder* in general. As God *opened his eyes he beheld wonders in his law;* and each discovery of this kind was like finding a prize.

Verse 163. *I—abhor lying*] Perhaps they might have made the confessions which the Chaldeans required, and by mental reservation have kept an inward firm adherence to their creed; but this, in the sight of the God of truth, must have been *lying;* and at such a sacrifice they would not purchase their enlargement, even from their captivity.

Verse 164. *Seven times a day do I praise thee*] We have often seen that *seven* was a number expressing *perfection, completion*, &c., among the Hebrews; and that it is often used to signify *many*, or an *indefinite number*, see Prov. xxiv. 16; Lev. xxvi. 28. And here it may mean no more than that his soul was filled with the spirit of gratitude and praise, and that he very frequently expressed his joyous and grateful feelings in this way. But *Rabbi Solomon* says this is to be understood literally, for they praised God *twice* in the morning before reading the decalogue, and *once* after; *twice* in the evening before the same reading, and *twice* after; making in the whole *seven* times. The Roman Church has prescribed a similar service.

In a manuscript Saxon Homily, Domin. 3, in Quadrag, A. D. 971, I find the following singular directions:—

eallum Cniptenum mannum er beboðen ᚦ hi ealne heopa licheman reoron riðum gebletrion miʋ Cnirtep noʋe tacns

1. æpept on anne mongen.
2. oþpe riðe on unðepn tiʋ.
3. ðpiðoan riðe on miʋne ðæg.
4. reopðan riðe on non tiʋ.
5. riftan riðe on æfen.
6. rixtan riðe on niht æp he repte.
7. reoðan riðe on uhtan hupu he hine goʋe be.

Every Christian man is commanded that he always his body seven times bless with the sign of Christ's cross.

1. First, at day-break.
2. Second time at undern tide, (nine o'clock in the morning.)
3. The third time at midday.
4. The fourth time at noon-tide, (3 o'clock P. M.)
5. The fifth time in the evening.

165 [d]Great peace have they which love thy law: and [e]nothing shall offend them.

166 [f]LORD, I have hoped for thy salvation, and done thy commandments.

167 My soul hath kept thy testimonies; and I love them exceedingly.

168 I have kept thy precepts and thy testimonies: [g]for all my ways *are* before thee.

ת TAU

169 Let my cry come near before thee, O LORD: [h]give me understanding according to thy word.

170 Let my supplication come before thee: deliver me according to thy word.

171 [i]My lips shall utter praise, when thou hast taught me thy statutes.

172 My tongue shall speak of thy word: for all thy commandments *are* righteousness.

173 Let thine hand help me; for [k]I have chosen thy precepts.

174 [l]I have longed for thy salvation, O LORD; and [m]thy law *is* my delight.

175 Let my soul live, and it shall praise thee; and let thy judgments help me.

176 [n]I have gone astray like a lost sheep: seek thy servant; for I do not [o]forget thy commandments.

---

[d]Prov. iii. 2; Isa. xxxii. 17——[e]Heb. *they shall have no stumbling block*——[f]Gen. xlix. 18; ver. 174 [g]Prov. v. 21——[h]Ver. 144——[i]Ver. 7

[k]Josh. xxiv. 22; Prov. i. 29; Luke x. 42——[l]Ver. 166 [m]Ver. 16, 24, 47, 77, 111——[n]Isa. liii. 6; Luke xv. 4, &c.; 1 Pet. ii. 25——[o]Ver. 16, 83, 93, 109, 141, 153

---

6. The sixth time at night ere he go to rest.
7. The seventh time at midnight. A good man would do so if he awoke.

It seems that the *sign of the cross* was thought sufficient, even without prayer.

Verse 165. *Great peace have they*] They have peace in their conscience, and joy in the Holy Spirit; and

Nothing shall offend] Stumble, or put them out of the way.

Verse 166. *Lord, I have hoped*] Thou hast promised deliverance, and I have *expected* it on the *ground* of that *promise*.

Verse 167. *My soul hath kept*] I have not attended to the *latter* merely, but my spirit has entered into the spirit and design of thy testimonies.

Verse 168. *For all my ways* are *before thee*.] Thou knowest that I do not lie; thy eye has been upon my heart and my conduct, and thou knowest that I have endeavoured to walk before thee with a perfect heart.

ANALYSIS OF LETTER SCHIN.—*Twenty-first Division*

In this section the psalmist shows,—
I. His love to God; and
II. The ardour and perfection of that love.
I. The *first* sign of his love was, that it stood in the midst of persecution.
1. "Princes have persecuted."
2. But "without a cause," though they pretended many.
3. "But my heart standeth in awe." My love and confidence have due respect to thy infinite justice and immaculate purity.

The *second* sign of his love is the *joy* and *delight* he took in *God's law;* it was greater than a conqueror could feel at the fortunate issue of a battle, and the spoils of the vanquished, howsover rich or immense.

The *third* sign was his *hatred to all inquity:* "I hate and abhor lying."

The *fourth* sign was his fervour and earnestness in devotion: "Seven times," &c.

The *fifth sign* was the satisfaction he took in the *welfare of others.*

1. "Great peace have they which love thy law."
2. "Nothing shall offend them." They go on their way rejoicing; and they that love God *rejoice with them that do rejoice.*
II. He shows the *perfection* of his love,—
1. By his *hope* and *confidence:* "Lord, I have hoped," &c.
2. By his *obedience:* "And done thy commandments."
3. By *keeping God's testimonies* with all *his soul.*

And this he repeats.
1. "I have kept thy precepts and thy testimonies."
2. I have *done* this through the *purest motives*, as thou knowest: "For all my ways are before thee." Whatever he did he did in God's sight; for he well knew that the eye of the Lord was constantly upon him.

For other particulars see the preceding notes.

LETTER ת TAU.—*Twenty-second Division*

Verse 169. *Let my cry come near before thee*] This is really a fine image; it is of frequent occurrence, and is little heeded. Here the psalmist's cry for deliverance is *personified;* made an intelligent being, and sent up to the throne of grace to negotiate in his behalf. He pursues this *prosopopœia* in the next verse, and sends his *supplication* in the same way. I have already had occasion to refer to a similar figure in *Homer*, where prayers are represented as the *daughters of Jupiter*. See on Psa. lxxxviii. 2.

Verse 171. *My lips shall utter praise*] תהלה *tehillah*, a song of praise.

Verse 172. *My tongue shall speak of thy word*] There is a curious *distinction* here. In the preceding verse he says, "My lips shall utter;" here no reference is made to *articulate sounds*, except as affixed to musical notes. In *this verse* he says, "My tongue shall speak;" here *articulate* and *intelligible* words are intended. He first utters sounds connected with words expressive of his grateful feelings; in the second he speaks words, principally those which God himself had spoken, containing promises of support, purposes relative to the redemption of his people, and denunciations against their enemies.

Verse 173. *Let thine hand help me*] Exert thy *power* in my defence.

Verse 175. *Let my soul live*] Let my *life* be *preserved*, and my *soul quickened!*

Verse 176. *I have gone astray like a lost sheep*] A sheep, when it has once lost the flock, strays in such a manner as to render the prospect of its own return utterly hopeless. I have seen them bleating when they have lost the flock, and when answered by the others, instead of turning to the *sound*, have gone on in the same direction in which they were straying, their bleatings answered by the rest of the flock, till they were out of hearing! This fact shows the propriety of the next clause.

Seek thy servant] I shall never find *thee;* come to the wilderness, take *me* up, and carry me to the flock. See the notes on the parable of *the lost sheep*, Luke xv. 4, &c. The psalmist began with "Blessed are the undefiled in the way, who walk in the law of the Lord;" and he concludes with "I have gone astray like a lost sheep; seek thy servant." And thus, conscious of the blessedness of those who are in the way or righteousness, he desires to be brought into it, that he may walk in newness of life. Ver. 1: "It is a good way, and they are blessed that walk in it." Verse the *last*, "Bring me into this way, that I may be blessed." And thus the Psalm, in sentiment, returns into itself; and the *latter* verse is so connected with the *former*, as to make the whole a perfect *circle*, like the serpent biting its own tail.

There is one extraordinary perfection in this Psalm: *begin* where you will, you seem to be at the commencement of the piece; *end* where you will, you seem to close with a complete *sense*. And yet it is not like the Book of *Proverbs*, a tissue of detached sentences; it is a *whole* composed of many *parts*, and all apparently as necessary to the perfection of the Psalm, as the different *alphabetical letters* under which it is arranged are to the formation of a complete alphabet. Though there be a continual recurrence of the *same words*, which would of itself prevent it from having a pleasing effect upon the ear, yet these words are so connected with a vast *variety* of others, which show their force and meaning in still new and impressive points of light, that *attention* is still excited, and *devotion* kept alive, during the whole reading. It is constructed with admirable art, and every where breathes the justest and highest encomiums on the revelation of God; shows the glories of the God who gave it, the necessities and dependence of his intelligent creatures, the bounty of the Creator, and the praise and obedience which are his due. It is elegant throughout; it is full of beauties, and I have endeavoured in the preceding notes to mark some of them; but the number might have been greatly multiplied. To no Psalm can its own words be better applied, ver. 18: "Open thou mine eyes, that I may behold wondrous things out of thy law."

ANALYSIS OF LETTER TAU.—*Twenty-second Division*

In this last section the psalmist seems to sum up all his preceding exercises.

I. He prays.

II. Gives thanks.

III. Confesses his errors.

IV. Craves mercy; and,

V. Promises obedience.

I. In the first two verses he *prays for his prayers*, begging God to accept them.

1. "Let my cry come near before thee!"

2. "Let my supplication come before thee!" This repetition shows his earnestness, fervency, importunity, and perseverance. See Luke xi. 1, &c.

That for which he prays is, 1. *Understanding;* 2. *Deliverance*.

1. "Give me understanding." I want more light.

2. Give me this "according to thy word." In the measure which thou hast promised.

3. And give it to me for this *end*, that I may know thy law, be obedient to its precepts, and finally, by thy mercy, obtain everlasting life.

4. "Deliver me according to thy word." I want *salvation*, and that *measure* of it which thy word promises.

II. He gives thanks.

1. "My lips shall utter praise." I will celebrate thy praises with songs.

2. "My tongue shall speak." I shall set forth thy wondrous deeds.

3. Shall show that all thy commandments are righteousness; just, holy, impartial.

4. But these things I cannot do till "thou hast taught me thy statutes."

III. He proceeds to other parts of prayer:—

1. "Let thy hand help me." My own *strength* will avail little.

2. "I have chosen thy statutes:" and without thy help I cannot obey them.

3. "I have longed for thy salvation." Thou knowest my heart is right with thee.

4. "And thy law is my delight." A man naturally *longs* for that which he delights to possess.

Here he notes *three* things:—

1. I have "chosen thy precepts."

2. I have "longed for thy salvation."

3. "Delighted in thy law;" therefore "let thy hand be with me."

He prays for,—

1. *Life:* "Let my soul live."

2. "And it shall praise thee." When the soul is dead to God, there is neither *gratitude* nor *obedience*.

3. "Let thy judgments help me." Cause the *merciful dispensations of thy providence* ever to work in my behalf. In this sense the word *judgments* is frequently taken in this Psalm.

IV. He confesses his errors.

1. "I have gone astray," departed from thee, my Shepherd.

2. "And like a lost sheep too." See the note.

3. My errors, however, have not been *wilful* and *obstinate*. I did not sufficiently watch and pray, and my *sheep-like simplicity* was practised upon by my arch enemy.

4. The consequence, however, has been, I am *lost*—far from thy fold. But thou didst come to seek and save that which was lost.

5. Therefore, O Lord, *seek me*. I am in the *wilderness;* leave the *ninety and nine* that do not need thee as I do, and seek me; for, by thy grace, I seek thee.

V. I look for thee in the spirit of *obedience*.

1. Seek thy *servant*. I am ready to do thy will, though I erred from thy ways.

2. "I do not forget thy commandments," though I have often come short of my duty.

These words may be very suitable to a person who has *backslidden,* and who is returning to God with a penitent and believing heart.

1. Though he had *fallen,* the light of God continued to shine into his conscience.

2. He had not *forgotten God's way,* nor lost sight of his own state. The word of the Lord, applied by his Spirit, 1. When he was slumbering, *awakened* him. 2. When he was dead, *quickened* him. 3. When he was in danger, *preserved* him. 4. When he was wounded, *cured* him. 5. When he was assailed by his foes,

armed and *defended* him. 6. And by this word he was *nourished* and *supported.* It was ever well with the psalmist, and it is ever well with all the followers of God, when *they do not forget God's word.*

It may be just necessary to note here, that if this Psalm be considered as belonging to the *times of the Babylonish captivity,* which it most probably does, the psalmist, though speaking in *his own person,* is ever to be considered as speaking *in the persons of all the captives in Babylon.*

PSALM CXX

The psalmist, in great distress, calls on the Lord for deliverance from calumny and defamation, 1, 2; shows the punishment that awaits his persecutor, 3, 4; deplores the necessity of his residence with the ungodly, 5–7.

XXVII. DAY. MORNING PRAYER

A Song of Degrees

I N ᵃmy distress I cried unto the Lord, and he heard me.

2 Deliver my soul, O Lord, from lying lips, *and* from a deceitful tongue.

3 ᵇWhat shall be given unto thee? or what shall be ᶜdone unto thee, thou false tongue?

ᵃPsa. cxviii. 5; Jonah iv. 2——ᵇOr, *What What shall it profit*

shall the deceitful tongue *give unto thee?* or, *thee?*——ᶜHeb. *added*

NOTES ON PSALM CXX

This Psalm, and all the rest that follow it, to the end of Psalm cxxxiv., *fifteen* in number, are called Psalms of Degrees; for thus the Hebrew title המעלות *hammaaloth* is generally translated, as coming from the root עלה *alah,* to *ascend* or *mount upwards.* Hence מעלות *maaloth, steps* or *stairs for ascending,* 1 Kings x. 19, 20; 2 Kings ix. 13. But as the word may be applied to *elevation* in general, hence some have thought that it may here signify the *elevation of voice;* "these Psalms being sung with the *highest elevations of voice and music.*" Others have thought the word expresses rather the *matter* of these Psalms, as being of peculiar *excellence:* and hence *Junius* and *Tremellius* prefix to each *Canticum excellentissimum,* "A most excellent ode."

R. D. Kimchi says, "There were *fifteen steps* by which the priests ascended into the temple, on each of which they sang one of these *fifteen* Psalms." This opinion I find referred to in the Apocryphal Gospel of *the birth of Mary:* "Her parents brought her to the temple, and set her upon one of the steps. Now there are *fifteen steps* about the temple, by which they go up to it, according to the *fifteen Psalms of Degrees.*" But the existence of such *steps* and *practices* cannot be proved.

Aben Ezra supposes that the word means some kind of *tune* sung to these Psalms. It is more likely, if the *title* be really *ancient,* that it was affixed to them on account of their being sung on the *return from the Babylonish captivity,* as the people were *going up* to Jerusalem; for though some of them are attributed

to *David,* yet it is very probable that they were all made long after his time, and probably during the captivity, or about the end of it. The author of these *fifteen* Psalms is not known; and most probably they were not the work of one person. They have been attributed to *David,* to *Solomon,* to *Ezra,* to *Haggai,* to *Zechariah,* and to *Malachi,* without any positive evidence. They are, however, excellent in their kind, and written with much elegance; containing strong and nervous sentiments of the most exalted piety, expressed with great felicity of language in a few words.

Verse 1. In my distress] Through the causes afterwards mentioned.

I cried unto the Lord] Made strong supplication for help.

And he heard me.] Answered my prayer by comforting my soul.

It appears to be a prayer of the *captives* in Babylon for complete liberty; or perhaps he recites the prayer the Israelites had made previously to their restoration.

Verse 2. Lying lips, and *from a deceitful tongue.*] From a people without faith, without truth, without religion; who sought by lies and calumnies to destroy them.

Verse 3. What shall be given unto thee?] Thou art worthy of the heaviest punishments.

Verse 4. Sharp arrows] The *Chaldee* has, "The strong, sharp arrows are like lightning from above, with coals of *juniper* kindled in hell beneath." On the *juniper,* see the note on Job xxx. 4, where this passage is explained. *Fiery arrows, or arrows wrapped about with inflamed combustibles,* were formerly used in sieges to set the places on fire. See my notes on Eph. vi. 16.

4 ^dSharp arrows of the mighty, with coals of juniper.

5 Wo is me that I sojourn in ^eMesech, ^f*that* I dwell in the tents of Kedar!

6 My soul hath long dwelt with him that hateth peace.

7 I *am* ^g*for* peace: but when I speak, they *are* for war.

---

^dOr, It is as *the sharp arrows of the mighty* man *with coals of juniper*——^eGen. x. 2; Ezek. xxvii. 13

^fGen. xxv. 13; 1 Sam. xxv. 1; Jer. xlix. 28, 29——^gOr, a man *of peace*

Verse 5. *That I sojourn in Mesech*] The *Chaldee* has it, "Wo is me that I am a stranger with the Asiatics, (אוסם *useey*,) and that I dwell in the tents of the Arabs." *Calmet*, who understands the Psalm as speaking of the state of the captives in *Babylon* and its *provinces*, says, "Meshec was apparently the father of the Mosquians, who dwelt in the mountains that separate Iberia from Armenia, and both from Colchis. These provinces were subjugated by Nebuchadnezzar; and it is evident from 2 Kings xvii. 23, 24, xviii. 11, xix. 12, 13, that many of the Jews were held in captivity in those countries. As to *Kedar*, it extended into *Arabia Petræa*, and towards the Euphrates; and is the country afterwards known as the country of the *Saracens*."

Verse 6. *My soul hath long dwelt with him that hateth peace.*] A restless, barbarous, warlike, and marauding people.

Verse 7. *I am for peace*] We love to be quiet and peaceable; but they are continually engaged in excursions of rapine and plunder. It is evident that the psalmist refers to a people like the *Scenitæ* or *wandering Arabs*, who live constantly in *tents*, and subsist by robbery; plundering and carrying away all that they can seize. The poor captives wished them to cultivate the arts of peace, and live quietly; but they would hear of nothing but their old manner of life.

ANALYSIS OF THE HUNDRED AND TWENTIETH PSALM

The psalmist in distress—
I. Flees to God by prayer.
II. Sets forth the miseries of a foul and deceitful tongue.
III. Complains of his banishment.
I. 1. He is in distress, and *cries* to the Lord; the surest and best way.

2. He tells us of the *success* of his prayer: "God heard him."
3. Of the matter of it: "Lord, I beseech thee deliver my soul!" 1. "From lying lips." Detractions, calumnies, and defamations. 2. From "a deceitful tongue," which, under the colour of friendship, covers deceit. A *detractor* does his mischief *openly,* a *flatterer* secretly; so that when *a deceitful tongue* is joined with *lying lips*, the mischief is intolerable.
II. He sets forth the evil that shall fall on such deceivers and slanderers.
1. *Arrows*—which wound afar off, suddenly and invisibly.
2. *Sharp arrows, well-headed* and *keen*, that can pierce deeply.
3. "Sharp arrows of the mighty," shot by a *strong hand*, and so much the more dangerous.
4. "With coals—inflamed arrows," such as set all things on *fire*.
5. "With coals of juniper," which of all coals are the *hottest*, and *keep fire the longest*.
III. The psalmist complains of his *banishment*.
1. He laments his situation on account of the wickedness of the people among whom he sojourned.
2. They were barbarous and inhuman, enemies to piety and civility.
3. His state was the more intolerable, as it had been of *long duration:* "My soul hath long dwelt," &c.
His *disposition* was quite contrary to theirs.
1. "I am for peace." I wish to live in peace, and cultivate it.
2. But when I *speak of peace*, they are *for war;* They are fierce and inhuman. It was said of the Macedonians in Philip's time, Illis pacem esse bellum et bellum pacem. "To them peace was war, and war was peace." Such were the people of the provinces, among whom many of the Israelites were in captivity.

PSALM CXXI

The resolution of a godly man, 1, 2. The safety and prosperity of such, as they and theirs shall be under the continual protection of God, 3–8.

A Song of Degrees

I ^aWILL lift up mine eyes unto the hills, from whence cometh my help.

2 ^bMy help *cometh* from the LORD, which made heaven and earth.

3 ^cHe will not suffer thy foot to be

---

^aOr, *Shall I lift up mine eyes to the hills? whence* cxxiv. 8——^c1 Sam.

should my help come? see Jer. iii. 23——^bPsa. ii. 9; Prov. iii. 23, 26

NOTES ON PSALM CXXI

This appears to be a prayer of the Jews in their captivity, who are solicitous for their restoration. It is in the form of a *dialogue*.

Ver. 1, 2. The person who worships God

speaks the *two* first verses, "I will lift up mine eyes—my help cometh,"—ver. 1, 2.
Ver. 3. The ministering priest answers him, "He will not suffer thy foot to be moved." "He that keepeth thee will not slumber," ver. 3.
To which the worshipper answers, that he

moved: ᵈhe that keepeth thee will not slumber.

4 Behold, he that keepeth Israel shall neither slumber nor sleep.

5 The LORD *is* thy keeper: the LORD *is* ᵉthy shade ᶠupon thy right hand.

6 ᵍThe sun shall not smite thee by day, nor the moon by night.

7 The LORD shall preserve thee from all evil: he shall ʰpreserve thy soul.

8 The LORD shall ⁱpreserve thy going out and thy coming in from this time forth, and even for evermore.

ᵈPsa. cxxvii. 1; Isa. xxvii. 3——ᵉIsa. xxv. 4——ᶠPsa. xvi. 8; cix. 31——ᵍPsa. xci. 5; Isa. xlix. 10; Rev. vii.

16——ʰPsa. xli. 2; xcvii. 10; cxlv. 20——ⁱDeut. xxviii. 6; Prov. ii. 8; iii. 6

---

knows that "he who keepeth Israel shall neither slumber nor sleep," ver. 4; but he seems to express a *doubt* whether *he* shall be an object of the Divine attention.

Ver. 5, &c. The priest resumes; and, to the conclusion of the Psalm, gives him the most positive assurances of God's favour and protection.

Verse 1. *Unto the hills*] Jerusalem was built upon a mountain; and Judea was a mountainous country; and the Jews, in their several dispersions, *turned towards* Jerusalem when they offered up their prayers to God.

Verse 2. *My help cometh from the Lord*] There is no help for me but in my God; and I expect it from no other quarter.

Verse 3. *He will not suffer thy foot to be moved*] The foundation, God's infinite power and goodness, on which thou standest, cannot be moved; and whilst thou standest on this basis, thy foot cannot be moved.

Verse 4. *He that keepeth Israel*] The Divine Being represents himself as a *watchman*, who takes care of the city and its inhabitants during the night-watches; and who is never overtaken with slumbering or sleepiness. There is a thought in the *Antigone* of *Sophocles*, that seems the counterpart of this of the psalmist.

> Ταν σαν, Ζευ, δυναμιν τις ανδρων
> 'Ὑπερβασια κατασχοι,
> Ταν ουθ' ὑπνος αἱ—
> ρει ποθ' ὁ παντογηρως,
> Ακαματοι τε θεων
> Μηνες;
>
> Antig. ver. 613, Edit. *Johnson.*

Shall men below control great Jove above,
   Whose eyes by all-subduing sleep
Are never closed, as feeble mortals' are;
   But still their watchful vigil keep
Through the long circle of th' eternal year?
                  FRANKLIN.

Verse 6. *The sun shall not smite thee by day*] Thus expressed by the *Chaldee:* "The morning spectres shall not smite thee by day, during the government of the sun; nor the nocturnal spectres by night, during the government of the moon." I believe the psalmist simply means, they shall not be injured by *heat* nor *cold;* by a *sun-stroke* by day, nor a *frost-bite* by night.

Verse 7. *The Lord shall preserve thee from all evil*] Spiritual and corporeal, *natural* and *moral.*

He shall preserve thy soul.] Take care of thy *life*, and take care of thy soul.

Verse 8. *Thy going out and thy coming in*] Night and day—in all thy business and undertakings; and this through the whole course of thy life: *for evermore.*

ANALYSIS OF THE HUNDRED AND TWENTY-FIRST PSALM

The scope of this Psalm is to show that God alone is the refuge of the distressed.

I. While some are looking for earthly comfort and support, "I will lift up mine eyes unto the hills," &c.

II. Faith sees God, the only helper; and says, "My help is the Lord."

And the *first* reason for this is given: God's omnipotence and sufficiency. "The Lord that made heaven and earth," and is consequently the author and dispenser of all spiritual and temporal blessings.

And the *second reason* is, his *grace* and *goodness;* "he will not suffer thy foot to be moved."

A *third reason* is, his watchful care: "He that keepeth thee will not slumber."

III. The *end* which God proposes in his watching,—to *keep them.*

1. He is the "Keeper of Israel." He guards his Church; he is as a wall of fire about it.

2. He is a *shade.* This certainly refers to that kind of *umbraculum*, or *parasol*, which was in very ancient use in the eastern countries. The sense of the passage is, Neither the day of prosperity nor the night of adversity shall hurt thee; nor the heat of persecution, nor the coldness of friends or relatives: all these shall work for thy good.

3. "He shall preserve thee from all evil;"—and,

4. Especially from every thing that might hurt thy *soul:* "He shall preserve thy soul."

The psalmist concludes with this encouraging assurance.

1. "The Lord shall preserve thy going out." We are always beginning or ending some action, going abroad or returning home; and we need the protecting care of God in all.

2. "From this time forth." Now that thou hast put thy whole trust and confidence in God, he will be thy continual portion and defence in all places, in all times, in all actions; in life, in prosperity, in adversity, in death, in time, and in eternity.

PSALM CXXII

The satisfaction of a gracious soul in the use of God's ordinances, 1, 2. Description of the internal government of Jerusalem, 3–5. Prayers for its peace and prosperity, 6–9.

A Song of Degrees of David

A. M. cir. 3468
B. C. cir. 536
Cyri,
R. Persarum,
cir. annum
primum

I WAS glad when they said unto me, ªLet us go into the house of the LORD.

2 Our feet shall stand within thy gates, O Jerusalem.

3 Jerusalem is builded as a city that is ᵇcompact together.

4 ᶜWhither the tribes go up, the tribes of the LORD, unto ᵈthe testimony of Israel, to give thanks unto the name of the LORD.

5 ᵉFor there ᶠare set thrones of judgment, the thrones of the house of David.

A. M. cir. 3468
B. C. cir. 536
Cyri,
R. Persarum,
cir. annum
primum

6 ᵍPray for the peace of Jerusalem: they shall prosper that love thee.

7 Peace be within thy walls, *and* prosperity within thy palaces.

8 For my brethren and companions' sakes, I will now say, Peace *be* within thee.

9 Because of the house of the LORD our God I will ʰseek thy good.

ªIsa. ii. 3; Zech. viii. 21——ᵇSee 2 Sam. v. 9——ᶜExod. xxiii. 17; Deut. xvi. 16——ᵈExod. xvi. 34

ᵉDeut. xvii. 8; 2 Chron. xix. 8——ᶠHeb. *do sit*——ᵍPsa. li. 18——ʰNeh. ii. 10

NOTES ON PSALM CXXII

In the preceding Psalms we find the poor captives crying to God for deliverance; here they are returning thanks that they find they are permitted to return to their own land and to the ordinances of their God.

Verse 1. *I was glad when they said*] When Cyrus published an edict for their return, the very first object of their thanksgiving was the kindness of God in permitting them to return to his ordinances.

Verse 2. *Our feet shall stand*] For *seventy* years we have been exiled from our own land; our *heart* was in Jerusalem, but our *feet* were in Chaldea. Now God has turned our captivity, and our *feet* shall shortly stand *within the gates of Jerusalem.* What a transition from misery to happiness! and what a subject for rejoicing!

Verse 3. *Jerusalem—compact together.*] It is now well rebuilt, every part contributing to the strength of the whole. It is also a state of great political and spiritual union. It is the *centre* of union to all the tribes, for each tribe has an equal interest in that God who is worshipped there.

Verse 4. *The testimony of Israel*] There is the *ark*, where the presence of God is manifested; there is the holy of holies; and there all the tribes assembled to worship Jehovah. He no doubt alludes to the assembling of the tribes *annually* at each of the *three* grand national festivals.

Verse 5. *There are set thrones of judgment*] There were the *public courts*, and thither the people went to obtain justice; and while the *thrones of the house of David* were there, they had justice.

Verse 6. *Pray for the peace of Jerusalem*] שלום *shalom* signifies both *peace* and *prosperity.* Let her *unanimity* never be *disturbed;* let her *prosperity* ever be on the *increase!*

They shall prosper that love thee.] In the peace and prosperity of the city, they shall find their peace and their prosperity; and even on this ground they should *love* the city, and

labour to promote its best interests. There is a remarkable *alliteration* in this verse, the letter ש *shin* frequently recurring.

שאלו שלום ירושלם ישליו אהביך

*Sh*aalu *sh*elom yeru*sh*alam yi*sh*layu ohabeycha.

"Ask ye the prosperity of Jerusalem; they shall be quiet that love thee."

There are remarkable specimens of similar *alliteration* to be found in *all poets*, ancient and modern. This formed the chief feature of our *ancient poetry.* Thus in *Peter the ploughman:*—

"In a *s*omers *s*eysoun whan *s*ete wa*s* the *s*onne
I *s*choop me in a *s*hrowde a*s* I a *s*heep were."

And the same manner often appears, even in Milton himself. See the *Il Penseroso:*—

"Oft, on a plat of rising ground,
I hear the *far-off curfew* sound
Over some wide-watered *s*hore,
*S*winging *s*low with *s*ullen roar."

Verse 7. *Peace be within thy walls*] This is the *form of prayer* that they are to use: "May *prosperity* ever reside within thy walls, on all the people that dwell there; and tranquillity within thy palaces or high places, among the *rulers* and *governors* of the people."

Verse 8. *For my brethren and companions' sakes*] Because this city is the abode of my kinsfolk and countrymen, I will wish it prosperity. I will promote its peace and tranquillity by all means in my power. I will affectionately say, *May peace be within thee!*

Verse 9. *Because of the house of the Lord our God*] Particularly will I wish thee well, because thou art the *seat of religion*, the place where our merciful God has condescended to dwell.

To the captives in Babylon the Prophet *Jeremiah* had given this charge, chap. xxix. 7: "And seek שלום *shalom*, the *prosperity* of the city, whither I have caused you to be carried captives, and pray unto the Lord for it; for in the *prosperity* thereof ye shall have *prosperity.*"

Was this a *duty* for the *captives?* Yes. And is it the duty of every man for his *own country?* God, nature, common sense, and self-interest say, YES! And what must we think of the wretches who not only do not thus pray, but labour to destroy the public peace, to subvert the government of their country, to raise seditions, and to destroy all its civil and religious institutions? *Think* of them! Why, that *hemp* would be *disgraced* by hanging them.

There is a fine picture given us here of the state of Jerusalem after the restoration of the Jews. The *walls* were finished, the *city* rebuilt, beautiful, strong, and regular; the temple and its worship were restored, the *courts of justice* were re-established, the *constituted authorities* in *Church* and *state* were doing their duty; and God was pouring out his blessing upon all. Who could see this without praying, May God increase thy peace, and establish thy prosperity for ever!

ANALYSIS OF THE HUNDRED AND TWENTY-SECOND PSALM

The psalmist, in the person of the people,—

I. Expresses his joy that he might join with the Church in God's service, ver. 1, 2.

II. Commends the Church, under the name of Jerusalem, for her unity, ver. 3; religious worship, ver. 4; civil and ecclesiastical policy, ver. 5.

III. Exhorts all to pray for its peace and prosperity, ver. 6; and puts the form of prayer into their mouths, ver. 7.

IV. Shows his own readiness to do this, and offers up his supplications, ver. 8, 9.

I. The psalmist congratulates himself and the people on the restoration of God's worship:—

1. He expresses his own joy: "I was glad."

2. To hear of the unanimity of the people mutually exhorting each other to it: "When they said unto me."

3. "Let us go into the house of the Lord." Let us *all* go, hear his word, give him thanks, and make prayers and supplications to him.

II. He commends Jerusalem *three* ways:—

1. For its *unity:* it was compact together; it was united in itself; and united, both in *politics* and *religion*, in its *inhabitants.*

2. For its being the *place of God's worship:* 1. For "thither the tribes go up" thrice in the year, as was ordained, Exod. xxiii. 14, to celebrate their deliverance from Egypt, in keeping the *passover.* 2. The giving of the law, in the feast of *pentecost.* 3. Their preservation in the wilderness, in the feast of *tabernacles.*

These tribes are "the tribes of the Lord." A very honourable title,

"Unto the testimony of Israel." To the ark of the covenant, the pledge of the covenant between God and the people.

The *end* for which they went up: "To give thanks unto the name of the Lord."

3. He commends Jerusalem for its civil and ecclesiastical policy: 1. "For there are set thrones of judgment." The tribunals and courts of justice are there. 2. "The thrones of the house of David." The court and throne of a legitimate sovereign.

III. He exhorts the tribes to *pray for* a continuance of its present happy state.

1. "Pray for the peace," &c. It is our duty to pray for the *prosperity* of the *nation* and of the *Church of God.*

2. "They shall prosper that love thee." Those who love both are *blessed*, those who do not are *cursed.*

3. And that we may know the prayer that God will hear, he puts one in our mouth, "Peace be within thy walls, and prosperity within thy palaces." It is well to join *peace* and *prosperity* together. *Peace* without *prosperity* is but a secure possession of *misery;* and *prosperity* without *peace* is but a dubious and uncertain *felicity.*

1. "Peace be within thy walls." Not only thy *fortifications, civil and religious institutions,* but also among all thy *officers, soldiers,* and *inhabitants,* for they constitute the strength and safety of the kingdom.

2. "And prosperity within thy palaces." In the king's house, his family, his ministers; if there be dissensions there, ruin will soon follow.

IV. The psalmist shows his own readiness to do this.

1. "I will now say, Peace be within thee." So should all the ministers of religion pray.

2. "I will seek thy good." So should the king and every officer of state resolve. All should be united in so good a work. They should not seek *their own good*, but the *good*, not the *goods*, of *the people.*

For this the psalmist gives *these* reasons:—

1. "For my brethren and companions' sakes." We are not only subjects of one king, citizens of the same city, but we have all one God and Father.

2. "Because of the house of the Lord." For the maintenance of true religion. If *religion* fail, the *kingdom* will fail; prosperity will be at an end; the nation will be divided, distracted, destroyed. Religion, the true religion in a country, is the *consolation* of the *good*, and the *bridle* that holds in the jaws of the *wicked.* Let us all pray for the prosperity of pure and undefiled religion, and the prosperity of the state!

PSALM CXXIII

The prayer and faith of the godly, 1, 2.   *They desire to be delivered from contempt,* 3, 4.

A Song of Degrees

UNTO thee ᵃlift I up mine eyes, O thou ᵇthat dwellest in the heavens.

2 Behold, as the eyes of servants *look* unto the hand of their masters, *and* as the eyes of a maiden unto the hand of her mistress; so our eyes *wait* upon the LORD our God, until that he have mercy upon us.

3 Have mercy upon us, O LORD, have mercy upon us: for we are exceedingly filled with contempt.

4 Our soul is exceedingly filled with the scorning of those that are at ease, *and* with the contempt of the proud.

ᵃPsa. cxxi. 1; cxli. 8

ᵇPsa. ii. 4; xi. 4; cxv. 3

NOTES ON PSALM CXXIII

This Psalm is probably a complaint of the captives in Babylon relative to the contempt and cruel usage they received. The author is uncertain.

Verse 1. *Unto thee lift I up mine eyes*] We have no hope but in thee; our eyes look upward; we have expectation from thy *mercy* alone.

Verse 2. *As the eyes of servants*] We now wait for thy commands, feeling the utmost readiness to obey them when made known to us. The words may be understood as the language of dependence also. As slaves expect their *support* from their masters and mistresses; so do we ours from thee, O Lord! Or, As servants look to their masters and mistresses, to *see how they do their work*, that they may do it in the same way; so do we, O Lord, that we may learn of thee, and do thy work in thy own Spirit, and after thy own method. Some think that there is a reference here to the *chastisement of slaves* by their masters, who, during the time they are receiving it, keep their eyes fixed on the hand that is inflicting punishment upon them, professing deep sorrow, and entreating for mercy. And this sense seems to be countenanced by the following words:—

Verse 3. *Have mercy upon us, O Lord*] Chastise us no more; we will no more revolt against thee.

We are exceedingly filled with contempt.] We not only suffer grievously from our captivity, but are treated in the most contemptuous manner by our masters.

Verse 4. *Those that are at ease*] The Babylonians, who, having subdued all the people of the neighbouring nations, lived *at ease*, had none to contend with them, and now became luxurious, *indolent*, and *insolent:* they were contemptuous and proud.

ANALYSIS OF THE HUNDRED AND TWENTY-THIRD PSALM

The oppressed followers of God make application to him for mercy. In this application they express *three* things:—

I. Their confidence in God.

II. Prayer for mercy.

III. An account of their oppressors.

I. Their trust in God.

1. "Unto thee lift I up mine eyes." We trust in thee *alone.*

2. "O thou that dwellest in the heavens." Infinitely raised above us; but affected with our miserable condition, and always ready to help us.

This he shows by a double similitude:—

1. "As the eyes of servants," i. e., *men-servants*, "look unto the hand of their masters."

2. "As the eyes of a maiden unto the hand of her mistress:" both might be beaten; and here both beg to be saved from farther stripes.

3. "So our eyes," &c. God's children are always looking up to him.

4. "Until that he have mercy;" abate his stripes, and take off his hand.

II. Their prayer for mercy.

1. Before they *lifted their eyes* to God, but now they *cry* for mercy.

For this *crying*, they give the following reasons:—

1. "We are exceedingly filled with contempt." To *suffer contempt* is *much;* to be *filled* with it is *more;* and to be *exceedingly filled* with it is *worst* of all.

2. We are *scorned:* they join *words* and *actions* to show how much they despise us.

III. They give the *character* of those by whom they suffer.

1. They are *at ease*—loaded with wealth, and sunk in indolence.

2. They are *proud*—puffed up with a sense of their own importance; and this leads them to despise others. Proud men are for the most part empty, shallow-pated men: and contempt and scorn from such wounds deeply; especially if they rise, as they often do, from the *dunghill.* The sick *lion* in the fable found it extremely galling to be kicked by the *foot* of an *ass.*

PSALM CXXIV

A thanksgiving of the godly for extraordinary deliverances, 1–6. The great danger they were in, 7. Their confidence in God, 8.

A Song of Degrees of David

A. M. cir. 3494
B. C. cir. 510
Assueri,
R. Persarum,
cir. annum
duodecimum

IF *it had not been* the LORD who was on our side, [a]now may Israel say;

2 If *it had not been* the LORD who was on our side, when men rose up against us:

3 Then they had [b]swallowed us up quick, when their wrath was kindled against us:

4 Then the waters had overwhelmed us, the stream had gone over our soul:

5 Then the proud waters had gone over our soul.

6 Blessed *be* the LORD, who hath not given us *as* a prey to their teeth.

A. M. cir. 3494
B. C. cir. 510
Assueri,
R. Persarum,
cir. annum
duodecimum

7 Our soul is escaped [c]as a bird out of the snare of the fowlers: the snare is broken, and we are escaped.

8 [d]Our help *is* in the name of the LORD, [e]who made heaven and earth.

---

[a]Psalm cxxix. 1——[b]Psalm lvi. 1, 2; lvii. 3; Proverbs i. 12

[c]Psa. xci. 3; Prov. vi. 5——[d]Psa. cxxi. 2——[e]Gen. i. 1; Psa. cxxxiv. 3

NOTES ON PSALM CXXIV

In our present Hebrew copies this Psalm is attributed to *David*, לדוד *ledavid;* but this inscription is wanting in *three* of *Kennicott's* and *De Rossi's* MSS., as also in the *Septuagint, Syriac, Vulgate, Æthiopic,* and *Arabic;* and in most of the ancient *fathers,* Greek and Latin, who found no other inscription in their copies of the text than *A Psalm of degrees.* It was composed long after David's days; and appears to be either a thanksgiving for their deliverance from the Babylonish captivity, or for a remarkable deliverance from some potent and insidious enemy after their return to Judea. Or, what appears to be more likely, it is a thanksgiving of the Jews for their escape from the general massacre intended by Haman, prime minister of Ahasuerus, king of Persia. See the whole Book of *Esther.*

Verse 1. *If it had not been the Lord*] If God had not, in a very especial manner, supported and defended us, we had all been swallowed up alive, and destroyed by a sudden destruction, so that not one would have been left. This might refer to the plot against the whole nation of the Jews by Haman, in the days of Mordecai and Esther; when by his treacherous schemes the Jews, wheresoever dispersed in the provinces of Babylon, were all to have been put to death in one day. This may here be represented under the figure of an earthquake, when a chasm is formed, and a whole city and its inhabitants are in a moment swallowed up alive.

Verse 5. *Then the proud waters*] The proud *Haman* had nearly brought the flood of desolation over our lives.

Verse 7. *Our soul is escaped as a bird out of the snare*] This is a fine image; and at once shows the *weakness* of the Jews, and the *cunning* of their adversaries. Haman had laid the snare completely for them; humanly speaking there was no prospect of their escape: but the *Lord was on their side;* and the providence that induced Ahasuerus to call for the book of the records of the kingdom to be read to him, as well indeed as the once very improbable advancement of Esther to the throne of Persia,

was the means used by the Lord for the preservation of the whole Jewish people from extermination. God thus *broke the snare,* and the *bird escaped;* while the poacher was caught in his own trap, and executed. See the Book of Esther, which is probably the best comment on this Psalm.

Verse 8. *Our help* is *in the name of the Lord*] בשום מימרא דיי *beshum meymra deyai,* Chaldee, "In the name of the WORD of the LORD." So in the second verse, "Unless the WORD of the LORD had been our Helper:" *the substantial* WORD; not a *word spoken,* or a *prophecy* delivered, but the person who was afterwards termed Ὁ Λογος του Θεου, *the* WORD OF GOD. This deliverance of the Jews appears to me the most natural interpretation of this Psalm: and probably *Mordecai* was the author.

ANALYSIS OF THE HUNDRED AND TWENTY-FOURTH PSALM

The people of God, newly escaped from some great danger, acknowledge it, and celebrate God as their Deliverer.

I. The psalmist begins abruptly, as is usual in pathetical expressions.

1. "If it had not been the Lord:" and so deeply was he affected with a sense of God's goodness, and the narrowness of the escape, that he repeats it: "Unless the Lord," &c. Nothing else could have saved us.

2. "Now may Israel say;" the whole body of the Jewish people may well acknowledge this.

3. "When men rose up:" when they were all leagued against us as one man to destroy us; and, humanly speaking, our escape was impossible.

II. This danger and escape the psalmist illustrates by *two metaphors:*—

1. The *first* is taken from *beasts* of prey: "They had swallowed us up quick." They would have rushed upon us, torn us in pieces, and swallowed us down, while life was quivering in our limbs.

This they would have done in their *fury.* The plot was laid with great *circumspection* and *caution;* but it would have been executed with a *resistless fury.*

2. The *second* similitude is taken from *waters* which had broken through dikes, and at once submerged the whole country: "The stream had gone over our soul;" the *proud waters,* resistless now the dikes were broken, would have *gone over our soul*—destroyed our life.

III. He next acknowledges the *deliverance.*

1. "We are not given a prey to their teeth."

2. It is the blessed God who has preserved us: "Blessed be God," &c.

As this deliverance was *beyond expectation,* he illustrates it by *another metaphor,* a *bird* taken in, but escaping from, a *snare.*

1. We were in "the snare of the fowler."

2. But "our soul is escaped."

3. And the fowler disappointed of his prey. The disappointment of Haman was, in all its circumstances, one of the most mortifying that ever occurred to man.

IV. He concludes with a grateful acclamation.

1. "Our help is in the name of the Lord." In open assaults, and in *insidious attacks,* we have no helper but God; and from him our deliverance must come.

2. This help is sufficient; for he made the *heaven* and *earth;* has both under his government; and can employ both in the support, or for the *deliverance,* of his followers.

Or, take the following as a plainer analysis:—

I. 1. The *subtlety* of the adversaries of the Church in laying snares to entrap it, as fowlers do birds, ver. 7.

2. Their *cruelty* in seeking to tear it to pieces, as some ravenous beasts of prey do; or, as mighty inundations that overthrow all in their way, ver. 3-6.

II. The cause of this subtlety and cruelty: wrath and displeasure, ver. 3.

III. The delivery of the Church from both, by the power and goodness of God, ver. 1, 2, 6, 7.

IV. The duty performed for this deliverance; praises to God, ver. 6.

PSALM CXXV

The safety of those who trust in God, 1, 2. *God's protecting providence in behalf of his followers,* 3. *A prayer for the godly,* 4. *The evil lot of the wicked,* 5.

A Song of Degrees

A. M. cir. 3559
B. C. cir. 445
Artaxerxis I.,
R. Persarum,
cir. annum
vigesimum

THEY that trust in the LORD *shall be* as Mount Zion, *which* cannot be removed, *but* abideth for ever.

2 *As* the mountains *are* round about Jerusalem, so the LORD *is* round about his people from henceforth even for ever.

3 For ªthe rod of ᵇthe wicked shall not rest upon the lot of the righteous; lest the righteous put forth their hands unto iniquity.

4 Do good, O LORD, unto *those that be* good

A. M. cir. 3559
B. C. cir. 445
Artaxerxis I.,
R. Persarum,
cir. annum
vigesimum

ªProv. xxii. 8; Isa. xiv. 5   ᵇHeb. *wickedness*

NOTES ON PSALM CXXV

This Psalm is without a *title:* it belongs most probably to the times after the captivity; and has been applied, with apparent propriety, to the opposition which *Sanballat* the Horonite, *Geshem* the Arabian, and *Tobiah* the Ammonite, gave to the Jews while employed in rebuilding the walls of Jerusalem, and restoring the temple.

Verse 1. *They that trust in the Lord*] Every faithful Jew who confides in Jehovah shall stand, in those *open* and *secret attacks* of the enemies of God and truth, as *unshaken* as *Mount Zion;* and shall not be moved by the power of any adversary.

Verse 2. As *the mountains* are *round about Jerusalem*] Jerusalem, according to *Sandys,* was situated on a rocky mountain every way to be ascended, except a little on the north, with steep ascents and deep valleys, naturally fortified. It is surrounded with other *mountains,* at no great distance, as if placed in the midst of an amphitheatre; for on the *east* is Mount

Olivet, separated from the city by the *valley of Jehoshaphat,* which also encompasses a part of the *north;* on the *south,* the mountain of *Offiner* interposed with the *valley of Gehinnom;* and on the *west* it was formerly fenced with the *valley of Gihon,* and the *mountains* adjoining. The situation was such as to be easily rendered impregnable.

The Lord is *round about his people*] He is *above, beneath, around* them; and *while they keep within it,* their fortress is impregnable, and they can suffer no evil.

Verse 3. *For the rod of the wicked shall not rest upon the lot of the righteous*] Rod, here, may be taken for *persecution,* or for *rule;* and then it may be thus interpreted: "The wicked shall not be permitted to *persecute always,* nor to have a *permanent rule.*" In our *liturgic version* this clause is thus rendered: "The rod of the ungodly cometh not into the lot of the righteous." "This," said one of our forefathers, "is neither *truth* nor *scripture.* First, it is not *truth;* for the rod of the wicked *doth come* into the inheritance of the righteous, and that *often.*

A. M. cir. 3559
B. C. cir. 445
Artaxerxis I.,
R. Persarum,
cir. annum
vigesimum
and to *them that are* upright in their hearts.

5 As for such as turn aside unto their ͨcrooked ways, the

LORD shall lead them forth with the workers of iniquity: *but* ͩpeace *shall be* upon Israel.

A. M. cir. 3559
B. C. cir. 445
Artaxerxis I.,
R. Persarum,
cir. annum
vigesimum

ͨProv. ii. 15

ͩPsa. cxxviii. 6; Gal. vi. 16

Secondly, it is not *scripture;* for the text saith, 'The rod of the wicked shall not rest there.' It may *come,* and stay for a time; but it shall not be permitted to abide."

This is only *one,* and not the *worst,* of the many sad blemishes which deform the Version in our national Prayer-book. In short, the Version of the Psalms in that book is wholly unworthy of regard; and should be thrown aside, and that in the *authorized Version* in the Bible substituted for it. The people of God are misled by it; and they are confounded with the *great* and *glaring differences* they find between it and what they find in their Bibles, where they have a version of a much better character, delivered to them by the authority of *Church* and *state.* Why do not our present excellent and learned prelates lay this to heart, and take away this sore stumbling-block out of the way of the people? I have referred to this subject in the *introduction to the Book of Psalms.*

Lest the righteous put forth] Were the wicked to *bear rule* in the Lord's vineyard, religion would soon become extinct; for the great mass of the people would conform to their rulers. Fear not your enemies, while ye fear God. Neither *Sanballat,* nor *Tobiah,* nor *Geshem,* nor any of God's foes, shall be able to set up their *rod,* their *power* and *authority,* here. While you are faithful, the Lord will laugh them to scorn.

Verse 4. *Do good, O Lord, unto* those that be *good*] Let the upright ever find thee his sure defence! Increase the *goodness* which thou hast already bestowed upon them; and let all who are *upright in heart* find thee to be their stay and their support!

Verse 5. *As for such as turn aside*] Who are not *faithful;* who *give way to sin;* who *backslide,* and walk in a *crooked way,* widely different from the *straight way* of the *upright,* ישָׁרִים *yesharim,* the *straight* in heart; they shall be *led forth* to punishment *with the* common *workers of iniquity.* Thus thy Church will be purified, and thy *peace* rest *upon* thy true *Israel.* Let him that readeth understand.

ANALYSIS OF THE HUNDRED AND TWENTY-FIFTH PSALM

It is the purpose of the psalmist to comfort the people of God,—

I. By an assurance of their perpetuity, both from God's presence and protection, ver. 1, 2.

II. That though he may permit them to be harassed by the wicked, yet he will not leave them under their rod, ver. 3.

III. He prays for the good; and,

IV. Sets down the portion of the wicked, ver. 4, 5.

I. A general promise of the perpetuity of the Church; that is, of them "that trust in God."

1. "They that trust in the Lord:" "The congregation of God's faithful people, who have the pure word of God preached, and the sacraments duly administered," Acts xix.

2. "Shall be as Mount Zion," secure and immovable; immovable, because a *mountain,*—a *holy* mountain,—and particularly *dear* to God.

3. "Which abideth for ever:" So surely as *Mount Zion* shall never be *removed,* so surely shall the *Church of God* be *preserved.* Is it not strange that wicked and idolatrous powers have not joined together, dug down this mount, and carried it into the sea, that they might nullify a promise in which the people of God exult! Till ye can carry Mount Zion into the Mediterranean Sea, the Church of Christ shall grow and prevail. Hear this, ye murderous Mohammedans!

4. "As the mountains are round about Jerusalem,"—to fortify it.

5. "So the Lord is round about his people"— to preserve them.

6. "From henceforth, even for ever:" Through both *time* and *eternity.*

II. 1. But the Church is often persecuted and harassed. Granted; for the "rod," the power and scourge, "of the wicked, may come into the heritage of the righteous."

2. But then may it not finally prevail? No: for though it *come,* it shall not *rest.*

3. And why? Because it might finally destroy the Church, pervert the good, and cause them to join issue with the ungodly. Therefore, "they shall not be tempted above that they are able."

III. Therefore the psalmist prays,—

1. "Do good to the good:" Give them *patience,* and keep them *faithful.*

2. And "to the upright in heart:" Let not the *weak* and the *sincere* be overcome by their enemies:

IV. He sets down the *lot of the ungodly:*—

1. "They turn aside."

2. They get into *crooked paths;* they get into the *spirit of the world,* and are *warped* into its *crooked* and *winding* ways.

3. They shall be condemned, and *then led forth to* punishment. The backslider in heart shall be filled with his own ways; he shall have *writhing* in pain, for *crooked walking* in sin.

4. But while this is their portion, "peace," prosperity, and blessedness, "shall be upon Israel."

PSALM CXXVI

The joy of the Israelites on their return from captivity, and the effect their deliverance had upon the heathen, 1–3.
The prayer which they had offered up, 4.   The inference they draw from the whole, 5, 6.

XXVII. DAY.   EVENING PRAYER

A Song of Degrees

A. M. cir. 3468
B. C. cir. 536
Cyri,
R. Persarum,
cir. annum
primum

WHEN the LORD ᵃturned again the captivity of Zion, ᵇwe were like them that dream. 2 Then ᶜwas our mouth filled

with laughter, and our tongue with singing: then said they among the heathen, The LORD ᵈhath done great things for them.

A. M. cir. 3468
B. C. cir. 536
Cyri,
R. Persarum,
cir. annum
primum

3 The LORD hath done great things for us; *whereof* we are glad.

ᵃHeb. *returned the returning of Zion;* Psa. liii. 6; lxxxv. 1; Hos. vi. 11; Joel iii. 1

ᵇActs xii. 9——ᶜJob viii. 21——ᵈHeb. *hath magnified to do with them*

NOTES ON PSALM CXXVI

This Psalm is not of David, has no title in the Hebrew or any of the Versions, and certainly belongs to the close of the captivity. It might have been composed by *Haggai* and *Zechariah*, as the *Syriac* supposes; or by *Ezra*, according to others. It is beautiful, and highly descriptive of the circumstances which it represents.

Verse 1. *When the Lord turned again the captivity*] When Cyrus published his decree in favour of the Jews, giving them liberty to return to their own land, and rebuild their city and temple.

We were like them that dream.] The news was so unexpected that we doubted for a time the truth of it. We believed it was too good news to be true, and thought ourselves in a dream or illusion. When the Romans had vanquished Philip, king of Macedon, they restored liberty to the Grecian cities by proclamation. It was done at the time of the Isthmian games, and by the crier, who went into the circus to proclaim them; none but the Roman general T. Quintius knowing what was to be done. Multitudes from all Greece were there assembled; and the tidings produced nearly the same effect upon them, according to Livy, that the publication of the decree of Cyrus did on the Jews, according to what is here related by the psalmist. I shall give the substance of this account from the Roman historian. When the Romans had sat down to behold the games, the herald with his trumpet went into the arena, according to custom, to proclaim the several games. Silence being obtained, he solemnly pronounced the following words:—

SENATUS ROMANUS ET T. QUINCIUS IMPERATOR, PHILIPPO REGE MACEDONIBUSQUE DEVICTIS; LIBEROS, IMMUNES, SUIS LEGIBUS ESSE JUBET CORINTHIOS, PHOCENSES, LOCRENSESQUE OMNES, ET INSULAM EUBŒAM, ET MAGNETAS, THESSALOS, PERRHÆBOS, ACHÆOS, PHTHIOTAS.

"The Roman Senate, and T. Quintius the general, having vanquished king Philip and the Macedonians, do ordain that the Corinthians, Phocensians, all the Locrensians, the island of Eubœa, the Magnesians, Thessalians, Perrhæbians, Acheans, and Phthiotians, shall be free, be delivered from all taxes, and live according to their own laws."

The effect that this produced on the astonished Grecians who were present, is related by this able historian in a very natural and affecting manner; and some parts of it *nearly in the words of the psalmist.*

Audita voce præconis, majus gaudium fuit, quam quod universum homines caperent. Vix satis se credere se quisque audisse: alii alios intueri mirabundi velut *somnii vanam speciem: quod ad quemque pertineret, suarum aurium fidei minimum credentes, proximos interroga-bant.* Revocatur præco, cum unusquisque non audire, sed videre libertatis suæ nuncium averit, iterum pronunciaret eadem. Tum ab certo jam gaudio tantus cum clamore plausus est ortus, totiesque repetitus, ut facile appareret, nihil omnium bonorum multitudini gratius quam LIBERTATEM esse.

T. LIV. *Hist.*, lib xxxiii., c. 32.

This proclamation of the herald being heard, there was such joy, that the people in general could not comprehend it. Scarcely could any person believe what he had heard. They gazed on each other, wondering as if it had been *some illusion, similar to a dream;* and although all were interested in what was spoken, none could trust his own ears, but inquired each from him who stood next to him what it was that was proclaimed. The herald was again called, as each expressed the strongest desire not only to hear, but see the messenger of his own liberty: the herald, therefore, repeated the proclamation. When by this repetition the glad tidings were confirmed, there arose such a shout, accompanied with repeated clapping of hands, as plainly showed that *of all good things none is so dear to the multitude* as LIBERTY.

O that God may raise up some other deliverer to save *these same cities* with their *inhabitants,* from a worse yoke than ever was imposed upon them by the king of Macedon; and from a servitude which has now lasted three hundred years longer than the *captivity* of the Israelites in the empire of Babylon!

Constantinople was taken by the *Turks* in 1453; and since that time till the present, (October, 1822,) three hundred and sixty-nine years have elapsed. Why do the *Christian* powers of Europe stand by, and see the ark of their God in captivity; the holy name by which they are called despised and execrated; the vilest indignities offered to those who are called Christians, by barbarians the most cruel, ferocious, and abominable that ever disgraced the name of man? Great God, vindicate the cause of the distressed Greeks as *summarily,* as *effectually,* as *permanently,* as thou once didst that of thy oppressed people the Jews! Let the *crescent* never more *fill* its *horns* with a *victory,* nor with the spoils of any who are called by the sacred name of JESUS: but let it *wane* back into total darkness; and know no

A. M. cir. 3468
B. C. cir. 536
Cyri,
R. Persarum,
cir. annum
primum

4 Turn again our captivity, O LORD, as the streams in the south.

5 ^eThey that sow in tears shall reap in ^fjoy.

6 He that goeth forth and weepeth, bearing ^gprecious seed, shall doubtless come again with rejoicing, bringing his sheaves *with him.*

A. M. cir. 3468
B. C. cir. 536
Cyri,
R. Persarum,
cir. annum
primum

eSee Jer. xxxi. 9, &c.

fOr, *singing*——gOr, *seed basket*

change for the better, till illuminated by the *orient splendour* of the *Sun of righteousness!* Amen! Amen!

How signally has this prayer been thus far answered! Three great Christian powers, the *British,* the *French,* and the *Russian,* have taken up the cause of the oppressed Greeks. The Turkish fleet has been attacked in the Bay of Navarino by the combined fleets of the above powers in October, 1827, under the command of the British Admiral, Sir Edward Codrington, and totally annihilated. After which, the Mohammedan troops were driven out of Greece and the Morea; so that the whole of Greece is cleared of its oppressors, and is now under its own government, protected by the above powers.—March, 1829.

Verse 2. *Then was our mouth filled with laughter*] The same effect as was produced on the poor liberated Grecians mentioned above.

Then said they among the heathen] The liberty now granted was brought about in so extraordinary a way, that the very *heathens* saw that the hand of the great Jehovah must have been in it.

Verse 3. *The Lord hath done great things for us*] We acknowledge the hand of our God. *Deus nobis hæc otia fecit,* "God alone has given us this enlargement."

We are glad.] This is a mere burst of ecstatic joy. O how happy are we!

Verse 4. *Turn again our captivity*] This is either a recital of the prayer they had used *before* their deliverance; or it is a prayer for those who *still remained* in the provinces beyond the Euphrates. The Jewish captives did not all return at *once;* they came back at different times, and under different leaders, Ezra, Nehemiah, Zerubbabel, &c.

As the streams in the south.] Probably the *Nile* is meant. It is now pretty well known that the Nile has its origin in the kingdom of *Damot;* and runs from *south* to *north* through different countries, till, passing through Egypt, it empties itself into the Mediterranean Sea. It it possible, however, that they might have had in view some *rapid rivers* that either rose in the south, or had a *southern* direction; and they desired that their return might be as rapid and as *abundant* as the waters of those rivers. But we know that the Nile proceeds from the south, divides itself into several *streams* as it passes through Egypt, and falls by *seven mouths* into the Mediterranean.

Verse 5. *They that sow in tears shall reap in joy.*] This is either a *maxim* which they gather from their own history, or it is a *fact* which they are now witnessing. We see the benefit of humbling ourselves under the mighty hand of God; we have now a sweet return for our bitter tears. Or, We *have* sown in tears; now we reap in joy. We are restored after a long and afflicting captivity to our own country, to peace, and to happiness.

Verse 6. *He that goeth forth and weepeth,*

bearing precious seed] The metaphor seems to be this: A poor farmer has had a very bad harvest: a very scanty portion of grain and food has been gathered from the earth. The *seed time* is now come, and is very unpromising. Out of the famine a little seed has been saved to be sown, in hopes of another crop; but the badness of the present season almost precludes the entertainment of hope. But he must sow, or else despair and perish. He carries his all, his *precious seed,* with him in his *seed basket;* and with a sorrowful heart commits it to the furrow, watering it in effect with his tears, and earnestly imploring the blessing of God upon it. God hears; the season becomes mild; he beholds successively the *blade,* the *ear,* and the *full corn* in the ear. The appointed weeks of harvest come, and the grain is very productive. He fills his arms, his carriages with the sheaves and shocks; and returns to his large expecting family in triumph, praising God for the wonders he has wrought. So shall it be with this handful of *returning Israelites.* They also are to be *sown*—scattered all over the land; the blessing of God shall be upon them, and their faith and numbers shall be abundantly increased. The return here referred to, *Isaiah* describes in very natural language: "And they shall bring all your brethren for an offering to the Lord out of all nations, upon horses, and in chariots, and in litters, upon mules, and upon swift beasts, to my holy mountain Jerusalem, saith the Lord, as the children of Israel bring an offering in a clean vessel into the house of the Lord," chap. lxvi., ver. 20.

ANALYSIS OF THE HUNDRED AND TWENTY-SIXTH PSALM

The parts of this Psalm are *three:*—
I. An expression of joy for their strange deliverance from captivity.
II. A prayer for the return of the remaining part.
III. A moral collected by the psalmist from it.
1. The psalmist celebrates their return, and amplifies it *three* ways:—
1. From the cause, *Jehovah.* Cyrus gave a commission for it; but it was the Lord who disposed his heart so to do: "When the Lord turned," &c.
2. From the *manner* of it. It was strange and wonderful; they could scarcely believe it.
3. From the *joy* at it, inward and external.
1. Their "mouths were filled with laughter."
2. Their "tongue with singing." A thankful tongue expressed the feelings of a thankful heart.
That God did this for them he proves by two evidences:—
1. The *heathen:* "Then said they among the heathen." They saw that they were permitted to return by virtue of a royal edict; that the

very king who gave the commission was named by a prophet; that they had rich gifts given them, the vessels of gold and silver restored, &c. Who could do all these things but GOD?

2. The *Jews*. It is true, said the Jews, what you acknowledge. 1. "The Lord hath done great things for us." Beyond our merit, beyond our hope. 2. "Whereof we are glad," for we are freed from a galling yoke.

II. But there were some Jews left behind, for whom they pray.

1. "Turn their captivity also." Put it in their hearts to join their brethren. Several, no doubt, stayed behind, because they *had married strange wives*, &c.

2. "Turn it as the streams in the south." Or, as some read it, *streams of water on a parched land*. Judea has been lying waste; we need many hands to cultivate it. When all join together in this work the land will become *fruitful*, like the parched ground when power-ful rivulets are sent through it in all directions.

III. The benefit of this will be great; for although it may cost us much *hard labour* and *distress* in the beginning, yet the maxim will hold good—"They who sow in tears shall reap in joy." Which the psalmist amplifies in the next verse.

1. "He that goeth forth and weepeth." The poor husbandman, for the reasons given above and in the notes, *bearing precious seed*—seed bought with a high price, which augments his grief, being so poor.

2. "He shall doubtless come again"—in harvest *with joy*, having a plentiful crop; for every grain sown at least one full-fed ear of corn, with at the lowest *thirty-fold*. Some maxims are to be gathered from the whole: Penitential sorrow shall be followed by the joy of pardoning mercy; he that bears the cross shall wear the crown; and, trials and difficulties shall be followed by peace and prosperity.

PSALM CXXVII

The necessity of God's blessing on every undertaking, without which no prosperity can be expected, 1, 2. Children are a heritage from the Lord, 3, 4. A fruitful wife is a blessing to her husband, 5.

A Song of Degrees ᵃfor Solomon

A. M. cir. 3559
B. C. cir. 445
Artaxerxis I.,
R. Persarum,
cir. annum
vigesimum

EXCEPT the LORD build the house, they labour in vain ᵇthat build it: except ᶜthe LORD keep the city, the watchman waketh *but* in vain.

2 *It is* vain for you to rise up early, to sit up late, to ᵈeat the bread of sorrows: *for* so he giveth his beloved sleep.

A. M. cir. 3559
B. C. cir. 445
Artaxerxis I.,
R. Persarum,
cir. annum
vigesimum

3 Lo, ᵉchildren *are* a heritage of the LORD: and ᶠthe fruit of the womb *is his* reward.

ᵃOr, *of Solomon*; Psa. lxxii. title——ᵇHeb. *that are builders of it in it*——ᶜPsa. cxxi. 3, 4, 5

ᵈGen. iii. 17, 19——ᵉGen. xxxiii. 5; xlviii. 4; Josh. xxiv. 3, 4——ᶠDeut. xxviii. 4

NOTES ON PSALM CXXVII

The *Hebrew*, *Chaldee*, and *Vulgate* attribute this Psalm to Solomon. The *Syriac* says it is "A Psalm of David concerning Solomon; and that it was spoken also concerning Haggai and Zechariah, who forwarded the building of the temple." The *Septuagint*, *Æthiopic*, *Arabic*, and *Anglo-Saxon* have no title, but simply "A Psalm of Degrees." It was most likely composed for the building of the second temple, under Nehemiah, and by some prophet of that time.

Verse 1. *Except the Lord build the house*] To build a house is taken in *three* different senses in the sacred writings. 1. To build the temple of the Lord, which was called הבית *habbeith*, *the house*, by way of eminence. 2. To build any ordinary house, or place of dwelling. 3. To have a numerous offspring. In this sense it is supposed to be spoken concerning the Egyptian midwives; that because they feared the Lord, therefore he built them houses. See the note on Exod. i. 21. But, however, the above passage may be interpreted, it is a fact that בֵן *ben*, a son, and בַת *bath*, a daughter, and בית *beith*, a house, come from the same root בנה *banah*, to build; because sons and daughters build up a household, or constitute a *family*, as much and as really as stones and timber constitute a *building*. Now it is true that unless the good hand of God be upon us we cannot prosperously build a place of worship for his name. Unless we have his blessing, a dwelling-house cannot be comfortably erected. And if his blessing be not on our children, the house (the family) may be built up, but instead of its being the house of God, it will be the synagogue of Satan. All marriages that are not under God's blessing will be a private and public curse. This we see every day.

Except the Lord keep the city] When the returned Jews began to restore the walls of Jerusalem, and rebuild the city, Sanballat, Tobiah, and others formed plots to prevent it. Nehemiah, being informed of this, set up proper watches and guards. The enemy, finding this, gathered themselves together, and determined to fall upon them at once, and cut them all off. Nehemiah, having gained intelligence of this also, armed his people, and placed them behind the wall. Sanballat and his company, finding that the Jews were prepared for resistance, abandoned their project; and Nehemiah, to prevent surprises of this kind, kept one-half of the people always under arms, while the other half was employed in the work. To this the psalmist alludes; and in effect says, Though you should watch constantly, guard every place, and keep on your armour ready to repel every attack, yet remember the success of all depends upon the presence and blessing of God. While, therefore, ye are not slothful in business, be fervent in spirit, serving the Lord; for there is no success either in spiritual or secular undertakings but in consequence of the benediction of the Almighty.

Verse 2. It is *vain for you to rise up early*]

A. M. cir. 3559
B. C. cir. 445
Artaxerxis I.,
R. Persarum,
cir. annum
vigesimum

4 As arrows *are* in the hand of a mighty man; so *are* children of the youth.

5 Happy *is* the man that ᵍhath

his quiver full of them: ʰthey shall not be ashamed, but they ˡshall speak with the enemies in the gate.

A. M. cir. 3559
B. C. cir. 445
Artaxerxis I.,
R. Persarum,
cir. annum
vigesimum

ᵍHeb. *hath filled his quiver with them*——ʰSee Job v. 4; Prov. xxvii. 11

ˡOr, *shall subdue*, as Psalm xviii. 47; or, *destroy*

There seems to be here an allusion to the daily and nightly watches which Nehemiah instituted. The people are worn out with constant labour and watching; he therefore divided them in such a manner, that they who had worked in the day should rest by night, and that they who worked by night should rest in the day; and thus *his beloved*, a title of the Jews, *the beloved of God*, got sleep, due refreshment, and rest. As for Nehemiah and his servants, they never put off their clothes day or night but for washing.

Verse 3. *Lo, children are a heritage of the Lord*] That is, To many God gives children in place of temporal good. To many others he gives houses, lands, and thousands of gold and silver, and with them the womb that beareth not; and these are their inheritance. The poor man has from God a number of children, without lands or money; these are his inheritance; and God shows himself their father, feeding and supporting them by a chain of miraculous providences. Where is the *poor man* who would give up his *six children*, with the prospect of having *more*, for the *thousands* or *millions* of him who is the *centre* of his *own existence*, and has neither *root* nor *branch* but his forlorn solitary self upon the face of the earth? Let the fruitful family, however poor, lay this to heart: "Children are a heritage of the Lord; and the fruit of the womb is his reward." And he who gave them will feed them; for it is a fact, and the *maxim* formed on it has never failed, "Wherever God sends mouths, he sends meat." "Murmur not," said an Arab to his friend, "because thy family is large; know that it is for *their sakes* that God feeds *thee*."

Verse 4. *As arrows are in the hand of a mighty man*] Each child will, in the process of time, be a *defence* and *support* to the family, as arrows in the quiver of a skilful and strong archer; the more he has, the more enemies he may slay, and consequently the more redoubted shall he be.

Children of the youth.] The children of *young people* are always more strong and vigorous, more healthy, and generally longer lived than those of *elderly*, or comparatively *elderly persons*. *Youth* is the time for marriage; I do not mean *infancy* or a comparative *childhood*, in which several fools join in marriage who are scarcely fit to leave the *nursery* or *school*. Such couples generally disagree; they cannot bear the *boyish* and *girlish* petulancies and caprices of each other; their own growth is hindered, and their offspring, (if any,) have never much better than an *embryo* existence. On the other hand *age* produces only a *dwarfish* or *rickety* offspring, that seldom live to procreate; and when they do, it is only to perpetuate deformity and disease. It would be easy to assign reasons for all this; but the interpretation of Scripture will seldom admit of *physiological details*. It is enough that God has said,

Children of the youth are strong and active, like arrows in the hands of the mighty.

Verse 5. *Happy is the man that hath his quiver full of them*] This is generally supposed to mean *his house full of children*, as his *quiver* if full of *arrows;* but I submit whether it be not more congenial to the metaphors in the text to consider it as applying to the *wife:* "Happy is the man who has a breeding or fruitful wife;" this is the *gravida sagittis pharetra* "the quiver pregnant with arrows." But it may be thought the metaphor is not natural. I think otherwise: and I know it to be in the *Jewish style*, and the style of the times of the captivity, when this Psalm was written, and we find the *pudendum muliebre*, or human *matrix*, thus denominated, Ecclus, xxvi. 12: Κατεναντι παντος πασσαλου καθησεται, και εναντι βελους ανοιξει φαρετραν. The reader may consult the place in the *Apocrypha*, where he will find the verse well enough translated.

With the enemies in the gate.] "When he shall contend with his adversaries in the gate of the house of judgment."—*Targum*. The reference is either to *courts of justice*, which were held at the *gates* of *cities*, or to *robbers* who endeavour to force their way into a *house* to spoil the inhabitants of their goods. In the *first case* a man falsely accused, who has a numerous family, has as many witnesses in his behalf as he has children. And in the *second case* he is not afraid of *marauders*, because his house is well defended by his active and vigorous sons. It is, I believe, to this last that the psalmist refers.

This Psalm may be entitled, "The Soliloquy of the happy Householder:—The poor man with a large loving family, and in annual expectation of an increase, because his wife, under the Divine blessing, is fruitful." All are blessed of the Lord, and his hand is invariably upon them for good.

ANALYSIS OF THE HUNDRED AND TWENTY-SEVENTH PSALM

The Jews were at this time very busy in rebuilding their temple, and the houses and walls of their city; and the prophet teaches them that, without the assistance of God, nothing will be blessed or preserved, and that their children are his especial blessing also. This the prophet shows by these words repeated, *nisi, nisi, frustra, frustra*, and proves it by an induction.

I. In civil affairs, whether in house or city.

1. "Except the Lord build the house," &c. God must be the chief builder in the family; his blessing and help must be prayed for, for the nourishment of wife, children, servants, cattle, &c.

2. "Except the Lord keep the city," &c. And so it is in kingdoms and commonwealths. The *Jews* had now a trowel in one hand, and a sword in the other, for fear of their enemies: but the prophet tells them that the Lord must be their

protector and keeper, else their watch, magistrates, judges, &c., would be of little value.

And this he illustrates by an elegant *hypothesis* of an industrious man who strives to be rich, but looks not to God.

1. "He riseth early." He is up with the rising of the sun.

2. "He sits up late." Takes little rest.

3. "He eats the bread of sorrow." Defrauds himself of necessary food. His mind is full of anxiety and fear: but all this without God's blessing is vain: "It is vain for you to rise up early," &c. On the contrary, he who loves and fears God has God's blessing: "For so he gives his beloved sleep," in the place of fear and distraction.

II. The prophet then sets down the blessing a man possesses in his children. In reference to their birth,

1. "Lo, children are a heritage," &c. They are alone the Lord's gift.

2. As regarding their education: being brought up in the fear of the Lord, they become generous spirits: "As arrows are in the hand of a mighty man," &c. enabled to do great actions, and to defend themselves and others.

And the benefit will redound to the father in his old age.

1. "Happy is the man that hath," &c. Of such good children.

2. "He shall not be ashamed," &c. He shall be able to defend himself, and keep out all injuries, being fortified by his children. And if it so happen that he has a cause pending in the gate, to be tried before the judges, he shall have the patronage of his children, and not suffer in his plea for want of advocates: his sons shall stand up in a just cause for him.

PSALM CXXVIII

The blessedness of the man that fears the Lord, 1. He is blessed in his labour, 2; in his wife and children, 3, 4; in the ordinances of God, 5; and in a long life and numerous posterity, 6.

A Song of Degrees

A. M. cir. 3559
B. C. cir. 445
Artaxerxis I.,
R. Persarum,
cir. annum
vigesimum

BLESSED [a]*is* every one that feareth the LORD; that walketh in his ways.

2 [b]For thou shalt eat the labour of thine hands: happy *shalt* thou *be,* and *it shall be* well with thee.

3 Thy wife *shall be* [c]as a fruitful vine by the sides of thine house: thy children [d]like

olive plants round about thy table.

4 Behold, that thus shall the man be blessed that feareth the LORD.

A. M. cir. 3559
B. C. cir. 445
Artaxerxis I.,
R. Persarum,
cir. annum
vigesimum

5 [e]The LORD shall bless thee out of Zion: and thou shalt see the good of Jerusalem all the days of thy life.

6 Yea, thou shalt [f]see thy children's children, *and* [g]peace upon Israel.

---

[a]Psa. cxii. 1; cxv. 13; cxix. 1——[b]Isa. iii. 10——[c]Ezek. xix. 10

[d]Psa. lii. 8; cxliv. 12——[e]Psa. cxxxiv. 3——[f]Gen. l. 23; Job xlii. 16——[g]Psa. cxxv. 5

NOTES ON PSALM CXXVIII

This Psalm has no *title,* either in the *Hebrew* or any of the *Versions;* though the *Syriac* supposes it to have been spoken of *Zerubbabel,* prince of Judah, who was earnestly engaged in building the temple of the Lord. It seems to be a continuation of the preceding Psalm, or rather the *second* part of it. The man who is stated to have a numerous offspring, in the *preceding Psalm,* is here represented as *sitting at table* with his large family. A person in the mean while coming in, sees his happy state, speaks of his comforts, and predicts to him and his all possible future good. And why? Because the man and his family "fear God, and walk in his ways."

Verse 2. *Thou shalt eat the labour of thine hands]* Thou shalt not be exempted from labour. Thou shalt *work:* But God will *bless* and *prosper* that work, and thou and thy family shall eat of it. Ye shall all live on the produce of your own labour, and the hand of violence shall not be permitted to deprive you of it. Thus,

Happy shalt *thou* be, *and* it shall be *well with thee.*] Thou shalt have prosperity.

Verse 3. *Thy wife* shall be *as a fruitful vine]* Thy *children,* in every corner and apartment of thy house, shall be the evidences of the fruitfulness of thy wife, as *bunches of grapes* on every *bough* of the vine are the proofs of its

being in a healthy thriving state. Being *about the house sides,* or *apartments,* is spoken of the *wife,* not the *vine;* being *around the table* is spoken of the *children,* not the *olive-plants.* It does not appear that there were any *vines* planted *against the walls* of the houses in Jerusalem, nor any *olive-trees* in *pots* or *tubs* in the inside of their houses; as may be found in different parts of Europe.

Verse 4. *Thus shall the man be blessed that feareth the Lord.*] A *great price* for a small consideration. Fear God, and thou shalt have as much domestic good as may be useful to thee.

Verse 5. *The Lord shall bless thee out of Zion]* In all thy approaches to him in his house by prayer, by sacrifice, and by offering, thou shalt have his especial blessing. Thou shalt thrive every *where,* and in all *things.*

And thou shalt see the good of Jerusalem] Thou shalt see the cause of God flourish in thy lifetime, and his Church in great prosperity.

Verse 6. *Yea, thou shalt see thy children's children]* Thou shall not die till thou have seen thy family all settled in the world, and those of them who may be *married* blessed with children.

And *peace upon Israel.*] This is the same conclusion as in Psa. cxxv.; and should be translated, *Peace be upon Israel!* May God favour his own cause, and bless all his people!

ANALYSIS OF THE HUNDRED AND TWENTY-EIGHTH PSALM

In this Psalm the prophet persuades men to fear God upon the several rewards that attend upon piety.

It is divided into *three* parts.

I. He describes the pious man, and pronounces him blessed, ver. 1.

II. He proposes the particulars of his blessing, ver. 2-6.

III. He gives his acclamation to it, ver. 4.

I. He describes the man who is to expect the blessing. Two qualities he must have:—

1. He must "fear the Lord." Fear, and not decline from him.

2. He must "walk in his ways." This is the true character of his fear.

3. This man shall be "blessed." Whether rich or poor, high or low; all such shall experience the blessing of the Lord.

II. And the blessedness consists in three particulars.

1. He shall enjoy those goods he has honestly obtained with his hands: "For thou shalt eat the labour of thine hands:" his happiness consists not in having much, but in enjoying what he has.

2. "Happy shalt thou be," &c. Able to help others, and leave to thy children.

3. Happy he shall be in his marriage, if his choice be prudent, and in the Lord: 1. "His wife shall be," &c. *Fetifera, non sterilis.* 2. Upon the walls of thy house. Staying at home, and caring for the things of the house, while her husband is taking care abroad.

4. Happy in his children: 1. "Thy children like olive-plants." Fresh, green, spreading, fruitful, and pledges of peace: not like sharp and prickly thorns. 2. "Round about thy table." Sit, eat, and converse with thee.

III. The acclamation follows these temporal blessings: "Thus shall the man be blessed," &c. In his goods, wife, and children.

But there is a blessing far beyond these, the sum of which is,—

1. God's blessing: "The Lord shall bless thee," &c. By a federal, a Church blessing.

2. "Thou shalt see the good of Jerusalem," &c. The prosperity of the Church.

3. "Yea, thou shalt see thy children's children."

Et natos natorum, et qui nascuntur ab illis.

"Thy children's children, and those born of *them.*"

4. "And peace upon Israel." A flourishing commonwealth and kingdom: for by peace is understood all prosperity.

PSALM CXXIX

The Jews give an account of the afflictions which they have passed through, 1–3. And thank God for their deliverance, 4. The judgments that shall fall on the workers of iniquity, 5–8.

A Song of Degrees

MANY ^aa time have they afflicted me from ^bmy youth, ^cmay Israel now say:

2 Many a time have they afflicted me from my youth: yet they have not prevailed against me.

3 The plowers plowed upon my back: they made long their furrows.

4 The LORD *is* righteous: he hath cut asunder the cords of the wicked.

5 Let them all be confounded and turned back that hate Zion.

ªOr, *Much*——ᵇSee Ezek. xxiii. 3; Hos. ii. 15; xi. 1——ᶜPsa. cxxiv. 1

NOTES ON PSALM CXXIX

This Psalm was written *after* the captivity; and contains a reference to the many tribulations which the Jews passed through from their *youth*, i. e., the earliest part of their history, their bondage in Egypt. It has no *title* in any of the *Versions*, nor in the *Hebrew text*, except the general one of *A Psalm of Degrees*. The *author* is uncertain.

Verse 1. *Many a time have they afflicted me*] The Israelites had been generally in affliction or captivity from the earliest part of their history, here called *their youth*. So Hos. ii. 15: "She shall sing as in the *days of her youth*, when she came up out of *the land of Egypt*." See Jer. ii. 2, and Ezek. xvi. 4, &c.

Verse 2. *Yet they have not prevailed*] They endeavoured to annihilate us as a people; but God still preserves us as his own nation.

Verse 3. *The plowers plowed upon my back*] It is possible that this mode of expression may signify that the people, during their captivity, were cruelly used by *scourging*, &c.; or it may be a sort of proverbial mode of expression for the most cruel usage. There really appears here to be a reference to a *yoke*, as if they had actually been *yoked to the plough*, or to *some kind of carriages*, and been obliged to draw like *beasts of burden*. In this way St. Jerome understood the passage; and this has the more likelihood, as in the next verse God is represented as *cutting them off* from these draughts.

Verse 4. *The Lord—hath cut asunder the cords of the wicked.*] The words have been applied to the sufferings of Christ; but I know not on what authority. No such scourging could take place in his case, as would justify the expression,—

"The ploughers made long furrows there,
Till all his body was one wound."

It is not likely that he received more than *thirty-nine* stripes. The last line is an unwarranted assertion.

Verse 5. *Let them all be confounded*] They shall be confounded. They who *hate Zion*, the Church of God, hate God himself; and all such must be dealt with as *enemies*, and be utterly *confounded*.

6 Let them be as ᵈthe grass *upon* the house-tops, which withereth afore it groweth up:

7 Wherewith the mower filleth not his hand; nor he that bindeth sheaves his bosom.

ᵈPsa. xxxvii. 2

Verse 6. *As the grass* upon *the housetops*] As in the east the roofs of the houses were *flat*, seeds of various kinds falling upon them would naturally vegetate, though in an imperfect way; and, because of the want of proper nourishment, would necessarily *dry* and *wither* away. If *grass*, the *mower* cannot make *hay* of it; if *corn*, the *reaper* cannot make a *sheaf* of it. Let the Babylonians be like such herbage—good for nothing, and come to nothing.

Withereth afore it groweth up] Before שלק *shalak*, it is *unsheathed;* i. e., before it *ears*, or comes to *seed*.

Verse 8. *Neither do they which go by say*] There is a reference here to the *salutations* which were *given* and *returned* by the reapers in the time of the *harvest*. We find that it was customary, when the master came to them into the field, to say unto the reapers, *The Lord be with you!* and for them to answer, *The Lord bless thee!* Ruth ii. 4. Let their land become desolate, so that no harvest shall ever more appear in it. No interchange of benedictions between owners and reapers. This has literally taken place: Babylon is utterly destroyed; no harvests grow near the place where it stood.

ANALYSIS OF THE HUNDRED AND TWENTY-NINTH
PSALM

The intent of the prophet in composing this Psalm is to comfort the Church in affliction, and to stir her up to glorify God for his providence over her, always for her good, and bringing her enemies to confusion, and a sudden ruin.

It is divided into *three* parts:—

I. The indefatigable malice of the enemies of the Church, ver. 1, 3.

II. That their malice is vain. God saves them, ver. 2, 4.

III. God puts into the mouth of his people

8 Neither do they which go by say, ᵉThe blessing of the LORD *be* upon you: we bless you in the name of the LORD.

ᵉRuth ii. 4; Psa. cxviii. 26

---

what they may say to their enemies, even when their malice is at the highest.

I. "Many a time have they afflicted me," &c. In which observe,—

1. That afflictions do attend those who will live righteously in Christ Jesus.

2. These afflictions are many: "Many a time," &c.

3. That they begin with the Church: "From my youth." Prophets, martyrs, &c.

4. This affliction was a heavy affliction: "The plowers plowed upon my back," &c. They dealt unmercifully with me, as a husbandman does with his ground.

II. But all their malice is to no purpose.

1. "Yet they have not prevailed against me." To extinguish the Church.

2. The reason is, "The Lord is righteous." And therefore he protects all those who are under his tuition, and punishes their adversaries.

3. "The Lord is righteous," &c. Cut asunder the ropes and chains with which they made their furrows: "He hath delivered Israel," &c.

III. In the following verses, to the end, the prophet, by way of prediction, declares the vengeance God would bring upon his enemies, which has *three* degrees:—

1. "Let them all be confounded," &c. Fail in their hopes against us.

2. "Let them be as the grass," &c. That they quickly perish. Grass on the housetops is good for nothing: "Which withereth afore it groweth up," &c. Never is mowed, nor raked together.

3. "Neither do they which go by say, The blessing of the Lord," &c. No man says so much as, God speed him! as is usual to say to workmen in harvest: but even this the enemies of the Church, and of God's work, say not, for they wish it not.

PSALM CXXX

The prayer of a penitent to God, with confession of sin, 1-3. Confidence in God's mercy, and waiting upon him,
4, 6. Israel is encouraged to hope in the Lord, because of his willingness to save, 7, 8.

A Song of Degrees

OUT ᵃof the depths have I cried unto thee, O LORD.

2 LORD, hear my voice: let thine ears

ᵃLam. iii. 55; Jonah ii. 2

NOTES ON PSALM CXXX

This Psalm has no title nor author's name, either in the Hebrew, or in any of the Versions; though the Syriac says it was spoken of Nehemiah the priest. It was most probably composed during the captivity; and contains the

be attentive to the voice of my supplications.

3 ᵇIf thou, LORD, shouldest mark iniquities, O LORD, who shall stand?

ᵇPsa. cxliii. 2; Rom. iii. 20, 23, 24

---

complaint of the afflicted Jews, with their hopes of the remission of those sins which were the cause of their sufferings, and their restoration from captivity to their own land. This is one of those called *penitential Psalms*.

Verse 1. *Out of the depths*] The captives in Babylon represent their condition like those

4 But *there is* ^cforgiveness with thee, that ^dthou mayest be feared.

5 ^eI wait for the LORD, my soul doth wait, and ^fin his word do I hope.

6 ^gMy soul *waiteth* for the LORD more than they that watch for the morning: ^hI *say,*

more *than* they that watch for the morning.

7 ⁱLet Israel hope in the LORD: for ^kwith the LORD *there is* mercy, and with him *is* plenteous redemption.

8 And ^lhe shall redeem Israel from all his iniquities.

---

^cExod. xxxiv. 7——^d1 Kings viii. 40; Psa. ii. 11; Jer. xxxiii. 8, 9——^ePsa. xxvii. 14; xxxiii. 20; xl. 1; Isa. viii. 17; xxvi. 8; xxx. 18——^fPsa. cxix. 81

^gPsa. lxiii. 6; cxix. 147——^hOr, *which watch unto the morning*——ⁱPsa. cxxxi. 1——^kPsa. lxxxvi. 5, 15; Isa. lv. 7——^lPsa. ciii. 3, 4; Matt. i. 21

---

who are in a prison—an abyss or deep ditch, ready to be swallowed up.

Verse 2. *Lord, hear my voice*] They could have no helper but God, and to him they earnestly seek for relief.

Verse 3. *If thou—shouldest mark iniquities*] If thou shouldst set down every deviation in thought, word, and deed from thy holy law; and if thou shouldst call us into judgment for all our infidelities, both of heart and life; O Lord, who could stand? Who could stand such a trial, and who could stand acquitted in the judgment? This is a most solemn saying; and if we had not the doctrine that is in the next verse, who could be saved?

Verse 4. *But* there is *forgiveness with thee*] Thou canst forgive; mercy belongs to thee, as well as judgment. The doctrine here is the doctrine of St. John: "If any man sin, we have an Advocate with the Father, Jesus Christ the righteous; and he is the propitiation for our sins; and not for ours only, but also for *the sins* of the whole world." "Hear, O heavens, and give ear, O earth; for the Lord hath spoken!" Jesus has died for our sins; therefore God *can be just, and yet the justifier of him who believeth in Jesus.*

Verse 5. *I wait for the Lord*] The word קוה *kavah,* which we translate *to wait,* properly signifies the *extension of a cord from one point to another.* This is a fine metaphor: *God* is one point, the *human heart* is the other; and the *extended cord* between both is the *earnest believing desire* of the soul. This *desire, strongly extended* from the *heart* to God, in every mean of grace, and when there is none, is the *active, energetic waiting* which God requires, and which will be successful.

Verse 6. More than *they that watch for the morning.*] I believe the original should be read differently from what it is here. The *Chaldee* has, "More than they who observe the morning watches, that they may offer the morning oblation." This gives a good sense, and is, perhaps, the true meaning. Most of the Versions have, "From the morning to the night watches." Or the passage may be rendered, "My soul waiteth for the Lord from the morning watches to the morning watches." That is, "I wait both day and night."

Verse 7. *Let Israel hope in the Lord*] This, to hope for salvation, is their *duty* and their *interest.* But what *reason* is there for this *hope?* A twofold reason:—

1. *With the Lord* there is *mercy*] החסד *hachesed,* THAT mercy, the fund, the essence of mercy.

2. *And with him* is *plenteous redemption.*] והרבה עמו פדות *veharabbah immo peduth;* and *that abundant redemption,* that to which there is none like, the *Fountain* of redemption, the

Lamb of God which taketh away the sin of the world. The article ה, both in הרבה *harabbah* and החסד *hachesed,* is very emphatic.

Verse 8. *He shall redeem Israel*] Και αυτος λυτρωσει, "He will make a ransom for Israel," He will *provide a great price* for Israel, and by it will *take away all his iniquities.* I would not restrict this to Israel in Babylon. Every *believer* may take it to himself. God perfectly justifies and perfectly sanctifies all that come unto him through the Son of his love.

ANALYSIS OF THE HUNDRED AND THIRTIETH PSALM

In this Psalm the Spirit of God proposes to us the case of a person oppressed with the wrath of God against sin, yet flying to him for comfort, remission, and purification.

I. Acknowledging his miserable condition, he prays to be heard, ver. 12.

II. He desires remission of sin, ver. 3, 4.

III. He expresses his hope and confidence, ver. 5, 6.

IV. He exhorts God's people to trust in him, ver. 7, 8.

I. The psalmist likens himself to a man in the bottom of a pit:—

1. "Out of the depths have I cried," &c. A true penitent cries out of the depth of his misery, and from the depth of a heart sensible of it.

2. "Lord, hear my voice." Although I be so low, thou canst hear me.

3. "Let thine ears be attentive," &c. Or I cry in vain.

II. But there was a reason why God should not hear. He was a grievous sinner; but all men are the same; therefore,

1. "If thou, Lord, shouldest mark iniquity." And I have nothing of my own but it to bring before thee, yet execute not thy just anger on account of my transgressions; for,

2. "There is mercy with thee," &c. True repentance requires two things, the recognition of our own misery and the persuasion of God's mercy. Both are needful; for if we know not the former, we shall not seek mercy; and if we despair of mercy, we shall never find it.

3. "That thou mayest be feared." Not with a servile but a filial fear, which involves prayer, faith, hope, love, adoration, giving of thanks, &c. This fear leads to God's throne as a merciful and pardoning God.

III. The method of God's servants in their addresses to heaven is, that they believe, hope, pray, and expect. Thus did the psalmist.

1. "I expect the Lord." In faith.

2. "My soul doth wait." His expectation was active and real, and proceeded from fervency of heart.

3. His expectation was not presumptive, but grounded upon God's word and promise: "In his word is my hope."

4. "My soul waiteth for the Lord." Which he illustrates by the similitude of a watchman who longs for the morning.

5. "I wait for the Lord more than they," &c. It was now night with him, darkness and misery were upon his soul; the morning he expected was the remission of his sins, which must come from God's mercy. For this he eagerly waited.

IV. He proposes his own example to God's people:—

1. "Let Israel hope in the Lord," like me, and cry from the depths.

2. "For with the Lord there is mercy." This is the reason and encouragement for the hope. Mercy flows from him.

3. "And with him is redemption." Which we need, being all sold under sin; and this redemption was purchased for us by the death of his Son.

4. And this redemption is *plentiful;* for by it he has redeemed the whole world, 1 John i. 2.

5. And this is to take effect upon Israel: "For he shall redeem Israel," &c. It is not, as the Jews expected, a temporal redemption, but a spiritual, as the angel told Joseph: "His name shall be called Jesus; for he shall save his people from their sins."

PSALM CXXXI

The psalmist professes his humility, and the peaceableness of his disposition and conduct, 1, 2. Exhorts Israel to hope in God, 3.

A Song of Degrees of David

LORD, my heart is not haughty, nor mine eyes lofty: [a]neither do I [b]exercise myself in great matters, or in things too [c]high for me.

2 Surely I have behaved and quieted [d]myself, [e]as a child that is weaned of his mother: my soul *is* even as a weaned child.

3 [f]Let Israel hope in the Lord [g]from henceforth and for ever.

---

[a]Rom. xii. 16——[b]Heb. *walk*——[c]Heb. *wonderful;* Job xlii. 3; Psa. cxxxix. 6

[d]Heb. *my soul*——[e]Matt. xviii. 3; 1 Cor. xiv. 20
[f]Psa. cxxx. 7——[g]Heb. *from now*

NOTES ON PSALM CXXXI

Some think that David composed this Psalm as a vindication of himself, when accused by Saul's courtiers that he affected the crown, and was laying schemes and plots to possess himself of it. Others think the Psalm was made during the captivity, and that it contains a fair account of the manner in which the captives behaved themselves, under the domination of their oppressors.

Verse 1. *Lord, my heart is not haughty*] The principle of *pride* has no place in my heart; and consequently the *high, lofty,* and *supercilious* look does not appear in my eyes. I neither *look up,* with desire to obtain, to the *state* of others, nor *look down* with contempt to the meanness or poverty of those below me. And the whole of my conduct proves this; for *I have not exercised myself*—walked, *in high matters,* nor associated myself with the higher ranks of the community, nor in *great matters,* נפלאות *niphlaoth, wonderful* or sublime things; *too high for me,* ממני *mimmeni, alien from me,* and that do not belong to a person in my sphere and situation in life.

Verse 2. *I have behaved and quieted myself, as a child*] On the contrary, I have been under the rod of others, and when chastised have not complained; and my *silence* under my affliction was the fullest proof that I neither *murmured* nor *repined,* but received all as coming from the hands of a just God.

My soul is *even as a weaned child.*] I felt I must forego many conveniences and comforts which I once enjoyed; and these I gave up without repining or demurring.

Verse 3. *Let Israel hope in the Lord*] Act all as I have done; trust in him who is the God of justice and compassion; and, after you have suffered awhile, he will make bare his arm and deliver you. Short as it is, this is a most instructive Psalm. He who acts as the psalmist did, is never likely to come to mischief, or do any to others.

ANALYSIS OF THE HUNDRED AND THIRTY-FIRST PSALM

I. The psalmist, having been accused of proud and haughty conduct, protests his innocence, states his humble thoughts of himself, and the general meekness of his deportment.

II. That his confidence was in God; in him he trusted, and therefore was far from ambition.

III. And by his own example calls on Israel to trust in God as he did.

I. He protests his humility.

1. There was no *pride* in his heart; and he calls God to witness it: "Lord, my heart is not haughty."

2. There was no *arrogance* in his carriage: "Nor mine eyes lofty."

3. Nor in his undertakings: "Neither do I exercise myself in great matters." He kept himself within his own bounds and vocation, and meddled not with state affairs.

II. What preserved him from *pride* was *humility*. He brought down his desires, and wants, and views to his circumstances.

1. "Surely I have behaved and quieted myself." Have I not given every evidence of my mild and peaceable behaviour? and I certainly never permitted a high thought to rise within me.

2. I acted as the *child weaned* from his mother. When once deprived of my comforts, and brought into captivity, I submitted to the will of God, and brought down my mind to my circumstances.

III. He proposes his own example of humility and peaceableness for all Israel to follow.

1. "Let Israel hope." Never despair of God's mercy, nor of his gracious providence. The storm will be succeeded by *fair* and *fine* weather.

2. "Let Israel hope in the Lord." Never content yourselves with merely supposing that in the course of things these afflictions will wear out. No; look to God, and depend on him, that *he* may bring them to a happy conclusion.

Remember that he is *Jehovah*.

1. Wise to plan.

2. Good to purpose.

3. Strong to execute, and will withhold no good thing from them that walk uprightly.

4. Trust *from henceforth*. If you have not begun before, begin now.

5. And do not be weary; trust *for ever*. Your case can never be out of the reach of God's power and mercy.

PSALM CXXXII

The psalmist prays that God would remember his promises to David, 1. His purpose to bring the ark of the Lord into a place of rest, 2–5. Where it was found, and the prayer in removing it, 6–9. The promises made to David and his posterity, 10–12. God's choice of Zion for a habitation, and his promises to the people, 13–17. All their enemies shall be confounded, 18.

XXVIII. DAY. MORNING PRAYER

A Song of Degrees

A. M. cir. 3489
B. C. cir. 515
Darii I.,
R. Persarum,
cir. annum
sextum

LORD, remember David, *and* all his afflictions:

2 How he sware unto the LORD *and* vowed unto *the mighty God* of Jacob;

3 Surely I will not come into the tabernacle of my house, nor go up into my bed;

4 I will *not give sleep to mine eyes, or* slumber to mine eyelids,

5 Until I *find out a place for the LORD, *a habitation for the mighty *God* of Jacob.

6 Lo, we heard of it *at Ephratah: *we found it *in the fields of the wood.

7 We will go into his tabernacles: *we will worship at his footstool.

8 *Arise, O LORD, into thy rest; thou, and *the ark of thy strength.

9 Let thy priests *be clothed with righteous-

A. M. cir. 3489
B. C. cir. 515
Darii I.,
R. Persarum,
cir. annum
sextum

---

*Psalm lxv. 1——*Gen. xlix. 24——*Prov. vi. 4
*Acts vii. 46——*Heb. *habitations*——*1 Sam. xvii. 12
*1 Sam. vii. 1

*1 Chron. xiii. 5——*Psa. v. 7; xcix. 5——*Num. x. 35; 2 Chron. vi. 41, 42——*Psa. lxxviii. 61——*Job xxix. 14; ver. 16; Isa. lxi. 10

NOTES ON PSALM CXXXII

Some attribute this Psalm to *David*, but without sufficient ground; others, to *Solomon*, with more likelihood; and others, to some inspired author at the conclusion of the captivity, which is, perhaps, the most probable. It refers to the building of the second temple, and placing the ark of the covenant in it.

Verse 1. *Lord, remember David*] Consider the promises thou hast made to this thy eminent servant, that had respect, not only to *him* and to his *family*, but to all the *Israelitish people*.

Verse 2. *How he sware unto the Lord*] It is only in this place that we are informed of David's vow to the Lord, relative to the building of the temple; but we find he had fully purposed the thing.

Verse 3. *Surely I will not come*] This must refer to the *situation* of the temple; or, as we would express it, he would not pass another day

till he had found out the *ground* on which to build the temple, and projected the *plan*, and devised *ways* and *means* to execute it. And we find that he would have acted in all things according to his oath and vow, had God permitted him. But even after the Lord told him that Solomon, not he, should build the house, he still continued to show his good will by collecting treasure and materials for the building, all the rest of his life.

Verse 5. *The mighty God of Jacob.*] עביר יעקב *abir yaacob*, the *Mighty One of Jacob*. We have this epithet of God for the first time, Gen. xlix. 24. Hence, perhaps, the *abirim* of the heathen, the stout ones, the *strong beings*.

Verse 6. *Lo, we have heard of it at Ephratah*] This may be considered as a continuation of David's vow; as if he had said: As I had determined to build a temple for the ark, and heard that it was at *Ephratah*, I went and found it in the *fields of Jaar*, יער;—not the wood, but Kirjath Jaar or Jearim, where the ark was then

A. M. cir. 3489
B. C. cir. 515
Darii I.,
R. Persarum,
cir. annum
sextum

ness; and let thy saints shout for joy.

10 For thy servant David's sake turn not away the face of thine anointed.

11 ⁿThe Lᴏʀᴅ hath sworn *in* truth unto David; he will not turn from it; ᵒOf the fruit of ᵖthy body will I set upon thy throne.

12 If thy children will keep my covenant and my testimonies that I shall teach them, their children shall also sit upon thy throne for evermore.

13 ᑫFor the Lᴏʀᴅ hath chosen Zion; he

A. M. cir. 3489
B. C. cir. 515
Darii I.,
R. Persarum,
cir. annum
sextum

hath desired *it* for his habitation.

14 ʳThis *is* my rest for ever: here will I dwell; for I have desired it.

15 ˢI ᵗwill abundantly bless her provision: I will satisfy her poor with bread.

16 ᵘI will also clothe her priests with salvation: ᵛand her saints shall shout aloud for joy.

17 ʷThere will I make the horn of David to bud: ˣI have ordained a ʸlamp for mine anointed.

18 His enemies will I ᶻclothe with shame: but upon himself shall his crown flourish.

ⁿPsa. lxxxix. 3, 4, 33, &c.; cx. 4——ᵒ2 Sam. vii. 12; 1 Kings viii. 25; 2 Chron. vi. 16; Luke i. 69; Acts ii. 30 ᵖHeb. *thy belly*——ᑫPsa. xlviii. 1, 2——ʳPsa. lxviii. 16 ˢPsa. cxlvii. 14

ᵗOr, *surely*——ᵘ2 Chron. vi. 41; ver. 9; Psa. cxlix. 4 ᵛHos. xi. 12——ʷEzek. xxix. 21; Luke i. 69——ˣSee 1 Kings xi. 36; xv. 4; 2 Chron. xxi. 7——ʸOr, *candle* ᶻPsa. xxxv. 26; cix. 29

---

lodged;—and having found it, he entered the tabernacle, ver. 7; and then, adoring that God whose presence was in it, he invited him to arise and come to the place which he had prepared for him.

Verse 8. *Arise, O Lord, into thy rest; thou and the ark of thy strength.*] Using the same expressions which Solomon used when he dedicated the temple, 2 Chron. vi. 41, 42. There are several difficulties in these passages. *Ephratah* may mean the *tribe of Ephraim;* and then we may understand the place thus: "I have learned that the ark had been in the tribe of Ephraim, and I have seen it at Kirjath-jearim, or *Field of the woods;* but this is not a proper place for it, for the Lord hath chosen Jerusalem." It is true that the ark did remain in that tribe from the days of Joshua to Samuel, during *three hundred and twenty-eight* years; and thence it was brought to Kirjath-jearim, where it continued *seventy* years, till the commencement of the reign of David over *all* Israel.

But if we take verses 6, 7, and 8, *not* as the continuation of David's vow, but as the *words of the captives in Babylon,* the explanation will be more plain and easy: "We have heard, O Lord, from our fathers, that thy tabernacle was formerly a long time at Shiloh, in the tribe of Ephraim. And our history informs us that it has been also at Kirjath-jearim, the fields of the wood; and afterwards it was brought to Jerusalem, and there established: but Jerusalem is now ruined, the temple destroyed, and thy people in captivity. Arise, O Lord, and reestablish thy dwelling-place in thy holy city!" See *Calmet* and others on this place.

Verse 9. *Let thy priests be clothed with righteousness*] Let them be as remarkable for *inward holiness* as they are for the splendour of their *holy vestments.*

Verse 10. *The face of thine anointed.*] David. Remember thy promises to him, that he may be restored to thee and to thy worship.

Verse 11. *The Lord hath sworn*] As David sware to the Lord, so the Lord swears to David, that he will establish his throne, and place his posterity on it: and that he had respect to David's Antitype, we learn from St. Peter, Acts

ii. 30, where see the note. This verse with the following refers to the spiritual David, and the Christian Church.

Verse 12. *If thy children will keep my covenant*] This was conditional with respect to the posterity of David. They have been driven from the throne, because they did not keep the Lord's covenant; but the true David is on the throne, and his posterity forms the genuine Israelites.

Verse 13. *The Lord hath chosen Zion*] Therefore neither *Shiloh* nor *Kirjath-jearim* is the place of his rest.

Verse 14. *This is my rest for ever*] Here the Christian Church is most indubitably meant. This is *God's place* for ever. After this there never will be another *dispensation;* Christianity closes and completes all communications from heaven to earth. God has nothing greater to give to mankind on this side heaven; nor does man need any thing better; nor is his nature capable of any thing more excellent.

Verse 15. *I will abundantly bless her provision*] There shall be an abundant provision of salvation made for mankind in the Christian Church. Our Lord's *multiplication of the loaves* was a *type* and *proof* of it.

Verse 16. *I will also clothe her priests*] All Christian ministers, *with salvation;* this shall appear in all their conduct. *Salvation—redemption from all sin* through the blood of the Lamb, shall be their great and universal message.

Verse 17. *There will I make the horn of David to bud*] *There,* in the *Christian Church,* the power and authority of the spiritual David shall appear.

I have ordained a lamp] I have taken care to secure a *posterity,* to which the promises shall be expressly fulfilled.

Verse 18. *His enemies will I clothe with shame*] Every opponent of the Christian cause shall be confounded.

But upon himself shall his crown flourish.] There shall be no end of the government of Christ's kingdom. From verse 11 to the end, the spiritual David and his posterity are the subjects of which the Psalm treats.

ANALYSIS OF THE HUNDRED AND THIRTY-SECOND PSALM

This Psalm is divided into *three* parts:—

I. A petition, before which is David's care and vow to settle the ark, and with what reverence they would settle it in the temple; and he sets down the solemn prayer then used, ver. 1-10.

II. An explication of the promises made unto David for the continuance of his kingdom in his posterity, ver. 11, 12, and God's love to his Church, ver. 13.

III. A prophecy, spoken in the person of God, for the stability of Christ's Church; and the blessings upon the people, the priests, and the house of David, from ver. 14 to the end.

I. In all prayer a man must reflect upon God's promise; otherwise he cannot pray in faith.

1. "Lord, remember David:" Thy promises made to him. First he prays for the king; then for the ecclesiastics, ver. 8, 9; then for the people, ver. 8.

2. "And all his afflictions:" Many he had before he was king; and one of the greatest was the settling of the ark.

Now this his ardent and sincere desire appears by his oath. And now,—

1. "How he sware unto the Lord," &c.

2. The substance of which was, "Surely I will not come," &c.

Now this is hyperbolical; for we must not conceive that he went not into his house or bed till he found out a place to build God's house. But see the note.

1. "I will not come into—my house:" So as to forget to build God's house.

2. "Nor go up into my bed:" Or let any thing make me forget the work.

3. "I will not give sleep," &c.: But make provision for building the temple.

And here the prophet inserts two verses by way of gratitude.

First, he exults for the news of the ark: "Lo, we heard of it at Ephratah," &c.

By *Ephratah* some understand the land of *Ephraim*, in which the ark remained at Shiloh. Being afterwards sent home, it was found in the field of Joshua; thence conveyed to the house of *Amminadab*, who dwelt in *Kirjath-jearim*, that signifies a *woody city*. Hence, David might well say, "And found it in the fields of the wood," &c.

And the place for the ark being found, he calls on Israel, saying,

1. "We will go into his tabernacles." Now the ark is rested in Mount Zion.

2. "And we will worship," &c. Not make rash approaches to the ark, but come with reverence, and bow in his presence.

The ark being brought into the temple, he uses this solemn form:—

1. "Arise, O Lord," &c. He prays and invites him to dwell in his temple.

2. "Into thy rest." To pass no more from place to place.

3. "Thou, and the ark of thy strength." Show thy power and strength, as thou didst at *Jordan*, &c.

Before the ark in the temple he prays,—

1. "Let thy priests be clothed," &c. Inwardly, in heart and soul.

2. "Let thy saints shout," &c. With a cheerful voice, for the ark rests.

3. "For thy servant David's sake," &c. 1. David is not here to be taken absolutely for his person only, as having the covenants and promises made to him, but for the promise' sake. 2. "Turn not away," &c. Suffer me not to depart from thy presence unheard.

II. The prophet now proceeds to count up the promises made to *David*, which God confirmed by oath, in which we are to observe, 1. The manner of the promise: "The Lord hath sworn in truth," &c. It was merciful to promise; but more so to bind himself by oath. 2. The matter of his oath expressed ver. 11-14.

1. For the seed of David, as respects Christ, is categorical and absolute: "Of the fruit of thy body," &c. Which word St. *Peter* refers to Christ, Acts ii. 30. According to the flesh he was David's seed; for by the *mother's* side Christ was to be David's seed, not by the father's.

2. For the seed of David, as it relates to his posterity, the oath is hypothetical and conditional: "If thy children will keep," &c.

As the external kingdom was by this oath annexed to one family, so the external worship was assigned by it to one place.

1. "For the Lord hath chosen Zion," &c.

2. "This is my rest for ever." Zion was the seat of the sanctuary till the coming of the Messiah. But Zion was but a type of Christ's Church, which he hath chosen to be his rest for ever.

III. The prophet represents God as promising good things to his Church.

1. Such abundance of temporal things that the poor shall not want: "I will abundantly bless her provision," &c.

2. That her "priests shall be clothed with salvation," &c.

3. "There will I make the horn of David to flourish," &c. That is, the kingdom of the Messiah.

4. The fourth benefit God promises is the confusion of their enemies, and the eternal authority in this kingdom: "His enemies will I clothe with shame, but upon himself shall his crown flourish."

PSALM CXXXIII

The comfort and benefit of the communion of saints, 1–3.

A Song of Degrees of David

A. M. cir. 3489
B. C. cir. 515
Darii I.,
R. Persarum,
cir. annum
sextum

BEHOLD, how good and how pleasant *it is* for [a]brethren to dwell [b]together in unity!

2 *It is* like [c]the precious ointment upon the head, that ran down upon the beard, *even* Aaron's beard: that went down to the skirts of his garments;

3 As the dew of [d]Hermon, *and as the dew* that descended upon the mountains of Zion: for [e]there the LORD commanded the blessing, *even* life for evermore.

A. M. cir. 3489
B. C. cir. 515
Darii I.,
R. Persarum,
cir. annum
sextum

[a]Gen. xiii. 8; Heb. xiii. 1——[b]Heb. *even together* [c]Exod. xxx. 25, 30

[d]Deut. iv. 48——[e]Lev. xxv. 21; Deut. xxviii. 8; Psa. xlii. 8

NOTES ON PSALM CXXXIII

There are different opinions concerning this Psalm; the most probable is, that it represents the priests and Levites returned from captivity, and united in the service of God in the sanctuary. This, the preceding, and the following, appear to make one subject. In the *one hundred and thirty-second*, the Lord is entreated to enter his temple, and pour out his benediction; in the *one hundred and thirty-third*, the beautiful order and harmony of the temple service is pointed out; and in the *one hundred and thirty-fourth*, all are exhorted to diligence and watchfulness in the performance of their duty. It is attributed to David by the Hebrew, the Syriac, and the Vulgate; but no name is prefixed in the Septuagint, Æthiopic, Arabic, and Anglo-Saxon.

Verse 1. *Behold, how good and how pleasant*] Unity is, according to this scripture, a *good* thing and a *pleasant;* and especially among *brethren*—members of the same family, of the same Christian community, and of the same nation. And why not among the great family of mankind? On the other hand, *disunion* is bad and hateful. The former is from heaven; the latter, from hell.

Verse 2. *Like the precious ointment*] The composition of this holy anointing oil may be seen, Exod. xxx. 23; *sweet cinnamon, sweet calamus, cassia lignea,* and *olive oil.* The odour of this must have been very agreeable, and serves here as a metaphor to point out the exquisite excellence of brotherly love.

Ran down upon the beard] The oil was poured upon the head of Aaron so profusely as to run down upon his garments. It is customary in the east to pour out the oil on the head so profusely as to reach every limb.

Verse 3. *As the dew of Hermon,* and as the dew *that descended upon the mountains of Zion*] This was not Mount Zion, צִיּוֹן *tsiyon,* in Jerusalem, but *Sion,* שִׂיאֹן which is a part of Hermon, see Deut. iv. 48: "Mount Sion, which is Hermon." On this mountain the dew is very copious. Mr. Maundrell says that "with this dew, even in dry weather, their tents were as wet as if it had rained the whole night." This seems to show the strength of the comparison.

For there] Where this *unity* is.

The Lord commanded the blessing] That is, an *everlasting* life. There he pours out his blessings, and gives a long and happy life.

For other particulars, see the commentators *passim,* and the following *analysis.*

ANALYSIS OF THE HUNDRED AND THIRTY-THIRD PSALM

In this Psalm the blessings of peace and unity are recommended and described, whether in the Church, family, or kingdom.

I. *It is,* says the prophet, *a good and pleasant thing,* &c., ver. 1.

II. He declares both by similitudes.

1. The pleasantness, by the *ointment* with which the high priest was anointed.

2. The goodness, by the *dew* which fell upon the mountains.

3. But in plainer terms, by the *blessing of God* upon the head of the peaceful.

1. The prophet begins with an encomium of peace, unity, and concord.

1. "Behold." Take notice of it in its effects.

2. "How good and pleasant," &c. He admires, but cannot express it.

3. The *encomium* itself is expressed by two epithets: 1. *It is good,* and brings much profit. 2. *It is pleasant,* and brings much content with it.

4. The concord itself is thus expressed: *Brethren,* either in a Church, family, or kingdom, should be of one soul, and intent on the common good.

II. The pleasantness is compared to "the precious ointment upon the head."

1. All benefit from this concord; princes, nobles, and people. *The head, beard,* and *skirts.*

2. It sends forth a sweet and reviving savour.

3. It is as balsam poured into wounds.

The profit he compares to the dews: "As the dew of Hermon," &c., gently descending, and fructifying and enriching the ground.

And this he sets down without any metaphor: "For there the Lord commanded the blessing," &c.; which approbation he manifests by the abundance he pours where concord and unity are found.

1. He commands his blessing. Makes all creatures useful to them.

2. His blessing is prosperity, good success. To bless is to benefit.

3. This he calls life; for with troubles, griefs, &c., a man's life is no life. A quiet life those shall have who live in peace, without dissensions respecting religion or in matters connected with the state.

PSALM CXXXIV

An exhortation to praise God in his sanctuary, 1-3.

A Song of Degrees

A. M. cir. 3489
B. C. cir. 515
Darii I.,
R. Persarum,
cir. annum
sextum

BEHOLD, bless ye the LORD, ^aall *ye* servants of the LORD, ^bwhich by night stand in the house of the LORD.

2 ^cLift up your hands ^din the sanctuary, and bless the LORD.
3 ^eThe LORD that made heaven and earth ^fbless thee out of Zion.

A. M. cir. 3489
B. C. cir. 515
Darii I.,
R. Persarum,
cir. annum
sextum

^aPsa. cxxxv. 1, 2——^b1 Chron. ix. 33——^c1 Tim. ii. 8

^dOr, in *holiness*——^ePsa. cxxiv. 8—— ^fPsa. cxxviii 5; cxxxv. 21

NOTES ON PSALM CXXXIV

This is the last of the fifteen Psalms called *Psalms of degrees.* Who was the author is uncertain; it is attributed to *David* only by the *Syriac;* it is intimately connected with the two preceding Psalms, and is an exhortation to the priests and Levites who kept nightly watch in the temple, to the assiduous in praising the Lord. It seems to consist of *two* parts: 1. An exhortation, probably from the high priest, to those priests and Levites who kept watch in the temple by night, to spend their time profitably, and duly celebrate the praises of God, ver. 1, 2. The *second* part, which is contained in the third verse, is the prayer of the priests and Levites for the *high priest,* who seems now to be going to his rest.

Verse 1. *Behold, bless ye the Lord*] I believe הנה *hinneh* should be taken here in the sense of *take heed!* Be upon your guard; you serve a jealous God; provoke him not.

Which by night stand] Who minister during the night.

Verse 2. *Lift up your hands* in *the sanctuary*] קדש *kodesh, "in* holiness:" or, as the SYRIAC, ܒܩܘܕܫܐ *lekoudishe, "to* holiness;" *in sancta,* VULGATE; and εις τα άγια, SEPTUAGINT; "in holy things;" or, as the ÆTHIOPIC, "in the house of the sanctuary." The expression seems very similar to that of St. Paul, 1 Tim. ii. 8: "Lifting up holy hands, without wrath and doubting."

Bless the Lord.] That is, speak good of his name: tell the wonders he has wrought, and show that his name is exalted.

Verse 3. *The Lord that made heaven and earth*] Who governs and possesses all things; and who can give you every spiritual and earthly blessing.

Bless thee out of Zion.] As if they had said, "We will attend to your orders; go in peace, and may God shower down his blessings upon you!" The blessing pronounced by the priests was the following: "The Lord bless thee and keep thee! The Lord make his face shine upon thee, and he gracious unto thee! The Lord lift up his countenance upon thee, and give thee peace!" Num. vi. 24-26.

ANALYSIS OF THE HUNDRED AND THIRTY-FOURTH PSALM

In this Psalm the prophet—

I. Exhorts the Levites and ministers of religion to attend the appointed hours of prayer.

II. Then the ministers bless the people.

1. 1. "Behold, bless ye the Lord."

2. Yet principally, "all ye servants of the Lord:" Choose out of the people to this service.

3. "Which by night stand in the house of the Lord," &c.: In the temple ye ought not to be sleepy, or forget your duty.

4. Therefore, "lift up your hands," &c., before the ark of the covenant which was the symbol of his presence.

5. "Bless the Lord," &c.

II. The other part of your office is to bless the people; let not that be forgotten, but say,—

1. "The Lord bless thee:" Let them know from whom the blessing comes.

2. "Out of Zion:" So long as they remain in the unity of the Church; there was none to be expected out of *Zion.*

3. "The Lord that made:" &c. He that hath power to bless hath given, and must give, his blessing to all creatures, without which they will not be blessed to thee; therefore, bless him.

PSALM CXXXV

An exhortation to praise God for his goodness and greatness, 1-5; for his wonders in nature, 6, 7; his wonders done in Egypt, 8, 9; in the wilderness, 10-12; for his goodness to his people, 13, 14. The vanity of idols, 15-18. Israel, with its priests and Levites, exhorted to praise the Lord, 19-21.

A. M. cir. 3489
B. C. cir. 515
Darii I.,
R. Persarum,
cir. annum
sextum

PRAISE ye the LORD. Praise ye the name of the LORD; [a]praise *him,* O ye servants of the LORD.

2 [b]Ye that stand in the house of the LORD, in [c]the courts of the house of our God,

3 Praise the LORD; for [d]the LORD *is* good: sing praises unto his name; [e]for *it is* pleasant.

4 For [f]the LORD hath chosen Jacob unto himself, *and* Israel for his peculiar treasure.

5 For I know that [g]the LORD *is* great, and *that* our LORD *is* above all gods.

6 [h]Whatsoever the LORD pleased, *that* did he in heaven, and in earth, in the seas, and all deep places.

7 [i]He causeth the vapours to ascend from the ends of the earth; [k]he maketh lightnings for the rain; he bringeth the wind out of his [l]treasuries.

8 [m]Who smote the first-born of Egypt, [n]both of man and beast.

A. M. cir. 3489
B. C. cir. 515
Darii I.,
R. Persarum,
cir. annum
sextum

9 [o]*Who* sent tokens and wonders into the midst of thee, O Egypt, [p]upon Pharaoh, and upon all his servants.

10 [q]Who smote great nations, and slew mighty kings;

11 Sihon king of the Amorites, and Og king of Bashan, and [r]all the kingdoms of Canaan:

12 [s]And gave their land *for* a heritage, a heritage unto Israel his people.

13 [t]Thy name, O LORD, *endureth* for ever; *and* thy memorial, O LORD, [u]throughout all generations.

14 [v]For the LORD will judge his people, and he will repent himself concerning his servants.

15 [w]The idols of the heathen *are* silver

---

[a]Psa. cxiii. 1; cxxxiv. 1——[b]Luke ii. 37——[c]Psa. xcii. 13; xcvi. 8; cxvi. 19——[d]Psa. cxix. 68——[e]Psa. cxlvii. 1 [f]Exod. xix. 5; Deut. vii. 6, 7; x. 15——[g]Psa. xcv. 3; xcvii. 9——[h]Psa. cxv. 3——[i]Jer. x. 13; li. 16——[k]Job xxviii. 25, 26; xxxviii. 24, &c.; Zech. x. 1——[l]Job xxxviii. 22——[m]Exod. xii. 12, 29; Psa. lxxviii. 51; cxxxvi. 10

[n]Heb. *from man unto beast*——[o]Exod. vii., viii., ix., x., xiv.——[p]Psa. cxxxvi. 15——[q]Num. xxi. 24, 25, 26, 34, 35; Psa. cxxxvi. 17, &c.——[r]Josh. xii. 7——[s]Psa. lxxviii. 55; cxxxvi. 21, 22——[t]Exod. iii. 15; Psa. cii. 12 [u]Heb. *to generation and generation*——[v]Deut. xxxii. 36 [w]Psa. cxv. 4, 5, 6, 7, 8

NOTES ON PSALM CXXXV

This Psalm is intimately connected with the preceding. It is an exhortation addressed to the *priests* and *Levites,* and to all *Israel,* to publish the praises of the Lord. The conclusion of this Psalm is nearly the same with Psalm cxv.; and what is said about *idols,* and the effects of the power of God, seems to be taken from it and the tenth chapter of Jeremiah; and from these and other circumstances it appears the Psalm was written *after the captivity;* and might, as *Calmet* conjectures, have been used at the dedication of the second temple.

Verse 1. *Praise ye the Lord*] This may be considered as the *title,* for it has none other.

Praise ye the name of the Lord] Perhaps the original הללו את שם יהוה *halelu eth shem Yehovah,* should be translated, *Praise ye the name Jehovah;* that is, Praise God in his infinite essence of being, holiness, goodness, and truth.

Verse 2. *Ye that stand*] Priests and Levites. For which he gives several reasons.

Verse 3. *The Lord is good*] Here is the *first* reason why we should be praised; and a *second* is subjoined:—

For it is *pleasant.*] It is becoming to acknowledge this infinite Being, and our dependence on him; and it is truly comfortable to an upright mind to be thus employed.

Verse 4. *For the Lord hath chosen Jacob*] This is a *third* reason. He has taken the Israelites for his peculiar people, סגלתו *segullatho,* his peculiar treasure; and now has brought them home to himself from their captivity and wanderings.

Verse 5. *The Lord is great*] Unlimited in his power: *another* reason.

Is above all gods.] Every class of *being,* whether idolized or not; because he is the Fountain of existence. This is a *fifth* reason.

Verse 6. *Whatsoever the Lord pleased*] All that he has done is *right,* and therefore it is *pleasing* in his sight. He is the author of all existence. Angels, men, spirits, the heavens, the earth, and all their contents, were made by him, and are under his control.

Verse 7. *He causeth the vapours to ascend*] Dr. Shaw thinks that the account here refers to the *autumnal* rains in the *east.* Of them he speaks as follows: "Seldom a night passes without much *lightning* in the north-west quarter, but not attended with *thunder;* and when this *lightning* appears in the west or south-west points, it is a sure sign of the approaching *rain,* which is often followed by *thunder.* A squall of wind and clouds of dust are the sure forerunners of the first rain." This account induces Mr. *Harmer* to believe that the word נשאים *nesiim,* should be translated *clouds,* not *vapours.* It shows that God—

Maketh lightnings for the rain] The squalls of wind bring on these *refreshing showers,* and are therefore *precious things* of the *treasuries of God;* and when he *thunders,* it is the *noise of waters in the heavens.* See Jer. x. 13, which contains almost the same words as those in this verse: "When he uttereth his voice, there is a multitude of waters in the heavens; and he causeth the vapours to ascend from the ends of the earth; he maketh lightnings with rain, and bringeth forth the wind out of his treasuries."

Verse 8. *Who smote the first-born of Egypt*] See the parallel passages.

Verse 14. *The Lord will judge his people*] He will do them justice against their enemies.

Verse 15. *The idols of the heathen*] This

A. M. cir. 3489
B. C. cir. 515
Darii I.,
R. Persarum,
cir. annum
sextum

and gold, the work of men's hands.

16 They have mouths, but they speak not; eyes have they, but they see not;

17 They have ears, but they hear not; neither is there *any* breath in their mouths.

18 They that make them are like unto them:

so is every one that trusteth in them.

A. M. cir. 3489
B. C. cir. 515
Darii I.,
R. Persarum,
cir. annum
sextum

19 ˣBless the LORD, O house of Israel: bless the LORD, O house of Aaron:

20 Bless the LORD, O house of Levi: ye that fear the LORD, bless the LORD.

21 Blessed be the LORD ʸout of Zion, which dwelleth at Jerusalem, ᶻPraise ye the LORD.

ˣPsa. cxv. 9, &c.——ʸPsa. cxxxiv. 3

ᶻJudg. v. 2; 1 Chron. xvi. 4; xxiii. 30; xxv. 3

---

verse and the following, to the end of the 18th, are almost word for word the same as verses 4-8 of Psalm cxv., where see the notes.

Verse 17. To this verse one of Kennicott's MSS. adds the 6th and 7th verses of Psalm cxv.

Verse 19. *Bless the Lord, O house, &c.*] See similar verses, Psa. cxv. 9-13, and the notes there.

Verse 21. *Blessed be the Lord out of Zion*] Who has once more restored our temple and city, and now condescends to *dwell* with us *in Jerusalem.*

ANALYSIS OF THE HUNDRED AND THIRTY-FIFTH PSALM

In this Psalm the prophet invites the servants of God, and especially his ministers, to praise God, ver. 1, 2, from arguments drawn,

I. From his goodness, particularly in choosing Israel, ver. 3, 4.

II. From the greatness and power showed in his works, ver. 5-8.

III. From his justice showed to the enemies of Israel, ver. 1-13.

IV. From his loving-kindness extended and promised still to his servants, ver. 13, 14.

V. Having derided the vanity of idols, ver. 15-19, he returns to his exhortation calling upon them to bless God, ver. 19-21.

I. He calls upon the ministers of religion especially to attend the recitation of Divine praises:—

1. "Praise ye the Lord," &c.

2. "Ye that stand."

And now, repeating his words again, he produces his reason of inducement:—

1. Because the Lord is worthy of praise: "For he is good," &c. Not comparatively, but absolutely good.

2. "Sing praises unto his name," &c. Because it is no painful duty, but pleasant.

3. Praise him for his love to Israel; for this you owe him gratitude: "For the Lord hath chosen Jacob," &c. 2. "And Israel for his peculiar treasure."

II. The next argument he uses is drawn from his greatness.

1. From his empire and universal dominion in heaven and earth: "Whatsoever the Lord pleased," &c. Nothing is impossible to him: but he does all from his free will, not from any necessity.

2. "He doth all things," &c. In all places; heaven, earth, seas, and hell.

And these last words the prophet amplifies,—

1. In the earth. Causing the vapours to

ascend from the ends of the earth, from all parts, which are endued with several qualities.

2. In the air. "He maketh lightning for rain."

3. In the water. "For he bringeth the winds out of his treasuries." Nothing is more obscure than the generation of the winds.

III. The fourth argument the prophet uses to persuade men to praise God, is from the vengeance he executes on the enemies of his people.

1. Upon the Egyptians. "Who smote the first-born of Egypt," &c.

2. "Who sent tokens and wonders," &c. "And he smote great nations," &c.

IV. To the commemoration of the justice God exercised upon their *enemies*, the prophet exhorts them to extol God.

1. "Thy name, O Lord," &c.

2. "And thy memorial," &c.

And the reason is drawn from his mercy.

1. "For the Lord will judge his people." Judge their cause, and deliver them.

2. "And he will repent himself," &c. If they repent, and turn to him.

The prophet, having proved that God is great in himself, now proves that he is above all gods, which are but vanity.

1. From their composition: "Silver and gold."

2. From their makers: "The work of men's hands."

3. From their impotency: "They have mouths," &c.

4. From the nature of their worshippers: "They that make them," &c.

Lastly, he invites all true worshippers of God to praise him, because they are lively images of the living God, from whom all their faculties have proceeded. To this he invites—

1. All *Israel:* "Bless the Lord, O house of Israel."

2. The priests: "Bless the Lord, O house of Aaron."

3. The Levites: "Bless the Lord, O house of Levi."

4. Lastly, all the laity: "Ye that fear the Lord bless the Lord."

To which he adds his own note, concluding—

1. "Blessed be the Lord out of Zion." Where he shows his presence by the ark.

2. "Which dwelleth at Jerusalem." Who, though in essence he is every where, yet more especially manifests his presence in his Church by his indwelling Spirit.

Therefore, let all the people bless the Lord for his great mercy: but let the citizens of *Zion* and *Jerusalem* never cease to praise him.

PSALM CXXXVI

An exhortation to give thanks to God for various mercies granted to all men, 1–9; particularly to the Israelites in Egypt, 10–12; at the Red Sea, 13–15; in the wilderness, 16–20; and in the promised land, 21, 22; for the redemption of the captives from Babylon, 23, 24; and for his providential mercies to all, 25, 26.

XXVIII. DAY. EVENING PRAYER

A. M. cir. 3489
B. C. cir. 515
Darii I.,
R. Persarum,
cir. annum
sextum

O ªGIVE thanks unto the Lord; for *he is* good: ᵇfor his mercy *endureth* for ever.

2 O give thanks unto ᶜthe God of gods: for his mercy *endureth* for ever.

3 O give thanks to the Lord of lords: for his mercy *endureth* for ever.

4 To him ᵈwho alone doeth great wonders: for his mercy *endureth* for ever.

5 ᵉTo him that by wisdom made the heavens: for his mercy *endureth* for ever.

6 ᶠTo him that stretched out the earth above the waters: for his mercy *endureth* for ever.

7 ᵍTo him that made great lights: for his mercy *endureth* for ever:

8 ʰThe sun ⁱto rule by day: for his mercy *endureth* for ever:

9 The moon and stars to rule by night: for his mercy *endureth* for ever.

A. M. cir. 3489
B. C. cir. 515
Darii I.,
R. Persarum,
cir. annum
sextum

10 ᵏTo him that smote Egypt in their first-born: for his mercy *endureth* for ever:

11 ˡAnd brought out Israel from among them: for his mercy *endureth* for ever:

12 ᵐWith a strong hand, and with a stretched-out arm: for his mercy *endureth* for ever.

13 ⁿTo him which divided the Red Sea into parts: for his mercy *endureth* for ever:

14 And made Israel to pass through the midst of it: for his mercy *endureth* for ever:

15 ᵒBut ᵖoverthrew Pharaoh and his host in the Red Sea: for his mercy *endureth* for ever.

ªPsa. cvi. 1; cvii. 1; cxviii. 1——ᵇ1 Chron. xvi. 34, 41; 2 Chron. xx. 21——ᶜDeut. x. 17——ᵈPsa. lxxii. 18 ᵉGen. i. 1; Prov. iii. 19; Jer. li. 15——ᶠGen. i. 9; Psa. xxiv. 2; Jer. x. 12——ᵍGen. i. 14——ʰGen. i. 16

ⁱHeb. *for the rulings by day*——ᵏExod. xii. 29; Psa. cxxxv. 8——ˡExod. xii. 51; xiii. 3, 17——ᵐExod. vi. 6 ⁿExod. xiv. 21, 22; Psa. lxxviii. 13——ᵒExod. xiv. 27; Psa. cxxxv. 9——ᵖHeb. *shaked off*

NOTES ON PSALM CXXXVI

This Psalm is little else than a repetition of the preceding, with the burden, כי לעולם חסדו *ki leolam chasdo,* "because his mercy endureth for ever," at the end of every verse. See below. It seems to have been a *responsive song:* the first part of the verse sung by the *Levites,* the burden by the *people.* It has no title in the Hebrew, nor in any of the Versions. It was doubtless written after the captivity. The *author* is unknown.

Verse 1. O give thanks unto the Lord: for he is good] This sentiment often occurs: the *goodness* of the Divine nature, both as a *ground* of *confidence* and of *thanksgiving.*

For his mercy endureth for ever] These words, which are the *burden* of every verse,

כי לעולם חסדו *ki leolam chasdo,* might be translated: "For his tender mercy is to the coming age:" meaning, probably, if the Psalm be *prophetic,* that peculiar display of his compassion, the redemption of the world by the Lord Jesus. These very words were prescribed by *David* as an acknowledgment, to be used continually in the Divine worship, see 1 Chron. xvi. 41: also by *Solomon,* 2 Chron. vii. 3. 6, and observed by *Jehoshaphat,* 2 Chron. xx. 21; all acknowledging that, however rich in mercy God was to them, the most extensive displays of his goodness were reserved for *the age to come;* see 1 Pet. i. 10-12: "Of which salvation the prophets have inquired, and searched diligently, who prophesied of the grace that should come unto you,—unto whom it was re-

vealed, that not unto themselves, but unto us, they did minister the things which are now reported unto you by them that preached the Gospel unto you by the power of the Holy Ghost sent down from heaven," &c.

Verse 2. The God of gods] לאדני האדנים *ladonai haadonim.* As *adonai* signifies *director,* &c., it may apply here, not to *idols,* for God is not their god; but to the priests and spiritual rulers; as *Lord* of *lords* may apply to *kings* and *magistrates,* &c. He is God and ruler over all the rulers of the earth, whether in things *sacred* or *civil.*

Verse 4. Who alone doeth great wonders] MIRACLES. No power but that which is *almighty* can work miracles, נפלאות *niphlaoth,* the inversion, or *suspension,* or *destruction* of the laws of nature.

Verse 5. By wisdom made the heavens] In the contrivance of the celestial bodies, in their relations, connexions, influences on each other, revolutions, &c., the wisdom of God particularly appears.

Verse 6. Stretched out the earth above the waters] Or, *upon the waters.* This seems to refer to a *central abyss of waters,* the existence of which has not been yet disproved.

Verse 7. Great lights] See the notes on the parallel passages in *Genesis,* &c.

Verse 10. Smote Egypt in their first-born] This was one of the heaviest of strokes: a great part of the rising generation was cut off; few but old persons and children left remaining.

Verse 13. Divided the Red Sea into parts] Some of the Jews have imagined that God made

A. M. cir. 3489
B. C. cir. 515
Darii I.,
R. Persarum,
cir. annum
sextum

16 qTo him which led his people through the wilderness: for his mercy *endureth* for ever.

17 rTo him which smote great kings: for his mercy *endureth* for ever:

18 sAnd slew famous kings: for his mercy *endureth* for ever:

19 tSihon, king of the Amorites: for his mercy *endureth* for ever:

20 uAnd Og the king of Bashan: for his mercy *endureth* for ever:

21 vAnd gave their land for a heritage:

for his mercy *endureth* for ever:

22 *Even* a heritage unto Israel his servant: for his mercy *endureth* for ever.

23 Who wremembered us in our low estate: for his mercy *endureth* for ever:

24 And hath redeemed us from our enemies: for his mercy *endureth* for ever.

25 xWho giveth food to all flesh: for his mercy *endureth* for ever.

26 O give thanks unto the God of heaven: for his mercy *endureth* for ever.

A. M. cir. 3489
B. C. cir. 515
Darii I.,
R. Persarum,
cir. annum
sextum

---

qExod. xiii. 18; xv. 22; Deut. viii. 15——rPsa. cxxxv. 10, 11——sDeut. xxix. 7——tNum. xxi. 21——uNum. xxi. 33

vJosh. xii. 1, &c.; Psa. cxxxv. 12——wGen. viii. 1; Deut. xxxii. 36; Psa. cxiii. 7——xPsa. civ. 27; cxlv. 15; cxlvii. 9

---

twelve paths through the Red Sea, that each tribe might have a distinct passage. Many of the *fathers* were of the same opinion; but is this very likely?

Verse 16. *Which led his people through the wilderness*] It was an astonishing miracle of God to support so many hundreds of thousands of people in a wilderness totally deprived of all necessaries for the life of man, and that for the space of *forty* years.

Verse 23. *Who remembered us in our low estate*] He has done much for our *forefathers;* and he has done much for us, in delivering us, when we had no helper, from our long captivity in Babylon.

Verse 25. *Giveth food to all flesh*] By whose *universal providence* every intellectual and animal being is supported and preserved. The appointing every *living thing* food, and that sort of food which is suited to its nature, (and the nature and habits of animals are endlessly diversified,) is an overwhelming proof of the wondrous providence, wisdom, and goodness of God.

The Vulgate, Arabic, and Anglo-Saxon, add a twenty-seventh verse, by repeating here ver. 3 very unnecessarily.

ANALYSIS OF THE HUNDRED AND THIRTY-SIXTH PSALM

This Psalm has the same argument with the preceding. It is divided into *three* parts:—

I. A general exhortation to praise God for his goodness and majesty, ver. 1, 2, 3.

II. A declaration of that goodness and majesty in their effects, ver. 4-10.

III. A conclusion fit for the exordium, ver. 26.

1. Of his creation, ver. 4-10.

2. Of his providence in preserving the Church, and punishing her enemies, ver. 10-25.

3. That his providence extends to all his creatures, ver. 25.

I. In the *three* first verses the prophet invites us to praise God for his mercy and goodness. And in these *three* verses expositors find the Trinity:—

1. *Jehovah.* God the Father, who is the Fountain of being.

2. *God the Son.* Who is God of gods, and over all.

3. *The Holy Ghost.* Who is Lord of lords.

The psalmist's reasons for calling upon us thus to praise him are, "for he is good: for his mercy endureth for ever."

The prophet now begins to praise God for his wonderful works, and which he alone was able to do.

1. "Who hath done wonderful things." Such as the work of creation.

2. "For his mercy endureth for ever." In sustaining and preserving all things.

"To him give thanks" for the wisdom manifested in the heavens; for, contemplate them as we may, they appear full of beauty, order, and splendour.

Praise him for the formation of the earth, as the mansion of man.

Give thanks "to him that stretched out," &c. Naturally this could not be, because the earth is heavier than water: but God hath made furrows for the waters to flow into, that man and beast might live on the earth.

"For his mercy endureth for ever." In this there was a threefold mercy:—

1. In reference to the *earth*. To make it something of nothing.

2. As respects the *water*. To prepare for it a settled place.

3. In regard to *man*. To whom he gave the earth uncovered from water, and yet plentifully supplied with rivers and fruits.

The third instance is the two great luminaries and the stars, in the three following verses. These do astonishingly adorn the heaven, and profit the earth. The sun and moon illuminate the earth, and comfort us. Perhaps the prophet instances these because they are alike blessings bestowed upon and shared by all the world.

II. From the wonderful works of the creation the prophet descends to those of his providence, in the preservation of the Church; and instances it in the redemption of his people *Israel* from the land of *Egypt*, &c., dwelling at large upon it, ver. 10-22.

In these verses the prophet records how God performed to *Israel* all the offices of a good Captain, Guide, Leader, and even Father; for he fed them with bread from heaven, gave them water out of the rock, caused that their clothes wore not out, cured their sick, defended them from their enemies, &c.

All this God did for them before they entered *Canaan.* And then the prophet reminds them how they rebelled against God, and he humbled them by bringing the *Philistines* and the *Babylonian* kings against them, who conquered and subjected them: but when they cried to him, he turned their captivity; for "he remembered us when we were in our low estate," &c.; "and hath redeemed us from our enemies," &c.

Lastly, that his goodness is not only extended over his people, but his *creatures;* to all *flesh,* which word signifies every thing that hath life.

III. He concludes as he began, "O give thanks unto the God of heaven," &c. The prophet calls him the *God of heaven,* because he alone made the heavens, and has his throne there, having the whole world under him; and by his wisdom and providence he preserves, moderates, and governs all things.

PSALM CXXXVII

The desolate and afflicted state of the captives in Babylon, 1, 2. *How they were insulted by their enemies,* 3, 4. *Their attachment to their country,* 5, 6. *Judgments denounced against their enemies,* 7–9.

B Y the rivers of Babylon, there we sat down, yea, we wept, when we remembered Zion.

2 We hanged our harps upon the willows in the midst thereof.

3 For there they that carried us away captive required of us [a]a song; and they that [b]wasted[c] us *required of us* mirth, *saying,* Sing us *one* of the songs of Zion.

4 How shall we sing the LORD's song in a [d]strange land?

5 If I forget thee, O Jerusalem, let my right hand forget *her cunning.*

6 If I do not remember thee, let my [e]tongue

---

[a]Heb. *the words of a song*——[b]Heb. *laid us on heaps*

[c]Psa. lxxix. 1——[d]Heb. *land of a stranger*——[e]Ezek. iii. 26

NOTES ON PSALM CXXXVII

The *Vulgate, Septuagint, Æthiopic,* and *Arabic,* say, ridiculously enough, a *Psalm of David for Jeremiah.* Anachronisms with those who wrote the *titles* to the Psalms were matters of no importance. *Jeremiah* never was at Babylon; and therefore could have no part in a Psalm that was sung on the banks of its rivers by the Israelitish captives. Neither the *Hebrew* nor *Chaldee* has any *title;* the *Syriac* attributes it to *David.* Some think it was sung when they returned from Babylon; others, while they were there. It is a matter of little importance. It was evidently composed *during* or at the *close* of the *captivity.*

Verse 1. *By the rivers of Babylon*] These might have been the *Tigris* and *Euphrates,* or their *branches,* or *streams* that flowed into them. In their captivity and dispersion, it was customary for the Jews to hold their religious meetings on the banks of rivers. Mention is made of this Acts xvi. 13, where we find the Jews of Philippi resorting to *a river side, where prayer was wont to be made.* And sometimes they built their synagogues here, when they were expelled from the cities.

Verse 2. *We hanged our harps upon the willows*] The עֲרָבִים *arabim* or *willows* were very plentiful in Babylon. The great quantity of them that were on the banks of the *Euphrates* caused Isaiah, chap. xv. 7, to call it *the brook* or *river of willows.* This is a most affecting picture. Perhaps resting themselves after toil, and wishing to spend their time religiously, they took their harps, and were about to sing one of the songs of Zion; but, reflecting on their own country, they became so filled with distress, that they unstrung their harps with one consent, and hung them on the willow bushes, and gave a general loose to their grief. Some of the Babylonians, who probably attended such meetings for the sake of the music, being present at the time here specified, desired them to *sing one of Zion's songs:* this is affectingly told.

Verse 3. *They that carried us away captive required of us a song*] This was as *unreasonable* as it was *insulting.* How could they who had reduced us to slavery, and dragged us in chains from our own beautiful land and privileges, expect us to sing a sacred ode to please them, who were enemies both to us and to our God? And how could those *who wasted us* expect *mirth* from people in captivity, deprived of all their possessions, and in the most abject state of poverty and oppression?

Verse 4. *How shall we sing the Lord's song*] איך נשיר *eich! nashir; O, we sing!* Who does not hear the *deep sigh* in the strongly guttural sound of the original איך *eich!* wrung, as it were, from the bottom of the heart? *Can* WE, in this state of *slavery,*—WE, *exiles,* from our *country,*—WE, *stripped* of all our *property,*—WE, reduced to *contempt* by our *strong enemy,*— WE, *deprived* of our *religious privileges,*—WE, *insulted* by our *oppressors,*—WE, in the land of *heathens,*—WE *sing,* or be *mirthful* in these *circumstances?* No: God does not expect it; man should not wish it; and it is base in our enemies to require it.

Verse 5. *If I forget thee, O Jerusalem*] Such conduct would be, in effect, a renunciation of our land; a tacit acknowledgment that we were reconciled to our bondage; a concession that we were pleased with our captivity, and could profane holy ordinances by using them as means of *sport* or *pastime* to the heathen. No: *Jerusalem!* we remember thee and thy Divine ordinances; and especially thy *King* and our

cleave to the roof of my mouth; if I prefer not Jerusalem above ᶠmy chief joy.

7 Remember, O LORD, ᵍthe children of Edom in the day of Jerusalem; who said, ʰRase *it,* rase *it, even* to the foundation thereof.

8 O daughter of Babylon, ˡwho art to be ᵏdestroyed; happy *shall he be,* ˡthatᵐ rewardeth thee as thou hast served us.

9 Happy *shall he be,* that taketh and ⁿdasheth thy little ones against ᵒthe stones.

ᶠHeb. *the head of my joy*——ᵍJer. xlix. 7, &c.; Lam. iv. 22; Ezek. xxv. 12; Obad. 10, &c.; 1 Esd. iv. 45 ʰHeb. *Make bare*——ⁱIsa. xiii. 1, 6, &c.; xlvii. 1; Jer. xxv. 12; l. 2

ᵏHebrew, *wasted*——ˡHebrew, *that recompenseth unto thee thy deed which thou didst to us*——ᵐJeremiah l. 15, 29; Rev. xviii. 6——ⁿIsaiah xiii. 16——ᵒHebrew, *the rock*

God, whose indignation we must bear, because we have sinned against him.

Let my right hand forget] Let me forget the use of my right hand. Let me forget that which is dearest and most profitable to me; and let me lose my skill in the management of my harp, if I ever prostitute it to please the ungodly multitude or the enemies of my Creator!

Verse 6. *Let my tongue cleave*] Let me lose my *voice,* and all its powers of *melody;* my *tongue,* and all its *faculty* of *speech;* my *ear,* and its *discernment* of *sounds;* if I do not prefer my *country,* my *people,* and the *ordinances of my God,* beyond all these, and whatever may constitute the *chiefest joy* I can possess in aught else beside. This is truly *patriotic,* truly noble and dignified. Such sentiments can only be found in the hearts and mouths of those slaves whom the grace of God has made *free.*

Verse 7. *Remember—the children of Edom*] It appears from Jer. xii. 6; xxv. 14; Lam. iv. 21, 22; Ezek. xxv. 12; Obad. 11-14; that the *Idumeans* joined the army of Nebuchadnezzar against their brethren the Jews; and that they were main instruments in rasing the walls of Jerusalem even to the ground.

Verse 8. *O daughter of Babylon, who art to be destroyed*] Or, *O thou daughter of Babylon the destroyer,* or, *who art to be ruined.* In being reduced under the empire of the Persians, Babylon was already greatly humbled and brought low from what it was in the days of Nebuchadnezzar; but it was afterwards so totally ruined that not a vestige of it remains. After its capture by Cyrus, A. M. 3468, it could never be considered a capital city; but it appeared to follow the fortunes of its various conquerors till it was, as a city, finally destroyed.

Rewardeth thee as thou hast served us.] This was Cyrus, who was chosen of God to do this work, and is therefore called *happy,* as being God's agent in its destruction. Greater desolations were afterwards brought upon it by *Darius Hystaspes,* who took this city after it had revolted, and slaughtered the inhabitants, men and women, in a barbarous manner. Herod. lib. iii.

Verse 9. *Happy—that taketh and dasheth thy little ones*] That is, So oppressive hast thou been to all under thy domination, as to become universally hated and detested; so that those who may have the last hand in thy destruction, and the total extermination of thy inhabitants, shall be reputed *happy*—shall be *celebrated* and *extolled* as those who have rid the world of a curse so grievous. These prophetic declarations contain no excitement to any person or persons to commit acts of cruelty and barbarity; but are simply *declarative* of what would take place in the order of the retributive providence and justice of God, and the general

opinion that should in consequence be expressed on the subject; therefore *praying for the destruction of our enemies* is totally out of the question. It should not be omitted that the Chaldee considers this Psalm a *dialogue,* which it thus divides:—The *three* first verses are supposed to have been spoken by the *psalmist, By the rivers,* &c. The Levites answer from the porch of the temple, in ver. 4, *How shall we sing,* &c. The voice of the *Holy Spirit* responds in ver. 5, 6, *If I forget thee,* &c. *Michael, the prince of Jerusalem,* answers in ver. 7, *Remember, O Lord,* &c. *Gabriel, the prince of Zion,* then addresses *the destroyer of the Babylonish nation,* in ver. 8, 9, *Happy shall be he that rewardeth thee,* &c. To slay all when a city was sacked, both male and female, old and young, was a common practice in ancient times. Homer describes this in words almost similar to those of the psalmist:—

Ὑίας τ' ολλυμενους, ἑλκυσθεισας τε θυγατρας,
Και θαλαμους κεραϊζομενους, και νηπια τεκνα
Βαλλομενα προτι γαιη εν αινῃ δηϊοτητι,
Ἑλκομενας τε νυους ολοῃς ὑπο χερσιν Αχαιων.

Il. lib. xxii., ver. 62.

My heroes slain, my bridal bed o'erturned;
My daughters ravished, and my city burned:
My bleeding infants dashed against the floor;
These I have yet to see; perhaps yet more.

POPE.

These excesses were common in all barbarous nations, and are only prophetically declared here. He shall be reputed *happy, prosperous,* and *highly commendable,* who shall destroy Babylon.

ANALYSIS OF THE HUNDRED AND THIRTY-SEVENTH PSALM

When this Psalm was composed, the *Jews* were in captivity in *Babylon,* far from their own country, the temple, and the public exercises of religion; and the scoff and scorn of their enemies; and they contrast what they were with what they are. This Psalm has *two* parts:—

I. The complaint of *Israel.* Because of the insults of the *Babylonians,* they deplore their sad condition, long for the temple, and their return to *Jerusalem,* ver. 1-7.

II. An imprecation or prayer for vengeance, on their persecutors, ver. 7-9.

I. Their complaint arises from their captivity, and it is aggravated.—

1. From the place, *Babylon:* "By the rivers of Babylon." A place far from their country; who were aliens from the covenant made by God with *Abraham,* scorners of their religion, had laid waste their city and forced them to base and servile labour.

2. From the continuance of their captivity

and misery: "There we sat down," &c. Took up the seats allotted to us, and that for *seventy* years.

3. From the effects it produced: "Yea, we wept," &c.

4. From the cause which drew these tears. The remembrance of what they had enjoyed, (now lost,) the services of religion: "We wept when we remembered Zion," &c.

5. From the intenseness of their grief, which was so great that they could not even tune their harps: "We hung our harps," &c.

That which increased their grief was the joy of their enemies manifested at it.

1. THERE, in a strange land, the place of our captivity.

2. "THEY that carried us away captive."

3. "They required of us a song." They required of us mirth, saying,

4. O thou *Jew* or captive, come now, "sing us one of the songs of Zion."

To this sarcasm the captive Jews return a double answer.

"How shall we sing the Lord's song in a strange land?" You are aliens, and this is a strange land; we cannot sing God's service there, which is destined to his honour, to you, or in this place without offending our God.

They reply by a protestation of their hope and constancy in religion, and accurse themselves if they do not continue in it.

1. "If I forget thee," &c. Forget the worship and feasts I kept there.

2. "If I do not remember thee," &c. If I do not prefer and make mention of Jerusalem, then "let my tongue cleave," &c. Let me no more have the use of that excellent organ of God's glory. It would be unworthy of my religion, and a dishonour to my God to sing the songs of Zion thus circumstanced, and to scoffers and aliens.

II. This seems to be the sense of the first part of the Psalm. The second part has reference to the imprecations poured out against *Edom* and *Babylon*, both persecutors of God's people. The Babylonians carried them away captive, and the *Edomites* persecuted their brethren with the sword, Amos i. 12.

1. Against Edom.

(1) "Remember, O Lord, the children of Edom," &c. How they carried themselves towards thy people on that day when thy anger smote against them, and the Babylonians carried us away.

(2) *Remember* how they added to our affliction, saying, "Rase it," &c.

2. Against *Babylon*. To her he turns his speech by an apostrophe; but at the same time foretells her ruin: "O daughter of Babylon," &c. Thou seemest to thyself to be most happy; but thy ruin approaches. Shortly after, the *Medes*, led by *Cyrus*, destroyed them.

(1) "Happy shall he be that rewardeth," &c. [See the notes.]

(2) "Happy shall he be that taketh and dasheth thy little ones," &c. [See the notes.]

PSALM CXXXVIII

The psalmist praises the Lord for his mercies to himself, 1–3. He foretells that the kings of the earth shall worship him, 4, 5. God's condescension to the humble, 6. The psalmist's confidence, 7, 8.

A Psalm of David

A. M. cir. 2956
B. C. cir. 1048
Davidis, Regis
Israelitarum,
cir. annum
decimum

I WILL praise thee with my whole heart: [a]before the gods will I sing praise unto thee.

2 [b]I will worship [c]toward thy holy temple, and praise thy name for thy loving-kindness and for thy truth: for thou hast [d]magnified thy word above all thy name.

A. M. cir. 2956
B. C. cir. 1048
Davidis, Regis
Israelitarum,
cir. annum
decimum

---

[a]Psa. cxix. 46——[b]Psa. xxviii. 2

[c]1 Kings viii. 29, 30; Psa. v. 7——[d]Isa. xlii. 21

NOTES ON PSALM CXXXVIII

The *Hebrew* and all the *Versions* attribute this Psalm to *David*, and it is supposed to have been made by him when, delivered from all his enemies, he was firmly seated on the throne of Israel. As the *Septuagint* and *Arabic* prefix also the names of *Haggai* and *Zechariah*, it is probable that it was used by the Jews as a *form of thanksgiving* for their deliverance from all their enemies, and their ultimate settlement in their own land, after Ahasuerus, supposed by Calmet to be *Darius Hystaspes*, had married *Esther*, before which time they were not peaceably *settled* in their own country.

Verse 1. *I will praise thee with my whole heart*] I have received the highest favours from thee, and my whole soul should acknowledge my obligation to thy mercy. The Versions and several MSS. add יהוה *Yehovah*, "I will praise thee, O LORD," &c.

Before the gods will I sing] נגד אלהים *neged Elohim*, "in the presence of Elohim;" most probably meaning before the ark, where were the sacred symbols of the Supreme Being. The *Chaldee* has, *before the judges*. The *Vulgate*, *before the angels*. So the *Septuagint*, *Æthiopic*, *Arabic*, and *Anglo-Saxon*. The *Syriac*, *Before kings will I sing unto thee*. This place has been alleged by the Roman Catholics as a proof that the holy angels, who are present in the assemblies of God's people, take their prayers and praises, and present them before God. There is nothing like this in the *text*; for supposing, which is not granted, that the word *elohim* here signifies *angels*, the praises are not *presented to them*, nor are *they requested to present them before God*; it is simply said, *Before elohim will I sing praise unto* THEE. Nor could there be need of any intermediate agents, when it was well known that God himself was present in the sanctuary,

A. M. cir. 2956
B. C. cir. 1048
Davidis, Regis
Israelitarum,
cir. annum
decimum

3 In the day when I cried thou answeredst me, *and* strengthenedst me *with* strength in my soul.

4 °All the kings of the earth shall praise thee, O LORD, when they hear the words of thy mouth.

5 Yea, they shall sing in the ways of the LORD: for great *is* the glory of the LORD.

6 ᶠThough the LORD *be* high, yet ᵍhath he respect unto the lowly: but the proud he knoweth afar off.

7 ʰThough I walk in the midst of trouble, thou wilt revive me: thou shalt stretch forth thine hand against the wrath of mine enemies, and thy right hand shall save me.

8 ⁱThe LORD will perfect *that which* concerneth me: thy mercy, O LORD, *endureth* for ever: ᵏforsake not the works of thine own hands.

A. M. cir. 2956
B. C. cir. 1048
Davidis, Regis
Israelitarum,
cir. annum
decimum

°Psalm cii. 15, 22——ᶠPsalm cxiii. 5, 6; Isa. lvii. 15
ᵍProv. iii. 34; James iv. 6; 1 Pet. v. 5

ʰPsa. xxiii. 3, 4——ⁱPsa. lvii. 2; Phil. i. 6——ᵏSee Job
x. 3, 8; xiv. 15

---

sitting between the cherubim. Therefore this opinion is wholly without support from this place.

Verse 2. *For thy loving-kindness*] Thy *tender mercy* shown to me; and for the fulfilment of thy *truth*—the promises thou hast made.

Thou hast magnified thy word above all thy name.] All the *Versions* read this sentence thus: "For thou hast magnified above all the name of thy holiness," or, "thy holy name." Thou hast proved that thou hast all *power* in heaven and in earth, and that thou art *true* in all thy words. And by giving the word of *prophecy*, and fulfilling those words, thou hast *magnified thy holy name above all things*—thou hast proved thyself to be *ineffably great*.

The original is the following: כי הגדלת על כל שמך אמרתך *ki higdalta al col shimcha, imrathecha*, which I think might be thus translated: "For thou hast magnified thy name and thy word over all," or, "on every occasion." *Kennicott* reads, "He preferred *faithfulness to his promise* to the attribute of his *power*." I believe my own translation to be nearest the truth. There may be some corruption in this clause.

Verse 3. *With strength in my soul.*] Thou hast endued my soul with many graces, blessings, and heavenly qualities.

Verse 4. *All the kings of the earth*] Of the land: all the neighbouring nations, seeing what is done for us, and looking in vain to find that any human agency was employed in the work, will immediately see that it was *thy hand;* and consequently, by *confessing* that it was *thou*, will give praise to thy name.

Verse 5. *They shall sing in the ways of the Lord*] They shall admire thy *conduct*, and the *wondrous workings* of thy providence; if they should not even unite with thy people.

Verse 6. *Though the Lord be high*] Infinitely *great* as God is, he regards even the lowest and most inconsiderable part of his creation; but the *humble* and *afflicted* man attracts his notice particularly.

But the proud he knoweth afar off.] He beholds them at a distance, and has them in utter derision.

Verse 7. *Though I walk in the midst of trouble*] I have had such experience of thy mercy, that let me fall into whatsoever trouble I may, yet I will trust in thee. Thou wilt *quicken* me, though I were *ready to die;* and thou wilt deliver me from the *wrath of my enemies.*

Verse 8. *The Lord will perfect*] Whatever is farther necessary to be done, he will do it.

Forsake not the works of thine own hands.] My body—my soul; thy work *begun in my soul;* thy work in *behalf of Israel;* thy work in the evangelization of the world; thy work in the salvation of mankind. Thou wilt not forsake these.

ANALYSIS OF THE HUNDRED AND THIRTY-EIGHTH PSALM

I. In the three first verses of this Psalm David promises a grateful heart, and to sing the praises of God, because he had heard his cries, and sent him comfort and deliverance.

II. In the three next he shows what future kings would do, when the works and truth of God should be made known to them.

III. In the two last verses he professes his confidence in God; shows what he hopes for from him; and, in assurance that God will perfect his works, prays him not to desert or forsake him.

I. The prophet shows his thankfulness, which he illustrates and amplifies.

1. "I will praise thee with my whole heart." Sincerely, cordially.

2. "Before the gods," &c. Publicly, before potentates, whether angels or kings.

3. "I will worship toward," &c. It is true God ruleth as King in his palace: there will I bow; it is the symbol of his presence.

4. "And praise thy name," &c. From a feeling sense of thy goodness. 1. "For thy loving-kindness," &c. In calling me to the kingdom from the sheepfold. 2. "And for thy truth." In performing thy promise. By which,

5. "Thou hast magnified," &c. This clause is differently read. "Thou hast magnified thy name in thy word; *by* performing thy word above all things." Or, "Thou hast magnified thy name and thy word above all things." See the notes.

6. "In the day when I cried," &c. Finite creatures as we are, we must sometimes faint in our temptations and afflictions, if not strengthened by God.

II. The prophet, having set down what God had in mercy done for him in calling him *from following the ewes*, &c., and *making him king*, and performing *his promises to him;* seeing all this, the prophet judges it impossible but that the neighbouring and future kings should acknowledge the miracle and praise God. This appears the literal sense: but it may have reference to the conversion of kings in future ages to the faith.

1. "All the kings of the earth," &c. Or the future kings of Israel.

2. "Yea, they shall sing in the ways," &c. His mercy, truth, clemency, &c.: "For great is the glory of the Lord." Righteous and glorious in all his works, of which this is one. "Though the Lord be high," &c. Of which David was an instance. "But the proud," &c., he removes far from him. Saul and others are examples of this.

III. Because *God who is high,* &c. And David, being conscious of his own humility of mind, confidently expects help from God.

1. "Though I walk," &c. Exposed on all sides to trouble.

2. "Thou wilt revive me." Preserve me safe and untouched.

3. "Thou shalt stretch forth thy hand," &c. Restrain the power of my enemies.

4. "And thy right hand," &c. Thy power; thy *Christ,* who, in Isa. liii. is called *the arm of the Lord.*

The last verse depends on the former. Because the prophet knew that many troubles and afflictions remained yet to be undergone; therefore he was confident that the same God would still deliver and make his work perfect.

1. "The Lord will perfect," &c. Not for my merits, but his mercy.

2. Of which he gives the reason: "Thy mercy, O Lord," &c. It does not exist only for a moment, but it is eternal.

3. And he concludes with a prayer for God to perfect his work: "Forsake not the work," &c. Thou who hast begun this work, increase and perfect it; because it is thy work alone, not mine. If we desire that God should perfect any work in us, we must be sure that it is his work, and look to him continually.

PSALM CXXXIX

A fine account of the omniscience of God, 1–6; of his omnipresence, 7–12; of his power and providence, 13–16. The excellence of his purposes, 17, 18. His opposition to the wicked, 19, 20; with whom the godly can have no fellowship, 21, 22.

XXIX. DAY. MORNING PRAYER

To the chief Musician, A Psalm of David

O LORD, [a]thou hast searched me, and known *me.*

2 [b]Thou knowest my downsitting and mine uprising, thou [c]understandest my thought afar off.

3 [d]Thou [e]compassest my path and my

---

[a]Psa. xvii. 3; Jer. xii. 3——[b]2 Kings xix. 27——[c]Matt. ix. 4; John ii. 24, 25——[d]Job xxxi. 4——[e]Or, *winnowest*

NOTES ON PSALM CXXXIX

The *title* of this Psalm in the *Hebrew* is, *To the chief Musician,* or, *To the Conqueror, A Psalm of David.* The *Versions* in general follow the Hebrew. And yet, notwithstanding these testimonies, there appears internal evidence that the Psalm was not written by *David,* but *during* or *after the time of the captivity,* as there are several *Chaldaisms* in it. See verses 2, 3, 7, 9, 19, 20, collated with Dan. ii. 29, 30; iv. 16; vii. 28; some of these shall be noticed in their proper places.

As to the *author,* he is unknown; for it does not appear to have been the work of *David.* The composition is worthy of him, but the language appears to be *lower* than his time.

Concerning the *occasion,* there are many conjectures which I need not repeat, because I believe them unfounded. It is most probable that it was written on *no particular occasion,* but is a moral lesson on the wisdom, presence, providence, and justice of God, without any reference to any circumstance in the *life of David,* or in the *history of the Jews.*

The Psalm is very sublime; the sentiments are grand, the style in general highly elevated, and the images various and impressive. The first part especially, that contains so fine a description of the wisdom and knowledge of God, is inimitable.

Bishop *Horsley's* account of this Psalm is as follows:—

"In the first twelve verses of this Psalm the author celebrates God's perfect knowledge of man's thoughts and actions; and the reason of this wonderful knowledge, *viz.,* that God is the Maker of man. Hence the psalmist proceeds, in the four following verses, 13, 14, 15, 16, to magnify God as ordaining and superintending the formation of his body in the womb. In the 17th and 18th he acknowledges God's providential care of him in every moment of his life; and in the remainder of the Psalm implores God's aid against impious and cruel enemies, professing his own attachment to God's service, that is, to the true religion, and appealing to the Searcher of hearts himself for the truth of his professions.

The composition, for the purity and justness of *religious sentiment,* and for the force and beauty of the images, is certainly in the very first and best style. And yet the frequent *Chaldaisms* of the diction argue *no very high antiquity.*

Verse 1. *O Lord, thou hast searched me*] חקרתני *chakartani;* thou hast *investigated* me; *thou hast thoroughly acquainted thyself* with my whole soul and conduct.

Verse 2. *My downsitting and mine uprising*] Even these inconsiderable and casual things are under thy continual notice. I cannot so much as *take a seat,* or *leave it,* without being marked by thee.

Thou understandest my thought] לרעי *lerei,* "my cogitation." This word is *Chaldee,* see Dan. ii. 29, 30.

Afar off.] While the figment is forming that shall produce them.

Verse 3. *Thou compassest my path*] זרית

lying down, and art acquainted *with* all my ways.

4 For *there is* not a word in my tongue, *but,* lo, O LORD, ᶠthou knowest it altogether.

5 Thou hast beset me behind and before, and laid thine hand upon me.

6 ᵍ*Such* knowledge *is* too wonderful for me; it is high, I cannot *attain* unto it.

7 ʰWhither shall I go from thy Spirit? or whither shall I flee from thy presence?

8 ⁱIf I ascend up into heaven, thou *art* there: ᵏif I make my bed in hell, behold thou *art there.*

9 *If* I take the wings of the morning, *and* dwell in the uttermost parts of the sea;

10 Even there shall thy hand lead me, and thy right hand shall hold me.

11 If I say, Surely the darkness shall cover me; even the night shall be light about me.

12 Yea, ˡthe darkness ᵐhideth not from thee; but the night shineth as the day: ⁿthe darkness and the light *are* both alike *to thee.*

13 For thou hast possessed my reins: thou hast covered me in my mother's womb.

14 I will praise thee; for I am fearfully *and*

ᶠHeb. iv. 13——ᵍJob xlii. 3; Psa. xl. 5; cxxxi. 1 ʰJer. xxiii. 24; Jonah i. 3——ⁱAmos ix. 2, 3, 4——ᵏJob xxvi. 6; Prov. xv. 11

ˡJob xxvi. 6; xxxiv. 22; Dan. ii. 22; Heb. iv. 13 ᵐHeb. *darkeneth not*——ⁿHebrew, *as is the darkness so is the light*

---

zeritha thou dost winnow, ventilate, or *sift* my path; and my lying down, רבעי *ribi*, my *lair,* my *bed.*

And art acquainted] *Thou treasurest up.* This is the import of סכן *sachan.* Thou hast the *whole number* of my ways, and the steps I took in them.

Verse 4. There is *not a word in my tongue*] Although (כי *ki*) *there be not a word in my tongue, behold, O Jehovah, thou knowest the whole of it,* that is, thou knowest all my *words before* they are *uttered,* as thou knowest all my *thoughts* while as yet they are *unformed.*

Verse 5. *Thou hast beset me behind and before*] אחור וקדם צרתני *achor vekodam tsartani,* "The hereafter and the past, thou hast formed me." I think Bishop Horsley's emendation here is just, uniting the two verses together. "Behold thou, O Jehovah, knowest the whole, the hereafter and the past. Thou hast formed me, and laid thy hand upon me."

Verse 6. Such *knowledge* is *too wonderful*] I think, with *Kennicott,* that פלאיה דעת *pelaiah daath* should be read פלאי הדעת *peli haddaath,* "THIS knowledge," ממני *mimmenni,* "is beyond or above me." This change is made by taking the ה *he* from the end of פלאיה *pelaiah,* which is really *no word,* and joining it with דעת *daath;* which, by giving it an *article,* makes it demonstrative, הדעת *haddaath,* "THIS knowledge." *This kind of knowledge,* God's knowledge, that takes in all things, and their reasons, essences, tendencies, and issues, is far beyond me.

Verse 7. *Whither shall I go from thy Spirit?*] Surely רוח *ruach* in this sense must be taken *personally,* it certainly cannot mean either *breath* or *wind;* to render it so would make the passage ridiculous.

From thy presence?] מפניך *mippaneycha,* "from thy faces." Why do we meet with this word so frequently in the *plural* number, when applied to God? And why have we his *Spirit,* and his *appearances* or *faces, both* here? A *Trinitarian* would at once say, "The plurality of persons in the Godhead is intended;" and who can *prove* that he is mistaken?

Verse 8. *If I ascend*] Thou art in *heaven,* in thy glory; in *hell,* in thy vindictive justice; and in all *parts of earth, water, space, place,* or *vacuity,* by thy *omnipresence.* Wherever I am,

there art thou; and where I cannot be, thou art there. Thou fillest the heavens and the earth.

Verse 11. *Surely the darkness shall cover me*] Should I suppose that this would serve to screen me, immediately this *darkness* is turned into *light.*

Verse 12. *Yea, the darkness hideth not from thee*] Darkness and light, ignorance and knowledge, are things that stand in relation to us; God sees equally in *darkness* as in *light;* and *knows* as perfectly, however man is enveloped in *ignorance,* as if all were *intellectual brightness.* What is to us *hidden* by *darkness,* or *unknown* through *ignorance,* is perfectly *seen* and *known* by God; because he is all sight, all hearing, all feeling, all soul, all spirit—*all* in ALL, and infinite in himself. He lends to every thing; receives nothing from any thing. Though his *essence* be *unimpartible,* yet his *influence* is *diffusible* through time and through eternity. Thus God makes himself known, seen, heard, felt; yet, in the infinity of his essence, neither angel, nor spirit, nor man can see him; nor can any creature comprehend him, or form any idea of the *mode* of his existence. And yet vain man would be wise, and ascertain his foreknowledge, eternal purposes, infinite decrees, with all operations of infinite love and infinite hatred, and their *objects specifically* and *nominally,* from all eternity, as if himself had possessed a being and powers co-extensive with the Deity! O ye wise fools! Jehovah, the fountain of eternal perfection and love, is as unlike your *creeds,* as he is unlike *yourselves,* forgers of doctrines to prove that ιthe source of infinite benevolence is a *streamlet of capricious love* to thousands, while he is an overflowing, eternal, and irresistible *tide* of *hatred* to millions of millions both of angels and men! The antiproof of such doctrines is this: he bears with such blasphemies, and does not consume their abettors. "But nobody holds these doctrines." Then I have written against *nobody;* and have only to add the prayer, May no such doctrines ever disgrace the page of history; or farther dishonour, as they have done, the annals of the Church!

Verse 13. *Thou hast possessed my reins*] As the Hebrews believed that the reins were the first part of the human fetus that is formed, it may here mean, thou hast laid the foundation of my being.

Verse 14. *I am fearfully* and *wonderfully*

wonderfully made; marvellous *are* thy works; and *that* my soul knoweth °right well.

15 ᵖMyᵠ substance was not hid from thee, when I was made in secret, *and* curiously wrought in the lowest parts of the earth.

16 Thine eyes did see my substance, yet being unperfect; and in thy book ʳall *my members* were written, ˢ*which* in continuance were fashioned, when *as yet there was* none of them.

17 ᵗHow precious also are thy thoughts unto me, O God! how great is the sum of them.

18 *If* I should count them, they are more in number than the sand: when I awake, I am still with thee.

°Heb. *greatly*——ᵖJob x. 8, 9; Eccles. xi. 5——ᵠOr, *strength* or *body*

ʳHeb. *all of them*——ˢOr, what *days they should be fashioned*——ᵗPsa. xl. 5

made] The texture of the human body is the most complicated and curious that can be conceived. It is, indeed, *wonderfully made;* and it is withal so exquisitely *nice* and *delicate*, that the slightest accident may impair or destroy in a moment some of those parts essentially necessary to the continuance of life; therefore, we are *fearfully made.* And God has done so to show us our *frailty*, that we should walk with *death*, keeping *life* in view; and feel the necessity of *depending* on the all-wise and continual superintending care and providence of God.

Verse 15. *My substance was not hid from thee*] עצמי *atsmi*, my *bones* or *skeleton*.

Curiously wrought] רקמתי *rukkamti*, embroidered, *made of needle-work.* These two words, says Bishop Horsley, describe the two principal parts of which the human body is composed; the *bony skeleton*, the *foundation* of the whole; and the *external covering* of muscular flesh, tendons, veins, arteries, nerves, and skin; a curious *web of fibres.* On this passage Bishop *Lowth* has some excellent observations: "In that most perfect hymn, where the immensity of the omnipresent Deity, and the admirable wisdom of the Divine Artificer in framing the human body, are celebrated, the poet uses a remarkable metaphor, drawn from the nicest tapestry work:—

> When I was formed in secret;
> When I was wrought, as with a needle, in the lowest parts of the earth.

"He who remarks this, (but the man who consults *Versions* only will hardly remark it,) and at the same time reflects upon the wonderful composition of the human body, the various implication of veins, arteries, fibres, membranes, and the 'inexplicable texture' of the whole frame; will immediately understand the beauty and elegance of this most apt translation. But he will not attain the whole force and dignity, unless he also considers that the most artful embroidery with the needle was dedicated by the Hebrews to the *service of the sanctuary;* and that the proper and singular use of their work was, by the immediate prescript of the Divine law, applied in a certain part of the *high priest's dress*, and in the *curtains* of the *tabernacle*, Exod. xxviii. 39; xxvi. 36; xxvii. 16; and compare Ezek. xvi. 10; xiii. 18. So that the psalmist may well be supposed to have compared the wisdom of the Divine Artificer particularly with that specimen of human art, whose dignity was through religion the highest, and whose elegance (Exod. xxxv. 30-35) was so exquisite, that the sacred writer seems to attribute it to a Divine inspiration."

In the lowest parts of the earth.] The womb of the mother, thus expressed by way of delicacy.

Verse 16. *Thine eyes did see my substance*] גלמי *golmi*, my *embryo state*—my yet indistinct mass, when all was *wrapped up* together, before it was gradually unfolded into the lineaments of man. "Some think," says Dr. Dodd, "that the allusion to *embroidery* is still carried on. As the embroiderer has still his work, pattern, or *carton*, before him, to which he always recurs; so, by a method as exact, were all my members *in continuance fashioned*, i. e., from the rude embryo or mass they daily received some degree of figuration; as from the rude skeins of variously coloured silk or worsted, under the artificer's hands, there at length arises an unexpected beauty, and an accurate harmony of colours and proportions."

And in thy book all my members *were written*] "All those members lay open before God's eyes; they were discerned by him as clearly as if the *plan* of them had been *drawn in a book*, even to the least figuration of the body of the child in the womb."

Verse 17. *How precious also are thy thoughts*] רעיך *reeycha*, thy *cogitations;* a *Chaldaism*, as before.

How great is the sum of them!] מה עצמו ראשיהם *mah atsemu rasheyhem; How strongly rational are the heads or principal subjects of them!* But the word may apply to the *bones*, עצמות *atsamoth*, the structure and uses of which are most curious and important.

Verse 18. If *I should count them*] I should be glad to enumerate so many interesting particulars: but they are beyond calculation.

When I awake] Thou art my Governor and Protector night and day.

I am still with thee.] All my steps in life are ordered by thee: I cannot go out of thy presence; I am ever under the influence of thy Spirit.

The subject, from the 14th verse to the 16th inclusive, might have been much more particularly illustrated, but we are taught, by the peculiar delicacy of expression in the Sacred Writings, to avoid, as in this case, the entering too minutely into *anatomical details.* I would, however, make an additional observation on the subject in the 15th and 16th verses. I have already remarked the elegant allusion to *embroidery*, in the word רקמתי *rukkamti*, in the astonishing texture of the human body; all of which is said to be done *in secret*, בסתר *bassether*, in the *secret place*, viz., *the womb of the mother*, which, in the conclusion of the verse, is by a delicate choice of expression termed *the lower parts of the earth.*

19 Surely thou wilt [u]slay the wicked, O God: [v]depart from me, therefore, ye bloody men.

20 For they [w]speak against thee wickedly, *and* thine enemies take *thy name* in vain.

21 [x]Do not I hate them, O LORD, that hate thee? and am not I grieved with those that rise up against thee?

22 I hate them with perfect hatred: I count them mine enemies.

23 [y]Search me, O God, and know my heart: try me, and know my thoughts:

24 And see if *there be any* [z]wicked way in me, and [a]lead me in the way everlasting.

---

[u]Isa. xi. 4——[v]Psa. cxix. 115——[w]Jude 15——[x]2 Chron. xix. 2; Psa. cxix. 151

[y]Job xxxi. 6; Psa. xxvi. 2——[z]Heb. *way of pain* or *grief* [a]Psa. v. 8; cxliii. 10

The *embryo* state, נלם *golem*, has a more forcible meaning than our word *substance* amounts to. נלם *galam* signifies *to roll* or *wrap up together;* and expresses the state of the fetus before the constituent members were developed. The best system of modern philosophy allows that *in semine masculino* all the members of the future animal are contained; and that these become slowly developed or *unfolded*, in the case of *fowls*, by *incubation;* and in the case of the more perfect *animals*, by gestation in the maternal matrix. It is no wonder that, in considering these, the psalmist should cry out, *How precious, how extraordinary, are thy thoughts! how great is the sum*—heads or outlines, *of them!* The *particulars* are, indeed, beyond comprehension; even the *heads*—the *general* contents, of thy works; while I endeavour to form any tolerable notion of them, *prevail over me*—they confound my *understanding*, and are vastly too multitudinous for my *comprehension.*

Verse 19. *Surely thou wilt slay the wicked*] The remaining part of this Psalm has no visible connexion with the preceding. I rather think it a *fragment*, or a part of some other Psalm.

Ye bloody men.] אנשי דמים *anshey damim, men of blood*, men *guilty of death.*

Verse 20. *Thine enemies take* thy name *in vain.*] Bishop *Horsley* translates the whole verse thus:—

"They have deserted me who are disobedient to thee;
"They who are sworn to a rash purpose—thy refractory adversaries."

The *original* is obscure: but I cannot see these things in it. Some translate the Hebrew thus: "Those who oppose thee iniquitously seize unjustly upon thy cities;" and so almost all the *Versions.* The words, thus translated, may apply to *Sanballat, Tobiah,* and the other enemies of the returned Jews, who endeavoured to drive them from the land, that they might possess the cities of Judea.

Verse 21. *Do not I hate them*] I hold their conduct in abomination.

Verse 22. *With perfect hatred*] Their *conduct*, their *motives*, their *opposition* to *thee*, their *perfidy* and *idolatrous purposes*, I perfectly abhor. With them I have neither part, interest, nor affection.

Verse 23. *Search me, O God*] Investigate my conduct, *examine* my *heart*, put me to *the test*, and *examine* my *thoughts.*

Verse 24. *If there be any wicked way*] דרך עצב *derech otseb: a way of idolatry*, or of *error.* Any thing false in *religious principle;* any thing contrary to *piety* to thyself, and love and benevolence to man. And he needed to offer

such prayer as this, while filled with indignation against the *ways* of the *workers of iniquities;* for he who hates, *utterly hates*, the practices of any man, is not far from hating the *man himself.* It is very difficult

"To hate the sin with all the heart,
And yet the sinner love."

Lead me in the way everlasting.] בדרך עולם *bederech olam, in the old way*—the way in which our *fathers* walked, who worshipped thee, the infinitely pure Spirit, in *spirit* and in *truth.* Lead me, guide me, as thou didst them. We have ארח עולם *orach olam*, the *old path*, Job xxii. 15. "The two words דרך *derech* and ארח *orach*, differ," says Bishop *Horsley*, "in their figurative senses: *derech* is the *right way*, in which a man *ought* to go; *orach* is the way, *right* or *wrong*, in which a man *actually goes by habit.*" The way that is right in a man's own eyes is seldom the way to God.

ANALYSIS OF THE HUNDRED AND THIRTY-NINTH PSALM

David, having had aspersions laid upon him, calls upon God in this Psalm to witness his innocency. Now, that this his appeal be not thought unreasonable, he presents God in his two especial attributes, omniscience and omnipresence; then he shows he loved goodness, and hated wickedness.

This Psalm is divided into four parts:—

I. A description of God's omniscience, ver. 1-7.

II. A description of his omnipresence, ver. 7-18.

III. David's hatred to evil and evil men, ver. 19-23.

IV. A protestation of his own innocency, which he offers to the trial of God, ver. 23, 24.

I. He begins with God's omniscience: "O Lord, thou hast searched me," &c. Examined me with scrutiny.

He searches and knows our actions.

1. "Thou knowest," &c. When and for what reasons I ever act.

2. "Thou understandest my thoughts," &c. Thou knowest my counsels and thoughts.

3. "Thou compassest my path," &c. The end I aim at.

4. "There is not a word," &c. Every word and thought thou knowest.

And for this he gives this reason: God is our Maker: "Thou hast beset me," &c. These *two* arguments prove that God knows all things.

1. God knows all the past and future: "Beset behind and before."

2. He governs man: "Thou God madest man,"

&c. The prophet concludes this Divine attribute, omniscience, with an acclamation: "Such knowledge," &c. It is beyond my reach and capacity.

II. From God's omnipresence the prophet argues that man cannot hide any thing from God, for he is every where present.

1. "Where shall I go," &c. That I may be hid from thy knowledge.

2. "Or whither shall I flee," &c. From thy face and eye.

There is no place that is not before thee.

1. "If I ascend up to heaven," &c.

2. "If I make my bed in hell," &c.

3. "If I take the wings of the morning," &c.

And among many instances that might be brought forward to prove God's omniscience and omnipresence, we may simply instance the formation of a child in the womb.

1. "Thou hast possessed my reins," &c. Thou hast undertaken wholly to frame, and cherish me when formed.

2. "Thou hast covered me," &c. Clothed me with flesh, skin, bones, &c.

Then the prophet breaks out in admiration of God's works.

1. "I will praise thee," &c.

2. "I am fearfully," &c. His works are enough to strike all men with reverential fear.

3. "Marvellous are thy works."

Then he proceeds with the formation of the infant embryo.

1. "My substance," &c. My strength, my essence. "Is not hid," &c.

2. "When I was made in secret," &c. In the secret cell of my mother's womb.

3. "And curiously wrought," &c. The word in the Hebrew signifies to interweave coloured threads. Man is a curious piece, and the variety of his faculties shows him such. [See the notes.]

4. "In the lowest parts of the earth," &c. In the womb, where it is as secret if God wrought it in *the lowest part of the earth.*

5. "Thine eyes did see my substance," &c. When in embryo, and without any distinct parts.

6. "And in thy book," &c. The idea of them was with thee, as the picture in the eye of the painter.

7. Which *in continuance,* &c.

The prophet closes this part with an exclamation.

1. "How precious also are thy thoughts," &c. In this and other respects.

2. "O how great is the sum of them." They are infinite.

3. And for this cause: "When I awake," &c., thy wisdom and providence are ever before my mind, and my admiration is full of them.

The prophet, having ended his discourse on the omniscience and omnipresence of God, justifies himself at God's tribunal.

1. "Surely thou wilt slay the wicked," &c. I dare not then associate with them.

2. "Depart, therefore, from me," &c. Keep at a distance.

3. "For they speak against thee wickedly," &c. Blaspheme my God.

So far from giving them the right hand of fellowship, he asks,—

1. "Do not I hate them, O Lord," &c. I hate them as sinners, but feel for and pity them as men.

2. Then he returns this answer to himself, "Yea, I hate them," &c. I count them my enemies, for they are thine.

IV. Lastly, it would appear that his heart was sincere and pure, or he would not abide such a trial.

1. "Search me, O God:" In the beginning of the Psalm he showed what God did; now he entreats him to do it.

2. "Try me," &c. Examine my heart and my ways.

3. "And see if there be any wicked way," &c. Presumptuous sins.

4. "And lead me in the way everlasting." This was the end proposed by his trial; that, if God saw any wickedness in him that might seduce him, he would withdraw him from it; and lead him to think, and devise, and do those things which would bring him to life eternal.

PSALM CXL

The psalmist prays against his enemies, 1-6; returns thanks for help, 7; describes his enemies, and prays farther against them, 8-11. His confidence in God, 12, 13.

To the chief Musician, A Psalm of David

A. M. cir. 2943
B. C. cir. 1061
Sauli, Regis
Israelitarum,
cir. annum
35

DELIVER me, O LORD, from the evil man: [a]preserve me from the [b]violent man;

2 Which imagine mischiefs in *their* heart; [c]continually are they gathered together *for* war.

3 They have sharpened their tongues like a serpent; [d]adders' poison *is* under their lips. Selah.

A. M. cir. 2943
B. C. cir. 1061
Sauli, Regis
Israelitarum,
cir. annum
35

---

[a]Ver. 4——[b]Heb. *man of violence*

[c]Psa. lvi. 6——[d]Psa. lviii. 4; Rom. iii. 13

NOTES ON PSALM CXL

The *Hebrew,* and all the *Versions,* attribute this Psalm to *David;* and it is supposed to contain his complaint when persecuted by Saul. The *Syriac* determines it to the time when Saul endeavoured to transfix David with his spear.

Verse 1. *From the evil man*] Saul, who was full of envy, jealousy, and cruelty against David, to whom both himself and his kingdom were under the highest obligations, endeavoured by every means to destroy him.

Verse 2. *They gathered together*] He and his courtiers form plots and cabals against my life.

Verse 3. *They have sharpened their tongues*] They employ their time in forging lies and

A. M. cir. 2943
B. C. cir. 1061
Sauli, Regis
Israelitarum,
cir. annum
35

4 ^eKeep me, O Lord, from the hands of the wicked; ^fpreserve me from the violent man; who have purposed to overthrow my goings.

5 ^gThe proud have hid a snare for me, and cords; they have spread a net by the wayside; they have set gins for me. Selah.

6 I said unto the Lord, Thou *art* my God: hear the voice of my supplication, O Lord.

7 O God the Lord, the strength of my salvation, thou hast covered my head in the day of battle.

8 Grant not, O Lord, the desires of the wicked: further not his wicked device; ^h*lest*ⁱ they exalt themselves. Selah.

9 *As for* the head of those that compass me about, ^klet the mischief of their own lips cover them.

A. M. cir. 2943
B. C. cir. 1061
Sauli, Regis
Israelitarum,
cir. annum
35

10 ^lLet burning coals fall upon them; let them be cast into the fire; into deep pits, that they rise not up again.

11 Let not ^man ⁿevil speaker be established in the earth: evil shall hunt the violent man to overthrow *him*.

12 I know that the Lord will ^omaintain the cause of the afflicted, *and* the right of the poor.

13 Surely the righteous shall give thanks unto thy name; the ^pupright shall dwell in thy presence.

---

^ePsa. lxxi. 4——^fVer. 1——^gPsa. xxxv. 7; lvii. 6; cxix. 110; cxli. 9; Jer. xviii. 22——^hOr, *let them not be exalted*——ⁱDeut. xxxii. 27——^kPsa. vii. 16; xciv. 23; Prov. xii. 13; xviii. 7——^lPsa. xi. 6

^mHeb. *a man of tongue*——ⁿOr, *an evil speaker, a wicked man of violence, be established in the earth; let him be hunted to* his *overthrow*——^o1 Kings viii. 45; Psa. ix. 4 ^pJob i. 1; Psa. lxviii. 10; Prov. ii. 21; xi. 20; xiv. 11

---

calumnies against me; and those of the most virulent nature.

Verse 4. *Preserve me from the violent man*] Saul again; who was as headstrong and violent in all his measures, as he was cruel, and inflexibly bent on the destruction of David.

Verse 5. *Have hid a snare for me*] They hunted David as they would a dangerous wild beast: one while striving to *pierce* him with the spear; another to *entangle* him in their snares, so as to take and sacrifice him before the people, on pretence of his being an *enemy to the state.*

Selah] This is the truth.

Verse 7. *Thou hast covered my head*] Not only when I fought with the proud blaspheming Philistine; but in the various attempts made against my life by my sworn enemies.

Verse 8. *Further not his wicked device*] He knew his enemies still desired his death, and were plotting to accomplish it; and here he prays that God may disappoint and confound them. The *Chaldee* understands this of *Doeg.*

Verse 10. *Let burning coals*] The *Chaldee* considers this as spoken against *Ahithophel,* who was head of a conspiracy against David; and translates this verse thus: "Let coals from heaven fall upon them, precipitate them into the fire of hell, and into miry pits, from which they shall not have a resurrection to eternal life." This is a proof that the Jews did believe in a resurrection of the body, and an eternal life for that body, in the case of the righteous.

Verse 11. *Let not an evil speaker be established*] אִישׁ לָשׁוֹן *ish lashon,* "a man of tongue." There is much force in the rendering of this clause in the *Chaldee* גְּבַר דְּמִשְׁתָּעִי לִישָׁן תְּלִיתִי *gebar demishtai lishan telithai,* "The man of detraction, or *inflammation,* with the *three-forked tongue.*" He whose tongue is *set on fire from hell;* the tale-bearer, slanderer, and dealer in scandal: *with the three-forked tongue;* wounding *three* at once: his *neighbour* whom he slanders; the *person* who receives the slander;

and *himself* who deals in it. What a just description of a character which God, angels, and good men must detest! Let not such a one be established in the land; let him be unmasked; let no person trust him; and let all join together to hoot him out of society. "He shall be hunted by the angel of death, and thrust into hell."—CHALDEE.

Verse 12. *The cause of the afflicted*] Every person who is *persecuted* for righteousness' sake has God for his *peculiar help* and *refuge;* and the *persecutor* has the same God for his *especial enemy.*

Verse 13. *The righteous shall give thanks*] For thou wilt support and deliver him.

The upright shall dwell in thy presence.] Shall be admitted to the most intimate intercourse with God.

The *persecuted* have ever been dear to God Almighty; and the *martyrs* were, in an especial manner, his delight; and in proportion as he loved *those,* so must he hate and detest *these.*

ANALYSIS OF THE HUNDRED AND FORTIETH PSALM

David, being persecuted by Saul, *Doeg,* and the men of *Ziph,* prays to God against their evil tongues. But the fathers apply it more largely to the Church, in its persecution by wicked men and devils.

The Psalm is divided into *four* parts:—

I. A petition to be delivered from his enemies, whom he describes, ver. 1-6.

II. A protestation of his confidence in God, ver. 6, 7.

III. A prayer against them, ver. 8-11.

IV. A manifestation of his hope, that God will maintain his just cause, ver. 12, 13.

I. He first summarily proposes his petition.

1. "Deliver me, O Lord," &c. From Saul, *Doeg,* or the devil.

2. "Preserve me," &c. From his violence and malice, and their effects. 1. Evil counsels, and wicked stratagems: "Which imagine mischief," &c. 2. From their evil words, which were consonant with their thoughts.

"They have sharpened their tongues," &c. With calumnies and frauds.

"Like a serpent," &c. Their bitter words are as the poison of the *viper* and *adder*, or the *asp*, which, without pain, extinguishes life.

He repeats his petition: "Keep me, O Lord," &c.

To move God, he shows their intentions.

1. "They have purposed," &c.: To make me walk slowly, or not at all, in the ways of God; to turn me back.

2. The method they took to attain their purpose: "The proud have laid a snare," &c.: as hunters do for birds and beasts. So the devil shows the bait, but hides the hook: under pleasure he hides the bitterness of its reward and consequences.

II. He implores aid from God against the evil and danger.

1. "I said unto the Lord," &c. I do not cast away my confidence.

2. "Hear the voice," &c.

Better to show the ground of his constancy, he declares,—

1. What esteem he had for his God: "Thou art the strength," &c. My fortification against all my enemies.

2. What he had formerly done for him: "Thou hast covered my head," &c.

III. The other part of his petition consists in praying against their plots.

1. "Grant not, O Lord," &c. Let them not have their wishes.

2. "Further not his wicked device," &c. Give them no prosperity in them.

3. "Lest they exalt themselves," &c. Triumph in my being conquered by them.

After praying against them, predicts their punishment: "As for the head of those that compass me about," &c.

1. "Let the mischief of their own lips," &c.

2. Deal severely with them: "Let burning coals," &c. Let them suffer extreme punishment: "Let them be cast into the fire," &c.

3. "Let not an evil speaker," &c.—a liar, flatterer, &c., "be established in the earth."

4. "Evil shall hunt," &c. Give no rest, but pursue the wicked man to his utter ruin; all those who persecute the Church, who write their laws in her blood.

IV. To the infliction of punishment on the wicked, he subjoins, by an antithesis, the promise of God for the defence of the righteous, and so concludes.

1. "I know," &c. Am certainly persuaded by my own experience, and the example of my forefathers, whom thou hast delivered in their trials and temptations.

2. "That the Lord will maintain," &c. He may defer his help and deliverance; but he will not take it from them.

And this he confirms and amplifies from the final cause, which is double.

1. That they praise him: "Surely the righteous shall give thanks," &c. Being delivered, they attribute the honour, not to themselves, or their innocency or merit, but give the glory of his grace and love to God alone.

2. That they remain before him in his Church militant and triumphant. That they may "dwell in thy presence," &c. Walk before his face here, dwell in his favour, and enjoy the beatific vision hereafter.

PSALM CXLI

The psalmist prays that his devotions may be accepted, 1, 2. That he may be enabled so to watch that he do not offend with his tongue; and that he may be preserved from wickedness, 3, 4. His willingness to receive reproof, 5. He complains of disasters, 6, 7. His trust in God, and prayer against his enemies, 8–10.

A Psalm of David

A. M. cir. 2943
B. C. cir. 1061
Sauli, Regis
Israelitarum,
cir. annum
35

LORD, I cry unto thee: [a]make haste unto me; give ear unto my voice, when I cry unto thee.

2 Let [b]my prayer be [c]set forth before thee [d]*as* incense; *and* [e]the lifting up of my hands *as* [f]the evening sacrifice.

3 Set a watch, O LORD, before my mouth; keep the door of my lips.

A. M. cir. 2943
B. C. cir. 1061
Sauli, Regis
Israelitarum,
cir. annum
35

[a]Psa. lxx. 5——[b]Rev. v. 8; viii. 3, 4——[c]Heb. *directed*
[d]Rev. viii. 3

[e]Psa. cxxxiv. 2; 1 Tim. ii. 8——[f]Exod. xxix. 39

NOTES ON PSALM CXLI

This Psalm is generally attributed to *David*, and considered to have been composed during his persecution by Saul. Some suppose that he made it at the time that he formed the resolution to go to *Achish, king of Gath;* see 1 Sam. xxvi. It is generally thought to be an *evening prayer*, and has long been used as such in the service of the Greek Church. It is in several places very obscure.

Verse 1. *Lord, I cry unto thee*] Many of David's Psalms begin with *complaints;* but they are not those of *habitual plaint* and *peevishness.* He was in frequent troubles and diffi-

culties, and he always sought help in God. He ever appears *in earnest;* at no time is there any evidence that the devotion of David was *formal.* He *prayed, meditated, supplicated, groaned, cried,* and even *roared,* as he tells us, for the disquietude of his soul. He had speedy answers; for he had much *faith,* and was always in *earnest.*

Verse 2. As *incense*] Incense was offered every morning and evening before the Lord, on the golden altar, before the veil of the sanctuary. Exod. xxix. 39, and Num. xxviii. 4.

As *the evening sacrifice.*] This was a burnt-offering, accompanied with flour and salt. But it does not appear that David refers to any

A. M. cir. 2943
B. C. cir. 1061
Sauli, Regis
Israelitarum,
cir. annum
35

4 Incline not my heart to *any* evil thing, to practise wicked works with men that work iniquity: [g]and let me not eat of their dainties.

5 [h]Let [i]the righteous smite me; *it shall be* a kindness: and let him reprove me; *it shall be* an excellent oil, *which* shall not break my head: for yet my prayer also *shall be* in their calamities.

6 When their judges are overthrown in stony places, they shall hear my words; for they are sweet.

A. M. cir. 2943
B. C. cir. 1061
Sauli, Regis
Israelitarum,
cir. annum
35

7 Our bones are scattered [k]at the grave's mouth, as when one cutteth and cleaveth *wood* upon the earth.

8 But [l]mine eyes *are* unto thee, O GOD the Lord: in thee is my trust; [m]leave not my soul destitute.

9 Keep me from [n]the snares *which* they have laid for me, and the gins of the workers of iniquity.

10 [o]Let the wicked fall into their own nets, whilst that I withal [p]escape.

---

[g]Prov. xxiii. 6——[h]Prov. ix. 8; xix. 25; xxiii. 12; Gal. vi. 1——[i]Or, *Let the righteous smite me kindly, and reprove me; let not* their *precious oil break my head,* &c.

[k]2 Cor. i. 9——[l]2 Chron. xx. 12; Psa. xxv. 15; cxxiii. 1, 2——[m]Heb. *make not my soul bare*——[n]Psa. cxix. 110; cxl. 5; cxlii. 3——[o]Psa. xxxv. 8——[p]Heb. *pass over*

---

sacrifice, for he uses not זבח *zebach,* which is almost universally used for a *slaughtered animal;* but מנחה *minchah,* which is generally taken for a *gratitude-offering* or *unbloody* sacrifice. The literal translation of the passage is, "Let my prayer be established for incense before thy faces; and the lifting up of my hands for the evening oblation." The psalmist appears to have been at this time at a distance from the sanctuary, and therefore could not perform the Divine worship in the way prescribed by the law. What could he do? Why, as he could not worship according to the *letter* of the law, he will worship God according to the *spirit;* then *prayer* is accepted in the place of *incense;* and the *lifting up of his hands, in gratitude and self-dedication* to God, is accepted in the place of the *evening minchah* or *oblation.* Who can deplore the necessity that obliged the psalmist to worship God in this way?

Verse 3. *Set a watch, O Lord, before my mouth*] While there are so many spies on my actions and words, I have need to be doubly guarded, that my enemies may have no advantage against me. Some think the prayer is against *impatience;* but if he were now going to Gath, it is more natural to suppose that he was praying to be preserved from *dishonouring the truth,* and from making *sinful concessions* in a heathen land; and at a court where, from his circumstances, it was natural to suppose he might be *tempted to apostasy* by the heathen party. The following verse seems to support this opinion.

Verse 4. *Let me eat not of their dainties.*] This may refer either to eating things *forbidden by the law;* or to the partaking in *banquets* or *feasts in honour of idols.*

Verse 5. *Let the righteous smite me*] This verse is extremely difficult in the original. The following translation, in which the *Syriac, Vulgate, Septuagint, Æthiopic,* and *Arabic* nearly agree, appears to me to be the best: "Let the righteous chastise me in mercy, and instruct me: but let not the oil of the wicked anoint my head. It shall not adorn (יני *yani,* from נוה *navah*) my head; for still my prayer shall be against their wicked works."

The oil of the wicked may here mean his *smooth flattering speeches;* and the psalmist intimates that he would rather suffer the cut-

ting reproof of the righteous than the *oily talk* of the flatterer. If this were the case, how few are there now-a-days of his mind! On referring to Bishop *Horsley,* I find his translation is something similar to my own:—

Let the just one smite me, let the pious remove me.
Let not the ointment of the impious anoint my head.
But still I will intrude in their calamities.

Verse 6. *When their judges are overthrown in stony places*] בידי סלע *biyedey sela,* "In the hands of the rock." Does this *rock* signify a *strong* or *fortified place;* and its *hands* the *garrison* which have occupied it, by whom these judges were overthrown? If we knew the occasion on which this Psalm was made, we might be the better able to understand the *allusions* in the text.

They shall hear my words; for they are sweet.] Some think there is here an allusion to David's generous treatment of Saul in the cave of En-gedi, and afterwards at the hill of Hachilah, in this verse, which might be translated: "Their judges have been dismissed in the rocky places; and have heard my words, that they were sweet." Or perhaps there may be a reference to the *death of Saul* and his *sons,* and the very disastrous defeat of the Israelites at *Gilboa.* If so, the *seventh* verse will lose its chief difficulty, *Our bones are scattered at the grave's mouth;* but if we take them as referring to the *slaughter of the priests at Nob,* then, instead of translating לפי שאול *lephi sheol, at the grave's mouth,* we may translate *at the command of Saul;* and then the verse will point out the *manner* in which those servants of the Lord were massacred; *Doeg cut them in pieces; hewed them down* as one cleaveth wood. Some understand all this of the *cruel usage* of the captives in Babylon. I could add other conjectures, and contend for my own; but they are all too vague to form a just ground for decided opinion.

Verse 8. *But mine eyes are unto thee*] In all times, in all places, on all occasions, I will cleave unto the Lord, and put my whole confidence in him.

Verse 10. *Let the wicked fall into their own*

nets] This is generally the case; those who lay snares for others fall into them themselves. *Harm watch, harm catch,* says the old adage. How many cases have occurred where the spring guns that have been set for thieves have shot some of the family! I have known some dismal cases of this kind, where some of the most amiable lives have been sacrificed to this accursed machine.

Whilst—I withal escape.] They alone are guilty; they alone spread the nets and gins; I am innocent, and God will cause me to escape.

ANALYSIS OF THE HUNDRED AND FORTY-FIRST PSALM

The contents and sum of the Psalm are the following:—

I. His prayer, ver. 1, 2.

II. That God would restrain his tongue, and compose his mind, that through anger or impatience he offend not, ver. 3, 4.

III. He prays that if he must be reproved, it be by the just, not the unjust man, ver. 5; whose judgment he declares, ver. 5, 6, and will not have any society with him.

IV. He shows the malice of the wicked to good men, ver. 6, 7.

V. He puts his trust in God, and prays to be delivered from snares, ver. 8-10.

I. 1. "Lord, I cry unto thee," &c. Speedily hear my prayer, which is fervently and affectionately addressed to thee.

2. "Let my prayer be set forth before thee," &c. Which was offered with the sacrifice. Why does David pray that his prayer might be accepted as the evening rather than the morning sacrifice? Perhaps the evening sacrifice might be more noble, as a figure of Christ's sacrifice on the cross, which was in the evening.

II. His second petition is, that God would restrain his tongue, that he might know when to speak and when to be silent. The metaphor is taken from the watch and gate of a city, which, to be safely kept, no one must be suffered to go in or out that ought not. The gate will not be sufficient without the watch; for it will be always shut, or ever open.

His third petition is for his heart, because it is deceitful above all things. Man is weak without the grace of God.

1. "Incline not my heart," &c. Suffer it not to be bent, or set on any evil thing.

2. "Incline not my heart to practices," &c. To do iniquity, being invited by their example.

3. "Let me not eat," &c. Partake with them in their feasts, doctrines, feigned sanctity, power, riches, or dignities.

III. His fourth petition is, that if reproved, it may be in the kindness of friendship, not revenge or bitterness.

1. "Let the righteous smite me," &c. Smite with a reproof.

2. "It shall be a kindness," &c. I shall account it an act of charity, and I will love him for it.

3. "And let him reprove me," &c. An excellent oil, to heal my wounds of sin.

IV. His next petition he prefaces thus: "Let my prayer," &c. "When their judges are overthrown," &c., refers to the judicature: the chief seats, authorities, &c., are swallowed up, as men are by the sea; as the ship is dashed against the rock, and broken to pieces.

And this sense the following verse will justify: "Our bones are scattered," &c. They beset me and my company so closely, that we despair of life; and our bones must be scattered here and there in the wilderness, except thou, O Lord, succour us.

V. Therefore he presents his last petition, which has two parts. 1. "But mine eyes are unto thee," &c. 2. "Leave not my soul destitute."

1. For his own safety: "Leave not my soul," &c. Let me not fall into their hands.

2. Which prayer is grounded on his confidence in God: "Mine eyes are unto thee," &c. I depend on and look to thee alone for deliverance.

3. "Keep me from the snares," &c. From their frauds and ambushes.

Lastly, he imprecates confusion on the heads of his enemies.

1. "Let the wicked fall," &c.

2. "Whilst that I withal escape." Pass by or through them unhurt.

PSALM CXLII

The psalmist, in great distress and difficulty, calls upon God, 1-7.

ᵃMaschil ᵇof David; A Prayer ᶜwhen he was in the cave

I ᵈCRIED unto the LORD with my voice; with my voice unto the LORD did I make my supplication.

2 ᵉI poured out my complaint before him; I showed before him my trouble.

3 ᶠWhen my spirit was overwhelmed within me, then thou knewest my path. ᵍIn the way wherein I walked have they privily laid a snare for me.

ᵃPsa. lvii. title——ᵇOr, A Psalm *of David, giving instruction*——ᶜ1 Sam. xxii. 1; xxiv. 3

ᵈ1 Sam. vii. 8; Psa. cvii. 19——ᵉPsa. cii. title; Isa. xxvi. 16——ᶠPsa. cxliii. 4——ᵍPsa. cxl. 5

NOTES ON PSALM CXLII

The title says, "An Instruction of David," or a Psalm of David giving instruction; "A Prayer when he was in the cave."

David was *twice* in great peril in *caves.*

1. At the cave of *Adullam,* when he fled from Achish, king of Gath, 1 Sam. xxii. 2. When he was in the cave of *En-gedi,* where he had taken refuge from the pursuit of Saul; and the latter, without knowing that David was in it, had gone into it on some necessary occasion,

4 [h]I [l]looked on *my* right hand, and beheld, but [k]*there was* no man that would know me: refuge [l]failed me; [m]no man cared for my soul.

5 I cried unto thee, O LORD: I said, [n]Thou *art* my refuge *and* [o]my portion [p]in the land of the living.

6 Attend unto my cry; for I am [q]brought very low: deliver me from my persecutors; for they are stronger than I.

7 Bring my soul out of prison, that I may praise thy name: [r]the righteous shall compass me about; [s]for thou shalt deal bountifully with me.

---

[h]Psa. lxix. 20——[i]Or, *Look on the right hand, and see* [k]Psa. xxxi. 11; lxxxviii. 8, 18——[l]Heb. *perished from me* [m]Heb. *no man sought after my soul*

[n]Psa. xlvi. 1; xci. 2——[o]Psa. xvi. 5; lxxiii. 26; cxix. 57; Lam. iii. 24——[p]Psa. xxvii. 13——[q]Psa. cxvi. 6 [r]Psa. xxxiv. 2——[s]Psa. xiii. 6; cxix. 17

---

1 Sam. xxiv. If the inscription can be depended on, the *cave of En-gedi* is the most likely of the two, for the scene laid here. But were there doubts concerning the legitimacy of the title, I should refer the Psalm to the state of the captives in Babylon, to which a great part of the Psalms refer. Bishop *Horsley* calls it "A Prayer of the Messiah taken and deserted." It may be so: but where is the *evidence*, except in the conjectural system of *Origen*.

Verse 1. *I cried unto the Lord*] See on the *first* verse of the preceding Psalm.

Verse 3. *Then thou knewest my path.*] When Saul and his army were about the cave in which I was hidden, *thou knewest my path*—that I had then no way of escape but by *miracle:* but thou didst not permit them to *know* that I was wholly in their power.

Verse 4. There was *no man that would know me*] This has been applied to the time in which our Lord was deserted by his disciples. As to the case of David in the cave of En-gedi, he had no refuge: for what were the handful of men that were with him to Saul and his army?

Verse 5. *Thou* art *my refuge*] Even in these most disastrous circumstances, I will put my trust in thee.

Verse 6. *I am brought very low*] Never was I so near total ruin before.

Deliver me from my persecutors] They are now in full possession of the only means of my escape.

They are stronger than I.] What am I and my men against this well-appointed armed multitude, with their king at their head?

Verse 7. *Bring my soul out of prison*] Bring נפשי *naphshi*, my *life*, out of this *cave* in which it is now *imprisoned;* Saul and his men being in possession of the entrance.

The righteous shall compass me about] יכתרו *yachtiru*, they *shall crown me;* perhaps meaning that the pious Jews, on the death of Saul, would cheerfully join together to make him king, being convinced that God, by his *bountiful dealings with him,* intended that it should be so. The *old Psalter,* which is imperfect from the *twenty-first* verse of Psalm cxix. to the end of Psalm cxli., concludes this Psalm thus: "Lede my saule oute of corrupcion of my body; that corrupcion is bodely pyne, in whilk my saule is anguyst; after that in Godes house, sal al be louyng (praising) of the."

ANALYSIS OF THE HUNDRED AND FORTY-SECOND PSALM

The substance of this Psalm is the earnest prayer of the psalmist that he might be delivered from the danger he was in.

The parts are,

I. An exordium; in which he

1. Shows what he did in his trouble; took himself to prayer, ver. 1, 2.

2. Then his consternation and anxiety of mind, which arose from the malice and craft of his enemies, and want of help from his friends, ver. 3, 4.

II. His address and petition to God, ver. 5-7.

1. The two first verses show the psalmist's intention. "I cried unto the Lord," &c. 2. "I poured out my supplication," &c.

This he amplifies,—

1. From his vehemence: "I cried, I supplicated."

2. From the object: "Unto the Lord." I invoked him, and no other.

3. From the instrument: "With my voice."

4. From his humility in prayer. It was a *supplication.*

5. From his free and full confession: "I poured out," &c.

6. From his sincerity and confidence in God. The reason was:—

1. This I did "when my spirit was overwhelmed," &c. There being no sufficiency in me, I betook myself to the all-sufficient God.

2. "For thou knowest my path," &c. My actions and intentions.

The craft and subtlety of his enemies, especially *Saul.*

1. "In the way wherein I walked," &c. My vocation.

2. "Have they privily laid," &c. Saul gave him his daughter *Michal* to be a snare to him; and a dowry he must have of a hundred foreskins of the Philistines, that David might fall by their hands.

His destitution in the time of trouble.

1. "I looked on my right hand," &c. But no friend was near: "There was no man," &c. The miserable have few friends.

2. "Refuge failed me," &c. I had no place of safety.

3. "No man cared," &c. Regarded my life, or cared if I perished.

II. The psalmist, having no human help, calls upon God.

1. "Thou art my refuge," &c. My hiding-place.

2. "Thou art my portion," &c. While I live in this world.

Then he sends up his prayer, fortified by a double argument.

1. From the lamentable condition he was brought into: "I was brought low," &c.

2. From the malice and power of his enemies: "Deliver me," &c.

Again he renews his prayer, and presses it from the final cause: "Bring my soul," &c.

Upon which follow two effects:—
1. His gratitude: "That I may praise thy name."
2. That of others: "The righteous shall compass me," &c. Come unto me.

3. The reason for this: "For thou shalt deal bountifully with me." Bestow favours upon me, having delivered me from my former miseries; which men seeing, who are commonly the friends of prosperity, will magnify and resort to me.

PSALM CXLIII

The psalmist prays for mercy, and deprecates judgment, 1, 2. His persecutions, 3. His earnest prayer for deliverance, 4–9. Prays for God's quickening Spirit, 10, 11. And for the total discomfiture of his adversaries, 12.

A Psalm of David

A. M. cir. 2981
B. C. cir. 1023
Davidis, Regis
Israelitarum,
cir. annum
33

HEAR my prayer, O LORD, give ear to my supplications: [a]in thy faithfulness answer me, *and* in thy righteousness.

2 And [b]enter not into judgment with thy servant: for [c]in thy sight shall no man living be justified.

3 For the enemy hath persecuted my soul; he hath smitten my life down to the ground; he hath made me to dwell in darkness as those that have been long dead.

4 [d]Therefore is my spirit overwhelmed within me; my heart within me is desolate.

A. M. cir. 2981
B. C. cir. 1023
Davidis, Regis
Israelitarum,
cir. annum
33

5 [e]I remember the days of old; I meditate on all thy works; I muse on the work of thy hands.

6 [f]I stretch forth my hands unto thee: [g]my soul *thirsteth* after thee, as a thirsty land. Selah.

7 Hear me speedily, O LORD: my spirit faileth: hide not thy face from me, [h]lest [i]I be like unto them that go down into the pit.

8 Cause me to hear thy loving-kindness [k]in the morning; for in thee do I trust: [l]cause me to know the way wherein I should walk; for [m]I lift up my soul unto thee.

---

[a]Psa. xxxi. 1——[b]Job xiv. 3——[c]Exod. xxxiv. 7; Job iv. 17; ix. 2; xv. 14; xxv. 4; Psa. cxxx. 3; Eccles. vii. 20; Rom. iii. 20; Gal. ii. 16——[d]Psa. lxxvii. 3; cxlii. 3

[e]Psa. lxxvii. 5, 10, 11——[f]Psa. lxxxviii. 9——[g]Psa. lxiii. 1——[h]Psa. xxviii. 1——[i]Or, *for I am become like*, &c.; Psa. lxxxviii. 4——[k]See Psa. xlvi. 5——[l]Psa. v. 8 [m]Psa. xxv. 1

NOTES ON PSALM CXLIII

The *Hebrew* and all the *Versions* attribute this Psalm to *David;* and the *Vulgate, Septuagint, Æthiopic* and *Arabic* state that it was composed on the rebellion of his son Absalom: nor is there any thing in the Psalm that positively disagrees with this inscription. This is the last of the seven Psalms styled *penitential.*

Verse 1. *In thy faithfulness answer me*] Thou hast promised to support me in my difficulties, and, though my children should forsake me, never to withdraw thy loving-kindness from me. See the present unnatural rebellion of my son. Lord, undertake for me!

Verse 2. *Enter not into judgment*] אל תבוא *al tabo.* Do not come into court, either as a *Witness* against me, or as a *Judge,* else I am ruined; for thou hast seen all my ways that they are evil, and thy justice requires thee to punish me. Nor can any soul that has ever lived be justified in the sight of thy justice and righteousness. Had I my desert from thee, I should have worse than even my unnatural son intends me. O what a relief is *Jesus crucified* to a soul in such circumstances!

Verse 3. *He hath made me to dwell in darkness*] Literally, *in dark places.* This may be understood of David's taking refuge in *caves* and *dens* of the earth, to escape from his persecuting son; yea, even to take refuge in the *tombs,* or *repositories* of the dead.

Verse 4. *Therefore is my spirit*] I am deeply depressed in spirit, and greatly afflicted in body.
My heart within me is desolate.] It has no companion of its sorrows, no sympathetic friend. I am utterly destitute of comfort.

Verse 5. *I remember the days of old*] Thou hast often helped me, often delivered me. I will therefore trust in thee, for thy mercy is not clean gone from me.

Verse 6. *I stretch forth my hands*] This is a natural action. All in distress, or under the influence of *eager desire,* naturally extend their hands and arms, as if to catch at help and obtain succour.
As a thirsty land.] Parched and burned by the sun, longs for rain, so does my thirsty soul for the living God.

Verse 7. *Hear me speedily*] מהר *maher, make haste* to answer me. A few hours, and my state may be irretrievable. In a short time my unnatural son may put an end to my life.

Verse 8. *Cause me to hear thy loving-kindness in the morning*] This petition was probably offered in the *night-season.* David had despatched his messengers in all directions; and prays to God that he might by the morning get some good news.
Cause me to know the way wherein I should walk] Absalom and his partisans are in possession of all the country. I know not in what direction to go, that I may not fall in with

A. M. cir. 2981
B. C. cir. 1023
Davidis, Regis
Israelitarum,
cir. annum
33
9 Deliver me, O Lord, from mine enemies: I [n]flee unto thee to hide me.

10 [o]Teach me to do thy will; for thou *art* my God: [p]thy Spirit *is* good; lead me into [q]the land of uprightness.

11 [r]Quicken me, O Lord, for thy name's sake: for thy righteousness' sake bring my soul out of trouble.
A. M. cir. 2981
B. C. cir. 1023
Davidis, Regis
Israelitarum,
cir. annum
33

12 And of thy mercy [s]cut off mine enemies, and destroy all them that afflict my soul: for [t]I *am* thy servant.

---

[n]Heb. *hide me with thee*——[o]Psa. xxv. 4, 5; cxxxix. 24
[p]Neh. ix. 20

[q]Isa. xxvi. 10——[r]Psa. cxix. 25, 37, 40, &c.——[s]Psa. liv. 5——[t]Psa. cxvi. 16

---

them: point out by thy especial providence the path I should take.

Verse 9. *I flee unto thee to hide me.*] That I may not be *found* by my enemies, who seek my life to destroy it.

Verse 10. *Teach me to do thy will*] רצונך *ret-sonecha*, thy *pleasure.* To be found doing the will of God is the only safe state for man.

Thy Spirit is *good*] The Author of every *good desire* and *holy purpose.*

Lead me] Let it lead me by its continued inspirations and counsels.

Into the land of uprightness.] "Into a right land," Chaldee. Into the place where I shall be safe. The old Psalter has, 𝔗𝔥𝔦 𝔤𝔬𝔰𝔱𝔢 𝔤𝔲𝔡𝔢 𝔰𝔞𝔩 𝔩𝔢𝔡𝔢 𝔪𝔢 𝔦𝔫𝔱𝔬 𝔯𝔶𝔤𝔱 𝔩𝔞𝔫𝔡𝔢.

Verse 11. *Quicken me*] I am as a dead man, and my hopes are almost dead within me.

Verse 12. *And of thy mercy*] To *me* and the *kingdom.*

Cut off mine enemies] Who, if they succeed, will destroy the very *form of godliness.* The steps he has already taken show that even *morality* shall have no countenance, if Absalom reign.

I am thy servant.] Whoever is disloyal to me, I will love and serve thee.

For a full explanation of this Psalm, as applied to penitents, see the analysis.

ANALYSIS OF THE HUNDRED AND FORTY-THIRD PSALM

David, being driven from *Jerusalem* by his son *Absalom*, wisely calls to mind his sin, as being the cause of it.

This Psalm has four parts:—

I. A prayer for remission of sin, grounded on God's promise, ver. 1; not on his own worthiness, ver. 2.

II. A narration of the sad state of his affairs, ver. 3, 4.

III. The comfort he received in his sad condition, and whence, ver. 5, 6.

IV. His petition, containing many particulars and reasons, ver. 7 to the end.

I. He prays for audience: "Hear my prayer, O Lord," &c. He does not plainly express the matter he prayed for; but it may be gathered from the context that it was for remission of sin.

1. "In thy faithfulness," &c. Thou art a faithful God, and hast promised to pardon the penitent. I am a penitent; have mercy on me.

2. "And in thy righteousness," &c. Which here signifies mercy, loving-kindness.

This sense appears more plainly from the next verse.

1. "And enter not into judgment," &c. Call me not to a strict account at the bar of thy justice. This he deprecates; so that *Justitia* in

the former verse could not be taken for that justice.

2. "For in thy sight," &c. Not I, nor any other man: pardon me, then, for the sake of thy mercy and promise, not my merits.

II. And now he enters upon the narration of his sad condition.

1. "For the enemy hath persecuted," &c. My son Absalom seeks my life: but it was Satan who enticed me to adultery and homicide.

2. "He hath smitten," &c. Humbled me; made me a lover of earth, vile in thy sight.

3. "He hath made me to dwell," &c. After Satan had entangled me with earthly pleasures, I was in spiritual darkness, and saw not the way of life, any more than those who have been long dead.

The effect this darkness produced was fear and consternation.

1. "Therefore is my spirit," &c. I suffered a kind of swoon in my soul; I was ready to faint when I considered thy holiness and my impurity.

2. "My heart within me," &c. Far from comfort in heavy trouble.

III. In this sadness of heart and mind,—

1. "I remember the days of old," &c. Thy past kindness to me and to others.

2. "I meditate," &c. I did not slightly run them over, but pondered on them.

And I derived great profit from my meditation; for,

1. "I stretch forth my hands," &c. I began earnestly to pray to thee.

2. "My soul thirsteth," &c. After thy righteousness, as the dry land wanting water. For as the earth without rain has no consistence, but is pulverized; so the soul not moistened with the grace of God falls on the right and left hand into temptation, and brings forth no fruit to God's glory.

IV. The sad case in which David was, upon a sense of God's indignation, makes him seek out a remedy.

1. "Hear me speedily," &c. And his reason for this is the sad condition in which he was till God was pacified for his sin.

2. "Hide not thy face," &c. Thy presence, thy favour.

His next petition resembles the former in substance.

1. "Cause me to hear," &c. Thy pardoning mercy out of thy word; it is thy Spirit which must work with it to save me.

2. "In the morning," &c. Betimes, speedily, quickly, &c.

3. His reason: "For in thee do I trust," &c. I did not let go my hold even in my extremity; but still hoped against hope.

His third petition is—

1. "Cause me to know," &c. The psalmist,

being truly penitent, fears to relapse into his pardoned sin, and prays to God for grace and direction.

2. His reason: "For I lift up my soul," &c. My purpose, to serve thee.

His fourth petition is—

1. "Deliver me, O Lord," &c. From the devil and all his temptations.

2. His reason: "I flee unto thee," &c. From them.

His fifth petition resembles his third.

1. "Teach me to do thy will," &c. Both by an active and passive obedience may I know thy will perfectly; in adversity, to submit to it; in prosperity, to do it without pride or presumption.

2. His reason: "For thou art my God." Who hast promised me thy help; and from whom all my good proceeds, being and well-being.

His sixth petition: "Thy Spirit is good." Not

mine. Let then thy good Spirit instruct and lead me in the right way.

His seventh petition is—

1. "Quicken me, O Lord," &c. Restore life; justify me fully.

2. "For thy name's sake." Not my merits, but thy mercy, and the glory that will accrue to thy name in pardoning a penitent soul.

3. He goes on: "For thy righteousness' sake," &c. Freedom he desires; but still at the hands of God's infinite mercy.

His last petition is for the destruction of Satan's kingdom.

1. "Of thy mercy cut off mine enemies," &c.

2. His reason: "For I am thy servant," &c. A follower; one under thy patronage and protection; one of thy family honoured with the dignity of being thy servant, and well contented and pleased to perform my duty and service.

PSALM CXLIV

The psalmist praises God for his goodness, 1, 2. *Exclamations relative to the vanity of human life,* 3, 4. *He prays against his enemies,* 5–8; *and extols God's mercy for the temporal blessings enjoyed by his people,* 9–15.

XXX. DAY. MORNING PRAYER
A Psalm of David

A. M. cir. 2981
B. C. cir. 1023
Davidis, Regis
Israelitarum,
cir. annum
33

BLESSED *be* the LORD [a]my strength, [b]which teacheth my hands [c]to war, *and* my fingers to fight:

2 [d]My [e]goodness, and my fortress; my high tower, and my deliverer; my shield, and

he in whom I trust; who subdueth my people under me.

A. M. cir. 2981
B. C. cir. 1023
Davidis, Regis
Israelitarum,
cir. annum
33

3 [f]LORD, what *is* man, that thou takest knowledge of him! *or* the son of man, that thou makest account of him!

4 [g]Man is like to vanity: [h]his days *are* as a shadow that passeth away.

---

[a]Heb. *my rock;* Psa. xviii. 2, 31——[b]2 Sam. xxii. 35; Psa. xviii. 34——[c]Heb. *to the war,* &c - —[d]2 Sam. xxii. 2, 3, 40, 48

[e]Or, *My mercy*——[f]Job vii. 17; Psa. viii. 4; Heb. ii. 6 [g]Job iv. 19; xiv. 2; Psa. xxxix. 5; lxii. 9——[h]Psa. cii. 11

NOTES ON PSALM CXLIV

The *Hebrew*, and all the *Versions*, attribute this Psalm to *David.* The *Vulgate, Septuagint, Æthiopic,* and *Arabic,* term it, *A Psalm of David against Goliath.* The *Syriac* says, "A Psalm of David when he slew Asaph, the brother of Goliath." *Calmet* thinks, and with much probability, that it was composed by David after the death of Absalom, and the restoration of the kingdom to peace and tranquillity. From a collation of this with Psa. xviii., of which it appears to be an *abridgment*, preserving the same ideas, and the same forms of expression, there can be no doubt of both having proceeded from the same pen, and that David was the author. There is scarcely an expression here of peculiar importance that is not found in the prototype; and for *explanation* I must refer generally to the above Psalm.

Verse 1. *Teacheth my hands to war*] To use *sword, battle-axe,* or *spear.*

And *my fingers to fight*] To use the *bow and arrows,* and the *sling.*

Verse 2. *Who subdueth my people*] Who has once more reduced the nation to a state of loyal obedience. This may refer to the peace after the rebellion of Absalom.

Verse 3. *Lord, what is man*] See the notes on Psa. viii. 4, 5. *What is Adam, that thou approvest of him?* Can he do any thing worthy of thy notice? Or *the son of feeble perishing man, that thou shouldest hold him in repute?* What care, love, and attention, dost thou lavish upon him!

Verse 4. *Man is like to vanity*] אדם להבל רמה *Adam lahebel damah,* literally, *Adam is like to Abel,* exposed to the same miseries, accidents, and murderers; for in millions of cases the hands of brothers are lifted up to shed the blood of brothers. What are wars but fratricide in the great human family?

His days are *as a shadow*] The life of *Abel* was promissory of much blessedness; but it afforded merely the *shadow of happiness.* He was pure and holy, beloved of his parents, and beloved of God; but, becoming the object of his brother's envy, his life became a sacrifice to his piety.

A. M. cir. 2981 B. C. cir. 1023 Davidis, Regis Israelitarum, cir. annum 33

5 [i]Bow thy heavens, O LORD,
and come down: [k]touch the
mountains, and they shall
smoke.
6 [l]Cast forth lightning, and scatter them:
shoot out thine arrows, and destroy them.
7 [m]Send thine [n]hand from above; [o]rid me,
and deliver me out of great waters, from the
hand of [p]strange children;
8 Whose mouth [q]speaketh vanity, and their
right hand *is* a right hand of falsehood.
9 I will [r]sing a new song unto thee, O God:
upon a psaltery *and* an instrument of ten
strings will I sing praises unto thee.
10 [s]*It is he* that giveth [t]salvation unto
kings: who delivereth David his servant from
the hurtful sword.
11 [u]Rid me, and deliver me from the hand
of strange children, whose mouth
speaketh vanity, and their right
hand *is* a right hand of falsehood:
12 That our sons *may be* [v]as plants grown
up in their youth; *that* our daughters *may be*
as corner stones, [w]polished *after* the similitude of a palace:
13 *That* our garners *may be* full, affording
[x]all manner of store: *that* our sheep may
bring forth thousands and ten thousands in
our streets:
14 *That* our oxen *may be* [y]strong to labour;
that there be no breaking in, nor going out;
that *there be* no complaining in our streets.
15 [z]Happy *is that* people, that is in such
a case: *yea,* happy *is that* people, whose
God *is* the LORD.

A. M. cir. 2981 B. C. cir. 1023 Davidis, Regis Israelitarum, cir. annum 33

---

[i]Psa. xviii. 9; Isa. lxiv. 1——[k]Psa. civ. 32——[l]Psa. xviii. 13, 14——[m]Psa. xviii. 16——[n]Heb. *hands* [o]Ver. 11; Psa. lxix. 1, 2, 14——[p]Psa. liv. 3; Mal. ii. 11 [q]Psa. xii. 2——[r]Psa. xxxiii. 2, 3; xl. 3

[s]Psa. xviii. 50——[t]Or, *victory*——[u]Ver. 7, 8——[v]Psa. cxxviii. 3——[w]Heb. *cut*——[x]Heb. *from kind to kind* [y]Heb. *able to bear burdens*, or *loaden* with flesh——[z]Deut. xxxiii. 29; Psa. xxxiii. 12; lxv. 4; cxlvi. 5

Verse 5. *Bow thy heavens*] See the note on Psa. xviii. 9.

Verse 6 *Cast forth lightning*] See the note, ib. ver. 13, 14.

Verse 7. *Deliver me out of great waters*] See the note, ib. ver. 16.

Verse 9. *I will sing a new song*] A song of peculiar excellence. I will pour forth all my *gratitude*, and all my *skill*, on its composition. See on Psa. xxxiii. 2, 3.

Verse 10. He *that giveth salvation unto kings*] *Monarchy*, in the principle, is from God: it is that *form of government* which, in the course of the Divine providence, has principally prevailed; and that which, on the whole, has been most beneficial to mankind. God, therefore, has it under his peculiar protection. It is by him that kings reign; and by his special providence they are protected.

Verse 12. *That our sons* may be *as plants*] God had promised to his people, being faithful, THREE *descriptions* of BLESSINGS, Deut. xxviii. 4. 1. The *fruit of the body*—sons and daughters. 2. The *fruits of the ground*—grass and corn in sufficient plenty. 3. *Fruit of the cattle*—"the increase of kine, and flocks of sheep." These are the blessings to which the psalmist refers here, as those in which he might at present exult and triumph: blessings *actually enjoyed* by his people at large; proofs of his mild and paternal government, and of the especial blessing of the Almighty. The people who *were in such a state*, and revolted, had no excuse: they were doubly guilty, as ungrateful both to *God* and *man*.

Verse 13. That *our garners, &c.*] *Our garners are full.* These are not *prayers* put up by David *for such blessings:* but *assertions*, that such blessings were actually in possession. All these expressions should be understood in the *present tense.*

Ten thousands in our streets.] בחצתינו *be-chutsotheynu* should be translated in our *pens* or *sheep-walks;* for *sheep bringing forth* in the *streets* of cities or towns is absurd.

Verse 14. *Our oxen* may be *strong to labour*] We have not only an abundance of cattle; but they are of the most strong and vigorous breed.

No breaking in] So well ordered is the *police* of the kingdom, that there are no depredations, no robbers, house-breakers, or marauding parties, in the land; no sudden incursions of neighbouring tribes or banditti breaking into fields or houses, carrying away property, and taking with them the people to sell them into captivity: there is no such *breaking in*, and no such *going out*, in the nation. My *enemies* are either become *friends*, and are united with me in political interests; or are, *through fear*, obliged to *stand aloof.*

Verse 15. *Happy* is that *people*] "O how happy are the people!" Such were his people; and they had not only all this secular happiness, but they had *Jehovah for their God;* and in him had a ceaseless fountain of strength, protection, earthly blessings, and eternal mercies! A people in such a case to rebel, must have the curse of God and man.

ANALYSIS OF THE HUNDRED AND FORTY-FOURTH PSALM

This Psalm is divided into *three* parts:—

I. A thanksgiving, ver. 1-5.

II. A petition, ver. 5-11.

III. A discussion on happiness, and in what it consists, ver. 12, to the end.

I. The prophet gives thanks, and praises God.

1. "Blessed be the Lord:" &c. Who has taught me in a general way the art of war, in a particular way the use of the sling; giving me skill, &c.

2. "He is my strength," &c. The strength I have is from him.

3. "My goodness," &c. Benignity or mercy.

4. "My fortress," &c. To him I fly as to a stronghold.

5. "And my Deliverer." Therefore will I trust in him.

From the consideration of so many benefits, the psalmist exclaims, "Lord what is man," &c. To which question he replies,—

1. "Man is like to vanity." If God be not his fulness and strength.

2. "His days," &c. God is always the same; but man changes every moment.

II. He prays for God's assistance: "Bow thy heavens," &c. "Cast forth lightning," &c. If men will not acknowledge thy mercy, let them see thy judgments. This first part of his petition against his enemies being ended, he prays,—

1. "Rid me, and deliver me:" &c. From dangers of men.

2. "From the hand of strange children:" &c. Moabites, Philistines, &c.

Upon whom he sets these two characters.

1. "Whose mouth speaketh vanity:" &c. Lies, insincere words.

2. "At their right hand:" &c. They use their power to oppress and deceive.

Then the psalmist exclaims, as in a short hymn—

1. "I will sing a new song," &c. And this I will do because "thou hast given victory," &c. "Thou hast delivered David," &c., from Saul, Absalom, &c.

2. And then he repeats, and concludes his petition as before: "Rid me," &c.

III. His petition being ended, he discourses on the nature of happiness, which is of two kinds, temporal and spiritual. The addition of temporal blessings is pleasant, and promised to the obedient: but godliness is the only safety in this, and especially in the life to come: "For godliness," &c. God created temporal *goods* not merely for the wicked; they are often the rewards of piety. The psalmist therefore prays,—

1. "That our sons," &c. They are the pillars of a house; let them be flourishing.

2. "That our daughters," &c. Stones that join the building, beautiful as well as useful.

3. "That our garners may be full," &c. That we may have abundance.

4. "That our sheep," &c. Our flocks' increase.

5. "That our oxen," &c. May be healthy and strong.

6. "That there be no breaking," &c. No plundering among us.

7. "That there be no complaining," &c. No want of bread, or any cause of tumult. David prays that, during his reign, the people may be happy, and enjoy the fruits of peace.

Then he concludes the Psalm with this acclamation:—

1. "Happy is that people," &c. Those he has described.

2. "Yea, happy," &c. That have the true God for their God; who know God to be their Father, and that he takes care of them, providing for their temporal necessities, and supplying all their spirtual wants. Others understand these words, not as prayers, but as a description of the state *David* and his people were then in. See the notes.

PSALM CXLV

God is praised for his unsearchable greatness, 1, 2; for his majesty and terrible acts, 3, 6; for his goodness and tender mercies to all, 7–9; for his power and kingdom, 10–13; for his kindness to the distressed, 14; for his providence, 15–17. He hears and answers prayer, 18–20. All should praise him, 21.

David's ªPsalm of praise

I WILL extol thee, my God, O King; and I will bless thy name for ever and ever.

2 Every day will I bless thee; and I will praise thy name for ever and ever.

3 ᵇGreat *is* the LORD, and greatly to be

ªPsa. c. title

ᵇPsa. xcvi. 4; cxlvii. 5

NOTES ON PSALM CXLV.

This Psalm is attributed to *David* by the *Hebrew* and all the *Versions*. It is the last of the *acrostic* Psalms; and should contain twenty-two verses, as answering to the twenty-two letters of the Hebrew alphabet; but the verse between the thirteenth and fourteenth, beginning with the letter נ *nun*, is lost out of the present Hebrew copies; but a translation of it is found in the *Syriac, Septuagint, Vulgate, Æthiopic, Arabic,* and *Anglo-Saxon.* See below. It is an incomparable Psalm of praise; and the

rabbins have it in such high estimation, that they assert, if a man with sincerity of heart repeat it three times a-day, he shall infallibly enjoy the blessings of the world to come. It does not appear on what particular occasion it was composed; or, indeed, whether there was any occasion but gratitude to God for his ineffable favours to mankind.

Verse 1. *I will extol thee*] I will raise thee on high, I will lift thee up.

I will bless thy name] לעולם ועד *leolam vaed, for ever and onward,* in this and the coming world. This sort of expressions, which are

praised; cand dhis greatness *is* unsearchable.

4 eOne generation shall praise thy works to another, and shall declare thy mighty acts.

5 I will speak of the glorious honour of thy majesty and of thy wondrous fworks.

6 And *men* shall speak of the might of thy terrible acts: and I will gdeclare thy greatness.

7 They shall abundantly utter the memory of thy great goodness, and shall sing of thy righteousness.

8 hThe LORD *is* gracious, and full of com-

passion; slow to anger, and lof great mercy.

9 kThe LORD *is* good to all: and his tender mercies *are* over all his works.

10 lAll thy works shall praise thee, O LORD; and thy saints shall bless thee.

11 They shall speak of the glory of thy kingdom, and talk of thy power;

12 To make known to the sons of men his mighty acts, and the glorious majesty of his kingdom.

13 mThy kingdom *is* nan everlasting king-

---

cHebrew, *and of his greatness* there is *no search*
dJob v. 9; ix. 10; Romans xi. 33——eIsaiah xxxviii.
19——fHebrew *things* or *words*——gHebrew *declare it*——hExodus xxxiv. 6, 7; Numbers xiv. 18; Psalm

lxxxvi. 5, 15; ciii. 8——iHebrew, *great in mercy*
kPsalm c. 5; Nahum i. 7——lPsalm xix. 1——mPsalm cxlvi. 10; 1 Timothy i. 17——nHebrew, *a kingdom of all ages*

---

very difficult to be translated, are on the whole well expressed by those words, in a hymn of Mr. Addison:—

> Through all eternity to thee
> A joyful song I'll raise;
> But O, eternity's too short
> To utter all thy praise!

This contains a strong *hyperbole;* but allowable in such cases.

Verse 3. *His greatness* is *unsearchable.*] Literally, *To his mightinesses there is no investigation.* All in God is *unlimited* and *eternal.*

Verse 4. *One generation*] Thy *creating* and *redeeming* acts are recorded in thy *word;* but thy *wondrous providential dealings* with mankind must be handed down by tradition, from generation to generation; for they are in continual occurrence, and consequently innumerable.

Verse 8. *The Lord* is *gracious*] His holy nature is ever *disposed* to show favour.

Full of compassion] Wherever he sees misery, his eye affects his heart.

Slow to anger] When there is even the *greatest provocation.*

Of great mercy.] Great in his *abundant mercy.* These *four* things give us a wonderful display of the goodness of the Divine nature.

Verse 9. *The Lord* is *good to all*] There is not a soul out of hell that is not continually under his *most merciful regards;* so far is he from *willing* or *decreeing before their creation* the damnation of any man.

His tender mercies] His *bowels of compassion* are over all his works; he feels for his intelligent offspring, as the most *affectionate mother* does for the child of her own bosom. And through this matchless mercy, these bowels of compassion, his son Jesus tasted death for every man. How far is all that is here spoken of the nature of God opposed to the Molochian doctrine of the eternal decree of reprobation!

> "His grace for every soul is free:
> For *his,* who forged the dire decree;
> For every reprobate and me."

Verse 10. *All thy works shall praise thee*] Whom? The God *who is good to all.*

Thy saints] חסידיך *chasideycha,* thy compassionate ones; those who are partakers of

thy *great mercy,* ver. 8. These shall *bless thee,* because they know, they *feel,* that thou willest the salvation of all. The dark, the gloomy, the hard-hearted, the narrow-minded bigots, who never have had thy love shed abroad in their hearts, can unfeelingly deal in the damnation of their fellows.

Verse 12. *To make known*] They delight to recommend their God and Father to others.

Verse 13. *Thy dominion* endureth] There is neither age nor people in and over which God does not manifest his *benignly ruling* power. As the above verse begins with the letter מ *mem,* the next in the order of the alphabet should begin with נ *nun:* but that verse is totally wanting. To say it never was in, is false, because the alphabet is not complete without it; and it is an unanswerable argument to prove the careless manner in which the Jews have preserved the Divine records. Though the *Syriac, Septuagint, Vulgate, Æthiopic, Arabic,* and *Anglo-Saxon,* have a verse, not in the Hebrew text, that answers to the נ *nun,* which is found in no printed copy of the Hebrew Bible; yet one MS., now in Trinity College, Dublin, has it thus, I suppose by correction, in the bottom of the page:—

נאמן יהוה בכל דבריו וחסיד בכל מעשיו:

Neeman Yehovah bechol debaraiv; vechasid bechol maasaiv.

"The Lord is faithful in all his words; and merciful in all his works."

Πιστος Κυριος εν τοις λογοις αυτου· και οσιος εν πασι τοις εργοις αυτου.—SEPTUAGINT.

Fidelis Dominus in omnibus verbis suis: et sanctus in omnibus operibus suis.—VULGATE.

These two Versions, the *Septuagint* and *Vulgate,* are the same with the Hebrew given above. The *Anglo-Saxon* is the same:—

ȝetrype Drihtn on eallum poꞃcum heoꞃa; ꞇ naliȝe on eallum ꞃeoꞃcum hiꞃ. "True Lord in all words his; and holy in all works his."

The *Latin* text in my old Psalter is the same with the present printed Vulgate: "Fidelis Dominus in omnibus verbis suis; et sanctus in omnibus operibus suis." Thus translated in the same MSS.: Lorde true in all his wordis; and holy in al his workes.

dom, and thy dominion *endureth* throughout
all generations.
14 The LORD upholdeth all that fall, and
[o]raiseth up all *those that be* bowed down.
15 [p]The eyes of all [q]wait upon thee; and
[r]thou givest them their meat in due season.
16 Thou openest thine hand, [s]and satisfiest
the desire of every living thing.
17 The LORD *is* righteous in all his ways,
and [t]holy in all his works.
18 [u]The LORD *is* nigh unto all them that call
upon him, to all that call upon him [v]in truth.
19 He will fulfil the desire of them that
fear him: he also will hear their cry, and will
save them.
20 [w]The LORD preserveth all them that
love him: but all the wicked will he destroy.
21 My mouth shall speak the praise of the
LORD: and let all flesh bless his holy name
for ever and ever.

[o]Psa. cxlvi. 8——[p]Psa. civ. 27——[q]Or, *look unto thee* [r]Psa. cxxxvi. 25——[s]Psa. civ. 21; cxlvii. 9

[t]Or, *merciful* or *bountiful*——[u]Deut. iv. 7——[v]John iv. 24——[w]Psa. xxxi. 23; xcvii. 10

It is remarkable that the whole verse is wanting in the *Vulgate*, as published in the *Complutensian* Polyglot, as also the *Antwerp* and *Paris* Polyglots, which were taken from it. It is wanting also in the Polyglot Psalter of *Porus*, because he did not find it in the Hebrew text.

Verse 14. *The Lord upholdeth all that fall*] נפלים *nophelim*, the *falling*, or those who are not able to keep their feet; the weak. He *shores* them up; he is their *prop*. No man falls through his own weakness *merely;* if he rely on God, the strongest foe cannot shake him.

Verse 15. *The eyes of all wait upon thee*] What a fine figure! The *young* of all animals look up to *their parents for food*. God is here represented as the *universal Father*, providing food for every living creature.

In due season] The kind of food that is suited to every animal, and to all the *stages of life* in *each animal*. This is a wonderful mystery. It is a fact that all are thus provided for; but *how* is it done? All expect it from God, and not one is dsappointed! For,

Verse 16. *Thou openest thine hand*] What a hand is this that holds in it all the food that meets the desires and necessities of the universe of creatures! A very large volume might be written upon this: The proper kinds of food for the various classes of animals.

Verse 17. *The Lord* is *righteous*] It was the similarity of *this* to the omitted verse, which should have been the *fourteenth*, that caused *it* to be omitted.

Verse 18. *The Lord* is *nigh*] Whoever calls upon God in truth, with a sincere and upright heart, one that *truly desires* his salvation, to that person *God is nigh*. The following verse shows he is not only *near* to praying people, but 1. He will *hear their cry*. 2. *Fulfil their desires*. 3. *Save them*. Reader, lift up thy soul in prayer to this merciful God.

Verse 20. *The Lord preserveth*] He is the keeper of all them that love him.

But all the wicked will be destroy.] They call not upon him; they fight against him, and he will confound and destroy them. There is something curious in the שומר *shomer*, the keeper or guardian of the pious; he is שמיד *shamid*, the destroyer of the wicked. The first word implies he is continually keeping them; the second, that he *causes* the others to be *destroyed*.

Verse 21. *Let all flesh bless his holy name*] He is good to all, wants to save all, actually feeds and preserves all. And as near as שמר *shamar* is to שמד *shamad*, so near is he a *Saviour* to those who stand on the brink of *destruction*, if they will look to him.

For the application of all this Psalm to the Church of Christ, see the *analysis*.

ANALYSIS OF THE HUNDRED AND FORTY-FIFTH PSALM

This hymn is most excellent, both as it regards matter and style. The matter is praise to God; the style, the Hebrew alphabet, the better to assist our memories in recording God's praise.

This Psalm contains,—

I. A proem, or protestation to praise God, ver. 1, 2.

II. A celebration of Divine praises through the whole Psalm, from these arguments:—

i. From the greatness of God, ver. 3.

ii. From his wonderful works, ver. 4, which he distinguishes under the following heads:—

1. They are glorious and beautiful, majestic and wonderful, ver. 5.
2. Marvellous, and full of terror, ver. 6.
3. Amiable, and full of goodness, ver. 7-9.

But all wonderful.

III. From his kingdom, and government of it, and in it, ver. 10-21.

IV. A conclusion, ver. 21, in which he performs his protestation of praising God.

I. In the two first verses the psalmist acquaints us what he will do with the whole.

1. "I will extol, I will bless, I will praise."

2. "Thee, my God, my King." I am thy servant, though an earthly king.

3. "Every day," &c. No day shall pass without my praising thee.

4. "For ever and ever." I shall now begin, and a succession of men will continue to hymn and praise thee till the consummation of all things.

II. The first thing he praises God for is his essence. *Great*.

i. "Great is the Lord, and greatly to be praised." Of course this follows:—

"And his greatness is unsearchable." Past our weak capacity to comprehend; higher than the heavens, deeper than hell, having no end. Or if *great* here refer to him as King, then in respect to the extension of his empire over every living creature, he is *great;* he rules over the hearts of the children of men, over their thoughts and affections, and nothing is hidden from his sight.

II. From the essence of God the psalmist passes to his works and effects, which yet set forth his praise: "One generation shall praise," &c. Each age is an eyewitness of thy mighty acts and mercy. From a general consideration of these works he then particularizes:—

1. "For the heavens declare," &c. The sun, moon, and stars, in their splendour, magnitude, and perpetual motion, show forth God's honour and majesty.

2. A second kind of works are the terrible acts of his justice, such as the deluge, the fire of Sodom, Pharaoh's overthrow in the Red Sea, the earth opening to swallow up *Korah, Dathan,* and *Abiram.*

Then there follow his acts of love and mercy, spoken of at large.

1. "Thy great works shall abundantly utter," &c. Thy bounty shall make all generations eloquent in thy praise, *and shall sing of thy righteousness,* in exhibiting thy promised blessings, in bestowing temporal benefits; but above all, in the gifts of thy grace:—In the incarnation, passion, resurrection, ascension, the coming of the Holy Ghost, calling of the Gentiles, justification, sanctification, and eternal life; for all these, and each of them, men shall abundantly utter thy righteousness.

2. "The Lord is gracious," &c.

3. "The Lord is good to all," &c.

4. "His tender mercies are over," &c. Even to the most wicked, God gives time and opportunity for repentance, before he cuts them off.

III. The prophet having sung of God's great works in glory, terror, and mercy, now adds, "All thy works shall praise thee, O Lord." And now he begins a new matter, the erection of his peculiar kingdom in his Church: "A peculiar people," &c. His saints. These will continue to mark thy wonders, and sing to thy glory: these, *thy saints, shall bless thee* for all and in all thy acts. "They shall speak of the glory of thy kingdom," &c. "To make known to the sons of men," &c. "Thy kingdom is an everlasting kingdom," &c. Now the power and glory of Christ's kingdom differ in a fourfold manner from that of the sons of men.

1. The kings on earth require obedience from their subjects; they exact subsidies, tributes, taxes, &c.

2. Earthly kings glory in their power, and rejoice in their dignity; but their crown is full of thorns, anxiety, care, &c.

3. Earthly kings reign but for a time, Christ for ever. 1. "They shall speak of the glory," &c. Excelling all others. 2. "To make known," &c. Thy acts far beyond theirs. 3. "Thy kingdom is an everlasting kingdom," &c. Not so theirs.

The prophet having described Christ's kingdom, begins to extol the qualities and virtues of a good king, which agrees with Christ.

I. His *veracity.*

II. His *probity:* "The Lord is faithful," &c.

III. This is another quality of a good king, so to govern his subjects that they fall not, or to raise them if fallen. Christ sustains and upholds his people, or restores them if they fall from him and return by repentance to him; this was exemplified in *David, Peter,* the *prodigal,* &c. "The eyes of all," &c. "Thou openest thine hand," &c.

IV. Liberality and bounty are excellent qualities in a king who cares for his subjects, and may properly be applied to Christ, who provides for his Church in all things. And—

1. "The eyes of all wait upon thee." In expectation.

2. "And thou givest," &c. It is a gift, not a debt.

3. "Their meat." Every thing fit for them.

4. "In due season." When fit and necessary.

5. "Thou openest thine hand." Givest bountifully.

6. "And satisfiest," &c. The covetous always want; content is from God.

7. "The desire of every living thing," &c. "The Lord is righteous," &c.

V. This is another virtue of a good king, and refers to Christ. "The Lord is nigh unto all them," &c.

VI. This is the sixth quality of a good king, to show himself ready of access to all who implore his aid.

1. *Faith.* For he that prays without it will not be answered.

2. *Hope and confidence.* He prays not seriously who hopes not to be heard.

3. *Love.* No man prays who hates God.

4. *Desire.* Nor that desires not to obtain.

5. *Attention and intention,* without which prayer is idle. "The Lord will fulfil," &c.

VII. The seventh quality of a good king is to grant petitions.

1. "He will fulfil," &c. But with limitation: "So they fear him."

2. "He also will hear their cry." When it is earnest and sincere.

3. "And will save them:" "The Lord preserveth all them," &c.

VIII. The eighth quality of a good king is to spare the humble and destroy the proud. *Parcere subjectis, et debellare superbos.*—VIRGIL. Which Christ will do; he preserves his martyrs in patience, and then receives them into glory.

IV. The conclusion is an acclamation, and answers to the beginning of the Psalm.

1. "My mouth shall speak," &c. This will I do while I live.

2. "And let all flesh," &c. And let all follow his example in giving due praise to this bountiful God.

PSALM CXLVI

The psalmist, full of gratitude, purposes to praise God for ever, 1, 2; and exhorts not to trust in man, not even the most powerful; for which he gives his reasons, 3, 4. The great advantage of trusting in God, 5. The mercies which they who trust in God may expect, 6–9. The Divine government is everlasting, 10.

PRAISE [a]ye the LORD. [b]Praise the LORD, O my soul.

2 [c]While I live will I praise the LORD: I will sing praises unto my God while I have any being.

3 [d]Put not your trust in princes, *nor* in the son of man, in whom *there is* no [e]help.

4 [f]His breath goeth forth, he returneth to his earth; in that very day [g]his thoughts perish.

5 [h]Happy *is he* that *hath* the God of Jacob for his help, whose hope *is* in the LORD his God:

6 [i]Which made heaven, and earth, the sea, and all that therein *is:* which keepeth truth for ever:

7 [k]Which executeth judgment for the oppressed: [l]which giveth food to the hungry. [m]The LORD looseth the prisoners:

8 [n]The LORD openeth *the eyes of* the blind: [o]the LORD raiseth them that are bowed down: the LORD loveth the righteous:

---

[a]Hebrew, *Hallelujah*——[b]Psalm ciii. 1——[c]Psalm civ. 33——[d]Psalm cxviii. 8, 9; Isaiah ii. 22——[e]Or, *salvation*——[f]Psalm civ. 29; Ecclesiastes xii. 7; Isaiah ii. 22——[g]See 1 Corinthians ii. 6——[h]Psalm cxliv. 15;

Jeremiah xvii. 7——[i]Genesis i. 1; Revelation xiv. 7 [k]Psalm ciii. 6——[l]Psalm cvii. 9——[m]Psalm lxviii. 6; cvii. 10, 14——[n]Matthew ix. 30; John ix. 7–32 [o]Psalm cxlv. 14; cxlvii. 6; Luke xiii. 13

NOTES ON PSALM CXLVI

This is the first of the Psalms called *Hallelujah* Psalms, of which there are *five,* and which conclude the book. No author's name is prefixed to this, either in the *Hebrew* or *Chaldee.* But the *Syriac, Vulgate, Septuagint, Æthiopic,* and *Arabic,* attribute it to *Haggai* and *Zechariah.* It was probably written after the captivity, and may refer to the time when Cyrus, prejudiced by the enemies of the Jews, withdrew his order for the rebuilding of the walls of Jerusalem, to which revocation of the royal edict the *third* verse may refer: *Put not your trust in princes,* &c.

Verse 2. *While I live will I praise*] The true feeling of a heart overpowered with a sense of God's goodness.

While I have any being.] בעודי *beodi,* in my continuance, in my progression, my eternal existence. This is very expressive.

Verse 3. *Put not your trust in princes*] This may refer, as has been stated above, to Cyrus, who had revoked his edict for the rebuilding of Jerusalem. Perhaps they had begun to suppose that they were about to owe their deliverance to the Persian king. God permitted this change in the disposition of the king, to teach them the *vanity of confidence in men,* and the necessity of *trusting in himself.*

Verse 4. *His breath goeth forth*] His existence depends merely, under God, on the *air* he breathes. When he ceases to *respire* he ceases to *live;* his body from that moment begins to claim its affinity to the earth; and all his thoughts, purposes, and projects, whether good or evil, come to nought and *perish.* He, then, who has no other dependence, must necessarily be *miserable.*

Verse 5. *Happy* is he *that* hath *the God of Jacob for his help*] While he that trusts in man is *miserable,* he that trusts in God is *happy.* *In the son of man,* בן אדם *ben Adam,* there is no help, תשועה *teshuah,* no *saving principle.* Every *son of Adam* naturally comes

into the world without this, and must continue so till the *Lord open the eyes of the blind,* ver. 8; but a measure of light is given from that true Light *which lighteth every man that cometh into the world.* This son of Adam returns to his earth, לאדמתו *leadmatho,* to *the ground,* from which he was taken; this refers directly to Gen. ii. 7; iii. 19. But he that has the God for his help who helped *Jacob* in his distress, and was with him, and sustained him in and through all adversities, can never be destitute; for this God *changes not;* he lives for ever, and his projects cannot perish. He has *purposed* that Israel shall be delivered from this captivity. *Cyrus may change, but God will not; trust therefore in* HIM. He has all power; he *made heaven and earth;* he has them under his government and at his disposal; and should *earth* itself fail, *heaven* endures. And he keeps his *truth for ever;* and therefore his promises must be fulfilled to them that trust in him. *Fear not.*

Verse 7. *Which executeth judgment for the oppressed*] For those who suffer by *violence* or *calumny.* This may refer to the Israelites, who suffered much by *oppression* from the Babylonians, and by *calumny* from the Samaritans, &c., who had prejudiced the king of Persia against them.

Giving food to the hungry.] No doubt he fed the poor captives by many displays of his peculiar providence.

The Lord looseth the prisoners] And as he has sustained you so long *under* your captivity, so will he bring you *out* of it.

Verse 8. *Openeth* the eyes of *the blind*] He brings us out of our prison-house, from the *shadow of death,* and *opens our eyes* that we may behold the *free light* of the day. And it is the Lord only that can open the eyes of any son of Adam, and give him to see his wretchedness, and where help and salvation may be found.

Raiseth them that are bowed down] Through a sense of their guilt and sinfulness.

9 ᵖThe Lᴏʀᴅ preserveth the strangers; he relieveth the fatherless and widow: ᑫbut the way of the wicked he turneth upside down.

10 ʳThe Lᴏʀᴅ shall reign for ever, *even* thy God, O Zion, unto all generations. Praise ye the Lᴏʀᴅ.

ᵖDeut. x. 8; Psa. lxviii. 5——ᑫPsa. cxlvii. 6

ʳExod. xv. 18; Psa. x. 16; cxlv. 13; Rev. xi. 15

The Lord loveth the righteous] These he makes partakers of a *Divine nature;* and he loves those who bear his own image.

Verse 9. *Preserveth the strangers*] He has *preserved you strangers* in a strange land, where you have been in captivity for *seventy* years; and though in an *enemy's country,* he has provided for the *widows* and *orphans* as amply as if he had been in the promised land.

The way of the wicked he turneth upside down.] He *subverts, turns aside.* They shall not do all the wickedness they wish; they shall not do all that is in their power. In their career he will either *stop* them, turn them *aside,* or *overturn* them.

Verse 10. *The Lord shall reign for ever*] Therefore he can never fail; and he is *thy God, O Zion.* Hitherto he has helped *you* and your *fathers;* and has extended that help from *generation to generation.* Therefore trust in him and bless the Lord.

ANALYSIS OF THE HUNDRED AND FORTY-SIXTH PSALM

The subject of this Psalm is the same with the former.

It is divided into *four* parts:—
I. An exhortation to praise God, ver. 1. Which the psalmist resolves to do, ver. 2.
II. A dehortation from confidence in man, ver. 3, 4.
III. He pronounces them happy who trust in God, ver. 5.
IV. And to persuade to this he uses every reason, ver. 6, to the end.
I. He begins with a dialogism.
1. "He speaks to all: "Praise ye the Lord."
2. Then by an apostrophe he truns to himself: "Praise the Lord, O my soul."
3. And his soul answers: "While I live," &c. While I am, while I shall be.

II. But the prophet, for fear men should trust too much in the great, and not rely wholly upon God, exhorts them: "Put not your trust in princes," &c.

He gives his reasons for the warning:—
1. Because of their impotency: "There is no help in them," &c.
2. Because of their mortality: "Their breath goeth forth," &c.
III. If a man will be happy, the prophet shows him that he must rely upon God alone; for,
1. "Happy is he that hath," &c. Him in whom *Jacob* trusted.
2. "And whose hope," &c. Not in short-lived man.

And this he confirms by many reasons:—
ɪ. From his omnipotence: "He is God the Creator," &c.
ɪɪ. From his veracity: "Who keeps truth for ever," &c. His word is passed for our protection, and he can and will keep it.
ɪɪɪ. From his justice: "He executeth judgment," &c.
ɪᴠ. From his mercy.
1. "He giveth food," &c. Relieves men in their necessities.
2. "The Lord looseth the prisoner." Another act of grace, again.
3. "The Lord openeth the eyes," &c. Whether spiritually or corporeally.
4. "The Lord raiseth them that are bowed down," &c. By sin or misery.
ᴠ. From his love: "The Lord loveth," &c. Of which the effects are:—
1. "The Lord preserveth," &c.
2. "He delivereth the fatherless," &c.
3. But the ungodly find a far different effect: "But the way of the wicked," &c. He makes their glory to perish utterly.

PSALM CXLVII

The psalmist praises God for his goodness to Jerusalem, 1–3; shows his great mercy to them that trust in him, 4–6; he extols him for his mercies, and providential kindness, 7–11; for his defence of Jerusalem, 12–15; for his wonders in the seasons, 16–18; and his word unto Jacob, 19, 20.

XXX. DAY. EVENING PRAYER

A. M. cir. 3485
B. C. cir. 519
Darii I.,
R. Persarum,
cir. annum
secundum

PRAISE ye the Lᴏʀᴅ: for ᵃ*it is* good to sing praises unto our God; ᵇfor *it is* pleasant; *and* ᶜpraise is comely.

2 The Lᴏʀᴅ doth ᵈbuild up Jerusalem: ᵉhe gathereth together the outcasts of Israel.
3 ᶠHe healeth the broken in heart, and bindeth up their ᵍwounds.

A. M. cir. 3485
B. C. cir. 519
Darii I.,
R. Persarum,
cir. annum
secundum

ᵃPsa. xcii. 1——ᵇPsa. cxxxv. 3——ᶜPsa. xxxiii. 1
ᵈPsa. cii. 16——ᵉDeut. xxx. 3

ᶠPsa. li. 17; Isa. lvii. 15; lxi. 1; Luke iv. 18——ᵍHebrew, *griefs*

NOTES ON PSALM CXLVII

This Psalm, which is without *title* in the *Hebrew, Chaldee,* and *Vulgate,* is attributed by the other *Versions* to *Haggai* and *Zechariah.* It

was probably penned after the captivity, when the Jews were busily employed in *rebuilding Jerusalem,* as may be gathered from the *second* and *thirteenth* verses. It may be necessary to remark that all the Versions, except the *Chal-*

A. M. cir. 3485
B. C. cir. 519
Darii I.,
R. Persarum,
cir. annum
secundum

4 [h]He telleth the number of the stars; he calleth them all by *their* names.

5 [l]Great *is* our LORD, and of [k]great power: [l]his [m]understanding *is* infinite.

6 [n]The LORD lifteth up the meek: he casteth the wicked down to the ground.

7 Sing unto the LORD with thanksgiving: sing praise upon the harp unto our God:

8 [o]Who covereth the heaven with clouds, who prepareth rain for the earth, who maketh grass to grow upon the mountains.

9 [p]He giveth to the beast his food, *and* [q]to the young ravens which cry.

10 [r]He delighteth not in the strength of the horse: he taketh not pleasure in the legs of a man.

11 The LORD taketh pleasure in them that fear him, in those that hope in his mercy.

A. M. cir. 3485
B. C. cir. 519
Darii I.,
R. Persarum,
cir. annum
secundum

12 Praise the LORD, O Jerusalem; praise thy God, O Zion.

13 For he hath strengthened the bars of thy gates; he hath blessed thy children within thee.

14 [s]He [t]maketh peace *in* thy borders, *and* [u]filleth thee with the [v]finest of the wheat.

15 [w]He sendeth forth his commandment *upon* earth: his word runneth very swiftly.

16 [x]He giveth snow like wool: he scattereth the hoar frost like ashes.

---

[h]See Gen. xv. 5; Isa. xl. 26——[i]1 Chron. xvi. 25; Psa. xlviii. 1; xcvi. 4; cxlv. 3——[k]Nah. i. 3——[l]Heb. *of his understanding* there is *no number*——[m]Isa. xl. 28 [n]Psa. cxlvi. 8, 9——[o]Job xxxviii. 26, 27; Psa. civ. 13, 14 [p]Job xxxviii. 41; Psa. civ. 27, 28; cxxxvi. 25; cxlv. 15

[q]Job xxxviii. 41; Matt. vi. 26——[r]Psa. xxxiii. 16, 17, 18; Hos. i. 7——[s]Heb. *Who maketh thy border peace* [t]Isa. lx. 17, 18——[u]Psa. cxxxii. 15——[v]Heb. *fat of wheat;* Deut. xxxii. 14; Psa. lxxxi. 16——[w]Psa. cvii. 20; Job xxxvii. 12——[x]Job xxxvii. 6

---

dee, divide this Psalm at the end of the *eleventh* verse, and begin a new Psalm at the *twelfth.* By this division the numbers of the Psalms agree in the Versions with the *Hebrew;* the former having been, till now, *one behind.*

Verse 1. *Praise is comely.*] It is decent, befitting, and proper that every intelligent creature should acknowledge the Supreme Being: and as he does nothing *but good* to the children of men, so they should *speak good of his name.*

Verse 2. *The Lord doth build up*] The psalmist appears to see the *walls* rising under his eye, because the *outcasts* of Israel, those who had been in *captivity,* are now *gathered together* to do the work.

Verse 3. *He healeth the broken in heart*] שבורי, *the shivered* in heart. From the root שבר *shabar,* to *break in pieces,* we have our word *shiver,* to break into *splinters,* into *shivers.* The heart broken in pieces by a sense of God's displeasure.

Verse 4. *He telleth the number of the stars*] He whose knowledge is so exact as to tell every star in heaven, can be under no difficulty to find out and collect all the scattered exiles of Israel.

Verse 5. *His understanding* is *infinite.*] To *his intelligence there is no number:* though he *numbers* the *stars,* his *understanding* is without *number.* It is infinite; therefore, he *can know,* as he *can do,* all things.

Verse 6. *The Lord lifteth up the meek*] The humbled, the afflicted.

Verse 7. *Sing unto the Lord*] ענו *enu,* sing a responsive song, sing in parts, answer one another.

Verse 8. *Who covereth the heaven with clouds*] Collects the vapours together, in order to cause it to rain upon the earth. Even the direction of the winds, the collection of the clouds, and the descent of the rain, are under the especial management of God. These things form a part of his *providential management of the world.*

Maketh grass to grow upon the mountains.] After this clause the *Vulgate,* the *Septuagint,*

Æthiopic, Arabic, and Anglo-Saxon, add, *and herb for the service of man.* It appears that a *hemistich,* or *half-line,* has been lost from the *Hebrew* text; which, according to the above *Versions,* must have stood thus: ועשב לעבדת האדם *veeseb laabodath haadam,* as in Psa. civ. 14: "And herbage for the service of mankind."

Verse 10. *He delighteth not*] The *horse,* among all animals, is most delighted in by man for *beauty, strength,* and *fleetness.* And a *man's legs,* if well proportioned, are more admired than even the finest features of his face. Though God has made *these,* yet they are not his peculiar delight.

Verse 11. *The Lord taketh pleasure in them that fear him*] That are truly religious.

In those that hope is his mercy.] Who are just beginning to seek the salvation of their souls. Even the *cry of the penitent* is pleasing in the ear of the Lord. With this verse the *hundred and forty-sixth* Psalm ends in all the *Versions,* except the *Chaldee.* And the *hundred and forty-seventh* commences with the 12th verse. I believe these to be two distinct Psalms. The subjects of them are not exactly the same, though something similar; and they plainly refer to different periods.

Verse 13. *He hath strengthened the bars of thy gates*] He has enabled thee to complete the *walls of Jerusalem.* From the former part of the Psalm it appears the *walls were then in progress;* from this part, they appear to be completed, and provisions to be brought into the city, to support its inhabitants. The *gates* were set up and well secured by *bars,* so that the grain, &c., was in safety.

Verse 14. *He maketh peace*] They were now no longer troubled with the Samaritans, Moabites, &c.

Verse 15. *He sendeth forth his commandment*] His substantial word. It is here personified, מימרא *meymra,* Chaldee; and appears to be a very active agent running every where, and performing the purposes of his will.

Verse 16. *He giveth snow like wool*] Falling

A. M. cir. 3485
B. C. cir. 519
Darii I.,
R. Persarum,
cir. annum
secundum

17 He casteth forth his ice like morsels: who can stand before his cold?

18 ʸHe sendeth out his word, and melteth them: he causeth his wind to blow, *and* the waters flow.

19 ᶻHe showeth ᵃhis word unto Jacob, ᵇhis statutes and his judgments unto Israel.

20 ᶜHe hath not dealt so with any nation: and *as for his* judgments, they have not known them. Praise ye the LORD.

A. M. cir. 3485
B. C. cir. 519
Darii I.,
R. Persarum,
cir. annum
secundum

ʸVer. 15; see Job xxxvii. 10——ᶻDeut. xxxiii. 2, 3, 4; Psa. lxxvi. 1; lxxviii. 5; ciii. 7

ᵃHeb. *his words*——ᵇMal. iv. 4——ᶜSee Deut. iv. 32, 33, 34; Rom. iii. 1, 2

---

down in large flakes; and in this state nothing in nature has a nearer resemblance to fine white *wool.*

Scattereth the hoar frost like ashes.] Spreading it over the whole face of nature.

Verse 17. He casteth forth his ice] קרחו *korcho,* (probably *hailstones,*) like crumbs.

Who can stand before his cold?] At particular times the cold in the *east* is so very intense as to kill man and beast. *Jacobus de Vitriaco,* one of the writers in the *Gesta Dei per Francos,* says, that in an expedition in which he was engaged against Mount Tabor, on the 24th of December, the cold was so intense that many of the poor people, and the beasts of burden, died by it. And *Albertus Aquensis,* another of these writers, speaking of the cold in Judea, says, that *thirty* of the people who attended Baldwin I. in the mountainous districts near the Dead Sea, were killed by it; and that in that expedition they had to contend with horrible hail and ice, with unheard-of *snow and rain.* From this we find that the winters are often very severe in Judea; and in such cases as the above, we may well call out, "Who can stand against his cold!"

Verse 18. He sendeth out his word] He gives a command: the *south wind* blows; the *thaw* takes place; and the *ice* and *snow* being liquefied, the *waters flow,* where before they were bound up by the ice.

Verse 19. He showeth his word unto Jacob] To no nation of the world beside had God given a revelation of his will.

Verse 20. And as for his judgments] The wondrous ordinances of his law, no nation had known them; and consequently, did not know the glorious things in futurity to which they referred.

ANALYSIS OF THE HUNDRED AND FORTY-SEVENTH PSALM

The parts of this Psalm are *two:*—

I. An exhortation to praise God, ver. 1, which is repeated, ver. 7 and 12.

II. The arguments to persuade to it: God's bounty, wisdom, power, providence, justice, and mercy; dwelt on through the whole Psalm.

I. The exhortation is briefly proposed, "Praise the Lord." Which the prophet, as the chanter of the choir, begins; and then more fully repeats, "Sing unto the Lord," &c. And again, "Praise the Lord, O Jerusalem," &c., ver. 12; where the *Arabic, Greek,* and *Latin* translators begin a new Psalm: but in the *Hebrew* they are conjoined, and form but one hymn.

The prophet, having ended his exhortation, adds his reasons for it.

1. It is pleasant and becoming.

2. His bounty in building *Jerusalem,* and bringing back the dispersed, ver. 2. In comforting the distressed, ver. 3. For his wisdom, ver.

4. For his power, ver. 5. For his mercy and justice, ver. 6.

His first arguments are drawn from the thing itself.

I. Good: "For it is good," &c.

For many reasons this may be called *good.*

1. For it is God's command, and must not be neglected.

2. It elevates the heart from earth to heaven.

3. Good again, because we are bound to it by obligations.

II. "To praise God is pleasant."

1. Because it proceeds from love.

2. Because it is pleasant to perform our duty, and the end of our creation.

3. Because God is pleased with it: "He that offereth me praise, glorifieth me," &c.

4. Because God is pleased with the virtues of faith, hope, charity, humility, devotion, &c., of which praise is the effect.

III. "It is comely." There is no sin greater than that of ingratitude.

These are the first arguments the prophet uses, and they are drawn from the nature of the thing itself: they may apply to all ages of the Church.

He dwells upon the deliverance of *Israel* from captivity.

1. "The Lord doth build up" his Church, the seat of his sanctuary. He hath restored our policy and religion.

2. "He gathereth together," &c. The banished and scattered ones; the Gentiles.

3. "He healeth the broken in heart," &c. Oppressed by captivity or sin.

4. "And bindeth up," &c. Like a good surgeon. The second argument is drawn from his *wisdom.*

1. "He telleth the number of the stars," &c. A thing to man impossible.

2. "He calleth them," &c. They are his army, and he knows them.

By the stars in this place some understand God's saints.

1. The stars are infinite in number. So are the saints.

2. Among them are planets. Saints have their circuits; and always revolve round him, the Sun of righteousness.

3. The stars shine clearest in the night. The saints in persecution.

4. One star differeth from another in glory. Some saints excel others in piety.

5. The stars are above. The saints' conversation is in heaven.

6. The stars are obscured by clouds. The Church is sometimes obscured by affliction and persecution.

His third argument is drawn from God's *power:* "Great is the Lord," &c.

His fourth argument is drawn from God's *justice* and *mercy.*

1. His mercy: "The Lord lifteth up the meek," &c. Sustains and exalts them.

2. His justice: "He casteth the wicked down," &c. They shall not always triumph.

But, before the prophet proceeds farther, he repeats:—

1. "Sing unto the Lord with thanksgiving." Do it in words.

2. "Sing praises upon the harp," &c. Do it in works.

Then he proceeds to argue from God's *providence*.

1. "Who covereth the heaven," &c. Not to obscure, but fructify the earth.

2. "Who maketh grass to grow," &c. By his blessing on the most barren places.

3. "He giveth to the beast," &c. They gather it from his supplies.

4. "And to the young ravens," &c. No bird suffers its young so soon to provide for themselves; but God hears and sends them food. *Christ* himself uses this argument to encourage us to rely on God's providence, Matt. vi.

Should the distrustful *Jew* argue, Alas, we have no strength, ammunition, horse, or armour, the prophet replies:—

1. "He delighteth not," &c. When used as a warlike creature.

2. "He taketh not pleasure," &c. In the nimbleness of man, when used for warlike preparations.

But he delights in his servants.

1. "The Lord taketh pleasure," &c. In those who obey and love him.

2. "In those that hope," &c. Have faith and confidence in him.

3. He again repeats his proposition, and calls upon the Church to perform it: "Praise the Lord, O Jerusalem," &c. "Thy God, O Zion." Should others be negligent, be not ye.

He then adds four reasons why *Zion* should praise him: 1. Security and defence. 2. Benediction. 3. Peace. 4. Substance.

1. Security: "For he hath strengthened," &c.

2. Benediction: "He hath blessed," &c. His officers with wisdom, &c.

3. Peace: "He maketh peace." *The vision of peace* is the literal interpretation of the word *Jerusalem*.

4. Provision: "Filleth thee with the finest of the wheat," &c.

That *God* has done this for Jerusalem, is evident from his general providence over the world. And this argument the prophet uses: "He sendeth forth his commandment upon earth," &c. For,

1. "He giveth snow like wool." Beautiful in appearance, and in order to preserve vegetables from the nipping but necessary frost, when long continued.

2. "He scattereth the hoar frost," &c. Thickening the air with it like ashes; freezing all the vapours that float in it.

3. "He casteth forth his ice," &c. Fragments of ice.

4. "Who can stand before his cold?" Endure it unprovided.

But having described all these powerful agents, the prophet next shows how easily they are governed by his *word*.

1. "He sendeth out his word, and melteth them."

2. "He causeth his wind to blow," &c. And the ice and snow return to water. All these are his, and on him we must depend for safety and comfort.

By these God teaches alike nations to acknowledge him.

But there are particular acts which refer to his people; for,

1. "He showeth his word," &c. By *Moses* and the prophets.

2. "He hath not dealt so," &c. None at that time, but since to his Church.

3. "As for his judgments," &c. His evangelical precepts. He is sending forth his word; the nations could not find out his precepts otherwise: therefore for this *praise ye the Lord*.

PSALM CXLVIII

The psalmist calls on all the creation to praise the Lord. The angels and visible heavens, 1–6; the earth and the sea, 7; the meteors, 8; mountains, hills, and trees, 9; beasts, reptiles, and fowls, 10; kings, princes, and mighty men, 11; men, women, and children, 12, 13; and especially all the people of Israel, 14.

A. M. cir. 3485
B. C. cir. 519
Darii I.,
R. Persarum,
cir. annum
secundum

P RAISE [a] ye the Lord. Praise ye the Lord from the heavens: praise him in the heights.

2 [b] Praise ye him, all his angels: praise ye him, all his hosts.

3 Praise ye him, sun and moon: praise him, all ye stars of light.

A. M. cir. 3485
B. C. cir. 519
Darii I.,
R. Persarum,
cir. annum
secundum

---

[a] Heb. *Hallelujah*

[b] Psa. ciii. 20, 21

NOTES ON PSALM CXLVIII

This Psalm has no title: but by the *Syriac* it is attributed to *Haggai* and *Zechariah;* and the *Septuagint* and the *Æthiopic* follow it. As a hymn of praise, this is the most sublime in the whole book.

Verse 1. *Praise ye the Lord from the heavens*] The *Chaldee* translates, "Praise the Lord, ye holy creatures from the heavens. Praise him, ye armies of supreme angels. Praise him, all ye angels who minister before him." מן השמים *min hashshamayim* signifies whatever belongs to the heavens, all their inhabitants; as מן הארץ *min haarets*, ver. 7, signifies all that belongs to the earth, all its inhabitants and productions.

Verse 3. *Praise ye him, sun and moon*] The meaning of this address and all others to *inanimate nature*, is this: Every work of God's hand partakes so much of his perfections, that

A. M. cir. 3485
B. C. cir. 519
Darii I.,
R. Persarum,
cir. annum
secundum

4 Praise him, °ye heavens of heavens, and ᵈye waters that *be* above the heavens.

5 Let them praise the name of the LORD: for ᵉhe commanded, and they were created.

6 ᶠHe hath also established them for ever and ever: he hath made a decree which shall not pass.

7 Praise the LORD from the earth, ᵍye dragons, and all deeps:

A. M. cir. 3485
B. C. cir. 519
Darii I.,
R. Persarum,
cir. annum
secundum

8 Fire, and hail; snow, and vapour; stormy wind ʰfulfilling his word:

9 ⁱMountains, and all hills; fruitful trees, and all cedars:

10 Beasts, and all cattle; creeping things, and ᵏflying ˡfowl:

11 Kings of the earth, and all people; princes, and all judges of the earth:

12 Both young men, and maidens; old men, and children:

ᶜ1 Kings viii. 27; 2 Cor. xii. 2——ᵈGen. i. 7——ᵉGen. i. 1, 6, 7; Psa. xxxiii. 6, 9——ᶠPsa. lxxxix. 37; cxix. 90, 91; Jer. xxxi. 35, 36; xxxiii. 25——ᵍIsa. xliii. 20

ʰPsa. cxlvii. 15–18——ⁱIsa. xliv. 23; xlix. 13; lv. 12 ᵏHeb. *birds of wing*——ˡGen. i. 26; ii. 19; vii. 23; viii. 17; ix. 2, 20; Deut. iv. 17; Ezek. xxxix. 17; Dan. vii. 6

---

it requires only to be studied and known, in order to show forth the manifold *wisdom, power,* and *goodness* of the Creator.

Sars of light] The brightest and most luminous stars: probably the planets may be especially intended.

Verse 4. Heavens of heavens] Heavens exceeding heavens. Systems of systems extending as far beyond the solar system, as it does beyond the lowest deeps. The endless systematic concatenation of worlds.

Ye waters that be above the heavens.] This refers to Gen. i. 7, where see the notes. Clouds, vapours, air, exhalations, rain, snow, and meteors of every kind.

Verse 5. He commanded, and they were created.] He spake the word expressive of the idea in his infinite mind; and they sprang into being according to that idea.

Verse 6. He hath also stablished them] He has determined their respective *revolutions,* and the *times* in which they are performed, so exactly to show his all-comprehensive wisdom and skill, that they have never passed the line marked out by his *decree,* nor intercepted each other in the vortex of space, through revolutions continued for nearly 6000 years.

Verse 7. Praise the Lord from the earth] As, in the first address, he calls upon the heavens, and all that *belong to them;* so here, in this second part, he calls upon the earth, and all *that belong to it.*

Ye dragons] תנינים *tanninim,* whales, porpoises, sharks, and sea-monsters of all kinds.

And all deeps] Whatsoever is contained in the sea, whirlpools, eddies, ground tides, with the astonishing flux and reflux of the ocean.

Every thing, in its *place* and *nature,* shows forth the perfections of its Creator.

Verse 8. Fire, and hail; snow, and vapours] All kinds of meteors, water, and fire, in all their forms and combinations. And *air,* whether in the gentle *breeze,* the *gale,* the *whirlwind,* the *tempest,* or the *tornado;* each accomplishing an especial purpose, and fulfilling a particular *will* of the Most High.

Verse 9. Mountains, and all hills] Whether *primitive, secondary,* or *alluvial;* of *ancient* or *recent formation,* with all their *contents,* quarries, mines, and minerals. But what a profusion of wisdom and skill is lavished on these! To instance only in the different metals, earths, and minerals; especially the precious stones.

Fruitful trees] עץ פרי *ets peri, fruit trees* of all kinds.

And all cedars] Every kind of *forest tree.* The formation of the *fruits,* their infinitely varied *hues* and *savours,* proclaim the unsearchable wisdom and goodness of God: not less so, the *growth, structure,* and *various qualities* and *uses* of the *forest trees.*

Verse 10. Beasts] החיה *hachaiyah, wild beasts* of every kind.

All cattle] בהמה *behemah,* all *domestic animals;* those used for the service of the *house,* and those for *agricultural* purposes.

Creeping things] All the class of *reptiles,* from the *boa constrictor,* that can combat, kill, and swallow whole the *royal tiger,* to the *cobra de manille,* a poisonous reptile as small as a *fine needle;* with those still smaller animals that are found in water, and require the power of the microscope to bring them to view. In the production, preservation, habits, and properties of all these, there is a profusion of wisdom and economy that would require ages to exhibit.

Flying fowl] The structure of fowls is astonishing; and the exact *mathematical manner* in which *flying fowls swim* the air, and steer their course 'wheresoever they will; the feathers, and their *construction,* with the *muscles* which give them motion; strike the observer of nature with *astonishment* and *delight.*

Verse 11. Kings of the earth] As being representatives of the Most High; and *all people*— the nations governed by them. *Princes,* as governors of provinces, and *all judges* executing those laws that bind man to man, and regulate and preserve civil society; *praise God,* from whom ye have derived your *power* and *influence:* for *by him kings reign.* And let the *people* magnify God for *civil* and *social institutions,* and for the *laws* by which, under him, their *lives* and *properties* are preserved.

Verse 12. Both young men, and maidens] Who are in the bloom of youth, and in the height of health and vigour; know that God is your Father; and let the morning and energy of your days be devoted to *him.*

Old men, and children] Very appropriately united here, as the *beginning* and *conclusion* of *life* present nearly the same passions, appetites, caprices, and infirmities: yet in both the beneficence, all-sustaining power, and goodness of God are seen.

A. M. cir. 3485
B. C. cir. 519
Darii I.,
R. Persarum,
cir. annum
secundum

13 Let them praise the name of the LORD: for ᵐhis name alone is ⁿexcellent; ᵒhis glory *is* above the earth and heaven.

14 ᵖHe also exalteth the horn of his people, ᑫthe praise of all his saints; *even* of the children of Israel, ʳa people near unto him. Praise ye the LORD.

A. M. cir. 3485
B. C. cir. 519
Darii I.,
R. Persarum,
cir. annum
secundum

ᵐPsa. viii. 1; Isa. xii. 4——ⁿHeb. *exalted*——ᵒPsa. cxiii.

4——ᵖPsa. lxxv. 10——ᑫPsa. cxlix. 9——ʳEph. ii. 17

Verse 13. *Let them*] All already specified, *praise the name of Jehovah,* because he excels all beings: and *his glory,* as seen in creating, preserving, and governing all things, is ‫בְּ‬ *al,* upon or over, the *earth* and *heaven.* All *space* and *place,* as well as the *beings* found in them, show forth the manifold wisdom and goodness of God.

Verse 14. *He also exalteth the horn*] Raises to power and authority *his people.*

The praise] Jehovah is the subject of the praise of all his *saints.*

A people near unto him.] The only people who know him, and make their approaches unto him with the *sacrifices* and *offerings* which he has himself prescribed. Praise ye the Lord!

O what a hymn of praise is here! It is a *universal chorus!* All created nature have a share, and all perform their respective parts.

All *intelligent beings* are especially called to praise him who made them in his love, and sustains them by his beneficence. *Man* particularly, in all the stages of his being—*infancy, youth, manhood,* and *old age:* all human beings have their peculiar interest in the great Father of the spirits of all flesh.

He loves *man,* wheresoever found, of whatsoever colour, in whatever circumstances, and in all the stages of his pilgrimage from his *cradle* to his *grave.*

Let the *lisp* of the *infant,* the *shout* of the *adult,* and the *sigh* of the *aged,* ascend to the universal parent, as a gratitude-offering. He guards those who *hang upon the breast;* controls and directs the *headstrong* and *giddy,* and sustains *old age* in its infirmities; and sanctifies to it the sufferings that bring on the termination of life.

Reader, this is thy God! How great, how good, how merciful, how compassionate! Breathe thy soul up to him; breathe it into him; and let it be preserved in his bosom till mortality be swallowed up of life, and all that is imperfect be done away.

Jesus is thy sacrificial offering; Jesus is thy Mediator. He has taken thy humanity, and placed it on the throne! He creates all things new; and faith in his blood will bring thee to his glory! Amen! hallelujah!

The beautiful morning hymn of Adam and Eve, (Paradise Lost, book v., line 153, &c.,)—

"These are thy glorious works, Parent of good;
Almighty, thine this universal frame," &c.—

has been universally admired. How many have spoken loud in its praises, who have never attempted to express their feelings in a stanza of the *hundred and forty-eighth* Psalm! But to the rapturous adorers of Milton's poetry what is the song of David, or this grand music of the spheres! Know this, O forgetful man, that *Milton's* morning hymn is a *paraphrase of this Psalm,* and is indebted to it for every excel-

lency it possesses. It is little else than the psalmist speaking in English instead of Hebrew verse.

ANALYSIS OF THE HUNDRED AND FORTY-EIGHTH PSALM

The psalmist calls upon the whole creation to be instrumental in praising God. By which he shows,—

I. His ardent desire that God be praised. As if creatures, endowed with reason, were too few, therefore he calls on inanimate things to join and be heralds of his wondrous works.

II. His intention; what he would and could have done.

III. That what could be done should be done.

IV. That all really do praise him in their kind and manner.

This Psalm is disposed into excellent distribution.

1. He calls upon celestial creatures in general; 2. In particular. 1. On angels: "Praise ye the Lord from the heavens," &c. Ye of celestial order. 2. "Praise him in the heights," &c. The heavens above. 3. "Praise him, all his hosts," &c. Which in St. Luke are called *the heavenly host.*

2. "Praise ye him, sun, moon, and stars." Though not with the voice, yet by your beauty, motion, light, efficacy, &c.

He mentions the whole body of the heavenly orbs.

1. "Praise him, ye heavens of heavens," &c. The highest state of bliss.

2. "And ye waters," &c. All the orbs above the air, in Scripture called *heavens;* and the *waters* that are above the firmament.

And in the two next verses he gives the reason.

1. "He commanded," &c. They are his creatures, therefore,—

2. "He hath established them," &c. They are incorruptible.

From the heavens he now descends to the earth, air, water, &c.: "Praise the Lord from the earth," &c. All ye elementary substances.

1. "Ye dragons." Whales, great fishes.

2. "All deeps." All kinds of waters.

3. "Fire and hail," &c. Meteors, &c.

4. "Mountains and hills," &c.

5. "Fruitful trees," &c. Trees fit to build with and fruit-trees.

6. "Beasts and all cattle." Both wild and tame.

7. "Creeping things," &c. Worms and serpents.

8. "And all flying fowls."

And, lastly, he cites all mankind to praise God.

1. "The highest kings," &c. They who command, and they who obey.

2. "Princes, and all judges," &c. All inferior magistrates.

3. "Both young men and maidens." Both sexes.

4. "Old men and children,"—all ages: "Let them praise the name of the Lord."

And for this reason:—

1. "For his name is excellent alone." No name is so sublime and worthy.

2. "His glory is above the earth and heaven." All good comes from him.

The prophet concludes this Psalm with God's goodness to the Church, which furnishes him with another reason:—

1. He also "exalts the horn," &c. The power and glory of his people.

2. "He is the praise," &c. The Guide of *Israel*.

3. "Even of the children of Israel," &c. A people consecrated to God. All which is to be understood not merely of *Israel* according to the flesh, but God's spiritual Church. Now those who are true *Israelites*, and those especially, he excites to sing,—

"Hallelujah! Praise ye the Lord!"

PSALM CXLIX

All the congregation are invited to praise God for his mercies, 1–3. Their great privileges, 4, 5. Their victories, 6–9.

PRAISE ^a^ye the LORD. ^b^Sing unto the LORD a new song, *and* his praise in the congregation of saints.

2 Let Israel rejoice in ^c^him that made him: let the children of Zion be joyful in their ^d^King.

3 ^e^Let them praise his name ^f^in the dance:

let them sing praises unto him with the timbrel and harp.

4 For ^g^the LORD taketh pleasure in his people: ^h^he will beautify the meek with salvation.

5 Let the saints be joyful in glory: let them ^i^sing aloud upon their beds.

---

^a^Heb. *Hallelujah*——^b^Psa. xxxiii. 3; Isa. xlii. 10 ^c^See Job xxxv. 10; Psa. c. 3; Isa. liv. 5——^d^Zech. ix. 9;

Matt. xxi. 5——^e^Psa. lxxxi. 2; cl. 4——^f^Or, *with the pipe* ^g^Psa. xxxv. 27——^h^Psa. cxxxii. 16——^i^Job xxxv. 10

NOTES ON PSALM CXLIX

This seems to be an *epinikion*, or *song of triumph*, after some glorious victory; probably in the time of the *Maccabees*. It has been also understood as predicting the success of the Gospel in the nations of the earth. According to the *Syriac*, it concerns the *new temple*, by which the *Christian Church* is meant. It has no *title* in the Hebrew, nor in any of the *Versions*, and no *author's* name.

Verse 1. *Sing unto the Lord a new song*] That is, as we have often had occasion to remark, an *excellent song*, the best we can possibly pronounce. So the word חדש *chadash* is often understood; and so the word *novus*, "new," was often used among the Latin writers:—

Pollio amat nostram, quamvis sit rustica, musam.
Pollio et ipse facit NOVA CARMINA.
         VIRG. Ecl. iii., ver. 84.

Pollio loves my lines, although rude:
Pollio himself makes *excellent* odes.

Tamely and inexpressively translated by Dryden:—

"Pollio my rural verse vouchsafes to read.
My Pollio writes himself."

O what a falling off is here!

Servius, in his comment on *nova*, says, *magna, miranda. Nova* means *great, admirable.*

So on *novum nectar*, Ecl. v., ver. 71, he says, id est, *magna dulcedo;* "nectar of EXCELLENT flavour."

Congregation of saints.] The *Israelites*, who were, by *profession* and *by injunction*, a *holy people.*

Verse 2. *In him that made him*] Let them remember in their exultations to give all glory to the *Lord;* for he is the Author of their *being* and their *blessings*. And let them know that he is their *King* also; and that they should submit to his *authority*, and be guided and regulated in their hearts and conduct by his *laws*.

Verse 3. *Let them praise his name in the dance*] במחול *bemachol, with the pipe*, or some kind of *wind music*, classed here with תף *toph*, the *tabor* or *drum*, and כנור *kinnor*, the *harp*. "מחול *machol*," says *Parkhurst*, "some *fistular wind-instrument of music, with holes*, as a *flute, pipe*, or *fife*, from חל *chal*, to make a hole or opening." I know no place in the Bible where מחול *machol* and מחלת *machalath* mean *dance* of any kind; they constantly signify some kind of *pipe*.

Verse 4. *The Lord taketh pleasure in his people*] The pleasure or good will of God is in his people: he loves them ardently, and will load them with his benefits, while they are *humble* and *thankful;* for,

He will beautify] יפאר *yephaer*, he will make *fair*, the *meek*, ענוים *anavim*, the *lowly*, the *humble with salvation*, בישועה *bishuah;* which St. Jerome thus translates, *Et exaltabit mansuetos in Jesu*, "And he will exalt the meek in Jesus." Whether this rendering be correct or not, there is no other way by which the *humble* soul can be exalted, but by JESUS, as the redeeming Saviour.

Verse 5. *Let the saints be joyful in glory*]

6 *Let* the high *praises* of God *be* [k]in their mouth, and [l]a two-edged sword in their hand;

7 To execute vengeance upon the heathen, *and* punishments upon the people;

8 To bind their kings with chains, and their nobles with fetters of iron;

9 [m]To execute upon them the judgment written: [n]this honour have all his saints. Praise ye the LORD.

---

[k]Heb. *in their throat*——[l]Heb. iv. 12; Rev. i. 16

[m]Deut. vii. 1, 2——[n]Psa. cxlviii. 14

Let them be gloriously joyful: seeing themselves so *honoured* and so *successful*, let them be joyful. God has put *glory* or *honour* upon them; let them give him the thanks due to his name.

Sing aloud upon their beds.] While they are reclining on their *couches*. At their festal banquets, let them shout the praises of the Lord. In imitation of this we often have at our public entertainments the following words sung, taken from the *Vulgate* of Psalm cxv. 1: Non nobis Domine non nobis; sed nomini tuo da gloriam! super misericordia tua et veritate tua. "Not unto us, O Lord, not unto us, but unto thy name give glory, for thy mercy and for thy truth's sake." Let them mingle their feasting with Divine songs. This reclining on couches, while they take their food, is still practised in Asiatic countries.

Verse 6. Let *the high* praises *of God*] Let them sing songs the most sublime, with the loudest noise consistent with *harmony*.

And a two-edged sword in their hand] Perhaps there is an allusion here to the manner in which the Jews were obliged to labour in rebuilding the walls of Jerusalem: "Every one with one of his hands wrought in the work, and with the other hand held a weapon," Neh. iv. 17.

The *two-edged sword*, in Hebrew, is פִיפִיּוֹת *pipiyoth*, "mouth mouths."

Verse 7. *To execute vengeance upon the heathen*] This may refer simply to their purpose of defending themselves to the uttermost, should their enemies attack them while building their wall: and they had every reason to believe that God would be with them; and that, if their enemies did attack them, they should be able to inflict the severest punishment upon them.

Punishments upon the people] The unfaithful and treacherous *Jews;* for we find that some, even of their *nobles*, had joined with *Sanballat* and *Tobiah;* (see Neh. vi. 17-19:) and it appears also that many of them had formed alliances with those heathens, which were contrary to the law; see Neh. xiii. 15-29.

Verse 8. *To bind their kings with chains, and their nobles with fetters of iron*] That is, if these kings, governors of provinces, and chiefs among the people, had attacked them, God would have enabled them to defeat them, take their generals prisoners, and lead them in triumph to Jerusalem. It is certain also that in the times of the *Maccabees* the Jews had many signal victories over the *Samaritans, Philistines,* and *Moabites;* and over *Antiochus,* king of *Syria.* See the Books of the *Maccabees.* To these the psalmist may here refer in a *hyperbolical* way, not unusual in poetry and in songs of triumph.

Verse 9. *To execute upon them the judgment written*] In Deut. vii. 1, &c., God promises his

people complete victory over all their enemies, and over the heathen. God repeatedly promises such victories to his faithful people; and this is, properly speaking, the *judgment written,* i. e., foretold.

This honour have all his saints.] They shall all be supported, defended, and saved by the Lord. Israel had this honour, and such victories over their enemies, while they continued faithful to their God. When they relapsed into iniquity, their enemies prevailed against them; they were defeated, their city taken, their temple burnt to the ground, more than a million of themselves slaughtered, and the rest led into captivity; and, scattered through the world, they continue without king, or temple, or true worship, to the present day.

"But do not these last verses contain a *promise* that all the nations of the earth shall be brought under the dominion of the *Church of Christ;* that all *heathen* and *ungodly kings* shall be put down, and *pious men* put in their places?" I do not think so. I believe God never intended that his Church should have the civil government of the world. His *Church,* like its *Founder* and *Head,* will never be a *ruler and divider among men.* The men who, under pretence of *superior sanctity,* affect this, are not of God; the truth of God is not in them; they are puffed up with pride, and fall into the condemnation of the devil. *Wo unto the inhabitants of the earth,* when the *Church* takes the *civil government* of the world into its hand! Were it possible that God should trust *religious people* with civil government, *anarchy* would soon ensue; for every professed believer in Christ would consider himself on a par with any other and every other believer, the *right to rule* and the *necessity to obey* would be immediately lost, and every man would do what was right in his own eyes; for, where the grace of God makes *all equal,* who can presume to say, I have Divine authority to govern my fellow? The Church of Rome has claimed this right; and the pope, in consequence, became a secular prince; but the nations of the world have seen the vanity and iniquity of the claim, and refused allegiance. Those whom it did govern, with force and with cruelty did it rule them; and the odious yoke is now universally cast off. Certain *enthusiasts* and *hypocrites,* not of that Church, have also attempted to set up a *fifth monarchy,* a *civil government* by the SAINTS! and diabolic saints they were. To such pretenders God gives neither countenance nor support. The secular and spiritual government God will ever keep distinct; and the Church shall have no power but that of *doing good;* and this only in proportion to its holiness, heavenly-mindedness, and piety to God. That the verses above may be understood in a *spiritual sense,* as applicable to the influence of the *word of God preached,* may be seen in the following analysis.

ANALYSIS OF THE HUNDRED AND FORTY-NINTH
PSALM

In this Psalm the saints of God are excited
to give due thanks.

I. For the grace and favour received from
God, ver. 1-5.

II. For the glory and privileges they shall
receive, ver. 5-9.

I. "Let Israel rejoice," &c. The saints.
Which he amplifies:

1. The saints: "For praise is not comely in
the mouth of sinners."

2. The quality of the song: "A new song."
By renewed men.

From the place in which it must be done.
The public congregation.

4. From the manner. With alacrity.

5. From the object. God, their Creator and
King: "Let Israel rejoice," &c.

And this part he concludes with a strong
reason:

1. "For the Lord taketh pleasure," &c. He
loves those who most resemble him in holiness
and purity.

2. "He will beautify the meek," &c. The
people who trust him he will save.

II. And now he describes their future
glory.

1. "Let the saints," &c. None others will
he beautify.

2. "Let them rejoice," &c. The mansions prepared for them in heaven. There they rest
from labour, but not from praise.

Their work is twofold: Present and future.

1. Present: "The high praises," &c. The
highest that can be thought of.

2. For the future: "Let a two-edged sword,"
&c. When Christ shall come to judgment, the
saints at the last shall be judges.

Then the exercise of this judiciary power
shall be,

1. "To execute vengeance," &c. To judge
them to punishment.

2. "To bind their kings with chains," &c.
The phrase is metaphorical. "Bind him hand
and foot," &c.; Matt. xxii. Christ's iron sceptre
shall bruise the head of his enemies.

3. "To execute upon them the judgment
written," &c. Against evil-doers.

He concludes with an acclamation. This
glory of sitting with Christ and judging the
world, is the glory of all saints. *Hallelujah.*

PSALM CL

*A general exhortation to praise God, 1, 2. With the trumpet, psaltery, and harp, 3. With the timbrel and dance,
stringed instruments and organs, 4. With the cymbals, 5. All living creatures are called upon to join in the
exercise.*

PRAISE [a]ye the LORD. Praise God in his
sanctuary: praise him in the firmament
of his power.

2 [b]Praise him for his mighty acts: praise
him according to his excellent [c]greatness.

3 Praise him with the sound of the [d]trum-

---

[a]Heb. *Hallelujah*——[b]Psa. cxlv. 5, 6

[c]Deut. iii. 24——[d]Or, *cornet;* Psa. xcviii. 6

NOTES ON PSALM CL.

This Psalm is without title and author in the
Hebrew, and in all the ancient versions. It is
properly the full chorus of all *voices* and *instruments* in the temple, at the conclusion of the
grand *Hallelujah,* to which the five concluding
Psalms belong.

Verse 1. *Praise God in his sanctuary*] In
many places we have the compound word
הללו־יה *halelu-yah,* praise ye Jehovah; but
this is the first place in which we find הללו־אל
halelu-el, praise God, or the strong God. Praise
him who is Jehovah, the infinite and self-existent Being; and praise him who is God, *El* or
Elohim, the great God in covenant with mankind, to bless and save them unto eternal life.

In his sanctuary—in the temple; in whatever
place is dedicated to his service. Or, *in his
holiness*—through his own holy influence in
your hearts.

The firmament of his power.] Through the
whole expanse, to the utmost limits of his
power. As רקיע *rakia* is the firmament of vast
expanse that surrounds the globe, and probably

that in which all the celestial bodies of the
solar system are included, it may have that
meaning here. Praise him whose power and
goodness extend through all worlds; and let
the inhabitants of all those worlds share in
the grand chorus, that it may be universal.

Verse 2. *For his mighty acts*] Whether
manifested in creation, government, mercy or
justice.

His excellent greatness.] כרב גדלו *kerob
gudlo,* according to the multitude of his magnitude, or of his majesty. Æᵹᶜᵉꞃ mæniᴣ ꝑeaꝇðnyꞃꝛe
muceꝇnyꞃꝛe hiꞃ; After the manyfoldness of his
mickleness.—Anglo-Saxon. After the mykelnes
of his greathede.—Old Psalter. Let the praise
be such as is becoming so great, so holy, and
so glorious a Being.

Verse 3. *The sound of the trumpet*] שופר
sophar, from its noble, cheering, and majestic
sound; for the original has this ideal meaning.

With the psaltery] נבל *nebel;* the nabla, a
hollow stringed instrument; perhaps like the
guitar, or the old *symphony.*

And harp.] כנור *kinnor,* another *stringed* instrument, played on with the *hands* or *fingers.*

pet: ᵉpraise him with the psaltery and harp.

4 Praise him ᶠwith the timbrel and ᵍdance: praise him with ʰstringed instruments and organs.

5 Praise him upon the loud ⁱcymbals: praise him upon the high-sounding cymbals.

6 Let every thing that hath breath praise the LORD. Praise ye the LORD.

ᵉPsa. lxxxi. 2; cxlix. 3——ᶠExod. xv. 20——ᵍOr, *pipe;* Psa. cxlix. 3

ʰPsa. xxxiii. 2; xcii. 3; cxliv. 9; Isa. xxxviii. 20——ⁱ1 Chron. xv. 16, 19, 28; xvi. 5; xxv. 1, 6

Verse 4. *Praise him with the timbrel*] תֹּף *toph, drum, tabret,* or *tomtom,* or *tympanum* of the ancients; a skin stretched over a broad hoop; perhaps something like the *tambarine.* Anglo-Saxon; 𝔤lig-beam, the *glad pipe. Taburne;* Old Psalter.

And dance] מָחוֹל *machol,* the *pipe.* The *croude* or *crowthe:* Old Psalter; a species of *violin.* It never means *dance;* see the note on Psa. cxlix. 3. *Crwth* signifies a *fiddle* in Welsh.

Stringed instruments] מִנִּים *minnim.* This literally signifies *strings put in order;* perhaps a *triangular kind of hollow instrument* on which the strings were regularly placed, growing *shorter* and *shorter* till they came to a *point.* This would give a variety of sounds, from a deep bass to a high treble. In an ancient MS. Psalter before me, David is represented in two places, playing on such an instrument. It may be the sambuck, or psaltery, or some such instrument.

Organs.] עוּגָב *ugab.* Very likely the *syrinx* or *mouth organ;* Pan's pipe; both of the ancients and moderns. The *fistula, septem, disparibus nodis conjuncta,* made of seven pieces of cane or thick *straw,* of unequal lengths, applied to the lips, each blown into, according to the *note* intended to be expressed. This instrument is often met with in the ancient *bucolic* or *pastoral* writers.

Verse 5. *Loud cymbals*] צִלְצְלִים *tseltselim.* Two hollow plates of brass, which, being struck together, produced a sharp clanging sound. This instrument is still in use. What the *high-sounding cymbals* meant I know not; unless those of a *larger make,* struck above the head, and consequently emitting a louder sound.

Verse 6. *Let every thing that hath breath*] Either to make a vocal noise, or a sound by blowing into *pipes, fifes, flutes, trumpets,* &c. Let all join together, and put forth all your *strength* and all your *skill* in sounding the praises of Jehovah; and then let a *universal burst* with HALLELUJAH! close the grand ceremony. It is evident that this Psalm has no other meaning than merely the summoning up all the *voices,* and all the *instruments,* to complete the service in FULL CHORUS.

Of such peculiar importance did the *Book of Psalms* appear to our blessed Lord and his apostles, that they have quoted nearly fifty of them several times in the New Testament. There is scarcely a state in human life that is not distinctly marked in them; together with all the variety of experience which is found, not merely among *pious Jews,* but among *Christians,* the most deeply acquainted with the things of Christ.

The minister of God's word, who wishes to preach *experimentally,* should have frequent recourse to this sacred book; and by consider-

ing the various parts that refer to Jesus Christ and the Christian Church, he will be able to build up the people of God on their most holy faith; himself will grow in grace, and in the knowledge of God; and he will ever have an abundance of the most profitable *matter* for the edification of the Church of Christ.

ANALYSIS OF THE HUNDRED AND FIFTIETH PSALM

This Psalm is the same with the former. In the *hundred and forty-eighth,* all creatures are invited to praise God; in the *hundred and forty-ninth,* men especially, and those who are in the Church; but in this, that they praise him with all kinds of instruments.

I. An invitation to praise God, which word he repeats thirteen times, according to the thirteen attributes of God, as the rabbins reckon them.

II. That this be done with all sorts of instruments, intimating that it is to be performed with all the care, zeal, and ardency of affection.

I. Throughout the Psalm he calls on men to praise God.

1. "Praise God in his sanctuary." Or in your hearts, which are the temples of the Holy Ghost.

2. "Praise him in the firmament," &c. His magnificence when he sits on his throne. Some understand the Church by it, in which his saints shine as stars in the firmament.

3. "Praise him for his mighty acts," &c. The works of his power.

4. "Praise him according," &c. Whereby he excels all things; he being absolutely great, they only comparatively so.

II. The prophet desires that no way be omitted by which we may show our zeal and ardency in praising him.

1. "Praise him with the sound of the trumpet," &c. An instrument used in their solemn feasts.

2. "Praise him with the psaltery," &c. And with these they sing, so that there is also music with the voice.

3. "Praise him with the timbrel," &c. In the choir with many voices.

4. "Praise him with stringed instruments," &c. Lutes, viols, organs, &c.

5. "Praise him upon the high-sounding cymbals," &c. An instrument which yields a loud sound, as bells among us.

His conclusion is of universal reference, "Let every thing," &c.

1. "Every thing that hath breath," &c. That hath faculty or power to do it.

2. "Every thing that hath life," &c. Whether spiritual, as angels; or animal, as man and beasts. Or, metaphorically, such as, though inanimate, may be said to praise God, because they obey his order and intention. Thus, all things praise God, because all things that have

life or being derive it immediately from him-self.

MASORETIC NOTES ON THE BOOK OF PSALMS

Number of verses, *two thousand five hundred and twenty-seven. Middle verse.* Psa. lxxviii. 36. *Sections, nineteen.*

At the end of the *Syriac* we have this colophon:—

"The hundred and fifty Psalms are completed. There are *five* books, *fifteen* Psalms of *degrees*, and *sixty* of *praises*. The number of verses is *four thousand eight hundred and thirty-two*. There are some who have added *twelve* others; but we do not need them. And may God be praised for ever!"

At the end of the *Arabic* is the following:—

The end of the *five books* of Psalms. The *first* book ends with the *fortieth* Psalm; the *second*, with the *seventieth* Psalm; the *third*, with the *eightieth* Psalm; the *fourth*, with the *hundred and fifteenth;* and the *fifth*, with the *last* Psalm, i. e., the *hundred and fiftieth*.

PSALM CLI

Besides these *hundred and fifty* Psalms, there is *one* additional in the *Syriac, Septuagint, Æthiopic*, and *Arabic*, of which it will be necessary to say something, and to give a translation.

1. The Psalm is not found in the *Hebrew*, nor in the *Chaldee*, nor in the *Vulgate*.

2. It is found, as stated, above, in the *Syriac, Septuagint, Æthiopic*, and *Arabic;* but not in the *Anglo-Saxon*, though *Dom. Calmet* has stated the contrary. But I have not heard of it in any MS. of that version; nor is it in Spelman's printed copy.

3. It is mentioned by *Apollinaris, Athanasius, Euthymius, Vigilius, Tapsensis*, and *St. Chrysostom*.

4. It has never been received either by the *Greek* or *Latin* Church; nor has it ever been considered as *canonical*.

5. It is certainly *very ancient*, stands in the *Codex Alexandrinus*, and has been printed in the *Paris* and *London Polyglots*.

6. Though the *Greek* is considered the most authentic copy of this Psalm, yet there are some things in the *Syriac* and *Arabic* necessary to make a full sense. The *Arabic* alone states the *manner* of Goliath's death.

The *title* is, "A Psalm in the handwriting of David, beyond the number of the Psalms, composed by David, when he fought in single combat with Goliath." I shall make it as complete as I can from the different versions.

I WAS the least among my brethren; and the youngest in my father's house; and I kept also my father's sheep.

2 My hands made the organ; and my fingers joined the psaltery.

3 And who told it to my LORD? [*Arab.:* And who is he who taught me?] The LORD himself, he is my Master, and the Hearer of all that call upon him.

4 He sent his angel, and took me away from my father's sheep; and anointed me with the oil of his anointing. [Others, *the oil of his mercy*.]

5 My brethren were taller and more beautiful than I; nevertheless the LORD delighted not in them.

6 I went out to meet the Philistine, and he cursed me by his idols.

7 [*Arab.:* In the strength of the LORD I cast three stones at him. *I smote* him in the forehead, and felled him to the earth.]

8 And I drew out his own sword from its sheath, and cut off his head, and took away the reproach from the children of Israel.

NOTES ON PSALM CLI.

If we were sure this was David's composition, we should not be willing to see it *out of the number of the Psalms*, or standing among the apocryphal writings. As a matter of *curiosity* I insert it; as, if a forgery, it is very ancient; and I leave it to the intelligent reader to add his own *notes*, and form his own *analysis*.

The subscription to the Syriac says some add *twelve* more. The *Codex Alexandrinus* has fourteen more. They are the following:—

1. The Song of Moses and the children of Israel, Exod. xv. 1, &c.

2. Ditto, from Deut. xxii. 1, &c.

3. The Song of Hannah, 1 Sam. ii. 1, &c.

4. The prayer of Isaiah, Isa. xxvi. 2, &c.

5. The prayer of Jonah, Jonah, ii. 3, &c.

6. The prayer of Habakkuk, Hab. iii. 2, &c.

7. The prayer of Hezekiah, Isa. xxxviii. 10, &c.

8. The prayer of Manasseh, see the *Apocrypha*.

9. The prayer of Azarias, or of the Three Children.—*Apocrypha*.

10. The Hymn of our Fathers, see the *Benedicite omnia opera* in the *Liturgy*.

11. The *Magnificat*, or Song of the Blessed Virgin, Luke i. 46, &c.

12. The *Nunc dimittis*, or Song of Simeon, Luke ii. 29, &c.

13. The prayer of Zacharias, Luke i. 68, &c.

14. The Ὕμνος ἑωθινος, or, Morning Hymn as used in the service of the *Greek Church*.

My old Psalter seems to have copied such authority as the *Codex Alexandrinus*, for it has added several similar pieces, after the *hundred and fiftieth* Psalm, where we read, *Explicit Psalmos, incipit canticum Ysaie.*

1. The Hymn of Isaiah, Isa. xii. 1, &c.
2. The Prayer of Hezekiah, Isa. xxxviii. 10-20, inclusive.
3. The Prayer of Hannah, 1 Sam. ii. 1, &c.
4. The Song of Moses at the Red Sea, Exod. xv. 1-19.
5. The Prayer of Habakkuk.
6. The Song of Moses, Deut. xxii. 1-43.
7. The *Magnificat*, or Song of the Blessed Virgin, Luke i. 46-55.
8. The ten commandments.

9. There are several curious maxims, &c., which follow the commandments, such as *Seven werkes of Mercy; Seven gastely werkes of Mercy; Seven Virtues; The keeping of the five senses; Fourteen points of trouthe.* Another head, which is torn off. Lastly, *some godly advices* in poetry, which terminate the book.

I suppose these hymns were added on the same principle that the general assembly of the Kirk of Scotland added, by an act of 1479 and 1750, a number of verses and portions of the sacred writings, among which are several of the above, to their authorized version of the Psalms of David in metre, to be sung in all kirks and families.

SKETCH

OF THE

LIFE AND CHARACTER OF DAVID

When the historical books of the Old Testament were under consideration, I formed the resolution to say but little on those parts where the history of David is concerned, till I should come to the end of the Psalms, where, if I did not give a general history of his life, I might at least draw his character. But so many facts in David's history were found to require illustration, I was obliged often to anticipate my design, and enter into discussions which I had hoped to be able to produce with good effect at the end of his writings. I must therefore refer back to several particulars in the Books of Samuel, Kings, and Chronicles, that concern the history of this most extraordinary man; and the objections produced against his spirit and conduct by persons not friendly to Divine revelation.

Where I have found David to blame, I have not palliated his conduct; and though it is with me a maxim to lean to the most favourable side when examining the characters of men, yet I hope I have nowhere served the cause of *Antinomianism*, which I abominate, nor endeavoured to render any thing, morally evil, venial, because it was found in the conduct of a religious man or a prophet. Vice must never be countenanced, though individuals, on the whole highly respectable, suffer by its disclosure, which disclosure should take place only when the interests of religion and truth absolutely require it.

David, Doud, or *Daoud,* דוד, the son of Jesse, of an obscure family in the tribe of Judah, and of the inconsiderable village of Bethlehem, in the same tribe, was born, according to the best accounts, A. M. 2919, B. C. 1085. He was the youngest of eight sons, and was keeper of his father's sheep. David was descended from *Jacob* by his son *Judah,* in that line which united both the *regal* and *sacerdotal* functions; and in his own person were conjoined the *regal* and *prophetic* offices. It is supposed he was anointed by Samuel, about A. M. 2934, when he was but about *fifteen* years of age; and that he slew Goliath in A. M. 2942, when

he was in the *twenty-third* or *twenty-fourth* year of his age. He became king of Judah after the death of Saul, A. M. 2949; and king of all Israel, A. M. 2956, when he was about *thirty-seven* years of age, and died A. M. 2989, B. C. 1015, when he was about *seventy-one* years old.

He is often mentioned by the *Asiatic* writers, and by *Mohammed,* in the *Koran,* in these words, "Daoud slew Geealout; (Goliath;) and God gave him a kingdom and wisdom, and taught him whatsoever he wished to know."

Hussain Vaez, one of the commentators on the Koran, observes on the above passage: "That Goliath was of such an enormous size that his armour, which was of *iron,* weighed *one thousand* pounds; and that his helmet alone weighed *three hundred;* nevertheless David slung a stone with such force as to break through the helmet, pierce the skull, and beat out the Philistine's brains.

"God gave him the gift of prophecy, and the Book *Ziboor;* (Psalms;) and taught him to make hair and sackcloth, which was the work of the prophets; and instructed him in the language of birds, which, with the stones of the field, were obedient to him, and iron was softened by his hands. During the *forty* days which he spent in bewailing his sins, plants grew where he watered the ground with his tears."

The Mohammedans all allow that the *Ziboor,* or Book of Psalms, was given to David by *immediate inspiration,* and that it contains 150 sourats or chapters. His skill in music is also proverbial among the Mohammedans. Hence some verses in the *Anvari Soheely,* which are to this effect: "You decide the greatest difficulties with as much ease as *Daoud* touched the chords of his lyre when he chanted his Psalms."

If we could persuade the Mohammedans that the *Book of Psalms* which we now possess was the real work of David, something would be gained towards their conversion. But they say the Jews have corrupted it, as the Christians have the *Angeel*, (Gospel,) and the book which they produce as the Psalms of David consists of extracts only from the Psalms, with a variety of other matters which have no relation either to David or his work.

In the sacred writings David is presented to our view—1. As a shepherd; 2. A musician; 3. A skilful military leader; 4. A hero; 5. A king; 6. An ecclesiastical reformer; 7. A prophet; 8. A type of Christ; 9. A poet; and 10. A truly pious man.

1. David stands before the world in his history and writings as a private person destitute of ambition, apparently in a low, if not mean, situation in life, contributing to the support of a numerous family, of which he formed a part, by keeping the sheep of his father in the wilderness or champaign country in the vicinity of Bethlehem. In those times, and in such a rocky and mountainous country as Judea, this situation required a person of considerable *address, skill, courage*, and *muscular strength*. The flock must not only be led out and in to find the proper pasture, but their maladies must be skilfully treated, and they defended against the attacks of wild beasts, than which none could be more formidable for rapacity and strength than the *lion* and the *bear*. These were among the savage inhabitants of the country of Judea, and were the destroyers of the flocks, and the terror of the shepherds. The land was also infested with *banditti*, or lawless solitary rovers, who sought by depredations among the flocks to live at the expense of others. The office therefore of a *shepherd* was neither *mean* nor *unimportant*, as a principal part of the property of the Jews consisted in their flocks.

From the ancient history of all civilized nations we learn that the persons thought qualified for it were such as had a liberal education, good natural parts, and were highly trustworthy and courageous. These most evidently were all combined in the character of David. That his *education* was good, his language and skill in music prove; and that his *mind* was highly cultivated, the depth, sublimity, and purity of his compositions demonstrate; and that his *courage* and *personal strength* must have been great, his slaying the lion and bear that had attacked the flock under his protection, are the clearest proofs.

2. His *skill in music* was so great as to be proverbial. In this curious art he excelled all his contemporaries, so as alone to acquire the character of the *sweet singer of Israel*. His success in quieting the turbulent and maniacal spirit of Saul by his performances on the lyre stand strongly marked in his history; and the effects produced were equal to any mentioned in the now fabulous histories of Greece or Rome. The wondrous harp of Orpheus, by which beasts and birds were enraptured, and the very stones and trees moved in harmony together, so as to compose of themselves the celebrated city of Thebes, we may well leave out of the question, as the fable is too gross to be credited, unless we take the exposition of an ancient author, *Philodemus*, some fragments of whose works have been recovered from the ruins of Herculaneum, from which we learn that the fable of the building of Thebes by the melody of his lyre arose from the fact that he was a musician who attended the builders, played to them during their labour, by whose contributions he earned a competent support, and caused them to go so lightly through their work, that he was hyperbolically said to have built the walls of the city by the power of his music. Nothing can be more natural than this explanation, nor could any thing serve better for the foundation of the fable. Indeed it has been conjectured by one of David's biographers, Dr. Delaney, that the history of David was the origin of that of Orpheus. The coincidence of the times, and the other circumstances alleged by this entertaining writer, have not served to persuade me of the truth of his hypothesis. We can amply support the credit of the Hebrew musician without impairing the credibility of the history and identity of the person of the ancient Greek lyrist.

It is not likely, however, that David was a performer on one kind of instrument only. There were many kinds of musical instruments in his time that were all used in the ordinances of religion, and apparently employed in those parts of it where the compositions of David were used. *Calmet* and others have properly divided these instruments into three classes. 1. STRINGED *instruments*. 2. WIND *instruments*. And 3. Such as were played on by a PLECTRUM.

I. STRINGED *instruments*. 1. The *nabla*, or psaltery. 2. The *kinnor*. 3. The *cythera* or *azur*, an instrument of ten chords. 4. The *symphony*. 5. The *Sambuck*. 6. The *minnim*.

II. WIND *instruments*. 1. The *chatsotserah*. 2. The *shophar*, or trumpet. 3. The *keren*, or horn. 4. The *ugab*, a species of organ. 5. The *mashrokitha*, or syrinx. 6. The *machalath*, a species of pipe or fife. 7. The *chalil*, or flute.

III. Instruments which required a PLECTRUM. 1. The *toph*, a drum, tomtom, or tambarine. 2. The *tseltselim*, or sistrum. 3. The *shalishim*, or triangle. 4. The *metsiltayim*, a species of bell.

As all these instruments were used in the service of God, and most of them are mentioned in the Psalms, it is very likely that such a consummate musician and poet played on the whole.

3. That David was a *skilful military leader*, requires little proof. When for the safety of his own life he was obliged to leave the court of Saul, and become an exile in the wilds of a country so much indebted to his courage and valour, he was under the necessity of associating to himself men of desperate fortunes and of no character. These, to the amount of *four hundred*, he so disciplined and managed, as to soften their lawless disposition, and repress their propensity to plunder and rapine, so that they never went on any expedition that was not under his direction, and made no inroads but what tended to strengthen the hands of his countrymen, and weaken those of their enemies. Neither by day nor night, so complete was his authority over them, were they permitted to take even a lamb or a kid from the flock of any man, though they had frequent opportunities of doing so in countries so thinly inhabited, and where the flocks were numerous. On the contrary they were *protectors* of the different herds which were fed in those parts of the wilderness where they were obliged to sojourn. To have succeeded in disciplining such a description of men is highly to the credit of his address and skill, especially when we consider that they were composed of such as had run away from the claims of their *creditors;* from the authority of their *masters; who*

were *distressed* in their circumstances, and *discontented* with the government, or their situation in life, 1 Sam. xxii. 2. I question much whether any of the heroes of the last or present century, from *Peter* and *Frederick* the Great down to Napoleon Bonaparte, destitute of all subsidiary authority, or their *other officer* to assist them in the command, could have disciplined *four hundred* such men, brought them under perfect obedience, and prevented them from indulging their restless and marauding spirit with so many temptations before their eyes, while prey was so easy to be acquired, and their general privations rendered such supplies necessary.

4. As a *hero*, David appears very conspicuous, if we take this word in its general acceptation, *a man eminent for bravery*. And here his proffering to fight with Goliath, the famous Philistine champion who had defied and terrified all the hosts of Israel, is at once a proof of his *bravery* and *patriotism*. In very remote times, and down to a late period, military etiquette permitted feuds and civil broils to be settled by single combat. In the presence of the hostile armies, previously to the shock of general battle, a man either stepped out from the ranks, or by a *herald* bid defiance to any person in the hostile army, and stipulated certain conditions of combat, in order to spare the effusion of blood; to the exact fulfilment of which he pledged himself and his party. This was done very circumstantially in the case before us. When the Israelites and the Philistines had drawn up their forces in battle array at Ephes-dammim, a champion of Gath called *Goliath*, of gigantic stature and strength, came out of the camp of the Philistines, and stood and cried unto the armies of Israel: "Why are ye come out to set your battle in array? Choose you a man for you, and let him come down to me. If he be able to fight with me, and to kill me, then will we be your servants; but if I prevail against him, and kill him, then shall ye be our servants, and serve us." And concluded with defying the armies of Israel. Saul, though he was a man of great personal courage, and the whole Israelitish army, were greatly dismayed at this challenge; and the more particularly so, because no man dared to take it up, notwithstanding the king had offered "to enrich the accepter with great gifts, give him his daughter in marriage, and make his father's house free in Israel;" 1 Sam. xvii. 1, &c. David had come to the camp with provisions for his brothers who were in Saul's army; (for it appears that the Israelitish militia bore their own expenses when their services were requisite for the safety of their country;) and hearing the defiance of the Philistine, proposed to take up the challenge; and having obtained Saul's consent, went forth, fought and slew the Philistine in the manner related in the chapter quoted above.

On numerous occasions he signalized himself in the same way; his natural courage, heightened by his constant dependence on God, never forsook him, and was always invincible. He was the life of his kingdom, and the soul of his army; knew well how to distinguish and employ eminent abilities, had the ablest generals, and the address to form a multitude of heroes like himself.

He had a company of champions, or as they are generally termed *worthies* or *mighty men*, to the number of thirty-seven. The account

given of these (2 Sam. xxiii.) would almost render credible the legend of King Arthur and the Knights of the Round Table; and it is probable that the first idea of that ancient romance was taken from the genuine history of David and his thirty-seven champions.

5. How David would have acquitted himself as a *lawgiver* we cannot tell; for God had taken care to leave nothing of this kind to the wisdom, folly, or caprice of any man. The laws were all made and the constitution framed by Jehovah himself; and no legitimate king of the Jews was permitted to enact any new laws, or abrogate or change the old. The faithful and constitutional king was he who ruled according to the laws already established, as well in religious as in civil matters; for although the Jewish theocracy was somewhat changed by the election of Saul, yet the monarch was considered only as the *vicegerent* of the Almighty; and David, taking care to abide by the laws as they then were, and governing his subjects accordingly, was said to be *after God's own heart*, or *a man after God's own heart:* and this is the sense in which this phrase is to be understood. And as David took great care that no innovation should be made in the *constitution*, that the law of God should be the law of the empire, and ruled according to that law, therefore he was most properly said to be *a man after God's own heart*, to fulfil all his counsels; and by this faithful attachment to the laws he was contradistinguished from Saul, who in several respects changed that law, and made not a few attempts to alter it in some of its most essential principles. On these grounds God rejected *him* and chose David.

But as a *civil magistrate* David's conduct was unimpeachable: his court was regulated according to the maxims of the Divine law; and the universal prosperity of his kingdom is a decisive proof that judgment and justice were faithfully administered in it. The *strong* did not oppress the *weak*, nor the *rich* the *poor;* and, although the empire was seldom at rest from war during his reign, yet it was so conducted that his subjects were neither *oppressed* nor *impoverished*. Many of his Psalms bear testimony to these matters, as they contain appeals to God relative to the sincerity of his heart, the uprightness of his conduct, and his impartiality in administering justice among the people. To David the cry of the distressed was never uttered in vain; and the curse of the widow and fatherless was never pronounced against him for a neglect of justice, or partiality in administering it according to the laws.

6. David, I think, may be fitly ranked among *ecclesiastical reformers;* for, although the *grand body* of the Jewish religion was so firmly fixed, that it could not be changed, yet there were *several circumstances* in the *form* of Divine worship that appear to have been left to the pious discretion of the Jewish prophets, priests, and kings, to improve as time and circumstances might require. That God might be constantly worshipped, that the Jewish ritual might be carefully observed, and all the Divinely appointed ecclesiastical persons have their proper share of the public service, David divided the *thirty-eight thousand Levites* into courses, assigning to each course its particular service, 1 Chron. xxiii. He did the same by the *priests, porters, singers*, &c.; and appointed *twelve captains* to serve each a month, and

have the rule and inspection of the different courses and orders, to see that the worship of God was properly conducted. The *twenty-third, twenty-fourth, twenty-fifth, twenty-sixth,* and *twenty-seventh* chapters of the *first* book of Chronicles, give a very detailed and circumstantial account of the improvements which David made in the *form* and *execution* of the different parts of public worship. Almost every pious king of Judah had matters of this kind to regulate and settle: but it appears that David's plan was so perfect, that it became a standard; and when any decay took place in the form of public worship, the chief aim of the succeeding kings was, to reduce every thing to the form in which David had left it. This is a full proof of the perfection of his plan.

7. That David was favoured with the *gift* of *prophecy*, is, I think, universally allowed. And although there have been prophets *pro tempore*, who were not remarkable for piety, yet there never was one on whom the prophetic Spirit *rested*, that was not truly pious. All such had deep communion with God: their souls were upright, and their bodies became temples of the Holy Ghost. This was most assuredly the case with David: the prophetic Spirit overshadowed and rested upon him; in general he held deep communion with God; and even in his Psalms, we can scarcely say *when* he does not prophesy. Some learned and very pious men consider the whole Psalter as a tissue of prophecies concerning Christ and his kingdom; and in this way our Lord and his apostles quote many of them. Could we really ascertain which were David's, perhaps we might find them all of this description; though the subjects to which they apply might not be so clearly distinct: but there were so many written *before, at, under,* and *after,* the Babylonish captivity, that are become so mixed with those of David, that it is difficult, and in some cases impossible, to ascertain them. Where he evidently prophesies of Christ and his Church, I have particularly remarked it in the notes. I have not gone so far as some learned and pious commentators have gone, in applying the Psalms to Christ and his Church, because I was not satisfied that they have such reference. Even those which are of David's composition, and have reference to Christ, are so mixed up with his own state, that it is often impossible to say when the Psalmist prophesies of the *Root of Jesse,* and when he simply refers to his own circumstances: and, on the whole, I am only sure of those which are thus quoted by our Lord and his apostles.

8. That David was a *type* of Christ is proved by the Scriptures themselves, see Jer. xxx. 9: "They shall serve the Lord their God, and David their king, whom I will raise up unto them;" Ezek. xxxiv. 23: "And I will set up one shepherd over them, and he shall feed them, even my servant David; he shall feed them, and he shall be their shepherd." Ver. 24: "And I the Lord will be their God, and my servant David a prince among them." See also Ezek. xxxvii. 24; and compare this with Jer. xxiii. 4, 5; John x. 11; Heb. xiii. 24; 1 Pet. ii. 25; and v. 5; Hosea, chap. iii. ver. 5, speaks in the same way: "Afterward shall the children of Israel return, and seek the Lord their God, and David their king; and shall fear the Lord and his goodness in the latter days." That none of these scriptures speak of *David, son of Jesse,* is evident from this, that Hosea lived three

hundred years *after* David, Jeremiah four hundred and seventy-three, and Ezekiel four hundred and ninety-three.

But in what was David a *type of Christ?* Principally, I think, in the *name* דויד *David,* which signifies *the beloved one,* that one more loved than any other; and this is what is expressed from heaven by God himself, when he says, *This is my Son,* Ὁ Ἀγαπητος, εν ᾧ ευδοκησα, THE BELOVED ONE, *in whom I have delighted.* This is the *genuine David;* the *man after my own heart.* He was his *type* also, in being a *royal prophet*—one in whom the Holy Spirit dwelt, and one who was a truly *spiritual king;* a character that seldom occurs in the history of the world.

Were we to consult those who have *laboured* on the *types,* we might find all the following resemblances *stated;* and, in their way, wondrously *proved!* David was a type of Christ, 1. In his originally mean appearance. 2. In his mean education. 3. In his unction. 4. In his eminent qualifications. 5. In his various persecutions. 6. In his enemies. 7. In his distresses. 8. In his deliverance. 9. "In his victories and conquests. And, 10. In his taking to wife the adulterous woman, and thereby bringing guilt upon himself." See *Parkhurst.* All the first *nine* particulars might be *controverted,* as not having any thing in them exclusively typical; and the *tenth* is horrible, if not blasphemous. No analogies, no metaphorical meanings can support this abominable position. I have already given my opinion: to elucidate the particulars above, I shall never attempt.

9. But the highest merit of David, and that which seems to have been almost exclusively *his own,* was his *poetic genius.* As a Divine poet, even God himself had created none greater, either *before* or *since.* In this science and gift he is therefore the *chef-d'œuvre* of the Almighty. *Moses* wrote some fine verses; *Solomon* two fine poems, an *ode* and an *elegy.* The prophets, particularly *Isaiah,* in several *chapters* of his prophecy; *Jeremiah,* in his book of *Lamentations;* and some of the *minor prophets,* in a few *select verses,* have given us specimens of a profound poetical genius; but we have no *whole* like that of David. The *sublimity,* the *depth,* the *excursive fancy,* the *discursive power,* the *vast compass* of *thought,* the knowledge of *heaven* and *earth,* of *God* and *nature,* the work of the Spirit, the endlessly varied temptations of Satan, the knowledge of the human heart, the travail of the soul, the full comprehension of the *prosopopœia* or *personification* of the whole of *inanimate nature,* of every *virtue,* and of every *vice,* the immense grasp of thought embodying and arranging, and afterwards clothing in suitable language, the vast assemblage of ideas furnished by the natural and spiritual world; in a word, the spirit of poetry, the true *genie createur,* the του ποιητου ποιησις, *framework of the framer, the poetry of the poet,* not the *fiction* of the *inventive* genius; but the production of truth, hidden before in the bosom of God and nature, and exhibited in the most pleasing colours, with the most impressive pathos and irresistible harmonic diction: these qualities, these supramundane excellences, are found in no other poet that ever graced the annals of the world; they exist in their perfection only in David king of Israel. What is peculiarly remarkable in David is, he has succeeded to the very high-

est degree in every species of poetic composition that has for its *object* the glory of God and the welfare of man; and there is not one poet who has succeeded him, that has not failed when he attempted to sing of God, the punishment and rewards of the future world, and the unsearchable riches of Christ.

The *hymns* which he produced have been the general song of the universal Church; and men of all nations find in these compositions a language at once suitable to their feelings, and expressive of their highest joys and deepest sorrows, as well as of all the endlessly varied wishes and desires of their hearts. Hail, thou sweet singer of Israel! thy voice is still heard in all the assemblies of the saints.

In my notes on different places of the Psalter I have taken the opportunity of pointing out some of the beauties of these incomparable productions. But I must here state that the true excellence of this work will never be fully known, till it be translated according to its *rythmical* order, or *hemistich plan*, in which the harmony of its versification will be felt, and the whole be much more easily apprehended and practically understood. Had we a second *Lowth* to take up *David*, as the *first* did *Isaiah*, the Church of God would have the utmost reason to rejoice; and each devout penitent and believer would be enabled to sing more with the *spirit* and the *understanding*, than they can possibly do in taking up the best translation of the Psalms, whether *metrical* or *prosaic*, now extant.

We have no less than *four* versions, *two in prose* and *two in verse*, given by public authority to the good people of this land. Of the former there is one in the public service of the Church, compiled out of various translations; and one by King James's translators, in the authorized version of the Bible: the latter indescribably the better of this class. The *two metrical* versions are by *Sternhold, Hopkins,* and *others,* and by *Brady* and *Tate.* The former is the most just and literal: but none of them worthy of the subject. All these have already passed under review.

10. That there should have been any doubt entertained as to the *piety of David* appears very strange: most certainly, no man ever gave more unequivocal proofs of piety and devotedness to God than he gave. It was utterly impossible that any man could have written such Psalms as David has, whose soul was not deeply imbued with the Spirit of holiness; and this appears, not only in his *writings,* but in his *general conduct.* That in some cases he grievously departed from God, who would attempt to deny? His adultery with Bathsheba, and the consequent murder of the brave Uriah, were crimes of a very deep dye. I can say no more on these, than I have said already in my notes on 2 Sam. xi., and in the observations at the end of that chapter; and to these I beg to refer the reader. His pretended *cruelty* to the *Ammonites* has been adduced as a proof of a *hard* and *wicked heart.* See the notes on 2 Sam. xii. 31, where this charge is shown to be *unfounded.* Whatever obliquities have been charged against him, from *facts* recorded in his history, have already been amply considered where the facts are mentioned. But all these, make the worst of them we can, are but *insulated facts;* they never existed in *habit,* they made no part of his *general character;* and his *repentance* on the account of that which was his great blot, was the deepest and most exemplary we have on record. If a man have fallen into sin, and made the speediest return to God by confession and repentance, he proves that that transgression *is no part of his character.* He does not *repeat* it; he loathes and abhors it. It requires *malice* against God's book to say this crime was a part of David's *character.* Adultery and murder were no part of the character of David; he fell *once* into the first, and endeavoured to cover it by the death of an innocent man; but who can prove that he ever *repeated* either? While it is granted that a man of God *should* never sin against his Maker, it must also be granted that, in a state of *probation,* a holy man *may* sin; that such *may* be renewed unto repentance, and sin against their God no more, are also possible cases. And it is not less possible that a holy man of God may fall into sin, continue in it, repeat it and re-repeat it, and rise no more. Of this dreadful possibility the Scripture gives ample proof. There are but few in the Church of God that have kept their garments unspotted from the world, and retained their first love: but it *should have been otherwise;* and had they watched unto prayer, they would not have fallen. I only contend for the *possibility,* not for the *necessity,* of the case. And I contend that, in the case of David, a life so long, so holy, so useful, and, except in these instances, so truly exemplary, entitles him to the character of *a holy man of God;* and, allowing but a little for the dispensation under which he lived, *one of the holiest, if not* THE *holiest,* that ever wore a crown, or wielded a sceptre. For the supposition that on his death-bed he retracted the promise of life to Shimei, see the notes on 1 Kings ii. 9, where he is amply vindicated.

On the whole, I can cheerfully sum up all in the words of Dr. *Delaney:* "David was a *true believer,* a *zealous adorer* of God, *teacher* of his *law* and *worship,* and *inspirer* of his *praise.* A glorious *example,* a *perpetual* and *inexhaustible fountain* of true piety. A consummate and unequalled *hero,* a skilful and fortunate *captain,* a steady *patriot,* a wise *ruler,* a faithful, generous, and magnanimous *friend;* and, what is yet rarer, a no less generous and magnanimous *enemy.* A true *penitent,* a *Divine musician,* a sublime *poet,* an inspired *prophet.* By birth a *peasant,* by merit a *prince.* In youth a *hero,* in manhood a *monarch,* and in age a *saint.*"

The matters of Bathsheba and Uriah are almost his only *blot.* There he sinned deeply; and no man ever suffered more in his body, soul, and domestic affairs, than he did in consequence. His penitence was as deep and extraordinary as his crime; and nothing could surpass both, *but* that eternal mercy that took away the guilt, assuaged the sorrow, and restored this most humbled transgressor to character, holiness, happiness, and heaven. Reader, let the God of David be exalted for ever!

Corrected for the Press, March 15th, 1829.—A. C.

INTRODUCTION

TO THE

PROVERBS OF SOLOMON,

THE SON OF DAVID, KING OF ISRAEL

THERE has scarcely been any dispute concerning either the *author* or *Divine authority* of this book, either in the *Jewish* or *Christian* Church: all allow that it was written by Solomon; and the general belief is, that he wrote the book by Divine *inspiration*.

It has, indeed, been supposed that Solomon *collected* the major part of these proverbs from those who had preceded him, whether *Hebrews* or *heathens;* but the latter opinion has been controverted, as derogating from the *authority* of the book. But this supposition has very little weight; for, whatever of *truth* is found *in* or *among* men, came originally from God; and if he employed an inspired man to collect those *rays of light*, and *embody* them for the use of his Church, he had a right so to do, and to claim his *own* wheresoever found, and, by giving it a *new authentication*, to render it more useful in reference to the end for which it was originally communicated. God is the *Father of lights*, and from him came all true wisdom, not only in its discursive teachings, but in all its detached maxims for the government and regulation of life. I think it very likely that Solomon did not *compose* them all; but he collected every thing of this kind within his reach, and what was according to the Spirit of truth, by which he was inspired, he condensed in this book; and as the Divine Spirit gave it, so the providence of God has preserved it, for the use of his Church.

That true Light, which lightens every man that cometh into the world, first taught men to acknowledge himself as the Fountain and Giver of all good; and then by *short maxims*, conveyed in terse, energetic words, taught them to regulate their conduct in life, in respect to the dispensations of his providence, and in reference to each other in domestic, social, and civil life; and this was done by such *proverbs* as we find collected in this book. The different changes that take place in society; the new relations which in process of time men would bear to each other; the invention of arts and sciences; and the *experience* of those who had particularly considered the ways of the Lord, and marked the operations of his hands; would give rise to many maxims, differing from the original stock only in their application to those *new relations* and *varying circumstances*.

The *heathen* who had any connection with the first worshippers of the Almighty would observe the maxims by which *they* regulated the affairs of life, and would naturally borrow from them; and hence those *original teachings* became diffused throughout the world; and we find there is not an ancient nation on earth that is without its *code of proverbs* or proverbial maxims. The ancient SANSCRIT is full of them; and they abound in the *Persian* and *Arabic* languages, and in all the *dialects* formed from these, in all the countries of the East. The HEETOPADESA of Vishnoo Sarma, the *Anvari Soheili*, the *Bahar Danush, Kalila we Dumna*, and all the other *forms* of that *original* work; the fables of *Lockman, Æsop, Phædrus, Avienus,* &c., are collections of proverbs, illustrated by their application to the most important purposes of domestic, social, and civil life.

Those nations with which we are best acquainted have their collections of proverbs; and perhaps those with which we are unacquainted have theirs also. Messrs. *Visdelou* and *Galand* formed a collection of *Asiatic* proverbs, and published it in their supplement to the *Bibliotheque Orientale* of *D'Herbelot*. This is a collection of very great worth, curiosity, and importance. Mr. J. *Ray*, F. R. S., formed a collection of this kind, particularly of such as are or have been in use in Great Britain: this is as curious as it is entertaining and useful.

The term PROVERB, *proverbium*, compounded of *pro*, for, and *verbum*, a word, speech, or saying, leads us to an original meaning of the thing itself. It was an *allegorical* saying, where "more was meant than met the eye"—a *short saying* that stood for a *whole discourse,* the words of which are metaphorical; e. g., this of the rabbins: "I have given thee my lamp: give me thy lamp. If thou keep my lamp, I will keep thy lamp; but if thou quench my lamp, I will quench thy lamp." Here the word *lamp* is a metaphor: 1. For *Divine revelation.* 2. For the *human soul.* I have given thee my *word* and *Spirit;* give me thy *soul* and *heart.* If thou *observe* my *word,* and *follow* the dictates of my *Spirit,* I will *regulate* thy *heart,* and *keep* thy *soul* from every evil; but if thou *disobey* my *word,* and *quench* my *Spirit,* I will withdraw my *Spirit,* leave thee to the *hardness* and *darkness* of thy own heart, and send thee at last into outer *darkness.* Such as this is properly the *proverb;* the *word* which stands *for* a *discourse.*

But the Hebrew משלים *meshalim,* from משל *mashal,* to *rule* or *govern,* signifies a set or collection of *weighty, wise,* and therefore *authoritative, sayings,* whereby a man's whole conduct, civil and religious, is to be governed; sayings containing rules for the government of life. Or, as the Divine author himself expresses it in the beginning of the first chapter, the design is to lead men "to know wisdom and instruction, to perceive the words of understanding; to receive the instruction of wisdom, justice, and judgment, and equity; to give subtilty to the simple, and to the young man knowledge and discretion," ver. 2, 3. This was the design of *proverbs;* and perhaps it would be impossible to find out a better definition of the design and object of those of Solomon, than is contained in the two preceding verses. See my Dissertation on Parabolical Writing, at the end of the notes on Matt. xiii.

Of the *three thousand proverbs* which Solomon spoke, we have only those contained in this book and in *Ecclesiastes;* and of the *one thousand and five songs* which he made, only the *Canticles* have been preserved: or, in other words, of all his numerous works in *divinity, philosophy, morality,* and *natural history,* only the *three* above mentioned, bearing his name, have been admitted into the sacred canon. His *natural history* of *trees* and *plants,* of *beasts, fowls,* and *fishes,* (for on all these he wrote,) is totally lost. *Curiosity,* which never says, *It is enough,* would give up the three we have for those on the *animal* and *vegetable kingdom,* which are lost. What God judged of importance to the eternal interests of mankind, is preserved; and perhaps we know the vegetable and animal kingdoms now as well through *Linnæus* and *Buffon,* and their *followers,* as we should have known them, had Solomon's books on natural history come down to our time. Others would investigate *nature,* and to them those researches were left. Solomon spoke by inspiration; and therefore to him *Divine doctrines* were communicated, that he might teach them to man. *Every man in his order.*

The book of *Proverbs* has been divided into *five* parts:

I. A *master* is represented as instructing his *scholar,* giving him admonitions, directions, cautions, and excitements to the study of wisdom, chap. i. to ix.

II. This part is supposed to contain the Proverbs of Solomon, *properly so called;* delivered in distinct, independent, general sentences. From chap. ix. to xxii. 17.

III. In this part the tutor again addresses himself to his pupil, and gives him fresh admonitions to the study of wisdom; which is followed by a set of instructions, delivered *imperatively* to the pupil, who is supposed all the while to be standing before him. From chap. xxii. 17 to chap. xxv.

IV. This part is distinguished by being a *selection* of Solomon's Proverbs, made by the *men of Hezekiah,* conjectured to be Isaiah, Hosea, and Micah, who all flourished under that reign. This part, like the *second,* is composed of distinct, unconnected sentences, and extends from chap. xxv. to xxx.

V. The *fifth* part contains a set of wise expostulations and instructions, which *Agur,* the son of *Jakeh,* delivered to his pupils, *Ithiel* and *Ucal,* chap. xxx. And the thirty-first chapter contains the instructions which a *mother,* who is not named, gave to *Lemuel* her son, being earnestly desirous to guard him against vice, to establish him in the principles of justice, and to have him married to a wife of the best qualities. These two last chapters may be considered a kind of *Appendix* to the book of Proverbs: see Dr. *Taylor;* but others suppose that the thirty-first chapter contains *Bathsheba's* words to *Solomon,* and his commendation of his mother.

There are many *repetitions* and some *transpositions* in the book of Proverbs, from which it is very probable that they were not all made at the same time; that they are the work of different authors, and have been collected by various hands: but still the sum total is delivered to us by Divine inspiration; and whoever might have been the original authors of *distinct parts,* the Divine Spirit has made them all its own by handing them to us in this form. Some attribute the collection, i. e., the formation of this collection, to *Isaiah;* others, to *Hilkiah,* and *Shebna* the scribe; and others, to *Ezra.*

That Solomon could have borrowed little from his predecessors is evident from this consideration, that all uninspired ethic writers, who are famous in history, lived *after his times.* Solomon began to reign A. M. 2989, which was 239 years before the *first Olympiad;* 479 before *Cyrus,* in whose time flourished the *seven wise men of Greece;* 679 before *Alexander the Great,* under whose reign flourished *Socrates, Plato,* and *Aristotle;* and 1011 before the *birth of Christ.* Therefore to the *Gentiles* he could be but little, if at all, indebted.

It is impossible for any description of persons to read the book of Proverbs without profit. *Kings* and *courtiers,* as well as those engaged in *trade, commerce, agriculture,* and the *humblest walks* of life, may here read lessons of instruction for the regulation of their conduct in their respective circumstances. *Fathers, mothers, wives, husbands, sons, daughters, masters,* and *servants,* may here also learn their respective duties; and the most excellent rules are laid down, not only in reference to *morality,* but to *civil policy* and *economy.* Many *motives* are employed by the wise man to accomplish the end at which he aims; motives derived from *honour, interest, love, fear, natural affection,* and *piety* towards God. The principal object he has in view is, to inspire a deep reverence for GOD, fear of his judgments and an ardent love for wisdom and virtue. He exhibits injustice, impiety, profligacy, idleness, imprudence, drunkenness, and almost every vice, in such livelycolours as to render every man ashamed of them who has any true respect for his interest, honour, character, or health. And as there is nothing so directly calculated to ruin young men, as *bad company, debauch,* and *irregular connections,* he labours to fortify his disciples with the most convincing reasons against all these vices, and especially against *indolence, dissipation,* and the company of *lewd women.*

Maxims to regulate life in all the conditions already mentioned, and to prevent the evils already described, are laid down so copiously, clearly, impressively, and in such *variety,* that every man who wishes to be instructed may take what he chooses, and, among multitudes, those which he likes best.

Besides the original *Hebrew,* the book of Proverbs exists in the following ancient versions: the *Chaldee, Septuagint, Syriac, Vulgate,* and *Arabic.* But the Septuagint takes greater liberty with the sacred text than any of the rest: it often *transposes, changes,* and *adds;* and all these to a very considerable extent. This is the version which is quoted in the *New Testament.* Several of these *additions,* as well as the most important *changes,* the reader will find noticed in the following notes; but to mark them all would require a translation of almost the whole *Greek text.* How our *forefathers* understood several passages will be seen by quotations from an ancient MS. in my possession, which begins with this book, and extends to the conclusion of the New Testament. It is well written upon strong vellum, in very large folio, and highly illuminated in the beginning of each book, and first letter of each chapter. The language is more antiquated than in the translation commonly attributed to Wiclif. It was once the property of *Thomas à Woodstock,* youngest son of Edward III., and brother of John of Gaunt and the Black Prince. I have often quoted this MS. in my notes on the New Testament.

A. CLARKE.

THE

PROVERBS

Year from the Creation, 3004.—Year before the birth of Christ, 996.—Year before the vulgar era of Christ's nativity, 1000.—Year since the Deluge, according to Archbishop Usher and the English Bible, 1348.—Year from the destruction of Troy, 185.—Year before the first Olympiad, 224.—Year before the building of Rome, 247.

CHAPTER I

The design of the proverbs, 1–6. An exhortation to fear God, and believe his word, because of the benefit to be derived from it, 7–9; to avoid the company of wicked men, who involve themselves in wretchedness and ruin, 10–19. Wisdom, personified, cries in the streets, and complains of the contempt with which she is treated, 20–23. The dreadful punishment that awaits all those who refuse her counsels, 24–33.

A. M. cir. 3004
B. C. cir. 1000
Ante I. Olymp.
cir. 224
Ante U. C. cir.
247

THE ªproverbs of Solomon the son of David, king of Israel;

2 To know wisdom and instruction; to perceive the words of understanding;

3 To ᵇreceive the instruction of wisdom, justice, and judgment, and ᶜequity;

4 To give subtilty to the ᵈsimple, to the young man knowledge and ᵉdiscretion.

A. M. cir. 3004
B. C. cir. 1000
Ante I. Olymp.
cir. 224
Ante U. C. cir.
247

ª1 Kings iv. 32; ch. x. 1; xxv. 1; Eccles. xii. 9——ᵇCh. ii.

1, 9——ᶜHeb. *equities*——ᵈCh. ix. 4——ᵉOr, *advisement*

NOTES ON CHAP. I

Verse 1. *The proverbs of Solomon*] For the meaning of the word *proverb*, see the *introduction;* and the *dissertation upon parabolical writing* at the end of the notes on Matt. xiii. Solomon is the first of the sacred writers whose name stands at the head of his works.

Verse 2. *To know wisdom*] That is, this is the design of parabolical writing in *general;* and the *particular* aim of the present work.

This and the two following verses contain the interpretation of the term *parable*, and the author's design in the whole book. The first verse is the *title*, and the next three verses are an explanation of the nature and design of this very important tract.

Wisdom] חכמה *chochmah* may mean here, and in every other part of this book, not only that Divine science by which we are enabled to *discover the best end*, and *pursue it by the most proper means;* but also the whole of that *heavenly teaching* that shows us both ourselves and God, directs us into all truth, and forms the whole of *true religion.*

And instruction] מוסר *musar*, the *teaching* that discovers all its parts; to *understand*, to *comprehend* the words or doctrines which should be comprehended, in order that we may become wise to salvation.

Verse 3. *To receive the instruction*] השכל

haskel, the deliberately *weighing* of the points contained in the *teaching*, so as to find out their *importance.*

Equity] משרים *mesharim*, *rectitude.* The pupil is to receive *wisdom and instruction, the words of wisdom and understanding, justice and judgment*, so perfectly as to excel in all. *Wisdom* itself, personified, is his teacher; and when God's wisdom teaches, there is no delay in learning.

Verse 4. *To give subtilty to the simple*] The word *simple*, from *simplex*, compounded of *sine*, without, and *plica*, a fold, properly signifies *plain* and *honest*, one that has no *by-ends* in view, who is *what he appears to be;* and is opposed to *complex*, from *complico*, to *fold together*, to make *one rope* or *cord* out of *many strands;* but because *honesty and plaindealing* are so rare in the world, and none but the *truly religious man* will practise them, farther than the *fear of the law* obliges him, hence *simple* has sunk into a state of progressive deterioration. At first, it signified, as above, *without fold, unmixed, uncompounded:* this was its *radical* meaning. Then, as applied to *men*, it signified *innocent, harmless, without disguise;* but, as such persons were rather an *unfashionable* sort of people, it sunk in its meaning to *homely, homespun, mean, ordinary.* And, as worldly men, who were seeking their portion in this life, and had little to do with religion, supposed that *wisdom, wit, and under-*

A. M. cir. 3004
B. C. cir. 1000
Ante I. Olymp.
cir. 224
Ante U. C. cir.
247

5 [f]A wise *man* will hear, and will increase learning; and a man of understanding shall attain unto wise counsels:

6 To understand a proverb, and [g]the interpretation; the words of the wise, and their [h]dark sayings.

7 [i]The fear of the LORD *is* [k]the beginning of knowledge: *but* fools despise wisdom and instruction.

A. M. cir. 3004
B. C. cir. 1000
Ante I. Olymp.
cir. 224
Ante U. C. cir.
247

8 [l]My son, hear the instruction of thy father, and forsake not the law of thy mother.

---

[f]1 Chron. xxvi. 14; chap. ix. 9; chap. xi. 30; xiii. 14, 20; xv. 2——[g]Or, *an eloquent speech*——[h]Psa. lxxviii. 2

[i]Job xxviii. 28; Psa. cxi. 10; chap. ix. 10; Eccles. xii. 13
[k]Or, *the principal part*——[l]Chap. iv. 1; vi. 20

---

standing, were given to men that they might make the best of them in reference to the *things of this life,* the word sunk still lower in its meaning, and signified *silly, foolish;* and there, to the dishonour of our language and morals, it stands! I have taken those acceptations which I have marked in Italics out of the *first dictionary* that came to hand—*Martin's;* but if I had gone to *Johnson,* I might have added to SILLY, *not wise, not cunning. Simplicity,* that meant at first, as MARTIN defines it, *openness, plaindealing, downright honesty,* is now degraded to *weakness, silliness, foolishness.* And these terms will continue thus degraded, till *downright honesty* and *plaindealing* get again into vogue. There are two Hebrew words generally supposed to come from the *same root,* which in our common version are rendered *the simple,* פתאים *pethaim,* and פתם or פתיים *pethayim;* the former comes from פתא *patha,* to be *rash, hasty;* the latter, from פתה *pathah, to draw aside, seduce, entice.* It is the first of these words which is used here, and may be applied to *youth;* the *inconsiderate,* the *unwary,* who, for want of knowledge and experience, act *precipitately.* Hence the *Vulgate* renders it *parvulis,* little ones, young children, or *little children,* as my old MS.; or *very babes,* as *Coverdale.* The *Septuagint* renders it ακακοις, those that are *without evil;* and the *versions* in general understand it of those who are *young, giddy,* and *inexperienced.*

To the young man] נער *naar* is frequently used to signify such as are in the *state of adolescence, grown up boys,* very well translated in my old MS. ȝunge fulwaxen; what we would now call the *grown up lads.* These, as being giddy and inexperienced, stand in especial need of lessons *of wisdom and discretion.* The Hebrew for *discretion,* מזמה *mezimmah,* is taken both in a *good* and *bad* sense, as זם *zam,* its root, signifies to *devise* or *imagine;* for the *device* may be either *mischief,* or the *contrivance* of some *good purpose.*

Verse 5. *A wise* man *will hear*] I shall not only give such instructions as may be suitable to the youthful and inexperienced, but also to those who have much knowledge and understanding. So said St. Paul: *We speak wisdom among them that are perfect.* This and the following verse are connected in the old MS. and in *Coverdale:* "By hearyinge the wyse man shall come by more wysdome; and by experience he shall be more apte to understonde a parable and the interpretation thereof; the wordes of the wyse and the darke speaches of the same."

Verse 6. *Dark sayings.*] חידת *chidoth,* enigmas or riddles, in which the Asiatics abounded. I believe *parables,* such as those delivered by our Lord, nearly express the meaning of the original.

Verse 7. *The fear of the Lord*] In the preceding verses Solomon shows the *advantage* of acting according to the dictates of wisdom; in the following verses he shows the *danger* of acting contrary to them. *The fear of the Lord* signifies that *religious reverence* which every intelligent being owes to his Creator; and is often used to express the *whole of religion,* as we have frequently had occasion to remark in different places. But *what is religion?* The love of God, and the love of man; the *former* producing *all* obedience to the *Divine will;* the *latter,* every *act of benevolence* to one's fellows. The love of God shed abroad in the heart by the Holy Spirit produces the deepest religious reverence, genuine piety, and cheerful obedience. To love one's neighbour as himself is the second great commandment; and as *love* worketh no ill to one's neighbour, *therefore it is said* to be *the fulfilling of the law.* Without *love,* there is no *obedience;* without *reverence,* there is neither *caution, consistent conduct,* nor *perseverance* in righteousness.

This fear or religious reverence is said to be *the beginning of knowledge;* ראשית *reshith,* the *principle,* the *first moving influence,* begotten in a tender conscience by the Spirit of God. No man can ever become *truly wise,* who does not begin with God, the fountain of knowledge; and he whose mind is influenced by the fear and love of God will learn more in a month than others will in a year.

Fools despise] אוילים *evilim,* evil men. Men of bad hearts, bad heads, and bad ways.

Verse 8. *My son, hear*] *Father* was the title of *preceptor,* and *son,* that of *disciple* or *scholar,* among the Jews. But here the reference appears to be to the *children of a family;* the *father* and the *mother* have the principal charge, in the first instance, of their children's instruction. It is supposed that these parents have, themselves, the fear of the Lord, and that they are capable of giving the best counsel to their children, and that they set before them a strict example of all godly living. In vain do parents give *good advice* if their own conduct be not consistent. The *father* occasionally gives *instruction;* but he is not always in the *family,* many of those occupations which are necessary for the family support being carried on abroad. The *mother*—she is constantly *within doors,* and to her the regulation of the family belongs; therefore she has and gives *laws.* The wise man says in effect to every child, "Be obedient to thy mother within, and carefully attend to the instructions of thy father, that thou mayest the better see the *reasons* of obedience; and learn from him how thou art to get thy bread honestly in the world."

A. M. cir. 3004
B. C. cir. 1000
Ante I. Olymp.
cir. 224
Ante U. C. cir.
247

9 For ^mthey *shall be* ⁿan orna-ment of grace unto thy head, and chains about thy neck.

10 My son, if sinners entice thee, ^oconsent thou not.

11 If they say, Come with us, let us ^play wait for blood, let us lurk privily for the innocent without cause:

12 Let us swallow them up alive as the grave; and whole, ^qas those that go down into the pit:

13 We shall find all precious substance, we shall fill our houses with spoil:

14 Cast in thy lot among us; let us all have one purse:

15 My son, ^rwalk not thou in the way with them; ^srefrain thy foot from their path:

A. M. cir. 3004
B. C. cir. 1000
Ante I. Olymp.
cir. 224
Ante U. C. cir.
247

16 ^tFor their feet run to evil, and make haste to shed blood.

17 Surely in vain the net is spread ^uin the sight of any bird.

18 And they lay wait for their *own* blood; they lurk privily for their *own* lives.

19 ^vSo *are* the ways of every one that is greedy of gain; *which* taketh away the life of the owners thereof.

20 ^wWisdom ^xcrieth without; she uttereth her voice in the streets:

21 She crieth in the chief place of concourse, in the openings of the gates: in the city she uttereth her words, *saying,*

---

^mChap. iii. 22——ⁿHebrew, *an adding*——^oGenesis xxxix. 7, &c.; Psalm i. 1; Ephesians v. 11——^pJeremiah v. 26——^qPsalm xxviii. 1; cxliii. 7——^rPsalm i. 1; chap. iv. 14——^sPsalm cxix. 101——^tIsaiah lix. 7;

Romans iii. 15——^uHebrew, *in the eyes of every thing that hath a wing*——^vChap. xv. 27; 1 Timothy vi. 10 ^wHebrew, *Wisdoms, that is, excellent wisdom*——^xChap. i. 8, &c.; ix. 3; John vii. 37

Verse 9. *An ornament of grace unto thy head, and chains*] That is, filial respect and obedience will be as ornamental to thee as *crowns, diadems,* and golden chains and pearls are to others.

Political dignity has been distinguished in many nations by a *chain of gold about the neck.* Solomon seems here to intimate, if we follow the metaphor, that the surest way of coming to distinguished eminence, in civil matters, is to act according to the principles of *true wisdom,* proceeding from the *fear of God.*

Verse 10. *If sinners entice thee, consent thou not.*] אל תבא *al tobe,* WILL—*not.* They can do thee no harm unless thy will join in with them. God's eternal purpose with respect to man is, that his *will* shall be *free;* or, rather, that the *will,* which is *essentially* FREE, shall never be forced nor be forceable by any power. Not even the devil himself can lead a man into sin till he *consents.* Were it not so, how could God judge the world?

Verse 11. *If they say, Come with us*] From all accounts, this is precisely the way in which the workers of iniquity form their partisans, and constitute their marauding societies to the present day.

Let us lay wait for blood] Let us rob and murder.

Let us lurk privily] Let us lie in ambush for our prey.

Verse 12. *Let us swallow them up alive*] Give them as hasty a death as if the earth were suddenly to swallow them up. This seems to refer to the destruction of a whole village. Let us destroy man, woman, and child; and then we may seize on and carry away the whole of their property, and the booty will be great.

Verse 14. *Cast in thy lot*] Be a *frater conjuratus,* a sworn brother, and thou shalt have an equal share of all the spoil.

Common sense must teach us that the words here used are such as must be spoken when a gang of cutthroats, pickpockets, &c., are associated together.

Verse 16. *For their feet run to evil*] The whole of this verse is wanting in the *Septuagint,* and in the *Arabic.*

Verse 17. *Surely in vain the net is spread in the sight of any bird.*] This is a *proverb* of which the wise man here makes a particular use; and the meaning does not seem as difficult as some imagine. The wicked are represented as *lurking privily* for the innocent. It is in this way alone that they can hope to destroy them and take their substance; for if their designs were *known,* proper precautions would be taken against them; for it would be *vain to spread the net in the sight of those birds* which men wish to ensnare. Attend therefore to my counsels, and they shall never be able to ensnare *thee.*

Verse 18. *They lay wait for their own blood*] I believe it is the *innocent* who are spoken of here, for whose *blood* and *lives* these *lay wait* and *lurk privily;* certainly not *their own,* by any mode of construction.

Verse 19. *Which taketh away the life*] A *covetous* man is in effect, and in the sight of God, a *murderer;* he wishes to get all the *gain* that can accrue to any or all who are in the same business that he follows—no matter to him how many families starve in consequence. This is the very case with him who sets up shop after shop in different parts of the same town or neighbourhood, in which he carries on the same business, and endeavours to *undersell* others in the same trade, that he may get all into his own hand.

Verse 20. *Wisdom crieth*] Here wisdom is again *personified,* as it is frequently, throughout this book; where nothing is meant but the *teachings* given to man, either by *Divine revelation* or the voice of the Holy Spirit in the heart. And this voice of *wisdom* is opposed to the *seducing language* of the wicked mentioned above. This voice is everywhere heard, in public, in private, in the streets, and in the house. Common sense, universal experience, and the law of justice written on the heart, as

A. M. cir. 3004
B. C. cir. 1000
Ante I. Olymp.
cir. 224
Ante U. C. cir.
247

22 How long, ye simple ones, will ye love simplicity? and the scorners delight in their scorning, and fools hate knowledge?

23 Turn you at my reproof: behold, ʸI will pour out my spirit unto you, I will make known my words unto you.

24 ᶻBecause I have called, and ye refused; I have stretched out my hand, and no man regarded;

25 But ye ᵃhave set at naught all my counsel, and would none of my reproof:

26 ᵇI also will laugh at your calamity; I will mock when your fear cometh;

27 When ᶜyour fear cometh as desolation, and your destruction cometh as a whirlwind, when distress and anguish cometh upon you.

28 ᵈThen shall they call upon me, but I will not answer; they shall seek me early, but they shall not find me:

A. M. cir. 3004
B. C. cir. 1000
Ante I. Olymp.
cir. 224
Ante U. C. cir.
247

29 For that they ᵉhated knowledge, and did not ᶠchoose the fear of the LORD:

30 ᵍThey would none of my counsel: they despised all my reproof.

31 Therefore ʰshall they eat of the fruit of their own way, and be filled with their own devices.

32 For the ⁱturning away of the simple shall slay them, and the prosperity of fools shall destroy them.

33 But ᵏwhoso hearkeneth unto me shall dwell safely, and ˡshall be quiet from fear of evil.

ʸJoel ii. 28——ᶻIsa. lxv. 12; lxvi. 4; Jer. vii. 13; Zech. vii. 11——ᵃPsa. cvii. 11; ver. 30; Luke vii. 30——ᵇPsa. ii. 4——ᶜCh. x. 24——ᵈJob xxvii. 9; xxxv. 12; Isa. i. 15; Jer. xi. 11; xiv. 12; Ezek. viii. 18; Mic. iii. 4; Zech. vii. 13; James iv. 3——ᵉJob xxi. 14; ver. 22——ᶠPsa. cxix. 173——ᵍVer. 25; Psa. lxxxi. 11——ʰJob iv. 8; ch. xiv. 14; xxii. 8; Isa. iii. 11; Jer. vi. 19——ⁱOr, *ease of the simple*——ᵏPsa. xxv. 12, 13——ˡPsa. cxii. 7

well as the law of God, testify against rapine and wrong of every kind.

Verse 22. *Ye simple ones*] פתים *pethayim*, ye who have been *seduced* and *deceived*. See on ver. 4.

Verse 23. *Turn you at my reproof*] לתוכחתי *lethochachti*, at my *convincing mode of arguing;* attend to my *demonstrations*. This is properly the meaning of the original word.

I will pour out my spirit unto you] "I wil expresse my mynde unto you;" COVERDALE. **Loo I shall bryngen forth to you my Spirit;** *Old MS. Bible.* If you will hear, ye shall have ample instruction.

Verse 24. *Because I have called*] These and the following words appear to be spoken of the persons who are described, ver. 11-19, who have refused to return from their evil ways till arrested by the hand of justice; and here the wise man points out their deplorable state.

They are now about to suffer according to the demands of the law, for their depredations. They now wish they had been guided by wisdom, and had chosen the fear of the Lord; but it is too late: die they must, for their crimes are proved against them, and *justice* knows nothing of *mercy*.

This, or something like this, must be the wise man's meaning; nor can any thing spoken here be considered as applying or applicable to the *eternal* state of the persons in question, much less to the case of any man convinced of sin, who is crying to God for mercy. Such persons as the above, condemned to die, may call upon justice for pardon, and they may do this *early, earnestly;* but they will call in vain. But no poor penitent sinner on this side of eternity can call upon God early, or seek him through Christ Jesus earnestly for the pardon of his sins, without being heard. Life is the time of probation, and while it lasts the vilest of the vile is within the reach of mercy. It is only in *eternity* that the state is irreversibly fixed, and where that which was guilty must be guilty

still. But let none harden his heart because of this longsuffering of God; for if he die in his sin, where God is he shall never come. And when once shut up in the unquenchable fire, he will not pray for mercy, as he shall clearly see and feel that the hope of his redemption is entirely cut off.

Verse 27. *Your destruction cometh as a whirlwind*] כסופה *kesuphah*, as the all-prostrating blast. *Sense* and *sound* are here well expressed. *Suphah* here is the gust of wind.

Verse 29. *They hated knowledge*] This argues the deepest degree of intellectual and moral depravity.

Verse 32. *For the turning away of the simple*] This difficult place seems to refer to such a case as we term *turning king's evidence;* where an accomplice saves his own life by impeaching the rest of his gang. This is called his *turning* or *repentance,* משובה *meshubah;* and he was the most likely to turn, because he was of the פתים *pethayim, seduced* or *deceived* persons. And this evidence was given against them when they were in their prosperity, שלוה *shalvah*, their *security*, enjoying the fruits of their depredations; and being thus in a state of fancied *security*, they were the more easily taken and brought to justice.

Verse 33. *But whoso hearkeneth unto me shall dwell safely*] The man who hears the *voice of wisdom* in preference to the *enticements* of the *wicked*. He shall dwell in *safety*, ישכן בטח *yishcan betach*, he shall *inhabit safety* itself; he shall be completely safe and secure; and *shall be quiet from the fear of evil*, having a full consciousness of his own innocence and God's protection. *Coverdale* translates, "And have ynough without eney feare of evell." What the just man has he got honestly; and he has the blessing of God upon it. It is the reverse with the thief, the knave, the cheat, and the extortioner: *Male parta pejus dilabuntur;* "Ill gotten, worse spent."

CHAPTER II

The teacher promises his pupil the highest advantages, if he will follow the dictates of wisdom, 1–9. He shall be happy in its enjoyment, 10, 11; shall be saved from wicked men, 12–15; and from the snares of bad women, 16–19; be a companion of the good and upright; and be in safety in the land, when the wicked shall be rooted out of it, 20–22.

A. M. cir. 3004
B. C. cir. 1000
Ante I. Olymp.
cir. 224
Ante U. C. cir.
247

MY son, if thou wilt receive my words, and ᵃhide my commandments with thee;

2 So that thou incline thine ear unto wisdom, *and* apply thine heart to understanding;

3 Yea, if thou criest after knowledge, *and* ᵇliftest up thy voice for understanding;

4 ᶜIf thou seekest her as silver, and searchest for her as *for* hid treasures;

5 Then shalt thou understand the fear of the Lord, and find the knowledge of God.

6 ᵈFor the Lord giveth wisdom: out of his mouth *cometh* knowledge and understanding.

7 He layeth up sound wisdom for the right-

eous: ᵉ*he is* a buckler to them that walk uprightly.

8 He keepeth the paths of judgment, and ᶠpreserveth the way of his saints.

9 Then shalt thou understand righteousness, and judgment, and equity; *yea,* every good path.

10 When wisdom entereth into thine heart, and knowledge is pleasant unto thy soul;

11 Discretion shall preserve thee, ᵍunderstanding shall keep thee:

12 To deliver thee from the way of the evil *man,* from the man that speaketh froward things;

13 Who leave the paths of uprightness, to

A. M. cir. 3004
B. C. cir. 1000
Ante I. Olymp.
cir. 224
Ante U. C. cir.
247

ᵃCh. iv. 21; vii. 1——ᵇHeb. *givest thy voice*——ᶜCh. iii. 14; Matt. xiii. 43——ᵈ1 Kings iii. 9, 12; James i. 5

ᵉPsa. lxxxiv. 11; chap. xxx. 5——ᶠ1 Sam. ii. 9; Psa. lxvi. 9——ᵍChap. vi. 22

NOTES ON CHAP. II.

Verse 1. *My son*] Here the *tutor* still continues to instruct his *disciple.*

Hide my commandments with thee] Treasure them up in thy *heart,* and then act from them through the medium of thy *affections.* He who has the rule of his *duty* only in his *Bible* and in his *head,* is not likely to be a steady, consistent character; his heart is not engaged, and his obedience, in any case, can be only *forced,* or done from a *sense of duty:* it is not the obedience of a *loving, dutiful child,* to an *affectionate father.* But he who has the word of God in his *heart,* works *from his heart;* his heart goes with him in all things, and he delights to do the will of his heavenly Father, because *his law is in his heart.* See chap. iii. 3.

Verse 4. *If thou seekest her as silver*] How do men seek money? What will they not do to get rich? Reader, seek the salvation of thy soul as earnestly as the covetous man seeks wealth; and be ashamed of thyself, if thou be less in earnest after the *true riches* than he is after *perishing wealth.*

Hid treasures] The original word signifies property of any kind *concealed* in the earth, in caves or such like; and may also mean *treasures,* such as the *precious metals* or *precious stones,* which are presumptively known to exist in such and such *mines.* And how are these sought? Learn from the following circumstance: In the Brazils *slaves* are employed to scrape up the soil from the bed of the Rio Janeiro, and wash it carefully, in order to find particles of *gold* and *diamonds;* and it is a law of the state, that he who finds a diamond of so many carats shall have his *freedom.* This causes the greatest ardour and diligence in

searching, washing out the soil, picking, &c., in order to find such diamonds, and the greatest anxiety for success; so precious is *liberty* to the human heart. This method of searching for gold and precious stones is alluded to in chap. iii. 13-15. In this way Solomon wishes men to seek for wisdom, knowledge, and understanding; and he who succeeds finds the *liberty* of the children of God, and is saved from the *slavery* of *sin* and the *empire of death.*

Verse 7. *He layeth up sound wisdom*] תושיה *tushiyah.* We have met with this word in Job: see chap. v. 12; vi. 13; xi. 6; xii. 16. See especially the note on Job xi. 6, where the different acceptations of the word are given. *Coverdale* translates, "He preserveth the welfare of the righteous." It is difficult to find, in any language, a term proper to express the original meaning of the word; its seems to mean generally the *essence* or *substance* of a thing, the thing itself—that which is *chief* of its *kind.* He layeth up what is essential for the *righteous.*

Verse 9. *Then shalt thou understand*] He who is taught of God understands the whole law of *justice, mercy, righteousness,* and *truth;* God has written this on his heart. He who understands these things by *books* only is never likely to practise or profit by them.

Verse 11. *Discretion shall preserve thee*] מזמה *mezimmah.* See on chap. i. 4. Here the word is taken in a good sense, a *good device.* The man *invents purposes* of good; and all his *schemes, plans,* and *devices,* have for their object God's glory and the good of man: he deviseth liberal things, and by liberal things he shall stand. *Coverdale* translates, "Then shall counsel preserve thee." A very good translation, much better than the present.

Verse 12. *The man that speaketh froward*

A. M. cir. 3004
B. C. cir. 1000
Ante I. Olymp.
cir. 224
Ante U. C. cir.
247

[h]walk in the ways of darkness;

14 Who [i]rejoice to do evil, *and* [k]delight in the frowardness of the wicked;

15 [l]Whose ways *are* crooked, and *they* froward in their paths:

16 To deliver thee from [m]the strange woman, [n]*even* from the stranger *which* flattereth with her words;

17 [o]Which forsaketh the guide of her youth, and forgetteth the covenant of her God.

18 For [p]her house inclineth unto death, and her paths unto the dead.

19 None that go unto her return again, neither take they hold of the paths of life.

20 That thou mayest walk in the way of good *men,* and keep the paths of the righteous.

21 [q]For the upright shall dwell in the land, and the perfect shall remain in it.

22 [r]But the wicked shall be cut off from the earth, and the transgressors shall be [s]rooted out of it.

A. M. cir. 3004
B. C. cir. 1000
Ante I. Olymp.
cir. 224
Ante U. C. cir.
247

---

[h]John iii. 19, 20——[i]Ch. x. 23; Jer. xi. 15——[k]Rom. i. 32——[l]Psa. cxxv. 5——[m]Chap. v. 20——[n]Chap. v. 3; vi. 24; vii. 5

[o]See Mal. ii. 14, 15——[p]Chap. vii. 27——[q]Psa. xxxvii. 29——[r]Job xviii. 17; Psa. xxxvii. 28; civ. 35
[s]Or, *plucked up*

---

things.] תהפכות *tahpuchoth,* things of *subversion;* from תפך *taphach,* to *turn* or *change* the *course of a thing.* Men who wish to subvert the *state* of things, whether *civil* or *religious;* who are seditious themselves, and wish to make others so. These speak much of *liberty* and *oppression,* deal greatly in *broad assertions,* and endeavour especially to corrupt the minds of *youth.*

Verse 16. *The stranger which flattereth with her words*] החליקה *hechelikah,* she that *smooths* with her words. The original intimates the *glib, oily* speeches of a *prostitute.* The English *lick* is supposed to be derived from the original word.

Verse 17. *Which forsaketh the guide of her youth*] Leaves her father's house and instructions, and abandons herself to the public.

The covenant of her God.] Renounces the *true religion,* and mixes with *idolaters;* for among them prostitution was enormous. Or by the *covenant* may be meant the *matrimonial contract,* which is a *covenant made in the presence of God between the contracting parties,* in which they bind themselves to be faithful to each other.

Verse 18. *For her house inclineth unto death*] It is generally in *by* and *secret places* that such women establish themselves. They go out of the *high road* to get a residence; and every step that is taken towards their house is a step towards *death.* The path of sin is the path of ruin: the path of duty is the way of safety. For *her paths* incline *unto the dead,* רפאים *rephaim,* the *inhabitants of the invisible world.*

The woman who abandons herself to prostitution soon *contracts,* and generally *communicates, that disease,* which, above all others, signs the speediest and most effectual *passport* to the *invisible world.* Therefore it is said,

Verse 19. *None that go unto her return again*] There are very few instances of prostitutes ever returning to the paths of sobriety and truth; perhaps *not one* of such as become prostitutes *through a natural propensity to debauchery.* Among those who have been *deceived, debauched,* and *abandoned,* many have been reclaimed; and to such alone *penitentiaries* may be useful; to the others they may only be incentives to farther sinning. *Rakes* and *debauchees* are sometimes converted: but most of them *never lay hold on the path of life;* they have had their *health* destroyed, and never *recover* it. The original, חיים *chaiyim,* means *lives;* not only the *health* of the *body* is destroyed, but the *soul* is *ruined.* Thus the unhappy man may be said to be *doubly* slain.

Verse 20. *That thou mayest walk*] Therefore thou shalt walk.

Verse 22. *Transgressors*] בוגדים *bogedim.* The *garment men,* the *hypocrites;* those who act *borrowed characters,* who go under a *cloak;* *dissemblers.* All such shall be *rooted out of the land;* they shall not be blessed with *posterity.* In general it is so: and were it not so, one evil offspring succeeding another, *adding* their *own* to their *predecessors'* vices, the earth would become so exceedingly corrupt that a *second flood,* or a *fire,* would be necessary to purge it.

CHAPTER III

An exhortation to obedience, 1–4; trust in God's providence, 5, 6; to humility, 7, 8; to charity, 9, 10; to submission to God's chastenings, 11, 12. The profitableness of wisdom in all the concerns of life, 13–26. No act of duty should be deferred beyond the time in which it should be done, 27, 28. Brotherly love and forbearance should be exercised, 29, 30. We should not envy the wicked, 31, 32. The curse of God is in the house of the wicked; but the humble and wise shall prosper, 33–35.

A. M. cir. 3004
B. C. cir. 1000
Ante I. Olymp.
cir. 224
Ante U. C. cir.
247

MY son, forget not my law; [a]but let thine heart keep my commandments:

2 For length of days, and [b]long life, and [c]peace, shall they add to thee.

3 Let not mercy and truth forsake thee: [d]bind them about thy neck; [e]write them upon the table of thine heart:

4 [f]So shalt thou find favour and [g]good understanding in the sight of God and man.

5 [h]Trust in the LORD with all thine heart; [i]and lean not unto thine own understanding.

A. M. cir. 3004
B. C. cir. 1000
Ante I. Olymp.
cir. 224
Ante U. C. cir.
247

6 [k]In all thy ways acknowledge him, and he shall [l]direct thy paths.

7 [m]Be not wise in thine own eyes: [n]fear the LORD, and depart from evil.

8 It shall be [o]health to thy navel, and [p]marrow [q]to thy bones.

---

[a]Deut. viii. 1; xxx. 16, 20——[b]Heb. *years of life* [c]Psa. cxix. 165——[d]Exod. xiii. 9; Deut. vi. 8; chap. vi. 21; vii. 3——[e]Jer. xvii. 1; 2 Cor. iii. 3——[f]Psa. cxi. 10; see 1 Sam. ii. 26; Luke ii. 52; Acts ii. 47; Rom. xiv. 18

[g]Or, *good success*——[h]Psa. xxxvii. 3, 5——[i]Jer. ix. 23 [k]1 Chron. xxviii. 9——[l]Jer. x. 23——[m]Rom. xii. 16 [n]Job i. 1; chap. xvi. 6——[o]Heb. *medicine*——[p]Heb. *watering* or *moistening*——[q]Job xxi. 24

NOTES ON CHAP. III

Verse 1. My son] The preceptor continues to deliver his lessons.

Forget not my law]. *Remember* what thou hast *heard*, and *practise* what thou dost *remember;* and let all obedience be *from the heart:* "Let thy heart keep my commandments."

Verse 2. For length of days] THREE eminent *blessings* are promised here: 1. ארך ימים *orech yamim*, long days; 2. שנות חיים *shenoth chaiyim*, years of lives; 3. שלום *shalom*, prosperity; i. e. health, long life, and abundance.

Verse 3. Let not mercy and truth forsake thee] Let these be thy constant *companions* through life.

Bind them about thy neck] Keep them constantly *in view. Write them upon the table of thine heart*—let them be thy *moving principles; feel* them as well as *see* them.

Verse 4. So shalt thou find favour] Thou shalt be acceptable to God, and thou shalt enjoy a sense of his approbation.

And good understanding] Men shall *weigh* thy character and conduct; and by this *appreciate* thy motives, and give thee credit for sincerity and uprightness. Though religion is frequently persecuted, and religious people suffer at first where they are not fully *known;* yet a truly religious and benevolent character will in general be prized wherever it is well known. The envy of men is a proof of the excellence of that which they envy.

Verse 5. Trust in the Lord with all thine heart] This is a most important precept: 1. God is the *Fountain* of all good. 2. He has made his intelligent creatures *dependent* upon himself. 3. He requires them to be *conscious* of that dependence. 4. He has *promised* to communicate what they need. 5. He commands them to *believe* his promise, and look for its fulfilment. 6. And to do this without doubt, fear, or distrust; "with their whole heart."

Lean not unto thine own understanding] אל תשען *al tishshaen*, do not *prop* thyself. It is on GOD, not on *thyself*, that thou art commanded to *depend*. He who trusts in his own heart is a fool.

Verse 6. In all thy ways acknowledge him] Begin, continue, and end every work, purpose, and device, with God. Earnestly pray for his *direction* at the *commencement;* look for his

continual *support* in the *progress;* and so begin and continue that all may terminate in his glory: and then it will certainly be to thy good; for we never *honour God*, without *serving ourselves*. This passage is well rendered in my old MS. Bible:—𝕳𝖆𝖇𝖊 𝖙𝖗𝖔𝖘𝖙 𝖎𝖓 𝖙𝖍𝖊 𝕷𝖔𝖗𝖉 𝖔𝖋 𝖆𝖑𝖑 𝖙𝖍𝖎𝖓 𝖍𝖊𝖗𝖙𝖊 𝖆𝖓𝖉 𝖓𝖊 𝖑𝖊𝖓𝖊 𝖙𝖍𝖔𝖚 𝖙𝖔 𝖙𝖍𝖎 𝖕𝖗𝖚𝖉𝖊𝖓𝖈𝖊: 𝖎𝖓 𝖆𝖑𝖑𝖊 𝖙𝖍𝖎 𝖜𝖊𝖞𝖘 𝖙𝖍𝖎𝖓𝖐 𝖍𝖞𝖒, 𝖆𝖓𝖉 𝖍𝖊 𝖘𝖍𝖆𝖑 𝖗𝖎𝖌𝖍𝖙 𝖗𝖚𝖑𝖊𝖓 𝖙𝖍𝖎 𝖌𝖔𝖞𝖓𝖌𝖊𝖘; 𝖓𝖊 𝖇𝖊 𝖙𝖍𝖔𝖚 𝖜𝖎𝖎𝖘 𝖆𝖓𝖊𝖓𝖙𝖎𝖘 𝖙𝖍𝖎𝖘𝖊𝖑𝖋. *Self-sufficiency* and *self-dependence* have been the ruin of mankind ever since the fall of Adam. The grand sin of the human race is their continual endeavour to *live independently of God*, i. e., to be *without God in the world. True religion* consists in considering God the fountain of all good, and expecting all good from him.

Verse 8. It shall be health to thy navel] We need not puzzle ourselves to find out what we may suppose to be a more *delicate* meaning for the original word שר *shor* than *navel;* for I am satisfied a more proper cannot be found. It is well known that it is by the *umbilical cord* that the *fetus* receives its nourishment all the time it is in the womb of the mother. It receives nothing by the *mouth*, nor by any other means: by *this* alone all nourishment is received, and the circulation of the blood kept up. When, therefore, the wise man says, that "trusting in the Lord with the whole heart, and acknowledging him in all a man's ways, &c., shall be health to the navel, and marrow to the bones;" he in effect says, that this is as essential to the life of God in the soul of man, and to the continual growth in grace, as the *umbilical cord* is to the *life* and *growth of the fetus* in the womb. Without the *latter*, no human being could ever exist or be born; without the *former*, no *true religion* can ever be found. *Trust* or *faith* in God is as necessary to derive grace from him to nourish the soul, and cause it to grow up unto eternal life, as the *navel string* or *umbilical cord* is to the human being in the first stage of its existence. I need not push this illustration farther: the good sense of the reader will supply what *he knows*. I might add much on the subject.

And marrow to thy bones.] This metaphor is not less proper than the preceding. All the larger *bones* of the body have either a large *cavity*, or they are *spongious*, and full of little cells: in both the one and the other the *oleaginous* substance, called *marrow*, is contained in proper vesicles, like the fat. In the larger *bones* the *fine oil*, by the gentle heat of the

A. M. cir. 3004
B. C. cir. 1000
Ante I. Olymp.
cir. 224
Ante U. C. cir.
247

9 [r]Honour the LORD with thy substance, and with the first-fruits of all thine increase:

10 [s]So shall thy barns be filled with plenty, and thy presses shall burst out with new wine.

11 [t]My son, despise not the chastening of the LORD: neither be weary of his correction:

12 For whom the LORD loveth he correcteth; [u]even as a father the son *in whom* he delighteth.

13 [v]Happy *is* the man *that* findeth wisdom, and [w]the man *that* getteth understanding.

A. M. cir. 3004
B. C. cir. 1000
Ante I. Olymp.
cir. 224
Ante U. C. cir.
247

14 [x]For the merchandise of it *is* better than the merchandise of silver, and the gain thereof than fine gold.

15 She *is* more precious than rubies: and [y]all the things thou canst desire are not to be compared unto her.

---

[r]Exod. xxii. 29; xxiii. 19; xxxiv. 26; Deut. xxvi. 2, &c.; Mal. iii. 10, &c.; Luke xiv. 13——[s]Deut. xxviii. 8——[t]Job v. 17; Psa. xciv. 12; Heb. xii. 5, 6; Rev. iii. 19

[u]Deut. viii. 5——[v]Ch. viii. 34, 35——[w]Heb. *the man that draweth out understanding*——[x]Job xxviii. 13, &c.; Psa. xix. 10; ch. ii. 4; viii. 11, 19; xvi. 16——[y]Matt. xiii. 44

---

body, is exhaled through the pores of its small vesicles, and enters some narrow passages which lead to certain fine canals excavated in the substance of the bone, that the marrow may supply the *fibres of the bones*, and render them less liable to break. *Blood-vessels* also penetrate the *bones* to supply this *marrow* and this *blood;* and consequently the *marrow* is supplied in the infant by means of the *umbilical cord.* From the *marrow* diffused, as mentioned above, through the *bones*, they derive their *solidity* and *strength.* A simple experiment will cast considerable light on the use of the *marrow* to the *bones:*—Calcine a *bone*, so as to destroy all the *marrow* from the cells, you will find it exceedingly *brittle.* Immerse the same bone in *oil* so that the cells may be all replenished, which will be done in a few minutes; and the bone reacquires a considerable measure of its *solidity* and *strength;* and would acquire the *whole*, if the *marrow* could be *extracted* without otherwise injuring the texture of the *bone.* After the calcination, the bone may be reduced to powder by the hand; after the *impregnation with the oil*, it becomes *hard, compact*, and *strong.* What the marrow is to the *support* and *strength* of the *bones*, and the *bones* to the *support* and *strength* of the *body;* that, *faith* in God, is to the *support, strength, energy*, and *salvation* of the *soul.* Behold, then, the force and elegance of the wise man's metaphor. Some have rendered the last clause, *a lotion for the bones.* What is this? How are the *bones washed?* What a pitiful destruction of a most beautiful metaphor!

Verse 9. *Honour the Lord with thy substance*] The מנחה MINCHAH or gratitude-offering to God, commanded under the *law*, is of endless obligation. It would be well to give a portion of the *produce* of *every article* by which we get our support to God, or to the *poor*, the representatives of Christ. This might be done either in *kind*, or by the *worth* in *money.* Whatever God sends us in the way of secular prosperity, there is a *portion of it* always for the poor, and for God's cause. When that *portion* is thus disposed of, the rest is *sanctified;* when it is *withheld*, God's curse is upon the whole. Give to the *poor*, and God will give to *thee.*

Verse 11. *Despise not the chastening of the Lord*] The word מוסר *musar* signifies *correction, discipline*, and *instruction. Teaching* is

essentially necessary to show the man the *way* in which he is to go; *discipline* is necessary to render that *teaching effectual;* and, often, *correction* is requisite in order to bring the mind into *submission*, without which it cannot acquire *knowledge.* Do not therefore reject this procedure of God; humble thyself under his mighty hand, and open thy eyes to thy own interest; and then thou wilt learn *specially* and *effectually.* It is of no use to *rebel;* if thou do, thou *kickest against the pricks*, and every act of rebellion against him is a *wound* to thine own *soul.* God will either *end* thee or *mend* thee; wilt thou then *kick* on?

Verse 12. *Whom the Lord loveth*] To encourage thee to bear correction, know that it is a proof of God's love to thee; and thereby he shows that he treats thee as a father does his son, even that one to whom he bears the fondest affection.

The last clause the *Septuagint* translate μαστιγοι δε παντα υιον ον παραδεχεται, "and chasteneth every son whom he receiveth;" and the *apostle*, Heb. xii. 6, quotes this *literatim.* Both clauses certainly amount to the same sense. *Every son whom he receiveth*, and *the son in whom he delighteth*, have very little difference of meaning.

Verse 13. *Happy is the man that findeth wisdom*] This refers to the advice given in chap. ii. 4; where see the note.

Verse 14. *For the merchandise*] סחר *sachar*, the *traffic*, the *trade* that is carried on by *going through countries* and *provinces* with such articles as they could carry on the backs of camels, &c.; from סחר *sachar*, to *go about, traverse.* **Chaffarynge;** Old MS. Bible.

And the gain thereof] תבואתה *tebuathah*, its *produce;* what is gained by the articles after all expenses are paid. The *slaves*, as we have already seen, got their *liberty* if they were so lucky as to find a diamond of so many carats' weight; he who *finds wisdom*—the *knowledge* and *salvation of God*—gets a greater prize; for he obtains the *liberty of the Gospel*, is adopted into the *family of God*, and made an *heir* according to the hope of an eternal life.

Verse 15. *She is more precious than rubies*] מפנינים *mippeninim.* The word principally means *pearls*, but may be taken for *precious stones* in general. The root is פנה *panah*, he *looked, beheld;* and as it gives the idea of the eye always being turned towards the observer, Mr. Parkhurst thinks that it means the *load-*

A. M. cir. 3004
B. C. cir. 1000
Ante I. Olymp. cir. 224
Ante U. C. cir. 247

16 ^zLength of days *is* in her right hand; *and* in her left hand riches and honour.

17 ^aHer ways *are* ways of pleasantness, and all her paths *are* peace.

18 She *is* ^ba tree of life to them that lay hold upon her: and happy *is every one* that retaineth her.

19 ^cThe LORD by wisdom hath founded the earth; by understanding hath he ^destablished the heavens.

20 ^eBy his knowledge the depths are broken up, and ^fthe clouds drop down the dew.

21 My son, let not them depart from thine eyes: keep sound wisdom and discretion:

22 So shall they be life unto thy soul, and ^ggrace to thy neck.

23 ^hThen shalt thou walk in thy way safely, and thy foot shall not stumble.

24 ⁱWhen thou liest down, thou shalt not

A. M. cir. 3004
B. C. cir. 1000
Ante I. Olymp. cir. 224
Ante U. C. cir. 247

---

^zChap. viii. 18; 1 Tim. iv. 8——^aMatt. xi. 29, 30 ^bGen. ii. 9; iii. 22——^cPsa. civ. 24; cxxxvi. 5; chap. viii. 27; Jer. x. 12; li. 15

^dOr, *prepared*——^eGen. i. 9——^fDeut. xxxiii. 28; Job xxxvi. 28——^gChap. i. 9——^hPsa. xxxvii. 24; xci. 11, 12; chap. x. 9——ⁱLev. xxvi. 6; Psa. iii. 5; iv. 8

---

stone; see the note on Job xxviii. 18, where this subject is considered at large. If the oriental *ruby,* or any other precious stone, be intended here, the word may refer to their being *cut* and *polished,* so that they present different *faces,* and reflect the light to you in whatever direction you may look at them.

All the things thou canst desire] Superior to every thing that can be an object of desire here below. But who believes this?

Verse 16. *Length of days is in her right hand*] A wicked man shortens his days by *excesses;* a righteous man prolongs his by *temperance.*

In her left hand riches and honour.] That is, her hands are full of the choicest benefits. There is nothing to be understood here by the *right hand* in preference to the *left.*

Verse 17. *Her ways are ways of pleasantness*] These blessings of true religion require little comment. They are well expressed by the poet in the following elegant verses:—

"Wisdom Divine! Who tells the price
Of Wisdom's costly merchandise?
Wisdom to silver we prefer,
And *gold* is *dross* compared to her.
Her hands are fill'd with length of days,
True riches, and *immortal praise;*—
Riches of Christ, on all bestow'd,
And honour that descends from God.

To purest joys she all invites,
Chaste, holy, spiritual *delights;*
Her ways are ways of pleasantness,
And *all her* flowery *paths are peace.*
Happy the man that finds the grace,
The blessing of God's chosen race;
The *wisdom coming from above,*
The *faith* that sweetly *works by love!"*
                  WESLEY.

Verse 18. *She is a tree of life*] עץ חיים *ets chaiyim,* "the tree of lives," alluding most manifestly to the tree so called which God in the beginning planted in the garden of Paradise, by eating the fruit of which all the wastes of nature might have been continually repaired, so as to prevent death for ever. This is an opinion which appears probable enough. The blessings which wisdom—true religion—gives to men, preserve them *in* life, comfort them *through* life, cause them to triumph in *death,* and ensure them a glorious *immortality.*

Verse 19. *The Lord by wisdom hath founded the earth*] Here wisdom is taken in its proper acceptation, for that infinite knowledge and skill which God has manifested in the creation and composition of the earth, and in the structure and economy of the heavens. He has established the *order* as well as the *essence* of all things; so that though they *vary* in their *positions,* &c., yet they never *change* either their *places,* or their *properties. Composition* and *analysis* are not *essential changes;* the original *particles,* their *forms* and *properties,* remain the same.

Verse 20. *By his knowledge the depths are broken up*] He determined in his wisdom how to *break up the fountains of the great deep,* so as to *bring a flood of waters upon the earth;* and by his knowledge those fissures in the earth through which *springs* of water arise have been appointed and determined; and it is by his skill and influence that *vapours* are exhaled, suspended in the *atmosphere,* and afterwards precipitated on the earth in *rain, dews,* &c. Thus the wisest of men attributes those effects which we suppose to spring from *natural causes* to the Supreme Being himself.

Verse 21. *Let not them depart from thine eyes*] Never forget that God, who is the author of nature, directs and governs it in all things; for it is no self-determining agent.

Keep sound wisdom and discretion] תושיה ומזמה *tushiyah umezimmah.* We have met with both these words before. *Tushiyah* is the *essence* or *substance* of a thing; *mezimmah* is the *resolution* or *purpose* formed in reference to something good or excellent. To acknowledge God as the author of all good, is the *tushiyah,* the *essence,* of a godly man's creed; to *resolve* to *act according* to the directions of his wisdom, is the *mezimmah,* the *religious purpose,* that will bring good to ourselves and glory to God. These bring *life to the soul,* and are *ornamental* to the man who acts in this way, ver. 22.

Verse 24. *When thou liest down*] In these verses (23-26) the wise man describes the confidence, security, and safety, which proceed from a consciousness of innocence. Most people are afraid of *sleep,* lest they should never awake, because they feel they are not prepared to appear before God. They are neither innocent nor pardoned. True believers know that God is their keeper night and day; they have

A. M. cir. 3004
B. C. cir. 1000
Ante I. Olymp.
cir. 224
Ante U. C. cir.
247

be afraid: yea, thou shalt lie down, and thy sleep shall be sweet.

25 [k]Be not afraid of sudden fear, neither of the desolation of the wicked when it cometh.

26 For the LORD shall be thy confidence, and shall keep thy foot from being taken.

27 [l]Withhold not good from [m]them to whom it is due, when it is in the power of thine hand to do *it*.

28 [n]Say not unto thy neighbour, Go, and come again, and to-morrow I will give; when thou hast it by thee.

29 [o]Devise not evil against thy neighbour, seeing he dwelleth securely by thee.

A. M. cir. 3004
B. C. cir. 1000
Ante I. Olymp.
cir. 224
Ante U. C. cir.
247

30 [p]Strive not with a man without cause, if he have done thee no harm.

31 [q]Envy thou not [r]the oppressor, and choose none of his ways.

32 For the froward *is* abomination to the LORD: [s]but his secret *is* with the righteous.

33 [t]The curse of the LORD *is* in the house of the wicked: but [u]he blesseth the habitation of the just.

34 [v]Surely he scorneth the scorners: but he giveth grace unto the lowly.

35 The wise shall inherit glory: but shame [w]shall be the promotion of fools.

---

[k]Psa. xci. 5; cxii. 7——[l]Rom. xiii. 7; Gal. vi. 10 [m]Heb. *the owners thereof*——[n]Lev. xix. 13; Deut. xxiv. 15——[o]Or, *Practise no evil*——[p]Rom. xii. 48——[q]Psa. xxxvii. 1; lxxiii. 3; chap. xxiv. 1

[r]Heb. *a man of violence*——[s]Psa. xxv. 14——[t]Lev. xxvi. 14, &c.; Psa. xxxvii. 22; Zech. v. 4; Mal. ii. 2 [u]Psalm i. 6——[v]James iv. 6; 1 Pet. v. 5——[w]Hebrew, *exalteth the fools*

---

strong confidence in him that he will be their director, and not suffer them to take any *false step* in life, ver. 23. They go to rest in perfect confidence that God will watch over them; hence their *sleep*, being undisturbed with foreboding and evil dreams, is *sweet* and refreshing, ver. 24. They are not apprehensive of any *sudden destruction*, because they know that all things are under the control of God; and they are satisfied that if *sudden destruction* should fall upon their wicked neighbour, yet God knows well how to preserve *them*, ver. 25. And all this naturally flows from the Lord being their confidence, ver. 26.

Verse 27. *Withhold not good from them to whom it is due*] מבעליו *mibbealaiv, from the lords of it.* But who are they? The *poor. And what art thou, O rich man?* Why, thou art a *steward*, to whom God has given substance that thou mayest divide with the poor. They are the right owners of every farthing thou hast to spare from thy own support, and that of thy family; and God has given the surplus for their sakes. Dost thou, by hoarding up this treasure, deprive the *right owners* of their property? If this were a *civil case*, the law would take thee by the throat, and lay thee up in prison; but it is a case in which GOD alone judges. And what will he do to thee? Hear! "He shall have judgment without mercy, who hath showed no mercy;" James ii. 13. *Read, feel, tremble, and act justly.*

Verse 28. *Say not unto thy neighbour*] Do not refuse a kindness when it is in thy power to perform it. If thou have the means *by thee*, and thy neighbour's necessities be pressing, do not put him off till the *morrow.* Death may take either him or thee before that time.

Verse 30. *Strive not with a man*] Do not be of a litigious, quarrelsome spirit. Be not under

the influence of too nice a sense of honour. If thou must appeal to judicial authority to bring him that wrongs thee to reason, avoid all enmity, and do nothing in a spirit of revenge. But, if he *have done thee no harm*, why contend with him? May not others in the same way contend with and injure *thee?*

Verse 31. *Envy thou not the oppressor*] O how bewitching is *power!* Every man desires it; and yet all hate *tyrants.* But query, if all had *power*, would not the major part be *tyrants?*

Verse 32. *But his secret*] סודו *sodo, his secret assembly;* godly people meet there, and God dwells there.

Verse 33. *The curse of the Lord*] No godly people meet in such a house; nor is God ever an *inmate* there.

But he blesseth the habitation of the just.] He considers it as his *own temple.* There he is worshipped in spirit and in truth; and hence God makes it his *dwelling-place.*

Verse 34. *Surely he scorneth the scorners; but he giveth grace unto the lowly.*] The *Septuagint* has Κυριος υπερηφανοις αντιτασσεται, ταπεινοις δε διδωσι χαριν. *The Lord resisteth the proud; but giveth grace to the humble.* These words are quoted by St. *Peter*, 1st Epist. v. 5, and by St. *James*, chap. iv. 6, just as they stand in the *Septuagint*, with the change of ὁ Θεος, *God*, for Κυριος, *the Lord.*

Verse 35. *The wise*] The person who follows the dictates of wisdom, as mentioned above, *shall inherit glory;* because, being one of the *heavenly family*, a *child of God*, he has thereby heaven for his *inheritance; but fools*, such as those mentioned chap. i. and ii., shall have *ignominy* for their *exaltation.* Many such fools as Solomon speaks of are exalted to the *gibbet* and *gallows.* The way to prevent this and the like evils, is to attend to the voice of wisdom.

CHAPTER IV

The preceptor calls his pupils, and tells them how himself was educated, 1–4; specifies the teachings he received, 5–19; and exhorts his pupil to persevere in well-doing, and to avoid evil, 20–27.

A. M. cir. 3004
B. C. cir. 1000
Ante I. Olymp.
cir. 224
Ante U. C. cir.
247

HEAR, [a]ye children, the instruction of a father, and attend to know understanding.

2 For I give you good doctrine, forsake ye not my law.

3 For I was my father's son, [b]tender and only *beloved* in the sight of my mother.

4 [c]He taught me also, and said unto me, Let thine heart retain my words: [d]keep my commandments, and live.

5 [e]Get wisdom, get understanding: forget *it* not; neither decline from the words of my mouth.

A. M. cir. 3004
B. C. cir. 1000
Ante I. Olymp.
cir. 224
Ante U. C. cir.
247

6 Forsake her not, and she shall preserve thee: [f]love her, and she shall keep thee.

7 [g]Wisdom *is* the principal thing; *therefore* get wisdom: and with all thy getting get understanding.

8 [h]Exalt her, and she shall promote thee:

---

[a]Psalm xxxiv. 11; chap. i. 8——[b]1 Chron. xxix. 1——[c]1 Chron. xxix. 9; Eph. vi. 4——[d]Chap. vii. 2

[e]Chap. ii. 2, 3——[f]2 Thess. ii. 10——[g]Matt. xiii. 44; Luke x. 42——[h]1 Sam. ii. 30

NOTES ON CHAP. IV

Verse 1. *Hear, ye children*] Come, my pupils, and hear how a father instructed his child. Such as *I* received from *my father* I give to you; and they were the teachings of a wise and affectionate parent to his only son, a peculiar object of his regards, and also those of a *fond mother.*

He introduces the subject thus, to show that the teaching he received, and which he was about to give them, was the most excellent of its kind. By this he ensured their attention, and made his way to their heart. Teaching by *precept* is good; teaching by *example* is better; but teaching *both by precept and example* is best of all.

Verse 4. *He taught me also, and said*] Open thy heart to receive my instructions—receive them with affection; w[h]en heard, retain and practise them; and thou shalt live—the great purpose of thy being brought into the world shall be accomplished in thee.

Verse 5. *Get wisdom*] True religion is essential to thy happiness; never *forget* its teachings, nor go *aside* from the path it prescribes.

Verse 6. *Forsake her not*] Wisdom personified is here represented as a *guardian* and *companion,* who, if not forsaken, will continue faithful; if loved, will continue a protector.

Verse 7. *Wisdom* is *the principal thing*] ראשית חכמה *reshith chochmah,* "wisdom is the principle." It is the *punctum saliens* in all religion to know the true God, and *what* he requires of man, and *for what* he has made man; and to this must be added, under the Christian dispensation, *to know Jesus Christ whom he hath sent,* and for *what end* HE was *sent,* the *necessity* of his being *sent,* and the *nature* of that *salvation* which he has *bought by his own blood.*

Get wisdom] Consider this as thy *chief gain;* that in reference to which all *thy* wisdom, knowledge, and endeavours should be directed.

And with all thy getting] Let this be thy *chief property.* While thou art passing through things temporal, do not lose those things which are eternal; and, while *diligent in business,* be *fervent in spirit, serving the Lord.*

Get understanding.] Do not be contented

with the lessons of wisdom merely; do not be satisfied with having a sound religious creed; *devils* believe and tremble; but see that thou properly *comprehend* all that thou hast learnt; and see that thou rightly apply all that thou hast been taught.

Wisdom prescribes the best end, and the means best calculated for its attainment. *Understanding* directs to the ways, times, places, and opportunities of practising the lessons of wisdom. *Wisdom* points out the *thing requisite; understanding* sees to the *accomplishment* and *attainment. Wisdom sees;* but *understanding feels.* One *discovers,* the other *possesses.*

Coverdale translates this whole verse in a very remarkable manner: "The chefe poynte of wyssdome is, that thou be wyllynge to opteyne wyssdome; and before all thy goodes to get the understandynge." This is *paraphrase,* not *translation.* In this version *paraphrase* abounds. The translation in my old MS. Bible is very simple: 𝕭𝖊𝖌𝖞𝖓𝖓𝖞𝖓𝖌𝖊 𝖔𝖋 𝖜𝖎𝖘𝖉𝖆𝖒, 𝖜𝖊𝖑𝖑𝖊 𝖙𝖍𝖔𝖚 𝖜𝖎𝖘𝖉𝖆𝖒: 𝖎𝖓 𝖆𝖑 𝖙𝖍𝖎 𝖜𝖎𝖘𝖉𝖆𝖒, 𝖆𝖓𝖉 𝖎𝖓 𝖆𝖑 𝖙𝖍𝖎 𝖕𝖔𝖘𝖘𝖎𝖔𝖚𝖓, 𝖕𝖚𝖗𝖈𝖍𝖆𝖘 𝖕𝖗𝖚𝖉𝖊𝖓𝖈𝖊. He is already wise who seeks wisdom; and he is wise who knows its value, seeks to possess it. The whole of this verse is wanting in the *Arabic,* and in the best copies of the *Septuagint.*

Instead of קנה חכמה *keneh chochmah, get wisdom,* the *Complutensian* Polyglot has קנה בינה *keneh binah, get understanding;* so that in it the verse stands, "Wisdom is the principle, get understanding; and in all thy getting, get understanding." This is not an error either of the *scribe,* or of the *press,* for it is supported by *seven* of the MSS. of *Kennicott* and *De Rossi.*

The *Complutensian, Antwerp,* and *Paris* Polyglots have the *seventh* verse in the *Greek* text; but the two latter, in general, copy the former.

Verse 8. *She shall bring thee to honour*] There is nothing, a strict life of piety and benevolence excepted, that has such a direct tendency to *reflect honour* upon a man, as the careful *cultivation of his mind.* One of *Bacon's* aphorisms was, *Knowledge is power;* and it is truly astonishing to see what *influence* true learning has. Nothing is so universally respected, provided the learned man be a *consis-*

A. M. cir. 3004
B. C. cir. 1000
Ante I. Olymp. cir. 224
Ante U. C. cir. 247

she shall bring thee to honour, when thou dost embrace her.

9 She shall give to thine head [l]an ornament of grace: [k]a crown of glory shall she deliver to thee.

10 Hear, O my son, and receive my sayings; [l]and the years of thy life shall be many.

11 I have taught thee in the way of wisdom; I have led thee in right paths.

12 When thou goest, [m]thy steps shall not be straitened; [n]and when thou runnest, thou shalt not stumble.

13 Take fast hold of instruction; let *her* not

go: keep her; for she *is* thy life.

A. M. cir. 3004
B. C. cir. 1000
Ante I. Olymp. cir. 224
Ante U. C. cir. 247

14 [o]Enter not into the path of the wicked, and go not in the way of evil *men*.

15 Avoid it, pass not by it, turn from it, and pass away.

16 [p]For they sleep not, except they have done mischief; and their sleep is taken away, unless they cause *some* to fall.

17 For they eat the bread of wickedness, and drink the wine of violence.

18 [q]But the path of the just [r]*is* as the

---

[i]Chap. i. 9; iii. 22——[k]Or, *she shall compass thee with a crown of glory*——[l]Chapter iii. 2——[m]Psalm xviii. 36——[n]Psalm xci. 11, 12——[o]Psalm i. 1; chap-

ter i. 10, 15——[p]Psalm xxxvi. 4; Isaiah lvii. 20 [q]Matthew v. 14, 45; Philippians ii. 15——[r]2 Samuel xxiii. 4

---

tent moral character, and be not proud and overbearing; which is a disgrace to genuine literature.

Verse 9. *A crown of glory*] A tiara, diadem, or crown, shall not be more honourable to the princely wearer, than sound wisdom—true religion—coupled with deep learning, shall be to the Christian and the scholar.

Verse 10. *The years of thy life shall be many.*] Vice and intemperance impair the health and shorten the days of the wicked; while true religion, sobriety, and temperance, prolong them. The principal part of our diseases springs from "indolence, intemperance, and disorderly passions." Religion excites to *industry*, promotes *sober habits*, and destroys *evil passions*, and *harmonizes* the soul; and thus, by preventing many diseases, necessarily prolongs life.

Verse 12. *Thy steps shall not be straitened*] True wisdom will teach thee to keep out of embarrassments. A man under the influence of true religion *ponders* his paths, and carefully *poises occurring circumstances;* and as the fear of God will ever lead him to act an upright and honest part, so his way in business and life is both *clear* and *large*. He has no *by-ends* to serve; he *speculates* not; he uses neither *trick* nor *cunning* to effect any purpose. Such a man can never be embarrassed. *His steps are not straitened;* he sees his way always plain; and when a favourable tide of Providence shows him the necessity of increased *exertion*, he *runs*, and is in no danger of *stumbling*.

Verse 13. *Take fast hold*] החזק *hachazek*, *seize it strongly*, and keep the hold; and do this as *for life*. Learn all thou canst, retain what thou hast learnt, and keep the reason continually in view—*it is for thy life*.

Verse 14. *Enter not into the path of the wicked*] Never *associate* with those whose life is irregular and sinful; never *accompany* them in any of their acts of transgression.

Verse 15. *Avoid it*] Let it be the serious purpose of thy soul to shun every appearance of evil.

Pass not by it] Never, for the sake of worldly gain, or through complaisance to others, *approach the way* that thou wouldst not wish to be found in when God calls thee into the eternal world.

Turn from it] If, through *unwatchfulness* or *unfaithfulness*, thou at any time get *near* or *into the way* of sin, *turn from it* with the utmost speed, and humble thyself before thy Maker.

And pass away.] Speed from it, run for thy life, and get to the utmost distance; eternally diverging so as never to come near it whilst thou hast a being.

Verse 16. *Except they have done mischief*] The *night* is their time for spoil and depredation. And they must gain some *booty*, before they *go to rest*. This I believe to be the meaning of the passage. I grant, also, that there may be some of so malevolent a disposition, that they cannot be easy unless they can injure others, and are put to excessive pain when they perceive any man in *prosperity*, or receiving a kindness. The address in *Virgil*, to an ill-natured shepherd is well known:—

Et cum vidisti puero donata, dolebas:
Et si non aliqua nocuisses, mortuus esses.
         Eclog. iii. 14.

"When thou sawest the gifts given to the lad, thou wast distressed; and hadst thou not found some means of doing him a mischief, thou hadst died."

Verse 17. *For they eat the bread of wickedness*] By *privately* stealing.

And drink the wine of violence.] By *highway* robbery.

Verse 18. *But the path of the just*] The path of the wicked is gloomy, dark, and dangerous; that of the righteous is open, luminous, and instructive. This verse contains a fine metaphor; it refers to the *sun* rising above the horizon, and the increasing twilight, till his beams shine full upon the earth. The original,

הולך ואור עד נכון היום *holech vaor ad nechon haiyom*, may be translated, "going and illuminating unto the prepared day." This seems plainly to refer to the progress of the rising *sun* while below the horizon; and the gradual increase of the light occasioned by the reflection of his rays by means of the *atmosphere*, till at last he is completely elevated above the horizon, and then the *prepared day* has fully taken place, the sun having risen *at the determined time*. So, the truly wise man is but in his twilight here below; but he is in a state

A. M. cir. 3004
B. C. cir. 1000
Ante I. Olymp.
cir. 224
Ante U. C. cir.
247

shining light, that shineth more and more unto the perfect day.

19 [s]The way of the wicked *is* as darkness: they know not at what they stumble.

20 My son, attend to my words; incline thine ear unto my sayings.

21 [t]Let them not depart from thine eyes; [u]keep them in the midst of thine heart.

22 For they *are* life unto those that find them, and [v]health [w]to all their flesh.

23 Keep thy heart [x]with all diligence; for out of it *are* the issues of life.

24 Put away from thee [y]a froward mouth, and perverse lips put far from thee.

25 Let thine eyes look right on, and let thine eyelids look straight before thee.

26 Ponder the path of thy feet, and [z]let all thy ways be established.

27 [a]Turn not to the right hand nor to the left: [b]remove thy foot from evil.

A. M. cir. 3004
B. C. cir. 1000
Ante I. Olymp.
cir. 224
Ante U. C. cir.
247

---

[s]1 Sam. ii. 9; Job xviii. 5, 6; Isa. lix. 9, 10; Jer. xxiii. 12; John xii. 35——[t]Chap. iii. 3, 21——[u]Chap. ii. 1 [v]Chap. iii. 8; xii. 18; [w]Heb. *medicine*——[x]Heb. *above all keeping*

[y]Heb. *frowardness of mouth, and perverseness of lips* [z]Or, *all thy ways shall be ordered aright*——[a]Deuteronomy v. 32; xxviii. 14; Josh. i. 7——[b]Isaiah i. 16; Rom. xii. 9

---

of glorious *preparation* for the realms of everlasting light; till at last, emerging from darkness and the shadows of death, he is ushered into the full blaze of endless felicity. Yet previously to his enjoyment of this glory, which is prepared for him, he is *going*—walking in the commandments of his God blameless; and *illuminating*—reflecting the light of the salvation which he has received on all those who form the circle of his acquaintance.

Verse 21. *Keep them in the midst of thine heart.*] Let them be wrapped up in the very *centre of thy affections;* that they may give spring and energy to every desire, word, and wish.

Verse 23. *Keep thy heart with all diligence*] "Above all keeping," guard thy heart. He who knows any thing of himself, knows how apt his affections are to go astray.

For out of it are *the issues of life.*] תוצאות חיים *totseoth chaiyim,* "the goings out of lives." Is not this a plain allusion to the *arteries* which carry the blood from the heart through the whole body, and to the utmost extremities? As long as the heart is capable of receiving and propelling the blood, so long *life* is continued. Now as the heart is the fountain whence all the streams of life proceed, care must be taken that the fountain be not stopped up nor injured. A double watch for its safety must be kept up. So in spiritual things: the heart is the seat of the Lord of life and glory; and the streams of spiritual life proceed from him to all the powers and faculties of the soul. Watch with all diligence, that this fountain be not sealed up, nor these streams of life be cut off. Therefore "put away from thee a froward mouth and perverse lips—and let thy eyes look straight on." Or, in other words, look *inward*— look *onward*—look *upward.*

I know that the *twenty-third* verse is understood as principally referring to the evils which proceed from the heart, and which must be guarded against; and the good purposes that must be formed in it, from which *life* takes its colouring. The former should be opposed; the latter should be encouraged and strengthened. If the heart be pure and holy, all its purposes will be just and good. If it be impure and defiled, nothing will proceed from it but abomination. But though all this be true, I have preferred following what I believe to be the *metaphor* in the text.

Verse 24. *A froward mouth*] Beware of hastiness, anger, and rash speeches.

And perverse lips] Do not delight in nor acquire the *habit* of *contradicting* and *gainsaying;* and beware of *calumniating* and *backbiting* your neighbour.

Verse 26. *Ponder the path of thy feet*] *Weigh* well the part thou shouldst act in life. See that thou contract no bad *habits.*

Verse 27. *Turn not to the right hand nor to the left*] Avoid all crooked ways. Be an upright, downright, and straight-forward man. Avoid *tricks, wiles,* and *deceptions* of this kind.

To this the *Septuagint* and *Vulgate* add the following verse: Αυτος δε ορθας ποιησει τας τροχιας σου, τας δε πορειας σου εν ειρηνη προαξει. Ipse autem rectos faciet cursus tuos; itinera autem tua in pace producet. "For himself will make thy paths straight and thy journeyings will he conduct in prosperity." The *Arabic* has also a clause to the same effect. But nothing like this is found in the *Hebrew, Chaldee,* or *Syriac;* nor in the *Vulgate,* as printed in the *Complutensian Polyglot;* nor in that of *Antwerp* or of *Paris;* but it is in the Greek text of those editions, in the *editio princeps* of the Vulgate, in *five* of my own MSS., and in the old MS. Bible. *De Lyra* rejects the clause as a *gloss* that stands on no authority. If an *addition,* it is certainly very *ancient;* and the promise it contains is true, whether the clause be authentic or not.

CHAPTER V

Farther exhortations to acquire wisdom, 1, 2. The character of a loose woman, and the ruinous consequences of attachment to such, 3–14. Exhortations to chastity and moderation, 15–21. The miserable end of the wicked, 22, 23.

A. M. cir. 3004
B. C. cir. 1000
Ante I. Olymp.
cir. 224
Ante U. C. cir.
247

MY son, attend unto my wisdom, *and* bow thine ear to my understanding:

2 That thou mayest regard discretion, and *that* thy lips may [a]keep knowledge.

3 [b]For the lips of a strange woman drop *as* a honey-comb, and her [c]mouth *is* [d]smoother than oil:

4 But her end is [e]bitter as wormwood, [f]sharp as a two-edged sword.

5 [g]Her feet go down to death; her steps take hold on hell.

6 Lest thou shouldest ponder the path of life, her ways are moveable, *that* thou canst not know *them*.

7 Hear me now therefore, O ye children,

and depart not from the words of my mouth.

8 Remove thy way far from her, and come not nigh the door of her house:

9 Lest thou give thine honour unto others, and thy years unto the cruel:

10 Lest strangers be filled with [h]thy wealth; and thy labours *be* in the house of a stranger;

11 And thou mourn at the last, when thy flesh and thy body are consumed,

12 And say, How have I [i]hated instruction, and my heart [k]despised reproof;

13 And have not obeyed the voice of my teachers, nor inclined mine ear to them that instructed me!

14 I was almost in all evil in the midst

A. M. cir. 3004
B. C. cir. 1000
Ante I. Olymp.
cir. 224
Ante U. C. cir.
247

---

[a]Mal. ii. 7——[b]Chap. ii. 16; vi. 24——[c]Heb. *palate*
[d]Psa. lv. 21——[e]Eccles. vii. 26——[f]Heb. iv. 12

[g]Chap. vii. 27——[h]Heb. *thy strength*——[i]Chap. i. 29
[k]Chap. i. 25; xii. 1

NOTES ON CHAP. V

Verse 1. *Attend unto my wisdom*] Take the following lessons from my *own experience*.

Verse 3. *The lips of a strange woman*] One that is not *thy own*, whether Jewess or heathen.

Drop as a honey-comb] She uses the most deceitful, flattering, and alluring speeches: as the droppings of the honey out of the comb are the sweetest of all.

Verse 4. *Bitter as wormwood*] כלענה *Kela-anah*, like the *detestable* herb *wormwood*, or something analogous to it: something as excessive in its *bitterness*, as *honey* is in its *sweetness*.

Verse 5. *Her feet go down to death*] She first, like a serpent, infuses her *poison*, by which the whole *constitution* of her paramour is infected, which soon or late brings on *death*.

Her steps take hold on hell.] First, the *death of the body;* and then the damnation of the soul. These are the *tendencies* of connections with such women.

Verse 6. *Lest thou shouldest ponder*] To prevent thee from reflecting on thy present conduct, and its consequences, *her ways are moveable*—she continually varies her allurements.

Thou canst not know them.] It is impossible to conceive all her tricks and wiles: to learn these in all their varieties, is a part of the *science* first taught in that infernal trade.

Verse 7. *Hear me—O ye children*] בנים *banim*, sons, *young men* in general: for these are the most likely to be deceived and led astray.

Verse 8. *Come not nigh the door of her house*] Where there are generally such exhibitions as have a natural tendency to excite impure thoughts, and irregular passions.

Verse 9. *Lest thou give thine honour*] The *character* of a *debauchee* is universally detested: by this, even those of *noble blood* lose their *honour* and *respect*.

Thy years unto the cruel] Though all the

blandishments of love dwell on the tongue, and the excess of fondness appear in the whole demeanour of the *harlot* and the *prostitute; yet cruelty* has its throne in their hearts; and they will *rob* and *murder* (when it appears to answer their ends) those who give their *strength*, their *wealth*, and their *years* to them. The unfaithful *wife* has often murdered her own husband for the sake of her paramour, and has given *him* over to justice in order to save herself. Murders have often taken place in brothels, as well as robberies; for the vice of *prostitution* is one of the parents of *cruelty*.

Verse 11. *When thy flesh and thy body are consumed*] The word שאר *shear*, which we render body, signifies properly the *remains, residue*, or *remnant* of a thing: and is applied here to denote the *breathing carcass, putrid* with the *concomitant disease* of debauchery: a public reproach which the justice of God entails on this species of iniquity. The *mourning* here spoken of is of the most excessive kind: the word נהם *naham* is often applied to the *growling of a lion*, and the *hoarse incessant murmuring* of the sea. In the line of my duty, I have been often called to attend the death-bed of such persons, where *groans* and *shrieks* were incessant through the *jaculating* pains in their bones and flesh. Whoever has witnessed a closing scene like this will at once perceive with what force and propriety the wise man speaks. And *How have I hated instruction*, and *despised the voice of my teachers!* is the unavailing cry in that terrific time. Reader, whosoever thou art, lay these things to heart. Do not *enter* into their sin: once *entered*, thy *return* is nearly hopeless.

Verse 14. *I was almost in all evil*] This vice, like a whirlpool, sweeps all others into its vortex.

In the midst of the congregation and assembly.] 𝕴𝖓 𝖙𝖍𝖊 𝖒𝖞𝖉𝖊𝖑 𝖔𝖋 𝖙𝖍𝖊 𝕮𝖚𝖗𝖈𝖍𝖊 𝖆𝖓𝖉 𝖔𝖋 𝖙𝖍𝖊 𝕾𝖞𝖓𝖆𝖌𝖔𝖌𝖊 —Old MS. Bible. Such persons, however sacred the place, carry about with *them eyes full of adultery, which cannot cease from sin*.

A. M. cir. 3004
B. C. cir. 1000
Ante I. Olymp.
cir. 224
Ante U. C. cir.
247
of the congregation and assembly.

15 Drink waters out of thine own cistern, and running waters out of thine own well.

16 Let thy fountains be dispersed abroad, *and* rivers of waters in the streets.

17 Let them be only thine own, and not strangers' with thee.

18 Let thy fountain be blessed: and rejoice with [l]the wife of thy youth.

19 [m]*Let her be as* the loving hind and pleasant roe; let her breasts [n]satisfy thee at all times; and [o]be thou ravished always with her love.

20 And why wilt thou, my son, be ravished with [p]a strange woman, and embrace the bosom of a stranger?

21 [q]For the ways of man *are* before the eyes of the LORD, and he pondereth all his goings.

22 [r]His own iniquities shall take the wicked himself, and he shall be holden with the cords of his [s]sins.

23 [t]He shall die without instruction; and in the greatness of his folly he shall go astray.

A. M. cir. 3004
B. C. cir. 1000
Ante I. Olymp.
cir. 224
Ante U. C. cir.
247

---

[l]Mal. ii. 14——[m]See Cant. ii. 9; iv. 5; vii. 3——[n]Heb. *water thee*——[o]Heb. *err thou always in her love*——[p]Ch. ii. 16; vii. 5

[q]2 Chron. xvi. 9; Job xxxi. 4; xxxiv. 21; chap. xv. 3; Jer. xvi. 17; xxxii. 19; Hos. vii. 2; Heb. iv. 13——[r]Psa. ix. 15——[s]Heb. *sin*——[t]Job iv. 21; xxxvi. 12

Verse 15. *Drink waters out of thine own cistern*] Be satisfied with thy own wife; and let the wife see that she reverence her husband; and not tempt him by inattention or unkindness to seek elsewhere what he has a right to expect, but cannot find, at *home*.

Verse 16. *Let thy fountains be dispersed abroad*] Let thy children lawfully begotten be numerous.

Verse 17. *Let them be only thine own*] The off-spring of a legitimate connection; a *bastard brood*, however numerous, is no credit to any man.

Verse 18. *Let thy fountain be blessed*] יהי מקורך ברוך *yehi mekorecha baruch. Sit vena tua benedicta.* Thy *vein;* that which carries off streams from the fountain of *animal life*, in order to *disperse them abroad*, and *through the streets*. How *delicate* and correct is the allusion here! But anatomical allusions must not be pressed into detail in a commentary on Scripture.

Verse 19. *The loving hind and pleasant roe*] By אילת *aiyeleth*, the *deer;* by יעלה *yaalah*, the *ibex* or mountain *goat*, may be meant.

Let her breasts satisfy thee] As the infant is satisfied with the breasts of its mother; so shouldst thou be with the wife of thy youth.

Verse 21. *For the ways of a man*] Whether they are public or private, God sees all the steps thou takest in life.

Verse 22. *He shall be holden with the cords of his sins.*] Most people who follow unlawful pleasures, think *they can give them up whenever they please;* but sin *repeated* becomes *customary;* custom soon engenders *habit;* and habit in the end assumes the form of *necessity;* the man becomes *bound with his own cords,* and so is *led captive by the devil at his will.*

Verse 23. *He shall die without instruction*] This is *most likely*, and it is a *general* case; but even *these* may repent and live.

CHAPTER VI

Exhortations against becoming surety for others, 1–5; against idleness, from the example of the ant, 6–11; description of a worthless person, 12–15; seven things hateful to God, 16–19; the benefits of instruction, 20–23; farther exhortations against bad women, and especially against adultery, 24–33; what may be expected from jealousy, 34, 35.

A. M. cir. 3004
B. C. cir. 1000
Ante I. Olymp.
cir. 224
Ante U. C. cir.
247
MY son, [a]if thou be surety for thy friend, *if* thou hast stricken thy hand with a stranger,

2 Thou art snared with the words of thy mouth, thou art taken with the words of thy mouth.

3 Do this now, my son, and deliver thyself when thou art

A. M. cir. 3004
B. C. cir. 1000
Ante I. Olymp.
cir. 224
Ante U. C. cir.
247

---

[a]Chap. xi. 15; xvii. 18; xx. 16; xxii. 26; xxvii. 13

NOTES ON CHAP. VI

Verse 1. *If thou be surety for thy friend*] לרעך *lereacha*, for thy *neighbour;* i. e., any person. If thou pledge thyself in behalf of another, thou takest the burden off him, and placest it on thine own shoulders; and when he knows he has got one to stand between him and the demands of law and justice, he will feel little responsibility; his spirit of exertion will become crippled, and listlessness as to the event will be the consequence. His own character will suffer little; his property nothing, for his friend bears all the burden; and perhaps the very person for whom he bore this burden treats him with neglect; and, lest the

A. M. cir. 3004
B. C. cir. 1000
Ante I. Olymp.
cir. 224
Ante U. C. cir.
247

come into the hand of thy friend; go, humble thyself, [b]and make sure thy friend.

4 [c]Give not sleep to thine eyes, nor slumber to thine eyelids.

5 Deliver thyself as a roe from the hand *of the hunter,* and as a bird from the hand of the fowler.

6 [d]Go to the ant, thou sluggard; consider her ways, and be wise:

7 Which having no guide, overseer, or ruler,

8 Provideth her meat in the summer, *and* gathereth her food in the harvest.

9 [e]How long wilt thou sleep, O sluggard? when wilt thou arise out of thy sleep?

A. M. cir. 3004
B. C. cir. 1000
Ante I. Olymp.
cir. 224
Ante U. C. cir.
247

10 *Yet* a little sleep, a little slumber, a little folding of the hands to sleep:

11 [f]So shall thy poverty come as one that travelleth, and thy want as an armed man.

12 A naughty person, a wicked man, walketh with a froward mouth.

13 [g]He winketh with his eyes, he speaketh with his feet, he teacheth with his fingers;

14 Frowardness *is* in his heart; [h]he deviseth mischief continually; [i]he [k]soweth discord.

---

[b]Or, *so shalt thou prevail with thy friend*——[c]Psa. cxxxii. 4——[d]Job xii. 7——[e]Chap. xxiv. 33, 34

[f]Ch. x. 4; xiii. 4; xx. 4——[g]Job xv. 12; Psa. xxxv. 19; ch. x. 10——[h]Mic. ii. 1——[i]Ver. 19——[k]Heb. *casteth forth*

---

restoration of the pledge should be required, will avoid both the sight and presence of his friend. *Give* what thou canst; but, except in extreme cases, be *surety* for no man. *Striking* or *shaking hands* when the *mouth had once made the promise,* was considered as the *ratification* of the engagement; and thus the man became *ensnared with the words of his mouth.*

Verse 3. *Do this—deliver thyself*] Continue to press him for whom thou art become surety, to pay his creditor; give him no rest till he do it, else thou mayest fully expect to be left to pay the debt.

Verse 5. *Deliver thyself as a roe*] צבי *tsebi,* the antelope. If thou art got into the snare, get out if thou possibly canst; make every *struggle* and *exertion,* as the antelope taken in the net, and the bird taken in the snare would, in order to get free from thy captivity.

Verse 6. *Go to the ant, thou sluggard*] נמלה *nemalah,* the *ant,* is a remarkable creature for *foresight, industry,* and *economy.* At the proper seasons they collect their food—not in the *summer* to lay up for the *winter;* for they sleep during the winter, and eat not; and therefore such hoards would be to them useless; but when the food necessary for them is most plentiful, then they collect it for their consumption in the proper seasons. No insect is more *laborious,* not even the *bee* itself; and none is more *fondly attached* to or more *careful* of its young, than the ant. When the young are in their *aurelia* state, in which they appear like a small *grain* of rice, they will bring them out of their nests, and lay them near their holes, for the benefit of the sun; and on the approach of *rain,* carefully remove them, and deposit them in the nest, the hole or entrance to which they will cover with a piece of thin stone or tile, to prevent the wet from getting in. It is a fact that they do not lay up any meat for winter; nor does Solomon, either here or in chap. xxx. 25, assert it. He simply says that they provide their food in summer, and gather it in harvest; these are the most proper times for a stock to be laid in for their consumption; not in *winter;* for no such thing appears in any of their nests, nor do they need it, as they *sleep* during that season; but for autumn, during which they wake and work. Spring, summer, and autumn, they are incessant in their labour;

and their conduct affords a bright example to men.

Verse 10. Yet *a little sleep, a little slumber*] This, if not the *language,* is the *feeling* of the sluggard. The *ant* gathers its food in summer and in harvest, and sleeps in winter when it has no work to do. If the sluggard would work in the day, and sleep at night, it would be all proper. The ant yields him a lesson of reproach.

Verse 11. *So shall thy poverty come as one that travelleth*] That is, with slow, but surely approaching steps.

Thy want as an armed man.] That is, with irresistible fury; and thou art not prepared to oppose it. The *Vulgate, Septuagint,* and *Arabic* add the following clause to this verse:—

"But if thou wilt be diligent, thy harvest shall be as a fountain; and poverty shall flee far away from thee."

It is also thus in the Old MS. Bible: 𝔍𝔣 𝔣𝔬𝔯-𝔰𝔬𝔱𝔥𝔢 𝔲𝔫𝔰𝔩𝔬𝔴 𝔱𝔥𝔬𝔲 𝔰𝔥𝔞𝔩 𝔟𝔢𝔫; 𝔰𝔥𝔞𝔩 𝔠𝔬𝔪𝔢𝔫 𝔞𝔰 𝔞 𝔴𝔢𝔩𝔩𝔢 𝔱𝔥𝔦 𝔯𝔦𝔭; 𝔞𝔫𝔡 𝔫𝔢𝔡𝔢 𝔣𝔢𝔯 𝔰𝔥𝔞𝔩 𝔣𝔩𝔢𝔢𝔫 𝔣𝔯𝔬 𝔱𝔥𝔢𝔢.

Verse 12. *A naughty person*] אדם בליעל *adam beliyal,* "Adam good for nothing." When he lost his innocence. 𝔄 𝔪𝔞𝔫 𝔞𝔭𝔬𝔰𝔱𝔞𝔱𝔞; Old MS. Bible.

A wicked man] איש און *ish aven.* He soon became a general transgressor after having departed from his God. All his posterity, unless restored by Divine grace, are men of Belial, and sinners by trade; and most of them, in one form or other, answer the character here given. They yield their members instruments of unrighteousness unto sin.

Verse 13. *He winketh with his eyes, he speaketh with his feet, he teacheth with his fingers*] These things seem to be spoken of debauchees; and the following quotation from Ovid, Amor. lib. i., El. iv., ver. 15, shows the whole process of the villany spoken of by Solomon:

Cum premit ille torum, vultu comes ipsa
    modesto
Ibis, ut accumbas: clam mihi *tange pedem.*
Me specta, *nutusque* meos, *vultum que loquacem*
    Excipe *furtivas,* et refer ipsa, *notas.*
Verba superciliis sine voce loquentia dicam
    Verba leges digitis, verba notata mero.
Cum tibi succurrit Veneris lascivia nostræ,
    Purpureas tenero *pollice tange genas,* &c., &c.

A. M. cir. 3004
B. C. cir. 1000
Ante I. Olymp.
cir. 224
Ante U. C. cir.
247

15 Therefore shall his calamity come suddenly; suddenly shall he [l]be broken [m]without remedy.

16 These six *things* doth the Lord hate: yea, seven *are* an abomination [n]unto him.

17 [o]A [p]proud look, [q]a lying tongue, and [r]hands that shed innocent blood,

18 [s]A heart that deviseth wicked imaginations, [t]feet that be swift in running to mischief,

19 [u]A false witness *that* speaketh lies, and he [v]that soweth discord among brethren.

20 [w]My son, keep thy father's commandment, and forsake not the law of thy mother:

21 [x]Bind them continually upon thine heart, *and* tie them about thy neck.

22 [y]When thou goest, it shall lead thee; when thou sleepest, [z]it shall keep thee; and *when* thou awakest, it shall talk with thee.

A. M. cir. 3004
B. C. cir. 1000
Ante I. Olymp.
cir. 224
Ante U. C. cir.
247

23 [a]For the commandment *is* a [b]lamp; and the law *is* light; and reproofs of instruction *are* the way of life:

24 [c]To keep thee from the evil woman, from the flattering [d]of the tongue of a strange woman.

25 [e]Lust not after her beauty in thine heart; neither let her take thee with her eye-lids.

26 For [f]by means of a whorish woman *a man is brought* to a piece of bread: [g]and [h]the

---

[l]Jer. xix. 11——[m]2 Chron. xxxvi. 16——[n]Heb. *of his soul*——[o]Psa. xviii. 27; ci. 5——[p]Heb. *Haughty eyes* [q]Psa. cxx. 2, 3——[r]Isa. i. 15——[s]Gen. vi. 5——[t]Isa. lix. 7; Rom. iii. 15——[u]Psa. xxvii. 12; chap. xix. 5, 9 [v]Ver. 14——[w]Chap. i. 8; Eph. vi. 1

[x]Chap. iii. 3; vii. 3——[y]Chap. iii. 23, 24——[z]Chap. ii. 11——[a]Psa. xix. 8; cxix. 105——[b]Or, *candle*——[c]Chap. ii. 16; v. 3; vii. 5——[d]Or, *of the strange tongue*——[e]Matt. v. 28——[f]Chap. xxix. 3——[g]Gen. xxxix. 14——[h]Heb. *the woman of a man, or a man's wife*

The whole *elegy* is in the same strain: it is translated in *Garth's* Ovid, but cannot be introduced here.

Verse 14. *He deviseth mischief*] He plots schemes and plans to bring it to pass.

He soweth discord.] Between men and their wives, by seducing the latter from their fidelity. See the preceding quotation.

Verse 15. *Suddenly shall he be broken*] Probably alluding to some punishment of the adulterer, such as being *stoned to death.* A multitude shall join together, and so overwhelm him with stones, that he shall have his flesh and bones broken to pieces; and there shall be *no remedy*—none to deliver or pity him.

Verse 16. *These six—doth the Lord hate*] 1. *A proud look*—exalted eyes; those who will not condescend to look on the rest of mankind. 2. *A lying tongue*—he who neither loves nor tells *truth.* 3. *Hands that shed innocent blood,* whether by murder or by battery. 4. *A heart that deviseth wicked imaginations*—the heart that *fabricates* such, lays the foundation, builds upon it, and completes the superstructure of *iniquity.* 5. *Feet that be swift in running to mischief*—he who works iniquity with greediness. 6. *A false witness that speaketh lies*—one who, even on his oath before a court of justice, tells any thing but the truth.

Seven are an abomination unto him] נבשׁו *naphsho*, "to his soul." The seventh is, *he that soweth discord among brethren*—he who troubles the peace of a family, of a village, of the state; all who, by lies and misrepresentations, strive to make men's minds evil-affected towards their brethren.

Verse 20. *Keep thy father's commandment*] See on Chap. i. 8.

Verse 21. *Bind them continually upon thine heart*] See on chap. iii. 3. And see a similar command, to which this is an allusion, Deut. vi. 6-8.

Verse 22. *When thou goest, it shall lead thee*] Here the *law* is *personified;* and is represented

as a nurse, teacher, and guardian, by night and day. An upright man never *goes* but as directed by God's word, and led by God's Spirit.

When thou sleepest] He commends his body and soul to the protection of his Maker when he lies down and sleeps in peace. And when he awakes in the morning, the promises and mercies of God are the first things that present themselves to his recollection.

Verse 23. *For the commandment is a lamp*] It illuminates our path. It shows us how *we should walk* and *praise God.*

And the law is light] A *general light,* showing the *nature* and *will* of God, and the *interest* and *duty* of man.

And reproofs of instruction] Or, that instruction which reproves us for our sins and errors leads us into the way of life.

Verse 24. *To keep thee from the evil woman*] Solomon had suffered sorely from this quarter; and hence his repeated cautions and warnings to others. The *strange woman* always means one that is not a man's own; and sometimes it may also imply a *foreign harlot,* one who is also a *stranger* to the God of Israel.

Verse 25. *Neither let her take thee with her eye-lids.*] It is a very general custom in the East to *paint the eye-lids.* I have many Asiatic drawings in which this is expressed. They have a method of *polishing the eyes* with a preparation of *antimony,* so that they appear with an indescribable lustre; or, as one who mentions the fact from observation, "Their eyes appear to be swimming in bliss."

Verse 26. *By means of a whorish woman*] In following lewd women, a man is soon reduced to poverty and disease. The *Septuagint* gives this a strange turn: Τιμη γαρ πορνης, ὁση και ἑνος αρτου. "For the price or hire of a whore is about one loaf." So *many* were they in the land, that they hired themselves out for a *bare subsistence.* The *Vulgate, Syriac,* and *Arabic,* give the same sense. The old MS. Bible has it thus: **The price forsothe of a strumpet is**

A. M. cir. 3004
B. C. cir. 1000
Ante I. Olymp.
cir. 224
Ante U. C. cir.
247

adulteress will [i]hunt for the precious life.

27 Can a man take fire in his bosom, and his clothes not be burned?

28 Can one go upon hot coals, and his feet not be burned?

29 So he that goeth in to his neighbour's wife; whosoever toucheth her shall not be innocent.

30 *Men* do not despise a thief, if he steal to satisfy his soul when he is hungry;

31 But *if* he be found, [k]he shall restore se-

venfold; he shall give all the substance of his house.

A. M. cir. 3004
B. C. cir. 1000
Ante I. Olymp.
cir. 224
Ante U. C. cir.
247

32 *But* whoso committeth adultery with a woman [l]lacketh [m]understanding: he *that* doeth it destroyeth his own soul.

33 A wound and dishonour shall he get; and his reproach shall not be wiped away.

34 For jealousy *is* the rage of a man: therefore he will not spare in the day of vengeance.

35 [n]He will not regard any ransom; neither will he rest content, though thou givest many gifts.

---

[i]Ezek. xiii. 18——[k]Exod. xxii. 1, 4——[l]Chap. vii. 7

[m]Heb. *heart*——[n]Heb. *He will not accept the face of any ransom*

---

unneth oon lof: the woman forsothe taketh the precious liif of a man. The sense of which is, and probably the sense of the *Hebrew* too, While the man hires the whore for a *single loaf* of bread; the woman thus hired taketh his *precious life*. She extracts his energy, and poisons his constitution. In the first clause אשה זונה *ishshah zonah* is plainly a *prostitute*; but should we render אשת *esheth*, in the second clause, an *adulteress?* I think not. The versions in general join אשת איש *esheth ish*, together, which, thus connected, signify no more than *the wife of a man;* and out of this we have made *adulteress*, and *Coverdale* a *married woman*. I do not think that the Old MS. Bible gives a good sense; and it requires a good deal of paraphrase to extract the common meaning from the text. Though the following verses seem to countenance the common interpretation, yet they may contain a complete sense of themselves; but, taken in either way, the sense is good, though the construction is a little violent.

Verse 27. *Can a man take fire*] These were proverbial expressions, the meaning of which was plain to every capacity.

Verse 29. *So he that goeth in to his neighbour's wife*] As sure as he who takes *fire into his bosom*, or who *walks* upon *live coals*, is burnt thereby; so sure he that seduces his neighbour's wife *shall be guilty*. That is, he shall be punished.

Verse 30. *Men do not despise a thief, if he steal*] Every man pities the poor culprit who was perishing for lack of food, and stole to *satisfy his hunger;* yet no law *clears* him: he is bound to make restitution; in some cases

double, in others *quadruple* and *quintuple;* and if he have not property enough to make restitution, to be sold for a *bondman;* Exod xxii. 1-4; Lev. xxv. 39.

Verse 32. But *whoso committeth adultery*] The case understood is that of a *married man:* he has a wife; and therefore is not in the circumstances of the *poor thief*, who stole to *appease his hunger*, having nothing to eat. In this alone the *opposition* between the two cases is found: the *thief had no food*, and he stole some; the married man had a *wife*, and yet went in to *the wife of his neighbour*.

Destroyeth his own soul.] Sins against *his life;* for, under the law of Moses, adultery was punished with *death;* Lev. xx. 10; Deut. xxii. 22.

Verse 33. *A wound and dishonour shall he get*] Among the *Romans*, when a man was caught in the fact, the injured husband took the law into his own hand; and a large *radish* was thrust up into the anus of the transgressor, which not only overwhelmed him with infamy and disgrace, but generally caused his death.

Verse 34. *Jealousy* is *the rage of a man: therefore he will not spare*] He will not, when he has detected the adulterer in the fact, wait for the slow progress of the law: it is then to him the *day of vengeance;* and in general, he avenges himself on the spot, as we see above.

Verse 35. *He will not regard any ransom*] This is an injury that admits of *no compensation*. No *gifts* can satisfy a man for the injury his honour has sustained; and to take a *bribe* or a *ransom*, would be setting up *chastity* at a price.

CHAPTER VII

A farther exhortation to acquire wisdom, in order to be preserved from impure connections, 1-5. The character of a harlot, and her conduct towards a youth who fell into her snare, 6-23. Solemn exhortations to avoid this evil, 24-27.

A. M. cir. 3004
B. C. cir. 1000
Ante I. Olymp.
cir. 224
Ante U. C. cir.
247

MY son, keep my words, and [a]lay up my commandments with thee.

2 [b]Keep my commandments, and live; [c]and my law as the apple of thine eye.

3 [d]Bind them upon thy fingers, write them upon the table of thine heart.

4 Say unto wisdom, Thou *art* my sister; and call understanding *thy* kinswoman:

5 [e]That they may keep thee from the strange woman, from the stranger *which* flattereth with her words.

6 For at the window of my house I looked through my casement,

7 And beheld among the simple ones, I discerned among [f]the youths, a young man [g]void of understanding,

8 Passing through the street near the corner; and he went the way to her house.

A. M. cir. 3004
B. C. cir. 1000
Ante I. Olymp.
cir. 224
Ante U. C. cir.
247

9 [h]In the twilight, [i]in the evening, in the black and dark night:

10 And, behold, there met him a woman *with* the attire of a harlot, and subtle of heart.

11 ([k]She *is* loud and stubborn; [l]her feet abide not in her house:

12 Now *is she* without, now in the streets, and lieth in wait at every corner.)

13 So she caught him, and kissed him, *and* [m]with an impudent face said unto him,

14 [n]*I have* peace-offerings with me; this day have I payed my vows.

15 Therefore came I forth to meet thee, diligently to seek thy face, and I have found thee.

---

[a]Chap. ii. 1——[b]Lev. xviii. 5; chap. iv. 4; Isa. lv. 3 [c]Deut. xxxii. 10——[d]Deut. vi. 8; xi. 18; chap. iii. 3; vi. 21——[e]Chap. ii. 16; v. 3; vi. 24——[f]Heb. *the sons* [g]Chap. vi. 32; ix. 4, 16

[h]Job xxiv. 15——[i]Heb. *in the evening of the day* [h]Chap. ix. 13——[l]1 Tim. v. 13; Titus ii. 5——[m]Hebrew, *she strengthened her face, and said*——[n]Hebrew, *Peace-offerings are upon me*

NOTES ON CHAP. VII

Verse 1. *My son, keep my words*] See chap. ii. 1.

Verse 2. *As the apple of thine eye.*] As the pupil of the eye, which is of such essential necessity to sight, and so easily injured.

Verse 3. *Bind them upon thy fingers*] See on chap. iii. 3.

Verse 4. *Thou* art *my sister*] Thou art my dearest friend, and I will treat thee as such.

Verse 5. *The strange woman*] The *prostitute*, the *adulteress*.

Verse 6. *I looked through my casement*] The *casement* is a small aperture in a large window, or a window opening on hinges. Here it means the *lattice*, for they had no *glass windows* in the East. And the *latticed* windows produced a *double* advantage: 1. Making the apartments sufficiently private; and 2. Admitting fresh air to keep them cool.

Verse 7. *Among the simple ones*] The inexperienced, inconsiderate young men.

A young man void of understanding] חסר לב *chasar leb*, "destitute of a heart." He had not wisdom to discern the evil intended; nor courage to resist the flatteries of the seducer.

Verse 8. *He went the way to her house.*] She appears to have had a corner house sufficiently remarkable; and a way from the main street to it.

Verse 9. *In the twilight, in the evening*] Some time after sun-setting; before it was *quite dark*.

In the black and dark night] When there were neither *lamps* nor *moon-shine*.

Verse 10. *A woman* with *the attire of a harlot*] It appears that sitting in some open place, and covering the face, or having a veil of a peculiar kind on, was the evidence of a harlot; Gen. xxxviii. 14, 15-19. No doubt, in Solomon's time, they had other distinctions. In all other countries, and in all times, *the*

show of their countenance did testify against them; they declared their sin as Sodom; they hid it not. However, this does not seem to have been a mere prostitute; for she was, according to her own declaration, a *married woman*, and kept house, ver. 19, if her assertions relative to this were not falsehoods, and calculated the better to render him secure, and prevent the suspicion of endangering himself by cohabiting with a common woman; which I am rather inclined to think was the case, for she was *subtle of heart*.

Verse 11. *She is loud and stubborn*] המיה *homiyah*, she is never *at rest*, always *agitated*; busily employed to gain her end, and this is *to go* into the *path of error*: סררת *sorereth*, "turning aside;" preferring any way to the right way. And, therefore, it is added, *her feet abide not in her house;* she gads abroad; and this disposition probably first led her to this vice.

Verse 12. *Now is she without*] She is continually exposing herself, and showing by her gait and gestures *what* she *is*, and *what* she *wants*. These two verses are a *parenthesis*, intended to show the character of the woman.

Verse 13. *So she caught him*] Laid *fast hold* on him, and *kissed him*, to show that she was affectionately attached to him.

And with an impudent face] העזה פניה *heezzah paneyha*, "she strengthened her countenance," assumed the most confident look she could; endeavoured to appear friendly and sincere.

Verse 14. *I have* peace-offerings *with me*] More literally, "the sacrifices of the peace-offerings are with me." *Peace-offerings* שלמים *shelamim*, were offerings the spiritual design of which was to make peace between God and man, to make up the *breach* between them which sin had occasioned; see the notes on Lev. vii., where every kind of sacrifice offered under the law is explained. When the *blood* of

A. M. cir. 3004
B. C. cir. 1000
Ante I. Olymp.
cir. 224
Ante U. C. cir.
247

16 I have decked my bed with coverings of tapestry, with carved *works,* with °fine linen of Egypt.

17 I have perfumed my bed with myrrh, aloes, and cinnamon.

18 Come, let us take our fill of love until the morning: let us solace ourselves with loves.

19 For the good man *is* not at home, he is gone a long journey:

20 He hath taken a bag of money ᴾwith him, *and* will come home at ᑫthe day appointed.

21 With ʳher much fair speech she caused him to yield, ˢwith the flattering of her lips she forced him.

22 He goeth after her ᵗstraightway, as an ox goeth to the slaughter, or as a fool to the correction of the stocks:

A. M. cir. 3004
B. C. cir. 1000
Ante I. Olymp.
cir. 224
Ante U. C. cir.
247

23 Till a dart strike through his liver; ᵘas a bird hasteth to the snare, and knoweth not that it *is* for his life.

24 Hearken unto me now, therefore, O ye children, and attend to the words of my mouth.

25 Let not thine heart decline to her ways, go not astray in her paths.

26 For she hath cast down many wounded: yea, ᵛmany strong *men* have been slain by her.

27 ʷHer house *is* the way to hell, going down to the chambers of death.

°Isa. xix. 9——ᴾHeb. *in his hand*——ᑫOr, *the new moon*
ʳChap. v. 3——ˢPsa. xii. 2

ᵗHeb. *suddenly*——ᵘEccles. ix. 12——ᵛNeh. xiii. 26
ʷChap. ii. 18; v. 5; ix. 13

---

these was poured out at the altar, and the *fat* burnt there, the *breast* and *right shoulder* were the priest's portion; but the rest of the carcass belonged to the sacrificer, who might carry it home, and make a feast to his friends. See Lev. iii. 1-11. Much light is cast on this place by the *fact* that the gods in many parts of the East are actually worshipped in *brothels,* and fragments of the *offerings* are divided among the wretches who fall into the snare of the prostitutes.—WARD'S *Customs.*

Have I payed my vows] She seems to insinuate that she had *made a vow for the health and safety of this young man;* and having done so, and prepared the sacrificial banquet, came actually out to seek him, that he might partake of it with her, ver. 15. But, as she intended to proceed farther than mere *friendship,* she was obliged to avail herself of the *night season,* and the *absence of her husband.*

Verse 16. *I have decked my bed*] עַרְשִׂי *arsi,* "my couch or sofa;" distinguished from מִשְׁכָּבִי *mishcabi,* "my bed," ver. 17, *the place to sleep on,* as the other was *the place to recline on* at meals. The tapestry, מַרְבַדִּים *marbaddim,* mentioned here seems to refer to the covering of the *sofa;* exquisitely *woven* and *figured* cloth. חֲטֻבוֹת אֵטוּן *chatuboth etun,* the *Targum* translates *painted carpets,* such as were manufactured in *Egypt;* some kind of *embroidered* or *embossed stuff* is apparently meant.

Verse 17. *I have perfumed my bed with myrrh*] מֹר *mor,* "aloes," אֲהָלִים *ahalim,* and "cinnamon," קִנָּמוֹן *kinnamon.* We have taken our names from the original words; but probably the *ahalim* may not mean *aloes,* which is no *perfume;* but *sandal wood,* which is very much used in the East. She had used every means to excite the passions she wished to bring into action.

Verse 18. *Come, let us take our fill of love*] נִרְוֶה דֹדִים *nirveh dodim,* "Let us revel in the breasts;" and then it is added, "Let us solace ourselves with loves," נִתְעַלְּסָה בָּאֳהָבִים *nithalesah boohabim;* "let us gratify each other with loves, with the utmost delights." This does not half express the original; but I forbear. The

speech shows the *brazen face* of this woman, well translated by the *Vulgate,* "Veni, inebriemur uberibus; et fruamur cupidinis amplexibus." And the *Septuagint* has expressed the spirit of it: Ἐλθε, και απολαυσωμεν φιλιας—δευρο, και εγκυλισθωμεν ερωτι. "Veni, et fruamur amicitia—Veni, et colluctemur cupidine." Though varied in the words, all the *versions* have expressed the same thing. In the old MS. Bible, the speech of this woman is as follows:— 𝔍 𝔥𝔞𝔟𝔢 𝔞𝔯𝔯𝔞𝔶𝔢𝔡 𝔴𝔦𝔱𝔥 𝔠𝔬𝔯𝔡𝔦𝔰 𝔪𝔶 𝔩𝔦𝔱𝔦𝔩 𝔟𝔢𝔡, 𝔞𝔫𝔡 𝔰𝔭𝔯𝔢𝔡 𝔴𝔦𝔱𝔥 𝔭𝔢𝔶𝔫𝔱𝔦𝔡 𝔱𝔞𝔭𝔢𝔱𝔦𝔰 𝔬𝔣 𝔈𝔤𝔦𝔭𝔱: 𝔍 𝔥𝔞𝔟𝔢 𝔰𝔭𝔯𝔦𝔫𝔤𝔦𝔡 𝔪𝔶 𝔩𝔦𝔤𝔤𝔦𝔫𝔤𝔢 𝔭𝔩𝔞𝔠𝔢 𝔴𝔦𝔱𝔥 𝔪𝔦𝔯𝔯𝔢 𝔞𝔫𝔡 𝔞𝔩𝔬𝔢𝔰 𝔞𝔫𝔡 𝔠𝔞𝔫𝔢𝔩𝔠𝔲𝔪, 𝔞𝔫𝔡 𝔟𝔢 𝔴𝔢 𝔦𝔫𝔴𝔞𝔯𝔡𝔩𝔶 𝔡𝔯𝔲𝔫𝔨𝔢𝔫 𝔴𝔦𝔱𝔥 𝔗𝔢𝔱𝔦𝔰, 𝔞𝔫𝔡 𝔲𝔰𝔢 𝔴𝔢 𝔱𝔥𝔢 𝔠𝔬𝔳𝔢𝔶𝔱𝔦𝔡 𝔠𝔩𝔦𝔭𝔭𝔦𝔫𝔤𝔦𝔰 𝔱𝔬 𝔱𝔥𝔢 𝔱𝔶𝔪𝔢 𝔱𝔥𝔞𝔱 𝔱𝔥𝔢 𝔡𝔞𝔦 𝔴𝔞𝔵 𝔩𝔦𝔤𝔥𝔱. The original itself is too gross to be literally translated; but quite in character as coming from the mouth of an abandoned woman.

Verse 19. *For the good man*] Literally, "For the man is not in his house."

Verse 20. *He hath taken*] Literally, "The money bag he hath taken in his hand." He is gone a journey of itinerant merchandising. This seems to be what is intended.

And *will come home at the day appointed.*] לְיוֹם הַכֵּסֶא *leyom hakkase,* the *time fixed* for a return from such a journey. The *Vulgate* says, "at the full moon." The *Targum,* "the day of the assembly." In other words, He will return by the *approaching festival.*

Verse 21. *With her much fair speech*] With her blandishments and lascivious talk, she overcame all his scruples, and constrained him to yield.

Verse 22. *As an ox goeth to the slaughter*] The original of this and the following verse has been variously translated. Dr. *Grey* corrects and translates thus: "He goeth after her straightway, as an ox goeth to the SLAUGHTER; as a DOG to the CHAIN; and as a DEER till the DART strike through his liver; as a BIRD hasteneth to the SNARE, and knoweth not that it is for its life." Very slight alterations in the Hebrew text produce these differences; but it is not necessary to pursue them; all serve to mark the stupidity and folly of the man who is led away by enticing women or who lives a life of intemperance.

Verse 24. *Hearken unto me now, therefore, O*

ye children] Ye that are young and inexperienced, seriously consider the example set before your eyes, and take warning at another's expense.

Verse 26. *For she hath cast down many wounded: yea, many strong men have been slain by her.*] That is, such like women have been the ruin of many. חללים *chalalim*, which we render *wounded*, also signifies *soldiers* or men of war; and עצמים *atsumim*, which we render *strong men*, may be translated *heroes*. Many of those who have distinguished themselves in the field and in the cabinet have been overcome and destroyed by their mistresses. History is full of such examples.

Verse 27. *Her house is the way to hell*] שאול *sheol*, the *pit*, the *grave*, the *place of the dead*, the *eternal* and *infernal world*. And they who, through such, fall into the *grave*, descend lower, into *the chambers of death;* the place where pleasure is at an end, and *illusion* mocks no more.

CHAPTER VIII

The fame and excellence of wisdom, and its manner of teaching, 1–4; *the matter of its exhortations,* 5–12; *its influence among men,* 13–21; *its antiquity,* 22–31; *the blessedness of attending to its counsels,* 32–35; *the misery of those who do not,* 36.

A. M. cir. 3004
B. C. cir. 1000
Ante I. Olymp.
cir. 224
Ante U. C. cir.
247

DOTH not [a]wisdom cry? and [b]understanding put forth her voice?

2 She standeth in the top of high places, by the way in the places of the paths.

3 She crieth at the gates, at the entry of the city, at the coming in at the doors.

4 Unto you, O men, I call; and my voice *is* to the sons of man.

5 O ye simple, understand wisdom: and ye fools, be ye of an understanding heart.

A. M. cir. 3004
B. C. cir. 1000
Ante I. Olymp.
cir. 224
Ante U. C. cir.
247

[a]Chap. i. 20; ix. 3   [b]Psa. cxix. 130; cxlvii. 5

NOTES ON CHAP. VIII.

Verse 1. *Doth not wisdom cry?*] Here wisdom is again *personified;* but the *prosopopœia* is carried on to a greater length than before, and with much more variety. It is represented in this chapter in a *twofold* point of view: 1. Wisdom, the *power of judging rightly,* implying *the knowledge of Divine and human things.* 2. As an *attribute* of God, particularly displayed in the various and astonishing works of *creation.* Nor has it *any other meaning* in this whole chapter, whatever some of the fathers may have dreamed, who find allegorical meanings every where. The wise man seems as if suddenly awakened from the distressful contemplation which he had before him,—of the ruin of young persons in both worlds by means of debauchery,—by the voice of wisdom, who has *lifted up her voice* in the most public places, where was the *greatest concourse* of the people, to warn the yet unsnared, that they might avoid the way of seduction and sin; and cause those who love her to *inherit substance,* and to have their *treasuries filled* with durable riches.

Verse 2. *In the places of the paths.*] בית נתיבת נצבה *beith nethiboth nitstsabah,* "The constituted house of the paths." Does not this mean the house of public worship? the tabernacle or temple, which stands a centre to the surrounding villages, the paths from all the parts leading to and terminating at it? In such a place, where the holy word of God is read or preached, there in a particular manner does wisdom *cry,* and *understanding lift up her voice.* There are the warnings, the precepts, and the promises of eternal truth; there the *bread of God* is broken to his children, and thither they that *will* may come and take the *water* of *life* freely.

Verse 3. *She crieth at the gates*] This might be well applied to the preaching of Jesus Christ and his apostles, and their faithful successors in the Christian ministry. He went to the *temple,* and proclaimed the righteousness of the Most High: he did the same in the *synagogues,* on the *mountains,* by the *sea-side,* in the *villages,* in the *streets* of the *cities,* and in *private houses.* His disciples followed his track: in the *same way,* and in the *same spirit,* they proclaimed the unsearchable riches of Christ. God's *wisdom* in the hearts of his true ministers directs them to go and to seek sinners. There are, it is true, temples, synagogues, churches, chapels, &c.; but hundreds of thousands never frequent them, and therefore do not hear the voice of truth: *wisdom,* therefore, *must go to them,* if she wishes them to receive her instructions. Hence the zealous ministers of Christ go still to the *highways* and *hedges,* to the *mountains* and *plains,* to the *ships* and the *cottages,* to persuade sinners to turn from the error of their ways, and accept that redemption which was procured by the sacrificial offering of Jesus Christ.

Verse 4. *Unto you, O men*] אישים *ishim,* men of *wealth* and *power, will I call;* and not to you alone, for my voice is אל בני אדם *al beney Adam,* "to all the descendants of Adam;" to the whole human race. As Jesus Christ tasted death for every man, so the Gospel proclaims salvation to all: *to* YOU—to every individual, my voice is addressed. *Thou* hast sinned; and *thou* must perish, if not saved by grace.

Verse 5. *O ye simple*] פתאים *pethaim,* ye that are *deceived,* and with flattering words and fair speeches deluded and *drawn away.*

Ye fools] כסילים *kesilim,* ye stupid, stiffnecked, senseless people. That *preaching* is never likely to do much good, that is not *pointed;* specifying and describing vices, and charging them home on the consciences of

A. M. cir. 3004
B. C. cir. 1000
Ante I. Olymp.
cir. 224
Ante U. C. cir.
247

6 Hear; for I will speak of [c]excellent things; and the opening of my lips *shall be* right things.

7 For my mouth shall speak truth; and wickedness *is* [d]an abomination to my lips.

8 All the words of my mouth *are* in righteousness; *there is* nothing [e]froward or perverse in them.

9 [f]They *are* all plain to him that understandeth, and right to them that find knowledge.

10 Receive my instruction, and not silver;

and knowledge rather than choice gold.

A. M. cir. 3004
B. C. cir. 1000
Ante I. Olymp.
cir. 224
Ante U. C. cir.
247

11 [g]For wisdom *is* better than rubies; and all the things that may be desired are not to be compared to it.

12 I wisdom dwell with [h]prudence, and find out knowledge of witty inventions.

13 [i]The fear of the LORD *is* to hate evil: [k]pride, and arrogancy, and the evil way, and [l]the froward mouth, do I hate.

14 Counsel *is* mine, and sound wisdom: I *am* understanding; [m]I have strength.

---

[c]Ch. xxii. 20——[d]Heb. *the abomination of my lips*
[e]Heb. *wreathed*——[f]Ch. xiv. 6——[g]Job xxviii. 15, &c.;
Psa. xix. 10; cxix. 127; ch. iii. 14, 15; iv. 5, 7; xvi. 16

[h]Or, *subtilty*——[i]Chapter xvi. 6——[k]Chapter vi. 17
[l]Chapter iv. 24——[m]Eccles. vii. 19; Psa. xviii. 1; xix.
14; xxii. 19; xxxi. 4

---

transgressors. Where this is *not done*, the congregation is unconcerned; no man supposes he has any thing to do in the business, especially if the preacher takes care to tell them, "These were the crimes of Jews, Romans, Greeks, of the people at Corinth, Philippi, Thessalonica, Laodicea, and of heathens in general; but I hope better things of you, who have been born in a Christian land, and baptized in the Christian faith." Thus he arms their *consciences* in double brass against the good effects of his own teaching.

Verse 6. *Hear; for I will speak of excellent things*] נגידים *negidim*, things which are pre-eminent, and manifestly superior to all others. The teaching is not *trifling*, though addressed to *triflers*.

The opening of my lips shall be right things.] מישרים *meysharim*, things which are calculated to correct your false notions, and set straight your crooked ways. Hence she declares,

Verse 7. *My mouth shall speak truth*] TRUTH, without *falsity*, or any mixture of *error*, shall be the whole matter of my discourse.

Verse 8. *All the words—are in righteousness*] בצדק *betsedek*, in justice and equity, testifying what man *owes* to his God, to his neighbour, and to himself; giving to each his *due*. This is the true import of צדק *tsadak*.

There is *nothing froward*] נפתל *niphtal*, tortuous, involved, or difficult.

Or perverse] עקש *ikkesh*, distorted, leading to obstinacy. On the contrary,

Verse 9. *They* are *all plain*] נבחים *nechochim*, straight forward, over against every man, level to every capacity. This is true of all that concerns the salvation of the soul.

To them that find knowledge.] When a man gets the *knowledge* of *himself*, then he sees all the *threatenings* of God to be *right*. When he obtains the knowledge of GOD in *Christ*, then he finds that all the *promises* of God are *right* —yea and amen.

Verse 10. *Receive my instruction, and not silver*] A Hebrew idiom; *receive my instruction in preference to silver*.

Verse 11. *Wisdom is better than rubies*] See on chap. iii. 15.

Verse 12. *I wisdom dwell with prudence*] Prudence is defined, *wisdom applied to practice;* so wherever true wisdom is, it will lead to action, and its activity will be always in

reference to the *accomplishment of the best ends by the use of the most appropriate means.* Hence comes what is here called *knowledge of witty inventions,* דעת מזמות אמצא *daath mezimmoth emtsa,* "I have found out knowledge and contrivance." The farther wisdom proceeds in man, the more *practical* knowledge it gains; and finding out the nature and properties of things, and the general course of providence, it can *contrive* by new combinations to produce new results.

Verse 13. *The fear of the Lord is to hate evil*] As it is impossible to hate *evil* without loving *good;* and as hatred to *evil* will lead a man to abandon the *evil way;* and *love to goodness* will lead him to do what is *right* in the sight of God, under the influence of that Spirit which has given the *hatred to evil,* and inspired the *love of goodness:* hence this implies the sum and substance of *true religion,* which is here termed *the fear of the Lord.*

Verse 14. *Counsel is mine*] *Direction* how to act in all circumstances and on all occasions must come from *wisdom:* the *foolish* man can give no *counsel,* cannot show another how he is to act in the various changes and chances of life. The wise man alone can give this counsel; and he can give it only as continually receiving instruction from God: for this Divine wisdom can say, תושיה TUSHIYAH, *substance, reality, essence,* all belong to me: I am the *Fountain* whence all are derived. Man may be wise, and good, and prudent, and ingenious; but these he derives from me, and they are *dependently* in him. But in *me* all these are *independently* and *essentially* inherent.

And sound wisdom] See above. This is a totally false translation: תושיה *tushiyah* means essence, substance, reality; the source and substance of good. How ridiculous the support derived by certain authors from this translation in behalf of their system! See the writers on and quoters of Prov. viii.

I have strength.] Speaking still of wisdom, as communicating rays of its light to man, it enables him to bring every thing to his aid; to construct machines by which *one man* can do the work of *hundreds.* From it comes all *mathematical learning,* all *mechanical knowledge;* from it originally came the *inclined plane,* the *wedge,* the *screw,* the *pulley,* in all its *multiplications;* and the *lever,* in all its

A. M. cir. 3004
B. C. cir. 1000
Ante I. Olymp.
cir. 224
Ante U. C. cir.
247

15 [n]By me kings reign, and princes decree justice.

16 By me princes rule, and nobles, *even* all the judges of the earth.

17 [o]I love them that love me; and [p]those that seek me early shall find me.

18 [q]Riches and honour *are* with me; *yea,* durable riches and righteousness.

19 My fruit *is* better than gold; yea, than fine gold; and my revenue than choice silver.

20 I [s]lead in the way of righteousness, in the midst of the paths of judgment:

21 That I may cause those that love me to inherit substance: and I will fill their treasures.

22 [t]The LORD possessed me in the beginning of his way, before his works of old.

23 [u]I was set up from everlasting, from

A. M. cir. 3004
B. C. cir. 1000
Ante I. Olymp.
cir. 224
Ante U. C. cir.
247

---

[n]Dan. ii. 21; Rom. xiii. 1——[o]1 Sam. ii. 30; Psa. xci. 14; John xiv. 21——[p]James i. 5——[q]Ch. iii. 16; Matt. vi. 33——[r]Chap. iii. 14; ver. 10——[s]Or, *walk* [t]Chap. iii. 19; Ecclus. xxiv. 9; John i. 1——[u]Psa. ii. 6

---

combinations and *varieties,* came from this wisdom. And as all these can produce prodigies of *power,* far surpassing all kinds of *animal energy,* and all the effects of the utmost efforts of muscular force; hence the maxim of Lord Bacon, "Knowledge is power," built on the maxim of the *tushiyah* itself; לי גבורה *li geburah,* MINE IS STRENGTH.

Verse 15. *By me kings reign*] Every wise and prudent king is such through the influence of Divine wisdom. And just laws and their righteous administration come from this source. In this and the following verse *five degrees* of *civil power* and *authority* are mentioned. 1. מלכים *melachim,* KINGS. 2. רזנים *rozenim,* CONSULS. 3. שרים *sarim,* PRINCES, CHIEFS of the people. 4. נדיבים *nedibim,* NOBLES. And 5. שפטים *shophetim,* JUDGES or CIVIL MAGISTRATES. All orders of government are from God. Instead of שפטי ארץ *shophetey arets,* "judges of the earth," שפטי צדק *shophetey tsedek,* "righteous judges," or "judges of righteousness," is the reading of *one hundred and sixty-two* of Kennicott's and De Rossi's MSS., both in the text and in the margin, and of several ancient editions. And this is the reading of the *Vulgate,* the *Chaldee,* and the *Syriac;* and should undoubtedly supersede the other.

Verse 17. *I love them that love me*] Wisdom shows itself; teaches man the knowledge of himself; shows him also the will of God concerning him; manifests the snares and dangers of life, the allurements and unsatisfactory nature of all sensual and sinful pleasures, the blessedness of true religion, and the solid happiness which an upright soul derives from the peace and approbation of its Maker. If, then, the heart embraces this wisdom, follows this Divine teaching, and gives itself to God, his love will be shed abroad in it by the influence of the Holy Spirit. Thus we love God because he hath first loved us; and the more we love him, the more we shall feel of his love, which will enable us to love him yet *more and more;* and thus we may go on increasing to eternity. Blessed be God!

And those that seek me early shall find me.] Not merely *betimes in the morning,* though he who does so shall find it greatly to his advantage; (see on Psa. iv.;) but early *in life*—in *youth,* and as near as possible to the first dawn of *reason.* To the *young* this gracious promise is particularly made: if *they* seek, they *shall find.* Others, who are old, may seek and find; but *never to such advantage* as they would have done, had they sought *early.* Youth is the *time* of *advantage* in every respect: it is the time of *learning,* the time of *discipline;* the time of *improvement,* the time of *acquiring useful, solid,* and *gracious habits.* As the *first-fruits* always belong to God, it is *God's time;* the time in which he is peculiarly gracious; and in which, to sincere youthful seekers, he pours out his benefits with great profusion. "They that seek me early shall find me."

Hear, ye *young,* and ye *little ones!* God offers himself now to *you,* with all his treasures of grace and glory. Thank him for his ineffable mercy, and embrace it without delay.

Verse 18. *Riches and honour are with me*] Often the wise, prudent, and discreet man arrives literally to *riches* and *honour;* but this is not *always* the case. But there are *other riches* of which he *never fails;* and these seem to be what Solomon has particularly in view, *durable riches and righteousness;* the treasure deposited by God in earthen vessels.

Verse 20. *I lead in the way of righteousness*] Nothing but the teaching that comes from God by his *word* and *Spirit* can do this.

Verse 22. *The Lord possessed me in the beginning of his way*] Wisdom is not *acquired* by the Divine Being; *man,* and even *angels,* learn it by *slow* and *progressive* degrees; but in God it is as eternally inherent as any other essential attribute of his nature. The *Targum* makes this wisdom a *creature,* by thus translating the passage: אלהא בראני ברייש בריתיה *Elaha barani bereish biriteiah,* "God created me in the beginning of his creatures." The *Syriac* is the same. This is as absurd and heretical as some modern glosses on the same passage.

Verse 23. *I was set up from everlasting*] נסכתי *nissachti,* "I was diffused or poured out," from נסך *nasach,* "to diffuse, pour abroad, as a spirit or disposition," Isa. xxix. 10. See *Parkhurst.* Or from סך *sach,* "to cover, overspread, smear over, as with *oil;*" to be *anointed* king. Hence some have translated it, *principatum habui,* I had the principality, or was a ruler, governor, and director, from eternity. All the schemes, plans, and circumstances, relative to creation, government, providence, and to all being, *material, animal,* and *intellectual,* were conceived in the Divine mind, by the Divine wisdom, from eternity, *or ever the earth was.* There was no *fortuitous creation,* no *jumbling concourse of original atoms,* that entered into the composition of *created beings;* all was the

A. M. cir. 3004
B. C. cir. 1000
Ante I. Olymp. was.
cir. 224
Ante U. C. cir.
247

the beginning, or ever the earth
was.

24 When *there were* no depths,
I was brought forth; when *there
were* no fountains abounding with water.

25 [v]Before the mountains were settled, before the hills was I brought forth:

26 While as yet he had not made the earth, nor the [w]fields, nor [x]the highest part of the dust of the world.

27 When he prepared the heavens, I *was* there: when he set [y]a compass upon the face of the depth:

A. M. cir. 3004
B. C. cir. 1000
Ante I. Olymp.
cir. 224
Ante U. C. cir.
247

28 When he established the clouds above: when he strengthened the fountains of the deep:

29 [z]When he gave to the sea his decree, that the waters should not pass his commandment: when [a]he appointed the foundations of the earth:

30 [b]Then I was by him, *as* one brought up *with him:* [c]and I was daily *his* delight, rejoicing always before him:

31 Rejoicing in the habitable part of his earth; and [d]my delights *were* with the sons of men.

---

[v]Job xv. 7, 8——[w]Or, *open places*——[x]Or, *the chief part*
[y]Or, *a circle*——[z]Gen. iv. 9, 10; Job xxxviii. 10, 11; Psa.

xxxiii. 7; civ. 9; Jer. v. 22——[a]Job xxxviii. 4——[b]John i.
1, 2, 18——[c]Matt. iii. 17; Col. i. 13——[d]Psa. xvi. 3

---

effect of the *plans* before conceived, laid down, and at last acted upon by God's eternal wisdom.

Verse 24. *When* there were *no depths*] תהמות *tehomoth,* before the original chaotic mass was formed. See Gen. i. 2.

I was brought forth] חוללתי *cholalti,* "I was produced as by labouring throes." Mr. *Parkhurst* thinks that the heathen poets derived their idea of *Minerva's* (wisdom's) being born of Jupiter's brain, from some such high poetic personification as that in the text.

Verse 26. *The highest part of the dust of the world*] ראש עפרות תבל *rosh aphroth tebel,* "the first particle of matter." The *prima materia,* the primitive atom. All these verses (3-29) are a periphrasis for *I existed before creation;* consequently before *time* was. I dwelt in God as a principle which might be communicated in its influences to intellectual beings when formed.

Verse 27. *When he prepared the heavens, I was there*] For there is no part of the creation of God in which wisdom, skill, contrivance, are more manifest, than in the construction of the visible heavens.

When he set a compass upon the face of the depth] Does not this refer to the establishment of the *law of gravitation?* by which all the particles of matter, tending to a *common centre,* would produce in all bodies the *orbicular* form, which we see them have; so that even the *waters* are not only retained within their boundaries, but are subjected to the *circular form,* in their great aggregate of seas, as other parts of matter are. This is called here *making a compass,* בחקו חוג *bechukko chug,* sweeping a circle; and even this on *the face of the deep,* to bring the chaotic mass into *form,* regularity, and order.

Verse 28. *The clouds above*] שחקים *shechakim,* "the ethereal regions," taking in the whole of the atmosphere, with all its meteors, clouds, vapours, &c.

Verse 29. *When he gave to the sea his decree*] When he assigned its limits, adjusted its saltness, and proportioned the *extent of the surface* to the quantity of *vapours* to be raised from it, for the irrigation of the terrene surface.

The foundations of the earth] Those irreversible laws by which all its motions are

governed; its annual and diurnal rotation, and particularly its *centrifugal* and *centripetal forces;* by the former of which it has its *annual motion* round the sun like all other planets; and by the *latter* all its particles are prevented from *flying off,* notwithstanding the great *velocity* of its motion round its own axis, which causes *one thousand and forty-two* miles of its equator to pass under any given point in the heavens in the course of a single *hour!* These are, properly speaking, *the foundations of the earth;* the *principles* on which it is constructed, and the *laws* by which it is governed.

Verse 30. *Then I was with him,* as *one brought up*] אמון *amon,* a *nursling,* a *darling* child. Wisdom continues its parable, says *Calmet;* and represents itself as a new-born child which is ever near its parent, and takes pleasure to see him act, and to sport in his presence. This is poetical and highly figurative; and they who think they find the deity of Jesus Christ in these metaphors should be very cautious how they apply such terms as these; so that while they are endeavouring to defend the truth, they *may do nothing against the truth,* in which most of them unhappily fail.

Rejoicing always before him] All the images in this verse are borrowed from the state and circumstances of a *darling,* affectionate, playful child; as any one will be convinced who examines the *Hebrew text.*

Verse 31. *Rejoicing in the habitable part of his earth*] There God displays especially his wisdom in ordering and directing *human beings,* and in providing for their wants. The *wisdom* of God is in an especial manner manifested in his *providence.*

My delights were *with the sons of men.*] This Divine wisdom, as it delighted in the creation of man, so it continues to delight in his *instruction.* Hence it is represented as offering its lessons of instruction continually, and using every means and opportunity to call men from folly and vice to sound knowledge, holiness, and happiness. It is to man that God especially gives *wisdom;* and he has it in the form of *reason* beyond all other creatures; therefore it is said, "My delights are with the sons of men;" to them I open my choicest treasures. They alone are capable of *sapience, intelligence,* and *discursive reason.*

A. M. cir. 3004
B. C. cir. 1000
Ante I. Olymp.
cir. 224
Ante U. C. cir.
247

32 Now therefore hearken unto me, O ye children: for [e]blessed *are they that* keep my ways.

33 Hear instruction, and be wise, and refuse it not.

34 [f]Blessed *is* the man that heareth me,

watching daily at my gates, waiting at the posts of my doors.

35 For whoso findeth me findeth life, and shall [g]obtain [h]favour of the LORD.

36 But he that sinneth against me [i]wrongeth his own soul: all they that hate me love death.

A. M. cir. 3004
B. C. cir. 1000
Ante I. Olymp.
cir. 224
Ante U. C. cir.
247

---

[e]Psa. cxix. 1, 2; cxxviii. 1, 2; Luke xi. 28——[f]Chap. iii. 13, 18——[g]Heb. *bring forth*——[h]Ch. xii. 2——[i]Ch. xx. 2

Verse 32. *Now therefore*] Since I delight so much in conveying instruction; since I have the happiness of the *children of Adam* so much at heart, *hearken unto me;* and this is for your own interest, for *blessed* are they who *keep my ways.*

Verse 34. *Watching daily at my gates*] Wisdom is represented as having a *school* for the instruction of men; and seems to point out some of the most *forward* of her *scholars* coming, through their intense desire to learn, even *before the gates were opened,* and waiting there for admission, that they might hear *every word* that was uttered, and not lose one accent of the heavenly teaching. *Blessed are such.*

Verse 35. *Whoso findeth me*] The wisdom that comes from God, teaching to avoid evil and cleave to that which is good; *findeth life*—gets that knowledge which qualifies him to answer the *purposes* for which he was *made;* for he is *quickened with* Christ, and made a partaker of the Divine life. *Christ dwells in his heart by faith;* he *lives a new life,* for Christ *liveth* in him; the law of the *spirit of life* in Christ Jesus makes him free from the *law* of *sin* and *death. And shall obtain favour of the Lord.* The more he walks after the Divine counsel, the more he obtains of the Divine image; and the more he resembles his Maker, the more he partakes of the Divine favour.

Verse 36. *Wrongeth his own soul*] It is not *Satan,* it is not *sin,* properly speaking, that hurts him; it is *himself.* If he received the teaching of God, *sin would have no dominion over him;* if he *resisted the devil,* the devil would *flee from him.*

Love death.] They do it in *effect,* if not in *fact;* for as they love sin, that leads to *death,* so they may be justly said to love *death,* the wages of sin. He that works in this case, works for wages; and he must love the *wages,* seeing he *labours* so hard in the *work.*

I HAVE gone through this fine chapter, and given the best exposition of it in my power. I have also, as well as others, *weighed every word,* and closely examined their *radical* import, their connection among themselves, and the connection of the subject of the chapter with what has gone before, and with what follows after; and I cannot come, conscientiously, to *any other* interpretation than that which I have given. I am thoroughly satisfied that it speaks not one word either about the *Divine* or *human nature of Christ,* much less of any *eternal filiation* of his *Divinity.* And I am fully persuaded, had there not been a preconceived creed, no soul of man, by fair criticism, would have ever found out that fond opinion of the eternal sonship of the Divine nature, which so many commentators persuade us they find here.

That it has been thus applied in *early ages,* as well as in *modern times,* I am sufficiently aware; and that many other portions of the Divine records have been appealed to, in order to support a particular opinion, and many that were false in themselves, must be known to those who are acquainted with the *fathers.* But many quote *them* who know nothing of them. As to the fathers in general, they were not all agreed on this subject, some supposing *Christ,* others the *Holy Spirit,* was meant in this chapter. But of these we may safely state, that there is not a *truth* in the most orthodox creed, that cannot be proved by their authority, nor a *heresy* that has disgraced the Romish Church, that may not challenge them as its abettors. In points of *doctrine,* their authority is, *with me,* nothing. On the WORD of GOD alone contains my creed. On a number of points I can go to the Greek and Latin fathers of the Church, to know what *they believed,* and what the *people of their respective communions* believed; but after all this I must return to *God's word,* to know what he would have ME to believe. No part of a *Protestant creed* stands on the decision of *fathers* and *councils.* By appealing to the Bible alone, as the only rule for the faith and practice of Christians, they confounded and defeated their papistical adversaries, who could not prove their doctrines but by *fathers* and *councils.* Hence their peculiar doctrines stand in their ultimate proof upon THESE; and *those* of Protestantism on the BIBLE. Some late writers upon this subject, whose names I spare, have presumed much on *what they have said on this subject;* but before any man, who seeks for sober truth, will receive any of their *conclusions,* he will naturally look whether their *premises* be sound, or whether from *sound principles* they have drawn *legitimate conclusions.* They say this chapter is a sufficient foundation to build their doctrine on. I say it is no foundation at all; that it never has been proved, and never can be proved, that it speaks at all of the doctrine in question. It has nothing to do with it. On this conviction of mine, their proofs drawn from this chapter must go with *me* for *nothing.* I have been even shocked with reading over some things that have been *lately written* on the subject. I have said in my heart, They have taken away my ETERNAL LORD, and I know not where they have laid him. I cannot believe their doctrine; I never did; I hope I never shall. I believe in the holy Trinity; in three persons in the Godhead, of which none is before or after another. I believe JEHOVAH, JESUS, the HOLY GHOST to be one infinite, eternal GODHEAD, subsisting ineffably in *three persons.* I believe Jesus the Christ to be, as to his *Divine nature,* as *unoriginated* and *eternal* as JEHOVAH himself; and with the *Holy*

Ghost to be one infinite Godhead, *neither* person being *created, begotten*, nor *proceeding*, more than another: as to its *essence*, but *one* TRINITY, in an infinite, eternal and inseparable UNITY. And this TRIUNE GOD is the object of my faith, my adoration, and my confidence. But I believe not in an eternal sonship or generation of the Divine nature of Jesus Christ. *Here* I have long stood, *here* I now stand, and *here* I trust to stand in the hour of death, in the day of judgment, and to all eternity. Taking the Scriptures in general, I find a *plurality* in the Divine nature; taking the grand *part* mentioned, Matt. iii. 16, 17, I find that *plurality* restrained to a *trinity*, in the most unequivocal and evident manner: Jesus, who was baptized in Jordan; the HOLY GHOST, who descended upon him who was baptized; and the FATHER, manifested by the VOICE from heaven that said, "This is my beloved Son, in whom I am well pleased." And how that person called JESUS the CHRIST, in whom dwelt all the fulness of the Godhead bodily, could be called the *Son of God*, I have shown in my note on Luke i. 35.

Some writers, in their defence of the doctrine above, which I venture to say *I do not believe*, have made reflections, in real or pretended pity, on the belief of their Trinitarian brethren, which have very little to do with candour: viz., "How the supporters of this hypothesis can avoid either the error of Tritheism on the one hand, or Sabellianism on the other, is difficult to conceive." Now, the supporters of the doctrine of the underived and unbegotten eternity of Christ's Divine nature might as well say of them: How the supporters of the eternal sonship of Christ can avoid the error of Arianism on the one hand, and Arianism on the other, it is difficult to conceive. But I would not say so; for though I know Arians who hold that doctrine, and express their belief nearly in the same words; yet I know many most conscientious Trinitarians who hold the doctrine of the eternal sonship, and yet believe in the proper deity, or eternal godhead, of Jesus Christ. After all, as a very wise and excellent man lately said: "While we have every reason to be satisfied of the soundness of each other's faith, we must allow each to explain his own sentiments in his own *words:* here, in the *words* used in explanation, a little latitude may be safely allowed." To this correct sentiment I only add:—

Scimus; et hanc veniam petimusque damus-
    que vicissim.—HORACE.

"I grant it; and the license give and take."

I have passed the *waters of strife*, and do not wish to recross them: the wrath of man worketh not the righteousness of God. I will have nothing to do with ill-tempered, abusive men; I wish them more light and better manners.

And while I am on this subject, let me add one thing, which I am sure will not please all the generation of his people; and it is this: that Jesus Christ, having taken upon him human nature, which was afterwards crucified, and expired upon the cross, did by those acts make a full, perfect, and sufficient offering, sacrifice, and atonement for the sin of the whole world. That he died, paid down the *redemption price*, for *every soul of man*, that *was ever born* into the world, and *shall ever be born* into it. That all who lay hold on the hope set before them shall be saved; (and all *may* thus lay hold;) and none shall perish but those who would not come to Christ that they might have life. And that men perish, not because they were not redeemed, but because they would not accept of the redemption.

To conclude on this subject, it will be necessary to refer the reader to the remarkable *opposition* that subsists between *this* and the *preceding chapter.* There, the *prostitute* is represented as *going out into the streets* to seek her prey; and the *alluring words* of *carnal wisdom* to excite the animal appetite to sinful gratification, which she uses: *here*, heavenly *wisdom* is represented as *going out* into the *streets*, to the *high places*, the *gates of the city*, to counteract 'her designs, and lead back the simple to God and truth.

These *personifications* were frequent among the Jews. In the Book of *Ecclesiasticus* we find a similar personification, and expressed in almost *similar terms;* and surely none will suppose that the writer of that Apocryphal book had either the Christian doctrine of the *Trinity*, or the *sonship of Christ* in view.

I will give a few passages:—

"WISDOM shall *glory* in the *midst of her people;* in the *congregation* of the Most High shall *she open her mouth*, and triumph before his power. I *came out of the mouth of the Most High*, and covered the earth as a cloud. I *dwelt in the high places;* I alone *compassed the circuit of the heaven*, and walked in the *bottom of the deep*, in the waves of the sea, and in all the earth. *He created me from the beginning, before the world;* and I shall never fail. I am the mother of fair love, and fear, and knowledge, and holy hope. I therefore, *being eternal*, am given to all my children which are named of him. *Come unto me*, and fill *yourselves with my fruits*. I also came out as a brook from a river, and a conduit into a garden," &c., &c., Eccl. xxiv. 1, &c. This kind of personification of wisdom we have had in the preceding chapters; and in the following chapter we shall find the figure still kept up.

CHAPTER IX

Wisdom builds her house, makes her provision for a great feast, calls her guests, and exhorts them to partake of her entertainment, 1–6. Different admonitions relative to the acquisition of wisdom, 7–12. The character and conduct of a bad woman, 13–18.

A. M. cir. 3004
B. C. cir. 1000
Ante I. Olymp.
cir. 224
Ante U. C. cir.
247

WISDOM hath ªbuilded her house, she hath hewn out her seven pillars:

2 ᵇShe hath killed ᶜher beasts; ᵈshe hath mingled her wine, she hath also furnished her table.

3 She hath ᵉsent forth her maidens: ᶠshe crieth ᵍupon the highest places of the city.

4 ʰWhoso *is* simple, let him turn in hither: *as for* him that wanteth understanding, she saith to him,

5 ⁱCome, eat of my bread, and drink of the wine *which* I have mingled.

A. M. cir. 3004
B. C. cir. 1000
Ante I. Olymp.
cir. 224
Ante U. C. cir.
247

ªMatthew xvi. 18; Ephesians ii. 20, 21, 22; 1 Pet. ii. 5——ᵇMatthew xxii. 3, &c.——ᶜHebrew, *her killing*——ᵈVerse 5; chapter xxiii. 30——ᵉRomans x. 15

ⁱChapter viii. 1, 2——ᵍVerse 14——ʰVerse 16; chapter vi. 32; Matthew xi. 25——ⁱVerse 2; Cant. v. 1; Isa. lv. 1; John vi. 27

NOTES ON CHAP. IX.

The same Wisdom speaks here who spoke in the preceding chapter. *There* she represented herself as manifest in all the *works of God* in the natural world; all being constructed according to counsels proceeding from an infinite understanding. *Here*, she represents herself as the great *potentate*, who was to rule all that she had constructed; and having an immense *family* to provide for, had made an abundant *provision*, and calls all to partake of it. This, says *Calmet*, is the continuation of the parable begun in the preceding chapter, where wisdom is represented as a venerable lady, whose real beauties and solid promises are opposed to the false allurements of PLEASURE, who was represented in the seventh chapter under the idea of a debauched and impudent woman. *This one*, to draw young people into her snares, describes the *perfumes*, the *bed*, and the *festival* which she has prepared. WISDOM acts in the same way: but, instead of the debauchery, the false pleasures, and the criminal connections which *pleasure* had promised, offers her guests a strong, well-built, magnificent palace, chaste and solid pleasures, salutary instructions, and a life crowned with blessedness. This is the sum and the substance of the parable; but as in the preceding part, so in this, men have produced strange creatures of their own brain, by way of explanation. One specimen of this mode of interpretation may suffice.

The *house* built by wisdom is the holy *humanity of Jesus Christ;* the *seven pillars* are the *seven sacraments*, or the *seven gifts of the Holy Ghost*, or the *whole of the apostles, preachers, and ministers of the Church;* the *slain beasts* are the *sacrifice of Christ's body* upon the cross; and the *bread* and *mingled wine* are the *bread* and *wine* in the *sacrament of the Lord's Supper!*—FATHERS and DOCTORS.

If we have recourse to any other particulars than those given above in the summary of the chapter, let us follow the first part of the parable, where wisdom is represented as laying the plan of the creation; and then perhaps we may say with safety, that wisdom, having *produced* the grand *ichnograph* or *ground plot* of the whole, with all the requisite *elevations* and *specifications of materials*, comes to show us, in this part, that the whole has been *constructed on this plan;* and specifies the *end* for which this august building has been raised.

Verse 1. *Wisdom hath builded her house*] The eternal counsel of God has framed the *universe.*

She hath hewn out her seven pillars] Every thing has been so constructed as to exhibit a scene of grandeur, stability, and durableness.

Verse 2. *She hath killed her beasts*] God has made the most ample provision for the innumerable tribes of animal and intellectual beings, which people the whole vortex of created nature.

Verse 3. *She hath sent forth her maidens*] The wisdom of God has made use of the *most proper means* to communicate Divine knowledge to the inhabitants of the earth; as a good and gracious Creator wills to teach them *whence* they *came, how* they are *supported, whither* they are *going*, and for what *end* they were formed. It is a custom to the present day, in Asiatic countries, to send their invitations to guests by a company of *females*, preceded by eunuchs: they go to the doors of the invited, and deliver their message.

Verse 4. *Whoso is simple*] Let the young, heedless, and giddy attend to my teaching.

Him that wanteth understanding] Literally, *he that wanteth a heart;* who is without *courage*, is *feeble* and *fickle*, and *easily drawn* aside from the holy commandment.

Verse 5. *Come, eat of my bread*] Not only receive my instructions, but *act* according to my directions.

Drink of the wine—I have mingled.] Enter into my counsels; be not contented with *superficial knowledge* on any subject, where any thing *deeper* may be attained. Go by the *streams* to the *fountain head*. Look into the *principles* on which they were formed; investigate their *nature*, examine their *properties*, acquaint thyself with their *relations, connections, influences*, and various *uses*. See the *skill, power*, and *goodness* of God in their creation. And when thou hast learned all within thy reach, know that thou knowest but little of the manifold wisdom of God. Let what thou hast learned humble thee, by showing thee how very little thou dost know. Thou hast drunk of the *provided wine;* but that *wine* was mingled with *water*, for God will hide pride from man. He dwells only on the surface of religious and philosophical learning, who does not perceive and feel that he is yet but a *child* in knowledge; that he *see through a glass darkly;* that he *perceives men like trees walking;* and that there are lengths, breadths, depths, and heights, in the works and ways of God, which it will require an eternity to fathom. Here below the pure wine is mingled with water: but this is God's work. Yet there is enough; do not therefore be contented with a little. To this subject the words of the poet may be well applied:—

A little learning is a dangerous thing;
Drink deep, or taste not the Pierian spring:
For *scanty draughts intoxicate* the brain,
But *drinking largely sobers* us again.

POPE

A. M. cir. 3004
B. C. cir. 1000
Ante I. Olymp. cir. 224
Ante U. C. cir. 247

6 Forsake the foolish, and live; and *go* in the way of understanding.

7 He that reproveth a scorner getteth to himself shame: and he that rebuketh a wicked *man getteth* himself a blot.

8 [k]Reprove not a scorner, lest he hate thee: [l]rebuke a wise man, and he will love thee.

9 Give *instruction* to a wise *man,* and he will be yet wiser: teach a just *man,* [m]and he will increase in learning.

10 [n]The fear of the LORD *is* the beginning of wisdom: and the knowledge of the Holy *is* understanding.

A. M. cir. 3004
B. C. cir. 1000
Ante I. Olymp. cir. 224
Ante U. C. cir. 247

11 [o]For by me thy days shall be multiplied, and the years of thy life shall be increased.

12 [p]If thou be wise, thou shalt be wise for thyself: but *if* thou scornest, thou alone shalt bear *it.*

13 [q]A foolish woman *is* clamorous: *she is* simple, and knoweth nothing.

14 For she sitteth at the door of her house, on a seat [r]in the high places of the city,

15 To call passengers who go right on their ways:

16 [s]Whoso *is* simple, let him turn in hither: and *as for* him that wanteth

---

[k]Matt. vii. 6——[l]Psa. cxli. 5——[m]Matt. xiii. 12
[n]Job xxviii. 28; Psa. cxi. 10; chap. i. 7

[o]Chap. iii. 2, 16; x. 27——[p]Job xxxv. 6, 7; chap. xvi. 26
[q]Chap. vii. 11——[r]Ver. 3——[s]Ver. 4

Among the ancient *Jews, Greek,* and *Romans,* wine was rarely drank without being mingled with water; and among ancient writers we find several ordinances for this. Some direct *three parts* of water to *one of wine;* some *five* parts; and *Pliny* mentions some wines that required *twenty* waters: but the most common proportions appear to have been *three parts of water* to *two of wine.* But probably the מסך יין *yayin masach,* mingled wine, was wine mingled, *not* with *water,* to make it *weaker;* but with *spices* and other ingredients to make it *stronger.* The ingredients were *honey, myrrh, mandragora, opium,* and such like, which gave it not only an *intoxicating* but *stupifying* quality also. Perhaps the *mixed wine* here may mean *wine* of the *strongest* and *best quality,* that which was good to cheer and refresh the heart of man.

If we consider the *mixed wine* as meaning this *strong wine,* then the import of the metaphor will be, a thorough investigation of the works of God will invigorate the soul, strengthen all the mental powers, enlarge their capacity, and enable the mind to take the most exalted views of the *wonders of God's skill* manifested in the *operations of his hand.*

Verse 6. *Forsake the foolish*] For the companion of fools must be a fool.

And live] Answer the *end* for which thou wert *born.*

Verse 7. *He that reproveth a scorner*] לץ *lets,* the person who *mocks* at sacred things; the *libertine,* the *infidel;* who turns the most serious things into ridicule, and, by his *wit,* often succeeds in rendering the person who reproves him ridiculous. Wisdom seems here to intimate that it is vain to attempt by reproof to amend such: and yet we must not suffer sin upon our neighbour; at all hazards, we must deliver our own soul. But no reproof should be given to any, but in the *spirit of love* and deep concern; and when they contradict and blaspheme, leave them to God.

Verse 9. *Give* instruction *to a wise* man] Literally *give to the wise, and he will be wise.* Whatever you give to such, they reap profit from it. They are like the bee, they extract honey from every flower.

Verse 10. *The fear of the Lord*] See on chap. i. 7. The knowledge of the holy; קדשים

kedoshim, of the holy ones: *Sanctorum,* of the saints.—*Vulgate.* Βουλη αγιων, the counsel of the holy persons.

Verse 11. *For by me thy days shall be multiplied*] Vice shortens human life, by a necessity of consequence: and by the same, righteousness lengthens it. There is a long addition here in the *Septuagint, Syriac,* and *Vulgate:* "He who trusts in falsity feeds on the winds; and is like him who chases the fowls of heaven. He forsakes the way of his own vineyard, and errs from the paths of his own inheritance. He enters also into lonely and desert places, and into a land abandoned to thirst; and his hands collect that which yieldeth no fruit."

Verse 12. *If thou be wise*] It is thy own interest to be religious. Though thy example may be very useful to thy neighbours and friends, yet the chief benefit is to *thyself.* But if thou *scorn*—refuse to receive—the doctrines of wisdom, and die in thy sins, *thou alone* shalt suffer the vengeance of an offended God.

Verse 13. *A foolish woman is clamorous*] Vain, empty women, are those that make *most noise.* And she that is *full* of clamour, has generally *little* or no *sense.* We have had this character already, see chap. vii. 11. The translation of the *Septuagint* is very remarkable: Γυνη αφρων και θρασεια, ενδεης ψωμου γινεται, "A lewd and foolish woman shall be in need of a morsel of bread."

Verse 14. *For she sitteth at the door of her house*] Her conduct here marks at once her *folly, impudence,* and *poverty.* See above on chap. vii. 6, &c., where the reader will find a similar character.

Verse 16. *Whoso is simple, let him turn in hither*] FOLLY or PLEASURE here personified, uses the very same expressions as employed by *Wisdom,* ver. 4. Wisdom says, "Let the simple turn in to me." No, says Folly, "Let the simple turn in to me." If he turn in to *Wisdom,* his folly shall be taken away, and he shall become wise; if he turn in to *Folly,* his darkness will be thickened, and his folly will remain.

Wisdom sets up her school to instruct the ignorant:

Folly sets her school up next door, to defeat the designs of Wisdom.

A. M. cir. 3004
B. C. cir. 1000
Ante I. Olymp.
cir. 224
Ante U. C. cir.
247

understanding, she saith to him,

17 [t]Stolen waters are sweet, and bread [u]*eaten* in secret is pleasant.

18 But he knoweth not that [v]the dead *are* there; *and that* her guests *are* in the depths of hell.

A. M. cir. 3004
B. C. cir. 1000
Ante I. Olymp.
cir. 224
Ante U. C. cir.
247

---

[t]Chap. xx. 17——[u]Heb. *of secrecies*

[v]Chap. ii. 18; vii. 27

Thus the saying of the satirist appears to be verified:—

"Wherever God erects a *house* of *prayer*,
The devil surely builds a *chapel* there.
And it is found upon examination,
The *latter* has the *larger congregation*."
DE FOE.

Verse 17. *Stolen waters are sweet*] I suppose this to be a proverbial mode of expression, importing that *illicit pleasures are sweeter than those which are legal*. The meaning is easy to be discerned; and the conduct of multitudes shows that they are ruled by this adage. On it are built all the *adulterous intercourses* in the land.

Verse 18. *But he knoweth not that the dead are there*] See on chap. ii. 18. He does not know that it was in this way the first apostates from God and truth walked. רפאים *rephaim;* γίγαντες, the GIANTS.—*Septuagint.* The *sons of men*, the *earth-born*, to distinguish them from the *sons of God*, those who were *born from above.* See the notes on Gen. vi. 1, &c.

Her guests are in the depths of hell.] Those who have been drawn out of the way of understanding by *profligacy* have in general lost their *lives*, if not their *souls*, by their folly. The *Septuagint, Syriac,* and *Arabic* make a long addition to this verse: "But draw thou back, that thou mayest not die in this place; neither fix thy eyes upon her; so shalt thou pass by those strange waters. But abstain thou from strange waters, and drink not of another's fountain, that thou mayest live a long time, and that years may be added to thy life." Of this *addition* there is nothing in the *Hebrew*, the *Chaldee*, or the *Vulgate*, as now printed: but in the *editio princeps* are the following words:—Qui enim applicabitur illi descendet ad inferos; nam qui abscesserit ab ea salvabitur. These words were in the copy *from which* my old MS. Bible has been made, as the following version proves: 𝕎ho forsoth schal ben joyned to hir, schal falle doun in to hell: for whi he that goth awai fro hir, schal be saved. Three of my own MSS. have the same reading.

CHAPTER X

It is impossible to give summaries *of such chapters as these, where almost* every verse *contains a separate subject. Our common version not being able to exhibit the contents as usual, simply says, "From this chapter to the five and twentieth are sundry observations upon moral virtues, and their opposite vices." In general the wise man states in this chapter the difference between the wise and the foolish, the righteous and the wicked, the diligent and the idle. He speaks also of love and hatred, of the good and the evil tongue, or of the slanderer and the peace-maker.*

A. M. cir. 3004
B. C. cir. 1000
Ante I. Olymp.
cir. 224
Ante U. C. cir.
247

THE proverbs of Solomon. [a]A wise son maketh a glad father: but a foolish son *is* the heaviness of his mother.

2 [b]Treasures of wickedness profit nothing: [c]but righteousness delivereth from death.

A. M. cir. 3004
B. C. cir. 1000
Ante I. Olymp.
cir. 224
Ante U. C. cir.
247

---

[a]Ch. xxv. 20; xvii. 21, 25; xix. 13; xxix. 3, 15——[b]Psa.

xlix. 6, &c.; ch. xi. 4; Luke xii. 19, 20——[c]Dan. iv. 27

NOTES ON CHAP. X.

Verse 1. *The proverbs of Solomon*] Some ancient MSS. of the *Vulgate* have *Proverbiorum liber secundus*, "The second book of the Proverbs." The preceding *nine* chapters can only be considered as an *introduction*, if indeed they may be said to make even a *part*, of the proverbs of Solomon, which appear to commence only at the tenth *chapter*.

A wise son maketh a glad father] The parallels in this and several of the succeeding chapters are those which *Bishop Lowth* calls the *antithetic;* when two lines correspond with each other by an opposition of *terms* and *sentiments;* when the second is contrasted with the first;

sometimes in *expression*, sometimes in *sense* only. Accordingly the degrees of antithesis are various; from an exact contraposition of *word* to *word*, through a whole sentence, down to a general *disparity*, with something of a *contrariety* in the two propositions, as:—

A wise son rejoiceth in his father.
But a foolish son is the grief of his mother.

Where *every word* has its *opposite;* for the terms *father* and *mother* are, as the logicians say, relatively opposite.

Verse 2. *Treasures of wickedness*] Property gained by wicked means.

Delivered from death] Treasures gained by

A. M. cir. 3004
B. C. cir. 1000
Ante I. Olymp. cir. 224
Ante U. C. cir. 247

3 ^dThe Lord will not suffer the soul of the righteous to famish: but he casteth away ^ethe substance of the wicked.

4 ^fHe becometh poor that dealeth *with* a slack hand: but ^gthe hand of the diligent maketh rich.

5 He that gathereth in summer *is* a wise son: *but* he that sleepeth in harvest *is* ^ha son that causeth shame.

6 Blessings *are* upon the head of the just: but ⁱviolence covereth the mouth of the wicked.

7 ^kThe memory of the just *is* blessed: but the name of the wicked shall rot.

8 The wise in heart will receive commandments: ^lbut ^ma prating fool ⁿshall fall.

9 ^oHe that walketh uprightly walketh surely: but he that perverteth his ways shall be known.

A. M. cir. 3004
B. C. cir. 1000
Ante I. Olymp. cir. 224
Ante U. C. cir. 247

10 ^pHe that winketh with the eye causeth sorrow: ^qbut a prating fool ^rshall fall.

11 ^sThe mouth of a righteous *man is* a well of life: but ^tviolence covereth the mouth of the wicked.

12 Hatred stirreth up strifes: but ^ulove covereth all sins.

13 In the lips of him that hath understanding wisdom is found: but ^va rod is for the back of him that is void of ^wunderstanding.

14 Wise *men* lay up knowledge: but ^xthe mouth of the foolish *is* near destruction.

---

^dPsa. x. 14; xxxiv. 9, 10; xxxvii. 25——^eOr, *the wicked for* their *wickedness*——^fCh. xii. 24; xix. 15 ^gCh. xiii.4; xxi.5——^hCh. xii.4; xvii. 2; xix. 26——ⁱVer. 11; Esth. vii. 8——^kPsa. ix. 5, 6; cxii. 6; Eccles. viii. 10 ^lVer. 10——^mHeb. *a fool of lips*——ⁿOr, *shall be beaten*

^oPsa. xxiii. 4; ch. xxviii. 18; Isa. xxxiii. 15, 16——^pCh. vi. 13——^qVer. 8——^rOr, *shall be beaten*——^sPsa. xxxvii. 30; ch. xiii. 14; xviii. 4——^tPsa. cvii. 42; ver. 6 ^uCh. xvii. 9; 1 Cor. xiii. 4; 1 Pet. iv. 8——^vCh. xxvi. 3 ^wHeb. *heart*——^xCh. xviii. 7; xxi. 23

---

robbery often bring their possessors to an untimely death; but those gained by righteous dealing bring with them no such consequences.

Verse 3. *But he casteth away the substance of the wicked.*] But instead of רשעים *reshaim*, the wicked, בוגדים *bogedim*, hypocrites, or perfidious persons, is the reading of *twelve* or *fourteen* of *Kennicott's* and *De Rossi's* MSS., and some *editions;* but it is not acknowledged by any of the ancient versions.

The righteous have God for their feeder; and because of his infinite bounty, they can never famish for want of the bread of life. On the contrary, the wicked are often, in the course of his providence, deprived of the property of which they make a bad use.

Verse 4. *He becometh poor*] God has ordered, in the course of his providence, that he who will not *work* shall not *eat.* And he always blesses the work of the *industrious* man.

Verse 5. *He that gathereth in summer*] All the work of the field should be done in the *season suitable to it.* If *summer* and *harvest* be neglected, in vain does a man expect the fruits of *autumn.*

Verse 6. *Violence covereth the mouth of the wicked.*] As *blessings shall be on the head of the just,* so the *violence of the wicked shall cover their face* with shame and confusion. Their own violent dealings shall be visited upon them. 𝕿𝖍𝖊 𝖒𝖔𝖚𝖙𝖍 𝖋𝖔𝖗𝖘𝖔𝖙𝖍 𝖔𝖋 𝖚𝖓𝖕𝖎𝖙𝖔𝖚𝖘 𝖒𝖊𝖓 𝖜𝖎𝖈𝖐𝖎𝖉𝖓𝖊𝖘𝖘𝖊 𝖈𝖔𝖛𝖊𝖗𝖊𝖙𝖍.—*Old MS. Bible.* "The forehead of the ungodly is past shame, and presumptuous."—*Coverdale.*

Verse 7. *The memory of the just is blessed*] Or, *is a blessing.*

But the name of the wicked shall rot.] This is another antithesis; but there are only two antithetic terms, for *memory* and *name* are synonymous.—*Lowth.* The very name of the wicked is as offensive as putrid carrion.

Verse 8. *A prating fool shall fall.*] This clause is repeated in the *tenth* verse. The *wise man will receive the commandment: but the*

shallow blabbing fool shall be cast down. See verse 10.

Verse 9. *He that walketh uprightly*] The upright man is always *safe;* he has not *two characters* to support; he goes straight forward, and is never afraid of *detection,* because he has never been influenced by *hypocrisy* or *deceit.*

Verse 10. *He that winketh with the eye*] Instead of the latter clause, on which see ver. 8, the *Septuagint* has, ὁ δὲ ἐλεγχων μετα παρρησιας ειρηνοποιει· "but he that reproveth with freedom, maketh peace." This is also the reading of the *Syriac* and *Arabic.* A faithful open reproving of sin is more likely to promote the peace of society than the passing it by slightly, or taking no notice of it; for if the wicked turn to God at the reproof, the law of *peace* will soon be established in his heart, and the law of kindness will flow from his tongue.

Verse 11. *The mouth of a righteous man is a well of life*] מקור חיים *mekor chaiyim,* is the *vein of lives;* an allusion to the *great aorta,* which conveys the blood from the heart to every part of the body. The latter clause of this verse is the same with that of verse 6.

Verse 12. *Hatred stirreth up strifes*] It seeks for occasions to provoke enmity. It delights in broils. On the contrary, love conciliates; removes aggravations; puts the best construction on every thing; and pours *water,* not *oil,* upon the *flame.*

Verse 13. *A rod is for the back of him*] He that *can learn,* and *will not learn,* should be *made to learn.* The rod is a most powerful instrument of knowledge. Judiciously applied, there is a lesson of profound wisdom in every *twig.*

Verse 14. *Wise men lay up knowledge*] They keep secret every thing that has a tendency to disturb domestic or public peace; but the foolish man blabs all out, and produces much mischief. Think much, speak little, and always think before you speak. This will promote your own peace and that of your neighbour.

A. M. cir. 3004
B. C. cir. 1000
Ante I. Olymp.
cir. 224
Ante U. C. cir.
247

15 ʸThe rich man's wealth *is* his strong city: the destruction of the poor *is* their poverty.

16 The labour of the righteous *tendeth* to life: the fruit of the wicked to sin.

17 He *is in* the way of life that keepeth instruction: but he that refuseth reproof ᶻerreth.

18 He that hideth hatred *with* lying lips, and ᵃhe that uttereth a slander, *is* a fool.

19 ᵇIn the multitude of words there wanteth not sin: but ᶜhe that refraineth his lips *is* wise.

20 The tongue of the just *is as* choice silver: the heart of the wicked *is* little worth.

21 The lips of the righteous feed many: but fools die for want ᵈof wisdom.

22 ᵉThe blessing of the LORD, it maketh rich, and he addeth no sorrow with it.

A. M. cir. 3004
B. C. cir. 1000
Ante I. Olymp.
cir. 224
Ante U. C. cir.
247

23 ᶠ*It is* as sport to a fool to do mischief: but a man of understanding hath wisdom.

24 ᵍThe fear of the wicked, it shall come upon him: but ʰthe desire of the righteous shall be granted.

25 As the whirlwind passeth, ⁱso *is* the wicked no *more:* but ᵏthe righteous *is* an everlasting foundation.

26 As vinegar to the teeth, and as smoke to the eyes, so *is* the sluggard to them that send him.

27 ˡThe fear of the LORD ᵐprolongeth days: but ⁿthe years of the wicked shall be shortened.

ʸJob xxxi. 24; Psa. lii. 7; ch. xviii. 11; 1 Tim. vi. 17——ᶻOr, *causeth to err*——ᵃPsa. xv. 3——ᵇEccles. v. 3——ᶜJames iii. 2——ᵈHeb. *of heart*——ᵉGen. xxiv. 35; xxvi. 12; Psalm xxxvii. 22——ᶠChap. xiv. 9; xv. 21

ᵍJob xv. 21——ʰPsa. cxlv. 19; Matt. v. 6; 1 John v. 14, 15——ⁱPsa. xxxvii. 9, 10——ᵏVer. 30; Psa. xv. 5; Matt. vii. 24, 25; xvi. 18——ˡChap. ix. 11——ᵐHeb. *addeth*——ⁿJob xv. 32, 33; xxii. 16; Psa. lv. 23; Eccles. vii. 17

Verse 15. *The rich man's wealth* is *his strong city*] Behold a mystery in providence; there is not a *rich man* on earth but becomes such by means of the *poor!* Property comes from the *labour* of the *poor*, and *the king himself is served of the field.* How unjust, diabolically so, is it to *despise* or *oppress* those by whose labour all property is acquired!

The destruction of the poor is *their poverty.*] A man in abject poverty never arises out of this pit. They have no nucleus about which property may aggregate. The poet spoke well:—

Haud facile emergunt, quorum virtutibus obstat
Res angusta domi.

"They rarely emerge from poverty, whose exertions are cramped by want at home."

Verse 16. *The labour of the righteous*] The good man labours that he may be able to *support life;* this is his *first* object: and then to have *something to divide with the poor;* this is his *next* object.

The fruit of the wicked to sin.] This man lives to eat and drink, and his property he spends in riot and excess. God's blessings are cursed to him.

Verse 17. *He* is in *the way of life*] The truly religious man accumulates knowledge that he may the better know how to live to God, and do most good among men.

Verse 18. *He that hideth*] This is a common case. How many, when full of resentment, and deadly hatred, meditating revenge and cruelty, and sometimes even murder, have pretended that they *thought nothing of the injury they had sustained;* had *passed by the insult*, &c.! Thus *lying lips* covered the malevolence of a wicked heart.

Verse 19. *In the multitude of words*] It is impossible to speak much, and yet speak nothing but truth; and injure no man's character in the mean while.

Verse 20. *The heart of the wicked* is *little worth*] כמעט *kimat*, is like little or nothing; or is *like dross*, while the tongue of the just is like *silver*. A sinner's heart is worth nothing, and is good for nothing; and yet because it is his most *hidden part*, he vaunts of its *honesty, goodness*, &c.! Yes, yes; it is very honest and good, only the devil is in it! that is all.

Verse 22. *The blessing of the Lord, it maketh rich*] Whatever we receive in the way of providence, has God's blessing in it, and will do us good. Cares, troubles, and difficulties come with all property not acquired in this way; but God's blessing gives simple enjoyment, and levies no tax upon the comfort.

Verse 23. It is *a sport to a fool to do mischief*] What a millstone weight of iniquity hangs about the necks of most of the *jesters, facetious* and *witty* people! "How many lies do they tell in jest, to go to the devil in earnest!"

Verse 24. *The fear of the wicked*] The wicked is full of fears and alarms; and all that he has dreaded and more than he has dreaded, shall come upon him. The righteous is always *desiring* more of the salvation of God, and God will exceed even his utmost desires.

Verse 25. *As the whirlwind passeth*] As tornadoes that sweep every thing away before them; so shall the wrath of God sweep away the wicked; it shall leave him neither branch nor root. But the righteous, being built on the *eternal foundation,* יסוד עולם *yesod olam,* shall never be shaken.

Verse 26. *As vinegar to the teeth*] The *acid* softening and dissolving the *alkali* of the bone, so as to impair their texture, and render them incapable of *masticating;* and as *smoke* affects the eyes, irritating their tender vessels, so as to give pain and prevent distinct vision; so the sluggard, the lounging, thriftless messenger, who never returns in time with the desired answer.

A. M. cir. 3004
B. C. cir. 1000
Ante I. Olymp. cir. 224
Ante U. C. cir. 247

28 The hope of the righteous
shall be gladness: but the [o]ex-
pectation of the wicked shall
perish.
29 The way of the LORD *is* strength to
the upright: but [p]destruction *shall be* to the
workers of iniquity.
30 [q]The righteous shall never be removed:
but the wicked shall not inhabit
the earth.
31 [r]The mouth of the just
bringeth forth wisdom: but the
froward tongue shall be cut out.
32 The lips of the righteous know what is
acceptable: but the mouth of the wicked
speaketh [s]frowardness.

---

[o]Job viii. 13; xi. 20; Psa. cxii. 10; chap. xi. 7——[p]Psa. i. 6; xxxvii. 20 — [q]Psa. xxxvii. 22, 29; cxxv. 1; ver. 25——[r]Psa. xxxvii. 30 — [s]Heb. *frowardness*

Verse 28. *The expectation of the wicked shall perish.*] A wicked man is always imposing on himself by the *hope of God's mercy* and *final happiness;* and he continues *hoping,* till he dies without receiving that *mercy* which alone would entitle him to that *glory.*

Verse 29. *The way of the Lord* is *strength*] In the path of *obedience* the upright man ever finds his *strength renewed;* the more he *labours* the *stronger* he grows. The same sentiment as that in Isa. xl. 31.

Verse 30. *The righteous shall never be removed*] Because he is built on the *eternal foundation.* See on ver. 25.

Verse 31. *The froward tongue shall be cut out.*] This probably alludes to the punishment of *cutting out the tongue* for *blasphemy, treasonable speeches, profane swearing,* or such like. **The tunge of schrewis schal perishen.**—Old MS. Bible. Were the tongue of every *shrew* or *scold* to be extracted, we should soon have much less *noise* in the world.

Verse 32. *The lips of the righteous know what is acceptable*] And what they believe to be most pleasing and most profitable, that they speak; but the wicked man knows as well what is *perverse,* and that he speaketh forth. As the love of God is not in his heart; so the law of kindness is not on his lips.

CHAPTER XI

A parallel of the advantages of the righteous and wise, opposed to the miseries of the wicked and the foolish. True and false riches.

A. M. cir. 3004
B. C. cir. 1000
Ante I. Olymp. cir. 224
Ante U. C. cir. 247

A [a]FALSE [b]balance *is* abomination to the LORD: but
[c]a just weight *is* his delight.
2 [d]*When* pride cometh, then
cometh shame: but with the lowly *is* wisdom.
3 [e]The integrity of the upright shall guide
them: but the perverseness of transgressors
shall destroy them.
4 [f]Riches profit not in the day of wrath:
but [g]righteousness delivereth
from death.
5 The righteousness of the perfect shall [h]direct his way: but
the wicked shall fall by his own wickedness.
6 The righteousness of the upright shall deliver them: but [i]transgressors shall be taken
in *their own* naughtiness.
7 [k]When a wicked man dieth, *his* expecta-

---

[a]Lev. xix. 35, 36; Deut. xxv. 13–16; ch. xvi. 11; xx. 10, 23——[b]Heb. *balances of deceit*——[c]Heb. *a perfect stone* — [d]Chap. xv. 33; xvi. 18; xviii. 12; Dan. iv. 30, 31 — [e]Chap. xiii. 6——[f]Chap. x. 2; Ezek. vii. 19; Zeph. i. 18; Ecclus. v. 8——[g]Gen. vii. 1——[h]Heb. *rectify* — [i]Chap. v. 22; Eccles. x. 8——[k]Chap. x. 28

NOTES ON CHAP. XI

Verse 1. *A false balance* is *abomination*] This refers to the balance itself deceitfully constructed, so that it is sooner turned at one end than at the other. This is occasioned by *one end* of the *beam* being *longer* than the other.

But a just weight] אבן שלמה *eben shelemah,* the *perfect stone,* probably because weights were first made of stone; see the law, Deut. xxv. 13-35.

Verse 2. When *pride cometh*] The proud man thinks much more of himself than any other can do; and, expecting to be treated according to his own supposed worth, which treatment he seldom meets with, he is repeatedly mortified, ashamed, confounded, and rendered indignant.

With the lowly] צנועים *tsenuim,* ταπεινων, the *humble,* the *modest,* as opposed to the *proud,* referred to in the first clause. The humble man looks for nothing but justice; has the meanest opinion of himself; expects nothing in the way of commendation or praise; and can never be disappointed but in receiving praise, which he neither expects nor desires.

Verse 4. *Riches profit not in the day of wrath*] Among men they can do all things; but they cannot purchase the remission of sins, nor turn aside the wrath of God when that is poured out upon the opulent transgressor.

Verse 7. *When a wicked man dieth*] HOPE is a great blessing to man in his present state of trial and suffering; because it leads him to expect a favourable termination of his ills. But *hope* was not made for the *wicked;* and yet

A. M. cir. 3004
B. C. cir. 1000
Ante I. Olymp.
cir. 224
Ante U. C. cir.
247

tion shall perish: and the hope of unjust *men* perisheth.

8 ¹The righteous is delivered out of trouble, and the wicked cometh in his stead.

9 A ᵐhypocrite with *his* mouth destroyeth his neighbour: but through knowledge shall the just be delivered.

10 ⁿWhen it goeth well with the righteous, the city rejoiceth: and when the wicked perish, *there is* shouting.

11 °By the blessing of the upright the city is exalted: but it is overthrown by the mouth of the wicked.

12 ᵖHe that is void of wisdom despiseth his neighbour: but a man of understanding holdeth his peace.

13 ۹A ʳtalebearer revealeth secrets: but he that is of a faithful spirit concealeth the matter.

14 ˢWhere no counsel *is,* the people fall: but in the multitude of counsellors *there is* safety.

15 ᵗHe that is surety for a stranger ᵘshall smart *for it:* and he that hateth ᵛsuretiship is sure.

16 ʷA gracious woman retaineth honour: and strong *men* retain riches.

17 ˣThe merciful man doeth good to his own soul: but *he that is* cruel troubleth his own flesh.

18 The wicked worketh a deceitful work: but ʸto him that soweth righteousness *shall be* a sure reward.

A. M. cir. 3004
B. C. cir. 1000
Ante I. Olymp.
cir. 224
Ante U. C. cir.
247

ˡChap. xxi. 18——ᵐJob viii. 13——ⁿEsth. viii. 15; chap. xxviii. 12, 28——°Chap. xxix. 8——ᵖHeb. *destitute of heart*——۹Lev. xix. 16; chap. xx. 19——ʳHeb. *He that walketh,* being *a talebearer*

ˢ1 Kings xii. 1, &c.; chap. xv. 22; xxiv. 6——ᵗChap. vi. 1——ᵘHeb. *shall be sore broken*——ᵛHeb. *those that strike* hands——ʷChap. xxxi. 30——ˣMatt. v. 7; xxv. 34, &c.——ʸHos. x. 12; Gal. vi. 8, 9; James iii. 18

---

they are the very persons that most abound in it! They hope to be saved, and get at last to the kingdom of God; though they have their face towards perdition, and refuse to turn. But their hope goes no farther than the *grave.* There the wicked man's expectation is cut off, and his hope perishes. But to the *saint,* the *penitent,* and the *cross-bearers* in general, what a treasure is *hope!* What a balm through life!

Verse 8. *The wicked cometh in his stead.*] Often God makes this distinction; in public calamities and in sudden accidents he rescues the righteous, and leaves the wicked, who has filled up the measure of his iniquities, to be seized by the hand of death. *Justice,* then, does its own work; for *mercy* has been rejected.

Verse 9. *A hypocrite with* his *mouth*] חנף *chaneph* might be better translated *infidel* than *hypocrite.* The latter is one that pretends to religion; that uses it for *secular purposes.* The former is one who *disbelieves* Divine revelation, and accordingly is *polluted,* and lives in *pollution.* This is properly the force of the original word. Such persons deal in calumny and lies, and often thus destroy the character of their neighbour. Besides, they are very zealous in propagating their own infidel notions; and thus, by this means, destroy their neighbour; but the experimental knowledge which the *just* have of God and his salvation prevents them from being ensnared.

Verse 10. *When it goeth well*] An upright, pious, sensible man is a great blessing to the neighbourhood where he resides, by his example, his advice, and his prayers. The considerate prize him on these accounts, and rejoice in his prosperity. But when the *wicked perish,* who has been a general curse by the contagion of his example and conversation, there is not only no regret expressed for his decease, but a *general joy* because God has removed him.

Verse 12. *He that is void of wisdom*] A

foolish man is generally abundant in his censures; he dwells on the *defects* of his neighbour, and is sure to bring them into the most prominent view. But a *man of understanding*—a prudent, sensible man, hides those defects wherever he can, and puts the most charitable construction on those which he cannot conceal.

Verse 13. *A talebearer*] הולך רכיל *holech rachil,* the walking busybody, the trader in scandal.

Revealeth secrets] Whatever was confided to him he is sure to publish abroad. The word means a *hawker,* or *travelling chapman.* Such are always great newsmongers; and will tell even their *own secrets,* rather than have nothing to say.

Verse 15. *He that is surety for a stranger shall smart* for it] He shall find evil upon evil in it. See on chap. vi. 1.

Verse 16. *A gracious woman retaineth honor*] Instead of this clause, the *Septuagint* have, Γυνη ευχαριστος εγειρει ανδρι δοξαν, "A gracious woman raiseth up honour to the man;" Θρονος δε ατιμιας γυνη μισουσα δικαια, "But she that hateth righteous things is a throne of dishonour." A good wife is an honour to her husband; and a bad wife is her husband's reproach: if this be so, how careful should a man be whom he marries!

Verse 17. *The merciful man doeth good to his own soul*] Every gracious disposition is increased while a man is exercised in showing mercy. No man can show an act of disinterested mercy without benefiting his own soul, by improving his moral feeling.

But he that is *cruel troubleth his own flesh.*] We seldom see a peevish, fretful, vindictive man either in good health, or good plight of body. I have often heard it observed of such, "He frets his flesh off his bones."

Verse 18. *Worketh a deceitful work*] An *unstable* work; nothing is durable that he does, except his crimes.

A. M. cir. 3004
B. C. cir. 1000
Ante I. Olymp. cir. 224
Ante U. C. cir. 247

19 As righteousness *tendeth* to life: so he that pursueth evil *pursueth it* to his own death.

20 They that are of a froward heart *are* abomination to the LORD: but *such as are* upright in *their* way *are* his delight.

21 *Though* hand *join* in hand, the wicked shall not be unpunished: but [a]the seed of the righteous shall be delivered.

22 *As* a jewel of gold in a swine's snout, *so is* a fair woman which [b]is without discretion.

23 The desire of the righteous *is* only good: *but* the expectation of the wicked [c]*is* wrath.

24 There is that [d]scattereth, and yet increaseth: and *there is* that withholdeth more than is meet, but *it tendeth* to poverty.

25 [e]The [f]liberal soul shall be made fat:

[g]and he that watereth shall be watered also himself.

A. M. cir. 3004
B. C. cir. 1000
Ante I. Olymp. cir. 224
Ante U. C. cir. 247

26 [h]He that withholdeth corn, the people shall curse him: but [i]blessing *shall be* upon the head of him that selleth *it*.

27 He that diligently seeketh good procureth favour: [k]but he that seeketh mischief, it shall come unto him.

28 [l]He that trusteth in his riches shall fall: but [m]the righteous shall flourish as a branch.

29 He that troubleth his own house [n]shall inherit the wind: and the fool *shall be* servant to the wise of heart.

30 The fruit of the righteous *is* a tree of life; and [o]he that [p]winneth souls *is* wise.

31 [q]Behold the righteous shall be recompensed in the earth: much more the wicked and the sinner.

---

[z]Chap. xvi. 5——[a]Psa. cxii. 2——[b]Heb. *departeth from*——[c]Rom. ii. 8, 9——[d]Psa. cxii. 9——[e]2 Cor. ix. 6, 7, 8, 9, 10——[f]Or, *The soul of blessing*——[g]Matt. v. 7 [h]Amos viii. 5, 6——[i]Job xxix. 13——[k]Esth. vii. 10; Psa. vii. 15, 16; ix. 15, 16; x. 2; lvii. 6

[l]Job xxxi. 24; Psa. lii. 7; Mark x. 24; Luke xii. 21; 1 Tim. vi. 17——[m]Psa. i. 3; lii. 8; xcii. 12, &c.; Jer. xvii. 8——[n]Eccles. v. 16——[o]Dan. xii. 3; 1 Cor. ix. 19, &c.; James v. 20——[p]Heb. *taketh*——[q]Jer. xxv. 29; 1 Pet. iv. 17, 18

Verse 19. *Righteousness* tendeth *to life*] True godliness promotes health, and is the best means of lengthening out life; but wicked men live not out half their days.

Verse 21. Though *hand* join *in hand*] Let them confederate as they please, to support each other, justice will take care that they escape not punishment. The Hindoos sometimes ratify an engagement by one person *laying his right hand on the hand of another.*—WARD.

Verse 22. *A jewel of gold in a swine's snout*] That is, beauty in a woman destitute of good breeding and modest carriage, is as becoming as a gold ring on the snout of a swine. *Coverdale* translates thus: "A fayre woman without discrete maners, is like a ringe of golde in a swyne's snoute." In Asiatic countries the *nose jewel* is very common: to this the text alludes.

Verse 24. *There is that scattereth, and yet increaseth*] The bountiful man, who gives to the poor, never turning away his face from any one in distress, the Lord blesses his property, and the bread is multiplied in his hand. To the same purpose the following verse.

Verse 25. *The liberal soul shall be made fat*] He who gives to the distressed, in the true spirit of charity, shall get a hundred fold from God's mercy. How wonderful is the Lord! He gives the *property*, gives the *heart* to use it aright, and *recompenses* the man for the deed, though all the fruit was found from himself!

He that watereth] A man who distributes in the right spirit gets more good himself than the poor man does who receives the bounty. Thus *it is more blessed to give than to receive.*

Verse 26. *He that withholdeth corn*] Who refuses to sell because he hopes for a dearth, and then he can make his own price.

The people shall curse him] Yes, and God shall curse him also; and if he do not return and repent, he will get God's curse, and the curse of the poor, which will be a *canker* in his *money* during *time*, and in his *soul* throughout *eternity*.

Verse 29. *Shall inherit the wind*] He who dissipates his property by riotous living, shall be as unsatisfied as he who attempts to feed upon *air.*

Verse 30. *The fruit of the righteous* is *a tree of life*] עץ חיים *ets chaiyim*, "the tree of lives." It is like that tree which grew in the paradise of God; increasing the bodily and mental vigour of those who ate of it.

He that winneth souls is *wise.*] Wisdom seeks to reclaim the wanderers; and he who is influenced by wisdom will do the same.

Verse 31. *Behold, the righteous shall be recompensed in the earth, &c.*] The *Septuagint, Syriac,* and *Arabic* read this verse as follows: "And if the righteous scarcely be saved, where shall the ungodly and the sinner appear?" And this St. Peter quotes *literatim,* 1st Epist. iv. 18, where see the note.

CHAPTER XII

Of the benefit of instruction, and the cultivation of piety. The virtuous woman. The different lot of the just and unjust. The humane man. The industrious man. The fool and the wise man. The uncharitable. The excellence of the righteous. The slothful is in want. Righteousness leads to life, &c.

A. M. cir. 3004
B. C. cir. 1000
Ante I. Olymp.
cir. 224
Ante U. C. cir.
247

WHOSO loveth instruction loveth knowledge: but he that hateth reproof *is* brutish.

2 ᵃA good *man* obtaineth favour of the LORD: but a man of wicked devices will he condemn.

3 A man shall not be established by wickedness: but the ᵇroot of the righteous shall not be moved.

4 ᶜA virtuous woman *is* a crown to her husband: but she that maketh ashamed *is* ᵈas rottenness in his bones.

5 The thoughts of the righteous *are* right:

but the counsels of the wicked *are* deceit.

6 ᵉThe words of the wicked *are* to lie in wait for blood: ᶠbut the mouth of the upright shall deliver them.

7 ᵍThe wicked are overthrown, and *are* not: but the house of the righteous shall stand.

8 A man shall be commended according to his wisdom: ʰbut he that is ⁱof a perverse heart shall be despised.

9 ᵏ*He that is* despised, and hath a servant,

A. M. cir. 3004
B. C. cir. 1000
Ante I. Olymp.
cir. 224
Ante U. C. cir.
247

ᵃChapter viii. 35——ᵇChapter x. 25——ᶜChapter xxxi. 23; 1 Corinthians xi. 7——ᵈChapter xiv. 30 ᵉChapter i. 11, 18——ᶠChapter xiv. 3

ᵍPsalm xxxvii. 36, 37; chapter xi. 21; Matthew vii. 24, 25, 26, 27——ʰ1 Samuel xxv. 17——ⁱHebrew *perverse of heart*——ᵏChapter xiii. 7

NOTES ON CHAP. XII

Verse 1. *Whoso loveth instruction*] מוסר *musar*, discipline or correction, *loves knowledge;* for correction is the way to knowledge.

But he that hateth reproof is brutish.] בער *baar*, he is a bear; and expects no more benefit from correction than the *ox* does from the *goad.*

Verse 2. *A good* man *obtaineth favour*] First, it is God who makes him *good;* for every child of Adam is *bad* till the grace of God changes his heart. Secondly, while he walks in the path of obedience he increases in *goodness,* and consequently in the *favour of the Lord.*

Verse 3. *A man shall not be established by wickedness*] Evil is always variable: it has no *fixed principle,* except the *root* that is in the human heart; and even that is ever assuming *new forms.* Nothing is *permanent* but *goodness;* and that is *unchangeable,* because it comes from GOD. The *produce* of goodness is *permanent,* because it has God's *blessing* in it: the *fruit* of *wickedness,* or the *property* procured by wickedness, is *transitory,* because it has God's curse in it. The righteous has his *root* in God; and therefore *he shall not be moved.*

Verse 4. *A virtuous woman* is *a crown to her husband*] אשת חיל *esheth chayil,* a *strong woman.* Our word *virtue* (*virtus*) is derived from *vir,* a *man;* and as *man* is the *noblest* of God's creatures, virtue expresses what is becoming to man; what is *noble, courageous,* and *dignified:* and as *vir,* a man, comes from *vis,* power or *strength;* so it implies what is *strong* and *vigorous* in principle: and as in uncivilized life *strength* and *courage* were considered the very highest, because apparently the most necessary, of all *virtues;* hence the term itself might have become the denomination of all *excellent moral qualities;* and is now applied to whatever constitutes the *system of morality* and *moral duties.* In some parts of the world, however, where *arts* and *sciences* have made little progress, *strength* is one of the first qualifications of a *wife,* where the labours of the field are appointed to them. It is not an uncommon sight in different parts of Africa, to see the wives (*queens*) of the kings and chiefs going out in the morning to the plantations, with

their mattock in their hand, and their youngest child on their back; and when arrived at the ground, lay the young *prince* or *princess* upon the earth, which when weary of lying on one side, will roll itself on the other, and thus continue during the course of the day, without uttering a single whimper, except at the intervals in which its mother gives it suck; she being employed all the while in such *labour* as we in Europe generally assign to our *horses.* In these cases, the *strong wife* is the highest acquisition; and is *a crown to her husband,* though he be *king of Bonny* or *Calabar.* It is certain that in ancient times the *women* in Judea did some of the severest work in the fields, such as *drawing water* from the wells, and watering the flocks, &c. On this account, I think, the words may be taken literally; and especially when we add another consideration, that a woman healthy, and of good *muscular powers,* is the most likely to produce and properly rear up a *healthy offspring;* and children of this kind are a *crown* to their parents.

Is as rottenness in his bones.] Does not this refer to a woman irregular in her manners, who by her *incontinence* not only maketh her husband *ashamed,* but contracts and communicates such diseases as bring *rottenness into the bones?* I think so. And I think this was the view taken of the text by *Coverdale,* who translates thus: "A stedfast woman is a crowne unto her hussbonde: but she that behaveth herself unhonestly is a corruption in his bones."

Verse 7. *The wicked are overthrown*] Seldom does God give such a long life or numerous offspring.

But the house of the righteous shall stand.] God blesses their progeny, and their families continue long in the earth; whereas the wicked seldom have many generations in a direct line. This is God's mercy, that the entail of iniquity may be in some sort cut off, so that the same vices may not be strengthened by successive generations. For generally the *bad root* produces not only a *bad plant,* but one *worse than itself.*

Verse 9. *He that is despised, and hath a servant*] I believe the *Vulgate* gives the true *sense* of this verse: Melior est pauper, et sufficiens sibi; quam gloriosus, et indigens pane.

A. M. cir. 3004
B. C. cir. 1000
Ante I. Olymp.
cir. 224
Ante U. C. cir.
247 *is* better than he that honoureth himself, and lacketh bread.

10 [1]A righteous *man* regardeth the life of his beast: but the [m]tender mercies of the wicked *are* cruel.

11 [n]He that tilleth his land shall be satisfied with bread: but he that followeth vain *persons* [o]*is* void of understanding.

12 The wicked desireth [p]the net of evil *men:* but the root of the righteous yieldeth *fruit.*

13 [q]The [r]wicked is snared by the transgression of *his* lips: [s]but the just shall come out of trouble.

---

14 [t]A man shall be satisfied with good by the fruit of *his* mouth: [u]and the recompense of a man's hands shall be rendered unto him. A. M. cir. 3004
B. C. cir. 1000
Ante I. Olymp.
cir. 224
Ante U. C. cir.
247

15 [v]The way of the fool *is* right in his own eyes: but he that hearkeneth unto counsel *is* wise.

16 [w]A fool's wrath is [x]presently known: but a prudent *man* covereth shame.

17 [y]*He that* speaketh truth showeth forth righteousness: but a false witness deceit.

18 [z]There is that speaketh like the piercings of a sword: but the tongue of the wise *is* health.

---

[1]Deut. xxv. 4——[m]Or, *bowels*——[n]Gen. iii. 19 [o]Chap. vi. 32——[p]Or, *the fortress*——[q]Heb. *The snare of the wicked is in the transgression of lips*——[r]Chap. xviii. 7——[s]2 Pet. ii. 9

[t]Chap. xiii. 2; xviii. 20——[u]Isa. iii. 10, 11——[v]Chap. iii. 7; Luke xviii. 11——[w]Chap. xxix. 11——[x]Heb. *in that day*——[y]Chapter xiv. 5——[z]Psa. lviii. 4; lix. 7; lxiv. 3

"Better is the poor man who provides for himself, than the proud who is destitute of bread." The versions in general agree in this sense. This needs no comment. There are some who, through *pride of birth,* &c., would rather starve, than put their hands to menial labour. Though they may be *lords,* how much to be preferred is the *simple peasant,* who supports himself and family by the drudgery of life!

Verse 10. *A righteous* man *regardeth the life of his beast*] One principal characteristic of a *holy man* is *mercy:* cruelty is unknown to him; and his benevolence extends to the meanest of the brute creation. Pity rules the heart of a pious man; he can do nothing that is *cruel.* He considers what is best for the comfort, ease, health, and life of the *beast* that serves him; and he knows that God himself *careth for oxen:* and one of the ten commandments provides *a seventh part of time* to be allotted for the *rest of labouring beasts* as well as for *man.*

I once in my travels met with the *Hebrew* of this clause on the *sign board* of a public inn: יודע צדיק נפש בהמתו *yodea tsaddik nephesh behemto.* "A righteous man considereth the life of his beast;" which, being very appropriate, reminded me that I should feed my horse.

The tender mercies of the wicked are cruel.] אכזרי *achzari,* are *violent, without mercy, ruthless.* The wicked, influenced by Satan, can show no other disposition than what is in their master. If they *appear* at any time *merciful,* it is a *cloak* which they use to cover purposes of cruelty. To accomplish its end, iniquity will assume any garb, speak mercifully, extol benevolence, sometimes even *give to the poor!* But, timeo Danaos, et dona ferentes. The *cry of fire at midnight,* provided it be in another's dwelling, is more congenial to their souls than the *cry of mercy.* Look at the *human fiends,* "out-heroding Herod," in *horse races, bruising matches,* and *cock fights,* and in wars for the extension of territory, and the purposes of ambition. The *hell* is yet undescribed, that is suited to such monsters in cruelty.

Verse 11. *He that tilleth his land*] God's

blessing will be in the labour of the honest agriculturist.

But he that followeth vain persons] He who, while he should be cultivating his ground, preparing for a future crop, or reaping his harvest, associates with *fowlers, coursers of hares, hunters of foxes,* or those engaged in any champaign amusements, is void of understanding; and I have known several such come to beggary.

To this verse the *Septuagint* add the following clause: Ὃς εστιν ἡδυς εν οινων διατριβαις, εν τοις εαυτου οχυρωμασι καταλειψει ατιμιαν. "He who is a boon companion in banquets, shall leave dishonour in his own fortresses." This has been copied by the *Vulgate* and the *Arabic.* That is, The man who frequents the ale-house enriches *that,* while he *impoverishes* his own *habitation.*

Verse 12. *The wicked desireth the net of evil* men] They applaud their ways, and are careful to imitate them in their wiles.

Verse 13. *The wicked is snared by the transgression of* his *lips*] A man who deals in *lies* and *false oaths* will sooner or later be found out to his own ruin. There is another proverb as true as this: *A liar had need of a good memory;* for as the *truth* is not in *him,* he *says* and *unsays,* and often *contradicts himself.*

Verse 16. *A fool's wrath is presently known*] We have a proverb very like this, and it will serve for illustration:—

A fool's bolt is soon shot.

A weak-minded man has no *self-government;* he is easily angered, and generally speaks whatever comes first to his mind.

Verse 18. *There is that speaketh*] Instead of בוטה *boteh, blabbing out, blustering,* several MSS. have בוטח *boteach,* TRUSTING: and instead of כמדקרות *kemadkeroth,* AS *the piercings,* seven MSS., with the *Complutensian Polyglot,* have במדקרות *bemadkeroth,* IN *the piercings.* "There is that *trusteth in* the piercings of a sword: but the tongue of the wise is health." But I suppose the *former* to be the true reading.

A. M. cir. 3004
B. C. cir. 1000
Ante I. Olymp.
cir. 224
Ante U. C. cir.
247

19 The lip of truth shall be established for ever: [a]but a lying tongue *is* but for a moment.

20 Deceit *is* in the heart of them that imagine evil: but to the counsellors of peace *is* joy.

21 There shall no evil happen to the just: but the wicked shall be filled with mischief.

22 [b]Lying lips *are* abomination to the LORD: but they that deal truly *are* his delight.

23 [c]A prudent man concealeth knowledge: but the heart of fools proclaimeth foolishness.

24 [d]The hand of the diligent shall bear rule: but the [e]slothful shall be under tribute.

25 [f]Heaviness in the heart of man maketh it stoop: but [g]a good word maketh it glad.

26 The righteous *is* more [h]excellent than his neighbour: but the way of the wicked seduceth them.

27 The slothful *man* roasteth not that which he took in hunting: but the substance of a diligent man *is* precious.

28 In the way of righteousness *is* life; and *in* the pathway *thereof there is* no death.

A. M. cir. 3004
B. C. cir. 1000
Ante I. Olymp.
cir. 224
Ante U. C. cir.
247

---

[a]Psa. lii. 5; chap. xix. 9——[b]Chap. vi. 17; xi. 20; Rev. xxii. 15——[c]Chap. xiii. 16; xv. 2

[d]Chap. x. 4——[e]Or, *deceitful*——[f]Chap. xv.43——[g]Isa 1. 4——[h]Or, *abundant*

Verse 19. *A lying tongue is but for a moment.*] *Truth* stands for ever; because its *foundation* is indestructible: but *falsehood* may soon be detected; and, though it gain credit for a while, it had that credit because it was supposed to be *truth*.

Verse 21. *There shall no evil happen to the just*] No, for all things work together for good to them that love God. Whatever occurs to a righteous man God turns to his advantage. But, on the other hand, the *wicked are filled with mischief:* they are hurt, grieved, and wounded, by every occurrence; and nothing turns to their profit.

Verse 23. *A prudent man concealeth knowledge*] "If a fool hold his peace he may pass for a wise man." I have known men of some learning, so intent on immediately informing a company how well cultivated their minds were, that they have passed either for *insignificant pedants* or *stupid asses*.

Verse 24. *The hand of the diligent shall bear rule*] And why? because by his *own industry* he is *independent;* and every such person is respected wherever found.

Verse 25. *Heaviness in the heart of a man maketh it stoop*] Sorrow of heart, hopeless love, or a sense of God's displeasure—these prostrate the *man*, and he becomes a *child* before them.

But a good word maketh it glad.] A single good or favourable word will remove despondency; and that word, "Son, be of good cheer, thy sins are forgiven thee," will instantly remove despair.

Verse 26. *The righteous is more excellent than his neighbour*] That is, if the neighbour be a wicked man. The spirit of the proverb lies here: The POOR *righteous man* is *more excellent* than his *sinful neighbour*, though *affluent* and *noble*. The *Syriac* has it, "The righteous deviseth good to his neighbour." A late commentator has translated it, "The righteous explore their pastures." How מרעהו can be translated THEIR *pastures* I know not; but none of the *versions* understood it in this way. The *Vulgate* is rather singular: Qui negligit damnum propter amicum, justus est. "He who

neglects or sustains a loss for the sake of his friend, is a just man." The *Septuagint* is insufferable: "The well-instructed righteous man shall be his own friend." One would hope these translators meant *not exclusively;* he should love his neighbour as himself.

Verse 27. *The slothful* man *roasteth not that which he took in hunting*] Because he is a *slothful* man, he does not hunt for prey; therefore gets *none*, and cannot *roast*, that he may *eat*. There is some obscurity in the *original*, on which the *versions* cast little light. *Coverdale* translates the whole verse thus: "A discreatfull man schal fynde no vauntage: but he that is content with what he hath, is more worth than golde." My old MS. Bible: 𝔗𝔥𝔢 𝔤𝔭𝔩. 𝔣𝔲𝔩 𝔪𝔞𝔫 𝔰𝔠𝔥𝔞𝔩 𝔫𝔬𝔱 𝔣𝔶𝔫𝔡 𝔴𝔭𝔫𝔫𝔭𝔫𝔤𝔢: 𝔞𝔫𝔡 𝔱𝔥𝔢 𝔰𝔲𝔟𝔰𝔱𝔞𝔫𝔠𝔢 𝔬𝔣 𝔞 𝔪𝔞𝔫 𝔰𝔠𝔥𝔞𝔩 𝔟𝔢𝔫 𝔱𝔥𝔢 𝔭𝔯𝔦𝔰 𝔬𝔣 𝔤𝔬𝔩𝔡.

By translating רמיה *remiyah* the *deceitful,* instead of the *slothful man,* which appears to be the genuine meaning of the word, we may obtain a good sense, as the *Vulgate* has done: "The deceitful man shall not find gain; but the substance of a (just) man shall be the price of gold." But our common version, allowing רמיה *remiyah* to be translated *fraudulent,* which is its proper meaning, gives the best sense: "The fraudulent man roasteth not that which he took in hunting," the justice of God snatching from his mouth what he had acquired *unrighteously.*

But the substance of a diligent man] One who by honest industry acquires all his property—*is precious,* because it has the blessing of God in it.

Verse 28. *In the way of righteousness is life*] חיים *chaiyim, lives; life* temporal, and *life* eternal.

And in *the pathway* thereof there is *no death.*] Not only do the *general precepts* and *promises* of God lead *to* life eternal, and promote *life temporal;* but every *duty,* every *act of faith, patience of hope,* and *labour of love,* though requiring much *self-abasement, self-denial,* and often an *extension of corporal strength,* all *lead to* life. For in every case, in every particular, "the path of duty is the way of safety." The latter clause is only a repetition of the *sense* of the former.

CHAPTER XIII

Various moral sentences; the wise child; continence of speech; of the poor rich man and the rich poor man; ill-gotten wealth; delay of what is hoped for; the bad consequences of refusing instruction; providing for one's children; the necessity of correcting them, &c.

A. M. cir. 3004
B. C. cir. 1000
Ante I. Olymp.
cir. 224
Ante U. C. cir.
247

A WISE son *heareth* his father's instruction: [a]but a scorner heareth not rebuke.

2 [b]A man shall eat good by the fruit of *his* mouth: but the soul of the transgressors *shall eat* violence.

3 [c]He that keepeth his mouth keepeth his life: *but* he that openeth wide his lips shall have destruction.

4 [d]The soul of the sluggard desireth, and *hath* nothing: but the soul of the diligent shall be made fat.

5 A righteous *man* hateth lying: but a wicked *man* is loathsome, and cometh to shame.

6 [e]Righteousness keepeth *him that is* upright in the way: but wickedness overthroweth [f]the sinner.

7 [g]There is that maketh himself rich, yet *hath* nothing: *there is* that maketh himself poor, yet *hath* great riches.

8 The ransom of a man's life *are* his riches: but the poor heareth not rebuke.

9 The light of the righteous rejoiceth: [h]but the [i]lamp of the wicked shall be put out.

10 Only by pride cometh contention: but

A. M. cir. 3004
B. C. cir. 1000
Ante I. Olymp.
cir. 224
Ante U. C. cir.
247

---

[a]1 Sam. ii. 25——[b]Chap. xii. 14——[c]Psa. xxxix. 1; chap. xxi. 23; James iii. 2——[d]Chap. x. 4

[e]Chap. xi. 3, 5, 6——[f]Heb. *sin*——[g]Chap. xii. 9 [h]Job xviii. 5, 6; xxi. 17; ch. xxiv. 20——[i]Or, *candle*

NOTES ON CHAP. XIII

Verse 1. *A wise son heareth his father's instruction*] The child that has had a proper *nurturing*, will profit by his father's counsels; but the child that is permitted to fulfil *its own will* and *have its own way*, will jest at the reproofs of its parents.

Verse 3. *He that keepeth his mouth keepeth his life*] How often have the foolish, headstrong, and wicked, forfeited their lives by the *treasonable* or *blasphemous* words they have spoken! The *government of the tongue* is a *rare* but useful talent.

But *he that openeth wide his lips*] He that puts no bounds to his loquacity, speaks on every subject, and gives his judgment and opinion on every matter. It has often been remarked that God has given us *two* EYES, that we may SEE *much;* two EARS, that we may HEAR *much;* but has given us but ONE *tongue*, and that fenced in with teeth, to indicate that though we *hear* and *see much*, we should *speak* but *little*.

Verse 4. *The soul of the sluggard desireth, and* hath *nothing*] We often hear many religious people expressing a *desire to have more of the Divine life*, and yet never get *forward* in it. How is this? The reason is, they *desire*, but do not *stir themselves up* to lay hold upon the Lord. They are always learning, but never able to come to the knowledge of the truth. They *seek* to enter in at the strait gate, but are not able, because they do not *strive*.

Verse 7. *There is that maketh himself rich*] That labours hard to acquire money, *yet hath nothing;* his excessive *covetousness* not being satisfied with what he possesses, nor permitting him to enjoy *with comfort* what he has acquired. The fable of *the dog in the manger* will illustrate this.

There is *that maketh himself poor, yet* hath *great riches*.] "As poor," said St. Paul, "yet making many rich; as having nothing, yet possessing all things." The former is the *rich poor* man; the latter is the *poor rich* man.

As the words are here in the *hithpael* con-

jugation, which implies *reflex action*, or the *action performed on one's self*, and often signifies *feigning* or *pretending* to be what one *is not*, or *not* to be what one *is;* the words may be understood of persons who *feign* or *pretend* to be either *richer* or *poorer* than they *really are*, to accomplish some particular purpose. "There is that *feigneth himself* to be *rich*, yet hath *nothing;* there is that *feigneth himself* to be *poor*, yet hath *great riches*." Both these characters frequently occur in life.

Verse 8. *The ransom of a man's life*] Those who have riches have often much trouble with them; as they had much trouble to *get* them, so they have much trouble to *keep* them. In despotic countries, a rich man is often accused of some capital crime, and to save his life, though he may be quite innocent, is obliged to give up his riches; but the *poor*, in such countries, are put to no trouble.

Verse 9. *The light of the righteous rejoiceth*] They shall have that measure of prosperity which shall be best for them; but the wicked, howsoever prosperous for a time, shall be brought into desolation. *Light* and *lamp* in both cases may signify *posterity*. The righteous shall have a joyous posterity; but that of the wicked shall be cut off. So 1 Kings xi. 36: "And unto his son will I give one tribe, that David my servant may have a *light* (נר) *ner*, a *lamp*) always before me." xv. 4: "Nevertheless for David's sake did the Lord give them *a lamp*, to set up his *son* after him." See also Psa. cxxxii. 17, and several other places.

Verse 10. *By pride cometh contention*] Perhaps there is not a *quarrel* among *individuals* in private life, nor a *war* among nations, that does not proceed from *pride* and *ambition*. Neither *man* nor *nation* will be content to be *less* than another; and to acquire the wished-for *superiority* all is thrown into general confusion, both in public and private life. It was to destroy this *spirit of pride*, that Jesus was manifested in the *extreme of humility* and *humiliation* among men. The salvation of Christ is a *deliverance* from *pride*, and a being clothed

A. M. cir. 3004
B. C. cir. 1000
Ante I. Olymp. cir. 224
Ante U. C. cir. 247

with the well advised *is* wisdom.
11 [k]Wealth *gotten* by vanity shall be diminished: but he that gathereth [l]by labour shall increase.
12 Hope deferred maketh the heart sick: but [m]*when* the desire cometh, *it is* a tree of life.
13 Whoso [n]despiseth the word shall be destroyed: but he that feareth the commandment [o]shall be rewarded.
14 [p]the law of the wise *is* a fountain of life, to depart from [q]the snares of death.
15 Good understanding giveth favour: but the way of transgressors *is* hard.
16 [r]Every prudent *man* dealeth with knowledge: but a fool [s]layeth open *his* folly.
17 A wicked messenger falleth into mischief but [t]a [u]faithful ambassador *is* health.

A. M. cir. 3004
B. C. cir. 1000
Ante I. Olymp. cir. 224
Ante U. C. cir. 247

18 Poverty and shame *shall be to* him that refuseth instruction: but [v]he that regardeth reproof shall be honoured.
19 [w]The desire accomplished is sweet to the soul: but *it is* abomination to fools to depart from evil.
20 He that walketh with wise *men* shall be wise: but a companion of fools [x]shall be destroyed.
21 [y]Evil pursueth sinners: but to the righteous good shall be repayed.
22 A good *man* leaveth an inheritance to his children's children: and [z]the wealth of the sinner *is* laid up for the just.

---

[k]Chap. x. 2; xx. 21——[l]Heb. *with the hand*——[m]Ver. 19——[n]2 Chron. xxxvi. 16——[o]Or, *shall be in peace* [p]Chap. x. 11; xiv. 27; xvi. 22——[q]2 Sam. xxii. 6 [r]Chap. xii. 23; xv. 2——[s]Heb. *spreadeth*

[t]Chap. xxv. 23——[u]Heb. *an ambassador of faithfulness*——[v]Chap. xv. 5, 31——[w]Ver. 12——[x]Heb. *shall be broken*——[y]Psa. xxxii. 10——[z]Job xxvii. 16, 17; chap. xxviii. 8; Eccles. ii. 26

---

with *humility*. As far as we are *humble*, so far we are *saved*.

Verse 11. *Wealth* gotten *by vanity*] Wealth that is not the result of *honest industry* and *hard labour* is seldom permanent. All fortunes acquired by speculation, lucky hits, and ministering to the pride or luxury of others, &c., soon become dissipated. They are not gotten in the way of Providence, and have not God's blessing, and therefore are not permanent.

Verse 12. *Hope deferred maketh the heart sick*] When once a *good* is discovered, *want* of it felt, *strong desire* for the possession excited, and the promise of attainment made on grounds unsuspected, so that the *reality* of the *thing* and the *certainity* of the *promise* are manifest, *hope* posts forward to *realize the blessing. Delay* in the gratification pains the mind; the increase of the delay prostrates and sickens the heart; and if *delay sickens the heart*, ultimate *disappointment kills* it. *But* when the thing desired, hoped for, and expected comes, it is a tree of life, עץ חיים *ets chaiyim*, "the tree of lives;" it comforts and invigorates both body and soul. To the tree of lives, in the midst of the gardens of paradise, how frequent are the allusions in the writings of Solomon, and in other parts of the Holy Scriptures! What deep, and perhaps yet unknown, mysteries were in this tree!

Verse 13. *Whoso despiseth the word*] The revelation which God has in his mercy given to man—*shall be destroyed;* for there is no other way of salvation but that which it points out.

But he that feareth the commandment] That respects it so as to obey it, walking as this revelation directs—*shall be rewarded;* shall find it to be his highest interest, and shall be in *peace* or *safety*, as the Hebrew word ישלם may be translated.

Verse 14. *The law of the wise* is *a fountain of life*] Perhaps it would be better to translate, "The law is to the wise man a fountain of life." It is the same to him as the "vein of lives," מקור חיים *mekor chaiyim*, the great *aorta* which transmits the blood from the heart to every part of the body. There seems to be here an allusion to the *garden of paradise*, to the *tree of lives*, to the *tempter*, to the baleful *issue* of that temptation, and to the *death* entailed on man by his *unwisely* breaking the *law* of his God.

Verse 15. *The way of transgressors* is *hard.*] Never was a truer saying; most sinners have *more pain* and *difficulty* to get their souls damned, than the righteous have, with all their cross-bearings, to get to the kingdom of heaven.

Verse 17. *A wicked messenger*] The *Septuagint:* Βασιλευς θρασευς, *a bold king;* instead of מלאך *malach*, a *messenger*, they had read מלך *melech*, a *king:* but they are singular in this rendering; none of the other versions have it so. He that betrays the counsels of his government, or the interests of his country, will sooner or later fall into mischief; but he that faithfully and loyally fulfils his mission, shall produce *honour* and *safety* to the commonwealth.

Verse 19. *The desire accomplished*] See on ver. 12.

Verse 20. *He that walketh with wise* men *shall be wise*] To *walk* with a person implies *love* and *attachment;* and it is impossible not *to imitate those we love.* So we say, "Show me his company, and I'll tell you the man." Let me know the company he keeps, and I shall easily guess his moral character.

Verse 22. *A good* man *leaveth an inheritance*] He files many a *prayer* in heaven in their behalf, and his good *example* and *advices* are remembered and quoted from generation to generation. Besides, whatever property he left was *honestly* acquired, and *well-gotten goods are permanent.* The general experience of men shows this to be a common case; and that *property ill-gotten seldom reaches to the third generation.* This even the *heathens* observed. Hence:

De male quæsitis non gaudet tertius hæres.

A. M. cir. 3004
B. C. cir. 1000
Ante I. Olymp.
cir. 224
Ante U. C. cir.
247

23 [a]Much food *is in* the tillage of the poor: but there is *that is* destroyed for want of judgment.

24 [b]He that spareth his rod hateth his son:

but he that loveth him chasteneth him betimes.

25 [c]The righteous eateth to the satisfying of his soul: but the belly of the wicked shall want.

A. M. cir. 3004
B. C. cir. 1000
Ante I. Olymp.
cir. 224
Ante U. C. cir.
247

---

[a]Chap. xii. 11——[b]Chap. xix. 18; xxii. 15; xxiii. 13; xxix. 15, 17——[c]Psa. xxxiv. 10; xxxvii. 3

"The third generation shall not possess the goods that have been unjustly acquired."

Verse 23. That is *destroyed for want of judgment.*] O, how much of the *poverty* of the *poor* arises from their own want of management! They have little or no economy, and no foresight. When they get any thing, they speedily spend it; and a *feast* and a *famine* make the chief *varieties* of their life.

Verse 24. *He that spareth his rod hateth his son*] That is, if he *hated* him, he could not do him a greater disservice than not to correct him when his *obstinacy* or *disobedience* requires it. We have met with this subject already, and it is a favourite with Solomon. See the places referred to in the margin.

The Rev. Mr. Holden makes some sensible observations on this passage: "By the neglect

of early correction the desires (passions) obtain ascendancy; the temper becomes irascible, peevish, querulous. Pride is nourished, humility destroyed, and by the habit of indulgence the mind is incapacitated to bear with firmness and equanimity the cares and sorrows, the checks and disappointments, which *flesh is heir to.*"

Verse 25. *To the satisfying of his soul*] His desires are all moderate; he is contented with his circumstances, and is pleased with the lot which God is pleased to send. The wicked, though he use all *shifts* and *expedients* to acquire earthly good, not sticking even at *rapine* and *wrong*, is frequently in real want, and always dissatisfied with his portion. *A contented mind is a continual feast.* At such feasts he eats not.

CHAPTER XIV

Various moral sentiments. The antithesis between wisdom and folly, and the different effects of each.

A. M. cir. 3004
B. C. cir. 1000
Ante I. Olymp.
cir. 224
Ante U. C. cir.
247

EVERY [a]wise woman [b]buildeth her house: but the foolish plucketh it down with her hands.

2 He that walketh in his uprightness feareth the LORD: [c]but *he that is* perverse in his ways despiseth him.

3 In the mouth of the foolish *is* a rod of

pride: [d]but the lips of the wise shall preserve them.

4 Where no oxen *are* the crib *is* clean: but much increase *is* by the strength of the ox.

5 [e]A faithful witness will not lie: but a false witness will utter lies.

6 A scorner seeketh wisdom, and *findeth it*

A. M. cir. 3004
B. C. cir. 1000
Ante I. Olymp.
cir. 224
Ante U. C. cir.
247

---

[a]Chap. xxiv. 3——[b]Ruth iv. 11——[c]Job xii. 4
[d]Chap. xii. 6

[e]Exod. xx. 16; xxiii. 1; chap. vi. 19; xii. 17; ver. 25

NOTES ON CHAP. XIV

Verse 1. *Every wise woman buildeth her house*] By her prudent and industrious management she *increases property* in the family, *furniture* in the *house*, and *food* and *raiment* for her household. This is the true *building of a house.* The *thriftless* wife acts differently, and the opposite is the result. Household *furniture*, far from being *increased*, is *dilapidated;* and her *household* are *ill-fed, ill-clothed,* and *worse educated.*

Verse 3. *The mouth of the foolish* is *a rod of pride*] The reproofs of such a person are *ill-judged* and *ill-timed,* and generally are conveyed in *such language* as renders them not only ineffectual, but displeasing, and even *irritating.*

Verse 4. *But much increase* is *by the strength of the ox.*] The *ox* is the most profitable of all the *beasts* used in *husbandry.* Except mere-

ly for *speed,* he is almost in every respect superior to the horse. 1. He is *longer lived.* 2. Scarcely liable to any *diseases.* 3. He is *steady,* and always *pulls fair* in his gears. 4. He *lives, fattens,* and *maintains* his strength on what *a horse will not eat,* and therefore is supported on one third the cost. 5. His *manure* is more profitable. And, 6, When he is worn out in his labour his *flesh* is good for the nourishment of man, his *horns* of great utility, and his *hide* almost invaluable. It might be added, he is *little or no expense* in shoeing, and his *gears* are much more *simple,* and much less *expensive,* than those of the *horse.* In all large farms *oxen* are greatly to be preferred to *horses.* Have but patience with this most patient animal, and you will soon find that *there is much increase by the strength* and labour *of the ox.*

Verse 6. *A scorner seeketh wisdom*] I believe the *scorner* means, in this book, the man

A. M. cir. 3004
B. C. cir. 1000
Ante I. Olymp.
cir. 224
Ante U. C. cir.
247

not; but ᶠknowledge is easy unto him that understandeth.

7 Go from the presence of a foolish man, when thou perceivest not *in him* the lips of knowledge.

8 The wisdom of the prudent *is* to understand his way: but the folly of fools *is* deceit.

9 ᵍFools make a mock at sin; but among the righteous *there is* favour.

10 The heart knoweth ʰhis own bitterness; and a stranger doth not intermeddle with his joy.

11 ⁱThe house of the wicked shall be over-

thrown: but the tabernacle of the upright shall flourish.

A. M. cir. 3004
B. C. cir. 1000
Ante I. Olymp.
cir. 224
Ante U. C. cir.
247

12 ᵏThere is a way which seemeth right unto a man, but the ˡend thereof *are* the ways of death.

13 Even in laughter the heart is sorrowful; and ᵐthe end of that mirth *is* heaviness.

14 The backslider in heart shall be ⁿfilled with his own ways; and a good man *shall be satisfied* from himself.

15 The simple believeth every word: but the prudent *man* looketh well to his going.

ⁱChap. viii. 9; xvii. 24——ᵍChap. x. 23——ʰHeb. *the bitterness of his soul*

ʲJob viii. 15——ᵏChap. xvi. 25——ˡRom. vi. 21
ᵐChap. v. 4; Eccles. ii. 2——ⁿChap. i. 31; xii. 14

---

that *despises* the *counsel of God;* the *infidel.* Such may *seek wisdom;* but he never can find it, because he does not seek it *where* it is to be found; neither in the *teaching of God's Spirit,* nor in the *revelation* of his *will.*

Verse 7. *When thou perceivest not—the lips of knowledge.*] Instead of רעת *daath,* knowledge, several MSS. have שקר *sheker,* a lie. How this reading came I cannot conjecture. The meaning of the adage is plain: Never associate with a vain, empty fellow, when thou perceivest he can neither *convey* nor *receive* instruction.

Verse 8. Is *to understand his way*] Instead of הבין *habin,* to *understand,* הכין *hachin,* to DIRECT his way, is found in one MS. It makes a very good sense.

Verse 9. *Fools make a mock at sin*] And only *fools* would do so. But he that makes a *sport* of *sinning,* will find it *no sport* to suffer the vengeance of an eternal fire. Some learned men by their criticisms have brought this verse into embarrassments, out of which they were not able to extricate it. I believe we shall not come much nearer the sense than our present version does.

Verse 10. *The heart knoweth his own bitterness*] מרת נפשו *morrath naphsho,* "The bitterness of its soul." Under spiritual sorrow, the *heart* feels, the *soul* feels; all the *animal* nature feels and suffers. But when the peace of God is spoken to the troubled soul, the joy is indescribable; the *whole man* partakes of it. And a stranger to these religious feelings, to the travail of the soul, and to the witness of the Spirit, does not *intermeddle* with them; he does not understand them: indeed they may be even foolishness to him, because they are spiritually discerned.

Verse 12. *There is a way which seemeth right unto a man*] This may be his *easily besetting sin,* the *sin of his constitution,* the *sin of his trade.* Or it may be *his own false views of religion:* he may have an *imperfect repentance,* a *false faith,* a *very false creed;* and he may persuade himself that he is in the direct way to heaven. Many of the papists, when they were burning the saints of God in the flames at Smithfield, thought they were doing God service! And in the late Irish massacre, the more of the Protestants they *piked to death,*

shot, or *burnt,* the more they believed they deserved of God's favour and their Church's gratitude. But cruelty and murder are the *short road,* the *near way,* to eternal perdition.

Verse 13. *Even in laughter the heart is sorrowful*] Many a time is a *smile* forced upon the *face,* when the heart is in *deep distress.* And it is a hard task to put on the *face of mirth,* when a man has a *heavy heart.*

Verse 14. *The backslider in heart shall be filled with his own ways*] 1. Who is the *backslider?* סוג *sug.* 1. The man who once walked in the ways of religion, but has *withdrawn* from them. 2. The man who once *fought manfully* against the world, the devil, and the flesh; but has *retreated* from the battle, or joined the enemy. 3. The man who once belonged to the congregation of the saints, but is now *removed* from them, and is set down in the synagogue of Satan.

2. But who is *the backslider in* HEART? 1. Not he who was *surprised* and *overcome* by the power of temptation, and the weakness of his own heart. 2. But he who drinks down iniquity with greediness. 3. Who gives cheerful way to the bent of his own nature, and now delights in fulfilling the lusts of the flesh and of the mind. 4. Who loves sin as before he loved godliness.

3. What are *his own ways?* Folly, sin, disappointment, and death; with the apprehension of the wrath of God, and the sharp twingings of a guilty conscience.

4. What is implied in being *filled with his own ways?* Having his soul *saturated* with folly, sin, and disappointment. At last ending here below in death, and then commencing an eternal existence where the *fire is not quenched,* and under the influence of that *worm that never dieth.* Alas, alas! who may abide when God doeth this?

And a good man shall be satisfied *from himself.*] 1. Who is the good man? (איש טוב *ish tob.*) 1. The man whose heart is right with God, whose *tongue* corresponds to his heart, and whose *actions* correspond to both. 2. The man who is every thing that the *sinner* and *backslider* are not.

2. *He shall be* satisfied *from himself*—he shall have the testimony of his own conscience, that in simplicity and godly sincerity, not with

A. M. cir. 3004
B. C. cir. 1000
Ante I. Olymp. cir. 224
Ante U. C. cir. 247

16 °A wise *man* feareth, and departeth from evil: but the fool rageth, and is confident.

17 *He that is* soon angry dealeth foolishly: and a man of wicked devices is hated.

18 The simple inherit folly: but the prudent are crowned with knowledge.

19 The evil bow before the good; and the wicked at the gates of the righteous.

20 ᵖThe poor is hated even of his own neighbour: but �q the rich *hath* many friends.

21 He that despiseth his neighbour sinneth: ʳbut he that hath mercy on the poor, happy *is* he.

22 Do they not err that devise evil? but

mercy and truth *shall be* to them that devise good.

A. M. cir. 3004
B. C. cir. 1000
Ante I. Olymp. cir. 224
Ante U. C. cir. 247

23 In all labour there is profit: but the talk of the lips *tendeth* only to penury.

24 The crown of the wise *is* their riches: *but* the foolishness of fools *is* folly.

25 ˢA true *witness* delivereth souls: but a deceitful *witness* speaketh lies.

26 In the fear of the LORD *is* strong confidence; and his children shall have a place of refuge.

27 ᵗThe fear of the LORD *is* a fountain of life, to depart from the snares of death.

28 In the multitude of people *is* the king's

°Chap. xxii. 3——ᵖChap. xix. 7——�qHeb. *many* are the lovers of the rich

ʳPsa. xli. 1; cxii. 9——ˢVer. 5——ᵗChap. xiii. 14

---

fleshly wisdom, but by the grace of God, he has his conversation among men.

3. He shall have God's Spirit to testify with his spirit that he is a child of God. He hath the witness in himself that he is born from above. The Spirit of God in his conscience, and the testimony of God in his Bible, show him that he belongs to the heavenly family. It is not from creeds or confessions of faith that he derives his satisfaction: he gets it from heaven, and it is sealed upon his heart.

Verse 16. *A wise* man *feareth*] He can never *trust in himself*, though he be *satisfied from himself.* He knows that *his sufficiency* is of GOD; and he has that *fear* that causes him to *depart from evil*, which is a guardian to the *love* he feels. Love renders him cautious; the other makes him confident. His *caution* leads him *from sin;* his *confidence* leads him *to God.*

Verse 17. *He that is soon angry*] קצר אפים *ketsar appayim,* "short of nostrils:" because, when a man is angry, his *nose is contracted,* and drawn up towards his eyes.

Dealeth foolishly] He has no time for reflection; *he* is *hurried* on by his passions, *speaks* like a *fool,* and *acts* like a *madman.*

Verse 19. *The evil bow before the good*] They are almost *constrained* to show them *respect;* and the *wicked,* who have wasted their substance with riotous living, *bow before the gates of the righteous*—of benevolent men—begging a morsel of bread.

Verse 20. *But the rich* hath *many friends.*] Many who *speak* to him the *language* of *friendship;* but if they profess *friendship* because he is *rich,* there is not *one real friend* among them. There is a fine saying of Cicero on this subject: Ut hirundines festivo tempore præsto sunt, frigore pulsæ recedunt: ita falsi amici sereno tempore præsto sunt: simul atque fortunæ hiemem viderint, evolant omnes.—Lib. iv., ad Herenn. "They are like *swallows,* who fly off during the winter, and quit our cold climates; and do not return till the warm season: but as soon as the winter sets in, they are all off again." So Horace:—

Donec eris felix, multos numerabis amicos:
Nullus ad amissas ibit amicus opes.

"As long as thou art prosperous, thou shalt have many friends: but who of them will regard thee when thou hast lost thy wealth?"

Verse 21. *He that despiseth his neighbor sinneth*] To despise a man because he has some natural blemish is *unjust, cruel,* and *wicked.* He is not the *author* of his *own imperfections;* they did not occur through his *fault* or *folly;* and if he *could,* he *would not retain them.* It is, therefore, *unjust* and wicked to despise him for what is not his *fault,* but his *misfortune.*

But he that hath mercy on the poor] Who reproaches no man for his *poverty* or *scanty intellect,* but divides his bread with the hungry—*happy is he;* the blessing of God, and of them that were ready to perish, shall come upon *him.*

Verse 23. *In all labour there is profit*] If a man work at his trade, he gains by it; if he cultivate the earth, it will yield an increase; and in *proportion* as he *labours,* so will be his *profit:* but he who *talks* much *labours* little. And a man *words* is seldom a man of *deeds. Less talk and more work,* is one of our own ancient advices.

Verse 24. But *the foolishness of fools* is *folly.*] The *Targum* reads, The *honour of fools is folly.* The fool, from his foolishness, produces acts of folly. This appears to be the meaning.

Verse 26. *In the fear of the Lord* is *strong confidence*] From this, and from genuine Christian experience, we find that the *fear of God* is highly consistent with the *strongest confidence* in his mercy and goodness.

Verse 27. *The fear of the Lord* is *a fountain of life*] מקור חיים *mekor chaiyim,* the *vein of lives.* Another allusion to the great *aorta* which carries the blood from the heart to all the extremities of the body. Of this phrase, and the *tree of lives,* Solomon is particularly fond. See on chap. iv. 23; x. 12.

Verse 28. *In the multitude of people*] It is the interest of every state to promote *marriage* by every means that is just and prudent; and to discourage, disgrace, and debase *celibacy;* to render *bachelors* incapable, after a given age, of all public employments: and to banish *nun-*

A. M. cir. 3004
B. C. cir. 1000
Ante I. Olymp.
cir. 224
Ante U. C. cir.
247

honour: but in the want of people *is* the destruction of the prince.

29 ᵘ*He that is* slow to wrath
is of great understanding: but *he
that is* ᵛhasty of spirit exalteth folly.

30 A sound heart *is* the life of the flesh:
but ʷenvy ˣthe rottenness of the bones.

31 ʸHe that oppresseth the poor reproacheth
ᶻhis Maker: but he that honoureth him hath
mercy on the poor.

32 The wicked is driven away in his wick-

edness: but ªthe righteous hath
hope in his death.

A. M. cir. 3004
B. C. cir. 1000
Ante I. Olymp.
cir. 224
Ante U. C. cir.
247

33 Wisdom resteth in the heart
of him that hath understanding;
but ᵇ*that which is* in the midst of fools is
made known.

34 Righteousness exalteth a nation: but sin
is a reproach ᶜto any people.

35 ᵈThe king's favour *is* toward a wise servant: but his wrath is *against* him that causeth shame.

ᵘChap. xvi. 32; James i. 19——ᵛHeb. *short of spirit*
ʷPsa. cxii. 10——ˣChap. xii. 4——ʸChap. xvii. 5; Matt.
xxv. 40, 45——ᶻSee Job xxxi. 15, 16; chap. xxii. 2

ªJob xiii. 15; xix. 26; Psa. xxiii. 4; xxxvii. 37; 2 Cor.
i. 9; v. 8; 2 Tim. iv. 18——ᵇChap. xii. 16; xxix. 11
ᶜHeb. *to nations*——ᵈMatt. xxiv. 45, 47

---

neries and *monasteries* from all parts of their
dominions;—they have ever, from their invention, contributed more to vice than virtue;
and are positively point blank against the law
of God.

Verse 29. That is *hasty of spirit*] קצר רוח
ketsar ruach, "the short of spirit;" one that is
easily irritated; and, being in a passion, he is
agitated so as to be literally *short of breath*.
Here put in opposition to ארך אפים *erech appayim*, *long of nostrils*; see on ver. 17; and
of the same import with St. Paul's μακροθυμια,
longsuffering, longmindedness. See on Eph. iv. 2.

Verse 30. *A sound heart* is *the life of the
flesh*] A healthy state of the *blood*, and a
proper *circulation* of that stream of life, is the
grand cause, in the hand of God, of *health* and
longevity. If the heart be diseased, *life* cannot be long continued.

Verse 31. *He that oppresseth the poor reproacheth his Maker*] Because the *poor*, or
comparatively *poor*, are, in the order of God,
a part of the inhabitants of the earth; and
every man who loves God will *show mercy to
the poor*, for with this God is peculiarly delighted. *The poor have we ever with us*, for the
excitement and exercise of those benevolent,
compassionate, and merciful feelings, without
which men had been but little better than
brutes.

Verse 32. *The wicked is driven away in his
wickedness*] He does not *leave life cheerfully*.
Poor soul! Thou hast no *hope* in the other
world, and thou leavest the present with the
utmost *regret!* Thou wilt not *go off*; but God
will *drive* thee.

But the righteous hath hope in his death.]
He rejoiceth to depart and be with Christ: to
him death is gain; he is not reluctant to *go*—
he *flies* at the call of God.

Verse 34. *But sin is a reproach to any people.*] I am satisfied this is not the sense of the

original, וחסד לאמים חטאת *vechesed leummim
chattath;* which would be better rendered, *And
mercy is a sin-offering for the people.* The
Vulgate has, *Miseros autem facit populos pec-
catum*, "sin makes the people wretched." Ελασ-
σονουσι δε φυλας αμαρτιαι; "But sins lessen the
tribes."—*Septuagint.* So also the *Syriac* and
Arabic. The plain meaning of the original
seems to be, *A national disposition to mercy
appears in the sight of God as a continual sin-
offering.* Not that it atones for the sin of the
people; but, *as* a sin-offering is pleasing in the
sight of the God of mercy, so is a merciful disposition in a nation. This view of the verse is
consistent with the purest doctrines of free
grace. And what is the true sense of the
words, we should take at all hazards and consequences: we shall never trench upon a *sound
creed* by a *literal interpretation* of God's words.
No nation has more of this *spirit* than the
British nation. It is true, we have too many
sanguinary laws; but the *spirit* of the people
is widely different.

If any one will contend for the *common version*, he has my consent; and I readily agree
in the saying, *Sin is the reproach of any people.* It is the *curse* and *scandal* of man.
Though I think what I have given is the true
meaning of the text.

Verse 35. *The king's favour is toward a wise
servant*] The king should have an intelligent
man for his *minister;* a man of deep sense,
sound judgment, and of a *feeling, merciful disposition.* He who has not the *former* will
plunge the nation into *difficulties;* and he
who has not the *latter* will embark her in
disastrous wars. Most wars are occasioned by
bad ministers, men of blood, who cannot be
happy but in endeavouring to unchain the spirit
of discord. Let every humane heart pray,
*Lord, scatter thou the people who delight in
war! Amen—so be it. Selah!*

CHAPTER XV

*The soft answer. Useful correction. Stability of the righteous. The contented mind. The slothful man. The
fool. The covetous. The impious. The wicked opposed to the righteous; to the diligent; and to the man who
fears the Lord.*

A. M. cir. 3004
B. C. cir. 1000
Ante I. Olymp.
cir. 224
Ante U. C. cir.
247

A [a]SOFT answer turneth away wrath: but [b]grievous words stir up anger.

2 The tongue of the wise useth knowledge aright: [c]but the mouth of fools [d]poureth out foolishness.

3 [e]The eyes of the LORD *are* in every place, beholding the evil and the good.

4 [f]A wholesome tongue *is* a tree of life: but perverseness therein *is* a breach in the spirit.

5 [g]A fool despiseth his father's instruction: [h]but he that regardeth reproof is prudent.

6 In the house of the righteous *is* much treasure: but in the revenues of the wicked is trouble.

7 The lips of the wise disperse knowledge: but the heart of the foolish *doeth* not so.

8 [i]The sacrifice of the wicked *is* an abomination unto the LORD: but the prayer of the upright *is* his delight.

9 The way of the wicked *is* an abomination unto the LORD: but he loveth him

that [k]followeth after righteousness.

A. M. cir. 3004
B. C. cir. 1000
Ante I. Olymp.
cir. 224
Ante U. C. cir.
247

10 [l]Correction *is* [m]grievous unto him that forsaketh the way; *and* [n]he that hateth reproof shall die.

11 [o]Hell and destruction *are* before the LORD; how much more then [p]the hearts of the children of men?

12 [q]A scorner loveth not one that reproveth him; neither will he go unto the wise.

13 [r]A merry heart maketh a cheerful countenance: but [s]by sorrow of the heart the spirit is broken.

14 The heart of him that hath understanding seeketh knowledge: but the mouth of fools feedeth on foolishness.

15 All the days of the afflicted *are* evil: [t]but he that is of a merry heart *hath* a continual feast.

16 [u]Better *is* little with the fear of the LORD, than great treasure and trouble therewith.

17 [v]Better *is* a dinner of herbs where love is, than a stalled ox and hatred therewith.

---

[a]Judg. viii. 1, 2, 3; chap. xxv. 15——[b]1 Sam. xxv. 10, &c.——1 Kings xii. 13, 14, 16——[c]Ver. 28; chap. xii. 23; xiii. 16——[d]Heb. *belcheth* or *bubbleth*——[e]Job xxxiv. 21; chap. v. 21; Jer. xvi. 17; xxxii. 19; Heb. iv. 14 [f]Heb. *The healing of the tongue*——[g]Chap. x. 1——[h]Ch. xiii. 18; ver. 31, 32——[i]Chap. xxi. 27; xxviii. 9; Isa. i. 11; lxi. 8; lxvi. 3; Jer. vi. 20; vii. 22; Amos v. 22——[k]Ch.

xxi. 21; 1 Tim. vi. 11——[l]Or, *Instruction*——[m]1 Kings xxii. 8——[n]Chap. v. 12; x. 17——[o]Job xxvi. 6; Psa. cxxxix. 8——[p]2 Chron. vi. 30; Psa. vii. 9; xliv. 21; John ii. 24, 25; xxi. 17; Acts i. 24——[q]Amos v. 10; 2 Tim. iv. 3——[r]Chap. xvii. 22——[s]Chap. xii. 25 [t]Chap. xvii. 22——[u]Psa. xxxvii. 16; Chap. xvi. 8; 1 Tim. vi. 6——[v]Chap. xvii. 1

NOTES ON CHAP. XV

Verse 1. *A soft answer*] Gentleness will often disarm the most furious, where positive derangement has not taken place; one angry word will always beget another, for the disposition of one spirit always begets its own likeness in another: thus kindness produces kindness, and rage produces rage. Universal experience confirms this proverb.

Verse 2. *Useth knowledge aright*] This is very difficult to know:—*when to speak*, and *when* to be *silent; what to speak*, and *what* to leave *unspoken;* the *manner* that is best and most suitable to the *occasion*, the *subject*, the *circumstances*, and the *persons*. All these are difficulties, often even to the wisest men. Even *wise counsel* may be *foolishly* given.

Verse 3. *The eyes of the Lord* are *in every place*] He not only sees all things, by his omnipresence, but his *providence* is everywhere. And if the consideration that *his eye is in every place*, have a tendency to *appal* those whose *hearts are not right before him*, and who seek for *privacy*, that they may *commit iniquity;* yet the other consideration, that his *providence* is *everywhere*, has a great tendency to encourage the upright, and all who may be in *perilous* or *distressing* circumstances.

Verse 4. *A wholesome tongue is a tree of life*] Here again is an allusion to the paradisiacal tree, עץ חיים *ets chaiyim*, "the tree of lives."

Verse 8. *The sacrifice of the wicked is an*

abomination] Even the most *sedulous attendance* on the *ordinances* of God, and *performance* of the *ceremonies of religion*, is an abomination to the Lord, if the *heart* be not right with him, and the observance do not flow from a principle of pure devotion. No *religious acts* will do in place of *holiness to the Lord.*

The prayer of the upright is *his delight.*] What a *motive* to be *upright;* and what a motive to the upright to *pray!* But who is the *upright?* The man who is *weary of sin*, and *sincerely desires* the salvation of God; as well as he who has already received a measure of that salvation. Hence it is said in the next verse, "He loveth him that followeth after righteousness."

Verse 11. *Hell and destruction*] שאול ואבדון *sheol vaabaddon.* *Hades*, the invisible world, the place of separate spirits till the resurrection: and *Abaddon*, the place of *torment;* are ever under the eye and control of the Lord.

Verse 13. *By sorrow of the heart the spirit is broken.*] Every kind of *sorrow worketh death*, but that which is the offspring of true repentance. This alone is healthful to the soul. The indulgence of a disposition to *sighing* tends to destroy life. Every *deep sigh* throws off a portion of the vital *energy.*

Verse 16. *Better* is *little with the fear of the Lord*] Because where the fear of God is, there are *moderation* and *contentment* of spirit.

Verse 17. *Better* is *a dinner of herbs*] Great

A. M. cir. 3004
B. C. cir. 1000
Ante I. Olymp. cir. 224
Ante U. C. cir. 247

18 ʷA wrathful man stirreth up strife: but *he that is* slow to anger appeaseth strife.

19 ˣThe way of the slothful *man is* as a hedge of thorns: but the way of the righteous ʸ*is* made plain.

20 ᶻA wise son maketh a glad father: but a foolish man despiseth his mother.

21 ᵃFolly *is* joy to *him that is* ᵇdestitute of wisdom: ᶜbut a man of understanding walketh uprightly.

22 ᵈWithout counsel purposes are disappointed: but in the multitude of counsellors they are established.

23 A man hath joy by the answer of his mouth: and ᵉa word *spoken* ᶠin due season, how good *is it!*

24 ᵍThe way of life *is* above to the wise, that he may depart from hell beneath.

25 ʰThe LORD will destroy the house of the proud: but ⁱhe will establish the border of the widow.

A. M. cir. 3004
B. C. cir. 1000
Ante I. Olymp. cir. 224
Ante U. C. cir. 247

26 ᵏThe thoughts of the wicked *are* an abomination to the LORD: ˡbut *the words* of the pure *are* ᵐpleasant words.

27 ⁿHe that is greedy of gain troubleth his own house: but he that hateth gifts shall live.

28 The heart of the righteous ᵒstudieth to answer: but the mouth of the wicked poureth out evil things.

29 ᵖThe LORD *is* far from the wicked: but ᑫhe heareth the prayer of the righteous.

30 The light of the eyes rejoiceth the heart: *and* a good report maketh the bones fat.

31 ʳThe ear that heareth the reproof of life abideth among the wise.

32 He that refuseth ˢinstruction despiseth his own soul: but he that ᵗheareth reproof ᵘgetteth understanding.

33 ᵛThe fear of the LORD *is* the instruction of wisdom; and ʷbefore honour *is* humility.

ʷChap. xxvi. 21; xxix. 22——ˣChap. xxii. 5——ʸHeb. is *raised up as a causey*——ᶻChap. x. 1; xxix. 3——ᵃCh. x. 23——ᵇHeb. *void of heart*——ᶜEph. v. 15——ᵈChap. xi. 14; xx. 18——ᵉChap. xxv. 11——ᶠHeb. *in his season* ᵍPhil. iii. 20; Col. iii. 1, 2——ʰChap. xii. 7; xiv. 11 ⁱPsa. lxviii. 5, 6; cxlvi. 9

ᵏChap. vi. 16, 18——ˡPsa. xxxvii. 30——ᵐHeb. *words of pleasantness*——ⁿChap. xi. 19; Isa. v. 8; Jer. xvii. 11——ᵒ1 Pet. iii. 15——ᵖPsa. x. 1; xxxiv. 16 ᑫPsa. cxlv. 18, 19——ʳVer. 5——ˢOr, *correction*——ᵗOr, *obeyeth*——ᵘHeb. *possesseth a heart*——ᵛChap. i. 7 ʷChap. xviii. 12

---

numbers of *indigent Hindoos* subsist wholly on *herbs*, fried in oil, and mixed with their rice.

Verse 19. *The way of the slothful* man *is as a hedge of thorns*] Because he is *slothful*, he imagines *ten thousand* difficulties in the way which cannot be surmounted; but they are all the creatures of his own *imagination*, and that imagination is formed by his *sloth.*

Verse 22. *But in the multitude of counsellors*] See note on chap. xi. 14. But רב יועצים *rob yoatsim* might be translated, chief or master of the council, the prime minister.

Verse 24. *The way of life* is *above to the wise*] There is a *treble* antithesis here: 1. The way of the *wise*, and that of the *fool.* 2. The one is *above*, the other *below.* 3. The one is of *life*, the other is of *death.*

Verse 25. *The house of the proud*] Families of this description are seldom continued long. The Lord hates *pride*; and those that will not be *humble* he will *destroy.*

Verse 27. *He that is greedy of gain*] He who *will* be rich; *troubleth his own house*—he is a torment to himself and his family by his avariciousness and penury, and a curse to those with whom he deals.

But he that hateth gifts] Whatever is *given* to pervert judgment.

Verse 28. *The heart of the righteous studieth to answer*] His tongue never runs before his wit; he never speaks rashly, and never unadvisedly; because he *studies*—ponders, his thoughts and his words.

Verse 29. *The Lord* is *far from the wicked*] He is neither near to *hear*, nor near to *help.*

Verse 30. *The light of the eyes rejoiceth the*

heart] Nature and art are continually placing before our view a multitude of the most resplendent images, each of which is calculated to give pleasure. The man who has a *correct judgment*, and an *accurate eye*, may not only *amuse*, but *instruct* himself endlessly, by the beauties of nature and art.

Verse 31. *The ear that heareth the reproof*] That receives it gratefully and obeys it. "Advice is for them that will take it;" so says one of our own old proverbs; and the meaning here is nearly the same.

Verse 32. *Despiseth his own soul*] That is, *constructively;* for if the instruction lead to the *preservation* of *life* and *soul*, he that neglects or despises it throws all as much in the way of danger as if he actually hated himself.

Verse 33. *The fear of the Lord*] See note on chap. i. 7. Much is spoken concerning this *fear;* 1. It is the *beginning of wisdom.* 2. It is also the *beginning of knowledge.* And, 3. It is the *instruction of wisdom.* Wisdom derives its most important lessons from the fear of God. He who fears God much, is well taught.

And before honour is *humility.*] That is, few persons ever arrive at *honour* who are not *humble;* and those who from low life have risen to places of trust and confidence, have been remarkable for humility. We may rest assured that the *providence* of God will never elevate a proud man; such God beholds *afar off.* He may get into places of trust and profit, but God will *oust* him, and the people will curse him, and curse his memory. So will it ever be with bad ministers and advisers of the crown.

CHAPTER XVI

Man prepares, but God governs. God has made all things for himself; he hates pride. The judgments of God. The administration of kings; their justice, anger, and clemency. God has made all in weight, measure, and due proportion. Necessity produces industry. The patient man. The lot is under the direction of the Lord.

A. M. cir. 3004
B. C. cir. 1000
Ante I. Olymp.
cir. 224
Ante U. C. cir.
247

THE [a]preparations [b]of the heart in man, [c]and the answer of the tongue, *is* from the LORD.

2 [d]All the ways of a man *are* clean in his own eyes: but [e]the LORD weigheth the spirits.

3 [f]Commit [g]thy works unto the LORD, and thy thoughts shall be established.

4 [h]The LORD hath made all *things* for himself: [i]yea, even the wicked for the day of evil.

A. M. cir. 3004
B. C. cir. 1000
Ante I. Olymp.
cir. 224
Ante U. C. cir.
247

---

[a]Ver. 9; chap. xix. 21; xx. 24; Jer. x. 23——[b]Or, *dis-posings*——[c]Matt. x. 19, 20——[d]Chap. xxi. 2——[e]1 Sam. xvi. 7

[f]Psa. xxxvii. 5; lv. 22; Matt. vi. 25; Luke xii. 22; Phil. iv. 6; 1 Pet. v. 7——[g]Heb. *Roll*——[h]Isa. xliii. 7; Rom. xi. 36——[i]Job xxi. 30; Rom. ix. 22

NOTES ON CHAP. XVI

Verse 1. *The preparations of the heart in man*] The Hebrew is לְאָדָם מַעַרְכֵי לֵב *leadam maarchey leb*, which is, literally, "To man are the dispositions of the heart; but from the Lord is the answer of the tongue." Man proposes his wishes; but God answers as he thinks proper. The former is the free offspring of the heart of man; the latter, the free volition of God. Man may *think* as he pleases, and *ask* as he lists; but God will *give*, or *not give*, as he thinks proper. This I believe to be the *meaning* of this shamefully tortured passage, so often vexed by critics, their doubts, and indecisions. God help them! for they seldom have the faculty of making any subject *plainer!* The text does not say that the "preparations," rather *dispositions* or *arrangements*, מַעַרְכֵי *maarchey*, "of the heart," as well as "the answer of the tongue, *is* from the Lord;" though it is generally understood so; but it states that the *dispositions* or *schemes* of the heart (are) man's; but the answer of the tongue (is) the Lord's. And so the principal *versions* have understood it.

Hominis est animam preparare; et Domini gubernare linguam.—VULGATE. "It is the part of man to prepare his soul: it is the prerogative of the Lord to govern the tongue." מִן בַּר נַשׁ

מִן בַּר נָשׁ תַּרְעִיתָא דְלִבָּא וּמִן יי מַמְלְלָא דְלִישָׁנָא *min bar nash taritha delibba; umin yeya mamlala delishana.*—CHALDEE. "From the son of man is the counsel of the heart; and from the Lord is the word of the tongue." The SYRIAC is the same. Καρδια ανδρος λογιζεσθω δικαια, ινα ὑπο του Θεου διορθωθῃ τα διαβηματα αυτη.—SEPTUAGINT. "The heart of man deviseth righteous things, that its goings may be directed by God."

The ARABIC takes great latitude: "All the works of an humble man are clean before the Lord; and the wicked shall perish in an evil day." 𝔒𝔣 𝔞 𝔪𝔞𝔫 𝔦𝔰 𝔱𝔬 𝔪𝔞𝔨𝔢𝔫 𝔯𝔢𝔡𝔶 𝔱𝔥𝔢 𝔦𝔫𝔴𝔦𝔱𝔱: 𝔞𝔫𝔡 𝔬𝔣 𝔱𝔥𝔢 𝔏𝔬𝔯𝔡𝔢 𝔱𝔬 𝔤𝔬𝔟𝔢𝔯𝔫𝔢 𝔱𝔥𝔢 𝔱𝔲𝔫𝔤𝔢.—Old MS. Bible.

"A man maye well purpose a thinge in his harte: but the answere of the tonge cometh of the Lorde."—COVERDALE.

MATTHEW's Bible, 1549, and BECKE's Bible of the same date, and CARDMARDEN's of 1566, follow *Coverdale.* The Bible printed by *R. Barker,* at Cambridge, 4to., 1615, commonly called the *Breeches Bible,* reads the text thus:—"The preparations of the hart *are* in man; but the answere of the tongue *is* of the Lord." So that it appears that our *first,* and all our *ancient versions,* understood the text in the same way; and this, independently of critical torture, is the genuine meaning of the *Hebrew text.* That very valuable version published in *Italian,* at Geneva, fol. 1562, translates thus: Le dispositioni del cuore sono de l'huomo; ma la risposta del la lingua è dal Signore. "The dispositions of the heart are of man; but the answer of the tongue is from the Lord."

The *modern European versions,* as far as I have seen, are the same. And when the word *dispositions, arrangements, schemes,* is understood to be the proper meaning of the *Hebrew term,* as shown above, the sense is *perfectly sound;* for there may be a *thousand schemes* and *arrangements* made in the heart of man, which he may earnestly wish God to bring to full effect, that are neither for *his good* nor *God's glory;* and therefore it is his interest that God has the *answer* in his own power. At the same time, there is no intimation here that *man can prepare his own heart to wait upon, or pray unto the Lord;* or that from the *human heart* any thing *good* can come, *without Divine influence;* but simply that he may have many *schemes* and *projects* which he may beg God to accomplish, that are not of *God,* but from *himself.* Hence our own proverb: "Man proposes, but God disposes." I have entered the more particularly into the consideration of this text, because some are very strenuous in the support of our vicious reading, from a supposition that the other defends the *heterodox* opinion of *man's sufficiency* to think any thing *as of himself.* But while they deserve due credit for their orthodox caution, they will see that no such imputation can fairly lie against the plain grammatical translation of the Hebrew text.

Verse 3. *Commit thy works unto the Lord*] See' that what thou doest is commanded; and then begin, continue, and end all in his name. *And thy thoughts shall be established*—these schemes or arrangements, though formed in the heart, are agreeable to the Divine will, and therefore shall be established. His *thoughts*—his meditations—are right; and he begins and ends his work in the Lord; and therefore all issues well.

Verse 4. *The Lord hath made all* things *for*

A. M. cir. 3004
B. C. cir. 1000
Ante I. Olymp.
cir. 224
Ante U. C. cir.
247

5 [k]Every one *that is* proud in heart *is* an abomination to the LORD:[l]*though* hand *join* in hand, he shall not be [m]unpunished.

6 [n]By mercy and truth iniquity is purged: and [o]by the fear of the LORD *men* depart from evil.

7 When a man's ways please the LORD, he maketh even his enemies to be at peace with him.

8 [p]Better *is* a little with righteousness, than great revenues without right.

9 [q]A man's heart deviseth his way: [r]but the LORD directeth his steps.

10 [s]A divine sentence *is* in the lips of the

A. M. cir. 3004
B. C. cir. 1000
Ante I. Olymp.
cir. 224
Ante U. C. cir.
247

---

[k]Chap. vi. 17; viii. 13——[l]Chap. xi. 21——[m]Heb. *held innocent*——[n]Dan. iv. 27; Tob. xii. 9; Luke xi. 41 [o]Chap. xiv. 16

[p]Psa. xxxvii. 16; Chap. xv. 16——[q]Ver. 1; chap. xix. 21——[r]Psa. xxxvii. 23; Prov. xx. 23; Jer. x. 24——[s]Heb. *Divination*

---

himself] He has so framed and executed every part of his creation, that it manifests his wisdom, power, goodness, and truth.

Even the wicked for the day of evil.] וגם רשע ליום רעה *vegam rasha leyom raah.* The whole verse is translated by the *Chaldee* thus: "All the works of the LORD are for those who obey him; and the wicked is reserved for the evil day."

As רעה *raah* literally signifies to *feed*, it has been conjectured that the clause might be read, *yea, even the wicked he feeds by the day*, or *daily.*

If we take the words as they stand in our present version, they mean no more than what is expressed by the *Chaldee* and *Syriac:* and as far as we can learn from their present *confused* state, by the *Septuagint* and *Arabic*, that "the wicked are reserved for the day of punishment." *Coverdale* has given, as he generally does, a good sense: "The Lorde doth all thinges for his owne sake; yea, and when he kepeth the ungodly for the daye of wrath." He does not *make* the *wicked* or *ungodly man;* but when *man has made himself* such, even *then* God bears with him. But if he repent not, when the measure of his iniquity is filled up, he shall fall under the wrath of God his Maker.

Verse 5. *Though hand* join *in hand, he shall not be unpunished.*] The day of wrath shall come on the wicked, whatever means he may take to avoid it. See chap. xi. 21.

Verse 6. *By mercy and truth iniquity is purged*] This may be misunderstood, as if a man, by *showing mercy* and *acting according to truth*, could atone for his own iniquity. The *Hebrew* text is not ambiguous: בחסד ואמת יכפר עון *bechesed veemeth yechapper avon;* "By mercy and truth he shall atone for iniquity." *He*—God, *by* his *mercy*, in sending his son Jesus into the world,—"shall make an atonement for iniquity" according to his *truth*—the word which he declared by his holy prophets since the world began. Or, if we retain the present version, and follow the *points* in יכפר *yecuppar*, reading "iniquity is purged" or "atoned for," the sense is unexceptionable, as we refer the *mercy* and the *truth* to GOD. But what an awful comment is that of *Don Calmet*, in which he expresses, not only his *own opinion*, but the *staple doctrine* of his own *Church*, the Romish! The reader shall have his own words: " 'L'iniquité se rachete par la misericorde et la verité.' On expie ses pechèz par des œuvres de *misericorde* envers le prochein; par la clemence, par la douceur, par compassion,

par les aumônes: et par la *verité*—par la fidelité, la bonne foi, la droiture, l'équité dans le commerce. Voyez Prov. iii. 3, xiv. 22, xx. 28." " 'Iniquity is redeemed by mercy and truth.' We expiate our sins by works of *mercy* towards our neighbour; by clemency, by kindness, by compassion, and by alms: and by *truth*—by fidelity, by trustworthiness, by uprightness, by equity in commerce." If this be so, why was Jesus incarnated? Why his agony and bloody sweat, his cross and passion, his death and burial, his resurrection and ascension? Was it only to *supply* a sufficient portion of *merit* for those who had *neglected to make a fund for themselves?* Is the guilt of sin so small in the sight of Divine justice, that a man can atone for it by *manifesting good dispositions towards his neighbours*, by *giving some alms*, and not doing those things for which he might be *hanged?* Why then did God make such a mighty matter of the redemption of the world? Why send his Son at all? An *angel* would have been *more* than sufficient; yea, even a *sinner*, who had been converted by his own compassion, alms-deeds, &c., would have been sufficient. And is not this the very doctrine of this most awfully fallen and corrupt Church? Has she not provided a *fund of merit* in her *saints*, of what was more than requisite for *themselves*, that it might be *given*, or *sold out*, to those who had not enough of their own? Now such is the doctrine of the Romish Church—grossly absurd, and destructively iniquitous! And because men cannot believe this, cannot believe these monstrosities, that Church will burn them to ashes. Ruthless Church! degenerated, fallen, corrupt, and corrupting! once a *praise*, now a *curse*, in the earth. Thank the blessed God, whose blood alone can expiate sin, that he has a Church upon the earth; and that the *Romish* is not the *Catholic* Church; and that it has not that political power by which it would subdue all things to itself.

Verse 7. *When a man's ways please the Lord*] God is the guardian and defence of all that fear and love him; and it is truly astonishing to see how wondrously God works in their behalf, raising them up friends, and turning their enemies into friends.

Verse 9. *A man's heart deviseth his way*] This is precisely the same sentiment as that contained in the first verse, on the true meaning of which so much has been already said.

Verse 10. *A divine sentence*] קסם *kesem*, "divination," as the margin has it. Is the meaning as follows? Though *divination* were applied to a righteous king's lips, to induce him

A. M. cir. 3004
B. C. cir. 1000
Ante I. Olymp.
cir. 224
Ante U. C. cir.
247
king: his mouth transgresseth not in judgment.

11 A 'just weight and balance *are* the LORD's: "all the weights of the bag *are* his work.

12 *It is* an abomination to kings to commit wickedness: for ᵛthe throne is established by righteousness.

13 ʷRighteous lips *are* the delight of kings; and they love him that speaketh right.

14 ˣThe wrath of a king *is as* messengers of death: but a wise man will pacify it.

15 In the light of the king's countenance *is* life; and ʸhis favour *is* ᶻas a cloud of the latter rain.

16 ᵃHow much better *is it* to get wisdom than gold? and to get understanding rather to be chosen than silver?

17 The highway of the upright *is* to depart from evil: he that keepeth his way preserveth his soul.

18 ᵇPride goeth before destruction, and a haughty spirit before a fall.

19 Better *it is to be* of an humble spirit with the lowly, than to divide the spoil with the proud.

A. M. cir. 3004
B. C. cir. 1000
Ante I. Olymp.
cir. 224
Ante U. C. cir.
247

20 ᶜHe that handleth a matter wisely shall find good: and whoso ᵈtrusteth in the LORD, happy *is* he.

21 The wise in heart shall be called prudent: and the sweetness of the lips increaseth learning.

22 ᵉUnderstanding *is* a well-spring of life unto him that hath it: but the instruction of fools *is* folly.

23 ᶠThe heart of the wise ᵍteacheth his mouth, and addeth learning to his lips.

24 Pleasant words *are as* a honey-comb, sweet to the soul, and health to the bones.

25 ʰThere is a way that seemeth right unto a man; but the end thereof *are* the ways of death.

26 ⁱHe ᵏthat laboureth, laboureth for himself; for his mouth ˡcraveth it of him.

27 ᵐAn ungodly man diggeth up evil: and

ᵗLev. xix. 36; chap. xi. 1——ᵘHeb. *all the stones*
ᵛChap. xxv. 5; xxix. 14——ʷChap. xiv. 35; xxii. 11
ˣChap. xix. 12; xx. 2——ʸChap. xix. 12——ᶻJob xxix.
23; Zech. x. 1——ᵃChap. viii. 11, 19——ᵇChap. xi. 2;
xvii. 19; xviii. 12——ᶜOr, *He that understandeth a matter*

ᵈPsa. ii. 12; xxxiv. 8; cxxv. 1; Isa. xxx. 18; Jer. xvii. 7
ᵉChap. xiii. 14; xiv. 27——ᶠPsa. xxxvii. 30; Matt. xii. 34
ᵍHeb. *maketh wise*——ʰChap. xiv. 12——ⁱSee chap. ix.
12; Eccles. vi. 7——ᵏHeb. *The soul of him that laboureth*
ˡHeb. *boweth unto him*——ᵐHeb. *A man of Belial*

---

to punish the innocent and spare the guilty, yet *would not his lips transgress in judgment;* so firmly attached is he to God, and so much is he under the Divine *care* and *influence.* Whatever judgment such a one pronounces, it may be considered as a decision from God.

Verse 11. *All the weights of the bag* are *his*] Alluding, probably, to the *standard weights* laid up in a bag in the *sanctuary,* and to which all weights in common use in the land were to be referred, in order to ascertain whether they were just: but some think the allusion is to the *weights* carried about by merchants in their *girdles,* by which they weigh the money, silver and gold, that they take in exchange for their merchandise. As the *Chinese* take no *coin* but *gold* and *silver* by weight, they carry about with them a sort of small *steelyard,* by which they weigh those metals taken in exchange.

Verse 12. *It is* an abomination to kings, *&c.*] In all these verses the wise man refers to *monarchical government rightly administered.* And the proverbs on this subject are all plain.

Verse 16. *How much better—to get wisdom than gold?*] Who believes this, though spoken by the wisest of men, under Divine inspiration?

Verse 17. *The highway of the upright*] The upright man is ever departing from evil; this is his *common road:* and by keeping *on* in this way, *his soul is preserved.*

Verse 18. *Pride goeth before destruction*] Here *pride* is personified: it walks along, and has destruction in its train.

And a haughty spirit before a fall.] Another

VOL. III

personification. A *haughty spirit* marches on, and *ruin* comes after.

In this verse we find the following *Masoretic* note in most Hebrew Bibles. חצי הספר *chatsi hassepher:* "the *middle* of the book." This verse is the *middle verse;* and the first *clause* makes the middle of the *words* of the book of Proverbs.

Verse 22. *Understanding is a well-spring of life*] מקור חיים *mekor chaiyim;* another allusion to the *artery* that carries the blood from the heart to distribute it to all the extremities of the body.

Verse 23. *The heart of the wise teacheth his mouth*] He has a wise heart; he speaks as it dictates; and therefore his speeches are all speeches of wisdom.

Verse 24. *Pleasant words* are as *a honey-comb*] The honey of which is *sweeter* than that which has been expressed from it, and has a much *finer flavour* before it has come in contact with the atmospheric air.

Verse 25. *There is a way that seemeth right*] This whole verse is precisely the same as that chap. xiv. 12.

Verse 26. *He that laboureth*] No thanks to a man for his labour and industry; if he do not *work* he must *starve.*

Verse 27. *An ungodly man diggeth up evil*] How will the following suit?

Effodiuntur opes irritamenta malorum

"*Wealth, the incitement to all evil, is digged up out the earth.*"

A. M. cir. 3004
B. C. cir. 1000
Ante I. Olymp.
cir. 224
Ante U. C. cir.
247

in his lips *there is* as a burning fire.

28 [n]And froward man [o]soweth strife: and [p]a whisperer separateth chief friends.

29 A violent man [q]enticeth his neighbour, and leadeth him in the way *that is* not good.

30 He shutteth his eyes to devise froward things: moving his lips he bringeth evil to pass.

---

[n]Chap. vi. 14, 19; xv. 18; xxvi. 21; xxix. 22——[o]Heb. *sendeth forth*

A wicked man labours as much to bring about an evil purpose, as the *quarryman* does to dig up stones.

In his lips—a burning fire.] His words are as *inflammable*, in producing *strife* and *contention* among his neighbours, as *fire* is in igniting dry stubble.

Verse 30. *He shutteth his eyes to devise, &c.*] He *meditates deeply* upon ways and means to commit sin. He shuts his eyes that he may shut out all other ideas, that his whole soul may be in this.

Verse 31. *The hoary head is a crown of glory*] The latter part of the verse is very well added, for many a *sinner* has a *hoary head.*

Verse 32. *He that ruleth his spirit, than he that taketh a city.*] It is much easier to subdue an enemy *without* than one *within.* There have been many kings who had conquered nations, and yet were slaves to their own passions. Alexander, who conquered the world, was a slave to *intemperate anger*, and in a fit of it slew *Clytus*, the best and most intimate of all his friends, and one whom he loved beyond all others.

The spirit of this maxim is so self-evident, that most nations have formed similar proverbs. The classical reader will remember the following in Hor., Odar. lib. ii., Od. 2:—

Latius regnes, avidum domando
Spiritum, quam si Libyam remotis
Gadibus jungas, et uterque Pœnus
             Serviat uni.

"By virtue's precepts to control
The furious passions of the soul,

A. M. cir. 3004
B. C. cir. 1000
Ante I. Olymp.
cir. 224
Ante U. C. cir.
247

31 [r]The hoary head *is* a crown of glory, *if* it be found in the way of righteousness.

32 [s]*He that is* slow to anger *is* better than the mighty; and he that ruleth his spirit, than he that taketh a city.

33 The lot is cast into the lap: but the whole disposing thereof *is* of the LORD.

---

[p]Chap. xvii. 9——[q]Chap. i. 10, &c.——[r]Chap. xx. 29
[s]Chap. xix. 11

Is over wider realms to reign,
Unenvied monarch, than if Spain
You could to distant Libya join,
And both the Carthages were thine."
                        FRANCIS.

And the following from OVID is not less striking:

—— Fortior est qui se, quam qui fortissima
       vincit
Mœnia, nec virtus altius ire potest.

"He is more of a hero who has conquered himself, than he who has taken the best fortified city."

Beyond this self-conquest the highest courage can not extend; nor did their philosophy teach any thing more sublime.

Verse 33. *The lot is cast into the lap*] On the *lot*, see the note on Num. xxvi. 55. How far it may be proper *now* to put difficult matters to the lot, after earnest prayer and supplication, I cannot say. *Formerly*, it was both lawful and efficient; for after it was solemnly cast, the decision was taken as coming immediately from the Lord. It is still practised, and its use is allowed even by writers on civil law. But those who need most to have recourse to the lot are those who have not *piety* to *pray* nor *faith* to trust to God for a positive decision. The lot should never be resorted to in indifferent matters; they should be those of the greatest importance, in which it appears impossible for human prudence or foresight to determine. In such cases the lot is *an appeal to God*, and he disposes of it according to his goodness, mercy, and truth. The result, therefore, cannot be *fortuitous.*

CHAPTER XVII

Contentment. The wise servant. The Lord tries the heart. Children a crown to their parents. We should hide our neighbour's faults. The poor should not be despised. Litigations and quarrels to be avoided. Wealth is useless to a fool. The good friend. A fool may pass for a wise man when he holds his peace.

A. M. cir. 3004
B. C. cir. 1000
Ante I. Olymp.
cir. 224
Ante U. C. cir.
247

BETTER *is* a [a]dry morsel, and quietness therewith, than a house full of [b]sacrifices *with* strife.

2 A wise servant shall have rule over [c]a son that causeth shame, and shall have part of the inheritance among the brethren.

A. M. cir. 3004
B. C. cir. 1000
Ante I. Olymp.
cir. 224
Ante U. C. cir.
247

---

[a]Chap. xv. 17——[b]Or, *good cheer*

NOTES ON CHAP. XVII

Verse 1. *Better is a dry morsel*] Peace and contentment, and especially *domestic peace*, are beyond all other blessings.

---

[c]Chap. x. 5; xix. 26

A house full of sacrifices] A Hindoo priest, who officiates at a festival, sometimes receives so many *offerings* that *his house is filled with them*, so that many of them are damaged before they can be used.—*Ward.*

A. M. cir. 3004 B. C. cir. 1000 Ante I. Olymp. cir. 224 Ante U. C. cir. 247

3 [d]The fining pot *is* for silver, and the furnace for gold: but the LORD trieth the hearts.

4 A wicked doer giveth heed to false lips; *and* a liar giveth ear to a naughty tongue.

5 [e]Whoso mocketh the poor reproacheth his Maker: *and* [f]he that is glad at calamities shall not be [g]unpunished.

6 Children's children *are* the crown of old men; and the glory of children *are* their fathers.

7 [i]Excellent speech becometh not a fool: much less do [k]lying lips a prince.

8 [l]A gift *is as* [m]a precious stone in the eyes of him that hath it: whithersoever it turneth, it prospereth.

9 [n]He that covereth a transgression [o]seeketh love: but [p]he that repeateth a matter separateth *very* friends.

10 [q]A reproof entereth more into a wise man, than a hundred stripes into a fool.

A. M. cir. 3004 B. C. cir. 1000 Ante I. Olymp. cir. 224 Ante U. C. cir. 247

11 An evil *man* seeketh only rebellion: therefore a cruel messenger shall be sent against him.

12 Let [r]a bear robbed of her whelps meet a man, rather than a fool in his folly.

13 Whoso [s]rewardeth evil for good, evil shall not depart from his house.

14 The beginning of strife *is as* when one letteth out water: therefore [t]leave off contention, before it be meddled with.

15 [u]He that justifieth the wicked, and he that condemneth the just, even they both *are* abomination to the LORD.

16 Wherefore *is there* a price in the hand of a fool to get wisdom, [v]seeing *he hath* no heart *to it?*

17 [w]A friend loveth at all times, and a brother is born for adversity.

18 [x]A man void of [y]understanding striketh

---

[d]Psa. xxvi. 2; chap. xxvii. 21; Jer. xvii. 10; Mal. iii. 3——[e]Chap. xiv. 31——[f]Job xxxi. 29; Obad. 12——[g]Heb. *held innocent*——[h]Psa. cxxvii. 3; cxxviii. 3——[i]Heb. *a lip of excellency*——[k]Heb. *a lip of lying*——[l]Chap. xviii. 16; xix. 6——[m]Heb. *a stone of grace*——[n]Chap. x. 12——[o]Or, *procureth*——[p]Chap. xvi. 28

[q]Or, *A reproof aweth more a wise man than to strike a fool a hundred times*——[r]Hos. xiii. 8——[s]Psa. cix. 4, 5; Jer. xviii. 20; see Rom. xii. 17; 1 Thess. v. 15; 1 Pet. iii, 9——[t]Chap. xx. 3; 1 Thess. iv. 11——[u]Exod. xxiii. 7. chap. xxiv. 24; Isa. v. 23——[v]Ch. xxi. 25, 26——[w]Ruth i. 16; ch. xviii. 24——[x]Ch. vi. 1; xi. 15——[y]Heb; *heart*

Verse 3. *The fining pot* is *for silver*] When *silver* is *mixed*, or suspected to be mixed, with *base metal*, it must be subjected to such a test as the *cupel* to purify it. And gold also must be purified by the action of the *fire*. So God tries hearts. He sends afflictions which penetrate the soul, and give a man to see his state, so that he may apply to the *spirit of judgment* and *the spirit of burning*, to destroy what cannot stand the fire, to separate and burn up all the dross.

Verse 4. *A wicked doer giveth heed*] An evil heart is disposed and ever ready to receive evil; and liars delight in lies.

Verse 5. *He that is glad at calamity*] He who is pleased to hear of the misfortune of another will, in the course of God's just government, have his own multiplied.

Verse 7. *Excellent speech becometh not a fool*] This proverb is suitable to those who affect, in public speaking, fine language, which neither comports with their ordinary conversation, nor with their education. Often *fine words* are injudiciously brought in, and are as unbecoming and irrelevant as a cart wheel among clockwork.

Verse 8. *A gift* is as *a precious stone*] It both enriches and ornaments. In the latter clause there is an evident allusion to *cut stones*. Whithersoever you *turn them*, they *reflect the light*, are *brilliant* and *beautiful*.

Verse 10. *A reproof entereth more*] Though the *rod*, judiciously applied, is a *great instrument of knowledge*, yet it is of no use where incurable dulness or want of intellect, prevails. Besides, there are *generous dispositions* on which *counsel* will work more than stripes.

Verse 12. *Let a bear robbed of her whelps*] At which times such animals are peculiarly fierce. See the note on 2 Sam. xvii. 8.

Verse 13. *Whoso rewardeth evil for good*] Here is a most awful warning. As many persons are guilty of the sin of *ingratitude*, and of paying *kindness* with *unkindness*, and *good* with *evil*, it is no wonder we find so much *wretchedness* among men; for God's word cannot fail; evil shall not depart from the houses and families of such persons.

Verse 14. *The beginning of strife* is as *when one letteth out water*] As soon as the smallest breach is made in the dike or dam, the water begins to *press* from all parts *towards the breach;* the resistance becomes too great to be successfully opposed, so that dikes and all are speedily swept away. Such is the beginning of contentions, quarrels, lawsuits, &c.

Leave off contention, before it be meddled with.] As you see what an altercation must lead to, therefore do not begin it. Before it be *mingled together*, התגלע *hithgalla*, before the spirits of the contending parties come into conflict—are joined together in battle, and begin to deal out mutual reflections and reproaches. When you see that the dispute is likely to take this turn, leave it off immediately.

Verse 17. *A friend loveth at all times*] Equally in *adversity* as in *prosperity*. And a *brother*, according to the ties and interests of consanguinity, is *born* to support and comfort a *brother* in *distress*.

Verse 18. *Striketh hands*] *Striking* each

A. M. cir. 3004
B. C. cir. 1000
Ante I. Olymp.
cir. 224
Ante U. C. cir.
247

hands, *and* becometh surety in the presence of his friend.

19 He loveth transgression that loveth strife: *and* [z]he that exalteth his gate seeketh destruction.

20 [a]He that hath a froward heart findeth no good: and he that hath [b]a perverse tongue falleth into mischief.

21 [c]He that begetteth a fool *doeth it* to his sorrow: and the father of a fool hath no joy.

22 [d]A merry heart doeth good [e]*like* a medicine: [f]but a broken spirit drieth the bones.

23 A wicked *man* taketh a gift out of the bosom [g]to pervert the ways of judgment.

24 [h]Wisdom *is* before him that hath understanding: but the eyes of a fool *are* in the ends of the earth.

A. M. cir. 3004
B. C. cir. 1000
Ante I. Olymp.
cir. 224
Ante U. C. cir.
247

25 [i]A foolish son *is* a grief to his father and a bitterness to her that bare him.

26 [k]Also to punish the just *is* not good, *nor* to strike princes for equity.

27 [l]He that hath knowledge spareth his words: *and* a man of understanding is of [m]an excellent spirit.

28 [n]Even a fool, when he holdeth his peace, is counted wise: *and* he that shutteth his lips *is* esteemed a man of understanding.

---

[z]Ch. xvi. 18——[a]Heb. *the froward of heart*——[b]James iii. 8——[c]Ch. x. 1; xix. 13; ver. 25——[d]Chap. xv. 13, 15; xii. 25——[e]Or, *to a medicine*——[f]Psa. xxii. 15

[g]Exod. xxiii. 8——[h]Ch. xiv. 6; Eccles. ii. 14; viii. 1 [i]Ch. x. 1; xv. 20; xix. 13; ver. 21——[k]Ver. 15; ch. xviii. 5 [l]James i. 19——[m]Or, *a cool spirit*——[n]Job xiii. 5

---

other's hands, or *shaking hands*, was anciently the *form* in concluding a contract. See notes on chap. vi. 1.

Verse 19. *He that exalteth his gate*] In different parts of Palestine they are obliged to have the doors of their courts and houses *very low*, not more than *three* feet high, to prevent the Arabs, who scarcely ever leave the backs of their horses, from *riding into the courts and houses*, and spoiling their goods. He, then, who, through pride and ostentation, made a *high gate*, exposed himself to *destruction;* and is said here to *seek it*, because he must know that this would be a necessary consequence of *exalting his gate.* But although the above is a fact, yet possibly *gate* is here taken for the *mouth;* and the *exalting of the gate* may mean proud boasting and arrogant speaking, such as has a tendency to kindle and maintain strife. And this interpretation seems to agree better with the scope of the context than the above.

Verse 22. *A merry heart doeth good* like *a medicine*] Instead of נהה *gehah*, a *medicine*, it appears that the *Chaldee* and *Syriac* had read in their copies נוה *gevah*, the body, as they translate in this way. This makes the apposition here more complete: "A merry heart doeth good to the *body;* but a broken spirit drieth the *bones.*" Nothing has such a direct tendency to ruin health and waste out life as grief, anxiety, fretfulness, bad tempers, &c. All these work *death.*

Verse 23. *A gift out of the bosom*] Out of his *purse;* as in their *bosoms*, above their girdles, the Asiatics carry their *purses.* I have often observed this.

Verse 24. *Are in the ends of the earth.*] Wisdom is within the *sight* and *reach* of every man: but he whose *desires* are scattered abroad, who is always aiming at impossible things, or is of an unsteady disposition, is not likely to find it.

Verse 26. *Nor to strike princes for equity.*] To fall out with the ruler of the people, and to take off his head under pretence of his not being a *just* or *equitable* governor, is *unjust.* To kill a king on the ground of justice is a most dreadful omen to any land. Where was it ever done, that it promoted the *public prosperity?* No experiment of this kind has ever yet succeeded, howsoever worthless the king might be.

Verse 28. *Even a fool*] He is counted wise as to that particular. He may know that he cannot speak well, and he has sense enough to keep from speaking. He is, as to that particular, a wise fool.

A man may be *golden-mouthed* and *silver-tongued* in eloquence; but to know *when* and *where* to *speak* and to be *silent*, is better than *diamonds.* But who that thinks he can speak well can refrain from speaking? His tongue has no rest.

CHAPTER XVIII

The man who separates himself and seeks wisdom. The fool and the wicked man. Deep wisdom. Contention of fools. The talebearer and the slothful. The name of the Lord. Pride and presumption because of riches. Hastiness of spirit. The wounded spirit. The influence of gifts. The lot. The offended brother. The influence of the tongue. A wife a good from God. The true friend.

A. M. cir. 3004
B. C. cir. 1000
Ante I. Olymp.
cir. 224
Ante U. C. cir.
247

THROUGH [a]desire a man, having separated himself, seeketh *and* intermeddleth with all wisdom.

2 A fool hath no delight in understanding, but that his heart may discover itself.

3 When the wicked cometh, *then* cometh also contempt, and with ignominy reproach.

4 [b]The words of a man's mouth *are as* deep waters, *and* [c]the well-spring of wisdom *as* a flowing brook.

5 [d]*It is* not good to accept the person of the wicked, to overthrow the righteous in judgment.

A. M. cir. 3004
B. C. cir. 1000
Ante I. Olymp.
cir. 224
Ante U. C. cir.
247

6 A fool's lips enter into contention, and his mouth calleth for strokes.

7 [e]A fool's mouth *is* his destruction, and his lips *are* the snare of his soul.

8 [f]The words of a [g]tale-bearer *are* [h]as wounds, and they go down into the [i]innermost parts of the belly.

---

[a]Or, *He that separateth himself, seeketh according to* his *desire,* and *intermeddleth in every business;* see Jude 19 [b]Chapter x. 11; xx. 5——[c]Psalm lxxviii. 2——[d]Leviticus xix. 15; Deuteronomy i. 17; xvi. 19; chapter xxiv.

23; xxviii. 21——[e]Chapter x. 14; xii. 13; xiii. 3; Ecclesiastes x. 12——[f]Chapter xii. 18; xxvi. 22——[g]Or, *whisperer*——[h]Or, *like as when men are wounded* [i]Heb. *chambers*

NOTES ON CHAP. XVIII

Verse 1. *Through desire a man, having separated himself*] The original is difficult and obscure. The *Vulgate, Septuagint,* and *Arabic,* read as follows: "He who wishes to break with his friend, *and* seeks occasions or pretences, shall at all times be worthy of blame."

My old MS. Bible translates, ꝺccasioun seeketh that wil go awei fro a freend: at al tyme he schal ben wariable.

Coverdale thus: "Who so hath pleasure to sowe discorde, piketh a quarrel in every thinge."

Bible by *Barker,* 1615: "Fro the desire *thereof* he will separate himself to seeke it, and occupie himself in all wisdome." Which has in the *margin* the following note: "He that loveth wisdom will separate himself from all impediments, and give himself wholly to seek it."

The Hebrew: לתאוה יבקש נפרד בכל תושיה יתגלע *lethaavah yebakkesh niphrad, bechol tushiyah yithgalla.* The nearest translation to the words is perhaps the following: "He who is separated shall seek the desired thing, (i. e., the object of his desire,) and shall intermeddle (mingle himself) with all realities or all essential knowledge." He finds that he can make little progress in the *investigation* of *Divine* and *natural* things, if he have much to do with *secular* or *trifling matters:* he therefore *separates himself* as well from *unprofitable pursuits* as from *frivolous company,* and then *enters into the spirit* of his pursuit; is not satisfied with *superficial* observances, but examines the *substance* and *essence,* as far as possible, of those things which have been the objects of his *desire.* This appears to me the best meaning: the reader may judge for himself.

Verse 2. *But that his heart may discover itself.*] It is a fact that most vain and foolish people are never satisfied in company, but in showing their own *nonsense* and *emptiness.* But this verse may be understood as confirming the view already given of the preceding, and may be translated thus: "But a fool doth not delight in understanding, though it should even manifest itself:" so I understand כי אם

בהתגלות *ki im behithgalloth.* The *separated person* seeks understanding in every hidden thing, and feels his toil well repaid when he finds it, even after the most painful and expensive search: the other regards it not, though

its *secret springs* should be *laid open to him* without toil or expense.

Verse 3. *When the wicked cometh, &c.*] would it not be better to read this verse thus? "When the wicked cometh contempt cometh; and with ignominy *cometh* reproach." A wicked man is despised even by the wicked. He who falls under ignominy falls under *reproach.*

Verse 4. *The words of a man's mouth*] That is, the wise sayings of a wise man are like *deep waters;* howsoever much you pump or draw off, you do not appear to lessen them.

The well-spring of wisdom] Where there is a *sound understanding,* and a deep, well-informed mind, its wisdom and its counsels are an incessant stream, מקור חכמה *mekor chochmah,* "the vein of wisdom," ever throwing out its healthy streams: but מקור חיים *mekor chaiyim,* "the vein of LIVES," is the reading of *eight* of *Kennicott's* and *De Rossi's* MSS., and is countenanced by the *Septuagint,* πηγη ζωης, "the fountain of life." And so the Arabic, عيسٮ

حٮٮة This is the more likely to be the *true reading,* because the *figure* of the heart propelling the blood through the great aorta, to send it to all parts of the animal system, is a favourite with *Solomon,* as it was with his father, *David.* See the note on Psa. xxxvi. 9; Prov. x. 11, &c.

Verse 5. *To accept the person of the wicked*] We must not, in judicial cases, pay any attention to a man's *riches, influence, friends, offices,* &c., but judge the case according to its own merits. But when the *wicked* rich man opposes and oppresses the poor *righteous,* then all those things should be utterly forgotten.

Verse 8. *The words of a tale-bearer*] דברי נרגן *dibrey nirgan,* "the words of the whisperer," the *busy-body,* the *busy, meddling croaker. Verba bilinguis,* "the words of the double-tongued."—*Vulgate.* Ꝥhe wordes of the twisel tunge.—Old MS. Bible. "The words of a slanderer."—*Coverdale.*

The words of a deceiver, the fair-spoken, deeply-malicious man, though they appear *soft* and *gracious,* are wounds deeply injurious.

The original word is כמתלהמים *kemithlahamim;* they *are as soft* or *simple,* or *undesigning.* But *Schultens* gives another meaning. He observes that לחם *lahamah* in *Arabic* signifies to "swallow down quickly or greedily." Such words are like dainties, eagerly swal-

A. M. cir. 3004
B. C. cir. 1000
Ante I. Olymp.
cir. 224
Ante U. C. cir.
247

9 He also that is slothful in his work is ^kbrother to him that is a great waster.

10 ^lThe name of the LORD *is* a strong tower: the righteous runneth into it, and ^mis safe.

11 ⁿThe rich man's wealth is his strong city, and as a high wall in his own conceit.

12 ^oBefore destruction the heart of man is haughty, and before honour *is* humility.

13 He that ^panswereth a matter ^qbefore he heareth *it,* it *is* folly and shame unto him.

14 The spirit of a man will sustain his infirmity; but a wounded spirit who can bear?

A. M. cir. 3004
B. C. cir. 1000
Ante I. Olymp.
cir. 224
Ante U. C. cir.
247

15 The heart of the prudent getteth knowledge; and the ear of the wise seeketh knowledge.

16 ^rA man's gift maketh room for him, and bringeth him before great men.

17 *He that is* first in his own cause *seemeth* just; but his neighbour cometh and searcheth him.

18 The lot causeth contentions to cease, and parteth between the mighty.

19 A brother offended *is harder to be won* than a strong city: and *their* contentions *are* like the bars of a castle.

20 ^sA man's belly shall be satisfied with the

---

^kChap. xxviii. 24——^l2 Sam. xxii. 3, 51; Psa. xviii. 2; xxvii. 1; lxi. 3, 4; xci. 2; cxliv. 2——^mHeb. *is set aloft* ⁿChap. x. 15——^oChap. xi. 2; xv. 33; xvi. 18

^pHeb. *returneth a word*——^qJohn vii. 51——^rGen. xxxii. 20; 1 Samuel xxv. 27; chap. xvii. 8; xxi. 14 ^sChap. xii. 14; xiii. 2

---

lowed, because inviting to the taste; like gingerbread, apparently *gilded* over, though with *Dutch leaf,* which is a preparation of *copper;* or *sweetmeats* powdered over with *red candied seeds,* which are thus formed by *red lead;* both deeply ruinous to the tender bowels of the poor little innocents, but, because of their *sweetness* and *inviting colour, greedily swallowed down.* This makes a good reading, and agrees with the latter clause of the verse, "they go down into the innermost parts of the belly."

Verse 9. *He also that is slothful*] A slothful man neglects his *work,* and the *materials* go to ruin: the *waster,* he destroys the *materials.* They are both destroyers.

Verse 10. *The name of the Lord is a strong tower*] The *name of the Lord* may be taken for the *Lord himself;* he is a *strong tower,* a *refuge,* and *place of complete safety,* to all that trust in him. What a strong fortress is to the besieged, the like is God to his persecuted, tempted, afflicted followers.

Verse 11. *The rich man's wealth*] See chap. x. 15.

Verse 12. *Before destruction*] See on chap. xi. 2; and xvi. 18.

Verse 13. *He that answereth a matter*] This is a common case; before a man can tell out his story, another will begin *his.* Before a man has made his *response,* the other wishes to confute *piecemeal,* though he has had his own speech already. This is foolishness to them. They are ill-bred. There are many also that *give judgment* before they hear the whole of the cause, and express an *opinion* before they hear the state of the case. How absurd, stupid, and foolish!

Verse 14. *The spirit of a man will sustain*] A man sustains the ills of his body, and the trials of life, by the strength and energy of his mind. But if the *mind* be *wounded,* if this be *cast down,* if slow-consuming care and grief have shot the dagger into the soul, what can then sustain the man? Nothing but the unseen God. Therefore, let the afflicted *pray.* A man's *own spirit* has, in general, sufficient fortitude to bear up under the *unavoidable* trials of life; but when the *conscience* is wounded by sin, and the soul is dying by iniquity, *who can lift him up?* God alone; for salvation is of the Lord.

Verse 16. *A man's gift maketh room for him*] It is, and ever has been, a base and degrading practice in Asiatic countries, to bring a gift or present to the great man into whose presence you come. Without this there is no audience, no favour, no *justice.* This arose from the circumstance that men must not approach the *altar of God* without an *offering.* Potentates, wishing to be considered as *petty gods,* demanded a similar homage:—

Munera, crede mihi, capiunt hominesque deosque;
Placatur donis Jupiter ipse suis.   OVID.

"Believe me, gifts prevail much with both gods and men: even Jupiter himself is pleased with his own offerings."

Verse 17. He that is *first in his own cause*] Any man may, in the first instance, make out a fair tale, because he has the choice of circumstances and arguments. But when the neighbour cometh and searcheth him, he examines all, dissects all, swears and cross-questions every witness, and brings out truth and fact.

Verse 18. *The lot causeth contentions to cease*] See note on chap. xvi. 33.

Verse 19. *A brother offended* is harder to be won *than a strong city*] Almost all the *versions* agree in the following reading: "A brother assisted by a brother, is like a fortified city; and their decisions are like the bars of a city." *Coverdale* is both plain and terse: "The unitie of brethren is stronger then a castell, and they that holde together are like the barre of a palace." The fable of the dying father, his sons, and the bundle of faggots, illustrates this proverb. Unity among brethren makes them invincible; small things grow great by concord. If we take the words according to the *common version,* we see them express what, alas! we know to be too generally true: that when brothers fall out, it is with extreme difficulty that they can be reconciled. And fraternal enmities are generally strong and inveterate.

Verse 20. *With the fruit of his mouth*] Our own words frequently shape our good or evil fortune in life.

A. M. cir. 3004
B. C. cir. 1000
Ante I. Olymp. cir. 224
Ante U. C. cir. 247

fruit of his mouth; *and* with the increase of his lips shall he be filled.

21 'Death and life *are* in the power of the tongue: and they that love it shall eat the fruit thereof.

22 ᵘ*Whoso* findeth a wife, findeth a good

thing, and obtaineth favour of the LORD.

A. M. cir. 3004
B. C. cir. 1000
Ante I. Olymp. cir. 224
Ante U. C. cir. 247

23 The poor useth entreaties; but the rich answereth ᵛroughly.

24 A man *that hath* friends must show himself friendly: ʷand there is a friend *that* sticketh closer than a brother.

ᵗMatt. xii. 37——ᵘChap. xix. 14; xxxi. 10

ᵛJames ii. 3——ʷChap. xvii. 17

Verse 21. *Death and life are in the power of the tongue*] This may apply to all men. Many have lost their lives by their tongue, and some have saved their lives by it: but it applies most forcibly to *public pleaders;* on many of their tongues hangs *life* or *death.*

Verse 22. *Whoso findeth a wife findeth a good* thing] *Marriage,* with all its troubles and embarrassments, is a blessing from God; and there are *few cases* where a *wife of any sort* is not better than none, because celibacy is an evil; for God himself hath said, "It is not good for man to be alone." None of the versions, except the *Chaldee,* are pleased with the naked simplicity of the Hebrew text, hence they all add *good:* "He that findeth a GOOD wife findeth a good thing;" and most people, who have not deeply considered the subject, think the assertion, without this qualification, is absurd. Some copies of the *Targum,* and apparently one of *Kennicott's* MSS., have the addition טובה *tobah, good;* but this would be an authority too slender to justify changing the Hebrew text; yet *Houbigant, Kennicott,* and other able critics argue for it. The *Septuagint* is not satisfied without an addition: "But he who puts away a good wife, puts away a good thing: and he that retains an adulteress, is a fool and wicked." In this addition the *Vulgate, Syriac,* and *Arabic,* agree with the *Septuagint.* The *Hebrew* text as it stands, teaches a *general doctrine* by a *simple* but general *proposition:* "He that findeth a wife findeth a good thing." So St. Paul: "Marriage is honourable in all." Had the world been left, in this respect, to the unbridled propensities of man, in what a horrible state would society have been—if indeed society could have existed, or civilization have taken place—if *marriage* had not obtained among men! As to *good wives* and *bad wives,* they are relatively so, in general; and most of them that have been *bad* afterwards, have been *good* at first; and we well know the best things may deteriorate, and the world generally allows that where there are matrimonial contentions, there are *faults on both sides.*

Verse 24. *A man that hath friends must show himself friendly*] Love begets love; and love requires love as its recompense. If a man do not maintain a friendly carriage, he cannot expect to retain his friends. Friendship is a good plant; but it requires cultivation to make it grow.

There is a kind of factitious friendship in the world, that, to show one's self *friendly* in it, is very expensive, and in every way utterly unprofitable: it is maintained by expensive *parties, feasts,* &c., where the table groans with dainties, and where the *conversation* is either *jejune* and *insipid,* or *calumnious;* backbiting, talebearing, and scandal, being the general topics of the different squads in company.

There is a friend that *sticketh closer than a brother.*] In many cases the genuine friend has shown more attachment, and rendered greater benefits, than the natural brother. Some apply this to *God;* others to *Christ;* but the text has no such meaning.

But critics and commentators are not agreed on the translation of this verse. The original is condensed and obscure. איש רעים להתרעע *ish reim lehithroea,* or *lehithroeang,* as some would read, who translate: *A man of friends may ring again;* i. e., he may boast and mightily exult: but there is a friend, אהב *oheb,* a *lover,* that sticketh closer, דבק *dabek,* is *glued* or *cemented,* מאח *meach, beyond,* or more than, a brother. The former will continue during *prosperity,* but the latter continues *closely united* to his friend, even in the most disastrous circumstances.

Hence that maxim of *Cicero,* so often repeated, and so well known:—

Amicus certus in re incerta cernitur.

"In doubtful times the genuine friend is known."

A late commentator has translated the verse thus:—

The man that hath many friends is ready to be ruined:
But there is a friend that sticketh closer than a brother. HOLDEN.

"A frende that delyteth in love, doth a man more frendship, and sticketh faster unto him, than a brother."—*Coverdale.*

"A man that hath friends *ought to* show himself friendly, for a friend is nearer than a brother."—BARKER'S *Bible,* 1615.

"𝔄 man ampable to felowschip, more a freend schal ben thanne a brother."—Old MS. Bible. The two last verses in this chapter, and the two first of the next, are wanting in the Septuagint and Arabic.

These are the principal varieties; out of them the reader may choose. I have already given my opinion.

CHAPTER XIX

The worth of a poor upright man. Riches preserve friends. False witnesses. False friends. A king's wrath. The foolish son. The prudent wife. Slothfulness. Pity for the poor. The fear of the Lord. The spendthrift son. Obedience to parents.

A. M. cir. 3004
B. C. cir. 1000
Ante I. Olymp.
cir. 224
Ante U. C. cir.
247

BETTER [a]*is* the poor that walketh in his integrity, than *he that is* perverse in his lips, and is a fool.

2 Also, *that* the soul *be* without knowledge, *it is* not good; and he that hasteth with *his* feet sinneth.

3 [b]The foolishness of man perverteth his way; [c]and his heart fretteth against the LORD.

4 [d]Wealth maketh many friends: but the poor is separated from his neighbour.

5 [e]A false witness shall not be [f]unpunished, and *he that* speaketh lies shall not escape.

6 [g]Many will entreat the favour of the prince: and [h]every man *is* a friend to [i]him that giveth gifts.

7 [k]All the brethren of the poor do hate him:

how much more do his friends go [l]far from him? he pursueth *them with* words, *yet* they are wanting *to him.*

A. M. cir. 3004
B. C. cir. 1000
Ante I. Olymp.
cir. 224
Ante U. C. cir.
247

8 He that getteth [m]wisdom loveth his own soul: he that keepeth understanding [n]shall find good.

9 [o]A false witness shall not be unpunished, and *he that* speaketh lies shall perish.

10 Delight is not seemly for a fool; much less [p]for a servant to have rule over princes.

11 [q]The [r]discretion of a man deferreth his anger; [s]and *it is* his glory to pass over a transgression.

12 [t]The king's wrath *is* as the roaring of a lion: but his favour *is* [u]as dew upon the grass.

13 [v]A foolish son *is* the calamity of his father: [w]and the contentions of a wife *are* a continual dropping.

---

[a]Chap. xxviii. 6——[b]Chap. xiv. 24; xv. 2, 14——[c]Psa. xxxvii. 7——[d]Chap. xiv. 20——[e]Ver. 9; Exod. xxiii. 1; Deut. xix. 16, 19; chap. vi. 19; xxi. 28——[f]Heb. *held innocent*——[g]Chap. xxix. 26——[h]Chap. xvii. 8; xviii. 16; xxi. 14——[i]Heb. *a man of gifts*——[k]Chap. xiv. 20

[l]Psa. xxxviii. 11——[m]Heb. *a heart*——[n]Ch. xvi. 20 [o]Ver. 5——[p]Ch. xxx. 22; Eccles. x. 6, 7——[q]Ch. xiv. 29; James i. 19——[r]Or, *prudence*——[s]Ch.xv i. 32——[t]Ch. xvi. 14, 15; xx. 2; xxviii. 15——[u]Hos. xiv. 5——[v]Ch. x. 1; xv. 20; xvii. 21, 25——[w]Ch. xxi. 9, 19; xxvii. 15

NOTES ON CHAP. XIX

Verse 1. *Better* is *the poor*] The upright poor man is always to be preferred to the rich or *self-sufficient* fool.

Verse 2. *Also, that the soul be without knowledge, it is not good*] Would it not be plainer, as it is more *literal*, to say, "Also, to be without knowledge, is not good for the soul?" The soul was made for God; and to be without his *knowledge*, to be *unacquainted with him*, is not only *not good*, but the *greatest evil* the soul can suffer, for it involves all other evils. The *Chaldee* and *Syriac* have: "He who knows not his own soul, it is not good to him." "Where no discretion is, there the soul is not well."— *Coverdale*.

And he that hasteth with his *feet sinneth.*] And this will be the case with him who is not Divinely instructed. A *child* does nothing *cautiously*, because it is uninstructed; a *savage* is also *rash* and *precipitate*, till *experience* instructs him. A man who has not the knowledge of God is incautious, rash, headstrong, and precipitate: and hence he *sinneth*—he is continually *missing the mark*, and wounding his own soul.

Verse 3. *The foolishness of man*] Most men complain of cross providences, because they get into straits and difficulties through the *perverseness of their ways;* and thus *they fret against God;* whereas, in every instance, they are the causes of their own calamities. O how inconsistent is man!

Verse 4. *The poor is separated from his neighbour.*] Because he has the "disease of all-shunned poverty."

Verse 7. *Do hate him*] They *shun* him as they do the person they *hate.* They neither *hate* him *positively*, nor *love* him: they *disregard*

him; they will have nothing to do with him. שׂנא *sana* signifies not only to hate, but to show a less degree of love to one than another. So Jacob loved Rachel, but hated Leah—showed her less affection than he did to Rachel.

Verse 10. *Delight is not seemly for a fool*] תענוג *taanug*, splendid or luxurious living, rank, equipage, &c. These sit ill on a *fool*, though he be by birth a *lord.*

For a servant to have rule over princes.] I pity the king who delivers himself into the hands of his own ministers. Such a one loses his character, and cannnot be respected by his subjects, or rather *their* subjects. But it is still worse when a person of mean extraction is raised to the throne, or to any *place of power;* he is generally cruel and tyrannical.

Verse 11. It is *his glory to pass over a transgression.*] "No," says what is termed a *man of honour;* "he must meet me as a gentleman; I must have his blood, let God say what he will." O poor, dastardly coward! thou canst not bear the reproach of poor, flimsy, paltry fellows who ridicule thee, because thou hast refused to commit murder. Such laws should be put down by law; and the man that *gives a challenge* should be hanged, because he *intends* to commit *murder.*

Verse 12. *The king's wrath is as the roaring of a lion*] There is nothing more dreadful than the roaring of this tyrant of the forest. At the sound of it all other animals tremble, flee away, and hide themselves. The *king* who is above law, and rules without law, and whose will is his own law, is like the *lion.* This is strongly descriptive of the character of *Asiatic* sovereigns.

Verse 13. *The contentions of a wife* are a *continual dropping.*] The man who has got such a wife is like a tenant who has got a *cottage* with

A. M. cir. 3004
B. C. cir. 1000
Ante I. Olymp.
cir. 224
Ante U. C. cir.
247
14 [x]House and riches *are* the inheritance of fathers: and [y]a prudent wife *is* from the LORD.

15 [z]Slothfulness casteth into a deep sleep; and an idle soul shall [a]suffer hunger.

16 [b]He that keepeth the commandment keepeth his own soul: *but* he that despiseth his ways shall die.

17 [c]He that hath pity upon the poor lendeth unto the LORD; and [d]that which he hath given will he pay him again.

18 [e]Chasten thy son while there is hope, and let not thy soul spare [f]for his crying.

19 A man of great wrath shall suffer punishment: for if thou deliver *him,* yet thou must [g]do it again.

20 Hear counsel, and receive instruction, that thou mayest be wise [h]in the latter end.

21 [i]*There are* many devices in a man's heart; nevertheless the counsel of the LORD, that shall stand.

22 The desire of a man *is* his kindness; and a poor man *is* better than a liar.

A. M. cir. 3004
B. C. cir. 1000
Ante I. Olymp.
cir. 224
Ante U. C. cir.
247
23 [k]The fear of the LORD tendeth to life: and *he that hath it* shall abide satisfied; he shall not be visited with evil.

24 [l]A slothful *man* hideth his hand in *his* bosom, and will not so much as bring it to his mouth again.

25 [m]Smite a scorner, and the simple [n]will [o]beware; and [p]reprove one that hath understanding, *and* he will understand knowledge.

26 He that wasteth *his* father, *and* chaseth away *his* mother, *is* [q]a son that causeth shame, and bringeth reproach.

27 Cease, my son, to hear the instruction *that* causeth to err from the words of knowledge.

28 [r]An ungodly witness scorneth judgment: and [s]the mouth of the wicked devoureth iniquity.

29 Judgments are prepared for scorners, [t]and stripes for the back of fools.

---

[x]2 Cor. xii. 14——[y]Chap. xviii. 22——[z]Ch. vi. 9
[a]Ch. x. 4; xx. 13; xxiii. 21——[b]Luke x. 28; xi. 28
[c]Chap. xxviii. 27; Eccles. xi. 1; Matt. x. 42; xxv. 40;
2 Cor. ix. 6, 7, 8; Heb. vi. 10——[d]Or, *his deed*——[e]Ch.
xiii. 24; xxiii. 13; xxix. 17——[f]Or, *to his destruction,* or
to cause him to die——[g]Heb. *add*——[h]Psa. xxxvii. 37

[i]Job xxiii. 13; Psa. xxxiii. 10, 11; ch. xvi. 1, 3; Isa. xiv.
26, 27; xlvi. 10; Acts v. 39; Heb. vi. 17——[k]1 Tim. iv. 8
[l]Ch. xv. 19; xxvi. 13, 15——[m]Ch. xxi. 11——[n]Heb. *will
be cunning*——[o]Deut. xiii. 11——[p]Ch. ix. 8——[q]Chap.
xvii. 2——[r]Heb. *A witness of Belial*——[s]Job xv. 16;
xx. 12, 13; xxxiv. 7——[t]Chap. x. 13; xxvi. 3

---

a *bad roof,* through every part of which the rain either *drops* or *pours.* He can neither *sit, stand, work,* nor *sleep,* without being exposed to these *droppings.* God help the man who is in such a case, with *house* or *wife!*

Verse 14. *A prudent wife* is *from the Lord.*] One who has a good understanding, אשה משכלת *ishshah mascaleth;* who avoids complaining, though she may often have cause for it.

Verse 15. *Into a deep sleep*] תרדמה *tardemah,* the same into which Adam was thrown, before Eve was taken from his side. Sloth renders a man utterly unconscious of all his interests. Though he has frequently felt hunger, yet he is regardless that his continual slothfulness must necessarily plunge him into more sufferings.

Verse 17. *Lendeth unto the Lord*] O what a word is this! God makes himself debtor for every thing that is given to the *poor!* Who would not *advance much* upon such *credit?* God will pay it again. And in no case has he ever forfeited his word.

Verse 18. *Let not thy soul spare for his crying.*] This is a hard precept for a *parent.* Nothing affects the heart of a parent so much as a child's *cries* and *tears.* But it is better that the *child* may be caused to *cry,* when the correction may be healthful to his soul, than that the parent should *cry* afterwards, when the child is grown to *man's* estate, and his evil habits are *sealed for life.*

Verse 19. *A man of great wrath*] He who is of an *irritable, fiery* disposition, will necessarily get himself into many broils; and he that is

surety for him once is likely to be called on again and again for the same friendly office.

Verse 21. There are *many devices, &c.*] The same sentiment as in chap. xvi. 1, where see the note.

Verse 24. *A slothful* man *hideth his hand in* his *bosom*] Is too lazy to feed himself. If he dip his hand *once* in the dish, he is too lazy to put it in a *second* time. It is a strange case that a man, through his excessive slothfulness, would rather starve than put himself to the trouble to eat.

Verse 26. *He that wasteth* his *father*] Destroys his substance by riotous or extravagant living, so as to embitter his latter end by poverty and affliction; and adds to this wickedness the *expulsion of his aged* widowed *mother* from the paternal house; *is a son of shame*—a most shameful man; and *a son of reproach*—one whose conduct cannot be sufficiently execrated. 𝔚𝔥𝔬 𝔱𝔬𝔯𝔪𝔢𝔫𝔱𝔦𝔱𝔥 𝔱𝔥𝔢 𝔣𝔞𝔡𝔢𝔯, 𝔞𝔫𝔡 𝔣𝔩𝔢𝔢𝔱𝔥 𝔱𝔥𝔢 𝔪𝔬𝔡𝔦𝔯, 𝔰𝔠𝔥𝔢𝔫𝔣𝔲𝔩 𝔰𝔠𝔥𝔞𝔩 𝔟𝔢𝔫, 𝔞𝔫𝔡 𝔲𝔫𝔟𝔩𝔦𝔰𝔣𝔲𝔩.—Old MS. Bible. The common reading of the *Vulgate* is, *et fugat matrem, and expels his mother;* but the *Old Bible* was taken from a copy that had *fugit matrem, shuns his mother, flees* away from her, *leaves her* to affliction and penury. It is prostitution of the term to call such, *man.*

Verse 27. *Cease, my son*] Hear nothing that would lead thee away from God and his truth.

Verse 29. *Stripes for the back of fools.*] Profane and *wicked* men expose themselves to the punishments denounced against such by just laws. Avoid, therefore, both their company and their end.

CHAPTER XX

Against wine and strong drink. We should avoid contentions. The sluggard. The righteous man. Weights and measures. Tale-bearers. The wicked son. The wise king. The glory of young men. The beauty of old men. The benefit of correction.

A. M. cir. 3004
B. C. cir. 1000
Ante I. Olymp.
cir. 224
Ante U. C. cir.
247

WINE [a]*is* a mocker, strong drink *is* raging: and whosoever *is* deceived thereby is not wise.

2 [b]The fear of a king *is* as the roaring of a lion: *whoso* provoketh him to anger [c]sinneth *against* his own soul.

3 [d]*It is* an honour for a man to cease from strife: but every fool will be meddling.

4 [e]The sluggard will not plough by reason of the [f]cold; [g]*therefore* shall he beg in harvest and *have* nothing.

5 [h]Counsel in the heart of man *is like* deep water: but a man of understanding will draw it out.

6 [i]Most men will proclaim every one his

own [k]goodness; but [l]a faithful man who can find?

7 [m]The just *man* walketh in his integrity: [n]his children *are* blessed after him.

A. M. cir. 3004
B. C. cir. 1000
Ante I. Olymp.
cir. 224
Ante U. C. cir.
247

8 [o]A king that sitteth in the throne of judgment scattereth away all evil with his eyes.

9 [p]Who can say, I have made my heart clean, I am pure from my sin?

10 [q]Divers [r]weights, *and* [s]divers measures, both of them *are* alike abomination to the LORD.

11 Even a child is [t]known by his doings, whether his work *be* pure, and whether *it be* right.

---

[a]Gen. ix. 21; chap. xxiii. 29, 30; Isa. xxviii. 7; Hos. iv. 11; [b]Chap. xvi. 14; xix. 12——[c]Chap. viii. 36——[d]Ch. xvii. 14——[e]Chap. x. 4; xix. 24——[f]Or, *winter*——[g]Ch. xix. 15——[h]Chap. xviii. 4——[i]Chap. xxv. 14; Matt. vi. 2; Luke xviii. 11——[k]Or, *bounty*——[l]1 Sam. xxii. 14; Psa. xii. 10; chap. xxviii. 20; Luke xviii. 8

[m]2 Cor. i. 12——[n]Psa. xxxvii. 26; cxii. 2——[o]Ver. 26 [p]1 Kings viii. 46; 2 Chron. vi. 36; Job xiv. 4; Psa. li. 5; Eccles. vii. 20; 1 Cor. iv. 4; 1 John i. 3——[q]Deut. xxv. 13, &c.; ver. 23; chap. xi. 1; xvi. 11; Mic. vi. 10, 11 [r]Heb. *A stone and a stone*——[s]Heb. *an ephah and an ephah*——[t]Matt. vii. 16

NOTES ON CHAP. XX

Verse 1. *Wine is a mocker*] It *deceives* by its *fragrance*, *intoxicates* by its *strength*, and renders the intoxicated *ridiculous*.

Strong drink] שכר *shechar*, any strong fermented liquor, whether of the *vine*, *date*, or *palm* species.

Verse 2. *The fear of a king*] Almost the same with chap. xix. 12, which see.

Verse 3. *It is an honour for a man*] The same sentiment as chap. xix. 11.

Verse 4. *The sluggard will not plough*] For other parts of this character, see the preceding chapter. It is seldom that there is a *season* of very cold weather in Palestine; very cold *days* sometimes occur, with wind, rain, and sleet. They begin their ploughing in the latter end of *September*, and sow their early wheat by the middle of *October*. And this is often the case in England itself. The meaning of the proverb is: the slothful man, under the pretence of unfavourable weather, neglects cultivating his land till the proper time is elapsed.

Verse 5. *Counsel in the heart of man*] Men of the deepest and most comprehensive minds are rarely apt, unsolicited, to join in any discourse, in which they might appear even to the greatest advantage; but a *man of understanding* will *elicit* this, by questions framed for the purpose, and thus *pump* up the salubrious waters from the deep and capacious well. The metaphor is fine and expressive.

Verse 6. *Most men will proclaim*] 𝕸𝖆𝖓𝖕 𝖒𝖊𝖓 𝖒𝖊𝖗𝖈𝖎𝖋𝖚𝖑 𝖇𝖊𝖓 𝖈𝖑𝖊𝖕𝖎𝖉: 𝖆 𝖋𝖊𝖎𝖙𝖍𝖋𝖚𝖑 𝖒𝖆𝖓 𝖋𝖔𝖗𝖘𝖔𝖙𝖍, 𝖜𝖍𝖔 𝖘𝖈𝖍𝖆𝖑 𝖋𝖎𝖓𝖉𝖊?—Old MS. Bible.

Verse 8. *A king that sitteth in the throne of*

judgment] Kings should see to the administration of the *laws*, as well as of the *state transactions*, of their kingdom. In the British constitution there is a *court* for the *king*, called the *King's Bench*, where he *should* sit, and where he is always *supposed* to be sitting. The *eyes*—the *presence*, of the monarch in such a place, *scatter evil*—he sees into the case himself, and gives right judgment, for he can have no *self-interest*. Corrupt judges, and falsifying counsellors, cannot stand before him; and the *villain* is too deeply struck with the *majesty* and state of the monarch, to *face out* iniquity before him.

Verse 9. *Who can say, I have made my heart clean*] No man. But thousands can testify that the blood of Jesus Christ has cleansed them from all unrighteousness. And he is *pure from his sin*, who is justified freely through the redemption that is in Jesus.

Verse 10. *Divers weights and divers measures*] 𝕬 𝖕𝖊𝖎𝖘𝖊 𝖆𝖓𝖉 𝖆 𝖕𝖊𝖎𝖘𝖊;—Old MS. Bible: from the French *pois*, weight. Hebrew: "A stone and a stone; an ephah and an ephah." One the *standard*, the other *below* it; one to *buy* with, the other to *sell* by.

Verse 11. *Even a child is known by his doings*] That is, in general terms, the *effect* shows the nature of the cause. "A childe is known by his conversation," says *Coverdale*. A child is easily detected when he has done evil; he immediately begins to excuse and vindicate himself, and profess his innocence, almost before accusation takes place. Some think the words should be understood, *every child will dissemble;* this amounts nearly to the meaning given above. But probably the principal thing

A. M. cir. 3004
B. C. cir. 1000
Ante I. Olymp.
cir. 224
Ante U. C. cir.
247

12 [u]The hearing ear, and the seeing eye, the LORD hath made even both of them.

13 [v]Love not sleep, lest thou come to poverty; open thine eyes, *and* thou shalt be satisfied with bread.

14 *It is* naught, *it is* naught, saith the buyer: but when he is gone his way, then he boasteth.

15 There is gold, and a multitude of rubies: but [w]the lips of knowledge *are* a precious jewel.

16 [x]Take his garment that is surety *for* a

stranger: and take a pledge of him for a strange woman.

A. M. cir. 3004
B. C. cir. 1000
Ante I. Olymp.
cir. 224
Ante U. C. cir.
247

17 [y]Bread [z]of deceit *is* sweet to a man; but afterwards his mouth shall be filled with gravel.

18 [a]*Every* purpose is established by counsel: [b]and with good advice make war.

19 [c]He that goeth about *as* a tale-bearer revealeth secrets: therefore meddle not with him [d]that [e]flattereth with his lips.

20 [f]Whoso curseth his father or his mother, [g]his [h]lamp shall be put out in obscure darkness.

---

[u]Exod. iv. 11; Psa. xciv. 9——[v]Chapter vi. 9; xii. 11; xix. 15; Rom. xii. 11——[w]Job xxviii. 12, 16, 17, 18, 19; chapter iii. 15; viii. 11——[x]Chapter xxii. 26, 27; xxxii. 13——[y]Chapter ix. 17——[z]Hebrew, *Bread of*

lying, or *falsehood*——[a]Chapter xv. 22; xxiv. 6 [b]Luke xiv. 31——[c]Chapter xi. 13——[d]Rom. xvi. 18 [e]Or, *enticeth*——[f]Exod. xxi. 17; Lev. xx. 9; Matt. xv. 4——[g]Job xviii. 5, 6; chapter xxiv. 20——[h]Or, *candle*

---

intended by the wise man is, that we may easily learn from the *child* what the *man* will be. In general, they give indications of those *trades* and *callings* for which they are adapted by nature. And, on the whole, we cannot go by a surer guide in preparing our children for future life, than by observing their early propensities. The future *engineer* is seen in the little *handicraftsman* of two years old. Many children are crossed in these early propensities to a particular calling, to *their* great prejudice, and the loss of their parents, as they seldom settle at, or succeed in, the business to which they are tied, and to which nature has given them no tendency. These infantine predilections to particular callings, we should consider as indications of Divine Providence, and its calling of them to that work for which they are peculiarly fitted.

Verse 12. *The hearing ear and the seeing eye*] Every *good* we possess comes from God; and we should neither use our *eyes*, nor our *ears*, nor *any thing* we possess, but in strict subserviency to his will.

Verse 13. *Love not sleep, lest thou come to poverty*] Sleep, indescribable in its nature, is an indescribable *blessing;* but how often is it turned into a *curse!* It is like *food;* a certain measure of it restores and invigorates exhausted nature; more than *that* oppresses and destroys life. A lover of sleep is a paltry, insignificant character.

Verse 14. It is *naught, it is naught, saith the buyer*] How apt are men to decry the goods they wish to purchase, in order that they may get them at a *cheaper rate;* and, when they have made their bargain and carried it *off,* boast to others at how much *less* than its *value* they have obtained it! Are such honest men? Is such knavery actionable? Can such be punished only in *another* world? St. Augustine tells us a pleasant story on this subject: A certain mountebank published, in the full theatre, that at the next entertainment he would *show to every man* present *what was in his heart.* The time came, and the concourse was immense; all waited, with deathlike silence, to hear what he would say to each. He stood up, and in a single sentence redeemed his pledge:—

VILI vultis EMERE, et CARO VENDERE.

"You all wish to BUY CHEAP, and SELL DEAR."

He was applauded; for every one felt it to be a description of his own heart, and was satisfied that all others were similar. "In quo dicto levissimi scenici omnes tamen conscientias invenerunt suas."—DE TRINITATE, lib. xiii., c. 3; OPER. vol. vii., col. 930.

Verse 15. *There is gold*] *Gold* is valuable, *silver* is valuable, and so are *jewels;* but the *teachings* of *sound knowledge* are more valuable than all.

Verse 16. *Take his garment that is surety for a stranger*] I suppose the meaning to be, If a stranger or unknown person become surety in a case, greater caution should be used, and such security taken from this *stranger* as would prevent him from running away from his engagements.

Verse 17. *Bread of deceit is sweet*] Property acquired by *falsehood, speculation,* &c., without labour, is pleasant to the unprincipled, slothful man; but there is a *curse* in it, and the issue will prove it.

Verse 18. *With good advice make war.*] Perhaps there is not a precept in this whole book so little regarded as this. Most of the *wars* that are undertaken are wars of injustice, ambition, aggrandizement, and caprice, which can have had no previous *good counsel.* A minister, who is perhaps neither a *good* nor a *great* man, counsels his king to make war; the *cabinet* must be brought into it, and a *sufficient number* out of the states of the kingdom gained over to support it. By and by, what was begun through *caprice* must be maintained through *necessity.* Places must be created, and offices must be filled with needy dependents, whose interest it may be to *protract the war,* till they get enough to pay their debts, and secure independence for life. And for these most important ends the blood of the country is spilled, and the treasures of the people exhausted! I have met with a fact precisely of this kind under the reign of Louis XIV.

Verse 20. *Whoso curseth his father*] Such persons were put to death under the law; see

A. M. cir. 3004
B. C. cir. 1000
Ante I. Olymp. cir. 224
Ante U. C. cir. 247

21 [i]An inheritance *may be* gotten hastily at the beginning; [k]but the end thereof shall not be blessed.

22 [l]Say not thou, I will recompense evil; *but* [m]wait on the LORD, and he shall save thee.

23 [n]Divers weights *are* an abomination unto the LORD; and [o]a false balance *is* not good.

24 [p]Man's goings *are* of the LORD; how can a man then understand his own way?

25 *It is* a snare to the man *who* devoureth *that which is* holy, and [q]after vows to make inquiry.

26 [r]A wise king scattereth the wicked, and bringeth the wheel over them.

27 [s]The spirit of man *is* the [t]candle of the LORD, searching all the inward parts of the belly.

28 [u]Mercy and truth preserve the king: and his throne is upholden by mercy.

29 The glory of young men *is* their strength: and [v]the beauty of old men *is* the gray head.

30 The blueness of a wound [w]cleanseth away evil: so *do* stripes the inward parts of the belly.

---

[i]Chap. xxviii. 20——[k]Hab. ii. 6——[l]Deut. xxxii. 35; chap. xvii. 13; xxiv. 29; Rom. xii. 17, 19; 1 Thess. v. 15; 1 Peter iii. 9——[m]2 Sam. xvi. 12——[n]Verse 10——[o]Heb. *balances of deceit*

[p]Psa. xxxvii. 23; chap. xvi. 9; Jer. x. 23——[q]Eccles. v. 4, 5——[r]Psa. ci. 5, &c.; ver. 8——[s]1 Cor. ii. 11——[t]Or, *lamp*——[u]Psa. ci. 1; chap. xxix. 14——[v]Ch. xvi. 31——[w]Heb. is *a purging medicine against evil*

Exod. xxi. 17; Lev. xx. 9; and here it is said, Their *lamp shall be put out*—they shall have no *posterity;* God shall cut them off both *root* and *branch.*

Verse 21. *An inheritance—gotten hastily*] Gotten by *speculation;* by *lucky hits;* not in the fair *progressive* way of *traffic,* in which money has its *natural increase.* All such inheritances are short-lived; God's blessing is not in them, because they are not the produce of *industry;* and they lead to *idleness, pride, fraud,* and *knavery.* A speculation in trade is a public nuisance and curse. How many honest men have been ruined by such!

Verse 22. *I will recompense evil*] Wait on the Lord; judgment is his, and his judgments are sure. In the mean time pray for the conversion of your enemy.

Verse 24. *Man's goings* are *of the Lord*] He, by his providence, governs all the great concerns of the world. Man often traverses these operations; but he does it to his own damage. An old writer quaintly says: "They who will carve for themselves shall cut their fingers."

Verse 25. Who *devoureth* that which is *holy*] It is a sin to take that which belongs to *God,* his *worship,* or his *work,* and devote it to one's own use.

And after vows to make inquiry.] That is, if a man be *inwardly* making a *rash vow,* the fitness or unfitness, the necessity, expediency, and propriety of the thing should be first carefully considered. But how foolish to make the vow first, and afterwards to inquire whether it was right in the sight of God to do it! This equally condemns all rash and inconsiderate conduct. My old MS. Bible translates, **Falling is of men often to bowen to seyntis, and after, the bowis is agen drawen.** Is it possible that *Wiclif* could have translated this verse thus? as it strongly countenances *vows to* and *invocations of saints.*

Verse 26. *Bringeth the wheel over them.*] He threshes them in his anger, as the *wheel does the grain on the threshing-floor.* Every one knows that grain was separated from its husks, in Palestine, by the feet of the oxen trampling among the sheaves, or bringing a rough-shod wheel over them. Asiatic kings often threshed their people, to bring out their property; but this is not what is intended here.

Verse 27. *The spirit of man* is *the candle of the Lord*] God has given to every man a *mind,* which *he so enlightens by his own Spirit,* that the man knows how to distinguish good from evil; and *conscience,* which springs from this, searches the inmost recesses of the soul.

Verse 28. *Mercy and truth preserve the king*] These are the brightest jewels in the royal crown; and those kings who are most governed by them have the stablest government.

Verse 29. *The glory of young men* is *their strength*] Scarcely any young man affects to be wise, learned, &c.; but all delight to *show their strength* and to be *reputed strong. Agility,* one evidence of strength, they particularly *affect;* and hence their various trials of strength and fleetness in public exercises.

And the beauty of old men is *the gray head.*] They no longer affect *strength* and *agility,* but they affect *wisdom, experience, prudent counsels,* &c., and are fond of being *reputed wise,* and of having respect paid to their *understanding* and *experience.*

Verse 30. *The blueness of a wound*] חברות *chabburoth,* from חבר *chabar,* to *unite,* to *join together.* Does it not refer to the cicatrice of a wound when, in its healing, the two lips are brought *together?* By this union the wound is *healed;* and by the previous discharge the lacerated ends of fibres and blood-vessels are purged away. So *stripes,* though they hurt for the time, become the means of *correcting* and *discharging* the *moral evil* of the inmost soul, the vice of the *heart,* the *easily-besetting sin.*

In this chapter, verses *fourteen* to *nineteen,* inclusive, are wanting in the *Septuagint* and *Arabic;* and the *tenth, eleventh, twelfth,* and *thirteenth,* come in after the *twenty-second.* It is difficult to account for these variations, unless they were occasioned by the change of leaves in MSS.

CHAPTER XXI

The king's heart is in the hand of God. We should practise mercy and justice. The lying tongue. The quarrelsome woman. The punishment of the wicked. The uncharitable. The private gift. The happiness of the righteous. The wicked a ransom for the righteous. The treasures of the wise. He who guards his tongue. Desire of the sluggard. The false witness. Salvation is of the Lord.

A. M. cir. 3004
B. C. cir. 1000
Ante I. Olymp.
cir. 224
Ante U. C. cir.
247

THE king's heart *is* in the hand of the LORD, *as* the rivers of water: he turneth it whithersoever he will.

2 ªEvery way of a man *is* right in his own eyes: ᵇbut the LORD pondereth the hearts.

3 ᶜTo do justice and judgment *is* more acceptable to the LORD than sacrifice.

4 ᵈA ᵉhigh look, and a proud heart, *and* ᶠthe ploughing of the wicked, *is* sin.

5 ᵍThe thoughts of the diligent *tend* only to plenteousness; but of every one *that is* hasty only to want.

6 ʰThe getting of treasures by a lying tongue *is* a vanity tossed to and fro of them that seek death.

A. M. cir. 3004
B. C. cir. 1000
Ante I. Olymp.
cir. 224
Ante U. C. cir.
247

7 The robbery of the wicked shall ¹destroy them; because they refuse to do judgment.

8 The way of man *is* froward and strange: but *as for* the pure, his work *is* right.

9 ᵏ*It is* better to dwell in a corner of the housetop, than with ¹a brawling woman in ᵐa wide house.

10 ⁿThe soul of the wicked desireth evil: his neighbour °findeth no favour in his eyes.

11 ᵖWhen the scorner is punished, the simple is made wise: and when the wise is

---

ªChap. xvi. 2——ᵇCh. xxiv. 12; Luke xvi. 15——ᶜ1 Sam. xv. 22; Psa. l. 8; chap. xv. 8; Isa. i. 11, &c.; Hos. vi. 6; Mic. vi. 7, 8——ᵈChap. vi. 17——ᵉHeb. *Haughtiness of eyes*——ᶠOr, *the light of the wicked*——ᵍChap. x. 4; xiii. 4

ʰCh. x. 2; xiii. 11; xx. 21; 2 Pet. ii. 3——ⁱHeb. *saw them*, or *dwell with them*——ᵏVer. 19; ch. xix. 13; xxv. 24; xxvii. 15——¹Heb. *a woman of contentions*——ᵐHeb. *a house of society*——ⁿJames iv. 5——°Heb. *is not favoured*——ᵖChap. xix. 25

NOTES ON CHAP. XXI

Verse 1. *The king's heart is in the hand of the Lord*] The Lord is the only ruler of princes. He alone can govern and direct their counsels. But there is an allusion here to the Eastern method *of watering their lands.* Several canals are dug from one stream; and by opening a particular sluice, the husbandman can direct a stream to whatever part he please: so the king's heart, wherever it turns; i. e., to whomsoever he is disposed to show favour. As the land is enriched with the streams employed in irrigation; so is the favourite of the king, by the royal bounty: and God can induce the king to give that bounty to whomsoever he will. See *Harmer.*

Verse 2. *The Lord pondereth the hearts.*] Every man feels strongly attached to his own opinions, modes of acting, &c.; and though he will not easily give up any thing to the judgment of a neighbour, whom he will naturally consider at least as fallible as himself, yet he should consider that the unerring eye of God is upon him; and he should endeavour to see that what he does is acceptable in the eye of his Maker and Judge.

Verse 3. *To do justice and judgment*] The words of Samuel to Saul. See note on 1 Sam. xv. 23.

Verse 4. *A high look*] The evidence of pride, self-conceit, and vanity. *A proud heart*, from which the *high look*, &c., come.

And *the ploughing*] נֵר *ner, lucerna*, the *lamp*, the prosperity and posterity of the wicked; *is sin*—it is evil in the *seed*, and evil in the *root*, evil in the *branch*, and evil in the *fruit*. They are full of sin themselves, and what they do is sinful.

Verse 6. *Of them that seek death*] Instead of מבקשי *mebakshey*, "them that seek," several MSS., some ancient editions, with *Symmachus*, the *Septuagint, Vulgate*, and *Arabic*, have מקשי *mokeshey*, the *snares*. He who gets treasures by a lying tongue, pursues vanity into the snares of death. Our common translation may be as good. But he who, by the snares of his *tongue*, endeavours to *buy* and *sell* to the best advantage, is *pursuing what is empty in itself;* and he is *ensnared* by *death*, while he is attempting to *ensnare* others.

Verse 7. *The robbery of the wicked*] The wicked shall be *terrified* and *ruined* by the means they use to aggrandize themselves. And as they refuse to do judgment, they shall have judgment without mercy.

Verse 9. *In a corner of the housetop*] A shed raised on the *flat roof:—a wide house;* בית חבר *beith chaber*, "a house of fellowship;" what we should call a *lodging-house*, or a *house occupied by several families.* This was usual in the *East*, as well as in the *West*. Some think a *house of festivity* is meant: hence my old MS. Bible has, **the house and feste.**

Verse 11. *When the scorner is punished*] When those who mock at religion, blaspheme against its Author, and endeavour to poison society, and disturb the peace of the community by their false doctrine, meet with that degree of punishment which their crimes, as far as they affect the public peace, deserve; then *the simple*, who were either led away, or in danger of being led away, by their pernicious doctrines, *are made wise.* And when those thus *made wise* are *instructed* in the important truths ·which have been decried by those unprincipled men, then they receive knowledge; and one

A. M. cir. 3004
B. C. cir. 1000
Ante I. Olymp.
cir. 224
Ante U. C. cir.
247

instructed, he receiveth knowledge.

12 The righteous *man* wisely considereth the house of the wicked: *but God* overthroweth the wicked for *their* wickedness.

13 ᑫWhoso stoppeth his ears at the cry of the poor, he also shall cry himself, but shall not be heard.

14 ʳA gift in secret pacifieth anger: and a reward in the bosom strong wrath.

15 *It is* joy to the just to do judgment: ˢbut destruction *shall be* to the workers of iniquity.

16 The man that wandereth out of the way of understanding shall remain in the congregation of the dead.

17 He that loveth ᵗpleasure *shall be* a poor man: he that loveth wine and oil shall not be rich.

18 ᵘThe wicked *shall be* a ransom for the righteous, and the transgressor for the upright.

19 ᵛ*It is* better to dwell ʷin the wilderness,

than with a contentious and an angry woman.

A. M. cir. 3004
B. C. cir. 1000
Ante I. Olymp.
cir. 224
Ante U. C. cir.
247

20 ˣ*There is* treasure to be desired and oil in the dwelling of the wise; but a foolish man spendeth it up.

21 ʸHe that followeth after righteousness and mercy findeth life, righteousness, and honour.

22 ᶻA wise *man* scaleth the city of the mighty, and casteth down the strength of the confidence thereof.

23 ᵃWhoso keepeth his mouth and his tongue keepeth his soul from troubles.

24 Proud *and* haughty scorner *is* his name, who dealeth ᵇin proud wrath.

25 ᶜThe desire of the slothful killeth him; for his hands refuse to labour.

26 He coveteth greedily all the day long: but the ᵈrighteous giveth and spareth not.

27 ᵉThe sacrifice of the wicked *is* abomination: how much more, *when* he bringeth ᶠit with a wicked mind?

ᑫMatt. vii. 2; xviii. 30, &c.; James ii. 13——ʳCh. xvii. 8, 23; xviii. 16——ˢCh. x. 29——ᵗOr, *sport*——ᵘCh. xi. 8; Isa. xliii. 3, 4——ᵛVer. 9——ʷHeb. *in the land of the desert*——ˣPsa. cxii. 3; Matt. xxv. 3, 4——ʸCh. xv. 9; Matt. v. 6

ᶻEccles. ix. 14, &c.——ᵃChap. xii. 13; xiii. 3; xviii. 21; James iii. 2——ᵇHeb. *in the wrath of pride*——ᶜChap. xiii. 4——ᵈPsa. xxxvii. 26; cxii. 9——ᵉPsa. l. 9; chap. xv. 8; Isa. lxvi. 3; Jeremiah vi. 20; Amos v. 22——ᶠHeb. *in wickedness*

---

such public example is made a blessing to thousands. But only *blasphemy* against *God* and the *Bible* should be thus punished. Private opinion the state should not meddle with.

Verse 12. *The righteous* man *wisely considereth*] This verse is understood as implying the *pious concern* of a righteous man, for a wicked family, whom he endeavours by his *instructions* to bring into the way of knowledge and peace.

Verse 13. *Whoso stoppeth his ears*] See the conduct of *the priest* and *Levite* to the man who *fell among thieves;* and let every man learn from this, that he who shuts his ear against the cry of the poor, shall have the ear of God shut against his cry. The words are quite plain; there is no difficulty here.

Verse 16. *The* man once enlightened, *that wandereth out of the way of understanding,* in which he *had* walked, *shall remain*—have a permanent residence—*in the congregation of the dead;* רפאים *rephaim, the lost;* either separate spirits in general, or rather the *assembly of separate spirits,* which had fallen from primitive rectitude; and shall not be restored to the Divine favour; particularly those sinners who were destroyed by the deluge. This passage intimates that those called *rephaim* are in a state of conscious existence. It is difficult to assign the true meaning of the word in several places where it occurs: but it seems to mean the state of separate spirits, i. e., of those separated from their bodies, and awaiting the judgment of the great day: but the *congregation* may also include the *fallen angels.* My old MS. Bible translates, 𝔗𝔥𝔢 𝔪𝔞𝔫 𝔱𝔥𝔞𝔱 𝔢𝔯𝔯𝔦𝔱𝔥 𝔣𝔯𝔬 𝔱𝔥𝔢 𝔴𝔢𝔦 𝔬𝔣 𝔡𝔬𝔠𝔱𝔯𝔦𝔫𝔢, 𝔦𝔫 𝔱𝔥𝔢 𝔣𝔢𝔩𝔬𝔴𝔰𝔠𝔥𝔦𝔭 𝔬𝔣 𝔤𝔢𝔞𝔫𝔱𝔦𝔰 𝔰𝔠𝔥𝔞𝔩 𝔴𝔬𝔫𝔫𝔢𝔫.

Verse 17. *He that loveth pleasure*] That follows gaming, fowling, hunting, coursing, &c., when he should be attending to the culture of the fields, *shall be a poor man;* and, I may safely add, shall be so deservedly poor, as to have none to pity him.

Verse 18. *The wicked* shall be *a ransom for the righteous*] God often in his judgments cuts off the *wicked,* in order to prevent them from destroying the *righteous.* And in general, we find that the wicked fall into the traps and pits they have digged for the righteous.

Verse 22. *A wise* man *scaleth the city of the mighty*] Wisdom is in many respects preferable to strength, even in the case of defence. See what skill does in the fortification and reduction of strong places.

Verse 25. *The desire of the slothful killeth him*] He desires to eat, drink, and be clothed: but as he does *not labour,* hence he dies with this desire in his heart, envying those who possess plenty through their labour and industry. Hence he is said to *covet greedily all the day long,* ver. 26, while the *righteous,* who has been *laborious* and diligent, has enough to *eat,* and some to *spare.*

Verse 27. When *he bringeth it with a wicked mind?*] If such a person even bring the sacrifices and *offerings* which God *requires,* they are an abomination to him, because the man is *wicked;* and if such offerings be *imperfect* in themselves, or of goods *ill-gotten,* or offered by *constraint of custom,* &c., they are doubly abominable.

A. M. cir. 3004
B. C. cir. 1000
Ante I. Olymp.
cir. 224
Ante U. C. cir.
247

28 ᵍA ʰfalse witness shall perish: but the man that heareth speaketh constantly.

29 A wicked man hardeneth his face: but *as for* the upright, he ⁱdirecteth his way.

ᵍChap. xix. 5, 9——ʰHeb. *A witness of lies*——ⁱOr, *considereth*——ᵏIsa. viii. 9, 10; Jer. ix. 23; Acts v. 39

Verse 29. *He directeth his way*] Instead of יכין *yachin*, he *directeth*, upwards of *fifty* of *Kennicott's* and *De Rossi's* MSS., several ancient *editions*, with some of the *versions*, read יבין *yabin*, he *understands;* and because he *understands* his way, he is able to *direct* himself in walking in it.

Verse 31. *The horse is prepared against the day of battle*] Horses were not used among the Jews before the time of *Solomon*. There was a Divine command against them, Deut. xvii. 16;

30 ᵏ*There is* no wisdom nor understanding nor counsel against the LORD.

31 ˡThe horse *is* prepared against the day of battle: but ᵐsafetyⁿ *is* of the LORD.

A. M. cir. 3004
B. C. cir. 1000
Ante I. Olymp.
cir. 224
Ante U. C. cir.
247

ˡPsalm xx. 7; xxxiii. 17; Isa. xxxi. 1——ᵐPsalm iii. 8
ⁿOr, *victory*

---

but Solomon transgressed it; see 1 Kings x. 29. But he here allows that a horse is a vain thing for safety; and that however strong and well appointed *cavalry* may be, still *safety, escape,* and *victory,* are of the Lord. Among the ancient Asiatics, the *horse* was used *only for war; oxen* laboured in the *plough* and *cart;* the *ass* and the *camel* carried *backloads;* and *mules* and *asses* served for *riding*. We often give the credit of a victory to *man*, when they who consider the circumstances see that it came from *God*.

CHAPTER XXII

A good reputation. The rich and the poor. The idle. Good habits formed in infancy. Injustice and its effects. The providence of God. The lewd woman. The necessity of timely correction. Exhortation to wisdom. Rob not the poor. Be not the companion of the froward. Avoid suretyship. Be honest. The industrious shall be favoured.

A. M. cir. 3004
B. C. cir. 1000
Ante I. Olymp.
cir. 224
Anti U. C. cir.
247

A ᵃ*GOOD* name *is* rather to be chosen than great riches, *and* ᵇloving favour rather than silver and gold.

2 ᶜThe rich and poor meet together: ᵈthe LORD *is* the Maker of them all.

3 ᵉA prudent *man* forseeth

A. M. cir. 3004
B. C. cir. 1000
Ante I. Olymp.
cir. 224
Ante U. C. cir.
247

ᵃEccles. vii. 1——ᵇOr, *favour is better than*, &c.——ᶜCh. xxix. 13; 1 Cor. xii. 21

ᵈJob xxxi. 15; chapter xiv. 31——ᵉChapter xiv. 16; xxvii. 12

NOTES ON CHAP. XXII

Verse 1. *A good name*] שם *shem*, a *name*, put for reputation, credit, fame. Used nearly in the same way that we use it: "He has got a name;" "his name stands high;" for "He is a man of credit and reputation." טבא *toba*, καλον, ܚܡܘܕ *hamood*, and *bonum*, are added by the *Chaldee, Septuagint, Arabic,* and *Vulgate,* all signifying *good* or *excellent*.

Is *rather to be chosen than great riches*] Because character will support a man in many circumstances; and there are many *rich* men that have *no name:* but the *word* of the man of character will go farther than all their riches.

Verse 2. *The rich and poor meet together*] עשיר *ashir*, the *opulent*, whether in money, land, or property; רש *rash*, the man that is destitute of these, and lives by his labour, whether a handicraftsman, or one that tills the ground. In the order of God, the rich and the poor live together, and are mutually helpful to each other. Without the *poor*, the *rich* could not be supplied with the articles which they consume; for the poor include all the labouring classes of society: and without the *rich*, the poor could get no *vent* for the *produce* of their *labour*, nor, in many cases, *labour* itself. The poor have more *time* to labour than the mere necessaries of life require; their *extra* time is employed in providing a multitude of things which are called the *superfluities* of life, and

which the *rich* especially consume. *All* the *poor man's time* is thus employed; and he is *paid* for his *extra labour* by the rich. The *rich* should not despise the *poor*, without whom he can neither have his *comforts*, nor *maintain* his *state*. The poor should not envy the *rich*, without whom he could neither get employment, nor the *necessaries of life*.

The Lord is the Maker of them all.] Both the *states* are in the order of God's *providence*, and both are *equally* important in his sight. Merely considered as *men*, God loves the *simple artificer* or *labourer* as much as he does the *king;* though the *office* of the latter, because of its entering into the plan of his government of the world, is of infinitely greatly consequence than the *trade* of the *poor artificer*. Neither should *despise* the *other;* neither should *envy* the *other*. Both are useful; both important; both absolutely necessary *to each other's welfare* and *support;* and both are accountable to God for the *manner* in which they acquit themselves in those *duties of life* which God has respectively assigned them. The *abject poor*—those who are destitute of *health* and the *means of life*—God in effect lays at the *rich man's door*, that by his *superfluities* they may be supported. How wise is that ordinance wnich has made the *rich* and the *poor!* Pity it were not better understood!

Verse 3. *A prudent* man *forseeth the evil*] God in mercy has denied man the knowledge of

---

A. M. cir. 3004
B. C. cir. 1000
Ante I. Olymp.
cir. 224
Ante U. C. cir.
247

the evil, and hideth himself: but the simple pass on, and are punished.

4 [f]By [g]humility *and* the fear of the Lord *are* riches, honour, and life.

5 [h]Thorns *and* snares *are* in the way of the froward: [i]he that doth keep his soul shall be far from them.

6 [k]Train [l]up a child [m]in the way he should go: and when he is old, he will not depart from it.

7 [n]The rich ruleth over the poor, and the

borrower *is* servant [o]to the lender.

8 [p]He that soweth iniquity shall reap vanity: [q]and the rod of his anger shall fail.

9 [r]He [s]that hath a bountiful eye shall be blessed; for he giveth of his bread to the poor.

10 [t]Cast out the scorner, and contention shall go out; yea, strife and reproach shall cease.

11 [u]He that loveth pureness of heart, [v]*for* the grace of his lips the king *shall be* his friend.

12 The eyes of the Lord preserve know-

A. M. cir. 3004
B. C. cir. 1000
Ante I. Olymp.
cir. 224
Ante U. C. cir.
247

---

[f]Psa. cxii. 3; Matt. vi. 33——[g]Or, *The reward of humility,* &c.——[h]Ch. xv. 19——[i]1 John v. 18——[k]Eph. vi. 4; 2 Tim. iii. 15——[l]Or, *Catechise*——[m]Heb. *in his way*——[n]James ii. 6——[o]Heb. *to the man that lendeth*

[p]Job iv. 8; Hos. x. 13——[q]Or, *and with the rod of his anger he shall be consumed*——[r]2 Cor. ix. 6——[s]Heb. *Good of eye*——[t]Gen. xxi. 9, 10; Psa. ci. 5——[u]Psa. ci. 6; chap. xvi. 13——[v]Or, *and hath grace in his lips*

---

futurity; but in its place he has given him *hope* and *prudence.* By *hope* he is continually expecting and anticipating *good;* by *prudence* he derives and employs *means* to secure it. His *experience* shows him that there are many *natural evils* in a current state, the course of which he can neither stem nor divert: *prudence* shows him beforehand the means he may use to step out of their way, and *hide* himself. The *simple*—the inexperienced, headstrong, giddy, and foolish—rush on in the *career of hope,* without *prudence* to regulate, chastise, and guide it; thus they commit many faults, make many miscarriages, and suffer often in consequence; and the commission of crimes leads to punishment.

Verse 5. *Thorns* and *snares*] Various difficulties, trials, and sufferings.

Verse 6. *Train up a child in the way he should go*] The Hebrew of this clause is curious: חנך לנער על פי דרכו *chanoch lannaar al pi darco,* "Initiate the child at the opening (the mouth) of his path." When he comes to the *opening of the way of life,* being able to walk alone, and to choose; stop at this entrance, and begin a series of instructions, how he is to conduct himself in every *step* he takes. Show him the *duties,* the *dangers,* and the *blessings* of the path; give him directions *how* to *perform* the *duties,* how to *escape* the *dangers,* and how to *secure* the *blessings,* which all lie before him. Fix these on his mind by *daily inculcation,* till their *impression* is become *indelible;* then lead him to *practice* by slow and almost imperceptible degrees, till each *indelible impression* becomes a *strongly radicated habit.* Beg incessantly the blessing of God on all this teaching and discipline; and then you have obeyed the injunction of the wisest of men. Nor is there any likelihood that such *impressions* shall ever be effaced, or that such *habits* shall ever be destroyed.

חנך *chanac,* which we translate *train up* or *initiate,* signifies also *dedicate;* and is often used for the *consecrating* any thing, house, or person, to the service of God. *Dedicate,* therefore, in the first instance, your *child* to God; and *nurse, teach,* and *discipline* him as God's child, whom he has intrusted to your care. These things observed, and illustrated by your own conduct, the child (you have God's word

for it) will never depart from the path of life. *Coverdale* translates the passage thus: "Yf thou teachest a childe what waye he shoulde go, he shall not leave it when he is olde." *Coverdale's* Bible, for generally giving the *true sense* of a passage, and in *elegant language* for the time, has no equal in any of the translations which have followed since. Horace's maxim is nearly like that of Solomon:—

Fingit equum tenera docilem cervice magister
Ire viam, quam monstrat eques; venaticus, ex
    quo
Tempore cervinam pellem latravit in aula,
Militat in sylvis catulus. Nunc adbibe puro
Pectore verba, puer; nunc te melioribus offer.
Quo semel est imbuta recens, servabit odorem
Testa diu.   Hor. Ep. lib. i., ep. 2, ver. 64.

"The docile *colt* is form'd with *gentle skill*
To *move obedient* to his *rider's will.*
In the *loud hall* the *hound* is taught to bay
The *buckskin trail'd,* then challenges his prey
Through the *wild woods.* Thus, in your *hour*
    of youth
From *pure instruction quaff the words of*
    truth:
The *odours* of the wine that *first* shall stain
The *virgin vessel,* it shall *long retain.*"
                      Francis.

Verse 7. *The rich ruleth over the poor*] So it is in the order of God, and may be a blessing to *both.*

Verse 8. *He that soweth iniquity*] The *crop* must be according to the *seed.* If a man sow *thistle seed,* is it likely he shall reap *wheat?* If he sow to the *flesh,* shall he not of the flesh reap *destruction?*

Verse 9. *A bountiful eye*] One that disposes him to help all that he sees to be in want; the *bountiful eye* means the *bountiful heart;* for the *heart* looks through the *eye.* The *merciful heart,* even when the *hand* has little or nothing to give, shall be blessed of the Lord.

Verse 11. *He that loveth pureness of heart*] Who aims to be what God would have him to be —the King of kings *shall be his Friend.* There is no class of men that value *uprightness* more than *kings;* as none stand so much in need of it in their *servants.*

Verse 12. *The eyes of the Lord*—(the Divine

A. M. cir. 3004
B. C. cir. 1000
Ante I. Olymp.
cir. 224
Ante U. C. cir.
247 ledge, and he overthroweth ʷthe words of the transgressor.

13 ˣThe slothful *man* saith, *There is* a lion without, I shall be slain in the streets.

14 ʸThe mouth of strange women *is* a deep pit: ᶻhe that is abhorred of the Lᴏʀᴅ shall fall therein.

15 Foolishness *is* bound in the heart of a child: *but* ᵃthe rod of correction shall drive it far from him.

16 He that oppresseth the poor A. M. cir. 3004
B. C. cir. 1000
Ante I. Olymp.
cir. 224
Ante U. C. cir.
247 to increase his *riches, and* he that giveth to the rich, *shall* surely *come* to want.

17 Bow down thine ear, and hear the words of the wise, and apply thine heart unto my knowledge.

18 For *it is* a pleasant thing if thou keep them ᵇwithin thee; they shall withal be fitted in thy lips.

19 That thy trust may be in the Lᴏʀᴅ, I

ʷOr, *the matters*——ˣChap. xxvi. 13——ʸChap. ii. 16; v. 3; vii. 5; xxiii. 27

ᶻEccles. vii. 26——ᵃCh. xiii. 24; xix. 18; xxiii. 13, 14; xxix. 15, 17——ᵇHeb. *in thy belly*

---

providence) *preserve knowledge.*] This providence has been wonderfully manifested in *preserving the sacred oracles,* and in *preserving many ancient authors,* which have been of great use to the *civil interests of man.*

Verse 13. *The slothful* man *saith,* There is *a lion without*] But *why* does he say so? Because he is a *slothful* man. Remove his slothfulness, and these imaginary difficulties and dangers will be no more. He will not *go abroad to work* in the fields, because he thinks there is a *lion in the way;* he will not *go out* into the *town* for employment, as he fears to be *assassinated* in the *streets!* From both these circumstances he seeks total cessation from *activity.*

Verse 14. *The mouth of strange women* is a *deep pit*] In chap. xxiii. 27, he says, A *whore* is a DEEP DITCH, and a *strange woman is a* NARROW PIT. The allusions in these *three* places are too plain to be misunderstood. Virgil's hell has been adduced in illustration:—

———————*Sate sanguine Divum,*
Tros Anchisiade, facilis descensus Averni;
Noctes atque dies patet atri janua Ditis:
Sed revocare gradum, superasque *evadere ad auras,*
Hoc ᴏᴘᴜꜱ; hic ʟᴀʙᴏʀ *est.* Pauci *quos ærquus amavit*
Jupiter, aut ardens evexit ad æthera virtus,
Dis geniti potuere.
            Vɪʀɢ. *Æn.* lib. vi., ver. 125.

"O glorious prince of brave Anchises' line!
Great godlike hero! sprung from seed divine,
Smooth lies the road to Pluto's gloomy shade;
And *hell's black gates* for ever *stand display'd:*
But 'tis a long unconquerable pain,
To climb to these *ethereal realms* again.
The choice-selected few, whom favouring Jove,
Or their own virtue, rais'd to heaven above,
From these *dark realms emerged again to day;*
The *mighty sons of gods,* and only *they.*
            PITT.

Verse 16. *He that oppresseth the poor*] He who, in order to obtain the favour of the *rich* and *great,* either *robs* or *cheats* the *poor,* to make those men *presents;* or gives *in presents* to them, for the sake of *honour* and *reputation,* what he should have given to the *poor, shall surely* come to *want.*

Verse 17. *Bow down thine ear*] From this to the end of ver. 21 are contained, not *proverbs,* but *directions* how to *profit* by that which *wisdom* has already delivered; the *nature* of the instruction, and the *end* for which it was given.

I shall give a paraphrase of this very important passage:—

I. Solomon addresses his pupils on the use of his past teachings. See on ver. 6.

1. The *wise* man speaks; and all his *words,* not merely his *sentiments,* are to be carefully heard.

2. He speaks *knowledge*—gives *doctrines* true in themselves, and confirmed by *observation* and *experience.*

3. These are to be *heard* with *humility* and deep *attention:* "Bow down thine ear."

4. They must not only be *heard,* but *meditated* and *pondered:* "Apply thine heart to my knowledge."

Verse 18. *For* it is *a pleasant thing if thou keep them within thee*]

II. The pleasure and profit which may be derived from an attentive hearing.

1. They should be *laid up in the heart*—stored, treasured up *within thee.*

2. This will yield high *satisfaction* and *happiness* to the soul: "For *it is* a pleasant thing if thou keep them within thee."

3. The man who thus attends to the teachings of wisdom shall gain an *experimental* knowledge of them, so as to be able to speak of them *suitably, pertinently* and *persuasively:* "They shall withal be fitted in thy lips."

Verse 19. *That thy trust may be in the Lord, I have made known, &c.*]

III. The END for which the wise man gives these instructions:—

1. "That thy trust may be in the Lord." That thou mayest acknowledge Hɪᴍ as the *Fountain* of all good; and refer every thing to *him.*

2. That this end may be *accomplished,* the instructions are *specific* and *particular:* "I have made known to thee, even to thee."

3. And this has not only been done in times past, "I have made known:" but even in the *present,* "I have made known this day!"

IV. An *appeal* is made to the person himself relative to the *matter* and *importance* of the teaching.

1. "Have I not written to thee excellent things;" שלשים *shalishim,* literally *threefold, thrice,* in *three different ways;* which some think refers to his three books:—1. *Canticles.* 2. *Koheleth,* or Ecclesiastes. And 3. *Proverbs.*

A. M. cir. 3004
B. C. cir. 1000
Ante I. Olymp.
cir. 224
Ante U. C. cir.
247

have made known to thee this day, ^ceven to thee.

20 Have not I written to thee ^dexcellent things in counsels and knowledge,

21 ^eThat I might make thee know the certainty of the words of truth: ^fthat thou mightest answer the words of truth ^gto them that send unto thee?

22 ^hRob not the poor, because he *is* poor: ⁱneither oppress the afflicted in the gate:

23 ^kFor the LORD will plead their cause, and spoil the soul of those that spoiled them.

24 Make no friendship with an angry man; and with a furious man thou shalt not go:

25 Lest thou learn his ways, and get a snare to thy soul.

26 ^lBe not thou *one* of them that strike hands, *or* of them that are sureties for debts.

27 If thou hast nothing to pay, why should

A. M. cir. 3004
B. C. cir. 1000
Ante I. Olymp.
cir. 224
Ante U. C. cir.
247

---

^cOr, trust *thou also*——^dChapter viii. 6——^eLuke i. 3, 4——^f1 Pet. iii. 15——^gOr, *to those that send thee* ^hExod. xxiii. 6; Job xxxi. 16, 21; Isa. x. 2; xvii. 14

ⁱZech. vii. 10; Mal. iii. 5——^k1 Sam. xxiv. 12; xxv. 39; Psa. xii. 5; xxxv. 1, 10; lxviii. 5; cxl. 12; ch. xxiii. 11; Jer. li. 36——^lChap. vi. 1; xi. 15

Others, understanding it of the voice of Divine wisdom, suppose the *three* grand divisions of the sacred oracles are intended; viz., 1. The *Law;* 2. The *Prophets;* and 3. The *Hagiographa.* And others interpret it of the *three* grand intellectual sciences:—1. *Morality*, or *Ethics.* 2. *Natural Philosophy*, or *Physics.* 3. *Theology*, or the science of *Divine things* as reported in the Scriptures. But Solomon's books of *Natural Philosophy* are lost.

And lastly, some of the *rabbins* and some Christians find in these *shalishim* the *three senses* of Scripture: 1. *Literal;* 2. *Figurative;* and 3. *Allegorical.*

After all, as we know the term *thrice* was used as the term *seven*, a *certain* number for an *uncertain*, (see Amos i. 11; 2 Cor. xii. 8,) it *may* mean no more here than, *I have written to thee often.* But perhaps it is safer to apply it to the *Scriptures*, and the excellent *doctrines* they contain: for שלשים *shalishim* signifies also *excellent, princely things;* things which become a *king to speak.* Indeed, it would not be difficult to prove that there is not one important *art* or *science* which is not alluded to in the Holy Scriptures, and used to illustrate and inculcate heavenly truths.

2. These *excellent, princely,* or *threefold teachings*, consist of two grand parts: 1. COUNSELS, מעצות *moetsoth, from* יעץ *yaats*, to give *advice, counsel,* or *information.* These (1) show thee what thou shouldst *know;* and (2) *advise* thee what thou shouldst do. 2. KNOWLEDGE, דעת *daath*, from ידע *yada*, to perceive, or *feel* by means of the senses and *internal perception;* viz., what should be *felt, experienced, known to be true by mental perception*, and by their *influence* on the *heart* and *affections.*

V. All this is done to give the pupil the *fullest satisfaction*, and most plenary *evidence* concerning the *truths* of God.

Verse 21. *That I might make thee know the certainty of the words of truth*]

1. These are words or doctrines of *truth:* 1. They are true in themselves. 2. Come from the God of truth. 3. Are truly *fulfilled* to all that believe.

2. These words of truth are *certain*, קשט *koshet*, they are not of dubious or difficult interpretation; they *point directly* to the great end for which God gave them; they *promise*, and they are *fulfilled.* He who pleads them by

faith, receives their *accomplishment* in the spirit and power of Divine love. The Scriptures, as far as they concern the salvation of the soul, are to be *experimentally* understood; and, by this experimental knowledge, every believer has the *witness in himself*, and knows the *certainty* of the words of truth.

VI. What we know ourselves to be true, and of infinite importance to the welfare of men in general, we should carefully proclaim and witness, that they also may believe.

That thou mightest answer the words of truth] 1. When the doctrine of salvation is preached, there will be many *inquirers.* What is this doctrine? Have any persons received these blessings—the remission of sins, witness of the Holy Spirit, purification of the heart, &c., &c.? *Who* are they? What are the collateral arguments that prove these things, and show us that you have not misapprehended the meaning of these Scriptures? 2. Inquiries of this kind should meet with the *speediest* and most distinct *answers;* and the *doctrines* of *truth* should be *supported* and *illustrated* with the *words of truth.* "That thou mightest answer the words of truth to them that send unto thee."

Verse 22. *Neither oppress the afflicted in the gate*] In judgment let the poor have a fair hearing; and let him not be borne down because he is *poor.* The reader has often seen that courts of justice were held at the *gates* of cities in the East.

Verse 23. *For the Lord will plead their cause*] Wo therefore to them that oppress them, for they will have *God*, not the *poor*, to deal with.

Verse 24. *Make no friendship with an angry man*] *Spirit* has a wonderful and unaccountable influence upon *spirit.* From those with whom we associate we acquire habits, and learn *their ways*, imbibe their *spirit*, show their *tempers*, and walk in their *steps.* We cannot be too choice of our *company*, for we may soon learn *ways* that will *be a snare to our soul.*

Verse 26. *That strike hands*] See on the parallel texts in the margin.

Verse 27. *If thou hast nothing to pay*] Should any man give security for more than he is *worth?* If he does, is it not a fraud on the very face of the transaction?

Why should he take away thy bed from under

A. M. cir. 3004
B. C. cir. 1000
Ante I. Olymp.
cir. 224
Ante U. C. cir.
247

he ^mtake away thy bed from under thee?

28 ⁿRemove not the ancient ^olandmark, which thy fathers have set.

29 Seest thou a man diligent in his business? he shall stand before kings; he shall not stand before ^pmean *men*.

A. M. cir. 3004
B. C. cir. 1000
Ante I. Olymp.
cir. 224
Ante U. C. cir.
247

---

^mChap. xx. 16——ⁿDeut. xix. 14; xxvii. 17; chap.

xxiii. 10——^oOr, *bound*——^pHeb. *obscure men*

---

thee?] The *creditor* will not pursue the *debtor* whom he knows to be worth nothing; but he will sue the *bail* or *bondsman*. And why shouldst thou put thyself in such circumstances as to expose thyself to the loss even of thy bed?

Verse 28. *Remove not the ancient landmark*] Do not take the advantage, in ploughing or breaking up a field contiguous to that of thy neighbour, to set the dividing stones *farther* into his *field* that thou mayest *enlarge thy own*. Take not what is not *thy own* in any case. Let all ancient *divisions*, and the *usages* connected with them, be held sacred. Bring in no new dogmas, nor *rites*, nor *ceremonies*, into *religion*, or the worship of God, that are not clearly laid down in the *sacred writings*. "Stand in the way; and see, and ask for the old paths, which is the good way, and walk therein; and ye shall find rest for your souls;" Jer. vi. 16. But if any *Church* have lost sight of the *genuine doctrines* of the Gospel, calling them back to these is not *removing the ancient landmarks*, as some have falsely asserted. God gave a law against removing the ancient landmarks, by which the inheritances of tribes and families were distinguished. See Deut. xix. 14, from which these words of Solomon appear to be taken.

Even among the *heathens* the *landmark* was sacred; so sacred that they made a *deity* of it. *Terminus* signifies the *stone* or *post* that served as a *landmark*. And *Terminus* was reputed a *god*, and had offerings made to him. Hence Ovid:—

Tu quoque sacrorum, Termine, finis eras.
    Fast. lib. i., ver. 50.

Nox ubi transierit, solito celebratur honore,
  Separat indicio qui Deus arva suo.
Termine, sive lapis, sive es defossus in agro
  Stipes, ab antiquis sic quoque Numen habes.
Te duo diversa domini pro parte coronant;
  Binaque serta tibi, binaque liba ferunt.——
Conveniunt, celebrantque dapes vicinia simplex;
  Et cantant laudes, Termine sancte, tuas.
Tu populos, urbesque, et regna ingentia finis:
  Omnis erit, sine te, litigiosus ager.
    Fast. lib. ii., ver. 639.

Here we find the owners of both fields bringing each his *garland* and *libation* to the honour of this god. They sung its *praises*, put on its top a *chaplet of flowers, poured out* the *libation* before it; and the inhabitants of the *country* held a *festival* in its honour. It was, in short, celebrated as the *preserver* of the *bounds* and territorial rights of tribes, cities, and whole kingdoms; and without its testimony and evidence, every field would have been a subject of litigation.

Verse 29. *He shall not stand before mean men.*] חשכים *chashukkim, dark* or *obscure persons;* men of no repute. Ꝥa ꝩe schal ben before un-noble men.—Old MS. Bible. "Not amonge the symple people."—*Coverdale.*

The general meaning of the proverb is, "Every diligent, active man, shall be at once independent and respectable."

CHAPTER XXIII

Sobriety in eating and drinking, especially at the tables of the great. Have no fellowship with the covetous. Remove not the ancient landmark. Children should receive due correction. Avoid the company of wine-bibbers. Obedience to parents. Avoid lewd connections. The effect of an unfeeling conscience.

A. M. cir. 3004
B. C. cir. 1000
Ante I. Olymp.
cir. 224
Ante U. C. cir.
247

WHEN thou sittest to eat with a ruler, consider diligently what *is* before thee:

2 And put a knife to thy throat, if thou *be* a man given to appetite.

3 Be not desirous of his dainties: for they *are* deceitful meat.

4 ^aLabour not to be rich: ^bcease from thine own wisdom.

A. M. cir. 3004
B. C. cir. 1000
Ante I. Olymp.
cir. 224
Ante U. C. cir.
247

---

^aChap. xxviii. 20; 1 Tim. vi. 9, 10

^bChap. iii. 5; Rom. xii. 16

NOTES ON CHAP. XXIII

Verse 1. *When thou sittest to eat with a ruler*] When invited to the table of thy betters, eat *moderately*. Do not appear as if half starved at home. Eat not of *delicacies* to which thou art not accustomed; they are *deceitful meat;* they please, but they do not profit. They are pleasant to the *sight*, the *taste*, and the *smell;* but they are injurious to *health*. These

are prudential cautions; and should be carefully observed by all who would avoid the conduct of a *clown*, and desire to pass for a *well-bred* man.

Verse 2. *Put a knife to thy throat*] Repress thy appetite, and do not be incontinent of speech. Eat, drink, and converse, under a *check*.

Verse 4. *Labour not to be rich*] Let not this be thy object. Labour to provide things *honest*

A. M. cir. 3004
B. C. cir. 1000
Ante I. Olymp.
cir. 224
Ante U. C. cir.
247

5 ^cWilt thou set thine eyes upon that which is not? for *riches* certainly make themselves wings; they fly away as an eagle toward heaven.

6 ^dEat thou not the bread of *him that hath* ^ean evil eye, neither desire thou his dainty meats:

7 For as he thinketh in his heart, so *is* he: Eat and drink, ^fsaith he to thee; but his heart *is* not with thee.

8 The morsel *which* thou hast eaten shalt thou vomit up, and lose thy sweet words.

9 ^gSpeak not in the ears of a fool: for he will despise the wisdom of thy words.

10 ^hRemove not the old ⁱlandmark; and enter not into the fields of the fatherless:

11 ^kFor their redeemer *is* mighty: he shall plead their cause with thee.

12 Apply thine heart unto instruction, and thine ears to the words of knowledge.

A. M. cir. 3004
B. C. cir. 1000
Ante I. Olymp.
cir. 224
Ante U. C. cir.
247

13 ^lWithhold not correction from the child: for *if* thou beatest him with the rod, he shall not die.

14 Thou shalt beat him with the rod, and ^mshalt deliver his soul from hell.

15 My son, ⁿif thine heart be wise, my heart shall rejoice, ^oeven mine.

16 Yea, my reins shall rejoice, when thy lips speak right things.

17 ^pLet not thine heart envy sinners: but ^q*be thou* in the fear of the LORD all the day long.

18 ^rFor surely there is an ^send; and thine expectation shall not be cut off.

19 Hear thou, my son, and be wise, and ^tguide thine heart in the way.

20 ^uBe not among winebibbers: among riotous eaters ^vof flesh:

21 For the drunkard and the glutton shall come to poverty: and ^wdrowsiness shall clothe *a man* with rags.

---

^cHeb. *Wilt thou cause thine eyes to fly upon*——^dPsa. cxli. 4——^eDeut. xv. 9——^fPsa. xii. 2——^gChap. ix. 8; Matt. vii. 6——^hDeut. xix. 14; xxvii. 17; chapter xxii. 28——ⁱOr, *bound*——^kJob xxxi. 21; chap. xxii. 23 ^lChap. xiii. 24; xix. 18; xxii. 15; xxix. 15, 17——^m1 Cor. v. 5

ⁿVer. 24, 25; chap. xxix. 3——^oOr, *even I* will rejoice——^pPsa. xxxvii. 1; lxxiii. 3; chap. iii. 31; xxiv. 1 ^qChap. xxviii. 14——^rPsa. xxxvii. 37; chap. xxiv. 14; Luke xvi. 25——^sOr, *reward*——^tChap. iv. 23——^uIsa. v. 22; Matt. xxiv. 49; Luke xxi. 34; Rom. xiii. 13; Eph. v. 18——^vHeb. *of their flesh*——^wChap. xix. 15

---

in the sight of God and all men; and if thou get wealth, do not forget the *poor*, else God's curse will be a canker even in thy *gold*.

Cease from thine own wisdom.] בִּינָתֶךָ *binathecha*, thy own *understanding* or *prudence*. The world says, "Get rich *if* thou canst, and *how* thou canst." Rem, si possis, recte; si non, quocunque modo rem; "Get a fortune *honestly* if thou canst; but if not, get one at all events." This is the devil's counsel, and well it is followed; but Solomon says, and God says, "Cease from thine own counsel." Thou hast an immortal soul, and shalt shortly appear before God. Lay up treasure for heaven, and be rich towards God.

Verse 6. *Of* him that hath *an evil eye*] Never eat with a covetous or stingy man; if he entertains you at his own expense, he grudges every morsel you put in your mouth. This is well marked by the wise man in the next verse: "Eat and drink, saith he: but his heart is not with thee."

Verse 8. *The morsel* which *thou hast eaten*] On reflection thou wilt even blame thyself for having accepted his invitation.

Verse 10. *Remove not the old landmark*] See the preceding chapter, ver. 28.

Enter not into the fields of the fatherless] Take nothing that belongs to an orphan. The heaviest curse of God will fall upon them that do so.

Verse 11. *For their redeemer is mighty*] גֹּאֲלָם *goalam*, their *kinsman*. The word means the person who has a right, being next in blood, to *redeem a field* or *estate*, alienated from the family; to avenge *the blood* of a murdered rela-

tive, by slaying the murderer; and to take *to wife* a brother's widow, who had died childless, in order to preserve the family. The *strength* here mentioned refers to the *justness* of his claim, the *extent* of his *influence*, and the powerful *abettors* of such a cause. But in reference to the orphans here mentioned, they having no *kinsman*, God takes up, vindicates, and avenges their cause.

Verse 14. *Thou shalt beat him with the rod*] A proper correction of children was a favourite point of discipline with Solomon. We have already seen how forcibly he speaks on this subject. See the notes on the places referred to in the margin.

Verse 18. *Surely there is an end*] יֵשׁ אַחֲרִית *yesh acharith*, there is *another* life; "and thy expectation" of the enjoyment of a blessed immortality "shall not be cut off." The Old MS. Bible reads thus: 𝔉𝔬𝔯 𝔱𝔥𝔬𝔲 𝔰𝔠𝔥𝔞𝔩𝔱 𝔥𝔞𝔟 𝔥𝔬𝔭 𝔦𝔫 𝔱𝔥𝔢 𝔩𝔞𝔰𝔱; 𝔞𝔫𝔡 𝔱𝔥𝔦𝔫 𝔞𝔟𝔦𝔦𝔡𝔦𝔫𝔤 𝔰𝔠𝔥𝔞𝔩 𝔫𝔬𝔱 𝔟𝔢𝔫 𝔱𝔞𝔨𝔢𝔫 𝔞𝔴𝔢𝔦. "For the ende is not yet come; and thy pacient abydinge shal not be in vayne."—COVERDALE.

Verse 20. *Be not among winebibbers*] There is much of this chapter spent in giving directions concerning *eating*, *drinking*, and *entertainments* in general. First, the pupil is directed relative to the manner in which he is to conduct himself in his visits to the tables of the *rich* and *great*. 2. Relative to the *covetous*, and his intercourse with them. And 3. To *public entertainments*, where there were generally riot and debauch. The reasons, says *Calmet*, which induced the wise man to give these directions were, 1. The useless expense. 2. The loss of time. 3. The danger from bad company. And 4. The danger of contracting irregular

A. M. cir. 3004
B. C. cir. 1000
Ante I. Olymp. cir. 224
Ante U. C. cir. 247

22 [x]Hearken unto thy father that begat thee, and despise not thy mother when she is old.

23 [y]Buy the truth, and sell *it* not; *also* wisdom, and instruction, and understanding.

24 [z]The father of the righteous shall greatly rejoice: and he that begetteth a wise *child* shall have joy of him.

25 Thy father and thy mother shall be glad, and she that bare thee shall rejoice.

26 My son, give me thine heart, and let thine eyes observe my ways.

27 [a]For a whore is a deep ditch; and a strange woman *is* a narrow pit.

28 [b]She also lieth in wait [c]as *for* a prey, and increaseth the transgressors among men.

29 [d]Who hath wo? who hath sorrow? who hath contentions? who hath babbling? who

hath wounds without cause? who [e]hath redness of eyes?

30 [f]They that tarry long at the wine; they that go to seek [g]mixed wine.

31 Look not thou upon the wine when it is red, when it giveth his colour in the cup, *when* it moveth itself aright.

32 At the last it biteth like a serpent, and stingeth like [h]an adder.

33 Thine eyes shall behold strange women, and thine heart shall utter perverse things.

34 Yea, thou shalt be as he that lieth down [i]in the midst of the sea, or as he that lieth upon the top of a mast.

35 [k]They have stricken me, *shalt thou say, and* I was not sick; they have beaten me, *and* [l]I [m]felt *it* not: [n]when shall I awake? I will seek it yet again.

A. M. cir. 3004
B. C. cir. 1000
Ante I. Olymp. cir. 224
Ante U. C. cir. 247

---

[x]Chapter i. 8; xxx. 17; Eph. vi. 1, 2——[y]Chapter iv. 5, 7; Matt. xiii. 44——[z]Chapter x. 1; xv. 20; ver. 15 [a]Chapter xxii. 14——[b]Chap. vii. 12; Eccles. vii. 26 [c]Or, *as a robber*——[d]Isa. v. 11, 22——[e]Gen. xlix. 12

[f]Chap. xx. 1; Eph. v. 18——[g]Psa. lxxv. 8; chapter ix. 2——[h]Or, *a cockatrice*——[i]Heb. *in the heart of the sea* [k]Jer. v. 3; chapter xxvii. 22——[l]Heb. *I knew it not* [m]Eph. iv. 19——[n]See Deut. xxix. 19; Isa. lvi. 12

---

habits, and of being induced to lead a voluptuous and effeminate life.

Verse 22. *Despise not thy mother when she is old.*] A very necessary caution, as *very old women* are generally helpless, useless, and burdensome: yet these circumstances do not at all lessen the child's *duty.* And this *duty* is strengthened by the Divine command here given.

Verse 23. *Buy the truth*] Acquire the *knowledge of God* at all events; and in order to do this, too much pains, industry, and labour, cannot be expended.

And sell it *not*] When once acquired, let no consideration deprive thee of it. Cleave to and guard it, even at the risk of thy life. *Coverdale* translates: "Labour for to get the treuth; sell not awaye wissdome."

Verse 26. *My son, give me thine heart*] This is the speech of God to every *human soul;* give thy *affections* to *God,* so as to love him with all thy heart, soul, mind, and strength.

And let thine eyes observe my ways.] Be obedient to me in all things. *My son,* thou believest that I AM, and that I AM the *Fountain of all good.* Give me thy *heart;* it is I alone who can make thee happy. *Observe my ways*—follow me; do what is right in my sight. This exhortation contains *three* words: BELIEVE, LOVE, OBEY! This is the *sum* of God's counsels to every child of man.

Verse 27. *For a whore is a deep ditch*] See on chap. xxii. 14.

Verse 28. *Increaseth the transgressors among men.*] More iniquity springs from this one source of evil, than from any other cause in the whole system of sin. *Women* and *strong drink* cause many millions to *transgress.*

Verse 29. *Who hath wo?*] I believe Solomon refers here to the natural effects of drunkenness. And perhaps אוי *oi,* which we translate

wo, and אבוי *aboi,* which we translate *sorrow,* are mere natural sounds or vociferations that take place among drunken men, either from illness, or the *nauseating* effects of too much liquor. As to *contentions* among such; *babblings* on a variety of subjects, which they neither understand nor are fit to discuss; *wounds,* got by falling out about nothing; and *red eyes,* bloodshotten with excess of drink, or *black* and *blue eyes* with fighting;—these are such common and general effects of these *compotations,* as naturally to follow from them. So that they who *tarry long at wine,* and use *mixed wine* to make it more inebriating, (see chap. ix. 2,) are the very persons who are most distinguished by the circumstances enumerated above. I need scarcely add, that by *wine* and *mixed wine* all inebriating liquors are to be understood.

Verse 31. *Look not thou upon the wine*] Let neither the *colour,* the *odour,* the *sparkling,* &c., of the wine, when poured out, induce thee to drink of it. However *good* and *pure* it may be, it will to thee be a snare, because thou art addicted to it, and hast no self-command.

Verse 33. *Thine eyes shall behold strange women*] Evil concupiscence is inseparable from drunkenness. Mr. *Herbert* shows these effects well:—

He that is *drunken* may his *mother* kill,
  Big with his sister: he hath lost the reins;
Is outlawed by himself. *All kinds of ill*
  Did, with his liquor, slide into his veins.
The drunkard forfeits *man;* and doth divest
All worldly right, save what he hath by *beast.*
HERBERT'S *Poems.—The Church Porch.*

Verse 34. *Lieth down in the midst of the sea*] He is utterly regardless of life; which is expressed very forcibly by one in a state of intoxication ascending the *shrouds,* clasping the mast-head, and there *falling asleep;* whence, in a few moments, he must either fall down upon the deck and be dashed to pieces, or fall into the sea and be drowned. Reader, if thou be a man given to this appetite, put a knife to thy throat.

Verse 35. *They have stricken me*] Though beat and abused, full of pain, and exhibiting a frightful figure; yet so drunk was he, as to be insensible who had struck him: still, after all this abuse and disgrace, he purposes to embrace the next opportunity of repeating his excesses! SIN makes a man *contemptible* in life, *miserable* in death, and *wretched* to all eternity. Is it not strange, then, that men should LOVE it?

CHAPTER XXIV

Do not be envious. Of the house wisely built. Counsel necessary in war. Save life when thou canst. Of honey and the honey-comb. Of the just that falleth seven times. We should not rejoice at the misfortune of others. Ruin of the wicked. Fear God and the king. Prepare thy work. The field of the sluggard, and the vineyard of the foolish, described.

A. M. cir. 3004
B. C. cir. 1000
Ante I. Olymp.
cir. 224
Ante U. C. cir.
247

BE not thou [a]envious against evil men, [b]neither desire to be with them.

2 [c]For their heart studieth destruction, and their lips talk of mischief.

3 Through wisdom is a house builded; and by understanding it is established:

4 And by knowledge shall the chambers be filled with all precious and pleasant riches.

5 [d]A wise man *is* [e]strong; yea, a man of knowledge [f]increaseth strength.

6 [g]For by wise counsel thou shalt make thy war: and in multitude of counsellors *there is* safety.

7 [h]Wisdom *is* too high for a fool: he openeth not his mouth in the gate.

A. M. cir. 3004
B. C. cir. 1000
Ante I. Olymp.
cir. 224
Ante U. C. cir.
247

8 He that [i]deviseth to do evil shall be called a mischievous person.

9 The thought of foolishness *is* sin: and the scorner *is* an abomination to men.

10 *If* thou faint in the day of adversity, thy strength *is* [k]small.

11 [l]If thou forbear to deliver *them that are* drawn unto death, and *those that are* ready to be slain;

12 If thou sayest, Behold, we knew it not: doth not [m]he that pondereth the heart consi-

---

[a]Psa. xxxvii. 1, &c.; lxxiii. 3; ch. iii. 31; xxiii. 17; ver. 19——[b]Ch. i. 15——[c]Psa. x. 7——[d]Ch. xxi. 22; Eccles. ix. 16——[e]Heb. is *in strength*——[f]Heb. *strengtheneth might*

[g]Chap. xi. 15; xiii. 22; xx. 18; Luke xiv. 31——[h]Psa. x. 5; chap. xiv. 6——[i]Rom. i. 30——[k]Heb. *narrow* [l]Psa. lxxxii. 4; Isa. lviii. 6, 7; 1 John iii. 16——[m]Chap. xxi. 2

NOTES ON CHAP. XXIV

Verse 3. *Through wisdom is a house builded*] That is, a family; household affairs. See the notes on chap. ix. 1, &c.

Verse 5. *A wise man is strong.* His wisdom enables him to construct a great variety of machines, by which, under his own influence, he can do the labour of a hundred or even a thousand men. But in all cases *wisdom* gives *power* and *influence;* and he who *is* wise to salvation can overcome even Satan himself. The *Septuagint* has: "The wise is better than the strong; and the man who has prudence, than a stout husbandman."

Verse 6. *By wise counsel thou shalt make thy war*] See note on chap. xx. 18.

Verse 7. *A fool—openeth not his mouth in the gate.*] Is not put into public offices of trust and responsibility.

Verse 9. *The thought of foolishness is sin*]

זמת אולת חטאת *zimmath ivveleth chattath.* "The device of folly is transgression;" or, "an evil purpose is sinful;" or, perhaps more literally, "the device of the foolish is sin." It has been variously understood by the *versions.*

"The cunning of the fool is sin."—*Targum.*

"The imprudent man (or fool, αφρων) shall die in sins."—*Septuagint.*

So the *Arabic.*

𝔗𝔥𝔢 𝔱𝔥𝔦𝔫𝔨𝔶𝔫𝔤𝔢 𝔬𝔣 𝔱𝔥𝔢 𝔣𝔬𝔬𝔩 𝔦𝔰 𝔰𝔶𝔫𝔫𝔢.—Old MS. Bible.

Fool is here taken for a *wicked* man, who is not only evil in his *actions*, but every thought of his heart is evil, and that continually. A simple thought *about* foolishness, or about *sin* itself, is not sinful; it is the *purpose* or *device*, the *harbouring* evil thoughts, and *devising how to sin*, that is criminal.

Verse 10. *If thou faint*] If thou give way to discouragement and despair *in the day of adversity*—time of trial or temptation.

Thy strength is small.] צר כחכה *tsar cochachah,* thy *strength* is *contracted.* So the old MS. Bible excellently: 𝔊𝔦𝔣 𝔰𝔩𝔦𝔡𝔢𝔫 𝔱𝔥𝔬𝔲 𝔡𝔦𝔰𝔭𝔢𝔦𝔯𝔢, 𝔦𝔫 𝔱𝔥𝔢 𝔡𝔞𝔦 𝔬𝔣 𝔞𝔫𝔤𝔲𝔭𝔱𝔰, 𝔰𝔠𝔥𝔞𝔩 𝔟𝔢 𝔪𝔞𝔡𝔢 𝔩𝔦𝔱𝔦𝔩 𝔱𝔥𝔶 𝔰𝔱𝔯𝔢𝔫𝔤𝔱𝔥𝔢. In times of trial we should endeavour to be doubly courageous; when a man loses his courage, his strength avails him nothing.

Verse 11. *If thou forbear to deliver*] If thou seest the innocent taken by the hand of lawless power or superstitious zeal, and they are about to be put to death, thou shouldst rise up in their behalf, boldly plead for them, testify to their innocence when thou knowest it; and thus thou wilt not be *guilty of blood;* which thou

A. M. cir. 3004
B. C. cir. 1000
Ante I. Olymp. cir. 224
Ante U. C. cir. 247

der *it?* and he that keepeth thy soul, doth *not* he know *it?* and shall *not* he render to *every* man [n]according to his works?

13.My son, °eat thou honey, because *it is* good; and the honey-comb, *which is* sweet [p]to thy taste.

14 [q]So *shall* the knowledge of wisdom *be* unto thy soul: when thou hast found *it,* [r]then

there shall be a reward, and thy expectation shall not be cut off.

A. M. cir. 3004
B. C. cir. 1000
Ante I. Olymp. cir. 224
Ante U. C. cir. 247

15 [s]Lay not wait, O wicked man, against the dwelling of the righteous; spoil not his resting place.

16 [t]For a just *man* falleth seven times, and riseth up again: [u]but the wicked shall fall into mischief.

17 [v]Rejoice not when thine enemy falleth,

---

[n]Job xxxiv. 11; Psa. lxii. 12; Jer. xxxii. 19; Rom. ii. 6; Rev. ii. 23; xxii. 12——°Cant. v. 1——[p]Heb. *upon thy palate*——[q]Psa. xix. 10; cxix. 103——[r]Chap. xxiii. 18 [s]Psa. x. 9, 10

[t]Job v. 19; Psa. xxxiv. 19; xxxvii. 24; Mic. vii. 8 [u]Esth. vii. 10; Amos v. 2; viii. 14; Rev. xviii. 21——[v]Job xxxi. 27; Psa. xxxv. 15, 19; chapter xvii. 5; Obadiah 12

---

wouldst be, if, through any pretence, thou shouldst neglect to save the life of a man unjustly condemned.

Verse 13. *And the honey-comb*] I have often had occasion to remark how much finer the flavour of honey is in the honey-comb than it is after it has been *expressed* from it, and exposed to the action of the air. But it has been asserted that the *honey-comb* is *never eaten;* it must be by those who have no acquaintance with the *apiary.* I have seen the *comb* with its contained honey eaten frequently, and of it I have repeatedly partaken. And that our Lord ate it, is evident from Luke xxiv. 42. Nor can any man who has not eaten it in this way feel the full force of the allusions to the *honey-comb* and its *sweetness* in several parts of the sacred writings. See 1 Sam. xiv. 27; Psa. xix. 10; Prov. v. 3; xvi. 24; xxvii. 7; Cant. iv. 11; v. 1; and the place before us.

Verse 14. *So* shall *the knowledge of wisdom* be *unto thy soul*] True religion, experimental godliness, shall be to thy soul as the honey-comb is to thy mouth.

Then there shall be a reward, and thy expectation shall not be cut off.] This is precisely the same with that in the preceding chapter, ver. 18, where see the note. The word אחרית *acharith,* we translate in the former place *an end,* and here we translate it a *reward;* but there is no place I believe in the sacred writings in which it has any such acceptation; nor can such a meaning be deduced from the root אחר *achar,* which always refers to *behind, after, extremity, latter part, time,* &c., but never carries the idea of *recompense, compensation,* or such like; nor has one of the *versions* understood it so. There is *another state* or *life,* and *thy expectation* of happiness in a *future world shall not be cut off.* In this sense the *versions* all understood it. I will take them as they lie before me.

"Which (wisdom) when thou shalt have found, thou shalt have hope in thy *last days;* and thy hope shall not perish."—*Vulgate.*

"And if thou find it, thou shalt have a *good death;* and hope shall not forsake thee."—*Septuagint.*

"Which, if thou have found, thy *latter days* shall be better than the former; and thy hope shall not be consumed."—*Chaldee.*

"There shall be *an end,* and thy hope shall not be cut off."—*Syriac.*

"For, if thou shalt find her, (wisdom,) *thy death shall be glorious,* and thy hope will not fail thee."—*Arabic.*

𝖂𝖍𝖎𝖈𝖍𝖊 𝖙𝖍𝖆𝖓 𝖙𝖍𝖔𝖚 𝖋𝖞𝖓𝖉𝖎𝖘𝖙 𝖙𝖍𝖔𝖚 𝖘𝖈𝖍𝖆𝖑𝖙 𝖍𝖆𝖓 𝖎𝖓 𝖙𝖍𝖊

𝖑𝖆𝖘𝖙 𝖙𝖍𝖎𝖓𝖌𝖎𝖘, 𝖍𝖔𝖕𝖊: 𝖆𝖓𝖉 𝖙𝖍𝖎𝖓 𝖍𝖔𝖕𝖊 𝖘𝖈𝖍𝖆𝖑 𝖓𝖔𝖙 𝖕𝖊𝖗𝖎𝖘𝖈𝖍𝖊𝖓. —Old MS. Bible.

"*And there* is GOOD HOPE; yee that hope shal not be in vayne."—*Coverdale.*

This rendering is indefinite, which is not the usual custom of the translator.

Verse 15. *The dwelling of the righteous*] צדיק *tsaddik,* the man who is walking unblameably in all the testimonies of God; who is rendering to every man his due.

Verse 16. *For a just* man] צדיק *tsaddik,* the *righteous,* the same person mentioned above.

Falleth seven times] Gets *very often* into distresses through his *resting place* being *spoiled* by the *wicked man,* the robber, the spoiler of the desert, *lying in wait* for this purpose, ver. 15.

And riseth up again] Though God permit the hand of *violence* sometimes to spoil his *tent, temptations* to assail his *mind,* and *afflictions* to press down his *body,* he constantly emerges; and every time he passes through the furnace, he comes out *brighter* and more refined.

But the wicked shall fall into mischief.] And there they shall *lie;* having no strong arm to uphold them. Yet,

Verse 17. *Rejoice not when thine enemy falleth,* (into this mischief,) *and let not thine heart be glad when he stumbleth*] When he meets with any thing that injures him; for God will not have thee to avenge thyself, or *feel any disposition* contrary to love; for if thou do, the Lord will *be angry,* and may *turn away his wrath from him,* and pour it out on thee.

This I believe to be the true sense of these verses: but we must return to the *sixteenth,* as that has been most sinfully misrepresented.

For a just man *falleth seven times.*—That is, say many, "the most righteous man in the world sins seven times a day on an average." Solomon does not say so:—1. There is not a word about *sin* in the text. 2. The word *day* is not in the Hebrew text, nor in any of the *versions.* 3. The word יפול *yippol,* from נפל *naphal,* to *fall,* is never applied to *sin.* 4. When set in opposition to the words *riseth up,* it merely applies to affliction or calamity. See Mic. vii. 8; Amos viii. 4; Jer. xxv. 27; and Psa. xxxiv. 19, 20. "The righteous falls into trouble." See above.

Mr. *Holden* has a very judicious note on this passage: "Injure not a righteous man; for, though he frequently falls into distress, yet, by the superintending care of Providence, 'he

A. M. cir. 3004
B. C. cir. 1000
Ante I. Olymp.
cir. 224
Ante U. C. cir.
247

and let not thine heart be glad when he stumbleth:

18 Lest the LORD see *it,* and ʷit displease him, and he turn away his wrath from him.

19 ˣFret ʸnot thyself because of evil *men,* neither be thou envious at the wicked;

20 For ᶻthere shall be no reward to the evil *man;* ᵃthe ᵇcandle of the wicked shall be put out.

21 My son, ᶜfear thou the LORD and the king: *and* meddle not with ᵈthem that are given to change:

22 For their calamity shall rise suddenly; and who knoweth the ruin of them both?

23 These *things* also *belong* to the wise. ᵉ*It is* not good to have respect of persons in judgment.

24 ᶠHe that saith unto the wicked, Thou *art* righteous; him shall the people curse, nations shall abhor him:

A. M. cir. 3004
B. C. cir. 1000
Ante I. Olymp.
cir. 224
Ante U. C. cir.
247

25 But to them that rebuke *him* shall be delight, and ᵍa good blessiᴜg shall come upon them.

26 *Every man* shall kiss *his* lips ʰthat giveth a right answer.

27 ⁱPrepare thy work without, and make it fit for thyself in the field; and afterwards build thine house.

28 ᵏBe not a witness against thy neighbour without cause; and deceive *not* with thy lips.

29 ˡSay not, I will do so to him as he hath done to me: I will render to the man according to his work.

30 I went by the field of the slothful, and by the vineyard of the man void of understanding;

ʷHeb. *it be evil in his eyes*——ˣPsa. xxxvii. 1; lxvii. 3; chap. xxiii. 17; ver. 1——ʸOr, *Keep not company with the wicked*——ᶻPsa. xi. 6——ᵃJob xviii. 5, 6; xxi. 17; chap. xiii. 9; xx. 20——ᵇOr, *lamp*——ᶜRomans xiii. 7; 1 Peter ii. 27——ᵈHeb. *changers*

ᵉLev. xix. 15; Deut. xi. 7; xvi. 19; chap. xviii. 5; xxviii. 21; John vii. 24——ᶠChap. xvii. 15; Isa. v. 23 ᵍHeb. *a blessing of good*——ʰHeb. *that answereth right words*——ⁱ1 Kings v. 17, 18; Luke xiv. 28——ᵏEph. iv. 25——ˡChap. xx. 22; Matt. v. 39, 44; Rom. xii. 17, 19

---

riseth up again,' is delivered from his distress, while the wicked are overwhelmed with their misfortunes. That this is the meaning is plain from the preceding and following verses: yet some expound it by the just man often relapsing into sin, and recovering from it; nay, it has even been adduced to prove the doctrine of the final perseverance of the elect. But נפל is never used for falling into sin, but into distress and affliction—as chap. xi. 5, 14; xiii. 17; xvii. 20; xxvi. 27; xxviii. 10, 14, 18."

Verse 18. *And he turn away his wrath from him.*] Wrath is here taken for the effect of wrath, punishment; and the meaning must be as paraphrased above—lest he take the punishment from *him,* and inflict it upon *thee.* And in this way *Coverdale* understood it: "Lest the Lorde be angry, and turn his wrath from him unto thee." Or we may understand it thus: Lest the Lord inflict on thee a *similar punishment;* for if thou get into his *spirit,* rejoicing in the calamities of another, thou deservest punishment.

Verse 20. *For there shall be no reward to the evil* man] אחרית *acharith.* There shall not be the *future state* of *blessedness* to the wicked. See the note on ver. 14. *His candle shall be put out;* his *prosperity* shall finally cease, or he shall have no *posterity.* Some have thought that this text intimates the *annihilation* of sinners; but it refers not to *being,* but to the *state* or *condition* of that being. The wicked shall *be;* but they shall not be HAPPY.

Verse 21. *My son, fear thou the Lord and the king*] Pay to each the homage due: to the LORD, Divine honour and adoration; to the *king,* civil respect, civil honour, and political obedience.

Meddle not with them that are given to change] עם שונים אל תתערב *im shonim al tith-arab:* "And with the changelings mingle not thyself." The *innovators;* those who are always for making experiments on modes of government, forms of religion, &c. The most dangerous spirit that can infect the human mind.

Verse 22. *The ruin of them both?*] *Of* them who do not *fear* the LORD; and of *them* that do not *reverence* the KING.

Verse 23. *These* things *also* belong *to the wise.*] גם אלה לחכמים *gam elleh lachachamim,* "These also to wise." This appears to be a *new section;* and perhaps, what follows belongs to *another collection.* Probably fragments of sayings collected by wise men from the Proverbs of Solomon.

It is *not good to have respect*] Judgment and justice should never be perverted.

Verse 26. *Kiss his lips*] Shall treat him with affection and respect.

Verse 27. *Prepare thy work without*] Do nothing without a *plan.* In *winter* prepare seed, implements, tackle, geers, &c., for *seed-time and harvest.*

Verse 28. *Be not a witness*] Do not be forward to offer thyself to bear testimony against a neighbour, in a matter which may prejudice him, where the essential claims of justice do not require such interference; and especially do not do this in a spirit of *revenge,* because he has injured thee before.

Verse 30. *I went by the field of the slothful*] This is a most instructive *parable;* is exemplified every day in a variety of forms; and is powerfully descriptive of the *state* of many a *blacksluder* and *trifler* in religion. *Calmet* has an excellent note on this passage. I shall give the substance of it.

A. M. cir. 3004
B. C. cir. 1000
Ante I. Olymp.
cir. 224
Ante U. C. cir.
247

31 And, lo, [m]it was all grown over with thorns, *and* nettles had covered the face thereof, and the stone wall thereof was broken down.

32 Then I saw, *and* [n]considered *it* well: I looked upon *it, and* received instruction.

A. M. cir. 3004
B. C. cir. 1000
Ante I. Olymp.
cir. 224
Ante U. C. cir.
247

33 [o]*Yet* a little sleep, a little slumber, a little folding of the hands to sleep:

34 So shall thy poverty come *as* one that travelleth; and thy want as [p]an armed man.

---

[m]Gen. iii. 18——[n]Heb. *set my heart*

[o]Chap. vi. 9, &c.——[p]Heb. *a man of shield*

Solomon often recommends diligence and economy to his disciples. In those primitive times when agriculture was honourable, no man was respected who neglected to cultivate his grounds, who sunk into poverty, contracted debt, or engaged in ruinous securities. With great propriety, a principal part of *wisdom* was considered by them as consisting in the *knowledge* of properly *conducting one's domestic affairs*, and duly cultivating the inheritances derived from their ancestors. Moses had made a law to prevent the rich from utterly depressing the poor, by obliging them to return their *farms* to them on the *Sabbatic year*, and to remit all debts at the *year of jubilee*.

In the civil state of the Hebrews, we never see those enormous and suddenly raised fortunes, which never subsist but in the ruin of numberless families. One of the principal solicitudes of this legislator was to produce, as far as possible in a monarchical state, an equality of property and condition. The ancient *Romans* held agriculture in the same estimation, and highly respected those who had applied themselves to it with success. When they spoke in praise of a man, they considered themselves as giving no mean commendation when they called him a *good husbandman*, an *excellent labourer*. From such men they formed their most valiant generals and intrepid soldiers. CATO *De Re Rustica*, cap. 1. The property which is acquired by these means is most innocent, most solid, and exposes its possessor less to envy than property acquired in any other way. See CICERO *De Officiis*, lib. 1. In Britain the *merchant* is all in all; and yet the waves of the sea are not more uncertain, nor more tumultuous, than the property acquired in this way, or than the agitated life of the speculative merchant.

But let us look more particularly into this very instructive parable:—

I. The owner is described. 1. He was איש עצל *ish atsel*, the loitering, sluggish, siothful man. 2. He was אדם חסר לב *adam chasar leb*, a man that wanted heart; destitute of courage, alacrity, and decision of mind.

II. His circumstances. This man had, 1st,

שדה *sadeh*, a sowed field, arable ground. This was the character of his estate. It was *meadow* and *corn* land. 2. He had כרם *kerem*, a *vineyard*, what we would call perhaps *garden* and *orchard*, where he might employ his skill to great advantage in raising various kinds of fruits and culinary herbs for the support of his family.

III. The state of this heritage: 1. "It was grown over with thorns." It had been long neglected, so that even *brambles* were permitted to grow in the fields: 2. "Nettles had covered the face thereof." It was not *weeded*, and all kinds of rubbish had been suffered to multiply: 3. "The stone wall was broken down." This belonged to the *vineyard: it* was neither *pruned* nor *digged;* and the *fence*, for want of timely repairs, had all fallen into ruins, ver. 31.

IV. The *effect* all this had on the attentive observer. 1. *I saw it,* אחזה אנכי *echezeh anochi*, I fixed my attention on it. I found it was no mere report. It is a fact. I myself was an eyewitness of it. 2. *I considered it well,* אשית לבי *ashith libbi*, I put my heart on it. All my feelings were interested. 3. *I looked upon it,* ראיתי *raithi*, I took an *intellectual* view of it. And 4. Thus *I received instruction,* לקחתי מוסר *lakachti musar*, I received a very important lesson from it: but the owner paid no attention to it. He alone was uninstructed; for he "slumbered, slept, and kept his hands in his bosom." Ver. 33. "Hugged himself in his sloth and carelessness."

V. The consequences of this conduct. 1. *Poverty* described as coming like a *traveller*, making sure steps every hour coming nearer and nearer to the door. 2. *Want,* מחסר *machsor*, total destitution; want of all the necessaries, conveniences, and *comforts* of life; and this is described as coming *like an armed man* כאיש מגן *keish magen*, as a man with a shield, who comes to destroy this unprofitable servant: or it may refer to a man coming with what we call an execution into the house, armed with the law, to take even his *bed* from the *slumberer*.

From this literal solution any minister of God may make a profitable discourse.

CHAPTER XXV

A new series of Solomon's proverbs. God's glory in mysteries. Observations concerning kings. Avoid contentions. Opportune speech. The faithful ambassador. Delicacies to be sparingly used. Avoid familiarity. Amusements not grateful to a distressed mind. Do good to your enemies. The misery of dwelling with a scold. The necessity of moderation and self-government.

A. M. cir. 3304
B. C. cir. 700
Ol. vigesimæ
cir. annum
primum
A. U. C. cir. 54

THESE [a]*are* also proverbs of Solomon, which the men of Hezekiah king of Judah copied out.

2 [b]*It is* the glory of God to conceal a thing: but the honour of kings *is* [c]to search out a matter.

3 The heaven for height, and the earth for depth, and the heart of kings *is* [d]unsearchable.

4 [e]Take away the dross from the silver,

and there shall come forth a vessel for the finer.

A. M. cir. 3304
B. C. cir. 700
Ol. vigesimæ
cir. annum
primum
A. U. C. cir. 54

5 [f]Take away the wicked *from* before the king, and [g]his throne shall be established in righteousness.

6 [h]Put not forth thyself in the presence of the king, and stand not in the place of great *men:*

7 [i]For better *it is* that it be said unto thee, Come up hither; than that thou shouldest be put lower in the presence of the prince whom thine eyes have seen.

---

[a]1 Kings iv. 32——[b]Deut. xxix. 29; Rom. xi. 33——[c]Job xxix. 16——[d]Heb. there is *no searching*

[e]2 Tim. ii. 21——[f]Ch. xx. 8——[g]Ch. xvi. 12; xxix. 14 [h]Heb. *Set not out thy glory*——[i]Luke xiv. 8, 9, 10

NOTES ON CHAP. XXV

Verse 1. *These* are *also proverbs of Solomon*] In my old MS. Bible, this verse concludes the preceding chapter. It seems that the remaining part of this book contains proverbs which had been collected by the order of King Hezekiah, and were added to the preceding book as a sort of supplement, having been collected from traditional sayings of Solomon. And as the men of Hezekiah may mean *Isaiah, Shebna,* and other *inspired* men, who lived in that time, we may consider them as of equal authority with the rest, else such men could not have united them to the sacred book. The chronological notes in the margin of this and the five following chapters denote the time when the proverbs contained in them were collected together in the reign of Hezekiah, about *two hundred and seventy years* after the death of Solomon.

Verse 2. It is *the glory of God to conceal a thing*] This has been understood as referring to the revelation of God's will in his word, where there are many things concealed in *parables, allegories, metaphors, similitudes,* &c. And it is becoming the majesty of God so to publish his will, that it must be *seriously studied* to be understood, in order that the truth may be more prized when it is discovered. And if it be God's glory thus partially to conceal his purposes, it is the glory of a king to search and examine this word, that he may understand how by Him kings reign and princes decree judgment. *Prophecies* are partially concealed; and we cannot fully know their meaning till their accomplishment; and then the *glory of God's wisdom* and *providence* will be more particularly evident, when we see the event correspond so particularly and exactly with the *prediction.* I know not, however, that there are not matters in the Book of God that will not be fully opened till mortality is swallowed up of life. For *here* we see through a glass darkly; but *there,* face to face: *here* we know in part; but *there* we shall know as we also are known.

On this subject I cannot withhold an extract of a letter sent to myself, by a *royal* and *learned* personage.[*]

"As far as I have presumed to dive into and occupy myself with the sacred volumes, I feel satisfied of their Divine origin and truth. And I am satisfied, likewise, that they contain more matter than any one, and myself in particular,

[*] His Royal Highness, the Duke of Sussex.

can ever aspire fully to understand. This belief, however, ought in nowise to slacken our diligence, or damp our ardour, in attempting a constant pursuit after the attainment of knowledge and truth; as we may flatter ourselves, although unable to reach the *gate,* we are still approaching nearer to its portals, which of itself is a great blessing." This sentiment will be approved by every pious and enlightened mind.

Verse 3. *The heaven for height*] The simple meaning of this is, the *reasons of state,* in reference to many acts of the *executive government,* can no more be fathomed by the *common people,* than the *height of the heavens* and the *depth of the earth.*

Verse 4. *Take away the dross from the silver*] You cannot have a *pure* silver vessel till you have purified the silver; and no nation can have a king a public blessing till the *wicked*—all bad counsellors, wicked and interested ministers, and sycophants—are banished from the court and cabinet. When the *wise* and *good* only are the king's ministers and advisers, then the throne will be established in righteousness, and his administration be a universal blessing.

Verse 7. *Come up hither*] Our Lord refers to this, see Luke xiv. 8, and the notes there. Be humble; affect not high things; let those who are desperate climb dangerous precipices; keep thyself quiet, and thou shalt live at ease, and in peace. Hear the speech of a wise *heathen* on this subject:—

Quid fuit, ut tutas agitaret Dædalus alas;
   Icarus immensas nomine signet aquas?
Nempe quod hic alte, dimissus ille volabat.
   Nam pennas ambo nonne habuere suas?
Crede mihi; bene qui latuit, bene vixit; et infra
   Fortunam debet quisque manere suam.
Vive sine invidia; mollesque inglorius annos
   Exige: amicitias et tibi junge pares.
       OVID, *Trist.* lib. [i]ii., El. 4, ver. 21.

"Why was it that *Dædalus* winged his way safely, while *Icarus* his son fell, and gave name to the Icarian sea? Was it not because the son flew aloft, and the father skimmed the ground? For both were furnished with the same kind of wings. Take my word for it, that he who lives privately lives safely; and every one should live within his own income. Envy no man; pray for a quiet life,

A. M. cir. 3304
B. C. cir. 700
Ol. vigesimæ
cir. annum
primum
A. U. C. cir. 54

8 [k]Go not forth hastily to strive, lest *thou know not* what to do in the end thereof, when thy neighbour hath put thee to shame.

9 [l]Debate thy cause with thy neighbour *himself;* and [m]discover not thy secret to another:

10 Lest he that heareth *it* put thee to shame, and thine infamy turn not away.

11 [n]A word [o]fitly spoken *is like* apples of gold in pictures of silver.

12 *As* an ear-ring of gold, and an ornament

of fine gold, *so is* a wise reprover upon an obedient ear.

13 [p]As the cold of snow in the time of harvest, *so is* a faithful messenger to them that send him: for he refresheth the soul of his masters.

14 [q]Whoso boasteth himself [r]of a false gift *is like* [s]clouds and wind without rain.

15 [t]By long forebearing is a prince persuaded, and a soft tongue breaketh the bone.

A. M. cir. 3304
B. C. cir. 700
Ol. vigesimæ
cir. annum
primum
A. U. C. cir. 54

---

[k]Chap. xvii. 14; Matt. v. 25——[l]Matt. v. 25; xviii. 15
[m]Or, *discover not the secret of another*——[n]Chap. xv. 23;
Isa. l. 4——[o]Heb. *spoken upon his wheels*

[p]Chap. xiii. 17——[q]Chap. xx. 6——[r]Heb. *in a gift of falsehood*——[s]Jude 12——[t]Gen. xxxii. 4, &c.; 1 Sam. xxv. 24, &c.; chap. xv. 1; xvi. 14

---

though it should not be dignified. Seek a friend, and associate with thy equals."

Verse 8. *Go not forth hastily to strive*] לרב *lerib*, to enter into a *lawsuit.* Keep from this *pit of the bottomless deep*, unless urged by the direst necessity.

Verse 9. *Debate thy cause with thy neighbour*] Take the advice of friends. Let both sides attend to their counsels; but do not tell the *secret* of thy business to any. After squandering your money away upon lawyers, both *they* and the *judge* will at last leave it to be settled by *twelve* of your fellow citizens! O the folly of going to law! O the blindness of men, and the rapacity of unprincipled lawyers!

On this subject I cannot but give the following extract from Sir *John Hawkins's* Life of Dr. Johnson, which he quotes from Mr. *Selwin*, of London: "A man who deliberates about going to law should have, 1. A good cause; 2. A good purse; 3. A good skilful attorney; 4. Good evidence; 5. Good able counsel; 6. A good upright judge; 7. A good intelligent jury; and with all these on his side, if he have not, 8. *Good luck*, it is odds but he miscarries in his suit." O the glorious uncertainty of the law!

Verse 11. *A word fitly spoken*] על אפניו *al ophannaiv, upon its wheels.* An observation, caution, reproof, or advice, that *comes in naturally, runs* smoothly along, is not *forced* nor *dragged* in, that appears to be without *design*, to rise out of the conversation, and though particularly relative to *one point*, will appear to the company to suit all.

Is like *apples of gold in pictures of silver.*] Is like the refreshing *orange* or beautiful *citron*, served up in *open work* or *filigree baskets*, made of *silver.* The Asiatics excel in *filigree silver work.* I have seen much of it, and it is exquisitely beautiful. The silver wire by which it is done they form into the appearance of numerous *flowers;* and though these wires are *soldered* everywhere at their junctions with each other, yet this is done with such *delicacy* and *skill* as to be scarcely perceptible. I have seen *animals* formed on this *filigree* work, with all *their limbs*, and every *joint* in its *natural play.* Fruit-baskets are made also in this way, and are exquisitely fine. The wise man seems to have this kind of work particularly in view; and the contrast of the *golden yellow fruit* in the exquisitely wrought *silver basket*, which may be all termed *picture work*, has a fine and pleasing effect upon the *eye*, as the contained

fruit has upon the *palate* at an entertainment in a sultry climate. So the word spoken judiciously and opportunely is as much in its place, as the *golden apples* in the *silver baskets.*

Verse 12. As *an ear-ring of gold*] I believe נזם *nezem* to mean the *nose-ring* with its *pendants;* the left nostril is pierced, and a ring put through it, as in the ear. This is very common in almost every part of the East, among women of condition. This is a farther illustration of the above metaphor.

Verse 13. As *the cold of snow*] That *snow* was frequent in *Judea*, is well known; and that in the East they have *snow-houses*—places dug under ground, where they lay up snow for *summer* use—is also a fact. By means of the mass of snow desposited in them the icy temperature is kept up, so that the snow is easily preserved. The *common method of cooling their wine*, which is as *easy* as it is *effectual*, is by dipping a cloth in *water*, wrapping it round the *bottle*, and then hanging the bottle in the *heat of the sun.* The strong *evaporation* carries off the *caloric* from the wine, and the repetition of the wet cloth in the same exposure, makes the wine almost as cold as *ice.*

How agreeable this must be in a burning climate, may be easily conceived. Perhaps it is this to which the wise man refers; for it is a fact that they could have no *snow in harvest*, unless such as had been *preserved* as mentioned above; but this could be only in a *few places*, and within the reach of a *very few persons.* But cooling their liquors by the *simple mode of evaporation* already explained, was within the reach even of the *labourers in the harvest field.* I think the text favours this supposition; for כצנת שלג *ketsinnath sheleg*, need not be referred to *snow itself* procuring cold, but to a *coldness like that of snow*, procured by *evaporation.* If this interpretation be allowed, all difficulty will be removed.

Verse 14. *A false gift*] מתת שקר *mattath shaker, a lying gift*, one *promised*, but never *bestowed.* "Whoso maketh greate boastes, and giveth nothing;" Coverdale. So the Vulgate: "Vir gloriosus, et promissa non complens;" "A bragging man, who does not fulfil his promises," is like *clouds* which appear to be laden with vapour, and like the *wind* which, though it blow from a rainy quarter, brings no moistness with it. So the vain boaster; he is big with promise, but performs nothing.

Verse 15. *A soft tongue breaketh the bone.*]

A. M. cir. 3304
B. C. cir. 700
Ol. vigesimæ
cir. annum
primum
A. U. C. cir. 54

16 [u]Hast thou found honey? eat so much as is sufficient for thee, lest thou be filled therewith, and vomit it.

17 [v]Withdraw thy foot from thy neighbour's house; lest he be [w]weary of thee, and *so* hate thee.

18 [x]A man that beareth false witness against his neighbour *is* a maul, and a sword, and a sharp arrow.

19 Confidence in an unfaithful man in time of trouble *is like* a broken tooth, and a foot out of joint.

20 *As* he that taketh away a garment in cold weather, *and as* vinegar upon nitre, so *is* he that [y]singeth songs to a heavy heart.

21 [z]If thine enemy be hungry, give him bread to eat; and if he be thirsty, give him water to drink:

22 For thou shalt heap coals of fire upon his head, [a]and the LORD shall reward thee.

A. M. cir. 3304
B. C. cir. 700
Ol. vigesimæ
cir. annum
primum
A. U. C. cir. 54

23 [b]The [c]north wind driveth away rain: so *doth* an angry countenance [d]a backbiting tongue.

24 [e]*It is* better to dwell in the corner of the house-top, than with a brawling woman, and in a wide house.

25 *As* cold waters to a thirsty soul, so *is* good news from a far country.

26 A righteous man falling down before the wicked *is as* a troubled fountain, and a corrupt spring.

27 [f]*It is* not good to eat much honey: so *for men* [g]to search their own glory *is not* glory.

28 [h]He that *hath* no rule over his own spirit *is like* a city *that is* broken down, *and* without walls.

---

[u]Ver. 27——[v]Or, *Let thy foot be seldom in thy neighbour's house*——[w]Heb. *full of thee*——[x]Psa. lvii. 4; cxx. 3, 4; chap. xii. 18——[y]Dan. vi. 18; Rom. xii. 15——[z]Exod. xxiii. 4, 5; Matt. v. 44; Rom. xii. 20——[a]2 Sam. xvi. 12

[b]Job xxxvii. 22——[c]Or, *The north wind bringeth forth rain; so doth a backbiting tongue an angry countenance*
[d]Psa. ci. 5——[e]Chap. xix. 13; xxi. 9, 19——[f]Verse 16
[g]Chap. xxvii. 2——[h]Chap. xvi. 32

This is similar to another proverb on the same subject: "A soft answer turneth away wrath." An *angry* word does nothing but *mischief*.

Verse 16. *Hast thou found honey?*] Make a moderate use of all thy enjoyments. "Let thy moderation be known unto all, and appear in all things."

Verse 17. *Withdraw thy foot*] Another proverb will illustrate this: "Too much familiarity breeds contempt."

Verse 20. As *vinegar upon nitre*] The original word נתר *nather* is what is known among chemists as the *natron* of the ancients and of the Scriptures, and *carbonate of soda*. It is found native in *Syria* and *India*, and occurs as an *efflorescence on the soil*. In *Tripoli* it is found in *crystalline incrustations* of from one third to half an inch thick. It is found also in solution in the water of some lakes in *Egypt* and *Hungary*. The borders of these lakes are covered with crystalline masses, of a grayish white or light brown colour; and in some specimens the *natron* is nearly *pure carbonate of soda*, and the *carbonate* is easily discovered by *effervescing* with an *acid*. It appears to have its Hebrew name from נתר *nathar*, to *dissolve* or *loosen*: because a solution of it in water is *abstersive*, taking out *spots*, &c. It is used in the East for the purposes of *washing*. If *vinegar* be poured on it, Dr. Shaw says a *strong fermentation* immediately takes place, which illustrates what Solomon says here: "The singing of songs to a heavy heart is like vinegar upon natron:" that is, "there is no *affinity* between them; and opposition, collucation, and strife, are occasioned by any attempt to unite them."

And poureth vyneger upon chalke.—COVERDALE. This also will occasion an *effervescence*. See Jer. ii. 22.

Verse 21. *If thine enemy be hungry*] See this and the next verse explained, Rom. xii. 20.

Verse 22. *Thou shalt heap coals of fire upon his head*] Not to *consume*, but to melt him into kindness; a metaphor taken from smelting metallic ores:—

So artists melt the sullen ore of lead,
By *heaping coals of fire upon its head:*
In the *kind warmth* the metal learns to *glow*,
And *pure from dross* the *silver* runs *below*.
                 S. WESLEY.

Verse 23. *The north wind driveth away rain*] The *margin* has, "The north wind bringeth forth rain." It is said that the "north wind brings forth rain at Jerusalem, because it brings with it the vapours arising from the sea that lies north of it." The marginal is the *true reading;* and is supported by the *Chaldee, Syriac*, and *Septuagint;* but the *Arabic* reads *south wind*.

A backbiting tongue] A *hidden tongue*.

Verse 24. It is *better to dwell in a corner*] See the note on chap. xxi. 9.

Verse 27. It is *not good to eat much honey*] *Coverdale* translates the whole passage thus: "Like as it is not good to eat to muche hony; even so, he that wyll search out hye thinges, it shal be to hevy for him." 𝔄𝔰 𝔥𝔢 𝔱𝔥𝔞𝔱 𝔢𝔱𝔦𝔱𝔥 𝔪𝔭𝔠𝔥𝔢 𝔥𝔬𝔫𝔭𝔢, 𝔞𝔫𝔡 𝔦𝔱 𝔦𝔰 𝔫𝔬𝔱 𝔱𝔬 𝔥𝔦𝔪 𝔤𝔬𝔬𝔡𝔢; 𝔰𝔬, 𝔱𝔥𝔞𝔱 𝔦𝔰 𝔞 𝔰𝔢𝔯𝔠𝔥𝔢𝔯 𝔬𝔣 𝔪𝔞𝔤𝔢𝔰𝔱𝔢, 𝔰𝔠𝔥𝔞𝔩 𝔟𝔢𝔫 𝔬𝔭𝔭𝔯𝔢𝔰𝔰𝔦𝔡 𝔬𝔣 𝔤𝔩𝔬𝔯𝔦𝔢—Old MS. Bible. He that searches too much into *mysteries*, is likely to be confounded by them. I really think this is the *meaning* of the place; and shall not puzzle either myself or my reader with the discordant explanations which have been brought forward with the hope of illustrating this passage.

CHAPTER XXVI

Honour is not seemly in a fool. The correction and treatment suitable to such. Of the slothful man. Of him who interferes with matters which do not concern him. Contentions to be avoided. Of the dissembler and the lying tongue.

A. M. cir. 3304
B. C. cir. 700
Ol. vigesimæ
cir. annum
primum
A. U. C. cir. 54

AS snow in summer, [a]and as rain in harvest; so honour is not seemly for a fool.

2 As the bird by wandering, as the swallow by flying, so [b]the curse causeless shall not come.

3 [c]A whip for the horse, a bridle for the ass, and a rod for the fool's back.

4 Answer not a fool according to his folly, lest thou also be like unto him.

5 [d]Answer a fool according to his folly, lest he be wise in [e]his own conceit.

6 He that sendeth a message by the hand of a fool cutteth off the feet, *and* drinketh [f]damage.

7 The legs of the lame [g]are not equal: so *is* a parable in the mouth of fools.

8 [h]As he that bindeth a stone in a sling, so *is* he that giveth honour to a fool.

A. M. cir. 3304
B. C. cir. 700
Ol. vigesimæ
cir. annum
primum
A. U. C. cir. 54

[a]1 Samuel xii. 17——[b]Numbers xxiii. 8; Deuteronomy xxiii. 5——[c]Psalm xxxii. 9; chapter x. 13 [d]Matthew xvi. 1–4; xxi. 24–27

[e]Hebrew, *his own eyes*——[f]Or, *violence*——[g]Hebrew, *are lifted up*——[h]Or, *As he that putteth a* precious *stone in a heap of stones*

NOTES ON CHAP. XXVI

Verse 1. *As snow in summer*] None of these is *suitable* to the *time;* and at this unsuitable time, both are *unwelcome: so a fool* to be in *honour* is *unbecoming.*

Verse 2. *As the bird*] צִפּוֹר *tsippor* is taken often for the *sparrow;* but means generally any small bird. As the *sparrow* flies about the house, and the *swallow* emigrates to strange countries; so an undeserved malediction may flutter about the neighbourhood for a season: but in a short time it will disappear as the bird of passage; and never take effect on the innocent person against whom it was pronounced.

Verse 3. *A whip for the horse*] Correction is as suitable to a fool, as a *whip* is for a horse, or a *bridle* for an ass.

Verse 4. *Answer not a fool*] On this and the following verse Bishop *Warburton*, who has written well on many things, and very indifferently on the doctrine of grace, has written with force and perspicuity: "Had this advice been given simply, and without circumstance, *to answer* the fool, and *not to answer* him, one who had reverence for the text would satisfy himself in supposing that the different directions referred to the *doing* a thing *in* and *out of season;* 1. The reasons given why a *fool should not be answered according to his folly*, is, "lest he (the answerer) should be like unto him." 2. The reason given why *the fool should be answered according to his folly*, is, "lest he (the fool) should be wise in his own conceit."

"1. The cause assigned for *forbidding to answer*, therefore, plainly insinuates that the defender of religion should not imitate the insulter of it in his modes of disputation, which may be comprised in sophistry, buffoonery, and scurrility.

"2. The cause assigned for directing *to answer*, as plainly intimates that the sage should address himself to confute the *fool* upon his own false principles, by showing that they lead to conclusions very wide from, very opposite to, those impieties he would deduce from them. If any thing can allay the *fool's vanity*, and prevent his being *wise in his own conceit*, it must be the dishonour of having his own principles turned against himself, and shown to be destructive of his own conclusions."—*Treatise on Grace. Preface.*

Verse 6. *Cutteth off the feet*] Sending by such a person is utterly useless. My old MS. Bible translates well: 𝕳𝖆𝖑𝖙 𝖎𝖓 𝖋𝖊𝖊𝖙 𝖆𝖓𝖉 𝖉𝖗𝖎𝖓𝖐𝖎𝖓𝖌 𝖜𝖎𝖈𝖐𝖎𝖉𝖓𝖊𝖘𝖘𝖊 𝖙𝖍𝖆𝖙 𝖘𝖊𝖓𝖉𝖎𝖙𝖍 𝖜𝖔𝖗𝖉𝖎𝖘 𝖇𝖎 𝖆 𝖋𝖔𝖔𝖑𝖊 𝖒𝖊𝖘𝖘𝖆𝖌𝖊𝖗. Nothing but *lameness* in *himself* can vindicate his sending it by such hands; and, after all, the expedient will be worse than the total omission, for he is likely to *drink wickedness*, i. e., the mischief occasioned by the fool's misconduct. *Coverdale* nearly hits the sense as usual: "He is lame of his fete, yee dronken is he in vanite, that committeth eny thinge to a foole."

Verse 8. *As he that bindeth a stone in a sling, so is he that giveth honour to a fool.*] It is entirely thrown away. This, however, is a difficult proverb; and the *versions* give but little light on the subject. The Hebrew may be translated, "As a piece of precious stone among a heap of stones, so is he that giveth honour to a fool." See the *margin*, and *Parkhurst:* but on this interpretation the meaning would rather be, "It is as useless to throw a jewel among a heap of stones to increase its bulk, as to give honour to a fool."

𝕬𝖘 𝖍𝖊 𝖙𝖍𝖆𝖙 𝖘𝖊𝖓𝖉𝖎𝖙𝖍 𝖆 𝖘𝖙𝖔𝖔𝖓 𝖎𝖓𝖙𝖔 𝖆 𝖍𝖊𝖕𝖊 𝖔𝖋 𝖒𝖔𝖓𝖊𝖊; 𝖘𝖔 𝖍𝖊 𝖙𝖍𝖆𝖙 𝖌𝖊𝖇𝖊𝖙𝖍 𝖙𝖔 𝖆𝖓 𝖚𝖓𝖜𝖎𝖎𝖘𝖒𝖆𝖓 𝖜𝖎𝖗𝖘𝖈𝖍𝖎𝖕.—Old MS. Bible.

"He that setteth a foole in hye dignite, that is even as yf a man dyd caste a precious stone upon the galous."—*Coverdale.* This translator refers to the custom of throwing a stone to the *heap* under which a *criminal lay buried.* The *Vulgate* gives some countenance to this translation: "He who gives honour to a fool is like one who throws a stone to Mercury's heap." *Mercury* was considered the deity who *presided over the highways;* and stones were erected in different places to guide the traveller. Hence those lines of Dr. *Young:*—

"Death stands like Mercuries in every way;
And kindly points us to our journey's end."

A. M. cir. 3304
B. C. cir. 700
Ol. vigesimæ
cir. annum
primum
A. U. C. cir. 54

9 *As* a thorn goeth up into hand of a drunkard; so *is* a parable in the mouth of fools.

10 [i]The great *God* that formed all *things* both rewardeth the fool, and rewardeth transgressors.

11 [k]As a dog returneth to his vomit; [l]*so* a fool [m]returneth to his folly.

12 [n]Seest thou a man wise in his own conceit? *there is* more hope of a fool than of him.

13 [o]The slothful *man* saith, *There is* a lion in the way; a lion *is* in the streets.

14 *As* the door turneth upon his hinges, so *doth* the slothful upon his bed.

15 [p]The slothful hideth his hand in *his* bosom; [q]it grieveth him to bring it again to his mouth.

16 The sluggard *is* wiser in his own conceit than seven men that can render a reason.

17 He that passeth by, *and* [r]meddleth with strife *belonging* not to him, *is like* one that taketh a dog by the ears.

18 As a mad *man* who casteth [s]firebrands, arrows, and death;

19 So *is* the man *that* deceiveth his neighbour, and saith, [t]Am not I in sport?

20 [u]Where no wood is, *there* the fire goeth out: so [v]where *there is* no [w]tale-bearer, the strife [x]ceaseth.

21 [y]*As* coals *are* to burning coals, and wood to fire; so *is* a contentious man to kindle strife.

22 [z]The words of a tale-bearer *are* as wounds, and they go down into the [a]innermost part of the belly.

23 Burning lips and a wicked heart *are like* a potsherd covered with silver dross.

24 He that hateth [b]dissembleth with his lips, and layeth up deceit within him:

25 [c]When he [d]speaketh fair, believe him not: for *there are* seven abominations in his heart.

26 [e]*Whose* hatred is covered by deceit, his wickedness shall be showed before the *whole* congregation.

27 [f]Whoso diggeth a pit shall fall therein: and he that rolleth a stone, it will return upon him.

28 A lying tongue hateth *those that are* afflicted by it; and a flattering mouth worketh ruin.

A. M. cir. 3304
B. C. cir. 700
Ol. vigesimæ
cir. annum
primum
A. U. C. cir. 54

---

[i]Or, *A great* man *grieveth all, and he hireth the fool, he hireth also transgressors*——[k]2 Peter ii. 22——[l]Exod. viii. 15——[m]Heb. *iterateth his folly*——[n]Chap. xxix. 20; Luke xviii. 11; Rom. xii. 16; Rev. iii. 17——[o]Chap. xxii. 13——[p]Chap. xix. 24——[q]Or, *he is weary*——[r]Or, *is enraged*——[s]Heb. *flames, or, sparks*——[t]Eph. v. 4

[u]Heb. *without wood*——[v]Chap. xxii. 10——[w]Or, *whisperer*——[x]Heb. *is silent*——[y]Chap. xv. 18; xxix. 22——[z]Chap. xviii. 8——[a]Heb. *chambers*——[b]Or, *is known*——[c]Psa. xxviii. 3; Jer. ix. 8——[d]Heb. *maketh his voice gracious*——[e]Or, *Hatred is covered in secret*——[f]Psa. vii. 15, 16; ix. 15; x. 2; lvii. 6; ch. xxviii. 10; Eccles. x. 8

Verse 10. *The great* God *that formed all things*] See the *margin*, where this verse is very differently translated. I shall add that of *Coverdale:* "A man of experience discerneth all thinges well: but whoso hyreth a foole, hyreth soch one as wyl take no hede." The רב *rab* may mean either the great God, or a great man: hence the two renderings, in the *text* and in the *margin*.

Verse 11. *As a dog returneth to his vomit*] See note on 2 Pet. ii. 22.

Verse 13. *The slothful* man *saith*] See the note on chap. xxii. 13.

Verse 16. *Than seven men that can render a reason.*] *Seven* here only means *perfection, abundance,* or *multitude.* He is wiser in his own eyes than a *multitude* of the wisest men. "Than seven men that sytt and teach."—*Coverdale;* i. e., than seven *doctors* of the *law,* or *heads* of the schools of the *prophets,* who always *sat* while they *taught.*

Verse 17. *He that passeth by*] This proverb stands true *ninety-nine* times out of a *hundred,* where people meddle with *domestic broils,* or differences between *men* and their *wives.*

Verse 19. *Am not I in sport?*] How many hearts have been made sad, and how many reputations have been slain, by this kind of *sport!* "I designed no harm by what I said;"

"It was only in jest," &c. *Sportive* as such persons may think their conduct to be, it is as ruinous as that of the *madman* who shoots *arrows,* throws *firebrands,* and projects in all directions *instruments of death,* so that some are wounded, some burnt, and some slain.

Verse 20. *Where no wood is,* there *the fire goeth out*] The tale-*receiver* and the tale-*bearer* are the agents of discord. If none received the slander in the *first* instance, it could not be propagated. Hence our proverb, "The receiver is as bad as the thief." And our *laws* treat them equally; for the *receiver* of stolen goods, knowing them to be stolen, is *hanged,* as well as *he who stole them.*

Verse 22. *The words of a tale-bearer*] The same with chap. xviii. 8, where see the note.

Verse 23. *Burning lips and a wicked heart*] Splendid, shining, smooth lips; that is, lips which make great professions of friendship are like a *vessel plated* over with *base metal* to make it resemble *silver;* but it is only a *vile pot,* and even the *outside* is not *pure.*

Verse 25. *When he speaketh fair*] For there are such hypocrites and false friends in the world.

Believe him not] Let all his professions go for nothing.

For there are *seven abominations in his heart.*] That is, he is *full of abominations.*

Verse 27. *Whoso diggeth a pit*] See note on Psa. vii. 15. There is a *Latin* proverb like this: *Malum consilium consultori pessimum,* "A bad counsel, but worst to the giver." *Harm watch; harm catch.*

Verse 28. *A lying tongue hateth* those that are *afflicted by it*] He that injures another hates him in proportion to the injury he has done him; and, strange to tell, in proportion to the *innocence* of the oppressed. The debtor cannot bear the sight of his creditor; nor the knave, of him whom he has injured.

CHAPTER XXVII

To-morrow is uncertain. Self-praise forbidden. Anger and envy. Reproof from a friend. Want makes us feel the value of a supply. A good neighbour. Beware of suretyship. Suspicious praise. The quarrelsome woman. One friend helps another. Man insatiable. The incorrigible fool. Domestic cares. The profit of flocks for food and raiment.

A. M. cir. 3304
B. C. cir. 700
Ol. vigesimæ
cir. annum
primum
A. U. C. cir. 54

BOAST [a]not thyself of [b]to-morrow; for thou knowest not what a day may bring forth.

2 [c]Let another man praise thee, and not thine own mouth; a stranger, and not thine own lips.

3 A stone *is* [d]heavy, and the sand weighty; but a fool's wrath *is* heavier than them both.

4 [e]Wrath *is* cruel, and anger *is* outrageous; but [f]who is *able* to stand before [g]envy?

5 [h]Open rebuke *is* better than secret love.

6 [i]Faithful *are* the wounds of a friend; but the kisses of an enemy *are* [k]deceitful.

A. M. cir. 3304
B. C. cir. 700
Ol. vigesimæ
cir. annum
primum
A. U. C. cir. 54

7 The full soul [l]loatheth a honey-comb; but [m]to the hungry soul every bitter thing is sweet.

8 As a bird that wandereth from her nest, so *is* a man that wandereth from his place.

9 Ointment and perfume rejoice the heart: so *doth* the sweetness of a man's friend [n]by hearty counsel.

---

[a]Luke xii. 19, 20; James iv. 13, &c.——[b]Heb. *to-morrow day*——[c]Chap. xxv. 27——[d]Heb. *heaviness* [e]Heb. *Wrath* is *cruelly, and anger an overflowing*——[f]1 John iii. 12

[g]Or, *jealousy;* chap. vi. 34——[h]Chap. xxviii. 23; Gal. ii. 14——[i]Psa. cxli. 5——[k]Or, *earnest,* or *frequent* [l]Heb. *treadeth under foot*——[m]Job vi. 7——[n]Heb. *from the counsel of the soul*

NOTES ON CHAP. XXVII

Verse 1. *Boast not thyself of to-morrow*] See note on James iv. 13, &c. Do not depend on any future moment for spiritual good which at present thou needest, and God is willing to give, and without which, should death surprise thee, thou must be eternally lost; such as repentance, faith in Christ, the pardon of sin, the witness of the Holy Spirit, and complete renovation of soul. Be incessant in thy application to God for these blessings.

My old MS. Bible translates thus: **Ne glorie thou into the morewenning.** Here we see the derivation of our word *morning;* morewenning, from *more,* and *wen* or *won,* to *dwell,* i. e., a *continuance* of time to *live* or *dwell* in your present habitation. Every man wishes to live longer, and therefore wishes for *to-morrow;* and when to-morrow comes, then to-morrow, and so on.

Verse 2. *Let another man praise thee, and not thine own mouth*] We have a similar proverb, which illustrates this: "Self-praise is no commendation."

Verse 4. *Who is able to stand before envy?*] The rabbins have a curious story on this subject, and it has been formed by the moderns into a fable. There were two persons, one *covetous* and the other *envious,* to whom a certain person promised to grant whatever they should ask; but *double* to him who should ask *last.* The covetous man would not ask *first,* because he wished to get the *double* portion; and the *envious* man would not make the first request because he could not bear the thoughts of thus benefiting his neighbour.

However, at last he requested that *one* of his eyes should be taken out, in order that his neighbour might lose both.

Verse 5. *Open rebuke is better than secret love.*] *Plutarch* gives an account of a man who, aiming a blow at his enemy's life, cut open an imposthume, which by a salutary discharge saved his life, that was sinking under a disease for which a remedy could not be found. *Partial friendship* covers faults; envy, malice, and revenge, will exhibit, heighten, and even multiply them. The former conceals us from ourselves; the latter shows us the worst part of our character. Thus we are taught the necessity of amendment and correction. In this sense *open rebuke is better than secret love.* Yet it is a *rough medicine,* and none can *desire* it. But the genuine open-hearted friend may be intended, who tells *you* your faults *freely,* but conceals them from all *others;* hence the *sixth* verse: "Faithful are the wounds of a friend."

Verse 8. *As a bird that wandereth from her nest*] Leaving her own brood, places of retreat, and feeding-ground behind, and going into strange countries, where she is exposed to every kind of danger. So is the man who leaves his family connections and country, and goes into strange parts to find employment, better his circumstances, make a fortune, &c. I have seen multitudes of such *wanderers from their place* come to great misery and wretchedness. God's general advice is, "Do good, and dwell in the land; and verily thou shalt be fed."

Verse 9. *Ointment and perfume*] Anointing

A. M. cir. 3304
B. C. cir. 700
Ol. vigesimæ
cir. annum
primum
A. U. C. cir. 54

10 Thine own friend, and thy father's friend, forsake not; neither go into thy brother's house in the day of thy calamity: *for* °better *is* a neighbour *that is* near, than a brother far off.

11 ᵖMy son, be wise, and make my heart glad, �qthat I may answer him that reproacheth me.

12 ʳA prudent *man* foreseeth the evil, *and* hideth himself; *but* the simple pass on, *and* are punished.

13 ˢTake his garment that is surety for a stranger, and take a pledge of him for a strange woman.

14 He that blesseth his friend with a loud voice, rising early in the morning, it

shall be counted a curse to him.

15 ᵗA continual dropping in a very rainy day and a contentious woman are alike.

16 Whosoever hideth her hideth the wind, and the ointment of his right hand, *which* bewrayeth *itself*.

17 Iron sharpeneth iron; so a man sharpeneth the countenance of his friend.

18 ᵘWhoso keepeth the fig tree shall eat the fruit thereof: so he that waiteth on his master shall be honoured.

19 As in water face *answereth* to face; so the heart of man to man.

20 ᵛHell and destruction are ᵂnever full, so ˣthe eyes of man are never satisfied.

A. M. cir. 3304
B. C. cir. 700
Ol. vigesimæ
cir. annum
primum
A. U. C. cir. 54

°Chap. xvii. 17; xviii. 24; see chap. xix. 7——ᵖChap. x. 1; xxiii. 15, 24——�q Psa. cxxvii. 5——ʳChap. xxii. 3——ˢSee Exodus xxii. 26; chap. xx. 16——ᵗChap.

xix. 13——ᵘ1 Corinthians ix. 7, 13——ᵛChap. xxx. 16; Habakkuk ii. 5——ᵂHebrew, *not*——ˣEcclesiastes i. 8; vi. 7

---

the head and various parts of the body with aromatic oil is frequent in the East, and fumigating the beards of the guests at the conclusion of an entertainment is almost universal; as is also sprinkling rose-water, and water highly ordoriferous. Two of the curious vessels which are used for this purpose are now before me; they hold some quarts each, and are beautifully inlaid with silver in the form of sprigs, leaves, &c.

Verse 10. *Thine own friend*] A well and long tried friend is invaluable. Him that has been a friend to thy *family* never *forget*, and never *neglect*. And, in the time of adversity, rather apply to such a one, than go to thy nearest relative, who keeps himself at a distance.

Verse 12. *A prudent* man *foreseeth the evil*] The very same as chap. xxii. 3.

Verse 13. *Take his garment*] The same as chap. xx. 16.

Verse 14. *He that blesseth his friend*] He who makes loud and public protestations of acknowledgments to his friend for favours received, subjects his *sincerity* to suspicion; and remember the Italian proverb elsewhere quoted:—"He who praises you more than he was wont to do, has either deceived you, or is about to do it." Extravagant public professions are little to be regarded.

Verse 15. *A continual dropping*] See chap. xix. 13.

Verse 16. *Whosoever hideth her hideth the wind*] You may as well attempt to repress the blowing of the wind, as the tongue of a scold; and to conceal this unfortunate propensity of a wife is as impossible as to hush the storm, and prevent its sound from being heard.

The ointment of his right hand] You can no more conceal such a woman's conduct, than you can the smell of the aromatic oil with which your hand has been anointed. The Hebrew is very obscure, and is variously translated. *Coverdale* thus: "He that refrayneth her, refrayneth the wynde; and holdith oyle

fast in his honde." That is, he attempts to do what is impossible to be done.

Verse 17. *Iron sharpeneth iron*] As *hard iron*, viz., *steel*, will bring a knife to a better edge when it is properly *whetted against* it: so one friend may be the means of *exciting* another to *reflect*, dive deeply into, and illustrate a subject, without which *whetting* or *excitement*, this had never taken place. Had *Horace* seen this proverb in the *Septuagint* translation when he wrote to the *Pisos?*

Ergo fungar vice cotis, acutum
Reddere quæ ferrum valet, exors ipsa secandi.
Hor. Ars. Poet., ver. 304.

"But let me sharpen others, as the hone
Gives edge to razors, though itself have none."
Francis.

Verse 19. *As in water face* answereth *to face*] All men's hearts are pretty nearly alike; water is not more like to water, than one heart is to another. Or, as a man sees his face perfectly reflected by the water, when looking into it; so the wise and penetrating man sees generally what is in the heart of another by considering the general tenor of his words and actions.

"Surely, if each man saw another's heart
There would be no commerce;
All would disperse,
And live apart."
Herbert.

Verse 20. *Hell and destruction are never full*] How hideous must the soul of a covetous man be, when God compares it to *hell and perdition!*

The eyes of man are never satisfied.] As the *grave* can never be filled up with *bodies*, nor *perdition* with *souls;* so the restless desire, the lust of power, riches, and splendour, is never satisfied. Out of this ever unsatisfied desire spring all the changing fashions, the varied amusements, and the endless modes of getting money, prevalent in every age, and in every country.

A. M. cir. 3304
B. C. cir. 700
Ol. vigesimæ
cir. annum
primum
A. U. C. cir. 54

21 [y]*As* the fining pot for silver, and the furnace for gold; so *is* a man to his praise.

22 [z]Though thou shouldest bray a fool in a mortar among wheat with a pestle, *yet* will not his foolishness depart from him.

23 Be thou diligent to know the state of thy flocks, *and* [a]look well to thy herds.

24 For [b]riches *are* not for ever: and doth the crown *endure* [c]to every generation?

25 [d]The hay appeareth, and the tender grass showeth itself, and herbs of the mountains are gathered.

26 The lambs *are* for thy clothing, and the goats *are* the price of the field.

27 And *thou shalt have* goats' milk enough for thy food, for the food of thy household, and *for* the [e]maintenance for thy maidens.

A. M. cir. 3304
B. C. cir. 700
Ol. vigesimæ
cir. annum
primum
A. U. C. cir. 54

---

[y]Ch. xvii. 3——[z]Isa. i. 5; Jer. v. 3; ch. xxiii. 35
[a]Heb. *set thy heart*——[b]Heb. *strength*——[c]Heb. *to gen-*

eration and generation; Psa. xxxiii. 11; xlv. 17; xlix. 11; lxxii. 5; lxxxv. 5; lxxxix. 1——[d]Psa. civ. 14——[e]Heb. *life*

Verse 21. As *the fining pot for silver*] As silver and gold are tried by the art of the refiner, so is a man's heart by the praise he receives. If he *feel* it not, he *deserves* it; if he be *puffed up* by it, he is *worthless.*

Verse 22. *Though thou shouldest bray a fool*] Leaving all other conjectures, of which commentators are full, I would propose, that this is a metaphor taken from *pounding metallic ores* in very large mortars, such as are still common in the East, in order that, when subjected to the action of the fire, the metal may be the more easily separated from the ore. However you may try, by *precept* or *example,* or both, to instruct a stupid man, your labour is lost; his foolishness cannot be separated from him. You may purge metals of all their dross; but you cannot purge the fool of his folly.

Verse 23. *The state of thy flocks*] The directions to the end of the chapter refer chiefly to *pastoral* and *agricultural* affairs. Do not trust thy flocks to the shepherd merely; number them thyself; look into their condition; see how they are tended; and when, and with what, and in what proportion, they are fed.

Verse 24. *For riches* are *not for ever*] All other kinds of property are very transitory. Money and the highest civil honours are but for a short season. Flocks and herds, properly attended to, may be multiplied and continued from generation to generation. The *crown* itself is not naturally so permanent.

Verse 25. *The hay appeareth*] Take care that this be timeously *mown,* carefully dried, and safely ricked or housed. And when the *tender grass* and the proper herbs *appear* in *the mountains* in the spring, then send forth the *lambs,* the young of the flock, that they may get suitable pasturage, without too much impoverishing the *home fields;* for by the sale of the *lambs* and *goats,* the *price of the field* is paid—all the landlord's demands are discharged. Either a certain number of lambs, goats, and other cattle, was given to the landlord; or so much money as so many lambs, &c., were then worth.

Verse 26. *The lambs* are *for thy clothing*] So many *fleeces* are given in some places as *rent* to the landlord.

Verse 27. *Goats' milk enough for thy food*] לחמך *lelachmecha,* "to thy bread;" for they ate the *bread* and *supped the milk* to assist mastication, and help deglutition. And it seems that *bread,* with *goats' milk,* was the general article of food for the *master* and his *family;* and for the *servant maids* who assisted in the household work, and performed the operations required in the *dairy.*

The reader who wishes to see these maxims detailed and illustrated at large, may consult the writers *De Re Rustica,* where he will find much curious information.

CHAPTER XXVIII

The timidity of the wicked. Quick succession in the government of a country is a punishment to the land. Of the poor who oppress the poor. The upright poor man is preferable to the wicked rich man. The unprofitable conduct of the usurer. The prosperity of the righteous a cause of rejoicing. He is blessed who fears always. A wicked ruler a curse. The murderer generally execrated. The faithful man. The corrupt judge. The foolishness of trusting in one's own heart. The charitable man. When the wicked are elevated, it is a public evil.

A. M. cir. 3304
B. C. cir. 700
Ol. vigesimæ
cir. annum
primum
A. U. C. cir. 54

THE [a]wicked flee when no man pursueth: but the righteous are bold as a lion.

2 For the transgression of a land many *are* the princes thereof: but [b]by a man of understanding *and* knowledge the state *thereof* shall be prolonged.

A. M. cir. 3304
B. C. cir. 700
Ol. vigesimæ
cir. annum
primum
A. U. C. cir. 54

---

[a]Lev. xxvi. 17, 36; Psa. liii. 5——[b]Or, *by men of under-*

standing and *wisdom shall they likewise be prolonged*

NOTES ON CHAP. XXVIII

Verse 1. *The wicked flee*] Every wicked man, however *bold* he may *appear,* is full of dreary apprehensions relative to both worlds. But the righteous has true courage, being conscious of his own innocence, and the approbation of his God. The unpitious fleeth.—Old MS.

A. M. cir. 3304
B. C. cir. 700
Ol. vigesimæ
cir. annum
primum
A. U. C. cir. 54

3 ᶜA poor man that oppresseth the poor *is like* a sweeping rain ᵈwhich leaveth no food.

4 ᵉThey that forsake the law praise the wicked: ᶠbut such as keep the law contend with them.

5 ᵍEvil men understand not judgment: but ʰthey that seek the LORD understand all *things*.

6 ᶦBetter *is* the poor that walketh in his uprightness, than *he that is* perverse *in his* ways, though he *be* rich.

7 ᵏWhoso keepeth the law *is* a wise son: but he that ˡis a companion of riotous *men* shameth his father.

8 ᵐHe that by usury and ⁿunjust gain in-

creaseth his substance, he shall gather it for him that will pity the poor.

A. M. cir. 3304
B. C. cir. 700
Ol. vigesimæ
cir. annum
primum
A. U. C. cir. 54

9 ᵒHe that turneth away his ear from hearing the law, ᵖeven his prayer *shall be* abomination.

10 ᑫWhoso causeth the righteous to go astray in an evil way, he shall fall himself into his own pit: ʳbut the upright shall have good *things* in possession.

11 The rich man *is* wise ˢin his own conceit: but the poor that hath understanding searcheth him out.

12 ᵗWhen righteous *men* do rejoice, *there is* great glory: but when the wicked rise, a man is ᵘhidden.

ᶜMatt. xviii. 28——ᵈHeb. *without food*——ᵉPsa. x. 3; xlix. 18; Rom. i. 32——ᶠ1 Kings xviii. 18, 21; Matt. iii. 7; xiv. 4; Eph. v. 11——ᵍPsa. xcii. 6——ʰJohn vii. 17; 1 Cor. ii. 15; 1 John ii. 20, 27——ᶦChap. xix. 1; ver. 18——ᵏChap. xxix. 3——ˡOr, *feedeth gluttons*

ᵐJob xxvii. 16, 17; chapter xiii. 22; Eccles. ii. 26 ⁿHeb. *by increase*——ᵒZech. vii. 11——ᵖPsa. lxvi. 18; cix. 7; chap. xv. 8——ᑫChap. xxvi. 27——ʳMatt. vi. 33 ˢHeb. *in his eyes*——ᵗVer. 28; chap. xi. 10; xxix. 2; Eccles x. 6——ᵘOr, *sought for*

Bible. This word is often used for *impious, wicked, ungodly;* hence it appears that our word *pity* anciently meant *piety* or *godliness.*

Verse 2. *Many are the princes*] Nations, as nations, cannot be judged in a future world; therefore, God judges them *here.* And where the *people* are very *wicked,* and the *constitution* very *bad,* the *succession of princes is frequent*—they are generally taken off by an untimely death. Where the people know that the constitution is in their favour, they seldom disturb the prince, as they consider him the guardian of their privileges.

But by a man of understanding] Whether he be a *king,* or the king's *prime minister,* the prosperity of the state is advanced by his counsels.

Verse 3. *A poor man that oppresseth the poor*] Our Lord illustrates this proverb most beautifully, by the parable of the *two debtors,* Matt. xviii. 23. One owed *ten thousand talents,* was insolvent, begged for time, was forgiven. A fellow servant owed this one *a hundred pence:* he was insolvent; but prayed his fellow servant to give him a little time, and he would pay it all. He would not, took him by the throat, and cast him into prison till he should pay that debt. Here the *poor* oppressed the *poor;* and what was the consequence? The oppressing poor was delivered to the tormentors; and the forgiven debt charged to his amount, because *he showed no mercy.* The *comparatively poor* are often shockingly uncharitable and unfeeling towards the *real poor.*

Like *a sweeping rain*] These are frequent in the East; and sometimes carry flocks, crops, and houses, away with them.

Verse 4. *They that forsake the law*] He that transgresses says, in fact, that it is *right to transgress;* and thus other wicked persons are encouraged.

Verse 5. *They that seek the Lord understand all* things.] They are wise unto salvation; they "have the unction from the Holy One, and they know all things," 1 John ii. 20, every

thing that is essentially needful for them to know, in reference to both worlds.

Verse 8. *He that by usury—increaseth his substance*] By taking unlawful interest for his money; *lending* to a man in great distress money, for the use of which he requires an *exorbitant sum.* O that the names of all those unfeeling, hard-hearted, consummate villains in the nation, who thus take advantage of their neighbour's necessities to enrich themselves, were published at every market cross; and then the delinquents all sent to their brother savages in New Zealand. It would be a happy riddance to the country.

Verse 9. *He that turneth away his ear from hearing the law*] Many suppose, if they *do not know their duty, they shall not be accountable for their transgressions;* and therefore avoid every thing that is calculated to enlighten them. They will not read the Bible, lest they should know the will of God; and they will not attend Divine ordinances for the same reason. But this pretence will avail them nothing; as he that *might have known* his *master's will,* but would not, shall be treated as he shall be who *did know* it, and disobeyed it. Even the *prayers* of such a person as this are reputed *sin* before God.

Verse 10. *Whoso causeth the righteous to go astray*] He who strives to pervert one really converted to God, in order that he may pour contempt on religion, shall fall into that hell to which he has endeavoured to lead the other.

Verse 12. *When righteous* men *do rejoice*] When true religion is no longer persecuted, and the word of God duly esteemed, *there is great glory;* for the word of the Lord has then free course, runs, and is glorified: but *when the wicked rise*—when they are *elevated* to places of trust, and put at the head of civil affairs, then the righteous man is obliged to hide himself; the word of the Lord becomes scarce, and there is no open vision. The *first* was the case in this country, in the days of EDWARD VI.; the *second* in the days of his suc-

A. M. cir. 3304
B. C. cir. 700
Ol. vigesimæ
cir. annum
primum
A. U. C. cir. 54

13 [v]He that covereth his sins shall not prosper: but whoso confesseth and forsaketh *them* shall have mercy.

14 Happy *is* the man [w]that feareth alway: [x]but he that hardeneth his heart shall fall into mischief.

15 [y]*As* a roaring lion, and a ranging bear; [z]*so is* a wicked ruler over the poor people.

16 The prince that wanteth understanding *is* also a great oppressor: *but* he that hateth covetousness shall prolong *his* days.

17 [a]A man that doeth violence to the blood of *any* person shall flee to the pit; let no man stay him.

18 [b]Whoso walketh uprightly shall be saved: but [c]*he that is* perverse *in his* ways shall fall at once.

19 [d]He that tilleth his land shall have plenty of bread: but he that followeth after vain *persons* shall have poverty enough.

20 A faithful man shall abound with blessings: [e]but he that maketh haste to be rich shall not be [f]innocent.

21 [g]To have respect of persons *is* not good; for, [h]for a piece of bread *that* man will transgress.

A. M. cir. 3304
B. C. cir. 700
Ol. vigesimæ
cir. annum
primum
A. U. C. cir. 54

22 [i]He [k]that hasteth to be rich *hath* an evil eye, and considereth not that poverty shall come upon him.

23 [l]He that rebuketh a man afterwards shall find more favour than he that flattereth with the tongue.

24 Whoso robbeth his father or his mother, and saith, *It is* no transgression; the same [m]*is* the companion of [n]a destroyer.

25 [o]He that is of a proud heart stirreth up strife: [p]but he that putteth his trust in the LORD shall be made fat.

26 He that trusteth in his own heart is a fool: but whoso walketh wisely, he shall be delivered.

27 [q]He that giveth unto the poor shall not lack: but he that hideth his eyes shall have many a curse.

28 [r]When the wicked rise, [s]men hide themselves: but when they perish, the righteous increase.

---

[v]Psa. xxxii. 3, 5; 1 John i. 8, 9, 10——[w]Psa. xvi. 8; chap. xxiii. 17——[x]Rom. ii. 5; xi. 20——[y]1 Pet. v. 8 [z]Exod. i. 14, 16, 22; Matt. ii. 16——[a]Genesis ix. 6; Exod. xxi. 14——[b]Chap. xix. 9, 25——[c]Ver. 6 [d]Chap. xii. 11——[e]Chap. xiii. 11; xx. 21; xxiii. 4; ver. 22; 1 Tim. vi. 9——[f]Or, *unpunished*

[g]Chap. xviii. 5; xxiv. 23——[h]Ezek. xiii. 19——[i]Or, *he that hath an evil eye hasteth to be rich*——[k]Ver. 20 [l]Chap. xxvii. 5, 6——[m]Chap. xviii. 9——[n]Heb. *a man destroying*——[o]Chap. xiii. 10——[p]1 Tim. vi. 6 [q]Deut. xv. 7, &c.; chap. xix. 17; xxii. 9——[r]Ver. 12; chap. xxix. 2——[s]Job xxiv. 4

---

cessor, MARY I. Popery, cruelty, and knavery, under her, nearly destroyed the Church and the State in these islands.

Verse 13. *He that covereth his sins*] Here is a general *direction* relative to *conversion.* 1. If the sinner do not *acknowledge* his sins; if he *cover* and *excuse* them, and refuse to come to the light of God's word and Spirit, lest his deeds should be reproved, he *shall find no salvation.* God will never admit a *sinful, unhumbled* soul, into his kingdom. 2. But if he confess his sin, with a penitent and broken heart, and, by *forsaking* every evil way, give this proof that he feels his own sore, and the plague of his heart, then he shall *have mercy.* Here is a doctrine of vital importance to the salvation of the soul, which the weakest may understand.

Verse 14. *Happy is the man that feareth alway*] That ever carries about with him that reverential and filial fear of God, which will lead him to avoid sin, and labour to do that which is lawful and right in the sight of God his Saviour.

Verse 16. *The prince that wanteth understanding*] A weak prince will generally have wicked ministers, for his weakness prevents him from making a proper choice; and he is apt to prefer them who flatter him, and minister most to his pleasures. The quantum of the king's intellect may be always appreciated by

the mildness or oppressiveness of his government. He who plunges his people into expensive wars, to support which they are burdened with taxes, is a prince without understanding. He does not know his own interest, and does not regard that of his people. But these things, though general truths, apply more particularly to those despotic governments which prevail in Asiatic countries.

Verse 17. *That doeth violence to the blood*] He who either *slays* the innocent, or procures his destruction, may flee to *hide* himself: but let none give him protection. The law demands his life, because he is a *murderer;* and let none deprive justice of its claim. Murder is the most horrid crime in the sight of God and man; it scarcely ever goes unpunished, and is universally execrated.

Verse 18. *Shall fall at once*] Shall fall *without resource, altogether.*

Verse 19. *He that tilleth his land*] See chap. xii. 11.

Verse 20. *He that maketh haste to be rich*] See chap. xiii. 11; xx. 21.

Verse 24. *Whoso robbeth his father*] The father's property is as much his own, in reference to the child, as that of the merest *stranger.* He who robs his parents is worse than a common robber; to the act of dishonesty and rapine he adds ingratitude, cruelty, and disobedience. Such a person is *the companion* of a destroyer; he may be considered as a murderer.

Verse 25. *Shall be made fat.*] Shall be prosperous.

Verse 26. *He that trusteth in his own heart*

is a fool] For his heart, which is deceitful and desperately wicked, will infallibly deceive him.

Verse 27. *He that giveth unto the poor*] See the notes on the passages referred to in the margin.

CHAPTER XXIX

We must not despise correction. The prudent king. The flatterer. The just judge. Contend not with a fool. The prince who opens his ears to reports. The poor and the deceitful. The pious king. The insolent servant. The humiliation of the proud. Of the partner of a thief. The fear of man. The Lord the righteous Judge.

A. M. cir. 3304
B. C. cir. 700
Ol. vigesimæ
cir. annum
primum
A. U. C. cir. 54

[a]HE, [b]that being often reproved hardeneth *his* neck, shall suddenly be destroyed, and that without remedy.

2 [c]When the righteous are [d]in authority, the people rejoice: but when the wicked beareth rule, [e]the people mourn.

3 [f]Whoso loveth wisdom rejoiceth his father: [g]but he that keepeth company with harlots spendeth *his* substance.

4 The king by judgment establisheth the land: but [h]he that receiveth gifts overthroweth it.

5 A man that flattereth his neighbour spreadeth a net for his feet.

6 In the transgression of an evil man *there is* a snare: but the righteous doth sing and rejoice.

7 [i]The righteous considereth the cause of the poor: *but* the wicked regardeth not to know *it.*

A. M. cir. 3304
B. C. cir. 700
Ol. vigesimæ
cir. annum
primum
A. U. C. cir. 54

8 [k]Scornful men [l]bring a city into a snare: but wise *men* [m]turn away wrath.

9 *If* a wise man contendeth with a foolish man, [n]whether he rage or laugh, *there is* no rest.

10 [o]The [p]bloodthirsty hate the upright: but the just seek his soul.

11 A [q]fool uttereth all his mind: but a wise *man* keepeth it in till afterwards.

12 If a ruler hearken to lies, all his servants *are* wicked.

13 The poor and [r]the deceitful man [s]meet together: [t]the LORD lighteneth both their eyes.

[a]Heb. *A man of reproofs*——[b]1 Sam. ii. 25; 2 Chron. xxxvi. 16; ch. i. 24–27——[c]Esth. viii. 15; ch. xi. 10; xxviii. 12, 28——[d]Or, *increased*——[e]Esth. iii. 15 [f]Ch. x. 1; xv. 20; xxvii. 11——[g]Ch. v. 9, 10; vi. 26; xxviii. 7; Luke xv. 13, 30——[h]Heb. *a man of oblations*

[i]Job xxix. 16; xxxi. 13; Psa. xli. 1——[k]Ch. xi. 11 [l]Or, *set a city on fire*——[m]Ezek. xxii. 30——[n]Matt. xi. 17——[o]Heb. *Men of blood*——[p]Gen. iv. 5, 8; 1 John iii. 12——[q]Judg. xvi. 17; chap. xii. 16; xiv. 33——[r]Or, *the usurer*——[s]Ch. xxii. 2——[t]Matt. v. 45

NOTES ON CHAP. XXIX

Verse 1. *Hardeneth his neck*] Becomes *stubborn* and *obstinate.*

Verse 3. *But he that keepeth company*] רעה roeh, he that *feedeth harlots,* יאבד yeabed, *shall utterly destroy* his substance. Has there ever been a single case to the contrary?

Verse 4. *He that receiveth gifts*] This was notoriously the case in this kingdom, before the passing of the *Magna Charta,* or *great charter of liberties.* Hence that article in it, Nulli vendemus justitiam; "We will not sell justice to any." I have met with cases in our ancient records where, in order to get his *right,* a man was obliged almost to ruin himself in *presents to the king, queen, and their favourites,* to get the case decided in his favour.

Verse 5. *Spreadeth a net for his feet.*] Beware of a flatterer; he does not flatter merely to please you, but to *deceive you* and *profit himself.*

Verse 9. *Whether he rage or laugh*] Coverdale translates, "Yf a wyse man go to lawe with a foole, whether he deale with him frendly or roughly he geteth no rest."

Verse 11. *A fool uttereth all his mind*] A man should be careful to keep his *own secret,* and never tell his whole mind upon any subject, while there are other opinions yet to be delivered; else, if he speak *again,* he must go over his old ground; and as he brings out nothing *new,* he injures his former *argument.*

Verse 12. *If a ruler hearken to lies*] Wherever the system of *espionage* is permitted to prevail, there the system of *falsity* is established; for he who is capable of being a *spy* and informer, is not only capable of telling and swearing lies, but also of cutting his king's or even his *father's* throat. I have seen cases, where the *same spy* received pay from both parties, and deceived both.

Verse 13. *The poor and the deceitful man*] It is difficult to fix the meaning of חככים techachim, which we here render the *deceitful man.* The TARGUM has, "The *poor* and the *man* of LITTLE WEALTH." The SEPTUAGINT, "The *usurer* and the DEBTOR." The VULGATE, "The *poor* and CREDITOR." COVERDALE, "The *poor* and the LENDER." OTHERS, "The *poor* and the RICH;" "The *poor* and the OPPRESSORS." I suppose the meaning may be the same as in chap. xxii. 2: "The rich and the poor meet

A. M. cir. 3304
B. C. cir. 700
Ol. vigesimæ
cir. annum
primum
A. U. C. cir. 54

14 [u]The king that [v]faithfully judgeth the poor, his throne shall be established for ever.

15 [w]The rod and reproof give wisdom: but [x]a child left *to himself* bringeth his mother to shame.

16 When the wicked are multiplied, transgression increaseth: [y]but the righteous shall see their fall.

17 [z]Correct thy son, and he shall give thee rest; yea, he shall give delight unto thy soul.

18 [a]Where *there is* no vision, the people [b]perish: but [c]he that keepeth the law, happy *is* he.

19 A servant will not be corrected by words: for though he understand he will not answer.

20 Seest thou a man *that is* hasty [d]in his words? [e]*there is* more hope of a fool than of him.

21 He that delicately bringeth up his servant from a child shall have him become *his* son at the length.

A. M. cir. 3304
B. C. cir. 700
Ol. vigesimæ
cir. annum
primum
A. U. C. cir. 54

22 [f]An angry man stirreth up strife, and a furious man aboundeth in transgression.

23 [g]A man's pride shall bring him low: but honour shall uphold the humble in spirit.

24 Whoso is partner with a thief hateth his own soul: [h]he heareth cursing, and bewrayeth *it* not.

25 [i]The fear of man bringeth a snare: but whoso putteth his trust in the LORD [k]shall be safe.

26 [l]Many seek [m]the ruler's favour: but *every* man's judgment *cometh* from the LORD.

27 An unjust man *is* an abomination to the just; and *he that is* upright in the way *is* abomination to the wicked.

---

[u]Chap. xx. 28; xxv. 5——[v]Psa. lxxii. 2, 4, 13, 14
[w]Ver. 17——[x]Chap. x. 1; xvii. 21, 25——[y]Psa. xxvii. 36;
lviii. 10; xci. 8; xcii. 11——[z]Chap. xiii. 24; xix. 18; xxii.
15; xxiii. 13, 14; ver. 15——[a]1 Sam. iii. 1; Amos viii. 11,
12——[b]Or, *is made naked*——[c]John xiii. 17; James i. 25
[d]Or, *in his matters*——[e]Chap. xxvi. 12

[f]Chap. xv. 18; xxvi. 21——[g]Job xxii. 29; chap. xv. 33;
xviii. 12; Isa. lxvi. 2; Dan. iv. 30, 31, &c.; Matt. xxiii.
12; Luke xiv. 11; xviii. 14; Acts xii. 23; James iv. 6, 10;
1 Pet. v. 5——[h]Lev. v. 1——[i]Gen. xii. 12; xx. 2, 11
[k]Heb. *shall be set on high*——[l]See Psalm xx. 9; chapter
xix. 6——[m]Heb. *the face of a ruler*

---

together; the Lord is the Maker of them all." Where see the note.

Verse 16. When the wicked are multiplied] That, in the *multiplication of the wicked transgression is increased*, requires no proof; but an important doctrine attaches to this. On this account wicked nations and wicked families are cut off and rooted out. Were it not so, righteousness would in process of time be banished from the earth. This will account for many of the numerous instances in which whole families fail.

Verse 18. Where there is *no vision*] My old MS. Bible, following the *Vulgate*, translates: **Whan prophecye schal fallen, the peple schal ben to scatered.** Where Divine revelation, and the faithful preaching of the sacred testimonies, are neither reverenced nor attended, the ruin of that land is at no great distance.

But he that keepeth the law, happy is *he.*] Go how it may with others, *he* shall be safe. So our Lord: "Blessed are they who hear the word of God, and keep it."

Verse 21. He that delicately bringeth up his servant] Such persons are generally forgetful of their obligations, assume the rights and privileges of children, and are seldom good for any thing.

Verse 22. An angry man stirreth up strife] His spirit begets its *like* wherever he goes.

And a furious man aboundeth in transgression.] His furious spirit is always carrying him into *extremes*, and each of these is a *transgression.*

Verse 23. A man's pride shall bring him low] A proud man is universally despised, and such are often exposed to great mortifications.

Verse 24. Hateth his *own soul*] נפשו

naphsho, his *life*, as the outraged law may at any time seize on and put him to *death.*

He heareth cursing] אלה *alah*, the *execration* or *adjuration*, (for all culprits were *charged, as before God*, to *tell the truth*,) ולא יגד *velo yaggid*, but HE *will not tell* IT. He has no fear of God, nor reverence for an oath, because his heart is hardened through the deceitfulness of sin.

Verse 25. The fear of man bringeth a snare] How often has this led weak men, though *sincere* in their general character, to deny their God, and abjure his people! See the case of *Peter;* and learn from this, O reader, that where the mighty have been slain, *thou* wilt fall, unless thou call on the Strong for *strength*, and for *courage* to use it. Be not ashamed of JESUS, nor of his *people*, nor of his *cross.* Glory in this, that thou knowest *him*, art joined to *them*, and art counted worthy to bear *it.*

Verse 26. Many seek the ruler's favour] To be screened from the punishment determined by the law; but should *he* grant the favour sought, and pardon the criminal, this takes not away his guilt in the sight of God, from whom all just judgment proceeds.

Verse 27. And he that is upright in the way] "But as for those that be in the right waye, the wicked hate them."—COVERDALE.

To this verse the VULGATE adds the following: *Verbum custodiens filius extra perditionem erit;* "The son that keeps the word shall not fall into perdition." This is not in *all* copies of the Vulgate: but it was in that from which my old MS. Bible was made, where it is thus translated: **The sone keping the worde schal ben out of perdicyon.** I believe *verbum* here is intended for the Divine *word;* the revelation from God.

CHAPTER XXX

Agur's confession of faith, 1–6. His prayer, 7–9. Of wicked generations, 10–14. Things that are never satis-
fied, 15, 16. Of him who despises his parents, 17. Three wonderful things, 18–20. Three things that dis-
quiet the land, 21–23. Four little but very intelligent animals, 24–28. Four things that go well, 29–31. A
man should cease from doing foolishly, and from strife, 32, 33.

A. M. cir. 3304
B. C. cir. 700
Ol. vigesimæ
cir. annum
primum
A. U. C. cir. 54

THE words of Agur the son of Jakeh, *even* [a]the pro-phecy: the man spake unto Ithiel, even unto Ithiel and Ucal,

2 [b]Surely I *am* more brutish than *any* man, and have not the understanding of a man.

3 I neither learned wisdom, nor [c]have the knowledge of the holy.

4 [d]Who hath ascended up into heaven, or descended? [e]who hath gathered the wind in his fists? who hath bound the

A. M. cir. 3304
B. C. cir. 700
Ol. vigesimæ
cir. annum
primum
A. U. C. cir. 54

---

[a]Chap. xxxi. 1——[b]Psa. lxxiii. 22——[c]Heb. *know*
[d]John iii. 13

[e]Job xxxviii. 4, &c.; Psa. civ. 3, &c.; Isa. xl.
12, &c.

NOTES ON CHAP. XXX

Verse 1. *The words of Agur the son of Jakeh*] The words *Agur, Jakeh, Ithiel,* and *Ucal,* have been considered by some as *proper names:* by others, as *descriptive characters.* With some, *Agur* is *Solomon;* and *Jakeh, David;* and *Ithiel* and *Ucal* are epithets of *Christ.*

The *Vulgate* translates, *Verba congregantis filii vomentis: visio, quam locutus est vir, cum quo est Deus, et qui Deo secum morante con-fortatus, ait.* "The words of the collector, the son of the vomiter: the vision of the man who has God with him, and who is fortified by God dwelling with him, saith."

COVERDALE makes the following words a *title* to the chapter:
"The wordes of Agur the sonne of Jake.
"The prophecie of a true faithfull man, whom God hath helped; whom God hath comforted and nourished."

The whole might be thus translated, keeping near to the *letter:—*
"The words of the epistle of the obedient son." Or,
"The words of the collector, the son of Jakeh. The parable which הגבר *haggeber,* the strong man, the hero, spake unto him who is God with me; to him who is God with me, even the strong God."

𝕿𝖍𝖊 𝖛𝖎𝖘𝖎𝖔𝖚𝖓 𝖙𝖍𝖆𝖙 𝖆 𝖒𝖆𝖓 𝖘𝖕𝖆𝖐𝖊 𝖜𝖎𝖙𝖍 𝖜𝖍𝖎𝖈𝖍𝖊 𝖎𝖘 𝕲𝖔𝖉, 𝖆𝖓𝖉 𝖙𝖍𝖆𝖙 𝕲𝖔𝖉 𝖜𝖎𝖙𝖍 𝖍𝖎𝖒, 𝖜𝖔𝖓𝖞𝖓𝖌 𝖈𝖔𝖓𝖋𝖔𝖗𝖙𝖎𝖇.—Old MS. Bible.

From this introduction, from the names here used, and from the style of the book, it appears evident that Solomon was not the author of this chapter; and that it was designed to be dis-tinguished from his work by this very preface, which specifically distinguishes it from the preceding work. Nor can the words in verses 2, 3, 8, and 9, be at all applied to Solomon: they suit no part of Solomon's *life,* nor of his *circumstances.* We must, therefore, consider it an *appendix* or *supplement* to the preceding collection; something in the manner of that part which the *men of Hezekiah, king of Judah, had collected.* As to *mysteries* here, many have been found by them who sought for noth-ing else; but they are all, in my view of the subject, hazarded and precarious. I believe *Agur, Jakeh, Ithiel,* and *Ucal,* to be the *names of persons* who did exist, but of whom we know nothing but what is here mentioned. *Agur*

seems to have been a public *teacher,* and *Ithiel* and *Ucal* to have been his *scholars;* and what he delivers to them was done by *prophecy.* It was what the prophets generally term משא *massa,* an ORACLE, something immediately de-livered by the *Holy Spirit* for the benefit of man.

Verse 2. *Surely I* am *more brutish*] These words can in no sense, nor by any mode of speech, be true of Solomon: for while he was the *wisest of men,* he could not have said that he *was more brutish than any man, and had not the understanding of a man.* It is saying nothing to the purpose, to say he was so *inde-pendently* of *the Divine teaching.* Had he put this in, even by innuendo, it might be legiti-mate: but he does not; nor is it by fair implica-tion to be understood. Solomon is not supposed to have written the Proverbs *after he fell from God.* Then indeed he might have said he *had been more brutish than any man.* But Agur might have used these words with strict propri-ety, for aught we know; for it is very probable that he was a *rustic,* without education, and without any human help, as was the prophet Amos; and that all that he knew now was by the *inspiration* of the Almighty, independently of which he was *rustic* and *uneducated.*

Verse 3. *I neither learned wisdom*] I have never been a scholar in any of those schools of the *wise men,* nor *have the knowledge of the holy,* קדשים *kedoshim,* of the *saints* or *holy persons.*

The *Septuagint* give this a different turn:
Θεος δεδιδαχε με σοφιαν, και γνωσιν ἁγιων εγνωκα;
"God hath taught me wisdom, and the knowl-edge of the saints I have known."

This may refer to the *patriarchs, prophets,* or *holy men,* that lived before the days of Solo-mon. That is, the translators might have had these in view.

Verse 4. *Who hath ascended up into heaven, or descended?*] *Calmet* paraphrases this pas-sage thus: "*Who hath* descended, &c. In order to show the truth of what he was about to say, he observes: *I have not the science of the saints;* for how could I have acquired it? Who is he who could attain to that? *Who has as-cended to heaven* to learn that science; and *who has descended* in order to publish it? Is the science of salvation one of those things that can be *apprehended* only by *study?* Is it not a pure gift of the goodness of God? Moses, after having shown to the people the will of

A. M. cir. 3304
B. C. cir. 700
Ol. vigesimæ
cir. annum
primum
A. U. C. cir. 54

waters in a garment? who hath established all the ends of the earth? what *is* his name, and what *is* his son's name, if thou canst tell?

5 [f]Every word of God *is* [g]pure: [h]he *is* a shield unto them that put their trust in him.

A. M. cir. 3304
B. C. cir. 700
Ol. vigesimæ
cir. annum
primum
A. U. C. cir. 54

6 [i]Add thou not unto his words, lest he reprove thee, and thou be found a liar.

7 Two *things* have I required of thee; [k]deny me *them* not before I die:

8 Remove far from me vanity and lies:

---

[f]Psalm xii. 6; xviii. 30; xix. 8; cxix. 140——[g]Heb. *purified*——[h]Psa. xviii. 30; lxxxiv. 11; cxv. 9, 10, 11

[i]Deut. iv. 2; xii. 32; Rev. xxii. 18, 19——[k]Heb. *withhold not from me*

God, said to them: 'This commandment which I command thee this day is not hidden from thee; neither is it far off. It is not in heaven, that thou shouldest say, Who shall go up for us to heaven, and bring it unto us, that we may hear it, and do it?' Deut. xxx. 11, 12. The person whose words we are here examining speaks a knowledge more sublime than that contained in the simple laws of the Lord, common to all the people of Israel. He speaks of the sublime science of the designs of God, of his ways, and of his secrets; and in this sense he affirms he has no knowledge."

Who hath gathered the wind in his fists?] It is as difficult for a mortal man to acquire this Divine science by his own reason and strength, as to collect the winds in his fists. And who can command the spirit of prophecy, so that he can have it whensoever he pleases?

What is *his name?*] Show me the nature of this Supreme Being. Point out his eternity, omniscience, omnipresence, omnipotence; comprehend and describe him, if thou canst.

What is *his son's name*] Some copies of the *Septuagint* have η τι ονομα τοις τικνοιο αυτου; "Or the name of his sons;" meaning, I suppose, the *holy angels*, called his *saints* or *holy ones*, ver. 3.

The *Arabic* has, *What is his name?* وما اسمه
والـ?, *and what is the name of his father?* him who *begat him*. But the *Chaldee*, the *Syriac*, and the *Vulgate*, read as the *Hebrew*.

Many are of opinion that Agur refers here to the *first* and *second persons* of the ever-blessed TRINITY. It *may* be so; but who would venture to rest the proof of that most glorious doctrine upon such a *text*, to say nothing of the *obscure author?* The doctrine is true, sublimely true; but many doctrines have suffered in controversy, by improper texts being urged in their favour. Every lover of God and truth should be very choice in his *selections*, when he comes forward in behalf of the *more mysterious doctrines* of the Bible. Quote nothing that is not clear: advance nothing that does not *tell*. When we are obliged to spend a world of critical labour, in order to establish the *sense* of a text which we intend to allege in favour of the doctrine we wish to support, we may rest assured that we *are going the wrong way to work*. Those who indiscriminately amass every text of Scripture *they think* bears upon the subject they defend, give their adversaries great advantage against them. I see many a sacred doctrine suffering through the bad judgment of its friends every day. The Godhead of Christ, salvation by faith, the great atoning sacrifice, and other essential doctrines of this class, are all suffering in this way. My heart says, with deep concern,

Non tali auxilio, nec defensoribus istis, Tempus eget.

When truth is assailed by all kinds of weapons, handled by the most *powerful foes*, injudicious defenders may be ranked among its enemies. To such we may innocently say, "Keep your cabins; you do assist the storm."

Verse 5. *Every word of God* is *pure*] כל
אמרת אלוה צרופה *col imrath eloah tseruphah*, "Every oracle of God is purified." A metaphor taken from the *purifying of metals*. Every thing that God has pronounced, every inspiration which the prophets have received, is pure, without mixture of error, without dross. Whatever trials it may be exposed to, it is always like *gold*: it *bears the fire*, and comes out with the same *lustre*, the same *purity*, and the same *weight*.

He is *a shield unto them*] And *this* oracle among the rest. "He is the defence of *all* them that put their trust in him." לכל *lechol, to all*, is added here by *nineteen* of *Kennicott's* and *De Rossi's* MSS.; for instead of לחסים *lachosim, to the trusters*, they read לכל החוסים *lechol hachosim*, "to EVERY ONE of them that trust." Where the *preposition* and *adjective* are not only added, but the *noun* is written *more full*, and more *emphatic*: but a translation cannot well express it without *paraphrase*.

Verse 6. *Add not thou unto his words*] You can no more increase their *value* by any *addition*, than you can that of *gold* by adding any *other metal* to it. Take care that you *do not* any thing that this word *forbids*, nor leave *undone* any thing that it *commands*: for this is *adding* and *diminishing* in Scripture phrase.

Lest he reprove thee] Lest he try *thy word by fire*, as his has been tried; and it appear that, far from *abiding* the test, the *fire* shows thine to be *reprobate silver;* and so thou be found a *falsifier of God's word*, and a *liar*. How amply has this been fulfilled in the case of the *Romish Church!* It has *added* all the *gross stuff* in the Apocrypha, besides innumerable *legends* and *traditions*, to the word of God! They have been tried by the *refiner's fire*. And this Church has been *reproved*, and *found to be a liar*, in attempting to filiate on the most holy God *spurious writings* discreditable to his nature.

Verse 7. *Two* things *have I required of thee*] These *two petitions* are mentioned in the next verse; and he wishes to have them answered *before he should die*. That is, he wishes the answer *now*, that he may live the rest of his life in the *state* he describes.

Verse 8. *Remove far from me vanity and lies.*] 1. שוא *shav,* all *false shows*, all *false*

A. M. cir. 3304
B. C. cir. 700
Ol. vigesimæ
cir. annum
primum
A. U. C. cir. 54

give me neither poverty nor riches; [l]feed me with food [m]convenient for me.

9 [n]Lest I be full, and [o]deny *thee,* and say, Who *is* the LORD? or lest I be poor and steal, and take the name of my God *in vain.*

10 [p]Accuse not a servant unto his master, lest he curse thee, and thou be found guilty.

11 *There is* a generation *that* curseth their father, and doth not bless their mother.

12 *There is* a generation [q]*that are* pure in their own eyes, and *yet* is not washed from their filthiness.

13 *There is* a generation, O how [r]lofty are their eyes! and their eyelids are lifted up.

14 [s]*There is* a generation, whose teeth *are as* swords, and their jaw teeth *as* knives, [t]to devour the poor from off the earth, and the needy from *among* men.

15 The horseleech hath two daughters, *crying,* Give, give. There are three *things that* are never satisfied, *yea,* four *things* say not, [u]*It is* enough:

16 [v]The grave; and the barren womb; the earth *that* is not filled with water; and the fire, *that* saith not, It *is* enough.

A. M. cir. 3304
B. C. cir. 700
Ol. vigesimæ
cir. annum
primum
A. U. C. cir. 54

---

[l]Matt. vi. 11——[m]Heb. *of my allowance*——[n]Deut. viii. 12, 14, 17; xxxi. 20; xxxii. 15; Neh. ix. 25, 26; Job xxxi. 24, 25, 28; Hos. xiii. 6——[o]Heb. *belie* thee [p]Heb. *Hurt not with thy tongue*——[q]Luke xviii. 11

[r]Psa. cxxxi. 1; chap. vi. 17——[s]Job xxix. 17; Psa. lii. 2; lvii. 4; chap. xii. 18——[t]Psa. xiv. 4; Amos viii. 4——[u]Hebrew, *Wealth*——[v]Chap. xxvii. 20; Hab. ii. 5

---

appearances of happiness, every *vain expectation.* Let me not set my heart on any thing that is not *solid, true, durable,* and *eternal.* 2. *Lies,* דבר כזב *debar cazab,* all *words of deception, empty pretensions, false promises, uncertain dependences,* and *words that* FAIL; *promises* which, when they become *due,* are like *bad bills;* they are *dishonoured* because they are found to be *forged,* or the *drawer insolvent.*

From the import of the original, I am satisfied that *Agur* prays against *idolatry, false religion,* and *false worship* of every kind. שׁוא *shav* is used for an *idol,* a *false god.* Jer. xviii. 15: "My people have forsaken me; they have burnt incense to VANITY;" לשׁוא *lashshav,* "to an IDOL." Psa. xxxi. 6: "I have hated them that regard lying VANITIES;" הבלי שׁוא *habley shave,* "vain IDOLS." See also Hos. xii. 11; Jonah ii. 8. And כזב *cazab,* a thing that *fails* or *deceives,* may well apply to the *vain pretensions, false promises,* and *deceptive religious rites* of idolatry. So Jer. xv. 18: "Wilt thou be unto me as a liar," כמו אכזב *kemo achzob,* like the false, failing *promises* of the *false gods;* "and as waters that fail;" לא נאמנו *lo neemanu,* that are not *faithful;* not like the *true* God, whose *promises never fail.* According to this view of the subject, *Agur* prays, 1. That he may be preserved from idolatry. 2. That he may put no confidence in any words but those *pure words* of God that never fail them that trust in him.

Give me neither poverty nor riches] Here are *three* requests: 1. *Give me not poverty.* The *reason* is added: *Lest,* being *poor, I shall* get into a covetous spirit, and, impelled by *want,* distrust my Maker, and take my neighbour's property; and, in order to excuse, hide, or vindicate my conduct, *I take the name of my God in vain;* תפשׁתי *taphasti,* "I catch at the name of God." Or, by swearing falsely, endeavour to make myself pass for innocent. Forswere the name of my God.—Old MS. Bible. *Coverdale,* "deny or apostatize from him."

2. *Give me not riches.* For which petition he gives a *reason* also: *Lest I be full,* and addict myself to luxurious living, pamper the flesh

and starve the soul, and so *deny thee,* the Fountain of goodness; and, if called on to resort to first principles, I say, *Who is Jehovah?* Why should I acknowledge, why should I serve him? And thus cast aside all religion, and all moral obligation.

3. The *third* request is, *Feed me with food convenient for me,* הטריפני לחם חקי *hatripheni lechem chukki;* the meaning of which is, "give me as prey my statute allowance of bread," i. e., my *daily bread,* a sufficient portion for each day. There is an allusion made to *hunting:* "Direct so by thy good providence, that I may each day find sufficient portion to subsist on, as a hunter in the forest prays that he may have good speed." It is the province of a *preacher* to show the importance and utility of such a *prayer,* and *dilate* the *circumstances,* and *expand* the *reasons,* after the *commentator* has shown the *literal sense.*

Verse 10. Accuse not a servant] Do not bring a *false* accusation against a *servant,* lest *thou be found guilty* of the falsehood, and he *curse thee* for having traduced his character, and in his turn traduce thine. In general, do not meddle with other people's servants.

Verse 11. There is *a generation*] There are *such persons* in the world. In this and the three following verses the wise man points out *four grand evils* that prevailed in his time.

The *first,* Those who not only did not *honour,* but who *evil-treated,* their *parents.*

Verse 12. The *second,* Those who were *self-righteous,* supposing themselves *pure,* and were *not so.*

Verse 13. The *third,* Those who were *full of vanity, pride,* and *insolence.*

Verse 14. The *fourth,* The *greedy, cruel,* and *oppressive,* and, especially, *oppressive to the poor.*

Verse 15. *The horseleech hath two daughters,* crying, *Give, give.*] "This horseleech," says *Calmet,* "is COVETOUSNESS, and her two daughters are *Avarice* and *Ambition.* They never say, It is enough; they are never satisfied; they are never contented."

Many explanations have been given of this verse; but as all the *versions* agree in render-

A. M. cir. 3304
B. C. cir. 700
Ol. vigesimæ
cir. annum
primum
A. U. C. cir. 54

17 ʷThe eye *that* mocketh at *his* father, and despiseth to obey *his* mother, the ravens of ˣthe valley shall pick it out, and the young eagles shall eat it.

18 There be three *things which* are too wonderful for me, yea, four which I know not:

ʷGen. ix. 22; Lev. xx. 9; chap. xx. 20; xxiii. 22

---

ing עֲלוּקָה *alukah* the *horseleech* or *bloodsucker*, the general meaning collected has been, "There are persons so excessively covetous and greedy, that they will scarcely let any live but themselves; and when they lay hold of any thing by which they may profit, they never let go their hold till they have extracted the last portion of good from it." *Horace* has well expressed this disposition, and by the *same emblem*, applied to a *poor poet*, who seizes on and extracts all he can from an *author of repute*, and obliges all to hear him read his wretched verses.

> Quem vero arripuit, tenet, occiditque legendo,
> Non missura cutem, nisi plena cruoris,
>   HIRUDO.   DE ARTE POET., ver. 475.

> "But if he seize you, then the torture dread;
> He fastens on you till he reads you dead;
> And like a LEECH, voracious of his food,
> Quits not his cruel hold till gorged with
>   blood."   FRANCIS.

The word אֲלוּקָה *alukah*, which we here translate *horseleech*, is read in no other part of the Bible. May it not, like *Agur, Jakeh, Ithiel*, and *Ucal*, be a *proper name*, belonging to some well-known *woman* of *his acquaintance*, and well known to the *public*, who had *two daughters* notorious for their *covetousness* and *lechery?* And at first view the following verse may be thought to confirm this supposition: "There are three things that are never satisfied, yea, four things say not, It is enough." the *grave*, the *barren womb*, the *earth*, the *fire*. What an astonishing similarity there is between this and the following *institute*, taken from the *Code of Hindoo Laws*, chap. xx., sec. i., p. 203.

"A *woman* is never satisfied with the copulation of man, no more than a *fire* is satisfied with burning *fuel;* or the *main ocean* is with receiving the *rivers;* or *death*, with the dying of *men* and *animals*." You can no more satisfy these two daughters of Alukah than you can the grave, &c.

Some of the rabbins have thought that *alukah* signifies *destiny*, or the *necessity of dying*, which they say has *two daughters, Eden* and *Gehenna*, paradise and hell. The former has never enough of *righteous souls;* the latter, of the *wicked*. Similar to them is the opinion of *Bochart*, who thinks *alukah* means *destiny*, and the *two daughters*, the *grave* and *hell;* into the *first* of which the *body* descends after death, and into the *second*, the *soul*.

The *Septuagint* gives it a curious turn, by connecting the *fifteenth* with the *sixteenth* verse: Τῇ Βδέλλῃ θυγατερες ησαν αγαπησει αγαπωμεναι, και αἱ τρεις αὐται ουκ ενεπιμπλασαν αυτην, και ἡ τεταρτη ουκ ηρκεσθη ειπειν· Ἱκανον; "The horseleech had three well-beloved daughters; and these three

A. M. cir. 3304
B. C. cir. 700
Ol. vigesimæ
cir. annum
primum
A. U. C. cir. 54

19 The way of an eagle in the air; the way of a serpent upon a rock; the way of a ship in the ʸmidst of the sea; and the way of a man with a maid.

20 Such *is* the way of an adulterous woman; she eateth, and wipeth her mouth,

---

ˣOr, *the brook*——ʸHeb. *heart*

---

were not able to satisfy her desire: and the fourth was not satisfied, so as to say, It is enough."

After all, I think my own conjecture the most probable. *Alukah* is a proper name, and the two daughters were of the description I have mentioned.

Verse 17. *The eye that mocketh at his father*] This seems to be spoken against those who *curse their father*, and *do not bless their mother*, ver. 11.

The ravens of the valley] Those which frequent the places where dead carcasses and offal are most likely to be found. The *raven*, the *crow*, the *rook*, the *daw*, the *carrion crow*, and the Cornish *chough*, appear to be all of the same genus. Some of them live on *pulse* and *insects;* others, the *raven* in particular, live on *carrion*.

The young eagles shall eat it.] The mother eagle shall scoop out such an eye, and carry it to the nest to feed her young. Many of the *disobedient to parents* have come to an *untimely end*, and, in the *field of battle*, where many a profligate has fallen, and upon *gibbets*, have actually become the prey of ravenous birds.

Verse 19. *The way of an eagle*] I borrow, with thanks, the very sensible note of the Rev. Mr. Holden on this passage.

"The particle כֵּן *ken* plainly shows that verses 19 and 20 are to be taken in connection; consequently, it is a comparison between the *way of an adulterous woman*, and the *way of the things* here described.

"The *adulterous woman* goes about in search of her deluded victim, like as the *eagle* takes its flight into the air to spy out its prey. She uses every species of blandishment and insinuation to allure and beguile, as the *serpent* employs its windings and sinuous motions to pass along the *rocks;* she pursues a course surrounded with danger, as *a ship in the midst of the sea* is continually exposed to the fury of the tempest, and the hazard of shipwreck; and she tries every means, and exercises all her sagacity, to prevent the discovery of her illicit enjoyments, as a man attempts to conceal his clandestine intercourse *with a maid*. Such is the conduct of a lewd woman, marked by specious dissimulation and traitorous blandishment; *she eateth and wipeth her mouth*—she indulges her adulterous lust, yet artfully endeavours to conceal it, and with unblushing countenance asserts her innocence, exclaiming, *I have done no wickedness*."

CHAUCER'S *January* and *May* is an excellent comment on such *wiles* and *protestations*.

The way of a man with a maid.] בְּעַלְמָה *bealmah* with or in a maid; but one of *De Rossi's* MSS. has בְּעַלְמָיו *bealmaiv*, in his

A. M. cir. 3304
B. C. cir. 700
Ol. vigesimæ
cir. annum
primum
A. U. C. cir. 54

and saith, I have done no wicked-ness.

21 For three *things* the earth is disquieted, and for four *which* it cannot bear.

22 [z]For a servant when he reigneth; and a fool when he is filled with meat;

23 For an odious *woman* when she is married; and a handmaid that is heir to her mistress.

24 There be four *things which are* little upon the earth, but they *are* [a]exceeding wise:

25 [b]The ants *are* a people not strong; yet they prepare their meat in the summer;

26 [c]The conies *are but* a feeble folk, yet make they their houses in the rocks;

27 The locusts have no king, yet go they forth all of them [d]by bands;

28 The spider taketh hold with her hands, and is in kings' palaces.

29 There be three *things* which go well, yea, four are comely in going:

A. M. cir. 3304
B. C. cir. 700
Ol. vigesimæ
cir. annum
primum
A. U. C. cir. 54

---

[z]Chap. xix. 10; Eccles. x. 7——[a]Heb. *wise, made wise*

[b]Chap. vi. 6, &c.——[c]Psa. civ. 18——[d]Heb. *gathered together*

---

youth; and with this the Septuagint, εν νεοτητι, the Vulgate, *in adolescentia,* the Syriac and the Arabic agree; and so also my own MS. Bible:—𝔗𝔥𝔢 𝔴𝔢𝔦𝔢 𝔬𝔣 𝔞 𝔪𝔞𝔫 𝔦𝔫 𝔥𝔦𝔰 𝔴𝔞𝔵𝔦𝔫𝔤 𝔭𝔬𝔲𝔱𝔥𝔢. Dr. *Kennicott,* in a *sermon preached at Oxford,* 1765, p. 46, has defended the reading of the *versions,* corroborating it by two MSS., one in the *Harleian,* and the other in the *Bodleian* library, besides that mentioned by *De Rossi.* See *De Rossi's* Var. Lect. Certainly the *way of a man in his youth* contains too many *intricacies* for human wisdom to explore. He only who searches the heart knows fully its various corrupt principles, and their productions. The common reading may refer to the formation of a child in the womb. But some have understood it of the *immaculate conception.* See my note on Matt. i. 23, where the subject is largely considered.

If we take the *four things* which Agur says were *too wonderful for him,* in their *obvious sense,* there is little difficulty in them. 1. The passage which a bird makes *through the air;* 2. That which is made by a *serpent on a rock;* and, 3. That *made by a ship through the sea,* are such as cannot be ascertained: for who can possibly show the *track* in which either of them has passed? And as to the *fourth,* if it refer to the *suspected incontinence* of one *reputed a virgin,* the *signs* are so *equivocal,* as to be absolutely unascertainable. The existence of the *hymen* has been denied by the ablest anatomists; and the signs of *continence* or *incontinence,* except in the most recent cases, are such as neither *man* nor *woman* can swear to, even to the present day; and they were certainly not less difficult to *Agur* and his *contemporaries.* I shall carry this matter no farther.

Verse 21. *For three* things *the earth is disquieted, and for four* which *it cannot bear*] This is another enigma. *Four* things insupportable to men. 1. A *slave, when he becomes ruler.* 2. An *overfed fool.* 3. An *ill-tempered woman, when mistress of a family.* And, 4. A *servant maid, when the rule of the house is committed* to her.

1. A *slave,* when he comes to *bear rule,* is an unprincipled *tyrant.* It has been often observed both in *America* and in the *West Indies,* when it was judged necessary to arm some of the most confidential slaves, that no regiments were used *so cruelly* in the *drill,* &c., as those *black regiments* that had *black officers.*

2. *The overfed fool.* The intellectually *weak man,* who has every thing *at his command,* has generally *manners* which none can bear; and, if a *favourite* with his *master,* he is insupportable to all others.

3. An *ill-tempered woman,* when she gets embarrassed with domestic cares, is beyond bearing.

4. A *servant maid,* when, either through the *death* of the mistress, or the sin of the husband, she is in fact exalted to be head over the family, is so insolent and impudent, as to be hateful to every one, and execrated by all.

Verse 24. *There be four* things] Of which it is said, they are *very little* but *very wise.* 1. The *ants.* 2. The *rabbits.* 3. The *locusts.* 4. The *spider.*

1. The *ants* show their wisdom by *preparing their meat in the summer;* seeking for it and storing it when it may be had; not for *winter consumption,* for they *sleep* all that time; but for *autumn* and *spring.* See the note on chap. vi. 6. The *ants* are a *people;* they have their *houses, towns, cities, public roads,* &c. I have seen several of these, both of the *brown* and large *black ant.*

2. The *rabbits* act curiously enough in the construction of their *burrows;* but the word שָׁפָן *shaphan* probably does not here mean the *animal* we call *coney* or *rabbit.* It is most likely that this is what Dr. *Shaw* calls the *Daman-Israel;* a creature very like a rabbit, but never burrowing in the ground, but dwelling in clefts and holes of *rocks.*

3. The *locusts.* These surprising animals we have already met with and described. Though they have no *leader,* yet they go forth by *troops,* some miles in circumference, when they *take wing.*

4. The *spider.* This is a singularly curious animal, both in the manner of *constructing her house,* her *nets,* and *taking* her *prey.* But the habits, &c., of these and such like must be sought in works on *natural history.*

Verse 29. *There be three* things *which go well*] Here is another set of *emblems; four* things which *walk beautifully* and *with majesty.* 1. The *lion.* 2. The *greyhound.* 3. The *he-goat.* And, 4. A *king.*

1. Nothing can be more majestic than the *walk of the lion.* It is deliberate, equal, firm, and in every respect becoming the king of the forest.

2. The *greyhound.* זַרְזִיר מָתְנַיִם *zarzir moth-*

A. M. cir. 3304
B. C. cir. 700
Ol. vigesimæ
cir. annum
primum
A. U. C. cir. 54

30 A lion, *which is* strongest among beasts, and turneth not away for any;

31 A [e]greyhound; [f]a he-goat also; and a king, against whom *there is* no rising up.

32 If thou hast done foolishly in lifting up thyself, or if thou hast thought evil, [g]*lay* thine hand upon thy mouth.

33 Surely the churning of milk bringeth forth butter, and the wringing of the nose bringeth forth blood: so the forcing of wrath bringeth forth strife.

A. M. cir. 3304
B. C. cir. 700
Ol. vigesimæ
cir. annum
primum
A. U. C. cir. 54

---

[e]Or, *horse*——[f]Heb. *girt in the loins*

[g]Job xxi. 5; xl. 4; Eccles. viii. 3; Mic. vii. 16

---

nayim, the *girt in the loins;* but what this beast is we do not distinctly know. It is *most likely* that this was the *greyhound*, which in the *East* are remarkably fine, and very *fleet*. Scarcely any thing can be conceived to *go* with greater fleetness, in full chase, than a grey-hound with its prey in view: it seems to *swim* over the earth.

3. The *goat*, תיש *tayish*. This is generally allowed to be the *he-goat;* and how he walks, and what *state* he assumes, in the presence of his part of the flock, every one knows, who has at all noticed this animal. The *ram* also, which some suppose to be intended, is both fierce and majestic at the head of the sheep.

4. *And a king, against whom* there is *no rising* up. That is, a king whose court, counsels, and troops, are so firmly united to him, as to render all hopes of successful conspiracy against him utterly vain. He walks boldly and majestically about, being safe in the affections of his people. But the *Hebrew* is singular; it makes but *two words;* and these are they, ומלך אלקום *umelech Alkum*, "and King Alkum." It is a doubt whether this may not be a *proper name*, as *Agur* abounds in them; see *Ithiel, Ucal*, and probably *Alukah*, ver. 15. But it is said, "We know nothing of a king named Alkum." True; nor do we know any thing of *Agur, Ithiel, Ucal*, to say nothing of *Alukah*.

And this might have been some remarkable *chieftain*, who carried his victories wherever he went, and was remarkably fortunate. If, however, we separate the word into אל *al*, "not," and קום *kum*, "he arose," we may make the interpretation above given.

Verse 32. *If thou hast done foolishly*] And who has not, at one time or other of his life?

Lay *thine hand upon thy mouth.*] Like the *leper;* and cry to God, *Unclean! unclean!* and *keep silence* to all besides. God will blot out thy offence, and neither the world nor the Church ever know it, for he is merciful; and man is rarely able to pass by a sin committed by his fellows, especially if it be one to which himself is by nature not liable or inclined.

Verse 33. *And the wringing*] 𝔚𝔥𝔬 𝔥𝔲𝔤𝔢𝔩𝔦 𝔰𝔫𝔭𝔱𝔦𝔱𝔥 𝔡𝔯𝔞𝔴𝔦𝔱𝔥 𝔬𝔲𝔱 𝔟𝔩𝔬𝔬𝔡.—Old MS. Bible. This is well expressed in homely phrase. The *Septuagint* have, "draw the milk, and you may have butter; if you press the nostrils you may bring out blood; and if you draw out your discourse to a great length, you may have strife and contention." Avoid, therefore, all strong *excitements* and irritations. *Coverdale's* translation of this verse is very simple: "Whoso chyrneth mylck maketh butter; he that rubbeth his nose, maketh it blede; and he that causeth wrath, bryngeth forth strife."

CHAPTER XXXI

The words and prophecy of King Lemuel, and what his mother taught him, 1, 2. Debauchery and much wine to be avoided, 3–7. How kings should administer justice, 8, 9. The praise of a virtuous woman and good housewife, in her economy, prudence, watchfulness, and assiduity in labour, 10–29. Frailty of beauty, 30, 31.

THE words of King Lemuel, [a]the prophecy that his mother taught him.

2 What, my son? and what, [b]the son of my womb? and what, the son of my vows?

---

[a]Chap. xxx. 1

[b]Isa. xlix. 15

NOTES ON CHAP. XXXI

Verse 1. *The words of King Lemuel*] דברי למואל מלך *dibrey lemuel melech*, "The words to Muel the king." So the *Syriac;* and so I think it should be read, the ל *lamed* being the article or *preposition*.

But who is *Muel* or *Lemuel? Solomon*, according to general opinion; and the *mother* here mentioned, *Bath-sheba*. I cannot receive these sayings; for 1. Whoever this was, he appears to have been the *first-born* of his mother:

called here emphatically בר בטני *bar bitni*, the *son of my womb;* which is not likely to be true of Solomon, as his mother had been the wife of Uriah, and possibly had borne that rough and faithful soldier some children. 2. It is intimated here that this son had come by a *lawful marriage:* hence בר נדרי *bar nedarai*, the *son of my vow*, her *matrimonial covenant;* for so it is most natural to understand the words. But is there any proper sense in which we can say that this was correct in reference to *David, Bath-sheba*, and *Solomon?* For although the son born in adultery died, it is by

3 [c]Give not thy strength unto women, nor thy ways [d]to that which destroyeth kings.

4 [e]*It is* not for kings, O Lemuel, *it is* not for kings to drink wine; nor for princes strong drink:

5 [f]Lest they drink, and forget the law, and [g]pervert the judgment [h]of any of the afflicted.

6 [i]Give strong drink unto him that is ready to perish, and wine unto those that be [k]of heavy hearts.

7 Let him drink, and forget his poverty, and remember his misery no more.

8 [l]Open thy mouth for the dumb [m]in the cause of all [n]such as are appointed to destruction.

9 Open thy mouth, [o]judge righteously, and [p]plead the cause of the poor and needy.

10 [q]Who can find a virtuous woman? for her price *is* far above rubies.

11 The heart of her husband doth safely trust in her, so that he shall have no need of spoil.

12 She will do him good and not evil all the days of her life.

---

[c]Chap. v. 9——[d]Deut. xvii. 17; Neh. xiii. 26; chap. vii. 26; Hos. iv. 11——[e]Eccles. x. 17——[f]Hos. iv. 11 [g]Heb. *alter*——[h]Heb. *of all the sons of affliction*——[i]Psa. civ. 15——[k]Heb. *bitter of soul;* 1 Sam. i. 10

[l]See Job xxix. 15, 16——[m]1 Samuel xix. 4; Esth. iv. 16 [n]Heb. *the sons of destruction*——[o]Lev. xix. 15; Deut. i. 16——[p]Job xxix. 12; Isa. i. 17; Jer. xxii. 16——[q]Chap. xii. 4; xviii. 22; xix. 14

---

no means likely that Bath-sheba made any particular *vows* relative to *Solomon;* for of her piety, so much vaunted of by some writers, we yet want the proofs.

But, however this may be, there is no evidence whatever that *Muel* or *Lemuel* means *Solomon;* the chapter seems to be much later than his time, and the several *Chaldaisms* which occur in the very opening of it are no mean proof of this. If *Agur* was not the author of it, it may be considered as another *supplement* to the book of Proverbs. Most certainly Solomon did not write it.

The prophecy that his mother taught him.] משא *massa* may here signify the *oracle;* the subject that came by *Divine inspiration;* see on chap. xxx. 1. From this and some other circumstances it is probable that *both* these *chapters* were written by the *same author. Houbigant* thinks that *Massa* here is the name of a *place;* and, therefore, translates, "The words of Lemuel, king of Massa, with which his mother instructed him."

Verse 2. *What, my son?*] The Chaldee בר *bar* is used twice in this verse, instead of the Hebrew בן *ben*, SON. This verse is very elliptical; and commentators, according to their different tastes, have inserted *words*, indeed some of them a whole *sentence*, to make up the sense. Perhaps *Coverdale* has hit the sense as nearly as any other: "These are the wordes of Kynge Lemuel; and the lesson that his mother taughte him. My sonne, thou son of my body, O my deare beloved sonne!"

The son of my vows?] A child born after vows made for offsprings is called the *child* of a person's *vows.*

Verse 3. *Give not thy strength*] Do not waste thy substance on *women.* In such intercourse the *strength* of *body, soul* and *substance* is destroyed. Such connections are those *which destroy kings,* מלכין *melachin*, the *Chaldee* termination instead of the *Hebrew.*

Verse 4. It is *not for kings—to drink wine*] An intemperate man is ill fit to hold the reins of government.

Verse 5. *Lest they drink, and forget the law*] When they should be administering justice, they are found incapable of it; or, if they go into the judgment-seat, may pervert justice.

Verse 6. *Give strong drink unto him that is ready to perish*] We have already seen, that inebriating drinks were mercifully given to condemned criminals, to render them less sensible of the torture they endured in dying. This is what was offered to our Lord; but he refused it. See note on Psa. civ. 15.

Verse 8. *Open thy mouth for the dumb*] For such accused persons as have no counsellors, and cannot plead for themselves.

Are appointed to destruction.] בני חלוף *beney chaloph*, variously translated, *children of passage*—indigent travellers; *children of desolation*—those who have no possessions, or *orphans.* I believe it either signifies those who are strangers, and are *travelling from place to place*, or those who are *ready to perish* in consequence of want or oppression.

Verse 10. *Who can find a virtuous woman?*] This and the following verses are *acrostic*, each beginning with a consecutive letter of the *Hebrew alphabet:* ver. 10, א *aleph;* ver. 11, ב *beth;* ver. 12, ג *gimel;* and so on to the end of the chapter, the last verse of which has the letter ת *tau.* From this to the end of the chapter we have the *character* of a woman of *genuine worth* laid down; *first, in general*, ver. 10, 11, and 12; *secondly*, in its particular or component parts, ver. 13-29; and, *thirdly*, the summing up of the character, ver. 30, 31.

I. Her *general character.*

1. She is a *virtuous woman*—a woman of power and strength. אשת חיל *esheth chayil*, a strong or virtuous wife, full of mental energy.

2. She is *invaluable;* her *price is far above rubies*—no quantity of precious stones can be equal to *her* worth.

Verse 11. *The heart of her husband*]

3. She is an *unspotted* wife. *The heart of her husband doth safely trust in her*—he knows she will take care that a proper provision is made for his household, and will not *waste* any thing. He *has no need for spoil*—he is not obliged to go out on predatory excursions, to provide for his family, at the expense of the neighbouring tribes.

Verse 12. *She will do him good*]

4. She has her husband's happiness in view constantly. She recompenses all his *kindness* to her in *beneficent acts.* For *kind words* she returns *kind deeds.* Her *good* is *unmixed;* she will *do him good*, and *not evil.* 2. *Her good* is

13 She seeketh wool, and flax, and ʳworketh willingly with her hands.

14 She is like the merchant's ships; she bringeth her food from afar.

15 ˢShe riseth also while it is yet night, and ᵗgiveth meat to her household, and a portion to her maidens.

16 She considereth a field and ᵘbuyeth it:

with the fruit of her hands she planteth a vineyard.

17 She girdeth her loins with strength, and strengtheneth her arms.

18 ᵛShe perceiveth that her merchandise *is* good: her candle goeth not out by night.

19 She layeth her hands to the spindle, and her hands hold the distaff.

ʳEccles. ix. 10; 2 Thess. iii. 10, 12——ˢRom. xii. 11

ᵗLuke xii. 42——ᵘHeb. *taketh*——ᵛHeb. *She tasteth*

---

not *capricious;* it is *constant* and *permanent,* while she and her husband live. *His heart safely trusts in her,* for *she will do him good all the days of her life.* This is her general character.

Verse 13. *She seeketh wool, and flax, and worketh willingly, &c.*]

II. This is the *second* part of her character, giving the *particulars* of which it is composed.

1. She did not buy *ready woven cloth:* she procured the *raw material,* if *wool,* most probably from her own *flocks;* if *flax,* most probably from her own *fields.*

2. Here she manufactured; for she *worketh willingly with her hands.* And all her labour is a *cheerful service;* her *will,* her *heart,* is in it.

It needs no arguments to prove that women, even of the highest ranks, among the Greeks, Romans, and Israelites, worked with their hands at every kind of occupation necessary for the support of the family. This kind of employment was not peculiar to the *virtuous woman* in the text.

Verse 14. *She is like the merchants' ships*]

3. She acts like merchants. If she buy any thing for her household, she sells sufficient of her *own manufactures* to pay for it; if she *imports,* she *exports:* and she sends articles of her own manufacturing or produce to distant countries; she traffics with the neighbouring tribes.

Verse 15. *She riseth also while it is yet night*]

4. She is an economist of *time;* and when the *nights* are *long,* and the *days short,* her family not only spend a part of the *evening* after sunset in domestic labour, but they all arise *before daylight,* and prepare the *day's* food, that they may not have their labour interrupted. To those who are going to the *fields,* and to the *flocks,* she gives the food necessary for the day: טרף *teref, prey,* a term taken from *hunting,* the object of which was, the supplying their natural wants: hence applied to *daily food.* See notes on chap. xxx. 8. And to the women who are to be employed within she gives חק *chok,* the *task*—the *kind* of work they are to do, the *materials* out of which they are to form it, and the *quantity* she expects from each. Thus all the servants are settled: their food, work, and tasks appointed. Every thing is done *orderly.*

Verse 16. *She considereth a field and buyeth it*]

5. She provides for the growing wants of her family. More land will shortly be needed, for the family is growing up; and having *seen a field* contiguous to her own, which was on sale,

she estimates its worth, and purchases it a good bargain; and she pays for it by the *fruit of her own industry.*

6. She does not restrict herself to the bare *necessaries* of life; she is able to procure some of its *comforts.* She plants a *vineyard,* that she may have wine for a *beverage,* for *medicine,* and for *sacrifice.* This also is procured of her own labour. Whatever *goes out* brings its worth *in;* and *barter,* not *buying,* is her chief mode of traffic.

Verse 17. *She girdeth her loins with strength*]

7. She takes care of her own health and strength, not only by means of useful labour, but by healthy exercise. She avoids what might enervate her body, or soften her mind—she is ever active, and *girt* ready for every necessary exercise. Her *loins* are *firm,* and her *arms strong.*

Verse 18. *She perceiveth that her merchandise is good*]

8. She takes care to manufacture the *best* articles of the kind, and to lay on a *reasonable price* that she may secure a *ready sale.* Her *goods* are in high repute, and she knows she can *sell* as much as she can *make.* And she finds that while she pleases her customers, she *increases her own profits.*

9. She is *watchful* and careful. Her *candle*— her *lamp,* burns all night, which is of great advantage in case of sudden alarms; and in the times and places where there were so many *banditti,* this was a very necessary family regulation. Perhaps some works were carried on *during the night,* those employed *sleeping in the daytime.* Thus labour never stood still; whilst some slept, others worked. This was no unusual thing in *ancient times;* and it prevails *now;* but alas! little children are often thus employed to help to support their indigent parents, and to fill the coffers of their unfeeling taskmasters.

Verse 19. *She layeth her hands to the spindle*]

10. She gives an example of *skill* and *industry* to her household. She takes the *distaff,* that on which the *wool* or *flax* was *rolled;* and the *spindle,* that by *twisting* of which she *twisted the thread* with the *right hand,* while she held the *distaff* in the *guard* of the left arm, and drew *down the thread* with the fingers of the left hand. Allowing that *spindle* and *distaff* are proper translations of כישור *kishor,* and פלך *pelech,* this was their *use,* and the *way* in which they were used. The *spindle* and *distaff* are the most *ancient* of all the instruments used for *spinning,* or making *thread.* The *spinning-wheel* superseded them in these countries; but still they were in considerable use till *spinning machinery* superseded both them and the *spinning-wheels* in general.

20 ^wShe ^xstretcheth out her hand to the poor; yea, she reacheth forth her hands to the needy.

21 She is not afraid of the snow for her household: for all her household *are* clothed with ^yscarlet.

22 She maketh herself coverings of tapestry; her clothing *is* silk and purple.

23 ^zHer husband is known in the gates, when he sitteth among the elders of the land.

24 She maketh fine linen, and selleth *it*; and delivereth girdles unto the merchant.

25 Strength and honour *are* her clothing; and she shall rejoice in time to come.

---

^wHeb. *She spreadeth*——^xEph. iv. 28; Heb. xiii. 16

^yOr, *double garments*——^zChap. xii. 4

Verse 20. *She stretcheth out her hand to the poor*]

11. She is truly charitable. She knows that in *every portion* of a man's *gain* God requires a *lot for the poor;* and if this is not given, God's blessing is not in the rest. And she is not contented to give common alms. While with *one hand* (יד *yad*) she relieves the *general poor*, with *both hands* (ידיה *yadeyha*) she gives *to the needy*, לעני *leaney*, to the *afflicted poor*.

Verse 21. *She is not afraid of the snow*]

12. She is not anxious relative to the health and comfort of her family in the winter season, having provided *clothes sufficient* for each in the cold weather, in addition to those which they wore in the warm season.

For all her household are *clothed with scarlet.*] Not *scarlet*, for the *colour* can avail nothing in keeping off the cold; nor would it be a proper colour for the bogs and dirt of winter. But שנים *shanim*, from שנה *shanah*, to *iterate*, to *double*, signifies not only *scarlet*, so called from being twice or doubly dyed, but also *double garments*, not only the *ordinary coat* but the *surtout* or *great-coat* also, or a *cloak* to cover all. But most probably *double garments*, or *twofold* to what they were accustomed to wear, are here intended. If the *general clothing* be intended, *scarlet* cannot be the meaning, nor did our translators entirely rely on it; and therefore put *double garments*, the true meaning, in the *margin*, from which it cannot be too speedily transferred to the *text*. The *Vulgate* has "duplicibus." And my old MS. very properly, 𝔄lle forsoth ꝟir ꝟoomli men, ben clotꝟid wiꝟ double. And *Coverdale*, with equal propriety, "For all hir householde folkes are duble clothed." But if her *husband* and *children* alone are referred to, *scarlet*, which is the general meaning of the term, may be proper enough; as even in *these countries* of ours, *scarlet*, as being a *lively bright* colour, is used in the *winter* dresses.

Verse 22. *She maketh herself coverings of tapestry*]

13. She is not regardless either of her own person, or of the decent, proper appearance of her presses and wardrobe. She has coverings or carpeting for her *guests to sit upon;* she has also tapestry, מרבדים *marbaddim*, either tapestry, carpeting, or quilted work for her *beds;* and her own *clothing* is שש *shesh*, fine flax, or linen cloth, and *purple;* probably for a cloak or mantle. The *fine linen* or *cotton cloth* of Egypt is probably intended. I have often seen it wrapping the bodies of mummies; it is something like our coarse calico. The *purple* was supposed to have been dyed by a precious liquor obtained from the *pinna magna*, a large shell-fish, of the *muscle* kind, found on the coast of the Mediterranean Sea. I have seen some of them nearly *two feet* in length. But it is a doubt whether any such liquor was ever obtained from this or any other fish; and the story itself is invented merely to *hide the secret*, the proper method of *dying purple;* which was kept so well that it certainly died with the ancients.

Verse 23. *Her husband is known in the gates*]

14. She is a loving wife, and feels for the *respectability* and *honour* of her husband. He is an *elder* among his people, and he sits as a *magistrate* in the *gate*. He is respected not only on account of the *neatness* and *cleanliness* of his *person* and *dress;* but because he is the husband of a woman who is justly held in universal esteem. And her complete management of household affairs gives him full leisure to devote himself to the civil interests of the community.

Verse 24. *She maketh fine linen, and selleth it*]

15. She is *here* remarkable for carrying on a traffic of *splendid* and *ornamental dresses*, or *habits*, as she is, ver. 13, for "a coarser manufacture." The סדן *sidon* is supposed to come from (Arabic) in Arabic; and to signify a kind of *loose inner garment*, shirt, chemise, or *fine muslin covering*. Some of these are so exceedingly fine, like the *abrooam*, that when spread on the grass, they are scarcely discernible. Some such garments as these are still worn by *ladies* in *India* and in *China*, and are so *thin* and *transparent*, that every part of the body may be seen through them. I have many representations of persons clothed in this way before me both of the *Chinese*, the *Hindoo*, and the *Malabar ladies*. Probably this eminent Jewish matron had such articles manufactured in her own house. She dealt also in *girdles*. These are still a very general and very expensive article of dress. I have seen them made of *silk*, and highly ornamented with *gold* and *silver thread*, worked into *flowers* and various *curious devices*. The *loose Eastern robe* is confined by these; and the word may also take in the *shawl* of the *turban*, which is often *superb* and *costly*. It is properly the *girdle* for the *head*. As these were generally woven, the consumption was great; and an able artist must have had a good trade.

The *Arabic* gives a remarkable translation of this verse: "She maketh towels, (or tablecloths,) and sells them to the inhabitants of Basra, (a city in Mesopotamia,) and fine linens, and sells them to the Canaanites." My old MS. Bible has, 𝔖andel sche made and sold, and a litil girdil sche toke to ℭhanane. Perhaps לכנעני *lakkenaani*, *for the merchant*, may stand here for לכנענים *lakkenaanim*, the Canaanites.

Verse 25. *Strength and honour are her clothing*]

26 She openeth her mouth with wisdom; and in her tongue *is* the law of [a]kindness.

27 She looketh well to the ways of her household, and eateth not the bread of idleness.

28 Her children arise up, and call her blessed; her husband *also,* and he praiseth her.

29 Many daughters [b]have done virtuously, but thou excellest them all.

30 Favour *is* deceitful, and [c]beauty *is* vain: *but* a woman *that* feareth the LORD, she shall be praised.

31 Give her of the fruit of her hands; and let her own works praise her in the gates.

---

[a]1 Tim. iii. 4——[b]Or, *have gotten riches*   [c]Isa. xxviii. 1, 4

---

16. All the articles manufactured by herself or under her care have a double perfection: 1. They are *strong.* 2. They are *elegant; Strength and honour are her clothing;* and on account of this *she shall rejoice in time to come;* she shall never have occasion to blush for any thing she has *made,* for any thing she or hers have *worn,* or for any thing she has *sold.* Besides, she has so conducted herself that she has reason to expect that the hand of the Lord shall be still with her, and shall keep her from evil that it may not grieve her.

Verse 26. She openeth her mouth with wisdom]

17. He comes now to the *moral management* of her family. 1. She is *wise* and *intelligent;* she has not neglected the cultivation of her *mind.* 2. She is amiable in her carriage, full of good nature, well tempered, and conciliating in her manners and address.

In her tongue is the law of kindness.] This is the most distinguishing excellence of this woman. There are very few of those who are called managing women who are not *lords* over their *husbands, tyrants* over their *servants,* and *insolent* among their *neighbours.* But this woman, with all her eminence and excellence, was of a *meek* and *quiet spirit.* Blessed woman!

Verse 27. She looketh well to the ways of her household]

18. She is a *moral* manager: she takes care that all shall behave themselves well; that none of them shall keep bad company or contract vicious habits. A religious industry, or an industrious religion, is the law of her house. She can instruct them in religion, as well as she can teach them in their labour. In her house, diligence in business, and fervency of spirit, serving the Lord, go hand in hand.

And eateth not the bread of idleness.]

19. She knows that *idleness* leads to *vice;* and therefore every one has *his work,* and every one has his *proper food.* That they may *work well, they are fed well;* and every one, at least, earns the bread that he eats—*eateth not the bread of idleness.*

Verse 28. Her children arise up, and call her blessed]

20. She considers a *good education* next to *Divine influence;* and she knows also that if she train up a child in the way he should go, when he is old he will not depart from it. 1. Her children are *well bred;* they *rise up* and pay *due* respect. 2. They are *taught the fear of the Lord,* and obedience to his *testimonies;* therefore they *call her blessed.* So they are of a decent, orderly, respectable, religious behaviour. 3. Her husband is so satisfied with her conduct towards *himself,* his *household,* his *business,* and their *children,* that he *praiseth her.* He shows himself sensible of her excellence, and

encourages her, in her work, by the *commendations* he bestows.

Verse 29. Many daughters have done virtuously] This is undoubtedly the speech of the husband, giving testimony to the excellence of his wife: "Her husband also, and he praiseth her, *saying,* 'many daughters,' *women,* 'have done virtuously,' with due propriety as wives, mistresses, and mothers; 'but THOU,' my incomparable wife, 'excellest them all;'ואת עלית על‎

כלנה‎ *veath alith al cullanah,* but THOU hast ascended above the whole of them—thou hast carried every duty, every virtue, and every qualification and excellency, to a *higher perfection,* than any of whom we have ever read or heard." And let the reader seriously consider the above particulars, as specified under the different heads and subdivisions; and he will be probably of the same mind. But high as the character of this Jewish matron stands in the preceding description, I can say that I have met at least *her equal,* in a *daughter* of the Rev. Dr. *Samuel Annesly,* the *wife* of *Samuel Wesley,* sen., rector of Epworth in Lincolnshire, and *mother* of the late extraordinary brothers, *John* and *Charles Wesley.* I am constrained to add this testimony, after having traced her from her *birth* to her *death,* through all the relations that a woman can bear upon earth. Her Christianity gave to her virtues and excellences a heightening, which the Jewish matron could not possess. Besides, she was a woman of great *learning* and information, and of a depth of mind, and reach of thought, seldom to be found among the daughters of Eve, and not often among the sons of Adam.

Verse 30. Favour is *deceitful, and beauty* is *vain, &c.*]

III. Here is the *summing up* of the character. 1. *Favour,* חן‎ *chen, grace* of manner may be *deceitful,* many a *fair appearance* of this kind is *put on,* assumed for certain secular or more unworthy purposes; it is learned by *painful drilling* in *polished seminaries,* and, being the effect of mere *physical discipline,* it continues while the *restraint* lasts; but it is שקר‎ *sheker,* a *lie,* a *mere semblance,* an *outward varnish.* It is not the *effect* of *internal moral regulation;* it is an *outside,* at which the *inside* murmurs; and which, because not *ingenuous,* is a *burden to itself.*

2. *Beauty,* היפי‎ *haiyophi,* elegance of shape, symmetry of features, dignity of mien, and beauty of countenance, are all הבל‎ *hebel, vanity; sickness* impairs them, *suffering* deranges them, and *death* destroys them.

3. "But a woman that feareth the Lord," that possesses *true religion,* has that *grace* that *harmonizes the soul,* that *purifies* and *refines* all the *tempers* and *passions,* and that *ornament*

of beauty, a *meek and quiet mind*, which in the sight of God *is of great price—*
She shall be praised.] This is the lasting grace, the unfading beauty.
Verse 31. *Give her of the fruit of her hands*] This may be a *prayer.* May she long enjoy the fruit of her labours! May she see her children's children, and peace upon Israel!
And let her own works praise her in the gates.] Let what she has done be spoken of for a memorial of her; let her bright example be held forth in the most *public places.* Let it be set before the eyes of every *female,* particularly of every *wife,* and especially of every *mother;* and let them learn from this exemplar, what men have a right to expect in their *wives,* the *mistresses* of *their families,* and the *mothers* of *their children.* Amen.

MASORETIC NOTES ON THIS BOOK

Number of verses in the book of Proverbs, 915.
Middle verse, chap. xvi. 18.
Sections, 8.
The Syriac reckons 1863 verses.
The Arabic concludes thus:—"The discipline of Solomon written out by the friends of Hezekiah, king of Judah, the interpretation or translation of which is extremely difficult, (but) is now completed by the assistance and influence of the Son of God."

IN the *introduction* to the book of Proverbs, among the several *collections* of a similar nature which are mentioned there, I have referred to M. Galand's *Maximes des Orientaux.* From this work, as contained in the supplement to the *Bibliotheque Orientale,* I have translated the following *selection.* They will serve to show the curious reader how many sayings similar to those of Solomon still abound in the East.

ASIATIC PROVERBS

I fear God; and beside him I fear none, but that man who fears him not.
He who knows not his Maker cannot know himself.
Godliness is the greatest wisdom, and impiety the greatest of follies.
The fear of God is the greatest safeguard.
To sin once is too much; but a thousand acts of devotion towards God are not sufficient to honour him.
If a man foresaw his end, and his exit from life, he would abhor his actions, and their deceitfulness.
Life is a sort of sleep, from which many awake not but in death.
The life of man is a path that leads to death.
The orphan is not the person who has lost his father; but he who has neither wisdom, nor a good education.
Want of good sense is worse than all the degrees of poverty.
Nothing so effectually hides what we are as *silence.*
He who has least wisdom has most vanity.
There is no greatness of soul in avenging one's self.
The heart of the fool is in his mouth, and the tongue of the wise man is in his heart.
He who runs with a slack rein, guided only by *hope,* encounters the last moment of his life, and falls.

Envy has no rest.
When you have once received a benefit, render yourself not unworthy of it, by a want of gratitude.
The desire of revenge is a constant hinderance to a happy and contented life.
When you have got an advantage over your enemy, pardon him, in returning God thanks for that advantage.
When you are in prosperity, you need seek no other revenge against him who envies you than the mortification he has from it.
How advantageous must wisdom be to its possessor, seeing it is of so great value as not to be purchased by money!
Nothing obtains pardon more speedily than repentance.
There is no disease so dangerous as the want of common sense.
Of all vices, vanity and a love of contention are the most difficult to be corrected.
Visiting your neighbour is no crime; but your visits should not be so often repeated, as to induce him to say, *It is enough.*
If a prince would worship God in truth, he must remain in his limits, be true to his treaties, be content with what he has, and suffer patiently the privation of what he has not.
Nothing so much resembles flowers planted on a dunghill, as the good which is done to an ignorant or worthless man.
In whatsoever company or society you be, engage not in those matters which concern the *whole;* for if you succeed, the whole company will attribute the success to itself; and if you succeed not, each person will lay the blame on *you.*
When the soul is ready to depart, what avails it whether a man die on a throne or in the dust?
Take and give with equity.
We need not be surprised when those who ask or seek for improper things, fall into misfortunes which they did not expect.
Riches dwell no longer in the hand of a liberal man, than patience in the heart of a lover, or water in a sieve.
As soon as a person takes pleasure in hearing slander, he is to be ranked in the number of slanderers.
That which a man suffers for this world, fills his heart with darkness; but that which he suffers for the other, fills it with light.
The greatest repose which a man can enjoy, is that which he feels in *desiring nothing.*
One seldom finds that which he seeks, when he searches for it with *impatience.*
Do not reproach a man for the sin which he has committed, when God has forgiven him.
He who pushes a jest farther than good breeding requires, shall never fail to be hated or despised.
He who is worthy of being called *a man,* is unshaken in adversity, humble in prosperity, active and bold in danger; and, if he be not learned, has at least a love for learning.
The man who is governed by his passions is in a worse state than the most miserable slave.
Men often give themselves much trouble to succeed in an affair from which they derive only vexation in the end.
He is a free man who desires nothing; and he is a slave who expects that which he wishes.
The advice of a wise man is to be considered as a *prediction.*

Be sincere, though your sincerity should cost you your life.

Live not on credit, and you shall live in liberty.

A wise man practises the three following things: he abandons the world before it abandons him; he builds his sepulchre before the time of entering it; and he does all with a design to please God, before entering into his presence.

He who lords it over those who are below him, shall one day find a master who will lord it over him.

Sin not, if you would have less vexation in the hour of death.

He who takes not counsel beforehand, will surely fail in accomplishing his projects.

Covetousness leads to poverty; but he is truly rich who desires nothing.

He who relates the faults of others to you, designs to relate yours to them.

Watch your friends; except those of whom you are certain; but know, that none can be a *true* friend but he who has the fear of God.

The most perfect pleasures in this world are always mingled with some bitterness.

He who considers consequences with too much attention, is ordinarily a man of no courage.

The world is the hell of the good, and the heaven of the wicked; i. e., it is all the evil that the former shall meet with, and all the good that the latter shall enjoy.

By doing good to those who have evil intentions against you, you thereby shut their mouth.

He who knows well what he is capable of, has seldom bad success.

He who has too good an opinion of himself, drives all others away from him.

He who loves jesting and raillery, brings himself into many troubles.

Partial knowledge is better than total ignorance; if you cannot get what you wish, get what you can.

He who has lost shame may bury his heart.

The poor should get learning in order to become rich; and the rich should acquire it for their ornament.

A man should accommodate himself to the weakness of his inferiors, in order to derive from them the services he requires.

An avaricious man runs straight into poverty. He leads a life of poverty here below; but he must give the account of a *rich man* in the day of judgment.

The greatest advantage that a man can procure for his children, is to have them well educated.

Do good to him who does you evil, and by this means you will gain the victory over him.

Men, because of *speech*, have the advantage over brutes; but beasts are preferable to men whose language is indecent.

If you can do good *to-day*, defer it not till *to-morrow*.

The excellence of many discourses consists in their brevity.

Two things are inseparable from lying; many promises and many excuses.

Deceivers, liars, and all persons who lead an irregular life, are intoxicated by the prosperity which smiles upon them in all things; but that intoxication is the just recompense of their evil actions.

He lives in true repose who bridles his passions.

It is in vain to expect these five things from the following persons: A present from a poor man; service from a lazy man; succour from an enemy; counsel from an envious man; and true love from a prude.

It is unbecoming the character of a wise man to commit the fault for which he reproves others.

A passionate man is capable of nothing; how unfit then is such a person for a governor!

A rich man who is not liberal, resembles a tree without fruit.

You cannot keep your own secret; what cause then have you to complain, if another to whom you have declared it should reveal it?

It is the same with the administration of the affairs of kings as with sea voyages; you may lose, gain, amass treasures, and lose your life.

He who submits to a voluntary poverty neither possesses, nor is possessed by, any thing.

A wicked man should be considered as dead while he is alive; but a good man lives even in the tomb.

No man should undertake any thing till he has thoroughly examined it.

He who possesses any art or science, is at least equal to a great lord.

Honours, employments, and dignities cannot recompense a man for the pains he has taken to acquire them.

On many occasions a good book supplies the place of an agreeable companion.

That day in which a man neither does some good action, nor acquires some useful knowledge, should not be (if possible) numbered in the days of his life.

He who is of a surly and unyielding disposition, never fails to excite troubles even among relatives and friends.

A great monarch should fix a *good reputation* as an object to which he should continually bend his pursuits; because, of all the grandeurs and eminences of this world, this is the only thing that shall survive him.

Leave not till to-morrow what you can perform to-day.

To have pity on one's enemy, when he is in distress, is the mark of a great soul.

He who does good shall not lose his reward. A good action never perishes, neither before God nor before men.

Covetousness proceeds *ad infinitum;* therefore, determine the bounds of your desires, and the objects of your pursuits. He who does not act thus shall never become either rich or happy.

A monarch who considers his own interest should ever abide in his kingdom, and consider himself as a *rose* in the midst of a garden, which continually reposes on *thorns.*

Never despise a man because his employment is mean, or his clothing bad. The *bee* is an insect which is not very pleasing to the sight, yet its hive affords abundance of honey.

The people enjoy *repose* when governed by princes who take none. The monarch who watches causes his people to repose in safety.

Confer your opinion with that of another, for truth is more easily discovered by two than one.

Do not rejoice at the death of your enemy; *your* life is not eternal.

Be always employed, that ye become not slothful; and refer to God all that you acquire by labour, otherwise you shall live in a continual and condemnable idleness.

It is extremely difficult to render him wise who knows nothing; because his ignorance causes him to believe that he knows more than he who attempts to instruct him.

One coat, one house, and one day's food, is enough for you; and should you die at noonday, you will have one half too much.

A covetous man is an enemy to all the poor; and is cursed both in this and the coming world.

Interested friends resemble dogs in public places, who love the bones better than those who throw them.

In order to live well, a man should die to all his passions and every thing that depends on them.

A thousand years of delight do not deserve the risk of our lives for a single moment.

You shall only receive in proportion to what you give.

The service of kings may be compared to a vast sea, where many merchants traffic, some of whom acquire great riches, and others are shipwrecked.

Fear the man who fears you.

Do nothing without design.

Humble yourself in asking, that you may be raised up in obtaining what you request.

A wicked woman in the house of a good man is a hell to him in this world.

It cannot be said of a miser that he possesses his riches, however attached he may be to them.

The thought of evil frequently derives its origin from idleness.

Kings and subjects are equally unhappy, where persons of merit are despised, and where ignorant men occupy the chief places of trust.

Answer those who ask questions of you in such a manner as not to offend them.

The most proper method of punishing an envious person is, to load him with benefits.

Prudence suffers between *impossibility* and *irresolution*.

When you speak, let it be in such a manner as not to require an explanation.

The most precious acquisition is that of a friend.

Never trust to appearance. Behold the *drum:* notwithstanding all its noise, it is *empty* within.

Keep not an evil conscience: but be diffident, to the end that you be never surprised nor deceived.

Nothing remains with punishment or reward.

A wise man by his speeches does things which a hundred armies conjoined could not execute.

Do not speak till you have thought on what you intend to say.

Those who believe they may gain by seditions and commotions never fail to excite them.

The best friends we have in this world are the spies of our actions, who publish our faults.

Hope for nothing from this world, and your soul will enjoy rest.

He who applies himself to acquire knowledge, puts himself in the capacity of possessing all good things.

He who does not succeed in the business in which he is employed, because he is incapable of it, deserves to be excused; for it is to be believed that he has done all he could to accomplish his end.

Every kind of employment requires a particular sort of genius.

Riches increase in proportion as you give to the poor.

The greatest reputation is frequently an embarrassment.

Do not despise a poor man because he is such: the lion is not less noble because he is chained.

A young man who has the wisdom of an old man is considered as an old man among those who are wise.

A righteous prince is the image and shadow of God upon earth.

As soon as virtue begins to discover itself, vice begins its insolent insults.

Can it be said that a man has wisely considered what he has done, when the end corresponds not with what he proposed?

To the end that what you desire may be advantageous to you, never desire any thing but that which is proper for you.

Those who will not forgive an offence are the most accursed of all men.

Though it be pretended that no man can shun his destiny, yet it is well to do nothing without precaution.

It is a double present when given with a cheerful countenance.

Nobility is nothing unless supported by good actions.

Evil speaking and calumny never quit their hold till they have destroyed the innocent on whom they have once seized.

Consider your estate, and leave playing and jesting to children.

Soft words may appease an angry man; bitter words never will.

Would you throw fire on a house in flames to extinguish them?

Continue to speak the truth, though you know it to be hateful.

It is a blessing to a house to have a number of guests at table.

Five things are useless when they are not accompanied each with another thing: advice without effect; riches without economy; science without good manners; almsgiving to improper objects, or without a pure intention; and life without health.

If you wish your enemy never to know your secret, never divulge it to your friend.

Art thou a man in honour? Wouldst thou live without inquietude or remorse? Then do actions worthy of thy character.

When subjects are ill treated by subaltern officers, and cannot make remonstrances to the prince, because the too great authority of ministers of state deprives them of the means; their lot is like to that of a man who, half dead with thirst, approaches the river Nile to drink; but perceiving a *crocodile*, is obliged to perish for lack of water, or submit to be devoured.

It is better to perish with hunger, than to deprive the poor of their bread.

If you be reproved for your faults, do not be angry with him who does it: but turn your anger against the things for which he has reproved you.

Poisonous food is preferable to bad discourse.

Do not discover the faults of others, if you be unwilling to have your own known.

Wage war against yourself, and you will thereby acquire true peace of soul.

One resembles those the company of whom he most frequents.

The best expended riches are those which are given for God's sake.

If you have a dispute with any person, take heed that you say not of him all the evil which you know; otherwise you will leave no room for accommodation.

Your conversation is the index of your intellect, and your actions show the bottom of your heart.

It is more difficult to manage riches well, than to acquire them.

The grandeur of kings is evidenced in the administration of justice.

Honour your parents, and your children will honour you.

Cultivate no friendship with him who loves your enemy.

If you have a friend who takes offence at trifles, break entirely with him, for he is not to be trusted.

The happiness of life is only to be found, when the conscience is pure and clean.

Measure every man with his own measure; i. e., "Do not expect or require from him more than is in him."

Can any man boast who considers what he is come from?

In whatever corner of the world you are, you will have something to suffer.

It will be more profitable for thee to adorn thy inside than thy outside.

The Words of Lockman to his Son

My son, I wish thee to observe these *six* maxims which comprehend all the morality of the ancients and moderns.

1. Have no attachment to the world, but in proportion to the short duration of thy life.

2. Serve God with all that fervour which the need thou hast of him demands.

3. Labour for the other life that awaits thee, and consider the time it must endure.

4. Strive to escape that fire, out of which those who are once cast in can never escape.

5. If thou hast temerity enough to sin, measure beforehand the strength thou shalt require to endure the fire of hell, and the chastisements of God.

6 When thou wishest to transgress, seek for a place where God cannot see thee.

The Words of Ali to his Sons

My sons, never despise any person: consider your superior as your father, your equal as your brother, and your inferior as your son.

Words addressed by a Mohammedan to the Messiah

The heart of the afflicted draws all its consolation from thy words.

The soul receives life and vigour at the bare mention of thy name.

If ever the human spirit be rendered capable of contemplating the mysteries of the Divinity, it is thou alone who givest it the light by which it understands, and the attractions by which it is penetrated.

INTRODUCTION

BOOK OF ECCLESIASTES

THE book, entitled *Koheleth*, or *Ecclesiastes*, has ever been received, both by the Jewish and Christian Church, as written under the *inspiration* of the Almighty; and was held to be properly a part of the sacred canon. But while this has been almost universally granted, there has been but little unanimity among learned men and critics as to its *author*. To *Solomon* it has been most generally attributed, both in ancient and modern times.

Grotius, however, conjectured that it was written a long time after Solomon; and he says, at the close of his notes on it, that it was revised in the days of *Zerubbabel* by some learned man, who in the twelfth verse of the last chapter addresses his son *Abihud*: "And farther, by these, my son, be admonished." But such a conjecture appears to have little foundation. This great man was more successful in his criticism on the *language* of the book; showing that there are many words in it which do not savour of the purity of the Hebrew tongue; and are found in the times of the *captivity* and *afterwards*, and such as appear principally in the books of *Ezra* and *Daniel*.

Calovius has on the other hand, not with so much success as he imagined, argued against *Grotius* for the *purity* of the language.

Mr. G. Zirkel of Wurtzburgh published an examination of this book in 1792, in which he endeavours to prove:—

1. That the *style* of Ecclesiastes is that of the *later Hebrew writers*, as appears by the *Chaldaisms*, *Syriasms*, and *Hellenisms* that occur in it.

2. That it may have been written between the years 380 and 130 before Jesus Christ, if not later.

The *Jena* reviewers seem to have thought it to be a *translation* from the *Greek*, and to have been written by a *Jew of Alexandria*, while the famous *library* was founding by *Ptolemy Philadelphus* king of Egypt, about the year 240 before Christ. And that it is to this circumstance that chap. xii. 12 alludes, "Of making many books there is no end;" which could not have entered into the head of a Palestine Jew; and such a person might speak with propriety of an *Israel in Jerusalem*, chap. i. 12, being acquainted with an *Israel in Alexandria*.

The Jews in general, and St. *Jerome*, hold the book to be the composition of *Solomon*, and the fruit of his repentance when restored from his idolatry, into which he had fallen through means of the strange or *heathenish women* whom he had taken for *wives* and *concubines*.

Others, of no mean note, who consider Solomon as the author, believe that he wrote it *before* his fall; there being no evidence that he wrote it afterwards; nor, indeed, that he ever recovered from his fall. Besides, it was in his *old age* that his wives turned away his heart from God; and the book bears too many evidences of mental *energy* to allow the supposition that in his *declining age*, after so deep a fall from God, he was *capable* of writing such a treatise. This opinion goes far towards destroying the *Divine inspiration* of the book; for if he did recover and repent, there is no evidence that God gave him back that *Divine inspiration* which he before possessed; for we hear of the Lord appearing to him *twice before his fall*, but of a *third* appearance there is no intimation. And lastly, Of the restoration of Solomon to the favour of God there is no proof in the sacred history; for in the *very place* where we are told that "in his old age his wives turned away his heart from the Lord," we are told of his *death*, without the slightest intimation of his *repentance*. See my character of Solomon at the end of 1 Kings xi.

Nothing, however, of this uncertainty can affect either the character, importance, or utility of the book in question. It is a production of singular worth; and the finest monument we have of the wisdom of the ancients, except the *book of Job*.

But the chief difficulty attending this book is the *principle* on which it should be interpreted. Some have supposed it to be a *dialogue* between a *true believer* and an *infidel*, which makes it to the unwary reader appear abounding with contradiction, and, in some instances, false doctrine; and that the parts must be attributed to their respective speakers, before interpretation can be successfully attempted. I am not convinced that the book has any such structure; though in some places the *opinions* and *sayings* of *infidels* may be quoted; e. g., chap. vii. 16, and in some of the following chapters.

In the year 1763, M. *Desvœux*, a learned foreigner then resident in England, and who was in the British service, wrote and published a *Philosophical and Poetical Essay* on this book, in which he endeavours to prove, that the design of the author was to *demonstrate the immortality of the soul;* and that it is on this principle alone that the book can be understood and explained.

As a late commentator on the Bible has adopted this plan, and interwoven the major part of this dissertation with his notes on the book, I shall introduce the whole of M. *Desvœux's analysis of its contents,* the *propositions, arguments, proofs, illustrations, corollaries,* &c., on the ground of which he attempts its illustration:—

The whole of the discourse (he says) may be reduced to the three following *propositions,* each of which is attended with its *apparatus* of *proofs* and *especial observations.*

PROPOSITION I

No labour of man in this world can render him contented, or give him true satisfaction of soul.

PROPOSITION II

Earthly goods and possessions are so far from making us happy, that they may be even viewed as real obstacles to our ease, quiet, and tranquillity of mind.

PROPOSITION III

Men know not what is or is not truly advantageous to them; because they are either ignorant or unmindful of that which must come to pass after their death.

The *three propositions,* with their *proofs* and *illustrations,* are contained in the following analysis:—

PROPOSITION I

Chap.	Ver.	
I.	2, 3.	No labour of man, &c.
	4–11.	First proof.—The course of nature.
	12, &c.	Second proof.—Men's occupations.
	16–18.	First head.—Wisdom or philosophy.
II.	1, 2.	Second head.—Pleasure.
	3–10.	Both jointly.
	11.	General conclusion of the second proof.
		A review of the second proof with special conclusions, relating to every particular therein mentioned, viz.,
	12–17.	I. Wisdom.
	18–23.	II. Riches.
	24–26.	III. Pleasure.
III.	1, &c.	Third proof.—Inconstancy of men's wills.
	9.	Conclusion of the third proof.
		A review of the second and third proofs, considered jointly, with special observations and corollaries.
	10, 11.	First observation.—God is inculpable.

Chap.	Ver.	
III.	12, 15.	Second observation.—God is the author of whatever befalls us in this world.
	16, 17.	First corollary.—God shall redress all grievances.
	18–21.	Second corollary.—God must be exalted, and man humbled.
	22.	Third corollary.—God allows men to enjoy the present life.
IV.	1.	Fourth proof.—Men's neglect of proper opportunities, evidenced in several instances, viz.,
	1–3.	I. Oppression.
	4.	II. Envy.
	5, 6.	III. Idleness.
	7–12.	IV. Avarice.
V.	13–19.	V. Misapplication of esteem and regard.
		N. B. 1–9 is a digression containing several admonitions, in order to prevent any misconstruction of the foregoing remarks.
	10–12.	IV. Expensive living.

PROPOSITION II.—Chap. v. 13

Chap. Ver.			Chap. Ver.		
v.	14–17.	First proof. Instability of riches.			him who lives without enjoying life.
vi.	18. 2.	Second proof. Insufficiency of riches to make men happy.	vi.	7–9.	Third proof. Men's insatiableness.
	3–6.	Corollary. The fate of an *abortive* is, on the whole, preferable to that of		10, 11.	General *conclusion* from the *first* and *second propositions.*

PROPOSITION III.—Chap. vi. 12

Chap. Ver.			Chap. Ver.		
vii.	1, &c.	First proof. Wrong estimation of things.	vii.	26–29.	i. Wickedness and ignorance.
		A *digression,* intended, like that ver. 1–9, to prevent any misconstruction of the preceding observations; and containing several *advices,* together with a strong commendation of him who gives them, in order to enforce the observation of the *rules* he lays down.	viii.	1–8.	ii. Wisdom.
					Second proof. Anticipated judgments.
				9–14.	i. That sin shall go unpunished, because it is so in this world.
			ix.	15–6.	ii. That life is preferable to death.
				7–9.	First corollary. Earthly enjoyments are not criminal.
	9–12.	First advice. Do not blame Providence.		10.	Second corollary. We must make a proper use of our faculties.
	13.	Second advice. Do not judge of Providence.		11–15.	Third proof. Judgments that are seemingly right, but entirely false.
	14, 15.	Third advice. Submit to Providence.		16, &c.	Fourth proof. Little regard paid to wisdom.
	16–20.	Fourth advice. Avoid excesses.		16.	i. Past services are forgotten.
	21, 22.	Fifth advice. Do not heed idle reports.			ii. The least fault is noticed.
	23–25.	Commendation of the foregoing advices from the author's application of every thing; and especially,	x.	5–19.	iii. Favour gets what is due to merit.
				20.	A caution to prevent the abuse of the preceding remarks.

PRACTICAL INFERENCES

Chap. Ver.			Chap. Ver.		
xi.	1–4.	i. From the *first* PROPOSITION,—We must give to earthly goods that stability of which they are capable.	xii.	7, 8.	iii. From the *three* PROPOSITIONS, but especially from the *third,* we must seek for happiness beyond the grave.
	5, 6.	ii. From the *first* and *second* PROPOSITIONS,—We must, in all our conduct, conform to the design of Providence, and leave the success to God.		9–12.	Commendation of the work, from several considerations.
				13, 14.	CONCLUSION of the whole.

This is the whole of M. *Desvœux's Analysis;* and I place it here, that the reader who approves of the *plan* may keep it in view while he is passing through the book. For my own part, I doubt whether the author made any such technical arrangement.

The three propositions which M. Desvœux lays down, and which are so essential to the interpretation he gives of the book, would have been expressly propounded by the inspired writer had he intended such; but they appear nowhere in it, and M. D. is obliged to *assume* or gather them from the general scope of the work. However, on his plan, he has certainly made a number of judicious observations on different passages, though his translations are *generally* too bold, and *seldom* well supported by the original text.

In 1768 was published "Choheleth, or the Royal Preacher, a Poetical Paraphrase of the Book of Ecclesiastes. Most humbly inscribed to the King." 4to. There is no name to this work. The late Rev. John Wesley gives the following account of the work and its author in his *Journals:*—

"Monday, Feb. 8, 1768. I met with a surprising poem, entitled, Choheleth, or the Preacher: it is a paraphrase in tolerable verse on the book of Ecclesiastes. I really think the author of it (a Turkey merchant) understands both the difficult expressions, and the connection of the whole, better than any other either ancient or modern writer whom I have seen. He was at Lisbon during the great earthquake, just then sitting in his night-gown and slippers. Before he could dress himself, part of the house he was in fell, and blocked him up. By this means his life was saved; for all who had run out were dashed to pieces by the falling houses."

Mr. W. seems to have known the author well, but did not like to tell his name. About the year 1789 that eminent man recommended the work to me, and told me several particulars relative to it, which have escaped my memory. I procured the book the first opportunity, and read it with great satisfaction; and from it derived no small portion of information. Having now examined it anew, I can most cordially subscribe to Mr. Wesley's opinion. I really believe that the author understood both the difficult expressions, and the connection of the whole, better than any other writer, whether ancient or modern, at least known to me. Had it comported with my plan, I should have thought a reprint of his work, with the *text*, which he does not insert, and a few philological notes, would have been quite sufficient to have given my readers a safe and general view of the whole work and its design; though I can by no means adopt the author's hypothesis, that the book was written by Solomon *after* he was restored from his grievous apostacy. This is an assumption that never was proved and never can be.

From the *preface* to this work I have selected some general observations, which I consider to be important, and subjoin to this introduction; and what I borrow from the *work* itself I mark with a C, not knowing the author's name. Of the *authenticity* of the book of *Ecclesiastes* I have no doubt; but I must say, the *language* and *style* puzzle me not a little. *Chaldaisms* and *Syriasms* are certainly frequent in it, and not a few *Chaldee words* and terminations; and the style is such as may be seen in those writers who lived at or after the captivity. If these can be reconciled with the age of Solomon, I have no objection; but the attempts that have been made to deny this, and overthrow the evidence, are in my view often trifling, and generally ineffectual. That Solomon, son of David, might have been the *author* of the whole *matter* of this, and a *subsequent writer* put it in his own language, is a possible case; and were this to be allowed, it would solve all difficulties. Let us place the supposition thus: Solomon said all these things, and they are highly worthy of his wisdom; and a Divine writer, *after his time*, who does not mention his name, gives us a faithful version of the whole in his own language.

On other subjects relative to this book, the author of Choheleth shall speak for me.

"I. Not to perplex our readers with the various expositions of the word *Choheleth*, the title of the book in the original, (for in truth we can find none better or more significant than that commonly received, viz., *Ecclesiastes, or the Preacher*,) let us now come to the book itself. Nothing can be more interesting than the subject it treats of, to wit, *the chief or sovereign good* which man, as a rational and accountable being, should here propose to himself. Every human creature, it is certain, naturally aims at happiness; but though all apply themselves with equal ardour to this desirable end, yet such is the violence of passion, and want of reflection in the generality of mankind, that the means they use for obtaining it, instead of conducting them to the safe and direct road, only serve to mislead and bewilder them in dark and intricate labyrinths, where it is impossible to find what they seek for. Now as it was absolutely necessary to convince such men of the vanity of their pursuits, in order to induce them to turn back in the right way, Solomon shows, in the first place, what is *not* happiness, and then what really *is*. Like a skilful physician, he searches deeply into the latent cause of the malady, and then prescribes a radical cure.

"II. In the former disquisition he enumerates all those particulars which mankind are most apt to fix their hearts upon, and shows, from his own dear-bought experience, and the transient and unsatisfactory nature of the things themselves, that no such thing as solid felicity is to be found in any of them. What he asserts on this head carries with it the greater weight, as no man upon earth was ever better qualified to speak decisively on such a subject, considering the opportunities he had of enjoying to the utmost all that this world affords. After having thus cleared away the obstacles to happiness, he enters on the main point, which is to direct us how and where it may be found. This he affirms, at the conclusion of the book, where he recapitulates the sum and substance of the sermon, as some not improperly have styled it, consists in a religious and virtuous life, with which, as he frequently intimates, a man in the lowest circumstances may be happy, and without which one in the highest must be miserable. As the whole book tends to this single point, so, in discussing thereof, many excellent observations are interpersed relating to the various duties of life, from the highest to the lowest station; the advantages resulting even from poverty, the genuine use of riches, and extreme folly of abusing them; the unequal dispensations of Divine Providence; the immortality of the human soul; and great day of final retribution. All these noble and important subjects are treated of in such a style and manner as nothing among the ancients can parallel.

"We have here given the genuine character of this inestimable piece; yet such has been the ignorance, inattention, or depravity of some persons, that it would be hard to find an instance of any thing written on so serious and interesting a subject, which has been so grossly misrepresented. How often has a handle been taken from certain passages, ill understood, and worse applied, to patronise libertinism, by such as pretend to judge of the whole from a single sentence, independent of the rest, without paying the least regard to the general scope or design! According to which rule the most pious discourse that ever was written may be perverted to atheism. Some fanatics have fallen into the contrary extreme; for, on reading that all here below was vanity, they have been so wrong-headed, as to condemn every thing as evil in itself. This world, according to them, cannot be too bitterly inveighed against; and man has nothing else to do with it, but to spend his days in sighing and mourning. But it is evident that nothing could be farther from the preacher's intention: for notwithstanding he speaks so feelingly of the instability and unsatisfactory nature of all sublunary things, and the vanity of human cares, schemes, and contrivances; yet, lest any one should mistake his meaning, he advises every man, at the same time, to reap the fruit of his honest labours, and take the comfort of what he possesses with a sober freedom and cheerful spirit. Not to harass and disturb his mind with anxious cares and restless solicitudes about future events; but to pass the short space which Heaven has allotted him here, as pleasantly as his station will admit, with a quiet conscience. He does not condemn the things themselves, such as science, prudence, mirth, riches, honours, &c.; but only their abuse, that is, the useless studies, unreasonable pursuits, and immoderate desires, of those who pervert God's blessings to their own destruction.

"On this head Solomon gives his sentiments, not only as a divine and philosopher, but like one thoroughly acquainted with the foibles of the human heart. It was not his design to drive people out of the world, or to make them live wretchedly in it; but only that they should think and act like rational creatures; or, in other words, be induced to consult their own happiness.

"There is nothing in the whole body of pagan philosophy so elevated and magnificent, as what some have written on the important subject of this poem: but we find their opinions so various and contradictory, and the most plausible so blended with errors, even those of the *divine Plato* not excepted, that their sublimest sentiments on the *sovereign good* or *ultimate happiness* of man, when compared with those of the royal preacher, not only appear cold and languid, but always leave the mind unsatisfied and restless. We are lost in a pompous flow of words; and dazzled, but not illuminated. One sect, by confining happiness to sensual pleasures, so greatly slackened the cord as to render it wholly useless: another, by their too austere and rigid maxims, stretched it so tight that it snapped asunder; though the experience of all ages has evinced that these latter imposed both on themselves and the world, when they taught that virtue, however afflicted here, was its own reward, and sufficient of itself to render a man completely happy. Even in the brazen bull of *Perillus*, truth will cry out from the rack against such fallacious teachers, and prove them liars. The extravagant figments, therefore, of the *stoical apathy*, no less than those of the *voluptuous epicurean*, both equally vanish at the splendour of the Divine truth delivered by Solomon.

He alone decides the great question in such a manner that the soul is instantly convinced; it need seek no farther.

"III. To prevent all misapprehensions, which a slight and cursory reading of this book is apt to raise in many persons, it will be requisite to observe two cautions: First, that Solomon, who tells us that he applied his heart not only to the search of wisdom and knowledge, but also of folly and madness, frequently speaks, not according to his own sentiments, though he proposes the thing in a naked and simple manner, designedly making use of such terms as might set the picture in a fuller and clearer light, so that we often meet with certain expressions which, unless we search into their true design, seem to have a quite different force and meaning from what the author really intended. We must therefore take particular care to distinguish the doubts and objections of others from Solomon's answers; the want of attending to which has made this book much more obscure than otherwise it would appear. Secondly, we should not judge of the entire discourse from some parts of it; since many things are pertinently said, according to the present subject, which, in themselves, and strictly taken, are far from true. In order to come at the genuine sense, we should form our opinion from the different circumstances of the matter treated of, comparing the antecedent with the consequent passages, and always considering the preacher's real scope and design. By carefully attending to these two cautions, this book will be seen in a very different light from what it now appears in to the generality of readers.

"IV. This book, besides the figurative and proverbial expressions to be found in no other part of the Scripture, is undoubtedly metrical; and, consequently, the grammatization, in many places, not a little perplexed, from the frequent ellipses, abbreviations, transposition of words, and other poetical licenses, allowed in all languages; to say nothing of the carelessness or ignorance of transcribers, as appears from the variety of readings. Yet, notwithstanding we are so little acquainted with the nature of the Hebrew metre, and the propriety of certain phrases which, at this vast distance of time, in a language that has been dead upwards of two thousand years, must unavoidably occasion the same difficulties and obscurities as occur in works of far less antiquity, and in languages more generally studied and better understood; notwithstanding this, I say, a diligent and attentive observer will always find enough to recompense his trouble; and, if he has any taste, cannot avoid being struck with the exquisite beauty and regularity of the plan.

"V. The most judicious commentators have remarked on this book, that we have here a conspicuous example of that form of disputing, which was so justly admired in the soundest of the pagan philosophers; particularly in Socrates, who, whilst others were taken up with abstruse speculations about the nature of things, and investigating the number, motions, distance, and magnitude of the stars, brought down philosophy from the upper regions, and fixed its abode on earth; that is, by teaching such precepts as served for the regulation of life and manners, by far the most useful of all sciences, as being most conducive to the welfare of society, and the general benefit of mankind. Of this we have a noble specimen in the memoirs of that ancient moralist, collected by Xenophon. It is, I think, beyond all contradiction, that no one ever made deeper researches into nature, or had made so great a progress in every branch of science, both speculative and experimental. But what, after all, was the result of his inquiries? A thorough conviction of the inutility of such studies, and how little they conduce towards the obtaining that peace and tranquillity of mind wherein true happiness consists. He applied himself, therefore, to that study which might produce a real and lasting advantage, namely, to render men wise to some purpose; that is, truly virtuous. The manner of his treating this important subject bears some resemblance to that of the celebrated Greek moralist. He does not give us a long roll of dry formal precepts, with which the mind is soon tired; but, to confirm the truth of every thing he says, appeals, not only to his own experience, but to the general sense of unbiassed reason. At the same time he sets before us, in the liveliest colours, the sad effects of vice and folly; and makes use of every incentive to engage the heart to be enamoured with virtue, and pursue its own interest. Whatever he intends to inculcate is first barely proposed, and then more accurately explained and illustrated, though by gentle and almost imperceptible transitions; with this peculiarity, that there is always much more implied than expressed; insomuch that the reader, from a slight hint given him, is left to draw such inferences as his own reflection must naturally suggest. Every thing, in short, is drawn, in this admirable composition, with equal simplicity and elegance; and hath as distinguished a superiority to whatever the best pagan philosophers have given us on the same subject, as the borrowed light of the moon is surpassed by that of the sun in his full meridian lustre; or, to use a still stronger comparison, as Solomon's knowledge of the one true God excelled the idle notion of their fictitious deities."

Some have supposed that the book of Ecclesiastes is a poem. That some poetic lines may be found in it, there is no doubt; but it has nothing in common with poetic books, nor does it exist in the hemistich form in any printed edition or MS. yet discovered. It is plain prose, and is not susceptible of that form in which the Hebrew poetic books appear.

The author already quoted thinks that the book of *Ecclesiastes* is *metrical*. I cannot see this: but it has what is essential to poetry, a truly dignified style; there are no mean, creeping words in it, whether pure Hebrew, or borrowed from any of its dialects. They are all well chosen, nervous, and highly expressive. They are, in short, such as become the subject, and are worthy of that inspiration by which the author was guided.

ECCLESIASTES;

OR,

THE PREACHER

Year from the Creation, according to Archbishop Usher, 3027.—Year from the Flood of Noah, according to the common Hebrew text, 1371.—Year before the birth of Christ, 973.—Year before the vulgar era of Christ's nativity, 977.—N. B. The time when this book was written is very uncertain: the above chronology is agreeable to that contained in the present authorized version.

CHAPTER I

The prophet shows that all human courses are vain, 1–4. The creatures are continually changing, 5–8. There is nothing new under the sun, 9–11. Who the prophet was, his estate and his studies, 12–18.

A. M. cir. 3027
B. C. cir. 977
Ante I. Olymp.
cir. 201
Ante U. C. cir.
224

THE words [a]of the Preacher, the son of David, king of Jerusalem.

2 [b]Vanity of vanities, saith the Preacher, vanity of vanities; [c]all *is* vanity.

3 [d]What profit hath a man of all his labour which he taketh under the sun?

4 *One* generation passeth away, and *another* generation cometh: [e]but the earth abideth for ever.

A. M. cir. 3027
B. C. cir. 977
Ante I. Olymp.
cir. 201
Ante U. C. cir.
224

---

[a]Ver. 2, 12; chap. vii. 27; xii. 8, 9, 10——[b]Psa. xxxix. 5, 6; lxii. 9; cxliv. 4; chap. ii. 1, 15, 19, 21, 23; iii. 19; iv. 8, 16; v. 10; vi. 2, 4, 9, 11; vii. 6, 15; viii. 10, 14; ix. 9; xi. 10; xii. 8; Isa. xxx. 28; xl. 17, 23; xli. 29; xliv. 9; lvii. 13; lviii. 9; lix. 4——[c]Rom. viii. 20——[d]Chap. ii. 22; iii. 9 [e]Psa. civ. 5; cxix. 90

NOTES ON CHAP. I

Verse 1. *The words of the Preacher*] Literally, "The words of Choheleth, son of David, king of Jerusalem." But the *Targum* explains it thus: "The words of the prophecy, which Choheleth prophesied; the same is Solomon, son of David the king, who was in Jerusalem. For when Solomon, king of Israel, saw by the spirit of prophecy that the kingdom of Rehoboam his son was about to be divided with Jeroboam, the son of Nebat; and the house of the sanctuary was about to be destroyed, and the people of Israel sent into captivity; he said in his word—*Vanity of vanities* is all that I have laboured, and David my father; they are *altogether vanity*."

The word קהלת *Koheleth* is a feminine noun, from the root קהל *kahal*, to collect, gather together, assemble; and means, *she who assembles* or *collects a congregation;* translated by the *Septuagint*, Εκκλησιαστης, a *public speaker, a speaker in an assembly;* and hence translated by us *a preacher.* In my old MS. Bible it is explained thus: **a talker to the peple; or togpber cleping.**

Verse 2. *Vanity of vanities*] As the words are an exclamation, it would be better to translate, *O vanity of vanities!* Emptiness of empti-

nesses. True, substantial good is not to be found in any thing liable to *change* and *corruption.*

The author referred to in the introduction begins his paraphrase thus:—

"O vain deluding world! whose largest gifts
Thine emptiness betray, like painted clouds,
Or watery bubbles: as the vapour flies,
Dispersed by lightest blast, so fleet thy joys,
And leave no trace behind. This serious truth
The royal preacher loud proclaims, convinced
By sad experience; with a sigh repeats
The mournful theme, that nothing here below
Can solid comfort yield: 'tis all a scene.
Of vanity, beyond the power of words
To express, or thought conceive. Let every
    man
Survey himself, then ask, what fruit remains
Of all his fond pursuits? What has he gain'd,
By toiling thus for more than nature's wants
Require? Why thus with endless projects
    rack'd
His heated brain, and to the labouring mind,
Repose denied? Why such expense of time,
That steals away so fast, and ne'er looks back?
    Could man his wish obtain, how short the
      space
For his enjoyment! No less transient here
The time of his duration, than the things

A. M. cir. 3027
B. C. cir. 977
Ante I. Olymp. cir. 201
Ante U. C. cir. 224

5 'The sun also ariseth, and the sun goeth down, and ᵍhasteth to his place where he arose.

6 ʰThe wind goeth toward the south, and turneth about unto the north; it whirleth about continually, and the wind returneth again according to his circuits.

7 ⁱAll the rivers run into the sea; yet the sea *is* not full; unto the place from whence the rivers come, thither they ᵏreturn again.

8 All things *are* full of labour; man can-

not utter *it:* ˡthe eye is not satisfied with seeing, nor the ear filled with hearing.

A. M. cir. 3027
B. C. cir. 977
Ante I. Olymp. cir. 201
Ante U. C. cir. 224

9 ᵐThe thing that hath been, it *is that* which shall be; and that which is done *is* that which shall be done: and *there is* no new *thing* under the sun.

10 Is there *any* thing whereof it may be said, See, this *is* new? it hath been already of old time, which was before us.

11 *There is* no remembrance of former

ᶠPsa. xix. 5, 6——ᵍHeb. *panteth*——ʰJohn iii. 8 ⁱJob xxxviii. 10; Psa. civ. 8, 9

ᵏHeb. *return to go*——ˡProverbs xxvii. 20——ᵐChapter iii. 15

Thus anxiously pursued. For, as the mind,
In search of bliss, fix'd on no solid point,
For ever fluctuates; so our little frames,
In which we glory, haste to their decline,
Nor permanence can find. The human race
Drop like autumnal leaves, by spring revived:
One generation from the stage of life
Withdraws, another comes, and thus makes room
For that which follows. Mightiest realms decay,
Sink by degrees; and lo! new form'd estates
Rise from their ruins. Even the earth itself,
Sole object of our hopes and fears,
Shall have its period, though to man unknown."

Verse 3. *What profit hath a man*] What is the sum of the real good he has gained by all his toils in life? They, in themselves, have neither made him *contented* nor *happy.*

Verse 4. One *generation passeth away*] Men succeed each other in unceasing generations: but the earth is still the same; it undergoes no change that leads to melioration, or greater perfection. And it will continue the same לעולם *leolam,* during the whole course of time; till the end of all things arrives.

Verses 5 and 6. These verses are confused by being falsely divided. The first clause of the *sixth* should be joined to the *fifth* verse.

"The sun also ariseth, and the sun goeth down, and hasteth to his place where he ariseth; going to the south, and circulating to the north."

Verse 6. "The wind is continually whirling about, and the wind returneth upon its whirlings."

It is plain, from the clause which I have restored to the *fifth* verse, that the author refers to the approximations of the sun to the *northern* and *southern* tropics, viz., of *Cancer* and *Capricorn.*

All the *versions* agree in applying the first clause of the *sixth* verse to the *sun,* and not to the *wind.* Our *version* alone has mistaken the meaning. My old MS. Bible is quite correct:

𝔗𝔥𝔢 𝔰𝔲𝔫𝔫𝔢 𝔯𝔦𝔦𝔰𝔦𝔱𝔥 𝔲𝔭, 𝔞𝔫𝔡 𝔤𝔬𝔱𝔥 𝔡𝔬𝔲𝔫, 𝔞𝔫𝔡 𝔱𝔬 𝔥𝔦𝔰 𝔭𝔩𝔞𝔠𝔢 𝔱𝔲𝔯𝔫𝔦𝔱𝔥 𝔞𝔤𝔢𝔦𝔫; 𝔞𝔫𝔡 𝔱𝔥𝔢𝔯𝔢 𝔞𝔤𝔢𝔦𝔫 𝔯𝔦𝔦𝔰𝔦𝔫𝔤, 𝔤𝔬𝔱𝔥 𝔞𝔟𝔬𝔲𝔱 𝔟𝔦 𝔱𝔥𝔢 𝔰𝔬𝔲𝔱𝔥, 𝔞𝔫𝔡 𝔱𝔥𝔢𝔫 𝔞𝔤𝔢𝔦𝔫 𝔱𝔬 𝔱𝔥𝔢 𝔫𝔬𝔯𝔱𝔥.

The author points out two things here: 1. Day and *night,* marked by the appearance of the sun above the horizon; proceeding *apparently* from *east to west;* where he sinks

under the horizon, and appears to be lost during the night. 2. His *annual course* through the twelve signs of the zodiac, when, from the equinoctial, he proceeds southward to the tropic of Capricorn; and thence turneth about towards the north, till he reaches the tropic of Cancer; and so on.

Verse 7. *All the rivers run into the sea; yet the sea* is *not full*] The reason is, nothing goes into it either by the *rivers* or by *rain,* that does not come from it: and *to the place whence the rivers come,* whether from the *sea* originally by evaporation, or immediately by *rain,* thither they return again; for the water exhaled from the sea by evaporation is collected in the *clouds,* and in rain, &c., falls upon the tops of the mountains; and, filtered through their fissures, produce *streams,* several of which *uniting,* make *rivers,* which flow into the sea. The water is again *evaporated by the sun;* the vapours collected are precipitated; and, being filtered through the earth, become *streams,* &c., as before.

Verse 8. *All things* are *full of labour*] It is impossible to calculate how much anxiety, pain, labour, and fatigue are necessary in order to carry on the *common operations of life.* But an *endless desire* of *gain,* and an *endless curiosity* to *witness* a variety of results, cause men to labour on. The *eye* sees much; but wishes to see more. The *ear* hears of many things; but is curious to have the actual knowledge of them. So *desire* and *curiosity* carry men, under the Divine providence, through all the labours and pains of life.

Verse 9. *The thing that hath been*] Every thing in the whole economy of nature has its *revolutions;* summer and winter, heat and cold, rain and drought, seedtime and autumn, with the whole system of *corruption* and *generation,* alternately succeed each other, so that *whatever has been* shall *be again.* There is really, physically, and philosophically, nothing absolutely new under the sun, in the course of sublunary things. The same is the case in all the revolutions of the heavens.

Verse 10. *Is there* any *thing, &c.*] The original is beautiful. "Is there any thing which will say, See this! it is new?" Men may say this of their discoveries, &c.; but universal nature says, It is not new. *It has been,* and it *will be.*

Verse 11. There is *no remembrance*] I believe the general meaning to be this: Multitudes of *ancient transactions* have been lost,

A. M. cir. 3027
B. C. cir. 977
Ante I. Olymp.
cir. 201
Ante U. C. cir.
224
things; neither shall there be *any* remembrance of *things* that are to come with *those* that shall come after.

12 [n]I the Preacher was king over Israel in Jerusalem.

13 And I gave my heart to seek and search out by wisdom concerning all *things* that are done under heaven: [o]this sore travail hath God given to the sons of man [p]to be exercised therewith.

14 I have seen all the works that are done under the sun; and, behold, all *is* vanity and vexation of spirit.

15 [q]*That which is* crooked cannot be made

straight: and [r]that which is wanting cannot be numbered.

A. M. cir. 3027
B. C. cir. 977
Ante I. Olymp.
cir. 201
Ante U. C. cir.
224

16 I communed with mine own heart, saying, Lo, I am come to great estate, and have gotten [s]more wisdom than all *they* that have been before me in Jerusalem: Yea, my heart [t]had great experience of wisdom and knowledge.

17 [u]And I gave my heart to know wisdom, and to know madness and folly: I perceived that this also is vexation of spirit.

18 For [v]in much wisdom *is* much grief: and he that increaseth knowledge increaseth sorrow.

---

[n]Verse 1——[o]Genesis iii. 19; chapter iii. 10——[p]Or, *to afflict them*——[q]Chapter vii. 13——[r]Hebrew, *defect*——[s]1 Kings iii. 12, 13; iv. 30; x. 7, 23; chapter ii. 9——[t]Hebrew, *had seen much*——[u]Chapter ii. 3, 12; vii. 23, 25; 1 Thessalonians v. 21——[v]Chapter xii. 12

---

because they were not *recorded;* and of many that have been recorded, the *records* are *lost.* And this will be the case with many others which are yet to occur. How many persons, not much acquainted with books, have supposed that certain things were their own discoveries, which have been *written* or *printed* even long before they were born! *Dutens,* in his *Origin of the Discoveries attributed to the Moderns,* has made a very clear case.

Verse 12. *I the Preacher was king*] This is a strange verse, and does not admit of an easy solution. It is literally, "I, Choheleth, have been king over Israel, in Jerusalem." This book, as we have already seen, has been conjectured by some to have been written about the time that *Ptolemy Philadelphus* formed his great library at Alexandria, about *two hundred and eighty-five* years before our Lord; and from the multitude of Jews that dwelt there, and resorted to that city for the sake of commerce, it was said there was an *Israel in Alexandria.* See the *introduction.*

It has also been conjectured from this, that if the book were written by *Solomon,* it was intended to be a *posthumous publication.* "I that *was* king, still continue to preach and instruct you." Those who suppose the book to have been written *after Solomon's fall,* think that he speaks thus through *humility.* "I was once worthy of the name of king: but I fell into all evil; and, though recovered, I am no longer worthy of the name." I am afraid this is not *solid.*

Verse 13. *And I gave my heart to seek and search*] While Solomon was faithful to his God, he diligently cultivated his mind. His giving himself to the study of natural history, philosophy, poetry, &c., are sufficient proofs of it. He had not intuitive knowledge from God; but he had a *capacity* to obtain every kind of knowledge useful to man.

This sore travail] This is the way in which knowledge is to be acquired; and in order to investigate the operations of nature, the most *laborious discussions* and *perplexing experiments* must be instituted, and conducted to their proper results. It is God's determination

that knowledge shall be acquired in no other way.

Verse 14. *Behold, all is vanity*] After all these discussions and experiments, when even the results have been the most successful, I have found only *rational satisfaction;* but not that *supreme good* by which alone the soul can be made happy.

O curas hominum! O quantum est in rebus inane!

"How anxious are our cares, and yet how vain The bent of our desires!"

PERS. *Sat.* i., v. 1.

Verse 15. That which is *crooked cannot be made straight*] There are many apparent irregularities and anomalies in nature for which we cannot account; and there are many *defects* that cannot be *supplied.* This is the impression from a *general view* of nature; but the more we study and investigate its operations, the more we shall be convinced that all is a *consecutive* and well-ordered whole; and that in the *chain of nature* not one *link* is broken, deficient, or lost.

Verse 16. *I communed with mine own heart*] Literally, "I spoke, I, with my heart, saying." When successful in my researches, but not happy in my soul, though easy in my circumstances, I entered into my own heart, and there inquired the *cause* of my discontent. He found that, though—1. He had gotten wisdom beyond all men; 2. Wealth and honours more than any other; 3. Practical wisdom more than all his predecessors; 4. Had tried *pleasure* and animal gratification, even to their extremes; yet after all this he had nothing but *vexation of spirit.* None of these *four* things, nor the *whole* of them *conjoined,* could afford him such a *happiness* as satisfies the soul. Why was all this? Because the soul was made for God, and in the possession of him alone can it find happiness.

Verse 17. *To know madness and folly*] הוללות ושכלות *holloth vesichluth.* Παραβολας και επιστημην, "Parables and science."—*Septuagint.* So the *Syriac;* nearly so the *Arabic.*

"What were error and foolishness."—*Coverdale.* Perhaps *gayety* and *sobriety* may be the better meaning for these two difficult words. I can scarcely think they are taken in that *bad sense* in which our translation exhibits them. "I tried pleasure in all its forms; and sobriety and self-abnegation to their utmost extent." Choheleth paraphrases, "Even fools and madmen taught me rules."

Verse 18. *For in much wisdom is much grief*] The more we know of *ourselves* the less satisfied shall we be with our own hearts; and the more we know of *mankind* the less willing shall we be to trust them, and the less shall we admire them.

He that increaseth knowledge increaseth sorrow.] And why so? Because, independently of God, the principal objects of knowledge are natural and moral evils.

The *Targum* gives a curious paraphrase here: "The man who multiplies wisdom, when he sins and is not converted to repentance, multiplies the indignation of God against himself; and the man who adds science, and yet dies in his childhood, adds grief of heart to his relatives." A man in science; a foolish child in conduct. How pained must they be who had the expense of his education! But there are many men-children of this sort in every age and country.

CHAPTER II

The vanity of human courses in the works of pleasure, planting, building, equipage, amassing wealth, &c., 1–11. Wisdom preferable to folly, 12–14; yet little difference between the wise and the foolish in the events of life, 15–17. The vanity of amassing wealth for heirs, when whether they will be foolish or wise cannot be ascertained, 18–21. There is much sorrow in the labour of man, 22, 23. We should enjoy what the providence of God gives, 25, 26.

A. M. cir. 3027
B. C. cir. 977
Ante I. Olymp.
cir. 201
Ante U. C. cir.
224

[a]I SAID in mine heart, Go to now, I will prove thee with mirth, therefore enjoy pleasure: and, behold, [b]this also *is* vanity.

2 [c]I said of laughter, *It is* mad: and of mirth, What doeth it?

3 [d]I sought in mine heart [e]to give myself unto wine, (yet acquainting mine heart with wisdom,) and to lay hold on folly, till I might

see what *was* that good for the sons of men, which they should do under the heaven [f]all the days of their life.

A. M. cir. 3027
B. C. cir. 977
Ante I. Olymp.
cir. 201
Ante U. C. cir.
224

4 I made me great works; I builded me houses; I planted me vineyards:

5 I made me gardens and orchards, and I planted trees in them of all *kind of* fruits:

6 I made me pools of water, to water therewith the wood that bringeth forth trees:

---

[a]Luke xii. 19——[b]Isa. l. 11——[c]Prov. xiv. 13; chap. vii. 6——[d]Chap. i. 17

[e]Heb. *to draw my flesh with wine*——[f]Heb. *the number of the days of their life*

NOTES ON CHAP. II

Verse 1. *I will prove thee with mirth*] This is well expressed by the author so often referred to. Having tried speculative knowledge in vain, passion and appetite whisper,—

"From the rugged thorny road
Of wisdom, which so ill repays thy toil,
Turn back, and enter pleasure's flowery paths.
Go, take thy fill of joy; to passion give
The reins; nor let one serious thought restrain
What youth and affluence prompt."

Verse 2. *I said of laughter, It is mad*] Literally, "To laughter I said, O mad one! and to mirth, What is this one doing?"

Solomon does not speak here of a sober enjoyment of the things of this world, but of *intemperate pleasure*, whose two attendants, *laughter* and *mirth* are introduced by a beautiful *prosopopœia* as two persons; and the contemptuous manner wherewith he treats them has something remarkably striking. He tells the *former* to her face that *she is mad*; but as to the *latter*, he thinks her so much beneath his notice, that he only points at her, and instantly turns his back.

Verse 3. *To give myself unto wine, (yet acquainting* [נהג *noheg*, "guiding"] *mine heart with wisdom,)*] I did not run into *extremes*, as when I gave up myself to *mirth* and *pleasure. There,* I threw off all restraint; *here,* I took the middle course, to see whether a *moderate* enjoyment of the things of the world might not produce that happiness which I supposed man was created to enjoy here below.

Verse 4. *I builded me houses*] Palace after palace; the house of the forest of Lebanon, 1 Kings vii. 1, &c.; a house for the queen; the temple, &c., 2 Chron. viii. 1, &c.; 1 Kings ix. 10, &c., besides many other buildings of various kinds.

Verse 5. *I made me gardens and orchards*] פרדסים *pardesim*, "paradises." I doubt much whether this be an original *Hebrew* word. فردوس *ferdoos*, is found in the *Persian* and *Arabic;* and signifies a *pleasant garden*, a *vineyard.* Hence our word *paradise*, a place *full of delights.* How well Solomon was qualified to form *gardens, orchards, vineyards, conservatories,* &c., may be at once conceived when we recollect his knowledge of *natural history;* and that he wrote treatises on vegetables and their properties, from the *cedar* to the *hyssop.*

Verse 6. *Pools of water*] Tanks and reservoirs.

A. M. cir. 3027
B. C. cir. 977
Ante I. Olymp. cir. 201
Ante U. C. cir. 224

7 I got *me* servants and maidens, and had [g]servants born in my house; also I had great possessions of great and small cattle above all that were in Jerusalem before me:

8 [h]I gathered me also silver and gold, and the peculiar treasure of kings and of the provinces: I gat me men singers and women singers, and the delights of the sons of men, *as* [i]musical instruments, and that of all sorts.

9 So [k]I was great, and increased more than all that were before me in Jerusalem: also my wisdom remained with me.

10 And whatsoever mine eyes desired I kept not from them, I withheld not my heart from any joy; for my heart rejoiced in all my labour: and [l]this was my portion of all my labour.

A. M. cir. 3027
B. C. cir. 977
Ante I. Olymp. cir. 201
Ante U. C. cir. 224

11 Then I looked on all the works that my hands had wrought, and on the labour that I had laboured to do: and, behold, all *was* [m]vanity and vexation of spirit, and *there was* no profit under the sun.

12 And I turned myself to behold wisdom, [n]and madness, and folly: for what *can* the man *do* that cometh after the king? [o]*even* that which hath been already done.

13 Then I saw [p]that wisdom excelleth folly, as far as light excelleth darkness.

---

[g]Heb. *sons of my house*——[h]1 Kings ix. 28; x. 10, 14, 21, &c.——[i]Heb. *musical instrument and instruments* [k]Ch. i. 16——[l]Ch. iii. 22; v. 18; ix. 9——[m]Ch. i. 3, 14

[n]Ch. i. 17; vii. 25——[o]Or, *in those things which have been already done*——[p]Heb. *that there is an excellency in wisdom more than in folly, &c.*

To water therewith the wood] Aqueducts to lead the water from the tanks to different parts.

Verse 7. Servants and maidens] For my works, fields, folds, and various domestic labours.

Servants born in my house] Besides those hired from without, he had *married couples* in the precincts of his grounds, palaces, &c., who, when their children grew up, got them employment with themselves.

Great and small cattle] Oxen, neat, horses, asses, *mules, camels,* and such like; with *sheep* and *goats*. And multitudes of most of these he needed, when we are told that his household consumed daily *ten stall-fed oxen, with twenty from the pasture, with a hundred sheep;* besides *harts, roebucks, fallow deer, fatted fowls,* and other kinds of provision. Probably, such another court for splendour and expense was not in the universe.

Verse 8. The peculiar treasure of kings and of the provinces] 1. The *taxes* levied off his subjects. 2. The *tribute* given by the neighbouring potentates. Both these make the "peculiar treasure of kings;" *taxes* and *tribute.*

Men singers and women singers] This includes all *instrumental* and *vocal* performers. These may be called the *delights* of the sons of men.

Musical instruments, and that of all sorts.] For these *seven* words, there are only *two* in the original, שדה ושדות *shiddah veshiddoth.* These words are acknowledged on all hands to be utterly unknown, if not utterly inexplicable. Some render them *male* and *female captives;* others, *cups* and *flagons;* others, *cooks* and *confectioners;* others, *a species of musical compositions* derived from a celebrated Phœnician woman named *Sido,* to whom Sanchoniatho attributes the invention of *music.* Others, with more probability, *wives* and *concubines;* of the *former* of whom Solomon had *seven hundred,* and of the *latter, three hundred;* and if these be not spoken of here, they are not mentioned at all; whereas music, and every thing connected with that, was referred to before. The author of *Choheleth* paraphrases thus:—

"To complete
This scene of earthly bliss, how large a span
Of that which most delights the sons of men
Fell to my portion! What a lovely train
Of blooming beauties, by *connubial* ties,
By *purchase,* or the *gifts* of neighbouring kings,
Or *spoils of war,* made mine."

If, after all this, I may add one *conjecture,* it shall be this; שדה *sadeh,* in Hebrew, is a *field,* and occurs in various parts of the Bible. שדות *sadoth* is *fields,* 1 Sam. xxii. 7, the *points* in such a case are of no consideration. May not Solomon be speaking here of *farms upon farms,* or *estates upon estates,* which he had added by purchase to the *common regal portion?* We know that a king of Israel (Ahab) once desired to have a vineyard (Naboth's) which he could not obtain: now, Solomon having spoken before of *gardens, orchards, and vineyards,* why may he not here speak of *supernumerary estates?* Perhaps every man who critically examines the place will be dissatisfied, and have a *conjecture* of his own.

Verse 10. I withheld not my heart from any joy] He had every means of gratification; he could desire nothing that was not within his reach; and whatever he wished, he took care to possess.

Verse 11. And, behold, all was *vanity*] Emptiness and insufficiency in itself.

And vexation of spirit] Because it promised the good I wished for, but did not, could not, perform the promise; and left my soul discontented and chagrined.

Verse 12. For what can *the man* do *that cometh after the king?*] I have examined every thing proposed by *science,* by *maddening pleasure,* and by more refined and regulated *mirth.* I seized on the whole, and used them to the uttermost; and so far, that none ever shall be able to exceed me; as none can, in the course of things, ever have such *power* and *means of gratification.*

Verse 13. Then I saw that wisdom excelleth folly] Though in none of these pursuits I found the *supreme good.* the happiness my soul longed

A. M. cir. 3027
B. C. cir. 977
Ante I. Olymp.
cir. 201
Ante U. C. cir.
224

14 �q The wise man's eyes *are* in his head; but the fool walketh in darkness: and I myself perceiveth also that ʳone event happeneth to them all.

15 Then said I in my heart, As it happeneth to the fool, so it ˢhappeneth even to me; and why was I then more wise? Then I said in my heart, that this also *is* vanity.

16 For *there is* no remembrance of the wise more than of the fool for ever; seeing that which now *is* in the days to come shall all be forgotten. And how dieth the ᵗwise *man?* as the fool.

17 Therefore I hated life; because the work that is wrought under the sun *is* grievous unto me: for all *is* vanity and vexation of spirit.

A. M. cir. 3027
B. C. cir. 977
Ante I. Olymp.
cir. 201
Ante U. C. cir.
cir. 224

18 Yea, I hated all my labour which I had ᵘtaken under the sun: because ᵛI should leave it unto the man that shall be after me.

19 And who knoweth whether he shall be a wise *man* or a fool? yet shall he have rule over all my labour wherein I have laboured, and wherein I have showed himself wise under the sun. This *is* also vanity.

20 Therefore I went about to cause my heart to despair of all the labour which I took under the sun.

21 For there is a man whose labour *is* in wisdom, and in knowledge, and in equity; yet to a man that hath not laboured therein shall he ʷleave it *for* his portion. This also *is* vanity and a great evil.

22 ˣFor what hath man of all his labour,

---

qProverbs xvii. 24; chapter viii. 1——rPsalm xlix. 10; chapter ix. 2, 3, 11——sHebrew, *happeneth to me, even to me*——tJob v. 13; Psalm xciv. 8; chapter ii. 15; vi. 8; vii. 16; Isa. xliv. 25——uHebrew, *laboured*——vPsalm xlix. 10——wHebrew, *give*——xChapter i. 3; iii. 9

---

after; yet I could easily perceive that wisdom *excelled* the *others*, as far as *light excels darkness*. And he immediately subjoins the reasons.

Verse 14. *The wise man's eyes, &c.*] Well expressed by *Choheleth*:—

"The wise are circumspect, maturely weigh
The consequence of what they undertake,
Good ends propose, and fittest means apply
To accomplish their designs."

But the fool walketh in darkness]

"But fools, deprived
Of reason's guidance, or in darkness grope,
Or, unreflecting like a frantic man,
Who on the brink of some steep precipice
Attempts to run a race with heedless steps,
Rush to their own perdition."

One event happeneth to them all.]

"Though wide the difference, what has human pride
To boast? Even I myself too plainly saw,
That *one event to both alike befalls;*
To various accidents of life exposed,
Without distinction: nor can *wisdom* screen
From *dangers, disappointments, grief*, and *pain*."

Verse 15. *As it happeneth to the fool*] Literally, "According as the event is to the fool, it happens to me, even me." There is a peculiar beauty and emphasis in the repetition of *me*. Having pointed out the advantages that wisdom has over folly, he takes this opportunity of reminding us of the danger of trusting too much to it, by showing that it is equally subject to the common accidents of life; and, therefore, incapable of making us completely happy. Having given his sentiments on this point in *general* terms, he proceeds to those *particular* instances wherein human prudence chiefly

exerts itself; and shows how egregiously it is mistaken in every one of them.—C.

Verse 16. There is *no remembrance*] The wise and the fool are equally subject to death; and, in most instances, they are equally forgotten. *Time* sweeps away all remembrances, except the very *few* out of *millions* which are preserved for a while in the *page of history*.

Verse 17. *Therefore I hated life*] את החיים *et hachaiyim, the lives*, both of the *wise*, the *madman*, and the *fool*. Also all the *stages* of life, the *child*, the *man*, and the *sage*. There was nothing in it worth *pursuing*, no *period* worth *re-living*, and no *hope* that if this were possible I could again be more successful.

Verse 18. *I hated all my labour*] Because, 1. It has not answered the end for which it was instituted. 2. I can enjoy the fruits of it but a short time. 3. I must leave it to others, and know not whether a *wise man*, a *knave*, or a *fool* will possess it.

Verse 19. *A wise* man *or a fool?*] Alas! Solomon, the *wisest* of all men, made the *worst use* of his wisdom, had *three hundred wives* and *seven hundred concubines*, and yet left but *one son* behind him, to possess his *estates* and his *throne*, and that one was the silliest of fools!

Verse 20. *I went about to cause my heart to despair*] What makes all worse, there is no remedy. It is impossible in the present state of things to prevent these evils.

Verse 21. *For there is a man*] Does he not allude to himself? As if he had said, "I have laboured to cultivate my mind in wisdom and in science, in knowledge of men and things, and have endeavoured to establish *equity* and dispense justice. And now I find I *shall leave* all the fruits of my labour to *a man that hath not laboured therein*, and consequently cannot prize what I have wrought." Does he not refer to his son *Rehoboam?*

Verse 22. *For what hath man of all his labour*] *Labour* of body, disappointment of

A. M. cir. 3027
B. C. cir. 977
Ante I. Olymp. cir. 201
Ante U. C. cir. 224
and of the vexation of his heart, wherein he hath laboured under the sun?

23 For all his days *are* ʸsorrows, and his travail grief; yea, his heart taketh not rest in the night. This is also vanity.

24 ᶻ*There is* nothing better for a man *than* that he should eat and drink, and *that* he ªshould make his soul enjoy good in his labour. This also I saw,

that it *was* from the hand of God.

A. M. cir. 3027
B. C. cir. 977
Ante I. Olymp. cir. 201
Ante U. C. cir. 224

25 For who can eat, or who else can hasten *hereunto,* more than I?

26 For *God* giveth to a man that *is* good ᵇin his sight, wisdom, and knowledge, and joy: but to the sinner he giveth travail, to gather and to heap up, that ᶜhe may give to *him that is* good before God. This also *is* vanity and vexation of spirit.

ʸJob v. 7; xiv. 1——ᶻChap. iii. 12, 13, 22; v. 18; viii. 15
ªOr, *delight his senses*

ᵇHeb. *before him;* Gen. vii. 1; Luke i. 6——ᶜJob xxvii. 16, 17; Prov. xxviii. 8

---

hope, and *vexation of heart,* have been all my portion.

Verse 23. *His days are sorrows*] What a picture of human life where the heart is not filled with the peace and love of God! All his *days* are *sorrows;* all his *labours griefs;* all his *nights restless;* for he has no portion but merely what *earth* can give; and that is embittered by the labour of *acquisition,* and the disappointment in the using.

This is also vanity.] Emptiness of good and substantial misery.

Verse 24. There is *nothing better for a man*] The sense of this passage is well expressed in the following lines:—

"For these disorders wouldst thou find a cure,
Such cure as human frailty would admit?
Drive from thee anxious cares; let reason curb
Thy passions; and with cheerful heart enjoy
That little which the world affords; for here,
Though vain the hopes of perfect happiness,
Yet still the road of life, rugged at best,
Is not without its comforts.——
Wouldst thou their sweetness taste, look up to heaven,
And praise the all-bounteous Donor, who bestows
The power to use aright."

Verse 25. *For who can eat—more than I?*] But instead of חוץ ממני *chuts mimmenni, more than I;* חוץ ממנו *chuts mimmennu, without* ʜɪᴍ, is the reading of *eight of Kennicott's* and *De*

Rossi's MSS., as also of the *Septuagint, Syriac,* and *Arabic.*

"For who maye eat, drynke, or bring enythinge to pass without him?"—Cᴏᴠᴇʀᴅᴀʟᴇ.

I believe this to be the true reading. No one can have a true relish of the comforts of life without the Divine blessing. This reading connects all the sentences: "This also I saw, that it was from the hand of God;—for who can eat, and who can relish without ʜɪᴍ? For God giveth to man that is good." It is through his liberality that we have any thing to eat or drink; and it is only through his blessing that we can derive good from the use of what we possess.

Verse 26. *Giveth—wisdom, and knowledge, and joy*] 1. God gives *wisdom*—the knowledge of himself, light to direct in the way of salvation. 2. *Knowledge*—understanding to discern the operation of his hand; *experimental acquaintance* with himself, in the dispensing of his *grace* and the *gifts of his Spirit.* 3. *Joy;* a hundred days of ease for one day of pain; *one thousand* enjoyments for one privation; and to them that believe, *peace of conscience,* and ᴊᴏʏ *in the Holy Ghost.*

But to the sinner he giveth travail] He has a life of labour, disappointment, and distress; for because he is an enemy to God, he travails in pain all his days; and, as the wise man says elsewhere, *the wealth of the wicked is laid up for the just.* So he loseth *earthly good,* because he would not take a *heavenly portion* with it.

CHAPTER III

Every thing has its time and season, 1–8. Men are exercised with labour, 9, 10. Every thing is beautiful in its season, 11. Men should enjoy thankfully the gifts of God, 12, 13. What God does is for ever, 14. There is nothing new, 15. The corruption of judgment; but the judgments of God are right, 16, 17. Man is brutish, and men and brutes die in like manner, 18–21. Man may enjoy the fruit of his own labours, 22.

A. M. cir. 3027
B. C. cir. 977
Ante I. Olymp.
cir. 201
Ante U. C. cir.
224
TO every *thing there is* a sea-son, and a [a]time to every purpose under the heaven.

2 A time [b]to be born, and a [c]time to die; a time to plant, and a time to pluck up *that which is* planted;

3 A time to kill, and a time to heal; a time to break down, and a time to build up;

4 A time to weep, and a time to laugh; a time to mourn, and a time to dance;

5 A time to cast away stones, and a time to gather stones to-gether; a time to embrace, and [d]a time [e]to refrain from embracing;

6 A time to [f]get, and a time to lose; a time to keep, and a time to cast away;

7 A time to rend, and a time to sew; [g]a time to keep silence, and a time to speak;

8 A time to love, and a time to [h]hate; a time of war, and a time of peace.

A. M. cir. 3027
B. C. cir. 977
Ante I. Olymp.
cir. 201
Ante U. C. cir.
224

---

[a]Ver. 17; chap. viii. 6——[b]Heb. *to bear*——[c]Hebrews ix. 27——[d]Joel ii. 16; 1 Cor. vii. 5

[e]Heb. *to be far from*——[f]Or, *seek*——[g]Amos v. 13
[h]Luke xiv. 26

NOTES ON CHAP. III

Verse 1. *To every* thing there is *a season, and a time to every purpose*] *Two* general remarks may be made on the first *eight* verses of this chapter. 1. God by his providence governs the world, and has determined particular *things* and operations to particular *times.* In those times such things may be done with propriety and success; but if we neglect the appointed sea-sons, we sin against this providence, and be-come the authors of our own distresses. 2. God has given to man that portion of duration called TIME; the space in which all the operations of nature, of animals, and intellectual beings, are carried on; but while nature is steady in its course, and animals faithful to their instincts, man devotes it to a great variety of purposes; but very frequently to that for which God never made *time, space,* or *opportunity.* And all we can say, when an evil deed is done, is, there was a *time* in which it was done, though God never made *it* for that purpose.

To say any farther on this subject is needless, as the words themselves give in general their own meaning. The Jews, it is true, see in these *times* and *seasons* all the events of their own nation, from the birth of Abraham to the pres-ent times; and as to *fathers* and their followers, they see all the events and states of the Chris-tian Church in them!

It is worthy of remark, that in all this list there are but *two* things which may be said to be done generally by the disposal of God, and in which men can have but little influence: the *time of birth,* and the *time of death.* But all the others are left to the option of man, though God continues to overrule them by his provi-dence. The following paraphrase will explain all that is necessary to be generally under-stood:—

Verse 2. *A time to be born, and a time to die —plant*]

"As in its *mother's womb* the *embryo* lies
A *space determined;* to full growth arrived,
From its dark prison *bursts,* and *sees the light;*
So is the period fix'd when man shall drop
Into the *grave.*—A *time there is to plant,*
And *sow;* another time to *pluck* and *reap.*
Even *nations* have their destined *rise* and *fall:*
Awhile they thrive; and for destruction ripe,
When grown, are rooted up like *wither'd
    plants.*"

Verse 3. *A time to kill,—heal,—break down,—build up.*

"The healing art, when out of season used,
Pernicious proves, and serves to hasten death.
But timely med'cines drooping nature raise,
And health restore.—*Now, Justice* wields her
    sword
With wholesome rigour, nor the offender
    spares:
But *Mercy* now is more expedient found.
On *crazy fabrics* ill-timed cost bestow'd
No purpose answers, when discretion bids
To *pull them down,* and wait a season fit
To *build anew.*"

Verse 4. *A time to weep,—laugh,—mourn,—dance*]

———————————— "When private *griefs* affect
The heart, *our tears with decent sorrow flow;*
Nor less becoming, when the *public mourns,*
To vent the *deepest sighs.* But all around
When things a *smiling aspect* bear, our souls
May *well exult;* 'tis then a time for *joy.*"

Verse 5. *A time to cast away stones,—to gather stones,—to embrace,—to refrain*]

"One while *domestic cares* abortive prove,
And then *successful.* Nature now invites
Connubial pleasures: but, when *languid* grown,
No less *rejects.*"

Verse 6. *A time to get,—to lose,—to keep,—to cast away*]

———————————— "*Commerce* produces wealth,
Whilst *time of gaining* lasts; from every point
Blow prosperous gales. Now heaven begins to
    lower,
And all our hopes are blasted. Prudence bids,
One while, our *treasure to reserve,* and then
With liberal hand to *scatter wide.* How oft
In raging storms, the owner *wisely casts
Into the deep* his precious merchandise,
To save the foundering bark!"

Verse 7. *A time to rend,—sew,—keep silence, —speak*]

———————————— "Intestine broils
And factions *rend a state:* at length the *breach*
Is *heal'd,* and rest ensues. Wisdom *restrains*
The *tongue,* when *words* are vain: but *now,*
'Tis *time to speak,* and silence would be
    criminal."

Verse 8. *A time to love,—hate,—of war,—of peace.*]

"*Love* turns to *hatred;* interest or caprice
Dissolves the firmest knot by *friendship* tied.
O'er *rival nations,* with *revenge* inflamed,
Or *lust of power,* fell *Discord* shakes awhile
Her *baleful torch:* now smiling *Peace* returns.

A. M. cir. 3027
B. C. cir. 977
Ante I. Olymp. cir. 201
Ante U. C. cir. 224

9 ¹What profit hath he that worketh in that wherein he laboureth?

10 ᵏI have seen the travail which God hath given to the sons of men to be exercised in it.

11 He hath made every *thing* beautiful in his time: also he hath set the world in their heart, so that ¹no man can find out the work that God maketh from the beginning to the end.

12 ᵐI know that *there is* no good in them, but for *a man* to rejoice, and to do good in his life.

13 And also ⁿthat every man should eat and drink, and enjoy the good of all his labour, it *is* the gift of God.

14 I know that whatsoever God doeth, it shall be for ever: ᵒnothing can be put to it, nor any thing taken from it: and God doeth *it,* that *men* should fear before him.

15 ᵖThat which hath been is now; and

A. M. cir. 3027
B. C. cir. 977
Ante I. Olymp. cir. 201
Ante U. C. cir. 224

ⁱChap. i. 3——ᵏChap. i. 13——ˡPsa. cxlv. 3; Isa. xl. 13; chap. viii. 17; Rom. xi. 33

ᵐVerse 22——ⁿChap. ii. 24——ᵒJames i. 17——ᵖChap. i. 9

The above paraphrase on the verses cited contains a general view of the *principal occurrences of time,* in reference to the human being, from his cradle to his grave, through all the operations of life.

Verse 9. *What profit hath he*] What real good, what solid pleasure, is derived from all the labours of man? *Necessity* drives him to the principal part of his *cares* and *toils;* he *labours* that he may *eat* and *drink;* and he *eats* and *drinks* that he may be preserved *alive,* and kept from *sickness* and *pain.* Love of *money,* the basest of all passions, and *restless ambition,* drive men to many labours and expedients, which perplex and often destroy them. He, then, who lives without God, travails in pain all his days.

Verse 10. *I have seen the travail*] Man is a sinner; and, because he is such, he suffers.

Verse 11. *Beautiful in his time*] God's works are well done; there are order, harmony, and beauty in them all. Even the *caterpillar* is a finished beauty in all the *changes* through which it passes, when its structure is properly examined, and the *end* kept in view in which each change is to issue. Nothing of this kind can be said of the works of man. The most finished works of art are bungling jobs, when compared with the meanest operation of nature.

He hath set the world in their heart] העולם *haolam,* that *hidden time—the period beyond* the present,—ETERNITY. The proper translation of this clause is the following: "Also that eternity hath he placed in their heart, without which man could not find out the work which God hath made from the commencement to the end." God has deeply rooted the idea of *eternity* in every human heart; and every considerate man sees, that all the operations of God refer to that endless duration. See ver. 14. And it is only in eternity that man will be able to discover what God has designed by the various works he has formed.

Verse 12. *I know that* there is *no good in them, but, &c.*] Since God has so disposed the affairs of this world, that the great events of providence cannot be accelerated or retarded by human cares and anxieties, submit to God; make a proper use of what he has given: do thyself *no harm,* and endeavour as much as possible to do others *good.*

Enjoy, and bless thyself; let others share
The transient blessing: 'tis the gift of God.

Verse 14. *I know that whatsoever God doeth, it shall be for ever*] לעולם *leolam,* for *eternity;* in reference to that grand consummation of men and things intimated in ver. 11. God has produced no being that he intends ultimately to destroy. He made every thing in reference to eternity; and, however matter may be changed and refined, animal and intellectual beings shall not be deprived of their *existence.* The brute creation shall be restored, and all human spirits shall live for ever; the *pure* in a state of supreme and endless blessedness, the *impure* in a state of indestructible misery.

Nothing can be put to it] No new order of beings, whether animate or inanimate, can be produced. God *will not* create more; man *cannot* add.

Nor any thing taken from it] Nothing can be *annihilated;* no power but that which can *create* can *destroy.* And whatever he has done, he intended to be a means of impressing a just sense of his being, providence, mercy, and judgments, upon the souls of men. A proper consideration of God's works has a tendency to make man a *religious creature;* that is, to impress his mind with a sense of the *existence* of the *Supreme Being,* and the *reverence* that is due to him. In this sense *the fear of God* is frequently taken in Scripture. The Hebrew of this clause is strongly emphatic: והאלהים עשה שיראו מלפניו *vehaelohim asah sheiyireu millephanaiv;* "And the gods he hath done, that they might fear from before his faces." Even the doctrine of the eternal *Trinity* in *Unity* may be collected from numberless appearances in *nature.* A consideration of the herb *trefoil* is said to have been the means of fully convincing the learned Erasmus of the truth of the assertion, *These Three are One:* and yet *three distinct.* He saw the *same root,* the *same fibres,* the same *pulpy substance,* the *same membraneous covering,* the *same colour,* the *same taste,* the *same smell,* in *every part;* and yet the *three leaves* distinct: but *each* and *all* a *continuation* of the *stem,* and proceeding from the *same root.* Such a fact as this may at least illustrate the doctrine. An intelligent shepherd, whom he met upon the mountains, is said to have exhibited the herb, and the illustration while discoursing on certain difficulties in the Christian faith. When a child, I heard a learned man relate this fact.

Verse 15. *That which hath been is now*] God

A. M. cir. 3027
B. C. cir. 977
Ante I. Olymp.
cir. 201
Ante U. C. cir.
224 that which is to be hath already been; and God requireth ᑫthat which is past.

16 And moreover ʳI saw under the sun the place of judgment, *that* wickedness *was* there; and the place of righteousness, *that* iniquity *was* there.

17 I said in mine heart, ˢGod shall judge the righteous and the wicked: for *there is* ᵗa time there for every purpose and for every work.

18 I said in mine heart concerning the estate of the sons of men, ᵘthat God might manifest them, and that they might see that they themselves are beasts.

19 ᵛFor that which befalleth the sons of men befalleth beasts; even one thing befalleth them: as the one A. M. cir. 3027
B. C. cir. 977
Ante I. Olymp.
cir. 201
Ante U. C. cir.
224 dieth, so dieth the other; yea, they have all one breath; so that a man hath no pre-eminence above a beast: for all *is* vanity.

20 All go unto one place; ʷall are of the dust, and all turn to dust again.

21 ˣWho knoweth the spirit ʸof man that ᶻgoeth upward, and the spirit of the beast that goeth downward to the earth?

22 ᵃWherefore I perceive that *there is* nothing better, than that a man should rejoice in his own works; for ᵇthat *is* his portion: ᶜfor who shall bring him to see what shall be after him?

ᑫHebrew, *that which is driven away*——ʳChapter v. 8
ˢRomans ii. 6, 7, 8; 2 Cor. v. 10; 2 Thess. i. 6, 7——ᵗVer.
1——ᵘOr, *that they might clear God, and see,* &c.
ᵛPsalm xlix. 12, 20; lxxiii. 22; chapter ii. 16——ʷGen-
esis iii. 19——ˣChapter xii. 7——ʸHebrew, *of the sons
of man*——ᶻHebrew, *is ascending*——ᵃChapter ii. 24;
v. 18; xi. 9——ᵇChapter ii. 10——ᶜChapter vi. 12;
viii. 7; x. 14

---

governs the world *now*, as he *has governed* it from the beginning; and the revolutions and operations of nature are the *same now*, that they have been from *the beginning.* What we see *now*, is the *same* as has *been seen* by those before us.

And God requireth that which is past] i. e., That it may return again in its proper order. The heavens themselves, taking in their great revolutions, show the same phenomena. Even comets are supposed to have their revolutions, though some of them are hundreds of years in going round their orbits.

But in the *economy of grace*, does not *God require that which is past?* Whatever blessing or influence God gives to the soul of man, he intends shall remain and increase; and it will, if man be faithful. Reader, canst thou produce all the secret inspirations of his Spirit, all the drawings of his love, his pardoning mercy, his sanctifying grace, the heavenly-mindedness produced in thee, thy holy zeal, thy spirit of prayer, thy tender conscience, the witness of the Spirit, which thou didst once receive and enjoy? WHERE are they? *God requireth that which is past.*

Verse 16. *The place of judgment, that wickedness* was *there*] The abuse of power, and the perversion of judgment, have been justly complained of in every age of the world. The following paraphrase is good:—

"But what enjoyment can our labours yield,
When e'en the *remedy* prescribed by heaven
To cure disorders proves our deadliest bane?
When God's vicegerents, destined to protect
The weak from insolence of power, to guard
Their lives and fortunes, impious robbers
  turn?
And, or by force or fraud, deprive of both?—
To what asylum shall the injured fly
From her tribunal, where perverted law
Acquits the guilty, the innocent condemns?"
                                  C.

Verse 17. *For there is a time there for every purpose*] Man has *his time* here below, and God shall have *his time* above. At his throne the judged shall be rejudged, and iniquity for ever close her mouth.

Verse 18. *That they might see that they themselves are beasts.*] The author of *Choheleth* has given a correct view of this difficult verse, by a proper translation: "I said in my heart, reflecting on the state of the sons of men, O that God would enlighten them, and make them see that even they themselves are like beasts." These words are to be referred to those in authority who abused their power; particularly to the corrupt magistrates mentioned above.

Verse 19. *For that which befalleth the sons of men befalleth beasts*] From the present comparison of *great men* to *beasts*, the author takes occasion to enforce the subject by mentioning the state of mankind in general, with respect to the *mortality* of their *bodies;* and then, by an easy transition, touches in the next verse on the point which is of such infinite consequence to religion.

As the one dieth, so dieth the other] Animal life is the same both in the *man* and in the *beast.*

They have all one breath] They respire in the same way; and when they cease to respire, animal life becomes extinct.

Befalleth beasts—This is wanting in six of *Kennicott's* and *De Rossi's* MSS.

Verse 20. *All go unto one place*]

          "Man was born
To die, nor aught exceeds in this respect
The vilest brute. Both transient, frail, and vain,
Draw the same breath; alike grow old, decay,
And then expire: both to one grave descend;
There blended lie, to native dust return'd."—C.

Verse 21. *Who knoweth the spirit of man*] I think the meaning of this important verse is well taken by the above able writer:—

The nobler part of *man*, 'tis true, survives
The frail corporeal frame: but who regards

The difference? Those who live like beasts,
  as such
Would die, and be no more, if their own fate
Depended on themselves. Who once reflects,
Amidst his revels, that the *human soul,*
Of origin celestial, *mounts aloft,*
While that of *brutes* to earth shall *downward*
  go?"

The word רוח *ruach,* which is used in this and the *nineteenth* verse, has two significations, *breath* and *spirit.* It signifies *spirit,* or an *incorporeal* substance, as distinguished from *flesh,* or a *corporeal* one, 1 Kings xxii. 21, 22, and Isa. xxxi. 3. And it signifies the *spirit* or *soul of man,* Psa. xxxi. 6, Isa. lvii. 16, and in this book, chap. xii. 7, and in many other places. In this book it is used also to signify the *breath, spirit,* or *soul* of a beast. While it was said in ver. 19, *they have all one breath,* i. e., the *man* and the *beast* live the same kind of animal life; in this verse, a proper distinction is made between the רוח *ruach,* or *soul* of man, and the רוח *ruach,* or *soul* of the beast: the one *goeth upwards,* the other *goeth downwards.* The literal translation of these important words is this: "Who considereth the (רוח *ruach*) immortal spirit of the sons of Adam, which ascendeth? it is from above; (היא למעלה *hi lemalah;*) and the spirit or breath of the cattle which descendeth? it is downwards unto the earth," i. e., it tends to the earth only. This place gives no countenance to the materiality

of the soul; and yet it is the strongest hold to which the cold and fruitless materialist can resort.

Solomon most evidently makes an *essential difference* between the human soul and that of brutes. Both have *souls,* but of different natures: the soul of man was made for *God,* and to *God* it shall return: *God is its portion;* and when a holy soul leaves the body, it goes to *paradise.* The soul of the beast was made to *derive its happiness* from this *lower world.* Brutes shall have a resurrection, and have an endless enjoyment in a *new earth.* The *body* of *man* shall arise, and join his *soul* that is already above; and both enjoy final blessedness in the fruition of God. That Solomon did not believe they had the *same kind of spirit,* and the same *final lot,* as some materialists and infidels say, is evident from chap. xii. 7: "The spirit shall return unto God who gave it."

Verse 22. A man should rejoice in his own works] Do not turn God's blessings into sin by perverseness and complaining; make the best of life. God will sweeten its bitters to you, if you be faithful. Remember this is the *state to prepare for glory;* and the evils of life may be so sanctified to you as to work for your good. Though even wretched *without,* you may be happy *within;* for God can make all grace to abound towards you. You may be happy if you please; cry to God, who never rejects the prayer of the humble, and gives his Holy Spirit to all them that ask him.

CHAPTER IV

The vanity of life is increased by oppression, 1–3; by envy, 4; by idleness, 5. The misery of a solitary life, and the advantages of society, 6–12. A poor and wise child; better than an old and foolish king, 13. The uncertainty of popular favour, 14–16.

A. M. cir. 3027
B. C. cir. 977
Ante I. Olymp.
  cir. 201
Ante U. C. cir.
  224

SO I returned, and considered all the [a]oppressions that are done under the sun: and behold, the tears of *such as were* oppressed, and they had no comforter; and on the [b]side of their oppressors *there was* power; but they had no comforter.

2 [c]Wherefore I praised the dead which are already dead more than the living which are yet alive.

3 [d]Yea, better *is he* than both they, which hath not yet been, who hath not seen the evil work that is done under the sun.

A. M. cir. 3027
B. C. cir. 977
Ante I. Olymp.
  cir. 201
Ante U. C. cir.
  224

4 Again, I considered all travail, and [e]every right work, that [f]for this a man is envied of his neighbour. This *is* also vanity and vexation of spirit.

5 The fool [g]foldeth his hands together, and eateth his own flesh.

---

[a]Chap. iii. 16; v. 8——[b]Heb. *hand*——[c]Job iii. 17, &c.
[d]Job iii. 11, 16, 21; chap. vi. 3

[e]Heb. *all the rightness of work*——[f]Heb. *this* is *the envy of a man from his neighbour*——[g]Prov. vi. 10; xxiv. 33

NOTES ON CHAP. IV

Verse 1. *Considered all the oppressions*] עשקים *ashukim* signifies any kind of *injury* which a man can receive in his *person,* his *property,* or his *good fame.*

On the side of their oppressors there was power] And, therefore, neither protection nor comfort for the oppressed.

Verse 2. *Wherefore I praised the dead*] I considered those happy who had escaped from the pilgrimage of life to the place where the wicked cease from troubling, and where the weary are at rest.

Verse 3. *Which hath not yet been*] Better never to have been born into the world, than to have *seen* and *suffered* so many miseries.

Verse 4. *For this a man is envied*] It is not by injustice and wrong only that men suffer, but through *envy* also. For if a man act uprightly and properly in the world, he soon becomes the object of his neighbour's envy and calumny too. Therefore the encouragement to do good, to act an upright part, is very little. This constitutes a part of the *vain* and *empty* system of human life.

Verse 5. *The fool foldeth his hands*] After all, without *labour* and *industry* no man can

A. M. cir. 3027
B. C. cir. 977
Ante I. Olymp. cir. 201
Ante U. C. cir. 224
6 [h]Better *is* a handful *with* quietness, than both the hands full *with* travail, and vexation of spirit.

7 Then I returned, and I saw vanity under the sun.

8 There is one *alone,* and *there is* not a second; yea, he hath neither child nor brother: yet *is there* no end of all his labour; neither is his [i]eye satisfied with riches; [k]neither *saith he,* For whom do I labour, and bereave my soul of good? This *is* also vanity, yea, it *is* a sore travail.

9 Two *are* better than one; because they have a good reward for their labour.

10 For if they fall, the one will lift up his fellow: but wo to him *that is* alone when he falleth; for *he hath* not another to help him up.

A. M. cir. 3027
B. C. cir. 977
Ante I. Olymp. cir. 201
Ante U. C. cir. 224
11 Again, if two lie together, then they have heat: but how can one be warm *alone?*

12 And if one prevail against him, two shall withstand him; and a threefold cord is not quickly broken.

13 Better *is* a poor and a wise child, than an old and foolish king, [l]who will no more be admonished.

14 For out of prison he cometh to reign; whereas also *he that is* born in his kingdom becometh poor.

15 I considered all the living which walk under the sun, with the [m]second child that shall stand up in his stead.

16 *There is* no end of all the people, *even* of all that have been before them: they also that come after shall not rejoice in him. Surely this also *is* [n]vanity and vexation of spirit.

---

[h]Prov. xv. 16, 17; xvi. 18——[i]Prov. xxvii. 20; 1 John ii. 16——[k]Psa. xxxix. 6

[l]Heb. *who knoweth not to be admonished*——[m]1 Kings xi. 43——[n]Chap. i. 2, 14

---

get any comfort in life; and he who gives way to idleness is the veriest of fools.

Verse 6. *Better* is *a handful* with *quietness*] These may be the words of the *slothful* man, and spoken in vindication of his idleness; as if he had said, "Every man who labours and amasses property is the object of *envy*, and is marked by the oppressor as a subject for spoil; better, therefore, to act as I do; gain little, and have little, and enjoy my handful with quietness." Or the words may contain Solomon's *reflection* on the subject.

Verse 8. *There is one* alone, *and* there is *not a second*] Here *covetousness* and *avarice* are characterized. The man who is the centre of his own existence; has neither wife, child, nor legal heir; and yet is as intent on getting money as if he had the largest family to provide for; nor does he only labour with intense application, but he even refuses himself the comforts of life out of his own gains! This is not only *vanity*, the excess of foolishness, but it is also *sore travail.*

Verse 9. *Two* are *better than one*] Married life is infinitely to be preferred to this kind of life, for the very reasons alleged below, and which require no explanation.

Verse 13. *Better* is *a poor and a wise child*] The *Targum* applies this to *Abraham.* "Abraham was a *poor child* of only *three* years of age; but he had the spirit of prophecy, and he refused to worship the idols which the *old foolish king*—Nimrod—had set up; therefore Nimrod cast him into a furnace of fire. But the Lord worked a miracle and delivered him. Yet here was no knowledge in Nimrod, and he would not be *admonished.*" The *Targum* proceeds:

Verse 14. *For out of prison he cometh to reign*] "Then Abraham left the country of the idolaters, where he had been *imprisoned*, and came and *reigned* over the land of Canaan; and Nimrod became *poor* in this world." This is

the *fact* to which the ancient rabbins supposed Solomon to allude.

Verse 15. *With the second child that shall stand up*] The *Targum* applies this to the case of *Jeroboam* and *Rehoboam.* History affords many instances of mean persons raised to sovereign authority, and of kings being reduced to the meanest offices, and to a morsel of bread. Agrippa himself ascended the throne of Israel after having been long in prison. See Josephus, Ant. lib. xviii. c. 8. This the heathens attributed to *fortune.*

Si fortuna volet, fies de rhetore consul;
Si volet hæc eadem, fies de consule rhetor.
Juv. Sat. vii., ver. 197.

Though I have given what the Jews suppose to be the allusion in these verses, yet the reader may doubt whether the reference be correct. There is a case implied, whether from *fact* or *assumption* I cannot say; but it seems to be this:

A king who had abused the authority vested in him by oppressing the people, had a son whose prudent conduct promised much comfort to the nation, when he should come to the throne. The father, seeing the popular wish, and becoming jealous of his son, *shut him up in prison.* In the interim the old king either *dies* or is *deposed,* and the son is brought *out of prison,* and *placed on the throne.* Then (ver. 15, 16) multitudes of the people flock to him, and begin to *walk under the sun;* i. e., the prosperous state to which the nation is raised by its redemption from the former tyranny. However, the wise man insinuates that this *sunshine* will not last long. The young king, feeling the reins in his own hands, and being surrounded by those whose interest it was to *flatter* in order to obtain and continue in court favour, he also becomes corrupted so that those who come after shall have no cause of rejoicing in him. This appears to be the case; and similar cases have frequently occurred, not only in *Asiatic*, but also in *European* history, I have, in another place, referred to the case of *Rushn Achter*, who was brought *out of prison*, and set upon the *throne of Hindoostan*. This is expressed in the following elegant Persian couplet, where his fortune is represented as similar to that of the patriarch *Joseph*:—

روشن اختر بود الٽون ماه شد

یوسف از زندن بر آمد شاه شد

"The *bright star* is now become a *moon:* Joseph is taken out of *prison*, and become a *king*."

Rushn Achter signifies a *bright* or *splendid star*.

Verse 16. There is *no end of all the people*] This is supposed to refer to the multitudes of people who hail the advent and accession of a new sovereign; for, as *Suetonius* remarks, *A plerisque adorari solem orientem*, "Most people adore the rising sun." But when the new king becomes old, very few regard him; and perhaps he lives long enough to be as much despised by the very persons who before were ready to worship him. This is also a miserable vanity. Thus the blooming heir—

"Shall feel the sad reverse: honoured awhile;
  Then, like his sire, contemn'd, abhorr'd, forgot."   C.

CHAPTER V

The reverence to be observed in attending Divine worship, 1–3. We should be faithful to our engagements, 4–7. The oppression of the innocent, 8. The king dependent on the produce of the soil, 9. Against covetousness, 10, 11. The peace of the honest labourer, 12. The evil effect of riches, 13, 14. Man cannot carry his property to the grave, 15–17. We should thankfully enjoy the blessings of God, 18–20.

A. M. cir. 3027
B. C. cir. 977
Ante I. Olymp.
cir. 201
Ante U. C. cir.
224

KEEP [a]thy foot when thou goest to the house of God, and be more ready to hear [b]than to give the sacrifice of fools: for they consider not that they do evil.

2 Be not rash with thy mouth, and let not thine heart be hasty to utter *any* [c]thing before God; for God *is* in heaven, and thou upon earth: therefore let thy words [d]be few.

3 For a dream cometh through the multi-tude of business; and [e]a fool's voice *is known* by multitude of words.

A. M. cir. 3027
B. C. cir. 977
Ante I. Olymp.
cir. 201
Ante U. C. cir.
224

4 [f]When thou vowest a vow unto God, defer not to pay it; for *he hath* no pleasure in fools: [g]pay that which thou hast vowed.

5 [h]Better *is it* that thou shouldest not vow, than that thou shouldest vow and not pay.

6 Suffer not thy mouth to cause thy flesh

---

[a]See Exod. iii. 5; Isa. i. 12, &c.——[b]1 Sam. xv. 22; Psalm l. 8; Prov. xv. 8; xxi. 27; Hos. vi. 6——[c]Or, *word* [d]Prov. x. 19; Matt. vi. 7

[e]Prov. x. 19——[f]Num. xxx. 2; Deut. xxiii. 21, 22, 23; Psa. l. 14; lxxvi. 11——[g]Psa. lxvi. 13, 14——[h]Prov. xx. 25; Acts v. 4

NOTES ON CHAP. V

Verse 1. *Keep thy foot*] This verse the *Hebrew* and all the *versions* join to the preceding chapter.

Solomon, having before intimated, though very briefly, that the only cure against human vanity is a due sense of religion, now enters more largely on this important subject, and gives some excellent directions with regard to the right performance of Divine service, the nature of vocal and mental prayer, the danger of rash vows, &c.—C.

The whole verse might be more literally translated thus:—

"Guard thy steps as thou art going to the house of God; and approach to hearken, and not to give the sacrifice of fools, for none of them have knowledge about doing evil." "They offer gifts for their sins, and do not turn from their evil works; for they know not (they distinguish not) between good and evil." See the *Chaldee*.

Verse 2. *Be not rash with thy mouth*] Do not hasten with thy mouth; weigh thy words, feel deeply, think much, speak little.

"When ye approach his altar, on your lips
  Set strictest guard; and let your thoughts
    be pure,

Fervent, and recollected. Thus prepared,
Send up the silent breathings of your souls,
Submissive to his will."   C.

Verse 3. *For a dream cometh*] That is, as *dreams* are generally the effect of the business in which we have been engaged during the day; so a *multitude of words* evidence the feeble workings of the foolish heart.

Verse 4. *When thou vowest a vow*] When in distress and difficulty, men are apt to promise much to God if he will relieve them; but generally forget the vow when the distress or trouble is gone by.

Verse 5. *Better is it that thou shouldest not vow, &c.*] We are under *constant obligations* to live to God; no *vow* can make it more so. Yet, there may be cases in which we should bind ourselves to take up some particular cross, to perform some particular duty, to forego some particular attachment that does not tend to bring our souls nearer to God. Then, if fully determined, and strong in faith relative to the point, *bind* and *hold fast*; but if not fully, rationally, and conscientiously determined, "do not suffer thy mouth to cause thy soul to sin."

Verse 6. *Neither say thou before the angel, that it was an error*] Nor think of saying "before the cruel angel, who shall exercise author-

A. M. cir. 3027
B. C. cir. 977
Ante I. Olymp.
cir. 201
Ante U. C. cir.
224
to sin; [1]neither say thou before the angel, that it *was* an error: wherefore should God be angry at thy voice, and destroy the work of thine hands?

7 For in the multitude of dreams and many words *there are* also *divers* vanities: but [k]fear thou God.

8 If thou [l]seest the oppression of the poor, and violent perverting of judgment and justice in a province, marvel not [m]at the matter: for [n]*he that is* higher than the highest regardeth; and *there be* higher than they.

9 Moreover the profit of the earth is for all; the king *himself* is served by the field.

10 He that loveth silver shall not be satisfied with silver; nor he that loveth abundance

with increase: this *is* also
A. M. cir. 3027
B. C. cir. 977
Ante I. Olymp.
cir. 201
Ante U. C. cir.
224
vanity.

11 When goods increase, they are increased that eat them: and what good is there to the owners thereof saving the beholding *of them* with their eyes?

12 The sleep of a labouring man *is* sweet, whether he eat little or much: but the abundance of the rich will not suffer him to sleep.

13 [o]There is a sore evil *which* I have seen under the sun, *namely,* riches kept for the owners thereof to their hurt.

14 But those riches perish by evil travail: and he begetteth a son, and *there is* nothing in his hand.

15 [p]As he came forth of his mother's womb, naked shall he return to go as he came, and

---

[i]1 Cor. xi. 10——[k]Chap. xii. 13——[l]Chap. iii. 16
[m]Heb. *at the will* or *purpose*

[n]Psa. xii. 5; lviii. 11; lxxxii. 1——[o]Chap. vi. 1——[p]Job
i. 21; Psa. xlix. 17; 1 Tim. vi. 7

---

ity over thee in the judgment of the great day, that thou didst it through ignorance."—*Chaldee.* I believe by the *angel* nothing else is intended than the *priest,* whose business it was to take cognizance of *vows* and *offerings.* See Lev. v. 4, 5. In Mal. ii. 7, the priest is called the "angel of the Lord of hosts."

Verse 7. *In—dreams—are—divers vanities; but fear thou God.*] If, by the disturbed state of thy mind during the day, or by Satanic influence, thou dream of evil, do not give way to any unreasonable fears, or gloomy forebodings, of any coming mischief:—FEAR GOD. Fear neither the *dream* nor its *interpretation;* God, will take care of and protect thee. Most certainly, he that fears God need fear nothing else. Well may an upright soul say to *Satan* himself, I fear God; and because I fear *him,* I do not fear *thee.*

Verse 8. *If thou seest the oppression of the poor*] For this was a frequent case under all governments; and especially in the *provinces* or *colonies* which being far from the *seat* of government, were generally oppressed by the sovereign's deputies.

Marvel not at the matter] החפץ *hachephets,* the *will,* i. e., of God; which permits such evils to take place; for all things shall work together for good to them that love him.

"Marvel not,
Ye righteous, if his dispensations here
Unequal seem. What, though disorders reign?
He still presides, and with unerring hand
Directs the vast machine. His wisdom can
From discord harmony produce; and make
Even vice itself subservient to his ends."

Verse 9. *The profit of the earth is for all*] The earth, if properly cultivated, is capable of producing food for every living creature; and without cultivation none has a right to expect bread.

The king himself *is served by the field.*] Without the field he cannot have supplies for his own house; and, unless *agriculture* flourish, the necessary expenses of the state cannot be defrayed. Thus, God joins the *head* and *feet* together; for while the peasant is protected by the king as executor of the laws, the king himself is dependent on the peasant; as the wealth of the nation is the fruit of the labourer's toil.

Verse 10. *He that loveth silver shall not be satisfied with silver*] The more he gets, the more he would get; for the saying is true:—

Crescit amor nummi, quantum ipsa pecunia crescit.

"The love of money increases, in proportion as money itself increases."

Verse 11. *When goods increase*] An increase of property always brings an increase of expense, by a multitude of servants; and the owner really possesses no more, and probably *enjoys* much less, than he did, when every day provided its own bread, and could lay up no store for the next. But if he have more *enjoyment,* his cares are multiplied; and he has no kind of profit. "This also is vanity."

Verse 12. *The sleep of a labouring man is sweet*] His labour is healthy exercise. He is without possessions, and without cares; his sleep, being undisturbed, is sound and refreshing.

Verse 13. *Riches kept for the owners thereof to their hurt.*] This may be the case through various causes: 1. He may make an improper use of them, and lose his health by them. 2. He may join in an unfortunate partnership and lose all. 3. His riches may excite the desire of the *robber;* and he may spoil him of his goods, and even take away his life. 4. Or, he may leave them to his son, who turns profligate, spends the *whole,* and ruins both his body and soul. I have seen this again and again.

Verse 14. *And he begetteth a son, and* there is *nothing in his hand.*] He has been stripped of his property by unfortunate trade or by plunderers; and he has nothing to leave to his children.

Verse 15. *As he came forth*] However it

A. M. cir. 3027
B. C. cir. 977
Ante I. Olymp.
cir. 201
Ante U. C. cir.
224

shall take nothing of his labour, which he may carry away in his hand.

16 And this also *is* a sore evil, *that* in all points as he came, so shall he go: and ^qwhat profit hath he ^rthat hath laboured for the wind?

17 All his days also ^she eateth in darkness, and *he hath* much sorrow and wrath with his sickness.

18 Behold *that* which I have seen: ^tit ^uis good and comely *for one* to eat and to drink,

and to enjoy the good of all his labour that he taketh under the sun ^vall the days of his life, which God giveth him: ^wfor it *is* his portion.

A. M. cir. 3027
B. C. cir. 977
Ante I. Olymp.
cir. 201
Ante U. C. cir.
224

19 ^xEvery man also to whom God hath given riches and wealth, and hath given him power to eat thereof, and to take his portion, and to rejoice in his labour; this *is* the gift of God.

20 ^yFor he shall not much remember the days of his life; because God answereth *him* in the joy of his heart.

---

^qChap. i. 3——^rProv. xi. 29——^sPsa. cxxvii. 2
^tChap. ii. 24; iii. 12, 13, 22; ix. 7; xi. 9; 1 Tim. vi. 17
^uHeb. there is *a good which is comely*, &c.

^vHeb. *the number of the days*——^wChap. ii. 10; iii. 22
^xChap. ii. 24; iii. 13; vi. 2——^yOr, *Though* he give *not much, yet he remembereth*, &c.

---

may be, he himself shall carry nothing with him into the eternal world. If he die worth millions, those millions are dead to him for ever; so he has had no real profit from all his labours, cares, anxieties, and vast property!

Verse 17. *All his days also he eateth in darkness*] Even his enjoyments are embittered by *uncertainty*. He fears for his goods; the possibility of being deprived of them fills his heart with anguish. But instead of יאכל *yochel*, "he shall eat," ילך *yelech*, "he shall walk," is the reading of several MSS. *He walks* in darkness—he has no evidence of salvation. There is no ray of light from God to penetrate the gloom; and all beyond life is darkness impenetrable!

And wrath with his sickness.] His *last hours* are *awful*; for,

"Counting on long years of pleasure here,
He's quite unfurnish'd for the world to come."
BLAIR.

He is full of anguish at the *thought* of death; but the *fear* of it is horrible. But if he have a sense of *God's wrath* in his guilty conscience,

what horror can be compared with his horror!

Verse 18. *Behold* that *which I have seen*] This is the result of my observations and experience. God gives every man, in the course of his providence, the necessaries of life; and it is his will that he should thankfully use them.

For it is *his portion.*] What is requisite for him in the lower world; without them his life cannot subsist; and earthly blessings are as truly the *portion* of his *body* and *animal life*, as the *salvation of God* is the portion of his soul.

Verse 20. *For he shall not much remember*] The person who acts in this way, extracts all the good requisite from life. He passes through things temporal so as not to lose those that are eternal:—

"Calm and serene, the road of life to him,
Or long or short, rugged or smooth, with thorns
O'erspread, or gay with flowers, is but a *road*.
Such fare as offers grateful he accepts,
And smiling to his *native home* proceeds."
C.

CHAPTER VI

The vanity of riches without use, 1, 2. Of children and of old age without riches and enjoyment, 3–7. Man does not know what is good for himself, 8–12.

A. M. cir. 3027
B. C. cir. 977
Ante I. Olymp.
cir. 201
Ante U. C. cir.
224

THERE ^ais an evil which I have seen under the sun, and it *is* common among men;

2 A man to whom God hath given riches, wealth, and honour, ^bso that he

wanteth nothing for his soul of all that he desireth, ^cyet God giveth him not power to eat thereof, but a stranger eateth it: this *is* vanity, and it *is* an evil disease.

A. M. cir. 3027
B. C. cir. 977
Ante I. Olymp.
cir. 201
Ante U. C. cir.
224

---

^aChap. v. 13——^bJob xxi. 10, &c.; Psa.

xvii. 14; lxxiii. 7——^cLuke xii. 20

NOTES ON CHAP. VI

Verse 2. *A man to whom God hath given riches*] A man may possess much earthly goods, and yet enjoy nothing of them. Possession and fruition are not necessarily joined together; and this is also among the *vanities* of life. It is worthy of remark, that it belongs

to God as much to give the power to enjoy as it does to give the earthly blessings. A wise heathen saw this:—

Di tibi divitias dederant, artemque fruendi.
HOR. Ep. lib. i., ep. 4, ver. 7.

"The gods had given thee riches, and the art to enjoy them."

A. M. cir. 3027
B. C. cir. 977
Ante I. Olymp.
cir. 201
Ante U. C. cir.
224

3 If a man beget a hundred *children,* and live many years, so that the days of his years be many, and his soul be not filled with good, and [d]also *that* he have no burial; I say, *that* [e]an untimely birth *is* better than he.

4 For he cometh in with vanity, and departeth in darkness, and his name shall be covered with darkness.

5 Moreover he hath not seen the sun, nor known *any thing:* this hath more rest than the other.

6 Yea, though he live a thousand years twice *told,* yet hath he seen no good: do not all go to one place?

7 [f]All the labour of man *is* for his mouth, and yet the [g]appetite is not filled.

8 For what hath the wise more than the fool? what hath the poor, that knoweth to walk before the living?

A. M. cir. 3027
B. C. cir. 977
Ante I. Olymp.
cir. 201
Ante U. C. cir.
224

9 Better *is* the sight of the eyes [h]than the wandering of the desire: this *is* also vanity and vexation of spirit.

10 That which hath been is named already, and it is known that it *is* man: [i]neither may he contend with him that is mightier than he.

11 Seeing there be many things that increase vanity, what *is* man the better?

12 For who knoweth what *is* good for man in *this* life, [k]all the days of his vain life which he spendeth as [l]a shadow? for [m]who can tell a man what shall be after him under the sun?

---

[d]2 Kings ix. 35; Isaiah xiv. 19, 20; Jeremiah xxii. 19 [e]Job iii. 16; Psa. lviii. 8; chapter iv. 3——[f]Proverbs xvi. 26——[g]Hebrew, *soul*——[h]Hebrew, *than the walking of the soul*

[i]Job ix. 32; Isa. xlv. 9; Jer. xlix. 19——[k]Heb. *the number of the days of the life of his vanity*——[l]Psa. cii. 11; cix. 23; cxliv. 4; James iv. 14——[m]Psa. xxxix. 6; chap. viii. 7

Verse 3. *If a man beget a hundre*d children] If he have the most numerous family and the largest possessions, and is so much attached to his riches that he grudges himself a monument; an *abortion* in the eye of reason is to be preferred to such a man; *himself* is contemptible, and his *life* worthless. The abortion *comes in with vanity*—baulks expectation, *departs in darkness*—never opened its eyes upon the light, and *its name is covered with darkness*—it has no place in the family register, or in the chronicles of Israel. This, that hath neither *seen the sun, nor known any thing* is preferable to the *miser* who has his coffers and granaries well furnished, should he have *lived a thousand years,* and had *a hundred children.* He *has seen*—possessed, no good; *and he and the abortion go to one place,* equally unknown, and wholly forgotten.

Verse 7. *All the labour of man*] This is the grand primary object of all human labour; merely to provide for the support of life by procuring things *necessary.* And life only exists for the sake of the soul; because man puts these things in place of *spiritual* good, the *appetite*—the intense desire after the *supreme good*—is not *satisfied.* When man learns to provide as distinctly for his *soul* as he does for his *body,* then he will begin to be happy, and may soon attain his end.

Verse 8. *For what hath the wise more than the fool?*] They must both labour for the same end. Both depend upon the labour of themselves or others for the necessaries of life. Both must eat and drink in order to live; and the rich man can no more eat two meals at a time, than he can comfortably wear two changes of raiment. The necessaries of life are the same to both, and their *condition* in life is nearly similar; liable to the same diseases, dissolution, and death.

Verse 9. *Better* is *the sight of the eyes than the wandering of the desire*] This is translated by the *Vulgate,* as a sort of adage: Melius est videre quod cupias, quam desiderare quod nescias; "It is better to see what one desires than to covet what one knows not." It is better to enjoy the present than to feed one's self with vain desires of the *future.* What we translate *the wandering of desire,* נפש מהלך *mehaloch nephesh,* is the *travelling of the soul.* What is this? Does it simply mean *desire?* Or is there any reference here to the state of *separate spirits?* It however shows the soul to be in a *restless state,* and consequently to be *unhappy.* If Christ dwell in the heart by faith, the soul is then at *rest,* and this is properly the *rest of the people of God.*

Verse 10. *That which hath been is named already*] The *Hebrew* of this verse might be translated, "Who is he who is? His name has been already called. And it is known that he is Adam; and that he cannot contend in judgment with him who is stronger than he."

"What is more excellent than man; yet can he not, in the lawe, get the victory of him that is mightier than he."—COVERDALE.

ADAM is his name; and it at once points out, 1. His *dignity;* he was made in the image of God. 2. His *fall;* he sinned against his Maker, and was cast out of Paradise. And 3. His *recovery* by *Christ;* the *second man (Adam) was the Lord from heaven,* and a *quickening Spirit.*

Verse 12. *For who knoweth what* is *good for man in* this *life*] Those things which we deem *good* are often *evil.* And those which we think *evil* are often *good.* So ignorant are we, that we run the greatest hazard in making a *choice.* It is better to leave ourselves and our concerns in the hands of the Lord, than to keep them in our own.

For who can tell a man what shall be after him] Futurity is with God. While he lives, man wishes to know what is before him. When he is about to die, he wishes to know what will be after him. All this is vanity; God, because he is merciful, will reveal neither.

CHAPTER VII

The value of a good name, 1. *Advantages of sorrow and correction,* 2–5. *The emptiness of a fool's joy,* 6. *Of oppression,* 7. *The end better than the beginning,* 8. *Against hastiness of spirit,* 9. *Comparison of former and present times,* 10. *Excellence of wisdom,* 11, 12. *Of the dispensations of Providence,* 13–15. *Against extremes,* 16–18. *The strength of wisdom,* 19. *Man is ever liable to sin and mistake,* 20. *We should guard our words,* 21, 22. *Difficulty of obtaining wisdom,* 23–25. *A bad woman dangerous,* 26. *There are few who are really upright,* 27–29.

A. M. cir. 3027
B. C. cir. 977
Ante I. Olymp.
cir. 201
Ante U. C. cir.
224

A [a]GOOD name *is* better than [b]precious ointment; and the day of death than the day of one's birth.

2 *It is* better to go to the house of mourning, than to go to the house of feasting: for that *is* the end of all men; and the living will lay *it* to his heart.

3 [c]Sorrow *is* better than laughter: [d]for by the sadness of the countenance the heart is made better.

4 The heart of the wise *is* in the house of

mourning; but the heart of fools *is* in the house of mirth.

A. M. cir. 3027
B. C. cir. 977
Ante I. Olymp.
cir. 201
Ante U. C. cir.
224

5 [e]*It is* better to hear the rebuke of the wise, than for a man to hear the song of fools.

6 [f]For as the [g]crackling of thorns under a pot, so *is* the laughter of the fool: this also *is* vanity.

7 Surely oppression maketh a wise man mad; [h]and a gift destroyeth the heart.

8 Better *is* the end of a thing than the beginning thereof: *and* [i]the patient in spirit *is*

---

[a]Proverbs xv. 30; xxii. 1——[b]Matthew xxvi. 7; Mark xiv. 3; Luke vii. 37——[c]Or, *Anger*——[d]2 Corinthians vii. 10——[e]See Psalm cxli. 5; Proverbs xiii.

18; xv. 31, 32——[f]Psalm cxviii. 12; chapter ii. 2 [g]Hebrew, *sound*——[h]Exodus xxiii. 8; Deuteronomy xvi. 19——[i]Proverbs xiv. 29

NOTES ON CHAP. VII

Verse 1. *A good name*] Unsatisfactory as all sublunary things are, yet still there are some which are of great consequence, and among them a good name. The place is well paraphrased in the following verses:

"A *spotless name,*
By virtuous deeds acquired, is sweeter far
Than fragant balms, whose odours round
   diffused
Regale the invited guests. Well may such
   men
Rejoice at death's approach, and bless the
   hours
That end their toilsome pilgrimage; assured
That till the race of life is finish'd none
Can be completely blest."

Verse 2. It is *better to go to the house of mourning*] Birthdays were generally kept with great festivity, and to these the wise man most probably refers; but according to his maxim, the miseries of life were so many and so oppressive that the day of a man's *death* was to be preferred to the *day of his birth.* But, independently of the allusion, it is much more profitable to visit the house of mourning for the dead than the house of festivity. In the *former* we find occasion for serious and deeply edifying thoughts and reflections; from the *latter* we seldom return with one profitable thought or one solid impression.

Verse 3. *Sorrow* is *better than laughter*] The reason is immediately given; for *by the sorrow of the countenance—the grief* of heart that shows itself in the countenance—

The heart is made better.] In such cases, most men try themselves at the tribunal of their own consciences, and resolve on amendment of life.

Verse 4. *The heart of the wise* is *in the house of mourning*] A wise man loves those occasions from which he can derive spiritual

advantage; and therefore prefers *visiting the sick,* and *sympathizing* with those who have *suffered privations* by death. But the *fool*—the gay, thoughtless, and giddy—prefers places and times of diversion and amusement. Here he is prevented from seriously considering either himself or his latter end. The grand fault and misfortune of youth.

Verse 6. *For as the crackling of thorns*] They make a great noise, a great blaze; and are extinguished in a few moments. Such, indeed, comparatively, are the joys of life: they are noisy, flashy, and transitory.

Verse 7. *Oppression maketh a wise man mad*] This has been translated with good show of reason, "Surely oppression shall give lustre to a wise man: but a gift corrupteth the heart." The chief difference here is in the word יהולל *yeholel,* which, from the root הלל *halal,* signifies to *glister, irradiate,* as well as to *move briskly,* to *be mad, furious,* in *a rage;* and certainly the former meaning suits this place best. We cannot think that the wise man—he that is truly religious, (for this is its meaning in the language of Solomon,) can be made *mad* by any kind of oppression; but as he trusts in God, so in patience he possesses his soul.

Verse 8. *Better* is *the end*] We can then judge of the whole, and especially if the matter relate to the conduct of Divine Providence. At the beginning we are often apt to make very rash conjectures, and often suppose that such and such things are against us; and that every thing is going wrong. Dr. *Byrom* gives good advice on such a subject:—

"With patient mind thy course of duty run:
God nothing does, nor suffers to be done,
But thou wouldst do thyself, couldst thou but
   see
The *end* of all events, as well as HE."

I may add, in the words of our paraphrast,—

A. M. cir. 3027
B. C. cir. 977
Ante I. Olymp.
cir. 201
Ante U. C. cir.
224

better than the [k]proud in spirit.

9 [l]Be not hasty in thy spirit to be angry: for anger resteth in the bosom of fools.

10 Say not thou, What is *the cause* that the former days were better than these? for thou dost not inquire [m]wisely concerning this.

11 Wisdom [n]*is* good with an inheritance: and *by it there is* profit [o]to them that see the sun.

12 For wisdom *is* a [p]defence, *and* money *is* a defence: but the excellency of knowledge

A. M. cir. 3027
B. C. cir. 977
Ante I. Olymp.
cir. 201
Ante U. C. cir.
224

is, that wisdom giveth life to them that have it.

13 Consider the work of God: for [q]who can make *that* straight, which he hath made crooked?

14 [r]In the day of prosperity be joyful, but in the day of adversity consider: God also hath [s]set the one over against the other, to the end that man should find nothing after him.

15 All *things* have I seen in the days of my vanity: [t]there is a just *man* that perisheth in his righteousness, and there is a wicked

---

[k]Prov. xxi. 4; xxviii. 25——[l]Prov. xiv. 17; xvi. 32; James i. 19——[m]Heb. *out of wisdom*——[n]Or, *as good as an inheritance; yea, better too*

[o]Chap. xi. 7——[p]Heb. *shadow*——[q]See Job xii. 14; chap. i. 15; Isa. xiv. 27——[r]Chap. iii. 4; Deut. xxviii. 47 [s]Heb. *made*——[t]Chap. viii. 14

"Wait the result, nor ask with frantic rage
Why God permits such things. His ways, though now
Involved in clouds and darkness, will appear
All right, when from thine eyes the mist is clear'd.
Till then, to learn submission to his will
More wisdom shows, than vainly thus to attempt
Exploring what thou canst not comprehend,
And God for wisest ends thinks fit to hide."
　　　　　　　　　　　　　　　　C.

Verse 9. *Anger resteth in the bosom of fools.*] A wise man, off his guard, may feel it for a moment: but in him it cannot *rest:* it is a *fire* which he immediately casts out of his breast. But the *fool*—the man who is under the dominion of his own tempers, harbours and fosters it, till it takes the form of malice, and then excites him to seek full revenge on those whom he deems enemies. Hence that class of *dangerous* and *empty fools* called *duellists.*

Verse 10. *The former days were better than these?*] This is a *common saying;* and it is as *foolish* as it is common. There is no weight nor truth in it; but men use it to excuse their crimes, and the folly of their conduct. "In former times, say they, men might be more religious, use more self-denial, be more exemplary." This is *all false.* In former days men were wicked as they are now, and religion was unfashionable: God also is the same *now* as he was *then;* as just, as merciful, as ready to help: and there is no depravity in the age that will excuse your crimes, your follies, and your carelessness.

Among the oriental proverbs I find the following:

"Many say, *This is a corrupt age.* This mode of speaking is not just; it is not the age that is corrupt, but the men of the age."

Verse 11. *Wisdom* is *good with an inheritance*] In this chapter Solomon introduces many observations which appear to be made by objectors against his doctrine; and as he was satisfied of their futility, he proposes them in their own full strength, and then combats and destroys them. It is quite necessary to attend to this; else we shall take the *objector's words* for *those* of *Solomon;* and think, as some have done, that the wise man contradicts and refutes himself. Observations, reflections, and objec-

tions of friends and adversaries are frequently introduced in the works of ancient authors, without mentioning them as such. This is frequent, more particularly in *ethic* writers; and we have many specimens in *Horace;* and without this distinction, it would be impossible to make sense of some of his writings. Here, an *objector,* who had listened to the wise man declaiming in favour of wisdom, suddenly interrupts him, and says in effect, "I grant the truth of what you have said. Wisdom is very good in its place; but what is it without property? A man who has a good inheritance may be profited by wisdom, because it will show him how to manage it to the best advantage."

Verse 12. *Wisdom* is *a defence*] To whom Solomon answers: All true *wisdom* is most undoubtedly a great advantage to men in all circumstances; and *money* is also of great use: but it cannot be compared to wisdom. *Knowledge* of Divine and human things is a great blessing. *Money* is the means of supporting our animal life: but *wisdom*—the religion of the true God—gives *life* to *them that have it. Money* cannot procure the favour of God, nor give *life* to the soul.

Verse 13. *Consider the work of God*] Such is the nature of his providence, that it puts money into the hands of few: but wisdom is within the reach of all. The first is not necessary to happiness; therefore, it is not offered to men; the latter is; and therefore God, in his goodness, offers it to the whole human race. The former can rarely be acquired, for God puts it out of the reach of most men, and you cannot *make that straight which he has made crooked;* the latter may be easily attained by every person who carefully and seriously seeks it from God.

Verse 14. *In the day of prosperity be joyful*] When ye receive these temporal gifts from God, enjoy them, and be thankful to the Giver: but remember, this sunshine will not *always* last. God has balanced *prosperity* and *adversity* against each other; and were it not so, how many would put the former in the place of God himself!

Verse 15. *There is a just* man *that perisheth*] This is another objection; as if he had said, "I also have had considerable experience; and I have not discovered any marked approbation of the conduct of the righteous, or disapprobation of that of the wicked. On **the**

A. M. cir. 3027
B. C. cir. 977
Ante I. Olymp. cir. 201
Ante U. C. cir. 224

man that prolongeth *his life* in his wickedness.

16 [u]Be not righteous overmuch: neither make thyself overwise: why shouldest thou [w]destroy thyself?

17 Be not overmuch wicked, neither be thou foolish: [x]why shouldest thou die [y]before thy time?

18 *It is* good that thou shouldest take hold of this; yea, also from this withdraw not thine hand: for he that feareth God shall come forth of them all.

19 [z]Wisdom strengtheneth the wise more than ten mighty *men* which are in the city.

A. M. cir. 3027
B. C. cir. 977
Ante I. Olymp. cir. 201
Ante U. C. cir. 224

20 [a]For *there is* not a just man upon earth, that doeth good, and sinneth not.

21 Also [b]take no heed unto all words that are spoken; lest thou hear thy servant curse thee:

22 For oftentimes also thine own heart knoweth that thou thyself likewise hast cursed others.

23 All this have I proved by wisdom; [c]I said, I will be wise; but it *was* far from me.

24 [d]That which is far off, and [e]exceeding deep, who can find it out?

---

[u]Prov. xxv. 16——[v]Ecclus. iii. 21, 22; Rom. xii. 3
[w]Heb. *be desolate*——[x]Job xv. 32; Psa. lv. 23; Prov. x. 27
[y]Heb. *not in thy time*——[z]Prov. xxi. 22; xxiv. 5; chap. ix. 16, 18

[a]1 Kings viii. 46; 2 Chron. vi. 36; Prov. xx. 9; Rom. iii. 23; 1 John i. 8——[b]Heb. *give not thine heart*
[c]Rom. i. 22——[d]Job xxviii. 12, 20; 1 Tim. vi. 16
[e]Rom. xi. 33

---

contrary, I have seen a righteous man perish, while employed in the work of righteousness; and a wicked man prosperous, and even exalted, while living wickedly. The former is indeed a victim to his righteousness, while the life and prosperity of the latter were preserved: hence I conclude, it is not prudent, whatever good there may be in religion, and whatever excellence in wisdom, that men should be overmuch righteous, or over-wise: for why should they by austerity and hard study destroy themselves?" So far the objector.

Verse 16. *Why shouldest thou destroy thyself?*] תשומם *tishshomem*, make thyself *desolate*, so that thou shalt be obliged to stand *alone;* neither make thyself over-wise, תתחכם *tithchaccam*, do not pretend to abundance of wisdom. Why shouldest thou be so singular? In other words, and in modern language, "There is no need of all this watching, fasting, praying, self-denial, &c., you carry things to *extremes*. Why should you wish to be reputed singular and precise?" To this the man of God answers:

Verse 17. *Be not overmuch wicked, neither be thou foolish: why shouldest thou die before thy time?*] אל תרשע הרבה *al tirsha harbeh.* Do not multiply wickedness; do not add direct opposition to godliness to the rest of your crimes. Why should you provoke God to destroy you before your time? Perdition will come soon enough. If you will not turn from your sins, and avoid it finally, yet keep out of it as long as you can.

It cannot be supposed, except by those who are totally unacquainted with the nature of true religion, that a man may have *too much holiness, too much of the life of God* in his soul! And yet a learned doctor, in three sermons on this text, has endeavoured to show, out-doing Solomon's infidel, "the *sin, folly,* and *danger* of being righteous overmuch." O rare darkness!

Verse 18. It is *good that thou shouldest take hold of this*] Do not let such an observation slip: *take hold of this; do not forget that.* Get what you can in an honest way; but do not forget to get true religion; for he that fears God will be saved from all evil.

Verse 19. *Wisdom strengtheneth the wise*] One wise, thoroughly learned, and scientific man, may be of more use in fortifying and defending a city, than ten *princes.* Witness the case of *Syracuse,* when attacked by the Romans both by sea and land. *Archimedes,* by his engines, burnt and dashed their fleet to pieces, and destroyed all that came near the walls. And had not the city been betrayed, and he killed, all their force and skill could not have taken it.

Verse 20. There is *not a just man upon earth, that doeth good, and sinneth not.*] לא יחטא *lo yechta,* that *may not sin.* There is not a man upon earth, however just he may be, and habituated to do good, but is *peccable*—liable to commit sin; and therefore should continually watch and pray, and depend upon the Lord. But the text does not say, the *just man does commit sin,* but simply that he *may sin;* and so our translators have rendered it in 1 Sam. ii. 25, twice in 1 Kings viii. 31, 46, and 2 Chron. vi. 36; and the reader is requested to consult the note on 1 Kings viii. 46, where the proper construction of this word may be found, and the doctrine in question is fully considered.

Verse 21. *Also take no heed unto all words that are spoken*] This is good advice, and much for every man's peace through life.

Thy servant curse thee] מקלל *mekallelecha,* make light of thee, speak evil of thee.

Verse 22. *Thou thyself—hast cursed others.*] קללת *kalalta,* thou hast spoken evil; hast vilified others. O, who is free from evil speaking; from uncharitable speaking; from detailing their neighbour's faults, from whispering, talebearing, and backbiting? Do not wonder if God, in his justice, permit *thee* to be calumniated, seeing thou hast so frequently calumniated others. See my discourse on Psa. xv. 1-5.

Verse 23. *All this have I proved by wisdom*] These rules I have laid down for my own conduct, and sought after more wisdom; but have fallen far short of what I wished to be.

Verse 24. *That which is far off*] Though the wisdom that is essential to our salvation may be soon learned, through the teaching of

A. M. cir. 3027
B. C. cir. 977
Ante I Olymp.
cir. 201
Ante U. C. cir.
224

25 ᶠI ᵍapplied mine heart to know, and to search, and to seek out wisdom, and the reason *of things,* and to know the wickedness of folly, even of foolishness *and* madness.

26 ʰAnd I find more bitter than death the woman, whose heart *is* snares and nets, *and* her hands as bands: ⁱwhoso pleaseth God shall escape from her; but the sinner shall be taken by her.

27 Behold, this have I found, saith ᵏthe Preacher, ˡcounting one by one, to find out the account:

A. M. cir. 3027
B. C. cir. 977
Ante I. Olymp.
cir. 201
Ante U. C. cir.
224

28 Which yet my soul seeketh, but I find not: ᵐone man among a thousand have I found; but a woman among all those have I not found.

29 Lo, this only have I found, ⁿthat God hath made man upright; but ᵒthey have sought out many ᵖinventions.

ᶠHeb. *I and my heart compassed*——ᵍChap. i. 17; ii. 12
ʰProv. v. 3, 4; xxii. 14——ⁱHeb. he that is *good before God*——ᵏChap. i. 1, 2

ˡOr, weighing *one thing after another, to find out the reason*——ᵐJob xxxiii. 23; Psa. xii. 1——ⁿGen. i. 27
ᵒGen. iii. 6, 7——ᵖPsa. xcix. 8; cvi. 29, 39; Prov. viii. 12

---

the Spirit of wisdom, yet in wisdom itself there are *extents* and *depths* which none can reach or fathom.

Verse 25. *I applied mine heart*] I cast about, סבותי *sabbothi*, I made a circuit; I circumscribed the ground I was to traverse; and all within my circle I was determined to *know,* and to *investigate,* and to *seek out wisdom,* and the *reason of things.* Has man *reason* and *understanding?* If so, then this is his work. God as much calls him to use these powers in this way, as to believe on the Lord Jesus that he may be saved; and he that does not, according to the means in his power, is a slothful servant, from whom God may justly take away the misemployed or not used talent, and punish him for his neglect. Every doctrine of God is a subject both for reason and faith to work on.

To know the wickedness of folly, even of foolishness and madness.]

"And my own heart, with scrutiny severe,
By far the harder task survey'd; intent
To trace that wisdom which from heaven descends,
Fountain of living waters, and to explore
The source of human folly, whose foul streams
Intoxicate and kill."—C.

Verse 26. *And I find more bitter than death the woman*] After all his investigation of the *wickedness of folly,* and the *foolishness of madness,* he found nothing equally dangerous and ruinous with the *blandishments of cunning women.* When once the affections are entangled, escape without ruin is almost impossible.

Whoso pleaseth God] The man who walks with God, and he alone, shall escape this sore evil: and even he that fears God, if he get with an artful woman, may be soon robbed of his strength, and become like other men. A bad or artful woman is represented as a *company of hunters,* with *nets, gins,* &c., to catch their prey.

Verse 27. *Counting one by one*] I have gone over every particular. I have compared one thing with another; man with woman, his wisdom with her wiles; his strength with her blandishments; his influence with her ascendancy; his powers of reason with her arts and cunning; and in a *thousand* men, I have found *one* thoroughly upright *man;* but among *one thousand* women I have not found *one such.* This is a lamentable account of the *state of morals* in Judea, in the days of the wise King

Solomon. Thank God! it would not be difficult to get a *tithe* of *both* in the same number in the present day.

The *Targum* gives this a curious turn:—
"There is another thing which my soul has sought, but could not find: a man perfect and innocent, and without corruption, from the days of Adam until *Abraham* the just was born; who was found faithful and upright among the thousand kings who came together to construct the tower of Babel: but a *woman* like to *Sarah* among the wives of all those kings I have not found."

Verse 29. *Lo, this only have I found, that God hath made man upright*] Whatever evil may be now found among men and women, it is not of God; for God made them all upright. This is a singular verse, and has been most variously translated: עשה האלהים את האדם ישר והמה בקשו חשבנות רבים *asah hælohim eth haadam yashar vehemhah bikkeshu chishbonoth rabbim.*

"Elohim has made mankind upright, and they have sought many computations."

"He hath meddled with endless questions."—VULGATE.

"Many reasonings."—SEPTUAGINT, SYRIAC, and ARABIC.

"They seek dyverse sotylties."—COVERDALE.

Anð he himself mengiðe with questions without enð.—Old MS. Bible.

The *Targum* considers the text as speaking of *Adam* and *Eve.*

"This have I found out, that the Lord made the first man upright before him, and innocent: but the serpent and Eve seduced him to eat of the fruit of the tree, which gave the power to those who ate of it to discern between good and evil; and was the cause that death came upon him, and all the inhabitants of the earth; and they sought that they might find out *many stratagems* to bring this evil upon all the inhabitants of the world."

I doubt much whether the word חשבנות *chishbonoth* should be taken in a *bad* sense. It may signify the whole of human *devices, imaginations, inventions, artifice,* with all their products; arts, sciences, schemes, plans, and all that they have found out for the destruction or melioration of life. God has given man wondrous faculties; and of them he has made strange uses, and sovereign abuses: and they have been, in consequence, at one time his help, and at another his bane. This is the fair way of understanding this question.

CHAPTER VIII

A man's wisdom makes his face shine, 1. Kings are to be greatly respected, 2–4. Of him who keeps the commandment; of the misery of man; of the certainty of death, 5–8. Of him that rules another to his own hurt, 9. The end of the wicked, 10. God's longsuffering, 11, 12. It shall be ill with wicked men, 13. Strange events in the course of Providence, 14, 15. God's works cannot be found out, 16, 17.

A. M. cir. 3027
B. C. cir. 977
Ante I. Olymp.
cir. 201
Ante U. C. cir.
224

WHO *is* as the wise *man?* and who knoweth the interpretation of a thing? [a]a man's wisdom maketh his face to shine, and [b]the [c]boldness of his face shall be changed.

2 I *counsel thee* to keep the king's commandment, [d]and *that* in regard of the oath of God.

3 [e]Be not hasty to go out of his sight:

stand not in an evil thing; for he doeth whatsoever pleaseth him.

A. M. cir. 3027
B. C. cir. 977
Ante I. Olymp.
cir. 201
Ante U. C. cir.
224

4 Where the word of a king *is, there is* power: and [f]who may say unto him, What doest thou?

5 Whoso keepeth the commandment [g]shall feel no evil thing: and a wise man's heart discerneth both time and judgment.

6 Because [h]to every purpose there is time

---

[a]Prov. iv. 8, 9; xvii. 24; see Acts vi. 15——[b]Heb. *the strength*——[c]Deut. xxviii. 50——[d]1 Chron. xxix. 24; Ezek. xvii. 18; Rom. xiii. 5——[e]Chap. x. 4——[f]Job xxxiv. 18——[g]Heb. *shall know*——[h]Chap. iii. 1

NOTES ON CHAP. VIII

Verse 1. *Who knoweth the interpretation*] פשר *pesher*, a pure *Chaldee* word, found nowhere else in the Bible but in the *Chaldee* parts of *Daniel*. "A man's wisdom maketh his face to shine." Every state of the heart shines through the countenance; but there is such an evidence of the contented, happy, pure, benevolent state of the soul in the *face* of a truly pious man, that it must be observed, and cannot be mistaken. In the Hebrew the former clause of this verse ends the preceding chapter. Who has ever been deceived in the appearance of the face that belonged to a savage heart? Those who represent, by painting. or otherwise, a *wise* man, with a *gravely sour face*, striking awe and forbidding approach, have either mistaken the man, or are unacquainted with some essential principles of their art.

The boldness of his face shall be changed.] Instead of ישׁנא *yeshunne*, which signifies *shall be hated*, many of *Kennicott's* and *De Rossi's* MSS. have ישׁנה *yeshunneh*, shall be *changed* or *doubled*. Hence the verse might be read, "The wisdom of a man shall illuminate his face; and the strength of his countenance shall be doubled." He shall speak with full confidence and conviction on a subject which he perfectly understands, and all will feel the weight of his observations.

Verse 2. *To keep the king's commandment*] This sentence would be better translated, *I keep the mouth of the king;* I take good heed not to meddle with state secrets; and if I know, to hide them. Or, I am obedient to the commands of the laws; I feel myself bound by whatever the king has decreed.

In regard of the oath of God.] You have sworn obedience to him; keep your oath, for the engagement was made in the *presence of God*. It appears that the Jewish princes and chiefs took an oath of fidelity to their kings. This appears to have been done to *David*, 2 Sam. v. 1-3; to *Joash*, 2 Kings xi. 17; and to *Solomon*, 1 Chron. xxix. 24.

Verse 3. *Be not hasty*] I consider the first *five* verses here as directions to *courtiers*, and the more immediate servants of kings.

Be steadily faithful to your sovereign. *Do not stand in an evil thing.* If you have done wrong, do not endeavour to vindicate yourself before him; it is of no use; his power is *absolute*, and *he will do what he pleases*. He will take his *own view* of the subject, and he will *retain* it. The language of a despotic sovereign was ever this, Sic volo sic jubeo, stat pro ratione voluntas; "I will this. I command that. No hesitation! My will is law!" Therefore it is added here, *Where the word of a king* is, there is *power*—influence, authority, *and* the sword. And *who may say unto him*, whether he acts right or wrong, *What doest thou?* ver. 4. No wonder in such governments there are so many *revolutions;* but they are *revolutions* without *amendment*, as it is one *tyrant* rising up to destroy *another*, who, when seated in authority, acts in the way of his predecessor; till another, like himself, do to him as he has done to the former. In our country, after a long trial, we find that a *mixed monarchy* is the safest, best, and most useful form of government: we have had, it is true, unprincipled ministers, who wished to turn our *limited* into an *absolute monarchy;* and they were always ready to state that an *absolute monarchy was best*. Granted; provided the monarch be as *wise*, as *holy*, and as *powerful* as God!

Verse 5. *Both time and judgment.*] It is a matter of great importance to be able to discern WHEN and HOW both to *speak* and *act;* but when *time* and *manner* are both determined, the *matter* comes next. WHAT shall *I speak?* WHAT shall *I do? When, how,* and *what*, answer to *time, manner,* and *matter.* To discern all these, and act suitably, is a *lesson* for a *philosopher*, and a *study* for a *Christian.*

Verse 6. *To every purpose there is time*] חפץ *chaphets*, every *volition*, every thing that *depends on the will of man.* He has generally the *opportunity* to do whatever he purposes; and as his purposes are frequently evil, his

A. M. cir. 3027
B. C. cir. 977
Ante I. Olymp.
cir. 201
Ante U. C. cir.
224

and judgment, therefore the misery of man *is* great upon him.

7 [i]For he knoweth not that which shall be: for who can tell him [k]when it shall be?

8 [l]*There is* no man that hath power [m]over the spirit to retain the spirit; neither *hath he* power in the day of death: and *there is* no [n]discharge in *that* war; neither shall wickedness deliver those that are given to it.

9 All this have I seen, and applied my heart unto every work that is done under the sun: *there is* a time wherein one man ruleth over another to his own hurt.

10 And so I saw the wicked buried, who had come and gone from the place of the holy, and they were forgotten in the city where they had so done: this *is* also vanity.

11 [o]Because sentence against an evil work

is not executed speedily, therefore the heart of the sons of men is fully set in them to do evil.

A. M. cir. 3027
B. C. cir. 977
Ante I. Olymp.
cir. 201
Ante U. C. cir.
224

12 [p]Through a sinner do evil a hundred times, and his *days* be prolonged, yet surely I know that [q]it shall be well with them that fear God, which fear before him:

13 But it shall not be well with the wicked, neither shall he prolong *his* days, *which are* as a shadow; because he feareth not before God.

14 There is a vanity which is done upon the earth; that there be just *men,* unto whom it [r]happeneth according to the work of the wicked; again, there be wicked *men,* to whom it happeneth according to the work of the righteous: I said that this also *is* vanity.

15 [s]Then I commended mirth, because a man hath no better thing under the sun, than to eat, and to drink, and to be merry; for that

---

[i]Proverbs xxiv. 22; chapter vi. 12; ix. 12; x. 14 [k]Or, *how it shall be*——[l]Psa. xlix. 6, 7——[m]Job xiv. 5 [n]Or, *casting off* weapons——[o]Psalm x. 6; l. 21; Isaiah xxvi. 10——[p]Isaiah lxv. 20; Romans ii. 5——[q]Psalm

xxxvii. 11, 18, 19; Proverbs i. 32, 33; Isaiah iii. 10, 11; Matthew xxv. 34, 41——[r]Psalm lxxiii. 14; chapter ii. 14; vii. 15; ix. 1, 2——[s]Chapter ii. 24; iii. 12, 22; v. 18; ix. 7

---

acts are so too: and in consequence his misery is great.

Verse 8. There is *no man that hath power over the spirit to retain the spirit*] The *Chaldee* has, "There is no man who can rule over the spirit of the breath, so as to prevent the animal life from leaving the body of man." Others translate to this sense: "No man hath power over the *wind* to restrain the wind; and none has power over *death* to restrain him; and when a man engages as a *soldier,* he cannot be discharged from the war till it is ended; and by wickedness no man shall be delivered from any evil." Taking it in this way, these are maxims which contain self-evident truths. Others suppose the verse to refer to the *king* who *tyrannizes* over and oppresses his people. He shall also account to God for his actions; he shall die, and he cannot prevent it; and when he is judged, his wickedness cannot deliver him.

Verse 9. *One man ruleth over another to his own hurt.*] This may be spoken of rulers generally, who, instead of *feeding, fleece the flock;* tyrants and oppressors, who come to an untimely end by their mismanagement of the offices of the state. All these things relate to *Asiatic* despots, and have ever been more applicable to *them* than to any other sovereigns in the world. They were despotic; they still are so.

Verse 10. *Who had come and gone from the place of the holy*] The place of the holy is the sacred office which they held, *anointed* either as *kings* or *priests* to God; and, not having fulfilled the holy office in a holy way, have been carried to their *graves* without *lamentation,* and lie among the dead without remembrance.

Verse 11. *Because sentence*] פתגם *pithgam,* a *Divine decree* or *declaration.* This is

no *Hebrew,* but a mere *Chaldee* word, and occurs only in the *later books* of the Bible—*Esther, Ezra* and *Daniel,* and nowhere else but in this place. Because God does not immediately punish every delinquency, men think he disregards evil acts; and therefore they are emboldened to sin on. So this longsuffering of God, which *leadeth to repentance,* is abused so as to *lead to farther crimes!* When men sin against the remedy of their salvation, how can they escape perdition?

Verse 12. *Though a sinner do evil a hundred times*] If God bear so long with a transgressor, waiting in his longsuffering for him to repent and turn to him, surely he will be peculiarly kind to them that *fear him,* and endeavour to walk uprightly before him.

Verse 13. *But it shall not be well with the wicked*] Let not the long-spared sinner presume that, because sentence is not speedily executed on his evil works, and he is suffered to go on to his *hundredth transgression,* God has forgotten to punish. No; *he feareth not before God;* and therefore he shall not ultimately escape.

Verse 14. *There be just* men] See on chap. vii. ver. 16.

Verse 15. *Then I commended mirth*] These are some more of the cavils of the infidel objector: "Since *virtue* is frequently under oppression, and *vice* triumphs in health, and rolls in wealth, I see plainly that we should not trouble ourselves about future things; and therefore should be governed by the maxim EDE, BIBE, LUDE. *Post mortem nulla voluptas.*"

> *Eat, drink,* and *play,*
> While here you may;
> For soon as death
> Has stopp'd your breath,
> Ye ne'er shall see a cheerful day.

A. M. cir. 3027
B. C. cir. 977
Ante I. Olymp.
cir. 201
Ante U. C. cir.
224

shall abide with him of his labour the days of his life, which God giveth him under the sun.

16 When I applied mine heart to know wisdom, and to see the business that is done upon the earth: (for also *there is that* neither day nor night seeth sleep with his eyes:)

ᵗJob v. 9; chap. iii. 11; Rom. xi. 33

Verse 16. *When I applied mine heart to know wisdom*] This is the reply of the wise man: "I have also considered these seeming contradictions. God governs the world; but we cannot see the reasons of his conduct, nor know why he does this, omits that, or permits a third thing. We may *study night* and *day*, and deprive ourselves of *rest* and *sleep*, but we shall never fathom the depths that are in the Divine government; but all is right and just. *This* is the state of *probation;* and in it neither can the wicked be punished, nor the righteous rewarded. But eternity is at hand; and then shall every man receive according to his works. He that spends his life in the *eat, drink,* and

17 Then I beheld all the work of God, that ᵗa man cannot find out the work that is done under the sun: because though a man labour to seek *it* out, yet he shall not find *it;* yea, farther; though a wise *man* think to know *it,* ᵘyet shall he not be able to find *it.*

A. M. cir. 3027
B. C. cir. 977
Ante I. Olymp.
cir. 201
Ante U. C. cir.
224

ᵘPsa. lxxiii. 16

---

play, will find in that day that he has lost the *time* in *which* he could have prepared for *eternity.*

Verse 17. *Then I beheld all the work of God, that a man cannot find out the work that is done under the sun*] I saw it to be of such a nature—1, That *a man cannot find it out.* 2. That if he *labour to find it out,* he shall not succeed. 3. That though he be *wise*—the *most instructed* among men, and *think* to find it out, he shall find *he is not able.* It is beyond the wisdom and power of man. How vain then are all your *cavils* about Providence. You do not understand it; you cannot comprehend it. Fear God!

CHAPTER IX

No man knows, by any present sign, what is before him, 1. All things happen alike to all, 2, 3. Comparison of the state of the dead and the living, 4–6. Enjoy God's mercies, and live to his glory, 7–10. The race is not to the swift, nor the battle to the strong, 11. Man is ignorant of futurity, 12, 13. The account of the little city, and the poor wise man, 14–18.

A. M. cir. 3027
B. C. cir. 977
Ante I. Olymp.
cir. 201
Ante U. C. cir.
224

FOR all this ᵃI considered in my heart even to declare all this, ᵇthat the righteous, and the wise, and their works, *are* in the hand of God: no man knoweth either love or hatred *by* all *that is* before them.

2 ᶜAll *things come* alike to all: *there is* one event to the righteous, and to the wicked; to the good and to the clean, and to the un-

---

ᵃHeb. *I gave* or *set to my heart*——ᵇChap. viii. 14

NOTES ON CHAP. IX

Verse 1. *The righteous, and the wise, and their works,* are *in the hand of God*] This is a continuation of the preceding subject; and here the wise man draws a conclusion from what he had seen, and from the well-known character of God, that the *righteous,* the *wise,* and *their conduct,* were all in *the hand of God,* protected by his power, and safe in his approbation: but we cannot judge from the occurrences which take place in life who are the objects of God's love or displeasure.

Verse 2. *All things come alike to all*] This is very generally true; but God often makes a difference; and his faithful followers witness many interventions of Divine Providence in their behalf. But there are general blessings, and general natural evils, that equally affect the just and the unjust. But in this all is right; the

clean; to him that sacrificeth, and to him that sacrificeth not: as *is* the good, so *is* the sinner; *and* he that sweareth, as *he* that feareth an oath.

A. M. cir. 3027
B. C. cir. 977
Ante I. Olymp.
cir. 201
Ante U. C. cir.
224

3 This *is* an evil among all *things* that are done under the sun, that *there is* one event unto all: yea, also the heart of the sons of men is full of evil, and madness *is* in their heart while

---

ᶜJob xxi. 7, &c.; Psa. lxxiii. 3, 12, 13; Mal. iii. 15

---

evils that are in *nature* are the effects of the FALL of man; and God will not suspend *general laws,* or *alter* them, to favour *individual* cases. Nor does he design that his approbation or disapprobation shall be shown by any of these occurrences. Every holy man has a testimony of God's approbation in his own heart; and this makes him truly happy, let outward things be as they may. And, in general, what the wicked suffer is the fruit of their own doings. But the general state of nature as to what are called *natural evils,* is just as it ought to be. There is *evil* enough to show that *man has fallen* from God, and *good* enough to show that God deals with him in *mercy.* I cannot see that there is any rational cause for me to stumble at the dispensations of Divine Providence on these accounts.

Verse 3. *The heart of the sons of men is full*

A. M. cir. 3027
B. C. cir. 977
Ante I. Olymp.
cir. 201
Ante U. C. cir.
224

they live, and after that *they go* to the dead.

4 For to him that is joined to all the living there is hope: for a living dog is better than a dead lion.

5 For the living know that they shall die: but ᵈthe dead know not any thing, neither have they any more a reward; for ᵉthe memory of them is forgotten.

6 Also their love and their hatred, and their envy, is now perished; neither have they any more a portion for ever in any *thing* that is done under the sun.

7 Go thy way, ᶠeat thy bread with joy, and drink thy wine with a merry heart; for God now accepteth thy works.

A. M. cir. 3027
B. C. cir. 977
Ante I. Olymp.
cir. 201
Ante U. C. cir.
224

8 Let thy garments be always white; and let thy head lack no ointment.

9 ᵍLive joyfully with the wife whom thou lovest all the days of the life of thy vanity, which he hath given thee under the sun, all the days of thy vanity: ʰfor that *is* thy portion in *this* life, and in thy labour which thou takest under the sun.

10 Whatsoever thy hand findeth to do, do

ᵈJob xiv. 21; Isa. lxiii. 16——ᵉJob vii. 8, 9, 10; Isa. xxvi. 14——ᶠChap. viii. 15

ᵍHebrews, *See* or *enjoy life*——ʰChap. ii. 10, 24; iii. 13, 22; v. 18

---

of evil] No wonder then that the curse of God should be frequent in the earth.

Verse 4. *For to him that is joined to all the living there is hope*] While a man lives he hopes to *amend*, and he hopes to have a *better lot;* and thus life is spent, hoping to *grow better*, and hoping to *get more*. The *Vulgate* has, "There is none that shall live always, nor has any hope of such a thing." Perhaps the best translation is the following: "What, therefore, is to be chosen? In him that is living there is hope." Then choose that eternal life which thou hopest to possess.

A living dog is better than a dead lion.] I suppose this was a proverb. The smallest measure of *animal* existence is better than the largest of *dead matter*. The poorest living peasant is infinitely above Alexander the Great.

Verse 5. *The living know that they shall die*] This is so self-evident that none can doubt it; and therefore all that have this conviction should prepare for death and eternal blessedness.

But the dead know not any thing] Cut off from *life*, they know nothing of *what passes under the sun*. Their day of *probation* is ended, and therefore they can have no farther *reward* in living a holy life; nor can they be liable to any *farther punishment* for crimes in a state of probation, that being ended.

Verse 6. *Also their love, and their hatred*] It is evident that he speaks here of the ignorance, want of power, &c., of the *dead*, in reference only to *this* life. And though they have no more a *portion* under the sun, yet he does not intimate that they have none anywhere else. A man threatens to conquer kingdoms, &c. He dies; what are his *threats?*

Verse 7. *Go thy way, eat thy bread with joy*] Do not vex and perplex yourselves with the dispensations and mysteries of Providence; enjoy the blessings which God has given you, and live to his glory; and then *God will accept your works*.

Verse 8. *Let thy garments be always white*] The Jews wore white garments on festal occasions, as emblems of joy and innocence. Be always pure, and always happy. The inhabitants of India are all dressed in clean *white cotton*, and to this is the allusion in the text.

The *Targum* says: "At all times let thy garments be washed and pure from the stain of

sin. Acquire a good name, which is likened to the oil of anointing, that blessings may be called down up thy head, and goodness not forsake thee."

Verse 9. *Live joyfully with the wife whom thou lovest*] Marry prudently, keep faithfully attached to the wife thou hast chosen, and rejoice in the labour of thy hands.

Some understand this as the words of the libertine objector: "Live joyfully with the woman whom thou lovest best." But this does not comport so well with the scope of the place.

Verse 10. *Whatsoever thy hand findeth to do*] Examine here the WHAT, the HOW, and the WHY.

I. *What* is necessary to be done in this life, in reference to another? 1. Turn from sin. 2. Repent. 3. Frequent the ordinances of God, and associate with the upright. 4. Read the Scriptures. 5. Pray for pardon. 6. Believe on the Lord Jesus, that thou mayest obtain it. 7. Look for the gift of the Holy Spirit. 8. Bring forth in their seasons the fruits of it—(1) Repentance; (2) Faith; and (3) The Holy Spirit. 9. Live to get good. 10. And to do good. 11. And refer every purpose and act to the eternal world.

II. *How* should these be done? *With thy might*. 1. Be fully convinced of the necessity of these things. 2. Be determined to act according to this conviction. 3. Then act with all thy strength; put forth all thy power in avoiding evil, repenting of sin, &c., &c.

III. *Why* should this be done? 1. Because thou art a dying man. 2. Thou art going into the grave. 3. When thou leavest this life, thy state of probation, with all its advantages, is eternally ended. 4. If thou die in sin, where God is thou shalt never come. For, 1. There is no *work* by which thou mayest profit; 2. No *device* by which thou mayest escape punishment; 3. No *knowledge* of any means of help; and, 4. No *wisdom*—restoration of the soul to the favour and image of God, *in that grave whither thou goest*. Therefore, work while it is called *to-day*.

My old MS. Bible translates this nervously: 𝔚𝔥𝔞𝔱𝔢𝔟𝔢𝔯 𝔱𝔥𝔦𝔫𝔤𝔢 𝔪𝔞𝔶 𝔱𝔥𝔦𝔫 𝔥𝔬𝔫𝔡 𝔡𝔬𝔫, 𝔟𝔢𝔰𝔦𝔩𝔶 𝔴𝔦𝔯𝔠𝔥: 𝔣𝔬𝔯 𝔫𝔬𝔲𝔱𝔥𝔢𝔯 𝔴𝔢𝔯𝔢, 𝔫𝔢 𝔯𝔢𝔰𝔬𝔲𝔫, 𝔫𝔢 𝔴𝔦𝔰𝔡𝔬𝔪, 𝔫𝔢 𝔨𝔢𝔢𝔫𝔫𝔶𝔫𝔤 𝔰𝔠𝔥𝔲𝔩𝔫 𝔟𝔢 𝔞 𝔫𝔢𝔫𝔱𝔦𝔰 𝔥𝔢𝔩𝔩, 𝔴𝔥𝔦𝔱𝔥𝔢𝔯 𝔱𝔥𝔬𝔲 𝔤𝔬𝔰𝔱. Properly speaking, every sinner is *going to hell*, and the wisdom of God calls upon him to turn and live.

A. M. cir. 3027
B. C. cir. 977
Ante I. Olymp. cir. 201
Ante U. C. cir. 224

it with thy might; for *there is* no work, nor device, nor knowledge, nor wisdom, in the grave, whither thou goest.

11 I returned, [i]and saw under the sun, that the race *is* not to the swift, nor the battle to the strong, neither yet bread to the wise, nor yet riches to men of understanding, nor yet favour to men of skill; but time and chance happeneth to them all.

12 For [k]man also knoweth not his time: as

the fishes that are taken in an evil net, and as the birds that are caught in the snare; so *are* the sons of men [i]snared in an evil time, when it falleth suddenly upon them.

A. M. cir. 3027
B. C. cir. 977
Ante I. Olymp. cir. 201
Ante U. C. cir. 224

13 This wisdom have I seen also under the sun, and it *seemed* great unto me:

14 [m]*There was* a little city, and few men within it; and there came a great king against it, and besieged it, and built great bulwarks against it:

---

[i]Amos ii. 14, 15; Jeremiah ix. 23——[k]Chapter viii. 7

[l]Prov. xxix. 6; Luke xii. 20, 39; xvii. 26, &c.; 1 Thess. v. 3——[m]See 2 Sam. xx. 16–22

Verse 11. *The race* is *not to the swift*] It is not by swiftness, nor by strength and valour, that races are gained and battles won. God causes the *lame* often to take the *prey*, the prize; and so works that the *weak* overthrow the *strong;* therefore, no man should confide in himself. All things are under the government, and at the disposal of God.

But time and chance] עת *eth,* time or opportunity, and פגע *pega,* incident or occurrence,—

Happeneth to them all.] Every man has what may be called *time* and *space* to act in, and *opportunity* to do a particular work. But in this TIME and OPPORTUNITY there is INCIDENT, what *may fall in;* and OCCURRENCE, what may *meet* and frustrate an attempt. These things should be wisely weighed, and seriously balanced; for those *four things* belong to every human *action.* While you have TIME, seek an OPPORTUNITY to do what is right; but calculate on *hinderances* and *oppositions,* because *time* and *opportunity* have their INCIDENT and OCCURRENCE. *Coverdale* translates this verse well: "I sawe that in runnynge, it helpeth not to be swift; in batayll, it helpeth not to be stronge; to fedynge, it helpeth not to be wyse; to riches, it helpeth not to be sutyll; to be had in favoure, it helpeth not to be connynge; but that all lyeth in time and fortune."

Verse 12. *As the birds that are caught*] Man acts so heedlessly, notwithstanding all his wisdom, and all his warnings, that he is often taken, as a *fish* is, by the baited hook; and the *bird* by the baited snare. And thus, *an evil time,* like the snare, gin, trap, hook, falleth suddenly upon them; and they are taken in a moment, and have no means of escaping. How frequently do we see these comparisons illustrated!

Verse 14. There was *a little city, and few men within it*] Here is another proof of the vanity of sublunary things; the *ingratitude of men,* and the *little compensation* that *genuine merit* receives. The little history mentioned here may have either been a *fact,* or intended as an instructive fable. A *little city,* with *few* to defend it, being besieged by a *great king* and a powerful army, was delivered by the *cunning and address of a poor wise man;* and afterwards his *townsmen* forgot *their obligation to him.*

Those who *spiritualize* this passage, making the *little city* the CHURCH, the *few men* the APOSTLES, the *great king* the DEVIL, and the *poor wise man* JESUS CHRIST, abuse the text.

But the *Targum* is not less whimsical: "The

little city is the human body; *few men in it,* few *good affections* to work righteousness; *the great king,* evil concupiscence, which, like a strong and powerful king, enters into the body to oppress it, and besieges the heart so as to cause it to err; *built great bulwarks against it*—evil concupiscence builds his throne in it wheresoever he wills, and causes it to decline from the ways that are right before God; that it may be taken in the greatest nets of hell, that he may burn it seven times, because of its sins. But there is *found in it a poor wise man*—a good, wise, and holy affection, which prevails over the evil principle, and snatches the body from the judgment of hell, by the strength of its wisdom. Yet, after this deliverance, the man did not remember what the good principle had done for him; but said in his heart, I am innocent," &c.

What a wonderful text has this been in the hands of many a modern *Targumist;* and with what force have the *Keachonians* preached Christ *crucified* from it!

Such a passage as this receives a fine illustration from the case of *Archimedes* saving the city of *Syracuse* from all the Roman forces besieging it by sea and land. He destroyed their ships by his *burning-glasses,* lifted up their galleys out of the water by his machines, dashing some to pieces, and sinking others. One man's wisdom here prevailed for a long time against the most powerful exertions of a mighty nation. In this case, wisdom far exceeded strength. But was not Syracuse taken, notwithstanding the exertions of this poor wise man? No. But it was *betrayed* by the baseness of *Mericus,* a Spaniard, one of the *Syracusan* generals. He delivered the whole district he commanded into the hands of *Marcellus,* the Roman consul, *Archimedes* having defeated every attempt made by the Romans, either by sea or land: yet he commanded no company of men, made no sorties, but confounded and destroyed them by his machines. This happened about 208 years before Christ, and nearly about the time in which those who do not consider Solomon as the author suppose this book to have been written. This wise man was *not remembered;* he was slain by a Roman soldier, while deeply engaged in demonstrating a new problem, in order to his farther operations against the enemies of his country. See *Plutarch,* and the historians of this *Syracusan* war.

When *Alexander* the Great was about to destroy the city *Lampsacus,* his old master *Anaxi-*

A. M. cir. 3027
B. C. cir. 977
Ante I. Olymp.
cir. 201
Ante U. C. cir.
224

15 Now there was found in it a poor wise man, and he by his wisdom delivered the city; yet no man remembered that same poor man.

16 [n]Then said I, Wisdom *is* better than strength: nevertheless [o]the poor man's wis-

dom *is* despised, and his words are not heard.

17 The words of wise *men are* heard in quiet, more than the cry of him that ruleth among fools.

18 [p]Wisdom *is* better than weapons of war: but [q]one sinner destroyeth much good.

A. M. cir. 3027
B. C. cir. 977
Ante I. Olymp.
cir. 201
Ante U. C. cir.
224

---

[n]Prov xxi. 22; xxiv. 5; chap. vii. 19; ver. 18   [o]Mark vi. 2, 3——[p]Ver. 16——[q]Josh. vii. 1, 11, 12

---

menes came out to meet him. Alexander, suspecting his design, that he would intercede for the city, being determined to destroy it, swore that he would *not* grant him any thing he should ask. Then said Anaximenes, "I desire that you *will destroy* this city." Alexander respected his oath, and the city was spared. Thus, says *Valerius Maximus*, the narrator, (lib. vii. c. iii., No. 4. Extern.,) by this sudden turn of sagacity, this ancient and noble city was preserved from the destruction by which it was threatened. "Hæc velocitas sagacitatis oppidum vetusta nobilitate inclytum exitio, cui destinatum erat, subtraxit."

A stratagem of *Jaddua*, the *high priest*, was the means of preserving *Jerusalem* from being destroyed by *Alexander*, who, incensed because they had assisted the inhabitants of Gaza when he besieged it, as soon as he had reduced it, marched against Jerusalem, with the determination to raze it to the ground; but Jaddua and his priests in their sacerdotal robes, meeting him on the way, he was so struck with their appearance that he not only prostrated himself before the high priest, and spared the city, but also granted it some remarkable privileges. But the case of *Archimedes* and *Syracuse* is the most striking and appropriate in all its

parts. That of Anaximenes and Lampsacus is also highly illustrative of the maxim of the wise man: "Wisdom is better than strength."

Verse 16. *The poor man's wisdom is despised, and his words are not heard.*] I cannot help pursuing this illustration a little farther. The soldier who found Archimedes busily employed in drawing figures upon the sand, put to him some impertinent question, withal rudely obtruding himself on his operations. To whom this wonderful mathematician replied, "Stand off, soldier, and do not spoil my diagram;" on which the bloody savage struck him dead!

Verse 17. *The words of wise men are heard in quiet*] In the tumult of war the words of *Archimedes* were not heard; and his *life* was lost.

Verse 18. *Wisdom is better than weapons of war*] So proved in the case of *Archimedes.*

But one sinner] Such as the Roman butcher above mentioned.

Destroyeth much good] Such as were the life and skill of the Syracusan mathematician. One sinner has often injured the work of God; one stumbling-block has sometimes destroyed a revival of religion. Sin acts like a ferment; whatever comes in contact with it, it assimilates to itself.

CHAPTER X

Observations on wisdom and folly, 1–3. Concerning right conduct towards rulers, 4. Merit depressed, and worthlessness exalted, 5–7. Of him who digs a pit and removes a landmark, 8, 9. The use of wisdom and experience, 10. Of the babbler and the fool, 11–15. The infant king, 16. The well-regulated court, 17. Of slothfulness, 18. Of feasting, 19. Speak not evil of the king, 20.

A. M. cir. 3027
B. C. cir. 977
Ante I. Olymp.
cir. 201
Ante U. C. cir.
224

DEAD [a]flies cause the ointment of the apothecary to send forth a stinking savour: *so doth* a little folly him that is in reputation for wisdom *and* honour.

2 A wise man's heart *is* at his right hand; but a fool's heart at his left.

3 Yea also, when he that is a fool walketh by the way, [b]his wisdom faileth

A. M. cir. 3027
B. C. cir. 977
Ante I. Olymp.
cir. 201
Ante U. C. cir.
224

---

[a]Heb. *Flies of death*   [b]Heb. *his heart*

NOTES ON CHAP. X

Verse 1. *Dead flies*] Any putrefaction spoils perfume; and so a foolish act ruins the character of him who has the reputation of being wise and good. Alas! alas! in an unguarded moment how many have tarnished the reputation which they were many years in acquiring! Hence, no man can be said to be safe, till he is taken to the paradise of God.

Verse 2. *A wise man's heart is at his right hand*] As the *right hand* is ordinarily the best

exercised, strongest, and most ready, and the *left* the contrary, they show, 1. The command which the wise man has over his own mind, feelings, passions, &c., and the prudence with which he acts. And, 2. The want of prudence and management in the fool, who has no restraint on his passions, and no rule or guard upon his tongue. The *right hand* and the *left* are used in Scripture to express *good* and *evil*. The wise man is always employed in doing *good;* the fool, in nonsense or evil.

Verse 3. *When—a fool walketh by the way*]

A. M. cir. 3027
B. C. cir. 977
Ante I. Olymp.
cir. 201
Ante U. C. cir.
224

him, cand he saith to every one that he *is* a fool.

4 If the spirit of the ruler rise up against thee, dleave not thy place; for eyielding pacifieth great offences.

5 There is an evil *which* I have seen under the sun, as an error *which* proceedeth ffrom the ruler:

6 gFolly is set hin great dignity, and the rich sit in low place.

7 I have seen servants iupon horses, and princes walking as servants upon the earth.

8 kHe that diggeth a pit shall fall into it;

and whoso breaketh a hedge, a serpent shall bite him.

9 Whoso removeth stones shall be hurt therewith; *and* he that cleaveth wood shall be endangered thereby.

10 If the iron be blunt, and he do not whet the edge, then must he put to more strength: but wisdom *is* profitable to direct.

11 Surely the serpent will bite lwithout enchantment; and a mbabbler is no better.

12 nThe words of a wise man's mouth *are* ogracious; but pthe lips of a fool will swallow up himself.

A. M. cir. 3027
B. C. cir. 977
Ante I. Olymp.
cir. 201
Ante U. C. cir.
224

---

cProv. xiii. 16; xviii. 2——dChap. viii. 3——e1 Sam. xxv. 24, &c.; Prov. xxv. 15——fHeb. *from before.* gEsth. iii. 1——hHeb. *in great heights*——iProv. xix. 10; xxx. 22

kPsa. vii. 15; Prov. xxvi. 27——lPsa. lviii. 4, 5; Jer. viii. 17——mHeb. *the master of the tongue*——nProv. x. 32; xii. 13——oHeb. *grace*——pProverbs x. 14; xviii. 7

In every act of life, and in every company he frequents, the irreligious man shows what he is. Vanity, nonsense, and wickedness are his themes: so that in effect *he saith to every one that he is a fool.*

Verse 4. *If the spirit of the ruler rise up against thee*] If the king get incensed against thee.

Leave not thy place] Humble thyself before him, that is *thy place* and duty; for yielding to him, and not standing stoutly in thy defence, pacifieth *great offences:* and then, when his anger is appeased, he will hear any thing in thy justification, if thou have any thing to offer. This is good advice to a *child* in reference to his *parents,* and to an *inferior* of any kind in reference to his *superiors.*

Several of the fathers understood this differently, *If the spirit of the ruler*—the influence of Satan—*hath risen up against* and prevailed over thee, to bring thee into some sin; *leave not thy place*—do not despair of God's mercy; humble thyself before him, and seek pardon through the Son of his love, and this will be מרפא *marpe,* a *remedy* or *cure* even for חטאים נדולים *chataim gedolim,* great errors or sins. All this is true in itself, whether found in this text or not.

Verse 5. *An error* which *proceedeth from the ruler*] What this error in the ruler is, the two following verses point out: it is simply this—an injudicious distribution of offices, and raising people to places of trust and confidence, who are destitute of *merit,* are neither of *name* nor *family* to excite public confidence, and are without *property;* so that they have no *stake in the country,* and their only solicitude must naturally be to enrich themselves, and provide for their poor relatives. This is frequent in the governments of the world; and *favouritism* has often brought prosperous nations to the brink of ruin. *Folly* was set in *dignity;* the man of property, sense, and name, in a *low place. Servants*—menial men, *rode upon horses*—carried every thing with a high and proud hand; and *princes,*—the nobles of the people, were obliged *to walk by their sides,* and often from the state of things to become in effect *their servants.* This was often the case in this country, during the reign of *Thomas à Becket,* and *Cardinal*

Woolsey. These insolent men lorded it over the whole nation; and the people and their gentry were raised or depressed according as their pride and caprice willed. And, through this kind of errors, not only a few sovereigns have had most uncomfortable and troublesome reigns, but some have even lost their lives.

Verse 8. *Whoso breaketh a hedge, a serpent shall bite him.*] While spoiling his neighbour's property, he himself may come to greater mischief: while pulling out the sticks, he may be bit by a serpent, who has his nest there. Some have supposed that נחש *nachash* here means a *thorn;* perhaps from the similarity of its *prick* to the serpent's *sting.* He who forces his way through a hedge will be pricked by the thorns.

Verse 9. *Whoso removeth stones*] This verse teaches care and caution. Whoever *pulls down* an old building is likely to be hurt by the stones; and in *cleaving wood* many accidents occur for want of sufficient caution.

Verse 10. *If the iron be blunt*] If the axe have lost its edge, and the owner do not sharpen it, he must apply the more strength to make it cut: but the *wisdom that is profitable to direct* will teach him, that he should *whet* his *axe,* and *spare* his *strength.* Thus, without wisdom and understanding we cannot go profitably through the meanest concerns in life.

Verse 11. *The serpent will bite without enchantment*] בלא לחש *belo lachash,* without *hissing.* As a snake may bite before it hiss, so also will the babbler, talkative person, or calumniator. Without directly speaking evil, he insinuates, by innuendoes, things injurious to the reputation of his neighbour. 𝔊𝔦𝔱 𝔱𝔥𝔢 𝔢𝔟𝔟𝔦𝔯 𝔟𝔦𝔱𝔢 𝔦𝔫 𝔰𝔦𝔩𝔢𝔫𝔠𝔢, 𝔫𝔬𝔱𝔥𝔦𝔫𝔤 𝔩𝔞𝔰𝔰𝔢 𝔱𝔥𝔞𝔫 𝔥𝔢 𝔥𝔞𝔱𝔥 𝔱𝔥𝔞𝔱 𝔭𝔯𝔦𝔳𝔦𝔩𝔶 𝔟𝔞𝔠𝔨𝔟𝔦𝔱𝔢𝔱𝔥.—Old MS. Bible. "A babbler of his tongue is no better than a serpent that styngeth without hyssynge."—COVERDALE. The *moral* of this saying is simply this: A calumniator is as dangerous as a poisonous serpent; and from the envenomed tongue of slander and detraction no man is safe. The comparing the serpent, נחש *nachash,* to a *babbler,* has something singular in it. I have already supposed that the creature mentioned, Gen. iii. 1, was of the genus *simia.* This has been ridiculed, but not *disproved.*

Verse 12. *The words of a wise man's mouth*]

A. M. cir. 3027
B. C. cir. 977
Ante I. Olymp.
cir. 201
Ante U. C. cir.
224

13 The beginning of the words of his mouth *is* foolishness: and the end of ᑫhis talk *is* mischievous madness.

14 ʳA fool also ˢis full of words: a man cannot tell what shall be; and ᵗwhat shall be after him, who can tell him?

15 The labor of the foolish wearieth every one of them, because he knoweth not how to go to the city.

16 ᵘWo to thee, O land, when thy king *is* a child, and thy princes eat in the morning!

17 Blessed *art* thou, O land, when thy king *is* the son of nobles, and ᵛthy princes eat in

due season, for strength, and not for drunkenness!

18 By much slothfulness the building decayeth; and through idleness of the hands the house droppeth through.

19 A feast is made for laughter, and ʷwine ˣmaketh merry: but money answereth all *things.*

20 ʸCurse not the king, no, not in thy ᶻthought; and curse not the rich in thy bedchamber: for a bird of the air shall carry the voice, and that which hath wings shall tell the matter.

A. M. cir. 3027
B. C. cir. 977
Ante I. Olymp.
cir. 201
Ante U. C. cir.
224

ᑫHeb. *his mouth*——ʳProv. xv. 2——ˢHeb. *multiplieth words*——ᵗChap. iii. 22; vi. 12; viii. 7——ᵘIsa. iii. 4, 5, 12; v. 11——ᵛProv. xxxi. 4

ʷPsalm civ. 15——ˣHeb. *maketh glad the life* ʸExodus xxii. 28; Acts xxiii. 5——ᶻOr, *conscience*, figure like, Luke xix. 40

Every thing that proceeds from him is decent and orderly; creditable to himself, and acceptable to those who hear him. But the *lips of the fool*, which speak every thing at random, and have no understanding to guide them, are not only not pleasant to others, but often destructive to himself.

Verse 14. A man cannot tell what shall be] A foolish babbling man will talk on every subject, though he can say as little on the *past*, as he can on the *future*.

Verse 15. He knoweth not how to go to the city.] I suppose this to be a proverb: "He knows nothing; he does not know his way to the next village." He may labour; but for want of *judgment* he wearies himself to no purpose.

Verse 16. Wo to thee, O land, when thy king is a child] *Minorities* are, in general, very prejudicial to a state. Regents either disagree, and foment civil wars; or oppress the people. Various discordant interests are raised up in a state during a minority; and the young king, having been under the tutelage of interested men, acts *partially* and *injuriously* to the interests of the people when he comes to the throne; and this produces popular discontent, and a troubled reign.

Thy princes eat in the morning!] They do nothing in order; turn night into day, and day into night; sleep when they should wake, and wake when they should sleep; attending more to chamberings and banquetings, than to the concerns of the state.

Verse 17. When thy king is the son of nobles] Τῖος ἐλευθερων, the son of freemen; persons well acquainted with the principles of civil liberty, and who rule according to them.—*Septuagint.* Such a one as comes to the throne in a legitimate way, from an ancient regal family, whose right to the throne is incontestable. It requires such a long time to establish a regal right, that the state is in continual danger from *pretenders* and *usurpers*, where the king is not the son of nobles.

And thy princes eat in due season] All persons in places of trust for the public weal, from the king to the lowest public functionary, should know, that the public are exceedingly scandalized at repeated accounts of entertain-

ments, where irregularity prevails, much money is expended, and no good done. These things are drawn into precedent, and quoted to countenance debauch in the inferior classes. The natural division of the day for necessary *repasts* is, BREAKFAST, *eight*, or *half after;* DINNER, *one*, or *half after;* SUPPER, *eight*, or *half after.* And these, or even *earliers* hours were formerly observed in these countries. Then we had scarcely any such thing as *gout*, and no *nervous disorders*.

In ancient nations the custom was to eat but *once;* and then about mid-day.

Verse 18. By much slothfulness] This is remarkably the case in some countries. Houses are not repaired till they almost fall about the ears of the inhabitants. We have an adage that applies to all such cases: "A stitch in time saves nine."

Verse 19. A feast is made for laughter] The object of it is to produce merriment, to banish care and concern of every kind. But who are they who make and frequent such places? Epicures and drunkards generally; such as those of whom *Horace* speaks:

Nos numerus sumus, et fruges consumere nati.
Epist. lib. i., ep. 2, ver. 27.

"Those whose names stand as indications of *men*, the *useless many;* and who appear to be born only to consume the produce of the soil."

But money answereth all] This saying has prevailed everywhere.

Scilicet uxorem *cum* dote, fidemque, *et* amicos,
Et genus, *et* formam REGINA PECUNIA *donat;*
Ac bene nummatum *decorat* Suadela, Venusque.
HOR. Ep. lib. i., ep. 6, ver. 36.

"For *gold*, the *sovereign* QUEEN of *all below,*
Friends, honour, birth, and *beauty,* can bestow.
The goddess of *persuasion* forms her train;
And *Venus* decks the *well-bemonied* swain."
FRANCIS.

Verse 20. Curse not the king] Do not permit thyself even to think evil of the king; lest thy tongue at some time give vent to thy thoughts, and so thou be chargeable with treason.

For a bird of the air shall carry the voice] Does he refer here to such fowls as the *carrier pigeon*, which were often used to carry letters under their wings to a great distance, and bring back answers? The *Targum* turns it curiously: "Do not speak evil of the king in thy conscience, nor in the secret of thy heart, nor in the most hidden place in thy house, curse not a wise man; for *Raziel* calls daily from heaven upon Mount Horeb, and his voice goes through the whole world; and *Elijah*, the great priest, goes, flying through the air like a winged eagle, and publishes the words which are spoken in secret by all the inhabitants of the earth."

Civil government is so peculiarly of God, that he will have it supported for the benefit of mankind; and those who attempt to disturb it are generally *marked* by his *strong disapprobation*. And though there have been multitudes of treasons hatched in the deepest secrecy; yet, through the providence of God, they have been discovered in the most singular manner. This shows God's care for government.

CHAPTER XI

Give alms to all, 1–4. The works of God unknown to man, 5. Diligence necessary, 6. Prosperity frequently succeeded by adversity, 7, 8. There will be a day of judgment, 9, 10.

A. M. cir. 3027
B. C. cir. 977
Ante I. Olymp.
cir. 201
Ante U. C. cir.
224

CAST thy bread [a]upon [b]the waters: [c]for thou shalt find it after many days.

2 [d]Give a portion [e]to seven, and also to eight; [f]for thou knowest not what evil shall be upon the earth.

3 If the clouds be full of rain, they empty *themselves* upon the earth: and if the tree fall toward the south, or toward the north, in the place where the tree falleth, there it shall be.

A. M. cir. 3027
B. C. cir. 977
Ante I. Olymp.
cir. 201
Ante U. C. cir.
224

4 He that observeth the wind shall not sow; and he that regardeth the clouds shall not reap.

5 As [g]thou knowest not what *is* the way of the spirit, [h]nor how the bones *do grow* in

---

[a]See Isa. xxxii. 20——[b]Heb. *upon the face of the waters*——[c]Deut. xv. 10; Prov. xix. 17; Matt. x. 42; 2 Chron. ix. 8; Gal. vi. 9, 10; Heb. vi. 10

[d]Psa. cxii. 9; Luke vi. 30; 1 Tim. vi. 18, 19——[e]Mic. v. 5——[f]Eph. v. 16——[g]John iii. 8——[h]Psalm cxxxix. 14, 15

NOTES ON CHAP. XI

Verse 1. *Cast thy bread upon the waters*] An allusion to the *sowing of rice;* which was sown upon muddy ground, or ground covered with water, and trodden in by the feet of cattle: it thus took root, and grew, and was *found after many days* in a plentiful harvest. Give alms to the poor, and it will be as seed sown in good ground. God will cause the *afterwards* to receive it with abundant increase. The *Targum* understands it of giving bread to poor sailors. The *Vulgate* and my *old Bible* have the same idea. 𝕾𝖊𝖓𝖉 𝖙𝖍𝖎 𝖇𝖗𝖊𝖉𝖊 𝖚𝖕𝖔𝖓 𝖒𝖊𝖓 𝖕𝖆𝖘𝖘𝖎𝖓𝖌 𝖜𝖆𝖙𝖊𝖗𝖘.

Verse 2. *Give a portion to seven*] Never cease giving while thou seest a person in distress, and hast wherewithal to relieve him.

Thou knowest not what evil] Such may be the change of times, that thou mayest yet stand in need of similar help thyself. *Do as thou wouldst be done by.*

Verse 3. *If the clouds be full of rain.*] Act as the clouds; when they are full they pour out their water indifferently on the *field* and on the *desert.* By giving charity indiscriminately, it may be that thou wilt often give it to the *unworthy;* but thou shouldst ever consider that he is an object of thy charity, who *appears* to be in real want; and better relieve or give to a *hundred* worthless persons, than pass by one who is in real distress.

Where the tree falleth, there it shall be.] Death is at no great distance; thou hast but a short time to do good. Acquire a heavenly *disposition* while here; for there will be no *change after this life.* If thou die in the love of God, and in the love of man, in that state wilt thou be found in the day of judgment. If a tree about to fall lean to the *north*, to the north it will fall; if to the *south*, it will fall to that *quarter.* In whatever *disposition* or *state of soul* thou diest, in that thou *wilt be found* in the *eternal world.* Death *refines nothing, purifies nothing, kills no sin, helps to no glory.* Let thy continual *bent* and *inclination* be to God, to holiness, to charity, to mercy, and to heaven: then, fall when thou mayest, thou wilt fall well.

Verse 4. *He that observeth the wind shall not sow*] The man that is too scrupulous is never likely to succeed in any thing. If a man neither plough nor sow till the weather is entirely to his mind, the season will in all probability pass before he will have done any thing: so, if thou be too nice in endeavouring to find out who are the *impostors* among those who *profess to be in want*, the real object may perish, whom otherwise thou mightest have relieved, and whose life might have been thereby saved. Those very punctilious and scrupulous people, who will *sift every thing* to the bottom in *every case*, and, before they will act, must be *fully satisfied* on all points, seldom do any good, and are themselves generally good for nothing. While they are *observing the clouds* and *the rain*, others have joined hands with God, and made a poor man live.

Verse 5. *As thou knowest not—the way of the spirit*] Why God should have permitted such an such persons to fall into want, and *how* they came into all their distresses, thou canst not tell, no more than thou canst how *their soul* is united to their body, how it came to *inform* that body, or how the *child* was formed in *the womb of its mother.* Nor canst thou discern the *end* which God has in view in these things. *He maketh all*, every thing is open to him; and take heed lest, while pretending motives of scrupulosity and prudence, in not relieving the distresses of those thou pre-

A. M. cir. 3027
B. C. cir. 977
Ante I. Olymp. cir. 201
Ante U. C. cir. 224

the womb of her that is with child: even so thou knowest not the works of God who maketh all.

6 In the morning sow thy seed, and in the evening withhold not thine hand: for thou knowest not whether [i]shall prosper, either this or that, or whether they both *shall be* alike good.

7 Truly the light *is* sweet, and a pleasant *thing it is* for the eyes [k]to behold the sun:

8 But if a man live many years, *and* re-

---

joice in them all; yet let him remember the days of darkness: for they shall be many. All that cometh *is* vanity.

A. M. cir. 3027
B. C. cir. 977
Ante I. Olymp. cir. 201
Ante U. C. cir. 224

9 Rejoice, O young man, in thy youth; and let thy heart cheer thee in the days of thy youth, [l]and walk in the ways of thine heart, and in the sight of thine eyes: but know thou, that for all these *things* [m]God will bring thee into judgment.

10 Therefore remove [n]sorrow from thy heart and [o]put away evil from thy flesh: [p]for childhood and youth *are* vanity.

---

[i]Heb. *shall be right*——[k]Chap. vii. 11——[l]Num. xv. 39 [m]Chap. xii. 14; Rom. ii. 6–11

[n]Or, *anger*——[o]2 Cor. vii. 1; 2 Tim. ii. 22——[p]Psalm xxxix. 5

---

tendest to suspect to be *unworthy*, he does not *see* that a *love of money* is the *motive* of thy conduct, and a *want of the bowels of mercy* the *cause* why thou drivest this *suspected* beggar from thy door.

Verse 6. *In the morning sow thy seed*] Be ready at *all times* to show mercy; begin in the *morning*, continue till the *evening*. Thou knowest not the most worthy object; it is enough that God knoweth; and if thy motive be *good*, he will applaud and reward thee; not according to the *worthiness* or *unworthiness* of the *object* of thy charity, but according to the *motive* which induced thee to relieve him.

Verse 7. *Truly the light is sweet*] Life is dear to every man as the *light of the sun* is to the *eye*. A man would give all that he has for his life; and it is particularly dear to him when he is in ease and affluence: but let each remember that,

Verse 8. *If a man live many years*] And even have *prosperity* through the whole; yet the *days of darkness*—times of affliction, weakness, and perhaps *old age, will be many.* If he die not a *violent* death, which no man can wish, he will die a *lingering death;* and this is ordinarily attended with many *pains*, and many *sorrows;* therefore let him prepare to meet his God; and to carry this thought through life,

---

that all must terminate in death. The writer of *Ecclesiasticus*, chap. vii. 36, has a good saying, similar to this: "Whatsoever thou takest in hand, remember *thy* END; and thou shalt never do amiss;" ουκ αμαρτησεις, *thou wilt not sin.*

Verse 9. *Rejoice, O young man, in thy youth*] *Youth* is devoid of cares; and, consequently, of many perplexities and distresses. Were it not so, we should have no *old men;* nay, perhaps not *one* even of *middle age.* It is in the order of a most gracious God, that the *young* should *rejoice* in their *youth;* but they should make such a moderate use of all their enjoyments, that they may not be confounded in the day of judgment. But, O young man, if thou wilt follow the propensities of thy *own heart*, the noisy mirth of the *fool*, and the dissipation of the *profligate*—*go on;* take thy full swing; but take this with thee, that "for all these things, God will judge thee;" and if the righteous are scarcely saved, where shall the *ungodly* and the *sinner* appear?

Verse 10. *Therefore remove sorrow*] כעם *caas, anger;* every kind of violent passion, all filthiness of *the flesh* and spirit. "Childhood and youth are vanity;" they pass away and come to nothing. Eternity alone is permanent; live for eternity.

CHAPTER XII

Youth should remember their Creator, 1. A description of old age and its infirmities, with the causes of death and dissolution, 2–9. How the Preacher taught the people knowledge, 9–11. General directions, and conclusion of the work, 12–14.

A. M. cir. 3027
B. C. cir. 977
Ante I. Olymp. cir. 201
Ante U. C. cir. 224

REMEMBER [a]now thy Creator in the days of thy youth, while the evil days come not, nor the years draw nigh, [b]when thou

---

shalt say, I have no pleasure in them.

A. M. cir. 3027
B. C. cir. 977
Ante I. Olymp. cir. 201
Ante U. C. cir. 224

2 While the sun, or the light, or the moon, or the stars, be not

---

[a]Prov. xxii. 6; Lam. iii. 27

[b]See 2 Sam. xix. 35

NOTES ON CHAP. XII

Verse 1. *Remember thy Creator*] בוראיך *Boreeycha*, thy CREATORS. The word is most certainly in the *plural* number in all our common Hebrew Bibles; but it is in the *singular*

---

number, בוראך *Borecha*, in *one hundred and seventy-six* of Dr. *Kennicott's* MSS., and *ninety-six* of *De Rossi's;* in many *ancient editions;* and in all the ancient *versions.* There is no dependence on the *plural* form in most of the modern editions; though there are some edi-

A. M. cir. 3027
B. C. cir. 977
Ante I. Olymp.
cir. 201
Ante U. C. cir.
224

darkened, nor the clouds return after the rain;

3 In the day when the keepers of the house shall tremble, and the

strong men shall bow themselves, and ᶜthe grinders cease because they are few, and those that look out of the windows be darkened,

A. M. cir. 3027
B. C. cir. 977
Ante I. Olymp.
cir. 201
Ante U. C. cir.
224

ᶜOr, *the grinders fail*, *because they* grind *little*

---

tions of great worth which exhibit the word in this form, and among them the *Complutensian, Antwerp, Paris,* and *London* polyglots.

The evidence, therefore, that this text is supposed to give to the doctrine of the *ever blessed Trinity,* is but precarious, and on it little stress can be laid; and no man who loves truth would wish to support it by dubious witnesses. Injudicious men, by laying stress on texts dubious in themselves, and which may be interpreted a different way, greatly injure the true faith. Though such in their hearts may be friends to the orthodox faith, they are in fact its *worst friends,* and their assistance is such as helps their *adversaries.*

But what does the text say? It addresses the *youth* of both *sexes* throughout the creation; and says in effect:—

I. You are not your own, you have no right to yourselves. God made you; he is your *Creator:* he made you that you might be happy; but you can be happy only *in him.* And as he *created* you, so he *preserves* you; he *feeds, clothes, upholds* you. He has *made* you capable of *knowing, loving,* and *serving* him in this world, and of *enjoying* him in his own glory for ever. And when you had *undone yourselves* by *sin,* he sent his Son to *redeem* you by his blood; and he sends his *Spirit* to *enlighten, convince,* and *draw you* away from childishness, from vain and trifling, as well as from sinful, pursuits.

II. *Remember* him; consider that he is your *Creator,* your *loving* and affectionate *Father.* In youth *memory is* strong and tenacious; but, through the *perversion of the heart* by *sin,* young people can *remember any thing* better than GOD. If you get a kindness from a friend, you can *remember* that, and *feel gratitude* for it; and the *person* is therefore *endeared* to you. Have any ever given you such *benefits* as your *Creator?* Your *body* and *soul* came from him; he gave you your *eyes, ears, tongue, hands, feet,* &c. What blessings are these! how *excellent!* how *useful!* how *necessary!* and will you *forget* HIM?

III. *Remember him in thy* YOUTH, in order that you may have a *long* and *blessed life,* that you may be saved from the corruption and misery into which young people in general run; and the evils they entail upon themselves by giving way to the sinful propensities of their own hearts. As in youth all the powers are more active and vigorous, so .hey are capable of superior enjoyments. *Faith, hope,* and *love,* will be in their best *tenor,* their greatest *vigour,* and in their *least encumbered state.* And it will be *easier* for you to *believe, hope, pray, love, obey,* and *bear your cross,* than it can be in old age and decrepitude.

IV. *Remember him* NOW, in *this part* of your *youth*—you have no certainty of life; *now* is yours, to-morrow may not be. You *are* young; but you may *never* be old. *Now* he waits to be gracious; *to-morrow* may be too late. God *now* calls; his *Spirit* now strives; his *minis-*

ters* now exhort. You have now *health;* sin has not now *so much dominion over you* as it will have, increasing by every future moment, if you do not give up your hearts to your Maker.

V. There is another consideration which should weigh with you: should you live to *old age,* it is a very disadvantageous time to begin to serve the Lord in. *Infirmities* press down both body and mind, and the oppressed nature has enough to do to bear its own infirmities; and as there is *little time,* so there is generally *less inclination,* to call upon the Lord. *Evil habits* are strengthened by long continuance; and every desire and appetite in the soul is a strong hold for Satan. There is little time for repentance, little for faith, *none* for obedience. The *evil days* are *come,* and the *years* in which you will feelingly be obliged to say, Alas! "we have no pleasure in them;" and, what is worse, the heart is hardened through the *deceitfulness of sin.*

Verse 2. *While the sun, or the light, or the moon, or the stars, be not darkened*] i. e., in the SPRING, prime, and prosperity of life.

Nor the clouds return] The infirmities of old age of which WINTER is a proper emblem, as *spring* is of *youth,* in the former clause of this verse.

Verse 3. *In the day when the keepers of the house*] The BODY of *man* is here compared to a. HOUSE:—mark the metaphors and their propriety.

1. *The keepers shall tremble*—the *hands* become paralytic, as is constantly the case, less or more, in old age.

2. *The strong men shall bow*] The *legs* become feeble, and unable to support the weight of the body.

3. *The grinders cease because they are few*] The *teeth* decayed and mostly lost; the *few* that remain being incapable of properly masticating hard substances or animal food. Anḋ so they *cease;* for soft or pulpy substances, which are requisite then, require little or no mastication; and these aliments become their ordinary food.

4. *Those that look out of the windows*] The *optic nerves,* which receive impressions, through the medium of the different *humours* of the eye, from surrounding objects—they *are darkened;* the humours becoming *thick, flat,* and *turbid,* they are no longer capable of transmitting those images in that clear, distinct manner, as formerly. There may be an allusion here to the *pupil* of the eye. Look into it, and you will see *your own image* in extreme minature *looking out* upon you; and hence it has its name *pupillus,* a *little child,* from *pupus,* a *baby,* a *doll;* because the image in the eye resembles such. The *optic nerve* being seated at the *bottom of the eye,* has the images of surrounding objects painted upon it; *it looks out through the different humors.* The different membranes and humours which compose the eye, and serve for vision, are, the *tunica con-*

A. M. cir. 3027
B. C. cir. 977
Ante I. Olymp. cir. 201
Ante U. C. cir. 224

4 And the ᵈdoors shall be shut in the streets, when the sound of the grinding is low, and he shall rise up at the voice of the bird, and all ᵉthe daughters of music shall be brought low;

5 Also *when* they shall be afraid of *that*

which *is* high, and fears *shall be* in the way, and the almond tree shall flourish, and the grass-hopper shall be a burden, and desire shall fail: because man goeth to ᶠhis long home, and ᵍthe mourners go about the streets:

A. M. cir. 3027
B. C. cir. 977
Ante I. Olymp. cir. 201
Ante U. C. cir. 224

ᵈPsa. cxli. 3——ᵉ2 Sam. xix. 35   ᶠJob xvii. 13——ᵍJer. ix. 17

---

junctiva, the *tunica sclerotica*, the *cornea*, the *iris*, the *pupil*, the *choroides*, and the *retina*. The *iris* is perforated to admit the rays of light, and is called the *pupil;* the *retina* is a diffusion of the *optic nerve* in the bottom of the eye, on which the images are painted or impressed that give us the *sensation* we term *sight* or *vision*. All these *membranes*, *humours*, and *nerves*, are more or less *impaired*, thickened, or rendered *opaque*, by *old age;* expressed by the metaphor, "Those that look out of the windows are darkened."

Verse 4. *And the doors shall be shut in the streets*]

5. The *doors*—the *lips*, which are the *doors* by which the *mouth* is *closed*.

6. *Be shut in the streets*] The *cavities* of the *cheeks* and *jaws*, through which the food may be said to *travel* before it is fitted by *mastication* or chewing to go down the *œsophagus* into the stomach. The *doors* or *lips* are *shut* to hinder the food in chewing from dropping out; as the *teeth*, which prevented that before, are now lost.

7. *The sound of the grinding is low*] Little noise is now made in eating, because the *teeth* are either lost, or become so infirm as not to suffer their being pressed close together; and the mouth being kept shut to hinder the food from dropping out, the *sound* in eating is scarcely heard. The *teeth* are divided into *three* kinds:—1. The *dentes incisores*, or *cutting teeth*, in the front of the jaw. 2. The *dentes canini*, or *dog teeth*, those in the sides of the jaws, for *gnawing*, or *tearing* and *separating* hard or *tough substances*. And, 3. *Dentes molares*, or *grinding teeth*, the posterior or *double teeth*, in both jaws, generally termed the *grinders;* because their office is to *grind down* the substances that have been *cut* by the *fore teeth*, *separated* into their parts or fibres by the *dog teeth*, and thus prepare it for digestion in the stomach.

8. *He shall rise up at the voice of the bird*] His sleep is not *sound* as it used to be; he *slumbers* rather than *sleeps;* and the *crowing of the cock* awakes him. And so much difficulty does he find to *respire* while in bed, that he is glad of the dawn to rise up and get some relief. The chirping of the sparrow is sufficient to awake him.

9. *All the daughters of music shall be brought low*] The VOICE, that wonderful *instrument*, almost endless in the *strength* and *variety* of its *tones*, becomes *feeble* and *squeaking*, and merriment and pleasure are no more. The tones *emitted* are all of the *querulous* or *mournful* kind.

Verse 5. *When they shall be afraid of that which is high*]

10. Being so *feeble*, they are afraid to trust themselves to *ascend steps*, *stairs*, &c., with-

out help. And when they *look upwards*, their heads turn giddy, and they are ready to fall.

11. *Fears shall be in the way*] They dare not walk *out*, lest they should meet some danger, which they have not *strength* to repel, nor *agility* to *escape*. A second childishness has taken place—apprehensions, fears, terrors, and weakness.

12. *The almond tree shall flourish*] יָנֵאץ *yenaets*, not *flourish*, but *fall off*. The *hair* begins to change, first *gray*, then *white;* it having no longer that supply of nutritive juices which it once had, this *animal vegetable withers* and *falls off*. The *almond tree*, having *white flowers*, is a fit emblem of a *hoary head;* or as *Hasselquist* says, who observed the tree in full flower in Judea, "like an old man with his *white locks*."

13. *The grasshopper shall be a burden*] Even such an inconsiderable thing as a *locust*, or a very small *insect*, shall be deemed burdensome, their strength is so exceedingly diminished. In cases of the *gout*, especially in *old men*, the *shadow* of a person passing by puts them to acute pain! How much less can they bear the smallest pressure! But probably the words refer to the man himself, who, bent at the loins, and his arms hanging down, exhibits some caricature of the animal in question. The poor grasshopper has become a burden to himself. Another interpretation has been given of the *grasshopper;* but I pass it by as impertinent and contemptible; such commentators appear as if they wished to render the text ridiculous.

14. *Desire shall fail*] Both *relish* and *appetite* for food, even the most *delicate*, that to which they were formerly so much *attached*, now *fails*. The *teeth* are no longer able to *masticate* the food, or have all *dropped out;* the stomach no longer able to digest any thing; and, as the body is no longer capable of receiving nourishment, *appetite* and *relish* necessarily fail.

15. *Because man goeth to his long home*] אֶל בֵּית עוֹלָמוֹ *el beith olamo*, "to the house of his age;" the place destined to receive him, when the *whole race* or *course* of life shall be *finished;* for עוֹלָם *olam* takes in the *whole course* or *duration of a thing;* if applied to a *dispensation*, such as the LAW, it takes in its *whole duration;* to the *life* of man, it takes in the *whole life;* to *time*, it includes its whole compass; to *eternity*, it expresses its infinite duration. So *old age* terminates the *olam*, the complete duration of human life; and when life is no longer desired, and nutrition ceases, the *olam* of man is terminated. My old MS. Bible translates it, 𝕿𝖍𝖊 𝖍𝖔𝖚𝖘 𝖔𝖋 𝖍𝖎𝖘 𝖊𝖇𝖊𝖗𝖑𝖆𝖘𝖙𝖎𝖓𝖌𝖓𝖊𝖘𝖘.

16. He is just departing into the invisible world; and this is known by the *mourners going about the streets*, the *long hollow groans* and *throat rattlings* which proceed from him;

A. M. cir. 3027
B. C. cir. 977
Ante I. Olymp. cir. 201
Ante U. C. cir. 224

6 Or ever the silver cord be loosed, or the golden bowl be broken, or the pitcher be broken at the fountain, or the wheel broken at the cistern.

7 [h]Then shall the dust return to the earth as it was: [i]and the spirit shall return unto God [k]who gave it.

---

[h]Gen. iii. 19; Job xxxiv. 15; Psa. xc. 3——[i]Chap. iii. 21——[k]Num. xvi. 22; xxvii. 16; Job xxxiv. 14; Isa. lvii. 16; Zech. xii. 1

---

8 [l]Vanity of vanities, saith the Preacher, all *is* vanity.

9 And [m]moreover, because the Preacher was wise, he still taught the people knowledge; yea, he gave good heed, and sought out, *and* [n]set in order many proverbs.

10 The Preacher sought to find out [o]ac-

A. M. cir. 3027
B. C. cir. 977
Ante I. Olymp. cir. 201
Ante U. C. cir. 224

---

[l]Psa. lxii. 9; chap. i. 2——[m]Or, *the more wise the Preacher was,* &c.——[n]1 Kings iv. 32——[o]Hebrew, *words of delight*

---

the sure prognostications of the extreme *debility* and *speedy cessation* of those essential animal functions next mentioned.

Verse 6. *Or ever the silver cord be loosed*] We have already *had* all the *external* evidences of *old age,* with all its attendant infirmities; next follow what takes place *in* the body, in order to produce what is called *death,* or the separation of body and soul.

1. *The silver cord.*—The *medulla oblongata* or *spinal marrow,* from which all the nerves proceed, as itself does from the *brain.* This is termed a *cord,* from its *exact similitude* to one; and a *silver cord,* from its *colour,* as it strikingly exhibits the *silver gray;* and from its *preciousness.* This is said to be *loosed;* as the *nervous system* became a little before, and at the article of death, wholly debilitated. The last *loosing* being the *fall of the under jaw,* the invariable and never-failing evidence of *immediate death;* a few struggles more, and the soul is dismissed from its clay tenement.

2. *The golden bowl be broken*] The *brain* contained in the *cranium,* or skull, and enveloped with the membranes called the *dura* and *pia mater;* here called a *bowl,* from its resemblance to such a vessel, the *container* being put for the *contained;* and *golden* because of its *colour,* and because of its exceeding *preciousness,* as has been noticed in the former case. *Broken*—be rendered *unfit to perform its functions,* neither supplying nor distributing any *nervous energy.*

3. *Or the pitcher be broken at the fountain*] The *vena cava,* which brings back the blood to the *right ventricle* of the heart, here called the *fountain,* המבוע *hammabbua,* the *spring* whence the water *gushes up;* properly applied here to the heart, which by its *systole* and *diastole* (*contraction* and *expansion*) sends out, and afterwards receives back, the blood; for all the blood flows from, and returns back to, the heart.

4. *The wheel broken at the cistern*] The *great aorta,* which receives the blood from the *cistern,* the *left ventricle* of the heart, and distributes it to the different parts of the system. These may be said, as in the case of the *brain* above, to be *broken,* i. e., rendered useless; when, through the *loosening of the silver cord,* the total relaxation of the *nervous system,* the *heart* becomes incapable of *dilatation* and *contraction,* so that the blood, on its return to the *right ventricle* of the heart, is not *received,* nor that already contained in the *ventricles* propelled into the great *aorta.* The *wheel* is used in allusion to the Asiatic *wheels,* by which they raise water from their wells and tanks, and deep cisterns, for domestic purposes, or to irrigate the grounds. Thus, then, the blood be-

comes stagnate; the lungs cease to respire; the blood is no longer *oxidized;* all motion, voluntary and involuntary, ceases; the body, the house of the immortal spirit, is no longer tenantable, and the soul takes its flight into the eternal world. The man D—I—E—S! This is expressed in the following verse:—

Verse 7. *Then shall the dust return to the earth as it was: and the spirit shall return unto God*]

5. Putrefaction and solution take place; the whole mass becomes decomposed, and in process of time is reduced to dust, from which it was originally made; while the spirit, הרוח *haruach,* that spirit, which God at first breathed into the nostrils of man, when he in consequence became a LIVING SOUL, an intelligent, rational, discoursing animal, returns to God who gave it. Here the wise man makes a most evident distinction between the body and the soul: they are not the same; they are not both matter. The body, which is matter, returns to dust, its original; but the spirit, which is *immaterial,* returns to God. It is impossible that two natures can be more distinct, or more emphatically distinguished. The author of this book was not a materialist.

Thus ends this affecting, yet elegant and finished, picture of OLD AGE and DEATH. See a description of old age similar, but much inferior, to this, in the Agamemnon of Æschylus, v. 76-82.

It has been often remarked that the *circulation of the blood,* which has been deemed a modern discovery by our countryman Dr. *Harvey,* in 1616, was known to Solomon, or whoever was the author of this book: the *fountains, cisterns, pitcher,* and *wheel,* giving sufficient countenance to the conclusion.

Verse 8. This affecting and minute description of *old age* and *death* is concluded by the author with the same exclamation by which he began this book: *O vanity of vanities,* saith Koheleth, *all is* vanity. Now that man, the masterpiece of God's creation, the delegated sovereign of this lower world, is *turned to dust,* what is there *stable* or worthy of contemplation besides? ALL—ALL is VANITY!

Verse 9. *Because the Preacher was wise, he still taught the people knowledge*] And in order to do this he took *good heed*—considered what would be most useful. *He set in order*—collected and arranged, many parables, probably alluding to the book over which we have already passed.

Verse 10. *He sought to find out acceptable words*] דברי חפץ *dibrey chephets,* words of desire, words of will; the best, the most suitable words; those which the people could best

A. M. cir. 3027
B. C. cir. 977
Ante I. Olymp.
cir. 201
Ante U. C. cir.
224 ceptable words: *and that which was* written *was* upright, *even* words of truth.

11 The words of the wise *are* as goads, and as nails fastened *by* the masters of assemblies, *which* are given from one shepherd.

12 And farther, by these, my son, be admonished: of making many books *there is* no end; and ᴾmuch �qstudy *is* a weariness of the flesh.

13 ʳLet us hear the conclusion of the whole matter: ˢFear God, and keep his commandments: for this *is* the whole *duty* of man.

14 For ᵗGod shall bring every work into judgment, with every secret thing, whether *it* be good, or whether *it* be evil.

A. M. cir. 3027
B. C. cir. 977
Ante I. Olymp.
cir. 201
Ante U. C. cir.
224

ᴾChap. i. 18——�q̇Or, *reading*——ʳOr, *The end of the matter, even* all that hath been heard, *is*——ˢDeut. vi. 2; x. 12

ᵗChap. xi. 9; Matt. xii. 36; Acts xvii. 30, 31; Rom. ii. 16 xiv. 10, 12; 1 Cor. iv. 5; 2 Cor. v. 10

---

understand. But these words were not such as might merely please the people; they were *words of truth;* such as came from God, and might lead them to him.

Verse 11. *The words of the wise*] Doctrines of faith, illustrated by suitable language, are *as nails fastened* by the *masters of assemblies,*

בעלי אספות *baaley asuphoth,* the *masters of collections,* those who had made the best collections of this kind, the *matter* of which was of the most excellent nature; every saying sinking as deeply into the mind, by the *force* of the *truth* contained in it, as a *nail* well *pointed* does into a *board,* when *impelled by the hammer's force.* These *masters of collections* have been supposed to be public persons appointed by the *prince* himself, the *sole shepherd,* to see that nothing was put into the people's hands but what would be profitable for them to read; and that, when any wise man gave public instructions, a good *scribe* sat by to take down the words; and then the master examined what he *had written,* to see that it was *upright,* and that the words were *doctrines of truth.* These were something like our *licensers of the press;* but the existence of such is little more than conjecture.

After all, *masters of assemblies* may mean *public teachers;* that *which was written,* the oracles of God, out of which they instructed the people; the *one Shepherd,* GOD ALMIGHTY, from whom they received their authority and unction to preach the truth; and by the energy of whose *Spirit* the heavenly teaching was fastened in their hearts, as a *well-driven nail* in a *sound piece of wood.*

Verse 12. *And farther, by these, my son, be admonished*] Hear such teachers, and receive their admonitions; and do not receive the grace of God in vain.

Of making many books there is *no end*] Two thousand years have elapsed since this was written; and since that time some millions of treatises have been added, on all kinds of subjects, to those which have gone before. The press is still groaning under and teeming with books, books innumerable; and no one subject is yet *exhausted,* notwithstanding all that has been written on it. And we who live in these *latter times* are no nearer an end, in the investigation of NATURE and its *properties;* of GOD, his attributes, his providence, his justice, and his mercy; of MAN, his animal life, his mode of nutrition and existence, and his soul and its powers; of JESUS, and the redemption by him; of ETERNITY, and what it implies as exhibiting to us the pains of the cursed, and the glories of the blessed. Of several of these we know no more than they who have lived *five thousand* years before us; nor do we know any thing *certainly* by the *endless books* that have been published, except what bears the seal of the God of heaven, as published in that word which was declared by his Spirit.

And much study is *a weariness of the flesh.*] O how true is this! Let the trembling knees, the palsied hands, the darkened eyes, the aching heart, and the puzzled mind of every real student declare! And should none more worthy of the name of student be within reach to consult, the writer of this work is a proof in point.

Verse 13. After all, the sum of the great business of human life is comprised in this short sentence, on which some millions of books have been already written!

FEAR GOD, AND KEEP HIS COMMANDMENTS

1. Know that HE IS, and that he is a rewarder of them that diligently seek him. 2. Reverence him; pay him adoration. 3. Love him, that you may be happy.

Keep his commandments] They are contained in two words: 1. "Thou shalt love the Lord thy God with all thy heart;" 2. "And thy neighbour as thyself." Blessed be God, much reading and much study are not necessary to accomplish this, which is called כל האדם *col haadam,* the whole of Adam; the whole that God required of the *first man* and of *all his posterity.* But the *Gospel* of Jesus Christ must be understood to comprehend the full force of this short saying.

The word *duty,* added here by our translators, *spoils,* if not PERVERTS, the sense.

The whole passage is rendered with great simplicity by *Coverdale:*—

"The same preacher was not wyse alone: but taught the people knowledge also. He gave good hede, sought out the grounde, and set forth many parables. His diligence was to fynde out acceptable wordes, right scripture, and the wordes of trueth. For the wordes of the wyse are like prickes and nales that go thorow, wherewith men are kepte together: for they are geven of one Shepherd onely. Therefore be warre (my sonne) that above these thou make thee not many and innumerable bookes, nor take dyverse doctrynes in hande, to weery thy body withall.

"Let us heare the conclucion of all thinges: Feare God, and kepe his comaundementes, for that toucheth all men; for God shall judge all workes and secrete thinges, whether they be good or evell."

I shall give the same from my old MS. Bible:—

And wan Ecclesiastes was most wiis he taght the peple, and told out what he had don, and enserchinge maade many parablis. He soght profitable wordis, and wrote most rigt sermons, and ful of trewth. The wordis of wismen as prickis and as nailis into herte pigt: that bi the counseyle of maisteris ben geben of oon scheperd. More thann thes sone mpn, ne seche thou; of making many bokes is noon eend, and oft bethinking is tormenting of the flesche. Eend of spekinge alle togydir heere mee. Drede God, and his hestis kepe; that is eche man. Alle thingis that ben maad he schal bringen into dome, for eche erid thinge, whithir good or ebyl it be.

Verse 14. *For God shall bring every work into judgment*] This is the *reason* why we should "fear God and keep his commandments." 1. Because there will be a *day of judgment.* 2. Every soul of man shall stand at that bar. 3. God, the infinitely wise, the heart-searching God, will be judge. 4. He will bring to light every *secret thing*—all that has been done since the creation, by all men; whether *forgotten* or *registered;* whether *done in secret* or *in public.* 5. All the works of the *godly*, as well as all the works of the *wicked*, shall be judged in that day; the *good* which the *godly* strove to *conceal*, as well as the *evil* which the *wicked* endeavoured to *hide.* This, then, will be the *conclusion* of the whole mortal story. And although in this world *all is vanity;* yet *there*, "vanities will be vain no more." Every thing, whether *good* or *evil*, will have its own proper, stable, eternal *result.* O God! prepare the reader to give up his accounts with joy in that day! Amen.

MASORETIC NOTES

Number of verses, 222.
Middle verse, chap. vi. 10.
Sections, 4.
The ARABIC subjoins this colophon:—"Praise be to God for ever and ever!"
"By the assistance of the Most High God this book of Ecclesiastes, which is vanity of vanities, written by Solomon the son of David, who reigned over the children of Israel, is completed."
The SYRIAC has, "The end of the book of Koheleth."
There are others, but they are of no importance.

INTRODUCTION

TO THE

CANTICLES, OR SONG OF SOLOMON

THE book before us is called in the Hebrew שיר השירים SHIR HASHSHIRIM, "The Song of Songs;" or, "An Ode of the Odes:" which might be understood, "An Ode *taken* or selected *from others* of a similar kind;" or, "An Ode the *most excellent* of all others;" this being an idiom common to the Hebrew language: e. g., the *God of gods* is the supreme God; the *Lord of lords*, the supreme Lord; the *King of kings*, the supreme King; the *heaven of heavens*, the supreme or highest heaven. It may therefore be designed to express "a song of the *utmost perfection; one of the best that existed, or had ever been penned.*" Perhaps the title may have a reference to the other poetical compositions of Solomon, which were no less than *one thousand and five;* and this was considered the *most excellent* of the whole, and the *only one* that remains, unless we suppose Solomon, with some of the Jews, to be the author of Psalms lxxii. and cxxvii.: but this cannot be proved.

There have been some doubts concerning the author of this book. Some of the rabbins supposed it to be the work of the prophet Isaiah; but this sentiment never gained much credit. Most have, without hesitation, attributed it to Solomon, whose name it bears; and if the book of Ecclesiastes be his, this will follow in course, as the *style* is exactly the same, allowing for the difference of the subject. Both books seem to have been written about the same *time*, and to have had the same *author.*

This book, if written by Solomon, could not have been written in his *old age*, as some have supposed the book of Ecclesiastes to have been; which sentiment is, I think, sufficiently disproved; for we find that long before Solomon's old age he had *three hundred* wives, and *seven hundred* concubines; but at the time this Song was written, Solomon had only *sixty* wives and *eighty* concubines. And the Song most certainly celebrates a *marriage;* whether between *Solomon* and the *daughter of Pharaoh*, or between him and some *Jewish princess*, has not been fully agreed on among critics and commentators. It is most likely to have been a *juvenile* or *comparatively juvenile* production; and indeed the high and glowing colouring, and the strength of the images, are full proofs of this. Though *Anacreon* made amatory odes when he was *bald-headed*, yet neither he nor *any one else*, humanly speaking, could have made such odes as the Canticles when stricken in years.

But to what denomination of writing do the Canticles belong? Are they mere *Odes*, or *Idyls*, or *Pastorals;* or are they an *Epithalamium?* Let us define these terms, and examine the Song of Solomon by them. 1. The ODE is generally understood to be a species of poetry containing sublime and important matter, always *sung*, or accompanied by the *harp*, or some proper *musical instrument*. 2. The IDYL implies a *short poem*, containing some *adventure*. 3. The PASTORAL contains what belongs to *shepherds*, and their *occupations*. 4. The EPITHALAMIUM is the congratulatory song, sung to a new married pair, wishing them abundant blessings, a numerous and happy offspring, &c. Strictly speaking, the book of Canticles falls under neither of these descriptions: it is rather a composition *sui generis*, and seems to partake more of the nature of what we call a MASK, than any thing else; an entertainment for the guests who attended the marriage ceremony, with a *dramatic cast* throughout the whole, though the *persons* who speak and act are not formally introduced. There are so many touches in the form and manner of this Song like those in the *Comus* of Milton, that it leads me to doubt whether the *English poet* has not taken the idea of his *mask* from the *Jewish*.

As to the *persons*, chiefly concerned, it is generally believed that *Solomon* and *Pharaoh's daughter* are the *bridegroom* and *bride;* with their proper *attendants*, viz., companions of the bridegroom, and companions of the bride, with certain *mutes*, who only appear, or are mentioned by others, without taking any particular part in the transactions.

But it is much more easy to be satisfied on the *species* of composition to which this book belongs, than on the *meaning* of the book itself. Is it to be understood in the *obvious manner* in which it presents itself? And are Solomon and his bride, their friends and companions, to be considered as mere *dramatis personæ?* Or are they *typical* or *representative* persons? Does this *marriage* represent a *celestial union?* Do the *speeches* of each contain Divine doctrines? Are the *metaphors*, taken from *earthly* things, to be understood of *spiritual* matters? In a word, does *Solomon* here represent *Jesus Christ?* Is the *daughter of Pharaoh* the *Christian Church;* or, according to some Roman Catholics, the Virgin Mary? Are *watchmen, vineyard-keepers, shepherds, &c.*, the *ministers* of the *Gospel? Wine* and *various fruits*, the *influences* and *graces* of the Divine Spirit? &c., &c. How multitudinous and *positive* are the *affirmative* answers to these questions! And yet, though the many agree in the general principle, how various their expositions of the different parts of the piece! And where, all this time, is the *proof* that the *principle* is not misunderstood? As to *conjectures*, they are as *uncertain* as they are endless; and what one pious or learned man may *think* to be the meaning, is no proof to any other that he should make up his mind in the *same way*.

Let us for a moment consider the different opinions held on this book, without entering into the discussion of their propriety or impropriety. They are the following:—

I. It is a plain *epithalamium* on the marriage of Solomon with the *daughter of Pharaoh*, king of Egypt; and is to be understood in no other way.

II. It is an *allegory* relative to the conduct of God towards the Hebrews, in bringing them out of Egypt, through the wilderness to the Promised Land.

III. It is intended to represent the *incarnation* of Jesus Christ, or his marriage with human nature, in reference to its redemption.

IV. It represents Christ's love to the Church or elected souls, and their love to him.

V. It is an *allegorical poem* on the glories of *Jesus Christ* and the *Virgin Mary*.

VI. It is a collection of sacred idyls; the spiritual meaning of which is not agreed on.

Now each of these opinions has its powerful supporters, and each of these has reasons to offer for the support of the opinion which is espoused; and nothing but a direct revelation from God can show us which of these opinions is the correct one, or whether any of them are correct.

The *antiquity* of an opinion, if that be not founded on a *revelation from God*, is no evidence of its truth; for there are many ungodly opinions which are more than a *thousand* years old. And as to *great men* and *great names*, we find them enrolled and arranged on each side of all controversies. It may be asked, What do Christ and his apostles say of it?

1. If Jesus Christ or any of his apostles had referred to it as an *allegory*, and told us the *subject* which it pointed out, the matter would have been *plain:* we should then have had *data*, and had only to proceed in the way of *elucidation*. But we find nothing of this in the New Testament.

2. If they had referred to it as an *allegory*, without intimating the *meaning*, then we should be justified in searching everywhere for that meaning; and *conjecture* itself would have been legal, till we had arrived at some *self-testifying issue*.

3. If they had referred to it at all, in connection with *spiritual* subjects, then we should

have at once seen that it was to be *spiritually understood;* and, comparing spiritual things with spiritual, we must have humbly sought for its spiritual interpretation.

4. Had the *Supreme Being* been introduced, or referred to in any of his *essential attributes,* or by any of the names which he has been pleased to assume in his revelations to men, we should have then seen that the writer was a *spiritual man,* and wrote probably in reference to a *spiritual end;* and, that we should pass by or through his *letter,* in order to get to the *spirit* concealed under it. But none of these things appear in this book: the *name of God* is not found in it; nor is it *quoted* in the *New Testament.* As to certain *references* which its allegorical expositors suppose are made to it, either in the *Gospels, Epistles,* or *Apocalypse,* they are not *express,* and do not, by any thing *in* or *connected with* them, appear *unequivocally* to point out this book. And after all that has been said, I am fully of opinion it is not once referred to in the New Testament. But this is no proof of its not being *canonical,* as there are other books, on which there is no doubt, that are in the same predicament. But still, if it refer so distinctly to Christ and his Church, as some suppose, it certainly would not have been passed over by both evangelists and apostles without pointed and especial notice; and particularly if it points out the *love of Christ to his Church,* and the whole *economy* of God's working in reference to the salvation of the souls of men.

From all this it will appear to the intelligent reader, that the *spiritual meaning* of this book cannot easily be made out: 1. Because we do not know that it is an *allegory.* 2. If one, the *principles* on which such allegory is to be explained do nowhere appear.

Whom then are we to follow in the interpretation of this very singular book? The *Targumist,* who applies it to God and the *Hebrews,* in their journeyings from Egypt to the promised land? *Origen,* who made it a Christian allegory? *Apponius,* who spiritualized it? *Gregory the Great,* who in the main copied them? The *good man,* who in 1717, at Paris, so illustrated it as "to induce men to devote themselves to Jesus Christ and the Virgin Mary?" Mr. *Durham,* Mr. *Robotham,* Mr. *Ainsworth,* Mr. *Romaine,* and Dr. *Gill,* who endeavoured to prove that it concerns *Christ* and *the elect?* Or Mr. *Harmer* and others who acknowledge it to be an inimitable composition, and to be understood only of Solomon and Pharaoh's daughter? Or, finally, Dr. *Mason Good,* who considers it a collection of sacred idyls, the spiritual interpretation of which is not agreed on?

I had for a long time hesitated whether I should say any thing on this book; not because I did not think I understood its chief design and general meaning, for of this I really have no doubt, but because I did not understand it as a *spiritual allegory,* representing the *loves of Christ and his Church.* I must own I see no indubitable ground for this opinion. And is it of no moment whether the *doctrines* drawn from it, by those who allegorize and spiritualize it, be indubitably founded on it or not? The doctrines may be true in themselves, (which is indeed more than can be said of those of most of its interpreters,) but is it not a very *solemn,* and indeed *awful* thing to say, *This* is the *voice* of *Christ* to his *Church, This* is the *voice* of the *Church* to *Christ,* &c., &c., when there is *no proof* from God, nor from any other portion of his word, that these things are so?

It is much better, therefore, if explained or illustrated at all, to take it in its *literal* meaning, and explain it in its *general* sense. I say *general* sense, because there are many passages in it which should not be explained, if taken literally, the references being too delicate; and Eastern phraseology on such subjects is too vivid for European imaginations. Let any sensible and pious medical man read over this book, and, if at all acquainted with Asiatic phraseology, say whether it would be proper, even in medical language, to explain all the descriptions and allusions in this poem.

After what I have said on the difficulty of interpreting this book in a *spiritual* way, it would not be fair to withhold from the reader the general *arguments* on which the *theory* of its allegorical meaning is founded. The principal part of the commentators on this book, especially those who have made it their *separate* study, have in general taken it for granted that their mode of interpretation is incontrovertible; and have proceeded to spiritualize every *figure* and every *verse* as if they had a Divine warrant for all they have said. Their conduct is dangerous; and the result of their well-intentioned labours has been of very little service to the cause of *Christianity* in general, or to the interests of true *morality* in particular. By their mode of interpretation an undignified, not to say mean and carnal, language has been propagated among many well-meaning religious people, that has associated itself too much with *selfish* and *animal affections*, and created feelings that accorded little with the dignified spirituality of the religion of the Lord Jesus. I speak not from report; I speak from observation and experience, and observation not hastily made. The conviction on my mind and the conclusion to which I have conscientiously arrived, are the result of frequent examination, careful reading, and close thinking, at intervals, for nearly *fifty* years; and however I may be *blamed* by some, and *pitied* by others, I must say, and I say it as fearlessly as I do conscientiously, that in this inimitably fine elegant Hebrew ode I see nothing of *Christ* and *his Church*, and nothing that appears to have been *intended* to be *thus* understood; and nothing, if applied in this way, that, *per se*, can promote the interests of vital godliness, or cause the simple and sincere not to "know Christ after the flesh." Here I conscientiously stand. May God help me!

The most rational view of the subject that I have seen is that taken by Mr. *Harmer*, who has indeed detailed and strengthened the arguments of his predecessors who have declared for the *spiritual* meaning. In his "Outlines of a Comment upon Solomon's Song," he supposes that the Song refers to *Solomon's marriage with the daughter of Pharaoh;* and that he had a *Jewish queen*, who is frequently referred to in the work; and that, unless this be allowed, there are several important passages in the book that cannot be understood; and indeed it is on this principle that he finds his chief ground for a *spiritual* and *allegorical* interpretation.

"Whatever was the intention of God," says he, "in bringing about this marriage, and in causing it to be celebrated in such an *extraordinary* manner, *by songs that were directed to be placed among the sacred writings*, it is certain there never was *any resemblance more striking* between the circumstances and transactions of any of the remarkable personages of the Old Testament and those of Messiah, than the *likeness* we may observe between *Solomon marrying a Gentile princess*, and making her *equal in honour and privileges* with his former *Jewish queen*, and in her being *frequently mentioned* afterwards in history, while the other is passed over in *total silence*, and the *conduct of the Messiah towards the Gentile and Jewish Churches*.

"The two remarkable things in the conduct of the Messiah towards the two Churches are the making the Gentiles *fellow heirs* of the same body and partakers of the promises, *without and difference;* and the *giving up to neglect* the Jewish Church, while that of the Gentiles has long flourished in great honour, and been the subject of many a history. St. Paul takes notice of both these circumstances with particular solemnity; of the first, in the *third* chapter of *Ephesians*, and elsewhere; of the other, in the *eleventh* chapter of *Romans*. They are points, then, that deserve great attention.

"They are both called *mysteries*, (Rom. xi. 25, Eph. iii. 3,) that is, things that had been concealed aforetime; but it by no means follows that there were no shadowy representations of these events in the preceding ages, only that they were not *clearly and expressly revealed*.

"*Kingdoms* and *cities* are frequently spoken of in holy writ as *women. Sacred* as well as secular bodies of men are represented under that image. *The universal Church* is spoken of under the notion of a *bride*, and the *Messiah* as her *husband*, Eph. v. The two Churches of Jews and Gentiles, or the Church under the Mosaic dispensation and the Church freed from those ceremonies, are represented as *two women*—the one formerly treated as the *principal wife;* and the second, as having been for a long time neglected, but afterwards producing a much more numerous issue than the first—by the prophet Isaiah in his *fifty-*

fourth chapter, according to the explanation St. Paul has given of that passage in Gal. iv. *Particular* Churches are mentioned after the same manner. So, concerning the Church at Corinth, St. Paul says, "I have espoused you to one husband, *that I may present you* as a chaste virgin to Christ;" 2 Cor. xi. 2.

"Since then it is common for the Scriptures to represent the Church of God under the notion of a *woman,* and the Messiah under that of a *husband;* since the two bodies of men —that which worshipped God according to the *Mosaic* rites, and that which observed them *not*—are compared to *two women;* and since the circumstances of these two Churches are such as I have given an account of from St. Paul, it must be acknowledged that there is a lively resemblance between Solomon's espousing the Egyptian princess and the Messiah's admitting the Gentiles to equal privileges with the Jews, whether it was or was not *designed* by God as an emblem and type of it: celebrated by his prophets for this cause, in holy songs; and those songs preserved with care to this day among writings of the *most sacred* kind on that account."

This is the whole of Mr. *Harmer's* argument; see his *Outlines,* pages 74–77. And *what* is proved by it? Nothing, in reference to this book. We know that the *Jewish people,* not the *Church* exclusively, are represented under the notion of a *woman afflicted,* and a *wife unfaithful, divorced,* and *forsaken,* &c.; and that the *Corinthians* were represented under the notion of a *chaste virgin espoused to Christ.* And we know that all this was done to show, that as the *marriage union* was the *closest, strictest,* and *most sacred* among men, the union of the soul to God, and its connection with him, might be most fitly represented by that union, and unfaithfulness to him by infidelity in the other case. But what has this to do with the *Canticles? Where is the intimation* that *Solomon* represents *Christ; Pharaoh's daughter,* the *Church* of the *Gentiles;* and the *Jewish queen,* the *Church* of the *Israelites?* Nowhere. Why then *assume* the thing that should be *proved;* and then build doctrines on it, and draw inferences from it, as if the *assumption* had been *demonstrated?*

Were this mode of interpretation to be applied to the Scriptures in general, (and why not, if legitimate here?) in what a state would religion soon be! Who could see any thing certain, determinate, and fixed in the meaning of the Divine oracles, when *fancy* and *imagination* must be the standard interpreters? God has *not* left his word to man's will in this way.

Every attempt, however well-intentioned, to revive this thriftless, not to say dangerous, *Origenian* method of seducing the Scriptures to particular creeds and purposes, should be regarded with jealousy; and nothing received as the *doctrine* of the Lord but what may be derived from those *plain words* of the Most High which lie most on a level with the capacities of mankind. Allegory, metaphor, and figures in general, where the design is clearly indicated, which is the case with all those employed by the sacred writers, may come in to *illustrate* and more forcibly to *apply* Divine truth; but to extort celestial meanings from *a whole book,* where no such *indication* is given, is most certainly not the way to arrive at the knowledge of the true God, and of Jesus Christ whom he has sent.

As the Jewish marriages were celebrated for *seven days,* it has been often observed that this Song divides itself into *seven periods,* and describes the *transactions* of each.

I. The FIRST *chapter* represents the *bridegroom* and *bride* as a *shepherd* and *shepherdess.* The bride asks her spouse where he takes his flock at noon, to preserve them from the excessive heat, lest she, in seeking him, should go astray into some strange pastures. After this day, the *first night* succeeds, which is pointed out chap. ii. 4, 5, 6. The bridegroom rises early in the morning, leaves the bride asleep, and goes hastily to the fields to his necessary occupations, ver. 7.

II. The SECOND *night* is pointed out chap. ii. 8, 9, &c. The bridegroom comes to the window of his spouse. She opens it, and he enters; and on the morrow, he returns to the fields to his flocks, ver. 17.

III. The THIRD *night*, the bridegroom having delayed his coming, the bride, being uneasy, arises from her bed, and goes out and inquires of the guards of the city, whether they had seen her beloved. She had not gone far from them till she met with him; she conducts him to her apartment, chap. iii. 1–4. Very early in the morning, he retires to the country, leaving the bride asleep, ver. 5. Afterwards she arises, and goes also to the fields, ver. 6.

The FOURTH *chapter* is an eulogium on the bride's beauty; and seems to be a conversation between the parties in the country. She invites the bridegroom to visit her, chap. v. 1. He leaves his friends, with whom he was feasting, and comes to the door of his spouse, ver. 2. She hesitating to let him in, he withdraws and goes to his garden. The bride follows; but, not knowing whither he had retired, asks the guards of the city, by whom she is maltreated; thence goes to the daughters of Jerusalem, and inquires of them, ver. 3, &c. At last she meets with him, chap. vi. 1, &c., and having spent some time with him, returns.

IV. Chap. vi. 9, points out the FOURTH *night* of the marriage.

V. The FIFTH *night* is pointed out chap. vii. 1, &c. The bridegroom gives his bride nearly the same praise and commendations which he had received from her in the preceding chapters; and early in the morning they go out together to the fields, ver. 11–13.

VI. The SIXTH *night* they pass at a village in the country, at the house of a person who is termed the bride's *mother*, chap. vii. 13, viii. 1–3. She invites her spouse thither, and promises to regale him with excellent fruits and choice wine; and early in the morning the bridegroom arises, leaves the bride asleep as formerly, and retires to the country, chap. viii. 4.

VII. The SEVENTH *night* is passed in the gardens. From chap. viii. 5, we have a series of dialogues between the bride and bridegroom. In the morning the bridegroom, having perceived that they were overheard, begs the bride to permit him to retire. She assents, ver. 13, 14, and exhorts him "to make haste, and be like a roe or a young hart on the mountains of spices."

This is the division, which is in the main most followed, especially by the best critics. But, besides this, several others have been proposed; and the reader, who wishes to enter more particularly into the subject, may consult Bishop *Bossuet, Calmet,* and Bishop *Lowth.* For my own part I doubt the propriety of this technical arrangement, and do not think that any thing of the kind was intended by the author. The division is not *obvious;* and therefore, in my apprehension, not *natural.* Of Dr. *Good's* division I shall speak below.

The *dramatis personæ* have been marked by some of the ancient interpreters, and the different portions of the whole Song appointed to several persons who are specified; and this division served for the *basis* of a *commentary.* The most regular division of this kind with which I have met is in a MS. of my own; the Bible which I have often quoted in my *comment.*

This, attributed by some to Wiclif, and by others to an older translator, I have carefully transcribed, with all the distinction of *parts* and *speeches.* The translation is very simple; and in many cases is much more faithful to the meaning of the *Hebrew* text, though in the main taken from the *Vulgate,* than our own version. It is a great curiosity, and certainly was never before printed; and is a fine specimen of our mother tongue as spoken in these countries in M.CCCLX., which may be about the date of this translation. On the common mode of interpretation I venture to assert that my readers will understand this Song ten times better from this translation and its *rubricks,* than they have ever done from all the forms in which it has been presented to them, to the present time. For this addition, I anticipate the thanks of every intelligent reader. The indications of the speakers, printed here in black letter, are all *rubrick,* in the beautiful original. I have added a short glossary on some of the more difficult or obsolete words, which will assist the less experienced reader, under whose notice such remote specimens of his own tongue seldom fall.

Between *twenty* and *thirty* years ago I received from India a *part* of the *Gitagovinda,* or

Songs of *Jayadeva.* This poet, the finest lyric poet of India, flourished before the Christian era; and the poem above, which makes the tenth book of the *Bhagavet,* was written professedly to celebrate the *loves* of *Chrishna* and *Radha,* or *the reciprocal attraction between the Divine goodness* and *the human soul.* The author leaves us in no doubt concerning the *design* of this little *pastoral drama;* for in the conclusion he thus speaks: "Whatever is delightful in the modes of music, *whatever is* DIVINE *in* MEDITATIONS on VISHNU, whatever is exquisite in the sweet art of love, whatever is graceful in the fine strains of poetry; all that, let the happy and wise learn from the Songs of Jayadeva, whose soul is united with the foot of *Narayan."* *Vishnu* and *Narayan* are epithets of *Chrishna,* or the supreme incarnated god of the Hindoos. I found the general phraseology of this work, and its imagery as well as its *subject,* to correspond so much with those of the *Canticles,* that in the short notes which I wrote on this book in 1798, I proposed the illustration of many of its passages from the *Gitagovinda;* and was pleased to find, several years after, that my view of the subject had been confirmed by that encyclopædia of learning and science, Dr. *Mason Good,* who in his translation of the *Song of Songs,* with *critical notes,* published 1803, 8vo., has illustrated many passages from the *Gitagovinda.*

After having made a selection from this ancient poet for the illustration of the *Canticles,* I changed in some measure my purpose, and determined to give the whole work, and leave it to my readers to apply those passages which they might think best calculated to throw light upon a book which professedly has the *wisest of men* for its *author,* and according to the opinion of many, the most *important doctrines* of the Christian religion for its *subject.* I have not followed the *metrical version* which I received from India, but rather the *prose translation* of Sir William Jones; dividing it into *parts* and *verses,* after the model of the metrical version above mentioned; and adding verbal interpretations of the principal proper names and difficult terms which are contained in the work.

Having been long convinced that the *Chaldee Targum* is at once the oldest and most valuable *comment* upon this book, I have also added this. And here I might say that I have not only followed my own judgment, but that also of a very learned divine, Dr. *John Gill,* who, having preached *one hundred and twenty-two* sermons on the Song of Solomon, to the Baptist congregation at *Horsleydown,* near London, embodied them all in what he calls *"An Exposition"* of this book; to which he added a *translation of the Targum,* with short *explanatory notes,* folio, 1728. This was, however, suppressed in all the later editions of this exposition; but why, I cannot tell. This piece I give to my readers, and for the same reasons alleged by this very learned and excellent man himself:—

"At the end of this exposition I have given," says he, "a version of the *Targum* or *Chaldee paraphrase* upon the whole book, with some notes thereon, induced hereunto by the following reasons:

"*First,* to gratify the curiosity of some who, observing frequent mention and use made of it in my exposition, might be desirous of perusing the whole.

"*Secondly,* for the profitableness thereof. Our learned countryman, Mr. *Broughton,* says, this paraphrase is worth our study both for delight and profit. It expounds several passages of Scripture, and some in the *New Testament,* which I have directed to in my notes upon it; and I am persuaded that the writings of the Jews, the ancient Jews especially, would give us much light into the phraseology and sense of abundance of texts in the New Testament."

It is certain that this paraphrase does very often direct us, or at least confirm us, as to the *persons speaking* in this Song, to know which is of very great use in the explication of it. I shall add another reason: I believe the book of Canticles refers more to the *Jewish* than to the *Christian Church,* and I think the *Targumist* has made a more rational use of it than any of his successors.

I have thus places within the reach of all my readers THREE *especial helps* towards a good understanding of this book: 1. The ancient English translation, with its curious *dramatis personæ*. 2. The *Gitagovinda*, a most curious poem of the spiritual and allegorical kind. 3. The *Chaldee Targum*, the oldest comment on this Song. And I add my prayer, May God guide the reader into all truth, through Christ Jesus! Amen.

On this part of the subject it would be almost criminal not to mention, still more particularly, Dr. *Mason Good's translation* and *notes* on the *Song of Songs*. He has done much to elucidate its phraseology, and his notes are a treasury of critical learning. He considers the book to be a collection of *Sacred Idyls, twelve* in number; and his division is as follows:

IDYL I

Royal Bride,	Chap. I.	Verses 2, 3, 4.
Attendant Virgins,	——	Part of the fourth verse, beginning, "We will exult."
Royal Bride,	——	Verses 5, 6, 7.
Attendant Virgins,	——	—— 8.

IDYL II

King Solomon,	Chap. I.	Verses 9, 10, 11.
Royal Bride,	——	—— 12, 13, 14.
King Solomon.	——	—— 15.
Royal Bride,	——	—— 16, 17. Chap. II. Ver. 1.
King Solomon,	—— II.	—— 2.
Royal Bride,	——	—— 3, 4, 5, 6, 7.

IDYL III

Royal Bride,	Chap. II.	Verses 8, 9, 10, 11, 12, 13, 14, 15, 16, 17.

IDYL IV

Royal Bride,	Chap. III.	Verses 1, 2, 3, 4, 5.

IDYL V

Scene, a Chiosk or Pavilion

Attendant Virgins,	Chap. III.	Verse 6.
Other Virgins,	——	—— 7, 8, 9, 10.
Royal Bride,	——	—— 11.
King Solomon,	—— IV.	—— 1, 2, 3, 4, 5, 6, 7.

IDYL VI

King Solomon,	Chap. IV.	Verses 8, 9, 10, 11, 12, 13, 14, 15.
Royal Bride,	——	—— 16.
King Solomon,	—— V.	—— 1.
Royal Bride,	——	Part of the first verse, beginning, "Eat, O my friends."

IDYL VII

Royal Bride,	Chap. V.	Verses 2, 3, 4, 5, 6, 7, 8.
Virgins,	——	—— 9.
Royal Bride,	——	—— 10, 11, 12, 13, 14, 15, 16.
Virgins,	—— VI.	—— 1.
Royal Bride,	——	—— 2, 3.
King Solomon,	——	—— 4, 5, 6, 7, 8, 9, 10.

IDYL VIII

Royal Bride,	Chap. VI.	Verses 11, 12.
Virgins,	——	—— 13.
Royal Bride,	——	Part of the thirteenth verse, beginning, "What do you expect?"
Virgins,	——	Latter part of the thirteenth verse, beginning "Fortitude."

IDYL IX

Virgins,	Chap. VII.	Verses 1, 2, 3, 4, 5.
King Solomon,	——	—— 6, 7, 8, 9.

IDYL X

Royal Bride,	Chap. VII.	Verses 10, 11, 12, 13.
	—— VIII.	—— 1, 2, 3, 4

IDYL XI

Virgins,	Chap. VIII.	Verse 5.
King Solomon,	——	Part of the fifth verse, beginning, "I excited thee."
Royal Bride,	——	Verse 6.
King Solomon,	——	—— 7.

IDYL XII

Royal Bride,	Chap. VIII.	Verse 8.
King Solomon,	——	—— 9.
Royal Bride,	——	—— 10, 11, 12.
King Solomon,	——	—— 13.
Royal Bride,	——	—— 14.

There have been various opinions on this division; and many will still think that much remains yet to be done. Dr. *Good* considers it a *spiritual allegory;* but he does not attempt a spiritual application of any part of it. This perhaps is no mean proof of his good sense and judgment. I have acted in the same way, though not so convinced of its spirituality as Dr. *Good* appears to be. If I took it up in this way, I should explain it *according to my own creed*, as others have done according to *theirs;* and could I lay it down as a maxim, that it is to be spiritually interpreted in reference to the Christian Revelation, I might soon show my reader that it points out the infinite love of God to every human soul, in the incarnation of Christ; the means he uses to bring all mankind to an acquaintance with himself; the redemption of true believers from all unrighteousness, through the inspiration of God's Holy Spirit; their consequent holy life, and godly conversation; the calling of the Gentiles; the restoration of the Jews; and the final judgment! And my comment on this plan would have just as *solid a foundation* as those of my predecessors, from *Origen* to the present day.

To conclude: I advise all young ministers to avoid preaching on Solomon's Song. If they take a text out of it, to proclaim salvation to lost sinners, they must borrow their doctrines from other portions of Scripture, where all is *plain* and *pointed*. And why then leave such, and go out of their way to find allegorical meanings, taking a whole book by storm, and leaving the word of God to serve tables?

It is curious to see the manner in which many preachers and commentators attempt to expound this book. They first assume that the book refers to Christ and his Church; his union with human nature; his adoption of the Gentiles; and his everlasting love to elect souls, gathered out of both people; then take the words bride, bridegroom, spouse, love, watchmen, shepherds, tents, door, lock, &c., &c., and, finding some words either *similar* or *parallel*, in other parts of the sacred writings, which have *there* an allegorical meaning, contend that those *here* are to be similarly understood; and what is spoken of *those* apply to *these;* and thus, in fact, are explaining other passages of Scripture in their own way, while professing to explain the *Canticles!* What eminent talents, precious time, great pains, and industry, have been wasted in this way! One eminent scholar preaches to his congregation *one hundred and twenty-two* sermons upon the Song of Solomon, while all this time the evangelists and apostles have been comparatively forgotten; except only as they are referred to in illustration of the particular creed which such writers and preachers found on this book. How can they account to God for so much time spent on a tract which requires all their ingenuity and skill to make edifying, even on their own plan; a text of which they are not permitted to allege, in controversy, to prove the truth of any disputed doctrine? This, however, is not the fault of any particular *class* of ministers *exclusively;* several of all classes, though of some more than of others, have been found, less or more, labouring at this thriftless craft. Some, having preached on it during the whole of their ministry, have carried it, in a certain way, beyond the grave. An aged minister once told me, in a very solemn manner, that as God had been exceedingly merciful to him in saving his soul, and putting him into the ministry, thus accounting him faithful, he hoped that, when called to the Church above, if any *funeral sermon* were preached for him, it should be from Canticles, chap. i. 8: "Go thy way forth by the footsteps of the flock, and feed thy kids beside the shepherds' tents." That he could have applied these words to his own state, and the use which should be made of his life and death, I have no doubt; but who, from this text, would have chosen to pronounce the funeral oration?

I repeat it, and I wish to be heard by young ministers in particular, take the plainest texts when you attempt to convince men of sin, and build up believers on their most holy faith; and thus show rather your love for their souls than your dexterity in finding out spiritual meanings for obscure passages, on the true signification of which few, either among the learned or pious, are agreed.

I now, according to my promise, lay before my readers a transcript from my own MS. Bible, which is most probably the first translation of this *Song* that was ever made into the English language. I have *added*, for the sake of reference, the *figures* for the present division into verses, in the *margin:* these are not in the MS. The *dramatis personæ*, here in *black* letter, are in *red* in the MS. The *orthography* is scrupulously followed.

THE
BOOK OF CANTICLES

[Carefully transcribed from a MS. of the fourteenth century in the Editor's possession]

Here begynnyth the Boke that is clepid Songis of Songis, of the Bridulis of Crist and of the Chirche.

CAP. I

The Chirche of the commyng of Crist, spekith sepinge,

2. Kysse he me with the cosse of his mouth.

The voice of the Fadir.

For better ben thi tetis thann wyn, smelling with best oynmentis.

The voice of the Chirche.

3. Oyle held oute thi name: there fore the yunge waxinge wymmen loviden thee ful myche.

The voice of the Chirche to Crist.

4. Drawe me after thee: we schul rennen in the smell of thin oynmentis.

The Chirche seyth of Crist.

Brogte me in the king into his celers. We schul ful out joyen and gladen in thee, myndful of thi tetis upon wyn, rigtmen loven thee.

The Chirche, of hir tribulacyouns.

5. O zee dogtris of Jerusalem, blac I am but schappli, as the tabernaculis of cedar, as
6. the skynnes of Salomon. Willith not beholden that I be broun; for discolord me hath the sunne. The sones of my modir fogten agein me: thei setiden me keper in vynes: my vyne gerde I kepte not.

The voice of the Chirche to Crist.

7. Schewe thou to me whom lovith my soule, where thou gevest leswe, where thou lygge in myd day: lest to gou vagraunt I begynne aftir the flockis of thi felawes.

The voice of Crist to the Chirche.

8. Gif thou knowest not thee, O thou fair most among wymmen; go oute, and go awei after the steppis of thi flockis and feed thi goot beside the tabernaculis of schepperdis.
9. To my ryding in charis of Pharao, I licned
10. thee, O my leef! Fair ben thy cheekis as
11. of a turture; thi necke as brochis. Golden ribanes we schul maken to thee maad furrede with sylvir.

The voice of the Chirche, of Crist.

12. Whan the king was in his lying place, my
13. maad encense gave his smell. A bundlet of mirre my lemman is to me: between my
14. tetis he schal dwellen. The cluster of cypre tree my lemman to me: in the vynes of Engaddy.

The voice of Crist to the Chirche.

15. Loo thou art fair my leef, loo thou fair: thin eegen of culveris.

The voice of the Chirche to Crist.

16. Loo thou art fair my lemman, and seemli; oure bed is schynynge. The trees of oure hous as cedre; oure couplis cypresse.

CAP. II

The voice of Crist, of him and of the Chirche.

1, 2. I the floure of the feeld, and the lilie of al valeys, as a lilie among thornes, so my leef among dogtris.

The voice of the Chirche, of Crist.

3. As an apple tree among the trees of wodis; so my lemman among sones. Undir the schadewe of him whom I hadde desirede, I satte: and his fruyte sweet to my throote.
4. The king ladde me into his wyne celere, he
5. ordeynede in me charite. Undir leye gee me with floures, settith me about applis; for I languych for love.

The voice of the Chirche, of Crist.

6. The left hond of him undir myn heued; and his rigt hond schal clippen me.

The voice of Crist, of the Chirche.

7. I adjure gou, gee dogtris of Jerusalem, by the capretis and the hertis of feeldis, ne rere gee, ne makith my leef to waken, to the time that sche wille.

The voice of the Chirche, of Crist.

8. The voice of my lemman: Loo, this commith lepinge in mounteynes, and over
9. lepinge hilles. Liic is my lemman to an capret and to an hert, calf of hertis. Loo, he stant behinden our wall beholding by the wyndowis a fer loking thurg the latises.
10. Loo my lemman spekith to me: Riis go thou my leef, my culver my schappli and

11. cum. Now forsothe wynter passide, wedir
12. geed fro, and is gon awei. Floures ap-
peereden in our lond—tyme of cutting is
cummen; the voice of the turtur is herd in
13. oure londe. The fiige tree brogt forth his
first fiigs: The vynes flouryng geven their
smell.

The voice of Crist to the Chirche.

14. Riis, go my leef, my schaply and cum thou
my culver, in the hoolis of the stoon wal.
Schewe thou to me thi face, and soun thi
voice in my eris; thi voice forsoth is sweet,
and thi face seemli.

The voice of Crist to the Chirche agein heryptikis.

15. Take gee to us litil foxis that destruyen
vynes: for oure vyne flourede.

The voice of the Chirche, of Crist.

16. My loved to me, and I to him, that is fed
among lilies, to the tyme that the day
17. springe, and schadewis ben bowed in. Turne
agein; liic be thou O my lemman to a
capret, and to the hert, calf of hertis, upon
the mounteynes of Bether.

CAP. III

The voice of the Chirche gedred togpder of Gentilis.

1. In my litil bed by nigtis, I sougt whom
lovede my soule: I sogte him, and I founde
2. not. I schal riisen and gon aboute the
cytee, by tounes and streetis: I schal
sechen whom loveth my soule. I sogt him
3. and found not. There founden me the
wacheris that kepen the cytee.

The Chirche seith of Crist, to the Apostlis.

Wheyther whom loveth my soule, gee
4. seegen? A litil whan I hadde passid hem,
I foond whom lovith my soule; I heeld him
and I schal not leven to the tyme that I
bringe him into the hous of my moder:
and into the bed of hir that gat me.

The voice of Crist, of the Chirche.

5. I adjure gou ge dogtris of Jerusalim, by
capretis and hertis of feeldis, ne reire gee,
ne make gee my leef to waken to the tyme
that sche wille.

The Synagoge, of the Chirche.

6. What is sche this that stiegeth up by
desert, as a litil gerde of smoke of the
swote spyces of mirre and of cense, and of
al pymentarie poudre?

The voice of the Chirche, of Crist.

7. Loo the litil bed of Salomon; sixti stronge
men compassen, of the most strong men of
8. Israel; the whiche alle ben holdinge
swerdis; and to bataile best tagt. Of eche
oon the swerd upon his hip, for the nigt
dredis.

Of Crist, and of the Chirche chosen of Gentilis.

9. A chaier King Salomon maad to him of the
10. trees of Liban. His pileers, he maade
sylveren; the lenying place, golden; the
steiging up, purpure; the myddis he en-
ournede with charite, for the dogteris of
Jerusalem.

The voice of the Chirche, of Crist.

11. Goth out and seeth gee dogtris of Syon,
Kyng Salomon, in the dyademe in the
whiche crowned him his modir, in the dai
of spousing of him; and in the dai of glad-
neese of his herte.

CAP. IV

The voice of Crist to the Chirche.

1. How fair art thou my leef, hou fair ert
thou! Thyn eegen of culveris, with out it
that with ine forth is hid. Thin heris as
the flockis of Got, that steigiden up fro the
the hill of Galaad.
2. Thi teeth as the flockis of clippid scheep
that steigeden up fro the wasching place.
Alle with double lombis in the wombe; and
3. bareyn is not there among hem. Als a
furred sylken fylet, thi lippis, and thy fair
speche swote. Als the brekyng of a powmgarnet, so thy cheekis; without it, that
4. withine forth litt hid. Als the tour of David thi neck that is bild out with pynaclis,
A thousand scheeldis hangen of it al the
5. armour of strong men. Thi two tetis as
two yunge capretis twynglingis of the
6. capret, that ben fed in lilies: to the tyme
that the day brethe out, and the schadewis
ben in bowid. I schal gou to the mount of
7. mirre, and to the hill of cens. Al fair thou
art my leef, and wemm is not in thee.
8. Cumm thou fro Libane my spouse, cumm
fro Liban; cum thou schalt ben crowned
fro the heued of Amana; fro the frount of
Sannir, and of Ermon: fro the couchis
9. liouns, and the hill of Paradise. Thou hast
woundid myn herte myn suster, my spouse,
thou hast woundide myn herte in oon of
thin eegen: and in oon here of thi neck.
10. Hou fair ben thi tetis my suster, my spouse,
fairer ben thi tetis than wyne: and the
smell of thin oynmentis, over alle spices.
11. A dropping honycomb thy lippis, spouse:
honey and mylc undir thi tunge; and the
smell of thi clothing is, as the smell of
12. cens. A closid garden my suster, spouse:
13. closid gardyn, a welle selid. Thin out send-
ingis is paradis of paumgarnetis: with thi
14. fruytis of applis. Of cypre tree with narde;
and narde with safrun, and fystula and
canel, with alle the trees of Liban, mirre
and aloes, with alle the first oynmentis.
15. The welle of gardynes, the pit of lyvyng
wateris that flowen with burre fro Liban,
Riis North, and cum South, blow thurg my
gardyn, and thei schul flowen swote spyces
of it.

CAP. V

The Chirche seith of Crist.

1. Cum my leef into his gardyn; and ete he
the fruyt of his applis.

Crist seith to the Chirche.

Cum into my gardyn, my sister, my spouse;
I have gadered my mirre with my swote
spices; I ette myn hony comb with myn
hony. I dranke my wyne with my mylc.

Crist to the Apostolis seith.

Etith gee freendis and drinkith: and gee
most derworth beth inwardli maad
2. drunken. I sleep and myn herte wakith.

The voice of the Chirche, of Crist.

The voice of my Lemman knockyng, open thou to me my sustir, my leef, my culver, my unwemmynd, for my heud is ful of dewe, and my temple heris of the droopis

3. of nigtis. I spoylide me my coote; hou schal I be clothid it? I waschide my feet,

4. hou schal I befoulen hem? my lemman putte his hond bi the hool; my wombe inwardly trembled at the touching of him.

5. I rose that I scholde opennen to my lemman. My hondis droppiden mirre; and my

6. fingris ful of best proved mirre. The lacche of my dore, I opened to my lemman; and he hadde bowid asyde and passide. My soule is moltyn as my lemman spac. I sogte and founde not him. I clepid and he

7. answered not to me. There founden me keperis that gon about the cytee. Thei smyten me, and woundiden me; takin my

8. mantill the keperis of the wallis. I adjure gou ye dogtris of Jerusalem, gif gee schul fynden my lemman, that gee telle to him, for I languisch for love.

The voice of freendis seith to the Chirche.

9. Whiche is thy lemman of the loved, O thou most fair of wymmen? Whiche is thy lemman of the loved? Forsoth thou hast adjured us.

The voice of the Chirche of Crist seith to the freendis.

10. My lemman whiit and roodi chosen of thou-
11. sandis. His heued, best gold; his her as bunchis of palmys, thick leved blac as a
12. crowe. His eegen as culveris upon litil ryvers. Of wateris that ben waschid with mylk; and sitte by the most full flowing of
13. wateris. The cheekis of litil flouris of
14. swote spices plaunted of pimentaries. His lippis dropping the first myrre; the hondis of him able to turnen about, golden and full of jacynctis. His wombe is yvren
15. depertid by saphiris. His lippis marbil pileeris, that ben foundid upon golden feet. His fairness as of Lyban, and chosen as of
16. cedre. The throot of him most swote; and he al desirable. Siche is my loved, and this is my lemman, gee dogtris of Jerusalem.

CAP. VI

The voice of holi soulis of the Chirche.

1. Whider grede awei thi lemman? O thou most fair of wymmen? Whither bowiden doun thi leef, and we schul sechen him with thee?

The voice of the Chirche, of Crist.

2. My leef went doun into his gardyne to the floore of swote spices: that there he fed in
3. the gardynes, and lilies he gadired. I to my leef, and my self, and my leef to me, that is fed among lilies.

The voice of Crist to the Chirche.

4. Fair thou art my leef; swote and fair as Jerusalem; ferful as the scheltrun of tentis
5. ordeyned. Turne awei thin eegen fro me; for thei maden me to fleen awei. Thin

6. heris as the flockis of sche got, that apeereden fro Galaad. Thi teeth as a floc of scheep that steigeden up fro the wasch-
7. ing place; al with double fruyt of wombe and bareyn there is not in hem. As the rynde of powmgarnet; so thi cheekis with-
8. out thin hid thingis. Sixty ben queenes, and eigty ben secundane wiives; and of yunge waxe wymmen there is no noumbre.
9. Oon is my culver, my perfite: oon is to hir modir, chosen of hir modir, chosen of hir that gat hir. There seegen hir the dogtris of Syon, and most blisful preisiden hir: the queenes and secundarie wiives preisiden
10. hir. What is sche this that goth forth as the morewtide, riising fair as the mone, chosen as the sunne; ferful as of tentis scheltrun ordeyned.

The voice of the Chirche, of the Synagoge.

11. I wente doun into my gardyne that I schulde seen the applis of valeys; and beholden gif the vynes hadden flouride, and
12. the poumgarnetis hadden burriouned, I wiste not, my soule distourbid me, for the foure horsid cartis of Amynadab.

The voice of the Chirche to the faith of the Natybyte.

13. Turne agein, turne agein Sunamytis; turne agein, turne agein that we beholden thee.

The voice of Crist to the Chirche, of the Synagoge.

What schalt thou seen in the Sunamyte, but queeris of tentis?

CAP. VII

The voice of Crist to the Chirche.

1. Hou fair ben thi goingis in schoon, thou dogtir of the prince? the jointures of thin hippis as broochis that ben forgid with
2. hond of the craftisman. Thin navel a turned cuppe, never needing drinkis. Thi wombe as an hepe of whete, of whete sett abouten
3. with lilies. Thy two tetis as two yunge
4. capretis, gemelwis of the sche capret. Thi necke as an yvren tour; thin eegen as the cysternys in Esebon; that ben in the gate of the dogtir of the multitude. Thi noose as the tour of Liban that beholdith ageins
5. damask. Thyn heued as Carmele, thin heris of thin heued as the purpure of the
6. kyng joined to watir pipis. Hou faire thou art, and hou seemli thou most derworthe
7. in delicis? Thi stature is lickened to a palme tree; and thi tetis to clusteris.

Crist, of the holi crosse seith.

8. I seide I schal steigen into a palme tree; and I schal taken the fruytis of it.

The voice of Crist to the Chirche.

And thi tetis schul ben as the clusteris of a vyne, and the smel of thi mouth as the smel of applis; and thi throot as best wyne.

The Chirche seith of Crist.

9. Worthi to my leef to drinken: to the lippis,
10. and to the teeth of him to chewen. I to my leef and to me the turnynge of him.

The voice of the Chirche to Crist.

11. Cum my leef, go we out into the feeld,
12. dwelle we togydir in townes: erli riise we to the vyne: see we gif the vyne flouride; gif the floures, fruytis bringen forth; gif
13. the poumgarnetis flouren? The mandraggis yeven their smel in oure yeatis. Alle appls newe and olde my leef, I kepte to thee.

CAP. VIII

The voice of Patriarkis, of Crist.

1. Who to me gevith thee my brother, souking the tetis of my modir, that I fynde thee aloon without forth and kysse thee, and
2. now, me, no man dispises. I schal taken thee and leiden into the hous of my modir, and into the bed place of hir that gat me. There thou shalt tecken me, and I schal geven to thee drinken of spycid wyne, and
3. of the must of my poumgarnetis. The left hond of him undir my heued, and the rigt hond of him schal clippen me.

The voice of Crist, of the Chirche.

4. I adjure you, gee dogtris of Jerusalem, ne rere gee, ne makith to wake my leef, to the tyme that sche will.

The voice of the Synagoge, of the Chirche.

5. What is sche this that steigith up fro desert, flowing delices, fast clevyng upon hir leef?

The voice of Crist to the Synagoge, of the holi Crosse.

Undir an apple tree I rered thee; there schent is thi modir: there defoulid is sche
6. that gat thee. Putte me as a brooche upon thi herte; putte me as a brooche upon thin arme; for strong as deth, love: hard as helle, gelousnesse: the lampis of it, the
7. lampis of fiir: and of flammes. Many wateris schal not mown quenchen oute charitee: ne floodis schal not throwen it doun. Gif a man gif al the substaunce of his hous for love, as nogt he dispisith it.

The voice of Crist, to the lynage of holi Chirche.

8. Our sustir a litil child; and tetis sche hath not. What schal we done to oure sustir, in the day whann sche is to be spoken to?
9. Gif a wal she is bilden we upon it sylveren pynnaclis. Gif a dore sche is, joyn we it with cedre tables.

The voice of the Chirche, answeeringe.

10. I, a wal; and my tetis as a tour; sythen I am maad be fore thee as pese receyvynge.

The Synagoge, of the Chirche seith.

11. Vyne sche was to pesyble, in hir that hath peplis; sche toke it to the keperis: a man takith awei for the fruyte of it, a thousand sylveren platis.

Crist to the Chirche seith.

12. My vyne before me is; a thousand thi
13. pesiblis; and two hundrith to hem that kepen the fruytis of it. The whiche dwellest in gardynes freendis herkenen thee: make me to heeren thi voice.

The voice of the Chirche to Crist.

14. Flee thou my leef, be thou lickened to a capret, and to an hert, calf of hertis, upon the mounteynes of swote spices.

Explicit Canticum

The above is taken, literatim, from an ancient MS. once the property of *Thomas à Woodstock*, youngest son of *Edward III.*, and brother to *Edward* the *Black Prince*.

Millbrook, Feb. 1, 1823.

EXPLANATION OF THE MOST DIFFICULT WORDS IN THE PRECEDING ANCIENT VERSION OF SOLOMON'S SONG

CHAP. I

Ver.
2	Cosse	kisses.
6	Fogten	fought.
7	Leswe	leisure or rest.
8	Goot	plural of *goat*.
9	Charis	chairs or chariots.
10	Leef	*love*, fem. as *lemman*, mas.
—	Turture	turtle dove.
11	Furrede	bordered.
13	Lemman	lover. See Leef.

CHAP. II

4	Throote	throat.
5	Gee	ye.
6	Heued	head.
—	Clippen	embrace.
7	Capretis	young goats, kids.
—	Rere	rear or raise.

CHAP. III

3	Sogt	sought, searched for.
4	Seegen	saw.
6	Stiegeth	ascendeth.
—	Gerde	rod or staff.
—	Swote	sweet.
—	Cense	incense.
—	Pymentarie	odoriferous.
8	Tagt	taught.
10	Enournede	strewed.

CHAP. IV

1	Eegen	eyes.
2	Clipped	shorne.
3	Swote	sweet.
6	Inbowid	declined.
—	Cens	incense.
7	Wemm	defect, wart, mole.

Ver.
8	Couchis	lairs or dens.
15	Burre	a rippling noise like waters.

CHAP. V

1	Derworth	most beloved.
2	Culver	dove.
6	Moltyn	melted.
13	Pimentaries	perfumers, confectioners.
14	Yvren	ivory.

CHAP. VI

4	Scheltrun	covering.
8	Secundane wiives	secondary wives, concubines.
9	Secundarie	*idem*.
10	Morewtide	to-morrow.
11	Burrouned	put forth buds.
13	Queeris	choirs.

CHAP. VII

3	Gemelwis	twins.
4	Yate	gate.
5	Heris	hairs.
—	Purpure	purple.
8	Tetis	teats, breasts.
12	Gif	if.
13	Yeven	give.

CHAP. VIII

2	Must	new wine.
3	Clippen	embrace.
5	Clevyng	holding on, leaning.
—	Schent	corrupted.
6	Gelousnesse	jealousy.
9	Pynnaclis	turrets, towers.
11	Pesyble	the peaceful man, i. e., Solomon.
13	Pesiblis	*idem*.

N. B.—There are many other words which, though they appear difficult, a little labour will make out as they differ more in the *spelling* than in the *sense*.

THE

SONG OF SOLOMON

Year from the Creation of the World, according to Archbishop Usher, 2990.—Year from the Flood of Noah, according to the common Hebrew text, 1334.—Year before the birth of Christ, 1010.—Year before the vulgar era of Christ's nativity, 1014.

CHAPTER I

The bride's love to her spouse, 1–5. She confesses her unworthiness; desires to be directed to the flock, 6, 7; and she is directed to the shepherds' tents, 8. The bridegroom describes his bride, and shows how he will provide for her, and how comfortably they are accommodated, 9–17.

A. M. cir. 2990
B. C. cir. 1014
Ante I. Olymp.
cir. 238
Ante U. C. cir.
261

THE ^asong of songs, which *is* Solomon's.

2 Let him kiss me with the kisses of his mouth: ^bfor ^cthy love *is* better than wine.

3 Because of the savour of thy good ^dointments, thy name *is as* ointment poured forth, therefore do the virgins love thee.

4 Draw me, ^ewe will run after thee: the king ^fhath brought me into his chambers: we will be glad and rejoice in thee, we will remember thy love more than wine: ^gthe upright love thee.

A. M. cir. 2990
B. C. cir. 1014
Ante I. Olymp.
cir. 238
Ante U. C. cir.
261

5 I *am* black, but comely, O ye daughters of Jerusalem, as the tents of Ke-

---

^a1 Kings iv. 32——^bChap. iv. 10——^cHeb. *thy loves*
^dHos. xi. 4; John vi. 44

^ePhil. iii. 12, 13, 14——^fPsa. xlv. 14, 15; John xiv. 2;
Eph. ii. 6——^gOr, *they love thee uprightly*

NOTES ON CHAP. I

Verse 1. *The song of songs*] A song of peculiar excellence. See the *Introduction.* The rabbins consider this superior to all songs. TEN *songs*, says the *Targum*, have been sung; but this excels them all. 1. The *first* was sung by *Adam* when his sin was pardoned. 2. The *second* was sung by Moses and the *Israelites* at the *Red Sea.* 3. The *third* was sung by the *Israelites* when they drank of the *rock* in the wilderness. 4. The *fourth* was sung by *Moses* when summoned to *depart* from this *world.* 5. The *fifth* was sung by *Joshua* when the *sun* and *moon stood still.* 6. The *sixth* was sung by *Deborah and Barak* after the defeat of *Sisera.* 7. The *seventh* was sung by *Hannah* when the Lord promised her a *son.* 8. The *eighth* was sung by *David* for all the *mercies* given him by God. 9. The *ninth* is the present, sung in the spirit of prophecy by *Solomon.* 10. The *tenth* is that which shall be sung by the *children of Israel* when restored from their *captivities.* See the *Targum.*

Verse 2. *Let him kiss me, &c.*] She speaks of the bridegroom in the *third* person, to testify her own *modesty*, and to show him the greater *respect.*

Thy love is better than wine.] The *versions* in general translate דדיך *dodeyca, thy breasts;* and they are said to represent, spiritually, the *Old* and *New Testaments.*

Verse 3. *Thy name is as ointment poured forth*] Ointments and perfumes were, and still are, in great request among the Asiatics. They occur constantly in their entertainments. Thy *name* is as refreshing to my heart, as the best perfumes diffused through a chamber are to the senses of the guests.

Therefore do the virgins love thee.] She means *herself;* but uses this *periphrasis* through modesty.

Verse 4. *Draw me*] Let me have the full assurance of thy affection.

We will run after thee] Speaking in the plural through modesty, while still *herself* is meant.

The king hath brought me] My spouse is a *potentate*, a mighty *king*, no ordinary person.

Into his chambers] He has favoured me with his utmost confidence.

The upright love thee.] The most perfect and accomplished find thee worthy of their highest esteem.

Verse 5. *I am black, but comely*] This is literally true of many of the Asiatic women; though *black* or *brown*, they are exquisitely beautiful. Many of the Egyptian women are still fine; but their *complexion* is much inferior to that of the Palestine females. Though black or swarthy in my complexion, yet am I *comely* —well proportioned in every part.

As the tents of Kedar] I am *tawny*, like the

A. M. cir. 2990
B. C. cir. 1014
Ante I. Olymp.
cir. 238
Ante U. C. cir.
261

dar, as the curtains of Solomon.

6 Look not upon me, because I *am* black, because the sun hath looked upon me: my mother's children were angry with me; they made me keeper of the vineyards; *but* mine own vineyard have I not kept.

7 Tell me, O thou whom my soul loveth, where thou feedest, where thou makest *thy flock* to rest at noon: for why should I be as ʰone that turneth aside by the flocks of thy companions?

A. M. cir. 2990
B. C. cir. 1014
Ante I. Olymp.
cir. 238
Ante U. C. cir.
cir. 261

8 If thou know not, ¹O thou fairest among women, go thy way forth by the footsteps of the flock, and feed thy kids beside the shepherds' tents.

9 I have compared thee, ᵏO my love, ¹to a company of horses in Pharaoh's chariots.

10 ᵐThy cheeks are comely with rows *of jewels,* thy neck with chains *of gold.*

ʰOr, *as one that is veiled*——ⁱChap. v. 9; vi. 1——ᵏChap. ii, 2, 10, 13; iv. 1, 7; v. 2; vi. 4; John xv. 14, 15

---

¹2 Chronicles i. 16, 17——ᵐEzekiel xvi. 11, 12, 13

---

tents of the *Arabians,* and like the pavilions of Solomon, probably covered by a kind of *tanned cloth.* The *daughters of Jerusalem* are said to represent the *synagogue;* the *bride,* the *Church of Christ.* It is easy to find spiritual meanings: every *creed* will furnish them.

Verse 6. *Because the sun hath looked upon me*] The bride gives here certain reasons why she was *dark complexioned.* "The sun hath looked upon me." I am sunburnt, tanned by the sun; being obliged, perhaps, through some domestic jealously or uneasiness, to keep much without: "My mother's children were angry; they made me keeper of the vineyards." Here the *brown complexion* of the Egyptians is attributed to the influence of the *sun* or *climate.*

My mother's children were angry with me] Acted *severely.* The bringing of a *foreigner* to the throne would no doubt excite jealousy among the Jewish females; who, from their own superior complexion, national and religious advantages, might well suppose that Solomon should not have gone to *Egypt* for a wife and queen, while *Judea* could have furnished him with every kind of superior excellence.

Verse 7. *Tell me—where thou feedest*] This is spoken as if the parties were shepherds, or employed in the pastoral life. But how this would apply either to *Solomon,* or the *princes of Egypt,* is not easy to ascertain. Probably in the marriage festival there was something like our *masks,* in which persons of quality assumed rural characters and their employments. See that fine one composed by *Milton,* called Comus.

To rest at noon] In hot countries the shepherds and their flocks are obliged to retire to shelter during the burning heats of the noonday sun. This is common in all countries, in the summer heats, where *shelter* can be had.

One that turneth aside] As a *wanderer;* one who, not knowing where to find her companions, wanders fruitlessly in seeking them. It was customary for shepherds to *drive their flocks together* for the purpose of *conversing, playing on the pipe,* or having *trials of skill* in *poetry* or *music.* So Virgil:—

Forte sub arguta consederat ilice Daphnis
Compulerantque greges Corydon et Thyrsis in
    unum:
Thyrsis oves, Corydon distentas lacte capellas;
Ambo florentes ætatibus, Arcades ambo,
Et cantare pares, et respondere parati.

                Ecl. vii. v. 1.

"Beneath a holm repair'd two jolly swains:
  Their sheep and goats together grazed the
    plains;
Both young Arcadians, both alike inspired
To sing and answer as the song required."
                    Dryden.

This does not express the *sense* of the original: from the different pastures in which they had been accustomed to feed their flocks, *they drove their sheep and goats together* for the purpose mentioned in the pastoral; and, in course, returned to their respective pasturages, when their business was over.

Verse 8. *If thou know not*] This appears to be the reply of the *virgins.* They know not exactly; and therefore direct the bride to the *shepherds,* who would give information.

Verse 9. *I have compared thee—to a company of horses*] This may be translated, more literally, "I have compared thee סֻסָתִי *lesusathi,* to *my mare,* in the chariots or courses of Pharaoh;" and so the *versions* understood it. Mares, in preference to *horses,* were used both for riding and for chariots in the East. They are much *swifter,* endure more *hardship,* and will go longer *without food,* than either the *stallion* or the *gelding.* There is perhaps no brute creature in the world so beautiful as a fine well-bred horse or mare; and the finest woman in the universe, *Helen,* has been compared to a *horse in a Thessalian chariot,* by *Theocritus.* Idyl. xviii. ver. 28:—

Ὧδε και ἁ χρυσεα Ἑλενα διαφαινετ' εν ἡμιν,
Πιειρη, μεγαλη, ἀτ' ανεδραμεν ογμος αρουρα,
Η καπῳ κυπαρισσος, η ἁρματι Θεσσαλος ἱππος.

"The golden Helen, tall and graceful, appears
  as distinguished among us as the furrow
  in the field, the cypress in the garden, or
  the *Thessalian horse in the chariot.*"

This passage amply justifies the Hebrew bard, in the simile before us. See Jer. vi. 2.

Verse 10. *Thy cheeks are comely*] D'Arvieux has remarked that "the Arabian ladies wear a great many *pearls* about their *necks* and *caps.* They have *gold chains* about their *necks* which hang down upon their *bosoms* with strings of coloured gauze; the gauze itself *bordered* with *zechins* and other pieces of *gold coin,* which hang upon their *foreheads* and both *cheeks.*

A. M. cir. 2990
B. C. cir. 1014
Ante I. Olymp.
cir. 238
Ante U. C. cir.
261

11 We will make thee borders of gold with studs of silver.

12 While the king *sitteth* at his table, my spikenard sendeth forth the smell thereof.

13 A bundle of myrrh *is* my well-beloved unto me; he shall lie all night betwixt my breasts.

14 My beloved *is* unto me *as* a cluster of

ⁿcamphire in the vineyards of En-gedi.

A. M. cir. 2990
B. C. cir. 1014
Ante I. Olymp.
cir. 238
Ante U. C. cir.
261

15 °Behold, thou *art* fair, ᵖmy love; behold, thou *art* fair; thou *hast* dove's eyes.

16 Behold, thou *art* fair, my beloved, yea, pleasant: also our bed *is* green.

17 The beams of our house *are* cedar, *and* our �q rafters of fir.

ⁿOr, *cypress;* chap. iv. 13——°Chap. iv. 1; v. 12

ᵖOr, *my companion*——�q Or, *galleries*

The ordinary women wear *small silver coins,* with which they cover their *forehead-piece* like *fish scales,* as this is one of the principal ornaments of their faces." I have seen their *essence bottles* ornamented with festoons of *aspers,* and small pieces of silver *pearls, beads,* &c. One of these is now before me.

Verse 11. *Borders of gold*] I have observed several of the *handkerchiefs,* shawls, and head attire of the Eastern women, curiously and expensively worked in the *borders* with *gold* and *silver,* and variously coloured silk, which has a splendid effect.

Verse 12. *While the king* sitteth *at his table*] במסבו *bimsibbo,* in his *circle,* probably meaning the circle of his friends at the marriage festivals, or a *round table.*

Verse 13. *He shall lie all night betwixt my breasts.*] Mr. *Harmer* contends that it is the *bundle of myrrh* which the bride says shall *lie all night betwixt her breasts,* to which she compares the bridegroom, his name being as pleasing and refreshing to her mind, as the myrrh or *stacte* was to her senses, by its continual fragrance.

Verse 14. *A cluster of camphire*] Mr. *Hasselquist* supposes this to mean a *bunch of the Cyprus grape;* but this is supposed to mean a *shrub* so called, not any production of the isle of *Cyprus;* the best kinds of which were found at *En-gedi.* This place belonged to the tribe of Judah.

Perhaps the poet alludes to the dark colour of the *hair,* which by the Greeks was not unfrequently compared to the *bunches of grapes;* by no means an unfit similitude for thick black

clustering curls. The following lines represent the same idea:—

وفوع يزين اضتنى اسود فاحم
اثيث كثن اللخلة اطتعتكل

"The dark black locks that ornament her neck
Hang thick and clustering like the branchy palm."

Verse 15. *Thou* hast *doves' eyes*] The large and beautiful dove of Syria is supposed to be here referred to, the eyes of which are remarkably fine.

Verse 16. *Also our bed* is *green.*] עֶרֶשׂ *eres,* from its use in several places of the Hebrew Bible, generally signifies a *mattress;* and here probably a *green bank* is meant, on which they sat down, being now on a walk in the country. Or it may mean a *bower* in a *garden,* or the nuptial bed.

Verse 17. *The beams of our house* are *cedar*] Perhaps it was under a *cedar tree,* whose vast limbs were interwoven with the ברות *beroth,* a tree of the *cypress* kind, where they now sat. And this natural bower recommended itself to the poet's attention by its strength, loftiness, and its affording them a *shady cover* and *cool retreat.* How natural to break out into the praise of a *bower,* by whose *branches* and *foliage* we are shielded from the intense heat of the sun! Even the *shelter of a great rock in a weary land* is celebrated by the pen of the first of *prophets* and greatest of *poets,* Isa. xxxii. 2.

With this chapter the *first* day of the marriage ceremonies is supposed to end.

CHAPTER II

A description of the bridegroom, and his love to the bride, 1–9. A fine description of spring, 10–13. The mutual love of both, 14–17.

A. M. cir. 2990
B. C. cir. 1014
Ante I. Olymp.
cir. 238
Ante U. C. cir.
261

I AM the rose of Sharon, *and* the lily of the valleys.

2 As the lily among thorns, so *is* my love among the daughters.

3 As the apple tree among the trees of the wood, so *is* my beloved among the sons. ᵃI sat down under his shadow with

A. M. cir. 2990
B. C. cir. 1014
Ante I. Olymp.
cir. 238
Ante U. C. cir.
261

ᵃHeb. *I delighted*

and sat down, &c.

NOTES ON CHAP. II

Verse 1. *I am the rose of Sharon*] *Sharon* was a very fruitful place, where David's cattle were fed, 1 Chron. xxvii. 29. It is mentioned as a place of excellence, Isa. xxxv. 2, and as a place of flocks, Isa. lxv. 10. Perhaps it would

be better, with almost all the *versions,* to translate, "I am the rose of the field." The bridegroom had just before called her *fair;* she with a becoming modesty, represents her beauty as nothing extraordinary, and compares herself to a *common flower of the field.* This, in the warmth of his affection, he denies, insisting that

A. M. cir. 2990
B. C. cir. 1014
Ante I. Olymp.
cir. 238
Ante U. C. cir.
261

great delight, [b]and his fruit *was* sweet to my [c]taste.

4 He brought me to the [d]banqueting house, and his banner over me *was* love.

5 Stay me with flagons, [e]comfort me with apples: for I *am* sick of love.

6 [f]His left hand *is* under my head, and his right hand doth embrace me.

7 [g]I [h]charge you, O ye daughters of Jerusalem, by the roes, and by the hinds of the field, that ye stir not up, nor awake *my* love, till he please.

8 The voice of my beloved! behold, he cometh leaping upon the mountains, skipping upon the hills.

A. M. cir. 2990
B. C. cir. 1014
Ante I. Olymp.
cir. 238
Ante U. C. cir.
261

9 [i]My beloved is like a roe, or a young hart: behold, he standeth behind our wall, he looketh forth at the windows, [k]showing himself through the lattice.

10 My beloved spake, and said unto me, [l]Rise up, my love, my fair one, and come away.

11 For, lo, the winter is past, the rain is over *and* gone;

---

[b]Rev. xxii. 1, 2——[c]Heb. *palate*——[d]Heb. *house of wine*
[e]Heb. *straw me with apples*——[f]Chap. viii. 3

[g]Heb. *I adjure you*——[h]Chap. iii. 5; viii. 4——[i]Ver. 17
[k]Heb. *flourishing*——[l]Ver. 13

---

she as much surpasses all other maidens as the flower of the *lily* does the *bramble,* ver. 2.

Verse 3. *As the apple tree*] The bride returns the compliment, and says, *As the apple* or *citron tree is among the trees of the wood,* so is the bridegroom among all other men.

I sat down under his shadow] I am become his spouse, and my union with him makes me indescribably happy.

Verse 4. *He brought me to the banqueting house*] Literally, *the house of wine.* The ancients preserved their wine, not in barrels or dark cellars under ground, as we do, but in large *pitchers,* ranged against the wall in some upper apartment in the house, the place where they kept their most precious effects. We have a proof of this in HOMER:—

Ως φαν· ὁ δ' ὑψοροφον θαλαμον κατεβησατο πατρος
Ευρυν, ὁθι νητος χρυσος και χαλκος εκειτο,
Εσθης τ' εν χηλοισιν, ἀλις τ' ευωδες ελαιον.
Εν δε πιθοι οινοιο παλαιου ἡδυποτοιο
Εστασαν, ακρητον θειον ποτον εντος εχοντες,
'Εξειης ποτε τοιχον αρηροτες· ειποτ' Οδυσσευς
Οικαδε νοστησειε, και αλγεα πολλα μογησας.
Κληϊσται δ' επεσαν σανιδες πυκινως αραρυιαι,
Δικλιδες· εν δε γυνη ταμιη νυκτας τε και ημαρ
Εσχ', κ. τ. λ.   Od. lib. ii., ver. 337.

Meantime the lofty rooms the prince surveys,
Where lay the *treasures* of th' Ithacian race.
Here, ruddy *brass* and *gold* refulgent blazed;
There, polished *chests embroider'd vestures* graced.
Here, *pots of oil* breathed forth a rich perfume;
There, *jars of wine* in rows adorn'd the dome.
(Pure flavorous wine, by gods in bounty given,
And worthy to exalt the feasts of heaven.)
Untouch'd they stood, till, his long labours o'er,
The great *Ulysses* reach'd his native shore.
A double strength of bars secured the gates;
Fast by the door wise *Euryclea* waits, &c.
                 POPE.

Verse 5. *Stay me with flagons*] I believe the original words mean some kind of *cordials* with which we are unacquainted. The *versions* in general understand some kind of *ointment* or *perfumes* by the first term. I suppose the good man was perfectly sincere who took this for his *text,* and, after having repeated, *Stay me with flagons, comfort me with apples, for I am sick of love* sat down, perfectly overwhelmed with

his own feelings, and was not able to proceed! But while we admit such a person's sincerity, who can help questioning his judgment?

Verse 7. *I charge you—by the roes*] This was probably some rustic mode of adjuration. The verses themselves require little comment. With this verse the *first night* of the *first day* is supposed to end.

Verse 8. *Behold, he cometh leaping*] This appears to be highly characteristic of the gambols of the shepherds, and points out the ecstasy with which those who were enamoured ran to their mates. It is supposed that the *second day's eclogue* begins at this verse. The author of what was then called *A New Translation of Solomon's Song,* observes, 1. The bride relates how the bridegroom, attended by his companions, had come under her window, and called upon her to come forth and enjoy the beauties of the spring, ver. 9, 10, 11, &c. 2. She then returns to her narration, chap. iii. 1. The bridegroom did not come according to her wishes. Night came on; she did not find him in her bed; she went out to seek him; found him, and brought him to her mother's pavilion, ver. 4; and then, as before, conjures the virgins not to disturb his repose, ver. 5.

Verse 9. *He standeth behind our wall*] This may refer to the *wall* by which the house was *surrounded,* the space between which and the house constituted the *court.* He was seen first *behind the wall,* and then in the *court;* and lastly came to the *window* of his bride's chamber.

Verse 11. *The winter is past*] Mr. *Harmer* has made some good collections on this part, from Drs. *Shaw* and *Russel,* which I shall transcribe. One part of the winter is distinguished from the rest of it by the people of the East, on account of the *severity of the cold.* At *Aleppo* it lasts about forty days, and is called by the natives *maurbanie.* I would propose it to the consideration of the learned, whether the word here used, and translated *winter,* may not be understood to mean what the *Aleppines* express by the term *maurbanie.* It occurs nowhere else in the Old Testament; and another word is used for the *rainy* part of the year in general. If this thought be admitted, it will greatly illustrate the words of the bridegroom: *Lo, the winter is past; the rain is over, and gone.* For then the last clause will not be explanatory of the first, and signify that the

A. M. cir. 2990
B. C. cir. 1014
Ante I. Olymp.
cir. 238
Ante U. C. cir.
261

12 The flowers appear on the earth; the time of the singing of birds is come, and the voice of the turtle is heard in our land;

13 The fig tree putteth forth her green figs, and the vines *with* the tender grape give a *good* smell. ᵐArise, my love, my fair one, and come away.

14 O my dove, *that art* in the clefts of the rock, in the secret *places* of the stairs, let me see thy countenance, ⁿlet me hear thy voice;

for sweet *is* thy voice, and thy countenance *is* comely.

A. M. cir. 2990
B. C. cir. 1014
Ante I. Olymp.
cir. 238
Ante U. C. cir.
261

15 Take us °the foxes, the little foxes, that spoil the vines: for our vines *have* tender grapes.

16 ᵖMy beloved *is* mine, and I *am* his: he feedeth among the lilies.

17 �q Until the day break, and the shadows flee away, turn, my beloved, and be thou ʳlike a roe or a young hart upon the mountains ˢof Bether.

ᵐVer. 10——ⁿChap. viii. 13——°Psa. lxxx. 13; Ezek. xiii. 4; Luke xiii. 32

ᵖChap. vi. 3; vii. 10——�q Chap. iv. 6——ʳVer. 9; chap. viii. 14——ˢOr, *of division*

---

moist part of the year was entirely past; with which, Dr. *Russel* assures us, all pleasantness withdraws at *Aleppo;* but the words will import: "The *maurbanie* is past and over; the weather is become agreeably warm; the rain too is just ceased, and consequently hath left us the prospect of several days of serenity and undisturbed pleasantness."

The weather of Judea was in this respect, I presume, like that at *Algiers;* where, after two or three days of rain, there is usually, according to Dr. *Shaw,* "a week, a fortnight, or more, of fair and good weather. Of such a sort of cessation of rain alone, the bridegroom, methinks, is here to be understood; not of the absolute termination of the rainy season, and the *summer droughts* being come on. And if so, what can the time that is *past* mean but the *maurbanie?* Indeed, Dr. *Russel,* in giving us an account of the excursions of the English merchants at *Aleppo,* has undesignedly furnished us with a good comment on this and the two following verses. These gentlemen, it seems, dine abroad under a tent, in spring and autumn on Saturdays, and often on Wednesdays. They do the same during the good weather in winter; but they live at the gardens in April, and part of May. In the heat of the summer they dine at the gardens, as once or twice a week they dine under a tent in autumn and spring." The cold weather is not supposed by Solomon to have been long over, since it is distinctly mentioned; and the *Aleppines* make these incursions very early; the *narcissus* flowers during the whole of the *maurbanie;* the *hyacinths* and *violets* at least before it is quite over. The appearing of flowers, then, doth not mean the appearing of the first and earliest flowers, but must rather be understood of the earth's being covered with them; which at *Aleppo* is not till after the middle of *February,* a *small crane's bill* appearing on the banks of the river there about the middle of *February,* quickly after which comes a profusion of flowers. The *nightingales,* too, which are there in abundance, not only afford much pleasure by their songs in the gardens, but are also kept tame in the houses, and *let out* at a small rate to divert such as choose it in the city; so that no entertainments are made in the *spring* without a concert of these birds. No wonder, then, that *Solomon* makes the bridegroom speak of the singing of birds; and it teaches us what these birds are, which are expressly distinguished from turtle doves.

Verse 13. *The fig tree putteth forth her green figs*] The fig tree in Judea bears *double* crops; the first of which is ripe in *spring.* But the tree, as I have elsewhere observed, bears figs all the year through, in the climes congenial to it. That is, the fig tree has always *ripe* or *unripe* fruit on it. I never saw a healthy tree naked. But in the beginning of spring they grow fast, and become turgid.

The vines with *the tender grape*] The versions understand this of the *flowers* of the vine. These were formerly put into the new wine (2 lbs. to every cask) to give it a fine flavour.

Verse 14. *My dove—in the clefts of the rock*] He compares his bride hiding herself in her secret chambers and closets to a *dove* in the clefts of the rock.

Verse 15. *Take us the foxes*] That these were ruinous to vines all authors allow. They love the vine, and they are eaten in autumn in some countries, according to *Galen,* when they are very fat with eating the grapes. They abounded in Judea; and did most damage when the clusters were young and tender. It is likely that these are the words of the *bridegroom* to his *companions,* just as he was entering the apartment of his spouse. "Take care of the vineyard: set the traps for the foxes, which are spoiling the vines; and destroy their *young* as far as possible."

Verse 16. *My beloved is mine*] The words of the *bride* on his entering: "I am thy own; thou art wholly mine."

He feedeth among the lilies.] The odour with which he is surrounded is as fine as if he passed the night among the sweetest scented flowers.

Verse 17. *Until the day break*] Literally, *until the day breathe;* until the first dawn, which is usually accompanied with the most refreshing *breezes.*

The shadows flee away] Referring to the *evening* or *setting of the sun,* at which all *shadows* vanish.

The mountains of Bether.] Translated also *mountains of division,* supposed to mean the mountains of *Beth-horon.*

There was a place called *Bithron,* 2 Sam. ii. 29, on the other side of Jordan; and as the name signifies PARTITION, it might have had its name from the circumstance of its being divided or separated from Judea by the river Jordan.

With this chapter the *second night* is supposed to **end.**

CHAPTER III

The bride mentions the absence of her spouse, her search after him, and her ultimate success, 1–5. A description of the bridegroom, his bed, chariot, &c., 6–11.

A. M. cir. 2990
B. C. cir. 1014
Ante I. Olymp.
cir. 238
Ante U. C. cir.
261

BY ᵃnight on my bed I sought him whom my soul loveth: I sought him, but I found him not.

2 I will rise now, and go about the city in the streets, and in the broad ways I will seek him whom my soul loveth: I sought him, but I found him not.

3 ᵇThe watchmen that go about the city found me: *to whom I said,* Saw ye him whom my soul loveth?

4 *It was* but a little that I passed from them, but I found him whom my soul loveth: I held him, and would not let him go, until I had brought him into my mother's house, and into the chamber of her that conceived me.

5 ᶜI charge you, O ye daughters of Jerusalem, by the roes, and by the hinds of the field, that ye stir not up, nor awake *my* love, till he please.

6 ᵈWho *is* this that cometh out of the wil-

derness like pillars of smoke, perfumed with myrrh and frankincense, with all powders of the merchant?

A. M. cir. 2990
B. C. cir. 1014
Ante I. Olymp.
cir. 238
Ante U. C. cir.
261

7 Behold his bed, which *is* Solomon's; threescore valiant men *are* about it, of the valiant of Israel.

8 They all hold swords, *being* expert in war: every man *hath* his sword upon his thigh because of fear in the night.

9 King Solomon made himself ᵉa chariot of the wood of Lebanon.

10 He made the pillars thereof *of* silver, the bottom thereof *of* gold, the covering of it *of* purple, the midst thereof being paved *with* love, for the daughters of Jerusalem.

11 Go forth, O ye daughters of Zion, and behold King Solomon with the crown wherewith his mother crowned him in the day of his espousals, and in the day of the gladness of his heart.

ᵃIsa. xxvi. 9——ᵇChap. v. 7——ᶜChap. ii. 7; viii. 4——ᵈChap. viii. 5——ᵉOr, *a bed*

NOTES ON CHAP. III

Verse 1. *By night on my bed I sought him*] It appears that the bridegroom only saw the bride *by night:* that on the night referred to here he did not come as usual. The bride, troubled on the account, rose and sought him; inquired of the city guards, and continued to seek till at last she found him, and brought him to her apartment, ver. 2-4.

Verse 4. *Into my mother's house*] The *women* in the East have all *separate apartments,* into which no person ever attempts to enter except the *husband.* We find *Isaac* bringing *Rebecca* into his *mother's tent,* when he made her his wife, Gen. xxiv. 67. What is here related appears to refer to the third night of the nuptials.

Verse 5. *I charge you*] The same adjuration as before, chap. ii. 7.

Verse 6. *Who is this that cometh out of the wilderness*] Going to Egypt was called *descending* or *going down,* coming from it was termed *coming up.* The bride, having risen, goes after her spouse to the country, and the clouds of incense arising from her *palanquin* seemed like *pillars of smoke;* and the appearance was altogether so splendid as to attract the admiration of her own women, who converse about her splendour, excellence, &c., and then take occasion to describe Solomon's nuptial bed and chariot. Some think that it is the *bridegroom* who is spoken of here.

With this verse the *third night* is supposed to end.

Verse 7. *Threescore valiant men*] These

were the *guards* about the pavilion of the bridegroom, who were placed there *because of fear in the night.* The *security* and *state* of the prince required such a guard as this, and the passage is to be *literally* understood.

Verse 8. *They all hold swords*] They are swordsmen. Every man has a sword, and is well instructed how to use it.

Verse 9. *Of the wood of Lebanon.*] Of the *cedar* that grew on that mount. It is very likely that a *nuptial bed,* not a *chariot,* is intended by the original word אפריון *appiryon.* *Montanus* properly translates it *sponsarum thalamum,* a nuptial bed. It may, however, mean a *palanquin.*

Verse 10. *The pillars—of silver*] The *bedposts* were made of silver, or *cased* with wrought silver plates, like the king's chairs brought from Hanover, now, in one of the staterooms in *Windsor Castle.*

The bottom thereof of gold] This may refer to *cords* made of *gold thread,* or to the *mattress,* which was made of cloth ornamented with gold.

The covering—of purple] Most probably the *canopy.*

The midst—paved with love] The *counterpane,* a superb piece of *embroidery,* wrought by some of the noble maids of Jerusalem, and, as a proof of their affection, respect, and love, presented to the bride and bridegroom, on their nuptial day. This is most likely to be the sense of the passage, though some suppose it to refer to the whole court.

A Turkish couch is made of wooden *lattices* painted and gilded; the inside is painted with baskets of flowers and nosegays, intermixed with *little mottoes* according to the fancy of the artist. Solomon's couch may have been of the same kind, and decorated in the same way; and the *paving with love* may refer to the amatory verses worked either on the counterpane, hangings, or embroidered carpet. And as this was done by the *daughters of Jerusalem*, they might have expressed the most striking parts of such a *chaste history of love* as Halaly's *Leely* and *Mejnoon* on the different parts. I see that Dr. *Good* is of this opinion. It is sufficiently probable.

Verse 11. *Go forth, O ye daughters of Zion*] This is the exhortation of the *companions* of the *bride* to the *females* of the *city* to examine the superb appearance of the bridegroom, and especially the *nuptial crown*, which appears to have been made by *Bathsheba*, who it is supposed might have lived till the time of Solomon's marriage with the daughter of Pharaoh. It is conjectured that the *prophet* refers to a *nuptial crown*, Isa. lxi. 10. But a *crown*, both on the *bride* and *bridegroom*, was common among most people on such occasions. The nuptial crown among the Greeks and Romans was only a chaplet or wreath of flowers.

In the day of the gladness of his heart.] The day in which all his wishes were crowned, by being united to that female whom beyond all others he loved.

Here the *third day* is supposed to end.

CHAPTER IV

The bridegroom's description of his bride, her person, her accomplishments, her chastity, and her general excellence, 1–16.

A. M. cir. 2990
B. C. cir. 1014
Ante I. Olymp. cir. 238
Ante U. C. cir. 261

BEHOLD, [a]thou *art* fair, my love; behold, thou *art* fair; thou *hast* doves' eyes within thy locks: thy hair *is* as a [b]flock of goats, [c]that appear from Mount Gilead.

2 [d]Thy teeth *are* like a flock *of sheep that are even* shorn, which came up from the washing; whereof every one bear twins, and none *is* barren among them.

3 Thy lips *are* like a thread of scarlet, and thy speech *is* comely: [e]thy temples *are* like a piece of a pomegranate within thy locks.

4 [f]Thy neck *is* like the tower of David

A. M. cir. 2990
B. C. cir. 1014
Ante I. Olymp. cir. 238
Ante U. C. cir. 261

---

[a]Chap. i. 15; v. 12——[b]Chap. vi. 5——[c]Or, *that eat of,* &c.——[d]Chap. vi. 6——[e]Chap. vi. 7——[f]Chap. vii. 4

NOTES ON CHAP. IV

Verse 1. *Thou* hast *doves' eyes within thy locks*] Perhaps this refers rather to a sort of veil worn by many of the Eastern women, but especially in Egypt. It is a species of black cloth made of the hair of some animal, probably the black goat; is suspended from the head by silken cords, one of which comes from the crown of the head, down the forehead, to the upper part of the nose, just under the eyes, at which place the veil begins; for the forehead and the eyes are uncovered, except the cord above mentioned, which is ornamented with gold, silver, and precious stones, according to the circumstances of the wearer. This partial veil not only covers all the face, the eyes and forehead excepted, but the neck also, and hangs loosely down over the bosom. One of them, lately brought from Egypt, now lies before me.

But the clause, *within thy locks,* מבעד לצמתך *mib-baad letsammathech,* is not well translated, either by ourselves or by the *versions.* Jerome's translation is an indication of the meaning: *Absque eo quod intrinsecus latet; without that,* or independently of that, *which lies hidden within.* The *Septuagint, Syriac,* and *Arabic* have, *besides thy silence.* *Calmet* contends that none of these gives the *true meaning,* and that *the word* צמת *tsemath* has not the meaning of *hair* or *locks* wherever it occurs, and has quite a different meaning in Isa. xlvii. 2. St. Jerome on this place expresses himself thus: *Nolentibus qui interpretati sunt transferre nomen quod in Sancta Scriptura sonat turpitudinem.*—Ergo צמתך *tsammathech, quod* Aquila *posuit,* verenda mulieris *appellantur cujus etymologia apud eos sonat* sitiens tuus. *Calmet* translates: *Vous êtes toute belle, mon amie; vous êtes toute belle: vos yeux sont des yeux de colombe; sans ce que la pudeur et la modestie tiennent caché.* I leave the translation of these to the learned reader. See another description under ver. 7.

As a flock of goats] Because it was *black* and sleek, as the hair of the goats of Arabia and Palestine is known to be; which, with its fine undulation, is supposed to bear some resemblance to the *curls* or *plaits* of a woman's tresses. The mountains of *Gilead* were beyond Jordan, on the frontiers of *Arabia Deserta.*

Verse 2. *Thy teeth are like a flock*] This comparison appears to be founded on the *evenness, neatness,* and *whiteness* of the *newly shorn* and newly *washed* sheep.

Verse 3. *Thy lips are like a thread of scarlet*] Both *lips* and *cheeks* were *ruddy; sicut fragmen mali punici.*—VULGATE. *Like the section of a pomegranate,* that side cut off on which is the *finest blush.* This is a good and apt *metaphor.* But the inside may be referred to, as it is finely streaked with red and white melting into each other. She had beautiful *hair,* beautiful *eyes,* beautiful *cheeks* and *lips,* and a most pleasing and dulcet *voice.*

Within thy locks.] See on ver. 1, and on ver. 7.

Verse 4. *Thy neck is like the tower of David*] It is certain that *bucklers* were frequently hung about towers, both for their ornaments, and to have them at hand when their use was required; see Ezek. xxvii. 10. But the allusion here may be to those *pillars* which are often seen in armouries on which weapons of

A. M. cir. 2990
B. C. cir. 1014
Ante I. Olymp.
cir. 238
Ante U. C. cir.
261 builded ᵍfor an armoury, whereon there hang a thousand bucklers, all shields of mighty men.

5 ʰThy two breasts *are* like
two young roes that are twins, which feed
among the lilies.

6 ¹Until the day ᵏbreak, and the shadows

flee away, I will get me to the A. M. cir. 2990
B. C. cir. 1014
Ante I. Olymp.
cir. 238
Ante U. C. cir.
261
mountain of myrrh, and to the
hill of frankincense.

7 ¹Thou *art* all fair, my love;
there is no spot in thee.

8 Come with me from Lebanon, *my* spouse,
with me from Lebanon: look from the top of

ᵍNeh. iii. 19——ʰSee Prov. v. 19; chap. vii. 3

¹Chap. ii. 17——ᵏHeb. *breathe*——¹Eph. v. 27

---

various kinds are hung, formed into a great
variety of shapes and very splendid. Whoever
has seen the *armoury* in the *tower* of London,
or such like places, has most probably seen
something very similar to that of which the
poet speaks.

Verse 5. *Thy two breasts are like two young
roes*] I have met with many attempts to support this *similitude*, or rather to show that there
is a *similitude;* but I judge them unworthy of
citation. The poet speaks the *language of
nature;* and in a case of this kind, where the
impassioned lover attempts to describe the different perfections of his bride, language often
fails him, and his comparisons and similitudes
are often without strict correctness. In love
songs we have heard ladies' *necks* compared to
that of the *swan*, not only for its *whiteness,*
but also for its *length!* The description here
shows more of *nature* than of *art*, which I consider a high recommendation.

Feed among the lilies.] It may be the *nipples*
especially, which the poet compares to the *two
young roes;* and the *lilies* may refer to the
whiteness of the *breasts* themselves.

Verse 6. *Until the day break*] Until the
morning *breeze.* See chap. ii. 17.

The shadows flee away] Till the *sun sets.*

Mountain of myrrh] Probably the same as
the mountains of *Bether*, chap. ii. 17. Mountains where the trees grew from which *myrrh*
and *incense* were extracted.

Verse 7. *Thou art all fair—there is no spot
in thee.*] "My beloved, every part of thee is
beautiful; thou hast not a single defect."

The description given of the beauties of
Daphne, by Ovid, Metam. lib. i. ver. 497, has
some similarity to the above verses:—

Spectat inornatos collo *pendere* capillos.
*Et, quid si comantur? ait. Videt igne micantes
Sideribus similes* oculos; *videt oscula, quæ non
Est vidisse satis. Laudat* digitosque, manusque,
Brachiaque, *et nudos media plus parte* lacertos.
Si qua latent *meliora putat.*

Her well-turn'd *neck* he view'd, (her neck was
    bare,)
And on her shoulders her *dishevell'd hair.*
O, were it comb'd, said he, with what a grace
Would every *waving curl* become her face!
He view'd her *eyes*, like heavenly lamps that
    shone,
He view'd her *lips*, too sweet to view alone;
Her taper fingers, and her panting *breast.*
He praises all he sees; and, for the rest,
Believes the *beauties yet unseen* the best.
                                    DRYDEN.

Jayadeva describes the beauty of Radha in
nearly the same imagery: "Thy *lips*, O thou
most beautiful among women, are a *bandhujiva*
flower; the lustre of the *madhuca* beams upon

thy *cheek;* thine *eye* outshines the blue *lotos;*
thy nose is a bud of the *tila;* the *cunda* blossom
yields to thy *teeth.* Surely thou descendedst
from heaven, O slender damsel! attended by a
company of youthful goddesses; and all their
beauties are collected in thee." See these
poems, and the short notes at the end.

The same poet has a parallel thought to that
in ver. 5, "Thy two breasts," &c. The companions of *Radha* thus address her: "Ask the
two round hillocks which receive pure dew
drops from the garland playing on thy neck,
and the *buds* on *whose tops* start aloft with
the thought of thy beloved."

Verse 8. *My spouse.*] The כלה *callah,*
which we translate *spouse*, seems to have a
peculiar meaning. Mr. Harmer thinks the
Jewish princess is intended by it; and this
seems to receive confirmation from the bridegroom calling her *sister*, ver. 9, that is, one of
the same stock and country; and thus different
from the Egyptian bride.

Mr. Harmer's opinion is very probable, that
TWO *queens* are mentioned in this song: one
Pharaoh's daughter, the other a Jewess. See
his *outlines.* But I contend for no system relative to this song.

Look from the top of Amana, &c.] Solomon,
says *Calmet*, by an admirable poetic fiction,
represents his beloved as a mountain nymph,
wholly occupied in hunting the lion and the
leopard on the mountains of Lebanon, Amana,
Shenir, and Hermon. As a bold and undisci-
plined virgin, who is unwilling to leave her
wild and rural retreats, he invites her to come
from those hills; and promises to deck her with
a crown and to make her his bride. Thus the
poets represent their goddess *Diana*, and even
Venus herself:—

Per juga, per sylvas, dumosaque saxa vagatur
Nuda genu, vestem ritu succincta Dianæ;
Hortaturque canes; tutæque animalia prædæ,
Aut pronos lepores, aut celsum in cornua
    cervum,
Aut agitat damas: at fortibus abstinet apris.
                            MET. lib. x., ver. 535.

Now buskin'd like the virgin huntress goes
Through woods, and pathless wilds, and moun-
    tain snows.
With her own tuneful voice she joys to cheer
The panting hounds that chase the flying deer.
She runs the labyrinth of the fearful hares,
But fearless beasts and dangerous prey forbears.

Mount *Libanus* separates Phœnicia from
Syria. *Amanus* is between Syria and Silicia.
Shenir and *Hermon* are beyond Jordan, to the
south of Damascus and Mount Libanus, and
northward of the mountains of Gilead. Hermon
and Shenir are but different parts of the same
chain of mountains which separates *Trachonitis,*

A. M. cir. 2990
B. C. cir. 1014
Ante I. Olymp. cir. 238
Ante U. C. cir. 261

Amana, from the top of Shenir [m]and Hermon, from the lion's dens, from the mountains of the leopards.

9 Thou hast [n]ravished my heart, my sister, *my* spouse; thou hast ravished my heart with one of thine eyes, with one chain of thy neck.

10 How fair is thy love, my sister, *my* spouse! [o]how much better is thy love than wine! and the smell of thine ointments than all spices!

11 Thy lips, O *my* spouse, drop *as* the honey-comb: [p]honey and milk *are* under thy tongue; and the smell of thy garments *is* [q]like the smell of Lebanon.

12 A garden [r]enclosed *is* my sister, *my* spouse; a spring shut up, a fountain sealed.

A. M. cir. 2990
B. C. cir. 1014
Ante I. Olymp. cir. 238
Ante U. C. cir. 261

13 Thy plants *are* an orchard of pomegranates, with pleasant fruits; [s]camphire, with spikenard.

14 Spikenard and saffron; calamus and cinnamon, with all trees of frankincense; myrrh and aloes, with all the chief spices:

15 A fountain of gardens, a well of [t]living waters, and streams from Lebanon.

16 Awake, O north wind; and come, thou south; blow up my garden, *that* the spices thereof may flow out. [u]Let my beloved come into his garden, and eat his pleasant fruits.

---

[m]Deut. iii. 9——[n]Or, *taken away my heart*——[o]Ch. i. 2——[p]Prov. xxiv. 13, 14; chap. v. 1

[q]Gen. xxvii. 27; Hos. xiv. 6, 7——[r]Heb. *barred*——[s]Or, *cypress;* ch. i. 14——[t]John iv. 10; vii. 38——[u]Ch. v. 1

---

or the country of *Manasses*, from Arabia Deserta. For these places, see 2 Kings v. 12, and Deut. iii. 9, where they are probably meant.

Verse 9. Thou hast ravished my heart] לבבתני *libbabtini,* "Thou hast hearted me," i. e., taken away my heart; as we say, "He has barked the tree," i. e., he has stripped it of its bark; "He has fleeced the flock," i. e., deprived them of their wool.

With one of thine eyes] באחד מעיניך *beachad meeynayich.* This has been thought a harsh expression, and various emendations have been sought. The *Masoretes* have put באחת *beachath,* "at once," in the margin; and this is confirmed by *twenty* of *Kennicott's* MSS.; but *De Rossi* does not notice it. It is scarcely necessary; the sense to me is clear and good without it. "Even one of thine eyes, or one glance of thine eyes, has been sufficient to deprive me of all power; it has completely overcome me;" for *glance* may be understood, and such forms of speech are common in all languages, when speaking on such subjects. If even taken *literally,* the sense is good; for the poet may refer to a *side glance,* shot in *passing by* or *turning away,* where only *one* eye could be seen. I think this a better sense than that which is obtained from the Masoretic emendation.

With one chain of thy neck] Probably referring to the play of the *cervical muscles,* rather than to *necklaces,* or *ringlets* of hair.

Verse 10. How much better is thy love] דדיך *dodayich;* Hebrew. Μαστοι σου; *Septuagint. Ubera tua; Vulgate.* "Thy breasts." And so all the *versions,* except the *Chaldee.*

Smell of thine ointments] Perfumes.

Verse 11. Thy lips—drop as the honey-comb] Thy words are as delicious to my heart as the first droppings of the honey-comb are to the palate.

Honey and milk are under thy tongue] Eloquence and persuasive speech were compared among the ancients to *honey* and *milk.*

Thus Homer, Iliad, lib. i., ver. 247:—

Τοισι δε Νεστωρ

Ηδυεπης ανορουσε, λιγυς Πυλιων αγορητης,
Του και απο γλωσσης μελιτος γλυκιων ρεεν αυδη.

Experienced Nestor, in *persuasion* skill'd,
Words sweet as honey from his lips distill'd.

But the figure is common to all writers and languages. A similar expression will be seen in the *Gitagovinda.*

Verse 12. A garden enclosed—a spring shut up, a fountain sealed.] Different expressions to point out the *fidelity* of the bride, or of the Jewish queen. See the *outlines.* She is *unsullied,* a chaste, pure *virgin.* None has ever *entered* into this *garden;* none has yet *tasted* of this *spring;* the *seal* of this *fountain* has never been *broken.* Among the Athenians, the interior part of the house, called the women's apartment, was not only locked but sealed; so Aristophan., Thesmoph. ver. 422:—

Ειτα δια τουτον ταις γυναικωνιτισιν
Σφραγιδας εμβαλλουσιν ηδη και μοχλους.

And on this account, to the women's apartment
They place seals as well as bolts.

And *seal,* as applicable to chaste conduct, is a phrase well known to the Greeks. Æschylus, in the Agamemnon, praises a woman, σημαντη ριον ουδεν διαφθειρασαν, who had not violated her seal of conjugal faith. But Nonnus, lib. ii., uses the form of speech exactly as Solomon does with reference to a pure virgin; he says, Αψαυστον εης σφρηγιδα κορειης; "She had preserved *the seal of her virginity untouched.*" All this is plain; but how many will make *metaphors* out of *metaphors!*

Verse 13. Thy plants are an orchard of pomegranates] This seems to refer to the *fecundity* of the bride or Jewish queen; to the former it would be a *prediction;* to the latter, a statement of *what had already taken place.* The word פרדס *pardes,* which we translate an *orchard,* is the same which has given birth to our *paradise,* a *garden of pleasure.* The other expressions, in this and the following verse, seem to refer wholly to matters of a connubial nature.

Verse 15. A fountain of gardens] Perhaps גנים *gannim,* "gardens," was originally חיים *chaiyim,* "lives," a living *fountain,* a *continual spring.* See *Houbigant.* But this is expressed afterwards; though there would be nothing improper in saying, "a living fountain, a well of living waters, and streams from Mount Lebanon." A fountain of gardens may mean one so abundant as to be sufficient to supply many gardens, to water many plots of ground, an exuberant fountain. This is the allusion; the reference is plain enough.

Verse 16. *Awake, O north wind; and come, thou south*] It is granted that the *south wind* in Palestine, in the summer, is *extremely hot and troublesome;* therefore, another interpretation of this passage has been proposed by Mr. *Harmer;* who thinks באי *boi*, which we render *come*, signifies *enter into thy repositories;* and, therefore, supposes the true interpretation of the words to be as follows: "Arise, thou north wind, (and retire, thou south,) blow upon my garden; let the spices thereof flow forth, that my beloved may come into his garden, invited by the coolness and fragrancy of the air, and

may eat his pleasant fruits; for, if the *south wind* blow, the *excessive heat* will forbid his taking the air, and oblige him to shut close the doors and windows of his apartments." Others think that he wishes the *winds* from *all directions* to carry throughout the land the *fume* of his spices, virtue, and perfections.

Let my beloved come into his garden] This is the invitation of the *bride:* and if we look not for far-fetched meanings, the sense is sufficiently evident. But commentators on this song sometimes take a *literal* sense where the *metaphor* is evident; at other times they build an *allegory* upon a *metaphor*. The *Gitagovinda* has an elegant passage similar to this. See the place, Part VII., beginning with *Enter, sweet Radha*.

The whole of this chapter is considered to be unconnected with any particular time of the marriage ceremonies.

CHAPTER V

The bridegroom calls on his spouse to admit him, 1–3. She hesitates; but arising finds him gone, seeks him, and is treated unworthily by the city watch, 4–7. Inquires of the daughters of Jerusalem, who question her concerning her beloved, 8, 9. This gives her occasion to enter into a fine description of his person and accomplishments, 10–16.

A. M. cir. 2990
B. C. cir. 1014
Ante I. Olymp. cir. 238
Ante U. C. cir. 261

I [a]AM come into my garden, my sister, *my* spouse: I have gathered my myrrh with my spice; [b]I have eaten my honeycomb with my honey; I have drunk my wine with my milk: eat, O [c]friends; drink, [d]yea, drink abundantly, O beloved.

2 I sleep, but my heart waketh: *it is* the voice of my beloved [e]that knocketh, *saying*, Open to me, my sister, my love, my dove, my undefiled: for my head is filled with dew, *and* my locks with the drops of the night.

3 I have put off my coat; how shall I put it on? I have washed my feet; how shall I defile them?

A. M. cir. 2990
B. C. cir. 1014
Ante I. Olymp. cir. 238
Ante U. C. cir. 261

[a]Chap. iv. 16——[b]Chap. iv. 11——[c]Luke xv. 7, 10; John iii. 29; xv. 14

[d]Or, *and be drunken* with *loves*——[e]Rev. iii. 20

NOTES ON CHAP. V

Verse 1. *I am come into my garden*] באתי *bathi*, I came, or have come; this should be translated in the *past* tense, as the other *preterite* verbs in this clause. I think the latter clause of the preceding verse should come in here: "Let my beloved come into his garden, and eat his pleasant fruits. I have come into my garden, my sister, callah, or spouse; I have gathered my myrrh," &c. I have taken thee for my spouse, and am perfectly satisfied that thou art pure and immaculate.

Eat, O friends—drink abundantly] These are generally supposed to be the words of the *bridegroom*, after he returned from the *nuptial chamber*, and exhibited those *signs* of his wife's *purity* which the customs of those times required. This being a cause of universal joy, the entertainment is served up; and he invites his companions, and the friends of both parties, to eat and drink abundantly, as there was such a universal cause of rejoicing. Others think that these are the words of the bride to her spouse: but the original will not bear this meaning; the verbs are all plural.

Verse 2. *I sleep, but my heart waketh*] This

is a *new part;* and some suppose that the *fifth* day's solemnity begins here. *Though I sleep, yet so impressed* is *my heart* with the excellences of my beloved, that my imagination presents him to me in the most pleasing *dreams* throughout the night. I doubt whether the whole, from this verse to the end of the *seventh*, be not a *dream:* several parts of it bear this resemblance; and I confess there are some parts of it, such as her hesitating to rise, his sudden disappearance, &c., which would be of easier solution on this supposition. Or part of the transactions mentioned might be the *effects of the dream* she had, as rising up suddenly, and going out into the street, meeting with the watchmen, &c., before she was well awake. And her being in so much *disorder* and *dishabille* might have induced them to treat her as a *suspicious person*, or one of questionable *character*. But it is most likely the whole was a *dream*.

For my head is filled with dew.] She supposed he had come in the night, and was standing without, *wet*, and exposed to the inclemency of the weather.

Verse 3. *I have put off my coat*] The bride must have been in a *dream*, or in much *disorder*

A. M. cir. 2990
B. C. cir. 1014
Ante I. Olymp.
cir. 238
Ante U. C. cir.
261

4 My beloved put in his hand by the hole *of the door,* and my bowels were moved [f]for him.

5 I rose up to open to my beloved; and my hands dropped *with* myrrh, and my fingers *with* [g]sweet-smelling myrrh, upon the handles of the lock.

6 I opened to my beloved; but my beloved had withdrawn himself, *and* was gone: my soul failed when he spake: [h]I sought him, but I could not find him; I called him, but he gave me no answer.

7 [i]The watchmen that went about the city found me, they smote me, they wounded me; the keepers of the walls took away my veil from me.

8 I charge you, O daughters of Jerusalem,

if ye find my beloved, [k]that ye tell him, that I *am* sick of love.

9 What *is* thy beloved more than *another* beloved, [l]O thou fairest among women? what *is* thy beloved more than *another* beloved, that thou dost so charge us?

A. M. cir. 2990
B. C. cir. 1014
Ante I. Olymp
cir. 238
Ante U. C. cir.
261

10 My beloved *is* white *and* ruddy, [m]the chiefest among ten thousand.

11 His head *is as* the most fine gold, his locks *are* [n]bushy, *and* black as a raven.

12 [o]His eyes *are* as *the eyes* of doves by the rivers of waters, washed with milk, *and* [p]fitly set.

13 His cheeks *are* as a bed of spices, *as* [q]sweet flowers: his lips *like* lilies, dropping sweet-smelling myrrh.

---

[f]Or, (as some read,) *in me*——[g]Heb. *passing* or *running about*——[h]1 Sam. x. 21; chap. iii. 1; Luke ii. 44, 45 [i]Chap. iii. 3——[k]Heb. *what*——[l]Chap. i. 8——[m]Heb. *a standard-bearer*

[n]Or, *curled*——[o]Chap. i. 15; iv. 1——[p]Heb. *sitting in fulness,* that is, *fitly placed, and set as a precious stone in the foil of a ring*——[q]Or, *towers of perfumes*

---

of mind to have made the frivolous excuses here mentioned. The words relate to the case of a person who had gone to take rest on his bed. As they wore nothing but sandals, they were obliged to wash their feet previously to their lying down. I have washed my feet, taken off my clothes, and am gone to bed: I cannot therefore be disturbed. A Hindoo always washes his feet before he goes to bed. If called from his bed, he often makes this excuse, *I shall daub my feet;* and the excuse is reasonable, as the floors are of earth; and they do not wear shoes in the house.—WARD.

Verse 4. *My beloved put in his hand*] If it were a *real scene,* which is mentioned in this and the two following verses, it must refer, from the well-known use of the *metaphors,* to matrimonial endearments. Or, it may refer to his *attempts to open the door,* when she hesitated to arise, on the grounds mentioned ver. 3. But this also bears every evidence of a *dream.*

Verse 5. *My hands dropped* with *myrrh*] It was a custom among the Romans, as *Brissonius, Isidore,* and others relate, to conduct the bride to the house of the bridegroom with lighted torches; and those who brought her *anointed the door-posts with fragant oils,* whence the name *uxor,* or as it was formerly written *unxor,* for a *wife* or *married* woman, because of the *anointing* which took place on the occasion; for sometimes the bride herself *anointed* the *door-posts,* and sometimes those who brought her; probably both at the same time. The same custom might have existed among the Jews. See *Vossius' Etymologicon.*

Verse 7. *Took away my veil*] They tore it off rudely, to discover who she was. See on ver. 2. To tear the veil signifies, in Eastern phrase, to deflower or dishonour a woman.

Verse 8. *I am* sick of love.] "I am exceedingly concerned for his absence; and am distressed on account of my thoughtless carriage towards him." The latter clause may be well translated, "What should ye tell him?" Why,

"that I am sick of love." This ends the transactions of the *third day* and *night.*

Verse 9. *What is* thy beloved more than another *beloved*] This question gives the bride an opportunity to break out into a highly wrought description of the beauty and perfections of her spouse.

Verse 10. *My beloved* is white and ruddy] *Red* and *white,* properly mixed, are essential to a *fine complexion;* and this is what is intimated: he has the *finest complexion among ten thousand persons;* not one in that number is equal to *him.* Literally, "He bears the standard among ten thousand men;" or "He is one before whom a standard is borne," i. e., he is *captain* or *chief* of the whole.

Verse 11. *His head* is as the most fine gold] He has the most beautiful head, fine and majestic. Gold is here used to express *excellence.*

His locks are *bushy*] Crisped or *curled.* This may refer to his mustachios.

Black as a raven.] His hair is black and glossy.

Verse 12. *His eyes* are as the eyes of doves] See on chap. iv. ver. 1.

Washed with milk] The *white* of the eye, exceedingly *white.* By the use of *stibium,* in the East, the eye is rendered very *beautiful;* and receives such *a lustre* from the use of this article, that, to borrow the expression of a late traveller, "their eyes appear to be swimming in bliss." I believe this expression to be the meaning of the text.

Fitly set.] Or, as the *margin,* very properly, *sitting in fulness;* not sunk, not contracted.

Verse 13. *His cheeks* are as a bed of spices] Possibly meaning a *bed in the garden,* where odoriferous herbs grew. But it has been supposed to refer to his *beard,* which in a *young well-made man* is exceedingly beautiful. I have seen young Turks, who had taken much care of their beards, mustachios, &c., look majestic. Scarcely any thing serves to set off the human face to greater advantage than the *beard,* when

A. M. cir. 2990
B. C. cir. 1014
Ante I. Olymp. cir. 238
Ante U. C. cir. 261

14 His hands *are as* gold rings set with the beryl: his belly *is as* bright ivory overlaid *with* sapphires.

15 His legs *are as* pillars of marble, set upon sockets of fine gold: his countenance *is*

---

[r] Heb. *His palate*

---

kept in proper order. Females admire it in their *suitors* and *husbands*. I have known cases, where they not only *despised* but *execrated* Europeans, whose faces were close shaved. The men perfume their beards often; and this may be what is intended by *spices* and *sweet-smelling myrrh*.

His lips like *lilies*] The שושנים *shoshannim* may mean any flower of the *lily* kind, such as the *rubens lilium*, mentioned by *Pliny*, or something of the *tulip* kind. There are tints in such flowers that bear a very near resemblance to a fine *ruby lip*.

Verse 14. *His hands—gold rings set with the beryl*] This really seems to refer to *gold rings* set with precious stones on the fingers, and perhaps to circlets or bracelets about the wrists. Some suppose it to refer to the roundness and exquisite symmetry of the hand and fingers. תרשיש *tarshish*, which we translate *beryl*, a gem of a sea-green tint, had better be translated *chrysolite*, which is of a *gold* colour.

His belly—bright ivory overlaid with *sapphires*.] This must refer to some *garment* set with *precious stones* which went round his

as Lebanon, excellent as the cedars.

16 [r] His mouth *is* most sweet: yea, he *is* altogether [s] lovely. This *is* my beloved, and this *is* my friend, O daughters of Jerusalem.

A. M. cir. 2990
B. C. cir. 1014
Ante I. Olymp. cir. 238
Ante U. C. cir. 261

---

[s] 2 Sam. i. 23

---

waist, and was peculiarly remarkable. If we take it *literally*, the sense is plain enough. His belly was beautifully white, and the blue veins appearing under the skin resembled the sapphire stone. But one can hardly think that this was intended.

Verse 15. *His legs* are as *pillars of marble*] Exquisitely turned and well-shaped; the *sockets of gold* may refer to his *slippers*. On these a profusion of gold and ornaments are still lavished in Asiatic countries.

His countenance is as *Lebanon*] As Lebanon exalts its head beyond all the other mountains near Jerusalem, so my beloved is tall and majestic, and surpasses in stature and majesty all other men. He is also as *straight* and as *firm* as the *cedars*.

Verse 16. *His mouth* is *most sweet*] His eloquence is great, and his voice is charming. Every word he speaks is sweetness, mildness, and benevolence itself. Then, her powers of description failing, and metaphor exhausted, she cries out, "The whole of him is loveliness. This is my beloved, and this is my companion, O ye daughters of Jerusalem."

CHAPTER VI

The companions of the bride inquire after the bridegroom, 1–3. A description of the bride, 4–13.

A. M. cir. 2990
B. C. cir. 1014
Ante I. Olymp. cir. 238
Ante U. C. cir. 261

WHITHER is thy beloved gone, [a] O thou fairest among women? whither is thy beloved turned aside? that we may seek him with thee.

2 My beloved has gone down into his garden,

to the beds of spices, to feed in the gardens, and to gather lilies.

3 [b] I *am* my beloved's, and my beloved *is* mine: he feedeth among the lilies.

4 Thou *art* beautiful, O my love, as Tirzah,

A. M. cir. 2990
B. C. cir. 1014
Ante I. Olymp. cir. 238
Ante U. C. cir. 261

---

[a] Chap. i. 8   [b] Chap. ii. 16; vii. 10

NOTES ON CHAP. VI

Verse 1. *Whither is thy beloved gone*] These words are supposed to be addressed to the *bride* by her own *companions*, and are joined to the preceding chapter by the *Hebrew* and all the versions.

Verse 2. *My beloved is gone down into his garden*] The answer of the *bride* to her companions.

Verse 4. *Beautiful—as Tirzah*] This is supposed to be the address of Solomon to the bride. Tirzah was a city in the tribe of Ephraim, (Josh. xii. 24,) and the capital of that district. It appears to have been *beautiful* in *itself*, and *beautifully situated*, for *Jeroboam* made it his residence before *Samaria* was built; and it seems to have been the ordinary residence of the kings of *Israel*, 1 Kings xiv. 17; xv. 53. Its *name* signifies *beautiful* or *delightful*.

Comely as Jerusalem] This was called *the perfection of beauty*, Psa. xlviii. 2, 3; l. 2. And thus the poet compares the bride's beauty to the two *finest places* in the land of Palestine, and the *capitals* of the two *kingdoms* of *Israel* and *Judah*.

Terrible as an army *with banners*.] This has been supposed to carry an allusion to the *caravans* in the East, and the manner in which they are conducted in their travels by night. The caravans are divided into *companies*, called *cottors*, according to *Thevenet;* and each company is distinguished by the *form* of the *brazier* in which they carry their *lights*. After night, these braziers are placed on the ends of long poles, and carried by a person who walks at the head of the company. Some have *ten* or *twelve* lights, and are of different forms; some triangular, or like an N; some like an M, by which each pilgrim readily knows

A. M. cir. 2990
B. C. cir. 1014
Ante I. Olymp.
cir. 238
Ante U. C. cir.
261
comely as Jerusalem, [c]terrible as *an army* with banners.

5 Turn away thine eyes from me, for [d]they have overcome me: thy hair *is* [e]as a flock of goats that appear from Gilead.

6 [f]Thy teeth *are* as a flock of sheep which go up from the washing, whereof every one beareth twins, and *there is* not one barren among them.

7 [g]As a piece of a pomegranate *are* thy temples within thy locks.

8 There are threescore queens, and fourscore concubines, and virgins without number.

9 My dove, my undefiled is *but* one; she *is* the *only* one of her mother, she *is* the choice one of her that bare her. The daughters saw

her, and blessed her; *yea, the*
A. M. cir. 2990
B. C. cir. 1014
Ante I. Olymp.
cir. 238
Ante U. C. cir.
261
queens and the concubines, and they praised her.

10 Who *is* she *that* looketh forth as the morning, fair as the moon, clear as the sun, [h]and terrible as *an army* with banners?

11 I went down into the garden of nuts to see the fruits of the valley, *and* [i]to see whether the vine flourished, *and* the pomegranates budded.

12 [k]Or ever I was aware, my soul [l]made me *like* the chariots of Amminadib.

13 Return, return, O Shulamite; return, return, that we may look upon thee. What will ye see in the Shulamite? As it were the company [m]of two armies.

---

[c]Ver. 10——[d]Or, *they have puffed me up*—— [e]Ch. iv. 1
[f]Ch. iv. 2——[g]Ch. iv. 3——[h]Ver. 4——[i]Ch. vii. 12

[k]Heb. *I knew not*——[l]Or, *set me on the chariots of my willing people*——[m]Or, *of Mahanaim;* Gen. xxxii. 2

---

his own company, both by *night* and *day.* A whole caravan, composed of many thousands of *hadgees* or *pilgrims,* divided into various *cottors* or companies, each having its own distinguishing brazier or *light,* must necessarily produce a very *splendid,* if not a *terrible,* appearance.

Verse 5. *Turn away thine eyes*] As the sight of so many fires after night was extremely *dazzling,* and the *eye* could not *bear* the sight, so the *look* of the bride was such as pierced the heart, and quite overwhelmed the person who met it. Hence the bridegroom naturally cries out, "Turn away thine eyes from me, for they have overcome me."

Thy hair is as a flock of goats] See on chap. iv. 1.

Verse 6. *Thy teeth*] See on chap. iv. 2.

Verse 7. *As a piece of a pomegranate*] See on chap. iv. 3.

Verse 8. *There are threescore queens*] Though there be *sixty queens,* and *eighty concubines,* or *secondary wives,* and *virgins innumerable,* in my *harem,* yet thou, *my dove, my undefiled, art* אחת *achath,* ONE, the ONLY ONE, she in whom I delight beyond all.

Verse 9. *The daughters saw her, and blessed her*] Not only the *Jewish women in general* spoke well of her on her arrival, but the *queens* and *concubines praised her* as the most accomplished of her sex.

With this verse the *fourth night* of the marriage week is supposed to end.

Verse 10. *Looketh forth as the morning*] The bride is as lovely as the *dawn* of day, the *Aurora,* or perhaps the *morning star,* VENUS. She is even more resplendent, she is as *beautiful as the* MOON. She even surpasses *her,* for she is as *clear* and *bright* as the SUN; and *dangerous* withal to look on, for she is as *formidable* as the vast collection of lights that burn by night at the head of every company in a numerous caravan. See the note on ver. 4. The comparison of a fine woman to the splendour of an unclouded *full moon* is continually recurring in the writings of the Asiatic poets.

Verse 11. *I went down into the garden of*

nuts] I believe this and the following verse refer at least to the preparations for a farther consummation of the marriage, or examination of the advancement of the bride's pregnancy. But many circumstances of this kind are so interwoven, and often *anticipated* and also *postponed,* that it is exceedingly difficult to arrange the whole so as to ascertain the several parts, and who are the actors and speakers. But other writers find no difficulty here, because they have their system; and that explains all things.

It is probably not the *hazel* but the *almond nut,* that is referred to here.

Verse 12. *The chariots of Amminadib.*] Probably for their great speed these chariots became proverbial. The passage marks a strong agitation of mind, and something like what we term palpitation of the heart. As I am not aware of any *spiritual* meaning here, I must be excused from commenting on that which is *literal. Amminadib* signifies *my noble* or *princely people;* but it may here be a proper name, and Amminadib might be celebrated for his skill and rapidity in driving, as Jehu was.

Verse 13. *Return, O Shulamite*] This appears to be addressed to the bride, as now the confirmed, acknowledged *wife of Solomon; for* שולמית *shulammith,* appears to be a *feminine* formed from שלמה *shelomoh,* or שלמון *shelomon,* as we form *Charlotte* from *Charles; Henrietta,* from *Henry; Janette,* from *John,* &c.

The company of two armies.] Or the *musicians of the camps.* She is as terrible as hosts of armed men, on the ground of what is said on verses 4, 5. The two armies may refer to the *choirs* of the bride's *virgins,* and the bridegroom's *companions;* but the similitude is not very perceptible. The *Targum* explains it of "the camps of Israel and Judah:" as if the bridegroom should say, "My beloved possesses all the perfections both of the Israelitish and Jewish women." But how little satisfaction do the best *conjectures* afford!

With this chapter the *fifth night* is supposed to end.

CHAPTER VII

A farther description of the bride, 1–9. Her invitation to the bridegroom, 10–13.

A. M. cir. 2990
B. C. cir. 1014
Ante I. Olymp.
cir. 238
Ante U. C. cir.
261

HOW beautiful are thy feet with shoes, ^aO prince's daughter? the joints of thy thighs *are* like jewels, the work of the hands of a cunning workman.

2 Thy navel *is like* a round goblet, *which* wanteth not ^bliquor: thy belly *is like* a heap of wheat set about with lilies.

3 ^cThy two breasts *are* like two young roes *that are* twins.

4 ^dThy neck *is* as a tower of ivory; thine eyes *like* the fish-pools in Heshbon, by the gate of Bath-rabbim: thy nose *is* as the tower of Lebanon, which looketh toward Damascus.

5 Thine head upon thee *is* like ^eCarmel, and the hair of thine head like purple: the king *is* ^fheld in the galleries.

A. M. cir. 2990
B. C. cir. 1014
Ante I. Olymp.
cir. 238
Ante U. C. cir.
261

6 How fair and how pleasant art thou, O love, for delights!

7 This thy stature is like to a palm tree, and thy breasts to clusters *of grapes.*

8 I said, I will go up to the palm tree, I will take hold of the boughs thereof: now also thy breasts shall be as clusters of the vine, and the smell of thy nose like apples;

9 And the roof of thy mouth like the best wine for my beloved, that goeth *down* ^gsweetly,

---

^aPsa. xlv. 13——^bHeb. *mixture*——^cChap. iv. 5

^dChap. iv. 4——^eOr, *crimson*——^fHeb. *bound*——^gHeb. *straightly*

NOTES ON CHAP. VII

Verse 1. *How beautiful are thy feet with shoes*] "How graceful is thy walking." In the *sixth* chapter the bridegroom praises the *Shulamite*, as we might express it, *from head to foot.* Here he begins a new description, taking her from *foot to head.*

The *shoes, sandals,* or *slippers* of the Eastern ladies are most beautifully formed, and richly embroidered. The *majestic walk* of a beautiful woman in such shoes is peculiarly grand. And to show that such a walk is intended, he calls her a *prince's daughter.*

The joints of thy thighs] Must refer to the ornaments on the beautiful *drawers,* which are in general use among ladies of quality in most parts of the East.

Verse 2. *Thy navel is like a round goblet*] This may also refer to some ornamental dress about the *loins.* These suppositions are rendered very probable from hundreds of the best finished and highly decorated drawings of Asiatic *ladies* in my own collection, where every thing appears in the drawings, as in nature.

A heap of wheat set about with lilies.] This is another instance of the same kind. The richly embroidered dresses in the above drawings may amply illustrate this also. Ainsworth supposes the metaphor is taken from a pregnant woman; the child in the womb being nourished by means of the *umbilical cord* or *navel string,* till it is brought into the world. After which it is fed 'by means of the mother's *breasts,* which are immediately mentioned. Possibly the whole may allude to the bride's *pregnancy.*

Verse 3. *Thy two breasts*] Where the hair and breasts are fine, they are the highest ornaments of the person of a female.

Verse 4. *Thy neck—as a tower of ivory*] High, white, and ornamented with jewellery, *as the tower of David* was with *bucklers.* See on chap. iv. 4.

The fish-pools in Heshbon] Clear, bright, and serene. These must have been very beautiful to have been introduced here in comparison. These two fountains appear to have been situ-

ated at the *gate* that led from *Heshbon* to *Rabba,* or *Rabboth Ammon.* There is a propriety in this metaphor, because *fountains* are considered to be the *eyes* of the *earth.*

Thy nose—as the tower of Lebanon] There was doubtless a propriety in this similitude also, which cannot now be discerned. If we are to understand the similitude as taken from the *projecting* form of the *nose,* even here I see nothing striking in the metaphor; for surely the tower of Lebanon did not *project* from the *mountain* as the human *nose* does from the *face.* It is better to acknowledge that there was undoubtedly some fit resemblances; but in what *circumstance* we know not. But some commentators are always extolling the correctness of the imagery in those very difficult places, where no soul sees the similitude but themselves.

Verse 5. *Thine head—like Carmel*] Rising majestically upon thy neck, and above thy shoulders, as Mount Carmel does in its district. Carmel was the name of the mountain where Elijah had his contest with the prophets of Baal. See 1 Kings xviii. 19, &c.

The hair of thine head like purple] Ornamented with *ribbons* and *jewellery* of this tint.

The king is held in the galleries.] Or is detained in the antechamber. His heart is captivated by thy person and conduct. Some understand the ringlets of the bride's hair.

Verse 6. *How fair and how pleasant*] Thou art every way beautiful, and in every respect calculated to inspire pleasure and delight.

Verse 7. *Like to a palm tree*] Which is remarkably *straight, taper,* and *elegant.*

And thy breasts to clusters of grapes.] *Dates* are the fruit of the palm tree; they grow in clusters; and it is these, not *grapes,* which are intended.

Verse 8. *I will go up to the palm tree*] I will take hold on the boughs of this tree, and climb up by them, in order to gather the clusters of dates at the top. The *rubric* here in the old MS. interprets this of the *cross of* '*Christ.*

Verse 9. *The roof of thy mouth like the best*

A. M. cir. 2990
B. C. cir. 1014
Ante I. Olymp.
cir. 238
A. U. C. cir.
261

causing the lips [h]of those that are asleep to speak.

10 [i]I *am* my beloved's, and [k]his desire *is* toward me.

11 Come, my beloved, let us go forth into the field; let us lodge in the villages.

12 Let us get up early to the vineyards; let us [l]see if the vine flourish, *whether*

---

[h]Or, *of the ancient*——[i]Chap. ii. 16; vi. 3——[k]Psa. xlv. 11

---

the tender grape [m]appear *and* the pomegranates bud forth: there will I give thee my loves.

A. M. cir. 2990
B. C. cir. 1014
Ante I. Olymp.
cir. 238
A. U. C. cir.
261

13 The [n]mandrakes give a smell, and at our gates [o]*are* all manner of pleasant *fruits,* new and old, *which* I have laid up for thee, O my beloved.

---

[l]Chap. vi. 11——[m]Heb. *open*——[n]Gen. xxx. 14
[o]Matt. xiii. 52

---

wine] The *voice* or *conversation* of the spouse is most probably what is meant.

Causing the lips of those that are asleep to speak.] As *good wine* has a tendency to cause the most backward to *speak fluently* when taken in moderation; so a sight of thee, and hearing the charms of thy conversation, is sufficient to excite the most taciturn to speak, and even to become eloquent in thy praises.

Verse 10. *I am my beloved's, and his desire is toward me.*] It is worthy of remark that the word which we translate *his desire* is the very same used Gen. iii. 16: *Thy desire,* thy ruling appetite, תשוקתך *teshukathech, shall be to thy husband, and he shall rule over thee.* This was a part of the woman's curse. Now here it seems to be *reversed;* for the bride says, *I am my beloved's,* and *his desire* or *ruling appetite* and *affection,* תשוקתו *teshukatho,* is עלי *ali,* UPON ME. The old MS. translates this with considerable force:—𝕴 to mp leef, anð to me the turnpnge of him.

Verse 11. *Let us go forth into the field*] It has been conjectured that the bridegroom arose

early every morning, and left the bride's apartment, and withdrew to the country; often leaving her asleep, and commanding her companions not to disturb her till she should awake of herself. Here the bride wishes to accompany her spouse to the country, and spend a night at his country house.

Verse 12. *Let us get up early to the vine-yards*] When in the country, we shall have the better opportunity to contemplate the progress of the spring vegetation; and there she promises to be peculiarly affectionate to him.

Verse 13. *The mandrakes give a smell*] See the note on Gen. xxx. 14, where the *mandrake* is particularly described; from which this passage will receive considerable light. The reader is *requested* to consult it.

All manner of pleasant fruits] Fruits *new* and *old; flowers* and *herbs* of every kind which the season could yield. The literal sense, allowing for the concealing metaphors, is, I believe, of a widely different nature from what is generally given. But this must be left to the reader's sagacity and prudence.

CHAPTER VIII

The love of the bride to her spouse, and the nature of that love, 1–7. The younger sister, 8–10. Solomon's vine-yard, 11, 12. The confidence of the bride and bridegroom in each other, 13, 14.

A. M. cir. 2990
B. C. cir. 1014
Ante I. Olymp.
cir. 238
A. U. C. cir.
261

O THAT thou *wert* as my brother, that sucked the breasts of my mother! when I should find thee without, I would kiss thee; yea, [a]I should not be despised.

2 I would lead thee, *and* bring thee into my mother's house, *who* would instruct me: I would cause thee to drink of [b]spiced wine

---

of the juice of my pomegranate.

A. M. cir. 2990
B. C. cir. 1014
Ante I. Olymp.
cir. 238
A. U. C. cir.
261

3 [c]His left hand *should be* under my head, and his right hand should embrace me.

4 [d]I charge you, O daughters of Jerusalem, [e]that ye stir not up, nor awake *my* love, until he please.

---

[a]Heb. *they should not despise me*——[b]Prov. ix. 2 [c]Chap. ii. 6

---

[d]Chap. ii. 7; iii. 5——[e]Heb. *why should ye stir up, or why,* &c.

NOTES ON CHAP. VIII

Verse 1. *O that thou wert as my brother*] The bride, fearing that her fondness for her spouse might be construed into too great a familiarity, wishes that he were *her little brother;* and then she might treat him in the most affectionate manner, and kiss him even in the *streets* without suspicion, and without giving offence to any one.

Verse 2. *Would—bring thee into my mother's house, who would instruct me*] She would

teach me how to conduct myself towards thee, as she would how to nurse a young child.

To drink of spiced wine] Wine rendered peculiarly strong and invigorating. The bride and bridegroom on the wedding day both drank out of the same cup, to show that they were to *enjoy* and equally *bear* together the *comforts* and *adversities* of life.

Verse 3. *His left hand*] See on chap. ii. 6.

With the *fourth* verse the SIXTH *night* of the marriage week is supposed to end.

A. M. cir. 2990
B. C. cir. 1014
Ante I. Olymp.
cir. 238
A. U. C. cir.
261
5 ⁱWho *is* this that cometh up from the wilderness, leaning upon her beloved? I raised thee up under the apple tree: there thy mother brought thee forth; there she brought thee forth *that* bare thee.

6 ᵍSet me as a seal upon thine heart, as a seal upon thine arm: for love *is* strong as death; jealousy *is* ʰcruel as the grave: the coals thereof *are* coals of fire, *which hath* a most vehement flame.

7 Many waters cannot quench love, neither

can the floods drown it: ⁱif a man would give all the substance of his house for love, it would utterly be contemned.

A. M. cir. 2990
B. C. cir. 1014
Ante I. Olymp.
cir. 238
A. U. C. cir.
261

8 ᵏWe have a little sister, and she hath no breasts: what shall we do for our sister in the day when she shall be spoken for?

9 If she *be* a wall, we will build upon her a palace of silver: and if she *be* a door, we will enclose her with boards of cedar.

10 I *am* a wall, and my breasts like tow-

ⁱCh. iii. 6——ᵍIsa. xlix. 16; Jer. xxii. 24; Hag. ii. 23

ʰHeb. *hard*——ⁱProv. vi. 35——ᵏEzek. xxiii. 33

Verse 5. *That cometh up from the wilderness*] Perhaps the words of the *daughters of Jerusalem*, who, seeing the bride returning from the country, leaning on the arm of her beloved, are filled with admiration at her excellent carriage and beauty.

I raised thee up under the apple tree] The original of this clause is obscure, and has given birth to various translations. The following is nearly literal: "Under the apple tree I excited thee (to espouse me:) there, thy mother contracted thee;—there, she that brought thee forth contracted thee (to me.) Or it may be understood of the following circumstance: The bridegroom found her once asleep under an apple tree, and awoke her; and this happened to be the very place where her mother, taken in untimely labour, had brought her into the world." And here the bridegroom, in his fondness and familiarity, recalls these little adventures to her memory.

The *Vulgate* gives this an abominable meaning.

Sub arbore malo suscitavi te: ibi corrupta est mater tua; ibi violata est genetrix tua; "I raised thee up under the apple tree: it was there that thy mother was corrupted; it was there that she who brought thee forth was violated." Spiritually, all this is applied to Eve losing her purity by sin; and Jesus as the promised seed *raising her up* by the promise of mercy, through the blood of his cross. But the *text* says nothing of this.

Verse 6. *Set me as a seal upon thine heart*] It was customary in the Levant and other places to make impressions of *various kinds* upon the *arms*, the *breast*, and other parts. I have seen these often: some slight punctures are made, and the place rubbed over with a sort of blue powder that, getting between the *cuticle* and *cutis*, is never discharged; it continues in all its distinctness throughout life. The figures of *young women* are frequently thus impressed on the *arms* and on the *breasts*. If the bride alludes to any thing of this kind, which is very probable, the interpretation is easy. Let me be thus depicted upon thine *arm*, which being constantly before thy eyes, thou wilt never forget me; and let me be thus depicted upon thy *breast*, the emblem of the share I have in thy *heart* and affections. Do this as a proof of the love I bear to thee, which is such as nothing but death can destroy; and do it to prevent any *jealousy* I might feel, which is as *cruel*

as the *grave*, and as deadly as *fiery arrows* or poisoned darts shot into the body.

A most vehement flame.] שלהבתיה *shalhebethyah*, "the flame of God;" for the word is divided שלהבת יה *shalhebeth Yah*, "the flame of Jehovah," by *one hundred and sixteen* of Dr. *Kennicott's* MSS., and by *one hundred and fourteen* of those of *De Rossi*. It may mean the *lightning;* or, as our text understands it, a most *vehement* or *intense* fire.

Verse 7. *Many waters*] Neither common nor uncommon *adversities*, even of the most *ruinous* nature, can destroy love when it is *pure;* and *pure love* is such that nothing can *procure* it. If it be not excited naturally, no money can purchase it, no property can procure it, no arts can persuade it. How vain is the thought of *old rich men* hoping to procure the affections of *young women* by loading them with *presents* and *wealth!* No woman can command her affections; they are not in her power. Where they do not rise spontaneously, they can never exist. "If a man would give all the substance of his house for love, it would be utterly contemned." Let the *old*, as well as the *gay* and the *giddy*, think of this.

Verse 8. *We have a little sister*] This young girl belonged most probably to the *bride*.

She hath no breasts] She is not yet marriageable.

What shall we do for our sister] How shall we secure her comfort and welfare?

In the day when she shall be spoken for?] When any person shall demand her in marriage.

Verse 9. *If she be a wall*] All these expressions, says Calmet, show that it was necessary to provide a husband for this young sister. For a *woman* without a *husband* is like a *wall* without *towers*, and without defence; is like a *gate* or *door* without *bar* or *lock;* and like a *city* without *walls*. They must therefore provide for their sister a *rich, powerful,* and *illustrious* man; qualities here figured by *towers* or *palaces* of silver, and *doors of cedar.* As it is customary to build *towers* upon a *wall*, and to put *bolts* and *bars* upon a *door* in order to secure it, so the expressions may point out the *defence, protection,* and *guardianship* which they imagined this young woman to require.

Verse 10. *I am a wall, and my breasts like towers*] I am become marriageable, and I stood in need of the *defence* I have now in my beloved; and as soon as I was so, and became

A. M. cir. 2990
B. C. cir. 1014
Ante I. Olymp.
cir. 238
A. U. C. cir.
261

ers: then was I in his eyes as one that found [1]favour.

11 Solomon had a vineyard at Baal-hamon; [m]he let out the vineyard unto keepers; every one for the fruit thereof was to bring a thousand *pieces* of silver.

12 My vineyard, which *is* mine, *is* before me: thou, O Solomon, *must have* a thousand,

and those that keep the fruit thereof two hundred.

A. M. cir. 2990
B. C. cir. 1014
Ante I. Olymp.
cir. 238
A. U. C. cir.
261

13 Thou that dwellest in the gardens, the companions hearken to thy voice: [n]cause me to hear *it*.

14 [o]Make [p]haste, my beloved, and [q]be thou like to a roe or to a young hart upon the mountains of spices.

---

[1]Heb. *peace*——[m]Matt. xxi. 33——[n]Chap. ii. 14

[o]See Rev. xxii. 17, 20——[p]Heb. *Flee away*——[q]Ch. ii. 17

---

pleasing in the eyes of my beloved, I was given to him in marriage, and have ever since *found favour in his sight.* As soon then as my sister is in my state, let a proper match be sought out for *her.* These expressions show the solicitude which the bride felt for her sister, and in her favour she wishes to interest her spouse.

Verse 11. *Solomon had a vineyard*] *Calmet* translates and paraphrases the *Hebrew* of these two verses thus: "Ver. 11. *Solomon has a vineyard at Baal-hamon: he has let it out to keepers, each of whom for the fruit of it was to bring a thousand pieces of silver.* Ver. 12. *As for me, my vineyard is before me;* that is, it is my own; I am its proprietor. *Keep thyself, O Solomon, thy thousand pieces of silver, and let those who dress* (thy vineyard) *have two hundred for their trouble.* I neither envy thee thy vineyard, nor them their profits. I am satisfied with my own. My beloved is my vineyard—my heritage; I would not change him for all the riches of the universe."

Some suppose that there is a reference here to some property which Pharaoh had given to Solomon with his daughter. See *Harmer's Outlines*, where this subject is considered at large.

Verse 13. *Thou that dwellest in the gardens*] This is supposed to refer to the bridegroom asking permission of his spouse early in the morning to retire, as was his usual custom. He intimates the *companions* were waiting to *hear*, and he wished to *hear it* in the way of *permission* to depart.

Verse 14. *Make haste, my beloved*] These appear to be the words of the bride giving permission, but entreating him to speed his *return*.

What these *mountains of spices* were, we cannot particularly tell; but they must have been thus named from their producing the *trees* on which the *spices* grew. They might have been the same as the *mountains of Bether*, chap. ii. 17, or the *mountains of myrrh*, chap. iv. 6; where see the notes.

Here ends the *seventh night* of the marriage week.

Thus ends this most singular book; the oldest *pastoral* in the world, if it may be ranked among this species of writing. To whatever species of composition it belongs, it is, beyond all controversy, the *finest*, the most *sublime* for *imagery* and *colouring*, that ever came from the pen of man.

In the preceding notes I have carefully avoided all attempts to *spiritualize* this song. My reasons I have already given in the *introduction;* and in the course of writing these short notes I have seen no cause to alter my opinion. Any man may *allegorize* it; that is an easy matter; for when he once considers it to be an *allegory*, his own *creed* will furnish him with enough to *say, write,* or *preach,* upon the *spiritual* meanings of every part, which will be an exhibition of his own *confession of faith!* But when he has finished his work, the question will recur, By what authority do you give it *these meanings?* And till the day of judgment none shall be able to say, "I have the authority of God for my exposition."

MASORETIC NOTES

Number of verses in Canticles, 117. Middle verse chap. iv. 14.

THE

TARGUM,[(a)] OR CHALDEE PARAPHRASE

ON THE

SONG OF SONGS

CHAPTER I

Verse 1. *The song of songs, &c.*] The songs and hymns which Solomon the prophet, king of Israel, delivered by the (b) spirit of prophecy, before Jehovah, the Lord of the whole world. Ten songs are sung in this world; but this is the most excellent of them all. The *first* song Adam sang, at the time when his sins were forgiven him; and when the Sabbath day came, he put a covering upon his lips, and sang (c) a psalm *or* song for the Sabbath day. The *second* song sang Moses with the children of Israel, at the time when the Lord of the world divided the Red Sea for them; *then* they all of them opened their mouths, and sang as one song, as it is written, (d) "Then sang Moses and the children of Israel." The *third* song the children of Israel sang at the time that the well of water was given to them, as it is written, (e) "Then sang Israel." The *fourth* song Moses the prophet sang, when his time was come to (f) depart out of the world, and in which he reproved the people of the house of Israel, as it is written, (g) "Give ear, O heavens, and I will speak." The *fifth* song Joshua the son of Nun sang, when he fought in *Gibeon*, and the sun and moon stood still for him (h) *thirty* and *six* hours: when they

ceased from singing, he himself opened his mouth, and sang this song, as it is written, (i) "Then sang Joshua before the Lord." The *sixth* song Barak and Deborah sang, in the day that the Lord delivered Sisera and his army into the hands of the children of Israel, as it is written, (k) "Then sang Deborah and Barak, the son of Abinoam." The *seventh* song Hannah sang, at the time when a son was given her by the Lord, as it is written, (l) "And Hannah prayed by the spirit of prophecy, and said." The *eighth* song David the king of Israel sang, on the account of all the wonders which the Lord did for him. He opened his mouth, and sang this song, as it is written, (m) "And David sang by the spirit of prophecy before the Lord." The *ninth* song Solomon the king of Israel sang by the Holy Spirit before Jehovah, the Lord of the whole world. And the *tenth* song the children of the captivity shall sing at the time when they shall come out of captivity; as it is written and explained by Isaiah the prophet, (n) This song shall be unto you for joy in the night, that the feast of the passover is kept holy, and gladness of heart; as *when* the people go to appear before the Lord, three times in the year, with *all*

(a) The word תרגום signifies an exposition, or interpretation, or a translation of one language into another; and here of the Hebrew text into the Chaldee language, with an explanation. The first use of these translations was after the return of the Jews from Babylon, where they had almost lost the Hebrew language; and, therefore, were necessary for the understanding the law and the prophets. The translation of the five books of Moses was done by Onkelos, and that of the prophets by Jonathan Ben Uzziel, the former of whom lived a little after Christ, and the latter a little before him: but the translation of the Hagiographa, among which is this book of Canticles, is generally thought to be done by R. Joseph Cæcus. The paraphrase on this book could not have been written till after the finishing of the Talmud, seeing express mention is made of it there.

(b) Which is the Holy Spirit, as it is afterwards explained. What the Targum says of this book is the mind of Jewish writers in general. *Vide* Mishna, Tract. Yadaim, c. 3, s. 5. Shirhashirim Rabba, in ver. 1. Midrash Koheleth, in ver. 1. Zohar, in Exod. fol. 59, 3. Jarchi and Aben Ezra, in Præfat. in Cant. Kimchi in 1 Reg. 11, 41.

(c) Psa. xcii., which Psalm many Jewish writers think was made by the first man Adam; so Targum in Psa. xcii. Zohar in Gen. fol. 43, 2. Vajikra Rabba, Parash. 10. But in Shemoth Rabba, Parash. 23, it is said that Adam never com-

posed any song: and that the song which Moses and the children of Israel sang at the Red Sea, was the first that ever was sung in the world; and, indeed, it is the first that is mentioned in Scripture.

(d) Exod. xv. 1.

(e) Num. xxi. 17.

(f) A phrase expressive of death. See Phil. i. 23.

(g) Deut. xxxii. 1.

(h) In Josh. x. 13, it is said, that "the sun stood still in the midst of heaven, and hasted not to go down כיום תמים, "about a whole day," or *a complete* day, which, if we understand of an artificial day, was but twelve hours; and if of a natural day, twenty-four hours. Kimchi, on Josh. x. 13, says that this miracle was wrought in the summer solstice, and on the longest day in the year, which in the land of Canaan consists but of fourteen hours; whereas the Targum here says, the sun stood still thirty-six hours, which makes three artificial days, or one natural day and a half. *Vide* Ecclus. xlvi. 5.

(i) So the Targum on Josh. x. 12.]

(k) Judg. v. 1.

(l) So the Targum on 1 Sam. ii. 1.

(m) So the Targum on 2 Sam. xxii. 1.

(n) Much to the same purpose is the Targum on Isa. xxx. 29.

kinds of music, and sound of the pipe, when they go up to the mountain of the Lord, to worship before the Lord, the mighty one of Israel.

Verse 2. *Let him kiss me, &c.*] Solomon the prophet said, "Blessed be the name of the Lord," who hath given us the law by the hands of Moses, (*o*) the great scribe, written upon two tables of stone, and the six parts of the (*p*) *Mishna* and *Talmud* (*q*) to study in; and he was speaking to us face to face, as a man kisseth his friend, because of the greatness of the love with which he loved us more than (*r*) the *seventy* nations.

Verse 3. *Because of the savour, &c.*] At the report of thy wonders and of thy power, which thou wroughtest for thy people the house of Israel. All the nations trembled who heard of the fame of thy greatness, and of thy favours; and thy holy name was heard in all the earth, which is more excellent than the anointing oil that was poured upon the heads of the kings and priests; and, therefore, the righteous love to walk in thy good way, that they may possess (*s*) this world, and the world to come.

Verse 4. *Draw me, &c.*] When the people of the house of Israel came out of Egypt, the *shechinah* of the Lord of the world went before them (*t*) in a pillar of cloud by day, and in a pillar of fire by night. The righteous of that generation said, Lord of all the world, draw us after thee, and we will run in thy good way; and bring us to the foot of Mount Sinai, and give us the law out of thy treasure house, the firmament; and we will rejoice and be glad, in the (*u*) *twenty-two* letters with which it is written; and we will remember them, and love thy deity; and will withdraw ourselves from the idols of the nations; and all the righteous which do what is right before thee shall fear thee, and love thy commandments.

Verse 5. *I am black, &c.*] When the house of Israel made the calf, their faces became black, like the sons of Cush, (*v*) which dwell in the tents of Kedar: but when they returned by repentance, and were forgiven, the brightness of the glory of their faces was increased, like the angels', because they made curtains for the tabernacle; therefore the *shechinah* of the Lord dwelt among them: and Moses, their master, went up into the (*w*) firmament, and made peace between them and their King.

Verse 6. *Look not upon me, &c.*] The congregation of Israel said before the nations, Do not despise me, because I am blacker than you, for I have done according to your works, and have (*x*) worshipped the sun and moon; for false prophets have been the cause that the fierce anger of the Lord hath come down upon me; and they taught me to worship your idols, and to walk in your laws: but the Lord of the world, who is my God, I have not served, nor walked in his commandments, nor have I kept his statutes and his law.

Verse 7. *Tell me, O thou, &c.*] When the time of Moses the prophet was come, to (*y*) depart out of the world, he said before the Lord, It is revealed unto me that this people will sin, and go into captivity; now show me how they shall be governed and dwell among the nations, whose decrees are grievous as the heat, and as the scorchings of the sun at noon, in the (*z*) summer solstice; and wherefore it is that they shall wander among the flocks of the sons of Esau and Ishmael, who join to thee their idols, for companions.

Verse 8. *If thou know not, &c.*] The holy blessed God said to Moses the prophet, It is their desire to smite the captivity of the congregation of Israel, which is like to a fair damsel: but my soul loveth her, *therefore* let her walk in the ways of the righteous, and let her order her prayer according to the direction of her governors, and let her lead her posterity, and teach her children, which are like to the kids of the goats, to go to the synagogue, and the school; and by that righteousness they shall be governed in the captivity, until the time that I send the King Messiah, and he shall lead them quietly to their habitations; *yea, he shall bring them to* the house of the sanctuary, which David and Solomon, the shepherds of Israel, built for them.

Verse 9. *To a company of horses, &c.*] When Israel went out of Egypt, Pharaoh and his host pursued after them with chariots and horsemen, and their way was shut up on the four sides of them; on the right hand and on the left were wildernesses full of fiery serpents, and behind them was wicked Pharaoh and his army, and before them was the Red Sea. What did the holy blessed God do? He was manifested in the power of his might upon the Red Sea, and dried the sea up; but the mud he did not dry up. The wicked and the mixed multi-

---

(*o*) So Ezra is called a "scribe of the law of the God of heaven," Ezra vii. 11, 12.

(*p*) The Mishna, which consists of six parts, is a collection of the traditions of the Jews, or their oral law, compiled by R. Judah, about the year of Christ 150.

(*q*) Or the Gemara, as it is read in Targum Triplex, printed with the Pentateuch. Of this Gemara, or Talmud, there are two sorts; the one is called the Jerusalem Talmud, which R. Jochanan collected together, about the year of Christ 230; the other is called the Babylonian Talmud, which was begun by R. Ase, in the year 367, who was succeeded in it by Maremar, in the year 427, and at last was finished by Avina, in the year 500. The former was written for the use of the Jerusalem Jews; the latter, for those in Babylon and other parts, and is most esteemed. It contains the disputations and decisions of the Jewish doctors upon the Mishna. *Vide* Buxtorf, Biblioth. Rab. p. 425.

(*r*) It is a generally received opinion among the Jews that seventy angels descended and confounded the language at Babel, from which time the earth was divided into seventy different nations, speaking seventy different languages. *Vide* Targum Jon. in Gen. xi. 7, 9.

(*s*) A like phrase see in Eph. i. 21; Matt. xii. 32.

(*t*) *Vide* Exod. xiii. 21, 22.

(*u*) The number of Hebrew letters in the alphabet. R. Isaac, in Shirhashirim Rabba in loc., gives the same sense of the words, which he collects from the word בָּךְ *bach, in thee,* בְּ *beth* standing numerically for two, and ךְ *caph,* for twenty.

(*v*) The Ethiopians. Shirhashirim Rabba in loc. explains the words by Amos ix. 7: "Are ye not as the children of the Ethiopians unto me," &c.

(*w*) It is a received opinion among the Jews that Moses went up into the firmament of heaven; though the Scriptures only signify that he went up into Mount Sinai, and was in the midst of the cloud with God there. So the Targum on ver. 11, 12, 14; and on Psa. lxviii. 18.

(*x*) So it is explained in Shirhashirim Rabba in loc. See Deut. xvii. 3; Job xxxi. 26, 27; 2 Kings xxiii. 5, 11; Ezek. viii. 16.

(*y*) See note on ver. 1.

(*z*) The Jews, as here and elsewhere, call it תְּקוּפַת תַּמּוּז, *tekuphath Tammuz,* "the revolution of Tammuz." The sun is so called Ezek. viii. 14, which was worshipped under this name; it answers in part to our June, when the sun enters into the tropic of Cancer, and is what is meant by this revolution, Maimon. Hilch. Kiddush Hachodesh, c. 9, s. 2. *Vide* Targum, Jon. in Gen. viii. 22.

tude, and the strangers which were among them, said, The waters of the sea he is able to dry up; but the mud he is not able to dry up. In that very hour the fierce anger of the Lord *came* upon them; and he sought to drown them in the waters of the sea, as Pharaoh and his army, his chariots, and his horsemen, and his horses, were drowned; had it not been for Moses, the prophet, who spread his hands in prayer before the Lord, and turned away the anger of the Lord from them. Then he and the righteous of that generation opened their mouths, and sang a song, and passed through the Red Sea on dry land, because of the righteousness of Abraham, Isaac, and Jacob, the beloved of the Lord.

Verse 10. *Thy cheeks are comely, &c.*] When they went out into the wilderness, the Lord said to Moses, How fair is this people; that the words of the law should be given unto them; and they shall be as bridles in their jaws, that they may not depart out of the good way, as a horse turneth not aside that has a bridle in his jaw; and how fair is their neck to bear (*a*) the yoke of my commandments; and it shall be upon them as a yoke upon the neck of a bullock, which plougheth in the field, and feeds both itself and its master!

Verse 11. *We will make thee borders of gold, &c.*] Then was it said to Moses, Go up into the firmament, and I will give thee the two tables of stone, hewed out of the (*b*) sapphire of the throne of my glory, shining as the best gold, disposed in rows, written with my finger, in which are engraven the (*c*) ten words, purer than silver that is purified seven times seven, which is the number of the things explained in them, (*d*) forty-nine ways; and they shall be given by thine hand unto the people of the house of Israel.

Verse 12. *While the king sitteth, &c.*] Whilst Moses their master was in the firmament, to receive the two tables of stone, and the law, and the commandments, the wicked of that generation, and the mixed multitude that was among them, rose up and made a golden calf, and caused their works to stink; and there went out an evil report of them in the world, for before this time a fragrant odour of them was diffused in the world: but afterwards they stank like (*e*) nard, whose smell is very bad; and the plague of leprosy came down upon their flesh.

Verse 13. *A bundle of myrrh, &c.*] At that time the Lord said unto Moses, Go down, for

the people have corrupted themselves; desist from *speaking to* me, and I will destroy them. Then Moses returned and asked mercy of the Lord; and the Lord remembered for them the (*f*) binding of Isaac, whom his father bound on (*g*) Mount Moriah, upon the altar; and the Lord turned from his fierce anger, and caused his shechinah to dwell among them as before.

Verse 14. *A cluster of camphire, &c.*] Lo, then went Moses down with the two tables of stone in his hands; and because of the sins of Israel his hands grew heavy, and they fell and were broken. Then went Moses, and ground (*h*) the calf to powder, and scattered the dust of it upon the river, and made the children of Israel drink *it*, and slew all that deserved to die, and went up a second time into the firmament, and prayed before the Lord, and made atonement for the children of Israel; then was he commanded to make a tabernacle and an ark. Immediately Moses hastened, and made the tabernacle, and all its furniture, and the ark; and he put in the ark two other tables, and appointed the sons of Aaron the priests to offer the offerings upon the altar, and to pour the wine upon the offerings: but from whence had they wine to pour? For in the wilderness they had no proper place for sowing, neither had they fig trees, nor vines, nor pomegranates; but they went to the vineyards of En-gedi, and took clusters of grapes from thence, and pressed wine out of them, and poured it upon the altar, the fourth part of a hin to one lamb.

Verse 15. *Behold, thou art fair, &c.*] When the children of Israel performed the will of their King, he (*i*) himself praised them, in the (*k*) family of the holy angels, and said, How fair are thy works, my daughter, my beloved, O congregation of Israel, in the time that thou doest my will, and studiest in the words of my law; and how well ordered are thy works and thy affairs, as young doves that are fit to be offered up upon the altar!

Verse 16. *Behold, thou art fair, &c.*] The congregation of Israel answered before the Lord of the world, and thus she said, How fair is the shechinah of thy holiness, when thou dwellest among us, and receivest our prayers with acceptance, and when thou dwellest in our beloved bed, and our children are multiplied in the world, and we increase and multiply like a tree that is planted by a fountain of water, whose leaf is fair, and whose fruit is plenteous!

Verse 17. *The beams of our house, &c.*] Solo-

(*a*) It is very common in Jewish writings to compare the law to a yoke; so Targum, in Lam. iii. 27. Mishna, Tract. Berac. c. 2, s. 2. Pirk. Aboth. c. 3, s. 5. Midrash Echa Rabbati, fol. 56, 3. Bereshith Rabba, Parash. 98. Bemidbar Rabba, Parash. 13. See Matt. xi. 29, and Acts xv. 10.

(*b*) So Targ. Jon. in Exod. xxxi. 18. Zohar in Exod. fol. 35, 1. Jarchi in Exod. xxxiv. 1. See Exod. xxiv. 10, and Ezek. i. 26.

(*c*) The decalogue or ten commandments.

(*d*) In Psa. xii. 6, the place here referred to, the "words of the Lord" are said to be "as silver purified seven times;" where by שבעתים *shibathayim* some of the Jewish rabbins, agreeably to the Targum here, understand *seven times seven*, which makes forty-nine; and so many ways they say the law is capable of being interpreted, and that he is a wise man who is acquainted with them. Midrash Agada in Jarchi, in Psa. xii. 6. Midrash Kohelet, in c. 8, v. 1. Vajikra Rabba, Parash. 26, and Yade Mose, in ib. Bemidbar Rabba, Parash. 19.

(*e*) In Buxtorf's Bible it is read כגידא *kegida*, "like wormwood," which, indeed, well agrees with what is said of it; though Matthiolus says of *nard*, that when it has lost its sweet smell it stinks exceedingly. His words are these:

Plerumque accidit dum per Indicum et Arabicum mare in Alexandriam defertur, et unde Venetias, ut ascito sibi maris humore (id namque facile sit quod nardus sit siccissima) vel situm contrahat, vel supputrescat: unde postea amissa suaveolentia, graviter oleat.—Matthiolus in Dioscor. l. 1, c. 6.

(*f*) The Jews suppose the binding of Isaac to be very meritorious, and that by virtue of it their sins are expiated and many blessings procured for them; and therefore in the beginning of the year they pray to God, that *in mercy to Israel* he would remember the binding of Isaac. Seder Tephillot, fol. 282, 1, 2. Edit. Basil. 1578. See Targum and Jarchi on Mic. vii. 20. Shirhashirim Rabba in c. 1, 14. Jarchi in Exod. xxxii. 13. Shemoth Rabba, Parash. 44.

(*g*) The Jews say, that in this same place Adam, Cain, Abel, and Noah built altars, and sacrificed. Maimon. Hilch. Beth. Habbechira, c. 2, s. 2. Targum Jon. in Gen. viii. 20, and xxii. 9. Here Solomon afterwards built the temple, 2 Chron. iii. 1.

(*h*) Exod. xxxii. 20.

(*i*) Ch. במימריה *bemeymreyh*, "by his word."

(*k*) The Latin word *familia* is here used by the paraphrast; compare with this Eph. iii. 15, Luke xii. 8.

mon the prophet said, How beautiful is the house of the sanctuary of the Lord, which is built by my hands of wood of (*l*) Gulmish: but far more beautiful will be the house of the sanctuary, which shall be built (*m*) in the days of the King Messiah, whose beams will be of the cedars of the garden of Eden, and whose rafters will be of brutine, fir, and box.

(*l*) A kind of cedar, see Eliæ Levitæ Methurgeman in voce. Targum Jon. in Num. xix. 6, and Ketoreth Hassammim, in ib.

(*m*) The Jews expect a third temple to be built in the days of the Messiah. See R. Abendan. not. in Miclol Yophi, and Abarbinel in Hagg. ii. 9. R. Isaac Chizuk Emun. par. 1, c. 34. Bemidbar Rabba, Parash. 14.

CHAPTER II

Verse 1. *I am the rose of Sharon, &c.*] The congregation of Israel said, When the Lord of the world causes his (*a*) shechinah to dwell in the midst of me, I am like the green daffodil of the garden of Eden, and my works are fair as the rose which is in the plain of the garden of Eden.

Verse 2. *As the lily among thorns, &c.*] But when I turn aside out of the way that is right before me, and he removes the shechinah of his holiness from me, I am like to a rose which flourishes among thorns, by which its leaves are pricked through and torn: even so am I pricked through and torn with wicked edicts, in the captivity among the (*b*) kings of the nations.

Verse 3. *As the apple tree among the trees, &c.*] As the pomecitron tree is beautiful, and to be praised among the unfruitful trees, and all the world knows it; so the Lord of the world was praised among the angels, when he was revealed on Mount Sinai, and gave the law unto his people; in that very hour I desired to sit under the shadow of his shechinah, and the words of his law were (*c*) fixed upon the roof of my mouth, and the reward of his commands is reserved for me in the world to come.

Verse 4. *He brought me, &c.*] The congregation of Israel said, The Lord brought me to the school which is in (*d*) Sinai, to learn the law from the mouth of Moses the great scribe; and the banner of his commandments I took upon me in love, and said, All that the Lord commandeth I will do, and will obey.

Verse 5. *Stay me with flagons, &c.*] But when I heard his voice, which spake out of the midst of the flame of fire, I trembled, and went backwards because of fear. Then I drew near to Moses and Aaron, and said unto them, Receive ye the voice of the words of the Lord, out of the midst of the fire, and bring me to the school, and sustain me with the words of the law on which the world is founded, and put veils upon my neck; *for* the interpretation of the holy words, which are sweet to my palate, are as the apples of the garden of Eden, and I will study in them: perhaps I may be healed by them, for I am sick of love.

Verse 6. *His left hand is under my head, &c.*] When the people of the house of Israel were travelling in the wilderness, they had (*e*) four clouds of glory at the four winds of the world round about them, that the (*f*) evil eye might not rule over them. There was one above them, that the heat and sun, as also the rain and hail, might not have power over them; and one below them, which carried them as a nurse carrieth her sucking child in her bosom; and another ran before them, at the distance of three days journey, (*g*) to level the mountains, and to elevate the plains; and it slew all the fiery serpents and scorpions which were in the wilderness; and it spied out a convenient place for them to lodge in, that they might study in the doctrine of the law, which was given them by the right hand of the Lord.

Verse 7. *I charge you, O ye daughters, &c.*] After that it was commanded Moses, by *the spirit of* prophecy from the Lord, to send spies to spy the land, and when they returned from spying it, they brought an evil report upon the land of Israel, wherefore they tarried forty years in the wilderness. Moses opened his mouth, and thus he said, I adjure you, O congregation of Israel, by the Lord of hosts, and by the fortresses of the land of Israel, that ye presume not to go up to the land of Canaan until it is the will of the Lord; lest the whole generation of warlike men perish from the camp, even as your brethren, the children of Ephraim, (*h*) who went out thirty years from

---

(*a*) The word shechinah comes from שכן *shachan*, which signifies *to dwell*, and Elias Levita, in his Methurgeman, says that their wise men called the Holy Spirit so, because it dwelt upon the prophets; though perhaps, he says, there may be another sense of it among the Cabalistic doctors, of which he declares himself ignorant. It seems to intend the glorious majesty and presence of God with his Church and people, and is the same with St. John's σκηνη του Θεου, tabernacle or *habitation of God*, which is said to be with men, Rev. xxi. 3; and may very well be applied to the Messiah, Jesus, who was made flesh, και εσκηνωσεν, *and dwelt* among us, John i. 14.

(*b*) In Buxtorf's Bible it is read פלכי *pilkey*, "the provinces of the nations."

(*c*) In Buxtorf's Bible it is read בסימן "*were sweet* to my palate, or taste."

(*d*) The same sense is given of those words in Shirhashirim Rabba in loc., and in Bemidbar Rabba, Parash. 2.

(*e*) The Jews are divided about the number of those clouds which they say attended the Israelites in their travels. R. Josiah says there were *five* of them, four at the four winds, and one went before them. R. Hoshea thinks there were *seven*, four at the four winds, one above, one below, and another that went before them; Bemidbar Rabba, Parash. 1.

(*f*) That is, envy or malice.

(*g*) The same is ascribed to this cloud in Bemidbar Rabba, *ubi supra*, and in Jarchi in Cant. iii. 6.

(*h*) The same story is reported in Targum Jon. in Exod. xiii. 7, where it is said that the number of the slain in this expedition was two hundred thousand mighty men, and that these are the dry bones Ezekiel saw in the valley, which upon his prophesying lived, and became an exceeding great army, Ezek. xxxvii. Something of this story is also hinted at in Shirhashirim Rabba, and Aben Ezra in loc. *Vide* 1 Chron. vii. 21, 22, and Kimchi, in *ibid*.

Egypt, before the time came, and they fell into the hand of the Philistines, which dwell in Gath, and they slew them: but tarry ye unto the end of forty years, and your children shall go up and inherit it.

Verse 8. *The voice of my beloved, &c.*] Solomon the king said, When the people of the house of Israel dwelt in Egypt, their cry went up to the highest heavens. Lo! then was the glory of the Lord revealed to Moses on Mount Horeb; and he sent him into Egypt to deliver them, and to bring them out of the oppression of the tyranny of Egypt; and he leaped over the appointed season through the righteousness of their fathers, who are like to mountains; and he skipped over the time of a hundred and ninety years' (*i*) servitude, through the righteousness of their mothers, who are like to hills.

Verse 9. *My beloved is like a roe, &c.*] The congregation of Israel said, When the glory of the Lord was revealed in Egypt, in the night of the passover, and slew all the first-born, he rode upon a swift cloud, and ran like a roe or a young hart, and protected the houses in which we were, and stood behind our wall, and looked out of the windows, and beheld through the lattices, and saw the blood of the sacrifice of the passover, and the blood of circumcision which was fixed upon our gates; and he hastened from the highest heavens, and saw his people, who eat of the sacrifice of the feast which was roasted with fire, with (*k*) Tamca and Ulshin, and unleavened bread; and he spared us, and did not give power to the destroying angel to destroy us.

Verse 10. *My beloved spake, and said unto me, &c.*] And in the morning my beloved answered, and said unto me, Arise, O congregation of Israel, my love, who *wast so* of old, and *who art* fair in *good* works; go, get thee out from the bondage of the Egyptians.

Verse 11. *For lo, the winter is past, &c.*] For behold, the time of bondage, which is like to winter, is ceased; and the years (*l*) which I spake of to Abraham between the pieces are at an end; and the tyranny of the Egyptians,

which is like to a violent rain, is over and gone; neither shall ye see them any more for ever.

Verse 12. *The flowers appear on the earth, &c.*] And Moses and Aaron, (*m*) who are like to branches of palm trees, appeared to do wonders in the land of Egypt; and the time of cutting the first-fruits is come, and the voice of the Holy Spirit of redemption, which I spake of to Abraham your father. Now ye hear what I said unto him; yea, the people whom ye shall serve I will judge, and after that ye shall come forth with great substance; and now it is my pleasure to do what I sware to him by my word.

Verse 13. *The fig tree putteth forth, &c.*] The congregation of Israel, which is like to the first-fruits of figs, opened her mouth, and sang a song at the Red Sea; yea, the babes and sucklings praised the Lord of the world with their tongues. Immediately the Lord of the world said unto them, Arise, O congregation of Israel, my love, and my fair one, and go from hence into the land which I have sworn unto thy fathers.

Verse 14. *O my dove, that art in the clefts of the rock, &c.*] And when wicked Pharaoh (*n*) pursued after the children of Israel, the congregation of Israel was like to a dove that is shut up in the clefts of the rock, when the serpent afflicts within, and the hawk oppresses without; even so the congregation of Israel was shut up on the four sides of the world, for before them was the sea, and behind them enmity (*o*) pursued; and on the two sides of them were the wildernesses, which were full of fiery serpents, which bite and kill the sons of men with their poison. And immediately she opened her mouth in prayer before the Lord, and Bath Kol (*p*) went out from the highest heavens, and thus it said, O thou congregation of Israel, who art like to a clean dove, and which is hid in the closure of the clefts of the rock, and in the secret places of the stairs, show me thy countenance, and thy works, which are right; cause me to hear thy voice, for thy voice is sweet in prayer in the house of the little sanctuary, and thy countenance is fair in good works.

(*i*) The Jews unanimously agree, that from the time of Jacob's going down into Egypt to the coming up of the Israelites from thence were just two hundred and ten years; Targum Jon. in Exod. xii. 40. Shirhashirim Rabba, in c. 2, ver. 11, 17. Shemoth Rabba, Parash. 13. Jarchi in Gen. xv. 13, and in Exod. xii. 40; which some of them collect from the word ‏רדו‎ *redu*, "get you down," used by Jacob, Gen. xiii. 2, when he ordered his sons to go down to Egypt, and buy corn, the letters of which word numerically make up 210. Bemidbar Rabba, Parash. 13. Jarchi in Gen. xlii. 2. R. Abendana not. in Miclol Yophi in Exod. xii. 40; to which two hundred and ten years if we add the one hundred and ninety, which the Targumist here says were skipped over in order to hasten the deliverance of the Israelites from their bondage, there will be just the four hundred years God spake of to Abraham, Gen. xv. 13, and mentioned by Stephen, Acts vii. 6, in which his seed should be a stranger, serve, be afflicted and evil entreated; which four hundred years may be reckoned after this manner: From the birth of Isaac to the birth of Jacob sixty years, Gen. xxv. 26; from thence to the coming of Jacob into Egypt one hundred and thirty years, Gen. xlvii. 9; and from thence to the coming of the children of Israel out of Egypt two hundred and ten years; which completes the number. And if we begin the date from Abraham's going out from Ur of the Chaldees, and allow five years for his dwelling in Haran, as the Jews do, see Aben Ezra in Exod. xii. 40; from whose departure from thence to the birth of Isaac were twenty-five years, Gen. xii. 4, and xxi. 5; which thirty years, being added to the above-said four hundred, make up the number given by Moses, Exod. xii. 40, and by the apostle Paul, Gal. iii. 17.

(*k*) The names of the bitter herbs with which the paschal lamb was eaten, Exod. xii. 8. The same are mentioned in Targum Jon. in Exod. xii. 8; and in some of their writings three other herbs are mentioned, the names of which are Chazareth, Charcabina, and Meror, by which they intend horehound, endive, wild lettuce, cichory, and such like herbs; for they themselves do not seem very well to understand them. See Misna Tract. Pesach. c. 2, s. 6. Jarchi ib., and Maimon. Tract. Chametz. Umetza, c. 7, s. 13.

(*l*) So it is explained in Shirhashirim Rabba, and by Jarchi in loc.

(*m*) So Shirhashirim Rabba, and Jarchi in loc.

(*n*) After the same manner Shirhashirim Rabba, and Jarchi in loc. Shemoth Rabba, Parash. 21.

(*o*) That is, the enemy; compare with this Rom. viii. 7.

(*p*) Frequent mention is made of this in the writings of the Jews. It was a voice from heaven which revealed secrets, foretold future events, decided controversies, and directed in difficult matters; it was used in the second temple in the room of prophecy, which the Jews say then ceased, Talmud Sota, fol. 48, col. 2, and Sanhedrin, fol. 2, col. 4. R. Saadiah Gaon in Dan. ix. 24. Shirhashirim Rabba in c. 8, 9. It is thought by R. Levi Ben. Gerson, in 2 Sam. i., s. 27, to be a more excellent and complete kind of divination; and indeed I am inclined to think that most of those voices which go under this name were the mere illusions of Satan, designed to deceive the people, and lessen the credit of those voices which were heard from heaven in the times of Christ. See Matt. iii. 17, and xvii. 5; John xii. 28.

Verse 15. *Take us the foxes, &c.*] After that they had passed through the sea, they murmured for water; then came wicked Amalek against them, who hated them on the account of the birthright and blessing which Jacob our father took away from Esau; and he came to make war with Israel, for they had made void the words of the law; and wicked Amalek (*q*) stole from under the wings of the clouds of glory *several* persons from the tribe of Dan, and slew them, because the idol of Micah was in their hand. In that very hour the house of Israel, which is like to a vineyard, was condemned to be destroyed, except the righteous of that generation, who were like to the best spice.

Verse 16. *My beloved is mine, &c.*] In that very hour they returned by repentance: then stood Moses the prophet, and prayed before the Lord; and Joshua his minister girded himself, and went out from under the (*r*) wings of the clouds of the glory of the Lord, and with him

mighty men that *were* righteous, who in their works are like to the rose; and they made war with Amalek, and they broke Amalek and his people with the anathema of the Lord, and with slaughter, and with breach, and with the edge of the sword.

Verse 17. *Until the day break, &c.*] But in a very few days the children of Israel made the golden calf, and the clouds of glory which covered them removed; and they were left open, and were spoiled of the apparatus of their armour, on which was engraven the Great Name, (*s*) that is explained by seventy names. And the Lord sought to destroy them out of the world; but that he remembered before him the oath which he sware to Abraham, to Isaac, and to Jacob, who were swift in their service, as a roe or a young hart, and the offering which Abraham offered up, *even* Isaac, his own son, on Mount Moriah, and where, before then, he had offered his offering, and divided them equally.

(*q*) In Targ. Jon. in Exod. xvii. 8, where the same story is mentioned, it is said that those men of the tribe of Dan whom Amalek took and slew, were such whom the cloud did not receive and protect because of their idolatry.

(*r*) So Targum Jon. and Jarchi in Exod. xvii. 9, and Shemoth Rabba Parash. 26.

(*s*) This is the name Jehovah, which the Jews think it unlawful to pronounce; and therefore explain it by other names, usually by Adonai or Elohim. Here it is said to be explained by seventy names, sometimes by seventy-two; of which see Galatinus de Arcanis Cath. ver. 1, 2, c. 17, and Schindler, Lex. Pentaglot., p. 1492.

CHAPTER III

Verse 1. *By night on my bed, &c.*] And when the people of the house of Israel saw that the clouds of glory were removed from them, and the holy crown (*a*) that was given to them at Sinai was taken from them, and they were left dark as the night; then they sought the holy crown, which was removed from them, but they found it not.

Verse 2. *I will rise now, &c.*] The children of Israel said one to another, Let us arise, and go and surround the tabernacle of the congregation, which Moses fixed without the camp; and let us seek instruction from the Lord, and the holy shechinah, which is removed from us. And they went about the cities, and in the streets, and in the broad places; but they found it not.

Verse 3. *The watchmen that go about the city, &c.*] The congregation of Israel said, (*b*) Moses and Aaron, and the Levites which keep the charge of the word of the tabernacle of the congregation, who go round about it, found me, and I inquired of them concerning the shechinah of the glory of the Lord, which was removed from me. Moses, the great scribe of Israel, answered, and thus he said: I will go up to the highest heavens, and I will pray before the Lord; perhaps atonement may be made for your transgressions, so that he may cause his shechinah to dwell among you as before.

Verse 4. *It was but a little that I passed,*

&c.] It was but a very little time, and the Lord turned from the fierceness of his anger, and commanded Moses the prophet to make the tabernacle of the congregation, and the ark, and caused his shechinah to dwell in it; and the people of the house of Israel offered their offerings, and studied in the words of the law in the chamber (*c*) of the school of Moses their master, and in the chamber of Joshua, the son of Nun, his minister.

Verse 5. *I charge you, &c.*] When the seven nations (*d*) heard that the children of Israel were about to possess their land, they arose as one *man*, and cut down the trees, and stopped up the fountains of water, and destroyed their cities, and fled. The holy blessed God said to Moses the prophet, I have sworn to their fathers, that I will bring their children to inherit a land flowing with milk and honey; but how shall I bring them to a land that is desolate and empty? Now, therefore, I will cause them to stay forty years in the wilderness, and my law shall be mixed with them, and after that those wicked nations shall build what they have destroyed. And then said Moses to the children of Israel, I charge you, O congregation of Israel, by the Lord of hosts, and by the fortresses of the land of Israel, that ye presume not to go up to the land of Canaan until the forty years are ended. When it shall be the good pleasure of the Lord to deliver the inhabitants of the land into your hands, then

---

(*a*) The same is mentioned in the Targums of Jon. and Jerus. in Exod. xxxii. 25. By this holy crown seems to be meant the shechinah or presence of God, and so it is explained in Shirhashirim Rabba in chap. iv. 12; or else the law, which is very frequently called so, Bemidbar Rabba, Parash. 4. Midrash Kohelet in c. 7, 1. Pirk. Aboth. c. 4, s. 13.

(*b*) These are also supposed to be intended by the watch-

men in Shirhashirim Rabba, and by Jarchi and R. Aben Ezra in loc.

(*c*) It was a common practice with the Jewish doctors to teach, dispute, and converse about religion in chambers or upper rooms. See Mishna Tract. Shabbath. c. 1, s. 4.

(*d*) The Hittites, the Girgashites, the Amorites, the Canaanites, the Perizzites, the Hivites, and the Jebusites, Deut. vii. 1.

shall ye pass over Jordan, and the land shall be subdued before you.

Verse 6. *Who is this that cometh out of the wilderness, &c.*] When the Israelites came up out of the wilderness, and passed over Jordan with Joshua the son of Nun, the people of the land said, Who is this choice nation which comes up out of the wilderness, perfumed with the sweet incense, and supported through the righteousness of Abraham, who worshipped and prayed before the Lord on Mount Moriah, and is anointed with the anointing oil, through the righteousness of Isaac, who was bound in that place of the sanctuary which is called the mountain of frankincense; for whom wonders are also wrought through the holiness of Jacob, who wrestled with him until the morning ascended, and prevailed over him, and was delivered, he and the twelve tribes?

Verse 7. *Behold his bed, which is Solomon's, &c.*] When Solomon, the king of Israel, built the house of the sanctuary of the Lord in Jerusalem, the Lord said by his word, How beautiful is the house of this sanctuary, which is built for me by the hands of King Solomon, the son of David! and how beautiful are the priests, when they spread their hands, and stand upon their desks, and bless the people of the house of Israel by the sixty letters (*e*) which were delivered to Moses their master, and with that blessing which surrounds them like a high and strong wall, and by which all the mighty men of Israel prevail and prosper!

Verse 8. *They all hold swords, &c.*] And the priests and the Levites, and all the tribes of Israel, all of them take hold of the words of the law, which are like to a (*f*) sword, in which they employ themselves as men that are expert in war; and every one of them has the (*g*) seal of circumcision sealed upon their flesh, even as it was sealed upon the flesh of Abraham; and by it they prevail as a man that has his sword girt upon his thigh, wherefore they are not afraid of noxious spirits (*h*) and apparitions, which walk in the night.

Verse 9. *King Solomon made himself a chariot, &c.*] King Solomon built for himself (*i*) a holy temple of the trees of (*k*) Zangebila, fir trees, and cedars, which came from Lebanon, and covered it with pure gold.

Verse 10. *He made the pillars thereof, &c.*] And after that he had finished it, he put in the midst of it the ark of the testimony, which is the pillar of the world; and in it the two tables of stone, which Moses placed there in Horeb, which are more precious than the best gold; and he spread and covered over it (*l*) the veil of blue and purple, and between the cherubims which are over the mercy-seat the shechinah of the Lord abode, whose name dwelleth in Jerusalem, above all the cities of the land of Israel.

Verse 11. *Go forth, O ye daughters of Zion, &c.*] When King Solomon came to make the dedication of the house of the sanctuary, a crier went forth in strength; and thus he said, Go forth and see, ye inhabitants of the provinces of the land of Israel, and ye people of Zion, the crown and diadem wherewith the people of the house of Israel crowned King Solomon in the (*m*) day of the dedication of the house of the sanctuary, when he rejoiced with the joy of the feast of tabernacles; for king Solomon kept at that time the feast of tabernacles (*n*) fourteen days.

(*e*) The same is mentioned in Shirhashirim Rabba in loc., and in Bemidbar Rabba, Parash. 11. There being just this number of letters in the forms of blessings with which the priests were to bless the people of Israel, in Num. vi. 24, 25, 26.

(*f*) The law is likewise compared to a sword, in Bereshith Rabba, Parash. 21. See Eph. vi. 17. Heb. iv. 12.

(*g*) The apostle Paul calls circumcision σημειον περιτομης, σφραγιδα της δικαιοσυνης της πιστεως, "the sign of circumcision, a seal of the righteousness of faith," Rom. iv. 11.

(*h*) So this "fear in the night" is interpreted by some of the rabbins in Shirhashirim Rabba in loc., and in Bemidbar Rabba, Parash. 11. Though others of them in the said places explain it of the fear of hell, which is like to the night; as they do also in Gemara Rab. Tract. Sanhedrin, c. 1, fol. 7, col. 1.

(*i*) By this chariot R. Aben Ezra also understands the house of the Lord; and in Shirhashirim Rabba, and by Jarchi in loc., it is interpreted of the tabernacle, as it is by some of the Jews, in Bemidbar Rabba, Parash. 12, though others think the ark is intended; and others in the same place would have the world meant, which way they explain it in Zohar in Gen. fol. 2, 1. The word אפריון very properly signifies "the marriage bed," so called from פרה which signifies "to fructify," or "to be fruitful." Hence אפריון לבנות is a very

usual phrase with the rabbins to express the celebration of marriage. *Vide* Buxtorf, epist. Heb. lib. 2, ep. 7.

(*k*) Elias Levita, in his Methurgeman on this word, says that this is cinnabar. He seems to mean a kind of red wood, which dyers use; but observes, that some say it is the spice we call ginger. So David de Pomis renders it in his Lex. Heb. fol. 54, 4; and indeed it is joined with pepper in Maimon. Tract. Shebitat Asur, c. 2, s. 6. Biath. Hamikdash, c. 7, s. 13, and Beracoth, c. 8, s. 7. It is most likely to be a kind of cedar.

(*l*) *Vide* Bemidbar Rabba, Parash. 12, Shirhashirim Rabba, and Jarchi in loc.

(*m*) Most of the Jewish writers refer this to the time of the giving of the law on Mount Sinai, and the setting up of the tabernacle by Moses; so Jarchi and Shirhashirim Rabba in loc. Shemoth Rabba, Parash. 52. Vajikra Rabba, Parash. 20, Bemidbar Rabba, Parash. 2 and 12. Præfat. Echa Rabbati. fol. 21, 2.

(*n*) In 1 Kings viii. 65, it is said that "Solomon held a feast seven days and seven days, even fourteen days;" the reason of which distinction is because the first seven days were kept for the dedication of the altar, and the other for the feast of tabernacles; see 2 Chron. vii. 8, 9: whereas our Targumist would have the feast of tabernacles kept the whole fourteen days, contrary to the command in Lev. xxiii. 34. *Vide* R. Levi Ben Gerson, and R. David Kimchi in 1 Reg. viii. 65.

CHAPTER IV

Verse 1. *Behold, thou art fair, &c.*] And in that day King Solomon offered up a (*a*) thousand burnt-offerings upon the altar, and his offerings were graciously accepted by the Lord.

(*a*) In 1 Kings viii. 63, the sacrifice of peace-offerings which Solomon offered was two and twenty thousand oxen, and a hundred and twenty thousand sheep: but the number of burnt-offerings is not mentioned.

Bath Kol (*b*) went forth from heaven; and thus it said, How fair art thou, O congregation of Israel, and how fair are the princes of the congregation and the wise men, (*c*) who sit in the sanhedrin, who enlighten (*d*) the world; the people of the house of Israel, and are like to young doves; yea, even the rest of the children of thy congregation; and the people of the earth are righteous, as the sons of Jacob, (*e*) who gathered stones, and made a heap *thereof* on the mount of Gilead!

Verse 2. *Thy teeth are like, &c.*] How fair are the priests and Levites, who offer up thine offerings, and eat the holy flesh, and the tithes, and the offering of fruits; and are pure from all oppression and rapine, even as clean as Jacob's flocks of sheep when they were shorn, and came up from the brook (*f*) Jabok, among whom there was no oppression or rapine, and they are all of them like to one another, and always bear twins; neither is any barren, or that miscarrieth among them.

Verse 3. *Thy lips are like a thread, &c.*] And the lips of the high priest inquire in prayer, on the day of atonement, before the Lord; and his words turn the transgressions of Israel, which are like to a thread of scarlet, and make them white (*g*) as pure wool; and the king, who is their head, is full of the commandments, as a pomegranate; besides the (*h*) Amarcalin and (*i*) Archonin, who are next the king, who are righteous; neither is there any iniquity in them.

Verse 4. *Thy neck is like the tower, &c.*] And the head of the school, who is thy master, is powerful in righteousness, and mighty in good works, as David king of Israel, by the word of whose mouth the world is restored, who in the doctrine of the law employs himself; *in which* the people of the house of Israel placing their confidence, overcome in war, as if they held in their hands all kinds of warlike instruments of mighty men.

Verse 5. *Thy two breasts, &c.*] Thy two Redeemers which shall redeem thee; (*k*) Messiah the son of David, and Messiah the son of Ephraim, are like to Moses and Aaron, the sons of Jochebed, who may be compared to young roes that are twins; who by their righteousness fed the people of the house of Israel forty years in the wilderness with manna, and with fatted fowls, and water of (*l*) the well of Miriam.

Verse 6. *Until the day break, &c.*] And all the time that the house of Israel held fast in their hands the religion of their righteous fathers, they drove away those noxious spirits that walk in the night-time, or in the morning, or at noonday; because that the shechinah of the glory of the Lord dwelt in the house of the sanctuary, which was built on Mount Moriah; for all the noxious and destroying spirits fled at the smell of the sweet incense.

Verse 7. *Thou art all fair, &c.*] And when thy people, the house of Israel do the will of the Lord of the world, he praises them in the highest heavens; and thus he saith, Thou art all fair, O congregation of Israel, and there is no (*m*) spot in thee.

Verse 8. *Come with me from Lebanon, &c.*] The Lord said by his word, Dwell with me, O congregation of Israel, who art like to a modest (*n*) damsel, and go up with me to the house of the sanctuary, where the heads of the people, which dwell by the river of (*o*) Amana, and the inhabitants that reside on the top of Mount (*p*) Talga, and the people which are in Hermon, shall bring gifts unto thee, and they that inhabit the strong fortified cities, which are as powerful as lions, shall pay tribute to thee; *yea*, an offering *shall be brought* from the cities of the mountains, which are mightier than the leopards.

Verse 9. *Thou hast ravished my heart, &c.*] Fixed upon the (*q*) table of my heart is thy love, O my sister, the congregation of Israel, who art like to a modest damsel; fixed upon the

---

(*b*) See note on chap. ii. 14.
(*c*) So the words are explained in Shirhashirim Rabba, in loc.
(*d*) So Christ calls his disciples the "light of the world," Matt. v. 14.
(*e*) This refers to the account that is given of what passed between Jacob and Laban, in Gen. xxxi. 46, 47. See Jarchi in loc.
(*f*) This is the ford Jacob passed over with his wives and children, when he went out to meet his brother Esau, Gen. xxxii. 22. Mention is made of it in several other places of Scripture: Deut. ii. 37, and iii. 16; Josh. xii. 2.
(*g*) The Jews say, that when the scape-goat was sent into the wilderness, a scarlet thread was tied to the temple door, which, as soon as the goat had arrived in the wilderness, turned white; which was not only a token to them of its arrival there, but was also an indication of their sins being forgiven; as it is said, "Though your sins be as scarlet, they shall be as white as snow," Isa. i. 18. See Mishna, Tract. Yoma, c. 6, s. 8, and Ez Chayim, *ibid.* This scarlet thread, they say, ceased turning white forty years before the destruction of the temple, which was about the time Jesus Christ, who was typified by the scape-goat, made atonement for sin; Talmud Yoma, fol. 39, col. 2. This tradition the Targumist seems to have in view here.
(*h*) These officers were of the tribe of Levi, Bemidbar Rabba, Parash. 3. Their number was never less than seven; their work was to take the care and charge of the keys of the court; and one might not open the door unless all seven were present, Mishna, Tract. Shekalim, c. 5, s. 2. Maimon. Hilch. Cele Hamikdash, c. 4, s. 17. Jarchi in 2 Reg. xii. 9; though Kimchi, in 2 Reg. xii. 9, and xxii. 4, thinks that they were treasurers, who had the charge of the public money. The etymology given of this word is very different. Baal Aruch says this officer was so called because he was מר על הכל *mar al haccol*, "lord over all:" the same is given in

Vajikra Rabba, Parash. 5, where Shebna the treasurer, Isa. xxii. 15, is said to be one of those officers. Elias Levita, in his Methurgeman, says he was so called because אומר כל *omar col*, "he said" or "prescribed" all things.
(*i*) This is from the Greek word Αρχων, and signifies princes, rulers, or governors.
(*k*) The Jews, observing different characters given of the Messiah, which they think irreconcilable in one person, have feigned two Messiahs; the one they call Messiah, the son of David, who shall be a potent, prosperous, and victorious prince; the other, Messiah the son of Ephraim, or Joseph, as he is sometimes called, who shall be exposed to many hardships and sufferings, and at last die in the war of Gog and Magog. Of these two Messiahs, see Talmud, Succah, fol. 52, col. 1. Zohar in Num. fol. 68, 3; 82, 2; 99, 4; and 101, 2. Jarchi in Isa. xxiv. 18. Kimchi, Jarchi, and Aben Ezra in Zech. xii. 10.
(*l*) It is an opinion which obtains among the Jews, that on account of the merits of Moses the manna was given; and on the account of those of Aaron, the clouds of glory; and for the sake of Miriam, the well of water, which they say they enjoyed all the forty years they were in the wilderness. Shirhashirim Rabba in loc. Bemidbar Rabba, Parash. 1 and 13. Targum Jon. and Jarchi in Num. xx. 2.
(*m*) Or plague.
(*n*) Here the Greek word νυμφη is used, as it is also in verses 9, 10, 11, 12, and chap. v. 1.
(*o*) This was one of the rivers of Damascus; see 2 Kings v. 12, where it is read Abana: but both the Masora and Targum read it Amana; and Kimchi thinks it was called by both names.
(*p*) Or "the mountain of snow." Elias Levita, in his Methurgeman, says that Mount Shenir was called so: perhaps Mount Salmon may be meant, which had snow continually upon it; see Psa. lxviii. 14, and R. Aben Ezra, *ibid.*
(*q*) Compare with this 2 Cor. iii. 3.

table of my heart is the love of the least of thy children, who is righteous as one of the great men of the sanhedrin, as one of the kings (*r*) of the house of Judah, on whose neck the crown of the kingdom is put.

Verse 10. *How fair is thy love, &c.*] How fair is thy love to me, my sister, the congregation of Israel, who art like to a modest damsel! How excellent is thy love to me, more than the (*s*) seventy nations; and the good (*t*) report of thy righteous ones is more excellent than all spices!

Verse 11. *Thy lips, O my spouse, &c.*] And when the priests pray in the holy court, their lips drop *as* the honey-comb; and so does thy tongue, O thou modest damsel, when thou deliverest songs and hymns, sweet as milk and honey; and the smell of the (*u*) priests' garments *is* as the smell of Lebanon.

Verse 12. *A garden enclosed, &c.*] Thy women, which are married to modest men, are as a modest damsel, and as the garden of Eden, into which no man hath power to enter except the righteous, whose souls are by angels (*v*) carried into it; and thy virgins are hid and concealed (*w*) in private chambers, and are sealed up because *they are* as a fountain of living water, which comes forth from under the tree, and is parted to the four heads (*x*) of the rivers: but if it is sealed with the great and holy name, it goes forth and flows, and overflows all the world.

Verse 13. *Thy plants are an orchard, &c.*] And thy young men are full of thy commands, as pomegranates, and love their wives, and beget children as righteous as themselves; and their smell, therefore, is as the excellent spices of the garden of Eden, even camphires with nards.

Verse 14. *Spikenard with saffron, &c.*] Nard, and saffron, and calamus, and cinnamon, with all trees of frankincense, pure myrrh, and lign aloes, with all kinds of spices.

Verse 15. *A fountain of gardens, &c.*] And the waters of Siloah (*y*) go softly, with the rest of the waters which flow from Lebanon, to water the land of Israel, for the sake of those who study in the words of the law, which are like to a well of living water; and on the account of the righteousness (*z*) of pouring of water, which they pour upon the altar in the house of the sanctuary, that is built in Jerusalem, which is called (*a*) Lebanon.

Verse 16. *Awake, O north wind, &c.*] And at the north side (*b*) was a table, and upon it (*c*) twelve loaves of shew-bread, and at the south side (*d*) was the lamp to give light; and upon the altar the priests offered up the offerings, and caused the sweet incense to ascend from thence. The congregation of Israel said, Let the merciful God come into the house of the sanctuary, and graciously accept the offerings of his people.

(*r*) Many of the kings of the house of Judah were holy and good men; so Aben Ezra in loc.

(*s*) See note in chap. i. 2.

(*t*) So Jarchi in loc.

(*u*) *Vide* Jarchi in loc.

(*v*) It was an ancient opinion of the Jews, that the ministry of angels was used in carrying the souls of saints to heaven. Thus in Debarim Rabba, Parash. 11, several angels are ordered by God to bring the soul of Moses to him. Agreeably to this notion, it is said in Luke xvi. 22, that "the beggar died, and was carried by the angels into Abraham's bosom.

(*w*) It was very usual with the Eastern people to keep their virgins, especially those of note and esteem, very recluse, and not admit them to public or common conversation; but oblige them to abide much within doors. Hence they are called in the Hebrew language עלמות, from the word עלם, which signifies to hide or cover, because they were not exposed to public view; wherefore the author of the second book of Maccabees calls them κατακλειστους παρθενους, "virgins that were shut up;" i. e., in the houses of their parents, in private chambers, as the Targumist here says. See 2 Macc. iii. 19.

(*x*) Regard seems to be had to the river which went out of Eden, mentioned in Gen. ii. 10, and was parted into four heads or rivers, the names of which were Pison, Gihon, Hiddekel, and Euphrates. The Cabalists suppose a great many mysteries to be contained therein; see Zohar in Gen. fol. 85, 2; in Exod. fol. 34, 3; 37, 2, and in Lev. fol. 24, 3, where the name of this river is said to be Jobel, according to Jer. xvii. 8; and so it is in Vajikra Rabba, Parash. 22, and in Bemidbar Rabba, Parash. 21.

(*y*) See Isa. viii. 6, and Aben Ezra upon it, who expounds the text in Isaiah by this in Canticles. Jarchi, in Isa. viii. 6 says the name of this fountain was Gihon. In the New Testament it is called Siloam, John ix. 7, 11; it was a fountain near Jerusalem, Neh. iii. 15.

(*z*) The paraphrast refers here to a ceremony used at the feast of tabernacles, when the people fetched water from Siloam, and brought it to the priest, who poured it upon the altar with the wine of the daily sacrifice; this they say Moses received from God at Mount Sinai, though it is not written. This ceremony of drawing and pouring water at those times was attended with all the demonstrations of joy imaginable, as shouting, leaping, dancing, singing, blowing of trumpets, throwing of citrons, illumination of houses, &c.; insomuch that they say, that those who never saw the rejoicing of drawing water never saw rejoicing in their lives, Mishna, Tract. Succa, c. 4, s. 9, 10, and c. 5, s. 1, 2, 3, 4, 5; Jarchi and Ez Chayim, *ibid.;* Maimon., Tract. Tamidin, c. 10, s. 6, 7, 8; Cele Hamikdash, c. 7, s. 8, and c. 8, s. 6. They fancied the Holy Ghost was much delighted with this vain joy of theirs; nay, that in drawing water they drew him, i. e., procured his descent upon them, and abode with them as a spirit of prophecy, which they say Jonah obtained at this time and in this way; and, therefore, whilst they were performing this ceremony, frequently used those words in Isa. xii. 3: "With joy shall ye draw water out of the wells of salvation;" which they understand of the Holy Ghost, Bereshith Rabba, Parash. 70. Midrash Ruth, fol. 32, 2. Jarchi and Ez Chayim in Mishna, *ubi supra.* To this ceremony Christ is thought to allude, "when in the last day, the great day of this feast of tabernacles, he stood and cried, saying, If any man thirst, let him come unto me and drink: he that believeth on me, as the Scripture hath said, out of his belly shall flow rivers of living water: but this spake he of the Spirit," &c. John vii. 37, 38, 39. *Vide* Tremell., *ibid.*

(*a*) So the temple is called in Zech. xi. 1: "Open thy doors, O Lebanon, that the fire may devour thy cedars," according to the mind of several Jewish interpreters, who, out of Talmud Yoma, fol. 39, 2, relate, that forty years before the destruction of the temple the doors thereof opened of themselves; at which Jochanan Ben Zaccai being affrighted, said, O temple, temple, now know I that thy destruction is at hand; for so prophesied Zechariah, the son of Iddo, of thee, Open thy doors, &c. *Vide* R. Abendam. Not. in Miclol Yophi; Jarchi and Kimchi in Zech. xi. 1.

(*b*) That is, of the sanctuary; see Exod. xl. 22, 23.

(*c*) Lev. xxiv. 5, 6.

(*d*) Exod. xl. 24, 25.

CHAPTER V

Verse 1. *I am come into my garden, &c.*] The holy blessed God said unto his people, the house of Israel, I am come into the house of my sanctuary, which thou hast built for me, O my sister, the congregation of Israel, who *art* like to a modest damsel: I have caused my shechinah to dwell with thee, (a) I have received thy sweet incense, which thou hast made on my account; I have sent fire from heaven, and it hath devoured thy burnt-offerings, and the holy drink-offerings; the libation of the red and white wine is graciously received by me, which the priests pour out upon mine altar. Now, *therefore*, come, ye priests that love my commandments, and eat what is left of the offerings, and delight yourselves with those good things which are prepared for you.

Verse 2. *I sleep, but my heart waketh, &c.*] After all these words the people of the house of Israel sinned, and he delivered them into the hand of Nebuchadnezzar, king of Babylon, who carried them into captivity; and they were in captivity like a man asleep, that cannot be awaked out of his sleep; wherefore the Holy Ghost warned them by the prophets, and awaked them out of the sleep of their hearts. *Then* answered the Lord of the whole world, and thus he said, Return by repentance, open thy mouth, rejoice and show forth my praise, my sister, my love, O congregation of Israel, who *art* like to a dove for the perfection of thy works; for the hair of my head is filled with thy tears, as a man the hair of whose head is wet with the dew of heaven; and my Nazaritical locks are filled with the drops of thine eyes, as a man whose Nazaritical locks are full of the drops of rain which descend in the night.

Verse 3. *I have put off my coat, &c.*] The congregation of Israel answered in the presence of the prophets, Behold, now have I removed from me the (b) yoke of his commandments, and have served the idols of the nations; wherefore, how can I have the face to return to him again? The Lord of the world answered them by the prophets, *saying*, And behold, now I also have removed my shechinah from thee; and how shall I return again, seeing thou hast done evil works? for I have washed my feet from thine uncleanness, and how shall I defile them in the midst of thee with thy evil works?

Verse 4. *My beloved put in his hand, &c.*] When it appeared manifest before the Lord that the people of the house of Israel would not repent and turn unto him, he stretched forth (c) his mighty arm against the tribes of Reuben and Gad, and the half tribe of Manasseh; on the other side of Jordan; and he delivered them into the hand of Sennacherib, the king of Assyria, who carried them into captivity, (d) to Lachlach, and Chabor, *and to the* rivers of Gozan, and cities of Media; and he took out of their hands the molten calf which Jeroboam, the wicked, set in Lesham-Dan, which was called (e) Pamias, in the days of Pekah, the son of Remaliah; and when I heard *it*, my bowels were moved towards them.

Verse 5. *I rose up to open to my beloved, &c.*] And when the mighty stroke of the Lord lay heavy upon me, I repented of my works; and the priests offered up offerings, and burnt the sweet incense: but it was not graciously received, for the Lord of the world shut the (f) doors of repentance to my face.

Verse 6. *I opened to my beloved, &c.*] The congregation of Israel said, I was willing to seek instruction from the Lord: but he removed his shechinah from me, and my soul desired the voice of his words. I sought the shechinah of his glory: but I found *it* not. I prayed before him: but he covered the heavens with (g) clouds, and did not receive my prayer.

Verse 7. *The watchmen that went about the city, &c.*] The (h) Chaldeans, which kept the ways, and besieged the city of Jerusalem all around, joined themselves to me. Some they slew with the sword, and others they carried into captivity. They took the crown royal off the neck of Zedekiah king of Judah, and carried him away to Ribla, (i) where the people of Babylon, who besieged the city and kept the walls, put out his eyes.

Verse 8. *I charge you, O daughters of Jerusalem, &c.*] The congregation of Israel said, I charge you, O ye prophets, by the decree of the word of the Lord, that, if your love manifests himself unto you, you tell him that I, who love him, am sick of love.

Verse 9. *What is thy beloved, &c.*] The prophets answered and said, unto the house of Israel, (k) Who is this God thou art seeking to worship, O congregation of Israel, *who art* fairer than all the nations? Who is this thou art desirous to fear, that thou dost so charge us?

Verse 10. *My beloved is white and ruddy,*

(a) These words are similarly paraphrased in Shirhashirim Rabba, and by Jarchi in loc., and in Bemidbar Rabba, Parash. 13.

(b) See note on chap. i. 10.

(c) Chald. The stroke of his might.

(d) See 2 Kings xvii. 6, and xviii. 11; 1 Chron. v. 26.

(e) Leshem being taken by the tribe of Dan, Josh. xix. 47, they call it Dan, after the name of their father; and it seems it was also called Pamias. Both Baal Aruch, and David de Pomis, say that פמיאס *Pamias* was a cave at the head of the river Jordan: and it is asserted by several of the rabbins, that Jordan took its rise from hence, who therefore say that the river was so called, שיורד מדן *sheiyored middan*, "because it descended from Dan," i. e., from Leshem, Dan, or Pamias, Talmud Baba Bathra, fol. 74, col. 2; and Bechoroth. fol. 55, col. 1; Jarchi in Deut. xxxiii. 22; Kimchi in Jos. xix. 47. This in Bereshith Rabba, Parash. 63, is called פמייס *Panias*, as it is also by Josephus, and no doubt is the same which Pliny, in Nat. Hist. 1. 5, c. 18, calls Pa-

neas, who also makes mention in c. 15 of a fountain of the same name, from whence he says the river Jordan sprung. The same is observed by Solinus, in his Polyhistor. c. 48, who calls it by the name of Peneas. Eusebius, in his Eccl. Hist. 1. 7, c. 17, says that the Phœnicians called Cæsarea Philippi Paneas, and speaks of a mountain called Paneius, from whence the river Jordan has its original.

(f) In Shirhashirim Rabba, in chap. 5, 2, mention is made of פתח של תשובה "the gate of repentance," which the Lord desired the Israelites to open to him. Agreeably to this phrase, it is observed, in Acts xiv. 27, that "God had opened unto the Gentiles θυραν πιστεως, the door of faith."

(g) See Lam. iii. 44.

(h) Jarchi by these watchmen understands Nebuchadnezzar and his army. R. Aben Ezra, the kings of Greece. Shirhashirim Rabba, the tribe of Levi.

(i) See Jer. iii. 7, 9, 11.

(k) *Vide* Jarchi, and Shirhashirim Rabba in loc.

&c.] Wherefore the congregation of Israel began to speak in the praise of the Lord of the world, and thus she said, That God I desire to serve, who in the day is covered with a garment (*l*) white as snow, (*m*) and the brightness of the glory of the Lord, whose face shines as fire, because of the greatness of wisdom and knowledge, for he is making new things every day, and will manifest them to his people in the (*n*) great day, and his banner is over ten thousand times ten thousand angels, who minister before him.

Verse 11. *His head is as the most fine gold, &c.*] His law, (*o*) which is more desirable than the best gold, and the interpretation of the words *thereof*, in which are senses, (*p*) heaps *upon* heaps, and the commandments to them that keep them *are* white as snow; but to those that do not keep them *are* black as the wings of a raven.

Verse 12. *His eyes are as the eyes of doves, &c.*] His eyes look continually (*q*) upon Jerusalem, to do good unto it, and to bless it, from the beginning of the year unto the end of the year, as doves which stand and look upon the water-courses, because of the righteousness of those who sit in the sanhedrin, who study in the law, and give light to a cause, that it may be smooth as milk; and they sit in the house of the school, and (*r*) wait in judgment until they have finished either for absolution or condemnation.

Verse 13. *His cheeks are as a bed of spices,*

&c.] The (*s*) two tables of stone which he gave unto his people are written in (*t*) ten lines, like to the rows of a spice garden, producing acute meanings and senses, even as a garden produces spices; and the lips of his wise men which study in the law, drop senses on every side, and the speech of their mouths is as the choice myrrh.

Verse 14. *His hands are as gold rings, &c.*] The twelve tribes of Jacob his servants are included in the plate of the holy crown of gold, and are engraven upon the twelve (*u*) precious stones with the three fathers of the world, Abraham, Isaac, and Jacob. Reuben is engraven on achmad, Simeon is engraven upon akik, Levi is engraven on barkan and affran, Judah is engraven on cachale, Issachar is engraven on ismorad, Zebulun is engraven on gihar, Dan is engraven on birla, Naphtali is engraven on esphor, Gad is engraven on tabeag, Asher is engraven on frozag, Joseph is engraven on meribag, Benjamin is engraven on apantor: these are like to the twelve celestial signs, shining as lamps, polished in their works like ivory, and bright as sapphires.

Verse 15. *His legs are as pillars of marble, &c.*] And the righteous they *are* the pillars of the world, set upon sockets of the best gold; these *are* (*x*) the words of the law, in which they study, and reprove the people of the house of Israel, that they may do his will who is filled with compassion to them, as an old man; and makes the transgressions of the house of Israel

---

(*l*) So the Ancient of days is represented in Dan. vii. 9.

(*m*) In some exemplars these following words are inserted:— "And studies in the twenty-four books of the law, and in the words of prophecy, and in the Holy Writings, and in the night-time employs himself in the six parts of the Mishna," which Buxtorf has omitted in his Bible, though he makes mention of them in his Recensio operis Talmud, p. 232; and indeed they greatly lessen the glory of the Divine Being, though they are designed to extol and magnify the Mishna or oral law.

(*n*) That is, the day of judgment, which in Jude, ver. 6, is called κρισις μεγαλης ημερας, "the judgment of the great day," when not only the hidden things of darkness and the counsels of the hearts will be made manifest, 1 Cor. iv. 5, but the judgments of God also, Rev. xv. 4.

(*o*) The same way the words are explained in Shirhashirim Rabba, and by Jarchi in loc., and in Vajikra Rabba, Parash. 19. By this head R. Aben Ezra understands the throne of glory.

(*p*) That is, a variety or great multitude of them; for the Jews suppose the law may be interpreted various ways, and that there is not the least thing in it but what contains a great many mysteries. See notes on chap. i. 11.

(*q*) *Vide* Shirhashirim Rabba in loc.

(*r*) That is, they proceed in trying causes slowly and gradually, and not rashly and precipitately, being willing to search thoroughly into them, that they may do justice and pass a right sentence; this is one of the three things the men of the great congregation advised to in Pirke Aboth, c. 1, s. 1, where they say הוו מתונין בדין *havu mittonin bedin*, "Be slow in judgment, settle many disciples, and make a hedge for the law."

(*s*) So Jarchi by "his cheeks" understands the words of Mount Sinai.

(*t*) Every commandment was written in a distinct line by itself, five on one table and five on the other.

(*u*) In the same order are the names of the twelve tribes as engraven on so many precious stones, mentioned in Targum Jerus. in Exod. xxviii. 17, 18, 19, 20; in Shemoth Rabba, Parash. 38; and in Bemidbar Rabba, Parash. 2. Though different names are given of the precious stones, the names of them in the Rabboth are the same with those in Exod. xxviii. In the Targum Jer. are Chaldee names, and in this paraphrase they are different from them. Reuben's stone was the Sardius, Heb. odem, Onk. samkan, Jon. semuktha, Jerus. samkatha. It is so called by all those names from the

redness of its colour; here it is called achmad, perhaps from חמד *chamad*, because it is very desirable. Simeon's stone was the topaz, Heb. pitdah, Onk. yarkan, Jon. and Jerus. yarketha, because of its green colour; here it is called akik: but what gem is intended by it is not certain. Levi's stone was the carbuncle, Heb. barketh, Jon. and Jerus, barketha, and here barkan, and so in Onk.; and is so called because of its bright and glistering light. Judah's stone was the emerald, Heb. nophec, Onk. ismaragdin, Jon. ismorad: both seem to mean the smaragd. Jerus. cadcedana, or the chalcedony; here it is called cachale; it is thought to be the smaragd. See Eliæ Levitæ Methurgeman, Buxtorf and Schindler *in voce*. Issachar's stone was the sapphire, Heb. saphir, Onk. shabzez, Jon. sapphirinon, Jerus. sampuryana: all intend the sapphire; here it is called ismorad, or the smaragd. Zebulon's stone was the diamond, Heb. yahalom, Onk. sabhalon; it bears those names from the hardness of it. Jon. cadcodin or chalcedony, Jerus. ein egla, the calves eye; here it is called gihar, which some think to be the jasper. See Buxtorf *in voce*. Dan's stone was the ligure, Heb. leshem, Onk. kankire, Jon. kankirinum, Jerus. zuzin; here it is called birla, which seems to be the beryl. Naphtali's stone was the agate, Heb. shebo, Onk. yarkia, Jon. arkin, Jerus. birzalin; and here it is called espor, which may be thought to be the sapphire. Gad's stone was the amethyst, Heb. achlamah, Onk. and Jon. ein egla, the calves eye, Jerus. smaragdin, the smaragd; and here it is called yabeag: but what is meant by it I know not. Asher's stone was the beryl, Heb. tarshish. Onk. Jon. and Jerus. crum yamma; here it is called frozag. Elias in his Methurgeman says, that a topaz, in the German language, is called frozam. Joseph's stone was the onyx, Heb. shoham, Onk. burla, Jon. berlevath; both seem to intend the beryl, Jerus. bdolcha or bdellium; here it is called meribag, which some take to be the onyx. See Buxtorf *in voce*. Benjamin's stone was the jasper, Heb. jashpeh, Jerus. margalita, a pearl, Onk. pantere, Jon. apanturin; and here apantor, which Elias in his Methurgeman says is so called because it comes from Pontus; but rather because some sorts of jaspers are variegated and spotted like panthers. In the same order were the names of the twelve tribes engraven both upon the stones in the breastplate, and on the two onyx stones upon the shoulders of the ephod, according to Maimon, Tract. Cele Hamikdash. c. 9, s. 1, 7, 9.

(*x*) So these sockets of fine gold are explained in Shirhashirim Rabba, and by Jarchi in loc., in Vajikra Rabba, Parash. 25, and in Bemidbar Rabba, Parash. 10.

as white as snow, and is ready to make victory and war among the nations who have transgressed his word, as a man who is strong and robust as the cedars.

Verse 16. *His mouth is most sweet, &c.*] The words of his mouth are sweet as honey, and all his commandments are more desirable to his wise men than gold and silver; this is the praise of God, who is my beloved, and this is the power of the mighty of the Lord, who is dear to me, O ye prophets who prophesy in Jerusalem.

CHAPTER VI

Verse 1. *Whither is thy beloved gone, &c.*] The prophets (a) replied, when they heard the praise of the Lord, from the mouth of the congregation of Israel, and thus they said, For what offence is the shechinah of the Lord removed from thee, O thou *who* art fairer in thy works than all the nations? and which way did thy beloved turn himself when he removed from thy sanctuary? The congregation of Israel said, Because of the sins, transgressions, and rebellion which were found in me. The prophets said, But now return by repentance, and let us arise, both thou and we, and we will pray before him, and seek mercy with thee.

Verse 2. *My beloved is gone down into his garden, &c.*] And the Lord of the world graciously received their prayer, and came down to the sanhedrin of the wise men at Babylon, and gave refreshment unto his people, and brought them out of their captivity by the hands of Cyrus, and Ezra, and Nehemiah, and Zerubbabel the son of Shealtiel, and the elders of Judah; and they built the house of the sanctuary, and appointed priests over the offerings, and Levites over the charge of the holy commandment; and he sent fire from heaven and graciously received the offerings, and the sweet incense; and as a man supplies his own beloved son with dainties, so did he deliciously feed them; and as a man that gathereth roses out of the plains, so did he gather them out of Babylon.

Verse 3. *I am my beloved's, &c.*] And when I served the Lord of the world, who is my beloved, my beloved caused the holy shechinah to dwell with me, and he fed me with dainties.

Verse 4. *Thou are beautiful, O my love, &c.*] The Lord said by his word, How fair art thou, my love, when thou art willing to perform my pleasure! beautiful is the sanctuary which thou hast built for me instead of the former sanctuary, which Solomon, king in Jerusalem, built for me, and thy dread was upon all the people in the day that thy four (b) standards marched in the wilderness.

Verse 5. *Turn away thine eyes from me, &c.*] Set thy doctors, the wise men of the great congregation, in a circle over against me, for these (c) made me *their* king in the captivity, and fixed the school, for the teaching of my law, and the rest of thy nobles, and the people of the earth justified me by the word of their mouth, as the sons of Jacob, who gathered stones and made a heap (d) upon the mount of Gilead.

Verse 6. *Thy teeth are as a flock of sheep, &c.*] And the priests and Levites, who eat thine offerings, and the holy tithes, and the oblation of fruits, are pure from all oppression and rapine, for they are as clean as Jacob's flocks of sheep, when they came up from the brook (e) Jabok, for there is no oppression or rapine in them: but they are all of them like one another, and they always bear twins, neither is there any that miscarrieth or is barren among them.

Verse 7. *As a piece of pomegranate, &c.*] And the kingdom of the house of the Hasmonæans (f) are all of them full of the commandments, even as a pomegranate; besides Matthias the high priest, and his sons, who are more righteous than them all, who very eagerly established the commandments and the words of the law.

Verse 8. *There are threescore queens, &c.*] At that time the Grecians arose and gathered sixty kings of the children of (g) Esau, clothed with coats of mail, riding upon horses, being horsemen, and eighty dukes of the children of Ishmael, riding upon elephants, besides the rest of the nations and languages, of which

---

(a) The persons here interrogating are said to be "the nations of the world," in Shirhashirim Rabba, and by Jarchi in loc.

(b) Which were those of Judah, Reuben, Ephraim, and Dan. See Num. ii., and Bemidbar Rabba, Parash. 2.

(c) So the word הרדיבני is paraphrased in Shirhashirim Rabba in loc.

(d) See note on chap. iv. 1.

(e) See note on chap. iv. 2.

(f) Schindler, in his Lex. Pentaglot. fol. 680, says that Mattathias and his posterity were so called from חשמון *Hasmon*, one of their ancestors, though I think there is no evidence of any of their ancestors being of that name. The Jewish writers pretty generally agree that they were so called from the word השמנים *Hashmannim*, which signifies *princes* or *great persons*, and is so used in Psa. lxviii. 32; for they had both the high priesthood and the princely government in their hands. So R. Aben Ezra, R. David Kimchi, and R. Sol. Ben Melec, in Psa. lxviii. 32. David de Pomis, Lex.

Heb. fol. 42, 1, and so likewise Scaliger de Emend. Temp. lib. 5, pp. 436, 437; who observes that Mattathias was never so called, nor was he a high priest, though the Targumist here calls him so, but a common priest of the course of Jehoiarib, and of the town of Moddin; (see 1 Mac. ii. 1;) and that this family began to be called by the name of the Hasmonæans, from the times of Simon Hyrcanus, who was both high priest and prince of the Jewish nation, which kind of government continued in that family unto the times of Herod the Great, who destroyed both it and them; and this well agrees with what the paraphrast here says, who manifestly distinguishes the kingdom of the house of the Hasmonæans from Mattathias and his sons, i. e., Judas Maccabæus and Jonathan. Of these Hasmonæans, Jarchi and Aben Ezra explain the 10th and 12th verses of this chapter.

(g) *Vide* Aben Ezra and Jarchi in loc., and Bemidbar Rabba, Parash. 14, where those sixty queens and eighty concubines are interpreted of the sons of Noah, Abraham, Ham, Ishmael, and Esau.

there is no number; and they appointed King Alexander to be the general over them, and they came to make war against Jerusalem.

Verse 9. *My dove, my undefiled, is but one, &c.*] And at that time the congregation of Israel, which is like to an unblemished dove, was serving her Lord with a single heart, and was united to the law, and studied in the words of the law with a perfect heart, and her righteousness was as pure as in the day when she came out of Egypt. Lo, the sons of the Hasmonæans, and Matthias, and all the people of Israel, went forth and made war with them, and the Lord delivered them into their hands; which, when the inhabitants of the provinces saw, they blessed them, and the kingdoms of the earth, and the governors, and they praised them.

Verse 10. *Who is she that looketh forth as the morning, &c.*] The nations said, How splendid are the works of this people as the morning; fair are their young men as the moon, and their righteousness as clear as the sun; and their dread was upon all the inhabitants of the earth, as in the time their (*h*) four standards marched in the wilderness!

Verse 11. *I went down into the garden of nuts, &c.*] The Lord of the world said, concern-

ing the second (*i*) temple, which was built (*k*) by the hands of Cyrus, I will cause my she-chinah to dwell *there*, to behold the good works of my people, and see whether the wise men, who are like to a vine, multiply and increase, and *whether* their branches are full of good works, as the pomegranates.

Verse 12. *Or ever I was aware, &c.*] And when it appeared manifest before the Lord that they were righteous, and studied in the law, the Lord said by his word, I will not humble them any more, yea, I will not consume them: but will consult with myself to do them good, and to set them, even their excellent ones, in the chariots of (*l*) kings, because of the worthiness of the righteous of that generation, who are like in their works to Abraham their father.

Verse 13. *Return, return, O Shulamite, &c.*] Return unto me, O congregation of Israel, return unto Jerusalem; return unto the house of the doctrine of the law; return to receive the prophecy from the prophets, who have prophesied in the name of the word of the Lord; for what is your goodness, ye lying prophets, to make the people of Jerusalem go astray by your prophecies? for ye speak perverse things against the word of the Lord, to profane the camp of Israel and Judah.

(*h*) See note on ver. 4.
(*i*) So Jarchi interprets this "garden of nuts;" though some of the rabbins in Shirhashirim Rabba think the world is meant; and by the vine, the schools and synagogues; and by the pomegranates, the students in the law.
(*k*) It is said to be built by Cyrus, because he gave the Jews liberty and encouragement to build it; see Ezra i. 2, 3, 4.

(*l*) In Shirhashirim Rabba in loc. these words are referred to the deliverance of the Israelites out of Egypt, and their exaltation over the nations in the land of Canaan; to the raising of David to the throne of Israel, after he had been persecuted by Saul; and to the advancement of Mordecai to great dignity in Babylon, after his mourning in sackcloth and ashes; all which are represented as severally surprising to them.

CHAPTER VII

Verse 1. *How beautiful are thy feet with shoes, &c.*] Solomon said, by the spirit of prophecy from the Lord, How beautiful are the feet of the Israelites, when they come up to appear before the Lord (*a*) three times a year, in sandals of badger *skin*, and offer up their vows and free-will offerings; and their sons which come out of their loins are fair as the gems which were fixed upon the holy (*b*) crown that Bezaleel the artificer made for Aaron the priest.

Verse 2. *Thy navel is like a round goblet, &c.*] And the head of thy school, by whose

righteousness all the world is nourished, even as the fetus receives its nourishment through its navel, in its mother's bowels; who shines in the law as the orb of the moon, when he comes to pronounce pure or unclean, to justify or condemn; neither do the words of the law ever fail from his mouth, even as the waters of the great river, which proceeds from Eden, never (*c*) fail; and the seventy wise men are round about him, as a round (*d*) floor, whose treasures are full of the holy tithes, and vows, and free-will offerings which Ezra the priest, and Zerubbabel, and Joshua, and Nehemiah, and

---

(*a*) That is, at the feast of the passover, at the feast of weeks or pentecost, and at the feast of tabernacles; see Exod. xxiii. 14, 15, 16, 17; 2 Chron. viii. 13. So the words are explained in Shirhashirim Rabba, and by Jarchi in loc.
(*b*) So the plate of gold was called, on which was inscribed "holiness to the Lord," which was fixed to the fore-front of the mitre on Aaron's forehead; see Exod. xxviii. 36, and xxxix. 30. This plate was two fingers broad, and reached from ear to ear; "holiness to the Lord" was written upon it in great letters, standing out, and that either in one line or in two lines; if in two lines, "holiness" was written below, and "to the Lord" above; Maimon. Hilch. Cele Hamikdash, c. 9, s. 1, 2; Ceseph Mishna in *ibid.*, and Jarchi in Exod. xxviii. 36.
(*c*) The same is said of them in Zohar in Exodus, fol. 34,

3, and xxxviii. 2: see Gen. ii. 10, and note on chapter iv. 12.
(*d*) The great sanhedrin consists of seventy persons, besides the nasi or prince, at whose right hand sat Ab Beth Din, or *the father of the house of judgment:* before them sat the two scribes, and the rest of the sanhedrin took their places according to their age or dignity, and sat in a semicircular form, or, as they express it, כחצי גורן עגולה *cachatsi goren agullah,* "as the half of a round corn floor," to which they compare this assembly. So that both the prince and father of the court could see them all, Mishna Tract. Sanhedrin, c. 4, s. 3. Jarchi and Ez Chayim, *ibid.* Maimon. Hilch. Sanhedrin, c. 1, s. 3, and Ceseph Mishna, *ibid.* Shemoth Rabba, Parash. 5. Vajikra Rabba, Parash. 11. R. Aben Ezra in loc. Midrash Echa Rabba Præfat. fol. 38, 4. Midrash Kohelet in chap. i. 11.

Mordecai Bilshan, men of the great (e) congregation who are like to roses, decreed for them, because they had strength to study in the law day and night.

Verse 3. *Thy two breasts are like two young roes, &c.*] Thy (f) two Redeemers which shall redeem thee, Messiah, the son of David, and Messiah, the son of Ephraim, are like to Moses and Aaron, the sons of Jochebed, who may be compared to two young roes that are twins.

Verse 4. *Thy neck is as a tower of ivory, &c.*] And (g) the father of the house of judgment, who determines thy causes, is mighty over thy people to bind them, and to bring him forth who is condemned in judgment, *even to* bring *him* forth, as Solomon the king, who made a tower of ivory, and subjected the people of the house of Israel, and returned them to the Lord of the world. Thy scribes are full of wisdom, as pools of water; and they know how to number the computations of the (h) intercalations; and they intercalate the years, and fix the beginning of the months and the beginning of the years at the gate of the house of the great sanhedrin, and the chief of the house of Judah is like to David the king, who built the fortress of Zion, which is called the tower of Lebanon, on which, whoever stands, may number (i) all the towers that *are* in Damascus.

Verse 5. *Thine head upon thee is like Carmel, &c.*] The king who is set over thee, a righteous head, *is* as (k) Elijah the prophet, who was jealous with a jealousy for the Lord of heaven, and slew the false prophets in the mount of Carmel, and reduced the people of the house of Israel to the fear of the Lord God; and the poor of the people, which go with a boweddown head because they are poor, shall be clothed in purple, as Daniel was clothed in the city of Babylon, and Mordecai in Shushan, because of the righteousness of Abraham, who long before consulted the Lord of the world; and because of Isaac, whom his father bound in order to offer him up; and because of the holiness of Jacob, who pilled the rods in the gutters.

Verse 6. *How fair and how pleasant art thou, &c.*] King Solomon said, How beautiful art thou, O congregation of Israel, when thou bearest upon thee the yoke of my kingdom, when I correct thee with chastisements for thy transgressions, and thou bearest them in love, and they appear in thy sight as delicious dainties.

Verse 7. *This thy stature is like to a palm tree, &c.*] And when thy priests (l) spread their hands in prayer, and bless their brethren, the house of Israel, their four hands are separated like the branches of the palm tree, and their stature is as the date; and thy congregations stand face to face over against the priests, and their faces are bowed to the earth like a cluster of grapes.

Verse 8. *I said, I will go up to the palm tree, &c.*] The Lord said by his word, I will go and try Daniel, and see whether he is able to stand in one temptation as Abraham his father, who is like to a palm tree branch, stood in (m) ten temptations; yea, I will also try Hananiah, Mishael, and Azariah, whether they are able to stand in their temptations; for the sake of whose righteousness I will redeem the people of the house of Israel, who are like to clusters of grapes; and the fame of Daniel, Hananiah, Mishael, and Azariah, shall be heard in all the earth; and their smell shall be excellent, like the smell of the apples of the garden of Eden.

Verse 9. *And the roof of thy mouth is like the best wine, &c.*] Daniel and his companions said, We will surely take upon us the decree of the word of the Lord, as Abraham our father, who may be compared to old wine, took it upon him; and we will walk in the way which is right before him, even as Elijah and Elisha the prophets walked, through whose righteousness the dead, which are like to a man asleep, were raised; and as Ezekiel, the son of Buzi, by the prophecy of whose mouth those who were asleep

---

(e) This was the sanhedrin or great council, collected by Ezra the scribe, after the return of the Jews from the Babylonish captivity, of which he was president. This assembly consisted of one hundred and twenty persons, of which these here mentioned were the chief. There are others reckoned with them by some, as the three prophets, Haggai, Zechariah, and Malachi, with Daniel, Hananiah, Mishael, Azariah, Seraiah, Relaiah, Mispar, Bigvai, Rehum, and Baanah: the last of this venerable body of men, they say, was Simeon the Just; who, about forty years after the building of the second temple, met Alexander the Great coming against Jerusalem, and appeased him. These men were called אנשי כנסת הגדולה *anshey keneseth haggedolah,* "the men of the great congregation," because they restored the law to its pristine glory, and purged the Jewish Church from those corruptions which had crept into it during the captivity in Babylon. They are said to have received the oral law from the prophets, who had received it from the elders, and they from Joshua, and Joshua from Moses, and to have transmitted it down to posterity, Pirke Aboth, c. 1, s. 1, 2, and Jarchi, *ibid.* Maimon. Præfat. in lib. Yad. *Vide* Buxtorfii Tiberiad. in c. 10.

(f) See note on chap. iv. 5.

(g) See note on ver. 2.

(h) The Jewish year consisted of twelve lunar months, and sometimes they intercalated a thirteenth month, which they called Veadar, or the second Adar, which was always done by the direction and at the pleasure of the sanhedrin; as also the fixing of the beginning of the months, by the phasis or first appearance of the moon, Maimon. Hilch. Kiddush Hachodesh, c. 1, s. 1, 2, 3, 4, 5, 6; c. 4, s. 1, 9, 10, 11, 13, and c. 5, s. 1, 2, 3, 4. The men of the tribe of Issachar were famous for their knowledge in these things, Bereshith Rabba, Parash. 72,

Bemidbar Rabba, Parash. 13. Midrash Esth. Parash. 4, and Kimchi in 1 Chron. xii. 32.

(i) Jarchi relates out of the Midrash, that from the house of the forest of Lebanon, which Solomon built, a man might number all the houses which were in Damascus.

(k) So these words are paraphrased in Shirhashirim Rabba in loc., and in Vajikra Rabba, Parash. 31.

(l) When the priests blessed the people, they stretched out their hands and lifted them above their heads, with their fingers spread out; only the high priest never lifted up his above the plate of gold upon the mitre; and though, at the time of blessing, the priests and people stood face to face, right over against each other, yet the priests never looked upon the people, but kept their eyes upon the ground, as in the time of prayer; nor might the people look in the faces of the priests, lest their minds should be disturbed thereby; which ceremony the Targumist here refers to, Maimon. Hilch. Tephila, c. 14, s. 3, 7, 9. Bemidbar Rabba, Parash. 11. Targum Jon. in Num. vi. 23.

(m) The same is said in Targum Jerus. in Gen. xxii. 1. Bereshith Rabba, Parash. 56. Bemidbar Rabba, Parash. 15. Pirke Aboth, c. 5, s. 3, and Jarchi, *ibid.*; where he, out of Pirke Eliezer, has given us an account of them in this following order, viz., 1st. Nimrod sought to kill him, and he was hid in a field thirteen years. 2. He cast him into Ur of the Chaldees, or into a furnace of fire. 3. He banished him from the land of his nativity. 4. The Lord brought a famine in his days. 5. Sarah was taken into the house of Pharaoh. 6. The kings came and carried Lot his brother's son away captive. 7. It was shown him between the pieces, that four kingdoms should rule over his children. 8. He was commanded to circumcise himself and his children. 9. To put away Ishmael and his mother. And 10. To slay his son Isaac.

were awaked, even the dead which were in the valley of (n) Dura.

Verse 10. *I am my beloved's, &c.*] Jerusalem (o) said, All the time that I was walking in the way of the Lord of the world, he caused his shechinah to dwell with me, and his desire was towards me: but when I turned aside out of his paths, he removed his shechinah from me, and carried me away among the nations; and they ruled over me as a man rules over his wife.

Verse 11. *Come, my beloved, let us go forth into the field, &c.*] When the people of the house of Israel sinned, the Lord carried them into captivity, into the land of Seir, the fields of Edom. The congregation of Israel said, I beseech thee, O Lord of the whole world, receive my prayer, which I have prayed before thee, in the cities of the captivity and in the provinces of the people.

Verse 12. *Let us get up early to the vine-yards, &c.*] The children of Israel said one to another, Let us get up early in the morning, and let us go to the synagogue and to the school, and let us search in the book of the law, and see whether (p) the time of the redemption of the people of the house of Israel, who are like to a vine, is come, that they may be redeemed out of their captivity; and let us inquire of the wise men, whether the righteousness of the righteous, who are full of the commandments as pomegranates, is made manifest before the Lord; whether the time is come to go up to Jerusalem, there to give praise to the God of heaven, and to offer up the burnt-offerings, and the holy drink-offerings.

Verse 13. *The mandrakes give a smell, &c.*] And when it is the pleasure of the Lord to redeem his people out of captivity, it shall be said to the King Messiah, Now is the end of the captivity completed, and the righteousness of the righteous is become sweet as the smell of balsam, and the wise men fix *their* habitations by the gates of the school; they study in the (q) words of the scribes, and in the words of the law. Arise now, take the kingdom which I have reserved for thee.

(n) In this valley Nebuchadnezzar set up his golden image. Dan. iii. 1. And here the Jews say the children of Ephraim were slain, who went out of Egypt before the time; as also the Israelites, whom the Chaldeans slew when they carried them captive; and that this is the valley Ezekiel was brought into by the Spirit of the Lord, Ezek. xxxvii. 1; and these the dry bones he prophesied over, which lived and stood upon their feet an exceeding great army, Targum Jon. in Exod. xiii. 17. R. Saadiah Gaon in Dan. iii. 1. Jarchi in Ezek. xxxvii. 1.

(o) That is, the inhabitants of Jerusalem, or the Shulamite the Church, as in chap. vi. 13. The Church is frequently called so in the Old Testament, and likewise in the New, see Gal. iv. 26; Heb. xii. 22; Rev. xxi. 2, 10.

(p) The Jews vainly expect the time of redemption by the Messiah to be future, when it is past many hundred years ago, as they might easily learn from the book of the law and the prophets; particularly from Jacob's prophecy in Gen. xlix. 10, from Haggai's in chap. ii. 6, 7, 8, and from Daniel's weeks in chap. ix. 24, 25, 26. See this fully proved in a book called "The prophecies of the Old Testament respecting the Messiah considered," &c. Chap. iii.

(q) The words of the scribes are mentioned before the words of the law, and are, indeed, by the Jews, preferred unto them. They say the words of the beloved, i. e., the wise men, are better than the wine of the law; so they paraphrase the words in Cant. i. 2: they assert that the law cannot be understood without the words of the scribes; that the oral law is the foundation of the written law, and not the written law the foundation of the oral law; and that he that transgresses the words of the wise men as much deserves death, as though he had been guilty of idolatry, murder, or adultery, or profanes the Sabbath; nay, that if these say their right hand is their left, and their left hand is their right, they are obliged to hearken to them, Shirhashirim Rabba, in c. 1, 2. Bemidbar Rabba, Parash. 14. Matteh Dan. Dialog. 3, fol. 31, 3. Jarchi in Deut. xvii. 11. *Vide* Buxtorf, Recensio Operis Talmud. pp. 222, 223, &c.

CHAPTER VIII

Verse 1. *O that thou wert as my brother, &c.*] And when the King Messiah (a) shall be revealed unto the congregation of Israel, the children of Israel shall say unto him, Be thou with us for a brother, and let us go up to Jerusalem, and let us suck with thee the senses of the law, as a sucking child sucketh the breasts of its mother; for all the time that I was wandering without my own land, whenever I remembered the name of the great God, and laid down my life for the sake of his Deity, even the nations of the earth did not despise me.

Verse 2. *I would lead thee, and bring thee, &c.*] I will lead thee, O King Messiah, and bring thee to the house of my sanctuary; and thou shalt teach me to fear the Lord, and to walk in his paths; and there will we keep (b) the feast of leviathan, and drink old wine, which has been reserved in its grapes ever since

---

(a) The Jews very seldom speak of the birth or nativity of the Messiah as future, but only of a revelation or discovery of him to them, which they expect; for they are under self convictions that he was born long since. Some of them say he was born on the day the house of the sanctuary was destroyed, but is hid because of their sins and transgressions, and that either in the sea, or the walks of the garden of Eden; and some say that he sits among the lepers at the gates of Rome, from whence they expect he will come unto them, R. Aben Ezra, in Cant. vii. 5. Targum in Mic. iv. 8. Talmud Sanhedrin, fol. 98, col. 2. Targum Jerus. in Exod. xii. 42.

(b) The Jews expect a very sumptuous feast to be made for the righteous in the days of the Messiah, which will consist of all sorts of flesh, fish, and fowl, of plenty of generous wine, and of a variety of the most delicious fruit; some particulars of which they have thought fit to give, and are as follow: 1. They say an exceeding large ox shall be served up, which they take to be the behemoth in Job xl., of which they say many things monstrous and incredible; as that it lies upon a thousand hills, and feeds upon them all, and drinks up all the waters which are gathered together in a year's time, in the river Jordan, at one draught, Vajikra Rabba, Parash. 22. Bemidbar Rabba, Parash. 21. Targum in Psa. l. 10. Jarchi in *ibid.*, and in Job xl. 20. 2. The next dish is the leviathan and his mate, which they say are "the great whales" mentioned in Gen. i. 21. The male, they say, God castrated, and the female he slew, and salted it against this feast, Talmud Baba Bathra, fol. 74. Targum Jon., Jarchi, and Baal Hatturim in Gen. i. 21. Vajikra Rabba, Parash. 13. Targum Sect. in Esth. iii. 7. Aben Ezra in Dan. xii. 2. 3. They speak of an exceeding large fowl, which they call Ziz, **that**

the day the world was created, and of the pomegranates, the fruits which are prepared for the righteous in the garden of Eden.

Verse 3. *His left hand should be under my head, &c.*] The congregation of Israel said, I am chosen above all people, because I have bound the tephillin (*c*) upon my left hand, and upon my head, and have fixed the mezuzah (*d*) on the right side of my door, in the third part thereof, over against my chamber, so that the noxious spirits have no power to destroy me.

Verse 4. *I charge you, O daughters of Jerusalem, &c.*] The King Messiah shall say, I adjure you, O my people, the house of Israel, wherefore do ye stir up yourselves against the people of the earth to go out of captivity? and why do ye rebel against the army of Gog and (*e*) Magog? tarry a little while until the people which come up to make war against Jerusalem are destroyed; and after that the Lord of the world will remember unto you the mercies of the righteous, and then it will be his good pleasure to redeem you.

Verse 5. *Who is this that cometh up from the wilderness, &c.*] Solomon the prophet said, When the dead shall live, the Mount of Olives shall be (*f*) cleaved asunder, and all the dead

of Israel shall come out from under it; yea, even the righteous, which die in captivity, shall pass through subterraneous (*g*) caverns, and come out from under the Mount of *Olives:* but the wicked which die and are buried in the land of Israel shall be cast away, (*h*) as a man casts a stone with a sling; then all the inhabitants of the earth shall say, What is the righteousness of this people, which ascend out of the earth, even ten thousand times ten thousand, as in the day they came up out of the wilderness to the land of Israel, and are deliciously fed by the mercies of the Lord, as in the day when they were hid (*i*) under Mount Sinai to receive the law; and in that very hour Zion, which is the (*k*) mother of Israel, shall bring forth her sons, and Jerusalem receive the children of the captivity.

Verse 6. *Set me as a seal upon thine heart, &c.*] The children of Israel said in that day unto their Lord, We pray thee, set us as the signature of a ring upon thine heart, as the signature of a ring upon thine arm, that we may not be carried captive any more; for strong as death is the love of thy Deity, and mighty as hell is the envy which the people bear unto us; and the hatred which they have reserved

---

shall be one part of this entertainment, of which they say many things incredible; as particularly, that when its feet are upon the earth its head reaches the heavens; and when it stretches out its wings, they cover the body of the sun, Baba Bathra, fol. 73, col. 2. Targum amd Kimchi in Psa. l. 10. Vajikra Rabba, Parash. 22. 4. After all this shall be served up a variety of the most pleasant and delightful fruits, which are in the garden of Eden, which the Targumist here speaks of. And lastly, the wine which will then be used will be generous old wine, which, as it is said here and elsewhere, was kept in the grape from the creation of the world, Zohar in Gen. fol. 81, 4. Targum Jon. in Gen. xxvii. 25, and Targum in Eccles. ix. 7. Something of this gross notion seems to have obtained among the Jews in the times of Christ; see Luke xiv. 15. *Vide* Buxtorf Synagog. Jud. c. 50.

(*c*) These were four sections of the law, written on parchments, folded up in the skin of a clean beast, and tied to the head and hand. The four sections were these following, viz.: The first was Exod. xiii. 2-11. The second was Exod. xiii. 11-17. The third was Deut. vi. 4-10. The fourth was Deut. xi. 13-22. Those that were for the head were written and rolled up separately, and put in four distinct places in one skin, which was fastened with strings to the crown of the head towards the face, about the place where the hair ends, and where an infant's brain is tender: and they take care to place them in the middle, that so they may be between the eyes. Those that were for the hand were written in four columns, on one parchment, which, being rolled up, was fastened to the inside of the left arm, where it is fleshy, between the shoulder and the elbow, that so it might be over against the heart. These they call tephillin, from the root פלל *phalal,* "to pray," because they use them in the time of prayer, and look upon them as useful to put them in mind of that duty; in Matt. xxiii. 5, they are called φυλακτηρια, *phylacteries,* because they think they *keep* men in the fear of God, are preservatives from sin, nay, from evil spirits, and against diseases of the body; they imagine there is a great deal of holiness in them, and value themselves much upon the use of them, Targum Jon. Jarchi and Baal Hatturim in Exod. xiii. 9, 10, and Deut. vi. 8. Maimon. Hilch. Tephilin, c. 1, s. 1; c. 2, s. 1; c. 3. 1, 2, 3, 4, 5, 6; and c. 4. 1, 2, 25. Matteh Dan. Dialog. 2, fol. 9, 4, and 10, 1. *Vide* Buxtorf Synagog. Jud. c. 9, and Leo Modena's History of the Rites, &c., of the Present Jews, par. 1, c. 11.

(*d*) These were two passages in the law, the one was Deut. vi. 4-10, the other was Deut. xi. 13-22, which were written on a piece of parchment in one column, which, being rolled up and put into a pipe of reed or wood, was fastened to the right side of the door-post: this they imagine was useful to put them in mind of the Divine Being, to preserve them from sin, and from evil spirits, Targum Jon. in Deut. vi. 9. Maimon. Hilch. Tephilin, c. 5, s. 1, 6, and 6, 13. *Vide* Buxtorf Synagog. Jud. c. 31.

(*e*) Magog was one of the sons of Japhet, Gen. x. 2, from whom very probably the people called by those two names sprung, who seem to be the Scythians or Tartars; for Josephus, Antiq. Jud. l. 1, c. 7, calls the Scythians Magogæ; and Hierapolis in Cœlesyria, Pliny (Nat. Hist. l. 5, c. 23) says, was called by the Syrians Magog: and Marcus Paulus Venetus, l. 1, c. 64, says that "the countries of Gog and Magog are in Tartary, which they call Jug (perhaps rather Gog) and Mungug." *Vide* Schindler, Lex. Pent. fol. 288. Mention is made of these in Ezek. xxxviii. and xxxix., Rev. xx. 8, 9; with which last text may be compared what the Targumist here says. The Jewish rabbins, in their writings, very frequently speak of the war of Gog and Magog, which they expect in the days of the Messiah. See Mr. Mede's works, book 1, disc. 48, p. 374, and book 3, pp. 713, 751.

(*f*) See Zech. xiv. 4.

(*g*) The Jews are of opinion, that those of their nation who die and are buried in other lands, at the resurrection of the dead shall not rise where they died and were buried; but shall be rolled through the caverns of the earth, into the land of Canaan, and there rise. This they call גלגול המתים *gilgul hammethim,* "the rolling of the dead," or גלגול המחילות *gilgul hammechiloth,* "the rolling through the caverns," which they represent as very painful and afflicting; and say that this was the reason that Jacob desired he might not be buried in Egypt, and is now one reason why the Jews are so desirous of returning to their own land: nay, at this time the more wealthy and religious among them go thither on this very account, especially when advanced in years, that they may die, and be buried there, and so escape this painful rolling under the earth, Bereshith Rabba, Parash. 96. Midrash Hannealam in Zohar in Gen. fol. 68, 4. Jarchi in Gen. xlvii. 29. Kimchi in Ezek. xxxvii. 12. *Vide* Buxtorf Synagog. Jud. c. 3, and Lex. Talmud, fol. 439.

(*h*) Though the resurrection of the dead is one of the thirteen articles of the Jewish creed, yet many of them are of opinion that it is peculiar to the righteous, and that the wicked shall have no share therein; but that their bodies perish with their souls at death, and shall never rise more, R. David Kimchi, in Psa. i. 5, and in Isa. xxvi. 19. R. Saadiah Gaon, in Dan. xii. 2. *Vide* Pocock. Not. Misc. c. 6, p. 180, &c.

(*i*) The Targumist here refers to a fabulous notion of the Jews, that when the people of Israel came to Mount Sinai to receive the law, the Lord plucked up the mountain, and removed it into the air, and set the people under it, where he gave the law unto them; this they collect from Exod. xix. 17, and Deut. iv. 11. And this, they say, is *the apple tree* under which the Church is here said to be *raised up,* Targum Jon. Jarchi and Baal Hatturim in Exod. xix. 17. Jarchi and Shirhashirim Rabba in loc.

(*k*) So Jerusalem is said to be "the mother of us all," in Gal. iv. 26.

for us is like to the coals of the fire of hell, (*l*) which the Lord created on the second (*m*) day of the creation of the world, to (*n*) burn therein those who commit idolatry.

Verse 7. *Many waters cannot quench love, &c.*] The Lord of the world said unto his people, the house of Israel, If all people (*o*) which are like to the waters of the sea, v hich are many, were gathered together, they could not extinguish my love unto thee; and if all the kings of the earth, which are like to the waters of a river that runs fiercely, they could not remove thee out of the world: but if a man will give all the substance of his house to obtain wisdom in the captivity, I will return unto him (*p*) double in the world to come; and all the spoils (*q*) which they shall take from the armies of Gog shall be his.

Verse 8. *We have a little sister, &c.*] At that time the angels of heaven shall say to one another, We have one nation in the earth, and her righteousness is very little, and the kings and governors do not bring her forth to make war with the armies of Gog. What shall we do for our sister, in the day when the nations shall speak of going up against her to war?

Verse 9. *If she be a wall, &c.*] Michael (*r*) the prince of Israel shall say, If she is fixed as a wall among the people, and gives silver to procure the (*s*) unity of the name of the Lord of the world, I and you, together with their scribes, will surround her as borders of silver, that the people may have no power to rule over her, even as a worm hath no power to rule over silver; and though she (*t*) is poor in the commandments, we will seek mercies for her from the Lord; and the righteousness of the law shall be remembered to her, in which infants study, being written upon (*u*) the table of the heart, and is placed over against the nations as a cedar.

Verse 10. *I am a wall, &c.*] The congregation of Israel answered and said, I am strong in the words of tne law as a wall, and my sons are mighty as a tower; and at that time the congregation of Israel found mercy in the eyes of her Lord, and all the inhabitants of the earth asked of her welfare.

Verse 11. *Solomon had a vineyard at Baalhamon, &c.*] One nation came up in the lot of the Lord of the world, (*v*) with whom is peace, which is like to a vineyard; (*w*) he placed it in Jerusalem, and delivered it into the hands of the kings of the house of David, who kept it as a vinedresser keeps his vineyard; after that Solomon king of Israel died, it was left in the hands of his son Rehoboam; Jeroboam, the son of Nebat, came and divided the kingdom with him, and took out of his hands ten tribes, according to the word of Ahijah of Shiloh, who was a great man.

Verse 12. *My vineyard, which is mine, &c.*] When Solomon, the king of Israel, heard the prophecy of Ahijah of Shiloh, he sought to (*x*) kill him; but Ahijah fled from Solomon, and went into Egypt. And at that time King Solomon was informed by prophecy that he should rule over the ten tribes all his days: but after his death Jeroboam, the son of Nebat, should rule over them; and the two tribes, Judah and Benjamin, Rehoboam, the son of Solomon, should reign over.

Verse 13. *Thou that dwellest in the gardens,*

(*l*) גהנם *gehinnom*, "the valley of Hinnom," where the idolaters caused their children to pass through the fire to Molech, and burned them, 2 Chron. xxviii. 3, and xxxiii. 6; Jer. vii. 31, and xxxii. 35. R. David Kimchi, in Psa. xxxix. 13, says that Gehinnom was a very contemptible place near Jerusalem, where all manner of filthiness and dead carcasses were cast; and that a continual fire was kept there to burn them: hence the word is used very frequently by the Jewish rabbins, to signify the place where the wicked are punished after death; and so the word γεεννα, is used in the New Testament; see Matt. v. 22, and x. 28, and elsewhere.

(*m*) The same is asserted in Talmud Pesach. fol. 54, 1. Bereshith Rabba, Parash. 4, and 11 and 21. Shemoth Rabba, Parash. 15. Zohar in Deut. fol. 120, 1. Jarchi in Isa. xxx. 33; and yet at other times they reckon hell among the seven things which were created before the world was, Talmud Pesach, fol. 54, 1, and Nedarim. fol. 39, 2. Zohar in Lev. fol. 14, 4. Targum Jon. in Gen. iii. 24. See Matt. xxv. 41.

(*n*) The punishment of the wicked in hell is very frequently expressed by Jewish writers, by their burning in fire and brimstone, Bereshith Rabba, Parash. 6 and 51. Zohar in Gen. fol. 71, 3. Raya Mehimna, *ibid*. in fol. 7, 2. Targum Jon. and Jerus. in Gen. iii. 24. Targum Jerus. in Gen. xv. 12. Targum in Eccles. viii. 10, and x. 11. Targum in Isa. xxxiii. 14. R. David Kimchi in Isa. xxx. 33. Thus idolaters, with others, are said to "have their part in the lake which burneth with fire and brimstone," Rev. xxi. 8.

(*o*) So the words are explained in Shemoth Rabba, Parash. 49. Bemidbar Rabba, Parash. 2. Zohar in Num. fol. 105, 3. Raya Mehimna, *ibid*. in Gen. fol. 51, 3. Shirhashirim Rabba, Jarchi and Aben Ezra in loc.

(*p*) See Mark x. 30; Luke xviii. 30.

(*q*) See Ezek. xxxix. 9, 10.

(*r*) See Dan. x. 13, 21, and xii. 1. The Jews suppose that every nation or kingdom has an angel set over it, to be its president, protector, and defender; and that Michael was he that presided over Israel.

(*s*) That is, the knowledge of the unity of God. The doctrine of the unity of the Divine Being is the second article of the Jewish creed, where they say that "God is one, and that there is no unity in any respect like his;" this they very much magnify and extol. Hence they often have those words in their mouths, "Hear, O Israel, the Lord our God is one Lord," Deut. vi. 4; which, they think, is entirely inconsistent with a trinity of persons. Hence, says Maimonides, (Hilch. Yesod Hattorah, c. 1, s. 4,) "This God is one, not two, or more than two; but one. For there is no unity like his in any of the individuals which are found in the world; neither is he one in species, which comprehends more individuals, nor one in body, which is divided into parts and extremes, but he is so one, that there is no other unity like it in the world." All which is not so much opposed to the polytheism of the heathens, as to the plurality of persons in the trinity, and the incarnation of Christ. But though modern Jews have exploded the doctrine of the trinity, as inconsistent with that of the unity of the Divine Being, yet their more ancient writers do very manifestly speak of it as the great mystery of faith, Zohar edit. Sultzbac. in Gen. fol. 1, col. 3; in Exod. fol. 18, 3, 4, fol. 58, 1, and fol. 66, 2, 3; in Lev. fol. 27, 2, and in Num. fol. 67, 3. Jetzira. edit. Rittangel. fol. 1, 4, 6, 38, 64. *Vide* Josep. de Voisin. Disp. Theolog. de S. Trinitate, Allix's judgment of the Jewish Church, against the Unitarians, c. 9, 10, 11.

(*t*) In Raya Mehimna in Zohar in Exod. fol. 38, 3, it is said that "no man is poor but he that is so in the law and in the commandments;" and that "the riches of a man lies in them;" and in Vajikra Rabba, Parash. 34, where those words in Prov. xxii. 2, "The rich and poor meet together," are mentioned, it is said, "The rich is he that is rich in the law, and the poor is he that is poor in the law;" see also Zohar in Num. fol. 91, 3; with all which compare 1 Tim. vi. 18.

(*u*) See note on chap. iv. 9.

(*v*) In Shirhashirim Rabba in loc. it is explained in the same way; R. Aben Ezra, by Solomon in the next verse, understands the King Messiah; though it is interpreted of Solomon, king of Israel, by the Targum and Jarchi in loc., by Maimon. Yesod Hattorah, c. 6, s. 12, and in Zohar in Exod. fol. 91, 3.

(*w*) So it is explained of the people of Israel, under the government of Solomon in Shirhashirim Rabba, and by Jarchi and Aben Ezra in loc.

(*x*) This is a very great mistake of the Targumist; for it was Jeroboam, and not Ahijah, who fled into Egypt, whom Solomon sought to kill; see 1 Kings xi. 40.

&c.] Solomon said at the end of his prophecy, The Lord of the world shall say to the congregation of Israel in the end of days, O thou congregation of Israel, which *art* like to a garden highly esteemed of among the nations, and sits in the school with the companions of the sanhedrin, and the rest of the people which hearken to the voice of the chief of the school, and learn from his mouth his words, cause me to hear the law, the voice of thy words, when thou sittest to justify and condemn, and I will consent to whatever thou dost.

Verse 14. *Make haste, my beloved, &c.]* In that very hour the elders of the congregation of Israel shall say, Flee, O my beloved, the Lord of the world, from this defiled earth, and cause thy shechinah to dwell in the highest heavens, and in the time of straits, when we pray before thee, be thou like a roe, which, when it sleeps, (*y*) has one eye shut and the other eye open; or as a young hart, which, when it flees, looks behind it; so do thou look upon us, and consider our sorrow and our affliction, from the highest heavens, until the time *comes* that thou wilt take pleasure in us, and redeem us, and bring us to the mountain of Jerusalem, where the priests shall offer up before thee the sweet incense.

(*y*) The same is mentioned in Shirhashirim Rabba in loc.

THE
GITAGOVINDA;

OR THE
SONGS OF JAYADEVA

A mystical poem, supposed to have a near resemblance to the Book of Canticles, many passages of which it illustrates.

PART I

The firmament is obscured by clouds, the woodlands are black with *Tamala* (1) trees.

That youth who roves in the forest must be fearful in the gloom of night.

Go, my daughter; bring the wanderer home to my rustic mansion.

Such was the command of Nanda, (2) the fortunate herdsman; and hence arose the loves of Radha (3) and Madhava, (4) who sported on the bank of *Yamuna*, (5) or hastened eagerly to the secret bower.

If thy soul be delighted with the remembrance of Heri, (6) or sensible to the raptures of love, listen to the voice of Jayadeva, whose notes are both sweet and brilliant.

O thou who reclinest on the bosom of Camala, (7) whose ears flame with gems, and whose locks are embellished with sylvan flowers;

Thou from whom the day-star derived his effulgence, who showedst the venom-breathing Caliya, (8) who beamedst like a sun on the tribe of Yadu, (9) that flourished like a lotos;

Thou, who sittest on the plumage of Garura, (10) who, by subduing demons, gavest exquisite joy to the assembly of immortals;

Thou, for whom the daughter of Janaca (11) was decked in gay apparel, by whom Dushana (12) was overthrown;

Thou, whose eye sparkles like the water-lily, who calledst three worlds into existence;

Thou, by whom the rocks of *Mandar* (13) were easily supported; who sippest nectar from the radiant lips of Pedma, (14) as the fluttering *Chacora* (15) drinks the moonbeams;

Be victorious, O Heri, *lord of conquest!*

Radha sought him long in vain, and her thoughts were confounded by the fever of desire.

She was roving in the vernal season, among the twining *Vasantis*, (16) covered with soft blossoms, when a damsel thus addressed her with youthful hilarity:

"The gale that has wantoned round the beautiful clove plant breathes from the hill of Maylaya; (17)

The circling arbours resound with the notes of the *Cocila*, (18) and the murmurs of honey-making swarms

Now the hearts of damsels, whose lovers are travelling at a distance, are pierced with anguish;

While the blossoms of *Bacul* (19) are conspicuous among the flowrets covered with bees.

The *Tamala*, with leaves dark and fragrant, claims a tribute from the musk, which it vanquishes;

And the clustering flowers of the *Cinsuca* (20) resembling the nails of *Cama*, (21) with which he rends the hearts of the young.

The full-blown *Cesara* (22) gleams like the sceptre of the world's monarch, love;

And the pointed thyrsus of the *Cetaci* (23) resembles the darts by which lovers are wounded.

See the bunches of *Patali* (24) flowers filled with bees, like the quiver of *Smara* (25) full of shafts,

While the tender blossom of the *Caruna* (26) smiles to see the whole world laying shame aside.

The far-scented *Madhavi* (27) beautifies the trees, round which it twines;

And the fresh *Malica* (28) seduces with rich perfume even the hearts of hermits;

While the *Amra* (29) tree with blooming tresses is embraced by the gay creeper *Atimucta*, (30)

And the blue streams of *Yamuna* wind round the groves of *Vrindavan*. (31)

In this charming season, which gives pain to separated lovers,

Young Heri sports and dances with a company of damsels.

A breeze, like the breath of love, from the fragrant flowers of the *Cetaci*, kindles every heart.

Whilst it perfumes the woods with the prolific dust, which it shakes from the *Mallica* (32) with half opened buds;

And the *Cocila* bursts into song, when he sees the blossoms glistening on the lovely *Rasala*." (33)

The jealous RADHA gave no answer;

And, soon after, her officious friend, perceiving the foe of MURA (34) in the forest, eager for the rapturous embraces of the herdman's daughters, with whom he was dancing,

Thus again addressed his forgotten mistress:

"With a garland of wild flowers, descending even to the yellow mantle that girds his azure limbs,

Distinguished by smiling cheeks, and by ear-rings that sparkle as he plays,

HERI exults in the assemblage of amorous damsels.

One of them presses him with her swelling breast, while she warbles with exquisite melody.

Another, affected by a glance from his eye, stands meditating on the lotos of his face.

A third, on pretence of whispering a secret in his ear, approaches his temples, and kisses them with ardour.

One seizes his mantle, and draws him towards her, pointing to the bower on the banks of *Yamuna*, where elegant *Vanjulas* (35) interweave their branches.

He applauds another who dances in the sportive circle, whilst her bracelets ring, as she beats time with her palms.

Now he caresses one, and kisses another, smiling on a third with complacency;

And now he chases her, whose beauty has most allured him.

Thus the wanton HERI frolics, in the season of sweets, among the maids of *Vraja*, (36)

Who rush to his embraces, as if he were pleasure itself assuming a human form;

And one of them, under a pretext of hymning his divine perfections, whispers in his ear,

'Thy lips, my beloved, are nectar.' "

PART II

RADHA remains in the forest: but, resenting the promiscuous passion of HERI, and his neglect of her beauty, which he once thought superior,

She retires to a bower of twining plants, the summit of which resounds with the humming of swarms engaged in their sweet labours;

And there, fallen languid on the ground, she thus addresses her female companion:

"Though he take recreation in my absence, and smile on all around him,

Yet my soul remembers him, whose beguiling reed modulates an air sweetened by the nectar of his quivering lip,

While his ear sparkles with gems, and his eye darts amorous glances;

Him, whose looks are decked with the plumes of peacocks resplendent with many-coloured moons,

And whose mantle gleams like a dark blue cloud illumined with rainbows;

Him, whose graceful smile gives new lustre to his lips, brilliant and soft as a dewy leaf, sweet and ruddy as the blossom of *Bandhujiva*, (37)

While they tremble with eagerness to kiss the daughters of the herdsmen;

Him, who disperses the gloom with beams from the jewels which decorate his bosom, his wrists, and his ankles;

On whose forehead shines a circlet of sandal wood, which makes even the moon contemptible, when it moves through irradiated clouds;

Him, whose ear-rings are formed of entire gems in the shape of the fish *Macara* (38) on the banners of love.

Even the yellow-robed god, whose attendants are the chief of deities, of holy men, and of demons;

Him who reclines under a gay *Cadumba* (39) tree, who formerly delighted me while he gracefully waved in the dance,

And all his soul sparked in his eye.

My weak mind thus enumerates his qualities; and, though offended, strives to banish offence.

What else can do it? It cannot part with its affection for CRISHNA, whose love is excited by other damsels and who sports in the absence of RADHA.

Bring, O my sweet friend, that vanquisher of the demon *Cesi* (40) to sport with me, who am repairing to a secret bower,

Who look timidly on all sides, who meditate with amorous fancy on his divine transfiguration.

Bring him, whose discourse was once composed of the gentlest words, to converse with me, who am bashful on his first approach,

And express my thoughts with a smile sweet as honey.

Bring him, who formerly slept on my bosom, to recline with me on a green bed of leaves just gathered, while his lips shed dew, and my arms enfold him.

Bring him, who has attained the perfection of skill in love's art, whose hand used to press these firm and delicate spheres, to play with me,

Whose voice rivals that of the *Cocila,* and whose tresses are bound with waving blossoms.

Bring him, who formerly drew me by the locks to his embrace, to repose with me whose feet tinkle, as they move, with rings of gold and of gems,

Whose loosened zone sounds, as it falls; and whose limbs are slender and flexible as the creeping plant.

That god, whose cheeks are beautified by the nectar of his smiles,

Whose pipe drops in his ecstasy from his hand, I saw in the grove encircled by the damsels of *Vraja,* who gazed on him askance from the corners of their eyes.

I saw him in the grove with happier damsels, yet the sight of him delighted me.

Soft is the gale which breathes over yon clear pool, and expands the clustering blossoms of the voluble *Asoca;* (41)

Soft, yet grievous to me in the absence of the foe of MADHU.

Delightful are the flowers of *Amra* trees on the mountain top, while the murmuring bees pursue their voluptuous toil;

Delightful, yet afflicting to me, O friend, in the absence of the youthful *Cesava.*"

PART III

Meantime, the destroyer of CANSA, (42) having brought to his remembrance the amiable RADHA, forsook the beautiful damsels of *Vraja.*

He sought her in all parts of the forest; his whole wound from love's arrow bled again;

He repented of his levity; and, seated in a bower near the bank of *Yamuna,* the blue daughter of the sun Thus poured forth his lamentation:

"She is departed; she saw me, no doubt, surrounded by the wanton shepherdesses;

Yet, conscious of my fault, I durst not intercept her flight.

Wo is me! she feels a sense of injured honour, and is departed in wrath.

How will she conduct herself? How will she express her pain in so long a separation?

What is wealth to me? What are numerous attendants?

What are the pleasures of the world? What joy can I receive from a heavenly abode?

I seem to behold her face with eyebrows contracting themselves through a just resentment;

It resembles a fresh lotos, over which two black bees are fluttering.

I seem, so present is she to my imagination, even now to caress her with eagerness.

Why then do I seek her in this forest? why do I lament her without cause?

O slender damsel, I know that anger has torn thy soft bosom;

But whither thou art retired, that I know not.

How can I invite thee to return?

Thou art seen by me, indeed, in a vision; thou seemest to move before me.

Ah! why dost thou not rush, as before, to my embrace?

Do but forgive me: never again will I commit a similar offence.

Grant me but a sight of thee, O lovely *Radhica;* for my passion torments me.

I am not the terrible *Mahesa:* (43) a garland of water-lilies with subtle filaments decks my shoulders, not serpents, with twisted folds.

The blue petals of the lotos glitter on my neck; not the azure gleam of poison.

Powdered sandal-wood is sprinkled on my limbs; not pale ashes.

O god of love, mistake me not for *Mahadeva.* (44)

Wound me not again; approach me not in anger;

I love already but too passionately; yet I have lost my beloved.

Hold not in thy hand that shaft barbed with an *Amra* flower.

Brace not thy bow, O conqueror of the world. Is it valour to slay one who faints?

My heart is already pierced by arrows from *Radha's* eyes, black and keen as those of an antelope;

Yet my eyes are not gratified with her presence.

Her eyes are full of shafts; her eyebrows are bows; and the tips of her ears are silken strings.

Thus armed by *Ananga,* (45) the god of desire, she marches, herself a goddess to ensure his triumph over the vanquished universe.

I meditate on her delightful embrace, on the ravishing glances darted from her eye,

On the fragrant lotos of her mouth, on her nectar-dropping speech,

On her lips, ruddy as the berries of the *Bimba* (46) plant;

Yet even my fixed meditation on such an assemblage of charms increases instead of alleviating the misery of separation."

PART IV

The damsel, commissioned by RADHA, found the disconsolate god under an arbour of spreading *Vaniras* by the side of *Yamuna;* where, presenting herself gracefully before him, she thus described the affliction of his beloved:

"She despises essence of sandal-wood, and even by moonlight sits brooding over her gloomy sorrow;

She declares the gale of *Malaya* to be venom; and the sandal-trees, through which it has breathed, to have been the haunt of serpents.

Thus, O MADHAVA is she afflicted in thy absence with the pain which love's dart has occasioned: her soul is fixed on thee.

Fresh arrows of desire are continually assailing her, and she forms a net of lotos leaves as armour for her heart, which thou alone shouldst fortify.

She makes her own bed of the arrows darted by the flowery-shafted god: but when she hoped for thy embrace, she had formed for thee a couch of soft blossoms.

Her face is like a water-lily, veiled in the dew of tears; and her eyes appear like moons eclipsed, which let fall their gathered nectar through pain caused by the tooth of the furious dragon.

She draws thy image with musk in the character of the deity with five shafts, having subdued the *Macar*, or horned shark, and holding an arrow tipped with an *Amra* flower; thus she draws thy picture, and worships it.

At the close of every sentence, O MADHAVA, she exclaims, At thy feet am I fallen, and in thy absence even the moon, though it be a vase full of nectar, inflames my limbs.

Then by the power of imagination she figures thee standing before her; thee, who art not easily attained;

She sighs, she smiles, she mourns, she weeps, she moves from side to side, she laments and rejoices by turns.

Her abode is a forest; the circle of her female companions is a net;

Her sighs are flames of fire kindled in a thicket; herself (alas! through thy absence) is become a timid roe; and love is the tiger who springs on her like YAMA, the genius of death.

So emaciated is her beautiful body, that even the light garland which waves over her bosom she thinks a load.

Such, O bright-haired god, is RADHA when thou art absent.

If powder of sandal-wood finely levigated be moistened and applied to her bosom, she starts, and mistakes it for poison.

Her sighs form a breeze long extended, and burn her like the flame which reduced CANDARPA (47) to ashes.

She throws around her eyes, like blue water-lilies with broken stalks, dropping lucid streams.

Even her bed of tender leaves appears in her sight like a kindled fire.

The palm of her hand supports her aching temple, motionless as the crescent rising at eve.

HERI, HERI, thus in silence she meditates on thy name, as if her wish were gratified, and she were dying through thy absence.

She rends her locks; she pants; she laments inarticulately;

She trembles; she pines; she muses; she moves from place to place; she closes her eyes;

She falls; she rises again; she faints: in such a fever of love she may live, O celestial physician, if thou administer the remedy;

But shouldst thou be unkind, her malady will be desperate.

Thus, O divine healer, by the nectar of thy love must RADHA be restored to health; and if thou refuse it, thy heart must be harder than the thunder-stone.

Long has her soul pined, and long has she been heated with sandal-wood, moonlight, and water-lilies, with which others are cooled;

Yet she patiently and in secret meditates on thee, who alone canst relieve her.

Shouldst thou be inconstant, how can she, wasted as she is to a shadow, support life a single moment?

How can she, who lately could not endure thy absence even an instant, forbear sighing now, when she looks with half-closed eyes on the *Rasala* with blooming branches, which remind her of the vernal season, when she first beheld thee with rapture?"

"Here have I chosen my abode: go quickly to RADHA; sooth her with my message, and conduct her hither."

So spoke the foe of MADHU (48) to the anxious damsel, who hastened back, and thus addressed her companion:

"Whilst a sweet breeze from the hills of *Malaya* comes wafting on his plumes the young god of desire,

While many a flower points his extended petals to pierce the bosoms of separated lovers,

The deity crowned with sylvan blossoms laments, O friend, in thy absence.

Even the dewy rays of the moon burn him; and as the shaft of love is descending, he mourns inarticulately with increasing distraction.

When the bees murmur softly, he covers his ears;

Misery sits fixed in his heart, and every returning night adds anguish to anguish.

He quits his radiant palace for the wild forest, where he sinks on a bed of cold clay, and frequently mutters thy name.

In yon bower, to which the pilgrims of love are used to repair, he meditates on thy form, repeating in silence some enchanting word which once dropped from thy lips, and thirsting for the nectar which they alone can supply.

Delay not, O loveliest of women; follow the lord of thy heart: behold, he seeks the appointed shade, bright with the ornaments of love, and confident of the promised bliss.

Having bound his locks with forest flowers, he hastens to yon arbour, where a soft gale breathes over the banks of *Yamuna;*

There, again pronouncing thy name, he modulates his divine reed.

Oh! with what rapture doth he gaze on the golden dust, which the breeze shakes from expanded blossoms:

The breeze which has kissed thy cheek!

With a mind languid as a drooping wing, feeble as a trembling leaf, he doubtfully expects thy approach, and timidly looks on the path which thou must tread.

Leave behind thee, O friend, the ring which tinkles on the delicate ankle, when thou sportest in the dance;

Hastily cast over thee thy azure mantle, and run to the gloomy bower.

The reward of thy speed, O thou who sparklest like lightning, will be to shine on the blue bosom of MU-RARI, (49)

Which resembles a vernal cloud, decked with a string of pearls like a flock of white water-birds fluttering in the air.

Disappoint not, O thou lotos-eyed, the vanquisher of MADHU; accomplish his desire.

But go quickly: it is night; and the night also will quickly depart.

Again and again he sighs; he looks around; he re-enters the arbour; he can scarce articulate thy sweet name;

He again smooths his flowery couch; he looks wild; he becomes frantic; thy beloved will perish through desire.

The bright-beamed god sinks in the west, and thy pain of separation may also be removed;

The blackness of the night is increased, and the passionate imagination of GOVINDA (50) has acquired additional gloom.

My address to thee has equalled in length and in sweetness the song of the *Cocila;* delay will make thee miserable, O my beautiful friend.

Seize the moment of delight in the place of assignation with the son of DEVACI, (51) who descended from heaven to remove the burdens of the universe.

He is a blue gem on the forehead of the three worlds, and longs to sip honey like the bee from the fragrant lotos of thy cheek."

But the solicitous maid, perceiving that RADHA was unable, through debility, to move from her arbour of flowery creepers, returned to GOVINDA, who was himself disordered with love, and thus described her situation:

"She mourns, O sovereign of the world, in her verdant bower;

She looks eagerly on all sides in hope of thy approach; then, gaining strength from the delightful idea of the proposed meeting, she advances a few steps, and falls languid on the ground.

When she rises, she weaves bracelets of fresh leaves; she dresses herself like her beloved, and looking at herself in sport, exclaims, 'Behold the vanquisher of MADHU!'

Then she repeats again and again the name of HERI, and catching at a dark blue cloud, strives to embrace it, saying, 'It is my beloved who approaches.'

Thus, while thou art dilatory, she lies expecting thee:·she mourns; she weeps; she puts on her gayest ornaments to receive her lord;

She compresses her deep sighs within her bosom; and then, meditating on thee, O cruel, she is drowned in a sea of rapturous imaginations.

If a leaf but quiver, she supposes thee arrived; she spreads her couch; she forms in her mind a hundred modes of delight;

Yet, if thou go not to her bower, she must die this night through excessive anguish."

PART V

By this time the moon spread a net of beams over the groves of *Vrindavan,*

And looked like a drop of liquid sandal on the face of the sky, which smiled like a beautiful damsel;

While its orb with many spots betrayed, as it were, a consciousness of guilt, in having often attended amorous maids to the loss of their family honour.

The moon, with a black fawn couched on its disk, advanced in its nightly course.

But MADHAVA had not advanced to the bower of RADHA, who thus bewailed his delay with notes of varied lamentations:

"The appointed moment is come; but HERI, alas! comes not to the grove.

Must the season of my unblemished youth pass thus idly away?

Oh! what refuge can I seek, deluded as I am by the guile of my female adviser?

The god with five arrows has wounded my heart; and I am deserted by him, for whose sake I have sought at night the darkest recess of the forest.

Since my best beloved friends have deceived me, it is my wish to die;

Since my senses are disordered, and my bosom is on fire—why stay I longer in this world?

The coolness of this vernal night gives me pain, instead of refreshment.

Some happier damsel enjoys my beloved; whilst I, alas! am looking at the gems of my bracelets, which are blackened by the flames of my passion.

My neck, more delicate than the tenderest blossom, is hurt by the garland that encircles it:

Flowers are, indeed, the arrows of love, and he plays with them cruelly.

I make this wood my dwelling: I regard not the roughness of the *Vetas trees;*

But the destroyer of MADHU holds me not in his remembrance!

Why comes he not to the bower of the blooming *Vanjulas,* assigned for meeting?

Some ardent rival, no doubt, keeps him locked in her embrace.

Or have his companions detained him with mirthful recreations?

Else why roams he not through the cool shades?

Perhaps, through weakness, the heart-sick lover is unable to advance even a step!"

So saying, she raised her eyes; and, seeing her damsel return silent and mournful, unaccompanied by MADHAVA, she was alarmed even to frenzy;

And, as if she actually beheld him in the arms of a rival, she thus described the vision which overpowered her intellect:

"Yes, in habiliments becoming the war of love, and with tresses waving like flowery banners,

A damsel, more alluring than RADHA, enjoys the conqueror of MADHU.

Her form is transfigured by the touch of her divine lover; her garland quivers over her swelling bosom;

Her face like the moon is graced with clouds of dark hair, and trembles while she quaffs the nectareous dew of his lip;

Her bright ear-rings dance over her cheeks, which they irradiate; and the small bells on her girdle tinkle as she moves.

Bashful at first, she smiles at length on her embracer, and expresses her joy with inarticulate murmurs;

While she floats on the waves of desire, and closes her eyes dazzled with the blaze of approaching CAMA:

And now this heroine in love's warfare falls, exhausted and vanquished by the resistless MURARI.

But alas! in my bosom prevails the flame of jealousy, and yon moon, which dispels the sorrow of others, increases mine.

See again, where the foe of MURA sports in yon grove, on the bank of the *Yamuna.*

See how he kisses the lip of my rival, and imprints on her forehead an ornament of pure musk, black as the young antelope on the lunar orb!

Now, like the husband of RETI, (52) he fixes white blossoms on her dark locks, where they gleam like flashes of lightning among the curled clouds.

On her breasts, like two firmaments, he places a string of gems like a radiant constellation.

He binds on her arms, graceful as the stalks of the water-lily, and adorned with hands glowing like the petals of its flower, a bracelet of sapphires, which resembles a cluster of bees.

Ah! see how he ties round her waist a rich girdle illumined with golden bells,

Which seem to laugh as they tinkle, at the inferior brightness of the leafy garlands, which lovers hang on their bowers to propitiate the god of desire.

He places her soft foot, as he reclines by her side, on his ardent bosom, and stains it with the ruddy hue of *Yavaca.*

Say, my friend, why pass I my nights in this tangled forest without joy, and without hope,

While the faithless brother of HALADHERA clasps my rival in his arms?

Yet why, my companion, shouldst thou mourn, though my perfidious youth has disappointed me?

What offence is it of thine, if he sport with a crowd of damsels happier than I?

Mark, how my soul, attracted by his irresistible charms, bursts from its mortal frame, and rushes to mix with its beloved.

She, whom the god enjoys, crowned with sylvan flowers,

Sits carelessly on a bed of leaves with him, whose wanton eyes resemble blue water-lilies agitated by the breeze.

She feels no flame from the gales of *Malaya* with him, whose words are sweeter than the water of life.

She derides the shafts of soul-born CAMA with him, whose lips are like a red lotos in full bloom.

She is cooled by the moon's dewy beams, while she reclines with him, whose hands and feet glow like vernal flowers.

No female companion deludes her, while she sports with him, whose vesture blazes like tried gold.

She faints not through excess of passion, while she caresses that youth who surpasses in beauty the inhabitants of all worlds.

O gale, scented with sandal, who breathest love from the regions of the south, be propitious but for a moment:

When thou hast brought my beloved before my eyes, thou mayest freely waft away my soul.

Love, with eyes like blue water-lilies, again assails me, and triumphs;

And, while the perfidy of my beloved rends my heart, my female friend is my foe;

The cool breeze scorches me like a flame, and the nectar-dropping moon is my poison.

Bring disease and death, O gale of *Malaya!* Seize my spirit, O god with five arrows!

I ask not mercy from thee: no more will I dwell in the cottage of my father.

Receive me in thy azure waves, O sister of YAMA, (53) that the ardour of my heart may be allayed."

PART VI

Pierced by the arrows of love, she passed the night in the agonies of despair, and at early dawn thus rebuked her lover, whom she saw lying prostrate before her, and imploring her forgiveness:

"Alas! alas! go, MADHAVA, depart, O CESAVA, (54) speak not the language of guile;

Follow her, O lotos-eyed god, follow her, who dispels thy care.

Look at his eye half opened, red with continual waking through the pleasurable night, yet smiling still with affection for my rival!

Thy teeth, O cerulean youth, are azure as thy complexion, from the kisses which thou hast imprinted on the beautiful eyes of thy darling, graced with dark blue powder;

And thy limbs, marked with punctures in love's warfare, exhibit a letter of conquest written on polished sapphires with liquid gold.

That broad bosom, stained by the bright lotos of her foot, displays a vesture of ruddy leaves over the tree of thy heart, which trembles within it.

The pressure of her lip on thine, wounds me to the soul.

Ah! how canst thou assert that we are one, since our sensations differ thus widely?

Thy soul, O dark-limbed god, shows its blackness externally.

How couldst thou deceive a girl who relied on thee; a girl who burned in the fever of love?

Thou rovest in the woods, and females are thy prey:—what wonder?

Even thy childish heart was malignant; and thou gavest death to the nurse, who would have given thee milk.

Since thy tenderness for me, of which these forests used to talk, has now vanished;

And since thy breast, reddened by the feet of my rival, glows as if thy ardent passion for her were bursting from it,

The sight of thee, O deceiver, makes my (ah! must I say it?) blush at my own affection."

Having thus inveighed against her beloved, she sat overwhelmed in grief, and silently meditated on his charms; when her damsel softly addressed her:

"He is gone: the light air has wafted him away. What pleasure, now my beloved, remains in thy mansion?

Continue not, resentful woman, thy indignation against the beautiful MADHAVA.

Why shouldst thou render vain those round, smooth vases, ample and ripe as the sweet fruit of yon *Tala* tree?

How often and how recently have I said, Forsake not the blooming HERI?

Why sittest thou so mournful? Why weepest thou with distraction, when the damsels are laughing around thee?

Thou hast formed a couch of soft lotos leaves: let thy darling charm thy sight, while he reposes on it.

Afflict not thy soul with extreme anguish: but attend to my words, which conceal no guile.

Suffer CESAVA to approach; let him speak with exquisite sweetness, and dissipate all thy sorrows.

If thou art harsh to him, who is amiable; if thou art proudly silent, when he deprecates thy wrath with lowly prostrations;

If thou showest aversion to him, who loves thee passionately; if, when he bends before thee, thy face be turned contemptuously away;

By the same rule of contrariety the dust of sandal-wood, which thou hast sprinkled, may become poison;

The moon, with cool beams, a scorching sun; the fresh dew, a consuming flame; and the sports of love be changed into agony."

MADHAVA was not absent long; he returned to his beloved; whose cheeks were healed by the sultry gale of her sighs.

Her anger was diminished, not wholly abated; but she secretly rejoiced at his return, while the shades of night also were approaching.

She looked abashed at her damsel, while he, with faltering accents, implored her forgiveness.

"Speak but one mild word, and the rays of thy sparkling teeth will dispel the gloom of my fears.

My trembling lips, like thirsty *Chacorus*, long to drink the moonbeams of thy cheek.

O my darling, who art naturally so tender-hearted, abandon thy causeless indignation.

At this moment the flame of desire consumes my heart. Oh! grant me a draught of honey from the lotos of thy mouth.

Or if thou beest inexorable, grant me death from the arrows of thy keen eyes.

Make thy arms my chains; and punish me according to thy pleasure.

Thou art my life; thou art my ornament; thou art a pearl in the ocean of my mortal birth:

Oh! be favourable now, and my heart shall externally be grateful.

Thine eyes, which nature formed like blue water-lilies, art become, through thy resentment, like petals of the crimson lotos.

Oh! tinge with their effulgence these my dark limbs, that they may glow like the shafts of love tipped with flowers.

Place on my head that foot like a fresh leaf: and shade me from the sun of my passion, whose beams I am unable to bear.

Spread a string of gems on those two soft globes; let the golden bells of thy zone tinkle, and proclaim the mild edict of love.

Say, O damsel, with delicate speech, shall I dye red with the juice of *Alactaca* those beautiful feet, which make the full blown land-lotos blush with shame?

Abandon thy doubts of my heart, now indeed fluttering through fear of thy displeasure, but hereafter to be fixed wholly on thee;

A heart, which has no room in it for another: none else can enter it, but love, the bodyless god.

Let him wing his arrows; let him wound me mortally; decline not, O cruel, the pleasure of seeing me expire.

Thy face is bright as the moon, though its beams drop the venom of maddening desire;

Let thy nectareous lip be the charmer, who alone has power to lull the serpent, or supply an antidote for his poison.

Thy silence afflicts me: Oh! speak with the voice of music, and let thy sweet accents allay my ardour.

Abandon thy wrath: but abandon not a lover, who surpasses in beauty the sons of men, and who kneels before thee, O thou most beautiful among women.

Thy lips are a *Bandhujiva* flower; the lustre of the *Madhuca* (55) beams on thy cheek;

Thine eye outshines the blue lotos; thy nose is a bud of the *Tila;* (56) the *Cunda* (57) blossom yields to thy teeth;

Thus the flowery-shafted god borrows from thee the points of his darts, and subdues the universe.

Surely thou descendest from heaven, O slender damsel, attended by a company of youthful goddesses; and all their beauties are collected in thee."

PART VII

He spake; and seeing her appeased by his homage, flew to his bower, clad in a gay mantle.

The night now veiled all visible objects; and the damsel thus exhorted *Radha*, while she decked her with beaming ornaments:

"Follow, gentle RADHICA, follow the son of MADHU;

His disclosure was elegantly composed of sweet phrases; he prostrated himself at thy feet, and he now hastens to his delightful couch by yon grove of branching *Vanjalas*.

Bind round thy ankle rings beaming with gems; and advance with mincing steps, like the pearl-fed *Marala*.

Drink with ravished ears the soft accents of HERI; and feast on love, while the warbling *Cocilas* obeys the mild ordinance of the flower-darting god.

Abandon delay: see the whole assembly of slender plants, pointing to the bower with fingers of young leaves agitated by the gale, make signals for thy departure.

Ask those two round hillocks, which receive pure dew-drops from the garland playing on thy neck, and the buds whose tops start aloft with the thought of thy darling;

Ask, and they will tell, that thy soul is intent on the warfare of love:

Advance, fervid warrior, advance with alacrity, while the sound of thy tinkling waist-bells shall represent martial music.

Lead with thee some favoured maid; grasp her hand with thine, whose fingers are long and smooth as love's arrows.

March; and with the noise of thy bracelets proclaim thy approach to the youth, who will own himself thy slave.

'She will come; she will exult in beholding me; she will pour accents of delight;

She will enfold me with eager arms; she will melt with affection.'

Such are his thoughts at this moment; and, thus thinking, he looks through the long avenue;

He trembles; he rejoices; he burns; he moves from place to place; he faints, when he sees thee not coming, and falls in his gloomy bower.

The night now dresses in habiliments fit for secrecy the many damsels, who hasten to their places of assignation;

She sets off with blackness their beautiful eyes; fixes dark *Tamala* leaves behind their ears;

Decks their locks with the deep azure of water-lilies, and sprinkles musk on their panting bosoms.

The nocturnal sky, black as the touchstone, tries the gold of their affections,

And is marked with rich lines from the flashes of their beauty, in which they surpass the brightest *Cashmirians*."

RADHA, thus incited, tripped through the forest: but shame overpowered her, when, by the light of innumerable gems on the arms, the neck, and the feet of her beloved,

She saw him at the door of his flowery mansion; then her damsel again addressed her with ardent exultation:

"Enter, sweet RADHA, the bower of HERI; seek delight, O thou whose bosom laughs with the foretaste of happiness.

Enter, sweet RADHA, the bower graced with a bed of *Asoca* leaves; seek delight, O thou whose garland leaps with joy on thy breast.

Enter, sweet RADHA, the bower illumined with gay blossoms; seek delight, O thou whose limbs far excel them in softness.

Enter, O RADHA, the bower made cool and fragrant by gales from the woods of *Malaya;* seek delight, O thou whose amorous lays are softer than breezes.

Enter, O RADHA, the bower spread with leaves of twining creepers; seek delight, O thou whose arms have been long inflexible.

Enter, O RADHA, the bower which resounds with the murmur of honey-making bees; seek delight, O thou whose embrace yields more exquisite sweetness.

Enter, O RADHA, the bower attuned by the melodious band of *Cocilas;* seek delight, O thou whose lips, which outshine the grains of the pomegranate, are embellished, when thou speakest, by the brightness of thy teeth.

Long has he borne thee in his mind; and now, in an agony of desire, he pants to taste nectar from thy lip.

Deign to restore thy slave, who will bend before the lotos of thy foot, and press it to his irradiated bosom.

A slave, who acknowledges himself bought by thee for a single glance from thy eye, and a toss of thy disdainful eyebrow."

She ended; and RADHA with timid joy, darting her eyes on GOVINDA, while she musically sounded the rings of her ankles, and the bells of her zone, entered the mystic bower of her only beloved.

There she beheld her MADHAVA, who delighted in her alone;

Who so long had sighed for her embrace; and whose countenance then gleamed with excessive rapture.

His heart was agitated by her sight, as the waves of the deep are affected by the lunar orb.

His azure breast glittered with pearls of unblemished lustre, like the full bed of the cerulean *Yamuna*, interspersed with curls of white foam.

From his graceful waste flowed a pale yellow robe, which resembled the golden dust of the water-lily scattered over its blue petals.

His passion was inflamed by the glances of her eyes, which played like a pair of water-birds with blue plumage, that sport near a full-blown lotos on a pool in the season of dew.

Bright ear-rings, like two suns, displayed in full expansion the flowers of his cheeks and lips, which glistened with the liquid radiance of smiles.

His looks, interwoven with blossoms, were like a cloud variegated with moonbeams;

And on his forehead shone a circle of odorous oil, extracted from the sandal of *Malaya*, like the moon just appearing on the dusky horizon;

While his whole body seemed in a flame from the blaze of unnumbered gems.

Tears of transport gushed in a stream from the full eyes of RADHA, and their watery glances gleamed on her best beloved.

Even shame, which before had taken its abode in their dark pupils, was itself ashamed, and departed, when the fawn-eyed RADHA gazed on the brightened face of CRISHNA.

While she passed by the soft edge of his couch, and the bevy of his attendant nymphs, pretending to strike the gnats from their cheeks in order to conceal their smiles, warily retired from the bower.

PART VIII

GOVINDA, seeing his beloved cheerful and serene, her lips sparking with smiles, and her eyes speaking desire, thus eagerly addressed her; while she carelessly reclined on the leafy bed strewn with soft blossoms.

Set the lotos of thy foot on this azure bosom; and let this couch be victorious over all who rebel against love.

Give short rapture, sweet RADHA, to NARAYAN, (58) thy adorer.

I do thee homage; I press with my blooming palms thy feet, weary with so long a walk.

O that I were the golden ring that plays round thy ankle!

Speak but one gentle word; bid nectar drop from the bright moon of thy mouth.

Since the pain of absence is removed, let me thus remove the thin vest that enviously hides thy charms.

Blest should I be, if those raised globes were fixed on my bosom, and the ardour of my passion allayed.

Oh suffer me to quaff the liquid bliss of those lips;

Restore with their water of life thy slave, who has long been lifeless, whom the fire of separation has consumed.

Long have these ears been afflicted in thy absence by the notes of the *Cocila*.

Relieve them with the sound of thy tinkling waist-bells, which yield music, almost equal to the music of thy voice.

Why are those eyes half closed? Are they ashamed of seeing a youth to whom thy careless resentment gave anguish?

Oh, let affliction cease, and let ecstasy drown the remembrance of sorrow.

PART IX

In the morning she rose disarrayed, and her eyes betrayed a night without slumber; when the yellow-robed god, who gazed on her with transport, thus meditated on her charms in his heavenly mind:

Though her locks be diffused at random; though the lustre of her lips be faded; though her garland and zone be fallen from their enchanting stations;

And though she hide their places with her hands, looking towards me with bashful silence, yet even thus disarrayed, she fills me with ecstatic delight.

But RADHA, preparing to array herself, before the company of nymphs could see her confusion, spake thus with exultation to her obsequious lover:

Place, O son of YADU, with fingers cooler than sandal-wood, place a circlet of musk on this breast, which resembles a vase of consecrated water, crowned with fresh leaves, and fixed near a vernal bower, to propitiate the god of love.

Place, my darling, the glossy powder, which would make the blackest bee envious, on this eye, whose glances are keener than arrows darted by the husband of RETI.

Fix, O accomplished youth, the two gems, which form part of love's chain, in those ears, whence the antelopes of thine eyes may run downwards, and sport at pleasure.

Place now a fresh circle of musk, black as the lunar spots, on the moon of my forehead; and mix gay flowers on my tresses with a peacock's feathers, in graceful order, that they may wave like the banners of CAMA.

Now replace, O tender-hearted, the loose ornaments of my vesture; and refix the golden bells of my girdle on their destined station, which resembles those hills where the god with five shafts, who destroyed SAMBARA, (59) keeps his elephant ready for battle.

While she spake the heart of YADAVA triumphed; and obeying her sportful behests, he placed musky spots on her bosom and forehead, dyed her temples with radiant hues, embellished her eyes with additional blackness, decked her braided hair and her neck with fresh garlands, and tied on her wrists the loosened bracelets, on her ankles the beamy rings, and round her waist the zone of bells, that sounded with ravishing melody.

Whatever is delightful in the modes of music, whatever is divine in meditations on VISHNU, (60) whatever is exquisite in the sweet art of love, whatever is graceful in the fine strains of poetry, all that let the happy and wise learn from the songs of JAYADEVA, (61) whose soul is united with the foot of NARAYAN.

THE GITAGOVINDA

May that HERI be your support, who expanded himself into an infinity of bright forms, when, eager to gaze with myriads of eyes, on the daughter of the ocean, he displayed his great character of the all-pervading deity, by the multiplied reflections of his divine person in the numberless gems on the many heads of the king of serpents, whom he chose for his couch;

That HERI, who removing his lucid veil from the bosom of PEDMA, and fixing his eyes on the delicious buds that grew on it, diverted her attention by declaring that, when she had chosen him as her bridegroom near the sea of milk, the disappointed husband of PERVATI (62) drank in despair the venom, which dyed his neck azure!

I HAVE now placed before my readers this extraordinary poem, which I believe will be considered by every adequate judge to be equal, if not superior, to every thing of the kind that has been produced, either by the ancients or moderns. The poem is confessedly *mystical*, relating to the pure and affectionate intercourse between the Deity and human souls; and is capable of a very extended comment, to illustrate its phraseology, and explain its almost numberless allusions to the mythological system of the Hindoos.

But the chief design of its introduction here is to illustrate the phraseology of the SONG OF SONGS. The most superficial reader cannot but be struck with the similarity of the language of the metaphors and imagery. There are few turns of thought in the *Song of Songs* that may not find a parallel in the *Gitagovinda;* and even the strongly impassioned language of *Solomon* may be everywhere supported by that of *Jayadeva*, and *vice versa*. Could it be proved that the love between Christ and the Church were really the subject of the *Canticles*, the *Gitagovinda* might be applied with the utmost success to illustrate and explain all its *imagery*, and all its allusions: but we have no key to unlock its reference; no *data* to which we can confidently refer; and though it be generally allowed to be a *mystic song*, yet all interpreters follow their own creed in its explanation; and it is only on the general subject that any two of them agree. As I am not satisfied that the common method used in its interpretation is either correct or genuine, I have simply avoided the rocks on which others have been wrecked, but have constructed no chart according to which a more prosperous voyage might be projected.

The late learned and pious Mr. *Romaine* seems to have thought that a competent knowledge of the original language might lead to its proper illustration; and is indignant at those who have attempted its explanation without this necessary qualification. Of his knowledge of the sacred language no man doubts. I, also, have brought some acquaintance with the original to bear on the subject; but, though perhaps as well acquainted with the meaning of the words as Mr. Romaine himself, I have not been able to discover his system in the poem; and I dare not by *conjecture* put a meaning on any thing that professes to be a revelation from God. I respect many of its interpreters for their piety and learning, but I cannot follow their steps; they have not proved to me that Solomon's Song refers to the love of Christ and his Church. Let this by my apology with the candid reader for not entering into a more extended comment on this extraordinary book.

ADAM CLARKE.

London, May 1, 1823.

To ascertain some of the *latter* PARTS of this poem, I have been obliged to trust to my own judgment; as Sir William Jones, from whom I have borrowed these, had not marked any division; and I have had the *original* of the four first PARTS only.

As to the *old version* of the Canticles which I have introduced, the reader will be pleased to observe, it is that which was used by our forefathers before and after the reformation: one word of which I would not presume to alter or change. It is sacred both by age and use.

NOTES ON THE GITAGOVINDA

(1) TAMALA TREE.—A dark-leaved tree, common in Mat'hura and other parts, but not found in Bengal.— The laurel.

(2) *Nanda.*—The foster father of Crishna.

(3) *Radha.*—One of the principal and favourite mistresses of Crishna.

(4) *Madhava.*—One of the names of Crishna, implying the possession of Ma or Lachmi, his heavenly consort.

(5) *Yamuna.*—Vulgarly called Jumna, the river which flows by Dehlee, Mat'hura, and Ayra.

(6) *Heri.*—A name of Crishna; importing the remover of sin and suffering.

(7) *Camala.*—A name of Lachmi, derived from the lotos.

(8) *Caliya.*—A huge snake, who from the Jumna infested the neighbourhood of Gocul till destroyed by Crishna.

(9) *Yadu.*—The name of a tribe, derived from Yadu, a celebrated Raja, famed to have been descended from the moon.

(10) *Garura.*—Not the vulture known by this name in Bengal; but a fabled bird, answering in some respects to the eagle of Jupiter, and described to be the bearer of Vishnu, the heavenly Crishna.

(11) *Janaca.*—A Raja of Tirhoot, whose daughter Suta was offered in marriage to whoever could draw a bow of immense size; and won by Crishna, in his incarnation of Ramehundra.

(12) *Dushana.*—A demon giant, slain by Crishna in the form of Rama.

(13) *Mandar.*—A mountain of immense size, with which Crishna is said to have churned the ocean in his second incarnation.

(14) *Pedma.*—A name of Lachmi, of the same meaning with Camala.

(15) *Chacora.*—A poetical bird, described like the partridge, but imagined to be enamoured of the moon, and to feed on her beams.

(16) *Vasanti.*—A vernal creeper, bearing a yellow and white flower.

(17) *Maylaya.*—A mountain in the Dekkan, on which sandal trees grow in abundance.

(18) *Cocila.*—An admired singing bird with green plumage, with red beak and feet, common in Mat'hura, and said to sing only in the spring season. The same name is given to a blackbird in Bengal, called the Rocil, which only sings in the night.

(19) *Bacul.*—A beautiful tree, commonly called orbicular, well known in Bengal, by the names of Moulseree and Boulseree.

(20) *Cinsuca.*—A broad-leaved tree, called also the Teisoo, bearing red flowers, shaped like nails.

(21) *Cama.*—The Hindoo god of love.

(22) *Cesara.*—A beautiful flower, with yellow and white petals, better known by the name of Nageisur.

(23) *Cetaci.*—The female Ceyora, a thorny shrub, whose flowers yield a fine perfume.

(24) *Patali.*—A large hollow flower, of which one species is red, the other white.

(25) *Smara.*—A name of the god of love, signifying *ideal*.

(26) *Caruna.*—A delicate creeper, with small red flowers, called in Persian Ishk-peiched, or love-tangler.

(27) *Madhavi.*—A creeper bearing small white flowers.

(28) *Malica.*—A species of jasmine.

(29) *Amra.*—The mango tree; with its flowers the god *Cama* tips his arrows.

(30) *Atimucta.*—A fragrant creeper, which runs to a great extent, called also Midmalut. It bears a flower of yellowish white, sometimes called also Madhavi.

(31) *Vrindavan.*—An extensive forest of Vraja.

(32) *Mallica.*—A species of jasmine, white and odoriferous.

(33) *Rasala.*—An epithet of the mango, implying replete with sweet juice.

(34) *Mura.*—A demon and giant slain by Crishna.

(35) *Vanjula.*—A large tree, called also Varvon, producing white flowers.

(36) *Vraja.*—A country about 170 miles in circumference, between Dehlee and Agra, including the city of Mat'hura, and intersected by the Jumna.

(37) *Bandhujiva.*—A red flower, named likewise Doperheca.

(38) *Macara.*—A horned fish, supposed to be the hammer shark.

(39) *Cadumba.*—A flower tree, vulgarly called Cuddum, very common in Bengal, and much esteemed by the Hindoos.

(40) *Cesi.*—A monster slain by *Vishnu.*

(41) *Asoca.*—A tall tree, somewhat resembling the beech, consecrated to Mahadeva.

(42) *Cansa.*—The maternal uncle of Crishna, destroyed by him for his iniquities.

(43) *Mahesa.*—Literally, mighty lord, an epithet of the god Shiva.

(44) *Mahadeva.*—The great deity; also an attribute of Shiva.

(45) *Ananga.*—A title of the god of love, implying incorporeal.

(46) *Bimba.*—A common plant, called also Cundooree, producing red berries which are eaten by the natives.

(47) *Candarpa.*—A name of *Cama*, the god of love, who having wounded *Siva* with one of his flowery arrows, was by him in revenge reduced to ashes.

(48) *Madhu.*—A giant destroyed by *Crishna.*

(49) *Murari.*—A name of *Crishna.*

(50) *Govinda.*—A name of *Crishna.*

(51) *Devaci.*—The mother of *Crishna.*

(52) *Reti.*—The wife of *Cama*, god of love.

(53) *Yama.*—The genius of Death.

(54) *Cesava.*—A name given to *Crishna*, on account of the fineness of his hair.

(55) *Madhuca.*—Bossia.

(56) *Tila.*—A grain called Sesamum.

(57) *Cunda.*—The jasmine.

(58) *Narayan.*—A name of *Crishna.*

(59) *Sambara.*—A tyrant destroyed by Cama.

(60) *Vishnu.*—A name of *Crishna.*

(61) *Jayadeva.*—A celebrated *Hindoo* poet, the author of the preceding poem.

(62) *Pervati.*—The consort of *Siva.*